THE TAPESTRY OF DELIGHTS

REVISITED

THE COMPREHENSIVE GUIDE TO BRITISH MUSIC OF THE BEAT, R&B, PYSCHEDELIC AND PROGRESSIVE ERAS 1963 - 1976

Written and compiled by Vernon Joynson

Consultants:-

Jon Newey, John Reed (Original Edition)

Richard Morton-Jack (Revised Edition)

This book is dedicated to rock and pop music collectors everywhere and to my wife Seonaid and children Jasmine and Jake for their support.

Published in Great Britain in 2006 by Borderline Productions. The original edition was published in September 1995.
This book is sold subject to the condition that it shall not be lent, resold, hired out or otherwise circulated in any form of binding or cover than that it is published in.

Reprinted 2008

Printed by Bell and Bain Ltd, 303 Burnfield Road, Thornliebank, Glasgow, G46 7UQ, Scotland.
Cover painting: Andrew Linsell, *Suncastle* (detail) 1991.

The Tapestry Of Delights
Revisited

THE COMPREHENSIVE GUIDE TO BRITISH MUSIC

OF THE BEAT, R&B, PSYCHEDELIC AND PROGRESSIVE ERAS

1963 - 1976

CONTENTS

AUTHOR'S NOTE

I have tried to ensure that this book is as accurate as possible, but some of the data it contains is difficult to verify, some entries are incomplete and doubtless there are omissions and errors. I would like to hear from anyone who is able to supply information that is missing in my book, correct errors or make suggestions for its improvement. If you can do any of these please contact me care of:

vernonjoynson@hotmail.co.uk

Vernon Joynson, May 2006.

DONOVAN - Barabajagal (CD).

DANTALIAN'S CHARIOT - Chariot Rising (CD).

FIRE - Underground And Overhead (CD).

DONOVAN - Mellow Yellow (CD).

MIKE STUART SPAN - Timespan (CD).

QUINTESSENCE - Epitaph For Tomorrow (CD).

FOREWORD

This book is the most detailed encyclopaedic guide on the market for record buyers and collectors of British rock between 1963 and 1976. It is intended as a companion volume to my earlier guide to American garage, psychedelic and hippie-rock, Fuzz Acid and Flowers - Revisited; but this book covers a much wider range of musical genres: mainstream rock and pop, folk, folk-rock, jazz-rock, blues-rock, psychedelia, freakbeat, Mersey-beat, R&B, glam-rock, progressive-rock - all are covered.

I hope this tome will bring to your attention many artists who didn't attract the publicity and acclaim they deserved first time around. Indeed, many of the artists featured had never appeared in music encyclopaedias before until the original edition of this book was published. After being out of print for some years it has now been comprehensively updated. Many entries have been rewritten and many artists originally omitted from the original volume have been included in this one.

The Remit Of This Book

As this is a guide to British rock and pop in this era, entries are largely confined to British-born artists. To qualify for an entry they had to release vinyl, or at least cut some demos. I've taken the liberty of including several musicians and bands from Ireland and I've also included a limited number of artists - such as Daevid Allen (Australian), Blossom Dearie (US), The Easybeats (Australian), Jimi Hendrix (US), Human Instinct (from New Zealand), Marsha Hunt (US), Alexis Korner (who had Greek/Turkish and Austrian parents), Harvey Matusow (US), Nanette (Canadian), Chiitra Neogy (Indian), Simple Image (from New Zealand), Sunforest (US), Gary Walker (US), Scott Walker (US), Gary Wright (US) and Mark Wirtz (German) - who weren't British by birth, but were based in Britain when they achieved their success and were an integral part of the tapestry of British rock and pop in this era. Where an artist is not British this is indicated in their entry. A case could possibly have been made for including several others, but constraint of space has made this impossible.

This is a vast volume, with over 3,300 entries and, for reasons of space, a comparatively limited number of mainstream pop artists (mostly ballad singers) have had to be omitted. Similarly, those punk acts, getting underway in 1976, which marked the start of another exciting era, are excluded (although you can read about them in my punk and new wave encyclopaedia 'Up Yours!'). Also excluded are ska, bluebeat, reggae and soul acts. The book has been updated until December 2005. Entries don't end abruptly at 1976 - where artists have remained active in the music business since then a brief overview of their post-1976 accomplishments is provided but not in the same detail as their pre-1976 exploits. A list of significant artists not included appears near the end of the book.

How To Use This Book

All bands and solo artists appear in alphabetical order. 'The' has been ignored as the first word of the band's name. Individual artists have been alphabetised under surnames, e.g. Mike Absalom appears in the 'A's.

Some entries are very brief, where bands or artists just released one 45 or appeared on a compilation, but for more prolific acts expect to see the following:-

Personnel Listings

Personnel are listed alphabetically by surname. Where more than one line-up occurs, these are indicated by the A-Z characters.

Personnel:	Name:	Instruments:	Line-up:
	MEMBER1	gtr, vcls	A
	MEMBER2	bs	AB
	MEMBER3	drms, vcls	A
	MEMBER4	keyb'ds	A
	MEMBER5	gtr, vcls	B
	MEMBER6	perc	B

Album Discographies

Where more than one has been released, they are listed in order of release. Line entries are as follows:-

ALBUMS:

No/Line-up *	Name	UK. Label & Cat No +
1(A)	A MUSICAL EVENING WITH MICK ABRAHAMS	(Chrysalis ILPS 9147) 1971 SC
2( )	AT LAST	(Chrysalis CHR 1005) 1972 R1

NB: * Where albums are known to have been reissued or pirated, this is indicated. + And Rarity rating / highest chart placing where applicable.

EP Discographies (where applicable)

Where more than one has been released, they are listed in order of release, in the same format as above.

45 Discographies

These are also listed in order of release. Line-up information is not supplied, but otherwise the same information is supplied as for album releases. 'c' before the year of release = circa or approximate and appears where the year of release is not known for sure.

Assorted Information About The Band Or Artist

In the text, the name(s) of other bands or artists who are featured in this book appear in bold to facilitate easy cross-reference. Where bands or artists have tracks which are also included on compilations these are also identified in italics as for all but the most ardent collector they will be the only means of accessing the song. Please note, though, that these references to compilation appearances are by no means comprehensive (that would be a practically impossible task!) A list of all compilation albums and CDs referred to, along with label details, catalogue numbers and year of release (where known), appears in the compilation section of this book. Some of these compilations had very limited pressings and are also rare now. Some additional compilations that may interest readers are also included in this section.

CD Releases

Many albums referred to in this book have now been repackaged on CD and this is often referred to in passing beneath the album discographies, where known. It has proved impossible to keep abreast of all these reissues so the information is not comprehensive. Many CD compilations are also appearing and those that are relevant and known to the author are included in the compilation section at the end of the book.

The Accent.

A Rarity / Sought-After Scale

Those albums, EPs and (for the first time in this edition) 45s, which are rare and sought-after (obviously there are some rare records that nobody wants) have been given a rating to the right of the year of release. The scale below can only give a rough banding guide to value and is provided for guidance only:-

SC	Scarce	£15 - 30
R1	Rare	£30 - 55
R2	Very Rare	£55 - 110
R3	Extremely Rare	£110 - 260
R4	Ultra Rare	£260 - 500
R5	Seldom offered for sale but very sought-after	£500 - £1,000
R6	Only a handful exist and they are very sought-after	£1,000 plus

PLEASE NOTE: - Any guide to the value of records is highly subjective. Any value will depend on the condition of the vinyl and sleeve, the local geographic scarcity, and the retail 'chain' (i.e. dealers will have a mark-up - they will offer less when buying an album than selling it). The value will also vary with time, and may go up or down. The values are based on records and their sleeves being in MINT condition. Ultimately the price at which you buy or sell any record is an individual decision, and Borderline Productions, its owners, employees and related companies cannot accept responsibility for the accuracy of this guide, or for any economic loss which may be encountered with regard to the use of this material.

Credits

This book was first published in September 1995. Further editions appeared in September 1996 and June 1998 but this edition is a radical rewrite.

The first edition of this book was a massive undertaking and many people helped to make it the book it was. Particular thanks are due to Erika and Ivor Trueman (typing/typesetting); Jon Newey (JN), John Reed (JR) (then of 'Record Collector') and Mike Warth (MWh), who spent several hours/days combing through the transcripts adding pieces and making improvements; Marcel Koopman (MK), who has reviewed some of those 'difficult to find' collector's albums; Jon Newey (JN), Max Waller (MW), Mike Warth (MWh) and Costas Arvanitis (CA) who supplied tapes and written entries; David Wells (data) and Phil Smee (illustrations); and Andy Linehan, Chris Mobbs and Tony Cadogan at the National Sound Archive Listening Service enabled me to hear many records I couldn't find elsewhere. Thanks also to Andrew Linsell (front and rear cover), Phil

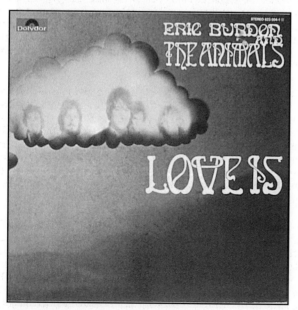

ERIC BUDON AND THE ANIMALS - Love Is... (2-LP).

Holden (tapes), George Lolos (tapes), Mark Paytress, Andy Davis, Brian Hogg, Alan Gowing, Gari Melville, Chris O'Malley, Peter Hughes, Alistair I.W. Campbell (tapes), Iain MacLean and sorry to anyone I've forgotten.

For the subsequent book editions, including this rewrite, aside from my all my own additions and updates, many people have either written to me with snippets of information or e-mailed us. Special thanks go to Richard Morton-Jack (RMJ) who edited the transcripts for 'The Tapestry Of Delights ... Revisited' and added several new entries, and to Louis Beheils and Marc 'Mushroom' Muijen who together supplied around 250 illustrations for the book.

Thanks also to:- Avo Adami (AA), Dave Allen (DA), Richard Allen (RA), Warren Allen (WA), Rob Almond (RA), Costas Arvanitis (CA), Nick Balaam (NB), Lee Beddow (LB), Joe Belde (JB), Ron Blackie (RB), Gary Brewer (GB), Tim Brigstocke (TB), Mick Buckley (MB), Keith Burns (KB), Ray Chan (RC), Andy Chrzanowski (AC), Peter Convey (PC), Peter Corney (PCr), Simon Coward (SC), Paul Cross (PCr), Peter Daltrey (PD), Zante Davide (ZD), Steve Davies (SD), Martyn Day (MD), Kai Drewitz (KD), Wolfgang Duringer (WD), H. Erka (HE), George Evers (GE), Peter Finberg (PF), Tony Fletcher (TF), Chris Gerbig (CG), Antonio Giordano (AG), Mike Godwin (MG), Edward Golga (EG), Ronald Halmen (RH), T. Hammond (TH), Anthony Harland (AH), Richard Havers (RH), Terence Hilton (TH), Hitomi Ishikawa (HI), Adrian M. Johnson (AJ), Daniel Jones (DJ), Stephen Jones (SJ), Francis Knight (FK), Pasi Koivu (PK), Marcel Koopman (MK), Sonja Kristina (SK), Pete Lawrence (PL), Richard Laws (RL), Victoria Ling (VL), Dr. Peter Martincek (PM), Gary Massucco (GM), Messmer Matthias (MM), Harvey Job Matusow (HJM), Jimmy McClernan (JMcC), Gillie McPherson (GMcP), Gari Melville (GM), Giuseppe Minetto (GMi), A. J. Moseley (AM), Brian Mugford (BM), Neil Murray (NM), Colin Nugent (CN), Anders Olson (AO), Robert Ommundsen (RO), R.N. Owens (RNO), Mark Paytress (MP), Richard Peabody (RP), Lorenzo Pittan (LP), Gavin Power (GP), Colette Randall (CR), Timo Rauhaniemi (TR), Rodney Rawlings (RR), Lori Reed (LR), Fred Rothwell (FR), Dr. H. Schwaller (DrS), Uygar Seu (US), Martin Shaer (MS), David Simon (DS), Leigh Smart (LS), Ian Southwood (IS), Bill Stow (BS), Martin Thornshom (MT), Gary Tibbs (GT), Allan Toombs (AT), Menachem Turchick (MT), Jens Unosson (JU), P.J. Van der Hoeven (Van H), Peter Viney (PV), Max Waller (MW), Mike Warth (MWh), David Wells (DW), Jon Williams (JW) and Lindsay Williams (LW) for supplying data.

When an earlier version of this book was online a few years back the following sent in significant (more than ten) e-mails containing data: Costas Arvanitis (CS), Gianpaolo Banelli (GB), Lukas Berny (LB), Arthur Davies (AD), Marcel Koopman (MK), Kim Lowden (KL), Barry Margolis (BM), Jim McMaster (JM), Neil Murray (NM), Jon Newey (JN), Stephane Rebeschini (SB), Dietmar Schwab (DS), Bill Stow (BS), Max Waller (MW), Mike Warth (MWh), and Vladimir Zhigulin (VZ).

Where people have contributed entries to the book their full name has been credited in abbreviated form at the end of the text e.g. Bill Stow (BS), Mike Warth (MWh). However, I cannot guarantee that this system is fullproof, so apologies to anyone not credited.

I am also grateful to the following sources:- Record Collector magazine; Record Collector: Rare Record Price Guides; Terry Hounsome's Rock Record and Single File; Guinness Book Of Hit Singles/Albums; Joel Whitburn's Top Pop Singles/Albums; Pete Frame's Rock Family Tree; Forbidden Fruit; Guinness Book Of Rock Stars; Brian Hogg's The History Of Scottish Rock And Pop; NME Encyclopaedia of Rock; Encyclopaedia Of British Beat Groups From The Sixties; M.C. Strong's The Great Rock Discography; Collectable 45s Of The Swinging Sixties Vol. 5 (A-F) and 6 (G-M); New Musical Express; Record Mirror; Melody Maker; 117 Magazine; 45 release sheets; The Rise and Fall Of Rock, Sequel, See For Miles and Bucketfull Of Brains and the All Music and various other artist-specific web sites.

INTRODUCTION

1963 might seem to be an arbitrary starting point for this book, but it was the year the British music industry underwent a revolution. Up until then the British pop industry had been based in London and the Charts had been dominated by balladeers, although the emergence of rock'n'roll in the mid-fifties and the impact of Elvis Presley, along with the success of Lonnie Donegan at the spearhead of skiffle music had all made their mark. Indeed skiffle - a combination of rhythm and blues and country music with a dash of folk - set the trend for the home-grown music of the late fifties as thousands of skiffle bands were formed in back rooms all over the country, often getting little further than that. The same era also saw the rise of the British answers to American rock'n'roll - Tommy Steele, Billy Fury, Marty Wilde and Cliff Richard (although Cliff never looked comfortable doing rock'n'roll and soon veered away towards softer material and a nice boy image). These rock'n'rollers provided a focal point for the teddy boy movement. By the early sixties traditional jazz was growing in popularity among the growing student population and instrumental groups like **The Shadows** and **The Tornados** were emerging.

The stage was set for a breakthrough into a completely new sound which came from Liverpool and became known as Merseybeat. The city's still thriving docks and clubs encouraged a lively music scene, many of the groups had formed during the skiffle era but became influenced by the imported American rhythm and blues records that came in by boat.

The standard beat group format was three guitarists - lead, rhythm and bass - and drums with lead vocalist being actively supported by at least one other backing singer. They played at clubs like the Iron Door, the Jacaranda, the Casbah, the Blue Angel and the Cavern. The Cavern is the most famous now because **The Beatles** enjoyed a residency there in their early days. The scene also spilled over into larger halls like the Empire and St Georges. Outside Liverpool opportunities were limited, although a thriving scene was developing for the more adventurous groups like **Tony Sheridan**, **Rory Storm and The Hurricanes** and **The Beatles** in the thriving German port of Hamburg where the atmosphere was considerably more decadent. The groups were also required to work harder at venues like the Star Club, the Indra and the Kaiser Keller but the experience sent the bands back to Liverpool all the tighter and better for it.

The Beatles were the first Merseybeat band to break into the charts - with *Love Me Do* in December 1962. At that stage there was no hint of what was to follow. It was the second single, *Please Please Me*, that opened the floodgates. **Gerry and The Pacemakers** were the first Merseybeat band to get to Number One, with *How Do You Do It?* a feat they later repeated with *I Like It* and *You'll Never Walk Alone*. **The Beatles** also scored three

Number Ones during 1963 with *From Me To You*, *She Loves You* and *I Wanna Hold Your Hand*. They were followed into the Charts by **The Searchers**, **Billy J Kramer and The Dakotas**, **The Swinging Blue Jeans**, and **Cilla Black** and by the end of 1963 A&R men from all the major record companies, particularly Decca, EMI, Fontana and Oriole - were scouring Liverpool signing literally dozens of bands.

In this book you'll find scores of them - the famous and the obscure. You'll discover that **Howie Casey and The Seniors** were the first Merseybeat band to issue records, that **The Big Three** are fondly remembered as the wildest and most raucous band (though they were never able to translate that onto vinyl), that **The Chants** were Liverpool's only all-black band who were heavily influenced by fifties vocal groups and that **The Riot Squad** were marketed by Larry Page as a London R&B band. And then see how many of the following you remember: **The Clayton Squares**, **Lee Curtis and The All Stars**, **The Dennisons**, **The Escorts**, **The Fourmost**, **Ian and The Zodiacs**, **Tony Jackson and The Vibrations**, **The Koobas**, **The Mojos**, **Mark Peters and The Silhouettes**, **Freddie Starr and The Midnighters** (the very same), **Kingsize Taylor and The Dominoes** and **The Undertakers**.

Merseybeat remains Britain's biggest ever musical explosion and spearheaded the export of British pop to America, changing the face of popular music as significantly as Elvis Presley had done nearly a decade earlier. Original records by Merseybeat groups have become collectable items, particularly those that capture the atmosphere of the era like Oriole's two *This Is Merseybeat* albums which feature live recordings from the Cavern Club.

It wasn't long before record companies started to look at other cities and sign up promising acts from the burgeoning group scenes developing elsewhere: **The Hollies** (the third most successful Chart act in this era behind **The Beatles** and **The Rolling Stones**) and **Freddie and The Dreamers** from Manchester, **The Animals** from Newcastle, **The Spencer Davis Group** from Birmingham, **Brian Poole and The Tremeloes** from Dagenham, **The Zombies** (arguably the most talented beat group after **The Beatles**) from St. Albans, and hundreds of others that released two or three singles before disappearing once again.

The Merseybeat phenomenon had to some extent overshadowed the vibrant London R&B scene which had been pioneered during the early sixties by **Alexis Korner** and Cyril Davies (who sadly died before it broke through nationally) and enthusiastically picked up by **The Rolling Stones**, **The Pretty Things**, **The Kinks**, **The Yardbirds**, **Georgie Fame and The Blue Flames** and **John Mayall's Bluesbreakers** at clubs like the Crawdaddy in Richmond, the Marquee, the Flamingo and Klooks Kleek. Behind them came another wave of R&B groups including **The Graham**

THE ZOMBIES - Begin Here (CD).

RUBBLE VOL. 4 - The 49 Minute Technicolour Dream Comp. LP.

Bond Organisation, **Zoot Money's Big Roll Band**, **Cliff Bennett & The Rebel Rousers**, **Bluesology** (featuring a young **Elton John**), **Steampacket** (featuring a young **Rod Stewart**) and **The Downliner's Sect**. The diversity of influences between London and Merseybeat bands can be partly explained by the fact that American records imported into London and Liverpool tended to come from different sources in the States.

During this era the rockers, who had descended from the teddy boy movement, emerged as a new cult, dressed in black leather and riding motorbikes. They preferred the rawer R&B sound of bands like **The Rolling Stones**, **The Pretty Things** and **The Animals**. In contrast, the mod cult was clean cut and fashion conscious, clad in long anoraks called parkas and riding Vespas or Lambretta motor scooters. The premier mod band was **The Who** who'd started out as **The High Numbers** whose first single, *I'm The Face/Zoot Suit* became an early mod anthem. Other significant mod acts included **The Small Faces**, **The Creation**, **The Action** even **Sandie Shaw**. The music was the soundtrack to a series of confrontations between mods and rockers at various seaside resorts around the country during the Summer of '63, '64 and '65. Between the mod groups and rocker groups however, there were a large number of bands whose pop music was derived from melodies and harmonies rather than from fashion or style. The most successful was undoubtedly **Herman's Hermits** who were almost teenybopper in format and achieved enormous success in America. Others included **The Fortunes**, **Unit 4 Plus 2**, **The Ivy League** and **The Easybeats** (who'd come over from Australia to join in the UK beat boom).

While the American Charts were filling up with **The Beatles**, **The Rolling Stones**, **The Dave Clark Five**, **Herman's Hermits** and **Gerry and The Pacemakers**, it was bands like **The Kinks**, **The Yardbirds** and **The Pretty Things** that were most influential on the countless garage bands that were being formed across the States. The black American R&B that had inspired

The Eyes.

the British groups was now being exported back to America by white English bands for white American bands.

This cross-fertilisation took another quantum leap forward with the arrival of marijuana and LSD during 1966 which had a dramatic effect on the music as bands of all styles, beat, R&B, blues, folk, etc began experimenting with psychedelic drugs, in some cases deconstructing the rhythms, chords and lyrics, creating something radically new and often more personal as a result.

The psychedelic era revolutionised rock and pop music all over again. A new range of instruments such as sitars, theramins, wind chimes and numerous electronic devices from fuzz-boxes to wah-wah pedals were introduced. On the American West Coast bands like The Doors, Jefferson Airplane, Grateful Dead and Country Joe and The Fish strove to push back the musical barriers beyond the three-minute pop format. It was also closely allied with the growth of the counter culture, centred in San Francisco during '66 and '67. The hippies had their own newspapers and shops as they espoused their alternative lifestyle to the rampant materialism prevalent throughout America. Free concerts and light shows became an integral part of the hippie experience with music providing the soundtrack to the cultural revolution.

In Britain, psychedelia was less associated with politics, perhaps because the issues of civil rights or the Vietnam war were not as directly relevant and the tradition of left-wing politics was already well established. Still it soon found its own cultural impetus as the underground movement reacted against the prejudices and hypocrisies of the British class system.

Arguably, the British approach to psychedelia was a more enlightened one. The term is used in this book in its broadest sense to refer to experimental beat music. Some people prefer to use the term freakbeat. Not surprisingly

PSYCHODELPHIA versus IAN SMITH GIANT FREAK OUT!

AT THE ROUNDHOUSE
CHALK FARM ROAD, N.W.1
DECEMBER 3rd, 10 p.m. on.
Screaming THOUSANDS, Underground Films, Poets, HAPPENINGS, with the PINK FLOYD and the RAM HOLDER MESSENGERS.
Bring your own happenings and ecstatogenic substances.
Drag optional

Tickets at Indica Books
Housemans, Better Books, and Collets

The Beatles led the way musically and lyrically with singles like *Day Tripper* and *I Feel Fine* while the *Rubber Soul* and *Revolver* albums contained heavy hints of what was to come. As **The Beatles** toiled away on the ground-breaking *Sgt. Pepper's Lonely Heart Club Band* album at London's Abbey Road studios early in 1967, in another studio down the corridor the little known **Pink Floyd** were working on their debut album, *Piper At The Gates Of Dawn*. While the former instantly became the most influential album of the sixties, the latter was adopted by the fast-growing UK underground scene which held court at London's UFO club, situated in a basement on Tottenham Court Road, every Friday night, parading top psychedelic bands like the house band **Pink Floyd**, **The Crazy World Of Arthur Brown**, **The Smoke**, **Pretty Things**, **Procol Harum**, **The Sam Gopal Dream**, **Tomorrow** and **Soft Machine** against a backdrop of light-shows and avant-garde or horror movies. As the movement spread, new clubs opened up like Middle Earth, Happening 44 and the Roundhouse, while even that old R&B stalwart the Marquee temporarily tarted itself up to reflect the colourful times. While Carnaby Street and

Kings Road became the fashion centres of "swinging London", the heart of the British underground lay closer to Portobello Road street market, around the streets of Notting Hill community-based groups like **Hawkwind** and **The Deviants** offered a harder social and political perspective.

The impact of the underground scene and **The Beatles'** *Sgt. Pepper* album swept through the music scene leaving no major band untouched. **The**

Rolling Stones responded with *Their Satanic Majesties Request*, **The Who** came up with singles like *I Can See For Miles* and *Pictures Of Lily* and **The Small Faces** unveiled *Here Comes The Nice* and *Itchycoo Park*. Other groups successfully adapted psychedelia to their own ends, including **The Move** (*I Can Hear The Grass Grow* and *Flowers In The Rain*) and **Procol Harum** (*Whiter Shade Of Pale* and *Homburg*), while even blatantly pop acts found plenty of opportunities, resulting in *King Midas In Reverse* by **The Hollies**, *Let's Go To San Francisco* by **The Flowerpot Men** (previously **The Ivy League** during the beat boom), *From The Underworld* by **The Herd** and even *Love Is All Around* by **The Troggs**. Disappointingly, however, there were very few genuine psychedelic albums, but let's not forget that there were classics like the ones by **Tomorrow**, **Apple**, **Kaleidoscope** and **The Open Mind**. Again, hundreds of psychedelic bands were formed during the late sixties but few survived beyond a couple of singles. Long lost bands like **The Birds**, **The Eyes**, **The Fleur de Lys**, **The Flies**, **Fire**, **Game**, **Tintern Abbey**, **One In A Million**, **Rupert's People**, **The Syn**, **The Tickle**, **The Shy Limbs**, **The Sands**, **Mike Stuart Span** and **The Voice** to name but a few were uncovered for the original edition of this book and their work appears on obscure compilations like *Chocolate Soup For Diabetics*, *The Perfumed Garden*, *The Rubble Collection*, *English Freakbeat* and *Electric Sugar Cube Flashbacks*.

Folk music may have been an unlikely psychedelic source but troubadours like **Donovan** fell under its spell with singles like *Sunshine Superman*, *Mellow Yellow*, *Jennifer Juniper* and *Hurdy Gurdy Man* as well as albums like *From A Flower To A Garden*. **The Incredible String Band** lapped up psychedelia for their *5,000 Spirits Or The Layers Of An Onion* album, to remarkable effect, while **Traffic** who'd grown out of **The Spencer Davis Group**, blended psychedelia with their folksy leanings to produce *Paper Sun*, *Hole In My Shoe* and *Here We Go Round The Mulberry Bush* and the

Mr. Fantasy album.

Fairport Convention were a regular attraction in London's pubs. In their early days they were influenced by US West Coast folk-rock. They found themselves infected by the spirit of the underground on albums like *What We Did On Our Holidays*.

The event which did most to spread the word about British psychedelia and the underground was the 14-Hour Technicolour Dream at London's Alexandra Palace between 28 - 30 April 1967 at which **Pink Floyd**, **The Crazy World Of Arthur Brown**, **The Social Deviants**, **Tomorrow**,

Tintern Abbey.

The Pretty Things, **The Purple Gang** and **The Syn** (who wrote a song about the event) were among 41 bands who played on two stages amid a carnival of light shows, posters, theatre groups and a fairground helter skelter while the audience included **John Lennon**. The show was a benefit for the underground newspaper, International Times, which had been busted by the Vice Squad and the establishment continued their harassing of the scene, busting several bands including **The Rolling Stones** and shutting down the pirate radio stations Radio London featuring John Peel's legendary 'Perfumed Garden' show, Radio Scotland and Radio 390 and 270 which had sprung up, broadcasting from boats out at sea, outside the British territorial waters. Still, Radio Caroline managed to defy the ban by moving its offices to Amsterdam and Paris. In response, the BBC set up Radio One but it was many years before UK radio enjoyed the range of music that has been part of the American way of life.

Meanwhile, blues-based bands were using the influence of psychedelia to expand their musical horizons. **Cream**, the first UK super-group featuring

Mighty Baby.

Eric Clapton, **Jack Bruce** and **Ginger Baker** refined their R&B roots to produce the *Disraeli Gears* album during '67 but the biggest star to emerge from that genre was **Jimi Hendrix** who was discovered in New York by ex-**Animals** bassist Chas Chandler and brought back to Britain where he flowered in the heady musical atmosphere, recording the epoch-making *Are You Experienced* and *Axis Bold As Love* albums during '67 as well as the single *Purple Haze* (named after the brand of acid produced for the Monterey Festival that year).

By '68 the pop charts were again reverting to teenybopper bands while the underground bands concentrated on albums rather than three-minute singles. The softer sound of British underground was represented by **The Idle Race**, **Nirvana**, **Honeybus**, **The Alan Bown Set**, **Tyrannosaurus Rex**, **World Of Oz** and **Kaleidoscope** while the heavier end found bands like **Jethro Tull**, **King Crimson**, **Blodwyn Pig**, **Spooky Tooth** and **The Edgar Broughton Band**. The continuing blues boom had yielded **Fleetwood Mac**, **Chicken Shack**, **Ten Years After**, **The Keef Hartley Band**, **The Groundhogs** and **The Savoy Blues Band** while the first glimmerings of "progressive" rock were being shed by the likes of **Audience**, **Arcadium**, **Affinity**, **Ben**, **Clear Blue Sky**, **Clouds**, **Cressida**, **Dogfeet**, **Dog That Bit People**, **Locomotive** and **Dr. 'Z'** to name a few.

The progressive movement proceeded in several different directions with some, like **Renaissance**, **Curved Air** and **The Moody Blues**, looking to classical music for their inspiration while others like **Genesis** and **Yes** headed off towards their own grandiose rhythmic and lyrical visions. **Pink Floyd**, who'd been among the leading psychedelic bands, evolved into a progressive band following the departure of their songwriter and guitarist **Syd Barrett**, Britain's most notable musical acid casualty. Open air festivals had become an increasing important part of the underground scene during the late sixties and early seventies. **Pink Floyd** had headlined the first free festival in London's Hyde Park in 1968 and they were soon followed by **Blind Faith** and **The Rolling Stones**. The Isle Of Wight festivals drew over 200,000 people in '69 to see Bob Dylan with The Band, **The Who**, **Moody**

Blues, **The Nice**, **Joe Cocker** and **King Crimson** and a bigger crowd the following year saw **Jimi Hendrix**, the Doors, Joni Mitchell, Sly and The Family Stone, **Free**, **Jethro Tull**, **The Who**, **Taste**, **Ten Years After** and **Emerson Lake and Palmer**.

The death of **Jimi Hendrix** two weeks after the '70 Isle Of Wight Festival and the break-up of **The Beatles** that year signalled another sea change in the direction of British rock, most notably with the rise of heavy rock pioneered by **Led Zeppelin** and **Deep Purple** and enthusiastically supported by bands like **Black Sabbath**, **Wishbone Ash**, **Uriah Heep** and **Atomic Rooster**.

The early seventies also saw the emergence of glam-rock with **David Bowie** leading the way as perhaps the most influential rock star of the decade. Others included **Roxy Music**, **T Rex**, **Wizzard**, **Mud**, **Slade**, **Sweet**, **Gary Glitter** and **The Rubettes**. By the mid-seventies live music was under threat from disco and live concerts were no longer so fashionable. Even then, down among the pubs and clubs of London something was stirring. Out of the spotlight, home-grown bands were exploring new musical areas like funk (**Kokomo**), reggae (G T Moore and The Reggae Guitars) and country (**Bees Make Honey**). There was also a renewed interest in R&B with a harder edge from **Dr. Feelgood**, Eddie and The Hotrods, **Graham Parker and The Rumour**, **Ducks Deluxe** and **Kilburn and The High Roads**, whilst **Kursaal Flyers** were R&B with a pop edge. This became known as the pub-rock movement and played a key role in creating a fresh interest in the ailing music form that was rock in the mid-seventies. It helped pave the way for the punk-rock explosion in late '76 and '77... but that's another story which you can read about in Vernon's punk and new wave 'Up Yours!' encyclopaedia.

Hopefully this brief introduction has helped to place the histories of the bands you'll go on to read about in this tome in a wider context. You'll also learn more about the lineage of the interwoven tapestry that was British rock and pop in this era and see how many of the musicians who were in the sixties bands resurfaced again over the years in different outfits. We hope you find it interesting.

Vernon Joynson and Hugh Fielder.

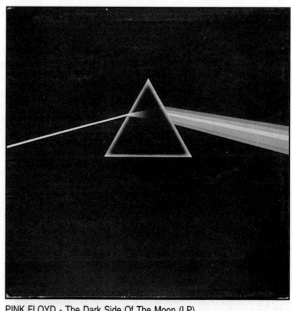

PINK FLOYD - The Dark Side Of The Moon (LP).

Aardvark

Personnel:
STAN ALDOUS	bs		A
FRANK CLARK	drms		A
STEVE MILLINER	keyb'ds, recorder, vibraphone		A
DAVE SKILLIN	vcls		A

ALBUM: 1(A) AARDVARK (Deram Nova SDN 17) 1970 R2

NB: (1) also released in mono (DN 17). (1) reissued on CD (Si-Wan SRMC 0056) 199?

A Midlands-based band, whose sole album presents us with the perennial problem of rock without guitars. As little instrumental interplay is possible, vocals, lyrics, compositions and above all the inventive use of keyboards become more important than ever. The result here is ambiguous. *Copper Sunset* has a nice title and a great 'wrong' and nagging bass-note in the chorus and *Many Things To Do* has nice harmonies, but this latter track is too long. Generally the music suffers from too many long extended tracks. The outstanding cut *Once Upon A Hill* is lovable, though, with great eclectic medieval stylings and effective celeste parts. Nice enough, but not brilliant.

Most songs on the album were written by Dave Skillin. They were mostly a studio band and made very few live appearances as they had enormous difficulties finding a keyboard player. Steve Milliner was previously in **Black Cat Bones**. Other keyboardists in the band were Paddy Coulter, Peter John Tdoof and Dave Watts, who was later in **Jackson Heights** and **Affinity**. Peter John Wood had played with The Trendsetters Soul Band and Hush and was later in **Sutherland Brothers and Quiver** and also played with **Al Stewart** and Natural Gas. Aldous had previously been in Odyssey and Skillen was later in Home. The album was produced by David Hitchcock, also responsible for LPs by **Caravan**, **Mellow Candle**, **Fuchsia** and others. (MK/VJ/RMJ)

A-Austr

Personnel:
BRIAN CALVERT	ld gtr, vcls, lute, voxhorn, voxtrombone		A
DENISE CALVERT	vcls, piano		A
YVONNE CARRODUS	vcls, triangle		A
CHRIS COOMBS	ld gtr, vcls, gtr, organ, voxhorn, hrmnca, perc		A
TED HEPWORTH	drms, water drm		A
MIKE LEVON	triangle, effects, electronics		A
BRIAN WILSON	bs, vcls, buzz gtr, organ, mandolin harp, cla		A

ALBUM: 1(A) A-AUSTR (Holyground HG 113) 1970 w/booklet R5

NB: (1) reissued (Magic Mixture MM1) 1989 (R1) and again (Holyground 010101LP) 1995 (SC). (1) also issued on CD (Kissing Spell KSD 002) 1995.

AARDVARK - Aardvark (LP).

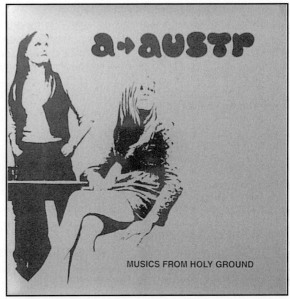

A-AUSTR - A-Austr (LP).

With an issue of only 99 copies, this is one of the rarest records to emerge from the UK that contains some interesting music. The elaborate packaging and the general care which went into the record betray, if nothing else, at least a heartfelt love of recorded music as a means of self-expression. Being a low-budget enterprise, a fact which is never really masked throughout the production, **A-Austr** went for diversity rather than sales figures. The music is strongly eclectic, with more influences than can be listed. No less than 15 tracks within a broad spectrum of styles can hardly be unanimously satisfying. In general the music is gentle and even folky, without drawing upon traditional material. At its best it's nothing less than brilliant, though in an unobtrusive sort of way. These highlights include almost all the songs which do not try to be "progressive" or severely emotional, but which instead opt for a simpler approach, thereby succeeding to convey a subtle and almost mythical atmosphere. As soon as the instrumentation gets denser, the sound tends to clog up or even becomes chaotic, being charming still, but nothing more than that. Definitely a very interesting record, though it's near to impossible to dig up an original. In 1989 a limited repro was manufactured, which now sells for a collector's price itself and is worth picking up.

Just 425 copies of the limited repressing appeared in the eighties on Magic Mixture. The album was reissued again by Holyground in 1995 with a fold-over gatefold sleeve and finally got a CD release on Kissing Spell the same year.

Many of the musicians on this album later figured on the **Astral Navigations** album. The Holyground label was owned by Mike Levon and Dave Wood and based in Wakefield, Yorkshire. (MK/VJ)

Abbey Road

Personnel:
RICK MANSWORTH	perc, vcls		A
STAN MOORE	drms, perc, vcls		A
KEN SALGREEN	bs, vcls		A
PERRY VALE	gtr, ukelele, vcls		A
ST. JOHN S. WOOD	piano, organ, vcls		A

45: Clunk-Click/Catamaran (Parlophone R 5989) 1973

The work of Abbey Road studio engineers and musicians working at the studio in the Summer of 1973, this was their sole vinyl offering, made in aid of a seat belt campaign. (VJ)

The Abdabs

Personnel:
ROGER 'SYD' BARRETT	gtr		A
BRIAN CLOSE	gtr		A
JULIETTE GALE	vcls		A
NICK MASON	drms		A
ROGER WATERS	bs		A
RICK WRIGHT	keyb'ds		A

Mason, Waters and Wright had all played together as Sigma 3 whilst studying at Regent Street Polytechnic. With the addition of **Barrett**, Gale and Close they became first the T-Set, then The Screaming Abdabs and finally **The Abdabs**. They played mostly R&B material and when Close left and Juliette Gale dropped out of the band they became **Pink Floyd**. (VJ)

Mick Abrahams (Band)

Personnel:	MICK ABRAHAMS	gtr, vcls	A
	RITCHIE DHARMA	drms	A
	WALT MONAHAN	bs	A
	BOB SARGEANT	keyb'ds, vcls	A

ALBUMS:	1(A)	A MUSICAL EVENING WITH MICK ABRAHAMS		
(up to		(Chrysalis ILPS 9147) 1971 SC
1975)	2( )	AT LAST	(Chrysalis CHR 1005) 1972 R1
	3( )	HAVE FUN LEARNING THE GUITAR	
		(SRT SRTM 73313) 1975 SC

NB: (3) original copies came with individually typed inserts. (2) reissued on CD (Edsel ED CD 335) 1991. (1) reissued on Beat Goes On (BGO CD 95) 1992.

Abrahams first played in a **Cream**-inspired blues band called McGregor's Engine before becoming a founder member of **Jethro Tull** in November 1967. He left a year later to join **Blodwyn Pig** but left them after two US tours in September 1970 to form the **Mick Abrahams Band,** with Walt Monaghan, the former bass player of Rust. Their debut album comprised a sort of jazzy R&B style rock. He rejoined a later **Blodwyn Pig** line-up in February 1974 but this soon petered out. **Abrahams** remained active in the music business, recording a third album in 1975, which was disappointing. Monaghan joined **If**.

Abrahams reformed **Blodwyn Pig** in 1988 and they released a well-received album entitled *All Said And Done*. The group later issued an album *Lies* in 1993, which many regarded as their best ever and they also issued a live album from their 1993 tour entitled *All Tore Down*. **Abrahams** remained active with **Blodwyn Pig** line-ups in the nineties. (VJ)

Mick Absalom

Personnel:	MIKE ABSALOM	gtr	ABC
	DIZ DIZLEY	gtr	B
	ERIC DILLON	drms	C
	RAY FENWICK	gtr	C
	JOHN PERRY	bs	C
	MIKE WEAVER	keyb'ds	C

ALBUMS:	1(A)	MIGHTY ABSALOM SINGS BATHROOM BALLADS	
		(Sportsdisc 1089) 1969 SC
	2(B)	SAVE THE LAST GHERKIN FOR ME	
		(Saydisc SDL 162) 1970 R2
	3(A)	MIKE ABSALOM	(Vertigo 6360 053) 1971 R2
	4(C)	HECTOR AND OTHER PECCADILLOS	
		(Philips 6308 131) 1972 SC

NB: (3) has been reissued on CD by Repertoire.

Mike Absalom was one of the real folk-singing characters of the seventies club and college music circuit. He was an ex-Oxford graduate and the son of a clergyman and spent many years after graduation travelling the world living on his wits and undertaking a variety of odd jobs including teacher, journalist, bodyguard, illegal liquor seller, tourist boat guide and busker, putting to good use his knowledge of eight foreign languages.

Returning to England in the late sixties, he joined the burgeoning club and college music circuit with an act based around the singing of mainly traditional bawdy rugby-style songs. An album of this material was released on the Sportsdisc label in 1969. He further developed his act and began to write his own material which largely consisted of his wry and humorous observations on various aspects of life but concentrating on sex, drugs and the church. This self-penned material first featured amongst the songs on his second album, which was entitled *Save The Last Gherkin For Me* on the collectable Saydisc label. Released in 1970, it also featured a well-known session guitarist of the time - Diz Dizley. In order to supplement the somewhat infrequent club and college bookings Mike was not averse to reverting to his busking past and could often be seen in and around the

Notting Hill area of London where he lived. It was during one such session that **Patrick Campbell - Lyons** of the group **Nirvana** spotted him and he was offered a deal with the legendary Vertigo label. His self-titled Vertigo album appeared in 1971 and featured an early Roger Dean designed fold-out sleeve based on the content of Mike's songs and was produced by **Campbell-Lyons**. It contained material based on drugs, sex, police corruption and politics humorously encapsulated in Mike's unique brand of storytelling poetry set to acoustic guitar. As background to understanding Mike's material it is important to remember that his formative years were in the swinging sixties and his audience was largely students. His work is full of essentially British-style humour and looks at the lighter side of drugs, sex, the church, politics and conflicts with authority which was well received on the college circuit. Mike's long hair, tall hat, hippie attire and engaging grin became a fixture in the early seventies. On his Vertigo album Mike created a series of characters for his drug-based tales including Ernie Plugg, John The Bog, Suzie Grapevine, Pusher Joe, Peaches Melba and Constable McLagen. As well as his drug-based material Mike also penned some serious folk songs based on love and life and also a humorous tale of the Arab/Israeli conflict (*Gaza Striptease*) and a tale of telephone tapping (*Don't Tell It On The Telephone*).

Mike continued this formula on his fourth album which came out on the Philips label in 1972 entitled *Hector And Other Peccadilos*. On this he introduced Hector the dope sniffing hound, WPC Sadie Stick and Flasher Jack as well as performing songs about a novel way to deal with the Taxman, his views on the Church and a song about the ancient Britons.

Mike Absalom may be an acquired taste but he is a taste worth acquiring. He followed in the long tradition of humorous music hall story-telling acts such as Flanders and Swann but took the genre into the sex, drugs and rock 'n' roll era of the seventies. His songs repay repeated listening as clever rhymes, puns and amusing storylines abound. He appeared on the Old Grey Whistle Test in 1972 performing songs from the *Hector...* album along with his band which consisted of Ray Fenwick (ex-**Quiver**), Eric Dillon, John Perry and Mike Weaver and continued on the college circuit until the mid-seventies. His Vertigo album, which is by far his strongest, has been released on CD by the Repertoire label.

He eventually emigrated to Canada where he took up several other instruments including the Celtic Harp. Various CDs of his material were issued in the nineties, including *Angels From Under My Feet* (APC04AFU) which is a mixture of Celtic harp and his mischievous wit and *Kettle Harp* (APC03KF), which features love songs and the Celtic harp. Apparently he never busked in London, although he did in lots of other countries, including Canada and France. (BS)

Academy

Personnel:	RICHARD COBBY	gtr	A
	DAMON J HARDY	vcls	A
	POLLY PERKINS	vcls	A
	DICK WALTER	flute	A

THE BRITISH PSYCHEDELIC TRIP 1966 - 1969 (Comp LP) including The Accent.

ALBUM: 1(A)   POP-LORE ACCORDING TO THE ACADEMY
                    (Morgan Bluetown BT 5001) 1969 R2

45:   α   Rachel's Dream/
          Munching The Candy   (Morgan Bluetown BTS 2) 1969
NB: α credited to Academy featuring Polly Perkins.

Sparsely but inventively instrumented folk-songs, with slight jazzy and psychedelic overtones are to be found on **Academy**'s sole album. The main attraction is the clear voice of Polly and the interesting woodwind parts. Male singer Hardy is less convincing, especially so on the trite *Anva*. *Poor Jean* has pretty harmonies but is marred by some out-of-key intonations. The best tracks are: *Munching The Candy* and *Rachel's Dream*, the latter starting sentimentally, but later on incorporating a lovely Russian theme. They were also issued on a 45. Interesting. **Polly Perkins** turned up occasionally as an actress in the following years. (MK)

The Accent

Personnel:	PETE BEETHAM	drms	A
	RICK BIRKETT	gtr	A
	ALAN DAVIES	bs	A
	JOHN HEBRON	vcls, gtr	A

45:   Red Sky At Night/Wind of Change   (Decca F 12679) 1967 R3

Originally from Yorkshire, where they were known as The Blue Blood Group, **Accent** moved to London in 1966 and recorded this 45 the following year having secured a residency at Billy Walker's Upper Cut Club. It was produced by Mike Vernon. The 'A' side contains some fine guitar work with bizarre sound effects and voices of doom. The flip is pretty good, too. A rather strange one this with galloping drums, relentless guitar and a rather eerie rhythm. The group recorded other tracks but this was the only one to make it onto vinyl.

Rick Birkett later released a solo album on Blue Horizon as **Rick Hayward** and was also later in **Jellybread** and **The Zombies**.

Compilation appearances have included:- *Red Sky At Night* on *The British Psychedelic Trip 1966 - 1969* (LP), *Chocolate Soup For Diabetics, Vol. 3* (LP), *Rubble Vol. 6: The Clouds Have Groovy Faces* (LP), *Rubble Vol. 4* (CD), *Glimpses, Vol. 3* (LP), *Perfumed Garden Vol. 2* (CD), *The Psychedelic Scene* (CD), *Chocolate Soup* (CD), *Illusions From The Crackling Void* (LP) and on the 4-CD box set, *Acid Drops, Spacedust & Flying Saucers*; and *Wind Of Change* on *Rubble Vol. 11: Adventures In The Mist* (LP), *Rubble Vol. 6* (CD), *Broken Dreams, Vol. 5* (LP), *Glimpses, Vol. 3* (LP), *Rare 60's Beat Treasures, Vol. 4* (CD) and *Visions Of The Past, Vol. 2* (LP & CD). (VJ)

Accolade

Personnel:	EDEN ABBA	double-bs	A
	BRIAN CRESSWELL	sax, flute	AB
	GORDON GILTRAP	gtr, vcls	A
	IAN HOYLE	drms	AB
	DON PARTRIDGE	gtr, vcls, vibraphone	AB
	MALCOLM POOLE	double-bs	B

ALBUMS: 1(A)   ACCOLADE   (Columbia SCX 6405) 1970 SC
            2(B)   ACCOLADE 2   (Regal Zonophone SLRZ 1024) 1971 R1
NB: (1) also released in the US (Capitol).

45:   Natural Day/Prelude To A Dawn   (Columbia DB 8688) 1969

Accolade were one of those short-lived late-'60s/early-'70s UK bands that attempted to expand musical boundaries, mixing traditional English folk with some rock influences. Prior to their collaboration in **Accolade**, both Giltrap and **Partridge** had enjoyed some solo recognition. Giltrap had released a pair of critically praised solo albums, while **Partridge** (who was actually working as a busker), enjoyed a fluke UK hit with the song *Rosie*.

Produced by Don Paul, 1969's *Accolade* is hard to accurately describe. The album exhibits a smooth and calming sound throughout. Largely acoustic, material such as *Maiden Flight Eliza* (featuring some weird Mamas and

ACE - Five Aside (LP).

Papas-styled harmonies), *Prelude To A Dawn* and *Never Ending Solitude* wasn't exactly mainstream rock, nor did it fall under the banner of **Fairport Convention**-styled folk. Imagine well crafted cocktail jazz with the addition of a touch of English folk (*Ulyssees*) and you'll get a feel for the LP. While that doesn't sound like a ringing endorsement, the result is actually a fascinating album that bears up to repeated plays. Abba's only contribution, the bluesy *Nature Boy* and the surprisingly hard rocking *Gospel Song*, are particularly noteworthy.

Following a shake-up of personnel that saw singer/guitarist Gordon Giltrap leave, the band returned with 1971's *Accolade 2*. Again produced by Don Paul, the band's sophomore effort was actually far stronger than the debut. With **Partridge** continuing to serve as chief writer (he's credited with six of the ten songs), his contributions were far more varied than on the first album. Musically the set was pretty entertaining, mixing acoustic folk and jazzy touches with occasional slices of more pop and rock-oriented material. Highlights included the opener *Transworld Blues* with its lyrics in six (!) languages, the surprisingly taunt rocker *The Spider To The Spy* (sporting inept harmony vocals), the bizarre *Cross Continental Pandemonium Theatre Company* and *William Taplin* which is a moving account of a man grown old. This is one of those albums that rewards patience. The first time around it doesn't sound like anything special, but with repeatedly play, it grows on you.

Malcolm Poole had been in **The Artwoods** and Gordon Giltrap went on to achieve solo success with acoustic-based material. (MK/SB)

Ace (1)

Personnel:	PAUL CARRACK	keyb'ds, vcls	ABCD
	TERRY 'TEX' COMER	bs, vcls	ABCD
	PHIL HARRIS	gtr, vcls	ABC
	BAM KING	gtr, vcls	ABCD
	STEVE WITHERINGTON	drms	A
	CHICO GREENWOOD	drms	B
	FRAN BYRNE	drms	CD
	JON WOODHEAD	gtr, vcls	D

ALBUMS: 1(C)   FIVE ASIDE   (Anchor ANCL 2001) 1974
            2(C)   TIME FOR ANOTHER   (Anchor ANCL 2013) 1975
            3(D)   NO STRINGS   (Anchor ANCL 2020) 1977
            4(-)   SIX ASIDE (Compilation)   (Polydor 2478 159) 1982
NB: (1) reissued on CD (Document CSAP CD 103) 1990. A later compilation is *The Best Of Ace* (See For Miles SEE 214 / SEE CD 214) 1988. Alternatively *How Long: The Best Of Ace* (Music Club MCCD 123) 1993 only duplicates seven songs from the earlier See For Miles collection.

HCP
45s: How Long/Sniffin' About   (Anchor ANC 1002) 1974 20
       I Ain't Gonna Stand For This/
       Rock And Roll Runaway   (Anchor ANC 1014) 1975 -
       No Future In Your Eyes/I'm A Man   (Anchor ANC 1024) 1975 -

3

You're All That I Need/Crazy World	(Anchor ANC 1036) 1977 -	
Found Out The Hard Way/		
Why Did You Leave Me	(Anchor ANC 1040) 1977 -	

Reissues: How Long/

I'm Not Taking It Out On You	(Polydor POSP 416) 1982 -	
How Long/(Flip by different artist)	(Old Gold OG 9392) 1984 -	
How Long/You're All That I Need	(Old Gold OG 9731) 1987 -	

Ace were formed by ex-**Action** member Alan 'Bam' King in December 1972. Tex Comer and Paul Carrack had previously played with **Warm Dust**. After earlier incarnations as Clat Thyger and Ace Flash and The Dynamoes, they finally settled for calling themselves simply **Ace**. They started playing on the pub circuit and their young drummer Steve Witherington was soon replaced by Chico Greenwood. They got a record deal with the new Anchor label in the late Summer of 1974 at which point Greenwood departed to be replaced by Fran Byrne from **Bees Make Honey**. They started work on an album and *How Long*, a gentle soulful classic culled from it reached No 20 in the UK Charts later in 1974 and topped the US Charts the following year. It would prove to be their finest moment and their only UK hit single. Their *Five A Side* album sold very well in the States - the two subsequent ones less so and they split in the Summer of 1977 with Carrack, Comer and Byrne all going on to play for **Frankie Miller**. Paul Carrack was subsequently involved in several other ventures.

The See For Miles compilation (available on album and CD) is a 14-track selection which confirms *How Long* as their finest moment but has several other high spots if mid-seventies pub-rock is your scene with *You're All That I Need* and *Time Ain't Long* among them.

Compilation appearances include: *How Long* on *Your Starter For Ten!!* (CD). (VJ)

Ace (2)

45:	Speed Freak/Aces Of Spades	(Decca F 13216) 1971

This was actually Barry Richards from Norwich where his father ran a garage. He owned a Harley Davidson and was leader of the Ace Angels, 40 leather boys. The record was said to be about a Norwegian woman who belonged to the Ace Angels. (VJ)

The Aces

Personnel:	ADRIAN GATIE	drms	A
	BRIAN GATIE	gtr	A
	ERIC LEE	gtr, hrmnca, vcls	A
	JOHN PATTERSON	bs	A

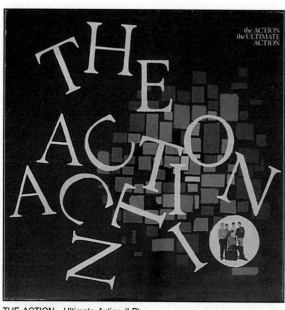

THE ACTION - Ultimate Action (LP).

THE ACTION - 16 Slices Of (LP).

45s:	Wait Until Tomorrow/	
	The Last One	(Parlophone R 5094) 1963 SC
	I Count The Tears/	
	But Say It Isn't So	(Parlophone R 5108) 1964 SC

This beat group was from Hull. Their second 45 was a Drifters number. (VJ/DD)

Aches and Pains

45:	There's No One Like Your Mother/	
	Again And Again	(Page One POF 008) 1966 SC

An obscure beat 45, from a London group. It was quite catchy. (VJ)

Acid Gallery

Personnel:	MIKE BLAKELY	drms, backing vcls	A
	VIC ELMES	lead gtr, lead vcls	A
	IAN JANSEN	gtr, backing vcls	A
	ALAN ROSS	bs	A

45:	Dance Around The Maypole/	
	Right Toe Blues	(CBS 4608) 1967 R1

The name may sound encouraging but don't be misled. The 45 is popish and disappointing. Not recommended but it has become collectable, because of **Roy Wood**'s (**Move**)'s involvement. This band had evolved out of **The Epics** and later became **Christie** of *Yellow River* fame. The 'A' side was written and produced by **Roy Wood** who also provided backing vocals along with Jeff Lynne.

See **The Epics** entry for further details.

You can also find *Dance Around The Maypole* on *Rubble Vol. 10* (CD), *The Best Of Rubble Collection, Vol. 2* (CD) and on the 4-CD *Nuggets 11* box set. (VJ)

The Act (1)

Personnel:	JOHN DENNIS	ld gtr	A
	MICHAEL GANGHAM	bs	A
	BRIAN PATTON	vcls	A
	DAVID SIMPSON	drms	A

45s:	Cobbled Streets/One Heart	(Columbia DB 8179) 1967 R1
	Here Come Those Tears Again/	

Without You	(Columbia DB 8261) 1967 SC
Just A Little Bit/	
Remedies Of Doctor Brohnicoy	(Columbia DB 8331) 1968 R1

An Essex-based beat group who were signed to Columbia for whom they recorded three 45s. None of them made much impression and they split in 1968 after being dropped by the label. Like **Game** showbiz personality **Kenny Lynch** took them under his own wing. Judging by their 3rd credible-enough mod-influenced 45, they must have sounded rather dated by 1968. The flip side was basically straight-forward pop.

Compilation appearances have included:- *I Just A Little Bit* on *Rubble Vol. 13*, *Freakbeat Fantoms* (LP), *Rubble Vol. 7* (CD) and *The Best Of Rubble Collection, Vol. 4* (CD); *Remedies Of Doctor Brohnicoy* on *Rubble Vol. 17*, *A Trip In A Painted World* (LP), *Rubble Vol. 10* (CD) and *The Best Of Rubble Collection, Vol. 6* (CD); and *Cobbled Streets* on *Justafixation II* (LP). (VJ)

The Act (2)

Personnel:	STUART ALDOUS	drms	A
	PAUL CRIBB	vcls	A
	DAVE FROMONT	bs	A
	DAVE RICHARDS	gtr	A
	ADRIAN TYNDALE	ld gtr	A

| EP: | 1(A) | THE ACT | (Oak Acetate EP RGJ 407) 1965 R3 |

A school outfit from Mitcham in South London who recorded a rather primitive five-track acetate EP for Oak. One of the tracks from it, *I Turn To Love You*, a rather amateurish harmony-pop effort, can also be heard on *Story Of Oak Records* (2-LP). When they split-up in March 1967, **Kenny Lynch**, who managed another slightly better-known Mitcham group, **Game** launched another group called **The Act** on Columbia. (VJ)

The Action

Personnel:	MIKE EVANS	bs	ABC
	ALAN BAM KING	gtr	ABC
	REG KING	vcls	ABC
	ROGER POWELL	drms	ABC
	PETE WATSON	gtr	A
	MARTIN STONE	gtr	BC
	IAN WHITEMAN	piano	C

ALBUMS:	1(A)	THE ULTIMATE ACTION	(Edsel ED 101) 1980 SC
	2( )	ACTION SPEAKS LOUDER THAN	
			(Castle DOJOLP 3) 1985 SC
	3(C)	BRAIN (THE LOST RECORDINGS)	
			(Autumn Stone Archives ASACD 01 /DIG005) 1996
	4(C)	ROLLED GOLD	(Dig The Fuzz DIG 025) 1998
	5( )	16 SLICES OF	(Carnaby Records CY 004) 2001

NB: (1) reissued on CD (Edsel CD 101) in 1990 with additional cuts. (2) is a five track 12". (4) is a reissue of (3), but taken from the mastertapes. (4) also issued on CD (Dig The Fuzz DISCD 01) 1998. *Rolled Gold* (Reaction REACT CD 001) 2002 is a remastered version of (3) and (4) from the mono mastertape with one bonus cut. *Uptight And Outasight* (Circle) 2005 is a 2-CD set with old live sessions on one disc and a late nineties live set on the other.

45s:	Land Of One Thousand Dances/	
	In My Lonely Room	(Parlophone R 5354) 1965 R2
	I'll Keep On Holding On/	
	Hey Sah-Lo-Ney	(Parlophone R 5410) 1966 R2
	Baby You've Got It/	
	Since I Lost My Baby	(Parlophone R 5474) 1966 R2
	Never Ever/Twenty Fourth Hour	(Parlophone R 5572) 1967 R2
	Shadows And Reflections/	
	Something Has Hit Me	(Parlophone R 5610) 1967 R2
Reissues:	I'll Keep Holding On/Wasn't It You (PS)	(Edsel E 5001) 1981
	Since I Lost My Baby/	
	Never Ever/Wasn't It You (PS)	(Edsel E 5002) 1981
	Shadows And Reflections/	
	Something Has Hit Me (PS)	(Edsel E 5003) 1981
	Hey Sah-Lo-Ney/	

| Come On, Come With Me (PS) | (Edsel E 5008) 1984 |

NB: They also recorded a German-only 45, *Harlem Shuffle/Wasn't It You* (Hansa 14 321 AT), whose flip side is highly rated.

The Action were one of the finest bands that **George Martin** signed to EMI in the mid-sixites. It's ironic that they never achieved a hit record when many lesser bands did.

Action were formed in 1963. They were previously known as **The Boys**, and under that name had also backed Sandra Barry on a 45. Based around the Kentish Town area of London they played an amalgam of R&B and high quality soul (in their later days). They enjoyed a strong mod following.

The Edsel compilation is a fine amalgam of British pop and soul. It includes all five of their Parlophone 45s, which range from powerhouse R&B (*I'll Keep On Holding On*), through excellent pop-soul (*Shadows And Reflections, Never Ever*) to the soul ballad (*Since I Lost My Baby*). Containing previously unissued cuts too, it is essential listening.

Watson left in 1966 to be replaced by Martin Stone, who was previously with the **Savoy Brown Blues Band** and **Stone's Masonry**. Ian Whiteman joined on piano in mid-1967. He had been on the **Ben Carruthers and The Deep** 45. They were thrown off EMI before their last planned 45, *Little Girl*, could be released. They taped lots of material for Giorgio Gomelsky. Martin Stone was in and out of the band in this era. In mid-1968, without **Reggie King**, who'd left to go solo and having briefly toyed with the name Azoth, they taped the Whiteman-dominated demos, which were issued belatedly on Dojo in 1985. These have a soft, West Coast psychedelic feel with very pleasant harmonies. In 1969 they evolved into **Mighty Baby**. Bam King was also later in **Ace**. Most of **The Action** returned for **Reggie King**'s eventual solo album.

Brain - The Lost Recordings features a series of demos from a shelved 1967 album project as the band gets to grips with psychedelia. The 15 tracks of demos, were mainly recorded at Polydor and Advision studios in '67/'68. The original release suffered from very poor sound quality. It was remastered and briefly reissued by Dig The Fuzz as *Rolled Gold* in 1998. More recently Reaction have remastered from the mono mastertape and added *In My Dreams* (arranged by George Martin as a bonus cut). There are sleevenotes from Alan 'Bam' King and Rhino archivist Andrew Sandoval and overall this is a fascinating psychedelic archive.

Compilation appearances have included: *Baby You've Got It* on *My Generation* (LP); *Land Of 1000 Dances* on *R&B At Abbey Road* (CD); and *Wasn't It You* on *Broken Dreams, Vol. 5* (LP). *Dustbin Full Of Rubbish* (LP) meanwhile gave an airing to *Brain* and *Little Boy*, two tracks from their shelved 1967 album project. *Shadows & Reflections* resurfaced on the *Nuggets 11* box set.

In 1985, Castle Communications issued a strange five-track 12" item, *Action Speaks Louder Than Words*. The cover was a tinted version of the

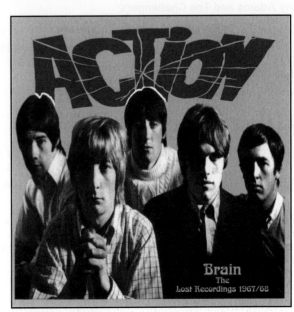

THE ACTION - Brain (CD).

Edsel insert. All five tracks were written by Ian Whiteman and comprise the floating, progressive music that **Mighty Baby** are remembered for. The likelihood is that they were demos dating from 1968 just before **Mighty Baby** got a deal with Head Records. The record company probably used the **Action** name because they were better known due to the Edsel reissues.

Uptight And Outasight is a live 2-CD set. The first disc collects their radio sessions for 'Saturday Club' and 'Pop North' during 1966 and 1967. There are good self-penned compositions here like *Never Ever* and *Love Is All* as well as superb covers like *Land Of 1,000 Dances* and *I'll Keep Holding On*. The second disc features a concert from the reformed band at the Boston Arms, London in 1998. It shows they can still hit the right buttons. (VJ)

The Actress

45:	It's What You Give/		
	Good Job With Prospects	(CBS 4016) 1969 R2	

This is now a collectable 45 but who were they? Both sides of the 45 were produced by Eddie Tre-Vett. *It's What You Give* is OK, but it's *Good Job With Prospects* that really excites fans of UK psychedelia with its strong vocals and superb guitar work.

Compilation appearances have included: *It's What You Give* on *Perfumed Garden Vol. 3* (CD); and *Good Job With Prospects* on *Circus Days Vol. 3* (LP & CD). (VJ)

Adam, Mike and Tim

Personnel:	TIM SAUNDERS (TIM)	vcls	A
	MIKE SEDGEWICK (MIKE)	vcls	A
	PETER SEDGEWICK (ADAM)	vcls	A

45s:	Little Baby/You're The Reason Why	(Decca F 12040) 1964
	That's How I Feel/It's All Too True	(Decca F 12112) 1965
	Little Pictures/Summer's Here Again	(Decca F 12221) 1965
	Flowers On The Wall/	
	Give That Girl A Break	(Columbia DB 7836) 1966
	A Most Peculiar Man/Wedding Day	(Columbia DB 7902) 1966

A Liverpool trio whose debut disc was an upbeat dance number written by Les Reed and Barry Mason. Subsequent recordings veered towards a folk-pop direction. Their best was *A Most Peculiar Man*, a Paul Simon song, on which they introduced a sitar.

Mike Sedgewick recorded a solo 45 in 1968. (VJ)

Danny Adams and The Challengers

45:	Bye Bye Baby, Bye Bye/	
	I'm So Proud Of You	(Philips BF 1346) 1964

This beat group hailed from Yorkshire. (VJ)

Derroll Adams

ALBUMS:	1	PORTLAND TOWN	(Ace Of Clubs 1227) c1967 R2
	2	FEELIN' FINE	(Village Thing VTS 17) 1973 SC

NB: There is also a German only album: *Movin' On* (Xenepton Ints 161014) 1974.

Adams sang and accompanied himself on banjo. In addition to the German album, *Songs Of The Banjoman* (Folk Freak FF 404016) 1984 contained old tracks from 1972 and 1976 on which he was accompanied by other folk artists like **Ian Anderson**, Maggie Anderson and **Wizz Jones**.

His rare debut album *Portland Town* was produced by **Mike Vernon** and engineered by Gus Dudgeon. (VJ/GB)

The Addicts

45:	That's My Girl/Here She Comes	(Decca F 11902) 1964 R1

This beat group operated out of Widnes in Lancashire.

Compilation appearances include: *That's My Girl* on *Beat Merchants* (2-LP). (VJ)

The Ad Libs

Personnel:	DAVE HARVEY	drms	A
	JOHN PAGE	organ	A
	STEVE RANCE	bs	A
	MIKE WARD	vcls, gtr	A
	TONY ?	conga drums	A
	(BOBBY WELLINS?	sax	A)

45:	Neighbour Neighbour/Lovely Ladies	(Fontana TF 584) 1965 R1

Another collectable one-off 45. Founded by Steve Rance, **The Ad Libs** line-up remained constant during their time together. Steve Rance:- "A manager who shall remain nameless saw us playing in the Zambesi Club in Earls Court sometime during 1963/64 and offered us a residency in the Ad Lib club just off Leicester Square. This was at the time of the top society club in the West End, with clientele such as the **Beatles**, **Stones** etc. and many film stars and actors. It was very expensive - I remember whisky and coke (the 'in' drink) was ten shillings a shot!"

"We changed our name to the **Ad Libs** (not to be confused with the American 'Adlibs') and did two sets a night, six nights a week at the club for a year or so, with a break for a few weeks whilst extra soundproofing was installed. The resident DJ, who sat behind a grand piano in which his record decks were installed, was a ultra-hip black guy who had access to all the latest American soul imports. At this time American record labels were desperate to sign British groups, and we were offered a deal by, I think it was Mercury. The club DJ lent us some LP's, from one of which we chose *Neighbour, Neighbour* and *Lovely Ladies*."

"When the record was released in this country on Fontana it was played on radio several times and we performed it live on the 'Club Edition' of 'Ready Steady, Go' on ITV. It got some good reviews, but everything came to a grinding halt when our manager disappeared with the fee from ITV, which I think was about £240. Shortly after this the Ad Lib club closed down permanently because of noise problems and the band split up."

"Mike Ward and I joined **Julian Covey and the Machine** for a while, and Dave Harvey played with **Them**. I haven't seen or heard of the others since 1965, but I am still playing on the Isle of Wight."

The sax solo on their sole record was played by a well known jazz session player, who Steve thinks might have been Bobby Wellins. (VJ/SR)

AFFINITY - Affinity (LP).

The Admirals

45:     Promised Land/Palisades Park   (Fontana TF 597) 1965 R1

A four-piece beat group from Stockport. The 'B' side was produced by Joe Meek.

Compilation appearances include: *In The Promised Land* on *Psychedelic Voyage Vol. 1* (LP) and *Psychedelic Voyage* (CD). (VJ)

Aerovons

Personnel incl:	TOM HARTMAN	gtr	A
	BILL LOMBARDO	bs	A
	MIKE LOMBARDO	perc	A

| 45s: | The Train/A Song For Jane | (Parlophone R 5790) 1969 R1 |
| | World Of You/Say Georgia | (Parlophone R 5804) 1969 R2 |

The Aerovons were actually from St. Louis, Missouri, but did all their recording in the UK. Their *World Of You*, is a magnificent orchestrated **Beatle**-pop moment. An album was recorded for Parlophone, but remains officially unissued, although test pressings still exist and a band-authorised counterfeit appeared some time ago, with an accompanying booklet detailing their history and containing photographs.

The band apparently sat in on some **Beatles** sessions (they sometimes sneaked one or two of their guitars out to take a photo with them but any rumours that they made off with their gear are unfounded - Tom Hartman tells us).

World Of You later resurfaced on *Fading Yellow* (CD). (GW/TH/VJ/RMJ)

A Fair Set

Personnel:	DENNIS McKEITH (KEITH DENNIS?)	bs	A
	KEITH McKENNA	drms	A
	MOORE		A
	WRIGHT		A

| 45: | Honey And Wine/Runaround | (Decca F 12168) 1965 |

A little known act that later became **The Caesers**. *Honey And Wine* is a reasonable, cheerie harmony pop effort. The flip sounds rather like a poor person's **Searchers**. (VJ/JM)

The Afex

| 45: | She's Got The Time/ | |
| | I Never Knew Love Was Like This | (King KG 1058) 1967 R2 |

The 'A' side to this 45, *She's Got The Time*, had previously been recorded by an obscure US band called The Poor. **The Afex** version is better and its mod feel has helped make it sought-after by collectors of freakbeat.

Compilation appearances include: *She's Got The Time* on *Rubble, Vol. 17 - A Trip In A Painted World* (LP), *Rubble, Vol. 10* (CD), *The Best Of Rubble Collection, Vol. 2* (CD) and *Electric Sugarcube Flashbacks, Vol. 2* (LP). (VJ)

Affinity

Personnel:	MO FOSTER	bs	A
	LINDA HOYLE	vcls	A
	MIKE JOPP	gtr	A
	LYNTON NAIFF	keyb'ds	A
	GRANT SERPALL	drms	A

| ALBUM: | 1(A) | AFFINITY | (Vertigo 6360 004) 1970 R2 |

NB: (1) issued on Paramount (PAS 5027) in the US. (1) reissued on CD (Repertoire REP 4349-WP) 1993 along with both sides of their 45 and again on CD (Angel Air SJPCD 111) 2001. *Live Instrumentals 1969* (Angel Air SJPCD 135) 2002 comprises a selection of instrumentals from gigs when **Linda Hoyle** was unable to sing after a throat operation. *Origins 65-67* (Angel Air SJPCD 167) 2004 explores the roots of the band at Sussex University.

45s:	I Wonder If I Care As Much/	
	Three Sisters	(Vertigo 6059 007) 1970 SC
α	Eli's Coming/United States Of Mind	(Vertigo 6059 018) 1970

NB: α credited to **Affinity** and **Linda Hoyle**.

Affinity was basically a blues-rock band with jazz influences. The music is very brassy and a bit like **Julie Driscoll** without soul. At least one beautiful atmospheric ballad *Night Flight* lightens the proceedings. They also slaughter Bob Dylan's *All Along The Watchtower*, while the non-album 45 falls short of Laura Nyro's original. **Linda Hoyle** recorded a blue-eyed blues album later on for Vertigo. Her vocals on the **Affinity** album have led some to regard the band as a British Jefferson Airplane.

They also recorded a 10" one-sided EMI disc acetate in 1969, when they formed out of the ashes of **The Ice**, in an attempt to win a recording contract. It featured three tracks - an amazing version of *I Am The Walrus* and the self-penned *You Met Your Match* and a different version of *All Along The Watchtower* to the one recorded a year later for their Vertigo album. It is bound to interest UK psychedelia fans.

Organist Lynton Naiff later played with **Toe Fat** and **Killing Floor**. In 1972 **Affinity** reformed, becoming **Mike D'Abo**'s backing band and performing on his *Down At Rachel's Place* album. Grant Serpall later ended up in **Sailor**.

Live Instrumentals 1969 comprises a selection of instrumentals from gigs when **Linda Hoyle** was unable to sing after an operation on her vocal chords. On offer are a number of jazz-prog instrumentals and a restructured instrumental version of **The Beatles** magnum opus *A Day In The Life*. Not an essential purchase unless you're heavily into jazz-prog.

They also had a track, *Three Sisters*, included on the *Vertigo Annual* (LP) compilation, but it's nothing special. (MK/VJ)

Agincourt

Personnel:	JOHN FERDINANDO	A
	PETER HOWELL	A
	LEE MENELAUS	A

| ALBUM: | 1(A) | FLY AWAY | (Merlin HF 3) 1970 R4 |

NB: (1) reissued on CD (Background HBG 123/6) 1994.

An ultra-rare privately-pressed album by the same group of people responsible for **Alice Through The Looking Glass**, **Ithaca** and **Tomorrow Come Some Day**.

AGINCOURT - Fly Away (CD).

AGNES STRANGE - Strange Flavour (LP).

This particular album is folkier than **Ithaca**, for example, but like the latter still has a strong **Moody Blues** influence, particularly on the best track *Through The Eyes Of A Lifetime*, which begins with a poem and ends with some lovely piano-dominated instrumentation. The opening cut *When I Awoke* is a very pleasant folky number with some lovely female vocals. Next up is *Though I May Be Dreaming*, which has a gorgeous acoustic guitar intro and more delicious female vocals. There's some nice flute work on instrumental *Joy In The Finding, Dawn* and *Kind Sir. All My Life* is a pleasant piano-led piece with a spooky sounding ending. All the material is written by either Ferdinando or Howell and whilst I'd be reluctant to recommend people to fork out hundreds on the album, the CD reissue is essential for fans of progressive folk. (VJ)

Agnes Strange

Personnel:	ALAN GREEN	bs	A
	DAVE RODWELL	drms	A
	JOHN WESTWOOD	gtr, vcls	A

ALBUM: 1(A) STRANGE FLAVOUR (Birds Nest BRL 9000) 1975 R2
NB: (1) reissued in the late eighties.

45s:	Clever Fool/Give Yourself A Chance	(Birds Nest BN1) 1975
	Can't Make Up My Mind /	
	Johnny B. Goode	(Baal BDN 38048) 1977

This bluesy hard-rock combo out of Southampton recorded an album, which is very sought-after by some. The small Birds Nest label was distributed by Pye and their second 45 was also on a Pye subsidiary label although strictly outside the book's time frame, both cuts are non-album and very rare. (VJ)

Airborne

| Personnel: | GERRY O'REGAN | gtr, hrmnca, kazoo | A |
| | ERIC WALES | gtr, mandolin | A |

45s:	Give It Up/Emily Jane	(Tiffany 6121 502) 1974
	Someone/Caroline	(Tiffany 6121 503) 1974
	Tell Me When/Goodbye Melanie	(RCA 2515) 1975

This electric folk duo came from Edinburgh. They formed around April 1972. The RCA 45 could be by a different band. (VJ)

The A-Jaes

| Personnel: | CHRISTOPHER MARCHANT | bs | A |
| | ALLEN RIMES | gtr | A |

	JOHN STEVENS	ld gtr	A
	STANLEY VILE	drms	A
	TONY WHITE	vcls	A

45: I'm Leaving You/Kansas City (Oak RGJ 132) 1964 R5

The 'A' side of this group's sole 45 - a good beat/R&B effort, was written by the band's vocalist Tony White and released back in 1964. It is extremely rare and copies change hands now for circa £1,000. Far worse recordings got a major label release at the time. In 1967 the group evolved into Candy Bus.

I'm Leaving You has been compiled on *Story Of Oak Records* (2-LP) and *The Story Of Oak Records* (CD). (VJ)

Albion Country Band

Personnel:	STEVE ASHLEY	gtr, vcls	A
	SUE DRAHEIM	fiddle	A
	ASHLEY HUTCHINGS	bs	ABC
	DAVE MATTACKS	drms	A
	SIMON NICOL	gtr, vcls	ABC
	ROYSTON WOOD	vcls	A
	SHIRLEY COLLINS	vcls, banjo	B
	ROGER SWALLOW	drms	BC
	LINDA THOMPSON	vcls	B
	RICHARD THOMPSON	gtr, vcls	B
	MARTIN CARTHY	gtr, vcls	C
	SUE HARRIS	vcls, oboe, dulcimer	C
	JOHN KIRKPATRICK	accordion, vcls, pi	C

ALBUM: 1(C) BATTLE OF THE FIELD (Island HELP 25) 1976

This outfit was formed by **Ashley Hutchings** after he left **Steeleye Span**. It was initially formed in April 1972 with the line-up including several folkies, but Mattacks was soon recruited from **Fairport Convention**. They were a popular attraction at colleges, universities and folk festivals and later in the year when the initial line-up split, the folk duo **Richard and Linda Thompson** were added. **Shirley Collins** was also briefly a member. They eventually packed up in August 1973 'cause they couldn't make a living, but their album was released retrospectively to satisfy demand from their fans. It had been recorded by line-up (C) but then shelved. **Hutchings** later played with **Shirley Collins** in The Etchingham Steam Band and then with Dave Mattacks in The Albion Dance Band, who fall outside the time frame of this book.

Steve Ashley also made some solo recordings. (VJ)

Alco

See **Threads Of Life**.

Steve Aldo and The Challengers

Personnel:	STEVE ALDO	vcls	A
	JOHN BEDSON	drms	A
	ROBIN GILMORE	lead gtr	A
	RAY PAWSON	bs	A
	PETE WILSON	gtr	A

NB: Other personnel included:- Tommy (Quickly) Quigley (vcls), Pat Quigley (vcls), Ray Shaw (vcls), Ian Bailey (drms) and Nobby Del Rosa (vcls).

45s:	Can I Get A Witness/	
	Baby What You Want Me To Do	(Decca F 12041) 1964 R2
α	Everybody Has To Cry/	
	You're Absolutely Right	(Parlophone R 5432) 1966 R3

NB: α **Steve Aldo** solo.

Both these 45s are now quite sought-after. **Aldo** was on the fringes of Merseybeat, though his first single is in a Tamla Motown vein. In fact both cuts are Marvin Gaye covers. The second 45, a solo effort, was pretty soulful. He was also briefly a vocalist with **The Fairies** in 1966 but didn't sing on any of their three 45s which predated his involvement.

Compilation appearances include: *Baby What You Want Me To Do* on *The Mod Scene* (CD), *English Freakbeat Vol. 6* (CD) and *Baby What You Want Me To Do* on *Pebbles, Vol. 6* (LP). (VJ/AD)

Clem Alford

ALBUMS: 1 MIRROR IMAGE - THE ELECTRONIC SITAR OF
            CLEM ALFORD   (Columbia SCX 6571) 1974 R1
         2 MUSIC LIBRARY ALBUM   (KPM) 1975 R1

NB: (1) reissued on CD as *Mirror Image - The Electronic Sitar Of Clem Alford*, with additional material (Magic Carpet MC 1003 CD) 1990.

Clem Alford was a classically-trained sitar player who spent time in India to enhance his knowledge of Indian classical music prior to joining the interesting but short-lived **Magic Carpet** in the early seventies. Upon their demise he recorded two solo albums of sitar music which are not easy to track down. The first is now a collector's item, and has been reissued on CD with additional material. The second, which is even harder to find, was recorded exclusively for use in music libraries. Prior to this in 1972 he'd recorded an album under the name **Sagram**.

In 1996, he teamed up with **Alisha Sufit** (who'd been the vocalist in **Magic Carpet**) to record *Once Moor* under the name Magic Carpet II, although none of the other original members of the band were involved in this project. (VJ)

Alice Through The Looking Glass

Personnel: JOHN FERNANDO   A
              PETER HOWELL   A

ALBUM: 1(A) ALICE THROUGH THE LOOKING GLASS
                                    (SNP no #) 1969 R5

NB: (1) has been counterfeited and also reissued officially on Tenth Planet (TP 032) 1997.

This concept album based upon the writings of Lewis Carroll was the work of the same persons responsible for **Agincourt**, **Ithaca** and **Tomorrow Come Some Day**. This album is reputedly the best of the four - an amalgam of folk and psychedelia with surrealistic lyrics.

David Wells' excellent sleeve-notes to the recent Tenth Planet reissue reveal more about the duo. In late 1968 they were approached by a local amateur dramatics group called The Ditching Players to provide a musical backdrop for a stage version of 'Alice Through The Looking Glass'. They used Lewis Carroll's surreal verse as the backdrop to the project and added a variety of studio trickery - backwards tapes, sound effects,

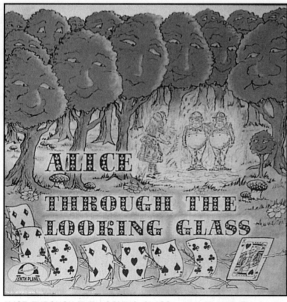

ALICE THROUGH THE LOOKING GLASS - Alice Through The Looking Glass (LP).

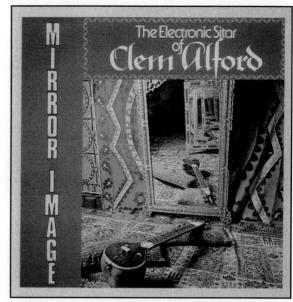

CLEM ALFORD - Mirror Image (The Electronic Sitar Of) (CD).

distorted vocals etc. - to create a uniquely English hybrid of folk and pastoral psychedelia. Fifty copies were pressed initially which sold quickly and the duo pressed a further twenty-thirty. The sleeve artwork utilised a sketch by Sir John Tennel (the original Alice illustrator) of Alice encountering Tweedledee and Tweedledum!

The duo continued to record a number of other albums over the next ten years - **Tomorrow Come Some Day** (a concept piece featuring a village threatened by motorway expansion), *To Fly Away* (credited to semi-ficticious group **Agincourt**) and *A Game For All Who Know* (credited to **Ithaca**). All had limited edition pressings of between fifty to a hundred. After a fifth album *Friends* the collaboration ended when Peter Howell, who composed all the music on *Alice Through The Looking Glass*, was offered a more demanding job at the BBC and ceased to have time to pursue his hobby with John Fernando. (VJ)

Alkatraz

Personnel: JIMMY DAVIES   vcls, gtr   A
              STUART HALLIDAY   drms   A
              JEFF SINGER   bs   A
              WILL YOUATT   gtr, vcls   A

ALBUM: 1(A) DOING A MOONLIGHT   (Rockfield UAS 30001) 1976

45:     Nito Bandito/Nobody Like You   (Rockfield ?) 1976

A Welsh band who formed in October 1975. Halliday and Youatt had both been in **The Neutrons** previously and Jimmy Davies was in **Quicksand**. (JM)

All Day

ALBUM: 1 YORK POP MUSIC PROJECT (Private Pressing) 1973 R3

This is a very rare privately-pressed limited issue album of folk, progressive and electronic music. David Wells tells me it was a compilation of tracks recorded by various students at the University of York, presumably as part of their music studies/thesis, which is why there's so many different musical styles. However, the album's not particularly good overall. (VJ)

Daevid Allen

ALBUMS: 1 BANANA MOON   (Caroline C 1512) 1975 R1
(up to   2 GOOD MORNING!   (Virgin V 2054) 1976
1976)

NB: (2) Credited to Daevid Allen and Euterpe. There's also a French import, *Banana Moon Gong* (Legend KZLM 15051) 1995, which compiles 19 of his previously

DAEVID ALLEN - Banana Moon (LP).

unissued recordings from the late sixties; and two compilations, *The Death Of Rock And Other Entrances* (Voiceprint VP 114CD) 1993 and *Live 1963* (Voiceprint CP 122CD) 1993.

Actually an Australian **Allen** was born in Melbourne in 1938. He was in the first **Soft Machine** line-up and later left to form **Gong**. He also recorded an album in 1971, *Obsolete*, which was credited to Dashiell Hedayat who added the vocals, but which

Daevid Allen's *Banana Moon* album was recorded back in 1971 and released in France on the Byg label. It came out in this country as a budget reissue on Virgin's Caroline subsidiary in 1975. He was helped on the album by Pip Pyle, Christian Tritsch and **Robert Wyatt**. On the album he not only sought to recreate the sound of Paris '68 with lots of improvisations but also produced material more in the mould of early **Soft Machine**.

After leaving **Gong** in April 1975, **Allen** went on to record a series of solo albums on which he was assisted by various bands. The first of these, *Good Morning!* in 1976, was recorded with a Spanish trio called Euterpe. The album comprised mostly acoustic material. Further details of **Allen**'s career with **Gong** and some of his later **Gong**-related projects can be found in the **Gong** entry. (VJ)

Dave Allen and The Exotics

Personnel:	IAN BROAD	drms	A
	BRIAN DANCER	sax	A
	RAY FAULKNER	gtr	A
	DAVE "ALLEN" FELLOWS	vcls	A
	BOB HOPKINS	keyb'ds, sax	A
	MALCOLM RARTRAY	bs	A

EP: 1 Un Hombre Respectable/She Walks/The Monkey/
Sweet Little Rock'n'roller (Hispavox) 1965

NB: (1) Spanish only.

45: The Monkey/Sweet Little Rock'n'roller (Derby DB 5144) 1966

NB: (1) Italian only.

This UK act headed for Spain where they recorded a Spanish language cover of **The Kinks**' *Well Respected Man*. They then moved to Italy where two tracks from the Spanish EP were released before they changed name to **Bigs**. (FB/CR/GB)

The Michael Allen Group

Michael Allen was of Irish descent, born on the Birkenhead side of the Mersey. He was in a band called The Abstracts before he started his own

group. They contributed four tracks: *Telegram, Evenin', I Can't Stand It* and *Trains And Boats And Planes* to *Liverpool Today - Live At The Cavern* (LP). (VJ/L)

Almond Lettuce

45s: The Tree Dog Song/
To Henry With Hope (Columbia DB 8442) 1968
Magic Circle/Twenty Weary Miles (Philips BF 1764) 1969 SC

A late sixties outfit whose two awful singles are often described as psychedelic but seem far from it.

Magic Circle can also be found on *Psychedelic Voyage Vol. 1* (LP) and *Psychedelic Voyage* (CD). (MWh)

Almond Marzipan

Personnel:	RICHARD BAINBRIDGE	sax	A
	PETER BETTIS	bs	A
	ALAN GRAVES	drms	A
	MICK KERR	gtr	A
	DAVE LAWSON	keyb'ds, vcls	A
	DAVE REED	organ	A

45s: Open Up Your Heart/Summer Love (Trend TNT 53) 1970
Marie Take A Chance/I'll Forget You (Trend TNT 55) 1970

This six-piece were **Long John Baldry**'s backing band during 1969/70. Dave Lawson had previously been in **Episode Six**. When Mick Kerr got married in February 1971, **Long John Baldry** was his best man. Lawson was later in **Web**.

Summer Love later resurfaced on *Fading Yellow, Vol 5* (CD). (VJ/JM)

Johnny Almond Music Machine

Personnel:	JIMMY CRAWFORD	gtr	A
	JON MARK	gtr	A
	ROGER SUTTON	bs	A
	ALAN WHITE	drms	A

ALBUMS: 1(A) PATENT PENDING (Deram SML 1043) 1969 SC
2(A) HOLLYWOOD BLUES (Deram SML 1057) 1970 R1

45: Solar Level/To R.K. (Deram DM 266) 1969 SC

A baritone/tenor jazz saxophonist who also played with **John Mayall and The Bluesbreakers** among others. The band played jazz/blues and came from Birmingham. Their producer was **Mike Vernon**. Alan White had drummed for **Alan Price** and Happy Magazine. He later drummed for **Griffin**, **Ginger Baker's Airforce**, Plastic Ono Band and **Balls**. **Johnny Almond** was also in **Zoot Money's Big Roll Band**, **Paul Williams Set** and **The Alan Price Set**. He later formed **Mark-Almond**. (VJ)

Alvyn

45: You've Gotta Have An Image/
Mind The Gap (Morgan Bluetown MR 185) 1969

This obscure 45 made no impact. (VJ)

Amaziah (featuring Derek Elliot)

Personnel:	JEREMY COAD	ld gtr, vcls	A
	DEREK ELLIOT	ld vcls	A
	RICHARD GRINTER	gtr, vcls	A
	PAUL LOADER	bs, vcls	A
	DAVE STEEL	keyb'ds	A
	PHIL WILLIAMS	drms, vcls	A

ALBUM: 1(A) STRAIGHT TALKER   (Sunrise SR 001) 1974 R3 w/insert
NB: (1) reissued in Canada (Tunesmith TS 6002) 1982.

A religious orientated hard-rock album - not really my scene. Musically and lyrically uninteresting. It was recorded in Bristol in the summer of 1979, and is often mistaken for a mid-seventies release. (VJ/JC)

Amazing Blondel

Personnel incl:	JOHN GLADWIN	vcls, gtr, bs	A
	TERRY WINCOTT	vcls, gtr, keyb'ds	AB
	(EDDIE BAIRD	vcls, gtr	AB)

ALBUMS: 1(A)	THE AMAZING BLONDEL AND A FEW FACES		
(up to		(Bell SBLL 131) 1970 R3
1976) 2(A)	EVENSONG	(Island ILPS 9136) 1970 SC
3(A)	FANTASIA LINDUM	(Island ILPS 9156) 1971 SC
4(A)	ENGLAND '72	(Island ILPS 9205) 1972 SC
5(B)	BLONDEL (THE PURPLE ALBUM)	
		(Island ILPS 9257) 1973 SC
6(B)	MULGRAVE STREET	(DJM DJLPS 433) 1974
7(B)	INSPIRATION	(DJM DJLPS 446) 1975
8(B)	BAD DREAMS	(DJM DJLPS 472) 1976

NB: (1) reissued on CD (Edsel EDCD), (2) reissued on CD by Edsel (EDCD 458), (3) reissued on CD by Edsel (EDCD 459) and (5) reissued on CD by Edsel (EDCD 460). *Going Where The Music Takes Me* (Shakedown SHAKEBX 1272) 2005 is a 2-CD anthology with a DVD.

45s:	Alleluia/Safety In God Alone	(Island WIP 6153) 1972
(up to	Be So Happy/Queen	(DJM DJS 10407) 1975
1976)	I'll Go The Way I Came/Liberty Belle	(DJM DJS 10661) 1976
	Mulgrave Street/	
	Sad To See You Go/Hole In The Head	(DJM DJX 503) 1976

This folk band was from Scunthorpe in Lincolnshire. Gladwin, Wincott and Baird had all previously played in an obscure band called **Methuselah**, whose sole album had appeared on Elektra in the US only in 1969. **Amazing Blondel** were notable for the use of several medieval instruments (krumhorns, lute, theorbo, dulcimers, flute, harpsichord, mellotron, tabor, cittern tubular, bells, glockenspiel and more) on their handful of albums for Island and DJM. Their very rare debut effort for Bell was an amalgam of folk and psychedelia on which *Saxon Lady* was the standout track.

Going Where The Music Takes Me compiles their music after they parted company with Island. Their beautiful vocal harmonies are evidenced on the tracks from a live gig at Croydon's Fairfield Hall, which is released for the first time. *Leaving Of A Country Love* stands out on this. The DVD consists of the band being interviewed telling their story.

The band reformed in the nineties recording three further albums: *English Musicke* (1993), *A Foreign Field That Is Forever England, Live Abroad* (1996) and *Restoration* (1997).

AMBROSE SLADE - Beginnings (LP).

Island's 1971 compilation *El Pea* included *Spring Season*, another of the band's better efforts. This is soft acoustic, melodic folk with harmony vocals. (VJ)

Amazing Friendly Apple

45: Water Woman/Magician   (Decca F 12887) 1969 R2

A one-off venture by an unknown group. The 45 was produced by **Tony Meehan**. The 'A' side, *Water Woman*, was taken from Spirit's first album. The flip is really a crossover between psychedelia and progressivism. The vocal style is quite commercial, the hammond organ is very much in the style of **The Nice** and the free-form saxophone definitely heralds the new progressive era.

Compilation appearances have included: *Magician* on *The British Psychedelic Trip 1966 - 1969* (LP), *The Great British Psychedelic Trip, Vol. 1* (CD) and the 4-CD box set, *Acid Drops, Spacedust & Flying Saucers*; and *Water Woman* on *British Psychedelic Trip, Vol. 4* (LP) and *Great British Psychedelic Trip, Vol. 2* (CD). (VJ)

Amber

Personnel:	MARTIN BERRY	bs	A
	DAVID GIBB	drms	A
	MIKE READ	gtr, vcls	A
	ALAN SMITH	gtr, vcls	A

This group is most notable for being future Radio DJ **Mike Read**'s first. They were together for about six months in 1968 and in this time cut three acetates at R.J. Jones' Oak Record's Morden studio. All three were recently brought to a wider audience by virtue of their inclusion on *Syde Trips, Vol. 2* (LP). *Time And Tide* was quite poppy, but *Yellow And Red* was rockier with some promising psychedelic guitar work from **Read**, while *Shirley* was more in the mould of The Loving Spoonful. *Yellow And Red*, the best of the three, can also be heard on *Story Of Oak Records* (2-LP) and *The Story Of Oak Records* (CD). **Mike Read** had earlier made solo recordings and was later in **The Lost** and **Just Plain Smith**. (VJ)

Ambrose Slade

Personnel:	DAVE HILL	gtr	A
	NODDY HOLDER	gtr, vcls	A
	JIM LEA	bs, violin	A
	DON POWELL	drms	A

| ALBUMS: 1(A) | BEGINNINGS | (Fontana STL 5492) 1969 R3 |
| 2(A) | BEGINNINGS OF SLADE | (Contour 6870 678) 1975 R1 |

NB: (2) was a reissue album, which was quickly withdrawn. (1) reissued on CD (Polydor 849 185-2) in 1991.

45: Genesis/Roach Daddy   (Fontana TF 1015) 1969 R3

Formed in the Wolverhampton area and originally known as **The In-Be-Tweens**, they started out as a cover band but were then 'discovered' by manager Chas Chandler. Their early image was of a skinhead group but after these recordings they shortened their name to **Slade** and the rest is history. Needless to say **Ambrose Slade**'s recorded output changes hands for hefty sums despite its mediocrity. Their *Genesis* 45 recalls **Fleetwood Mac's** *Albatross*, but interspersed with louder, phased segments. Their album includes cover versions of Steppenwolf's *Born To Be Wild*, The Amboy Dukes' *Journey To The Center Of The Mind* and Zappa's *Ain't Got No Heart*. (VJ)

Amen Corner

Personnel:	DENNIS BYRON	drms	A
	ANDY FAIRWEATHER-LOW	vcls	A
	ALLAN JONES	sax	A
	NEIL JONES	ld gtr	A
	MIKE SMITH	sax	A
	CLIVE TAYLOR	bs	A
	BLUE WEAVER	organ	A

ALBUMS: 1(A) ROUND AMEN CORNER
                        (Deram DML/SML 1021) 1968 SC 26
      2(A) EXPLOSIVE COMPANY (NATIONAL WELSH
            COAST LIVE)   (Immediate IMSP 023) 1969 SC 19
      3(A) FAREWELL TO THE REAL MAGNIFICENT SEVEN
                    (Immediate IMSP 028) 1969 SC -
      4(A) WORLD OF AMEN CORNER (Compilation)
                    (Decca SPA 33) 1969 -
      5(A) RETURN OF THE MAGNIFICENT SEVEN
                    (Immediate IM 1004) 1976 -
      6(A) GREATEST HITS   (Immediate IM 2004) 1978 -

NB: (1) reissued on CD (Deram 820 918-2) 1990, with four additional cuts. (2) reissued on CD (Repertoire REP 4227-WY) 1993 with eight previously unissued bonus tracks. (3) reissued on CD (Repertoire REP 4291-WY) 1993 also with several bonus tracks. *The Best Of Amen Corner* (Repertoire REP 4819-WG) 1999 is a compilation of their post-Deram hits and selective album cuts. *If Paradise Was Half As Nice - The Immediate Anthology* (Immediate CMDDD 056) 2001 is a collection, which only covers their Immediate material. *The Collection* (Spectrum 544 630 2) 2002 is a budget priced compilation, but does not cover their output for Immediate.

45s: Gin House Blues/I Know   (Deram DM 136) 1967 12
       The World Of Broken Hearts/Nema   (Deram DM 151) 1967 26
       Bend Me, Shape Me/
       Satisnek The Job's Worth   (Deram DM 172) 1968 3
       High In The Sky/Run, Run, Run   (Deram DM 197) 1968 6
       The World Of Broken Hearts/
       Gin House Blues   (Deram DM 228) 1969 -
       (If Paradise Is) Half As Nice/
       Hey Hey Girl   (Immediate IM 073) 1969 1
       Hello Susie/Evil Man's Gonna Win (Immediate IM 081) 1969 4
       Get Back/
       Farewell To The Magnificent Seven (Immediate IM 084) 1969 -
α So Fine   (Immediate AS 3) 1969 SC -
Reissues: High In The Sky/Gin House   (Decca F 13634) 1976 -
       (If Paradise Is) Half As Nice/
       When We Make Love   (Immediate IMS 103) 1976 34
       (If Paradise Is) Half As Nice/Bend Me Shape Me/
       Hello Susie/High In The Sky (dbl 7") (PS)
                    (Immediate SV 104) 1976 -
       Bend Me Shape Me/High In The Sky/Gin House Blues/
       The World Of Broken Hearts (PS)   (Decca F 13897) 1980 -
       Bend Me Shape Me/Gin House   (Old Gold OG 9354) 1983 -
       (If Paradise Is) Half As Nice/
       Hello Susie   (Old Gold OG 9469) 1985 -

NB: α This was a 'promo-only' single sampler for their second album.

Forming in Cardiff in 1967 **Amen Corner** enjoyed a hit with the slow, bluesy *Gin House Blues* the following year. They employed a brass section which gave them a different sound from most of their contemporary beat groups. They also had a distinctive vocalist in **Andy Fairweather-Low**. A

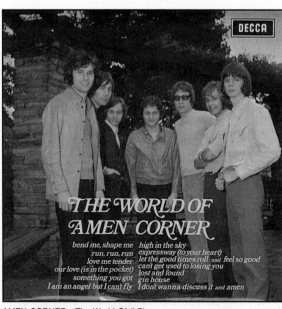

AMEN CORNER - The World Of (LP).

string of hits followed of which *Bend Me, Shape Me* (recorded by The American Breed in the US), *High In The Sky* and *(If Paradise Is) Half As Nice* were the most memorable. By the time of the last one, they'd switched to **Andrew Oldham**'s new Immediate label. When the label collapsed in 1969 the group splintered with the brass section forming **Judas Jump** and the remainder becoming **Fairweather**.

Andy Fairweather-Low later had a patchy solo career and Blue Weaver became a sessionman for a number of acts including **The Strawbs** and **Mott The Hoople**.

The CD reissue of their original album, which was primarily comprised of soul covers and ballads, also included four additional cuts: *World Of Broken Hearts*, their second 45, and its flip, *Nema* and two other 'B' sides, *Satisnek The Job's Worth*, a rather psychedelic number and *I Know*.

The CD reissue of their second album, which was a mixture of their hits like *(If Paradise Is) Half As Nice*, *High In The Sky* and *Bend Me, Shape Me* and cover versions of songs like *Stag-O-Lee*, *Baby Do The Philly Dog*, *Penny Lane* and an instrumental cover of *MacArthur Park*, includes eight previously unissued bonus tracks, including different takes of *(If Paradise Is) Half As Nice* and *Hello Susie* and the band's version of *Natural Sinner*, which **Fairweather-Low** later enjoyed a solo hit with.

The CD reissue of their third album comes with a handful of 'A' and 'B' 45 sides, a previously unissued backing track *Long Chocolate Limousine* and an alternate version of *Natural Sinner*.

If Paradise Was Half As Nice is an anthology, which only covers their material released on Immediate. *The Collection*, released in 2002, includes their Decca hits and flops but is not definitive because it omits their output for Immediate.

Bend Me, Shape Me also figured on *The World Of Hits, Vol. 2* back in 1969 and *Hello Susie* got a further airing on *Juke Box Jive* in 1976.

Other compilation appearances have included: *Expressway To Your Heart* on *The Mod Scene* (CD); *(If Paradise Is) Half As Nice* on *Immediate Single Collection, Vol. 1* (CD), *No 1s & Million Sellers Vol 4* (CD), the 2-CD set *60 Number Ones Of The Sixties* and on the 2-CD set *45s - 45 Classic No 1's*; *Hello Suzie* on *Immediate Single Collection, Vol. 2* (CD), *Hits Of The Swinging Sixties* (CD) and *The Greatest Sixties Album Of All Time Vol 2* (CD); *Get Back* and *Evil Man's Gonna Win* on *Immediate Single Collection, Vol. 3* (CD) and on *Rock Of Ages, Four Decades Of Heavy Rock 1962-2002*; and finally *Farewell To The Real Magnificent Seven* figured on *Immediate Single Collection, Vol. 4* (CD) and *Run, Run, Run* on *Pop-In, Vol 1* (CD). (VJ)

Amm

Personnel: CORNELIUS CARDEW   A
               LOU GARE   A
               KEITH ROWE   A
               LAWRENCE SHEAFF   A
               EDDIE PROVOST   A

ALBUM: 1(A) AMM MUSIC   (Elektra EUKS 7256) 1967 R2
NB: (1) reissued on CD with 24 page booklet, (ReR AMMCD) 1996.

EP: 1   AT THE ROUND HOUSE   (Incus EP1) 1972 R3

This group of musicians played strange free-form improvised music with cellos, sax and an assortment of strange instruments, often at London's Marquee. Some of the members were also in The Scratch Orchestra. The group was only a duo on the EP. In 1980, Rowe, Provost and Gare cut an LP *It Has Been An Ordinary Day* (Japo 60031) calling themselves Amm 111. (VJ)

Amsterdam Lil

Personnel: GRAHAM DEAN   bs   A
               JIM GRIERSON   vcls, flute A
               PETER GRISAFFI   organ   A
               STEVE PARKINSON lead gtr   A
               DAVE SKOLFIELD   drms   A

ALBUM: 1(A) EVOLUTION KID   (?) 1973

This was a folk-rock band. Grierson was later in **Pete Brown's** Flying Tigers. (JM)

Anan

Personnel: PETER HUMPHREYS
              PHILIP REED

45s: Haze Woman/
        I Wonder Where My Sister's Gone   (Pye 7N 17571) 1968 R1
        Madena/Standing Still   (Pye 7N 17642) 1968 SC

Anan was a little known ballad duo. *Haze Woman* is a pleasant commercial psych-pop number, but its flip side *I Wonder Where My Sister's Gone* is rated by some collectors and it's certainly weird and off beat. When neither of their 45s sold plans for a projected album were shelved. They first worked as Cowboys on a holiday ranch!

Compilation appearances include: *I Wonder Where My Sister's Gone* on *Paisley Pop - Pye Psych (& Other Colours) 1966-1969* (CD), *We Can Fly* (CD) and *Hot Smoke & Sassafras - Psychedelic Pstones Vol One* (CD); whilst *Haunted - Psychedelic Pstones Vol Two* (CD) gave a further airing to *Medena* and *Haze Woman*. (VJ)

The Anchormen

45:    Oh Alice/Anchor   (Anchor ANC 1006) 1975

This group were the staff of Anchor records. Their sole vinyl offering was produced by Charlie Ainley (of **Charlie and The Wide Boys**). (VJ)

Ancient Grease

Personnel: GARETH 'MORTY' MORTIMER   vcls   A
              JACK BASS   bs   A
              DICK 'FERNDALE' OWEN   drms   A
              GRAHAM WILLIAMS   gtr   A

ALBUM: 1(A) WOMEN AND CHILDREN FIRST
                               (Mercury 6338 033) 1970 R1

NB: (1) reissued on CD by Repertoire (REP 4359-WP) 1993 with one extra track.

When Welsh-based covers band Strawberry Dust got some gigs supporting **The Eyes Of Blue** they impressed John Weathers and he approached their then record company boss, Lou Reizner, about signing them. This he did but he changed their name to **Ancient Grease**. When they entered the studio to record *Women And Children First* Weathers and other **Eyes Of**

AMM - Amm Music (CD).

ANCIENT GREASE - Women And Children First (LP).

Blue members also helped out. After the album was released in July 1970 the band reverted to its original monicker, Strawberry Dust, and spent a short while in Hamburg. They disintegrated on their return but Mortimer and Williams later lined up in **Racing Cars**. Gary Pickford Hopkins was later involved in lots of other projects including Cutting Crew, Drivers, etc

The recent CD reissue includes a previously unreleased alternate take of *Freedom Train*.

Mercury's 1970 compilation *Dimension of Miracles* included *Women And Children First*, which was one of the band's better efforts. (VJ)

Ian (A.) Anderson

ALBUMS: 1 THE INVERTED WORLD
(up to   (Saydisc Matchbox SDM 159) 1968 R1
1976)   2 STEREO DEATH BREAKDOWN
                        (Liberty LBS 83242E) 1969 R1
         3 BOOK OF CHANGES   (Fontana STL 5542) 1970 SC
         4 ROYAL YORK CRESCENT (Village Thing VTS 3) 1970 SC
         5 A VULTURE IS NOT A BIRD YOU CAN TRUST
                        (Village Thing VTS 9) 1971 SC
         6 SINGER SLEEPS ON AS BLAZE RAGES
                        (Village Thing VTS 18) 1972

NB: (1) with **Mike Cooper**. (2) as Ian Anderson Country Blues Band. (3) catalogue number was only briefy "STL 5542", it then became "6309 001", the first of the new PHILIPS numbering system.

EP: 1 ALMOST THE COUNTRY BLUES
                        (Saydisc EP SD 134) 1969 R1

NB: (1) with Elliot Jackson.

45:      One More Chance/
         Policeman's Ball   (Village Thing VTSX 1002) 1971

Born on 26 July 1947 in Weston-Super-Mare, Somerset, **Anderson** (who was not the same guy that fronted **Jethro Tull**) was a bottleneck and slide guitarist. Indeed from 1970 he added the 'A' between his names to avoid confusion with the **Jethro Tull** frontman. He'd been in a local R&B band at school, but from 1966 started playing folk and blues clubs around Bristol. He contributed two tracks to the *Blues Like Showers Of Rain* compilation album, released on Saydisc Matchbox in 1967. He also recorded an EP the following year with **Al Jones** and Elliot Jackson, *Anderson, Jones, Jackson* (Saydisc 33 SD 125) 1968. The same year he began touring nationally as part of the British blues boom with artists like **Mike Cooper** and **Jo-Ann Kelly**. Indeed he recorded *The Inverted World* with **Mike Cooper** on his own Matchbox label. He then formed Ian Anderson's Country Blues Band, which included Paul Rowen (hrmnca) and Bob Rowe (bs). Their album was a good example of this genre and one of its cuts, *My Babe She Ain't Nothing But A Doggone Crazy Fool Mumble*, was also featured on the *Son Of Gutbucket* sampler. From 1970 he worked as a solo artist, forming his own Village Thing label. *One More Chance* from his fifth album appeared on the *Us* sampler. His albums featured mostly self-penned material. In 1973 he formed **Hot Vultures** with his wife Maggie Holland. Later **Anderson** projects included English Country Blues Band and Tiger Moth in the eighties.

Ian founded his own folk magazine 'Southern Rag' which later changed it name to 'Folk Roots', which is now one of the UK's major music magazines. (VJ)

Jon Anderson

			HCP
ALBUM:	1	OLIAS OF SUNHILLOW	(Atlantic K 50261) 1976 8

45:	Flight Of The Moorglade/	
	To The Runner	(Atlantic K 10840) 1976

Jon Anderson, who was born on 25 October 1944 in Lancashire, is best known as the vocalist with **Yes**. Back in 1964 he was in a beat group called **The Warriors**. In 1968 he recorded two 45s for Parlophone using the name **Hans Christian**. Later in the year he was a founding member of **Yes**, which had evolved out of **Mabel Greer's Toyshop**. **Yes** took a rest for most of 1975 and, as with many big name bands, some members concentrated on solo recordings. **Anderson**'s name and attractive vocals helped *Olias Of Sunhillow* achieve the UK Top Ten. It also climbed to No 47 in the US.

Anderson went on to make several solo recordings in the post-1976 era. In 1980 he left **Yes**, after teaming up with Greek keyboardist Vangelis. In the late eighties he was in Anderson, Bruford, Wakeman and Howe. He is still touring in 2005. (VJ)

Miller Anderson

ALBUM:	1	BRIGHT CITY	(Deram SDL 3) 1971 SC

NB: (1) reissued on CD (Repertoire REP 4524-WP) 1995.

45:	Bright City/Another Time, Another Place	(Deram DM 337) 1971

This significant Scottish-born guitarist may have only issued two solo albums, *Dream City* in 1971 and *Celtic Moon* in 1988, but he's been involved with many influential musicians and bands over more than three decades of rock. His early bands were **The Voice** and **At Last The 1958 Rock 'n' Roll Show** (which also included **Ian Hunter**), but his first well known one was **The Keef Hartley Band**, a jazzy, progressive era rock outfit. When he left it, after differences with **Hartley**, he set about recording these solo efforts, assisted by **Madeline Bell**, Lyn Dobson and Mick

ANDROMEDA - Andromeda (LP).

Weaver (**Wynder K. Frog**). Indeed Weaver's keyboards and **Anderson**'s soulful voice were distinguishing features on his typical progressive era rock album, which was reissued on the prolific German-based Repertoire label. The non-album 45 'B' side doesn't appear on the CD either.

After this solo effort **Anderson** formed **Hemlock**, then he teamed up again with **Hartley** in **Dog Soldier**. He was later in **T. Rex** in its final days and formed the Dukes in the late seventies together with Ronnie Leahy, Jimmy McCulloch and Charlie Tumahai. Their self-titled album (Warner Brothers K 56710) 1979 also featured Barry de Souza and Morris Pert.

In the eighties **Anderson** was with Stan Webb's Speedway, **Chicken Shack**, Mountain and a reformed version of **The Spencer Davis Group**, which recorded one album, *Extremely Live* in Birmingham Town Hall. He also worked with Pete York and Superblues. In 1988, he recorded a second mostly acoustic solo album *Celtic Moon* with **The Spencer Davis Group**.

In the nineties, he performed solo at Blackheath Concert Hall in South London in 1993 in a show which also featured the likes of **John Renbourn**, **Davey Graham** and **Bert Jansch**. He also played several shows with **Jansch** before resuming his solo career in January 1994. (VJ)

The Andicaps

This British group didn't release anything here in the UK but it did release a single in Finland: *You Make Me Happy/It's So Fine* (Sonet T 6513) in 1966. (VJ/TR)

Chris Andrews

		HCP
45s:	Yesterday Man/	
	Too Bad You Don't Want Me	(Decca F 12236) 1965 3
	To Whom It Concerns/	
	It's All Up To You Now	(Decca F 22285) 1965 13
	Something On My Mind/	
	I'll Do The Best I Can	(Decca F 22365) 1966 41
	What'cha Gonna Do Now?/	
	Lady Oh Lady	(Decca F 22404) 1966 40
	Stop That Girl/	
	I'd Be Far Better Off Without You	(Decca F 22472) 1966 36
	That's What She Said/Write It Down	(Decca F 22521) 1966 -
	I'll Walk To You/	
	They've All Got Their Eyes On You	(Decca F 22597) 1967 -
	Hold On/Easy	(Decca F 22668) 1967 SC -
	Man With The Red Balloon/	
	Keep Your Mind On The Right Side	(Pye 7N 17617) 1968 -
	Pretty Belinda/Make No Mistakes	(Pye 7N 17727) 1969 -
	Yo Yo/Hey Babe	(Pye 7N 17958) 1970 -
	Rainstorm/Old Fool	(Epic EPC 5248) 1977 -
Reissues:	To Whom It Concerns/Stop That Girl/Pretty Belinda/	
	Yesterday Man/The First Time	(Scoop SC/SR 5001) 1984 -
	Yesterday Man/	
	To Whom It Concerns	(Old Gold OG 9257) 1985 -
	Yesterday Man/	
	(Flip by different artist) (7" and 12")	(PRT PYT/S 6) 1988 -

NB: He also had a number of albums and EPs in Europe which are not listed above. There are various compilations of his material: *20 Greatest Hits* (Repertoire REP 4233 WG)1993 on German import and *Swinging Sixties Hit Man - The Anthology* (Repertoire REP 4504), also on German import.

Chris Andrews was a talented songwriter as well as a vocalist. Apart from writing his own hits of which *Yesterday Man* and *To Whom It Concerns* were the most successful and best known, he also wrote hits for the likes of **Sandie Shaw**, Adam Faith, **The Roulettes** etc.

The CD compilation, *20 Greatest Hits* is a good and obvious way to get to hear most of his 45 releases but for completists there's also a 2-CD set *Swinging Sixties Hit Man - The Anthology* available, which includes all you'd want to hear and more! **Andrews** also figures on the *Sons And Lovers* compilation in 1993 and also recorded as **Chris Ravel and The Ravers**.

Hold On has been compiled on *Oddities, Vol 2* (LP) and *Jagged Time Lapse, Vol 3* (CD). (VJ)

ANDROMEDA - Return To Sanity (CD).

John Andrews and The Lonely Ones

Personnel incl: JOHN ANDREWS   A

45:      A Rose Growing In The Ruins/
         It's Just Love   (Parlophone R 5455) 1966 R1

This one-off 45 is now quite collectable. (VJ)

Tim Andrews (and Paul Korda)

45s: Sad Simon Lives Again/
         You Won't Be Seeing Me Anymore   (Parlophone R 5656) 1967
         (Something About) Surburbia/
         Your Tea Is Strong   (Parlophone R 5695) 1968
    α   Smile If You Want To/
         Makin' Love To Him   (Parlophone R 5714) 1968
    α   Angel Face/Waiter Get Me A Drink (Parlophone R 5746) 1968
    α   How Many More Hearts Must Be Broken/
         Discovery   (Parlophone R 5769) 1969

NB: α credited to **Tim Andrews and Paul Korda**.

Perhaps this guy's main claim to fame was that he nearly joined The Monkees. Unfortunately for him the people assembling the group decided one English guy (**Davy Jones**) was enough. He was often referred to as 'Tiny Tim' on account of his diminutive height (5 foot, 5 inches). As a solo artist and with **Paul Korda** he failed to achieve any significant commercial success.

Compilation appearances include: (Something About) Suburbia on Sixties Lost And Found, Vol. 1 - 1964-1969 (LP); and Angel Face on 60's Back Beat (LP). (VJ)

Andromeda

Personnel: JOHN CANN   gtr, vcls   A
             MICK HAWKSWORTH   bs, vcls   A
             IAN McLANE   drms   A

ALBUMS: 1(A) ANDROMEDA   (RCA SF 8031) 1969 R3
        2(A) 7 LONELY STREET
                      (Reflection/Music Mixture MM 026) 1990 R1
        3(A) RETURN TO SANITY   (Background HBG 122/5) 1992
        4(A) ANTHOLOGY   (Kissing Spell KSCD 9492) 1994
        5(A) LIVE AT MIDDLE EARTH
                              (Kissing Spell KSLP 9497) 1995
        6(A) BBC TOP GEAR SESSION '68 / LIVE AT MIDDLE
              EARTH '67   (Kissing Spell KSCD 9594) 1995

NB: (1) repressed (Eclipse 88) in the late eighties and reissued on CD (Repertoire GTR 024) with eight bonus tracks:- Go Your Way, Keep Out 'Cos I'm Dying, Garden

Of Happiness, Exodus, Journey's End, Let's All Watch The Sky Fall Down, Darkness Of Her Room and See Into The Stars. (1) reissued (Get Back GETLP 561). (2) is an album of previously unreleased material. Just 450 copies were issued although the material was also released on CD as (3). (4) is a CD release which includes material from their early years including eight previously unreleased tracks. (6) includes a BBC session from November '68, and a live rehearsal which had earlier been released as (5). Definitive Collection (Angel Air SJP CD 053) 2000 is a 2-CD compilation set.

45:      Go Your Way/Keep Out 'Cos I'm Dying   (RCA 1854) 1969 SC

This is a crossover band which transcends the psychedelic and progressive era. The band was formed by John (Du) Cann, who'd earlier been in **The Attack**. Indeed, their sole 45 Go Your Way had previously been recorded by **The Attack**, but that version was not released. Originals of the album are not easily come by but you'll notice it has been re-issued. The album's finest moments are Day Of The Change, which features some fine discordant guitar work and great vocals, and Return To Sanity, which opens with a guitar-driven instrumental passage similar to Mars from Holst's Planets suite and contains some fine guitar work throughout. By contrast there are a couple of more mellow, laid back numbers of note - And Now The Sun Shines and The Reason - but most of the remaining tracks are expendable.

After they disbanded at the end of 1969 Cann went on to form **Atomic Rooster** playing on their Tomorrow Night and Devil's Answer 45. He later formed **Hard Stuff**. Hawksworth formed **Fuzzy Duck** and was later in Ten Years Later with **Alvin Lee**. John Cann used his original name John Du Cann for a minor hit, Don't Be A Dummy in 1979 and later was involved in reforming **Atomic Rooster** with organist **Vincent Crane**.

Definitive Collection comprises their eponymous album and non-album 45 for RCA along with demos, outtakes, live recordings and a session from John Peel's 'November 1968 'Top Gear' show.

Day Of The Change can also be heard on Broken Dreams, Vol. 3 (LP) and Go Your Way, a later version of their rare 45, can be heard on Circus Days, Vol. 4 (LP) and Circus Days Vol's 4 & 5 (CD). This is a really punchy number with some great guitar work which wasn't on their album and it's well worth a spin. (VJ/FC)

Andwellas Dream

Personnel: GORDON BARTON   drms   ABC
             DAVE LEWIS   gtr, piano, organ, vcls   ABC
             NIGEL SMITH   bs, vcls   ABC
             DAVE McDOUGALL   keyb'ds   BC
             JACK McCULLOCH   drms   C
             DAVE STRUTHERS   bs, vcls   C

ALBUMS: 1(A) LOVE AND POETRY   (CBS 63673) 1968 R4
        2(B) WORLD'S END   (Reflection REF 1010) 1970 SC

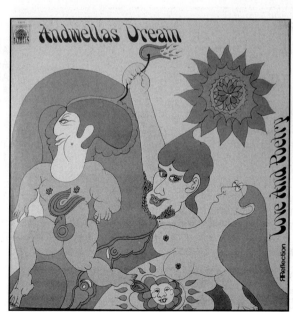

ANDWELLAS DREAM - Love And Poetry (LP).

3(C)   PEOPLE'S PEOPLE   (Reflection REFL 10) 1971 SC

NB: (1) reissued on CD (Fingerprint No #) 1995 and again (Vinyl Japan) 2004. (2) and (3) credited to **Andwella**.

45s:	Sunday/Midday Sun	(CBS 4301) 1968 R1
	Missus Man/Felix	(CBS 4469) 1968 R2
	Mister Sunshine/Shades Of Grey	(CBS 4634) 1969 R1
	Every Little Minute/Michael Fitzhenry	(Reflection RS 1) 1970
	Are You Ready / People's People	(Reflection RS 6) 1970

This band started life as a trio from Northern Ireland called **Method**, changing their name to **Andwella's Dream** after moving to London in 1968. After the first album they were known simply as Andwella.

Love And Poetry is a highly-rated psychedelic album, which featured guest artist **Bob Downes** playing sax, flute etc. All the songs were written by **Dave Lewis**. The highlights are the opening track, *The Days Grew Longer For Love*, which like most tracks is slow and melodic but with killer guitar leads; the heavier psychedelic number *Sunday* (which was their first and strongest 45 'A' side) and *Cocaine* and *Shades Of Grey*, two tracks which veer towards progressive rock with plenty of organ and jazzy guitar. CBS released three singles from the album including two non-album sides: *Missus Man* and *Mister Sunshine*. Of these, *Sunday* is a superb slice of psychedelic rock with some **Hendrix**-influenced guitar work.

In 1970 they switched to Reflection for whom they recorded two albums, neither of which matched their first effort and two 45s. *The World's End* album was also comprised entirely of **Dave Lewis** compositions, but most of the tracks were more mainstream with string orchestrations, brass arrangements and background vocals. The best tracks are the mid-tempo R&B influenced *I Got A Woman* with flute solo, jazzy piano and guitar; two tracks (*Reason For Living* and *Shadow Of The Night*), which sound similar to **Traffic** and the slow instrumental *Michael Fitzhenry* which featured some good guitar work and flute. On the down side *Back On The Road* was a pale imitation of The Band's *The Weight*. The flip side of their first 45 was an instrumental credited to Andwella. A Mike Fitzhenry appears on the credits of the first album as one of the recording engineers.

Lewis was a multi-instrumentalist and an acclaimed songwriter who also recorded a privately-pressed album in 1970. He also made further solo albums. McCulloch had previously played with **One In A Million**, **Thunderclap Newman** and with Struthers had been with short-lived group 'McCullochs, Struthers and Patterson' (the other members being Jimmy McCulloch and Robbie Patterson). After **Andwella** he went on to a group called 'White Line', with his brother Jimmy. McDougall went on to work with Speedy Keen (ex-**Thunderclap Newman**), while Smith joined **Khan**.

Compilation appearances have included: *Felix* on *Perfumed Garden Vol. 3* (CD); and *Sunday* on *Rubble, Vol. 17 - A Trip In A Painted World* (LP), *Rubble, Vol. 10* (CD) and *The Best Of Rubble Collection, Vol. 5* (CD). (VJ/MWh/CA/JM)

Angel

Personnel:	BRIAN JOHNSON	ld vcls	AB
	MARTIN KEMP	bs	AB
	STEVE RICKARD	drms	AB
	JOE RYAN	ld gtr	A
	BOB BANASIAK	ld gtr	B

45s:	Good Time Fanny/	
(up to	Who D'Ya Think Your Fooling	(Cube BUG 41) 1974
1976)	Little Boy Blue/Tragedy Queen	(Cube BUG 51) 1974

This Essex band were originally called The Pebbles, and apparently had a hit in New-Zealand with the song *Stand Up And Be Counted*. They changed their name to **Angel** in 1974, encouraged by Mick Tucker and Andy Scott of the **Sweet**, who became their new producers. As Andy Scott had a lot unreleased songs, he decided to let **Angel** record them. Then, **Angel** consisted of four members with a similar look to **Sweet**.

Their first single was a catchy tune in the style of *Ballroom Blitz*, with **Sweet** type harmonies. The 'B' side was composed by the band and is a boogie in the vein of **Status Quo**. It reached No 6 in the German charts. The same year, **Angel** issued a second single (with Banasiak now on lead

PERFUMED GARDEN VOL. 3 (Comp CD) includes Andwellas Dream.

guitar) also produced by Scott and Tucker. Written by Scott, *Little Boy Blue* was re-recorded some time later by **Sweet** under the title *Fox On The Run* and became a hit single in 1975! The 'B'-side is another group composition with some excellent guitar work. As the two singles did nothing, the band disbanded in late 1974. (CSx/VJ/MK)

Angel and Eighleen

| 45: | Midnight Flyer/Flight | (Rak RAK 137) 1972 |

This 45 was recorded in the Island record studios and produced by Mickie Most. The music papers of the era described it as an unusually bad disc - something not generally associated with Most. (VJ)

Angela and Her Fans

| 45: | Love Ya Illya/I Know You | (Pye 7N 7108) 1966 SC |

This was a novelty record - recorded as a tribute to David McCallum (of 'The Man From U.N.C.L.E.'). (VJ)

Angelina

| 45: | I Just Don't Know How/ | |
| | Wishing My Life Away | (Fontana TF 648) 1965 |

A one-off teenbeat disc. (VJ)

Angel Pavement

Personnel:	DANNY BECKERMAN
	TERRY MORRIS
	CLIVE SHEPPARD
	PAUL SMITH

45s:	Baby You've Gotta Stay/	
	Green Mello Hill	(Fontana TF 1059) 1969
	Tell Me What I've Got To Do/	
	When Will I See June Again	(Fontana TF 1072) 1970

NB: *Maybe Tomorrow* (Tenth Planet TP 057) 200? compiles their recorded output and had a limited edition of 1,000 numbered copies released on 190gm vinyl. *Maybe Tomorrow* (Wooden Hill WHCD 014) 2005 compiles their complete recordings on CD with additional tracks.

A York outfit that included Danny Beckerman who was also in **Fortes Mentum** and later **Pussy**. Their *Baby You've Gotta Stay* was written by

Beckerman and arranged by Geoff Gill of **The Smoke**. Gill supervised their recordings when they returned to England in the summer of 1969 after a tour to Mexico, when they became part of producer Monty Babson's Morgan Bluetown stable of artists in the late sixties. It's pure harmony-pop with a feel similar to US band Left Banke in places but is nothing special. Despite further singles and an album being scheduled from these sessions, it all remained in the can until much later.

Maybe Tomorrow, initially released on Tenth Planet on vinyl rectified this. The later CD release on Wooden Hill includes all the material from the Morgan Bluetown sessions as well as some earlier demos, including the superb *Tootsy Wootsy Feelgood*.

Compilation appearances have included: *Baby You've Gotta Stay* on *Morgan Blue Town* (LP) and *Beat Merchants* (CD); *Green Mello Hill* and *Baby You've Gotta Stay* on *Collecting Peppermint Clouds, Vol. 1* (LP) and *When Will I See June* again on *Fading Yellow, Vol 5* (CD). (VJ)

The Angellettes

45s:	Don't Let Him Touch You/Rainy Day	(Decca FR 13284) 1972
	Popsicles And Icicles	(UK UK 11) 1972
	Do You Love Me/	
	I Just Want To Say Thank You	(UK UK 26) 1973
	I Surrender/Goodbye Jon	(Mooncrest MOON 35) 1974

Despite having **Jonathan King** as their writer and producer, this all-girl group remained anonymous. They also recorded two of their earlier singles on his UK Records label. (VJ)

The Anglians

45:	A Friend Of Mine/Daytime Lover	(CBS 202489) 1967 SC

Hailed from Norwich and were originally known as Gary Freeman and The Contours (but did not record under that name). They later became **The Moving Finger**. (VJ)

The Anglos

45s:		Incense/You're Fooling Me	(Brit WI 004) 1965 R1
		Incense/You're Fooling Me	(Fontana TF 589) 1965 SC
α		Incense/You're Fooling Me	(Sue WI 4003) 1967
		Incense/You're Fooling Me	(Island WIP 6061) 1969

NB: α Unreleased. The Fontana and Island 45s were reissues of the Brit release.

The fact that this band was rumoured to have included **Stevie Winwood** has ensured the Brit and Fontana releases are now quite collectable. The 45 was produced by Larry Tallon and Jimmy Miller. They may have been American, nobody seems sure. (VJ)

The Animals

Personnel:

ERIC BURDON	vcls		ABC
CHAS CHANDLER	bs		ABC
ALAN PRICE	keyb'ds		A
JOHN STEEL	drms		AB
HILTON VALENTINE	gtr		ABC
DAVE ROWBERRY	keyb'ds		BC
BARRY JENKINS	drms		C

HCP

ALBUMS:	1(A)	THE ANIMALS	(Columbia 33SX 1669) 1964 R2 6
	2(A)	ANIMAL TRACKS	(Columbia 33SX 1708) 1965 R1 6
	3(A/B)	MOST OF THE ANIMALS	(Columbia SX 6035) 1966 SC 4
	4(C)	ANIMALISMS	(Decca LK 4797) 1966 R1 4
	5( )	THE ANIMALS	(EMI Regal SREG 104) 196? SC -
	6( )	IN CONCERT FROM NEWCASTLE	
			(DJM DJSL 069) 1976 -

NB: (5) Export only. (1) reissued on CD (EMI DORIG 125) 1997 but in mono only. They also had some US-only albums- *Get Yourself A College Girl* (Soundtrack)

(MGM E/SE 4273) 1964; *The Animals On Tour* (MGM E/SE 4281) 1965; *The Best Of The Animals* (MGM E/SE 4324) 1966; *Animalization* (MGM E/SE 4384) 1966; *The Best Of The Animals, Vol. 2* (MGM E/SE 4454) 1967 and appeared on two other US Soundtrack albums - *The Dangerous Christmas Of Red Riding Hood* (ABC-Paramount 536/S-536) 1965 and *The Biggest Bundle Of Them All* (MGM E/SE 4446) 1967. As one would expect several of their albums have been reissued and repackaged. (2) reissued on Starline (SRS 5006) in 1969 and on CD digipack (EMI 498 9362) 1999. (3) reissued on Music for Pleasure (MFP 5218) in 1973. It reached No 18 in the Charts. There have also been numerous compilations. More recent ones have included *The EP Collection* (See For Miles (SEE 244) in 1988, (SEE CD 244) in 1989. Also relevant is *Live At The Club-A-Go-Go, Newcastle* (Decca LIK 46) 1989, which features live material from late 1963 and *The Most Of The Animals* (Australia: Raven RVCD 005) 1989, an excellent CD which includes tracks from throughout the band's sixties career. *The Animals With Sonny Boy Williamson* (Decal CD CHARLY 215) 1990 is a CD of two separate albums recorded in December 1963, one is an Animals set, the other features Sonny Boy Williamson with **The Animals** supporting him. *The Complete Animals* (EMI EM 1367) 1990 compiles all their EMI recordings from 1964 and 1965. *Roadrunners* (Raven/Topic RVCD-11) 1991 is a 19-track set of live and previously unissued studio recordings from Melbourne, Monterey, London and Stockholm between 1966-68, which fans will love. *Trackin' The Hits* (Decal CD LIK 72) 1991, is a 19-track selection of their Columbia singles. *Inside Looking Out* (Sequel NEX CD 153) 1991 collects material released in the UK during 1965 and 1966. *The Very Best of The Animals* (Spectrum) 1998 documents the band in transition *from Inside Looking Out* in 1965 to *Ring Of Fire* in 1968. *Club Au Go-Go 30th December 1963* (Get Back GET 580) 2000 is a 10" vinyl LP available on import. *Gunsight!* (Akarma AK 074) 2001 is a 9-track CD compilation of both both incarnations of the band with an alternate mix of *House Of The Rising Sun* and the non-LP *Sky Pilot*. *The Best Of The Animals* (EMI EMI 527 0842) 2000 is a 20-track compilation. *Don't Bring Me Down* (Castle Music CMRCD 766) 2003 is a 22-track compilation of the 1965-1966 Decca output. *Gratefully Dead 1964-1968* (Raven RVCD 194) 2004 compiles some of the best of their R&B and early forays into psychedelia.

EPs:	1(A)	I JUST WANNA MAKE LOVE TO YOU	
			(Graphic Sound ALO 10867) 1963 R4
	2(A)	THE ANIMALS IS HERE	(Columbia SEG 8374) 1964 SC
	3(A)	THE ANIMALS (BOOM BOOM)	
			(Columbia SEG 8400) 1965 R1
	4(A)	THE ANIMALS No 2 (I'M IN LOVE AGAIN)	
			(Columbia SEG 8439) 1965 R1
	5(C)	THE ANIMALS ARE BACK	(Columbia SEG 8452) 1966 R1
	6(A)	IN THE BEGINNING THERE WAS EARLY ANIMALS	
			(Decca DFE 8643) 1966 R1
	7(C)	ANIMAL TRACKS	(Columbia SEG 8499) 1966 R1

NB: (1) was a one-sided 12" EP privately-pressed and credited to Alan Price Rhythm and Blues Group. Just 99 copies were pressed originally. It was later reissued as (6). *The EP Collection* (See For Miles SEECD 244) 1999 rounds up their five Columbia EPs from 1964 and 1965.

HCP

45s:	Baby Let Me Take You Home/	
	Gonna Send You Back To Walker	(Columbia DB 7247) 1964 21
	The House Of The Rising Sun/	
	Talkin' Bout You	(Columbia DB 7301) 1964 1
	I'm Crying/Take It Easy	(Columbia DB 7354) 1964 8
	Don't Let Me Be Misunderstood/	

THE ANIMALS - Club Au Go-Go, 30th December 1963 (10").

Club-A-Go-Go	(Columbia DB 7445)	1965 3
Bring It On Home To Me/		
For Miss Caulker	(Columbia DB 7539)	1965 7
We've Gotta Get Out Of This Place/		
I Can't Believe It	(Columbia DB 7639)	1965 2
It's My Life/		
I'm Going To Change The World	(Columbia DB 7741)	1965 7
Inside - Looking Out/Outcast	(Decca F 12332)	1966 12
Don't Bring Me Down/Cheating	(Decca F 12407)	1966 6
Help Me Girl/See See Rider	(Decca F 12502)	1966 14

Reissue: The House Of The Rising Sun/
α Don't Let Me Be Misunderstood/
I'm Crying   (Rak RR 1) 1972 25

NB: α Reissued in 1982 and climbed to No. 11.

THE ANIMALS - Animal Tracks (CD).

The Animals were one of the very best British R&B bands and **Eric Burdon** was a superb blues vocalist.

Their roots lay in The Alan Price Combo (line-up: Price, Chandler, Steel and Valentine), a Newcastle-based R&B band. Not long after **Eric Burdon** joined their line-up in 1962 the group, who were known locally as 'the animals' on account of their wild stage act, renamed themselves **The Animals** during 1963. They also moved from a residency at the Downbeat club to the larger, more prestigious and central Club A-Go-Go. The name change was a carefully calculated ploy and it got them into immediate difficulties. They had been booked to appear on 'Saturday Club' as The Alan Price Combo and the BBC took some persuasion to feature a group called **The Animals**! The name change also coincided with a deal their manager had done with **The Yardbirds'** management for the two bands to do a swap i.e. **The Yardbirds** would tour that part of England that was **The Animals'** stomping ground and **The Animals** would take over **The Yardbirds'** residency in London.

The group relocated to London in January 1964 and were soon signed by producer Mickie Most who got them a record deal with EMI's Columbia label. Quickly capitalising on the R&B boom Most found them a traditional blues song, first recorded by Snooks Eaglin, called *Moma, Don't You Tear My Clothes*, which had recently been released in the US by Bob Dylan and titled *Baby Can You Follow Me Down*. The lyrics' sexual nature meant the song had to be cleaned up for Britain and the title was changed to *Baby Let Me Take You Home*. The end result was a pleasant enough amalgam of early sixties pop, beat music and the blues which just missed the Top 20, peaking at No 21 in the UK. On 9 May 1964 they commenced a long-awaited UK tour with Chuck Berry. There were 21 scheduled dates and they were second on a Bill which included **The Swinging Blue Jeans**, Carl Perkins, **Kingsize Taylor**, **The Nashville Teens** and **The Other Two**. During their tour **Eric Burdon** had discovered a song called *The House Of The Rising Sun* on Bob Dylan's first album. They persuaded Mickie Most to let them record a 4 minute 20 second rearrangement of it (making it the longest single to date) for their next 45. The song, about a New Orleans brothel, was ideally suited to the band's raw style and Eric's vocals. Their manager told them that even though they all had a hand in arranging the old blues tune (especially Hilton), all of their names wouldn't fit on the record label. They were told **Alan Price's** name would be put on the label

THE ANIMALS - THE ANIMALS (CD).

for the sake of convenience. It entered the UK Charts at No 15 but after selling 1/4 million copies within three days shot to No 1 the following week. The disc was their finest moment. In the US it was released in a shortened version of 2 minutes 58 seconds to fit in with American jukeboxes and sold 150,000 copies within two weeks of its release. It went on to top the Charts there too. On the back of this success their debut 45 was reissued in the US, although it was the flip side *Gonna Send You Back To Walker* (a cover version of an American hit by R&B artist Timmy Shaw in which Walker-on-Tyne, Eric's birthplace, was substituted for Georgia) which got into the Charts peaking at No 57.

Their third single was a self-penned number *I'm Crying*, which was co-written by **Burdon** and **Price**. This seemed a logical step as **The Beatles** were by now writing their own songs and **The Rolling Stones** were beginning to try to too. It was a catchy, straightforward, upbeat rock song, though it lacked the atmosphere of *House Of The Rising Sun*. It only got to No 6 here and No 19 in the US. Their management and producer Mickie Most kept pushing outside writers, but the band were clear that they did not want to keep recording other people's songs.

Their debut album, *The Animals*, was recorded in February 1964 before their first single. It was released in the US (although the titles were slightly different) to coincide with their US tour in September 1964 and climbed to No 17. It wasn't released in the UK until November 1964. Primarily comprised of blues songs from their live set it got to No 6 over here. The only original on the album was **Burdon**'s *The Story Of Bo Diddley*, which related the history of the blues from Bo Diddley to **The Beatles** and **Rolling Stones** accompanied by an infectious rhythm. The remaining material included fine covers of three John Lee Hooker numbers *Boom Boom, I'm Mad Again* and *Dimples*; Fats Domino's *I've Been Around* and *I'm In Love Again* and Chuck Berry's *Memphis Tennessee* and *Around And Around*. *Boom Boom* was also released as a US-only 45, but only climbed to No 43.

1965 began with the release of an EP, *The Animals Is Here*. It consisted of four previously issued tracks:- *House Of The Rising Sun, Gonna Send You Back To Walker, I'm Crying* and *Baby Let Me Take You Home* but spent four weeks at No 3 in the EP Charts. Sales were limited, though.

Their fourth 45 was a powerful cover of Nina Simone's *Don't Let Me Be Misunderstood*. It was a powerful pop song with an infectious chorus which built up to a climax ideally suited to **Burdon**'s punchy vocals. Most insisted that the song was speeded up for the British Charts but the band and Nina Simone, who described it as the worst version of the song she'd ever heard, were very unhappy at the end result. The punters gave it the thumbs up though and it got to No 4 here and No 15 in the US.

Their next 45 was a rework of Sam Cooke's straightforward soul/blues song *Bring It On Home To Me*. Again it was ideally suited to **Burdon**'s voice and climbed to No 4 here, though it only got to No 32 in the US.

Alan Price left the band in Spring 1965 going on to enjoy a successful solo career. He was replaced by ex-**Mike Cotton Sound** pianist Dave Rowberry (although a guy called Mickey Gallagher from the **Chosen Few** subbed on several gigs until Rowberry was available). **Price** did play on the *Animals*

Tracks album, which was recorded before he left. Again it consisted of re-workings of old blues standards. Highlights included covers of Chuck Berry's *How You've Changed*, Ray Charles' *Hallelujah I Love Her So* and *I Believe To My Soul*; Jimmy Reed's *Bright Lights, Big City* and Bo Diddley's *Roadrunner*. It also came in an unusual cover which pictured the group dressed in army uniforms and helmets squatting on a railway track. Like their first album it got to No 6 in the UK, but only managed No 57 in the US, where it was preceded by the US-only album *The Animals On Tour*, which had got to No 99 over there.

Their next 45 was a Barry Mann/Cynthia Weil composition *We've Gotta Get Out Of This Place*, which seemed ideal for a raw group from Newcastle given that the lyrics related the austerity of working-life for many people in the affluent sixties. **Burdon** was allowed to use his own composition, a melancholic blues song *I Can't Believe It*, on the flip side. The 'A' side was, in the final analysis, a powerful and gutsy pop song, and it got to No 3 here and No 13 in the US (a considerable improvement on their recent efforts).

In October 1965 a second EP, *The Animals Are Back*, was released. Again it contained four previously issued tracks:- *Bring It On Home To Me, Don't Let Me Be Misunderstood, We've Gotta Get Out Of This Place* and *Club A-Go-Go* and was a case of the record company cashing in. It got to No 8 in the EP Charts.

Their final Columbia 45 was the Roger Atkins/Carl D'Errico song *It's My Life*. Built around guitar-bass interplay and featuring **Burdon**'s typically howling vocals it was a catchy song and got to No 7 in the UK and No 23 in the US. The 'B' side was another **Burdon** composition, *I'm Going To Change The World*, which was interesting for being his first socio-political composition - there would be many to come.

By now Eric, in particular, was determined to move away from Mickie Most and EMI feeling that the material on offer wasn't that adventurous. So he refused to re-sign the group's contract with Most and EMI and the group signed to Decca. Most remained very unhappy about this saying that **The Animals** were his favourite group of all and believing that he could have enjoyed several more hits with them.

With Tom Wilson producing *Inside Looking Out* (an old **Jackie** and Alan **Lomax** song) was chosen as their first single for Decca. Far less commercial than their previous more pop-based singles this song concerned a prisoner's lament about conditions in a 'burning oven' of a jail and was dominated by thumping drums, and harsh guitar. It was released to mixed reviews but got to No 12 here and No 34 in the US. After this John Steel left the band in mid-February 1966 signing over his royalty rights in return for £4,000. His replacement was Barry Jenkins of **The Nashville Teens**. They were near the end of the road and the 'Best Of' albums began to appear. In the US *The Best Of The Animals* (an US-only compilation) became their best selling album over there, rising to No 6 and spending over 100 weeks in the Charts. In the UK a compilation, *The Most Of The Animals*, which compiled the Mickie Most-produced singles up to *It's My Life*, got to No 4.

They recorded what would prove to be their final UK single, *Don't Bring Me Down*, in the Bahamas during an US tour. A melodic Goffin/King rock song it proved to be one of their best for a while and peaked at No 6 here and

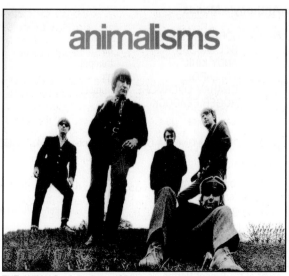

THE ANIMALS - Animalisms (CD).

No 12 in the States. The flip side was an offbeat **Burdon**/Chandler composition that veered towards reggae.

May 1966 also saw the release of their third proper UK studio album, *Animalisms*. The title was the term used in George Orwell's 'Animal Farm' to describe the principles on which the new liberal society of animals would operate. It included a higher percentage of rock songs than their previous albums such as an atmospheric version of Screamin' Jay Hawkins' *I Put A Spell On You*, a cover of Joe Tex's *One Monkey Don't Stop No Show* and a gentle self-penned ballad *You're On My Mind*. The blues were represented by songs like John Lee Hooker's *Maudie* and the classic *Gin House Blues*. The album got to No 4 but the group was now in rapid decline with a rift developing between **Eric Burdon** and Barry Jenkins, who were now heavily into acid and the rest of the group who weren't. They finally split on 5 September 1966 at the end of an American tour although a final US-only 45, *See See Rider*, and an US-only album, *Animalization*, both by the original group, reached No 10 and 12 respectively in the US.

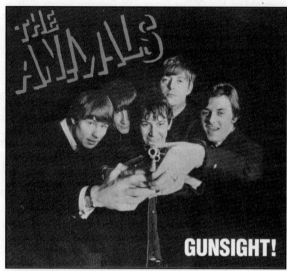

THE ANIMALS - Gunsight (CD).

The split had come after non-stop touring /recording had begun to take its toll and the band had divided into two camps. Some wanted to continue the tried and tested formula, while others wanted to get back to their roots. Both camps were unanimous in wanting new management. After a particularly heated meeting, it was decided to split rather than continue with the internal bickering.

Burdon and Jenkins stayed together to form a new group, The New Animals, and Hilton Valentine, after his attempt to establish himself as a folk singer failed, fled to a Buddhist monastery in Scotland. Chas Chandler, meanwhile, developed a new career as a producer/manager.

In September 1966 Columbia issued a further cash-in EP, *Animal Tracks*, even though the group had now split, and it still got to No 7 in the EP Charts.

In January 1967 **Burdon** formed a new group, **Eric Burdon And The Animals**. (See entry for details).

The original **Animals** reunited in 1976 for a critically acclaimed album *Before We Were So Rudely Interrupted*, which failed to sell well. A more successful reformation followed in 1983 between the original members augmented by **Zoot Money** (keyb'ds). They recorded an album *Ark* entirely of new material that was more successful and embarked on a world tour, but when this venture lost momentum they called it a day for good.

See For Miles' *The EP Collection* draws its material from their five EMI Columbia EPs and includes all their early hits apart from *It's My Life*. The *Live At The Club-A-Go-Go* album predates their early hits but is full of raw and exciting material. Highpoints include covers of John Lee Hooker songs like *Dimples* and *Boom Boom*.

Don't Bring Me Down compiles much of their 1965-66 output for Decca. It includes their *Animalisms* album, which largely contained fairly benign R&B covers, a rare limited pressing EP recorded in 1963 by the Alan Price Rhythm & Blues Combo and the 1966 single *Inside-Looking Out*.

The Best Of The Animals is a 20-track compilation containing all their Columbia 1964-1965 era 'A' sides and their last two 1966 Decca singles, *Inside Looking Out* and *Don't Bring Me Down*.

Club Au Go-Go 30ᵗʰ December 1963 is a 10" vinyl album containing six tracks of their primal R&B from their heyday.

Don't Let Me Be Misunderstood resurfaced on *The Woodstock Generation* (CD) although **The Animals** predated 'Woodstock' and **Eric Burdon And The Animals** never played there! They contributed one side each to *The Roots Of British Rock, Vols 1* and *2* (a live recording of them at the Club A Go Go, Newcastle from December 1963). Other compilations appearances have included:- *Boom Boom* on *Tough Rock* (LP); *Talkin' 'Bout You* on *Sounds Of The Sixties* (2-LP) and *Sixties Archive Vol. 1* (CD); *Bring It On Home To Me* and *The House Of The Rising Sun* on *Mickie Most Presents: British Go-Go* (LP), *U.K. No 1 Hits Of The 60's* (CD) and on *The Best Summer Ever!* (CD); *Don't Bring Me Down* on *A Whiter Shade Of Pale* (LP); *We're Gonna Howl* on *English Freakbeat, Vol. 2* (LP); *Don't Let Me Be Understood* on *Hits Of The Sixties - 20 Swinging Sounds* (CD); *House Of The Rising Sun* and *We've Got To Get Out Of This Place* on the 2-CD set *Stars And Stripes*; *It's My Life* and *We've Gotta Get Out Of This Place* on *Go... With An All Star* (LP).

More recently, *We've Gotta Get Out Of This Place* resurfaced on the 6-CD collection *Best Of Driving Rock*, *Hits Of The 60's Vol 2* (CD) and on *Full Throttle - 60 Original Driving Classics*; *We've Gotta Get Out Of This Place* (alternate take) on the 2-CD set *Greatest Hits Of The Sixties*; *Bring It On Home To Me* has been compiled on the 2-CD set *Greatest Hits Of The 60's Vol 4*; *I'm Crying* can be found on *Super Hits Of The 60s - Vol 2* (CD); *Don't Let Me Be Misunderstood* has been compiled on *Super Hits Of The 60s - Vol 3* (CD) and *House Of The Rising Sun* can also be found on the 2-CD set *45s - 45 Classic No 1's*, *Dizzy* (CD), *Super Hits Of The 60s - Vol 1* (CD), *Best Of British Rock* (CD) and on the 2-CD set *Sixties Summer Love*. (VJ/JM)

Anno Domini

Personnel:			
	JOHN JONES	gtr	A
	TREVOR JONES	bs	A
	DAVE MERCER	gtr, bs, vcls	A
	KERRY SCOTT	vcls, hrmnca, perc	A
	TIGER TAYLOR	gtr, vcls	A

ALBUM: 1(A) ON THIS NEW DAY (Deram SML-R 1085) 1971 R3

Formed in Ireland by Taylor (ex-**Eire Apparent**) their mildly flavoured folksy album is surprisingly hard to find. Not that locating it would be a very rewarding musical experience. The music is gentle, almost bland and although it contains some nice melodic patterns, you're bound to have forgotten them quickly. They were obviously influenced by The Byrds. The album begins with a good version of their *Rock And Roll Star* and *June Tremayne* and *The Badlands Of Ardguzth* are full of ringing guitars. Best of the melodic, folky songs are *The Trapper* and *The Good Life I Have Known*. There's also a heavy rockin' version of Dion's *Daddy Rollin'*. This is only recommended for fans of melodic acoustic folk.

John Jones and his brother Trevor had earlier played in the Australian band Sweatty Betty. When group split, the Jones brothers formed **Jonesy**, Taylor joined Brown and O'Brien, Mercer went solo and Scott joined T.F. Much then Bruno AD. (VJ)

The Answers

Personnel incl:	TONY HILL	ld gtr		A

45s:	(It's) Just A Fear/		
	You've Gotta Believe Me	(Columbia DB 7847) 1966 R3	
	That's What You're Doing To Me/		
	Got A Letter From My Baby	(Columbia DB 7953) 1966 R1	

This Newcastle group is most noteworthy for including brilliant guitarist Tony Hill, who was later in **The Misunderstood** and then formed **High Tide**. Their finest moment *(It's) Just A Fear* (a Hill composition) is pretty compelling stuff:- punchy with some inevitably driving guitar work. The first 45 is by far the most sought-after and valuable of the two.

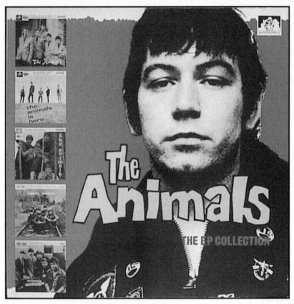

THE ANIMALS - The EP Collection (LP).

Compilation appearances have included:- *You've Gotta Believe Me* on *Magic Spectacles* (CD); *Just A Fear* on *Rubble, Vol. 13 - Freak Beat Fantoms* (LP), *Rubble, Vol. 7* (CD), *That Driving Beat* (CD), *The Best Of Rubble Collection, Vol. 4* (CD), *English Freakbeat, Vol. 3* (LP & CD) and *It's Only A Passing Phase* (LP); and *Tawny Wood* on *Circus Days Vol's 4 & 5* (CD) and *Circus Days, Vol. 4* (LP). (VJ)

The Anteeeks

45: I Don't Want You/Ball And Chain (Philips BF 1471) 1966 R3

They did have three e's in their name and this was their sole vinyl offering. The 'A' side was an organ-led mod-influenced stomper, written by **Pete Dello** of **Honeybus** fame. The flip was a cover of a song by Canadian band Great Scots.

Compilation appearances have included: *I Don't Want You* on *Psychedelia, Vol. 3* (LP) and *Hen's Teeth, Vol. 3* (CD); and *Ball and Chain* on *Beat It* (3-CD). (VJ/MWh)

Dave Anthony

45: Race With The Wind/Hide And Seek (Mercury MF 1031) 1968

Dave Anthony once played circa 1961 with **Zoot Money** in a **Shadows**-like band. (VJ)

Dave Anthony's Moods

Personnel:			
	JOHN DE VEREY	drms	A
	BILL JACOBS	bs	A
	ANDY KIRK	trumpet	A
	TIM LARGE	gtr	A
	GRAHAM LIVERMORE	trumpet	A
	ROGER PEACOCK	vcls	A

(UK)
45: New Directions/Give It A Chance (Parlophone R 5438) 1966 R1

(Italian)
45s:	My Baby/Fading Away	(Joker M 7000) 1967
	A Whiter Shade Of Pale/	
	Talking To The Rain	(Joker M 7001) 1967

A beat group originally from Bournemouth, which was formed by **Roger Peacock** (ex-**Cheynes/Mark Leeman Five**). After relocating to Italy, they released a good hard beat 45, *My Baby*, and their second Italian only 45 was a cover of the **Procol Harum** classic.

Their line-up, also included Chris Dennis (b) (ex-Nomadi) and Robert Henry Kenneth MacMaels (keyb'ds) at some point.

After the band split, **Peacock** remained in Italy for a while.

The 1968 compilation *Weekend In Musica* (Ricordi) also includes *Jumbo* (a **Bee Gees** cover) credited to Moods. (MWh/FB/CR/GB)

Rey Anton

45s:			
	Hey Good Looking/Mary Lou	(Oriole CB 1771)	1962
α	Peppermint Man/		
	Can't Say More Than That	(Oriole CB 1811)	1963
β	You Can't Judge A Book By The Cover/		
	It's Cold Outside	(Parlophone R 5132)	1964 SC
β	Heard It All Before/I Want You	(Parlophone R 5172)	1964 SC
β	Wishbone/Kingsway	(Parlophone R 5245)	1965 SC
β	Girl You Don't Know Me/		
	Don't Treat Me Bad	(Parlophone R 5274)	1965 SC
β	Nothing Comes Easy/Breakout	(Parlophone R 5310)	1965 SC
χ	Premeditation/Now That It's Over	(Parlophone R 5350)	1966 R1
χ	Don't You Worry Boy/		
	Hold It Babe	(Parlophone R 5420)	1966 SC
χ	Things Get Better/Newsboy	(Parlophone R 5487)	1966 SC

NB: α with The Batons. β with The Peppermint Men. χ with Pro Formula.

Anton came from Bournemouth. After recording two beat 45s for Oriole he switched to Parlophone recording a series of 45s first with The Peppermint Men and then with The Pro Formula. His best effort is generally considered to be his version of the R&B number *You Can't Judge A Book By The Cover*, which can also be heard on *English Freakbeat, Vol. 5* (CD).

Chris Burrows (later of **Circus**) played on the *Things Get Better* 45. (VJ)

Anvil Flutes and Capricorn Voices

ALBUM:	1	SOMETHING NEW IS COMING		
		(Deram DML/SML 1026)	1968 SC

45:	April Showers/Jolie Gendarme	(Deram DM 208)	1968

Put together by Irving Martin and Pete Smith this album consists of new arrangements of popular songs like *Never My Love, April Showers, Jezamine, Step Inside Love* and *March Of The Siamese Children* based around flutes and ethereal voices with extra tone colours of Spanish guitars, harp and percussion. The end result isn't at all convincing, making this definitely an album to avoid. The two 45 cuts are from the album and are similar in style. (VJ)

The Apex Rhythm and Blues All Stars

Personnel incl: IAN HUNTER

EP:	1	APEX RHYTHM AND BLUES ALL STARS		
		(John Lever Records)	1968 R3

Operating out of Northampton this band's main claim to fame was the inclusion of **Ian Hunter** who later found fame and fortune in **Mott The Hoople**. As you'd expect the EP is now extremely rare, sought-after and expensive. It featured four cuts:- *Tall Girl, Reeling And Rocking, Down The Road Again* and *Sugar Shack*. (VJ)

Apostolic Intervention

Personnel incl: JERRY SHIRLEY   drms   A

45:	(Tell Me) Have You Ever Seen Me?/		
	Madame Garcia	(Immediate IM 043)	1967 R3

This band were originally called RAF when they were signed to Immediate. There's a strong **Small Faces** involvement in the project because **Stevie Marriott** and **Ronnie Lane** wrote and produced the 45. The group members were great **Small Faces** fans. Like **The Small Faces** the band was also from London's East End. The 'A' side is a great mod-influenced stomper with some catchy drumming and effective organ backing. The 45 is very collectable.

Jerry Shirley later teamed up with **Stevie Marriott** in **Humble Pie**.

Compilation appearances have included: *(Tell Me) Have You Ever Seen Me* on *Immediate Alternative* (LP & CD), *Immediate Single Collection, Vol. 1* (CD); *Madame Garcia* on *Immediate Single Collection, Vol. 3* (CD); and *(Tell Me) Have You Ever Seen Me* and *Madame Garcia* on *Immediate Single Anthology, Vol. 1 - Rarities* (CD). (VJ)

Apple

Personnel:	DAVID BRASSINGTON	drms	AB
	JEFF HARROD	bs	AB
	ROBBO INGRAM	gtr	AB
	DENIS REGAN	vcls	AB
	CHARLIE BARBER	piano	B

ALBUM: 1(B)   AN APPLE A DAY (some w/insert)
(Page One POLS 016) 1969 R5

NB: (1) R4 without insert. (1) reissued on CD (Repertoire REP 4366-WP) 1994 along with the original single mixes of their two UK 45s and on Essex (ESSEX 1001 CD) 1994.

45s:	α	Thank U Very Much/		
		Your Heart Is Free Just Like The Wind	(Smash S-2143)	1968
		Let's Take A Trip Down The Rhine/		
		Buffalo Billycan	(Page One POF 101)	1968 R2
		Doctor Rock/The Otherside	(Page One POF 110)	1968 R2

NB: α only appeared in the US and Holland (Philips 320 269 BF), with picture sleeve.

One of the few interesting psychedelic bands about whom nothing is known to this day, the best of **Apple**'s material is up there with the cream of British psychedelia.

The band came to the attention of producer Larry Page on the strength of their US and Dutch-only cover of **Scaffold**'s hit *Thank U Very Much*. Their album was produced by Caleb Quaye (himself responsible for a very rare psych 45 as **Caleb**). A fine amalgam of psychedelia and heavy R&B, it's well-established as one of the most sought-after of all UK psych albums, and even came with a free leaflet from the Apple And Pear Marketing Board of Great Britain! Though not all the material is good, at its best it's nothing short of superb. *Buffalo Billycan* was a strange psychedelic pop

APPLE - An Apple A Day (LP).

ARCADIUM - Breathe Awhile (LP).

song, and *The Otherside*, a meditation on life and death with a piercing riff, is one of the few really moving songs to emerge from the UK psychedelic boom. Both appeared on 45s as well as the album. The album also contained *Doctor Rock* and *Let's Take A Trip Down The Rhine*, which were straight-ahead rockers, and competent covers of the **Yardbirds**' *Rock Me Baby* and *Psycho Daisies* and the Lovin' Spoonful's *Sporting Life*.

Compilation appearances have included: *The Other Side* and *The Buffalo Billycan* on *The Best Of Rubble Collection, Vol. 6* (CD); *The Otherside* on *Chocolate Soup* (CD), *Chocolate Soup For Diabetics, Vol. 1* (LP) and on the 4-CD box set *Acid Drops, Spacedust & Flying Saucers*; and *Buffalo Billy Can* on *Chocolate Soup For Diabetics, Vol. 2* (LP). (VJ/RMJ)

The Applejacks

Personnel:	MARTIN BAGGOTT	gtr	A
	PHIL CASH	gtr	A
	MEGAN DAVIES	bs	A
	GERRY FREEMAN	drms	A
	DON GOULD	keyb'ds	A
	AL JACKSON	vcls	A

| ALBUM: | 1(A) | THE APPLEJACKS | (Decca LK 4635) 1964 R2 |

NB: There's also a CD compilation, *Tell Me When* (Deram 820 968-2) 1990.

			HCP
45s:	Tell Me When/Baby Jane	(Decca F 11833) 1964	7
	Like Dreamers Do/		
	Everybody Fall Down	(Decca F 11916) 1964	20
	Three Little Words/		
	You're The One For Me	(Decca F 11981) 1964	23
α	Chim Chim Chiree/		
	It's Not A Game Anymore	(Decca F 12050) 1965	-
	It's Not A Game Anymore/Bye Bye Girl	(Decca F 12106) 1965	-
	I Go To Sleep/		
	Make Up Or Break Up	(Decca F 12216) 1965	SC -
	I'm Through/We Gotta Get Together	(Decca F 12301) 1965	-
	You've Been Cheating/		
	Love Was In My Eyes	(CBS 202615) 1967	-
Reissue:	Tell Me When/(Flip by different artist)	(Old Gold OG 9353) 1983	-

NB: α for export release only, but no-one's ever seen a copy!

This wimpy pop group hailed from Solihull, where they were previously known as The Crestas and The Jaguars, and had the novelty appeal of a female bassist in Megan Davies. Their best known recording was *Tell Me When*, which made the Top Ten. The follow-ups *Like Dreamers Do* and *Three Little Words* were minor hits, but their subsequent career was a rapid slide down pop's slippery pole. Very few people bought their album at the time, and it now changes hands for considerable sums.

The *Tell Me When* compilation consists of the album, both sides of their second 45, a 1964 flip side *You're The One For Me* and a 1965 'A' side, *I Go To Sleep*, a Ray Davies' composition.

They had one cut, *Baby's In Black* on Decca's 1964 compilation, *Fourteen, Lord Taverners* (LP). Retrospective compilation appearances have included: *Tell Me When* on *Hits Of The 60's - Save The Last Dance For Me* (CD) and on *Dizzy* (CD); and *Like Dreamers Do* on *Pop Inside The '60s, Vol. 2* (CD), *Sixties Lost & Found, Vol. 2* (LP), *Songs Lennon And McCartney Gave Away* (LP) and *Sixties Explosion, Vol. 1* (CD). (VJ/RMJ)

Aquarian Age

Personnel:	CLEM CATTINI	drms	A
	NICKY HOPKINS	piano	A
	TWINK (JOHN ALDER)	multi-instrumental	A
	JOHN 'JUNIOR' WOOD	bs	A

| 45: | 10,000 Words In A Cardboard Box/Good Wizard | | |
| | Meets Naughty Wizard | (Parlophone R 5700) 1968 | R3 |

Twink, who later achieved some fame with **The Pretty Things** and **Pink Fairies**, was the brainchild behind this superb slice of orchestrated psychedelia with nonsensical lyrics, which was produced by **Mark Wirtz** and released in June 1968. **Wirtz** later re-recorded it under the title *Love And Occasional Rain* on his *Come Back And Shake Me* album and **Twink** also reworked it for his *Think Pink* album. The flip is a novelty throw-away effort. **Twink** went on to join **The Pretty Things** and appeared with them in the Norman Wisdom comedy 'What's Good For The Goose'. He also played on their psychedelic rock opera *S.F. Sorrow*.

Compilation appearances include: *10,000 Words In A Cardboard Box* on *Psychedelia At Abbey Road* (CD), *Rubble, Vol. 3 - Nightmares In Wonderland* (LP), *Rubble, Vol. 2* (CD), *Illusions From The Crackling Void* (LP) and on the 4-CD box set, *Acid Drops, Spacedust and Flying Saucers*. (VJ)

Aquila

Personnel:	RALPH DENYER	vcls, gtr	A
	JAMES SMITH	drms	A
	MARTIN WOODWARD	organ	A
	(PHIL CHILDS	bs, keyb'ds	A)
	(GEORGE LEE	woodwind	A)

| ALBUM: | 1(A) | THE AQUILA SUITE | (RCA SF 8126) 1970 R2 |

NB: (1) reissued on CD by TRC.

The album, which came in a gatefold sleeve, is now a collectable. Musically, it is progressive rock with slight jazz tinges, produced by **Patrick Campbell-Lyons**. All of the songs on the album were composed by Ralph Denyer, who had previously been with **Blonde On Blonde**. In the nineties he published some books about guitar playing.

George Lee was later in a touring line-up of **Arrival**. (VJ/JM)

Arc

Personnel:	TOM DUFFY	bs, vcls	ABC
	MICKEY GALLAGHER	keyb'ds	ABC
	DAVE TRUDEX	drms	A
	JOHN TURNBULL	gtr, vcls	ABC
	ROB TAIT	drms	B
	DAVID MONTGOMERY	drms	C

| ALBUM: | 1(C) | ARC... AT THIS | (Decca SKL-R 5077) 1971 R1 |

NB: (1) reissued on CD (Green Tree Records GTR022) 1994.

This progressive blues/rock album involved some former members of **Skip Bifferty** and is now a minor collectable. They formed the band in 1970 when **Graham Bell** joined from **Every Which Way** but never really made a living on their own and later joined **Graham Bell** in **Bell and Arc**.

Three parts Scottish and one part Australian their band now clearly stands up as a progressive rock outfit, but manages to avoid most of its pitfalls and the results are generally rather impressive. Most importantly they succeed in restraining themselves, without losing any emotional impact. They have the ability to write memorable tunes and arrange them well. The vocals are a strong point, often oddly harmonized and never overstated. Heavier tracks alternate with more poetic ones, although this at times acts to the detriment of the album's coherence. All in all a very pleasant album to listen to, but not essential to own. (MK/VJ)

Arcadium

Personnel:	GRAHAM BEST	bs, vcls	A
	ALAN ELLWOOD	keyb'ds, vcls	A
	ROBERT ELLWOOD	vcls, gtr	A
	JOHN ALBERT PARKER	drms	A
	MIGUEL SERGIDES	vcls, gtr	A

ALBUM: 1(A) ARCADIUM (BREATH AWHILE)
(Middle Earth MDLS 302) 1969 R3

NB: (1) released on Vogue in France in 1969. Also reissued in the late eighties on vinyl and CD with two bonus tracks.

45: Sing My Song/Riding Alone (Middle Earth MDS 102) 1969 R1

All tracks (composed by Miguel Sergides) on their extremely rare album are filled with an atmosphere of anguish and despair, even in their quieter moments. Both lyrics and music are struggling for expression, to the effect of creating a very dense and at times impenetrable album, which is worth your while nonetheless. Although barely escaping perennial threats of murkiness and even sloppiness, the convincing emotional contents save the day for this album. Especially impressive are the longer tracks like the opening *I'm On My Way* with its telling title, in which the song structure gets blown to pieces by emotional outbursts on guitar, leading into an altogether strange and hitherto uncharted territory. This track was also issued on the rare label sampler *Earthed* from 1970. Due to mediocre vinyl, there are practically no copies to be found in truly excellent condition. Now their 45 is also hard to find. The 'A' side is nicely paced with subtle guitar work whilst the flip is gently pleasing and atmospheric.

They also appeared on an EP, *Aries 1969* and *Poor Lady* can be found on *Progressive Music* (LP). (MK/MWh)

Neil Ardley

ALBUMS:	1	WESTERN UNION	(Decca SKL 4690) 1965 R3
	2	DEJEUNER SUR L'HERBE	(Verve SVLP 9236) 1969 R3
	3	GREEK VARIATIONS	(Columbia SCX 6414) 1970 R3
	4	A SYMPHONY OF AMARANTHS	
			(Regal Zonophone SLR2 1028) 1972 R3

ARGENT - Argent (LP).

ARGENT - Ring Of Hands (LP).

5	WILL POWER (2-LP)	(Argo ZDA 164/5) 1974 R2
6	KALEIDOSCOPE OF RAINBOWS	
		(Gull GULP 1018) 1975 R1
7	HARMONY OF THE SPHERES	
		(Decca TXS-R 133) 1978 SC

NB: (3) With Ian Carr and Don Rendell. (5) With Ian Carr, Stan Tracey and Mike Gibbs. (7) Featuring **John Martyn**.

A keyboard/synthesizer jazz player who has also written non-fiction books for children which adorn school libraries. His earlier albums, in particular, are now very hard to find and sought-after by collectors of British progressive jazz.

He also made an album for library use in 1971 on the KPM label entitled *Mediterranean Intrigue*. It is one of his more obscure releases and therefore difficult to find.

Ardley spent much of the eighties writing about music, including the excellent 1986 publication Music: An Illustrated Encyclopaedia. He became interested in choral music in the 2000's and died in February 2004, soon after completing a new choral composition. (VJ/MWh/BS)

Argent

Personnel:	ROD ARGENT	keyb'ds, vcls	AB
	RUSS BALLARD	gtr	A
	ROBERT HENRIT	drms	AB
	JIM RODFORD	bs	AB
	JOHN GRIMALDI	gtr	B
	JOHN VERITY	gtr	B

				HCP
ALBUMS:	1(A)	ARGENT	(CBS 63781) 1970 SC	-
(up to	2(A)	RING OF HANDS	(Epic EPC 64190) 1971	-
1976)	3(A)	ALL TOGETHER NOW	(Epic EPC 64962) 1972	13
	4(A)	IN DEEP	(Epic EQ 31295/Q 65475) 1973 SC	49
	5(A)	NEXUS	(Epic EPC 65924) 1974	-
	6(A)	ENCORE (2-LP)	(Epic EPC 88063) 1974	-
	7(B)	CIRCUS	(Epic EPC 80691) 1975	-
	8(B)	COUNTERPOINT	(RCA RS 1020) 1975	-

COMPILATION:

				HCP
ALBUMS:	9(-)	BEST OF ARGENT	(Epic EPC 81321) 1976	-
	10(-)	HOLD YOUR HEAD UP	(Embassy 31640) 1978	-
	11(-)	ANTHOLOGY. THE BEST OF ARGENT		
			(Epic EPC 3257) 1984	-

NB: (1) reissued on CD (Beat Goes On BGOCD 110) 1991. (1) and (2) reissued as a 2-CD set (Beat Goes On CD 480) 2000. (3) reissued on CD (Epic 477377 2) 1994. (4) also released in quadrophonic and reissued on CD (Epic 480529 2) 1997. (5) reissued on CD (Epic) 1998 at mid-price. There's also a CD compilation, *The Best Of Argent* (Epic 902293 2) 1990. Also relevant are the CD *In Concert* (Windsong WINCD 067) 1995, featuring material from a 1972 show and *The BBC*

ARGENT - All Together Now (LP).

Sessions (BBC Worldwide / Strange Fruit) 1997, which combines radio recordings from 1970 - 73, including unissued versions of *Tragedy*, *Hold Your Head Up* and *God Gave Rock 'n' Roll To You*.

			HCP
45s:	Celebration/Kingdom	(Epic EPC 5423) 1971	-
(up to	Hold Your Head Up/		
1976)	Closer To Heaven (PS)	(Epic EPC 9135) 1971	5
	Hold Your Head Up/		
	Closer To Heaven/Keep On Rollin' (PS)	(Epic EPC 9135) 1971	-
	Tragedy/Rejoice	(Epic EPC 8115) 1972	34
	God Gave Rock 'N' Roll To You/		
	Christmas For The Free	(Epic EPC 1243) 1973	18
	It's Only Money (Part 2)/		
	Candle On The River	(Epic EPC 1628) 1973	-
	Thunder And Lightning/		
	Keeper Of The Flame	(Epic EPC 2147) 1974	-
	Man For All Seasons/		
	Music From The Spheres	(Epic EPC 2448) 1974	-
	Highwire/Circus	(Epic EPC 3047) 1975	-
	Hold Your Head Up/		
	God Gave Rock 'N' Roll To You	(Epic 152332) 1975	-
	Rock 'N' Roll Show/It's Fallen Off	(RCA 2624) 1975	-
Reissues:	God Gave Rock 'n' Roll To You/		
	Hold Your Head Up	(Epic EPC 3954) 1976	-
	Hold Your Head Up/It's Only Money	(Epic EPC 4321) 1976	-
	Hold Your Head Up/Tragedy	(Epic EPC 7062) 1979	-
	Hold Your Head Up/		
	Dance In The Smoke	(Old Gold OG 9187) 1982	-
	Hold Your Head Up/		
	God Gave Rock 'n' Roll To You	(CBS A 4580) 1984	-

Rod Argent formed this band in 1969 following the break-up of **The Zombies**. The remaining line-up consisted of his cousin Jim Rodford and former **Roulettes Russ Ballard** and Bob Henrit.

Their debut album **Argent** was very much in **The Zombies'** mould. One of its stronger tracks was *Dance In The Smoke* which brought the band to the attention of a much wider audience by virtue of its inclusion on the 2-LP budget compilation, *Fill Your Head With Rock*. Another of its songs, *Liar*, was covered by Three Dog Night in the US, where it became a hit, whilst *Cast Your Spell Uranus* was included on the *Together!* (LP) compilation.

Ring Of Hands was more cohesive as an album and had several memorable moments. *Sweet Mary* and *Celebration* were both blues-influenced tracks.

Their subsequent albums were heavier in style but yielded two UK hits:- the classic *Hold Your Head Up* and *God Gave Rock 'N' Roll To You*. The *All Together Now* and *In Deep* albums sold well in this country.

In May 1974 **Russ Ballard** left the band to pursue a solo career, releasing a solo album *Winning* (Epic SEPC 69210) in 1976. He was replaced by

guitarist John Grimaldi and John Verity. Following the flop of their *Circus* album, they switched to RCA for *Counterpoint*, which fared no better and in 1976 they split.

Rod Argent went on to pursue a solo career. Henrit opened a drum shop in London's West End and played in a band called Phoenix, with Rodford before they both joined **The Kinks**. (VJ)

Argosy

Personnel:	ROGER HODGSON	vcls	A
	ELTON JOHN	piano	A
	NIGEL OLSSON	drms	A
	CALEB QUAYE	lead gtr	A

45:	Mr. Boyd/Imagine	(DJM DJS 214) 1969

Imagine is orchestrated pop with 'flower power' lyrics, whilst *Mr. Boyd* is more straight-forward pop. Hodgson had previously been in **People Like Us** and would of course go on to **Supertramp**.

Compilation appearances have included:- *Imagine* and *Mr. Boyd* on *Incredible Sound Stories, Vol. 6* (LP); and *Imagine* on *Rubble Vol. 10* (CD) and *The Best Of Rubble Collection, Vol. 3* (CD). (VJ)

The Aristocrats

Personnel:	RUSTY BROWN	lead gtr, vcls	A
	JACK GARDNER	drms	A
	DAVE GRAHAM	gtr, vcls	A
	MEL JAMES	vcls	A
	CHRIS ROBERTS	bs, vcls	A

45:	Girl With The Laughing Eyes/	
	I Picked You	(Oriole CB 1928) 1964

This London-based band were originally known as Mel James and The Meltones and played harmony/beat ballads. Their manager Max Diamond wrote the 'A' side of this disc. (VJ)

Arizona Swamp Company

45:	Train Keeps Rollin'/	
	Tennessee Woman	(Parlophone R 5841) 1970 SC

This was **The Nashville Teens** under a pseudonym. The 'A' side of this 45, a pretty good rendition with an extended guitar instrumental in the middle, can also be heard on *Rubble Vol. 13: Freakbeat Fantoms* (LP), *Rubble Vol. 7* (CD) and *The Best Of Rubble Collection, Vol. 6* (CD). Both sides can also be found on *Rare 60's Beat Treasures, Vol. 1* (CD). (VJ)

ARGENT - In Deep (LP).

ARMAGEDDON - Armageddon (CD).

Deke Arlon (And The Offbeats)

Personnel:	DEKE ARLON		
	(aka ANTHONY HOWARD WILSON)	vcls	A
	ALAN EDWARDS	drms	A
	RAY MILLS	ld gtr	A
	BOBBY ROSS	bs	A
	BRIAN TYRELL	gtr	A

45s:	I Must Go And Tell Her/I Need You	(HMV POP 1340) 1964 SC
	I'm Just A Boy/	
	Can't Make Up My Mind	(Columbia DB 7194) 1964 R1
	If I Didn't Have A Dime/	
	Gotta Little Girl	(Columbia DB 7487) 1965
α	Little Piece Of Paper/I've Been Away	(Columbia DB 7753) 1965
α	Hard Times For Young Lovers/	
	Little Boy	(Columbia DB 7841) 1966 SC

NB: α **Deke Arlon** solo efforts.

This band's first two 45s were produced by Joe Meek who also wrote *Can't Make Up My Mind*. The band are still active as **The Offbeats** and are reputedly very good!

Compilation appearances include: *Hard Times For Young Lovers* on *60's Back Beat* (LP). (VJ/KL/JM)

Armageddon

Personnel:	BOBBY CALDWELL	drms, vcls	A
	LOUIS CENNAMO	bs	A
	MARTIN PUGH	gtr	A
	KEITH RELF	vcls, hrmnca	A

ALBUM: 1(A) ARMAGEDDON   (A&M AMLH 64513) 1975 SC

NB: (1) reissued on A&M (A&M SP 4513) and on CD (TRC Records TRC031) 1993. (1) reissued again on CD (Repertoire PMS 7089 -WP) 1998 on German import with extensive liner notes by Chris Welch.

This was a sort of hard-rock supergroup. **Relf** had previously been with **The Yardbirds**, **Renaissance** and recorded two solo 45s in 1966. Cennamo and Pugh had been with **Steamhammer** and Caldwell had played with Captain Beyond and The Johnny Winter Band. Their album is now a minor collectable, which has been likened to **T2**. Given the experience of the musicians it's disappointing and filled with boring minimalistic guitar riffs and flat melody lines. There are some good instrumental breaks but only *Buzzard*, a hard-rockin' number with fast **Ritchie Blackmore**-like guitar work which culminates with some bluesy harmonica from **Keith Relf** and the slow, melodic *Silver Tightrope* are worth a listen.

Louis Cennamo also played in **Renaissance**, **Chicago Line** and **Jody Grind**. Their career was effectively ended when **Relf** accidentally electrocuted himself on 14 May 1976. (VJ/CA)

Paul Arnold

45s:	Somewhere In A Rainbow/Got A Feeling	(Pye 7N 17317) 1967
	Bon Soir Dame/Don't Leave	(Pye 7N 17473) 1968

This London-based singer had previously been in **The Overlanders**. These 45s are beat ballads.

Somewhere In A Rainbow and *Got A Feeling* have been compiled on *Ripples, Vol. 6* (CD).

Vance Arnold and The Avengers

45:	I'll Cry Instead/Those Precious Words	(Decca F 11974) 1964

Joe Cocker recorded his first single using this name. The 'A' side is a **Beatles'** song.

Arrival

Personnel:	DYAN BIRCH	vcls	AB
	CARROLL CARTER	vcls	A
	FRANK COLLINS	vcls	AB
	LLOYD COURTENAY	drms	A
	DON HUME	bs	A
	PADDY McHUGH	vcls	AB
	TONY O'MALLEY	vcls, keyb'ds	AB
	GLEN LE FLEUR	drms, perc	B
	RAPHAEL PEREIRA	gtr	B
	LEE SUTHERLAND	bs	B

ALBUMS:	1(A)	ARRIVAL	(Decca SKL 5055) 1970 SC
	2(B)	ARRIVAL	(CBS 64733) 1972

45s:	Friends/Don't Turn His Love Away	(Decca F 12986) 1969 8
	I Will Survive/See The Lord	(Decca F 13026) 1970 16
	Let My Life Be Your Love Song/	
	Out Of Desperation	(CBS 7035) 1971 -
	Family Tree/Part Of My Dream	(CBS 7617) 1971 -
	(The Theme From) Heartbreak Kid/	
	Sweet Summer	(CBS 1350) 1973 -
	Mr. Know It All/Not Gonna Worry	(Epic EPC 1821) 1973 -
Reissues:	I Will Survive/See The Lord	(Decca F 13593) 1975 -
	Friends/I Will Survive	(Decca F 13763) 1978 -

A pop/rock band from Liverpool who enjoyed Top 20 hits with *Friends* and *I Will Survive*. On the CBS album the stronger tracks like *Glory Be* and *Family Tree* have quite a strong black/gospel influence. Also of note for Birch's vocals are the melancholic *Part Of My Dream*, *So It Is Written* and *Not Preconceived*.

Their original bassist was Don Hume and original drummer was Lloyd Courtenay ex-Casuals and **Lace**, both appeared on all Decca material and first two CBS singles before they left in 1972. They were replaced by Lee Sutherland (ex-Sunburst / pre **Cross & Ross**), Steve Chapman (drums) (ex-**Distant Jim**) and George Lee (sax) (ex-**Aquila**). Chapman only stayed briefly, leaving for **Coast Road Drive** and in turn being replaced by Glen Lefleur (ex-Legend). Pereira then joined and the recording of the CBS album *Arrival* commenced. Sutherland had also left prior to its recording and Phil Chen (ex-**Graham Bond's Magick**) joined to complete the album. Chen then left to join The Butts Band (US) and Lee left too. Pereira switched to bass. Birch, Collins and McHugh went on to **Kokomo**, O'Malley initialy joined Mick Cox then went to **Kokomo**, Lefleur went on to Gonzales. (VJ/JM)

The Arrivals

45:	Scooby Doo/She's About A Mover	(Pye 7N 17761) 1969 SC

This soulish beat group was originally known as Kevin Kane and Arrivals.

Arrows

45:     Mercy/See Saw   (Pye 17756) 1969

This seems to have been a one-off venture. The 'A' side is a Ohio Express song and the flip a Dan Covey composition. (GT)

Art

Personnel: LUTHER GROSVENOR   gtr   A
             MIKE HARRISON   vcls, keyb'ds   A
             MIKE KELLIE   drms   A
             GREG RIDLEY   bs   A

ALBUM: 1(A)   SUPERNATURAL FAIRY TALES (Island ILP 967) 1967 R2

NB: (1) reissued on Ariola in Germany in 1975 and on Island in the UK the same year (SC). Later re-issued on Lott (NR 51422) 1987. It's also available on CD.

45s: What's That Sound (For What It's Worth)/
        Rome Take Away Three   (Island WIP 6019) 1967 SC
   α   Room With A View/
        (flip by **Spooky Tooth**)   (Island WIP 6048) 1969
        What's That Sound/Flying Anchors (Island WIP 6224) 1975

NB: α Promo only.

A 'progressive' outfit **Art** later evolved into **Spooky Tooth** in October 1967 with the addition of Gary Wright. Their finest moment was *What's That Sound*, which was a rehash of Buffalo Springfield's superb *For What It's Worth*. It's now quite hard to obtain but was included on Island's *You Can All Join In* (LP) compilation. The flip side is constructed around a heavy guitar riff.

Their album is adventurous and quite unique British psychedelic rock. It's quite primitive in places, but utilises a wide range of instruments with plenty of sound effects and variety, although side two is a bit nondescript. Guy Stevens handled the production duties. It's well worth a spin.

In its pre-**Art** days the band was known as **The V.I.P.'s**. *Rome Take Away Three* can also be heard on *Jagged Time Lapse, Vol 4* (CD). (VJ/MWh)

Art Movement

Personnel incl: KEITH HEDLEY   keyb'ds   X
                  BOB MUNDY   drms   X
                  ALAN POINTER   gtr   X
                  TERRY WIDLAKE   bs   X

NB: 'X' 1969 line-up.

ART - Supernatural Fairy Tales (LP).

45s: The Game Of Love/
        I Love Being In Love With You   (Decca F 12768) 1968
        Loving Touch/Such A Happy Song   (Decca F 12836) 1968
        Yes Sir, No Sir/
        Sally Goes Round The Moon   (Columbia DB 8602) 1969
        For As Long As You Need Me/
        Nice 'N' Easy   (Columbia DB 8651) 1969
        The Sooner I Get You/Morning Girl (Columbia DB 8697) 1970

Yes Sir, No Sir can also be heard on the *Not Just Beat Music 1965-70* (LP) compilation. Although it's sometimes described as psychedelic the band was little more than a reasonable pop group. Their better moments included *Loving Touch*, a well-produced pop song with a catchy chorus.

Art Movement backed Roy Orbison during his 1970 and 1971 gigs in the UK and Europe. Widlake had been in **The Overlanders**. (MWh/VJ/JM)

Art Nouveaux

45:     Extra Terrestrial Visitations/
        Way To Play It   (Fontana TF 843) 1967 SC

An obscure one-off 45. (VJ)

THE ARTWOODS - Art Gallery (LP).

The Artwoods

Personnel: DEREK GRIFFITHS   gtr   A
             KEEF HARTLEY   drms   A
             JON LORD   organ   A
             MALCOLM POOL   bs   A
             ARTHUR WOOD   vcls   A

ALBUMS: 1(A)   ART GALLERY   (Decca LK 4830) 1966 R4
        2(A)   THE ARTWOODS   (Spark SRLM 2006) 1973 R1
        3(A)   100 OXFORD STREET   (Edsel ED 107) 1983

NB: (1) reissued on Decca Eclipse (ECS 2025) in different sleeve (SC). (3) also issued on CD. There's also a more recent compilation, *Art Gallery* (Repertoire REP 4533-WP) 1995.

EP: 1   JAZZ IN JEANS   (Decca DFE 8654) 1966 R4

NB: There also is a rare French EP (Decca 457.076) which contains their first two UK 45s.

45s: Sweet Mary/
        If I Ever Get My Hands On You   (Decca F 12015) 1964 R1
        Oh My Love/Big City   (Decca F 12091) 1965 R1
        Goodbye Sisters/
        She Knows What To Do   (Decca F 12206) 1965 R1

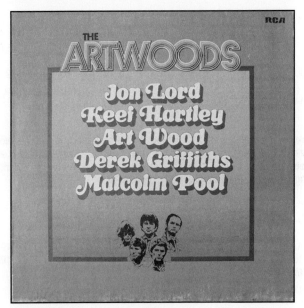

THE ARTWOODS - The Artwoods (LP).

I Take What I Want/I'm Looking For A Saxophonist Doubling
French Horn Wearing Size 37 Boots   (Decca F 12384) 1966 R1
I Feel Good/
Molly Anderson's Cookery Book   (Decca F 12465) 1966 R2
What Shall I Do/In The Deep End (Parlophone R 5590) 1967 R3

The Artwoods formed in London in 1964. Arthur Wood (the eldest brother of **Rolling Stones** and **Faces** guitarist Ronnie) had previously played with The Art Wood Combo, a swing and blues band, and was later a member of **Blues Incorporated**. Indeed, Wood used the name The Art Wood Combo for an earlier line-up of **The Artwoods** which featured Reg Dunnage on drums, though by the time their name was shortened to **The Artwoods** he'd been replaced by **Keef Hartley** from **Rory Storm and The Hurricanes**. By now the band had secured a residency at London's 100 Club and a recording deal with Decca. Decca decided not to release their first recording, a cover of Muddy Waters' *Hoochie Coochie Man*, and surviving acetates are very expensive collectors' items. Instead a Leadbelly cover, *Sweet Mary*, was chosen as their first single. Although it failed to chart, it got sufficient airplay to bring them a lot of live work and an appearance on the first live edition of 'Ready, Steady, Go!' The follow-up, *Oh My Love*, was another blues cover with a **Jon Lord** composition on the flip. It didn't chart but they continued to get plenty of live work, touring England with P.J. Proby, Europe with Petula Clark and backing US blues singer Mae Mercer. Their third single was *Goodbye Sisters*, a smoother R&B number backed by a group composition. It also failed to chart, but they finally achieved some commercial success with their fourth 45, a pulsating cover of Sam and Dave's *I Take What I Want*.

The *Jazz In Jeans* EP consisted of three cover versions - *Our Man Flint*, *These Boots Are Made For Walking* and *A Taste Of Honey* - and one original, *Routine*. Originally recorded for release in France, it didn't comprise their usual R&B covers and its release in England could easily have damaged the band's R&B credentials. It's now their rarest and most expensive item.

The *Art Gallery* album was entirely comprised of cover versions and sold badly, as did the *I Feel Good* single which was used to promote it. However, *I Feel Good* was definitely one of their more interesting singles. In view of their disappointing sales the band were dropped by Decca at the end of 1966, but negotiated a one-off deal with Parlophone, who didn't take up the option to extend it when the *What Shall I Do* 45 flopped.

The group finally split on a tour of Denmark but returned to the UK to find that their booking agent had secured another one-off deal with Fontana. To honour this the group were relaunched under the new name of **St. Valentine's Day Massacre**. It was to be their final 45 as they split shortly after its release.

Keef Hartley, who was sacked in the final days of **The Artwoods** later joined **John Mayall's Bluebreakers** and then formed his own **Keef Hartley Band**. He later formed **Dog Soldier** who also included guitarist Derek Griffiths who in the interim had played with **Mike Cotton Sound** and **Satisfaction**. Malcolm Pool played with Jon Hiseman's **Colosseum** and the

Don Partridge Band and then started a graphic design studio in Hillingdon. **Jon Lord**, of course, was later in **Deep Purple** and Whitesnake. Art Wood formed the short-lived **Quiet Melon**, who later had two tracks issued on CD in April 1995, and he then quit the music business eventually to become a graphic designer. He later re-emerged to make the occasional recording and was a member of the revived **Downliners Sect** in recent decades.

For those into mega collectables, there's an unissued album, *Zetas Twigs*, a mix of R&B, music hall and Art's zany Goon Show type humour and also a one-sided acetate of *What Shall I Do Now* on EMI. Various members of the band also appeared uncredited on the album *The Fantastic Freddie Mack Show* on Raynik Records in 1966. **Freddie Mack** was managed by Johnny Jones, **The Artwoods**' manager, who produced this 'live' recording. Various session men were required to improve the performance of Freddie's original band - enter **The Artwoods**. The album, a R&B style offering with a **Geno Washington** feel flopped.

There's also one fake 'collectable' - an acetate of the band playing live in a club in North Wales which was sold by a dealer a few years back for big money. This gig was actually recorded in 1964 by an aquaintance of the band and copied to the band members. Subsequently someone has made an acetate from a couple of tracks on the tape and passed it off as an old demo. Further live tapes do exist.

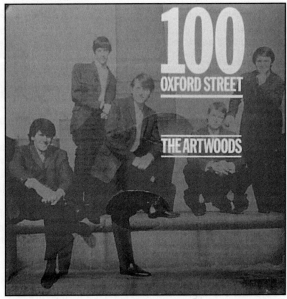

THE ARTWOODS - 100 Oxford Street (LP).

It's really been the subsequent success of **Jon Lord** and **Keef Hartley** that has kept some level of interest in **The Artwoods**. Decca reissued the *Art Gallery* album on their budget Eclipse label in 1970. In 1973 Spark put out a compilation comprising eight songs from *Art Gallery* and all the tracks (except *These Boots Are Made For Walking*) from the *Jazz In Jeans* (EP). Ten years later, Edsel released a 16-track compilation consisting of all their Decca 'A' and 'B' sides (except *Molly Anderson's Cookery Book*) and seven cuts from the *Art Gallery* album. The album came with a four-page history of the group written by former member, Derek Griffiths. Repertoire too have an excellent 26-track CD compilation entitled *Art Gallery*.

Compilation appearances have included: *Shake* on *Justification* (LP); *What Shall I Do* on *My Generation* (LP); *Chicago Calling* and *Hoochie Coochie Man* on *Made In England, Vol. 2* (CD) and *Incredible Sound Show Stories, Vol. 5* (LP); and *In The Deep End, What Shall I Do, Daytripper, Steady Getting' It* and *Devil With The Blue Dress On/Good Golly Miss Molly* on *Deep Purple - Odd Ditties* (CD). (VJ)

Arzachel

Personnel: CLIVE BROOKS (BASIL DOWLING)   drms   A
            MONT CAMPBELL
            (NJEROGI GATEGAKA)   bs, vcls A
            STEVE HILLAGE
            (SIMON SASPARELLA)   gtr, vcls A
            DAVE STEWART (SAM LEE-UFF)   keyb'ds   A

ARZACHEL - Arzachel (LP).

ALBUM: 1(A) ARZACHEL   (Evolution Z 1003) 1969 R4

NB: (1) Also issued in the US (Roulette 42036); by Vogue (LDVS 17218) in France; by CBS in Italy in 1971; and by Bellaphon in Germany in 1972, also with a different cover. (1) has also been pirated on vinyl several times and reissued officially on CD (Demon/Drop Out DOCD 1983) 1994.

This spacey psychedelic album is notable for the involvement of **Steve Hillage**. Musically it's at times a little over the top. But, the opening cut, *Garden Of Earthly Delights* is of interest and *Azathoth* has a rich 'church' organ backing. On side two *Clean Innocent Fun* previews **Hillage**'s fine guitar work and *Metempsychosis* opens full of weirdness and sound effects (which recur at regular intervals throughout) before pursuing a similar vein. The latter track, in particular, begs comparison with **Pink Floyd** around the *Saucerful Of Secrets* era. *Arzachel* is a very keyboard-dominated album.

The group was known as Uriel until July 1968 when **Hillage** went off to college. The others formed **Egg** (July '68 - May '72) and the **Arzachel** album was recorded by **Egg** with help from **Steve Hillage**. When **Hillage** left college in April 1971 and returned to London he formed **Khan**.

Compilation appearances have included: *Garden Of Earthly Delights* on *Circus Days Vol. 1 & 2* (CD) and *Circus Days, Vol. 1* (LP); and *Queen Street Gang* on *Instro-Hipsters A Go-Go* (CD). (VJ/JR/JM/GB)

Asgard

Personnel:	TED BARTLETT	vcls	A
	DAVE COOK	bs	A
	RODNEY HARRISON	gtr, vcls	A
	PETER ORGIL	violin	A
	JAMES SMITH	vcls	A
	IAN SNOW	drms	A

ALBUM: 1(A) IN THE REALM OF ASGARD (Threshold THS 6) 1972 R1

NB: (1) reissued on CD in Japan (JPHCR4238).

45s: Friends/Children Of A New Born Age   (Threshold TH 10) 1972
        In The Realm Of Asgard/Town Crier(Threshold TH 15) 1973

This album, which is a cross between **Fantasy** and **The Moody Blues**, is worth checking out. **Asgard** came from the West Country and their first 45 was produced by Tony Clarke. They were also one of the first bands signed by Gerry Hoff, head of The **Moody Blues**' Threshold label.

Rod Harrison had previously played in **Please** and **Bulldog Bread**, whilst James Smith and Ian Snow went on to **Stonehouse**. (VJ)

Ashkan

Personnel: STEVE BAILEY   vcls   A

RON BENDING	bs, vcls	A
TERRY SIMS	perc, drms	A
BOB WESTON	gtr, vcls, mandolin	A

ALBUM: 1(A) IN FROM THE COLD   (Decca Nova SDN-R 1) 1969 R1

NB: (1) also issued in the US (Sire). (1) reissued on CD (World Wide Records SPM-WWR-CD-0053) 1993.

Basically a hard-blues album and the first to be issued on Decca's Nova imprint. Bob Weston went on to play with Ashman-Reynolds and **Fleetwood Mac**. One of the cuts, *Practically Never Happens*, got a further airing on *Broken Dreams, Vol. 6* (LP). (MK/SB/RMJ)

Steve Ashley

ALBUMS:	1	STROLL ON	(Gull GULP 1003) 1974
(up to	2	SPEEDY RETURN	(Gull)1976
1976)			

NB: (1) reissued on CD (Market Square MSMCD 104) 1999.

45s:	α	No Smoke Without Fire/	
(up to		Only One Love, Never Two	(Columbia DB 8827) 1971
1976		Old Rock 'n' Roll/Fire And Wine	(Gull GULS 9) 1974

NB: α released as Ashley.

Steve Ashley has been an influential member in the evolution of British folk over four decades.

Steve Ashley was born in London in March 1946. His musical career began on two radically opposed fronts in the emerging roots of music of the early sixties. The first was as a singer of traditional songs and the second was as a vocalist/harmonica player in an art college blues band. The synthesis of these and other styles inspired a songwriting career which began in 1967 in a folk duo with Dave Menday called The Tinderbox.

In 1969, **Ashley** appeared singing on **Shirley and Dolly Collins**' *Anthems In Eden* album. In 1971, he co-founded **The Albion Country Band** with ex-**Fairport Convention** members **Ashley Hutchings**, Simon Nichol and Dave Mattocks plus Royston Wood from **The Young Tradition** and the American fiddler Sue Draheim.

In 1972 he formed his own band Ragged Robin with whom he recorded an album with **Anne Briggs**.

His 1974 debut album *Stroll On* was released on the Decca subsidary, Gull Records. It was critically acclaimed and 'Folk Review' heralded it as 'Contemporary Album of the Year'. It was also the Sunday Telegraph's recommended folk album of the year. It was produced by Austin John Marshall using arrangements by Robert Kirby.

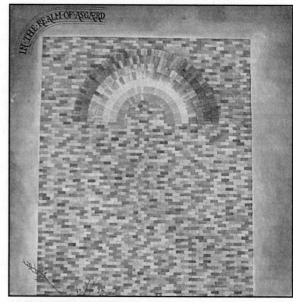

ASGARD - In The Realm Of Asgard (LP).

ASHKAN - In From The Cold (LP).

The Kirby-produced follow-up *Speedy Return* consolidated his reputation as a songwriter who reflected English life and culture in a very individual way and both his albums were released in the US by Motown. They both feature appearances from some of folk's key names, such as Danny Thompson, **Dave Pegg**, **Barry Dransfield** and Dave Mattacks. Robert Kirby, incidentally, was best known for his work with **Nick Drake**.

Ashley toured Europe and the States until 1978 when he took a rest after failing to find a label for his third album *Rare Old Men*. However, he returned with a concept album of songs relating to each member of a typical English family. *The Family Album* was released on **Dave Pegg's** Woodworm label in 1982 to a warm reception.

In the eighties his music became more political - he recorded a cassette album *Demo Tapes* (1981) as a fundraiser for CND and a further set, *More Demo Tapes* followed in 1985. The nineties saw further albums and he played at festivals including Cropredy, Glastonbury and Cambridge. In April 2001 he released a new solo album *Everyday Lives*.

The first 45 is reputedly by a different artist. (VJ/RMJ)

Ashman - Reynolds

Personnel:	ALIKI ASHMAN	vcls	A
	KEITH BOYCE	drms	A
	ROD EDWARDS	keyb'ds	A
	MICKEY KEEN	gtr	A
	HARRY REYNOLDS	vcls, bs	A
	BOB WESTON	gtr, vcls	A

| ALBUM: | 1(A) | STOP OFF | (Polydor) 1972 |

| 45: | Taking Off/Long Long Road | (Polydor) 1972 |

All of the above (except Keen, who had played with **Alex Harvey**) had been in **Long John Baldry's** band. After this brief venture, Weston joined **Fleetwood Mac** in September 1972; Ashman joined **Casablanca**; Boyce played with **The Heavy Metal Kids** and Edwards went on to session work. (JM)

Mark Ashton

| 45: | Get Up And Groove/Barking Dogs | (United Artists 35390) 1972 |

Ashton had left **Rare Bird** shortly before making this 45, which also featured Cyril Jordan on slide guitar. As many of you will know Cyril was a member of The Flamin' Groovies who were touring England at the time. (VJ)

Ashton, Gardner and Dyke

Personnel:	TONY ASHTON	keyb'ds, vcls	A
	ROY DYKE	drms	A
	KIM GARDNER	bs	A

ALBUMS:	1(A)	ASHTON, GARDNER AND DYKE	
(up to			(Polydor 583 081) 1969 SC
1976)	2(A)	THE WORST OF ASHTON, GARDNER AND DYKE	
			(Capitol EST 563) 1971
	3(A)	WHAT A BLOODY LONG DAY IT'S BEEN	
			(Capitol EAST 862) 1972

NB: (1) reissued on CD Line (LMCD 9.51136) 1992. (1), (2) and (3) reissued on CD (Repertoire REO 4565-WY, REP 4458-WY and REP 4457-WY respectively) 1994. *Let It Roll! Live On Stage* (Purple PUR 307) 2001 captures their live legacy for the first time. Also of interest is *The Last Rebel* (Purple PUR 309) 2002, a reissue of an original soundtrack album featuring Tony Ashton and Jon Lord, which originally had a very limited US-only pressing.

HCP

45s:	Maiden Voyage/		
	See The Sun In My Eyes	(Polydor 56306) 1969 R1 -
	Resurrection Shuffle/		
	Hymn To Everyone	(Capitol CL 15665) 1970 3
	Can You Get It/Delirium	(Capitol CL 15684) 1971 -

This was something of a supergroup. Kim Gardner had been in **The Birds, Creation** and **Quiet Melon** prior to joining this band. Tony Ashton was previously in The New Dakotas and Roy Dyke had been in **The Remo Four**. All three were part of PP Arnold's backing band for her January - February European tour. Their debut album lacked a certain amount of verve but was liberally laced with R&B influenced compositions and they scored an unexpected hit with the goodtime rock 'n' blues song *Resurrection Shuffle* in 1971.

Their second album explored a range of soul-flavoured rock styles with lyrics that often reflected on the evils of war. **Eric Clapton** and **George Harrison** guested on one of its better moments, *I'm Your Spiritual Breadman* and **Chicken Shack**'s Stan Webb played guitar on another, *Let It Roll*. The final album was less political and more personal than the predecessor. Musically we're talking blues-rock here with the occasional track which veers more towards jazz-rock.

Tony Ashton and Jon Lord also collaborated on the original soundtrack album to a 1971 western called *The Last Rebel*. It's the story of Joe Nemeth, a famous American footballer of the era. It's a largely instrumental album, although Ashton does sing in some places. There are lots of orchestrated passages and some Purplesque-style too. The original album had a limited US-only release and is now scarce. The CD reissue includes sections that were edited out of the original soundtrack and a few alternate versions to provide an extra half hour of additional material and detailed sleevenotes. This will interest serious **Deep Purple** fans and those who liked Tony Ashton.

ASHTON GARDNER AND DYKE - Ashton Gardner And Dyke (CD).

ASHTON GARDNER AND DYKE - The Worst Of (CD).

ASHTON GARDNER AND DYKE - What A Bloody Long Day It's Been . (CD).

After their demise Tony Ashton went on to play for **Medicine Head** and was briefly in **Family** before teaming up with **Deep Purple**'s **Jon Lord** in Ashton and Lord. He died on 28 May 2001 aged 55 from cancer. Kim Gardner was later in **Badger**. He also died from cancer on 24 October 2001. Roy Dyke joined Angel Dust (which became **Badger**).

The trio was also featured on a couple of compilations:- *Supergroups, Vol. 2* (LP) included *Rolling Home* and *Rock Party* (LP) contained *Maiden Voyage*. (VJ/JM)

Astral Navigations

Personnel: (**Lightyears Away**)

BRIAN CALVERT	vcls, gtr, piano, bs	A
CHRIS CARRODUS COOMBS	gtr, vcls	A
TED HEPWORTH	drms	A
BILL NELSON	gtr, vcls	A
MARTIN SNELL	piano	A
BRIAN WILSON	bs	A
and other guests		A

Personnel: (**Thundermother**)

DAVID JOHN	vcls	A
FRED KELLY	drms	A
DAVE MILLEN	gtr, vcls	A
FRANK NEWBOULD	gtr, bs	A
DAVE SMITH	bs	A
DAVE WILKINSON	piano	A

ALBUM: 1(A) ASTRAL NAVIGATIONS
(Holyground HG 114/NSR 172) 1971 R4

NB: (1) reissued (Magic Mixture (MM 2) 1989, with a booklet and just 425 copies (R1). (1) reissued on CD (Holyground HBG 122/1 CD) 1992 (SC). The CD reissue is limited to 1,000 copies and includes two bonus tracks, *Rock Me Babe*, and a spacey version of *Come On Home*.

These two bands share a side each of this album which is a nice mixture of folk and psychedelia with lots of fuzz guitar. A very difficult record to find now, the original came with a poster cover and booklet and the reissue came with a booklet and was lavishly repackaged. The five **Lightyears Away** tracks are mostly quite folky and melodic with pleasant male vocals and the occasional female voice too. The exception is *Yesterday* which begins with a recording of a space launch which leads into lots of fuzz guitar work.

Thundermother were a studio creation and their contribution was recorded over a weekend (mostly on acid). They were an amalgam of various Preston artists:- David John (**David John and The Mood**), Fred Kelly (**Rare Bird**), Dave Millen (**The Puppets**) and Frank Newbould (**Little Free Rock**). To my ears the three **Thundermother** tracks are better. *Today, Tomorrow, Someday* and *Country Lines* are both notable for some

discordant instrumental work whilst on the first cut the vocals are rather folky. The magnum opus, though, is the extended and highly experimental finale *Boogie Music*, which is imaginative with lots of good fuzzy guitar work - it's one of Holyground's finest moments.

The album got a welcome limited reissue on vinyl in 1989 and a limited CD reissue in 1992.

Thundermother has also been the focus of another CD retrospective *No Red Rowan* (Kissing Spell KSG 003) 1995, which features material recorded between '70-'71. You can also hear **Thundermother**'s *Boogie Music* and *Rock Me Babe* on *Loose Routes* (LP).

Bill Nelson went on to found **Be-Bop Deluxe**. (VJ)

The Athenians

45s:			
	You Tell Me/		
	Little Queenie (Edinburgh Students Charities Appeal 1) 1964 R1		
	I've Got Love If You Want It/		
	I'm A Lover Not A Fighter		
	(Some PS)	(Waverley SLP 532) 1964 R3/R2	
	Thinking Of Your Love/Mercy		
	Mercy (some custom sleeve)	(Waverley SLP 533) 1965 R2/R1	

This was the first Scottish-based beat group to record a single. The Edinburgh band recorded *You Tell Me* to help the student's annual charities appeal and was also sold at the University Shop. It's reputedly poor. The follow-up, a Slim Harpo song, was a big improvement and came in a picture bag. Their final effort, *Thinking Of Your Love*, was a **Shadows'** song, but after this and various line-up changes they fell apart.

Compilation appearances include: *I'm A Lover Not A Fighter* on *Rare 60's Beat Treasures, Vol. 4* (CD); and *Louie Louie* on *That Driving Beat* (CD). (VJ)

Glenn Athens and The Trojans

Personnel incl: GLENN ATHENS

EP: 1 GLENN ATHENS AND THE TROJANS
(Spot 7E 1018) 1965 R4

This group won a Surrey Beat Group contest in 1964 which enabled them to record this very rare four-track EP. The stand-out track on this was the slow bluesy number *Let Me Show You How*, which came with fuzzy guitar and garage-style vocals. The remaining cuts comprised a brief instrumental *Guillotine* and a couple of pleasant but mundane beat ballads, *You're The One* and *Don't Say That Word*.

Let Me Show You How can also be heard on *Perfumed Garden Vol. 2* (LP & CD) and *English Freakbeat, Vol. 2* (LP & CD). (VJ)

Pete Atkins

ALBUMS:	1	BEWARE OF THE BEAUTIFUL STRANGER	
(up to			(Fontana 6309 011) 1970
1976)	2	DRIVING THROUGH MYTHICAL AMERICA	
			(Philips 6308 070) 1971
	3	A KING AT NIGHTFALL	(RCA SF 8336) 1973
	4	THE ROAD OF SILK	(RCA LPLI 5014) 1974
	5	SECRET DISASTER	(RCA LPLI 5062) 1974
	6	LIVE LIBEL	(RCA RS 1013) 1975

NB: There was also a compilation, *Master Of Revels* (RCA PL2 5041) 1977. (1) reissued on vinyl (RCA SF 8387) 1974 with one different track. (2) reissued on vinyl (RCA SF 8386) 1974. (1) and (2) reissued on one CD (See For Miles C5HCD) 1999.

Pete Atkins was a pianist composer who worked with Clive James (yes the Australian chat show king) who wrote the lyrics on their albums. Their song writing partnership was critically acclaimed in the music press but commercial success always proved more elusive for them to achieve.

They first met as members of the Cambridge Footlights Revue that spawned such British comedy talent as 'Beyond The Fringe' and 'Monty Python'. This connection later resulted in **Atkins** and James being invited to perform at various Amnesty International benefits that were subsequently released on DVD under the Secret Policeman's Ball titles.

Beware Of The Beautiful Stranger was originally recorded as a collection of demos to display their talents as songwriters to other artists but BBC DJ Kenny Everett liked the album's opening track and played it on his show and Philips decided to issue the album on its Fontana label. The same year future 'Evita' star Julie Covington released an album *Beautiful Changes* that was almost entirely comprised of **Atkins**/James songs.

Their second album *Driving Through Mythical America* was more rock-oriented but the punters showed little interest and they switched to RCA for further albums but with little success. On 1975's *Live Libel* they sent-up other artists including Leonard Cohen, James Taylor and Clive James made his vocal debut on a spoof of the Telly Savalas hit *If*. This proved to be their final album for RCA, aside from a couple of compilations.

Atkins became a radio producer with the BBC and still continued to gig occasionally in small folk clubs. James became a household name for his television appearances, but excelled as a writer, critic and poet as well. His autobiography 'Unreliable Memoirs' was extremely amusing in places and became a best-seller.

In the late nineties **Atkins** began to perform regularly again and was soon joined by Clive James. As a result his back catalogue was reissued on CD and in 2001 he released a pair of albums *The Lakeside Sessions, Vol. 1*

and *Vol. 2*, which contained new recordings of many of his songs left over from the seventies. His composing partnership with James was reinvigorated too and the result was an album *Winter/Spring* in 2003 containing brand new material, which was funkier in style. (VJ/AH)

Atlantic Bridge

Personnel:	MIKE McNAUGHT	keyb'ds	A
	JIM PHILLIPS	flute, sax	A
	DARRYL RUNSWICK	double bs, bs	A
	MIKE TRAVIS	drms	A

ALBUM: 1(A) ATLANTIC BRIDGE   (Dawn DNLS 3014) 1970 SC

NB: (1) reissued on vinyl (Get Back GET 552).

EP: 1(A)   I CAN'T LIE TO YOU   (Dawn DNX 2507) 1971

While making another UK "jazz" album on a progressive label, this crew testified their closeness to rock by playing exclusively tracks such as Jimmy Webb's *MacArthur Park*, **Harrison**'s *Something* and **Lennon**'s *Dear Prudence*. Still, those songs were better served by the originals than by these re-makes. Double bass player Runswick executed a few beautiful bowed passages, but on the whole this fell between the chairs of jazz and rock and hit the floor with a nondescript thud. Buy yourself a Sonny Rollins album instead.

Mike Travis had earlier played in **Buzz** and went on to **Gilgamesh**.

They also figure on Dawn's 1971 *Dawn Takeaway Concert* (LP) compilation playing *Childhood Room (Exit Waltz)*. (MK)

Atlas

Personnel:	RONNIE CHARLES	vcls	AB
	LES GOUGH	bs	AB
	TERRY SLADE	drms	A
	GLEN TURNER	gtr, vcls	A
	ERIC CAIRNS	drms	B
	BRIAN HOLLOWAY	gtr	B
	GARY MOBERLEY	keyb'ds	B

ALBUM: 1(A) ROCK'N'ROLL WIZARDS   (Reprise) 1974

45:    Rock 'n' Roll Wizards/Military Rag   (Reprise) 1974

This UK/Australian heavy rock band was based in the UK. Ronnie Charles was something of a heartthrob down under in the sixties being in an outfit called The Groop, who were rarely out of the Aussie charts in the 1965 - 1967 era. Prior to joining **Atlas** he was in Captain Australia and Honky Tonk (back in Australia). Brian Cadd is one of Australia's best known

ASTRAL NAVIGATIONS - Astral Navigations (CD).

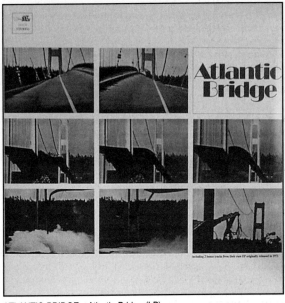

ATLANTIC BRIDGE - Atlantic Bridge (LP).

songwriters. He was also a member of The Groop. Les Gough had been in Aussie band Heart & Soul and the two Brits (Slade and Turner) were in **Sunshine**. After recording the album and 45 Slade departed to The George Hatcher Band and Turner joined **Tundra**. They were replaced by Australians Eric Cairn (ex-Company Caine) and Gary Moberley (ex-John Rupert Group) and former **Esperanto Rock Orchestra** member Brian Holloway.

After the group split Cairns returned to Australia to join Red Hot Peppers. Holloway went on to the **Kiki Dee** Band. Ronnie Charles was later in a studio group called White Light Orchestra and then Turbo Love (Luv) Nuns. (JM)

At Last The 1958 Rock 'n' Roll Show

Personnel incl:	MILLER ANDERSON	A
	IAN HUNTER (PATTERSON)	A
	FREDDIE 'FINGERS' LEE	A
	PETE PHILIPS	

| 45: | I Can't Drive/Working On The Railroad | (CBS 3349) 1968 SC |

A one-off project most likely to be of interest to **Mott The Hoople** fans since **Ian Hunter** played on the 45, which was issued around the same time the band appeared in a film documentary. The 'A' side *I Can't Drive* is the exact same recording of the 'B' side by **Fingers Lee**. This same band recorded a second single in August 1968, but under a new name Charlie Woolfe (*Dance Dance Dance/Home* (NEMS 56-3675)). **Miller Anderson** was later with **Savoy Brown**, **Keef Hartley**, **Hemlock** and **Broken Glass**, among others. (VJ/JP)

Atomic Rooster

Personnel:	VINCE CRANE	keyb'ds	ABCDEFG H I
	NICK GRAHAM	bs, vcls	A
	CARL PALMER	drms	A
	RICK PARNELL	drms	B EFG
	JOHN CANN		
	(aka DU CANN)	vcls, gtr	CD H
	PAUL HAMMOND	drms	CD H
	PETE FRENCH	vcls	D
	STEVE BOLTON	gtr	EF
	CHRIS FARLOWE	vcls	EF
	BILL SMITH	bs	EFG
	JOHN MANDELLA	gtr	FG
	BRIAN JUNIPER	sax	G
	TONY SUPER-SMOOTH	sax	G
	GINGER BAKER	drms	I
	JOHN MIZAROLLI	gtr	I

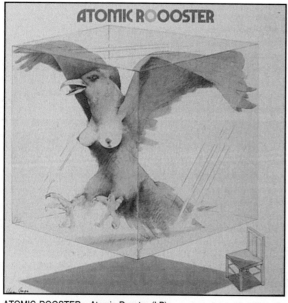

ATOMIC ROOSTER - Atomic Rooster (LP).

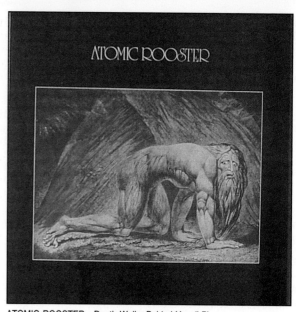

ATOMIC ROOSTER - Death Walks Behind You (LP).

HCP

ALBUMS:	1(A)	ATOMIC ROOSTER	(B+C CAS 1010) 1970 R1 49
(up to	2(C)	DEATH WALKS BEHIND YOU	
1977)			(B+C CAS 1026) 1970 SC 12
	3(D)	IN HEARING OF ATOMIC ROOSTER	
			(Pegasus PEG 1) 1971 SC 18
	4(E)	MADE IN ENGLAND	(Dawn DNLS 3038) 1972 R1 -
	5(E)	NICE 'N' GREASY	(Dawn DNLS 3049) 1973 R1 -
	6(-)	ASSORTMENT (Compilation)	(B+C CS 9) 1974 -
	7(-)	HOME TO ROOST (2-LP) (Compilation)	
			(Mooncrest CDR 2) 1977 -

NB: (1), (2) and (3) reissued on CD by Repertoire (REP 4135 WZ, REP 4069 WZ and REP 4563 WY respectively) 1995. (1) reissued on CD (Receiver RRCD 277 Z) 1999, with one bonus track *Play The Game*. (3) reissued again on CD (Castle CMQCD 926) 2004, with several additional tracks, including some live BBC recordings and lots of sleevenotes. (4) reissued on CD (Repertoire REP 4165-WZ). (4) reissued again on CD (Castle CMQCD 927) 2004 , with several additional tracks, including some live BBC recordings and lots of sleevenotes. (4) and (5) reissued on CD Sequel (NEM CD 610) and (NEM CD 611) in 1991. (4) also issued in the U.S.A. with a different cover (Elektra 75039) 1972. (5) reissued on CD (Akarma AK 178) and again on CD (Sanctuary/Castle CMQCD 1004) 2004 plus the two alternate tracks from the US version of the album and two from the 1980 reunion with original guitarist John Cann. (5) also issued in the USA under the alternative title *Atomic Rooster IV* and with different artwork (Elektra 75074) 1973. (7) later reissued on Rawpower (RAWLP 027) in 1986 and again with the same catalogue number, but a different cover in 1989. The band reformed in 1980 recording *Atomic Rooster* (EMI EMC 3341) that year. It was later reissued on Charisma (CHC 58) in 1986. The reformed band also recorded *Headline News* (Towerbell TOWLP 004) in 1983. The *Devil Hits Back* (Demi-Monde DMLP 1023) 1989 is an album of live material mostly from the 1980 **Atomic Rooster** comeback album and is not recommended. Compilations include: *The Collection* (Object Enterprises ORO138) 1991, *In Satan's Name: The Definitive Collection* (Recall) 1997 compiles the better cuts from their first five albums and *Devil's Answer - BBC Sessions* (Hux HUX 005) 1998. *The First Ten Explosive Years* (Angel Air SJPCD 038) 1999 is a 16-track compilation covering their output from 1970-1972 and their second 1979-1982 incarnation. *Rarities* (Angel Air SJPCD 069) 2000 will appeal to diehard fans of the band. *The First Ten Explosive Years: Volume 2* (Angel Air SJPCD 086) 2001 comes with sleevenotes that provide a good band history. *Heavy Soul* (Sanctuary CMDDD364) 2001 is a 2-CD compilation, which concentrates on their early seventies material.

HCP

45s:	Friday The 13th/Banstead	(B+C CB 121) 1970 -
(up to	Tomorrow Night/Play The Game	(B+C CB 131) 1971 11
1976)	Devil's Answer/The Rock	(B+C CB 157) 1971 4
	Stand By Me/Never To Lose	(Dawn DNS 1027) 1972 -
	Save Me/Close Your Eyes	(Dawn DNS 1029) 1972 -
α	Tell Your Story (Sing Your Song)/	
	O.D.	(Decca FR 13503) 1974 -
Reissues:	Devil's Answer/The Rock	(Mooncrest MOON 52) 1976 -
	Devil's Answer/Tomorrow Night/	
	Can't Take You No More	(B+C BCS21) 1980 -
	Devil's Answer/Tomorrow Night	(Old Gold OG9391) 1984 -

NB: α as **Vincent Crane's Atomic Rooster**.

Atomic Rooster was an important thread in the tapestry of early seventies progressive rock. The central figure throughout the many line-ups of Atomic Rooster was Vince Crane, who'd previously played for The Crazy World Of Arthur Brown. Drummer, Carl Palmer, (ex-Chris Farlowe's Thunderbirds) had previously played with Crane on The Crazy World's US tour. They seem to have taken their name from an album by the American group Rhinoceros and, having quickly established themselves on the club and college circuit, issued a debut album *Atomic Rooster* in 1970, which was well received and sold enough copies to make the Top 50. A couple of tracks were also put out on a 45 but these failed to make much impact. The first of these *Friday The 13th* is pretty rocky and *Winter* veers towards progressive rock. By contrast *Before Tomorrow* was extremely frantic. Their promising start was rapidly arrested in 1970 when Nick Graham departed for Skin Alley, being replaced by John Cann (ex-Andromeda). In June, Carl Palmer also left, to became one third of Emerson, Lake and Palmer. He was replaced briefly by Rick Parnell (ex-Horse).

In the Autumn of 1970 Vince Crane brought in former Farm drummer Paul Hammond to replace Parnell. This line-up played a much heavier brand of rock which proved popular with the punters. The *Death Walks Behind You* album made the UK Top 20 and they also enjoyed two Top 20 UK hit singles with *Tomorrow Night* and their best known song *Devil's Answer*, which peaked at No 4.

In 1971 they signed to Pegasus Records and with the addition of vocalist Pete French (ex-Big Bertha/Leaf Hound) they recorded the *In Hearing Of* album, which many consider to be their finest. Once again their progress was halted when John Cann and Paul Hammond left in September 1971 to form Bullet. Parnell rejoined with Steve Bolton (ex-Wide Open) and vocalist Paul French departed in February 1972 to the U.S. band Cactus.

The next line-up Crane pieced together (E) raised a few eyebrows by virtue of the inclusion of R&B singer Chris Farlowe (ex-Jon Hiseman's Colosseum). Supplemented by two girl backing vocalists Liza Strike and Doris Troy they changed from their previous hard-rock format to a sort of soul-funk recording a couple of albums and singles for Dawn. Earlier copies of *Made In England* came in a denim cover and, along with *Nice 'n' Greasy* (on which guitarist John Mandella also played), these are their rarest items. The *Save Me* 45 was also a non-album cut at the time. *Nice'n'Greasy* had some good cuts, particularly *Save Me* and *Ear In The Snow*. However, the sales of the two Dawn albums were disastrous and taking the view that the band's fortunes were in irreversible decline Crane disbanded them in 1973. The inevitable compilations appeared over subsequent years of which the *Home To Roost* double set was the most worthwhile.

During this period, Bolton left in Dec '72 to Headstone, being replaced by Mandella (aka Johnny Goodsall ex-Alan Bown). Farlowe left in May '73 to tour with a pickup band as Chris Farlowe and The Thunderbirds to promote an album.

For live appearances, they were joined by sax players Brian Juniper and Tony Super-Smooth (both ex-Grand Stamp). Parnell then joined Al Matthews' Last Word and Mandella/Goodsall joined Brand X.

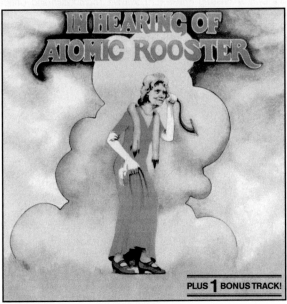

ATOMIC ROOSTER - In Hearing Of (CD).

ATOMIC ROOSTER - Nice 'N' Greasy (LP).

Having done some further work with Arthur Brown in the interim Crane reformed the band in 1979 reuniting with John Cann and drummer Preston Hayman. They recorded an album and a couple of singles for EMI and then, with Hayman having been replaced by previous member Paul Hammond, a couple of singles for Polydor and an album for Towerbell. After the latter made no impact at all Vince Crane decided to bring the Atomic Rooster story to an end for good. He was briefly a member of Dexy's Midnight Runners.

Heavy Soul, Sanctuary's 2001 compilation concentrates on their early seventies material. It features the 'B' side *Friday 13th* for the first time on CD. The tracks are all remastered and the sleevenotes are very detailed, making this a delight both for serious and more casual collectors. Angel Air's *Rarities* collection will excite diehard fans. It's full of alternate takes, demos and unreleased tracks.

Vincent Crane committed suicide on 14 February 1989. He'd suffered from anxiety and depression.

Stand By Me can also be heard on Ronco's *20 Star Tracks* and two Atomic Rooster tracks written by John duCann, previously unreleased elsewhere, *Take It For Granted* and *Sleepless Nights* can be found on *Kiss Yer Skull Goodbye* (LP). More recently, *Death Walks Behind You* got a further airing on *Rock Of Ages, Four Decades Of Heavy Rock 1962-2002* (LP) and *Devil's Answer* figured on the 3-CD box set *Radio Caroline Calling - 70's Flashback*, on the 3-CD box set *Ars Longa Vita Brevis: A Compendium Of Progressive Rock 1967-1974* (which also included *Tomorrow Night*) and on *70's FAB FAV's - Classic 70's Hits* (CD). (VJ/FC/VS/JM)

The Attack

Personnel incl:			
GERRY HENDERSON	bs	ABCD	
BOB HODGES	organ	ABCD	
DAVEY O'LIST	ld gtr	AB	
RICHARD SHERMAN	vcls	ABCD	
BOB TAYLOR	gtr	ABCD	
ALAN 'NODDY' WHITEHEAD	drms	A	
BARNY BARNFIELD	drms	B	
BRIAN DAVIDSON	drms		C
JOHN DU CANN	gtr		D
KEVIN FLANAGAN			
DENNIS HOOKER			

ALBUM: 1( ) MAGIC IN THE AIR (Reflection MM 08) 1990 SC

NB: (1) reissued on CD (Aftermath AFT 1001) 1992. *The Complete Recordings From 1967-1968* (ACME Deluxe Series ADLP 1026) 2000 contains everything the band recorded on one album. *Final Daze* (Get Back GET 602) 2001 is a compilation of 17 unreleased tracks from between 1968-1969. It later appeared on CD (Angel Air SJPCD-080) 2001.

45s: Try It/We Don't Know   (Decca F 12550) 1967 R3
        Anymore Than I Do/
        Hi Ho Silver Lining   (Decca F 12578) 1967 R1
        Created By Clive/Colour Of My Mind   (Decca F 12631) 1967 R2
        Neville Thumbcatch/Lady Orange Peel (Decca F 12725) 1968 R2
    α   Hi Ho Silver Lining/Anymore Than I Do   (Decca F 13353) 1972
NB: α not released.

The Attack who played a form of guitar-driven mod-rock were one of the finest examples of what is now termed freakbeat. The level of interest now in this musical genre and the resulting reissue of their material in recent years has meant that, in common with many other bands of this genre, they have a far larger fan base now than they enjoyed back in the sixties.

Originally known as The Soul System this group signed to Decca late in 1966, having chosen the new name of **The Attack**. They seem to have undergone several line-up changes although vocalist Richard Sherman and bassist Gerry Henderson appear to have been core members throughout. Their first 45 was a reasonable attempt at the Standells' classic punk song, which had also been tackled in the US by The Ohio Express. At this point Alan Whitehead departed for **Marmalade** and Barny Barnfield replaced him on drums.

Their next release *Hi Ho Silver Lining* lost out in the Chart battle to **Jeff Beck**'s version and also led them into controversy in the music press when they claimed **Beck** had nicked the song from them. The flip side, a frantic hard-edged rocker with some fine guitar work, was adapted by John Peel for one of his Radio London jingles. At this point Davey O'List left to join **The Nice**. Brian Davidson came in briefly on drums, but he left very soon to join O'List in **The Nice**.

Surprisingly, having already been bruised by the **Jeff Beck** clash, their record label had the lack of foresight to issue their version of *Created By Clive* on the same day that **The Syn**'s version appeared on their Deram subsidiary. The result was stalemate when in actual fact the song deserved better. The 45 spawned another strong flip side - *Colours Of My Mind* - great vocals, prominent organ and some sitaresque guitar work.

Their final 45, *Neville Thumbcatch*, which tells the story of a man and his allotment is frankly awful. The flip, *Lady Orange Peel* was a slow, rather offbeat effort, which came with a short guitar solo but really weak vocals. Not surprisingly, it met with little commercial success. In fact *Magic In The Air* had been intended for 45 release prior to this but was rejected as too heavy. Guitarist John Du Cann joined around this period.

Despite their lack of 45 success the band began work on an album which was to have been called *Roman Gods Of War*. According to Record Mirror it was scheduled for release on 15 March 1968, but it never appeared. A final 45 Feel Like Flying/Freedom For You was also projected for release but never appeared. Sadly, the band were no more and all we have to remember them by are their four 45s which fortunately have been well covered on recent compilations and the various retrospective releases.

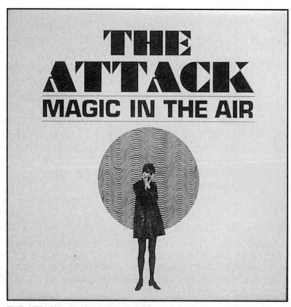

THE ATTACK - Magic In The Air (LP).

THE ATTACK - Final Daze (LP).

John Du Cann did work on an album with **Five Day Week Straw People** in 1968. He later formed **Andromeda** who issued a new version of **The Attack's** *Go Your Way* as their first single. In the seventies Du Cann joined **Atomic Rooster**.

The 1990 Reflection album *Magic In The Air* is comprised of rarities by the band, mostly taken from acetates. It includes a different version of *Hi Ho Silver Lining*, the swinging sixties style *Neville Thumbcatch*, the psychedelic *Lady Orange Peel* and what some would term freakbeat compositions like *Anymore Than I Do* and *Try It*.

In 2000 Acme released a compilation *The Complete Recordings From 1967-1968*, which comprised the above album plus three additional songs to ensure that everything they had recorded was finally contained on one album.

The 2001 *Final Daze* release contains 17 mostly mono, previously unreleased tracks, recorded between 1968-69. Clearly demonstrating the band's transition away from psychedelic pop and into the heavier **Andromeda** style rock, it's worth hearing and includes renditions of *Go Your Way* and an acoustic *Magic In The Air*.

Compilation coverage has included:- *We Don't Know* on *The Mod Scene* (CD); *Try It* on *Mod Scene, Vol. 2* (CD); *Colour Of My Mind* on *Electric Sugarcube Flashbacks, Vol. 1* (LP), *The Psychedelic Scene* (CD) and on the 4-CD box set *Acid Drops, Spacedust & Flying Saucers*; *Anymore Than I Do* and *Try It* on *Rubble, Vol. 5 - The Electric Crayon Set* (LP), *Rubble, Vol. 3* (CD); *Anymore Than I Do*, *Colours Of My Mind* and *Try It* on *Broken Dreams, Vol. 1* (LP); *Anymore Than I Do* on *The Freakbeat Scene* (CD) and *It's Only A Passing Phase* (LP); *Neville Thumbcatch* and *Created By Clive* on *Rubble, Vol. 6 - The Clouds Have Groovy Faces* (LP) and *Rubble, Vol. 4* (CD); *Colours Of My Mind* and *Lady Orange Peel* on *Rubble, Vol. 11 - Adventures In The Mist* (LP) and *Rubble, Vol. 6* (CD); *Created By Clive* on *The British Psychedelic Trip 1966 - 1969* (LP); and *Hi Ho Silver Lining* on *The World Of Hits, Vol. 2*. (VJ/BM)

The Attraction

Personnel: FEZ HARRIS   drms   A
              DEAN MAVERICK   vcls   A
              GEOFF WARREN   ld gtr   A
              KEITH WASTELL   gtr   A
              BRIAN YOUNG   bs   A

45s: Stupid Girl/Please Tell Me   (Columbia DB 7936) 1966 R1
        Party Line/She's A Girl   (Columbia DB 8010) 1966 R2

Despite this band's specialisation in cover versions (*Stupid Girl* was a **Rolling Stones** song and *Party Line* a **Kinks** composition), these 45s are very collectable now.

They hailed from Romford in Essex and **Dave Davies** produced *Party Line*. The flip side, *She's A Girl*, is basically a British form of garage music.

Compilation appearances have included: *She's A Girl* on *Rubble, Vol. 13 - Freak Beat Fantoms* (LP), *Rubble, Vol. 7* (CD), *That Driving Beat* (CD) and *English Freakbeat, Vol. 3* (LP & CD); *Party Line* and *She's A Girl* on *Rare 60's Beat Treasures, Vol. 1* (CD); and *Stupid Girl* on *Go... With An All Star* (LP). (VJ/JM)

Aubrey Small

Personnel:	ALAN CHRISTMAS	gtr	A
	GRAHAM HUNT	drms, gtr, vcls	A
	PETER PINCKNEY	gtr, vcls	A
	ROD TAYLOR	keyb'ds, vcls	A
	DAVID YEARLEY	bs	A
	DAVE YOUNG	flute	A

ALBUM: 1(A)   AUBREY SMALL (w/insert)   (Polydor 2383 048) 1971 R2

NB: (1) reissued on CD (Elergy E610/1)

45:   Loser/Oh What A Day It's Been   (Polydor 2058 204) 1972

A quite well regarded song-based melodic progressive album, by a South Coast band. Pinckney had previously been in **Lace**. (VJ)

Audience

Personnel:	TONY CONNOR	drms	AB
	KEITH GEMMELL	woodwind	AB
	HOWARD WERTH	gtr, vcls	AB
	TREVOR WILLIAMS	bs, keyb'ds, vcls	AB
	NICK JUDD	keyb'ds	B
	BOBBY KEYS	sax	B
	JIM PRICE	horns	B

ALBUMS:	1(A)	AUDIENCE	(Polydor 583 065) 1969 R2
	2(A)	FRIEND'S FRIEND'S FRIEND	(Charisma CAS 1012) 1970 SC
	3(A)	THE HOUSE ON THE HILL	(Charisma CAS 1032) 1971 SC
	4(B)	THE LUNCH	(Charisma CAS 1054) 1972
	5(-)	YOU CAN'T BEAT THEM (Compilation)	(Charisma CS 7) 1973

NB: (1) reissued as *The First Audience Album* (RPM 148) 1995. Complete with detailed sleevenotes, it also contains a couple of out-takes. (1) later reissued on CD (Luminous Records LCD 003) 2000, with three bonus tracks from 1969. (3) reissued on CD (Virgin CASCD 1032) 1990. (2) reissued on CD (Virgin CASCD 1012) 1992. (4) reissued on CD (Virgin CASCD 1054) 1991. There's also a later compilation, *Unchained* (Virgin CDVM 9007) 1992.

AUBREY SMALL - Aubrey Small (LP).

AUDIENCE - Audience (LP).

45s:	Belladonna Moonshine/The Big Spell	(Charisma CB 126) 1971
	Indian Summer/ It Brings A Tear/Princess (PS)	(Charisma CB 141) 1971
	You're Not Smiling/Eye To Eye	(Charisma CB 156) 1971
	Stand By The Door/ Thunder And Lightnin'	(Charisma CB 185) 1972

A London-based art-rock band who were popular on the club and college circuit. After an album for Polydor, which is now rare and sought-after because it was withdrawn soon after its release, they were signed to Charisma after they were spotted by the label's boss Tony Stratton-Smith supporting **Led Zeppelin** at the Lyceum in London. The debut album blended sax, flute and acoustic guitar, and some favourably likened it to **Traffic** at the time. In terms of style the album veers between folk, R&B, Latino and baroque pop.

Friend's Friend's Friend and *The House On The Hill* were both creative and worthwhile rock albums. Both, especially the former, are dominated by the outstanding sax and flute playing of Keith Gemmell and **Werth**'s strong and rather unusual vocals. Shel Talmy was lined up to produce the *Friend's Friend's Friend* album but declined at the last moment because he didn't like some of the material. He was looking for a big commercial album and while tracks like *Belladonna Moonshine* and *It Brings A Tear* probably appealed to him many of the others (e.g. *Raid*) were more experimental and didn't. As a result the band ended up producing the album themselves. Their *Indian Summer* 45, which sold quite well in the States, and the *House On The Hill* album were produced by Gus Dudgeon. This had a cover version (*I've Put A Spell On You*) but otherwise, like the first two, was made up of self-penned material including the R&B *Jackdaw* and the gentler *I Had A Dream*.

The band toured America with **The Faces** and built up a good underground following there. The line-up was augmented for the *Lunch* album by Nick Judd and American sessionmen Bobby Keys and Jim Price. This was probably their magnum opus but after its release personality rifts, particularly between Keith Gemmell and the rest of the band, ripped them apart.

They also performed the score for the 'Bronco Bullfrog' movie (also released under the name 'Angel Lane') which was written by **Howard Werth**. It was a film shot in the East End with a team of kids from a theatre, none of whom were professional actors.

After the band split, Gemmel joined **Sammy**; **Werth** recorded a solo album and went to the US in an attempt to make music with the surviving Doors members, before returning to the UK. In 1975 he recorded as **Howard Werth and The Moonbeams**. Trevor Williams went on to **Judas Jump**, **Jonathan Kelly's Outside**, and then **The Nashville Teens**; Connor first joined Jackson Heights and then **Hot Chocolate**; and Judd joined first **Sharks** (May '73 - Jul '74), then **The Andy Fraser Band** and **Casablanca**. He eventually become a session musician. Both Bobby Keys and Jim Price became respected session musicians too. Judd has played for **Eric Clapton**, **Joe Cocker**, **George Harrison**, **Rod Stewart**, **Peter Frampton**

AUDIENCE - Friends Friends Friend (LP).

and **Dr. John** as well as being in **Ashton, Gardner and Dyke** and **Heavy Jelly** - he also made solo albums in his own right.

Their debut album was reissued in 2000 with three bonus cuts: *Troubles*, a previously unfinished track which **Werth** added vocals to 30 years later; *The Going Song*, a previously unheard song from a film soundtrack and *Paper Round*, an outtake from the album sessions.

The *Unchained* compilation featured their Charisma material between 1970-72 and came with quite informative sleevenotes. They also figured on compilations at the time:- *Banquet* on *Rock Party* (LP), and *House On The Hill* on *Way Into The 70s* (LP). (VJ/LP/JM)

Mick Audsley

ALBUMS: 1 DARK AND DEVIL WATERS
                        (Sonet SNTF 641) 1973 with insert
         2 STORYBOARD   (Sonet SNTF 679) 1974

45s: Mr. Landlord/The Commissioner, He Come (Sonet 2035) c1974
        Mistah Foghorn Likes Bananas/Red Biddy (Sonet 2040) 1974

A gently rocking singer-songwriter assisted by a host of regular session people, including **Mick Hugg** and Hughie Flint of **Manfred Mann**. The first album is produced by Robert Kirby who also worked with the likes of **Nick Drake** and **Shelagh McDonald** at around the same period, leading to rumours that **Drake** may have contributed guitar to a couple of tracks on it. **Audsley**'s voice is light and pleasant, sounding a bit like **Mike Heron** in places. Some of the tunes are quite interesting. The lyrics have a highly visual quality ("underground trains come rising through the ground" for example), which may be appropriate if this is indeed the same **Mick Audsley** whose name now appears as a film editor in productions such as "My Beautiful Launderette", "The Avengers", and many others. Come to think of it, "storyboard" is a movie word, too. (NM/GB/RMJ)

Brian Auger (and The Trinity)

ALBUMS: 1 DEFINITELY WHAT!   (Marmalade 607 003) 1968 R1
(up to   2 DON'T SEND ME NO FLOWERS
1976)   (Marmalade 608 004) 1969 R1
         3 THE BEST OF BRIAN AUGER AND THE TRINITY
                        (Polydor 2334 004) 1969 SC
         4 BEFOUR   (RCA SF 8101) 1970 SC
         5 OBLIVION EXPRESS (RCA SF 8170) 1971 SC
         6 BETTER LAND   (Polydor 2383 062) 1971 SC
         7 SECOND WIND   (Polydor 2383 104) 1972 SC
         8 CLOSER TO IT   (CBS 65625) 1973
         9 STRAIGHT AHEAD   (CBS 80058) 1974
        10 LIVE OBLIVION   (RCA APLI-0645) 1974
        11 JAM SESSIONS   (Charly 30011) 1975

NB: (1) reissued on CD (Disconforme DISC 1004 CD) 1999 and later on vinyl (Disconforme SI DISC 1903 LP) 2001. (3) reissued on CD (Disconforme DISC 1008 CD) 1999 and later on vinyl (Disconforme SI DISC 1908 LP) 2001. (5) reissued on CD (Disconforme SI DISC 1009 CD) 2001. (7) reissued on CD (Disconforme SI DISC 1011 CD) 2001. (8) reissued on CD (Castle Music CMRCD 1101) 2005 in an expanded edition. (9) reissued on CD (Disconforme SI DISC 1014 CD) 2001.

45s: α Fool Killer/Let's Do It Tonight   (Columbia DB 7590) 1965 R2
(up to α Green Onions '65/Kiko   (Columbia DB 7715) 1965 R1
1976) α Tiger/Oh Baby, Won't You Come Back
          Home To Croydon, Where Everybody
          Beedle's And Bo's   (Columbia DB 8163) 1967 R1
       α Red Beans And Rice Pts 1 & 2   (Marmalade 598 003) 1967 R1
       α I Don't Know Where You Are/
          A Kind Of Love In   (Marmalade 598 006) 1968
       α What You Gonna Do?/
          Bumpin' On Sunset   (Marmalade 598 015) 1968 SC
       α I Want To Take You Higher/
          Just Me Just You   (RCA RCA 1947) 1970
       β Maria's Wedding/Tomorrow City   (Polydor 2058.133) 1971
       β Inner City Blues/Light On The Path   (CBS 1444) 1973
       β Straight Ahead / Change   (CBS 2309) 1974

NB: α as **Brian Auger and The Trinity**. β as Brian Auger's Oblivion Express.

Born in London in 1939 **Auger** started out as a jazz pianist. He quit the jazz genre in 1964 in favour of the emerging R&B movement forming The Trinity with Phil Kinnora (drms), Rick Laird (bs), **John McLaughlin** (gtr) and Glen Hughes (sax). This line-up only lasted a few months but **McLaughlin** and Laird would later re-emerge in the mid-seventies in the **Mahavishnu Orchestra**.

Auger then formed a second line-up with Vic Briggs (gtr), Rick Brown (bs) and Mickey Waller (drms), with himself switching from piano to organ. This line-up cut the two 45s for Columbia in 1965 but then got sucked into **The Steampacket** roadshow. When **Steampacket** folded in July 1966, Rick and Mickey were then replaced by Roger Sutton (bs) and Clive Thacker (drms). Vic Briggs then left in October 1966 to join **Eric Burdon and The Animals**, with Gary Boyle coming on board. Roger Sutton, too, left at some later point, being replaced by Dave Ambose.

In the subsequent few years **Auger** teamed up with **Julie Driscoll** and continued to release discs with The Trinity (of which she was a sometime member). After the Trinity broke up in mid-1970 he formed Oblivion Express who released several more jazz-rock orientated albums primarily targeted at the US market.

Auger moved to the US in 1975 and lived in the San Francisco Bay area. He switched to Warner Brothers recording further albums *Happiness Heartache* in 1977 and *Encore* a live reunion with Julie Tippetts (nee **Driscoll**), but after this he dissolved Oblivion Express and recorded less frequently. In 1990 he worked with **Eric Burdon** and the pair toured together over the next four years releasing an album *Access All Areas* in

BRIAN AUGER & THE TRINITY - Definitely What! (LP).

1993. He reformed Oblivion Express in 1995 and his daughter Savannah was included in the 2000 line-up that issued the album *Voices Of Other Times*.

Compilation appearances have included: *I Am A Lonesome Hobo* and *Red Beans And Rice (Part 1 and 2)* on *The Marmalade Record Co. Show Olympia 68* (LP); and *Gatto Negro* on *14 Groovy Sounds From The Blow Up* (LP). (VJ)

Cliff Aungier

ALBUM: 1   LADY FROM BALTIMORE   (Pye NSPL 18294) 1969 SC

NB: (1) reissued on CD (Castle) 2003.

45s:	Time/Fisherboy	(Polydor 56250) 1968
(Some)	My Love/Abigail	(RCA RCA 1730) 1968
	Lady From Baltimore/	
	Back On The Road Again	(Pye 7N 17753) 1969
	Good, Good/Beat Routes	(Pye 7N 17915) 1970

Performing from the mid-sixties onwards, **Aungier** was a folk singer/songwriter and guitarist who was a notable performer in the burgeoning sixties folk scene.

Aungier grew up in the Croydon area of London. His influences ranged from American blues legends to fellow folk artists like **Ralph McTell** and **Bert Jansch**. In 1963 he began performing at venues like the Marquee, 100 Club and (as a duo with harmonica player Royd Rivers) at The Half Moon. He produced a series of singles (not all of which are listed above) and in 1967 contributed a few tracks to the album *Alex Campbell And His Friends*.

His *Lady From Baltimore* album contained eight of his own compositions alongside two **Bee Gees** and Bob Dylan covers and the Tim Hardin-penned title track. It attracted some interest but he was poorly advised by his management and failed to build on this. Disillusioned he opted out of the music business for a considerable time.

He re-emerged in the mid-eighties with *Full Moon*, a live performance which included contributions from has old mates **Ralph McTell**, **Bert Jansch** and Albert Lee. Further albums followed, including *The Acoustic Blues* and his first album was reissued on CD in 2003.

Although suffering from serious alcohol problems for years, he is said today to be recovering and still performs often as part of a duo/trio. (VJ/JRy)

The Australian Playboys

Personnel:	TREVOR GRIFFIN	keyb'ds	AB
	BRIAN PEACOCK	bs, vcls	AB

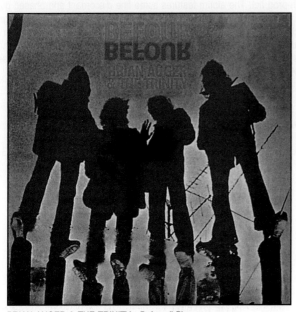

BRIAN AUGER & THE TRINITY - Befour (LP).

BRIAN AUGER'S OBLIVION EXPRESS - Second Wind (LP).

	ROD STONE	gtr	A
	GRAEME TROTTMAN	drms	AB
	MICK ROGERS	gtr, vcls	B

45:     Black Sheep RIP/Sad   (Immediate IM 054) 1967 R5

This is an extremely rare one-off 45 which changes hands for quite hefty sums. *Black Sheep RIP* is a bizarre version of the nursery rhyme, which is full of loud wailing guitar and culminates in a haze of feedback. *Sad* features some good psychedelic guitar work but doesn't really gel together as a song too well.

The band was originally known as The Playboys and originated from Melbourne, Australia. Like many of their (successful) contemporaries they came to the UK for a short spell, and the above 45 included pommie Trevor Griffin (ex-The Question Marks), plus ex-Librettos (New Zealand) members Griffin and Stone.

When Stone returned to Australia he was replaced by another pom Mick Rogers (ex-Vision), however the band split in October 1967. Rogers later moved back to the UK and eventually joined forces with **Manfred Mann's Earth Band**. The remaining members returned to Australia to form Procession. For more information see the "Dreams, Fantasies and Nightmares" book.

Sad has been compiled on *Chocolate Soup* (CD), *Chocolate Soup For Diabetics, Vol. 3* (LP) and on the 4-CD *Nuggets* box set. (VJ/JM)

Automatic Fine Tuning

Personnel:	DAVE BALL	drms, vcls	A
	ROBERT CROSS	gtr	A
	TREVOR DARKS	bs	A
	PAUL A. MacDONNELL	gtr	A

ALBUM: 1(A)   A.F.T.   (Charisma CAS 1122) 1976

A short-lived progressive outfit who recorded this album shortly before punk broke. Both sides of the album have two tracks with the majority of activity devoted to *The Great Panjandrum Wheel Parts One And Two*. Long guitar based solos are the norm and these become a little boring after a while but the album is worth a spin for progressive music fans. (BS)

Autumn

Personnel:	DAVE CHARLWOOD	drms	A
	JOHN COURT	gtr	A
	PETER CRAMER	bs, vcls	A
	KEITH PARSONS	gtr	A
	RON SHAUGHNESSY	gtr, vcls	A

45s:	My Little Girl/Sun, Sunshine	(Pye 7N 45090) 1970 37
	Not The Way She Looks/Stood Up	(Pye 7N 45144) 1970 -
	Down, Down, Down/October	(Pye 7N 45249) 1973 -

HCP

A semi-professional five-piece, from Brighton, who formed in late 1968. They scored a contract with Pye in 1970 and had a minor hit with the **Tony Rivers** composition *My Little Girl*.

Compilation appearances have included: *My Little Girl* on *Ripples, Vol. 1* (CD); *Sun Sunshine* on *Ripples, Vol. 2* (CD); and an acetate track *Shy Fly*, which has resurfaced on *Mynd The Gap* (LP) also may be by this act. (VJ/JM)

Avalanche

45:	Finding My Way Home/Rabbits	(Parlophone R 5890) 1971 R1

This 45 was actually by **The Norman Haines Band** with both tracks taken from their *Den Of Iniquity* album. *Rabbits* can also be found on *We Can Fly, Vol 2* (CD). (VJ)

The Avalons

45:	Everyday/I Love You	(Island WI 263) 1966 SC

A Liverpool band, who played at The Star Club in Hamburg in their time. (VJ)

The Avengers

Personnel incl:	TREVOR BRICE	A
	TONY GOULDEN	A
	TONY JARRETT	A

45:	Everyone's Gonna Wonder/	
	Take My Hand	(Parlophone R 5661) 1968

A harmony beat band from the Medway towns in Kent. All three personnel listed above later formed **Vanity Fair**. (VJ/JM/MGn)

Alan Avon and The Toy Shop

Personnel:	ALAN AVON (ALAN DUTTON)	vcls	A
	MAURICE COPE	bs	A
	ROGER JONES	drms	A
	TONY TODD	ld gtr	A

45s:	These Are The Reasons/	
	Night To Remember	(Concord CON 005) 1970 R3
α	Before I Ever Get Much Older/	
	Time To Love You	(Philips 600 6279) 1973

NB: α **Alan Avon** solo 45.

Alan Avon and The Toyshop were formed in February 1969 in the Stoke on Trent area. They were signed and produced by Terry Kennedy who was at the time one of the UK's top producers. He was responsible for **Donovan**, **The Flowerpot Men** and **The Ivy League** to name but a few. The band toured extensively and played at some of the country's top venues including The Cavern and Electric Garden City. They were regularly featured on Radio One and were seen by a number of top DJ's as being one of the UK's most promising groups.

The 'A' side of the first 45, *These Are The Reasons*, is eminently forgettable but the flip is a haunting slice of psychedelia - a sort of musical documentary about the sinking of the Titanic with some good psychedelic guitar work. The 45 was recorded at Central Sound Studios, Denmark Street, London in December 1969. The band played their final gig at Northampton during September 1971. Two members of the band, Tony Todd and Roger Jones have sadly passed away but the other two are still active as musicians.

KEVIN AYERS - Joy Of A Toy (CD).

A Night To Remember can also be heard on *Psychedelia, Vol. 1* (LP), *The Best Of Rubble Collection Vol. 1* (CD) and *Hen's Teeth Vol. 1* (CD). (VJ/MC)

Away From The Sand

ALBUM:	1	AWAY FROM THE SAND	(Beaujangle DB 0003) 197? R1

This is a privately pressed very English sounding rural progressive effort with both folk and rock elements. (VJ)

Axe

Personnel:	A. BARFORD	ld gtr	A
	S. GORDON	perc	A
	M. NOBBS	bs	A
	VIVIENNE	vcls	A
	(R. HILLIARD	acc. gtr	A)

CD:	1(A)	LIVE & STUDIO	(Kissing Spell KSCD 9579) 199?

This little known outfit appear to have come from Northampton and at the turn of the decade supported acts such as **Free** and **The Who**. They also recorded an acetate album in 1970, the tapes for which have subsequently resurfaced on the *Live & Studio* CD and which show **Axe** to a competent psych-prog act. The album features some fine discordant and phased guitar work, particularly on *Abinam Take II*, which also uses phasing to great effect and *Another Sunset, Another Dawn*. Other cuts are quieter, with the female vocals in a Jefferson Airplane / Art Of Lovin / Peanut Butter Conspiracy mould, particularly effective on their cover of Love's *A House Is Not A Motel*, and the live bonus track *Here To There*. (VJ)

Kevin Ayers (and The Whole World)

Personnel:	KEVIN AYERS	gtr, vcls	ABCDEF G H
	DAVID BEDFORD	piano	ABC
	LOL COXHILL	bs	AB
	MICK FINCHER	drms	A
	MIKE OLDFIELD	bs	ABC
	DAVE DUFORT	drms	B
	WILLIAM MURRAY	drms	C
	ANDY ROBINSON	bs	C
	ARCHIE LEGGET	bs, vcls	DEF
	EDDIE SPARROW	drms	DEF
	STEVE HILLAGE	gtr	E
	RABBIT BUNDRICK	keyb'ds	F
	OLLIE HALSALL	gtr	F G

FREDDIE SMITH	drms	F
ZOOT MONEY	keyb'ds	G H
TONY NEWMAN	drms	G
RICKY WILLS	bs	G
CHARLIE McCRACKEN	bs	H
ANDY SUMMERS	gtr	H
ROB TOWNSEND	drms	H

ALBUMS: 1(-) JOY OF A TOY (Harvest SHVL 763) 1969 R1
(up to 2(A) SHOOTING AT THE MOON
1976) (Harvest SHSP 4005) 1970 R1
3(-) WHATEVERSHEBRINGSWESING
(Harvest SHVL 800) 1972 SC
4(D) BANANAMOUR (Harvest SHVL 807) 1973 R1/SC
5(-) THE CONFESSIONS OF DR. DREAM AND
OTHER STORIES (Island ILPS 9263) 1974 SC
6(F) JUNE 1st, 1974 (Island ILPS 9291) 1974
7(G) SWEET DECEIVER (Island ILRS 9322) 1975
8(-) ODD DITTIES (Harvest SHSP 2005) 1976
9(H) YES WE HAVE NO MANANAS (Harvest SHSP 4057) 1976

NB: Some copies of (4) came with a booklet. (1) and (2) reissued as a double set on Harvest (SHDW 407) in 1975. (4) reissued on Harvest (EMS 1124) in 1986. (3), (2) and (1) reissued on Beat Goes On (BGOLP 11, 13 and 78) in 1988, 1989 and 1989 respectively. (5) reissued (Beat Goes On BGOLP 86) in 1989, also on CD (BGOCD 86) 1990. A recommended compilation is *The Kevin Ayers Collection* (See For Miles CM 117) 1983. This has been reissued in 1986 and 1990 (also on CD, SEE CD 117). There's also *The Best Of Kevin Ayers*, a double compilation (Harvest EM 2032) 1989. All of these albums are available on CD. *BBC Radio One Live In Concert* (Windsong WINCD 018) 1992 is from a 1972 'In Concert' broadcast. *Too Old To Die Young* (Hux HUX 006) 1998 is a 2-CD set compiled from BBC recordings. *Banana Follies* (Hux HUX 007) 1998 was recorded after the demise of The Whole World and credited to **Ayers** and Archibald. *Didn't Feel Lonely Till I Thought Of You: The Island Record Years* (Edsel MEDCD 749) 2004 is a mid-price 2-CD set which compiles his three albums for Island plus the singles previously unavailable on CD.

45s: α Singing A Song In The Morning/
(up to Eleanor's Cake Which Ate Her (Harvest HAR 5011) 1970
1976) Butterfly Dance/Puis-Je? (Harvest HAR 5027) 1970
Stranger In Blue Suede Shoes/Stars (Harvest HAR 5042) 1971
Oh! Wot A Dream/
Connie On A Rubber Band (Harvest HAR 5064) 1972
Caribbean Moon/Take Me
To Tahiti (Some in PS) (Harvest HAR 5071) 1973 SC/-
The Up Song/ Everybody's Sometimes And Some People's
All The Time Blues (Island WIP 6194) 1974
After The Show/Thank You Very Much (Island WIP 6201) 1974
Caribbean Moon/Take Me To Tahiti (Harvest HAR 5100) 1975
Falling In Love Again/
Everyone Knows The Song (Island WIP 6271) 1976
Stranger In Blue Suede Shoes/
Fake Mexican Tourist Blues (Harvest HAR 5107) 1976
Caribbean Moon/
Take Me To Tahiti (PS) (Harvest HAR 5109) 1976 SC

KEVIN AYERS - Whatevershebringswesing (CD).

KEVIN AYERS - Bananamour (CD).

NB: α acetates exist of an extended version of "Singing A Song In The Morning" entitled "Religious Experience", which includes **Syd Barrett** on guitar and backing vocals. **Barrett**'s contribution was deemed too non-comercial at the time, and was mixed out from the final single release, with **Kevin Ayers** contributing the ragged solo midway through the song, in the style of **Syd Barrett**.

Kevin Ayers has been an important and innovative figure in the evolution of progressive rock. Aside from his significance as a solo artist, he helped to launch **Soft Machine** as their original bassist and worked with significant progressive musicians including **Mike Oldfield**, **Steve Hillage** and **Lol Coxhill**.

Kevin Ayers is a native of Kent, where he was born at Herne Bay on 16th August 1944, although he spent part of his important formative years in Malaysia, where his father was a District Officer. Back in England in his youth he integrated into the local Bohemians who were into art, poetry and avant-garde jazz. He was a member of **The Wilde Flowers** in 1963, but left them in 1965 to travel to Ibiza with **Daevid Allen**. He returned in 1966 to help form **The Soft Machine** and was extremely influential in their early years but left at the end of 1968, after the release of the band's debut album, exhausted from the continual travelling. He again headed for the then tranquil island of Ibiza. When he returned to London he pieced together a series of demos in a tiny London flat which led to his *Joy Of A Toy* album which is full of wistful melodies, but did not sell well at the time as it was only marketed in the underground press.

In March 1970 **Ayers** formed a backing group called The Whole World. Their *Shooting The Moon* album was inconsistent but had its moments, particularly on *May I?* and *Lunatic Lament*. The *Butterfly Dance* 45 is of interest to collectors because it wasn't on the album. The Whole World fell apart in the Summer of 1971 and **Ayers** briefly joined **Gong**. His *Whatevershebringswesing* album was recorded with members of The Whole World and **Gong**. Again it was inconsistent but the superb title track, the demented *Song From The Bottom Of A Well* and *There Is Loving* were among the high points. Overall it mixed experimental cuts with idyllic, poignant pieces.

His *Oh! Wot A Dream* single was a tribute to **Syd Barrett** whilst the catchy *Caribbean Moon* was a clear attempt to achieve commercial success and it could easily have been a hit. *Bananamour* is generally considered one of his best loved albums. It highlights included the rousing *Shouting In A Bucket Blues*, *When Your Parents Go To Sleep*, notable for its strong backing vocals, *Hymn*, with **Robert Wyatt** on vocals and *Oh! Wot A Dream*, a bizarre little song about **Syd Barrett**. The follow-up *The Confessions Of Dr. Dream And Other Stories*, which was cut using session musicians, suffered as a result. **Kevin Ayers** formed The Soporifics initially as a road band to push the *Dr. Dream* album but he subsequently made the *June 1st, 1974* and *Sweet Deceiver* albums with them. In fact part of the first one contained live material from a *Rainbow Concert* with other Island artists, **Eno**, **John Cale** and Nico. The *Sweet Deceiver* album was received like a lead balloon by the critics and suffered from weak material and poor production - **Ayers** fled to the sun again after this. Harvest successfully kept interest alive in him by a budget reissue of his first two

KEVIN AYERS - The Radio Sessions (LP).

45s: Eeny Meeny/Peep My Love   (Fontana TF 627) 1965
         Only Love Can Save Me Now/
         Celebration Of The Year   (Polydor 56276) 1968 R1
         Another Night/
         Taking The Sun From My Eyes   (Polydor 56302) 1969
         Farewell/The Best Years Of My Life (Harvest HAR 5073) 1973

Ayshea Brough was just 16 when she recorded her first 45. In the early seventies she had her own TV show for children, 'Lift Off With Ayshea'. She also appeared on 'Top Of The Pops' as one of the backing vocalists on a **Wizzard** single (she was romantically involved with **Roy Wood**). Her first husband Chris Brough was a staff producer for Polydor (he produced the first **Audience** album), which is presumably why **Ayshea**'s first album appeared on Polydor. (VJ/DW)

albums and the *Odd Ditties* retrospective album which contained singles and unreleased material from 1969-73. As we leave the time span of this book **Ayers** had re-emerged with one of his finest albums yet, *Yes We Have No Mananas* on which he was assisted by the new Kevin Ayers Band, which included **Zoot Money** and Andy Summers (both ex-**Dantalian's Chariot** and **Zoot Money's Big Roll Band**), Rob Townsend (ex-**Family**) and Charlie McCracken (formerly of **Taste**).

Ayers only recorded sporadically after 1980, although he remained active in the nineties mostly in Europe.

In recent years most of **Ayers**' albums have been reissued on the Beat Goes On label. There are also compilations of his material on the See For Miles and Harvest labels. The See For Miles compilation covers the entirety of his solo career between 1969 and 1980. The compilation includes tracks from each of his albums and several songs like *Caribbean Moon, Puis-Je?* and *After The Show*, which were previously only issued as 45s. *Didn't Feel Lonely Till I Thought Of You: The Island Record Years* is a mid-price package reissuing all three of his albums plus the singles (previously unavailable on CD) *The Up Song* and *After The Show*, along with the 'B' side *Thank You Very Much*. It comes with a booklet full of information about the albums, the musicians who played on it and an appraisal of **Kevin Ayers**' period with Island.

In 1998 Hux released two live albums compiled from BBC sessions. *Too Old To Die Young* is a 2-CD set. Disc one dates from January 1972 and captures him in top form supported by a 16-year-old **Mike Oldfield**, **David Bedford** and **Lol Coxhill** on some tracks. The highlight is perhaps The Whole World's version of *Why Are We Sleeping?* (a song from his **Soft Machine** days). The second disc contains material from 1975 and 1976. This is disappointing and more in a pub-rock format. *Banana Follies* presents a cabaret revue at Hampstead Theatre Club in 1972, after the demise of The Whole World, which was also performed for the BBC. It also contains spoken word passages and old-time songs.

Back in 1970 *Eleanor's Cake That Ate Her* was included on Harvest's *Picnic* (2-LP) compilation. **Ayers**' remains a largely under-rated talent who has never enjoyed commercial success commensurate with his undoubted abilities. (VJ/LP/RDk)

Ayshire Folk

ALBUM: 1   AYRSHIRE FOLK   (Deroy) 1974 R2

A rare privately-pressed folk album. (VJ)

Ayshea

ALBUMS: 1   AYSHEA   (Polydor 2384 026) 1970 R1
         2   LIFT OFF WITH AYSHEA   (DJM DJLPS 445) 1974 SC

THE ATTACK - The Complete Recordings From 1967 - 68 (LP).

ATOMIC ROOSTER - Nice & Greasy (LP).

Babe Ruth

Personnel:	DICK POWELL	drms	A
	JANITA 'JENNY' HAAN	vcls	ABCD
	DAVE HEWITT	bs	ABCD
	DAVE PUNSHON	keyb'ds	AB
	ALAN SHACKLOCK	gtr	A
	CHRIS HOLMES	keyb'ds	B
	ED SPEVOCK	drms	BCDE F
	STEVE GURL	keyb'ds	CDE F
	BERNIE MARSDEN	gtr	DE
	ELLIE HOPE	vcls	E F
	RAY KNOTT	bs	E F
	ALLAN ROSS	gtr	F
	SID TWINEHAM	gtr	F

ALBUMS:	1(A)	FIRST BASE	(Harvest SHSP 4022) 1972 SC
	2(B)	AMAR CABALLERO	(Harvest SHVL 812) 1973 SC
	3(C)	BABE RUTH	(Harvest SHSP 4038) 1975 SC
	4(D)	STEALIN' HOME	(Capitol 11451) 1975
	5(E)	KID'S STUFF	(Capitol 23739) 1976
	6(-)	BEST OF	(Harvest SHSM 2019) 1977

NB: (1) reissued on CD with both sides of their first 45 (Repertoire REP 4554-WP) 1995. (1) and (2) reissued as a 2-on-1 CD (BGOCD 382) 1998. (3) and (4) reissued on one CD (BGOCD 491) 2000. (1), (2) and (3) also reissued on CD in Japan. (1) and (3) reissued in the USA. Also of note is the compilation, supervised by Alan S. himself, *Grand Slam*, (Harvest CZ-538) 1994, which provides a fairly definitive overview of albums (1)-(3). This has been reissued (EMI 5428442).

45s:	Wells Fargo/Few Dollars More	(Harvest HAR 5061) 1972
	Ain't That Livin'/We Are Holding On	(Harvest HAR 5072) 1973
	If Heaven's On Beauty's Side/	
	Doctor Love	(Harvest HAR 5082) 1974
	Wells Fargo/Mexican	(Harvest HAR 5087) 1974
	Private Number/Somebody's Nobody	(Harvest HAR 5090) 1975
	The Duchess Of New Orleans/	
	The Jack O Lantern/Tyrquoise	(Harvest SPSR 377) 1976
	Elusive/Say No More	(Capitol CL 15689) 1976

This progressive rock outfit formed in 1971 in Hatfield, Hertfordshire. They were originally known as Shacklock after their founder member Alan Shacklock (ex-**Juniors** and **Chris Farlowe and the Thunderbirds**), but adopted the name **Babe Ruth** after the legendary American baseball player after the release of their debut album. The album didn't make much impression here in the UK but went gold in Canada. Pushon and Powell left after the first album (although Powell is credited with playing on the second album). Their sound is quite guitar-driven and features some fine blues singing from Jenny Haan.

Ed Spevock (ex-**Bond and Brown**) and Chris Holmes (ex-**Timebox**) both joined the group in August 1973 for their second album.

Holmes left in October 1974 and was replaced by Steve Gurl, formerly of **Wild Turkey**, shortly prior to the release of their third album which climbed to No 75 in the US Charts. It starts with the powerful *Dancer* and the beefed up version of *A Fistful Of Dollars* also catches the ears.

The band was now under considerable demand to tour the US but these demands gradually brought about their demise. Firstly, their founder Alan Shacklock left in 1975 to be replaced by Bernie Marsden (who was also formerly with **Cozy Powell's Hammer**), and then after the *Stealin' Home* album had met with some success here in the UK both Jenny Haan and Dave Hewitt left in short succession in January 1976 and ended up in a group called Lion later that year. *Stealin' Home* is a rock album with a bit of blues and slide guitar.

Ray Knott and Ellie Hope, who'd played with an obscure girl group Ellie, were enlisted in February 1976 in their place and this line-up recorded *Kid's Stuff*, which proved to be their final album, aside from the obligatory *Best Of* compilation. Finally **Allan Ross** (ex-Ross) replaced Bernie Marsden and Sid Twineham also joined on guitar just before the band split in 1976. Marsden joined **Paice - Ashton - Lord** in October 1976 and then Whitesnake in January 1978.

After their demise Spevock joined **Chicken Shack**, Gurl went on to Fletcher and Gurl and **Ross** went solo. Both Ray Knott and Ellie Hope were in Liquid Gold in the late seventies. Ellie Hope also later recorded a solo single. Janita 'Jenny' Haan also sang on **Strider**'s 1974 album, *Misunderstanding*.

Private Number was included on *Harvest Heritage - 20 Greats* (LP). (VJ/JHs/MD/JM)

Baby Ruth

| 45: | Rupert's Magic Feather/Flood | (Decca F 13234) 1971 |

Previously listed as **Babe Ruth**, this 45 was probably the work of session musicians. The 'A' side was written by Ian Southern and John House, and the 'B' side was penned by **Jonathan King**. *Rupert's Magic Deather* is a country and western song. (MD)

Babylon

| Personnel incl: | CAROL GRIMES | vcls |
| | LEWIS RICH | keyb'ds |

| 45: | Into The Promised Land/Nobody's Fault | |
| | But Mine (Some PS) | (Polydor BM 56356) 1969 R1/SC |

This short-lived rock band was most significant for the inclusion of **Carol Grimes** who later played in Delivery and **Uncle Dog** among others. Rich had previously been in **The Herd** and with **Cliff Bennett**. (VJ)

Baby Sunshine

| ALBUM: | 1 | BABY SUNSHINE | (Deroy DER 1301) (w/insert) 1975 R2 |

This privately-pressed album was recorded at Deroy Sound Studios. Just 150 copies were pressed and musically the menu is acoustic folk with lots of flute. The magnum opus is a track called *Ity's Is Lost*. Two tracks from this album also appear on a related album by **Fairy's Moke**. (VJ)

Back Alley Choir

| ALBUM: | 1 | BACK ALLEY CHOIR | (York FYK 406) 1972 R3 |

| 45: | Smile Born Of Courtesy/ | |
| | Why Are You Here | (York SYK 517) 1972 R1 |

This studio band's folk album is a mediocre amalgam of cover versions and original material. Only 500 copies were pressed and it's now very hard to find. (VJ)

BABE RUTH - First Base (LP).

Back Door

Personnel incl:

RON ASPERY	sax, flute	A B C
TONY HICKS	drms	A B
COLIN HODGKINSON	bs, gtr, vcls	A B C
PETER THORUP	vcls gtr	B
ADRIAN TILBROOK	drms	C

ALBUMS: 1(A) BACK DOOR (Blakey BLP 5989) 1972 R1
(up to 2(A) BACK DOOR (Warner Bros K 46231) 1973
1976) 3(A) 8TH STREET NITES (Warner Bros K 46265) 1973
4(B) ANOTHER FINE MESS (Warner Bros K 56098) 1975
5(C) ACTIVATE (Warner Bros K 56243) 1976

NB: *Human Bed* (Hux HUX 031) compiles BBC Radio 1 sessions recorded between 1973-1974 and is accompanied by a booklet with extensive liner notes from Colin Hodkinson.

45: The Dashing White Sargeant/
The Spoiler (Warner Bros K 16490) 1975

A jazz-rock trio from Blakey in Yorkshire whose debut album was originally issued on a small local label but caused considerable excitement when it was discovered by the music press. This led to its reissue on the Warner Brothers label and much wider exposure for Colin Hodgkinson's unique bass-playing. Aspery and Hodgkinson penned all the compositions on their all instrumental debut but somehow their subsequent albums never reached quite the same heights.

Hodgkinson and Aspery had previously played with Eric Delaney, whilst Hicks was ex-Assegai. In January 1974, Peter Thorup (ex-Snape) joined and Adrian Tilbrook later replaced Tony Hicks on drums. Their final album was produced by Carl Palmer.

Tony Hicks later played with Pure Chance and Pacific Eardrum. Hodgkinson joined Whitesnake for a brief period in early 1984 before joining Blues Reunion. Aspery also later joined Planet Earth.

More recently The Beastie Boys sampled **Back Door**'s *Slivadiv* on their *The Blue Nun* song from the *Check Your Head* CD. (VJ/MR/JM)

Backstreet Band

Personnel:

NORMAN BELL		
RUSS HARNESS	vcls	
JOHN PHILIPS		
ALAN STEVENSON	drms	A

45s: This Ain't The Road/Daybreak (Ember EMBS 277) 1969
This Ain't The Road/She's Clean (Ember EMBS 286) 1970

A short-lived rock group. *This Ain't The Road* was a **Mike Berry** composition and the reissue the following year was a re-written and rearranged version.

They also figure on Ember's *New Faces For The 70s* (LP) compilation. (VJ)

Back Street Crawler

Personnel:

TONY BRAUNAGEL	drms	A B
PAUL KOSSOFF	gtr	A
MICHAEL MONTGOMERY	keyb'ds	A B
TERRY WILSON	bs	A B
TERRY WILSON-SLESSOR	vcls	A B

ALBUMS: 1(A) THE BAND PLAYS ON (Atlantic K 50173) 1975
2(A) SECOND STREET (Atlantic K 50267) 1976

NB: (1) reissued on CD by (Repertoire REP 4265 WY) and again on CD (Wounded Bird WOU 125). (2) reissued on CD (Repertoire REP 4376-WY) and again on CD (Wounded Bird WOU 138).

This band was formed by ex-**Free** member **Paul Kossoff** after he had been out of the music business for a couple of years fighting drug addiction and associated ill health. He named the band after a solo album he'd recorded back in 1973. Shortly after the release of the first album he suffered a serious heart attack and almost died (he was kept alive on a heart machine). They delayed a planned UK tour to promote the album although he recovered sufficiently to play a limited number of gigs. Ironically after his doctors had given the go-ahead for a UK tour in the April of 1976, he died in his sleep in a plane en route to New York on 19 March 1976 from a further heart attack. The *Second Street* album had for the most part been recorded prior to his death but fellow former **Free** member John Bundrick appeared on some tracks and with the addition of former **If** member Geoff Whitehorn the remaining members continued as Crawler.

Terry Wilson-Slessor had earlier been with **Beckett**, whilst the other. (VJ/SR)

Bacon Fat

ALBUMS: 1 GREASE ONE FOR ME (Blue Horizon 7-63858) 1970 R1
2 TOUGH DUDE (Blue Horizon 2431 001) 1971 R1

NB: (1) reissued on CD (Walhalla WH 90341). (2) has been reissued on CD.

45s: Nobody But You/Small On 53rd (Blue Horizon 57-3171) 1970 SC
Evil/Blues Feeling (Blue Horizon 57-3181) 1970 SC

This blues-rock group featured Rob Piazzo (from big band **Ten Wheel Drive**). (VJ/CG)

The Bad Boys

Personnel:

RONNIE HANSON	gtr	A B C
TONY JORDAN	bs	A B C
ROGER MARSH	drms	A
WALLY SCOTT	gtr, vcls	A B
BERNIE MARTIN	drms	B C
ROGER DEAN	ld gtr	C

ALBUM: 1(B) BEST OF THE BAD BOYS (Style STLP 8061) 1966 R4

NB: (1) was an Italian only release.

45s: Owl And The Pussycat/
(UK) That's What I'll Do (Piccadilly 7N 35208) 1964 SC
Satisfaction/Mr. Tambourine Man (Pye NP 5078) 1965

45s: Gol/She's A Breakaway (Style STMS 633) 1966
(Italian) Balliamo il Jerk/Finch t'incontrer (Style STMS 634) 1966
Kicks/She's A Breakaway (Style STMS 635) 1966
Summertime Blues/Wishin' and Hopin' (Style STMS 641) 1966
Il Mio Amore E' Un Capellone/
Runnin' And Hidin' (Style STMS 643) 1967
Shaly n.1/Quel Ragazzo Triste Sono Io (Style STMS 648) 1967
Cerco La Verit/Che Vita La Mia (Style STMS 658) 1967
Da Da Da/Nasco Da Oggi (City C 6215) 1968

BACK DOOR - 8th Street Nites (LP).

A R&B combo whose Italian-only album contains savage R&B in **The Pretty Things** vein, with the occasional nod and wink towards pop art. There's a lively version of the Paul Revere classic *Kicks* and a frantic cover of *Milk Cow Blues* and *Crawling Up A Hill*. There are also some good originals, too, especially *Runnin' And Hidin'* and *She's A Breakaway*, both are in the freakbeat mould.

The band was formed in 1964 at the Elliotts Green Grammar School by Wally Scott (from Greenford), Ron Hanson (Eton), Tom Jordan (Northolt) and Roger Marsh. After their second 45 their manager Leo Wachter, arranged for them to go to Italy. Here, after supporting Italian beat group New Dada they got a deal for their album.

After the album, (which is rich with covers and features only three tracks sung in Italian), they were forced to record more melodic Italian songs. *Shaly n.1* was the most successful, but they split soon after.

Hanson, Jordan and Martin were also involved in recording early releases by Francesco Guccini, an important Italian songwriter.

Bernie Martin and Roger Dean had both previously played in **The Nu Notes**.

Compilation coverage has included:- *Owl And The Pussycat* on *Turds On A Bum Ride, Vol. 6* (CD); *That's What I'll Do* on *Turds On A Bum Ride, Vol. 5* (CD); and *She's A Breakaway* on *Red With Purple Flashes, Vol. 1* (LP) and *Incredible Sound Show Stories, Vol. 9* (LP). (VJ/FB/CR/GB/RD)

Bad Company

Personnel:

BOZ BURRELL	bs	A
(up to	SIMON KIRKE	drms, vcls	A
1976)	MICK RALPHS	gtr, vcls	A
	PAUL RODGERS	vcls	A

			HCP
ALBUMS: 1(A)	BAD COMPANY	(Island ILPS 9279) 1974	3
(up to 2(A)	STRAIGHT SHOOTER	(Island ILPS 9304) 1975	3
1976) 3(A)	RUN WITH THE PACK	(Island ILPS 9346) 1976	4

NB: (1) reissued on CD (Swan Song 7567924412). (2) and (3) reissued on CD (Swan Song SS 8502-2 and SS 8503-2 respectively) 1988. 10 from 6 (WEA 781 625-2) 1986 may also be of interest. (2) and (3) reissued on CD again digitally remastered (Swan Song 7567-92436-2 and 7567 92435-2) 1994. *The Original Bad Company Anthology* (Elektra) 1999 is a 2-CD set.

			HCP
45s:	Can't Get Enough (Of Your Love)/		
(up to	Little Miss Fortune	(Island WIP 6191) 1974	15
1976)	Good Lovin' Gone Bad/Whisky Bottle	(Island WP 6223) 1975	31
	Feel Like Makin' Love/		
	Wild Fire Woman	(Island WIP 6242) 1975	20
	Run With The Pack/		
	Do Right By Your Woman	(Island WIP 6263) 1976	-

Formed in August 1973. Ralphs had been a founder member of **Mott The Hoople**; Rodgers and Kirke had both played together earlier in **Free** and Burrell had learnt to play bass in **King Crimson**. Essentially a 'supergroup', they made a widely-publicised debut at Newcastle City Hall on 8 March 1974 and enjoyed a meteoric rise to fame and fortune, which was further enhanced by a US tour later the same year. They had a lot going for them with Ralphs' considerable songwriting talents and Rodgers' superb vocal ability. They played a brand of hard-rock that was extremely popular at this time.

Their debut album and a track from it, *Can't Get Enough*, which Ralphs had written during his time with **Mott The Hoople**, topped both the US Albums and Singles Charts. In the UK the album peaked at No 3 and the 45 made No 15. They were both the most popular new band in Britain and the most successful new British band in the States. In fact they could do little wrong. The *Straight Shooter* and *Run With The Pack* albums were also both extremely successful and they enjoyed further hits with *Feel Like Makin' Love* and *Run With The Pack*, which were very much in the same vein as *Can't Get Enough*. They became the first band to sign to the **Led Zeppelin** vanity label Swan Song. **Page** and Plant jammed with them at a few of their gigs.

BAD COMPANY - Striaght Shooter (LP).

In 1986 Ralphs and Kirke returned with a new **Bad Company** line-up with former Ted Nugent vocalist Brian Howe replacing Rodgers. A whole series of albums followed: *Fame And Fortune* (1984) which flopped, *Dangerous Age* (1988) met with some success and *Holy Water* (1990) did better and spawned a Top 20 single with the power ballad *If You Needed Somebody*. *Here Comes Trouble* (1992) went platinum and produced a Top 40 hit *How About That*. In 1993 the reformed trio became a quintet with Rick Willis (bs) and Dave Coldwell (gtr) and a live retrospective *The Best Of Bad Company Live...What You Hear Is What You Get* was released. Two more albums were recorded *The Company Of Strangers* (1995) and *Stories Told And Untold* (1996). In 1988, the original line-up of Rodgers, Ralphs, Kirke and Burrell reunited for a reunion tour.

The Original Bad Company Anthology is a 30-track collection compiling their hit singles, a selection of 'B' sides and it also includes two unreleased *Straight Shooter* era tracks, *Superstar Woman* and *Smokin'*. The set is accompanied by a 44-page booklet with unreleased pictures and lyrics. (VJ)

The Badd Boys

45s:	α	Never Going Back To Georgia/	
		River Deep Mountain High	(Epic 10119) 1967
	α	Folks In A Hurry/I Told You So	(Epic 10165) 1967

NB: α are US releases.

Originally thought to be American, Mike Markesich informs us that the copyright info on the above 45s says otherwise. Whatever, the band were good enough to get signed by a major label in the 'States and these guys have made a couple of retrospective compilation appearances:- *I Told You So* on *Psychedelic Unknowns, Vol 7* (LP) and *Never Going Back To Georgia* on both *Boulders, Vol 4* (LP) and *Searching For Love* (LP). (MW/MMh)

Badfinger

Personnel:

TOM EVANS	bs, vcls	AB
MIKE GIBBINS	drms	AB
RON GRIFFITHS	bs, vcls	A
PETE HAM	vcls, gtr	AB
JOEY MOLLAND	gtr, vcls	B
BOB JACKSON	keyb'ds	C

ALBUMS: 1(A)	MAGIC CHRISTIAN MUSIC	(Apple SAPCOR 12) 1970	R2
(up to 2(B)	NO DICE	(Apple SAPCOR 16) 1970	R1
1976) 3(B)	STRAIGHT UP	(Apple SAPCOR 19) 1972	R2
4(B)	BADFINGER	(Warner Brothers K 56023) 1973	SC
5(B)	ASS	(Apple SAPCOR 27) 1974	R1
6( )	WISH YOU WERE HERE		
		(Warner Brothers K 56076) 1975	R2

NB: (1) reissued on CD, vinyl and cassette by Apple in 1991 and again (Apple CDSAPCOR 12) 2004. (2) reissued on CD (Apple CDP 7 98698 2) 1992 with five additional and previously unreleased cuts and on CD (Apple CDSAPCOR 16) 2004. (3) reissued on CD (Apple CDSAPCOR 19, also on vinyl) 1993 along with six bonus tracks and again on CD (CDSAPCOR 19) 2004. (4) reissued on CD (Apple CDSAPCOR 27). *Shine On* (Edsel ED 302) 1989 compiles material from (5) and (6). *The Best Of Badfinger, Vol. II* (Rhino RZ 70978) 1990 is a CD compilation of material from their Warner Brothers' era. *Day After Day* (Essential/Castle ESSCD 135) 1990, is an official release of recordings from a 1974 show at Cleveland Agora, which had previously been in circulation as a bootleg. It's a punchy set mostly comprising of material from their Apple albums. *Apple Daze* (Raven RVCD 250) 1992 is an Australian interview disc with former member and main songwriter Tom Evans, who later committed suicide. Another compilation is *Come And Get It: The Best Of Badfinger* (Apple CD SAPCOR 28) 1995. *BBC In Concert* (Strange Fruit SFRSCD 031) 1997 captures their Radio 1 In Concert performances from 1972 and 1973. None of their Apple singles were featured in either set - the only well known numbers being two **Dave Mason** songs *Only You Know And I Know* and *Feelin' Alright*. At the end of the CD is a 1970 TV performance of *Come And Get It* - which is what we all remember them for. Turning Point put out digitally remastered audiophile double vinyl editions of these CDs in 1999. In 2002 Snapper released a 2-CD compilation, *Head First*.

45s:		HCP	
	Come And Get It/Rock Of All Ages (PS)	(Apple 20) 1969	4
(up to	No Matter What/Better Days (PS)	(Apple 31) 1970 SC	5
1974) α	Name Of The Game/Suitcase	(Apple APPLE 35) 1971	-
β	Baby Blue/Flying	(Apple APPLE 42) 1972	-
	Day After Day/		
	Sweet Tuesday Morning (PS)	(Apple 40) 1972 SC	10
	Love Is Easy/		
	My Heart Goes Out	(Warner Brothers K 16323) 1973	-
	Apple Of My Eye/Blind Owl	(Apple 49) 1974 SC	-

NB: α Unreleased. β Unreleased in the UK.

Badfinger, who were the most successful non-**Beatles** related band signed to the Apple label, began life as **The Iveys** in Swansea in the mid-sixties. The name change came in 1969 and around the same time the band was invited to contribute three tracks to the soundtrack of a movie based on a novel, 'The Magic Christian', written by Terry Southern. The three tracks, *Come And Get It, Rock Of All Ages* and *Carry On Till Tomorrow*, were all contained on their first album as well. The first of them was a highly commercial song, written by **Paul McCartney** and after its release, in December 1969, it rocketed up the Charts peaking at No 4 in the UK and No 7 in the US. Around the same time Ron Griffiths left the band and was replaced by Joey Molland who'd previously played with **The Masterminds**, **The Merseys** and **Gary Walker and The Rain**. It was Griffiths who had played on most of these tracks when they were originally recorded, but Joey Molland, who looked a little like **Paul McCartney** who helped promote them. The finest track on the album was *Maybe Tomorrow*, but several of Pete Ham's other whimsical tunes like *Crimson Ship* and *Dear Angie*, which was written by Ron Griffiths, were fine examples of sixties pop. However, in the progressive era of the early seventies the album sounded rather dated and didn't sell too well, only charting in the US, where it peaked at No 54.

Their next 45, the self-composed *No Matter What*, was much heavier and made the Top 10 on both sides of the Atlantic. The follow-up album, *No Dice*, again sold better in the States. It contained some good rockers like *Better Days* and *Love Me Do* (not **The Beatles** song) and a Ham/Evans ballad, *Without You*, that would later top the UK Charts when covered by Harry Nillson.

Their next album was scheduled to be produced by **George Harrison** but he became understandably preoccupied with the 'Concert for Bangladesh' and **Badfinger** appeared, as back-up musicians at Madison Square Garden. Apple also rejected many of the initial compositions for the album, which was eventually produced by Todd Rundgren and contained several slickly produced soft-rock songs. Again *Straight Up* sold better abroad than here, peaking at No 31 in the US. One of the **Harrison** productions, *Day After Day*, was released as a single (he actually played on the guitar intro) and it made the Top Ten on both sides of the Atlantic. In the States to capitalise on this another track, *Baby Blue*, was taken from the album and made the US Top 20, but for some unknown reason no follow-up issue was put out here.

It would be fair to say that Apple didn't do the band too many favours over the years - **Badfinger** set out to produce the next album themselves but Apple rejected it and whilst it was put on hold (much of it was being remixed) the band's business manager negotiated them a new contract with Warner Brothers. They got to work on a new album, releasing *Love Is Easy*

BAKER GURVITZ ARMY - Baker Gurvitz Army (CD).

as a 45. It was more rock 'n' roll orientated. Probably a little out of pace with the current fad and released almost two years after their previous 45 when any momentum they'd previously enjoyed was lost, it missed out. Before the Warners album could be put out Apple released the *Ass* album. One of its tracks, *Apple Of My Eye*, was released as a 45 but flopped only making No. 102 in the US. The album was less immediate in its appeal than their previous efforts and it made little impact. It did, however, result in Warner Brothers delaying the release of their album, which in the end was simply entitled *Badfinger*. It included that earlier *Love Is Easy* 45 but no new 45 was released to help promote it and in fact the album was hastily put together and sounded like it.

Most people regard *Wish You Were Here* as their finest album, but by the time of its release any popular base of support they had was eroded. It contained some excellent Pete Ham compositions like *Know One Knows, Dennis* and *Just A Chance*, as well as strong numbers like *Some Other Time* and *In The Meantime*. Some of the arrangements were complex and Chris Thomas, who Warner had assigned to produce the album, had done a far better job than on the previous effort. Despite the release of no 45 to help promote it, it sold well in the US, climbing to No. 60 when Warner Brothers withdrew it from sale. An investigation was launched to establish why advance monies had gone missing, the band were cleared of any culpability, but the progress of the album, which was only released briefly here where it is their rarest album, was halted as a result and thoroughly frustrated Joey Molland left the group at the end of 1974. The remaining members recorded an album entitled *Head First* during the early months of 1975, but it was shelved in April of that year when Pete Ham committed suicide. Pete was really the band's major talent and after his death the band split up.

Joey Molland, who in the interim had had spells with **Blue Goose** and **Natural Gas**, reformed the band with a new line-up in 1978 and they re-recorded *Come And Get It* for the *Hits Reunion* (LP) compilation. They used the funds from this to record demos for Elektra. This led to a recording contract and a further album and 45 in 1979. Incidentally, the new recording of *Come And Get It* was later included on *The Legendary Sixties* (Arcade ADEH 453) compilation. However, the band later fell apart after a problematic American tour in 1983 and in November of that year Tom Evans, who returned to England to find himself in severe financial difficulties, committed suicide too. The remaining members have occasionally embarked on Sixties revival tours but in reality **Badfinger** was now dead too - the band had never really fulfilled its early promise.

The recent CD reissue of *Straight Up* includes five tracks from the original version of the album which was rejected by Apple (*Money, Flying, Suitcase, Name Of The Game* and *Perfection*) along with an US 45 version of *Baby Blue*. These six tracks appear on a separate 12" single which accompanies the vinyl reissue. Mike Gibbins, their drummer, sadly die in Oviedo, Florida on 4 October 2005, aged 56.

Come And Get It has been compiled on *The Seventies Vol 2* (CD) and on *70's FAB FAV's - Classic 70's Hits* (CD). (VJ)

Badger

Personnel:
ROY DYKE	drms	AB
DAVID FOSTER	bs, vcls	A
TONY KAYE	keyb'ds	AB
BRIAN PARRISH	gtr, vcls	A
KIM GARDNER	bs	B
JACKIE LOMAX	vcls	B
PAUL PILNICK	gtr	B

ALBUMS: 1(A) ONE LIVE BADGER (Atlantic K 40473) 1973 SC
2(B) WHITE LADY (Epic EPC 80009) 1974

NB: (1) reissued on CD (Repertoire REP 4373) and again (Wounded Bird WOU 7022)..

45: White Lady/Don't Pull The Trigger (Epic EPC 2326) 1974

Initially christened Angel Dust, **Badger** were formed in 1973 after Kaye had left **Flash**. Foster had previously worked with **Jon Anderson** in **The Warriors** and Roy Dyke had been part of **Ashton, Gardner and Dyke**. Their debut album, *One Live Badger* was a largely instrumental and recorded at London's Rainbow Theatre.

In November 1973, when Parrish and Foster left, Pilnick (ex-**Stealer's Wheel**), Gardner (ex-**Ashton, Gardner and Dyke**) and **Jackie Lomax** were recruited. **Jackie Lomax** wrote much of their second album, which was more soulful and had **Jeff Beck** as a guest. Several addition backing musicians were also utilised on the album.

Parrish went on to work with **Eric Burdon**; Kaye went on to **David Bowie**, Detective, **Badfinger** (1979-1983), then **Yes**; Dyke went on to Swallow then Pat Travers Band; and Pilnick joined **Deaf School** (Nov 1975 - Jun 1976).

Kim Gardner died on 24 October 2001 after losing a three year battle with cancer. (VJ/JM)

Ginger Baker

HCP
ALBUMS: 1 GINGER BAKER'S AIRFORCE 1 (2-LP)
(up to (Polydor 2662 001) 1970 SC 37
1977) 2 AIRFORCE 2 (w/insert) (Polydor 2383 029) 1970 SC -
3 STRATAVARIOUS (Polydor 2383 133) 1972 SC -
4 FELA RANSOME KUTI AND AFRICA BAND
(Royal Zonophone SLRZ 1023) 1972 SC -
5 AT HIS BEST (Compilation) (Polydor 2659 023) 1973 -
6 ELEVEN SIDES OF BAKER (Compilation)
(Mountain 5005) 1977 -

NB: (1) as Ginger Baker's Airforce. A further compilation is, *The Album* (ITM 1469) 1992, a selection of off-cuts from his career.

45s: α Man Of Constant Sorrow/Doin' It (Polydor BM 53680) 1970
(up to β Atunde! (We Are Here)/Part 2 (Polydor 2058 107) 1972
1977) Don Dorango/Candlestick Taker (Mountain TOP 23) 1977

NB: α as Ginger Baker's Airforce. β As Ginger Baker Drum Choir.

Ginger Baker was rock's first superstar drummer and arguably the most influential drummer of the sixties.

Ginger Baker was born in Lewisham during 1939. His first instrument was the trumpet but later he switched to drums and played in several jazz bands including Terry Lightfoot's and Acker Bilk's before joining Blues Incorporated in 1962. In February 1963 he was in The Graham Bond Trio and later the **Graham Bond Organisation** before joining **Cream** in 1966.

Upon **Cream**'s demise in late 1968 he was involved in the short-lived **Blind Faith** venture. When they split in January 1970 he formed Ginger Baker's Airforce, which included Ric Grech (ex-**Family** and **Blind Faith**), **Stevie Winwood** (ex-**Traffic** and **Spencer Davis Group**), **Graham Bond**, **Denny Laine**, Chris Wood (also ex-**Traffic**) and Remi Kabaka. They released two pretty awful albums (the second one is a live recording) and when the group collapsed **Baker** headed for Africa.

In 1971 **Baker** actually bought some land in Akeja, Nigeria, and built a recording studio. It eventually opened in January 1973. He recorded *Stratavarious* and *Fela Ransome* whilst in Nigeria and briefly played in a predominantly Nigerian band called Salt. He eventually returned to England to form **Baker-Gurvitz Army**.

He re-appeared in 1986 on the album *Horses And Trees* with bassist/guitarist Bill Laswell. He was involved in subsequent projects including Ginger Baker's African Force and Middle Passage mixing African and Western influences. Then in 1991 he re-emerged with a free-form, almost entirely acoustic album *Unseen Rain*. In 1994 he returned to his jazz roots for *Going Back Home* which included The Ginger Baker Trio. Then he linked up with jazz trumpeter Ron Miles for *Coward Of The County*, which was very successful and jazzy and included a tribute to Cyril Davies.

Ginger Baker's Airforce also appear on Polydor's 1971 *Bombers* (LP) compilation singing *Sweet Wine*; on *Rock Party* (2-LP) playing *Man Of Constant Sorrow* and on *Supergroups, Vol. 2* (LP) playing *Doin' It*. (VJ/JM)

Baker-Gurvitz Army

Personnel:
GINGER BAKER	drms	ABC
ADRIAN GURVITZ	gtr	ABC
PAUL GURVITZ	bs	ABC
SNIPS	vcls	BC
PETER LEMER	keyb'ds	B

HCP
ALBUMS: 1(A) BAKER-GURVITZ ARMY (Vertigo 9103.201) 1974 SC 22
(up to 2(B) ELYSIAN ENCOUNTER (Mountain TOPS 101) 1975 -
1976) 3(C) HEARTS ON FIRE (Mountain TOPS 111) 1976 -

NB: (1) issued on Janus in the US. (2) and (3) issued on Atco. (1) reissued on CD (Repertoire REP 4163-WZ) 1991. (2) reissued on CD (Repertoire REP 4388-WP) 1993. (3) reissued on CD (Repertoire REP 4605-WZ). *The Collection* (Receiver CD 267 Z) 1999 is a 16-track anthology. *Live In Derby '75* (MLP 08 CD) 2005 comprises of live renditions of 12 previously unreleased tracks by the band. *Flying In And Out Of Stardom* (Castle CMEDD 769) is a 30-track 2-CD anthology. *Live* (CD) (Revisited SPV085304232) is a previously unreleased live album.

45s: Help Me/I Wanna Live Again (Vertigo 6078211) 1975
(up to Space Machine/The Dreamer (Mountain TOP 2) 1975
1976) The Gambler/Time (Mountain TOP 4) 1975
Tracks Of My Life/Artist (Mountain TOP 10) 1976
Dancing The Night Away/Night People (Mountain TOP 15) 1976

Baker joined the Gurvitz brothers in late 1974. They were then playing in a band called **Three Man Army** but had previously played in **Gun** in the late sixties. The new band became known as **Baker-Gurvitz Army** and played pretty decent hard-rock. For the *Elysian Encounter* album Snip was recruited from **Sharks** (who backed **Chris Spedding**) and Peter Lemer joined from **Seventh Wave**, although he later moved on to Barbara Thompson's Paraphenalia then Ascend before *Hearts On Fire*.

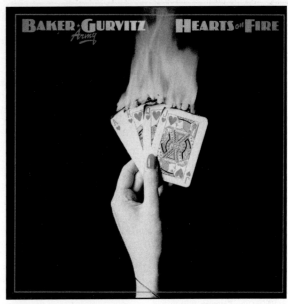

BAKER GURVITZ ARMY - Hearts On Fire (CD).

The previously unreleased *Live* (CD) comprises two tracks from their first album, three from the second along with two previously unreleased tracks *Freedom* and *Whatever It Is*. *Live In Derby* was originally recorded for a radio broadcast when they were promoting their second album. It contains material from this and their first album, some singles, **Cream** covers (*White Room* and *Sunshine of Your Love*) and some previously unrecorded songs. It comes with a 12-page booklet of previously unseen photos and sleevenotes by the band. (VJ/JM)

Bakerloo

Personnel:	KEITH BAKER	drms	A
	DAVE CLEM CLEMPSON	gtr, keyb'ds, hrmnca	A
	TERRY POOLE	bs	A
	JERRY SALISBURY	trumpet	A

| ALBUM: | 1(A) | BAKERLOO | (Harvest SHVL 762) 1969 R2 |

NB: (1) has been counterfeited in 1987 and reissued on CD (Repertoire REP 4358-WP) 1993 and again (Repertoire REP 4870). (1) also reissued on CD and vinyl (Akarma AK 261).

| 45: | Driving Backwards/ |
| | Once Upon A Time | (Harvest HAR 5004) 1969 SC |

Another blues-rock/progressive outfit whose album is of interest to collectors. We're talking a typical and average British blues album here which included a version of Willie Dixon's *Bring It On Home* and *Big Bear Ffolly*, a fast bluesy instrumental with **Alvin Lee**-like guitar work. Side two is dominated by two long tracks: *This Worried Feeling*, a typical slow bluesy number, and the heavier *Son Of Moonshine*.

The Tamworth-based outfit began life as The Bakerloo Blues Line. Keith Baker and Terry Poole had both been in **May Blitz**. Some critics likened the band's sound to **Cream**. They were also afforded the honour of supporting **Led Zeppelin** at their Marquee debut. Musically the format is quite good jazz/blues rock. They also had a cut, *This Worried Feeling*, on Harvest's *Picnic* (2-LP) compilation.

The band split up when Clempson accepted a very attractive offer to join **Colosseum**. Baker played on **Uriah Heep**'s *Salisbury* album and then, along with Poole, later played with **Graham Bond**. (VJ/CA)

Balance

Personnel:	IAN BRIGHTON	gtr	AB
	RADU MALFATTI	trombone, recorder, khene	AB
	FRANK PERRY	drms, perc	AB
	PHIL WACHSMANN	violin	A
	(COLIN WOOD	cello	AB)

BAKERLOO - Bakerloo (LP).

ALBUMS: 1(A)	BALANCE	(Incus INCUS 11) 1973 R2
(up to 2( )	IN FOR THE COUNT	(Private Pressing) 1973 SC
1976)		

NB: (1) reissued on vinyl (Portrait) 1981 (SC). (2) reissued on vinyl (Portrait) 1982.

These jazz fusion albums may be of minor interest to some collectors. They featured, Austrian Radu Malfatti, who was based in the UK at the time and was already well-known as a member of Brotherhood Of Breath and **Elton Dean**'s Ninesense. He later played with Louis Moholo's Spirits Rejoice but by the early 1980s was working more in mainland Europe than in Britain.

Phil Wachsmann had earlier played with Chamberpot and went on to make his mark with String Thing, Iiska 1903 (new version) and Barry Guy's London Jazz Composers Orchestra. Ian Brighton went on to play with String Thing and **Lol Coxhill**. Frank Perry also played with **Keith Tippett**'s experimental band **Ovary Lodge**. Colin Wood later appeared with the **Spontaneous Music Ensemble** and **Lol Coxhill**.

Incus was a small independent company best known for releasing many albums by Derek Bailey. Their first album, was recorded on 11th - 12th October 1973.

This act should not be confused with the US band Balance who did not form/record until the early 1980s. The US band who, apart from (ex-Blues Magoo) Pepe Castro, also included ex-Good Rats and Lou Reed guitarist Bob Kulick. (VJ/RR/IM)

'Long' John Baldry

ALBUMS:	1	LONG JOHN'S BLUES (United Artists ULP 1081) 1964 R2
(up to	2	LOOKING AT LONG JOHN
1976)		(United Artists SULP 1146) 1966 R1
	3	LET THE HEARTACHES BEGIN
		(Pye NSPL 18208) 1968 SC
	4	LET THERE BE LONG JOHN
		(mono/stereo) (Pye N(S)PL 18228) 1968 SC
	5	LONG JOHN BALDRY AND THE
		HOOCHIE COOCHIE MEN (Hallmark HM 560) 1969 SC
	6	WAIT FOR ME
		(mono/stereo) (Pye N(S)PL 18306) 1969 SC
	7	IT AIN'T EASY (Warner Brothers K 46008) 1971 SC
	8	EVERYTHING STOPS FOR TEA
		(Warner Brothers K 46160) 1972 SC
	9	HEARTACHES (GOLDEN HOUR) (Pye GH 572) 1974

NB: (1) With The Hoochie Coochie Men. (1) and (2) reissued on one CD (Beat Goes On BGODCD 2) 1990. (3) and (5) reissued on one CD (Beat Goes On BGOCD 272) 1995. CD compilations include *Let The Heartaches Begin* (PRT PYL 4018) 1988, *A Golden Hour Of Long John Baldry* (Knight KGHCD 127) 1990, although it's already deleted, and *Mexico* (Spectrum 55 0757-2) 1995, which is a mid-price collection of material from 1967-70. *The Very Best Of Long John Baldry* (Music Club MCCD 306) 1997 is a 20-track collection which demonstrates the wide range of material he could tackle from hard-rock to soul and quality pop. It comes with extensive liner notes from Spencer Leigh. *Let The Heartaches Begin (Pye Anthology)* (Sequel NEECD 298) 1998 is a 2-CD collection.

| EP: | 9 | LONG JOHN'S BLUES |
| | | (United Artists UEP 1013) 1964 R2 |

NB: (1) With The Hoochie Coochie Men.

HCP

45s:	α	Up Above My Head/
(up to		You'll Be Mine	(United Artists UP 1056) 1964 R1
1976)		I'm On To You Baby/
		Good Bye Baby	(United Artists UP 1078) 1965 -
		House Next Door/
		How Long Will It Last?	(United Artists UP 1107) 1965 R1
		Unseen Hands/
		Turn On Your Lovelight	(United Artists UP 1124) 1966 -
		The Drifter/Only A Fool Breaks
		His Own Heart	(United Artists UP 1136) 1966 R1
		Cuckoo/
		Bring My Baby Back To Me	(United Artists UP 1158) 1967 -
		Only A Fool Breaks His Own Heart/Let Him
		Go (And Let Me Love You)	(United Artists UP 1204) 1967 SC
		Let The Heartaches Begin/Annabella (Who

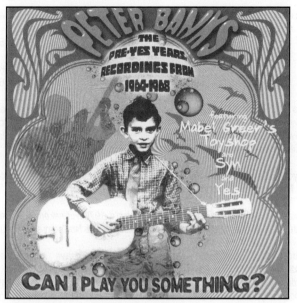

PETER BANKS - Can I Play You Something? (CD).

	Flies To Me When She's Lonely)	(Pye 7N 17385) 1967	1
	Hold Back The Daybreak/		
	Since I Lost You Baby	(Pye 7N 17455) 1968	-
	Mexico/We're Together	(Pye 7N 17563) 1968	15
	When The Sun Comes Shinin' Thru/		
	Wise To The Ways Of The World	(Pye 7N 17593) 1968	29
	It's Too Late Now/		
	Long And Lonely Nights	(Pye 7N 17664) 1969	21
	Wait For Me/Don't Pity Me	(Pye 7N 17815) 1969	-
	Well I Did It/		
	Setting The Tail Of A Fox On Fire	(Pye 7N 17921) 1970	-
	When The World Is Over/		
	Where Are My Eyes?	(Pye 7N 45007) 1970	-
β	Rock Me When He's Gone/		
	Flying	(Warner Brothers K 16105) 1971	-
α	Iko Iko/Mother Ain't Dead	(Warner Brothers K 16175) 1972	-
	Everything Stops For Tea/		
	Hambone	(Warner Brothers K 16217) 1972	-
	Let Me Pass/Let's Go	(GM GMS 15) 1974	-
	Crazy Lady/End Of Another Day	(ABC ABC 4016) 1974	-
	The Boy's In Love Again/		
	Song For Martin Luther King	(GM GMS 9043) 1976	-
Reissues:	Let The Heartaches Begin/Mexico	(Pye 7N 46098) 1978	-
	Mexico/Let The Heartaches Begin	(PRT 7P 356) 1986	-

NB: α With **Rod Stewart**. β as John Baldry.

Born in London in January 1941 and standing 6 feet 7 inches tall this guy cut a commanding figure. He also played a significant role in the development of British R&B and blues.

He began singing in folk clubs and coffee bars in the late fifties and in 1961 fronted **Alexis Korner's Blues Incorporated**. He appeared on **Korner**'s *R&B At The Marquee* album the following year. After spending some time on the Continent he returned to the UK in 1963 and became a member of Cyril Davies' All Stars. Davies sadly died in 1964 and **Baldry** became the band's leader, re-christening them The Hoochie Coochie Men. **Rod Stewart** was recruited as a second vocalist. The *Long John's Blues* album compiles recordings from this era.

Baldry's next venture was to help form **Steampacket** in 1965, although it was during this era that he recorded a number of mostly R&B style solo singles for United Artists, although some, like *Cuckoo*, were Tom Jones-ish. When **Steampacket** quit he formed a new backing group, **Bluesology**, which included a certain Reg Dwight (**Elton John**) among its members.

In 1967 he switched to Pye and with the change of labels came an abrupt change of style. **Baldry** now turned his back on his R&B and blues roots in favour of some pretty sickly easy-listening ballads. At first this brought him Chart success, most notably a No 1 with *Let The Heartaches Begin*. He cut *It Ain't Easy* in 1971 with **Rod Stewart** and **Elton John** but he couldn't sustain his earlier success during the seventies and moved to Canada in 1980. He played the blues and folk circuits, continued to record and loaned

his voice to various Canadian adverts. He also supplied the voice for 'Sonic The Hedgehog's' computer game character Robotnik and Disney's 'Winnie The Pooh recordings.

The 1988 compilation, *Let The Heartaches Begin*, concentrates on his pop recordings from the 1967-68 era. The later Sequel 2-CD *Let The Heartaches Begin* compiles singles, album tracks and eight unissued songs. These include versions of **Cream's** *Sunshine Of Your Love*, Ike and Tina Turner's *River Deep Mountain High* and Richard Harris's *Macarthur Park*.

Back in 1972 he had one track, *Seventh Son*, on Warner Brothers' *Fruity* (LP) compilation. Other compilation appearances have included: *Hoochie Coochie Man* on *R&B At Abbey Road* (CD); *Goin' Out Of My Head* on *Ripples, Vol. 4* (CD); *The 2.19* on *The First British R&B Festival, February 28, 1964* (LP) and *Let The Heartaches Begin* on the 2-CD set *No 1s & Million Sellers Vol 2*.

'Long' John Baldry died in Vancover, Canada after a chest infection on 21 July 2005, aged 64. His last European tour was in 2003. (VJ)

David Ballantyne

45s: I Can't Express It/Ginger Eyes   (Columbia DB 7807) 1966
         I Love Around The World/Wonder Full
         Of Woman   (Columbia DB 7896) 1966

These are solo efforts by **Ballantyne** who was also in **Espirit De Corps**. (VJ)

David Ballantyne and Solitude

45:    Roof Above Our Head/
       Sad Song Of A Sad Man   (Regal Zonophone RZ 3046) 1972

This disc was made to assist Shelter's National Campaign for the homeless. (VJ)

Russ Ballard

ALBUM: 1   WINNING   (Epic SEPC 69210) 1976
(up to 1976)

45:    Loose Women/Danger Zone Part 1   (Epic S EPC 3122) 1974
(up to 1976)

Russ Ballard was in **The Roulettes**, **Unit Four Plus Two** (briefly) and **Argent** prior to launching a solo career, which continued into the eighties. (VJ)

The Balloon Busters

45:    Alcock And Brown/Bluer Than Blue   (Pye 7N 17748) 1969

A happy-go-lucky style pop outfit. *Alcock And Brown* was a Howard-Blaikley-Mason composition. (VJ)

Balls

Personnel:			
	TREVOR BURTON	bs, vcls	A B C
	STEVE GIBBONS	vcls	A C
	DENNY LAINE	gtr, vcls	A B C
	DAVE MORGAN	bs	A
	KEITH SMART	drms	A
	RICHARD TANDY	keyb'ds	A
	ALAN WHITE	drms	B
	MIKE KELLIE	drms	C

NB: Line-up 'A' may not have existed, or may have been very short-lived. Some references also say **Jackie Lomax** was a member, but this appears to be false.

45: Fight For My Country/Janie Slow Down   (Wizard WIZ 101) 1971

When **Trevor Burton** quit **The Move** to replace Willie Hammond in **The Uglys**, the latter changed name to **Balls** in February 1969 and spent eighteen months rehearsing material in a country retreat. Gigs were infrequent for the new combo despite containing a talented array of musicians, **Denny Laine** (ex-**Moody Blues**), **Steve Gibbons** and **Trevor Burton**. White left on the eve of the band's UK live debut around Christmas 1969 and Laine and Burton worked as an acoustic duo until Kellie and Gibbons joined.

Between January-June 1970 **Denny Laine** was also in Airforce as was **Trevor Burton** briefly.

The band's lone single featured Burton's 'A' Side and the Laine-White collaboration on the flip. It was recorded in 1970 but was not issued until the following year, by which time the band had split. Melody Maker claimed in August 1970 that the band had recorded twelve tracks for an album, although they didn't actually have a deal at the time. Ric Grech apparently appeared on some tracks. The same magazine also reported that the 45 was issued in France in August 1970 by Byg Records. The 45 was later reissued under **Burton**'s name, but in a heavily edited down form. Reputedly the track also garnered a third issue, this time credited to B.L.G. and titled *Live In The Mountains*.

Gibbons recorded a solo album for Wizard in the Summer of 1970. When **Balls** split, **Burton** played briefly with **Pink Fairies** and **Steve Gibbons** was briefly in **Idle Race** but, before long, the two had re-united in The Steve Gibbons Band. **Denny Laine** went on to **Wings** and Alan White was later in **Yes**.

Fight For My Country later resurfaced on *Jagged Time Lapse, Vol 2* (CD). (VJ/NW/BM)

Bambis

45s:		
Not Wrong/Handle With Care	(Oriole CB 1965) 1964	R1
Baby Blue/If This Is Love	(CBS 201778) 1965	R1

A beat group. *Baby Blue* was an old Gene Vincent number.

Compilation appearances have included: *Not Wrong* and *Handle With Care* on *Rare 60's Beat Treasures, Vol. 4* (CD); *Baby Blue* and *If This Is Love* on *Rare 60's Beat Treasures, Vol. 5* (CD); and *Not Wrong* on *Visions Of The Past, Vol. 3* (LP & CD). (VJ)

The Bamboo Shoot

45:		
The Fox Has Gone To Ground/		
There And Back Again	(Columbia DB 8370) 1968	R4

An unknown group was responsible for this now extremely rare and collectable 45. It is a complex song with a mod-influenced intro and **Steve Marriott**-style vocals which give way to religious-style chanting and a gong. It got a few plays on John Peel's 'Top Gear' but sold in predictably minuscule quantities.

The Fox Has Gone To Ground later resurfaced on *Rubble, Vol. 3 - Nightmares In Wonderland* (LP), *Rubble, Vol. 2* (CD) and on the 4-CD box set *Acid Drops, Spacedust & Flying Saucers*. (VJ)

A Band Of Angels

Personnel:			
	MIKE D'ABO	vcls, piano	AB
	ERIC FORD	bs	A
	CHRISTIAN (JOHN) GAYDON	gtr, vcls	AB
	BOBBY GRAHAM	drms	A
	BIG JIM SULLIVAN	gtr	A
	JOHN BAKER	gtr	B
	JAMES RUGGE-PRICE	drms	B
	DAVE WILKINSON	bs	B

45s:			
Not True As Yet/Me	(United Artists UP 1049) 1964	SC
Gonna Make A Woman Of You/		
She'll Never Be You	(United Artists UP 1066) 1965	SC
Leave It To Me/		
Too Late My Love	(Piccadilly 7N 35279) 1966	SC
Invitation/Cheat And Lie	(Piccadilly 7N 35292) 1966	SC

This was a soulful pop band, which failed to break into the big time. Its members had all been together at Harrow public school and usually sported straw boaters on stage. The group split in 1966 when **Mike D'Abo** replaced **Paul Jones** as lead vocalist in **Manfred Mann**.

Gaydon later linked up with the band's manager David Enthoven to become EG Management. Their portfolio included **King Crimson** and **T Rex**.

Invitation was also included on Marble Arch's 1970 *Hitmakers* compilation. Both sides of this, their final 45 were popular on the Northern soul circuit.

Retrospective compilation appearances include: *Leave It To Me* on *Piccadilly Story* (CD); *Leave It To Me* and *(Accept My) Invitation* on *The Sixties File* (2-LP); *(Accept My) Invitation* on *Doin' The Mod, Vol. 1* (CD); *(Accept My) Invitation* and *Cheat And Lie* on *Footsteps To Fame, Vol. 2* (CD); and their first two singles on *The Ember Years II* (CD); *Invitation, Too Late My Love, Cheat And Lie, Leave It To Me, She'll Never Be You, Gonna Make A Woman Of You, Me; Not True As Yet* on *Sixties Years, Vol. 3 - French 60's EP Collection* (CD) and *Invitation* on the 2-CD set *We Love The Pirates: Charting The Big 'L' Fab 40*. (VJ)

Band Of Joy

Personnel:			
	JOHN BONHAM	drms	A
	CHRIS BROWN	keyb'ds	A
	KEVIN GAMMOND	gtr	A
	PAUL LOCKEY	bs	A
	ROBERT PLANT	vcls	A

Most notable for including future **Led Zeppelin** members **Robert Plant** and John Bonham, **Band Of Joy**'s story is nonetheless surprisingly murky. It seems that there were at least two (and probably three) versions of the band, with **Plant** being recruited to the first in 1966 only to be fired shortly thereafter. **Plant** then formed an alternative **Band Of Joy**, which soon folded. He then rejoined the third version, with the line-up listed above. Roger Beamer (bs) and John Crutchley (gtr), who had played in **Listen** (another of **Plant**'s bands of the era), are also sometimes also quoted as members, but it's not thought they were part of **The Band Of Joy**. Bonham and Gammond had earlier played in The Crawling Kingsnakes.

The above line-up were together between 1967 and May 1968 and cut at least four demos at Regent Sound Studios in early 1968. These contain some wonderful heavy rock-blues, with **Plant** displaying his full vocal range. *Memory Lane* was planned to be released as a 45, but this never

BARCLAY JAMES HARVEST - Barclay James Harvest (LP).

happened and the song remains uncirculated. The remaining three tracks were a storming version of *Hey Joe*, a cover of Buffalo Springfield's *For What It's Worth* and *Adriatic Sea View* (often mis-credited as *Got To Find My Baby*). *Adriatic Sea View* can be found (as *I Got To Find My Baby*) on the mostly US compilation *Turds On A Bum Ride, Vol. 5* (CD), whilst *Vol. 6* of the same series includes *Hey Joe* and *For What It's Worth*.

In 1976 **The Band Of Joy** reunited with the following line-up: Kevin Gammond (guitar, vocals); Paul Lockey (guitar, vocals); John Pasternak (bass, vocals); Michael Chetwood (keyboards) and Francesco Nizza (drums). They released a self-titled album in 1978 (Polydor 2310 588); **Plant** and Bonham planned to guest on the album, but the idea was scrapped. The reformed **Band Of Joy** also released a second album in 1983, titled *24K* (Thunderbolt THBL 003).

One of the group's pre-Bonham drummers was Peter Robinson, who would later join Gammond and Pasternak in the early seventies band **Bronco**. When the group recorded their *Band Of Joy* album in 1978, Robinson played on most of the tracks, following Francesco Nizza's return to Italy.

It's also been rumoured that some of members were part of **Alexis Korner**'s backing group and also played on **Robert Plant**'s rare 1966 singles. This hasn't been substantiated.

Bonham and Gammond had earlier played in The Crawling Kingsnakes and Gammond was also previously in Bronco.

The *Nowhere Men, Vol. 2* (CD) compilation contains two **Band Of Joy** tracks - *Long Time Coming* and *I've Got A Secret*, though whether by the same act is unconfirmed. (SS/VJ/KP/JA)

Peter Banks

ALBUMS: 1 PETER BANKS AND JAN AKKERMAN
                           (Sovereign SVNA 7250) 1972
          2 PETER BANKS   (Sovereign SVNA 7256) 1973 SC

NB: Also relevant is *Can I Play You Something?* (Blueprint BP 301CD) 2000 is a 22-track compilation.

These were later solo efforts by **Banks** who'd earlier been in **The Syn**, **Neat Change**, **Mabel Greer's Toy Shop**, **Yes** and **Blodwyn Pig**.

Can I Play You Something? comprises 22 tracks, mostly from the 1964-1968 era. Material by **The Syn** and **Mabel Greer's Toy Shop** features quite heavily and this will mostly interest collectors of psychedelia, although the live title tracks dates from 1980 and there are a few other short more recent recordings. (VJ)

The Banshees

Personnel:	MEL AUSTIN	vcls	ABC
	WESLEY BLACK	gtr, keyb'ds	ABC
	PETER DOUGLAS	gtr	ABC
	FRED HULL	gtr	AB
	DES McALEA	sax	ABC
	GERRY McAULEY	drums	ABC
	DINKY O'DAY	vcls	ABC
	DAVE 'TIGER' TAYLOR	bs, gtr	ABC
	PAUL STEVENS		B
	TOM McGRATH	bs	C

45s:	I Got A Woman/Don't Say Goodnight		
	And Mean Goodbye	(Columbia DB 7361) 1964 R1
	Big Buildin'/Mockingbird	(Columbia DB 7530) 1965 SC
	I'm Gonna Keep On Loving You/	
	Yes Indeed	(Columbia DB 7752) 1965 SC

An Irish showband who didn't made much impact at the time. *I Got A Woman* was a Ray Charles song. Paul Stevens was later in The Gibsons and then went solo.

It would appear that this act is unconnected to the Newcastle-based Banshees who included **Bryan Ferry**.

Big Buildin' later appeared on *Sixties Lost And Found, Vol. 1* (LP). (VJ/JM)

BARCLAY JAMES HARVEST - Once Again (LP).

Barclay James Harvest

Personnel:	LES HOLROYD	bs	A
	JOHN LEES	gtr, vcls	A
	MEL PRITCHARD	drms	A
	STUART 'WOOLY' WOLSTENHOLME	keyb'ds, vcls	A

				HCP
ALBUMS:	1(A)	BARCLAY JAMES HARVEST		
(up to			(Harvest SHVL 770) 1970	SC -
1976)	2(A)	ONCE AGAIN	(Harvest SHVL 788) 1971	SC -
	3(A)	BARCLAY JAMES HARVEST AND OTHER		
		SHORT STORIES	(Harvest SHVL 794) 1971	SC -
	4(A)	EARLY MORNING ONWARDS (Compilation)		
			(EMI Starline SRS 5126) 1972	
	5(A)	BABY JAMES HARVEST	(Harvest SHSP 4023) 1972	-
	6(A)	EVERYONE IS EVERYBODY ELSE		
			(Polydor 2383 286) 1974	-
	7(A)	BARCLAY JAMES HARVEST LIVE (2-LP)		
			(Polydor 2683 052) 1974	40
	8(A)	TIME HONORED GHOSTS	(Polydor 2383 361) 1975	32
	9(A)	OCTOBERON	(Polydor 2442 144) 1976	19

NB: (2) reissued (Harvest Q4SHVL 788) 1972 (SC). (1) and (2) reissued on one CD (Beat Goes On BGOCD 152) 1993 and (3) and (5) reissued on one CD (Beat Goes On BGOCD 160) 1993. (1) reissued again on CD (EMI 538 4052) 2002, with 11 bonus tracks. (2) reissued again on CD (Brimstone BRIM002) 1998 and again on CD (EMI 538 4062) 2002, remastered with five bonus cuts. (3) reissued again on CD (EMI 538 4072) 2002, remastered with six bonus cuts. (4) reissued on CD (Brimstone BRIM001) 1998. (5) reissued again on CD (EMI 538 4082) 2002, remastered with eight bonus tracks. (6) reissued on CD (Polydor 8334 482) 1992. (7) reissued on CD (Eclectic ECLCD 1028) 2005. (8) reissued on CD (Polydor 8315 432) 1984 and again remastered. (9) reissued on CD (Polydor 8219 302) 1984 and again remastered (Polydor 0653992). Other CDs on Polydor are: - *Eyes Of The Universe* (Polydor 8215 912) 1992, *Face To Face* (Polydor 8314 83-2) 1992 and *Glasnost* (Polydor 8355 902) 1992. Other relevant CD compilations are: - *The Best Of Barclay James Harvest* (LP) (Harvest SHSM 2013), *The Best Of Barclay James Harvest, Vol 2* (Harvest SHSM 2023), *Another Arable Parable* (Harvest CDP 746 709 2) 1987, *Alone We Fly*, (Connoisseur Collection VSOP CD 140/LP 140) 1990, *Barclay James Harvest Live* (Connoisseur Collection VSOPCD 164) 1991 and *The Harvest Years* (Harvest CDEN 5014) 1991. *The Best Of Barclay James Harvest* (EMI CTMCD 309) 1996 compiles cuts from their 1968 - 1973 Harvest catalogue plus John Lees' 1977 solo 45, *Child Of The Universe*. *Four Barclay James Harvest Originals* (EMI 7243 8 34476 2 6) 1995 compiles their first four albums in a CD box-set format housed in their original gatefold sleeves with a fold-out poster sleeve. *Mockingbird - The Best Of* (EMI Harvest 7243 5 29542) 2001 is a 17-track compilation of material from their four Harvest albums. *BBC In Concert 1972* (EMI 07243 538980 2) 2002 is a 2-CD set originally issued in 1972. *All Is Gathered Safely In* (5-CD set) (Eclectic ECLBOX 1) 2005 is a deluxe set and is the first time that tracks from their EMI Harvest and Polydor eras have been compiled together.

45s:	Early Morning/Mr. Sunshine	(Parlophone R 5693) 1968 SC
(up to	Brother Thrush/Poor Wages	(Harvest HAR 5003) 1969 SC
1976)	Taking Some Time On/	
	The Iron Maiden	(Harvest HAR 5025) 1970 SC
	Mocking Bird/Vanessa Simmons	(Harvest HAR 5034) 1971

I'm Over You/Child Of Man	(Harvest HAR 5051)	1972
α	Breathless/When The City Sleeps	(Harvest HAR 5056)	1972
Thank You/Medicine Man	(Harvest HAR 5058)	1972
Rock And Roll Woman/The Joker (PS)	(Harvest HAR 5068)	1973
Poor Boy Blues/Crazy City	(Polydor 2058 474)	1974
Mocking Bird/Galadriel	(Harvest HAR 5094)	1975
Titles/Song For You	(Polydor 2058 660)	1975

NB: α Later reissued as Harvest (HAR 5095) in 1975. It was originally issued under the pseudonym of **Bombadil**.

Barclay James Harvest was a significant progressive rock band that could pen hook-laden songs with gorgeous melodies and harmonies. Somehow they never achieved the success their talent merited.

The roots of this band lie in the Oldham-based mid-sixties R&B groups, The Blues Keepers, and Heart and Soul and The Wickeds. These merged into a six-piece Blues Keepers which in 1966 became a four-piece. Then after John Crowther, a local businessman, became their manager they were installed in an 18th century farmhouse in Saddleworth Moor, adopting the new name of **Barclay James Harvest**.

Their first single, *Early Morning*, was crisp, clear and harmonious. It got quite a lot of airplay from John Peel at the time but didn't sell in any quantities and is now quite hard to find. The follow-up, *Brother Thrush*, was similar but had a fuller sound and a wider appeal. However, in terms of sales, it fared no better than its predecessor. Shortly after its release they met **Robert John Godfrey**, who helped them assemble The Barclay James Harvest Orchestra. This basically consisted of a loose knit group of classical music students who accompanied the band at live concerts and on recordings.

Now signed to EMI's new progressive Harvest label the band recorded its first album at the famous Abbey Road Studios. Their earlier simple harmonies were now augmented by complex orchestral arrangements and rock which had more cutting edge. The result was a fine album whose highlights included the finale, *Dark Now My Sky, Taking Some Time On* and *Mother Dear*, which was more in the style of their first two 45s.

Their follow-up album, *Once Again*, made more impact and included the classic *Mocking Bird*. This was another exquisitely beautiful song and was their best known recording from their early years. Harvest later released a quadrophonic version of this album, which first time around had bolstered their cult following.

Unfortunately their next effort, *Barclay James Harvest And Other Short Stories*, did not continue this progression. Indeed the band let it be known that they were not happy with the final product. Nonetheless it still had some fine tracks, particularly *Medicine Man, Song With No Meaning* and *After The Day*. By now though, the band was beginning to get into financial difficulties as a result of their lack of commercial success, the high cost of keeping an orchestra on the road and mismanagement. They even returned from an European tour with their equipment impounded as a result of a border dispute and unpaid by one of their concert promoters.

The *Baby James Harvest* album, which had been hastily recorded with no producer, was a real low point in their career. It met with poor reviews and sales and led to them being dropped by EMI, who a few weeks before its release had released a budget-priced compilation, *Early Morning Onwards*, which is a very good introduction to their earlier recordings. They were also involved in a bitter split with their management.

Eventually they secured new management, got a recording contract with Polydor and unable to afford the cost of a touring orchestra reproduced the orchestral arrangements on their own instruments, giving them a unique sound even in the progressive era when many bands had a strong classical influence on their music. Their first album for Polydor, *Everyone Is Everybody Else*, was greeted to critical acclaim. Indeed they built up a strong live following and capitalised on this with the issue of a double live album in 1974. This 11-song collection captured them in top form. It contains the politically charged *Summer Soilder;* the gorgeous beauty of songs like *Mockingbird, Medicine Man* and *Crazy;* the apocalyptic *After The Day* and the psychedelic nugget *Galadriel*. The album did effectively mark the end of their orchestral period, though.

Their next album, *Time Honored Ghosts*, recorded in San Francisco, with producer Elliott Mazer, marked the start of a period of steady growth in their popularity which continued well beyond the time frame of this book.

BARCLAY JAMES HARVEST - Early Morning Onwards (LP).

They never realised their full commercial potential in Britain but went on to become enormously popular in Europe.

They recorded a whole series of albums throughout the seventies, eighties and nineties and celebrated their 25th anniversary with a concert in Liverpool and then went on tour to promote a new compilation, *The Best Of Barclay James Harvest*.

Robert John Godfrey issued a solo album in 1974 on the Charisma label entitled *Fall Of Hyperion* which is becoming hard to find. Recently there has been a falling out between **Godfrey** and the band culminating in a court case from which neither side emerged victorious.

John Lees went on to record a solo album and a couple of 45s in the mid-seventies. 'Wooly' Wolstenholme cut a solo album, *Maestoso*, for Polydor in 1980.

If you're not familiar with the band, *Mockingbird - The Best Of* is a good introduction to songs from their four Harvest albums. It includes elegant rock classics like *Mockingbird* and *She Said*; the ethereal *Moonwater* incorporating strings; the majestic *After The Day* and the pastoral *Early Morning*.

In 2002 EMI reissued their first four studio albums on CD, each with a liberal splattering of bonus cuts. The deluxe 5-CD set *All Is Safely Gathered In* is their most definitive release so far. It features 11 previously unreleased recordings, three tracks previously unreleased outside of Germany and one track not released on CD before. The set is accompanied by a lavish 80-page book which tells the band's story in the words of **John Lees**, Wolly Wostenholme, Les Holroyd and Mel Pritchard.

Harvest's 1970 *Picnic* (2-LP) compilation included *Mother Dear* and you'll also find *After The Day* on the *Harvest Bag* (LP) and *Galadriel* on *Harvest Heritage - 20 Greats* (LP) compilations. More recently *Child Of The Universe* and *Medicine Man* got further airings on *Radio Caroline Calling - 70's Flashback* (CD) and *Pools Of Blue* on the 4-CD box set *Acid Drops, Spacedust & Flying Saucers*.

Mel Pritchard died of a suspected heart attack on 27 January 2004, aged 56, just days after performing with his colleague Les Pritchard in Switzerland. A drummer with a sound reputation - he had played on all their classic albums. (VJ)

Timothy Barclay

45:	Catch The Wind/		
	Girl From Indiana	(Penny Farthing PEN 740)	1970

This is in fact **Mike Berry** and the 'A' side is probably the **Donovan** song. (VJ)

50

Pete Bardens

ALBUMS:	1	THE ANSWER	(Transatlantic TRA 222) 1970 SC
(up to	2	PETER BARDENS	(Transatlantic TRA 243) 1971 SC
1976)	3	VINTAGE '69 (comp)	(Transatlantic TRANSAM 36) 1976

NB: (1) reissued on CD (Breathless 52010) in three-fold digipak. (2) also issued in the US as *Write My Name In Dust* (Verve/MGM). (2) reissued on Line (TACD 90559) 1991, and (Get Back GETLP 574). (3) also featured **Peter Green**. Some copies on clear vinyl. There's a good 2-CD compilation, *Write My Name In The Dust: The Anthology 1963-2002* (Castle CMEDD 1070) 2005.

Peter Bardens first worked at The Marquee with Hamilton King's Blues Messengers and The Peter Bardens Trio. He also managed **The Cheynes** at the time, and in July 1963 joined them too. In April 1965 he left **The Cheynes** for **Them**, and formed **Peter B's (Looners)** in February 1966. The following May, after **Rod Stewart** and **Beryl Marsden** joined, they became **Shotgun Express**.

In 1969 he formed **Village**, who also backed him on his first solo album *The Answer*. It features **Steve Ellis** and **Linda Lewis** on vocals and some superb acid-blues playing from **Peter Green**. The second, featured "Peter Bardens' On". Both are dope-infested in sound and are a bit primitive in production. Long instrumental improvisation dominated both albums, but his keyboard playing was always impressive. **Peter Green** is credited as guitarist on *Vintage 69*, though it doesn't say on which tracks.

In 1972 **Bardens** formed **Camel**, which at least matched the success of **Them**. Leaving **Camel** in 1978 **Bardens** later recorded several albums which were at the forefront of the 'new age' music genre of the late eighties. He also has played on numerous sessions and was a member of studio group Keats.

Alan Marshall, who played on the early **Pete Bardens** albums, later played for **Zzebra**. The anthology *Write My Name In The Dust* traces his recordings with **The Cheynes**, **Peter B. Looners**, **Shotgun Express** and **Village**. It also includes his 1970 solo effort *The Answer* in its entirety, along with his eponymous 1971 release. Then it's on to some of his finest moments with **Camel** before ending with tracks from *The Art Of Levitation*, which was released after his death in 2002. This compilation serves as an excellent testimony to his talents.

Compilation appearances include *The Answer* on *The Transatlantic Story* CD box set. and on the 3-CD box set *Ars Longa Vita Brevis: A Compendium Of Progressive Rock*. (VJ/JM)

Barney J. Barnes and The Intro

Personnel:	BARNEY J. BARNES	vcls	A
	GLEN CURRAN	bs	A
	PETER DAVIES	tenor sax	A
	FRANK HODGES	drms	A

PETE BARDENS - Peter Bardens (LP).

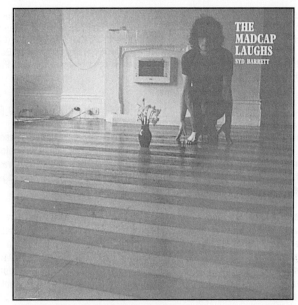

SYD BARRETT - The Madcap Laughs (LP).

	DON HUNTER	baritone sax	A
	BRIAN SHEPHERD	gtr	A
	PETER WOOD	organ	A

45:	It Must Be Love/Can't Stand The Pain	(Decca F 12 662 1967

Featured in a 1966 edition of 'Valentine' magazine, we can only speculate that Frank Hodges could be the same guy who later played with **Magna Carta** in 1970. Similarly, Peter Wood could possibly be the same P. Wood who went on to Vigrass and Osbourne, etc. (JM/KS)

Richard Barnes

ALBUM:	1	RICHARD BARNES	(Philips 630 8027) 1970 SC

				HCP
45s:	Woman, Woman/The Princess And The Soldier		(Columbia DB 8436) 1968	-
	Look Away/Mr In Between		(Columbia DB 8507) 1968	-
	Take To The Mountains/But It's Now I Need Your Love		(Philips BF 1840) 1970	35
	Go North/So Will I		(Philips 6006 039) 1970	38
	Coldwater Morning/Suddenly I Know		(Bronze WIP 6104) 1971	-
	Take To The Mountains/ I'll Never Tell You		(Bronze BRO 6) 1973	-

Barnes had been in **The Quiet Five**. *Fading Yellow, Vol 5* includes his *High Flyin' Electric Bird*. (VJ)

Syd Barrett

ALBUMS:	1	THE MADCAP LAUGHS	(Harvest SHVL 765) 1970 R1 40
	2	BARRETT	(Harvest SHSP 4007) 1970 R1 -

NB: (1) and (2) reissued by Harvest as a double set (SHDW 404) in 1974 (SC) and on CD in 1987 and subsequently (EMI 582346ZPMI). (1) reissued on vinyl (Harvest 7423 855663 18) 1997 and again on vinyl (Simply Vinyl 289) 2000. (1) reissued on CD (EMI 7243 8 25906 2 1) 1994. (2) reissued on vinyl (Harvest 7423 821450 11) 1997, again on vinyl (EMI LPCENT 24) 1997 and again on vinyl (Simply Vinyl 281) 2000. (2) reissued on CD (EMI 7243 8 28907 2 0) 1994. Also of interest is *Opel* (Harvest SHSP 4126) 1988, a collection of outtakes from 1968-1970. *Opel* reissued again as a 2-LP set with *Crazy Diamond* tracks (Harvest SVLP 153) 1999 and again on a single vinyl album (Simply Vinyl SVLP 153) 1999. *Opel* also reissued on CD (Harvest 7243 28908 2 9 respectively) 1994. *Crazy Diamond* (EMI SYD BOX1) 1993, which contains his two official albums, the *Opel* collection and bonus tracks of alternate versions of his songs. Also relevant are *The Peel Session* (EP) (Strange Fruit SFPS 043) 1988 (SC), also on CD (SFPSCD 043) 1988. *The Peel Session* (Strange Fruit SFPSCD 043) 1995 includes versions of *Terrapin*, *Gigolo Aunt*, *Baby Lemonade* and *Effervescent Elephant* and the non-album cut *Two Of A Kind*, written by **Pink Floyd**'s Rick Wright, all originally taped for a John Peel session in February 1970. There's also an unofficial box set, *The Madcap Laughs* (UFO MROK 1), which includes the original EMI CD, a 48-page book, a reproduction of Syd's shirt and a postcard, which was released in a print run of 2,500 in the late nineties. *Radio One Sessions* (CD) (Strange Fruit SFRCD 127) compiles two lost recordings on which he is accompanied by David Gilmour and Jerry Shirley. The recordings were made off air so the recording quality is poor. *Return Of The Crazy Diamond* (LP) compiles unearthed demos and rarities from the 1968-1970 era. *Wouldn't You Miss Me* (CD) (EMI 532302) is a 22-track compilation. *A Fish Out Of Water* (CD) (Sonic Book SBK2) is an audio book that is accompanied by a CD containing two rare early **Pink Floyd** tracks.

45: Octopus/Golden Hair   (Harvest HAR 5009) 1969 R3

Founder of **Pink Floyd** and visionary songwriter on their early releases, **Syd Barrett** went on to record two fragmentary solo albums before becoming the ultimate example of the 'acid casualty'. Later new wave psychedelic acts like Julian Cope and Robyn Hitchcock have acknowledged **Barrett**'s enormous influence on their work.

Roger Keith Barrett was born in Cambridge in January 1946, and always displayed an aptitude for painting. As an art student in London he became interested in the blues, and eventually formed **Pink Floyd**. He wrote or co-wrote all but one track on their classic *Piper At The Gates Of Dawn* album, as well as both sides of their first two hit singles, *Arnold Layne* and *See Emily Play*, and their third 45, *Apples And Oranges*. All are essential British psychedelic recordings.

Sadly, however, in early 1968 **Barrett**'s prodigious intake of hallucinogenic drugs had led to a nervous breakdown. By April of that year he'd become such a liability that the band were forced to replace him with David Gilmour. Prior to his departure he recorded the legendary *Scream Thy Last Scream* and *Vegetable Man*, which went unreleased. **Pink Floyd** arguably never reached quite the same standards of inventiveness without him, and has always acknowledged his huge influence over their progress.

Since then his recordings have been confined to one 45 and two albums. *The Madcap Laughs* is generally considered the finer of the two, and contains several nuggets including *Terrapin*, *Octopus* and *Golden Hair*. **Roger Waters** and Dave Gilmour, who encouraged him to record the album, guested on it, and he's backed by **The Soft Machine** on *No Good Trying*. **Waters** and Gilmour also guested on his next effort, *Barrett*, along with Jerry Shirley, drummer with **Humble Pie**. By now, however, he'd lost any enthusiasm for recording and much of it had was padded with demos. *Dominoes* and *Baby Lemonade* were the best moments on a relatively disappointing album.

In 1972 he joined **Twink** (see **Pink Fairies**) and Jack Monck (ex-Delivery) in Cambridge-based trio Stars, which only managed three gigs before disbanding. Other than that, he's spent his life since 1970 shut away in Cambridge, though he surfaced in 1975 when **Pink Floyd** were mixing *Shine On You Crazy Diamond*, a tribute to him which appeared on their *Wish You Were Here* album. More recently they dedicated *Wish You Were Here* to him at the Live 8 concert in July 2005.

The Peel Session was recorded in February 1970 and first released as a 12" EP in 1988. The initial batch had a metallic finish sleeve, but it was reissued on CD with revised artwork in 1995. *Opel* is a collection of

BARRETT - Barrett (LP).

SYD BARRETT - The Madcap Laughs And Barrett (LP).

outtakes from 1968-70, and aimed at die-hard **Barrett** fans. It certainly has its moments, however, such as the haunting title track, *Birdy Hop*, *Milky Way* and *Word Song*.

Wouldn't You Miss Me is a 22-track compilation. Seven songs come from *The Madcap Laughs*, nine from *Barrett*, four from *Opal*, there's another (*Two of A Kind*) from a Peel session and the set is rounded off by a previously unreleased track *Bob Dylan Blues*. It's a fitting epitaph to the man and comes with a 12-page booklet with lots of information about the tracks and more. *A Fish Out Of Water* is an Italian audio book with an interview with Syd's sister, the story of Syd's career and a full discography and the CD that comes with it features two rare early **Pink Floyd** cuts.

Return of The Crazy Diamond collects unearthed demos and rarities from the 1968 - 1970 period. Many tracks feature **Barrett** playing acoustic guitar with some accompaniment. It includes versions of *Gigolo Aunt*, *Baby Lemonade* and *It's Obvious*. He is a true legend.

Terrapin was also included on Harvest's *Picnic* (2-LP) compilation. More recently, *Baby Lemonade* seems very out of place on the CD compilation, *The Age Of Enlightenment - Prog Rock, Vol. One*; *Octopus* appears on *Harvest Heritage - 20 Greats* (LP) and on the 4-CD box set *Acid Drops, Spacedust & Flying Saucers*; and *Golden Hair* on *Psychedelia At Abbey Road* (CD). (VJ/RMJ)

The Barrier

Personnel incl:	ALAN BROOKS	drms	A
	DEL DWYER	ld gtr	A
	ALAN FRANCIS	bs	A
	ERIC FRANCIS	vcls, organ	A

45s:	Georgie Brown/Dawn Breaks		
	Through (some PS)	(Eyemark EMS 1013) 1968 R3/R2
	The Tide Is Turning/	
	Place In Your Heart	(Philips BF 1692) 1968
	Spot The Lights/Uh	(Philips BF 1731) 1968 R1

Fulham in South London was this band's home turf and their debut 45 was released on a small blues label. The flip side, which was also recorded by **The Purple Barrier** for the same label suggesting that the two bands may have been the same, was good psychedelic pop but untypical of their style. They were then signed to Philips producing two lively pop 45s with Howard and Blaikley producing. *Georgie Brown* is a naff song a few copies of which appeared in a now horrendously rare picture sleeve, but the flip *Dawn Breaks Through* is superb with a fine vocal, ravaging lead guitar, insistent drumming and upfront bass - all in all a fine slice of psych-pop. The follow-up *Tide Is Turning* was recorded by session musicians whilst the band was touring abroad and this is not recommended. *Spot The Lights* with its great discordant intro gives way to a pretty upbeat pop 45 with some good fuzz guitar and drumming which would have benefited from stronger vocals.

Alan Brooks was later in **Punchin' Judy**.

Incredible Sound Show Stories, Vol. 1 (LP) also includes a harpsichord-dominated acetate, *Shapes And Sounds*, by this band. It seems this may have been the subject of a small demo run. The sleevenotes reveal that they also recorded four songs for a Stuart Henry Radio One show in 1967, which have yet to be tracked down.

Other compilation appearances include: *Dawn Breaks Through* on *Psychedelia, Vol. 3* (LP), *Hen's Teeth, Vol. 3* (CD), *Incredible Sound Show Stories, Vol. 1* (CD); *Rubble, Vol. 11* (CD) and *The Best Of Rubble Collection, Vol. 3* (CD); *Spot The Lights* on *English Freakbeat, Vol. 3*, *Rubble Vol. 17: A Trip In A Painted World* (LP) and *Rubble Vol. 10* (CD); *Shapes And Sounds* (acetate) on *Incredible Sound Show Stories, Vol. 1*; *Foxy Lady* and *Toad* on *Alphabet (Pop Psych and Prog 1967-1970)*(LP) and (CD) and *Uh!* on *Jagged Time Lapse, Vol 4* (CD). (VJ)

Barron Knights

Personnel:

BUTCH BAKER (LESLIE JOHN BAKER)	vcls, gtr	A
DAVE BALLINGER	drms	A
DUKE D'MOND (RICHARD PALMER)	vcls, gtr	A
PETER 'P'NUT' LANGFORD	vcls, gtr	A
"BARRON" ANTHONY OSMOND	vcls, bs	A

ALBUMS: 1(A) CALL UP THE GROUPS   (Columbia 33SX 1648) 1964
(up to 2 (A) THE BARRON KNIGHTS   (Columbia SX 6007) 1966
1976) 3 (A) SCRIBED   (Columbia SX/SCX 6176) 1967
       4 (A) ONE MAN'S MEAT   (Penny Farthing PGC 1012) 1972
       5 (A) SONGS FROM THEIR SHOWS   (Tavern MTA 1001) 1972
       6 (A) BARRON KNIGHTS   (Tavern STA 1003) 1973
       7 (A) ODDS-ON FAVOURITES   (Tavern STA 1005) 1974
       8 (A) KNIGHTS OF LAUGHTER
                                    (Penny Farthing PAGS 533) 1975
       9 (A) THE BARRON KNIGHTS   (Tavern STA 1010) 1975
     10 (A) THE BARRON KNIGHTS   (Tavern STA 1015) 1976

NB: (4) reissued again on vinyl (Penny Farthing PELS 536) 1975. (8) reissued again on vinyl (Pickwick SHM 981) 1979. There's also a 2-LP set *The Best Of The Barron Knights* (Warwick WW 5128/9) 1982. CD compilations include: *The Best Of The Barron Knights* (Tring QED 103) 1996, *The Best Of The Barron Knights* (Hallmark 306382) 1997, *The Best Of The Barron Knights* (Prestige CDSGP 0338) 1997 and *The Two Sides Of The Sensational Barron Knights* (See For Miles C5CD 572) 1997.

EPs: 1 (A) GUYING THE TOP POPS   (Columbia SEG 8424) 1965
(up to   2 (A) THOSE VERSATILE BARRON NIGHTS
1977)   (Columbia SEG 8526) 1966
        3 (A) CALL UP THE GROUPS + 3   (EMI 2697) 1977

                                               HCP
45s: Let's Face It/Never Miss Chris   (Fontana H 368) 1962 -
        Jo-Anne/That's My Girl   (Columbia DB 7108) 1963 -

SYD BARRETT - Opel (LP).

Comin' Home Baby/Peanut Butter	(Columbia DB 7188)	1964 -
Call Up The Groups (Parts 1 & 2)	(Columbia DB 7317)	1964 3
Come To The Dance/		
Choose Me Tonight	(Columbia DB 7375)	1964 42
The House Of Johann Strauss/		
She's The One	(Columbia DB 7427)	1964 -
Pop Go The Workers (Parts 1 & 2)	(Columbia DB 7525)	1965 5
It Was A Very Good Year/		
Worry And Wonder	(Columbia DB 7698)	1965 -
Merry Gentle Pops (Parts 1 & 2)	(Columbia DB 7780)	1965 9
Round The World Rhythm And Blues/Where		
There's A Will There's A Way	(Columbia DB 7884)	1965 -
Doing What She's Not Supposed To Do/		
Every Night	(Columbia DB 7933)	1966 -
Under New Management		
(Parts 1 & 2)	(Columbia DB 8071)	1966 15
Lazy Fat People/In The Night	(Columbia DB 8161)	1967 -
Here Come The Bees/It's A Sin	(Columbia DB 8280)	1967 -
I Never Will Marry/		
A Cold In My Nose	(Columbia DB 8423)	1968 -
An Olympic Record (Tracks 1 & 2)	(Columbia DB 8485)	1968 35
Love, And The World Loves With You/		
Along Come Those Summer Days	(Columbia DB 8612)	1969 -
Traces/Awake	(Columbia DB 8679)	1970 -
α If You Jumbo Jet Me/Peaceful Life	(Plexium PXM 21)	1971 -
Hey Ho! Europe/I'm Gonna Give		
My Love To You	(Penny Farthing PEN 768)	1971 -
Popumentary (Parts 1 & 2)	(Penny Farthing PEN 777)	1971 -
You're All I Need/Nothin' Doin'	(Penny Farthing PEN 786)	1972 -
To The Woods/		
Turning My Back On You	(Penny Farthing PEN 797)	1972 -
Turning My Back On You/		
Oh Little Girl	(Penny Farthing PEN 818)	1973 -
The Ballad Of Frank Spencer/		
Pardon Me	(Penny Farthing PEN 854)	1974 -
β Hatters, Hatters/We Are Luton		
Town, You Know	(Tavern STA 1007)	1974 -
χ Danny's Song/		
Me And My Guitar	(Penny Farthing PEN 881)	1975 -

NB: α 'B' side by The Wings Of The Dove. β 'B' side with the Luton Town Squad. χ 'B' side by Pete Langford.

The Barron Knights were an unique and successful comedy and beat group of the sixties who survived with an unchanged line-up for two decades and made a chart comeback in the eighties.

The group formed in Leighton Buzzard in Bedfordshire in 1960. When Antony Osmond brought himself out of the RAF he decided to form a group, having previously produced stage shows. He acquired the nickname of 'The Baron' and the group's original name was The Knights Of The Round Table. It was Osmond's father Wing Commander C.P. Osmond who converted it to **The Barron Knights**.

Initially the group when through several drummers and guitarists before stabilising into a line-up that lasted for over twenty years. Pete Langford was from Durham, Leslie John Baker came from Amersham in Buckinghamshire originally, Richard Palmer (who adopted the name Duke D'Mond) was from Dunstable in Bedfordshire, Ballinger from Slough and Osmond himself had been born in Abingdon, Berkshire. They had a spell in Hamburg, Germany when they were developing as a close harmony act. Their set then comprised material from the Coasters and other black groups, but they gradually introduced a humorous side to their act.

In 1962 they recorded a Pete Langford song *Let's Face It* for Fontana. The label dropped them shortly after its release and it is now their most collectable single. They soon got a deal with Columbia and it was their parodies of the top beat groups of the day that developed their distinctive identity and brought them chart success. The five double-sided singles in question were *Call Up The Groups*, *Pop! Go The Workers*, *Merry Gentle Pops*, *Under New Management* and *An Olympic Record*. Their first album *Call Up The Groups* contained a mix of straight songs and humorous ones. Their second album included no parodies at all. It included covers of **The Beatles**' *She's A Woman*, and The Four Season's *Big Girls Don't Cry* as well as *With Her Head Tucked Underneath Her Arm*, a music hall favourite. Their third album *Scribed* had no comedy material either but 10 of the 12 songs on it were self-penned.

Their only none parody single for EMI to make the charts was *Come To The Dance*, which climbed to a modest No 42 in 1964. 45 sides of some note include: *The House Of Johann Strauss* (an amalgam of classical music and rock'n'roll), *Lazy Fat People* (a **Pete Townsend** composition), a couple of folky numbers *I Never Will Marry* and *It Was A Very Good Year* and the witty *Cold In My Nose*.

They also recorded a one-off protest single *If You Jumbo Jet Me* for Plexium in 1971 against a proposed airport in Wing, Bedfordshire under the pseudonym **Wings Of A Dove**. It's worth noting that the airport was never built!

In 1971 they signed to Larry Page's Penny Farthing label. Their debut effort *Hey Ho! Europe* was written to celebrate our entry into the Common Market. The follow-up *Popumentary 1971* included *Did You Ever* sung as a duet between then premier Edward Heath and opposition leader Harold Wilson. Pete Langford was also the only **Barron Knight** to record a solo single - a version of *Danny's Song* in 1975.

They set up Tavern Records in the seventies to make records to sell at gigs and they also recorded other performers on a direct sales basis. One of the novelty records released on this label was *Hatters, Hatters* to celebrate Luton Town's promotion to the First Division in 1974, which they recorded with the Luton Town squad.

They continued to flourish long beyond the time span of this book. *Live In Trouble* was one of the Christmas hits of 1977 and included a hilarious version of The Floaters' *Float On*. In 1978, they climbed to No 3 with *A Taste Of Aggro* and an album of the same name gave them their first Top 20 album. Despite the Englishness of their humour, they even made the US charts in 1979 with a parody of **Supertramp's** *The Logical Song* called *The Topical Song*. The group is still active today, making records and touring all over the world with a line-up containing three members from their definitive sixties line-up. (VJ)

The Baskervilles

Personnel:	PETER BERRYMAN	vcls	A
	LESTER DINNEY	drms	A
	WILL SLATER	gtr	A
	BRIAN TATUM	organ, vcls	A
	RED ?	bs	A

This act played R&B with harmony vocals and evolved from Sudbury band Brian and The Comets. They were proteges of **The Pretty Things'** Phil May, but split in 1966 and had no known recorded output.

Tatum went on to play for Feel For Soul and then **Mooche**. Is Pete Berryman the same guy as in **The Famous Jug Band**? (JM)

Baskin and Copperfield

Personnel:	JOHN RICHARDSON
	ALAN WILLIAMS

45s:
The Long And Winding Road/	
Beautiful Blue Eyes	(Decca F 13053) 1970
I Never See The Sun/	
Stranger On The Ground	(Decca F 23079) 1970
Moonbeams/Long Grass	(Decca F 23131) 1971
Roly Poly/We Got Love	(Decca F 23174) 1971

Richardson and Williams later found fame in **The Rubettes**. As **Baskin and Copperfield** they were the Simon and Garfunkel of London's East End. The debut 45 was **The Beatles'** cover. (VJ)

Shirley Bassey

HCP

ALBUMS:	1	THE FABULOUS SHIRLEY BASSEY			
(up to		(Columbia SCX 3287) 1959 12			
1976)	2	SHIRLEY	(Columbia 33SX 1286/SCX 3352) 1961 9		

3	SHIRLEY BASSEY		
	(Columbia 33SX 1382/SCX 3419) 1962 14		
4	LET'S FACE THE MUSIC		
	(Columbia 33SX 1454/SCX 3454) 1962 12		
5	SHIRLEY STOPS THE SHOWS		
	(Columbia 33SX 1691/SCX 3543) 1965 -		
6	SHIRLEY BASSEY AT THE PIGALLE		
	(Columbia 33SX 1787/SCX 3577) 1965 16		
7	THE BEST OF SHIRLEY BASSEY (Wing WL 1079) 1966 -		
8	I'VE GOT A SONG FOR YOU		
	(United Artists (S)ULP 1142) 1966 26		
9	AND WE WERE LOVERS		
	(United Artists (S)ULP 1160) 1967 -		
10	TWELVE OF THOSE SONGS		
	(Columbia SX/SCX 6204) 1968 38		
11	THIS IS MY LIFE	(United Artists (S)ULP 1210) 1968 -	
12	THE GOLDEN HITS OF SHIRLEY BASSEY		
	(Columbia SCX 6294) 1968 28		
13	DOES ANYBODY MISS ME		
	(United Artists UAS 29039) 1969 -		
14	LIVE AT THE TALK OF THE TOWN		
	(United Artists UAS 29095) 1969 38		
15	SOMETHING	(United Artists UAS 29100) 1970 5	
16	SOMETHING ELSE	(United Artists UAG 29149) 1971 7	
17	THE SHIRLEY BASSEY COLLECTION (2-LP)		
	(United Artists UAD 60013/14) 1972 37		
18	I CAPRICORN	(United Artists UAS 29246) 1972 13	
19	AND I LOVE YOU SO (United Artists UAS 29385) 1972 24		
20	BROADWAY BASSEY'S WAY		
	(Columbia SCX 6515) 1973 -		
21	NEVER NEVER NEVER		
	(United Artists UAS 29471) 1973 10		
22	LIVE AT CARNEGIE HALL (2-LP)		
	(United Artists UAD 301/2) 1974 -		
23	THE VERY BEST OF SHIRLEY BASSEY		
	(Columbia SCX 6569) 1974 -		
24	THE SHIRLEY BASSEY SINGLES ALBUM		
	(United Artists UAS 29728) 1975 2		
25	GOOD BAD BUT BEAUTIFUL		
	(United Artists UAS 29881) 1975 13		
26	LOVE, LIFE AND FEELINGS		
	(United Artists UAS 29944) 1976 13		
27	THOUGHTS OF LOVE		
	(United Artists UAS 30011) 1976 15		

NB: (16) is a reissue of (15). Vinyl compilations include: *25th Anniversary Album* (2-LP) (United Artists SBTV 60147/48) 1978 (No 3), *21 Hit Singles* (EMI EMTC 105) 1979, *Born To Sing The Blues* (2-LP) (Connoisseur VSOPLP 110) 1987 and *This is Shirley Bassey* (2-LP) (EMI DL 1140) 1988. CD compilations include: *Daimonds (The Best Of Shirley Bassey)* (EMI CDP 790 469-2), *This Is Shirley Bassey* (EMI CDDL 1140) 1988, *Solid Gold* (CD set) (Telstar STACD 027/8) 1992, *Collection: Shirley Bassey* (EMI CDDL 1239) 1993, *Shirley Bassey: 40 Great Songs* (Target/BMG DBP 102002) 1993, *Classic Tracks* (PolyGram 514 347-2) 1994, *Born To Sing* (Polygram 550 185-2) 1994, *Bassey - The EMI/UA Years 1959-1979* (5-CD box set) (EMI BASSEY 1) 1994 and *20 Of The Best* (EMI CDMFP 6252) 1996.

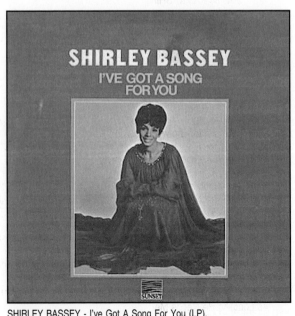

SHIRLEY BASSEY - I've Got A Song For You (LP).

SHIRLEY BASSEY - I Capricorn (CD).

EPs:
1 AT THE CAFÉ DE PARIS LONDON
    (Philips BBE 12113) 1957
2 AS I LOVE YOU   (Philips BBE 12212) 1958
3 BLUES BY SHIRLEY BASSEY   (Philips BBE 12232) 1959
4 LOVE FOR SALE   (Philips BBE 12321) 1959
5 THE FABULOUS SHIRLEY BASSEY
    (Columbia SEG 8027/ESG 7819) 1959
6 BLUES BY SHIRLEY BASSEY NO 2
    (Philips BBE 12408) 1960
7 AS LONG AS HE NEEDS ME
    (Columbia SEG 8063) 1960
8 THE FABULOUS SHIRLEY BASSEY NO 2
    (Columbia SEG 8068/ESG 7840) 1960
9 SHIRLEY NO 1   (Columbia SEG 8098/ESG 7854) 196?
10 SHIRLEY NO 2   (Columbia SEG 8116/ESG 7865) 1961
11 SHIRLEY NO 3   (Columbia SEG 8149/ESG 7869) 1961
12 SHIRLEY BASSEY (Columbia SEG 8165/ESG 7879) 196?
13 TILL AND OTHER GREAT SONGS
    (Columbia SEG 8200) 196?
14 SHIRLEY BASSEY NO 2
    (Columbia SEG 8232/ESG 7889) 196?
15 THE HITS OF SHIRLEY BASSEY
    (Columbia SEG 8252) 1963
16 IN OTHER WORDS   (Columbia SEG 8258) 1963
17 LET'S FACE THE MUSIC
    (Columbia SEG 8273/ESG 7899) 1963
18 I (WHO HAVE NOTHING)   (Columbia SEG 8296) 1964
19 SHIRLEY'S MOST REQUESTED SONGS
    (Columbia SEG 8315) 1964
20 THE DYNAMIC SHIRLEY BASSEY
    (Columbia SEG 8365) 1964
21 LET'S FACE THE MUSIC NO 2
    (Columbia SEG 8404) 1964
22 SHIRLEY STOPS THE SHOW (Columbia SEG 8446) 196?

HCP

45s: α The Banana Boat Song/Tra La La   (Philips JK 1006) 1957 8
(up to α If I Had A Needle And Thread/
1976)   Tonight My Heart She Is Crying   (Philips JK 1018) 1957 -
  α Puh-Leeze! Mister Brown/Take My Love,
  Take My Love   (Philips JK 1018) 1957 -
  As I Love You/Hands Across The Sea   (Philips PB 845) 1958 1
  Kiss Me, Honey Honey, Kiss Me/There's
  Never Been A Night   (Philips PB 860) 1958 3
  Love For Sale/Crazy Rhythm   (Philips PB 917) 1959 -
  My Funny Valentine/How About You?   (Philips PB 919) 1959 -
  Night And Day/The Gypsy In My Soul   (Philips PB 975) 1959 -
  If You Love Me/Count On Me   (Columbia DB 4344) 1959 -
  With These Hands/
  The Party's Over   (Columbia DB 4421 1960 31
  The Birth Of The Blues/
  The Careless Love Blues   (Philips BF 1091) 1960 -
  As Long As He Needs Me/

So In Love   (Columbia DB 4490) 1960 2
You'll Never Know/Hold Me Tight   (Columbia DB 4643) 1961 6
Reach For The Stars/
Climb Every Mountain   (Columbia DB 4685) 1961 1
I'll Get By/Who Are We?   (Columbia DB 4737) 1961 10
Tonight/Let's Start All Over Again   (Columbia DB 4777) 1962 21
Ave Maria/You'll Never Walk Alone   (Columbia DB 4816) 1962 34
Far Away/My Faith   (Columbia DB 4836) 1962 24
What Now My Love?/
Above All Things   (Columbia DB 4882) 1962 5
What Kind Of Fool Am I?/Till   (Columbia DB 4974) 1963 47
I (Who Have Nothing)/
How Can You Tell?   (Columbia DB 7113) 1963 6
Puz-Leeze! Mister Brown/
The Wayward Wind   (Philips 3265565 BF) 1963 -
My Special Dream/You   (Columbia DB 7185) 1964 32
Gone/Your Love   (Columbia DB 7248) 1964 36
Who Can I Turn To?/
To Be Loved By A Man   (Columbia DB 7337) 1964 -
Goldfinger/
Strange How Love Can Be   (Columbia DB 7360) 1964 21
Now/How Can You Believe   (Columbia DB 7423) 1964 -
No Regrets/Seesaw Of Dreams   (Columbia DB 7535) 1965 39
It's Yourself/Secrets   (Columbia DB 7759) 1966 -
The Liquidator / Sunshine   (Columbia DB 7811) 1966 -
Don't Take The Lovers From The World/
Take Away   (United Artists UP 1134) 1966 -
Shirley/Who Could Love Me?   (United Artists UP 1148) 1966 -
The Impossible Dream/
Do I Look Like A Fool?   (United Artists UP 1173) 1966 -
If You Go Away/
Give Him My Love   (United Artists UP 1176) 1967 -
Big Spender/Dangerous Games(United Artists UP 1192) 1967 21
This Is My Life/Without A Word   (United Artists UP 1207) 1968 -
To Give/
My Love Has Two Faces   (United Artists UP 2254) 1968 -
Does Anybody Miss Me/
Fa Fa Fa   (United Artists UP 35083) 1968 -
Doesn't Anybody Miss Me/
Now You Want To Be Loved   (United Artists UP 35015) 1969 -
As I Love You/
Kiss Me, Honey Honey, Kiss Me   (Philips BF 1782) 1969 -
Sea & Sand/What About Today (United Artists UP 35094) 1970 -
Something/Easy To Be Hard   (United Artists UP 35125) 1970 4
Fool On The Hill/What Are You
Doing The Rest   (United Artists UP 35165) 1971 48
Where Do I Begin (Love Story)/
For The Love Of Him   (United Artists UP 35165) 1971 34
For All We Know/
What's Done Is Done   (United Artists UP 35267) 1971 6
Diamonds Are Forever/
Pieces Of My Dreams   (United Artists UP 35293) 1972 38
I've Never Been A Woman Before/The Greatest
Performance Of My Life   (United Artists UP 35270) 1972 -
And I Love You So/I Don't Know How
To Love Him   (United Artists UP 35479) 1972 -
Ballad Of The Said Young Man/
If I Should Find Love Again   (United Artists UP 35479) 1972 -
Never Never Never/
Day By Day   (United Artists UP 35490) 1973 8
Make The World A Little Younger/
The Old-Fashioned Way   (United Artists UP 35557) 1973 -
When You Smile/The Trouble
With Hello Is Goodbye   (United Artists UP 35649) 1974 -
Good, Bad But Beautiful/
I'm Nothing Without You   (United Artists UP 35837) 1975 -
Living/
Everything That Touches You   (United Artists UP 36007) 1975 -
Natali/Runaway   (United Artists UP 36102) 1976 -
Can't Take My Eyes Off You/
Born To Lose   (United Artists UP 36200) 1976 -

NB: α Jukebox edition.

Shirley Bassey is a great entertainer. She oozes style, sexuality and sensuality and is Wales's leading woman vocalist. Her incredible vocal flexibility has brought her success over three years with rock'n'roll, soul and pop.

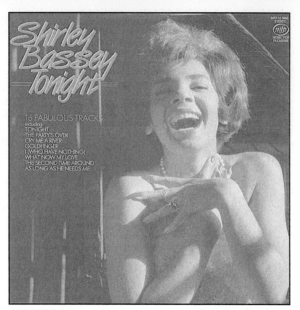

SHIRLEY BASSEY - Tonight (LP).

She was born as Shirley Veronica Bassey on 8 January 1937 in Tiger Bay, Cardiff, Wales, the youngest of seven children. Her parents, a Nigerian sailor and an English woman, divorced before she was three years old, but generally they kept the family together and once Shirley overcame her shyness she began to sing at family parties, often performing duets with her brother. When she left school she worked in factories by day and sang at smoke-filled workingmen's clubs by night. Aged just 16 in 1953 she made her professional debut in a touring revue called 'Memories Of Jolson'. This was followed by a five-month stint in 'Hot From Harlem', but she became homesick and returned to Wales (still only 17) to work as a waitress.

Her mother persuaded her to return and, after being spotted at London's Albany Club by band leader Jack Hylton, she was placed in the year-long revue 'Such Is Life' at London's Aldelphi Theatre with comedian Al Read. The show ran for a year and won her a contract for Philips Records. Her debut *(Who's Going To) Burn My Candle* generated radio interest, although it failed to chart. The follow-up calypso style *Banana Boat Song* climbed to No 8 in the charts in 1957. She headlined a season at the Hippodrome Theatre in London's West End and topped the bill on a series of regional tours. In late 1968 she had two records in the same Top Ten - *As I Love You* and *Kiss Me, Honey Kiss Me* peaked at No's 1 and 3 respectively.

In 1959 she signed a long-term deal with EMI's Columbia where Norman Newell produced most of her subsequent sixties hits. In 1961, *With These Hands* charted on three separate occasions. Then *As Long As He Needs Me* (from the highly successful musical 'Oliver') stayed in the Top 50 for 30 weeks, peaking at No 2. In July 1962 her double 'A' side *Reach For The Stars/Climb Every Mountain* occupied the No 1 slot for 16 weeks. She was a superb live performer and was loved in the US where her concerts rapidly became sell-outs. Indeed her highly-touted live show won her headlining spots in both Las Vegas and New York in the early sixties and she also sang for President John F. Kennedy at the White House. Here in the UK she was a popular fixture at the Variety Performances and much-liked by the Royal Family.

In 1964 she was chosen to sing the theme song for the latest (and one of the best) Bond movies *Goldfinger*, which became a worldwide hit and sold more than a million copies in the US. It climbed to No 8 in the States but strangely missed the Top 20 here in Britain. She enjoyed some big selling albums too. *The Fabulous Shirley Bassey* and *Let's Face The Music* were both arranged by Nelson Riddle (Sinatra's arranger) and set her on course for her international success. *Shirley Stops The Shows* and *Live At The Pigalle* were big band sound albums that generated big sales.

No Regrets was a minor hit in 1965 and was to prove her last for Columbia. In 1966, in an attempt to increase her US record sales, she signed to the US label United Artists and set out on a new phase of her recording career. Her first single for them, the Jack Gold produced *Don't Take The Love From The World* failed to chart, but the following year the brassy belter *Big Spender* rose to No 21. Her first album for United Artists *I've Got A Song For You* was produced by her then husband Kenneth Hume. On this her vocals revealed a decidedly seductive drawl. She

recorded three further albums between 1966 and 1969 which delighted her fans, but it was her acclaimed version of **George Harrison's** *Something*, a No 4 hit in 1970, that introduced her to a wider audience. The same year she returned from abroad (where she lived and worked as a tax exile) for a sell-out season at the 'Talk Of The Town' nightclub. The *Something* album was released in August 1970 and became her best-selling one to date peaking at No 2 and spending six months in the charts. Other highlights included fine versions of The Doors' *Light My Fire* and Blood Sweat and Tears' *Spinning Wheel*. A succession of hits followed and two of them *For All We Know* and *Never Never Never* brought her more Top Ten hits, climbing to No's 6 and 8 respectively. When the disco craze arrived in 1975 **Bassey** contributed *Can't Take My Eyes Off You* in 1976 and *You Take My Heart Away* in 1977, although neither of them charted.

Bassey's achievements won her much acclaim. She was nominated the Best Female Singer by the 'TV Times' in 1962 and 1963. In 1976 she was voted Best Female Entertainer by the American Guild of Variety Artists and the following year Britannia voted her Best Female Singer Of The Last 50 Years. She had a highly-rated BBC TV show in the late seventies, but in 1981 entered semi-retirement in Switzerland. But she returned periodically, most notable in 1987 to enjoy a minor hit with *The Rhythm Divine* when she was backed by Swiss synth-pop group Yello. She also recorded several TV specials.

In the nineties **Bassey** raise her profile again, embarking on several world tours and opening a nightclub in Cardiff. In 1993 she received a CBE and in 1995 she was awarded the Variety Club Of Great Britain's Show Business Personality Of The Year. (VJ)

The Bats

Personnel:	PAUL DITCHFIELD	bs	A
	JIM DUNNING	ld gtr	A
	EDDIE ECKSTEIN	drms	A
	BARRY JORMAN	gtr	A

45s:	Accept It/Lovers Lie Sleeping	(Columbia DB 7429) 1964 SC
	Listen To My Heart/Stop, Don't Do It	(Decca F 22534) 1966
	You Will Now, Won't You/	
	You Look Good Together	(Decca F 22568) 1967 SC
	Hard To Get Up In The Morning/	
	Take Me As I Am	(Decca F 22616) 1967 SC

A soft beat group. Their first 45 was produced by Mickie Most. Erroneously listed as being from Ireland in the earlier edition - they in fact came from South Africa. Band members Paul Ditchfield and Eddie Eckstein both had successful careers as television presenters in South Africa and the band reformed circa 200 to release *Not Out*, which was essentially a novelty album in praise of the South African cricket team.

Compilation appearances include: *On The Waterfront* on *Belfast Beat Maritime Blues* (CD); *Stop, Don't Do It* on *Colour Me Pop, Vol 1* (CD) and *You Look Good Together* on *Colour Me Pop, Vol 3* (CD). (VJ/JM)

THE BATTERED ORNAMENTS - Mantle-piece (CD).

Mike Batt

45s: (up to 1976)	Mister Poem/Fading Yellow	(Liberty LBF 15093) 1968
	I See Wonderful Things In You/	
	Mary Goes Round	(Liberty LBF 15122) 1968
	Your Mother Should Know/Suddenly	(Liberty LBF 15210) 1969
	All The Way Down/Wendy	(DJM DJS 10246) 1972
	Your Mother Should Know/Suddenly	(UA UP 35696) 1974
	All The Way Down/Wendy	(DJM DJS 10316) 1974
	Madhouse Rag/Joker's Song	(Epic EPC 3321) 1975

Born in Southampton, **Batt**'s first venture was as a staff songwriter with Liberty records for whom he also recorded a few early 45s. He later became their A&R Manager and produced **The Groundhogs**' first album as well as putting together **Hapshash and The Coloured Coat**. He also worked as an independent writer/producer - his credits included the strings on **Family**'s *Music In A Doll's House* album and several advertising jingles for the likes of Guinness and Smarties. However, his most successful venture and the one which made him famous was The Wombles, which also spurred him on to a few minor hits in his own name. He was also the man behind **Phase 4**. His career continued to blossom well beyond the time span of this book.

Fading Yellow can also be found on *Fading Yellow* (CD) and *Wendy* on *Fading Yellow, Vol 5* (CD). (VJ)

Battered Ornaments

Personnel:	PETE BAILEY	perc, vcls	A
	NISAR AHMED KHAN	flute, vcls	A
	ROGER POTTER	bs, vcls	A
	CHRIS SPEDDING	gtr, keyb'ds, vcls	A
	ROB TAIT	drms, vcls	A

| ALBUM: | 1(A) | MANTLE PIECE | (Harvest SHVL 758) 1969 R3 |

NB: (1) reissued on CD (Repertoire REP 4405-WY) 1994 with two previously unissued outtakes.

| 45: | Goodbye We Loved You (Madly)/ | |
| | (Flip side by Chris Spedding) | (Harvest HAR 5013) 1969 SC |

When **Pete Brown** was kicked out of the band, **Chris Spedding** took over the vocal role for this now very rare album. *Twisted Track* is a standout cut, which also got an airing on Harvest's *Picnic* (2-LP) sampler. Other highlights include *Turned On To The Earls Court Scene* and there's also some good interplay between the band, particularly **Spedding** and Khan, throughout.

After this album, **Spedding** concentrated on session work and also pursued a solo career. The remaining members formed **The People Band**, cutting one album on Transatlantic. (VJ)

Dave Baxter

| ALBUM: | 1 | GOODBYE DAVE | (Reflection REFL 9) 1970 SC |

This singer / songwriter's album features **Dave Lewis** and **Andwella's Dream**. **Baxter** was a hippie poet and the album is an interesting period piece. (BS)

Bay City Rollers

Personnel: (up to 1976)	NOBBY CLARKE	vcls	AB
	JOHN DEVINE	gtr	AB
	ALAN LONGMUIR	bs	ABC
	DEREK LONGMUIR	drms	ABCD
	ERIC FAULKNER	gtr	BCD
	LESLIE McKEOWN	vcls	CD
	STUART WOOD	gtr	CD
	IAN MITCHELL	bs	D

BAY CITY ROLLERS - Rollin' (LP).

				HCP
ALBUMS:	1(C)	ROLLIN'	(Bell BELLS 244) 1974	1
(up to	2 (C)	ONCE UPON A STAR	(Bell SYBEL 8001) 1975	1
1976)	3 (C)	WOULDN'T YOU LIKE IT	(Bell SYBEL 8002) 1975	3
	4 (D)	DEDICATION	(Bell SYBEL 8005) 1976	4

NB: (1) reissued on CD (BMG 82876 608212) 2004. (2) reissued on CD (BMG 82876 608202) 2004. (3) reissued on CD (BMG 82876 608222) 2004. (4) reissued on CD (BMG 82876 608552) 2004. Other CD releases covering pre-1976 material include *Bay City Rollers* (Ariola Express 295588) 1992, *Greatest Hits* (Tring JHD 025) 1992, *Absolute Rollers* (Arista 74321265752) 1996, *Bye Bye Baby* (Tring QED 106) 1996, *Greatest Hits* (BR Music RM 1551) 1997, *The Very Best Of The Bay City Rollers* (A-Play Collection 100602) 1997, *Shang-A-Lang* (Camden 743215696025) 1998 and *The Very Best Of The Bay City Rollers* (Hallmark 309062) 1998.

			HCP
45s:	Keep On Dancing/Alright	(Bell BLL 1164) 1971	9
(up to	Manana/Because I Love You	(Bell BLL 1262) 1972	-
1976)	Saturday Night/Het C B	(Bell BLL 1319) 1973	-
	Remember (Sha-La-La-La)/		
	Bye Bye Barbara	(Bell BLL 1338) 1974	6
	Shang-A-Lang/Are You Ready For		
	That Rock & Roll	(Bell BLL 1355) 1974	2
	Summerlove Sensation/		
	Bringing Back The Good Times	(Bell BLL 1369) 1974	3
	All Of Me Loves All Of You/The Bump	(Bell BLL 1382) 1974	4
	Bye Bye Baby/It's For You	(Bell BLL 1409) 1975	1
	Give A Little Love/		
	She'll Be Crying Over You	(Bell BLL 1425) 1975	1
	Money Honey / Maryanne	(Bell BLL 1461) 1975	3
	Love Me Like I Like You/Mama U	(Bell BLL 1477) 1976	4
	I Only Want To Be With You/		
	Rock & Roller	(Bell BLL 1493) 1976	4

The Bay City Rollers were the archetypal teenybopper band. The Scottish pop/rock band enjoyed an impressive following amongst teenage girls in the seventies, but their hits were largely cover versions and their success was out of proportion to their talent.

The origins of the group lay in the duo the Longmuir Brothers who formed in the late sixties. Drummer Derek Longmuir was born on 19 March 1952 in Edinburgh and his bassist brother Alan was born in Edinburgh on 20 June 1953. They eventually changed their name to Saxon and added singer Nobby Clarke and guitarist John Devine to their line-up at around the same time. Wanting to change their name to something more American, they decided to stick a pin in a map of the United States and see where it landed. The first attempt landed in Arkansas, which they decided wasn't sexy enough. Continuing this random approach the first place that appealed to them was Bay City, Mitchigan. The suffix 'Rollers' was added to complete the new name.

A local entrepreneur Tam Paton was able to get them gigs in the Edinburgh area and he became their manager by default. They developed a good live reputation in Southern Scotland and the north of England. Eventually, he invited Dick Leahy, the top man at Bell Records to see them in action. He later confided that he couldn't hear them play a note because of the sheer hysteria and signed them on the strength of the audience reaction.

Their debut single was a cover of The Gentry's *Keep On Dancing* produced by **Jonathan King**, which reached No 9 in September 1971. However, their next three releases - *Manana*, *We Can Make Music* and *Saturday Night* - all flopped. During this period the band underwent further line-up changes. In June 1972, guitarist Eric Faulkner was recruited to supplement the line-up. Then, in January 1973, singer Leslie McKeown and guitarist Stuart Wood (both from Edinburgh) replaced Clarke and Devine.

In a desperate attempt to raise their profile Paton circulated their photos to fan clubs and magazines and to adopt a fresh image the band had adopted tartan clothing to emphasise their Scottish-ness. They finally hit the Top Ten again with *Remember* in February 1974, which rose to No 6 and stayed three months in the charts. The follow-up, *Shang-A-Lang* built on this further climbing to No 2 and a band that had been heading nowhere was as a result of effective marketing hot property. Their faces adorned the pop magazines, their merchandise was selling in quantities and they were a regular TV attraction. Their next effort *Summerlove Sensation* climbed to No 3 in July 1974 and when *All Of Me Loves All Of You* peaked at No 4 they had enjoyed four Top Ten hits in a seven month period during 1974. However, privately the band was less than happy with their fourth 1974 45 *All Of Me Loves All Of You* which they described as 'rubbish teeny fodder' as they had wanted the 'B' side, *The Bump* (which was a dance craze at the time) issued as the 'A' side. Revelations that session men often played on their records because it was cheaper and more efficient led to them sacking their producers Martin and Coulter. This was a gamble for the band as they had penned all four of their 1974 hits. They now teamed up with Phil Wainman. Their rather rushed debut album *Rollin'* included their first three 1974 45s along with other Martin/Coulter songs. It topped the album charts and spent over a year in the charts.

Their next single, a cover of The Four Season's *Bye Bye Baby*, was probably their best. They also ensured that no session musicians were involved in its recording. It climbed to No 1 in March 1975, spent six weeks at the top and sold a million copies. The band was now at the zenith of its career - not since the days of **The Beatles** had such mayhem and hysteria been seen. There was a succession of sell-out tours and concerts were often stopped or cancelled altogether because of fan hysteria - the press termed this phenomenon "Rollermania".

Give A Little Love reached No 1 for three weeks in July 1975 and their second album *Once Upon A Star* topped the album charts too. It included favourites like *Bye Bye Baby*, *Angel Baby*, *Marlina* and *Let's Go*. Their final single of 1975, *Money Honey* which climbed to No 3 in November 1975, had a harder edge as the band developed artistically.

As 1975 drew to a close **The Bay City Rollers** embarked on a determined mission to crack the US market. They appeared on 'Saturday Night Live' singing *Saturday Night* - a flopped single from 1973. Given a fresh US release it reached No 1 there in January 1976. It was followed by the Top

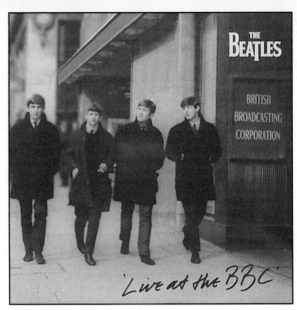
THE BEATLES - Live At The BBC (LP).

Ten hits *Money Honey* and *You Made Me Believe In Magic*. They went on to enjoy five gold albums in the US: *Bay City Rollers*, *Rock'n'Roll Love Letter*, *Dedication*, *It's A Game* and *Greatest Hits*. The mayhem of "Rollermania" was now repeated in the States and Canada as they embarked on an exhaustive programme of concerts, TV appearances and magazine interviews but to a much larger captive audience. Then they focused their sights on Australia where the same sequence of events followed.

Back here in Britain *Love Me Like I Love You* and their cover of **Dusty Springfield's** *I Only Want To Be With You* brought them two further Top Ten hits in 1976, but they would prove to be their last. *Wouldn't You Like It?* and *Dedication* became their next Top Ten albums. *Wouldn't You Like It?* was notable for the rather punkish vocals in the title track. Other highlights include: *Give A Little Love*, *Maybe I'm A Fool To Love You* and *Don't Stop The Music*. *Dedication* was recorded after the emergence of punk and a line-up change. Its highlights are the title track, *Yesterday's Hero*, *You're A Woman* and *Rock'n'Roll Love Letter*.

As we leave the time span of this book their sales were in decline. Alan Longmuir departed in June 1976. His replacement Ian Mitchell was from Downpatrick in County Down in Northern Ireland. Mitchell only survived until June 1977 when he was replaced by another Edinburgh lad Pat McGlynn. It was a different story in Japan though where "Rollermania" reached heights never experienced in the UK and US combined.

In their later years The Rollers were victims of the emergence of punk and their rather lightweight sound placed them squarely in the 'boring old fart' category. Later 1977 singles *It's A Game* and *You Made Me Believe In Magic* could only climb to No's 16 and 34 respectively and their final album *It's A Game* only made it to No 18. In 1978, Longmuir returned to the fold. The same year McKeown was replaced by Duncan Faure and Faulkner left to go solo.

From late 1977 onwards they recorded more adult-orientated material. Audiences in Britain weren't interested but their later albums *Voxx*, *Strangers On The Wind*, *Elevator* and *Ricochet* sold well in other parts of the world. As they became increasingly frustrated the band fragmented. There was an on stage fight in Japan and court cases when two splinter groups, led by Les McKeown and Eric Faulkner fought for rights to use the group's name. McKeown was charged with reckless driving after he knocked over and killed a 75-year old woman. Eric Faulkner and Alan Longmuir attempted suicide and Paton was jailed for committing indecent acts with underage teenagers.

They reformed in 2000 to record an album and tour in an attempt to resolve their differences and claim the millions they allege was due to them in royalties. Derek Longmuir was found guilty of possessing 6,000 images of child pornography downloaded form the internet. He was sentenced to 300 hours of community service.

Compilation appearances include *Bye Bye Baby* on the 2-CD set *45 Classic No 1's* on *UK No 1 Hits Of The 70's* (CD), *30 Years Of Number 1*

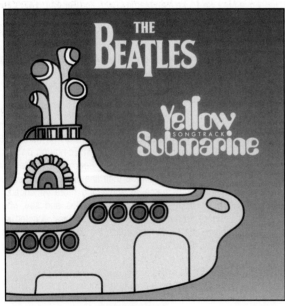
THE BEATLES - Yellow Submarine (CD).

Hit Singles 1960/1989 (CD) and on *Number 1 Hits Of The 70's & 80's* (CD); *Love Me Like I Love You* on *The Seventies, Vol 2* (CD); *You Made Me Believe In Magic* on *The Seventies, Vol 2* (CD); *I Only Want To Be With You* on *The Seventies, Vol 2* (CD) and on *Love Is All Around* (CD); *Keep On Dancing* on *Hits Of The 70's* (CD) and on UK No 1 Hits Of The 70's (CD) and *The Super 70's Vol 2* (CD); and *Shang-a-Lang* on *The Best Summer Ever!* (CD) and *The Super 70's Vol 1* (CD). (VJ)

Baytown Singers

45:      Walkin' Down The Line/
         Let My Feet Fall On The Ground   (Decca F 12160) 1965

This obscure folk 45 is of little interest to collectors. The 'A' side was a Dylan song which had not been committed to vinyl until now and the 45 was produced by Nick Venet and Tony Calder. (VJ)

Baz

Personnel: CHICO GREENWOOD
             BRUCE THOMAS
             JOHN WEIDER
             KEITH WEST

45:      Portrait/Castle   (Dawn DNS 1084) 1974

A minor supergroup here! Greenwood ex-Trifle, Thomas ex-**Sutherland Brothers and Quiver**, Weider, a veteran of **The Animals** and **Family** and of course **Keith West** had been in **Tomorrow** and recorded solo.

They later became Moonrider. (VJ)

B.B. Blunder

Personnel: BRIAN BELSHAW   bs, vcls   AB
             BRIAN GODDING   gtr, vcls, keyb'ds AB
             REG KING   vcls   AB
             KEVIN WESTLAKE   drms, gtr   A
             CHRIS HUNT   drms   B
             ALAN KING   gtr   B

ALBUM: 1(A) WORKER'S PLAYTIME
                               (United Artists UAG 29156) 1971 SC

NB: (1) Reissued as *New Day* (Decal LIK 48) 1989 and credited to Blossom Toes '70.

45s: Sticky Living/
         Rocky Yagbatee Yagbag   (United Artists UP 35203) 1971
    α   Little Boy/10,000 Miles (United Artists UP 35204) 1971

NB: α issued as **Reg King** and **B.B. Blunder**.

This was a later progressive rock venture for Godding (ex-**Keith Tippett Big Band**), Belshaw (ex-**Blossom Toes**), King (ex-**Mighty Baby**) and **Westlake** (ex - **Blossom Toes** and **Eclection**). **Kevin Westlake** had released a solo album.

Westlake left and joined **Ronnie Lane's Slim Chance** in September 1973. Chris Hunt (ex-**Thunderclap Newman**) and Alan King (ex-**Mighty Baby**) then joined. Reg King left in February 1972 and went onto Clat Tyger where he was later joined by Alan King. Godding joined German rock band Magma and Belshaw headed for **Ronnie Lane's Slim Chance** in May 1974. Hunt went on to **Meal Ticket**.

They also have a cut, *Seed*, on United Artists' 1971 double compilation *All Good Clean Fun*.

The album indicates that although the band's music was still progressive in style it was now punctuated by funkier passages. (VJ/NR/JM)

The wrap-around picture sleeve for the first UK Beatles Fan Club Christmas flexi-disc, sent out at the end of 1963.

George Bean

45s: Secret Love/Lonely Weekends   (Decca F 11762) 1963 SC
         Will You Be My Lover Tonight?/
         It Should Be You   (Decca F 11808) 1964
         A Sad Story/Er Um Er   (Decca F 11922) 1964
    α   She Belongs To Me/
         Why Must They Criticise?   (Decca F 12228) 1965 SC
         The Candy Shop Is Closed/Smile From Sequin (CBS 2801) 1967
         Bring Back Lovin'/Floatin'   (CBS 3374) 1968 SC

NB: α as George Bean and The Runners.

A garage-folk artist, pretty lightweight, but one who might have prospered in the protest era of the mid-sixties. One of his best efforts, *Why Must They Criticise?*, was covered in November 1965 by **The In Crowd** (who later became **Tomorrow**). **George Bean** also sang *Onward Christian Soldiers* in the movie 'Privilege' and later formed **Trifle** but died before their 1971 album was released.

Floatin', the 'B' side to his final single, was a decent pop/psych number.

Compilation appearances have included:- *Floatin'* on *Psychedelia, Vol. 4* (LP) and *Hen's Teeth, Vol. 3* (CD); *Will You Be My Lover Tonight* and *Lonely Weekends* on *Pop Inside The '60s, Vol. 2* (CD) and *Sixties Explosion, Vol. 1* (CD); *Er Um Er* on *Rare 60's Beat Treasures, Vol. 4* (CD); *Lonely Weekends, Secret Love* and *It Should Be You* on *Rolling Stones Connection 1963-66* (CD) and *Will You Be My Lover Tonight?* on *Rolling Stones Connection 1963-66* (CD); *Will You Be My Lover Tonight* on *Sixties Lost & Found, Vol. 2* (LP); *Lonely Weekends* on *Sixties Lost And Found, Vol. 3* (LP); and *Why Must They Criticize?* on *English Freakbeat, Vol. 5* (LP & CD). (VJ)

Bean and Loopy's Lot

45:      Stitch In Time/Hay Wire   (Parlophone R 5458) 1966 SC

This group may have included **George Bean**.

A Stitch In Time later appeared on *Diggin' For Gold, Vol. 6* (LP).

The Beat Boys

Personnel incl: RONNIE CARR   bs, vcls   A
                 MAL GRUNDY   gtr   A
                 ALAN PARKINSON   gtr, vcls
                 KENNY POWELL   gtr, vcls
                 RONNIE SIMS   drms   A

45:      That's My Plan/Third Time Lucky   (Decca F 11730) 1963 R1

A Sheffield beat group whose 45 was produced by Joe Meek. A Canadian only album, *Beatlemania* (Kent 253) 196? has the liner notes "On this album, a popular English group, The Beat Boys, do some of the big tunes made popular by the **Beatles**, plus several other big hits of their own". It's not known whether this is the same act, however, as the album doesn't include any credits.

Compilation appearances include: *That's My Plan* and *Third Time Lucky* on *RGM Rarities, Vol. 2* (CD); and *Third Time Lucky* on *Sixties Lost And Found, Vol. 3* (LP) and *The Beat Scene* (CD). (VJ/VZ)

Beat Brothers

45:     Nick Nack Hully Gully/
        Lantern Hully Gully   (Polydor NH 52185) 1964 R1

At one time they were **Tony Sheridan**'s backing band. (VJ)

Beat Chics

Personnel incl: ANN BRIDGEMAN
              CHRISTINE LEE

45:     Skinny Minnie/Now I Know   (Decca F 12016) 1964 SC

A female beat group, who once played at The Star Club in Hamburg. *Skinny Minnie* was an old Bill Haley number.

Now I Know later emerged on *Pop Inside The '60s, Vol. 2* (CD), *Sixties Lost & Found, Vol. 2* (LP), *Sixties Explosion, Vol. 1* (CD) and *The Beat Scene* (CD). (VJ)

The Beatles

Personnel:			
PETE BEST	drms		AB
GEORGE HARRISON	vcls, ld gtr		ABC
JOHN LENNON	vcls, gtr		ABC
PAUL McCARTNEY	vcls, gtr, bs		ABC
STU SUTCLIFFE	bs		A
RINGO STARR	drms		C

                                      HCP

ALBUMS: 1(C) PLEASE PLEASE ME (mono/stereo)
              (Parlophone PMC 1202/PCS 3042) 1963 R1/R2 1
       2(C) WITH THE BEATLES (mono/stereo)
              (Parlophone PMC 1206/PCS 3045) 1963 R1/R2 1
       3(C) A HARD DAY'S NIGHT (Soundtrack) (mono/stereo)
              (Parlophone PMC 1230/PCS 3058) 1964 R1/R2 1

THE BEATLES - Please Please Me (LP).

THE BEATLES - The 1964 Christmas Fan Club flexi disc.

    4(C) BEATLES FOR SALE (mono/stereo)
              (Parlophone PMC 1240/PCS 3062) 1964 R1/R2 1
    5(C) HELP! (Soundtrack) (mono/stereo)
              (Parlophone PMC 1255/PCS 3071) 1965 R1 1
    6(C) RUBBER SOUL (mono/stereo)
              (Parlophone PMC 1267/PCS 3075) 1966 R1 1
    7(C) REVOLVER
        (mono/stereo)   (Parlophone PMC/PCS 7009) 1966 R1 1
    8(C) A COLLECTION OF BEATLES OLDIES
        (mono/stereo)   (Parlophone PMC/PCS 7016) 1967 R1 7
    9(C) SGT. PEPPER'S LONELY HEARTS CLUB BAND
        (mono/stereo) (w/insert)
              (Parlophone PMC/PCS 7027) 1967 R1 1
   10(C) THE BEATLES (2-LP) (mono/stereo) (w/insert & poster)
              (Apple PMC/PCS 7067/8) 1968 R1 1
   11(C) YELLOW SUBMARINE (Soundtrack)
              (Apple PMC/PCS 7070) 1969 R1 3
   12(C) ABBEY ROAD   (Apple PCS 7088) 1969 SC 1
   13(C) LET IT BE   (Apple PCS 7096) 1970 SC 1
   14(C) FROM THEM TO YOU (THE BEATLES' CHRISTMAS
        ALBUM)   (Apple/Lyntone LYN 2154) 1970 R4 -

NB: (14) Fan club issue - Mail order only. Stereo versions of (1) (Parlophone OCS 3042) 1963, with black and gold labels are among the rarest UK releases and worth in excess of £3,000. There are various collectable versions of (10), notably low number copies below 0000010, in mono or stereo with the top-opening Garrard & Lofthouse gatefold sleeve, black inners, the poster and four colour prints and dark green label with "Sold in the UK?" text were valued in the December 2004 issue of 'Record Collector' at £10,00; the above but numbered between 0000011 & 0000100 at £1,000. The export issue of the album with yellow and black labels and the Decca pressing fetch £4,000 and the original export album is worth £1,200 according to 'Record Collector' at December 2004 prices. A version of (11) (Odeon PPCS 7070) 1969 was pressed for export to countires like Holland and Denmark with an Odeon sticker on the rear of the Apple sleeve. Copies are extremely rare and valued at £2,000 plus. Some export versions of (12) (Parlophone P-PCS 7088) 1969 come with distinctive yellow and black labels and no stamper letters at three o'clock to the matrix number. These are valued at £3,000. Another pressing (Parlophone 7088) was made for export to countries with limited pressing power. It comes in an Apple sleeve, but is a Parlophone pressing and should have a Parlophone sticker on the rear of the sleeve. These are worth circa £1,200. There's a very rare export version of (13) (Parlophone 7096) 1970, which comes with no notable text differences to other export issues and bears the normal yellow and black export labels. Copies are valued at in excess of £1,200.

(1) reissued on CD (Parlophone 746 435 2) 1987. (2) reissued on CD (Parlophone CDP 746 436 2) 1987. (3) reissued on CD (Parlophone CDP 746 437 2) 1987. (4) reissued on CD (Parlophone CDP 746 438 2) 1987. (5) reissued on CD (Parlophone CDP 746 439 2) 1987. (6) reissued on CD (Parlophone CDP 746 440 2) 1987. (7) reissued on CD (Parlophone CDP 746 441 2) 1987. (9) reissued on CD (Parlophone CDP 746 442 2) 1987. (10) reissued as a CD set (Parlophone CDS 746 443 8) 1987. (11) reissued on CD (Parlophone CDP 746 445 2) 1987. (12) reissued on CD (Parlophone CDP 746 446 2) 1987. (13) reissued on CD (Parlophone CDP 746 447 2) 1987.

There have also been numerous compilations and live recordings including:- *The Beatles 1962-66* (2-LP) (Apple PCSPR 717) 1973 (No 3), reissued as a CD set on Parlophone (CDPCSP 7231) 1991; *The Beatles 1967-70* (2-LP) (Apple PCSPR 718) 1973 (No 2), reissued as a CD set on Parlophone (CDPCSP 7241) 1991; *Rock'n'Roll Music* (Parlophone PCSP 719) 1976 (No 11); *The Beatles Tapes*

(Polydor 2683 068) 1976 (No 45); *The Beatles Live At The Hollywood Bowl* (EMI EMTV 4) 1977 (No 1) later reissued on Music For Pleasure (1983); *Live At The Star Club, Hamburg,* Germany 1962 (Bellaphon 15233) 1977 later reissued on CD (Spectrum SPEC 85025) 1988; *Love Songs* (Parlophone PCS 7211) 1977 (No 7); *Rarities* (Parlophone PCM 1001) 1979 (No 71); *The Beatles Collection* (all the original albums boxed) (Parlophone BC 13) in 1978; *Beatles Ballads* (Parlophone PCS 7214) 1980 (No 17); *Reel Music* (Parlophone) 1982; *The Beatles Mono Collection* (Parlophone BMC 10) 1982 (red vinyl) (R3); *20 Greatest Hits* (2-LP) (Parlophone PCTC 260) 1982 (No 10); *Hamburg Tapes Vol's 1, 2 and 3* (Breakaway) 1983; *Past Masters, Vol. 1* (Parlophone CDBPM 1) 1988 (No 49), also on CD (Parlophone CDP 790 043 2) 1988; *Past Masters, Vol. 2* (Parlophone CDBPM 2) 1988 (No 46), also on CD (Parlophone CDP 790 044 2) 1988; *Past Masters (Vol's 1 and 2)* (EMI (Japan) JBCDBOX 5) 1988; *The CD Singles* Collection (Parlophone CDBSC 1) 1989; *The Beatles - The Ultimate Box Set* (CD) (Parlophone CDS 791 302 2) 1988; *Beatles Tapes* (David Wigg Interviews 1969-73) (CD set) (Polydor 847 185-2) 1990; *Decca Sessions (1/1/62)* (CD) (Topline TOP CD 523) 1987; *Introspective: Beatles* (CD) (Baktabak CINT 5004) 1991; the CD set *It Was Twenty Years Ago Today* (EMI (Japan) JBCDBOX 3) 1988; *Live Recordings* (1962) (Baktabak CTAB 5001) 1988; *Magical Mystery Tour* (Soundtrack) (CD) (Parlophone CDP 748 062 2) 1987, this was earlier available on vinyl in album format in 1976. It consisted of their *Magical Mystery Tour* (EP) and their 1967 singles; *Rockin' At The Star Club, 1962* (Columbia 4689502) 1992; *The Savage Young Beatles* (Charly CFM 101) 1982 reissued as *The Beatles Featuring Tony Sheridan, Hamburg* (Topline TOP CD 108) 1987 and finally there's *The Beatles Live At The BBC* (EMI 7243 8 31796 1 9) 1994, the first album of new Beatles material since 1977.

Two interview excerpts have recently appeared which may be of interest to **Beatles'** obsessives. *In Their Own Words - A Rockumentary* (5-CD box set, Laserlight 15968) is an audio anthology comprising material from interviews, press releases etc. *Inside Interviews* (5-CD box set, Laserlight 15981) traces their career through a series of interviews not all of which have appeared on interview discs before. *1* (Apple 743 5 299702 2) 2000 compiles 27 No 1 singles on one CD. *The Beatles First!* (Polydor 9821323) credited to The Beatles Featuring Tony Sheridan includes six tracks recorded during their visits to Hamburg when they played as **Tony Sheridan's** back-up band. It includes six tracks with them backing Sheridan and two of them playing on their own. *The Capitol Albums Vol 1* (Capitol CPT 1234) 2004 is a 4-CD set containing their first four albums for Capitol.

HCP

EPs:
1(C)	TWIST AND SHOUT	(Parlophone GEP 8882) 1963	SC	2
2(C)	THE BEATLES' HITS	(Parlophone GEP 8880) 1963	SC	14
3(C)	THE BEATLES (No 1)			
		(Parlophone GEP 8883) 1963	SC	19
4(C)	ALL MY LOVING	(Parlophone GEP 8891) 1964	SC	12
5(C)	LONG TALL SALLY	(Parlophone GEP 8913) 1964	SC	14
6(C)	EXTRACTS FROM THE FILM 'A HARD DAY'S NIGHT'			
		(Parlophone GEP 8920) 1964	SC	34
7(C)	EXTRACTS FROM THE ALBUM 'A HARD DAY'S NIGHT'			
		(Parlophone GEP 8924) 1964	R1	-
8(C)	BEATLES FOR SALE	(Parlophone GEP 8931) 1965	SC	-
9(C)	BEATLES FOR SALE No.2			
		(Parlophone GEP 8938) 1965	R1	-
10(C)	THE BEATLES' MILLION SELLERS			
		(Parlophone GEP 8946) 1965	R1	-
11(C)	YESTERDAY	(Parlophone GEP 8948) 1966	R2	-
12(C)	NOWHERE MAN	(Parlophone GEP 8952) 1966	R2	-
13(C)	MAGICAL MYSTERY TOUR (2-EP) (PS)			
	(mono/stereo)	(Parlophone (S)MMT-1) 1967	R1/R2	2

THE BEATLES - Past Masters Volume One (CD).

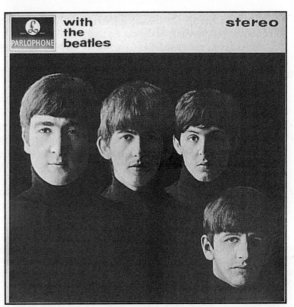

THE BEATLES - With The Beatles (LP).

NB: They had an EP, *Golden Discs* (Parlophone GEP 8891) 1964 (R5), which was never released. It comprised 2 x one-sided test pressings and one set of label proofs. It was intended to release four of their million selling singles: *She Loves You, I Want To Hold Your Hand, Can't Buy Me Love* and *I Feel Fine* but was withdrawn to avoid affecting the sales of *A Hard Days Night*. 'Record Collector' in December 2004 valued this item at £2,000 minus the label proofs. (13) reissued in 197?. There was also a 14 EP box set, *The Beatles EP Collection* (Parlophone BEP 14) 1981 with a bonus EP, *The Beatles*. (R1). This was later available as a CD set (Parlophone CDBEP 14) 1992.

HCP

45s:	α	Love Me Do/P.S. I Love You	(Parlophone R 4949) 1962	17
	β	Please Please Me/Ask Me Why	(Parlophone R 4983) 1963	2
	χ	From Me To You/Thank You Girl	(Parlophone R 5015) 1963	1
	δ	She Loves You/I'll Get You	(Parlophone R 5055) 1963	1
	ε	I Want To Hold Your Hand/This Boy	(Parlophone R 5084) 1963	1
	φ	Cry For A Shadow/		
		Why (Can't You Love Me Again)	(Polydor NH 52275) 1964	-
	φ	Ain't She Sweet/		
		If You Love Me, Baby	(Polydor NH 52317) 1964	29
	γ	Can't Buy Me Love/		
		You Can't Do That	(Parlophone R 5114) 1964	1
	η	A Hard Day's Night/		
		Things We Said Today	(Parlophone R 5160) 1964	1
	ι	I Feel Fine/She's A Woman	(Parlophone R 5200) 1964	1
	φ	Ticket To Ride/Yes It Is	(Parlophone R 5265) 1965	1
	κ	Help!/I'm Down	(Parlophone R 5305) 1965	1
	λ	We Can Work It Out/Day Tripper	(Parlophone R 5389) 1965	1
	μ	Paperback Writer/Rain	(Parlophone R 5452) 1966	1
	ν	Yellow Submarine/Eleanor Rigby	(Parlophone R 5493) 1966	1
	o	Penny Lane/Strawberry Fields		
		Forever (Some PS)	(Parlophone R 5570) 1967	2
	π	All You Need Is Love/		
		Baby You're A Rich Man	(Parlophone R 5620) 1967	1
	θ	Hello Goodbye/I Am The Walrus	(Parlophone R 5655) 1967	1
	ρ	Lady Madonna/The Inner Light	(Parlophone R 5675) 1968	1
	σ	Hey Jude/Revolution	(Apple R 5722) 1968	1
	τ	Get Back/Don't Let Me Down	(Apple R 5777) 1969	1
	υ	The Ballad Of John And Yoko/		
		Old Brown Shoe	(Apple R 5786) 1969	1
	ϖ	Something/Come Together	(Apple R 5814) 1969	4
	ω	Let It Be/You Know My Name	(Apple R 5833) 1970	2

Christmas flexidiscs:
The Beatles' Christmas Record (PS) (Lynton LYN 492) 1963 R2
Another Beatles Christmas Record (PS)
    (Lynton LYN 757) 1964 R1
The Beatles' Third Christmas Record (PS)
    (Lynton LYN 948) 1965 R1
Pantomime: Everywhere It's Christmas (PS)
    (Lynton LYN 1145) 1966 R2
Christmas Time (Is Here Again) (PS)
    (Lynton LYN 1360) 1967 R2
The Beatles' Sixth Christmas Record (PS) (Some with 'Super

Pix' sales insert)   (Lynton LYN 1743/4) 1968 R2/R1
The Beatles' Seventh Christmas Record (PS) (Some with 2x
foolscap fan club newsletter) (Lynton LYN 1970/1-IL) 1969 R2/R1

Reissues: Yesterday/I Should Have Known Better   (Apple R 6013) 1976 8
Back In The U.S.S.R./
Twist And Shout   (Parlophone R 6016) 1976 19
Medley of Songs for "Rock 'n' Roll Music" (excerpts)
(promo only)   (EMI SPSR) 1976 -
Twist And Shout/Falling In Love Again   (Lingasong NB 1) 1977 -
Sgt. Pepper's Lonely Hearts Club Band/With A Little Help From
My Friends/A Day In The Life (PS) (Parlophone R 6022) 1978 63
Searching/Twist And Shout/
Til There Was You (PS)   (AFE FAS 1) 1982 -
Beatles Movie Medley   (Parlophone R 6055) 1982 10
Love Me Do/P.S. I Love You   (Parlophone R 4949) 1982 4

NB: α Rose to No. 4 when reissued in 1982. Any demo versions of these 45s are collector's items nowadays, but demos of *Love Me Do* change hands for in excess of £3,000. φ Flip sides credited to Tony Sheridan and The Beatles. All of The Beatles' original singles were reissued as CD singles in 1988/89. α on Parlophone (CD3R 4949) 1988. β on Parlophone (CD3R 4983) 1988. χ on Parlophone (CD3R 5015) 1988. δ on Parlophone (CD3R 5055) 1988. ε on Parlophone (CD3R 5084) 1989. γ on Parlophone (CD3R 5114) 1989. η on Parlophone (CD3R 5160) 1989. ι on Parlophone (CD3R 5200) 1989. φ on Parlophone (CD3R 5265) 1989. κ on Parlophone (CD3R 5305) 1989. λ on Parlophone (CD3R 5389) 1989. μ on Parlophone (CD3R 5452) 1989. ν on Parlophone (CD3R 5493) 1989. o on Parlophone (CD3R 5570) 1989. π on Parlophone (CD3R 5620) 1989. θ on Parlophone (CD3R 5655) 1989. ρ on Parlophone (CD3R 5675) 1989. σ on Parlophone (CD3R 5722) 1989. τ on Parlophone (CD3R 5777) 1989. υ on Parlophone (CD3R 5786) 1989. ϖ on Parlophone (CD3R 5814) 1989. ω on Parlophone (CD3R 5833) 1989. They'd earlier been reissued on vinyl during 1983/84 and most of them re-entered the Charts as minor hits. In the 1980s their singles were reissued as picture discs. These are not listed below. The first four Apple 45s (including *Hey Jude*) were released in a presentation pack as *Our First Four* to celebrate Apple's launch. This set (the other discs were **Mary Hopkins**' *Those Were The Days*, *Sour Milk Sea* by **Jackie Lomax** and *Thingumybob* by the Black Dyke Mills Band) now fetches circa £1,000. During their career they also recorded seven 7" Christmas flexi-discs, which were mailed to fan club members. These are listed in the discography above, and Record Collector No. 112 (December 1988) included a detailed article about them. As the band had split by Christmas 1970, remaining fan club members were given a hard-vinyl album instead. Entitled *From Them To You* here in the UK and *The Beatles' Christmas Album* in the States, both variants comprised all seven flexi-discs, and are now extremely rare and sought-after.

What is there left to say about **The Beatles**? Many of the acts featured in this book wouldn't have picked up an instrument without them, and much of the music they made was directly inspired by them. In **John Lennon** and **Paul McCartney** they possessed the two most consistently inventive songwriters of the era, and **George Harrison** also contributed increasingly sophisticated and ground-breaking material. But their appeal transcends the purely musical - many people's memory of the 1960s is inextricably linked to the band, which came to symbolise all the optimism, experimentalism and, ultimately, despair of the decade. Put simply, they shaped and influenced the evolution and development of British pop, rock and youth culture more than any other artists in this book, leaving behind a canon that has never been rivalled and probably never will be.

THE BEATLES - A Hard Day's Night (LP).

John Lennon and **Paul McCartney** were both members of The Quarrymen whilst at school in Liverpool. **George Harrison** joined on guitar in August 1958, but they disbanded in late 1959. In April 1960 John, Paul and George reformed the band as Long John and The Silver Beatles, with **Pete Best** (drms) and an art school friend of John's, Stu Sutcliffe (gtr). They dropped the 'Long John' almost immediately. In May 1960 they employed Alan Williams as their manager and he got them some gigs around the Liverpool clubs. They also undertook a brief tour of Scotland, backing Johnny Gentle as The Silver Beatles. That August they set sail for Hamburg, whose tough clubs were a tried and tested environment for bands to hone their repertoires in. By the time they set sail they'd dropped the 'Silver' from their name and were known as simply **The Beatles**.

On this trip, which lasted from August to December, they played the Indra, Kaiserkeller and Top Ten clubs, but had to return to the UK when George was deported for being underage. The punishing sets they were expected to play had made them rawer and more inventive, and upon their return to the UK they built up a good reputation for themselves in the North West. They made their first appearance at Liverpool's legendary Cavern Club on 21 March 1961.

In April 1961 they returned to Hamburg for a second three month stint, and the following month undertook their first recording session, backing cabaret-style singer **Tony Sheridan** for Polydor. They also cut two tracks without him - *Ain't She Sweet* and *Cry For A Shadow*. By now Sutcliffe, who was barely competent as a bassist, had fallen in love with a German girl and wanted to leave the band to get married and stay in Germany. Despite much resistance from John, who desperately wanted his best mate in the band, he left in June 1961 and remained in Hamburg to study art and be with his new wife. On 10 April 1962 he would tragically die there of a brain haemorrhage.

When they returned to Liverpool, local record shop owner Brian Epstein (who'd been inundated with requests for their record) became their manager after seeing them play a lunchtime set in the Cavern. With Paul having switched to bass, they remained a four-piece. Epstein arranged for them to record a demo for Decca in London on New Year's Day, 1962. Worse for wear from an overnight journey, however, they performed below their best and A&R men Dick Rowe and Mike Smith signed **Brian Poole and The Tremeloes** instead.

They returned to Hamburg on 11 April 1962 (not knowing that Sutcliffe had died the previous day), to play a seven-week residency at Hamburg's Star Club. Soon afterwards Epstein wired them with the exciting news that EMI producer **George Martin** liked their demo tapes and had arranged a recording session for them. On 18 August John, Paul and George decided to fire their quiet drummer **Pete Best** (probably at Epstein's instigation) and replace him with **Ringo Starr**, whom they'd met when he was playing with fellow Liverpudlians **Rory Storm and The Hurricanes**. Five days later John married fellow art student Cynthia Powell, with Paul as his best man.

The release of *Love Me Do* in October 1962 attracted little attention, but Brian Epstein heavily promoted it in the North and it rose to No. 17 in the

THE BEATLES - For Sale (LP).

UK Charts that December. Later that month **The Beatles** made their final visit to Hamburg, playing two weeks at The Star Club. In hindsight this trip can be seen as the final phase of their preparation for world domination, and several live recordings from this era have since been issued.

1963 was the year **The Beatles** really broke big. Their second 45, *Please Please Me*, charted almost immediately and went on to peak at No. 1 on three of the UK charts and No. 2 on the fourth. Their debut album, *Please Please Me*, was released in the UK in March 1963 and is solid testament to the long hours they'd worked in Hamburg. It opens with the brilliant rocker *I Saw Her Standing There*, one of eight **Lennon/McCartney** originals, including both sides of their first two 45s. The six cover versions include *Baby, It's You* (a US hit for The Shirelles in the summer of 1962), the Goffin/King composition *Chains* and the popular standard *A Taste Of Honey*. Also present were live favourites such as the fast rocker *Boys* and raucous closer *Twist And Shout*, which features a stunningly raw **Lennon** vocal. Though a highly enjoyable and fresh debut, it was very much a statement of where they'd come from rather than where they were headed. Still, it topped the UK album charts for 30 weeks from 11 May 1963, and what became known as 'Beatlemania' was well underway.

In the summer of 1963 *Introducing... The Beatles* was released in the States, commencing the frustrating practice of issuing different albums in the US to the UK which would continue for the next few years. Typically the US releases were shorter than the UK ones, and contained the group's singles. With an almost identical track listing to *Please Please Me*, *Introducing?* rose to No. 2 there in February 1964. Their third single, *From Me To You*, made No. 1 after just two weeks in April 1963, and hysteria started to accompany their every move. During May and June they embarked on their first headlining UK tour, supported by their hero Roy Orbison and fellow Liverpudlians **Gerry and The Pacemakers**. In July their first EP, *Twist And Shout*, was released and got to No. 2. All four tracks were from the *Please Please Me* album (the other three being *A Taste Of Honey*, *Do You Want To Know A Secret?* and *There's A Place*).

By now their distinctive brand of melodic pop was at the forefront of what was being heralded as the exciting new 'Merseybeat' sound. Their fourth 45, *She Loves You*, was another excellent song with an unforgettable vocal refrain. Released in August, it had massive advance orders and was another long-lived No. 1. Their second album, *With The Beatles*, was released in November 1963 with advance orders of 300,000. It contained some powerful **Lennon/McCartney** compositions like *It Won't Be Long*, *All My Loving* and *I Wanna Be Your Man*, as well as a few slower ones like *Not A Second Time*, *Little Child* and *All I've Got To Do*. The album was rounded off with some favourites from their live act - covers of The Marvelettes' *Please Mr. Postman*, Chuck Berry's *Roll Over Beethoven*, The Miracles' *You Really Got A Hold On Me*, The Donays' *Devil In Her Heart*, the much-recorded *Money* and the ballad *Till There Was You*, from the show 'The Music Man'. The album was also notable for featuring **George Harrison**'s first recorded composition, *Don't Bother Me*, a fast number with a haunting tune. The album topped the UK charts for 21 weeks from 7 December 1963.

THE BEATLES - 1965 Christmas Fan Club flexi disc.

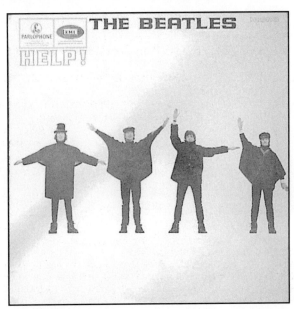

THE BEATLES - Help (LP).

Their fifth 45, *I Want To Hold Your Hand*, instantly replaced *She Loves You* at No. 1 in the UK charts in December 1963. The disc was rush-released by Capitol in the US the following month, as part of a massive campaign to sell the group to American audiences. Three weeks later it was at the top of the US charts too. *She Loves You* and *Please Please Me* were also released and charted instantly. *Meet The Beatles* (with a similar track listing to *With The Beatles*) topped the US album charts, with *Introducing... The Beatles* at No 2. On 7 February 1964 they flew to New York amidst more 'Beatlemania', and made their USA TV debut on the Ed Sullivan Show a couple of days later, to unprecedented viewing figures. During 1964 three US-only singles were also released - *I'll Cry Instead*, *And I Love Her* and *Matchbox*, which got to No.'s 25, 12 and 17 respectively.

Their sixth UK 45, *Can't Buy Me Love* (yet another excellent song), topped the UK and US charts simultaneously. Indeed on 4 April 1964 they achieved the extraordinary and never-repeated feat of holding all top five places in the US singles chart, with *Can't Buy Me Love* (1), *Twist And Shout* (2), *She Loves You* (3), *I Want To Hold Your Hand* (4) and *Please Please Me* (5). After several months of relentless touring, they withdrew from the limelight in March to begin work on their first feature film, 'A Hard Day's Night', in Twickenham, South-West London, directed by Dick Lester. Alun Owen's much-praised script illustrated the band's lifestyle and attitude in greater depth than was customary for pop cash-in movies, and the result (which premiered in London in July 1964) was a commercial and critical hit worldwide.

The accompanying album and title track occupied the No. 1 spots in their respective charts on both sides of the Atlantic. *A Hard Day's Night* (a phrase coined by Ringo) was their first album comprised entirely of **Lennon/McCartney** originals. Side 1 contained the seven songs used in the film (*A Hard Day's Night*, *I Should Have Known Better*, *If I Fell*, *I'm Happy Just To Dance With You*, *And I Love Her*, *Tell Me Why* and their earlier hit, *Can't Buy Me Love*). Side 2 contained six new **Lennon/McCartney** songs which couldn't be fitted into the film (*Any Time At All*, *I'll Cry Instead*, *Things We Said Today*, *When I Get Home*, *You Can't Do That* and *I'll Be Back*). All were excellent, making it a consistently superb album.

I Feel Fine, released in November 1964, was yet another fine single, notable for the guitar feedback in its intro. It followed the now familiar pattern of topping the US and UK charts simultaneously. The flip, *She's A Woman*, was pretty good too - in fact, it got to No. 4 in its own right in the States. 1964 ended with the release of their fourth album, *Beatles For Sale*. Surprisingly, this didn't contain all new material (as *A Hard Day's Night* had done) but reverted to the format of their first two albums by mixing originals (eight in all) with covers. Though it had its moments, it wasn't one of their better efforts. That said, **John Lennon**'s *I'm A Loser* pointed the way towards a the more personal material they'd soon start writing, and *Eight Days A Week* climbed to No. 1 when released as a 45 in the States the following February. *Words Of Love* and *Rock And Roll Music* were also among its better songs. It replaced *A Hard Day's Night* at the top of the UK Charts on 19 December 1964, but didn't stay there for nearly as long. In the US, *Beatles '65*, which had a similar track listing, topped the charts after just two weeks.

THE BEATLES - Rubber Soul (LP).

On 11 February 1965 Ringo married his long-time sweetheart, hairdresser Maureen Cox. At the end of the month the band began work on a new movie with Lester, 'Help'. While it was being made, *Ticket To Ride* (one of the songs they'd written for the film) was released as a 45 and topped the US and UK charts, as did the title track when released as a 45 a couple of months later. This was John's first really personal work, and hinted at the vulnerability behind his caustic facade. The excellent *Help!* album was released in July 1965. It contained 10 **Lennon/McCartney** compositions. Aside from the two 45s just mentioned, highlights were **Lennon**'s Dylan-inspired *You've Got To Hide Your Love Away*, the melodic pop ballad *You're Going To Lose That Girl* and Paul's ever-popular *Yesterday*, which topped the US charts when released as a 45 there a couple of months later. The remaining tracks included two **George Harrison** compositions (*I Need You*, notable for some pleasant guitar, and *You Like Me Too Much*, a reasonable mid-tempo song) and two cover versions (*Act Naturally* and *Dizzy Miss Lizzy*). The album sold extremely well, topping both the US and UK album charts, though in the States it had to wait for the US-only *Beatles VI* album, released the same month, to get there first. The 'Help' film, meanwhile, was a forgettable farce but featured some good performance footage.

As 1965 drew to an end, there were signs that **The Beatles** were about to enter a new stage of their musical evolution. In December their first double 'A' sided single, *Day Tripper/We Can Work It Out*, was released. They'd been experimenting with marijuana during the year, at Bob Dylan's instigation, and the new perspective it had given them meant their days of relentless touring, playing hits to halls full of screaming fans, were limited. The relentlessly catchy *Day Tripper*, in particular, made ambiguous use of the word 'trip' as it taunted a 'weekend hippie'. Their next album, *Rubber Soul*, released in December, represented a distinct musical progression on what had gone before. The music was more sophisticated and the lyrics more poignant and personal. The album comprised 12 **Lennon/McCartney** compositions, including the beautiful *Michelle*, propulsive *Drive My Car*, **John**'s autobiographical trio of *In My Life*, *Nowhere Man* and *Norwegian Wood*, the superb ballad *Girl* and rocker *Run For Your Life*. The sentiments of *Nowhere Man* and *The Word*, as well as George's sitar work on the delightful *Norwegian Wood*, certainly indicated a broadening of horizons. George also contributed two compositions - *If I Needed Someone*, duly covered by **The Hollies**, and *Think For Yourself* (whose title reflected their increasing self-awareness). Overall the material was mellower than on their previous albums, and certainly more reflective.

On 21 January 1966 George married model Patti Boyd at Epsom, leaving Paul the only unmarried Beatle (though he had a long-standing girlfriend, actress Jane Asher). In February 1966, *Nowhere Man* was released as a US-only 45 and climbed to No. 3. On March 4th John gave an interview to The Evening Standard's Maureen Cleave in which he remarked that **The Beatles** were 'probably bigger than Jesus right now'. When this was picked up on (out of context) by a US teen magazine and then proliferated, a colossal backlash ensued in America. Though John apologised, the damage was done. Public burnings of **Beatles** records and merchandise were held, radio stations refused to play their music, death threats were received and, perhaps most significantly, the band began to question the point in continuing to tour.

By the middle of 1966 the band had begun to flirt with LSD, and their music was quick to reflect the fact. June 1966 saw the release of *Paperback Writer*, which - in terms of lyrical and technical sharpness - continued where *Rubber Soul* had left off. Its flip, the brilliant *Rain*, was significant for being the first record to make use of backwards tape, helping to produce an other-worldly quality aimed at recreating the acid experience. Needless to say, it continued their tradition of topping the charts on both sides of the Atlantic. At the same time a compilation album, *Yesterday and Today*, was released in the States. This album was originally issued in the controversial 'butcher cover', depicting the band grinning in lab coats draped with raw meat, and holding dismembered dolls. When shops declined to stock it, it was hastily withdrawn and substituted with a bland image of the foursome posing in and on some outsized suitcases. Original 'butcher covers' are now the most prized record among Beatles collectors. The album's contents, meanwhile, included four recent US hits - *Yesterday, We Can Work It Out, Day Tripper* and *Nowhere Man* - and it quickly climbed to No. 1, despite the furore over **Lennon**'s 'bigger than Jesus' remark. On 23 June they flew to Germany for the first stage of what would prove their final world tour (it was when they landed in Chicago on 12 August that **John Lennon** apologised at a hastily assembled news conference).

August 1966 saw the release of *Revolver*, which many regard as their single greatest achievement. Housed in an attractive Klaus Voorman-designed cover, it was a considerable progression on *Rubber Soul* and introduced many exciting new sounds to pop music. *I'm Only Sleeping* evoked the drowsy effects of mind-altering drugs, *She Said She Said* was inspired by a shared acid trip with members of The Byrds and Peter Fonda in August 1965, *And Your Bird Can Sing* was allegedly a dig at **Mick Jagger** and *Dr. Robert* commemorated the exploits of a certain practitioner's mind-altering prescriptions. *Revolver* also contained brilliant commercial pop songs like *Here, There and Everywhere*, *Good Day Sunshine* and the brassy *Got To Get You Into My Life*, and also marked George's emergence as a major songwriter - *Love You To* was one of the first pop songs written for Indian instruments (with him playing the sitar again), his punchy *Taxman* was covered by a number of other bands and *I Want To Tell You* was notable for some catchy piano work. The final track, *Tomorrow Never Knows*, was, however, the album's most startling moment. A visionary slice of early psychedelia, its backward guitars, distorted vocals and hypnotic drum beat pointed firmly in the direction pop would go in the months ahead. The album also spawned their second double 'A' sided 45, *Yellow Submarine/Eleanor Rigby*, which topped the charts on both sides of the Atlantic. *Eleanor Rigby* was a melancholic, orchestrated number with cryptic lyrics, while *Yellow Submarine* was a very light-hearted, fun song aimed at children and sung with typical charm by Ringo. In short, *Revolver* is an absolutely essential artefact of sixties pop and rock.

It should also be pointed out here that **George Martin**, the **Beatles**' producer, played a colossal and ever-growing role in helping to translate the band's ideas onto tape, and more than anyone deserves the epithet 'fifth Beatle'.

The Beatles played their final US concert at San Francisco's Candlestick Park on 29 August 1966 and, in September; John began filming Dick

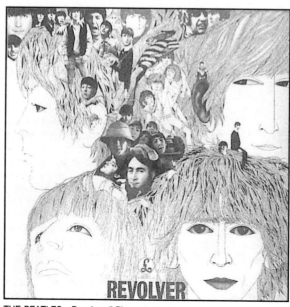

THE BEATLES - Revolver (LP).

Christmas 1966 Fan Club flexi, which took the form of a specially-written Christmas pantomime. Paul McCartney designed the picture sleeve.

Lester's 'How I Won The War' in Germany and Spain. An anti-war farce, it was premiered in London on 18 October 1967. In the absence of a new Christmas release, in December a UK-only compilation album, *A Collection Of Beatles Oldies*, appeared. Housed in a pop art cover by David Christian, it contained all their UK 45 'A' sides to date, along with two album favourites, *Michelle* and *Yesterday* and one surprise - the previously unavailable *Bad Boy* (which had appeared on *Beatles VI* in the US). The album was a decent summation of their career to date.

Penny Lane/Strawberry Fields Forever, their third double 'A' sided 45, was released in February 1967 and has been called the finest pop single of all time. *Penny Lane* was a joyous celebration of Paul's Liverpool childhood, while John's *Strawberry Fields Forever* was dreamy psychedelia, laden with manipulated tapes. Though it topped the US charts, it was their first 45 to miss the top in the UK since *Please Please Me*, being held off by Englebert Humperdinck's *Release Me*. Indeed, it is important to remember that at the height of psychedelia, muzak was as commercially prevalent as ever.

In May 1967 the band announced it wouldn't be performing live again, but focusing on recording. They underscored the decision the following month by releasing an unqualified masterpiece, *Sgt. Pepper's Lonely Hearts Club Band*. Paul's initial concept was for *Pepper* to be a mock variety concert, with **The Beatles** playing the part of an Edwardian band, but this was soon jettisoned in favour of their most eclectic selection of songs yet. If nothing else, the album is testament to the staggering variety of songwriting genres **Lennon** and **McCartney** had mastered, from the hard-rocking title track and psychedelic haze of *Lucy In The Sky With Diamonds* to the faux-music hall whimsy of *When I'm Sixty-Four*, winsome pop of *With A Little Help From My Friends* and carnivalesque *Being For The Benefit Of Mr. Kite*. George contributed just one track, the droning *Within You Without You*, which has been called the most influential piece of 'world music' ever recorded on account of its sheer proliferation. Perhaps the album's highlight, however, was its finale, *A Day In The Life*. A genuine **Lennon/McCartney** collaboration, it captured the band at their creative zenith and culminated in a mind-blowing orchestral climax.

The album's impact went beyond its music, though. Its packaging was revolutionary, for instance - Peter Blake's iconic front cover showed cut-outs of Bob Dylan, James Dean and Mae West alongside a cross-section of political, cultural and religious figures and two sets of **Beatles**, indicating just how far the band had come in the preceding three years. It was also one of the first albums to have a gatefold, an insert, a printed inner sleeve or the lyrics printed on the sleeve. Taken as a whole, *Pepper* indicated two vital facts that are now taken as read - that pop didn't have to appeal to the young alone, and that it could be taken seriously as an art form. Probably the most influential album of the decade and the band's magnum opus for many, it entered the UK charts at No. 1 and soared to pole position in the US in its second week.

Their next 45, **Lennon**'s *All You Need Is Love*, perfectly captured the sentiments of the 'summer of love'. The final session was broadcast live from Abbey Road to a record TV audience worldwide. Musically, though, it

had its shortcomings, with an overlong and repetitive fade. Its flip, *Baby You're A Rich Man*, was an inspired, if slight, slice of psychedelia. The 45 topped the charts on both sides of the Atlantic in July 1967.

By August 1967 **The Beatles** seemed unassailable, but two events occurred which were to have a profound influence on their future. On 25 August they went to Bangor in Wales with friends including **Mick Jagger** to study transcendental meditation with Maharishi Mahesh Yogi, and two days later (on 27 August) their manager Brian Epstein, who had played such a key role in forging their success, died in bed of a drug overdose after a period of deep depression. Following his death **The Beatles** resolved to manage their own business affairs but, heavily into Eastern mysticism and its related values, and befuddled by a wide array of drugs, they made a series of misjudgements.

Much of September 1967 was spent filming the improvised 'Magical Mystery Tour' at various locations around the UK. Essentially Paul's brainchild, the venture was equally inspired by Ken Kesey's recent exploits with The Merry Pranksters on America's West Coast and the working class 'mystery tour' tradition.

If the 'A' side of their next single, *Hello Goodbye*, was relatively straightforward, John's flip, *I Am The Walrus*, was a peerless work of psychedelia, incorporating many of the techniques they'd developed in the studio and showcasing his inimitable imagination and humour. The single topped the charts in both the UK and US. In fact *I Am The Walrus* was also John's major contribution to the *Magical Mystery Tour* soundtrack EP, which climbed to no. 2 in the UK. The title cut, one of Paul's few inroads into psychedelia, was a fresh and dynamic, introduction to what followed - the melodic *Fool On The Hill*, the gentle instrumental *Flying* (one of just three compositions credited to all four **Beatles** and perhaps a collective tribute to their LSD experiences), George's superbly sinister *Blue Jay Way*, which - laden with phasing, backward tapes and double tracking - was his psychedelic tour de force, Paul's endearingly lightweight *Your Mother Should Know* and Lennon's aforementioned masterpiece *I Am The Walrus*. In the States, the EP was released as an album, incorporating their 1967 singles. The package, which reached No. 1 there, wasn't released in the UK until 1976, though it was heavily imported and still got to No. 31.

The verdict on the film (which premiered on British TV on Boxing Day 1967) was less effusive. Many critics condemned it as self-indulgent, ill-conceived drivel. To an extent this missed its point - to be as shapeless and unpredictable as an acid trip - but it was palpably unsuitable for family viewing, and the first **Beatles** project to be widely criticised.

Perhaps stung by its reception, in February 1968 the foursome flew to Northern India to join a meditation group (including **Donovan** and Mike Love of the Beach Boys) at Maharishi's retreat in Rishikesh, though Ringo couldn't stand it for long. Eventually the others returned, disillusioned, to focus on launching the Apple empire. The basic idea was to create a series of companies under one liberal umbrella, providing an environment for all sorts of creativity to flourish away from the clutches of men in suits. Hopelessly idealistic, the project haemorrhaged money via a series of

THE BEATLES - Sgt. Pepper's Lonely Hearts Club Band (LP).

ill-advised ventures - clothing, electronics, films and so forth - and eventually limited itself to its only profitable aspect - music.

Their next 45, the thumping, piano-led *Lady Madonna*, was their last on Parlophone and a partial return to their earlier, immediately catchy sound. Its flip, *The Inner Light*, was virtually a **George Harrison** solo number (John and Paul's vocal overdubs were added at the final stage) and another of his Indian-influenced compositions - it was in fact a product of a five-day visit to Bombay, where he'd begun work on his *Wonderwall Music* solo album. The single shot to No. 1 here, but only reached No. 4 in the US.

In June 1968 **The Beatles** announced that all their future recordings would be on the Apple label. The following month the feature-length cartoon 'Yellow Submarine', directed by George Dunning, was premiered in London. A trippy folly centring on the band's attempts to escape 'the Blue Meanies', it featured a number of new songs and footage of the real **Beatles** at the end, singing *All Together Now*. At the end of July their Apple boutique in London (already the subject of controversy owing to a colossal psychedelic mural on its outside wall) closed due to mounting debts and the entire stock was given away. At this juncture the band was at a crossroads. Years of fame had denied them the opportunity to mature as individuals, and suddenly they found their personalities diverging.

They were also undergoing huge changes in their personal lives. Paul (who'd announced his engagement to Jane Asher on Christmas Day 1967) had met Linda Eastman whilst on a business trip to the States in June 1968. The following month he broke off his engagement to Asher, and at the end of the month Eastman moved to the UK to live with him. They eventually married at Marylebone Registry Office in London on 12 March 1969. John, meanwhile, had started an affair with Japanese avant-garde artist Yoko Ono after a long flirtation, and on 22 August Cynthia Lennon named her in divorce proceedings, On 8 November John and Cynthia were divorced, enabling John to marry Yoko in Gibraltar on 20 March 1969. Six days later they began their first 'bed-in' at Amsterdam's Hilton Hotel. Henceforth John's behaviour was increasingly defined by radical politics.

The Beatles' first Apple 45, *Hey Jude/Revolution*, appeared in August 1968. Its A-side was a cryptic message of solidarity from Paul to John's young son Julian, and is notable for its length and infectious singalong fade. *Revolution*, meanwhile, set John's growing political interests to a rollicking rock and roll beat, and features a scorching fuzz-guitar intro. Not only did the single top the UK and US charts, it was also their biggest-selling latter-day hit. The single was, however, only a taster of the banquet they were readying - in November they released their self-titled double album, commonly known as 'The White Album', an embarrassment of riches that contained some of the best songs they ever produced.

Much of the material had been written while the group was studying meditation together in India, but discerning listeners could hear their coming disintegration spread over its four sides. Unlike their previous offerings, it was essentially a collection of fine solo performances rather than a group effort. The **Lennon/McCartney** contributions were a beautiful blend of rock

THE BEATLES - Magical Mystery Tour (LP).

The 1967 Christmas Fan Club flexi. Ringo Starr created the collage for this. Note the similarities to the "Sgt. Pepper" album cover.

numbers like *Back In The USSR, Revolution* and *Helter Skelter* and aching ballads such as *Julia, Mother Nature's Son* and *Blackbird*. The album contained surprisingly little evidence of psychedelia, excepting John's dreamy *Dear Prudence* and self-referential *Glass Onion* and Paul's crazed *Helter Skelter*. John also contributed the sound collage *Revolution # 9*, probably the best-known piece of avant-garde music ever recorded. Given the album's length, there are remarkably few throwaway songs, though Paul's ultra-commercial *Ob-La-Di, Ob-La-Da* (which **Marmalade** took to No. 1) grates after a few plays. **Harrison** contributed four songs - the majestic *While My Guitar Gently Weeps* (featuring a memorable guitar solo from **Eric Clapton**), *Long, Long, Long, Savoy Truffle* and the ridiculous *Piggies*, later cited by the Manson 'family' as a catalyst for their crimes. Even Ringo weighed in with his first composition for the band, the good-timey *Don't Pass Me By*.

It is perhaps also worth pointing out that the album shows up the error of labelling John the firebrand and Paul the soppy balladeer - the former was responsible for the saccharine, orchestrated closer *Goodnight*, while the latter produced the ultra-raw punk of *Helter Skelter*, for example.

The album's plain white cover was a tongue-in-cheek riposte to *Pepper*'s riot of colours, though each copy did come complete with a top-loading gatefold sleeve, custom-made inners, a poster and a print of each **Beatle**. Each copy was also stamped with a number, and low examples are now highly-prized by collectors. The band themselves took numbers 1 to 4, though it's uncertain whether the different pressing plants all numbered from scratch or not.

Though *The White Album* was in many respects a triumph, it also indicated that the group was starting to fragment, and indeed Ringo did leave at one point during the sessions, only to return following conciliation from his bandmates. In January 1969 the *Yellow Submarine* soundtrack was released, featuring one side of **Beatles** recordings and one of **George Martin**'s original score. Though it can't be regarded as a **Beatles** album proper, it did contain some excellent material. As well as John and Paul's title cut and *All You Need Is Love*, there were two notable compositions by George - *Only A Northern Song* (whose title referred to **Lennon** and **McCartney**'s publishing firm, Northern Songs) had originally been intended for *Sgt. Pepper*, and was thus full of psychedelic effects, including the sound of an orchestra being dragged across the studio floor, and *It's All Too Much*, which also dated from the same period. The bouncy **Lennon** rocker *Hey Bulldog* was enjoyable too, and helped the album reach no. 4 in the UK and No. 2 in the US.

At the turn of the year relations within the band had become more tense than ever, leading Paul to urge them to undertake an ambitious project to be entitled 'Get Back'. This would involve being filmed rehearsing for a one-off live gig, perhaps to be held at London's Roundhouse, which would then form the climax of the movie. An album comprising the best of the rehearsals and subsequent gig would also be released. He hoped that a return to the urgency of their early days would revive their enthusiasm for playing together, but the idea fizzled out and only a series of rather gloomy

The 1968 Christmas flexi disc was recorded by the four Beatles working separately. The late Kenny Everett then edited the tapes together.

and uninspired rehearsals were filmed, and later released as the album and film *Let It Be*. They sounded like the work of a band that had run out of ideas, as well as the enthusiasm to work together as a cohesive unit. On 30 January 1969, however, they were filmed performing four songs on the roof of the Apple building in Savile Row, with Billy Preston guesting on organ, and the results are highly enjoyable. One of these, Paul's bouncy rocker *Get Back*, was released as their next 45 in April, along with John's soulful *Don't Let Me Down*. It topped both the UK and US charts, indicating that the public's appetite for the band was far from sated. It was followed in May by *The Ballad Of John And Yoko*, which conveyed a sense of the strife within the band and, in fact, only featured John and Paul. It climbed to No. 1 in the UK, though the inclusion of the exclamation 'Christ' in the lyrics led to airplay problems.

In place of the chaotic *Get Back* sessions, the band agreed to set aside their differences in order to make another studio album. The result was the marvellous *Abbey Road*, released in September. Side one included excellent songs such as John's *Come Together*, Paul's *Oh Darling*, George's brilliant *Something* and even Ringo's *Octopus' Garden*. The second side was organised into a suite of sorts, incorporating the other-worldly *Because*, the beautiful *Golden Slumbers* and eccentric *Mean Mr. Mustard*, culminating in the hard-rocking *The End*. Though not flawless (Paul's *Maxwell's Silver Hammer*, in particular, can become irritating), the album showed their creative powers to be far from diminished. It was, however, to be their final recording. As the year progressed, relationships in the band had become increasingly strained, and by the New Year it was fairly clear that they'd come to the end of the road together.

The *Get Back* tapes were handed over to Phil Spector, against Paul's wishes, and eventually released as *Let It Be* in May 1970, though *Across The Universe* had already appeared on the World Wildlife Fund compilation *No One's Gonna Change Our World* in December 1969, and the title track had been issued as a 45 in March, peaking at No. 2 here and No. 1 in the US. It was a far weaker album than the subsequently-recorded *Abbey Road*, and contained just three truly outstanding cuts, all by Paul - the title track, the earlier *Get Back* 45 and the atmospheric *The Long And Winding Road*, which was appropriately issued as the band's final 45 in the US, where it got to No. 1. Early pressings came in a presentation box containing a lavish book of photographs. These are now understandably rare.

By now all four members were concentrating on solo projects, and the 'Let It Be' movie, also released in May (for whose title song **Lennon** and **McCartney** won the best original song Oscar), was regarded by many as a chronicle of their break-up, which was announced shortly afterwards. Lawsuits soon began to fly, a sorry ending to the first chapter of pop's greatest fairytale. Of course, that wasn't the end of the story - for details of their subsequent careers see the entries for **John Lennon**, **Paul McCartney**, **George Harrison** and **Ringo Starr**.

Needless to say, their recordings - including those left in the can - have been extensively reissued and repackaged ever since. Perhaps the most

significant subsequent releases have been the following three albums. Firstly, *The Beatles Live At The BBC* double (Apple, 1994) probably comes closer than anything to capturing the sheer excitement of their early live performances. Secondly, *The Beatles Anthology* (three double albums of out-takes and unreleased material released concurrently with a superb book and documentary series of the same name in 1994-5) made it clear just how creative and productive the band had been. To help launch the project, Paul, George and Ringo collaborated on two 'new' songs, *Free As A Bird* and *Real Love*, which were in fact solo demos by John. Neither was especially brilliant, but they were bought in predictably huge numbers. Thirdly, in 2003 Paul oversaw *Let It Be? Naked*, a remixed and much-altered version of their final album, featuring the songs as he'd originally envisaged them. The result is arguably superior to the original version, but revisionist history and still not up there with the band's best work.

In 1973 Apple released two comprehensive compilations of **Beatles** material, which proved very popular - *The Beatles 1962-66* and *The Beatles 1967-70*. These were followed over the next few years by the double *Past Masters* sets, which included rarities such as German renditions of *She Loves You* and *I Wanna Hold Your Hand*.

May 1977 saw the worldwide release of *The Beatles Live At The Hollywood Bowl*, featuring previously unissued live tapes from 23 August 1964 and 30 August 1965. Promoted through a TV campaign in the UK, it soon topped the charts.

In 1978 EMI issued all **The Beatles**' original albums in stereo form as *The Beatles Collection*. The set also included *The Rarities* album, which was subsequently released by itself the following year and climbed

In 1982 EMI began a massive reissue project of each of the original **Beatles** singles on their twentieth birthdays, commencing with *Love Me Do*, which got to No. 4 in the UK, 13 places higher than its peak when originally released back in 1962. Each was available as a picture disc too. EMI also packaged a box set of the original 22 singles, each with a new picture sleeve. All charted.

Less successful was EMI's attempt to promote the *Reel Music* album in 1982 with the dire *Beatles Movie Medley* 45, which included snippets of several songs that had featured in their films. The 45 managed No. 10 here and No. 12 in the US, but the album didn't make the charts at all here, though it did get to No. 19 in the States. 1982 also saw the release of *20 Greatest Hits* (No. 10 UK, No. 50 US), which compiled *Love Me Do* and all their No 1s. Two years later EMI allowed Marks and Spencers to issue a tape, *The Beatles: Their Greatest Hits*, which contained the same tracks as *A Collection Of Beatles Oldies* plus a 64-page history of the group. The publishers of 'The History Of Rock' also featured similar **Beatles** material in their series of mail order compilations.

During 1987 each original **Beatles** album was reissued on CD and re-entered the charts in both the UK and US. In 1988 the aforementioned *Past Masters* compilations were released, but perhaps the ultimate **Beatles**

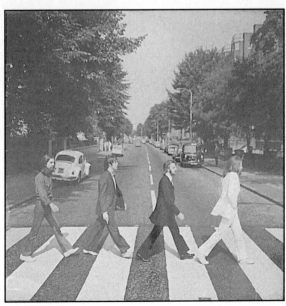

THE BEATLES - Abbey Road (LP).

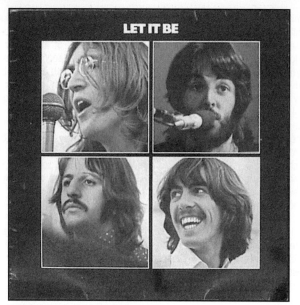

THE BEATLES - Let It Be (LP).

reissue was the October 1988 box set, which not only included all their original albums but also *Past Masters* - their entire EMI catalogue, in other words. The albums were available as a complete set on vinyl, cassette or CD in a sturdy wooden box, as well as individually.

During 1988 and 1989 all **The Beatles'** original 45s were released as CD singles. There have also been various interview albums, beginning with a double set of David Wigg's conversations with all four **Beatles** during the late sixties and early seventies, entitled *The Beatles Tapes* (Polydor 2683 068). In 1981 Charly reissued a US promo-only album, originally issued on Vee Jay. Baktabak have also issued several interview albums of **The Beatles'** 1964 Australian tour.

A recent release has again highlighted the significant role that **Tony Sheridan** played in their early career. *The Beatles' First!* (which is credited to The Beatles featuring Tony Sheridan) was recorded in June/July 1961 and April 1962 and originally issued in 1964 with Beatlemania at its height. Now remastered and given a deluxe 2-CD release, it contains six tracks on which **The Beatles** played as **Sheridan's** support band and two on which **The Beatles** play alone. These are the raucous *Ain't She Sweet* with **Lennon** on lead vocals and a **Lennon/Harrison** twangy guitar instrumental called *Cry For A Shadow*. As bonus tracks there are two versions of *My Bonnie* (one with an English and the other with a German intro). This will interest fans interested in **The Beatles'** Hamburg era.

The Capitol Albums Vol.1 is a 4-CD box set containing their first four US albums. *Meet The Beatles* contained material from *Please Please Me* and *With The Beatles* plus *I Want To Hold Your Hand*; *The Beatles Second Album* featured cuts from *With The Beatles*, the *Long Tall Sally* EP and *She Loves You*; *Something New* includes the remainder of the *Long Tall Sally* EP, cuts from *A Hard Days Night* and *Komm, Gob Mir Deine Hand*; and, finally, *Beatles '65* contained tracks from *Beatles For Sale* and the *I Feel Fine* 45. All songs have been remastered, and the Capitol mixes are possibly more powerful than any previous releases. The sleeves reproduce the original US cover art, and sleevenotes are from the world's pre-eminent **Beatles** expert, Mark Lewisohn. Certainly, this is a must for serious **Beatles** collectors.

Compilation appearances include: *She Loves You* and *I Want To Hold Your Hand* on *Mersey Beat* (LP); and *Misery* on *Twist A La Star Club* (LP). (VJ/RMJ)

The Beatmen

Personnel:	BARRY HEALD	sax	A
	BILL BRAZIER	ld gtr	A
	BILL MOSELY	gtr, vcls	A
	PAUL MOUNTAIN	bs	A
	PHIL SEVERN	drms	A

| 45s: | You Can't Sit Down/ | | |
| | Come On Pretty Baby | (Pye 7N 15659) 1964 SC |

Now The Sun Has Gone/Please Believe   (Pye 7N 15792) 1965

A beat outfit as their name suggests. *You Can't Sit Down*, is a cover of the classic organ-driven instrumental by the Phil Upchurch Combo. The band hailed from Nottingham and *Now The Sun Has Gone* is highly-rated and not dissimilar to **The Poets**. They formed back in 1960 and did a four month stint in Hamburg in their early days.

Compilation appearances have included: *You Can't Sit Down* on *The R&B Era, Vol. 1* (CD) and *It Happened Then* (LP); and *Now The Sun Has Gone* on *Ripples, Vol. 3* (CD) and *Watch Your Step* (LP & CD). (VJ)

The Beat Merchants

Personnel:	CHRIS BOYLE	vcls	A
	GAVIN DANESKI	gtr	A
	GEOFF FARNDELL	bs	A
	VIC SENDALL	drms	A
	RALPH WORMAN	ld gtr	A

| 45s: | Pretty Face/Messin' With The Man | (Columbia DB 7367) 1964 R1 |
| | So Fine/She Said Yeah | (Columbia DB 7492) 1965 R1 |

A hard-edged R&B band from the South Coast area who got to appear on ITV's 'Thank Your Lucky Stars' to promote their first powerful R&B single *Pretty Face*. Their two fine and inevitably collectable R&B singles are recommended for fans of the genre.

Compilation appearances have included: *Pretty Face* on *Maximum R'n'B* (CD), *R&B At Abbey Road* (CD), *Beat Merchants* (2-LP), and *English Freakbeat, Vol. 1* (LP & CD). (VJ)

The Beat Six

| Personnel incl: | JOHN BURNESS |
| | RICKY BURNESS |

| 45: | Bernadine/The River And I | (Decca F 12011) 1964 SC |

An obscure beat group. The 45 was a ballad. The Burness brothers were later in **Guys**. (VJ)

The Beatstalkers

Personnel:	EDDIE CAMPBELL	organ	AB
	DAVIE LENNOX	vcls	AB
	ALAN MAIR	bs	A

THE BEATLES - Live At The Hollywood Bowl (LP).

RONNIE SMITH	gtr, vcls	AB
'TUDGE' WILLIAMSON	drms	A
JEFF ALLEN	drms	B
JOE GAFFNEY	bs	B

45s:
Everybody's Talking 'Bout My Baby/ Mr. Disappointed	(Decca F 12259) 1965 R1
Left Right Left/ You'd Better Get A Better Hold On	(Decca F 12352) 1966 R1
A Love Like Yours/Base Line	(Decca F 12460) 1966 SC
My One Chance To Make It/Ain't Got No Soul (Left In These Old Shoes)	(CBS 2732) 1967 R1
Silver Treetop School For Boys/ Sugar Coated Man	(CBS 3105) 1967 R1
Rain Coloured Roses/ Everything Is For You	(CBS 3557) 1968 R1
When I'm Five/Little Boy	(CBS 3936) 1969 R1

This Glasgow band was sometimes referred to as The Scottish Beatles in their early days, although when they signed to Decca in 1965, they moved down to London. In their early days their live repertoire was drawn from originals, black America and less well known **Rolling Stones** cuts. They had a mod image and built up a very loyal audience around Glasgow before moving South.

Their debut disc *Everybody's Talking About My Baby* had a distinctive organ riff and some good offbeat vocals. The record sold very well in their native Scotland but didn't make sufficient impact South of the Border to chart. Thereafter they seem to have been forced by their record company into recording pop material which was far removed from their live set. This was typified by their next 'A' side, *Left Right Left*, although tucked away on the flip was a song by Joe South, *You'd Better Get A Better Hold On*, which with its stomping beat and rabid fuzz guitars must have been nearer to their live act. *A Love Like Yours* was a Holland/Dozier/Holland composition not particularly well delivered. *Ain't Got No Soul (Left In These Old Shoes)* was a Major Lance composition and a popular Northern soul number.

1967 saw a label change to CBS and a new line-up 'B'. In their later days they were managed by Kenneth Pitt who also looked after **David Bowie**'s affairs. At Pitt's suggestion they recorded some of **Bowie**'s songs:- *Silver Treetop School For Boys*, *Everything Is You* and *When I'm Five*. The latter typified the rubbish he was writing at the time and was probably the worst disc they recorded. Their final flip side, *Little Boy*, was a version of the unreleased last **Action** single. **Bowie** also sang backing vocals on *Silver Treetop School For Boys*. By now they were in terminal decline and when their van was stolen with all their equipment in it the obvious thing to do was to pack up.

Eddie Campbell was later in **Tear Gas** and Jeff Allen went on to play for **Dr. K's Blues Band** and then **East Of Eden**. Mair eventually joined The Only Ones when they reformed in 1975 and is now a studio engineer. Lennox was a member of The Joe O'Donnell Band in 1978.

Compilation appearances have included: *Left Right Left* on *Justification* (LP); *You Better Get A Better Hold On* on *Beat Us If You Can! Vol. 1* (LP) and *The Freakbeat Scene* (CD); and *Little Boy* on *Jagged Time Lapse, Vol 1* (CD). (VJ/JM)

Beau

Personnel:	C.J.T. (BEAU) MIDGLEY	gtr, vcls	AB
	STEVE CLAYTON		B
	JIM MILNE		B

ALBUMS:	1(A)	BEAU	(Dandelion S 63751) 1969 SC
	2(B)	CREATION	(Dandelion DAN 8006) 1971 SC

NB: (1) and (2) reissued on one CD by See For Miles.

45:	1917 Revolution/Sleeping Town	(Dandelion S 4403) 1969

Beau was the pseudonym of C.J.T. Midgley, a folk-styled artist from Leeds who was backed on his second album by **The Way We Live**. His finest moment was *1917 Revolution*, with its fine 12-string guitar work, but on the whole his material would have benefited from better arrangements.

BEAU - Creation (LP).

Sleeping Town can be heard on the *Dandelion Rarities* (CD), and *Time* is featured on the budget *Dandelion Sampler 1969-1972* (CD) sampler. (VJ)

The Beazers

Personnel incl: CHRIS FARLOWE

45:	The Blue Beat/I Wanna Shout	(Decca F 11827) 1964 R1

Chris Farlowe was involved in this cash-in disc in the brief ska/bluebeat craze of 1964. The band was based in Ipswich and their 45 was written and produced by Cyril Stapleton.

Blue Beat has been compiled on *The R&B Scene* (CD). (VJ)

Be-Bop Deluxe

Personnel:	RICHARD BROWN	keyb'ds	A
	ROBERT BRYAN	bs, vcls	AB
	NICHOLAS CHATTERTON-DEW	drms	AB
	NICK CLARK	gtr	A
	BILL NELSON	gtr, vcls	ABCDE
	IAN PARKIN	gtr	B
	SIMON FOX	drms	CDE
	PAUL JEFFREYS	bs	C
	MILTON REAME-JAMES	keyb'ds	C
	CHARLIE TUMAHAI	bs	DE
	ANDY CLARKE	keyb'ds	E

				HCP
ALBUMS: 1(B)	AXE VICTIM	(Harvest SHVL 813) 1974	-
(up to 2(D)	FUTURAMA	(Harvest SHSP 4045) 1975	-
1976) 3(E)	SUNBURST FINISH	(Harvest SHSP 4053) 1976	17
4(E)	MODERN MUSIC	(Harvest SHSP 4058) 1976	12

NB: (1) and (2) later reissued as a double set (Harvest EDP 154 679-3) 1983. (3) reissued on Fame (FA 3004) in 1982. (1) - (4) reissued on Harvest (CDP 7947262), (CDP 7920742), (CDP 7947272) and (CDP 7947312) on CD in 1991. (1) reissued again on CD (EMI CDP 7947262) 2004, with three bonus tracks. (2) reissued again on CD (EMI CDP 7920742) 2004, with three bonus tracks. (3) reissued again on CD (EMI CDP 7947272) 2004, with three bonus tracks. (4) reissued again on CD (EMI CDP 7947312) 2004, with three bonus tracks. Also relevant on vinyl is *The Best And The Rest Of Be-Bop Deluxe* (2-LP) (Harvest SHOW 410) 1978; *Singles A's and B's* (Harvest SHSM 2034) 1992 and *Rading The Divine - The Best Of Be-Bop Deluxe* (Harvest EMS 1130) 1987. CD retrospectives include: *Rading The Divine - The Best Of Be-Bop Deluxe* (Emi CZ 296) 1994, with four additional tracks to the vinyl version; *Singles A's and B's* (See For Miles SEECD 336) 1992; and *Air Age Anthology* (2-CD) (EMI CDEM 1602) 1997. *Tramcar To Tomorrow* (Hux HUX) 1998 is a collection of BBC radio sessions between 1974 and 1978, which includes the previously unreleased *15th of July (Invisibles)*. *Postcards From The Future* (EMI 590 9762) 2004 is an 18-track compilation of their material from their albums, which also contains a single recorded and released prior to their EMI days.

BE-BOP DELUXE - Axe Victim (LP).

EP: 1(C) HOT VALVES *HCP*
(Harvest HAR 5117) 1976 36

NB: (1) contains *Maid In Heaven*, *Blazing Apostles*, *Jet Silver and The Dolls Of Venus* and *Bring Back The Spark*.

HCP

45s:			
(up to	Teenage Archangel/Jets At Dawn	(Smile LAFS 001) 1972 SC	-
1976)	Jet Silver (And The Dolls Of Venus)/		
	Third Floor Heaven	(Harvest HAR 5081) 1974	-
α	Between The Worlds/Lights	(Harvest HAR 5091) 1975 R1	-
	Maid In Heaven/Lights	(Harvest HAR 5098) 1975	-
	Ships In The Knight/		
	Crying To The Sky	(Harvest HAR 5104) 1976 23	
	Kiss Of The Light/		
	(Flip side by different artist)	(Harvest HAR 5110) 1976	-

NB: α withdrawn.

This band's founder **Bill Nelson** had been involved with the highly collectable Wakefield-based Holyground label in the early seventies, which had been responsible for releases like **A-Austr** and **Astral Navigations**. He also released a solo album *Northern Dream* in 1971. He was a fine guitarist and the band started out playing slick guitar-based rock. Keyboardist Richard Brown and guitarist Nick Clarke left shortly before the release of their debut album *Axe Victim*, which was a promising start. **Nelson** penned all the material on their debut album, except for *Rocket Cathedral's*, which was written and sung by their bassist Rob Bryan. The album is full of **Nelson**'s blistering guitar playing.

In 1974 the band embarked on their first major tour as support to **Cockney Rebel**. **Bill Nelson** disbanded the group in August of that year because of dissatisfaction with its progress and thus former members of **Cockney Rebel**, also in a period of transition, Milton Reame-James and Paul Jeffreys, were recruited for the new line-up (C) along with ex-**Hackensack** drummer Simon Fox. Jeffreys and Reame-James soon left but with the addition of Charlie Tumahai, a New Zealander, the band continued as a three-piece. The line-up recorded *Futurama*, which was produced by **Queen** producer Ray Thomas Baker. The album's highlights include *Maid In Heaven* and *Sister Seagull*. A new version of the track *Between The Worlds* was recorded for 45 release, but only a few copies made it into the shops before it was withdrawn because the band weren't happy with it. It was replaced by *Maid In Heaven*, produced by Roy Thomas Baker (Nick Mobbs had produced the withdrawn single).

Keyboardist Andy Clarke (aka Simon Andrew-Clarke ex-**Upp**) was recruited in mid-1975 and with **Nelson** himself handling production duties they recorded the ambitious *Sunburst Finish* the following year. Despite considerable promotion it didn't bring them the success many had predicted. It did provide their most successful single *Ships In The Night* and they appeared (for the only time) on 'Top Of The Pops' to help promote it. It secured them their first US release and they spent the next two years frantically touring the States.

Modern Music was written whilst they toured the States. The title track is as strong dreamy pop song, but much of the rest of the material was rather pompous and laboured. They split after two further albums *Live! In The Air Age* (1977) and *Drastic Plastic* (1978). **Nelson** later worked as Red Noise and then recorded a plethora of solo material throughout the eighties.

Reame-James and Jeffreys later joined Chartreuse. Jeffreys was tragically killed in the Lockerbie air disaster in 1989.

You can also find *Night Creatures* on *Loose Routes* (2-LP). (VJ/JM)

Be-Bop Preservation Society

Personnel:	SPIKE HEATLEY	bs	A
	PETE KING	alto sax	AB
	BILL SAGE	piano, vibes	A
	HANK SHAW	trumpet	A
	BRIAN SPRING	drms	A

ALBUM: 1(A) THE BE-BOP PRESERVATION SOCIETY
(Dawn DNLS 3027) 1971 SC

This five-piece band also figured on the Dawn *Takeaway Concert* (LP) compilation playing *One Bass Hit*, a cut from their album. They played progressive jazz in the **Mike Westbrook** mould.

There are lots of good piano parts on the album, which is recommended to fans of the genre. (VJ)

Gordon Beck Trio/Quartet

Personnel:	GORDON BECK	gtr, vcls	A
	JEFF CLYNNE	bs	A
	TONY OXLEY	drms	A

ALBUMS:	1(A)	GYROSCOPE	(Morgan MJ 1) 1969 R4
	2(-)	EXPERIMENTS WITH POP	
			(Major Minor MMLP/SMLP 21) 1969 R3
	3	HALF A JAZZ SIXPENCE	
			(Major Minor MMLP/SMLP 22) 1969 R3
	4	DR. DOOLITTLE LOVES JAZZ	
			(Major Minor SMLP 88) 1969 R1
	5	BECK - MATTHEWSON - HUMAIR TRIO	
			(Dire FO 341) 1972 R1

NB: (1) credited to Gordon Beck Trio. (2) credited to Gordon Beck Quartet.

Gordon James Beck was born in London on 16 September 1935. He studied classical piano and also spent two months in Monte Carlo playing

BE-BOP DELUXE - Futurama (LP).

BE-BOP DELUXE - Sunburst Finish (LP).

with Tony Crombie. When he returned to England he played with the Vic Ash/Harry Klein Quartet and then joined The Tubby Hayes Quintet in 1962. In 1969 he teamed up with Clynne and Oxley to record *Gyroscope*. The 7-track album is his rarest item by some way, but all of the above arouse interest from jazz enthusiasts. (VJ)

Jeff Beck

				HCP
ALBUMS:	1	TRUTH	(Columbia S(C)X 6293) 1968	R1 -
(up to	2	BECK-OLA	(Columbia S(C)X 6351) 1969	R1 39
1976)	3	THE MOST OF JEFF BECK		
			(Music For Pleasure MFP 5219) 1971	-
	4	ROUGH AND READY	(Epic Q 64619) 1974	SC -
	5	JEFF BECK GROUP	(Epic 64899) 1974	SC -
	6	BLOW BY BLOW	(Epic 69117) 1975	-
	7	WIRED	(Epic 86012) 1976	38

NB: (4) also issued in quadrophonic (Epic EQ 30973) 1972 (SC). (5) also issued in quadrophonic (CBS EQ 31331) 1974 (SC). (1) reissued on vinyl (Epic 26413) 2005. (1) reissued on CD (EMI 873 7492) 2005 remastered and with eight bonus tracks. (1) and (2) reissued on one CD (EMI C2 374) 1991. (3) is a reissue of (2), which was also reissued on Epic (32367) in 1983. (2) reissued on vinyl (Epic 26478) 2005. (2) reissued again on CD (EMI 5787502) 2004. (4) reissued on (CBS 32037) in 1984. (4) and (5) reissued on vinyl (That's Original/Castle TFOLP 019) in 1989. (5) also issued on CD (Epic 469 0122) 1999. (6) reissued on vinyl (Epic 33409) 2005. (6) also issued on CD (Epic 4690122) and later remastered and reissued (Sony/Epic 502181-2) 2001. (7) reissued on vinyl (Epic 32067) in 1982 and on CD in 1988. (7) remastered and reissued on CD (Sony/Epic 502182 2) 2001. A recommended retrospective compilation is *Masters Of Rock* (EMI 054 92207) in 1974. *Beckology* (Epic 4692622) 1992 is a 3-CD set anthology of his career weighted towards his years with **The Yardbirds**. Alternatively you may prefer the one-CD or cassette set *Best Of Beckology* (Epic 4713482) 1992. Also of interest may be *Late 60s With Rod Stewart* (EMI CZ 130) 1988. *Shapes Of Things - 60s Groups & Sessions* (Castle CMQCD 702) 2003 compiles his work with groups and sessions up to his solo album.

			HCP
45s:	Hi-Ho Silver Lining/		
(up to	Beck's Bolero	(Columbia DB 8151) 1967	SC 14
1976)	Tallyman/Rock My Plimsoul	(Columbia DB 8227) 1967	SC 30
	Love Is Blue/I've Been Drinking	(Columbia DB 8359) 1968	23
	Plynth/Hangman's Knee	(Columbia DB 8590) 1969	-
	Got The Feeling/Situation	(Epic EPC 7720) 1972	-
α	Hi Ho Silver Lining//Beck's Bolero		
	Rock My Plimsoul (pic disc and 7")	(Rak RR 3) 1972	17
	I've Been Drinking/		
	Morning Dew/Greensleeves	(Rak RR 4) 1973	27
	Black Cat Moon/Livin' Alone	(Epic EPC 1251) 1973	-
	She's A Woman/		
	It Doesn't Really Matter	(Epic EPC 3334) 1975	-

NB: α Reissued in 1982 as a picture disc (RRP 3).

Beck is one of rock's finest guitarists. Indeed few have surpassed him for imagination and inventiveness and he deserved much greater success than he actually achieved.

Born in Surrey in June 1944, he later studied at Wimbledon Art College. His first live appearances were at Eel Pie Island in Twickenham but in March 1965 he joined **The Yardbirds** in a stint lasting through until November 1966 when he left to form his own group, having by then established himself as one of Britain's top rock guitarists.

Shortly after forming his new band he enjoyed a hit single with the completely out of character *Hi Ho Silver Lining*. Recorded during a drunken studio session it became an all time classic and a very popular party record. Produced by Mickie Most, as was all his Columbia material, the 'A' side was recorded with sessionmen. The flip featured **Keith Moon, Jimmy Page, John Paul Jones** and **Nicky Hopkins**. After this he put together his own Jeff Beck Group (**Rod Stewart** (vcls), Ron Wood (bs) and **Aynsley Dunbar** (drms)) which featured on the flip side of the *Tallyman* 45. The 'A' side, which was a minor hit, was recorded with sessionmen.

The first two albums were patchy but excellent in places. Musically they comprised a sort of bluesy hard-rock. They built up a live reputation, mostly by touring in the States. *Love Is Blue*, a rather bizarre instrumental recorded with sessionmen, gave them another UK hit. **Nicky Hopkins**, who joined the group in October 1968 in preference to **Led Zeppelin**, played on the flip side to this. Micky Waller also replaced **Aynsley Dunbar** on drums.

The group never really fulfilled its potential because of internal tensions that emerged and a self-destructive tendency to cancel tours and gigs at the last minute. When **Rod Stewart** and Ron Wood quit to join **Quiet Melon** and then **The Faces**, **Beck** was all set to join former Vanilla Fudge member Tim Bogert and Carmine Appice in a new venture, **Beck, Bogert and Appice**, but a bad car crash put **Beck** out of action for eighteen months. Meanwhile Bogert and Appice had formed Cactus, so **Beck** put together another Jeff Beck Group with Clive Chapman (bs), Max Middleton (piano), **Cozy Powell** (drms) and Bob Tench (vcls). They signed to Epic and recorded the *Rough And Ready* and *Jeff Beck Group* albums, which both made the American Charts. Musically they veered towards jazz/funk/rock fusion. Whilst Americans bought them in vast quantities, British audiences weren't roused. **Beck** wasn't entirely satisfied with either album and when Cactus split up he did actually join **Beck, Bogert and Appice**. When this venture folded in 1974 little was heard of **Beck** until *Blow By Blow* was released in March 1975. Produced by **George Martin**, he was assisted on it by sessionmen Richard Bailey (drms), Philip Chen (bs) and Max Middleton (keyb'ds). It sold very well in the States rising to No 4 in the Charts there. It included versions of **Lennon** and **McCartney's** *She's A Woman* and Stevie Wonder's *Thelonius*. The follow-up, *Wired*, was also produced by **Martin** and recorded with sessionmen, including Jan Hammer, whose band **Beck** later joined. It featured Charlie Mingus' *Goodbye Pork Pie Hat* and also demonstrated heavier influences and a reggae feel.

Beck retired to his estate outside London in the late seventies but re-emerged in 1980 with *There And Back*, which included contributions from

BE-BOP DELUXE - Modern Music (LP).

Hammer and rose to No 38 in the UK charts. He toured to promote this but then hibernated for a further five years. He returned with a pop-rock album *Flash* that featured a number of different vocalists. This only made the lower reaches of the UK album charts but did produce a minor hit *People Get Ready* with **Rod Stewart** on vocals. It also included *Escape*, which won the Grammy Award for Best Rock Instrumental. He played lead guitar on **Mick Jagger**'s 1987 *Primitive Cool* solo album. **Beck** returned in 1989 with *Jeff Beck's Guitar Shop With Terry Bozzio And Tony Hymas*, which wasn't a big seller but did contain another instrumental *Guitar Shop* that won a Grammy Award for Best Rock Instrumental. He toured with guitarist Stevie Ray Vaughan to promote the album and then slipped away from the public eye. He returned from semi-retirement since with Gene Vincent tribute *Crazy Legs* (1993), *Who Else* (1999) and *You Had It Coming* (2001).

Shapes Of Things - 60s Groups & Sessions is a fascinating 26-track anthology of his early years. There are **Yardbirds**' classics *Shapes Of Things*, *Heart Full Of Soul* and *Evil Hearted You*; **The Nighshifts**' *Stormy Monday*, *Dracula's Daughter* with **Screaming Lord Sutch and The Savages** captures him in more offbeat mode; whilst *Steelin'* and *Chuckles* (both recorded with **Jimmy Page**) showcase him closer to Chicago blues. Of course *Hi Ho Silver Lining* is here and other acts he played with featured include **Donovan**, **John's Children**, **Paul Jones** and the GTO's.

Compilation appearances include: *Chuckles* and *Steelin'* by the Jeff Beck All Stars on *Jimmy Page - Hip Young Guitar Slinger* (2-CD); *Beck's Bolero* on the 3-CD set *Guitar Heroes - Rock The Night Away* and *Hi-Ho Silver Lining* on *60's Mix* (CD). (VJ)

Beck, Bogert and Appice

Personnel:			
CARMINE APPICE	drms, vcls		AB
JEFF BECK	gtr		AB
TIM BOGERT	bs, vcls		AB
MAX MIDDLETON	piano		A

HCP
ALBUM: 1(B)   BECK, BOGERT AND APPICE   (Epic 65455) 1973 SC 28
NB: (1) reissued in quadrophonic (Epic Q 65455) 1975 SC and on CD (Essential ESSCD 011) 1989. (1) reissued again on CD (Phony 4680242).

45:      Black Cat Moan/Livin' Alone   (Epic EPC 1251) 1973

Line-up (A) lasted for just one month and also briefly featured vocalist Kim Milford. **Beck** had seen him playing Jesus in 'Jesus Christ Superstar' in Washington D.C. Milford, didn't fit into the group and returned to his career in acting and films and by September Middleton had left too so the band was down to a trio. Although their sole album sold well in the States, they never achieved their full potential. Instrumentally they were first rate and on stage they were exciting but they lacked enough decent songs. After they split in April 1974 a *Live In Japan 1993* (Epic/Sony ECPO 58) album was released in the Far East only. **Beck** meanwhile put together another Jeff Beck Group. (VJ)

Beckett

Personnel:			
ROBERT BARTON	gtr, vcls		AB
KEITH FISHER	drms		AB
FRANK GIBBONS	bs		A
KENNY MOUNTAIN	gtr, keyb'ds, vcls		ABCD
TERRY WILSON-SLESSER	vcls		ABCD
IAN MURRAY	bs		BC
(TIM HINKLEY	keyb'ds		B)
BARRY BLACK	drms		CD
ARTHUR RAMM	gtr		CD
JIMMY WILEY	bs		D

ALBUM: 1(B) BECKETT   (Raft RA 48502) 1974
NB: (1) also issued on CD (Raft RA 48502), with the Raft flexi-disc as a bonus.

45s: Little Girl/My Lady   (Raft RA 18506) 1973
   α   My Lady   (Raft/Lyntone LYN 2842) 1973
NB: α was a flexidisc.

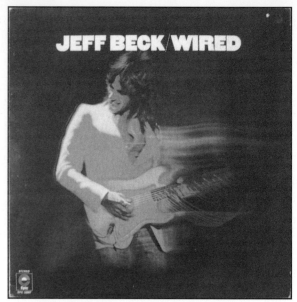
JEFF BECK - Wired (LP).

This progressive rock outfit from Newcastle formed in 1970. Wilson-Slesser had previously played with the Les Humphries Singers and Ken Mountain was ex-**Yellow**. After their *Little Girl* flexi, Gibbons left to join Halfbreed and was replaced by Ian Murray (ex-Music, Goblin).

Their album is very much in the progressive genre with a pop/rock edge. There's plenty of experimentation with lush strings, etc. After their album, which was produced by Roger Chapman of **Family**, Barton and Fisher left, being replaced by Arthur Ramm (ex-Les Humphries Singers) and Barry Black (ex-**John Miles** Set). Then Ian Murray departed, to be replaced by Jimmy Wiley (ex-**Icarus**).

After the band split, Wilson-Slesser went on to **Back Street Crawler**, Wiley and Barton ended up in Captain Whizzo (1976) and Black rejoined **John Miles**. (JM/VJ/MWh)

David Bedford

ALBUMS:	1	MUSIC FOR ALBION MOONLIGHT	
			(Argo ZRG 638) 1970 SC
	2	NURSE'S SONG WITH ELEPHANTS	
			(Dandelion 2310 165) 1972 SC
	3	STAR'S END	(Virgin V 2020) 1974
	4	ORCHESTRAL TUBULAR BELLS	(Virgin V 2026) 1975
	5	THE RIME OF THE ANCIENT MARINER	
			(Virgin V 2038) 1975
	6	THE ODYSSEY	(Virgin V 2070) 1976

NB: (1) Side 1 of this album was by Elizabeth Lutyens. (2) reissued on CD (Voiceprint VP 116CD) 1993. (3) reissued on CD (Virgin CDV 2020) 1997. (5) and (6) reissued on CD (Virgin CDOVD 443 and 444 respectively) 1994.

David Bedford was born in London in 1937. His grandmother was the composer Liza Lehmann and his mother, Lesley Duff, was a member of the English Opera Group just after the war and was involved in several Britten premieres. So it's no surprise that he became a talented and interesting music composer/arranger. Indeed, he began composing at the age of seven and studied at the Royal Academy of Music. A grant from RAM in 1961 enabled him to study in Venice with Luigi Nono.

He first came to light working on **Kevin Ayers**' *Joy Of A Toy* album and then joined **Kevin Ayers**' The Whole World as their keyboardist from March 1970 until they broke up in August 1971. He then formed the Coxhill/Bedford Duo with fellow Whole World musician **Lol Coxhill**. This produced just one 45 before **Bedford** embarked on a solo career.

His first recording venture had been to contribute half a side to *Music For Albion Moonlight*, but he signed to John Peel's Dandelion label for his first solo album proper. He was assisted in this by **Kevin Ayers** and **Mike Oldfield**. He returned the compliment by arranging some of their subsequent recordings. Indeed, he was widely used as an arranger in this era, working with **Edgar Broughton Band** and **Roy Harper** among others.

He signed to Virgin for the *Star's End* album. He'd been commissioned by the Royal Philharmonic Orchestra to write this music which was performed live at the London Festival Hall in November 1974. **Mike Oldfield** played guitar on the album version.

His next vinyl venture was an orchestral arrangement of **Mike Oldfield**'s *Tubular Bells*. Later the same year he put Samuel Coleridge's *Rime Of The Ancient Mariner* to record and the narrative was provided by actor Robert Powell. **Mike Oldfield** added some effective guitar work. His next effort *The Odyssey* was symphonic progressive rock.

An avant-garde artist worth investigating, he later collaborated with Elvis Costello, Frankie Goes To Hollywood, Propaganda, China Crisis, Enya, Billy Bragg and many more. He's also done the orchestrations for a number of films, including 'The Killing Fields', 'Supergrass', Absolute Beginners', 'Meeting Venus', 'Orlando' and was Choral Coordinator for 'The Mission'. He's also written the original music for many of the Hammer House of Mystery and Suspense TV series. (VJ)

Bedlam

Personnel:

FRANK AIELLO	vcls		A
DAVE BALL	gtr		A
DENNIS BALL	bs		A
COZY POWELL	drms		A

ALBUM: 1(A) BEDLAM (Chrysalis CHR 1048) 1973

NB: (1) reissued on CD (Zoom Club ZCR CD 8) 1998. *Anthology* (??) is a 2-CD set and *Live In London* (??) features previously unreleased live recordings from London during 1973.

45: I Believe In You/Whiskey And Wine (Chrysalis CFB 1) 1973

The antecedent of this band is a Cirencester-based group called The Sorcerers, who worked the German night clubs extensively in the late sixties and who seem to have been **Cozy Powell**'s first band. Prior to **Bedlam** (who were originally known as Beast between Nov. '72 - May '73) **Powell** and the Ball brothers were in **Ace Kefford Stand** and **Big Bertha** and **Powell** also had a spell in **Jeff Beck**'s group and a very short spell in the LA band, Spirit. Dave Ball also had a spell in **Procol Harum** and in **Long John Baldry**'s group for a couple of months prior to joining **Bedlam**. Frank Aiello was in **Truth**.

Bedlam lasted for about eighteen months, splitting in April '74, but never seemed to get going. Musically they veered towards hard-rock and it's worth noticing that their album was produced by Mountain's Felix Pappalardi (who also produced **Cream**). This offered a range of tidy rock on tracks like *Sweet Sister Mary* and *Sarah*. *Believe You* was a space-rock track and *Putting On The Flesh* is a moody, riffy song. When they split the Ball brothers quit the music business, with Dennis starting a limo business and David supposedly joining the army. **Powell** stuck with Aiello for Cozy

BEE GEES - Bee Gees First (LP).

Powell's Hammer. **Powell** later went on to achieve considerable success as a member of **Ritchie Blackmore**'s Rainbow and was later tragically killed in a car accident on the M4 in April 1998.

The *Anthology* (2-CD) set contains early demos and outtakes on disc one and disc two contains a legendary 1974 New York City FM live broadcast recorded at the end of a very lengthy **Black Sabbath** tour. *Live In London 1973* features live performances of nine cuts mostly from their album. (VJ/JM)

The Bedrocks

Personnel:

REG CHALLENGER	drms		A
PAUL DOUGLAS	sax		A
WILLIAM HIXON	ld gtr		A
LE ROY MILLS	trumpet		A
OWEN WISDOM	bs		A
TREVOR WISDOM	organ, vcls		A

HCP

45s: Ob-La-Di, Ob-La-Da/Lucy (Columbia DB 8516) 1968 20
The Lovedene Girls/I've Got A Date (Columbia DB 8539) 1969 -
Wonderful World/Before You Came (Columbia DB 8620) 1969 -
Hit Me On The Head/Musical Clowns (Columbia DB 8669) 1970 -
Stone Cold Dead In The Market/
Every Night And Every Day (Columbia DB 8699) 1970 -

A group of West Indians based in the UK who were unfortunate to release their version of *Ob-La-Di, Ob-La-Da* around the same time as **Marmalade**. It can also be found on See For Miles' *20 One Hit Wonders* (LP). (MW/GT)

The Bee Gees

Personnel:

BARRY GIBB	vcls, gtr	ABCDEFG H I
MAURICE GIBB	vcls	ABCDEFG H I
ROBIN GIBB	vcls	ABC FG H I
VINCE MELOUNEY	gtr	B
COLIN PETERSON	drms	BCD
GEOFF BRIDGEFORD	drms	G
ALAN KENDALL	ld gtr	G H I
DENNIS BRYON	drms	I

HCP

ALBUMS: 1(A) BEE GEES FIRST (Polydor 583 012) 1967 SC 8
(up to 2(B) HORIZONTAL (Polydor 582/583 020) 1968 SC 16
1975) 3(A) RARE, PRECIOUS AND BEAUTIFUL
  (Polydor 236 221) 1968 SC -
  4(B) IDEA (Polydor 582/583 036) 1968 4
  5(A) RARE, PRECIOUS AND BEAUTIFUL, VOL 2
  (Polydor 236 513) 1968 SC -
  6(A) RARE, PRECIOUS AND BEAUTIFUL, VOL 3
  (Polydor 236 556) 1969 SC -
  7(C) ODESSA (2-LP) (Polydor 583 049/050) 1969 SC 10
  8(-) THE BEST OF THE BEE GEES (Polydor 583 063) 1969 7
  9(E) CUCUMBER CASTLE (Polydor 2383 010) 1970 SC 57
  10(F) TWO YEARS ON (Polydor 2310 069) 1970 SC -
  11(G) TRAFALGAR (Polydor 2383 052) 1971 -
  12(H) TO WHOM IT MAY CONCERN (Polydor 2283 139) 1972 -
  13(-) MASSACHUSETTS (Contour 2870 196) 1972 -
  14(H) LIFE IN A TIN CAN (RSO 2394 102) 1973 -
  15(-) BEST OF THE BEE GEES, VOL 2 (RSO 2394 106) 1973 -
  16(I) MR. NATURAL (RSO 2394 132) 1974 -
  17(-) GOTTA GET A MESSAGE TO YOU
  (Contour 2870 404) 1974 -
  18(A) MAIN COURSE (RSO 2394 150) 1975 -

NB: (3), (5) and (6) were reissued on the budget Hallmark label in 1979 as *The Early Days, Vol. 1, 2 and 3* (Hallmark SHM 971, 973 and 982 respectively). Beware the corresponding volume numbers aren't the same as the originals. *Vol. 1* of *The Early Days* is *Vol. 3* of *Rare, Precious And Beautiful; Vol. 2* is the original *Vol. 1* and *Vol. 3* is the original *Vol. 2*. *Vol. 1* and *2* of *Rare, Precious And Beautiful* were also repackaged as a double set *Bee Gees Bonanza* (Pickwick PDA 048) in 1978. (1) reissued on CD (Polydor 825 220-2), (2) on CD (Polydor 833 659-2), (4) on CD (Polydor 833 660-2), (7) on CD (Polydor 825 451-2), (9) on CD (Polydor 833 783-2) 1989, (10) and (11) on CD (Polydor 833 785 2 and 833 786 2 respectively) 1990. *Tales From The Brothers Gibb: A History In Song 1967-1990* (Polydor 843 911-2) 1990, a 4-CD set, tells their story through their singles and hits. It does also contain a few rare 'B' sides and previously unissued tracks (though these had appeared on a Japanese rarities CD). There have been several other CD compilations of their earlier pop material including *Best Of The Bee Gees, Vol. 1* (Polydor 831 594-2) and *Vol. 2* (Polydor 831 960-2) 1988 and *The Very Best Of The Bee Gees* (Polydor 847 339 2) 1990. *Brilliant From Birth* is a 2-CD 62-track compilation featuring material from the 1961-1966 era.

			HCP
45s:	Spicks And Specks/I Am The World	(Polydor 56727) 1967	-
(up to	New York Mining Disaster 1941/		
1975)	I Can't See Nobody	(Polydor 56161) 1967	12
	To Love Somebody/Close Another Door	(Polydor 56178) 1967	41
	Massachusetts/Barker Of The U.F.O.	(Polydor 56192) 1967	1
	World/Sir Geoffrey Saved The World	(Polydor 56220) 1967	9
	Words/Sinking Ships	(Polydor 56229) 1968	8
	Jumbo/The Singer Sang His Song	(Polydor 56242) 1968	25
	I've Gotta Get A Message To You/		
	Kitty Can	(Polydor 56273) 1968	1
	First Of May/Lamplight	(Polydor 56304) 1969	6
	Tomorrow Tomorrow/		
	Sun In My Morning	(Polydor 56381) 1969	23
	Don't Forget To Remember/The Lord	(Polydor 56343) 1969	2
	I.O.I.O./Sweetheart	(Polydor 56377) 1970	49
	Lonely Days/Man For All Seasons	(Polydor 2001 104) 1970	33
	How Can You Mend A Broken Heart/		
	Country Woman	(Polydor 2058 115) 1971	-
	My World/On Time	(Polydor 2058 185) 1972	16
	Run To Me/Road To Alaska	(Polydor 2058 255) 1972	9
	Alive/		
	Papermache Cabbages And Kings	(Polydor 2058 304) 1972	-
	Saw A New Morning/		
	My Life Has Been A Song	(RSO 2090 105) 1973	-
	Wouldn't I Be Someone/Elisa	(RSO 2090 111) 1973	-
	Mr. Natural/		
	It Doesn't Matter Much To Me	(RSO 2090 128) 1974	-
	Charade/Heavy Breathing	(RSO 2090 136) 1974	-
	Jive Talkin'/Wind Of Change	(RSO 2090 160) 1975	5
	Nights On Broadway/		
	Edge Of The Universe	(RSO 2090 171) 1975	-

The Bee Gees operated over four decades and appealed to a very wide range of punters. In the sixties they achieved considerable success as a pop band, but they surpassed this success in the mid to late seventies at the forefront of the disco movement. Their talent as vocalists was exceptional.

Although some people mistakenly think of them as Australian the Gibb brothers grew up in Manchester, although they were actually born in the Isle of Man, which was a popular holiday resort with their parents. Barry was born on 1 September 1946 and Robin and Maurice were twins on 22 December 1949. They were born into a musical family. Their dad was a bandleader who also did a bit of drumming and their mum was an ex-jazz singer. With this sort of background they were inevitably going to be encouraged to sing and play almost as soon as they could talk and,

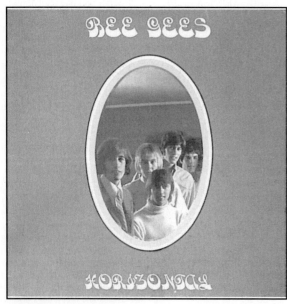

BEE GEES - Horizontal (LP).

indeed, they made a few childhood appearances on stage in Manchester before their parents emigrated to Brisbane in Australia in 1958. To get themselves established they had to move to Sydney and it was there that **The Bee Gees** were born and the band started recording 45s. They were signed by Leedon Records, a subsidiary of one of Australia's largest labels, Festival Records. Out in Australia they recorded a couple of albums and a series of Australian-only 45s. Success came very slowly at first - some of their early 45s sold poorly - but eventually their penultimate Australian 45, *Spicks And Specks*, rocketed to No 1 and by 1966 they were regarded as Australia's top group.

By now they realised their future lay in Britain and they returned there in January 1967. Almost immediately they were tracked down by Robert Stigwood and signed a recording deal with Polydor. *Spicks And Specks* was rapidly issued as a 45 but made little impact. Two Australians, Vince Melouney and Colin Peterson, were added to the line-up for their next 45, *New York Mining Disaster 1941*, which was a big hit both in the US and the UK and eventually became a million-seller. The follow-up, *To Love Somebody*, superbly showcased their vocal talents, although surprisingly it was only a minor hit in Britain. It was a Top 20 hit in the US, though.

Their debut album was warmly welcomed by the music press. Comparisons to **The Beatles**, the greatest compliment they could have received, were commonplace. Some tracks like *Red Chair Fadeaway* were very Beatleish, indeed the album was full of strong melodies and imaginative string arrangements. Other highlights included *Holiday*, *Every Christian Lion Hearted Man Will Show You* and *Turn Of The Century*.

Massachusetts, an instantly commercial single which again showcased their vocal talents, gave them a UK No 1 and follow-up *World*, a song which had some interesting tempo changes and was in many respects quite different from *Massachusetts*, also made the UK Top Ten.

Their second album, *Horizontal*, proved another diverse selection of strong material. Jose Feliciano covered one of the finer tracks, *And The Sun Will Shine*, enjoying a UK hit in the process. Among its many other highlights were *Really And Sincerely*, *Day Time Girl* and *Lemons Never Forget*. It comfortably made the Top 20 in the Album Charts on both sides of the Atlantic.

Barry Gibb put in a superb vocal performance in a breathy style on *Words*, another big ballad, which soon gave them another UK hit. Although the follow-up, *Jumbo*, flopped commercially, *I've Gotta Get A Message To You*, their next effort, was again ideally suited to the band and gave them another No 1.

The next album, *Idea*, was their most successful of the sixties. Like its predecessors, it was full of varied and melodic first rate pop songs. One of its finest moments, *I Started A Joke*, was released as a US 45 and later covered by many artists including **Lulu**.

After the *Idea* album guitarist Vince Melouney left the group to pursue an independent musical direction.

Their next 45, *The First Of May*, again made the UK Top Ten, although it sold less well in the US. Again it was a pop ballad ideally suited to their distinctive vocal style. The double album set, *Odessa*, appeared a month later and whilst it contained several songs in the usual pop style, it also contained three longish instrumentals (*Seven Seas Symphony*, *The British Opera* and *With All Nations*), as well as a country blues-influenced number, *Marley Purt Drive* and *Give Your Best*, which featured a couple of bluegrass musicians. *Odessa* made the UK Top 10 and the US Top 20, not a bad performance for a double album.

Despite or perhaps because of their rapid rise to fame and fortune the band became increasingly prone to internal strife. The big split happened in March 1969 when Robin left to pursue a solo career. Initially Robin scored a solo success with *Saved By The Bell*, which climbed to No 2 but his next effort failed to chart at all. Whilst the **Bee Gees'** first single without Robin, *Tomorrow, Tomorrow*, sold disappointingly, their pretty awful country-ballad, *Don't Forget To Remember* made No 2. After this Colin Peterson left the group reducing Barry and Maurice to a duo.

Around this time **Maurice Gibb** appeared with Steve Kipner (of **Tin Tin**) on a 45, *Have You Heard The Word*, credited to an outfit called **The Fut**. Issued on the obscure Beacon label it's now quite collectable. Its appearance on **Beatles** bootlegs led many people erroneously to believe that it had **Beatles** involvement, which it didn't.

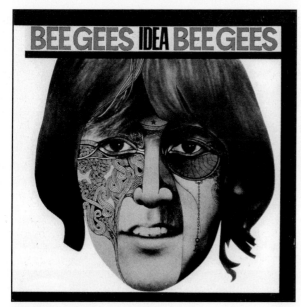

BEE GEES - Idea (CD).

The next **Bee Gees**' 45 was only a minor hit. They named their next album, *Cucumber Castle*, after a song title from their first album. **Barry Gibb**'s songwriting ability is again in evidence on tracks like *I Was The Child* and *If Only I Had My Mind On Something Else*. The country influence was also evident on *Sweetheart* and *The Lord*. The album peaked at No 57 in the UK and managed No 94 in the US. It did inspire a TV comedy spectacular featuring the two brothers, Vincent Price, Spike Milligan and Frankie Howard. However, the brothers weren't impressed with the end result.

Now with the band marking time both Maurice and Barry began to concentrate on solo ventures, though with little success. Robin's solo ventures had also been unsuccessful of late and in many respects everybodies face was saved when they all agreed to settle their differences and reform as a trio in December 1970.

In the UK their popularity had been damaged by all the squabbles and when *Lonely Days* from their next album, *Two Years On*, was released as a 45 it only managed No 33 here, although it peaked at No 3 in the US. The album, which only charted in the US, was their weakest yet and no other singles were taken off it.

In 1971 a number of the band's old songs and a re-recording of *In The Morning* were included on the Soundtrack to the film 'Melody' along with orchestral music by Richard Hewson and Crosby, Stills, Nash and Young's *Teach Your Children* from their *Deja Vu* album. This helped to keep the band in the public eye. In the US, meanwhile, *How Can You Mend A Broken Heart*, which wasn't released here, made No 1.

Drummer Geoff Bridgeford and guitarist Alan Kendall joined the line-up for their Trafalgar album. This was an improvement on the *Two Years On* album featuring two strong **Barry Gibb** ballads, *The Greatest Man In The World* and *Don't Wanna Live Inside Myself*. This last one was issued as a US-only 45 in edited form where it was a minor hit. Shortly after, they returned to the UK Charts with a non-album 45, *My World*. However, their final album on Polydor, *To Whom It May Concern*, was disappointing and is worth avoiding. Geoff Bridgeford quit during the recording sessions and **Clem Cattini** drummed on most of the tracks.

Their next UK release was the budget compilation, *Massachusetts*, which was worthwhile since it included a number of cuts not released in the UK previously. *Live In A Tin Can* was released on Robert Stigwood's RSO label. A second *Best Of* collection followed and the band also recorded several tracks for an album which was to have been called, *A Kick In The Head (Is Worth Eight In The Pants)*, but never made the shops. The next album, *Mr. Natural*, was made with a new producer, Arif Mardin and featured their new drummer, Dennis Byron. It was really a transitional album for the band and is certainly not essential. The title track was a very minor US hit.

A second budget compilation, *Gotta Get A Message To You*, followed. Again it was quite an interesting collection with a very different version of the flip side of *Mr. Natural (It Doesn't Matter Much To Me)*, it also included some of the Gibbs' solo singles.

1975 saw the band joined by ex-**Strawbs** keyboardist Blue Weaver and was very much the dawning of a new era for the band as they set about moulding the R&B feel under Arif Mardin's direction which would see them so closely associated with the depressing but phenomenally successful disco movement of the late seventies. This was a new phase in the band's career, but is beyond the remit of this book, which is why I've ended their discography and history at 1975.

When the disco era ended they fell out of favour, although they attempted various comebacks and remained active as a unit until the death of **Maurice Gibb** in January 2003. He suffered a cardiac arrest whilst receiving treatment for an intestinal blockage and died aged 53. Robin and Barry decided to wind up **The Bee Gees** after this.

Appearances on Various Artists' compilations in their early years included *Marley Purt Drive* on *No-One's Gonna Change Your World* (LP) and *I.O.I.O* on *Pop Party* (LP). More recently, *Spicks And Specks* has resurfaced on *Here Comes Summer (CD)*; *Sir Geoffrey Saved The World* can be heard on *Pop-In, Vol 1* (CD); *I've Gotta Get A Message To You* can be heard on the 2-CD set *Sixties Summer Love* and they supplied *Sitting In The Meadow* (Coke Ad #1) to *Spinning Wheel, Vol 1* (CD). (VJ)

Bees Make Honey

Personnel:			
	BOB LEE	drms	A
	DEKE O'BRIEN	gtr, vcls	AB
	RUAN O'LOCHLAINN	piano, gtr, sax	A
	MICK MOLLOY	gtr, vcls	AB
	BARRY RICHARDSON	bs, vcls, sax	ABC
	FRANK BYRNE	drms	BC
	ROD DEMICK	bs, vcls	BC
	ED DEAN	gtr	C
	WILLIE FINLAYSON	gtr, vcls	C
	KEVIN McALEA	piano	C

ALBUM:	1(A)	MUSIC EVERY NIGHT	(EMI EMI 3013) 1973 SC

45:		Knee Trembler/Caldonia	(EMI EMI 2078) 1973

Formed in the Summer of 1972 by Barry Richardson this band was an important part of the pub-rock scene of the early seventies. Their name was suggested by Ruan's wife Jackie. By September 1973 Ruan had departed and Bob Lee headed for **Supertramp** in the Autumn of that year. Keyboardist Malcolm Marley (who is not listed above) was also in the band for three months at the end of 1973 in between his time with **Help Yourself** and **Man**. Rod Demick, who joined during 1973, had previously been with **The Wheels** and Demick and Armstrong.

Considering they were together for at least two years the band's vinyl output was minimal. They played good music but lacked the image or management to achieve success beyond the pub circuit. Their debut 45 *Knee Trembler* was a fifties-influenced song.

BEGGAR'S OPERA - Act One (CD).

The enlistment of Ed Dean and Kevin McAlea in the Spring of 1974 brought some new life into the band and they recorded albums for EMI and DJM but when neither saw the light of day they called it a day in the Autumn of 1974.

Barry Richardson formed the Barry Richardson Band; Willie Finlayson and Rod Demick joined Meal Ticket; Frank Byrne joined **Ace** and Kevin McAlea played piano for Kate Bush. (VJ)

Beggars Hill

ALBUM: 1   BEGGARS HILL   (Moonshine MS 60) 1976 R3

This highly-touted privately-pressed album was recorded by a Surrey-based folk-rock band. The musical format is superb cover versions of **Fairport Convention**, **Bridget St. John** and **Dransfield** Brothers songs. (VJ)

Beggar's Opera

Personnel:			
	MARSHALL ERSKINE	bs, flute	AB
	RICKY GARDINER	gtr, vcls	ABCD
	MARTIN GRIFFITHS	vcls, perc	ABC
	ALAN PARK	keyb'ds	ABCD
	RAYMOND WILSON	drms	ABC
	GORDON SELLAR	bs, gtr, vcls	BCD
	PETE SCOTT	vcls, perc	
	COLIN FAIRLEY	drms	D
	LINNIE PATTERSON	vcls	D
	(VIRGINIA SCOTT	keyb'ds, vcls	D)

ALBUMS:			
1(A)	ACT ONE	(Vertigo 6360 018) 1970 SC
2(B)	WATERS OF CHANGE	(Vertigo 6360 054) 1971 R1
3(C)	PATHFINDER	(Vertigo 6360 073) 1972 SC
4(D)	GET YOUR DOG OFF ME	(Vertigo 6360 090) 1973 SC
5(-)	SAGITTARY	(Ariola 88907) 1974
6(-)	BEGGARS CAN'T BE CHOOSERS	(Ariola 27702) 1975

NB: (1) reissued on CD (Repertoire REPUK 1036). (2) and (3) were reissued by Line in 1992 and on CD by Repertoire (EMS 7029 and IMS 7028, respectively) in 1995.(4) reissued on CD (Repertoire REP 4994). (5) and (6) were only released in Germany. *Time Machine* (Zounds 2700020 113 B) is a rare 2-CD import compilation which draws material from all four of their Vertigo albums.

45s:		
	Sarabande/Think	(Vertigo 6059 026) 1970 SC
	Hobo/Pathfinder	(Vertigo 6059 060) 1972
	Two Timing Woman/Lady Hell Of Fire	(Vertigo 6059 088) 1973
	Classical Gas/Sweet Blossomed Woman	(Vertigo 6059 105) 1974

This Glasgow-based band, founded by Ricky Gardiner, was signed to the progressive Vertigo label. They specialised in flashy instrumentation but were somewhat short on melody. Their name was derived from the 17th century opera. They moved down to London and became friendly with

BEGGAR'S OPERA - Waters Of Change (CD).

BEGGAR'S OPERA - Time Machine (CD).

Radio 1 DJ's Mike Harding and the late Stuart Henry. They also had a big Continental hit with the non-album 45 *Sarabande*. Its non-album flip side *Think* is another strong track. Overall, the *Act One* album attempted to fuse classical and post-psychedelic progressive rock - none too successfully.

Their next album effort, *Waters Of Change*, is usually considered a progression on their first effort. It is similar in style, possibly less frantic. One cut *Time Machine* 34 years later provided the title cut to the recent 3-CD Vertigo box set.

Pathfinder was their magnum opus. It was issued in a memorable large poster sleeve. It opened with the sad tale of *Hobo* and also contained a superb cover version of **Richard Harris**'s *MacArthur Park*, which was probably its highlight. By now they had discarded their earlier keyboard-dominated sound for West Coast influenced harmonies and *Get Your Dog Off Me* was a very disappointing effort.

When Griffiths left in July 1972 he was replaced by Pete Scott. Scott and Wilson left in May 1973 to be replaced by Linnie Patterson (ex-**Writing On The Wall**) and Colin Fairley (ex-Chris McClure Section). Virginia Scott was employed as a session singer shortly before the band split.

The band also recorded two German-only albums, *Sagittary* and *Beggar's Can't Be Choosers*.

Park and Sellar joined **Ronnie Lane's Slim Chance** in July 1974 and Fairly went on to **String Driven Thing.** In 1976 Park replaced Dave McCrae in **Tiger** for their second album

In the mid-seventies Gordon Sellar put together a band under the **Beggar's Opera** name and recorded a further album *Lifeline* for Vertigo in 1980. This has been reissued as *Final Curtain* on CD and contains a bonus in unreleased tracks from 1980-1991. Ricky Gardiner toured with **David Bowie** in this era and also worked with Iggy Pop. Their keyboardist and founder member Alan Park became Sir Cliff Richard's musical director. (VJ/JM)

Belfast Gypsies

Personnel:			
	JACKIE McAULEY	vcls	A
	PAT McAULEY		A
	KEN McCLEOD		A
	MIKE SCOTT		A

ALBUM: 1(A)   BELFAST GYPSIES   (Grand Prix GP 9923) 1967

NB: (1) Swedish only release. Reissued as *Them Belfast Gypsies* (Sonet SNTF 738) in 1977 (R1) and reissued on CD (Rev-Ola 49) 2003 for the first time in the UK.

45:     Gloria's Dream/Secret Police   (Island W1 3007) 1967 R1

Belfast Gypsies was formed by Pat and **Jackie McAuley** after they left **Them** in 1965. Under the guidance of producer Kim Fowley they recorded an album, which was only released in Sweden, prior to its reissue in 1977. The album was somewhat bizarre. Totally over-the-top and fuelled by **Jackie McAuley**'s gutbucket vocals they played a weird brand of punk, folk, rock and blues, which didn't really catch on. Their philosophy on the album was captured on tracks like the Bo Diddley-inspired *People Let's Freak Out*, featuring Kim Fowley and the frantic garage punk renditions of standards like *Gloria* and *Midnight Train*. Tracks like *The Crazy World Inside Of Me* and *Secret Police* are often likened to The Seeds in style and vocal delivery.

After this Pat McAuley dropped out of the music business and later tragically drowned in Donegal in 1984. Jackie was later in **Trader Horne**, recorded a solo album and was in an outfit called Poor Mouth.

The album finally received a UK release in 2003 on CD accompanied with detailed sleevenotes, including an interview with Kim Fowley about the making of the album.

Compilation appearances have included *The Gorilla* (taken from a French EP on Vogue) on *Sound Of The Sixties* (2-LP), *Sixties Archive, Vol. 1* (CD), *Incredible Sound Show Stories, Vol. 1* and *Psychedelic Archives, Vol. 7* and both sides of a US-only single (*People Let's Freak Out/Portland Town*) on the *Garage Zone, Vol. 1* (LP). *The Gorilla* is a good mod/R&B number with fuzz guitar and distorted organ.

They also recorded a 45 as **Freaks Of Nature**, which was released as by **The Belfast Gypsies** in the US. Its flip side (*The Shadow Chasers*) was simply the 'B' side of the first single (*Secret Police*) under a different name. (VJ)

Graham Bell

ALBUM: 1   GRAHAM BELL   (Charisma CAS 1061) 1972 SC

45s: How Do You Say I Don't Love You/
       If You're Gonna Go   (Polydor BM 56067) 1966
       Too Many People/Before You're A Man (Charisma CB 201) 1972
       60 Minute Man/
       The Whole Town Wants You Hung   (Charisma CB 209) 1973
       You Need A 60 Minute Man/
       That's The Way It Is   (Charisma CB 250) 1975

Bell first came to some attention as lead singer of underground band **Skip Bifferty** (who briefly became **Heavy Jelly**), though prior to this he'd recorded a ballad 45 for Polydor. Then after being in **Every Which Way** and **Bell and Arc** he embarked on a solo career that spawned the above vinyl but brought him little commercial success. His album was recorded and mixed at Island Studios, London and Nashville, USA. It contained covers of B.B. *King's The Thrill Is Gone*, J.J. Cale's *After Midnight*, Bob

BELFAST GYPSIES - Them Belfast Gypsies (LP).

Dylan's *Watching The River Flow* and Kris Kristofferson's *So Black And So Blue*. The remaining six songs were written or co-written by **Bell**. Much of this material sounds like an inferior version of **Elton John**, but the opening track, *Before You Can Be A Man*, is a good vocal performance. (VJ)

Madeline Bell

ALBUMS:			
(up to	1	BELLS A POPPIN'	(Philips (S)BL 7818) 1967 SC
1976)	2	DOIN' THINGS	(Philips SBL 7865) 1968 SC
	3	MADELINE BELL	(Philips 6308 053) 1971
	4	16 STAR TRACKS BY MADELINE BELL	
			(Philips 6308 066) 1971
	5	COMIN' ATCHA	(RCA SF 8393) 1974
	6	THIS IS ONE GIRL	(Pye NSPL 18483) 1976

NB: (6) reissued on CD (Sequel NEMCD 457) 1999.

45s:	I Long For Love/	
(up to	Because You Didn't Care	(HMV POP 1215) 1963
1976)	You Don't Love Me No More/Don't Cross	
	Over To My Side Of The Street	(Columbia DB 7257) 1964
	Daytime/Don't Cry My Heart Out	(Columbia DB 7512) 1965
	What The World Needs Now Is Love/	
	I Can't Wait To See My Baby's Face	(Philips BF 1448) 1965 SC
	Don't Come Running To Me/	
	I Got Carried Away	(Philips BF 1501) 1966 SC
	One Step At A Time/You Won't See Me	(Philips BF 1526) 1966
	Climb Every Mountain/	
	It Makes No Difference Now	(Philips BF 1596) 1967
	Picture Me Gone/Go Ahead On	(Philips BF 1611) 1967 R1
	I'm Gonna Make You Love Me/	
	I'm Gonna Leave You	(Philips BF 1656) 1968
	Thinkin'/Don't Give Your Love Away	(Philips BF 1688) 1968
	Hold It/What Am I Supposed To Do	(Philips BF 1726) 1968
	We're So Much In Love/	
	How Much Do I Love You	(Philips BF 1799) 1970
	If You Didn't Hear Me The First Time/	
	You Walked Away	(Philips 6006 082) 1971
	I'm So Glad/Another Girl	(RCA RCA 2440) 1973

American by birth **Madeline Bell** arrived in the UK in 1962 from New Jersey. She established herself as a session vocalist, working particularly closely with **Dusty Springfield**, who became the President of her fan club and also did backing vocals on some of **Bell**'s solo records, which were mostly soul ballads. She was later in **Blue Mink** and **Seven Ages Of Man**. Her 1969 45, *Hold It*, was written by **John Paul Jones** who later found fame in **Led Zeppelin**. (VJ)

Maggie Bell

ALBUMS:	1	QUEEN OF THE NIGHT	(Polydor 2383 239) 1974
(up to	2	SUICIDE SAL	(Polydor 2383 313) 1975
1976)			

NB: (1) reissued on CD (Repertoire REP 4661-WY). (2) reissued on CD (Repertoire REP 4663-WY) 2000. *Coming On Strong* (Recall SNDCD 519) 2004 is a 2-CD live set.

45:	Oh My My/	
(up to	As The Years Go Passing By	(Polydor 2058 447) 1974
1976)		

A Glaswegian, **Maggie Bell** was born on 12 January 1945 in one of the city's many mean areas. She quit school at 15 working as a window dresser by day and a musician by night, eventually fronting **Stone The Crows**. Upon their demise she embarked upon a solo career, but despite her powerful gutbucket vocals and much critical acclaim in the music press, she made little impression as a solo artist. *Queen Of The Night*, her first album, is usually considered her best.

Coming On Strong collects her live material from the seventies. The first CD features her playing with **Stone The Crows** at Montreal in 1972. It is poorly recorded and pretty heavy-going. The second CD is from London's Rainbow Theatre in 1974 after she has turned solo. This captures her at her best. The support band includes **Pete Wingfield** on keyboards and Brian Breeze on guitar. It includes superb versions of her *Suicide Sal* and **Free**'s *Wishing Well* and culminates in a rousing gospel medley.

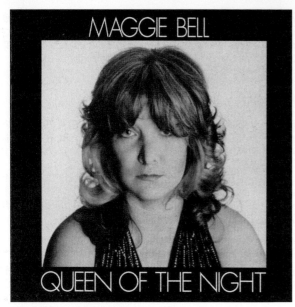

MAGGIE BELL - Queen Of The Night (CD).

She enjoyed two hits after the time span of this book with *Hazell* (No 37 in 1978) and a duet *Hold Me* (No 11 in 1981) with B. A. Robertson. (VJ)

Bell and Arc

Personnel:	GRAHAM BELL	vcls	ABCD
	TOMMY DUFFY	bs	ABCD
	MICKEY GALLAGHER	keyb'ds	ABCD
	ROB TAIT	drms	A
	JOHN TURNBULL	gtr, vcls	ABCD
	JOHN WOODS	drms	B
	ALAN WHITE	drms	C
	IAN WALLACE	drms	D

ALBUM: 1(A/B) BELL AND ARC   (Charisma CAS 1053) 1971 SC

45:    She Belongs To Me/Dawn   (Charisma CB 170) 1971

Bell, Gallagher and Turnbull had all previously played together in **Skip Bifferty** and Gallagher and Turnbull were both in **Arc** when **Graham Bell** who'd gone solo after he left **Skip Bifferty** asked them to back him on demos for a new solo album. In the end everything was so hunky dory that they combined as **Bell and Arc** and produced the above album and 45.

Tait left during the recording of the album to be replaced by John Woods (ex-**Jackson Heights**); when Woods left to join **Vinegar Joe**, Alan White deputised for the Nov-Dec '71 leg of a US tour; he then left to go on to session work, a tour with Chris Stainton and finally **Yes**; Ian Wallace, who was in **King Crimson** at the time, drummed with them until they split in February 1972. In the final month of the band Gallagher was replaced by Ken Craddock (ex-**Ginger Baker's Airforce**).

After the band's demise, John Turnbull joined **Glencoe**, **Graham Bell** continued as a solo artist releasing an album in 1973. Gallagher eventually recorded and toured with **Parrish and Gurvitz** before joining **Peter Frampton**. Duffy went on to **Gary Wright**'s **Wonderwheel** and Craddock recorded/toured with **The Alan White Band**.

She Belongs To Me has resurfaced on *One More Chance*. (VJ/JM)

George Bellamy

45s:	Where I'm Bound/How Could I Ever	(Parlophone R 5282) 1965
(up to	Maman/Come To The Party	(Chapter One CH 167) 1972
1976)		

George Bellamy was rhythm guitarist with The Tornados. In addition to these two solo 45s recorded after he left them in the Summer of 1963, he also went on to run a record pressing factory. (VJ)

Peter Bellamy

ALBUMS:	1	MAINLY NORFOLK	(Argo) 1968 SC
(up to	2	FAIR ENGLAND'S SHORE	(Xtra XTRA 1075) 1969 R1
1976)	3	THE FOX JUMPS OVER THE PARSON'S GATE	
			(Topic 12T 200) 1969 SC
	4	OAK, ASH AND THE THORN	(Argo ZFB 11) 1970 SC
	5	WON'T YOU GO MY WAY	(Argo ZFB 37) 1971 SC
	6	MERLIN'S ISLE OF GRAMARYE	(Argo ZFB 81) 1972 SC
	7	TELL IT LIKE IT IS	(Trailer LER 2089) 1974

Peter Bellamy was a significant vocalist in the English folk movement. He was born in Norfolk in 1944 but moved to London in early 1965. He joined a trio that adopted the moniker **The Young Tradition**. After their demise he embarked on a solo career and in 1970 began to put Kipling poems to music. Five albums of Kipling songs resulted. He also recorded a ballad opera *The Transports* with input from the likes of **Martin Carthy**, Cyril Tawney, Nic Jones and A.L. Lloyd which was released in 1977 and performed on stage. In the eighties his shows were multimedia historical presentations as he tried to reach beyond traditional folk audiences but by the nineties he had returned to a more traditional repertoire again. He committed suicide in 1991. (VJ)

Ben

Personnel:	PETER DAVEY	sax, clarinet	A
	ALEX MACLEERY	keyb'ds	A
	GERRY REID	gtr	A
	DAVID SHEEN	drms, perc, vcls	A
	LEN SURTEES	bs	A

ALBUM: 1(A) BEN   (Vertigo 6360 052) 1971 R3

NB: (1) counterfeited in limited quantities in Italy during the eighties. (1) reissued on CD (Repertoire REP 4195-WP) 1991 and again on CD and vinyl (Akarma AK 247).

Apart from being one of the rarest albums on the eagerly collected Vertigo label, there is little to say in favour of this jazz combo's sole album. Most of its contents are an uninteresting mixture of jazz and progressive rock, while the vocals are downright grating. The (mostly long) pieces have little development, and the decent instrumental ability is quite wasted. Especially boring is *Christmas Execution*, a lesson in futile riffing. This is definitely one to avoid, unless you're a fusion connoisseur.

Ben supported **The Groundhogs** and **Van Der Graaf Generator** on tour. Their drummer David Sheen had been with **Graham Bond's** Initiation and, after **Ben** split, worked with **Jonathan Kelly's** Outside.

They contributed one cut *The Influence* to the retrospective *Time Machine* (CD) compilation. (MK/VJ)

MAGGIE BELL - Suicide Sal (CD).

Bobby Bennett

45s:	Just Say Goodbye/She Believes In Me	(CBS 202511) 1967
	All My Life Is You/	
	To Give (The Reason I Live)	(Columbia DB 8435) 1968
	Music Mother Made/	
	You're Ready Now	(Columbia DB 8532) 1969 SC

Bobby Bennett is a long-forgotten solo artist. *You're Already Now* was Frankie Valli's Northern soul favourite. (VJ)

Cliff Bennett (and The Rebel Rousers)

Personnel:	FRANK ALLEN	bs	A
	CLIFF BENNETT	vcls	ABC
	MICK BURT	drms	ABC
	MOSS GROVES	sax	ABC
	SID PHILLIPS	sax	ABC
	DAVE WENDELLS	gtr	AB
	ROY YOUNG	keyb'ds, vcls	ABC
	BOBBY THOMPSON	bs	B
	JOHN GOLDEN	trumpet	C
	CHAS HODGES	bs	C

HCP

ALBUMS:	1(A)	CLIFF BENNETT AND THE REBEL ROUSERS	
		(Parlophone PMC 1242) 1964 R1 -	
	2(C)	DRIVIN' YOU WILD	
		(Music For Pleasure MFP 1121) 1966 SC 25	
	3(C)	GOT TO GET YOU INTO OUR LIVE	
		(Parlophone PCS 70517) 1968 R1 -	
COMPS:	4(-)	CLIFF BENNETT AND THE REBEL ROUSERS	
		(EMI NUT 14) 1978 -	
	5(-)	GOT TO GET YOU INTO MY LIFE	
		(See For Miles CM 108) 1982 -	
	6(-)	SLOW DOWN	(Edsel ED 148) 1986 -

NB: (2) also released on Regal Zonophone (REG 1035) in 1966. (5) was reissued in 1986. There's also a CD compilation *The Best Of The EMI Years: Cliff Bennett* (EMI CDEMS 1450) 1992. *Got To Get You Into Our Life/Cliff Bennett Branches Out* (Beat Goes On BGOCD 473) 2000 puts his third album and his **Cliff Bennett Band** album in stereo on one CD.

EPs:	1	CLIFF BENNETT AND THE REBEL ROUSERS	
		(Parlophone GEP 8923) 1964 SC	
	2	TRY IT BABY	(Parlophone GEP 8936) 1965 SC
	3	WE'RE GONNA MAKE IT	(Parlophone GEP 8955) 196 R1

HCP

45s:	You've Got What I Like/	
	I'm In Love With You	(Parlophone R 4793) 1961 R1 -
	That's What I Said/	
	When I Get Paid	(Parlophone R 4836) 1961 R1 -
	Poor Joe/Hurtin' Inside (Twist)	(Parlophone R 4895) 1962 R1 -
	Everybody Loves A Lover/	
	My Old Stand-By	(Parlophone R 5046) 1962 SC -
	You Really Got A Hold On Me/	
	Alright	(Parlophone R 5080) 1963 -
	Poor Joe/Hurtin' Inside (Twist) (export	
	issue, black label)	(Parlophone DP 560) 1963 SC -
α	When I Get Paid/	
	That's What I Said	(Parlophone DP 561) 1963 SC
	Got My Mojo Working/	
	Beautiful Dreamer	(Parlophone R 5119) 1964 -
	One Way Love/Slow Down	(Parlophone R 5173) 1964 9
	I'll Take You Home/	
	Do You Love Him?	(Parlophone R 5229) 1965 42
	Three Rooms Of Running Water/	
	If Only You'd Reply	(Parlophone R 5259) 1965 -
	I Have Cried My Last Tear/	
	As Long As She Looks Like You	(Parlophone R 5317) 1965 -
	You Can't Love 'Em All/	
	Need Your Loving Tonight	(Parlophone R 5406) 1966 -
	Eyes For You/Hold On I'm Coming	(Parlophone R 5466) 1966 -
	Got To Get You Into My Life/	
	Baby Each Day	(Parlophone R 5489) 1966 6
	Never Knew Lovin' Could Be So Doggone Good/	

Cliff Bennett and The Rebel Rousers with dancer 1967.

Don't Help Me Out	(Parlophone R 5534) 1966 -
I'm Sorry/Take Good Care Of You	(Parlophone R 5565) 1967 -
I'll Be There/Use Me	(Parlophone R 5598) 1967 -

NB: α Export issue with black label.

Bennett came from Slough (so it has some claim to fame) and formed the **Rebel Rousers** back in 1961, having previously sung in various obscure late fifties acts. Their early 45s (circa 1961-62) were produced by Joe Meek. Eventually they were seen by a talent spotter from the Star Club in Hamburg and enticed over there, where they played with many of the top acts of the era. The talent spotter was veteran keyboardist **Roy Young** who'd led the Star Club's house band for several years - in late 1963 he joined their line-up. They built up a solid reputation but hit singles continued to elude them. In July 1964 Frank Allen left to join **The Searchers** and Bobby Thompson took over bass duties. Eventually *One Way Love* gave them a Top Ten hit.

In June 1965 the line-up changed again when Wendells was sacked for being drunk and disorderly (he ended up with **Lulu**'s Luvvers) and Thompson who wasn't suited to the band's strict discipline and clean cut image joined **The Rockin' Berries**.

Chas Hodges (from The Outlaws) and later John Golden joined for what was their most durable and successful line-up (C). With Brian Epstein as their manager their fortunes improved and they achieved their commercial zenith with a cover of **Paul McCartney**'s *Got To Get You Into My Life*, which he also produced for them.

In early 1968 Cliff wanted to change the band's style to keep apace with the rapidly changing musical world. The remainder of the band was unenthusiastic and when he was sent to Germany to do some TV promotional work he was ousted as frontman by **Roy Young** and the outfit became **The Roy Young Band**.

When **Bennett** returned he formed a new **Cliff Bennett Band** and was later in **Toe Fat**. In 1971 he released **Cliff Bennett**'s *Rebellion* (CBS S 64487), whose sleevenotes say it was a collaboration between **Bennett** and a group called **Spiggy Topes**.... It has an excellent version of Green's *Sandy Mary*.

Much later in 1975 **Bennett** formed the short-lived **Shanghai**, before quitting the music business in 1976. Although he returned in the mid-eighties with a new version of The Rebel Rousers and their 1964 hit *One Way Love* was revised by Dexy's Midnight Runners.

Of the retrospective compilations the ones on EMI and See For Miles concentrate on their hits and more commercial material. *Slow Down* compiles some of their early singles, flip sides and album tracks and is altogether more obscure and not recommended for first timers. It comes with the detailed sleevenotes one would expect from Brian Hogg.

Compilation appearances have included: *If Only You'd Reply* on *Liverpool '65* (LP); *Got To Get You Into My Life* on *60's Mix* (CD); *Got To Get You Into My Life* and *634-5789* on *R&B At Abbey Road* (CD); *You Make Me Happy* on *Sixties Lost And Found, Vol. 1* (LP); *That's What I Said* on *Twist A La Star Club* (LP); *You Really Got A Hold On Me* on *Beat Merchants* (2-LP); and *Got To Get You Into My Life* on *Juke Box Jive*. (VJ/MF)

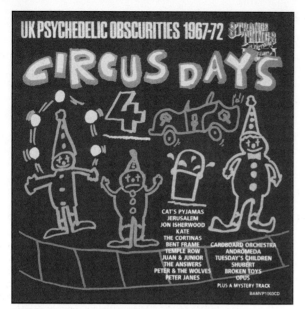

CIRCUS DAYS Vol. 4 (Comp CD) includes Bent Frame.

Cliff Bennett Band

Personnel:

MIKE BAILEY	trumpet	A	
CLIFF BENNETT	vcls	ABC	
JOHN BENNETT	trombone	A	
ADRIAN DROVER	sax	A	
FRANK FARLEY	drms	ABC	
MICK GREEN	gtr	AB	
STUART HAMER	trumpet	A	
ROBIN MacDONALD	bs	AB	
PAUL BASS	bs	C	
KEN HENSLEY	gtr	C	

ALBUM: 1(A) CLIFF BENNETT BRANCHES OUT
(mono/stereo)   (Parlophone PMC/PCS 7054) 1968 R1

NB: *Got To Get You Into Our Life/Cliff Bennett Branches Out* (Beat Goes On BGOCD 473) 2000 puts his third Rebel Rousers album and (1) in stereo on one CD.

45s: Take Your Time/
House Of A Thousand Dolls   (Parlophone R 5666) 1968
You're Breaking Me Up/
I Hear Her Voice   (Parlophone R 5691) 1968
Lonely Weekends/Good Times   (Parlophone R 5711) 1968
One More Heartache/
Nobody Runs Forever   (Parlophone R 5728) 1968 SC
Back In The USSR/This Man   (Parlophone R 5749) 1968 SC
Memphis Streets/But I'm Wrong   (Parlophone R 5792) 1969

Upon the demise of **Cliff Bennett and The Rebel Rousers** in the Summer of 1968, **Bennett** formed a new band. MacDonald, Farley and Green had previously comprised **Billy J. Kramer**'s backing band **The Dakotas** but **Bennett** also added a brass section comprising some pretty talented players although for some reason it didn't gel. By the Autumn he'd dispensed with the brass section who'd reverted back to session/studio work but the new quartet only managed a cover of **The Beatles**' high energy rocker *Back In The USSR* before MacDonald and Green left to join Englebert Humperdinck's cabaret band! Line-up (C) recorded the *Memphis Streets* 45, but when Frank Farley left to get married in the Summer of 1969 **Bennett** helped to form **Toe Fat**.

In 1971 he formed **Cliff Bennett's Rebellion**. (VJ)

Cliff Bennett's Rebellion

Personnel:

CLIFF BENNETT	vcls	A	
JOHN GREY	bs	A	
MERLICK KLUCXYNSKI	woodwinds	A	
BOB SMITH	gtr	A	
DEREK WEIR	drms	A	

ALBUM: 1 REBELLION   (CBS S 64487) 1971 SC

NB: (1) reissued on CD (Repertoire RES 2319) 2005.

45: Amos Moses/Movin' And Travelin' On   (CBS 7231) 1971

Formed in 1971 after **Cliff Bennett** had left **Toe Fat**, Weir, Klucxynski and Grey were all ex-**Spiggy Topes**. Their album includes an excellent version of **Peter Green's** *Sandy Mary* and the **Eric Clapton**/Leon Russell's *Blues Power*, as well as a number of **Bennett's** own compositions. The album is melodic and workman-like. The Repertoire reissue includes the 1971 single as a bonus.

On the above May 1971 45 he was backed by **Skid Row** (who included a young **Gary Moore** on guitar). In 1973, **Cliff Bennett** linked up with ex-members of The Hot Shots as The High Shots (aka The Hi-Spots).

In June 1975, **Cliff Bennett** joined **Shanghai** after which he quit the music business in 1976. He did return in the mid-eighties with a new Rebel Rousers line-up. (JM)

Duster Bennett

ALBUMS: 1 SMILING LIKE I'M HAPPY
(Blue Horizon 7-63208) 1968 R1
2 BRIGHT LIGHTS   (Blue Horizon 7-63221) 1969 R1
3 12 DB's   (Blue Horizon 7-63868) 1970 R1

NB: (1) and (3) were reissued on Line (OLLP 5289) and (OLLP 5312) in Germany in the 1980s. He also had a couple of US-only albums *Justa* and *Bennett* and an Australian release, *Fingertips*, (Toadstool L 35436) in 1974. *Jumpin' At Shadows* (Indigo IGOCD 2010) 1995 is a CD retrospective and *The Complete Blue Horizon Sessions* (2-CD) (Blue Horizon/Columbia 518517 2) 2005 is an 11-track live recording..

45s: It's A Man Down There/
Things Are Changing   (Blue Horizon 57-3141) 1968 SC
Raining In My Heart/
Jumpin' For Joy   (Blue Horizon 57-3148) 1968 SC
Bright Lights, Big City/
Fresh Country Jam   (Blue Horizon 57-3154) 1969 SC
I'm Gonna Wind Up Endin' Up Or I'm Gonna
End Up Windin' Up With You/
Rock Of Ages, Cleft For Me   (Blue Horizon 57-3164) 1969 SC
I Chose To Sing The Blues/If You Could Hang Your Washing
Like You Hang Your Lines   (Blue Horizon 57-3173) 1970
Act Nice And Gentle/
I Want You To Love Me   (Blue Horizon 57-3179) 1970
Comin' Home/Pretty Little Thing   (Rak RAK 177) 1974 SC

This Surrey-born guy was basically a sort of one-man blues-band, although he also played with **John Mayall's Bluesbreakers** and **Fleetwood Mac** in the late sixties.

Raining In My Heart also featured on Blue Horizon's *In Our Own Way (Oldies But Goodies)* compilation and *Jumping At Shadows* can also be found on *Super Duper Blues*. Fans will also be interested in two CD retrospectives: *Jumpin' At Shadows* and *The Complete Blue Horizon Sessions* which features 11 live cuts clearly recorded in a small venue

He was sadly killed in a car accident in 1976 aged 29 when he fell asleep at the wheel. (VJ/JM)

Barry Benson

45s: Stay A Little While/That's For Sure   (Parlophone R 5446) 1966
Not A One Guy Girl/Sunshine Child   (Parlophone R 5484) 1966
Always Waitin'/My Friend And I   (Parlophone R 5544) 1966
Cousin Jane/Meet Jacqueline   (Parlophone R 5578) 1967
I Can't Wait/Oh No   (Page One POF 034) 1967

Barry Benson is another long-forgotten solo artist. He was P.J. Proby's personal hairdresser. Most of his recordings were beat ballads. *Stay A Little While* was a **Peter Lee Stirling** composition and *Cousin Jane* and *Meet Jacqueline* were by **The Troggs**. (VJ)

Bent Frame

A very obscure group whose previously unreleased *Fairylights*, which had competent vocals and some good guitar/piano interplay, can now be heard on *Circus Days, Vol. 4* (LP) and *Circus Days Vol's 4 & 5* (CD). It's not known whether this is the same **Bent Frame** which included Jack McCulloch, the older brother of Jimmy and tour-drummer with **Thunderclap Newman**. Jack later went on to Wild Country, McCullochs Struthers and Patterson, **Andwella**, White Line etc.

One **Bent Frame** has a track, *It's Only Me* on the Track compilation *Backtrack 7 - Mixed Bag*. This is written by Hetherington and is reputedly produced by **Roger Daltrey**. It has been suggested that the band also had a 45 for Track, although we haven't been able to find reference to it. (JM/VJ/BMo)

Berlin

ALBUM: 1   ALL RIGHT 'ACK?   (Deroy) 1970 R3

This was a demo pressing in a plain white sleeve with a handwritten title in thought bubble on the front sleeve and song titles / musician credits handwritten on the back sleeve. It features **Soft Machine** - style jazzy progressive sounds but also the occasional **Hendrix**-style fuzz and wah-wah guitar leads. All the material is self-penned and the **Hendrix** influence is evident on *Cake Shop Blues* and the full scale freakout *Pink Aires*. Other tracks like *Tibetan Walk*, *Funeral* and *Abe's Blues* evoke a stoned dreaminess á la It's A Beautiful Day or **Pink Floyd**. (VJ)

Kenny Bernard

45s:	α	The Tracker/You Gotta Give	(Pye 7N 15920) 1965
		Nothing Can Change This Love/	
		What Love Brings	(Pye 7N 17131) 1966
		Ain't No Soul (Left In These Old Shoes)/	
		Hey Woman	(Pye 7N 17233) 1967
		I Do/Isn't That A Good Idea	(Pye 7N 17284) 1967
		Somebody/Pity My Feet	(CBS 2936) 1967
		Victim Of Perfume And Lace/	
		A Change Is Gonna Come	(CBS 3860) 1968

NB: α with The Wranglers.

Many of these 45s are now quite collectable. They were R&B and soulish. *Nothing Can Change This Love* was an old Sam Cooke song. *Ain't No Soul (Left In These Old Shoes)* was a Major Lance track and *Pity My Feet* was a Northern soul favourite.

Compilation appearances have included: *The Tracker* on *Quick Before They Catch Us* (CD) and *Ripples, Vol. 5* (CD); and *Hey Woman* on *Ripples, Vol. 6* (CD). (VJ)

DAVE BERRY - This Strange Effect (LP).

Bernie and The Buzz Band

45s:	α	The House That Jack Built/	
		(Flip by different artist)	(Decca F 22829) 1968 SC
		When Something's Wrong With My Baby/	
		Don't Knock It	(Deram DM 181) 1969 R1

NB: α Export only.

This eight-piece band from Liverpool recorded cheerful-sounding songs. (VJ)

Dave Berry

ALBUMS:	1	DAVE BERRY	(Decca LK 4653) 1964 R1
	2	THE SPECIAL SOUND OF DAVE BERRY	
			(Decca LK 4823) 1966 SC
	3	A DOZEN BERRY'S	(Ace Of Clubs SCL 1218) 1966 SC
	4	DAVE BERRY '68	(Decca LK/SLK 4932) 1968 R1
COMPS:	5	REMEMBERING	(Decca REM 3) 1976
	6	THE CRYING GAME	(Decca TAB 69) 1983
	7	THIS STRANGE EFFECT	(See For Miles CM 122) 1983

NB: (1) and (3) reissued on one CD (BGO BGOCD 643) 2005. (7) reissued in 1986. (7) reissued on CD as *The Best Of Dave Berry* (See For Miles SEECD 384) 1993. Also of interest is the CD compilation *Berry's Best* (Deram 820 633-2) 1989 and *The Very Best Of Dave Berry* (Spectrum) 1998. *The Singles* (BR Music BX 536 2) 2000 collects his hits and misses.

EPs:	1	DAVE BERRY	(Decca DFE 8601) 1964 SC
	2	CAN I GET IT FROM YOU	(Decca DFE 8625) 1965 SC

HCP

45s:	α	Memphis Tennessee/	
		Tossin' And Turnin'	(Decca F 11734) 1963 19
	β	My Baby Left Me/	
		Hoochie Coochie Man	(Decca F 11803) 1964 37
		Baby It's You/Sweet And Lovely	(Decca F 11876) 1964 24
		The Crying Game/	
		Don't Gimme No Lip, Child	(Decca F 11937) 1964 5
		One Heart Between Two/	
		You're Gonna Need Somebody	(Decca F 12020) 1964 41
		Little Things/	
		I've Got A Tiger By The Tail	(Decca F 12103) 1965 5
		This Strange Effect/Now	(Decca F 12188) 1965 37
		I'm Gonna Take You There/	
		Just Don't Know	(Decca F 12258) 1965 -
		If You Wait For Love/Hidden	(Decca F 12337) 1966 -
		Mama/Walk, Walk, Talk, Talk	(Decca F 12435) 1966 5
		Picture Me Gone/Ann	(Decca F 12513) 1966 -
		Stranger/Stick By The Book	(Decca F 12579) 1967 -
		Forever/And I Have Learned To Dream	(Decca F 12651) 1967 -
		Just As Much As Ever/I Got A Feeling	(Decca F 12739) 1968 -
		(Do I Still Figure) In Your Life/	
		Latisha	(Decca F 12771) 1968 -
	χ	Oh What A Life/Huma Luma	(Decca F 12905) 1969 -
		Change Our Minds/Long Walk To DC	(Decca F 12999) 1970 -
		Chaplin House/Trees	(Decca F 13080) 1970 -
		Moving On/Don't Bring Me Down	(CBS 7780) 1972 -
Reissues:		Crying Game/	
		Don't Give Me No Lip, Child	(Decca F 13608) 1975 -
		Little Things / Heartbeat	(Decca F 13673) 1976 -
		Crying Game/(Flip by different artist)	(Old Gold OG 9393) 1984 -

NB: α with The Cruisers. β 'B' side by The Cruisers. χ 'A' side by Dave Berry and Sponge.

Dave Berry was born David Holgate Grundy in Beighton, near Sheffield, in 1941. By the time he was 18 he was working as an electric welder and had entered music as half of an Everly Brothers-type duo. He started using his stage surname when he was invited to front The Cruisers, a R&B group inspired by Chuck Berry (which was where the stage name came from) which had emerged out of the ashes of another local group, The Chuck Fowler R'n'B Band.

Berry and The Cruisers soon became a popular attraction in the Sheffield area, playing a repertoire largely based around the Chicago blues and achieving a residency at The Esquire Club in Sheffield. They went on to play at other clubs in the north of England and their break came when they were spotted by Mickie Most (then a freelance talent scout). Most spotted them playing at a Doncaster club and supervised the taping of a demo recording for Decca, which eventually led to a record contract.

Their debut disc (and the only one to feature The Cruisers, who subsequently only backed him on stage) was a revival of Chuck Berry's *Memphis Tennessee*. Its release prompted the reissue of Chuck's original version which won the Chart battle, getting to No 6 but **Dave Berry**'s version still squeezed into the Top 20 at No 19. The Cruisers, incidentally, were prevented from playing on future discs by Decca recording manager Mike Smith, who was horrified that it took them eight hours to record the 45.

For future discs top studio members Big Jim Sullivan and future **Led Zeppelin** members **Jimmy Page** and **John Paul Jones** were used. Covers of Elvis Presley's *My Baby Left Me* and The Shirelles' *Baby It's You* were minor hits but it was *The Crying Game*, a tear-jerking ballad by Geoff Stephens with a distinctive guitar part by **Jimmy Page** that gave him his first Top 5 hit. **Berry** used the considerable TV exposure it ensured to fashion the image he wanted as a black-clad, slinky, mysterious performer. He perfected this style for the duration of his career. The follow-up, another Geoff Stephens' ballad, *One Heart Between Two*, suffered from being too similar to its predecessor and narrowly missed the Top 40.

Towards the end of 1964 he released an album, *Dave Berry*, but in common with all his subsequent albums it didn't sell well enough to chart. *One Dozen Berries* included some pre-*Crying Game* material and *Girl From The Fair Isle* (which had also been on his debut album).

His magnum opus was a cover of Bobby Goldsboro's US hit, *Little Things*, which gave him his second Top 5 hit and seemed ideally suited to that finger curling that was such an important part of his live act.

The follow-up, a Ray Davies' song, *This Strange Effect*, could only manage the Top 40 here but was a No 1 in Holland and in Belgium, where a prize-winning performance at the Knokke Song Festival earlier in the year had helped establish him as a star. He went on to enjoy huge success in Europe, though his next two UK 45s flopped. When he finally returned to the Top 5 here it was with the awful *Mama*, a cover of a US hit by B.J. Thomas. It proved to be his final UK hit. Subsequent 45s included a **Bee Gees**' song *Forever* and **Pete Dello**'s ballad, *Do I Figure In Your Life* (which had fared no better when recorded by **Dello**'s own band, **Honeybus**).

In 1972 he signed to CBS but this didn't bring about an upturn in his fortunes and he drifted, like many of his peers, into the world of cabaret and clubs. Later, he became a frequent attraction on sixties revival tours.

The Sex Pistols covered his toughest track *Don't Gimme No Lip Child* and in 1992 *The Crying Game* was used as the thme song for one of the years most successful films.

THE R&B SCENE (Comp CD) including Dave Berry.

For those unfamiliar with his music See For Miles' 1983 album would be a good starting point as it includes a good cross-section of his material. Aside from the title track (a **Kinks** cover), there's a couple of his Top Ten hits, *Mama* and *The Crying Game*; some of his best rock material (*Memphis, My Baby Left Me, Hoochie Coochie Man, Don't Gimme No Lip Child* and *Diddley Daddy*) as well as some of his better later beat ballads (*I'm Gonna Take You There* and *Picture Me Gone*). The sleevenotes also feature his comments on many of the tracks.

The CD compilation *Berry's Best* traces his career from 1963-70 and is quite an enjoyable slice of British sixties pop. *The Singles* collates his hits and misses.

He can also be heard singing *Little Queenie* and *Diddley Daddy* on Decca's rare 1964 *At The Cavern* (LP) album, which was reissued on vinyl by See For Miles in 1985 and on CD as *Live At The Cavern*, and *Original Liverpool Sound* (LP). Decca's 1964 *Fourteen, Lord Taverners* (LP) compilation featured him singing *He's With You* and he performs *Memphis Tennessee* on *Saturday Club* (LP).

Retrospective compilation appearances include: *My Baby Left Me* on *Hard-Up Heroes* (2-LP), *James Patrick Page: Session Man, Vol. 1* (CD) and *James Patrick Page, Session Man* (2-LP); *Don't Gimme No Lip, Child* on *Jimmy Page, Session Man* (CD); *Not Fade Away* and *Don't Gimme No Lip, Child* on *The R&B Scene* (CD); *Mama* on *A Whiter Shade Of Pale* (LP); *The Moonlight Skater* on *Beat Merchants* (CD); *Memphis, Tennessee* on *Beat Merchants* (2-LP); *The Crying Game* on *Hits Of The 60's - Save The Last Dance For Me* (CD) and *Remember The 60's* (CD); *And I Have Learned To Dream* on *Fading Yellow, Vol 4* (CD); *Forever* on *Colour Me Pop, Vol 3* (CD); *Latisha* on *Jagged Time Lapse, Vol 5* (CD); *Little Things* on *The Swinging Sixties - 18 Classic Tracks* (CD) and there's an alternate take of *Little Things* on the 2-CD set *Greatest Hits Of The 60's*. (VJ)

Mike Berry

ALBUM:	1	AMBUSH	(York FYK 409) 1972 SC

EPs:	1	IT'S TIME FOR MIKE BERRY	(HMV 7EG 8793) 1963 R1
	2	A TRIBUTE TO BUDDY HOLLY	(HMV 7EG 8808) 1963 R1

NB: (1) with The Outlaws: Chas Hodges (bs); Bill Kuy (lead gtr); Reg Hawkins (rhythm gtr) and Bobbie Graham (drms).

HCP

45s:		My Little Baby/			
(1963		You'll Do It, You'll Fall In Love	(HMV POP 1142) 1963 SC	34
onwards)		It Really Doesn't Matter/		
		Try A Little Bit Harder	(HMV POP 1194) 1963 SC	-
	β	This Little Girl/On My Mind	(HMV POP 1257) 1964 SC	-
		Lovesick/Letter Of Love	(HMV POP 1284) 1964 SC	-
	α	Who Will It Be/Talk	(HMV POP 1314) 1964 SC	-
		Don't Try To Stand In My Way/		
		Two Lovers	(HMV POP 1362) 1964	
		That's All I Ever Wanted From You/		
		She Didn't Care	(HMV POP 1449) 1965	
		It Comes And Goes/Gonna Fall In Love	(HMV POP 1494) 1965	
		Warm Baby/Just Thought I'd Phone	(HMV POP 1530) 1966	
		Raining In My Heart/Eyes	(Polydor 56182) 1967	

NB: α with **The Innocents**. β 'B' side with **The Innocents**.

A well-known early sixties crooner who'd earlier fronted The Outlaws and had achieved a minor UK hit (No 24) in this capacity in 1961 with *Tribute To Buddy Holly* and reached No 6 with them early in 1963 with *Don't You Think It's Time*, which had been released at the tail-end of 1962. He achieved a minor solo hit with *My Little Baby*, the first of three 45s up to *This Little Girl* produced by Joe Meek. Best of the above was the beat material recorded with **The Innocents**. Much later in 1981 he achieved a hit (No 9) with *The Sunshine Of Your Smile*, from the album of the same name, which got to No 63. He had a couple more minor 45 hits in this era too.

Compilation appearances have included: *Tribute To Buddy Holly* on *Twist A La Star Club* (LP) and it's also been compiled on the 2-CD set *Greatest Hits Of The 60's Vol 4*; *Don't You Think It's Time* on *Twist A La Star Club* (LP); and *Don't Ever Change* on *The Youngblood Story Vol. 1* (CD). (VJ/MWh/KL)

THE BETTERDAYS - Here 'Tis (CD).

Jon Best

45: Young Boy Blues/Living Without Love (Decca F 12077) 1965 SC

The 'A' side is a blues-tinged Spector/Pomus ballad. The flip is a pretty dreadful Billy Fury-styled song. Not recommended. (VJ)

Pete Best Four

Personnel:	PETE BEST	drms	ABCD
	FRANK BOWEN	lead gtr	A
	WAYNE BICKERTON	bs	ABCD
	TONY WADDINGTON	gtr, lead gtr	ABCD
	TOMMY McGURK	lead gtr	B
	TREVOR BROWNE	baritone sax	CD
	BILLY BURTON	tenor sax	C
	BILLY WESLEY	tenor sax	D

45: I'm Gonna Knock On Your Door/
Why Did I Fall In Love With You (Decca F 11929) 1964 R2

NB: *Beyond The Beatles - 1963 to 1968* (CD) (Cherry Red CDMRED 124) features all the singles he released in this period.

Pete Best was, as many of you will know, ousted as drummer with **The Beatles** to make way for **Ringo Starr**. Decca was quick to sign his new outfit, but it lacked the talent to make it. **Best** also recorded 45s and albums in the US, for labels like Cameo, Mr. Maestro and Happening. One of his best, *The Way I Feel About You*, was a pretty grungy beat-punk effort.

Wayne Bickerton had previously played in Steve Bennett and The Syndicate. Tony Waddington was in Gene Day and The Jango-Beats. They were then all in **Lee Curtis and The All-Stars** and then left Lee Curtis and became The Original All-Stars. After **The Beatles** success, they changed names to **Pete Best's** Original All-Stars, then **Pete Best's** All Stars and in September 1963 **The Pete Best Four**. Bowen left and was replaced by Tommy McGurk (also from Gene Day and The Jango Beats). Waddington became lead guitarist. After touring Germany, they travelled to the USA where they released six singles between 1965-1966 and one album called *Best Of The Beatles* (Savage BM71/2) 1965. **Best** also made some recordings with Joe Meek shortly after departing **The Beatles**, however none have subsequently seen the light of day.

Beyond The Beatles - 1963 to 1968 (CD) features all the singles he released in this period and they have never been released in Europe or on CD before. The CD comes with a booklet that contains a full **Pete Best** discography.

Compilation appearances have included: *I'm Gonna Knock On Your Door* and *Why Did I Fall In Love With You* on *Liverpool 1963-1964, Vol. 2* (LP) and *Mersey Sounds* (2-LP); *I'm Gonna Knock On Your Door* on *Mersey*

Beat (2-LP) and *The Beat Scene* (CD); *Why Did I Fall In Love With You* on *Rare 60's Beat Treasures, Vol. 4* (CD); *The Way I Feel About You* on *English Freakbeat, Vol. 5* (LP & CD) and *Garage Music For Psych Heads, Vol. 1* (cassette); and, finally, *The Way I Feel About You* and *If You Can't Get Her* on *Psychedelic Archives, Vol. 7* (LP). (VJ/KL/AD/L)

The Betterdays

Personnel:	RICHARD BROCZEK	ld gtr	A
	MIKE 'SHANE' HAYNE	vcls	A
	BOB PITCHER	gtr, piano	A
	FRANK TYLER	drms	A
	MIKE WESTON	bs	A

45s: α Here 'Tis/Crackin' Up/Aw Shucks, Hush Your Mouth (Oak) 1964
β Don't Want That/Here 'Tis (Polydor BM 56024) 1965

NB: α Acetate only. β an acetate also exists of the 'A' side with a different 'B' side, *Honey What's Wrong*. *Here 'Tis* (Aftermath AFT 1002) CD 1992 compiles their existing studio recordings, plus a couple of tracks by a reformed line-up, whilst *No Concessions* (Aftermath NAFT 1001) CD 1994, contains studio material recorded in the early nineties plus a live track from 1963.

This R&B band hailed from the West Country, where they were a big live attraction. They started life as The Saints Beat Combo, a four-piece, but changed their name to **The Betterdays** in early 1964 when Bob Pitcher was added to their line-up. The new name was taken from an American blues song by Sonny Terry and Brownie McGee. The rest of 1964 was spent consolidating their live reputation, but they also recorded a three-track acetate for R.G. Jones' legendary Oak label. The two or three copies still in existence would change hands for small fortunes today, as would copies of a second EMIDISC acetate (*Don't Want That/Honey What's Wrong*), cut earlier in 1965, which prompted Polydor to sign them. Collectors also pay a lot for the **Stones**-ish R&B single they released on the label. Its 'A' side has strong vocals and good mouth harp, whilst the flip is a frantic version of Bo Diddley's *Here 'Tis*. Undoubtedly talented, they deserved to do better but suffered from being stuck out in the West Country, a lack of strong management and main songwriter Bob Pitcher's ill health.

In the nineties the band released two EPs of their mid-sixties recordings - *Howl Of The Streets* (*Honey What's Wrong, Don't Want That, Here 'Tis, Aw Shucks Hush Your Mouth*) (N.T.B. 001) 1991 and *Down On The Waterfront* (*Crackin' Up*, the Oak acetate version of *Here 'Tis* and the EMIDISC version of *Don't Want That*) (N.T.B. 1002) 1992. The band also re-recorded an album's worth of their old material in the early nineties.

Compilation appearances include: *Don't Want That* on *Maximum R'n'B* (CD), *Beat It* (3-CD) and *English Freakbeat, Vol. 1* (LP); and whilst *Don't Want That* and *Here 'Tis* can be heard on *Nowhere Men Vol. 1* (LP & CD). (VJ)

Beverley

45s: Happy New Year/
Where The Good Times Are (Deram DM 101) 1966 SC
Museum/(Flip by a different artist) (Deram DM 137) 1967 SC

Beverley Kutner had been in **Levee Breakers** and also played at the Monterey Festival in the States, probably due to her connection with Paul Simon. Her finest moment, *Happy New Year*, was a melodic, up-tempo number with a complex arrangement, and the very first release on Deram. Her second 45, *Museum*, was a **Donovan** song and influenced by Dixieland jazz. A small number of acetates of further songs have surfaced since. **Beverley** later married guitarist **John Martyn**, and the two recorded as **John and Beverley Martyn**.

Happy New Year can also be heard on *Deram Dayze* (LP), *Jagged Time Lapse, Vol 3* (CD) and *Where The Good Times Are* got a further airing on *Jagged Time Lapse, Vol 5* (CD). (VJ/RMJ)

Big Bertha

Personnel:	DAVE BALL	gtr	AB
	DENNIS BALL	bs	AB
	PETE BALL	keyb'ds	AB

COZY POWELL	drms		A
DAVE McTAVISH	vcls		A
FRANK AIELLO	vcls		B
MAC POOLE	drms		B

45: This World's An Apple/
Gravy Bobby Jam   (Atlantic 584 298) 1969 SC

NB: *Live In Hamburg 1970* (Zoom Club Records ZCRCD 17) 1999 reissued again (Majestic Rock MAJCD 033) 2004 is a 2-CD live set .

Formed late in 1969 in Birmingham. The Ball brothers and **Powell** had all previously been with **Ace Kefford Stand**.

The Live In Hamburg 1970 set was recorded in December 1970, shortly before **Cozy Powell** left to join **The Jeff Beck Group**. They played blues-rock and the set featured a cover of **Cream's** *Crossroads*. The recording quality of this live set is not great, but it does include useful sleevenotes from Dennis Ball.

In 1973 the Ball brothers and **Cozy Powell** teamed up again with vocalist Frank Aiello in **Bedlam**.

Pete French went on to join **Atomic Rooster** and Cactus. In addition to the 45 listed, they had another 45, *Munich City*, released on the Continent. *Gravy Bobby Jam* was recorded with **Ace Kefford**. (VJ)

Big Boris

45: Big Country/Devil's Drive   (RCA RCA 2197) 1972

This is another obscure 45. The instrumental 'A' side had been used as the theme tune to 'Laramie'. The flip side is a beaty orchestrated instrumental. (VJ)

Big Boy Pete

ALBUMS: 1 HOMAGE TO CATATONIA(Tenth Planet TP 026) 1996 SC
         2 RETURN TO CATATONIA   (Tenth Planet TP 035) 199?

NB: (1) ltd edition of 1,000 copies. Later reissued on CD (Dionysus BA 1123) 1998. (2) ltd edition of 1,000 copies, also issued on CD (Gear Fab GF-139). Also relevant is *The Magnetic Demos* (CD) (Gear Fab GF 206), which contains unreleased tracks from the 1966-1968 era and *World War IV* (LP) (Gear Fab/Comet GF 157).which was a previously unreleased album.

45: Cold Turkey/
My Love Is Like A Spaceship   (Camp 602 005) 1968 R2

Big Boy Pete was former Peter Jay and The Jaywalkers member Pete Miller who also cut *Baby I Got News For You* as **Miller**, recording under a pseudonym. He first played in a rock n roll combo called The Offbeats, who recorded a six-song EP *Introducing The Offbeats* in 1958, before joining Peter Jay and The Jaywalkers in 1961. His work with the Jaywalkers included a number of singles, produced by Joe Meek, from whom **Pete** would learn many recording techniques. In October 1965, he quit the band to concentrate on recording demos, alongside session work. During this period, over 100 of his songs were accepted by major publishing houses in London.

Returning to his native Norwich, **Pete** continued to record demos - influenced by the contemporary sounds, of *Sgt. Pepper, Satanic Majesties* and *Axis Bold As Love*, and although rejected for being too far-out for the mainstream publishing houses, many of these tracks have now been compiled on the *Homage To Catatonia* and *Return To Catatonia* retrospectives.

However **Big Boy Pete** is best remembered for *Cold Turkey* which is an interesting and unusual psychedelic record well worth getting to hear. When the single started to create a buzz, **Pete**, tired of touring from his days with The Jaybirds, refused to go out gigging to support the single so a 'bogus' **Big Boy Pete** was enlisted to do the dirty work.

Big Boy Pete later relocated to the 'States, where he runs his own Recording Studio, and record label. There have been a few retrospective releases: *The Magnetic Demos* contain 23 previously unreleased tracks

recorded between 1966-1968; titles include *L.S.D., Watch Your Step, For The Love Of Three, Funny World* and more. *World War IV* subtitled 'A Symphonic Poem' is full of weirdness and lyrical word poetry, it veers more towards progressive rock than his other works. Recorded in 1968, it was almost released by Apple in 1969, but has now been unearthed and remastered by Gear Fab.

Compilation appearances have included: *My Love Is Like A Spaceship* on *Visions Of The Past, Vol. 2* (LP & CD); and *Cold Turkey* on *Chocolate Soup For Diabetics, Vol. 2* (LP), *Electric Sugar Cube Flashbacks* (CD) and *Electric Sugar Cube Flashbacks, Vol. 4* (LP). (VJ)

Big Carrot

45:     Blackjack/Squint Eye Mangle   (EMI EMI 2047) 1973 R1

This instrumental was actually a **Marc Bolan/T Rex** 45 put out under a pseudonym. (VJ)

Big John's Rock 'n' Roll Circus

Personnel:	COLIN FLETCHER	gtr, bs	A
	JOHN GOODISON	vcls	A
	MICHAEL GREGORY	drms	A
	PHIL WAINMAN	drms, vcls	A
	PIP WILLIAMS	gtr	A

ALBUMS: 1(A)	ACT ONE	(DJM DJLPS 438) 1974
(up to 2 (A)	ACT TWO	(DJM DJLPS 463) 1975
1976)		

45s:	Lady/Love	(DJM DJS 10301) 1974
	When Will You be Mine/	
	I'm In The Army Now	(DJM DJS 10329) 1974

Big John's Rock 'n' Roll Circus was an Anglo-American rock and roll band. Several members had played with **Duster Bennett** and the vocalist also appeared on **Deep Purple's Roger Glover's** *Butterfly Ball* concept album. They made a further album *On The Road* (DJM DJF 30511) in 1977. (BS/VJ)

Bigroup

ALBUM: 1( )   HAMMER (Peer International Library Ltd PIL 009) 1971 R3

This obscure album now changes hands for quite high prices. (VJ)

BIG BOY PETE - Homage To Catatonia (LP).

Bigs

Personnel:	IAN BROAD	drms	A
	BRIAN DANCER	sax	A
	RAY FAULKNER	gtr	A
	DAVE "ALLEN" FELLOWS	vcls	A
	BOB HOPKINS	keyb'ds, sax	A
	MALCOLM RARTRAY	bs	A

45:   α   Nella Gabbia/Rido e Rider   (Derby DB 5153) 1966

NB: α Italian only.

This UK band had recorded earlier as **Dave Allen and The Exotics**. In addition to this Italian language 45, they reputedly also recorded a version of *Penny Lane*. (FB/CR/GB)

Big Sleep

Personnel:	RITCHIE FRANCIS	bs, piano, vcls	A
	GARY PICKFORD HOPKINS	vcls, gtr	A
	PHIL RYAN	keyb'ds	A
	JOHN WEATHERS	drms	A
	RAY TAFF WILLIAMS	gtr	A

ALBUM: 1(A) BLUEBELL WOOD   (Pegasus PEG 4) 1971 R1

NB: (1) also released on Global in Germany. (1) has been reissued on CD (Walhalla WH 90334), which is a Korean label.

This rather unusual progressive effort is interesting mainly because of its above average arrangements, which include some very fine strings, and for its thoughtful atmosphere. None of the tracks are very heavy and with four vocalists there is quite a lot of diversity of interpretation. John Weathers, between his stints in **Eyes of Blue** and **Gentle Giant**, proves that even he can sing and write. Not all of the songs are particularly good, though. The album starts off interestingly enough, but as almost all cuts are in minor keys and glide along at the same quiet pace, there isn't always enough going on to keep the ear attentive. Side two, with the extensive title track which isn't very good, confirms this impression. This is undoubtedly worthwhile, but nothing stunning.

Ray Williams and Phil Ryan were later in the Welsh band **Man**. Hopkins, Ryan and Weathers had all been in **The Eyes Of Blue** and were later in **Ancient Grease**. (MK)

The Big Three

Personnel:	ADRIAN BARBER	ld gtr	AB	
	JOHNNY GUSTAFSON	bs, vcls	AB	E
	JOHNNY HUTCHINSON	drms	ABCD	
	BRIAN GRIFFITHS	gtr, vcls	B	E
	PADDY CHAMBERS	bs, vcls	C	
	BILL FARON	gtr, vcls	CD	
	PAUL PILNICK		D	
	NIGEL OLSSON	drms		E

ALBUM: 1(E) RESURRECTION   (Polydor 2383 199) 1973 SC

EP: 1   THE BIG THREE AT THE CAVERN
                               (Decca DFE 8552) 1963 SC

NB: (1) reissued in 1981. In 1985 See For Miles added this EP to Decca's original *At The Cavern* album to make an extra long compilation (SEE 58) 1985. In 1995 the E.P. was reissued on CD, together with all their 45s, and two unreleased cuts as *Cavern Stomp* (Deram 844 006-2) 1995.

                                          HCP

45s: Some Other Guy/
        Let True Love Begin   (Decca F 11614) 1963 SC 37
        By The Way/Cavern Stomp   (Decca F 11689) 1963 22
        I'm With You/Peanut Butter (Decca F 11752) 1963 SC -
        If You Ever Change Your Mind/You've Got
        To Keep Her Under Hand   (Decca F 11927) 1964 SC -
        Some Other Guy//Let It Rock / If You Gotta Make
        A Fool Of Somebody   (Polydor 2058 343) 1973 -

BIG BOY PETE - Return To Catatonia (LP).

The group was earlier known as Cass and The Casanovas when it was fronted by lead singer and rhythm guitarist Brian Casser back in 1959. Casser was a poor singer and the other members soon ousted him. He left to form **Casey Jones and The Engineers** (who briefly included **Eric Clapton** in their line-up). Later he became a TV actor and fronted another group Casey Jones and The Governors, which worked in Germany with some success.

Meanwhile back on Merseyside The Casanovas became **The Big Three** and soon established a good reputation as a live act playing loud R&B material with Hutchinson's unusually raucous drumming for the times. They often backed local solo singers like **Cilla Black**.

They met Brian Epstein in 1961 and he arranged for them to do the obligatory spell in Hamburg. Brian Griffiths (formerly of **Howie Casey and The Seniors**) was added to the line-up because the Germans insisted on a four-piece group. They enjoyed a residency at Hamburg's Star Club for several months. Adrian Barber left the group in August 1962 and around this time Johnny Hutchinson briefly drummed for **The Beatles** after **Pete Best** was sacked and before **Ringo Starr** joined.

The Big Three was in many ways a classic case of a group who couldn't transfer its exciting live act onto vinyl. The debut 45, *Some Other Guy*, a Richie Barrett composition, was recorded early one morning after the group had travelled back overnight from Hamburg. It was a poor representation of the group's ability but it still became a minor hit. The flip, a ballad, *Let True Love Begin*, had earlier been a hit for Nat 'King' Cole. The follow-up was a tuneful Mitch Murray song, *By The Way*, which narrowly missed the Top 20. Like their third 45, *I'm With You*, which didn't make the Charts, it was very poppy and far removed from the wilder R&B material the group used to play, although this can be found on flip sides like *Cavern Stomp*.

Their live sound is captured best on their *Live At The Cavern* EP, which is their most collectable disc. It features covers of Ray Charles' *What'd I'd Say*, Chuck Berry's *Reelin' And Rockin'*, *Zip-A-Dee-Doo-Dah* and the group's own song *Don't Start Running Away*. They also recorded another live set at The Oasis Club in Manchester, but it never made it onto vinyl.

Eventually Brian Epstein dropped them from his management because of their wild behaviour! They moved to another agency but their original line-up split in November 1963 and it was left to Johnny Hutchinson to put together a new line-up with Faron (of **Faron's Flamingoes**) and another Flamingo member Paddy Chambers. The new line-up (C) recorded a live version of *You Better Move On* for the *Live At The Cavern* album. Chambers and Hutchinson didn't get on and Chambers left after a few months. He later joined The Dominoes (**Kingsize Taylor**'s backing band) before forming **Paddy, Klaus and Gibson**. He was replaced by Paul Pilnick (formerly of **Lee Curtis and The All Stars**, he was later in **Stealer's Wheel**). This line-up (D) recorded a version of Sam Cooke's *Bring It On Home To Me* entitled *If You Ever Change Your Mind*, which was a good arrangement and their only disc to feature strings. Neither this or Sam Cooke's original version made the UK Charts, though **The Animals** later had a hit with it in 1965.

By 1964 **The Big Three** had split for good. By then **Johnny Gustafson** had joined **The Merseybeats**. He also released two solo 45s for Polydor in 1964 and 1965. Then in 1965 he worked briefly with Brian Griffiths as The Johnny Gus Set. Later in 1973 the two teamed up again with Nigel Olsson of **Elton John**'s band and using **The Big Three** name recorded an album, *Resurrection*. It didn't sell and afterwards Brian Griffiths emigrated to Canada and **Johnny Gustafson** returned to his career as a session musician. His credits include albums with **Roxy Music**, **Ian Hunter**, Gene Pitney and **Shirley Bassey**. He was also on the original album cast of Jesus Christ Superstar. Paddy Chambers died of throat cancer on 28 September 2000.

Back in 1964 the band had one cut, *Bring It On Home To Me*, on Decca's *At The Cavern* (LP) compilation. In 1985 See For Miles reissued this compilation on vinyl with *The Big Three At The Cavern* EP added to it, and again in 1994 on CD as *Live At The Cavern*. More recently, Deram have issued a CD retrospective, *Cavern Stomp* (Deram 844 006-2) 1995, which compiles their *Live At The Cavern* (EP), their 45s and two previously unreleased tracks:- an alternate take of *Bring It On Home To Me* and a version of Jerry Lee Lewis' *High School Confidential*.

Other compilation appearances by the band include *I'm With You* on *Ready, Steady, Go!* (LP) back in 1964; *You've Gotta Keep Her Underhand*, *What'd I Say* and *If You Ever Change Your Mind (Bring It On Home To Me)* on *Liverpool 1963-1964, Vol. 2* (LP); *Some Other Guy* and *Reelin' And A Rockin'* on *Mersey Beat* (2-LP); *Cavern Stomp*, *By The Way*, *I'm With You*, *Don't Start Running Away* and *Reelin' And A Rockin'* on *Mersey Sounds* (2-LP); *Some Other Guy*, *Peanut Butter* and *I'm With You* on *Mersey Beat 1962-1964* (2-LP); *You've Gotta Keep Her Underhand* on *The R&B Scene* (CD); *Bring It On Home To Me*, *What'd I Say*, *Don't Start Running Away*, *Zip-A-Dee-Doo-Dah* and *Reelin' And A Rockin'* on *At The Cavern* (LP); *By The Way* on *Thank Your Lucky Stars, Vol. 2* (LP); *Some Other Guy* on *Weekend Starts Here* (LP), *Hits Of The Mersey Era, Vol. 1* (LP) and *Hard-Up Heroes* (2-LP); *What'd I Say* on *Beat Merchants* (2-LP); four tracks on *Cavern Stomp* (LP) (1982); and one track on the 2-LP compilation *Made In Britain* (1983).

The band's widespread compilation coverage lends weight to the view that it never achieved the recognition it deserved at the time. (VJ)

Trevor Billmuss

ALBUM: 1   FAMILY APOLOGY   (Charisma CAS 1017) 1970

45s: Whoops Amour!/?   ( ) 197?
        English Pastures/?   (B+C) 197?

This obscure album was produced by John Anthony. The second 45 was produced by Tony Stratton-Smith and issued well after the album was released. **Trevor Billmuss** was managed by Marquee Artists Management

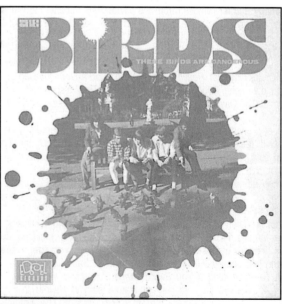

THE BIRDS - These Birds Are Dangerous (Mini LP).

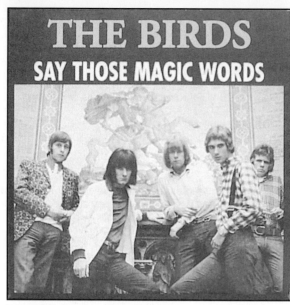

THE BIRDS - Say Those Magic Words (LP).

and his fifteen minutes of fame were split: five minutes worth playing warm-up for **Blodwyn Pig** at the Marquee Club, London without getting throttled; five minutes worth playing warm-up for **Yes** also at the Marquee without incident and a final five minutes at the "10th National Jazz & Blues Festival" at Plumpton Race Course with a jolly good write up in a local rag the next day.

He then moved to America and informs us that today he is a very happy "unfamous" man. (VJ)

The Birds

Personnel:	KIM GARDNER	bs	A
	PETE McDANIELS	drms	A
	ALISTAIR McKENZIE	vcls	A
	TONY MONROE	gtr	A
	RONNIE WOOD	gtr	A

ALBUMS: 1(A)   THESE BIRDS ARE DANGEROUS
                               (Demon WEST 901) 1985 SC
       2(A)   SAY THOSE MAGIC WORDS (Beat Records BLP 3) 1997
       3(A)   THE COLLECTORS' GUIDE TO RARE
             BRITISH BIRDS (CD)   (Deram 564 139 2) 1999

NB: (1) is a mini-LP. (3) is a Dutch CD release, including numerous backing tracks, unreleased mixes, acetates etc. There's also a good vinyl compilation *Birds*, which includes all their 7" tracks including their rare French-only EP from 1966 and a couple of unreleased studio tracks and alternate versions.

                                               HCP

45s: You're On My Mind/
        You Don't Love Me (You Don't Care)(Decca F 12031) 1964 R3 -
        Leaving Here/Next In Line   (Decca F 12140) 1965 R2 45
        No Good Without You Baby/
        How Can It Be   (Decca F 12257) 1965 R2 -
   α   Say Those Magic Words/
        Daddy Daddy   (Reaction 591 005) 1966 -
   β   Leaving Here/
        (Flip by different artist)   (Decca FR 13864) 1979 -

NB: α as Birds Birds. β is a reissue.

Although this West Drayton band, originally known as the Thunderbirds, set out playing R'n'B and Motown-influenced music some of their later records will be of interest to collectors of psychedelia. All of their 45s are now rare and sought-after, especially the Reaction one.

The Bird's three 45s feature frantic guitar work and together with McKenzie's powerful vocals, confirm them as one of the most talented UK mid-sixties bands. In 1966 they changed their name to **Birds Birds** to record the now mega-rare *Say Those Magic Words* 45, which also features additional guitar work on the flip from **Jeff Beck**.

The band attracted public attention as a result of a legal battle with America's Byrds over the rights to the name and also appeared in a horror movie, 'The Deadly Bees' singing *That's All I Need You For*. When they split in 1966 Gardner and Wood joined **Creation**. Later Gardner achieved some success with **Ashton, Gardner and Dyke**. Wood, of course, achieved fame with **The Jeff Beck Group**, **The Faces** and **The Rolling Stones**.

In Australia, a group using **The Birds** name, recorded versions of *No Good Without You* and *(Say Those) Magic Words*, but were otherwise unconnected with the UK band.

In 1985 Edsel compiled a 12" EP/mini-album comprising **The Bird's** three 45s, whilst these tracks plus the **Birds Birds** 45 and acetate demos of *You Don't Love Me*, *You're On My Mind*, *Daddy Daddy* and *The Doll Who Said No* have also resurfaced on the recent *Say Those Magic Words* (LP). Even better however, is the Deram CD, *Collectors Guide To...*, which includes eighteen tracks - all their singles, early demos and plenty of unreleased material/backing tracks, etc.

Kim Gardner died on 24 October 2001 after losing a three year battle with cancer.

Not surprisingly, given their good reputation, their work has featured quite prominently on compilations:- *You Don't Love Me* on *Maximum R'n'B* (CD); *Leaving Here* on *Mod Scene, Vol. 2* (CD), *Weekend Starts Here* (LP) and *Hard-Up Heroes* (2-LP); *Say Those Magic Words* and *Daddy Daddy* on *Nowhere Men Vol. 1* (LP & CD) and *English Freakbeat, Vol. 1* (CD); *Say Those Magic Words* and *No Good Without You Baby* on the 4-CD box set *Nuggets 11*; *No Good Without You Baby* on *Perfumed Garden, Vol. 1* (LP & CD), *The Freakbeat Scene* (CD); *You're On My Mind* on *Pop Inside The '60s, Vol. 2* (CD), *Sixties Explosion, Vol. 1* (CD) and *Sixties Lost And Found, Vol. 3* (LP); *You're On My Mind* and *You Don't Love Me* on *Broken Dreams, Vol. 2* (LP), *Incredible Sound Show Stories, Vol. 5* (LP), *The R&B Scene* (CD) and *Sixties Years, Vol. 2 - French 60's EP Collection* (CD); *Say Those Magic Words* on *The Seventh Son* (LP); *How Can It Be* and *No Good Without You Baby* on *Broken Dreams, Vol. 4* (LP); *You Don't Love Me*, *Say Those Magic Words* and *You're On My Mind* on *Beat It* (CD); and *You're On My Mind*, *You Don't Love Me*, *No Good Without You Baby*, *How Can It Be*, *Leaving Here*, *Next In Line*, *Say Those Magic Words*, *Daddy Daddy* and *The Doll Said No* on *Hard Up Heroes, Vol. 6* (CD). (VJ/GMs/JM)

Birds Of A Feather

Personnel: DOREEN CHANTER
              IRENE CHANTER

ALBUM: 1 BIRDS OF A FEATHER   (Page One POLS 027) 1970 R1

45s: Blacksmith Blues/
        Sing My Song And Pray   (Page One POF 156) 1969
        All God's Children Got Soul/
        Get It Together   (Page One POF 179) 1970
        You Know Me Better/Summer Has Gone   (Jam JAM 23) 1972
        Thank You/
        Baby Don't You Bring Me Down   (DJM DJS 10243) 1972

Originally known as **The Chanters**, the group came from Fulham in London. In the sixties and seventies, apart from **Sue and Sunny**, they were one of the most prolific vocal backing teams in the UK working with everybody from **John Cale** to Stomu Yamashta. Their singing credits are awesome and include another three albums as The Chanter Sisters. (MK/JM)

Jane Birkin and Serge Gainsbourg

ALBUM: 1 JANE BIRKIN AND SERGE GAINSBOURG
                              (Fontana STL 5493) 1969 R1

NB: (1) reissued (Philips 558 830-2) 1998

HCP

45s: Je T'Aime Moi Non Plus/
        Jane B (Some P/S)   (Fontana TF 1042) 1969 2
        Je T'Aime Moi Non Plus/Jane B   (Major Minor MM 645) 1969 1
        Je T'Aime Moi Non Plus/Jane B (PS)   (Antic K 11511) 1974 31

Jane Birkin was British - hence their inclusion here. *Je T'Aime*, inevitably banned by the BBC, was the ultimate slow, smoochy, party record in this era. It was very catchy and very sexy. It does not feature on the album, which includes the 'B' side *Jane B*. It and another cut *La Chanson de Slogan* are equally erotic and both are also duets. The remainder of the album alternates between solo contributions from the two singers.

Birkin recorded a further album *Di Doo Dah* in 1973, which was also reissued (Philips 558 829-2) in the late nineties. (VJ)

Birmingham

Personnel incl: DAVE PEACE   A

ALBUM: 1(A)   BIRMINGHAM   (Grosvenor GRS 1011) 1971 R2

A privately-pressed ultra-rarity by yes (a Birmingham-based outfit), which included **Dave Peace** who'd recorded an album for Saga with **The Dave Peace Quartet** a couple of years earlier. The *Birmingham* album is according to 'Record Collector' an uneasy mixture of pop, blues, soul and heavy rock. There's an hilarious attempt at **Hendrix**'s *Stone Free* but a spirited attempt at **Trapeze**'s *Black Cloud*. (VJ)

Birth

Personnel:			
PAUL DAVIS	drms	AB
BRUCE GOODING	gtr, vcls	AB
BILL FORD	vcls, hrmnca	A
MIKE WILBAND	bs, vcls	AB
KEITH ASHWIN	vcls	B

Birth formed in Bath in mid-1968 as Revolution, a band influenced initially by the likes of Jefferson Airplane and **Tomorrow**. Their early shows featured mime, lights, smoke bombs and other props as they performed their self-penned song cycle *The Alchemist*. In 1969 under new management they signed up with Bristol promoters Plastic Dog who also had **Stackridge** on their books at the time. They changed their name to **Birth** and gigged across the UK supporting the likes of **The Who** and **Yes.** By now their music had hardened up to become a sot of proto-punk, which suited their stage antics. After a very successful Marquee debut in early 1970 Bill Ford left thinking the band were becoming too commercial. He was replaced by Keith Ashwin, who sadly died in 2000. The band soldiered on for a couple of years with various line-up changes, adding a female vocalist at one point, before splitting up.

Although they never recorded, apart from a few private pressing they were said to be a great, if unpredictable, live act considered by many to be ahead of their time. Punk would have suited them well.

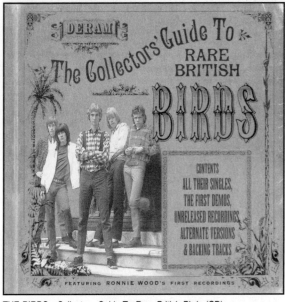

THE BIRDS - Collectors Guide To Rare British Birds (CD).

All continued in the music business sporadically but not for a career, except for Gooding who became a sough-after Sound Engineer and Tour Manager. In 1999 they reformed for a one-off concert in Bath, which was a huge success. (BF)

Tommy Bishop's Ricochets

45:    I Should Have Known/
On The Other Hand   (Decca F 12238) 1965 SC

A little known beat group. (MWh)

Cilla Black

HCP

ALBUMS: 1 CILLA (mono/stereo)
(up to   (Parlophone PMC1243/PCS 3063) 1965 SC 5
1976)   2 CILLA SINGS A RAINBOW
    (mono/stereo)   (Parlophone PMC/PCS 7004) 1966 SC 4
  3 SHER-OO!
    (mono/stereo)   (Parlophone PMC/PCS 7041) 1968 SC 7
  4 THE BEST OF CILLA BLACK (compilation)
    (mono/stereo)   (Parlophone PMC/PCS 7041) 1968 SC 21
  5 SURROUND YOURSELF WITH CILLA
    (mono/stereo)   (Parlophone PMC/PCS 7079) 1968 SC -
  6 SWEET INSPIRATION   (Parlophone PCS 7103) 1969 42
  7 IMAGES   (Parlophone PCS 7128) 1970 -
  8 YOU'RE MY WORLD (compilation)
        (Regal Starline SRS 5044) 1970 -
  9 YESTERDAY (compilation)
        (World Record Club ST 1100) 1971 -
  10 DAY BY DAY WITH CILLA (Parlophone PCS 7155) 1973 -
  11 IN MY LIFE   (EMI EMC 3031) 1974 -
  12 IT MAKES ME FEEL GOOD
        (EMI EMC 3108) 1976 - (with inner sleeve)

NB: (1) issued in mono/stereo on a yellow/black label. (1) reissued on vinyl (World Record Club STP 1036) 1969. (2) issued in mono/stereo on a yellow/black label. (2) reissued on vinyl (Sounds Superb SPR 90062) 1973. (3) issued in mono/stereo on a yellow/black label. (3) reissued on vinyl as *Step Inside Love* (Sounds Superb SPR 90019) 1973. (4) issued in mono/stereo on a yellow/black label. (9) reissued on vinyl (C5 C5 547) 1989. *25 Wonderful Tracks* (Regal Starline TC EXC 1009) 1972 is also worth a mention. It's a cassette compilation of (2) and (5) above. There have also been some vinyl compilations: *The Very Best Of Cilla Black* (EMI EMTV 38) 1983 (No 20), which was reissued again (Music For Pleasure MFP 41 5663) 1984 and *25th Anniversary Album* (2-LP) (Music For Pleasure DI 1134) 1988. CD compilations have included: *The Best Of The EMI Years* (EMI CDEMS 1140) 1991, *Love, Cilla* (EMI CDEMS 1508) 1993, *Cilla's World* (Silva Treasury SILVAD 3004) 1993, *Simply The Best* (Disky WM 860022) 1995 and *The George Martin/Abbey Road Decade - 1963-1973* (3-CD box set) (EMI 7243 8 57053 28) 1997, which comes with a booklet. *The Best Of 1963-1978* (EMI 584 1242) 2004 is a definitive 3-CD collection.

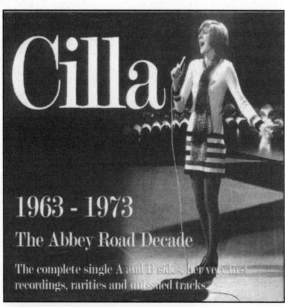

CILLA BLACK - The Abbey Road Decade (CD).

HCP

EPs: 1 ANYONE WHO HAD A HEART (Anyone Who Had A
(up to   Heart/Just For You/Love Of The Loved/Shy Of Love)
1977)   (Parlophone GEP 8901) 1964 SC 5
     2 IT'S FOR YOU (It's For You/He Won't Ask Me/You're My
       World/Suffer Now I Must)
           (Parlophone GEP 8916) 1964 SC 12
     3 CILLA'S HITS (Don't Answer/The Right One Is
       Left/Alfie/Night Time Is Here)
           (Parlophone GEP 8954) 1966 SC 6
     4 TIME FOR CILLA (Abyssinian Secret/Trees And
       Loneliness/There I Go/Time)
           (Parlophone GEP 8967) R1 1967
     5 YOU'RE MY WORLD (You're My World/It's For
       You/Alfie/Love's Just A Broken Heart)
           (EMI 'Nut Series' EMI 2698) (PS) 1977

HCP

45s: Love Of The Loved/Shy Of Love (Parlophone R 5065) 1963 35
(up to Anyone Who Had A Heart/
1976)   Just For You   (Parlophone R 5101) 1964 1
      You're My World/Suffer Now I Must (Parlophone R 5133) 1964 1
      It's For You/he Won't Ask Me   (Parlophone R 5162) 1964 7
      You've Lost That Loving Feeling/
      Is It Love?   (Parlophone R 5225) 1965 2
      I've Been Wrong Before/
      I Don't Want To Know   (Parlophone R 5265) 1965 17
      Love's Just A Broken Heart/
      Yesterday   (Parlophone R 5395) 1966 5
      Alfie/Night Time Is Here   (Parlophone R 5427) 1966 9
      Don't Answer Me/
      The Right One Is Left   (Parlophone R 5463) 1966 6
      A Fool Am I (Dimmelo Parlami)/
      For No One   (Parlophone R 5515) 1966 13
      What Good Am I?/Over My Head (Parlophone R 5608) 1967 24
      I Only Live To Love You/
      From Now On   (Parlophone R 5652) 1967 26
      Step Inside Love/
      I Couldn't Take My Eyes Off You (Parlophone R 5674) 1968 8
      Where Is Tomorrow/
      Work Is A Four Letter Year (Parlophone R 5706) 1968 39
      Surround Yourself With Sorrow/
      London Bridge   (Parlophone R 5759) 1969 3
      Conversations/Liverpool Lullaby (Parlophone R 5785) 1969 7
      If I Thought You'd Ever Change Your Mind/
      It Feels So Good   (Parlophone R 5820) 1969 20
      Child Of Mine/
      That's Why I Love You   (Parlophone R 5879) 1970 -
      Something Tells Me (Something's Gonna Happen Tonight)/
      La La La Lu   (Parlophone R 5924) 1971 3
      The World I Wish For You/
      Down In The City   (Parlophone R 5924) 1972 -
      You, You, You/Silly Wasn't It? (Parlophone R 5972) 1972 -
      Baby We Can't Go On/Someone   (EMI EMI 2107) 1974 36
      I'll Have To say I Love You In A Song/
      Never Run Out (Of You)   (EMI EMI 2169) 1974 -
      He Was A Writer/
      Anything That You Might Say (EMI EMI 2227) 1974 -
      Alfie Darling/Little Bit Of Understanding (EMI EMI 2278) 1975 -
      I'll Take A Tango/
      To Know Him Is To Love Him (EMI EMI 2328) 1975 -
      Little Things Mean A Lot/It's Now (EMI EMI 2438) 1976 -
      Easy In Your Company/I Believe (EMI EMI 2532) 1976 -

NB: The flexidisc *The Sound Of The Stars* (Lyntone LYN 995) 1966 which was available through 'Disc and Music Echo' includes excerpts of **Cilla** talking to The Bachelors.

Cilla Black was the first and only woman performer to emerge from Liverpool in the Merseybeat era. Indeed the first lady of Liverpool also had the distinction of sharing the same manager (Brian Epstein), producer (**George Martin**) and stage as **The Beatles** and **Paul McCartney** also wrote songs for her. She was also the second biggest selling music star to come out of Liverpool after **The Beatles**. When she was past her prime as a recording artist she became one of Britain's most popular television stars.

Cilla Black was born on 27 May 1943 as Priscilla White in Liverpool. It was whilst working as a cloak room attendant in her lunch hour at Liverpool's Cavern Club in 1963 whilst working as a typist that **Cilla**

CILLA BLACK - Surround Yourself With Cilla (LP).

appeared as a guest singer with various groups (including **The Big Three** and **Rory Storm and The Hurricanes**) and Brian Epstein got to hear of her. On of her admirers was Bill Harry who published the music paper 'Mersey Beat' at the time. She was not a natural singer or performer and her 'girl next door' look presented a challenge which Epstein rose to with perfection. **George Martin**'s role as her producer was also crucial in her success. It was really Epstein's management skills, **Martin**'s production skills and her tenacity that made her a formidable ballad singer.

Her debut single was a brassy re-work of a second-rate **Lennon-McCartney** song *Love Of The Loved*. Nonetheless, it entered the lower reaches of the charts. It was a style change to the Burt Bacharach/Hal David song (previously recorded by Dionne Warwick) *Anyone Who Had A Heart* that witnessed her emergence as a powerful ballad singer. Not only was it a No 1, the single became the biggest-selling by a female artist in England, selling 800,000 copies in England and a further million internationally. The follow-up *You're My World* was an English version of a song originally written in Italian. The passionate, orchestrated ballad brought her another massive No 1.

Her fourth single was another **Paul McCartney** composition, this time a jazz waltz ballad called *It's For You*, although it didn't sell as well as its two predecessors peaking at No 7. By now, though, she was firmly established as one of the best female singers of the sixties. In late 1964 she made her film debut in 'Ferry Cross The Mersey', which starred **Gerry and The Pacemakers**. **Cilla** sang *Is It Love?* in the film and this can be heard on the soundtrack *Ferry Cross The Mersey* (Columbia 33SX 1693/SCX 3544) released in 1965. The record has been reissued on a number of occasions on vinyl (Castle Showcase SHLP 102) 1986 and (BGO BGOLP 10) 1988 and on a digipak CD (EMI DORIG 114) 1997.

One of her best singles was her soulful cover of The Righteous Brothers' *You've Lost That Lovin' Feelin'*, which propelled her to the No 2 spot in the charts in early 1965. She followed this with a fine interpretation of Randy Newman's *I've Been Wrong Before*, which reached No 17. However, for the remainder of 1965 she stopped recording to work on what would be her only film 'Work Is A Four Letter Word'. This was a futurist science-fiction adventure involving the use of hallucinogenic mushrooms based on a play by Henry Livings, in which she co-starred with David Warner, although it wasn't well received when it was finally released in 1967. She also went to the States in 1965, appearing on 'The Ed Sullivan Show' and 'The Tonight Show'. Here in the UK, she performed on a late 1965 TV Special 'The Beatles: The Music Of Lennon and McCartney'. By now she was one of only two acts still personally managed by Brian Epstein. Indeed, after **The Beatles**, she was the most successful act from Liverpool.

Black enjoyed two major hits in 1966, *Alfie* and *Don't Answer Me*, which both made the UK Top Ten. It seems she was beginning to develop doubts about Epstein's management and considered, but initially shelved, plans to switch to Robert Stigwood. Of course, this all became irrelevant with Epstein's death in the summer of 1967. The songwriter Bobby Willis, whom she later married in 1969, now guided her career towards television work and she launched her own successful variety series 'Cilla'. It was another

Paul McCartney song *Step Inside Love* that revived her singing career, taking her back into the Top Ten in 1968. Further Top Ten hits followed in 1969 with *Surround Yourself With Sorrow* and *Conversations*. Her final Top Ten hit was *Something Tells Me (Something's Gonna Happen Tonight)*, which peaked at No 3 in late 1971.

Black continued to record throughout the seventies, but the focus of her career switched from the recording studio to the television commitments and live performances. Of her seventies albums *In My Life* is a notable collection of her past songs. Most people, though, will now associate her with two major TV shows 'Surprise, Surprise' and 'Blind Date', which made her one of the most popular and highest paid family entertainers in the music business. The latter secured her an award from the British Academy of Film and Television Arts.

In 1993, she released an album, a retrospective video, published a book and presented an anniversary special - all to commemorate her 30 years in the music business. Each entity was entitled *Through The Years*. The 3-CD retrospective *The George Martin/Abbey Road Decade: 1963-1973* contains 14 of her Top 20 hit singles, including the highly-touted Beat-era ballads *Anyone Who Had A Heart* and *You're My World*. It also contains lots of harder-to-track-down 'B' sides, EP and album tracks and there's a whole disc of previously unreleased or very rare material, including **Paul McCartney's** original demo for *Step Inside Love*.

In 2003, during her 40th year in showbiz, EMI released a 80-track definitive set *The Best Of 1963-1978*. As well as her hit singles, this includes several covers - most of which come off well. Harry Nillson's *I'll Take A Tango*, David Cassidy's *Day Dreamer*, **Badfinger's** *Without You* and Bread's *Make It With You* are prime examples of this. Following its release she re-signed to the label and recorded her 15th studio album *Beginnings*. She also published a revealing autobiography 'What's It All About?' which became a Top Five best-seller.

In 2004, she became a grandmother and gave a number of impromptu performances with her friend Sir Cliff Richard. She also starred in a specially commissioned 2-hour Christmas spectacular 'Cilla Live' for the digital channel LIVINGtv. She remains one of Britain's most popular entertainers. (VJ)

Tony Blackburn

ALBUMS: 1 TONY BLACKBURN SINGS   (MGM C(S) 8062) 1968 SC
(up to   2 TONY BLAKBURN MEETS MATT MONRO
1976)   (Fontana SFL 13161) 1970

NB: On (2) **Blackburn** and Matt Monro contribute six tracks each.

HCP

45s:	Don't Get Off That Train/		
(up to	Just To Be With You Again	(Fontana TF 562) 1965	-
1976)	Is There Another Way To Love You/		
	Here Today Gone Tomorrow	(Fontana TF 601) 1965	-
	Green Light/Winter Is Through	(Fontana TF 729) 1966	-
	So Much Love/In The Night	(MGM MGM 1375) 1967	31
	She's My Girl/Closer To A Dream	(MGM MGM 1394) 1968	-
	It's Only Love/Janie	(MGM MGM 1467) 1969	42
	Blessed Are The Lonely/Wait For More	(Polydor 56360) 1969	-
	Is It Me Is It You/Happy	(RCA RCA 2067) 1971	-
	Chop Chop/You Were A Dream	(RCA RCA 2109) 1971	-

Tony Blackburn was born as Kenneth Blackburn on 29 January 1943 in Guilford, Surrey. He first became involved in the music scene in the late fifties as rhythm guitarist and singer in the Jan Ralfini Orchestra. **Al Stewart** was the lead guitarist in the same band. He was a dancehall singer in Bournemouth in the early sixties but then joined pirate radio station Radio Caroline partly in the hope of getting closer to record companies so he could record. It worked, too, mainly because he was a DJ record companies approached him. There was a little flurry in the late sixties of DJs recording discs and at the time he was a very high profile DJ. As a singer he recorded some pretty undistinguished pop songs, two of which were minor hits and a couple of albums (including one shared with Matt Monro). On the albums he tried to record some of his favourite songs but it doesn't come off. More significant was his career as a pirate radio DJ in the sixties. First with Radio Caroline and then with Radio London he played a key role in introducing black music to this country. When the

Wilson government outlawed pirate radio he transferred to Radio One and had the distinction of playing its first record - **The Move's** *Flowers In The Rain*. He continued to advocate soul music at Radio One and also advanced the disco movement in the mid-seventies. After leaving Radio One in 1984 he worked for Capital Radio for 19 years. He's also worked for London's Capital Gold and Manchester's Jazz FM. In the eighties he pioneered pop-soul, but when he was becoming less prominent in the public eye a successful appearance on 'I'm A Celebrity.?.Get Me Out Of Here' (the reality TV show set in the Australian outback) in 2002 made him a household name again and he enjoyed the same profile for a while as he had as a 'Top Of The Pops' presenter. (VJ)

Black Cat Bones

Personnel:	DEREK BROOKS	gtr	A
	STUART BROOKS	bs	A
	PHIL LENOIR	drms	A
	STEVE MILLINER	piano	A
	SIMON KIRKE	drms	A
	PAUL KOSSOFF	gtr	A

ALBUM: 1(A) BARBED WIRE SANDWICH (Nova SDN 15) 1970 R2
NB: (1) issued on Decca in Germany. Much later it was repressed in limited quantities in the USA. (1) reissued on CD (See For Miles SEECD 405) 1994.

This hard-rock/blues outfit is principally notable for the presence of **Paul Kossoff** and Simon Kirke, who later formed **Free**. Their album, overseen by Decca's in-house hippie David Hitchcock (**Mellow Candle**, **Caravan**, **Aardvark**), is rare but unexceptional.

Fans might also want to track down *Come Aboard QE2!* (Sceptre SALR 1216), an obscure promotional album designed to promote the launch of the QE2 cruise ship in 1969. Though mostly spoken, when the tour reaches the on-board discotheque the DJ announces a blistering piece of psych from the band, which is not on their album.

Some band members were later involved in **Leaf Hound** and Steve Milliner went on to **Aardvark**. Paul Tiller, long-time harpist for **Downliners Sect**, also joined **Black Cat Bones** for a while.

They contributed a typical British blues cut, *Please Tell Me Baby*, to *The Nova Sampler* (LP) in 1970. More recently, *Warmth Of The Day* has been compiled on *Alphabeat (Pop, Psych and Prog 1967-1970)* (CD). (VJ/RMJ)

Black Claw

Personnel:	MIKE BURT	drms	A
	HARVEY HINSLEY	gtr	A
	CHRIS 'CHAS' HODGES	piano, gtr	A
	DAVE PEACOCK	bs	A

ALBUM: 1(A) COUNTRY PIE (Bell) 1970

45: Across The Great Divide/Sally (Bell BLL 1089) 1970

Black Claw is most notable for including future **Heads, Hands and Feet** member Chris Hodges and **Hot Chocolate** member Harvey Hinsley.

Chris Hodges, and Dave Peacock eventually found fame and fortune as Chas & Dave. Mike Burt also went on to play with Chas & Dave. (VJ/JM)

Black Country Three

| Personnel incl: | JON RAVEN | A |
| | MICHAEL RAVEN | A |

ALBUM: 1(A) BLACK COUNTRY THREE
(Transatlantic TRA 140) 1966 R3

This is one of the rarest Transatlantic albums and the group's vinyl debut. Fans of this genre consider this one of the hidden treasures of the mid-sixties British folk scene. (VJ)

Black Dyke Mills Band

45: Thingumybob / Yellow Submarine (Apple APPLE 4) 1968 R1

Both of these jazzy instrumentals were written and produced by **Paul McCartney**. The 45 reflected his nostalgic fondness for traditional brass bands. (VJ/RMJ)

Blackfoot Sue

Personnel:	DAVE FARMER	drms	A
	TOM FARMER	bs, keyb'ds, vcls	A
	EDDIE GOLGA	lead gtr, keyb'ds	A
	ALAN JONES	gtr, vcls	A

ALBUMS:	1(A)	NOTHING TO HIDE	(Jam JAL 104) 1973 SC
(up to	2( )	STICK WITH ME AND YOU'LL WEAR DIAMONDS	
1976)			(DJM) 1973
	3( )	STRANGERS	(Jam) 1974
	4(A)	GUN RUNNING	(DJM DJLPS 455) 1975 R1

HCP

45s:	Standing In The Road/Celestial Pain	(Jam JAM 13) 1972 4
(up to	Sing Don't Speak/2 B Free	(Jam JAM 29) 1972 36
1976)	Summer/Morning Light	(Jam JAM 44) 1973 -
	Get It All To Me/My Oh My	(Jam JAM 53) 1973 -
	Bye Bye Birmingham/Messiah	(DJM DJS 10296) 1974 -
	You Need Love/Tobago Rose	(DJM DJS 10326) 1974 -
	Moonshine/Corrie	(DJM DJS 10411) 1975 -
Reissue:	Standing In The Road/Summer	(Old Gold OG 9037) 1979 -

This Birmingham band was centred around the Farmer brothers and originally known as Gift. For a while, particularly with *Standing In The Road*, they successfully appealed to both rock and pop audiences, but the onset of punk in 1977 killed them off. Their *Gun Running* album is of interest to collectors because it was withdrawn soon after release.

Tom Farmer and Eddie Golga later formed the band Liner and released an album *1979* (Atlantic K 50553) in 1979. (VJ/JM)

The Black Knights

Personnel:	KENNY GRIFFITHS	lead gtr	AB
	BILL KENNY	bs	AB
	DEREK SMALLRIDGE	drms	A
	ALLAN SCHRODER	drms	B

45: I Gotta Woman/Angel Of Love (Columbia DB 7443) 1965 SC

An undistinguished Merseybeat group whose main claim to fame was an appearance as an 'up and coming' beat group in the film 'Ferry Cross The Mersey'. Both songs were written by Ken Griffiths.

BLACK SABBATH - Black Sabbath (LP).

Compilation appearances have included: *I Gotta Woman* and *Angel Of Love* on *Liverpool 1963-1968* (CD) and *Liverpool 1963-1968, Vol. 1* (LP); and *I Gotta Woman* on *Beat At Abbey Road* (CD) and *Ferry Cross The Mersey* (LP). (VJ/AD)

Ritchie Blackmore Orchestra

45:	Getaway/Little Brown Jug	(Oriole CB 314) 1965	R3

This obscure 45 was the first solo recording by this future **Deep Purple** member who, of course, later went on to have his own band Ritchie Blackmore's Rainbow. Inevitably, it's now ultra-rare and extremely expensive to purchase. Mick Underwood and Chas Hodges, who'd earlier played with **Blackmore** in The Outlaws were also on the 45. Both sides were terrible instrumentals. *Little Brown Jug* was a Glenn Miller tune.

There are also a couple of CDs of his sixties recordings - *Rock Profile* (Connoisseur Collection) 199? and *Take It! - Sessions 63/68* (r.p.m. RPM 120) 1994, which includes many obscurities that were only issued abroad at the time.

Compilation appearances include: *Getaway* and *Little Brown Jug* on *Ritchie Blackmore - Rock Profile, Vol. 2* (CD) and *Ritchie Blackmore - Take It! - Sessions 63 - 68* (CD). (VJ)

Black Sabbath

Personnel:

GEEZER (TERRY) BUTLER	bs	A
TONY IOMMI	gtr	A
OZZY OSBOURNE	vcls	A
BILL WARD	drms	A

					HCP
ALBUMS:	1(A)	BLACK SABBATH	(Vertigo VO 6) 1970	R1	8
(up to	2(A)	PARANOID	(Vertigo 6360 011) 1970	R1	1
1976)	3(A)	MASTER OF REALITY			
		(w/poster)	(Vertigo 6360 050) 1971	R2	5
	4(A)	BLACK SABBATH, VOLUME 4			
			(Vertigo 6360 071) 1972	R1/SC	8
	5(A)	SABBATH BLOODY SABBATH	(Vertigo 6360 115) 1973		4
	6(A)	SABOTAGE	(NEMS 9119 001) 1975		7
	7(A)	WE SOLD OUR SOULS FOR ROCK'N'ROLL			
		(2-LP Compilation)	(NEMS 6641 335) 1975		35
	8(A)	TECHNICAL ECSTACY	(Vertigo 9102 750) 1976		13

NB: (1)-(5) reissued on WWA in 1973 and by NEMS in 1976 and again in 1980. *Technical Ecstacy* also reissued on vinyl (Vertigo PRICE 40) in 1983 and on CD (Essential! ESM CD 328) 1995. There's also a *Greatest Hits* compilation issued by NEMS (NEL 6009) in 1977 and then reissued again in 1980 and *Blackest Sabbath* (Vertigo 838 818 1) 1989. (1) reissued on CD (Sanctuary CMTCD 003) 2000. (2) reissued on CD (Sanctuary CMTCD 004) 2000 and again on CD (Sanctuary SMRCD 032). (3) reissued on CD (Sanctuary CMTCD 005) 2000 and again on CD (Sanctuary SMRCD 033). (4) reissued on CD (Sanctuary CMTCD 006) 2000 and again on CD (Sanctuary SMRCD 034). (5) reissued on CD (Sanctuary CMTCD 028) 2000. (6) reissued on CD (Sanctuary CMTCD 029) 2000. (8) reissued on CD (CMTCD 030) 2000. There's a 7-LP box set *The Sabbath Collection* (Nems BSBLP 001) 1985 and a limited edition (3,000 numbered copies) 6-CD box set complete with a badge and book, *The Black Sabbath CD Collection* (Castle BSBCD 001) 1988. *The Ozzy Osbourne Years* (Essential! ESBCD 142) 1991 squeezes their first six albums onto three CDs and comes with an informative 20-page booklet about the band. Alternatively (1)-(8) are all available individually on CD. People wanting an introduction to their music should check out *Between Heaven And Hell: 1970-1983* (Raw CD 104) 1995, which covers most of their prime cuts. *Live At Last* (Essential! ESMCD 331) 1996, which was recorded during the band's *Vol. 4* tour but was not released until 1980, is now available on CD. Many of the tracks come, as one would expect, from *Vol. 4*, but a few classics like *Paranoid*, *Sweet Leaf* and a preview of *Killing Yourself To Live* are thrown in too. The recording quality could be better. All eight albums are available on an 8-CD set (Castle CMXBX 305). *Under The Wheels Of Confusion* (Essential ESMCD 419) 2005 is a 4-CD box set with a 60-page colour booklet.

				HCP
45s:	Evil Woman/Wicked World	(Fontana TF 1067) 1970	R2	-
(up to	Evil Woman/Wicked World	(Vertigo V 2) 1970	SC	-
1976)	Paranoid/The Wizard	(Vertigo 6059 010) 1970	SC	4
	Tomorrow's Dream/			
	Laguna Sunrise	(Vertigo 6059 061) 1972	SC	-
α	Children Of The Grave/			
	(flip by **Status Quo**)	(Phonogram DJ 005) 1972	R4	

BLACK SABBATH - Paranoid (LP).

	Sabbath Bloody Sabbath/Changes	(WWA WWS 002) 1973 -
	Am I Going Insane (Radio)/	
	Hole In The Sky	(NEMS 6165 300) 1975 -
Reissue:	Paranoid/Sabbath Bloody Sabbath	(NEMS NES 112) 1976 -

NB: α 100 promo copies only.

Black Sabbath has been enormously influential in the development of heavy metal music. Building on the blues-rock of late sixties bands like **Cream** and Blue Cheer they developed a heavy, doom-laden yet ingenious form of rock that became known as heavy metal a style that continues to appeal to millions of music fans today.

Black Sabbath began their long musical journey in 1967 in Birmingham when schoolmates Iommi, Butler, Osbourne and Ward formed a blues band called Polka Tulk, although they soon changed their name to Earth. By now they were playing a sort of jazz-blues fusion and toured the UK and Europe extensively. Back in London their manager Jim Simpson encouraged them to change name again in 1969 to **Black Sabbath** (the title of one of their early songs) in view of their interest in the occult which fitted in well with the emerging underground movement's interest in mysticism.

After a further year's hard touring during most of 1969 they signed to Philips' Records' subsidiary Fontana in December of that year. Their debut single in January 1970, *Evil Woman*, was a blues/pop style song, which had been a US hit for Crow. By no means exceptional it made little impact here, despite a reissue on Philips' new 'progressive' Vertigo label a few months later.

The reception that awaited their debut album *Black Sabbath* was a very different story. Full of occult imagery it was a prototype heavy metal album. Despite receiving awful reviews the fans the band had built up during their relentless gigging rushed out to buy the album. It got to No 9 in the UK Charts and stayed in them for the next five months. Musically it was pretty clumsy, full of megalithic riffs, though these would become the band's trademark. Aside from the title track other stronger moments included a 10-minute bluesy workout and doomy version of *The Warning*, which had earlier been a 45 for **Aynsley Dunbar's Retaliation**. Evil Woman is a weak attempt at commercial rock and nowhere near as good as the later song of the same name by **Electric Light Orchestra**.

Their second album, *Paranoid*, did even better. By the time of its release the title track was already a Top 5 hit single in the UK. It's a three-minute high energy assault on the senses. The album, which also contained previous live favourites like *War Pigs* and *Iron Man*, topped the UK Charts for two weeks and is generally regarded as an early heavy metal classic.

Next came the inevitable attempt to crack the US market. It's very riffy on tracks like *Sweet Leaf*, *Lord Of This World* and *Children Of The Grave*; *Embryo* and *Orchid* are acoustic and *Solitude* is melancholic. They toured American colleges in late 1970 and then Warner Brothers released their debut album which climbed to No 23, staying in the US Charts for 65 weeks. *Paranoid* climbed to No 12 and was in the Charts for as long as its

BLACK SABBATH - We Sold Our Soul For Rock 'N' Roll (2-LP).

predecessor and the title track had preceded it to No 61 in the Singles Chart.

Their third album, *Master Of Reality* in June 1971, contained their popular anthem, *Children Of The Grave*, which was preceded by a brief classical guitar instrumental, *Orchid* on which Tony Iommi turned in a good performance. Certainly a varied album, it contains arse-kickers like *Sweet Leaf* and the slower, almost ballad-like *Solitude* as well as a couple of short instrumentals. The first pressings came in a box sleeve but subsequent reissues came in regular packaging. Copies with the elusive poster are quite collectable. It peaked at No 5 here and No 8 in the US.

A 45, *Tomorrow's Dream*, their first for two years, was released in October 1972 as a prelude to their fourth album. It was pretty standard fare but surprisingly failed to chart. The flip side, *Laguna Sunrise*, was an out of character acoustic instrumental! The 45 is now scarce.

Early pressings of *Black Sabbath, Volume 4* came with a free colour booklet with great live shots of the band, which is now hard to locate. The album appeared very briefly on a 'spaceship' label and copies of this are very collectable and in the R3 category. The subsequent 'spiral' issue is R1. The title was a direct lift from **Led Zeppelin**'s numbering system and musically the band seems on this album to be heading in that direction. It's more melodic than its predecessors. *Wheels Of Confusion* has a slow bluesy opening. *Supernaut* is a funky, rocky number and *Snowblind* is based on a simple progression. This was originally to have been the title of the album, but with its link to a powdery stimulant someone clearly had second thoughts. Its epic is usually considered to be a lumbering ballad called *Changes,* which is full of piano and mellotrons. *FX* experiments with echo chambers. *Cornucopia* sets out riffy but then becomes melodic and the closing cut *Under The Sun* is a slow bombastic number. Again the album sold well, peaking at No 8 in the UK and No 13 in the US.

After this the band replaced manager Jim Simpson with Patrik Meehan and recorded *Sabbath Bloody Sabbath*. Originally intended for issue on Vertigo, it actually appeared a few months later with the rest of their album back catalogue on the newly formed WWA (World Wide Artists) label. Many fans cite this album as their favourite. The title cut contains a memorable riff. *A Natural Acrobat*, *Killing Yourself To Live* and *Looking For Today* all feature fine wah wah guitar from Iommi. **Rick Wakeman** added keyboards to good effect on *Sabbra Cadabra* and *Spiral Architect* utilises orchestral effects. The album peaked at No 4 here and No 11 in the US. WWA also released the title track on a 45 backed by *Changes* from the previous album, but it sold poorly.

The band again changed management replacing Meehan with Don Arden, whilst Jim Simpson took legal action over what he considered to be a breach of contract. This effectively prevented the band either recording or performing for almost two years during which their new WWA label went under.

When matters were finally resolved in September 1975, their UK contract (and back catalogue) was transferred to NEMS and they embarked on a

major UK tour. Their next album, *Sabotage*, which appeared the same month, was certainly their most disappointing to date. Aside from the lengthy *Megalomania*, the only other track of note was *Am I Going Insane (Radio)*, which was also released in edited form as a 45. The 45 flopped but the album got to No 7 in the UK and No 28 in the US, although it didn't spend many weeks in either Chart.

The relationship with NEMS also proved brief, ending when the label reissued the first four Vertigo albums and a double-CD compilation, *We Sold Our Souls For Rock'n'Roll*, without even consulting the band! It only achieved No 35 here in the UK and No 48 in the US and wasn't in the shops for long but early copies came with a colour booklet which contained good photos of the band and some dreadful sleeve artwork - a badly made-up 'corpse' lying in a coffin with a crucifix.

Returning to Vertigo they released *Technical Ecstacy*. Musically this was another disappointment, perhaps because there had been much friction during the recording. This largely resulted from Iommi's determination to experiment with more complex arrangements, overdubs and horns, which led to much friction with Ozzy Osbourne, who eventually went on to leave the band the following year because of unhappiness about their musical direction. He rejoined a couple of months later but left for good in January 1979 to form Blizzard Of Oz and launch a successful solo career.

Most people agree the best thing about the album was the sleeve which showed two robots fucking one another on an elevator. The Sanctuary reissue CD includes Kipper Williams' cartoons satirising the cover.

As we leave the time frame of this book, **Black Sabbath** were clearly established as the archetypal heavy metal band leading a cliche lifestyle of sex, drink, drugs and endless touring. They continued to prosper well into the new millennium and there've been some pretty good compilations of their material which are detailed in the discography.

The *Vertigo Annual 1970* (2-LP) included *Behind The Walls Of Sleep*. More recent compilation appearances have included: *Paranoid* on *Axe Attack, Vol 1* (LP); *Die Young on Axe Attack, Vol 2* (LP); *Heaven And Hell* on the 2-CD *Rock Resurrection*; *Paranoid* and *War Pigs* on *The Best Heavy Metal Album In The World? Ever*! (CD); *Paranoid* on *Kerrang! The Album* (2-CD); *Snowblind* and *Killing Yourself To Live* on *Metal Gods* (LP); *War Pigs* and *Killing Yourself To Live* on the 3-CD set *Metal* and a live version of *Paranoid* on *Guitar Anthems* (CD). (VJ)

The Blackwells

Personnel:	ALBIE GORNELL	gtr	A
	TEX McDERMOTT	lead gtr	A
	ROY LITTLE	drms	A
	DAVE TRIMHALL	bs	A

45:	Why Don't You Love Me/		
	All I Want Is Your Love	(Columbia DB 7442) 1965 R1

BLACK WIDOW - Sacrifice (LP).

This Merseybeat group climbed onto the post-**Beatles** roller coaster but lacked the talent to stay on it for long. They appeared in the 'Ferry Cross The Mersey' film playing the R&B flavoured 'A' side of this 45. The flip was a routine beat ballad.

Compilation appearances include: *Why Don't You Love Me?* on *Liverpool 1963-1968* (CD), *Liverpool 1963-1968, Vol. 1* (LP) and *Ferry Cross The Mersey* (LP); and *All I Want Is Your Love* on *Rare 60's Beat Treasures, Vol. 2* (CD). (VJ/AD)

Black Widow

Personnel:

BOB BOND	bs	A	
CLIVE BOX	drms	A	
JIM GANNON	vcls, gtr, vibes	AB	
CLIVE JONES	wind	ABC	
ZOOT TAYLOR	keyb'ds	ABC	
KIP TREVOR	vcls, gtr	ABC	
ROMEO CHALLENGER	drms	BC	
GEOFF GRIFFITHS	bs	BC	
JOHN CULLEY	gtr, vcls	C	

				HCP
ALBUMS: 1(A)	SACRIFICE	(CBS 63948)	1970 SC	32
2(B)	BLACK WIDOW	(CBS 64133)	1970 SC	-
3(C)	BLACK WIDOW THREE	(CBS 64562)	1971 SC	-

NB: (1) and (2) reissued on CD (Repertoire REP 4067-WZ and REP 4031-WZ respectively) 1991. (1) reissued on vinyl (Get Back GET 531) and on CD (Essential ESM CD 711). It has been remastered and sounds much better than the first Repertoire reissue. (2) reissued on CD (Essential ESM CD 711) 1999. (2) also reissued on vinyl (Akarma AK 326). (3) reissued on vinyl (Get Back GET 571) and on CD (Repertoire REP 4241-WZ). *Black Widow IV* (Mystic Records MYS CD 117) 1997 is their fourth album recorded back in 1972. *Return To The Sabbat* (Mystic Records MYS CD 129) 1998 gave an airing to the first acetate recording of *Sacrifice* back in November 1969. *Come To The Sabbat - The Anthology* (Sanctuary CMEDD 661) 2003 collects many of their better-known songs and rarities. *The Ultimate Sacrifice* (Castle CMQCD 1048) 2005 comprises the original *Sacrifice* album and five demos by the pre-CBS band, featuring their original vocalist Kay Garret. It comes with comprehensive sleevenotes.

45s:	Come To The Sabbat/Way To Power	(CBS 5031)	1970 SC
	Wish You Would/Accident	(CBS 7596)	1971

Essentially a satanist hard-rock outfit on their debut album, collectors are showing more interest in their albums now. They evolved out of a band called **Pesky Gee**. Indeed their first single was originally recorded as **Pesky Gee**.

They made their first recording of *Sacrifice* featuring Kay Garret on vocals alongside Kip Trevor in November 1969. One acetate of the recording was made and it was finally released as *Return To The Sabbat* on Mystic Records in 1998. An interesting document it is more like a live version of their first album, with no string arrangements. On *Sacrifice* the hard-rock influence is most evident on *Attack Of The Demon*, which is something of a

BLACK WIDOW - III (LP).

BLACK WIDOW - IV (LP).

keyboard-driven epic. There are also pastoral interludes and moments of progressive experimentation on the album too. Their best known song was *Come To The Sabbat*, by virtue of its inclusion on the budget *Fill Your Head With Rock* (2-LP) compilation. It's also included on their second album, which has its moments, but is rather patchy overall.

Black Widow Three is a charming melodic rock album with great vocal harmonies and many people think it is their best. However, despite endless touring to support each release, sales were disappointing. By the Summer of 1972, the impetus was beginning to drain from **Black Widow**. The band was tired, dispirited and without a record label, having been dropped by CBS.

With the future looking increasingly bleak they entered D.T. Studios in Kettering to begin recording their fourth album. The irony of the situation was that the band, due to the circumstances prevailing at the time, was left to produce the record themselves, something they had requested in the past but never been allowed to do. The end result was that it was the best album they ever recorded - but it would never see the light of day until 1997. Their fourth album is a melodic progressive recording and there are really no songs about Black Magic! Musically we're talking melodic progressive music with strong vocal harmonies and lots of flute. Shortly after the album was recorded Kip Trevor left the band to be replaced by an American singer called Rick 'E'. It contains four demos put together by the band in December 1972.

Come To The Sabbat - The Anthology released by Sanctuary in 2003 is the best introduction to their music now. It's attractively packaged, full of illustrations of some of their rarer releases, includes press cuttings which many of you like me may find visually challenging, and sleevenotes from Clive Jones, the band's leader. It contains their finer moments and rarities.

The Ultimate Sacrifice comprises the *Sacrifice* album plus five demos from their pre-CBS days, which will interest their fans. Their finest moments like *Come To The Sabbat*, *In Ancient Days* and , of course, the title track, are all their.

Gannon later played with **Fox** and Yellow Dog. Challenger later drummed for **Showaddywaddy**.

Later compilation appearances have included *Come To The Sabbat* on *Rock Of Ages, Four Decades Of Heavy Rock* (CD) and on the 3-CD set *Ars Longa Vita Brevis: A Compendium Of Progressive Rock 1967-1974*. (VJ/PK)

Howard Blaikeley Orchestra

ALBUM:	1 SILHOUETTES OF SUCCESS	(RIM)	1968 SC

The album, issued on a small label, contains instrumental versions of hits, including **The Herd**'s *From The Underworld*, **Dave Dee etc.'s** *Zabadak* and a number of misses too, delivered in a Swingin' London style. (VJ)

BLIND FAITH - Blind Faith (LP).

Y Blew

Personnel:	GERAINT EVANS	drms	A
	DAFYDD IFANS	bs	A
	RICHARD LLOYD	gtr	A
	MALDWYN PATE	vcls	A

45:    Maes B/
       Beth Sy'n Dod Rhyngom Ni (PS)   (Qualiton QSP 7001) 1967

Y Blew was the first authentic Welsh language rock band. It was heavily influenced by the **Spencer Davis Group** and mod-orientated black R'n'B. Their first and only release featured a cover of Curtis Mayfield and The Impressions' *You Must Believe Me* (also covered by the **Spencer Davis Group**). The 'A' side, *Maes B* was a totally different kettle of fish. This slab of psychedelic tom-foolery conjuring up through its lyrics tales of fairies and clocks striking 13 o'clock was perfectly in tune with the Summer of Love. Unfortunately Wales was not and the band split soon after. Played on a record review programme on Radio One soon after its release, it was met with the comment, "Do you think this gimmick will work?" (i.e. a song in Welsh). (GM)

Bley-Peacock Synthesizer Show

Personnel:	PAUL BLEY
	ANNETTE PEACOCK

ALBUMS:	1	REVENGE	(Polydor 2425 043) 1972 R1
	2	DUAL UNITY	(Polydor 2383 105) 1974

NB: (2) as **Bley and Peacock**.

Revenge is an experimental album which is now a collectors' item. **Bley** also cut a solo album, *Touching* (Fontana SFJL 929), which was credited to the Paul Bley Trio and Annette Peacock went on to make several solo albums in the seventies and eighties. (VJ)

Blind Faith

Personnel:	GINGER BAKER	drms	A
	ERIC CLAPTON	gtr	A
	RIC GRECH	bs	A
	STEVIE WINWOOD	keyb'ds, vcls	A

ALBUM: 1(A) BLIND FAITH   (Polydor 583 059) 1969 SC 1

NB: (1) reissued on RSO (2394 142) in 1977 and at budget price on RSO (SPELP 14) in 1983. Also on CD (Polydor 825 094-2) in 1986 and at mid-price (Polydor 825 094-2) 1995. The album was originally released on Atco (33304) in the US. There's also a re-vamped 2-CD reissue of the album (Polydor 549 5292) 2001.

45:        Change Of Address From June 23 1969 (promo only)
                               (Island) 1969 R4

This rock supergroup was formed with **Ginger Baker** and **Eric Clapton** who'd both come from **Cream**), **Stevie Winwood** (formerly of **Spencer Davis Group** and **Traffic**) and Ric Grech (of **Family**). They spent much of early 1969 rehearsing, before giving a free concert in Hyde Park in June 1969 before 100,000 people They whole concert was filmed in colour by Mike Mansfield, but only brief extracts have ever found their way onto the screen. The band was reputedly the worse for some potent weed, and it was a variable and rather lacklustre performance. Prior to their album, 500 copies of an instrumental promotional single were pressed, to notify the press of their change of address from 23 June 1969. It is now by far their most sought-after record.

The album's cover depicted a naked 11-year old girl holding a model aeroplane and was the subject of controversy, causing a different design to be used on most US copies. Though many regarded the album as disappointing at the time, it's actually quite good. Highlights included **Winwood**'s *Sea Of Joy* and *Can't Find My Way Home* and **Clapton**'s *Presence Of The Lord*. It also contained a good cover of Buddy Holly's *Well All Right*, but **Baker**'s *Do What You Like* (marred by a long drum solo) dragged a bit. Nonetheless, the album went to No. 1 on both sides of the Atlantic.

After just one US tour, however, the band split. **Winwood** rejoined **Traffic**, **Clapton** took a liking to the soul music Delaney and Bonnie (one of their support acts) were playing and became their lead guitarist, and **Baker** formed **Ginger Baker's Airforce**.

The CD issue of their earlier album included two bonus tracks - *Exchange And Mart* (the Island promo single with a new name) and *Spending All My Days*.

Polydor's *Supergroups* (LP) compilation included *Well All Right* and *Rock Party* (2-LP) featured *Can't Find My Way Home*. (VJ)

The Blinkers

45:    Original Sin/Dreams Secondhand   (Pye 7N 17752) 1969 R2

Original Sin is a fine driving blues number with great guitar work and superb vocals. The flip side is more commercial but a good song.

Compilation appearances include: *Dreams Secondhand* on *Paisley Pop - Pye Psych (& Other Colours) 1966-1969* (CD) and *Original Sin* on *We Can Fly, Vol 2* (CD). (MWh/VJ)

Bliss

Personnel:	MARTIN BERRY	vcls, gtr	A
	ROGER HURN	perc	A
	ANDY PEGG	vcls, gtr	A

45:    Court Yards In Castille/Lifetime   (Chapter One CH 107) 1969

The band wrote all their own material with Hurn writing the lyrics and Berry and Pegg handling the composing. On the single they were joined by the flautist **Harold Macnair**, the string section of the London Symphony Orchestra and bassist Nick South (**Alexis Korner**'s New Church and **Vinegar Joe**). Chris Welch's review in Melody Maker stated "The singer sounds like Donovan with a head cold". Anyway on offer is melodic, orchestrated pop.

Berry later played in an excellent band called Slender Loris and Pegg played in various jazz-rock bands including Gamelan, Naiad, Incognito and World Service.

Lifetime can also be heard on *Fading Yellow, Vol 1* (CD). (VJ/AP)

Blodwyn Pig

Personnel:	MICK ABRAHAMS	gtr	ABC
	RON BERG	drms	AB

JACK LANCASTER	woodwind	ABC
ANDY PYLE	bs	ABC
GRAHAM WALLER	keyb'ds	B
PETER BANKS	gtr, vcls	B
CLIVE BUNKER	drms	C

				HCP
ALBUMS:	1(A)	AHEAD RINGS OUT	(Island ILPS 9101) 1969	SC 9
	2(A)	GETTING TO THIS	(Chrysalis ILPS 9122) 1970	SC 8

NB: (1) reissued on vinyl (Beat Goes On BGOLP 54) 1990. (2) reissued on vinyl (Beat Goes On BGOLP 81) 1990 and CD (BGOCD 81) 1990. There's also a live CD, *The Modern Alchemist* (Indigo Delux IGOXCD 507), thought to date from 1969/1970. *The Basement Tapes* (Hux HUX 019) 2000 compiled material from previously unavailable BBC sessions. *All Said And Done* (Snapper SBOX 003) 2005 is a 2-CD set which includes on one disc his re-recordings of his contributions to **Jethro Tull's** *This Was* album with a patched up band and on the other re-recordings of old **Blodwyn Pig** material.

45s:	Dear Jill/Sweet Caroline	(Island WIP 6059) 1969
	Walk On The Water/Summer Day	(Island WIP 6069) 1969
	Same Old Story/Slow Down	(Island WIP 6078) 1970

Blodwyn Pig was formed in November 1968 by **Mick Abrahams** after he left **Jethro Tull**. They recorded two good rock albums and toured the US. Their first album had a pig's head on the front cover with a ring through its nose, a fag in its mouth, sunglasses and headphones. The playing on the album is good but it isn't always matched by the material. Still, it had its moments, listen out particularly for some classic progressive rock on *The Modern Alchemist* and *Ain't Ya Coming Home, Babe?* which conclude each side of the album. Their second album saw them move away from their blues roots towards a more soulful sound. The See For Miles CD reissue of this contains two additional cuts, both sides of their second 45. In September 1970, after Abrahams had left, **Pete Banks** joined from **Yes** but the new line-up just didn't gel and the band split up at the end of 1970. Jack Lancaster was a very good brass player who could play two reed instruments at the same time.

Mick Abrahams formed his own band. Andy Pyle joined **Savoy Brown** and was then in a later incarnation of **Juicy Lucy** with Ron Berg.

The band reformed briefly in 1974 (line-up C) but had no vinyl output. **Abrahams** was part of a different line-up that reformed in the late eighties and issued albums in the nineties. Clive Bunker had been in **Jethro Tull**.

The Basement Tapes compiles material from previously unavailable BBC sessions recorded between 1969 and 1974 plus two new tracks from 1996.

The 2005 2-CD set *All Said And Done* is not essential. One CD contains his contributions to **Jethro Tull's** *This Was* album and although the songs themselves are strong - the re-recordings include some tedious over-long solos. The second CD features rehashes of old **Blodwyn Pig** songs. The set comes with an interview DVD, which may interest fans of **Jethro Tull**.

BLODWYN PIG - Ahead Rings Out (LP).

BLONDE ON BLONDE - Rebirth (LP).

Compilation appearances included *Send Your Son To Die* on *Bumpers* (2-LP) and *Sing Me A Song That I Know* on *Nice Enough To Eat* (LP). More recently, *See My Way* has resurfaced on *The Age Of Enlightenment - Prog Rock, Vol. One* (CD). (VJ/HW)

Blonde On Blonde

Personnel:	RALPH DENYER	gtr, vcls	AB
	LES HICKS	perc, drms	ABCD
	RICHARD HOPKINS	bs, keyb'ds	ABC
	GARETH JOHNSON	gtr	ABCD
	SIMON LAWRENCE	gtr	A
	DAVE THOMAS	hrmnca, bs, vcls, gtr	CD
	GRAHAM DAVIES	banjo, vcls, gtr, bs	D
	KIP	mellotron	D

ALBUMS:	1(B)	CONTRASTS	(Pye NSPL 18288) 1969	R2
	2(C)	REBIRTH	(Ember NR 5049) 1970	R1
	3(D)	REFLECTIONS ON A LIFE	(Ember NR 5058) 1971	R1
	4(-)	BLONDE ON BLONDE	(Ember LP 7005) 197?	R2

NB: (1) was released on Janus (3003) in the US. (4) Unissued. Test pressings only. (1) reissued on vinyl (Abraxas 42044). (1) reissued on CD (Earmark 42044) 2005. (3) reissued on CD (Repertoire REP 4308-WP) 1993. (1) reissued on CD as *Contrasts... Plus* (See For Miles SEECD 406) 1994 and (Repertoire REP 4521-WP) 1995, with the addition of the band's debut 45 on Pye and recently on CD again (Castle CMRCD 257). (2) reissued on CD (TKO Magnum CDTB 206) 2000 and again on CD (Spalax 14525). (3) reissued on CD (Spalax 14526).

45s:	All Day All Night/Country Life	(Pye 7N 17637) 1968	R1
	Castles In The Sky/Circles (Some PS)	(Ember EMB S 279) 1970	
	Sad Song For An Easy Lady/		
	Happy Families	(Ember EMB S 316) 1972	

Named after the title of Bob Dylan's 1965 album, this short-lived and little known Welsh outfit stands as one of the better 'unknown' bands. Even though they enjoyed strong reviews from music critics and achieved massive exposure playing before gigantic crowds at the 1969 Isle of Wight festival (coincidently headlined by Dylan), they never managed to generate much in the way of sales. Best of all - their three albums sported a tremendously talented guitarist in Gareth Johnson.

Formed in Newport, South Wales in 1967, the initial **Blonde On Blonde** line-up featured the talents of singer/guitarist Ralph Denyer, drummer Les Hicks, bassist/keyboard player Richard Hopkins and guitarist Johnson. Simon Lawrence (another guitarist) also played on their first single *All Day All Night*. This blends acoustic guitar and sitar to give an Indian-influenced sound and the flip recalls **The Moody Blues'** sound. Convinced they could make it in the big leagues, in 1968 the quartet packed up their gear, leaving Wales for London. Playing clubs such as London's Middle Earth generated a groundswell of publicity, with Pye Records eventually signing the band.

Contrasts, released in 1969 and produced by Barry Murray, has been described as progressive. To some degree, that's a major misnomer and disservice to the band. While there are some true progressive leanings, the majority of the set is simply too diverse to be dumped under such a broad and meaningless genre. These guys rather effortlessly manage to cover a wide range of genres, including hard-rock (the leadoff jam *Ride With Captain Max*), folk (*Island On An Island*), psych (Johnson's *Spinning Wheel* sports a great sitar solo), and conventional pop (*Jeanette Isabella* and *Goodbye* - the latter featuring a beautiful harpsichord-propelled melody which would have made for a wonderful radio hit). Elsewhere, the album included a pair of the **Robin Williamson** covers *No Sleep Blues* and a blazing, feedback propelled *I Need My Friend*. A personal favourite was Denyer's hysterical *Conversationally Making The Grade*. Among the few blatant missteps was a needless horn enhanced cover of **The Beatles** *Eleanore Rigby*. Ralph Denyer left the group after recording the first album and he formed **Aquila**, who released an eponymous album on RCA in 1970.

1970's *Rebirth* was released in the wake of a heavy touring schedule and a massive personal upheaval that saw singer/guitarist Ralph Denyer replaced by school friend David Thomas. (For some reason bassist Hopkins was also credited as 'Richard John'.) In the role of lead vocalist, Thomas was considerably more talented than his predecessor. The extra firepower provided by Thomas' versatile chops was apparent in the form of a tougher, rock-oriented sound. That said, like the debut, their sophomore set was fairly varied, including stabs at **Moody Blues**-styled ballads (*Castles In The Sky*, which was initially a **Simon Dupree And The Big Sound** outtake), progressive romps (*You'll Never Know Me/Release*) and fuzz-propelled rockers (*November*). As before, Johnson's versatile guitar provided many of the highlights - check out his scorching solos on *Circle* and *Colour Question*.

The group was the house band on the TV programme 'How Late It Is'. Ralph Denyer later went on to **Aquila**.

Compilation appearances include: *All Day And All Night* on *Justafixation II* (LP), *We Can Fly, Vol 2* (CD) and on *Hot Smoke & Sassafras - Psychedelic Pstones Vol 1* (CD); *Ride With Captain Max* and *Conversationally Making The Grade* on *Progressive Music* (CD); *Castles In The Sky* and *Circles* on *Circus Days Vol. 1 & 2* (CD) and *Circus Days, Vol. 2* (LP); *Spinning Wheel* on *Electric Psychedelic Sitar Headswirlers, Vol. 1* (CD) and *Country Life* and *Spinning Wheel* also resurfaced on *Haunted - Psychedelic Pstones Vol 2* (CD). *Castles In The Sky* was also earlier included on an Ember compilation. (SB/VJ)

Bloontz

Personnel:			
	TONY BRAUNAGEL	drms	A
	ANDY CHAPMAN	vcls	A
	MARGARET DORN	vcls	A
	LINDA LAWLEY	vcls	A
	MIKE MONTGOMERY	keyb'ds	A
	STEVE RADNEY	gtr	A
	SHARON REDD	vcls	A
	TERRY WILSON	bs, gtr	A

ALBUM: 1(A) BLOONTZ   (Evolution 3020) 1973
NB: (1) US pressing.

Bloontz was a little known rock group with female vocals. Tony Braunagel and Terry Wilson would later join **Paul Kossof** in **Back Street Crawler**. (SR)

The Blossoms

Personnel incl: MIKE BLAKELY

45:        Twiddy Dee/You Got Me Humming   (MGM MGM 1435) 1968

This London band was notable for including Mike Blakely who later played in **Christie**. (VJ)

Blossom Toes

Personnel:			
	BRIAN BELSHAW	bs	ABC
	BRIAN GODDING	gtr, vcls	ABC
	JIM CREGAN	gtr, vcls	ABC
	KEVIN WESTLAKE	drms	A
	POLI PALMER	drms, flute, vibes, harp	B
	BARRY REEVES	drms	C

ALBUMS: 1(A) WE ARE EVER SO CLEAN (Marmalade 607 001) 1967 R2
        2(A) IF ONLY FOR A MOMENT (Marmalade 608 010) 1969 R2
        3(A) THE PSYCHEDELIC SOUND OF BLOSSOM TOES
                              (Toes Records BT 102) 196?

NB: (1) and (2) have had limited repressings in Germany. (1) has also been issued on CD in Japan (Polydor POCP-2190) 1995. (1) reissued on vinyl (Astra Zombie AZ 2). (2) reissued on CD (Polydor POCP 2191). (1) and (2) have also been reissued together with *Workers Playtime* as a double CD package from Germany. (1) and (2) also reissued on CDR (Two Of Us 003). (3) Swedish only release. (3) pirated in 1980's with orange cover. There's also a compilation, a double set *Blossom Toes Collection* (Decca LIKD 43) 1988. *New Day* (Decal LIK 48) 1989 is actually a reissue of the **B.B. Blunder** album *Workers Playtime* as explained in the article.

45s: Look At Me I'm You / What On Earth / Mrs Murphy's
         Budgerigar (Some PS)   (Marmalade 598 002) 1967 R2/SC
         I'll Be Your Baby Tonight/Love Is (Marmalade 598 009) 1968 SC
         Postcard/
         Everyone's Leaving Me Now   (Marmalade 598 012) 1968 SC

BLONDE ON BLONDE - Reflections On A Life (CD).

BLOSSOM TOES - We Are Ever So Clean (LP).

BLOSSOM TOES - Collection (LP).

	Peace Loving Man/Up Above My Hobby Horse's Head	(Marmalade 598 014) 1969 SC
α	New Day/Love Bomb	(Marmalade 598 022) 1969 R2

NB: α Unissued, existence unconfirmed.

This talented but largely overlooked late sixties outfit centred on Brian Godding and Brian Belshaw, who'd met as apprentices at the Hilger and Watts scientific instrument factory at Highbury, Islington in 1962. They formed a group called The Grave Diggers and evolved into R&B outfit The Ingoes, who took their name from an obscure Chuck Berry number, *Ingo*. The Ingoes persuaded **Yardbirds** manager Giorgio Gomelsky to take them on, and he arranged for them to go to Paris. There they developed a strong cult following and, after a short interlude in London (where they recruited Jim Cregan, who had played in various R&B outfits) they returned for a second spell in Paris.

At this time The Ingoes recorded an EP for the Riviera label (cat no 231141) and a single version of *Help*, sung in Italian for the Italian market. Shortly after their return to London, drummer Colin Martin left to be replaced by **Kevin Westlake**, who'd been in Johnny B. Great and The Quotations (which included future Rockpile guitarist Billy Bremner). Around the same time The Ingoes signed to Gomelsky's fledling Marmalade imprint and adopted the suitably psychedelic moniker of **Blossom Toes**.

Their debut 45, *Look At Me I'm You*, with its melee of backwards tapes, swirling xylophone, brass and clear production, flopped at the time but is now recognised as a defining moment of UK psychedelia.

Gomelsky installed the band in Holmead Road, Fulham, and before long they entered the studio to record their first album. It was full of quirky, rather naive psychedelic pop songs with *I'll Be Late For Me* among the best. Also of note are the beautiful cello parts in *Love Is*, the hook-ladened *Telegram Tuesday* and the eerie *What On Earth*. To their consternation, much of the backing was provided by an orchestra and sessionmen, and their live act suffered from the difficulty of reproducing it live. During 1967 they also had a three week residency at Stockholm's leading psychedelic club, the Merry Hassan. *The Psychedelic Sound Of Blossom Toes* album is a largely unimpressive bootleg culled from one of their Swedish shows, and is full of Beefheart numbers, though it does include *Listen To The Silence*, which ended up on their next album.

Late in 1967 **Kevin Westlake** left, to be replaced by Poli Palmer, who had played in several Midlands bands including **Deep Feeling**, and had latterly been in a duo with **Gordon Jackson**. A multi-instrumentalist, he would soon find his role restricted. In March 1968 the band released an uninspired version of Dylan's *I'll Be Your Baby Tonight*, backed by *Love Is*, but their next 45, October's *Postcard/Everyone's Leaving Me Now*, was much better. The 'A' side was catchy and the jazzy flip side featured Palmer on vocals, as well as playing harpsichord and vibes. 1969's *If Only For A Moment* album was much heavier than their debut and relied too much on melodramatic vocals. It had moments of brilliance, but was disappointing overall.

Shortly afterwards Palmer left to join **Eclection** and then **Family**. He was replaced by Barry Reeves from the soul band **Ferris Wheel**. Jim Cregan went on to play in **Stud** and then **Family**, before joining **Cockney Rebel** and later still becoming a member of **Rod Stewart**'s backing band. Brian Godding and Brian Belshaw, meanwhile, formed **B.B. Blunder**, who made one album in 1970, *Workers Playtime*, which - though still progressive - was interspersed by funkier passages.

The 1988 *Blossom Toes Collection* double set is a good introduction to their music with informative sleeve-notes by John Platt.

New Day is actually a reissue of the 1971 **B.B. Blunder** album *Workers Playtime* (who comprised the creative part of **Blossom Toes** (Brian Godding and Brian Belshaw)). By now, although the band still had a 'progressive' sound, it was interspersed by funkier passages. Again the album comes with extensive sleeve-notes by John Platt.

I'll Be Your Baby Tonight and *Love Is* can also be heard on the 1968 *The Marmalade Record Co. Show Olympia 68* album, and *King Of Confusion* on *Marmalade - 100 Proof*, a 1969 compilation.

Retrospective compilation appearances have included: *Mister Pitiful* and *Jump Back* as The Ingoes on *Made In England, Vol. 2* (CD); *In The Midnight Hour* as The Ingoes on *Sounds From The Sixties* (2-LP) and *Sixties Archive Vol. 1* (CD); *I'll Be Your Baby Tonight* on *Hard Up Heroes, Vol. 2* (CD); *Postcard* on *Jagged Time Lapse, Vol 1* (CD); *Telegram Tuesday* on *Jagged Time Lapse, Vol 4* (CD) and *When The Alarm Clock Rings* on the 4-CD *Nuggets* 11 box set. (VJ/RMJ)

Blue

Personnel:	TIMMY DONALD	drms	AB
(up to	IAN MacMILLAN	bs, vcls	AB
1976)	HUGH NICHOLSON	gtr, vcls	AB
	ROBERT 'SMIGGY' SMITH	gtr	B

ALBUMS:	1(A)	BLUE	(RSO 2394 105) 1973 SC
(up to	2(B)	LIFE IN THE NAVY	(RSO 2394 133) 1974
1976)			

45s:	Little Jody/The Way Things Are	(RSO 2090 114) 1973
(up to	Lonesome/Max Bygraves	(RSO 2090 130) 1974
1976)	Too Many Cookies In The Jar/	
	Don't Let This Feeling Go	(RSO 2090 154) 1975
	Round And Round/I Know How It Feels	(RSO 2090 163) 1975

This Glasgow band formed in 1973. Donald had previously been with **White Trash**, whilst MacMillan and Nicholson had both played in **The Poets**. Nicholson had also been in **Marmalade** briefly and their debut album recalled the melodic rock style of that band. *For Life In The Navy* 'Smiggy' Smith was added to the line-up but the end result was relatively

BLOSSOM TOES - The Psychedelic Sound Of (LP).

disappointing and the band split up. They re-emerged in 1977 for a more successful period, including a Top 20 single, *Gonna Capture Your Heart*, but that is really beyond the remit of this book. (VJ)

Timothy Blue

45:     The Room At The Top Of The Stairs/
        She Won't See The Light   (Spark SRL 1014) 1968

This is a highly-rated pop-psych 45. (VJ)

Blue Aces

45s: Land Of Love/Love Song Of The Waterfall (Pye 7N 15672) 1964
        I Beat You To It/
        I Just Can't Help Loving You   (Pye 7N 15713) 1964
        Ain't What I Say/You Don't Care   (Pye 7N 15821) 1965
        Tell Me What You're Gonna Do/
        All I Want   (Columbia DB 7755) 1965 R2
   α   That's All Right/
        Talk About My Baby   (Columbia DB 7954) 1966 R2

NB: α has been reissued in a limited edition of 500 with a large centre hole.

This outfit started out as an Irish Showband in Waterford. Formed in 1958 and managed by Billy Mulcahy, like most showbands of the time, they travelled all over Ireland playing in ballrooms, marquees and parish-halls. Their line-up in these days included Charlie Cheevers (tenor sax), Larry Barry (tpt), John Cooney (piano), Michael Gilligan (gtr), Seamus Carew (bs), Tony Dalton (trombone), Jerry O'Shea (drms) and Michael O'Meara (trombone). In these early years Barry and Gilligan were replaced by Tony Condon and Tony Walsh. Sometime later, Walsh moved to trombone and Jimmy Phelan came in on guitar. Saxophonist Neil McMahon also joined around this time and later Condon joined The Paragon 7 and was replaced by Ron Carthy.

In 1964 the band relocated to London to try to make a breakthrough in the British charts. Things went well for them at first, they were featured in a few BBC shows and in pop magazines such as "Fabulous", "Record Song Book" and "Boyfriend". Their first single *Land Of Love*, featuring Charlie Cheevers on vocals, was played on all the pop stations. During their time in London, original members Cooney, Carew and Phelan decided to return to Ireland, but the band continued with British replacements Ron Ryan, Geoff Foote, Mike Kellecher and Keith Field. Unfortunately the big breakthrough never came, and in 1966, the band returned to Waterford, with some of them joining other showbands. Tony Condon, Ron Carthy and Tony Walsh are now deceased, whilst some other band members are still involved in the music business.

BLUE MINK - Real Mink (LP).

The compilation *Diggin' For Gold, Vol. 1* (LP & CD) features *That's Alright*, a thumpin' good thrash with crashin' chords (despite the brass). Of their other 45s, *All I Want*, was a great soul/mod track.

You can also check out *That's Alright* on *Rare 60's Beat Treasures, Vol. 4* (CD). (FK/VJ/MW)

The Blueberries

Personnel: JEFF FOUNTAIN   gtr, bs   A
             IAN LEE   vcls   A
             JIM McGUIRE   bs, sax   A
             DAVID McPHIE   drms   A
             NEIL MULLINS   perc   A
             ANDREW PEPPITT   ld gtr   A

45:     It's Gonna Work Out Fine/
        Please Don't Let Me Know   (Mercury MF 894) 1965 R1

This obscure Chesterfield outfit recorded just this one soul-flavoured R&B 45 and then returned to oblivion.

Compilation appearances have included: *Please Don't Let Me Know* and *It's Gonna Work Out Fine* on *Nowhere Men, Vol. 4* (CD) and *English Freakbeat, Vol. 2* (CD); and *Please Don't Let Me Know* on *English Freakbeat, Vol. 2* (LP). (VJ/JM)

Blue Chips

45s: I'm On The Right Side/
        You're Good To Me   (Pye 7N 15970) 1965 SC
        Some Kind Of Lovin'/I Know A Boy (Pye 7N 17111) 1966 SC
        Tell Her/Good Lovin' Never Hurt (Pye 7N 17155) 1966 SC

This beat group's three 45s are quite collectable. *Tell Her* was a Billie Davis number.

You'll also find *I'm On The Right Side* on *Doin' The Mod, Vol. 2* (CD). (VJ)

Blue Epitaph

Personnel: JAMES GORDON   A
             PETE HOWELLS   A
             (RICH ROBINSON   bs   A)
             (PAUL TODD   drms   A)

ALBUM: 1(A) ODE BY... BLUE EPITAPH (Holyground HG 117) 1974 R3

NB: (1) reissued with same cat. no. (1991) (SC) and on CD, as *Ode (The Works, Vol 7)* (Kissing Spell KSG 013).

Just 99 copies of this album were pressed making it ultra-rare and expensive. It was recorded by a folk duo who put out a second album as Magus several years later.

On the album James Gordon and Pete Howells were assisted by Paul Todd and Rich Robinson. It was produced by Mike Levon and recorded at the Holyground Studio, Wakefield.

Ffief has been compiled on *The History Of U.K. Underground Folk Rock 1968-1978 Vol. 2* (CD). (VJ/RB)

Blue Goose

Personnel: ALLAN CALLAN   gtr, vcls   AB
             EDDIE CLARKE   gtr   A
             NICKY HOGARTH   keyb'ds   AB
             CHRIS PERRY   drms   AB
             NICK SOUTH   bs   AB
             MIKE TODMAN   gtr   B

ALBUM: 1(B) BLUE GOOSE   (Anchor ANCLP 2005) 1975

45:   α   Loretta/Call On Me   (Anchor ANC 1015) 1975

NB: α both sides also included on their album.

Blue Goose was most notable for including Eddie Clarke who was later in Motorhead. Clarke, Perry and Hogarth had previously been in Curtis Knight and Zeus. Clarke and Hogarth's next venture was a band called Continuous Performance, who had no waxings.

By the time of their album Eddie Clarke had been replaced by Mike Todman. The album includes both their 45 cuts. (VJ/VZ)

Blue Jeans

45:   Hey Mrs Housewife/Sandfly   (Columbia DB 8555) 1969 SC

See also **Swinging Blue Jeans** and **Ray Ennis and The Blue Jeans**. Yes, this was a later version of **The Swinging Blue Jeans**. The 'A' side is straightforward commercial pop, the flip a reasonably good slightly summery ditty.

Compilation appearances include: *Sandfly* on *Psychedelia, Vol. 1* (LP) and *Hens Teeth, Vol. 1* (CD) and *Hey Mrs Housewife* on *Pop In, Vol 1* (CD). (VJ)

Blue Mink

Personnel:	ROGER COOKE	piano, vcls	AB
	MADELINE BELL	vcls	A
	ROGER COULAM	keyb'ds	AB
	HERBIE FLOWERS	bs	AB
	BARRY MORGAN	drms	AB
	ALAN PARKER	gtr	AB
	RAY COOPER	perc	B
	ANN ODELL	keyb'ds	B

ALBUMS:	1(A)	OUR WORLD	(Philips 6308 024) 1970
(up to	2(A)	MELTING POT	(Philips SBL 1029) 1970
1977)	3(A)	LIVE AT THE TALK OF THE TOWN	
			(Regal Zonophone SLRZ 1029) 1972
	4(A)	A TIME OF CHANGE	(Regal Zonophone SRZA 8507) 1972
	5(A)	BEST OF BLUE MINT	(Philips 6382 077) 1973
	6(A)	ONLY WHEN I LAUGH	(EMI EMA 756) 1973
	7(B)	FRUITY	(EMI EMC 3021) 1974
	8(-)	THE BEST OF BLUE MINK	(EMI EMC 3043) 1974
	9( )	HIT MAKING WORLD OF BLUE MINK	
			(Decca SPA 437) 1975
	10( )	HIT MAKING SOUND	(Gull GULM 500) 1977

NB: There's a comprehensive budget-priced CD collection, *The Best Of Blue Mink* (Music Club MCCD 117) 1993, which included all their hits and more. More recent releases are *Melting Pot/The Very Best Of Blue Mink* (Sequel NEMCD 456) 2000 and *Good Morning Freedom - The Anthology* (Castle CMDD 530).

HCP

45s:	Melting Pot/Gimme Reggae	(Philips BF 1818) 1969	3
(up to	Good Morning Freedom/ Mary Jane	(Philips BF 1838) 1970	10
1976)	Our World/Pastures New	(Philips 6006 042) 1970	17
	Time For Winning/		
	Many-Loving Things	(Philips 6006 084) 1970	-
	The Banner Man/		
	Mind Your Own Business	(Regal Zonophone RZ 3034) 1971	3
	Sunday/One Smart Fellow	(Regal Zonophone RZ 3041) 1971	-
	Count Me In/Did You Get It	(Regal Zonophone RZ 3043) 1972	-
	Wacky, Wacky, Wacky/		
	We'll Be There	(Regal Zonophone RZ 3053) 1972	-
	Stay With Me/		
	We'll Be There	(Regal Zonophone RZ 3064) 1972	11
	By The Devil/I Can't Find The Answer	(EMI EMI 2007) 1973	26
	Randy/John Brown's Down	(EMI EMI 2028) 1973	9
	Quackers/		
	Mind If I Stand And Watch Here	(EMI EMI 2109) 1974	-
	Get Up/I Wanna Be Around	(EMI EMI 2145) 1974	-
	Another Without You Day/		
	Yesterday's Gone	(EMI EMI 2214) 1974	-
Reissues:	Melting Pot/Gimme Reggae	(Gull GULS 11) 1975	-

BLUE PHANTOM - Distortions (LP).

Melting Pot/Gimme Reggae	(Old Gold OG 9035) 1979	-
The Banner Man/Stay With Me	(Old Gold OG 9275) 1983	-

One of the best-loved early seventies pop groups, **Blue Mink** was formed in 1969 by a group of session musicians and singers. Roger Cooke was a talented songwriter and they stormed up the Charts with their first record, *Melting Pot*, a classic inter-racial song.

The project was never a full-time occupation for any of the band's members - **Madeline Bell** was a solo artist in her own right, releasing several singles during the sixties and early seventies. She had also starred in the 'Black Nativity' stage show, sang with **Judd** and was later in **Seven Ages Of Man**.

Herbie Flowers and Alan Parker also played in Rumplestiltskin and Barry Morgan came from **Gulliver's People**.

Roger Coulam ceased to be a member of **Blue Mink** in April 1973 although he appeared on *Only When I Laugh* which was released the following September. His place was taken by Ann Odell, with percussionist Ray Cooper also joining.

Madeline Bell toured and recorded with **Chris Farlowe** in 1975, whilst Cooper became a member of **Elton John**'s backing band. Herbie Flowers toured and recorded with **David Bowie**. Ann Odell later joined Chopyn.

Sequel's *Very Best Of Blue Mink* includes all their 'A' sides along with some more obscure 'B' sides and album tracks. However, the most comprehensive retrospective of their work is Castle's *Good Morning Freedom - The Anthology*.

Compilation appearances have included *Melting Pot* on Philips' *Sixteen Star Tracks Of The Sixties* (LP) in 1971. (VJ/JM)

The Blue Mountain Boys

45:   Drop Me Gently/
      One Small Photograph Of You   (Oriole CB 1774) 1963

From Liverpool, this appears to be the band's only recording. (LBy)

Blue Phantom

Personnel: No credits on record.

ALBUM: 1   DISTORTIONS   (Kaleidoscope KAL 101) 1972 R2

NB: (1) reissued on CD (Golden Classics Rebirth GCR 013) 1997.

Very trendy track titles such as *Distillation*, *Equivalence* and *Psychonebulous* (all credited to H. Tical), as well as the lack of info on the sleeve, are more often than not a bad omen. This all-instrumental exploitation album, however, has some hidden surprises for us. The ridiculous liner-notes (mentioning life before birth, no less) notwithstanding, almost each and every track is a short heavy acid-rock symphony which make the title of the album ring true. Disturbing, subtly dissonant and even downright menacing, I wouldn't recommend listening to this daily, but I would certainly recommend it in small doses. A good soundtrack to your worst expectations, this is an unclassifyable hybrid of orchestrated pop and trips gone awry. This is for the strong-souled among us.

The "Tical" monicker is thought to be a pseudonym and as the album and a 45 with two non album tracks were issued in Italy on the Spider label (distributed by Vedette), it's probable that this album was the work of an Italian artist. (MK/GB)

Blue Rondos

Personnel incl:	MICK COOK	drms	A
	ROGER HALL	ld gtr	A
	BILLY PITT-JONES	bs	A
	MICK STUBBS	gtr	A

45s:	Little Baby/Baby I Go For You	(Pye 7N 15734) 1964
	Don't Want Your Lovin' No More/	
	What Can I Do	(Pye 7N 15833) 1965

This band's first 45 sold well and almost made it into the Charts. Its flip side featured some fine guitar work and was a blues number produced by Joe Meek. Dealers have subsequently speculated that **Jimmy Page** was responsible for the axework, to the extent that the track appeared on **Jimmy Page** themed compilations. In fact, band member Roger Hall was responsible for the fretwork.

The band was originally known as The Moonrakers. Stubbs was later in **The Syndicats** and went on to form **Home** with Mick Cook - who sadly died many years later, as did Stubbs from cancer on 5 May 1999, aged 51.

Compilation appearances have included: *Baby I Go For You* on *James Patrick Page: Session Man, Vol. 2* (LP & CD), *Trans-World Punk Rave-Up!, Vol. 1* (LP), *The Joe Meek Story: The Pye Years, Vol. 2* (CD) and *Freakbeat Freakout* (CD); *Baby I Go For You* and *Little Baby* on *Jimmy's Back Pages - The Early Years* (CD); *Little Baby* on *English Freakbeat, Vol. 2* (CD) and *Little Baby* on *The Joe Meek Story: The Pye Years* (2-CD). (VJ/KL)

Blues and Roots

This R&B outfit from Nottingham recorded four tracks onto tape in 1964 before eventually splitting. The organ-driven instrumental *Gettin' It* has resurfaced on *Incredible Sound Show Stories, Vol. 1* (LP & CD) and *Leaving Here* on *Incredible Sound Show Stories, Vol. 5* (LP). (VJ)

Blues By Five

Personnel:	LEN ASHLEY	vcls	A
	JOHN BLISSETT	piano, keyb'ds	A
	DICK BRICE	drms	A
	NOEL CHARTRES McMANUS	sax	A
	RON McQUEEN	lead gtr	A
	MICK WRIGHT	bs	A

| 45: | Boom Boom/I Cried | (Decca F 12029) 1964 R2 |

The band came from London and their 45 is sought-after. The 'A' side was a powerful rendition of John Lee Hooker's R&B classic. The flip was an **Andrew Loog Oldham**/Mike Leander song.

Compilation appearances include: *Boom, Boom* on *R&B Scene, Vol. 2 - 1963-1969* (LP), *The R&B Scene* (CD), *Weekend Starts Here* (LP), *British R'n'B Explosion, Vol. 1* (CD), *Beat Merchants* (2-LP), *English Freakbeat Vol. 6* (CD) and *Pebbles, Vol. 6* (LP); and *Boom, Boom* and *I Cried* on *Broken Dreams, Vol. 2* (LP). (VJ)

Jimmy Page Session Man Vol. 2 (Comp CD) includes Blue Rondos.

Blues Council

Personnel:	BILLY ADAMSON	drms	AB
	FRASER CALDER	vcls	A
	JAMES GIFFEN	bs	A
	LESLIE HARVEY	lead gtr	AB
	JOHN McGINNIS	piano	AB
	BILL PATRICK	sax	AB
	LARRY QUINN	alto sax	AB
	BILL PATRICK		B
	BOBBY WISHART	tenor sax	B

| 45: | Baby Don't Look Down/ | |
| | What Will I Do | (Parlophone R 5264) 1965 R2 |

A Scottish mod band that was formed by Bill Patrick who'd previously worked as a band leader in a Glasgow ballroom. They used an electric keyboard and had a couple of sax players. They were quickly signed up by EMI and their debut 45, now a sought-after collector's item, was promising. The urban blues influence of Chicago was clearly there but tempered by a swing influence too. They appeared to have a bright future ahead which was cruelly curtailed when their van was involved in a crash in the early hours of 12 March 1965 on the way home from a gig and Calder and Giffen were killed. The remaining members did regroup (line-up B) but the crash had knocked the stuffing out of the band which disintegrated a few weeks later. (VJ)

Bluesology

Personnel:	REX BISHOP	bs	AB
	STUART BROWN	gtr	AB
	REGGIE DWIGHT	keyb'ds	AB
	MICK INKPEN	drms	AB
	MARK CHARIG		B
	ELTON DEAN	sax	B
	PETE GAVIN		B
	NEIL HUBBARD	gtr	B
	CALEB QUAYE	gtr	B

45s:	Come Back Baby/	
	Time's Getting Tougher Than Tough	(Fontana TF 594) 1965 R4
	Mister Frantic/	
	Everyday (I Have The Blues)	(Fontana TF 668) 1966 R4
α	Since I Found You Baby/	
	Just A Little Bit	(Polydor 56195) 1967 R4

NB: α as Stu Brown and Bluesology.

This Middlesex band formed in 1961 and soon worked the London club circuit, playing blues and R&B covers. They also often backed visiting US stars and often toured the Continent. Eventually, they became **Long John**

Baldry's backing band but when he switched from the R&B circuit to big ballads and cabaret their days were clearly numbered. By now **Baldry** had expanded the group into a nine-piece.

Meanwhile Reg Dwight was becoming disillusioned with the music **Baldry** was playing and auditioned for Liberty Records. A few months later he changed his name to **Elton John** and began a slow and steady claim to superstardom.

Needless to say these three **Bluesology** 45s are now extremely expensive collector's items. *Come Back Baby* was written and performed by Reg Dwight. *Times Getting Tougher* was their interpretation of a Jimmy Witherspoon blues composition. *Mr Frantic* was another Dwight number, but when it flopped Philips didn't renew their option on the band's output. Instead they obtained a one-off deal with Polydor in the summer of 1967. This time they opted for a Kenny Lynch penned-and-produced single *Since I Found You Baby*, but it met the same fate.

Caleb Quaye later released a rare 45 as **Caleb** and joined **Hookfoot**, whilst **Elton Dean** joined **Soft Machine**.

They also contributed one track, *Just A Little Bit*, to the *Rare Tracks* (LP) 1975 compilation. *The Fontana Singles Box Set Volume 1 - Hits And Rarities* includes *Come Back Baby* and *Time's Getting Tougher*. They also feature on the 3-CD set *The 60s and 90s Collection*. (VJ)

Blue Stars

An early sixties beat band from Birmingham, who should not be confused with the savage R&B bunch from New Zealand. The Brummie outfit had three cuts on the rare sixties *Brum Beat, Vol. 2* compilation, *I Saw You Yesterday*, *Yours Forever* and *School Day*, although none are particularly outstanding. Still, you can also find them on *Brumbeat* (CD).

The New Zealand **Bluestars**, were the first NZ act to have a UK release, (*Please Be A Little Kind/I Can Take It* (Decca F 12303) 1965) (R2), which has led to some confusion on our part... More recently both sides of the 45 have also appeared on *Broken Dreams, Vol. 2* (LP) and you can also check out *I Can Take It* on *Trans-World Punk, Vol. 2* (LP). The NZ **Bluestars** were later responsible for the garage gem *Social End Product*, also featured on *Trans-World Punk, Vol. 2* (LP) and *Ugly Things, Vol. 3* (LP). You can also check out all their material on an excellent retrospective album from *Dig The Fuzz* (DIG 020), also available on CD. *Social End Product* can also be heard on the 4-CD box set *Nuggets 11*. (VJ)

Blue Yogurt

| 45: | Lydia/Umbrella Man | (Penny Farthing PEN 732) 1976 |

An obscure pop group whose *Lydia* can also be heard on *Circus Days, Vol. 5* (LP) and *Circus Days Vol's 4 & 5* (CD), but it's of no special note. (VJ/BH)

BRUMBEAT (Comp CD) including The Blue Stars.

Colin Blunstone

ALBUMS:	1	ONE YEAR	(Epic 64557) 1971 SC
(up to	2	ENNISMORE	(Epic 65278) 1973 SC
1976)	3	JOURNEY	(Epic 65805) 1974
	4	PLANES	(Epic 81592) 1976

NB: (1) reissued on CD in a digipak. (2) reissued on CD in a digipak. There's also a CD, *Colin Blunstone Sings His Greatest Hits* (Essential ESSCD 139) 1991. *Live At The BBC* (Windsong WINCD 079) 1995 contains some of his finest moments - two versions of his Top 20 hit *Say You Don't Mind*, *I Don't Believe In Miracles*, re-recordings of **Zombies'** classics *Time Of The Season* and *She's Not There* and several other later gems. *Greatest Hits* (Mystic MYS CD 138) 1999 actually comprises reworks of some of his favourite tunes and he's assisted by his old mates like Don Airey and **Cozy Powell**. *Some Years: It's The Time Of Colin Blunstone* (Legacy/Epic 489 487 2) 2000 compiles the best tracks from his three early seventies albums for Epic.

HCP

45s:	Caroline Goodbye/	
(up to	Though You Are Far Away	(Epic EPC 7520) 1971 -
1976)	Say You Don't Mind/	
	Let Me Come Closer	(Epic EPC 7765) 1972 15
	I Don't Believe In Miracles/	
	I've Always Had You	(Epic EPC 8434) 1972 31
	How Could We Dare Be Wrong?/	
	Time's Running Out	(Epic EPC 1197) 1973 45
	Wonderful/Beginning	(Epic EPC 1775) 1973 -
	It's Magical/Summersong	(Epic EPC 2413) 1974 -
	When You Close Your Eyes/	
	Good Guys Don't Always Win	(Epic EPC 4576) 1976 -
	Planes/Dancing In The Dark	(Epic EPC 4752) 1976 -

Colin Blunstone was born on 24 June 1945 in Hatfield, Hertfordshire. In March 1963 he became a founder member of **The Zombies**. After the group's demise he embarked on a successful solo career. In fact, in 1968 he enjoyed a minor hit with a remake of *She's Not There* under the pseudonym **Neil MacArthur**. His first album *One Year* spawned his first solo hit under his own name with a cover of **Denny Laine**'s *Say You Don't Mind*. Other highlights included *Caroline Goodbye* and *Let Me Come Closer To You*. The album, which took a year to record is generally considered to be his finest.

Ennismore included the hit singles *How Could We Be Wrong* and *I Don't Believe In Miracles*. **Rod Argent**, **Russ Ballard**, Phil Dennys, Mike Snow and **Pete Wingfield** all guested on the album. He also recorded an exquisite version of Tim Hardin's *Misty Roses*.

After his second album he formed a backing group - Derek Griffiths (gtr), Terry Poole (bs), Jim Toomey (drms), Pete Wingfield (piano) - which stayed together until after the *Journey* album. His live appearances in this era were consequently pretty rocky in contrast to his recorded work, which was often orchestrated to showcase his floating vocals.

His vocals were later featured on many of The Alan Parsons Project albums. He was also a member of the eighties supergroup Keats, who were produced by and sounded like The Alan Parsons Project. (VJ)

Bo and Peep

| 45: | Young Love/ | |
| | The Rise Of The Brighton Surf | (Decca F 11968) 1964 R1 |

This project was the result of a collaboration between **The Rolling Stones** and Kim Fowley.

Compilation appearances include: *Young Love* and *Rise Of The Brighton Surf* on *English Freakbeat Vol. 6* (CD); and *Young Love* on *Pebbles, Vol. 6* (LP). (VJ)

Bobcats

Personnel:	DAVE COWLEY	gtr, vcls	A
	LES FORTNAM	drms	A
	GARY HEDGES	bs, vcls	A
	PAUL WILLINGTON	gtr, vcls	A

45: Can't See For Looking/Let Me Get By (Pye 7N 17242) 1967 SC

Signed by Pye records in 1966 after winning two band competitions at the Locarno in Birmingham and the Adelphy in West Bromwich, Cowley and Fortnam were aged 12 at the time and Hedges and Willington were 14. They appeared on Blue Peter and the David Frost Show in 1967.

Can't See For Looking can also be heard on *Purple Pill Eaters* (LP & CD) and on *Haunted - Psychedelic Pstones Vol 1* (CD). (VJ/DC)

Bodast

Personnel:	DAVE CURTIS	bs, vcls	AB
	BOBBY CLARKE	drms	AB
	STEVE HOWE	gtr	AB
	CLIVE SKINNER	vcls	B
	(BRUCE THOMAS	bs	B)

NB: No recorded output at the time. They recorded an album for MGM who folded before it could be issued. It later emerged on *The Bodast Tapes Featuring Steve Howe* (Cherry Red BRED 12) 1982. A later compilation, credited to Steve Howe and Bodast is *The Early Years* (CS C5-528) 1983. *Spectral Nether Street* (RPM RPM 198) 2000 gives another airing to the tapes first released in 1982 but this time in its original mix, with the addition of four more tracks. It includes all of their recorded output.

This progressive rock outfit was operative from May 1968 to December 1969. Prior to joining **Bodast**, **Howe** had been in **The Syndicats**, **The In Crowd** and **Tomorrow**. The band's name took the first two letters of the three founding members' Christian names. They recorded an album of psychedelia-tinged progressive rock for MGM, but the label folded before it could be issued. **Howe**, of course, went on to become guitarist in **Yes**.

Their album eventually emerged as *The Bodast Tapes Featuring Steve Howe* (Cherry Red BRED 12) 1982. A later compilation, *The Early Years* (CS C5-528, 1983), credited to **Steve Howe** and **Bodast**, includes two previously unissued tracks - *Nothing To Cry For* and *I Want You*. *Spectral Nether Street* (RPM RPM 198, 2000) gives another airing to the tapes first released in 1982, but in their original mix with the addition of four more tracks.

Beyond Winter, *Nothing To Cry For* and *Nether Street* have all been compiled on *Steve Howe - Mothballs* (CD). (VJ)

J.P. Boddy

45: Stop Me Spinning/
Song Without A Word (Columbia DB 8989) 1973

This one 45 was **J.P. Boddy's** sole vinyl excursion. (VJ)

Rubble Vol. 14 (Comp LP) includes Boeing Duveen & The Beautiful Soup.

BODAST - Spectral Nether Street (CD).

Bodkin

Personnel:	BILL ANDERSON	bs	A
	ZEIK HUME	vcls	A
	MICK RIDDEL	gtr	A
	DOUGIE ROME	keybd's	A
	DICK SNEDDON	drms	A

ALBUM: 1(A) BODKIN (West CSA 104) 1972 R4

NB: (1) reissued on CD (Witch and Warlock Records W&W 001) 1989 and again on CD (World Wide Records W&W 001) 1991. (1) reissued on vinyl (Akarma AK 125 LP) and CD (AK 125) 2001.

This privately-pressed early seventies collectable now changes hands for substantial sums. The band was Scottish and the album consists of five extended tracks of superb heavy organ and guitar work. In addition to the three members listed above there was also a drummer. Originally issued in a plain white sleeve, unsold copies were according to 'Record Collector' acquired by a German dealer a few years back who designed a new sleeve to enhance the album's appeal. Recommended. (VJ/BL)

Boeing Duveen and The Beautiful Soup

45: Jabberwock/
Which Dreamed It (Some P/S) (Parlophone R 5696) 1968 R3/R2

This 45 is extremely rare and collectable, partly because the man behind it was a certain Sam Hutt (the gynaecologist better known to many as Hank Wangford). Wangford, of course, became quite a popular country and western artist in the eighties.

Some copies of the *Jabberwock* 45 came in picture sleeves and these are particularly rare and sought-after. It's one of those records that defies description, it's worth hearing but certainly not worth what you'd have to pay for the original 45. The flip side was a psychedelic sitar number.

Compilation appearances have included:- *Jabberwock* on *Rubble Vol. 14: The Magic Rocking Horse* (LP), *Rubble Vol. 8* (CD), *The Best Of Rubble Collection, Vol. 5* (CD), *Head Sounds From The Bam-Caruso Waxworks, Vol. 1* (CD) and *Electric Sugarcube Flashbacks, Vol. 1* (LP); and *Which Dreamed It* on *Perfumed Garden Vol. 3* (CD), *Justavibration* (LP) and *The Best Of Rubble Collection Vol. 1* (CD). (VJ)

Marc Bolan

ALBUMS:	1	THE BEGINNING OF DOVES (Track 2410 201) 1974 SC
	2	YOU SCARED ME TO DEATH (Cherry Red ERED 20) 1981
	3	BEYOND THE RISING SUN (2-LP)(Cambra DR 115) 1984

NB: (1) Reissued on Media Motion (MEDIA 2) in 1988, on CD (Receiver RRCD 152) 1991, again (Media Motion MEDIACD 2) 1989 and again (Castle Music CMRCD

491) 2002, with 17 additional tracks. (2) Some copies came as picture discs (PERED 20). Early copies of (2) came with a booklet stapled to a gatefold sleeve. Later copies came with a loose booklet. There's also a CD release of his solo work, *Love And Death* (Cherry Red CBRED 70) 1985, reissued in 1991 and again in 1998 as a mid-price collection of his early recordings captured by his manager Simon Napier-Bell, who unearthed them in 1981 and added new instrumental tracks. He also recorded an unreleased album, *Hard On Love* (Track 2406 009) 1972 (R5). He blocked the release because he felt it was unrepresentative of his material at the time, but two-sided acetates exist of this release, which include **Bolan** swearing in the introduction (R6). Also of relevance is *Rarities, Vol. 1* (SPS 3) 1991, which is an excellent package of his more obscure material, also on CD (SPS CD3) 1991, along with *Rarities, Vol. 2* (SPS 4CD) 1991. *Anthology* (Essential ESBCD 965) 1991 is a three-CD set traces his career from 1968-77. Disc one mostly comprises material from his **Tyrannosaurus Rex** days while the other two cover the **T Rex** years. One to avoid is *Acoustic Warrior* (Telstar TCD 2858) 1996, a budget-priced collection of seventies tapes of material which most of his fans will have on other collections. *Spaceball* (New Millennium Communications PILOT 21) 1997 is a 2-CD set of all **Bolan**'s surviving sessions for American radio. It also comes with a well illustrated booklet and extensive sleeve notes from Cliff McLenehan.

45s:		
	The Wizard/Beyond The Rising Sun	(Decca F 12288) 1965 R4
	The Third Degree/San Francisco Poet	(Decca F 12413) 1966 R4
	Hippy Gumbo/Misfit	(Parlophone R 5539) 1966 R5
	Jasper C Debussy//Hippy Gumbo/The Perfumed	
	Garden Of Gulliver Smith (PS)	(Track 2094 013) 1974 R2
	You Scared Me To Death/The Perfumed	
	Garden Of Gulliver Smith	(Cherry Red CHERRY 29) 1981
α	Cat Black/Jasper C. Debussy	(Cherry Red CHERRY 32) 1981
	The Wizard//Beyond The Rising Sun	
	Rings Of Fortune (PS)	(Cherry Red CHERRY 39) 1982
	The Road I'm On (Gloria) (PS)	(Archive Jive TOBY 1) 1990

NB: α 1st 10,000 copies came with an interview disc. There was also a picture disc release (P29). (9) Limited edition of 1,500 only sold by mail order.

Bolan's real name was Mark Feld and he was born in Hackney, East London in 1948. He became something of a face around London's mod scene in the mid-sixties, worked as a male model for a while and also spent a couple of years in France.

His first recording was thought to be a demo from early 1965 when he was using the name Toby Tyler. The song *The Road I'm On (Gloria)* appeared on a one-sided Emidisc acetate but was reissued as a numbered limited edition of 1,500 by a **Bolan** fan in 1990. A second acetate surfaced a year later backed by a pop-folk version of Dylan's *Blowin' In The Wind*. Then in 1992 a reel-to-reel master tape surfaced featuring three other alternate and previously unissued versions of *The Road I'm On* and six of Dylan's *Blowin' In The Wind*. What amounted to one of **Bolan**'s first recording sessions was released as a CD single *Blowin' In The Wind* (Zinc Alloy ZAR CDS 9005) 1993 and is a must for his fans. It's also rumoured that he recorded a third acetate around this time of Betty Everett's *You're No Good* (later a hit for **The Swinging Blue Jeans**) but no copies have ever been found. **Bolan** is also known to have recorded some material with Joe Meek, and an acetate of *Mrs. Jones* has recently been discovered, which may yet be earlier than the Toby Tyler material.

BODKIN - Bodkin (LP).

MARC BOLAN - Love And Death (CD).

By the time of his first single release in November 1965, Marc had changed his name to **Bolan** and was managed by Mike Purskin. On the acetates of *The Wizard* 45 his name is misspelt as Bowland. The song was a simple composition, although it was filled out with some heavy orchestration and fairy-story lyrics. The end result was something too complex for the singles market at that time and, despite an appearance on 'Ready Steady Go' to promote it, it failed to sell. Inevitably, given his premature death, this (and his other solo singles) is now extremely expensive to find and hard to purchase. The follow-up, *The Third Degree*, was pretty different, a driving R&B number, but again, it sank without trace. Nowadays it is a ridiculously priced rarity.

The first big break in his career came when he linked up with **Yardbird**'s producer Simon Napier-Bell. Under Napier-Bell's guidance he recorded a number of songs in one or two sessions, which were just him singing and playing acoustic guitar. There is some uncertainty as to precisely which songs these were but they are thought to have included *Jasper C. Debussy*, *Eastern Spell*, *Cat Black*, *Black And White Incident*, *You Got The Power*, *Observations*, *Pictures Of Purple People*, *Jasmine '49*, *Charlie*, *Mustang Ford* and *Hippy Gumbo*. *Hippy Gumbo* was re-recorded shortly after with some sparse string accompaniment and striking acoustic guitar. On this his distinctive warbling vocal style came into its own. Despite another preview on 'Ready Steady Go' and some airplay on John Peel's 'Perfumed Garden' it failed to sell and is now his rarest 45. It was also his first to feature distinctively his warbled vocal style. The remaining songs recorded in this early session or sessions did not resurface until *The Beginning Of Doves* album in 1974, after he'd become famous. All of the **Bolan** 'A' and 'B' sides are included on the Australian triple album, *20th Century Boy*.

In the Spring of 1967 Napier-Bell persuaded **Bolan** to join the mod soon to become psychedelic group, **John's Children**. He later unsuccessfully tried to form a five-piece electric band but when the HP company repossessed the equipment, he and **Steve Peregrin Took** started working as an acoustic duo, **Tyrannosaurus Rex**, which eventually became **T Rex**.

On 16 September 1977 after a long night out clubbing with his then girlfriend Gloria Jones he was killed when his car left the road at a bend on Barnes Common, London, and crashed into a tree. Inevitably much of his material has been repackaged since his death. See the discographies at the start of this article and the **Tyrannosaurus Rex** and **T Rex** entries for details.

The Third Degree later emerged on *The Freakbeat Scene* (CD). (VJ/KL)

Bombadil

45:	Breathless/When The City Sleeps (PS)	(Harvest HAR 5056) 1972
Reissue:	Breathless/When The City Sleeps (PS)	(Harvest HAR 5095) 1975

This 45 was by **Barclay James Harvest** recording under a pseudonym, but has yet to attain any collectable value. (VJ)

Graham Bond (Organisation)

Personnel:

GINGER BAKER	drms	A
GRAHAM BOND	keyb'ds, sax, vcls	A B
JACK BRUCE	bs	A
DICK HECKSTALL-SMITH	sax	A
JOHN McLAUGHLIN	gtr	A
DIANE STEWART	vcls	B

plus several session artists and guests.

ALBUMS:

HCP

1(A)	THE SOUND OF '65	(Columbia 33SX 1711) 1965	R2	-
2(A)	THERE'S A BOND BETWEEN US	(Columbia 33SX 1750) 1966	R2	-
3(A)	SOLID BOND (dbl)	(Warner Bros 3001) 1970	SC	40
4(B)	HOLY MAGICK	(Vertigo 6360 021) 1971	SC	-
5(B)	WE PUT OUR MAGICK ON YOU	(Vertigo 6360 042) 1971	SC	-
6(B)	BOND IN AMERICA (dbl)	(Philips 6499 200/1) 1971	SC	-
7(B)	THIS IS GRAHAM BOND	(Philips 6382 010) 1972	-	
8(-)	LIVE AT KLOOKS KLEEK (Live '65 set reissue)	(Decal LIK 47) 1988	-	
9(-)	SOUND OF '65/THERE'S A BOND BETWEEN US (Two LP reissue)	(Edsel DED 254) 1988	-	

NB: (1) and (2) reissued on one CD (BGO BGOCD 500) 2000. (4) as Graham Bond and Magick. (4) reissued (BGO BGOLP 35) 1988. (5) as Graham Bond with Magick. (5) reissued (BGO BGOLP 73) in 1990. (4) and (5) reissued on CD (Repertoire REP 4016-WP and 4107-WP respectively) 1991. (4) and (5) reissued as a 2-CD set (BGO BGOCD 483) 2000. (6) and (7) **Graham Bond** solo efforts recorded whilst he was living in America. *Love Is The Law* and *Mighty Graham Bond* (originally issued on Pulsar) are now available as individual CDs. (8) reissued on CD (Decal CDCHARLY 214) 1988. (9) reissued on CD (Decal CD 214) in 1990.

45s:

	Long Tall Shorty/Long Legged Baby	(Decca F 11909) 1964 R1
	Tammy/Wade In The Water	(Columbia DB 7471) 1965 R1
	Tell Me (I'm Gonna Love Again)/ Love Come Shining Through	(Columbia DB 7528) 1965 R1
	Lease On Love/ My Heart's In Little Pieces	(Columbia DB 7647) 1965 R1
	Saint James' Infirmary/Soul Tango	(Columbia DB 7838) 1966 R1
	You've Gotta Have Love Babe/ I Love You	(Page One POF 014) 1967 R1
α	Walking In The Park/ Springtime In The City	(Warner Bros 8004) 1970

NB: α a solo 45.

First coming to prominence as a jazz saxophonist **Bond** was an important individual in the sixties R&B movement. His first band formed in 1963 evolved out of **Alexis Korner's Blues Incorporated**. Although they started out playing jazz they soon built up a reputation for playing really raw R&B.

Bond was also a significant innovator - the first British musician to use the Hammond organ and Leslie speaker (in a R&B context); the first to build in electric keyboard and the first to use a mellotron.

The Sound of '65 featured a rhythm section of **Jack Bruce** and **Ginger Baker**, with **Bond** on Hammond organ and Dick Heckstall-Smith on bass. On offer was an abrasive jazzy R&B delivered in an uncompromising style by **Bond**. The album includes excellent versions of standards like *Got My Mojo Working* and *Neighbour Neighbour*.

Upon the demise of the **Graham Bond Organisation**, he made a couple of weird moody albums for Pulsar in 1968 whilst living in the USA. *Love Is The Law* is an occult-tinged collection of blues, jazz and progressive soulish rock with lots of keyboards and mellotron. *Mighty Graham Bond* featured Harvey Mandel and is another dark progressive jazz/blues offering with lots of spooky organ and mellotron and occult references. **Bond** also did some session work. He then joined **Ginger Baker's Airforce**.

He then formed **Bond and Brown** with **Pete Brown** recording one progressive album and a 45. Then, having married singer Diane Stewart upon his return from America, he formed and disbanded several groups with her including Holy Magick, which recorded the *Holy Magick* and *We Put Our Magick On You* albums. These combined jazz, soul, and Afro rhythm into a song format. On *Holy Magick* they are supported by a large jazz-rock ensemble. **Bond** believed himself to be the illegitimate son of Aleister Crowley and these albums reflect an obsession with the occult. The resulting mysticism is pretty hard going at times for the listener though. *We Put Our Magick On You* is more accessible than its predecessor but still based around the mysticism of the occult.

By 1973 his finances and marriage were in deep trouble. He formed a band called Magus with folkie **Carolanne Pegg**, which was forced to disband before it even recorded, largely because of lack of finance. He had also become a junkie and was heavily into the occult. On 8 May 1974 he died, just 37 years old, under a tube train at Finsbury Park. He was thought to have been off drugs at the time but whatever the case it was a sad loss to the British R&B / rock scene.

Live At Klooks Kleek features the band's classic line-up (A). The menu is a mixture of R&B classics like *What'd I Say* and *Big Boss Man* and self-arranged traditional songs.

Compilation appearances have included:- *Hoochie Coochie Man* and *Harmonica* (which had previously only appeared on the *Gonks Go Beat* (LP) soundtrack) on *R&B Scene, Vol. 2 - 1963-1969* (LP); *Little Girl* and *Strut Around* on *The Soul Of British RnB 1962-68* (LP); *Little Girl* on *The Mod Scene* (CD); *Long Legged Baby* on *Mod Scene, Vol. 2* (CD) and *Sixties Lost And Found, Vol. 3* (LP); *Long Tall Shorty* and *Long Legged Baby* on *Pop Inside The '60s, Vol. 2* (CD) and *Sixties Explosion, Vol. 1* (CD); *Long Tall Shorty* on *The R&B Scene* (CD), *Sixties Lost And Found, Vol. 2* (LP) and *Hard-Up Heroes* (2-LP); *Wade In The Water* on *R&B At Abbey Road* (CD); *Little Girl*, *Strut Around* and *Harmonica* on *British R'n'B Explosion, Vol. 1* (CD); and *Long Tall Shorty*, *Long Legged Baby*, *High Heeled Sneakers*, *Hoochie Coochie Man*, *Little Girl*, *Strut Around*, *Harmonica* and *Wade In The Water* on *Broken Dreams, Vol. 7* (LP). They also have a live set featured on side two of *The Roots Of British Rock, Vol 3* (LP), whilst *The Roots Of British Rock, Vol 4* (LP) includes the band

THE GRAHAM BOND ORGANIZATION - The Sound Of '65 (LP).

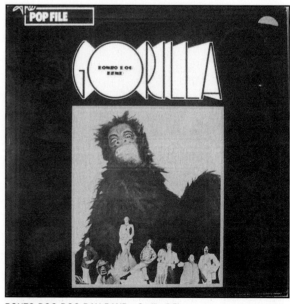

BONZO DOG DOO DAH BAND - Gorilla (LP).

playing *The First Time I Met The Blues*, *Stormy Monday*, *What'd I'd Say*, *Train Time* and a rave up finale. (VJ)

Graham Bond and Pete Brown

ALBUM: 1   TWO HEADS ARE BETTER THAN ONE
(Chapter One CHSR 813) 1972 R2

NB: Issued by Harvest in France. Reissued as *Two Heads Are Better Than One... Plus* (See For Miles SEECD 345) 1992 and *Two Heads Are Better Than One*, including *Maltamour Soundtrack* (Repertoire REP 4271) 1992.

45:        Lost Tribe//Macumbe
           Milk Is Turning Sour In My Shoes (Greenwich G 55104) 1972 SC

This album and 45 were the result of a collaboration between R&B bandleader **Graham Bond and Pete Brown**, leader of **Battered Ornaments** and **Piblokto!**, who'd also written lyrics for **Cream** and was a bit of a poet. The album ranged from R&B material, reminiscent of **The Graham Bond Organisation**, to more ambitious mid-seventies style jazz-rock with elements of funk. It has become a minor collector's album but the recent CD reissues have made it accessible to a wider audience once again.

The See For Miles reissue comes with additional cuts and the usual excellent sleevenotes from Brian Hogg based on an interview with **Pete Brown**. The Repertoire release comes with notes penned by **Pete Brown** and material from the 'Maltamour' soundtrack that the two collaborated on. (VJ)

Bonzo Dog Doo Dah Band

Personnel:			
NEIL INNES	keyb'ds, bs, gtr, vcls	ABC
BOB KERR	hrmnca, vcls	A
VERNON NOWELL	bs, banjo	A
RODNEY SLATER	sax	ABC
LARRY SMITH	drms	ABC
ROGER RUSKIN SPEAR	sax	ABC
SAM SPOONS	perc	A
VIV STANSHALL	vcls, trumpet	ABC
DAVE CLAGUE	bs	B
DENNIS COWAN	bs, vcls	C

HCP

ALBUMS: 1(A) GORILLA   (Liberty LBS 83056) 1967 R1 -
        2(B) THE DOUGHNUT IN GRANNY'S GREENHOUSE
                                 (Liberty LBS 83158) 1968 R1 40
        3(C) TADPOLES   (Liberty LBS 83257) 1969 R1 36
        4(D) KEYNSHAM   (Liberty LBS 83290) 1969 R1 -
        5(-) THE BEST OF THE BONZOS (Liberty LBS 83332) 1970 -
        6(-) LET'S MAKE UP AND BE FRIENDLY
                                 (United Artists UAS 29288) 1972 -

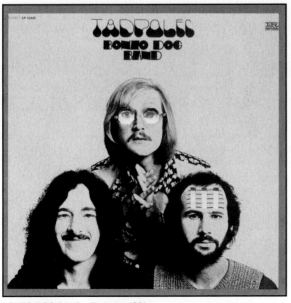

BONZO DOG BAND - Tadpoles (CD).

BONZO DOG BAND - Keynsham (LP).

        7(C) URBAN SPACEMAN   (Sunset SLS 50418) 1973 SC -
        8(-) THE HISTORY OF THE BONZOS (2-LP)
                                 (United Artists UAS 60071/2) 1974 SC 41
        9(-) VERY BEST OF THE BONZOS
                                 (Music For Pleasure 4156801) 1984 -

NB: (1) later reissued in Britain on Sunset (1970), United Artists (1980), Beat Goes On (BGOLP 82) 1990, also on CD (BGOCD 82) 1990. (2) later reissued in Britain on Sunset (1971) and Edsel (XED 209) 1987. (4) later reissued in Britain on Sunset (1975), United Artists (1980) and Edsel (1987). (6) reissued on Awareness (AWL 1004) 1986. (3) reissued on Edsel (XED 186) in 1986. (3) and (4) reissued as *The Outro* (Music For Pleasure CDMFP 6311) 199?. There's also some later compilations *The Bestiality Of The Bonzo Dog Band* (EMI EMS 1335) 1990 and *The Best Of The Bonzo Dog Band* (Rhino R2 71006) 1991. *A History Of The Bonzos* (Beat Goes On BGO 376) is a 2-CD compilation. *Anthropology* (Voiceprint DJC 008) is an alternative compilation. *Cornology* (EMI CD DOG 1) 1992 is a three-CD boxed set compilation including all of (1), (2), (3), (4) and (6) plus some early singles and other rarities like a German language version of *Mr. Apollo*. A more recent compilation is *New Tricks* (Sanctuary MRCD 199) 2001. Also of interest is *The Complete BBC Recordings* (Strange Fruit SFRSCD 108) 2002.

HCP

45s: My Brother Makes The Noises For The Talkies/I'm Gonna
         Bring A Watermelon To My Gal Tonight
                                 (Parlophone R 5430) 1966 -
         Alley Oop/Button Up Your Overcoat (Parlophone R 5499) 1966 -
         Equestrian Statue/
         The Intro And The Outro   (Liberty LBF 15040) 1967 -
         I'm The Urban Spaceman/
         Canyons Of Your Mind   (Liberty LBF 15144) 1968 5
         Mister Apollo/Ready Mades   (Liberty LBF 15201) 1969 -
         I Want To Be With You/
         We Were Wrong   (Liberty LBF 15273) 1969 -
         You Done My Brain In/
         Mr. Slater's Parrot   (Liberty LBF 15314) 1970 -
Reissues: The Intro And The Outro/
         Hello Mabel   (United Artists UP 35602) 1973 -
         Mr. Slater's Parrot/
         Noises For The Leg   (United Artists UP 35662) 1974 -
         The Intro And The Outro/
         Hello Mabel   (United Artists UP 36002) 1975 -
         I'm The Urban Spaceman/The Intro And The Outro/
         Strain   (United Artists UP 36397) 1978 -
         I'm The Urban Spaceman/
         The Intro And The Outro   (EMI G 4533) 1984 -

The Bonzos formed in Goldsmith's College, South London, in late 1965. They'd originally been known as The Bonzo Dog Dada Band, but the name was soon changed to save them the trouble of continually having to explain who or what Dada was. They recorded a couple of singles for Parlophone in 1966 but neither made any impact.

In 1967 they were signed by Liberty (after appearing in **The Beatles'** 'Magical Mystery Tour' film) and recorded the *Gorilla* album, which was a mixture of jazz and eccentricity. *Equestrian Statue* was culled from the

105

BONZO DOG BAND - Let's Make Up And Be Friendly (CD).

album and issued as a 45, but made little impact. This album included several of what would become their cult favourites:- *Cool Britannia, The Intro And The Outro, Jollity Farm, The Sound Of Music*, and *Mickey's Son And Daughter*.

Their most successful recording was *I'm The Urban Spaceman*, a typically eccentric song ladened with drug references, that somehow managed not to get banned. The producer, one *Apollo C. Vermouth* according to the record, was in fact **Paul McCartney**. The flip side was pretty memorable too, a sort of love song in which parts of the body were likened to geographical features.

Their next album, *The Doughnut In Granny's Greenhouse*, begs some comparison to Frank Zappa with tracks like *We Are Normal, My Pink Half Of The Drainpipe* and *Rhinocratic Oaths*. It peaked at No 40 in the UK Album Charts.

Their finest 45, *Mr. Apollo*, with some fine spacey guitar work and a strong chorus, surprisingly flopped but their strongest album, *Tadpoles*, did prove their most successful commercially. Aside from containing both sides of the *Urban Spaceman* 45 and *Mr. Apollo* it was their most consistent effort and definitely worth tracking down.

Their fourth album, *Keynsham*, also had its moments, particularly on *You Done My Brain In*, which was released as a 45, and *Mr. Slater's Parrot*.

Early in 1970 they split and all worked on solo projects, although they reformed in 1972 for a reunion album, *Let's Make Up And Be Friendly*, which wasn't bad as reunion albums go. However, it wasn't long-lasting and within a year **Neil Innes** had joined **Grimms**. He later recorded solo albums and singles, created The Rutles (a take-off of **The Beatles**) with Monty Python's Eric Idle and got his own TV show 'The Innes Book of Records' in 1979. **Roger Ruskin Spear** became a popular live performer with his Giant Kinetic Wardrobe of home made robots, and **Viv Stanshall** made a couple of solo albums. He tragically died after a fire at his Muswell Hill flat in March 1995.

Most of their albums have been reissued more than once since and the double album compilation, *The History Of The Bonzos*, is a fine epitaph. The 1990 compilation *The Bestiality Of Bonzo Dog Band* also demonstrates that some of their humour and music has aged better than one might have expected. It contains many of their better known songs like *Canyons Of Your Mind, Shirt*, the bluesy *Can Blue Men Sing The Whites*, the slightly psychedelic *We Are Normal* and the rather soulful *Trouser Press*. The 1991 CD compilation duplicates some of these but contains 20 tracks in all.

The 2001 Sanctuary compilation is an enjoyable listen but omits a few tracks, such as *Mr Apollo* (their follow-up 45 to *I'm An Urban Spaceman*), which one would expect to find on a definitive compilation of the band.

The *Complete BBC Recordings* is not quite what it purports to be as several of their BBC recordings have disappeared so this comprises what remains. However, there's enough here to whet the appetite. *Anthropology*

has been compiled from rehearsals, demos and works in development from the 1967 through to 1968 era. *New Tricks* is a 21-track compilation of their material.

Bob Kerr went on to form his Whoopee Band which has over the years recorded several albums and which still performs today mainly in and around the London area. Ex-members of the **Bonzos** occasionally perform in his band which is a less zany version of the early **Bonzos** but which is nonetheless still a good act to watch live.

Their appearances on Various Artists' compilations include: *Can Blue Men Sing The Whites* on *Gutbucket* (LP); *I'm The Urban Spaceman* on See For Miles' *20 One Hit Wonders* (LP); *Help* and *Ready Mades* on *Hard Up Heroes, Vol. 2* (CD). (VJ)

The Boomerangs (1)

Personnel:	RAY ARNFIELD		A
	DAVE BLAKEY	lead gtr	A
	BERNIE BYRNES		A
	CEC MOSELY		A
	ALF SAYERS		A

45s:	Rockin' Robin/		
	Don't Let Her Be Your Baby	(Fontana TF 507) 1964 R1
	Another Tear Falls/Fun Fun Fun	(Fontana TF 555) 1965 SC

A Manchester-based beat group. The first 45 was a Contours song - the second a Bacharach/David number. (VJ)

The Boomerangs (2)

45:	Dream World/Upgraded	(Pye 7N 17049) 1966

This was a different but equally obscure band, this time from Ireland. *Dream World* was a folk protest song.

Compilation appearances include: *Dream World* on *Ripples, Vol. 7 - Rainbows* (CD); whilst *Dream World* and *Upgraded* can be found on *Irish Rock - Ireland's Beat Groups 1964-1969* (CD). (VJ)

Boots

45s:	Even The Bad Times Are Good/	
	The Animal In Me	(CBS 3550) 1968 SC
	Keep Your Lovelight Burning/	
	Give Me One More Chance	(CBS 3833) 1968 SC

BONZO DOG BAND - Urban Spaceman (CD).

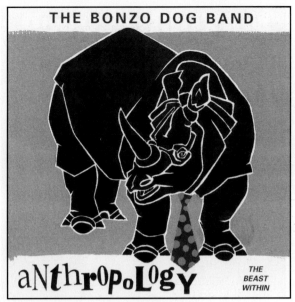

BONZO DOG BAND - Anthropology (CD).

An Edinburgh band, they were previously known as The Beachcombers. They actually recorded *Even The Bad Times Are Good* before the **Tremeloes** released their version. Their drummer Eccles was perhaps one of the first Scottish drummers to use two bass drums and had the words 'Protected by Batman' on them!

Another **Boots**, or possibly the same act recorded one 45 *You'd Better Run* (Youngblood YB 1018) 1970. This featured a good cover of the Young Rascals on the 'A' side, with a group composition on the 'B' side. Originally known as Gregorian Chant, they consisted of: - Don Wright (ld gtr), Dave Bower (or Bown) (gtr, vcls), Terry Bower (or Bown) (bs) and possibly John Wilson (drms)(ex-**Them**, pre-**Taste**) or someone with the surname White. Can anyone confirm whether or not the CBS act is the same band?

Gaby and *But You'll Never Do It Baby* can also be heard on the 4-CD box set *Nuggets 11*. (VJ/JM/GB/RP)

The Boston Crabs

Personnel:	FRED DRIEDLIN	vcls, gtr, hrmnca	A
	IAN JACK	gtr	A
	SIMON JONES	bs	A
	GEOFF MOTT	gtr	A
	ALAN TAYLOR	drms	A

45s:	Down In Mexico/Who?	(Columbia DB 7586) 1965 SC
	As Long As I Have You/Alley Oop	(Columbia DB 7679) 1965 SC
	Gin House/	
	You Don't Have To Be So Nice	(Columbia DB 7830) 1966 SC

This Cambridge band's cover of **Amen Corner**'s *Gin House* resurfaced on EMI's *My Generation* (LP) compilation in 1976 and *Down In Mexico* got a further airing on *R&B Scene, Vol. 1* (LP) and *R&B At Abbey Road* (CD). (VJ)

The Boston Dexters

Personnel:	ALAN COVENTRY	bs	A
	TOTO McNAUGHTON	drms	A
	JOHNNY TURNBULL	gtr	A
	TAM WHITE	vcls	A

45s:	Matchbox/La Bamba	(Contemporary CR 101) 1964 R3
	You've Been Talking About Me/	
	Nothing's Gonna Change Me	(Contemporary CR 102) 1964 R2
	What Kind Of Girl Are You/	
	I've Got Troubles Of My Own	(Contemporary CR 103) 1964 R2
	I Believe To My Soul/	
	I've Got Something To Tell You	(Columbia DB 7498) 1965 R1
	Try Hard/No More Tears	(Columbia DB 7641) 1965 R1

The Boston Dexters (named after thirties gangsters) hailed from Edinburgh and usually appeared on stage dressed as Chicago gangsters. They played urban-styled R&B and the owner of a club they regularly played at put up the cash for them to record six demos which were pressed as three limited-issue singles on the Contemporary label. They were signed to EMI's Columbia label after an audition in January 1965 but it was the usual story; they were given a post-Merseybeat pop composition to record, *I've Got Something To Tell You*, which was untypical of their raw R&B style. This was more evident on the flip. After a further and better 45 the band returned to Edinburgh, disillusioned by the fact they were made to record material that differed from their live repertoire, and broke up soon after.

Tam White and Johnny Turnbull later resurfaced in **Buzz** in 1966. A second version of **The Boston Dexters** was formed by drummer Toto McNaughton in 1966 with a line-up that included Linnie Patterson but they weren't in the same class as the original line-up and fell apart after about nine months. Tam White is still singing the blues in the 21st century.

You can also find *I Believe To My Soul* on *R&B At Abbey Road* (CD). (VJ)

The Bo Street Runners

Personnel:	DAVE CAMERON	bs	ABCD
	JOHN DOMINIC	vcls, hrmnca	ABC
	NIGEL HUTCHINSON	drms	A
	GARY THOMAS	gtr	ABCD
	BOBBY O'BRIEN	keyb'ds	A
	ROY 'FINGERS' FRY	keyb'ds	B
	GLYN THOMAS	drms	B
	MICK FLEETWOOD	drms	C
	TIM HINKLEY	keyb'ds, bck vcl	CD
	MIKE 'TOO MUCH' PATTO	vcls	D
	BARRY WILSON	drms	D

| EP: | 1(A) | BO STREET RUNNERS | (Oak RGJ 131) 1964 R6 |

NB: (1) contains: *Lonely Avenue, Bo Street Runner, Shame, Shame, Shame* and *I Just Wanna Make Love To You*. (1) reissued (Beat Records BEAT 1) 1996. There's also a French CD *I Just Want* (LCD LCD 23-2) that includes all of their 45s and all of the **Soul Agents** 45s - note the sleevenotes are in French!

45s:	Bo Street Runner/Tell Me	(Decca F 118096) 1964 R1
	Tell Me What You're Gonna Do/	
	I Do Just What I Want	(Columbia DB 7488) 1965 R2
	Baby Never Say Goodbye/	
	Get Out Of My Way	(Columbia DB 7640) 1965 R1
	Baby You Can Drive My Car/	
	So Very Woman	(Columbia DB 7901) 1966 R2

NB: There is a 500 copies limited edition pressing of their second single which is a reproduction of the original French jukebox pressing.

BONZO DOG BAND - Cornology (CD Box Set).

The Bo Street Runners existed for barely three years yet within that time thirteen musicians, including five drummers, came and went. It isn't surprising then that references to the band, on sleeve notes and in magazines present a confused history. The following has been written, by band member Gary Thomas in an attempt to remedy this.

The band's genesis came in 1963 within a mainstream jazz group composed of young musicians from the London suburbs of Wembley and Harrow. The band was called Group Indigo (no prizes for guessing their signature tune) and amongst its members were Nigel Hutchinson (drums), John Jenkinson (vocs) and Gary Thomas (bass). At this time, with the ascendance of **The Beatles** the general popularity of jazz was on the wane and as with other bands an interval group developed within Group Indigo which was to play RnB; and usually to receive a much warmer reception than the main band. At the core of this splinter group, largely inspired by **Alexis Korner** and Cyril Davies, were John, Gary and Nigel. With the increasing popularity of R&B in the London area it soon became obvious that this was the direction to develop. Group Indigo was bid farewell and the former interval group become The Road Runners (after the Bo Diddley number) with Gary Thomas switching to guitar, a schoolmate of Gary's, Dick Connor, being brought in on bass and a keyboard player, Bobby O'Brien, was duly recruited. The band found its style of music increasingly popular and began playing regularly in pubs, schools and colleges around the NW London area.

At the end of 1963 Dick Connor left, to live in Denmark and a replacement bassist, Dave Cameron recruited and a name change was decided upon: **Bo Street Runners**, and this was to be the original line-up. Again the Bo Diddley reference as a greater part of the band's repertoire consisted of Diddley songs and much wielding of maracas was to be seen during their performances!

During the winter 63/64 the **'Runners** had set up a residency at a popular music venue of that era, the Railway Hotel in Wealdstone, Harrow. Interestingly this was also to become the launching pad of another unknown West London group **The High Numbers** before changing their name to become **The Who**. The back entrance to the Railway was immortalized as the centre spread of **The Who**'s album *Meaty, Beaty, Big & Bouncy*. The weekly Sunday night sessions had initially been organised by the Wembley branch of the Young Communists League (YCL) and the proceeds from each gig were to be split 50/50 between the band and the YCL. If you were a North London mod during this period the place to be on Sunday nights was the Railway and after a few weeks the pub's car park would be wheel to wheel with chrome adorned Vespas and Lambrettas and the cloakroom stuffed with fur-trimmed anoraks. The gig became so popular that Gary recalls earning more each Sunday night than he received in a weekly student grant.

In the spring of 1964 the ultra-hip TV rock show "Ready Steady Go" announced a competition, Ready Steady Win! for unrecorded amateur groups whose modest intention was to 'find the next Beatles'. Unknown to the boys in the band Dave's mother sent for an application to enter the competition which then required the band to produce a demo recording. As

BO STREET RUNNERS / SOUL AGENTS - I Just Want (CD).

MAXIMUM R'N'B (Comp CD) including The Bo Street Runners.

there was a growing demand from fans for a disc it was decided to kill two birds with one stone and produce not just a single but a 4-track EP. The studio selected was that of RG Jones of Morden, South West London, which had become a popular one amongst aspiring R&B groups. In a short session the 'Runners whacked down a selection of their repertoire; *Lonely Avenue, Bo Street Runner, Shame, Shame, Shame* and *Love To You*. A limited pressing was made, probably just 100, and the disc was issued on the Oak label with a sleeve, hand produced by John, showing the group lined up in a sprinters crouch on a starting line. The EP was rapidly sold to fans at the band's gigs.

The EP has, in the last ten years, become highly collectable with a value of £1,500 attached to it according to a recent (December 2004) issue of Record Collector magazine! (This wasn't the band's first studio outing for a few months previously they had recorded a Diddley inspired jingle for Schmirnoff Vodka to be broadcast on Radio Luxemburg.)

The demo found favour at the TV company and the band was invited to the first round of the competition which was organised as a series of four knockout heats broadcast live from Redifussion TV's Wembley studios. Being local lads the band was able to take along a wild army of fans from the Railway Hotel whose fanatical support in the studio lifted the band's performances and enabled them to reach the final of the competition in the Autumn of that year.

This final round took place at the end of October 1964 at the TV company's Kingsway studios and again spurred on by the Mods the band pulled of a final victory before a judges panel which included the **Beatles**' manager Brian Epstein. At the studio party, which followed the win, Epstein expressed an interest in taking the **'Runners** under his wing; an offer which the band's current manager at the time curiously failed to pursue!

The winners' prize included a recording contract with Decca Records, a publishing deal with Keith Prowse Music (KPM), an agency tie-up with London's biggest agent, Harold Davidson and £1,000 towards new instruments. The latter meant a new p.a. for John, new bass for Dave and a Gretsch Country Gentleman guitar for Gary. Christmas and birthday rolled into one or what? So it seemed, at the time, that the gravy train had arrived and a rosy future lay ahead for the band; but remember the musician's adage 'Don't give up your day job'

During the night of the "Ready Steady Win" final the band cut a second version of the winning number, *Bo Street Runner*, together with the self-penned B-Side, *Tell Me*, for an immediate rush release on the Decca label. The competition had created a great wave of interest amongst a wide cross section of TV viewers and had attracted a huge nationwide audience; it was anticipated the single would sell well. In the event the release didn't chart but did sell a healthy 20,000 copies.

It's interesting at this point to reflect on the reasons for the group's early success. Listening to tracks of groups that competed against the **Bo Street Runners** on the *Ready Steady Win!* vinyl album it's clear that they were in the same amateur league as most of the other bands with no particular musical genius cutting through. Perhaps where they did score was in their live performances and in particular with the image projected by the band's driving force, John Dominic. Also their style of music, London R&B, was clearly definable and quite different to the other groups who were still locked into the Merseyside 'beat' mode.

It was now decision time for the band. Their new agent had already lined up several prestigious gigs; a concert at the Albert Hall with Cliff Richard and **The Shadows**, another at the Empire Pool Wembley with a host of chart toppers and at the end of that year "Ready Steady Go's New Year's Eve Party" with the 'Stones and other big acts from 1964. It was evident that the growing number of commitments, including touring around the country and a number of TV shows could not be undertaken by a part-time group.

John, Gary, and Dave decided to take the plunge and did give up their day jobs whilst Nigel and Bobby O'Brien took the safer option of pursuing their careers. The empty drum and keyboard seats were taken over by two established London jazzmen, Glyn Thomas who also recruited Roy 'Fingers' Fry to the band. Thomas had already played with **Long John Baldry**, **Brian Auger** and Bob Stuckey among others.

A limited company was formed with the three original members as company directors, names were changed, John was reborn as John Dominic and Gary as Gary Lewis, and the "Bo Street Runners Fan Club" was launched. Thomas and Fry also became directors of the band. With precious little time to rehearse the new line up, now full-time, embarked on a busy schedule of radio and TV shows and gigs up and down the country.

The introduction of the two out and out jazzers into the line up had a radical effect on the bands repertoire and overall sound. Several Jimmy Smith instrumental numbers entered the programme and the sound became less raw and more sophisticated. These early months, bowling along on the massive publicity created by the "Ready Steady Win" success were exciting times even though outside the R&B club scene of the South East the reception the band was receiving was sometimes less than ecstatic. Part of the problem lay in the fact that the 'Runners were now working the 'pop' circuit which mainly consisted of gigs in large dancehalls throughout the provinces. Their music, largely made up of covers of Muddy Waters, Jimmy Reed and Bo Diddley tunes, plus the new jazz influence, was alien to teenage ears north of Watford who were more accustomed to gyrating to Merseyside chart groups. However for a while the work kept coming in and the money was good.

In early 1965 it was clear that a follow up release was going to be needed and having no more original songs in the pipeline the band began looking around for a suitable number. The coming man at this time who was beginning to make waves in the UK was James Brown and by a lucky chance the 'Runners publisher, KPM Music, held the publishing rights, for his work. Under pressure from KPM, who would benefit considerably from a James Brown cover hit, the group decided on recording the jazzy *Tell Me What You Gonna Do* as an 'A' side with Brown's more funky *I Do Just What I Want* as the flip. To enhance the soul groove that the band was moving into, jazz saxist Dave Quincy was brought into the band and so for the first time the **Bo Street Runners** had a six piece line up.

This second recording was to be released on the Columbia label and was recorded at their Portland Place studio being produced by the pop hit maker Mickie Most. Not overimpressed by the musicianship within the group and following common practice at that time, Most hired several session musicians for the recording, including Big Jim Sullivan who played a blistering guitar solo on the 'A' side. The single was released and received favourable reviews on both radio and TV shows and in the press. Sadly the record buying public were not interested, however, and the disc bombed. Although musically both sides were streets ahead of the first release the band's new sound bore no resemblance to the old with only John Dominic's powerful vocals providing continuity.

Not long after this disappointment the jazzers decided to cut their losses leaving John, Gary and Dave to find replacements. Adverts in 'Melody Maker' found a young and talented keyboard player, Tim Hinkley and a search of the Charing Cross Road music shops' noticeboards unearthed an even younger drummer, Mick Fleetwood, who had just parted company with the popular club band **The Cheynes**. This move was to be just one small step in Mick's rise to mega-stardom in later years. The bizarre introduction he had to gigs with the band is recounted in **Bob Brunning's** book, 'Blues, the British Connection' (Blandford Press 1986).

So once again the band underwent a change of line-up and a shift in style. It was less jazzy now but funkier, particularly when Tim Hinkley invested in a Hammond organ with its giant Leslie speaker which gave the group a new soulful sound. Gigs kept coming in but lacking a hit record there was an inevitable downsizing in the kind of venues being played. Gone were the big, well paid dates on the Rank dancehall circuit and in came the less lucrative, but in many ways more enjoyable small club gigs. A weekly residency was established at London's 100 Club where the support band, **Bluesology**, featured the unassuming, bespectacled keyboards player Reg Dwight who would later emerge from his caccoon as **Elton John**.

By the time summer 1965 arrived Apollo Music had taken over as the band's management and agent and again the search was on for the elusive hit tune. Amongst the groups that Apollo represented was **Unit 4 + 2** who had had a huge hit with their original composition *Concrete And Clay* written by group member Tommy Moeller. It wasn't surprising then for Apollo to offer another of Moeller's compositions *Baby Never Say Goodbye* to the 'Runners as their next release. This well structured and catchy tune was very much in the vein of *Concrete And Clay* and appeared to everyone concerned to provide the hit the band so needed. It's curious, in retrospect, that Unit 4 + 2 didn't use the number as a follow up to their first success.

So into a budget studio this time and without a name producer the **Bo Street Runners** recorded their third single. Unfortunately the quality of the final mix reveals the cost cutting and it sounds more like a demo disc than a finished product. In the weeks following its release it received a few airplays and reached the mid-twenties in the pirate radio ship 'Radio London's' chart. In retrospect the song was a strange one to have chosen having nothing in common with the group's style or musical roots; not a hint of blues, soul or jazz but pure pop.

Perhaps record buyers sensed this mis-match and the record would certainly not have appealed to the band's R&B fans anyway, the upshot was poor sales and so back to touring on the club circuit. Shortly afterwards Mick Fleetwood said farewell and joined **Pete B's Looners** a band led by his old musical mate **Peter Bardens** and was replaced, briefly, by Alan Turner. A couple of months on singer John Dominic decided that his future wasn't to be in the world of music and returned to his job in an advertising agency though keeping his links with the group as co-manager.

Replacing John was to prove fairly straightforward for during that summer the band had been supported at a gig somewhere in the wilds of Norfolk by a local band, The Bluebottles, which had featured the impressive soul singer **Mike Patto**. Contact was made and after competing at an audition with a number of other hopefuls **Patto** joined the 'Runners bringing with him his Norwich drummer, Barry Wilson.

So New Year 1966 saw yet another line up with only two members of the original group still in place; Gary Thomas on guitar and Dave Cameron on bass. With the arrival of **Patto** came another change of management with the band now being handled by Stephen Komlosy from his Gerard Street office. The band's programme shifted once again; out went the remaining

RARE SIXTIES BEAT TREASURES VOL. 1 (Comp CD) including The Bo Street Runners.

blues standards of Muddy Waters and Jimmy Reed and in came numbers by Wilson Pickett, Otis Reading and Booker T which more suited Mike's voice. Gigs were still coming in and the band settled into the London and provincial club circuit once more. These modestly paid bread and butter venues were topped up with more prestigious dates at universities and colleges where the 'Runners usually played support to bigger names such as **John Mayall**, **Manfred Mann** or **Steampacket**. Fronted by the dynamic **Mike 'Too Much' Patto**, and with a developing musicality within the band, respect and interest from both the 'soul' audiences and fellow musicians began too grow. All the group needed now was a successful single. Sadly with virtually no airplay and thin press coverage the record was destined for oblivion alley.

This then was to be the final chapter in the **Bo Street Runner** story for without chart success the group was condemned to a continuing circuit of small venues which only just provided a living wage. After a series of disasters involving band wagons and a number of let downs by dodgy promoters at the end of that autumn the group members decided to call it a day and the band was quietly put to sleep.

Of the final line-up **Mike Patto** went on to form his own bands to record and write. Tim Hinkley to carve a career as session player whilst the two remaining original runners, Gary and Dave returned to their respective day jobs as a teacher and aircraft engineer.

At the end of the seventies, with a return of interest by the public in Chicago style R&B, Gary Thomas returned to the music scene and by the early eighties had formed the highly-rated London blues band The Radical Sheiks who can be sampled only their the vinyl mini album (Red Door Records AB 1). Throughout the eighties he was also playing as sideman with eccentric harmonica player and singer Wolfie Witcher; dubbed as 'The Clown Prince of RnB'. As a result of these activities in 1992 he was approached by the organiser of a neo-mod club in North London with the idea of organising a **Bo Street Runners** reunion gig. The 'Runners, by this time, had achieved a mythical reputation amongst the new generation of mods. John Dominic agreed to the project and a new line up was formed which included a top rhythm section of Andy 'Wally' Coughlan on bass, Sam Kelly drums, augmented by John Gourd on guitar and Doc Docherty keyboards. So almost thirty years on the 'Runners trod the boards once more though admittedly in the backroom of a seedy pub in the Archway. However inspired by a warm reception the outing was repeated a few months later at the more prestigious Rock Garden club this time with two other 'Runners, Tim Hinkley and Dave Cameron sitting in for a couple of numbers. Sadly Mick Fleetwood was unable to wing over from LA to complete the line-up!

Compilation appearances have included:- *Bo Street Runner*, *Tell Me What You Gonna Do*, *I Do Just What I Want*, *Baby Never Say Goodbye* and *Get Out Of My Way* on *Ready Steady Win* (LP & CD), an album released by Columbia after the competition, and subsequently reissued by See For Miles; *Bo Street Runner* on *Maximum R'n'B* (CD), *The Demention Of Sound* (LP), *Bo Street Runner* on *Sixties Lost And Found, Vol. 3* (LP) and *Weekend Starts Here* (LP); *I Just Wanna Make Love To You*, *Lonely*

DAVID BOWIE - The Man Who Sold The World (LP).

Avenue, *Bo Street Runner* and *Shame Shame Shame* on *Rare 60's Beat Treasures, Vol. 1* (CD).

Glyn Thomas moved to California in 1981 to launch Simmons Electronic Drums on the USA music scene - it was so successful that in 1988 he sold the company and retired. Roy Fry tragically died of a heart attack aged 27 a couple of years after leaving the band. (© Gareth Thomas/VJ)

Simon Boswell

ALBUM: 1   THE MIND PARASITES   (Transatlantic TRA 307) 1975

Simon Boswell was an **Al Stewart**-like folk artist. *The Mind Parasites* can also be heard on *The Transatlantic Story* CD box set. (MWh)

The Bow Bells

Personnel incl: GLEN STUART
                  TERRY WALE
                  NOLA YORK

45s: Not To Be Taken/
           I'll Try Not To Hold It Against You   (Polydor 56030) 1965
           Belinda/When You're In   (Parlophone R 5520) 1966

The Bow Bells was a pretty mainstream dance-pop combo from Liverpool. York had recorded a solo 45 the previous year and recorded ballads throughout the decade. (VJ)

David Bowie

HCP

ALBUMS:			HCP
(up to	1	DAVID BOWIE (mono/stereo)	
1976)		(Deram DML/SML 1007) 1967	R3 -
	2	DAVID BOWIE (Philips SBL 7912) 1967	R3 -
	3	THE WORLD OF DAVID BOWIE	
		(Decca SPA 58) 1967	SC -
	4	THE MAN WHO SOLD THE WORLD	
		(Mercury 6338 041) 1970	R3 -
	5	HUNKY DORY (RCA SF 8244) 1971	3
	6	THE RISE AND FALL OF ZIGGY STARDUST	
		AND THE SPIDERS FROM MARS (RCA SF 8267) 1972	5
	7	SPACE ODDITY (RCA LSP 4813) 1972	17
	8	THE MAN WHO SOLD THE WORLD	
		(RCA LSP 4816) 1972	26
	9	ALLADDIN SANE (RCA RS 1001) 1973	1
	10	PIN-UPS (RCA RS 1003) 1973	1
	11	DIAMOND DOGS (RCA APL 1-0576) 1974	1
	12	DAVID LIVE (2-LP) (RCA APL 2-077) 1974	2
	13	YOUNG AMERICANS (RCA APL 1-1006) 1975	2
	14	IMAGES 1966-67 (2-LP) (Decca DPA 3017/8) 1975	-
	15	STATION TO STATION (RCA APL 1-1327) 1976	5
	16	CHANGES ONE BOWIE (RCA RS 1055) 1976	2

NB: (7) was a reissue of (2). (6), (15) and (9) later reissued on RCA International INTS (5063), (5064) and (5067) respectively. (14) comprised material from the same period as (1). (10), (13) and (14) reissued on RCA LP (3004), (3009) and (3013) respectively. (4), (5) and (7) reissued on CD by EMI (1990). (5) reissued on vinyl (EMI LPCENT 21) 1997. (6) reissued on CD (EMI CDP 79 4400 2) in 1990, followed by (9) and (10) (EMI CDEMC 3579 and 3580) also in 1990. (9) reissued on vinyl (EMI 7243 4 99463 1 6) 1999. (11) and (12) reissued on CD and album (EMI EMC 3584) and (EMI DBLD 1) respectively in 1990. (12) reissued again on CD (EMI) 2005, with bonus tracks. (15) reissued on CD at mid-price (EMI) 1998. His later albums, *Low* (EMI CDEMD 1027), *Heroes* (EMI CDEMD 1025) and *Lodger* (EMI CDEMD 1026) were all reissued on CD in 1991 with some bonus tracks. *The Collection* (Castle CCSCD 118) 1992 concentrated on material from his early years. *Santa Monica '72* (Golden Years GY 002) 1994 is a legitimate issue of his legendary 20 October 1972 concert at the Santa Monica Civic Auditorium. It comes with a 16-page booklet full of photos and memorabilia. (15) and (16) reissued on CD (EMI CDEMD 1020) 1991 and (RCA PD 81732) 1984, but deleted in 1986. The CD *David Bowie* (Deram 800 087-2) 1988 features all his 1967 recordings for Deram. *Early On (1964-66)* (Rhino RZ 70526) 1991 (VS CD) is a very comprehensive look at his early career and includes five previously unissued tracks making it an essential item for Bowie fans. There's also *1966: David Bowie* (Castle Communications CLACD 154) 1989 and a 2-CD set, *Best Of Bowie* (EMI 539 8212) 2002. *The Best Of 1969 - 1974* (EMI CDPP 029) 1997 could well be the best 20-track CD compilation of his material from this era to date and includes the full length studio version of *All The Young Dudes*. *I Dig Everything: The 1966 Pye Singles* (Essential ESMCD 712) 1999 documents his early recordings. *Changesbowie* (EMI DB TV 1) is a double-LP hits

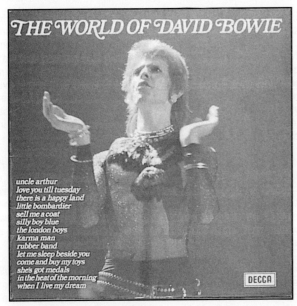

DAVID BOWIE - The World Of (LP).

collection, which still manages to omit four of his Top Ten hits:- *Sorrow, Knock On Wood, Boys Keep Swinging* and *Drive-In Saturday*. *Diamond Dogs 30th Anniversary Edition* (EMI 5778572) 2004 is a 2-CD set with lots of additional tracks but few treats. *Platinum Collection* (EMI 331 3142) 2005 is a 3-CD set with some nice surprises, but it only covers his material with EMI.

45s:				HCP
δ	Can't Help Thinking About Me/			
(up to	And I Say To Myself	(Pye 7N 17020)	1966	R3 -
1976)	Do Anything You Say/			
	Good Morning Girl	(Pye 7N 17079)	1966	R3 -
	I Dig Everything/I'm Not Losing Sleep	(Pye 7N 17157)	1966	R3 -
	Rubber Band/The London Boys	(Deram DM 107)	1966	R3 -
α	The Laughing Gnome/			
	The Gospel According To Tony Day	(Deram DM 123)	1967	R2 6
	Love You Till Tuesday/			
	Did You Ever Have A Dream?	(Deram DM 135)	1967	R3 -
β	Space Oddity/Wild-Eyed Boy From			
	Freecloud (mono and stereo)	(Philips BF 1801)	1969	5
	The Prettiest Star/			
	Conversation Piece	(Mercury MF 1135)	1970	R3 -
	Memory Of A Free Festival (Part 1)/			
	(Part 2)	(Mercury 6052 026)	1970	R3 -
	Holy Holy/Black Country Rock	(Mercury 6052 049)	1971	R3 -
	Changes/Andy Warhol	(RCA 2160)	1972	-
	Starman/Suffragette City (Some P/S)	(RCA 2199)	1972	R2/- 10
χ	John I'm Only Dancing/			
	Hang On To Yourself	(RCA 2263)	1972	12
	Do Anything You Say//I Dig Everything/			
	Can't Help Thinking About Me			
	I'm Not Losing Sleep (P/S)	(Pye 7NX 8002)	1972	-
	The Jean Genie/Ziggy Stardust	(RCA 2302)	1972	2
	Drive-In Saturday/Round And Round	(RCA 2352)	1973	3
	Life On Mars/			
	The Man Who Sold The World (Some P/S)	(RCA 2316)	1973	3
	Sorrow/Amsterdam	(RCA 2424)	1973	3
	Rebel Rebel/Lady Grinning Soul	(RCA APBO 0287)	1974	5
	Rock'n'Roll Suicide/Quicksand	(RCA LPBO 5021)	1974	22
	Diamond Dogs/Holy Holy	(RCA APBO 0293)	1974	21
	Knock On Wood (live)/			
	Panic In Detroit (live)	(RCA 2466)	1974	10
	Bowie's Greatest Hits (flexidisc with Record Mirror)			
		(Lyntone LYN 2929)	1974	-
	Young Americans/Suffragette City	(RCA 2523)	1975	18
	The London Boys/Love You Till Tuesday	(Decca F 13579)	1975	-
	Fame/Right	(RCA 2579)	1975	17
	Space Oddity/			
	Changes/Velvet Goldmine (Some P/S)	(RCA 2593)	1975	1
	Golden Years/Can You Hear Me	(RCA 2640)	1975	8
	TVC-15/We Are The Dead	(RCA 2682)	1976	33
	Suffragette City/Stay (Some P/S)	(RCA 2726)	1976	SC -

NB: δ with The Lower Third. α This was not a hit until 1973. Some picture sleeves were printed to promote β and then not distributed, just two or three copies are

known to have survived and these are valued at in excess of £3,000. χ Later reissued in 1973 with an alternative version of the 'A' side. PRT have subsequently reissued **Bowie**'s 1966 singles several times. There's also a 12" picture disc issue containing all three 45s (PRT PYX 6001) 1988.

Few rock stars have had the lasting impact that **David Bowie** has. His career has passed through several phases and all of them have successfully engaged the record buying public. A mod in the mid-sixties, he re-emerged with his Ziggy Stardust persona in the early seventies to capture the imagination of the record-buying public, redefine glam-rock and become an international star. *Young Americans*, a funky soul-oriented album marked another change of direction in the mid-seventies to what he termed 'plastic soul'. Towards the end of the decade he flirted with more avant-garde experimental electronic music. He was always trying something new and interesting.

David Bowie was born on 8th January 1947 in Brixton, London. His real name was David Jones. He sang and occasionally played sax in a part-time group The Kon-Rads during 1962/63 but his first full-time band was **Davie Jones and The King Bees**, which he formed with George Underwood in 1964. When the group split up at the end of 1964 **Bowie** moved to **The Manish Boys**, although they lasted only a few months, but issued one single.

In June 1965 **Bowie** formed a new outfit The Lower Third. After releasing a 45 for Parlophone *You've Got A Habit Of Leaving* the band was spotted playing at London's Marquee by Ken Pitt who became their manager. **Bowie** also penned an earlier single for them, *Born Of The Night*, which may exist in acetate format. By now David Jones was using the name **David Bowie**. The first single, *Can't Help Thinking About Me*, was one of the best of his early days. A beautiful song with idiosyncratic lyrics it got considerable airplay on pirate station Radio London but failed to become a hit. The group split up after this and **Bowie** advertised in the music press to form a new outfit The Buzz (line-up: Derek Boyles (organ), John Eager (drms), Dek Fearnley (bs) and John Hutchinson (gtr), who was later replaced by Billy Gray). They weren't credited on the next soul-influenced single *Do Anything You Say*. The follow-up *I Dig Everything* was a more mod-influenced recording with some distinctive organ, recorded without assistance from The Buzz, who disbanded shortly after its release. After this Pye didn't extend his contract and he was back in the studio recording demos which included *Please Mr. Gravedigger*, *The London Boys* and *Rubber Band*. He took these round the record companies and won a contract with Deram in September 1966. There's also an Oak album of jingles which Ken Pitt owns.

His debut 45 *Rubber Band* was a novelty song with rather sentimental lyrics. The flip slide was the much more interesting *The London Boys*, about the obsessive side of Swinging London, which had some haunting organ work. This is considered by many to be his magnum opus for Deram. He'd earlier recorded a version produced by Tony Hatch in 1965 for a possible single, which was shelved. *Love You Til Tuesday* (later issued by Decca in 1975) was first recorded in 1965 and acetates are believed to exist.

DAVID BOWIE - Hunky Dory (LP).

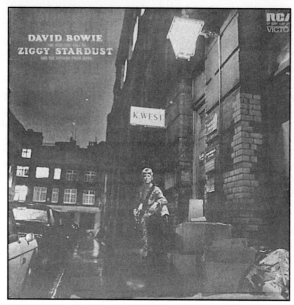

DAVID BOWIE - The Rise And Fall Of Ziggy Stardust... (LP).

Another **Bowie** song, *Over The Wall*, was covered by one **Oscar (Paul Nicholas)**, who later went on to enjoy a successful acting career. Meanwhile, **Bowie**'s next 45 was an unashamedly ultra-commercial load of rubbish, *The Laughing Gnome*, a novelty song sung in a sort of Anthony Newley style. It wasn't a hit on this occasion but later proved a considerable embarrassment to **Bowie** when it was reissued in 1973 and rose to No 6 in the Charts.

His debut album, *David Bowie*, released in June 1967, included his early single *Rubber Band* alongside a collection of pop songs and some vaudeville-inspired songs. One of the better cuts, *Love You Till Tuesday*, was later issued as a 45. This is now one of his more collectable singles. The album got promising reviews but the sales didn't take off and after Decca rejected the next three singles that Pitt submitted for **Bowie** (*Let Me Sleep Beside You, When I Live My Dream* and *In The Heat Of The Morning*) Pitt decided to terminate the contract with Deram. There are various acetates in existence from **Bowie**'s time with Deram which now sell for several hundred pounds. Original pressings of the *David Bowie* album are now very rare.

After his association with Deram ended **Bowie** took mime and dance lessons from Lindsay Kemp and went on to appear in Kemp's mime production of 'Pierrot In Turqoise' in Oxford. He also worked with producer Tony Visconti on a number of tracks for BBC's 'Top Gear' and played a minor role in the film 'The Virgin Soldiers'.

His next band was a short-lived vocal trio called Turquoise, which soon changed its name to Feathers. The other members of the trio were **Bowie**'s girlfriend, Hermione and former Buzz guitarist John Hutchinson.

When Feathers disbanded in February 1969 **Bowie** made a 30-minute film with Pitt, which was designed for TV; auditioned for the rock musical 'Hair'; toured the UK as a support act for **Tyrannosaurus Rex** and recorded an early demo of *Space Oddity*, which was used to secure a new contract with Philips on 20 June. He re-recorded a version of it the same day with producer Gus Dudgeon. He got a big break when the BBC used the song during their coverage of the first moon landing the following month. This almost certainly aided its breakthrough into the Charts where it eventually peaked at No 5.

The success of *Space Oddity* prompted Decca to issue *The World Of Davie Bowie* compilation in 1970. In addition to some cuts from the original *David Bowie* album, it contained *The London Boys* (the flip side of his debut 45 for Deram) and three previously unissued tracks - *Karma Man, In The Heat Of The Morning* and *Let Me Sleep Beside You*. The album was one of the last Decca ones issued in both mono and stereo versions and the mono releases are now quite collectable. It didn't sell well at the time but was later repackaged in 1973 at the prime of the Ziggy Stardust era with a Ziggy-type picture on the sleeve which sold much better.

Aside from its Chart success *Space Oddity* was widely recognised for its originality and received an award from the UK Songwriters in recognition of this.

In February 1970 **Bowie** formed a new backing band called Hype, comprising John Cambridge (drms), **Mick Ronson** (gtr) and Tony Visconti (bs). For his next 45 he chose *The Prettiest Star*, which he had written for his future wife Angie Barnet. The disc was issued in March 1970 and the couple married at Bromley Registry Office on 20 March. David had met Angie at a reception at the Speakeasy Club in London the previous Summer. The 45 attracted very little interest and shortly after its release **Bowie** parted company with Ken Pitt who **Bowie** felt was holding him back. His new manager was Tony De Fries, who'd originally been drafted in to handle **Bowie**'s financial affairs.

For the next 45 a lengthy re-recorded version of *Memory Of A Free Festival* was selected. It had originally appeared on his first album and was now split over both sides of the 45, making it a strange choice for release. Mick 'Woody' Woodmansey had replaced John Cambridge on drums in Hype by the time of this recording. Sales were disappointing and this was a major factor (as with his previous and successive single) in explaining why it's an expensive purchase nowadays.

His next album, *The Man Who Sold The World*, was issued in the US in November 1970 in a cartoon cover. It sold very few copies and Mercury arranged for a tour to help promote it early the following year. Work permit difficulties prevented David from playing live but his penchant for wearing dresses during the visit in Texas and LA won him much publicity. Whereas *Space Oddity* had been a largely acoustic set this album was full of dark doom-laden music punctuated by **Ronson**'s incisive guitar riffs with a backing which included a moog synthesizer. **Bowie**'s vocals were cold and impersonal but his voice and the music were ideally suited to the subject matter of many of the songs whose characters were often on the verge of insanity. It's an excellent album and anyone not familiar with it should investigate it immediately. The title track, in particular, was one of **Bowie**'s finest moments. Boosted by his promotional visit it helped establish him as a cult figure in the States. When it was later released here in the UK in April 1971 early copies came with a different sleeve with **Bowie** wearing a dress. This was quickly withdrawn and, as many of you will know; original pressings bearing this sleeve are now major collectors' items. A non-album 45, *Holy Holy*, was also released but flopped. Another **Bowie** song, *Oh! You Pretty Things* (which would appear on his next album) was recorded by Peter Noone and became a Top Ten hit.

The early seventies were a particularly creative period for **Bowie** and he formed a new act **Arnold Corns**, based around his dress designer Freddi Buretti to help market his material. Three demos were sold to B&C Records:- *Hang Onto Yourself, Man In The Middle* and *Moonage Daydream*. These were released on two 45s: *Moonage Daydream/Hang Onto Yourself* and *Hang Onto Yourself/Man In The Middle*. Neither single sold at all and consequently original pressings are now very hard to track down. The other member of this band was Mark Carr Pritchard (bs) but the backing on these tracks was provided by **Ronson**, Woodmansey and former **Rat** Trevor Bolder.

The Man Who Sold The World album was eventually issued here in the UK in April 1971 in a sleeve showing **Bowie** in a dress. The album was later

DAVID BOWIE - Pin-Ups (LP).

withdrawn and copies of these original pressings, which only sold in small quantities, are now highly prized collectors' items. (The album was later reissued by RCA in September 1972).

Arnold Corns split up in March 1971 after the failure of their single and Tony De Fries, having pressed 500 copies of a promo album which featured **Bowie** on one side and **Dana Gillespie** on the other, used it to win **Bowie** a new record contract with RCA. A demo 45, *Bombers/Eight Line Poem*, was put out only in the US. Needless to say, it is now very rare and sought-after by **Bowie** collectors. December 1971 saw the release of *Hunky Dory*. The album didn't sell well at first and was patchy, but it did contain some of his finest moments in *Changes, Life On Mars?*, which both had considerable commercial potential (indeed the former was his next single), the more sensitive *Quicksand* and *Queen Bitch*. It also contained *Oh! You Pretty Things*. More irritating was *Andy Warhol*, a song **Bowie** had originally written for **Dana Gillespie**. Although the *Changes* single failed to Chart here it did get to No 66 in the US.

He toured the UK in February 1972, now naming his backing band (Trevor Bolder (bs), **Mick Ronson** (gtr, vcls) and Woody Woodmansey (drms)) The Spiders. In the US, meanwhile, *Hunky Dory*, belatedly entered the Charts, creeping to No 93 in April, whilst here in the UK *Starman* was released as a single, eventually climbing to No 10 here and No 65 in the US. It was followed in June by *The Rise And Fall Of Ziggy Stardust And The Spiders From Mars*, the album which gave him his big breakthrough in the UK where it climbed to No 5 (it reached No 75 in the US). This was a much more consistent album than *Hunky Dory*, though similar in style. Again it contained several classic **Bowie** songs - *Suffragette City, Rock'n'Roll Suicide, Five Years, Moonage Daydream*, the title track and *Starman*. It also introduced **Bowie** acting the role of Ziggy, a sort of bisexual otherworldly astronaut, a prophet of both doom and extravagance - it all made for wonderful rock theatre.

Bowie was now a household name and the less interesting but weird *John I'm Only Dancing* 45 was released as a 45 in the UK climbing to No 12. Hard on the heels of the success with *Ziggy Stardust* his previous album *Hunky Dory* belatedly climbed to No 3 in the UK Album Charts. RCA were quick to reissue *The Man Who Sold The World* and his first album, retitled as *Space Oddity*. They climbed to No 26 and 17 in the UK and 105 and 16 in the US. *The Jean Genie*, a pulsating rock song with a great beat, was released the same month. Written during a US tour and recorded in New York it was another big hit here (No 2) but only managed No 71 in the US, where it was left to a reissue of the *Space Oddity* 45 to give him his first Top 20 hit.

On 25th January 1973 **Bowie** embarked on a 100-day World Tour which included the US and Japan. His next album, *Alladin Sane*, was an enormous commercial success (UK No 1, US No 12) but suffered from being rushed out in the wake of his megastar status. Still, the title track was stunning with some captivating piano playing and it also included another massive UK hit, *Drive-In Saturday* (No 3) and his earlier 45 release *The Jean Genie*.

When **Bowie** completed his World Tour he embarked on a UK tour during which *Life On Mars* (from *Hunky Dory*) was released as a 45 by popular demand. It climbed to No 3. The UK tour closed at the Hammersmith Odeon, London, on 3 July 1973, when **Bowie** announced he had retired from live performing. In fact it later transpired that it was Ziggy **Bowie** was retiring.

During his 'retirement' Deram reissued his *Laughing Gnome* 45, causing him considerable embarrassment, particularly since it got to No 6 in the UK Charts. **Bowie** also recorded a new (and very disappointing) album of his versions of some of his favourite sixties acts' songs. Whilst it contained several classics his treatment of many of them was very disappointing. Despite this, given his popularity and that of many of the songs the album, *Pin-Ups*, topped the UK Charts. About the best cover version, that of **The Merseys'** *Sorrow*, was issued as a 45 peaking at No 3 in the UK.

After this **Bowie** pursued stage ambitions but when they collapsed he concentrated on his *Diamond Dogs* album. Only **Aynsley Dunbar** from his earlier backing band appeared on this album and **Bowie** took on the lead guitar role. The album had been preceded by the *Rebel Rebel* 45, which featured superb lead guitar work from **Bowie** and made the UK Top 5. Surprisingly *Rock'n'Roll Suicide* (from *Ziggy Stardust*) was belatedly selected by RCA for the follow-up 45 and it got to No 22 in the UK. In between these two releases **Bowie** moved to the US to live in April 1974.

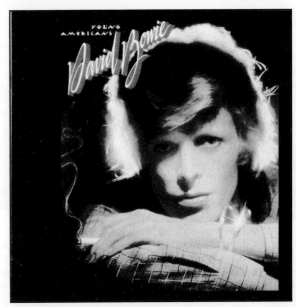

DAVID BOWIE - Young Americans (CD).

To help promote the *Diamond Dogs* album **Bowie** embarked on a 'Diamond Dogs' tour, a highly theatrical spectacle which developed some of the concepts on the album further. The album was packaged in a controversial sleeve painting by the Belgium artist Guy Peelaert, which displayed genitalia by the half-Ziggy, half-something else entity on the sleeve. Later copies were altered by RCA but some of the uncensored versions got into circulation and these are now very collectable. The album was another enormous commercial success, topping the Charts here and peaking at No 5 in the US. The title track was issued as a 45 but only charted here, where it climbed to No 21. The 'Diamond Dogs' tour, which had opened in Montreal, Canada, on 14 June, closed at Madison Square Gardens in New York on 20 July 1974. Plans to transfer it to London had to be abandoned because the enterprise didn't seem financially viable.

As 1974 drew to a close **Bowie** enjoyed another Top Ten hit here in Britain with his cover of Eddie Floyd's *Knock On Wood* and the *David Live* album, a double set which had been recorded at The Tower, Philadelphia, during the 'Diamond Dogs' tour, rose to No 2 in the UK and No 8 in the US. This was significant for representing the first signs of his gradual shift towards R&B and soul music. In the US, meanwhile, *Changes* was belatedly issued as a 45 climbing to No 41.

To many **Bowie** seemed in decline at the start of 1975. There were question marks against his health and he was becoming increasingly dissatisfied with his manager Tony De Fries, from whom he eventually broke away after a prolonged legal dispute. **Bowie** surprised many when he bounced back with *Young Americans*, a funky soul-orientated album which featured **John Lennon** on a couple of tracks. The album sold very well climbing to No 2 in the UK and No 9 in the US. The title track was released as a 45 making the Top 20 here and No 28 in the US. This was followed by *Fame* (one of the tracks co-written with **Lennon**), which again made the Top 20 but did much better in the US, where it held the No 1 spot for two weeks. He also belatedly began an acting career appearing in the Nicholas Roeg-directed movie 'The Man Who Fell To Earth'. The film was premiered the following year (on 18 March 1976) in London, though **Bowie** wasn't present - he was touring the US at the time.

He topped the UK 45 Charts for the first time in October 1975 when *Space Oddity* was reissued on a three cut 45 with *Changes* and the previously unreleased *Velvet Goldmine*.

The soul/funk influence continued in **Bowie**'s music. 1976 began with the *Golden Years* 45 making the Top Ten on both sides of the Atlantic. It was taken from his *Station To Station* album which was another big commercial success peaking at No 5 here and No 3 in the US. To help promote the album, he'd embarked on another World Tour commencing in Vancouver, Canada, on 2 February. Later in May he played six shows at Wembley, which would be his first in the UK since his 'retirement' announcement in July 1973.

TVC-15 was a minor UK hit (No 33) in the Summer of 1976, but this was **Bowie** well below his best. The compilation of past hits *Changesonebowie*, which had been compiled by **Bowie**, served to keep him in the public eye reaching No 2 here and No 10 in the US.

As we leave the time frame of this book, **Bowie** had moved to live in West Berlin for a while as a semi-recluse. He would continue to be an extremely successful rock star - his next couple of albums marked a change of musical direction again towards a synthesized 'European' sound. That was **Bowie** all over - there were the prevailing musical fads and trends of the time and there was **David Bowie** who could usually be relied upon to come up with something different and interesting.

Even when he was less fashionable in the eighties and nineties he remained influential and he has continued to record into the millennium.

EMI's 2002 2-CD set *Best Of Bowie* concentrates on most of his 45 hits, although *The Laughing Gnome* is a notable absentee - perhaps that's quality control at work! The 2005 3-CD *Platinum Collection* contains one CD covering the late sixties and early seventies; one covering the mid-late seventies and a third covering the eighties. It's basically another 'best of' and contains mostly what one might expect, although it is confined to the material he recorded for EMI. Unexpected inclusions are a 1975 cover of Bruce Springsteen's *It's Hard To Be A Saint In The City*, *Underground* from the *Labyrinth* soundtrack and *Can You Hear Me* from his *Young Americans* album.

Bowie's appearance on Various Artists' compilations have included:- *Width Of A Circle* on Mercury's *Dimension Of Miracles*; *Can't Help Thinking About Me* (with The Lower Third) on *Hitmakers* (LP), *Maximum '65* (LP) and more recently on the 2-CD set *We Love The Pirates: Charting The Big 'L' Fab 40*; *Space Oddity* on *Sixteen Star Tracks Of The Sixties*; *The London Boys* on *The London Boys* on *Pop Inside The '60s, Vol. 2* (CD), *Sixties Lost And Found, Vol. 2* (LP), *Sixties Explosion, Vol. 1* (CD) and *Hard-Up Heroes* (Dble LP); *Good Morning Girl* on *Doin' The Mod, Vol. 1* (CD); *I'm Not Losing Sleep* on *Doin' The Mod, Vol. 2* (CD); *Can't Help Thinking About Me* on *Rock Of Ages, Four Decades Of Heavy Rock 1962 - 2002*; *The Man Who Sold The World* (with Lulu) on *Best Sellers Of The 70's - Vol 1* (CD) and *I Dig Everything* on the 2-CD set *We Love The Pirates: Charting The Big 'L' Fab 40*. (VJ)

The Alan Bown (Set)

Personnel:			
ALAN BOWN	trumpet		ABCD
STAN HALDANE	bs, vcls		ABC
JOHN HELLIWELL	sax		ABCD
ROBERT PALMER	vcls		AB
VIC SWEENEY	drms		ABCD
TONY CATCHPOLE	gtr		BCD
JESS RODEN	vcls		B
GORDON NEVILLE	vcls		CD
ANDY BROWN	bs, vcls		D

ALBUMS: 1(B)   OUTWARD BOWN
(mono/stereo)   (Music Factory MF 12000) 1967 R1

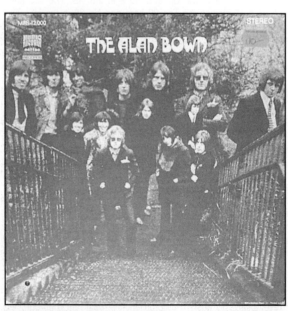

THE ALAN BOWN - Outward Bown (LP).

2(B)	THE ALAN BOWN		
	(mono/stereo)	(Deram DML/SML 1049)	1968 R1
3(C)	LISTEN	(Island ILPS 9131)	1970 SC
4(D)	STRETCHING OUT	(Island ILPS 9163)	1971

NB: (1) reissued (Tenth Planet TP027)1997 limited to 1,000 copies. (2) reissued as *The Early Years* (CS 501) in 1987 and credited to Robert Palmer with Alan Bown. *Emergency 999* (Sequel/Sanctuary KEMCD 483) 2000 is a compilation of their material.

45s:	Can't Let Her Go/I'm The One	(Pye 7N 15934) 1965 R1
	Baby Don't Push Me/	
	Everything's Gonna Be Alright	(Pye 7N 17084) 1966 R1
	Headline News/Mister Pleasure	(Pye 7N 17148) 1966 R1
	Emergency 999/Settle Down	(Pye 7N 17192) 1966 R2
	Gonna Fix You Good (Everytime You're Bad)/	
	I Really Really Care	(Pye 7N 17256) 1967 R1
	We Can Help You/	
	Magic Hankerchief	(Music Factory CUB 1) 1967
	Toyland/Technicolour Dream	(MGM 1355) 1967
	Story Book/Little Lesley	(MGM 1387) 1968
	Still As Stone/Wrong Idea	(Deram DM 259) 1969
	Gypsy Girl/All I Can	(Deram DM 278) 1969
	Pyramid/Crash Landing	(Island WIP 6091) 1971
	Rockford Files/I Don't Know	(CBS 3721) 1975

This was a long running soul and blues influenced outfit that was very popular on the club circuit. Perhaps their finest moment was *We Can Help You*, a whimsical slice of late sixties pop, which surprisingly wasn't a hit - it reached No. 26 in the NME chart, leading to an appearance on "Top of The Pops", but in the week of their appearance, the company pressing the single was on strike, and consequently there were no singles in the shops! Of their other releases, *Headline News* was an Edwin Starr cover; *Emergency 999* was played on the Northern soul scene and *Gonna Fix You Good* was a Little Anthony and The Imperials cover.

As you can see from the line-up information some pretty prestigious musicians passed through **Bown**'s band. When he called it a day in 1974 he played in **Jonesy** and went to work for CBS Records A&R Department.

The reissue of *Outward Bown* on Tenth Planet includes *We Can Help You*, along with their version of *All Along The Watchtower*, which impressed **Hendrix** sufficiently enough for Jimi to start including it in his set, plus other goodies such as **The Bee Gees** influenced *Sally Green*. The album failed to happen, and **Jess Roden** left to pursue a solo career, with the band taking on a more 'progressive' sound.

The Early Years is a reissue of their Deram album and includes both sides of the *Still As Stone* 45 on which **Jess Roden** rather than **Robert Palmer** sings vocals.

Compilation appearances have included: *Baby Don't Push Me* on *The R&B Era, Vol. 2* (LP & CD); *All I Can Do* on *Broken Dreams, Vol. 6* (LP) and on *Fading Yellow, Vol 4* (CD); *Emergency 999* on *Doin' The Mod, Vol. 1* (CD);

THE ALAN BOWN - Listen (LP).

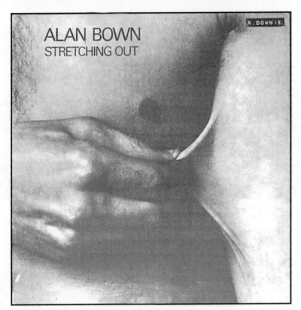

THE ALAN BOWN - Stretching Out (LP).

Baby Don't Push Me and *Everything's Gonna Be Alright* on *Doin' The Mod, Vol. 2* (CD); *I Really Really Care* on *Echoes From The Wilderness - Sixteen UK R&B Freakbeat Trippers* (LP & CD); *Can't Let Her Go* and *I'm The One* on *Footsteps To Fame, Vol. 2* (CD); *Techinicolour Dream* on *Pop-In, Vol 1* (CD); *We Can Help You* on *Pop-In, Vol 2* (CD); *Story Book, Toyland* and *Technicolour Dream* on *Lovely Summer Days* (CD) and *Headline News* on the 2-CD set *We Love The Pirates: Charting The Big 'L' Fab 40*. (VJ)

Andy Bown

ALBUMS:	1	GONE TO MY HEAD	(Mercury 6310 002) 1972
(up to	2	SWEET WILLIAM	(GM GML 1001) 1973
1976)	3	COME BACK ROMANCE ALL IS FORGIVEN	
			(EMI EMC 3176) 1976

45s:	Tarot/Lulli Rides Again	(Parlophone R 5856) 1970
(up to	Sweet William/I Won't Let You Down	(GM GMS 1) 1973
1976)	New York Satyricon Zany/Party Games	(GM GMS 19) 1974
	Supersonic / Feeling Better	(GM GMS 9039) 1975

Aside from these solo efforts **Andy Bown** was in **The Herd** and **Judas Jump**. He also became an associate of **Status Quo** in 1973, though he didn't become an official member until the eighties when Rossi and Parfitt reformed the band. His *Gone To My Head* album contains some good progressive tunes.

The 'A' side to his first solo 45, *Tarot* was the theme to an early seventies TV series "Ace Of Wands", whilst the 'B' side is an instrumental, which was also used as incidental music in the same series.

The *Reading Festival 1973* (CD) compiles his *Long Legged Linda* performance from that particular festival. You can also find *Tarot* on *Justavibration* (LP). (VJ)

Boxer

Personnel:	KEITH ELLIS	bs	A B
	OLLIE HALSALL	gtr, keyb'ds	A B
	TONY NEWMAN	drms	A B
	MIKE PATTO	vcls, keyb'ds	A B C
	CHRIS STAINTON	keyb'ds	A B C
	BOZ BURRELL	vcls	B
	TIM HINKLEY	keyb'ds	B
	BOB TENCH	vcls	B
	NIGEL THOMAS	perc	B
	TIM BOGERT	bs, vcls	C
	ADRIAN FISHER	gtr	C
	EDDIE TUDURI	drms	C

ALBUMS:	1(A)	BELOW THE BELT	(Virgin V 2049) 1975

	2(B)	BLOODLETTING	(Virgin V 2073) 1976 R2
	3(C)	ABSOLUTELY	(Epic EPC 82151) 1977

NB: (1) also released in the US (Virgin PZ 34115) 1975. (2) withdrawn, later issued on CD (Virgin 7243844341) 1997. (3) also released in the US (Epic PE 34812) 1977.

45s:	All The Time In The World/Don't Wait	(Virgin VS 135) 1976
	Everybody's A Star/	
	Can't Stand What You Do	(Epic EPC 5540) 1977
α	Hey Bulldog/Loony Ali	(Virgin 9509) 1978

NB: α US release.

Boxer was notable for their inclusion of **Mike Patto** and **Ollie Halsall**. Their album *Below The Belt* ran into censorship problems as the cover had a picture of a naked lady with a strategically placed boxing glove, the reverse had no such glove - sexist rubbish! The album had its moments musically as all albums featuring **Patto** and **Halsall** do. Both are now sadly not with us.

In 1976 **Boxer** had their *Bloodletting* album withdrawn and consequently it has become sought-after. It was reissued on CD in 1997.

Mike Patto played with **Centipede**, **Bo Street Runners**, **Chicago Blues Line**, **Timebox**, **Spooky Tooth** and **Patto**. **Ollie Halsall** played with **Kevin Ayers**, **Grimms**, **Rhythm and Blues Inc.**, **Tempest**, **Patto** and **Timebox**. **Keith Ellis** played with **Juicy Lucy**, **Spooky Tooth** and **Van der Graaf Generator**. Tony Newman was with **Sounds Incorporated**, **Jeff Beck**, **May Blitz**, **David Bowie**, **T. Rex**, **Three Man Army** and **Driftwood**. Chris Stainton was previously with **Grease Band** / **Joe Cocker**. Adrian Fisher was a former Sparks band member. Tim Bogert also previously played with Cactus and **Beck, Bogert and Appice**. (VJ/LS)

The Boys (1)

45:	It Ain't Fair/I Want You	(Pye 7N 15726) 1964 R2

This Kentish Town outfit evolved into **The Action** after recording this now collectable 45. They also recorded a 45 backing Sandra Barry, a beat girl from London, *Really Gonna Shake/When We Get Married* (Decca F 11851) 1964.

Compilation appearances include: *It Ain't Fair* on *Watch Your Step* (LP & CD); and *It Ain't Fair* and *I Want You* on *Footsteps To Fame, Vol. 2* (CD). (VJ)

The Boys (2)

45:	Polaris/Jumpin'	(Parlophone R 5027) 1963 SC

A different sixties band. (VJ)

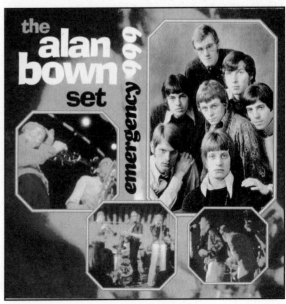

THE ALAN BOWN SET - Emergency 999 (CD).

The Boys Blue

45:      You Got What I Want/Take A Heart   (HMV POP 1427) 1965 R2

This raw and powerful Coventry R&B band's sole 45 is now very collectable. Both sides were written and produced by **Miki Dallon** who was also **The Sorrows'** producer. No surprise then that both of these songs would later be recorded by **The Sorrows**, who, of course, enjoyed a minor hit with *Take A Heart*. As for **The Boys Blue** versions, well they sank without trace.

Compilation appearances have included: *Take A Heart* and *You Got What I Want* on *Nowhere Men Vol. 1* (CD), *Rubble, Vol. 13 - Freak Beat Fantoms* (LP) and *Rubble, Vol. 7* (CD); and *You Got What I Want* on *Searching In The Wilderness* (LP & CD). (VJ)

The Boz

Personnel:	BOZ BURRELL	vcls	A
	IAN MacLAGAN	keyb'ds	A
	IAN WHITEMAN	ld gtr	A

45s:	You're Just The Kind Of Girl I Wanted/	
	Isn't That So	(Columbia DB 7832) 1966
	Meeting Time/	
	No (Ah) Body Knows The Blues	(Columbia DB 7889) 1966
	Pinnochio/Stay As You Are	(Columbia DB 7941) 1966
	The Baby Song/Carry On Screaming	(Columbia DB 7972) 1966
	I Shall Be Released/	
	Down In The Flood	(Columbia DB 8406) 1968
	Light My Fire/Back Against The Wall	(Columbia DB 8468) 1968

This was a London-based band. Their singles included covers of Bob Dylan's *I Shall Be Released* and The Doors' *Light My Fire*. Musically they were very varied. Boz Burrell was later in **King Crimson** and **Bad Company**; Ian MacLagan went on to **The Small Faces** and **The Faces** and Ian Whiteman was later in **The Action**.

Compilation appearances have included: *I Shall Be Released* on *Ritchie Blackmore - Rock Profile, Vol. 1* (CD); and *Down In The Flood* on *Ritchie Blackmore - Take It!- Sessions 63 - 68* (CD). (VJ)

Phil Brady and The Ranchers

Personnel incl:	PHIL BRADY	vcls, acc. gtr	ABC
	DAVE FIDLER	drms	BC
	PAUL KIRBY	bs	BC
	PHIL MORRIS	gtr	BC
	PAUL 'MITCH' MITCHELL	pedal steel	C

NB: Line-up 'B' 1971.

BRAM STOKER - Heavy Rock Spectacular (LP).

45s:	α	An American Sailor At The Cavern Club/	
		Sidetracked	(Cavern Sound IMSTL 2) 1965
		Little Rosa/Just One More Time	(Rex R 11011) 1965

NB: α credited to The Ranchers.

The group's debut, a novelty song about Liverpool's famous Cavern Club, was one of a small number issued on the Cavern Club's own label. Normally their music veered towards country - their second 45 came out on an Irish label.

Phil Brady continued to perform with different Ranchers into the seventies. Paul Kirby, who may also have been with the earlier incarnations of the band, was later in a country duo with his girlfriend/singer Little Ginny (Brown). (VJ/PM)

Brain

Personnel:	MIKE GILES	A
	PETE GILES	A
	ROBERT FRIPP	A

45s:		Nightmares In Red/	
		Kick The Donkey	(Parlophone R 5595) 1967 R2
	α	Nightmares In Red/	
		(Flip by different artist)	(Bam-Caruso OPRA 63) 1987

NB: α a limited edition jukebox release.

Yep, this project was actually **Giles, Giles and Fripp** before they switched to Deram in mid-1968. Prior to this the Giles brothers had been in **Trendsetters Limited** and Robert Fripp had been in **The League Of Gentlemen**, a mid-sixties soul band. Both sides of the 45 were written by the Giles brothers.

Nightmares In Red is three minutes of sheer lunacy, nonsensical lyrics, discordant orchestration, snoring? Total mayhem. Inevitably, given Robert Fripp and Mike Giles' later success with **King Crimson**, this obscure single is now very rare and collectable. The 'A' side was reissued by Bam-Caruso in 1987, though, and it also figures on *Rubble Vol. 3: Nightmares In Wonderland* (LP) and *Rubble Vol. 2* (CD). The group was from Bournemouth. (VJ)

Bram Stoker

Personnel incl: T. BRONSDON

ALBUM: 1 HEAVY ROCK SPECTACULAR
                  (Windmill WMD 117) 1972 SC

NB: (1) reissued on CD as *Poltergeist* (Audio Archives) 1998 and again on vinyl (Black Widow BWR 042) 2000.

This rare progressive rock album is now a minor collectors' item. Musically we're talking excellent atmospheric organ-led progressive rock. In particular, *Blitz*, a haunting, doomy track, is memorable and the band could be considered to have a sort of heavy **Nice** sound. *Extensive Corrosion* contains some great psychedelic guitar work and *Born To Be Free* sounds like it was modelled on *Born To Be Wild*. All the tracks were written by T. Bronsdon, who presumably led the band and it's surprising that they weren't snapped up by a major label. Had they been they might have fared better.

Although their album appeared on Windmill, a budget label sold through Woolworths, this was a gigging act, rather than a bunch of session musicians. (VJ/JS)

The Brand

45s:	α	I'm A Lover Not A Fighter/	
		Hear 'Em Talking	(Piccadilly 7N 35216) 1964
		I'm A Lover Not A Fighter/	
		Zulu Stomp	(Piccadilly 7N 35216) 1964 R3

NB: α unissued.

The Brand was a raw and wild R&B band from Birmingham whose solo vinyl offering was right out of the top drawer. It is now extremely rare and collectable for R&B fans. *Zulu Stomp* is a frenetic R&B instrumental and *I'm A Lover Not A Fighter* was an R&B standard.

Compilation appearances include: *I'm A Lover Not A Fighter* on *Maximum R'n'B* (CD), *The R&B Era, Vol. 1 - A Shot Of Rhythm And Blues* (LP & CD) and *Freakbeat Freakout* (CD); *Zulu Stomp* on *Trans-World Punk Rave-Up!, Vol. 2* (LP), *Watch Your Step* (LP & CD); and *I'm A Lover Not A Fighter* and *Zulu Stomp* on *Nowhere Men, Vol. 3* (CD), *Electric Sugarcube Flashbacks, Vol. 2* (LP) and *Electric Sugarcube Flashbacks, Vol. 3* (LP). (VJ)

The Brandy Boys

45:     Gale Winds/
        Don't Come Knocking At My Door   (Columbia DB 7507) 1965

The 'A' side was a Tornados-style instrumental. (VJ)

Brass Alley

Personnel incl: DAVEY DITCHBURN   vcls

This band has a heavy rock song entitled *Dr. Beecham's Pink Pills*, written by Ken Mountain, on a four-track EP, *Hart Rock '71*, which came out on the Abreaction label. The EP is a collection of four songs by four different bands recorded at Multichord Studios in Sunderland. The other tracks are by **Yellow**, **Lucas Tyson** and **Trilogy**. *Pink Pills* is the best of the four with good instrumentation. You'll also find it on *Syde Trips, Vol. 4* (LP). Mountain's Alan Clarke was an occasional keyboard player for this band. (MWh)

Brass Monkey

Personnel:			
	BEN CASE	vcls	A
	LES HURDLE	bs	A
	MIKE MORGAN	gtr	A
	KEN SUMMER	gtr	A
	DOUGIE WRIGHT	drms	A

ALBUM: 1 (A) BRASS MONKEY   (Philips 6303 025) 1971 R1

This rare and utterly obscure studio effort is a mixed bag – some songs are trite, but others contain surprisingly hard-edged guitar work and complex arrangements. Behind it were Guy Fletcher and Doug Flett, who were responsible for Britain's Eurovision entries in the period! The best numbers are the mellow ballad *Goodbye Birds*, menacing instrumental *Strange Days* and a tough rendition of Sonny and Cher's *Bang Bang*, Other songs are truly pedestrian, however, and it's anyone's guess what market projects like

BREAD, LOVE AND DREAMS - Bread Love And Dreams (CD).

this were aimed at. Engineering duties were carried out by **John Pantry**, well-known to psych fans for his involvement with **The Factory**, **Peter And The Wolves** and others. (RMJ)

Brass Tacks

45s:	I'll Keep Holding On/		
	Let The Sunshine In	(Big T BIG 110) 1968 SC	
	Maxwell Ferguson/		
	Sunshine After The Rain	(Big T BIG 114) 1968 R1	

This is a long forgotten single. The 'A' side was a Marvelletes song covered by **The Action**. The flip was done by **Georgie Fame** among others.

The oddball *Maxwell Ferguson*, is one of the weirdest psychedelic records, on *The Electric Lemonade Acid Test, Vol. 2* (LP). (VJ)

Brave

45s:	Please Let Me Love You/	
	Stay With Me Forever	(Polydor 2058 154) 1971
	My Brother Your Son/Don't Be Wrong	(Polydor 2058 198) 1972

These two 45s were this obscure band's sole vinyl offering. (VJ)

Bread and Beer Band

Personnel:			
	BERNIE CALVERT	bs	A
	REG DWIGHT	keyb'ds	A
	ROGER POPE	drms	A
	CALEB QUAYE	gtr	A
	ROLFO	perc	A
	LENNOT	perc	A

ALBUM: 1 THE BREAD AND BEER BAND
                              (Private Pressing) 1969 R5

NB: (1) has been pirated on CD.

45:	Dick Barton Theme (The Devil's Gallop)/	
	Breakdown Blues	(Decca F 12891) 1969 R2
Reissue:	Dick Barton Theme (The Devil's Gallop)/	
	Breakdown Blues	(Decca F 13354) 1972 R1

Primarily of interest because Reg Dwight (**Elton John**) was in this band, just one copy of their album was pressed. This consists entirely of cover versions, with all except a cover of The Box Tops' *The Letter* being instrumentals.

Breakdown Blues is a pleasant number, on which **Caleb Quaye**'s guitar work and Reg Dwight's piano playing, were very evident.

Rolfo and Lennot were Jamaican percussionists.

You van also hear *Breakdown Blues* on *Mod Scene, Vol. 2* (CD) and *R&B Scene, Vol. 2 - 1963-1969* (LP). (VJ)

Bread, Love and Dreams

Personnel:			
	CAROLYN DAVIS	gtr, vcls	A
	DAVID McNIVEN	vcls, keyb'ds, gtr	AB
	ANGIE REW	vcls, flute	AB

ALBUMS:	1(A)	BREAD LOVE AND DREAMS	
		(mono/stereo)	(Decca LK/SKL 5008) 1969 R2
	2(B)	STRANGE TALE OF CAPTAIN SHANNON AND	
		THE HUNCHBACK FROM GIGHA	
		(mono/stereo)	(Decca LK/SKL 5048) 1970 R2
	3(B)	AMARYLLIS	(Decca SKL 5081) 1971 R3

NB: (1) reissued on CD (HMP HMPCD 006). (2) reissued on CD (Si-Wan SRMC 0059). (3) reissued in on CD Korea (Si-Wan SRML 0035) 1996 and again (Won Sin W8856582).

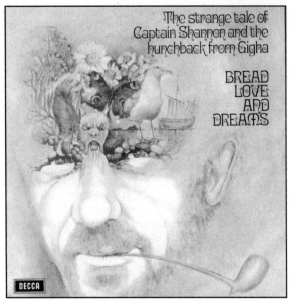

BREAD, LOVE AND DREAMS - Strange Tale Of Captain Shannon... (LP).

45:       Virgin Kiss/Switch Out The Sun   (Decca F 12958) 1969 SC

This Edinburgh act was responsible for some of Britain's best 'acid folk'.

They were spotted by Decca staff producer Ray Horricks at the Edinburgh Festival in 1968, and swiftly became his favourite group. He brought them down to London to make their debut early in 1969. An enjoyable collection of self-penned folk ballads with some orchestration, it sold poorly and Davis decided to leave. Decca wanted to drop the band at this point, but Horricks intervened and grudging permission was given for further material to be taped. McNiven and Rew recorded *Captain Shannon* and *Amaryllis* in a single four day session in the summer of 1970. They were originally intended as a double album, but separated at Decca's insistence.

Captain Shannon begins with the wistful *Hymn For Sylvia*, but rocks out on the following track, *Masquerade*. Other highlights are Rew's enchanting *Butterflyland* and McNiven's lengthy title track. It came in a beautiful psychedelic sleeve, but also failed to sell. *Amaryllis* appeared just a few months later, and is considered their finest work by many. On it the duo was augmented by musicians including Terry Cox and Danny Thompson of **Pentangle** and **Alan Trajan**. The ambitious title track accounted for the whole of side one, while side two consisted of the sprightly *Time's The Thief* (about McNiven's attempt to win a place at RADA as a teenager), Rew's unforgettable *Brother John* (inspired by a childhood trip to the ruins of a hermit's shelter in Mexico), *My Stair-Cupboard At 3am* (an unsettling song about isolation and paranoia, set to a jaunty tune) and *Circle Of The Night* (written for friends and labelmates **Human Beast**, for whose *Volume One* album McNiven wrote lyrics).

They performed *Amaryllis* at Edinburgh and The Royal Court Theatre, but when it sold even more poorly than the others they were dropped by Decca. In fact, it is thought that *Amaryllis* was released solely as a tax loss. Certainly it vies with **Leaf Hound**'s *Growers of Mushroom* as the rarest progressive release on the label.

McNiven and Rew continued to tour and work in theatre, eventually joining Edinburgh rock band Mama Flier in the mid-seventies. A popular support band, and live attraction in their own right, they made various recordings, none of which were released. A married couple, they continue to perform to this day. (VJ/RMJ)

The Breakaways

Personnel:	VICKI BROWN	vcls	A
	JEAN HAWKER	vcls	A
	MARGOT QUANTRELL	vcls	A

45s:	He's A Rebel/Wishing Star	(Pye 7N 15471) 1962 SC
	That Boy Of Mine/Here She Comes	(Pye 7N 15585) 1963 SC
	That's How It Goes/	

	He Doesn't Love Me	(Pye 7N 15618) 1964 SC
	Danny Boy/Your Kind Of Love	(Pye 7N 15973) 1965 SC
	Sacred Love/Don't Be A Baby	(CBS 2833) 1967 SC
	Santo Domingo/So In Love Are We	(MCA MV 1018) 1968

This vocal trio, who formed in 1962, were all married to showbiz husbands. Vicky was married to Joe Brown. Jean wed Mike Hawkes, a successful songwriter and Margot tied the knot with **Tony Newman**. Their first-ever session was *I Wonder Who's Kissing Her Now* with Emile Ford. Then they recorded an album with Joe Brown. All three hailed from Liverpool and they also did a lot of session work.

Here She Comes has been compiled on *Ripples, Vol. 4* (CD). (VJ)

Breakthru'

45:       Ice Cream Tree/Julius Caesar   (Mercury MF 1066) 1968

An obscure pop band Julius Caesar has a nice organ sound but was nothing too special.

Compilation appearances include: *Julius Caesar* on *Magic Spectacles* (CD); *Ice-Cream Tree* and *Julius Caesar* on *Nowhere Men, Vol. 4* (CD) and *Here Comes The End* and *Spoonful* on *Alphabeat (Pop, Psych and Prog 1967-1970)* (LP) and (CD). (MWh)

Paul Brett('s Sage)

Personnel:	PAUL BRETT	gtr, vcls	A
	DICK DUFALL	bs	A
	NICK HIGGINBOTTOM	flute, soprano sax	A
	BOB VOICE	drms	A

ALBUMS:	1(A)	PAUL BRETT SAGE	(Pye NSPL 18347) 1970 SC
(up to	2(A)	JUBILATION FOUNDRY	(Dawn DNLS 3021) 1971 SC
1976)	3(A)	SCHIZOPHRENIA	(Dawn DNLS 3032) 1972 SC
	4(-)	PAUL BRETT	(Bradley's BRADL 1001) 1973 SC
	5(-)	CLOCKS	(Bradley's BRADL 1004) 1973 SC
	6(-)	PHOENIX FUTURE	(Private Pressing) 1975 SC
	7(-)	MUSIC MANIFOLD	(Private Pressing) 197? SC

NB: (4) - (6) **Paul Brett** solo recordings. (7) was a library issue.

45s:	Three D Mona Lisa/	
(up to	Mediterranean Lazy Heat Wave	(Pye 7N 17974) 1970
1976)	Good Old-Fashioned Funky Kind Music/	
	Goodbye Forever	(Dawn DNS 1010) 1970
	Reason For Your Askin'//Everlasting Butterfly/Savannah Ladies	
	To Everyman (Freedom) (PS)	(Dawn DNX 2508) 1971

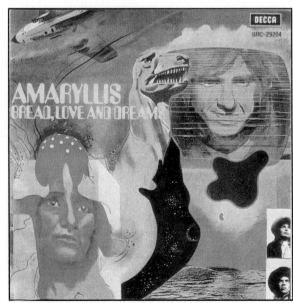

BREAD, LOVE AND DREAMS - Amaryllis (CD).

α	Mr. Custer/Good Times Hard Times	(Bradley's BRAD 301) 1973
α	Summer Driftin'/Clocks (PS)	(Bradley's BRAD 305) 1973
α	Soho Jack/Captain Dan	(Bradley's BRAD 7405) 1974

NB: α **Paul Brett** solo recordings.

Paul Brett had been a guitarist with **Elmer Gantry's Velvet Opera**. He was later in **Fire** with future **Strawbs**' member Dave Lambert. Later in 1970 he formed **Paul Brett's Sage** with former **Fire** members Dick Dufall and Bob Voice. After three reasonable rock albums with this outfit he went solo. *Phoenix Future*, was a privately-pressed effort, just 500 copies were issued but it's yet to interest collectors much. He also recorded a library-only album, *Music Manifold*, during the seventies.

Brett went on to record further progressive rock solo albums in the late seventies: *Earthbirth* (1977), *Interlife* (1978) and *Eclipse* (1979). (VJ)

Steve Brett and Mavericks

Personnel:	PETE BICKLEY	bs	A
	STEVE BRETT	vcls	A
	PHIL BURNELL	lead gtr, organ	A
	NEVILLE (NODDY) HOLDER	gtr	A
	GERRY KIBBLE	drms	A
	TERRY ?	sax	A

45s:	Wishing/		
	Anything That's Part Of You	(Columbia DB 7470) 1965 R2
	Sad, Lonely And Blue/Candy	(Columbia DB 7581) 1965 R2
	Chains On My Heart/Sugar Shack	(Columbia DB 7794) 1965 R3

This Wolverhampton band's most notable for the inclusion of Holder, who played guitar and sang backing vocals on their third 45. His next venture was **The In-Be-Tweens** who later became **Ambrose Slade** and then **Slade**. Because of this these 45s are obviously very sought-after by **Slade** collectors. Musically they were very varied: the first was a ballad, the second was folky and the third bluesy.

Compilation appearances include: *Wishing, Anything That's Part Of You, Sad, Lonely and Blue, Candy, Chains On My Heart, Sugar Shack* and *Hurting Inside* on *The Genesis Of Slade* (CD). (VJ/AD)

Brewers Droop

Personnel:	MALCOLM BARRETT	bs, violin	A
	STEVE DARRINGTON	keyb'ds, vcls, hrmnca	A
	PETE DUNCAN	horns	A
	DAVE GELLY	sax	A
	JOHN McKAY	gtr, vcls	A
	BOB WALKER	drms, perc	A
	RON WATTS	vcls, perc	A
	JOHN WILLIAMS	sax	A

ALBUM:	1(A)	OPENING TIME	(RCA SF 8301) 1972 SC

NB: There's also a retrospective of unreleased material, *Booze Brothers* (Red Lightnin RL 0077) 1989, also issued on CD (Red Lightnin RLCD 0079).

45:	Sweet Thing//Heart Of Stone		
	It Ain't The Meat - It's The Motion (PS)	(RCA 2216) 1972

This was a pub-rock outfit whose album is now a minor collectors' item. They came from the High Wycombe area and played an earthy sort of music which probably went down well on the Rugby Club circuit.

They later made a further 45 as **Droop**.

Mark Knopfler was in the band for a few months before they disbanded in August 1974. Steve Darrington recalls:- "We shared a house together in Amersham, Buckinghamshire. During this period we went to Rockfield Studios and recorded the second **Brewers Droop** album *The Booze Brothers*, which features Mark Knopfler, **Dave Edmunds** and Pick Withers (on drums and spoons!). This was lost for nearly 20 years and not released till about 1994, when 'Music Week' amongst other magazines stated that "this is the original Dire Straits!". (VJ/MW)

Ripples Vol. 4 (Comp CD) includes The Breakaways.

Marc Brierley

ALBUMS:	1	WELCOME TO THE CITADEL	(CBS 63478) 1967 R3
	2	HELLO	(CBS 63835) 1969 R1

EP:	1	MARC BRIERLEY	(Transatlantic TRA EP 147) 1966 R2

45s:	Hold On, Hold On, The Garden Sure Looks Good		
	Spread On The Floor/Autograph Of Time	(CBS 3857) 1968
	Stay A Little Longer Merry Ann/Flaxen Hair	(CBS 4191) 1969
	Lady Of The Light/Sunny Weather	(CBS 4632) 1969
	Be My Brother/If You Took The Bandage Off	(CBS 5266) 1970

Having trained to be a teacher, **Marcus Brierley** gravitated towards London's folk clubs in the mid-sixties and was eventually offered a deal by Transatlantic, who released his stark, though appealing, EP in the autumn of 1966. Stung by comparisons to **Bert Jansch**, **Brierley** spent 1967 expanding his musical horizons and soon outgrew Transatlantic's folky profile. As such he spent well over a year searching for another deal, including a near-miss with Apple. Finally CBS took the bait and he spent a week in the autumn of 1968 making *Welcome To The Citadel*. A superb piece of jazzy psych-folk, directly influenced by his experiments with LSD, it is now very rare and much sought-after.

When it failed to sell, his publisher hooked him up with **Donovan**'s ex-manager Ashley Kozak, who produced *Hello* in 1969. Smoother and more varied than its predecessor, it contained arguably **Brierley**'s finest moment, the beguiling *A Presence (I Am Seeking)* and featured Dudley Moore, of all people, on piano. It too died a commercial death, prompting him to move to Birmingham and raise a family. When a deal with Island fell through, he gave up on music altogether and became a photographer instead.

Both sides of his second and fourth singles were non-album. These, together with the EP and both albums, were issued on CD by Sanctuary in 2005, with notes by **Brierley** himself. This release comes highly recommended for fans of **Nick Drake** and the like. (VJ/RMJ)

Anne Briggs

ALBUMS:	1	ANNE BRIGGS	(Topic 12TS 207) 1971 R3
	2	THE TIME HAS COME	(CBS 64612) 1971 R2

EP:	1	THE HAZARDS OF LOVE	
		(w/insert)	(Topic TOP 94) 1963 R3

NB: *A Collection* (Topic TSCD 504) 1999 compiles material of hers between 1963 and 1971.

A true legend of British folk, **Anne Briggs** is a wandering spirit who recorded sporadically and only on her own terms, rather akin to America's

119

Karen Dalton. She was an important influence on almost all other contemporary female British folk singers, including **Sandy Denny** of **Fairport Convention**, Maddy Prior of **Steeleye Span** and **Linda Thompson**, and indeed **Denny**'s own *The Pond and the Stream* was about her.

Briggs was born in Nottinghamshire in 1944, and began singing in folk clubs while still a teenager. In 1962 she joined the 'Centre 42' tour, an attempt to disseminate left-wing culture nationwide. Local talent would audition for support slots, and **Briggs**' potential was spotted by seasoned folkie Ewan MacColl, who persuaded her to leave school and sing full-time. **Briggs** soon met MacColl's friend and associate Bert Lloyd, who recorded her debut EP. **Briggs**, however, disliked recording and spent much of the decade travelling instead, occasionally with her sometime boyfriend **Bert Jansch**. In this time she contributed occasional tracks to folk compilations, but made no full-length recordings.

Slowly her legend grew, and she was finally persuaded to make an album in 1971. Her self-titled debut album is an austere collection of traditional songs, some of which are sung entirely unaccompanied. It will not appeal to fans of psychedelic folk, but has some extremely appealing and artless performances on it. Later that year she made a follow-up for CBS, who were cultivating a folk catalogue, signing **COB**, **the McLynns**, **Wizz Jones** and others at much the same time. Eight of its thirteen songs were composed by **Briggs**, with the title track, *Ride Ride* and *The Sandman's Song* the highlights. Covers include songs by **Jansch**, Steve Ashley and Henry McCulloch. Less stark than its predecessor, it's the best starting point for the curious.

In March 1973 she made another album, which went unreleased for over twenty years, supposedly because of her own reservations about her singing. These fears were shown to be groundless when *Sing A Song For You* (Fledgling CD 3008) finally appeared in 1997. On it she flirts with fuller-rock backing to worthwhile effect, and it is well-worth investigating. Having recorded it, however, she withdrew from music and now lives reclusively on a Scottish island.

A Collection mostly comprises unaccompanied traditional folk songs, including all of her debut album. Later **Pentangle** also recorded a version. (VJ/AH/RMJ)

The Brighton Horns

45:     Surf Dell'amore/High Midnight   (Stateside SS 526) 1966

Surf Dell'amore is a good-time sounding brass-based song. (VJ)

Brimstone

45s: Keyhole Jake/Monkey Song   (Deram DM 522) 1971
        If You Ever See Me/Work Out   (Decca F 13222) 1971

Keyhole Jake is a catchy pop number. (VJ)

Brindley Brae

ALBUM: 1   VILLAGE MUSIC   (Harmony DB 0002) 197? R1

This privately-pressed folk music album is quite collectable. It was a Bev Pegg project. He was a **Clifford T. Ward** sideman. (VJ)

Brinsley Schwarz

Personnel:	BOB ANDREWS	keyb'ds, vcls	AB
	BILLY RANKIN	drms	AB
	NICK LOWE	bs, vcls	AB
	BRINSLEY SCHWARZ	gtr, vcls	AB
	IAN GOMM	gtr, vcls	B

ALBUMS:	1(A)	BRINSLEY SCHWARZ		
		(w/insert)	(United Artists UAS 29111) 1970	R1
	2(A)	DESPITE IT ALL	(Liberty LBG 83427) 1970	SC
	3(B)	SILVER PISTOL		
		(Some w/poster)	(United Artists UAS 29217) 1972	SC

BRINSLEY SCHWARZ - Hens' Teeth (CD).

4(B)	NERVOUS ON THE ROAD		
		(United Artists UAS 29374) 1972	SC
5(B)	PLEASE DON'T EVER CHANGE		
		(United Artists UAS 29489) 1973	SC
6(-)	ORIGINAL GOLDEN GREATS (Compilation)		
		(United Artists USP 101) 1974	
7(B)	THE NEW FAVOURITES OF BRINSLEY SCHWARZ		
		(United Artists UAS 29641) 1974	
8(-)	15 THOUGHTS OF BRINSLEY SCHWARZ (Compilation)		
		(United Artists UAK 30177) 1978	

NB: (3) reissued on Edsel (ED 190) 1986. (3) and (5) reissued on CD (Edsel EDCD 190 and EDCD 237 respectively) in 1990 and again (BGO BGOCD 642) 2004. (4) and (7) reissued on one CD (Beat Goes On BGOCD 289) 1995. There's also a 20-track CD compilation *Surrender To The Rhythm* (EMI CDP 7 96746 2) 1991. (1) reissued on CD (Repertoire REP 4421-WY) 1994. (1) and (2) later reissued on one CD (BGO BGOCD 239) 1994. *Original Golden Greats* and *15 Thoughts Of Brinsley Schwarz* reissued on one CD (BGO BGOCD 476) 2000. *Hen's Teeth* (Edsel EDCD 546) 2001 is a CD compilation of early **Brinsley Schwarz** and **Kippington Lodge** tracks. *Cruel To Be Kind* (BBC/Hux HUX 052) 2004 compiles 19 previously unreleased studio sessions from 1971-75.

45s:	Shining Brightly/		
	What Do You Suggest	(United Artists UP 35118)	1970
	Country Girl/Funk Angel	(Liberty LBY 15419)	1970
	Country Girl/Funk Angel	(United Artists UP 35312)	1972
	Speedo/I Worry	(United Artists UP 35588)	1973
	I've Cried My Last Tear/		
	Bringdown	(United Artists UP 35642)	1974
	(What's So Funny 'Bout) Love, Peace And Understanding/		
	Since You're Gone	(United Artists UP 35700)	1974
	Everybody/		
	I Like You, I Don't Love You	(United Artists UP 35768)	1975
	There's A Cloud In My Heart/		
	I Got The Real Thing	(United Artists UP 35812)	1975
	Country Girl//Hooked On Love		
	Surrender To The Rhythm	(United Artists UP 36409)	1978
	(What's So Funny 'Bout) Love, Peace And Understanding/		
	I've Cried My Last Tear	(United Artists UP 36446)	1978

This group was an important part of the 'pub-rock' phenomenon in Britain in the seventies - Andrews, Lowe and **Schwarz** had all previously been with **Kippington Lodge**, a harmony band that **Mark Wirtz** had signed up to EMI's Parlophone label in the mid-sixties.

As is well known now the band were subjected to one of the biggest hypes in rock history - a planeload of music journalists were flown across the Atlantic to see their debut at New York's Fillmore East, but were unimpressed with the then unknown band. The inevitable press slagging did the band irreparable damage, although their debut album, an amalgam of 'heavy' blues and harmony folk-rock, had its moments. *Despite It All* showed promise too, but failed to undo the damage done by all the earlier 'hype'.

After the second album Ian Gomm was added providing a fuller guitar sound and the band reacted against all the 'hype' of their early days by becoming as anti-commercial as possible, accepting a residency at the Tally Ho in London's Kentish Town in the Summer of 1972. Their next album, *Silver Pistol*, was very laid back, almost mellow. Over the next two and a half years they were at the forefront of the 'pub rock' scene and helped to bring it to the attention of the music press and a wider audience. They often appeared under a pseudonym to keep the crowds down. Nick Lowe blossomed as a songwriter and they made a number of musically diverse albums which won critical acclaim and good singles, like *What's Funny 'Bout Peace Love And Understanding* and *Cruel To Be Kind*) but failed to sell. This eventually led them to split after a Marquee gig on 18 March 1975.

Schwarz and Andrews went on to join **Graham Parker**'s backing band The Rumour. Rankin joined Terraplane and Big Jim Sullivan's **Tiger** before retiring from the music business. Gomm and Lowe both went solo. Lowe tried his hand at production too. One of Lowe's biggest hits *Cruel To Be Kind* in 1979 was a Brinsley song that they had never recorded.

The 1974 *Original Golden Greats* compilation was a budget-priced attempt to generate the band some record sales. *15 Thoughts Of Brinsley Schwarz* was a later retrospective compilation, which included seven cuts from *Original Golden Greats*. Beat Goes On ironed out the duplication at the turn of the Millennium and reissued both on one CD.

In addition to the above discography they have five tracks (*Wonder Woman, It's Just My Way Of Saying Thank You, I'm Ahead If I Can Quit While I'm..., Midnight Train* and *Surrender To The Rhvt*) on *The Greasy Truckers Party* (2-LP) and one cut on the *Glastonbury Fayre* (3-LP) set. *Funk Angel* can also be heard on *All Good Clean Fun* (2-LP). More recently *Surrender To The Rhythm* and *What's So Funny 'Bout Peace Love And Understanding* were included on the 3-CD set *Radio Caroline Calling - 70's Flashback*.

They also recorded as **The Hitters**, The Electricians (with **Dave Edmunds**) and possibly too as **The Limelight**.

After their demise Nick Lowe and Ian Gomm both became solo artists. Bob Andrews and **Brinsley Schwarz** resurfaced in **Graham Parker and The Rumour** and Billy Rankin joined fellow pub-rockers **Ducks Deluxe**. (VJ)

Britt

45:     You Really Have Started Something/
        Leave My Baby Alone   (Piccadilly 7N 35273) 1966

A teenbeat 45 - the 'A' side was written by Carter-Lewis. **Britt** was actually Britt Ekland, who later married Peter Sellers and **Rod Stewart**. (VJ)

Buddy Britten and The Regents

45s: My Pride, My Joy/
        Long Gone Baby   (Piccadilly 7N 35075) 1962 SC
        Don't Spread It Around/
        The Beat Of My Heart   (Decca F 11435) 1962
        If You Gotta Make A Fool Of Somebody/
        Money   (Oriole CB 1827) 1963 SC
        Hey There/I'll Cry No More   (Oriole CB 1839) 1963 SC
        My Resistance Is Low/
        When I See You Smile   (Oriole CB 1859) 1963 SC
        Money/Sorrow Tomorrow   (Oriole CB 1889) 1963 SC
        I Guess I'm In The Way/
        Zip-A-Dee-Doo-Dah   (Oriole CB 1911) 1964 SC
        She's About A Mover/
        Since You've Gone   (Piccadilly 7N 35241) 1965 SC
        Right Now/Jailer Bring Me Water (Piccadilly 7N 35257) 1965

This Liverpool band's story is a bit of a hard luck one. **Freddie and The Dreamers** put out their version of *If You Gotta Make A Fool Of Somebody* one week earlier which effectively put pay to their chances of a hit. A few months later the same thing happened with *Money*, a strong Motown favourite and they lost out to **Bern Elliot and The Fenmen**. Even when they switched to Piccadilly and recorded a cover of Sir Douglas Quintet's

US hit *She's About A Mover* its release coincided with a version by James Royal and The Hawks. Of course groups who wrote their own material didn't have these problems but after three years of recording this lot had achieved little.

The band also released a 45 in 1963 as The Regents. On *She's About A Mover* they were backed by Nick Simper (bs), who later joined **The Flowerpot Men**.

Realm's 1963 compilation, *Group Beat '63* (LP), included two cuts:- *If You Gotta Make A Fool Of Somebody* and *I'll Cry No More*, by the band. More recently, *Since You've Been Gone* has resurfaced on Sequel's *Hippy Hippy Shake* (CD); *Long Gone Baby* on *Piccadilly Story* (2-CD); and *Right Now* on *Doin' The Mod, Vol. 1* (CD). (VJ)

Terry Britten

45:     α 2,000 Weeks/Bargain Day   (Columbia DB 8580) 1969
NB: α demo only.

Terry Britten was leader of The Twilights, one of Australia's better sixties bands. This solo 45 didn't get beyond the demo stage. *2,000 Weeks* sounds a little like **Elmer Gantry's Velvet Opera**'s *Mary Jane* and *Bargain Day* recalls **The Smoke** circa 1968-69. He went on to join **Quartet**, who released a 45 and recorded an album for Decca. Later he penned *Devil Woman*, a hugely successful hit for Cliff Richard. (VJ/RMJ)

Chris Britton

ALBUM: 1   AS I AM   (Page One POLS 022) 1969 R3

This, the sole solo album by the **Troggs**' lead guitarist, is now almost impossible to find. Produced by 'the Troggs' George Martin', Colin Frechter, some popsike fans swear by it while others dismiss it as overblown pap. As usual, the truth lies somewhere between. *Sit Down Beside Me* is a feast of raunchy guitar, honking brass, blaring organ and funky drums, and the relentless *Fly With Me* is made for dancefloors, while other numbers, such as the mellow *Will It Last?* and lo-fi closer *Learn To Love Life*, capture him in a more languid mood. Elsewhere there are lesser tracks, but overall this is a varied and unfairly neglected piece of the psych-pop jigsaw. (VJ/RMJ)

The Broadsiders

45s: The Shores Of Amerkay/Bottle Of Wine   (Pye 7N 17382) 1967
        Grandfather's Will / Deportees   (Pye 7N 17548) 1968

This Irish group's recordings are of no significance to collectors. Musically they veered towards folk. (VJ)

Brodie Brothers

45:     If You Only Loved Me/Strange   (Columbia DB 8105) 1967

This Irish group's 45 recalls The Batchelors. (VJ)

Broken Glass

Personnel: ROBBIE BLUNT   gtr   A
              MAC POOLE   drms   A
              ROB RAWLINSON   bs   A
              STAN WEBB   vcls, gtr, dobro A

ALBUM: 1(A)   BROKEN GLASS   (Capitol E-ST 11510) 1975

Miller Anderson did session work on this album. Stan Webb came from **Chicken Shack** and **Savoy Brown**'s "Boogie Brothers" and Robbie Blunt from **Bronco**. Mac Poole was from **Warhorse**. The album was produced by

Tony Ashton, but despite the excellent pedigree of the musicians and the fine blues guitar the group failed to break through. (CG)

Broken Toys

A twee pop outfit whose previously unreleased *Broken Toys* gets an airing on *Circus Days, Vol. 4* (LP) and *Circus Days Vol's 4 & 5* (CD). Not recommended. (VJ)

John Bromley

ALBUM:	1	SING	(Polydor 583 048) 1969 SC

45s:	What A Woman Does/My My	(Polydor 56224) 1968
	And The Feeling Goes/	
	Sweet Little Princess	(Polydor 56287) 1968
	Melody Fayre/Sugar Love	(Polydor 56305) 1969 R1
	Hold Me Woman/Weather Man	(Polydor 56340) 1969
	Kick A Tin Can/Wonderland Avenue USA (Atlantic 584289) 1969

John Bromley was a songwriter who Polydor encouraged to put his songs on vinyl. The album was a collection of 45s with extra tracks added. **The Fleur de Lys** were called in to provide the backing on some, including *So Many Things*, which can also be heard on *Rubble Vol. 16: Glass Orchid Aftermath* (LP) and *Rubble Vol. 9* (CD). Despite this added dimension the album didn't sell well. He'd been with **The Three People** in 1966/67. He wrote *Come On Down* for Jackie De Shannon and *This World's An Apple* for the **Ace Kefford Stand**.

If You Are There With Me later resurfaced on *Fading Yellow, Vol 4* (CD); *Sugar Love* on *Pop-In, Vol 2* (CD); *Melody Fayre* on *Colour Me Pop, Vol 2* and *Wonderland Avenue* on *Colour Me Pop, Vol 3* . (VJ)

Bronco

Personnel:	JEFF BANNISTER	piano	A
	ROBBIE BLUNT	gtr, vcls	AB
	KEVIN GAMMOND	gtr, vcls	ABC
	JOHN PASTERNAK	bs	ABC
	PETE ROBINSON	drms	ABC
	JESS RODEN	vcls	AB
	CLIFFORD T. WARD	vcls	A C
	(TERRY ALLEN	keyb'ds	B)
	(PAUL DAVENPORT	piano	B)
	(IAN HUNTER	keyb'ds	B)
	(TREVOR LUCAS	vcls	B)
	(MICK RALPHS	keyb'ds	B)
	DAN FONE	gtr, keyb'ds, hrmnca, vcls	C
	RICHARD HEWSON	strings	C
	SIMON LANZON	keyb'ds	C
	PAUL LOCKEY	gtr, vcls	C

ALBUMS:	1(A)	COUNTRY HOME	(Island ILPS 9124) 1970 SC
	2(B)	ACE OF SUNLIGHT	(Island ILPS 9161) 1971 SC
	3(C)	SMOKIN' MIXTURE	(Polydor 2383 215) 1973 SC

45s:	Lazy Now/Matter Of Perspective	(Chrysalis WIP 6096) 1971
	Traveller/Steal That Gold	(Polydor 2058 395) 1973

Notable for including **Jess Roden**, formerly of **The Alan Bown Set**, they made little impression, probably because their brand of US-influenced rock lacked any originality. They contributed one track, *Sudden Street*, to Island's *El Pea* (2-LP) compilation.

On *Ace Of Sunlight* they were assisted by **Mott The Hoople**'s **Ian Hunter** and Mick Ralphs and **Trevor Lucas** of **Fotheringay**.

When **Roden** embarked on a solo career, Pasternak, Gammond and Robinson teamed up with Dan Fone (gtr) and Paul Lockey (gtr, vcls), who had sung with **The Equals** a bit, to form **Band Of Joy**. **Band Of Joy** was, of course, **Robert Plant**'s old band and Gammond earlier had been in this band with **Plant**. They released one eponymous album on Polydor which

bombed. Robinson then went back to work in the nuts and bolts factory. Pasternak and Gammond later formed Pictures In A Darkroom which had one self-released single called *Animals In Music* which was horrendous but now seems ahead of its time, in that it sounded like Prodigy! Pasternak died of a heart attack in 1987. Gammond now teaches music in Kidderminster.

Blunt was later in **Silverhead** and went on to work for **Robert Plant** as well as **Chicken Shack**, Clannad, **Steve Gibbons** and The Jeff Healey Band. John Pasternak had also earlier played with **Band of Joy**. (VJ/KP)

Bronx Cheer

Personnel:	BRIAN COOKMAN	gtr, vcls, hrmnca	A
	CHAS JOHNSTON	piano, gtr, vcls	A
	TONY KNIGHT	drms	A
	JOHN REED	gtr, mandolin	A

ALBUM:	1(A)	GREATEST HITS, VOL. 3	(Dawn DNLS 3004) 1972 SC

EP:	1(A)	Barrell House Player/Surprising Find/Whether Or Not/	
		Party For One (PS)	(Dawn DNX 2512) 1971

45s:	Drive My Car/Foxtrot	(Parlophone R 5865) 1970
	Hold On To Me/Late Date	(Dawn DNS 1019) 1972

Bronx Cheer was a jug band in the **Mungo Jerry** mould. They originally recorded a 45 as a trio as **Jug Trust**. They added a pianist and changed name to **Bronx Cheer**. Brian Cookman wrote most of their material. (VJ)

Tony Brook and The Breakers

Personnel incl: TONY BROOK

45s:	Meanie Genie/	
	Ooh Poo Pah Doo (Some PS)	(Columbia DB 7279) 1964 R3/R2
	Love Dances On/I Won't Hurt You	(Columbia DB 7444) 1965 SC

The 'A' side to their first 45 was a bluesy, organ-dominated number, which is now collectable. Some copies come in a rare promotional picture sleeve (probably for export) and these are particularly collectable.

Meanie Genie and *Ooh Poo Pah Doo* have been compiled on *R&B Scene, Vol. 1* (LP). (VJ)

Elkie Brooks

ALBUM:	1	RICH MAN'S WOMAN	(A&M AMLH 64554) 1975

(up to 1976)

NB: (1) reissued on CD (Pickwick PWKS 553) 1989. Also of interest is *The Early Years 1964-66* (C5 C5 506) 1987, The Best Of Elkie Brooks (Spectrum) 1998 is an 18-track compilation and *The Very Best Of....* (CD) (Polygram CD 5407122).

45s:	Something's Got A Hold On Me/	
(up to	Hello Stranger	(Decca F 11928) 1964 SC
1976)	Nothing Left To Do But Cry/	
	Strange Though It Seems	(Decca F 11983) 1964 SC
	The Way You Do The Things You Do/	
	Blue Tonight	(Decca F 12061) 1965 SC
	He's Gotta Love Me/	
	When You Appear	(HMV POP 1431) 1965 SC
	All Of My Life/	
	Can't Stop Thinking Of You	(HMV POP 1480) 1965
	Baby Let Me Love You/Stop The Music	(HMV POP 1512) 1966
	Come September/If You Should Go	(NEMS 56-4136) 1969
	Rescue Me/Sweet Nuthin's	(Island WIP 6187) 1974
α	Sacrifice/(flip by Alice Cooper) (PS)	(Chrysalis CHS 2069) 1974

NB: α promo only.

Elkie Brooks first came to public attention as part of the Merseybeat scene

- along with **Cilla Black** and **Beryl Marsden** she was one of the very few female singers connected with Merseybeat. None of her singles sold particularly well, though, and she moved down to London working first with Eric Delaney's dance band, touring Poland with **The Artwoods** in 1965 and then working with Humphrey Lyttleton as a jazz singer. Indeed she is more significant for her jazz roots and good voice. Of her 45s, *Hello Stranger* was a Barbara Lewis track; *The Way You Do The Things You Do* was a Temptations' number and *Rescue Me* was a Fontella Bass soul favourite. Some of her 45s were picked up on the Northern soul scene.

In 1969 she recorded a version of **The Mindbenders**' *Groovy Kinda Love* with Jamaican reggae legend Owen Gray for the Revolution label as Elki and Owen. There's also a 45 with Alice Cooper from a dreadful space age rock opera, which is very rare and was recently reissued by r-p-m.

At the start of the seventies she re-emerged in an experimental 12-piece jazz-rock band called **Dada**, which recorded one album for Atlantic. After **Dada**'s demise she was in **Vinegar Joe**, which proved a tailor-made showcase for her bluesy and jazzy vocal style.

After they disbanded in 1974 she embarked on a solo career, achieving considerable success although that career falls beyond the time span of this book, she is still going strong in the new millennium. She also sang on **Keef Hartley**'s final unreleased album.

An early compilation appearance for Elkie was on Island's *British Blue-Eyed Soul* (LP) back in 1968 singing *God Bless The Child*. Also of interest is the See For Miles C5 subsidiary compilation of material from the 1964-66 era when she was one of the countries' best white R&B singers. Basically the compilation includes both sides of all her singles from this era plus a few other tracks. Much of the material is strong cover versions of black R&B hits and the first three Decca 45s came across the best. (VJ)

Joey Brooks and The Baroque Folk

45:     I Ain't Blamin' You/
        Nobody Waved Goodbye   (Decca F 12328) 1966

This obscure folk 45 is of no significance to collectors. (VJ)

Brotherhood

Personnel:	DON PARTRIDGE	vcls	A
	PAT PARTRIDGE	vcls	A

ALBUM: 1(A)	BROTHERHOOD	(Fontana TL 5390) 1967

NB: (1) reissued in 1968 with the same label number but titled *Singin' 'N' Sole-In*.

45:	Paper Man/Give It To Me Now	(Philips BF 1760) 1969

Brotherhood is notable for the inclusion of Don Partridge, who later went solo. (VJ)

Brotherhood Of Man

Personnel:	TONY BURROWS		vcls	A
	TONY HILLER		vcls	A
	MARTIN LEE		vcls	B
	LEE SHERIDAN	vcls		B
	NICKY STEVENS	vcls		B
	SANDRA STEVENS	vcls		B

HCP

ALBUMS:
(up to	1 (A)	UNITED WE STAND	(Deram SML 1066) 1970 SC -
1976)	2 (A)	BROTHERTHOOD OF MAN	(Deram SML 1089) 1972 SC -
	3(B)	LOVE AND KISSES FROM THE BROTHERHOOD	
		OF MAN	(Pye NSPL 18490) 1976 20

NB: Vinyl compilations include: *Brotherhood Of Man* (K-Tel BML 7980) 1978 (No 6), *Sing 20 Number One Hits* (Warwick WW 5087) 1980 (No 14) and *The Best Of Brotherhood Of Man* (Pye) 1983. CD compilations include: *20 Great Hits* (Prestige

CDPT 817) 1992 and 1996, *Best Of Brotherhood Of Man* (16 Super Hits) (Laserlight 12210) 1994, *United We Stand* (Deram 8206232)1996 and *Very Best Of Brotherhood Of Man* (Emporio EMPRCD 654) 1996.

HCP

45s:	Love One Another/Little Bit Of Heaven	(Deram DM 276) 1969 -
(up to	United We Stand/Say A Prayer	(Deram DM 284) 1970 10
1976)	Where Are You Going To My Love	(Deram DM 298) 1970 22
	This Boy/You Can Depend On Me	(Deram DM 317) 1970 -
	Reach Out Your Hand/Better Tomorrow	(Deram DM 327) 1971 -
	You And I/Sing In The Sunshine	(Deram DM 335) 1971 -
	California Sunday Morning/	
	Do Your Thing	(Deram DM 341) 1971 -
	Say A Prayer/Follow Me	(Deram DM 361) 1972 -
	Rock My Baby/Hang On	(Deram DM 366) 1972 -
	Happy Ever After/We Can Make It	(Deram DM 385) 1973 -
	Our World Is Love/Maybe The Morning	(Deram DM 393) 1973 -
	United We Stand/Follow Me	(Deram DM 404) 1973 -
	When Love Catches Up On You/	
	How Can Love Love	(Dawn DNS 1055) 1974 -
	Lady/Love's Bound To Get Ya	(Dawn DNS 1072) 1974 -
	Lady, Lady, Lady Lay/Join The Party	(Dawn DNS 1091) 1974 -
	Spring Of 1912/Movin' With Susan	(Dawn DNS 1099) 1975 -
	Kiss Me Kiss Me Baby/	
	Put Out The Fire	(Dawn DNS 1111) 1975 -
	Save Your Kisses For Me/	
	Let's Love Together	(Pye 7N 45569) 1976 1
	My Sweet Rosalie/Sugar Honey Love	(Pye 7N 45602) 1976 30
Reissue:	Save Your Kisses For Me/Oh Boy	(Old Gold OG 9127) 1982 -

Brotherhood Of Man was a vocal pop group originally formed in London in 1969 by songwriter Tony Hiller. In the original line-up the main vocalist was Tony Burrows, who'd been in **The Ivy League**, **The Flower Pot Men** and **Edison Lighthouse**. They enjoyed early success with *United We Stand* and *Where Are You Going To My Love*, which peaked at No's 10 and 22 respectively. They made a number of further recordings with changing personnel for Deram and Dawn, which did not build on their early chart success.

The band's big break came when it was re-modelled on the style and two-boy two-girl approach of the Swedish group Abba, who had won the Eurovision song contest in 1974. The format (line-up B above) worked because they won Eurovision in 1976 with *Save Your Kisses For Me*, which brought them the first of three UK No 1's. Indeed it was an international hit and even made the US Top 30. They enjoyed further UK hits beyond the time span of this book, including two more No 1's with *Angelo* (1977) and *Figuro* (1978), but could not sustain this success beyond 1978. By the eighties they were playing the lower grade nightclub circuit, although they returned in 1982 with a minor hit *Lightning Flash*.

Save Your Kisses For Me has been compiled on several compilations, including *Nothing But Number 1 Love Songs* (CD). (VJ)

EDGAR BROUGHTON BAND - Sing Brother Sing (CD).

Brothers and Sisters

ALBUM: 1   ARE WATCHING YOU   (Private Pressing) 1968 R3

As this is a privately-pressed album it is obviously quite expensive and sought-after by some collectors. Not to be confused with an American band of the same name who recorded the Dylan's *Gospel* album. This one was recorded by various students at Sussex University. It is collectable because of its limited edition (99 copies) release and because it bears a passing resemblance to **Sandy Denny's Fairport Convention**. (VJ/BS)

Brothers Grimm

| 45s: | Lost Love/Make It Or Break It | (Decca F 12224) 1965 |
| | A Man Needs Love/Looky Looky | (Ember EMB 222) 1966 R2 |

Brothers Grimm was a beat group whose second 45 is very collectable because it is a massive Northern soul favourite. They also recorded a surf 45 as Barry and Tony. (VJ)

Brothers Kane

Personnel incl:	EDEN KANE (RICHARD SARSTEDT)	A
	CLIVE 'WES' SANDS (CLIVE SARSTEDT)	A
	PETER LINCOLN (PETER SARSTEDT)	A

| 45: | Walking In The Sand/ | |
| | Won't You Stay Awhile | (Decca F 12448) 1966 SC |

As you can see this venture is far more significant historically for who it involved rather than the end result, which was a sing-along type 45. In addition to the above pseudonyms, Clive Sarstedt was also known as Robin S. Clive also had a record called *There's Lots Lots More Where This Came From/Three Cups* (Columbia DB4996) 1963, which was produced by Joe Meek. (VJ/KL)

Brothers William

| 45: | Honey Love/Linda Jane Blues | (Parlophone R 5293) 1965 |

A folk-blues 45 produced by Giorgio Gomelsky. (VJ)

The Edgar Broughton Band

Personnel:	EDGAR BROUGHTON	vcls, gtr	ABCD
(up to	STEVE BROUGHTON	vcls, drms, perc, piano	ABCD
1976)	ARTHUR GRANT	bs, gtr, vcls	ABCD
	VICTOR UNITT	vcls, gtr, hrmnca, piano, organ	B
	JOHN THOMAS	gtr, vcls	C

EDGAR BROUGHTON BAND - Edgar Broughton Band (CD).

ALBUMS:	1(A)	WASA WASA	(Harvest SHVL 757) 1969 SC -
(up to	2(A)	SING BROTHER SING	(Harvest SHVL 772) 1970 SC 18
1976)	3(B)	THE EDGAR BROUGHTON BAND	
			(Harvest SHVL 791) 1971 SC 28
	4(B)	INSIDE OUT	(Harvest SHTC 252) 1972 SC -
	5(B)	OORA	(Harvest SHVL 810) 1973 SC -
	6(C)	BANDAGES	(NEMS NEL 6006) 1975 -
	7(D)	BUNCH OF 45's	(Harvest SHMS 2001) 1975 -

NB: (2) reissued on Beat Goes On (BGOLP 7), 1983 and (4) on Beat Goes On (BGOLP 59) 1989. (1), (2) and (3) reissued on CD (Beat Goes On BGOCD 129, 7, and 114 respectively) 1992. (3) reissued on CD (Repertoire REP 4409-WY) 1993 with some bonus tracks. (3) and (4) reissued on one CD (Beat Goes On BGOCD 179) 1994. (4) also reissued on CD (Repertoire REP 4410-WY) 1994 with four additional non-album cuts: *Hotel Room, Call Me A Liar, Someone* and *Mr. Crosby*. (4) reissued again on CD (EMI 8661742) 2004. (6) reissued on CD (Repertoire REP 4201-WY) 1992. *Document Series Presents The Edgar Broughton Band* (Document CSAP CD 109) 1992 is a compilation of their better album and single tracks between 1969-73. A second CD compilation is *As Was (The Best Of The Edgar Broughton Band)* (EMI 790 963 Z) 1988, although it was deleted in 1990. An earlier vinyl compilation is *The Best Of The Edgar Broughton Band* (Harvest EMS 1122) 1986. There's also a live album entitled *Live Hits Harder* recorded at the end of the eighties and issued in Europe. They also recorded two albums as **The Broughtons**: *Parlez Vous Anglais* (Babylon Z 80007) 1979 and *Superchip* (Sheet SHEET 2) 1982 SC. The latter has also been reissued on CD as *Superchip... Plus* (See For Miles SEECD 464). *Chilly Morning Mama* (Receiver Records RRCD 262 Z) 1998 is a CD release of a live performance from 1972. *Demons At The Beeb* (Hux HUX 020) 2000 compiles their BBC sessions and will attract completists. *Out Demons Out* (EMI 531 0672) 2001 is a compilation of their better known songs. *Keep Them Freaks A'Rollin: Live At Abbey Road* (EMI 8661782) 2004 is a live recording of the band from December 1969.

45s:	Evil/Death Of An Electric Citizen	(Harvest HAR 5001) 1969 -
	Out Demons Out/Mamma's Reward	(Harvest HAR 5015) 1970 39
	Up Yours!/Officer Dan	(Harvest HAR 5021) 1970 -
	Apache Drop Out/Freedom	(Harvest HAR 5032) 1971 33
	Hotel Room/Call Me A Liar	(Harvest HAR 5040) 1972 -
	Gone Blue/Someone Mr. Crosby	(Harvest HAR 5049) 1972 -

Originally from Warwick, **The Edgar Broughton Band** were an important part of the underground scene in the late sixties and early seventies. The **Edgar Broughton Band**'s vocal style was undoubtedly influenced by the growling Captain Beefheart and their first two albums as a three-piece, while containing some interesting ideas lyrically, were patchy musically. Highlights included *Death Of An Electric Citizen* and *American Boy Soldier* from *Wasa Wasa* and *Aphrodite, Momma's Reward* and *The Moth* from *Sing Brother Sing*. Recruitment of Victor Unitt (formerly connected with **The Pretty Things**) led to a more accessible style musically but they remained an underground politico / rock band. Their third album, the infamous meat cover self-titled album remains their supreme achievement. In particular Side One is a tour de force of evocative lyrics, good rock music and an excellent acoustic track *Poppy* - a 1971 equivalent of The Stranglers' *Golden Brown*.

EDGAR BROUGHTON BAND - Inside Out (CD).

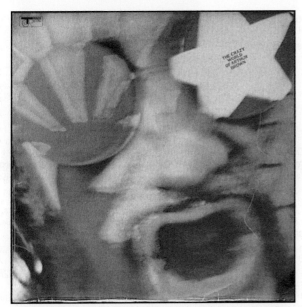

ARTHUR BROWN - THE CRAZY WORLD OF ARTHUR BROWN (LP).

ARTHUR BROWN - The Lost Ears (2-LP).

Their fourth album has a gimmick cover (hence the title *Inside Out*) and is stronger lyrically than musically. Highlights are *Get Out Of Bed* and *Homes Fit For Heroes* and an interesting song about the sexual possibilities of a rake. Their fifth album and last to feature Victor Unitt - *Oora* - is more mainstream rock and makes use of girl backing singers. Highlights are *Hurricane Man*, *Things On My Mind* and *Exhibits From A New Museum*. The band then had a three year sabbatical from recording and even then *Bandages* was delayed a further year due to legal wrangles. Highlights were *I Want To Lie* and *Signal Inspector*. Their seventh studio album *Parlez Vous Anglais* was recorded in 1979 and their eighth *Superchip* in 1982. Neither of the last two can be recommended even if Peter Hope-Evans of **Medicine Head** played harmonica on two tracks of the *Parlez Vous Anglais* album. **The Edgar Broughton Band** may not have made it big but they endeared themselves to the early seventies concert-going public because of their extensive gigging and appearances at most of the UK open-air festivals of the time. They were very popular on the Continent, particularly Germany, and with the **Broughton**'s mum driving the tour bus they became known as the 'Legendary' **Edgar Broughton Band**.

Their manager was killed in a tour bus road accident, Edgar suffered mental health problems but the band survived and was still touring in the early nineties when Edgar had become a social worker. All their studio albums are now available on CD. Incidentally Steve Broughton appeared on **Mike Oldfield**'s *Tubular Bells*.

John Thomas also recorded as **Creepy John Thomas**. Steve Broughton went on to form **City Boy**.

Fans of the band will love the recently unearthed live Abbey Road set from December 1969, *Keep Them Freaks A'Rollin*. It contains a pulsating version of *Smokestack Lightning* and favourites like *Out Demons Out*, an early version of *What Is A Woman For* and the biting *American Soldier Boy*. The package is completed with a booklet with pictures from the session.

EMI's *Out Demons Out* compilation in 2001 contains many of their better known songs like *Apache Dropout*, *Evening Over Rooftops* and, of course, the title track. This is a good introduction to the band's music.

Appearances on Various Artists' compilation included *Old Gopher* on *Picnic* (2-LP); *Call Me A Liar* on *Harvest Bag*; and *Momma's Reward (Keep Them Freaks A Rollin')* on *Harvest Heritage - 20 Greats* (LP). More recently, *Hotel Room* has appeared on the 3-CD set *Guitar Heroes - Rock The Night Away* and *Apache Dropout* can be found on the 3-CD set *Radio Caroline Calling - 70's Flashback*. (BS/VJ)

(The Crazy World Of) Arthur Brown

Personnel:

ARTHUR BROWN	vcls		AB
VINCE CRANE	keyb'ds		AB
DRACHEN THEAKER	drms		A
CARL PALMER	drms		B

HCP

ALBUMS: 1(A) THE CRAZY WORLD OF ARTHUR BROWN
(Track 612 005/613 005) 1967 R1/SC 2
2(-) DANCE (w/insert) (Gull GULP 1008) 1974 -
3(-) THE LOST EARS (2-LP) (Gull GUD 2003/4) 1977 -
4(-) CHISHOLM IN MY BOSOM (Gull GULP 1023) 1978 -
5(-) STRANGELANDS (Reckless RECK 2) 1988 -

NB:(1) Both Nick Greenwood (bs) and John Marshall (drms) also appeared on the first album. (1) reissued on CD (Polydor 833 736 2) 1991. (1) also issued on CD in the US (Touchwood TWCD-2012) 1997 with three non-album bonus cuts: *Devil's Grip*, *Give Him A Flower* and *What's Happening?*. (5) is a retrospective release of the band's previously unreleased second album, also available on CD (Reckless CDRECK 2) 1989. *Fire! The Story Of Arthur Brown* (Sanctuary CMEDD 674) 2003 is a 2-CD compilation.

EP: SIX-PACK / SIX TRACK (Gull SIX/PACK 4) 1977

HCP

45s: α You Don't Know/You'll Be Mine (Lyntone LYN 770/1) 1965 R2 -
Devil's Grip/Give Him A Flower (Track 604 008) 1967 -
Fire/Rest Cure (Track 604 022) 1968 1
β Nightmare/What's Happening (Track 604 026) 1968 -
Gypsies/Dance (Gull GULS 4) 1974 -
We Gotta Get Out Of This Place/
Here I Am (Gull GULS 13) 1975 -
Woman In My Life/Isn't It Amazing (DJM DJS 10619) 1975 -
Reissues: Fire (Track 209 4017) 1975 -
Fire (Old Gold OG 9427) 1984 -

NB: α 'A' side credited to Arthur Brown and The Diamonds. 'B' side credited to The Diamonds. This was a Reading University Rag Week flexidisc. β Some copies had *Music Man* on the flip.

Arthur Brown (real name Arthur Wilton) was born in Whitby, England, on 24th June 1944 and was undoubtedly one of the memorable figures of British psychedelia. His first vinyl excursion was a Reading University flexidisc which is now sought-after. The 'A' side, *You Don't Know* is bluesy. Even harder to track down are two tracks he contributed to a Soundtrack for a 1966 Roger Vadim film. The French title of the film was 'La Cure', although it was released in the States as 'The Game Is Over'. The Arthur Brown Set (backed by The Sharks) recorded two songs for Vadim, *Baby You Know What You're Doing* and *Don't Tell Me*, which were quite close to the sound of the **Crazy World Of Arthur Brown** a year later but with some soul/James Brown influence. The two songs featured on a French EP (Barclay 71 026) and a US Soundtrack album (Atco 33-205) and the sleeves feature slightly different pictures of Jane Fonda nude. The bulk of the music on the US album, though, was provided by the French musicians Jean-Pierre Boutayre and Jean Bouchty and is of little interest.

The **Crazy World Of Arthur Brown**'s debut 45, *Devil's Grip*, made little impression but the follow-up, *Fire*, became a UK No 1 in July 1968 and also climbed to No 2 in the USA. Even before this they had become a very popular attraction around London's underground clubs, like the UFO, in this era. They had a flamboyant stage act which often involved **Brown** appearing in a flaming helmet with bizarre facial make-up. Indeed, their act

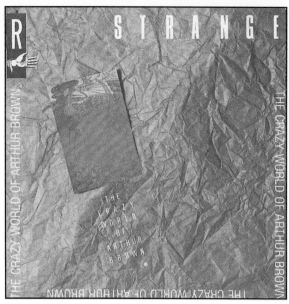

ARTHUR BROWN - Strangelands (CD).

was so expensive to stage that **Brown** eventually became broke. Their (first) album was built around **Brown**'s screaming vocal style and is certainly worth a spin. Also of interest was *Rest Cure*, the flip side to their international hit. They failed to consolidate on their sudden and phenomenal commercial success and, after the failure of their third 45, they split in the wake of a US tour. The second album they'd been working on remained unreleased until Reckless Records issued it in 1988.

Carl Palmer and **Vincent Crane** went on to form **Atomic Rooster** and Palmer later became a member of **Emerson, Lake and Palmer**. **Brown** re-emerged in 1971 with **Kingdom Come** - another theatrical rock outfit. In 1975 he recorded a cover of **The Animals**' *We Gotta Get Out Of This Place*. Also, back in 1964/5, he recorded a R&B album with a London group called South West Five, which has yet to be released. He told 'Record Collector' in an interview in its September 1993 edition that it 'was mainly covers - James Brown, Bobby Bland, Ray Charles - but we did a few originals as well.'

Strangelands was an album of 'Post' **Crazy World** recordings from 1969. Musically the material veers nearer to his work with **Kingdom Come** than **The Crazy World Of Arthur Brown** (though the album is credited to the latter). We're talking vintage progressive rock here - lots of keyboard and up-front guitar. Worth seeking out though.

Brown is still going strong in the new millennium and his voice sounds as good as ever. He acted as narrator when **The Pretty Things** performed their rock opera *S. F. Sorrow* live a few years back and had the audience on their feet with his rendition of *Fire* at the end of the show.

Fans of **Arthur Brown** will also be interested in three later CDs released on Voiceprint in 1993:- *Requiem* (VP 125 CD), *Speak No Tech* (VP 124 CD) and *Order From Chaos - Live 1993* (VP 144 CD). **Brown** also makes a guest appearance on Mandragora's *Pollen* album (Delerium DELEC CD 070) 1998.

Fire!: The Story Of Arthur Brown compiles his career commencing with his version of Peggy Lee's *You Don't Know* for a University of Reading 1965 flexidisc and includes a number of tracks taped prior to his recording contract with Track. Obviously *Fire* (the disc that propelled him to stardom) is here, but more recent material includes a 2002 version of *Silver Machine* with **Hawkwind**; a re-work of *Fire!* with German outfit Die Krupps and there's a predominantly acoustic version of *Heartaches* from 2003's *Tantric Lover* album.

Back in the late sixties *Devil's Grip* and *Fire* were included on *Backtrack 1* (LP) and *Nightmare* got an airing on *Vol. 2* (LP) of the same series. Other compilation appearances include *Prelude-Nightmare*, *Fanfare-Fire Poem* and *Fire* on *Deep Overground Pop* (LP); *You Don't Know* from the Reading University flexi-disc on *Visions Of The Past, Vol. 3* (LP & CD) and *Incredible Sound Show Stories, Vol. 1* (LP & CD); *Don't Tell Me* and *Baby You Know What You're Doing* on *Made In England, Vol. 2* (CD) and *Fire* on the 3-CD box set *Ars Longa Vita Brevis: A Compendium Of Progressive Rock 1967-1974*. (VJ)

Pete Brown and His Battered Ornaments

Personnel:	PETE BAILEY	perc	A
	PETE BROWN	vcls, perc	A
	CHARLIE HART	keyb'ds	A
	DICK HECKSTALL-SMITH	sax	A
	GEORGE KHAN	sax	A
	ROGER POTTER	bs	A
	CHRIS SPEDDING	gtr	A
	ROB TAIT	drms	A

ALBUMS: 1(A) A MEAL YOU CAN SHAKE HANDS WITH IN THE DARK
                                                   (Harvest SHVL 752) 1969 R2
         2(A) MANTLEPIECE   (Harvest SHVL 758) 1969 R2

NB: (1) reissued on CD (Repertoire REP 4406-WY) 1994 with additional tracks. (1) and (2) reissued on a 2-CD set (BGO BGOCD 489). A good compilation is *Before Singing Lessons* (LP) (Decal LIKD 7) 1987.

45:        The Week Looked Good On Paper/Morning
        Call (Some PS, promo)   (Parlophone R 5767) 1969 R2/SC

NB: Those promo 45s issued in a picture sleeve are R2.

Pete Brown was a Londoner and a veteran of the underground scene. Born in 1940, he first came to prominence as a poet. He was just 14 when his first poem appeared in 'Evergreen Revue' in the US. Then in the early sixties he worked alongside another British poet Mike Horowitz. His direct involvement with rock music came when he was asked to form a songwriting partnership with **Jack Bruce** to write lyrics for **Cream** and the partnership proceeded to produce the lyrics for many of their finest songs:- *Wrapping Paper, I Feel Free, Sunshine Of Your Love* and *White Room*. After the demise of **Cream**, **Brown** continued to write with **Bruce** but also began his own recording career with **The Battered Ornaments** who included **Chris Spedding**. After an initial 45, which with its wailing saxes and effective vocals was underrated, the band recorded this album which was a mixture of jazz-rock and blues. *Dark Lady, The Old Man* and *Station Song* were among the fine tracks and the latter later got a further airing on the *Before Singing Lessons* compilation. *Station Song* and *Dark Lady* had earlier featured along with *Travelling Blues* on the ultra-rare promo-only *Harvest Sampler* (LP) in 1969.

Brown then suffered the humiliation of being thrown out of the band the night before they had a Hyde Park gig with **The Rolling Stones**. **Brown**'s response was to form a new band, **Piblokto!**

Pete Bailey went on to work with **Graham Bond**. Charlie Hart formed Juice On The Loose in the eighties and worked with **Ronnie Lane's Slim Chance**, Townsend-Lane and Matchbox, amongst others. Dick Heckstall-Smith had an illustrious career with **Colosseum**, **Neil Ardley**, **Alexis Korner**, **John Mayall**, **Chicken Shack**, **Locomotive**, **Peter Green** and **Sweet Pain** amongst others. He also made solo albums. Roger Potter played with **Chris Spedding** and was also active as a session musician. **Chris Spedding** was one of the most respected session guitarists of the

PETE BROWN AND HIS ORNAMENTS - A Meal You Can Shake Hands With In The Dark (CD).

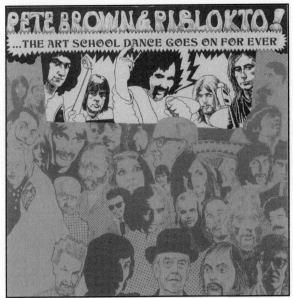

PETE BROWN AND PIBLOKTO - Things May Come And Things May Go But The Art School Dance Goes On Forever (CD).

era and was in **Sharks**, **Nucleus** and **Solid Gold Cadillac**, as well as working with **Paul Korda** and **Jack Bruce** amongst a host of others. He also made solo albums. George Khan went on to **Formerly Fat Harry** and worked with Annette Peacock, **Robert Wyatt**, **Solid Gold Cadillac**, **Arthur Brown** and **The People Band**. Rob Tait drummed with **Kevin Ayers** on his first album, he was in **Piblokto!**, **Bell and Arc**, **Vinegar Joe** and **Paul Korda** and played with Dick Heckstall-Smith.

The *Before Singing Lessons* compilation covers **Brown**'s career during the 1969-77, so it not only contains material from his time with **Pete Brown and The Battered Ornaments** but also material from **Pete Brown and Piblokto!**, **Pete Brown and Graham Bond** and Back To Front. An essential purchase for his fans it includes a considerable amount of previously unissued material, some of his more obscure singles and fine sleeve notes from John Platt. (VJ/BS)

Pete Brown and Graham Bond

Personnel:	GRAHAM BOND	vcls	A
	PETE BROWN	vcls	A

ALBUM: 1(A) TWO HEADS ARE BETTER THAN ONE
(Chapter One CHS R 813) 1972 R2

NB: (1) reissued on CD (See For Miles SEECD 345-A) 19??, with extra tracks.

45:	Lost Tribe//Milk Is Turning Sour In My Shoes		
	Macumba	(Decca/Greenwich GSS 104) 1972

After the break up of **Piblokto!**, **Brown** began to work with **Graham Bond** in a jazz-tinged R&B project, which included assistance on occasions from **Jack Bruce** but was prematurely ended by **Bond**'s death. The album is certainly worth tracking down and only *Lost Tribe* also appeared on the 45 - this was one of their finer songs. *Lost Tribe* and *Mass Debate* are, along with *Amazing Grass*, the strongest tracks on the album but it maintains a consistent standard throughout.

Brown and Bond also recorded almost half an hour music for the soundtrack to 'Maltamour'. One track, *Spend My Nights In Armour*, later reappeared on *Before Singing Lessons* (LP), and the See For Miles reissue of *Two Heads*....

After **Bond**'s death, **Brown** formed a studio group, Brown and Friends. He was later in Flying Tigers and the *Before Singing Lessons* compilation features demos by both of these ventures.

In 1973 **Brown** recorded a spoken word album, *The Not Forgotten Association*, which comprised poems from his early career. In 1976 he recorded demos with Back To Front, two of which figure on *Before Singing Lessons*. The following year he recorded an album with the band's keyboardist Ian Lynn, *Party In The Rain*, which was not released until 1982 on Discs International (INTLP 1).

In the nineties **Brown** teamed up with keyboardist Phil Ryan, who'd played with **Man**, **The Eyes Of Blue** and the final **Piblokto!** line-up for two albums - *Ardours Of The Lost Rake* and *Coals To Jerusalem*. In the late nineties he formed Interoceters to perform songs from throughout his career. He's often worked with **Jack Bruce** and appeared on lots of other artists albums.

Brown's definitely one of the most interesting figures of the British rock scene and his albums are well worth investigation. (VJ)

Pete Brown and Piblokto!

Personnel:	PETE BROWN	vcls, perc	ABC
	ROGER BUNN	bs	A
	JIM MULLEN	gtr, bs	AB
	ROB TAIT	drms	AB
	DAVE THOMPSON	drms	AB
	STEVE GLOVER	perc, bs	BC
	BRIAN BREEZE	ld gtr	C
	PHIL RYAN	keyb'ds	C
	JOHN PUGWASH-WEATHERS	drms	C

ALBUMS: 1(A) THINGS MAY COME AND THINGS MAY GO BUT THE ART SCHOOL DANCE GOES ON FOREVER
(Harvest SHVL 768) 1970 R2
2(B) THOUSANDS ON A RAFT (Harvest SHVL 782) 1970 R2
3(-) MY LAST BAND (Comp.) (Harvest SHSM 2017) 1977 SC

NB: (1) reissued on CD (Repertoire REP 4407-WY). (2) reissued on CD (Repertoire REP 4408-WY) 1994 with additional tracks (both sides of the *Can't Get Off The Planet* album).

45s:	Living Life Backwards/		
	High Flying Electric Bird	(Harvest HAR 5008) 1969 SC
	Can't Get Off The Planet/		
	Broken Magic	(Harvest HAR 5023) 1970 SC
	Flying Hero Sandwich/		
	My Last Band	(Harvest HAR 5028) 1970 SC

Brown formed **Piblokto!** after he'd been asked to leave **Battered Ornaments**. **Piblokto**'s debut album was much more accessible than any of the **Battered Ornaments**' output. The title track was inventive; *My Love's Gone Far Away* featured some effective organ work; *High Flying Electric Bird* (from the 'B' side of their first 45) featured **Brown** on a Cornish slide whistle which sounded like a chirping bird; *Firesong* was a folky, relaxed number and the magnum opus was definitely the gentle *Golden Country Kingdom*. Overall the songs were more commercial than those on **The Battered Ornaments**' album.

By the time of the second album Steve Glover had replaced **Bunn** on bass. Overall this was a patchier effort, although the title track was one of its finest moments: beginning at a slow tempo it builds into an impressive

PETE BROWN AND PIBLOKTO - Thousands On A Raft (CD).

127

climax and is full of atmosphere. The opening track, *Aeroplane Head Woman*, gives an impressive nod and wink in the direction of heavy rock and *Station Song Platform Two* is quite jazzy. Unfortunately, the instrumental *Highland Song*, which closed side one was too long and though the songs on side two were pleasant enough none were in any way exceptional. The album was housed in a clever sleeve which depicted Concorde and the Titanic sinking into the sea whilst thousands of baked beans escaped on rafts of toast!

After the release of the second album, **Brown** disbanded the band and put together a new line-up (C). This line-up recorded the *Flying Hero Sandwich* 45. When a deal for **Piblokto!** to tour the States fell through the band disintegrated. The *My Last Band* album is a compilation, which includes all their singles. After their demise **Brown** began collaboration with **Graham Bond**.

Golden Country Kingdom has been compiled on *Picnic* (2-LP); and you can check out *Living Life Backwards* on *Harvest Heritage - 20 Greats* (LP). (VJ)

Polly Brown

| ALBUMS: | 1 | POLLY BROWN | (Pye NSPL 18396) 1973 |
| | 2 | SPECIAL DELIVERY | (GTO GTLP 003) 1975 |

NB: *Bewitched - The Polly Browne Story* (CD) (RPM RPM 143) is the first compilation of her work.

		HCP
45s:	The Feeling Alright/	
(up to	I Can't Do Without You	(Pye 7N 45148) 1970 -
1976	I'll Cry My Heart Out for You/	
	Teardrops Will Fall	(Pye 7N 45197) 1970 -
	Amoureuse/Crazy Love	(Pye 7N 45283) 1973 -
	So Much In Love/	
	I Can't Go On Living Without You	(Pye 7N 45246) 1973 -
	Up In A Puff Of Smoke/	
	I'm Saving All My Love	(GTO GT 2) 1974 14
	Dial For Love//Love Lovin' You	(GTO GT 14) 1975 -
	You're My Number One/S.O.S.	(GTO GT 20) 1975 -
	Special Delivery/Am I Losing My Touch	(GTO GT 38) 1975 -
	Do You Believe In Love At First?/	
	Shot Down In Flames	(GTO GT 54) 1976 -
	Love Bug/ Love Bug Buzzin'	(GTO GT 61) 1976 -

A solo album from the vocalist of **Pickettywitch**, who recorded several singles too. *Bewitched - The Polly Browne Story* (CD) (RPM RPM 143) is the first compilation of her work and she helped to write the comprehensive sleevenotes. It features singles from **Pickettywitch** as well as solo efforts including *Up In A Puff Of Smoke*, which made the US Top 20 in 1975. (BS/VJ)

Stu Brown and Bluesology

See **Bluesology**.

Duncan Browne

Personnel:	DUNCAN BROWNE	gtr, vcls	AB
	JOHN "RABBIT" BUNDRICK	keyb'ds	B
	TONY CARR	vcls	B
	ROBERT HENRIT	drms	B
	KEITH HODGE	vcls	B
	SUZI QUATRO	vcls	B
	JIM RODFORD	bs	B

ALBUMS:	1(A)	GIVE ME TAKE YOU	
(up to		(w/insert)	(Immediate IMSP 018) 1968 R3
1976	2(B)	DUNCAN BROWNE	(Rak SRKA 6754) 1973 SC

NB: (1) reissued on CD (Castle Music CMRCD 057) and again on CD (Immediate CMRCD 057) 2000. *Journey: The Anthology 1967-1993* (Castle CMEDD 753) 2004 is a 2-CD set.

DUNCAN BROWNE - Give Me Take You (CD).

		HCP
45s:	On The Bombsite/Alfred Bell	(Immediate IM 70) 1968 -
(up to	Resurrection Joe/Final Asylum	(Bell BLL 1119) 1970 -
1976)	Journey/?	(Rak RAK 135) 1972 23
	Send Me The Bill/My Only Son	(Rak RAK 162) 1973 -

Born on 25th March 1947 **Browne** was a singer/songwriter originally signed to Immediate as part of a flower-pop duo called Lorel (the other member was Davy Morgan). Lorel recorded a projected single - *Here And Now* - produced by **Mike D'Abo** but it was never released. Disillusioned, Morgan departed but Immediate owner **Andrew Loog Oldham** agreed to release an album of **Browne**'s material with a new partner David Bretton writing the lyrics.

Give Me Take You met with much critical acclaim at the time. There's some pleasant late sixties baroque pop in evidence on tracks like *Dwarf In A Tree (A Cautionary Tale)*, *Ninepence Worth Of Walking* and *Walking You (Parts 1&2)*. A single, *On The Bombsite*, was taken from it (you'll also find it on *The Immediate Alternative* (LP)), but neither sold. Both were pleasant enough but lacked that distinctive ingredient which may have guaranteed success and may have suffered from excessive use of strings. His second solo album was recorded with two members of **Argent** (Rodford and Henrit). He enjoyed a hit with *Journey* in 1972 which contained a strange mix of classical guitar, Farfisa organ and mixed choir (the last two probably courtesy of Mickie Most's production).

Browne recorded spasmodically during the seventies, with the group Metro in 1977 and two other solo albums in 1978 (*Wild Places*) and 1979 (*Streets Of Fire*) but these ventures also sank without trace and he eventually quit the music business. He sadly died in May 1993 of cancer.

Browne can also be found on **Tom Yates'** *Love Comes Well Armed* (1973) and **Colin Blunstone**'s *Journey* (1974). **David Bowie** covered **Browne**'s *Criminal World* on his *Let's Dance* album.

Journey: The Anthology 1967-1993 traces his career from the early dream-like pop of *Here And Now* and the angst of *Alfred Bell*, through the glam-like **Mickie Most**-produced hit *Journey*, through his flirtation with Japan-esque Europop (as Metro) to atmospheric rock on *Scull Twins*.

Compilation appearances include: *On The Bombsite* on *Immediate Alternative* (LP & CD) and *Journey* on the 3-CD set *Radio Caroline Calling - 70's Flashback*. (VJ/JM/SR)

Friday Brown(e)

| ALBUM: | 1 | FRIDAY BROWN | (Philips 6308074) 1971 |

45s:	α	Getting Nowhere/	
		And (To Me He Meant Everything)	(Parlophone R 5396) 1966
		32nd Love Affair/Born A Woman	(Fontana TF 736) 1966 R1

Ask Any Woman/Outdoor Seminar	(Fontana TF 851) 1967
Stand By Your Man/I Want To Rain	(Fontana H 996) 1969
Groovy Kind Of Love/Salford	(Philips 6006 324) 1973

NB: α as **Friday Browne**.

This Manchester-based pop singer failed to achieve any commercial success. She was also involved in **Manchester Mob**, a studio combo which included **Graham Gouldman**. For her final two 45s she covered Tammy Wynette's *Stand By Your Man* and **The Mindbenders'** *Groovy Kind Of Love*.

Back in 1964 she'd been **Marianne** in **Marianne and Mike**. (VJ)

Thomas F. Browne

ALBUM: 1 WEDNESDAY'S CHILD   (Vertigo 6325 250) 1972 R1

This obscure singer/songwriter had previously been in Nero and The Gladiators, an early sixties instrumental outfit who recorded for Decca. He was supported by **Gary Wright** and Mickey Jones (of **Spooky Tooth** and Foreigner) on this album but it's eminently forgettable. He later rejoined The Gladiators (along with Mick Jones) and they both backed French singer Johnny Halliday and wrote several hits for him. They then recorded under the pseudonym **The State Of Mickey and Tommy**. Nothing has been heard of **Browne** since he wrote a song for **Chris Andrews** in the early seventies. (VJ)

Brownhill Stamp Duty

45s:	Maxwell's Silver Hammer/	
	My Woman's Back	(Columbia DB 8625) 1969
	Hey There Lonely Girl/Caroline	(Pye 7N 45217) 1970
	Kyrie Elison/Who's Got The Love	(Pye 7N 45324) 1974
	Pigeon/Fill My Boots	(Pye 7N 45386) 1974

A pop outfit who covered **The Beatles'** *Maxwell's Silver Hammer* for their debut 45 and the Eddie Holman hit, *Hey There Lonely Girl* for the follow-up. So clearly they relied a lot on cover versions. (VJ)

Jack Bruce

HCP
ALBUMS:	1	SONGS FOR A TAILOR	(Polydor 583 058) 1969 SC 6
(up to	2	THINGS WE LIKE	(Polydor 2343 033) 1970 SC -
1976)	3	HARMONY ROW	(Polydor 2310 107) 1971 -
	4	OUT OF THE STORM (w/insert)	(RSO 2394 143) 1974 -

NB: (1) reissued on CD (Polydor 835 242-2) but deleted at the end of 1989. (1) reissued again on CD (Polydor/Universal 065 603-2) 2003, remastered with a demo and alternate takes of three album tracks as bonuses. (2) reissued on vinyl (Polydor 2310 070) 1971. (2) reissued on CD (Polydor/Universal 065 604-2) 2003, remastered with one bonus track. (3) reissued on CD (Polydor/Universal 065 605-2) 2003, remastered with bonus alternate and instrumental takes. (4) reissued on CD (Polydor/Universal 065 606-2) 2003, remastered with five bonus cuts. There's also *Willpower* (Polydor 837 806-1) 1987, a 73-minute double album or single CD anthology of his career and *The Collection* (Castle CCSSMC 326, also on CD) 1992 includes some of his better-known material with **Cream** and the best moments from his early solo career. *Live In Concert* (Windsong WINCD 076) 1995 contains a 1971 live BBC TV special by a very short-lived **Bruce** band, which featured Carla Bley, Mick Taylor (gtr), John Marshall (drms), **Chris Spedding** (gtr) and Art Theman (alto player). *The Jack Bruce Collectors Edition* (Times Square/Silver Screen TSQCD 9046) is a 14-track collection compiling many of his best solo tracks.

45s:	I'm Getting Tired (Of Drinking And Gambling)/	
	Rootin' Tootin'	(Polydor BM 56036) 1965 R1
	The Consul At Sunset/	
	Letter Of Thanks	(Polydor 2058 153) 1971 SC
	Keep It Down/Golden Days	(RSO 2090 141) 1974

Clearly a very talented bass guitarist, **Bruce** only really enjoyed the success he was capable of for short spells of his career.

Bruce entered the world at Bishopbriggs, Lanarkshire on 14th May 1943. Growing up in his native Scotland he played bass in Jim McHarg's Scotsville Jazzband and was also a regular attraction in Glasgow's

dancehalls. His early musical influences seem to have been Scottish folk, jazz and classical - he actually won a scholarship to the Royal Scottish Academy of Music.

In the early sixties he headed for London, playing in **Alexis Korner's Blues Incorporated** and then attracting attention in the **Graham Bond Organisation**. He later had short spells with **John Mayall's Bluesbreakers** and **Manfred Mann** before forming **Cream** with **Ginger Baker** and **Eric Clapton**.

He recorded his first 45, which is now an expensive collectors' item, whilst still with the **Graham Bond Organisation** back in 1965, so after the demise of **Cream** it was no major surprise that he chose to work on a solo career.

In November 1969 he put together **Jack Bruce and Friends** to promote his critically acclaimed *Songs For A Tailor* album with Larry Coryell, **Chris Spedding** and Jon Hiseman. Its finer moments include the **Procol Harum**-like piano piece, *Theme From An Imaginary Western* and *Rope Ladder To The Moon*, with its nasal vocals.

His second album, *Things We Like*, which featured **Dick Heckstall-Smith**, Jon Hiseman and **John McLaughlin** made less impact. To promote it **Spedding** and Hiseman were replaced by Mike Mandel and Mitch Mitchell. This album is very jazzy and, as one might expect, utilises lots of brass.

In October 1970, **Bruce** joined **Tony Williams' Lifetime**.

Bruce put together a new tour band in April 1971 with **Spedding**, John Marshall, Art Theman and **Graham Bond**. This band may have also promoted **Bruce**'s third album *Harmony Row*. This marked a further change of style, containing 11 rock songs. *The Consul At Sunset* features some Latin favela-style shuffling and *Smiles And Grins* is a notable keyboard-dominated track.

His next venture was a collaboration with Carla Bley and Paul Haines on *Escalator Over The Hill*, a jazz-rock album. He spent from 1972-73 in West, Bruce and Laing, but in the summer of 1974 formed a new tour band with Mick Taylor (ex-**Rolling Stones**), Bruce Gary (drms), Carla Bley (keyb'ds) and Max Middleton - although Middleton only rehearsed with them and was replaced by Ronnie Leahy. This band promoted *Out Of The Storm* and stayed together until July 1975.

In January 1977 he put together another band with Hughie Burns, Tony Hymas and Simon Phillips to promote *How's Tricks* (March 1977). In 1981, he then formed BLT with **Robin Trower**.

Always innovative throughout the five decades he's been active in the music business, **Bruce** drove himself into uncharted waters with his jazz and folk-rock songs. He also recorded some significant bluesy albums with **Cream**, **Robin Trower**, West Bruce and Laing and several of his solo albums from the eighties and early nineties and he's still going strong today.

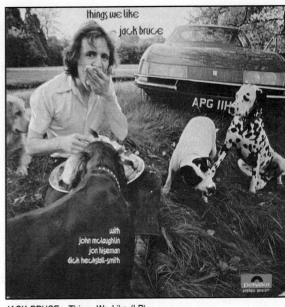

JACK BRUCE - Things We Like (LP).

Bruce can also be heard playing *Never Tell Your Mother She's Out Of Tune* on Polydor's 1971 compilation *Bombers* (LP); *Rope Ladder To The Moon* on *Rock Party* (LP); *Clearout* on *Supergroups* (LP); *I'm Getting' Tired (Of Drinkin' And Gamblin' Etcetera)* and *Rootin' Tootin'* on *Rare Tracks* (LP); and *Never Tell Your Mother* on *Supergroups, Vol. 2* (LP). *Willpower*, the anthology set, covers his career up to 1978. More recently, the *Prime Cuts* compilation includes *Pieces Of Mind* from 1974.

He also played on several cuts from 1966/67, which were unissued until they appeared on the new 1995 **Duffy Power** CD, *Just Stay Blue*, released on r-p-m's new mid-price label. (VJ/JM)

The Bruisers

Personnel incl:	DON McGINTY	drms	A

			HCP
45s:	Blue Girl/Don't Cry	(Parlophone R 5042) 1963 SC	31
	Your Turn To Cry/Give It To Me	(Parlophone R 5092) 1963 SC	-

A Birmingham beat group. **Peter Lee Stirling** handled the vocals on both these singles and the band backed him. They also performed as backing artists for Tommy Bruce, an early sixties ballad singer, and on some of **Cilla Black**'s first beat recordings.

Blue Girl can also be heard on *Twist A La Star Club* (LP). (VJ/JM/LBy)

The Brumbeats (1)

Personnel:	JOHN HANCOX	drms	A
	NORMAN HAINES	organ	A
	GRAHAM HILL	lead gtr	A
	TONY QUINN	bs	A

NB: Other personnel included Terry Guy (bs), Alan Madden (drms) and stand-in bassist Colin Timmins.

A mid-sixties outfit from Birmingham, most significant for including Terry Guy later joined **Ghost** and **Norman Haines** who found brief fame in **Locomotive** and later pursued a solo career recording a horrendously rare album. (VJ/AD)

The Brumbeats (2)

Personnel:	BUDDY ASH	vcls	A
	DAVID CARTER	sax	A
	ALLAN EASTWOOD	drms	A
	GRAHAM GALLERY	bs	A
	ROGER HILL	gtr	A

45:	Cry Little Girl, Cry/I Don't Understand	(Decca F 11834) 1964 SC

A different mid-sixties Birmingham-based pop outfit who veered more towards R&B as their career progressed. Their 45, which is of no particular significance, is not easy to find.

Hill later went on to **The Uglys**, etc and Gallery linked up with **Wizzard** in 1977. (VJ/JM)

Beau Brummel Esquire

45s:	I Know You Know/Shoppin' Around	(Columbia DB 7447) 1965
	The Next Kiss/Come And Get Me	(Columbia DB 7538) 1965
	A Better Man Than I/Teardrops	(Columbia DB 7675) 1965
	You Don't Know What You've Got/	
	Take Me Like I Am	(Columbia DB 7878) 1966

A South African called Mike Bush, he originally settled in the UK in 1961. One of the true characters of the mid-sixties music scene - he carried a gold topped walking cane and was always colourful on stage during his short career. He tended to use backing vocalists 'cos he couldn't sing much... and lacked the talent (though not the front) to make much impact. His vocal limitations could also explain the band's reputation for high volume, and the 53 takes required for his first 45, *I Know You Know*.

His backing band, called The Noblemen operated under pseudonyms: - Earl Ketley, Count Bernard, The Hon. Bryan Dray Stevens, Baron Laroche and Lord Chuck. (VJ/JM)

Brunning (Hall) Sunflower Blues Band

Personnel	BOB BRUNNING	bs	ABC
	PETER FRENCH	vcls	A
	BOB HALL	piano	ABC
	MICK HALLS	gtr	A
	COLIN JORDAN	gtr	A C
	JEFF RUSSEL	drms	A
	PAT GOWER	vcls, gtr	B
	BARRIE GUARD	drms	B
	JO ANN KELLY	vcls	B
	LEO MANNING	drms	B
	KEITH NELSON	banjo	B
	JOHN O'LEARY	hrmnca	B
	STEVE RYE	hrmnca	B
	PETER BANHAM	drms	C
	PETER GREEN	gtr, vcls	C

ALBUMS:	1(A)	BULLEN ST. BLUES	(Saga FID 2118) 1968 SC
	2(B)	THE BRUNNING HALL SUNFLOWER BLUES BAND	
			(Gemini GM 2010) 1969 R2
	3(C)	TRACKSIDE BLUES	(Saga EROS 8132) 1969 R1
	4(-)	I WISH YOU WOULD	(Saga EROS 8150) 1970 R1

NB: (3) and (4) reissued in Italy (Appaloosa AP 031) and (AP 035) respectively. (1) and (4) reissued in one CD in Italy (Appaloosa AP 035-2)1999. (2) and (4) reissued on one CD (Indigo IGOCD 2113 Z) 1999. *Long Road* (Akarma AK 246/3) 2003 is a 3-CD box set, available on Italian import, which compiles their material.

This blues band's recordings are now pretty rare and, as you can see, the seminal duo of Brunning and Hall were assisted on them by some of the famous blues artists of the period. **Peter Green**, for example, is better known as a founder of **Fleetwood Mac** and Steve Rye was with **Groundhogs**.

Musically they played a sort of big belly bar-room blues which had nothing to distinguish it from several of the other artists which made up the British blues boom.

Slide guitarist J.B. Hutto showcased his talents on the third CD of the *Long Road* set. (VJ)

Bruno

45s:	Wander Boy/Window In My Room	(Parlophone R 5450) 1966
	The English Girl/The Driver	(Parlophone R 5507) 1966

This guy's two easy listening pop 45s are of no lasting significance. (VJ)

BUDGIE - Budgie (LP).

Brute Force

45:     King Of Fuh/Nobody Knows   (Apple APPLE 8) 1969 R5

This was allocated a catalogue number but remains unissued. Any copies would be exceedingly rare. (VJ)

Bryan and The Brunelles

| Personnel incl: | BRIAN BURKE | vcls | A |
| | SNIP TURNER | gtr | A |

45:     Jacquelline / Louie, Louie   (HMV POP 1394) 1965

The A side to this, their sole 45, is a catchy but slow beat tune with some fine vocals. You can also find it on *English Freakbeat, Vol. 3* (LP & CD), which states that the band evolved out of an act called The Hangmen. (MS)

Calum Bryce

45:     Lovemaker/I'm Glad   (Condor PS 1001) 1968 R3

Condor was a short-lived label established by Howard Conder, who was involved with **Rupert's People**. This was its most sought-after release and unusual slice of pop-psych and the royalties (such as they were) went to the victims of the Biafra disaster. (VJ)

Bubblegum

45:     Little Red Bucket/
        With The Sun In Your Hair   (Philips BF 1677) 1968

A five-piece beat group. *Little Red Bucket* was a Vanda-Young composition. (VJ)

The Buckinghams

45s: I'll Never Hurt You No More/She Lied   (Pye 7N 15848) 1965
        To Be Or Not To Be/I Was Your First Guy (Pye 7N 15921) 1965

This UK band was unconnected to their better-known US namesakes from Chicago. From Islington in North London they played slow beat tunes. (VJ)

Sean Buckley and The Breadcrumbs

Personnel:	COLIN BANYARD	gtr	A
	SEAN BUCKLEY	ld vcls	A
	VINCE NICHOLS	gtr	A
	KEVIN SHEEHAN	gtr	A
	DAVID SIMMONDS	drms	A

NB: Presumably one of the guitar players listed above is actually the bassist.

45:     It Hurts Me When I Cry/
        Everybody Knows   (Stateside SS 421) 1965 R2

A sought-after 45 whose flipside is a slow beat number, produced by Shel Talmy. Given the label, this could have been a US band, although they were featured in 'Valentine' magazine as a UK act.

Everybody Knows later turned up on *James Patrick Page: Session Man, Vol. 2* (CD), *Searching In The Wilderness* (LP & CD) and *Beat It* (3-CD). (VJ/JM)

Budgie

Personnel:	TONY BOURGE	gtr, vcls	ABC
	RAY PHILLIPS	drms	A
	BURKE SHELLEY	bs, vcls	ABC
	PETE BOOT	drms	B
	STEVE WILLIAMS	drms	C

BULLDOG BREED - Made In England (CD).

			HCP
ALBUMS:	1(A)	BUDGIE (MCA MKPS 2018) 1971	SC -
(up to	2(A)	SQUAWK (MCA MKPS 2023) 1972	SC -
1976)	3(A)	NEVER TURN YOUR BACK ON A FRIEND (MCA MDKS 8010) 1973	SC -
	4(B)	IN FOR THE KILL (MCA MCF 2546) 1974	29
	5(C)	BANDOLIER (MCA MCF 2723) 1975	36
	6(-)	THE BEST OF (MCA MCF 2766) 1975	-
	7(C)	IF I WAS BRITANNIA I'D RULE THE WAVES (A&M AMLH 68377) 1976	-

NB: (1) First pressings issued with a poster, these are R1. (1), (2), (3), (4) and (5) reissued on CD in Germany by Repertoire (REP 4012-WZ, 4026-WZ, 4013-WZ, 4027-WZ and 4100-WZ) in 1992. (7) reissued on CD (MCA DMCL 1637) 1989, but deleted in 1992. There's also a double CD retrospective: *An Ecstacy Of Fumbling - The Definite Anthology* (Repertoire REP 4435-WO1/2) 1995. *Heavier Than Air: Rarest Eggs* (Burning Airlines PILOT 42) 1998 is a 2-CD set comprising a collection of sessions taped for radio.

45s:	Crash Course In Brain Surgery / Nude	
(up to	Disintegrating Parachutist Woman	(MCA MK 5072) 1971 SC
1976)	Whisky River/Guts	(MCA MK 5085) 1972
	Zoom Club/	
	Wondering What Everyone Knows	(MCA MCA 133) 1974
	I Ain't No Moutain/Honey	(MCA MCA 175) 1975

A rather pedestrian heavy rock outfit who formed in Cardiff in 1968. What I've heard of their music is rather tedious and unimaginative and I can't commend them to you. Their music is highly-rated by the heavy rock fraternity, though. (VJ)

John Bull Breed

45:     Can't Chance A Breakup/
        I'm A Man   (Polydor BM 56065) 1966 R4

This R&B group came from Birmingham and they recorded a rare and expensive 45. The 'A' side of their 45 was pretty beaty but the real jewel for many will be the deranged interpretation of the R&B classic, *I'm A Man*, on the flip, which builds into a furious climax.

You'll also find *Can't Chance A Break-up* on *Rare 60's Beat Treasures, Vol. 3* (CD). (VJ)

Bulldog

45:     Glancy/In The City   (Cube BUG 44) 1974

Originally from Stanely in Co. Durham, this group won an EMI audition following a talent search. In August 1973, they entered the recording studio. I don't know if this was the same band that recorded for Decca. (VJ)

Bulldog Breed

Personnel incl:

PETER DUNTON	drms	A
KEITH CROSS	ld gtr	A
BERNIE JINKS	bs	AB
ROD HARRISON	gtr	B
ROB HUNT	flute, vcls	B
LOUIS FARRELL	drms	B

ALBUM: 1(B) MADE IN ENGLAND (Deram Nova (S)DN 5) 1969 R2

NB: (1) reissued on CD (World Wide Records SPM-WWR-0052) 1993. (1) reissued again on CD (Acme Gramophone ACLN 104 CD) and on vinyl (with their 45 as a bonus) (Acme Deluxe ADLP 1036).

45: Portcullis Gate/Halo In My Hair (Deram DM 270) 1969 R1

An obscure psych-prog outfit from the Woodford Green area of London whose album is now a minor collectable. Farrell had previously been with **Gun** and other members had played with **Please**. *Portcullis Gate*, which was inspired by the image on the reverse of a three penny bit, veered towards progressive rock, while its punchy flip owed more to early **Pink Floyd**. It is now rare and expensive. Despite its date, *Made In England*'s short, snappy songs sound more psychedelic than progressive, and the album sold as badly as everything else on Nova.

After they split, Keith Cross and Bernie Jinks formed **T2**. Cross later formed **Cross and Ross**. Rod Harrison played with **Asgard** (who re-recorded **Bulldog Breed**'s *Austin Osman Spare*), and other members ended up working for **The Moody Blues**, **Robert Plant** and even Tony Hatch. Robin Hunt died circa 1998.

Compilation appearances have included: - *Portcullis Gate* on *Rubble Vol. 12: Staircase To Nowhere* (LP) and *Rubble Vol. 6* (CD); *Halo In My Hair* on *Deram Dayze* (LP); *Portcullis Gate* and *Halo In My Hair* on *Psychedalia - Rare Blooms From The English Summer Of Love* (CD); and *Friday Hill*, a track from their album on *Broken Dreams, Vol. 6* (LP) and *Jagged Time Lapse, Vol 2* (CD). (VJ/JM/RH)

Bullet

Personnel:

JOHN CANN	gtr	A
JOHNNY GUSTAFSON	bs	A
PAUL HAMMOND	drms	A
AL SHAW	vcls	A

45: Hobo/Sinister Minister (Purple PUR 101) 1971

This was an offshoot of **Atomic Rooster** formed in August 1971 by John Cann and Paul Hammond with **Johnny Gustafson** (ex-**Quatermass**). They were originally known as "An", but quickly renamed themselves as **Bullet** when Al Shaw was recruited on vocals. In April 1972, they changed name

ROGER BUNN - Piece Of Mind (CD).

to Bulldog and then, following the departure of Al Shaw in June 1972, became **Hard Stuff**, who had a couple of albums on the Purple label.

The groups of this name who recorded on Philips and Alaska were US bands, however 'Billboard' magazine described these three 45s as by the UK act.

			HCP
45s:	White Lies, Blue Eyes/		
	Changes Of Mind	(Big Tree 123) 1972	28
	Hittin On You/		
	Will Power Weak, Temptation Strong	(Big Tree 131) 1972	96
	Little Bit Of Soul/Up Your Sleeve	(Big Tree 140) 1972	-

Is anyone able to confirm whether Billboard was correct? None of the Big Tree titles appear on the first **Hard Stuff** *Bulletproof* album, whereas both *Hobo* and *Sinister Minister* do. Big Tree was a subsidiary label of Atlantic, which hyped quite a number of Canadian artists, so they could have been by a Canadian act. *White Lies, Blue Eyes* was a mild chart hit in the US.

Gustafson had also been in **The Big Three** and **The Merseybeats**. (VJ/JM/Br)

The Bullring

Personnel:

LEN BEDDOW	ld gtr, vcls	A
ALAN LACEY	drms	A
HERBIE (DANNY ROBINSON)	ld vcls	A
MICK TAYLOR	gtr, vcls	A
PETE STEVENS	bs, vcls	A

45: Birmingham Brass Band /
Lady Of The Morning Sun (CBS 4881) 1970

This was actually **Herbie's People** under a pseudonym. It was featured on the British TV quiz show "The Golden Shot" in the musical part of the show, with the band filmed in Brass Band outfits at various points of local interest around Birmingham! (LB)

The Bumbles

Personnel incl: PETER ROBINSON keyb'ds

45: Beep Beep/
Buzz Off (Some in promo-only PS) (Purple PUR 107) SC/- 1972

Musically this 45 is pure unadulterated bubblegum music, á la 1910 Fruitgum Co. etc. It's about a guy driving on the motorway who sees a woman driving past in a new car. A juniors choice record. It was produced by Dave Atkins and John Cann (of **Bullet**) who co-wrote the song. Some copies were issued in a picture sleeve. (VJ)

The Bunch (1)

45s:	We're Not What We Appear To Be/		
	You Never Came Home	(CBS 202506) 1967	R1
	Don't Come Back To Me/		
	You Can't Do This	(CBS 2740) 1967	SC
	Looking Glass Alice/Spare A Shilling	(CBS 3060) 1967	R2
	Birthday/Still	(CBS 3692) 1968	SC
Reissue:	Birthday/Still	(CBS 3709) 1968	

This Bournemouth-based band played at The Star Club in Hamburg in the course of their career. Their first 45 was experimental beat music. Some of their later 45s were more psychedelic. This was the case with *Looking Glass Alice*. They later had a horn section.

Compilation appearances include: *Looking Glass Alice* on *Justafixation II* (LP) and *We Can Fly, Vol 1* (CD); *Spare A Shilling* on *The Upside Down World Of John Pantry* (LP); *Spare A Shilling* and *Looking Glass Alice* on *Artefacts From The Psychedelic Dungeon* (CD); *We're Not What We Appear To Be* on *Yellow Elektric Years* (LP) and *Jagged Time Lapse, Vol 3*

(CD); *You Can't Do This* on *Colour Me Pop, Vol 1* (CD) and *Birthday* on *Colour Me Pop, Vol 2* (CD). (VJ)

The Bunch (2)

Personnel:			
	ROGER BALL	sax	A
	GERRY CONWAY	drms	A
	TONY COX	piano	A
	SANDY DENNY	vcls	A
	PAT DONALDSON	bs	A
	MALCOLM DUNCAN	sax	A
	ASHLEY HUTCHINGS	vcls	A
	TREVOR LUCAS	gtr, vcls	A
	DAVE MATTACKS	drms	A
	MIKE ROSEN	trumpet	A
	LINDA THOMPSON	vcls	A
	RICHARD THOMPSON	gtr, vcls	A
	IAN WHITEMAN	piano	A

ALBUM: 1(A) THE BUNCH ROCK ON   (Island ILPS 9189) 1972 SC

NB: (1) Some issued with a one-sided flexi-disc *Let There Be Drums* (Island WI 4002). These are R1.

45:      When Will I Be Loved/
         Willie And The Hand Jive   (Island WIP 6130) 1972

This was not a group but more a **Fairport Convention** project incorporating the top drawer of the UK folk scene - the personnel just reads like a roll call of honour! Early copies of the album came with a one-sided flexidisc *Let There Be Drums* and inevitably they have a higher value. Ian Whiteman had previously been with **Mighty Baby**. (VJ)

The Bunch Of Fives

Personnel incl:			
	RICHARD DALLING	bs	A
	MIKE DOCKERS	vcls	A
	VIV PRINCE	drms	A
	DAVE STEWART	organ	A
	MICK WAYNE	ld gtr	A

45:      Go Home Baby/At The Station   (Parlophone R 5494) 1966 R2

This short-lived venture was formed by **Viv Prince** after he left **The Pretty Things**, but it soon fell apart. The 45 remains quite sought-after by collectors, though.

Prince later played for **Vamp**, **Denny Laine** and **Kate** and Dave Stewart went on to **Egg** and **Hatfield and The North**. Mick Wayne had joined from **The Hullaballoos** and was later in **Juniors Eyes**.

Compilation appearances include: *Go Home Baby* on *60's Back Beat* (LP); and you'll find *At The Station* on *Visions Of The Past, Vol. 3* (LP & CD) and *Beat It* (3-CD). (VJ)

Bundle

45:      Dirty La Rue/
         Progressive Underground   (Polydor 2058 029) 1970 SC

This is an uptempo folk disc. Nothing is known about the band. (VJ)

Roger Bunn

ALBUM: 1 PIECE OF MIND   (Major Minor SMLP 70) 1970 R1

NB: (1) also released in Germany on Ohr (56009) in 1971 and reissued on CD (Shagadelic SDCD 9). (1) reissued on CD (Roller Coaster Records) 2005.

The back of **Roger Bunn**'s only album describes him as 'a 27 year-old

VASHTI BUNYAN - Just Another Diamond Day (CD).

English composer/lyric-writer/singer/guitarist and a genius besides.' Whilst this might be a shade hyperbolic, he certainly had one of pop's more interesting careers, spanning work with dance orchestras, blues bands and jazz groups as well as artists as varied as **David Bowie**, **Pete Brown**, **Roxy Music** (from November 1970 - September 1971, before they made it onto vinyl), and even Billy Idol. For obscure reasons, *Piece Of Mind*, an enjoyably bizarre mixture of funky pop, freeform poetry and orchestrated ballads, was recorded in Holland with the Dutch National Orchestra. It originally appeared on the continent in a gatefold, but the UK version has a single sleeve.

In more recent years **Bunn** became active in the field of human rights, founding MIHRA (the Music Industry Human Rights Association) and campaigning tirelessly on behalf of exploited musicians. Sadly he died in July 2005, just after completing work on the long-awaited reissue of *Piece of Mind*. (VJ/MWh/RMJ)

Bob Bunting

ALBUM: 1 YOU'VE GOT TO GO DOWN THIS WAY
                              (Transatlantic TRA 166) 1968 R1

Bob Bunting is an obscure electric folk artist whose album may be of interest to folkies. (VJ)

Vashti Bunyan

ALBUM: 1 JUST ANOTHER DIAMOND DAY
                              (Philips 6308 019) 1971 R5

NB: (1) has been bootlegged but more recently officially reissued on CD (Spinney 001 CD) 2000 and on vinyl plus a 7" (B980272). It compiles material she recorded with the help of **Fairport Convention's** Dave Swarbrick and Simon Nicol and Robin Williamson (of **The Incredible String Band**). The 7" contains some earlier solo material and a home demo of one album track *Iris's Song For Us*.

45s: Some Things Just Stick In Your Mind/
         I Want To Be Alone   (Decca F 12157) 1965
         Train Song/Love Song   (Columbia DB 7917) 1966

NB: These 45s were credited to **Vashti**.

Vashti Bunyan grew up in the heart of London, dreaming of pop stardom. When she was expelled from art school in Oxford, discovered by **Andrew Loog Oldham** and given a **Jagger**/Richard composition to record for her first 45, it all seemed set to come true. But the single (produced in typically overblown fashion by **Oldham**) was not a hit and Decca soon lost interest. Its B-side, a haunting self-penned number, is in fact superior. The following year she recorded a sparse follow-up for Columbia, with Canadian Peter Snell producing. The flip was co-written with **Alasdair Clayre**, a friend from student days, but it was even less successful than her debut. Though further recordings were made in this period, only an edited rendition of *Winter Is Blue* got released, as part of the *Tonite Let's All Make Love In London* (LP) soundtrack album. She can also be heard contributing backing vocals to *The Coldest Night Of The Year* on **Twice As Much**'s second album *That's All*, though even she was unaware of this till recently.

Frustrated by the continual shelving of her own recordings, in 1968 she turned her back on London and, accompanied by her boyfriend Robert, Bess, the horse and Blue the dog, she embarked on a horse-drawn journey to the Hebrides with the initial intention of joining a commune led by **Donovan** on the Isle of Skye. One can't help admiring the sheer audacity of the venture - living on the road with no money except what they earned from painting farms and digging gardens, frequently cold and wet and occasionally mocked or insulted, but writing songs in defiance of it all.

During a break in the journey she met Joe Boyd at London's ICA, and he showed interest in recording the songs she'd been penning en route. Sessions were held at Christmastime, 1969 and the result, the hauntingly melodic *Just Another Diamond Day*, is simply magical. An account of her travels and travails, backed by top folk figures including **Fairport Convention**'s Simon Nicol and **Dave Swarbrick** and **the Incredible String Band**'s **Robin Williamson**, every track is a gem. Hard as it is to isolate highlights on such a consistent album, the soothing title track, beautifully subdued *Timothy Grub* and powerfully evocative *Rose Hip November* spring to mind.

The album was originally slated for release on Island, via Boyd's Witchseason imprint, but in the event he moved back to the States and it languished for a full year before creeping out on Philips at the end on 1970. Barely anyone bought it (a sales figure of just 50 has been mentioned by one label employee), making it ultra-rare and sought-after today.

Stung by its reception, **Vashti** abandoned music and travelled around Ireland and elsewhere instead, eventually coming to a halt in Scotland, where she still lives. Following the ecstatic response to *Just Another Diamond Day*'s reissue (in 2004 the Observer named it one of the top 100 British albums of all time), however, in mid-2005 she completed work on a superb follow-up, *Lookaftering* (Fat Cat FATCD 38).

You can also find *Some Things Just Stick In Your Mind* on *Pop Inside The 60s Vol. 1* (CD), *Rolling Stones Connection 1963-66* (CD) and *Rolling Stones Works* and *Winter Is Blue* on *Spinning Wheel* (CD). The previously unreleased *I'd Like To Walk Around In Your Mind*, recorded with Mike Hurst for Andrew Oldham in '67, has appeared on *Circus Days Vol. 1 & 2* (CD) and *Circus Days, Vol. 1* (LP), though how it got there is a mystery, as **Vashti** gave the only copy (on acetate) to an old lady in the Hebrides. Even more curious is the fact that the track was covered in 1996 by Lush as the 'B' side to their *500* single and on their *Topolino* album in Japan and Canada. *Winter Is Blue* also turned up on *Gather In The Mushrooms* CD (Sanctuary) 2003. (VJ/RMJ)

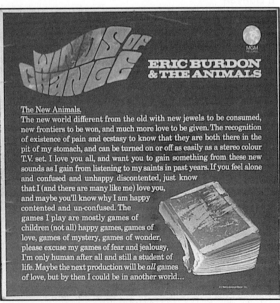

ERIC BURDON - Winds Of Change (LP).

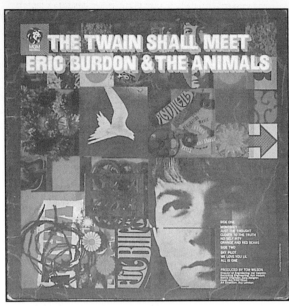

ERIC BURDON - Twain Shall Meet (LP).

Eric Burdon and The Animals

Personnel:			
VIC BRIGGS (ANTION MEREDITH)	gtr, piano vibes	AB
ERIC BURDON	vcls	ABC
BARRY JENKINS	drms	ABC
DANNY McCULLOCH	bs	AB
JOHN WEIDER	gtr, violin	ABC
GEORGE BRUNO (ZOOT MONEY)	keyb'd s, piano, vcls, bs	BC
ANDY SUMMERS	gtr, vcls	C

ALBUMS:				
1(A)	WINDS OF CHANGE	(MGM CS 8052)	1967	SC
2(A)	THE TWAIN SHALL MEET	(MGM CS 8074)	1968	SC
3(B)	EVERY ONE OF US	(MGM SE 4553)	1968 - US only	
4(C)	LOVE IS	(MGM CS 8105)	1968	SC
5(C)	LOVE IS (2-LP)	(MGM 2354 006/7)	1968	SC

NB: (1) reissued on CD (Polydor 825 712-2) 1985, but deleted in 1992. (2) reissued on CD. (3) reissued on CD (One Way OW 30337) 1994 and again (Repertoire) 2005, with bonus tracks. (4) reissued on CD (Repertoire) 2005, with bonus tracks. See comments on *Greatest Hits* (Bigtime 2415255) 1989 at the end of this article. A more credible compilation is *Greatest Hits: Eric Burdon* (Compact Collection 2415255) 1987.

HCP

45s:	α	Mama Told Me Not To Come/		
		See See Rider	(Decca F 12502)	196? -
		Help Me Girl/See See Rider	(Decca F 12502)	1966 14
		When I Was Young/		
		A Girl Named Sandoz	(MGM MGM 1340)	1967 45
		Good Times/Ain't That So	(MGM MGM 1344)	1967 20
		San Franciscan Nights/		
		Gratefully Dead	(MGM MGM 1359)	1967 7
		Sky Pilot Parts 1 & 2	(MGM MGM 1373)	1967 40
		Monterey/Anything	(MGM MGM 1412)	1968 -
		Ring Of Fire/I'm An Animal	(MGM MGM 1461)	1968 SC 35
		River Deep Mountain High/		
		Help Me Girl	(MGM MGM 1481)	1969 SC -
Reissues:		Good Times/San Franciscan Nights	(MGM 2006 028)	1972 -
		Good Times/San Franciscan Nights	(Polydor POSP 534)	1982 -

NB: α Unreleased, but some demos may exist.

When **The Animals** split, **Eric Burdon** quit England for San Francisco and put together the above line-up. The four albums listed were made on the West Coast of America and illustrate his experimentation with acid rock. He also underwent a complete change of character, sacrificing his old boozing image for the love and peace vibes of San Francisco. Apart from a version of **Jagger**/Richard's *Paint It Black*, the debut album *Winds Of Change* contained all original compositions full of social comment on the changing times, which were expressed most cogently on *Good Times*, which was also culled for 45 release.

ERIC BURDON - Every One Of Us (LP).

Good Times and *San Franciscan Nights* both became hit singles, reaching No's 20 and 7 respectively in the UK. Also of note were mellow numbers like *Hotel Hell, Anything* and *Poem By The Sea*. Two other tracks, *The Black Plague* and *Man-Woman*, though musically sparse, consisted of **Burdon**'s spoken commentaries. However, many of his fans back in England were disappointed by an album they did not understand.

Their follow-up album, *The Twain Shall Meet*, contained *Monterey*, a song the band had written in honour of the previous year's festival and another semi-successful hit single *Sky Pilot* (No 40 in the UK). Other tracks, notably *Just The Thought* and *Orange And Red Beams*, were full of flower-power ideology and psychedelic backing. His preoccupation with 'message songs' was evident to on *No Self Pity*, which expressed the sentiment that no matter how low you are there's also someone lower. The closing track, *All Is One*, which had an unusual bagpipe introduction and Eastern backing, expounded the hippie 'love everybody' philosophy.

Like its predecessor, this album sold better in the USA, for acid-rock had not really caught on in quite the same way in the UK and consequently, the band's next album, *Every One Of Us*, was only released in America. This featured George Bruno (**Zoot Money**) for the first time. But it became evident that the band was running out of ideas. *The Immigrant Lad*, dealing with the problems of a young Geordie adjusting to life in London, was unusual, but most of the other material was arguably dispensable.

Andy Summers (gtr) (later with The Police) replaced Briggs on the final album *Love Is*. This was a double album in America and a single album in Britain. It contained the band's final hit *Ring Of Fire*, which also reached No 35 over here, and poor cover versions of **The Bee Gees**' *To Love Somebody*, **Traffic**'s *Coloured Rain* and Ike and Tina Turner's *River Deep - Mountain High*. The strongest tracks were *Madman*, which Summers and **Money** had earlier recorded with **Dantalion's Chariot** and *Gemini*. Overall, though, the album was a disappointment and **Burdon** split the band at the end of 1968, vanishing for a couple of years with drug and marriage problems. Two years later he teamed up with War, a black progressive band. **Danny McCulloch** went on to release at least one solo album.

Eric Burdon later fulfilled a personal dream when he recorded an album, *Guilty* (United Artists UAG 29251) in 1971 with blues hero Jimmy Witherspoon.

The *Greatest Hits* CD compilation released in 1989 is very misleading. The photo on the front is of the band's 1963/4 line-up, yet the album is credited to **Eric Burdon and The Animals**, suggesting it might be the late sixties line-up. In fact the material comes from Eric Burdon and War in 1970 and The Eric Burdon Band in 1974. So beware!

Vic Briggs had earlier played with **Peter's Faces**, **Dusty Springfield** and **Brian Auger and The Trinity**. He later went into production including **Zoot Money**'s US-only album *Welcome To My Head* and one solo album by **The Animals**' guitarist Hilton Valentine. **Burdon** also released an album of new material *My Secret Life*.

Compilation appearances include: *Gratefully Dead* on *Hide & Seek Again (Vol. 2)* (LP); *Sky Pilot* on the 4-CD box set *Acid Drops, Spacedust & Flying Saucers*; *House Of The Rising Sun* on the *Greatest Sixties Album Of All Time Vol 2* (CD); *Sky Pilot Pts 1 & 2* on the *Lovely Summer Days* (CD) and *Help Me Girl* on the 2-CD set *We Love The Pirates: Charting The Big 'L' Fab 40*. (VJ)

Trevor Burton

| 45: | Fight For My Country/ | | |
| | Janie Slow Down | (Wizard WIZ 103) 1972 SC |

Trevor Burton was in **The Move**. The 'A' side was also recorded by **Balls** on the same label. (VJ)

Butterscotch

Personnel:	CHRIS ARNOLD	A
	DAVID MARTIN	A
	GEOFF MORROW	A

| ALBUM: | 1(A) | DON'T YOU KNOW | (RCA LSA 5000) 1970 |

HCP

45s:	Don't You Know/The Closer To You	(RCA RCA 1937) 1970	17
	Surprise, Surprise/		
	In The World Of Loving You	(RCA RCA 1983) 1970	-
	All On A Summer's Day/		
	Things I Do For You	(Bell BLL 1166) 1971	-
	Can't You Hear The Song/		
	All I Ever Wanna Do	(Jam JAM 15) 1972	-
	Sunday Won't Be Sunday Anymore/		
	This Way That Way	(Ammo AMO 112) 1974	-

This band played lightweight studio pop that's just as saccharin as the band's name implies. (RMJ)

Buzz (1)

Personnel:	BRIAN HENDERSON	bs	A
	MIKE TRAVIS	drms	A
	JOHNNY TURNBULL	gtr	A
	TAM WHITE	vcls	A

| 45: | α You're Holding Me Down/ | | |
| | I've Gotta Buzz | (Columbia DB 7887) 1966 R3 |

NB: α has been reissued (Columbia DB 7887) in a limited edition of 500 in a reproduction of the French jukebox release.

This was a later version of Edinburgh's **The Boston Dexters**, which Turnbull and White had previously been in. This 45 was produced by Joe Meek. *You're Holding Me Down* is a frantic piece which almost borders on total mayhem at times, the vocals are great and it's understandably very sought-after by collectors.

Mike Travis later drummed with **Atlantic Bridge** and **Gilgamesh**.

Compilation appearances have included: *You're Holding Me Down* on *Rubble, Vol. 13 - Freak Beat Fantoms* (LP), *Rubble, Vol. 7* (CD), *Searching In The Wilderness* (LP & CD) and *The Best Of Rubble Collection, Vol. 2* (CD); *I Gotta Buzz* on *Yellow Elektric Years* (LP) and *Beat It* (3-CD); and you can hear *You're Holding Me Down* and *I Gotta Buzz* on *RGM Rarities, Vol. 2* (CD). (VJ)

Buzz (2)

Personnel:	PHIL LANCASTER	drms	A
	GRAHAM RIVERS	bs	A
	T-CUP TAYLOR	ld gtr	A

This was **David Bowie**'s backing band in early 1966. They appeared on at least one Oak acetate with **David Bowie**. (VJ)

Bye Laws

45s:	Then You Can Tell Me Goodbye/		
	Come On Over To My Place	(Pye 7N 17481)	1968
	Run Baby Run/To Sir With Love	(Pye 7N 17701)	1969

A long forgotten harmony pop group, who seem to have relied on cover versions. *Come On Over To My Place* was a Drifters favourite. *Run Baby Run* was a hit for The Newbeats and *To Sir With Love* was a **Lulu** film theme.

Compilation appearances have included: *Run Baby Run* on *Ripples, Vol. 7* (CD); and *Run Baby Run* and *Deep Water* on *Irish Rock - Ireland's Beat Groups 1964-1969* (CD). (VJ)

Anne Byrne

| ALBUM: | 1 | I CHOSE THE GREEN | (EMI Waverley) 1967 R3 |

There's an Irish influence on many of her folk songs, but her strong female vocals reach their zenith on the beautiful *Come By The Hills*. (VJ)

The Bystanders

Personnel:	GERRY BRADEN	vcls	A
	JEFF PARLS	drms	AB
	RABIN J. SELBY	bs	AB
	MARK ST. JOHN	keyb'ds	AB
	MIKE STEEL	gtr	AB
	VIC OAKLEY	vcls	B

			HCP
45s:	That's The End/This Time	(Pylot WD 501) 1966 R3	-
	(You're Gonna) Hurt Yourself/		
	Have I Offended The Girl	(Piccadilly 7N 35330) 1966 SC	-
	My Love - Come Home/		
	If You Walk Away	(Piccadilly 7N 35351) 1966 R1	-
	98.6/Stubborn Kind Of Fellow	(Piccadilly 7N 35363) 1967 SC	45
	Royal Blue Summer Sunshine Day/		
	Make Up Your Mind	(Piccadilly 7N 35382) 1967 SC	-
	Pattern People/Green Grass	(Piccadilly 7N 35399) 1967 SC	-
	When Jesamine Goes/		
	Cave Of Clear Light	(Pye 7N 17476) 1968 R1	-
	This Is My World/Painting The Time	(Pye 7N 17540) 1968 SC	-

NB: There's also a compilation, *Birth Of Man* (See For Miles SEE 301) 1990, also on CD (SEE CD 301) 1990.

Formed in Merthyl Tydfil during the early sixties, this harmony vocal act was of no particular significance in themselves but in 1968 when Vic Oakley became a resident Top Rank vocalist the remaining members, whose real names were Micky Jones, Clive John, Ray Williams and Jeff Jones, evolved into **Man**.

Their debut 45 on Pylot is now an ultra rarity. It was on the strength of this that they secured a record contract with Pye. Some of their subsequent 45s were quite good and narrowly missed the Charts. They did a good cover of the Keith hit *98.6*; a lively version of Marvin Gaye's *Stubborn Kind Of Fellow*; an appealing version of The Fifth Dimension's harmony-pop *Pattern People* and *When Jesamine Goes* was the same song as *Jesamine*, **The Casuals**' hit. On the flip of this was *Cave Of Clear Light*, an inventive little gem with more than a hint of psychedelia. Possibly their finest effort was *Royal Blue Summer Sunshine Day*, a **Kinks**-influenced slice of psych-pop.

Given the rarity of their original 45 releases, See For Miles' 1990 compilation was very welcome and is undoubtedly the best way to access the band's recordings. *Petal Pushers* (LP), a US compilation back in 1967, included *Royal Blue Summer Sunshine Day*, *Make Up Your Mind* and *Pattern People*.

Retrospective compilation appearances have included: *Cave of Clear Light* on *Paisley Pop - Pye Psych (& Other Colours) 1966-1969* (CD), *Pop Inside The Sixties, Vol. 3* (CD); *We Can Fly, Vol 2* (CD) and on *Hot Smoke & Sassafras - Psychedelic Pstones Vol 1* (CD); *98.6* on *The Sixties File* (LP)

and *Piccadilly Story* (CD); *Pattern People* on *Quick Before They Catch Us - The Pop Era Volume 1* (LP & CD); *You're Gonna Hurt Yourself* on *Ripples, Vol. 4* (CD); *Painting The Time* on *Ripples, Vol. 6* (CD); *Royal Blue Summer Sunshine Day* and *98.6* on *Ripples, Vol. 1* (CD); *Pattern People* and *Make Up Your Mind* on *Ripples, Vol. 2* (CD); and you'll find *You're Gonna Hurt Yourself* and *Have I Offended The Girl?* on *Footsteps To Fame, Vol. 1* (CD). (VJ)

Byzantium

Personnel:	STEVE CORDUNER	drms	AB
	CHAS JANKEL	gtr, vcls	AB
	ROBIN LAMBLE	bs, gtr, vcls	AB
	NICO RAMSDEN	gtr, vcls	A
	MICK BARAKAN	gtr, vcls	B
	JAMIE RUBINSTEIN	gtr, vcls	B
	(B.J. COLE	steel gtr	B)
	(DAVID HENTSCHEL	synth	B)
	(FRANK RICOTTI	perc	B)
	(ROBIN SYLVESTER	synth	B)

ALBUMS:	1(-)	LIVE AND STUDIO	(Private Pressing) 1972 R3
	2(A)	BYZANTIUM	(A&M AMLS 68104) 1972 SC
	3(B)	SEASONS CHANGING	(A&M AMLH 68163) 1972 R1

NB: (1) reissued on CD (Byzantium BYZ 001) in a limited edition of 500. (1) issued as a 2-LP set (Akarma AK 332/2). Some copies of (2) came with a poster - these are R1. (3) was issued in a poster sleeve.

| 45: | What A Coincidence/ | | |
| | My Seasons Changing With The Sun | (A&M AMS 7064) 1973 |

Formed in the summer 1971, Jamie Rubinstein and Robin Sylvester had earlier been involved in **Ora**. The band was famously left off the *Greasy Truckers* album due to a power cut. Their first album was a private pressing demo of just 100 copies and featured 12 cuts recorded in 1972. Not surprisingly it is now their rarest item. At this stage a very US West Coast-influenced blend of spacey rock was on offer, which was much better than their subsequent A&M releases.

After *Byzantium*, Ramsden was replaced with Barakan and Rubenstein. He later worked with **Andy Bown**. When the band split in 1973, Chis Jankel worked with **Jonathan Kelly's Outside**, before moving into session work and ultimately becoming a top producer for Ian Dury and Madness among others. Corduna and Barakan joined Dana Gillespie's backing band, whilst Lamble went on to back **Al Stewart**.

Of the session players featured on *Seasons Changing*, **B.J. Cole** recorded a solo album, *New Hovering Dog*, for United Artists in 1972 and was also in **Cochise**. David Hentschel also issued a solo album of synthesiser based tunes entitled *Startling Music* (RingO 2017101) 1975. From this album he had a minor hit with the **Ringo Starr** tune *Oh My My*. (VJ/JM)

BYZANTIUM - Live And Studio (CD).

C Jam Blues

| Personnel incl.: | CECIL JAMES | vcls |
| | MELVIN BUCKLEY | gtr |

45: Candy/Stay At Home Girl (Columbia DB 8064) 1966 SC

A beat group from London whose 45 was in **The Tremeloes** mould. The A-side was a Stax number and the B-side was co-written by guitarist Melvin Buckley and the group's manager Andrew Lauder, who went on to oversee many vital underground releases for UA, Liberty and others. Buckley and singer 'Sir' Cecil James formed **Someones Band** a couple of years later, who made an excellent album on Deram. (MWh/RMJ)

Cado Belle

Personnel:	ALAN DARBY	gtr	A
	GAVIN HODGSON	bs	A
	STUART MACKILLOP	keyb'ds	A
	MAGGIE REILLY	vcls	A
	DAVY ROY	drums, perc	A
	COLIN TULLY	sax, flute	A

| ALBUM: | 1 CADO BELLE | (Anchor ANCL 2015) 1976 |

| EP: | 1 CADO BELLE EP | (Anchor AN 1) 1977 |

| 45: | Got To Love/Paper In The Rain | (Anchor 1033) 1976 |

An album of funky rock played and sung pretty well, with backing from strings and horns, by this Scottish band. All the tunes come from Mackillop or Tully, with lyrics by Alasdair Robertson. The bands 12" maxi-single release *Cado Belle E.P.* is worth tracking down, demonstrating a wide range of styles despite only having four tracks, with its standout cut being Alan Darby's composition *September*. Here the band gives vent to mellow guitar and sax, with a great vocal from Maggie Reilly. They had some success with a second 45 *Stones Throw From Nowhere/Airport Shutdown* (Anchor ANC 1038) in 1977. She, of course, later enjoyed considerable chart success with **Mike Oldfield**. (NM/BS)

The Caesars

Personnel:	KEITH DENNIS		A
	MOORE		A
	PLUTO ROLLS	drms	A
	WRIGHT		A

45s:	On The Outside Looking In/	
	Can You Blame Me?	(Decca F 12251) 1965
	Five In The Morning/It's Superman	(Decca F 12462) 1966

The first 45 was a Four Seasons-style effort and on the evidence of this, they had little to commend them.

The group was originally known as **A Fair Set**. (VJ/JM)

Café Society

Personnel:	RAY DOYLE	gtr, vcls	A
	HEREWARD KAYE	gtr, piano, vcls	A
	TOM ROBINSON	vcls, gtr, bs, piano	A

| ALBUM: | 1(A) CAFÉ SOCIETY | (Konk KONK 102) 1975 |
| (up to 1976) | | |

| 45s: | Whitby Two-Steps/Maybe It's Me | (Konk KOS 5) 1975 |
| (up to 1976) | | |

A melodic folk-based rock band which was notable for being one of the few bands to be signed to **The Kinks**' Konk label and for being one of the first

vehicles for Gay Rights activist Tom Robinson. He later enjoyed success with The Tom Robinson Band and as a solo performer. **Ray Davies** and other members of **The Kinks** performed on the album. (BS/VJ)

Cain

| 45: | Her Emotion/ | |
| | Take Me Back One Time | (Page One POF 054) 1968 R1 |

This single is quite collectable and you can also check out *Her Emotion* on the *Voyage Through The Sugarcube* (CD). (VJ)

Cajun Moon

Personnel:	DICK CADBURY	gtr, vcls	A
	JOHN GILLESPIE	keyb'ds	A
	BRIAN GOLBEY	gtr	A
	MADDY PRIOR	vcls	A
	DAVE MATTACKS	drms	A
	ALLEN TAYLOR	gtr, vcls	A
	JOHN WOOD	perc	A

| ALBUM: | 1 (A) CAJUN MOON | (Chrysalis CHR 1116) 1976 SC |

A folk-rock album notable for the inclusion of **Steeleye Span** vocalist **Maddy Prior** and **Fairport Convention** drummer Dave Mattacks. All the band are respected folk artists. (BS)

John Cale

ALBUMS:	1	VINTAGE VIOLENCE	(CBS 64256) 1970 SC
(up to	2	CHURCH OF ANTHRAX	(CBS 64259) 1971 SC
1976)	3	ACADEMY IN PERIL	(Reprise K 44212) 1972
	4	PARIS 1919	(Reprise K 44239) 1973
	5	FEAR	(Island ILPS 9301) 1974
	6	SLOW DAZZLE	(Island ILPS 9317) 1975
	7	HELEN OF TROY	(Island ILPS 9350) 1975

NB: (2) with Terry Riley. (1) and (3) reissued on CD (Edsel EDCD 230) 1988 and (Edsel EDCD 182) 1989. (1) later reissued on a mid-price CD (Columbia 477356 2) 1994. (5) reissued on CD (Island IMCD 140) 1991. (6) reissued on CD (Island CID 9317) 1987, but deleted in 1990. It was reissued on CD (Island IMCD 202) in 1994. There's also a two CD set of his recordings *Seducing Down The Door: A Collection 1970-1990* (Rhino R2 71685) 1994, available here as a US import. It comes with a booklet that gives a good overview of his career.

| 45: | The Man Who Couldn't Afford To Orgy/ | |
| | Sylvia Said | (Island WIP 6202) 1974 |

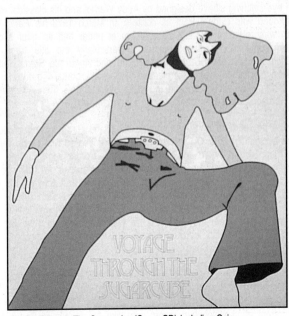

Voyage Through The Sugarcube (Comp CD) including Cain.

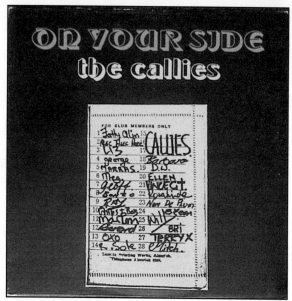

THE CALLIES - On Your Side (LP).

John Cale's contribution to rock is not easy to summarise. Influential as an underground rock musician and an influence on punk and new wave, he was schooled in avant-garde and classical music yet much of his output was song-oriented and veered towards the mainstream. Much of his music was too offbeat to achieve commercial success without being adventurous enough to make him one of rock's greatest innovators.

Cale was born on 4 December 1940 at Garnant, Wales. He studied classical piano as a child, first composed for the BBC at the age of 8 and later studied viola and piano at London's Guildhall School of Music. In 1963 he moved to New York's Eastman Conservatory, studying avant-garde music under a scholarship from the Leonard Bernstein Foundation. Whilst there he became involved in a project with La Monte Young called 'The Dream Academy' which later influenced his work with Velvet Underground. He joined The Velvet Underground after meeting Lou Reed at a New York party in 1965. He played electric viola, bass and keyboards with them, leaving after their second album in March 1968 because of a growing personality clash with Lou Reed.

Upon leaving The Velvets Cale produced Nico's second album, The Marble Index. It didn't sell well but Elektra's Jac Holzman liked the production and commissioned Cale to produce The Stooges' first album.

He then signed to CBS/Columbia to record Vintage Violence assisted by Grinderswitch. The album contained a number of uncharacteristically clean pop songs.

His next effort, Church Of Anthrax, with Terry Riley was much more avant-garde. The follow-up, Academy In Peril, was in similar style. It came in an eye-catching sleeve designed by Andy Warhol and his classical music background was evident from its content. In March 1973 his Paris 1919 album was released. A very short album at under half an hour it does contain some of his finest moments, particularly the title track, the autobiographical Child's Christmas In Wales and Antarctica Starts Here. A limited edition album was also released in Germany containing on one side half of the Paris album and on the other side extracts from Academy In Peril. It also had a poster designed by a German artist.

In 1974 he returned to Britain signing for Island Records and produced Nico's album, The End. On 1 June 1974, Cale appeared with Kevin Ayers, Eno, Nico, Robert Wyatt and others in a concert organised by Island. The occasion was captured on a rush-released album, June 1st 1974, a few weeks later. He used the services of Roxy Music and Eno on his next album, Fear. It was accompanied by Hear Fear, a limited promotional album, which contained an interview as well as music and was limited to a pressing of 200. Fear also included his first 45, The Man Who Couldn't Afford To Orgy, which featured a seductive vocal performance by Judy Nylon but just failed to Chart.

He undertook his first major European tour in 1975 with a band comprising Timi Donald, Pat Donaldson, Chris Spedding and Chris Thomas. This line-up also appeared on his next album, Slow Dazzle. This was an inconsistent effort which had some highs like Mr. Wilson (a Beach Boys

parody/tribute) and Darling I Need You. His final album for Island (and the final one that came within the time span of this book), Helen Of Troy, which featured Phil Collins on drums, suffered from the fact that he'd had to go on an Italian tour midway through its recording, only to return and find that the record company had effectively released the demos. He also produced Patti Smith's debut album, Horses.

Cale has continued to record throughout the eighties, nineties and into the new millennium on a variety of labels.

Extremely talented and always imaginative Cale is one of the more interesting people you'll read about in this book. (VJ)

Caleb

Personnel:	CALEB QUAYE	vcls, gtr	A

45:	Baby Your Phrasing Is Bad/ A Woman Of Distinction	(Philips BF 1588) 1967 R4

This was Caleb Quaye backed by some Fontana label house musicians who included David Hynes (of The Mirage). It's also strongly rumoured that Elton John was the keyboardist on this rare and expensive disc.

Baby Your Phrasing Is Bad, is a very fuzzy guitar driven song, whilst the flip side, although notable for its distorted vocals, isn't nearly as good.

Caleb Quaye later had his own band Hookfoot but also became a top session man. He also worked with Elton John.

Compilation coverage has included:- Baby Your Phrasing Is Bad on Rubble Vol. 4: 49 Minute Technicolour Dream (LP), Rubble Vol. 3 (CD) and on the 4-CD box set Acid Drops, Spacedust & Flying Saucers; and Woman Of Distinction on Rubble Vol. 1: The Psychedelic Snarl (LP) and Rubble, Vol. 1 (CD). (VJ)

The Californians

Personnel:	MIKE BROOKES	A
	P.J. HABBERLY	A
	JOHN O'HARA	A
	ROBERT TREWIS	A

45s: (up to 1976)	Golden Apples /Little Ship With A Red Sail	(CBS 2263) 1967 R1
	Follow Me/What Love Can Do	(Decca F 12678) 1967
	Sunday Will Never Be The Same/ Can't Get You Out Of My Mind	(Decca F 12712) 1967
	Congratulations/What Is Happy Baby	(Decca F 12758) 1968
	Out In The Sun/The Sound	(Decca F 12802) 1968
	Mandy/ The Cooks Of Cakes And Kindness	(Fontana TF 991) 1968 R2

ROBERT CALVERT - Captain Lockheed And The Starfighters (CD).

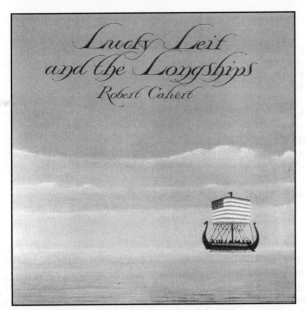

ROBERT CALVERT - Lucky Leif And The Longships (CD).

Sad Old Song/Weep No More	(Fontana TF 1052)	1969
Golden Apples/Little Ship With A Red Sail	(CBS 2663)	1969
You've Got Your Troubles/		
Early Morning Sun	(Chapter One CH 112)	1969

This Midlands band looked very straight in their white pullovers and slacks but tucked away in between their increasingly MOR singles output were a few gems. *Golden Apples*, is a pleasant piece of Middle-Eastern-influenced pop. The follow-up was their version of US songwriter Warren Zevon's *Follow Me*. Zevon's own version featured his folk-rock duo, Lyme and Cybelle, but **The Californians**' effort is certainly worth a spin. They followed this with a cover of Spanky and Our Gang's big US hit *Sunday Will Never Be The Same*. Although their later singles are less interesting, *The Cooks Of Cakes And Kindness* verged towards psychedelia and featured some incisive guitar work. John O'Hara was also in **O'Hara's Playboys**.

Compilation coverage has included:- *Follow Me* on *British Psychedelic Trip, Vol. 3* (LP), *Great British Psychedelic Trip, Vol. 1* (CD), *Rubble Vol. 11: Adventures In The Mist* (LP) and *Rubble Vol. 6* (CD); *The Cooks Of Cakes And Kindness* on *Rubble Vol. 4: 49 Minute Technicolour Dream* (LP) and *Rubble Vol. 3* (CD); *Golden Apples* on *Rubble Vol. 17: A Trip In A Painted World* (LP), *Rubble Vol. 10* (CD) and *The Best Of Rubble Collection, Vol. 4* (CD) and *Can't Get You Out Of My Mind* on *Fading Yellow, Vol 4* (CD). (VJ)

The Callies

Personnel:	WILL BROWELL	banjo, gtr, vcls	A
	BILL MITCH MITCHELL	vcls, gtr, mandolin, harp	A
	RAY TWEEDY	12-string gtr, mandolin,	
		vcls	A

ALBUM:	1(A)	ON YOUR SIDE	(Rubber RUB 002) 1971 SC

The Callies were an under-rated folk-rock band whose album, on this small Newcastle-based label, comprises mostly original material. There are versions of the traditional song *Peggy Gordon* and Tim Hardin's *Reason To Believe*, but the better tracks are originals like *Rocking Chair, Monty's Song, Is It Surprising, A Change Of Mind* and the melancholic *Turning Into Winter*. (VJ)

Callinan-Flynn

ALBUM:	1	FREEDOM'S LAMENT	(Mushroom 150 MR 18) 1972 R3

This Irish duo is supplemented by other musicians on their now ultra-rare album, which was only pressed in very small quantities (around 200) by Mushroom. It contained 12 folk-rock cuts, nine of which were written by the band. I haven't heard it but reputedly it's a good example of the genre. (VJ)

Robert Calvert

ALBUMS:	1	CAPT. LOCKHEED AND THE STARFIGHTERS	
		(United Artists UAG 29507) 1974 SC	
	2	LUCKY LEIF AND THE LONGSHIPS	
		(United Artists UAG 29852) 1975 SC	

NB: (1) and (2) reissued on CD by Beat Goes On (BGOCD 5 and 2 respectively) in 1988.

45:	α	Ejection/Catch A	
		Falling Starfighter (PS)	(United Artists UP 35543) 1973 SC

NB: α there was also a version with a different mix of the 'A' side and no picture sleeve.

Calvert is probably best known for his connection with **Hawkwind** but his two albums are now both minor collectables. He was assisted on them by a wide array of personnel which inevitably included **Hawkwind** members like Dave Brock and Nik Turner. Both albums were mini-rock operas. He later recorded a 45, *Lord Of The Hornets* for Flicknife in 1980.

Originally born in South Africa in 1945, he'd grown up in Margate, England. He died in the late eighties. (VJ)

Camel

Personnel:	PETE BARDENS	keyb'ds	A
	DOUG FERGUSON	bs	A
	ANDY LATIMER	gtr	A
	ANDY WARD	drms	A

				HCP
ALBUMS:	1(A)	CAMEL	(MCA MUPS 473) 1973 SC	-
(up to	2(A)	MIRAGE (w / insert)	(Deram SML 1107) 1974	-
1976)	3(A)	THE SNOW GOOSE		
		(w / insert)	(Deram SKLR 5207) 1975	22
	4(A)	MOONMADNESS	(Deram TXSR 115) 1976	15

NB: (1) reissued on CD (Universal 882 925 2) 2002. (2) - (4) released on Janus in the USA. (2) reissued on CD Deram (820 613-2) in 1989 and again (Universal 882 929 2) 2002. (3) reissued on CD (Deram 800 080-2) 1988, but deleted in 1991. (3) reissued again on CD (Universal 882 930 2) 2002. (4) reissued on CD (Decca 810 879-2) 1983, but deleted in 1989. (4) reissued again on CD (Universal 882 931 2) 2002. There's also *Collection: Camel* (Castle Collector Series CCSCD 116) 1986 and a 2-CD set *A Live Record* (Universal 882 927 2) 2002, first issued in 1978.

45s:	Never Let Go/Curiosity	(MCA MUPS 1177) 1972
(up to	Flight Of The Snow Goose/Rhayader	(Decca FR 13581) 1975
1976)	Snow Goose/Free Fall	(Decca FR 13603) 1975
	Another Night/Lunar Sea	(Decca FR 13656) 1976

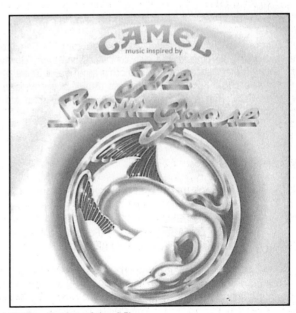

CAMEL - The Snow Goose (LP).

Camel was a significant progressive rock band that developed a strong cult following without achieving the mass popularity of bands like **Yes** or **Genesis**.

Pete Bardens was actually a veteran R&B artist. He played with **Them**, **Peter B's**, **Shotgun Express** and **Village** before forming **Camel** in 1972. He also recorded several solo albums. The other three members had previously played together in a band called Brew and also worked with **Philip Goodhand-Tait**.

Their debut album features elegant instrumental passages and mellow progressive elements with both funk and jazz undertones. There are some delicate synthesizer moments and plenty of luscious flute and eloquent guitar playing. Overall it was a promising start.

The majestic playing is also evident on their second album *Mirage*, which had its moments too with the instrumental *Supertwister*, the gentle *Nimrodel* trilogy and *Lady Fantasy* suite and the rockier *Freefall*. This was another strong album.

It was the instrumental album, *The Snow Goose*, which really put the group into the big time. It was inspired by Paul Gallico's novel 'The Snow Goose' and was undoubtedly one of the finest classical-influenced albums of the seventies - beautifully soothing and relaxing in places. They also performed it live at the Albert Hall in October 1975, backed by the London Symphony Orchestra conducted by **David Bedford**.

Moonmadness contained rich flute passages, pleasing keyboards and cascading electric guitar. This was their tour de force and best-seller. Richard Sinclair replaced Doug Ferguson on bass (and some vocals) for 1977-78 (and two more albums).

Camel continued throughout the eighties and nineties, recording occasionally and touring in areas of the world where they still had a big fan base.

The first four albums and *A Live Record* were reissued in 2002 and all contain bonus tracks. (VJ)

John Cameron (Quartet)

Personnel:

JOHN CAMERON	piano	AB
TONY CARR	drms	B
HAROLD McNAIR	sax	B
DANNY THOMPSON	bs	B

ALBUMS: 1(A) COVER LOVER   (Columbia SCX 6116) 1967 SC
2(B) OFF CENTRE   (Deram SML 1044) 1969 R2
NB: (1) credited to John Cameron.

45s: α Walk Small/You Owe Me   (Columbia DB 8120) 1967
Troublemaker / Off Centre   (Deram DM 256) 1969 R2
NB: α credited to John Cameron.

The Columbia recordings were solo efforts by **Cameron**. The Deram ones were the work of the quartet, who also contributed one track, *Go Away, Come Back Another Day* to Decca's 1969 compilation *Wowie Zowie! World Of Progressive Music* (LP). His material was usually bluesy or jazz. He later joined **CCS**. **Harold McNair** recorded a number of solo albums. Danny Thompson was also in **Pentangle**. (VJ)

Alex Campbell

ALBUMS: (up to 1976)
1 WAY OUT WEST   (Society SOC 912) 1963 SC
2 FOLK SESSION   (Society SOC 960) 1963 SC
3 ALEX CAMPBELL   (Xtra XTRA 1064) 1964 SC
4 IN COPENHAGEN   (Polydor 623 035) 1965 SC
5 ALEX CAMPBELL AND HIS FRIENDS
      (Saga ERO 8021) 1967 R1
6 THIS IS ALEX CAMPBELL 1
      (Ad-Rhythm-Tepee ARPS-1) 1971 R1
7 THIS IS ALEX CAMPBELL 2
      (Ad-Rhythm-Tepee ARPS-2) 1971 R1

8 AT HIS BEST   (Boulevard 4073) 1972
9 NO REGRETS   (Look LK LP 6043) 1976
NB: (2) reissued on vinyl (Fidelity FID 2171) 1964. (3) with **Martin Carthy**. (5) with **Sandy Denny**. (6) and (7) reissued as a double album *With The Greatest Respect* (Sundown SDLP 2048) 1987. *Been On The Road So Long* (Castle CMDRCD 1168) 2005 is a 23-track compilation of his material.

EP: 1 OUT WEST WITH ALEX CAMPBELL   (Arc ARC 36) 1963

45s: Been On The Road So Long/
Night Visiting Song (Some PS)   (Transatlantic TRASP 4) 1965
Victoria Dines Alone/Pack Up Your Sorrows (Saga OPP 2) 1968

Alex Campbell was one of the stalwarts of the British folksong revival during the fifties and sixties and one of Scotland's finest folk musicians. His 1967 album included **Sandy Denny**.

In 1971 Dave Travis set out to document **Campbell**'s life story. The idea was to record an album of folk songs from the British Isles and the States. The album also featured **Barry Dransfield**, **Dave Cousins** and Joe Locker and captured **Campbell** on top form. Sadly Tony Pike's Tepee label, which was to have released the album, didn't survive to do so and the material for the double set was only released as test pressings in 1971 as two separate discs on the amalgamated Ad-Rhythm/Tepee label. Only around 200-300 copies of each were pressed and very few copies reached the shops, making them extremely rare and elusive. Both were eventually reissued on one double album, *With The Greatest Respect*, in 1987 with different cover artwork to the original release but this item is now deleted.

The *No Regrets* album was released on a small independent Golcar, Huddersfield, West Yorkshire, label. It too is hard to find now. It also featured Tom McCanville, Nick Strutt, Roger Sutcliffe, Dave Townsend and Gordon Tyrell.

Campbell died in Denmark in January 1987. *Been On The Road Again* is a 23-track compilation of his material. It contains a mixture of this sixties folk stalwart's originals along with arrangements of mainly traditional material and, of course, the title track featured **Sandy Denny**. (VJ)

David Campbell

ALBUMS:
1 DAVID CAMPBELL   (Transatlantic TRA 141) 1967 SC
2 YOUNG BLOOD   (Transatlantic TRA 153) 196?
3 SUN WHEEL   (Decca SKL 5139) 1972 SC

This Canadian-born artist of Scottish/Guyanese parents recorded these folk albums in England. **Campbell** was educated in Toronto and then worked mostly in Stockholm. One track on his first album *Cane Cutter* was directly influenced by his Guyana childhood. On *Young Blood* there were three - the uptempo calypso *Rock Me Home*, *Brown Boy* and *Guyana Brothers*. The better tracks are *Sleep Talk*, *It's Only Morning*, *Requiem In September* and the title cut. (VJ)

IAN CAMPBELL FOLK GROUP - This Is... (LP).

Ian Campbell Folk Group

Personnel incl:
IAN CAMPBELL	vcls		A
LORNA CAMPBELL	vcls		A
BRIAN CLARK	vcls, gtr		A
JOHN DUNKERLEY	banjo, mandolin		A
DAVE SWARBRICK	fiddle, mandolin		A

ALBUMS: 1(A) THIS IS THE IAN CAMPBELL FOLK GROUP!
                                    (Transatlantic TRA 110) 1963 R1
2 ACROSS THE HILLS   (Transatlantic TRA 118) 1964 SC
3 COALDUST BALLADS   (Transatlantic) 1965 SC
4 CONTEMPORARY CAMPBELLS (Transatlantic) 1966 SC
5 TAM O'SHANTER   (Transatlantic XTRA 1074) 1968 SC
6 THE CIRCLE GAME   (Transatlantic TRA 163) 1968 SC
7 THIS IS THE IAN CAMPBELL FOLK GROUP!
                                    (Transatlantic TRASAM 9) 1969 SC
8 SAMPLER 2   (Transatlantic TRASAM 12) 1969
9 IAN CAMPBELL AND FOLK GROUP WITH
    DAVE SWARBRICK
                            (Music For Pleasure SMFP 1349) 1969
10 THE SUN IS BURNING   (Argo 2FB 13) 1970 R1
11 SOMETHING TO SING ABOUT (Pye PKL 5506) 1972 SC

NB: (1) reissued as *Presenting The Ian Campbell Folk Group* (Contour 2870 314) 1964. (8) As The **Ian Campbell** Folk Four. (5) As **Ian Campbell** and John Dunkerley. (7) is a reissue of (1). (1) has also been reissued on Contour (2870 314) in 1964. (1) and (2) reissued on one CD as *The Ian Campbell Folk Group* (Essential! ESM CD 567) 1996. *The Times They Are A-Changin* (Castle CMDDD 1072) 2005 is a 2-CD anthology of their recordings forTtransatlantic.

EPs: 1 SONGS OF PROTEST   (Topic TOP 82) 1962 SC
         2 IAN CAMPBELL FOLK GROUP
                                    (Decca DFE 8592) 1964 SC
         3 SAMPLER   (Transatlantic TRAEP 128) 1965

                                                            HCP

45s: The Sun Is Burning/
        The Crow On The Cradle (Some PS) (Topic STOP 102) 1964 -
        Marilyn Monroe/The Bells Of Rhymney (Decca F 11802) 1964 -
    α   Kelly From Killane/
        Boys Of Wexford   (Transatlantic TRASP 2) 1965 -
        The Times They Are A-Changin'/
        Across The Hills (Some PS) (Transatlantic TRASP 5) 1965 42
        Come Kiss Me/The First Time Ever
        I Saw Your Face (Some PS) (Transatlantic TRASP 6) 1966 -
        Guantanemera/Mary Anne   (Transatlantic TRASP 7) 1966 -
    β   One Eyed Reilly/
        Snow Is Falling   (Transatlantic TRASP 10) 1966 -
    χ   Lover Let Me In/Private Harold Ham's (Big T BIG 103) 1967 -
    β   Break My Mind/
        Govan Cross Special   (Major Minor MM 639) 1969 -

NB: α with the Boys From Wexford. β **Ian Campbell** solo. χ as **Ian Campbell** Four. Singles issued in PS are SC.

Progressive Pop Inside The Seventies (Comp CD) including Junior Campbell.

This folk group has had a prolific output but it's only recently attracted much interest from folk collectors.

There weren't many folk groups in London in the early sixties. Liverpool had The Spinners and Birmingham The Ian Campbell Four, who played regularly at The Crown in Station Street. They made a big impact when they moved down to London on a musical scene which mostly consisted of solo singers and skiffle groups. Their debut album, which was recorded live by line-up (A) showcased their musical discipline and the quality of their instrumentation which was exceptional for the times. They were assisted on the album by Dave Phillips (bs) and Brian Brocklehurst (bs). **Dave Swarbrick** went on to become extremely influential in British folk circles both as a solo artist and as a member of **Fairport Convention**.

The Times They Are A-Changin is a 2-CD anthology comprising material from the 10 albums they released for Transatlantic and provides a good overview of their career.

Compilation appearances include *Across The Hills*, *Johnny Lad* and *The D-Day Dodgers* on *The Transatlantic Story* CD box set. (MWh)

Jimmy Campbell

ALBUMS: 1 SON OF ANASTASIA   (Fontana STL 5508) 1969 SC
          2 HALF BAKED   (Vertigo 6360 010) 1970 SC
          3 JIMMY CAMPBELL'S ALBUM (Philips 6308 100) 1972 SC

45s: On A Monday/Dear Marge (Some PS) (Fontana TF 1009) 1969
        Lyanna/Frankie Joe   (Fontana TF 1076) 1970
        Don't Leave Me Now/
        So Lonely Without You   (Fontana 6007 025) 1970

Yorkshire-man **Campbell** first came to prominence as a singer/songwriter on the folk-club scene. He originally signed for Fontana, recording an album and three 45s for them before switching to Vertigo. The finest moment on *Half Baked* was the title track, which can also be heard on *The Vertigo Annual* compilation, but the album has never become particularly collectable as it was printed in larger quantities than many of its Vertigo label mates. **Campbell** then formed **Rockin' Horse** whose 1971 album for Philips has become very collectable, but after one further solo album for Philips, his career as a recording artist ended. He now lives in Liverpool and continues to write songs.

Vertigo's *Heads Together, First Round* (2-LP) compilation includes *Lonely Norman*. (VJ)

Junior Campbell

Personnel:
JUNIOR CAMPBELL	keyb'ds, gtr, hrmnca,		
	vcls		A
RAYMOND DUFFY	drms		A
RICK WEST	bs		A
PETE ZORN	sax, flute		A

ALBUM: 1(A) SECOND TIME AROUND   (Deram SML 1106) 1974 SC

                                                            HCP

45s: Goodbye Baby Jane/If I Call Your Name (Deram DM 344) 1971 -
(up to Hallelujah Freedom/Alright With Me   (Deram DM 364) 1972 10
1976)   Sweet Illusion/Ode To Karen   (Deram DM 387) 1973 15
        Help Your Fellow Man/Pretty Belinda (Deram DM 403) 1973 -
        Sweet Lady Love/
        If I Could Believe You Darlin'   (Deram DM 414) 1974 -
        Ol' Virginia/Willie Sings The Blues   (Deram DM 421) 1974 -
        Carobino Lady/Southern Man   (Rocket ROKN 509) 1976 -
        Here Comes The Band/Pick Up (Rocket ROKN 514) 1976 -
        Baby Hold On/Pick Up   (Rocket ROKN 518) 1976 -
Reissue: Hallelujah Freedom/Sweet Illusion (Old Gold OG 9358) 1983 -

Scot **Junior Campbell** was lead guitarist with **Dean Ford and The Gaylords** and then **Marmalade**. When he launched a solo career he enjoyed hits with *Hallelujah Freedom* and *Sweet Illusion* as well as recording the above solo album. On this his four-piece was supplemented by various studio musicians. This contains both hits and some other ditties in the same vein, almost all adorned with an excruciating female choir. The track *Pretty Belinda* is not the same as the **Chris Andrews** hit, which in comparison is a minor masterpiece. It also contains dreadful cover versions of **The Beatles**' *Drive My Car* and Dylan's *Positively 4th Street*. Definitely one to avoid. He later composed the theme tune to 'Thomas The Tank Engine', a children's TV series.

Goodbye Baby Jane and *Sweet Illusion* have both been compiled on *Progressive Pop Inside The Seventies* (CD). (VJ)

Patrick Campbell-Lyons

ALBUM: 1   ME AND MY FRIEND   (Sovereign SVNA 7258) 1973 R2

45s:	Everybody Should Fly Like A Kite/		
	I Think I Want Him To	(Sovereign SOV 115) 1973 SC
	Out On The Road/		
	Me And My Friend	(Sovereign SOV 119) 1973 SC

These solo ventures by the former **Nirvana** leader are worth tracking down, although all sold poorly and were quickly deleted. Prior to forming **Nirvana**, **Campbell-Lyons** had been vocalist in Second Thought, a group which didn't make it onto vinyl but later evolved in **July** who recorded one of the most sought-after albums of the late sixties.

In **Nirvana**'s later years **Campbell-Lyons** worked as a talent spotter and producer for Vertigo records. He compiled their 1971 compilation *Heads Together, First Round* (2-LP), which aside from *Home* from **Nirvana**'s *Local Anaesthetic* album included two of his other songs:- *Compositions*, performed by Sunbird and *Brothers*, sung by Lassoo. His other production credits with Vertigo were **Clear Blue Sky**, **Mike Absalom** and **Dr. 'Z'** (a professor from North Wales called Keith Keyes).

Campbell-Lyons was a real talent who deserved greater recognition. He recorded occasionally in the late seventies and early eighties, but these efforts, too, passed largely unnoticed. He was also involved in several pseudonym records like **Hat and Tie**, Patrick O'Magic and **Picca**.

The *Me And My Friend* album was available directly from him in the nineties and he and Spyropoulos appeared as a support act in London during the nineties. (VJ)

Canaan

Personnel:	GUS EYRE	lead gtr, vcls	AB
	BOB FRASER	lead vcls, gtr	AB
	DAVE LEWIS	gtr, hrmnca, mandolin, vcls	AB
	DAVE LLOYD	bs, vcls	AB
	NIGEL STEWART	drms	B

NB: Line-up 'A' up to 1976, Line-up 'B' 1977.

ALBUMS: 1(A)	CANAAN	(Dovetail DOVE 3) 1973 R1
(up to 2(A)	OUT OF THE WILDERNESS	(Myrrh MYR 1042) 1976 SC
1976)		

Formed in 1970, **Canaan** were, particularly in the early seventies, one of England's leading gospel-rock bands, whose musical style reflected that of the early albums by the Eagles and similar American country-rock harmony groups. Their debut album is now a significant collector's item. Sometimes described as a poor-man's Eagles, but with some fairly good cuts including *Follow Me*, this was produced by **John Pantry**, with John assisting on keyboards and Mick Wade filling in on drums.

The second album, *Out Of The Wilderness*, was produced by Gordon Miller, with Gordon Miller on drums, and various other session musicians and backing singers, including **B.J. Cole** making a lovely contribution on pedal steel guitar.

Of the two, *Canaan* was the more consistent, polished production, presenting the band much as they sounded live, but with some subtle enhancements. *Out Of The Wilderness* was more ambitious in its sound, using elements new to the band such as pedal steel guitar, piano, strings and female backing singers, but was a somewhat more patchy production overall.

Both Dovetail and Myrrh, were religious/Christian music labels.

The band, who came from genteel coastal town of Lytham St. Annes (a bit south of Blackpool), performed primarily in the North-West, with occasional forays further afield. Their line-up remained unchanged until 1977, when Nigel Stewart joined on drums, the band having been without a drummer until then (session drummers were used on the records). In 1979 the band split into the Gus Eyre Band (later New Citizens Band) and Portrait.

The Dave Lewis in this band is not the same guy who led **Andwella's Dream**. (PWr/VJ)

The Candles

Personnel incl: JOHN WILKINSON   vcls   A

A six-piece Essex group, whose style was similar to **Cliff Bennett**. They played a more commercial R'n'B sound. The vocalist modelled himself on Rufus Thomas. In February 1965 they recorded two demo discs for Pye, but they don't appear to have released any 45s. (VJ)

Candlewick Green

Personnel incl:	ANDY BALL	keyb'ds, vcls	A
	DEREK CLEARY	gtr, vcls, piano	A
	ALAN LEYLAND	drms, vcls	A
	JIMMY NUNNEN	bs, vcls, gtr	A
	TERRY WEBB	lead vcls	A
	LENNIE COSWELL	ld gtr	A

ALBUM: 1 (A)   WHAT KIND OF SONGS   (Decca SKLR 5195) 1974

HCP

45s:	Doggie/Like We Still Do	(Decca F 13379) 1973 -
(up to	Sunday Kinda Monday/I Found My Way	(Decca F 13405) 1973 -
1976)	Who Do You Think You Are/		
	Fingers In Your Ears	(Decca F 13480) 1974 21
	Leave A Little Love/Jimmy	(Decca FR 13512) 1974 -
	Everyday Of My Life/You Play	(Decca FR 13540) 1974 -
	Last Bus Home/Things That We Said	(Buk BUK 3019) 1975 -
	Sign Of The Times/You Don't Know	(Decca FR 13648) 1976 -

A pop group from Liverpool who were literally 'one hit wonders' and now long forgotten by most rock and pop fans. Jimmy Nunnen was ex-Gospel Folk, Alan Leyland ex-Dee Jays, and Terry Webb ex-Blue Rhythms and Heatwave. Ball joined **Mud** in late 1974. (VJ/JM/G)

Candy Choir

| 45s: | Silence Is Golden/Shake Hands | (Parlophone R 5472) 1966 SC |
| | Children and Flowers/Marianne | (CBS 3061) 1967 |

CANDLEWICK GREEN - What Kind Of Songs (LP).

Alexander's Ragtime Band/No Grey Skies   (CBS 3305) 1968
Why Do You Cry My Love/Lucky Jim   (Polydor 56369) 1970

A four-piece harmony beat group from London.

Shake Hands (And Come Out Crying) has been compiled on *Go... With An All Star* (LP). (VJ)

Candy Dates

45s: A Day Just Like That/Well I Do   (Pye 7N 15944) 1965
     Some Other Time/Show Me How To Live (Pye 7N 17000) 1965

This folk/beat group with a girl vocalist gained exposure via 'Opportunity Knocks', but never achieved a commercial breakthrough. They contributed *Don't Let Me Down* to *Oddities, Vol 2* (CD). (VJ)

Capability Brown

Personnel:			
	TONY FERGUSON	vcls, gtr, bs	A
	DAVE NEVIN	keyb'ds, gtr, vcls, bs	A
	KENNY ROWE	bs, vcls, perc	A
	GRAHAME WHITE	vcls, gtr, bs	A
	JOE WILLIAMS	vcls, perc	A
	ROGER WILLIS	vcls, drms, keyb'ds	A

ALBUMS:	1(A)	FROM SCRATCH	(Charisma CAS 1056) 1972 SC
(up to	2(A)	VOICE	(Charisma CAS 1068) 1973 SC
1976)	3(A)	LIAR (Compilation)	(Charisma CS 5) 1976

45s:	War (PS)	(Charisma BCP 7) 1971
	Wake Up Little Sister/Windfall	(Charisma CB 193) 1972
	Midnight Cruiser/Silent Sounds	(Charisma CB 207) 1973
	Liar/Keep Death Off The Road	(Charisma CB 217) 1973

This band's staple diet was mainstream rock with some arty pop leanings. Their *From Scratch* album had a couple of tracks with more progressive leanings:- *Rayge* and *Sole Survivor*. This latter song was about the escape from the coming war with a time machine and culminated in some fine guitar work imitating time machine travel! There are reasonable stabs at **Rare Bird**'s *Beautiful Scarlet* and Russ Bolland's *Liar*. They also covered another **Rare Bird** song *Redman*, which dealt with the fate of the American Indian. The *Liar* album is a compilation of their recordings from 1972 and 1973.

Kenny Rowe had earlier been in The Moments and both he and Tony Ferguson had been in **Harmony Grass**. Joe Williams and Dave Nevin may also have been later members of **Harmony Grass**, whilst Roger Willis had played with The Gremlins. Willis, White and Ferguson went on to Krazy Kat in 1976.

Wake Up Little Sister later surfaced on the *One More Chance* (LP) compilation. (VJ/CA/JM)

Jim Capaldi

ALBUMS:	1	OH HOW WE DANCED	(Island ILPS 9187) 1972
(up to	2	WHALE MEAT AGAIN	(Island ILPS 9254) 1974
1976)	3	SHORT CUT DRAW BLOOD	(Island ILPS 9336) 1975

			HCP
45s:	Eve/Going Down Slow All The Way	(Island WIP 6127) 197?	-
(up to	Tricky Dicky Rides Again/		
1976)	Oh How We Danced	(Island WIP 6165) 1973	-
	It's All Up To You/		
	Whale Meat Again	(Island WIP 6198) 1974	27
	Love Hurts/Sugar Honey	(Island WIP 6246) 1975	4
	Goodbye Love/It's Alright	(Island WIP 6269) 1976	-
	Talkin' About My Baby/Still Talkin'	(Island WIP 6299) 1976	-

Born in Evesham, Worcestershire, on 24 August 1944, **Capaldi**'s first band was **Deep Feeling**, but then he became a founding member of **Traffic**. He wrote their lyrics and was their drummer.

CAPABILITY BROWN - Liar (LP).

His first solo album, *Oh How We Danced*, was well received and their debut 45, *Eve*, taken from it was a minor hit peaking at No 91 in the US.

His follow-up album, a couple of years later, *Whale Meat Again*, was very ecologically orientated. The same year he enjoyed his first Top 30 UK hit, *It's All Up To You*; but the following year he made the UK Top 10 with oldie revival, *Love Hurts*. With the album, *Short Cut Draw Blood*, creeping into the US Top 200, **Capaldi** had laid firm foundations on which to build his future career.

Capaldi sadly died on 28 January 2005 of cancer. (VJ)

Cape Kennedy Construction Co

45:   The First Steps On The Moon/
     Armageddon   (President PT 265) 1969 R1

A totally obscure group and a weird and wonderful 45. Just check out *Armageddon*, where a church organ type intro leads into a slowed down recitation from the Book of Revelation. Thereafter the vocals and organ backing and occasional, upfront guitar are interrupted by intermittent sounds of a rocket launching and the record ends with church bells ringing.

Compilation appearances have included: *Armaggedon* on *Psychedelia, Vol. 1* (LP); and *Armaggedon* and *The First Step On The Moon* on *The Electric Lemonade Acid Test, Vol. 1* (LP) and *Sometimes I Wonder* (CD). (VJ)

The Capitols

45:   Honey And Wine/Boulavogue   (Pye 7N 17025) 1966

This seems to have been a one-off venture. The band shouldn't be confused with the US band of the same name who recorded on Capitol. (VJ)

Capricorn

Personnel incl:	SUE AVORY	ld vcls
	UNWIN BROWN	drms
	COLIN TRAVERS	gtr
	STEVE PRYOR	bs

45s:	α	Liverpool Hello/How Did You Find Me	(MCA MK 5050) 1970
	β	Goodbye Today, Hello Tomorrow/	
		Shine A Little Light On Me	(CBS 7481) 1971
	χ	Feeling/Falling For That Feeling	(CBS 1130) 1973
		Life Is What You Make It/Stop Running Around	(CBS 1422) 1973

I Got It Bad Boy/
Leave It To The Indians   (Epic EPC 1801) 1973
Don't You Know It's Magic/
Shake The City   (Epic EPC 2432) 1974

NB: α also issued in Japan (MCA D-1084). β issued in Japan (Epic 83011). χ issued in Japan (ECPA 52).

A little known act in the UK, who featured ex-**Trees** drummer Unwin Brown, who were much more successful in Japan. Their debut 45, which featured music used as a BBC TV theme tune was a No. 1 hit in Japan. *Liverpool Hello* was composed by Ronny Scott/Marty Wild and produced by Marty Wild. The follow-up, a Carter-Lewis composition reached No. 27 in Japan, and with the third, *Feeling*, they won the 1972 'World Popular Song Festival' in Tokyo and also reached No. 3 in the Japanese charts. (IS)

Captain Noah and His Floating Zoo

Personnel:

ALF BIGDEN	drms		A
STEVE GRAY	keyb'ds		A
JOSEPH HOROVITZ	keyb'ds		A
ROY JONES	drms		A
THE KING'S SINGERS	vcls		A
BRIAN ODGES	bs		A
DARYL RUNSWICK	bs		A

ALBUM: 1(A)   CAPTAIN NOAH AND HIS FLOATING ZOO
      (Argo ZDA 149) 1972 SC

A perfectly silly album with the King's Singers' incredible vocal techniques squandered to the deplorable concept of a musical interpretation of the big flood, as well as of the story of holy Moses. If you feel that utter squareness is also a kind of psychedelia, then look no further. (MK)

Caravan

Personnel:

RICHARD COUGHLAN	drms	ABCDEFG
PYE HASTINGS	gtr, vcls	ABCDEFG
(STEVE MILLER	piano, vcls	AB)
DAVID SINCLAIR	keyb'ds	AB DEF
RICHARD SINCLAIR	bs, vcls	ABC
PHIL MILLER	gtr	B
DEREK AUSTIN	keyb'ds	C
STUART EVANS	bs	C
GEOFF RICHARDSON	violin	CDEFG
JOHN PERRY	bs, vcls	D
MIKE WEDGWOOD	bs, vcls	EF
JAN SCHELHAAS	keyb'ds	FG

CARAVAN - Caravan (LP).

ALBUMS: 1(A)   CARAVAN   (Verve 6011) 1968 R3 -
(up to   2(A)   IF I COULD DO IT ALL OVER AGAIN
1976)   (Decca SKL 5052) 1970 R1 -
      3(A)   IN THE LAND OF GREY AND PINK
                   (Deram SLDR 1) 1971 SC
      4(B)   WATERLOO LILY   (Deram SDL 8) 1972 SC
      5(D)   FOR GIRLS WHO GROW PLUMP IN THE NIGHT
                   (Deram SDL 12) 1973 SC
      6(D)   CARAVAN AND THE NEW SYMPHONIA
                  (Deram SML 1110) 1974 SC
      7(E)   CUNNING STUNTS   (Decca SKL 5210) 1975 50
      8(F)   BLIND DOG AT ST. DUNSTAN'S
                   (BTM BTM 1007) 1976 53
      9(-)   THE CANTERBURY TALES (2-LP) (Compilation)
                  (Decca DKL 81/82) 1976
    10(G)   LIVE FROM THE BBC STUDIOS, LONDON '76
                  (Transcription Disc) 1976

NB: (1) reissued on MGM (2353 058) in 1972 (R1), later on Polydor Select and again (Verve/Universal 882 958 2) 2002. (2) - (6) issued by London in the USA. Most albums were also issued in France by various labels. (7) reissued on Request (RR 003) in 1988. (1) reissued on CD (HTD CD 65) 1996. (3) re-issued on CD (Deram 820 520-2) in 1989. (5) reissued on Deram (820 971-2) in 1991. (2) reissued on CD (Deram 820 521-2) 1989. (7) reissued on CD (Repertoire REP 4494-WY) and (8) also (REP 4501-WP), both in 1994. (9) reissued on CD (Virgin 5155222). Other CD compilations include *Best Of Caravan* (See For Miles CSCD-505) 1987 and *Canterbury Collection* (Kingdom CD KVL 9028) 1987. There's also *Caravan In Concert* (Windsong WINCD 003) 1991 and *Songs For Oblivion Fisherman* (Hux HUX 002) 1998, which compiles recordings from session work they did for Radio 1 between 1970-74. Earlier vinyl compilations have included *The Show Of Our Lives* (Decca TAB 23) 1981, *And I Wish I Were Stoned, Don't Worry* (See For Miles SEE 46) 1985 and *The Best Of Caravan* (CS 505) 1987. *Songs For Oblivion Fisherman* (Hux HUX 002) 1998 complies material recorded at the BBC between 1970 and 1974. *Either Way* (Hux HUX 013) 1998 brings some pretty bland sessions from the mid-seventies to a wider audience. *Live At Fairfield Halls, 1974* (Decca/Universal 882 902 2) 2002 will also delight fans.

45s: A Place Of My Own/Ride   (Verve VS 1518) 1969 R1
(up to   If I Could Do It All Over Again, I'd Do It All Over You/
1976)   Hello, Hello   (Decca F 13063) 1970 SC
        Love To Love You/
        And Tonight Pigs Will Fly/Golf Girl   (Decca F 23125) 1971 SC
        Stuck In A Hole/Cover   (Decca FR 13599) 1971
        All The Way/Chiefs And Indians (PS)   (BTM SBT 104) 1976

Caravan emerged from the now-legendary Canterbury music scene to become a vital part of the British underground in the late sixties and early seventies, though real commercial success eluded them.

Richard Coughlan, David Sinclair and Pye Hastings had all played in **The Wilde Flowers** and formed **Caravan** early in 1968. They soon earned a contract from MGM/Verve, for whom they recorded their eponymous debut the same year. By turns gentle and heavy, this hypnotic album endeared itself to underground audiences but only sold in small numbers and is very hard to find today. All tracks were originals except for *Where But For*

CARAVAN - If I Could Do It All Over Again (LP).

144

CARAVAN - In The Land Of Grey And Pink (CD).

CARAVAN - Waterloo Lily (CD).

Caravan Would I, which was written by Hastings' older brother Jimmy and Brian Hopper (who'd been in **The Wilde Flowers**). Its highlights included the beautiful *Love Song With Flute* and instantly-memorable *Place Of My Own*, which appeared on a rare 45 backed by *Ride*.

When the Verve label folded, they moved to Decca for their second album, which was enjoyably jazzy and offbeat. The title track and *Hello Hello* were culled for a second 45, but the most popular track with their fans proved to be *For Richard*. They were switched to Decca's progressive Deram label for their third album, one side of which was taken up with the epic *Nine Feet Underground*. Two other cuts were put out as their third 45. A couple of months after its release David Sinclair quit the band to work with **Robert Wyatt**, so Steve Miller from **Carol Grimes' Delivery** came in as a replacement.

Their fourth album, *Waterloo Lily*, is largely expendable but for the title track and *Love In Your Eye*. Shortly after its release, Richard Sinclair and Steve Miller left. Miller initially reformed Delivery, with whom he'd worked previously, then worked with **Lol Coxhill**. Sinclair formed **Hatfield and The North**. They were replaced by relative unknowns Evans and Austin, and the band became a quintet with the addition of electric viola player Geoff Richardson. This line-up wasn't together long enough to record, as Evans and Austin both left after an unsuccessful Australian tour.

John Perry was then recruited from **Spreadeagle**, and David Sinclair rejoined the band, having left **Hatfield and The North**. Their next album, *For Girls Who Grow Plump In The Night*, was heavily orchestrated and included lots of brass. It was well received and included another of their classic songs, *Hoedown*. The original sleeve, which depicted a naked, pregnant woman, was vetoed by Decca, and in the final version the she wore flimsy nightwear.

On *Caravan And The New Symphonia* the band re-recorded many of their earlier songs live at the Theatre Royal, Drury Lane, on 28 September 1973 with the New Symphonia conducted by Martin Ford. Only two new songs were included - *Mirror For The Day* and *Virgin On The Ridiculous*. In July 1974 Mike Wedgwood, who'd previously worked with **Kiki Dee** and **Curved Air**, replaced Perry in the band. Perry first concentrated on session work, then made a solo album and later joined the pop band **Quantum Jump**.

In commercial terms, **Caravan**'s most successful album was *Cunning Stunts*, whose sleeve was designed by Hipgnosis and which peaked at No 124 in the US and No 50 in the UK. It also spawned a 45, *Stuck In A Hole*, backed by a Mike Wedgwood ballad, *Lover*, but unlike the album it only sold in small quantities. In late 1975 Dave Sinclair left the band to go solo and was replaced by keyboardist Jan Schelhass, previously of **National Head Band**. This new line-up recorded *Blind Dog At St Dunstan's*, which was certainly rockier than any previous effort. *Chiefs And Indians* was released on a 45, backed by an edited version of another album cut *All The Way*, but it met the same fate as all their previous singles.

Caravan went on to record albums into the eighties, reforming at least once, in 1982, before finally calling a halt to their activities, following the

release of *The Album* and *Back To Front*, which were released on Kingdom Records, which was owned by their former manager Terry King. In 1990 the original quartet (line-up A) reunited for a one-off TV concert, but it attracted some acclaim and the sales of the resulting live album were so encouraging that they have been together in one line-up or another ever since.

There are plenty of compilations to interest the collector:- *Canterbury Tales - The Best Of Caravan* was a double compilation of material from their 1970-75 period put out by Decca in 1976; *The Show Of Our Lives* contained similar material and comprehensive sleeve notes by Roger Milne or more recently See For Miles have done their customary good job with *And I Wish I Were Stoned, Don't Worry*. The *Best Of Caravan* features material from their years with Decca.

Songs From Oblivion Fishermen compiles some of their BBC sessions between 1970 and 1974. Their 'Top Of The Pops' recordings include *If I Could Do It All Over Again I'd Do It All Over You* and also included are four stereo recordings for John Peel in 1974.

Compilation appearances have included: *Feelin', Reelin', Squealin'* and *Summertime* on *Canterburied Sounds Vol. 1* (CD); *Carazobe, As I Feel I Die* and *Where But For Caravan Would I* on *Canterburied Sounds Vol. 2* (CD); and *If I Could Do It All Over Again I'd Do It All Over You* on *Canterburied Sounds Vol. 3* (CD). (VJ/RMJ)

The Caravelles

Personnel:	ANDREA SIMPSON	vcls	AB
	LYNNE WILKINSON	vcls	A
	LYNNE HAMILTON	vcls	B

ALBUM:	1(A)	THE CARAVELLES	(Decca LK 4565) 1963 R1

45s:	You Don't Have To Be A Baby To Cry/	
	The Last One To Know	(Decca F 11697) 1963 6
	I Really Don't Want To Know/	
	I Was Wrong	(Decca F 11758) 1963 -
	Have You Ever Been Lonely?/	
	Gonna Get Along Without Ya Now	(Decca F 11816) 1964 -
	You Are Here/How Can I Be Sure?	(Fontana TF 466) 1964 -
	I Don't Care If The Sun Don't Shine/	
	I Like A Man	(Fontana TF 509) 1964 -
	True Love Never Runs Smooth/	
	Georgia Boy	(Polydor NH 59034) 1964 -
	Hey Mamma You've Been On My Mind/	
	New York	(Polydor 56137) 1966 -
	I Want To Love You Again/	
	I Had To Walk Home Myself	(Polydor 56156) 1967 -
	The Other Side Of Love/	
	I Hear A New Kind Of Music	(Pye 7N 17654) 1968 -

The original duo Lois Ann Wilkinson and Andrea Simpson were both born in Barnet, Hertfordshire. *You Don't Have To Be A Baby To Cry* made No 6 in the UK and No 3 in the US in 1963 (where an album of the same name reached No 127). Later *Have You Ever Been Lonely?* crept into the US No 84 slot.

In late 1965 Wilkinson left to go solo as **Lois Lane**. She went on to record solo 45s for RCA and Mercury in the sixties and DJM, Disneyland, Buk and Gold in the seventies. Her replacement was Lynne Hamilton who emigrated to Australia after the duo split and had a huge solo hit with the theme song from an Australia TV series "Prisoner Cell Block H" called *On The Inside* in 1979.

You Don't Have To Be A Baby To Cry can also be found on *Thank Your Lucky Stars, Vol. 2* (LP). (VJ/JM)

Cardboard Orchestra

Personnel:	KEITH BONSOR	vcls, gtr, keyb'ds	A
	VIC COLLINS	bs	A
	MARK WESLEY	vcls	A
	ROGER ?	drms	A

45s:	Zebady Zak/Mary Tell Me Why	(CBS 4176) 1969
	Nothing But A Sad Sad Show/	
	Yes I Heard A Little Bird	(CBS 4633) 1969

An experimental mid-sixties outfit from Southend. Bonsor had earlier been in a local R&B band The Essex Five and was later in **Zior**. Collins was later in **The Kursaal Flyers** and Wesley went on to become a dee-jay on 'Radio Luxembourg'. CBS forced them to record pop-orientated material and one such example *Yes I Heard A Little Bird* has later resurfaced on *Circus Days Vol's 4 & 5* (CD) and *Circus Days, Vol. 4* (LP). (VJ)

The Cardinals

| ALBUMS: | 1 | SWEET AND REFRESHING | (Nelmwood Audio) 1970 R2 |
| | 2 | ON TOP OF THE WORLD | (Nelmwood Audio) 1972 SC |

These are privately-pressed folk albums with lovely female vocals. *Sweet And Refreshing* has been likened to **Faraway Folk**, especially on standout cut *Summer Wine*. The use of tablas on *Morning Please Don't Come* gives the track an Eastern folk-psych feel and there's also a nice version of *Last Night They Burnt Atlanta*. (VJ)

Dave Carlsen

| ALBUM: | 1 | PALE HORSES | (Spark SRLP 110) 1973 R1 |

A rare hard-rock album with **Keith Moon** on drums, **Noel Redding** on bass, **Henry McCullough** on guitar and the presence of **Spencer Davis**. (SR)

Carmen

Personnel:	ANGELA ALLEN	vcls, keyb'ds	A
	DAVID ALLEN	gtr, vcls	A
	ROBERTO AMARAL	vcls, perc	A
	PAUL FENTON	drms	A
	JOHN GLASCOCK	vcls	A

ALBUMS: 1(A)	FANDANGOES IN SPACE	
(up to	(Regal Zonophone SRZA 8518) 1973 SC
1976) 2(A)	DANCING ON A COLD WIND	
	(Regal Zonophone SLRZ 1040) 1975 R1
3(A)	THE GYPSIES	(Mercury SRMI 1047) 1976

NB: (1) issued on Dunhill (DP 50192) in the US. (1) and (2) reissued on one CD (Line LICD 92 1150) 1992. (3) US only release.

RUBBLE Vol. 7 (Comp LP) including Carnaby.

| 45s: | Flamenco Fever/Lonely House | (Regal Zonophone RZ 3086) 1974 |
| | Bulerias/Stopping Stone | (Regal Zonophone RZ 3090) 1974 |

Angella Allen, David Allen and Roberto Amaral originally came from Los Angeles, California, and **Carmen** are regarded as one of the first flamenco-rock groups from the West Coast. Drummer Paul Fenton had been with **Christie**. The drummer Paul Fenton was English and later drummed with **T. Rex**. They received a boost early in their career when they were endorsed by **David Bowie**. Angela later played on **Jethro Tull**'s *Too Old To Rock 'n' Roll, Too Young To Die* album. John Glasock, who also played bass with **Carmen** had previously been with **Chicken Shack** on *Imagination Lady*, **Ken Hensley**'s **Gods** and **Toe Fat** (on *Toe Fat Two*) and later, from 1976 - 79, with **Jethro Tull**. Glasock sadly died after heart surgery in 1979. (VJ/JM/BS)

Carnaby

Personnel:	ANDY ANDREWS	bs	A
	JOHN CAHILLANE	vcls	A
	STEVE MINERS	gtr	A
	RONNIE ROSS	drms	A
	KIP SMITH	gtr	A

| 45: | Jump And Dance/ | |
| | My Love Will Stay | (Piccadilly 7N 35272) 1965 R2 |

A fashionable, mid-sixties, London-based mod group who all worked in various Carnaby Street clothes stores and dressed in all the latest gear but made little impact with their sole 45. Now, forty years later it's became quite collectable and expensive. *Jump And Dance* is a popular mod club favourite, hence its high value.

Jump And Dance can also be heard on *Maximum '65* (CD), *Rubble, Vol. 7 - Pictures In The Sky* (LP), *Watch Your Step* (LP & CD), *Doin' The Mod, Vol. 2* (CD) and *Freakbeat Freakout* (CD). (VJ)

Carnaby Street Pop

| ALBUM: | 1 | CARNABY STREET POP ORCHESTRA AND CHOIR |
| | | (Carnaby CNLS 6003) 1969 R2 |

NB: (1) reissued as *The London Theme* (Recur ECD 702) 1999.

Arranged, produced and conducted by Keith Mansfield, this exploitation album contains easy listening versions of songs like *Puppet On A String*, *Congratulations* and *Boom Bang-A-Bang*. The opening track, *Young Scene*, was used as the theme for one of ITV's early seventies football programmes. Not recommended. The reissue on Recur includes eight bonus tracks, which are all similar in style to the original release. (VJ)

Sasha Caro

Personnel:	SASHA CARO (CARO MINAS)	gtr, piano, hrmnca, vcls	A

45s:	Grade 3 Section 2/Little Maid's Song	(Decca F 12687) 1967
	Molotov Molotov/Never Play A B Side	(Decca F 12744) 1968

Sasha Caro, whose real name was Caro Minas, was discovered/produced by **Cat Stevens**. Both 45s flopped, but the second features **Stevens**' *Never Play A B Side* on the flip, and has Cat doing a "Russian" spoken intro on the 'A' side.

Caro was born in Rangoon in 1940, but fled to India with his family when Burma was invaded by the Japanese. Aged 15 he came to England to study engineering and in 1965 he opened a recording studio and began writing and producing songs. Several of his compositions were recorded by other artists, including **Graham Bond**. (GBn)

Carol and The Memories

45:	Tears On My Pillow/Crying My Eyes Out	(CBS 202086) 1966

This was a long-forgotten and short-lived pop combo, from Liverpool. The 45 was produced by **Scott Walker**. (VJ)

The Carolines

45:	Love Made A Fool Of Me/ Believe In Me	(Polydor BM 56027) 1965

This is another obscure and long forgotten pop 45 by an all girl group. (VJ)

The Carolls

45:	Give Me Time/ Darling I Want You So Much	(Polydor 56046) 1965

This band later recorded as **The Carrolls** and **The Carols**. (VJ)

The Carols

45:	Everyday I Have To Cry Some/ (flip by Fire Session)	(Revolution REV 013) 1970

This band had earlier recorded as **The Carolls** and **The Carrolls**. (VJ)

Johnny Carr and The Cadillacs

Personnel:	MERVYN ALEXANDER	bs	A
	JOHNNY CARR (CON O'SULLIVAN)	vcls	A
	DAVE PURSLOW	drms	A
	RAY TRUSCOTT	gtr	A

45s:	Remember That Night/Respectable	(Decca F 11854) 1964 SC
	Do You Love That Girl?/ Give Him A Little Time	(Fontana TF 600) 1965 SC
α	Then So Do I/I'm Just A Little Bit Shy	(Fontana TF 681) 1966
α	Things Get Better/You Got Me Baby	(Fontana TF 823) 1967

NB: α as **Johnny Carr**.

This Bristol-based band formed in 1958 as a rock'n'roll band, but by the mid-sixties they'd changed to an R&B style and spent much of their time like many other British beat and R&B acts of this era in Hamburg. *Do You Love That Girl?* was their most successful 45, reaching No. 30 in the NME chart. In their later days they became **Zombies**' impersonators. (VJ/JM)

The Carolls

45s:	Surrender Your Love/The Folk I Love	(Polydor BM 56081) 1966
	So Gently Falls The Rain/ Nice To See You Darling	(CBS 3414) 1968
	Ever Since/Come On	(CBS 3710) 1968
	A Lemon Balloon And A Blue Sky/ Make Me Belong To You	(CBS 3875) 1968
	We're In This Thing Together/We Know Better	(CBS 4401) 1968

This sixties pop outfit also recorded as **The Carols** and **The Carolls** and may have been American. (VJ)

Carriage Company

This band's *Feel Right*, is an appealing piece of experimental pop with good vocals and effective use of echo. You can also find it on *Rubble Vol. 16: Glass Orchid Aftermath* (LP) and *Rubble Vol. 9* (CD). *In Your Room* has resurfaced on *Jagged Time Lapse, Vol 4* (CD). (VJ)

Ben Carruthers and The Deep

Personnel:	BEN CARRUTHERS	vcls	A
	PETE HODGKINSON	drms	A
	BENNY KERN	gtr	A
	IAN WHITEMAN	keyb'ds	A
	?????	bs	A
	(JIMMY PAGE	gtr	A)
	(NICKY HOPKINS	piano	A)

45:	Jack O'Diamonds/ Right Behind You	(Parlophone R 5295) 1965 R1

Ben Carruthers was a half-cast actor friend of Dylans. The 'A' side of this highly collectable 45, was written by Benny Kern and consists of an extract from the sleevenotes of Bob Dylan's *Another Side* album put to music. It was recorded for use in a TV play 'A Man With No Papers' in which **Carruthers** appeared. The end result is an impressive folk-rock cut. The flip side is more jazzy with a substantial injection of R&B.

The session was produced by Shel Talmy in IBC in Portland Place and featured session men **Jimmy Page** and **Nicky Hopkins**.

Ian Whiteman, who went on to play with **The Action**, **Mighty Baby** and others, recalls:- "We were all students at the Architectural Association in Bedford Square. Nicky Hopkins played piano on the session and I played Wurlitzer organ!!! Benny Carruthers was also one of the first 'Dirty Dozen' cast along with Lee Marvin and John Cassavetes (who incidentally had directed Benny in the cult movie 'Shadows' in the very early '60s). Benny

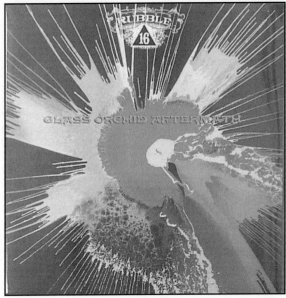

RUBBLE Vol. 16 (Comp LP) including Carriage Company.

had been at the Lee Strasbourg school of method acting with Marilyn Monroe and was the ultimate lanky cool half black half Hispanic kid (hence Benito Carruthers). He loved everything jazzy as well as soul music like Otis Redding (hence the 'B' side which was a King Pleasure number I do recall) and tried really hard to swing it as a singer in the UK but had no musical discipline. I used to have a picture of him with Bob Dylan in the Savoy when Dylan gave him the lyrics for the song. I believe he died from liver failure recently. There is little on record about him, but he was an enigmatic and tragic character."

Both sides of the 45 can be heard on *R&B Scene, Vol. 1* (LP) 1985 compilation. (VJ/IW/RMJ)

John Carter and Russ Alquist

| 45: | The Laughing Man/ | |
| | Midsummer Dreaming | (Spark SRL 1017) 1968 R1 |

NB: *Measure For Measure: The John Carter Anthology 1961-1977* (RPM RPMD 268) 2003 is a mid-price 2-CD set chronically his career.

These songwriters wrote and produced several 45s during the period of this book. **Carter** had earlier been in Carter-Lewis and The Southeners, **The Ivy League** and **The Flowerpot Men**. They decided to record this bizarre 45 themselves.

The Laughing Man was a few minutes of wackiness, which recently got a further airing on *Psychedelia, Vol. 2* (LP) and the equivalent CD compilation, *Hen's Teeth Vol. 1*. If you like a few minutes weirdness this one could be for you.

Measure For Measure: The John Carter Anthology 1961-1977 chronicles his career as a performer and features many of his hits with **The Ivy League**, **The Flowerpot Men**, **First Class** and others. It's an excellent compilation and showcases his talent superbly. (VJ)

Nick Carter

This guy was responsible for the privately-pressed experimental instrumental, *Prayer To St. Peter*, in the mid-seventies which was brought to the attention of a slightly wider audience by virtue of its recent inclusion on *Psychedelic Salvage Co. Vol. 1* (LP & CD) and *Electric Psychedelic Sitar Headswirlers Vol. 4* (CD). Recommended for fans of progressive/electronic rock, there's a clear **Pink Floyd** influence here. (VJ)

Sheila Carter and Episode Six

| 45: | I Will Warm Your Heart/Incense | (Pye 7N 17194) 1966 R1 |

This 45 is now quite sought-after by collectors. The 'A' side is a Charles Aznavour ballad. See **Episode Six**. **Sheila Carter** played keyboards.

Incense later resurfaced on *Doin' The Mod, Vol. 1* (CD). (VJ)

Martin Carthy (and Dave Swarbrick)

ALBUMS:	1	MARTIN CARTHY	(Fontana STL 5269) 1965 SC
(up to	2	SECOND ALBUM	(Fontana STL 5362) 1966 SC
1976)	3	BYKER HILL	(Fontana STL 5434) 1967 SC
	4	BUT TWO CAME BY	(Fontana STL 5477) 1968 SC
	5	PRINCE HEATHEN	(Fontana STL 5529) 1969 SC
	6	LANDFALL	(Philips 6308 049) 1971 SC
	7	SELECTIONS	(Pegasus PEG 6) 1971 SC
	8	SHEARWATER	(Pegasus PEG 12) 1972
	9	THIS IS MARTIN CARTHY	(Philips 6282 022) 1972
	10	SWEET WIVELFIELD	(Deram SML 1111) 1974

NB: (2) - (5) and (7) were made with **Dave Swarbrick**. (1) - (6) reissued on Topic in 1977. (1) reissued on CD (Topic TSCD 340) 1993. (2) reissued on CD (Topic TSCD 341) 1994. (3) reissued on CD (Topic TSCD 342) 1991. (8) reissued on CD (Castle CMQCD 1096) 2005 with three bonus cuts.

| EP: 1 | NO SONGS | (Fontana TE 17490) 1967 R1 |

NB: (1) with **Dave Swarbrick**.

PSYCHEDELIA VOL. 2 (Comp LP) including John Carter and Russ Alquist.

Carthy was the third most influential UK folk artist after **Bert Jansch** and **Davy Graham**. His first band was **Three City Four**, who cut an album in 1965 shortly before **Carthy** released his first album. It was **Carthy**'s reinterpretation of the traditional folk tune *Scarborough Fair* which Simon and Garfunkel went on to enjoy a massive hit with.

By the time of his second album he'd been joined by violinist **Dave Swarbrick**. The album basically consists of traditional folk ballads although **Carthy**'s haunting vocals gave them a new slant. As you can see he went on to record several more albums, many with **Swarbrick** before playing for the **Albion Country Band** in 1973. One of the best was *Shearwater* released in 1972 which contained his first experiments with overdubbing different instrumental textures into his distinctive guitar/vocal arrangements of traditional folk material. The magnum opus on the album is *Famous Flower Of Serving Men*, a nine-minute story of bloody revenge, which was quite effectively promoted by the late John Peel. The reissue on Castle includes three bonus cuts: *King Henry*, *The False Lover Won Back* and *Trindon Grange*. All three were from a 1972 Peel session.

Carthy revived his partnership with **Dave Swarbrick** in the eighties and recorded in the nineties on the Green Linnet label. **Carthy** and **Swarbrick** continue to perform and record together

He contributed tracks to the *Rave On* (LP) compilation. (VJ)

Cartoone

Personnel:	MIKE ALLISON	lead gtr	A
	CHICK E. COFFILS	drms	A
	DEREK CREIGAN	vcls, bs	A
	CHARLES 'MO' TROWERS	lead vcls, gtr	A
	(JIMMY PAGE	gtr	A)

| ALBUM: 1(A) | CARTOONE | (Atlantic 588 174) 1969 SC |

| 45: | A Penny For The Sun / Knick Knack Man (Atlantic 584240) 1969 |

This obscure and otherwise forgettable album was notable for the inclusion of **Jimmy Page** on a number of tracks and has therefore become a minor collectable.

The band was from Scotland and recorded its album in London. (BS/SS/SR/JM)

Dave Cartwright

ALBUMS:	1	MIDDLE OF THE ROAD	
(up to		(w/insert)	(Harmony DB 0001) 1970 R1
1976)	2	A LITTLE BIT OF GLORY	
			(Transatlantic TRA 255) 1972

	3	BACK TO THE GARDEN	(Transatlantic TRA 267) 1973
	4	DON'T LET YOUR FAMILY DOWN	
			(Transatlantic TRA 284) 1975
	5	MASQUERADE	(DJM DJF 20489) 1976

45s:	My Delicate Skin/Angeline	(Big T BIG 510) 1972
	Have You Seen Saphi Dance/	
	Stage Fright	(DJM DJS 10725) 1976

Dave Cartwright is a friendly, but mostly uninspired sort of British James Taylor. Though his observations on life sometimes strike an interesting line or two, his music has nothing to separate it from countless other bands in the same vein. His backing bands are always competent, but never compelling. Stick to **Richard Thompson**, I'd say. (MK)

Casablanca

Personnel:	ALIKI ASHMAN	vcls	AB
	CHARLIE CHARLES	drms	AB
	BARRY CLARKE	gtr, vcls	AB
	DAVID COSTA	gtr, vcls	AB
	MICK FEAT	bs	A
	JUANITA FRANKLIN	vcls	AB
	LUIS JARDIM	perc	A
	PAUL VIGRASS	vcls	A
	EARL ROBINSON		B

ALBUM:	1	CASABLANCA	(Rocket PIGL 7) 1974 SC

NB: (1) issued in die-cut sleeve with inner lyric sleeve.

This band was signed to **Elton John**'s Rocket label on the strength of demos they had recorded. Their smooth brand of funk surprisingly failed to make any commercial impact and the band didn't gig much. Their second album, *The Lost Funk*, has only recently appeared (Second Sight, 2003). Ashman was ex-**Graham Bond**, **Airforce** and **Ashman-Reynolds**, Charles had been in **Kingdom Come** and Costa and Clarke had been in **Trees**, from where Clarke had gone on to join Vigrass & Osbourne's backing group. Most of the lead vocals on the album are provided by Vigrass. Jardim went on to play with **Eric Clapton, The Rolling Stones, Bryan Ferry** and others. When Feat left to join **Rare Bird,** he was replaced by Earl Robinson. Charles joined **Loving Awareness** in March 1974, and Robinson went on to the Real Thing. (RMJ/JM)

Howie Casey and The Seniors

Personnel:	STAN FOSTER	piano	ABCD
	DEREK GILL	drms	ABC
	BILLY HUGHES	lead gtr	ABCD
	STAN JOHNSON	gtr	ABC
	JIMMY O'CONNOR	vcls	ABC
	HOWIE CASEY	sax	BCDEFG H
	BRIAN GRIFFITHS	lead gtr	CDEFG H I
	DERRY WILKIE	vcls	CDEFG H
	JEFF WALLINGTON	drms	D
	PHIL WHITEHEAD	bs	DE
	FREDDIE FOWELL		
	(STARR)	vcls	EFG H
	FRANK WIBBERLEY	drms	EFG
	LU WALTERS	bs	F
	FRANK BOWEN	bs	G
	KENNY HARDIN	drms	H
	JOHN O'HARA	bs	H
	IAN BROAD	drms	I
	JOHNNY GUSTAFSON	bs	I

NB: Line-ups 'A' - 'C' as The Hy-Tones.

ALBUMS:	1( )	TWIST AT THE TOP	(Fontana TFL 5108) 1962 R2
	2( )	LET'S TWIST	(Wing WL 1022) 1965 SC

45s:	Double Twist/True Fine Mama	(Fontana H 364) 1962 SC
	I Ain't Mad At You/Twist At The Top	(Fontana H 381) 1962 SC
	The Boll Weevil Song/Bony Moronie	(Fontana TF 403) 1963 SC

PSYCHEDELIC SALVAGE COMPANY VOL. 1 (Comp CD) including Castle Farm.

Although, they technically pre-date this book playing and recording in 1962, they are worthy of a mention since, aside from **The Beatles**' spell as **Tony Sheridan**'s backing group, this was the first Merseybeat group to record. They were originally led by Derek Wilkie, who ended up fronting The Pressmen. Their first two 45s were very much in the 'twist' style and Wilkie and a very young **Freddie Starr** shared lead vocals on them. The third 45 was issued a few months after they'd split to capitalise on the success of **The Beatles, The Searchers** and **Gerry and The Pacemakers**.

Howie Casey went on to become a famous session saxophonist, marrying **Bridget St. John** in 1967. **Freddie Starr** (whose real name was Freddie Fowell) went on to front another Merseybeat group, **Freddie Starr and The Midnighters** before going solo.

The Boll Weevil Song and *Bony Moronie* were originally released and is included on the *Beat Battle At The Star-Club, Vol. 1* (live) (LP) 1986 compilation. The 'A' side, which is better known done by Eddie Cochran, is a very good R&B number. Their cover of Little Richard's *Hey Hey Hey Hey*, released only in Germany in 1963, is on the (2-LP) compilation *Beat In Star Club*.

Retrospective compilation appearances have included: *Bony Moronie* on *Mersey Beat* (2-LP); and *I Ain't Mad At You* on *Mersey Beat 1962-1964* (2-LP). (VJ/AD)

Lee Castle and The Barons

Personnel:	TOMMY BENNETT	bs	A
	LEE CASTLE	vcls	A
	JOHNNY FALLON	lead gtr	A
	BOB O'HANLON	drms	A
	MIKE (SNOW) LISTON	organ, gtr	A

NB: Other personnel included: Frank Knight (gtr, vcls), Les Saint (gtr), Jimmy Martin (lead gtr), Les Stewart (lead gtr), Mel Preston (drms) and Graham Hodgson (drms).

45: A Love She Can Count On/Foolin' (Parlophone R 5151) 1964 SC

An undistinguished and short-lived Merseybeat group. (VJ/AD)

Castle Farm

Mascot, this band's privately-pressed 45 from 1972 recently got a further airing on *Psychedelic Salvage Co. Vol. 1* (LP & CD). We're talking rather pedestrian instrumental progressive rock here. (VJ)

CATAPILLA - Catapilla (LP).

The Casuals

Personnel:
HOWARD NEWCOMB	gtr, vcls	A
ROB O'BRIEN	drms	A
ALAN TAYLOR	flute, bs, vcls	A
JOHN TEBB	vcls, organ	A
STEVE WALLACE	bs	A

ALBUM: 1(A) HOUR WORLD (Decca SKLR 5001) 1969 R1

NB: There's are also two CD compilations, *Jesamine* (Deram 820 990-2) 1991 and *The Very Best Of The Casuals* (Spectrum) 1998, a 20-track set.

			HCP
45s:	If You Walk Out/Please Don't Hide	(Fontana TF 635) 1965	-
	Adios Amor/Don't Dream Of Yesterday	(Decca F 12737) 1968	-
	Jesamine/I've Got Something To	(Decca F 22784) 1968	2
	Toy/Touched (Some PS)	(Decca F 22852) 1968	30
	Fool's Paradise/Seven Times Seven	(Decca F 22900) 1969	-
	Sunflower Eyes/Never My Love	(Decca F 22943) 1969	-
	Caroline/Naughty Boy	(Decca F 22969) 1969	-
	My Name Is Love/I Can't Say	(Decca F 23027) 1970	-
	Someday Rock'N'Roll Lady/		
	Letter Every Month	(Decca F 23112) 1971	-
	Tara Tiger Girl/Nature's Child	(Parlophone R 5959) 1972	-
	Witch/Good Times	(Dawn DNS 1069) 1974	-
Reissue:	Jesamine/(Flip by different artist)	(Old Gold OG 9347) 1983	-

The Casuals came from Lincoln. They formed back in 1961. They played a lot in Italy, where they had a number of hits in that language. Here they are best remembered for their hit single *Jesamine*, which was a beautifully crafted three minute pop song. The follow-up *Toy*, which was similar in style, but not as good, just made the UK Top 30 and thereafter their short spell in the limelight was over. *Caroline*, one of their later 45s, was produced by **Roy Wood**.

O'Brien had been in **The Riot Squad**.

Retrospective compilation appearances have included *Jesamine* on *20 Hits Of The 60's* (CD), *Best Of British Rock* (CD), *Hits Of The 60's - Save The Last Dance For Me* (CD), the 2-CD set *Sixties Summer Love* and on *Remember The 60's* (CD); and *Naughty Boy* on *Pop-In, Vol 2* (CD). (VJ)

Catapilla

Personnel:
ROBERT CALVERT	sax	AB
HUGH EAGLESTONE	sax	A
MALCOLM FRITH	drms	A
BRYAN HANSON	drms	B
ANNA MEEK	vcls	AB
RALPH ROLINSON	keyb'ds	B
THIERRY RHEINHARDT	woodwind	A
DAVE TAYLOR	bs	A
CARL WASSARD	bs	B
GRAHAM WILSON	gtr	AB

ALBUMS: 1(A) CATAPILLA (Vertigo 6360 029) 1971 R2
2(B) CHANGES (Vertigo 6360 074) 1972 R3

NB: (1) also issued in the US. (1) reissued on CD (Green Tree GTR 009) 1993. (1) reissued on vinyl (Akarma AK 131) and on CD (Akarma 00012116). (2) reissued on vinyl (Akarma AK 132).

Built around the nucleus of Wilson, **Calvert** and Meek, this unusual progressive band opts for long tracks, not too clearly structured, but with a unique and quite eerie atmosphere. At times the substance is necessarily overstretched, but mostly it works well and steers clear from any tedious soloing. If the music is spiritually inclined, it is at least never sugar-coated and the piercing, witch-like voice of Anna Meek creeps under your very skin. Purgatoric elements are present throughout, stronger even on *Changes*, which carries a telling track title: *Thanks Christ For George*. They have a rare quality: they do not sound like anybody else.

Both albums are particularly collectable coming in the original spiral Vertigo label with the spiral inner sleeve but the second one is particularly difficult to find. (MK)

Cat's Eyes

45s:	Smile Girl For Me/In A Fantasy World	(Deram DM 190) 1968
	I Thank You Marianne/Turn Around	(Deram DM 209) 1968
	Where Is She Now?/Tom Drum	(Deram DM 251) 1969 SC
	The Loser/Circus	(MCA MK 5028) 1970
	Lucille/Circus	(MCA MK 5043) 1970
	The Wizard/Hey Open Your Eyes	(MCA MK 5056) 1970

Despite quite a prolific output this group failed to make an impact. They played a commercial form of toy shop psychedelic pop, with *Hey Open Your Eyes* perhaps their most interesting offering. They originated from Evesham in Worcestershire. *Come Away Melinda* got a further airing on *Fading Yellow, Vol 5* (CD) and *The Loser* resurfaced on *Jagged Time Lapse, Vol 2* (CD). (VJ)

Cat's Pyjamas

Personnel:
KENNY BERNARD	vcls	A
ALAN GRIFFIN	lead gtr	A
PHIL LANZON	organ	A
ROY MANDERSON	drms	A
COLIN PULLEN	bs	A

45s:	Virginia Water/Baby I Love You	(Direction 58-3235) 1968 SC
	Camera Man/House For Sale	(Direction 58-3482) 1968 SC

A very obscure band whose music bridged psychedelia and progressivism. *Virginia Water*, which features some strong vocals and good guitar/organ interplay can also be heard on *Circus Days, Vol. 4* (LP) and *Circus Days, Vol. 3* (CD). *Baby I Love You* was the old Ronettes song. *Camera Man*, their second 'A" side is also worth a spin. It got a further airing on *Oddities, Vol 1* (CD) and on *Jagged Time Lapse, Vol 3* (CD). **Kenny Bernard** had earlier cut a handful of solo 45s and been in The Wranglers. (VJ/CP)

Clem Cattini Ork

45:	No Time To Think/Impact	(Decca F 12135) 1965 R1

Clem Cattini was originally the drummer in the early sixties instrumental combo The Tornados. This 'solo' 45 made after their demise attracts some interest from collectors. It was an instrumental beat effort recorded whilst he was with **The Ivy League**.

He was later involved in **Twink**'s **Aquarian Age** project. He also did lots of session drumming for Joe Meek. (VJ)

Eddie Cave and The Fyx

45:      Fresh Out Of Tears/It's Almost Good   (Pye 7N 17161) 1966 R1

This R&B disc is now quite a sought-after and expensive 45. **Chris Curtis** (of **The Searchers**) wrote *It's Almost Good.*

It's Almost Good re-emerged on *Doin' The Mod, Vol. 1* (CD) and *Oddities, Vol 2* (CD). (VJ)

CCS (Collective Consciousness Society)

| Personnel incl: | ALEXIS KORNER | vcls, gtr | A |
| | PETER THORUP | vcls | A |

Plus several of the country's top jazz musicians depending on their availability

			HCP
ALBUMS: 1(A)	C.C.S. aka WHOLE LOTTA LOVE		
		(Rak SRKA 6751) 1970	SC -
2(A)	C.C.S. 2	(Rak SRAK 503) 1972	SC 23
3(A)	THE BEST BAND IN THE LAND		
		(Rak SRAK 504) 1973	SC -

NB: There's also a compilation, *The Best Of C.C.S.* (Rak SRAK 527) 1977. (1) reissued on CD as *Whole Lotta Love* (EMI CDEMS 1426) 1991.

			HCP
45s:	Whole Lotta Love/Boom Boom	(Rak RAK 104) 1970	13
	Walking/Salome	(Rak RAK 109) 1971	7
	Tap Turns On The Water/		
	Save The World	(Rak RAK 119) 1971	5
	Brother/Mister What You Can't Have	(Rak RAK 126) 1972	25
	Sixteen Tone/This Is My Life	(Rak RAK 141) 1972	-
	The Band Played The Boogie/		
	Hang It On Me	(Rak RAK 154) 1973	36
	Hurricane Coming / Dragster	(Rak RAK 172) 1974	-
Reissues:	Whole Lotta Love/Boom Boom	(Rak RR 5) 1973	-
	Brother/Primitive Love	(EMI RR 7) 1977	-
	Whole Lotta Love/Walking	(EMI G 4520) 1984	-

CCS formed in 1970 around bluesman **Alexis Korner** and Peter Thorup. The rest of the line-up was rather loose and depended on people's availability but it included the likes of Tony Carr (drms), Harold Beckett (trumpet), Herbie Flowers (bs), **Henry Lowther** (trumpet) and **Harold McNair** (woodwind) to name but a few. They were among the first groups to record on Mickie Most's new Rak label and **John Cameron** arranged their albums. They had several hit singles, commencing with a cover of **Led Zeppelin**'s *Whole Lotta Love*, which was used as the theme for BBC's 'Top Of The Pops' in this era. This also got to No 58 in the US, where their debut album made No 197. Their music was characterised by **Korner**'s

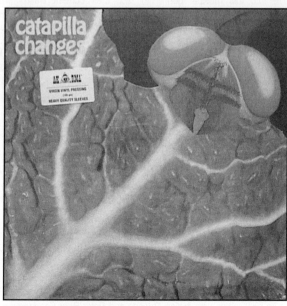

CATAPILLA - Changes (LP).

unique growling vocals. They split in 1973 when **Korner** and Thorup teamed up with former **King Crimson** members Boz Burrell and Ian Wallace to form Snape.

Compilation appearances have included *Whole Lotta Love* on *Classic Rock - cd3,* the 3-CD set *Guitar Heroes - Rock The Night Away;* the 6-CD box set *Best Of Driving Rock* and on the 3-CD set *Radio Caroline Calling - 70's Flashback.* (VJ)

The Cedars

45s:	For Your Information/		
	Hide If You Want To Hide	(Decca F-22720) 1968	R1
	I Like The Way/I Don't Know Why	(Decca F-22772) 196?	R1

From Lebanon originally, this act relocated to the UK and were originally known as **The Sea-ders**. This 45 was recorded in the UK and produced by Tony Clarke. *For Your Information* is a cool mid-tempo number with balalaikas as the lead instrument and great harmonies too.

For Your Information can also be found on *Exploiting Plastic Inevitable, Vol. 1* (LP) and *Perfumed Garden Vol. 3* (CD); *Hide If You Want To Hide* is on *Pebbles, Vol. 12* (CD), *Collecting Peppermint Clouds, Vol. 2* (LP) and on *We Can Fly, Vol 2* (CD). (BM/MW)

Centipede

Personnel:	ROY BABBINGTON	bs	A
(partial list)	IAN CARR	trumpet	A
	ELTON DEAN	sax, cello	A
	KARL JENKINS	oboe	A
	JOHN MARSHALL	drms	A
	ZOOT MONEY	vcls	A
	MIKE PATTO	vcls	A
	ALAN SKIDMORE	sax	A
	JULIE TIPPETT	vcls	A
	KEITH TIPPETT	keyb'ds	A
	ROBERT WYATT	drms	A

NB: Around 40 musicians are featured in total.

ALBUM: 1(A) SEPTOBER ENERGY (2-LP)   (RCA Neon NE9) 1971 R2
NB: (1) reissued on RCA (DPS 5042) 1974 (SC).

Whatever happened to producer **Robert Fripp** during the sessions for this horrible over-indulgent would-be-jazz? They probably stuffed his ears with impenetrable wax, or maybe he earned a million pounds to overhear the proceedings. There can be no excuse for this. To be avoided at all cost! (They even failed to give the tracks individual titles!) (MK)

Rob Chance and The Chances-R

Personnel incl: RON CHANCE

45:      At The End Of The Day/I've Got The Power   (CBS 3130) 1967

This was a slightly later version of the previous outfit. (VJ)

Chances Are

Personnel incl:	ROSCO BIRCHMORE	bs	A
	DICK SMITH	vcls	A

45:      Fragile Child/What Went Wrong   (Columbia DB 8144) 1967 R1

An obscure group whose soul-styled version of San Francisco's Golliwogs (who later became Creedence Clearwater Revival) *Fragile Child* can also be found on *Rubble Vol. 3: Nightmares In Wonderland* (LP) and *Rubble Vol. 2* (CD). (VJ)

Chances-R

45s: Talking Out The Back Of My Head/
         I Aimed Too High   (CBS 202614) 1967
         Do It Yourself/Turn A New Leaf Over   (CBS 2940) 1967

This was a four-piece soul/pop outfit from Southampton. The second 45 was produced by **Dave Dee**.

Talking Out The Back Of My Head has been compiled on *Magic Spectacles* (CD). (VJ)

The Chanters

Personnel incl: DOREEN CHANTER
                    IRENE CHANTER

45s: Every Night (I Sit And Cry)/Where   (CBS 202454) 1967
         You Can't Fool Me/All Day Long   (CBS 202616) 1967
         What's Wrong With You/Right By Your Side   (CBS 3400) 1968
         My Love Is For You/Mississippi Paddleboat (CBS 3668) 1968

A seven-piece band from Fulham, London. It comprised five brothers and two sisters. The sisters later became **Birds Of A Feather**. (VJ)

The Chants

Personnel: EDDIE AMOO   vcls   A
           EDDIE ANKRAH   A
           JOE ANKRAH   A
           ALAN FIELDING (ALAN HARDING??)   A
           NAT SHALMA (NAT SMEDA??)
           RONNIE BONNIE
           BOB CONRAD
           BOBBY JAMES
           HARRY KENNER

45s: I Don't Care/Come And Go With Me   (Pye 7N 15557) 1963 SC
         I Could Write A Book/
         A Thousand Stars   (Pye 7N 15591) 1964 SC
         She's Mine/Then I'll Be Home   (Pye 7N 15643) 1964
         Sweet Was The Wine/One Star   (Pye 7N 15691) 1964
         Come Back And Get This Loving Baby/
         Love Light   (Fontana TF 716) 1966
         A Love's Story/Wearing A Smile   (Decca F 12650) 1967
         Ain't Nobody Home/For You   (Page One POF 016) 1967
         A Man Without A Face/
         Baby, I Don't Need Your Love   (RCA RCA 1754) 1968 R1
         I Get The Sweetest Feeling/Candy (RCA RCA 1823) 1969

MICHAEL CHAPMAN - Fully Qualified Survivor (LP).

A Liverpool soul/pop band, but these were different from the rest in that they were black. They were also durable, their recording career spanned most of the decade, although none of their singles got into the Charts. In the seventies Eddie Amoo finally found success with The Real Thing.

The Ankrah brothers went on to a group called Ashanti.

Compilation appearances have included: *A Thousand Stars* on *Mersey Beat* (2-LP); *I Could Write A Book* on *Beat Merchants* (CD); *She's Mine* on *Ripples, Vol. 4* (CD) and *The Sixties File* (LP); *Come Go With Me* and *She's Mine* on *Pop Inside The Sixties, Vol. 3* (CD); *I Don't Care* and *Come Go With Me* on *Ripples, Vol. 5* (CD); *Come Go With Me, I Could Write A Book* and *She's Mine* on *Some Other Guys* (2-LP); *I Don't Care, A Thousand Stars, One Star, Sweet Was The Wine* and *Then I'll Be Home* on *Merseybeat Nuggets, Vol. 2* and *What About Us* (CD). (VJ/JM)

Michael Chapman

                                                       HCP
ALBUMS: 1   RAINMAKER   (Harvest SHLV 755) 1969 SC -
(up to   2   FULLY QUALIFIED SURVIVOR
1977)   (Harvest SHVL 764) 1969 SC 45
        3   WINDOW   (Harvest SHVL 786) 1971 SC -
        4   WRECKED AGAIN   (Harvest SHVL 798) 1971 SC -
        5   MILLSTONE GRIT   (Deram SML 1105) 1973 -
        6   DEAL GONE DOWN   (Deram SML 1114) 1974 -
        7   SAVAGE AMUSEMENT (Decca SKLR 5242) 1976 -
        8   THE MAN WHO HATED MORNINGS
                          (Decca SKLR 5290) 1977 -
        9   MICHAEL CHAPMAN LIVED HERE (Cube GNAT 1) 1977 -
       10   GUITARS   (Standard ESL 146) 197? -

NB: (1) and (2) reissued on CD (BGO BGOCD 554) 2005, with full sleevenotes. (2) reissued on (CS 527) 1988 and on CD (C5CD 527) 1991. (3) and (4) reissued on CD (BGO BGOCD 555) 2005. (5) was a library issue.

There's also *The Best Of Michael Chapman* (See For Miles SEE 230) 1988, which is a reissue of (9). *BBC Sessions 69-75* (Strange Fruit SFRSCD 060) 1998 draws from a 1969 'Top Gear' performance and two Peel sessions in 1973 and 1975. *Pleasures of The Street* (Mooncrest CRESTCD 047-2) 2000 is a reissue of live material from 1975 with lots of bonus tracks. *Dangerous When Sober* (Sanctuary CMDD 993) 2004 is a 2-CD set, which compiles studio demos and live cuts recorded between 1966 and 1980.

45s: It Didn't Work Out/
(up to   Mozart Lives Upstairs   (Harvest HAR 5002) 1969
1977)   Banjo Song/Dumplings   (Deram DM 407) 1974
         Lovin' Dove/Steel Bonnets   (Decca FR 13658) 1976

Born in Leeds on 24th January 1941 **Chapman** was an important figure in the singer/songwriter phenomenon of the seventies. He'd originally worked as an art and photography teacher in Hull, but gave this up in 1967 to become a folkie. He soon secured a contract with EMI's new progressive Harvest label and recorded a series of albums which you need to check out if you're into this musical genre. In fact, their content wasn't entirely confined to solo folk singer material. **Chapman** pulled in a number of session musicians and acquaintances to assist on these albums including Rick Kemp who later played with **Steeleye Span**; **Mick Ronson**, who was later guitarist for **David Bowie** and drummers Richie Dharma and **Keef Hartley**. As a consequence many of these albums included guitar instrumentals and rock as opposed to folk material. After he signed to Decca his work veered further towards rock.

Rainmaker features some superb eastern-influenced guitar work. The opening cut *It Didn't Work Out* is the finest on the album, but there's some simple but beautiful music here.

Fully Qualified Survivor is generally considered his magnum opus. It includes his most acclaimed song *Postcards Of Scarborough*, whilst *Soulful Lady* showcases his rockier side and *Kodak Ghosts* captures him in reflective mood.

When *Window* was first released, **Chapman** disowned it because it was pressed whilst he was away on tour. It still has its moments, though, on tracks like *A Scholarly Man* and the funky *Last Lady Song*.

Wrecked Again is more electric than his earlier albums. The title track is among its best, along with *Indian Queens* and *Polar Bear Fandango*.

Chapman never attained much more than a cult following over here but on the Continent, where he had a live album issued (in Germany), *Pleasures Of The Street*, he was much more popular. This live album was recorded in Onkel Po's Hamburg where he used an electric band featuring **Keff Hartley** and German Krautrock guru Achim Reichel. The material is a kind of soulful funk-rock.

Chapman's contract with Decca ended in 1977 and he secured a new deal with Criminal Records. Both labels released *The Man Who Hated Mornings*, his album of that year. He continued to record and gig consistently sometimes with a full group and others just with Rick Kemp (his bassist for many years). He released a guitar instruction record and after the release of *Heartbeat* in 1987 experimented with self-released records. His albums continue to receive acclaim, although this is not reflected in the sales.

The *Best Of Michael Chapman* compilation had originally appeared on Cube in 1977 as *Michael Chapman Lived Here*. Over 45 minutes in length it compiles material from his first four albums. The See For Miles compilation comes with a new cover displaying the four original albums and reasonably good sleeve notes.

Dangerous When Sober compiles studio demos and live recordings between 1966 and 1980. Some were previously included on the *Growing Pains 1* and *2* compilations and a German-only 1975 live set *Pleasures Of The Street*. The set comes with interesting sleevenotes and at 150 minutes length offers good value.

Michael Chapman's production credits included Preston singer/guitarist Dave Gardner, who's very much in the Tim Buckley mould.

Back in 1969 **Chapman** had had three cuts:- *No Song To Sing, You Say* and *Thank You P.K. 1944*, featured on the very rare promo-only *Harvest Sampler* (LP), whilst *Postcards Of Scarborough* was included on their easier to find *Picnic* (2-LP) compilation. (VJ)

Chapter Five

Personnel incl: JOHN RITSON   vcls

45s: Anything That You Can Do/
      You Can't Mean It   (CBS 202395) 1967 R5
  α   One In A Million/Hey Hey   (CBS 2696) 1967 R3

NB: α demo only.

This British soul band, from Barrow-in-Furness is a marginal case for inclusion in this book. *You Can't Mean It* was a very significant disc in British soul music and commands a high price (circa £550 according to Record Collectors' 'Rare Record Price Guide 2006') on the collector's market. Their second 45, *One In A Million*, is actually harder to find as it was shelved when an alternative version by Karol Keyes was released first and was consequently only available in demo form. (VJ)

Chapter Four

45: In My Life/
     In Each Other's Arms   (United Artists UP 1143) 1966 R3

This is a very rare and collectable single. The 'A' side has some great discordant guitar work and can also be heard on *Chocolate Soup For Diabetics, Vol. 3* (LP) or the *Chocolate Soup* (CD). The sleevenotes claim that this is the work of the US band Jay and The Americans, but I've left this entry in the book so this fact will become more widely known. (VJ)

The Chapters

45: Can't Stop Thinking About Her/
     Dance Little Lady   (Pye 7N 15815) 1965 R1

An excellent beat group from Bradford, whose *Can't Stop Thinking About Her* is a powerful example of what began to happen to the tried and tested beat formula during the 1965/66 period.

INCREDIBLE SOUND SHOW STORIES VOL. 2 (Comp LP) including Charge.

Can't Stop Thinking About Her can also be heard on *Pop Inside The Sixties, Vol. 3* (CD) and *Quick Before They Catch Us* (LP & CD). (MWh)

Charge (1)

Personnel: ANDY   ld gtr   A
            CHRIS   bs   A
            PAUL   organ, gtr   A
            SLIM   drms   A

45: Zeugma / Boring Song (Art sleeve)   (No label) 1970 SC

Incredible Sound Show Stories, Vol. 2 (LP) includes *Boring Song*, an early **Floyd** influenced psych number, which was recorded by Derby Art College students in their college library. (VJ)

Charge (2)

Personnel incl: SMILEY DE JONES   perc
                 RIC GRECH   violin, gtr, bs
                 IAN GREEN   keyb'ds
                 ROSETTA HIGHTOWER   vcls
                 NEIL HUBBARD   gtr
                 GODFREY McLEAN   drms
                 ALAN SPENNER   bs
                 LEE VAN DER BILT   vcls, perc
                 MIKE WOODS   gtr

ALBUM: 1 CHARGE   (Fresh Air 6308900) 1974

45: Can You Feel It/Every Mother's Son   (Fresh Air 6121112) 1974

Here is another of those one-off studio bands who only did a few gigs to promote a hastily put together album, which in turn didn't sell many copies. Still they did feature some well-known musicians:- Alan Spenner and Neil Hubbard were both ex-**Joe Cocker's Mad Dogs**; Ric Grech was ex-**Family**; Rosetta Hightower and Ian Green ex-Hightower; Mike Woods was ex-**Eclection**; Smiley De Jones was ex-**Maggie Bell** and Godfrey McLean was ex-**Hummingbird**. All but Grech, Green and McLean appeared on the album and the live line-up varied a little from the musos featured on their recordings.

The album consists of a loud, blistering sonic attack that rarely relents. Half the recording is an extended piece called *Child Of Nations*.

Spenner and Hubbard went on to **Kokomo**, Grech joined KGB, McLean joined Gonzales, Woods joined Swallow, Van der Bilt joined **Elkie Brooks**. Spenner and Hubbard were the first to jump ship being replaced by Andy Dalby who went on to **Arthur Brown**'s **Kingdon Come**. (VJ/RR/JM)

Charge (3)

Personnel incl: ELLIS   A

ALBUM: 1(A)   CHARGE   (SRT no #) 1973 R5

NB: (1) reissued (Kissing Spell KSLP 9205) 1992 in a limited pressing of 500 and on CD (Kissing Spell KSCD 9419) 1992.

An obscure privately-pressed progressive-rock album, but only one copy is known to exist. Its magnum opus is probably the opening cut *Glory Boy* with its wild guitar, whilst a lot of the other material veers towards space-rock territory. All the songs were penned by band member Ellis, but nothing more is known about him or the band. The limited edition reissue by Kissing Spell in 1992 brought it to the attention of a wider audience. (VJ)

Charlie

Personnel:			
JOHN ANDERSON	bs, vcls	ABC
STEVE GADD	drms	ABC
MARTIN SMITH	gtr, vcls	A
TERRY THOMAS	ld vcls, gtr	ABC
JULIAN COLBECK	keyb'ds	BC
EUGENE ORGAN	gtr, vcls	C

ALBUMS: 1(A)	FANTASY GIRLS	(Polydor 2383 373) 1976
(up to 2(B)	NO SECOND CHANCE	(Polydor 2383 422) 1977
1977)		

45s:	First Class Traveller/TV Dreams	(Polydor 2058 863) 1976
(up to	Turning To You/Love Is Alright	(Polydor 2058 783) 1976
1976)		

A band who just squeeze into the tail end of our time frame; the second album makes it as it was mainly recorded in 1976. They had good harmony vocals and some soaring guitar lines. A certain sparkle is sometimes lacking, but there is also a glossy artfulness which can't help being reminiscent of a kind of heavy **10cc**. Their best songs are self-mocking or have targets such as narcissistic rock stars (*Guitar Hero, False Messiah*), those in love with money (the jaunty *First Class Traveller*), and, (ahem, cough) obsessive music fans (*Greatcoat Guru*)!

The main man creatively here is Terry Thomas - composer, lyricist, lead vocalist and guitarist. He had also been in a late version of **Bad Company**. **Charlie** made at least another five albums and existed at least into the early eighties. Currently unfashionable, these albums can be picked up and enjoyed for next to nothing. Side two of the second album is particularly recommended. They appear to have been popular in the U.S. where they regularly charted with both singles and albums even having a No. 38 hit in 1983. Their later UK albums included:- *Lines* (Polydor 2383 487) 1978, *Fight Dirty* (Polydor 2443 161) 1979, *Good Morning America* (RCA RCALP 5040) 1981, and *Here Comes Trouble* (Polydor POLS 1053) 1982.

SYDE TRYPS VOL. 3 (Comp LP) including Charlotte Black.

After Martin Smith left in September 1976 to join U-Boat, Julian Colbeck (ex-Greep) came in to replace him. (NM/JM)

Charlie and The Wide Boys

Personnel:			
CHARLIE AINLEY	vcls, gtr	AB
NIGEL CHAPPELL	bs	AB
SIMON FRASER	gtr	AB
ANDY McDONALD	drms	A
GREG PHILLIPS	vcls, perc	AB
RICHARD WORTHY	gtr, vcls	AB
GUY EVANS	drms	B

ALBUM: 1(B)   GREAT COUNTRY ROCKERS
                     (Anchor / Music For Pleasure MFP 50293) 1976

EP: 1(B)   Gilly I Do/Oh Sweet Annie/Love Me Real/Wahtusi
                                                    (Anchor) 1974

NB: There was also a German 45 *Gilly I Do/Love Me Real* (Anchor) 1974.

A Cornish group with two vocalists who were only together for about eighteen months. Charlie Ainley also produced a 45 for **The Anchormen**.

Their original drummer, Andy McDonald (ex-**Andwella**) quit in July 1974 and was replaced by Guy Evans (ex-**Van der Graaf Generator**). When they split in February 1975, Evans rejoined **Van der Graaf Generator**, and Ainley and Worthy went solo. (VJ/JM/WH)

Charlotte Black

A Tonbridge-based group who recorded an acetate which coupled **Jason Crest**'s Terry Clark and Terry Dobson's *Charge Of The Light Brigade*, which featured some reasonable fuzz guitar work, with a weak cover of The Byrds' seminal *So You Want To Be A Rock 'n' Roll Star*. Both efforts can also be heard on *Syde Trips, Vol. 3* (LP). (VJ)

The Chasers

Personnel:			
LENNY BUTCHER	drms	ABCDE
JACK CHAMBERS	bs	A
LEN TUCKEY	gtr	ABCDE
TONY WADLOW	sax, flute, bs	BCDE
ROGER PINCOTT	vcls	C
BOBBY RIO	vcls	D

45s:	Hey Little Girl/That's What They	
	Call Love (Some PS)	(Decca F 12302) 1965 R2/R1
	Inspiration/She's Gone Away	(Parlophone R 5451) 1966 R2
	The Ways Of A Man/Summer Girl	(Philips BF 1546) 1967 SC

The group formed in 1960 at Chase Cross School, Romford (line-up A) as a four-piece with a rhythm guitarist (name unknown). They played at the school's music festival and continued with gigs at youth clubs etc.

During the 1961/62 era Tony Wadlow replaced Chambers and also brought sax and flute to the sound. They were playing further a field by now and their set included mainly instrumentals. By late 1962 and during 1963 they changed to a R&B sound which helped them get more gigs, a number supporting **The Downliners Sect**.

Following local friend **Chris Andrews** to Germany they played at the 'Liverpool Club' in Düsseldorf. **Andrews** became their producer and they cut demos of *Hey Little Girl* and *Hey Baby*. Then, with Tuckey's father acting as their manager, they got *Hey Little Girl* released by Decca with a Tony Wadlow song, *That's What They Call Love*, on the flip. It was played on 'Juke Box Jury' and Radio Caroline as a 'power play' but got little promotion from Decca.

In 1966 they switched to Parlophone releasing a laid back, experimental 45, *Inspiration*, backed by *She's Gone Away*, a Lenny Butcher/Tony Wadlow song. New vocalist Roger Pincott sang on this 45 but left soon after. The band supported **Shotgun Express** and **Cops 'n' Robbers** at Southend's Studio Club the same year.

ENGLISH FREAKBEAT VOL. 1 (Comp CD) including The Chasers.

In late 1966 a new singer, **Bobby Rio** from **Bobby Rio and The Revelles**, was recruited and they changed labels again to Philips. Their final 45, *The Ways Of A Man*, was another **Chris Andrews**' composition with another Tony Wadlow flip. Frankly this effort is best avoided and when commercial success wasn't forthcoming **Rio** departed and the group became a trio. When Tuckey left soon after to join **The Riot Squad** the band folded. Tuckey, incidentally, is the husband of Suzi Quatro.

Compilation coverage has included:- *Hey Little Girl* on *Garage Punk Unknowns, Vol. 1* (LP), *Justification* (LP), *The R&B Scene* (CD) and *Maximum R'n'B* (CD); and *Inspiration* on *English Freakbeat, Vol. 1* (LP & CD), *Rubble Vol. 16: Glass Orchid Aftermath* (LP) and *Rubble Vol. 9* (CD). (VJ/MWh)

The Cheatin' Hearts

45:     Zip-Tease/The Bad Kind   (Columbia DB 8048) 1966

This was a short-lived beat group. (VJ)

The Checkmates

Personnel:	PETER CARTER	lead gtr	AB
	RAYE DUVAL	drms	A
	REX GATES	bs	A
	JOHN CUFFLEY	drms	BC
	LES HART	sax	B
	ALAN HAWKSHAW	keyb'ds	BCD
	DAVE SWEETNAM	baritone sax	BCD
	STEVE BROWN	lead gtr	C
	KEN STREET	lead gtr	C
	GEORGE FORD	bs	D
	BARRY REEVES	drms	D

ALBUM:	1 THE CHECKMATES	(Pye NPL 18061) 1961 R1

45s:	Rockin' Minstrel/Pompeii	(Piccadilly 7N 35010) 1961
	You've Gotta Have A Gimmick Today/	
	Westpoint	(Decca F 11603) 1963 SC
	Sticks And Stones/	
	Please Listen To Me	(Decca F 11844) 1964 SC
	Around/I've Got To Know Now	(Decca F 12114) 1965 SC
	Stop That Music/	
	I've Been In Love Before	(Parlophone R 5337) 1965 SC
	(You've Got) The Gamma Goochie/	
	It Ain't Right	(Parlophone R 5402) 1966 SC
	Every Day Is Just The Same/	
	I'll Be Keeping The Score	(Parlophone R 5495) 1966 SC

A quite prolific beat group who also recorded 45s in 1962 and 1963 as The Original Checkmates. They also recorded as the backing group for Emile Ford between 1959 - 63 and their three Decca 45s were produced by Joe Meek.

George Ford and Barry Reeves all went on to **Ferris Wheel**, whilst Alan Hawkshaw later worked with **The Shadows**.

Compilation appearances have included: *Sticks And Stones*, *I've Got To Know Now* and *Around* on *Mersey Sounds* (2-LP); and *Sticks And Stones* on *RGM Rarities, Vol. 2* (CD). (VJ/MWh/JM/AD)

The Cheetahs

Personnel:	RAY BRIDGER	vcls, gtr	A
	EVAN ROSE	drms	A
	NIGEL WRIGHT	gtr	A
	RODNEY WRIGHT	bs	A

			HCP
45s:	Mecca/Goodnight Kiss	(Philips BF 1362) 1964	36
	Soldier Boy/Johnny	(Philips BF 1383) 1965	39
	Goodbye Baby (Baby Goodbye)/		
	That's How It Goes	(Philips BF 1412) 1965	-
	Whole Lotta Love/Party	(Philips BF 1453) 1965	-
	The Russian Boat Song/Gamble	(Philips BF 1499) 1966	-

A pop group who enjoyed some commercial success with their first two 45s. Hailing from Birmingham they wore cheetah suits on stage! They also released a 45, *Beg Borrow Or Steal/Only The Beginning* (Columbia DB 7162) 1963 as Carl and The Cheetahs.

Russian Boat Song and *The Gamble* can both be heard on *The Star-Club Singles Complete, Vol. 8* (LP & CD). (VJ/MWh)

The Chelsea Lads

45:     English Teas/Hump A Dink   (CBS 202047) 1966

A little known instrumental beat group. (MWh)

The Cherokees

Personnel:	DAVE BOWER	gtr	A
	JIM GREEN	drms	A
	JOHN KIRBY	vcls	A
	TERRY STOKES	gtr	A
	MIKE SWEENEY	bs	A

			HCP
45s:	You've Done It Again Little Girl/		
	Girl Girl Girl	(Decca F 11915) 1964	-
	Seven Daffodils/		
	Are You Back In My World Now	(Columbia DB 7341) 1964	33
	Wondrous Place/		
	Send Me All Your Love	(Columbia DB 7473) 1965	-
	I Will Never Turn My Back On You/		
	Dig A Little Deeper	(Columbia DB 7704) 1965	-
	Land Of A 1000 Dances/		
	Everybody's Needs	(Columbia DB 7822) 1966 SC	-

Mickie Most was this Leeds-based band's producer and their version of *Seven Daffodils* was a minor hit, selling better than the one by the better-known **Mojos**.

Dave Bower, John Kirby and Terry Stokes all later played in **New York Public Library**.

Compilation appearances have included: *I Will Never Turn My Back On You* and *Rejected* on *Mickie Most Presents: British Go-Go* (LP); *Dig A Little Deeper* on *Rare 60's Beat Treasures, Vol. 1* (CD); *I Will Never Turn My Back On You* on *Rare 60's Beat Treasures, Vol. 5* (CD); *Everybody Needs* on *Beat Us If You Can! Vol. 1* (LP); and *Wondrous Place* on *Psychedelic Unknowns, Vol. 6*. (VJ)

Cherry Smash

Personnel:
JOHN CURTIS		AB
MICK GILL		A
GRAHAM HUNT		AB
BRYAN SEBASTIAN	vcls, gtr	AB
MARK TUDDENHAM	vcls	AB

45s:
Sing Songs Of Love/Movie Star	(Track 604 017) 1967	
Goodtime Sunshine/		
Little Old Country Home Town	(Decca F 12838) 1968 SC	
Fade Away Maureen/Green Plant	(Decca F 12884) 1969 SC	

Formed in Gosport, Hampshire, **Cherry Smash** are best remembered for *Sing Songs Of Love*, which was written by **Mike Hugg** (who was Sebastian's brother) and Mick Gill. The pretty slushy pop song was taken to a wider audience by virtue of its inclusion on **Manfred Mann**'s 'Up The Junction' soundtrack and later on Track's *Backtrack, 2* (LP) compilation. Gill left after this and wasn't replaced. The follow-up, *Goodtime Sunshine*, was a **Mike Hugg** composition as was their final effort, *Fade Away Maureen*. This had commercial potential with quite a memorable guitar riff but sounds distinctly wimpy now. The flip side, a song about an office plant, is for me their best composition but they aren't essential listening.

Compilation appearances have included:- *Fade Away Maureen* on *Rubble, Vol. 11 - Adventures In The Mist* (LP), *Rubble, Vol. 6* (CD), *British Psychedelic Trip, Vol. 4* (LP), *Broken Dreams, Vol. 5* (LP) and *Great British Psychedelic Trip, Vol. 2* (CD); and *Green Plant* on *British Psychedelic Trip, Vol. 3* (LP). (VJ)

The Chevlons

45: Too Long Alone/It's My Problem   (Pye 7N 17145) 1966

A harmony beat group from Glasgow.

Too Long Alone can also be heard on *Ripples, Vol. 1* (CD). (VJ)

The Cheynes

Personnel:
PETER BARDENS	organ, vcls	A
PETER HOLLIS	bs	A
MICK FLEETWOOD	drms	A
ROGER PEACOCK	vcls	A
PHIL SAWYER	gtr	A

45s:
Respectable/		
It's Gonna Happen To You	(Columbia DB 7153) 1963 R2	
Going To The River/		
Cheyne-Re-La	(Columbia DB 7368) 1964 R2	

NOWHERE MEN VOL. 1 (Comp CD) including The Cheynes.

Down And Out/
Stop Running Around   (Columbia DB 7464) 1965 R2

This London-based R&B band had pedigree and were reputedly excellent. Their founder was **Peter Bardens**, who also acted as their manager. Mick Fleetwood met **Bardens** via his sister and got invited to join. Their three 45s were all pretty raw R&B and included a cover of The Isley Brothers' *0.* *Stop Running Around* was also written by **Bill Wyman**.

After the band's demise in mid-1965, **Bardens** and Fleetwood went on to play together in **Peter B's** and **Shotgun Express**. Then in 1967 Mick Fleetwood was a founder member of **Fleetwood Mac**. Phil Sawyer later played with **The Fleur De Lys** and **Spencer Davis Group**. **Bardens** was later in **Them** and **Camel**. **Roger Peacock** rcorded a solo 45 before replacing **Mark Leeman** in the **Mark Leeman Five**.

Compilation coverage has included:- *0* on *On The Scene* (CD); *Respectable*, *It's Gonna Happen To You*, *Going To The River*, *Cheyne-Re-La*, *Down And Out* and *Stop Running Around* on *Nowhere Men, Vol. 1* (CD); and *Respectable* on *That Driving Beat* (CD), *Pebbles, Vol. 6* (LP) and *English Freakbeat Vol. 6* (CD). (VJ)

Chicago Line (Blues Band)

Personnel incl:
LOUIS CENNAMO	bs	A
MIKE FELLANA	trumpet	A
TIM HINKLEY	keyb'ds	A
MIKE PATTO	vcls	A
VIV PRINCE	drms	A

45:
Shimmy Shimmy Ko Ko Bop/		
Jump Back	(Philips BF 1488) 1966 R2	

A short-lived 1966 outfit which evolved out of **The Bo Street Runners**. Their single fetches high prices among collectors. Cennamo and Fellana went on to do session work, whilst **Patto** later had his own band before forming **Boxer**. *Shimmy Shimmy Ko Ko Bop* was a heavy dance number. *Jump Back* was a bluesy interpretation of a Rufus Thomas song.

Viv Prince was **The Pretty Things'** drummer and also recorded a solo 45 in 1966.

Compilation appearances include: *Shimmy Shimmy Ko Ko Bop* and *Jump Back* on *English Freakbeat Vol. 6* (CD), *Electric Sugarcube Flashbacks, Vol. 2* (LP) and *Electric Sugarcube Flashbacks, Vol. 3* (LP); and *Shimmy Shimmy Ko Ko Bop* on *Echoes From The Wilderness* (LP & CD). (VJ)

Chicken Shack

Personnel:
ANDY SILVESTER	bs	ABCD
AL SYKES	drms	A
STAN WEBB	gtr, vcls	ABCDEFG
DAVE BIDWELL	drms	BCD
CHRISTINE PERFECT	piano, vcls	C
PAUL RAYMOND	keyb'ds	D
PAUL HANCOCK	drms	EF
JOHN GLASCOCK	bs	E
TONY ASHTON	piano	E
BOB DAISLEY	bs	F
CHRIS MERCER	sax	F
ROB HULL	bs	G
ALAN POWELL	drms	G
DAVE WILKINSON	keyb'ds	G

HCP

ALBUMS:
1(C)	FORTY BLUE FINGERS FRESHLY PACKED AND READY TO SERVE			
		(Blue Horizon 7-63203) 1968 R1 12		
2(C)	O.K. KEN?	(Blue Horizon 7-63209) 1969 R1 9		
3(D)	100 TON CHICKEN	(Blue Horizon 7-63218) 1969 R1 -		
4(D)	ACCEPT	(Blue Horizon 7-63861) 1970 R1 -		
5(E)	IMAGINATION LADY	(Deram SDL 5) 1972 R1 -		
6(F)	UNLUCKY BOY	(Deram SML 1100) 1973 R1 -		
7(G)	GOODBYE CHICKEN SNACK (live)			
		(Deram Nova SDL 8008) SC 1974 -		

ECHOES FROM THE WILDERNESS (Comp CD) including Chicago Line.

NB: These albums were also released in the USA and most were released in Germany too. They have all subsequently been repackaged and reissued. (1) reissued on CD by Blue Horizon (477357 2) 1994. (2) reissued on Beat Goes On (BGOCD 186) 1993. (5) reissued on CD (Indigo Delux IGOX CD 506) 199?. (6) reissued on CD (Indigo IGO XCD 520 Z UK) 1999 with four additional bonus tracks. A good compilation of their material is *Collection: Chicken Shack* (Castle Communications CCSCD 179) 1990. *On Air* (Strange Fruit SFRSCD 045) 1998 only features four cuts from their **Perfect**-era line-up and suffers from a lack of sleevenotes. *On Air* (Band Of Joy BOJOLP 002) 1991, also on CD, is a 12-track compilation of their BBC Radio performances which includes many of their best songs. *Going Up Going Down - The Anthology 1968-2001* (Sanctuary CMDDD 948) 2004 is a 2-CD anthology. *Poor Boy In Concert 1973 and 1981* (Indigo IGOXDC 532Z) 2000 contains two live sets.

HCP

45s:	It's Okay With Me Baby/			
	When My Left Eye Jumps	(Blue Horizon 57-3135)	1967	SC -
	Worried About My Woman/			
	Six Nights In Seven	(Blue Horizon 57-3143)	1968	SC -
	When The Train Comes Back/			
	Hey Baby	(Blue Horizon 57-3146)	1968	-
	I'd Rather Go Blind/			
	Night Life	(Blue Horizon 57-3153)	1969	14
	Tears In The Wind/			
	Things You Put Me Through	(Blue Horizon 57-3160)	1969	29
	Maudie/Andalucian Blues	(Blue Horizon 57-3168)	1970	-
	Sad Clown/Tired Eyes	(Blue Horizon 57-3176)	1970	-
	As Time Goes Passing By/Poor Boy	(Deram DM 381)	1973	-
	You Know You Could Be Right/			
	The Loser	(Deram DM 396)	1973	-
Reissues:	I'd Rather Go Blind/Sad Clown	(CBS 1832)	1974	-
	I'd Rather Go Blind/			
	Tears In The Wind	(Old Gold OG 9201)	1982	-

Chicken Shack were part of the late sixties blues boom. They were quite popular for a while, although they were overshadowed by the likes of **Fleetwood Mac** who their keyboard player **Christine Perfect** later joined. In Stan Webb they had a guitarist who could excite audiences.

Chicken Shack formed in April 1965 in Birmingham, but had a long residency at the Star Club in Hamburg in its early days. Their first break came when **Mike Vernon** signed them to his new Blue Horizon label along with **Fleetwood Mac**. Their second break came when **Christine Perfect**, who'd previously played for an outfit called Sound Of Blue, joined them in April 1967, for she was considered to be one of Britain's finest female blues singers. Along with **Fleetwood Mac** for the next couple of years they were at the forefront of the British blues boom, cutting a couple of good albums in *40 Blue Fingers...* and *O.K. Ken* and enjoying a couple of big hits with their classic cover of Elta James' R&B ace *I'd Rather Go Blind* and *Tears In The Wind*. These two singles really represented the more commercial side of their music.

After **Christine Perfect** left the band in August 1969 to join her husband John McVie in **Fleetwood Mac** they were never the same force. They

maintained a good live reputation, though, based around Stan Webb's theatrics. He was really one of the unsung guitar heros of the British blues boom and was their lead vocalist too. Sure he lacked the flair of **Peter Green** but their first three albums are essential for blues fans. Indeed, he kept them together through many line-up changes. They developed quite a strong club following in the early seventies.

Unlucky Boy leads off with *You Know You Could Be Right* and features a fine version of Lonnie Johnson's *Too Late To Cry*. There are a couple of pulsating live numbers too, but eventually they split at the end of 1973 after a German tour which was full of strife and conflict. Webb later reformed them in the late seventies, having been with **Broken Glass** in the interim.

Webb kept **Chicken Shack** going with a range of musicians into the eighties, although he briefly disbanded the band to join **Savoy Brown** for a while in the mid-seventies.

Going Up Going Down is a 36-track anthology that showcases their material over four decades and Stan Webb's guitar playing stands out.

Their appearances on Various Artists' compilations include *Hey Baby, It's Okay With Me Baby* and *When My Left Eye Jumps* on Blue Horizon's 1969 *In Our Own Way (Oldies But Goldies)* (LP) and *What You Did Last Night* and *I Wanna See My Baby* on the same label's *Super Duper Blues* (LP). More, recently *Daughter Of The Hillside* has been compiled on the 3-CD box set *Ars Longa Vita Brevis: A Compendium Of Progressive Rock 1967-1974*. (VJ/FC)

Chicory Tip

Personnel:	DICK FOSTER	gtr	A
	PETER HEWSON	vcls	AB
	BARRY MAYGER	bs	AB
	BRIAN SHEARER	drms	AB
	ROD CLOUTT	lead gtr, synthesizer, organ	B

ALBUM: 1(A) SON OF MY FATHER (CBS 64871) 1972

NB: *The Very Best Of Chicory Tip* (Sounds Media SUMCD 4099) 199? and *The Best Of Chicory Tip* (Repertoire REP 4816 WG) 1999 compile their better songs.

HCP

45s:	Monday After Sunday/			
	Pride Comes Before A Fall	(CBS 5056)	1970	-
	My Girl Sunday/Doctor Man	(CBS 7118)	1971	-
	Excuse Me Baby/The Devil Rides Tonight	(CBS 7312)	1971	-
	I Love Onions/Don't Hang Jack	(CBS 7595)	1971	-
	Son Of My Father/Pride Comes Before A Fall	(CBS 7737)	1971	1
	What's Your Name/Memory	(CBS 8021)	1972	13
	The Future Is Past/Big Wheels Rolling	(CBS 8094)	1972	-
	Good Grief Christina/Move On	(CBS 1258)	1973	17
	Cigarettes, Women And Wine/I See You	(CBS 1668)	1973	-
	I.O.U./Join Our Gang	(CBS 1866)	1973	-
	Take Your Time Caroline/Me And Stan Foley	(CBS 2507)	1974	-
	Survivor/Move On	(Route RT 1)	1975	-
Reissue:	Son Of My Father/			
	What's Your Name	(Old Gold OG 9003)	1978	-

From Maidstone in Kent, **Chicory Tip** are best remembered for their catchy pop song, *Son Of My Father*, which topped the Charts for three weeks early in 1972. It also got to No 91 in the States, where they were known as simply Chicory. The band was formed by vocalist Peter Hewson in 1968. Their big break came when *Son Of My Father*, written by Giorgio Moroder, who went on to become a successful disco producer (the synthesizer on the song was played by another future producer Chris Thomas), latched them onto the glam-rock movement for a few years, but after a couple more hits they fizzled out.

Their better moments have now been compiled on *The Very Best Of Chicory Tip* and *The Best Of Chicory Tip* - so take your pick! Some of them still play at parties and functions as Chicory.

Son Of My Father can be found on several compilations including *Hits Of The 70's Vol 2* (CD), *Hits Of The 70's Vol 3* (CD), *Number 1 Hits Of The 70's and 80's* (CD), *Seventies Legends* (CD), *30 Years Of Number 1 Hit*

Singles - 1960/1989 (CD) and *UK No 1 Hits Of The 70's* (CD). They have been compiled singing a version of *Let's Go To San Francisco* on *Perfect Day* (CD). (VJ)

Chili Charles

Personnel:			
	PAT ARNOLD	vcls, bs	A
	ROBERT BAILEY	electric piano	A
	PHIL BECQUE	bs	A
	CHILI CHARLES	drms, perc, moog	A
	KENNY COLE	vcls	A
	JOE JAMMER	gtr	A
	DEL RICHARDSON	gtr	A
	FUZZY SAMUELS	bs	A
	GORDON SMITH	slide gtr	A

ALBUM: 1(A) BUZY CORNER   (Virgin V2009) 1973

A predominantly instrumental album combining pub-rock with white soul, recorded with excellent musicians (members of **Bad Company**, **King Crimson**, etc) but it's not memorable at all. (SR)

Chilli Willi and The Red Hot Peppers

Personnel:			
	PHIL 'SNAKEFINGER' LITHMAN	gtr, fiddle, piano, vcls	AB
	MARTIN STONE	gtr, mandolin, vcls	AB
	PAUL 'DICE MAN' BAILEY	gtr, sax, banjo	B
	PAUL RILEY	bs	B
	PETE THOMAS	drms	B

ALBUMS: 1(A) KINGS OF THE ROBOT RHYTHM
                    (Revelation REV 002) 1972 SC
          2(B) BONGOS OVER BALHAM   (Mooncrest CREST 21) 1974

NB: (2) issued on Nova in Germany and reissued on CD (Total CRESTCD 007) 1991.

45:      Breathe A Little/Friday Song   (Mooncrest MOON 40) 1975

Lithman and Stone had both been in Junior's Blues Band, an early sixties outfit. Lithman later moved to San Francisco, whilst Stone played in **The Savoy Brown Blues Band, The Action** and **Mighty Baby**. They teamed up again in 1972 and were assisted on *Kings Of The Robot Rhythm*, a US country-ish influenced album, by **Jo-Ann Kelly** and various members of **Brinsley Schwarz**. In December 1972, they were expanded into a five-piece and evolved into a popular live attraction. Indeed, it is as a live band they are best remembered and their musical repertoire was very diverse incorporating rock, country, blues and R&B. Their *Bongos Over Balham* album failed to capture the energy of their live show and in February 1975 they split up.

After their demise, Martin Stone was in **The Pink Fairies** but then drifted out of the music scene. Lithman returned to San Francisco, where as 'Snakefinger', he played in The Residents. Thomas was later in The Attractions (Elvis Costello's backing band) and Riley was in **Graham Parker**'s band. (VJ)

Chillum

Personnel: No credits on cover.   A

ALBUM: 1   CHILLUM (w/insert)   (Mushroom 100 Mr. 11) 1971 R2
NB: (1) has been reissued on CD as *Chillum... Plus* with five unreleased tracks.

This is supposed to be the 3rd **Second Hand** album and surely the organ parts sound like it. On the other hand there isn't much coherence between the players, so the music comes forth in uncontrolled spurts, leaving it to coincidence whether it coagulates or not. Too much of the insanity of **Second Hand**'s *Death May Be Your Santaclaus* and too little of the solidity of *Reality* makes it hard on the ears. A full-blown drum solo doesn't improve things either. Funny insert, though. (MK)

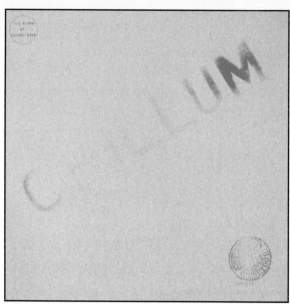

CHILLUM - Chillum (LP).

Chimera

Personnel:			
	LISA BANKOFF	vcls	A
	FRANCESCA GARNETT	vcls	A
	NICK SOUTH	bs	A
	ROY TEMRO	drms	A
	BOB WESTON	gtr	A

ALBUM: 1(A) CHIMERA   (Tenth Planet TP 054) 2002

An obscure band whose *Peru*, features distinctive high-pitched vocals somewhere between **Fairport Convention** and **Trees**. They meet **The Beatles** and almost signed to Apple but **George Harrison** wasn't keen so they didn't. Then they meet Nick Mason at a **Pink Floyd** gig and he agreed to manage them. Amazingly they cut 20 tracks of their superb psychedelic folk for Morgan Bluetown but had nothing released. Had they been they would have pre-dated **Fairport Convention** and **Mellow Candle** An album's worth of material was compiled in the eighties for possible release, but it too remained unissued until Tenth Planet released it in 2002. Tracks like *Come Into The Garden*, *The Grail* (which featured Nick Mason who produced many of the other tracks) and *Sad Song For Winter* showcase Bankoff's delightful vocals augmented by some fine guitar and sometimes melodramatic piano and keyboard work. **Pink Floyd** fans will also be interested in *Lady With Bullets In Her Hair* because Rick Wright plays on it.

Bob Weston later played with **Fleetwood Mac**, Nick South (ex-**Alexis Korner**), went on to play with **Elkie Brooks** and Roy Temro sadly died some time ago. Lisa Bankoff was the group's songwriter:- "The project fell to pieces mainly because I had a car accident shortly after the recordings were finished and couldn't walk for a couple of years. Our producer was called Mal Luker."

Reputedly, **Cliff Wade** and Danny Beckerman were involved in some way too, although this may be incorrect.

Lisa Bankoff now lives in Perth, Western Australia and still writes songs and plays "a little bit here and there". She and Francesca have recently written a book about their life in London during the late sixties / early seventies called "Making It! Famous Names and Silly Girls".

Peru has been compiled on *Morgan Blue Town* (LP) and *Best And The Rest Of British Psychedelia* (CD). (VJ)

Chimes Featuring Denise

Personnel incl: GENE COBEN   vcls   A

45s: Say It Again/Can This Be Love?   (Decca F 11783) 1963
         I'll Be Waiting I'll Be Here/
         Hello Heartache   (Decca F 11885) 1964

A short-lived Manchester beat-pop outfit, whose *Say It Again* also got an airing on Decca's 1964 *Saturday Club* (LP) compilation. Denise also recorded as Little Frankie. (VJ)

Chitinous Ensemble

ALBUM: 1 CHITINOUS   (Deram SML 1093) 1971 R4

This album is a rare and sought-after collectable. Musically, it's progressive jazz with a cast of thousands led by Paul Buckmaster, who'd arranged classic albums for **The Rolling Stones**, **Elton John** and **David Bowie**. Buckmaster spent four years at The Royal Academy of Music and also toured as a cellist with **The Bee Gees**, before joining **The Third Ear Band**. **Chitinous** is powerful and eerie (apparently it was originally conceived as 'The Intergalactic Music Festival' featuring music from different planets performed by their inhabitants). The album didn't sell and is hardly ever seen nowadays, though it has recently been reissued on CD by Vocalion. (VJ/RMJ)

Choc

45:    Way Of Life/I Want You To Be My Girl   (Decca F 23106) 1970

This 45 was this pop outfit's sole vinyl excursion. (VJ)

The Chocolate Frog

Personnel:	TAGO BYERS	bs	A
	KEITH GUSTER	drms	A
	BRYN HAWORTH	gtr	A
	TONY HEAD	vcls	A

45:    Butchers And Bakers/I Forgive You   (Atlantic 584 027) 1968 SC

You may recognise the above names - they went on to become the 1969 line-up of **The Fleur de Lys**, so obviously the 45 will interest some collectors. I'm unsure why this 45 was recorded under a different name.

Butchers And Bakers later resurfaced on *Beat It* (3-CD). (VJ)

The Chocolate Watchband

| Personnel: | JACK OLIVER | | A |
| | GARY OSBORNE | | A |

45s:	The Sound Of The Summer/	
	The Only One In Sight	(Decca F 12649) 1967 SC
	Requiem/What's It To You	(Decca F 12704) 1967 SC

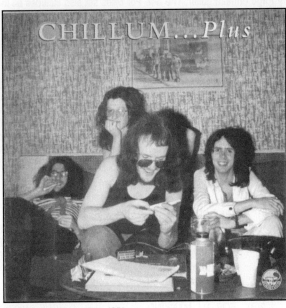

CHILLUM - Chillum... Plus (CD).

Not to be confused with the better-known US band of this name, this outfit played a pretty commercial form of pop which could easily have brought hit singles with slightly stronger material. These singles were the first productions by Sandy Roberton, who went on to work with **Shelagh McDonald**, **Synanthesia**, **Steeleye Span**, **Al Jones**, **Keith Christmas** and others. *Requiem* has got a further lease of life on *Broken Dreams, Vol. 5* (LP), *British Psychedelic Trip, Vol. 4* (LP) and *Great British Psychedelic Trip, Vol. 2* (CD), but it's one of several songs on this and many similar British sixties compilations which stretch the term 'psychedelic' beyond its limits. (VJ)

Choise

45:    Cecilia/She's A Man   (Page One POF 168) 1970

A Leicester band. The 'A' side of their 45 was a cover of the Simon and Garfunkel song. (VJ)

Chopyn

Personnel:	DENNY McCAFFREY	vcls	A
	SIMON COLCLOUGH	gtr	A
	CLYDE McMULLEN	bs, vcls	A
	ANN ODELL	keyb'ds, vcls	A
	SIMON PHILLIPS	drms	A
	RAY RUSSELL	gtr, vcls, sitar	A

ALBUM: 1(A) GRAND SLAM   (Jet LPO 8) 1975

| 45s: | In The Midnight Hour/Funky Lady | (Jet JET 751)1975 |
| | Wasting Time/If It Feels Good Do It | (Jet JET 752)1975 |

Chopyn was a studio-based heavy-rock band who recorded for Jet. Odell had been with **Blue Mink**, Russell with **Alan Bown** and Philips with Dana Gillespie. Indeed, Russell was a session guitarist of some note. Phillips left in September to tour with **Chris Farlowe and the Thunderbirds** and Odell went on to tour with the **Brian Ferry Band** in January 1977. (JM/BS)

Chords Five

Personnel:	GEOFF GILL	drms	A
	MAL LUKER	gtr	A
	JOHN 'ZEKE' LUND	bs	A
	MICK ROWLEY	vcls	A

45s:	I'm Only Dreaming/Universal Vagrant	(Island W1 3044) 1967 R2
	Same Old Fat Man/	
	Hold On To Everything You've Got	(Polydor 56261) 1968 R1
	Some People/Battersea Fair	(Jay Boy BOY 6) 1969 SC

This band also recorded as **The Smoke**. Their first two 45s are rare and quite sought-after, the first is uptempo beat in style, but the third is less interesting.

Compilation appearances include: *Universal Vagrant* on *Beat It* (3-CD) and *14 Groovy Sounds From The Blow Up* (LP); and *Some People* on *The Electric Lemonade Acid Test, Vol. 1* (LP) and *Sometimes I Wonder (CD)*. (VJ)

The Chosen Few

Personnel:	BUMPER BROWN	bs	A
	MICKEY GALLAGHER	keyb'ds	AB
	RON HOOD	vcls	A
	ALAN HULL	gtr, vcls	A
	TOMMY JACKMAN	drms	AB
	ERNIE BELL	vcls	B
	COLIN GIBSON	bs	B
	JOHN TURNBULL	gtr, vcls	B

45s: I Won't Be Around You Anymore/
Big City   (Pye 7N 15905) 1965 SC
So Much To Look Forward To/
Today, Tonight And Tomorrow   (Pye 7N 15942) 1965 SC

Originally formed in Newcastle in 1962. In their early days they played a mixture of compositions penned by Hull and Tamla covers at local residencies like The Key Clubs and Manhole. They also briefly had a Radio Luxembourg show. All four songs were written by **Alan Hull**. When **Hull** left to become a folk singer in 1965 (he later joined **Lindisfarne**) this prompted further line-up changes and the following year they evolved into **Skip Bifferty**.

Compilation appearances include: *Today Tonight and Tomorrow* on *The R&B Era, Vol. 1* (LP & CD); and *I Won't Be Around Anymore* and *So Much To Look Forward To* on *Ripples, Vol. 2* (CD). (VJ)

Peter Chris and Outcasts

Personnel incl: PETER CHRIS   A

45:   Over The Hill/
The Right Girl For Me   (Columbia DB 7923) 1966 R1

This is quite a collectable mid-sixties 45, probably because Joe Meek handled the production and wrote the 'B' side. The 'A' side was written by Mike Batory who also co-wrote **The Riot Squad**'s *It's Never Too Late To Forgive*, with Brian McKay. (MWh)

Hans Christian

45s: All Of The Time/Never My Love   (Parlophone R 5676) 1968 R1
(The Autobiography Of) Mississippi Hobo/
Sonata Of Love   (Parlophone R 5698) 1968 R2

These were both solo efforts by **Jon Anderson**, who was also with **Mabel Greer's Toy Shop** and **Yes**, so they're obviously now quite collectable and expensive items. His cover of The Association's *Never My Love* later resurfaced on *60's Back Beat* (LP) in 1985.

The name is related to the Danish poet who was best known for writing fairytales. (VJ)

Neil Christian and The Crusaders

Personnel:			
NEIL CHRISTIAN	vcls	ABCDEFG H	
TORNADO EVANS	drms	ABCD G	
JIMMY PAGE	gtr	A	
JUMBO SPICER	bs	AB	
ALBERT LEE	gtr	B	

PAISLEY POP (Comp CD) including Neil Christian and The Crusaders.

DAVID ANDERSON	bs	CD	G
TONY MARSH	piano	C	G
PHIL McPILL	gtr	C	
RITCHIE BLACKMORE	gtr	D	G H
MICK ABRAHAMS	gtr	EF	
DAVE CAKEBREAD	bs	E	
GRAHAM HALL	drms	E	
STAN THOMAS	sax	E	
ALEX DMCHOWSKI	bs	F	
CARLO LITTLE	drms	F	H
GRAHAM WALLER	keyb'ds	F	
MATT SMITH	piano		H
TONY DANGERFIELD	bs		H

EP: 1   LITTLE BIT OF SOMETHING ELSE
(Columbia SEG 8492) 1966 R2

NB: There are two retrospective compilations of his material, *That's Nice* (Repertoire REP 4164-WY) 1992 and *Neil Christian And The Crusaders 1962-1973* (See For Miles SEECD 342) 1992.

HCP

45s: The Road To Love/
The Big Beat Drum   (Columbia DB 4938) 1962 R1 -
A Little Bit Of Someone Else/
Get A Load Of This   (Columbia DB 7075) 1963 SC -
Honey Hush/One For The Money   (Columbia DB 7829) 1964 -
That's Nice/She's Got The Action   (Strike JH 301) 1965 14
Oops/She Said Yeah   (Strike JH 313) 1966 -
Two At A Time/Wanna Lover   (Strike JH 319) 1966 -
You're All Things Bright And Beautiful/
I'm Gonna Love You Baby   (Pye 7N 17372) 1967 SC -

This group were around for several years without ever achieving any notable success. As you can see several people passed through their ranks including a very youthful **Jimmy Page** prior to his years with **The Yardbirds** and **Led Zeppelin**. Later Albert Lee was in the line-up briefly but he left before the band made a disc. In 1965 many of the earlier members joined **Lord Sutch's Savages** and **Christian** pulled in an entirely new line-up, taking over a Luton group called The Hustlers. Their most successful song was *That's Nice*, which made the UK Top 20. *Two At A Time* was a big hit for them in Germany where **Christian** developed a big following and went on to release material which never made it onto vinyl in the UK.

He later moved to Vogue for whom he recorded a 45 with a reformed Crusaders which included a certain **Ritchie Blackmore** on guitar and then to Metronome. In the early seventies he worked for **Young Blood** but none of the fruits of his labour got an airing at the time. He recorded a 45 for Satril in Germany and since then has worked spasmodically on the live circuit.

The Repertoire compilation contains all the UK singles, a German language version of his German hit *Two At A Time*, two German-only releases from 1969 and 1975 and a Crusaders' instrumental, *Crusading*, from 1964 with **Jimmy Page** on lead guitar. The See For Miles set also includes all the UK singles plus a 1962 pre-Columbia demo, *Feel The Mood*, and some hitherto unissued seventies cuts.

Compilation appearances have included: *Honey Hush* and *I Like It* on *James Patrick Page: Session Man, Vol. 2* (LP & CD); *Get A Load Of This*, *Honey Hush* and *Crusading* on *Jimmy Page Studio Works 1964-1968* (CD); *Crusading* on *Jimmy Page, Session Man* (CD); *Get A Load Of This* on *James Patrick Page, Session Man* (LP); *You're All Things Bright & Beautiful* on *Paisley Pop - Pye Psych (& Other Colours) 1966-1969* (CD); *I'm Gonna Love You Baby* on *Doin' The Mod, Vol. 2* (CD) and *Oops* on the 2-CD set *We Love The Pirates: Charting The Big 'L' Fab 40*. (VJ)

Christie

Personnel:			
MIKE BLAKELY	drms	A	
JEFF CHRISTIE	vcls, bs	ABC	
VIC ELMES	gtr	ABC	
PAUL FENTON	drms	BC	
LEN LUBIN		C	

ALBUMS: 1(B) CHRISTIE   (CBS 64108) 1970
2(B) FOR ALL MANKIND   (CBS 64397) 1971

NB: (1) reissued on CD (Repertoire RES 2304) 2005 with bonus tracks. (2) reissued on CD (Repertoire 2305) 2005.

			HCP
45s:	Yellow River/Down The Mississippi Line	(CBS 4911) 1970	1
	San Bernadino/Here I Am	(CBS 5069) 1970	7
	Man Of Many Faces/Country Sam	(CBS 7081) 1971	-
	Everything's Gonna Be Alright/		
	Freewheelin' Man/Magic Highway (PS)	(CBS 9130) 1971	-
	Iron Horse/Every Now And Then	(CBS 7747) 1972	47
	The Dealer/Pleasure And Pain	(CBS 1438) 1973	-
	Alabama/I'm Alive	(Epic EPC 2044) 1974	-
	Peace Lovin' Man/Picture Painter	( ) 197?	-
	Fools Gold/Born To Lose	( ) 197?	-
	Most Wanted Man In The USA/Rockin Suzanna	( ) 197?	-
Reissues:	Yellow River/Iron Horse	(CBS 1145) 1973	-
	Yellow River/(Flip by different artist)	(Epic 152315) 1975	-
	Yellow River/Iron Horse	(CBS 5960) 1978	-
	Yellow River/San Bernadino	(Old Gold OG 9301) 1983	-

A pop group best remembered for their No 1 hit *Yellow River*, a song originally written for **The Tremeloes** (who featured Mike Blakely's brother Alan). When **The Tremeloes** procrastinated Jeff Christie, who'd written the song, decided to record it himself and the rest is history. In fact the band was not formed until after *Yellow River* became a hit. It was recorded by Jeff Christie with backing by **The Tremeloes**. **Christie** had evolved out of **The Epics** and Jeff Christie himself had earlier been in several bands including **The Outer Limits**. Mike Blakely had been in **The Blossoms**. *San Bernadino*, another highly commercial song, gave them another Top Ten hit, but after one further minor hit *Iron Horse*, they faded from the spotlight. Their debut album comprised hummable country-pop that was too inoffensive to make much lasting impact. The recent Repertoire reissue features all three of their hit singles in an expanded format.

Blakely left in late 1970 and was replaced by Fenton. Trevor St John played with them for a short while (he went on to the oddly named Ragnarok) before Lubin joined. He'd been in **Unit 4 + 2** and a jazz-rock band called Satisfaction. Jeff Chrsitie moved to keyboards in this later line-up, which recorded the *Iron Horse* 45.

Their 45s *Man Of Many Faces*, *Magic Highway* and *Peace Lovin' Man* were all taken from their second album, *For All Mankind*. Aside from the title track, which has been described as outstanding, other strong tracks are *Picture Painter* (which recalls the mid-sixties **Who**) and *Martian King*. This album is very different to their debut with lots of extended riffing and bluesy guitar solos and the Repertoire reissue again adds lots of bonus tracks.

After they disbanded, Jeff Christie released two solo 45s: *Both Ends Of The Rainbow* and *Tightrope*. Fenton went on to **Carmen**.

Yellow River later resurfaced on *The Best Summer Ever!* (CD), *The Seventies, Vol 2* (CD), *Hits Of The 70's* (CD), *Hits Of The 70's Vol 3* (CD), the 2-CD set *Good Times - Best Of The 70's*, *Number 1 Hits Of The 70's & 80's* (CD) and on *UK No 1 Hits Of The 70's* (CD). (VJ/RC/JM)

David Christie

45:	Love And The Brass Band/	
	Penelope Breedlove	(Mercury MF 1028) 1968

Mike Warth tells me that, whilst the 'A' side is typical British commercial pop, the flip is an altogether more thoughtful quality pop song. (VJ)

Tony Christie (and the Trackers)

Personnel:	TONY CHRISTIE	vcls	A
	HARRY CROFT	gtr	A
	MICHAEL RYAL	bs	A
	BARRY WOOTTON	drms	A

45s:	Life's Too Good To Waste/	
	Just The Two Of Us	(CBS 202097) 1966
	Turn Around/	
	When Will I Ever Love Again?	(MGM MGM 1365)1967

	I Don't Want To Hurt You Anymore/	
	Say No More	(MGM MGM 1386) 1968
	My Prayer/I Need You	(MGM MGM 1440) 1968

No other details are known on this band. It could have included the **Tony Christie** who had the solo hits with *Is This The Way To Amarillo?* etc. (VJ/JM)

Tony Christie

				HCP
ALBUMS:	1	I DID WHAT I DID FOR MARIA		37
(selective)			(MCA MKPS 2016) 1971	
(up to	2	WITH LOVING FEELING	(MCA MUPS 468) 1973	19
1976)	3	TONY CHRISTIE - LIVE	(MCA MCF 2703) 1975	33
	4	BEST OF TONY CHRISTIE	(MCA MCF 2769) 1976	28

NB: There's also a CD The Best Of Tony Christie (Music Club MCCD 185) 1994.

			HCP
45s:	God Is On My Side/Thing Called Love	(MCA MK 5049) 1970	-
(up to	Las Vegas/?	(MCA MK 5049) 1970	21
1976)	I Did What I Did For Maria/		
	Give Me Your Love Again	(MCA MK 5064) 1971	2
	Is This The Way To Amarillo?/		
	Love Is A Friend Of Mine	(MCA MK 5073) 1971	18
	Don't Go Down To Reno/		
	Sunday Morning	(MCA MK 5089) 1972	-
	My Love Song/Celia	(MCA MK 5095) 1972	-
	Avenues and Alleyways/		
	I Never Was A Child	(MCA MKS 5101) 1973	37
	Life Without You/		
	Love And Rainy Weather	(MCA MU 1199) 1973	-
	You Don't Have The Magic Anymore/		
	By Tomorrow	(MCA MU 1217) 1973	-
	I Did What I Did For Maria/Don't Go	(MCA MCA 108) 1974	-
	Lover's Question/		
	Underneath The Covers	(MCA MCA 123) 1974	-
	Happy Birthday Baby/		
	Who Am I Fooling	(MCA MCA 157) 1974	-
	Easy To Love/Now My World Is Yours	(MCA MCA 212) 1975	-
	Drive Safely Darlin'/		
	Sweet Summer Souvenirs	(MCA MCA 219) 1975	35
	Queen Of The Mardi Grass/		
	Wall Of Silence	(MCA MCA 231) 1976	-
Reissue:	I Did What I Did For Maria/		
	Is This The Way To Amarillo?	(Old Gold OG 9212) 1982	-

Tony Christie was born as Anthony Fitzgerald on 25 April 1944 in Conisborough, Yorkshire. He became a professional pop singer in 1964 and his attractive voice attracted interest from songwriters Mitch Murray and Peter Callender who penned his first hit *Las Vegas*. *I Did What I Did For Maria* gave him a UK No 2 and *Is This The Way To Amarillo* (written by Howard Greenfield and Neil Sedaka) became a million-seller, topping charts across Europe. His *With Loving Feeling* album was well-received and he enjoyed a couple of further minor hits. He also appeared on the *Evita* soundtrack but by the eighties had switched to the cabaret circuit. He returned with a series of albums in the nineties. In 2005 he achieved a massive UK No 1 with a re-recorded version of *Is This The Way To Amarillo*, which became the biggest selling single of the year in the UK. (VJ)

Keith Christmas

ALBUMS:	1	STIMULUS	(RCA Victor SF 8059) 1969	R2
(up to	2	FABLE OF THE WINGS	(B&C CAS 1015) 1970	SC
1976)	3	PIGMY	(B&C CAS 1041) 1971	SC
	4	BRIGHTER DAY	(Manticore K 53503) 1974	SC
	5	STORIES FROM THE HUMAN ZOO		
			(Manticore K 53509) 1976	

NB: (1) with **Mighty Baby**.

Christmas made his debut album with members of **Mighty Baby**, played acoustic guitar on **David Bowie**'s second album and appeared at the first Glastonbury festival. During the seventies he toured with and supported acts like **The Who**, **King Crimson**, **Ten Years After**, Frank Zappa and **Roxy Music**.

In 1992 he released a blues album *Weatherman* and in 1996 *Love Beyond Deals* (HTD). In 1997 he started playing the folk circuit with his wife Julia (nee Julia Howe ex-*Divine Light*) as *Magic*. (VJ)

Chucks

EP: 1   THE CHUCKS   (Decca DFE 8562) 1964

                                                  HCP
45s: Loo-Be-Loo/Anytime Is The Right Time (Decca F 11569) 1963 22
       Mulberry Bush/That's All I Need   (Decca F 11617) 1963 -
       The Hitch-Hiker/Humpity Dumpity   (Decca F 11777) 1963 -

A session group with three girls put together by Ivor Raymonde, who sang the vocals on their sole hit *Loo-Be-Loo*.

The Hitch Hiker also appeared on *Ready, Steady, Go!* (LP). (VJ)

Chick Churchill

ALBUM: 1   YOU AND ME   (Chrysalis CHR 1051) 1973 SC

45:      Broken Engagements/
        Dream Of Our Maker Man   (Chrysalis CHS 2019) 1973

These were solo efforts by the former **Ten Years After** member. (VJ)

The Circles

Personnel: TONY DANGERFIELD   bs   A
           BRIAN KEITH   vcls   A
           CARLO LITTLE   drms   A
           BILL PARKINSON   gtr   A
           PAUL RAYMOND   organ   A

45:      Take Your Time/
        Don't You Love Me No More   (Island WI 279) 1966 R2

This 45 was made by **Screaming Lord Sutch**'s backing group The Savages recording under another name. (VJ)

CIRCUS - Circus (LP).

Circus

Personnel: CHRIS BURROWS   drms   A
           MEL COLLINS   sax   AB
           IAN JELFS   gtr, vcls   AB
           KIRK RIDDLE   bs   AB
           ALAN BUNN   drms   B

ALBUM: 1(A)   CIRCUS   (Transatlantic TRA 207) 1969 R1
NB: (1) issued on Metronome (15360) in Germany. Reissued on vinyl (Get Back GET 562) 1999. Reissued on CD (Essential ESMCD 926) 2000.

45s: α   Sink Or Swim/Gone Are The
          Songs Of Yesterday   (Parlophone R 5633) 1967 SC
          Do You Dream?/House Of Wood (Parlophone R 5672) 1968 R1
NB: α also in the USA (USA 903) 1968.

This band was first called The Stormeville Shakers. Their rare progressive album is now of minor interest to collectors. Mel Collins was later in **King Crimson** and **Kokomo**. **Philip Goodhand-Tait** had earlier recorded three 45s for Parlophone and after his spell with **Circus** he went on to record several solo albums. Chris Burrows had earlier played with **Ray Anton and The Proform**, and later had some involvement with **Spirit Of John Morgan** and **Arthur Brown**'s **Kingdom Come**.

Do You Dream? is a delightful piece of psychedelic pop and their first 45 was produced by **Mike D'Abo**.

Chris Burrows later became a Buddhist monk, releasing four CDs of Buddhist percussion/chanting for the New Beginnings label.

Compilation appearances have included: *Father Of My Daughter* and *Norwegian Wood* on *Children Of The Sun* (CD); *Don't Make Promises* on *The Transatlantic Story* CD box set; *Do You Dream?* on *Spinning Wheel, Vol 1* (CD) and *Sink Or Swim* on *Colour Me Pop, Vol 2* (CD). (VJ/SP/JM)

Cirkus

ALBUM: 1   CIRKUS ONE   (RCB 7) 1971 R3
NB: (1) reissued on Five Hours Back (TOCK 1) 1986 and also on CD with bonus tracks taken from the Melissa EP plus two extra tracks recorded in 1971 (Audio Archives AACD 009) 1995.

EP: 1   Melissa / Amsterdam / Pick Up A Phone
                                (Guardian GRCA 4) 1976 R2

The album is a significant collector's item among fans of progressive music. The Geordie band financed the album themselves and paid for 1,000 copies to be released. Musically it's competent progressive symphonic rock with mellotrons etc. very much in the mould of bands like **Yes**. The later reissue on Five Hours Back should be easier to obtain and will save you quite a lot of money. It retained the original gatefold sleeve and more recently the album has been issued on CD with bonus tracks. They also recorded a second album *Future Shock* (Shock SHOCK 1) (R1) 1977.

Amsterdam, which dates from 1976, can also be found on *Circus Days, Vol. 2* (LP) and *Circus Days, Vol. 3* (CD). It's certainly worth a spin as it contains attractive vocals and good choppy guitar work. (VJ/SP)

The Citations

45:      Moon Race/Slippin' And Slidin'   (Columbia DB 7068) 1963 SC

Although essentially an early sixties instrumental group, their manic version of Little Richard's *Slippin' And Slidin'* came with vocals and sax. (VJ/MWh)

City Boy

Personnel: STEVE BROUGHTON   ld vcls, gtrs, mandolin,
                              perc   A
           CHRIS DUNN   bs, vcls, acoustic gtr   A
           ROGER KENT   drms, perc   A

CIRKUS - Cirkus One (LP).

LOL MASON	ld vcls, perc	A
MIKE SLAMER	vcls, gtrs, perc	A
MAX THOMAS	vcls, keyb'ds, 12-string gtr, perc	A

ALBUMS: 1(A) CITY BOY (Vertigo 636 0126) 1976
(up to 2(A) DINNER AT THE RITZ (Vertigo 636 0136) 1976
1976)

NB: (1) issued in the US (Mercury 1098) 1976. (2) issued in the US (Mercury 1182) 1976.

45s: Shake My Head & Leave/Tele-hula (Vertigo 6059 128) 1975
(up to Surgery Hours/Deadly Delicious (Vertigo 6059 132) 1976
1976) Hap Ki Do Kid/Possessed (Vertigo 6059 137) 1976

Steve Broughton had previously been in the **Edgar Broughton Band**. Their first album features some acoustic guitar and vocal harmonies. They are usually considered to have been an art-rock outfit in the mould of **10CC** and Split Enz. They went on to make four further albums before dissolving in the early eighties. Their main claim to fame was a later hit single *5705* in 1978. (CG/VJ)

City Smoke

45: Sunday Morning/A Little Bit Of Love (Mercury MF 971) 1966

A short-lived pop outfit. Both sides of this 45 were written by Peter Morris, who was quite a prolific songwriter, also responsible for *Pictures Of Today* by Paul and **Barry Ryan** and other compositions by the likes of **Orange Seaweed**. (MWh)

City Waites

Personnel: LUCIE FINCH AB
JOSEPH SKEAPING A
ROD SKEAPING violin AB
DOUG WOOTON A
KEITH THOMPSON B

ALBUMS: 1(A) A GORGEOUS GALLERY OF GALLANT INVENTIONS
(EMI EMC 3027) 1974 R1
2(B) THE CITY WAITES (Decca SKL 5264) 1976 R1

45: The Fox/One Of My Aunts (EMI EMI 2149) 1974

An obscure outfit, whose albums are now very hard to find. Both albums consist of medieval folk influenced music.

They returned with a further album *How The World Wags* (Hyperion A 66008) in 1981. (VJ)

The Clague

45: Bottle Up And Go/Mandy Lee (Dandelion S 4493) 1970

This 45 was recorded on dee-jay John Peel's Dandelion label with assistance from **Kevin Coyne**. (VJ)

Clancy

Personnel: COLIN BASS bs, vcls AB
BARRY FORD drms, vcls AB
ERNIE GRAHAM gtr, vcls AB
GASPAR LAWAL perc, vcls AB
DAVE SKINNER keyb'ds, vcls AB
DAVE VASCO gtr, vcls AB
SAM MITCHELL dobro B
(JIM CUOMO sax AB)

ALBUMS: 1(A) SERIOUSLY SPEAKING (Warner Bros K 56103) 1975
2(B) EVERYDAY (Warner Bros K 56206) 1975

45s: Back On Love/Steal Away (Warner Brothers K 16491) 1974
(up to Baby Don't You Do It/
1976) Everything's Gonna Be Fine (Warner Brothers K 16579) 1975
Good Judgement/Leavin' Town (Warner Brothers K 16626) 1975
You Have Made My Life So Sweet/
Stealaway (Warner Brothers K 16760) 1976

Clancy were formed circa July 1973 by Ernie Graham (ex-**Eire Apparent**, **Help Yourself** and various solo ventures), Colin Bass (ex-**Foundations**, **Velvet Opera**), Dave Vasco (ex-**Foundations**, Johnny Johnson's Band-wagon), Jon Glemser (gtr,vcls) (ex-**Help Yourself**) and Steve Brendall (d) (ex-Matchbox). In September 1973, Brendall left and was replaced by George Butler (ex-**Uncle Dog**). The following December, Glemser was replaced by Dave Skinner (ex-**Uncle Dog**) and finally George Butler quit for McSmith and was replaced by Barry Ford (ex-**Noir**) and Gaspar Lawal (ex-**Graham Bell**).

Gasper Lawal played with virtually everybody during the seventies and early eighties including Joan Armatrading, **Babe Ruth**, **Vinegar Joe** and **Wishbone Ash**, to name but a few. Dave Skinner went on to work with **Bryan Ferry**, Phil Manzanera, the reformed **Roxy Music** and later Chris Rea. He was also part of **Twice As Much**. Colin Bass later played with **Pete Barden**'s **Camel** and **Steve Hillage**. Jim Cuono did some work with **Marianne Faithful** in the late seventies and was regularly featured as a session man on Charisma. In the late seventies, he got involved with Pacific Eardrum, the band fronted by Dave Macrae after the demise of **Matching Mole**, following **Robert Wyatt**'s accident. Barry Ford went on to a band called Merger.

File **Clancy** under pub-rock. (VJ/JM)

Eric Clapton

HCP
ALBUMS: 1 ERIC CLAPTON (Polydor 2383 021) 1970 17
(up to 2 ERIC CLAPTON AT HIS BEST
1976) (Polydor 2659 025) 1972 -
3 HISTORY OF ERIC CLAPTON (RSO 2659 012) 1972 20
4 ERIC CLAPTON'S RAINBOW CONCERT
(RSO 2394 116) 1973 -
5 461 OCEAN BOULEVARD (RSO 2479 118) 1974 3
6 THERE'S ONE IN EVERY CROWD
(RSO 2479 132) 1975 15
7 E.C. WAS HERE (RSO 2394 160) 1975 14
8 THE BLUES WORLD OF ERIC CLAPTON
(Decca SPA 387) 1975 -
9 NO REASON TO CRY (RSO 2479 179) 1976 8

NB: (1), (4) - (7) and (8) were all reissued by RSO in 1983. There are also CD compilations *The Best Of Eric Clapton* (Polydor 511 072-2) 1991; *The Early Clapton Collection* (Castle CCSCD 162) 1992, which was issued on vinyl in 1988, and *Cream Of Eric Clapton* (Polydor 833 519-2) 1987. (5) reissued on CD Polydor (839 874 2) 1989 and again as a 2-CD set (Polydor 9825246) 2004 with a bonus live disc to commemorate its 30th anniversary. (6) reissued on CD (Polydor 829 649 2) 1986, but deleted in 1988. (9) reissued on CD (Polydor 813 582 2) 1986, but deleted in 1988. Additional "remastered" CD reissues include: (5) (Polydor 5318212) 1996; (1)

as (Polydor 531819-2) 1996; (6) as (Polydor 531822-2) 1996; (7) as (Polydor 531823-2) 1996 and (9) as (Polydor 531824-2) 1996.

				HCP
45s:	α	Lonely Years/Bernard Jenkins	(Purdah 45-3502) 1966	R4 -
(up to	β	I Am Yours	(Polydor 2001 096) 1970	-
1976)		After Midnight/Easy Now	(Polydor 2001 096) 1970	-
		I Shot The Sheriff/Give Me Strength	(RSO 2090 132) 1974	9
		Willie And The Hand Jive/		
		I Can't Hold Out Much Longer	(RSO 2090 139) 1974	-
		Swing Low Sweet Chariot/		
		Pretty Blue Eyes	(RSO 2090 158) 1975	19
		Knockin' On Heaven's Door/		
		Someone Like You	(RSO 2090 166) 1975	38
		Hello Old Friend/All Our Pastimes (PS)	(RSO 2090 208) 1976	-
Reissues:		I Shot The Sheriff/Cocaine/		
		Knockin' On Heaven's Door (PS)	(RSO 880 1982	64
		I Shot The Sheriff/		
		Knockin' On Heaven's Door	(Old Gold OG 9586) 1986	-

NB: α with **John Mayall** 500 copies only. β Unissued.

Clapton was one of the very best rock guitarists of his generation and by the time he launched his solo career in mid-1970 he was an established star by virtue of his involvement in **The Yardbirds**, **John Mayall's Bluesbreakers**, **Cream** and **Blind Faith**.

Born on 30th March 1945 in Ripley, Surrey, **Clapton** was the product of a broken home. When his parents separated he was brought up by his grandparents who gave him his first guitar when he was seventeen and studying stained glass design at Kingston Art School. In these early days he did a bit of busking and developed an interest in the blues and R&B. By the end of 1962 he was working on a building site in the daytime and playing in local bands by night.

His career began to take off in 1963; he joined the London-based R&B band The Roosters in January, then spent two weeks with the Merseybeat-style **Casey Jones and The Engineers** in August before replacing lead guitarist **Tony 'Top' Topham** in **The Yardbirds** in October 1963. The group had recently taken over **The Rolling Stones'** residency at The Crawdaddy Club in Richmond and his playing ability and dress sense was soon instrumental in their and his development. It was also during his time with **The Yardbirds** that their manager Giorgio Gomelsky nicknamed him 'slowhand'. By March 1965 he'd become disillusioned by their movement away from R&B towards more commercial pop and he parted company with them - again working on a building site for a while before being invited to join **John Mayall's Bluesbreakers**. When **Mayall** later sacked him in July 1966 he formed **Cream** with **Ginger Baker** and **Jack Bruce**. This relationship brought considerable commercial success and made **Clapton** a superstar. During his time with **Cream Clapton** was much sought-after to play on other session musician's albums. Credits included The Mother Of Invention's *We're Only In It For The Money*, **George Harrison**'s *Wonderwall Music* and his *While My Guitar Gently Weeps* (on **The Beatles'** *White Album*).

PAISLEY POP (Comp CD) Including Neil Christian and The Crusaders.

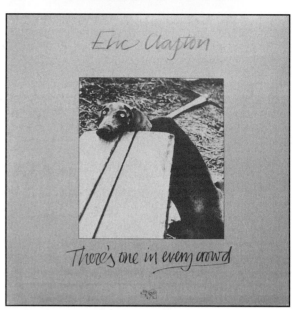

ERIC CLAPTON - There's One In Every Crowd (LP).

Cream eventually disbanded in November 1968 and in February 1969 he formed the disappointing and short-lived **Blind Faith** with **Ginger Baker** and **Stevie Winwood**.

After **Blind Faith**'s demise in January 1970 he joined and helped finance American white gospel duo "Delany and Bonnie and Friends" US tour appearing on the associated album. He recorded his first solo album in LA in March 1970, *Eric Clapton* with assistance from the touring band. The album eventually climbed to No 17 in the UK and No 30 in the US.

In June 1970 he formed **Derek And The Dominoes**. They played on **George Harrison**'s *All Things Must Pass* album with Phil Spector producing and went on to record a double album which was patchy but did include some of **Clapton**'s finest music. In October 1970 his version of J.J. Cale's *After Midnight* (from the *Eric Clapton* album) gave him a Top 20 US hit, peaking at No 18.

After an unsatisfactory live album **Derek and The Dominos** split up in May 1971 and **Clapton**, who was by now suffering from heroin addiction, withdrew from the public eye until 1974, except for his performance at **George Harrison**'s Bangla Desh concert in August 1971, an unannounced guest appearance at Leon Russell's concert at London's Rainbow Theatre in December of that year and his own concert at London's Rainbow Theatre on 13 January 1973 which was organised for him by **The Who**'s **Pete Townshend**. The concert was recorded and released as *Eric Clapton's Rainbow Concert*, but the end result was unsatisfactory and **Clapton** remained a recluse. By the end of the year though **Clapton** sought assistance from an electro-acupuncture therapist to overcome his heroin addiction. It almost certainly saved his life.

During **Clapton**'s period in exile a number of compilations were released to help maintain interest in his music. The first of these, *The History Of Eric Clapton*, was a collection of his work with **The Yardbirds**, **John Mayall's Bluesbreakers**, **Cream**, **Blind Faith**, **Derek and The Dominos** and Delaney and Bonnie. It sold best in the States, where it rose to No 6, but also got to No 20 here, where *Layla* (his finest moment) climbed to No 7 in the 45 Charts. Polydor, meanwhile, released *Eric Clapton At His Best*, a collection of songs from the *Eric Clapton* and *Layla* albums, which reached No 87 in the US, where the 45 *Let It Rain* was also a minor hit. Later in February 1973 Polydor put out a second retrospective album, simply titled *Clapton*, which again sold better in the States where it climbed to No 67 and the 45 *Bell Bottom Blues* got to No 78.

He returned in 1974 with a new group - Yvonne Elliman (vcls), Jamie Oldaker (drms), Carl Radle (bs), Dick Sims (keyb'ds) and George Terry (gtr) and a new album *461 Ocean Boulevard*. The album, which topped the US Charts and got to No 3 here, established him as a significant singer and songwriter and featured his biggest hit single of the seventies, a version of Bob Marley's *I Shot The Sheriff*, which topped the US Charts and peaked at No 9 here. The album was also successful in overcoming the guitar hero image which he was so keen to rid himself of.

There's One In Every Crowd (US No 21, UK No 15), released in Spring 1975, can be seen as a consolidation of the progress made by the previous album. He toured the World extensively that year and achieved further UK hits with his interpretation of the spiritual *Swing Low Sweet Chariot* and *Knockin' On Heaven's Door*. However, the live album *E.C. Was Here* was disappointing (his popularity ensured it got to No 14 here and No 20 in the US) and evidence that his recorded output remained erratic in quality.

The Blues World Of Eric Clapton includes tracks from his days with **John Mayall**, plus other rarities from early recordings he did with Otis Span and Champion Jack Dupree. The outstanding cut on the album is a live version of *Stormy Monday Blues* by The Bluesbreakers.

His 1976 *No Reason To Cry* album included guest appearances from Bob Dylan and The Band. It peaked at No 8 here and No 15 in the US. Later in the year **Clapton** returned the compliment by performing *Further On Up The Road* at The Band's "The Last Waltz" farewell concert. He also made a number of session appearances that year.

The Best Of Eric Clapton CD compilation contains most of his best known recordings from the seventies:- *Layla*, *I Shot The Sheriff*, *Knockin' On Heaven's Door*, *After Midnight*, *Badge* and *Sunshine Of Your Love* all figure.

Polydor reissued *461 Ocean Boulevard* as a 2-CD set with a bonus disc to commemorate its 30th anniversary. The bonus disc is compiled from concerts **Clapton** embarked on across the UK (including two Hammersmith Odeon gigs) to promote the album.

Erratic and overrated (in my view his best work was with **Cream** and **Derek and The Dominos**) **Clapton** has continued to record, with varying degrees of success, until the present day.

Back in 1971 he was included on Polydor's compilation *Bombers* (LP) playing *After Midnight*. Earlier in 1967 he'd played *Lonely Years* and *Bernard Jenkins* on Ace Of Club's *Raw Blues* (LP) (and supported by Powerhouse) and *I Want To Know*, *Crossroads* and *Steppin' Out* on Elektra's 1967 *Good Time Music* (LP). Decca's 1969 *World Of Blues Power* included him playing *All Your Love* and *Steppin' Out*, and, finally, *Rock Party* (LP) includes *Bottle Of Red Wine*. More recently *Prime Cuts* (LP) includes *Smile*.

Retrospective compilation appearances include: *Draggin' My Tail*, *Miles Road*, *Freight Loader*, *Choker*, *Snake Drive*, *Tribute To Elmore* and *West Coast Idea* on *Jimmy Page Studio Works 1964-1968* (CD) and *Jimmy Page - Hip Young Guitar Slinger* (Dble CD). (VJ)

Dave Clark Five

Personnel:	DAVE CLARK	drms	A
	LENNY DAVIDSON	gtr, vcls	A
	RICK HUXLEY	bs	A
	DENNY PAYTON	sax	A
	MIKE SMITH	keyb'ds, vcls	A

DAVE CLARKE FIVE - 25 Thumping Great Hits (LP).

ALBUMS:
1(A)	A SESSION WITH THE DAVE CLARK FIVE (Columbia 33SX 1598) 1964 R1 3
2(A)	THE DAVE CLARK FIVE AND THE WASHINGTON DC'S (Ember FA 2003) 1964 R1 -
3(A)	CATCH US IF YOU CAN (Soundtrack) (Columbia SX 1756) 1965 R1 8
4(A)	THE DAVE CLARK FIVE'S GREATEST HITS (Columbia SX 6105) 1967 SC -
5(A)	EVERYBODY KNOWS (Columbia SX 6207) 1968 R1 -
6(A)	5 BY 5 1964 - 1969: 14 TITLES BY DAVE CLARK (Columbia SX 6309) 1968 R1 -
7(-)	IF SOMEBODY LOVES YOU (Columbia SCX 6437) 1971 SC -
8(A)	PLAYS GOOD OLD ROCK 'N' ROLL (Starline SRS 5090) 1971 -
9(A)	25 THUMPING GREAT HITS (Polydor POLTV 7) 1978 7

NB: (1) reissued on Music For Pleasure (MFP 1260) in 1968. (8) reissued on Music for Pleasure (MFP 50197) in 1972. *Glad All Over Again* (EMI CDEMTV 75) 1993 is a CD compilation of his hits. (7) **Dave Clark** solo.

EPs:
1(A)	THE DAVE CLARK FIVE (Columbia SEG 8289) 1964 SC
2(A)	THE HITS OF DAVE CLARK FIVE (Columbia SEG 8381) 1965 SC
3(A)	WILD WEEKEND (Columbia SEG 8447) 1965 R1

NB: Teen Scene '64 (Ember EM 4540) 1964 also included two tracks by the band.

45s:
Chaquita/In Your Heart	(Ember EMB S 156) 1962 R1 -
I Knew It All The Time/ That's What I Said	(Piccadilly 7N 35500) 1962 R1 -
First Love/I Walk The Line	(Piccadilly 7N 35088) 1962 R1 -
The Mulberry Bush/Chaquita	(Columbia DB 7011) 1963 SC -
Do You Love Me/Doo-Dah	(Columbia DB 7112) 1963 30
Glad All Over/I Know You	(Columbia DB 7154) 1963 1
Bits And Pieces/All Of The Time	(Columbia DB 7210) 1964 2
Can't You See That She's Mine/ Because	(Columbia DB 7291) 1964 10
Thinking Of You Baby/ Whenever You're Around	(Columbia DB 7335) 1964 26
Any Way You Want It/ Crying Over You	(Columbia DB 7377) 1964 25
Everybody Knows (I Still Love You)/ Say You Want Me	(Columbia DB 7453) 1965 37
Reelin' and Rockin'/ Little Bitty Pretty One	(Columbia DB 7503) 1965 24
Come Home/Mighty Good Loving (Some PS)	(Columbia DB 7580) 1965 SC/- 16
Catch Us If You Can/Move On	(Columbia DB 7625) 1965 5
Over And Over/I'll Be Yours	(Columbia DB 7744) 1965 45
Try Too Hard/All Night Long	(Columbia DB 7863) 1966 -
Look Before You Leap/ Please Tell Me Why	(Columbia DB 7909) 1966 50
Nineteen Days/I Need Love	(Columbia DB 8028) 1966 -
You Got What It Takes/ Sitting Here Baby	(Columbia DB 8152) 1967 28
Tabatha Twitchit/Man In A Pin-Striped Suit (Some in export PS)	(Columbia DB 8194) 1967 SC/-
Everybody Knows/ Concentration Baby	(Columbia DB 8286) 1967 2
No One Can Break A Heart/ You Don't Want My Lovin'	(Columbia DB 8342) 1968 28
The Red Balloon/Maze Of Love	(Columbia DB 8465) 1968 7
Live In The Sky/Children	(Columbia DB 8505) 1968 39
Mulberry Tree/Small Talk	(Columbia DB 8545) 1969 -
α Get It On Now/Maze Of Life	(Columbia DB 8591) - -
Put A Little Love In Your Heart/ 34-06	(Columbia DB 8624) 1969 31
Good Old Rock'n'Roll Medley Part 1 & 2 (PS)/ Good Old Rock'n'Roll Medley Part 1 & 2 (PS)	(Columbia DB 8638) 1969 7
Everybody Get Together/ Darling I Love You	(Columbia DB 8660) 1970 8
Julia/Five By Five	(Columbia DB 8681) 1970 -
β Here Comes Summer/ Break Down And Cry	(Columbia DB 8689) 1970 44
More Good Old Rock'n'Roll Medley Parts 1 & 2 (PS)/	

CLARK-HUTCHINSON - A=MH² (LP).

More Good Old Rock'n'Roll Medley		
Parts 1 & 2 (PS)	(Columbia DB 8724) 1970	34
Southern Man/		
If You Wanna See Me Cry	(Columbia DB 8749) 1970	-
Won't You Be My Lady/		
Into Your Life	(Columbia DB 8791) 1971	-
All Time Greats Medley/		
Wild Weekend (PS)	(Columbia DB 8963) 1972	-
Everybody Knows/Always Me (PS)	(Polydor 2058 953) 1977	-

NB: α Unreleased but acetates do exist. β Reissued on EMI (2307) in 1975.

The Dave Clarke Five was one of Britain's top beat groups - indeed for two or three years it was among the biggest pop bands in the world.

The origins of this band go back to 1958 when **Dave Clark** (born in Tottenham, London on 15 December 1942) and a bassist called Chris Walls advertised in 'Melody Maker' for musicians to form a band. The original line-up consisted of **Clark**, Walls, Rick Huxley on rhythm guitar, Mick Ryan on lead and a singer/sax player Stan Saxon. Operating as **The Dave Clark Five featuring Stan Saxon**, Walls was the first to depart, with Rick Huxley switching to bass and Mike Smith being recruited on keyboards/vocals. When Stan Saxon failed to appear one night, Mike Smith took over lead vocals and further shake-ups in personnel occurred with Denny Payton joining and Lenny Davidson eventually replacing Mick Ryan, who'd quit to become a doctor. According to Peter Bruce (the original guitarist with successful Australian band The Groop), Bruce also had a spell in the embryonic band (when they were called The Dave Clark Six), after emigrating to the UK. By 1961, however, the line-up had stabilised and the band was on track for a highly successful career.

Their first recording was *Chaquita*, an instrumental which **Dave Clark**, who proved to be an astute businessman over the years sold the master of to Ember Records in 1962. They released it in August, but meanwhile the band had signed to Pye's Piccadilly label and released the vocal single *I Knew It All The Time*. The follow-up was another instrumental, *First Love*, but again made little impression and the Piccadilly deal was terminated.

It could have been a future of complete obscurity for the band but an EMI A&R man spotted them playing at their residency, the Municipal Baths, and signed them up to EMI's Columbia label. Their first record, a rock version of a nursery rhyme, *The Mulberry Bush*, didn't Chart, but their next release, a cover of The Contour's *Do You Love Me?*, crept into the UK Top 30, although **Brian Poole and The Tremeloes** concurrent release of the same song made No. 1.

Next came the two records for which the band are best remembered, although by now they'd already won the Mecca Gold Cup being voted the best band of 1963 on the ballroom circuit. *Glad All Over*, released in late 1963, written by **Clark** and Smith, had immediate commercial appeal and a pounding beat. It knocked **The Beatles**' *I Want To Hold Your Hand* from the top of the Charts and prompted speculation in the press that London would replace Liverpool as the centre of the beat music revolution. The

follow-up, *Bits And Pieces*, was similar in style and every bit as good. It had a stomping break which inspired dancers to stomp their feet in time with the music and also led to it being banned by many ballroom managers who feared for their wooden dancefloors. It peaked at No. 2 in the UK.

1964 saw the release of their first album, *Session With The Dave Clark Five* in the UK and marked the beginning of their onslaught on America. On May 30th they appeared at New York's Carnegie Hall, followed by a slot on the 'Ed Sullivan Show' the following day. The tour was a phenomenal success. Indeed they went on to enjoy 24 U.S. hits over the next three years and for the first two of these rivalled **The Beatles** for popularity. Their U.S. discography is very different and included several U.S.-only albums, which would only have been available here as imports.

In 1965, partly inspired by **The Beatles**' successes, they made a film, 'Catch Us If You Can'. It was a success and had its risque moments. The title track made No. 5 in the U.K., where the soundtrack movie peaked at No. 8. In the US the movie was released as 'Having A Wild Weekend' and climbed to No. 15. The title track, still known as *Catch Us If You Can*, peaked at No 4.

In 1967 the band formed its own film company, Big Five Films, to make low-budget features and documentaries. The first, a profile of the band itself, was sold to U.S. TV.

Even with the onset of the psychedelic era their records still sold - they even peaked at No. 2 in December 1967 of that year with *Everybody Knows*, a ballad written by Les Reed and **Barry Mason**, on which Lenny Davidson sang lead. A couple of years later their medley, *Good Old Rock'n'Roll Parts 1 & 2* put them back in the Top 10 again. It featured rock oldies like *Blue Suede Shoes*, *Lucille* and *Long Tall Sally*. Their last U.K. Top 10 hit was *Everybody Get Together*, a cover of The Youngbloods' U.S. hippie anthem, *Get Together*. One of their most interesting latterday releases was the 45, *Southern Man*, a cover of the Neil Young composition treated very differently by the band.

When the band broke up in September 1970, Rick Huxley went on to join **The Barron Knights** for a short time. **Clark** continued to record with Mike Smith as **Dave Clark and Friends** and he also went to drama school and spent six years writing the musical 'Time'. In April 1986 it was premiered at London's Dominion Theatre with Cliff Richard in the lead role. It had a long and successful run with David Cassidy later taking over the lead.

Interestingly **Clark** ensured he owned the rights to all the band's songs. This enabled him to compile the 1978 *25 Thumping Hits* compilation himself and a CD compilation, *Glad All Over Again* in 1993. A boxed set with an anthology video to accompany it followed.

Ever the astute businessman **Clark** also purchased the rights to the 'Ready, Steady, Go!' TV shows back in the late sixties when the IBA gave Thames and London Weekend the London TV franchise and all the old Rediffusion shows were canned. Later in the eighties he sold some of the shows to the Japanese video market and he also sold a limited number to Channel 4.

CLARK-HUTCHINSON - Retribution (CD).

Clark has resisted all pressure, including several lucrative offers, to reform the band. In any case, their place in the annals of rock history is assured as one of Britain's top beat groups - indeed for two or three years they were among the biggest pop bands in the world.

Compilation appearances on Various Artists' albums have included *I Walk The Line* on Marble Arch's 1970 *Hitmakers* (LP); *That's What I Said* on Pye *Golden Guinea's Package Tour* (LP); *I Knew It All The Time* on Sequel's two-CD set, *The Piccadilly Story*; *Come Home* on *Liverpool '65* (LP); *Do You Love Me* on *Twist A La Star Club* (LP); *Maze Of Love* on *Electric Sugar Cube Flashbacks* (CD); *Electric Sugar Cube Flashbacks, Vol. 4* (LP) and *Jagged Time Lapse, Vol 3* (CD); *Concentration Baby* on *Jagged Time Lapse, Vol 1* (CD); *Look Before You Leap* and *Over And Over* on *Go... With An All Star* (LP) and *Five By Five* on *Jagged Time Lapse, Vol 4* (CD). (VJ/JM/JN)

Dave Clark and Friends

Personnel incl:
DAVE CLARK		A
MIKE SMITH		A

ALBUM: 1(A) DAVE CLARK AND FRIENDS
(Columbia SCX 6494) 1972 SC

45s:	Draggin' The Line/One-Eyed Blues Suited,	
	Gun Totin' Man	(Columbia DB 8834) 1971
	Think Of Me/Right Or Wrong	(Columbia DB 8862) 1972
α	Rub It In/I'm Sorry Baby	(Columbia DB 8907) 1972
	Sweet City Woman/Love Comes But Once	(EMI EMI 2013) 1973
	Sha-Na-Na-Na / I Don't Know	(EMI EMI 2082) 1973

NB: α reissued on EMI (EMI 2205) in 1974.

After the demise of the **Dave Clark Five**, **Clark** and Smith recorded under this name. *Draggin' The Line* was a cover of a Tommy James US hit and *Sweet City Woman* had earlier been a US hit for the Stampeders.

After their demise Mike Smith became involved in promotional work and wrote commercial jingles. He also figured briefly in a duo with ex-**Manfred Mann** vocalist **Mike D'Abo**. **Clark**'s later exploits are covered in the **Dave Clark Five** entry. (VJ)

Clark-Hutchinson

Personnel:
ANDY CLARK	vcls, keyb'ds	AB
MICK HUTCHINSON	gtr	AB
STEPHEN AMAZING	bs	AB
DEL COVERLY	perc	B

ALBUMS:	1(A)	A = MH²	(Decca Nova (S)DN-R 2) 1970 R1
	2(A)	RETRIBUTION	(Deram SML 1076) 1970 R1
	3(B)	GESTALT	(Deram SML 1090) 1971 R1
	4(C)	BLUES	(Little Wing LW 2042) 1994 SC

NB: (1) and (2) issued on Nova in Germany and (1) later reissued on Teldec in Germany in 1973. (3) reissued on CD (HF 9554) 199? (4) recorded in 1968, but not released until 1994.

This early seventies outfit was most notable for Mick Hutchinson's fine guitar work. Clocking in at 50 minutes their debut album was certainly good value in terms of length. It can only be recommended to those of you interested in clever guitar instrumentals. The band didn't deploy vocals and the tracks on this album are long, Eastern-influenced and slightly mystical with titles like *Impromptu In 'E' Minor* and *Improvisation On An Indian Scale*. Hutchinson's and Clarke's other outfits included **Sam Gopal Dream**, **Vamp** and Dogs, which became **Clark-Hutchinson**.

'Ptolemaic Terrascope #9' contains an article about the band and Hutchinson also had one track, *Ragamag*, on the EP which accompanied the magazine.

The *Blues* album was recorded in 1968 before *A=MH2* and featured Andy Clark, Mick Hutchinson, Walt Monahan (bs) and Franco Franco (drms). It was released by the German label Little Wing.

Stephen Amazing and Andy Clark later played in a mid-seventies combo called **Upp**. (VJ)

CLARK-HUTCHINSON - Gestalt (CD).

The Classmates

45s:	Let's Get Together Tonight/It's No Game	(Decca F 11736) 1963
	Go Tell It On The Mountain/	
	Give Me A Girl	(Decca F 11779) 1963
	In Morocco/I Feel	(Decca F 11806) 1964
	Go Away/Pay Day	(Decca F 12047) 1964

A gospel beat group who attained no commercial success. (VJ)

Alasdair Clayre

ALBUMS:	1	ALASDAIR CLAYRE	(Elektra EUK 255) 1967 R1
	2	ADAM AND THE BEASTS	(Acorn CF 252) 1976 SC

NB: (2) reissued in 1978 on Folkways in the USA.

Alasdair Clayre was a brilliantly talented academic, novelist, poet and singer who won a highly prestigious prize fellowship of All Souls, Oxford on the strength of his outstanding performance in his final examinations. He'd been friends at Oxford with **Vashti Bunyan**, with whom he wrote her second and final single, *Train Song*. His debut was Joe Boyd's first production for Elektra in the UK, and followed the inclusion of two of his songs on the rare 1966 compilation *A Cold Wind Blows* (LP). It's an eccentric collection, much of which is mildly grating, though it contains beautiful tracks such as the spellbinding *Lullaby and Come Afloat*. Support comes from Leon Rosselson and Peggy Seeger, and the liner notes are by Iris Murdoch! His second album was made a decade later for a local Oxfordshire label, and features re-recordings of numerous tracks from his debut, alongside other material with a fuller electric backing and vocal support from Emma Kirkby. One of the founders of the Open University and a noted television producer, after his second album **Clayre** immersed himself in *The Heart Of The Dragon*, an epic television series and accompanying book about China. His perfectionism and fears about its reception contributed towards his much-lamented suicide under a London tube train in late 1984. The series went on to win a posthumous Emmy award.

According to Dr. Sidney Blatts's (sidney.blatt@yale.edu) excellent article "The Destructiveness of Perfectionism" Vol 32, No 12, pp 1004-1005, **"Alasdair Clayre**... was considered an all-around "golden boy" - someone who had not only academic abilities of the highest order, but who also represented the highest values of (Oxford) and excelled at sports.... **Clayre** had "manifold gifts" and was especially interested in moral philosophy... **Clayre** wrote several other books, produced television programmes, delivered lectures for the Open University, and for a while was a folksinger who published and recorded his own songs."

Clayre's best-known track *Adam And The Beasts* was covered by Shusha and **The Dransfield**s and his translation/arrangement of Jacques Brel's 'The Dove' was recorded by Joan Baez and Judy Collins. (RMJ/VJ/GB/JL)

ALASDAIR CLAYRE - Alasdair Clayre (LP).

The Clayton Squares

Personnel:	PETE DUNN	lead gtr	ABC
	MIKE EVANS	tenor sax	ABCDE
	TERRY HINES	vcls	AB
	ARTHUR MEGGINSON	bs	A
	BOBBY SCOTT	drms	ABCDE
	BROOK WILLIAMS	vcls, gtr	AB
	GEOFF JONES	bs	BCDE
	DENNY ALEXANDER	gtr, vcls	CDE
	LES SMITH	tenor sax	CD
	DAVE IRVING		D
	BARRY WOMERSLEY	lead gtr	DE
	ALBIE DONNELLY	tenor sax	E
	MIKE HART	gtr, vcls	
	ANDY ROBERTS	gtr	
	KARL TERRY	gtr	

| 45s: | Come And Get It/And Tears Fall | (Decca F 12250) 1965 R1 |
| | There She Is/Imagination | (Decca F 12456) 1966 R3 |

A short-lived Liverpool band, who arrived on the scene a little too late for their own good. They played a form of R&B with horns to the fore. Barry Womersley was ex-R&B Inc and **Big Three**, Mike Hart ex-**Roadrunners** and Karl Terry ex-Cruisers. Hart and **Roberts** later found a little more success accompanying **Scaffold** and in **Liverpool Scene** and Donnelly was later in the late seventies act Supercharge. **Roberts** also recorded solo albums. (VJ/AD)

Clear Blue Sky

Personnel:	MARK SHEATER	bs	A
	JOHN SIMMONS	gtr	A
	KEN WHITE	drms	A

ALBUM: 1(A) CLEAR BLUE SKY   (Vertigo 6360 013) 1971 R2

NB: (1) also issued in Europe as *Play It Loud*. (1) reissued on CD (Repertoire REP 4110-WP) 1990. *Destiny* (Saturn Records SRLP 101) 1990 comprises recordings made after their Vertigo album. Also of interest is *Out Of The Blue - Live And Unreleased* (Aftermath AFT 1009) 2002.

This hard-rock/progressive album is now quite sought-after by collectors. The semi-pro band from Acton, West London was discovered by **Patrick Campbell-Lyons** of **Nirvana**, playing in a local youth club. They were originally known as X. **Campbell-Lyons** signed them to Vertigo in 1970 and the three members were only eighteen when they recorded the above album. In Europe it was retitled *Play It Loud* and issued in a different sleeve.

They split in 1973 and John Simms went on to **Tangerine Peel**, The Needle, Separate Energy and ended up in **Ginger Baker**'s touring band.

Clear Blue Sky reformed in 1990 and they issued an album of post-1973 outtakes entitled *Destiny*.

In the nineties they reformed (Ted Landon (bs), Adam Lewis (keyb'ds) Kranet Montpellier (bs), John Simmons (gtr, vcls), Ken White (drms)) and released a CD, *Cosmic Crusader* (Aftermath) 1996.

Out Of The Blue released in 2002 is disappointing for its lack of sleevenotes or any information really considering it's intended to be a historically significant release.

They also had one cut, *Bird Catcher*, on Vertigo's 1971 *Heads Together, First Round* (2-LP) compilation. (VJ/PM)

Clearways

45:    I'll Be Here/I Just Got A Letter   (Columbia DB 7333) 1964

A short-lived beat group. They sang ballads and sounded similar to **The Applejacks**. (VJ)

The Climax (Chicago) Blues Band

Personnel:	COLIN COOPER	sax, vcls	ABCDE
	PETE HAYCOCK	gtr, vcls	ABCDE
	DEREK HOLT	bs	ABCDE
	GEORGE NEWSOME	drms	ABC
	ARTHUR WOOD	keyb'ds	ABC
	RICHARD JONES	bs, keyb'ds	B DE
	ANTON 'HUMPTY' FARMER	keyb'ds	C
	JOHN CUFFLEY	drms	DE

HCP

ALBUMS: 1(A)	CLIMAX CHICAGO BLUES BAND		
(up to		(Parlophone PMC/PCS 7069) 1969 R1 -
1976) 2(B)	PLAYS ON	(Parlophone PCS 7084) 1969 R1 -
3(C)	A LOT OF BOTTLE	(Harvest SHSP 4009) 1970 SC -
4(D)	TIGHTLY KNIT	(Harvest SHSP 4015) 1971 SC -
5(D)	RICH MAN	(Harvest SHSP 4024) 1972 SC -
6(E)	FM/LIVE	(Polydor 2883 259) 1974 -
7(E)	SENSE OF DIRECTION	(Polydor 2883 291) 1974 -
8(?)	STAMP ALBUM	(BTM 1004) 1975 -
9(B)	1969/72	(Harvest SHSM 2003) 1975 -
10(E)	GOLD PLATED	(BTM 1009) 1976 56

NB: Their albums were released on Sire in the US. Also relevant is *Loosen Up* (See For Miles CM 128) 1984, *Couldn't Get It Right* (C5 C5 508) 1988 (also on CD, See For Miles CD 222) 1988, and *Live Plus* (See For Miles 279) 1990, a reissue of (6) with two additional cuts:- *Let's Work Together* and *Standing By A River*. (6) was originally released as a double album in the US and the CD reissue (SEE CD 279) 1990 includes the full original double album. (3) reissued on CS (C5-548) 1990 with two additional cuts. (5) reissued on CD in Germany (Repertoire RR 4045-C) 1990. (1), (2), (4), and (5) reissued on C5 (C5 555, 556, 557 and 553 respectively) in

CLEAR BLUE SKY - Clear Blue Sky (CD).

CLIMAX CHICAGO BLUES BAND - Climax Chicago Blues Band (LP).

1990, all four are also available on CD. (1) reissued on vinyl (Akarma AK 142). (2) reissued on vinyl (Akarma AK 143). (8) reissued on CD (Repertoire) 1998. *The Harvest Years* (See For Miles SEE CD 316) 1991 is a 16-cut compilation of material from their first five albums.

45s:	Like Uncle Charlie/Loving Machine	(Parlophone R 5809) 1969 -
(up to	Reap What I've Sowed/Spoonful	(Harvest HAR 5029) 1970 -
1976)	Towards The Sun/Everyday	(Harvest HAR 5041) 1971 -
	Mole On The Dole/	
	Like Uncle Charlie	(Harvest HAR 5065) 1973 -
	Shake Your Love/You Make Me Sick	(Harvest HAR 5067) 1973 -
	Sense Of Direction/Bird To Whistle	(Polydor 2058 512) 1974 -
	Couldn't Get It Right/Fat Maybellene	(BTM SBT 105) 1976 10
Reissue:	Couldn't Get It Right/	(Old Gold OG 9642) 1986 -

Colin Cooper had earlier fronted **the Hipster Image**, who had recorded a rare single for Decca in 1965. Although their material, particularly in their early days, was strongly influenced by the Chicago blues scene they were, despite their name, from the Stafford area. They formed there in 1969 and were really 'Johnny Come Latelys' on the tail end of the British blues boom. This probably accounted for the band's low profile over most of their long career here in the UK, although *Shoot Her If She Runs* was included on the *Harvest Bag* (LP) compilation back in 1971.

The 'Chicago' was dropped from their name, but once the British blues boom eroded they concentrated on the American market and their albums achieved modest commercial success there in the seventies. By then, their original bassist Richard Jones had left (after their first album) to go to Cambridge University, although he later rejoined the band in 1975, after a spell in **Principal Edwards Magic Circus** the previous year.

The *Live/FM* album recorded in New York got to No 107 Stateside and they became big FM radio favourites but it wasn't until the release of the catchy and accessible *Couldn't Get It Right* that they were drawn to wider attention in the UK. Their *Sense Of Direction* Album climbed to No 37 in the States, where *Stamp Album* got to No 69 and *Gold Plated* was their most successful of all at No 27.

Always a tight sounding band they were unfortunate not to have achieved more success over here, although they continued to record well into the eighties. There's a See For Miles compilation of some of their 1974-76 material, *Loosen Up* with material from their *Sense Of Direction, Stamp Album* and *Gold Plated* albums. This shows them to have been more influenced by funk than the blues. For the most part the songs are pretty ordinary and uninspired. No better is the later compilation on C5 which confirms them as 'also-runs'. This is a view reinforced by C5's reissue of *A Lot Of Bottle*, which comes with two additional tracks: covers of Willie Dixon's *Seventh Son* and Muddy Waters' *Louisiana Blues*.

Compilation appearances include: *Looking For My Baby* on *Harvest Heritage - 20 Greats* (LP) and *Couldn't Get It Right* on *Classic Rock - cd2*. (VJ/JM/RMJ)

The Clique

Personnel:	PETER WESTGARTH	vcls	AB
	JOHNNY ROWE	lead gtr	AB
	TREVOR	drms	A
	JOHN KITCH	gtr	AB
	ADRIAN STAMBACH	bs	AB
	BRIAN MORRIS	drms	B

ALBUM:	1	THE COMPLETE RECORDINGS	
		(Dig The Fuzz Dig 003) 1996	

EP:	1	THE CLIQUE	(Private Pressing) 1964 R5

45s: She Ain't No Good/Time Time Time   (Pye 7N 15786) 1965 R2
We Didn't Kiss, Didn't Love, But Now We Do/
You've Been Unfair   (Pye 7N 15853) 1965 R3

This UK five-piece outfit was unconnected to the US band who made an album on White Whale. Their two 45s are now rare, expensive and sought-after, especially the second. The 'A' side to the first, *She Ain't No Good* was a mod-influenced song. The second, *We Didn't Kiss, Didn't Love But Now We Do*, was a highly-touted, experimental and rather bluesy effort, which now fetches very big money on the collector's market. When they toured Scotland in 1965 with new drummer Brian Morris they were under the management of Larry Page, who managed **The Troggs** and **The Kinks**. Page also produced their two 45s.

Prior to these 45s the band released a privately pressed promotional EP of which only a handful of copies were pressed. Its collectable value is in excess of £550. Fortunately, the four tracks it contained, along with a previously unreleased version of *Leaving Here* and *I Left My Heart* have been compiled alongside both 45s on the *Complete Recordings* retrospective.

Adrian Stambach had earlier been in The Cravattes with John Hector of the **Hammersmith Gorillas**. Although John Hector was not a member of **The Clique**, he did jam with them on many occassions, and this has led to rumours that he was once a member of the band.

Compilation appearances include: *We Didn't Kiss, Didn't Love But Now We Do* on *Maximum '65* (CD), *Rubble, Vol. 10 - Professor Jordan's Magic Sound Show* (LP), *The R&B Era, Vol. 1* (LP & CD); *She Ain't No Good* on *Watch Your Step - The Beat Era Vol. 1* (LP & CD); *She Ain't No Good* on *The Demention Of Sound* (LP), *English Freakbeat, Vol. 4* (CD); and *We Didn't Kiss, Didn't Love But Now We Do* and *She Ain't No Good* on *Freakbeat Freakout* (CD). (VJ/KM)

Clockwork Oranges

45: Ready Steady/After Tonight   (Ember S 227) 1966 SC

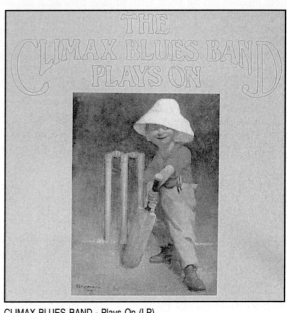

CLIMAX BLUES BAND - Plays On (LP).

THE CLIQUE - Complete Recordings 1964/1965 (LP).

A surf-mod four-piece. *Ready Steady* combines **Beatles** beat with Beach Boys style harmonies - quite an unusual song, which you can also find it on *Turds On A Bum Ride Vol. 4* (CD). (VJ)

The Clouds

Personnel:	IAN ELLIS	gtr, bs, vcls	A
	HARRY HUGHES	drms	A
	BILLY RITCHIE	keyb'ds, gtr, bs, vcls	A
	PETER BANKS	gtr,vcls	

ALBUMS:	1(A)	SCRAPBOOK	(Island ILPS 9100) 1969 R1
	2(A)	UP ABOVE OUR HEADS	(Deram DES 18044) 1969
	3(A)	WATERCOLOUR DAYS	(Island ILPS 9151) 1971 SC

NB: (2) US only. (3) issued on Deram in the USA. (1) and (3) reissued on one CD (Beat Goes On BGOCD 317) 1997.

45s:	Heritage/Make No Bones About It	(Island WIP 6055) 1969 SC
	Scrapbook/Carpenter	(Island WIP 6067) 1969 SC

A Scottish trio from Edinburgh, who were originally known as 1-2-3, they'd been renamed **The Clouds** by Terry Ellis after he'd become their manager and agent having spotted them playing in a tiny South London club. Although the title track of their debut album was heavily orchestrated much of the remaining material was in a progressive vein. The most commercial track, *I'll Go Girl*, was included on the *You Can All Join In* budget compilation ensuring considerable airplay. This was a pop song with nicely sculptured melodies and the album achieved some commercial success but the band's response was to record an album of stage favourites, *Up Above Our Heads*, which was only released in the USA and Canada. They toured with **Jethro Tull** and **Free** but *Watercolour Days* was a less satisfactory attempt to blend pop and progressivism and they split up soon afterwards. They also appeared on Island's 1970 compilation, *Bumpers* (2-LP), singing *Take Me To Your Leader*, which seemed to be publicised for 45 release in November 1969 but never appeared.

Peter Banks (ex-**Blodwyn Pig**) joined the band for a short time but then left to join **Flash**. Ellis departed for **Steamhammer** in April 1972 and was also in **Savoy Brown**. Hughes went on to a band called Mahatma Kane Jeeves. (VJ/JM)

Clover

An obscure group who have two versions of *Ice Cream Man*, which sounds like (but I'm not saying it was) an outtake from the **Keith West/Mark Wirtz** *Teenage Opera* project, on the *Circus Days* compilation series. The one on *Circus Days, Vol. 1* (LP) and *Circus Days, Vol. 1 & 2* (CD) is straight-forward pop. There's an alternate and better mildly psychedelic version of the same song on *Circus Days, Vol. 5* (LP) and *Circus Days*

Vol's 4 & 5 (CD). *Circus Days, Vol. 6* (CD) and *Circus Days, Vol. 5* (LP) also contains *Dream, Dream, Dream*, which is pure pop. A free EP (STFREE 301) given away with 'Strange Things Are Happening' magazine also included a version of *Ice Cream Man*.

This **Clover** were not the same band as the US bunch who relocated to the UK and which included Huey Lewis, (of Californian band Huey Lewis and The News and Elvis Costello fame). (VJ)

C.M.J.

ALBUM:	1	C.M.J. LIVE AT THE BANKHOUSE	
			(Impression IMPL 1001) 1969 R3
EP:	1	THE C.M.J. TRIO	(Impression EPIM 501) 1965 R2

45:	I Can't Do It All By Myself/	
	Nothing At All	(Impression IMP 102) 1968 R1
	La, La, La/Step Around It	(Mother MOT 3) 1971

A Worcester-based trio whose album and 45s were privately-pressed and the former, in particular, is expensive and sought-after by a few collectors. The album's an odd combination of psychedelic soul and ballads. Its finest moment, is a cover of *In The Midnight Hour*.

The second 45, isn't as sought-after as their earlier release and was reissued later again in 1971 year using the same number.

Compilation appearances have included: *I Can't Do It All By Myself* on *Return Of The Amphetamine Generation* (LP); and *In The Midnight Hour* on *Syde Trips, Vol. 4* (LP). (VJ)

Coast Road Drive

Personnel:	STEVE CHAPMAN	drms	A
	CHARLIE HARRISON	gtr, bs, vcls	A
	STEVE KRIEGER	gtr, vcls	A
	LES NICOL	gtr, vcls	A

ALBUM:	1(A)	DELICIOUS AND REFRESHING	
			(Deram SML 1113) 1974 R1

A laid back progressive album which now interests collectors. Steve Kreiger was the main writer and vocalist behind the band, somewhat in the style of Lowell George. Kreiger had previously been in the Californian US band The Grassroots. Nicol had been in **Kala**, Chapman in **Arrival** and Harrison's previous band was **Tundra**. Nicol also did some work with Dana Gillespie during the brief lifespan of this group. All except for Krieger moved on to back Leo Sayer. (VJ/JM)

THE CLOUDS - Scrapbook (LP).

COB - Spirit Of Love (LP).

COB (Clive's Original Band)

Personnel:	MICK BENNETT	perc, vcls, keyb'ds	AB
	JOHN BIDWELL	banjo, keyb'ds, vcls	AB
	CLIVE PALMER	banjo, vcls, gtr	AB
	RALPH McTELL	gtr, drms	AB
	STEVE BONNETT	bs	A
	URSULA SMITH	cello	A
	DANNY THOMPSON	bass	B
	DEMELZA VAL BAKER	perc	B
	GENEVIEVE VAL BAKER	perc, sax	B]

ALBUMS:	1(A)	SPIRIT OF LOVE	(CBS 69010) 1971 R1
	2(B)	MOYSHE McSTIFF AND THE TARTAN LANCERS OF THE SACRED HEART	
			(Polydor Folk Mill 2383 161) 1972 R3

NB: Both (1) and (2) have been counterfeited, the second in Italy. *Spirit of Love* is available on CD on BGO. *Moyshe McStiff* has recently been remastered and officially reissued on CD and vinyl by Radioactive.

45:	Blue Morning / Bones	(Polydor 2058 260) 1972 SC

After leaving **The Incredible String Band** because they were getting too far-out for him, **Clive Palmer** travelled to India, then moved to Penzance and immersed himself in the fertile local music scene, centring on the Folk Cottage club, outside Newquay. Having made an album with **The Famous Jug Band**, he formed the US country-styled Stockroom Five and Eastern-flavoured **Temple Creatures** before settling into a trio with vocalist Mick Bennett and multi-instrumentalist John Bidwell. They named themselves **Clive's Original Band** (*not* 'Clive's Own Band'), though the name was always shortened to COB, pronounced 'cob'. Living together in a caravan in the woods, they began to produce a haunting, mystical and deeply beautiful strain of folk music, much assisted by the dulcitar, an instrument invented by Bidwell and **Palmer** that combined the dulcimer and sitar to eerie, droning effect.

Their great friend and champion **Ralph McTell**, then at the peak of his own success, quickly found them a deal with CBS and produced their debut, **Spirit of Love**. A superb collection of predominantly original material, it appeared to rapturous reviews that December. Relocating to London, they gigged tirelessly, but when it didn't sell they moved to Polydor, which released their uncharacteristically jolly, reggae-tinged 45 the following June. Though that also failed to catch on, they returned to the studio in August to make their masterpiece, *Moyshe McStiff*. Again produced by **McTell**, its ten songs draw on Haile Selassie and The Old Testament as well as Middle Eastern and British folk traditions to create a spellbinding atmosphere of joy and sorrow, hope and resignation. Bennett's singing is powerfully moving throughout, and the musicianship is exemplary. It appeared in October, clad in a lurid gatefold sleeve depicting a dragon-slaying knight, and they embarked on a national tour with **Pentangle** to support it. It too failed to sell, however, and money troubles compelled them to split the following spring.

Palmer went on to several solo projects, including reunions with **The Incredible String Band**. Bidwell joined **Wizz Jones** in **Lazy Farmer** before leaving music for academia. Bennett remained in Cornwall, where he played in a wide variety of subsequent bands. **COB** have subsequently acquired a mystique and reputation that arguably outstrips that of any other contemporary UK folk act. The albums were near-impossible to obtain until the recent reissues appeared, and have served as a major inspiration to the current wave of US 'alt-folk' singers such as Devendra Banhart, Joanna Newsom and Espers.

Compilation appearances include: *Let It Be You* on *Electric Psychedelic Sitar Headswirlers, Vol. 1* (CD); and *Music Of The Ages* on *Electric Psychedelic Sitar Headswirlers Vol. 4* (CD). (RMJ/MK/VJ/JM)

Cochise

Personnel:	STEWART BROWN	vcls, gtr	A
	B.J. COLE	steel gtr	ABC
	MICK GRABHAM	gtr, keyb'ds, vcls	ABC
	RICK WILLS	bs, vcls	ABC
	JOHN WILLIE WILSON	drms	AB
	(STEVE MARRIOTT	piano, vcls	B)
	JOHN GILBERT	vcls	BC
	ROY O'TEMRO	drms	C

ALBUMS:	1(A)	COCHISE	(United Artists UAS 29177) 1970 SC
	2(B)	SWALLOW TALES	(Liberty LBG 83428) 1970 SC
	3(C)	SO FAR	(United Artists UAS 29286) 1972 SC

NB: (1) reissued on CD (Spiral SCD 935) 2002. (2) reissued on CD (Spiral SCD 936) 2002. (3) reissued on CD (Spiral SCD 937) 2002.

45s:	Watch This Space/	
	59th Street Bridge Song	(United Artists UP 35134) 1970
	Love's Made A Fool Of You/	
	Words Of A Dying Man	(Liberty LBF 15425) 1970
	Why I Sing The Blues/Jed Collder	(Liberty LBF 15460) 1971

This band is more significant for who they included than what they produced. **Grabham** had been in **Plastic Penny**, Brown in **Bluesology**, Wills and Wilson in **Jokers Wild**. Brown and Wilson left prior to the release of *Swallow Tales* but appeared on some tracks. John Gilbert and Roy O'Temro (ex-**Herbie Goins and the Nighttimers**) replaced them.

They played a distinctly British form of country-rock characterised by the steel guitar of **B.J. Cole** and the inspirational guitar playing of **Mick Grabham**. Their debut album sounds inspired by the then recently released Neil Young *After The Goldrush* album.

Swallow Tales is a mixture of hard-rock and subtle instrumental interplay.

COB - Moyse McStiff And The Tartan Lancers Of The Sacred Heart (CD).

So Far was released as they were splitting up. Its highlights include an adventurous cover of Crazy Horse's *Dance Dance Dance* and the final cut *Midnight Moonshine*.

After their demise in December 1971, **Mick Grabham** made a solo album in 1972 and joined **Procol Harum** the following year. **Cole** (who did a tour with **Tony Hazzard** whilst the group was still viable) joined the US group The Lee Riders, along with O'Temro. He also recorded a solo album in 1972 before becoming an important session musician. **Stevie Marriott** was in **The Small Faces** and **Humble Pie**. He also made solo recordings. Wills toured with **Parrish and Gurvitz** before joining **Peter Frampton** and Gilbert went on to **Pluto**.

Cochise have one cut, *Home Again*, on United Artists' 1971 compilation *All Good Clean Fun* (2-LP). (VJ/JM)

Dib Cochran and The Earwigs

Personnel: MARC BOLAN   gtr   A
             JOHN CAMBRIDGE   drms   A
             TONY VISCONTI   vcls   A
             RICK WAKEMAN   keyb'ds   A

45:     Oh Baby/Universal Love   (Bell BLL 1121) 1970 R5

This 45 is a major collector's item now but was totally ignored by the record buying public at the time of its release. It was a **Marc Bolan** project after **Tyrannosaurus Rex** and prior to the release of the first **T Rex** single *Ride A White Swan*. As you can see **Bolan**'s producer Tony Visconti handled the vocals and a youthful **Rick Wakeman** was the keyboardist. John Cambridge was **David Bowie**'s drummer. The teen-pop 45 really previewed **Bolan**'s new musical direction with **T Rex**, though it was also notable for its use of strings. (VJ)

Joe Cocker

ALBUMS:				HCP
(up to	1	WITH A LITTLE HELP FROM MY FRIENDS		
1976)		(Regal Zonophone SLRZ 1006) 1969 R1 -		
	2	JOE COCKER! (Regal Zonophone SLRZ 1011) 1969 R1 -		
	3	MAD DOGS AND ENGLISHMEN (2-LP)		
		(A&M AMLD 6002) 1971 16		
	4	COCKER HAPPY	(Fly HIFLY 3) 1971 -	
	5	JOE COCKER/WITH A LITTLE HELP FROM		
		MY FRIENDS (Double Back TOOFA 1/2) 1972 29		
	6	SOMETHING TO SAY	(Cube HIFLY 13) 1973 -	
	7	I CAN'T STAND A LITTLE RAIN (Cube HIFLY 18) 1974 -		
	8	JAMAICA SAY YOU WILL	(Cube HIFLY 20) 1975 -	
	9	STINGRAY	(A&M AMLH 64574) 1976 -	
	10	LIVE IN LA	(Cube HIFLY 23) 1976 -	

NB: Most of his albums were released by A&M in the US. (1) reissued on CD (Castle CLACD 172) 1990 and again (A&M 490 419 2) 2000, with two bonus tracks. (2) reissued on CD (A&M 490 420 2) 2000, with two bonus tracks. (3) reissued on CD (A&M 490 449 2) 2000, with two bonus tracks. (3) scheduled for release as 2-CD deluxe edition (Universal) 2006. (2) reissued on CD (Castle Communications CLACD 236) 1991. (3) reissued on CD (A&M CDA 6002) 1988. (4) reissued on CD (Castle Communications CLACD 238) 1991. (6) reissued on CD (Castle Communications CLACD 207) 1990. (7) reissued on CD (Castle Communications CLACD 144) 1989. (8) reissued on CD (Castle Communications CLACD 237) 1991. (8) and (4) reissued on one CD (That's Original TFOCD 4) 1988. (10) reissued on CD (Castle Communications CLACD 189) 1990. *Cocker Happy* (Castle CLACD 238) 1991 is a 12-track 'Best Of' compilation. *Connoisseur's Cocker* (Raven/Topic RVCD 16) 1991 concentrates on some of his more obscure album cuts and does not include his hit singles. *On Air* (Strange Fruit SFRCD 036) 1997 compiles material from a wealth of BBC recordings. *Anthology* (A&M 490 390 2) 2000 is a 2-CD set.

EP: 1   RAG GOES MAD AT THE MOJO
                        (Action ACT 002EP) 1967 R2

NB: (1) this 33 rpm EP featured two tracks by the Joe Cocker Blues Band and came free with 'Twikker', the Sheffield University rag magazine. Rumours that **Joe Cocker** recorded an EP for Oak in the sixties have never been substantiated.

			HCP
45s:	I'll Cry Instead/Precious Words	(Decca F 11974) 1964 R2 -	
(up to	Marjorine/		
1976)	The New Age Of The Lily	(Regal Zonophone RZ 3006) 1968 48	
	With A Little Help From My Friends/		

Something's Coming On	(Regal Zonophone RZ 3013) 1968 1
Delta Lady/	
She's So Good To Me	(Regal Zonophone RZ 3024) 1969 10
The Letter/Space Captain	(Regal Zonophone RZ 3027) 1970 39
Cry Me A River/Give Peace A Chance (PS)   (Fly BUG 3) 1970 -
High Time We Went/Black-Eyed Blues	(Fly BUG 9) 1971 -
Woman To Woman/Midnight Rider	(Cube BUG 25) 1972 -
Pardon Me Sir/She Don't Mind	(Cube BUG 28) 1973 -
Put Out The Light/If I Love You	(Cube BUG 47) 1974 -
Love Live On/On My Way To You	(MCA MCA 129) 1974 -
You Are So Beautiful/I Get Mad	(Cube BUG 57) 1975 -
It's All Over But The Shouting/	
Sandpaper Cadillac	(Cube BUG 61) 1975 -
Jealous Kind/You Came Along	(A&M AMS 7243) 1976 -
I Broke Down/You Came Along	(A&M AMS 7257) 1976 -

Reissues:	With A Little Help From My Friends/Delta Lady/	
	The Letter (PS)	(Magni Fly ECHO 103) 1972 -
	With A Little Help From My Friends/	
	Delta Lady	(Old Gold OG 9232) 1982 -
	You Are So Beautiful/Marjorine (PS)	(Cube BUG 97) 1983 -
	With A Little Help From My Friends/Marjorine/Delta Lady/	
	The Letter	(Archive 4) 1986 -

Joe Cocker was born as John Cocker in Sheffield on 20th May 1944. When he left school he worked initially as a gas fitter and played in his brother Victor's skiffle group The Cavaliers at night. By 1963 The Cavaliers had changed name to **Vance Arnold and The Avengers** and **Cocker** was fronting them as their vocalist.

In 1964, following an audition in Manchester, the band was offered a contract by Decca and travelled down to Decca's London studio to record. In the event Decca liked **Cocker**, but not the band and he ended up recording a solo 45, a cover of **Lennon/McCartney**'s *I'll Cry Instead*. **The Ivy League** and session guitarist Big Jim Sullivan supplied the backing but the 45 flopped. Thereafter **Cocker** briefly joined The Big Blues, touring the UK and US army bases in France before returning back to Sheffield to his own job. His career was dormant for a while but then in 1965 he formed **The Grease Band** with Chris Stainton. The band played soul material in pubs and clubs all over the North of England for the next year or so. Its first recording, a live version of the blues standard, *Saved*, appeared on a free flexi-disc given away with 'Twikker', the Sheffield University rag magazine in 1966.

The Grease Band began experimenting with original material during 1967 and a demo of *Marjorine* was passed to producer Denny Cordell via a Chesterfield dee-jay. This led to another recording opportunity, although of the other **Grease Band** members only Chris Stainton was allowed to play on the session. The remaining instrumentation was provided by none other than **Jimmy Page** and Albert Lee on guitars and **Clem Cattini** on drums. *Marjorine* just crept inside the UK Top 50.

For his follow-up **Cocker** recorded a distinctive cover of **The Beatles**' *With A Little Help From My Friends* which shot him to the top of the UK Charts and reached No 68 in the US. It seemed **The Beatles** liked his effort, too,

JOE COCKER.

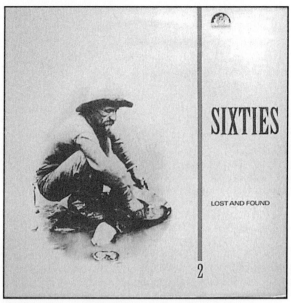
SIXTIES LOST AND FOUND VOL. 2 (LP) including Joe Cocker.

for they sent him a congratulatory telegram and placed adverts in the music press, praising his effort. It was certainly a powerful gutbucket vocal performance. His debut album, on which he was assisted by **Jimmy Page** and **Stevie Winwood**, was a mixture of **Cocker**/Stainton originals and **Cocker**'s unique interpretations of other people's songs.

In August 1969 **The Grease Band** underwent some personnel changes with Kenny Slack (drms) leaving for session work and Tommy Eyre (keyb'ds) joining **Aynsley Dunbar**. Alan Spenner (bs) and Bruce Rowlands (drms) came in and the band headed for a US tour which included an appearance at the 'Woodstock Festival', which was captured on the album and film of the festival and was the zenith of **Cocker**'s career. **Cocker** delivered another fine vocal performance on the *Joe Cocker* album. It was recorded in LA at A&M studios under supervision from Leon Russell (whom **Cocker** had met at Woodstock) and Denny Cordell. Inexplicably it only sold a few thousand copies over here but in the States it reached No 11. **Cocker**'s recording of Russell's *Delta Lady* did give him another Top 10 UK hit but sadly it was his last with **The Grease Band**. They and **Cocker** parted company just prior to a US tour in early 1970.

With help from Russell and Cordell **Cocker** assembled an ungamely array of 21 musicians which became known as Mad Dogs and Englishmen. They honoured **Cocker**'s US tour commitment in a private aircraft, recorded a live double album and there was also a feature film of the tour. They also managed some hits with a cover of The Box Tops' *The Letter; Cry Me A River* (No 11 in the US); and a double-A side *High Time We Went/Black-Eyed Blues* (US No 22).

The *Cocker Happy* album, released in 1971, was a compilation of his early hits. **Cocker** was by now thoroughly sick of the music business but in early 1972 he was persuaded out of hibernation to front the **Chris Stainton Band**. They toured the UK as a 12-piece **Joe Cocker** and The **Chris Stainton Band**. By now though, **Cocker** was the worse for wear, often unable to remember his words. He was arrested for dope possession in Australia and was consequently unable to tour the US. The group, which had managed a poor album, *Something To Say*, and a US hit single, *Midnight Rider/Woman To Woman*, soon fell apart after this tour.

By now **Cocker** was very wasted - unable to cope, it seems, with his sudden rise to fame; he had become a classic case of drug and alcohol abuse. The final effort from his collaboration with **Chris Stainton** was *Pardon Me Sir*, which was a minor hit in the US but when **Stainton** joined **Tundra Cocker** headed for LA. There, producer Jim Price attempted to revive his career. Although he was well past his prime he did achieve further success in the US. By contrast in Britain he was very much a 'has been'. He proceeded through various incarnations of **Joe Cocker Band**'s and then in 1976 formed **Joe Cocker** and Stuff with some of the finest session men in New York. They perfected a sorta soul-funk style and the resulting album, *Stingray*, marked a return to form. This line-up played 62 dates across America and at a festival in Marseilles. Inevitably only a short-term venture, this split up at the end of 1976 as we reach the end of this book's time span but Joe continued to record with various bands throughout the seventies and eighties.

He continued to enjoy chart success in the nineties, although with less frequency than in the seventies and eighties. He continues to work in the new millennium and recent albums have been *Respect Yourself* (2002) and a covers album *Heart And Soul* (2004).

Anthology (2000) is a 2-CD set which mostly concentrates on compiling material from his first three albums.

Compilation appearances have included:- *With A Little Help From My Friends* on *The Woodstock Generation* (CD) 1994; *Marjorine, With A Little Help From My Friends* and *Bye Bye Blackbird* on *Jimmy Page Studio Works 1964-1968* (CD); *I'll Cry Instead, Precious Words* and *Something's Coming On* on *Jimmy Page, Session Man* (CD); *I'll Cry Instead* on *Pop Inside The '60s, Vol. 2* (CD), *Sixties Lost And Found, Vol. 2* (LP), *Sixties Explosion, Vol. 1* (CD), *The Beat Scene* (CD) and *Hard-Up Heroes* (2-LP); and *Precious Words* on *British R'n'B Explosion, Vol. 1* (CD) and *The Soul Of British RnB 1962-1968* (CD). (VJ)

The Cockneys

45s: α After Tomorrow/I'll Cry Each Night   (Philips BF 1303) 1964 SC
I Know You're Gonna Be Mine/
Oh No You Won't   (Philips BF 1360) 1964 SC
NB: α reissued on Philips (1338) 1964 (SC).

Apparently, this beat band wore pearly king costumes on stage. (VJ)

Cocktail Cabinet

Personnel:	GEORGE BROWN	piano	A
	PHIL COULTER		A
	BILL MARTIN	vcls	A

45: Puppet On A String/
Breathalyser   (Page One POF 23046) 1967 SC

This was a satirical cover of the song that **Sandie Shaw** won the Eurovision Contest with. George Brown was an American producer and Bill Martin, an American singer - so a marginal case for inclusion.

Breathyliser resurfaced on *Yellow Elektric Years* (LP) and *Instro-Hipsters A Go-Go* (CD). (VJ)

Cody

Personnel:	IAN CLEWS	vcls	A
	TIMI DONALD	drms	A
	RONNIE LEAHY	keyb'ds	A
	NODDY McKENZIE	ld gtr	A
	IAN McMILAN	bs, ld gtr	A

45: I Belong With You/
Wanna Make You Happy   (Polydor 2058 100) 1971

A Scottish country-rock band. All the members except for McMilan had been in **White Trash** (**Trash**). Their name is a North Country name for a miner. Noddy McKenzie had also been in **The Poets** and Ian McMilan was with them too prior to joining **Trash**.

Leahy went on to play with **Stone The Crows** and Donald left to tour with **Sandy Denny** before rejoining the group just prior to their split. Donald and McMilan then joined **Blue**. (VJ/JM)

Peter and Chris Coe

Personnel:	CHRIS COE	vcls	A
	PETER COE	vcls	A

ALBUMS:	1	OPEN THE DOOR	(Leader LER 2077) 1972 SC
(up to	2	OUT OF THE SEASON, OUT OF RHYME	
1976)			(Leader LER 2098) 1976 SC

A respected folk duo, whose 1972 album features another folk stalwart **Steve Ashley**. They recorded a further album, *Game Of All Fours* (Highway SHY 7007) in 1979. (BS)

Coffee Set

45s:	Dicky Boy/Georgia On My Mind	(Mercury MF 1076) 1969
	Happy Birthday	(Mercury MF 1113) 1969

Insignificant late sixties pop. Nine vocalists backed by the Frank Barber Orchestra. (VJ)

B.J. Cole

ALBUM: 1   NEW HOVERING DOG   (United Artists UAS 29418) 1972

Cole had previously played with **Cochise**. This solo album made little impact, but he went on to become a significant pedal steel guitar session man. Having already worked for **Dave Edmunds** and **Elton John** in 1971, later session credits included **Nazareth** and **Uriah Heep** (1972), **Trapeze** (1973), **Procol Harum** (1974) and **Ray Thomas** (1975). There were several others, too, post-1976. (VJ)

The College Boys

Personnel:	MICKY ASTOR	A
	RODOLPHE 'ROO' D'ERLANGER	A
	JAMIE GRAHAM	A
	NICK ROBINSON	A
	DAVID WARD	A

45s:	I Just Don't Understand/I'm Gonna Cry	(Columbia DB 7306) 1964
	Good Times/San Antonio Rose	(Pye 7N 17294) 1967
	Simon Says/White Cliffs Of Dover	(Dolphin DOS 3) 1968

This was a group of Eton College pupils who played cover versions.

Good Times can also be found on *Ripples, Vol. 5* (CD). (VJ)

Peter Collins

ALBUM: 1   FIRST ALBUM   (Decca Nova SDN 21) 1970 SC

45:     Get In A Boat/Girl By The Sea   (Decca F 13048) 1970

SHIRLEY COLLINS - Sweet England (LP).

SHIRLEY COLLINS AND DAVY GRAHAM - Folk Roots, New Routes (CD).

Produced by Mel Collins, this became the sole vinyl outing for Peter, when he was still a teenager. It's heavily orchestrated and features some of the UK's finest jazz and session musicians. It has won some acclaim amongst fans of psych-pop. When it failed to sell, **Collins** became a jingle writer and later became a producer for Rush, Bon Jovi, Alice Cooper and others. (VJ)

Shirley Collins

ALBUMS:	1	FALSE TRUE LOVERS	(Folkways FG 3564) 1959 R3
(up to	2	SWEET ENGLAND	(Argo RG 150) 1960 R3
1976)	3	FOLK ROUTES, NEW ROUTES	(Decca LK 4652) 1964 R3
	4	THE SWEET PRIMEROSES	(Topic 12TS 170) 1967 R1
	5	THE POWER OF THE TRUE LOVE KNOT	
			(Polydor 583 025) 1968 R2
	6	ANTHEMS IN EDEN	(Harvest SHVL 754) 1969 R1
	7	LOVE, DEATH AND THE LADY	
			(Harvest SHVL 771) 1970 R2
	8	NO ROSES	(Pegasus PEG 7) 1971 R1
	9	ADIEU TO OLD ENGLAND	(Topic 12TS 238) 1974 R1
	10	A FAVOUR GARLAND (BEST OF)	
			(Deram SML 1117) 1975 R1
	11	AMARANTH	(Harvest SHSM 2008) 1976 SC

NB: (3) recorded with **Davy Graham**. (3) reissued on CD (Fledgling FLED 3502) 2005. (5) with **The Incredible String Band**. (6) & (7) recorded with Dolly Collins. (8) recorded with the **Albion Country Band**. (5) reissued on Hannibal in 1988. (6) reissued by See For Miles in 1985. (7) reissued in 1987. (7) reissued on EMI (EMI 8 29860 2) 1995, with four previously unreleased tracks from the same era and again (Fledg'ling FLED 3039) 2003, with four extra cuts and sleevenotes by Shirley and David Suff. (6) reissued on CD (Harvest 0777 7 81473 29) 1993, along with several cuts from (11). (7) reissued on CD (EMI 8 29860 2) 1995, with four previously unissued tracks. (8) reissued on CD (Mooncrest CRESTCD 11) 1991 and again (Sanctuary CMRCD 951) 2004. *Fountain Of Snow* (Durtro 010 CD) 1992 is a 75-minute CD compilation of material from 1967, 1974 and 1978 plus all four tracks from her very rare 1963 *Heroes In Love* (EP).

EPs:	1	SINGS IRISH	(Collector JEB 1508) 1960 R2
	2	THE FOGGY DEW	(Collector JEB 3) 1960 R2
	3	ENGLISH SONGS	(Collector JEB 5) 1960 R2
	4	HEROES IN LOVE	(Topic TOP 95) 1963 R2
	5	ENGLISH SONGS, VOL 2	(Collector JEB 9) 1964 R2

NB: (5) with Robin Hall.

A folky who was also in the **Albion Country Band** (in 1972) and The Etchingham Steam Band. Her albums are all collectable and some change hands for considerable sums.

Her first recording was a folk album issued back in 1959. Expect to pay a three figure sum for this ultra-rarity. Equally rare and sought-after is her *Sweet England* album from the following year. Also highly desirable is the 1964 album she recorded with **Davy Graham** and her early sixties EPs.

The Power Of The True Love Knot, on which she was backed by members of **The Incredible String Band**, contained songs highly evocative of medieval England and was something of a landmark in her recording career.

By the time of the *Anthems In Eden* album she'd been joined by her sister Dolly on harmonium and organ. The album was originally designed for a radio broadcast in 1968. The material on side one, which is this time evocative of Olde England, is the most memorable.

The **Collins**' sisters' 1970 set *Love, Death And The Lady* follows the format of its predecessors and is full of traditional folk material. Overall, though, it didn't match the standard of *Anthems In Eden* and after its release Dolly opted out of the music business. Shirley went on to record the *No Roses* (with the **Albion Country Band**) and *Adieu To Old England* albums.

Amaranth featured recordings by members of The Albion Dance Band, whom **Collins** was a vocalist with, on one of its sides. A good introduction to her music would be *A Favourite Garland*, a compilation covering the 1964-74 period.

Back in 1969 Shirley and Dolly had three cuts - *God Dog, A Leavetaking - Pleasant And Delightful* and *Bonny Cuckoo*, included on the very rare promo-only *Harvest Sampler* (LP). Harvest's *Picnic* (2-LP) sampler from 1970 included *Picnic* and *Black Joker / Black, White, Yellow And Green* also appears on *Harvest Heritage - 20 Greats* (LP). She also provided two tracks to the *Rave On* (LP) compilation. (VJ)

Colonel Bagshot

Personnel:

DAVE DOVER	vcls, bs, keyb'ds	A
BRIAN FARRELL	vcls, gtr, stylophone	A
TERRY McCUSKER	vcls, drms	A
KEN PARRY	vcls, gtr, keyb'ds	A

ALBUM: 1 OH! WHAT A LOVELY WAR (Cadet Concept 50010) 1971

45s: Georgia Fireball/One Look To Her Eyes (Parlophone 5893) 1971
Smile/Heading Home (Parlophone 5910) 1971
She's My Sun/Meet Down The Middle (Polydor 2058 381) 1973

Brian Farrell wrote all bar one track on this U.S. released album with Ken Parry providing the remaining credit but it's unexceptional and not particularly recommended. From Liverpool, they had at least three singles issued in UK, all of them containing non-album tracks, and usually more country-oriented. The album is not so bad, it does have at least 3/4 good songs, especially on the first side.

Dover, McCusker and Parry were all part of **Eric Burdon's** touring band from September - October 1976. (VJ/RR/MSs/GB/JM)

SHIRLEY COLLINS - The Power Of The True Love Knot (LP).

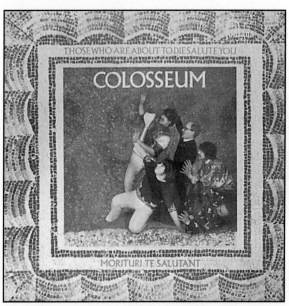

COLOSSEUM - Those Who Are About To Die Salute You (LP).

Colonel Murphy's Electric Trousers

ACETATE: 1 COLONEL MURPHY'S ELECTRIC TROUSERS
(No label) 1969 R4

This discovery, in a beautiful silk-screen sleeve, will interest those into strange, stoned, music. The four-piece band operate a guitar, bass, drums, piano format, sometimes supplemented by a second guitarist. The acetate contains group originals, like the title cut, *Pilkington's Wonderful Greaseless Hair Restorer* and *Blues For Colonel Murphy*. It also includes three **Idle Race** covers and a **Bonzo Dog Band** cover, *Death Cab For Cutie* - in fact they're quite an influence. (VJ)

The Colorados

45: Lips Are Redder On You/
Who You Gonna Hurt? (Oriole CB 1972) 1964 SC

A forgotten beat group. *Their Lips Are Redder On You* is a Joe Meek production and was also recorded by Gene Pitney. (MWh)

The Colors of Love

Personnel incl: JOAN KNIGHTON
JILL LONGSTAFFE
ELAINE PAGE
JOHN SHEPHERD
RUSSEL STONE

45s: I'm A Train/Up On A Cotton Cloud (Page One POF 060) 1968
Just Another Fly/Twenty Ten (Page One POF 086) 1968
Mother Of Convention/Music Mother (Page One POF 124) 1969

Late sixties folky pop thought to have been based in Mansfield, who played across the North and Midlands. Knighton and Stone both became session vocalists and, of course, Elaine Page enjoyed a solo career. (VJ)

Colosseum

Personnel:

DAVE GREENSLADE	organ, vcls	ABCD
DICK HECKSTALL-SMITH	sax	ABCD
JOHN HISEMAN	drms	ABCD
TONY REEVES	bs	ABC
JAMES LITHERLAND	gtr, vcls	AB
JIM ROCHE	gtr	A
MARK CLARKE	bs, vcls	D
DAVE CLEMPSON	gtr, vcls	D
CHRIS FARLOWE	vcls	D

COLOSSEUM - Valentyne Suite (LP).

Their follow-up album, *Valentyne Suite*, was their magnum opus. It was also the first release on the then new Vertigo label which showcased so much good progressive rock. The title track was an ambitious 16-minute composition taking up the whole of side two. However, its *Elegy, Butty's Blues* and *The Machine Demands A Sacrifice* on side one that really showcase the band at their best.

Not long after the release of *Valentyne Suite*, Litherland left to form **Mogul Thrash** whilst Tony Reeves left to do production work with various Danish bands. Newcomers were Mark Clarke (bs), Dave Clempson (ex-**Bakerloo**) and veteran R&B vocalist **Chris Farlowe**. This line-up produced *Daughter Of Time*, which was another strong album with the epic finale *Time Machine* and *Take Me Back To Doomsday* the highlights. It climbed to No 23 in the UK Album Charts but proved to be the band's last album for Vertigo as they signed up to the newly-established Bronze label.

Bronze almost immediately released a budget-priced double live album, *Live*, which consisted of six lengthy tracks recorded at Manchester University and the Big Apple, Brighton, in March 1971. They split at the end of 1971 without ever recording a studio album for Bronze, which perhaps explains why the label wasted little time in putting out a compilation, *Collectors Colosseum*, which included several previously unreleased cuts alongside many of their finest songs. The label later reissued all of their albums, except *Daughter Of Time*.

Upon their demise Mark Clarke joined **Uriah Heep**; Clem Clempson replaced **Peter Frampton** in **Humble Pie**; **Chris Farlowe**'s next stop was **Atomic Rooster**; **Dick Heckstall-Smith** went on to record a solo album and later played for many London pub bands and **Dave Greenslade** formed his own band.

Jon Hiseman has for a number of years recently played in his wife's Barbara Thompson's various bands including Paraphenalia.

The US edition of *Those Who Are About To Die Salute You / Morituri Te Salutant* (Dunhill DS 50062) is a strange mixture of material from their first two British albums. It came in a different gatefold cover and includes on the 'A' side *The Kettle* (from the UK *Valentyne Suite*), *Plenty Hard Luck, Debut* and *Those About To Die* (from the UK *Those About To Die...*). Side 'B' consists of the *Valentyne Suite* and *Walking In The Park*. However, the US version of *Valentyne Suite* differs from the UK one. *Theme Three* on the UK one is the *Grass Is Always Greener*, but the US version omits this and *Theme Two* leads straight into *Beware The Ides Of March* (from the UK version of *Those About To Die...*).

Anthology is a 2-CD compilation, which includes their highlights from their first three albums.

Elegy, one of their finest moments from *The Valentyne Suite* album, can also be heard on *Vertigo Annual* (2-LP) 1970. More recently *The Kettle* was included on *Rock Of Ages, Four Decades Of Heavy Rock 1962-2002.*; *Walking In The Park* has been compiled on the 3-CD box set *Ars Longa Vita Brevis: A Compendium Of Progressive Rock 1967-1974*;

ALBUMS: 1(B) THOSE WHO ARE ABOUT TO DIE SALUTE YOU

                                            (Fontana STL 5510) 1969 SC 15

HCP

2(B) VALENTYNE SUITE   (Vertigo VO 1) 1969 R1 15
3(D) DAUGHTER OF TIME   (Vertigo 6360 017) 1970 R1 23
4(D) COLOSSEUM LIVE (2-LP)   (Bronze ICD 1) 1971 17
5(D) COLLECTORS COLOSSEUM (Bronze ILPS 9173) 1971 -

NB: These albums were also issued in Germany, where 'Live' (Club Issue), a double LP, was also issued on S International in 1970. (1) reissued (Get Back GETLP 554) and on CD (Sanctuary SMQCD 096) 2004, with four BBC sessions of album tracks. (1) reissued again on CD (Essential ESMCD 643) 2005. (2) reissued on Bronze (HELP 4) 1972 and again on Bronze (BRNA 214) in 1977. (2) reissued on CD (Sanctuary SMEDD 097) 2004, with bonus tracks. (2) reissued again on CD (Essential ESMCD 642) 2005. (3) reissued on CD (Sequel 1007-2) 1996. (3) reissued on CD (Sanctuary CMRCD 119) 2004, with bonus tracks and new sleevenotes and again on CD (Essential ESMCD 644) 2005 and again on CD (Essential ESMCD 641) 2005. (4) reissued on Bronze (BRSP 2) in 1977 and on CD (Sanctuary CMRCD 118) 2004, with bonus tracks and new sleevenotes. (5) reissued on Bronze (BRON 173) in 1977. (1) and (2) have been issued together on CD (Sequel NEX CD 161) 1990, as have (4) (Sequel NEX CD 201) 1992, which included a previously unissued cut, *I Can't Live Without You*, and (5) (Castle CCSCD 287) 1991. (3) and (5) reissued on CD (Sequel NEX CD 256 and 255 respectively). Three compilations are *Epitaph* (Raw Power RAWLP 014) in 1986 (also on CD); *The Golden Decade Of Colosseum* (CD) (Knight KNCD 10016) 1990 and *The Ides Of March* (Karussek/Spectrum 550 734-2) 1995 (CD) from the 1969-71 era. *Anthology* (Castle Music CMDDD 075) 2000 is a 2-CD collection.

45:      Walking In The Park/
       Those About To Die   (Fontana TF 1029) 1969

Colosseum was at the forefront of the fusion of progressive rock, jazz and blues in the late sixties and was in many respects one of the most ambitious groups of that era.

Hiseman and **Heckstall-Smith** had both previously been with the **Graham Bond Organisation** and they also played with **John Mayall** on his *Bare Wires* album. Hiseman also played on **Howard Riley**'s ultra-rare privately-pressed *Discussions* album.

The original **Colosseum** line-up (A) was gelled together in late 1968 and they signed to Fontana. Their debut album featured some pleasant organ work and effectively blended jazz, rock and the blues with some classical influences. It even climbed to No 15 in the UK Album Charts. Their only 45 ever released, *Walking In The Park*, was an organ-led R&B effort, written by **Graham Bond**, which sank without trace. They really were more suited to the album market.

They developed a good live reputation, assisted by an appearance in the 'Supersession' rock film.

COMPLEX - Complex (LP).

COMPLEX - The Way We Feel (LP).

Dick Heckstall-Smith sadly died on 18 December 2004, aged 70, after suffering from long-term cancer. (VJ)

Colourful Seasons

45:    Out Of The Blue/It's Gonna Break My Back   (MGM 1433) 1968

No other information on these I'm afraid. They may even be American. (VJ)

Christopher Colt

45:    Virgin Sunrise/Girl In The Mirror   (Decca F 12726) 1968 SC

The above 45 was this obscure vocalist's sole platter. Still, *Virgin Sunrise* is a fine slice of pop with a tinge of psychedelic influence, which you can also check out on *Rubble Vol. 17: A Trip In A Painted World* (LP) and *Rubble Vol. 10* (CD). (VJ)

Tony Colton's Big Boss Band

45s: α Lose My Mind/
         So Used To Loving You   (Decca F 11879) 1964 SC
         I Stand Accused/
         Further On Down The Track   (Pye 7N 15886) 1965 R2
         You're Wrong There Baby/
         Have You Lost Your Mind   (Pye 7N 17046) 1966 SC
         I've Laid Some Down In My Time/
         Run Poney Rider   (Pye 7N 17117) 1966 R1
      α In The World Of Marnie Dreaming/
         Who Is She?   (Columbia DB 8385) 1968

NB: α **Tony Colton** solo 45s.

Tony Colton is best known as the vocalist of **Heads Hands And Feet**, a multi-faceted band comprised of some of the country's best early seventies sessionmen. After the demise of The Big Boss Band, whose 45s, particularly, *I Stand Accused*, which was a big Northern soul rarity, is now collectable, **Colton** was in Real McCoy and **Poet and One Man Band** prior to joining **Heads Hands And Feet**. He was also a noted songwriter, for example, with **Zoot Money**.

Compilation appearances have included: *You're Wrong There Baby* on *The R&B Era, Vol. 2* (LP & CD); *I Stand Accused* on *Watch Your Step* (LP & CD); *I've Laid Some Down In My Time* on *Diggin' For Gold, Vol. 4* (LP & CD); *You're Wrong There Baby* and *Further On Down The Track* on *Doin' The Mod, Vol. 1* (CD); *Run Pony Rider* on *Doin' The Mod, Vol. 2* (CD); and *I Stand Accused* and *Further On Down The Track* on *Footsteps To Fame, Vol. 1* (CD). (VJ)

Colts

45:    San Miguel/Where Has Our Love Gone?   (Pye 7N 15955) 1965

A mid-sixties beat group from Essex. (VJ)

Columbia Boys

45s: Baby Come Back/Born To Lose   (Pye 7N 17513) 1968
        That's My Pa/She Thinks I Still Care   (Pye 7N 17763) 1969

Columbia Boys was a show band. *Baby Come Back* was **The Equals'** song. (VJ)

Columbus

45:    Everybody Loves The US Marshall/Tired   (Deram DM 294) 1970

This was an obscure pop 45 from the early seventies. (VJ)

Commanches

45:    Tomorrow/Missed Your Loving   (Pye 7N 15609) 1964

This beat band had previously been the backing band for early sixties vocalist Bobby Allen. *Tomorrow* can also be heard on Sequel's *Hippy Hippy Shake* (CD) compilation. (VJ)

The Committee (1)

45:    Sleep Tight Honey/Memories Of Melinda   (Pye 7N 12826) 1969

A short-lived pop outfit. (VJ)

The Committee (2)

45:    Hard Way/Hey You   (Liberty LBF 15154) 1968

Another late sixties pop outfit, probably unconnected to the previous one. (VJ)

Complex

Personnel: STEVE COE   organ   A
             LANCE FOGG   bs, vcls   AB
             BRIAN LEE   gtr, vcls   AB
             TONY SHAKESPEARE   vcls, drms   AB

ALBUMS: 1(A) COMPLEX   (CLPM 001) 1970 R5
        2(A) THE WAY WE FEEL   (Deroy no #) 1971 R5

NB: (1) has been counterfeited. (1) reissued on vinyl (Tenth Planet TP 038) 1998 and on CD (Wooden Hill WHCD 008) 2000. (2) reissued on vinyl (Tenth Planet TP 039) 1998 and on CD (Wooden Hill WHCD 009) 2000.

These two psychedelic albums are among the most sought-after artefacts of British psychedelia. Only 99 copies of each album by this Blackpool-based band were pressed. Despite the fact the debut album was recorded in November 1970 it sounds like it's straight out of the Summer of love. Basically we're talking echo-laden organ-driven garage psychedelia which is marred only by poor sound quality. Eight of the eleven compositions were penned by Steve Coe and a guy called Mitchell, two were Steve Coe compositions and the finale, *Live For The Minute*, was the product of a Coe-Shakespeare songwriting collaboration. This has lots of fine guitar organ interplay. Other highlights are *Witch's Spell* and *Storm On The Way*, both notable for some punchy organ work and strong vocals and *Self Declaration*, which has lots of fuzzy guitar and cheesy organ. A couple of tracks, *Josie* and *Madamoiselle Jackie* veer more towards pop with a commercial edge.

Despite its rarity and value many collectors regard *The Way We Feel*, which was recorded at Deroy Sound Studios the following year, as an anti-climax. A few songs, particularly *Moving Moor* and *We Don't Exist*, are on a par with the debut album, but overall the quality of material is comparatively disappointing. Soon after the release of this album the band's main songwriter Steve Coe departed. Several years later he re-emerged in Monsoon. The remaining members recorded a five-track acetate for a third album, which remains unreleased, before disbanding.

Both these albums were treated to limited edition vinyl reissues (1,000 copies of each) in the late nineties and later got a CD reissue - both courtesy of labels run by psych/prog rock connoisseur David Wells.

Witch's Spell can also be heard on *Syde Trips, Vol. 4* (LP). (VJ)

Compromise

45:        You Will Think Of Me/Love Minus Zero   (CBS 202050) 1966

A folky beat outfit from the mid-sixties. (VJ)

Comus

Personnel: GLEN GORING   gtr, vcls   A
             COLIN PEARSON   violin   A B
             BOBBIE WATSON   vcls, perc   A B C
             ROGER WOOTTON   gtr, vcls   A B C
             ROB YOUNG   perc, oboe, flute A B
             LINDSAY COOPER   C
             ANDY HELLABY   bs   C

ALBUMS: 1(B)   FIRST UTTERANCE
               (w/insert)   (Dawn DNLS 3019) 1971 R2
        2(C)   TO KEEP FROM CRYING (Virgin V 2018) 1974 SC

NB: (1) reissued on CD (Beat Goes On BGOCD 275) 1995 and with extensive liner notes and bonus tracks on Sanctuary (2005). (1) reissued on vinyl (Earmark 42075) 2005. *Songs To Comus* (Castle CMEDD 1121) 2005 is a 2-CD set which compiles their entire output.

45:    Diana / In The Lost Queen's Eyes /
       Winter Is A Coloured Bird (PS)   (Dawn DNX 2506) 1971

Comus was a drummer-less folk-rock group, formed in South-East London. They honed their material at the legendary Beckenham Arts Lab, curated by **David Bowie**, whom they supported live on various occasions in 1969. Goring left the band before the recording of *First Utterance*. Taking British

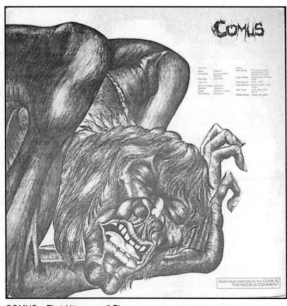

COMUS - First Utterance (LP).

folk as point of departure, it twists and oozes like a vile bunch of snakes, pairing gorgeous melodies and expert playing with ecstatically altered vocals and vicious lyrics. Rape, murder, witchcraft and abuse are main ingredients, which are cooked with raging madness, but still manage to taste delicately composed. The opening cut *Diana* is very strange and appealing, *The Herald* is beautifully fragile, with strings and woodwind, *Drip Drip* is a decidedly weird series of rantings and ramblings. The four tracks on side two essentially continue the challenging tapestry of beautiful woodwind, strings and unorthodox vocals. One of the very few British folk albums that creates a totally original atmosphere, this dark, haunting and bizarre psychedelic folk masterpiece is recommended. The rare 'maxi-single' (Dawn DNX 2506) combines a slightly more subdued version of *Diana* with two excellent non-album cuts, the melodic *Winter Is A Coloured Bird* and dramatic *In The Lost Queen's Eyes*.

Pearson and Young departed in August 1971, when ex-**Strawbs** member Lindsay Cooper joined and the band signed to Virgin when Dawn declined to extend their contract. By comparison with its predecessor, the second album cannot but disappoint. Recorded by line-up (C) and supplemented by session musicians, it's more commonplace both in sound and content, but is still a nice folk album with some good tracks, though nothing superb. Their leader Roger Wootton changed his surname to Raven and moved to Sweden in the late seventies, though he is now back in the UK. Cooper later joined **Henry Cow**.

Comus featured in Lindsay Shonteff's low-budget 1971 UK film 'Permissive', about the perils of being a groupie and their compilation appearances include *The Herald* on *Gather In The Mushrooms* (CD) and *Diana* on the 3-CD Box Set *Ars Longa Vita Brevis: A Compendium Of Progressive Rock 1967-1974*. (RMJ/MK/VJ/JM)

The Con-Chords

45:    You Can't Take It Away/
       Let Me Walk With You   (Polydor 56059) 1966 SC

A Birmingham-based beat group. (VJ)

Brian Connell and Round Sound

45s: Just My Kind Of Loving/
       Something You've Got   (Mercury MF 956) 1966
       The Same Thing's Happened To Me/
       Mister Porter   (Mercury MF 991) 1966
       What Good Am I/
       Just Another Wedding Day   (Philips BF 1661) 1968
       I Know/Mister Travel Company (Philips BF 1718) 1968

A pop group which made little impact at the time. **Brian Connell** worked at Harrod's during 1968. (VJ)

Brian Connolly

CD: 1   68 WAS 68   (Malibu BCCD 01) 2001

The above CD compiles a handful of poor quality demo recordings dating from 1967/68 by future **Sweet** front man **Brian Connelly**. It's poorly packaged, the material is weak (except for the final cut - an embryonic version of **The Sweet's** debut single *Slow Motion*) and this cannot be recommended. (VJ)

Tony Conrad and Faust

Personnel: TONY CONRAD   A
             WERNER DIERMAIER   A
             JEAN HERVE PERON   A
             RUDOLF SOSSNA   A

ALBUM: 1(A)   OUTSIDE THE DREAM SYNDICATE
                              (Caroline C1501) 1972 SC

RIPPLES VOL. 7 (Comp CD) including Consortium.

A marginal case for inclusion here in the UK section, as Faust were a German band and **Tony Conrad** an American. **Conrad**, a violinist and minimalist composer, was a member of La Monte Young's Dream Syndicate in New York in the mid-sixtiess, who were a seminal group in the history of minimalist music (**John Cale** was also a member). A lot of **Conrad**'s work with Dream Syndicate was tied up for years in some sort of legal dispute with Young. Recently, **Conrad** has put out records on Table Of Elements, an avant-garde label out of Atlanta and may have also collaborated with Jim O'Rourke.

Although down as a Caroline release the album actually came with a Virgin catalogue number and label. It comprised two sides of bass and drums (presumably Faust) playing a monotonously slow one note beat and a violin (presumably **Conrad**) screeching away over the top, holding a single note for minutes at a time. The two side-long tracks were called *The Side Of Man and Womankind* and *The Side Of The Machine*. (VJ/Es/GB)

Consortium

Personnel:	JOHN BARKER	bs, trombone	A
	BRIAN BRONSON	gtr	A
	RUBBIE FAIR	vcls	A
	JOHN PODBURY	drms	A
	GEOFFREY SIMPSON	organ, lead gtr	A

HCP

45s:	All The Love In The World/		
	Spending My Life Saying Goodbye	(Pye 7N 17635) 1968 22	
	When The Day Breaks/		
	Day The Train Never Came	(Pye 7N 17725) 1969 -	
	Beggar Man/Cynthia Serenity	(Pye 7N 17797) 1969 -	
	I Don't Want Her Any More/		
	The House Upon The Hill	(Pye 7N 17841) 1969 -	
	Melanie Cries Alone/		
	Copper Coloured Years	(Trend TNT 52) 1970 -	
	Annabella/Tell Me My Friend	(Trend 6099 004) 1971 -	

This was a pretty decent harmony-pop group from London previously known as **West Coast Consortium**. Their finest moment was *All The Love In The World*, which was distinctive for its falsetto vocals and narrowly missed giving them a Top 20 hit.

Compilation appearances include: *The Day The Train Never Came* on *Justafixation* (CD) and *Haunted - Psychedelic Pstones, Vol 2* (CD); *All The Love In The World* on *Paisley Pop - Pye Psych (& Other Colours) 1966-1969* (CD) and *Pop Inside The Sixties, Vol. 3* (CD); *When The Day Breaks* and *I Don't Want Her Anymore* on *Ripples, Vol. 7* (CD); and *All The Love In The World, Spending My Life Saying Goodbye, When The Day Breaks* and *The Day The Train Never Came* on *Sixties Years, Vol. 5* (CD). (VJ)

Contemporary Music Unit (CMU)

Personnel:	JAMES GORDON	vcls, perc	AB
	IAN HAMLETT	gtr, flute	AB
	ED LEE	bs	AB
	TERRY MORTIMER	gtr, keyb'ds, viola,	
		vcls	A
	LARRAINE ODELL	vcls	ABCD
	ROGER ODELL	drms	ABCD
	LEARY HASSON	keyb'ds	CD
	RICHARD JOSEPH	vcls, gtr	CD
	STEVE COOK	bs	D
	FRANK ROBERTS	keyb'ds	D

ALBUMS:	1(B)	OPEN SPACES	(Transatlantic TRA 237) 1971 R1
	2(C)	SPACE CABARET	(Transatlantic TRA 259) 1972 R1

NB: (1) and (2) reissued on one CD (See For Miles SEECD 373) 1994.

45:	Heart Of The Sun/Doctor Am I Normal?	(Big T BIG 508) 1972

Mortimer left the band before they recorded. Hamlett, Gordon and Lee left during the recording of the first album and were replaced by Joseph and Hasson. Hasson had previously been in **Marsupilami**. On **CMU**'s first effort, voodoo blues wrestles with cocktail jazz, mock-Japanese melodies and British pop for a place to live, thereby creating an interesting but rather uneven album. The long, vaguely experimental *Chantecleer*, with its dual guitar harmonies stands out.

Roberts and Cook also joined, but Roberts left shortly after to join Cirrus. The second album is far better, largely due to the beneficial influence of Richard Joseph who wrote almost all of side one. The songs (!) are catchier, more coherent, and yet do not lose the variety from the first album. The mellotron-laden *Archway 272* is downright brilliant with quick shifts of atmosphere as if two bands alternate on this track. Side two is less poppy with two long tracks. Undoubtedly nice records. The 'A' side of their 45 does not feature on either of their albums making it quite collectable too.

Cook went on to play with **Gilgamesh** and Roger Odell joined Shakatar. (MK/VJ/JM)

Continuum

Personnel:	MIKE HART	double-bs	A
	YOEL SCHWARCZ	gtr, flute, recorder,	
		hrmnca	A
	JOHN WARREN	gtr	A
	DICK WILDMAN	drms, perc	A

ALBUMS:	1	CONTINUUM	(RCA SF 8157) 1970
	2	AUTUMN GRASS	(RCA SF 8196) 1971

Not too many bands have attempted a fusion of 'classical' with 'blues' styles, as **Continuum** have! A jazzy feel is in evidence on much of the opening side of the first album, with arrangements of works by J.S Bach and Handel. Part of Bach's "Lute Suite Number 1" gets an usual blues harmonica treatment. Side two is taken up by a lengthy concept piece in five parts inspired by Byron's poem "Childe Harold's Pilgrimage". Here strings and electronics are used interestingly, and this effort may be worth a footnote by any budding historians of early progressive music. The second album, which is the rarer of the two, has a gatefold sleeve like the first, and musically follows the same pattern. This time Byrd and Vivaldi are the classical composers given the **Continuum** treatment, and there is again a lengthy original piece on the second side.

The band was centred around Yoel Schwarcz, who was apparently of Hungarian extraction. Part of the engineering at Morgan Studios was undertaken by Mike Bobak of **Motherlight**. This Mike Hart should definitely not be confused with the other **Mike Hart** (of **Liverpool Scene**). (NM)

Contraband

Personnel:	ALEX BAIRD	drms	A
	PETER CAIRNEY	gtr, bs	A
	BILLY JACKSON	bs	A

GEORGE JACKSON	keyb'ds, mandolin	A
JOHN MARTIN	violin	A
MAE McKENNA	lead vcls	A

ALBUM: 1(A) CONTRABAND   (Transatlantic TRA 278) 1974 SC

45:      Lady For Today/On The Road   (Transatlantic BIG 518) 1974

An electric folk-rock band from Glasgow. They formed in 1971 and recorded their album in late 1973. It was finally released in May 1974.

They finally quit in May 1975 due to financial problems shortly after Mae McKenna decided to leave to go solo. She is the sister of Hugh. Alex Baird went on to join **Gryphon**. (VJ/JM)

The Contrasts (featuring Bob Morrison)

45s: I Can't Get You Out Of My Mind/
         Click When You're In Love   (Parlophone R 5095) 1964
         Call Me/Come On Let's Go   (Parlophone R 5190) 1964
         What A Day/Lonely Child   (Monument MON 1018) 1968

A little known beat group from Huddersfield. (MWh)

Roger (James) Cook

ALBUMS: 1 STUDY   (Columbia SCX 6388) SC 1970
         2 MEANWHILE BACK AT THE WORLD
                             (Regal Zonophone SRZA 8508) 1972 SC
         3 MINSTREL IN FLIGHT
                             (Regal Zonophone SLRZ 1035) 1973 SC
         4 ALRIGHT   (Polydor 2383 357) 1976

45s: Not That It Matters Anymore/
         Paperchase   (Columbia DB 8510) 1969
         Stop/Someday   (Columbia DB 8556) 1969
         Smiling Through My Tears/
         Ain't That A Wonderful Thing   (Columbia DB 8596) 1969

NB: (3) with Eve Graham.

Roger Cook was earlier David (of **David and Jonathan**) and he'd also gone on to form **Blue Mink** before recording these solo albums, which are now scarce and attract interest from some collectors.

Cook also wrote material for **The Fortunes**.

NB: This artist should not be confused with Roger James, a 'light' reggae artist with at least one 45: *If I Didn't Have You/I Know It's You* (Nems NEMS 3719) 1968. (VJ/JHn)

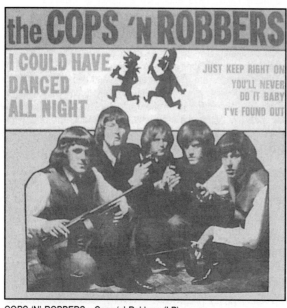

COPS 'N' ROBBERS - Cops 'n' Robbers (LP).

Cool

ALBUM: 1 POP SOUNDS   (DeWolf DW/LP 3136) 1969 R1

This was a music library album. (VJ)

Mike Cooper

ALBUMS: 1 THE INVERTED WORLD (Matchbox SDM 159) 1968 R1
         2 OH REALLY!?   (Pye NSPL 18281) 1969 SC
         3 DO I KNOW YOU?   (Dawn DNLS 3005) 1970
         4 TROUT STEEL
            (Some with poster insert) (Dawn DNLS 3011) 1970 SC
         5 PLACES I KNOW (w/insert)   (Dawn DNLS 3026) 1971
         6 THE MACHINE GUN COMPANY (Dawn DNLS 3031) 1972
         7 LIFE AND DEATH IN PARADISE
                                   (Fresh Air 6370 500) 1974

NB: (1) recorded with **Ian A. Anderson**.

EP: 1 UP THE COUNTRY BLUES   (Saydisc SD 137) 196? R2

45s: Your Lovely Ways, Parts 1 and 2/
         Watching You Fall, Parts 1 and 2 (PS)   (Dawn DNX 2501) 1970
         Too Late Now//The Ballad Of Fulton Allen
         Good Times (PS)   (Dawn DNX 2511) 1971
         Time In Hand/Schaabisch Hall   (Dawn DNX 1022) 1972

A contemporary folk/blues artist who was based in Reading, Berkshire. He was at the forefront of the folk/blues movement in the UK in the sixties and early seventies and ran a popular folk/blues club in Reading. He helped found the Matchbox label, for whom he recorded his debut album, along with **Ian A. Anderson**. His second album *Oh Really!?* Is acclaimed as one of the best acoustic blues albums of the period. He also played guitar on some of **Anderson**'s recordings, as well as on some by **John Dummer** and **Heron**. **Cooper** used an impressive array of artists on his recordings.

The five solo albums he recorded in the early 1970s chronicle, through his own songwriting, a shift from pure blues through to free jazz. Collaborating with jazz, improvising and avant-garde musicians he produced some of the first and finest rogue folk. His maxi singles for Dawn are recommended. *Your Lovely Ways* features excellent instrumentation with **Cooper**'s wavering vocals.

In the late seventies he went on to establish himself on the free-improvised music scene, working with members of the London Musicians Collective such as Keith Rowe, Max Eastety, Steve Beresford, Paul Burwell, Eddy Prevost, David Toop and dancer Joanna Pyne. (VJ/MWh)

Copperfield

Personnel: DEREK ARNOLD   bs   A
            JOHN COPE   drms   A
            BOB DAFFURN   gtr   A
            MIKE HOPKINS   ld gtr A
            DERRY RYAN   vcls   A

45s: Any Old Time/I'm No Good For Her   (Instant IN 004) 1969
         I'll Hold Out Of My Hand/
         Far Away Love   (Parlophone R 5818) 1970

This was a soul/beat band from Birmingham. Arnold and Hopkins later reappeared in Quartz in the late seventies/early eighties. (VJ)

Cops 'n' Robbers

Personnel: TERRY FOX   organ   AB
            HENRY HARRISON   drms   AB
            BRIAN ';SMUDGER' SMITH vcls   A
            STEVE SMITH   bs   AB
            DANE STEPHENS   vcls   B

ALBUM: 1(-) COPS 'N' ROBBERS   (Distortions DR 1036) 1998

NOWHERE MEN VOL. 3 (Comp CD) including Cops 'n' Robbers.

45s: St. James Infirmary/
        There's Gotta Be A Reason   (Decca F 12019) 1964 R1
        Just Keep Right On/
        I Could Have Danced All Night   (Pye 7N 15870) 1965 SC
        It's All Over Now Baby Blue/
        I've Found Out   (Pye 7N 15928) 1965 SC

This R&B band from Watford was a popular act on the club circuit during the mid-sixties. They tended to record cover versions and their cover of Bob Dylan's *It's All Over Now Baby Blue* sold well without entering the Charts.

Their first 45 was decidedly bluesy and they later recorded other bluesy numbers, *You'll Never Do It Baby* and *I've Found Out*, which were only available on a French EP.

Vocalist Brian 'Smudger' Smith had previously sung with and later returned to **The Fairies**. Upon their demise Henry Harrison formed **The New Vaudeville Band**.

Distortions have recently issued a retrospective album, *Cops 'n' Robbers*, which compiles rare acetates, European EP cuts and 45 tracks. There's also detailed liner notes from R&B guru Mike Stax, which reveal that **Donovan** was an early fan of the band and later helped set up their deal with Pye.

Compilation appearances have included: *St. James Infirmary, There's Got To Be A Reason, I've Found Out* (two versions), *I Could Have Danced All Night, Just Keep Right On, You'll Never Do It Baby* and *It's All Over Now (Baby Blue)* on *Nowhere Men Vol. 3* (CD); *I Could Have Danced All Night* on *Pop Inside The Sixties, Vol. 3* (CD) and *Hippy Hippy Shake* (CD); *St. James Infirmary* on *Pop Inside The '60s, Vol. 2* (CD), *Sixties Lost And Found, Vol. 3* (LP) and *Sixties Explosion, Vol. 1* (CD); *There's Got To Be A Reason* on *The R&B Scene* (CD) and *Broken Dreams, Vol. 2* (LP); *It's All Over Now (Baby Blue)* on *Ripples, Vol. 6* (CD) and *Watch Your Step* (CD); *Harlem Shuffle* and *It Hurts Me So* on *Bits And Pieces - Lost And Found* (LP & CD); and *I've Found Out* and *You'll Never Do It Baby* on *English Freakbeat, Vol. 4* (LP & CD). (VJ)

Phil Cordell

45:    Pumping The Water/Red Lady   (Warner Bros WB 8001) 1969

Phil Cordell had previously been with **Thursday's Children**. *Red Lady* later resurfaced on *Fading Yellow, Vol 1* (CD). (VJ)

The Cordes

Personnel: DAVE DOVER   bs   A
                DEREK FULLWOOD gtr   A
                STEVE LISTER   lead gtr A
                CLIVE SMITH   drms   A

45:    Give Her Time/She's Leaving (Cavern Sound IMSTL 1) 1965 R2

This short-lived band's sole recording came out on Liverpool's seminal Cavern Club's own label. (VJ/AD)

The Corduroys

45:    Tick Tock/Too Much Of A Woman   (Planet PLF 122) 1966 R1

This 45 is now a minor collectable but the band remains unknown. It was produced by Shel Talmy.

Too Much Of A Woman has been compiled on *The Best Of Planet Records* (CD). (VJ)

Arnold Corns

Personnel incl: DAVID BOWIE

45s: α   Moonage Daydream/Hang Onto Yourself (B&C CB 149) 1971 R2
            Hang Onto Yourself/Man In The Middle (B&C CB 189) 1971 R1
Reissue: Hang Onto Yourself/
           Man In The Middle   (Mooncrest MOON 25) 1974
NB: α credited to **The Arnold Corns**.

These recordings were the work of **David Bowie** and various **Spiders From Mars** working under a pseudonym and the first, in particular, is now quite collectable. (VJ)

The Corsairs

45:    Pay You Back With Interest/
        I'm Gonna Shut You Down   (CBS 202624) 1967 SC

This was a one-off venture and the band should not be confused with a US band of the same name from La Grange, North Carolina whose records were released on Pye International here and a Jamaican band who recorded on Unity. (VJ)

The Cortinas

45:    Phoebe's Flower Shop/
        Too Much In Love   (Polydor 56255) 1968 SC

A one-off late sixties project from Hatfield. The 'A' side, *Phoebe's Flower Shop* is an innocuous, bouncy little ditty with some commercial appeal.

COSMIC EYE - Dream Sequence (CD).

Phoebes Flower Shop has resurfaced on *Circus Days Vol's 4 & 5* (CD) and *Circus Days, Vol. 4* (LP). (VJ)

Cosmic Eye

Personnel:	JOHN MAYER	violin	A
	ALAN BRANSCOMBE	sax	A
	TONI CAMPO	bs	A
	AMANCIO D'SILVA	gtr	A
	DAVE GROSSMAN	alto flute	A
	VIRAM JASANI	sitar	A
	KESH SATHIE	tambourine	A
	RAY SWINFIELD	flute	A
	C. TAYLOR	bs, flute	A
	D. WRIGHT	drms	A

ALBUM: 1(A) DREAM SEQUENCE
(Regal Zonophone SLRZ 1030) 1972 R3

This instrumental album was jazz heavyweight John Mayer's foray into progressive rock, and has only one track, spread over two sides. It attempts a metamorphosis and blending of different atmospheres into a sequence of musical styles. There is some bebop jazz, some Indian music augmented with electric guitar, some which could easily pass for New Age music, and some which is totally unclassifiable. Although pretentious by its very nature, the album has its moments, but suffers from a shortage of good ideas. Rather half-baked. (MK)

Day Costello

45: Long And Winding Road/
Free (Unlimited Horizons) (Spark SRL 1042) 1970

This was a one-off 45 by the father of Elvis Costello Presley. The 'A' side is presumably **The Beatles'** song. (VJ)

Mike Cotton Sound

Personnel incl:	MIKE COTTON	trumpet, hrmnca	ABC
	STU MORRISON	bs	A
	TONY PITT	ld gtr	A
	DAVE ROWBERRY	organ	A
	JOHN BEECHAM	trumpet, piano, bs	BC
	JOHN CROCKER	sax	BC
	JIMMY GARFORTH	drms	B
	ERIC HEESE		B
	JIM RODFORD	bs	BC
	BERNIE BYRNES	drms	C

THE MIKE COTTON SOUND - The Mike Cotton Sound (LP).

ALBUM: 1   MIKE COTTON SOUND   (Columbia 33SX 1647) 1964 R3
NB: (1) reissued as a limited edtion of 500 (Beat Records BLP 2) 1997.

EPs: 1   COTTON PICKING   (Columbia SEG 8144) 1962 SC
2   THE WILD AND THE WILLING
(Columbia SEG 8190) 1963 SC

45s: α Swing That Hammer/Heartaches   (Columbia DB 7029) 1963 36
β Midnite Flyer/One Mint Julep   (Columbia DB 7134) 1963 -
I Don't Wanna Know/
This Little Pig   (Columbia DB 7267) 1964 R1
Round And Round/Beau Dudley   (Columbia DB 7382) 1964 R1
Make Up Your Mind/
I've Got My Eye On You   (Columbia DB 7623) 1965 R1
Harlem Shuffle/Like That   (Polydor BM 56096) 1966 SC -
Step Out Of Line/
Ain't Love Good, Ain't Love Proud   (Pye 7N 17313) 1967 -
NB: α as Mike Cotton Jazzmen. β as Mike Cotton Band.

Mike Cotton had fronted a jazzband since the late fifties. After their only hit in 1963 with *Swing That Hammer*, the Mike Cotton Jazzmen became The Mike Cotton Band in 1963 and then the **Mike Cotton Sound**. Aside from backing other artists like **Lucas** they also recorded a number of their own 45s and their music veered more towards blues and soul. Rodford had been in **Casey Jones and The Governors** (or Engineers) and went on to join **Argent**; Byrnes was ex-**Boomerangs**; **Cotton**, Beecham and Byrnes joined **Zoot Money's** Money Music Band and, following that were the founders of **Satisfaction**. Rowberry replaced **Alan Price** in **The Animals** (and was in turn replaced by **Zoot Money).** Finally, Crocker joined Chris Barber's band in April 1972.

I Don't Wanna Know can also be heard on *Rare 60's Beat Treasures, Vol. 2* (CD) and *That Driving Beat* (CD). (VJ/JM)

The Cougars

Personnel:	DAVE HACK	drms	A
	ADRIAN MORGAN	bs	A
	KEITH (RED) OWEN	lead gtr	A
	DAVE TANNER	gtr	A

EP: 1   SATURDAY NIGHT WITH THE COUGARS
(Parlophone GEP 8886) 1963 R1

HCP

45s: Saturday Nite At The Duck Pond/
See You In Dreamland   (Parlophone R 4989) 1963 SC 33
Red Square/Fly By Night   (Parlophone R 5038) 1963 SC -
Caviare And Chips/
While The City Sleeps   (Parlophone R 5115) 1964 SC -
Reissue: Saturday Nite At The Duck Pond/See You In Dreamland/
Red Square/Fly By Night   (EMI EMI 2833) 1978 -

A Bristol band who attracted a little limelight when their instrumental, *Saturday Nite At The Duck Pond*, adapted from *Swan Lake*, was a minor hit. It can also be heard on See For Miles' *20 One Hit Wonders* (LP) compilation. (VJ/AD)

Dennis Couldry (and Smile)

45s: α James In The Basement/
I Am Nearly There   (Decca F 12734) 1968
Penny For The Wind/
Tea & Toast Mr. Watson?   (Decca F 12786) 1968 SC
NB: α 'A' side **Dennis Couldry** solo, 'B' side credtied to **Dennis Couldry** & Next Collection.

Couldry had been the organist in **Felius Andromeda**. You'll also find *Tea & Toast Mr. Watson?* on *Oddities, Vol 1* (CD) and *Am I Nearly There* on the *Freakbeat Scene* (CD). (VJ)

ENGLISH FREAKBEAT VOL. 3 (Comp CD) featuring The Couriers.

Coulson, Dean, McGuiness, Flint

Personnel:	DENNIS COULSON	vcls	A
	DIXIE DEAN	bs	A
	HUGHIE FLINT	drms	A
	TOM MCGUINESS	gtr	A

ALBUM: 1(A) LO AND BEHOLD   (DJM DJLPS 424) 1972 SC

45:     I Wanna Be Your Lover T Montgomery/
        Lay Down Your Weary Tune   (DJM DJS 10267) 1972

This was an offshoot of **McGuiness Flint** formed when songwriters Benny Gallagher and Graham Lyle left the band. Dixie Dean joined on bass. Hughie Flint had played with **John Mayall's Bluesbreakers** and Tom McGuiness had been in **Manfred Mann**. Their album comprised Dylan covers and is considered one of the best of its type. They later became known as **McGuiness Flint** (Mark 2). (VJ)

Country Fever

Personnel:	PAT DONALDSON	bs	A
	JON DEREK	ld vcls	AB
	JERRY HOGAN	steel gtr	AB
	JED KELLY	drms	AB
	ALBERT LEE	gtr, vcls	A
	ROGER DEAN	ld gtr	B
	PETER OAKMAN (aka OAKES)	bs	B

ALBUMS: 1(B) COUNTRY FEVER   (Pye/Lucky LUS 3003) 1970
         2(B) A NEW DIMENSION   (Pye/Lucky LUS 3013) 1970

45s: Pictures Of You/Too Far Gone   (Pye 7N 17963) 1970
        I'm Sorry/   ( ) 1972

A country-rock band from London who formed during 1968. Roger Dean had earlier played with **The Nu-Notes**, **Ronnie Jones with The Blue Jays** and **John Mayall's Bluesbreakers**. Jerry Hogan had earlier played in **The Flintlocks** who became **Jamie's People**. Albert Lee had previously been with **Chris Farlowe and The Thunderbirds**; and Donaldson's was in **Dantalian's Chariot**. Lee and Donaldson left in April 1969. Lee initially joined **The Steve Gibbons Band**, but then teamed up with Donaldson in **Poet and The One Man Band**. Their first album includes covers of *Ruby*, *Listen To The Band*, *You Ain't Going Nowhere* and *Come Stay With Me*. Their second album contained tracks like *Rocky Top*, *You Won't Get Away With It* and *Picture Of You*.

Their 1972 single *I'm Sorry* was produced by Ray Dorset of **Mungo Jerry**. Peter Oakman had been with Joe Brown and The Bruvvers. In October 1971, he became a sideman of Brown's again in Brown's Home Brew. Then in early 1972 he joined Easy, who soon changed names to Harley Quinn.

Roger Dean:- "Albert Lee played lead on the *Country Fever* album. When Albert is around in the studio, it's a good idea to let him get on with it!! I played lead on *A New Dimension*. We also recorded an album with Marvin Rainwater (of *Whole Lotta Woman* fame), but it's too long ago and I can't remember the details."

Jed Kelly departed in late 1970. In 1971, he became part of an early line-up of **Bees Make Honey** and was also with **Gracious**. He soon left for spells with Easy and **Harley Quinne** (like Oakman). In March 1973, he joined **Bees Make Honey** again only to leave them in October 1973. (VJ/RD/JM)

The Country Gentlemen

Personnel:	PETER COWAP	lead gtr	AB
	NICK DUVALL	bs	A
	LEO LARTI	drms	AB
	TERRY MORTON	bs	B

45:     Greensleeves/Baby Jean   (Decca F 11766) 1963 R1

A short-lived Manchester beat group whose 45 is now quite desired. They were connected to **High Society** and possibly **Friday Browne**, **Graham Gouldman** and the **Manchester Mob**. Cowap was later with **Herman's Hermits**.

Baby Jean reappeared on *Beat Merchants* (2-LP). (VJ/DH/AD)

The Couriers

Personnel:	BARRY ASHBY	vcls	A
	PETER FAIRWEATHER	bs	A
	BILL KIMBER	vcls, gtr	A
	RICHARD LAWS	ld gtr	A
	ALLAN TURNER	drms	A

45:     Take Away/
        Done Me Wrong (Some PS)   (Ember EMB S 218) 1966 R3/SC

This group came from fashionable Chelsea in London. Some copies of their 45 came in a picture sleeve which bore a photo of the group. These are particularly collectable, although copies of disc in ordinary sleeves are also quite sought-after too. The group wrote the flip side, the R&B number, *Done Me Wrong*, themselves. The 'A' side, is a reasonable **Zombies**'-type beat number.

Group member William E. Kimber later launched his own solo career, recording a 45, *Kilburn Towers/Goodbye* (Parlophone R 5735) 1968, which was withdrawn.

Session keyboardist Roy Budd did the piano track on their 45. Richard Laws went on to work with P.J. Proby and Tommy Roe.

Compilation appearances include: *Done Me Wrong* on *Beat It* (3-CD) and *English Freakbeat, Vol. 1* (LP & CD); and *Take Away* on *English Freakbeat, Vol. 3* (LP & CD). (VJ)

The Cousins

45:     Yes Sir That's My Baby/
        Two Lovely Black Eyes   (Decca F 11924) 1964

This was an obscure one-off venture. (VJ)

Dave Cousins

ALBUM: 1 TWO WEEKS LAST SUMMER
                              (A&M AMLS 68118) 1972 SC

45:     Going Home/Ways And Means   (A&M AMS 7032) 1972

Cousins recorded this album and 45 whilst with **The Strawbs**. (VJ)

Julian Covey and Machine

Personnel incl:	JULIAN COVEY	vcls, drms	A
	JOHN HOLLIDAY	bs	A
	JOHN MORESHEAD	gtr	A
	PETER SHELLY	keyb'ds	A
	KEITH WEBB	drms	A

45:	A Little Bit Hurt/Sweet Bacon	(Island WIP 6009) 1967 R1
Reissue:	A Little Bit Hurt/Sweet Bacon	(Island WIP 6442) 1967

A progressive rock/blues group of some pedigree whose 45 is of some interest to collectors. **Julian Covey**'s real name was Phil Kinorra and he'd played with **Brian Auger** in his early days. John Moreshead had played with Johnny Kidd and The Pirates and **Shotgun Express**. He later played for **Aynsley Dunbar**. The group also included **Pete Bardens**, Jim Creagan (later of **Blossom Toes** and **Family**) and **Dave Mason** at various times. The 45 bears distinct similarity to a passage of Stravinsky's *Rite of Spring* that also served as inspiration for **Soft Machine**'s *I Did It Again*.

Compilation appearances include: *A Little Bit Hurt* on *Rare 60's Beat Treasures, Vol. 3* (CD) and *Beat It* (3-CD) and *Sweet Bacon* on *Jagged Time Lapse, Vol 3*. (VJ/RMJ)

Billy Cox's Nitro Function

Personnel:	BILLY COX	bs	A
	ROBERT TARRANT	drms	A
	CHAR VINNEDGE	gtr, vcls	A

ALBUM:	1(A)	NITRO FUNCTION
		(Pye International NSPL 25158) 1971 R1

NB: (1) has been counterfeited on CD.

This album cover was by Roger Dean. There's no band photo but one of **Cox**, Mitch Mitchell and a silhouette, which must be **Hendrix**. All tracks except *You Really Got Me* and *You Got A Hold On Me* (Cox) and *Let Me Do What I Want To Do* (Cox - Vinnedge), were written by Char Vinnedge. The record starts promisingly but then lapses into an inevitable **Hendrix** tribute (*42-70*). Once the lyrics are over the guitar-playing is a more fitting tribute. When Char quit the group her place was taken by Pat Quatro (Suzi's sister) who went on to **Fanny**. (VJ/JM)

Lol Coxhill

ALBUMS:	1	EAR OF THE BEHOLDER (2-LP)	
(up to			(Dandelion 69001) 1971 R2
1976)	2	TOVERBAL SUITE	(Mushroom 150 Mr. 23) 1972 R2
	3	COXHILL MILLER	(Caroline C 1503) 1973 SC
	4	THE STORY SO FAR ... OH REALLY (1 SIDE)	
			(Caroline C 1507) 1974 SC

	5	LOL COXHILL AND WELFARE STATE	
			(Caroline C 1514) 1975 SC
	6	FLEAS IN CUSTARD	(Caroline C 1515) 1975 SC
	7	DIVERSE	(Ogun OG 510) 1976 SC

NB: (3) and (4) with **Stephen Miller**. (1) reissued on See For Miles (SEECD 414) 199? (2) reissued on CD with one bonus track.

EP:	1	MURDER IN THE AIR (12") (Chiltern Sound CS 100) 1978

Coxhill is a veteran saxophonist who has been involved in groups going back to the late sixties. In 1970 he briefly played with **Carol Grimes and Delivery** before joining **Kevin Ayers (and The Whole World)**. The following year he was involved in D.C. and The MBs, who never really got off the ground. An early signing to John Peel's Dandelion label in 1971, Peel had discovered him busking in London's Piccadilly Circus.

His first solo album, *The Ear Of The Beholder*, featured guest appearances from **Kevin Ayers**, **David Bedford**, **Mike Oldfield** and **Robert Wyatt**. Well worth seeking out; it was the only double album on the Dandelion label.

Coxhill's *Toverbal Suite* album is his rarest and most sought-after, but of course Mushroom was an obscure and is now a very collectable label.

He went on to record on specialist jazz labels, was featured on a London Weekend Television documentary and has guested for several other artists including The Damned (Captain Sensible was a great admirer of his work).

Dandelion Sampler 1969-1972 (CD) features *Little Triple One Shot*. (VJ)

Coxhill Bedford Duo

Personnel:	LOL COXHILL	A
	DEVID BEDFORD	A

45s:	Pretty Little Girl (Parts 1 & 2)	(Polydor 2001 253) 1971
	Mood/	
	(flip by Dandy and The Dandylettes)	(Dandelion 2058 214) 1972

These 45s were joint ventures by **Lol Coxhill** and **David Bedford**. See their solo entries for further details of their careers.

Dandelion Rarities (CD) compiles *Pretty Little Girl* by the **Coxhill-Bedford Duo**. (VJ)

Kevin Coyne

HCP

ALBUMS:	1	CASE HISTORY	(Dandelion 2310 228) 1972 R1
(up to	2	MARJORY RAZORBLADE (2-LP)	(Virgin VD2501) 1973 SC
1976)	3	BLAME IT ON THE NIGHT	(Virgin V 2012) 1974 -

BILLY COX'S NITRO FUNCTION - Nitro Function (CD).

LOL COXHILL - Fleas In Custard (LP).

184

KEVIN COYNE - Case History (LP).

KEVIN COYNE - Marjory Razorblade (2-LP).

4	MATCHING HEAD AND FEET	(Virgin V 2033) 1975 -
5	HEARTBURN	(Virgin V 2047) 1976 -
6	IN LIVING BLACK AND WHITE (2-LP)	
		(Virgin VD 2505) 1976 -

NB: (3) reissued on Virgin (CDVM 2051) in 1990, with both sides of the *Lovesick Fool* 45 added. (6) reissued on CD (Virgin CDVM 2505) in 1991. The *Peel Sessions* (Strange Fruit SFRCD 112) 1991 compiles recordings from his many BBC sessions. The material is mostly from 1973-74 but some later recordings are included. (2) reissued on CD (Virgin CDVM 2501) 1990. (4) reissued on CD (Virgin CDV 2033) 1991. (5) reissued on CD (Virgin CDVM 2047) 1991. There's a (3-LP) box set, *The Dandelion Years* (Butt BUTBOX 1) 1982. *Case History... Plus* (See For Miles SEECD 410) 1995 includes all of (1) plus two non-album tracks, *I'm All Aching* and *A Leopard Never Changes Its Spots.*

45s:	Cheat Me/Flowering Cherry	(Polydor 2001 357) 1972
	Marlene/Everybody Says	(Virgin VS 102) 1973
	Lovesick Fool/Sea Of Love	(Virgin VS 104) 1973
	I Believe In Love/	
	Queenie Queenie Caroline	(Virgin VS 107) 1974
	Rock'n'Roll Hymn/It's Not Me	(Virgin VS 119) 1975
	Lorna/Shangri La	(Virgin VS 126) 1975
	Don't Make Waves/	
	Mona, Where's My Trousers	(Virgin VS 136) 1976
	Walk On By/Shangri La	(Virgin VS 148) 1976
	Fever/Daddy	(Virgin VS 160) 1976
	Merlene/England Is Dying	(Virgin VS 175) 1977
	Amsterdam/I Really Love You	(Virgin VS 203) 1978
	I'll Go To/Having A Party	(Virgin VS 255) 1979
	So Strange/	
	Father Dear Father (PS)	(Cherry Red CHERR 49) 1982

One of the more interesting characters of this era, **Coyne** entered the world on 27 January 1944 in Derby. He went to Art College there and later worked as a social therapist in the Whittington Hospital (a Preston mental hospital) from 1965.

In 1968 he relocated to London, working as a social worker in Camden and beginning to pursue a music career. He soon became vocalist for **Siren**, but when they split he quit his day job, too, concentrating on a solo career.

Snapped up by Dandelion he put out a debut album which was full of his eccentricities and is now cherished by collectors. Much of his music was totally anti-commercial and entirely lacking in conventional song structures.

In 1973 he signed to Virgin who put out a double album of his work, *Marjory Razorblade*. This was a classic seventies **Coyne** album. It included the magnum opus *House On The Hill*, a story of institutional life, and the lively *Marlene*.

In 1974 he formed a support band to play dates in Britain and Europe. After it collapsed he put together an enlarged band in January 1975 comprised of Archie Legget (bs) (ex-**Kevin Ayers** & Soporifics), Tim Penn (keyb'ds), Gordon Smith (slide gtr) (ex-**Demick and Armstrong**), Andy

Summers (gtr), Steve Thompson (bs) and Peter Woolf (drms). Summers and Woolf had been playing with **David Essex**. The resulting album, *Matching Hands And Feet*, was not one of his best though. In April 1975 Penn and Smith went on their way to form The Smiggs Band and the slimmed down band embarked on a long UK tour and recorded a further album, *Heartburn*. *In Living Black And White*, a live album, included **Zoot Money** and Andy Summers in the line-up. It also featured extended versions of two of his finest works, *House On The Hill* and *Marjory Razorblade*. Leget left in August 1976 and was replaced by Thompson (ex-Alvin Lee). However, by April 1976 it had become apparent that **Coyne**, whose music was always an acquired taste, couldn't afford to keep a band on the road and he was forced back to a solo format. So Summers and Money went on to the **Kevin Ayers Band**, Thompson to Mick Taylor Band and Woolf to session work. **Coyne** continued to record as a cult figure. He embarked on a small tour of the UK in March 2002.

He can also be heard playing *Saviour* on the 1975 Chrysalis compilation album *Over The Rainbow* (LP). More recently *Sand All Yellow* has made an appearance on the *Dandelion Rarities* (CD).

Kevin Coyne died on 2 December 2004, aged 60. Despite suffering from respiratory ailments, he continued to perform and played at the 100 Club in London and other UK venues just weeks before his death. He will be lovingly remembered as a distinctive singer-songwriter. (VJ/JM)

Coyne-Clague

45:     The Stride/I Wonder Where   (Dandelion S 4494) 1970

This 45 released on John Peel's Dandelion label featured **Kevin Coyne** and members of **Clague**. (VJ)

The Crackers

45:     Honey Do/It Happens All The Time   (Fontana TF 995) 1968

This was **The Merseys** recording their final single for Fontana under a pseudonym but sadly for them it met with the same fate as their later efforts as **The Merseys**. The 'B' side was written by **Vincent Crane** prior to his days with **Atomic Rooster**. The 'A' side was a cover of a song by US band The Strangeloves. (VJ)

Craig

Personnel:	GEOFF BROWN	vcls, gtr	A
	LEN COX	bs	A
	CARL PALMER	drms	A
	RICK PANNELL	lead gtr	A

45s: A Little Bit Of Soap/
              Ready Steady Let's Go   (Fontana TF 665) 1966 R1
              I Must Be Mad/Suspense   (Fontana TF 715) 1966 R4

This Birmingham band may have evolved out of The King Bees according to the sleeve notes to *The Psychedelic Snarl* compilation. Their first 45 had a pretty forgettable cover of Jimmy Justice's *A Little Bit Of Soap* on the 'A', but a beaty flip side. However, their magnum opus was without doubt *I Must Be Mad*, which was produced by Larry Page. It's full of clanging chords and screeching guitar work - an essential slab of British psychedelia. The 45 was released in Germany on the Hansa label in an art sleeve with a much stronger flip side, *Dancing Down In New Orleans* than it had in the UK. Pannell and Brown went on to **Galliard**, which evolved into Helicopter.

Compilation coverage has included:- *I Must Be Mad* on *Rubble Vol. 1: The Psychedelic Snarl* (LP), *Rubble Vol. 1* (CD), *Chocolate Soup For Diabetics, Vol. 2* (LP), *Chocolate Soup* (CD), *Perfumed Garden, Vol. 1* (CD), *Pebbles, Vol. 7* (LP) and on the 4-CD box set *Nuggets 11*; *Dancing Down In New Orleans* on *Purple Heart Surgery, Vol. 1* (LP) and *Hens Teeth Vol. 2* (CD); *Suspense* on *Yellow Elektric Years* (LP); *Ready Steady Let's Go* on *Purple Pill Eaters* (CD); and *I Must Be Mad*, *Suspense* and *Dancing Down In New Orleans* on *Rare 60's Beat Treasures, Vol. 2* (CD). (VJ)

Don Craine's New Downliners Sect

Personnel: BARRY 'BAZ' COOPER   keyb'ds,   A
              DON CRAINE   vcls   A
              KEVIN FLANAGAN   drms   A
              KEITH GRANT   bs   A
              BOB TAYLOR   ld gtr   A

45:      I Can't Get Away From You/Roses   (Pye 7N 17261) 1967 R3

The original **Downliners Sect** had folded by the end of 1966 following their final single, *The Cost Of Living*, which had been made as a contractual obligation. By 1967 **Craine** had put together a new band which recorded this 45. They also briefly included **Matthew Fisher** (later of **Procol Harum**) but he did not play on the single. After a year of touring **Craine** packed it in although Grant continued and cut a few tracks for a set of Swedish Juke Box EPs in 1968/69 with the band reverting to the shorter **Downliners Sect** name. Some while later **Craine** and Keith Grant rejoined and the band has continued until the present day.

There is a compilation CD (See For Miles SEECD 398) 1994 focusing on the original **Downliners Sect** which covers some of this band's recordings. Compilation appearances include: *Roses* on *Quick Before They Catch Us* (LP & CD) and *Freakbeat Freakout* (CD); *I Can't Get Away From You* on *The R&B Era, Vol. 2* (LP & CD), *Voyage Through The Sugarcube* (LP & CD) and, more recently, on *Rock Of Ages, Four Decades Of Heavy Rock 1962-2002*.. (MWh/VJ/BC)

CREAM - Fresh Cream (LP).

CREAM - Disraeli Gears (LP).

Tony Crane

45s: Even The Bravest/I Still Remember   (CBS 202 022) 1965
(up to   Ideal Love/Little You   (Polydor BM 56008) 1965
1976)   Anonymous Mr. Brown/In This World   (Pye 7N 17337) 1967
              Scratchin' Ma Head/Patterns In The Sky   (Pye 7N 17517) 1968
              If I Ever Get To Saginaw Again/
              Winds Of Change   (Pye 7N 17645) 1968

These were solo efforts by the man better known as lead vocalist with **The Merseybeats**.

Anonymous Mr. Brown later turned up on *Petal Pushers* (LP). (VJ)

Vincent Crane and Chris Farlowe

45:      Can't Find A Reason/Moods   (Dawn DNS 1034) 1972

This 45 was the product of a one-off venture by former **Crazy World Of Arthur Brown** and **Atomic Rooster** member **Crane** and sixties R&B veteran **Farlowe**. *Visions Of The Past, Vol. 3* (LP & CD) incidentally features a previously unissued cut, *Little Girl* by The Vincent Crane Big Sound. (VJ)

Crazy Feelings

45:      Please Lie/Time Is Running Out   (Polydor BM 56723) 1967

A later beat era group. (MWh)

Crazy Mabel

ALBUM: 1   CRAZY MABEL   (Bellaphon 19016) 1970
NB: (1) German release.

This English blues-rock quintet released the above album in Germany. (VJ)

Cream

Personnel: GINGER BAKER   drms   A
              JACK BRUCE   bs, vcls   A
              ERIC CLAPTON   gtr, vcls   A

                                                      HCP
ALBUMS: 1(A)   FRESH CREAM   (Reaction 593/4 001) 1966 R1 6
        2(A)   DISRAELI GEARS   (Reaction 593/4 003) 1967 R1 5
        3(A)   WHEELS OF FIRE (2-LP)
                                 (Polydor 582/3 031/2) 1968 R1 3

4(A)	WHEELS OF FIRE - IN THE STUDIO			
		(Polydor 582/3 033)	1968	7
5(A)	WHEELS OF FIRE - LIVE AT THE FILLMORE			
		(Polydor 582/3 040)	1968	-
6(A)	CREAM ON TOP	(Polydor 2855 002)	1969	R2 -
7(A)	GOODBYE	(Polydor 583 053)	1969	1
8(A)	BEST OF CREAM	(Polydor 583 060)	1969	6
9(A)	LIVE CREAM	(Polydor 2383 016)	1970	4
10(A)	LIVE CREAM, VOL 2	(Polydor 2383 119)	1972	15
11(A)	HEAVY CREAM (2-LP)	(RSO/Polydor 2659 022)	1973	-
12(A)	CREAM, VOL 2 (Comp.)	(RSO 2479 701)	1978	-

NB (1) reissued as *Cream* (Polydor 2384 067) 1975 with two extra tracks and again (Polydor SPELP 42) 1983. (1) also reissued on CD (Polydor 927 576-2) 1987 and again remastered (Polydor 531 810-2) 1998 and also as a gold limited edition CD (Polydor 559 429-2) 1998. (1) reissued on vinyl (DCC Compact Classics LPZ 2015) 1997. (2) reissued (RSO 2394 129) 1977 and on CD (Polydor 8236362) 1990 and again remastered (Polydor 531 811-2) 1998, also as a limited edition gold CD (Polydor 559 428-2) 1998 and later as a 2-CD set *Disraeli Gears: Deluxe Edition* (Polydor 9819312) 2004 (3) reissued (Polydor 2612 001) 1972 and (RSO 2671 109) 1977 and again (RSO SPDLP 2) 1984. (3) also reissued on CD (Polydor 827 578-2) 1987, again (Polydor 8275782) 1990 and again remastered (Polydor 531 812-2) 1998, also as a limited edition gold CD (Polydor 559 425-2) 1998. (4) reissued (RSO 2394 136) 1977 and on a 2-CD set (Polydor 825 414-2) 1987. (5) reissued (RSO 2394 137) 1977. (6) Mail order only. (7) reissued (RSO 2394 179) 1975 in a gatefold sleeve, again (RSO 2394 178) 1977 and again (RSO SPELP 75) 1984. (7) also reissued on CD (Polydor 823 660-2) 1988 and again remastered (Polydor 531 815-2) 1998. (8) reissued (RSO 2394 131) 1977, again (Arude MG ADAH 427) 198? and issued as a limited edition gold CD (Polydor 559 430-2) 1998. (9) reissued (RSO 2394 154) 1977 and (RSO SPELP 93) 1985. (9) also reissued on CD (Polydor 927577-2) 1987 and again remastered (Polydor 531 816-2) 1998, also as a limited edition CD (Polydor 559 432-2) 1998. (10) reissued (RSO 2394 155) 1977. (10) also reissued on CD (Polydor 823 661-2) 1987 and again remastered (Polydor 531 817-2) 1998. *Cream* (RSO 2658 142) 1980 is a 7-LP box set including *Fresh Cream, Disraeli Gears, Wheels Of Fire, Goodbye, Live Cream* and *Live Cream Vol 2*. *Strange Brew - The Very Best Of Cream* (RSO RSD 5021) 1983 was a compilation, later issued on CD (RSO 811 639-2) 1990. *Crossroads* (Polydor 835 263-1/2) 1988 is a 5-LP or 3-CD **Eric Clapton** package, which features unissued **Cream** BBC session tracks, *Lawdy Mama* and *Steppin' Out*. *The Alternative Album* (ITM 960002) 1992 consists largely of alternate takes of songs which appeared on their debut album and a few previously unissued numbers, including *You Make Me Feel*, a different version of *The Coffee Song*, an instrumental version of *I Feel Free* and a much later alternate version of *White Room*. *Deserted Cities: The Cream Collection* (Pickwick PWKS 4127 P) 1992 is a good budged-priced CD compilation of live and studio recordings. *Cream In Gear* (UFO CR1) 1992 is a 96-page photo book packaged with the *Disraeli Gears* CD. *Those Were The Days* (Polydor 539 002-2) 1997 is a 4-CD compilation. *At The BBC* (Polydor 760482) 2003 is comprised of 22 almost entirely previously unreleased versions of their shorter songs from 1966/67.

HCP

45s:	Wrapping Paper/Cat's Squirrel	(Reaction 591 007)	1966	SC 34
	I Feel Free/N.S.U.	(Reaction 591 011)	1966	11
	Strange Brew/			
	Tales Of Brave Ulysees	(Reaction 591 015)	1967	17
	Anyone For Tennis/			
	Pressed Rat And Warthog	(Polydor 56258)	1968	40
	Sunshine Of Your Love/SWLABR	(Polydor 56286)	1968	25

CREAM - Wheels Of Fire (2-LP).

CREAM - Goodbye (LP).

	White Room/Those Were The Days	(Polydor 56300)	1969	28
α	Strange Brew/Wrapping Paper	(Polydor 56315)	1969	-
	Badge/What A Bringdown	(Polydor 56315)	1969	18
Reissues:	I Feel Free/Wrapping Paper	(Polydor 2058 120)	1971	-
	Badge/What A Bringdown	(Polydor 2058 285)	1972	42
	Badge/Tales Of Brave Ulysees	(RSO RSO 91)	1982	-
	Badge/Tales Of Brave Ulysees/			
	White Room (12")	(RSO HSOX 91)	1982	-
	I Feel Free/Wrapping Paper	(Old Gold OG 9423)	1984	-
	Strange Brew/			
	Tales Of Brave Ulysees	(Old Gold OG 9424)	1984	-
	White Room/Badge	(Old Gold OG 9425)	1984	-
	Sunshine Of Your Love/			
	Anyone For Tennis	(Old Gold OG 9426)	1984	-
	I Feel Free/Badge	(RSO POSP 812)	1986	-
β	I Feel Free/Badge	(Lyntone no #)	1986	-

NB: α Unissued. β Flexi free with Sunday colour supplement.

This hard-rock/blues band was formed in July 1966. Although the term was not used at the time, **Cream** was effectively the first supergroup. **Clapton**, from Ripley, Surrey, had played for The Roosters, **Casey Jones and The Engineers**, **The Yardbirds**, and **John Mayall's Bluesbreakers**. **Bruce**, from Lanarkshire, had played in several groups including **Alexis Korner's Blues Incorporated** and The Graham Bond Quartet (which later became **The Graham Bond Organisation**). **Baker**, from New Eltham, had played in The Storyville Jazzmen and later in **Alexis Korner's Blues Incorporated**.

Cream set out as a blues band, but their early singles, *Wrapping Paper* and *I Feel Free*, were quite popish.

A 1967 tour of America appears to have been a turning point in their career. Confronted by vast audiences they began playing powerhouse rock with extended and experimental solos. Their *Disraeli Gears* album was actually recorded in the US at Atlantic Studios, New York. Its cover and, to a lesser degree, its contents were very much a product of the psychedelic era. It included some of their classic songs like *Sunshine Of Your Love, Swablr* and *Tales Of Brave Ulysees*. 1967 also saw them produce an interesting hit single in *Strange Brew*.

By the time that *Wheels Of Fire* was released, in August 1968, the hard-rock band was beginning to feel that it had taken things musically as far as it could. *Wheels Of Fire* consisted of a studio album and a live album, recorded at The Fillmore in San Francisco. It was an enormous transatlantic success. Each album was also packaged separately. The 'live' set contained extended versions of *Toad* and *Spoonful*. Much of the album can be viewed as self-indulgent though, and its massive sales may be partly attributable to their plans to split and stage a farewell extravaganza at the Albert Hall on 26 November 1968. After this, the *Goodbye* album appeared and it became their most successful of all. This was followed by a series of 'live' albums, compilations and bootlegs, which are of less relevance here.

Clapton and **Baker** went on to play in **Blind Faith** and **Bruce** embarked on a solo career. Later, **Baker** had rather unsuccessful encounters with Ginger Baker's Airforce and **Baker-Gurvitz Army**. Meanwhile, **Clapton** adopted a low profile with Delaney and Bonnie before forming **Derek and The Dominos**.

Cream were enormously important as founders of heavy rock style imitated by countless bands, such as Mountain, although much of the material is overlooked by collectors. Readers who are not familiar with *Disraeli Gears*, in particular, should find it worth checking out.

The *Deserted Cities* CD compilation is a good introduction to their music. It includes both live and studio material which ranges from popish moments like *Wrapping Paper* and *I Feel Free* to their extended rock/blues compositions like *Toad* and *NSU*. To worldwide astonishment, the trio reformed in May 2005 for a strictly one-off week of gigs at the Albert Hall, which were rapturously received by press and public alike, with tickets changing hands for stupendous sums.

Compilation appearances have included: *Politician* and *Passing The Time* on *Deep Overground Pop* (LP); *Lawdy Mama* on *Rock Party* (2-LP); *Doing That Scrapyard Thing* on *Supergroups* (LP); and *Anyone For Tennis* on *Rare Tracks* (LP). (VJ)

The Creation

Personnel:	BOB GARNER	bs, vcls	ABC
	JACK JONES	drms	ABC
	EDDIE PHLLIPS	ld gtr	AB
	KENNY PICKETT	vcls	A C
	KIM GARDNER	bs	BC
	RONNIE WOOD	ld gtr	B

ALBUMS:	1(A)	WE ARE PAINTERMEN	(Hit-ton 340037) 1967 R4
	2( )	BEST OF	(Pop-Schallplatten 101678) 1968 R3
	3( )	THE CREATION '66-67	(Charisma Perspective CS 8) 1973 R1

NB: (1) and (2) were German only releases. (1) was reissued in 1982 (OutLine OLLP 5234 AS). A companion volume of their non-LP cuts and rarities entitled *The Rest Of The Creation* (Outline OLLP 5242 AS), collected together most of their other recordings using a similar cover to (2). Other compilations have included: *Creation '66-'67* (Charisma CS 8) 1973 R1; *The Mark Four/The Creation* (Eva 12005) 1983; *How Does It Feel To Feel* (Edsel ED 106) 1982, later reissued on CD (Edsel EDCD 106) 1990 with four extra cuts; *Painter Man* (Edsel NESTCD 904) 1993 - a mini-CD which duplicates much of the superior *How Does It Feel To Feel* compilation. Finally there's *Creation - The Complete Collection, Vol. 1 (Making Time)* (Retroactive RECD 9002) 1998, *Our Music Is Red With Purple Flashes* (Diablo DIAB 857) 1998 and *Creation - The Complete Collection, Vol. 2 (Biff Bang Pow)* (Retroactive RECD 9003) 1998 which collect together **all** the existing **Creation** recordings from the '60s, including rare stereo mixes, previously unreleased and live material. *Psychedelic Rose* (Cherry Red CDM RED 256) 2004 collects tracks intended for a mid-eighties album, which was never released.

THE CREATION - We Are Paintermen (LP).

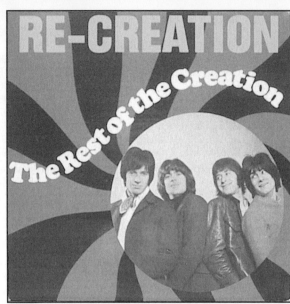

CREATION - The Rest Of (LP).

HCP

45s:	α	Making Time/Try And Stop Me	(Planet PLF 116) 1966 R1 49
	α	Painter Man/Biff Bang Pow	(Planet PLF 119) 1966 R1 36
		If I Stay Too Long/Nightmares	(Polydor 56177) 1967 R1 -
		Life Is Just Beginning/ Through My Eyes	(Polydor 56207) 1967 R2 -
		How Does It Feel To Feel/Tom Tom	(Polydor 56230) 1968 R1 -
		Midway Down/The Girls Are Naked	(Polydor 56246) 1968 R1 -
Reissues:		Making Time/Painter Man	(Charisma CB 213) 1973 -
		Making Time/Painter Man	(Raw RAW 4) 1977 -
		Making Time/Uncle Bert (PS)	(Edsel E 5006) 1984 -

NB: α Some in company sleeve.

This group evolved out of a mainly R&B oriented group **The Mark Four**, which featured Phillips, Pickett and Jones, with John Dalton on bass. **The Mark Four** recorded four singles, which are now very sought-after, primarily because they were the first recordings by this personnel. When Dalton departed to join **The Kinks**, Bob Garner joined from **Tony Sheridan**'s Band as a replacement.

The group then changed their name to **The Creation** and had two minor UK hits with *Making Time*, which reached No 49 in July 1966 and *Painter Man*, a No 36 in November 1966. Both featured fine guitar work from Phillips who was the first musician to use a violin bow on his guitar. Both were reissued on a double-sided single in 1973 and 1977. They appeared at the 14-Hour Technicolour Dream in London's Alexander Palace in May '67.

Kenny Pickett now left the group for a while. Bob Garner took over on vocals and Kim Gardner (from **The Birds**) came in on bass.

After Planet folded they switched to Polydor for whom they released four further singles. All of **The Creation**'s singles are sought-after.

The Creation made far more impact on the Continent, where two albums were issued, than in the UK. Both albums are good, containing many of their singles and other strong material such as *Hey Joe, Nightmares* and *Can I Join Your Band?*

In 1968, Ronnie Wood (later of **The Faces** and **Rolling Stones**) replaced Phillips on guitar, although later that year the whole group disintegrated. They made a further single, *For All That I Am/Uncle Bert*, which was not released in Britain, before splitting in the Summer of 1968. Both of their Continental albums are extremely rare, particularly copies of *We Are Paintermen*. However, for the less affluent, there have been a number of compilations, and any of these will serve as a good introduction to the band.

The Creation were rather special and this explains collectors' interest in them. They were innovative and talented. Pickett's vocals were powerful, Phillips' guitar work was inventive and they composed some excellent songs. They were a theatrical live attraction, too, Pickett often sprayed aerosol paint onto a white screen and burnt it. It is surprising that the success they achieved on the Continent eluded them here - perhaps they spent too little time in the UK.

After they split, Kenny Pickett co-wrote Clive Dunn's 1970 No 1 *Grandad!* and was a roadie for **Led Zeppelin**. Gardner later became part of **Ashton, Gardner and Dyke** who had a 1971 hit with *Resurrection Shuffle*.

The Creation reformed in May 1987 and issued a single, *A Spirit Of Love*, backed by an update of their sixties hit, *Making Time*. They reformed again in the nineties (line-up Bob Garner, Eddie Phillips, Kenny Pickett and Jack Jones) issuing a live album, *Lay The Ghost* (Cohesion COCRE 1) 1993, which captures their excellent re-union gig at London's Mean Fiddler venue that year. The CD package comes in an album-sized sleeve, with a pop-art poster and detailed liner notes by Kenny Pickett. The band also recorded a single *Creation*, in 1994 and started recording an album of new studio material in 1995. They've also did some further gigs and had a BBC Radio One session on 'The Mark Radcliffe Show'.

Cherry Red's 2004 *Psychedelic Rose* compilation collects tracks intended for a mid-eighties album, which never materialised. The riffy *Lay The Ghost* is the stand-out track on this. The title track harps back to the hazy sixties and *Radio Beautiful* is very catchy. The release comes with a CD-ROM of *Painter Man* and a spoken word book relaying part of the band's history.

Sadly, Kenny Pickett, the band's much loved singer and principal songwriter died on 10th January, 1997. He was followed by Kim Gardner, who died on 24 October 2001, after losing a three year battle with cancer.

Compilation appearances have included: *Painter Man* and *That's How Strong My Love Is* (both live from German TV) on *Made In England, Vol. 1* (CD); and *Making Time*, *How Does It Feel To Feel* and *Biff! Bang! Pow!* on the 4-CD *Nuggets* 11 box set. (VJ/WD)

Creepy John Thomas

Personnel:	ANDY MARX	bs, gtr	AB
	HELMUT POHL	drms	A
	CREEPY JOHN THOMAS	gtr, vcls	AB
	DAVE HUTCHINS	bs	B
	ROY OCTEMRO	drms	B

| ALBUMS: | 1(A) | CREEPY JOHN THOMAS | (RCA SF 8061) 1969 R2 |
| | 2(B) | BROTHER BAT BONE | (Telefunken) 1970 R2 |

NB: (1) and (2) reissued on one CD (Fingerprint CDCJ 421) 1992 in Germany.

45:      Ride A Rainbow/Moon And Eyes Song   (RCA RCA 1912) 1969

A little known and underrated talent. **John Thomas** had two hits with The Flies in Australia before coming to London to form his own band in 1969. Both albums are consistently good, strong material and raw vocals, which suit the guitar-driven musical format. There's some good guitar work on both albums. *Ride A Rainbow* is certainly the most commercial track on the first album but *Trippin' Like A Dog And Rockin' Like A Bitch* is really the magnum opus. The second album is excellent too. The opening cut *Down In The Bottom* sets the tone for more guitar driven hard-rock from which the title track, *Brother Bat Bone*, is really the highlight, but dig the melodic guitar work on *This Is My Body* and *Standin' In The Sunshine* illustrates his mellower side. This is slightly the stronger of two but both are recommended.

Unfortunately the German release of the first album wrongly states that Kiernan O'Conner (drms) and George Hart (bs) were members of the group. Both were only in the live band for a brief period.

Line-up 'B' stayed together for more than two years. **John Thomas** later played for **Edgar Broughton** in 1975 and now lives in Berlin, running a band called Johnny and The Drivers.

Moon And Eyes recorded by line-up 'A' later resurfaced on *Broken Dreams, Vol. 3* (LP). (VJ)

Cressida

Personnel:	IAN CLARK	drms	AB
	ANGUS CULLEN	vcls, gtr	AB
	JOHN HEYWORTH	gtr	A
	PETER JENNINGS	keyb'ds	AB
	KEVIN McCARTHY	bs	AB
	JOHN CULLEY	gtr	B
	HAROLD McNAIR	flute	B

| ALBUMS: | 1(A) | CRESSIDA | (Vertigo VO 7) 1970 R1 |
| | 2(B) | ASYLUM | (Vertigo 6360 025) 1971 R2 |

NB: (1) also reissued on CD (Repertoire REP 4299-WY) 1992 and on vinyl (Akarma AK 182) 2001. (2) also reissued on CD (Repertoire REP 4105-WP) 1990. (1) and (2) reissued on 2-CD set (Gott Discs GOTTCD 002)

Both **Cressida** albums can be used as an example of what is interesting and worthwhile about UK progressive rock. Although freely borrowing from almost any style imaginable, the band manages to create a unique atmospheric blend of seriousness and light-heartedness, more often than not with a melancholic touch not unlike **Spring**. The music on the first album is slightly more song-orientated and simply spills over from memorable and simultaneously sad and beautiful melodies. Singer Cullen possesses one of the few agreeable voices from the prog-rock scene, totally devoid of any style-bound mannerisms. The music is intelligently played throughout, most notably on the title track and the aching *Down Down*, although it's hard to choose any favourite tracks. The second album relies a bit more on instrumental passages and tends more to elaborate arrangements, without ever getting pompous. A superb track is *Munich* with great and subtle organ parts and good dual lead guitar as well. Wholeheartedly recommended. Originals are on the swirl label.

CREEPY JOHN THOMAS - Creepy John Thomas (CD).

CRESSIDA - Cressida (LP).

CRESSIDA - Asylum (LP).

Ian Clark went on to **Uriah Heep** from September 1970 - November 1971. He is now a teacher. John Culley went on to **Black Widow** and McCarthy to **Tranquility** (as guitarist).

The *Vertigo Annual* (2-LP) also included their *To Play Your Little Game*. More recently acetate versions of *Lights In My Mind* and *Depression* have resurfaced on *Mynd The Gap* (LP). (VJ/JM)

The Cresters (aka The Crestas)

Personnel incl:	JOHNNIE CASSON	drms	A
	MALCOLM CLARKE	gtr, vcls	A
	JOHN HARDING	bs	A
	RICHARD HARDING	lead gtr	A

45s:	To Be Loved/When I Fall In Love	(Fontana TF 551) 1965 SC
	I Just Don't Understand/I Want You	(HMV POP 1249) 1964 SC
	Put Your Arms Around Me/	
	Do It With Me	(HMV POP 1296) 1964 SC

A beat group from Bramley in Yorkshire. They actually shared the bill with **The Beatles** at Doncaster Baths and with **The Rolling Stones** at Leeds Town Hall. Their guitarist Richard Harding had made an instrumental single back in 1961, *Jezebell Temptation* (HMV POP 8871). They did not disband until 1984. Johnnie Casson is now a well known celebrity comedian.

I Just Don't Understand has been compiled on *R&B Scene, Vol. 1* (LP) and *Beat Merchants* (2-LP). (MWh/VJ/JM/RD)

Crew

Personnel:	JOHN CHICHESTER	gtr	A
	JON NEWEY	congas, perc	A
	TONY PERRY	organ	A
	IAN RUTTER	bs	A
	MARTIN SAMUEL	drms	A
	JOHN WRIGHT	vcls, perc	A

45s:	Marty/Dangersigns	(Plexium PXM 12) 1969
	Cecilia/1970	(Decca F 13000) 1970
	Lady Of The Night/Today	(Orange Music acetate no #) 1971

A London-based percussive, heavy, progressive group fronted by vocalist 'Big' John Wright, who had worked with soul giant James Brown. Chichester came from **Siren** and Newey came from **They Bite** along with Rutter. **Crew** folded in 1972. Wright went to work for DJ Emperor Rosko, Chichester became roadie for **Greg Lake** in **Emerson Lake and Palmer** and Newey formed **England's Glory**.

Their second 45 was produced by **Jonathan King** and featured a version of Simon and Garfunkel's *Cecilia* on the 'A' side. Dave Neal, who was born at Woolwich in South East London on 24th April 1952 was in **Justin Tyme** previously and later drummed for Suzi Quatro. (VJ)

Crocheted Doughnut Ring

Personnel:	GEORGE BIRD	bs	A
	JOHN CHAPEL	keyb'ds	A
	RICK MILLS	vcls	A
	BERT PULHAM	gtr	A
	DAVE SKATES	drms	A

45s:	Two Little Ladies (Azeila And	
	Rhododendren)/Nice	(Polydor 56204) 1967 R1
	Havana Anna/Happy Castle	(Deram DM 169) 1967 R1
	Maxine's Parlour/	
	Get Out Your Rock And Roll Shoes	(Deram DM 180) 1968 SC

A very obscure outfit whose *Happy Castle*, seems to be influenced by the US West Coast and UK outfits like **The Small Faces**. The 'A' side of the follow-up 45 was quite classically influenced.

The band evolved from a beat group called **Force Five** (Bert Pulham used the name Bert Ash whilst in this band). He was born in Liverpool in April 1943. Skates was known as Dave Skinner whilst in **Force Five** and was born in Eton, Berkshire in April 1941. The **Force Five** released five singles for United Artists. Vocalist Rick Mills was from **The Fingers**, who recorded on Columbia. *Havana Anna* actually reached No 2 in the Japanese Top 10 in 1968, but a prospective tour of Japan fell through due to financial management problems. They appeared on 'Dee Time' playing *Maxine's Parlour*, which was written by **Bill Fay,** prompting Dee to remark 'that was the **Crocheted Doughnut Ring**. Doughnut ring us, we'll ring you.' Their final 45 *Nice* was a bizarre instrumental full of studio effects, which was created by their producer Peter Eden whilst the band was away. They also recorded a 45 as **Doughnut Ring**.

In the 1990s Mojo magazine printed a letter, with a bogus band history.

Bert Pulham joined **Gulliver's People** and is now a taxi driver. George Bird is a driving instructor and Dave Skates sadly died.

Compilation appearances have included: *Two Little Ladies (Azalea and Rhododendron)* and *Nice* on *Nice* (LP); *Happy Castle* on *British Psychedelic Trip, Vol. 3* (LP) and *Great British Psychedelic Trip, Vol. 2* (CD); and *Get Out Your Rock'n'Roll Shoes* on *Jagged Time Lapse, Vol 1* and *Maxine's Parlour* on *Colour Me Pop, Vol 2* (CD). (VJ/MWh/JM/RMJ)

Cromwell

Personnel:	PATRICK BRADY	vcls, gtr	A
	DEREK DAWSON	drms	A
	JOLYON JACKSON	keyb'ds	A
	JOHN KEOGH	keyb'ds	A
	MICHAEL KIELLY	vcls, bs, gtr, keyb'ds	A
	FININ O'CALLAGHAN	gtr	A
	JOHN O'CALLAGHAN	keyb'ds	A

| ALBUM: | 1 | AT THE GALLOP | (Cromwell WELL 005) 1975 R3 |

| 45: | First Day | (Cromwell WELL 006) 1975 |

A privately-pressed album from an Irish rock outfit who apparently sounded very much like **The Rolling Stones** and Thin Lizzy. It's reputedly good. Some band members were later involved in an outfit called Establishment, appearing on their *Unfree Child* (EMI (Ireland) SPLEAF 7018) 1977 album. (MK)

(Keith) Cross and (Peter) Ross

| Personnel: | KEITH CROSS | | A |
| | PETER ROSS | | A |

| ALBUM: | 1(A) | BORED CIVILIANS | (Decca SKL 5129) 1972 R1 |

NB: (1) also reissued on the Korean label Si-Wan.

45s:

Can You Believe It?/		
Blind Willie Johnson	(Decca F 13224)	1972
Peace In The End/Prophets Guiders	(Decca F 13316)	1972

Prior to this project **Keith Cross** had been a member of **T2**. These recordings aren't in the same league. Both **Cross** and **Ross** had earlier played in a band called **Sunburst**. (VJ)

The Crossbeats

Personnel:	EDDIE BOYES	lead gtr	A
	JOHN BOYES	bs	A
	ERIC KNOWLES	drms	A
	TONY MATHIAS	lead vcls	A
	SAM PENNINGTON	gtr	A

ALBUM: 1(A) CRAZY MIXED UP GENERATION
(Pilgrim KLP 12) 1967 SC

45s:			
If Only/He Wants To Know	(Pilgrim PSR 7001)	196?	
I Know/He Waits	(Pilgrim PSR 7002)	1965	
Step Aside/Forgive Me	(Pilgrim PSR 7003)	1967	
Busy Man/Change (PS)	(Pilgrim PSR 7004)	196?	

A gospel beat group. All the songs on their album were self-penned. (VJ/Lukas)

The Cruisers

Personnel:	PETER CLIFFE	bs	A
	JOHN RILEY	drms	A
	ALAN TAYLOR	gtr	A
	FRANK WHITE	vcls, gtr	A

45: It Ain't Me Babe/
Baby What Do You Want Me To Do (Decca F 12098) 1965 SC

This was a one-off project by **Dave Berry**'s backing band. The 'A' side was a Bob Dylan song.

You can also check out *Baby What You Want Me To Do* on *R&B Scene, Vol. 2* (LP). (VJ)

Crushed Butler

Personnel:	ALAN BUTLER	bs	A
	JESSE HECTOR	gtr, vcls	ABC

KEITH CROSS AND PETER ROSS - Bored Civilians (CD).

DARRYL READ	drms		ABC
STAN ALDOUS	bs		B
BARRY MITCHELL	bs		C

NB: (1) a 10" featuring six songs from various acetates recorded between 1969 and 1971.

A proto-punk outfit that lasted from the summer of 1969 through to 1971. Despite a number of terrific demos and gigs with **Atomic Rooster**, **Mott The Hoople**, **Slade** and **Kevin Ayers**, the band never got a record deal and split soon after.

Of **Crushed Butler**'s acetates, the first in October 1969 was recorded at Regent Sound Studios (*It's My Life*) with Alan Butler. In 1970, Stan Aldous (ex-**Aardvark**) came on the bass for a second session at EMI's Manchester Square studios. Two songs were recorded, the hard *Factory Grimes* and *Love Is All Around Me*. Further acetates were recorded with a new bassist called Barry Mitchell, like *My Son's Alive* and *Love Fighter* at Decca Studios (Broadhurst Gardens, West Hampstead)... and still unsigned, Alan Butler came back in on bass in 1971 for final recording at Marquee Studios, *High School Dropout*, under a new name, "Tiger".

Jesse Hector and Alan Butler were more successful with their next venture, the now legendary **Hammersmith Gorrillas**. (CSx)

Cryin' Shames

Personnel:	PAUL CRANE	vcls	A
	CHARLIE GALLAGHER	drms	A
	JOEY KEEN	vcls	A
	PHIL ROBERTS	organ	A
	GEORGE ROBINSON	bs	A
	RICHARD 'RITCHIE' ROUTLEDGE	ld gtr	A

HCP

45s:	Please Stay/What's New Pussycat (Decca F 12340) 1966	SC 26	
	Nobody Waved Goodbye/You (Decca F 12425) 1966	R1	
Reissue:	Please Stay/ (Old Gold OG 9357) 1983	-	

Completely unconnected with the similarly-named US band from Chicago, this mob, originally known as The Bumbles, made the lower reaches of the Charts with *Please Stay*. Both of this Merseybeat group's 45s (and a subsequent one credited to **Paul and Ritchie and Cryin' Shames**) were produced by Joe Meek. *Please Stay* was a straight-forward cover of a Drifter's song, but tucked away on the flip side is a snarling garage-sounding Dylan-type folk-punker, which sounds far more American than British.

In Germany, a book with an EP called *Beat In Liverpool* was released. It included three tracks by **The Cryin' Shames**: *Watch Your Step*, *Hey Good-Looking* and *Tell Me How You Feel* along with two by another Liverpool group, **The Hideways**.

Compilation appearances include: *Please Stay* on *Mersey Beat* (2-LP); *What's New Pussycat?* on *Mod Scene, Vol. 2* (CD), *Pop Inside The '60s, Vol. 2* (CD), *Sixties Lost And Found, Vol. 3* (LP), *Sixties Explosion, Vol. 1* (CD) and *English Freakbeat, Vol. 5* (LP & CD); and *Please Stay*, *What's New Pussycat?* and *Nobody Waved Goodbye* on *Nowhere Men, Vol. 4* (CD). (VJ/CRr/Lukas)

Cupid's Inspiration

Personnel:	WYNDHAM GEORGE	ld gtr	A
	ROGER GRAY	drms	AB
	LAUGHTON JAMES	bs	A
	TERRY RICE-MILTON	vcls	AB
	GARFIELD TONKIN	keyb'ds	AB
	GORDON HASKELL	bs	B
	BERNIE LEE	ld gtr	B

ALBUM: 1 YESTERDAY HAS GONE (NEMS 6-63553) 1968

NB: (1) credited to **Cupid's Inspiration** featuring T.Rice-Milton. (1) has been reissued on CD (Repertoire REP 4543-WY) 1995.

45s:	Yesterday Has Gone/Dream	(NEMS 56-3500) 1968 4
	My World/Everything I Meant To Be	(NEMS 56-3702) 1968 33
	Sad Thing/Look At Me	(Bell BLL 1069) 19?? -
	Without Your Love/Different Guy	(CBS 4722) 1970 -
	Are You Growing Tired Of My Love/Sunshine (CBS 4994) 1970 -
Reissues:	Yesterday Has Gone/My World	(DJM DJS 10300) 1974 -
	Yesterday Has Gone/My World (Some PS)	(NB NB 5) 1987 -
	Yesterday Has Gone/My World	(MBS 001) 1987 -

Every so often a group produces a record that is almost timeless. *Yesterday Has Gone* was one such record - full of atmosphere and featuring a powerful vocal performance by Terry Rice-Milton, who later pursued a solo career with surprisingly little success. *Dream* and *My World* weren't bad compositions either. A band who could have been much bigger. Their sole album, *Yesterday Has Gone* has now been reissued on CD and is a strange mixture of American soul covers, plush orchestration and lightweight hard-rock. Still, it comes with six bonus tracks, including the excellent *Dream* - hidden away on the flip side to their debut 45.

Gordon Haskell had been involved in **The Flowerpot Men** and **Fleur de Lys** and went on to sing on a session with **King Crimson,** who he eventually joined as bassist/singer in August - October 1970 before going solo. Bernie Lee may have been in **Paper Blitz Tissue** and then **Orange Bicycle**. He went on to a group called **Onyx**.

Compilation appearances have included: *Different Guy* on *Justafixation* (CD); *Dream* on *Magic Spectacles* (CD) and *Voyage Through The Sugarcube* (CD) and *Yesterday Has Gone* on *20 Hits Of The 60's* (CD), *60's Love Songs* (CD) and *Hits Of The Sixties - 20 Swinging Sounds* (CD). (VJ)

Cup O'Kindness

| 45: | Please Don't Sell My Daddy No More/ | |
| | The Tattooed Lady Of Main Street | (Parlophone R 5467) 1966 |

A short-lived group, their 45 is harmony folk in The Rooftop Singers vein. (MWh)

Cuppa T

| Personnel: | VIV LYTHGOE | A |
| | TERRY WIDLAKE | A |

| 45s: | Miss Pinkerton/Brand New World | (Deram DM 144) 1967 |
| | Streatham Hippodrome/One Man Band | (Deram DM 185) 1968 |

An obscure flower-pop outfit whose best offering, *Miss Pinkerton*, got a further airing several years later on *British Psychedelic Trip, Vol. 3* (LP) (and *Vol. 1* of the corresponding CD). They basically played good-time

RUBBLE VOL. 1 (Comp LP) including Martin Cure and The Peeps.

music, punctuated by the occasional Indian-style note and exaggerated Cockney lyrics which on this occasion dealt with the boredom of office life. The second 45, *Streatham Hippodrome*, applied similar ingredients, less successfully and then they were heard of no more. Lythgoe and Widlake were both former members of **The Overlanders**. Prior to this Widlake had been in The Sherwoods. Widlake joined **The Art Movement**. (VJ)

The Cups

| 45: | Good As Gold/Life And Times | (Polydor BM 56777) 1969 |

This 45 also got a US release on the Tetragrammaton label (T-1538) in 1968. *Good As Gold* is reasonable late sixties more rock-than-pop fodder, written by **Gallagher and Lyle** and published by Apple Music. The flip was very different written by 'Van Zwanenberg' and published by Ganja Music. (VJ)

Martin Cure and The Peeps

Personnel:	ROY ALBRIGHTON	gtr	A
	GRAHAM AMOS	bs	A
	MARTIN CURE	vcls	A
	PAUL WILKINSON	drms	A

| 45: | It's All Over Now/ | |
| | I Can Make The Rain Fall Up | (Philips BF 1605) 1967 R1 |

The Peeps came from Coventry and formed there in 1965. See **The Peeps** entry for details of the four 45s made under that name. This was a slightly later effort with a rather slow, bluesy flip. It's certainly not essential listening, though.

With the addition of a keyboard player they went on to record two singles in 1969 as the **Rainbows**. Albrighton later played for **Nektar** and **Quantum Jump**. Wilkinson went on to **Flying Machine**.

You can also find *It's All Over Now* on *Rubble Vol. 1: The Psychedelic Snarl* (LP) and *Rubble, Vol. 1* (CD). (VJ)

Curiosity Shoppe

| 45: | Baby I Need You/So Sad | (Deram DM 220) 1968 R2 |

A Liverpool group whose sole vinyl offering seems to have been this one 45. The 'A' side has an organ-driven rave-up rather similar to **Deep Purple**'s *Hush* and it's now a minor collectable. It builds up to quite an impressive crescendo and is well worth a listen.

Baby I Need You later resurfaced on *The Psychedelic Scene* (CD), *Rubble, Vol. 14 - The Magic Rocking Horse* (LP), *Rubble, Vol. 8* (CD) and *Broken Dreams, Vol. 1* (LP). (VJ)

Current Kraze

Personnel:	ROGER COOK	
	JOHNNY GOODMAN	
	ROGER GREENAWAY	

| 45: | Lady Pearl/ | |
| | Breaking The Heart Of A Good Man | (Deram DM 292) 1970 |

This was a one-off pop project by Roger Greenaway, Johnny Goodman and **Roger Cook**. (VJ)

Chris Curtis

| 45: | Aggravation/ | |
| | Have I Done Something Wrong | (Pye 7N 17132) 1966 R1 |

Chris Curtis was born Christopher Crummey in Oldham in 1941. He joined **The Searchers** in 1960 and played a key role in helping to select the blend of American R&B and country-tinged material which after **The Beatles** made them the best Liverpudlian band of the beat era. **The Searchers** enjoyed several early and mid-sixties hits, but he left the group in 1966. The above 45 was a solo venture recorded after he left.

The following year he was involved in **The Flowerpot Men**, who enjoyed a massive hit with *Let's Go To San Francisco*. He then formed **Roundabout** (embryonic **Deep Purple**) with his brother Dave. He also did some production work for Pye and **Paul and Barry Ryan** were among his credits. He then joined the Civil Service, but when ill health forced him to retire he sang with the charity group The Merseycats.

Both sides of his rare 45 can also be heard on the German-based Repertoire label's CD compilation *German, French and Rare Recordings* (RR 4102-WZ) 1991. *Aggravation* also appeared on *Some Other Guys* (2-LP), *It Happened Then* (EP) and on the 2-CD set *We Love The Pirates: Charting The Big 'L' Fab 40*.

Curtis died in February 2005, aged 63, after a long illness. (VJ)

Jeff Curtis and The Flames

Personnel:

JEFF CURTIS	vcls		AB
CB	sax		AB
KEITH GARDINER	gtr		AB
LOUIS McKELVEY	lead gtr		AB
DAVE WIGGINGTON	bs		AB
MALCOLM TOMLINSON	drms		B

Formed in 1961/62. **Jeff Curtis and The Flames** are best known as the house band at the Ealing Jazz Club. With the addition of Tomlinson, the group recorded a demo with the legendary Joe Meek.

Tomlinson left in 1964 to tour Germany with James Deane and The London Cats and was later a member of **The Motivation**, **The Penny Peeps** and **Gethsemane** before moving to Canada to play with Milkwood in early 1969. McKelvey dropped out in the summer of 1965 and travelled to South Africa where he recorded with The Upsetters and The A-Cads before returning to the UK in the Spring of 1966. He subsequently moved to Montreal where he played with Our Generation (1966) and Influence (1967 - 1968) and then reunited with Tomlinson in Milkwood.

The remaining members, with new additions, continued to play the London club scene, including a date supporting Edwin Starr at Tiles in Oxford Street in late 1966. The following year the band changed name to The Jeff Curtis Set and performed at the Upper Cut in Forest Gate, London. (NW)

Lee Curtis and The All Stars

Personnel:

WAYNE BICKERTON	bs		AB
FRANK BOWEN	lead gtr		AB
PETER (LEE) FLANNERY	vcls		ABCDEFG H
BERYL MARSDEN	vcls		A F
BERNIE ROGERS	drms		A
TONY WADDINGTON	gtr		AB
PETE BEST	drms		B
DON ALCYD	drms		C
DAVE (MUSY) COOPER	bs		C
GEORGE PECKHAM	gtr		C
PAUL PILNICK	lead gtr		C E
MIKE BANKS	bs		D
MIKE CUMMINGS	lead gtr		D
SIMON HIND	gtr		D
JOE WALSH	drms		DEF
CHRIS DENNIS	organ		E
BOB GARNER	bs		EF
DAVE McSHANE	sax		E
SCOTTISH DAVE	lead gtr		F
FRANK JARNACH	organ		F
JIMMY CAVE	lead gtr		G H
ARTHUR DAVIES	drms		G H
BILL GOOD	bs		G
KEITH ROBERTS	bs		H

THE PSYCHEDELIC SCENE (Comp CD) including Curiosity Shoppe.

45s:	α	Little Girl/Just One More Dance	(Decca F 11622) 1963 SC
		Let's Stomp/Poor Unlucky Me	(Decca F 11690) 1963 SC
		What About Me/	
		I've Got My Eyes On You	(Decca F 11830) 1964 SC
		Ecstasy/	
		A Shot Of Rhythm And Blues	(Philips BF 1385) 1965 SC

NB: α credited to **Lee Curtis**.

A Merseyside group. **Lee Curtis** (real name Peter Flannery) had earlier cut a solo disc, *Little Girl*. Their debut *Let's Stomp* is regarded as a classic of the genre. The drummer on this track was former **Beatle Pete Best**. The band also released several records in Germany which didn't get an airing here in the UK. They can also be heard playing *Skinny Minnie* and *Jezebel* on Decca's 1964 *At The Cavern* (LP) compilation.

Curtis also recorded two albums and many 45s for the Star-Club label. These have all been re-released on CD by Repertoire (IMS 7012/7013), along with all his Decca recordings.

Compilation appearances have included: *Skinnie Minnie* (live) on *Liverpool 1963-1964, Vol. 2* (LP); *Let's Stomp* on *Mersey Beat* (2-LP); *Skinny Minny, I've Got My Eyes On You* and *Let's Stomp* on *Mersey Sounds* (2-LP); *Skinnie Minnie* and *Let's Stomp* on *Mersey Beat 1962-1964* (2-LP); *Jezebel* on *Original Liverpool Sound* (LP); *Shot Of Rhythm And Blues* and *Ecstacy* on *The Star-Club Singles Complete, Vol. 1* (LP & CD); *Shame And Scandal In The Family* and *Nobody But You* on *The Star-Club Singles Complete, Vol. 6* (LP & CD); *Kelly* and *Mohair Sam* on *The Star-Club Singles Complete, Vol. 7* (LP & CD); *Shot Of Rhythm And Blues* on *Star-Club Show* (LP) and *Beat Battle At The Star-Club, Vol. 1* (LP); *Come On Down To My Boat* and *Concerto For Her* on *The Star-Club Singles Complete, Vol. 12* (LP & CD); *Ecstacy* on *Sweet Beat* (LP) and *Beat Battle At The Star-Club, Vol. 1* (LP); *Um Um Um Um Um Um* on *Star Club Scene '65* (LP); *Mess Of Blues* on *The Star-Club Anthology, Vol. 1* (LP); *Blue Suede Shoes* on *The Star-Club Anthology, Vol. 4* (LP); *Skinny Minny* and *Jezebel* on *At The Cavern* (LP) and *Live At The Cavern* (CD); and finally *Boy* on *Beat Im Star Club* (LP). (VJ/AD)

Dave Curtiss and The Tremors

Personnel incl: DAVE CURTISS

45s:	You Don't Love Me/Sweet Girl Of Mine	(Philips BF 1257) 1963
	What Kind Of Girl Are You?/	
	Dreamer's Funfair	(Philips BF 1285) 1963
	Summertimes Blues/	
	I'm A Hog For You Baby	(Philips BF 1330) 1964

Hailed from Clacton in Essex. They are best remembered for their cover of Eddie Cochran's *Summertime Blues. What Kind Of Girl Are You?* is a Ray Charles number.

After the Tremors split up Dave formed Curtiss and Co.

Summertime Blues has been compiled on *Beat Merchants* (2-LP). (VJ/CS)

Curtiss Maldoon

Personnel:	DAVE CURTISS	vcls, gtr, piano, perc	A
	CLIVE SKINNER		
	aka CLIVE MALDOON	vcls, gtr, perc	A

ALBUMS: 1(A) CURTISS MALDOON   (Purple TPS 3501) 1971
        2(A) 1972 CURTISS MALDOON   (Purple TPS)1971

NB: (2) as Maldoon.

45s: You Make Me Happy/
        Amber Man   (Regal Zonophone RZ 3038) 1971
        One Way Ticket/ Next Time   (Purple PUR 106) 1972

These two formed their duo from contacts made around the setting up of **Deep Purple** and then the Purple label. The Purple label was not ready to be launched at the time of their first single so it came out on Regal Zonophone, another EMI outlet. The first album was promoted in the States on a tour with **Badfinger**, when the duo's touring band included drummer Liam Genocky, who later played with **Sonja Kristina** and **Steeleye Span**, to name just two. The album features a host of well-known musicians and has a variety of styles, but throughout has a relaxed hippie feel. Nothing really stands out except the final track *Find A Little Peace* which has some terrific **Steve Howe** guitar work and also features **Tony Ashton** on organ. The sleeve has line drawings of **Curtiss and Maldoon** by a Judith Mackenzie - presumably the singer **Judy Mackenzie**?

Curtiss was apparently unhappy with the second album and insisted on his name being removed from it, leading to the curiosity of an album by a duo but with only one member credited! The band was already defunct at the time of Maldoon's accidental death in 1976. **Curtiss** finally had his delayed fifteen minutes of fame - and some royalties! - in 1998 when the song *Sepheryn* from the first album was taken up by Madonna and recorded by her under the title *Ray Of Light*. (NM)

Curved Air

Personnel:	SONJA KRISTINA	vcls	ABCDEFG H I
	ROBERT MARTIN	bs	A
	FRANCIS MONKMAN	keyb'ds	ABC E
	FLORIAN		
	PILKINGTON-MIKSA	drms	ABC E
	DARRYL WAY	violin	ABC EFG H
	IAN EYRE	bs	B

CURVED AIR - Airconditioning (LP).

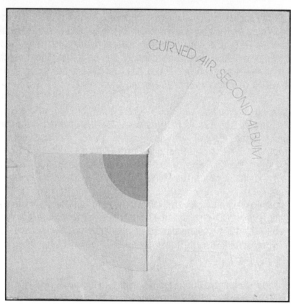

CURVED AIR - Second Album (LP).

MIKE WEDGWOOD	bs	CD
KIRBY GREGORY	gtr	D
EDDIE JOBSON	violin, synth	D
JIM RUSSELL	drms	D
PHIL KOHN	bs	EF
STEWART COPELAND	drms	FG H I
MIKE JACQUES	gtr	FG H I
JOHN PERRY	bs	G
TONY REEVES	bs	H I
ALEX RICHMAN	keyb'ds	I

HCP

ALBUMS: 1(A) AIR CONDITIONING
                 (Warner Brothers WS 3012) 1970 SC 8
        2(B) SECOND ALBUM   (Warner Brothers K 46092) 1971 11
        3(C) PHANTASMAGORIA
                 (Warner Brothers K 46158) 1972 SC 20
        4(D) AIR CUT   (Warner Brothers K 46224) 1973 SC
        5(E) CURVED AIR LIVE   (Deram SML 1119) 1975 -
        6(G) MIDNIGHT WIRE   (BTM 1005) 1975 -
        7(-)   THE BEST OF CURVED AIR
                 (Warner Brothers K 36015) 1976 -
        8(H) AIRBORNE   (BTM 1008) 1976 -

NB: (1) catalogue number changed to K 56004 in 1971, following the Warner Bros / Elektra / Reprise merger. (1) was also the first ever album to be issued as a picture disc (WSX 3012) (R1). (5) was also issued on BTM (5001) in 1975. (5) reissued on CD (Deram 820 522-2) 1988, (Repertoire REP 4514-WY) 1995 and (HTD CD 49) 1995. (6) reissued on CD (Repertoire REP 4499-WY) 1995 and (HTD CD 50) 1995. (8) reissued on CD (Repertoire REP 4493-WY) 1994. Fans of the band will also want to check out *Live At The BBC* (Band Of Joy BOJCD 014) 1995, which contains versions of some of their finest moments:- *Vivaldi*, *Stretch*, *It Happened Today*, etc. The CD *Lovechild* (Castle ESSCD 024) 1990 contains material dating from early 1973 and is short on playing time. *Lovechild* (Snapper Music SMMCD 609) 2000 is a set of demos from Spring 1973 (around the time their *Air Cut* album was released).

HCP

45s: It Happened Today//Vivaldi
        What Happens When You Blow
        Yourself Up?   (Warner Brothers WB 8023) 1971 -
        Back Street Luv/Everdance (Warner Brothers WB 8029) 1971 4
        Sarah's Concern/
        Phantasmagoria   (Warner Brothers K 16164) 1972 -
        Back Street Luv//It Happened Today/Marie Antoinette
        Ultra Vivaldi   (Warner Brothers K 16412) 1974 -
        Back Street Luv/Everydance (Warner Brothers K 16092) 1974 -
   α Back Street Luv/
        It Happened Today (live)   (Deram DM 426) 1975 -
        Desiree/Kids To Blame   (BTM SBT 103) 1976 -
        Baby Please Don't Go/Broken Lady   (BTM SBT 106) 1976 -
        Renegade/We're Only Human   (Pearl Key PK 07350) 1984 -

NB: α Reissued on Decca (F 13911) in 1981.

A talented and rather underrated progressive rock band **Curved Air** formed in March 1970. **Sonja Kristina**, their lead vocalist and sex symbol, had previously made a handful of TV appearances as a teenager in the 'Song and Story' series. She then worked her way on to the folk circuit and later appeared in 'Hair' providing the lead vocals on *Frank Mills*, which not only appeared on the Soundtrack album, but was also released as a 45. **Darryl Way** had met Francis Monkman by chance in a music shop, whilst **Way** was studying at the Royal College of Music. Monkman was currently playing with an outfit called Sisyphus. He also chose the band's name because he was captivated by Terry Riley's *Rainbow In Curved Air* album at the time.

Their debut album was released to enormous hype and a large promotional budget. Aside from the ordinary release, a substantial number were issued as picture discs - indeed it was one of the first and has inevitably become a minor collector's item. They were carefully packaged to appeal to the prevailing progressive rock genre - using the in vogue violin and synthesizer with quasi-classical material and a sexy female vocalist to provide an additional ingredient. The album's finest moment was *Vivaldi*, a seven-and-a-half minute reinterpretation of *The Four Seasons* by **Darryl Way**, which includes some superb violin playing, but other highs on what was an imaginative debut include the uptempo *Propositions* and the rather mournful, offbeat *Screw*. One of the less strong cuts, *It Happened Today*, was released as a 45 and the 'B' side included *What Happens When You Blow Yourself Up?*, which did appear on their album.

In 1971 the band toured America although they never cracked the lucrative US market and only attained a cult following. Indeed only their first three albums were released there. Shortly after they returned they enjoyed their only UK hit when *Back Street Luv* (later included on their *Second Album*) climbed to No 4 in the Summer of that year on the crest of the progressive rock wave. Ian Eyre replaced Robert Martin on bass at around this time.

The *Second Album* was another fine slab of vinyl, in many respects a progression on their innovative debut. The opener *Young Mother* showcased **Kristina**'s vocal talents admirably as well as **Way**'s songwriting talents. Indeed, all the songs on side one were his - and whilst *You Know* may have been rather below par, the dream-like *Jumbo* and *Puppets* were both rather sensitive, melodic songs with **Kristina**'s vocals at their most delectable. Francis Monkman wrote all the material on side two, with the lengthy *Piece Of Mind* the imaginative highlight. Indeed, this highly complex, innovative song was one of the finest moments of their six year career and possibly of UK progressive rock.

In January 1972 Mike Wedgwood replaced Ian Eyre on bass and the third album was preceded by a single, *Sarah's Concern*, which made so little impression it was excluded from the *Phantasmagoria* album. For many (though not for me) this was their finest work. Again **Way** was responsible for most of the material on side one and the rather tedious *Marie Antoinette* became a favourite of the fans though to me **Kristina**'s gentle, dreamlike *Melinda (More Or Less)* was far superior. The side closed with **Way**'s *Ultra-Vivaldi*. On side two *Whose Shoulder Are You Looking Over Anyway* consisted of Sonja's voice fed through a computer and accompanied by a

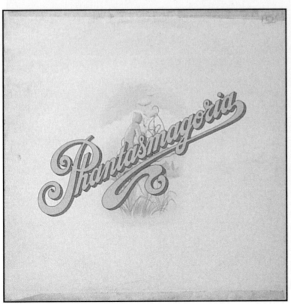

CURVED AIR - Phantasmagoria (LP).

CURVED AIR - Air Cut (LP).

synthesizer. The long Monkman track this time, *Over And Above*, was jazzier than anything the band had done previously, whilst the finale, the fun-loving *Once A Ghost Always A Ghost* was an assortment of percussion, brass and various noises. To me that album was hardly a progression on their previous works.

After *Phantasmagoria* 'personality clashes and musical disagreements' tore the band apart. **Darryl Way** left to form **Darryl Way's Wolf**, Monkman went into session work and Florian Pilkington-Miksa later played with **Kiki Dee**'s backing group. This left **Kristina** to build a new band around herself and Wedgwood (line-up D). The most significant recruit was 17 year old Eddie Jobson, a young keyboard wizard. This line-up recorded *Air Cut*, an inconsistent album though arguably their most underrated. The band took on a rockier sound now that the **Way**/Monkman influence was no longer around, although the instrumental *Armin* sounded like an imitation of a **Darryl Way** composition. If *World* was a throwaway number and *The Purple Speed Queen* and *U.H.F.* were rather nondescript, these were countered by **Kristina**'s upbeat *Easy* and gentle, mournful *Elfin Boy*. However, tucked away on this rather erratic album was for me the band's finest work, Jobson's keyboard-driven *Metamorphosis*, which showcased Sonja's crystal clear vocals at their most childlike and innocent and Jobson's keyboard dexterity as he plays the grand piano, electric piano, organ, VC S3, synthesizer and mellotron in the course of this extended delight. This line-up was short-lived, disbanding when Jobson left to replace **Eno** in **Roxy Music**. Kirby Gregory and Jim Russell formed **Stretch** and Wedgwood joined **Caravan**. In 2000 Snapper released *Lovechild*, a set of demos from Spring 1973. The title track and *Seasons* were the best of Sonja Kristina's four contributions and Jobson's *Paris By Night* is a fine keyboard-driven piece.

Sonja briefly returned to 'Hair' for three months in the Summer of 1974 but by September of that year apparently faced by a large unpaid VAT bill four of the five original members (line-up E) relaunched the band to make enough bread to pay off the debt. During an intensive three week UK tour *Curved Air Live* was recorded and featured strong versions of some of the band's stage favourites:- *Vivaldi* (now complete with a vocal section and highland fling), *Back Street Luv*, *Young Mother* and an extended version of *Propositions*. A live 45 was issued, coupling their first two singles:- *It Happened Today* and *Back Street Luv*, but it failed to sell. After the tour Monkman went off to form Sky and Pilkington/Minsa drifted out of the music scene.

Anxious to keep the band on the road Sonja and **Darryl Way** drafted in their road manager for the reunion tour; Stewart Copeland on drums, and guitarist Mike Jacques. Bassist Phil Kohn, who'd been recruited for the tour to augment the original quartet, was made permanent but left in August 1975. He was replaced by John Perry (ex-**Caravan**) who sat in on the recording of *Midnight Wire*. The highlight of this rockier album was undoubtedly the title track. Co-written by **Way** and lyricist Norma Tager, who co-wrote all the material on the album, it featured another superb vocal performance from **Kristina** and more of **Way**'s fine violin playing. Other highlights were the upbeat *Woman On A One Night Stand* and the gentle, romantic *Dance Of Love*. No expense was spared in making the album but

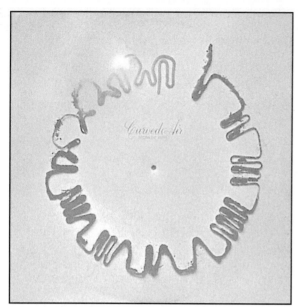

CURVED AIR - Midnight Wire (LP).

possibly because it was out of step with the times it didn't sell. Once the album was complete Perry departed to **Quantum Jump** and enjoyed brief success. Tony Reeves from **Greenslade** replaced him.

The band spent much of its final year on the road but managed to find time to record a final album, *Airborne*. It passed unnoticed at the time but is worth investigating. The album is dominated by **Kristina**'s vocals. The highlights are three **Darryl Way** compositions, *Juno*, *Moonshine* and *Dazed*; the sad and gentle *Broken Lady* and the summery *Touch Of Tequila*. However, the rather mundane *Desiree* was chosen for a 45 and not surprisingly made little impact.

Darryl Way left to go solo before *Airborne* was released. Alex Richman (ex-Butts Band) became the final member to be recruited to the band, who decided they had got as far as they could at the end of 1976. Two weeks later Stewart Copeland met Sting and Police was formed. Some rock books suggest that **Curved Air** should have been laid to rest a couple of years earlier but those last two albums contained some lovely songs.

The Best Of Curved Air features a fairly random selection of material from their first four albums only. A bootleg, *Live In London*, from the mid-seventies includes material from *Midnight Wire* and *Marie Antoinette* (from *Phantasmagoria*).

In 1984 **Kristina** and **Way** re-united for a one-off single for the Pearl Key label, which was released in limited quantities and isn't easy to find. Since **Curved Air**'s demise Sonja has had lots of children (she is married to Stewart Copeland), occasionally returning to the music scene with Sonja Kristina's Escape (late seventies), she recorded solo albums in 1980 and 1992, occasional singles and had a band called Tunis. Two of her later CDs were *Songs From The Acid Folk*, with Tylor and Friends, and *Harmonics Of Love* with Cloud Ten. Both have been re-released on Mystic Records.

Eddie Jobson went on to play for **Roxy Music, UK** and **Jethro Tull.** He also released a solo album in 1983 and became a LA session man. **Way** pursued a solo career, worked with several other artists and even recorded a concert with Francis Monkman for the 'South Bank Show'. Monkman went on to work mainly with electric orchestras. Monkman recorded two solo albums in the eighties after leaving Sky. In 1998, he released a CD *21st Century Blues* as by "Francis Monkman & The Virtuous-Realiti Band". With nearly 80 minutes of original material it also includes a short snippet of Country Joe & The Fish's *Section 43*.

The original quartet of **Kristina**, **Way**, Monkman and Pilkington-Miksa reunited in 1990 for a show at London's Town & Country 2. Featuring one new track, the opener *20 Years On*, the concert was captured on the *Alive 1990* album.

Phantasmagoria figured on Warner's 1972 *Fruity* (LP) compilation, whilst more recently *Back Street Luv* has been compiled on *Progressive Pop Inside The Seventies* (CD). (VJ)

Custer's Track

45:      On The Run/Hello Heaven   (Major Minor MM 698) 1970

This was an obscure band, whose vinyl output seems to have been confined to this one 45. The group comprised five guys. *On The Run* later resurfaced on *Oddities, Vol 1* (CD). (VJ)

Ivor Cutler

ALBUMS: (up to 1976)			
	1	WHO TORE YOUR TROUSERS?	(Decca LK 4405) 1961 R2
	2	LUDO	(Parlophone PCS 7040) 1967 R1
	3	DANDRUFF	(Virgin V 2021) 1974
	4	VELVET DONKEY	(Virgin V 3027) 1975
	5	JAMMY SMEARS	(Virgin V 2065) 1976

NB: (3) - (5) reissued by Virgin (OVED 33, 34 and 12 respectively) in 1984 and on CD in 1992. Also relevant is *Peel Session* (Strange Fruit SFPS 068) 1989. *An Elpee And Two Epees* (Decca 9826606) 2005 is an anthology of his first album and his two EPs below.

EPs:	1	OF Y'HUP	(Fontana TFE 17144) 1959 SC
	2	GET AWAY FROM THE WALL	
			(Decca DFE 6677) 1961 SC

45:      I Had A Little Boat/
            Great Grey Grasshopper   (Parlophone R 5624) 1967

Cutler wasn't just a songwriter and performer, he was also a poet, humorist, cartoonist and teacher. He taught at A.S. Neill's Summerhill in 1950-1 and latterly taught music, drama and poetry at various Inner London schools.

His albums are weird, usually full of short compositions and sparse instrumentation, often interspersed by poems. Certainly imaginative but something of an acquired taste.

The Peel Sessions album dates from an August 1977 session. The 2005 collection *An Elpee And Two Epees*, which compiles his first album and his first two EPs, is a timely reminder of the appeal of his gentle, eccentric stories and songs. (VJ)

Cyan Three

45:      Since I Lost My Baby/
            Face Of A Loser   (Decca F 12371) 1966 SC

This is a soul/beat offering. (VJ)

CURVED AIR - Airborne (LP).

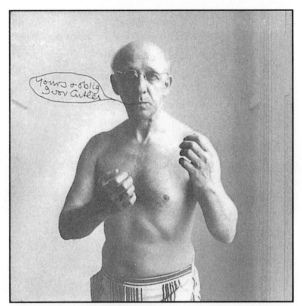

IVOR CUTLER - Jammy Smears (LP).

The Cyclones

Personnel:	FRANK DUDLEY	bs	ABCDE
	PETER FLEMING	vcls	ABCD
	STEVE FLEMING	keyb'ds	ABCD
	VIC GRACE	lead gtr	A
	LES WATKINS	drms	ABC
	KENNY FOGARTY	lead gtr	B
	FRANK BOWEN	lead gtr	C
	ROY CRESSWELL	drms	DE
	TONY WEBSTER	lead gtr	DE
	BILLY BURTON	tenor sax	E

45:     Nobody/Little Egypt   (Oriole CB 1898) 1964 R1

A Liverpool band whose sole vinyl offering passed largely unnoticed. Peter and Steve Fleming had previously played with **Mark Peters and The Silhouettes**, whilst Frank Bowen was ex-**Lee Curtis and The All Stars**. The band are also said to have backed **Peter and Gordon**.

When line-up 'E' recruited Fred Ennis on bass (Frank Dudley having joined The St Louis Checks), they changed names to The Few. (Billy Burton (tenor sax), Roy Cresswell (drms), Tony Webster (lead gtr) and Fred Ennis (bs)). (VJ/AD)

The Cymbaline

Personnel:	PHILIP CHESTERTON	drms	A
	STUART CLAVER	vcls	A
	JOHN HOLLIS	gtr	A
	GERALD MORRIS	bs	A
	TERRY MORTLOCK	ld gtr	A

45s:	Please Little Girl/Coming Home Baby	(Pye 7N 15916) 1965 SC
	Top Girl/Can You Hear Me?	(Mercury MF 918) 1965 SC
	I Don't Want It/	
	Where Did Love Go Wrong	(Mercury MF 961) 1966
	Peanuts And Chewy Macs/	
	Found My Girl	(Mercury MF 975) 1966
	Matrimonial Fears/	
	You Will Never Love Me	(Philips BF 1624) 1967 SC
	Down By The Seaside/Fire	(Philips BF 1681) 1968 SC
	Turn Around/Come Back Baby	(Philips BF 1749) 1969

A good, if rather lightweight, pop group from Essex. In addition to the above, they also had a bassist called Brian Gill in the mid-sixties. In Stuart Calver they had a vocalist with a very attractive voice and they were perhaps a bit unlucky that commercial success eluded them. *Matrimonial Fears*, is a well-crafted pop song with a gimmicky introduction and this was their finest moment .

Philip Chesterton later drummed with **Marc Ellington** and Stuart Calver sang as a backing vocalist for several artists including **Roger Daltrey**, **Steve Harley and Cockney Rebel** and **Linda Lewis**.

Compilation appearances have included: *Matrimonial Fears* on *Rubble, Vol. 4 - The 49-Minute Technicolour Dream* (LP) and *Rubble, Vol. 3* (CD); *Fire* on *Circus Days, Vol. 6* (CD) and *Incredible Sound Show Stories, Vol. 6* (LP); *Coming Home Baby* on *Doin' The Mod, Vol. 1* (CD) and *Down By The Seaside* on *Pop-In, Vol 2* (CD). (VJ)

The Cymerons

Personnel:	BRIAN CUSICK	A
	JOHN 'PEDRO' DEARDEN	A
	TERRY HOWARD	A
	PHILIP 'SPIKE' POULSON	A

45s:	I'll Be There/Making Love To Another (Decca F 11976) 1964 SC
	I Can See You/Everyday Will Change (Polydor BM 56098) 1966

The Cymerons' 45s were produced by Mike Leander, but they made no lasting impression. (VJ).

Czar

Personnel:	DEL GOUGH	drms	A
	BOB HODGES	keyb'ds, vcls	A
	PAUL KENDRICK	bs, vcls	A
	MICK WARE	gtr, vcls	A

ALBUM: 1(A) CZAR   (Fontana 6309 009) 1970 R3

NB: (1) counterfeited on CD (Fingerprint no #) 1995, with two bonus tracks *Oh Lord I'm Getting Heavy* and *Why Don't We Be A Rock'n'Roll Band*.

45:	Oh Lord I'm Getting Heavy/Why Don't	
	We Be A Rock'n'Roll Band	(Philips 6006 071) 1970 SC

A keyboard-driven album, admittedly derivative of bands like **King Crimson**, it is probably essential for fans of keyboard-dominated progressive rock. The opening and closing cuts:- *Tread Softly On My Dreams* and *A Day In September* capture the band at its best, but *Cecelia* features some melodramatic instrumentation and by way of contrast *Today* is a rather sentimental ballad. A clever counterfeit exists, which is discernable only by the too new-looking label and the slightly vague edges of the corner. Beware! The bonus tracks on the CD are below par compared to the original album. (MK/VJ)

CZAR - Czar (LP).

CREAM - Best Of (LP).

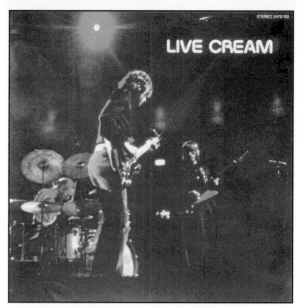
CREAM - Live Cream (CD).

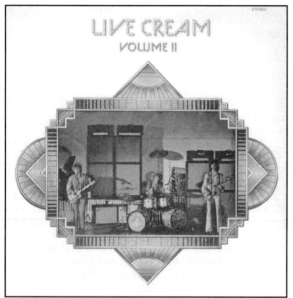
CREAM - Live Cream Vol. 2 (LP).

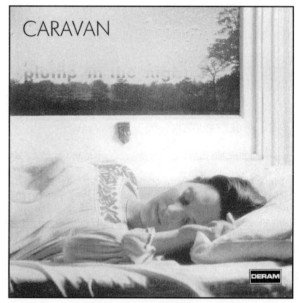
CARAVAN - For Girls Who Grow Plump In The Night (CD).

CARAVAN - Cunning Stunts (CD).

CREATION - Biff Bang Pow! (CD).

Kim D

Personnel incl: KIM DAVIES   vcls   A

45:      The Real Thing/Come On Baby   (Pye 7N 15953) 1965 SC

This was **Kim Davies** recording under a shorter name. *The Real Thing* was a soul record originally recorded by Tina Britt. (VJ)

Tony D and The Shakedowns

Personnel:			
	KEITH GRESTY	lead gtr	ABC
	PETER WALSH	drms	ABC
	TERRY YORKE	bs	ABC
	DAVE TOMLINSON	organ	BC
	LORRAINE GRAY		C

45:      Is It True/Let Her Go   (Piccadilly 7N 35168) 1964

This is a long-forgotten beat group. Compilation appearances include: *Is It True* on *Piccadilly Story* (CD). (VJ/AD)

Mike D'Abo

ALBUMS:	1	D'ABO	(Uni UNLS 114) 1970 SC
(up to	2	DOWN AT RACHEL'S PLACE	(A&M AMLH 68097) 1972
1976)	3	BROKEN RAINBOWS	(A&M AMLH 63634) 1974
	4	SMITH AND D'ABO	(CBS 81583) 1976

NB: *A Little Misunderstood: Collection, Volume Two* (RPM RPM 264) 2003 is a 21-track retrospective.

45s: (See The Little People) Gulliver's Travels/Anthology
          Of Gulliver's Travels Part 2   (Immediate IM 075) 1969 SC
          Let It Roar/California Line   (Uni UNS 525) 1970
          Miss Me In The Morning/
          Arabella, Cinderella   (Bell BLL 1134) 1970
          Fuel To Burn/Hold On Darlin'   (A&M AMS 7121) 1974

These were solo efforts by **D'Abo** who was born on 1st March 1944 in Betchworth, Surrey. He was a pupil at Harrow School, where he joined **A Band Of Angels**. Then in 1966, he replaced **Paul Jones** in **Manfred Mann**. He also had considerable songwriting skills, writing *Build Me Up Buttercup* for **The Foundations** and *Handbags And Gladrags*. He also appeared in a new style pantomime, 'Gulliver's Travels', which resulted in his first solo 45 release.

In 1969 he sang the role of Herod in 'Jesus Christ Superstar' and the following year he recorded his debut album for UNI. In 1972 **Affinity**

GULLIVER'S TRAVELS (Comp CD) featuring Mike D'Abo.

became his backing band and they are featured on his most celebrated solo album, *Down At Rachel's Place*. He was also assisted on this by young record producer Chris Demetriou.

In 1976, **D'Abo** linked up with former **Dave Clarke Five** vocalist and keyboard player Mike Smith for a composing and recording partnership which resulted in the *Smith And D'Abo* album the same year. However, neither this or subsequent efforts attracted much interest from the punters. In the seventies and eighties, **D'Abo** also busied himself writing songs for commercials and had a notable success with a jingle for Cadbury's chocolate. He also played in a band called Beat Goes On that recorded a live album at Ronnie Scott's and in a top dance band called Mike D'Abo & His Mighty Quintet as well as working as a deejay and hosting a couple of radio programmes. In the nineties he rejoined a reunited version of his old sixties band **Manfred Mann**, which was known as The Manfreds.

A Little Misunderstood: Collection, Volume Two is a 21-track retrospective of some of his material from his three solo albums and songs like *Running Away From Love*, from his short-lived collaboration with former **Dave Clark Five** member Mike Smith. If you're into singer/songwriter material this has some merit. (VJ)

Terry Dactyl and The Dinosaurs

Personnel:			
	PETE GIBSON	trombone, vcls, perc	A
	GRAHAM HINE	gtr, vcls	A
	JOHN LEWIS		
	(JONA LEWIE)	keyb'ds, vcls	A
	JIM PITTS	gtr, vcls, hrmnca	A
	BIG JOHN RANDALL	perc	A
	KEITH TRUSSELL	perc	A

			HCP
45s:	Sea Side Shuffle/Ball And Chain	(UK UK 5) 1972	2
(up to	On A Saturday Night/		
1976)	Going Round The World	(UK UK 21) 1972	45
	She Left I Died/Too Self Centred	(UK UK 39) 1973	-
Reissues:	Sea Side Shuffle/Ball And Chain	(Sonet SON 2027) 1974	-
	Sea Side Shuffle/Ball And Chain	(UK UK 133) 1976	-

This was **Brett Marvin and The Thunderbolts** operating under a pseudonym. **Terry Dactyl** was actually Jona Lewie, who later enjoyed a solo career. Initially, under this guise, they enjoyed considerable success when *Sea Side Shuffle* climbed to No 2, but when follow-up releases failed to repeat this success they reverted back to their original moniker.

Dada

Personnel:			
	ELKIE BROOKS	vcls	A
	MALCOLM CAPEWELL	woodwind	A
	JIMMY CHAMBERS	vcls, perc	A
	BARRY DUGGAN	woodwind	A
	PETE GAGE	gtr, bs	A
	MARTYN HARRYMAN	drms	A
	PAUL KORDA	vcls	A
	ERNIE LAUCHLAN	horns	A
	DON SHINN	keyb'ds	A
	ROBERT PALMER	vcls	A

ALBUM: 1(A) DADA   (Atco 2400 030) 1970 SC

This group was most notable for being a particularly early outing for **Elkie Brooks** and **Robert Palmer** who were later in **Vinegar Joe**. This is probably why the album has become a very minor collector's item. Peter Gage was also in **Vinegar Joe**.

They also have one cut on the *Age Of Atlantic* (LP) compilation, *Last Time*. (VJ)

Daddy Longlegs

Personnel:			
	MOE ARMSTRONG	vcls	A
	CLIF CARRISON	drms	ABCD
	STEVE HAYTON	gtr, vcls	AB
	STEPHEN MILLER	keyb'ds	AB

KURT PALOMAKI	bs, vcls	ABCD
PETER ARNESEN	keyb'ds	CD
GARY NORTON HOLDERMAN		CD
(IVAN CHANDLER	keyb'ds	)

ALBUMS:	1(A)	DADDY LONGLEGS	(Warner WS 3004) 1970 SC
	2(B)	OAKDOWN FARM	(Vertigo 6360038) 1971 R1
	3(C)	THREE MUSICIANS	(Polydor 2371261) 1972
	4(D)	SHIFTING SANDS	(Polydor 2371323) 1972

NB: (2) reissued on CD (Repertoire REP 4350-WP) 1993.

45:	High Again/	
	To The Rescue (Wet Patso)	(Warner Bros WB 3004) 1970

Formed in 1968, they released their first album in March 1970 and played a mixture of blues and rock with country influences. Stephen Miller of **Caravan** played on their first albums, which rarely turn up. (SR)

Daddy's Act

45:	Eight Days A Week/	
	Gonna Get You	(Columbia DB 8242) 1967 SC

This was a one-off venture. The 'A' side is a well-known **Beatles** song. (VJ)

The Cyril Dagworth Players

Personnel:	PETER FRAMPTON	A
	GEORGE GLOVER	A
	GLENN MORGAN	A
	DES (DAVE) PARTON	A
	RON SMITH	A
	JOHN WRIGHT	A

ALBUM:	1(A)	THE CYRIL DAGWORTH PLAYERS
		(Pye NSPL 18499) 1976

A one-off Des Parton project. The albums features an Edwardian style cover and the music is rather bland melodic rock, almost pop-rock in places.

The Peter Frampton in question here was not the **Peter Frampton** but another guy who played in a folk band called Poacher, and who later had a R&B band called Escape Comittee.

George Glover later played keyboards for the **Climax Blues Band**. (BS/DL)

WE CAN FLY VOL. 2 (Comp CD) includes A.P. Dangerfield.

The Dakotas

Personnel:	RAY JONES	bs	A
	TONY MANSFIELD	drms	AB
	MIKE MAXFIELD	ld gtr	AB
	ROBIN McDONALD	gtr, bs	AB
	MICK GREEN	gtr	B

EP:	1(A) MEET THE DAKOTAS	(Parlophone GEP 8888) 1963 R1

		HCP
45s:	The Cruel Sea/The Millionaire	(Parlophone R 5044) 1963 18
	Magic Carpet/Humdinger	(Parlophone R 5064) 1963 -
	Oyeh/My Girl Josephine	(Parlophone R 5203) 1964 SC -
	I'm 'n' 'Ardworkin' Barrow Boy/	
	Seven Pounds Of Potatoes	(Page One POF 018) 1967 SC -
	I Can't Break The News To Myself/	
	The Spider And The Fly	(Philips BF 1645) 1968 R2 -

This initially instrumental band operated around the Manchester area. They started out as The Dakotas with Pete McClaine in 1960. They had a regular slot at a local nightclub called The Oasis. In 1963 they were spotted playing by Brian Epstein who arranged for them to become **Billy J. Kramer**'s backing band. Around the same time Pete McClaine departed - he went on to form Pete McClaine and The Clan.

They returned from a spell at The Star Club in Hamburg to record a couple of instrumentals written by Mike Maxfield. The 'A' side was (at the time) an exciting guitar melody which got to No 18 in the Charts. The follow-up, *Magic Carpet*, was quite a catchy number penned by **George Martin** though it wasn't a hit.

The Meet The Dakotas EP comprised their first two 45s and is now one of the rarest EP releases from this era.

Before their next 45 Ray Jones left to be replaced by Mick Green, who'd previously been with Johnny Kidd and The Pirates and was later in a re-formed Pirates in 1977. The next 45, *Oyeh*, was a pretty frantic 12-bar effort. The 45s on Page One and Philips were vocal rather than instrumental efforts recorded with a different line-up.

The Spider And The Fly, their final 'B' side is a notable psychedelic/ freakbeat number with several strong riffs.

Compilation coverage has included:- *Oyeh* on *20 Classic Instrumental Rarities* (LP); *The Spider And The Fly* on *Rubble Vol. 1: The Psychedelic Snarl* (LP), *Rubble Vol. 1* (CD) and *Rare 60's Beat Treasures, Vol. 3* (CD); *Cruel Sea* on *Beat At Abbey Road* (CD); and *Seven Pounds Of Potatoes* is on *English Freakbeat, Vol. 2* (LP & CD), but be warned it's pretty dire.

Guitarist Mick Green was also a big influence on Wiko Johnson and later worked with **Johnny Gustafson**. (VJ)

Miki Dallon

45s:	Do You Still Call That Love?/	
	Apple Pie	(RCA RCA 1438) 1965 SC
	I Care About You/I'll Give You Love	(RCA RCA 1478) 1965 R2
	Cheat And Lie/(I'm Gonna Find A) Cave	(Strike JH 306) 1966 SC
	What Will Your Mama Say Now?/	
	Two At A Time	(Strike JH 318) 1966

A songwriter/producer who also had this brief career as a solo artist. His first break came when he wrote and produced **The Boys Blue**'s *Take A Heart/You Got What I Want*, which was subsequently made famous by **The Sorrows**, for whom he wrote several other R&B songs. He was also backed by **The Sorrows** on *I'll Give You Love*, a pretty broody R&B number. He later owned the Youngblood label and also part-owned Strike.

Compilation coverage has included: *I'll Give You Love* on *English Freakbeat, Vol. 1* (LP & CD) and *Rare 60's Beat Treasures, Vol. 1* (CD); *Do You Call That Love* and *Apple Pie* on *Nowhere Men, Vol. 1* (LP & CD); *I'll Give You Love* and *I Care About You* on *Nowhere Men, Vol. 2* (CD).

DANDO SHAFT - Dando Shaft (LP).

Roger Daltrey

			HCP
ALBUMS:	1	DALTREY	(Track 2406 207) 1973 -
(up to			
1976)	2	RIDE A ROCK HORSE	(Polydor 2442 135) 1975 14

NB: (1) reissued on CD (Polydor 527 259-2) 1995 and again on Repertoire in 1998 remastered with their singles from the period added as bonuses. (2) reissued on CD on Repertoire in 1998 remastered with their singles from the period added as bonuses. There's also two CD compilations *Best Of Rockers And Ballads* (Polydor 847 855-2) 1991 and *Martyrs And Madmen: The Best Of* (Rhino RZ 72846) 1997. Also now on CD is the Soundtrack *McVicar* (Polydor 527 341-2) 1995 in which **Daltrey** played the lead role. The movie was about one of Britain's most infamous criminals. *Anthology* (Repertoire REP 4670 WY) 2000 is a 20-track compilation available on CD on German import. *Just A Boy* (Sanctuary SMEDD 013) 2004 is a 2-CD compilation of his solo work, including lots of **Who** songs. *Moonlighting - The Anthology* (Sanctuary) 2005 is a 2-CD collection of his material.

			HCP
45s:	I'm Free/Overture (PS)	(Ode ODS 66302) 1972 13
(up to	Giving It All Away/	
1976)	The Way Of The World	(Track 2094 110) 1973 5
	Thinking/There Is Love	(Track 2094 014) 1973 -
	It's A Hard Life/One Man Band	(Track 2094 016) 1973 -
	Orpheus Song/Love's Dream	(A&M AMS 7206) 1975 -
	Get Your Love/World Over	(Polydor 2058 593) 1975 -
	Walking The Dog/Crowd	(Polydor 2058 628) 1975 -

Roger Daltrey was born in London on 1st March 1944. In 1962, having left Acton Grammar School, he formed a band called The Detours, which he invited **Pete Townshend** and **John Entwistle** to join. By 1964 they'd incorporated **Keith Moon** into the line-up, changing their name first to **The Who** then to **The High Numbers** later that year. In November 1964 they became **The Who** again and began to embark on an enormously successful career. However, by the early seventies there was considerable scope for the individual members of the band to pursue their own solo careers. **Daltrey**'s was in many respects more successful than one might have anticipated. His debut album, produced by David Courtney and Adam Faith, using material written by Courtney and Leo Sayer, sold promisingly and also spawned a Top 10 UK hit single with *Giving It All Away*.

The following year **Daltrey** embarked on an acting career playing lead roles first in Ken Russell's 'Tommy' and then in 'Lisztomania'. *Ride A Rock Horse* proved to be another successful album and as we leave the period of this book **Daltrey** had also established his own Goldhawke Records - a bright future lay ahead.

Anthology is a 20-track compilation of his solo career between 1973 and 1987. *Moonlighting* is a 2-CD anthology of his recording career.

Sanctuary's compilation *Just A Boy* compiles his solo work but confirms that his best work was as a member of **The Who**. (VJ)

Dando Shaft

Personnel:	ROGER BULLEN	bs	AB
	DAVE COOPER	gtr, vcls	ABCD
	KEVIN DEMPSEY	gtr, vcls	ABCD
	MARTIN JENKINS	vcls, mandolin, violin	ABCD
	TED KAY	perc	ABCD
	POLLY BOLTON	vcls	BCD
	ROD CLEMENTS	bs	D
	PAUL DUNMAL	sax	D
	TOMMY KEARTON	keyb'ds	D
	JON STEVENS	drms	D
	DANNY THOMPSON	bs	D

ALBUMS:	1(A)	AN EVENING WITH DANDO SHAFT	
(up to		(Youngblood SSYB 6) 1970 R1
1977)	2(B)	DANDO SHAFT	(RCA Neon NE 5) 1971 R1
	3(C)	LANTALOON (initially w/ poster)	
		(RCA Victor SF 8256) 1972 R2/R1
	4(D)	KINGDOM	(Rubber RUB 034) 1977 SC

NB: (1) released on Decca (75217) in the US. *Reaping The Harvest* (See For Miles SEE 291) 1990 includes all their second album and highlights from the third. Alternatively *Early Dando Shaft* (In Respect 847 446) 1994 compiles (1) and (2) on one CD. (2) reissued on CD (Repertoire REP 4470-WP) 1994 with four bonus cuts.

45s:	Cold Wind/Cat Song	(Youngblood YB 1012) 1970
	Sun Clog Dance/This Gift	(RCA RCA 2246) 1972

Starting as a five-piece folk-band, **Dando Shaft** initiated a completely unique mixture of acoustic folk (none of the instruments are electrically amplified!) with driving rhythms and impeccable inventive musicianship. The lyrics are largely concerned with the relationship between man and nature, resulting in song-titles such as *Rain, Cold Wind* and *September Wine* as the first three tracks on their first album. They marvel in complicated structures and textures and are able to weave very intricate patterns, especially between mandolin (played in a highly original manner), guitar and violin. Very characteristic is also the combination of hand-beaten percussion and double-bass. After a change of label they acquired the services of a female singer, Polly Bolton, who had a pure and very expressive voice. Their second album brings in some elements of Bulgarian folk-music (asymmetrical time-measures) but is very much stamped by Polly's vocals and superb original compositions such as *Whispering Ned*, a rather funny drug-song and above all the achingly beautiful *Riverboat*. Preoccupation with travelling becomes discernable in *Railway* (a live favourite) and *Kallyope Driver*. After Neon folded they made another album on RCA, very much continuing in the same direction, although not as good as their previous effort. *Road Song* is another pulsating travel-song and *Black Prince Of Paradise* equals any track on the second album. Rumour has it, that another album was recorded for RCA, but due to lack of commercial success it never saw the light of day. Some seven years later some kind of reunion was attempted, but with the usual ambiguous results. Nevertheless, the magic returned for full on *Stroller In The Air*, an excellent composition and, at least partly, on *Trees*, a deceptively simple track with great atmosphere. Judging from a BBC Transcription disc, they were also a good live band. All their albums are worth investigation. (MK)

Patrick Dane

45s:	In My Baby's Eyes/Only One	(Columbia DB 7485) 1965
	Go Out And Get Somebody/	
	Go Your Way	(Columbia DB 7749) 1965
	When You Lose The One You Love/	
	Home	(MGM MGM 1403) 1968

Patrick Dane was a beat singer from London. He's backed by **The Quiet Five** on the first disc. The 'A' side was a Goffin/King number. Club '69 backed him on the second and Mark 7 on the third. (VJ)

A.P. Dangerfield

45:	Conversations (In A Station Refreshment Bar)/	
	Further Conversations	(Fontana TF 935) 1968 SC

Both sides of this collectable 45 received a further airing on *We Can Fly, Vol 2* (CD). (VJ)

Keith Dangerfield and The Way Ahead

45:      No Life Child/She's A Witch   (Plexium P 1237) 1968 R3

There has been speculation that this was **Keith Relf** recording under a pseudonym, but 'Record Collector' magazine has revealed that this is not the case. Curiously, *No Life Child* is almost a note for note and word for word rip off of **The Riot Squad**'s *How It Is Done* 45 from 1966. The 45 is extremely rare.

Compilation appearances include: *No Life Child* on *Story Of Oak Records* (2-LP); and *She's A Witch* on *The Story Of Oak Records* (CD) and *Beat It* (3-CD). (VJ/KL)

Tony Dangerfield and The Thrills

Personnel: JOHNNY BEDDER   gtr   A
             TONY DANGERFIELD   vcls   A
             RON 'THE ELF' BLACKIE bs   A
             NEIL NORMAN   drms   A
             MIKE BENSON   piano   A

45:      I've Seen Such Things/
         She's Too Way Out   (Pye 7N 15695) 1964 SC

Dangerfield was with The Savages when Joe Meek signed him as a solo artist. He had dyed blonde hair (although Meek made him dye it black so as not to clash with **Heinz**, another of his solo artists). The band worked mostly in Germany, where their 45 did well. It's now quite a sought-after collectable. The flip side, *She's Too Way Out*, is a sort of rockabilly/R&B fusion.

The band also cut two other tracks at Joe Meek's studio; a version of *Who Do You Love?* the old blues standard and a track written by Joe Meek which included the immortal line "Big fat spider flying by and by". Mike Benson was the band's pianist, and he now manages a country band. In Germany they shared a venue with **Ted (Kingsize) Taylor** for a month. Tony also used "Cheap Thrills" as an alternative nickname. Ron (The Elf) Blackie still plays double bass in orchestras. He was in Birmingham Philharmonic between 1979 - 86 and bassist in a blues-rock band called Pigs In Aspic.

Compilation appearances have included: *I've Seen Such Things* on *The R&B Era, Vol. 1* (CD); and *She's Too Way Out* on *English Freakbeat, Vol. 4* (LP & CD), *Freakbeat Freakout* (CD) and on Sequel's two-CD set, *The Joe Meek Story, The Pye Years*. (VJ)

Dantalian's Chariot

Personnel: COLIN ALLEN   drms   A
             PAT DONALDSON   bs   A
             ZOOT MONEY   keyb'ds, vcls A
             ANDY SUMMERS   gtr   A

ALBUM: 1(A)   CHARIOT RISING   (Tenth Planet TP 015) 1995 SC
NB: (1) Limited edition of 1,000 numbered, also available on CD with an extra track (Wooden Hill WHCD 005) 1997.

45:      The Madman Running Through The Fields/The Sun
         Came Bursting Through My Cloud (Columbia DB 8260) 1967 R3

When **Money** broke up The Big Roll Band, he formed this suitably named psychedelic outfit who performed frequently at London's Middle Earth and UFO clubs. They were certainly a talented outfit. Andy Summers, of course, later played with The Police, and Colin Allen went on to play with **John Mayall** and **Stone The Crows**. They recorded just one single for Columbia, *The Madman Running Through The Fields*. Penned by **Money** and Andy Summers it was perhaps one of the finest pieces of psychedelia recorded in the UK, this single is now very sought-after. The song was later covered by **Eric Burdon and The Animals** (with a line-up including **Zoot Money** and Andy Summers) on their *Love Is* album and is also on *Transition* (Direction 863231) 1968 by **Zoot Money**. The 45's flip side was a **Tony Colton**/Ray Smith ballad with appealing vocals.

Dantalion's Chariot's live appearances were amazing. They took to the stage in white robes and had what was generally regarded as the best light show in town. The only problem was this ensured they made heavy financial loses with every appearance. They also appeared in 'Pop Down', a Fred Marshall film about the excesses of Swingin' London seen through the eyes of two visitors from outer space named Sagittarius and Aries. The film, by all accounts, was appalling but it did feature music from **Blossom Toes** and an embryonic **Idle Race** as well.

Rumours of an unreleased **Dantalion's Chariot** album were untrue, but in 1995 David Wells' Tenth Planet label pieced together an album of previously unreleased material by the band, plus both sides of their 45. *Soma*, which appeared in two parts, one on each side of the album, with Andy Summers (who co-wrote it with his tutor Narzir Jarazbhoy) on sitar, was a fine Eastern-sounding remnant from 1967. *Fourpenny Bus Ride* and, to a lesser degree, *Four Firemen* were reasonable examples of whimsical psychedelic pop, but of the previously unissued material the jarring *World War Three* and jazz-tinged *High Flying Bird* (not the popular US West Coast standard), although it is an ode to the beautiful people of San Francisco, both **Money**/Summers collaborations, are the high points. By contrast *Coffee Song* and *Recapture The Thrill* were inconsequential mainstream recordings. However, overall this album is recommended.

Compilation coverage has included:- *The Madman Running Through The Fields* on *Chocolate Soup For Diabetics, Vol. 1* (LP), *Rubble Vol. 8: All The Colours Of Darkness* (LP), *Rubble Vol. 5* (CD) and on the 4-CD box set *Nuggets 11*; and *This Island* on *Electric Psychedelic Sitar Headswirlers Vol. 4* (CD). (VJ)

Troy Dante (and The Infernos)

45s: Golding Earings/Milord   (Decca F 11639) 1963
     α   It's Alright/Tell Me   (Decca F 11746) 1963
     α   Tell Me When/I Had To Be   (Fontana TF 445) 1964
     α   This Little Girl/Loving Eyes (Fontana TF 477) 1964 SC
          Baby/Tell Me Now   (Fontana TF 498) 1964
          I Wish I Knew/Sad Tears   (Fontana TF 541) 1965
          I'll Never Know/Security   (Polydor NH 56110) 1966
          My Friend The Scarecrow/
          Emma May Kingston   (Columbia DB 8381) 1968
          These Are Not My People/Little Star   (MCA MU 1056) 1969
          Behold/It's About Time   (MCA MK 5093) 1969

NB: α with The Infernos.

Troy Dante had quite a prolific 45s output, although they seemed to make little impact at the time and even less of a lasting impression. The ones with The Infernos were mostly beat, his latter efforts were ballads. He was managed by Diana Dors. (VJ)

DANTALIAN'S CHARIOT - Chariot Rising (LP).

DARK - Round The Edges (LP).

Anthony Dares Progress

Personnel incl: DAVE GAUNT

A four-piece from the Midlands who cut a two track acetate in 1966. One side, *Devil*, which has some quite good fuzz guitar moments, has resurfaced on *Incredible Sound Show Stories, Vol. 1* (LP & CD). (VJ)

Darien Spirit

Personnel:			
	DENNIS COWEN	bs, vcls	A
	HARRY MacDONALD	gtr, keyb'ds, vcls	A
	JACK McALLISTER	gtr, vcls, hrmnca	A
	FRANK RICCOTTI	perc, vibes	A
	ALAN WATERSON	drms, vcls	A

ALBUM: 1(A) ELEGY TO MARILYN (Charisma CAS 1065) 1973

Nice pleasant soft-harmony rock from an obscure band on the Charisma label. Dennis Cowan was in the **Bonzo Dog Band** and **The World** and sadly died some years ago. **Frank Riccotti** is a well-known session musician who recorded albums in his own right. All songs were McAllister / MacDonald compositions. (BS)

Dark

Personnel:			
	BRUCE DUNCAN	bs, gtr, vcls	A
	STEVE GILES	gtr	ABC
	CHARLES HIAMS	drms	A
	MARTIN MOLONEY	organ, vcls	A
	CARL BUSH	bs	BC
	CLIVE THORNEYCROFT	drms	AB
	RONALD JOHNSON	bs	C
	(MARTIN WEAVER	gtr	C)

Line-up A 1969-1970, line-up B 1971, line-up C 1971-1972.

ALBUM: 1(B/C) DARK ROUND THE EDGES (SIS 0102) 1972 R6

NB: (1) reissued on Swank (250 copies only) in 1990 (R1) and on Swank/Darkside 001 (250 copies only) in 1991 with lyric sheet. (1) reissued on CD (Kissing Spell KSCD 9204) 1992 (SC) with four bonus tracks: *In The Sky, Wasting Your Time, Could Have Sworn* and an old version of *Maypole* (which is unlisted). The bonus tracks only feature Steve Giles on lead and vocals, Clive Thorneycroft on drums and a bass player called Carl Bush. Neither Martin Weaver nor Ron Johnson feature on these added tracks. (1) also reissued on vinyl in a repro of the original sleeve 1998. There have been a number of additional retrospective releases: *Anonymous Days* (Darkedge Records DRCD 2371), is the twenty-five year follow-up to *Round The Edges*. Recorded between 1994 and 1996 it features the original band with tracks written both in the '70s and the '90s; *Dark / Tarsus* (Kissing Spell KSCD 9494) features a long jam which the band recorded for their own interest in 1975. It features Steve on lead, Clive on drums, Martin on lead, Ron on acoustic and electric guitars, and a couple of friends on bass and bongos. It is not one of their better jams. It also features a couple of tracks from Tarsus, a local band who disappeared

in the early '70s. Their tracks are pretty poor. The **Dark** jam has also been issued on CD as *The Jam*. Another CD *Teenage Angst* (Kissing Spell KSCD 9402) 1994, features only Steve of the **Dark** line-up and was recorded on amateur equipment in a church hall. From all accounts it is pretty poor. *Artefacts From A Black Museum* (Acme) is thought to only feature Steve and possibly Clive and is not very good. There is also an acetate single on a New York label in existence. It features Steve Giles on lead and Clive Thorneycroft on drums and Carl Bush on bass. The tracks are believed to be *RC8* and *In The Sky*. There are only two copies in existence and the band has one of them.

This legendary progressive rock band, which was responsible for the UK's most expensive album, was formed by Steve Giles whilst at school in Northampton in 1968. They met local entrepreneur Alan Bowley who'd recently converted a derelict house into a recording studio and this led to four acetates of *R.C.8* and *In The Sky*.

They perfomed at a few local gigs and as their playing got tighter decided to go into SIS Studios, Northampton with engineer Alan Bowley to record an album. The six tracks, written and arranged by the band were recorded over a weekend in 1972 and consist of melodic progressive rock laced with lots of fuzzy guitar riffs. Only a handful of copies were pressed and Giles, who had a strong interest in photography, made the first twelve copies into full-colour gatefold sleeves, complete with booklets of photographs stapled together, augmented with handwritten notes. They were handed out to band members and their girlfriends! Copies which came with a black and white gatefold sleeve are more sought-after and valuable than those which came in a single black and white sleeve. A total of 65 copies were reissued in all and each came with a lyric booklet and were sold originally for £3.

The band then split with Clive and Martin going their own ways and Steve and Ron continuing to record for their own pleasure until 1977 when Ron married and moved to Cornwall.

Kissing Spell traced the band in 1991 to tell them the original album was worth a small fortune, and offered to re-issue it on vinyl and CD. A re-issue had been done on vinyl in the States, followed by Kissing Spell's efforts. The members then got back together, and decided to see if they could still play. Previously unrecorded tracks were dusted off, more material written, and **Dark** re-entered the studio world in 1994 at Outrider Studios, Northampton, over twenty years after their first outing. A couple of tracks were laid down before the studio went bust, and **Dark** moved on to Far Heath Studios in Guilsborough, where the album *Anonymous Days* was completed in 1996. It was issued on CD in a limited edition of 500, twenty-five years after *Round The Edges*. Word got around that the band were playing again and offers of live gigs started to come in. They decided to do just one hail/farewell gig, which turned out to be the Northampton Beer Festival, on May 31st 1997. The local brewery, Frog Island, brewed a special limited edition bottled beer in the gig's honour, which sold for £2.50. The label being a copy of the CD cover of *Round The Edges*.

If you want to discover what their music was like track down one of the relatively recent vinyl or CD reissues of the original *Round The Edges* before investigating any of plethora of retrospectives.

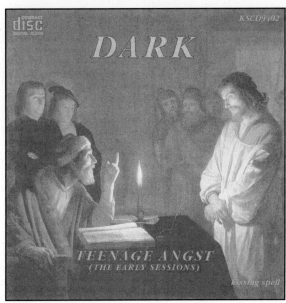

DARK - Teenage Angst (CD).

Kissing Spell, have also incidentally, issued a CD by Martin Weaver's power trio **Wicked Lady**, entitled *The Axeman Cometh* (Kissing Spell KSCD 9307) 1993. Weaver was an ancillary member of **Dark**. (VJ)

Darwin's Theory

45:      Daytime/Hosanna   (Major Minor MM 503) 1967 R1

The 'A' side of this combo's 45 was first recorded by **Hedgehoppers Anonymous**.

Compilation appearances have included: *Daytime* and *All The Time Clementine* on *Rare 60's Beat Treasures, Vol. 3* (CD); *Hosanna* on *Twisted Teenage Screaming Fuzzbusters* (LP) and *That Driving Beat* (CD); and *Daytime* on *English Freakbeat, Vol. 5* (LP & CD). (VJ)

Dave Davani and D Men

Personnel incl: DAVE DAVANI
                  BERYL WAYNE

45s: Don't Fool Around/
         She's The Best For Me   (Columbia DB 7125) 1963 SC
         Midnight Special/
         She Knew A Lot About Love   (Decca F 11896) 1964 SC

This beat group later became the **Dave Davani Four**. (VJ)

Dave Davani Four

Personnel incl: DAVE DAVANI
                  BERYL WAYNE

ALBUM: 1   FUSED   (Parlophone PMC 1258) 1965 R2

45s: Top Of The Pops/Workin' Out   (Parlophone R 5329) 1965 SC
         Tossin' And Turnin'/Jupe   (Parlophone R 5490) 1966 R1
    α   One Track Mind/
         On The Cooler Side   (Parlophone R 5525) 1966 R1
    α   King Kong Blues/Come Back Baby   (Philips 6006 195) 1971
NB: α Dave Davani solo efforts.

This is a later version of **Dave Davani and D Men**. The album and the singles on Parlophone are now minor collectables. (VJ)

THAT DRIVING BEAT (Comp CD) including Darwin's Theory.

Dave and The Diamonds

Personnel incl: DAVE RUSSELL   vcls

45:      I Walk The Lonely Night/
         You Do Love (Some PS)   (Columbia DB 7692) 1965 R1/SC

This was a short-lived beat group. Dave Russell also released a ballad 45 the following year. (VJ)

David and The Embers

45:      What Is This/Teddy Beat Special   (Decca F 11717) 1963

A beat group from Edinburgh. The Embers had earlier released a 45 for Decca. (VJ)

David and Jonathan

Personnel: DAVID (ROGER COOK)   A
                JONATHAN (ROGER GREENAWAY)   A

ALBUM: 1(A)   DAVID AND JONATHAN
                 (mono/stereo)   (Columbia SX/SCX 6031) 1967 SC
NB: There's also a compilation, *Lovers Of The World Unite*, (See For Miles CM 129) 1984 and a CD compilation, *The Very Best Of David and Jonathan* (C5 C5CD 507) 1990.

                                                                    HCP

45s: Laughing Fit To Cry/
         Remember What You Said   (Columbia DB 7717) 1965 -
         Michelle/
         How Bitter The Taste Of Love   (Columbia DB 7800) 1966 11
         Speak Her Name/
         Take It While You Can   (Columbia DB 7873) 1966 -
         Lovers Of The World Unite/
         Oh My Word   (Columbia DB 7950) 1966 7
         Ten Storeys High/
         Looking For My Life   (Columbia DB 8035) 1966 -
         Gilly Gilly Ossenfeffer Katzenellenbogen By The Sea/
         Scarlet Ribbons For Her Hair (Columbia DB 8167) 1966 -
         She's Leaving Home/
         One Born Every Minute   (Columbia DB 8208) 1967 -
         Softly Whispering I Love You/
         Such A Peaceful Day   (Columbia DB 8287) 1967 -
         You Ought To Meet My Baby/
         I've Got That Girl On My Mind   (Columbia DB 8428) 1968 -

These two, whose real names are given in brackets, were songwriters and session singers who formed a fairly successful duo in 1965. Their big breakthrough came when their cover of **The Beatles'** *Michelle* made the Charts and the subsequent success of *Lovers Of The World Unite* proved they were no 'one hit wonders' - just 'two hit wonders' instead! They were talented songwriters in their own right, though, and credits included *You've Got Your Troubles* (a massive hit for **The Fortunes**). **Cook** went on to form **Blue Mink** in 1969.

The See For Miles compilation consists of 20 tracks - mostly breezy pop songs, including their version of *You've Got Your Troubles* and *This Golden Ring* (another **Fortunes**' hit), *Softly Whispering I Love You* (a subsequent hit for The Congregation) and a cover of **Paul McCartney**'s *She's Leaving Home*, arranged by **George Martin**. For fans of sixties pop only and even then not essential. The later C5 CD compilation includes similar material.

Lovers Of The World Unite has been compiled on *Beat Generation - Ready Steady Go* (CD). David went on to record a number of solo albums in the seventies under his real name **Roger Cook**. Roger Greenaway experienced considerable success as a composer (sometimes in collaboration with **Cook**). His credits included **The Hollies'** *Long Cool Woman...*, Gene Pitney's *Something Gotten Hold Of My Heart* and **Whistling Jack Smith**'s *I Was Kaiser Bill's Batman* to name but a few! (VJ)

SPENCER DAVIS GROUP - I'm A Man (CD).

David and Rozza

Personnel incl: DAVID ESSEX
ROZZA WORTHAM

45s: Time Of Our Life/
We Can Reach An Understanding (Philips 6006 040) 1970 SC
The Spark That Lights The Flame/
Two Can Share (Philips 6006 094) 1971 SC

This was an early **David Essex** project. Their 45s are only really of much interest to his fans. (VJ)

Alun Davies

ALBUM: 1 DAYDO (CBS 65108) 1972

45: One Day Soon/
Pretend You Don't See Her (Mercury MF 1043) 1968

From Wales, this album was made by **Cat Stevens'** backing guitarist. It features mainly self-written songs and was produced by himself and Paul Samwell-Smith, the former **Yardbirds'** member who was **Cat Stevens'** producer. It's no surprise therefore that there is a strong **Cat Stevens** influence on the album, which also features a cover of Buddy Holly's *I'm Gonna Love You Too*. **Cat Stevens** also played some back-up piano on the album.

Davies also appeared on the 'Opportunity Knocks' TV show.

Back in 1963, **Davies** had released a folk/skiffle album as half of **Jon and Alun**. The pair also later worked together in **Sweet Thursday**, and the **Mark-Almond** band.

Another 45, *Girls Were Made To Love And Kiss/Rose Marie* (Parlophone R 5384) 1965, is by a different **Alun Davies** - a Welsh operatic singer. (VJ/GBn)

Bryan Davies

45: Tell The Other Guy/My Dream Of You (Columbia DB 7345) 1964

The 'A' side is a good uptempo beat song and the 'B' side a very passable Cliff Richard-like melody. The backing is arranged and conducted by Norrie Paramor. (VJ)

Dave Davies

EP: 1 DAVE DAVIES HITS (Pye NEP 24289) 1968 R4

NB: (1) reissued along with the five original **Kinks** EPs on *The EP Collection* (See For Miles SEE 295) 1990, also on CD (SEE CD 295). There's also *Dave Davies Anthology: Unfinished Business* (Essential ESSCD 584) 1998, which compiles all his solo work, except *Funny Face*.

HCP

45s: Death Of A Clown/
Love Me Till The Sun Shines (Pye 7N 17356) 1967 3
Susannah's Still Alive/Funny Face (Pye 7N 17429) 1967 20
Lincoln County/
There's No Life Without Love (Pye 7N 17514) 1968 SC -
Hold My Hand/Creeping Jean (Pye 7N 17678) 1969 SC -
α Drivin'/Mindless Child Of Motherhood (Pye 7N 17776) 1969 -
α Shangri-La/This Man He Weeps Tonight (Pye 7N 17812) 1969 -
Reissue: Death Of A Clown/
Susannah's Still Alive (Old Gold OG 9128) 1982 -

NB: All of the above were also released as promo copies with yellow labels and are collectable now. The 'B' sides of α were **Kinks** songs originally intended as **Dave Davies** solo recordings.

Dave Davies was born on 3 February 1947 at Muswell Hill, London. In 1963 he was playing in a R&B outfit, The Ravens, with his brother Ray and later that year in **The Kinks**. In the late sixties, whilst still with **The Kinks**, Dave enjoyed a brief solo career, reaching No 3 with *Death Of A Clown*, written by his brother Ray, backed by **The Kinks** and produced by Shel Talmy. He returned to the Top 20 later in the year with *Susannah's Still Alive*. There the success ended, although much later in 1980 Dave released his first solo album, *AFLI-3603* (which was titled after the disc's catalogue number).

A good compilation of his material is *The Album That Never Was* (PRT PYL 6012) 1988, which contains both sides of his four singles and two **Kinks** songs originally intended as solo recordings:- *This Man He Weeps Tonight* and *Mindless Child Of Motherhood*. *Creeping Jean* the menacing flip side of *Hold My Hand* is worth a spin.

Various artists compilation appearances include: *Creeping Jean* on *Pop Inside The Sixties, Vol. 3* (CD); *Quick Before They Catch Us* (LP & CD) and *Hot Smoke And Sassfras - Psychedelic Pstones, Vol 1* (CD) and *Love Me Till The Sun Shines* on *Rock Of Ages, Four Decades Of Heavy Rock 1962-2002*. (VJ)

Clifford Davis

45s: Before The Beginning/
Man Of The World (Reprise RS 27003) 1969
Man Of The World/Before The Beginning (Reprise K 14282) 1973

Clifford Davis was the manager of **Skid Row**, **Curved Air**, **Gary Moore** and **Fleetwood Mac**. The above songs were all written and produced by **Peter Green**, who also plays most of the instruments as well, with **Cliff Bennett** providing the vocals.

When **Davis** also put together a bogus **Fleetwood Mac** to tour the States (later called **Stretch**), *Why Did You Do It?* was written about him. (VJ)

Kim Davis

Personnel incl: KIM DAVIS vcls A
MIKE TULLOCH drms A
COLIN WOODLAND gtr A

ALBUM: 1 KIM DAVIS (Ariola 86 683 IT) 1973

45s: Don't Take Your Lovin' Away/
Feelin' Blue (Decca F 12387) 1966 SC
Tell It Like It Is/Losing Kind (CBS 202568) 1967
Until It's Time For You To Go/
I Hold No Grudge (CBS 3260) 1968
Are You Ready For Love/Taste Of Excitement (CBS 4210) 1969

An R&B artist from Newcastle whose *Feelin' Blue* got a further airing on *R&B Scene, Vol. 2* (LP) and *British R'n'B Explosion, Vol. 1* (CD). She earlier recorded a 45 as **Kim D**. (VJ/CW)

Sandy Davis

Personnel:

MARTIN BRILEY	gtr	A
ALAN COWDERROY	gtr	A
PAUL "SANDY" DAVIS	multi-instruments	A
PETER SKELLERN	piano	A
ANDREW BRYCE JACKMAN	keyb'ds, recorder	A

ALBUM: 1(A) INSIDE EVERY FAT MAN (EMI ECM 3029) 1974

45: Inside Every Fat Man/Share A Little Love (EMI EMI 2181) 1974

A 'solo' outting by former **Gracious** member **Paul "Sandy" Davis**, with former band-mate Alan Cowderoy featured on one track and Henri Spinnetti and Roy Babbington involvement.

Davis wrote all songs on the album except *He Gives Us All His Love* by Randy Newman. (VZ)

Spencer Davis Group

Personnel:

SPENCER DAVIS	gtr, vcls	ABCDE
MUFF WINWOOD	bs, vcls	A
STEVIE WINWOOD	keyb'ds, gtr, vcls	A
PETER YORK	drms	ABC
EDDIE HARDIN	organ, vcls	BC
PHIL SAWYER	ld gtr	B
RAY FENWICK	gtr, vcls	CDE
DEE MURRAY	bs	DE
DAVE HYNES	drms	D
(KIRK DUNCAN	keyb'ds	D)
NIGEL OLSSON	drms	E

HCP

ALBUMS:				
1(A)	THEIR FIRST LP	(Fontana TL 5242) 1965	R1	6
2(A)	THE SECOND ALBUM	(Fontana TL 5295) 1966	R1	3
3(A)	AUTUMN '66	(Fontana TL 5349) 1966	R1	4
4(B)	HERE WE GO ROUND THE MULBERRY BUSH (Soundtrack)			
	(mono/stereo)	(United Artists (S)ULP 1186) 1967	R1	-
5(C)	WITH THEIR NEW FACE ON			
	(mono/stereo)	(United Artists SULP 1192) 1968	SC	-
6(A)	THE BEST OF THE SPENCER DAVIS GROUP			
	(mono/stereo)	(Island ILP 970/ILPS 9070) 1968	SC	-
7( )	LETTERS FROM EDITH	(CBS 63842) 1969	R3	-
8( )	IT'S BEEN SO LONG	(United Artists UAS 29177) 1971	-	
9( )	GLUGGO	(Vertigo 6360 088) 1973	-	
10( )	LIVING ON A BACK STREET	(Vertigo 6360 105) 1974	-	

NB: Line-up D recorded an album in 1969 *Letters From Edith*. Line-up E has not recorded. Tracks from *Letters From Edith* were later available on the compilation *The*

SPENCER DAVIS GROUP - Best Of (LP).

SPENCER DAVIS GROUP - Gluggo (LP).

Spencer Davis Group: Taking Out Time 1967-1969 (rpm RPM 127) 1994, which also includes 12 tracks recorded by line-up C. (1) reissued as *Every Little Bit Hurts* (Wing WL 1165) 1968. (7) unissued. 50 white label test pressings only. (9) reissued on CD (Repertoire) 1998, with three additional different tracks from the US edition, a forgotten 'B' side and two previously unissued mixes.

There's also two excellent compilations: *Best Of The Spencer Davis Group* (Rhino RNLP 117) 1984; and *Eight Gigs A Week: The Stevie Winwood Years* (Island CRNCD 5) 1995, which includes all but one of the band's recordings with **Winwood** on Fontana and Island and two previously unissued blues numbers, *Oh Pretty Woman* and *Kansas City*. r-p-m have also issued a CD of previously unissued material from 1968/69 in 1994. *Mulberry Bush* (Get Back GET 548) 2000, a vinyl release on Italian import, contains the tracks from the *Here We Go Round The Mulberry Bush* soundtrack plus some singles and alternate versions. *Mojo Rhythms And Midnight Blues, Vol 1: Sessions '65-'68* (RPM RPM 207) 2000 is a 23-track compilation, which includes sessions from programmes like 'Saturday Club'. *Gimme Some Lovin'* (Sundazed SC 11103) 2001 and *I'm A Man* (Sundazed SC 1104) 2001, which are both available as US imports, are reissues of their original US releases of their Fontana material supplemented by eight bonus tracks. *Funky* (Angel Air SJPCD 021) 2002 is an album of material recorded in 1969 for an intended release on CBS which did not happen. *Keep On Running 40th Anniversary* (Cherry Red CMRED 250) 2004 is a retrospective set.

EPs:			
1(A)	YOU PUT THE HURT ON ME	(Fontana TE 17444) 1965	SC
2(A)	EVERY LITTLE BIT HURTS	(Fontana TE 17450) 1965	SC
3(A)	SITTIN' AND THINKIN'	(Fontana TE 17463) 1966	R1
4( )	KEEP ON RUNNING/SOMEBODY HELP ME/EVERY LITTLE BIT HURTS/I'M A MAN	(Island IEP 10) 1978	

HCP

45s:			
	Dimples/Sittin' And Thinkin'	(Fontana TF 471) 1964	SC
	I Can't Stand It/Midnight Train	(Fontana TF 499) 1964	SC 47
	Every Little Bit Hurts/ It Hurts Me So	(Fontana TF 530) 1965	41
	Strong Love/This Hammer	(Fontana TF 571) 1965	44
	Keep On Running/High Time Baby	(Fontana TF 632) 1965	1
	Somebody Help Me/Stevie's Blues	(Fontana TF 679) 1966	1
	When I Come Home/Trampoline	(Fontana TF 739) 1966	12
	Gimme Some Loving/Blues In F	(Fontana TF 762) 1966	2
	I'm A Man/I Can't Get Enough Of It	(Fontana TF 785) 1967	9
	Time Seller/Don't Want You No More	(Fontana TF 854) 1967	30
	Mr. Second Class/ Sanity Inspector	(United Artists UP 1203) 1967	35
	After Tea/Moonshine	(United Artists UP 2213) 1968	-
	Short Change/ Picture Of Heaven	(United Artists UP 2226) 1968	-
	Catch You On The Rebop/The Edge	(Vertigo 6059 076) 1972	
α	Don't Let It Bring You Down/World	(Vertigo) 197?	
	Mr. Operator/Touching Cloth	(Vertigo 6059 082) 1973	-
	Living In A Back Street/ Helping Hand	(Vertigo 6059 087) 1973	-
Reissues:	Gimme Some Loving/ When I Come Home	(Island WIP 5001) 197?	-
	Gimme Some Loving (two versions)	(Island WIP 6318) 197?	-

NB: α Unreleased. The US 45 *Gimme Some Lovin'/Blues In F* (United Artists 50108) 1966 features a completely different version to the UK release.

At their best **The Spencer Davis Group** merged black and white music and **Stevie Winwood**'s superb vocal performances (he was only in his teens at the time) are living proof that white men can sing the blues.

This exciting Birmingham R&B group came about after the Winwood brothers and York (playing as The Muff-Woody Jazz Band) shared the bill with **Spencer Davis**, who was doing acoustic country blues music at the time, at a Birmingham pub, The Golden Eagle.

They formed as the **Spencer Davis Group** in 1963. Although they took their name from **Davis**, it was teenage guitarist and vocalist **Stevie Winwood**, who gave the band their special ingredient. Indeed, he wrote much of their material. After signing to Fontana, their career took a little while to get started. Their debut 45, *Dimples*, flopped and *I Can't Stand It*, *Every Little Bit Hurts* (a slow, soulful ballad written by Ed Cobb) and *Strong Love* (a faster R&B number) were all minor hits. It was two songs by Jamaican singer Jackie Edwards, which were perfectly suited to **Winwood**'s strong blues voice, which catapulted the band to the top of the UK Charts - *Keep On Running* and *Somebody Help Me*. Both were among the finest 45s of the mid-sixties. Almost as strong were *When I Come Home*, another Edwards song adapted by **Winwood** and the self-penned *Gimme Some Lovin'*. The final hit of this their most successful period was **Stevie Winwood**'s adaptation of *I'm A Man*.

In early 1967 Stevie left to form **Traffic** and Muff departed to work with Chris Blackwell at Island. Hardin and Sawyer were drafted in as replacements from **The Cheynes** and **The Fleur de Lys** respectively, but the band was never really as good. Of their later singles by far the most interesting was *Time Seller*, which became a minor hit and saw the band flirting with psychedelia. *Mr. Second Class* is worth a spin, but after that they really lost direction.

Check out the *Here We Go Round The Mulberry Bush* soundtrack, which is an important sixties artefact. Tracks like *Virginal's Dream* and *Taking Out Time* capture the band in reflective mood, whilst *Possession* and *Looking Back* are more beaty. The soundtrack also includes music from **Traffic** and **Andy Ellison**. In October 1968 Hardin and York left to form Hardin and York and Dee Murray and Nigel Olsson came in to replace them. **Davis** kept the band on the road until the Summer of 1969 when he brought it to an end. Murray and Olsson both later played for **Elton John**. **Davis** headed for California, working first with Alun Davis, in an acoustic partnership, then later with Peter Jameson. In 1973 he reformed a new **Spencer Davis Group**, although it was short-lived and he ended up working at Island Records with Muff Winwood.

The three albums by the original line-up sold well and are worth checking out, alternatively a good introduction to their music is *The Best Of The Spencer Davis Group* on Island Records, or the similarly titled 1984 compilation on Rhino. This has a great colour cover and sleevenotes written by **Davis** himself. It also includes a couple of tracks:- *Midnight Special* and *The Hammer Song* with **Davis** in the vocal role.

SPENCER DAVIS GROUP - Mulberry Bush (LP).

SPENCER DAVIS GROUP - Gimme Some Lovin' (CD).

The band also appeared back in 1968 on Island's *British Blue-Eyed Soul* (LP) compilation playing *Stevie's Blues, Let Me Down Easy* and *Sittin' And Thinkin'*. They're also responsible for the *Great Shakes Ad* on the *Great Shakes* EP from 1967. Island's 1969 *You Can All Join In* (LP) included *Somebody Help Me* and the band contributed *Taking Out Time, Every Little Thing, Virginals Dream, Looking Back, Picture Of Her, Just Like Me, Waltz For Caroline* and *Possession* to the soundtrack album *Here We Go 'Round The Mulberry Bush* (LP).

In 1994 r-p-m issued a CD of unissued material from 1968/69. *Funky* comprises material from 1969 intended for CBS release, which didn't come about because the band was on the brink of splitting. However, some test pressings saw the light of day and there was a US release on the Date label. It contains some interesting material but falls short of classic status.

Get Back's vinyl release *Mulberry Bush* takes the eight tracks from the original soundtrack and adds very different versions of four of them and some singles from the same period.

Mojo Rhythms And Midnight Blues, Vol 1: Sessions '65-'68 has excellent sound quality and incorporates radio sessions from programmes like 'Saturday Club'.

In 2001, Sundazed reissued their two original US albums *Gimme Some Lovin'* and *I'm A Man* of their Fontana material, each supplemented by eight bonus tracks. Both have excellent sound quality and sleevenotes relaying **Spencer Davis's** memories of their golden years.

The *Keep On Running 40th Anniversary* retrospective highlights **Stevie Winwood's** talent on tracks like John Lee Hooker's *Dimples* (BBC 1965 session), the live version of Ed Cobb's *Every Little Bit Hurts* (Marquee 1965) and *I'm A Man* (from 1967).

Retrospective compilation appearances have included: *When A Man Loves A Woman* and *When I Come Home* on *Made In England, Vol. 1* (CD); *I'm A Man* on *Made In England, Vol. 2* (CD); *After Tea* on *Rubble, Vol. 2 - Pop Sike Pipe Dreams* (LP), *Rubble, Vol. 2* (CD) and on the Bam-Caruso *Psych-Out* flexi; *Night Time Is The Right Time* on *The First British R&B Festival, February 28, 1964* (LP); *Great Shakes* on *Great Shakes Shake-Out* (EP); *I'm A Man* and *Gimme Some Lovin'* on the US compilation *The Golden Archive Series Sampler* (LP); *Gimme Some Lovin'* on *Frat Rock! The Greatest Rock 'n' Roll Party Tunes Of All Time* (LP); *Keep On Running* on the 2-CD set *45s - 45 Classic No 1's* and on the 2-CD set *60 Number Ones Of The Sixties* and *Time Seller* on the 4-CD box set *Acid Drops & Flying Saucers*. (VJ/BM)

Dawn and The Deejays

45:     These Are The Things About You/
        I Will Think Of You   (RCA RCA 1470) 1965

This beat group came from Lincolnshire. (VJ)

The Dawnbreakers

Personnel incl: JIM ATKINSON   bs   A

45:        Let's Live/Lovin' For You   (Decca F 12110) 1965

This long forgotten one-off 45 was a gentle ballad. The group came from Leeds. (VJ)

The Dawn Chorus

45:        A Night To Be Remembered/
           Crying All Night   (MCA MK 5004) 1969

This was a Carter-Lewis creation. You'll also find the 'A' side on Sequel's recent CD compilation, *Carter-Lewis Story*. (VJ)

Dawnwind

Personnel: JON HARFLETT   vcls, gtr   A
                JOHN PERKINS   gtr, hrmnca, vcls   A

ALBUM: 1(A)   LOOKING BACK ON THE FUTURE
                                  (Amron ARN 5003) 1976 R3

This privately-pressed album now changes hands for three figure sums. The band played a form of folk-rock on the album which is characterised by rather surreal lyrics over a slightly melancholic accompaniment. Their magnum opus was a cut called *Dogs Of War*, but the album, which includes a cover version of John Prine's *Sam Stone*, attains a consistently good standard throughout.

Dawnwind were formed in 1968 by Jon Harflett and John Perkins. Originally the pair performed as Harflett and Perkins, playing mainly in the Midlands as a semi-professional act. The duo went full-time in 1970 and changed name to **Dawnwind**. They were signed up as songwriters by Carlin Music Company and represented by Nucleus who also represented **The Pretty Things**, **UFO** and others.

In the early seventies they built a fairly solid reputation as a live act on Club/University/College scene. They also got to tour in the USA, Germany and Holland.

The band's recording history is quite complicated. An album was recorded for the Eden label in 1970, *Natural Born Ramblers* and although some copies were pressed Eden went bust before the album could be released. EMI then began to show some interest but although John Perkins sat in playing guitar on Sam Parry's album and Jon Harflett wrote liner notes for a couple of albums, their management Nucleus never managed to get a deal.

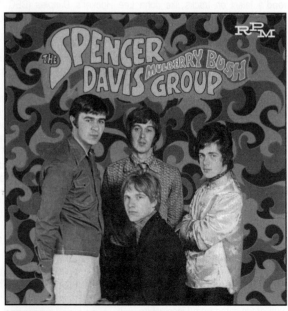

SPENCER DAVIS GROUP - Mulberry Bush (CD).

In 1974, Norman Davies of Amron approached **Dawnwind** about making an album, and it was recorded in 1975 at the Mid-Wales Sound Studio, with Norman producing and Alan Green as engineer.

Dawnwind was always a duo but many guests appeared at gigs, people could be forgiven for thinking of them as a band. For the *Looking Back On The Future* album, they used Dana Simmons (American) and Alistair Leacock on back-up guitars and Will Thomas on fiddle and mandolin. Dana sang high harmony on *Street-Singer*. Jon Harflett was lead vocalist on all tracks except *Man Of Stars*, *Concrete Circles* and *I'm Sentimental Too*. In addition to the tracks used on the album they also recorded a version of Steve Goodman's *City Of New Orleans*. Both Harflett and Perkins were responsible for the musical arrangements.

Jon Harflett:- "The first pressing was 500 copies for sale in clubs but then everything got very complicated. Norman Davies either sold or just gave up on Amron. Copies of the album then started to turn up in shops (and were still turning up circa 1978). It was fairly widely availible in Germany, where it was also bootlegged. It was bootlegged too in the USA in the mid-nineties. Nobody really knows how many copies were printed or sold in total but it's a lot more than most people think despite it being rare now."

Dawnwind split up as a working duo in 1976 but have remained friends to this day. Jon Harflett continued a solo career in and around London until the eighties and then became a University Teacher until ill health forced him into retirement. He has written an autobiography, 'Dancing With The Moon'. John Perkins later founded his own label (Check out White Eagle Records on the Net). They have been known to turn up in folk clubs just for old time's sake but have no interest in bringing **Dawnwind** back. Both are frankly amazed that the album should have become a collector's item.

Jon:- "We have been approached several times about a CD issue but there is a tangled web of copyrights involved and it's never seemed worth it. There are about fourteen sites on the Net with information about **Dawnwind** - most of it wrong. The only thing that really annoys the two Johns is when we're described as a Welsh Band." (VJ/JHt)

John Dawson Read

Personnel: JOHN DAWSON READ   acc. gtr   A
                LES HURDLE   bs   A
                MIKE MORAN   keyb'ds   A
                BARRY MORGAN   drms   A
                FRANK RICOTTI   perc   A

ALBUMS: 1(A)   A FRIEND OF MINE   (Chrysalis CHR 1075) 1975
(up to   2(A) READ ON   (Charisma CHR 1102) 1976
1976)

45:        Friend Of Mine/Superficial Thing   (Chrysalis CHS 2067) 1975

This is singer / songwriter fare from an obscure artist. The seventies had legions of such artists who recorded pleasant enough but fairly average material and often the supporting band members were of more interest as is the case here. Barry Morgan drummed with **Blue Mink**, **Brian Protheroe**, **Gullivers People** and **Whistler**. Mike Moran was a well-known session musician, he was on the **Howard Werth** album for instance and **Frank Ricotti** recorded solo albums, played in **Byzantium** and appeared on hundreds of albums as one of the premier percussionists of this era. (BS)

Daylight

Personnel: TONY CARR   drms   A
                LYN DOBSON   woodwind   A
                STEVE HAYTON   gtr, mandolin, vcls   A
                SPIKE HEATLEY   bs   A
                CHRISSIE QUAYLE   gtr, vcls   A
                MIKE SILVER   gtr, vcls   A

ALBUM: 1(A)   DAYLIGHT   (RCA SF 8194) 1971 R1

45:        Lady Of St. Clare/Wednesday People   (RCA 2106) 1971

A short-lived hippie folk-rock outfit from Penzance in Cornwall, whose album was produced by Tony Cox, also responsible for albums by **Trees**, **Amory Kane**, **Caravan** and others. Tony Carr had been in **CCS** and later played with **Alan Price** and in **Power Pack**. Lyn Dobson had been in **Soft Machine** and **The Keef Hartley Band**. Steve Hayton had been in **Daddy Longlegs** and recorded solo. He was later in Amalgam. Spike Heatley has played with **Donovan**. Chrissie Quayle sang back-up on **COB**'s *Spirit of Love* album. (VJ/JN/RMJ)

Dead Sea Fruit

Personnel:			
	SI CLIFFORD	keyb'ds	A
	CHRISTOPHER HALL	bs, gtr, vcls	A
	CLIVE KENNEDY	vcls	A
	CHRIS LANSDOWN	bs, vcls	A
	DAVE 'BEANO' LASHMAR	gtr, vcls	A
	JOHN ERRINGTON-TOWNSEND	perc, vcls	A

ALBUM: 1(A) DEAD SEA FRUIT (Camp 603 001) 1967 R2

45s: Kensington High Street/
Put Another Record On (Camp 602 001) 1967
Love At The Hippiedrome/
My Naughty Bluebell (Camp 602 004) 1968

Dead Sea Fruit's album is quite strange, which makes it hard to tell whether its makers were serious or not. Vocals and lyrics are so totally deadpan, that comparisons to **Bonzo Dog Band** or even **The Barron Knights** are unavoidable. They also seem to parody older musical styles like music-hall, calypso and fifties rock like the above bands do. Still, some of the songs do have a very slight psychedelic atmosphere, especially *Mr. Coffee Pot*, which sounds like **The Kinks** and features a tambura in the backing. A period piece no doubt, this shouldn't be confused with psychedelic music.

Dave Lashmar owns Beano's, Britains self-proclaimed largest second hand record shop.

Kensington High Street was later compiled on *Magic Spectacles* (CD). (MK)

Deadwood

45s: The Turning Of Them All/
That Don't Help Me None (Decca F 13109) 1971
Me And My Friends/Little Joe (Decca F 13179) 1971

The first 45 is a mixture of **Marmalade** and bubblegum. (VJ)

Deaf School

Personnel:			
	ANN BRIGHT	vcls	A
	BETTE BRIGHT	vcls	A
	HAZEL BARTRAM	vcls	A
	ENRICO CADILLAC		
	(aka STEVE ALLEN)	gtr	A
	MIKE EVANS	sax	A
	CLIFF HANGAR		
	(aka CLIVE LANGER)	gtr	A
	ROY HOLDER	gtr	A
	PAUL PILNICK	gtr	A
	MR AVERAGE		
	(aka STEVE LINDSAY)	gtr	A
	REVEREND MAX RIPPLE		
	(aka JOHN WOOD)	gtr	A
	IAN RITCHIE	sax	A
	ERIC SHARK	vcls	A
	TIM WHITAKER	drms	A

ALBUM: 1 SECOND HONEYMOON (Warner Bros) 1976
(up to 1976)

DEAF SCHOOL - Second Honeymoon (LP).

45: What A Way To End It All/
(up to Nearly Moonlit Night Motel (Warner Bros K 16812) 1976
1976)

Deaf School was an art-rock band from Liverpool with a theatrical stage act and very fluid personnel. The band was named after the place where they used to rehearse. An early influence on new wave, they went on to make two further albums: *Don't Stop The World* in 1977 and *English Boys Working Girls* in 1978, along with further singles too. Many of them went on to greater things including Clive Langer as a producer, Steve Allen in Original Mirrors and Steve Lindsay in Big In Japan, Secrets and The Planets. Bette Bright later married Suggs of Madness. (VJ)

Alan Dean and His Problems

Personnel incl: ALAN DEAN

45s: The Time It Takes/Dizzy Heights (Decca F 11947) 1964 SC
Thunder And Rain/As Time Goes By (Pye 7N 15749) 1965 R2

Back in the fifties **Dean** had been a solo artist. Their records were produced by Joe Meek, who wrote the 'B' side of *Thunder And Rain*.

Compilation appearances include: *The Time It Takes* on *Mod Scene, Vol. 2* (CD), *British R'n'B Explosion, Vol. 1* (CD) and *The Sound Of British RnB 1962-68*; *Thunder And Rain* on *The Joe Meek Story: The Pye Years* (2-CD); and *As Time Goes By* on *The Joe Meek Story: The Pye Years, Vol. 2* (LP). (VJ)

Elton Dean

ALBUM: 1 ELTON DEAN (CBS 64539) 1971 R1

Born in Nottingham, **Elton Dean** was a jazz musician who first played with **Bluesology**. He was then in the **Keith Tippett Sextet** playing on their *You Are Here, I Am There* 1969 album for Polydor. He next played on **Julie Driscoll**'s 1969 album. In October 1969 with Nick Evans and Marc Charig (who'd also played with him in the **Keith Tippett Sextet**) he joined **The Soft Machine** for sessions, which were eventually released on *Triple Echo* (Harvest). Whilst involved in work for the *Third* **Soft Machine** album, **Dean** formed *Just Us* in 1970. He also played on **Robert Wyatt**'s *End Of An Ear* album and **Keith Tippett**'s *Dedicated To You But You Weren't Listening*.

His 1971 solo album was made mainly with members of Just Us and he was one of many musicians to play on **Centipede**'s *Septober Energy* that year. He also played on **Head, Hands and Feet**s' debut album, **Reg King**'s only solo album and **Mike Hugg**'s *Somewhere* album.

After Just Us folded in 1972 **Dean** joined Supersister, a Dutch fusion band in 1973 and also contributed to **Hugg**'s *Stress And Strain* album the same year.

DECAMERON - Mammoth Special (CD).

In 1974 **Dean** left Supersister to join up with **Hugh Hopper** on the *Monster Band* album (Atmosphere IRI 5003), which was taken from a gig in Bordeaux. The line-up included Mike Travis on drums and two French musicians. **Dean** also played with **Georgie Fame's Blue Flames** for a tour and on **Alexis Korner**'s *Mr. Blues* album.

In 1975 **Dean** formed Ninesense who made an album, *Oh For The Edge*, on Ogun Records. In 1977, he released a further album *The Cheque's In The Mail* (Ogun OG 610) 1977 with Joe Gallivan and Kenny Wheeler. He later worked with **Gilgamesh**, National Health and Soft Heap. (MWh)

Paul Dean

45s: α   You Don't Own Me/Hole In The Head (Decca F 12136) 1965 SC
       β   She Can Build A Mountain/
           A Day Gone By   (Reaction 591 002) 1966 SC

NB: α as Paul Dean and Thoughts. β as Paul Dean and Soul Savages.

The Thoughts later cut a 45 without **Paul Dean**, who was the son of **The Who**'s lawyer Oscar Beuselinck. Based in London. He later recorded as **Oscar** and **Paul Nicholas**. (VJ)

Blossom Dearie

ALBUMS: 1   SWEET BLOSSOM DEARIE   (Fontana TL 5399) 1967 SC
          2   BLOSSOM TIME AT RONNIE'S
                                         (Fontana TL 5352) 1967 R1
          3   SOON IT'S GONNA RAIN   (Fontana STL 5454) 1967 SC
          4   THAT'S JUST THE WAY I WANT TO BE
                                         (Fontana 6309 015) 1970 R1

45s: I'm Hip/
          Wallflower Lonely, Cornflower Blue   (Fontana TF 719) 1966
          Sweet Georgie Fame/One Note Samba   (Fontana TF 788) 1967
          Moonlight Saving Time/
          On A Clear Night You Can See Forever   (Fontana TF 813) 1967
          Sunny/Once I Loved   (Fontana TF 886) 1967
          The Music Played/Discover Who I Am   (Fontana TF 934) 1968
          Hey John/59th Street Bridge Song   (Fontana TF 986) 1968

NB: *Blossom Dearie Live In London Volume 2* (Harkit HRKCD 8066) 2004 compiles material from a Ronnie Scott's concert in February 1966.

A jazz/pop singer, who may be best known for her 1967 single *Sweet Georgie Fame*. One of her better efforts was *The Music Played*, which benefited from quite a grandiose arrangement, but commercial success always eluded her. *Sweet Georgie Fame* and *Hey John* were tributes to **Georgie Fame** and **John Lennon**. From the USA originally, she came to live in the UK in this era and is therefore a marginal case for inclusion. Of the many albums she recorded, the two listed above will be of the greatest interest to readers of this book. The latter is especially sought after because it contains the superb pop-funk tune *I Like London In The Rain* and features musicians including Ian Carr, **Harold McNair** and Kenny Wheeler. (VJ/RMJ).

Dear Mr. Time

ALBUM: 1   GRANDFATHER   (Square SQA 101) 1970 R2

45:   Prayer For Her/Light Up A Light   (Square SQ 3) 1970

This is an obscure progressive concept album which now interests some collectors. It is similar at times to **The Moody Blues**, and the project featured comment on the life of one man from the turn of the century until the time of his death.. The 45 *Prayer For Her* was a track from the album. (VJ)

The Debonaires

45s: A Love Of Our Own/
       The Night Meets The Dawn   (Pye 7N 17151) 1966
       Crying Behind Your Smile/Forever More (Pye 7N 17204) 1966

This short-lived beat group from Ireland made little impact. (VJ)

The Debonairs

Personnel: CHARLES COLLIER   gtr   A
             JOHN COLLIER   drms   A
             GEORGE GILL   ld gtr   A
             DAVIS RILEY   bs   A

45:   That's Right/
      When True Love Comes Your Way   (Parlophone R 5054) 1963

This was a Sheffield-based beat group. (VJ)

Decameron

Personnel: DAVE BELL   gtr, bs   ABCD
             JOHN COPPIN   gtr, keyb'ds   ABCD
             AL FENN   hrmnca, gtr, bs   BCD
             GEOFF MARCH   keyb'ds, vcls, sax BCD
             DIK CADBURY   bs, gtr, vcls   CD
             BOB CRITCHLEY   drms, vcls   D

ALBUMS: 1(B)   DECAMERON - SAY HELLO TO THE BAND
(up to   (Vertigo 6360 097) 1973
1976)   2(C)   MAMMOTH SPECIAL   (Mooncrest CREST 19) 1974
        3(C)   BEYOND THE LIGHT (Mooncrest CREST 28) 1975
        4(C)   THIRD LIGHT   (Transatlantic TRA 304) 1975
        5(D)   TOMORROW'S PANTOMIME
                                 (Transatlantic TRA 325) 1976

NB: There's also a 2-CD collection *Paraboala Road - The Decameron Anthology* (Sanctuary CMDDD 929) 2004.

45s: Stoats Grope (All I Need)/
(up to   Friday Night At The Regal   (Vertigo 6059 086) 1973
1976)   Rock And Roll Away/
          Twinset And Pearls   (Mooncrest MOON 34) 1974
          Breakdown Of The Song/
          Twinsets And Pearls   (Mooncrest MOON 45) 1975
          Trapeze/Saturday   (Mooncrest MOON) 1975
          Falling Over/Rock 'n' Roll Away (Mooncrest MOON) 1976
          Dancing/Single Handed   (Transatlantic BIG 557) 1976

Formed in 1968 this band was based in Cheltenham, Gloucestershire. They played a sort of contemporary folk-rock. The 'A' side of their debut 45 had a more country feel to it with some nice violin. They also recorded two singles for Transatlantic in a 'doo wop' style as The Magnificent Mercury Brothers. The singles in question were *New Girl In School* in 1975 and a cover of *Why Do Fools Fall In Love* in 1976. Fenn, Cadbury and March left in July 1976 but appeared on *Tomorrow's Pantomime*, which came out in September 1976. When they split in 1976 Coppin pursued a solo folk career and went on to record a string of interesting and unusual albums. Cadbury went on to **Cajun Moon** and Critchley worked with the **Dransfield** brothers for a short time.

Saturday was later compiled on *The Transatlantic Story* CD box set. (MWh/VJ/JM)

Dedicated Men's Jug Band

45s: Boodle-Am-Shake/Come On Boys (Piccadilly 7N 35245) 1965
      Don't Come Knocking/
      Out Time Blues (Piccadilly 7N 35283) 1966

This seven-piece jug band made little lasting impression. *Don't Come Knocking* was an old Fats Domino song. *Boodle-Am-Shake* can also be heard on *The R&B Era, Vol. 2* (LP & CD). (VJ)

Dave Dee

			HCP
45s:	My Woman's Man/		
	Gotta Make You Part Of Me	(Fontana TF 1074) 1970	42
	Everything About Her/		
	If I Believed In Tomorrow	(Philips 6006 061) 1970	-
	Wedding Bells/Sweden	(Philips 6006 100) 1970	-
	Hold On/Mary Morning, Mary Evening	(Philips 6006 154) 1971	-
	Swingy/		
	Don't You Ever Change Your Mind	(Philips 6006 180) 1971	-
	Annabella/Kelly	(Fontana 6007 021) 1974	-

In 1969 **Dave Dee** left **Dave Dee, Dozy, Beaky, Mick and Tich** to go solo and try his hand at acting. Neither was very successful, although *My Woman's Man* was a minor hit. In 1973 he became A&R Chief for WEA Records and the following year the band reformed for a one-off single on a WEA subsidiary. (VJ)

Dave Dee, Dozy, Beaky, Mick and Tich

Personnel:	IAN 'TICH' AMEY	ld gtr	A
	TREVOR 'DOZY' DAVIES	bs	A
	JOHN 'BEAKY' DYMOND	gtr	A
	'DAVE DEE' HARMAN	vcls	A
	MICK WILSON	drms	A

				HCP
ALBUMS:	1(A)	DAVE DEE, DOZY, BEAKY, MICK AND TICH		
(up to			(Fontana TL 5350) 1966 SC	11
1976)	2(A)	IF MUSIC BE THE FOOD OF LOVE... PREPARE		
		FOR INDIGESTION		
		(mono/stereo)	(Fontana (S)TL 5388) 1966 SC	27
	3(A)	GOLDEN HITS		
		(mono/stereo)	(Fontana (S)TL 5441) 1967	-
	4(A)	WHAT'S IN A NAME	(Fontana 858 000) 1967	-
	5(A)	IF NO ONE SANG		
		(mono/stereo)	(Fontana (S)TL 5471) 1968 SC	-
	6(A)	GREATEST HITS	(Fontana SFL 13002) 1968 SC	-
	7(B)	TOGETHER	(Fontana SFL 13173) 1969	-
	8(B)	LEGEND OF	(Fontana SFL 13063) 1969	-
	9(A)	GREATEST HITS	(Philips SON 015) 1976	-

NB: (5) reissued on CD (Repertoire REPUK 1013) 2004, with 11 bonus tracks and an informative 12-page booklet. (7) reissued on CD (BR Music BX 436-2) 1997 with no less than twelve bonus tracks. CD compilations include, *Greatest Hits: Dave Dee, Dozy, Beaky, Mick and Tich* (Design DSK 123) 1988; *The Very Best Of Dave Dee, Dozy, Beaky, Mick and Tich* (Spectrum 551 823-2) 1998 and 2-CD *The Complete Collection* (Mercury 534 068-2) 1996. The latter pads out their hits with 'B' sides and a selection of album tracks. *Boxed* (BR Music Box 1009 2) 1999 is a 100-track 4-CD box set.

				HCP
EP:	1(A)	LOOS OF ENGLAND	(Fontana TE 17488) 1967	-

			HCP
45s:	No Time/Is It Love	(Fontana TF 531) 1965 SC	-
(up to	All I Want/It Seems A Pity	(Fontana TF 586) 1965 SC	-
1976)	You Make It Move/I Can't Stop	(Fontana TF 630) 1965	26
	Hold Tight!/You Know What I Want	(Fontana TF 671) 1966	4
	Hideaway/Here's A Heart	(Fontana TF 711) 1966	10
	Bend It/She's So Good	(Fontana TF 746) 1966	2
	Touch Me, Touch Me/Marina	(Fontana TF 798) 1967	13
	Okay/He's A Raver	(Fontana TF 830) 1967	4
	Zabadak/The Sun Goes Down	(Fontana TF 873) 1967	3
	The Legend Of Xanadu/Please	(Fontana TF 903) 1968	1
	Last Night In Soho/Mrs. Thursday	(Fontana TF 953) 1968	8
	The Wreck Of The Antoinette/		
	Still Life	(Fontana TF 971) 1968	14
	Don Juan/Margaretta Lidman	(Fontana TF 1000) 1969	23
	Snake In The Grass/Bora Bora	(Fontana TF 1020) 1969	23
	Tonight Today/Bad News	(Fontana TF 1061) 1969	-
	She's My Lady/Babeigh	(Antic K 11510) 1974	-
Reissues:	The Legend Of Xanadu/Zabadak	(Old Gold OG 9243) 1982	-
	Hold Tight/Bend It	(Old Gold OG 9472) 1985	-

This combo, which proved to be one of the most successful pop bands of the late sixties, started out in Salisbury as Dave Dee and The Bostons and had a comic image. In 1964 they met Ken Howard and Alan Blaikley, the songwriting duo, who became their managers and provided them with a string of hit songs with immediate commercial appeal. **Dave Dee**'s real name was David Harman. The pick of the pack (and probably the most inventive) was *The Legend Of Xanadu*, although *The Wreck Of The Antoinette* is worth a spin and *Hideaway* featured some good fuzz guitar. There's no denying either that *Hold Tight!* was an excellent pop song but some of their other material was rubbish. Their first three 45s are now scarce.

In 1969 **Dave Dee** went solo and the group soldered on but less successfully as **Dozy, Beaky, Mick and Tich**. There were brief reformations of the band in 1974 and the early eighties. The latter resulted in a single, *Staying With It / Sure Thing* in 1983.

Boxed is a 100-track, 4-CD Dutch box set. Whilst the hit singles provide the meat in the collection, there are some hidden gems in 'B' sides like *The Sun Goes Down* and the hook-ridden *Please*, a host of mostly self-penned album tracks and a splattering of out-takes. The package is accompanied by a luscious 64-page booklet and will pleasantly surprise those who buy it, although inevitably with a collection of this size you'll want to skip some of the tracks after one play.

Bend It was also included on Regal Starline's 1970 compilation *No-One's Gonna Change Our World* (LP) and on Philips *Sixteen Star Tracks Of The Sixties* (LP). More recently *Do Wah Diddy* has been compiled on See For Miles *The Youngblood Story Vol. 1* (LP).

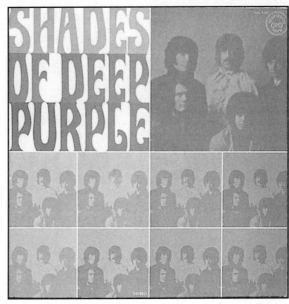

DEEP PURPLE - Shades Of (LP).

Other compilation appearances have included: *Bend It* on *Made In England, Vol. 1* (CD); *Touch Me, Touch Me* on *Made In England, Vol. 2* (CD); *Save Me* and *Shame* on *The Star-Club Singles Complete, Vol. 10* (LP & CD); *Touch Me, Touch Me, Marina, Okay!* and *He's A Raver* on *The Star-Club Singles Complete, Vol. 11* (LP & CD); *Hideaway* and *Here's A Heart* on *The Star-Club Singles Complete, Vol. 8* (LP & CD); *Bend It, You Make It Move, Hard To Love You* and *No Time* on *The Star-Club Singles Complete, Vol. 9* (LP & CD); *Hideaway* on *Star-Club Show* (LP); *Zabadak, Nose For Trouble, The Legend Of Xanadu* and *Please* on *The Star-Club Singles Complete, Vol. 12* (LP & CD); *Hold Tight* on *Beat Im Star Club* (LP); *He's A Raver* on *English Freakbeat, Vol. 3* (CD); *The Legend Of Xanadu* on *U.K. No 1 Hits Of The 60's* (CD), *Best Of British Rock* (CD), *30 Years Of Number 1 Hit Singles - 1960/1989* (CD) and on the 2-CD set *60 Number Ones Of The Sixties*; *Still Life* on *Pop-In, Vol 1* (CD); *Shame* on *Spinning Wheel* (CD); and *The Sun Goes Down* on *Jagged Time Lapse, Vol 3* (CD). (VJ)

Kiki Dee

ALBUMS:
(up to 1976)

1	I'M KIKI DEE		
	(mono/stereo)	(Fontana (S)TL 5455)	1968 R1
2	GREAT EXPECTATIONS		
		(Tamla Motown STML 11158)	1970 R1
3	LOVING AND FREE	(Rocket PIGL 5)	1973
4	I'VE GOT THE MUSIC IN ME	(Rocket PIGL 10)	1974
5	KIKI DEE	(Sounds Superb SPR 9000)	1974
6	PATTERNS	(Philips International 6382 079)	1974

NB: (4) reissued on vinyl (Rocket ROLL4) 1976. (3) reissued on vinyl (Rocket ROLL5) 1976. Also relevant is *Kiki Dee's Greatest Hits* (LP) (Warwick WW5092) 1980, *Spotlight On Kiki Dee Greatest Hits* (CD) (Rocket 8483592) 1991 and *The Very Best Of Kiki Dee* (CD) (Rocket 5167282) 1994.

EPs:
(up to 1976)

1	KIKI DEE	(Fontana TE 17443)	1965 R1
2	KIKI DEE IN CLOVER	(Fontana TE 17470)	1965 SC
3	KIKI DEE	(Rocket ROKN 515)	1976

NB: (3) contains *Loving And Free/Amoureuse/I've Got The Music In Me*.

45s:
(up to 1976)

		HCP
Early Night/Lucky High Heels	(Fontana TF 394) 1963	-
I Was Only Kidding/		
Don't Put Your Heart In His Hand	(Fontana TF 414) 1963	-
Miracles/That's Right, Walk On By	(Fontana TF 443) 1964	SC -
Baby I Don't Care/How Glad I Am	(Fontana TF 490) 1964	-
Runnin'/ Out Of Fools/There He Goes	(Fontana TF 596) 1965	-
Why Don't I Run Away From You?/		
Small Town	(Fontana TF 669) 1966	-
I'm Going Out (The Same Way I Came In)/		
We've Got Everything Going For Us	(Fontana TF 792) 1967	-
I/Stop And Think	(Fontana TF 833) 1967	-
Excuse Me/Patterns	(Fontana TF 870) 1967	-

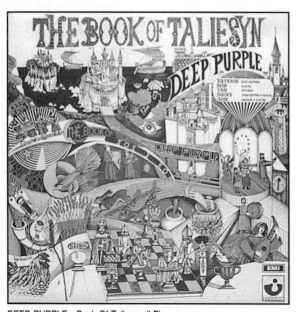

DEEP PURPLE - Book Of Taliesyn (LP).

Can't Take My Eyes Off You/		
Hungry Heart	(Fontana TF 926)	1968 -
Now The Flowers Cry/		
On A Magic Carpet Ride	(Fontana TF 983)	1968 R2 -
The Day Will Come (Between Sunday And Monday)/		
My Whole World Ended (The Moment You Left Me)	(Tamala Motown TMG 739)	1970 -
Lonnie And Josie/		
The Last Good Man In My Life	(Rocket PIG 2)	1973 -
Amoureuse/Rest My Head	(Rocket PIG 4)	1973 13
Excuse Me/Patterns	(Philips 6006 352)	1974 -
Hard Luck Story/		
Everyone Should Have Their Way	(Rocket PIG 10)	1974 -
I've Got The Music In Me/		
Simple Melody	(Rocket PIG 12)	1974 19
(You Don't Know) How Glad I Am/		
Peter	(Rocket PIG 16)	1975 33
Once A Fool/Someone To Me	(Rocket ROKN 501)	1975 -
α Don't Go Breaking My Heart/		
Snow Queen	(Rocket ROKN 512)	1976 1

NB: α with **Elton John**.

A Bradford lass whose real name was Pauline Matthews, she changed her name when she met songwriter Mitch Murray and moved down to London in 1964. She's rather a marginal case for inclusion here because most of the string of singles she recorded in the sixties were Motown in style and in 1970 she actually became the first English white singer to be signed by the Motown label, although it failed to bring her any more success. *Why Don't I Run Away From You* and *On A Magic Carpet Ride* were popular Northen soul numbers. Her 1974 album for Sounds Superb was full of Motown material.

It wasn't until returning from a tour of Australia and South Africa in 1972 and signing to **Elton John**'s Rocket label the following year that her career really took off. She enjoyed real stardom as *Amoureuse, I've Got The Music In Me* and *How Glad I Am* all made the Charts and in 1976 her duo with **Elton John** enjoyed a No 1 with *Don't Go Breaking My Heart*. However, that remains the high point of her career commercially.

Later she sought to establish a career in acting, appearing in the London stage musical 'Pump Boys and Dinettes' in 1984 and later still in London's West End in Willy Russell's musical 'Blood Brothers'. In 1993, she and **Elton John** sang another duet on Cole Porter's *True Love*. (VJ)

Dee and The Quotum

45:	Someday You'll Need Someone/	
	Send Some Flowers To Julie	(Jay Boy BOY 8) 1969

The 'A' side of this obscure 45 has a good lead vocal and makes imaginative use of studio effects. Jay Boy was a President subsidiary. (VJ)

The Deejays

Personnel:

PETE CLINTON	ld gtr		AB
ERIE MORGAN	drms		AB
JOHN MURRAY	gtr, vcls		AB
BUZZ NELSON	bs		AB
JOHNNY VALLONS	ld gtr		A
CLIVE SANDS	ld gtr		B

45s:

Dimples/Coming On Strong	(Polydor BM 56034) 1965 R1
Blackeyed Woman/		
I Just Can't Go To Sleep	(Polydor BM 56501) 1966 R2

A British group who were more active in Sweden. They were originally known as Johnny Vallons and The Deejays. They split from a girl singer of the time (Billy Davies) and went to Sweden as an exchange for the Swedish band The Spotnicks in 1964. They took up residency and enjoyed some success on the Swedish circuit playing fifties and early sixties rock'n'roll. Their debut 45, *Dimples*, was a John Lee Hooker song given R&B treatment, backed by a beat number *Coming On Strong*. Their finest moment however, is usually considered to be the follow-up, a pounding R&B stomper, *Blackeyed Woman*, although, the flip is a rather disappointing cover version of a **Kinks**' song.

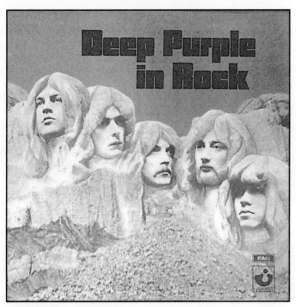

DEEP PURPLE - In Rock (LP).

Only these two 45s were released here in Britain and both, particularly the second, are much sought-after by collectors. Over in Sweden, however, they had a six-track EP released on the Swe Disc label as well as several singles and albums. One rare album was also released in Germany (Polydor International LPHM 46254), as was a 45 *Tobacco Road*.

After they'd moved from the U.K. they originally backed an English vocalist Johnny Vallons. By 1967 he'd been replaced by Clive Sands, the brother of English pop artists Eden Kane and Peter Sarstedt. The change of vocalist certainly resulted in a much softer sound although one of their rarest 45s, *Incrowd Hangout* is more in the psychedelic pop mould. Between 1964 - 67 John Murray handled their vocals as well as playing guitar. He also wrote most of the band's own material, although this was mixed in with a liberal splashing of covers of the R&B standards of the time. They enjoyed quite a few hits there before splitting up in 1968.

Many of their pounding beat and R&B songs were pretty inventive and well worth a listen - the band have been heavily compiled and there's also a Swedish CD compilation of their material, *Best Of 1964-68* (EMI).

Compilation coverage has included: *You Must Be Joking* and *Dimples* on *Nowhere Men, Vol. 2* (CD); *Blackeyed Woman* on *Maximum R'n'B* (CD), *Trans-World Punk Rave-Up!, Vol. 1* (LP), *The Best Of Rubble Collection, Vol. 2* (CD), *Rubble Vol. 13: Freakbeat Fantoms* (LP) and *Rubble Vol. 7* (CD); *Incrowd Hangout* on *Pebbles, Vol. 20* (LP); *Tobacco Road* on *Pebbles, Vol. 18* (LP); *Skinni Minni* on *Swedish Beat, Vol. 1*; *You Must Be Joking* (from 1965), *Not That Girl* (previously only on a German compilation) and *Striped Dreams* (from their 1967 Swedish-only album) on *Pebbles, Vol. 28* (LP); *I Just Can't Go To Sleep, Farmer John* and *Long Tall Shorty* on *Go Go Go* (LP); and a version of *In The Midnight Hour* on *Twisted Teenage Screaming Fuzzbusters* (LP). (VJ/JM)

Deep Feeling (1)

Personnel:	JIM CAPALDI	drms	A
	LUTHER GROVENOR	gtr, vcls	A
	GORDON JACKSON	gtr, vcls	A
	DAVE MASON	gtr, vcls	A
	POLI PALMER	vibes	A
	CHRIS WOOD		

This Birmingham-based mid-sixties group was more notable for including **Capaldi** and **Mason** who were in **Traffic**. **Gordon Jackson** had made solo recordings in the late sixties. **Luther Grosvenor** had been in **Spooky Tooth** and later made solo recordings.

They played acid rock and two of their most popular but never released numbers were *Pretty Colors* and *The Ruin*. They contributed two cuts: *Poltergeist Of Alice* and *Pretty Colours* to *The Roots Of British Rock, Vol 8*. (VJ)

Deep Feeling (2)

Personnel:	DAVE CLARKE	drms	A
	RON COCKFIELD	sax, flute	A
	DEREK ELSON	keyb'ds	A
	DAVE GREEN	bs, vcls, flute	A
	MARTIN JENNER	gtr, vcls	A
	JOHN SWAIL	vcls	A

ALBUM: 1(A) DEEP FEELING (DJM DJLPS 419) 1971 R1

HCP

45s:	Do You Love Me/Move On	(Page One POF 165) 1970 34
	Skyline Pigeon/	
	We've Thrown It All Away	(Page One POF 177) 1970 -
	Do You Wanna Dance/	
	The Day My Lady Cried	(DJM DJS 10231) 1971 -
	Sweat, Dust And Red Wine/	
	Tum Around	(DJM DJS 10237) 1972 -
	Country Heir/We've Thrown It All Away	(DJM DJS 10257) 1972 -
	Let's Spend The Night Together/	
	Avalon	(Santa Ponsa PNS 12) 1974 -

Formed in the Summer of 1969. All five members were session musicians. John Swail (real name Guy Darrell) met Dave and Martin on sessions when Guy was singing and then the other two came along so they recorded as The Guy Darrell Syndicate for about nine months. They had a minor hit with a cover of *Do You Love Me* in 1970.

During 1971 the line-up changed, Guy re-started his solo career again during the early seventies and made many more singles up to the mid-seventies.

The *Rock Generation* (LP) compilation contains two tracks by a **Deep Feeling** - these are rumoured to the Jim Capaldi **Deep Feeling**. (VJ)

Deep Purple

Personnel:	RITCHIE BLACKMORE	gtr	ABC
	ROD EVANS	vcls	A
	JON LORD	keyb'ds	ABCD
	IAN PAICE	drms	ABCD
	NICK SIMPER	bs, vcls	A
	ROGER GLOVER	bs, vcls	B
	IAN GILLAN	vcls	B
	GLENN HUGHES	bs, vcls	CD
	DAVID COVERDALE	vcls	CD
	TOMMY BOLIN	gtr	D

HCP

ALBUMS:	1(A)	SHADES OF DEEP PURPLE (mono/stereo)	
(up to		(Parlophone PMC/PCS 7055) 1968 R2/R1 -
1976)	2(A)	BOOK OF TALIESYN	(Harvest SHVL 751) 1969 R1 -
	3(A)	DEEP PURPLE	(Harvest SHVL 759) 1969 R1 -
	4(B)	CONCERTO FOR GROUP AND ORCHESTRA	
			(Harvest SHVL 767) 1970 SC 26
	5(B)	DEEP PURPLE IN ROCK	(Harvest SHVL 777) 1970 SC 4
	6(B)	FIREBALL	(Harvest SHVL 793) 1971 1
	7(B)	MACHINE HEAD	(Purple TPSA 7504) 1972 1
	8(B)	WHO DO YOU THINK WE ARE	
			(Purple TPSA 7508) 1973 4
	9(C)	BURN	(Purple TPS 3505) 1974 3
	10(C)	STORMBRINGER	(Purple TPS 3508) 1974 6
	11( )	COME TASTE THE BAND	(Purple TPSA 7515) 1975 19
	12( )	24 CARAT PURPLE	(Purple TPSM 2002) 1975 14
	13( )	MADE IN EUROPE (LIVE)	(Purple TPSA 7517) 1976 12

NB: (1) - (3) released on Tetragrammaton in the US. A tiny original mono pressing of (1) also exists (R4). (4) - (11) and (13) released on Warner Brothers in the US. (1) reissued on vinyl (EMI LPCENT 25) 1997. (1) reissued on CD Parlophone (7 92407-1) 1989 and again remastered with five bonus tracks and exemplary sleevenotes (EMI EMI 7243 4 98336 2 3) 2000. (2) reissued on vinyl (EMI 7243 4 99469 1 0) 1999. (2) reissued on CD Harvest (7 92408-1) 1989 and again remastered with five bonus tracks and exemplary sleevenotes (EMI EMI 7243 5 21608 2 2) 2000. (3) on CD Harvest (7 92409-1), also in 1989 and again remastered with five bonus tracks and exemplary sleevenotes (EMI EMI 7243 5 21597 2 7) 2000. (4) reissued on CD (EMI CDP 794 886 2) 1990. (5) reissued on CD (Fame CDFA 3011) 1988 and (Harvest CDP 746 239 2) 1988, but deleted in 1989. (6) reissued on CD (EMI CZ 30) 1988. (7) reissued on CD (EMI CZ 83) 1987, but

DEEP PURPLE - Made In Japan (2-LP).

deleted in 1989 and (Fame CDFA 3158) 1989. (8) reissued on CD (EMI CDP 748 273 2 and CZ 6) 1987. (9) reissued on CD (Purple CDP 792 6112 and CZ 203) 1989 and again (EMI) 2004 to celebrate its 30th Anniversary with remixes and improved sound quality. (10) reissued on CD (EMI CDP 791 084 2 and CZ 142) 1988. (11) reissued on CD (EMI CDP 794 032 2 and CZ 343) 1990. (12) reissued on CD (Fame CDM 752 020 2 and CDFA 3132) 1987 and (13) reissued on CD (EMI CDP 793 796 2 and CZ 344) 1990. (5), (6) and (7) reissued in 1985 on EMI (EJ 26 0343 0 - EJ 26 0345 0) respectively with designs based on their original covers, as picture discs and each comes with a giant free poster.

Also of interest will be *The Anthology* (EMU PUR 1) 1985. *Scandinavian Night* (Connoisseur Collection DP VSOP LP 125) 1988 is a double set from a Stockholm concert on 12 November 1970, also available on one CD. *Anthology* (EMI CDS 7 96129 2) 1991 is a double CD set of the band's best tracks from 1968-70 and is much better than EMI's earlier *Anthology* album. *Purple Rainbows* (EMI/Polygram TV 845 534-2) 1991 is a beginners guide CD compilation of the band's best known tracks as well as famous songs by associated projects like Rainbow and Whitesnake. *Knebworth '85* (Connoisseur Collection CD VSOP CD 163) 1991 is a double CD set of a 1985 reunion concert by the band previously broadcast by the BBC and bootlegged. *In Concert* (EMI CDS 7981812) 1992 is a definitive compilation of the band's live 1970 and 1972 shows for the BBC's 'In Concert' series. The two tracks missing from a 1980 album release of these concerts are included here. *Singles A's and B's* (EMI 0777 7 81009 2 8) 1993 is, as its title suggests, although some of their less interesting 'B' sides are omitted in favour of various other non-album rarities. The package comes with a wonderfully detailed booklet which documents their 45 history. *The Family Album* (Connoisseur Collection VSOP CD 187) 1993 is a selection of **Deep Purple** material, including samples from pre- and post-**Purple** projects, over the past 25 years. *The Gemini Suite Live* (RPM RPM 114) 1993 is a CD set of a September 1970 performance of the band tackling this orchestral composition by Jon Lord. An earlier compilation is *The Best Of Deep Purple* (Telstar TCD 2312) 1987. *The Collection* (EMI Gold 7243 8 55077 2 4) 1997 is a hotch potch CD collection of material from their 1970-76 era. *Machine Head* (EMI DEEPP 3) 1997 is available as a 2-LP set on purple vinyl and as a 2-CD box set - the first disc features the 1997 remixes of the whole album plus the non-LP flip, *When A Blind Man Cries*. The second disc includes the music in remastered form plus quadrophonic mixes of *Maybe I'm A Leo* and *Lazy* with different **Richie Blackmore** guitar solos. *Fireball: 25th Anniversary Edition* (EMI CDDEEP 2) 1996 comprises the original 1971 album, remastered by Glover, along with forty minutes worth of bonus material. The package comes with a thirty-six page booklet, full of rare photos, which details the band's history. *Made In Japan* (EMI) 1997 has been reissued on CD in remastered format along with a bonus CD of previously unreleased encores. The *Odd Ditties* CD (Backdoor Possibilities ARF 2) 1995 includes lots of pre-**Deep Purple** material. Three tracks by **The Maze** are featured:- *Harlem Shuffle*, *Aria Del Sud* and *Non Fatemi Odiare* (the last two being from an Italian-only 45) as well as three by **Episode Six**:- *I Hear Trumpets Blow*, *Gentlemen Of The Park* and *Morning Dew*, which was from a BBC session. It also contains the following **Artwoods** tracks, all from a 1967 session for the Beeb, *In The Deep End*, *What Shall I Do*, *Daytripper*, *Devil With The Blue Dress On - Good Golly Miss Molly* (medley). *This Time Around - Live In Tokyo, 1975* (Purple PUR 321 D) 2001 is a 2-CD set, whilst *On The Road* (Connoiseeur Collection DPBOX 400) 2001 is a 4-CD box set. *UK Singles Anthology 68/77* (EMI 550 3892) 2002 is an 11-CD singles box set. *Listen, Learn, Read On* (EMI 540 9732) 2002 is a 6-CD box set. *Live In Denmark '72* (Purple PUR 203) 2002 captures a live performance from March 1972.

HCP

45s:	Hush/One More			
(up to	Rainy Day (promo) (PS)	(Parlophone R 5708)	1968	R4 -
1976)	Hush/One More Rainy Day	(Parlophone R 5708)	1968	R1 -
α	Kentucky Woman/			
	Wring That Neck	(Parlophone R 5745)	1968	R1 -
	Emmaretta/Wring That Neck	(Parlophone R 5763)	1969	R1 -
	Hallelujah (I Am The Preacher)/			
	April Part 1 (promo) (PS)	(Harvest HAR 5006)	1969	R3 -
	Hallelujah (I Am The Preacher)/			
	April Part 1	(Harvest HAR 5006)	1969	SC
	Concerto For Group And Orchestra			
	(two versions)	(Harvest PSR 325)	1970	SC
	Black Night/Speed King	(Harvest HAR 5020)	1970	-
	Strange Kind Of Woman/I'm Alone	(Harvest HAR 5033)	1971	8
	Fireball/Demon's Eye	(Harvest HAR 5045)	1971	15
	Never Before/			
	When A Blind Man Cries	(Purple PUR 102)	1971	35
	Might Just Take Your Life/			
	Coronarias Redig	(Purple PUR 117)	1974	-
	You Keep On Moving/Love Child	(Purple PUR 130)	1976	-
Reissues:	Black Knight/Strange Kind Of Woman (also in 12")			
		(Harvest HAR 5178)	1979	-
	Black Knight/Speed King (live) (PS)	(Harvest HAR 5210)	1980	43
	Black Knight/Speed King/			
	Into The Fire (12")	(Harvest HAR 5233)	1985	-
	Hush (live)/Dead Or Alive	(Poydor PO 4)	1988	62
	Hush/Dead Or Alive/Bad Attitude (12")	(Polydor PZ 4)	1988	-

NB: α withdrawn.

Deep Purple is lovingly remembered as one of the finest and most influential heavy rock bands in the World, along with **Led Zeppelin** and **Black Sabbath**.

Deep Purple evolved out of **Roundabout** who had been set up when two London businessmen, Tony Edwards and John Coletta decided to invest in a pop group. The name change to **Deep Purple** took place in April 1968 and coincided with their live debut in Tastrup, Denmark. The following month they recorded *The Shades Of Deep Purple* album, which was influenced by US band Vanilla Fudge. It included re-works of well-known songs, including *Hey Joe* and *Hush*. Musically they followed a pretty straight-forward pop format and the album peaked at No 24 in the US, although it didn't make the UK Charts at all. Similarly, their first single, *Hush*, a revival of a Joe South song with lots of great guitar work, rose to No 4 in the US singles Charts but failed to gain a Chart placing over here. A cover of Neil Diamond's *Kentucky Woman* gave them another minor US hit, but over here it was withdrawn shortly after its release. All this led them to court the emerging American concert circuit.

In 1969 they were signed by EMI's then new progressive Harvest label. They had *Exposition/We Can Work It Out* and *Wring That Neck* included on the very rare promo-only *Harvest Sampler* (LP) album. Their first album for Harvest, *The Book Of Taliesyn*, followed a similar format to their first album, with several excellent re-works, including Neil Diamonds' *Kentucky Woman*. *Look, Listen, Read On* with its echoed vocals saw them flirt with psychedelia and the album has a good cover of **The Beatles'** *We Can*

DEEP PURPLE - Burn (LP).

Work It Out and a version of the *Theme from 2001*. Again, it fared better in the States, climbing to No. 54. A cover of Ike and Tina Turner's *River Deep, Mountain High* culled from the album, gave them another minor US hit, peaking at No 53.

Deep Purple, released in 1969, marked the end of their pop phase. It included a good version of **Donovan**'s *Lalena*. *The Painter* and *Why Didn't Rosemary* certainly hinted at the heavier sound to come. Most of side two was taken up by the experimental and classically-influenced extended track *April*. After this the Tetragrammaton label folded and Simper and Evans were sacked departing for **Warhorse** and Captain Beyond respectively.

Ian Gillan and Roger Glover from **Episode Six** came in as replacements to form what is generally considered to be the strongest of the band's four line-ups. Musically this new line-up veered towards a much heavier sound. However, *Concerto For Group And Orchestra*, the new line-up's first album, attempted to merge rock and classical music with the band being supported by the Royal Philharmonic Orchestra at the Albert Hall. It gave the group their UK Chart debut, peaking at No 26 and, unusually for them did much better than in the US, where it only got to No 143.

They worked immensely hard in this phase of their career and gradually it began to pay off with *Black Night*, a superb slice of heavy rock, rising to No 2 to give them their first UK hit single.

Deep Purple In Rock was really their magnum opus. It became a million seller, climbing to No 4 in the UK (but only managing No 142 in the US). This album really is worth checking out with tracks like *Speed King, Child In Time, Into The Fire, Living Wreck* and *Hard Lovin' Man* epitomising all that was good about their frenetic brand of heavy rock. Their popularity in the UK was increasing and *Black Night*, a 1970 single, reached No 2 in the charts.

However, there were signs that Ian Gillan, at least, was becoming restless. On 27 October he played the part of Jesus in a live performance of Tim Rice and Andrew Lloyd Webber's 'Jesus Christ Superstar' at St Peters Lutheran Church in New York and he'd also played Jesus on the original album.

1971 saw the release of a new album, *Fireball*, which was similar in style to its predecessor. It topped the UK Album Charts and reached No 32 in the US. The title track peaked at No 15 in the UK 45 Charts at the end of the year, to give them their second Top 20 hit. *Strange Kind Of Woman* had made the UK Top Ten back in March. On 3 December Montreux Casino in Switzerland burnt down during a Frank Zappa set whilst the band were recording there, this led the band to write another classic song, *Smoke On The Water*, which was included on their next album, *Machine Head*. This was another mega seller, topping the UK Charts for three weeks and later climbing to No 7 in the US. In April 1972 *Never Before* from the album gave them a minor UK hit, climbing to No 35. The same month **Jon Lord** released an album, *Gemini Suite*, with the London Symphony Orchestra.

By now the band was deservedly one of the top live attractions in the

DEEP PURPLE - Stormbringer (CD).

DEEP PURPLE - Come Taste The Band (CD).

World - playing the first night at the resurrected Rainbow Theatre in June 1972 and touring Japan in August of that year, where they were extremely popular. Material from some of the concerts on this tour was later released on the *Live In Japan* album, which later climbed to No 16 in the UK and No 6 in the US. Towards the end of 1972 Warner released *Purple Passages*, a US-only compilation of material from their three Tetragrammaton albums, and it peaked at No 57.

By now Gillan had made up his mind to leave the group because he felt the band was ceasing to progress, although he remained with the band until 29 June 1973 to honour touring commitments in Japan, where the band members were idolised. He later formed his own band. Roger Glover followed him shortly after, initially becoming the Purple label's A&M man and later pursuing a solo career. The following month their classic song, *Smoke On The Water* (from *Machine Head*) was released as a 45 in the US, becoming a million-seller and peaking at No 4.

The previously unknown David Coverdale, who'd been working in a menswear shop in Redcar, Yorkshire, was brought in, along with ex-**Trapeze** bassist Glenn Hughes, after responding to an advert placed by the band. This new line-up was responsible for the *Burn* and *Stormbringer* albums, which were both successful commercially, but this particular incarnation of the band was brought to a conclusion when **Ritchie Blackmore** announced his departure to form Rainbow on 7 April 1975. His replacement was Tommy Bolin, formerly with The James Gang. *Burn* has its moments with the title track showcasing the vocal talents of David Coverdale and Glenn Hughes and Blackmore's fine guitar playing. *Might Just Take Your Life* is an appealing dual-vocalled number, whilst *Mistreated* with its phasing and climatic chorale crescendo is another highlight.

This final line-up recorded a studio album, *Come Taste The Band*, and embarked on a World Tour of Australia, New Zealand, Hawaii, Japan, Hong Kong, America and Europe. However, it was proving increasingly difficult for the band to harness the undoubted talent of its individual members to best effect and they finally split in June 1976 following a farewell UK tour. Inevitably there have been several posthumous releases and compilations.

Upon their demise Coverdale embarked on a solo career later forming Whitesnake; **Lord** and Paice became two of the trio known as Paice, Ashton and Lord; Hughes rejoined **Trapeze** and Tommy Bolin formed his own band back in the US. He later died of a heroin overdose on 4 December 1976.

A series of 'best of' and archive releases kept the band in the public eye and kept up pressure for a reformation. This happened in 1984 when Gillian, **Lord**, **Blackmore**, Paice and Glover came together to record *Perfect Strangers* (1984) and *The House Of Blue Light* (1987). Bad feeling between Gillan and **Blackmore** led to the former's departure after *Nobody's Perfect*, which captured them in concert was released in 1988. Ex-Rainbow vocalist Joe Lynn Turner came on board for 1990's *Slaves And Masters*.

Gillan rejoined in 1993, but quit shortly after and **Blackmore** followed him the following year. He was replaced by Joe Satrini briefly. In the late

DEEP PURPLE - Made In Europe (CD).

nineties, a line-up comprising **Lord**, Gillan, Glover, Paice and Steve Morse recorded *Purpendicular* (1996) and *Abandon* (1998). Come the millennium and **Lord** retired - he was replaced by rock veteran Don Airey and he was included on their 2003 studio album, *Bananas*.

For a good retrospective collection try *The Anthology*, released in 1985. This doesn't just follow the 'greatest hits' type format - it mixes the best known material with the obscure. In the latter category are three previously unissued tracks:- *Freedom*, recorded as a follow-up single to *Strange Kind Of Woman* in 1971, which never saw the light of day until 1985 and two tracks from the 'Roundabout' acetate in 1968 (*Love Help Me* and *Shadows*), before the group had chosen the **Deep Purple** name. Some of their rare 45s (*Hush, Emmaretta* and *Hallelujah*) are included, too, and there are plenty of stage favourites like *Woman From Tokyo, Black Night, Child In Time* and *Strange Kind Of Woman*.

This Time Around - Live In Tokyo, 1975 is a 2-CD set containing 17 cuts (seven of which are previously unreleased). Classics like *Burn, Lady Luck, Smoke On The Water, Stormbringer* and *Soldier Of Fortune* are here and of the new material *This Time Around* is strong vocally and *You Keep On Moving* is a cutting mellow composition.

The 4-CD *On The Road* box set contains some of their more obscure live releases and it came with a booklet full of memorabilia.

Still on the road in 2002 - the year saw the release of two CD box sets (*UK Singles Anthology 68/77* and *Listen, Learn, Read On*) and the band embark on a huge tour. The latter 6-CD box set comprises 74 tracks of rarities and album highlights accompanied by a 120-page colour booklet containing detailed profiles of all ten band members between 1968 and 1976. There's also a discography, loads of contemporary reviews and photos. **Deep Purple** fans will be particularly interested in the first 10 tracks of CD1, which feature tracks future band members played on before joining **Deep Purple**. So you can hear Simper in Johnny Kidd and The Pirates, Gillan and Glover in **Episode Six** and David Coverdale impersonating Neil Diamond on a bizarre cabaret piece *Does Anybody Know What Time It Really Is?* There are plenty of live tracks from BBC Sessions and live concerts that haven't been released before making this a must for fans.

Appearances on Various Artists' compilations have included *Into The Fire* (from the *Deep Purple In Rock* album) on Harvest's 1970 *Picnic* (2-LP) compilation; and *Hush* on *Harvest Heritage - 20 Greats* (LP). More recent appearances have been: *Shield* on the CD *The Age Of Enlightenment - Prog Rock, Vol. 1*, *Strange Kind Of Woman* and *Smoke On The Water* on the 3-CD set *Guitar Heroes - Rock The Night Away*; *Strange Kind Of Woman* on *Classic Rock - cd3*; *Black Night* on the 3-CD set *Full Throttle - 60 Original Driving Classics* and *Classic Rock - cd2*; *Highway Star* and *Hush* on the 2-CD set *Stars And Stripes*; *Woman From Tokyo* and *Highway Star* on *Guitar Anthems* (CD); *Strange Kind Of Woman* on *Greatest Hits Of The 70's - cd3*; *Hush* on the 2-CD set *Greatest Rock*; *Hush* and *Speed King* on *Rock Resurrection* (CD); *Burn* and *Smoke On The Water* on *The Best Heavy Metal Album In The World.... Ever* (CD); *Smoke On The Water* and *Child In Time* on the CD box set *Radio Caroline Calling - 70's*

Flashback; *Smoke On The Water* and *Black Night* on the 6-CD box set *Best Of Driving Rock*; *Smoke On The Water* on *Kerrang! The Album* (CD); and *Somebody Stole My Guitar* on *Best Of Heavy Metal* (CD). (VJ)

Deep Set

45s: That's The Way Life Goes/Hallo Amy (Pye 7N 17594) 1968
I Started A Joke/Spicks And Specks (Major Minor MM 607) 1969

This late sixties pop outfit from Ireland failed to achieve any commercial success. Both sides of the second 45 were **Bee Gees**' songs. *That's The Way Life Goes* can also be heard on Sequel's CD compilation, *Irish Rock - Ireland's Beat Groups 1964-1969*. (VJ)

Deep Water

45: Take A Look Around/Poor Little Me (Pye 7N 17946) 1970

A semi-rock 45. (VJ)

Pete Dello and Friends

ALBUM: 1 INTO YOUR EARS (Nepentha 6437 001) 1971 R3
NB: *Into Your Ears Plus* (See For Miles SEE 257) 1989 is a reissue of (1) plus two tracks **Dello** issued under the name **Magic Valley** in 1969 and two previously unissued solo tracks from 1972. It was also available on CD (SEE CD 257) 1989.

Pete Dello was the creative force behind **Honeybus**, which he unexpectedly left just as they were taking off. After releasing numerous singles under pseudonyms such as **Lace**, **Red Herring** and **Magic Valley**, he made this charming and very rare solo album. It's a laid-back, acoustic effort featuring heartfelt ballads like *Taking The Heart Out Of Love* alongside other tracks which display a penchant for the whimsical, such as *Harry the Earwig and Uptight Basil*. A version of **Honeybus**' second 45 *(Do I Still) Figure In Your Life* is also included, though it barely differs from the original. Soon after the album was released, **Dello** reformed the original line-up of **Honeybus**.

The late eighties reissue on See For Miles included some additional cuts as pointed out in the discography above. (RMJ/VJ)

Dennis D'ell (real name Dennis Dalzeal)

45s: α It Breaks My Heart In Two/
Better Use Your Head (CBS 202605) 1967 R3
β A Woman Called Sorrow/
The Night Has A Thousand Eyes (Decca F 12647) 1967
χ Home Is Home/Morning Without You (Polydor 2058 715) 1976
NB: α withdrawn. β credited to Dennis D'ell. χ as Dennis D'ell.

These were solo efforts by the former lead singer of **The Honeycombs**. As the first one was withdrawn shortly after release copies are very hard and expensive to find. There are also some demos of this disk, which are easier to find. The interest in it results largely from the flip side which was a version of Little Anthony and The Imperial's *Better Use Your Head*. This has gradually become a favourite on the Northern soul circuit. (VJ)

The Del Renos

This beat band had tracks on both of Oriole's *This Is Merseybeat* albums - *Sigh Cry Almost Die* on *Vol. 1* and *When Will I Be Loved* on *Vol. 2*. Both were also included on Columbia's 1964 compilation *The Exciting New Liverpool Sound*. (VJ)

The Deltones

45: Gimme Some Lovin'/
Have A Little Talk With Myself (Columbia DB 8719) 1970 SC

This with a one-off venture and they should not be confused with a Jamaican band of the same name. (VJ)

Demick and Armstrong

Personnel: ROD DEMICK   gtr, vcls, steel gtr, h,
                                          banjo   A
                   HERBIE ARMSTONG   gtr, vcls, bs   A

ALBUMS: 1(A) WEE WILLIE RAMBLER   (Mam MAM-AS 1001) 1971
                2(A) LOOKIN' THROUGH   (A & M AMLH 68908) 1972

45s: α   We're On The Right Track/Dreaming   (Decca F 13056) 1970
               If I Ever Get To You/Girl   (Mam MAM 10) 1971

NB: α as Demick - Armstrong.

Rod Demick and Herbie Armstrong were both previously in **The Wheels** and had also recorded as The James Brothers, in which they were joined by former **Flaming Youth** member Gordon Smith. On the first album they were assisted by David Watkins (keyb'ds) and Tony Knight (drms). Drummer Henry Spinetti, who'd played with **Mike D'Abo** assisted on their second album. After this venture **Demick** joined **Bees Make Honey** in January 1974. Armstrong worked as a session musician and then joined **Fox** in late 1974. In June 1974 Spinetti joined **Tundra** and Smith went on to work for **Kevin Coyne**. (JM/VJ)

Roger Denison

45s: I'm On An Island /
            I'm Running Out Of Time   (Parlophone R 5545) 1966
            This Just Doesn't Seem To Be Me My Day /
            She Wanders Through My Mind   (Parlophone R 5566) 1967

Roger Denison was the pseudonym of Roger Watson, a youthful Decca plugger who stage-managed **the Beatles'** now-legendary concert at Stowe School as a schoolboy in 1963. A DJ called Phil Jay heard him playing at a party soon afterwards, took him into the studio and financed his debut, a **Ray Davies** song which attracted some attention at the time. He had to adopt a pseudonym because all the DJs knew him in his professional capacity. He mimed to it on various shows but it didn't sell. His follow-up, whose 'B' side was co-written by legendary folk producer Sandy Roberton, was a moody folk-psychedelic piece which now commands considerable interest from collectors. Watson went on to produce albums by **Zakarrias, G.F. FitzGerald** and others before becoming a senior figure in the music industry.

She Wanders Through My Mind can also be heard on *Justavibration* (LP). (RMJ)

The Dennisons

Personnel: CLIVE HORNBY   drms   ABC
                   STEVE McLAREN   ld gtr   ABC
                   EDDIE PARRY   vcls   AB
                   RAY SCRAGG   gtr   ABC
                   ALLAN WILLIS   bs   A
                   TERRY CARSON   bs   BC
                   COLIN ARYEETY   C

                                                             HCP
45s: (Come On) Be My Girl/
            Little Latin Lupe Lu   (Decca F 11691) 1963 SC 46
            Walkin' The Dog/
            You Don't Know What Love Is (Decca F 11880) 1964 SC 36
            Lucy (You Sure Did It This Time)/
            Nobody Like Me Babe   (Decca F 11990) 1964 SC -

A Liverpool beat group who had some minor chart success but failed to make it into the big time. Their debut disc was self-penned but they scored their biggest success with a cover of Rufus Thomas's *Walkin' The Dog*. The 'B' side of this, *You Don't Know What Love Is* was written especially for the group by Ben E. King, who they had toured with. Apparently he liked them a lot. Willis left in December 1972 as he didn't want to turn professional and was replaced by Carson. Parry, who was 16 when they debuted at the Cavern Club in Liverpool, left in March 1965 after their third single failed to make much impact. They continued as a four piece until

SANDY DENNY - Sandy Denny And The Strawbs (CD).

Colin Aryeety (ex-Almost Blues) joined. Hornby quit in 1966 to go on to fame as 'Jack Sugden' in TV's "Emmerdale Farm". Aryeety went solo and recorded for Deram. Their last 45 was produced by Shel Talmy.

They also had two cuts, *Devoted To You* and *You Better Move On* on Decca's 1964 *At The Cavern* (LP) compilation, which has subsequently been reissued by See For Miles (on vinyl and as *Live At The Cavern* on CD); one track, *Be My Girl*, on Decca's 1963 *Thank Your Lucky Stars, Vol. 2* (LP) compilation and three *Walkin' The Dog, Lucy (You Sure Did It This Time)* and *Be My Girl* on *Liverpool 1963-64*.

Retrosepctive compilation appearances have included: *Walking The Dog, Lucy (You Sure Did It This Time)* and *Be My Girl* on *Liverpool 1963-1964, Vol. 2* (LP); *Ain't Nobody Like Me Babe* on *Mersey Beat* (LP); *Be My Girl* and *Devoted To You* on *Mersey Sounds* (2-LP); *Be My Girl* and *Walking The Dog* on *Mersey Beat 1962-1964* (2-LP); *You Better Move On* on *Original Liverpool Sound* (LP); *Devoted To You* and *You Better Move On* on *At The Cavern* (LP); and *Little Latin Lupe Lu* on *Weekend Starts Here* (LP).

McLaren contracted multiple sclerosis and died in 1993. Parry died of a heart attack aged 50 in 1995. (VJ/JM)

Sandy Denny

                                                                                  HCP
ALBUMS: 1   SANDY AND JOHNNY   (Saga EROS 8041) 1967 R1 -
(up to   2   SANDY DENNY   (Saga EROS 8153) 1970 R1 -
1977)   3   THE NORTH STAR GRASSMAN AND THE RAVENS
                                                    (Island ILPS 9165) 1971 SC 31
                4   SANDY   (Island ILPS 9207) 1972 SC -
                5   LIKE AN OLD-FASHIONED WALTZ
                                                    (Island ILPS 9258) 1974 SC -
                6   RENDEZVOUS   (Island ILPS 9433) 1977 -

NB: (1) with Johnny Silvo. (2) reissued on Mooncrest (CREST 28) in 1978 (SC) with one additional track. (3) reissued on CD (Island IMCD 313) 2005, with bonus tracks. (4) reissued on CD (Island IMCD 314) 2005, with bonus tracks. (5) reissued on CD (Island IMCD 316) 2005, with bonus tracks. There's also a four vinyl album collection of her material *Who Knows Where The Time Goes?* (Island SDSP 100) 1986, also released as a 3 CD set (Hannibal HNCD 5301). Also of interest is *Sandy Denny and The Strawbs* (Hannibal HNCD 1361) 1991. There are three 'Best Of' compilations issued on Island (CDSD 100) 1987, Hannibal (HNCD 1328) 1989 and *The Best Of Sandy Denny* (Island IMCD 217) 1995, which covers the pick of the crop from her time with **Fairport Convention** and **Fotheringay**, as well as some of the cream of her solo career. *Dark Of The Night* (Nixed 006) CD, contains BBC World Service and Home demos from 1966, together with two BBC 'Sounds Of The Seventies' sessions and two tracks from the rare and gorgeous EP, *Pass Of Arms* (Island WIP 6141). This EP was recorded as a soundtrack to the film of the same name from 1972. There's also a CD called *Attic Tracks* (Special Delivery SPDCD 1052). The latter beats the boxed set for unreleased gems. Devotees of **Fairport Convention, Strawbs** and **Fotheringay** as well as her own fans will want to seek out *The BBC Sessions 1971-1973* (Strange Fruit SFRSCD 006) 1997, which contains material recorded during her solo period between 1971 - 73. *Listen Listen: An Introduction To*

217

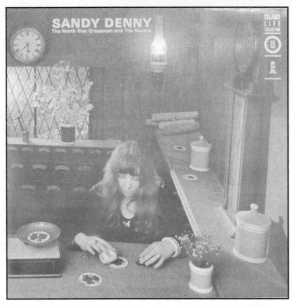

SANDY DENNY - The North Star Grassman And The Ravens (LP).

Sandy Denny (Island IMCD 524 5112) 1999 was the first compilation to concentrate solely on her solo work. *A Boxful Of Treasures* (Fledg'Ling) 2004 is a 5-CD set, which aims to be the definitive collection of her material. *Where The Times Goes* (Castle CMRCD 1181) 2005 is an 18-track compilation of her earliest studio recordings from 1967.

45s:	α	Here In Silence/	
(up to		Man Of Iron (Some PS)	(Island WIP 6141) 1972 R1/SC
1977)		Listen Listen/Tomorrow Is A Long Time	(Island WIP 6142) 1972
		Whispering Grass/Friends (Some PS)	(Island WIP 6176) 1973
	β	Like An Old Fashioned Waltz	(Island WIP 6195) 1974
		Make Me A Pellet On Your Floor/	
		This Train	(Mooncrest MOON 54) 1976
	χ	Candle In The Wind/	
		Still Waters Run Deep	(Island WIP 6391) 1977 SC

NB: α This was the theme from the 'Pass Of Arms' film and is her rarest item. β Unissued. χ Unissued, promo only.

Sandy was the foremost female folk singer in Britain in the late sixties and early seventies. She was born in Wimbledon, London, on 6 January 1947. Her real name was Alexandra Elene Maclean Denny (no wonder she simplified it!). After studying at Kingston Art College she got to perform a diverse set of eclectic material on London's burgeoning folk circuit at venues like Bunjies, Les Cousins and Scots House. There are two 1967 albums, *Sandy and Johnny* (the Johnny in question was Johnny Silvo) and *Alex Campbell and His Friends*, which feature her work from this period. After a short spell with **The Strawbs** she joined **Fairport Convention** in May 1968 winning fame and fortune until she quit them in December 1969. Her next venture **Fotheringay** was less successful, although in *The Sea, The Pond And The Stream* and *Nothing More* their album included some of her best work. She then embarked on a series of solo albums which were well received and achieved some commercial success.

Her first solo album proper was *North Star Grassman And The Ravens*. Like all her subsequent efforts it featured **Richard Thompson** on guitar. Its highlights included *Late November* on which **Thompson's** incisive guitar work complements her vocals beautifully; the orchestrated title track; the Irish ballad *Blackwaterside* and the lengthy *John The Gun*, but most of the material was good.

The follow-up album, *Sandy*, was every bit as good, with **Thompson** backing her again and with Pete Kleinow on pedal steel guitar. The record was allocated a healthy budget and energetically promoted but sales were surprisingly disappointing. Particularly noteworthy was *It'll Take A Long Time*, a beautiful, haunting song, *The Lady* with its discordant harmonies and *Quiet Joys Of Brotherhood* are in a folkier vein.

Like An Old Fashioned Waltz completed her trio of solo albums from this era and in *Solo* included another of her finest moments. Again assisted by **Thompson** and various **Fairport Convention** members and lush orchestration **Denny** was breaking further away from her folk routes, especially on tracks like the keyboard-driven *Dark The Night*.

In 1973 she married **Trevor Lucas** and in Spring 1974, having assisted them on a World Tour in the Winter of 1973-74 she rejoined **Fairport Convention**, only to leave again in February 1976 to work as a duo with **Trevor Lucas** and pick-up on her earlier solo career. She recorded a further solo album, *Rendezvous* (Island ILPS 9433) in 1977, but this was overshadowed by the emergence of punk and to many she was a musical 'has been'. She was also increasingly the worse for drink and drugs and died, aged just 31, on 21 April 1978 and from the resultant brain haemorrhage after falling down stairs at a friend's house.

A widely acclaimed folk singer with a beautiful voice she never made a bad album and any or all of these are recommended. Alternatively you may be sufficiently keen to purchase the four album set *Who Knows Where The Time Goes?*, which features 43 tracks in all, including ten previously unreleased songs and ten others not released previously in the same form as on this album. It also includes material from her spell with **The Strawbs** and **Fotheringay** as well as less accessible material from her time with **Fairport Convention**. All in all this is a collection which does real justice to this talented singer.

Also of interest to **Sandy Denny** and **Strawbs** fans will be *Sandy Denny and The Strawbs* which is a CD reissue of an album originally only issued in Denmark in 1967 which was later issued in Britain in the early seventies under the title *All Our Own Work*. The CD reissue includes one extra cut, *Two Weeks Last Summer*.

Listen Listen: An Introduction To Sandy Denny was the first compilation to concentrate solely on her solo work. The material is moving but melancholic. It's well arranged and sung with real feeling.

A Boxful Of Treasures is a 5-CD set exquisitely remastered and luxuriously presented, which aims to be the definitive compilation of her material. Its 88 tracks include 28 previously unreleased performances (six studio mulit-tracks, four live recordings, 13 home demos, four studio demos and one BBC radio session). There is also a 56-page booklet with rare images and an essay about her by Jim Irvin.

Where The Time Goes is a 18-track compilation of her earliest studio recordings from 1967. Compiled by her biographer Clinton Heylin it includes a number of alternate takes. The highlights are the breathtaking title cut and *Two Weeks Last Summer*.

Back in 1971 she had one cut, *Late November*, on Island's *El Pea* compilation. This was in fact an outtake from the aborted second **Fotheringay** album (though credited to **Sandy Denny**). It sounds very different from the take on her first solo effort. (VJ)

The Deputies

45:     Given Half A Chance/Where Do People Go (Strike JH 305) 1966

Quite a sought-after fast tempo beat single. (MWh)

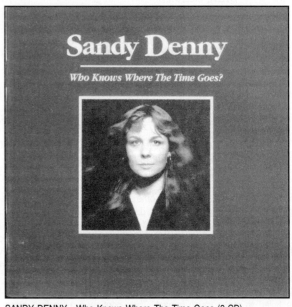

SANDY DENNY - Who Knows Where The Time Goes (3-CD).

Derek and The Dominos

Personnel:
ERIC CLAPTON	gtr, vcls	A
JIM GORDON	drms	A
CARL RADLE	bs	A
BOBBY WHITLOCK	keyb'ds, vcls	A
(DUANE ALLMAN	slide gtr	A)

HCP
ALBUMS: 1(A) LAYLA AND OTHER ASSORTED LOVE SONGS (2-LP)
(Polydor 2625 005) 1971 -
2(B) DEREK AND THE DOMINOS LIVE IN CONCERT (2-LP)
(Polydor 2659 020) 1973 36

NB: *The Layla Sessions* (Polydor 847 083-2) 1990 is a three-set CD. (1) reissued on CD (RSO 8232772) 1984.

HCP
45s: α	Tell The Truth/Roll It Over	(Polydor 2058 057) 1970 R2 -
	Layla/Bell Bottom Blues	(Polydor 2058 130) 1971 7
	Why Does Love Got To Be So Sad/	
	Presence Of The Lord	(RSO 2090 104) 1974 -
Reissues:	Layla/Wonderful Tonight (PS)	(RSO 87) 1982 -
	Layla/Only You And I Know	(Old Gold OG 9422) 1984 -
	Layla/ (also in 12")	(Old Gold OG 4046) 1987 -

NB: α withdrawn.

Formed by **Clapton** in May 1970, they evolved out of Delaney and Bonnie and Friends, who I've counted as an American band. **Clapton**'s main intention in forming the band was to play a charity concert in London in June 1970 (and this line-up included **Dave Mason**) but he kept the band on the road for a low key British tour which was punctured by a trip to Miami to record *Layla And Other Short Stories*, which proved a significant showcase for **Clapton**'s talents as a songwriter and vocalist, as well as a guitarist. Also of note is Duane Allman's slide guitar playing. It also spawned a hit single from the classic title track, which has been reissued several times since. A live album was recorded during a US trip in 1971 (although it was not released until 1973), but was frankly tedious and overrated (as live albums often are). The group eventually split in April 1971 following severe disagreements during the recording of a second studio album.

After the demise of **Derek and The Dominos**, Bobby Whitlock went solo and Jim Gordon did session work. Carl Radle worked for Leon Russell for a while before rejoining **Clapton** in the **Eric Clapton Band**. Radle and **Clapton** also both played in **George Harrison**'s Bangladesh Concert Group.

The band can be heard playing *Bell Bottom Blues* on Polydor's 1971 compilation *Bombers* (LP) and *Layla* on *Stardust* (2-LP).

The 3-CD set, *The Layla Sessions*, aside from a reissue of the original double album comes with two other disappointing CDs of outtakes from the session, *The Jams and Alternate Masters, Jams And Outtakes*. It's for archivists only. (VJ)

Derrick and The Sounds

45s:	Power Of Love/I'll Take You Home	(Pye 7N 17601) 1968
	My Sly Sadie/I Can't Lose That Girl	(Pye 7N 17709) 1969
	Morning Papers And Margarine/	
	Winter Of Your Love	(Pye 7N 17801) 1969

This late sixties pop group failed to attract much interest. (VJ)

The Descendants

45:	Garden Of Eden/Lela	(CBS 202345) 1967

This 45 is now expensive to obtain. *Lela* later resurfaced on *Justification* (LP). (VJ)

DEREK AND THE DOMINOES - Live In Concert (2-LP).

Design

Personnel:
BARRY ALEXANDER	vcls, gtr	AB
GABRIELLE FIELD	vcls	A
KATHY MANUELL	vcls	AB
JEFF MATTHEWS	gtr	AB
JOHN MULCAHY-MORGAN	vcls, gtr	AB
GEOFF RAMSEYER	vcls, gtr	A

ALBUMS: 1(A) DESIGN (Epic EPC 64322) 1970 SC
(up to 2(A) TOMORROW IS SO FAR AWAY
1976) (Epic EPC 64653) 1971 R1
3(A) DAY OF THE FOX
(Regal Zonophone SLRZ 1037) 1973 R1
4(A) IN FLIGHT (EMI EMC 3032) 1974
5(B) BY DESIGN (EMI EMC 3113) 1976

45s:	Willow Stream/Coloured Mile	(CBS 5112) 1970
(up to	Jet Song/Minstrel's Theme	(Epic EPC 7119) 1971
1976)	Colour All The World/	
	Lazy Song	(Regal Zonophone RZ 3044) 1972
	Mayday/Yellow Bird	(Regal Zonophone RZ 3060) 1972
	One Sunny Day/	
	End of The Party	(Regal Zonophone RZ 3082) 1973
	Second Love/Once Upon a Time	(EMI EMI 2122) 1974
	Losing You/I Am the Greene Man	(EMI EMI 2146) 1974
	Sing the World a Song/So Be It Baby	(EMI EMI 2199) 1974
	Pullin' Away/You Take My Breath Away	(EMI EMI 2324) 1975
	Bangin On the Old Piano/	
	Won't You Say You Love Me	(EMI EMI 2360) 1975
	Michael Angelo/Never Need Another Love	(EMI EMI 2430) 1976
	You're So Good To Me/	
	Never Been a Love Like This	(EMI EMI 2529) 1976

Sometimes classed as a folk-rock band, no doubt due to their battery of acoustic guitars, **Design**'s covers of songs by the likes of **The Beatles**, Steely Dan, **Roy Wood** and Carole King actually outnumbered their attempts at folk material. They did, admittedly, record Tom Paxton's *You'd Better Believe It* and the atmospheric *Pisces Hymn* by Dave Shannon of the folk band **Therapy**. Most of their songs were original, however - classy mainstream pop numbers with intricate and appealing harmonies and an interesting psychedelic twist, which sometimes gave way to tweeness. The albums hint at something like a British equivalent of the American group Fifth Dimension. Their amplified backing came from such musicians as Clem Cattini, Herbie Flowers and **Chris Spedding**. Pictures of the band in concert show the men dressed casually, while the visual flair came from the blonde Gabrielle, the dark-haired Kathy and their colourful gowns. Chart success always eluded them but they persevered, as the list of singles shows. By the time of their final album the group had begun to break up and the material moved more towards the middle of the road. Recommended as an introduction is their almost a capella version of *Strawberry Fields* from their second album. *The Minstrel's Theme* got fresh exposure on *Fading Yellow, Vol 5* (CD). (NM/VJ)

THE DEVIANTS - Ptooff! (LP).

Andy Desmond

ALBUM: 1 LIVING ON A SHOESTRING   (Konk KONK 103) 1975

45s: So It Goes/She Can Move Mountains   (Konk KOS 2) 1975
(up to   Beware/Only Child   (Konk KOS 4) 1975
1976)

Desmond had played with the Hertfordshire duo **Gothic Horizon** in the early seventies. He recorded these solo releases on the **Kinks**' - owned Konk label. (VJ)

The Detours

Personnel:	BILLY CHURCHILL	lead gtr	ABCD
	CHARLIE CHEZ KING	bs	ABC
	JOHN D. PUDIFER	drms	ABC
	RITCHIE QUILLAN	gtr	ABCD
	LEE CURTIS	vcls	B
	JIMMY CONNELL	bs	D
	KENNY GUY	drms	DE
	RICKY YATES	vcls	DE
	TOMMY HUSKEY	sax	E
	VINNY ISMAEL	lead gtr	E
	SID ?	bs	E

45s: Run To Me Baby/Hanging Up   (CBS 3213) 1968 SC
           Whole Lot Of Lovin'/Pieces Of You   (CBS 3401) 1968 R1

This Liverpool group also backed **Gene Latter** on his first single.

Pieces Of You has been compiled on *The Seventh Son* (LP). (VJ/AD)

Deuce Coup

45:     A Clown In Town/Angela (PS)   (Mercury MF 1013) 1967

This short-lived surf combo hailed from Leicester. They also recorded as **Bubblegum**. (VJ)

Deuce of Hearts

45:     Closer Together/
        The Times They Are A Changin'   (CBS 202345) 1966

This was a boy and girl duo. (VJ)

The Deviants

Personnel:	SID BISHOP	gtr	ABC
	MICK FARREN	vcls	ABCD
	RUSSELL HUNTER	drms	ABCDE
	CLIVE MALDOON	gtr	A
	PETE MONROE	bs	A
	CORD REES	bs	AB
	MICHAEL McDONNELL	bs	A
	DENNIS HUGHES	keyb'ds	C
	DUNCAN SANDERSON	bs, vcls	CDE
	PAUL RUDOLPH	gtr, vcls	DE

ALBUMS:	1(B)	PTOOFF	(Impressarios IMP 1) 1967 R3
(up to	2(B)	DISPOSABLE	(Stable SLP 7001) 1968 R2
1976)	3(B)	PTOOFF	(Decca SKLR 4993) 1969 R1
	4(D)	DEVIANTS THREE	(Transatlantic TRA 204) 1969 R1

NB: (1) and (3) are the same album which was also reissued on Logo (MOGO 4001) 1978 and Psycho (16) 1983 (SC). (2) reissued on (Drop Out/Transatlantic TRANDO 8) in 1988. (1) reissued on CD (Drop Out DOCD 1988) 1993 along with a foldout sleeve reproducing the album's original artwork and again on (Alive Records CD 00014) 1995. (2) reissued on CD (Fingerprint no Cat #) 1995. (4) reissued on CD (Line TACD 9.00619 O) 1988 and (Captain Trip CTCD 061) 1997. A good collection is *The Best Of The Deviants and Mick Farren* (Essential ESMCD 746) 1999.

45:     You Got To Hold On/
        Let's Loot The Supermarket   (Stable STA 5601) 1968 R1

Originally known as The Social Deviants (line-up 'A') this was a London-based community underground band that grew up in the Notting Hill area. **Farren** and Russell ran into a 21-year-old millionaire who put up £700 to finance their first album on their own Underground Impressarios label. This was distributed by mail order through 'Oz' and 'The International Times' and sold sufficiently well for Decca to reissue it.

The material on their three albums was variable. The first included harsh punk (*I'm Coming Home*), percussion dominated progressivism (*Nothing Man*) as well as long gimmicky diatribes interspersed with none too imaginative music. *Child Of The Sky* and *Bun* were evidence of a softer side, but *Deviation Street* summarized their intent with a series of political slogans, sound effects and a variety of musical approaches which have not stood the test of time well.

Disposable had its moments, notably with good rock songs like *Slum Lord*, *Jamie's Song*, *You've Got To Hold On*, *Fire In The City* and *Guaranteed*. The remainder of the album was eminently disposable, however.

The Deviants also issued a single, which is now a rare collectors' item. After a disappointing third album the band disintegrated during an American tour. The remaining members plus **Twink** formed **Pink Fairies**. Rudolph also had a spell with **Hawkwind**.

In 1977 **Farren** reformed the band with a new line-up including Andy Colquhoun on bass/vcls and issued an EP for Stiff, entitled *Stiff EP*. In the same year their first album was reissued on Logo. Readers may also be interested in *Human Garbage* (Psycho 25), another 1984 reunion album, with a line-up of **Farren** (vcls), Sanderson (bs), Larry Wallis (gtr), Wayne Kramer (gtr) ex-MC5, and George Butler (drms). Recapturing the band's original sound and spirit quite well, it includes a re-work of *Ramblin' Rose*, Wallis' *Police Car* and Zappa's *Trouble Coming Every Day*. This has also been reissued on CD (Captain Trip CTCD 092) 1998.

Also on Psycho was a **Farren** solo re-release *Mona* (Psycho 20).

1996 saw a further re-incarnation as **Deviants IXVI** with an album *Eating Jello With A Heated Fork* (Alive Records 1022), and a CD as **Mick Farren and The Deviants** entitled *Fragments Of Broken Probes* on Captain Trip Records, from Japan. The band also played the Ptolemaic Terrascope festival in New York on April 25-27th 1997, with **Mick Farren**, Andy Colquhoun, Nick Saloman (Bevis Frond) and others.

Compilation appearances include: *I'm Coming Home* on *Perfumed Garden Vol. 2* (LP); *First Line (Seven The Row)*, *Billy The Monster* and *Death Of A Dream Machine* on *The Electric Lemonade Acid Test, Vol. 2* (LP); *Billy The Monster* on the 3-CD Box Set *Ars Longa Vita Brevis: A Compendium Of Progressive Rock 1967-1974* and *Death Of A Dream Machine* on *The Transatlantic Story* CD box set. (VJ)

Devoted

| 45: | I Love George Best/ | |
| | United (Initially PS) | (Page One POF 076) 1968 SC/- |

A novelty beat 45 in awe of the talented and wayward footballer. (VJ)

Dharma Blues Band

Personnel:	GARY COMPTON	hrmnca	A
	JOHN HILLARY	gtr, vcls	A
	MIKE KING	keyb'ds	A

ALBUM: 1(A) DHARMA BLUES (Major Minor SMPC 5017) 1969 R2

NB: (1) reissued on CD (Forgotten Jewels FJ 003) in 1991.

This blues-rock album is now rare and sought-after by collectors. It's rumoured to have included **Hawkwind**'s Dave Brock playing under a pseudonym, but I can't confirm this. The album's value seems more due to its rarity than its music, for it consists of blues standards and the playing isn't wonderful. Beware of the quality of the CD reissue, which isn't from the masters.

Some tracks, (*Come On, My Baby's Gone, Dealing With The Devil* and *Roll 'em Pete*) have also resurfaced on the *Dawn Of Hawkwind* CD, compiled by Dave Brock. (VJ/DS)

Brian Diamond and The Cutters

Personnel incl: BRIAN DIAMOND

45s:	Jealousy Will Get You Nowhere/	
	Brady Brady	(Decca F 11724) 1963 SC
	Shake, Shout And Go/	
	Whatcha Gonna Do Now Pretty Baby	(Fontana TF 452) 1964 SC
	Big Bad Wolf/See If I Care	(Pye 7N 15779) 1965 SC
	Bone Idol/Sands Of Time	(Pye 7N 15952) 1965 SC

None of these 45s seems to have made much impact. They were mostly beat. The group played a lot in Germany, where it also recorded two German language tracks, *Keine Angst, Little Woman* and *Daisy Lu.*

Compilation appearances have included: *Big Bad Wolf* on *Rare 60's Beat Treasures, Vol. 3* (CD); *See If I Care* on *Hippy Hippy Shake* (CD); and *Keine Angst, Little Woman* and *Daisy Lu* on *1000 Nadelstiche, Vol. 6 (Beat)* (CD). (VJ/DS)

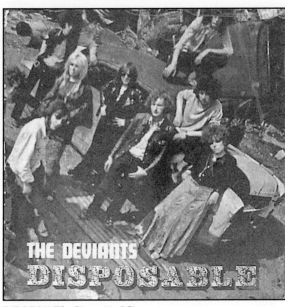

THE DEVIANTS - Disposable (LP).

THE DEVIANTS - 3 (LP).

The Diamond Twins

| 45: | Crying The Night Away/ | |
| | Start The World Spinning Again | (HMV POP 1508) 1966 |

This was a short-lived pop girl duo. (VJ)

Diane and The Javelins

Personnel incl: DIANE PARRY-HUSBANDS vcls

| 45: | Heat And Soul/Whose The Girl | (Columbia DB 7819) 1966 R1 |

This is now quite a collectable 45, largely because it was produced by Joe Meek. A bluebeat-style record, it is a marginal case for inclusion. (VJ/KL)

Charles Dickens

HCP

45s:	That's The Way Love Goes/In The City	(Pye 7N 15887) 1965 37
	I Stand Alone/Hey Little Girl	(Pye 7N 15938) 1965 -
	So Much In Love/	
	Our Soul Brothers	(Immediate IM 025) 1966 SC -

This was actually a London-based fashion photographer, David Anthony, who tried to become a pop star. His first disc sold quite well but when the next two failed to make much impact he reverted back to his career in photography. He was backed by **The Habits** who at one time included future **Nice** drummer Brian Davidson.

So Much In Love, the 'A' side of his Immediate 45, is a distinctly unexceptional pop singalong effort.

Compilation appearances have included: *Hey Little Girl* on *Ripples, Vol. 1* (CD); *I Stand Alone* and *Hey Little Girl* on *Footsteps To Fame, Vol. 2* (CD); *So Much In Love* on *Immediate Alternative* (LP), *Immediate Single Anthology, Vol. 1 - Rarities* (CD) and *Immediate Single Collection, Vol. 3* (CD); *So Much In Love* and *Our Soul Brothers* on *Immediate Alternative* (CD); and *Our Soul Brothers* on *Immediate Single Collection, Vol. 4* (CD). (VJ)

Barbara Dickson

ALBUMS:	1	THE FATE O' CHARLIE	(Trailer LER 3002) 1969 R1
(up to	2	THRO' RECENT YEARS	(Decca SKL 5041) 1970 R1
1976)	3	DO RIGHT WOMAN	(Decca SKL 5058) 1970 R1
	4	FROM THE BEGGAR'S MANTLE	(Decca SKL 5116) 1972 R1

```
    5   JOHN, PAUL, GEORGE, RINGO AND BERT
                                (RSO 2394 141) 1974 SC
    6   ANSWER ME           (RSO 2394 167) 1976
```
NB: (2) with Archie Fisher. (5) with London Cast. (6) reissued on RSO (SPELP 5) in 1983. *For The Record* (Eagle Rock EDGCD 188) 2002 is a 2-CD set

			HCP
45s:	Here Comes The Sun/		
(up to	Long And Winding Road	(RSO 2090 144) 1974	-
1976)	Blueskies/Fine Feathers	(RSO 2090 161) 1975	-
	Answer Me/From Now On	(RSO 2090 174) 1975	9
	People Get Ready/Give Me Space	(RSO 2090 186) 1976	-
	Out Of Love With Love/		
	Boys From The Men	(RSO 2090 194) 1976	-

I don't propose to deal with Barbara in any detail here but she started out as a folk singer in her native Scotland and there's growing interest now in her albums. She often worked with others in this circle. *The Fate O' Charlie* consisted of songs from the period of the Jacobite rebellions from the late 17th century to middle 18th century. You don't need to be a genius to work out that these songs were about events which changed the course of Scottish history. The album was recorded with **Archie Fisher** and John MacKinnon. *Thro' Recent Years* was recorded with Archie and he and **Rab Noakes** were also heavily involved on *Do Right Woman*, an album which is becoming particularly elusive now.

She went on to sing a duet *I Know Him So Well* with Elaine Page in 1985. In the nineties she recorded an album of Dylan songs *Don't Think Twice It's Alright* and an album of traditional tunes from the Celtic Isles called *Parcel Of Rogues*.

She made her acting debut in Willy Russell's musical 'John, Paul, George, Ringo… And Bert' in 1974 and later received a Society of West End Theatre Award as 'Best Actress In A Musical' for her appearance in his production 'Blood Brothers'. After a long lay-off she returned in late-1977 in a new production of 'The Seven Ages Of Woman' that premiered at Liverpool Playhouse. She received a 'Best Actress In The Theatre' Award from Liverpool Echo Arts and Entertainment for this effort.

For The Record, the 2002 2-CD set comprises one disc of studio recordings, including covers of Dylan's *Blowin' In The Wind* and *The Times They Are A-Changing*; and **The Beatles**' *A Day In The Life* and *She's Leaving Home*, along with some old standards. Disc Two features classics like *Another Suitcase In Another Hall* and some live versions of her new songs.

Her version of *With A Little Help From My Friends*, dating from 1974, on the *Prime Cuts* (LP) compilation may also be of interest. (VJ)

Richard Digance

ALBUMS:	1	ENGLAND'S GREEN AND PLEASANT LAND	
(up to		(Transatlantic TRA 277) 1974	
1975)	2	HOW THE WEST WAS LOST	
		(Transatlantic TRA 289) 1975	
	3	TREADING THE BOARDS	(Transatlantic TRA 306) 1975

NB: There's also a compilation *The Best Of The Transatlantic Years* (Essential ESMCD 497) 2005.

This folk / poet / songwriter was born on 24 February 1949 in Plaistow, East London. He went on to become a TV personality and comedian. (VJ/DS)

The Dimensions

Personnel:	JIMMY CLARK	bs	ABCDE
	MIKE EASTHOPE	drms	ABCDE
	RAY JONES	gtr	A
	KENNY McGONAGEL	lead gtr	A
	GRAHAM PUGH	gtr	B
	ARTHUR RAYNOR	lead gtr	B
	IRENE TIFFANY GREEN	vcls	BC
	DENNIS SWALE	gtr	CD
	LES WILLIAMS	lead gtr	CDE

45:	Tears On My Pillow/		
	You Don't Have To Whisper	(Parlophone R 5294) 1965 R1

A Liverpool-based group who tried to reproduce an American soul sound on this their sole 45, which was produced by **George Martin**. *Tears On My Pillow* was a Little Anthony number.

Tears On My Pillow can also be heard on *Mersey Beat* (2-LP). (VJ/AD)

The Dimples

Personnel:	CRAIG AUSTIN	bs, vcls	A
	JOHN GLADWIN	vcls	A
	STUART SMITH	drms	A
	GREG TOMLINSON	lead gtr, vcls	A
	TERRY WINCOTT	gtr, vcls	A

45:	Love Of A Lifetime /		
	My Heart Is Tied To You	(Decca F 12537) 1966 R1

This group was part of the Don Arden "Galaxy" stable in Carnaby Street alongside the **Small Faces**, **Nashville Teens**, **The Move**, **The Attack** and **Chris Jagger** etc. They were originally a Scunthorpe-based blues/soul band, formed by Gladwin and Wincott in 1964. In 1965 they were joined by Greg Tomlinson from the Chechakos and Craig Austin from the Imps (who also included **Ian Matthews** of **Matthews Southern Comfort** / **The Pyramid** / **Faiport Convention** and **Plainsong**). The above 45 was recorded after the band had turned down the chance to record *Hi Ho Silver Lining*.

The Dimples later became hotel trashing pioneers, resident at London's infamous Madison Hotel in Sussex Gardens and regularly worked the Marquee, Flamingo and other major London blues haunts. In their time they also played the College Circuit, Mecca and Top Rank Ballrooms, 76 Club, Golden Torch, Nottingham's Boat Clubs, Newcastle's Go-Go and Key (Quay?) Club. They also appeared on Granada TV's "Scene At Six Thirty".

Perhaps they're most notable historical footnote, however, is that they made the first live radio gig at Tiles in Oxford Street on "Ready Steady Radio" with Pete Murray.

Eventually the band evolved into psychedelic harmony soul band **Gospel Garden** with various personnel changes. Gladwin, Wincott and Austin later played in **Methuselah** before John Gladwin and Terry Wincott formed **Amazing Blondell**. (VJ)

Dirty Tricks

ALBUM:	1	DIRTY TRICKS	(Polydor 2383 351) 1975 SC
(up to 1976)			

45s:	Call Me Up For Love/Hire Car	(Polydor 2058 640) 1975
(up to 1976)	I'm Gonna Get Me A Gun/Night Man	(Polydor 2058 739) 1976

Dirty Tricks was a heavy rock group who made a second album *Night Man* in 1977. They also made a further 45 *Too Much Wine* in 1977. (VJ/CG)

The Discs

45:	Not Meant To Be/Come Back To Me	(Columbia DB 7477) 1965

This six-piece band came from Kent. (VJ)

Distant Jim

Personnel:	CRAIG AUSTIN	bs, vcls	A
	STEVE CHAPMAN	drms	A
	LES NICOL	gtr, vcls	A

45:	Just A Little Bit/Cosmarama	(N/K) 1969

Dr. STRANGELY STRANGE - Heavy Petting (LP).

In late 1968, Bassist Craig Austin and guitarist Les Nicol, renegades from recently disbanded Elektra folk-rock group **Methuselah** joined former **Junior's Eyes** drummer Steve Chapman. Throughout 1969, **Distant Jim** were writing original material and performing at Klooks Kleek and other now long forgotten North London venues. During the psychedelic mayhem that ensued, a single for Dutch label Negram, as well as an album were somehow recorded at Morgan Studios by producer "Saint" Geoff Gill of **Smoke** fame. Because of gross obscenity, the single was banned in UK and released only in Holland where it was a huge flop. The 'B' side *Cosmarama* had its moments. Consequently the album (if it was actually ever finished?) was never released and after a brief period of total insanity the trio split. Craig Austin became the Loonpant King and is now writing and producing for V8 Music. Les Nicol joined **Coast Road Drive**, Leo Sayer, **Dana Gillespie** and American glam-rockers Magnet. Steve Chapman also joined **Coast Road Drive**, Leo Sayer, and then **Sutherland Brothers and Quiver**. Later he went to the America with fellow Brit Charlie Harrison joining Poco and eventually **Al Stewart**. He now runs a successful management agency in LA. (VJ)

Doctor Father

45:     Umbopo/Roll On   (Pye 7N 17977) 1970

This 45 was a spin-off from **Graham Gouldman**'s time with Kasenatz-Katz. The 'A' side was penned by Godley and Creme. All are better-known for their involvement in **10cc**. (VJ)

Dr. Feelgood

Personnel:	LEE BRILLEAUX	vcls, slide gtr	A
	WILKO JOHNSON	gtr, vcls	A
	JOHN B. SPARKES	bs	A
	THE BIG FIGURE	drms, vcls	A

HCP

ALBUMS: 1(A) DOWN BY THE JETTY (United Artists UAS 29727) 1975 -
(up to 2(A) MALPRACTICE   (United Artists UAS 29880) 1975 17
1976)   3(A) STUPIDITY   (United Artists UAS 29990) 1976 1
NB: (1) reissued on vinyl (Fame FA 3029) 1982 and again (Grand GRAND 05) 1990. (2) reissued on vinyl (Grand GRAND 09) 1990. (3) was initially issued with stickered covers and a free live 7" 45 *Riot In Cell Block No 9/Johnny Be Goode* (Feel 1). (3) reissued on vinyl (Liberty ED 260 634-1) 1985. (1) and (2) reissued on CD on Grand (GRAND CD 05 and 06 respectively) 1990. Also relevant are *Case History - The Best Of Dr Feelgood* (EMI CDP 746 711-2) 1987 and *Singles - The U.A. Years* (Liberty CDEM 1332) 1989. For a comprehensive overview of the band try *Looking Back* (Liberty ACDFEEL 195) 1995, a 5-CD box set. A good introduction to their material is the two CD set *Twenty Five Years Of Dr. Feelgood* (GRAND CD 20) 1997. *Live At The BBC, 1974-1975* (Grand GRAND CD 22) 1999 is a remastered, previously unreleased collection of blues-rock, with a splattering of skiffle and rockabilly. *Going Back Home - Live At The Kursaal, Southend, 1975* (EMI) 2004 is a CD and DVD captures their live act in form.

HCP

45s: Roxette/
(up to   (Get Your Rocks On) Route 66 (United Artists UP 35760) 1974 -
1976)   She Does It Right/I Don't Mind (United Artists UP 35815) 1975 -
           Back In The Night/I'm A Man   (United Artists UP 35857) 1975 -
           Roxette(live)/
           Keep It Out Of Sight (Live)   (United Artits UP 36171) 1976 -

Dr Feelgood were relative latecomers to the London pub-rock movement, but their power-driven rhythm and blues took the scene by storm. They originated from Canvey Island near Southend. Full of energy and great live, Lee Brilleaux's vocals and Wilko Johnson's manic guitar playing were a breath of fresh air to the mid- seventies live scene.

Their debut album was produced by Vic Maile. Its black and white sleeve captured their musical format superbly. The *Malpractice* album consolidated their reputation. It featured classics like *Back In The Night* (which was put out as a 45) and *Going Back Home*. Also on the album was *Riot In Cell Block No 9*, a Leiber and Stroller composition, which was a show-stopping part of their live act.

Live shows at Sheffield (in May 1975) and Southend's Kursaal (November 1975) had also been recorded and it was the live album *Stupidity* that catapulted them up to the top of the charts.

Wilko Johnson departed (to his Solid Senders) and while he was missed the **Feelgood**'s endured into the nineties. Unfortunately Lee Brilleaux is no longer with us but the **Feelgood**'s deserve a mention in any UK rock history.

Milk And Alcohol has since resurfaced on the 3-CD set *Guitar Heroes*, the 3-CD collection *Full Throttle - 60 Original Driving Classics*, the 3-CD box set *Radio Caroline Calling - 70's Flashback* and on *Greatest Hit Of The 70's - cd3*; *Get Your Kicks On Route 66* on the 2-CD set *Stars And Stripes* and *She's A Wind Up* and *Roxette* can be heard on the 6-CD box set *Best Of Driving Rock*. (BS/VJ)

Dr. K's Blues Band

Personnel:	MICK HASSE	vcls, hrmnca	ABC
	ASHLEY HUTCHINGS	bs	A
	DR K (RICHARD KAY)	piano	ABC
	GEOFF KRIVIT	gtr, bs	ABC
	ERIC PEACHEY	drms	AB
	ROGER ROLT	gtr	ABC
	HAROLD VICKERS	bs	BC
	JEFF ALLEN	drms	C

ALBUM: 1(B) DR K'S BLUES BAND   (Spark SRLP 101) 1968 R2
NB: (1) issued on World Pacific (21903) in the USA. Reissued on CD as *Rock The Joint* (See For Miles SEE CD 361) 1992.

As the name suggests, this was a blues band - a solid but not particularly original one. **Dr. K's** real name was/is Richard Kay. The band was originally called Blue Reeds and then Still Waters. **Ashley Hutchings** left to form **Fairport Convention** in November 1967 and was replaced by Vickers. Krivit spent a short time in late 1965 with **John Mayall's Bluesbreakers** subbing for **Eric Clapton** until he returned to the fold. Peachey was replaced by ex-Beatstalker Jeff Allen, who went on to play for **East of Eden** when the band split.

Their album contains a fair number of blues standards and particularly noteworthy is the piano boogie *Crippled Clarence*. Geoff Krivit had been in **John Mayall's Bluesbreakers**. Eric Peachey subsequently joined **Steve Hillage**'s band **Khan**. (VJ/JM)

Dr. Marigold's Prescription

Personnel:	ALAN FRENCH	keyb'ds	A
	BILL FRENCH	bs	A
	DAVE MORRIS	drms	A
	FRED RADLEY	gtr, vcls	A
	DOMINIC GRANT		

ALBUMS: 1(A) PICTURES OF LIFE   (Marble Arch MALS 1222) 1969
        2( ) HELLO GIRL   (Pye PNL 501) 1973

45s: My Old Man Is A Groovy Old Man/
        People Get Ready   (Pye 7N 17493) 1969
        You've Got To Build Your Love/
        My Picture Of Love   (Pye 7N 17832) 1969
        Breaking The Heart Of A Good Man/
        Night Hurries On By   (Bell BLL 1096) 1970
        Sing Along, Sing Along, Sing Along/
        Father Jim   (Bell BLL 1126) 1970
        Muddy Water/Come With Me   (Bell BLL 1149) 1971
        Friend Of Mine/In Your Own Sweet Way (CBS 7286) 1971
        Time To Rock/Tokens   (CBS 8313) 1972
        March Hare/Crazy Love   (Santa Ponsa PNS 5) 1973
        March Hare/Pride Comes Before A Fall (Route RT 21) 1975

A fairly middle of the road outfit although the name promises better. Their albums comprised decent but utterly predictable pop songs. Dominic Grant who was also once a member had been a solo artist and was later in Guys and Dolls. (VJ)

Dr. Strangely Strange

Personnel: TIM GOULDING   vcls, keyb'ds   AB
             TIM BOOTH   vcls, gtr   AB
             IVAN PAWLE   vcls, bs, keyb'ds   AB
             NEIL WOOD   drms   A
             (LINUS   perc, vcls   AB
             (JAY MYRDAL   glockenspiel   AB)
             (JOHN MOYNIHAN   bazouki   B)
             (DAVE MATTACKS   drms   B)
             (GARY MOORE   ld gtr   B)
             (ANDY IRVINE   mandolin   B)
             (BRENDAN SHIELS   bs   B)
             (HEATHER, JOHANNA
             and ANNIE   vcls   B)
             TERRY WOODS
             GAY WOODS

ALBUMS: 1(A) KIP OF THE SERENES   (Island ILPS 9106) 1969 R2
        2(B) HEAVY PETTING   (Vertigo 6360 009) 1970 R2

NB: (2) reissued in Holland (Frizzbee 5) 1985 and on CD (Repertoire REP 4273-WP) 1992, again on CD (Airmail Archives AIRAC 1048) and again on CD (Progressive Line PL 572) 2002.

The original pressings of both these albums have become rare and sought-after. Originals of the first came with a pink label. Originals of the second came with a swirl label with a gimmix cover.

Often compared with **The Incredible String Band**, with whom they share the opportunism and their wilful approach to folk music, this band managed

Dr. 'Z' - Three Parts To My Soul (LP).

to deliver two completely unique albums in a style of their own. The attitude towards making music is an altogether spontaneous one, which makes for both hilarious mistakes (not mixed away in the control-room, of course) and highly inventive half-improvised parts. Most readers will at least be acquainted with *Strangely Strange But Oddly Normal* from the first album, as this cut was included on the much cherished sampler *Nice Enough To Eat* (LP) from 1968, a track with an eerie beauty, which never managed to get clear outlines. More of the same, hardly rock music, but very psychedelic nonetheless, is featured on *Kip*. The lyrics are partly very wise, partly utter nonsense. (Which is which, is up to you). Unexpected twists and turns are scattered across almost all songs. The music is acoustic throughout, almost amateurish, but continuously charming.

The second album gives more of the same, but this time augmented with sharpness and a 'rock' feel, due to the powerful drumming of Mattacks (who sometimes can hardly keep order among the players) and incisive guitar soloing by the very young **Gary Moore**. Outstanding track is the 8 minute 34 seconds *Sign On My Mind*, with great melodies which are delivered with confidence. Original pressings of this album come on the Vertigo swirl label in an elaborate gatefold sleeve. Counterfeits both with and without the gimmix sleeve are known to exist. Definitely worth a try, if you like psych which is close to nature and 'elevates' you without using any technical equipment to reach this aim.

The core group comprised Booth, Goulding, Pawle and Neil Wood and the others listed on their second album were all session players. **Terry and Gay Woods** were in **Dr. Strangely Strange** between April 1970 until they split in May 1971. **Terry** and **Gay Woods** then formed **The Woods Band**.

Gary Moore, of course, later achieved greater fame with **Skid Row**, Colosseum II and **Thin Lizzy**, before pursuing a solo career. Dave Mattacks joined **Fairport Convention**, Irvine had earlier played with **Sweeney's Men**. A further compilation appearance was *Summer Breeze* on *Vertigo Annual 1970* (2-LP).

In 1997 the band reformed for a third album *Alternative Medicine* (Big Beat WIKCD) 1997. (MK/VJ/JM)

Doctors Of Madness

Personnel: URBAN BLITZ   gtr, vcls   A
             COLIN 'STONER' BROWN   bs, vcls   A
             PETER DILEMNA   drms, vcls   A
             RICHARD 'KID' STRANGE   gtr, vcls   A

ALBUMS: 1(A) LATE NIGHT MOVIES   (Polydor 2383 378) 1976
(up to   2(A) FIGMENTS OF EMANCIPATION (Polydor 2383 403) 1976
1976)

An idiosyncratic rock band with theatrical leanings led by the larger than life highly individualistic persona of "Kid" Strange. A third album appeared in 1977 entitled *Sons Of Survival* and "Kid" Strange went on to solo success in the eighties. (BS)

Doc Thomas Group

Personnel: BOB HALL
             MIKE RALPHS
             DAVE TEDSTONE
             STAN TIPPINS
             PETE WATTS

ALBUM: 1 DOC THOMAS GROUP   (Interrecord 280) 1966
NB: (1) was an Italian only release.

An R&B band. They came from Hereford and gigged around the Welsh borders circa '66, before recruiting Stan Tippins and heading for Italy, where the above album was released. Hall later joined **The Savoy Brown Blues Band** and Tedstone was later in **Juicy Lucy**. **The Doc Thomas Group** then became The Shakedown Sound (Ralphs, Watts, Verden Allen, Dale Griffin and **Jess Roden**). After **Roden** left, they became Silence and, with the addition of **Ian Hunter**, they became **Mott The Hoople**. (JM/VJ/HI)

DOGFEET - Dogfeet (LP).

Dr. 'Z'

Personnel:	KEITH KEYES	keyb'ds, vcls	A
	BOB WATKINS	drms	A
	ROB WATSON	bs	A

ALBUM: 1(A) THREE PARTS TO MY SOUL (Vertigo 6360 048) 1971 R3
NB: (1) reissued on CD (Vertigo/Second Battle SB 012) 1991.

45: Lady Ladybird/People In The Street (Fontana 6007 023) 1970 R1

Only around 80 copies were reputedly sold of this keyboard-dominated progressive album, making it one of the most difficult major label releases to trace. It is, however, better than its reputation would suggest. The main concept is the division of human nature in three parts which are inimical to each other and this philosophical point of view is strongly reflected in the lyrics:-

'The more I live, to love, caress and tend
The more I know the need to rave and rip and rend
So liberate my soul, come see the trinity
- Neither good nor bad
It's dead - that makes you free.'

Although this inevitably hangs heavy on the music, the careful approach applied to most of it saves a lot. The parts where the shadow-side of the soul plays the cardinal role are full of real despair and get a convincing musical treatment. The sparse instrumentation, virtually without guitar, is skilfully used. If you don't mind being showered with philosophical content while listening to rock, then this comes recommended.

The 1991 CD reissue came in two formats and included both sides of their earlier non-album 45, which was a fine example of inventive late sixties pop. Aside from the straight-forward CD reissue, there's also a lavish 7" sleeve CD package which tries to replicate the original open-out sleeve which had been designed by Barney Bubbles who was better known for designing **Hawkwind**'s sleeves.

Robbie Watson was later in The Speedometers in 1979. The band was the musical vehicle of a North Wales professor called Keith Keyes. It was signed to Vertigo by **Patrick Campbell-Lyons** after he'd been sent a tape of Keyes' singing accompanied only by a piano. (MK/VJ)

Dodo Resurrection

| Personnel incl: | MARK BRADBURY | gtr |
| | JONATHAN KEIRAN | organ |

ALBUM: 1(A) NOSTRADAMUS (Elegiac SNT 7926) 1972 R6

Just 99 copies of this album were made and sent to various record labels as the Kettering, Northants quintet sought a deal. The band split in 1973 and nothing more was heard of them until a copy of their album surfaced in London in 1992 and was traded for spiralling prices. 'Record Collector' revealed that the album is of interest to occultists because it apparently guides the listener through a series of rituals designed to climax in the physical manifestation of the Goatfoot God. The finale to the 10-track collection, *Key Of Solomon* culminates in a chant with lots of wah-wah guitar and tambourines. Highly-touted by both progressive rock collectors and occultists the album is a very rare and expensive item.

The band split in 1973 and Jonathan Keiran was found dead in a burnt out shed in the nineties. (VJ/BS)

Dogfeet

Personnel:	DAVE NICHOLS	bs	A
	ALAN PEAVE	gtr, vcls	A
	DUCK PERRY	drms	A
	TREVOR POVEY	gtr, vcls	A

ALBUM: 1(A) DOGFEET (Reflection REFL 8) 1970 R4
NB: (1) reissued on Kissing Spell (CD version CA 36002, has extra tracks, including studio demos for the 1970 album and two live tracks from 1991).

45s: Sad Story/On The Road (Reflection HRS 7) 1971 R1
Since I Went Away/Evil Woman (Reflection HRS 12) 1971 R1

This 'progressive' album, produced by Andrew Cameron Millar, is now a major collectable and similar to **Wishbone Ash**. On the heavyish side, it's vastly overrated and I couldn't even recommend the recent reissue on Kissing Spell, unless you're heavily into this type of music. (VJ)

Doggerel Bank

Personnel:	SUSAN BAKER	violin, hrmnca	AB
	GARY BOYLE	gtr	AB
	TONI CAMPO	bs	A
	JIM PARKER	keyb'ds	AB
	TOM PARKER	keyb'ds	AB
	ANDREW STEELE	drms	A
	WILLIAM WRIGHT	vcls	AB

ALBUMS: 1(A) SILVER FACES (Charisma CAS 1079) 1973
2(B) MISTER SKILLCORN DANCES
(Charisma CAS 1102) 1975 SC

45: Tiny Seed Of Love/Down On The Farm (Charisma CB 220) 1973

This was a wacky folk-rock group that also went in for some poetry. They were assisted by several other artists on the second album and the above personnel were in a number of other bands: Susan Baker, Jim Parker and William Wright had been in The Barrow Poets. Gary Boyle (who was a member of **Isotope** at the same time as this band) had been in **Eclection** and played with **Brian Auger**. Toni Campo was ex-**Greenslade**. He was later in **Rock Workshop**. Andrew Stock had been with **The Herd**. (VJ)

Dog Rose

ALBUM: 1 ALL FOR THE LOVE OF DOGROSE
(Satril SALP 4001) 1972 SC

45: All For The Love Of City Lights/
Each Other (Satril SAT 6) 1973

This duo recorded on a small label. The record was produced by Dave Paramour (who also worked with **The Gods**, **Head Machine** and **Mike Stuart Span** etc.). There's a strong *Abbey Road* - era **Beatles** influence with winsome harmonies and melodies but some typically early seventies progressive fuzz leads and a rural rock feel too at times. (VJ)

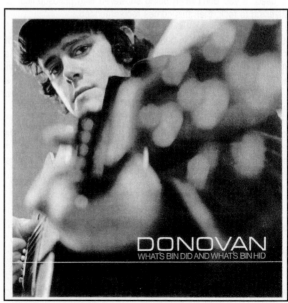

DOG THAT BIT PEOPLE - Dog That Bit People (CD).

Dog Soldier

Personnel:
MILLER ANDERSON	gtr, vcls	ABCD
PAUL BLISS	bs	AB
DEREK GRIFFITHS	gtr	ABC
KEEF HARTLEY	drms	A
MEL SIMPSON	keyb'ds	ABCD
ERIC DILLON	drms	BC
JIMMY LEVERTON	bs	CD
PHIL PALMER	gtr	D

ALBUM: 1(A) DOG SOLDIER (United Artists UAS 29769) 1975

45: Pillar To Post/Several People (United Artists UP 35847) 1975

A short-lived mid-seventies outfit formed by **Keef Hartley**, who'd been in **The Artwoods**, **John Mayall's Bluesbreakers** and had later formed his own **Keef Hartley Band**. Most recently he had toured with **Mike Chapman**. Derek Griffiths had also been in **The Artwoods,** Atlantic Flight and was later with **Mike Cotton Sound** and **Satisfaction** prior to joining this band. **Miller Anderson** had also been in the **Keef Hartley Band** as well as **The Voice**, **At Last The 1958 Rock 'n' Roll Show** and **Hemlock**. He also had a brief solo career in 1971.

Hartley left shortly after their album was released in May 1975 to tour with **Mike Chapman** again. His replacement was Eric Dillon, formerly of **Savoy Brown**. Bliss then left in June 1975 citing 'musical differences'. He then formed The Paul Bliss Band in 1977 with Andy Brown and Alan Park (from **Tiger**). He was replaced by Jimmy Leverton, another ex-**Savoy Brown** man. Griffiths then joined the Australian band The Aztecs and was replaced by Phil Palmer (the nephew of **Ray** and **Dave Davies**).

After they split, Anderson went on to **T. Rex**; Leverton toured and recorded with Leo Sayer; Palmer toured with **Chris Farlowe** and Dillon joined a band called Lion. (VJ/JM)

Dog That Bit People

Personnel:
JOHN CASWELL	vcls, gtr	A
MICHAEL HINCKS	vcls, bs	A
BOB LAMB	drms	A
KEITH MILLAR	vcls, gtr, keyb'ds	A

ALBUM: 1(A) DOG THAT BIT PEOPLE (Parlophone PCS 7125) 1971 R3
NB: (1) reissued on CD (Shoestring BL 003) 1995.

45: Lovely Lady / Merry-Go-Round (Parlophone R 5880) 1971 SC

Hincks and Lamb were left over from **Locomotive** after **Norman Haines** had left and they formed this interesting outfit which is very much a progressive rock outfit playing short songs. The album opens mellowly with *Goodbye Country*, featuring a nice melody, but gets heavier on the somewhat prototypical *The Monkey And The Sailor*. This track has an unexpected middle 8, though. *Lovely Lady* sounds like **The Honeybus** and *Sound Of Thunder* again lives from an odd juxtaposition between verse and chorus, a recipe which is some kind of trademark on this album. *Someone Somewhere* should have been sung by Ringo and boasts a horrible guitar solo which should have been played by George. *A Snapshot Of Rex* sounds like **Joe Cocker** but suffers from the absence of **Joe Cocker**, while *Mr. Sunshine* clearly tries to be **Traffic**. *Tin Soldier* is not the **Small Faces'** song, but is an agreeable tune, albeit with embarrassing lyrics. The concluding *Reptile Man* has, predictably enough, doctored vocals above a repeated jungle riff and is the only truly black spot on the album, though hard progressive fans will argue otherwise. All in all a nice effort, but not worth the price tag it now commands. The 45 has an undistinguished non-album 'B' side.

Michael Hincks and Bob Lamb both went on to play with **Raymond Froggatt**. (MK)

The Dollies

Personnel:
RAIE BANCROFT		A
JILL DAVIES		A
GERI OSWALD		A
CAROL PARKES		A

45: You Touch Me Baby/I Can't Go On (CBS 201788) 1965

This teenage girl group came from Cheshire. They backed Del Shannon in his 1965 tour of the UK and also played once at the Star Club in Hamburg. The 45 is a cheerful beat single. (VJ)

Don Bradshaw Leather

Personnel incl: ROBERT JOHN GODFREY A

ALBUM: 1(A) DISTANCE BETWEEN US (2-LP) (Distance no #) 1972 R1

This is a strange occult-influenced double album, which was reputedly recorded by future Enid member **Robert John Godfrey**. (VJ)

Donovan

				HCP
ALBUMS:	1	WHAT'S BIN DID AND WHAT'S BIN HID		
(up to			(Pye NPL 18117) 1965	SC 3
1976)	2	FAIRYTALE	(Pye NPL 18128) 1965	SC 20
	3	SUNSHINE SUPERMAN	(Pye NPL 18181) 1967	SC 25
	4	UNIVERSAL SOLDIER	(Marble Arch MAL 718) 1967	5

DONOVAN - What's Bin Did And What's Bin Hid (CD).

5	A GIFT FROM A FLOWER TO A GARDEN (2-LP box set)		
		(Pye NPL 200000) 1968 R1 13	
6	DONOVAN IN CONCERT		
	(mono/stereo)	(Pye N(S)PL 18237) 1968 SC -	
7	DONOVAN GREATEST HITS LP		
	(mono/stereo)	(Pye N(S)PL 18283) 1969 -	
8	WORLD OF DONOVAN	(Marble Arch MAL 1168) 1969 -	
9	OPEN ROAD	(Dawn DNLS 3009) 1970 SC 30	
10	GOLDEN HOUR OF DONOVAN	(Pye GH 506) 1971 -	
11	HMS DONOVAN (2-LP)	(Dawn DNLP 4001) 1971 R1 -	
12	COLOURS	(Hallmark HMA 241) 1972 -	
13	COSMIC WHEELS	(Epic SEPC 65450) 1973 15	
14	ESSENCE TO ESSENCE	(Epic SEPC 69050) 1973 -	
15	FOUR SHADES	(Pye 11PP 102) 1973 -	
16	COSMIC WHEELS	(Epic EPC 65490) 1973 -	
17	7 - TEASE	(Epic SEPC 69104) 1974 -	
18	SLOW DOWN WORLD	(Epic SEPC 86011) 1976 -	

NB: (1) reissued on Marble Arch (MAL 795) in 1968. *Catch The Wind* originally a US-only release in 1965 was issued on Hallmark (HMA 200) in 1971. (2) also released as *Songs For Sunshine* (Pye 2053) in 1965 with one different track. (2) reissued on Marble Arch (MAL 867) in 1969 and on CD (Castle CLACD 226) in 1991. A slightly later compilation was *Donovan File* (Pye FILD 004) 1977, but this was bettered by *Greatest Hits And More* (EMI EMS 1333) 1989, also on CD. (3) reissued on CD (Beat Goes On BGOCD 58) 1990. *The Collection* (Castle CCSCD 276, also on cassette) 1990 is probably the most interesting and wide ranging of his compilations. (6) reissued (Beat Goes On BGOLP 90) 1991, also on CD (BGOCD). (10) reissued on CD (Knight KGHCD 107) 1990. (12) reissued on CD (PRT AYC 7004) 1987. (14) reissued on CD (Epic) 1998 at mid-price. (15) is a 4-LP box set (*H.M.S. Donovan/Greatest Hits/Open Road*). (17) and (18) reissued on one CD (Edsel DIAB 8052) 2004. (17) reissued again on CD (Repertoire) 2005. Also on CD is *Introspective* (Baktabak CINT 5007) 1992. *Four Donovan Originals* (EMI DONOVAN 1) 1994 is a 4-CD set of his *Sunshine Superman, Mellow Yellow, Hurdy Gurdy Man* and *Barabajagal* albums in the form they were originally issued in the US. **Donovan** fans who don't already have the US issues will probably want this well-packaged set. All four were individually issued again with bonus tracks: *Sunshine Superman* (EMI 873 5662) 2005, *Mellow Yellow* (EMI 873 5672) 2005, *Hurdy Gurdy Man* (EMI 873 5682) 2005 and *Barabajagal* (EMI 873 5692) 2005. *Sunshine Superman* (Sundazed LP 5028) 2005, also reissued on vinyl. *Universal Soldier* (Spectrum 550 721-2) 1995, is a compilation which concentrates on material from his early years as a folksinger. There's also a live album that has been issued in recent years as *In Concert* (Happy Price Records), *Colours Live* (Magnum Force) and *The Very Best Of Donovan* (Artful CD 5) 1997. *Colours* (2-CD) (Recall) 1997 compiles material from his early folk protest period. *Anthology - Summer Day Reflection Songs* (Essential ESDCD 861) 2000 is a 2-CD set containing everything he recorded in 1965. *Rising Again* (NMC) issued in the mid-eighties is a 2-CD live hits package. *Greatest Hits Live* (Varese Sarabande 302 066 259 2) 2001 is a single CD collection featuring similar material. *Sixty Four: The Donovan Archive Volume 1* (Donovan Discs DDCD 0001) 2004 is only available via his official website (www.donovan.ie) and is the first release from his own label. *Best Of Live* (Artful PBZ 009) 2004 contains 18 tracks from a 1971 US tour. *Summer Day Reflection Songs* (Sanctuary ESDCD 861) 2005 is a reissue of the earlier 2-CD set on Essential, which compiles his first two albums, EP and three hit singles from 1965 and has been repackaged for his 2005 UK tour. *Try For The Sun: The Journey Of Donovan* (Epic/Legacy EK-94446) 2005 is a 3-CD set with a bonus DVD.

EPs:	1	THE UNIVERSAL SOLDIER	(Pye NEP 24219) 1965

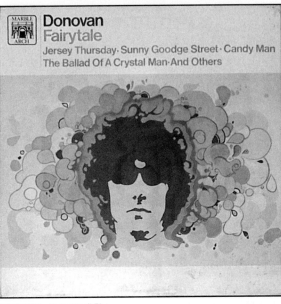

DONOVAN - Fairytale (LP).

DONOVAN - Sunshine Superman (US) (LP).

2	COLOURS	(Pye NEP 24299) 1966 SC
3	DONOVAN, VOLUME ONE	(Pye NEP 24239) 1966 SC
4	CATCH THE WIND	(Pye NEP 24287) 1968 SC
5	HURDY GURDY DONOVAN	(Pye NEP 24299) 1968 SC

NB: These are compiled on *The EP Collection* (See For Miles SEE 300) 1990, also on CD (SEE CD 300) 1990.

HCP

45s:		Catch The Wind/		
(up to		Why Do You Treat Me Like You Do	Pye 7N 15801) 1965 4	
1976)		Colours/To Sing For You	(Pye 7N 15866) 1965 4	
		Turquoise/Hey Gyp (Dig The Slowness)	(Pye 7N 15984) 1965 30	
		Josie/Little Tin Soldier	(Pye 7N 17067) 1966 -	
	α	Remember The Alamo/		
		The Ballad Of A Crystal Man	(Pye 7N 17088) 1966 -	
		Sunshine Superman/The Trip	(Pye 7N 17241) 1967 2	
		Mellow Yellow/Preachin' Love	(Pye 7N 17267) 1967 8	
		There Is A Mountain/Sand And Foam	(Pye 7N 17403) 1967 8	
		Jennifer Juniper/Poor Cow	(Pye 7N 17457) 1968 5	
		Hurdy Gurdy Man/Teen Angel	(Pye 7N 17537) 1968 4	
	α	To Susan On The West Coast/Atlantis	(Pye 7N 17660) 1969 -	
		Atlantis/I Love My Shirt	(Pye 7N 17660) 1969 23	
	β	Goo Goo Barabajagal (Love Is Hot)/		
		Bed With Me	(Pye 7N 17778) 1969 12	
	χ	Riki Tiki Tavi/Roots Of Oak	(Dawn DNS 1006) 1970 -	
	δ	Celia Of The Seals/Mr. Wind	(Dawn DNS 1007) 1970 -	
		I Like You/Earth Sign Man	(Epic EPC 1471) 1973 -	
		Maria Magenta/		
		The Intergalactic Laxative (PS)	(Epic EPC 1644) 1973 -	
		Sailing Homeward/Lazy Daze (PS)	(Epic EPC 1960) 1973 -	
		Rock And Roll With Me/		
		Divine Daze Of Deathless Delight	(Epic EPC 2661) 1974 -	
		Rock And Roll Souljer/Love Of My Life	(Epic EPC 3037) 1975 -	
Reissues:		There Is A Mountain/Jennifer Juniper/Sunshine Superman/		
		Mellow Yellow	(Pye PMM 104) 1971 -	
		Sunshine Superman/Mellow Yellow	(Epic 152251) 1975 -	
		Jennifer Juniper/Hurdy Gurdy Man	(Epic 152280) 1975 -	
		Colours/Universal Soldier	(Pye 7N 46105) 1978 -	
		Catch The Wind/Colours	(Old Gold OG 9134) 1982 -	
		Mellow Yellow/Sunshine Superman	(EMI G 4545) 1985 -	
		Jennifer Juniper/(Flip by different artist)	(Fontana SYP 1) 1990 68	

NB: α and α withdrawn. β with **The Jeff Beck Group**. χ as **Donovan** with **Open Road**. δ as **Donovan** with Danny Thompson. There's also a CD single, *Sunshine Superman* (EMI CD EM 98) 1989 which contains *Wear Your Love Like Heaven*, *Jennifer Juniper* and *Mellow Yellow*, in addition to the title track.

Although some saw **Donovan** at the time of his emergence as the British answer to Bob Dylan his recordings lacked the bleakness of Dylan's. In fact they perfectly captured the optimism of the peace and love vibes of the flower-power movement and many are significant remnants of the psychedelic era.

DONVAN - A Gift From A Flower To The Garden (2-LP).

Donovan was born in Glasgow on 10 May 1946. He was hanging around the South with a guitar when he was discovered in early 1965 and given a residency on ITV's brand new rock programme, 'Ready Steady Go'. In these early days he played a form of gentle, melodic folk and was inevitably dismissed as a poor man's Dylan. He also carved a distinctive image with his blue denim cap. Without the exposure on 'Ready Steady Go' it's doubtful if his career would have gone anywhere, but with TV exposure *Catch The Wind* and *Colours* were both catapulted high up the Charts as was his first EP, which also included Buffy Sainte-Marie's *Universal Soldier*. However, by the Autumn of 1965 there were signs that the frequent and unfavourable comparisons with Dylan were beginning to harm him. His first folkie album had sold well but the more reflective *Fairytale* only peaked at No 20 and his third single, *Turquoise*, peaked at No 30. These factors led the singer to change musical direction and to this end he enlisted the assistance of producer Mickie Most and musical director John Cameron. However, a legal battle between his new management and his previous management agency froze his progress initially. To maintain public interest in him, *Josie* from his first album was issued as a 45 in February 1966 but it made little impression. Another EP was put out, too, and *Remember The Alamo* was released and then withdrawn.

The legal battle delayed the release of *Sunshine Superman* in Britain from January 1966 until December of that year. Along with *Eight Miles High* by The Byrds it was one of the first psychedelic singles to be recorded and when it was released in America in July 1966 it climbed to No 1 in a few weeks. It's reference to 'blowing your mind' was ideally suited to those heady days. It was a classic 45 with its distinctive guitar work, whilst the flip was more uptempo R&B.

The legal disputes also delayed the release of the *Sunshine Superman* album, which had climbed to No 11 in the US after its release in July 1966 in the US. It's certainly well worth checking out. Highlights included *Seasons Of The Witch*, a chilling song with a sparse arrangement later covered by Vanilla Fudge; *Fat Angel*, which became a big favourite for Jefferson Airplane and was covered by them on their *Bless It's Pointed Little Head* live album (**Donovan** referred to the band in the lyrics 'fly Jefferson Airplane, getcha there on time'); *Legend Of A Girl Child Linda*, a fairytale set to a string backing with lots of harpsichord and woodwind; *Bert's Blues*, a jazzy song which acknowledged his influence on **Donovan**'s music and the beautiful finale *Celeste*.

His follow-up 45, *Mellow Yellow*, came out in November 1966 in the US and was almost as good as *Sunshine Superman*. It again had a very catchy intro tapped out on drums but was essentially a jazzy sorta pop song, with lots of brass and percussion. The flip side, *Sunny South Kensington*, was similar in style to *The Trip*. A sorta R&B style description of swinging London with references to Mary Quant. In the US it climbed to No 2. In the UK it was not released (because of the legal wrangle) until February 1967 and came with a different flip side, *Preachin' Love*, a jazzy number which was also used to back **Donovan**'s next US single, *Epistle To Dippy*, which featured trippy lyrics but was weaker than its two predecessors. It was not released in the UK presumably because of its lyrics.

His *Mellow Yellow* album (a US-only release) came out in March 1967 and climbed to No 14 in the US Charts. Aside from the title track other highlights were *Sunny Goodge Street* (later covered by **Marianne Faithful** on her *Country Maid* album); *Hampstead Incident, Sand And Foam* (about smugglers in Mexico); *Young Girl Blues* (a song about bedsitter living) and *Museum*, which had an unusual string accompaniment and was later covered by **Herman's Hermits** and **Beverly (Martyn)**.

When the *Sunshine Superman* album was eventually released in the UK in May 1967 it comprised a selection of tracks from **Donovan**'s US *Sunshine Superman* and *Mellow Yellow* albums. Inevitably much good material was omitted, including *The Trip* and *Fat Angel* (from the US *Sunshine Superman*) and *Museum, Sunny South Kensington* and the title track (from *Mellow Yellow*) and readers are recommended to buy the two US releases.

Donovan's next 45 was the calypso-style *There Is A Mountain*, which marked a further change in musical direction away from his early more psychedelic sound. It peaked at No 11 in the US and No 8 in the UK. This was unusual for he was far more popular in the States than in his homeland. Indeed, he toured the States regularly in this era and his next *Donovan In Concert* album used material from a performance at the Anaheim Convention Centre in LA.

In December 1967 **Donovan** provided three songs for the Soundtrack of the film 'Poor Cow':- *Colours, Be Not Too Hard* and the title cut itself.

His next album, *A Gift From A Flower To A Garden*, was a double package which was also available separately (each album had its own title). The first, *Wear Your Love Like Heaven*, was named after his next US-only single. It tended to consist of fairly simple rock numbers and the better tracks included *There Was A Time*; the organ-driven *The Land Of Doesn't Have To Be* and *Someone Singing*, which featured some nice horns, strings and harp and **Jack Bruce** on bass. The second disc, *For Little Ones*, contained twelve charming songs including *The Tinker And The Crab* and *Epistle To Derroll*, a lengthy nursery tale. Lavishly packaged, this double set is generally regarded as an essential item of the flower power era. In the UK it was preceded by the lovely love song *Jennifer Juniper*, which climbed to No 5 in the Charts. The 'B' side, *Poor Cow*, was a folk-influenced song.

Donovan's next UK single, *Hurdy Gurdy Man*, was arguably his finest moment. The backing marked a return to the heavier psychedelic sound of *Sunshine Superman* and his vibrato vocals were near to perfection. It was later covered by **Steve Hillage**. *Hurdy Gurdy Man* was allegedly written by the Danish band *Hurdy Gurdy*, who allowed **Donovan** the rights to the song in exchange for **Donovan** paying their fare to London. The non-album 'B' side was a sad love song with a sparse backing. Peaking at No 4 it was his second most successful UK single to *Sunshine Superman*. It also climbed to No 5 in the US. It was followed by a US-only single, *Lalena*, which was less striking than its predecessors and only climbed to No 33. This was followed by a US-only album, *Hurdy Gurdy Man*, which was rather patchy. Aside from the title track and *Jennifer Juniper*, other more notable tracks were the psychedelic *Peregrine*, with its Celtic and

DONOVAN - Live 1968 (LP).

DONOVAN - Open Road (LP).

Eastern-style instrumental backing; *The River Song* and the jazz-influenced *Get Thy Bearings*.

His next single, *Atlantis*, was five minutes long and featured a lengthy spoken intro which then gave way to a repetitive chant rather reminiscent of *Hey Jude*, indeed **Paul McCartney**, even contributed to its backing vocals. Backed by the inane *I Love My Shirt* in the UK it climbed to No 23. In the US *Atlantis* was originally the flip side to a Vietnam-related song, *To Susan On The West Coast Waiting*, which managed to climb to No 35 before the record company flipped the disc and *Atlantis* achieved the No 7 spot.

Released in March 1969 *Donovan's Greatest Hits* climbed to No 4 in the US but surprisingly didn't Chart in the UK. It included the original unedited version of *Sunshine Superman* and rerecorded versions of *Catch The Wind* and *Colours* that were very different from the originals. In fact, given that it contained most of his hits the album is a good first purchase for anyone unfamiliar with **Donovan**'s material.

For his next single **Donovan** joined forces with **The Jeff Beck Group** to record *Barabajagal (Love Is Hot)*. This was one of his finest moments and certainly his heaviest offering climaxing (after a guitar intro) into a wall of sound. Other points of note about the single were the female backing vocalist and the brief frenzied spoken passage. Early copies in the UK saw its flip side *Trudi* entitled *Bed With Me*. Unusually, it was more successful in the UK, where it climbed to No 12 than in the US, where it could only manage No 36. He also had another US-only album *Barabajagal*, which was variable in content but included both sides of his last two US singles.

With the onset of the seventies **Donovan**'s popularity began to wane. *Open Road* sold quite well but spawned no hit singles. The follow-up, *HMS Donovan*, sold poorly and financial problems forced him to become a tax exile living in Ireland, although he later retreated to Joshua Tree in California. However, he did write a few movie scores:- 'If It's Tuesday, It Must Be Belgium', 'The Pied Piper' (1972) in which he starred and 'Brother Sun Sister Moon' (1973).

His last album to obtain any sort of commercial success was *Cosmic Wheels* in 1973, but his albums and singles back in the sixties are essential ingredients in any collection of sixties folk and psychedelia. He also contributed *Jersey Thursday* to Marble Arch's 1970 *Hitmakers* (LP) compilation.

Donovan's career was revived in 1991 when the Happy Mondays named a song in his honour on their *Pills'n'Thrills & Bellyaches* album and he later toured with the group too. In 1996 he released a comeback album *Sutras* but it made little impact. He went missing again, but re-appeared with a collection of largely original songs on *Beat Café* in 2004 produced by John Chelew. The album also included a spoken-word rendition of Dylan Thomas' *Do Not Go Gentle* and a fine version of the traditional tune *Cuckoo*.

A good introduction to his music for those of you who missed out first time around is undoubtedly EMI's 1989 *Greatest Hits And More* compilation,

which includes his hits, some of his better album tracks and a few rarities not previously issued in the UK (*To Susan On The West Coast Waiting*, *Happiness Runs* and *Superlungs My Supergirl*) before. **Donovan** collectors should note EMI's 1994 4-CD set mentioned in the earlier discography.

Another interesting fact is that he provided co-lead vocals for Alice Cooper's 1973 *Billion Dollar Babies* track, which reached No. 57 in the US single charts.

The Very Best Of? (on Artful), *In Concert* (on Happy Price Records) and *Colours Live* (on Magnum Force) are basically all the same live recording.

Sixty Four: The Donovan Archive Volume, released on his own label and only available via his website, includes early demos recorded at Southern Music's London studios in 1964 (*Freedom Road*, *Talkin' Pop Star Blues*, *Isle Of Sadness* and *Darkness Of My Mind*). *Isle Of Sadness* later became *Belated Forgiveness Plea* on his second album *Fairytale* and *Darkness Of My Night* got an airing as *Breezes Of Patchouli* on his box set *Troubadour: The Definitive Collection 1964-76*.

Best Of Live contains 18 tracks from a 1971 US tour, but is poorly packaged and contains no information about the songs included.

Summer Day Reflection Songs is a 2-CD set containing everything he recorded in 1965, including both of his albums, all his singles and an obscure track *Every Man Has Had His Chain*, which appeared on a French EP. It's accompanied by detailed sleevenotes from Lorne Murdoch and rare photos. Originally released in 2000, it was reissued and repackaged in 2005 as part of the EMI repackages and to coincide with his 2005 UK tour.

Try For The Sun: The Journey Of Donovan is a 60-track 3-CD career-spanning set containing 13 previously unreleased songs which comes with a bonus DVD of his 1970 documentary 'There is An Ocean'. It's a feast of delights for his fans. There are mono recordings of many of his early singles on disc one, some previously unavailable recordings and plenty of live material too.

Retrospective compilation appearances have included: *Sunshine Superman* on *Jimmy's Back Pages - The Early Years* (CD) and on *Psychedelia and The Underground* (CD); *Universal Soldier* on *No 1s & Million Sellers, Vol 4* (CD) and the 2-CD set *We Love The Pirates: Charting The Big 'L' Fab 40*; *Hey Gyp (Dig The Slowness)* on *Maximum '65* (CD), *Ripples, Vol. 6* (CD) and *Your Starter For Ten!!* (CD); *Sunshine Superman* and *Sunny South Kensington* on *Psychedelia At Abbey Road* (CD); *Catch The Wind* on *No 1s & Million Sellers, Vol 1* (CD) and *Brit Pop* (CD); *The Sunny Day Reflection Song* on *Ripples, Vol. 3* (CD); *Jennifer Juniper* on *Hard Up Heroes, Vol. 2* (CD) and *Love Is All Around* (CD); *Colours* on *Hits Of The Swinging Sixties* (CD) and *Celeste* and *Hurdy Gurdy Man* on the 4-CD *Acid Drops, Spacedust & Flying Saucers* box set. (VJ/RH)

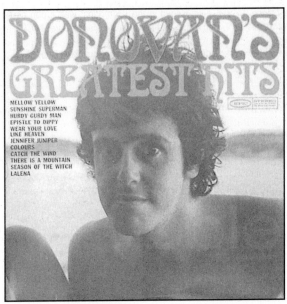

DONOVAN - Greatest Hits (LP).

Ray Dorset

ALBUM: 1 COLD BLUE EXCURSION (Dawn DNLS 3033) 1972 SC

45: Cold Blue Excursion/I Need It (Dawn DNS 1018) 1971
(up to
1976)

Dorset, born in Ashford, Middlesex, on 21st March 1946, was the lead singer of **Mungo Jerry**. This solo album, which experimented largely unsuccessfully with a variety of musical styles was **Dorset**'s response to critics who described **Mungo Jerry**'s music as monotonous.

His previous bands included The Buccaneers, Concords, Trammps, Sweet And Sour Band, Camio Reale and **Good Earth**. (VJ)

Double Feature

Personnel: BILL HALL A
　　　　　　BRIAN LANE A

45s: Baby Get Your Head Screwed On/
　　　 Come On Baby (Deram DM 115) 1967 R1
　　　 Handbags And Gladrags/
　　　 Just Another Lonely Night (Deram DM 165) 1967 SC

A short-lived Birmingham-based duo. For their first 45 they added wailing fuzz guitars and **ELO**-style cello to a **Cat Stevens** pop-soul composition, *Baby Get Your Head Screwed On*. Not a bad effort, the vocals are pretty gritty, too, but somehow it isn't entirely convincing. The follow-up, a cover of **Mike D'Abo's** *Handbags And Gladrags*, produced by Mark Leander, marked their transition from soul-tinged psychedelia to pure soul, but it also proved to be their final vinyl offering.

Compilation appearances include: *Baby Get Your Head Screwed On* on *Mod Scene, Vol. 2* (CD), *Psychedalia - Rare Blooms From The English Summer Of Love* (CD), *British Psychedelic Trip, Vol. 4* (LP) and *Great British Psychedelic Trip, Vol. 2* (CD); *Come On Baby* on *Colour Me Pop, Vol 1* (CD) and *Just Another Lonely Night* on *Colour Me Pop, Vol 2* (CD). (VJ)

Doughnut Ring

Personnel: GEORGE BIRD bs A
　　　　　　JOHN CHAPEL keyb'ds A
　　　　　　RICK MILLS vcls A
　　　　　　BERT PULHAM gtr A
　　　　　　DAVE SKATES drms A

45: Dance Around Julie/The Bandit (Deram DM 215) 1968 R1

Their *Dance Around Julie*, issued in the late sixties, was a pop single with a psychedelic taint. You'll also find it on *Colour Me Pop, Vol 1* (CD).

They had earlier recorded as **Crocheted Doughnut Ring**. (VJ)

Carl Douglas and The Big Stampede

Personnel incl: CARL DOUGLAS

45s: Crazy Feeling/(Flip by different artist) (Go AJ 11401) 1966 SC
　　　 Let The Birds Sing/
　　　 Something For Nothing (Go AJ 11408) 1967 R1
　 α Nobody Cries/
　　　 Serving A Sentence Of Life (United Artists UP 1206) 1967 R2
　　　 Sell My Soul To The Devil/
　　　 Good Hard Worker (United Artists UP 2227) 1968 SC
　 α Do You Need My Love/Lean On Me (CBS 7101) 1971
　 β Somebody Stop This Madness/
　　　 Ain't No Use (Blue Mountian BM 1007) 1972

NB: α **Carl Douglas** solo. β as Karl Douglas.

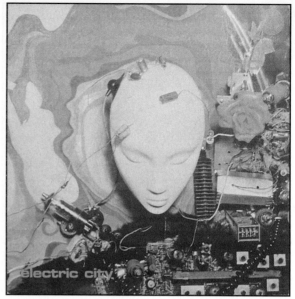

BOB DOWNES - Open Music (LP).

Before achieving Chart success with the awful *Kung Fu Fighting* **Carl Douglas** (who came to Britain from California in 1958) fronted a soul/pop/beat band and recorded these singles (including one solo effort). The first two were on the tiny Go label, a small subsidary of CBS, which also featured **Scots Of St. James**.

In the early to mid-seventies he was vocalist in Gonzales.

Crazy Feeling has resurfaced on *The Youngblood Story, Vol. 1* (CD). (MWh)

Rob & Dean Douglas

Personnel: DEAN DOUGLAS
　　　　　　ROB DOUGLAS

45: I Can Make It With You/Phone Me (Deram DM 132) 1967 R1

This is an obscure and collectable 45. You can also check out *Phone Me* on *Oddities, Vol 2* (CD). (VJ)

The Dowlands

Personnel: DAVID DOWLAND vcls A
　　　　　　GORDON DOWLAND vcls A

　　　　　　　　　　　　　　　　　　　　　　　HCP
45s: α Little Sue/Julie (Oriole CB 1748) 1962 R1 -
　　　　 Big Big Fella/Don't Ever Change (Oriole CB 1781) 1962 R3 -
　　　　 Break Ups/A Love Like Ours (Oriole CB 1815) 1963 R1 -
　　　　 Lucky Johnny/
　　　　 Do You Have To Make Me Blue? (Oriole CB 1892) 1963 R5 -
　　　 α All My Loving/Hey Sally (Oriole CB 1897) 1964 SC 33
　　　　 I Walk The Line/Happy Endings (Oriole CB 1926) 1964 R1 -
　　　　 Wishing And Hoping/
　　　　 You Will Regret It (Oriole CB 1947) 1964 R2 -
　　　　 Don't Make Me Over/
　　　　 Someone Must Be Feeling Sad (Columbia DB 7547) 1965 R1 -

NB: α As Dowlands and Soundtracks.

A harmony vocal duo from Bournemouth. They enjoyed a minor hit with their cover of **The Beatles'** *All My Loving* and were largely reliant on cover versions. None of their subsequent efforts repeated this success.

The music on their records was provided by The Soundtracks who were actually an integral part of the band - no-one knows why they were only credited on three of their records. Their line-up included Roy Phillips on guitar. (VJ/KL)

Bob Downes

ALBUMS:
1	ELECTRIC CITY	(Vertigo 6360 005)	1970 R1
2	DEEP DOWN HEAVY	(Music For Pleasure MFP 1412)	1970
3	OPEN MUSIC	(Philips SBL 7922)	1970 R2
4	DIVERSIONS	(Ophenian BDOM 001)	1974 SC
5	EPISODES AT 4 A.M.	(Ophenian BDOM 002)	1974 SC
6	HELLS ANGELS	(Ophenian BDOM 003)	1975 SC

NB: (1) reissued on CD on Repertoire (REP 4451-WP) 1994.

45:        No Time Like The Present/
           Keep Off The Grass   (Vertigo 6059 011) 1970

Bob Downes was an established session man, playing for **Manfred Mann**, **Chris Andrews** and later for **Egg**, **Andwella's Dream**, **Dada** and **Rock Workshop**. This progressive/avant-garde jazz artist has been assisted by a wide variety of artists on his releases. *Electric City* wasn't enhanced by **Downes'** singing. Only *Open Music* has really attracted much interest from collectors to date. Ophenian was his own record label. He also went on to compose music for the ballet 'Rambert'. He was one of the country's top flautists but moved to live on the continent in the late eighties.

The *Deep Down Heavy* album is interesting, being an amalgam of **Bob Downes'** music and Robert Cockburn's poetry. They collaborated on most tracks but also had their own moments; Cockburn, for example, reading extracts from his poetry. One memorable track, entitled *Poplar Cheam*, includes references to more than 40 underground stations. An underrated album for sure and something of a surprise on the Music For Pleasure label. **Downes** now lives in Germany.

Vertigo Annual 1970 (2-LP) included his *No Time Like The Present*, but this is only likely to appeal to fans of avant-garde jazz. (VJ/MWh)

The Downliners Sect

Personnel:
DON CRANE	vcls	ABCDEF
KEITH GRANT	vcls, bs	ABCDEF
MEL	gtr	A
JOHN SUTTON	drms	ABC F
TERRY GIBSON	gtr	BC F
RAY STONE	mouth organ	C
MATTHEW FISHER	keyb'ds	D
KEVIN FLANAGAN	drms	DE
BOB TAYLOR	gtr	DE
BARRY COOPER	keyb'ds	E

ALBUMS:
1( )	THE SECT	(Columbia 33SX 1658)	1964 R2
2( )	THE COUNTRY SECT	(Columbia 33SX 1745)	1965 R2
3( )	THE ROCK SECT'S IN	(Columbia 33SX 6028)	1966 R2

NB: (1), (2) and (3) reissued on Charly (CR 30122, CR 30137 and CR 30140) in 1977, 1977 and 1978 respectively. Three compilations worth checking out are *Be A Sect Maniac* (Line OLLP 5183 A5) 1983, *Cross Section* (Decal LIK 10) 1987 and the CD set *The Definitive Downliners Sect - Singles A's And B's* (See For Miles SEECD 398) 1994.

EPs:
1	NITE IN GT. NEWPORT STREET	
	(Contrast Sound RBCSP 001)	1964 R4
2	THE SECT SING SICK SONGS	
	(Columbia SEG 8438)	1965 R3

45s:
Baby What's Wrong/	
Be A Sect Maniac	(Columbia DB 7300) 1964 SC
Little Egypt/Sect Appeal	(Columbia DB 7347) 1964 SC
Find Out What's Happening/	
Insecticide	(Columbia DB 7415) 1964 SC
Wreck Of The Old '97/	
Leader Of The Sect	(Columbia DB 7509) 1965 SC
I Got Mine/	
Waiting In Heaven Somewhere	(Columbia DB 7597) 1965 SC
Bad Storm Coming/	
Lonely And Blue	(Columbia DB 7712) 1965 SC
All Night Worker/	
He Was A Square	(Columbia DB 7817) 1966 SC
Glendora/I'll Find Out	(Columbia DB 7939) 1966 SC

The Cost Of Living/	
Everything I've Got To Give	(Columbia DB 8008) 1967 SC
Reissues: Little Egypt/Sect Appeal (PS)	(Charly CYS 1020) 1976
Showbiz/Killing Me	(Raw RAW 10) 1977
α Cadillac/Roll Over Beethoven	(Lava LC 5749) 1979 - German
Colour Coded Red/	
You Ain't Doing Me Right	(Inner Mystique IM 5082) 1985 - US

NB α 1963 demos.

The roots of this band go back to a late fifties Twickenham outfit known simply as The Downliners that **Craine** had earlier played in. **The Downliners Sect** was formed in 1963 when The Downliners disintegrated and **Craine** recruited a new line-up out of people he met at various R&B and blues clubs in London.

Their first recording - a live EP on the independent Contrast Sound label in January 1964 - is now very collectable and expensive. It included a cover of Booker T and The MG's *Green Onions*. A few months later, mouth organist Ray Stone was added to their line-up and they were signed by Columbia. For their first 45 they covered Jimmy Reed's *Baby What's Wrong* and put a self-penned composition, *Be A Sect Maniac*, on the flip.

Their debut album, *The Sect*, was largely comprised of enthusiastically delivered Chuck Berry and Bo Diddley songs. The highlight was perhaps their cover of Bo Diddley's *Cops And Robbers*. There was also lots of fine guitar work on the album.

Their second 45 was a chirpy revival of The Coasters' *Little Egypt*, which topped the Swedish hit parade, although it went largely unnoticed over here. Subsequent singles fared less well. *Wreck Of The Old '97* was rather unusual in that it was a sort of countryfied skiffle-styled song.

The *Country Sect* album was an ill-timed attempt by the band to experiment with other musical styles. It included covers of Little Jimmy Dickens' novelty country and western song *May The Bird Of Paradise Fly Up Your Nose!* After this failure *The Rock Sect's In* marked a return to a basic R&B format. It included the first cover of Reed-Cale's *Why Don't You Smile Now?* released in Britain. Once again, though, the sales were disappointing.

By the time of *The Cost Of Living* 45 only Keith Grant and **Don Craine** remained in the band. However, **Craine** and Grant reformed the band under the name **Don Craine's New Downliners Sect** for a one-off, *I Can't Get Away From You/Roses* (Pye 7N 17261), in 1967. This was line-up D and E (which recorded the disc). Matthew Fisher was later in **Procol Harum**. The 45 flopped and **Craine** quit but a further line-up recorded three quasi-psychedelic Swedish Juke Box EPs:- *Spider* (JSEP 5580), *Lord Of The Ring* (JSEP 5584) and *White Caterpillar* (JSEP 55), all in 1968. The band had earlier had an album of their material *Downliners Sect* (HMV SGLP 534) released in Sweden back in 1966. It consisted of material from their various Columbia output. Earlier the same year a different take of *All Night Worker* (with an additional guitar solo not on the UK release) had been issued as a 45 in Sweden, with an alternate take of *Outside* from their third album on the flip.

In the seventies **Don Craine** joined Finnegan's Wake and he was later in a duo with Paul Tiller called Loose End. The almost inevitable reformation of **The Downliners Sect** came in 1976 (line-up F) as they sought to plug into

THE DOWNLINERS SECT.

the pub-rock circuit. Their three original albums were reissued by Charly. A new single, *Showbiz* (the title track of a German-only album) was released. Two demos from 1963, *Cadillac/Roll Over Beethoven*, were put out by the German Lava label in 1979. However, they weren't much in demand and after a US-only 45, *Colour Coded Red*, and the 1986 *Live In The 80s* album was released in Sweden the reformed group began to lose members, but still they soldiered on recording a further album, *Savage Return* (Promised Land 456780) in 1991. **Craine** and Grant also became involved in the British Invasion All-Stars along with former members of **The Yardbirds**, **Nashville Teens** and **Creation**. There's also a **Downliners Sect** album called *The Birth Of Suave* on the Hangman label and at the end of the century **Don Craine** became a some-time member of **Thee Headcoat Sect**, along with cult-garage guru Billy Childish (ex-Milkshakes, Mighty Caesers and current Headcote), who happens to be a big **Downliners Sect** fan.

Those of you into videos should also check out *The Downliners Sect Story - Colour Coded Red* (Brisk Productions EAGLE 12) 1990.

The CD compilation *The Definitive Downliners Sect - Singles A's And B's* includes all the bands 45s and a few of their album tracks too. This band was still inspiring audiences in 2004.

Compilation appearances have included: *Baby What's Wrong* on the *On The Scene* (EP) - they also figured on an album of that name; *Glendora* on *My Generation* (LP) and *Go... With An All Star* (LP); *Break Up* on *Beat Merchants* (CD); *Baby What's Wrong* on *Beat Merchants* (2-LP); *Shake*, *Glendora* and *Living In The USA* on *Hard Up Heroes, Vol. 2* (CD); *Glendora* and *Why Won't You Smile Now* on the 4-CD box set *Nuggets 11*; *The Cost Of Loving* on *Colour Me Pop, Vol 3* (CD); and *White Caterpillar*, *Spider* and *Lord Of The Rings* (three of the psychedelic Swedish Juke-box tracks) on *Incredible Sound Show Stories, Vol. 2* (LP). (VJ)

Dozy, Beaky, Mick and Tich

Personnel:
IAN 'TICH' AMEY	ld gtr		A
TREVOR 'DOZY' DAVIES	bs		A
JOHN 'BEAKY' DYMOND	gtr		A
MICK WILSON	drms		A

ALBUM: 1(A) FRESH EAR (Philips 6308 029) 1970 SC

		HCP
45s:	Tonight Today/Bad News	(Fontana TF 1061) 1970 -
	Mr. President/Frisco Annie(	Fontana 6007 022) 1970 33
	Festival/	
	Leader Of A Rock 'n' Roll Band	(Philips 6006 066) 1970 -
	I Want To Be There/	
	For The Use Of Your Son	(Philips 6006 114) 1970 -
	They Won't Sing My Song/Soukie	(Philips 6006 198) 1972 -

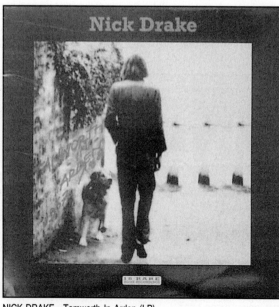

NICK DRAKE - Tamworth In Arden (LP).

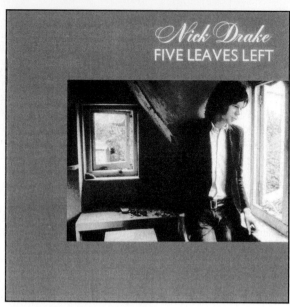

NICK DRAKE - Five Leaves Left (CD).

As the name suggests this was a later version of **Dave Dee, Dozy, Beaky, Mick and Tich** after **Dave Dee** left to go solo. Whilst they didn't achieve the kind of success that they had previously, many **Dave Dee, Dozy, Beaky, Mick and Tich** fans rate *Fresh Ear* very highly.

In 1974, the band also made further recordings for a proposed album called *Tracker*, but these were never completed. You can check out *Mr. President* on *Pop-In, Vol 2* (CD). (VJ/SH/RC)

Dragonfly

ALBUM: 1 ALMOST ABANDONED (Retreat RTL 6002) 1974 SC

45s:	Gondola/Almost Abandoned (demo)	(Retreat RTS 257) 1974 SC
	Driving Around The World/	
	Since I Left My Home	(Retreat RTS 261) 1975

This **Dragonfly** included personnel from **The Alan Bown Set** and is generally described as a hard-rock band. (CG)

Nick Drake

ALBUMS:	1	FIVE LEAVES LEFT	(Island ILPS 9105) 1969 R3
	2	BRYTER LAYTER	(Island ILPS 9134) 1970 R3
	3	PINK MOON	(Island ILPS 9184) 1972 R3
	4	FRUIT TREE (triple LP + booklet)	
			(Island NDSP 100) 1979 R1
	5	HEAVEN IN A WILD FLOWER	
			(Island ILPS 9826) 1985 SC
	6	FRUIT TREE (4-LP box set + booklet)	
			(Hannibal HNBX 5302) 1986 R1
	7	TIME OF NO REPLY	(Hannibal HNBL 1318) 1987 SC

NB: First pressings of (1) came with pink label with black 'circle' logo and gatefold sleeve (R4). Second pressings in gatefold sleeve with pink rim label and palm tree logo (R3). (1) reissued on vinyl (Island ILPS 9105) 1989 (SC) with blue and white palm tree label. (2) issued with pink rim label and palm tree logo (R3). (2) reissued on vinyl (Island ILPS 9134) 1989 (SC) with blue and white palm tree label. (3) issued with pink rim label and palm tree logo (R3). (3) reissued on vinyl (Island ILPS 9184) 1989 (SC) with blue and white palm tree label. All of the above are also available on CD. (1), (2) and (3) on Island (IMCD 8, IMCD 71, and IMCD 94 respectively) 1989. (1) reissued again on CD digitally remastered (Island 8 842 915 2) 2000. (2) reissued again on CD digitally remastered (Island IMCD 71 846 005 2) 2000. (3) reissued again on CD digitally remastered (Island 94 842 923 2) 2000. (7) on (Hannibal HNCD 1318) 1989. Also of interest is *Tamworth In Arden 1967/68* (Anthology ANT 15.00) CD 1998, which compiles eighteen rare recordings made at home, prior to his deal with Island. *Made To Love Magic* (Universal/Island ILPS 8141/986 631-9) 2004 is an album of rarities and remixes. *A Treasury...The Best Of Nick Drake* (Island CID 8149) 2004 is an official 'best of' collection of his songs.

45:	Introduction/Hazy Jane II/Time Has Told Me/Fruit Tree/	
	Rider On The Wheel (one-sided promo-only	
	'Fruit Tree' sampler)	(Island RSS 7) 1979 R3

Nick Drake was born in Burma in 1948 to a very upper-middle class British family. When his parents returned to England half a dozen years later, he spent his childhood at Tamworth-in-Arden (to the northwest of Stratford) initially moving on to a Surrey preparatory school and later to Marlborough Public School. His sister Gabrielle was in the TV soap 'Crossroads'. In 1967 he won a scholarship to read English at Fitzwilliam College, Cambridge, although he preferred to write songs and develop his guitar playing than study. He gave some public performances whilst he was at Cambridge and was eventually recommended by **Ashley Hutchings** (of **Fairport Convention** and **Steeleye Span** fame) to Joe Boyd's Witchseason Productions, who were offering a comprehensive management package-agency, publishing and recording. On the basis of a demo tape **Drake** was rapidly offered a recording contract.

His debut album was in many respects stunning, full of haunting, dream-like melodies and unusual guitar work. The best known track is *Time Has Told Me* by virtue of its inclusion on Island's *Nice Enough To Eat* (LP) sampler. It was later included on a promo-only release in 1986, *Island Life* (Island ISLAND MP1). The sales from the album were sufficient to encourage **Drake** to leave Cambridge to concentrate on a music career, although it passed unnoticed by the majority of the record buyers. To promote the album he did a limited number of 'live' performances which seem to have been much appreciated by the small numbers of people who had the privilege to hear him. Generally, though, he had no enthusiasm for touring.

His second album, *Bryter Layter*, was largely comprised of songs written in his spartan bedsitter in Hampstead. It took over a year to complete because he was very fussy about the musicians who he wanted to work with him on the album. **Richard Thompson** and others connected with **Fairport Convention** were heavily involved and **John Cale** played on two tracks, *Fly* and the shimmering love song *Northern Sky*. Other highlights included *At The Chime Of A City Clock* and *Hazey Jane I*. The critics considered the album magnificent but sadly it was too esoteric to achieve the widespread interest and mass sales that some predicted.

Shortly after *Bryter Layter* Joe Boyd paired Nick up with **Vashti Bunyan** to see whether they could write as a duo, but nothing came of it. The fact that people didn't buy the album in great numbers was a major blow and may have been a contributory factor in his growing depression, which was exacerbated by his producer Joe Boyd's move to Los Angeles to work for Warner Brothers. However, Boyd sold Witchseason to Island and made them agree to release any album **Drake** made as part of the contract. As he became ill **Drake** quit London to return to his parents' home. He recovered enough to rent a flat in Muswell Hill to record his third album, *Pink Moon*. Recorded in just two sessions the album was short and very stark compared to his earlier efforts. It just consists of his vocals, guitar and a piano overdub on one cut. Far less accessible than his earlier two albums it inevitably sold in small quantities and is consequently the hardest of his three albums to find. The songs are full of impending doom and depression, but full of creativity and some of his finest guitar playing. Get to hear *From The Morning* and *Place To Be*. Another stunning track was the unnervingly delightful *Thing Behind The Sun*.

NICK DRAKE - Bryter Later (CD).

NICK DRAKE - Pink Moon (CD).

After recording *Pink Moon* Nick suffered a nervous breakdown and was hospitalised on a voluntary basis for a few weeks. He had become withdrawn from society and was increasingly difficult to communicate with. He recovered sufficiently to record four tracks for a future album, which he later decided to scrap. He possibly intended to re-record them later, but after a short break in Paris he returned to try out new material but tragically died from an overdose of Tryptizol, which he may well have taken to try and get off to sleep.

In addition to his released material, Nick is known to have contributed guitar parts to *Interplay One*, an educational double album recorded by Longman publishers in 1971/2 for use in schools. Only a handful of copies have ever surfaced, and details are available at http://www.michaelorgan.org.au/drake3.htm.

A small number of cover versions of his songs appeared in his lifetime, including *Mayfair* by **Millie**, *Saturday Sun* by **Alexis Korner**, *Time Has Told Me* by **Andrew Johns** and *Free Ride* by **Tir Na Nog**.

Later in 1979 Island produced a box set, *Fruit Tree - The Complete Recorded Works*, compiling his three albums with the four tracks which had been laid down at his final session. It came with a lavish booklet and an extensive biography. There was also a much rarer five track Island promo sampler consisting of *Introduction, Hazy Jane II, Time Has Told Me, Fruit Tree* and *Rider On The Wheel*. In 1985 Island released a 14-track compilation, *Heaven In A Wild Flower*, but the best retrospective collection of his material is the 4-LP box set *Fruit Tree* released by Joe Boyd in 1986 on his own Hannibal label. The extra album consisted of five tracks which had been recorded for the *Five Leaves Left* album but never used, some alternate versions of album tracks and the four songs from his final session. This album was released as a separate item and entitled *Time Of No Reply* in 1987.

The *Made To Love Magic* album compiles rarities and remixes and the previously unreleased song *Tow The Line* (recorded back in 1974). The recordings were made by fellow university student Robert Kirby in spring 1968. They contain the earliest known version of *Mayfair* and an un-orchestrated *River Man*. *A Treasury?The Best Of Nick Drake* is an official 'best of' collection of his songs.

Other compilation appearances have been *Hazy Jane I* on *Bumpers* (2-LP), a double budget priced compilation released in 1970, *One Of These Things First* on *El Pea* (2-LP), another double set released in 1971 and much more recently *Black Eyed Dog* appeared on the CD and cassette version of *Voices* (Hannibal HNCD 8301) in 1990. Collectors may be interested in a US-only compilation comprised of eight tracks from his first two albums and entitled *Nick Drake* (Island ILPS 9307). It came out in 1972 and is hard to find. Also of interest is *Tamworth In Arden 1967/68* (CD), which compiles eighteen rare recordings made at home, prior to his deal with Island.

Those of you who didn't get to hear **Drake**'s stunning work the first time round and who have any appreciation of folk music should be sure to investigate his music now. (VJ/RMJ)

Barry Dransfield

ALBUM: 1 BARRY DRANSFIELD
(up to   (Polydor Folk Mill 2383 160) 1972 R3
1976)

NB: (1) reissued on CD (Spinney 003 CD) 2003

Barry was better known as a member of **The Dransfields**. This debut solo album, which is full of beautiful and enchanting folk music, is one of the most sought-after major label UK folk albums. Highlights include versions of David Ackles' *Be My Friend* and Michael Hurley's *The Werewolf*. The recent Spinney CD reissue will now enable more people to hear it. (VJ/RMJ)

The Dransfields

Personnel:	BARRY DRANSFIELD	vcls, gtr, fiddle	A
	ROBIN DRANSFIELD	vcls, gtr	A
	BRIAN HARRISON	drms	A
	CHARLIE SMITH	vcls, bs, keyb'ds	A

ALBUM: 1(A) THE FIDDLERS DREAM (Transatlantic TRA 322) 1976 SC

NB: (1) reissued on CD (Essential! ESMCD 462) 1997. Unfortunately, the original album artwork has been severely and unnecessarily diminished in size, but there are new sleevenotes from Robin Dransfield. (1) reissued again (Castle CMEDD 943) 2004 as a 2-CD set, the second comprising BBC session and concert tracks.

On offer here is basically folk-rock, with stringed accompaniments, three-part harmonies and a violin. The band recorded on into the eighties. See the **Robin and Barry Dransfield** and **Barry Dransfield** entries for more details.

Compilation appearances include *The Handsome Meadow Boy* on *The Transatlantic Story* CD box set. (VJ)

Robin and Barry Dransfield

ALBUMS: 1 THE ROUT OF THE BLUES (Trailer LER 2011) 1970 SC
(up to   2 LORD OF ALL I BEHOLD   (Trailer LER 2026) 1971 SC
1976)

See also **The Dransfields**. These brothers were talented folk musicians from Harrogate in North Yorkshire. Both albums came on the original red Trailer label and are hard to find now. They feature some fine fiddle playing from Barry who'd been tutored by various friends in Leeds' Irish community. (VJ)

The Dreamers

45:      The Maybe Song/The Long Road   (Columbia DB 8340) 1968

A novelty 45 by Freddie Garrity's backing group. (VJ)

The Dream Police

Personnel incl:	DAVE BATCHELOR	vcls	A
	TED McKENNA	drms	AB
	HAMISH STUART	vcls, gtr	ABC
	JOE BREEN	bs	ABC
	MATT IRVING	organ, gtr	ABC
	CHARLIE SMITH	drms	C

45s: I'll Be Home/Living Is Easy   (Decca F 12998) 1970
        Our Song/Much Too Much   (Decca F 13078) 1970
        I've Got No Choice/
        What's The Cure For Happiness   (Decca F 13105) 1970

A Glasgow-based band, many of whose members went on to greater things. Dave Batchelor and Hugh McKenna who became producer and keyboardist for **Alex Harvey** and McIntyre and Stuart were later in The

THE GREAT BRITISH PSYCHEDELIC TRIP Vol. 2 (Comp CD) including The Dream Police.

Average White Band. Batchelor left to join **Tear Gas** in 1969 before the band recorded. When McKenna departed to the same band in 1970, Charlie Smith joined and they began to record for Decca.

Musically **Dream Police** played an adventurous amalgam of psychedelic and progressive rock. It was **Junior Campbell** who recommended the band to Decca and he produced their debut 45 *I'll Be Home*, which had a melodramatic orchestrated arrangement. The flip side was a more atypical progressive effort. Their third 45 was more in a country-rock style but by now Decca had decided not to extend their option on the band which fragmented soon after.

When the band split up Hamish Stuart and Matt Irving formed a group called The Beserk Crocodiles then a trio who became a trio with Steve Tilson (gtr, vcls). Irving later joined **Longdancer** and Squeeze and Breen and Smith joined **The Poets**. Hamish Stuart later resurfaced in the **Paul McCartney Band**.

Compilation appearances have included: *Living Is Easy* on *Rubble, Vol. 5 - The Electric Crayon Set* (LP), *Rubble, Vol. 3* (CD) and *Broken Dreams, Vol. 3* (LP); and *I'll Be Home (In A Day Or So)* on *British Psychedelic Trip, Vol. 4* (LP) and *Great British Psychedelic Trip, Vol. 2* (CD). (VJ/JM)

The Dreams

ALBUMS: 1 DREAMS   (CBS 64203) 1970
         2 IMAGINE MY SURPRISE   (CBS 64597) 1972

45s: I Will See You There/
         A Boy Needs A Girl   (United Artists UA 2249) 1968
         Baby I'm Your Man/Softly, Softly   (CBS 4247) 1969
         Casatschok/Don't You Ask Me   (Dolphin 4432) 1969

This Irish band was originally known as The Blarney Boys. The story goes that **The Tremeloes** met them whilst in Ireland and Alan Blaikey and 'Chip' Hawkes wrote the 'A' side of the United Artists 45 for them, which not surprisingly sounds similar to **The Tremeloes** at this time.

Softly Softly also appears on *Rubble Vol. 16: Glass Orchid Aftermath* (LP) and *Rubble Vol. 9* (CD). (VJ)

John Drevar('s Expression)

Personnel:	KEITH BENNETT	sax	A
	JOHN DREVAR	vcls	A
	DEREK EDMUNDS	drms	A
	MELV McCRAE	gtr	A
	GEOFF SHAW	organ	A
	COLIN WILSHER	bs	A

The Closer She Gets/
When I Come Home   (MGM MGM 1367) 1967 R2
α   What Greater Love/I've Decided   (Polydor BM 56290) 1968

NB: α as **John Drevar**.

A Southampton Tamla Motown-influenced soul/R&B group who played a lot in Germany. *The Closer She Gets* is a Northern soul rarity.

Driftwood

Personnel: NEIL ALFORD   gtr, vcls   A
            NEIL HARRISON   keyb'ds, vcls   A
            NICK HARRISON   gtr, vcls, hrmnca A
            TONY NEWMAN   drms   A

ALBUM: 1(A) DRIFTWOOD   (Decca SKL 5069) 1970 R1

45s: Shylock Bay/The Wind Cried Above You (Decca F 13084) 1970
      Say The Right Things/
      Still I'll Stay With You   (Decca F 13139) 1971

Neil Harrison, who also made an album for Deram (SML 1115) in 1974, is responsible for most of these songs which never made **Paul McCartney**'s first solo album. They are so inoffensive that they border on insulting the listener. Maybe some find them "poetic". They definitely are not. On the album the band is assisted by three session men: Alan Jones (bs), Zack Laurence (keyb'ds) and Daryl Runswick (bs).

Newman had been in **Sounds Incorporated** and went on to **May Blitz**. Zack Laurence was later with Mr. Bloe. Daryl Runswick had played with **Ray Russell** and backed **Bill Fay** on his second album. He went on to **The Henry Lowther Band** and **Atlantic Bridge**. (MK/JM)

Julie Driscoll

ALBUM: 1   JULIE DRISCOLL - 1969   (Polydor 2480 074) 1971 R1

NB: (1) reissued on Polydor (2383 077) in 1972 (SC).

45s: Take Me By The Hand/
      Stay Away From Me   (Columbia DB 7118) 1963 R1
      Don't Do It No More/I Know You (Parlophone R 5296) 1965 R1
      I Didn't Want To Have To Do It/
      Don't Do It No More   (Parlophone R 5444) 1966 SC
      I Know You Love Me Not/
      If You Should Ever Leave Me (Parlophone R 5588) 1967 SC
      Save Me Pts 1 & 2   (Marmalade 598 005) 1968 SC

Born in London on 8 June 1947 **Julie**'s first connection with the music world was as fan club secretary for **The Yardbirds**, but then producer Georgio Gomelski suggested she would make an excellent member for **Steampacket**, which she joined in 1964. Having already recorded a solo 45 in 1963, when **Steampacket** folded she tried her hand at some more though none of them are particularly memorable. When she became vocalist for the **Brian Auger Trinity** she gained far greater exposure becoming one of the sex symbols and best female singers of the late sixties.

For her solo album *Julie Driscoll - 1969* she enlisted help from members of **Soft Machine** and **Blossom Toes** and it marked a move from pop towards progressive jazz. **Keith Tippett** was also on the record; she later married him, became Julie Tippett and played with his avant-garde ensembles **Centipede** and **Ovary Lodge**.

Her innovative 1974 album *Sunset Glow* (recorded under her married name) ranged from folk to free jazz. In 1976, she formed the experimental vocal quartet Voice with Brian Ely, Phil Minton and Maggie Nicols. She duo'd with Nicols two years later on the album *Sweet and s'Ours*. In the eighties, she released *Couple In Spirit* with her husband. In 1991, she was involved with musicians from the UK and Georgia (from the former USSR) in the Mujician/Georgian Ensemble. She re-recorded her classic song *This Wheel's On Fire* as the theme to the highly successful BBC comedy 'Absolutely Fabulous' the following year.

Compilation appearances include: *This Wheel's On Fire* on *The Marmalade Record Co. Show Olympia 68* (LP) and *Don't Do It No More* and *I Didn't Want To Have To Do It* on *Hippy Chick* (CD). (VJ)

Julie Driscoll, Brian Auger and The Trinity

Personnel: DAVE AMBROSE   bs   A
            BRIAN AUGER   keyb'ds, vcls   A
            GARY BOYLE   gtr   A
            JULIE DRISCOLL   vcls   A
            DAVE THACKER   drms   A

                                      HCP
ALBUMS: 1(A) OPEN
          (mono/stereo)   (Marmalade 607/608 002) 1967 R2 12
      2(A) JOOLS/BRIAN (Music For Pleasure MFP 1265) 1968 SC -
      3(A) STREETNOISE (2-LP)   (Marmalade 608 005/6) 1969 R3 -

NB: (3) was also available as two single albums *Part One* (Marmalade 608 014) 1969 (R2) and *Part Two* (Marmalade 608 015) 1969 (R2). (1) and (3) issued on Atco in the US. (3) reissued on CD (Polydor 843 999 2) 1990, but deleted in 1992. (1) reissued on CD (Disconforme DISC 1002 CD) 1999 and on vinyl (Disconforme SL DISC 1901 LP) 2001. (3) reissued on CD (Disconforme DISC 1005 CD) 1999 and on vinyl (Disconforme SL DISC 1905 LP) 2001. *The Mood Years* (Disconforme SL DISC 1922 LP) 2001 is a 2-LP set.

                                        HCP
45s: This Wheel's On Fire/
      A Kind Of Love-In   (Marmalade 598 006) 1968 5
      The Road To Cairo/
      Shadows Of You   (Marmalade 598 011) 1968 -
      Take Me To The Water/
      Indian Rope Man   (Marmalade 598 018) 1968 SC -
Reissues: This Wheel's On Fire/
      The Road To Cairo   (Polydor 2058 119) 1971 -
      This Wheel's On Fire   (Old Gold OG 9427) 1984 -

Sadly short-lived, but the combination of **Driscoll**'s vocals and sex appeal and **Auger**'s musicianship was stunning for a while. The organ-driven *This Wheel's On Fire* (a Dylan composition) was a massive international hit and *The Road To Cairo* was similar and almost as good. However, she left the band in 1968 during an American tour and after starring in a TV play 'The Season Of The Witch' recorded her solo album in 1969. Then she faded from the limelight re-appearing just occasionally in the seventies to play with her husband **Keith Tippett**'s **Centipede** in the early seventies and to make a solo album under her married name, *Sunset Glow* (Utopia UTS 601) in 1976.

Completists will be interested in seeking out the Italian issue of the *Open* album, for the version of *Black Cat* which is sung in Italian by **Auger**.

The band can also be heard on a number of compilations:- *Marmalade - 100 Proof* (LP) included *Let The Sunshine In*, *Tropic Of Capricorn* and

JULIE DRISCOLL, BRIAN AUGER AND THE TRINITY - Open (CD).

Word About Colour, *Deep Overground Pop* (LP) featured *Kind Of Love-In* and *Season Of The Witch*; *Supergroups* (LP) included *Indian Ropeman* and *Take Me To The Water* can be heard on *Rock Party* (2-LP). More recently, *This Wheel's On Fire* and *Road To Cairo* have been compiled on the 3-CD box set *Ars Longa Vita Brevis: A Compendium Of Progressive Rock 1967-1974*. (VJ/PV)

Droop

45:      Louise/Caught Us Doin' It   (RCA RCA 2411) 1973

For this one and only single **Brewers Droop** shortened their name to **Droop**. (VJ)

Druid

Personnel:	NEIL BREWER	bs	ABC
	DANE STEVENS	gtr, vcls	ABC
	CEDRIC SHARPLEY	drms, perc	ABC
	MALCOLM	sax	A
	PETE	organ	A
	ANDREW McCRORIE - SHAND	keyb'ds	C

ALBUMS:	1(C)	TOWARDS THE SUN	(EMI EMC 3081) 1975
	2(C)	FLUID DRUID	(EMI EMC 3128) 1976

NB: (1) and (2) reissued on one CD (Beat Goes On BGOCD 285) 1995.

Druid evolved out of a three-piece, consisting Brewer, Sharpley and someone called Robin, who in 1970 was known as Maggot. They soon added a sax player called Malcolm, and shortly after an organist (Pete) before changing names to **Druid**. They gigged in their local area of Berkhamstead, Herts. Robin left in 1971, to be replaced by Dane Stevens. The following year Malcolm and Pete left too, and from then on the line-up stabilised as 'B'.

In June 1974 they won the 'Melody Maker' Rock & Folk Contest and with the prize money of £800 bought some new equipment. Soon after the contest McCrorie-Shand became their final keyboard player.

Both of their albums of melodic and carefully constructed pop/progressivism (very close to **Yes** in their sound) have now been reissued on CD, and it's worth noticing that the Beeb's Bob Harris handled production duties on the first.

The Beat Goes On 2-on-1 CD has lots of good background information on this band which would have attracted much more attention if it had been around a few years earlier. (VJ)

Druid Chase

45:      Take Me In Your Garden/
            I Wanna Get My Hands On You   (CBS 3053) 1967 SC

A hopelessly obscure band but you can at least hear the 'A' side of this disc, which is now a minor collectable, on *Circus Days Vol. 3* (LP & CD). **Druid Chase** were also responsible for an unreleased acetate *Druid Chase* in 1967. In addition to both sides of their 45 it contains lots of other Swinging London pop with female vocals like *Child Of Summer*, *In The Half Light*, *Pass The Peace Pipe* and *Find Brown Frame*. (VJ)

The Druids

Personnel:	JOHN ADAMS	vcls, mandolin, bs	A
	DAVE BROUGHTON	fiddle, accordian	A
	MICK HENNESSY	vcls, bs	A
	KEITH KENDRICK	vcls, gtr, banjo	A
	JUDI LONGDEN	vcls	A

ALBUMS:	1(A)	BURNT OFFERING	(Argo ZFB 22) 1970 R2
	2(A)	PASTIME WITH GOOD COMPANY	
			(Argo ZFB 39) 1972 R2

A folk band who formed in Derby in 1969. Their first album came in a striking sleeve and both are now hard to find. Musically, though, they are unexceptional and full of rehashes of traditional material. Some members went on to play in **Giles Farnaby's Dream Band** and Muckram Rakes. (VJ)

The Druids

Personnel:	KEN GRIFFITHS	gtr	A
	JEFF KANE	drms	A
	GEARIE KENTWORTHY	bs	A
	BRIAN MIXTER	lead gtr	A

45s:	Long Tall Texan/Love So Blue	(Parlophone R 5097) 1963 R3
	See What You've Done/	
	It's Just A Little Bit Too Late	(Parlophone R 5134) 1964 R3

An R&B band from Chingford in Essex who played a lot in Hamburg. Kentworthy was originally born in Canada and is thought to have joined **Simon Dupree and The Big Sound**, as Geary Kenworthy for a short period. (JM/VJ)

Dry Ice

Personnel incl:	PAUL GARDNER	
	TERRY SULLIVAN	drms

45:	Running To The Convent/	
	Nowhere To Go	(B&C CB 115) 1970 SC

A very obscure group but the 'A' side to this 45, *Running To The Convent*, is really very good - great vocals and very bouncy instrumentation. Paul Gardner was later in **Pluto**.

Compilation appearances include: *Running To The Convent* on *Circus Days Vol. 1 & 2* (CD) and *Circus Days, Vol. 1* (LP) and *Nowhere To Go* on *Jagged Time Lapse, Vol 4* (CD).

Ducks Deluxe

Personnel:	MARTIN BELMONT	gtr, vcls	ABCDE
	NICK GARVEY	bs, vcls	ABC
	TIM ROPER	drms	ABCD
	SEAN TYLA	gtr, vcls	ABCDE
	KEN WHALEY	bs, vcls	A
	ANDY McMASTERS	keyb'ds, vcls	C
	MICKY GROOME	bs, vcls	DE
	BILLY RANKIN	drms	E
	BRINSLEY SCHWARTZ	gtr, vcls	E

DUCKS DELUXE - Ducks Deluxe (LP).

```
ALBUMS: 1(A)   DUCKS DELUXE            (RCA LPLI 5008) 1974
(up to   2(C)   TAXI TO THE TERMINAL ZONE   (RCA SF 8402) 1975
1976)    3(-)   DON'T MIND ROCKIN' TONITE   (RCA PLZ 25132) 1978
```

NB: (1) and (2) reissued on CD (Mau Mau/Demon MAU CD 610) 1992 and again on a 2-CD set (BGO BGOCD 539) 2002. Also relevant is *Last Night Of A Pub Rock Band* (Blue Moon BMLP 001)1979.

```
EP:      1(D)   JUMPIN'                 (Skydog EP 005) 1975
```

```
45s:     Coast To Coast/
(up to   Bring Back That Packard Car    (RCA RCA 2438) 1973
1976)    Fireball/Saratoga Suzie        (RCA LPBO 5019) 1974
         Love's Melody/Two Time Twister (RCA RCA 2477) 1974
         I Fought The Law/Cherry Pie    (RCA RCA 2531) 1975
```

Ducks Deluxe was part of the London pub-rock scene. They formed in August 1972 and soon got a residency at the Tally Ho twice a week. After signing to RCA they cut a debut album in 1974, which was well received. It featured most of the live material they had been playing at gigs prior to its release in 1973. Highlights from this include the **Beatles'**-influenced *Please Please Please* and *Fireball*, complete with its nasal style vocals.

Taxi To The Terminal Zone is similar in style to their debut but doesn't reach the same heights.

Last Night Of A Pub Rock Band is a double album recorded live at the 100 Club, London, on 1 July 1975.

Ken Whaley departed to rejoin **Help Yourself** in December 1972. He was later in **Man**. With the addition of Scotsman Andy McMasters, who'd previously been in **The Sabres**, they recorded a second album which was nowhere as good as the first. With the band's fortunes on a downward edge Nick Garvey, who'd once been The Flamin' Groovies road manager, departed to form Snakes. McMasters also left and was later in The Motors with Nick Garvey. The remaining three soldiered on with the addition of Micky Groome, who'd once been in **The Nashville Teens**, but they were dropped by RCA and reduced to recording an EP, *Jumpin'* on Skydog. Former **Brinsley Schwarz** members **Brinsley Schwarz** and Billy Rankin supplemented the band in their final months. On the Continent they had built up a good following but their recording career was going nowhere and they finally called it a day in the Summer of 1975.

Sean Tyla went on to form The Tyla Gang, who also included Ken Whaley. **Brinsley Schwarz** and Martin Belmont went on to play for **Graham Parker and The Rumour**.

They can also be heard singing *Boogaloo Babe* on the *Christmas At The Patti* (2x10") compilation.

Micky Groome later released two solo CDs *Yo!* and *Soul Rider*. The 2002 2-CD remastered release of their first two albums comes with detailed sleevenotes. (VJ/HS)

Duffy

```
ALBUM:   1   SCRUFFY DUFFY       (Chapter One CHSR 814) 1973 R2
```

```
45:      The Joker/Running Away  (Chapter One CH 184) 1973 SC
```

This band also released a second European-only album, *Just In Case You're Interested*. This was released on Ariola (85 846) in Italy. (VJ)

Duffy's Nucleus

```
Personnel:   TERRY COX          drms        A
             JOHN McLAUGHLIN    gtr         A
             DANNY THOMPSON     double bs   A
             DUFFY POWER        vcls        A
```

```
45:      Hound Dog/Mary Open The Door   (Decca F 22547) 1967 R1
```

An R'n'B band whose haunting, jazzy, slowed down rendition of Elvis Presley's *Hound Dog* later resurfaced on *R&B Scene, Vol. 2* (LP) and *British R'n'B Explosion, Vol. 1* (CD). *Mary Open The Door* can also be

DULCIMER - And I Turned As I Had Turned As A Boy (LP) (US cover).

heard on *The Soul Of British R'n'B 1962-68* and *British R'n'B Explosion, Vol. 1* (CD). It was a **Duffy Power** song. More recently another version of *Hound Dog* has appeared on Edsel's 1992 CD *Little Boy Blue*. **Duffy Power** also made solo recordings.

Duffy's Nucleus also had a 1967 French-only EP, which in addition to both sides of the UK 45 included, *It's Funny*, a song he wrote with **John McLaughlin** and his own composition, *Little Boy Blue* (Decca 457 142 M). Their UK 45 was reissued in Germany in 1971 in an attractive art sleeve (Philips 6003 066). (VJ)

Don Duggan and The Savoys

```
45:      Let Her Dance/Westmeath Bachelor   (Pye 17633) 1968
```

Let Her Dance is a pleasant version of a Bobby Fuller number. The 'B' side is a traditional Irish song suggesting this was probably an Irish show band. (VJ)

Dukes Noblemen

```
45:      City Of Windows/
         Thank You For Your Loving   (Philips BF 1691) 1968
```

This 45 was the band's sole vinyl offering. (VJ)

Dulcimer

```
Personnel:   RICHARD DODD    vcls                   A
             DAVE EVES       gtr, hrmnca, recorder  A
             PETE HODGE      gtr, dulcimer          A
             JEM NORTH       bs, perc               A
```

```
ALBUM:   1(A)   AND I TURNED AS I HAD TURNED AS A BOY
                                 (Nepentha 6437 003) 1971 R2
```

NB: (1) issued on Mercury (61355) in the US and reissued on See For Miles (SEE 266) 1989 and on CD (SEE CD 266) in 1992. *Room For Thought* (Background HBG 122/6) 1992 gave a CD release to their previously unreleased second album.

This folk-rock album is now quite sought-after by collectors. It was produced by Larry Page (the man behind **The Troggs**), but is simply pleasant but unexceptional folk music, somewhat marred by Richard Todd reciting poetry over the opening track on each side. The band was from Gloucestershire and two of the album's stronger tracks are *Gloucester City* and *Fruit Of The Musical Tree*, an effective English folk Indian raga fusion.

They also recorded a second album, *Room For Thought*, funded by Larry Page in 1971, but it remained unissued until 1992, when Background put it out on CD with the original artwork. Earlier in 1980 a privately-pressed album, *A Land Fit For Heroes* was released. (VJ)

Dum

45:    In The Mood/Watching The Clock   (Rak RAK 179) 1974

This was actually **Mud** using a pseudonym. Both sides can also be heard on *The Singles '67 - '78* (CD) 1998. *Watching The Clock* was a mediocre piece, almost identical to another **Mud** 'B' side, *Watching The Clock Again*. (VJ)

John Dummer (Blues Band)

Personnel:			
JOHN DUMMER	drms	ABCD
DAVE KELLY	gtr, vcls	ABCD
ROGER PEARCE	gtr	A
STEVE RYE	harp, vcls	A
TONY WALKER	bs	A
BOB HALL	piano	BC
JOHN O'LEARY	harp	BC
THUNDER THOMPSON	bs	BCD
TONY McPHEE	gtr	C
ADRIAN PIETRYGA	gtr	D

ALBUMS:	1(C)	CABAL	(Mercury SMCL 20136) 1969 R2
	2(C)	JOHN DUMMER BLUES BAND	(Mercury SMCL 20167) 1969 R3
	3(D)	FAMOUS MUSIC BAND	(Philips 6309 008) 1970 R1
	4( )	NINE BY NINE	(Philips 6382 039) 1972 R1
	5( )	BLUE	(Vertigo 6360 055) 1972 R2
	6( )	OOBLEEDOOBLEE JUBILEE	(Vertigo 6360 083) 1973 R1
	7( )	TRY ME ONE MORE TIME	(Philips 6382 040) 1973 R1
	8( )	VOLUME II	(Philips 6382 083) 1973 SC

NB: (1) reissued on CD as *Cabal... Plus* with eight bonus tracks (See For Miles SEECD 456). (5) reissued on CD (Repertoire REP 4450-WP) 1994.

45s:	Travellin' Man/Forty Days	(Mercury MF 1040) 1969
	Try Me One More Time/ Riding At Midnight	(Mercury MF 1119) 1969
α	Nine By Nine/Going In The Out	(Philips 600 6111) 1970
β	Oobleedooblee Jubilee/ The Monkey Speaks His Mind	(Vertigo 6059 074) 1972

NB: α as John Dummer Famous Music Band. β as John Dummer Oobleedooblee Band.

This blues outfit formed in the Summer of 1967 in London. By the beginning of 1968 Tony Walker and Roger Pearce had both quit the music business. Line-up (B) played a solid Chicago-styled blues. In July 1968 they turned professional. By now Steve Rye had departed for Simon and Steve and **Tony McPhee**, a friend of **Dave Kelly's**, came in on guitar. However, **McPhee**'s stay was brief - a few month later he left to join **The**

Groundhogs. Their two albums for Mercury are the most sought-after by collectors.

Dummer followed this with Music Band, a venture with violinist Nick Pickett, which achieved little here but had a French hit with *Nine By Nine*.

Shortening their name to **John Dummer** they signed to Vertigo recording *Blue*, with a cover designed by Roger Dean. The music was still competent blues-rock, but nowhere near as good as their earlier late sixties offerings on Mercury. Then, teaming up again with his original guitarist Dave Kelly, **Dummer** recorded *Oobleedooblee Jubilee* with a country-influenced band. This was a dreadful album and **Dummer** went on to hit the skins for another appalling (if commercially successful band) Darts.

Only his early albums are recommended. John Dummer's Famous Music Band's French hit *Nine By Nine* can also be heard on Vertigo's 1971 compilation *Heads Together, First Round* (2-LP). (VJ)

Aynsley Dunbar

Personnel:			
VICTOR BROX	trumpet, keyb'ds, vcls	ABC
AYNSLEY DUNBAR	drms	ABC
JOHN MOORSHEAD	gtr, vcls	ABC
KEITH TILLMAN	bs	A
ALEX DMOCHOWSKI	bs	BC
TOMMY EYRE	keyb'ds	C

ALBUMS:	1(B)	AYNSLEY DUNBAR'S RETALIATION	(Liberty LBL/LBS 83154) 1968 R1
	2(B)	DR. DUNBAR'S PRESCRIPTION	(Liberty LBS 83177) 1969 R1
	3(B)	TO MUM FROM AYNSLEY AND THE BOYS	(Liberty LBS 83223) 1969 R1
	4(C)	REMAINS TO BE HEARD	(Liberty LBS 83316) 1970 R1
	5(C)	BLUE WHALE	(Warner Bros WS 3010) 1970 SC

NB: (5) Catalogue number changed to (K 46062) in 1971, following the Warner Bros / Elektra / Reprise merger. (1) to (3) issued by Blue Thumb in the USA and by Byg in France.

45s:	Warning/Cobwebs	(Blue Horizon 57-3109) 1967
	Watch'n'Chain/Roamin' And Ramblin'	(Liberty LBF 15132) 1967
	Watch'n'Chain/Roamin' And Ramblin'	(Liberty LIB 15132) 1968

Liverpudlian **Dunbar** had played with **The Mojos**, **John Mayall** and **Jeff Beck** prior to forming his own blues-based band in 1967. An early version of the band comprised **Dunbar**, **Peter Green**, **Jack Bruce** and **Rod Stewart** recording a song called *Stone Crazy* for Blue Horizon but it was not issued at the time. It appeared several years later on *History Of British Blues* along with *Cobwebs*, the flip of their first 45.

The early albums are fairly routine blues records. *Blue Whale* veered more towards progressive rock with lots of improvisation. It includes four long

AYNSLEY DUNBAR - Retaliation (CD).

AYNSLEY DUNBAR - Dr. DUNBAR'S PRESCRIPTION (CD).

AYNSLEY DUNBAR - TO MUM FROM AYNSLEY AND THE BOYS (CD).

tracks written by the band's vocalist Paul Williams and a version of Frank Zappa's *Willie The Pimp*. The best track is *It's Your Turn*.

Later in the seventies he moved to America. First, joining The Mothers Of Invention, then subsequently moving into session work for **David Bowie** among others. In 1974 he filled the drummer slot in Journey, a San Franciscan band, and in 1979 fulfilled the same role for Jefferson Starship.

The band also cropped up on a number of compilations. You'll find *Call Me Woman* on *Gutbucket* (LP); *Cobwebs Warning* on *In Our Own Way (Oldies But Goodies)* (LP) and *Sugar On The Line* on *Son Of Gutbucket* (LP). (VJ)

Lesley Duncan

ALBUMS:	1	SING CHILDREN SING	(CBS 64202) 1971
(up to	2	EARTH MOTHER	(CBS 64807) 1972
1977)	3	EVERYTHING CHANGES	(GM GML 1007) 1974
	4	MOONBATHING	(GM GML 1017) 1975
	5	MAYBE IT'S LOST	(GM GML 1019) 1977

NB: (1) and (2) issued on CD (Demon/Edsel).

45s:	α	I Want A Steady Guy/Movin' Away	(Parlophone R 5034) 1963
(up to		Tell Me/You Kissed Me Boy	(Parlophone R 5106) 1964
1977)		When My Baby Cries/Did It Hurt	(Mercury MF 830) 1964
		Just For The Boy/See That Guy	(Mercury MF 847) 1965
		Run To Love/Only The Lonely And Me	(Mercury MF 876) 1965
		Hey Boy/Go To Sleep	(Mercury MF 939) 1965
		Lullaby/I Love You I Love You	(RCA RCA 1746) 1968
		Sing Children Sing/Exactly Who Are You	(CBS 4585) 1969
		Road To Nowhere/Love Song	(RCA RCA 1783) 1969
		Sing Children Sing/Emma	(CBS 7493) 1971
		Earth Mother/Love Will Never Loose You	(CBS 8362) 1972
		Watch The Tears/Sam	(GM GMS 16) 1974
		Everything Changes/Love Melts Away	(GM GMS 22) 1974
		I Can't See Where I'm Going/Heaven Knows	(GM GMS 36) 1975
		Could've Been A Winner/Moonbathing	(GM GMS 9040) 1975
		Maybe It's Lost/Another Rainy Day	(GM GMS 9046) 1977
		Sky's On Fire/Don't Worry 'Bout It	(GM GMS 9048) 1977

NB: α as Lesley Duncan and The Jokers.

This singer/songwriter folk artist began her career singing pop songs in the sixties with her group The Jokers. She was also one of Britain's top session vocalists. She sang on recordings by **Michael Chapman**, **Dave Clark Five**, **Elton John**, **Pink Floyd** and on the soundtrack of *Jesus Christ Superstar*. Her songs were covered by **Elton John**, **Long John Baldry** and Olivia Newton-John. Her albums are pleasant if a bit bland.

Her early singles made little commercial impact. Her first break came when **Elton John** included her composition *Love Song* on his *Tumbleweed*

Connection album. This led to her getting a contract with CBS and her debut album's title track featured **Elton John** on piano. She collaborated again with John on her *Moonbathing* album, which included them performing a live duet version of *Love Song*. She never made it as a solo artist and was dropped by MCA in 1976 because of poor album sales. She continued to record as a singles artist working with producer Tony Cox until 1986.

She continues to perform with her husband Jimmy Horowitz (keyb'ds) and **Chris Spedding** (gtr). (VJ/BS)

Pete Dunton

45:	Taking Time/Still Confused	(Rockfield ROC 3) 1973

This was a solo effort by the drummer of **Gun** and **T2**. It was produced by **Dave Edmunds**. (VJ)

Simon Dupree and The Big Sound

Personnel:	ERIC HINE	keyb'ds	AB
	PETE O'FLAHERTY	bs	A
	TONY RANSLEY	drms	A
	DEREK SHULMAN	vcls	AB
	PHIL SHULMAN	sax	AB
	RAY SHULMAN	bs, gtr, vcls	AB
	GEARY KENWORTHY	bs	B
	MARTIN SMITH	drms	B
			HCP

ALBUMS:	1(A)	WITHOUT RESERVATIONS		
		(Parlophone PMC/PCS 7029) 1967	R1	39
	2(A)	AMEN	(See For Miles CM 109) 1982	-

NB: (1) repressed (Parlophone PCS 7029) 1969 (SC) with a silver and black label. (1) originally issued with a yellow and black label. (2) later reissued in 1986 as *Kites* and on CD (SEE CD 368) in 1993. *Part Of My Past: The Simon Dupree and The Big Sound Anthology* (EMI 5937272) 2004 is a 2-CD set.

EP:	1	SIMON DUPREE AND THE BIG SOUND	
			(EMI EMI 2893) 1978

NB: (1) contains *Kites/For Whom The Bell Tolls/I See The Light/Reservations*.

			HCP
45s:	I See The Light/It Is Finished	(Parlophone R 5542) 1966	-
	Reservations/You Need A Man	(Parlophone R 5574) 1967	-
	Day Time, Night Time/		
	I've Seen It All Before	(Parlophone R 5594) 1967	-
	Kites/Like The Sun Like The Fire	(Parlophone R 5646) 1967	9

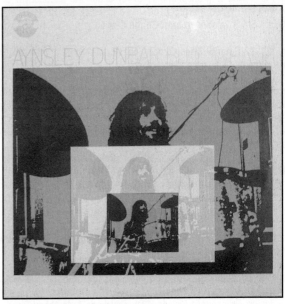

AYNSLEY DUNBAR - Blue Whale (LP).

239

For Whom The Bell Tolls/Sleep	(Parlophone R 5670)	1968 43
Part Of My Past/		
This Story Never Ends	(Parlophone R 5697)	1968 -
Thinking About My Life/		
Velvet And Lace	(Parlophone R 5727)	1968 -
Broken Hearted Pirates/		
She Gave Me The Sun	(Parlophone R 5757)	1969 -
The Eagle Flies Tonight/		
Give It All Back	(Parlophone R 5816)	1969 -
Reissue: Kites/(Flip by different artist)	(Old Gold OG 9655)	1987 -

Simon Dupree started out The Howling Wolves and later became The Road Runners, a Portsmouth-based R&B band. 'Simon Dupree' was actually vocalist Ray Shulman and the band got the new name in 1966. Their early music was almost entirely soul, mostly Wilson Pickett and Otis Redding covers.

Their debut 45, *I See The Light*, was a good stomping R&B number, but it made little impression on the record buying public. The flip side was more soul-based with lots of brass. Their follow-up, *Reservations*, was an uptempo, organ-driven R&B number, which was certainly one of their better singles. It's sales were quite encouraging although it failed to make the Charts. The flip side, *You Need A Man*, was frankly nondescript.

Their next release, *Day Time, Night Time*, was another organ-led R&B belter. A fine record of its type but again it failed to Chart. The flip side was similar in style but a weaker composition. At this time the band was the subject of a surprisingly explicit BBC 'Man Alive' documentary entitled 'The Ravers', focusing on girls who 'collect groups like autographs'. Details and stills are available at http://homepages.ihug.co.nz/~peterkin/simon-dupree-the-ravers-doco.htm.

Their album, *Without Reservations*, released at the start of August 1967, included much of the material from their live act. There's the soul medley, *60 Minutes Of Your Love/A Lot Of Love*, a cover of Sam Cooke's *Amen*, as well as some self-penned compositions like *Who Cares* and *Get Off My Bach*. The only remotely psych-pop track was *There's A Little Picture Playhouse* and the album certainly isn't worth purchasing for connoisseurs of psychedelia, but it is if soul or R&B is your scene.

The release of the quasi-psychedelic *Kites* in October 1967 marked a drastic change of image and musical direction. Recorded at the Abbey Road studios it's full of interesting sound effects and instruments like the mellotron, gongs and vibraphone. It shot them into the Top Ten but gave them an image that was at odds with their R&B roots which they had difficulty reconciling themselves to. The flip side, *Like The Sun Like The Fire*, also had a hint of *Sgt. Pepper* about it but wasn't quite as good.

From here on the band's career was in decline through their failure to score another Top Twenty hit. Of their later singles, *For Whom The Bell Tolls* and *Broken Hearted Pirates*, are the most interesting. The former did reach No 43 in the Charts in April 1968. It features some pleasant flamenco-style guitar and another strong vocal performance from Ray Shulman as well as tolling bells, naturally. They also recorded a single called *We Are The Moles Pts 1 And 2* (Parlophone R 5743) under the pseudonym of **The Moles** in 1968. When the group dissolved in 1969, the Shulman brothers and Martin Smith went on to form **Gentle Giant**.

Amen, a 1982 See For Miles compilation, included most of their 'A' and 'B' sides and many tracks from their album.

A second unreleased album of **Simon Dupree and The Big Sound** material was recorded and titled, *Once More Into The Breach Dear Friends*. This would have featured the original version of *Castle in The Sky* (later recorded by **Blonde On Blonde**), but this album was shelved when the singles stiffed.

In 1978 EMI devoted one of their NUT EP series to the band. The four track EP included their two hits:- *Kites* and *For Whom The Bell Tolls* and their first two are 'A' sides:- *I See The Light* and *Reservations* - four of the songs the band are best remembered for.

The 2-CD anthology *Part Of My Past* suggest that their strengths were confined largely to their 45s.

Compilation appearances have included: *Kites* and *We Are The Moles* on *Not Just Beat Music 1965-70* (LP); *We Are The Moles* on *My Generation* (LP); *Kites* on *Psychedelic Visions* (CD), *Psychedelia At Abbey Road* (CD),

British Psychedelic Trip, Vol. 2 (LP), *Great British Psychedelic Trip, Vol. 3* (LP), *Psychedelia and The Underground* (CD) and on the 4-CD box set *Acid Drops, Spacedust & Flying Saucers*; *Part Of My Past, I See The Light, Thinking About My Life* and *Velvet And Lace* on *Sixties Years, Vol. 5* (CD). *Thinking About My Life* can also be heard on *Colour Me Pop, Vol 1* (CD); *Day Time, Night Time* has been compiled on *Colour Me Pop, Vol 2* (CD); and *I've Seen It All Before* resurfaced on *Jagged Time Lapse, Vol 4* (CD). (VJ/RMJ)

Judith Durham

ALBUMS:	1	FOR CHRISTMAS WITH LOVE	
			(Columbia SCX 6374) 1969 SC
	2	GIFT OF SONG	(A&M AMLS 967) 1970 SC
	3	CLIMB EV'RY MOUNTAIN	(A&M AMLS 2011) 1971

HCP

45s:	The Non Performing Lion Quickstep/	
	The Olive Tree	(Columbia DB 8207) 1967 33
	Again And Again/Memories	(Columbia DB 8290) 1967 -
	I Wanna Dance To Your Music/	
	Mama's Got The Blues	(Pye 7N 45312) 1974 -
	What'll I Do/The Hottest Band In Town	(Pye 7N 45365) 1974 -
	It's Gonna Be A Beautiful Day/	
	Chase The Blues Away	(Pye 7N 45389) 1974 -

The Australian-born former vocalist with The Seekers **Judith Durham** was the woman with the crystal clear voice who was partly responsible for their success. These discs were the product of her unsuccessful attempt to launch a solo career. (VJ)

Terry Durham

ALBUM:	1	CRYSTAL TELEPHONE (mono/stereo)	
		(w/insert)	(Deram DML/SML 1042) 1969 SC

This was an early solo outing for **Durham**, who was later in **Storyteller**. It largely consists of spoken poetry, with a soft jazzy background that occasionally sparks into something groovier. (VJ/RMJ)

SIMON DUPREE AND THE BIG SOUND - Kites (LP).

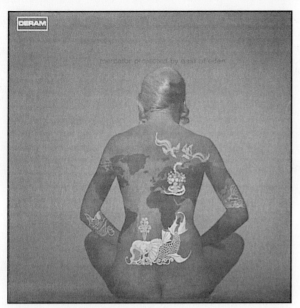

EAST OF EDEN - Mercator Projected (LP).

Gus Eadon Band

Personnel incl: GUS EADON   vcls

45:       Times Are Hard Now, Ain't They/
          Ladybird   (Dawn DNS 1043) 1973

Gus Eadon had replaced **Steve Ellis** as vocalist in **The Love Affair** prior to setting up his own band. (VJ)

Earth

Personnel:			
DAVID BALITO			A
RANGFORD			A
PETER SPEARING			A
GREG VANDYKE	keyb'ds		A

45s: Resurrection City/Comical Man   (CBS 4671) 1969 R1
          Stranger Of Fortune/
          Everybody Sing The Song   (Decca F 22908) 1969 SC

This group was from Plymouth. You can get to hear *Resurrection City* with its good guitar work on *Circus Days Vol. 3* (LP & CD). The first is the most sought-after of their two quite collectable 45s. The second was recorded by a modified line-up.

Greg Vandyke is now a record dealer in Plymouth. (VJ)

The Earthlings

45:       Landing Of The Daleks/
          March Of The Robots   (Parlophone R 5242) 1965 R1

This was an instrumental combo from Birmingham. (VJ)

East of Eden

Personnel incl:			
DAVE ARBUS	violin, flute	ABCDE
RON CAINES	sax	AB
DAVE DUFONT	drms	A
GEOFF NICHOLSON	ld gtr	AB
STEVE YORK	bs	A
GEOFF BRITTON	drms	B
ANDY SNEDDON	bs	B
DAVID JACKS	vcls	CD F
JIM ROCHE	gtr	CD
JEFF ALLEN	drms	DEF
DAVE WELLER	sax	D F
MARTIN FISHER		E
JOE O'DONNELL	violin	E
GARTH WATT ROY	gtr	E
LES DAVIDSON	gtr	F
PETER FILLEUL	keyb'ds	F
DEAN FORD	vcls	F
GEORGE HOWDEN	trumpet	F

			HCP
ALBUMS: 1(A)	MERCATOR PROJECTED		
(up to		(Deram DML/SML 1038) 1969	R1 -
1976) 2(B)	SNAFU	(Deram SML 1050) 1970	SC 29
3(C)	EAST OF EDEN	(Harvest SHVL 792) 1971	SC -
4(D)	NEW LEAF	(Harvest SHVL 796) 1971	SC -
5(-)	WORLD OF	(Decca SPA 157) 1971	-
6(-)	JIG-A-JIG	(Deram NDM 674) 1971	
7(A/B)	SNAFU/MERCATOR PROJECTED (2-LP)		
		(Deram SDM 30131 2) 1975	
8(E)	ANOTHER EDEN	(EMI 97101) 1975	
9(-)	MASTERS OF ROCK	(EMI 06295117) 1975	
10(F)	HERE WE GO AGAIN	(EMI 06298065) 1976	
11(-)	THINGS	(Nova 628367) 1976	

NB: (1) reissued on CD 199? and again (Eclectic Discs ECLCD 1012) 2005, with bonus tracks and extensive sleevenotes. (2) reissued on CD (Deram 820 617-2) 1990 and again (Eclectic Discs ECLCD 1013) 2005, with bonus tracks and extensive sleevenotes. (6) and (11) German only compilations. (8) German only release. (9) European compilation. (10) European only release

			HCP
45s:	King Of Siam/Ballad Of Harvey Kaye	(Atlantic 584198) 1968	SC -
	Northern Hemisphere / Communion	(Deram DM 242) 1969	SC -
	Jig A Jig/Marcus Junior	(Deram DM 297) 1970	7
	Ramadhan/In The Snow For A Blow/Better Get It In Your Soul/		
	Have To Whack It Up A Bit	(Deram DM 338) 1971	SC -
	Boogie Woogie Flu/		
	Last Dance Of The Clown (PS)	(Harvest HAR 5055) 1972	-
	Sin City Girls/		
	All Our Yesterdays	(United Artists UP 35567) 1973	-

A 'progressive' band formed in Brighton in 1968 by violinist and multi-instrumentalist Dave Arbus. Their novelty hit with the instrumental *Jig A Jig* was completely untypical of their usual musical style, progressive rock with lots of hard-rock guitar and Dave Arbus' wild violin work.

The band was very popular in London's underground clubs. *King Of Siam* was a promising debut single. The follow-up *Northern Hemisphere* captures them at their most inventive with echoed vocals and treated voices backed by a full guitar sound.

Their debut album came in an outstanding sleeve and was the best example of their Eastern-influenced rock. Guitarist/vocalist Nicholson left after this along with drummer Dufont and bassist York (who joined **Manfred Mann's Chapter 3**).

Snafu veered more towards jazz-rock but was their most successful album commercially getting into the Top 30. It was also a big success on the Continent as was their *Ramadhan* 45.

In 1970 they signed to Harvest but their first album for them was rather mundane having sacrificed their earlier Eastern influence for a country sound. *New Leaf* was slightly better and certainly the opening cut *Bradshaw The Bison Hunter* is worth a spin. After this Arbus quit though he later reappeared on **Roger Daltrey**'s self-titled solo album. The band carried on replacing him with former **Mushroom** violinist Joe O'Donnell. This line-up recorded a couple of further albums which only appeared on the Continent before splitting up in 1978.

Hemisphere can also be heard on *Rubble Vol. 12: Staircase To Nowhere* (LP) and *Rubble Vol. 6* (CD). It was based around a distinctive guitar riff topped with Arbus' frenetic violin work and has a rather hypnotic ending with good flute and effects. Earlier in 1971 *Harvest Bag* (LP) included *Ain't Gonna Do You No Harm* and two years earlier *Communion* was featured on *Wowie Zowie! World Of Progressive Music* (LP). More recently, *The Ballad Of Harvey Kaye* has received further exposure on *Talking About The Good Times* (CD).

Eclectic Discs have recently reissued their first two albums. *Mercator Projected* is now supplemented by three previously unissued tracks and comes with extensive sleevenotes. *Snafu* comes with an additional eight tracks of previously unreleased material.

Geoff Britton later played with **Wings**, whilst Joe O'Donnell made several solo albums in the seventies and eighties, many of which feature guest appearances by **Rory Gallagher**. Les Davidson went to Sniff 'n' The Tears ended up doing session work in London in mid eighties. Jeff Allen runs Sensible Music and still plays drums. Les Davidson runs People Studios with his son Tom and still plays guitar. (VJ/TW/LD)

The Easybeats

Personnel:

DICK DIAMONDE	bs		AB
GORDON FLEET	drms		A
HARRY VANDA	ld gtr		AB
STEVIE WRIGHT	vcls		AB
GEORGE YOUNG	gtr		AB
TONY CAHILL	drms		B

ALBUMS:				
1(A)	GOOD FRIDAY	(United Artists (S)ULP 1167) 1967	R2
2(B)	VIGIL	(United Artists (S)ULP 1193) 1968	R1
3(B)	FRIENDS	(Polydor Special 2482 010) 1970	R1

NB: (1) reissued on vinyl (Hallmark HM 609) 197? They also had a couple of US-only albums, *Friday On My Mind* (United Artists UAS 6588) 1967 and *Falling Off The Edge Of The World* (United Artists UAS 6667) 1968. There's a 'Greatest Hits' compilation, *Friday On My Mind* (Fan Club FC 014) 1985, also on CD. *Easy As Can Be* (Fan Club FC 019) is a collection of some of their less well known songs. The German line-ups of (1) and (2) have been reissued on CD by Repertoire (REP 4162-WY) and (REP 4240-WY) respectively with additional cuts. (3) reissued on CD by Repertoire (REP 4278-WY) 1992 with additional tracks. Repertoire has also issued two of the Australian-only albums on CD, which were recorded before they came to the UK in 1966, *It's 2 Easy* (Repertoire REP 4302-WZ) and *Volume 3* (Repertoire REP 4303-WY) along with *The Shame Just Drained* (Repertoire REP 4304-WY) 1993, a collection of previously unissued rarities which first appeared on vinyl in 1977. All three CDs came with plethora of bonus tracks. Another CD import is *Collection: Easybeats* (Impact IMCD 900823) 1989. 1995 saw the release of another CD compilation, *The Best Of The Easybeats* (Repertoire REP 4542-WG), which concentrates on their freakbeat and more experimental pop efforts. *Gonna Have A Good Time* (Sin-Drome/Retroactive SD 8936) 2000 is a more recent compilation. *The Singles As & Bs* (Repertoire REP 50939) 2005 is a 2-CD chronological retrospective of all their UK and Aussie A and B sides plus the title track to their retrospective *Friends* album. *Friday On My Mind* (Repertoire REP 5038) 2005 is basically a reissue of their first album with 12 bonus tracks added including some of their later singles.

45s:			HCP
	Come And See Her/Maybe You		
	Feel Alright (Women)	(United Artists UP 1144) 1966	SC -
	Friday On My Mind/		
	Made My Bed, Gonna Lie In It	(United Artists UP 1157) 1966	6
	Who'll Be The One?/		
	Saturday Night	(United Artists UP 1175) 1967	-
	Heaven And Hell/Pretty Girl	(United Artists UP 1183) 1967	-
	The Music Goes Round My Head/		
	Come In, You'll Get Pneumonia	(United Artists UP 1201) 1967	-
	Hello, How Are You?/Falling Off		
	The Edge Of The World	(United Artists UP 2205) 1968	20
	The Land Of Make-Believe/		
	We All Live Happily	(United Artists UP 2219) 1968	-
	Good Times/		
	Lay Me Down And Die	(United Artists UP 2243) 1968	-
	St. Louis/Can't Find Love	(Polydor 56335) 1969	-
	(Who Are My) Friends?/		
	Rock'n'Roll Boogie	(Polydor 2001 028) 1970	-
Reissues:	Friday On My Mind/Hello, How Are You	(EMI G 4537) 1985	-
	Friday On My Mind/		
	Hello, How Are You	(Old Gold OG 9548) 1985	-

NB: There are a few 45s, which were recorded in the UK but not issued here. Of particular interest are:- *Heaven And Hell*/*Pretty Girl* (United Artists 50187) 1967, a US release with different lyrics on the 'A' side; *Hello, How Are You?*/*Come In You'll Get Pneumonia* (United Artists 67116) 1968, a Dutch release with a different recording of the 'B' side; and *Hello, How Are You?*/*The Music Goes Round My Head* (United Artists 3137) 1968, an Italian 45 with a different recording of the 'B' side.

The Easybeats were all sons of parents who'd emigrated to Australia (although Diamonde and Vanda were Dutch). By the time they headed for England in mid-1966 they'd had four No 1s in Australia in the past year. Their first release here in the UK, *Come And See Her*, made little

EAST OF EDEN - Jig-A-Jig (CD).

impression but the follow-up, a classic pop song, *Friday On My Mind*, had immediate appeal and climbed to No 6 in the UK, No 16 in the US and gave them another Chart topper back in Australia. Its expression of teenage frustration with the nine-to-five routine uniquely captured the feelings of many throughout the world, but their career took a downward spiral when they were unable to provide strong enough follow-ups. Fleet left the grouping 1967 and eventually became a builder in Perth, Western Australia. He was replaced by Tony Cahill, who'd been with Brisbame, Queensland group The Purple Hearts.

Their albums were a curious mixture of easy listening songs and mildly psychedelic offerings like *We All Live Happily Together*. Their second album, *Vigil* spawned a couple of further minor UK hits, *The Music Goes Round My Head* and *Hello, How Are You?* *St. Louis* was a very minor hit in the US in 1969. **My Dear Watson**, a Scottish group, also appeared on their second album.

After they split in 1970 Vanda and Young formed Band Of Hope and then the Marcus-Hook Roll Band before returning to Australia where they later concentrated on production work and songwriting masterminding the success of AC/DC for whom Young's brothers Angus and Malcolm were guitarists. Stevie Wright joined a series of groups that went nowhere and also held a few manual day jobs. He auditioned for the Australian production of "Jesus Christ Superstar" in 1972 and for two years played the part of Simon Ziolotes. After leaving the show he went solo and enjoyed some Aussie chart successes during 1974-75. Since that his career went downhill, not helped by drink and drug problems.

George Young was the younger brother of George Alexander, a guitarist, singer and songwriter who fronted **Grapefruit**.

Friday On My Mind can also be heard on *Absolute Anthology* (Albert Productions) 1980.

The Easy As Can Be compilation includes some of the band's finest moments:- *Falling Off The Edge Of The World*, *Come In You'll Get Pneumonia*, *Peculiar Hole In The Sky* and *Saturday Night*. It also includes *Who'll Be The One*, their follow-up 45 to *Friday On My Mind*, which flopped badly.

The additional cuts on the CD reissue of *Friends* were alternate mixes of *Pretty Girl* and *Remember Sam*; the weird *Peculiar Hole In The Sky* and an instrumental version of *Gonna Make It*. *Gonna Have A Good Time* is a more recent compilation. *The Singles As and Bs* is a chronological retrospective on which you can hear every A and B side they ever released here or in Australia, with the title cut of their posthumous album *Friends* thrown in for good measure! This is a worthwhile release and demonstrates their talent admirably.

Friday On My Mind and *Heaven And Hell* can also be heard on *Nuggets* (CD) and *Friday On My Mind* can also be found on *60's Mix* (CD) and *Best Of British Rock* (CD). For those of you who are interested, a number of their Australian releases have been compiled too. You'll find *All Gone By* (from an Australian EP) on *Albert's Archives* (EMI APLP 037) along with a previously unreleased version of *She's So Fine*. *More Nuggets, Vol. 2* (CD) contains *Gonna Have A Good Time*. *Ugly Things, Vol. 1* (LP) includes *Goin' Out Of My Mind* and you'll find *For My Woman* on *Vol. 3* (LP) of the same series. *Get Ready To Love* has appeared on *The Youngblood Story Vol. 1* (CD). There's also a live version of *River Deep Mountain High* on *The Early Days Of Rock, Vol. 2* (CD); *Sorry* and *Friday On My Mind* have resurfaced on the 4-CD *Nuggets 11* box set and *What In The World* can be heard on *Colour Me Pop, Vol 3* (CD). (VJ/BM/JM)

The Ebonies

45:	Never Gonna Break Your Heart/	
	Shoeshine Boy	(Philips BF 1648) 1968

This is another long-forgotten outfit. The 'A' side was an upbeat pop song, the flip was heavier with quite a strong vocal performance (similar to **Stevie Winwood**), but was rather limited instrumentally. (VJ)

The Eccentrics

Personnel:	JOHN KERRISON	drms	A
	MICK LIDDELL	vcls	A
	PETE MAGGS	lead gtr	A
	ROY ROBINSON	bs	A
	BRUCE WATTS	gtr	A

45:	What You Got/Fe Fi Fo Fum	(Pye 7N 15850) 1965 R1

This was an R&B band. *What You Got* was a Goffin/King composition but didn't Chart. It's now quite sought-after.

Compilation appearances include: *What You Got* on *That Driving Beat* (CD). (VJ/RR)

Eclection

Personnel:	GERRY CONWAY	drms	AB
	GEORGE HULTGREN	bs, vcls	AB
	TREVOR LUCAS	gtr, vcls	AB
	KERILEE MALE	vcls	A
	MIKE ROSEN	gtr, vcls	AB
	DORRIS HENDERSON	vcls	B
	POLI PALMER	keyb'ds	B

ALBUM:	1(A)	ECLECTION	(Elektra EKS 4023) 1968 R2

45s:	Nevertheless/Mark Time	(Elektra EKSN 45033) 1968
	Another Time, Another Place/	
	Betty Brown	(Elektra EKSN 45040) 1968
	Please/Saint George And	
	The Dragon	(Elektra EKSN 45042) 1968
	Please (Mark II)/In The Early Days	(Elektra EKSN 45046) 1968
	Nevertheless/Please	(Elektra K 12196) 1976

This interesting folk-rock group from Birmingham failed to achieve any commercial success despite quite a lot of media attention. When Kerilee Male vanished in October 1968, Dorris Henderson, a vibrant vocalist from LA was drafted in as a replacement. She was an ex-folk club singer who had recorded two albums, *There You Go* and *Watch The Stars* with one time partner **John Renbourn**. The new line-up recorded a strong 45, *Please*, but success continued to elude them and, even now, their album is only of minor interest to collectors. **Eclection** split in October 1969, although Dorris Henderson did make an unsuccessful attempt to revive the band in the early 1970s. When they split Poli Palmer later joined **Family**, George Hultgren changed his name to George Kajanus and later enjoyed a certain amount of fame with **Sailor**. Australian **Trevor Lucas** and Gerry Conway later joined **Fotheringay** and Mike Rosen resurfaced in an outfit called **Mogul Thrash**.

Eclection can be heard singing *Confusion* on Elektra's 1969 *Begin Here* (LP) compilation and *Nevertheless* on *Elektrock The Sixties* (LP). (VJ)

PURPLE PILL EATERS (Comp LP) featuring Jason Eddie and The Centremen.

Jason Eddie (and The Centremen)

45s:	Whatcha Gonna Do Baby/	
	Come On Baby	(Parlophone R 5388) 1965 R3
	Singing The Blues/True To You	(Parlophone R 5473) 1966 R3
α	Heart And Soul/	
	Playing The Clown	(Tangerine DP 0010) 1969 R1

NB: α **Jason Eddie** solo disc.

Jason Eddie was Billy Fury's younger brother. His real name was Al Wycherley. These first two 45s are very sought-after. *Whatcha Gonna Do Baby* is very organ driven and has a haunting feel to it. The flip side is quite frenetic. The follow-up, *Singing The Blues*, was produced by Joe Meek and is more frantic than their debut effort. **Eddie**'s later solo effort in 1969 is less interesting.

Compilation appearances have included: *Watcha Gonna Do Baby* on *Purple Pill Eaters* (LP & CD); *Whatcha Gonna Do Baby*, *Come On Baby*, *True To You* and *Singing The Blues* on *RGM Rarities, Vol. 2* (CD); *Come On Baby* on *English Freakbeat, Vol. 5* (LP & CD); *Singing The Blues* on *Pebbles, Vol. 6* (LP), *English Freakbeat Vol. 6* (CD) and *Rare 60's Beat Treasures, Vol. 4* (CD).

The complete songs of **Jason Eddie** were released as bonus tracks on the CD, *Billy Fury Sings A Buddy Holly Song* (Ozit 0056) 2001. (VJ/L)

Eddie's Crowd

45:	Baby Don't Look Down/	
	Take It Easy Baby	(CBS 202078) 1966 R2

The 'A' side of this R&B band's 45 was a Randy Newman number. (VJ)

Eddie West

45:	All The Children Sleep/Desolation	(Columbia DB 8174) 1967

This was a group (not a guy) from Bristol. The 'A' side was penned by **Kevin Westlake** and Mickie Most. (VJ)

Graeme Edge Band

Personnel:	MICK GALLAGHER	keyb'ds	A
	GRAEME EDGE	drms, vcls	A
	ADRIAN GURVITZ	gtr, vcls	A
	PAUL GURVITZ	bs	A

ALBUM: 1 (A)   KICK OFF YOUR MUDDY BOOTS
(up to   (Threshold THS 15) 1974
1976)

45s: We Like To Do It/Shotgun   (Threshold TH 18) 1974
(up to   Tunnel/Bareback Rider   (Threshold TH 22 1975
1976)

Edge teamed up with the **Gurvitz** brothers for this solo effort during **The Moody Blues** years. He recorded a second album *The Paradise Ballroom* in 1978. (CG)

Edison Lighthouse

Personnel incl: TONY BURROWS   ld vcls

                                                              HCP
45s: Love Grows (Where My Rosemary Goes)/
            Every Lonely Day   (Bell BLL 1091) 1970 1
            It's Up To You Petula/
            Let's Make It Up   (Bell BLL 1136) 1971 49
            What's Happening/Take A Little Time   (Bell BLL 1153) 1971 -
            Find Mr. Zebedee?/
            Reconsider, My Belinda   (Bell BLL 1206) 1972 -
Reissues: Love Grows/
            It's Gonna Be A Lonely Summer   (GTO GTO 32) 1975 -
            Love Grows/It's Up To You Petula   (Old Gold OG 9316) 1983 -

This studio group (a Cook-Greenaway creation) is best remembered for their middle-of-the-road hit *Love Grows*. *It's Up To You Petula* also enjoyed promising sales, but the whole venture is eminently forgettable. Burrows was also involved with **The Brotherhood Of Man**, **First Class**, **The Pipkins** and **White Plains**. In addition, he recorded a solo album for Bell in 1970.

Compilation appearances include *Love Grows (Where My Rosemary Goes)* on *Nothing But No.1 Love Songs (CD)*, *The Seventies Vol 2 (CD)*, *Hits Of The 70's Vol 3 (CD)*, *Number 1 Hits Of The 70's & 80's (CD)*, *UK No 1 Hits Of The 70's (CD)*, *Best Sellers Of The 70's - Vol 1 (CD)*, *Perfect Day (CD)*, *The Super 70's Vol 2 (CD)*, *60's Love Songs (CD)*, *70's Love Songs (CD)*, *Seventies Legends (CD)* and *20 Hits From The 70's (CD)*. (VJ)

Dave Edmunds (and Rockpile)

ALBUMS: 1   ROCKPILE   (Regal Zonophone SLRZ 1026) 1972 R1
(up to   2   SUBTLE AS A FLYING MALLET
1976)   (Rockfield RRL 101) 1975 SC
NB: Also of interest may be *The Best Of Dave Edmunds* (Swan Song SSK 59413) 1981. (1) was reissued on EMI in Europe in 1983. (1) reissued as *The Original Rockpile* (Harvest EMS 1126) in 1987. Also relevant is *Singles A's And B's* (See For Miles SEE 282) 1990, which was earlier issued on Harvest (SHSM 2032) 1980. *The Dave Edmunds Anthology (1968-90)* (Rhino R2 71191) 1993 is a 2-CD set which traces his career from his days with **Love Sculpture** to the start of the decade. Also relevant is *The Complete Early Edmunds* (EMI CDEM 1406) 1991. *Chronicles* is a 20-track hits and more package spanning *Sabre Dance* to eighties material, whilst there's now a 22-track album *Rockin' - The Best Of* (Camden 74321451922) 199?. which includes over twenty minutes of quality live in concert recordings. *I Hear You Knocking* (EMI 7243 8 55079 2 2) 1997 is another CD collection of his material with **Love Sculpture** and Rockpile. *A Pile Of Rock* (Essential ESMCD 876) 2000 is a live collection.

                                                              HCP
45s: I Hear You Knocking/Black Bill   (Mam MAM 1) 1970 1
(up to   I'm Coming Home/
1976)   Country Roll   (Regal Zonophone RZ 3032) 1971 SC -
            Blue Monday/
            I'll Get Along   (Regal Zonophone RZ 3037) 1971 SC -
            Down Down Down/
            It Ain't Easy   (Regal Zonophone RZ 3059) 1972 SC -
            Baby I Love You/Maybe   (Rockfield ROC 1) 1973 8
α   Born To Be With You/Pick Axe Rag   (Rockfield ROC 2) 1973 5
            Needs A Shot Of Rhythm And Blues/
            Let It Be Me   (Rockfield ROC 4) 1974 -
            I Ain't Never/Some Other Guy   (Rockfield ROC 6) 1975 -
            Here Comes The Weekend/
            As Lovers Do   (Swan Song K 19408) 1976 -

            Where Or When/
            New York's A Lonely Town   (Swan Song K 19409) 1976 -
Reissues: I Hear You Knocking/Black Bill   (Blue Print BW 2010) 1980 -
β   I Hear You Knocking/Sabre Dance   (EMI G 452) 1984 -
            I Hear You Knocking   (Old Gold OG 9711) 1987 -
NB: α flip with Mickey Gee. β 'B' side by **Love Sculpture**.

Edmunds was born in Cardiff, Wales, on 15 April 1944. He first came to public attention as a member of **Love Sculpture** in 1968. They had originally been known as **Human Beans**. After they disbanded he returned to Wales with Kingsley Ward and built his own recording studio, Rockfield. He spent several months there experimenting and producing his own unique sound. His first solo single, a cover of a Smiley Lewis song, *I Hear You Knocking*, shot to No 1 in the UK and No 8 in the US. This was a tribute to his idols of the fifties.

He then recorded the *Rockpile* album with assistance from John Williams, who'd also been in **Love Sculpture**. *Rockpile* was a patchy album which did not include his first two rather ordinary 45s for Regal Zonophone. Its finer moments included *Down Down Down*, the opening track, which was written by Trevor Burton of **The Move**; his earlier hit, *I Hear You Knocking*, Ron Davies' *It Ain't Easy*, which was later recorded by **David Bowie** and a version of Neil Young's *Dance Dance Dance*. **Andy Fairweather-Low** and Terry Williams toured with the duo to help promote the album. When the two of them left to work together Dave recruited Nick Lowe, Billy Bremner and Terry Williams to record and tour as Rockpile. Terry Williams also worked with **Deke Leonard's** Iceberg for a short time during this period. Due to **Edmunds'** subsequent success the album is now quite a significant collectors' item. Neither the album nor his three singles for Regal Zonophone sold particularly well and when EMI released him from his contract Kingsley Ward signed him to his new Rockfield label which had a distribution deal with RCA. **Edmunds** then set about glorifying the Phil Spector sound on a couple of 45s. First off was *Baby I Love You*, a cover of the old Ronettes hit, which made No 8 in the UK. Then later in 1973 *Born To Be With You*, originally recorded by the Chordettes, made No 5. The flip side, was an instrumental recorded with Mickey Gee.

During 1973 he also appeared on the live *Christmas At The Patti* (2x10") playing *Run Rudolph Run*.

In February 1974 **Edmunds** appeared in 'Stardust' and also produced most of the music for the film. This was performed by **Edmunds** in a fictitious band called The Stray Cats, which included **David Essex** and **Keith Moon**. In addition it included *Da Doo Ron Ron* recorded with **Brinsley Schwarz** using the pseudonym Dave Edmunds and The Electricians. He was also asked to produce **Brinsley Schwarz'** forthcoming album, *New Favourites*, on which he provided some vocals and formed what would become an important working relationship with Nick Lowe.

His long awaited second album, *Subtle As A Flying Mallet*, did not sell particularly well and as we leave the time span of this book, **Edmunds** had signed to **Led Zeppelin's** Swan Song label and produced The Flamin' Groovies' *Shake Some Action* album. Rosier times lay ahead...

EGG - Egg (CD).

EGG - The Polite Force (CD).

Edmunds formed and recorded with a new backing band Rockpile who earned rave reviews in the UK music press, who tended to categorise the band in with the new wave movement because of its energy. This period was a high point of **Edmunds'** career and *Repeat Where Necessary* in 1979 gave him a Top 40 album that generated major hits with *Girls Talk* (No 4) and *Queen Of Hearts* (No 11), both in 1979. Rockpile recorded *Seconds Of Pleasure* in their own right in 1980, which was also a UK Top 40 album, but after tensions between Lowe and **Edmunds** emerged, the group split. He continued to record throughout the eighties, achieving further moderate success with *Twangin'* (1981) and *DE7* (1982). He working with Jeff Lynne for 1983's *Information* and Lynne's influence resulted in a more measured sound. The album introduced synthesizers and drum machines to his sound and was better received in the States than here. The same formula was repeated for 1984's *Riff Raff*, which flopped commercially. **Edmunds** also produced records for The Stray Cats (a rockabilly revival band) in this period, he also produced The Everly Brothers' comeback record *EB 84*. In the mid-eighties he concentrated more on production but returned with the live *I Hear You Rockin'* in 1987. *Closer To The Flames*, a 1990 studio album met with a mixed reception. 1994's *Plugged In* was his first set of one-man-band material since 1975. This was critically acclaimed and he toured for the first time for years to promote the album. He has continued to record into the new millennium.

Four tracks from the *Rockpile* album were included on *The Classic Tracks 1968-72*, a 1974 **Love Sculpture** compilation. A later **Love Sculpture** compilation, *The Singles A's And B's* (Harvest SHSM 2032) 1980 included both sides of all four **Dave Edmunds and Rockpile** 45s.

The 2-CD *Dave Edmunds Anthology (1968-1990)* is a pretty good guide to his career. Incidentally, *Pebbles, Vol. 4* (LP) includes *London's A Lonely Town*, a previously unreleased track by **Dave Edmunds** and he can be heard on *Stardust* (2-LP), singing The Crystals' hit *Da Doo Ron Ron* with The Electricians.

I Hear You Knocking has been compiled on the 6-CD set *Best Of Driving Rock*, *Radio Caroline Calling - 70's Flashback* and the 3-CD set *Full Throttle- 60 Original Driving Classics*. (VJ/JM/BM)

Edward H. Dafis

Personnel:			
	CHARLIE BRITTON	drms	AB
	HEFIN ELIS	gtr, keyb'ds	AB
	JOHN GRIFFITHS	bs	AB
	DEWI MORRIS	vcls, gtr	AB
	CLEIF HARPWOOD	vcls	B

ALBUMS:	1(B)	YR HEN FFORD GYMREIG O FYW		
(up to			(Sain SAIN 1016 M) 1974 R2	
1976)	2(B)	FFORDD NEWYDD EINGL AMERICANAIDD		
		GRET O FYW	(Sain SAIN 1043 M) 1975 R1	
	3(B)	'SNEB YN BECSO DAM	(Sain SAIN 1053 M) 1976 R1	

EP:	1(B)	DYMA'R URDD (PS)	(Sain SAIN 61 E) 1976 R3
(up to			
1976)			

45s:		Ffarwel I Langyfelach Lon/	
(up to		Gwrandewch (PS)	(Sain SAIN 38 E) 1973 R3
1976)		Singl Tragwyddol/Ar Y Ffordd (PS)	(Sain SAIN 63 S) 1976 R2

Edward H. Dafis was formed in 1973 by Dewi Morris (ex-Y Tebot Piws) and Hefin Elis (ex-Y Nhw), who both had their roots in the Welsh language folk-rock scene. **Edward H. Dafis** played an exhilarating brand of folk-rock. Their first single whilst the 'A' side was a standard folk number, the 'B' side was full blown psychedelic rock. Cleif Harpwood joined for the recording of the first album which is generally considered to be a landmark in the history of Welsh language rock. By the time the band released their second album they were playing to huge audiences in Wales and had acquired a fanatical following especially from a group of fans called Bois Ffostrasol who followed them from gig to gig. At the height of their popularity in 1976 they decided to split but not before releasing what many consider to be their finest album, *'Sneb Yn Becso Dam*. This was a first for Welsh language rock in that it was a concept album, tracing the progress of an innocent young country girl and her seduction into the wildest excesses of city life. John Peel played a couple of tracks and it received critical acclaim at home. They finished the year playing to a capacity audience of 1,500 at Corwen Pavilion. This gig was filmed and transmitted by H.T.V.. They reformed later in 1978 and released two further albums before calling it a day in 1981. (GM)

Edwards Hand

Personnel incl:	ROD EDWARDS	vcls, gtr, keyb'ds
	ROGER HAND	gtr, vcls

ALBUMS:	1	STRANDED	(RCA SF 8154) 1971 SC
	2	RAINSHINE	(Regal Zonophone SRZA 8513) 1973 R2

NB: (2) unissued, demos only.

These two albums were the work of ex-**Piccadilly Line** members Rod Edwards and Roger Hand. (VJ)

Eddie Edwards and The Alamo

Personnel:		
	EDDIE EDWARDS	A
	JIM JACQUES	A
	EDDIE LE SURF	A
	TONY LE SURF	A

EP:	1	(The Golden Days Of Summer/Windy And Warm/	
		Love You Like I Used To/The Soldier)	(SRT 73314) 1975

A four track folk/country 45, which is an interesting obscurity, though of no special merit. (MWh)

Ian Edward and The Zodiacs

45:	Just The Little Things/	
	This Won't Happen To Me	(Fontana TF 548) 1965 R1

See also **Ian and The Zodiacs**. (VJ)

Edwick Rumbold

45s:	Specially When/Come Back	(CBS 202393) 1966 R2
	Shades Of Grey/Boggle Woogle	(Parlophone R 5622) 1967 R2

Both of this obscure London's group's 45s are now rare and sought-after. The flip side to the first, *Come Back*, is attractive to collectors of freakbeat, whilst *Shades Of Grey* is more psychedelic. *Boggle Woogle* features 'swinging' Carnaby Street type lyrics. The group had four members but their identity remains unknown. *Specially When* was co-written and produced by Johnny Flux and Paul Rodriguez (of **The Manish Boys**).

Compilation appearances have included: *Shades Of Grey* on *Rubble, Vol. 3 - Nightmares In Wonderland* (LP) and *Rubble, Vol. 2* (CD); *Come Back* on *Echoes From The Wilderness - Sixteen UK R&B Freakbeat Trippers.* (LP & CD); and you'll find *Boggle Woggle* on *Psychedelia, Vol. 2* (LP) and *Hen's Teeth Vol. 1* (CD). (VJ)

Egg

Personnel:	CLIVE BROOKS	drms	A
	MONT CAMPBELL	bs, vcls	A
	DAVE STEWART	organ	A

ALBUMS:	1(A)	EGG	(Deram Nova SDN 14)	1970	SC
	2(A)	THE POLITE FORCE	(Decca SML 1074)	1971	SC
	3(A)	THE CIVIL SURFACE	(Caroline C 1510)	1974	SC

NB: (1) reissued on CD (Eclectic Discs ECLCD 1015) 2005, with bonus cuts and extensive sleevenotes. (2) reissued on CD (Eclectic Discs ELCD 1016) 2005. (3) reissued on CD (Charisma CACD 1510) 1990. There's also a compilation, *Seven Is A Jolly Good Time* (See For Miles/Charly SEE 47) 1985, which consists of their first album and their 45. A later CD, *Egg Featuring Dave Stewart* (Deram 844 168-2) 1992 covers the same ground.

| 45: | Seven Is A Jolly Good Time/ | | |
| | You Are All Princes | (Deram DM 269) | 1969 SC |

This trio had previously been in a flower-power outfit with **Steve Hillage** called Uriel, which ended in 1968 when **Hillage** went off to college. **Egg**'s first incarnation lasted from July 1968 to May 1972 and the two albums they recorded were in the progressive mould and are now of minor interest to collectors. They were characterised by rather jazzy, esoteric music, which took extremely difficult time sequences as its basis.

Egg veers into **Pink Floyd** territory, particularly on the opening cut *Bulb*, whilst the second side comprises improvised music based on the works of Grieg and Stravinsky. In fact the first version of the album was cancelled before release when Stravinsky's estate objected and only a handful of finished copies exist.

The Polite Force contains just seven tracks and the longest *Long Piece No 3* is just over 20 minutes.

They also contributed two tracks, *Song Of McGillicude The Pussillanimous* and *I Will Be Absorbed* to *The Nova Sampler* (LP) in 1970. Dave Stewart's next outfit was **Khan** with **Steve Hillage**, formed when he returned to London from college. He was later in **Hatfield and The North**, National Health and Bruford before 'going commercial' with a series of covers with Barbara Gaskin (ex-**Spirogyra** and **Hatfield and The North**). Clive Brooks went on to join **Groundhogs** and Mont Campbell was later in National Health. **Egg** did reform briefly in 1974 to cut the third album. (VJ)

EGG - The Civil Surface (CD).

EIRE APPARENT - Sun Rise (CD).

Eggs Over Easy

Personnel:	AUSTIN de LONE	keyb'ds, gtr, vcls	A
	BILL FRANC	drms	A
	BRIEN HOPKINS	keyb'ds, bs, gtr, vcls	A
	JACK O'HARA	gtr, bs, hrmnca, vcls	A

| ALBUM: | 1 | GOOD 'N' CHEAP | (A&M 4366) 1972 |

NB: (1) reissued on Edsel (ED 199).

Although from the New York originally, **Eggs Over Easy** was an integral part of the pub-rock scene frequently gigging with bands like **Help Yourself**, **Ducks Deluxe** and **Bees Make Honey**.

They originally came to Britain to record an album in 1970 at Olympic Studios with **Chas Chandler** for Mercury Records. The sessions happened, but back in New York something went wrong with their business affairs and they were advised to stay in London until the problems were resolved. They secured a couple of gigs at their local jazz pub and debuted at The Tally Ho in Kentish Town on 13 May 1971. Their large song repertoire included great Motown, **Stones** and Band covers and they soon secured a residency at the pub. Musically, their own material veered towards country-rock and soul. They undertook a brief UK tour supporting **John Mayall**, before returning to New York to record their album that was eventually released in 1972.

Housed in a cover inspired by Edward Hopper paintings, their album features good pub-rock with vocal harmonies and some country rock influences. All their material was written by the group members, except for *Song Is Born Of Riff And Tongue* penned by Robert Fraker. Their album was produced by Link Wray and the strongest tracks are *The Factory* and *Night Flight*, both with good guitar work and clever lyrics.

Austin de Lone later became a session men, working with British pub rockers (like **Nick Lowe**) and later with Dan Hicks in the Christmas Jug Band. (VJ/SR)

The Eggy

Personnel:	BILLY CAMPBELL	bs	A
	NIGEL LOMAS	drms	A
	ROGER LOMAS	gtr	A
	BILL PASTE	vcls	A

| 45: | Hookey/You're Still Mine | (Spark SRL 1024) 1969 SC |

Roger Lomas had been in **The Sorrows** prior to joining **The Eggy**, who came from Coventry. He wrote the 'A' side to their 45. Lomas also played in a band called Dodger with Bob Jackson and Paul Hooper (both formerly of **Indian Summer**) who recorded albums and singles between 1977-79. Jackson and Hooper were later both members of **The Fortunes**. After leaving **The Eggy** Roger Lomas became a full-time freelance record producer and has to date notched up eighteen hit singles which include hits by Bad Manners, Selector, The Bodysnatchers, Modettes and **Roy Wood**. In addition to these his album credits include The Specials, **Groundhogs**, Desmond Dekker, Specialbeat, Laurel Aitken and Reluctant Stereotypes.

The flip side to their 45, *You're Still Mine*, is nothing special but contains some reasonably good guitar work. The 45 was leased to Imperial for a US release.

Compilation appearances include: *You're Still Mine* on *Circus Days Vol. 1 & 2* (CD), *Circus Days, Vol. 2* (LP), *English Freakbeat, Vol. 5* (LP & CD) and on a free EP with the good but short-lived 'Strange Things Are Happening' (STFREE 301) magazine. (LS/VJ)

Eire Apparent

Personnel incl:	MICHAEL COX	gtr, flute	A
	ERNEST GRAHAM	vcls	A
	DAVE LUTTON	drms	A
	CHRIS STEWART	bs	A

ALBUM: 1(A) SUN RISE   (Buddah 203 021) 1969 R2

NB: (1) reissued on Sequel (NEX CD 199) 1992 and on Repertoire (REP 4174-WZ) 199? with one bonus track *Rock 'n' Roll Band*.

45s:	Follow Me/Here I Go Again	(Track 604 019) 1967 SC
	Rock 'n' Roll Band/	
	Yes I Need Someone	(Buddah 201 039) 1969 SC
Reissue:	Rock 'n' Roll Band/	
	Yes I Need Someone	(Buddah 2011 117) 1972

This Irish band toured the States with **Jimi Hendrix** in 1967 and as a consequence he produced their album and played on it. The tracks he played on were: *Yes I Need Someone* (with Michael Cox on rhythm guitar); *The Clown* (Michael Cox on rhythm guitar); *Captive In The Sun* (Michael Cox is on lead guitar - Jimi plays the guitar on the bridge) and *Let Me Stay* (Michael and Jimi alternate between playing lead guitar). They were managed by Chas Chandler. **Eire Apparent**'s album is now quite collectable - veering towards psychedelia with lots of phasing and effects; it is worth seeking out. Try the Sequel CD reissue.

After the short-lived venture folded **Graham** had spells with **Clancy** and **Help Yourself**, and made a highly-regarded solo album, Tolson joined **The Edgar Broughton Band** and a later **Pretty Things** line-up and McCullogh joined **The Grease Band** and was later in **Wings**; Chris Stewart was later with **Spooky Tooth** and Dave Lutton was in **Ellis**.

Compilation appearances have included: *Yes, I Need Someone* on *Psychedelic Visions* (CD); *Morning Glory* on *Broken Dreams, Vol. 3* (LP); *Follow Me* on *Backtrack 1* and *The Clown* on *Jagged Time Lapse, Vol 5* (CD). (VJ/JO/RMJ)

ELASTIC BAND - Expansions On Life (LP).

The Elastic Band

Personnel:	SEAN JENKINS	drms	A
	ANDY SCOTT	ld gtr	A
	MIKE SCOTT	bs	A
	AUGUSTE (TED) YEADON	vcls, organ	A
	DAVE SCOTT	drms	A

ALBUM: 1(A) EXPANSIONS ON LIFE   (Decca Nova SND 6) 1969 R1

45s:	Think Of You Baby/	
	It's Been A Long Time Baby	(Decca F 12763) 1969 SC
	Do Unto Others/	
	Eight And A Half Hours Of Paradise	(Decca F 12815) 1969 SC

Originally known as The Silverstone Set this band gigged around the Midlands and North Wales. They also appeared on 'Opportunity Knocks', apparently they won five times! This helped secure a contract with Decca. They played a sort of blue-eyed soul and in Ted Yeadon's vocals they had quite an asset. The 'A' side of their second 45, *Do Unto Others*, was taken from the 'Mr. Rose' TV series and the flip was also quite an appealing piece of blue-eyed soul. Their sole album was a bit inconsistent. One of the tracks from it, *Has Anybody Seen Her?*, was also included on *Nova Sampler* (LP) in 1970.

Andy Scott later became **Sweet**'s lead guitarist. Dave Scott was later in **Northwind**. They also went on to back **Scaffold**, **The Love Affair** and **Henry Cow**.

Compilation appearances have included: *8 And A Half Hours To Paradise* on *Rubble, Vol. 6 - The Clouds Have Groovy Faces* (LP), *Rubble, Vol. 4* (CD), *British Psychedelic Trip, Vol. 4* (LP) and *Great British Psychedelic Trip, Vol. 2* (CD); *Mother Goose* and *Has Anybody Seen Her?* on *Broken Dreams, Vol. 3* (LP) and *Think Of You Baby* on *Colour Me Pop, Vol 2* (CD). (VJ)

Elcort

| Personnel incl: | KENNY CRADDOCK | organ | A |
| | DEREK RUTHAN | gtr | A |

45:     Tammy/Searchin'   (Parlophone R 5447) 1966

This four-piece from Newcastle played a jazz/blues style on their Parlophone 45. (MWh)

Electric Banana

See **Pretty Things** entry.

ELECTRIC BANANA - Blows Your Mind (LP).

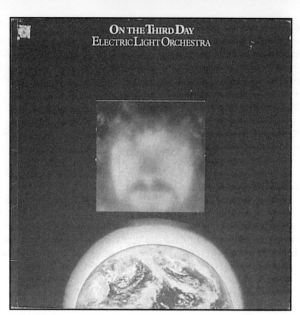

ELO - On The Third Day (LP).

Electric Light Orchestra (ELO)

Personnel:	BEV BEVAN	drms, vcls	ABCD
(up to	ANDY CRAIG	cello	A
1976)	WILF GIBSON	violin	AB
	BILL HUNT	keyb'ds,	
		french horn	A
	JEFF LYNNE	gtr, vcls	ABCD
	HUGH McDOWELL	cello	A
	RICHARD TANDY	bs, vcls	ABCD
	ROY WOOD	cello, vcls	A
	MICHAEL DE		
	ALBUQUERQUE	bs, vcls	BC
	MIKE EDWARDS	cello	BC
	COLIN WALKER	cello	B
	MIK KAMINSKI	violin	CD
	MELVYN GALE	cello	D
	KELLY GROUCUTT	bs, vcls	D

				HCP
ALBUMS:	1(A)	ELECTRIC LIGHT ORCHESTRA		
(up to			(Harvest SHVL 797) 1971	32
1976)	2(B)	ELO 2	(Harvest SHVL 806) 1973	35
	3(C)	ON THE THIRD DAY	(Jet LP 202) 1973	-
	4(-)	SHOWDOWN (Compilation)	(Harvest SHSP 4037) 1974	-
	5(C)	ELDORADO	(Jet LP 203) 1974	-
	6(D)	FACE THE MUSIC	(Jet LP 201) 1975	-
	7(D)	A NEW WORLD RECORD	(Jet LP 204) 1976	6

NB: There have been several compilations including *The Light Shines On* (Harvest SHSM 2015) 1977, *The Light Shines On, Vol. 2* (Harvest SHSM 2027) 1979, the US-only *OLE ELO* (United Artists UALA 630) 1976, *ELO's Greatest Hits* (Jet JET LX 525) 1979, *The First Movement* (Harvest EMS 1128) 1986, *The Greatest Hits* (Telstar STAR 2370) 1989 and *Electric Light Orchestra, Part 2* (Telstar STAR 2503) 1991. They also had a live album, *The Night The Light Went On Long Beach* (Warner K 56058) in 1974, which was released worldwide but NOT in the UK or US. (3), (5) and (6) also released as 3-LP box set, Also of interest is *Three Light Years* (Jet JETBX 1) in 1978. *Early ELO (1971-1973)* (EMI CDS 79 7471 2) 1991 is a two CD compilation containing the whole of (1) and (2) and five previously unissued outtakes from the band's final months with EMI. (5), (7) and *Out Of The Blue* reissued as a three CD budget boxed set (Epic EPC 472267 2) in 1992. A further compilation is *The Very Best Of The Electric Light Orchestra* (Dino DINCD 90) 1994. (1) reissued (EMI Harvest 533 3730) 2001 as a 2-CD set with a bonus CD to celebrate its 30th anniversary.(2) reissued (EMI 7423 5 43328 2 1) 2003 as a 2-CD set with a bonus CD to celebrate its 30th anniversary and again on CD (EMI EMI 5433292) 2005. (6) reissued on CD (Pickwick 982596 2) 1991. (7) reissued on CD by Jet (CD 32545) 1989, but deleted 1990 and Pickwick (902198 2) 1990. For a good introduction to their material, check out the compilation CD, *The Gold Collection* (EMI 7243 8 37162 2 7) 1996. *Light Years: The Very Best Of Electric Light Orchestra* (Sony 489039 2/4) 1997 contains all of their twenty-nine UK hits digitally remastered on a 2-CD collection. *The Night The Light Went On (In Long Beach)* (Epic 491103 2) 1998 is a live set from 1974 in Long Beach, California. *Live At Winterland 1976* (Eagle EAMCD 038) 1998 comes from a U.S. radio transcription broadcast.

			HCP
45s:	10538 Overture/First Movement	(Harvest HAR 5053) 1972	9
(up to α	Roll Over Beethoven/		
1976)	Queen Of The Hours	(Harvest HAR 5063) 1973	6
	Showdown/In Old England Town	(Harvest HAR 5077) 1973	12
	Ma-Ma-Ma-Belle/Can't Find The Title	(Warner K 16439) 1974	22
	Can't Get It Out Of My Head/		
	Illusions In G Major	(Warner K 16510) 1974	-
	Evil Woman/10538 Overture (live)	(Jet JET 764) 1975	10
	Night Rider/Daybreaker	(Jet JET 769) 1976	-
	Strange Magic/Showdown (live)	(Jet JET 779) 1976	38
	Livin' Thing/Far On High	(Jet UP 36184) 1976	4
Reissues:	β Showdown/Roll Over Beethoven	(Harvest HAR 12-5121) 1977	
	χ Can't Get It Out Of My Head/Evil Woman	(Jet ELOJB 1) 1978	
	Showdown/Roll Over Beethoven	(Harvest HAR 125179) 1979	
	10538 Overture/Roll Over Beethoven	(EMI G 4522) 1984	

NB: α early copies came with a different 'B' side, *Manhattan Rumble (49th Street Massacre)*. β 12" picture sleeve. χ also issued on an EP (Jet ELO 1) with two additional tracks, *Strange Dream* and *Ma-Ma-Ma Belle*.

Inventive and imaginative the **Electric Light Orchestra** (hereafter ELO) was one of Britain's most successful progressive rock acts of the seventies.

Our story of the **Electric Light Orchestra** begins with Jeff Lynne, a Brummie born there on 30 December 1947. Originally in **The Nightriders** who evolved into an interesting quasi-underground band, **Idle Race**, Lynne had been invited to join another Birmingham band, **The Move**, on two occasions. In 1969 he turned them down but in 1970, when their vocalist **Carl Wayne** left to pursue a solo career in cabaret, he accepted on the condition that he could also be involved in the new group **The Move**'s vocalist **Roy Wood** was planning, which was going to play a form of orchestrated free-form music influenced as much by jazz and classical music as by rock. The experiment was financed by **The Move**'s manager, Don Arden, who got the new outfit a record contract with EMI's new 'progressive' Harvest label.

Contractual problems and some late (and perhaps rather surprising) hits for **The Move** delayed the experiment getting off the ground but the band eventually made their live debut at Croydon's Greyhound pub. An experimental album, *The Electric Light Orchestra*, was recorded over a long period. Highlights include *10538 Overture*, a daring and lavish magnum opus; *Nellie Takes Her Bow*, a piano-based ballad and *Mr Radio*, a fairly commercial pop song. It met with considerable critical acclaim and sold quite well, too, climbing to No 32 in the UK. It also spawned a hit single, Jeff Lynne's *10538 Overture*, which made the UK Top Ten. In the US it was titled *No Answer* because United Artists trying to contact Arden to discover the album's title got a message back from his secretary, saying 'No Answer', because she couldn't track him down, but assumed this to be the album's title. It peaked at No 196 in the US.

Already at this early stage the group's two main creative forces - **Wood** and Lynne - were clashing but there was widespread surprise when **Wood** left the group in August 1972, taking Hunt and McDowell with him, to form the more commercial rock'n'roll revival group **Wizzard** - after all he'd been planning **ELO** for several years. Andy Craig quit the music business altogether.

The new line-up (B) made its debut at The Reading Rock Festival the same month. One of the newcomers Michael De Albuquerque had released a solo 45 in 1970. Their first 45 was a heavily orchestrated version of Chuck Berry's *Roll Over Beethoven*, which had a quasi-classical intro. Ambitious it certainly was but the end result was a classic rock single and they were rewarded with a Top Ten hit here (it later climbed to No 42 in the US). The accompanying album, *ELO II*, was less enthusiastically received but climbed to No 35 here and No 62 in the US, where the group commenced a 40 venue tour on 2 June, 1973.

September 1973 saw further line-up changes with Kaminski (who'd earlier played with **Zoot Money**) joining and McDowell rejoining from **Wizzard** and Gibson and Walker leaving (line-up C). This line-up's first album was a concept one, *On The Third Day*, which only charted in the States where it peaked at No 52. It was an excellent album with no really weak cuts. Side two, in particular, contained an appealing song in *Daybreaker*, the rocky *Ma-Ma-Ma Belle* and *In The Hall Of The Mountain King*, which is from Grieg's *Peer Gynt*. Their next hit single was *Showdown*, which by veering towards black American soul, displayed their versatility. It climbed to No 12 here and No 53 in the US.

In March 1974 *Ma-Ma-Ma Belle* (a UK-only release) climbed to No 22 in the Charts, while in the States *Daybreaker* (No 87) was a more minor hit a couple of months later. Their next album, *Eldorado*, was billed as 'A Symphony By The Electric Light Orchestra'. It got to No 16 in the US going gold but failed to chart here at all. One of its highlights, *Can't Get You Out Of My Head*, utilised a 30-piece string section and also gave them their first US Top Ten hit (peaking at No 9). Kelly Groucutt who joined the group in October 1974 was a member of the Birmingham group **Sight'n'Sound** in the early seventies.

In November 1974 Warner Brothers issued a live album, *The Night The Light Went On In Long Beach*, worldwide except in the UK and US. The same month Harvest issued a compilation album, *Showdown*, comprising singles and tracks from their first two albums. The year ended with further personnel changes, Albuquerque and Edwards leaving to be replaced by Kelly Groucutt (formerly of Barefoot) and cellist Melvyn Gale, who'd been with the London Palladium Orchestra.

This latest line-up (D) produced less experimental but extremely distinctive music characterised by Lynne's fresh vocals and lots of strings. The band's next album, *Face The Music*, was their most commercial to date. Comprised of reasonably short orchestrated rock songs it attracted considerable radio play. In the UK three singles were taken off it (*Evil Woman, Night Rider* and *Strange Magic*) and two of them were hits. In the US too, where the album climbed to No 8, *Evil Woman* and *Strange Magic* climbed to Nos 10 and 14 respectively in the Singles Chart. Hot on their heels, *Showdown*, was reissued and got to No 59.

A New World Record developed the successful formula of the previous album. By now Jeff Lynne was very much the dominant force in the group - he wrote, arranged and produced the whole album. It was a massive success, climbing to No 6 in the UK and No 5 in the US and selling over five million copies worldwide. It also spawned three further excellent hit singles - *Livin' Thing, Rockaria* and *Telephone Line*, which were innovative, orchestrated and dominated by Lynne's keen vocals.

The Night The Light Went Out On (In Long Beach) is a reissue of an album recorded live in 1974, which wasn't reissued in the US or UK at the time. It did get a brief issue in those countries in 1985 but soon disappeared, making it scarce since. The sound has been fully remastered and the four edited tracks on the original vinyl release have been restored to full length. The set, which captures them on form and closes with a barnstorming version of *Roll Over Beethoven*, is accompanied by detailed liner notes from **ELO** fanzine editor Rob Caiger.

Live At Winterland 1976 comes from a previously bootlegged U.S. radio transcription broadcast. It captures them in form and includes superb versions of *Eldorado* and *Ma Ma Ma Belle*.

EMI Harvest reissued their debut album in 2001 to celebrate its 30th anniversary. The lavishly-packaged release was available for a limited period and included a bonus CD of alternate versions, live performances and a small number of quadraphonic mixes.

ELO - Face The Music (LP).

Appearances on Various Artists' compilations have included: *Queen Of The Hours* on *Harvest Bag* (LP); *Showdown* on *Harvest Heritage - 20 Greats* (LP); *Roll Over Beethoven* on the 3-CD set *Full Throttle - 60 Original Driving Classics*, the 2-CD set *Stars And Stripes* and on the 3-CD box set *Radio Caroline Calling - 70's Flashback*, along with *Showdown*; *On Tight* on *Seventies Legends 1* (CD), and *Don't Bring Me Down* on the 2-CD set *Good Times - Best Of 70's* and on *Rock The Night* (CD).

As we leave the period covered by this book **ELO** would go on to enjoy many more successes well into the eighties. (VJ/JM/WB)

Janet and Diane Elergi

ALBUM: 1 THE ANSWER (Fanfare FR 2196) 1974 R2

This Christian female folk obscurity was strongly influenced by **Shirley Collins**. The title track has menacing organ and echo-laden acid guitar with eerie female vocals. There's another track almost on a par with this too. (VJ)

Elf

Personnel:	RONNIE JAMES DIO	vcls	A
	GARY DRISCOLL	drms	A
	STEVE EDWARDS	gtr	A
	CRAIG GRUBER	bs	A
	MARK NAUSSEEF	perc	A
	MICKEY LEE SOULE	keyb'ds	A

ALBUM: 1(A) CAROLINA COUNTRY BALL (Purple TPS 3506) 1974 SC
NB: They also had some US-only albums: *Elf* (Epic 31789) 1972, *Trying To Burn The Sun* (MGM M3G 4994) 1975 and *Live* (MGM) 1976.

45: LA 59/Ain't It All Amusing (Purple PUR 118) 1974

A heavy-rock outfit formed in 1970. Roger Glover (of **Deep Purple**) took to their mixture of hard-rock, boogie and blues signing them to Purple Records. They also got to support **Deep Purple** on their 1974 tour which was an ideal opportunity for them to promote their *Carolina County Ball* album. This was their best effort, subsequent US-only albums paled by comparison but in any case when **Ritchie Blackmore** hired Dio, Soule, Edwards and Gruber to help him record his solo Ritchie Blackmore's Rainbow album the band became defunct. (VJ)

Elias Hulk

Personnel:	GRANVILLE FRAZER	gtr	A
	JAMES HAINES	bs	A
	BERNARD JAMES	drms	A
	NEIL TATUM	gtr	A
	PETER THORPE	vcls	A

ALBUM: 1(A) ELIAS HULK UNCHAINED (Youngblood SSYB 8) 1970 R3
NB: (1) reissued on See For Miles (SEE LP 286) or (SEE CD 286) 1990.

This rare hard-rock album, very much in the mould of **Leaf Hound**, now changes hands for considerable sums. It's full of endless riffs, tortured blues vocals and drum and bass solos. Frankly, I found this all rather tedious! (VJ)

Elio Karfenetti

This weird group from 1967 played with **The Soft Machine** and other psychedelic bands at odd events and underground clubs. Nothing else is known about them. (JN)

Marc Ellington

ALBUMS:	1	MARC ELLINGTON		
		(mono/stereo)	(Philips (S)BL 7883) 1969 SC
	2	RAINS, REINS OF CHANGES	(B&C CAS 1033) 1971 SC

	3	A QUESTION OF ROADS	(Philips 6308 120) 1972 SC
	4	RESTORATION	(Philips 6308 143) 1972 SC
	5	MARC TIME	(Transatlantic Xtra 1154) 1972 SC

NB: (5) with **Fairport Convention**.

45s:	I Shall Be Released/Mrs Whittle	(Philips BF 1665) 1968
	Did You Give The World Some Love Today Baby?/	
	Bless The Executioner	(Philips BF 1742) 1969
	Peggy Day/Four In The Morning	(Philips BF 1779) 1969
	Alligator Man/Song For A Friend	(B&C CB 161) 1971
	Please Be My Friend/Four Rode By	(Philips 600 6221) 1972
	Good Love Is Like A Good Song/	
	Just Let The Music Bring You Back	(Philips 600 6272) 1973
	Stealin'/Answer Is You	(Philips 600 6323) 1973

Ellington was a folk-rock singer-songwriter. He was American but based himself in the UK, hence his inclusion here. His albums, which are all now quite rare, are always in demand by folk collectors. They also feature several other prominent folk musicians:- **Richard Thompson**, **Linda Thompson**, **Dave Pegg**, Dave Mattacks, Pat Donaldson, Simon Nicol, Gerry Conway and **Gordon Huntley** to name a few. His *Marc Time* album veered more towards country and featured steel guitarist and dobro player **B.J. Cole**. **Ellington** also did session work and played on albums by **Matthews Southern Comfort** and **Fairport Convention**. *Yarrow* from his second album appeared on the Peg label folk sampler *Clogs* (LP) in 1972. He is now resident in Scotland, where he was recently appointed a High Sheriff! (RMJ/VJ)

Bern Elliot and The Fenmen

Personnel:	WALLY ALLEN	vcls	A
	BERN ELLIOT	vcls	A
	ALAN JUDGE	ld gtr	A
	JOHN POVEY	drms	A
	ERIC WILMER	bs, vcls	A

EP:	1(A)	BERN ELLIOT AND THE FENMEN	
			(Decca DFE 8561) 1964 SC

NB: There's also a compilation, *The Beat Years* (See For Miles SEE 239) 1988, reissued on CD (SEECD 239) 1993.

			HCP
45s:	Money/Nobody But Me	(Decca F 11770) 1963	14
	New Orleans/		
	Everybody Needs A Little Love	(Decca F 11852) 1964	24
	Good Times/		
α	What Do You Want With Me Baby	(Decca F 11970) 1964	-
β	Guess Who/Make It Easy On Yourself	(Decca F 12051) 1965	-
β	Lipstick Traces/Voodoo Woman	(Decca F 12171) 1965	-

NB: α as Bern Elliot and The Clan. β **Bern Elliot** solo efforts.

Formed in Erith, Kent, in 1961, this outfit cut its teeth on the Hamburg club circuit. Their cover of **The Beatles**' *Money* gave them a Top 30 hit and the following year their cover of *New Orleans* repeated the success. After an EP the group split and **Elliot** initially got together a backing group called The Klan. He then recorded a couple of solo singles and **The Fenmen** also carried on making discs including a cover of The Four Seasons' *Rag Doll*. Allen and Povey later joined **The Pretty Things** in 1968.

The band also featured on Decca's rare 1964 *At The Cavern* (LP) compilation, playing two tracks:- *I'm Talking About You* and *Little Egypt*; on *Fourteen, Lord Taverners* (LP) (1964) playing *Forget Her* and their version of *Money* can be heard on *Ready, Steady, Go!* (LP) (1964).

Recent compilation coverage has included: - *Money* on *Sixties Lost And Found, Vol. 2* (LP) and *Beat Merchants* (2-LP); *Money* and *Please Mr. Postman* on *Pop Inside The '60s, Vol. 2* (CD) and *Sixties Explosion, Vol. 1* (CD); *Please Mr. Postman* on *Sixties Lost And Found, Vol. 3* (LP); and *I'm Talking About You* and *Little Egypt* on *At The Cavern* (LP) and *Live At The Cavern* (CD).

The See For Miles compilation includes the band's two 45s and their EP, the 45 **Elliot** recorded with his new backing band, The Clan, and his two solo 45s, the first of which was a big production number. (VJ)

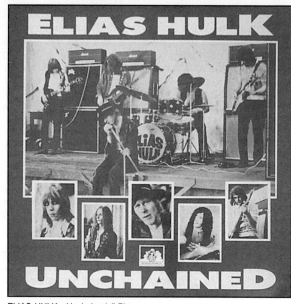

ELIAS HULK - Unchained (LP).

Bill Elliot and The Elastic Oz Band

Personnel incl:	BILL ELLIOT
	CHARLES SHAAR MURRAY

45:	God Save Us/	
	Do The Oz (Initially with PS)	(Apple APPLE 36) 1971 R1/SC

A **John Lennon** project designed to raise money for 'Oz' magazine when it was facing an obscenity charge. The Elastic Oz Band was a mixture of 'Oz' journalists and musicians including the rock journalist Charles Shaar Murray. (VJ)

Dave Elliot

ALBUMS:	1	DAVE ELLIOT	(Atlantic K 40374) 1972
	2	SOLID GROUND	(Atlantic K 40527) 1973

45s:	Dear Mary/Kid's Stuff	(Atlantic K 10146) 1972
	Railway Line/Key West	(Atlantic K 10366) 1973
	I Read The News/I Can't Go Home	(Atlantic K 10384) 1973

Dave Elliot is a singer/songwriter. On his albums he is assisted by such luminaries as **B.J. Cole**, **Mike Grabham** and Chris Karan. (BS/VJ)

Elliot's Sunshine

45:	Is It Too Late?/Cos I'm Lonely	(Philips BF 1649) 1968

A short-lived pop group whose heavily orchestrated *Cos I'm Lonely* was one of several non-psychedelic recordings to find its way onto the *British Psychedelic Trip* series (*British Psychedelic Trip, Vol. 3*) of the vinyl series, although it seems to have been omitted from the corresponding CD series. More recently, you'll find it on *Fading Yellow, Vol 1* (CD). *Is It Too Late* is a romantic ballad and much less impressive than the 'B' side. (VJ/JO)

Ellis

Personnel:	STEVE ELLIS	vcls	ABC
	ANDY GEE	gtr	ABC
	ZOOT MONEY	keyb'ds, vcls	AB
	JIMMY LEVERTON	bs	A
	DAVE LUTTON	drms	ABC
	NICK SOUTH	bs	BC
	ALAN CALLAN	gtr	C

ALBUMS:	1(A)	RIDING ON THE CREST OF A SLUMP	
			(Epic 64878) 1972 SC
	2(B)	WHY NOT?	(Epic 65650) 1973 SC

NB: They also recorded an unissued album for Ariola *The Last Angry Man* in 1978. There's also a 2-CD anthology *An Everlasting Soul (The Anthology)* (Castle CMEDD 1047) 2005.

45s:	Good To Be Alive/Morning Paper	(Epic EPC 8318) 1972
	El Doomo/Your Game	(Epic EPC 1052) 1973
	Open Road/Leaving In The Morning	(Epic EPC 1627) 1973
	Loud And Lazy Love Songs/	
	Goodbye Boredom	(Epic EPC 1803) 1973

A hard-rock band formed in 1972 by **Steve Ellis** (ex-**Love Affair**), with **Zoot Money** who'd just finished touring and recording with **Grimms**. Andy Gee was ex-**Springfield Park**, whilst bassist Jimmy Leverton had played with **Juicy Luicy** and Dave Lutton had been with **Heavy Jelly**.

Leverton departed to **Hemlock** following their first album and was replaced by Nick South (ex-**Vinegar Joe**). **Mike Patto**, Roger Chapman and **Maggie Bell** also assisted on their albums.

They have one track *El Doomo*, written by **Steve Ellis** on a K-Tel compilation. It's a slow floating number with strong vocals by **Steve Ellis**.

Money later rejoined **Grimms**, being replaced by Alan Callan. **Ellis** split in January '74, with **Steve Ellis** forming **Widowmaker**, Gee joining **Thin Lizzy**, Lutton **T-Rex** and South **Murray Head**'s group.

An Everlasting Soul is a 2-CD anthology, which collects the best of his material with **The Love Affair**, **Ellis**, **Widowmaker** plus his solo work. (VJ/JM)

Matthew Ellis

ALBUMS:	1	MATTHEW ELLIS	
		(Regal Zonophone SRZA 8501) 1971 SC	
	2	AM I?	(Regal Zonophone SRZA 8505) 1971 R1

NB: (1) with **Chris Spedding**.

45s:	Avalon/You Are	(Regal Zonophone RZ 3033) 1971
	Birthday Song/Salvation	(Regal Zonophone RZ 3039) 1971
	Palace Of Plenty/Two By Two	(Regal Zonophone RZ 3045) 1972

Matthew Ellis was also connected with **Procol Harum**. The first album is pleasant early seventies singer / songwriter fare. He was a multi-instrumentalist and there is orchestral backing on several of the tracks. An American compilation of his first two albums also exists. (VJ)

Steve Ellis

45s:	Loot/More More More	(CBS 4992) 1970
(up to	Evie/Fat Cow	(CBS 5199) 1970
1976)	Take Your Love/Jingle Jangle Jasmine	(CBS 7037) 1971
	Hold On/	
	Goody Goody Dancing Shoes	(CBS 7411) 1971
	El Doomo/Your Game	(Epic EPC 4525) 1976

NB: There's also a 2-CD anthology *An Everlasting Soul (The Anthology)* (Castle CMEDD 1047) 2005.

These were solo efforts by **The Love Affair**'s former vocalist and founder of **Ellis**. He also cut a couple of 45s for Ariola in 1978 and a withdrawn one for Ocean in 1988. However, his solo career never really got off the ground. **The Love Affair**'s *Singles A's and B's* includes half a dozen of his tracks from the early seventies.

An Everlasting Soul is a 2-CD anthology, which collects the best of his material with **The Love Affair**, **Ellis**, **Widowmaker** plus his solo work. (VJ/JM)

Andy Ellison

45s:	α	It's Been A Long Time/Arthur Green	(Track 604 018) 1967 R2
		Fool From Upper Eden/Another Lucky Lie	(CBS 3357) 1968 R1
	β	You Can't Do That/Casbah	(S.N.B. 55-3308) 1968 R2

NB: α flip was by **John's Children**. β Promo-only copies exist of *Casbah* coupled with *Cornflake Zoo* (R2).

Ellison is best known as vocalist with **John's Children** (who reformed in the nineties) and later resurfaced in **Jet** and later in Radio Stars in the late seventies. All three 45s are now quite collectable and expensive.

It's Been A Long Time, an orchestrated pop number and a pretty weak one too, can also be found on *Backtrack 1* (LP), the *Here We Go 'Round The Mulberry Bush* soundtrack (LP) and on *Pop-In, Vol 2* (CD). *Electric Sugar Cube Flashbacks* (CD) and *Electric Sugar Cube Flashbacks, Vol. 4* (LP) include a version of *Cornflake Zoo*, an excellent composition which also appeared on a bootleg release on **John's Children**'s *Midsummer Night Scene* (EP) from 1979 and on a **John's Children** bootleg album, *Instant Action* (Hawkeye 010) 1984. **Arthur Green** has re-emerged on *Oddities, Vol 2* (CD), while *Fool From Upper Eden* can also be heard on *Colour Me Pop, Vol 1* (CD). (VJ)

Jeff Elroy and The Boys Blue

Personnel incl:	JEFF ELROY		A

45:	Honey Machine/Three Woman	(Philips BF 1533) 1966 SC

This was a bluesy ballad. **The Boys Blue** also had solo recordings. (VJ)

The Emeralds

45s:	Don't Listen To Your Friends/	
	Say You're Mine	(Decca F 12096) 1965
	King Lonely The Blue/	
	Someone Else's Fool	(Decca F 12304) 1965 R1

There was also an American band of this name who had a 45 on London, but this outfit came from Farnborough in Hampshire. Most of their material comprised beat-ballads, but their final effort, *King Lonely The Blue*, was a cut above the rest. Produced by former **Shadow Tony Meehan** it was basically a heavy re-work of **The Sorrows**' *Take A Heart* and is now quite collectable. This band later became **Wishful Thinking**.

Compilation appearances include: *King Lonely The Blue* on *The R&B Scene* (CD); and you'll find *Someone Else's Fool* on *Rare 60's Beat Treasures, Vol. 5* (CD). (VJ)

Emerson, Lake and Palmer

Personnel:	KEITH EMERSON	keyb'ds	A
	GREG LAKE	bs, gtr, vcls	A
	CARL PALMER	drms	A

EMERSON LAKE AND PALMER - Emerson Lake And Palmer (LP).

ALBUMS: 1(A) EMERSON, LAKE AND PALMER
(up to   (Island ILPS 9132) 1970 SC 4
1976) 2(A) TARKUS   (Island ILPS 9155) 1971 1
       3(A) PICTURES AT AN EXHIBITION (live)
                                (Island HELP 1) 1971 3
       4(A) TRILOGY (w/poster) (Island ILPS 9186) 1972 2
       5(A) BRAIN SALAD SURGERY
             (w/poster)   (Manticore K 53501) 1973 SC 2
       6(A) WELCOME BACK MY FRIENDS TO THE
             SHOW THAT NEVER ENDS (Manticore K 63500) 1974 5

NB: (1) reissued on vinyl (Get Back GETLP 528). (1) reissued on CD (Warner 191
20 2) (live triple) 1988 and again (Essential CMRCD 165) 2001. (2) reissued on CD
(WEA K 7815202) 1989, again on CD (Essential CMRCD 166) 2001, again
(Essential CMTCD 434) 2002 and again on CD (Essential ESMCD 341) 2005. (3)
reissued on (WEA K 781 521-2) 1989, again on CD (Essential CMRCD 167) 2001,
with a bonus rendition of the title track and again (Essential ESMCD 342) 2005. (4)
reissued on (WEA K 781 522-2) 1989, again on CD (Essential CMTCD 435) 2002
and again on CD (Essential ESMCD 343) 2005. (5) reissued on (WEA 781 523-2)
1989 and again (Essential CMTCD 433) 2002. Also relevant is *The Best Of
Emerson, Lake And Palmer* (Manticore K2 50757) 1983. *The Best Of Emerson, Lake
And Palmer* (Essential! ESS CD 296) 1995 includes their explosive reworking of
Jerusalem, their 45 version of *Fanfare For The Common Man*, the title cuts of their
Tarkus and *Trilogy* albums, *Still... You Turn Me On*, the melodic opening cut, *In The
Beginning*, a later techno-rock 45, *Black Moon* and ends with **Greg Lake**'s hit, *I
Believe In Father Christmas*. Talking of which, Christmas 1995 also saw the release
of a 5-track CD EP, *I Believe In Father Christmas* (Rhino R2 72242, import only).
Aside from two versions of the title track, it featured the trio's live version of B.
Bumble and The Stinger's *Nutrocker* plus Profokiev's *Troika* and **Lake**'s *Humbug*.
The Return Of The Manticore (Essential! ESFCD 421) 1996 is a 4-CD set of their
finest moments. Also of interest is *The Very Best Of ELP* (Rhino R2 79777) 2001.
The Original Bootleg Series From The Manticore Vaults Vol One (Sanctuary SRG
CMXBX 309) 2001 is a 7-CD box set of the band's live material and *Vol Two*
(Sanctuary SRG CMXBX 330) 2001 is an 8-CD box set of the same. The Original
Live At The Isle Of Wight Festival, 1970 (Castle CMRCD 458) 2002 captures the
band's second gig, which was originally available in 1997 via the band's website. *An
Introduction To Emerson Lake and Palmer* (Sanctuary SMRCD 001) 2004 compiles
some of their hits and some of their lesser-known moments. *The Ultimate Collection*
(Sanctuary TDSAN 009) 2004 is a 2-CD collection that could prove definitive.

45:     Jerusalem/
        When The Apple Blossoms Bloom   (Manticore K 13503) 1973

A popular techno-rock outfit at the time **Emerson, Lake and Palmer** have
not stood the test of time as well as many of their less revered colleagues.
Only their debut album is really recommended listening and then only for
fans of progressive techno-rock.

Keith Emerson, who was born on 2 November 1944, had previously
played with **The T-Bones**, **The V.I.P.'s** and **The Nice**. **Greg Lake**, born on
10 November 1948 in Bournemouth, had recently parted company with
King Crimson and, after auditioning for a drummer, they recruited Carl
Palmer from the recently defunct **Atomic Rooster**. Prior to this Palmer had
been with **Chris Farlowe's Thunderbirds** and later **Arthur Brown**.

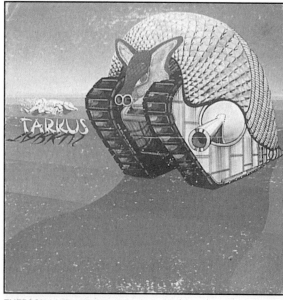

EMERSON LAKE AND PALMER - Tarkus (LP).

After making their live debut at the Guildhall, Portsmouth, on 25 August
1970, they played on the penultimate day of the Isle of Wight festival on 29
August.

Their debut album, which was released by Island in December 1970, was
very typical of their musical style. The album was technically excellent and
full of virtuoso instrumentation and rock/classical fusion but lacking in
feeling. With that qualification it certainly had its moments - *The Barbarian*
was awash with rousing keyboard work from **Emerson**, who, after **Hendrix**,
was one of rock's premier showmen. Indeed, their whole live act was based
around his organ-vaulting acrobatics. *Take A Pebble* was a much gentler,
softer track but still based (as most of their work) around **Emerson**'s
keyboards. The final track on side one, *Knife-Edge*, heralded a return to the
rousing keyboard theatrics of the opener. Side two opened with **Emerson**'s
The Three Fates, a rock/classical instrumental trilogy which opened with the
Royal Festival Hall organ on *Clotho*, which was followed by a piano solo on
Lachesis and a piano trio on *Atropos*. The piano trio is one of the album's
finest moments whilst the next cut, *Tank*, veered towards the tedious and
was further marred by the drum solo that seemed to be almost compulsory
on albums of this type in this era. The album concluded with a vocal cut,
Lucky Man. This was one of two **Lake** compositions on the album (the
other being *Take A Pebble*). The album sold well at the time peaking at No
4 in the UK and No 16 in the US.

The follow-up album, *Tarkus*, was a concept one - all about a mechanized
armadillo which engages the Manticore (a mythical beast) in battle. It sold
even better than their debut, actually reaching No 1 for a week in the UK
and peaking at No 9 in the US. Again it has not aged well. Only
occasionally does **Emerson**'s rousing organ work relieve the overall tedium
of the record.

Back on 26 March 1971 they'd been recorded playing their arrangement of
Mussorgsky's *Pictures At An Exhibition* at Newcastle City Hall and this was
later released as their third album. Establishing them firmly as one of the
country's leading techno-rock acts it peaked at No 3 in the UK and No 10
in the US. Their cover of B. Bumble and The Stingers *Nutrocker*, which
was also included on this album, was later extracted and issued as a
US-only single. It made No 70 in their Charts.

In April 1972 their performance of *Take A Pebble/Lucky Man* was recorded
at the Mar-Y-Sol festival in Puerto Rico for a live album of the event.

Their subsequent albums became increasingly self-indulgent and are
certainly not recommended. *Trilogy* sold quite well peaking at No 2 in the
UK and No 5 in the US and another US-only 45 taken from it, *From The
Beginning*, achieved more minor Chart success in the US peaking at No
39.

1973 saw the band embark on a US tour. The *Lucky Man* 45 was reissued
to help promote them and it re-entered the US Charts peaking at No 50.
The film 'Pictures At An Exhibition', which featured the band in a concert
performance of the title piece, helped to give them further exposure. The
same year they formed their own Manticore label (the name was taken
from the beast in *Tarkus*) and their next album, *Brain Salad Surgery*, and
their debut UK single from it, *Jerusalem*, were released on this label. The
single failed to Chart but the album made it to No 2 in the UK and No 11 in
the US.

The obligatory triple live set, *Welcome Back My Friends...*, followed and got
to No 5. *Works* a 2-LP set from 1977 was the album that proved to be their
downfall. It consisted of three solo sides and a fourth side on which the
group collaborated on two extended tracks *Pirates* and *Fanfare For The
Common Man*. Ponderous and self-indulgent, the album was released in a
year that saw a change in public taste with the emergence of punk and
disco and it sold poorly. Dedicating three of its four sides to solo projects
had done little for the group's harmony and it was never the same again.
Works, Vol 2 followed later the same year, but as a collection of obscure
'B' sides and odd tracks from over the last four years did nothing to stop
their decline and on their own admission on *Love Beach* (1978) the band
was merely going through the motions to honour its contractual obligations.
ELP disbanded in 1979.

Lake embarked on a moderately successful solo career. However, his most
successful venture commercially remained his 45 *I Believe In Father
Christmas* back in 1975. An uncharacteristic record for him it reached No 2
in the UK and tends to sell well every Christmas. **Emerson** concentrated
on composing film scores, but also embarked on the occasional solo
project. After a short spell with the band P.M., Palmer joined the

in the beginning...

THE END

THE END - In The Beginning (LP).

supergroup Asia. In the mid-eighties **Emerson** and **Lake** linked up with drummer **Cozy Powell** to form Emerson, Lake and Powell releasing an eponymous album, which climbed to No 35 in the UK album charts in the summer of 1986. The original trio of **ELP** reunited for a new album *Black Moon* (1992) followed by a fairly successful promotional tour. *Live At The Royal Albert Hall* followed in 1993, but their attempts to record another new album *In The Hot Seat* were thwarted when **Emerson** required surgery for repetitive stress disorder in one hand and restricted their ability to record or perform. The album was eventually completed in 1994, but all their subsequent recordings have been live ones.

The Very Best Of ELP is nicely packaged with good sleevenotes and it shows their worst excesses and some of their finest moments.

The Return Of The Manticore is a deluxe 4-CD set with a booklet. Aside from compiling their essential material, it is notable for re-recordings of *Pictures At An Exhibition* and *I Believe In Father Christmas* and for recordings of three pre-ELP classics: **The Nice's** *Hang On To A Dream*, **Arthur Brown's** *Fire* and **King Crimson's** *21st Century Schizoid Man*.

The Original Bootleg series put out in 2001 is exhaustive but marred by dodgy recording quality and will probably only interest diehard fans of the band.

Live At The Isle Of Wight Festival, 1970 is a five-track set plus an interview. It opens with the thundering *Barbarian*, followed by an elongated 11-minute version of the acoustic guitar and piano-backed *Take A Pebble*. Also of note is a 35-minute version of *Pictures At An Exhibition*, which is probably the stand-out track.

An Introduction To Emerson, Lake And Palmer compiles some of their hits alongside some of their more creative but lesser-known songs, so cuts like *Take A Pebble* and *Bennie The Bouncer* are featured, whereas *Fanfare For The Common Man* and *Karn Eveil 9* aren't.

The Ultimate Collection includes many of their finer moments, including a 10-minute version of *Fanfare For The Common Man* and a 20-minute bombastic version of *Tarkus*.

Compilation appearances include: *Barbarian* on *Rock Of Ages*, *Four Decades Of Heavy Rock* and *Lucky Man* and *Karn Evil 9 (First Impression Part 2)* on the 3-CD Box Set *Ars Longa Vita Brevis: A Compendium Of Progressive Rock 1967-1974*. (VJ/CG)

Keith Emerson

HCP

| 45: | Honky Tonk Train Blues/ | | |
| | Barrelhouse Shake Down | (Manticore K 13513) 1976 | 21 |

NB: There is a 2-CD set, *Hammer It Out - The Anthology* (Sanctuary CMEDD 1111) 2005, which traces his career and includes some output that is pre-1976.

As mentioned above by the mid-seventies **E.L.P.**'s members were beginning to work on solo projects. **Keith Emerson** went on to record several discs but only this 45, which narrowly missed the Top 20, came within the time frame of this book. (VJ)

Emmet Spiceland

| Personnel incl: | DONAL LUNNY | A |

| ALBUM: | 1 | THE FIRST | (Page One POLS 011) 1968 R2 |

NB: (1) reissued on vinyl *The Emmet Spiceland Album* (Hawk HALP 166) 1977.

| 45: | So Long Marianne/Ballad Of Franklin (Page One POF 143) 1968 |

This obscure late sixties album is now of some minor collectable value. The band was an Irish folk trio. (VJ)

The Emotions

| 45: | Lonely Man/Live Shooter | (Polydor BM 56025) 1965 |

Again there were other bands of this name including one from Jamaica and a black female trio from Chicago, USA. This one was from the UK. (VJ)

Enchanted Forest

Personnel:	SANNA GROSETH	vcls, bs	A
	SALLY HALBERT	drms	A
	JUDY HUNTER	lead gtr, vcls	A
	LAURIE STANTON	tambourine, vcls	A

| 45: | α | You're Never Gonna Get My Lovin'/ | |
| | | Suzanne | (Stateside SS 2080) 1968 |

NB: α issued on Bell in the USA.

A girl harmony-pop group, most probably from New York. They didn't include the Janis Ian (as is sometimes alleged), but were managed by Kenny Lynch who co-wrote the 'A' side, and were presumably based in the UK at the time. (VJ/Cn)

The End

Personnel:	DAVE BROWN	bs, vcls	ABCDE
	NICK GRAHAM	keyb'ds, vcls	ABCDE
	COLIN GIFFIN	steel gtr, vcls	ABCD
	ROGER GROOM	drms	A
	JOHN HORTON	sax	A

THE END - Retrospection (LP).

HUGH ATTWOOLL	drms	BCD
GORDON SMITH	sax	C
TERRY TAYLOR	gtr	DE
PAUL FRANCIS	drms	E

ALBUM: 1(C) INTROSPECTION (Decca LK-R/SKL-R 5015) 1969 R2
(up to 1976)

NB: (1) reissued on CD (Decca SRMC 0065) 1997. (1) reissued on CD in Korea (Si-Wan SRMC 0065) 1997. Also of interest are: *In The Beginning* (Tenth Planet TP025) 1996 (SC) is a Ltd edition compilation of previously unreleased demos, single and rare EP tracks; *Retrospection* (Tenth Planet TP033) 1998 (SC), a Ltd edition album of outtakes etc. and *The Last Word* (Tenth Planet TP 047) 2002 features post-*Introspection* sessions from 1968-69 before they evolved into **Tucky Buzzard**.

45s: I Can't Get Any Joy/Hey Little Girl (Philips BF 1444) 1965 SC
(up to Shades Of Orange/
1976) Loving Sacred Loving (Decca F 22750) 1968 R1

Managed by **Rolling Stone**, **Bill Wyman**, both Charlie Watts and **Nicky Hopkins** played on a track a piece on the *Introspection* album, which is very much a product of the psychedelic late sixties and is good. *Dreamworld* and *Don't Take Me* have sleepy harmonies, and other tracks like *What Does It Feel Like?* have some nice organ work. However, success eluded them and they eventually evolved into **Tucky Buzzard** who made three albums produced by **Bill Wyman** in the 1970's.

Dave Brown and Colin Griffin formed **The End** in 1965 following the demise of **The Innocents**. Nicky Graham and John Horton were drafted in from Dickie Pride's backing group The Original Topics, and the line-up completed by former Tuxedos drummer Roger Groom. They set about recording at R.G. Jones' Morden studio, and **Bill Wyman** arranged for them to tour with **The Rolling Stones** to coincide with their first 45. They also appeared with **Spencer Davis** on ITV's 'Thank Your Lucky Stars' playing *Hallelujah I Love Her So*. Following the tour Roger Groom quit, to be replaced by Hugh Attwooll, a former schoolfriend of Nicky Graham. John Horton also quit although the split was amicable and he helped out on their second single *Shades Of Orange*. Cut by **Bill Wyman** during the sessions for **The Rolling Stones**' *Their Satanic Majesties Request* album, the song, has an almost hypnotic, dreamlike quality, and featured Charlie Watts on tabla.

Following the release of *Shades Of Orange*, Gordon Smith too called it a day, and was replaced by former Mode guitarist Terry Taylor. This signalled a change in musical emphasis, more towards the style of their *Introspection* album, release of which was delayed for over a year, due to fallout from the '**Stones** bust-up with Allen Klein.

The band decamped to Spain, where several singles were released domestically, including *Why*, with which they scored a Top Five hit in April 1967.

THE END - Introspection (LP).

By Christmas 1968, both Colin Giffin and Hugh Attwooll had left, and although a new drummer, Paul Francis, was enlisted the writing was on the wall... and with the arrival of another Mode refugee Jim Henderson, they metamorphosed into **Tucky Buzzard**.

Also look out for two albums on the excellent Tenth Planet label. *In The Beginning... The End* 1996 is an 18-track anthology of their recordings they cut between 1964-67. It charts their development from the beat era, mod-tinged R&B, wild freakbeat and blue-eyed soul, culminating in a previously unissued mix of their superb psychedelic 45 *Shades Of Orange*, which was written by **Bill Wyman** and featured Charlie Watts on tabla. It also includes both sides of their 1965 single for Philips but 10 of the 18 tracks are previously unreleased. Also featured are both sides of two Spanish singles *You'd Better Believe It, Baby / Please Do Something* (Sonoplay SN-20,002), originally released January 1967, and *Why / Yo-Yo* (Sonoplay SN-20,014), originally released in March 1967.

Retrospection 1997 is a collection of outtakes from the *Introspection* sessions including the 45 version of *Loving Sacred Loving*, a US-only remix of *Shadows Of Orange*, two tracks only issued at the time in Spain and a further 10 previously unissued tracks. All the material was produced by **Bill Wyman** and the album comes in a stunning full colour sleeve. Only 1,000 copies were pressed of each album, which are bound to be of great interest to collectors of UK pop-psych.

The Last Word 2002 is compiled from post-*Introspection* sessions in 1969-1970. All of the tracks, apart from a Spanish 'B' side (a jazzy instrumental *Smartypants*), were previously unreleased. *North Thames Gas Board* features Ian 'Stu' Stewart (the sixth **Rolling Stone**) on piano. *So Free* has lovely harmonies. *For Eleanor* is an acoustic number and there's just one cover version - a rather mundane offering of Dan Penn/Spooner Oldham's *Do Right Woman*.

Compilation coverage has included:- *Jacob's Bladder* and *Introspection, Part 2* on Broken Dreams, Vol. 3 (LP); *Shades Of Orange* on The Psychedelic Scene (CD), The British Psychedelic Trip 1966 - 1969 (LP), Great British Psychedelic Trip Vol. 1 (CD), Rubble Vol. 6: The Clouds Have Groovy Faces (LP), Rubble Vol. 4 (CD) and on the 4-CD box set Acid Drops, Spacedust & Flying Saucers; *Loving Sacred Loving* on Jagged Time Lapse, Vol 1 (CD) and *Why* is on Visions Of The Past, 3 (LP & CD). (VJ)

England

Personnel:	OLLY ALCOCK	gtr, ld vcls	A
	PHIL COOK	drms	A
	BEN EGGLESTON	bs, vcls	A

ALBUM: 1(A) ENGLAND (Deroy DER 1356) 1976 R4
NB: (1) has been reissued on Audio Archives.

England's privately-pressed hard-riffing guitar rock album featured some fine guitar work and some strong material with *The Osprey* and *How Does It Feel* among the highlights. Worth seeking out but not easy to find. In addition to the above Paul Rossiter played sax on two tracks. (VJ/PM)

England's Glory

Personnel:	DAVID CLARKE	ld gtr	A
	HARRY KAKOULLI	bs, backing vcls	A
	JON NEWEY	drms, perc	A
	PETER PERRETT	vcls, gtr	A
	(MICHAEL KEMP	piano, organ	A)

ALBUM: 1(A) ENGLAND'S GLORY (promo only)
(Private Pressing) 1973 R3

NB: Reissued on Five Hours Back (TOCK 4) 1987 and on CD Anagram (CD MGRAM 73) 1994 and on vinyl and CD by Skyclad in the US-only in 1991. *The First And Last* (Diesel Motor MOTORCD 1020) 2005 contains four songs from the band's second May 1973 studio demo and nine previously unreleased tracks.

England's Glory was a short-lived but significant band. They were Peter Perrett's band prior to the formation of The Only Ones. A Dylan obsessive Perrett had released an acoustic demo in the Spring of 1972. Harry

ENGLAND - The Last Word (LP).

Kakoulli, a talented bass player who later played with Squeeze before recording two albums, completed the line-up together with Jon Newey and David Clarke who'd earlier played in an early seventies acid-rock group, **They Bite**. This outfit had been a regular attraction at underground clubs and student union gigs during 1970/71 supporting bands like **Stone The Crows**, **T2** and Uriel. Jon Newey, incidentally, went on to work for 'Sounds' and was later publisher of Tower Records' 'Top Magazine'.

England's Glory had the enterprise to finance their own album. Initially eight acetates bearing a blank, light blue label were pressed up and then 25 vinyl copies were privately pressed. They bore a pink label with the matrix number VEN 105. The album was heavily bootlegged in Australia in the late seventies/early eighties, where The Only Ones enjoyed cult status, but it's been officially issued here since in 1987 and reissued again on CD in 1994. It's well worth acquiring a copy. Almost all the material on the album is good, the stand-out track being the fast, rather punkish *City Of Fun*. Perrett's distinctive vocals shine through, the instrumentation is catchy and the disc sounds very much like the early Only Ones.

The First And Last, compiled by their former drummer Jon Newey as a sequel to the *Legendary Lost Album*, contains four songs from their second May 1973 studio demo and nine previously unreleased, remastered rehearsal tapes from 1972. The material is laid back, darkly romantic with a stoned feel and the set is accompanied by extensive sleevenotes. (VJ)

English Rose

Personnel incl: LYNTON GUEST   organ

45s:	Yesterday's Hero/To Jackie	(Polydor 2058 040) 1970
	Why Shouldn't I/Fairytale	(Electric WOT 3) 1976

Formed in June 1970 by Lynton Guest, who had been the organist in **The Love Affair**, they were featured in the film 'Groupie Girl', in which the band both acted and performed. A track from the film, *Yesterday's Hero* was released as a 45, although it is commercial pop with no stand-out features. The flip side, *To Jackie*, was orchestrated pop with good vocals.

There was another unconnected act by this name floating around in 1976. (VJ)

Ray Ennis and The Blue Jeans

45:	What Have They Done To Hazel?/	
	Now That You've Got Me (You Don't Seem To Want Me)	
		(Columbia DB 8431) 1968 SC

See **Swinging Blue Jeans**.

Brian Eno

ALBUMS:	1	NO PUSSYFOOTING	(Island HELP 16) 1973 -	HCP
(up to	2	HERE COME THE WARM JETS		
1976)			(Island ILPS 9268) 1974	26
	3	TAKING TIGER MOUNTAIN BY STRATEGY		
			(Island ILPS 9309) 1974	-
	4	ANOTHER GREEN WORLD	(Island ILPS 9351) 1975	-
	5	EVENING STAR	(Island/HELP 22) 1975	-
	6	DISCREET MUSIC	(Island/OBSCURE OBS 3) 1975	-
	7	801 LIVE	(Island ILPS 9444) 1976	-

NB: (1) and (5) with Robert Fripp. *More Blank Than Frank* (EG EGLP 65) 1986 is a compilation. (1) and (5) released on Antilles in the US. (1) and (5) reissued on CD (Editions E.G. Records EEGCD 2 and EEGCD 3 respectively) 1987. (2) reissued on CD (EG EGCD 11) 1986, deleted 1991. (3) reissued on CD (EG EGCD 17) 1986, deleted 1991. (4) reissued on CD (EG EGCD 21) 1987. (5) reissued on CD (EG EGCD 23) 1987. Also of interest is *Working Backwards 1983 - 1973* a 9-LP box set (EG EGBS 002) 1983.

45s:	Seven Deadly Finns/Later On	(Island WIP 6178) 1974
	The Lion Sleeps Tonight (Wimoweh)/	
	I'll Coming Running	(Island WIP 6233) 1975

Brian Eno has been an immensely influential and prolific pioneering figure in the history of rock as an innovative avant-garde and glam-rock performer, a hit producer, a multi-media artist and more.

Born Brian Peter George St John le Baptiste de la Salle Eno in Suffolk in 1948, **Brian Eno** (as he became known) later joined Winchester College of Art in 1966 and went on to become Student Union President. Whilst there he met Andy Mackay, a saxophonist, who would be an important future influence on his life. He quickly became an electronics whizzkid and a dab hand on the synthesizer and after joining **Roxy Music** in 1971 he was largely responsible for their radical new sound.

He left **Roxy Music** in 1973 after disagreements with **Bryan Ferry** and collaborated with **King Crimson**'s Robert Fripp on the *No Pussyfooting* album. It was very avant-garde and influenced by Terry Riley. Fripp also played guitar on **Eno**'s first solo album, *Here Come The Warm Jets*, as did **Roxy Music**'s Phil Manzanera. Although the end product was rather an anti-climax it did climb to No 26 in the UK Album Charts and No 151 in the US. Three months after its release, on 1 June 1974, he took part in a concert at London's Rainbow Theatre with **John Cale**, **Kevin Ayers** and Nico, which was released later in the month as *June 1st 1974*.

He continued to make creative albums like *Taking Tiger Mountain By Strategy* and *Another Green World* as well as *Evening Star*, which was the result of another collaboration with Robert Fripp. Sadly these works were mostly ignored by the public at large. However, **Eno** was far more than just a recording artist - he contributed to other people's albums (**John Cale**'s *Slow Dazzle* and *Helen Of Troy*, **Robert Wyatt**'s *Ruth Is Stranger Than Richard* and Phil Manzanera's *Diamond Head* album); produced **Robert**

ENO - Here Come The Warm Jets (LP).

ENO - Another Green World (CD).

Calvert's album *Lucky Lief And The Longships*; made a lecture tour of UK universities; undertook a tour with pub-rock outfit The Winkies and issued a boxed set of writings, 'Oblique Strategie' - phew, what a dynamic guy! That wasn't all - at the end of 1975 he started working on his own studio with Manzanera and **Wyatt** and launched his own record label, Obscure, which he secured a distribution deal for through Island. His first release on this label was *Discreet Music*, which was quite a bit different from what he'd done previously.

During 1976 he formed a group called 801 with Phil Manzanera, which had its final of three concerts at London's Queen Elizabeth Hall recorded for the *801 Live* album. 1977's pop-based *Before And After Science* was one of his best efforts but amongst his more interesting ambient projects were: *Music For Films* (1978), an experimental collection of pieces of music compiled as soundtracks for imaginary motion pictures, *Music For Airports* (1978) an ambient collection designed to calm air passengers' fears of flying and crashing and his collaborations with the minimalist composer Harold Budd (*The Plateaux Of Mirror*) and avant-garde trumpeter Jon Hassell (*Possible Musics*). In 1981 he recorded a ground-breaking album *My Life In The Bush Of Ghosts* with Talking Head's vocalist David Byrne that fused electronic music with Third World percussion.

Eno also became a much sought-after producer - his credits included the ground-breaking **Bowie** album trilogy - *Low*, *Heroes* and *Lodger*; the German group Cluster; Talking Heads (he also co-wrote with the band's David Byrne all but one track on their 1980 *Remain In Light* album); the highly-acclaimed *No New York* compilation; **John Cale**'s 1989 solo album *Words For The Dying*; and he worked with Acadian producer Daniel Lanois on a series of records for the Irish band U2 (including *The Joshua Tree* and *Achtung Baby*).

More ambient recordings followed in the eighties: *On Land* (1982), the spaced-themed *Apollo: Atmospheres & Sountracks* (1983) on which his brother Roger assisted and *Thursday Afternoon* (1985), a soundtrack to a VHS cassette of "video paintings" by artist Christine Alicino. In 1986 **Eno** put together a compilation *More Blank Than Frank*, which contains many of his favourite songs. This contains a lot of material from *Another Green World* and one of his best post-1976 albums, *Before And After Science*. He remained prolific in the nineties, teaming up with **John Cale** for *Wrong Way Up* (1990), subsequent albums included *The Shutov Assembly* and *Nerve Net* (1992), *Neroli* (1993), and 1994's *Glitterbug* was a soundtrack to a film by Derek Jarman. In 1999 *Sonora Portraits* was released. This collection of previous ambient tracks was accompanied by a 93-page booklet. In the late nineties, **Eno** was working in the world of art installations and his installation soundtracks were released usually in extremely limited editions with the result that they became instant collectors' items. In 2000 he collaborated with the German deejay Peter Schwalm on *Music For Onmyo-Ji*, which was only released in Japan. In 2004 many of his early EG albums were reissued and a new **Eno** solo album *Another Day On Earth* was released in 2005. (VJ)

Enough's Enough

45:    Please Remember/
       Look Around You Baby   (Tattoo TT 101) 1968 R4

Please Remember has strong vocals, and *Look Around You Baby* the better instrumentation of the two tracks. The group was probably from the Dublin area of Eire.

Compilation appearances have included: *Please Remember* on *Psychedelia, Vol. 1* (LP); *Look Around You Baby* on *Psychedelia, Vol. 2* (LP); and *Please Remember* and *Look Around You Baby* on *Syde Trips, Vol. 3* (LP) and *Hen's Teeth Vol. 1* (CD). (VJ)

John Entwistle

ALBUMS: 1 SMASH YOUR HEAD AGAINST THE WALL
(up to   (Track 2406 005) 1971 SC
1976)   2 WHISTLE RHYMES   (Track 2406 104) 1972 SC
         3 MAD DOG   (Decca TXS 114) 1975 SC

NB: (3) as John Entwistle's Ox. (1) and (2) were issued on Decca and MCA in the US. (1) reissued on CD (Castle Music CMRCD 1152) 2005. (2) reissued on CD (Castle Music CMRCD 1153) 2005. ((3) reissued on CD (Repertoire REP 4629 WY) 1996. *Anthology* (Repertoire REP 4600 WY) 1996 compiles material from the five albums he issued between 1971-81 in chronological order. *Thunderfingers: The Best Of John Entwistle* (Rhino R2 72570) 1996 is an import-only collection of similar material, but more weighted towards the early seventies. *King Biscuit Hour* (1998) features him in concert in 1975.

45s: I Believe In Everything/My Size   (Track 2094 008) 1970
    α   Mad Dog/Cell No 7   (Decca FR 13567) 1975

NB: α as John Entwistle's Ox.

Entwistle was born in Hammersmith, London, on 9 October 1944. His father John Alec Entwistle had played trumpet in the Royal Navy and his mother played piano and ensured her son took lessons from the age of seven. Although his parents separated when he was young their encouragement paid off and by his early teens John was proficient on piano, trumpet and French horn. However, he ended up playing bass and carved his first model from a piece of plywood.

Whilst at Acton Grammar School he met **Roger Daltrey** and **Pete Townshend** and played with them in The Detours who became **The High Numbers** and later **The Who**. In 1971 he became the first member of the band to achieve solo success when his debut album peaked at No 126 in the US. It included a re-work of *Heaven And Hell*, the flipside to **The Who**'s *Summertime Blues*, which had also been included on *The Ox* album. Frankly, though, it was pretty limited and his second effort, *Whistle Rhymes* was a big improvement although it didn't translate into greater Chart success. It just peaked at No 138 in the US. The outstanding track on this was the weird and discordant *Nightmare*, although *I Found Out* was a rather appealing, accessible song.

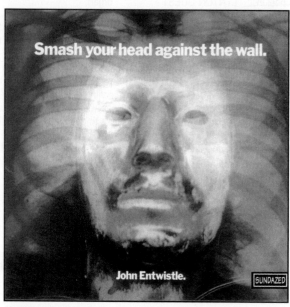

JOHN ENTWISTLE - Smash Your Head Against The Wall (CD).

JOHN ENTWISTLE - Whistle Rhymes (CD).

In 1973 he formed a studio band called **Rigor Mortis** who were infamously loud to record a further album and the following year he compiled a collection of previously unreleased **Who** material, *Odds And Sods*, which turned out to be surprisingly successful. His next recording venture was a new band, John Entwistle's Ox. The Ox's line-up included Ashton, Casey and Deacon (from his earlier band **Rigor Mortis**) plus Jim Ryan (gtr) and Mike Wedgewood (gtr) together with a handful of backing vocalists and session musicians including Eddie Jobson, who was with **Roxy Music** at the time. They toured the US in February/March 1975 and later recorded *Mad Dog*, which again was more successful in the US, where it peaked at No 192. *Mad Dog* was an arse-kicking hard-rock album which must have captured the band's live material pretty well. **Entwistle**'s solo ventures have been pretty spasmodic since, though he recorded *Too Late The Hero* for WEA in 1981.

His 1998 *King Biscuit Hour* release captures him in concert in 1975. It also includes a brief interview with him and a version of *Boris The Spider*.

He died of a heart attack at the Hard Rock Hotel, Las Vegas, on 27 June 2002, aged 57, just a day before a reconstituted **Who** was due to embark on an extensive US tour.

The Ox compilation ('Ox' was his nickname) released in 1971 collected some of his finer compositions for **The Who** including *Boris The Spider*, *Fiddle About* and *Cousin Kevin*, the last two being his contributions to 'Tommy'. (VJ)

The Envoys

Personnel:

JAN CUTTS	vcls		A
ALEC HITCHCOK	drms		A
GWILYM HITCHCOCK	ld gtr		A
GEOFF SHEARN	gtr, ld vcls		A
ROSEMARY SUTTON	vcls		A
DAVE TAYLOR	bs, vcls		A

EP: 1(A) THE ENVOYS (XPR 3048) 196?

A gospel beat combo who recorded this superb four-track EP. All tracks contain "the message" - two are very good musically. Indeed *Danger* is on a par with many other beat songs of the era. (VJ)

The Epics

Personnel:

MIKE BLAKELY	drms, backing vcls		A
VIC ELMES	lead gtr, lead vcls		A
IAN JANSEN	gtr, backing vcls		A
STUART TANN	bs, lead vcls		A

45s: There's Just No Pleasing You/
My Little Girl (Pye 7N 15829) 1965
Just How Wrong You Can Be/
Blue Turns To Grey (Pye 7N 17053) 1966
Travelling Circus/Henry Long (CBS 3564) 1968

This band included the brother of **Tremeloes**' Alan Blakely and evolved into **Acid Gallery** and then bubblegum outfit **Christie** of *Yellow River* fame. Their very competent melodic version of **Jagger**-Richards' *Blue Turns To Grey* is well worth a spin.

The Epics started life in the early sixties as The 4 Zodiacs with Vic Elmes (lead gtr, vcls), Ian Jansen (gtr, vcls), Bill Fifield (drms, vcls) and Stuart Tann (bs, vcls). Influenced by the skiffle craze they played at parties, weddings and pubs and were managed by Ian's Mum! She made a good job of it too - as the band was working most weekends, no doubt improving musically as they got more and more bookings in clubs and dance halls. They also got to play a few one-nighters backing established artists such as John Leyton, Billie Davis and Millie.

When Bill left, his replacement was Mike Blakley (**Tremelo** Alan's younger brother) and the band was signed shortly afterwards to Starlite Enterprises - **The Tremeloes** management/booking agency. They then became **The Epics**. Bill Fifield, meanwhile later changed his surname to Legend and resurfaced as drummer with **T Rex**.

Stuart Tann recalls:- "Not long after this we got to record for Pye (what a fantastic experience) under recording manager Tony Hatch. We released two records at Pye, *Just No Pleasing You*, written by Jackie De-Shannon and *Just How Wrong You Can Be*, by P.F Sloane. The 'B' side of *Just How Wrong....* was *Blue Turns To Grey*, by messers **Jagger** & Richards. This was to have been our next single, but we were prevented from releasing it because Cliff Richard was about to!!"

"By now we were all getting a bit despondent, neither disc had done anything chart wise, so when our contract with Pye was not renewed, we moved to CBS with recording manager Mike Smith. *Travelling Circus* was the only release and, despite TV appearances on the prime time Simon Dee show "Thank Your Lucky Star's" and radio's "Jimmy Young Show", the record only managed to 'bubble under'."

"During this time we were touring in Europe, particularly in Denmark where we had some chart success with a cover version of **Chris Andrews**' *Yesterday Man*, with our Danish road manager Johan Lind, on lead vocals. This record was released on the Metronome label and was in fact Denmark's first stereo single release."

"A little later **The Epics** became 'Blossom', for a very short period (flower-power and all that!) and it wasn't until I left the band in late 1968, that they became **Acid Gallery**."

"Auditions were held to find my replacement and, out of the many, John Barber, previously lead singer with **The Overlanders** on there hit cover

RIPPLES VOL. 6 (Comp CD) including The Epics.

257

version of **The Beatles** *Michelle*, was chosen. This union only lasted a few weeks and soon John was replaced by Alan Ross. The music too changed.... becoming heavier hard-rock and blues."

"**Acid Gallery** recorded *Dance Round The Maypole*, written and produced by **Roy Wood** at CBS studios, along with Jeff Lynne. Both Roy and Jeff sang backing vocals on the disc and the unmistakeable sound of **The Move** permeates the record."

"**Acid Gallery** didn't last long, and when Ian Jansen left in 1970, Vic, Mike and Alan were joined by Jeff Christie and... **Christie** was born.... but that's another story."

Vic Elmes later did some session work in Germany and has had several CD's released there. He married Dee Anderson, daughter of Gerry and Sylvia Anderson of "Thunderbirds" fame, and composed some of the music for one of the series.

Compilation coverage has included:- *Blue Turns To Grey* on *Let's Go Get Stoned (The Songs Of Jagger And Richards)* (LP), *The Roots Of Rock* (LP), *Hippy Hippy Shake* (CD) and *Rubble, Vol. 7 - Pictures In The Sky* (LP); *Just How Wrong..* on *Ripples, Vol. 6* (CD); *How Wrong Can You Be?* and *Blue Turns To Grey* on *Footsteps To Fame, Vol. 2* (CD) and *Henry Long* on *Oddities, Vol 2* (CD), *Jagged Time Lapse, Vol 4* (CD) and *Fading Yellow, Vol 4* (CD). (VJ/ST/IJ)

Episode Six

Personnel:

GRAHAM CARTER - DIMMOCK	gtr, vcls	ABCDEF
SHEILA CARTER - DIMMOCK	organ, vcls	ABCDEF
ROGER GLOVER	bs	ABCD
TONY LANDER	ld gtr	ABCDEF
ANDY ROSS	vcls	A
HARVEY SHIELDS	drms	AB
IAN GILLAN	vcls	BCD
JOHN KERRISON	drms	C
MICK UNDERWOOD	drms	D
JOHNNY GUSTAFSON	vcls, bs	E
PETE ROBINSON	keyb'ds	E
JOHN BANKS	drms	F
TONY DANGERFIELD	vcls, bs	F
DAVE LAWSON	keyb'ds	F

ALBUMS: 1(-) PUT YOURSELF IN MY PLACE (PRT PYL 6026) 1987
2 THE ROOTS OF DEEP PURPLE: THE COMPLETE
EPISODE SIX (CD) (Sequel NEX CD 156) 1991

NB: (1) also released on CD (PYC 6026) 1987. There's also an earlier retrospective release *Episode Six* (Pye 260404), however this is a pirate and is inferior to (2) or (3). *The Radio One Club Sessions Live 1968/1969* (RPM RPM 178) 1998 includes them being interviewed by **Tony Blackburn**! *Cornflakes And Crazy Foam* (Purple PUR 319 D) 2002 is a 2-CD 51-track set. *Love, Hate, Revenge* (Castle/Sanctuary CMEDD 894) is an exhaustive 2-CD 44-track collection of their material.

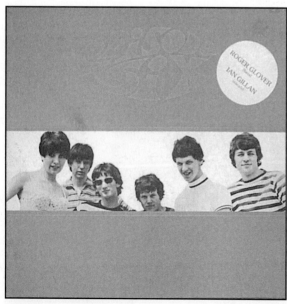
EPISODE SIX - Episode Six (LP).

EPISODE SIX - Put Yourself In My Place (LP).

45s:

	Put Yourself In My Place/	
	That's All I Want	(Pye 7N 17018) 1966 SC
	I Hear Trumpets Blow/	
	True Love Is Funny That Way	(Pye 7N 17110) 1966 SC
	Here, There and Everywhere/	
	Mighty Morris Ten	(Pye 7N 17147) 1966 SC
α	I Will Warm Your Heart/Incense	(Pye 7N 17194) 1966 SC
β	Love, Hate, Revenge/Baby Baby Baby	(Pye 7N 17244) 1967 SC
	Morning Dew/Sunshine Girl	(Pye 7N 17330) 1967 SC
χ	I Won't Hurt You/U.F.O.	(Pye 7N 17371) 1967 SC
	I Can See Through You/	
	When I Fall In Love	(Pye 7N 17376) 1967 SC
δ	Little One/Wide Smiles	(MGM 1409) 1968 SC
	Lucky Sunday/Mr. Universe	(Chapter One CH 103) 1968 SC
	Mozart vs. The Rest/Jak D'Or	(Chapter One CH 104) 1969 SC

NB: α credited to **Sheila Carter and Episode Six**. β also issued in the US (Elektra EK 45617) 1967, but with a completely different middle section to the UK version consisting of a weird electronic freakout. χ credited to **Neo Maya**, but this was a pseudonym used by Graham Carter-Dimmock. δ credited to Episode.

The roots of this band lie in two Harrow County Grammar School bands, The Madisons (who included Glover, Lander and Shields in their personnel) and The Lightnings (who featured the Carter-Dimmocks and Andy Ross). As the members of both bands began to leave school and drift away from the bands the remaining members decided that their best chance was to merge, which they did in October 1963 as The Lightnings initially, although by July 1964 they had changed to the rather more hip name of **Episode Six**. They got plenty of live work including a four week assignment at a Frankfurt club. Their music was essentially melodic ballads with lavish harmonies, but after the Frankfurt trip they underwent their first line-up change when Andy Ross quit the music business to get married. His replacement was one Ian Gillan, who, of course would go on to find fame and fortune with **Deep Purple** and later form his own band.

Their first 45, *Put Yourself In My Place*, was a **Beatles**-influenced song, although a catchy **Roger Glover** song was used on the flip. The follow-up, *I Hear Trumpets Blow*, was a cover of an old Tokens song and again a self-penned number, this time by drummer Harvey Shields, was used on the flip. Their third 45 was a very good cover of **The Beatles'** *Here, There And Everywhere* with another **Roger Glover** song on the flip. There is a very rare French EP which contains their second and third singles. This changes hands for a lot of money. Still the sad fact was that after three singles the band had made little impact and their manager, Gloria Bristow, decided to try something different - a pretty awful cover of Charles Aznavour's *I Will Break Your Heart* which was credited to **Sheila Carter and Episode Six** and did nothing to assist the band's cause.

The band spent the Christmas of 1966 working in Beirut and some Eastern influence is evident on *Love, Hate, Revenge*, which was their next 45 release and one of their better offerings. After their next effort, a cover of Tim Rose's *Morning Dew*, Harvey Shields left the band to form a duo with a belly dancer he'd met during their spell in Beirut. He was replaced by John Kerrison.

The first recording by the new line-up was actually a single, *I Won't Hurt You*, credited to **Neo Maya** (which was a pseudonym used by Graham Carter-Dimmock). Since no one had heard of **Neo Maya** very few people bought it and it's their hardest UK release to track down. Their next 'group' release, *I Can See Through You*, was the first self-penned song they'd been allowed to use as an 'A' side. Written by **Roger Glover**, there was a hint of psychedelia in its powerful backing, which was ideally suited to late 1967 when the single came out. It also featured a powerful vocal performance by Ian Gillan. Surprisingly it wasn't a hit and the group's dissatisfaction with Pye's distribution of it led them to sign a new record deal with MGM. Their first single for their new label, *Little One*, featured lots of brass and was very different to its predecessor, one thing both had in common though was poor sales. However, the band continued to believe they were on the verge of a breakthrough for Ian Gillan turned down the chance to join his old mate Nick Simper (who he'd worked with previously) in an embryonic **Deep Purple** line-up. One member who did part company with the band was John Kerrison after a dressing room row - at his final appearance with them at The Boathouse Kew, he set up his drum-kit at the opposite end of the hall from the rest of the band. He was replaced by ex-**Herd** member Mick Underwood.

The band changed labels again to new Decca subsidiary Chapter One, but their first effort was of more interest for the Ian Gillian-written 'B' side *Mr. Universe* than the uninspired 'A' side. Of more interest was the band's final 45, an uptempo over-the-top guitar instrumental, *Mozart vs. The Rest*, probably inspired by **Love Sculpture**'s *Sabre Dance*.

In April 1969 the band entered the studio to begin recording tracks for a long-delayed album which had a working title of *The Story So Far* but it wasn't to be. Ian Gillan was lured away to replace **Deep Purple**'s departing vocalist Rod Evans and **Roger Glover** joined him in **Deep Purple** a few days later. They were initially replaced by Pete Robinson (ex-James Royal Set) and Johnny Gustafson (ex-**Questions**). Having not played any live dates, Robinson, Gustafson and Underwood left to form **Quartermass**. They were replaced by Tony Dangerfield, John Banks (both ex-**Rupert's People**) and Dave Lawson. This line-up did a brief residency in Beirut and on their return, Lander joined Johnny Quantrell and the Confederates before turning to interior decorating, Dangerfield joined **Alan Bown** and Lawson went on to **Almond Marzipan**. Of the remaining members the Carter-Dimmocks went out to Beirut briefly to work as **Episode Six** but she returned to the UK later marrying **Harmony Grass**' Tom Marshall and Graham became a booking agent arranging for bands to tour Middle East hotels. John Kerrison, who'd been in The Pirates (the final line-up put together after Johnny Kidd's death), went on to the Rockin' Eccentrics.

Back in 1968 the band recorded one track, *Gentlemen Of The Park*, for the soundtrack to a short B-movie entitled 'Les Bicyclettes de Belsize'. It was included, along with songs from another film, 'The Twisted Nerve', on *Music From Twisted Nerve And Les Bicyclettes De Belsize* (Polydor 583 728) in 1969.

The Radio One Club Sessions Live 1968/69 features the band mostly performing covers of sixties classics like Lorraine Ellison's *Stay With Me*

Baby, The Door's *Light My Fire* and *Spanish Caravan*, Love's *The Castle*, Tim Rose's *Morning Dew*, Gene Pitney's *Something's Gotten Hold Of My Heart* and a **Rolling Stones** medley. It's packaged in a fold-out sleeve and there is **Tony Blackburn** interviewing the band.

The 2-CD compilation *Cornflakes And Crazyfoam* is a 51-track selection of early demos, unreleased singles, radio spots, live concert and rehearsal material. It's accompanied by a 24-page booklet with biographies and photos. In addition to their own material, they do quite a lot of covers, including **Sandie Shaw's** *Always Something There To Remind Me*; **The Beatles**' *Here There And Everywhere*; Harry Belafonte's *Island In The Sun*; a **Rolling Stones** medley and numbers by US band like The Doors, Love and Moby Grape.

The retrospective album, released on PRT in 1987 only includes their Pye singles whereas the CD release on Sequel goes further by including their MGM and Chapter One singles too, as well as a demo from 1964, *My Babe*, and some outtakes from the mid-sixties. All in all a worthy acquisition for fans of sixties pop. Fans will also be interested in *The Radio One Club Sessions Live 1968/69* (CD) 1998 which includes an interview with **Tony Blackburn** and the band's interpretation, usually based around Ian Gillan and Sheila Carter's twin vocal attack, of classics such as **The Rolling Stones**' *Satisfaction* and *Paint It Black*, The Doors' *Light My Fire* and *Spanish Caravan*, Tim Rose's *Morning Dew*, Lorraine Ellison's *Stay With Me Baby*, Gene Pitney's *Something's Gotten Hold Of My Heart*, Love's *The Castle* and Simon and Garfunkel's *Hazy Shade Of Winter*.

Love, Hate, Revenge is a 2-CD set with very concise sleevenotes which help to clarify their history. It includes live recordings, rarities, 'A' and 'B' sides and demos of 13 previously unreleased recordings. **Deep Purple**/Ian Gillan fans will want this.

Retrospective compilation appearances have included: *Love, Hate, Revenge* on *Quick Before They Catch Us* (LP & CD), *We Can Fly* (CD) and the 4-CD *Nuggets 11* box set; *Put Yourself In My Place* and *Sunshine Girl* on *Ripples, Vol. 1* (CD); *Morning Dew* and *Here, There And Everywhere* on *Ripples, Vol. 3* (CD); *Mighty Morris Ten* on *Ripples, Vol. 5* (CD) and *Hang II - Mutant Surf Punks*; *I Hear Trumpets Blow* on *Ripples, Vol. 2* (CD); *I Can See Through You* on *The Sound Of The Sixties* (2-LP), *Sixties Archive Vol. 1* (CD), *Hot Smoke & Sassfras - Psychedelic Pstones Vol 1* (CD), *Jagged Time Lapse, Vol 1* (CD) and *Rock Of Ages, Four Decades Of Heavy Rock 1962-2002*; *Put Yourself In My Place* on *Watch Your Step* (CD); *Morning Dew, I Hear Trumpets Blow* and *Gentleman Of The Park* on *Deep Purple - Odd Ditties* (CD); *Morning Dew* and *I Hear Trumpets Blow* on *The Early Days Of Rock, Vol. 2 - Live In Concert 1964 - 1968* (CD); *Put Yourself In My Place* and *That's All I Want* on *Footsteps To Fame, Vol. 1* (CD); *Plastic Love* and *Time And Motion Man* on *Haunted - Psychedelic Pstones, Vol 2*; *Mr. Universe* on *Incredible Sound Show Stories Vol. 11* (LP) and *I Hear Trumpets Blow* and *Morning Dew* on the 2-CD set *Ars Longa Vita Brevis: A Compendium of Progressive Rock 1967-1974*. (VJ/BM/JM)

The Equals

Personnel:			
	LINCOLN GORDON	gtr	ABCD
	DERVIN GRAHAM	vcls	ABCD
	EDDY GRANT	vcls, gtr	A
	JOHN HALL	drms	ABC
	PAT LLOYD	gtr	ABCD
	JIMMY HAYNES	vcls	B
	DAVE MARTIN	vcls	CD
	NEIL McBAIN	drms	D

				HCP
ALBUMS:	1(A)	UNEQUALLED EQUALS	(President PTL 1006) 1967	SC 10
(up to	2(A)	EQUALS EXPLOSION	(President PTL 1015) 1968	SC 32
1976)	3(A)	SENSATIONAL EQUALS		
			(President PTL(S) 1020) 1968	SC -
	4(A)	EQUALS SUPREME	(President PTL(S) 1025) 1968	SC -
	5(A)	THE EQUALS STRIKE AGAIN		
			(President PTLS 1030) 1969	SC -
	6(A)	BEST OF THE EQUALS	(President PTLS 1050) 1969	
	7(A)	AT THE TOP	(President PTLS 1038) 1970	SC -
	8(-)	GREATEST HITS (Music For Pleasure MFP 50153) 1974		
	9( )	BORN YA	(Mercury 9109 601) 1976	SC -

NB: (1) and (2) reissued on one CD (Repertoire REP 45730-WY) 1995. (3) and (4)

EPISODE SIX - The Roots Of Deep Purple (CD).

reissued on one CD together with three bonus EP cuts: *I Can't Let You Go, Lonely* and *Don't Throw Your Love Away* (Repertoire REP 4673 WP) 1998. A couple of vinyl retrospectives that may be of interest are *Best Of* (Astan 20048) 1984 and *20 Greatest Hits* (Astan 20050) 1984. Their most definitive compilation is on CD though, *The Very Best Of The Equals* (See For Miles SEE CD 374) 1993. Other CD compilations are *20 Greatest Hits: Equals* (Mainline 266 201 2) 1990, *The Ultimate Hit Collection* (Repertoire REP 4214-WZ) 1991 and *All The Hits Plus More* (Prestige CDPT 001) 1992.

				HCP
EPs:	1(A)	BABY COME BACK	(President PTE 1) 1968	SC -
	2(A)	THE EQUALS	(President PTE 2) 1968	SC -

			HCP
45s:	I Won't Be There/Fire	(President PT 117) 1968	-
(up to	Baby Come Back/Hold Me Closer	(President PT 135) 1968	1
1976)	Give Love A Try/		
	Another Sad And Lonely Night	(President PT 158) 1968	-
	I Get So Excited/Skies Above	(President PT 180) 1968	44
	Laurel And Hardy/		
	The Guy Who Made Her A Star	(President PT 200) 1968	35
	Softly Softly/Lonely Rita	(President PT 222) 1968	48
	Michael And The Slipper Tree/		
	Honey Gum	(President PT 240) 1969	24
	Viva Bobby Joe/I Can't Let You Go	(President PT 260) 1969	6
	Rub A Dub Dub/		
	After The Lights Go Down Low	(President PT 275) 1969	34
	I Can See But You Don't Know/		
	Gigolo Sam	(President PT 303) 1970	R2 -
	Black Skin Blue Eyed Boys/		
	Happy Birthday Girl	(President PT 325) 1970	9
	Stand Up And Be Counted/		
	What Would You Do To Survive	(CBS 7874) 1972	-
	Diversion/		
	Here Today, Gone Tomorrow	(President PT 414) 1973	-
	Georgetown Girl/		
	We've Got It Worked Out	(President PT 436) 1975	-
	Kaiwana Sunshine Girl/Soul Mother	(Mercury 6007 104) 1976	-
	Funky Like A Train/		
	If You Didn't Miss Me	(Mercury 6007 106/7) 1976	-
Reissues:	Baby, Come Back/Hold Me Closer	(Old Gold OG 9021) 1979	-
	Viva Bobby Joe/I Can't Let You Go	(Old Gold OG 9025) 1979	-
	Black Skinned Blue Eyed Boy/		
	Happy Birthday Girl	(Old Gold OG 9033) 1979	-

This London group is most notable now for the fact it had Eddie Grant as its lead vocalist. It was also an interracial group, which was reasonably rare at the time - they consisted of three West Indians and two British guys. They played a form of very accessible pop/rock (almost bubblegum) and are best remembered for *Baby, Come Back*, which gave them a UK No 1. Over the next few years they enjoyed other Chart entries - most notably *Viva Bobby Joe* and *Black Skinned Blue Eyed Boy* - but in June 1972 Eddy Grant left initially to a group called 90 Degrees Inclusive and then to go

THE EQUALS - Sensational Equals (LP).

solo. After this, their days as a Chart force were over, although they continued to record well into the late seventies. *Funky Like A Train* was an excellent club track. *The Skies Above* is a slightly unusual track.

I Can See But You Don't Know, which features aggressive loud guitar work, later resurfaced on *Electric Sugarcube Flashbacks, Vol. 2* (LP); *The Skies Above* gets a further airing on *Jagged Time Lapse, Vol 3* (CD); *Baby Come Back* got fresh exposure on *60's Mix* (CD); *and Viva Bobby Joe* and *Baby Come Back* can also be heard on *Here Comes Summer* (CD) and *Brit Pop* (CD).

Grant was an in-house producer for President and was responsible for lots of other acts including **Little Grants and Eddie**. (VJ/JM)

Equinox

ALBUM:	1	HARD ROCK	(Boulevard 4118) 1973 SC

This heavy rock outfit's album is presently only of minor interest to collectors. (VJ)

The Escorts

Personnel incl:	PETE CLARKE	drms	A
	MICK GREGORY	bs	ABC
	JOHN KINRADE	ld gtr	ABC
	TERRY SYLVESTER	gtr, vcls	ABC
	JOHNNY STICKS	drms	AB
	PADDY CHAMBERS	gtr	C
	TOM KELLY	drms	C

			HCP
45s:	Dizzy Miss Lizzy/All I Want Is You	(Fontana TF 453) 1964	SC -
	The One To Cry/Tell Me Baby	(Fontana TF 474) 1964	SC 49
	I Don't Want To Go On Without You/		
	Don't Forget To Write	(Fontana TF 516) 1965	SC -
	C'mon Home Baby/		
	You'll Get No Lovin' That Way	(Fontana TF 570) 1965	SC -
	Let It Be Me/Mad Mad World	(Fontana TF 651) 1966	SC -
	From Head To Toe/Night Time	(Columbia DB 8061) 1966	R1 -

One of the better Liverpool groups to come out of the Merseybeat boom, their progress may have been undermined by the several personnel changes they underwent during their three year career.

Their version of *Dizzy Miss Lizzy* was pretty good and they also enjoyed a minor hit with *The One To Cry*. *I Don't Want To Go On Without You* was also recorded by **The Moody Blues**, who had the hit and **Paul McCartney** played tambourine on their final 45, *From Head To Toe*.

Their days were probably numbered when Sylvester and Gregory departed to join **The Swinging Blue Jeans** (Sylvester was later in **The Hollies**) but they soldiered on until late 1966 when they finally gave up the ghost. Paddy Chambers died of throat cancer on 28 September 2000.

Compilation appearances include: *The One To Cry* on *Mersey Beat* (2-LP); *Dizzy Miss Lizzie* and *The One To Cry* on *Mersey Beat 1962-1964* (2-LP); *Dizzy Miss Lizzie* and *C'mon Home Baby* on *The Star-Club Singles Complete, Vol. 5* (LP & CD); and you can check out *All I Want Is You* on *Beat Merchants* (2-LP). (VJ)

Esperanto Rock Orchestra

Personnel:	BRIGETTE Du DOIT	vcls	ABC
	TONY HARRIS	viola	ABC
	BRIAN HOLLOWAY	gtr	AB
	TIM KRAEMER	cello	ABC
	BRUNO LIBERT	keyb'ds, vcls	ABC
	GINO MALISAN	bs	ABC
	TONY MALISON	drms	ABC
	GODFREY SALMON	violin, vcls	ABC
	GLENN SHORROCK	vcls	ABC
	JANICE SLATER	vcls	A

RAYMOND VINCENT	violin	ABC
KEITH CHRISTMAS	vcls	B
ROGER MEAKIN	gtr	C
KIM MOORE	vcls	C

ALBUMS: 1(A) ESPERANTO ROCK ORCHESTRA
(A&M AMLH 68175) 1973
   2(B) DANSE MACABRE   (A&M AMLH 63624) 1974
   3(C) LAST TANGO   (A&M AMLH 68294) 1975

NB: (1) - (3) also released in the US and (1) and (3) in Germany.

45s:	Danse Macabre/Castle	(A&M AMS 7104) 1974
	Last Tango/Obsession	(A&M AMS 7154) 1975
	Last Tango/Obsession	(A&M AMS 7291) 1977

Brian Holloway left the UK for Australia in 1968, where he was involved in some of their most successful chart acts. He moved back to the UK and linked up with **Glenn Shorrock** in The **Glenn Shorrock Group** from late 1971. They recorded a couple of singles for MAM before **Shorrock**, Slater and Holloway joined **Esperanto**. This was a complex multi-national progressive outfit. For example, Raymond Vincent was previously in Belgium's Wallace Connection and **Glenn Shorrock** later formed Australia's Little River Band. Many consider *Danse Macabre* to be their best album but their version of *Eleanor Rigby* on *Last Tango* is astonishing with manic violins and strong female vocals by Kim Moore, but with the exception perhaps of the lengthy *The Rape* their own compositions on *Last Tango* aren't so good. This was an erratic outfit.

In addition to the personnel listed above, Joy Yates (vcls) was also a member for a short time - she was replaced by Allison MacCallum who had been touring the UK to promote her then Australian hit *Superman*. MacCallum and Slater returned to Australia and did session work and solo recordings before joining a trio called The Hooter Sisters. Holloway joined up with the expatriate Aussie Ronnie Charles in a group called **Atlas** and later worked with **Kiki Dee**, before returning to Australia where he is still active. **Shorrock** also returned to Australia to join the Little River Band.

Keith Christmas also recorded several solo albums and made a comeback playing local folk clubs in the nineties. (VJ/CA/JM)

Esprit De Corps

Personnel incl: DAVID BALLANTYNE   A
               MIKE READ   A

45s:	If (Would It Turn Out Wrong)/	
	Picture On The Wall	(Jam JAM 24) 1973 SC
	Lonely/Do You Remember Me	(Jam JAM 32) 1973

A psych-pop outfit (despite the late date of these releases) who included deejay **Mike Read** in their ranks, together with four other personnel including producers, arrangers, session men and multi-instrumentalists. Formed out of a group called Saturday comprising Read, Ballantyne and Dave Mindel, Saturday had recorded a whole album which has never been released.

If (Would It Turn Out Wrong), which was written by Dave Mindel was brought to a wider audience by virtue of its inclusion on *Rubble Vol. 14: The Magic Rocking Horse* (LP), *Rubble Vol. 8* (CD), *The Best Of Rubble Collection Vol. 1* (CD) and *It's Only A Passing Phase* (LP).

Dave Ballantyne also wrote and released two further singles *I Can't Express It* and *Love Around The World*. The later reached No 2 in Radio London's Fab 40. (VJ/DB)

David Essex

HCP
ALBUMS:	1	ROCK ON	(CBS 65823) 1973 7
(up to	2	DAVID ESSEX	(CBS 69088) 1974 2
1976)	3	ALL THE FUN OF THE FAIR	(CBS 69160) 1975 3
	4	ON TOUR	(CBS 95000) 1976 51
	5	OUT ON THE STREET	(CBS 86017) 1976 31

NB: In 2004, Edsel Records began reissuing all his CBS albums on CD in beautifully remastered editions.

Inevitably there have been several compilations including: - *The Very Best Of David Essex* (TV Records TVA 4) 1982, *Centre Stage* (K-Tel ONE 1333) and *His Greatest Hits* (Mercury 5103081) 1991. CD compilations include *The Collection* (Castle CCSCD 248) 1990, *Best Of* (Columbia 9822734 2) 1994 which concentrates on the 1973-74 era; *Best Of* (Pickwick 9827342) 1992 and *The Best Of David Essex* (Columbia 481036 2) 1995.

HCP
45s:	And The Tears Came Tumbling Down/	
(up to	You Can't Stop Me Loving You	(Fontana TF 559) 1965 R1 -
1976)	Can't Nobody Love You/	
	Baby I Don't Mind	(Fontana TF 620) 1965 R1 -
	This Little Girl Of Mine/	
	Brokenhearted	(Fontana TF 680) 1966 R1 -
	Thigh High/De Bloom Lay Bloom	(Fontana TF 733) 1966 R1 -
	Love Story/Higher Than High	(Uni UN 502) 1968 SC -
	Just For Tonight/Goodbye	(Pye 7N 17621) 1968 SC -
	That Takes Me Back/	
	Lost Without Linda	(Decca F 12935) 1969 R1 -
	The Day The Earth Stood Still/	
	Is It So Strange?	(Decca F 12967) 1969 R1 -
	Rock On/On And On (PS)	(CBS 1693) 1973 3
	Lamplight/We All Insane (PS)	(CBS 1902) 1973 7
	America/Dance Little Girl	(CBS 2176) 1974 32
	Gonna Make You A Star/Window	(CBS 2492) 1974 1
	Stardust/Miss Sweetness (PS)	(CBS 2828) 1974 7
	Rolling Stone/Coconut Ice	(CBS 3425) 1975 5
	Hold Me Close/Good Ol' Rock And Roll	(CBS 3572) 1975 1
	If I Could/Funfair	(CBS 3776) 1975 13
	City Lights/St Amie	(CBS 4050) 1976 24
	Coming Home/Won't Get Burned Again	(CBS 4486) 1976 24
Reissues:	Gonna Make You A Star/Window	(CBS 5952) 1978 -
	Gonna Make You A Star/Hold Me Close	(CBS A 4588) 1984 -
	Gonna Make You A Star/Rock On	(Old Gold OG 9553) 1985 -

David Essex entered the world as David Cook on 23rd July 1947 in East London. A keen footballer in his youth he even got to play for West Ham Juniors. When he left school his first job was at a local factory as an apprentice but he was soon playing drums in a local dance band and later joined the semi-professional East London band called The Everons in 1964. They later changed name to The China Plates Blues Band and before long David took over the vocal duties as well. It soon became apparent that this band was going nowhere fast and by the end of the year it had split up freeing David to pursue a solo career under a new name **David Essex**.

His debut disc, *And The Tears Came Tumbling Down*, was a ballad written by Perry Ford of **The Ivy League** and he was accompanied by a 35-piece orchestra with an enormous string section all of which was far removed from the music he'd been singing with his earlier blues group. It flopped. His next effort, *Can't Nobody Love You*, was a blues-tinged single, which did get to No 17 in the Radio London Charts but overall its sales disappointed as did those of follow-ups *This Girl Of Mine* and *Thigh High*. After four poorly selling singles it was little surprise that Fontana released him from his contract.

BEST OF RUBBLE COLLECTION VOL. 1 (CD) including Espirit De Corps.

In the short term he played with The Anzaks and later toured Britain and Europe with a Stevanage group Mood Indigo.

In 1967 he was signed by MCA recording two songs (*She's Leaving Home* from *Sgt. Pepper* and *He's A Better Man Than Me*) for release on the UNI label in the States. Again the record failed to sell in any numbers. Despondent he turned to acting but still played with Mood Indigo. After getting a very small part in the film 'Smashing Time' he became run down, the constant touring had affected his health and he eventually caught pneumonia, which sidelined him for six weeks). After he'd recovered he was chosen to play the lead part in 'The Fantasticks' and then appeared in another musical 'Oh Kay'. His next 45 was a Randy Newman song, *Love Story*, but it fared no better than his earlier ones and a switch to Pye, for whom he recorded *Just For Tonight*, couldn't achieve a breakthrough.

After a few more months acting **Essex** signed for Decca in June 1969. The first single, *That Takes Me Back*, made little impact, although the flip, *Lost Without Linda*, later resurfaced on *Pop Inside The '60s, Vol. 1* (CD). The follow-up, *The Day The Earth Stood Still*, also made no impact but has subsequently been included on a Decca compilation, *Golden Decade 1968-69* (LP) in 1977. **Essex** also recorded two other tracks whilst with Decca, which were never released at the time but have subsequently surfaced on the double compilation *Lost And Found* (LP) in 1980. The compilation consists of rare tracks by well-known artists. The two **David Essex** tracks concerned were *So-Called Loving* and *Never Mind It's Only Love*.

David returned to acting; first as understudy to Tommy Steele in the pantomime 'Dick Whittington' at the London Palladium in 1969; then he took a post in 'Ten Years Hard', a revue at London's Mayfair Theatre. On the recording front he teamed up with black singer Rozza Wortham in 1970 to record two 45s (the second in 1971) under the name **David and Rozza**. Neither 45 sold well. He took any acting parts he was offered and played Dandini in 'Cinderella' at Manchester Opera House. He was literally living on the bread line with his pregnant wife when his big break came - he successfully auditioned to play the role of 'Jesus' in Jean Michael Tebelak's religious rock musical 'Godspell'. The show was a big success and his performance eventually led to him landing the lead part in David Puttnam's 'That'll Be The Day', a film about a would-be pop star which was an instant box office success.

In September 1973 he signed to CBS, now a significant stage and screen success. His first 45 for them, *Rock On*, successfully recalled the nostalgia of his recent movie and made the UK Top Five. It also became a massive hit and a million-seller in the US. The album of the same name also made No 7 here and No 22 in the US. He proceeded to release a string of singles, skilfully produced by ex-jingle writer Jeff Wayne, which reached the higher echelons of the UK Charts. In America he was far less successful. *Lamplight*, his second 45, which got to No 71, was his final US hit.

He starred in 'Stardust', which was the sequel to 'That'll Be The Day', and showed the would-be pop star (Jim MacLaine) rise to dizzy heights before excesses lead to his destruction. It was another outstanding financial success.

DAVID ESSEX.

By the mid-seventies **Essex** had established himself as a teenybopper hero with several hits and two No 1s (*Gonna Make You A Star* and *Hold Me Close*) to his credit. After so many false starts the boy from the East End had well and truly become a superstar. Later in his career, appearances in 'Evita' (as Che in 1978) and 'A Winter's Tale' and an ambitious concept album, *Mutiny*, helped to rid him of his teenybopper image. Only some of his early 45s (particularly the four on Fontana which are now minor collectables) are really likely to interest the record collector.

By the mid-nineties, his success in Sir Peter Hall's 'She Stoops To Conquer' fully established him as a respected actor. He also composed the ballet 'Beauty And The Beast' in 1995 and resumed his recording career in the same period with *Back To Back* (1995) and *Missing You* (1996). He's also become involved in charitable work with the Gypsy Council and Voluntary Service Overseas, and has done educational and charitable work in African countries including Zimbabwe and Uganda. In recognition of his stage, screen and music career and charitable work, he was awarded the Order of the British Empire by the Queen in 1999. (VJ)

The Etceteras

Personnel:	ANDREW GWEE	gtr	A
	JOHN GWEE	drms	A
	GEORGE TEO	ld gtr	A
	SAM YOUNG	bs	A

| 45s: | Where Is My Love/Bengawon Solo | (Oriole CB 1950) 1964 SC |
| | Little Lady/Now I Know | (Oriole CB 1973) 1964 SC |

This London Chinese group was from Hampstead. They came to Britain from Singapore in 1962. *Where Is My Love* is an organ-dominated ballad. *Bangawan Solo* has a standard, if rather primitive, Merseybeat tune, with much guitar work and would be a fairly unremarkable piece of beat music for 1964 were it not largely sung in a completely strange language! (VJ/CR)

Euphoria

A London-based band whose *Hangman's Rope* originally appeared on the *Transworld* promo album. See the **Free Expression** or **Kat** entries for further details. *Hangman's Rope* is pretty undistinguished progressive rock.

Compilation appearances include: *Hangman's Rope* on *Syde Tryps, Vol. 1* (LP & CD) and *The Best Of Rubble Collection, Vol. 6* (CD). (VJ)

Bryan Evans

| 45: | We're Going Wrong/Paradise Lost | (CBS S 5392) 1971 |

The 'A' side is a brassy version of a **Jack Bruce** song which actually works quite well. (MWh)

Dave Evans

ALBUMS:	1	THE WORDS IN BETWEEN	(Village Thing VTS 6) 1971
	2	ELEPHANTASIA	(Village Thing VTS 14) 1972
	3	SAD PIG DANCE (w/booklet)	
			(Kicking Mule SNKF 107) 1974

An important part of the Bristol folk scene **Dave Evans** was on a par with **Steve Tilston**. (VJ)

Rod Evans

| 45: | Hard To Be Without You/ | |
| | You Can't Love A Child Like A Woman | (Capitol 545-75210) 1970 |

After his stint with **Deep Purple** and prior to joining **Captain Beyond**, **Evans** recorded this single for Capitol. It's unclear whether it was just a demo or was actually issued. The 'A' side was penned by T. Powers-G. Fischoff and the 'B' side was written by Barry Gordon. (CG)

Kenny Everett

45s:	It's Been So Long/Without Her	(MGM MGM 1421) 1968
(up to	Nice Time/	
1976)	And Now For A Little Train Number	(Deram DM 245) 1969

Kenny Everett was a popular deejay. He started out on pirate radio and had a successful show with Dave Cash on Radio London. They'd recorded a 45 in 1965 as **Kenny and Cash**. He was working with Radio One when he recorded these two efforts. He also recorded a 45 with **Mike Vickers** *Captain Krenmen/Retribution* (DJM DJS 10810) 1977 and returned with a few more efforts in the eighties. He later died of AIDS. (VJ)

Roy Everett

45:	Turn On Your Own Heat/	
	Look At That Old Bird	(Parlophone R 5857) 1970

Roy Everett was the original vocalist in **Locomotive** but left to become a greengrocer! On this 45 he was backed by people like Roger Coulam, Herbie Flowers, **Chris Spedding** and **Caleb Quaye**.

I Believe was also included on *Brum Beat, Vol. 1* (LP). (VJ)

Everybody

45:	The Shape Of Things To Come/	
	Do Like The Children Do	(Page One POF 163) 1970

Another little known act **Everybody** recorded on Larry Page's label. (VJ)

Everyone

Personnel:	JOHN PEARSON	drms	A
	JOHN PORTER	gtr	A
	DAVE RICHARDS	vcls, bs, keyb'ds	A
	ANDY ROBERTS	gtr, vcls, violin	A
	BOB SARGEANT	gtr, vcls, keyb'ds, hrmnca	A

ALBUM:	1(A)	EVERYONE	(B&C CAS 1028) 1971
	2(A)	EVERYONE	(Polydor 2310068) 1971

NB: (1) released as ANDY ROBERTS WITH EVERYONE (Ampex 10117) 1971 in the US. (2) is the same album as (1), but replaces *Trouble At The Mill* and *Don't Get Me Wrong* with an otherwise unavailable cover of Neil Young's *Cowgirl In The Sand*.

45:	Trouble At The Mill/Radio Lady	(B&C CB 146) 1971
	Trouble At The Mill/Radio Lady (PS)	(Polydor 2001186) 1971

This folk-rock outfit's album was produced by Sandy Robertson. They were fronted by **Andy Roberts** who'd previously been with **Liverpool Scene** and was later with **Plainsong**. One of their best efforts was *Radio Lady*.

They played just one gig - the 1970 Isle of Wight Festival - before releasing their eponymous album. It included four songs with **Andy Roberts** on vocals - *Midnight Shift* (a Buddy Holly cover), and three originals *Don't Get Me Wrong* (dealing with the recent US student revolts against the Vietnam War), *Sitting On A Rock* and *Radio Lady*, which became the 'B' side of a later picture sleeve 45.

Tragically this group was cut short by an accident involving their road crew on the A33 in November 1970. Their van and gear were destroyed and Paul Scard, **Andy Roberts**' roadie was killed. After this **Roberts** concentrated on solo material for a while. (VJ/MWh)

SYDE TRYPS VOL. 1 (CD Comp) including Euphoria.

Everyone Involved

ALBUM:	1 EITHER OR (w/inserts)	(Arcturus ARC 4) 1972 R3

45:	The Circus Keeps On Turning/	
	Motor Car Madness	(Arcturus ARC 3) 1972 R1

This was a privately issued album, just 100 copies were pressed, so not surprisingly it's very rare indeed. Copies change hands for lots of money.

Heavily influenced by psychedelic folk acts like **The Incredible String Band**, **Dr Strangely Strange** and **Forest** the album was the work of a London-based hippie commune who gave all the copies of their album away. Look out for the limited edition CD reissue - original copies of the album came in an embossed plain white sleeve. (VJ)

Every Which Way

Personnel:	GRAHAM BELL	vcls	A
	ALAN CARTWRIGHT	bs	A
	BRIAN DAVISON	drms	A
	GEOFF PEACH	flute	A
	JOHN HEDLEY	gtr	A

ALBUM:	1(A) EVERY WHICH WAY	(Charisma CAS 1021) 1970

45:	Go Placidly	(Charisma BD 1) 1969

A short-lived act formed by former **Nice** drummer Brian Davison in May 1970. Vocalist **Graham Bell** had previously been with **Skip Bifferty**. He wrote most of the material on their album which was essentially an amalgam of jazz-rock and fantasy. They were managed by Tony Stratton-Smith and expanded to include guitarist John Hedley but their music never really caught on. In 1971 **Bell** joined **Arc** and Cartwright departed to **Procol Harum**. Davison was later in **Refugee**. (VJ)

Excelsior Spring

Personnel incl: MIKE FINESILVER

45:	Happy Miranda/It	(Instant IN 002) 1969 SC

Both sides of this trio's sole 45 got a further airing on *Immediate Alternative* (LP & CD) compilation. *Happy Miranda*, in particular, is a pleasant pop song though its style was a little passé by 1969. *It* can also be found on *Jagged Time Lapse, Vol 1* (CD). Mike Finesliver went on to **Heron**. (VJ)

The Exception(s)

Personnel incl:	BUGSY EASTWOOD	vcls	A
	ROGER HILL	gtr	A
	DAVE PEGG	bs	A

ALBUM: 1 THE EXCEPTIONAL EXCEPTION
                    (President PTLS 1026) 1969 SC

45s:	The Eagle Flies On Friday/Girl Trouble	(CBS 202632) 1967 R1
	Garberdine Saturday Night Street Walker/	
	Sunday Night At The Prince Rupert	(CBS 2830) 1967 SC
	Rub It Down/	
	It's Snowing In The Desert	(President PT 181) 1968
	Helicopter/Back Room	(President PT 205) 1968
	Tailor Made Babe/Turn Over The Soil	(President PT 218) 1968
	Jack Rabbit/Keep The Motor Running	(President PT 236) 1969
	Pendulum/Don't Torture Your Mind	(President PT 271) 1969

NB: Early 45s were recorded as **The Exception**, they then added an **s**.

This Birmingham band was formed after Hill had left **The Uglys** in August 1967. Pegg joined from **Way Of Life**, but he too had been with **The Uglys** earlier. They recorded a number of commercial pop singles, which are now of little interest, although we're told that *Don't Torture Your Mind* was in a different class to anything else they made.

Roger Hill went on to join **Mongrel** then **Fairport Convention** (from November 1971 - June 1972). Pegg joined **Fairport Convention** in December 1969 (replacing **Ashley Hutchings**). Eastwood also joined **Fairport Convention** and he and Pegg were both later in **Fotheringay**. Eastwood also had a solo 45, *Blackbird Charlie/My Sun* (President PT 209) in 1968.

Compilation appearances have included: *The Eagle Flies On Friday* and *Girl Trouble* on *Rare 60's Beat Treasures, Vol. 5* (CD); *Don't Torture Your Mind* on *The Electric Lemonade Acid Test, Vol. 1* (LP) and *The Best Of President, Vol. 2* (LP); *Don't Torture Your Mind, Jack Rabbit* and *Woman Of The Great Lantern* all resurfaced on *Sometimes I Wonder* (CD) and *The Eagle Flies On Friday* on *Oddities, Vol 1* (CD). (VJ/MWh/JM)

The Excheckers

Personnel:	PHIL BLACKMAN	organ	ABC
	PETER JOHNSON	lead gtr	A
	JOHN PICKETT	bs	ABC
	GEORGE ROBERTS	drms	A
	AYNSLEY DUNBAR	drms	B
	JOHN BELL	drms	C

45:     All The World Is Mine/It's All Over   (Decca F 11871) 1964 SC

A Liverpool beat group, who'd backed Jimmy Justice. (VJ/AD)

The Executive(s)

Personnel:	ROY CARR	vcls	A
	DON ELD	bs	A
	DEREK FELL	drms	A
	PETER FIELDING	lead gtr	A
	COLIN McLAREN	vcls, gtr	A
	PETER NUGENT	gtr	A
	REG POWELL	organ	A

NB: Eugene "Genie" Carberry may also have played drums.

45s:	March Of The Mods/Why, Why, Why	(Columbia DB 7323) 1964
	Strictly For The Beat/	
	No Room For Squares	(Columbia DB 7393) 1964
	It's Been So Long/You're For Me	(Columbia DB 7573) 1965
	Return Of The Mods/How Sad	(Columbia DB 7770) 1965
	Lock Your Door/In My Arms	(Columbia DB 7919) 1966
	Smokey Atmosphere/Sensation	(CBS 202652) 1967
	Ginza Strip/I'll Always Love You	(CBS 3067) 1967

	Tracy Took A Trip/		
α	Gardena Dreamer (some P/S)	(CBS 3431) 1968 R1/SC
α	I Ain't Got Nobody/To Kingdom Come	(CBS 4013) 1969

NB: α as **The Executive**.

An instrumental combo, originally, this band was led by NME member Roy Carr. They tended to play soul on stage but on disc they were persuaded to play pop in the quest for the breakthrough which never came. Their best known song is now *Tracy Took A Trip*, which certainly had the commercial potential to give them a hit in the 'Summer of Love', but the BBC banned it presumably because of its title which helped ensure they remained in relative obscurity. The flip was less impressive. *Smokey Atmosphere* features good guitar work but the vocals are not so hot.

Return Of The Mods is also rumoured to be a Joe Meek production, and consequently is particularly collectible. Their bassist Don Eld was from Blackpool and the drummer on some recordings Eugene Caberry hailed from Preston, making it likely that this was a Lancastrian group. Roy Carr later edited New Musical Express.

Compilation appearances have included:- *Tracy Took A Trip* on *Rubble Vol. 2: Pop-Sike Pipe-Dreams* (LP), *Rubble Vol. 1* (CD); *Gardena Dreamer* on *Rubble Vol. 3: Nightmares In Wonderland* (LP) and *Rubble Vol. 2* (CD); *It's Been So Long* on *Yellow Elektric Years* (LP); *Sensations* on *Beat Us If You Can! Vol. 1* (LP) and *I Ain't Got Nobody (For Real)* on *Jagged Time Lapse, Vol 5* (CD). (VJ/KL/AD)

The Exiles

Personnel:	BOBBY CAMPBELL	vcls	A
	ENOCH KENT	vcls	A
	GORDON McCULLOCH	vcls	A

| ALBUMS: | 1(A) | FREEDOM, COME ALL YE | (Topic 12T 143) 1966 SC |
| | 2(A) | THE HALE AND THE HANGED | (Topic 12T 164) 1967 SC |

This Glaswegian folk group utilised three vocalists on its albums, which are now scarce and may be of interest to folk collectors. (VJ)

The Exotics (1)

45:     Cross My Heart/Ooh La La   (Decca F 11850) 1964

This is a long forgotten band. Both sides of the 45 can also be heard on *The Soul Of British RnB 1962-1968* and *Cross My Heart* can be found on *The R&B Scene* (CD). (VJ)

THE ELECTRIC LEMONADE ACID TEST (Comp LP) including The Exceptions.

THE EYES - Blink (CD).

The Exotics (2)

45:       Don't Lead Me On/You Can Try   (Columbia DB 8418) 1968

This is a different, but equally obscure band. (VJ)

Explosive

45s: Crying All Night/I Close My Eyes   (President PT 221) 1968
            Cities Make The Country Colder/
            Step Out Of Line   (President PT 244) 1969 SC
            (Who Planted Thorns In) Miss Alice's Garden/
            I Get My Kicks From Living   (President PT 262) 1969
   α   Hey Presto, Magic Man/Get It Together (Plexium PXM 20) 1971
   α   Love Doesn't Come Easy/
            See You In The Morning   (Plexium PXM 24) 197?

NB: α may be by a different band.

This soulish quartet also backed Watson T. Browne.

Compilation appearances have included: *Cities Make The Country Colder* and *(Who Planted Thorns In) Miss Alice's Garden* on *The Electric Lemonade Acid Test, Vol. 1* (LP); *Cities Make The Country Colder* on *The Best Of President, Vol. 2* and *(Who Planted Thorns In) Miss Alice's Garden*, *Step Out Of Line* and Cities *Make The Country Colder* can all be found on *Sometimes I Wonder* (CD). (VJ)

The Extreem (1)

45:       On The Beach/Don't Ignore Me   (Strike JH 236) 1966

It is unclear whether this 45 was by the band below. (VJ)

The Extreem (2)

This group was responsible for an unreleased acetate *The Extreem* in 1969. On the musical menu is heavy psychedelic / progressive rock. It opens with the superb *Out Of The Sky* followed by *Desolation City* and *Mal's Blues* is a slow agonised blues psych offering. There is also an impressive heavy version of *Meet On The Ledge* and a wild rehash of *Day Tripper*. They may have had pre-**Budgie** connections.

Out Of The Sky has been compiled on *Syde Trips, Vol. 3* (LP). (VJ)

The Eyes (1)

Personnel:	BARRY ALLCHIN	bs	AB
	BRIAN CORCORAN	drms	AB
	PHIL HEATLEY	gtr	A
	CHRIS LOVEGROVE	ld gtr	AB
	TERRY NOLDER	vcls	AB
	STEVE VALENTINE	gtr	B

ALBUMS: 1(A) BLINK   (Bam-Caruso KIRI 028) 1984 SC
        2(A) SCENE BUT NOT HEARD
                       (Bam-Caruso MARI 038) 1987 SC

NB: (1) and (2) reissued on one CD (Essex 1007 CD) 1995. (1) was released in two different sleeves. (2) is a mini album.

EP: 1(A) THE ARRIVAL OF THE EYES
                       (Mercury 10035 MCE) 1966 R4

45s: When The Night Falls/I'm Rowed Out (Mercury MF 881) 1965 R3
          The Immediate Pleasure/
          My Degeneration   (Mercury MF 897) 1966 R3
          Man With Money/You're Too Much (Mercury MF 910) 1966 R3
          Good Day Sunshine/
          Please Don't Cry   (Mercury MF 934) 1966 R2

The Eyes came from the Ealing area of West London. The band evolved out of an outfit called The Renegades, an instrumental combo, who, when they added a vocalist, became known as Gerry Hart and The Hartbeats. The name change to **The Eyes** came during 1964.

An article in Record Collector No 144 revealed that prior to their first 45 they recorded a four-track demo at Rayrik Sound Studios in Central London. It consisted of a cover of Johnny Kidd and The Pirates' *Shakin All Over* and three originals:- *When The Night Falls, The Immediate Pleasure* and *I'm Rowed Out*. They also recorded a 30 second version of *Route 66* as a Radio London jingle. Demo discs from these sessions now change hands for in excess of £200. Only five were ever pressed!

One of these earlier demos, *When The Night Falls*, was eventually put out as their debut 45 and it is a fine example of what is now termed mid-sixties freakbeat. It got quite a lot of airplay at the time but sadly failed to make any inroads into the Charts.

The second 45 comprised two more self-penned songs. The flip, *My Degeneration*, was a response to **The Who**'s mod classic *My Generation* and also became a popular mod anthem. Again it enjoyed good sales but failed to make the Charts.

For the third 45 their record company insisted that they use a cover of The Everly Brothers' *Man With Money*. It made little difference in terms of commercial success but the flip side, *You're Too Much* with some ace fuzz lead guitar work was probably their finest moment.

THE EYES - Arrival Of The Eyes (LP).

Their final 45, *Good Day Sunshine*, was of course a **Beatles**' cover and once again the record company did them no favours in refusing to let them record a band original. In 1967 Phil Heatley quit the band to be replaced by Steve Valentine but shortly after, having failed to make a commercial breakthrough, they split. Terry Nolder, after a brief spell with **Andromeda**, later joined Entire Sioux Nation. The remaining members drifted out of the music business.

The Arrival Of The Eyes EP is now extremely collectable. Housed in a colourful picture sleeve it contained both sides of their first two singles. They were also approached by Philips to record a **Rolling Stones** tribute album. This was done in six hours and released under a pseudonym **The Pupils** (*Tribute To The Rolling Stones* (Wing WL 1150) 1966). Copies are now very rare and quite sought-after.

The best introduction to the band is undoubtedly the Bam-Caruso album *Blink*, which includes all their recordings and two tracks from **The Pupils** album. This should be an essential purchase for freakbeat fans. The mini-album *Scene But Not Heard* contains the band's demo recordings and the Radio London jingle but suffers from poor recording quality.

Compilation appearances have included: *Good Day Sunshine* on *Made In England, Vol. 1* (CD); *When The Night Falls* on *Perfumed Garden Vol. 2* (LP & CD), *Head Sounds From The Bam-Caruso Waxworks, Vol. 1* (CD), and *Illusions From The Crackling Void* (LP); *When The Night Falls* and *I'm Rowed Out* on the 4-CD *Nuggets 11* box set; *You're Too Much* on *Perfumed Garden, Vol. 1* (LP & CD); and *When The Night Falls* and *I'm Rowed Out* on *Relics* (LP). (VJ)

The Eyes (2)

Personnel:			
PADDY CHAMBERS	gtr		A
JOHN FRANKLAND	gtr		A
GIBSON KEMP	drms		A
KLAUS VOORMAN	bs		A

45: α She/Peanut Butter   (Star-Club 148519) 1965
NB: α German only 45.

This band had their roots in Liverpool and their sole 45 was only released in Germany. *She* was a typical mid-tempo Merseybeat track penned by Chambers and the 'B' side was a cover of the song - written by the US songwriters Fred Smith and Cliff Goldsmith - which is better known with different lyrics as *Hully Gully* (which was recorded by The Olympics, Delbert McClinton, The Beach Boys etc). *Peanut Butter* had previously been covered in the UK by **The Big Three**. **The Eyes** played at the famous Star-Club in Hamburg (Klaus Voorman's home) in 1965 and then came to England and started to record - minus Frankland - as **Paddy, Klaus and Gibson**. Paddy Chambers died of throat cancer on 28 September 2000.

Lewis Collins (ex-The Mojos, later Bodie in seventies cop series 'The Professionals') is said to have been a member of this group at some point.

Compilation appearances have included: *Baby, Baby* and *Another Saturday Night* on *Beat* (Elite Special) 1965, *Rare And Raw Beat From The Sixties, Vol. 1* (CD) and *Bits And Pieces - Lost And Found* (LP & CD); *Twenty Flight Rock* and *Love Is A Swinging Thing* on *Rare And Raw Beat From The Sixties, Vol. 4* (CD); *A Stitch In Time*, *I Take What I Want* and *6-3-4-5-7-8-9* on *Rare And Raw Beat From The Sixties, Vol. 7* (CD); *Peanut Butter* on *Star-Club Show* (LP) and *Star Club Scene '65* (LP); and you can check out *Peanut Butter* and *She* on *Beat Battle At The Star-Club, Vol. 1* (LP) and *The Star-Club Singles Complete, Vol. 3* (LP & CD). (MK/LBy)

The Eyes of Blue

Personnel:			
RITCHIE FRANCIS	gtr		AB
GARY PICKFORD HOPKINS	vcls		AB
PHIL RYAN	keyb'ds		AB
WYNDHAM REES	drms		A
RAY WILLIAMS	bs		A
RAY BENNETT	bs		B
JOHN WEATHERS	drms		B

ALBUMS:	1(A)	THE CROSSROADS OF TIME	
		(Mercury SMCL 20134) 1968	R1
	2(B)	IN FIELDS OF ARDATH	(Mercury SMCL 20164) 1969 R1

NB: (1) has been reissued on CD. (2) reissued on CD (Black Rose Records BR 114) 1997

45s:	Heart Trouble/Up And Down	(Deram DM 106) 1966 SC
	Supermarket Full Of Cans/Don't Ask Me	
	To Mend Your Broken Heart	(Deram DM 114) 1967 SC
	Largo/Yesterday	(Mercury MF 1049) 1968

Starting out as a soul-based band from Neath, the **Eyes Of Blue** gradually turned to the American West Coast sound. All of their recordings are quite collectable.

In collaboration with Quincy Jones they contributed to the 'Toy Grabbers' film score and they later appeared in the film 'Connecting Rooms'. Their albums are diverse with pop, R&B, jazz, classical, psychedelic and Eastern influences. The best tracks on the first one are two R&B **Graham Bond** songs (he also wrote the sleevenotes) *Love Is The Law* and *Crossroads Of Time*. It also included good versions of Love's *7 And 7 Is* and **The Beatles**' *Yesterday*. Also noteworthy are their own *Inspiration For A New Day* and *Prodigal Son*, which feature some Eastern-sounding psychedelic guitar work.

Their second album is more progressive. The best tracks are *Merry Go Round* (from the 'Toy Grabbers' Soundtrack), which is a keyboard-dominated progressive piece with some good guitar breaks and much classical influence; **Graham Bond**'s *Spanish Blues*, with some jazzy organ; *Door*, with its spooky vocals, which along with the dreamy title cut indicated the band's interest in the supernatural and the occult (especially reincarnation).

They also recorded an album in October 1968 as the backing band to American singer-songwriter Buzz Linhart, *Buzzy*. Highlights included a very good R&B version of Tim Hardin's *Yellow Cab* and Linhart's *Willie Jean* and *End Song*. There's a long track on side two which they don't play on which is also very good. On this Linhart is backed by Big Jim Sullivan (gtr) and Keshav Sathe (tabla).

Phil Ryan later played in **Man**, whilst Weathers went onto play with **Pete Brown and Piblokto!** and **Gentle Giant**. Ray Bennett was later in **Flash**. **Ritchie Francis** later made a solo album in 1971. The band later recorded as **Big Sleep** and aided **Ancient Grease** on their sole album.

Deram Dayze (LP) and *The Mod Scene* (CD) both include *Supermarket Full Of Cans*, a pop-soul number with just a hint of psychedelia; their debut 45, *Heart Trouble*, has resurfaced on *Broken Dreams, Vol. 5* (LP) and you'll also find *QIII*, a rare 'B' side from an American 45, on *Rubble Vol. 16: Glass Orchid Aftermath* (LP) and *Rubble Vol. 9* (CD). It's an organ-driven instrumental. Finally, there's *Prodigal Son* on *Rubble Vol. 8: All The Colours Of Darkness* (LP) and *Rubble Vol. 4* (CD) and *Don't Ask Me To Mend Your Broken Heart* can be found on *Colour Me Pop, Vol 1* (CD). (VJ/CA)

EYES OF BLUE - Crossroads Of Time (LP).

Fable

Personnel:
MAC BAILEY	gtr		A
PETER GOALBY	lead vcls, gtr, mandolin		A
PETER MACKIE	bs, vcls		A
PAUL ROBBINS	keyb'ds, bs, vcls		A
KEITH TULLY	drms		A

ALBUM: 1(A) FABLE (Magnet MAG 5002) 1974

45s:
Minstrel Boy/She Said Yes	(Penny Farthing PEN 735) 1970	
With A Boy Like You/		
She Said Yes	(Penny Farthing PEN 751) 1971	
See My Face/Thick As A Plank	(Magnet MAG 3) 1973	
Madolin/Thick As A Plank	(Magnet MAG 6) 1974	
Motorbike/Gotta Getaway	(Magnet MAG 9) 1975	

The band on Magnet was from Wolverhampton. It's possible that the discs on Penny Farthing were by a different group. Bailey, Robbins and Tully had all been recording with First Chapter previously. *She Said Yes* was a **Honeybus** cover, whilst *With A Boy Like You* was a cover of the old **Troggs** song *With A Girl Like You*, but the version by **Fable** was sung by a girl. This again adds weight to the different group theory as the above personnel consists of male vocalists. The album was recorded during August 1973, but not released until 1974. The Magnet label was owned by Alvin Stardust.

Their album comprises pleasant, tight melodic rock and was recorded before Goalby and Mackie moved onto **Trapeze**. Goalby eventually ended up in **Uriah Heep**. The best track is probably *Madolin* on side two.

She Said Yes can also be heard on *Pop-In, Vol 2* (CD). (VJ)

The Faces

Personnel:
KENNY JONES	drms, vcls		AB
RONNIE LANE	bs, vcls		A
IAN McLAGAN	keyb'ds, vcls		AB
ROD STEWART	vcls		AB
ROD WOOD	gtr, vcls		AB
TETSU YAMAUCHI	bs		B

					HCP
ALBUMS: 1(A)	FIRST STEP	(Warner Bros WS 3000) 1970	SC	45
(up to 2(A)	LONG PLAYER	(Warner Bros WS 3011) 1971	SC	31
1977) 3(A)	A NOD'S AS GOOD AS A WINK			
	(Some w / poster)	(Warner Bros K 56006) 1971		2
4(A)	OOH-LA-LA	(Warner Bros K 56011) 1973		1
5(B)	COAST TO COAST OVERTURE AND BEGINNERS			
		(Mercury 9100 011) 1974		3
6(-)	SNAKES AND LADDERS (A Best Of)			
		(Warner Bros K 56172) 1976		-

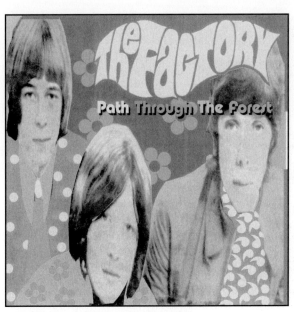

THE FACTORY - Path Through The Forest (CD).

7(-)   THE BEST OF THE FACES   (Riva RVLP 3) 1977 24

NB: (1) and (2) Catalogue number changed to K 46053 and K 46064 respectively in 1971, following the Warner Bros / Elektra / Reprise merger. (1) and (2) reissued as a double set in 1977. (5) credited to **Rod Stewart** and **The Faces**. (1) also reissued on Edsel (ED 240) in 1987 and on CD (ED CD 240) in 1991. *Five Guys Walk Into A Bar* (Warners/Rhino) 2004 is a worthwhile compilation.

EP: 1   STAY WITH ME   (Riva RIVA 8) 1977 41

NB: (1) features *Memphis/You Can Make Me Dance Sing Or Anything/Stay With Me/Cindy Incidentally*.

			HCP
45s:	Flying/		
	Three-Button Hand-Me-Down	(Warner Bros WB 8005) 1970	-
	Had Me A Real Good Time/		
	Rear Wheel Skid	(Warner Bros WB 8018) 1971	-
	Stay With Me/Debris	(Warner Bros K 16136) 1971	6
	Cindy Incidentally/Skewiff	(Warner Bros K 16247) 1973	2
	Pool Hall Richard/		
	I Wish It Would Rain	(Warner Bros K 16341) 1973	8
	Cindy Incidentally//Memphis		
	Stay With Me/Pool Hall Richard	(Warner Bros K 16406) 1974	-
α	You Can Make Me Dance Sing Or Anything/		
	As Long As You Tell Him	(Warner Bros K 16494) 1974	12

NB: α as **Rod Stewart** and **The Faces**.

The Faces formed in June 1969 when three former **Small Faces** (Lane, McLagan and Jones) joined forces with former **Jeff Beck Group** members **Rod Stewart** and Ron Wood. From their inception **Stewart** also pursued a solo career signing a separate recording contract with Mercury. Indeed, aside from their highly-touted live performances, **Stewart**'s fame when *Maggie May* became a massive hit in 1971, was a major factor in their success.

The musical offering was a brand of boozy, easy-going rock that sounded better live than on vinyl. They made their debut at Cambridge University in 1969 as part of **Quiet Melon** with Kim Gardner and Art Wood and were promoted as The Small Faces for their debut album in the US. Their first three albums were frankly patchy but sold quite well and their recorded work was mostly overshadowed by **Rod Stewart**'s solo exploits. The group often backed him and found itself being billed as Rod Stewart and The Faces, which caused a degree of bitterness. *The First Step* album had a raunchy R&B flavour but was short on strong material. The strongest song was **Ronnie Lane**'s *Stone*. *A Nod's As Good As A Wink* was their best and most successful album, peaking at No 2 in the UK and No 6 in the US. In particular it featured a ball crunching rework of Chuck Berry's *Memphis Tennessee*, which was probably their finest moment. Their best remembered 45, though, has to be *Stay With Me*, which captured **Stewart**'s vocals at their best and climbed to No 6 in the UK and No 17 in the US. This was the band in their heyday.

By contrast *Ooh La La* was a poor album and **Stewart**, whose commitment to the whole project was becoming increasingly questionable, even made his dislike of the album public. This didn't stop it selling, though: it topped the UK Album Charts and climbed to No 21 in the US. Shortly after its release **Ronnie Lane** parted company with the band going on to form **Ronnie Lane and Slim Chance** and his replacement was a Japanese bassist Tetsu Yamauchi (ex-**Free**).

This new line-up went on to achieve more Chart success in the UK, initially with the double 'A' side 45, *Pool Hall Richard/I Wish It Would Rain*, which peaked at No 8 in the UK in January 1974, and later in December of that year with *You Can Make Me Dance Sing Or Anything*, which made it to No 12. Between time they put out a live album, *Coast To Coast Overture And Beginners*, which sold well in the UK rising to No 3 but less well in the US where it could only manage No 63.

When **Rod Stewart** was forced to leave Britain for tax reasons in April 1975 this inevitably threatened the group's future. A couple of months later Ron Wood guested for **The Rolling Stones** on a US tour and when **Stewart** announced he was quitting the band in December 1975, Wood joined **The Rolling Stones** on a permanent basis. Jones and McLagan made an abortive attempt to relaunch **The Small Faces** the following year and Yamauchi headed back to Japan. In 1979 **Kenny Jones** became **The Who**'s drummer. The inevitable 'Best Of' albums followed the band's disintegration but they rarely ever captured the excitement and raucousness of their live act on vinyl. They can also be heard playing *Around The Plynth* on Warner Brothers' *Going Home* (LP) compilation and *Maybe I'm Amazed* on the same label's *Fruity* compilation. More recently *Reading Festival 1973* (CD) has captured their version of *Losing You* from the festival of the same name. (VJ)

The Factory (1)

Personnel:	JACK BRAND	vcls, bs	A
	BILL MacLEOD	drms	A
	IAN OATES	ld gtr	A

45s:	Path Through A Forest/Gone	(MGM MGM 1444) 1968 R5
	Try A Little Sunshine/Red Chalk Hill	(CBS 4540) 1969 R3

Originally known as The Souvenir Badge Factory, this band's two 45s are classic slices of British psychedelia. They scored a deal, when studio engineer Brian Carroll met 17-year-old Ian Oates at a party. *Path Through A Forest*, their first recording, started life as an acoustic folk demo, by an unknown writer and is unusual for its distorted vocals and great guitar. In fact, the band had intended to include a barrage of weird sound effects on the single, in a similar manner to **Pink Floyd**, but the 'suits' at the time said no.

On their second 45, *Try A Little Sunshine* the vocals are more poppy and it again features some great guitar work, but with it's suggestive lyrics ('Sunshine' was slang for L.S.D.) resulted in a BBC ban, and like it's predecesor it failed to happen commercially. Both 45s are now very sought-after by collectors of psychedelia and you can expect to pay in excess of £100 for either. *Gone*, the flip to their first 45, was a cover of a track from a Paul Revere and The Raiders album. Both sides of their second 45 were written by studio engineer **John Pantry**.

Try A Little Sunshine can also be heard on *Perfumed Garden, Vol. 1* (LP & CD) and *Electric Sugar Cube Flashbacks, Vol. 4* (LP) compilations and *Path Through A Forest* has resurfaced on *Chocolate Soup For Diabetics, Vol. 3* (LP), *Chocolate Soup* (CD), *Beat It* (3-CD), *Artefacts From The Psychedelic Dungeon* (CD), Lovely Summer Days (CD) and on the 4-CD *Nuggets 11* box set. There's also a demo version of *Red Chalk Hill* on the CD compilation *Circus Days, Vol. 6*, although according to Brian Carroll, this was written and performed by **John Pantry** without the involvement of the band. Other compilation appearances have included:- *Try A Little Sunshine* and *Red Chalk Hill* on *The Upside Down World Of John Pantry* (LP); *Path Through The Forest* (two versions), *Gone*, *Mr. Lacey*, *Try A Little Sunshine*, *Red Chalk Hill* and *Second Generation Woman* on *Hard Up Heroes, Vol. 6* (CD) and *Gone* on *Jagged Time Lapse, Vol 1* (CD).

Both sides of the MGM and CBS 45s can also be heard on a mini-CD *Path Through The Forest* along with rare demo versions of **Fairport Convention**'s *Mr. Lacey* and **Family**'s *Second Generation Woman*. All of these tracks, plus a re-creation of the *Path Through The Forest* with the original sound effects added back in, can also be heard on *The Complete Recordings* (Heads Together HT 0) 1996.

Jack Brand went on to a band called Meal Ticket in the mid-seventies. (VJ/JM)

The Factory (2)

Personnel:	LAURIE COOKSEY	drms	AB
	GEOFF 'JAFFA' PECKHAM	bs	A
	ANDY QUNTA	ld vcls	AB
	TONY QUNTA	12-string acoustic gtr	AB
	STEVE KINCH	bs	B

45:	Time Machine/Castle On The Hill	(Oak RGJ 718) 1971 R3

A different band from the above who recorded a very different sounding 45 on the highly collectable Oak label, in January 1971. Expect to pay in excess of £100 for this too (largely because of the label). The Qunta brothers had previously recorded an Oak acetate *Stones* and *Perfect Turkey Blues* as members of a school band Perfect Turkey in the late sixties. As **The Factory** they cut four songs - *Time Machine*, *Castle On The Hill*, *Mr. Jones* and *Road Sweeper Joe* - in January 1971 and the first

two tracks were issued on an Oak single. All 99 copies sold within weeks. *Time Machine*, written by Tony Qunta, features harsh vocals from brother Andy, a prototype heavy metal sound and lyrics in keeping with its science fiction-derived title. Geoff Peckham had been replaced by Steve Kinch when the band finally split in 1976. The Qunta brothers and Kinch were later in a band called Head On until 1979, when Kinch and Andy Qunta played with Hazel O'Conner. Post-1982 Tony Qunta became a session guitarist. One of **The Factory**'s final gigs had featured a bunch of misfits called The Sex Pistols as support band!

Compilation appearances have included: *Castle On A Hill* on *Psychedelia, Vol. 3* (LP) and *Hen's Teeth, Vol. 3* (CD); and *Time Machine* on *Story Of Oak Records* (2-LP). (VJ)

The Factotums

Personnel:	STEVEN KNOWLES	bs	A
	JEFF LEES	gtr	A
	ANDY LYNCH	drms	A
	NIGEL THOMAS	gtr	A

45s:	In My Lonely Room/Run In The Green	
	And Tangerine Flaked Forest	(Immediate IM 009) 1965 R1
	You're So Good To Me/	
	Can't Go Home Anymore My Love	(Immediate IM 022) 1966 R1
	Here Today/In My Room	(Piccadilly 7N 35333) 1966 SC
	I Can't Give You Anything But Love/	
	Absolutely Sweet Marie	(Piccadilly 7N 35355) 1966 SC
	Cloudy/Easy Said, Easy Done	(Pye 7N 17402) 1967 SC
	Mr. And Mrs. Regards/Driftwood	(CBS 4140) 1969

A Manchester-based four-piece whose debut 45, *In My Lonely Room*, a Martha and The Vandellas cover, is quite an adventurous harmony pop effort. For the follow-up they covered The Beach Boys' *You're So Good To Me*, but commercial success continued to elude them although they soldiered on for the remainder of the decade. A later effort, *Cloudy*, is pretty naff and twee pop. A sort of poor man's **Ivy League** in the final analysis.

Compilation appearances include: *Can't Go Home Anymore My Love* on *Jimmy Page - Hip Young Guitar Slinger* (2-LP); *Here Today* on *Quick Before They Catch Us* (LP & CD) and *Ripples, Vol. 1* (CD); *Cloudy* on *Rubble, Vol. 7 - Pictures In The Sky* (LP) and *Ripples, Vol. 3* (CD); *Absolutely Sweet Marie* on *Ripples, Vol. 6* (CD); *In My Room* and *Easy Said Easy Done* on *Ripples, Vol. 2* (CD); *In My Lonely Room* on *Immediate Alternative* (LP); *In My Lonely Room* and *Run In The Green And Tangerine Flaked Forest* on *Immediate Alternative* (CD); *You're So Good To Me* on *Immediate Single Collection, Vol. 4* (CD); *In My Lonely Room* and *Can't Go Home Anymore My Love* on *Immediate Single Collection, Vol. 5* (CD); and *Absolutely Sweet Marie* on *The Songs Of Bob Dylan* (CD). (VJ/JM)

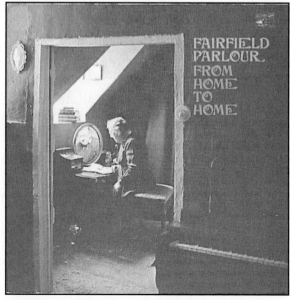

FAIRFIELD PARLOUR - From Home To Home (LP).

Nowhere Men Too
Rare British Beat 64-67

The DEE JAYS • MIKI DALLON & The SOLBOWS • The BALLSKINNERS
JIMMY WINSTON & the REFLECTIONS • The TALES OF the CITY
The TASTE • The BAND OF JOY • The FAIRIES

NOWHERE MEN VOL. 2 (Comp CD) including The Fairies.

Fairfield Parlour

Personnel:	DANNY BRIDGMAN	vcls, drms	A
	STEVE CLARK	bs, flute	A
	PETER DALTREY	vcls, keyb'ds	A
	EDDIE PUMER	vcls, keyb'ds, gtr	A

ALBUM: 1(A)   FROM HOME TO HOME   (Vertigo 6360 001) 1970 R2

NB: (1) was reissued on vinyl in the late nineties (U.F.O. no #) (SC) and again more recently by Si-Wan in Korea. (1) reissued on CD (Blast From The Past BFP 003CD) 1991 and by Repertoire (REP 4144 WP) 1994 and again (Repertoire REPUK 1044) 2005. (1) also reissued as part of a 2-CD set, *Kaleidoscope: The Fairfield Parlour Years* (NMC) 2000. The remainder of the package consists of their *White Faced Lady* album, all A + B sides of single releases as **Fairfield Parlour**, the previously unreleased film theme, 'Eyewitness', the **I Luv Wight** single, *Let The World Wash In* and a new recording of *Bordeaux Rose*.

45s:	Bordeaux Rose/Chalk On The Wall	(Vertigo 6059 003) 1970 SC
	Just Another Day//Caraminda	
	I Am All The Animals/Song For You	(Vertigo 6059 009) 1970 SC
Reissues:	Bordeaux Rose/Baby Stay For Tonight	(Prism PRI 1) 1976
α	Bordeaux Rose/	
	Overture To The White Lady	(Decca) 1976

NB: α is an Australian release.

This was **Kaleidoscope** recording under a new name, although in the interim they recorded a one-off disc - a theme tune for the 1970 Isle Of Wight Festival - using the name **I Luv Wight**. Indeed, **Fairfield Parlour**'s involvement with the festival enabled them to appear as its opening act. They also recorded a live album whilst there but the tapes subsequently disappeared.

The group also recorded the theme song for the 1970 film 'Eyewitness', which starred Mark Lester, Lionel Jeffries and Susan George. A handful of acetates of the song were also made.

Their first 45 as **Fairfield Parlour**, *Bordeaux Rose*, was an appealing ballad with a very commercial chorus. Despite considerable airplay, the disc failed to chart. The band later reissued it in 1976 on their own label with a different flip side, which was the product of a brief reunion in 1972.

Their album, *From Home To Home*, was a pretty good amalgam of sixties-influenced pop (*The Glorious House Of Arthur* and *In My Box*) and sombre songs (*Aries* and *The Drummer Boy Of Shiloh*). It is now quite a significant collectable, particularly for **Kaleidoscope** fans.

Their second Vertigo 45 contained four non-album tracks, one of which (*Just Another Day*) featured **Graeme Edge** of **The Moody Blues** on drums and a certain Reg Dwight (**Elton John**) on piano. The other three songs were short gentle numbers. The disc is now hard to find. It was also issued in a picture sleeve in Germany - these issues are more collectable.

After this they parted company with Vertigo and financed the recording of a double album, *White Face Lady*, which was loosely based on the life of Marilyn Monroe. This remained unissued until it was finally released in the early nineties by Imaginary Records' new Triad label. One track, *Nursey, Nursey*, had earlier been given away free with Issue 29 of 'Bucketfull Of Brains' and an instrumental, *Overture To The White Faced Lady*, appeared in 1976 on the flip side to an Australian Decca release of *Bordeaux Rose*. The project, which featured the London Symphony Orchestra, contained arguably their finest work and is worth investigating.

In My Box was also included on *Vertigo Annual 1970* (2-LP). More recently *Bordeaux Rose* has re-emerged on *Pop-In, Vol 2* (CD).

In the nineties, Peter Daltrey was still actively recording, with four solo albums: *Dream On* (Voiceprint VP 182) 1995, *English Roses* (Evangel Records EV 001) 1995 (Japan), *When We Were Indians* (Evangel Records EV 003) 1996 (Japan) and *Heroine* (Chelsea Records) 2001.

Sadly, on 1st May 1999, Steve Clarke was killed by a car as he walked across Chelsea Bridge in London. (VJ)

Fairfield Sky

ALBUM: 1   FAIRFIELD SKY   (OR OR 012) 1996

This progressive rock combo recorded three metal acetates in 1973 at Trident Studios. The sparse hand-written back cover notes credit each track to "Nigel and the group". The recent reissue on US Indianapolis-based label OR has brought it to a wider audience. Side one is the best, with *Silver Tavern* at times recalling **Forever Amber**, *Circus* showing traces of **Deep Purple** and the stand-out track *Would You Mind/The Writer* will appeal to those of you who like sound effects and psychedelic vocals. (VJ)

The Fairies

Personnel:	JOHN ACUTT	ABC
	JOHNNY 'TWINK' ALDER	ABC
	JOHN GANDY	ABC
	DANE STEPHENS (DOUGIE ORDE)	A C
	MICK WEAVER	ABC
	NICK WYMER	BC

45s:	Don't Think Twice, It's Alright/	
	Anytime At All	(Decca F 11943) 1964 R2
	Get Yourself Home/I'll Dance	(HMV POP 1404) 1965 R3
	Don't Mind/Baby Don't	(HMV POP 1445) 1965 R2

A R&B crew from Colchester in Essex. They were originally known as Dane Stephens and The Deep Beats in 1963, but changed name to **The Fairies** in 1964 after getting a recording contract with Decca. Their first 45 was a Dylan cover, which, like their other two, is now rare, sought-after and expensive to obtain. In fact, it was pretty weak, but the flip was a strong R&B number. Stephens left the band temporarily after this and was replaced by Nick Wymer for their next single, *Get Yourself Home*, which is now the most expensive of the three because it was one of the high points of British R&B although he later returned for their final effort, *Don't Mind*, whose flip side was notable for some good feedback.

After their demise '**Twink**' Alder went on to enjoy an often controversial career. He initially joined a group called The Santa Barbara Machine before joining **The In Crowd**. Later ventures were **Tomorrow**, **The Pretty Things** and **The Pink Fairies**; Dane Stephens (real name Dougie Orde) joined **Cops 'n' Robbers** as their vocalist and Mick Weaver went on to play for several seventies bands. Nick Wymer played in **Them** and also cut a demo single with **Jimmy Page** and **Jeff Beck**. He is still playing today with The Nick Wymer Band.

Compilation coverage has included:- *I'll Dance* and *Anytime At All* on *Maximum R'n'B* (CD); *Anytime At All* on *Broken Dreams, Vol. 2* (LP), *British R'n'B Explosion, Vol. 1* (CD), *R&B Scene, Vol. 2* (LP) and *The R&B Scene* (CD); *Get Yourself Home*, *I'll Dance* and *Anytime At All* on *Pebbles, Vol. 6* (LP) and *English Freakbeat Vol. 6* (CD); *Get Yourself Home* on *Maximum Freakbeat* (CD) and on the 4-CD box set *Nuggets 11*; *Don't Mind* on *60's Back Beat* (LP); and *Don't Think Twice, It's Alright, Anytime At All, Get Yourself Home, I'll Dance, Don't Mind* and *Baby Don't* on *Nowehere Men, Vol. 2* (CD). (VJ/JM/NW)

FAIRPORT CONVENTION - Fairport Convention (LP).

Fairport Convention

Personnel:				
(up to	JUDY DYBLE	vcls	A	
1976)	ASHLEY HUTCHINGS	bs	ABCD	
	MARTIN LAMBLE	drms	ABC	
	IAN MATTHEWS	vcls	AB	
	SIMON NICOL	gtr, vcls	ABCDEF	
	RICHARD THOMPSON	gtr, vcls	ABCDE	
	SANDY DENNY	vcls	BCD	KLM
	DAVE MATTACKS	drms	DEFG	JK
	DAVE SWARBRICK	fiddle, vcls	DEFGHIJ	KLMN
	DAVE PEGG	bs, vcls	EFGHIJ	KLMN
	ROGER HILL	gtr, vcls	GH	
	TOM FARNALL	drms	HI	
	DAVE REA	gtr	I	
	JERRY DONAHUE	gtr		JKLM
	TREVOR LUCAS	gtr, vcls		JKLM
	PAUL WARREN	drms		L
	BRUCE ROWLAND	drms		MN
	BOB BRADY	piano		N
	DAN AR BRAS	gtr		N
	ROGER BURRIDGE	mandolin, fiddle		N

HCP

ALBUMS:	1(A)	FAIRPORT CONVENTION (mono/stereo)		
(up to			(Polydor 582/583 035) 1968	R2 -
1976)	2(B)	WHAT WE DID ON OUR HOLIDAYS		
			(Island ILPS 9092) 1969	R1/SC -
	3(C)	UNHALFBRICKING	(Island ILPS 9102) 1969	SC 12
	4(D)	LEIGE AND LIEF	(Island ILPS 9115) 1969	SC 17
	5(E)	FULL HOUSE	(Island ILPS 9130) 1970	13
	6(E)	LIVE AT THE L.A. TROUBADOUR		
			(Island HELP 28) 1976	SC -
	7(F)	ANGEL DELIGHT	(Island ILPS 9162) 1971	8
	8(F)	BABBACOMBE LEE	(Island ILPS 9176) 1971	-
	9(-)	THE HISTORY OF FAIRPORT CONVENTION		
			(Island ICD 4) 1972	SC -
	10(J)	ROSIE	(Island ILPS 9208) 1973	-
	11(J)	NINE	(Island ILPS 9246) 1973	-
	12(K)	LIVE CONVENTION	(Island ILPS 9285) 1974	SC -
	13(M)	RISING FOR THE MOON	(Island ILPS 9313) 1975	52
	14(N)	GOTTLE O'GEER	(Island ILPS 9389) 1976	-

NB: First and second pressings of (2) with pink label and black 'circle' or 'block' logos are R1. Third pressing with 'i' logo (SC) and fourth pressing with pink rim label and palm tree logo (SC). (5) reissued on Hannibal (HNBL 4417) 1987. (1) reissued on CD (Polydor 835 230 2) 1990. (2), (3) and (4) reissued on CD (Island IMCD 97) 1990, (IMCD 61) 1989 and (IMCD 60) 1989 respectively. (4) reissued on CD again (Universal/Island IMCD 291) 2002. (5) reissued on CD (Hannibal HNCD 4417) 1991. (6) reissued on CD as House Full (Live In LA) (Hannibal HNCD 1319) 1990. (7) reissued on CD (Island IMCD 307) 2004, remastered and with bonus tracks. (8) reissued on CD (Island IMCD 308) 2004, remastered and with bonus tracks. (9) reissued on CD (Island IMCD 128) 1991. (10) reissued on CD (Island IMCD 309) 2004, remastered and with bonus tracks. (11) reissued on CD (Island IMCD 310) 2005, remastered with four bonus tracks. (12) reissued on CD (Island IMCD 95)

1990 and again on CD (Island IMCD 311) 2005, remastered and with three previously unreleased live recordings added. (13) reissued on CD (Island IMCD 312) 2005, remastered and with four bonus tracks (a B side and three **Sandy Denny** demos). (14) reissued on CD (Island IMCD 546 4202) 1999. Also relevant is Heyday (BBC Radio Sessions) (Hannibal HNCD 1329) 1987, which was reissued again (Universal IMCD 290) 2001, remastered and with eight bonus tracks. Before The Moon is a 2-CD recording of the band in concert in Colorado in 1974, after **Sandy Denny** had returned to the line-up. Meet On The Ledge: The Classic Years 1967-1975 (Island 564 6872) 1999 is a 2-CD compilation set. What We Did On Our Holiday - An Introduction To Fairport Convention (Island IMCD 564 7722) 1999 is an alternative compilation. Unconventional (Free Reed FRQ CD 35) 2002 is a 4-CD collection. The Airing Cupboard Tapes '71-'74 (Talking Elephant TECD 046) 2002 is a collection of live recordings. Shines Like Gold (Talking Elephant EURBOX 1) 2003 is a 3-CD box of live material, which should only interest diehard fans. Chronicles (Universal 9822557) 2005 is a 2-CD set compiling tracks they recorded for Island between 1968 and 1976. Who Knows? - The Woodworm Archive Series 1 (Talking Elephants TECD 072) 2005 is a 13-song set recorded by a line-up of the band containing no original members.

HCP

45s:	If I Had A Ribbon Bow/If (Stomp)	(Track 604.020) 1967	R1 -
(up to	Meet On The Ledge/		
1976)	Throwaway Street Puzzle	(Island WIP 6047) 1968	-
	Si Tu Dois Partir/Genesis Hall	(Island WIP 6064) 1969	21
	Sir B. McKenzie's Daughter Lament/		
	Now Be Thankful	(Island WIP 6089) 1970	-
	If (Stomp)/Chelsea Morning	(Polydor 2058 014) 1970	-
	John Lee/The Time Is Near (Some PS)	(Island WIP 6128) 1972	-
	Rosie/Knights Of The Road	(Island WIP 6155) 1973	-
	White Dress/Tears (Some PS)	(Island WIP 6241) 1975	-

Few would dispute that **Fairport Convention** was the best British folk-rock band in this book's era. They successfully drew on and re-interpreted traditional British folk material, but were talented songwriters too penning some fine original material. In **Sandy Denny** they possessed one of the finest British vocalists of this era.

Coming together in the Muswell Hill area of London, **Fairport Convention** were heavily influenced in their early days by US West Coast outfits like Jefferson Airplane. From the Spring of 1967 through till November of the same year they were a regular attraction at London's Underground venues like The Middle Earth and The UFO Club.

After their interesting debut album Judy Dyble departed to form **Trader Horne**, being replaced by **Sandy Denny** from **The Strawbs**. What We Did On Our Holidays was an excellent and diverse album, but it marked the start of their movement towards traditional British music, which led **Ian Matthews** to depart and form **Matthews Southern Comfort**. A month before the release of Unhalfbricking the band's van was involved in a motorway crash in which Martin Lamble was killed. However, they survived this major setback. **Dave Swarbrick** came in, initially as a session man, but he became a permanent member. Dave Mattacks replaced Lamble on drums. This revised line-up produced Liege And Lief, which is regarded by some as the finest British folk-rock album.

FAIRPORT CONVENTION - Heyday (LP).

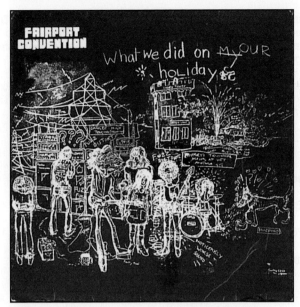

FAIRPORT CONVENTION - What We Did On Our Holidays (LP).

In November 1969 **Ashley Hutchings** left the band to form a new group which didn't really get off the ground because he suffered a nervous breakdown. From now on **Fairport Convention**'s fortunes became decidedly patchy. Line-up E lasted a little over a year and recorded two albums - *Full House* and *Live At The LA Troubadour* - but then **Richard Thompson** left to do solo and session work and Simon Nicol took over on lead guitar. *Full House* was notable for a nine-minute version of *Sloth*, a mini-epic reflecting on War on which **Swarbrick** and **Thompson** alternate verses before the song builds up to an impressive crescendo of guitar and fiddle. The 1971 line-up recorded a couple more albums - *Angel Delight* and *Babbacombe Lee* - but then Simon Nicol left and shortly after joined the **Albion Country Band**. The next year was a particularly unstable one for the band. Roger Hill, a veteran of the Birmingham rock scene replaced him, but returned to the Midlands just a few months later. Dave Mattacks also decided to leave and Tom Farnall, who had played in Midland dance bands, came in to replace him but he, too, made tracks back to Birmingham after just three months. David Rea was then flown in from California to replace Roger Hill on guitar, but his style was too American to gel with the rest of the band and he was on his way after little more than a month, too. Eventually, in August 1972, Dave Mattacks rejoined the band and **Trevor Lucas** (formerly in **Fotheringay**, who he had left to become a producer for Island Records) came in on guitar along with Jerry Donahue, who'd also played in **Fotheringay** - the band had found a stable line-up at last. The *Rosie* and *Nine* albums were recorded and *The History Of Fairport Convention* was released in this period too. *Nine* is a mixture of folk-rock and US country-rock. It's inconsistent but includes a couple of their best songs - *Hexingham Lass* and *Polly On The Shore*. The recent Island CD reissue comes with four bonus tracks comprising three unreleased countryish live recordings and a 'B' side *Fiddlestix*.

In March 1974 **Sandy Denny** returned to the fold, having played in **Fotheringay** and enjoyed a three year solo career. She married **Trevor Lucas**. The two had been together for some time. She had guested on their 1973/74 world tour and is featured on their *Live* album. This doesn't capture them at their prime, but the recent CD reissue of this album on Island includes five previously unissued live cuts from a concert at Sydney Opera House.

Dave Mattacks left again in January 1975 becoming part of the Sussex-based folk band Etchingham Steam Band, which also included **Ashley Hutchings** and later evolved into Albion Dance Band. With a European tour in the offering Paul Warren was recruited on a temporary basis but left immediately the tour was over. He was replaced by drummer Bruce Rowland (previously with **Joe Cocker** and **Ronnie Lane**) for *Rising For The Moon*. Produced by Glyn Johns, it has its moments but fell short of the classic album the band required at this time. Again the recent CD reissue includes four bonus tracks (three **Sandy Denny** demos and a 'B' side).

After this album, **Denny**, Donahue and **Lucas** all left and the band dropped Convention from their name (not for long though, it was re-adopted in March 1977) and recruited three newcomers for the *Gottle O'Geer* album (line-up N), though they didn't hang around long afterwards. Roger Burridge

and Dan Ar Bras both went on to play for Alan Stirell and former **Wizzard** piano man Bob Brady headed back to Birmingham.

Sandy Denny sadly died of a brain haemorrhage on 21 April 1978 after falling down the stairs at a friend's home. The band continued to record albums throughout the eighties, nineties and was still going strong in 2005.

Fans of **Fairport Convention** should try tracking down *Tour Sampler* (Island ISS 2) 1975. This was pressed to help publicise the band's British tour from October to early November 1975 drawing on their back catalogue and their then latest album *Rising For The Moon*. It didn't contain any exclusive material but did feature a good cross-section of their work. Five hundred copies of the radio sampler were given away free as prizes in a competition organised by NME.

From 1969 onwards **Fairport Convention**'s career was distinctly chequered, but in those early days they were one of Britain's best Underground bands. Some of their material has been reissued in recent years, including *Heyday* (Hannibal HNBL 1329) 1987, on their producer Joe Boyd's label, which features their BBC recordings between May 1968 - March 1969.

Heyday - BBC Sessions 1968-69 recorded for John Peel's Top Gear radio show first received an official CD release in 1987. It comprised covers of (among others) *Suzanne* and *Bird On A Wire* (Leonard Cohen); *Percy's Song* (Bob Dylan); *Gone, Gone, Gone* (The Everley Bros); *I Don't Know Where I Stand* (Joni Mitchell) alongside originals like *Shattering Life Experience*, *You Know It Can't be Wrong* and *It Feels So Good*. In 2001 Universal remastered and reissued it with eight bonus tracks including: *Nottmun Town*, *Fotheringay*, *Si Tu Dois Partir*, *Cajun Woman*, *Autopsy From Unhalfbricking*, *Reynardine* and *Tam Lin*.

Liege and Lief was remastered and reissued in 2002, with detailed liner notes from **Ashley Hutchings**.

Before The Moon is a 2-CD set, which captures the band live in Colorado. **Sandy Denny** had just returned to the line-up and lively versions of classics like *Matty Groves*, *Dirty Linen* and *Who Knows Where The Time Goes* are included. Also featured is a new interview with Dave Pegg.

Meet On The Ledge: The Classic Years 1967-1975 is a 2-CD set compiling material from their Island years plus *Chelsea Morning* from their debut album on Polydor. *What We did On Our Holidays* (although sporting the same title as their second album) is an alternative compilation covering much the same era. Both compilations feature sleevenotes penned by Patrick Humphries and well-illustrated booklets.

Unconventional is a 4-CD 72-track box set and the first 5,000 copies received a bonus disc entitled *The Best Of The Guests*, which included guest performances from 20 years of re-union concerts.

The Airing Cupboard Tapes '71-'74 comprises live recordings from the early seventies. The sound quality leaves a bit to be desired in some places.

FAIRPORT CONVENTION - Liege And Lief (LP).

Highlights include a lovely version of **Sandy Denny's** *It'll Take A Long Time* and a lively version of *Walk Awhile*. Four bonus tracks are added to the original collectors tape that this release was taken from.

Who Knows? is a live performance by the *Rising For The Moon* line-up, which included none of the band's original members. It's not known where it was recorded (possibly at a University gig), but it includes a 15-minute version of *Sloth* and other favourites like *Sir B. MacKenzie*, *John The Gun* and *Hexhamshire Lass*. It also contains **Sandy Denny** tracks such as *Who Knows Where The Time Goes?* and *One More Chance*. This is one for the band's diehard fans.

Ashley Hutchings went on to form **Steeleye Span. Fairport Convention** have continued to play live and every year there is a big festival at Cromarty where thousands of fans gather to hear their music and listen to spin off bands and musicians like **Richard Thompson**.

Compilation appearances have included *Walk Awhile* on *Bumpers* (2-LP); *Cajun Woman* on *Nice Enough To Eat* (LP); *Meet On The Ledge* on *You Can All Join In* (LP); *If (Stomp)* on *Pop Party* (LP); *If I Had A Ribbon Bow* on *Backtrack 2* (LP) and *Rare Tracks* (LP); and *Lord Marlborough* on *El Pea* (LP). (VJ)

Fair Weather

Personnel:	DENNIS BRYON	drms	A
	ANDY FAIRWEATHER - LOW	vcls, gtr	A
	NEIL JONES	gtr	A
	CLIVE TAYLOR	bs	A
	BLUE WEAVER	keyb'ds	A

ALBUM: 1(A) BEGINNING FROM AN END (RCA Neon NE 1) 1971 R1

NB: (1) reissued on CD (Akarma AK 296) 2005, with six bonus tracks.

			HCP
45s:	Natural Sinner/Haven't I Tried	(RCA 1977) 1970 6	
	Road To Freedom/Tutti Frutti	(RCA 2040) 1971 -	
	Lay It On Me/		
	Looking For The Red Label, Pt 2	(RCA Neon 1000) 197? -	

This was a progressive outfit formed by **Andy Fairweather-Low** who'd previously been with **Amen Corner** and who subsequently enjoyed a reasonably successful solo career in the mid-seventies. On initial live dates, they were accompanied by a 6-piece brass section. On latter dates, this was reduced to a 3-piece.

They scored a sizeable hit with *Natural Sinner*, but the group which was formed out of the remains of **Amen Corner** couldn't shake off the 'teenybopper' tag and broke up after just one album. The album is a pleasant enough blend of vocal harmonies and R&B, with an occasional

taint of hard-rock. **Fairweather-Low** then initially worked with **Dave Edmunds'** Rockpile before pursuing a solo career. Blue Weaver joined **The Strawbs** and also became a significant session musician. Byron became a long-time drummer with **The Bee Gees** (1975 - 79).

Akarma reissued their sole album in 2005, with six bonus tracks including *Lay It On Me*, *Tutti Fruitti*, *Natural Sinner* and *Looking For The Red Label Part 11*. (VJ/JM)

Andy Fairweather-Low

ALBUMS:	1	SPIDER JIVING	(A&M AMLH 68263) 1974
(up to	2	LA BOOGA ROOGA	(A&M AMLH 68328) 1975
1976)	3	BE BOP 'N' HOLLA	(A&M AMLH 64602) 1976

NB: *Wide Eyed And Legless: The A&M Recordings* (Edsel MEDCD 748) 2004 is a 2-CD set compiling his three solo albums.

			HCP
45s:	Reggae Tune/Same Old Story	(A&M AMS 7129) 1974 10	
(up to	Mellow Down/Light Is Within	(A&M AMS 7136) 1975 -	
1976)	La Booga Rooga/Halfway To Everything	(A&M AMS 7192) 1975 -	
	Wide Eyed And Legless/Grease It Up	(A&M AMS 7202) 1975 6	
	Champagne Melody/		
	Inner Man Highwayman	(A&M AMS 7214) 1976 -	
	Travellin' Light/If I Ever Get Lucky	(A&M AMS 7248) 1976 -	
	Be Bop 'n' Holla/Lighten Up	(A&M AMS 7268) 1976 -	

Fairweather-Low was from Cardiff, Wales, and was born in 1948. After the demise of **Amen Corner**, **Andy Fairweather-Low**, who initially formed **Fairweather** set about trying to consolidate on his earlier success with *Natural Sinner* and establish himself as a solo artist. His nasal-inflected vocals gave him a unique sound and *Spider Jiving*, which saw him playing guitar as well as handling the vocals, also spawned a hit single, *Reggae Tune*. He enjoyed other spasmodic success with his laid-back vocal style most notably with *Wide Eyed And Legless* and *Be Bop 'n' Holla*.

Spider Jiving highlighted his vocal range and excellent guitar playing - the material is largely good-time and eclectic.

He returned in 1980 with a new album *Mega Shebang*, but in later years worked more as a sideman for other British musicians like **Pink Floyd's Roger Waters**. Since touring Japan with **George Harrison** and **Eric Clapton** in 1991, he has been in **Clapton's** back-up band. (VJ)

Fairy's Moke

ALBUM: 1 FAIRY'S MOKE (Deroy No #) 1975 R3

This very rare privately-pressed album was recorded by Deroy at a university folk club and includes two tracks which also appear on the **Baby Sunshine** album. (VJ)

The Fairytale

Personnel:	BILLY FAGG	drms	A
	CHADDY PENKETH	bs	A
	MALLY RABBIT	organ	A
	JOHN WESTON	ld gtr	A

45s:	Guess I Was Dreaming/Run And Hide	(Decca F 12644) 1967 R2
	Lovely People/Listen To Mary Cry	(Decca F 12665) 1967 R2

A short-lived Lancastrian outfit who formed in Warrington in March 1967 and tended to blend pop psychedelia with a taint of punk-rock on their two 45s, which are both very rare and sought-after now by collectors of this genre.

Guess I Was Dreaming was quite an interesting debut of flowery psychedelia with some distinctive piano. The flip side, *Run And Hide* was more upfront with a distinctive drumbeat and much the stronger of the two

RUBBLE VOL. 11 (Comp LP) including The Fairytale.

sides to my mind. The follow-up, released just a month later, *Lovely People*, is typically whimsical British psych-pop and altogether too twee. Its flip side, *Listen To Mary Cry*, is probably the least interesting of the four.

When neither of their 45s 'happened' **Fairytale** had called it a day by 1968.

Compilation coverage has included:- *Guess I Was Dreaming* and *Listen To Mary Cry* on *Rubble Vol. 11* (LP), *Adventures In The Mist* (LP) and *Rubble Vol. 6* (CD); *Guess I Was Dreaming* on *Illusions From The Crackling Void* (LP) and *The Psychedelic Scene* (CD); *Listen To Mary Cry* on *Electric Sugarcube Flashbacks, Vol. 2* (LP); *Run And Hide* on *The British Psychedelic Trip* (LP), *Rubble Vol. 5: The Electric Crayon Set* (LP), *Rubble Vol. 3* (CD), *Freakbeat Scene* (CD) and on the 4-CD box set *Acid Drops, Spacedust and Flying Saucers*; and *Lovely People* can also be found on *Rubble Vol. 6: The Clouds Have Groovy Faces* (LP) and *Rubble, Vol. 4* (CD). (VJ)

Marianne Faithfull

				HCP
ALBUMS:	1	COME MY WAY	(Decca LK 4688) 1965 R1 12	
(up to	2	MARIANNE FAITHFULL	(Decca LK 4689) 1965 R1 15	
1976)	3	NORTH COUNTRY MAID	(Decca LK 4778) 1966 R1 -	
	4	LOVE IN A MIST	(Decca LK/SLK 4854) 1967 R2 -	
	5	WORLD OF MARIANNE FAITHFULL		
		(mono/stereo)	(Decca (S)PA 17) 1969 SC/- -	
	6	DREAMIN' MY DREAMS	(Nems NEL 6007) 1976 SC -	

NB: (1) reissued on CD (Deram 820 629-2) 1991 with bonus tracks. (2) reissued on CD (London 820 630-2) 1988. (3) reissued on CD (London 820 631-2) 1990. (4) reissued on CD (Decca 820 632-2) 1988, but deleted 1991. (6) reissued on CD (Castle CMRCD 988) 2005, with four additional tracks. *The Very Best Of Marianne Faithfull* (London 820 482-2) 1987 is a CD compilation. *Rich Kids Blues* (Demon) 1998 is a selection of tracks from her time with Mike Leander in the early seventies. A more recent CD compilation is *Faithfull: A Collection Of Her Best Recordings* (Island CIDX 8023) 1994. *A Stranger On Earth :An Introduction To Marainne Faithfull* (Universal 585 1152 2) 2001 is a good introduction to her music.

EP:	1	MARIANNE FAITHFULL (GO AWAY FROM MY WORLD)	(Decca DFE 8624) 1965 R1

			HCP
45s:	As Tears Go By/Greensleeves	(Decca F 11923) 1964 9	
(up to	Blowin' In The Wind/		
1976)	The House Of The Rising Sun	(Decca F 12007) 1964 -	
	Come And Stay With Me/		
	What Have I Done Wrong?	(Decca F 12075) 1965 4	
	This Little Bird/Morning Sun	(Decca F 12162) 1965 6	
	Summer Nights/The Sha La La Song	(Decca F 12193) 1965 10	
	Yesterday/Oh Look Around You	(Decca F 12268) 1965 36	
	Tomorrow's Calling/That's Right Baby	(Decca F 12408) 1966 -	
	Counting/I'd Like To Dial Your Number	(Decca F 12443) 1966 -	
	Is This What I Get For Loving You?/		
	Tomorrow's Calling	(Decca F 12524) 1967 43	
α	Something Better/Sister Morphine	(Decca F 12889) 1969 R1 -	
	Dreamin' My Dreams/Lady Madalene	(Nems NES 4) 1975 -	
	All I Wanna Do In Life/		
	Wrong Road Again	(Nems NES 13) 1976 -	
Reissues:	As Tears Go By/Come And Stay With Me/		
	This Little Bird/Summer Nights (PS)	(Decca F 13890) 1980 -	
	As Tears Go By/		
	Come And Stay With Me	(Old Gold OG 9335) 1983 -	
	As Tears Go By/Trouble In Mind (PS)	(Island IS 323) 1987 -	
	As Tears Go By/Trouble In Mind/		
	This Hawk El Galvion (PS) (12")	(Island IS 323) 1987 -	

NB: α withdrawn.

Marianne Faithfull was born on 29 December 1946 into a very well-to-do Hampstead family. Her father was a university lecturer and her mother an Austrian Baroness. She was still at St Joseph's Convent School in Reading when she was taken to a London party by artist John Dunbar, her boyfriend, where she met **Andrew Loog Oldham**, the **Rolling Stones'** manager, who, impressed by her looks and aspirations to become a folk singer, signed her to the Decca label and gave her the **Mick Jagger**/Keith Richards' song *As Tears Go By* for her first single. With her own feminine

MARIANNE FAITHFULL - The World Of... (LP).

interpretation of it she took it to No 9 in the UK Charts (it later made No 22 in the US). However, the follow-up, a cover of Bob Dylan's *Blowing In The Wind*, failed to Chart. Her most successful 45 here in the UK was Jackie de Shannon's *Come Stay With Me*. It climbed to No 4 and later managed No 26 in the US Charts.

Extremely attractive and with a delicate, wistful voice she charmed her way onto many record decks in the mid-sixties. Her voice was ideally suited to her next 45, *This Little Bird*, which climbed to No 6 in the UK and No 36 in the US. Her first two albums, which were released on the same day also sold well in the UK. *Come My Way*, the folkier of the two made it to No 12 in the Album Charts and *Marianne Faithfull*, which included her first two hit singles peaked just three places behind at No 15, but was by far the most successful of the two in the US, where it climbed to No 12.

Her last big UK hit was *Summer Nights* (No 10) - once again a song that was ideally suited to her. It also got to No 24 in the US Charts. Thereafter her commercial success began to wane and so had her marriage to John Dunbar, who she'd married in May 1965. Her cover of **The Beatles'** *Yesterday* was outmanoeuvred in the UK Charts by Matt Monro's and, after a US-only album and 45, *Go Away From My World*, had only met with moderate success her next UK album, the folky *North Country Maid*, registered disappointing sales. Her follow-up, *Love In A Mist*, fared little better.

By now she was shacked up with **Mick Jagger** and her career was veering away from music towards films and the stage. She appeared with Oliver Reed in 'I'll Never Forget Whatsisname' in 1967 and in 'Girl On A Motorcycle' in 1968, which was ravaged by the critics. On the stage she played Orphelia in Nicol Williamson's 'Hamlet' in 1970 and in Chekhov's 'The Three Sisters'. She also achieved some notoriety for being with **Mick Jagger** when he was busted at Keith Richards' house in West Wittering, Sussex, on 12 February 1967, although unlike the other two she wasn't charged.

In March 1967 she enjoyed a minor hit with her cover of The Ronettes' *Is This What I Get For Loving You*. After suffering a miscarriage in late November 1968 she starred in the filming of **The Rolling Stones'** 'Rock And Roll Circus' musical extravaganza, which never got the TV airing that had been intended for it.

Her final single for Decca came in February 1969 and was produced by **Mick Jagger**, its 'B' side, *Sister Morphine*, a **Jagger**/Richard composition, was one of her best recordings, although it was withdrawn not long after its release. It was her last record for several years as she strove to develop her acting career. However, her relationship with **Mick Jagger** ensured she was never long out of the news. They were both arrested in May 1969 at their London home for dope possession, one month after the inevitable *Marianne Faithfull Greatest Hits* collection had peaked at No 171 in the US Charts. Worse was to follow, on 8 July 1969, having flown to Australia to co-star with **Mick Jagger** in the film 'Ned Kelly', she was discovered in a coma after a drug overdose, withdrawn from the film and received hospital treatment for heroin addiction. Indeed her drug problems continued to plague her throughout the early seventies and it was a series of affairs rather than the development of her acting career that won her publicity. In the mid-seventies she made a recording comeback, initially with a cover of Waylon Jennings' *Dreaming My Dreams*, which showed her voice to have lost all of its youthful innocence.

Broken English (1979) was the album that returned her to the charts and by now she was writing much of her own material. *Dangerous Acquaintances* (1981) was a Top 50 album for her and *A Child's Adventure* (1983) spent a week at No 99. 1987's *Strange Weather*, a Hal Willner-produced collection of standards and contemporary songs, was her most successful album of the eighties. In 1994, her eponymous autobiography was published, but she recorded only spasmodically in the nineties. She returned in 2002 with *Kissin' Time*, a collection of songwriting collaborations with stars like Beck, Jarvis Cocker, Damon Alban and others. 2004's *Before The Poison* followed a similar format with contributions from Nick Cave and The Bad Seeds, Damon Alban and P.J. Harvey (among others) but with more success.

The Very Best Of Marianne Faithfull is a good CD hits collection which covers the whole of her period with Decca. The *A Stranger On Earth* compilation includes early tracks like *I'm A Loser*, *Is This What I Get For Loving You* and a version of *House Of The Rising Sun*. There's a re-recording of *As Tears Go By* and a superb version of *Sister Morphine*, alongside her interpretations of *Monday Monday* and *Reason To Believe*. This, too, is a good introduction to her music.

Her debut album was reissued on CD in 1991 with four bonus tracks:- *Blowin' In The Wing*, *That's Right Baby*, *Sister Morphine* (from 1969) and *Et Maintenant (What Now My Love?)*. Most of her other albums are available on CD too.

Rich Kids Blues is a selection of tracks from her sessions with **Mike Leander** in the early seventies. It includes a version of **George Harrison's** *Beware Of Darkness* and renditions of *It's All Over Now Baby Blue*, *Visions Of Johanna* and *Mud Slide Slim*.

The recent Island CD collection includes only one track, *As Tears Go By*, from her sixties output. The remaining material is all post-1979 making the collection's title a misleading one.

Compilation appearances have included: *Sister Morphine* on *Sixties Lost And Found, Vol. 2* (LP) and *Sixties Explosion, Vol. 1* (CD); and *Something Better* on *Sixties Lost And Found, Vol. 3* (LP). (VJ)

The Falcons

45: Stampede / Kazutzka (Philips BF 1297) 1964 SC

This was an obscure one-off venture. (VJ)

RUBBLE VOL. 6 (Comp LP) including The Falling Leaves.

The Falling Leaves

Personnel:			
	LARRY NEDEL	drms	A
	WILL PATRICK	ld gtr	A
	NEIL STANLEY	organ	A
	ROD STEPHENS	vcls	A
	MAL WEST	bs	A

45s:	She Loves To Be Loved/		
	Not Guilty	(Parlophone R 5233) 1964	R2
	Beggar's Parade/Tomorrow Night	(Decca F 12420) 1966	R1

This band hailed from Oxford. *She Loves To Be Loved* was slightly bluesy with some good organ, but their later release on Decca was much more poppy. You'll also find *Beggar's Parade*, which did have some pleasant vocal harmonies and distinctive electric piano, on *Rubble Vol. 6: The Clouds Have Groovy Faces* (LP) and *Rubble Vol. 4* (CD). In 1964 they entered a 'best unknown group' competition held by TV series 'Ready Steady Go' and their performance of *She Loves To Be Loved* and *Not Guilty* taken from the show has been compiled on See For Miles' *Ready Steady Win* (LP & CD). (VJ)

Georgie Fame (and The Blue Flames)

Personnel:			
	MICK EVE	sax	A
	GEORGIE FAME	piano, vcls	A
	COLIN GREEN	gtr	A
	TONY MAKINS	bs	A
	RED REECE	drms	A

HCP

ALBUMS: (up to 1976)	1	RHYTHM AND BLUES AT THE FLAMINGO (Columbia 33SX 1599)	R2	-
	2	FAME AT LAST (Columbia 33SX 1638) 1964	SC	15
	3	SWEET THING (Columbia SX 6043) 1966	R1	6
	4	SOUND VENTURE (Columbia SX 6076) 1966	R1	9
	5	HALL OF FAME (Columbia SX 6120) 1967	SC	12
	6	TWO FACES OF FAME (CBS (S)BPG 63018) 1967	SC	22
	7	THE THIRD FACE OF FAME (CBS (S) 63293) 1968	SC	
	8	DOES HIS OWN THING WITH STRINGS (CBS (S) 63650) 1969	SC	-
	9	SEVENTH SON (CBS 63786) 1969	SC	-
	10	GEORGIE FAME (Starline SRS 5002) 1969		
	11	GOING HOME (CBS 64350) 1971	SC	-
	12	FAME AND PRICE (CBS 64392) 1971		
	13	ALL ME OWN WORK (Reprise K 44183) 1972	SC	-
	14	FAME AGAIN (Starline SR5 5107) 1972		
	15	THE BALLAD OF BONNIE AND CLYDE (Embassy 31033) 1973		-
	16	GEORGIE FAME (Island ILPS 9293) 1974	SC	-

NB: *The First 30 Years* (Connoisseur Collection VSOP LP 144) 1989 is a double set compiling his classic sixties recordings alongside lesser known material from the seventies and eighties, also available on CD (VSOPCD 144) 1989. (6) reissued on CD (Columbia Rewind 477850 2) 1995. *The Very Best Of Georgie Fame And The Blue Flames* (Spectrum) 1998 is a mid-price compilation.

EPs:	1	RHYTHM AND BLUEBEAT (Columbia SEG 8334) 1964	R1
	2	RHYTHM AND BLUES AT THE FLAMINGO (Columbia SEG 8382) 1964	R1
	3	FAME AT LAST (Columbia SEG 8393) 1964	SC
	4	FATS FOR FAME (Columbia SEG 8406) 1965	SC
	5	MOVE IT ON OVER (Columbia SEG 8454) 1965	SC
	6	GETAWAY (Columbia SEG 8518) 1966	SC
	7	KNOCK ON WOOD (CBS EP 6363) 1967	SC

HCP

45s: (up to 1976)	α	J.A. Blues/Orange Street	(R&B JB 114) 1963	-
	α	Stop Right Here/Rik's Tune	(R&B JB 126) 1963	-
		Do The Dog/Shop Around	(Columbia DB 7193) 1964	-
		Do-Re-Mi/Green Onions	(Columbia DB 7255) 1964	-
		Bend A Little/I'm In Love With You	(Columbia DB 7328) 1964	-
		Yeh Yeh/Preach And Teach	(Columbia DB 7428) 1964	1
		In The Meantime/Telegram	(Columbia DB 7494) 1965	22
		Like We Used To Be/It Ain't Right	(Columbia DB 7633) 1965	33
		Something/Outrage	(Columbia DB 7727) 1965	23
		Get Away/El Bandido	(Columbia DB 7946) 1966	1
	β	Sunny/Don't Make Promises	(Columbia DB 8015) 1966	13

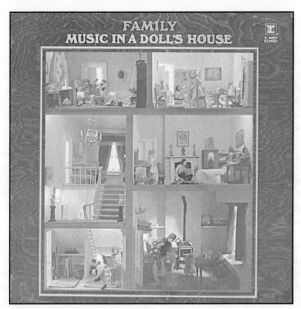
FAMILY - Music In A Doll's House (LP).

β Sitting In The Park/
   Many Happy Returns   (Columbia DB 8096) 1966 12
   Because I Love You/Bidin' My Time (PS) (CBS 202587) 1967 15
   Try My World/No Thanks (PS)   (CBS 2945) 1967 37
   Ballad Of Bonnie And Clyde/
   Beware Of The Dog   (CBS 3124) 1967 1
   By The Time I Get To Phoenix/
   (Flip by Simon Garfunkel)   (CBS Special Prod. WB 732) 1968 -
   By The Time I Get To Phoenix/
   For Your Pleasure   (CBS 3526) 1968 -
   Peaceful/Hideaway   (CBS 4295) 1969 16
   Seventh Son/Fully Booked   (CBS 4659) 1969 25
   Somebody Stole My Thunder/
   Entertaining Mr. Sloane   (CBS 5035) 1970 -
   Fire And Rain/Someday Man   (CBS 5131) 1970 -
   Hey Baby I'm Getting Ready/
   City Hicker   (Reprise K 14191) 1972 -
   Everlovin' Woman/
   That Ol' Rock And Roll   (Island WIP 6213) 1974 -
   Ali Shuffle/Round Two   (Island WIP 6218) 1974 -
   Yes Honestly/Lily   (Island WIP 6279) 1976 -
   Sweet Perfection/Thanking Heaven (Island WIP 6311) 1976 -
Reissues: Ballad Of Bonnie And Clyde/
   Seventh Son (PS)   (CBS 1151) 1973 -
   Ballad Of Bonnie And Clyde/
   Beware Of The Dog   (Epic 152298) 1975 -
   Yeh Yeh/Getaway (PS)   (RSO 58) 1980 -
   Yeh Yeh/Getaway   (Old Gold OG 9588) 1986 -

NB: α as The Blue Flames. β solo singles.

Fame's name by birth was Clive Powell and he was born on 26 June 1943 in Leigh, Lancashire. He played piano in various local groups before moving down to London in 1959. There he was spotted by songwriter Lionel Bart who recommended him to top rock manager Larry Parnes. Parnes took him under his wings, renamed him **Georgie Fame** and used him to back various singers including Marty Wilde and Vince Eager, prior to **Fame** joining Billy Fury's backing band The Blue Flames in June 1961. After at the end of 1961, Billy Fury replaced The Blue Flames with The Tornadoes as his backing band, **Georgie Fame and The Blue Flames** secured a residency at a jazz cellar in London's West End called The Flamingo. Initially they played twist sessions but they soon built up a cult following with their blend of jazz, rock and blue beat.

They signed to EMI Columbia in September 1963 and recorded a debut album live at the Flamingo club which came out the following year and helped to 'spread the word'. Their early singles flopped, although their second album, Fame At Last, climbed to No 15 in the UK Album Charts. It was his rework of an Afro-Cuban song by Lambert, Hendricks and Ross, called Yeh Yeh, that thrust him into the limelight when it became a UK No 1 (and also reached No 21 in the US) becoming a million seller. From hereon he was widely respected as a leading exponent of the burgeoning R&B movement. He enjoyed other notable hits with In The Meantime,

Something, Getaway (another No 1, which was every bit as good as Yeh Yeh) and a cover of Bobby Hebb's Sunny. His Sweet Thing and Sound Venture albums also sold well, both making the Top Ten in the UK Album Charts.

In September 1966 he disbanded The Blue Flames to go solo. He used a wide range of musicians and a very flexible line-up to back him in subsequent years including **John McLaughlin**, Jon Hiseman and Mitch Mitchell. He also veered away from the R&B sound he'd been closely associated with in favour of a pretty commercial brand of pop, this almost certainly cost him part of his audience. However, his initial 45, a cover of Billy Stewart's Sitting In The Park was a reasonably big hit and subsequent 45s, the self-penned Because I Love You and Try My World did quite well as did his Hall Of Fame and Two Faces Of Fame albums. The latter comprised a live side and a studio side, giving a well balanced picture of his music. In December 1967 he enjoyed his third UK No 1 with The Ballad Of Bonnie And Clyde, which had been written by Mitch Murray and Peter Callender. The song had been inspired by the hit movie of the same name. It also made No 7 in the US becoming another million seller.

Thereafter his career declined. He formed a partnership with ex-**Animals** organist **Alan Price** which was very MOR, aimed at the TV and cabaret circuit. It produced three 45s, in addition to the Fame And Price album, which are not shown in the earlier discography but are set out below:-

                                               HCP
45s: Rosetta/John And Mary   (CBS 7108) 1971 11
       Follow Me/Sergeant Jobsworth   (CBS 7602) 1971 -
       Don't Hit Me When I'm Done/
       Street Lights   (Reprise K 14230) 1972 -

All were awful. Rosetta was subsequently coupled with The Ballad Of Bonnie And Clyde and reissued by CBS in 1984 and on Old Gold in 1985. This alliance with **Price** ended in late 1973.

In mid-1974 **Fame** attempted to revive his old R&B heyday by signing to Island and forming a new Blue Flames, which only featured Colin Green from the original line-up. The resulting album, Georgie Fame, made little impact, being rather passé for the times and he tended to spend the subsequent years writing jingles for TV commercials, occasionally appearing in TV commercials and numerous variety shows. His album releases in the nineties struck a chord with an AOR/blues audience, however, and he also found success as musical director of **Van Morrison**'s band, as well as garnering respect from the jazz fraternity for his work with Count Basie and BBC Big Bands.

Compilation appearances include: Something and Getaway on Go... With An All Star (LP); Yeh Yeh has resurfaced on the 2-CD set 60 Number Ones Of The Sixties and Sitting In The Park can also be found on the 2-CD set Sixties Summer Love. From the seventies Rosetta (recorded with **Alan Price**) was compiled on the 2-CD set Good Times - Best Of 70's. (VJ/AR)

Family

Personnel: ROGER CHAPMAN   vcls   ABCDE
            RIC GRECH   bs, vcls, violin A
            JIM KING   sax, flute   AB
            ROB TOWNSEND   drms   ABCDE
            CHARLIE WHITNEY gtr   ABCDE
            JOHN WEIDER   bs, violin   BC
            POLI PALMER   keyb'ds, vibes CD
            JOHN WETTON   bs, vcls   D
            TONY ASHTON   keyb'ds   E
            JIM CREGAN   bs, gtr   E

                                             HCP
ALBUMS: 1(A) MUSIC IN A DOLL'S HOUSE (w/insert)
           (mono/stereo)   (Reprise R(S)LP 6312) 1968 R2/R1 35
      2(A) FAMILY ENTERTAINMENT (Some w/ poster)
           (mono/stereo)   (Reprise R(S)LP 6340) 1969 R1/SC 6
      3(C) A SONG FOR ME   (Reprise RSLP 9001) 1970 SC 4
      4(C) ANYWAY   (Reprise RSX 9005) 1970 7
      5(C) OLD SONGS NEW SONGS - COMPILATION
                       (Reprise RSLP 9007) 1971 -
      6(D) FEARLESS   (Reprise K 54003) 1971 14

FAMILY - Family Entertainment (LP).

| 7(D) | BANDSTAND | (Reprise K 54006) 1972 15 |
| 8(E) | IT'S ONLY A MOVIE | (Raft RA 58501) 1973 30 |

NB: Only original pressings of (1) and (2), which came with a steamboat design are scarce. (1) - (4) reissued by Reprise in 1971 and (1) - (2) reissued by See For Miles in 1987, also on CD (SEECD 100) 1987 and (SEECD 200) 1987. (1) reissued on CD (See For Miles SEECD 100H) 1998 remastered and with enhanced packaging. (2) reissued on CD (See For Miles SEECD 200H) 1998 remastered and with enhanced packaging. (1) and (2) also issued on a 2-CD set (See For Miles SFM 1968) 1999. This release was lavishly packaged as a hardback book and comes with a 40-page booklet containing extensive sleevenotes. (5) Catalogue number changed to (K 34001) 1971, following the Warner Bros / Elektra / Reprise merger. (3), (7) and (4) reissued on See For Miles (SEE 240, 241 and 245). They are also available on CD. (3) reissued on CD (Castle ESMCD 616) 1998. (4) reissued on CD (Castle ESMCD 615) 1998. The Peel Sessions (Strange Fruit SFPS 061) 1988 is based on a 1973 recording containing songs from the It's Only A Movie era. There's also The Best Of Family... Plus (See For Miles SEE 330) 1991, also on CD (SEE CD 330). As And Bs (Castle CCSCD 354) 1992 contains most but not all of their 'A' and 'B' sides and one cut from their Strange Band (EP). (5) reissued on CD (See For Miles SEECD 334) 1991. (6) and (8) reissued on one CD (That's Original TFOCD 22) 1989, but deleted in 1992. (6), (7) and (8) all reissued on CD (Castle) 1997, with bonus cuts and liner notes from Roger Chapman. Also of interest is Family In Concert (Windsong WINCCD 001) 1991. A Family Selection - The Best Of Family (Essential ESDCD 839) 2000 is a 2-CD set taken from their post-1969 albums, which comes with detailed sleevenotes. The 1973 BBC Radio Show (Turning Point TPM 00204v) 2000 is a 2-LP set available as an Italian import. BBC Radio Vol 1 1968-1969 (CD) (Hux HUX ?) 2004 and BBC Radio Vol 2 1971-73 (CD) (Hux HUX 060) 2004 collects the best of their live BBC recordings from these eras.

HCP

45s:	Scene Through The Eyes Of A Lens/		
	Gypsy Woman	(Liberty LBF 15031) 1967 R3 -
	Me My Friend/Hey Mr. Policeman	(Reprise RS 23270) 1968 SC -
	Second Generation Woman/		
	Home Town	(Reprise RS 23315) 1968 SC -
	No Mule's Fool/Good Friend Of		
	Mine (initially PS)	(Reprise RS 27001) 1969 SC/- 29
	Today/		
	Song For Lots (initially PS)	(Reprise RS 27005) 1970 SC/- -
	Strange Band//The Weaver's Answer		
	Hung Up Down (initially PS)	(Reprise RS 27009) 1970 11
	In My Own Time/Seasons (initially PS)	(Reprise K 14090) 1971 4
α	Larf And Sing/Children	(Reprise SAM 1) 1971 -
	Burlesque/The Rockin' R's	(Reprise K 14196) 1972 13
	My Friend The Sun/Glove	(Reprise K 14218) 1973 -
	Boom Boom/Stop This Car	(Raft RA 18501) 1973 -
	Sweet Desiree/Drink To You	(Raft RA 18503) 1973 -
Reissues:	My Friend The Sun/Burlesque	(Reprise K 14378) 1974 -
	Burlesque/In My Own Time/		
	Weaver's Answer	(Reprise K 14487) 1978 -
	Burlesque/My Friend In The Sun	(Rebecca) 1982 -

NB: α Early copies in picture sleeves. Promo only.

Notable for the rasping vocals of Roger Chapman, their superb live act and Charlie Whitney's often superb guitar work, **Family** was one of the most interesting progressive rock bands. Much cherished in Britain and Europe,

they failed to achieve the breakthrough their quality merited in the States, where they only achieved a cult following.

Formed in Leicester in 1967 **Family** evolved out of **The Farinas**, a R&B group who recorded for Fontana and were also known as The Roaring Sixties, but probably not the same band who in 1966 had recorded the then topical We Love The Pirates for Marmalade. **The Farinas** had been going since 1962 when Charlie Whitney had founded them at Leicester Art College.

In mid-1967 **The Farinas** moved to London and met up with American producer Kim Fowley who persuaded them to change their name to **Family**. They signed a one-off deal with Liberty in September 1967 for whom they cut a superb psychedelic single, Scene Thru' The Eyes Of A Lens, which also offered a foretaste of Chapman's unique vocals. It did not sell and is now extremely rare.

Their debut album, Music In A Doll's House (co-produced by **Traffic**'s **Dave Mason**) was a brilliant mind-expanding effort, full of new ideas and diversity. It surely must rate as one of the best debut albums of the sixties. **Family** at this time was an important part of London's underground circuit along with **Pink Floyd**, **Soft Machine**, **Tomorrow** et al. Their stage act was electric, the charismatic Chapman would contort around the stage in a demented haze and considerable use was made of light shows and smoke clouds.

Music In A Doll's House was self-penned, save for one **Mason** composition, Never Like This, and contained daringly innovative material like The Chase, Mellowing Grey, Winter, See Through Windows, New Songs Old Songs and Peace Of Mind. This was mind-expanding music that highlighted Chapman's raucous vocal dexterity and utilized a wide range of instruments. Every track was a winner. Around this time the band achieved the dubious distinction of being the anonymous subjects of Jenny Fabian's novel 'Groupie'.

Family's reputation as one of Britain's leading rock bands was consolidated by their follow-up album, which was produced by John Gilbert and Glyn Johns. Although less consistent than the debut it contained some of their most powerful work, particularly on The Weaver's Answer which captures Chapman's vocals at their most manic, Hung Up Down and Observations From A Hill (Side one's three opening tracks). The album made No 6 in the UK Charts. After a series of unsuccessful 45s (in commercial terms, at any rate) 45 Chart success eventually came in 1969 when No Mule's Fool reached No 29 in the November of that year. 1969 was a tumultuous year, for the band witnessed the first of a series of personnel changes. Ric Grech left during their first US tour to join **Blind Faith**. John Weider, who was then playing with an LA-based club band Stonehenge but who had previously been with **Eric Burdon and The Animals** flew out to replace him. During the tour the group got into a misunderstanding with America's top promoter at the time, Bill Graham, and they never did make it big in the States probably as a consequence of that. When they returned to Britain they parted company with Jim King too. He was ousted due to some rather unpredictable behaviour and went on to play for an outfit called Ring Of Truth.

FAMILY - A Song For Me (LP).

FAMILY - Bandstand (LP).

Upon King's departure, Poli Palmer, who had played in various Birmingham-area bands including Bakerloo Blues Line and **Deep Feeling** joined. The band now enjoyed its most commercially successful, if not its most innovative, period. Not only did *A Song For Me* and *Anyway* reach numbers 4 and 7 in the Album Charts respectively, they also enjoyed three hit singles. In June 1971 John Weider left to join **Stud**, who having recorded an album for Deram earlier that year, went on to record a couple for the German BASF label which weren't released in Britain. John Wetton came in to replace him from **Mogul Thrash** but left 15 months later for **King Crimson**. However, in this time the band produced two albums:- *Fearless* and *Bandstand*, which not only gave them more success in the UK Album Charts reaching Nos 10 and 15 respectively but also gave them their only US success making Nos 177 and 183 respectively in the Album Charts over there. After these Poli Palmer left to start a new band with Ric Grech which never got off the ground. Tony Ashton was drafted in as a replacement on keyboards, and Jim Cregan joined from **Stud** but by now the band was past its prime. A switch from Reprise to Raft for their final album, *It's Only A Movie*, did not ebb the tide and by October 1973 they were gone for good. Roger Chapman and Charlie Whitney later teamed up in **Streetwalkers**. Rob Townsend re-emerged in **Medicine Head** and was later in The Blues Band.

Fans of Roger Chapman may (or may not) know that one of his best vocal performances was *Shadow On The Wall* from **Mike Oldfield**'s *Crises* album. It's a killer. He now lives in Germany, where he has a flourishing solo career. Charlie Whitney plays in a low profile country/bluegrass band Los Rackateeros. Ric Grech was plagued by drink problems and died from liver failure in 1990. Tony Ashton died on 28 May 2001, aged 55 from cancer.

See For Miles' 1991 *The Best Of Family... Plus* compilation would be a good introduction to the band for those unfamiliar with their music. It includes a good selection of their finest moments including the seminal *Weaver's Answer*.

The 1973 BBC Radio Show is available on Italian import and captured their exciting live act effectively.

BBC Radio Vol 1 1968-69 features several of their tracks not available on CD before including their rare coveted first 45 *Scene Through The Eyes Of A Lens*, and their only official release of the old blues number *I Sing Um The Way I Feel*. The five sessions contained on this CD date from the period between September 1968 - July 1969 and are mastered from the original BBC transcription tapes. The package comes with a 12-page booklet. *BBC Radio Vol 2 1971-73* also captures the band in fine fettle. This package also includes a 12-page booklet containing many previously unseen band photos and excellent sleevenotes.

In their prime they were giants - powerful, gritty, rough and original - for my money one of the best British bands of the progressive era.

Compilation appearances have included: *The Weavers Answer* on *Your Starter For Ten!!* (CD); *Scene Thru' The Eye Of A Lens* on *Electric Sugar*

Cube Flashbacks (CD) and *Electric Sugarcube Flashbacks, Vol. 1* (LP); and *Face In The Clouds* on *Electric Psychedelic Sitar Headswirlers Vol. 6* (CD). (VJ)

Family Affair

ALBUM: 1   FAMILY AFFAIR   (Saga 2124) 1968

The album sleeve shows this band as a Hispanic-like pop group on stage. (VJ)

Family Dogg

Personnel:	DOREEN DE VEUVE		A
	ALBERT HAMMOND	gtr, vcls	ABCDE
	MIKE HAZELWOOD		ABCDE
	STEVE ROWLAND	vcls	ABCDE
	ZOOEY VAN ZUILECOUR		AB
	CHRISTINE HOLMES		BCD
	BILLIE COX		C
	IRENE SHEER		DE
	LESLEY DUNCAN		E
	CAROL FORBES		

ALBUMS: 1( ) A WAY OF LIFE   (Bell SBLL 122) 1969 SC
        2( ) VIEW FROM ROWLAND'S HEAD
                                  (Polydor 2318 061) 1972 SC

		HCP
45s:	Family Dogg/Storm	(MGM 1360) 1967 -
	I Wear A Silly Grin/Couldn't Help It	(Fontana TF 921) 1968 -
	Brown-Eyed Girl/Let It Rain	(Fontana TF 968) 1968 -
	A Way Of Life/Throw It Away	(Bell BLL 1055) 1969 6
	Arizona/House In The Heather	(Bell BLL 1077) 1969 -
	When Tomorrow Comes Today/	
	This Unhappy Heart Of Mine	(Bell BLL 1100) 1970 -
	Coat Of Many Colours/Jesus Loves You	(Bell BLL 1139) 1971 -
	Sweet America/Rikers Island	(Buddah 2011 143) 1972 -

This five-piece was put together by Steve Rowland and aside from himself consisted of two guys and two girls. They are best remembered for the well crafted pop song *A Way Of Life*, which was a Top Ten hit in 1969. They were unable to attain such dizzy heights in the future and despite the fact that Steve Rowland tried different line-ups under the same name in 1970 and 1976 they are remembered as 'one hit wonders'.

De Veuve was sacked in July 1969, after *A Way Of Life* had charted. She was replaced by Christine Holmes. Van Zuilecour was replaced by Billie Coe who in turn was replaced by Irene Sheer. Holmes was later replaced by **Lesley Duncan**. Carol Forbes was a member of the 1976 line-up.

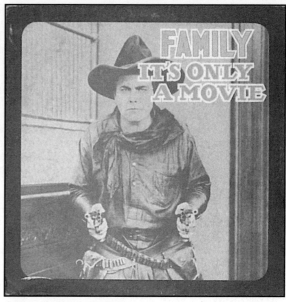

FAMILY - It's Only A Movie (LP).

FANTASY - Paint A Picture (LP).

Christine Holmes went on to host 'Crackerjack' briefly, recorded some naff singles under the name Kristine Sparkle and did impersonations for the TV series 'Who Do You Do' under the name Kristine. Several people passed through the band over the years and their album includes performances by **Led Zeppelin** members **Page**, Bonham and **Jones**. (VJ/JM)

Famous Jug Band

Personnel:	HENRY VIII BARTLETT	vcls, jug, perc	AB
	PETE BERRYMAN	gtr, vcls	AB
	JILL JOHNSON	vcls, gtr	AB
	CLIVE PALMER	dulcimer, gtr, vcls	A

| ALBUMS: | 1(A) | SUNSHINE POSSIBILITIES | (Liberty LBS 83263) 1969 R1 |
| | 2(B) | CHAMELEON | (Liberty LBS 83355) 1970 SC |

NB: (1) reissued on CD (Wooden Hill HILL CD 25) 1999.

| 45: | The Only Friend I Own/ | |
| | A Leaf Must Fall | (Liberty LBF 15224) 1969 |

Though their name may have been intended to sound ironical, this more or less folky outfit is now at least famous for providing a station for the restless **Clive Palmer**, who came from **The Incredible String Band**. On their first album an unobtrusive influence of the blues is mixed with moderate success into typical British folk. *Palmer*'s two contributions are very wistful indeed, but unfortunately on *Nickolson Sq.* the two male voices do not blend very well with the fabulously pure vocals of Johnson. *A Leaf Must Fall* is very sad and very quiet. Main songwriter Berryman offers more diversity: some folk-blues, some bluegrass, some well-meant philosophy. The production is extremely natural with no studio tricks at all. They became the house band at the Folk Cottage Club outside Falmouth in Cornwall.

Palmer then left to form the Stockroom Five and **Temple Creatures**, neither of whom made it on to vinyl. He then formed **C.O.B.** (Clive's Original Band). **The Famous Jug Band** soldiered on undefeated to produce the much stranger *Chameleon*, an uneven but at its best highly underrated and interesting effort. By now they sound quite close to Mormos, spicing their increasingly idiosyncratic songs with unexpected harmonic twists to great effect. This isn't much evident on side one, but it comes to full bloom on side two, which must be counted among the most fragile and intimate sequences of folk songs from the UK. It is only marred by an unnecessary cover of **Michael Chapman**'s *Rabbit Hills*. Otherwise this comes recommended.

Sunshine Possibilities can also be heard on Liberty's *Son Of Gutbucket* (LP) sampler. (MK/RMJ)

Fancy

Personnel:	LES BINKS	drms	A
	RAY FENWICK	gtr	A
	MO FOSTER	bs	A
	ANNIE KAVANAUGH	vcls	A

ALBUMS:	1(A)	WILD THING	(Atlantic K 51502) 1974
(up to	2 (A)	SOMETHING TO REMEMBER	(Arista ARTY 102) 1975
1976)	3 (A)	TURNS YOU ON	(RCA Victor 1482) 1976

45s:	Wild Thing/Fancy (some PS)	(Atlantic K 10383) 1973
(up to	Touch Me/I Don't Need Your Love	(Atlantic K 111514) 1974
1976)	I Was To Love Him/Stop	(Arista ARIST 15) 1975
	Music Maker/Blue Bird	(Arista ARIST 32) 1976

Fancy are rather forgotten now. Formed by three session musicians, they achieved a big US hit with their re-styled version of **The Troggs**' *Wild Thing*. Ray Fenwick was later in the Ian Gillan Band and Les Binks banged the skins for metal messiahs **Judas Priest**. (VJ/CG)

Fantasy

Personnel:	PETER JAMES	gtr	A
	PAUL LAWRENCE	vcls, gtr	AB
	DAVID METCALFE	keyb'ds	A
	DAVID READ	bs	AB
	JON WEBSTER	drms	A
	MALCOLM PAGE	drms	B
	NICK PAGE	piano	B
	GEOFF WHITEHORN	gtr	B

| ALBUM: | 1(A) | PAINT A PICTURE | (Polydor 2383 246) 1973 R3 |

NB: (1) reissued on vinyl (Second Battle 843 263-1) 1990 in Germany and on CD (Polydor/Edison ERC-29229) 1990 in Japan. There's also a second album, *Beyond The Beyond*, which was recorded in 1974 and intended as a follow-up to (1) but never released until 1992 on CD (Audio Archives AACD 001) in the UK and vinyl (Colours COSLP 014/CTM 5) 1993 in Norway. Then in 1994 came *Vivariatum* (Audio Archives AACD 004), a CD comprised of four songs recorded in 1970 by the embryonic stage of the band and six by a reformed line-up (B) in 1976.

| 45: | Politely Insane/I Was Once Aware | (Polydor 2058 405) 1973 R1 |

A progressive rock outfit who originally formed in Kent as Chapel Farm with a gritty vocalist called Paul Petley. Four tracks from a 10" acetate in this period (*Fire-Fire, Vacuum, Alone* and *Afterthought*) can now be heard on the *Vivariatum* CD and all four are pleasant but unexceptional keyboard-driven progressive rock.

Original vocalist Paul Petley left in 1971 to be replaced by Paul Lawrence. Then in 1972 they changed name briefly to Firequeen before switching again to **Fantasy** in 1973.

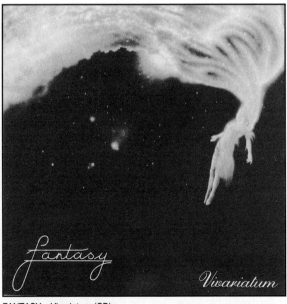

FANTASY - Vivariatum (CD).

DON FARDON - I've Paid My Dues (LP).

Fantasy's *Paint A Picture* album is now very rare and their 45 is pretty elusive too. The best tracks on the album were the title cut with its gentle, melodic vocals and the livelier *Circus*, with its good guitar work and swirling keyboards. *Award, Icy River* and *Young May's Fortune* are also worth a listen.

The first incarnation of the band split in 1974 before a projected second album, *Beyond The Beyond*, could be released, although it is now available as the discography notes explain.

There was a reformation (line-up B) in 1976 and six tracks from this reincarnation can also be heard on the *Vivariatum* CD. Personally I prefer the ones from 1970. (VJ)

Faraway Folk

ALBUMS:	1	LIVE AT THE BOLTON	(RA LP 6006ST) 1970 R2
	2	TIME AND TIDE	(RA LP 6012ST) 197? R2
	3	ON THE RADIO	(RA LP 6019) 1974 SC
	4	ONLY AUTHORISED EMPLOYEES TO BREAK BOTTLES	
			(RA LP 6022) 1974 R1
	5	SEASONAL MAN	(RA LP 6029) 1975 R3

NB: (4) with Harry H. Corbett. There was also a later cassette-only release, *Battle Of The Dragons*, in the eighties.

EP: 1 INTRODUCING THE FARAWAY FOLK (RA EP 7001) 197? R1

45: Shadow Of A Pie//Folsom Prison Blues
Rent A Man/Soulful Shade Of Blue (Tabitha TAB 3) 197?

An electric folk outfit who, as you can see, released several privately-pressed albums. The *On The Radio* album includes songs recorded for a local BBC Radio broadcast. *Seasonal Man* is reputedly the best of the bunch - very much in the style of **Steeleye Span**. (VJ)

Don Fardon (and The Soul Machine)

ALBUMS:	1	LAMENT OF THE CHEROKEE INDIAN (GNP 2044) 1968
	2	I'VE PAID MY DUES (Youngblood SYB 4) 1970 SC
	3	RELEASED (Youngblood SSYB 13) 1970 SC

NB: (1) US release. There's also a compilation, *Indian Reservation* (C5 C5 540) 1989, also issued on CD as *The Best Of...* (C5 C5CD 540) in 1989.

HCP

45s: (The Lament Of The Cherokee) Indian Reservation/
Dreamin' Room (Pye International 7N 25437) 1967 -
(The Lament Of The Cherokee) Indian Reservation/
Dreamin' Room (Pye International 7N 25475) 1968 -
We Can Make It Together/

Coming On Strong (Pye International 7N 25483) 1969 -
Good Lovin'/
Ruby's Picture On My Wall (Pye International 7N 25486) 1969 -
I Follow Your Drum/
Get Away John (Young Blood YB 1027) 1971 -
Girl/Sandiago (Young Blood YB 1021) 1972 -
Belfast Boy/
Echoes Of The Cheers (Young Blood YB 1010) 1972 SC 32
Delta Queen/Hometown Baby (Young Blood YB 1013) 1972 -
Indian Reservation/Hudson Bay (Young Blood YB 1015) 1972 3
Lady Zelda/Louisiana (Young Blood YB 1055) 1973 -
Running Bear/St Matthew, St Mark,
St Luke, St John (Young Blood YB 1071) 1974 -
It's Been Nice Loving You/
Let The Love Live (Young Blood YB 1007) 1975 -
I'm Alive/Keep On Loving Me (Young Blood YB 1003) 1975 -
Judy Mae/Dady's Song (MCA MCA 233) 1976 -
Reissue: Indian Reservation/Dreamin' Room (Old Gold OG 9034) 1979 -

Fardon's real name was Don Maughn and he was born in Coventry and first caught the public eye as lead singer of **The Sorrows**. After their demise he had a soul act called **Don Fardon and The Soul Machine**, which had a good reputation as a live band. Then he embarked on a solo career enjoying a major hit with *Indian Reservation* and a minor hit with *Belfast Boy*.

The C5 compilation, aside from his two hits, includes reworked versions of **The Sorrows**' *Take A Heart* and Johnny Preston's *Running Bear* and some pretty undistinguished cover versions of US popular bubblegum hits like *The Letter* and *Gimme Gimme Good Lovin'*. Not recommended. *Let the Love Live* has been compiled on *The Youngblood Story Vol. 1* (CD).

Indian Reservation has been compiled on *Best Sellers Of The 70's, Vol 1* (CD) and on *Sunshine Day A Taste Of The 70's* (CD). (VJ)

The Farinas

Personnel:	TIM KIRCHIN	bs	A
	JIM KING	sax	ABC
	HARRY OVERNALL	drms	ABC
	CHARLIE WHITNEY	gtr, vcls	ABC
	RIC GRECH	bs	BC
	ROGER CHAPMAN	vcls	C

45s: Bye Bye Johnny/All You Gotta Do/
Twist And Shout (Victor Buckland Studio Sound) 1964 R5
α You'd Better Stop/I Like It Like That (Fontana TF 493) 1964 R2
NB: α as James King & Farinas.

A R&B outfit formed in 1962 by Whitney at Leicester Art College. They were heavily influenced by late fifties US rockers like Chuck Berry and The Coasters at first but later got into blues and soul. Ric Grech replaced Kirchin in 1965 a year after they recorded their sole 45, which is now quite collectable of course. The 'A' side was a good bluesy number and the flip was a very credible cover of a Chris Kenner song. Roger Chapman joined them in 1966 and they became known as The Roaring Sixties for a while before changing their name to **Family** at Kim Fowley's suggestion.

Compilation appearances have included: *You'd Better Stop* on *Visions Of The Past, Vol. 3* (LP & CD); and *I Like It Like That* on *Beat Merchants* (2-LP). (VJ)

Chris Farlowe (and The Thunderbirds)

Personnel:	RICKY CHAPMAN	bs	A
	CHRIS FARLOWE	vcls	ABC
	DAVE GREENSLADE	organ	AB
	ALBERT LEE	gtr	ABC
	JOHNNY WISE	drms	A
	IAN HAGUE	drms	B
	JERRY TEMPLE	congas	B
	BUGS WADDELL	bs	B
	CARL PALMER	drms	C
	PETE SOLLEY	keyb'ds	C

NB: Although not listed above Alan Shacklock (ex-**Juniors**, pre-**Babe Ruth**) plays guitar on the *Paint It Black* 45.

ALBUMS:				
(up to 1976)	1( )	CHRIS FARLOWE AND THE THUNDERBIRDS (Columbia SX 6034)	1966	R3 -
	2( )	14 THINGS TO THINK ABOUT (Immediate IMLP 005)	1966	R2 19
	3( )	THE ART OF CHRIS FARLOWE (Immediate IMLP 006)	1966	R2 37
	4( )	THE BEST OF CHRIS FARLOWE (Immediate IMLP/IMCP 010)	1968	R1 -
	5( )	THE LAST GOODBYE (Immediate IMLP 021)	1969	R2 -
	6( )	FROM HERE TO MAMA ROSA (Polydor 2425 029)	1970	SC -
	7(-)	CHRIS FARLOWE BAND LIVE (Polydor 2469 259)	1975	SC -
	8(-)	OUT OF TIME/PAINT IT BLACK (Charly CR 300020)	1976	-

NB: (6) as **Chris Farlowe** and Hill. (1) reissued as *Stormy Monday* (Music For Pleasure MFP 1186) in 1966. (2) reissued on CD (Repertoire REP 4280-WY) 1993 with 12 bonus tracks, comprising 'B' sides and EP cuts from his years with Immediate. (3) reissued on CD (Repertoire REP 4292-WY) 1993 with 11 bonus tracks. CD compilations include:- *I'm The Greatest* (See For Miles SEE CD 396) 1994 and *Mr. Soulful* (Castle Showcase SHCD 156) 1987. *BBC In Concert* (Windsong WINCD 081) 1995 comprises material from 1976 and four previously unissued studio tracks dating from circa 1969/70. *Hits* (Repertoire REP 4834-WG) 1999 on German import is a good round-up of his material. *The Very Best Of* (Camden/BMG) 2002 is a 20-track collection of his material spanning 1966-1968. *Rock'n'Roll Soilder: Anthology 1970-2004* (Delicious) 2004 is a 3-CD compilation of his output. *Handbags And Gladrags - The Immediate Collection* (Castle) 2004 gives a good overview of his music and contains his hits.

EPs:				
	1( )	CHRIS FARLOWE (Decca DFE 8665)	1965	R2
	2( )	FARLOWE IN THE MIDNIGHT HOUR (Immediate IMEP 001)	1965	R1
	3( )	STORMY MONDAY (Island IEP 709)	1966	R3
	4( )	CHRIS FARLOWE'S HITS (Immediate IMEP 004)	1966	R1

45s:					
(up to 1976)		Air Travel/ Why Did You Break My Heart?	(Decca F 11536)	1962	R1 -
	α	I Remember/Push Push	(Columbia DB 7120)	1963	SC -
	α	Girl Trouble/Itty Bitty Pieces	(Columbia DB 7237)	1964	SC -
	α	Just A Dream/ What You Gonna Do?	(Columbia DB 7311)	1964	SC -
	α	Hey, Hey, Hey, Hey/Hound Dog	(Columbia DB 7379)	1964	SC -
	α	Buzz With The Fuzz/ You're The One (Withdrawn)	(Columbia DB 7614)	1965	R3 -
		The Fool/Treat Her Good	(Immediate IM 016)	1965	-
		Think/Don't Just Look At Me	(Immediate IM 023)	1966	37
		Out Of Time/Baby Make It Soon	(Immediate IM 035)	1966	1
		Just A Dream/Hey, Hey, Hey, Hey	(Columbia DB 7983)	1966	-
		Ride On Baby/Headlines	(Immediate IM 038)	1966	31
		My Way Of Giving/ You're So Good To Me	(Immediate IM 041)	1967	48
		Yesterday's Papers/ Life Is But Nothing	(Immediate IM 049)	1967	-
		Moanin'/What Have I Been Doing?	(Immediate IM 056)	1967	46
		Handbags And Gladrags/ Everyone Makes A Mistake	(Immediate IM 065)	1967	33
	β	The Last Goodbye/ Paperman Fly In The Sky	(Immediate IM 066)	1968	-
		Paint It Black/ I Just Need Your Lovin'	(Immediate IM 071)	1968	-
		Dawn/April Was The Month	(Immediate IM 074)	1969	-
		Black Sheep/Fifty Years	(Polydor 2066 017)	1971	-
	χ	Put Out The Light/Questions	(Polydor 2066 046)	1971	-
		We Can Work It Out/ Only Women Bleed	(Polydor 2066 650)	1975	-
Reissues:		Out Of Time/Ride On Baby	(Immediate IM 078)	1969	-
		Out Of Time/Handbags And Gladrags/Yesterday's Papers/ Ride On Baby (double pack)	(Virgin SV 102)	1975	-
		Out Of Time/My Way Of Giving	(Immediate IMS 101)	1975	44
		Out Of Time/Think	(Old Gold OG 9468)	1985	-

NB: α As Chris Farlowe and The Thunderbirds. β B-side with Thunderbirds. χ As Chris Farlowe and Hill.

Chris Farlowe's real name was John Deighton and he was born on 13 October 1940. Before forming **The Thunderbirds** in 1964 he'd played in a number of skiffle acts including The John Henry Skiffle Group. **The Thunderbirds** were reputedly a first rate R&B band, one of the best on the circuit in the mid-sixties, but they got little recognition at the time. They featured a certain Albert Lee on guitar who went on to play in several other bands including **Heads Hands and Feet**, **Joe Cocker** and The Cock'n'Bull Band and he also had his own studio-only Albert Lee Band in 1975. Their organist Dave Greenslade also went on to greater things with **The Ram Jam Band** and **Colosseum**.

After a one-off release for Decca, *Air Travel*, passed largely without notice, **The Thunderbirds** released some first rate R&B singles for EMI's Columbia label, which were ideally suited to **Farlowe**'s powerful rasping vocal style. The rarest and most sought-after of these is *Buzz With The Fuzz*, which was withdrawn shortly after its release because EMI objected to some of the mod slang in the lyrics. Following this **Farlowe** released *Stormy Monday Blues* under the pseudonym of Little Joe Cook on the Sue label. At the time everyone thought the 45 was the work of an obscure black US blues singer.

It wasn't until **Farlowe** and his band signed to the new Immediate label that they began to enjoy the success they really deserved. The first 45, *The Fool*, produced by **Eric Burdon** of **The Animals** missed out; the follow-up, *Think*, a **Jagger**/Richard composition due to be included on the forthcoming **Rolling Stones**' *Aftermath* album was a minor hit but the big breakthrough came with another **Jagger**/Richard number, *Out Of Time*, which was also on the *Aftermath* album and shot him to No 1. He later achieved a minor hit with *Ride On Baby*, another **Jagger**/Richard song which hadn't made it onto *Aftermath*.

His two albums around this time, *14 Things To Think About* and *The Art Of Chris Farlowe*, which veered more towards soul and R&B both sold pretty well and he continued to enjoy further 45 successes during 1968 with **The Small Faces**' *My Way Of Giving* produced by **Marriott** and **Lane** and a cover of the jazz standard *Moanin'* and *Handbags And Gladrags*, which had been written by **Manfred Mann**'s **Mike D'Abo**. Following this brace of minor hits he disbanded **The Thunderbirds** and took a two year sabbatical from the music scene. During this time he channelled much of his energy into building up his Islington-based collection of Nazi World War II memorabilia. When he returned in the Autumn of 1970 he briefly fronted a band called Hill and then did short stints as vocalist for **Colosseum** and **Atomic Rooster**. Then in 1975 after the revived Immediate label reissued some of his old discs he formed a new band for a national tour, resulting in a live album for Polydor, but it made little impression with the punters. Since then his recording forays have been spasmodic. In early 1978 he sang the theme tune to the BBC's crime series 'Gangsters'. In 1982 he sang two cuts, 'Who's To Blame' and 'Hypnotising Ways' on the musical score for Charles Bronson's 'Death Wish II'. Later that year he appeared in the 'Heroes and Villains' charity concert at London's Hammersmith Odeon along with several other sixties stars. This revival in his fortunes spurred him to release a cover of **Long John Baldry**'s *Let The Heartaches Begin*, which failed to sell in any great quantities.

CHRIS FARLOWE - From Here To Mama Rosa (LP).

280

Back in 1968 he'd appeared on Island's *British Blue-Eyed Soul* (LP) compilation playing *Stormy Monday Blues Pts. 1 and 2*, and in 1971 with The Hill Polydor's *Rock Party* (LP) compilation featured *Black Sheep Of The Family*.

Other compilation appearances have included: *Out Of Time* on *Jimmy Page Studio Works 1964-1968* (CD), the 2-CD set *60 Number Ones Of The Sixties*, *The Greatest Sixties Album Of All Time Vol 2* (CD) and *Juke Box Jive* (EP); *Moanin'* on *Jimmy Page - Hip Young Guitar Slinger* (2-CD); *Air Travel* on *The Mod Scene* (CD); *Handbags And Gladrags* on *Maximum '65* (CD), *Hits Of The Swinging Sixties* (CD) and *Radio Two: Sound Of The Sixties* (CD); *Air Travel* on *A Whiter Shade Of Pale* (LP); *Out Of Time* and *Paint It Black* on *Tonite Let's All Make Love In London* (LP); *She's Alright* (a cut from his *Stormy Monday* EP) on *Broken Dreams, Vol. 4* (LP); *You're So Good For Me*, *Life Is But Nothing* and *Dawn* on *Immediate Single Collection, Vol. 1* (CD); *Paint It Black*, *Yesterday's Papers*, *April Was The Month* and *I Just Need Your Loving* on *Immediate Single Collection, Vol. 2* (CD); *Ride On Baby*, *Handbags And Gladrags* and *My Way Of Giving* on *Immediate Single Collection, Vol. 3* (CD); *Baby Make It Soon* and *Think* on *Immediate Single Collection, Vol. 4* (CD); *Out Of Time*, *The Last Goodbye* and *Paperman Fly In The Sky* on *Immediate Single Collection, Vol. 5* (CD). *Handbags And Gladrags* can also be found on *Rock Of Ages, Four Decades Of Heavy Rock 1962-2002* and you'll also find *Think* and *Out Of Time* on the 2-CD set *We Love The Pirates: Charting The Big 'L' Fab 40*.

Peter Solley later played with **Fox**, **Paladin**, **Gravy Train** and **Procol Harum**. (VJ)

Giles Farnaby's Dream Band

Personnel:

ANNE CROZIER	concertina, bowed psalbery	A
TREVOR CROZIER	ba, gtr, hrmnca	A
JEFF CLYNE	bs	A
VIC GAMMON	gtr	A
FRANK GRUBB	recorder	A
JOHN GRUBB	lube harp-zither	A
DEREK HARRISON	rebec	A
JOHN LAWES	crumbhorn, recorder	A
DAVE MAcCRAE	piano	A
MIKE OXENHAM	clarinet, recorder	A
JOHN SOTHCOTT	recorders	A
TREVOR TOMKINS	drms	A
LEILA WARD	recorders, crumblehorns	A

ALBUM: 1 (A)   GILES FARNABY'S DREAM BAND
(Argo ZDA 158) 1973 R2

45:   Newcastle Brown/29th Of May   (Argo AFW 112) 1973

A rare and sought-after album, which came about as a result of a collaboration between Trevor Crozier's Broken Consort, (who'd recorded an album called *A Parcel Of Old Crams* for Argo) and St Georges Canzona, a medieval group. **The Druids** guested on two songs. The record was a studio-only concept album but Trevor Crozier did take a band called Lyonesse on the road playing similar material. Crozier later made a solo album, *Trouble Over Bridgwater*, for EMI's One-Up label.

Giles Farnaby's Dream Band is full of medieval folk music and includes a version of *Greensleeves*. (VJ/BS)

Faron's Flamingoes

Personnel:

NICKY CROUCH	lead gtr	ABCD
BILL FARON RUFFLEY	vcls, bs	ABCDEFG H I J KL
BILLY JONES	gtr	AB
TREVOR MORAIS	drms	ABCD
ERIC LONDON	bs	B
PADDY CHAMBERS	lead gtr	CD
DAVE 'MUSHY' COOPER	bs	C
ARTHUR DAVIES	drms	E
PETE JONES	lead gtr	EF

THE MOD SCENE (Comp CD) including Chris Farlowe.

KEITH TAYLOR	bs	E
KEITH KARLSEN	bs	F
JOHNNY JAY RATHBONE	drms	F
MOGSY COOK	vcls, dancer	G
PETER COOK	lead gtr	G
PETER COOK Jnr	bs	G
BRIAN JONES	sax	G H I
DEREK SMALLRIDGE	drms	G H I J
DENNIS ?	lead gtr	H
OWEN ROBERTS	bs	H I J
TERRY ?	lead gtr	I
CHRIS EVANS	lead gtr	J K
STEVE ROBERTS	sax	J
COLIN DRUMMOND	keyb'ds	K
RONNIE PLUMMER	sax	K
BERNIE ROGERS	drms	K

45s: Do You Love Me?/See If She Cares   (Oriole CB 1834) 1963
          Shake Sherry/Give Me Time   (Oriole CB 1867) 1963

Nicky Crouch, Trevor Morais, Billy Jones and Eric London were known as The Ravens and were joined by Billy 'Faron' Russley upon his return from a residency in Germany with **Gerry and The Pacemakers**. They took the name **Faron's Flamingos** after a suggestion by the DJ Bob Wooler. The band turned professional in January 1962 (except for London, who joined the semi-pro group Group One). He was replaced by ex-**Undertaker** Dave 'Mushy' Cooper. Jones left in July 1962 and was replaced by Paddy Chambers, who had been playing with a jazz trio in Paris and had previously been with Steve Bennett and The Syndicate. Cooper left in January 1963 to join The Renegades and Russley moved to bass.

The Liverpool group produced two of Merseybeat's finest singles. Many regard their version of *Do You Love Me?* as more arse-kicking than either of the hit versions by **Brian Poole** or **Dave Clark**. *Do You Love Me?* and *Shake Sherry* were both Motown covers originally recorded by The Contours which, coincidentally enough, both came out here on Oriole.

When the band split in November 1963, Paddy Chambers and Bill Faron Ruffley went on to join **The Big Three** whilst Nicky Crouch was later in **The Mojos**. Morais did session work until joining **The Peddlers.**

Paddy Chambers died of throat cancer on 28 September 2000.

Compilation appearances have included: *Let's Stomp*, *Do You Love Me?*, *Shake Sherry* and *See If She Cares* on *Let's Stomp!* (LP); *Do You Love Me?* on *Mersey Beat* (2-LP); *Shake Sherry*, *Let's Stomp* and *Do You Love Me?* on *Mersey Beat 1962-1964* (2-LP); *See If She Cares* on *Beat Merchants* (2-LP); *Let's Stomp* and *Talkin' 'Bout You* on *The Exciting New Liverpool Sound* (LP) and *This Is Merseybeat, Vol. 1* (LP); *Shake Sherry* and *So Fine* on *This Is Merseybeat, Vol. 2* (LP); *Do You Love Me?* and *See If She Cares* on Realm's *Group Beat '63* (LP). (VJ/AD/JM)

MICK FARREN - Mona The Carnivorous Circus (LP).

Wayne Faro's Schmaltz Band

45:      There's Still Time/Give It Time   (Deram DM 222) 1969

This was an obscure one-off 45. (VJ)

Gary Farr (and The T-Bones)

Personnel: GARY FARR   vcls   ABCD
             STU PARKES   bs   ABC
             ANDY McKECHNIE   gtr   AB
             BRIAN WALKELEY   drms   A
             WINSTON WEATHERILL   lead gtr ABCD
             ANDREW STEELE   drms   BCD
             KEITH EMERSON   keyb'ds   CD
             KEITH 'LEE' JACKSON bs   D

ALBUMS: 1   TAKE SOMETHING WITH YOU
                                   (Marmalade 608 013) 1969 R2
          2   STRANGE FRUIT   (CBS 64138) 1971 R1
          3   ADDRESSED TO THE CENSORS OF LOVE (US only)
                                   (Atco SD 7034) 1973
          4   LONDON 1964/65   (Charly CR 300015) 1977
          5   DEM BONES   (Eva EVA 12041) 1984

NB: (2) reissued on CD (Columbia 483672 2) 1995.

EP: 1(A)   DEM BONES, DEM BONES, DEM T-BONES
                                   (Columbia SEG 8414) 1965 R3

45s: α   Give All She's Got/
           Don't Stop And Stare   (Columbia DB 7608) 1965 R1
       β   Everyday/Green   (Marmalade 598 007) 1969
           Hey Daddy/
           The Vicar And The Pope   (Marmalade 598 017) 1969 SC
           Revolution Of The Season/Old Man Boulder   (CBS 5330) 1971
           Revolution Of The Season/Old Man Boulder   (CBS 5430) 1971

NB: α with **The T-Bones**. β with **Kevin Westlake**.

Gary Farr formed **The T-Bones** in Worthing, Sussex, in 1963. He was the son of boxer Tommy Farr and his brother Ricky was one of the leading pop promoters of the period, and went on to organise the Isle Of Wight festivals in the late sixties. The band was a raw R&B outfit who were very popular in the clubs and made an appearance on 'Ready Steady Go'. See **The T-Bones** entry for details of their records under this name. After their demise, Emerson left for **The VIP's** and Jackson (who'd previously been with Von Dykes) went to **Hedgehoppers Anonymous**. Weatherill was later in **The Fox** and Steele went on to **The Herd**.

After disbanding **The T-Bones** in 1967, **Farr** recorded a single with **Kevin Westlake** (featuring Martin Stone of **Mighty Baby** on lead guitar) and an

excellent album for the Marmalade label, which was folk-rock tinged with psychedelia, *Take Something With You* is a decent reflection of its era. He was backed on this now rare album by other members of **Mighty Baby** and **Blossom Toes**. Next he recorded *Strange Fruit*, which is quite rare but not especially interesting, with the exception of the anthemic *In the Mud*. **Richard Thompson** played lead guitar and again **Mighty Baby** (without Stone) provided the backing. It was produced by Fritz Fryer, a former member of **The Four Pennies** and also producer of the **Open Mind**'s *Magic Potion* 45. Next he headed for the States, where his US-only Atco album was made. It's largely typical of the US singer/songwriter genre, but surprisingly good in places. In the early eighties he formed Lion, who issued an unsuccessful album before **Farr** largely quit music in favour of photography and family. His premature death from a heart attack in 1984 deprived pop of one of its better voices.

The band can also be heard on *The Roots Of British Rock, Vol 7* (LP). (VJ/JM/RMJ)

Mick Farren

ALBUMS: 1   MONA (THE CARNIVOROUS CIRCUS)
                                   (Transatlantic TRA 212) 1970 R2
          2   VAMPIRES STOLE MY LUNCH MONEY
              (w/lyric insert)   (Logo LOGO 1010) 1978 R1

NB: (1) reissued on vinyl (Psycho PSYCHO 20) in 1984 and reissued again on CD as *Partial Recall* (Transatlantic/Drop Out DOCD 1989) 1992, with extra tracks. A good collection is *The Best Of The Deviants and Mick Farren* (Essential ESMCD 746) 1999. *People Call You Crazy : The Story Of Mick Farren* (Sanctuary CMQCD 731) 2003 is an overview of his recording career.

45s: Half Price Drinks/
          I Don't Want To Go This Way (PS)   (Logo GO 321) 1978
          Broken Statue/It's All In The Picture   (Logo GO 345) 1979

Mick Farren was a raucous charismatic vocalist who founded **The Deviants** in 1967. These were his spasmodic solo efforts, but he also went on to become quite a successful writer and a central part of London's Ladbroke Grove underground scene.

Mona was comprised largely of heavy metal reinterpretations of R&B standards with quite a few spoken passages and has not aged at all well. The CD reissue, *Partial Recall*, not only gives *Mona* yet another airing (it was originally reissued by Psycho in 1984) it also includes a couple of tracks from *Deviants 3* and three songs from **Farren**'s later *Vampire Stole My Lunch Money* album.

People Call You Crazy is an attempted overview of his career, which surprisingly omits *You Got To Hold On*. Still there's much good music to listen to on this.

Compilation appearances include *Summertime Blues* on *The Transatlantic Story* CD box set and on *Rock Of Ages, Four Decades Of Heavy Rock 1962-2002*. (VJ)

MICK FARREN - Vampire Stole My Lunch Money (CD).

Fat Graple

Personnel incl: EDDIE JOBSON

45:     Happy In The Lord/
        My Friends And I   (United Artists UP 35590) 1973

This Newcastle band included future **Curved Air** member Eddie Jobson from 1971 until early 1973. He had left before they recorded this 45. (VJ)

Fat Mattress

Personnel: ERIC DILLON   drms   AB
            NEIL LANDON   vcls   AB
            JAMES LEVERTON   bs   AB
            NOEL REDDING   gtr, bs, vcls   A
            STEVE HAMMOND   gtr   B
            (MIKE WEAVER   keyb'ds   B)

ALBUMS: 1(A) FAT MATTRESS   (Polydor 583 056) 1969 SC
        2(B) FAT MATTRESS TWO   (Polydor 2383 025) 1970 SC

NB: (1) and (2) reissued on CD (Sequel NEXCD 196 and 197 respectively) 1992. There's also a 2-CD compilation *The Black Sheep Of The Family - The Anthology* (Essential ESDCD 865) 2000.

45s: Naturally/Iridescent Butterfly   (Polydor 56352) 1969
        Magic Lanterns/Bright New Way   (Polydor 56367) 1970
        Highway/Black Sheep Of The Family (Polydor 2058 053) 1970

This band burst onto the scene with considerable publicity in 1968 on account of **Redding** being the bassist with **The Jimi Hendrix Experience**. **Landon** was a former session singer and also one of **The Flowerpot Men**. His extensive vocal range gave the band's music much of its flavour. Leverton and Dillon had previously been with Englebert Humberdinck's Band O' Men. They issued three singles which met with no success in the UK, although *Magic Lanterns* was a No. 1 hit in Holland and their druggy music featured in these singles and on album tracks like *Mr. Moonshine* may be of interest to readers.

Steve Hammond (ex-**Johnny Almond's Music Machine**) joined the band just prior to **Noel Redding's** departure half way through the second album to go to the States to front a US/UK band called Road. He later formed the **Noel Redding Band** in 1975. Mick Weaver joined the band after the demise of Mason Wood Capaldi Frog. **Redding**'s departure ultimately meant disintegration for the band. Leverton joined **Juicy Lucy** and later became a member of **Savoy Brown's Boogie Brother**'s with Eric Dillon, whose next band was **Miller Anderson**. Landon headed for **Noel Redding and Friends**; Weaver to **Keef Hartley** and Hammond became a member of Chris Barber's Jazz Band.

The 2-CD anthology *The Black Sheep Of The Family* includes both the original albums and all the surviving out-takes, but it portrays them as a solid but uninspired band.

FAT MATTRESS - Fat Mattress (LP).

FAT MATTRESS - The Black Sheep Of The Family (2-CD).

Fat Mattress had one cut, *Everything's Blue*, on Polydor's 1970 *Supergroups* (LP) and 1971 *Rock Party* (2-LP) compilations. More recently, *The Storm* was included on *Rock Of Ages, Four Decades Of Heavy Rock 1962-2002*. (VJ/JM)

Favourite Sons

45:     That Driving Beat/
        Walkin' Walkin' Walkin'   (Mercury MF 911) 1965 R3

Favourite Sons hailed from Hatfield, Hertfordshire. The 'A' side of this 45 is a competent R&B standard penned by Willie Mitchell; the flip, which was written by their producer Mike Hurst (once of The Springfields), has a simple but great guitar intro.

Compilation appearances have included: *Walking, Walking, Walking* on *Psychedelia, Vol. 2* (LP), *English Freakbeat, Vol. 3* (CD) and *Hen's Teeth Vol. 1* (CD); and *That Driving Beat* on *That Driving Beat* (CD). (VJ)

Bill Fay

Personnel incl.: BILL FAY   piano, vcls   AB
                  RAY RUSSELL   gtr   AB
                  DARYL RUNSWICK   bs   B
                  ALAN RUSHTON   drms   B

ALBUMS: 1 BILL FAY   (Deram Nova SDN 12) 1970 R1
         2 TIME OF THE LAST PERSECUTION
                                       (Deram SML 1079) 1971 R3

NB: (1) and (2) were reissued on a single CD by See For Miles in the 1990s, and have recently appeared on single CDs (1) (Eclectic Discs ECLCD 1022) 2005 and (2) (Eclectic Discs ECLCD 1023) 2005. *From The Bottom Of An Old Grandfather Clock* (Wooden Hill CD) 2004 is a collection of his 1960s demos. *Tomorrow, Tomorrow And Tomorrow* (Durtro/Jnana 1976 CD) 2005 comprises songs he recorded himself between 1978 and 1981.

45:     Some Good Advice/
        Screams In The Ears   (Deram DM 143) 1967 R1

Bill Fay recorded two of the most beguiling and original albums of their time. A Londoner who'd studied electronics at Bangor University before deciding to pursue a career in music, he came to Decca's attention via **Honeybus**'s manager Terry Noon early in 1967 and his sole single, *Some Good Advice*, appeared that August. It's now one of the hardest Deram 45s to locate. Backed by **The Fingers** and produced by Peter Eden, who'd discovered **Donovan** and was later to produce **The Crocheted Doughnut Ring**, **Heron** and others, it was a haunting message song whose surreal piano-led flipside hinted at the darker themes he'd later explore. Decca declined to issue a follow-up, so **Fay** accepted a bizarre range of temporary jobs while continuing to write. His demos from the time are compiled on the excellent *From The Bottom Of An Old Grandfather Clock* compilation and include the memorable *Maxine's Parlour*, recorded by **Pinkerton's Assorted Colours**.

Eden hadn't forgotten **Fay**, however, and when Decca announced its budget Nova series in 1969, he negotiated him an album deal. Recording of his debut began with **Honeybus** backing him, but when **Pete Dello** left the band the sessions were started again, this time with orchestral arrangements courtesy of Mike Gibbs (a jazzman who made a couple of rare Deram albums himself). Though it was largely recorded in a day, and with no second takes, it's delightfully original and rounded, containing excellent songs like the dramatic *The Sun Is Bored*, the aching *Cannons Plain* and the beautiful *Be Not So Fearful*. **Fay** barely played live, however, and radio play proved elusive, so it slipped into obscurity despite being relaunched in the late summer of 1970 following a glowing review in ZigZag.

All was not lost, though. **Fay**'s friendship with **Dello** had awakened an interest in religion and philosophy that guitarist **Ray Russell** (who'd played on his debut and went on to form **Running Man** and **Mouse**, among many other projects) had encouraged. When Decca authorised a follow-up, Eden suggested **Russell** produce it in his place. The result, the partly-improvised *Time Of The Last Persecution*, was recorded in a single day in October 1970 and stands as one of the more challenging and personal records to emerge from England in the period. Showcasing **Fay**'s warm singing and delicate piano playing alongside **Russell**'s astounding guitar style and some remarkably powerful drumming from Alan Rushton, it's an often unbearably intense and poignant account of his personal, political and spiritual struggles, alternating simple songs of great beauty (*I Hear You Calling*) with squalling epics (*Till The Christ Come Back*) and unreservedly recommended to anyone with adventurous tastes.

The band played a handful of gigs and radio sessions in the album's support, but it failed to sell and originals are now near-impossible to locate. **Fay** inevitably parted with Decca and, unable to find a deal elsewhere, he continued to write and record privately whilst working in various other fields. By the early eighties he'd completed another album, recorded with the Acme Quartet, but it was rejected by various labels and emerged only recently as *Tomorrow, Tomorrow & Tomorrow*. A worthy companion to his earlier work, it has helped to stimulate a resurgence of interest in **Fay**, including articles in magazines such as Mojo, Record Collector and Wire and welcome reissues of his albums.

Compilation appearances have included *Be Not So Fearful* on the Nova Sampler (LP); *Garden Song*, *The Sun Is Bored* and *The Room* on *Nice* (Tenth Planet LP); *Scream In The Ears* and *Some Good Advice* on *Psychedalia - Rare Blooms From The English Summer Of Love* (CD); *Some Good Advice* on *Deram Dayze* (LP); and *Scream In The Ears* on *Fading Yellow* (CD) and on the 4-CD box set *Acid Drops, Spacedust & Flying Saucers*. (RMJ/VJ/CA)

F.B.I. (Folk Blues Inc.)

45s:	Don't Hide/		
	When The Ship Comes In	(Eyemark EMS 1006) 1966 SC	
	I Wonder What She's Doing Tonight/		
	Boogaloo Boo-Boo	(A&M AMS 7050) 1973	

This folk trio recorded on the obscure Eyemark label along with **The Barrier**. A band of this name also released an album and further 45s in the mid-seventies. *When The Ship Comes In* was a Dylan song. (VJ/MWh)

Fearns Brass Foundry

45s:	Don't Change It/John White	(Decca F 12721) 1968 SC
	Love, Sink And Drown/	
	Now I Taste The Tears	(Decca F 12835) 1968

A Midlands-based blues group, whose music was popular on the Northern soul circuit. (VJ)

The Federals

Personnel incl: TONY KAYE   organ

PSYCHEDALIA (Comp CD) including Felius Andromeda (CD).

45s:	Brazil/In A Persian Market	(Parlophone R 4988) 1963 SC
	Boot Hill/	
	Keep On Dancing With Me	(Parlophone R 5013) 1963 SC
	The Climb/Dance With A Dolly	(Parlophone R 5100) 1964 SC
	Marlena/Please Believe Me	(Parlophone R 5139) 1964 SC
	Twilight Time/Lost And Alone	(Parlophone R 5193) 1964 SC
	Bucket Full Of Love/Leah	(Parlophone R 5320) 1965 SC

A beat group from Watford. Some songs are instrumentals. Tony Kaye was later in **Winston's Fumbs** and **Yes**.

Compilation appearances have included: *Twilight Time* on *Rare 60's Beat Treasures, Vol. 2* (CD); and *Marlena* on *60's Back Beat* (LP). (VJ)

Felder's Orioles

Personnel:	NICK O'BRIEN	bs	A
	JOHN HALSEY	drms	A
	BARRY HEIBAND	vcls, organ	A
	PAUL HODGSON	gtr	A
	ROD MEALESTON	baritone sax	A
	PETER NEWMAN	tenor sax	A

45s:	Down Home Girl/Misty	(Piccadilly 7N 35247) 1965 R1
	Sweet Tasting Wine/	
	Turn On Your Lovelight	(Piccadilly 7N 35269) 1965 SC
	I Know You Don't Love Me No More/	
	Only Three Can Pay	(Piccadilly 7N 35311) 1966 SC
	Back Street/Something You Got	(Piccadilly 7N 35332) 1966 SC

A London-based R&B band which operated between 1965-67. *Down Home Girl* was an Alvin Robinson track also done by **The Rolling Stones** and *Turn On Your Lovelight* was the Bobby Bland classic. John Halsey was later in **Timebox** and **Patto**.

Compilation appearances have included: *I Know (You Don't Love Me No More)* on *Piccadilly Story* (CD); *Turn On Your Lovelight* on *The R&B Era, Vol. 1* (LP & CD) and *Doin' The Mod, Vol. 1* (CD); and *Down Home Girl* and *Misty* on *Footsteps To Fame, Vol. 2* (CD). (VJ/MWh)

Felius Andromeda

Personnel incl:	DENNIS COULDRY	organ	A
	BILL HAINE	vcls	A
	ALAN MORGAN	bs	A
	PETE PARKS	gtr	A
	MICK RICHARDSON	drms	A

| 45: | Meditations/ | |
| | Cheadle Heath's Delusions | (Decca F 12694) 1967 R1 |

The 'A' side of this their sole 45, *Meditations*, is a **Procol Harum**-style ballad, which begins with some brief meditative chanting. Very atmospheric... very 1967.

The band members mainly came from North West London, but were living in a flat in Pimlico when they we made the record.

Alan Morgan recalls:- "Mick Richardson and myself went to school together and initially formed a blues band called Morgans Roots with Pete Parks. We played all the blues venues in and around London my favourite being the Witches Cauldron at Belzise Park and Eel Pie Island Twickenham. We also got to play the universities occasionally."

"Denis Cauldry and Bill Haine were not original members of the band but were musicians on Vic Keary's books and added by him. We recorded *Meditations* at Maximum Sound Studios on the Old Kent Road with Vic producing. The organ was recorded at a church in Willesden. When Vic sold the studios to **Manfred Mann** we later recorded at Chalk Farm opposite the Roundhouse."

Mediations was written by Alan Morgan with the record producers girlfriend Pam Barry. The 'B' side was written and sung by Denis Cauldry.

"I remember we dressed in monks robes as I wanted to create a "mystery image" and made a promo film for TV to accompany the record. We were so confident that the record would be a success, when it failed, disillusionment took over and we drifted apart rather than split."

"Denis I believe went back to Manchester and Bill to Cheltenham. I tried with Mick to kick-start the band with Adrian Gurvitz, (pre-**Gun**) and later without Mick with Steve Webber (organ) and **Pete Banks** (ld gtr), but nothing materialised. Funnily enough, Mick had played with **Pete Banks** in **The Syn**. Afterwards Pete Parks went on to **Warhorse** and Mick to a band called Black August, both with some success."

"I started writing with Bill Haine for Louvigny Music (Radio Luxemburg's publishers) and later with Steve Webber for Apple Publishing. One commercial record was released under the name of **Promise** on Nems. I later started writing again with Paul Greedus and when we released *After The Storm* (Cactus) 19??, we actually shortened the name to Andromeda."

"We later recorded a song written by myself and Paul Greedus called *The Funeral Of Us All* for Mushroom Records. Our version was not released, but another of Vic's groups **Second Hand** released it on their *Death May Be Your Santa Claus* album. I think it was a better song than *Meditations*! Paul carried on writing and also writes TV music."

Meditations has been compiled on *Chocolate Soup For Diabetics, Vol. 3* (LP), *Psychedalia - Rare Blooms From The English Summer Of Love* (CD), *The Psychedelic Scene* (CD), and on the 4-CD box set *Acid Drops, Spacedust & Flying Saucers*. (VJ/AM)

Jaymes Fenda and The Vulcans

Personnel incl:	TREVOR FAULL		
	JOHN FORD	bs	
	MIKE PIERCE	vcls	

| 45: | Mistletoe Love/The Only Girl | (Parlophone R 5210) 1964 SC |

A long forgotten beat group from South London. Faull left before the 45 was recorded. John Ford was later in **Elmer Gantry's Velvet Opera**, **The Strawbs** and **Hudson-Ford**.

Their performances of *Mistletoe Love* and *The Only Girl*, taken from a 'best unknown group' competition held by 'Ready Steady Go' TV show, can be heard on See For Miles *Ready Steady Win* (LP & CD). (VJ/MWh)

The Fenmen

Personnel:	WALLY ALLEN	gtr	A
	BERN ELLIOTT	vcls	A
	ALAN JUDGE	ld gtr	A
	ERIC WILLMER	bs	A
	JOHN POVEY	drms	A

45s:	Rag Doll/Be My Girl	(Decca F 11955) 1964 SC
	I've Got Everything You Need Babe/	
	Every Little Day Now	(Decca F 12269) 1965
	California Dreamin'/Is This Your Way	(CBS 202075) 1966
	Rejected/Girl Don't Bring Me Down	(CBS 202236) 1966 SC

A Kent outfit who'd earlier spent time in Germany and were also known as **Bern Elliott and The Fenmen**. Their records included covers of The Four Season's *Rag Doll* and The Mamas and The Papas' *California Dreamin'*. When they split up in 1968 Povey and Allen joined **The Pretty Things**.

You can also check out *Rejected* on *Circus Days Vol. 3* (LP & CD). (VJ)

Andy Fernbach

| ALBUM: | 1 | IF YOU MISS YOUR CONNEXION | |
| | | (Liberty LBL/LBS 83233) 1969 R2 |

A blues singer and guitarist from Bournemouth whose first recordings on *Me And The Devil* compilation (LP) 1968; *Duckin' And Dodgin'*, *Broken Down Engine* and *Hard Time Killing Floor* (he's backed by Nick Whiffen on harmonica on the first two) were interesting arrangements of traditional tunes. Particularly notable was *Hard Time Killing Floor*, a long solo acoustic piece with echoed vocals creating a lost and lonely atmosphere. His own album with the Connexion (sic) (Philip Crowther (drms), J.D. Langer (gtr) and Rob Rowe (bs)) comprised six of his own compositions and two traditionals. Those featuring J.D. Langer on guitar are ideal accompaniment for his flowing vocal delivery and acoustic guitar. The partnership continued onto *I Asked For Water And She Gave Me Gasoline* (LP) 1969 blues compilation to which he contributed two cuts; *She's Gone* and *Built My Hopes Too High*. Both were self-penned. The last one was a long mellifluous number that builds up to a peak as it unfolds. **Fernbach** now owns and runs Jacob's Studios near Farnham in Surrey, one of the UK's leading independent recording facilities. (VJ/RMJ)

Ferris Wheel

Personnel:	DENNIS ELLIOT	drms	AB
	DIANA FERRIS	vcls	A
	LINDA LEWIS	vcls	AB
	MICHAEL SNOW	vcls, gtr, keyb'ds	AB
	DAVID SWEETNAM FORD	sax	AB
	GEORGE SWEETNAM FORD	bs, vcls	AB
	BERNIE HOLLAND	gtr	B

| ALBUMS: | 1(A) | CAN'T BREAK THE HABIT | (Pye NPL 18203) 1967 SC |
| | 2(B) | FERRIS WHEEL | (Polydor 583 086) 1970 |

| 45s: | I Can't Break The Habit/Number One Guy | (Pye 7N 17387) 1967 |
| | Let It Be Me/You Look At Me | (Pye 7N 17538) 1968 |

ACID DROPS AND FLYING SAUCERS (Comp CD Set) including Felius Andromeda.

The Na Na Song/Three Cool Cats	(Pye 7N 17631) 1968
Can't Stop Now/I Know You Well	(Polydor 56366) 1970

A club band who failed to make any significant impact in terms of record sales in the late sixties. Bernie Holland went on to play for **Jody Grind**, **Linda Lewis** enjoyed a successful solo career in the mid-seventies and Dennis Elliot went on to **If** and Foreigner. **Marsha Hunt** was also a vocalist with this outfit briefly.

Compilation appearances have included: *Can't Stop Now* on Polydor's *Way Into The '70s* (LP); *Movie Queen* on *Rock Party* (2-LP); *Three Cool Cats* on Sequel's *The Songs Of Leiber and Stoller* (CD); *The 'Na Na' Song* on *Doin' The Mod, Vol. 1* (CD); and *I Can't Break The Habit* on *Doin' The Mod, Vol. 2* (CD).

They also appeared in the 1968 film 'The Touchables' along with **Wynder K. Frog**. (VJ/LP)

Bryan Ferry

				HCP
ALBUMS:	1	THESE FOOLISH THINGS	(Island ILPS 9249) 1973	5
(up to	2	ANOTHER TIME, ANOTHER PLACE		
1976)			(Island ILPS 9284) 1974	4
	3	LET'S STICK TOGETHER	(Island ILPS 9367) 1976	19

NB: There was an unissued version of (1) in a gatefold sleeve (R1). (1) also issued on CD in 1984 (Polydor 823 021 2), but deleted in 1989 and reissued again on E.G. Records (EGCD 9) 1991. (2) reissued on Polydor (8136 542) in 1977 but deleted in 1988 and reissued again on E.G. Records (EGCD 14) 1991. Also relevant is *Ultimate Collection* (Bryan Ferry and Roxy Music) (E.G. Records EGCTV 2) 1988.

			HCP
EP:	1	EXTENDED PLAY EP (PS)	(Island IEP 1) 1976	7

			HCP
45s:	A Hard Rain's Agonna Fall/2hb	(Island WIP 6170) 1973	10
(up to	The 'In' Crowd/Chance Meeting (PS)	(Island WIP 6196) 1974	13
1976)	Smoke Gets In Your Eyes/		
	Another Time, Another Place	(Island WIP 6205) 1975	17
	You Go To My Head/		
	Re-Make Re-Model	(Island WIP 6234) 1975	33
	Let's Stick Together/Sea Breezes	(Island WIP 6307) 1976	4
	The Price Of Love/		
	Shame Shame Shame	(Island WIP 6320) 1976	-

Although he is best remembered as frontman for **Roxy Music**, the sophisticated **Bryan Ferry** has also enjoyed a successful solo career spanning three decades and a number of memorable moments.

Bryan Ferry was born on 26 September 1945 in Washington, County Durham. He formed his first band in Sunderland in 1964. They were called

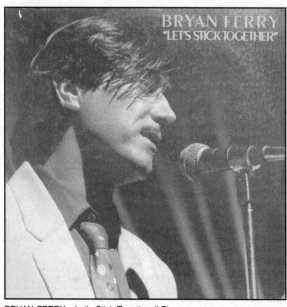

BRYAN FERRY - Let's Stick Together (LP).

The Banshees but he didn't play on their 45s. However, a few months later he moved to Newcastle University to study fine art. Whilst there he became vocalist with a local R&B band, The Gas Works, and worked as a deejay.

When he graduated from University in 1968 with a degree he moved down to London. He took jobs as a van driver and an antiques restorer before getting a job as a ceramics teacher at a Hammersmith girls school which he later lost because the authorities objected to him turning the lessons into music classes. By now he was writing songs and had taught himself how to play piano. In 1971 he formed **Roxy Music** to play the songs he wrote. Although the band became his prime concern for the next few years he also began a solo career.

In October 1973 he released *These Foolish Things* on which he was assisted by session musicians. The album was a collection of cover versions of his favourite old songs. It sold well, partly on the strength of **Roxy Music**'s popularity, climbing to No 5 in the Album Charts and a cover of Bob Dylan's *A Hard Rain's Agonna Fall* culled from it also made the Top Ten.

Over the subsequent couple of years he continued to achieve commercial success with his unique brand of cover versions of Dobie Gray's *The "In" Crowd* and The Platters' *Smoke Gets In Your Eyes*. His next album, *Another Time, Another Place*, followed the same formula as his first effort aside from the self-penned title track. It made the Top 5 here but failed to Chart in the US.

His next 45, *You Go To My Head*, was only a minor hit but is one of his more interesting discs. His next album, *Let's Stick Together*, was roughly a 50:50 mix of cover versions and his own compositions. It made the Top 20 in the Album Charts over here and was a very minor hit (but his first Chart entry) in the US. The title track, a cover of a Wilbert Harrison R&B song, made the UK Top 5. A couple of months later his *Extended Play* EP, which included four cover versions from his latest album (*Heart On My Sleeve*, *The Price Of Love* (an old Everly Brothers' song), *Shame Shame Shame* (a Jimmy Reed number) and *It's Only Love*) became the first EP to enter the UK Top Ten since **The Beatles**' *Magical Mystery Tour* back in 1967.

As we leave the time span of this book **Bryan Ferry** had just put together his own Bryan Ferry Band and would go on to enjoy considerable success in the eighties. Indeed he has continued to record into the new millennium.

Compilation appearances include *Let's Stick Together* on the 3-CD set *Full Throttle - 60 Original Driving Classics* and on the 6-CD box set *Best Of Driving Rock*. (VJ)

Fever

45:	The Moth And The Flame/It's So Peaceful (Decca F 23156) 1971

This was an obscure one-off single. (VJ)

Fickle Finger

45:	Fickle Lizzie-Anne/	
	Cellophane Mary Jane	(Page One POF 150) 1969

A forgotten 45. (VJ)

Fickle Pickle

Personnel incl.:	WIL MALONE
	GEOFF GILL
	CLIFF WADE
	STEVE HOWDEN

ALBUM:	1	SINFUL SKINFUL (Explosion EQ 20-049) 1972 R2

45s:	Millionaire/Sam And Sadie	(Fontana TF 1069) 1970
	American Pie/Blown Away	(B&C CB 177) 1972
	California Calling/Doctor Octopus	(B&C CB 178) 1972

A studio band centred on London's legendary Morgan Studio and featuring the talents of **Wil Malone**, previously a member of **Orange Bicycle**,

Motherlight and a solo artist in his own right, alongside **Smoke**'s Geoff Gill and others. Their music is light-hearted and tends towards the novelty end of the spectrum. The album was only released in Northern Europe and is scarce but mediocre. Their cover of **Paul McCartney**'s *Maybe I'm Amazed* was a hit in Holland, perhaps accounting for the album's appearance. The flower pop song *Sam And Sadie* has resurfaced on *Psychedelic Voyage Vol. 1* (LP) and *Psychedelic Voyage* (CD). (RMJ/VJ)

Fields

Personnel:	ALAN BARRY	gtr, vcls, bs, synth	A
	GRAHAM FIELD	keyb'ds	A
	ANDY McCULLOCH	drms	A

ALBUM: 1(A) FIELDS (Some w/poster)   (CBS 69009) 1971 R1/SC

NB: (1) also issued in the US on Epic. A few UK copies of their album came with a free poster. These are now R1.

45:      Friends Of Mine/Three Minstrels   (CBS 7555) 1971

Graham Field had previously been in **Rare Bird**. Andrew McCulloch played in **King Crimson** and Alan Barry had been with the Giles brothers. (VJ)

The Fife Reivers

Personnel incl:	JIM LAING	vcls, gtr	A
	MAUREEN LAING	vcls	A
	RUSSELL LAING	ld gtr, banjo, mandolin	A

ALBUM: 1(A)   THE FIFE REIVERS   (Columbia SCX 6371) 1969 SC

45:      Dry Leaves / Spring   (Columbia) 1969

This obscure Scottish folk band was notable for the very gifted 12-year old Russell Laing whose lead guitar, banjo and mandolin playing defines the whole album. His dad was a schoolteacher and his mum a midwife. Most of the material was self-penned, though there are a few traditional folk songs too. On offer are Jim Laing's appealing voice, beautiful harmonies and some exquisite instrumentation. They apparently toured with **David Bowie** in 1969, but soon returned to obscurity. (RMJ)

Fifth Avenue

| Personnel: | DENVER GERRARD | A |
| | KENNY ROWE | A |

45:      The Bells Of Rhymney/
         Just Like Anyone Would Do   (Immediate IM 002) 1965 SC

Quite a sought-after 45 by an obscure harmony duo. The 'A' side is a folky cover of The Byrds, according to '117' zine and it has a nice flip which is "largely **Jimmy Page** by all accounts".

This duo later recorded with **Andrew Oldham**'s Immediate label as **The Warm Sounds** and **Tony Rivers and The Castaways**.

Compilation appearances include: *The Bells Of Rhymney* and *Just Like Anyone Would Do* on *Jimmy Page - Hip Young Guitar Slinger* (CD); and *Just Like Anyone Would Do* on *James Patrick Page, Session Man* (2-LP). (MW)

Fifth Column

Personnel:	D. BELL	A
	JOE EGAN	A
	GERRY RAFFERTY	A

45:      Benjamin Day/
         There's Nobody Here   (Columbia DB 8068) 1966 SC

A folky trio. **Gerry Rafferty**, of course, was later in **Stealer's Wheel** along with Joe Egan. (VJ)

SIMON FINN - Pass The Distance (CD).

Fifth Form

Personnel incl: KEN LEWIS

45:      Back At School/Darling   (Dawn DNS 1079) 1974

This obscure band was most notable for featuring Ken Lewis who was with **The Ivy League**. (VJ)

Pauline Filby

ALBUM: 1   SHOW ME A RAINBOW   (Herald LLR 567) 1969 R3

EP: 1   MY WORLD BY PAULINE FILBY
                              (Herald ELR 1081) 1968 SC

45:      I'm Hungry/
         (flip by Nardia Cattouse)   (Church Miss. Soc. LIV/SP/81) 196?

Pauline Filby's solo album is very rare. She was later in **Narnia** and also played with **Gordon Giltrap**. (VJ)

Finbar and Eddie Furey

Personnel:	BRIAN BROCKLEHURST	double bs	A
	EDDIE FUREY	gtr, mandolin, perc, whistle	A
	FINBAR FUREY	vcls, pipes, banjo, violin, whistle	A

ALBUMS: 1(A)   FINBAR AND EDDIE FURAY
                              (Transatlantic TRA 168) 1968 SC
        2(A)   TRADITIONAL IRISH PIPE MUSIC
                              (Xtra XTRA 1077) 1969 SC
        3(A)   THE LONESOME BOATMAN
                              (Transatlantic TRA 191) 1969 SC
        4(A)   THE DAWNING OF THE DAY
               (w/lyric insert)   (Dawn DNLS 3037) 1972 SC

45:      Her Father Didn't Like Me Anyway/
         Reynardine   (Dawn DNS 1025) 1972

This was a traditional folk band. Basically *The Dawning Of The Day* is an average traditional folk album with well-known material such as *Reynardine*, *Farewell To Tarwathy* and *William Hollander*, but occasionally it drifts into **C.O.B.** - style sadness and despair. It not only is very well executed but acquires an extra quality on some cuts, due to its deep-felt emotion, taking this almost into the vicinity of **The Peelers**. They also include a cover of **The Humblebums**' *Her Father Didn't Like Me Anyway*. (MK/VJ)

FIRE - Magic Shoemaker (LP)

Finders Keepers

Personnel incl: ALAN CLEE
JOHN ELCOCK
MEL GALLEY   gtr   A
GLENN HUGHES   bs   A
ROY KENT
IAN LEES
PHILIP OVERFIELD
DAVID WILLIAMS

45s:	α	Light/Power Of Love	(CBS 202249) 1966 R2
		Light/Come On Now	(CBS 202249) 1966 SC
		On The Beach/	
		Friday Kind Of Monday	(Fontana TF 892) 1967 SC
		Sadie (The Cleaning Lady)/	
		Without Her	(Fontana TF 938) 1968 SC

NB: α withdrawn.

This Wolverhampton-based band had a rather fluctuating line-up. *On The Beach* is an inventive pop-psych effort with harpsichord, organ and brass. They are most notable for including future **Deep Purple** member Glenn Hughes who joined from a Birmingham group The News and left with Mel Galley to form a teen group called **Trapeze**.

None of their 45s are particularly memorable but you can check out *On The Beach* on *Rubble Vol. 4: 49 Minute Technicolour Dream* (LP) and *Rubble Vol. 3* (CD), we're talking straight-forward pop really. *Light* has resurfaced on *Fading Yellow, Vol 4* (CD). (VJ)

The Fingers

Personnel incl: BOB CLOUTER   drms   A
RICK MILLS   vcls   A
JOHN ROBIN   bs   A
MO WITHAM   gtr   A

45s:	I'll Take You Where The Music's Playing/	
	My Way Of Thinking	(Columbia DB 8026) 1966
	All Kinds Of People/	
	Circus With A Female Clown	(Columbia DB 8112) 1967 SC

A Southend-based pop outfit, whose *Circus With A Female Clown*, produced by Peter Eden has pop-psych leanings but is eminently forgettable. The 'A' side was a Carter-Lewis composition. They also backed **Bill Fay** on his 45. Bob Clouter was later in **Legend**. Richard Mills was later in **Crocheted Doughnut Ring**.

Compilation appearances have included: *Just Like Loving You Baby, I Go To Sleep, Look Away, I Hear The Sun* and *Oh* on *Nice* (LP); *Most Likely You Go Your Way And I'll Go Mine* and *What Is The Reason* on *Nowhere*

Men, Vol. 4 (CD); and *Circus With A Female Clown* on *Psychedelia At Abbey Road* (CD), *Circus Days Vol. 1 & 2* (CD) and *Circus Days, Vol. 2* (LP). (VJ/RJM)

Mickey Finn and The Blue Men

See **Mickey Finn** entry.

Simon Finn

Personnel incl: SIMON FINN   vcls, gtr, perc   A
DAVID TOOP   gtr, mandolin, bs, flute
violin, keyb'ds, perc   A
PAUL BURWELL   dulcimer, perc   A
ROB BUCKLIN   recorder   A
KEN ELLIOT   organ   A

ALBUM: 1   PASS THE DISTANCE
(Mushroom 100 MR 2) 1970 R3 (with insert)

NB: (1) reissued on CD (Durtro / Jnana) 2004. A new album, *Magic Moments*, is due on Durtro/Jnana in 2005.

The son of two actors, **Simon Finn** was raised by his grandparents in Surrey. In 1967 he ran away from his public school armed with thirty pounds and a cheap guitar. His money was soon spent, but he landed a slot opening for **Al Stewart** at the Marquee's weekly folk night, earning a pound a gig. At the time his material was simple, melodic and influenced by **Donovan**. Times grew hard and he soon found himself sleeping rough. A regular gig in Knightsbridge's Borscht and Tears restaurant the following year allowed him to move into a squalid Kensington bedsit, where his songwriting took a darker turn. By early 1969, when he met engineer Vic Keary, he had a collection of spooky, downbeat songs ready to go. Keary, in the process of opening a studio opposite the Roundhouse in Chalk Farm, offered him a weekly £10 retainer, with an album in mind. Shortly afterwards **Finn** encountered Toop and Burwell at the Roundhouse, where the trio successfully jammed together. A week later they found themselves recording in Keary's studio. The result, *Pass The Distance*, is one of the most unusual and demanding albums of the period. Formal song structures are jettisoned in favour of free-form playing that combines with **Finn**'s impassioned singing to create a uniquely compelling and unsettling experience. The album is frequently described as 'nightmarish,' 'menacing' or 'sinister', words that ignore the fragility and bemusement underlying the songs. Though guitars are out of tune, song structures are blissfully ignored and dissonances occur constantly, it stands as a deeply personal statement about troubles both private and political and can be compared to **Bill Fay**'s *Time of the Last Persecution* and **Nick Drake**'s *Pink Moon*. Its striking sleeve, designed by Toop, sadly bore similarities to the logo for Start-Rite shoes, causing predictable legal difficulties and its withdrawal from sale. **Finn** eventually moved to the US and Canada, where he has been farming, writing and teaching ever since. One of many overlooked talents who only came to realise their standing with the advent of the internet, **Finn** has recently recorded a belated follow-up as well as participating in an excellent reissue of *Pass The Distance*. (RMJ/VJ)

Fire

Personnel incl: DAVID LAMBERT   vcls, gtr, keyb'ds   A
DICK DUFALL   bs, vcls   A
BOB VOICE   drms, vcls   A

ALBUMS: 1(A) THE MAGIC SHOEMAKER   (Pye NSPL 18343) 1970 R4
2(A) UNDERGROUND AND OVERHEAD:
THE ALTERNATE FIRE   (Tenth Planet TP 029) 1997 SC

NB: (1) had a limited reissue by PLM records in Germany and was later issued on See For Miles (SEE 294) 1990, also on CD (SEE 294 CD) 1990. (1) reissued on CD (Sanctuary CMRCD 620) 2002. (2) is a ltd retrospective including alternate versions, demos etc. It was reissued on CD (Wooden Hill WHCD 010) 2001, with more sleevenotes from David Wells.

45s: Father's Name Is Dad/
Treacle Toffee World   (Decca F 12753) 1968 R3
Round The Gum Tree/Toothie Ruthie (Decca F 12856) 1968 SC

Formed in Hounslow, Middlesex, in 1966, they were originally known as Friday's Chyld. Prior to recording their first 45, they cut some demos in early 1967 at R.G. Jones' Morden studio, and auditioned for Decca with demo versions of *Father's Name Is Dad* and *Treacle Toffee World*. Suitably smitten, Decca offered them a deal, and on the strength of the recordings, they were also signed by Apple Publishing.

Their first 45, released in March 1968, many months after it had been recorded, was a fine slice of pop psychedelia complete with frantic chord changes and a catchy tune on the 'A' side, whilst the 'B' side was almost as good. Two versions of the 'A' side exist - after **Paul McCartney** heard it on the radio, he arranged for the band to recut the 'A' side with backing vocals, and doubled guitar riffs an octave higher... It didn't make much difference however, although both versions have now been preserved on the *Underground and Overhead* album. Following this failure, the band recorded a number of demo tracks, many of which are again featured on the *Underground...* retrospective, before being forced into recording the second 45.

Rather inexplicably, both sides of the *Round The Gum Tree* were written by Mike Berry, head of Apple Publishing, after he had rejected all of **The Fire**'s demos as 'unsuitable'. The band refused to play on the disc, and **The Fire**'s contribution to the 45 is limited to Lambert's vocal on the 'A' side. It lacked the sparkle of the first and is consequently far less sought-after and expensive to obtain.

With their relationship with Decca and Apple Publishing damaged, the band set about demo'ing tracks for what would become *The Magic Shoemaker* a concept album that revolved around a cobbler and a pair of magic shoes.

In January 1970 they started work on the album with the aid of **Strawbs** frontman **Dave Cousins** and **Velvet Opera** guitarist **Paul Brett**. It was composed and narrated by David Lambert who was very much the brains behind the group. The album's finer moments include the opening cut, *Children Of Imagination*; the R&B tinted *I Can See The Sky*, the experimental passage between *Reason For Everything* and *Only A Dream*. However, buy one of the reissues as it's not good enough to justify the ridiculous price originals now command.

Even better is the retrospective *Underground and Overhead* album which contains alternative versions of *Father's Name Is Dad*, the 'B' side, plus many excellent demo tracks. As always with Tenth Planet releases, there are excellent sleeve notes as well.

After the band's demise in 1970 Voice and Dufall joined **Paul Brett's Sage** and Dave Lambert later joined **The Strawbs** in 1972 and recorded a solo album, *Framed*, (Polydor) in 1979.

Compilation coverage has included:- *Father's Name Is Dad* on *The Freakbeat Scene* (CD), *The British Psychedelic Trip* (LP), *Broken Dreams, Vol. 1* (LP), *Chocolate Soup For Diabetics, Vol. 1* (LP), *Chocolate Soup* (CD), *Rubble Vol. 5: The Electric Crayon Set* (LP), *Rubble Vol. 3* (CD), the 4-CD *Nuggets 11* box set and on the 4-CD box set *Acid Drops, Spacedust*

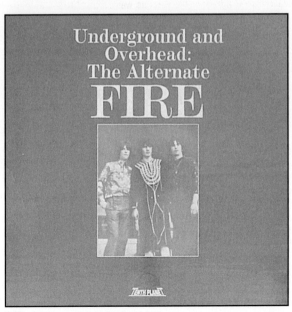

FIRE - Underground And Overhead (LP).

& Flying Saucers; *Treacle Toffe World* on *Rubble Vol. 11: Adventures In The Mist* (LP) and *Rubble Vol. 6* (CD); *Man In The Teapot* on *Psychedelia, Vol. 3* (LP) and *Hen's Teeth, Vol. 3* (CD) and *I Can See The Sky* on *Hot Smoke & Sassafras - Psychedelic Pstones, Vol 1* (CD).

Dave Lambert now divides his time between teaching music at his home studio and working as a ski instructor in Austria. (VJ)

Fire Session

45s:	Souvenir/Bad Girl	(Revolution REV 10) 1970
	Sleeping Reggae/	
	Everyday I Have To Cry Some	(Revolution REV 13) 1970
	Death Of The Ugly One/Big Feet	(Revolution REV 14) 1970

A forgotten late sixties/early seventies combo. (VJ)

Firing Squad

Personnel incl:	KEVIN NALLY	bs	A
	BERNARD SHELMERDINE	ld gtr, vcls	A
	FRANK SHELMERDINE	drms	A

| 45: | A Little Bit More/Bull Moose | (Parlophone R 5152) 1964 SC |

A little known beat group from Hampstead. Shel Talmy produced their 45.

Bull Moose and *A Little Bit More* can also be found on *Rare 60's Beat Treasures, Vol. 1* (CD). (VJ)

First Class

Personnel incl:	CLIVE BARRETT	keyb'ds	
	TONY BURROWS	vcls	
	JOHN CARTER	vcls	
	SPENCER JAMES	gtr	A
	DEL JOHN	vcls	
	CHAS MILLS	vcls	
	EDDIE RICHARDS	drms	A
	ROBIN SHAW	bs	A

ALBUMS: 1( )	THE FIRST CLASS	(UK UKAL 1008) 1974 SC
(up to 2( )	S.S.T.	(UK UKAL 1022) 1976 SC
1976)		

NB: (1) and (2) have been reissued on one CD *First Class / SST... Plus* (See For Miles SEECD443). *Summer Sound Sensations* (RPM RPM 301) 2005 is a 21-track collection, which takes the best material from their two albums and adds five tracks from what should have been their third.

			HCP
45s:	Beach Baby/Both Sides Of The Story	(UK UK 66) 1974	13
(up to	Bobby Dazzler/Lavender Man	(UK UKR 73) 1974	-
1976)	Dreams Are Ten A Penny/Long Time Gone	(UK UKR 82) 1974	-
	What Became Of Me/		
	Won't Somebody Help Me	(UK UKR 90) 1975	-
	Life Is Whatever You Want It To Be/		
	I Was Always A Joker	(UK UKR 96) 1975	-
	I Was A Star/7-10 To Nowhere	(UK UK 107) 1975	-
	Ain't No Love/Long Time Gone	(UK UK 130) 1976	-
	Child's Play/Old Time Love	(UK UK 152) 1976	-
Reissues:	Beach Baby/Both Sides Of The Story	(UK UK 144) 1976	-
	Beach Baby/Bobby Dazzler	(Old Gold OG 9097) 1982	-

This was one of a series of studio groups put together by John Carter and Ken Lewis, who'd previously been in Carter-Lewis and The Southerners and **The Ivy League**. The artists listed above were assembled to record *Beach Baby*, which proved to be an ideal summery hit in 1974. Subsequent efforts flopped and the group was dissolved in 1976. Carter went on to form another studio group **Ice** and in the early eighties the **First Class** name was used again by Carter and colleagues for a version of Brenton Wood's *Gimme Little Sign*.

FIVE DAY RAIN - Five Day Rain (LP).

On the first album there's a cover of **The Ivy League**'s *Funny How Love Can Be* and a number of Beach Boys influenced summer pop offerings. The second was basically top quality melodic pop and there's the bonus of a previously unreleased tune, *Wake Up America*.

Their ability to write well constructed and professionally executed songs is evident on the *Summer Sound Sensations* collection. It takes the best material from their two albums, including their hit *Beach Baby*, *Bobby Dazzler*, *Dreams Are Ten A Penny* and *What Became Of Me* (which were their first four 'A' sides). There are five bonus tracks too as well as *Silver Surfer*, which was recorded in the eighties. (VJ)

First Gear

Personnel incl:

PHIL BIRKENSHAW	gtr, vcls	A
IAN COLLING	drms	A
MICHAEL RYAL	bs, vcls	A
RAYMOND WAFER	gtr	A
DAVE WALTON	vcls	A

45s:			
	A Certain Girl/Leave My Kitten Alone	(Pye 7N 15703) 1964	R3
	The 'In' Crowd/		
	Gotta Make Their Future Bright	(Pye 7N 15763) 1965	R1

From Barnsley in South Yorkshire, this band debuted with fine cover versions of Little Willie John's *Leave My Kitten Alone*, for which **Jimmy Page** guested on guitar, and Ernie K. Doe's *A Certain Girl*. This song was also recorded by **The Paramounts** and **The Yardbirds**. The 45 is now extremely collectable and expensive. They followed this with a cover of Dobie Gray's *The 'In' Crowd*. Their 45s were produced by Shel Talmy.

Compilation appearances have included: *A Certain Girl* and *Leave My Kitten Alone* on *James Patrick Page: Session Man, Vol. 1* (LP & CD), *James Patrick Page, Session Man* (2-LP) and *Footsteps To Fame, Vol. 1* (CD); *A Certain Girl*, *Leave My Kitten Alone*, *The "In" Crowd* and *Gotta Make Their Future Bright* on *Jimmy Page - Hip Young Guitar Slinger* (2-CD) and *Jimmy's Back Pages - The Early Years* (CD); *A Certain Girl* on *The R&B Era, Vol. 2* (LP & CD); *Gotta Make Their Future Bright* on *Ripples, Vol. 6* (CD); *Leave My Kitten Alone* on *Pebbles, Vol. 6* (LP), *Watch Your Step* (LP & CD) and *Freakbeat Freakout* (CD); *The "In" Crowd* on *Doin' The Mod, Vol. 1* (CD) and *Leave My Kitten Alone* on the CD-set *Rock Of Ages, Four Decades Of Heavy Rock 1962-2002*. (VJ)

First Impression

ALBUM: 1	BEAT CLUB	(Saga SOC 1045) 1967 SC

In addition to releasing this album **First Impression** also shared half of the *Swinging London* (Saga FID 2117) 1968 album with **Good Earth**. (VJ)

First Impressions

Personnel incl: PETE WATKINSON   vcls

45:	Looking For Her/I'm Coming Home	(Pye 7N 15797) 1965

This band was later known as **The Legends**. It came from Hayes in West London. (VJ)

Archie Fisher

ALBUMS:	1	ARCHIE FISHER	(Xtra XTRA 1070) 1968 SC
	2	ORFEO	(Decca SKL 5057) 1970 SC

NB: (1) reissued (Celtic Music CM 007) 1982.

Archie Fisher has been described as the godfather of Scottish folk. His debut album was a traditional folk set on which he played sitar and guitar. *Orfeo* is generally regarded as his finest moment, especially the atmospheric and melodic title track. He also recorded an album with **Barbara Dickson** *Thro' Recent Years* for Decca in 1970. He later became heavily involved in Scottish radio and TV.

Bogie's Bonny Belle has been compiled on *The Transatlantic Story* CD box set. (VJ)

Matthew Fisher

ALBUMS:	1	JOURNEY'S END	(RCA SF 8380) 1973 SC
	2	I'LL BE THERE	(RCA APLI 0325) 1974

45:	Suzanne/Seperation	(RCA RCA 2406) 1973

Solo ventures from **Fisher**, formerly of **Procol Harum**, **Lord Sutch**'s band and National Anthem.

John Fitch and Associates

Personnel incl: JOHN FITCH

45:	Romantic Altitude/ Stoned Out Of It	(Beacon BEA 118) 1971 SC

John Fitch had been the guitarist on The Showstoppers' 1968 hit *Ain't Nothing But A Houseparty*. He recorded this 45 whilst here in the UK, but hailed from Philadelphia originally. *Romantic Altitude*, which vocally at least is very much in a pop-soul style, surprisingly found its way onto *Rubble Vol. 15:5,000 Seconds Over Toyland* (LP), *Rubble Vol. 8* (CD) and *The*

FIVE DAY WEEK STRAW PEOPLE - Five Day Week Straw People (LP).

Best Of Rubble Collection, Vol. 4 (CD) - presumably on the strength of its good guitar solo. The flip side *Stoned Out Of It* also blends rock and soul with some **Hendrix**-style guitar work. This can be found on *We Can Fly, Vol 2* (CD) and *Jagged Time Lapse, Vol 3* (CD). The single is yet to interest collectors much. (VJ)

G.F. Fitzgerald

ALBUM: 1   MOUSEPROOF   (MCA UNLS 115) 1970 R2

G.F. Fitzgerald was an American resident in London who was part of the UK's psychedelic scene in the late sixties. On his album he was assisted by **Sam Gopal**, Geoff Leigh, Rick Kenton and **B.J. Cole** among others. The music on the album is best described as psychedelic folk with progressive leanings and is an interesting period piece. This album is recommended but it's becoming difficult to track down.

On tour he named his band Mouseproof and it included Geoff Leigh (sax, flute), Alan Place (gtr), Alan Smith (bs) and Tony Turnball (gtr).

G.F. Fitzgerald later played with **Lol Coxhill** and Fred Frith. (BS)

Five and a Penny

45:      You Don't Know Where Your Interest Lies/
         Mary Go Round   (Polydor BM 56282) 1968

An obscure 45. (VJ)

Five Day Rain

Personnel incl:			
CLIVE BURGESS	bs		A
GRAHAM MAITLAND	gtr, vcls		A
RICK SHARP	gtr		A
KIM	drms		A

ALBUM: 1(A)   FIVE DAY RAIN   (Private Pressing) 1969 R5

NB: (1) has been repressed in signed, numbered sleeves, 25 only (R2). Reissued on CD (Background HBG 123/1 CD) 1994. Also available on vinyl (HBG 123) 1994.

One of the rarest UK albums; just 15 copies of this album were put out but soon after someone circulated 'white label' copies of it so beware of these.

Graham Maitland had earlier been in **Scots Of St James** and **Hopscotch**. He was also in **The Fleur de Lys** in their final days. The album contained some adventurous pop compositions often with a taint of psychedelia but it was eventually put out as a private pressing in a plain white cover because no label was interested in it. Notable cuts are the 11-minute instrumental *Rough Cut Marmalade*, which is the album's most psychedelic offering; the catchy *Sea Song* and keyboard driven *Leave It At That.*

The CD reissue omitted *Too Much Of Nothing* and tampered with *Marie's A Woman*. Graham Maitland was later in **Glencoe** but the other members quit the music business. (VJ)

Five Day Week Straw People

Personnel incl: JOHN DU CANN   gtr A

ALBUM: 1   FIVE DAY WEEK STRAW PEOPLE
                                     (Saga FID 2123) 1968 R2

NB: This album was repressed in the late 1980s and issued on CD (Merlin MER II) 199? (1) reissued again on CD (Angel Air SJPCD 059) 2000 and again on CD (Akarma AK 218) 2002, each time with nine bonus tracks from **The Attack**, another of John Du Cann bands.

A fine slice of sixties psychedelia which attains a pretty good standard throughout with some fine guitar work on tracks like *I'm Going Out Tonight* and *Gold Digger*, whilst there's some interesting echoed vocals on *Sunday*

Morning, Does It Rain is a sensitive slice of pop psych and *If You Were Around* is another slower, more sensitive number with a catchy drum roll. An album well worth obtaining, it was apparently recorded in four hours in a children's nursery in London's St John's Wood. It successfully covers a person's activities over a weekend and makes excellent use of sound effects, although it's a pity it was pressed on low grade vinyl as this does make copies very vulnerable to surface noise. (VJ)

Five of Diamonds

EP: 1   FIVE OF DIAMONDS   (Oak RGJ 150 FD) 1965 R4

This now highly collectable four track EP featured a cover of Bobby Troupe's *Route 66*; *Good Morning Blues*; *Summertime* and a disappointing attempt at Tommy Tucker's *High Heel Sneakers*.

Compilation appearances have included: *Good Morning Blues* on *Return Of The Amphetamine Generation* (LP); and *Route 66* on *Story Of Oak Records* (2-LP) and *The Story Of Oak Records* (CD). (VJ)

Five Steps Beyond

Personnel incl:			
DARYL HITCH	gtr		AB
EVAN IRWIN	drms		ABC
PAUL QUINTON	ld vcls		A
IAN SHORT	bs		ABC
ROGER WINWARD	ld gtr		ABC
RAY SEDDON	gtr		C

ALBUMS: 1( )   FAINT HEARTS AND FAIR MAIDS
                                  (Tenth Planet TP 019) 1995
        2( )   SMILE   (Tenth Planet TP 021) 1996

45:      Not So Young Today/
         Meanwhile Back In My Heart   (CBS 202490) 1967

This London harmony pop quintet seems to have derived inspiration from US West Coast bands like The Beach Boys and The Association. They recorded two unreleased acetate EPs for Oak in May 1965 and February 1966 prior to signing with CBS for their 1967 45. In early '67 Paul Quinton and Daryll Hitch quit, and the band was dropped by CBS. Regrouping around the nucleus of Short, Winward and Irwin, rhythm guitarist Ray Sneddon was recruited to help flesh out their sound, but by the end of 1967, the band had called it a day.

Story Of Oak Records (2-LP)/*The Story Of Oak Records* (CD) include Roger Winward's *Faint Heart*, which was recorded as an intended follow-up but never released at the time.

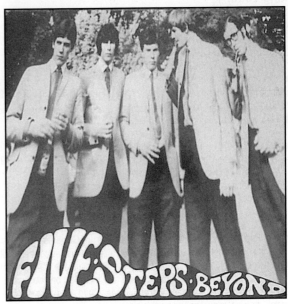

FIVE STEPS BEYOND - Faint Hearts And Fair Maids (LP).

Tenth Planet have now issued two albums worth of material. *Faint Hearts And Fair Mads* features pleasant, but lightweight sugary pop. There's a mixture of self-penned material (including eight Roger Winward compositions - *Baby Mine, Don't Let It Worry You, In Finding Love, Heartbreak Love Or Paradise, You've Cooled, Love Me Faint Heart* and *Waited For Her*); three Paul Quinton/Ian Short songs and a few covers, including a brave attempt at the Shangri-Las hit *Remember (Walking In The Sand), Come On Back* which first appeared on the flip to **The Hollies**' *We're Through* and *Sunshine Girl*, which had been a minor US hit in 1967 for Californian studio band The Parade.

After the group disbanded in 1967, Roger Winward and his wife Lesley Blake concentrated on their management / songwriting / production company, recording material at R.G. Jones' Mordern studio, before developing their own home studio, and recording demos for publishing companies - both alone and with fellow **Five Steps Beyond** members Short and Irwin. Many of these have subsequently resurfaced on the *Smile* retrospective and are in a similar harmony pop vein as the earlier **Five Steps Beyond** recordings. (VJ/RW)

Five Towns

| 45: | It Isn't What You've Got/Advice | (Direction 58-3115) 1967 |

This was another obscure outfit. (VJ)

Five's Company

Personnel incl:	E. BROADRIDGE	piano, vcls	A
	BOB BRUNNING	bs	A
	COLIN JORDAN	vcls, gtr	A
	EDDIE St. JOHN	organ	A

| ALBUM: | 1(A) | THE BALLAD OF FRED THE PIXIE | |
| | | (Saga FID 2151) 1969 SC | |

45s:	Sunday For Seven Days/The Big Kill	(Pye 7N 17118) 1966
	Some Girls/Big Deal	(Pye 7N 17162) 1966
	Session Man/Dejection	(Pye 7N 17199) 1966 SC

This outfit is probably most notable for including Bob Brunning on bass. He also had his own **Brunning Hall Sunflower Blues Band** (which included Colin Jordan) and later joined **Fleetwood Mac**. Nowadays the album's probably of most interest to **Fleetwood Mac** completists. *Session Man* was a **Kinks**' number.

Dejection can also be found on *Ripples, Vol. 6* (CD). (VJ)

Flaming Youth

Personnel incl:	RONNIE CARYL	bs, 12-string gtr, vcls	A
	BRIAN CHATTEN	organ, piano, vcls	A
	PHIL COLLINS	drms, percsn, vcls	A
	(FLASH) GORDON SMITH	gtr, 12-string gtr, bs, vcls	A

| ALBUM: | 1(A) | ARK II | (Fontana STL 5533) 1969 R1 |

NB. (1) reissued in Japan (Fontana PHCR-2005) with a booklet containing lyrics in both English and Japanese.

45s:	Guide Me Orion/From Now On	(Fontana TF 1057) 1969 SC
	Every Man Woman And Child/ Drifting	(Fontana 6001 002) 1970 SC
	From Now On/Space Child	(Fontana 6001 003) 1970 SC

Originally known as **Hickory**, this rock outfit is now most notable for containing Phil Collins, who was later of course in **Genesis**. The first 45 had a slight classical influence and their album was a concept album featuring the story of a second flood and second ark in the 20th Century. In addition to the band members, many horns are included on the album too. Of their 45 tracks, *Guide Me Orion, Space Child* and *From Now On (Immortal Invisible)* also appear on the album.

Brian Chatten was later in **Jackson Heights** and went on to play in many bands before starting a solo career in 1980. Gordon Smith also started a solo career and went to Holland in the eighties. (VJ/RK)

Flash

Personnel incl:	PETER BANKS	banjo, gtr, vcls, synth	AB
	RAY BENNETT	keyb'ds, bs, gtr, vcls, sax	AB
	COLIN CARTER	vcls, drms	AB
	MIKE HOUGH	drms, perc	AB
	TONY KAYE	keyb'ds	A

ALBUMS:	1(A)	FLASH	(Sovereign SVNA 7251) 1972 SC
	2(B)	FLASH IN THE CAN	(Sovereign SVNA 7255) 1972 SC
	3(B)	OUT OF OUR HANDS	(Sovereign SVNA 7260) 1973 SC

NB: These albums were released on Capitol in the US.

| 45s: | Small Beginnings/Morning Haze | (Sovereign SOV 105) 1972 |
| | Watch Your Step/Lifetime | (Sovereign SOV 116) 1973 |

This outfit's main claim to fame was that it included **Peter Banks** who was once in **Yes** and also recorded a solo album in 1973 for Sovereign.

Their albums were progressive rock in style comprising compositions with symphonic overtones, not unlike **Yes**. Tony Kaye had also been in **Yes**. He left to join **Badger** after the first album and they continued as a four-piece. Their music never sold in significant quantities here but in the US their first 45, *Small Beginnings*, got to No 29.

Upon their demise, **Banks** recorded an album with Focus guitarist Jan Akkerman prior to his solo efforts. Hough resurfaced in the short-lived Fast Bucks. Colin Carter sang with Coconut Mushroom, who did sign to Apple and did record, although no vinyl output seems to have emerged. (VJ)

Fleetwood Mac

Personnel:	BOB BRUNNING	bs	A
	MICK FLEETWOOD	drms	ABCDEF G H I J
	PETER GREEN	gtr, vcls	ABC
	JEREMY SPENCER	gtr, vcls	ABCDE
	JOHN McVIE	bs	BCDEF G H I J
	DANNY KIRWAN	gtr, vcls	CDEF
	CHRISTINE McVIE	keyb'ds, vcls	EFG H I J
	BOB WELCH	gtr, vcls	FG H I
	DAVE WALKER	vcls	G
	BOB WESTON	gtr, vcls	G H
	LINDSEY BUCKINGHAM	gtr, vcls	J
	STEVIE NICKS	vcls	J

FLEETWOOD MAC - Mr Wonderful (LP).

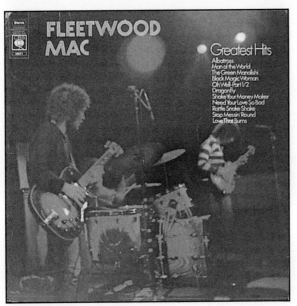

FLEETWOOD MAC - Greatest Hits (LP).

ALBUMS: 1(B) FLEETWOOD MAC   (Blue Horizon 7-63200) 1968 R1 4
(up to   2(B) MR WONDERFUL   (Blue Horizon 7-63205) 1968 R1 10
1976)   3(C) PIOUS BIRD OF GOOD OMEN (Compilation)
                                  (Blue Horizon 7-63215) 1969 SC 18
         4(C) THEN PLAY ON   (Reprise RSLP 9000) 1969 SC 6
         5(C) BLUES JAM AT CHESS (Blue Horizon 7-66227) 1969 -
         6(D) KILN HOUSE   (Reprise RSLP 9004) 1970 SC 39
         7(B) BEFORE THE SPLIT (Compilation)
                                  (CBS 63875) 1971 SC -
         8(F) FUTURE GAMES   (Reprise K 44153) 1971 -
         9(C) GREATEST HITS   (CBS 69011) 1971 36
         10(F) BARE TREES   (Reprise K 44181) 1972 SC -
         11(G) PENGUIN   (Reprise K 44235) 1973 -
         12(H) MYSTERY TO ME   (Reprise K 44248) 1974 -
         13(I) HEROES ARE HARD TO FIND
                                  (Reprise K 54026) 1974 -
         14(J) FLEETWOOD MAC   (Reprise K 54043) 1975 23

NB: (1) reissued on CD (Blue Horizon 477358 2) 1994 and again on CD (Columbia) 2004. (2) reissued on Essential (ESSLP 010) in 1990, also on CD (ESSCD 010) 1990 and again on CD (Columbia) 2004. (3) reissued on CD (WEA 927448 2) 1988, also on (Columbia Rewind 480524 2) 1995 and again on CD (Columbia) 2004. (9) reissued on CD (CBS 4607042) 1989 and again (Columbia 460704 9) 1998 at mid-price to celebrate the band's 30th anniversary. (14) reissued on CD (Warner Bros 254043) 1985 and earlier on Reprise (K 254 043) 1983. (14) later reissued (Warners 8122738812) 2004 as a deluxe 2-CD set. There have been several repackages. One of the first was *Vintage Years* (CBS 88227) 1975 (issued by Sire in the US), which was later reissued by CBS (22122) in 1982. Others included *Man Of The World* (CBS 83110) 1978 and the budget-priced *Albatross* (Embassy 31569) 1977. Also of interest may be *Live In Boston* (Shanghai HAI 107) 1985, which was taped during their 1969 US tour. It is an extremely good set. *London Live '68* (Thunderbolt THBL 1038) suffers from poor recording quality but contains many songs not available elsewhere. *The Blues Collection* (Castle Communication CCSCD 216) 1989 is a 76-minute long CD compilation of their material, which is also available on vinyl (CCSLP 216). A budget-priced compilation, *Looking Back On* (Pickwick SHM 3268) 1989 contains several of their earlier hits and some of their early album tracks. It was later issued on CD (Essential ESSCD 026) 1990. *Boston Live* (Castle Classics CLACD 152) 1989 is not such a good purchase as five of its seven cuts had previously appeared on their earlier *Blues Collection* compilation. The two tracks appearing on *Boston Live* but not on *Blues Collection* are *Can't Hold On* and *Only You*. The material on the CD is from a 1970 *Boston Tea Party* concert. The *Original Fleetwood Mac* (Essential ESSCD 026) 1990 is a CD of unusual and previously unissued material, which was reissued on (Columbia) 2004. As was *Blues Jam in Chicago* (Columbia) 2004. *Like It This Way* (Elite 008 CD) 1991 is a budget-priced compilation. *Live At The Marquee* (Sunflower SF-CD 104) 1992 features the second ever live performance by the band's original line-up but is marred by poor sound quality. It was also issued on vinyl (Receiver RRLP 157) 1992 *The Blues Years* (Essential ESBCD 138) 1991 is an extremely comprehensive multi-CD collection of their early years. *Albatross* (*Fleetwood Mac and Christine Perfect*) (Columbia CD 31569) 1991 is also a relevant CD collection. The repackaging on CD continues with *The Fleetwood Mac Family Album* (Connoisseur VSOP CD 222) 1995 and *The Best Of Fleetwood Mac* (Columbia 483724 2), which is misleadingly titled as it's confined to material they recorded for Blue Horizon. Still, many of their early classics, *Black Magic Woman*, *Need Your Love So Bad* and *Albatross*, are included. Fans of the early **Peter Green** line-up, will also be interested in a *Live At The BBC* 2-CD set (Essential! EDF CD 297) 1995, which includes 36 tracks. *The Vaudeville Years Of Fleetwood Mac: 1968-1970* (Receiver RDPCD 14 Z)

1998 is a 2-CD set of out-takes. *Live In Boston Volume 1 & 2* (Snapper Music SMMCD 555/556) 1999 is a 2-CD live set compiling three nights of them performing in Boston in July 1970. *The Best Of Peter Green's Fleetwood Mac* (Columbia 510155 2) 2002 is an eclectic collection and *The Very Best Of Fleetwood Mac* (Warners 8122 73635 2) 2002, which essentially comprises *Rumours* plus some of their other more significant tracks and hit singles released either side of *Rumours*.

45s: α   I Believe My Time Ain't Long/Rambling
(up to   Pony (initially with PS)   (Blue Horizon 57-3051) 1967 R2/SC -
1976)   Black Magic Woman/
            The Sun Is Shining   (Blue Horizon 57-3138) 1968 37
            Need Your Love So Bad/
            Stop Messin' Around   (Blue Horizon 57-3139) 1968 31
            Albatross/Jigsaw Puzzle Blues (Blue Horizon 57-3145) 1968 1
        β   Man Of The World/Somebody's Gonna
            Get Their Head Kicked In Tonight   (Immediate IM 080) 1969 2
            Oh Well Pts 1 & 2   (Reprise RS 27000) 1969 2
            The Green Manalishi (With The Two-Prong Crown)/World
            In Harmony (initially with PS) (Reprise RS 27007) 1970 SC/- 10
            Dragonfly/The Purple Dancer (Reprise RS 27010) 1971 -
            Sunny Side Of Heaven/
            Spare Me A Little Of Your Love (Reprise K 14194) 1972 -
            Did You Ever Love Me/The Derelict (Reprise K 14280) 1973 -
            Black Magic Woman/Stop Messin' Around   (CBS 1722) 1973 -
            For Your Love/Hypnotised   (Reprised K 14315) 1974 -
            Heroes Are Hard To Find/
            Born Enchanter   (Reprise K 14388) 1975 -
            Warm Ways/Blue Letter (PS) (Reprise K 14403) 1975 -
            Over My Head/I'm So Afraid (Reprise K 14413) 1976 -
            Rhiannon/Sugar Daddy (PS)   (Reprise K 14430) 1976 -
            Say You Love Me/Monday Morning (Reprise K 14447) 1976 40
Reissues: I Beleive My Time Ain't Long/Rambling Pony (CBS 3051) 1969 -
            Need Your Love So Bad/
            No Place To Go   (Blue Horizon 57-3157) 1969 32
            The Green Manalishi/Oh Well (Reprise K 14174) 1972 -
            Albatross/Need Your Love So Bad (PS)   (CBS 8306) 1973 2
        β   Man Of The World/Somebody's Gonna Get Their Head Kicked
            In Tonight   (DJM DJS 10620) 1975 -
            Albatross/Need Your Love So Bad   (CBS 5957) 1978 -
            Man Of The World/Second Chance (Epic EPC 6466) 1978 -
            Albatross/Need Your Love So Bad   (CBS 7066) 1979 -
            Albatross/Man Of The World (CBS A 4578) 1984 -
            Man Of The World/
            (Flip by different artist) (Old Gold OG 9529) 1985 -

NB: α as Peter Green's Fleetwood Mac. β flip side credited to Earl Vince and The Valiants, but this was actually **Fleetwood Mac** under a pseudonym.

Fleetwood Mac has been around for five decades and the only constants during this period have been drummer Mick Fleetwood and bassist John McVie - the rhythm section that the band took its name from. Despite this, it was other members that passed through the band who influenced their

FLEETWOOD MAC - Complete Blue Horizon Sessions (CD Box Set).

radical shifts in musical styles. In the late sixties they spearheaded the British blues boom, but by the mid-seventies the band had transformed into a polished pop/rock act whose music was tailor-made for US radio.

Mick Fleetwood, a Londoner born on 24th June 1942 (previously of **The Cheynes** and **The Bo Street Runners**) first teamed up with **Peter Green** in **Peter B's Looners** (who were later known as **The Peter B's**). They also played together in **Shotgun Express** and **John Mayall's Bluesbreakers** (who also featured John McVie), but when Fleetwood and **Green** were fired within a month of one another from **John Mayall's Bluesbreakers** they formed **Fleetwood Mac** in July 1967.

The new blues group made a publicised debut at the Windsor Jazz and Blues Festival in August 1967. The other two members were Jeremy Spencer who'd been introduced to Fleetwood and **Green** by Blue Horizon label owner **Mike Vernon** and Bob Brunning (who was really filling in until John McVie decided whether to leave **John Mayall's Bluesbreakers** too). In September 1967 McVie made the break so Brunning left to form his own band, the **Brunning Sunflower Blues Band**.

They released their debut disc, *I Believe My Time Ain't Long*, billed as Peter Green's Fleetwood Mac. They also became the house band for the Blue Horizon label backing several blues artists on a variety of albums.

Their debut album was a mixture of originals and covers of classic blues numbers. Entitled simply *Fleetwood Mac* it made the Top Five here and crept to No 198 in the US. The band was at the forefront of the British Blues Boom, which hit the UK in 1968. Their next single, **Peter Green**'s *Black Magic Woman* gave them their first hit, climbing to No 37. (Featuring some nice guitar moments, this was later covered by US group Santana, who enjoyed a No 4 hit with it in January 1971). This was followed by the bluesy *Need Your Love So Bad*, a song originally performed by Little Willie John. The song featured a skilful arrangement by Mickey Baker (of Mickey and Sylvia) and gave the band another minor hit.

Mr. Wonderful was similar in style to their debut album. It climbed to No 10 in the UK and was also notable for featuring future band member **Christine Perfect** (later McVie) on piano, though she was still with **Chicken Shack** at this time.

The *Before The Split* album issued by CBS in 1971 compiled material by this line-up.

In August 1968 a third guitarist, ex-Boilerhouse member Danny Kirwan (a Londoner), was added to the group. A month later they recorded **Peter Green**'s haunting guitar-led instrumental *Albatross*, which topped the UK chart and marked the group's movement out of the blues genre to a more widely commercially acceptable style of music. *Albatross* is one of those classic records with a timeless quality. It was a hit again when it was re-released in 1973 and has been a popular slow dance number over the years. The follow-up, another **Peter Green** original, *Man Of The World*, which was very similar in style, was another massive UK hit (No 2). By now their contract with Blue Horizon had expired and they'd signed a one-off deal with **Andrew Loog Oldham**'s Immediate label. Meanwhile their old label, Blue Horizon, cashing in on the band's enormous popularity, reissued their third single (*Need Your Love So Bad*) and it was a minor hit once again. Blue Horizon also put out a compilation (*Pious Bird Of Good Omen*) and repromoted *Need Your Love So Bad* for a third time causing it to chart again, but this time its best position was No 42.

Their first album on their new label Reprise, *Then Play On*, marked the culmination of the movement towards a more melodic three guitar sound and away from the twelve bar blues format they had started out with. **Green** was also getting into religion (he'd renounced his Jewish faith in favour of Christianity). Their next 45, the double-sided *Oh Well* was full of religious overtones. Hearing it today it seems remarkable that such an uncommercial sound could have gotten to No 2 in the charts - but this only serves to illustrate how hot **Fleetwood Mac** were at the time. It even went on to rise to No 55 in the US too.

Blue Horizon, meanwhile, released *Blues Jam At Chess*, an album of material recorded live in Chicago the previous year when the band were nearing the end of their twelve bar blues format.

In Spring 1970 **Peter Green**, who'd been finding the pressures of stardom increasingly hard to cope with and had been thinking of leaving the band for some time, finally quit. He made his decision in Munich during the middle of a European tour, but completed all the contracted gigs. The final

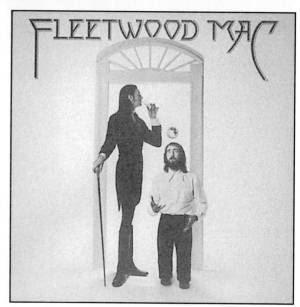

FLEETWOOD MAC - Fleetwood Mac (LP).

single he wrote for the band, *The Green Manalishi (With The Two-Prong Crown)*, was another fairly uncommercial number with some great three-part guitar work. The lyrics sound rather autobiographical - an insight into what was by now a pretty tortured mind. In any event the single, which got to No 10, would prove to be their last hit (excluding reissues) for six years. He went on to record a solo album.

Green's replacement was John McVie's wife Christine (ex-**Chicken Shack**) who'd been voted female vocalist of the year by Melody Maker. Minus their leader the band searched hard for a new direction. **Jeremy Spencer** was the main creative force on their next album, *Kiln House*. Peaking at No 39 here and No 69 in the US it would be their last UK Chart album (excluding compilations) for six years. Then **Jeremy Spencer** walked out on the band during a US tour to join a religious cult 'The Children Of God'. He went on to record an album with them in 1973 and a solo album in 1979. This left the group in some disarray, having lost its two main songwriters and guitarists in the space of a year. It was Judy Wong (wife of **Jethro Tull**'s Glenn Cornick) who suggested Bob Welch, an American working at an R&B club in Paris, and within a couple of months with Welch in the line-up the band set about recording a new album with Welch, Kirwan and **Christine McVie** sharing the songwriting between them. By now they were pretty much permanently touring in the US and their next two albums (*Future Games* and *Bare Trees*) made the lower echelons of the US charts (91 and 70), whilst in the UK only their *Greatest Hits* album charted.

Their next single, *Dragonfly* (co-written by Danny Kirwan and W.H. Davies), featured more pleasant melodic guitar work, but neither this nor successive efforts interested the punters in sufficient numbers. To make matters worse another member, Danny Kirwan, was feeling the strain of relentless touring. He had to be fired for refusing to appear on stage and after going on to record unsuccessfully for DJM, ended up in a mental hospital. **Long John Baldry**'s sideman Bob Weston and **Savoy Brown** vocalist Dave Walker were recruited as replacements.

The new line-up (G) recorded a promising and complex album, *Penguin*, which got to No 49 in the US and included a guest appearance from **Peter Green**. The reissue of *Albatross*, which this time reached No 2 in the UK, kept them in the public eye, but Walker left the band at this point which reverted to a five-piece.

Mystery To Me was a disappointing album and to make matters worse considerable personality clashes (Weston was having an affair with Fleetwood's wife Jenny) meant the band was in considerable disarray. This led to Weston's departure soon after the release of the album and after this the group pulled out of the tour. Angered by this **Fleetwood Mac**'s manager, **Clifford Davis**, assembled a bogus band to honour the remaining engagements. This inevitably led to a bitter legal battle, which took several months to resolve. The members of this bogus combo eventually turned up in the group **Stretch**.

Reduced now to a foursome the band managed to put another album out, *Heroes Are Hard To Find*. Again the album made no impression here but achieved modest success in the US, where it peaked at No 34. The relative success of their recent albums in the States was almost certainly a factor in their deciding to move permanently to California in November 1974. A couple of months later Bob Welch left the band for Paris. He also went on to enjoy solo successes. Ironically, when the band was at its lowest ebb, a chance meeting between Mick Fleetwood and Lindsey Buckingham at Sound City studios in Van Nuys, California, which Fleetwood was considering as a future recording venue, led to the two building up a friendship which soon resulted in Buckingham and his lover Stevie Nicks being invited to join the band. (Buckingham and Nicks were playing as a duo at the time but their 1973 album for Polydor had passed largely unnoticed).

The rejuvenated line-up achieved massive success over the next few years. Along with Christine McVie, Buckingham and Nicks proved to be talented songwriters, whilst Stevie Nicks' vocals were ideally suited to the new MOR sound tailor-made for US radio, which the band now created. The new line-up's first album, *Fleetwood Mac*, eventually got to No 1 in the US Charts, going platinum. It also produced a trio of US hits:- *Over My Head* (No 20), *Rhiannon* (No 11) and *Say You Love Me* (No 11). The last one was also a minor hit over here, where the album eventually climbed to No 23. Aside from the 45 releases the album was an excellent collection of strong songs superbly delivered. The exquisite *Landslide* remains a personal favourite but it was one of the most consistent albums of the decade. Yet all of this was bettered by their next release, *Rumours* (1977), which eventually sold in excess of 25 million copies worldwide.

The Vaudeville Years Of Fleetwood Mac is a 2-CD set of out-takes, which includes alternate versions of *Oh Well, Green Manalishi, Man Of The World* and a fine version of *Do You Give A Damn For Me.*

Live In Boston Volume 1 & 2 is a 2-CD set capturing them in blistering form over three nights in Boston in July 1970. Highlights include crisp versions of *Black Magic Woman*, a 25-minute version of *Rattlesnake Shake* and the previously unreleased *Got To Move*. The finale *Encore Jam* builds up to a memorable crescendo.

The Very Best Of Fleetwood Mac essentially comprises *Rumours* plus some of their other more significant tracks and hit singles released either side of *Rumours*. The UK pressing also includes a few cuts from the **Peter Green** era **Fleetwood Mac** and if you like these check out the 2002 release *The Very Best Of Peter Green's Fleetwood Mac.*

It had been a long, long journey, but as we leave the time frame of this book, the band was at the pinnacle of its career. Only Mick Fleetwood had survived from the original line-up (although John McVie had been present for all but the first three months too). Some members had played a high price during the long struggle towards success. Just as *Rumours* was released **Peter Green** (the band's earliest creative force and songwriter) became the second former member (the other being Kirwan) to end up in a mental hospital after attacking his accountant with an air rifle. Luckily it wasn't a permanent story and he returned with a solo instrumental album two years later.

They continued to prosper for many years beyond the time span of this book. *Tusk* was a UK No 1 album in 1979 and 1980's *Fleetwood Mac Live* narrowly missed the Top 30. *Mirage* (1982) was a Top 5 UK album and 1987's *Tango In The Night* and *Behind The Mask* (1990) both topped the album charts here in Britain. After touring to promote the album Stevie Nicks and Christine McVie announced they would continue to record with the group, but not tour any more. In 1992, the box set *25 Years - The Chain* was released. The classic line-up of Fleetwood, the McVies, Buckingham and Nicks reformed to play at President Clinton's inauguration early in 1993. Within the year, Nicks and Christine McVie had both left to concentrate on their solo careers and a new line-up went in tour and released a new album *Time*, which met with little commercial success. They are still going strong in the new millennium and *Say You Will* (2003) was their first studio album for 15 years.

Appearances on Various Artists' compilations have included: *Rollin' Man, Long Grey Mare* and *Shake Your Moneymaker* on *Super Duper Blues* (LP); *Sentimental Lady* on *Fruity* (LP); and *Man Of The World* on *Immediate Single Anthology, Vol. 1* (CD). More recently, *Man Of The World* has resurfaced on the 3-CD set *Guitar Heroes - Rock The Night Away*; on *No 1s & Million Sellers Vol 4* (CD), *Hits Of The Swinging Sixties* (CD), the 2-CD set *Sixties Summer Love*; on *The Greatest Sixties Album Of All Times Vol 2* (CD) and on the CD-set *Rock Of Ages, Four Decades Of Heavy Rock 1962-2002*; whilst *Albatross* can be found on *45s - 45 Classic No 1's* and on the 2-CD set *60 Number Ones Of The Sixties. Man Of The*

World and *The Green Manalishi* have been compiled on the 3-CD box set *Ars Longa Vita Brevis: A Compendium Of Progressive Rock 1967-1974.* (VJ)

The Fleur de Lys

Personnel:	ALEX CHAMBERLAIN	organ	A
	GARY CHURCHILL	bs	A
	KEITH GUSTER	drms	ABCDEFG H I
	FRANK SMITH	gtr, vcls	A
	GORDON HASKELL	bs	BCDEF
	PHIL SAWYER	gtr	B
	PETE SEARS	keyb'ds	BCD
	CHRIS ANDREWS	vcls	CDE
	BRYN HAWORTH	gtr	DEFG
	TAGO BYERS	bs	G H I
	TONY HEAD	vcls	G H I
	GRAHAM MAITLAND	gtr	I

ALBUM: 1 REFLECTIONS - 1965-1969 (FDL 1005) 1996

NB: (1) is a compilation of material from their 45s and other related projects on CD and LP. The CD version includes seven extra tracks, and the original CD issue (FDL 1005) was later reissued by Blueprint (BP 256CD) in 1997.

45s:	Moondreams/Wait For Me	(Immediate IM 20) 1965 R3
	Circles/So Come On	(Immediate IM 32) 1966 R5
	Mud In Your Eye/I've Been Trying	(Polydor 56124) 1966 R4
	I Can See A Light/Prodigal Son	(Polydor 56200) 1967 R2
	Gong With The Luminous Nose/	
	Hammer Head	(Polydor 56251) 1968 R2
	Stop Crossing The Bridge/	
	Brick By Brick (Stone By Stone)	(Atlantic 584 193) 1968 R1
	You're Just A Liar/One City Girl	(Atlantic 584 243) 1969 R2

NB: Their second 45 has been reissued in a limited edition pressing of 500 copies. The reproduction is taken from the original French jukebox pressing.

The Fleur de Lys was one of the most talented underground guitar bands of the sixties and deserve far more recognition than they have received to date. They underwent many line-up changes and their story is a complex one.

They originally formed (line-up A) as Les Fleur de Lys in Southampton during the Autumn of 1964. They established a small following locally, playing at youth clubs, parties and pubs, but were signed by Immediate in 1965 after being spotted at a London gig. With a young **Jimmy Page** in charge of their recording sessions, the outcome was a beat version of Buddy Holly's *Moondreams*. It made little impression and disillusioned, the group disintegrated, leaving Keith Guster (the only ever-present member in their various line-ups) to reform the band with line-up (B). Phil Sawyer had previously been in **The Cheynes** and **Shotgun Express**. With this new

THE FLEUR DE LYS - Reflections (CD).

line-up and **Page** again producing, they recorded a superb version of **Pete Townshend**'s *Circles*, which was notable for some fine psychedelic guitar work from Sawyer. By now the group was known as **The Fleur de Lys** and building up a good reputation on the club circuit. Indeed **The Animals'** Hilton Valentine got them involved in a session he was producing with fellow **Animals'** recent discovery **Jimi Hendrix**. Two tracks were put down, one was a cover of The Impressions' *Amen*, but they weren't used, although Pete Sears has a copy of the recordings in his own collection.

To give the group an up-front vocalist Chris Andrews, who'd been a child actor (his roles included The Artful Dodger in the London production of 'Oliver' in 1964), was added to the line-up (C) and the group signed to Polydor in the Summer of 1966. Pete Sears left soon after to join **The Sam Gopal Dream**. He later went to the US West Coast and progressed through Stoneground, Silver Metre and Copperhead finally ending up in Jefferson Starship. Phil Sawyer joined the new-look **Spencer Davis Group** and, briefly, the group were a three-piece prior to **Bryn Haworth** being recruited. He'd previously played with a number of local bands in Darwin (near Blackburn), including The Mustangs, The Railroaders and The Mike Taylor Combo, but none of them made it onto vinyl. With line-up (E) *Mud In Your Eye* was recorded, featuring **Haworth**'s fine guitar work.

A chance meeting with producer/manager Frank Fenter led to the group backing young South African singer Sharon Tandy on studio and live work. As a session group they also toured Holland with Aretha Franklin, backed Isaac Hayes and recorded an album with Barney Kessel in this era. It was also Fenter who arranged for the group to embark on a new psychedelic project, **Rupert's People**. With friend and guitarist Rod Lynton they wrote and recorded *Hold On*. Lynton came up with the **Procol Harum**-influenced *Reflections Of Charles Brown* to accompany it, but only Chris Andrews liked the song so he left to continue with the **Rupert's People** project and the band continued as a three-piece.

Line-up (F) re-cut *Hold On* in the studio, with Sharon Tandy on vocals. They also recorded *Daughter Of The Sun* at the same session. *Hold On* figured as the 'B' side to her next single but both songs were coupled on a 1968 45. There's no Sharon Tandy entry in this book so here's the discographical details of this line-up's involvement with her:-

| 45s: | Stay With Me/Hold On | (Atlantic 584 124) 1967 |
| | Hold On/Daughter Of The Sun | (Atlantic 584 219) 1968 |

The band guested on John Peel's 'Top Gear' radio programme in October 1967, along with Sharon Tandy. **The Fleur de Lys** performed *Neighbour, Neighbour*, *Go Go Power* and *Cross Cut Saw* and backed Sharon Tandy on *Always Something There To Remind Me*, *Our Day Will Come* and a belting version of *Hold On*.

Line-up F's other recordings were the *I Can See A Light* 45 (with **Bryn Haworth** on vocals) and a 45 under the pseudonym of **Shyster** (*Tick-Tock*), both in September' 1967.

In 1968 they started work on an album. Their next 45, *Gong With The Luminous Nose*, a **Gordon Haskell** song based on the famous nonsense rhyme of Edward Lear, came from this session, with **Haskell** handling the vocals. Again featuring ace guitar work from **Haworth**. The 'album' included many cover versions from Ray Charles to The Young Rascals, but it was never issued and the tapes have never been relocated. The group did, however, complete an album with **John Bromley**, backed Donnie Elbert on an album and worked with William E. Kimber on a rare and beautiful single as **Waygood Ellis** (which may be another pseudonym).

Gordon Haskell left the group during 1968, eventually joining **King Crimson** in late 1969. He also cut a solo album in 1970. **The Fleur de Lys**, now with line-up (G), switched to Atlantic and released a Stax-style 45 *Stop Crossing That Bridge*. Shortly after, they released a second 45, *Butchers And Bakers*, under yet another pseudonym, **Chocolate Frog**. There was also a version by **The Staccatos** (which may have been **The Creation** in disguise), but the song wasn't too good and both versions sold poorly. Line-up (G) also backed Sharon Tandy on some of her 45s and a Tony and Tandy collaboration, *Two Can Make It Together* (Atlantic 584 262) 1969. **The Fleur de Lys** are credited on its 'B' side, *The Bitter And The Sweet*. The 'Tony' in question here was **Fleur de Lys'** Tony Head.

The Fleur de Lys' final 45, *You're Just A Liar*, penned by **Haworth** and Polydor songwriter Brian Potter, saw them go out on a high in a haze of hot guitar work. **Haworth** left and headed for America's West Coast, where he formed a band with ex-Blue Cheer member Leigh Stephens, recording

an album which was never released. Former **Scots Of St. James'** member Graham Maitland joined the band in its final days and he was later in **Five Day Rain**.

Look out for the *Reflections* compilation of their recordings. The CD version includes *Sugar Love* and *So Many Things* recorded with **John Bromley**; *Hold On* and *Daughter Of The Sun* with Sharon Tandy; *Tick Tock* recorded using **The Shyster** pseudonym; both sides of **The Chocolate Frog** 45; both sides of the first **Rupert's People** 45 and *I Like What I'm Trying To Do* by **Waygood Ellis**. The vinyl version omits seven tracks.

Compilation coverage has included:- *Gotta Get Enough Time* (Sharon Tandy) on *Justafixation* (CD); *Circles* and *So Come On* on *Jimmy Page Studio Works 1964-1968* (CD), *Broken Dreams, Vol. 1* (LP) and *Immediate Alternative* (LP & CD); *Moondreams, Wait For Me, Circles* and *So Come On* on *Jimmy Page - Hip Young Guitar Slinger* (2-CD) and *Immediate Single Anthology, Vol. 1* (CD); *Circles, So Come On* and *Moondreams* on *Jimmy's Back Pages - The Early Years* (CD); *So Come On* on *Immediate Single Collection, Vol. 2* (CD); *Circles* on *Maximum '65* (LP), *Chocolate Soup For Diabetics, Vol. 2* (LP), and *Immediate Single Collection, Vol. 1* (CD); *Liar* and *Mud In Your Eye* on *Perfumed Garden Vol. 2* (CD); *Liar* on *Perfumed Garden, Vol. 2* (LP); *Hold On* and *Daughter Of The Moon* (both with Sharon Tandy) on *Rubble, Vol. 8 - All The Colours Of Darkness* (LP); *Gong With A Luminous Nose* on *Rubble, Vol. 13 - Freak Beat Fantoms* (LP), *Rubble, Vol. 7* (CD), *The Best Of Rubble Collection Vol. 1* (CD), *Electric Sugar Cube Flashbacks* (CD), *Electric Sugar Cube Flashbacks, Vol. 4* (LP) and *Electric Sugarcube Flashbacks, Vol. 1* (LP); *Hold On* (with Sharon Tandy) on *Rubble, Vol. 4* (CD); *Daughter Of The Moon* (with Sharon Tandy) on *Rubble, Vol. 5* (CD) and *Visions Of The Past, Vol. 2* (LP & CD); *So Come On, Mud In Your Eye, You're Just A Liar* and *Hammer-Head* on *Beat It* (3-CD); *Circles* and *Mud In Your Eye* on *Chocolate Soup* (CD); *Mud In Your Eye* on *Chocolate Soup For Diabetics, Vol. 3* (LP) and *Circles* can also be heard on *Rock Of Ages, Four Decades Of Heavy Rock 1962-2002* and on the 4-CD *Nuggets 11* box set. (VJ)

The Flies

Personnel incl: PETER DUNTON

| ALBUM: | 1 COMPLETE COLLECTION | (Acme ADLP 1030) 2001 |

NB: (1) Also on CD (Acme ADCD 1030) with five additional tracks.

45s:	I'm Not Your Stepping Stone/	
	Talk To Me	(Decca F 12533) 1966 R3
	The House Of Love/It Had To Be You	(Decca F 12594) 1967 R2
	The Magic Train/Gently As You Feel	(RCA RCA 1757) 1968 R1

Notable for their outrageous stage act, **The Flies** recorded a psychedelic version of The Monkees' 'B' side, *I'm Not Your Stepping Stone*, in 1966, which was written by Tommy Boyce and Bobby Hart. Their next 'A' side, *The House Of Love*, is a more restrained song in a pop-soul style. They

THE FLIES - Complete Collection (LP).

appeared at the '14-Hour Technicolour Dream' with painted faces and wearing palm leaf skirts, and can be seen in the BBC's 'Man Alive' documentary film of the event. The lead singer was notable for some particularly bizarre antics.

Acme's *Complete Collection* includes all their 45 tracks, plus unreleased songs and a different version of *I'm Not Your Stepping Stone*.

Compilation appearances have included: *I'm Not Your Stepping Stone* and *House Of Love* on *Rubble, Vol. 5 - The Electric Crayon Set* (LP) and *Rubble, Vol. 3* (CD), whilst *I'm Not Your Steppin' Stone* can also be heard on *Freakbeat Scene* (CD) and on the 4-CD box set *Acid Drops, Spacedust & Flying Saucers*.

Peter Dunton was later in Pleace and **T2**. (VJ)

Flintlock

Personnel:	MIKE HOLOWAY	vcls, drms	A
	DEREK PASCOE	vcls, sax	A
	BILL RICE	keyb'ds, vcls	A
	JAMIE STONE	bs, vcls	A
	JOHN SUMMERTON	gtr, vcls	A

ALBUMS: 1(A)	ON THE WAY	(Pinnacle PLP 8307) 1975
(up to 2 (A)	HOT FROM THE LOCK	(Pinnacle PLP 8309) 1976
1976)		

			HCP
45s:	Learn To Cry/I'm Going Home	(Pinnacle P8409) 1975	-
(up to	Little Bit Of Lovin'/Sooner Or Later	(Pinnacle P8417) 1976	-
1976)	Dawn/Thunderman	(Pinnacle P8419) 1976	30
	Sea Of Flame/I've Got My Eye On You	(Pinnacle P8428) 1976	-
	Russian Roulette/Saddle My Horse	(Pinnacle P8438) 1976	-

This teenage pop band was formed around mid-seventies TV heartthrob Mike Holoway. They enjoyed a Top 30 hit with *Dawn* and made a final album *Stand Alone* in 1979. (BS)

The Flintlocks

45:	What Goes On?/	
	I Walked Right Into A Heaven	(Decca F 12412) 1966

No other information on this one. (VJ)

Flip and The Dateliners

Personnel incl:	VIVIEN CHERING (FLIP)	vcls, gtr	ABC
	DAVE CHERING	bs (organ/sax)	ABC
	DAVE DONNISON	drms	A
	GRAHAM SHARP	ld gtr	ABC
	MIKE COOKE	drms	BC
	ROB DEKA	organ	BC
	JIM ENGLISH	bs	C

45:	My Johnny Doesn't Come Around Anymore/	
	Please Listen To Me	(HMV POP 1359) 1964 R2

This teenbeat 45 was produced by Joe Meek. The flip featured backing vocals by the group, with most of the remainder consisting of Meek indulging in his usual frenzy of overdubs. A third track, *Mama Didn't Lie*, recorded in 1964 finally got released on the 1995 CD *Joe's Girls*.

Drummer Dave Donnison explains:- "In 1962 I was eighteen, and living in Tottenham in north London, when I put together a traditional jazz band called 'The Barrelhouse Seven'. Unlike most similar bands of the day I didn't want a banjo in the rhythm section, but preferred the richer sound of a guitar, and that's how I came to meet Graham Sharp, who was then sixteen years old. Graham had a fine ear for chords, and outside of jazz we also liked the rock 'n roll of people like Chuck Berry. The band broke up after about a year, and the electrician at the company I worked for - Dave Chering - asked me to join the group he had with his sister Viv and a guitarist named Ken, called 'The Davernettes'."

THE FREAKBEAT SCENE (Comp CD) including The Flies.

"Dave played bass guitar and Viv played rhythm guitar and sang. Ken's style was very much based on **Hank Marvin**, so we did plenty of **Shadows** songs - and sounded like all the other British groups of the time. Viv's material was mainly of the singalong pub variety, *Memories, Who's Sorry Now* etc.

"After a few weeks Ken left the band and I suggested Graham as a replacement, and he joined us at the 'Prince Albert'. Our own musical tastes rather changed the style of the group toward rock 'n roll and a little blues. We then became resident band at a pub called the 'Hornsey Wood Tavern' in Seven Sisters Road, playing four nights a week and completely filling the place. On a Saturday night all the seats were taken an hour or more before we started playing. Graham and I were doing many of the vocals by this time, almost entirely rock or rhythm and blues material."

"In the later part of 1963 we went to a recording studio called 'City of London Studios' and cut four sides, two vocals by Viv and two instrumentals. Dave Chering took these to Joe Meek to show what sort of band we were, and Joe gave us a demo of *My Johnny* to work on. In 1964 we changed our name to **The Dateliners** (we were sitting around at Dave and Viv's house trying to think up a new name for the band. The TV was on and a news programme came on called 'Dateline') and went into the studio in Holloway Road on several occasions and recorded four tracks, *My Johnny Doesn't Come Around, Listen To Me, Mama Didn't Lie* (which after hearing the playback in the studio I didn't hear again for about thirty years when the tapes were discovered and I was asked to identify and confirm that it was us playing!) and another track which I've completely forgotten. Incidentally, carrying a drum kit up those three flights of narrow wooden stairs from the street was no joke, and when we arrived to record *Listen To Me* Heinz' band was there, and their drummer had heard some of our work and said some nice things about my drumming. He asked me if I would like to borrow his kit - a beautiful Rogers drum kit already set up in the studio - to save me having to bring mine up. As he was of course a professional musician making this offer to someone he had only just met I thought this was very kind and generous. I hope I did it justice! We had a few plays on Radio Luxembourg but not enough to get the single moving - if only the pirates had been in full swing by then!"

"I then was faced with one of the most difficult decisions of my life. I had changed my job and joined the GPO as a telephone engineer, when the group was offered a tour of Germany. My simple choice was to leave the job or leave the group. My decision to leave the group turned out to be absolutely right, but it was a very hard thing to do at the time."

Two new members then joined the band, Mick Cooke (drms) and Rob Deka (organ). Later, Dave Chering switched to tenor sax and a bass guitarist called Jim English also joined. The tour of Germany was a disaster with the group having to take the German club owner to court to get paid in order to get home. After this the band broke up.

Dave Donnison later played in a pick-up band from 1977 - 1979 with Graham Sharp, at the 'Thatched House' pub in Barking. Mike Cook, was later in **Home**. (VJ/DD)

The Floribunda Rose

45:      One Way Street/
        Linda Loves Linda   (Piccadilly 7N 35408) 1967 SC

A little known band, they were also known as **Scrugg**. South African John Kongos wrote both sides of a **Scrugg** 45 and had earlier released a 45 on Piccadilly, *I Love Mary/Good Time Party Companion*, as John T. Kongos which has led some to speculate that he may have been involved in **The Floribunda Rose**. Anyway, *Linda Loves Linda*, a pop-psych effort which culminates in a free-form ending later resurfaced on *Rubble, Vol. 10 - Professor Jordan's Magic Sound Show* (LP) but it is inane pop which is best forgotten. (VJ)

The Flowerpot Men

Personnel:	TONY BURROWS	vcls		A
	PERRY FORD	vcls		A
	NEIL LANDON	vcls		A
	PETER LANDON	vcls		A

			HCP
45s:	Let's Go To San Francisco (Part 1)/		
	(Part 2)	(Deram DM 142) 1967	4
	A Walk In The Sky/Am I Losing You?	(Deram DM 160) 1967	-
	A Man Without A Woman/		
	You Can Never Be Wrong	(Deram DM 183) 1968	-
	In A Moment Of Madness/		
	Young Birds Fly	(Deram DM 248) 1969	-
Reissue:	Let's Go To San Francisco/		
	Sweet Baby Jane	(Penny Farthing PEN 847) 1974	-

NB: *Let's Go To San Francisco* (C5 526) 1988 is a good compilation of their material. There's also a later CD compilation, *Let's Go To San Francisco* (Repertoire REP 4344-WZ) 1993 which adds several previously unreleased cuts to C5's earlier vinyl collection. Their finer moments are also compiled on *The Very Best Of The Flowerpot Men* (Sounds & Media SUMCD 411) 199? *Peace Album/Past Imperfect* (Repertoire REP 4883) 2000 consists of two albums recorded in 1969 but not given an airing until now. *Midsummer Dreaming* (*Let's All Go To San Francisco*) (Tenth Planet TP 051) 2002 is a compilation of rarities, 'B' sides and previously unreleased tracks.

The Flowerpot Men were arguably the nearest the UK got to the Beach Boys and John Carter and his colleagues haven't received the acclaim they deserved.

These three session singers successfully articulated the sentiments of the flower-power movement with *Let's Go To San Francisco*, which climbed to No 4. The follow-up, *A Walk In The Sky*, also captured the feel of the flower-power era but didn't sell as well. Their later efforts were more ordinary and even a change of name to **Friends** late in 1968 failed to revive their fortunes. Inevitably, perhaps, this act were destined to be

THE FLOWERPOT MEN - Midsummer Dreaming (LP).

one-hit wonders and after their demise in 1969 Burrows went on to join **Edison Lighthouse** after a brief stab at a solo career, whilst **Landon** departed to **Fat Mattress**. All three had previously been involved in **The Ivy League**.

The *Let's Go To San Francisco* compilation features both sides of their four Deram singles on side one and an interesting selection of material on side two including both sides of the 1968 single the trio recorded as **Friends** (*Piccolo Man* and *Mythological Sunday*) and some other previously unissued songs, including the psychedelic *Blow Away* and two songs dating from the seventies, *Journey's End* and *Silicon City*.

The later CD compilation on Repertoire adds several previously unreleased and somewhat rockier tracks including an eight-minute mini-epic *Children Of Tomorrow*. This is recommended for anyone wanting a complete rundown of their music. *Peace Album/Past Imperfect* were two albums recorded in 1969, but not given an airing until now. On offer are 21 tracks superbly packaged and arranged with a wide range of layered harmonies, which shine through on tracks like *White Dove*. There's also a skiffle version of **Donovan's** *Colours*.

Midsummer Dreaming (Let's All Go To San Francisco) is a compilation of rarities, 'B' sides and previously unreleased tracks. It also includes some studio experimentation. If you like mid to late sixties pop music you'll enjoy this CD.

The Sequel CD, *Carter-Lewis Story* gives a further airing to *Let's Go To San Francisco*, *Let's Go Back To San Francisco*, *A Walk In The Sky*, *Blow Away* and *White Dove*. You can also find *Let's Go To San Francisco* on *Your Starter For Ten!!* (CD). (VJ)

Flying Machine

Personnel:	STUART COLEMAN	bs	A
	STEVE JONES	ld gtr, vcls	A
	SAM KEMPE	vcls	A
	TONY NEWMAN	vcls	A
	PAUL WILKINSON	drms	A

ALBUM: 1(A) DOWN TO EARTH WITH THE FLYING MACHINE
                              (Pye NSPL 18328) 1970 SC

NB: There's also a double CD compilation *Flight Recorder* (Sequel NECD 290) 1998, and double LP compilation *Down To Earth With - The Complete Recordings* (Get Back GET 555) 2000, which was available as an Italian import.

45s:	Smile A Little Smile For Me/	
	Maybe We've Been Loving Too Long	(Pye 7N 17722) 1969
	Baby Make It Soon/	
	Smile A Little Smile For Me	(Pye 7N 17722) 1969
	Send My Baby Home Again/	
	Look At Me, Look At Me	(Pye 7N 17811) 1969
	Hanging On The Edge Of Sadness/	
	Flying Machine	(Pye 7N 17914) 1970
	The Devil Has Possession Of Your Mind/	
	Hey Little Girl	(Pye 7N 45001) 1970
	Yes I Understand/Pages Of Your Life	(Pye 7N 45093) 1970

This was a studio project of songwriters Tony Macauley and Geoff Stevens. The touring group featured **Tony Newman** as lead vocalist. He and the other members (except Wilkinson) had earlier been in **Pinkerton's Assorted Colours** (later known as simply Pinkerton's).

Musically they were pop-oriented and *Smile A Little Smile For Me* portrayed this most effectively, although by the time of *The Devil Has Lost Possession Of My Mind* they had developed a more psychedelic edge.

Sequel's double CD retrospective *Flight Recorder* compiles everything that they recorded for Pye between '67 - '71, plus sixteen previously unreleased cuts including demos of their Decca hits as **Pinkerton's Assorted Colours**. *Down To Earth With - The Complete Recordings* the 2-LP compilation contains all their output and showcases their harmony-pop style perfectly.

Compilation appearances have included: *Smile a Little Smile for Me* on *Paisley Pop - Pye Psych (& Other Colours) 1966-1969* (CD); *The Flying Machine* on *Rubble, Vol. 7 - Pictures In The Sky* (LP) and *Haunted -*

FLIGHT RECORDER

from PINKERTON'S (Assort.) COLOURS to THE FLYING MACHINE

*includes previously unreleased material

THE FLYING MACHINE - Flight Recorder (CD).

Psychedelic Pstones Vol, 1 (CD); *The Devil Has Possession Of Your Mind* on *Pop-In, Vol 2* (CD) and *Hey Little Girl* and *Smile A Little Smile For Me* on *Ripples, Vol. 7* (CD). (VJ)

Steve Flynn

45s: Mister Rainbow/
        Let's Live For Tomorrow   (Parlophone R 5625) 1967 SC
        Your Life, My Life/Come Tomorrow   (Parlophone R 5689) 1968

An obscure sixties singer from Chelsea whose *Mister Rainbow* was a spin-off from the ill-fated **Keith West** *Teenage Opera* project. It's an interesting mixture of experimentation and harmonies which deserved to sell better.

Mr Rainbow can also be heard on *60's Back Beat* (LP), *A Teenage Opera - The Original Soundtrack Recording* (CD) and *Fading Yellow* (LP). (VJ)

Focal Point

Personnel:	TED HESKETH	drms	A
	DAVE RHODES	lead gtr	A
	DAVE SLATER	bs	A
	PAUL TENNANT	gtr, vcls	A
	TIM WELLS	keyb'ds	A

45:    Love You Forever/Sycamore Sid   (Deram DM 186) 1968 R1

The flip side to this obscure 45 is typical British whimsical flower-pop. They came from Liverpool and **Paul McCartney** arranged for them to record this 45. Brian Epstein chose their name. **John Lennon** loved their work and was the main reason the band were signed by Apple publishing. One great song he raved about was called *Hassle Castle* - a true sixties style recording ala *Strawberry Fields*. They also spent some time backing **Jackie Lomax** in the studio.

Compilation appearances include: *Love You Forever* and *Sycamore Syd* on *Nowhere Men, Vol. 4* (CD); whilst *Sycamore Syd* can be found on *Psychedalia - Rare Blooms From The English Summer Of Love* (CD) and *Deram Dayze* (LP). (VJ/BP/PT)

Focus Three

45:    10,000 Years Behind My Mind/
        The Sunkeeper   (Columbia DB 8279) 1967 R1

The 'A' side of their sole 45, *10,000 Years Behind My Mind*, is a ballad with strong soulful lead vocals rumoured to be those of **Liza Strike**, later a backing vocalist on **Pink Floyd**'s *Dark Side Of The Moon*.

10,000 Years Behind My Mind has been compiled on *Psychedelia At Abbey Road* (CD), *Rubble, Vol. 3 - Nightmares In Wonderland* (LP), *Rubble, Vol. 2* (CD) and on the 4-CD box set *Acid Drops, Spacedust & Flying Saucers*. (VJ)

Fogg

Personnel:	CHRIS McPHERSON	vcls	A
	ROBERT PORTEOUS	drms	AB
	DAVID/DAVY ROBSON	bs	AB
	DEREK ROOTHAM	ld gtr	AB
	DAVE DITCHBURN	ld vcls	B

ALBUM: 1(A)   THIS IS IT FOGG   (EMI EMD-06155) 1974
NB: (1) was a German release.

45s: Doing The Best I Can/You'll Be Free   (EMI EMI 2108) 1974
        Water In My Wine/Just Like Me   (EMI EMI 2182) 1974
        Wind It Up/Northern Song   (EMI EMI 2225) 1974

A Newcastle pop/rock band formed in early 1973. They had plans for an album, which was only finally released in Germany in 1974.

McPherson left in 1975 and Dave Ditchburn came in as a replacement. (VJ)

Foggy

ALBUMS:	1( )	SIMPLE GIFTS (w/insert)	(York FYK 411) 1972 R1
(up to	2( )	PATCHWORK	(Canon No #) 1973 R1
1976)	3( )	EXPORT	(Norwegian Box) 1976 R3

NB: (1) was recorded with **The Strawbs**. (3) private Norwegian release.

45s: How Come The Sun/Take Your Name   (York SYK 534) 1972
        Kitty Starr/She's Far Away (PS)   (York SYK 542) 1973

A psychedelic folk outfit who utilised a wide range of instruments, including a sitar, psaltery, tabla and mellotron on their *Simple Gifts* album. This was their best album and the finest cut on it was *She's Far Away*. Their third release *Export* was on a private Norwegian label in a unique silver/grey demo sleeve. It includes material like *Blind Beggar Man, Black Rose, First Love Song* etc. (VJ)

Foggy Dew-O

Personnel:	DANNY CLARKE	A
	LENNY WESLEY	A

ALBUMS:	1(A)	FOGGY DEW-O	(Decca LK/SKL 4940) 1968 SC
	2(A)	BORN TO TAKE THE HIGHWAY	
			(Decca SKL 5035) 1969

NB: (1) reissued on vinyl (Decca Eclipse ECS 2118) 1971.

45s: Reflections/Grandfather's Clock   (Decca F 12776) 1968
        Me And Bobby McGee/Feelin' Groovy   (York SYK 503) 1971

This quaint folk duo came from Yorkshire. (VJ)

Foghat

Personnel:	ROGER EARL	drms	ABC
	DAVE PEVERETT	gtr, vcls	ABC
	ROD PRICE	gtr, vcls	ABC
	TONE STEVENS	bs	A
	NICK JAMESON	bs	B
	CRAIG McGREGOR	bs	C

ALBUMS:	1(A)	FOGHAT	(Bearsville K 45503) 1972 SC
(up to	2(A)	FOGHAT (ROCK 'N' ROLL)	(Bearsville K 45514) 1973
1976)	3(A)	ENERGISED	(Bearsville K 55500) 1974
	4(B)	ROCK 'N' ROLL OUTLAWS	(Bearsville K 55502) 1974
	5(B)	FOOL FOR THE CITY	(Bearsville K 55507) 1975

NB: (2) and (3) reissued on a 2-CD set (Essential ESACD 741) 1999. (4) and (5) reissued on a 2-CD set (Essential ESACD 742) 1999. There are also three CD compilations, *The Best Of Foghat* (Sequel NEX CD 141) 1991, *The Best Of Foghat, Vol. 2* (Rhino RZ 705160) 1992 and *The Best Of Foghat* (Rhino RZ 71030) 1994. Now deleted but released in 1990 was *Foghat Live* (Sequel NEXCD 112) 1990. *Anthology* (Castle CCSCD 834) 1999 is a 2-CD collection.

45s:	What A Shame/Hole To Hide	(Bearsville K 15501) 1972
(up to	Long Way To Go/Ride Ride Ride	(Bearsville K 15511) 1974
1976)	Step Outside/Maybellene	(Bearsville K 15517) 1974
	Slow Ride/	
	Save Your Lovin' (For Me)	(Bearsville K 15522) 1976

Formed in December 1970, Peverett, Earl and Stevens had all previously played in **Savoy Brown**. They were 'unknowns' here in the UK, but enjoyed considerable popularity in the US where they toured continuously and were one of the biggest grossing acts on the US stadium circuit. Their musical style was a sort of blues/boogie similar to **The Climax Blues Band**.

Tone Stevens left the band early in 1975 and was replaced by Nick Jameson from Missouri. They also relocated to New York State the same year. They recorded into 1983 and also reformed for *Return Of The Boogie Men* (Modern) 1994.

Their music hasn't aged well and they're perhaps now best forgotten, but they were a good live act in their day. Dave Peverett died from cancer on 7 February 2000.

Anthology consists of their experimental first album on one disc and a selection of the best of their other material on the other. This consists mostly of blues-rock and driving hard-rock.

They turn up on a lot of compilations including: *Slow Ride* on *70's Arena Rockers* (CD); *Driving Wheel* on the 3-CD set *Metal*; *Live Now - Pay After* on the 12" LP *Double Hard*; and *Eight Days On The Road* can be heard on the CD-set *Rock Of Ages, Four Decades Of Heavy Rock 1962-2002*. (VJ)

Folkal Point

Personnel inc:	CHERIE MUSIALIK	vcls		A

ALBUM:	1 FOLKAL POINT	(Midas MR 003) 1972 R5

One of the more legendary UK folk private pressings, this Bristol band's sole outing features the attractively pure vocals of Cherie Musialik on an often unimaginative selection of material (Joan Baez's *Sweet Sir Galahad*, Joni Mitchell's *Circle Game*, Bob Dylan's *You Ain't Goin' Nowhere*, Tom Paxton's *Victoria Dines Alone*). The sparse acoustic backing is deft and beautifully recorded, but as a whole the album is let down by a lack of original songs or musical flourishes. Midas was a tiny local label, also responsible for ultra-rarities by **Gallery** and **The Oldest Profession**. It is rumoured that many of the original 500 copies of *Folkal Point* were swept away in a flood - a copy today would cost you well into four figures, anyway. Musialik is still playing around the Bristol area in a duo with Julian Reason. (RMJ)

A Folk Passion

ALBUM:	1 A FOLK PASSION	(Country) 1969 R4

This is an ultra-rare privately-pressed folk album with female vocals, electric guitar, organ, bass and drums format. There are some very strange instrumental parts and some traditional folk passages. Only a handful of copies are thought to exist. They came with a paste-on home-made sleeve and a twenty-page booklet. (VJ)

Wayne Fontana

ALBUM:	1 WAYNE ONE	(Fontana (S)TL 5351) 1966 SC

NB: (1) was reissued on Fontana (SFL 13144) in 1969 and on CD as *Wayne One Plus* (Beat Goes On BGOCD 663) 2005, a 2-CD set.

45s:	It Was Easier To Hurt Her/		
	You Made Me What I Am Today	(Fontana TF 642) 1965 36	
	Come On Home/		
	My Eyes Break Out In Tears	(Fontana TF 684) 1966 16	
	Goodbye Bluebird/		
	The Sun's So Hot Today	(Fontana TF 737) 1966 49	
	Pamela Pamela/		
	Something Keeps Calling Me Back	(Fontana TF 770) 1966 11	
	24 Sycamore/From A Boy To A Man	(Fontana TF 827) 1967 -	
	The Impossible Years/In My World	(Fontana TF 866) 1967 -	
	Gina/We All Love The Human Race	(Fontana TF 889) 1967 -	
	Storybook Children/		
	I Need To Love You	(Fontana TF 911) 1968 -	
	The Words Of Bartholomew/		
	Mind Excursion	(Fontana TF 933) 1968 -	
	Never An Everyday Thing/		
	Waiting For A Break In The Clouds	(Fontana TF 976) 1968 -	
	Dayton Ohio 1903/		
	Say Goodbye To Yesterday	(Fontana TF 1008) 1969 -	
	We're Building A Love/Charlie Cass	(Fontana TF 1054) 1969 -	
α	Charlie Cass/Linda	(Fontana TF 1054) 1969 SC -	
α	Give Me Just A Little More Time/		
	I'm In Love	(Philips 6006 035) 1970 SC -	
	Together/One Man Woman	(Warner Bros K 16269) 1973 -	
Reissue:	Pamela Pamela	(Old Gold OG 9473) 1985 -	

NB: α withdrawn.

After splitting from **The Mindbenders** in November 1965 **Wayne Fontana** embarked on a solo career, becoming a somewhat smoother pop singer. Relying on cover versions he found it difficult to establish himself as a successful solo artist. Early on he achieved modest success with covers of Garnett Mimms' *It Was Easier To Hurt Her*, Jackie Edwards' *Come On Home* and *Goodbye Bluebird*, it was not until **Graham Gouldman**'s *Pamela Pamela* that he achieved a really big hit. The truth was that his solo efforts lacked a cutting edge without **The Mindbenders** and despite a string of subsequent singles none of them was able to return him to the charts. By 1970 he'd abandoned his singing career in favour of songwriting for Chappell music publishers.

His album, originally issued in 1966, but reissued in 1969 was an unconvincing blend of originals, soul ballads and MOR pop.

Little more was heard of Wayne until 1973 when he put together a New Mindbenders who figured in the 'English Invasion Revival' tour of the US that year along with several old contemporaries. Later, after an unsuccessful comeback 45 for Polydor (*Last Bus Home* in 1976) he got together a new Mindbenders group in 1979 to perform his old hits. In 1982 he re-emerged in 'Heroes and Villains' nostalgia concert to celebrate 15 years of Radio One. In later years he was banished to the cabaret circuit but received more exposure in 1988 when *The Game Of Love* was featured in 'Good Morning Vietnam', a Robin Williams movie. You can also find it on *Remember The 60's* (CD) and on *The Swinging Sixties - 18 Classic Tracks*

FOLKAL POINT - Folkal Point (LP).

300

(CD); *Goodbye Bluebird* on *Made In England, Vol. 1* (CD); *A Groovy Kind Of Love* on *Everlasting Love* (CD), *60's Love Songs* (CD), *Brit Pop* (CD), *Dizzy* (CD), *Hits Of The 60's Vol 2* (CD) and on *Love Songs* (CD); *The Impossible Years* and *In My World* on *Fading Yellow, Vol 4* (CD); *The Words Of St Bartholomew* has resurfaced on *Pop-In, Vol 1* (CD); *Pamela Pamela* on *The Greatest Sixties Album Of All Times Vol 2* (CD); *Come On Home* and *Pamela Pamela* have resurfaced on *Hits Of The Sixties - 20 Swinging Sounds* (CD), whilst *Um, Um, Um, Um, Um* got a further airing on *Hits Of The 60's - Save The Last dance For Me* (CD). There's also an alternate take of *Pamela Pamela* on the 2-CD set *Greatest Hits Of The 60's*.

The *Wayne One Plus?* 2-CD set contains the album on one CD and his A and B sides on the other disc. (VJ)

Wayne Fontana and The Mindbenders

Personnel:
WAYNE FONTANA	vcls		A
BOB LAND	bs		A
RICK ROTHWELL	drms		A
ERIC STEWART	gtr		A

HCP

ALBUMS: 1(A) WAYNE FONTANA AND THE MINDBENDERS
(Fontana TL 5230) 1964 R2 18
2(A) ERIC, RICK, WAYNE, BOB - IT'S WAYNE FONTANA AND THE MINDBENDERS
(Fontana TL 5257) 1965 R1 -

NB: (1) reissued on Fontana (SFL 13106) in 1969 and on Wing (WL 1166) in 1967. (SC).

EPs: 1(A) ROAD RUNNER (Fontana TE 17421) 1964 R1
2(A) UM, UM, UM, UM, UM, UM (Fontana TE 17435) 1964 SC
3(A) THE GAME OF LOVE (Fontana TE 17449) 1965 SC
4(A) WALKING ON AIR (Fontana TE 17453) 1965 R1

HCP

45s: Hello! Josephine/Road Runner (Fontana TF 404) 1963 SC 46
For You, For You/Love Potion No. 9 (Fontana TF 418) 1963 -
Little Darlin'/Come Dance With Me (Fontana TF 436) 1964 -
Stop Look And Listen/Duke Of Earl (Fontana TF 451) 1964 37
Um, Um, Um, Um, Um, Um/
First Taste Of Love (Fontana TF 497) 1964 5
The Game Of Love/
Since You've Been Gone (Fontana TF 535) 1965 2
It's Just A Little Bit Too Late/
Long Time Comin' (Fontana TF 579) 1965 20
She Needs Love/Like I Did (Fontana TF 611) 1965 32
Reissues: Um, Um, Um, Um, Um, Um/
The Game Of Love (Fontana H 1022) 1969 -
The Game Of Love (Old Gold OG 9266) 1982 -
The Game Of Love (A&M AM 435) 1988 -

Wayne Fontana (whose real name was Glyn Ellis) formed his first outfit, The Jets, a semi-professional combo that worked the Manchester club circuit, whilst working as a telephone engineer. Prior to this he'd played in a school skiffle group, The Velfins. Their first break came when this rough and ready group was spotted playing at Manchester's Oasis Club by Fontana Records talent scout Jack Baverstock. However, at the sound check only Wayne and drummer Rick Rothwell had shown up and they'd had to frantically recruit a couple of substitutes, bassist Robert Land and guitarist Eric Stewart, to complete the band. Basically, the band members were competent musicians though a little short on imagination. **Fontana** decided to name his new backing group **The Mindbenders** after a psychological horror movie playing at his local cinema.

Predictably they made their vinyl debut with a series of cover versions. First off was their revival of Bo Diddley's *Hello Josephine*, which scraped into the lower reaches of the Top 50. Their next two discs, *For You, For You* and *Little Darlin'*, failed to capitalise on their limited early success, and it wasn't until their cover of Ben E. King's *Stop Look And Listen* that they enjoyed some further modest Chart success.

Their heady days began when they covered Major Lance's US hit, *Um, Um, Um, Um, Um, Um*, which had been written by Curtis Mayfield. It propelled

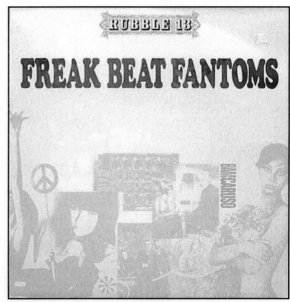

RUBBLE VOL. 13 (Comp LP) including Force Five.

them to No 5 in the UK Charts and the more accomplished follow-up, *Game Of Love*, a Hank Ballard Junior composition, won them international acclaim climbing to No 2 in the UK and No 1 in the US, where it became a million-seller. However, their opportunity to capitalise on their US success was largely frustrated by the US Immigration Authorities reluctance to grant them performance visas in the States until they had obtained evidence from 'Billboards' and 'Cash Box' magazines that their single was the topselling US record!

Their debut album consisted mostly of songs from their live act and a couple of originals including Eric Stewart and **Wayne Fontana**'s *One More Time*. The sales were promising and it peaked No 18 in the UK and No 58 in the US (where it was issued with slightly different tracks).

In retrospect their big error came when they turned down another Hank Ballard Junior composition on which they had first refusal (*I'm Alive*, which was later taken to No 1 by **The Hollies**) in favour of *It's Just A Bit Too Late*, which was only a minor hit on both sides of the Atlantic. When their self-penned follow-up, *She Needs Love*, was even less successful, the singer and group blamed each other for the decline in their fortunes and went their separate ways in November 1965. By that time their second album had been recorded, although it was not released until after they'd split and this was undoubtedly a factor in why it passed largely unnoticed.

For details of their future careers see the **Wayne Fontana** and **Mindbenders** entries.

Compilation appearances have included: *It's Just A Little Bit Too Late* and *Long Time Comin'* on *The Star-Club Singles Complete, Vol. 5* (LP & CD); *Love Potion Number Nine* on *Star-Club Show* (LP); *The Game Of Love* and *Since You've Been Gone* on *The Star-Club Singles Complete, Vol. 3* (LP & CD); *Um Um Um Um Um Um* on *Sweet Beat* (LP) and *Sixteen Star Tracks Of The Sixties* (LP) 1971; *The Game Of Love* on *The Star-Club Anthology, Vol. 1* (LP), *Best Of British Rock* (CD) and on the 2-CD set *Sixties Summer Love*; *It's Just A Little Bit Too Late* on *The Star-Club Anthology, Vol. 3* (LP); *A Groovy Kind Of Love* on *Cruisin' Classics* (CD); and *Road Runner* on *Beat Im Star Club* (2-LP) and *Beat Merchants* (2-LP). (VJ)

Force Five

Personnel:
RON GENT	vcls		A
PETE GOSLING	gtr		A
DAVE OSBOURNE	bs		A
BERT PULHAM	ld gtr		A
DAVE SKATES	drms		A

45s: Don't Make My Baby Blue/
Shaking Postman (United Artists UP 1051) 1964 SC
Yeah, I'm Waiting/I Don't Want
To See You Again (United Artists UP 1089) 1965 SC
Baby Don't Care/
Come Down To Earth (United Artists UP 1102) 1965 SC

FOREST - Forest (LP).

I Want You Babe/		
Gee Too Tiger	(United Artists UP 1118) 1965 R1	
Don't Know Which Way To Turn/		
Baby Let Your Hair Down	(United Artists UP 1141) 1966 R1	

Starting out as The Shadows in 1960, this band quickly changed name to The Whirlwinds. They became **Force Five** with the above line-up in 1962 and drew crowds at local gigs by playing covers of chart hits. Their second single was plugged on 'Ready Steady Go' but otherwise this beat group attracted little attention. They did back American singer Bobby Goldsboro, who was using the same studio as them at the time, on a 1966 'B' side, *No Fun At The Fair*. They later evolved into **Crocheted Doughnut Ring** with Rob Mills on vocals. He made a solo release in 1967 calling himself Daddy Linberg.

Their finest moment was *Yeah I'm Waiting* with its catchy chorus. Their fourth 45 got a US release on Ascot (2206) in 1966.

Compilation appearances have includes: *Yea I'm Waiting* on *Rubble, Vol. 13 - Freak Beat Fantoms* (LP), *Rubble, Vol. 7* (CD) and *The Best Of Rubble Collection, Vol. 4* (CD); *Don't Know Which Way To Turn* on *Yellow Elektric Years* (LP); and *Gee Too Tiger* on *Beat Us If You Can! Vol. 1* (LP). (VJ)

Force West

Personnel incl: DANNY CLARKE   vcls

45s:	I Can't Give What I Haven't Got/	
	Why Won't She Stay?	(Decca F 12223) 1965
	Gotta Find Another Baby/	
	Talkin' About Our Love	(Columbia DB 7908) 1966 SC
	When The Sun Comes Out (Weatherman)/	
	Gotta Tell Somebody	(Columbia DB 7963) 1966
	All The Children Sleep/Desolation	(Columbia DB 8174) 1967 SC
	I'll Walk In The Rain/What's It To Be	(CBS 3632) 1968
	I'll Be Moving On/Like The Tide The Ocean	(CBS 3798) 1968
	Sherry/Mr. Blue	(CBS 4385) 1969

Bristol was this band's home turf but they failed to make it into the big time. Their first 'A' side was written by Clive Westlake and featured him on piano.

Talkin' About Our Love has been compiled on *Beat Us If You Can! Vol. 1* (LP). (VJ)

Dean Ford and The Gaylords

Personnel:	JUNIOR CAMPBELL	gtr	AB
	RAYMOND DUFFY	drms	AB
	PAT FAIRLEY	gtr	AB
	DEAN FORD (THOMAS MacALEESE)	vcls	AB
	BILLY IRVING	bs	A
	GRAHAM KNIGHT	bs	B

ALBUM:	1	DEAN FORD	(EMI EMC 3079) 1975

NB: (1) is a solo album.

45s:	Twenty Miles/	
	What's The Matter With Me?	(Columbia DB 7264) 1964 SC
	Mr. Heartbreak's Here Instead/	
	I Won't	(Columbia DB 7402) 1964 SC
	The Name Game/	
	That Lonely Feeling	(Columbia DB 7610) 1965 SC
α	He's A Good Face (But He's Down And Out)/	
	You Know It Too	(Columbia DB 7805) 1966

NB: α credited to The Gaylords.

A Glasgow band who formed in 1963. Initially influenced by Cliff Richard and The Shadows they gradually expanded their live show to include an increasing number of black R&B songs, including a number of Stax and Motown favourites. By 1964 they were weekly guests on 'Come Thursday', a BBC Scotland TV magazine show and appeared regularly at The Picasso (Glasgow's top club in this era) with the **Alex Harvey Soul Band** among others. Down in London they often shared bills with **Brian Poole and The Tremeloes** whose manager, Peter Walsh, secured them a deal with EMI's Columbia label. For their debut disc they recorded Chubby Checker's *Twenty Miles*, which had been a mainstay of their live act backed by their own group composition, *What's The Matter With Me?* The follow-up *Mr. Heartbreak's Here Instead*, an early **Gallagher and Lyle** composition was weak and like their next 45, a cover of Shirley Ellis's *The Name Game*, attracted little attention. They abbreviated their name to The Gaylords for *He's A Good Face (But He's Down And Out)*, a popular mod song which did attract more airplay than the previous three efforts.

Duffy left in 1967 and they moved to CBS, changing name to **Marmalade**.

He's A Good Face, which was something of a minor mod classic, later resurfaced on *60's Back Beat* (LP). You can also find *The Name Game* on *Beat At Abbey Road* (CD) and *That Lonely Feeling* on *Fading Yellow* (CD). (VJ)

Ricky Ford (and The Tennesseans)

Personnel:	RICKY FORD	vcls	A
	DANNY DAVIS	ld gtr	A
	BARRY SARGEANT	drms	A
	KENNY SHERRATT	bs	A

45s:	Sweet And Tender Romance/	
	Cheat Cheat	(Parlophone R 5018) 1963
α	You Are My Love/	
	Long Way From Home	(Parlophone R 5230) 1964

NB: α with The Tennesseans.

Ricky Ford's backing band, The Tennesseans, actually comprised three of the five Marauders. Ricky was originally with **The Cyclones**, who later backed **Peter and Gordon**. (VJ)

The Forerunners

45:	Bony Moronie/Pride	(Solar SRP 100) 1964 R1

This was a short-lived beat group. *Bony Moronie* was a much covered Larry Williams number. (VJ)

Forest

Personnel:	DEREK ALLENBY	keyb'ds, vcls, hrmnca,	
		perc	AB
	MARTIN WELHAM	vcls, gtr, perc	AB
	HADRIAN WELHAM	gtr, keyb'ds, vcls,	

		hrmnca, perc	AB
(HUNTLEY GORDON		steel gtr	B)

ALBUMS: 1(A) FOREST   (Harvest SHVL 760) 1969 R2
        2(B) FULL CIRCLE   (Harvest SHVL 784) 1970 R2

NB: (1) and (2) reissued on one CD (Beat Goes On). (1) also reissued on Radioactive (LP & CD) 2005. (2) reissued on vinyl (Zap! ZAP 3) 1988.

45:      Searching For Shadows/Mirror Of Life (Harvest HAR 5007) 1969

Brothers Martin & (H)Adrian Welham had started playing folk music with their friend Dez Allenby while still schoolboys in Grimsby. Moving to the tiny village of Walesby in the mid-sixties, they named themselves The Foresters of Walesby and became regulars on the local club circuit, playing folk songs with their own distinctive brand of vocal harmonies. Dez and Martin went to Birmingham University in the autumn of 1967, but continued to play live and communicate with Adrian via tapes. Under the influence of the psychedelic movement they moved away from traditional material and began to devise their own idiosyncratic style, involving diverse instrumentation and more complex arrangements.

Moving to London under the patronage of John Peel, after a triumphant gig in Notting Hill's All Saints Hall they were offered a management deal with Blackhill Enterprises (home to **Pink Floyd** and **Roy Harper** amongst others) and soon afterwards got signed to EMI's nascent Harvest label. Their debut was made early in 1969 under the supervision of its head, Malcolm Jones, and turned out to be something special. In place of traditional material are their own uncommon compositions, most of which rely on strangely-sculpted melodies and partly-improvised accompaniment. Neither as malicious as **Comus**, nor as ironic as **Dr. Strangely Strange**, **Forest** manage to capture one of the essentials of British folk: closeness to the spirit of nature. A rare single featuring the non-album *Searching For Shadows* didn't help sales, but they played various BBC sessions and became regulars on the college circuit and festival scene, touring in what Peel's sleevenotes call 'a succession of the most absurd vans in living memory.'

Despite warm reviews their 1970 follow-up, *Full Circle*, also failed to sell, prompting Allenby's departure. On *Full Circle* the playing is more inspired and less sloppy, the melodies are better (check out the wriggling, shifting harmonies on *Don't Want To Go*) and the arrangements are inventive and sympathetic to the material. Overall it's nearly as strong as the debut, but the addition of steel guitar soups up the sound and partly destroys its magic. A few excellent tracks are still to be found, though, notably *Hawk The Hawker*, *Graveyard* and *Famine Song*. Naturally, it made no commercial impact whatsoever.

The brothers struggled on till 1973, but progressive rock was overshadowing the folk scene and when it became clear that EMI didn't intend to authorise a third album, they reluctantly called it a day.

A Glade Somewhere later resurfaced on Harvest's compilation, *Picnic* (2-LP). (MK/VJ/RMJ)

FOREST - Full Circle (LP).

The Foresters

Personnel incl: BERNIE HOLLAND   ld vcls

45s:	Broken Hearted Clown/Lonely Boy	(Polydor 56038) 1965
	How Can I Tell Her/So Shy(	Polydor 56057) 1965
	Early Morning Hours/World Is Mine	(Polydor 56104) 1966
α	Sometimes When You're Lonely/	
	Today Or Tomorrow	(Columbia DB 8040) 1966
	Mr. Smith/Ship On The Sea	(Columbia DB 8086) 1966
	Comin' Home In The Evening/	
α	Sunshine's On Its Way	(Columbia DB 8176) 1967

NB: α as The Forresters.

The band's lead vocalist could have been Bernie Holland who was later with **Ferris Wheel**. (VJ)

Forever Amber

Personnel:	BARRY BROAD	drms	A
	CHRISTOPHER JONES	gtr, vcls	A
	RICHARD LANE	ld gtr, vcls	A
	ANTHONY MUMFORD	bs, vcls	A
	CHRISTOPHER PARREN	organ, piano,	
		harpsichord, vcls	A
	MICHAEL RICHARDSON	vcls	A
	(JOHN M. HUDSON	piano, harpsichord	A)

ALBUM: 1(A) THE LOVE CYCLE   (Private Pressing) 1969 R6

NB: (1) reissued on Swank (VPAG LP 5299) in 1990 and on CD (Background HBG 122/7) 1992.

An absolute mega privately-pressed rarity - 99 copies were pressed originally and these change hands for around £1,000 or more. Its value is entirely due to its rarity: the vinyl contains pleasant enough concept pop with taints of psychedelia but it's nothing to rave about.

All the words and music on the album were written by John M. Hudson, who handled the vocal and instrumental arrangements with the group. Chris Parren later played piano on George Michael's *Careless Whisper*.

The Swank reissues (only a little over 100 were pressed) weren't taken from the original master tapes, which can't be traced and inevitably the quality suffers as a result. These, too, are now rare, but beware this album is no lost psychedelic nugget. The sound quality on the Background CD release is better, however. (VJ)

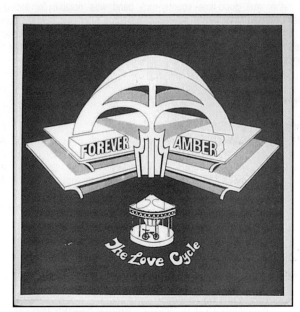

FOREVER AMBER - The Love Cycle (LP).

Forever More

Personnel:
ALAN GORRIE	lead vcls, bs, piano, teapot		A
STEWART FRANCIS	drms, vcls		A
ONNIE MAIR	gtr, bs, vcls		A
MICK TRAVIS	ld vcls, gtr		A

ALBUMS: 1(A) YOURS FOREVER MORE (RCA SF 8016) 1970 SC
2(A) WORDS ON BLACK PLASTIC (RCA LSA 3015) 1971 SC

45: Put Your Money On A Pony/Yours (RCA RCA 2024) 1970

A Scottish group based in London. Stewart was earlier in **Hopscotch**. They cut two good albums. The first had a red valentine heart cover in the USA and a black and white cover labelled "Paint It Yourself" in the UK. The album's standout track was *Back In The States Again*.

Molly Duncan played sax on one track on *Words On Black Plastic*, which was produced by Simon Napier-Bell.

Alan Gorrie and Onnie Mair (aka McIntyre) later formed Average White Band with Hamish Stuart (later of **Wings**) and Roger Ball and Molly Duncan (ex-**Mogul Thrash**). There was a Dundee connection between **Forever More** and Molly Duncan and Roger Ball. Stewart Francis formed **Glencoe**. (VJ/SR)

Format

Personnel:
JOEY BOWERS	gtr	A
BILLY HATTON	bs	A
DAVE LOVEDAY	drms	A
BRIAN O'HARA	vcls, ld gtr	A

45: Maxwell's Silver Hammer/Music Man (CBS 4600) 1969

A short-lived project by **The Fourmost** under a different name, which covered *Maxwell's Silver Hammer* from **The Beatles**' *Abbey Road* album. (VJ)

Formerly Fat Harry

Personnel:
LAURIE ALLEN	drms	A
BRUCE BARTHOL	bs	A
PHIL GREENBERG	vcls, gtr	A
GEORGE KHAN	sax	A
GARY PETERSON	vcls, gtr, keyb'ds, perc	A

ALBUM: 1(A) FORMERLY FAT HARRY (Harvest SHSP 4016) 1971 SC
NB: (1) issued on Capitol in the US.

This rather dull good-time country-rock band was notable for including former **Battered Ornaments**' saxophonist George Khan and former Country Joe and The Fish bassist Bruce Barthol. The album was eminently forgettable and the band was soon forgotten too. It split up soon after the album's release. (VJ)

Formula

Personnel:
BRUCE CAREY	bs	A
MARTIN FALLON	lead gtr	A
TOMMY GUTHRIE	drms	A
MIKE HARPER	vcls	A
KRU ZAKKES	sax, vcls	A

45: Close To Me/If Ever (HMV POP 1438) 1965

This is another forgotten mid-sixties band. (VJ)

Formula I

45: I Just Can't Go To Sleep/
Sure Know A Lot About Love (Warner Bros WB 155) 1965 SC

A different four-piece from Birmingham. The 'A' side was a **Kinks**' cover. (VJ)

Andy Forray

45s: Sarah Jane/Don't Care Anymore (Parlophone R 5715) 1968
The Proud One/
Messin' Round With Me (Parlophone R 5729) 1968
Epitaph To You/Dream With Me (Decca F 12733) 1968 R1
Let The Sun Shine In/Baby Is Coming (Fontana TF 999) 1969

Of **Andy Forray's** four singles it's the Decca one that excites collectors the most. *Dream With Me* can also be heard on *The Psychedelic Scene* (CD). (VJ)

Fortes Mentum

Personnel incl: DANNY BECKERMAN lead vcls A

45s: Saga Of A Wrinkled Man/Mister Partridge
Passed Away Today (Parlophone R 5684) 1968 SC
I Can't Go On Loving You/
Humdiggle We Love You (Parlophone R 5726) 1968
Gotta Go/Marrakesh (Parlophone R 5768) 1969

This group evolved into **Pussy**. *Saga Of A Wrinkled Man* is worth hearing - a lovely piano intro gives way to some choppy organ and then some typical 1968 pop-psych. Lead vocalist Danny Beckerman wrote their material.

Saga Of A Wrinkled Man has been compiled on *Morgan Blue Town* (LP) and *Best And Rest Of British Psychedelia* (CD). (VJ)

The Fortunes

Personnel:
ROD ALLEN	bs	ABCD
ANDY BROWN	drms	ABCD
DAVID CARR	keyb'ds	AB
GLEN DALE	gtr	A
BARRY PRITCHARD	gtr	ABCD
SHEL MACRAE	gtr, vcls	BCD
GEORGE McALLISTER		D

ALBUMS: 1(A) THE FORTUNES (mono/stereo)
(Decca LK/SKL 4736) 1965 R1/R2
2(B) THE FORTUNES (Capitol ST 21891) 1972 SC

NB: Compilations have included:- *Remembering The Fortunes* (Decca REM 2) 1976, *Hit Collection* (Eclecstar VCL 3) 1984 and the CD set *You've Got Your Troubles* (Deram 820 920-2) 1990, an excellent collection but it is confined to their recordings with Decca in the sixties. There's also a Dutch import, *Greatest Hits: Fortunes* (BR Music BRCD 27) 1988 and *Here It Comes Again* (CD) (Deram 844 011-2) 1995 is another compilation of their material. *Storm In A Teacup / Here It Comes That Rainy Day Feeling Again* (Beat Goes On BGOCD 310) 1996 repackages two of their US cash-in albums on one CD with sleevenotes by Alan Clayson.

EP: 1 YOU'VE GOT YOUR TROUBLES (Decca F 13891) 1980

HCP

45s: α Summertime Summertime/
I Love Her Still - some (PS) (Decca F 11718) 1963 R1/SC
Caroline/If You Don't Want Me Now (Decca F 11809) 1964 SC -
I Like The Look Of You/Come On Girl (Decca F 11912) 1964 -
Look Homeward Angel/
I'll Have My Tears To Remind Me (Decca F 11985) 1964 -
You've Got Your Troubles/
I've Got To Go (Decca F 12173) 1965 2
Here It Comes Again/
Things I Should Have Known (Decca F 12243) 1965 4
This Golden Ring/Someone To Care (Decca F 12321) 1966 15
You Gave Me Somebody To Love/
Silent Street (Decca F 12429) 1966 -
Is It Really Worth Your While?/
Am I Losing My Touch (Decca F 12485) 1966 -
Our Love Has Gone/Truly Yours (Decca F 12612) 1967 -
The Idol/His Smile Was A Lie (United Artists UP 1188) 1967 -

Loving Cup/		
An Hour At The Movies	(United Artists UP 2218) 1968	-
Seasons In The Sun/Louise	(United Artists UP 2239) 1968	-
Ballad Of The Alamo/		
Save A Little Dream	(United Artists UP 35027) 1969	-
β Lifetime Of Love/		
Sad Sad Sad	(United Artists UP 35054) 1970	-
Books And Films/Sad Sad Sad	(United Artists UP 35054) 1970	-
Here Comes That Rainy Day Feeling/		
Bad Side Of Town	(Capitol CL 15671) 1971	-
Freedom Come, Freedom Go/		
There's A Man	(Capitol CL 15693) 1971	6
Storm In A Teacup/		
I'm Not Following You	(Capitol CL 15707) 1972	7
Baby By The Way/Long Way Home	(Capitol CL 15719) 1972	-
Everything Is Out Of Season/		
Don't Sing To Me	(Capitol CL 15732) 1972	-
I Can't Remember When The Sun Went/		
Secret Love	(Capitol CL 15739) 1972	-
These Are The Good Old Days/		
Holy Roller	(Mooncrest MOON 51) 1975	-
I Can't Believe It's Over/		
Kentucky Girl	(Target TGT 135) 1977	-

Reissues: Here It Comes Again/
Our Love Has Gone   (Decca F 12874) 1969 -
You've Got Your Troubles/
You've Got To Go   (Decca F 12173) 1974 -
Seasons In The Sun/
Save A Little Dream   (United Artists UP 35663) 1974 -

NB: α as The Fortunes and The Cliftones. β Withdrawn. There's also a non-UK 45 of particular interest:- *Fire Brigade/Painting A Shadow* (United Artists 50280) 1968. Issued in the US, this is one of their better rock efforts, with a cover of **The Move** on the 'A' side.

This harmony-driven, Merseybeat-influenced beat band had its moments in the sun before retiring, like many of its contemporaries to the nostalgia circuit.

This Birmingham-based group was originally known as The Cliftones when it formed in September 1963 and their debut 45, a cover of the Jamies' *Summertime, Summertime* was credited to The Fortunes and The Cliftones.

They projected a clean cut image and sang a form of harmony pop which was typified by their next release, *Caroline*, a song which, despite its strong commercial appeal and regular airplay on Radio Caroline (which adopted it as its theme tune), surprisingly did not chart.

They had to wait until their fifth 45, *You've Got Your Troubles*, to enjoy a hit, but a sizeable hit it was, climbing to No 2 in the UK and No 7 in the US. Essentially a strong but inoffensive pop song it was a recipe for success which was repeated with *Here It Comes Again* and *This Golden Ring*, although the latter would prove to be their last hit for over five years. It followed a US tour with **Peter and Gordon** and **The Moody Blues**.

FOTHERINGAY - Fotheringay (LP).

In July 1966 Glen Dale left to go solo and was replaced by Scotsman Shel MacRae. The first 45 by the new line-up was *Is It Really Worth Your While?*, but it didn't quite make it into the Charts.

In August 1967 the group switched to United Artists. Their first release on the new label was a strong song, *The Idol*, which was inventive enough to deserve to be a hit, but perhaps because of their failure to come to terms with the onset of the psychedelic era it wasn't. Their subsequent singles for United Artists sold poorly but the group compensated for this by recording advertising jingles including *It's The Real Thing* for Coca Cola and touring the northern club circuit. Carr left the band in August 1968, leaving them to continue as a four-piece.

In June 1970 they recorded a cover of **Pickettywitch**'s *That Same Old Feeling*, which was a US-only release on World Pacific Records. It peaked at No 62 in the US Singles Chart.

1971 saw a switch to Capitol Records with writer/producer **Roger Cook** and Roger Greenaway being assigned to them. The first 45 from this new partnership, *Here Comes That Rainy Day Feeling*, didn't sell well here in the UK but it reached No 15 in the US. However, the follow-up, *Freedom Come, Freedom Go*, made the UK Top Ten, but could only manage No 72 in the US. They repeated their success in the UK with *Storm In A Teacup* and in truth their style had changed little from the mid-sixties. At this point Scotsman George McAllister joined their line-up but subsequent singles, including a version of *Seasons In The Sun*, failed to Chart. However, they went on to trade their harmony pop sound around the UK clubs for many years to come.

Barry Pritchard died on 11 January 1999. Rod Allen still leads a version of the band on the nostalgia circuit.

The band also featured on Decca's rare *At The Cavern* (LP) compilation, which was later reissued by See For Miles (on CD as *Live At The Cavern*), playing *She's Sure The Girl I Love* and *You've Really Got A Hold On Me*. *You've Got Your Troubles*, probably their best known number, can also be heard on *Stardust* (2-LP). Other compilation appearances have included:- *Caroline* on *Sixties Lost And Found, Vol. 3* (LP), *Pop Inside The '60s, Vol. 2* (CD) and *Sixties Explosion, Vol. 1* (CD); *You've Got Your Troubles* on *Best Of British Rock* (CD), *The Greatest Sixties Album Of All Time Vol 2* (CD), *The Swinging Sixties - 18 Classic Tracks* (CD), *Brit Pop* (CD) and *Hits Of The 60's Vol 2* (CD); *Here It Comes Again* on *A Whiter Shade Of Pale* (LP), *Hits Of The 60's Vol 2* (CD) and on *Hits Of The Sixties - 20 Swinging Sounds* (CD); *The Idol* on *Pop-In, Vol 2* (CD); *Cygnet Twitch* resurfaced on *Brum Beat, Vol. 1* (LP); *Here Comes That Rainy Day Feeling* can be heard on *70's Remembered* (CD) and *The Seventies Vol 2* (CD); *Freedom Come, Freedom Go* has resurfaced on *Hits Of The 70's* (CD) and you can check out *Storm In A Teacup* on *Hits Of The 70's Vol 2* (CD). (VJ/BM)

Fotheringay

Personnel:	GERRY CONWAY	drms	A
	SANDY DENNY	vcls	A
	JERRY DONAHUE	gtr, vcls	A
	PAT DONALDSON	bs	A
	TREVOR LUCAS	gtr, vcls	A

ALBUM: 1(A) FOTHERINGAY (Island ILPS 9125) 1970 R1/SC 18

NB: Original issues of (1) with 'i' logo R1, later issues with 'palm tree' logo SC. (1) issued on A&M in the US. Reissued on Hannibal (HNBL 4426) in 1987 and on CD (Hannibal HNCD 4426) in 1989. (1) reissued on CD again (Fledg'ling FLED 3044) 2004, remastered and with additional previously unreleased live cuts.

45:      Peace In The End/Winter Winds   (Island WIP 6085) 1970

This folk-rock group was formed by Australian **Trevor Lucas** when his previous group **Eclection** split. His then girlfriend, **Sandy Denny**, left **Fairport Convention** to set up the new band with him. However, despite Sandy being at the peak of her popularity - she was voted Britain's No 1 girl singer in a Melody Maker poll in 1970 - the band was relatively short-lived, lasting from March 1970 - January 1971, because it didn't enjoy the commercial success one might have expected. Sandy then embarked on a solo career before rejoining **Fairport Convention** in 1974. Donahue, Conway and Donaldson (who'd previously been with **Zoot Money**) became part of Mick Greenwood's backing group and **Trevor Lucas** became a producer for Island Records.

The *Fotheringay* album is by now considered to capture Denny's vocals at their best. Trevor Lucas (her husband) also sings on a lot of the tracks and provides a distinct contrast to her vocals. Sandy is probably at her very best on the exquisite traditional song *Banks Of The Nile*.

The band can also be heard playing *The Sea* on the *Bumpers* (2-LP) compilation. (VJ)

The Foundations

Personnel:

ERIC ALLENDALE	trombone	AB
PAT BURKE	sax	AB
CLEM CURTIS	vcls	A
MIKE ELLIOT	sax	A
TONY GOMEZ	organ	AB
TIM HARRIS	drms	AB
PETER MACBETH	bs	AB
ALLAN WARNER	lead gtr, vcls	AB
COLIN YOUNG	gtr, vcls	B

ALBUMS:
1(A) FROM THE FOUNDATIONS   (Pye NPL 18206) 1967 SC
2(A) ROCKING THE FOUNDATIONS
                (Pye NPL 18227) 1968 SC
3(A) THE FOUNDATIONS   (Marble Arch MALS 11571) 1968
4(B) DIGGING THE FOUNDATIONS
                (Pye N(S)PL 18290) 1969 SC
5(-) GOLDEN HOUR OF THE FOUNDATIONS
                (Pye GH 574) 1973

NB: US releases were different:- *Baby Now That I've Found You* (Uni 73016) 1967 and *Build Me Up Buttercup* (Uni 73043) 1968. (4) was also released in the US on Uni. (1) and (4) reissued on CD (Repertoire REP 4182-WZ) 1991 with all their non-album 45s from the period. There have also been two 'Best Of' collections on CD:- *Best Of The Foundations* (PRT PYC 4003) 1987 and *Golden Hour Of The Foundations Greatest Hits* (Knight KGHCD 104) 1990, but this was deleted in 1992. *Baby Now That I've Found You* (Sequel NEECD 300) 1998 is a 2-CD set. *Build Me Up Buttercup* (Castle CMETD 961) 2004 is a 3-CD set comprising all their Pye releases plus Clem Cutis's solo singles and a one-off recording by a New Foundations.

EPs: 1(A) IT'S ALL RIGHT   (Pye NEP 24297) 1968 SC

		HCP
45s:	Baby, Now That I've Found You/	
	Come On Back To Me (Pye 7N 17366) 1967	1
	Back On My Feet Again/	
	I Can Take Or Leave Your Loving (Pye 7N 17417) 1967	18
	Any Old Time (You're Lonely And Sad)/	
	We Are Happy People (Pye 7N 17503) 1968	48
	Build Me Up Buttercup/New Direction (Pye 7N 17636) 1968	2
	In The Bad Bad Old Days/Give Me Love (Pye 7N 17702) 1969	8
	Born To Live, Born To Die/	
	Why Did You Cry (Pye 7N 17809) 1969	46
	Baby I Couldn't See/Penny Sir (Pye 7N 17849) 1969	-
	Take A Girl Like You/	
	I'm Gonna Be A Rich Man (Pye 7N 17904) 1970	-
	I'm Gonna Be A Rich Man/	
	In The Beginning (Pye 7N 17956) 1970	-
	Stoney Ground/I'll Give You Love (MCA MCA 5075) 1971	-
Reissues:	Baby, Now Take I've Found You/Build Me Up Buttercup/	
	In The Bad Bad Old Days/	
	I Can Take Or Leave Your Loving (Pye BD 107) 1977	-
	Baby, Now That I've Found You/	
	Build Me Up Buttercup (Pye FBS 6) 1979	-
	Baby, Now That I've Found You/	
	Build Me Up Buttercup (Old Gold OG 9407) 1984	-
α	Baby, Now That I've Found You/	
	Build Me Up Buttercup (PRT 7 P 372) 1987	-

NB: α also issued in 12" format.

This multi-racial pop group hailed from London with personnel from London, Barbados, Ceylon (now Sri Lanka), Dominica and Jamaica. They were managed by Tony Macauley who wrote their material, some of it with John MacLeod. They enjoyed a string of hits with a series of straightforward pop songs with immediate commercial appeal and a soulful flavour. The most memorable of these were their debut 45, *Baby, Now That I've Found You*

(a No 1), *Build Me Up Buttercup* and *In The Bad Bad Old Days*. In 1968 Elliot left and Curtis was replaced by Colin Young, but by 1970 their appeal had eroded and they broke up. Despite their popularity at the time few people took much interest for some years afterwards.

In late 1998 *Build Me Up Buttercup* was repromoted on account of its appearance in the movie 'There's Something About Mary' and this prompted the release of the Sequel CD *Baby Now That I've Found You*, which combined their *From The Foundations* and *Digging The Foundations* albums and added another 20 bonus tracks, including the previously unreleased *Where The Fire Burns*.

Alan Warner was later in **Pluto**. *Baby, Now That I've Found You*, one of their finest moments, has resurfaced on Sequel's CD set, *Radio Two: Sound Of The Sixties, Nothing But No. 1 Love Songs* (CD), *U.K. No. 1 Hits Of The 60's* (CD), *Hits Of The 60's - 20 Swinging Sounds* (CD), *No 1s & Million Sellers Vol 2* (CD), *Here Comes Summer* (CD), *60's Mix* (CD), *Hits Of The 60's Vol 2* (CD), *Hits Of The 60's - Save The Last Dance For Me* (CD); *Love Is All Around* (CD); the 2-CD set *60 Number Ones Of The Sixties* and on *Remember The 60's* (CD). In addition, an alternate take of *Baby Now That I've Found You* can be heard on the 2-CD set *Greatest Hits Of The Sixties*. *Build Me Up Buttercup*, another of their best-known songs, has got fresh exposure on *The Best Summer Ever!* (CD), *Everlasting Love* (CD), *Super Hits Of The 60s - Vol 3* (CD), *No 1s & Million Sellers Vol 1* (CD), *20 Hits Of The 60's* (CD), *Here Comes Summer* (CD), *Brit Pop* (CD), *Hits Of The 70's* (CD), and *Hits Of The 70's Vol 3* (CD). You can also find *Jerkin' The Dog* (from their first album) on *Doin' The Mod, Vol. 2* (CD) and *In The Bad Bad Old Days* on *Hits Of The Swinging Sixties* (CD). (VJ)

The 4

45:    It's Alright/There's Nothing Like It   (Decca F 11999) 1964 SC

This was a short-lived beat group. *It's Alright* was an Impressions track. (VJ)

The Four Just Men

See **The Just Four Men**. (VJ)

The Four Kingsmen

Personnel:

REG AYERS	bs, vcls	A
ANDREW CULVERWELL	electric piano, vcls	A
DON MORGAN	drms	A
MIKE TOZER	ld gtr, vcls	AB
CHRIS ALLEN	drms	B
ANDY LEGG	bs	B

EPs: 1(A) WHEREVER HE GOES   (Herald ELR 1080) 196?
       2(B) THE FOUR KINGSMEN   (Cathedral CRL 1013) 196?

A gospel beat group from Wells in Somerset. I'm unsure which order the EPs were released in. Both featured four cuts. Aside from the title track, *Wherever He Goes* featured *My Wondrous Friend*, *Tra-La-La* and *I'll Go To Cavalry*. The eponymous EP contained *That's How The World Goes Around*, *Prayer*, *Watcha Gonna Do* and *The Joy Of Living*. They frequently visited prisons, borstals, remand homes, churches, halls, coffee-bars, dance halls and clubs and took part in a "Sunday Break" programme for Channel Television during "Crusade '65". (VJ)

The Four Kinsmen

45:    It Looks Like The Daybreak/
       Forget About Him   (Decca F 22671) 1967

This was another short-lived and obscure sixties combo. *It Looks Like The Daybreak* can also be heard on *Spinning Wheel* (CD). (VJ)

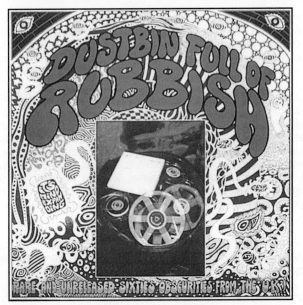

DUSTBIN FULL OF RUBBISH (Comp LP) including Four Leaved Clovers.

Four Leaved Clovers

Personnel:
PAUL CHELTON	drms		A
DES GATES	gtr		A
TONY PIPE	ld gtr		A
DENNIS SABOURN	bs		A

45:    Alright Girl/Why   (Oak RGJ 207) 1965 R4

A Kingston-Upon-Thames beat group who cut this obscure 45 which was released in an edition of just 200 copies on the now highly collectable Oak label. *Why* was a harmony-tinged pop number, *Alright Girl* veered towards the emerging mod style of bands like **The Who** and **The Small Faces**. Inevitably it's now an ultra-rarity. The group's name was misspelt on the 45 with the 's' being omitted from the end of Clover.

Alright Girl has been compiled on *Story Of Oak Records* (2-LP)/*The Story Of Oak Records* (CD) and *Dustbin Full Of Rubbish* (LP). (VJ)

The Four Macs

Personnel:
DAVID BOOKER	gtr		A
RON BROWN	drms		A
PETER DUDMAN	piano		A
TOMMY QUARTER	bs		A

45:    Come Back Silly Girl/Darlin'   (Parlophone R 5204) 1964

An Ealing-based beat group that later became **The Sands Of Time**. (VJ)

The Four Matadors

45:    A Man's Gotta Stand Tall/
Fast Cars And Money   (Columbia DB 7806) 1966 R2

Another forgotten band. This mid-tempo beat effort was produced by Joe Meek.

You'll also find *A Man's Gotta Stand Tall* on *RGM Rarities, Vol. 2* (CD). (VJ)

The Fourmost

Personnel:
BILLY HATTON	bs		AB
DAVE LOVELADY	drms		AB
MIKE MILLWARD	gtr		A
BRIAN O'HARA	lead gtr		AB
BILL PARKINSON	gtr		B

ALBUMS: 1(A) FIRST AND FOURMOST (Parlophone PMC 1259) 1965 R2
        2( ) THE FOURMOST   (Fourmost SOF 001) 1975

NB: (1) reissued on See For Miles (CM 104) 1982 and Beat Goes On (BGOLP 51) 1989. (1) reissued as a digipak CD, combining both mono and stereo versions (EMI DORIG 116) 1997. There's also a compilation, *Best Of The EMI Years: Fourmost* (EMI CDEMS 1449) 1992.

EPs: 1(A) THE SOUND OF THE FOURMOST
            (Parlophone GEP 8892) 1964 R2
        2(A) THE FOURMOST   (Parlophone GEP 8917) 1964 R2

HCP

45s:			
	Hello Little Girl/Just In Case	(Parlophone R 5056) 1963	9
	I'm In Love/Respectable	(Parlophone R 5078) 1963	17
	A Little Loving/Waitin' For You	(Parlophone R 5128) 1964	6
	How Can I Tell Her/		
	You Got That Way	(Parlophone R 5157) 1964	33
	Baby I Need Your Loving/		
	That's Only What They Say	(Parlophone R 5194) 1964	24
	Everything In The Garden/		
	He Could Never	(Parlophone R 5304) 1965	-
	Girls Girls Girls/		
	Why Do Fools Fall In Love	(Parlophone R 5379) 1965	33
	Here, There And Everywhere/		
	You've Changed		
	(Parlophone R 5491) 1966 -		
	About Maggie's Remedy/		
	Turn The Lights Down	(Parlophone R 5528) 1966 SC -	
	Apples, Peaches, Pumpkin Pie/		
	He Could Never	(CBS 3814) 1968 SC -	
	Rosetta/Just Like Before	(CBS 4041) 1969 SC -	
	Easy Squeezy/Do I Love You	(CBS 4461) 1969 SC -	
Reissue:	Hello Girl/I'm In Love/A Little Lovin'/		
	I Need Your Loving	(EMI EMI 2695) 1977 -	

The roots of this Merseybeat band go back to Liverpool's Bluecoat Grammar School where Liverpudlians Hatton and O'Hara were in a part-time band known as The Four Jays in the late fifties and early sixties. The Four Jays' great claim to fame is that they debuted at Liverpool's Cavern Club on 1 March 1961, 20 days before **The Beatles'** first appearance there. They also got to back Billy Fury on his 1960 debut album *Sound Of Fury*. By September 1962 Millward (the only non-Liverpudlian in the band - he came from Cheshire) and Lovelady had been recruited when the guitar and the drum slots became vacant and by November that year they had turned professional changing their name to The Four Mosts.

Their big break came in June 1963 when Brian Epstein became their manager, modifying their name to **The Fourmost** and getting them a contract with EMI's Parlophone label. The Epstein connection ensured them relatively strong material and for their first single they recorded a **Lennon/McCartney** song which had previously been offered to **Gerry Marsden**. It made the Top 10. Epstein was also careful to exploit **The Beatles'** connection in their favour and they supported **The Beatles** in their Christmas show at The Finsbury Park Astoria in December 1963. The follow-up was another **Lennon/McCartney** composition, albeit a lightweight soft-rocker, *I'm In Love*, which stiffed at No 17, in 1964. Later in the year they enjoyed an eight-months residency with **Cilla Black** in the 'Startime' variety show at the London Palladium. During this time they achieved their biggest hit with Russ Alquist's *A Little Loving*, which achieved the No 6 spot. Thereafter, it was all downhill really, in commercial terms at least. *How Can I Tell Her* didn't quite make the Top 30 but is of some interest for its rather unusual march time. Their replica of The Four Tops' first UK 45, *Baby I Need Your Loving* did return them to the Top 30, though it couldn't manage the Top 20, but caused some dissent by breaking an agreement that EMI, as Motown's UK distributor, would not release singles which were cover versions of Motown's singles.

January 1965 saw the group appear in **Gerry and The Pacemakers'** film 'Ferry Cross The Mersey'. They played *I Love You Too*, portraying the losers in a Battle of the Bands competition. In April 1965 they toured the UK with **Cilla Black** and P.J. Proby, but by now the Merseybeat sound was in decline and their next 45, *Everything In The Garden*, sold disappointingly as did their album, *First And Fourmost*. The album, which was largely comprised of cover versions of US rock and pop songs, is now very hard to track down and an expensive purchase. Their final Chart success was *Girls Girls Girls*, a Leiber/Stoller song earlier recorded by Elvis Presley and The Coasters, which reached No 33.

By 1966 the band's progress was further impeded by the fact that Mike Millward had developed leukaemia. He was soon forced to leave the band and was replaced by Bill Parkinson. (Sadly, Millward died within the year). By now the band had lost all momentum and not even a cover of **The Beatles**' *Here There And Everywhere* was able to propel them back into the charts. In the wake of **The New Vaudeville Band**'s old tyme revival of *Winchester Cathedral*, **The Fourmost** turned next to George Formby's *Aunt Maggie's Remedy*, but again the punters were no longer interested.

In 1967 the group switched to CBS but their subsequent singles, including a cover of Jay and The Techniques' US hit, *Apples, Peaches, Pumpkin Pie*, and the **Paul McCartney**-produced *Rosetta*, also failed. The group continued for a few years on the cabaret circuit before its members drifted away from the music business altogether. They also recorded a 1969 45 for CBS as **Format**.

Compilation appearances have included: *Everything In The Garden* on *Liverpool 1963-1968* (CD) and *Liverpool 1963-1968, Vol. 1* (LP); *Baby, I Need Your Loving* on *Mersey Beat* (2-LP) and *Beat Generation - Ready Steady Go* (CD); *I'm In Love* and *Hello Little Girl* on *Songs Lennon And McCartney Gave Away* (LP); *I'm In Love* on *Beat At Abbey Road* (CD); *I Love You Too* on *Ferry Cross The Mersey* (LP); *Hello Little Girl* on *Hits Of The Mersey Era, Vol. 1* (LP); *A Little Loving* (alternate take) on the 2-CD set *Greatest Hits Of The Sixties*; *A Little Loving* on *Hits Of The 60's Vol 2* (CD) and *Dizzy* (CD), whilst *A Little Loving* and *Hello Little Girl* have been complied on *Hits Of The 60's - Save The Last Dance For Me* (CD) and the 2-CD set *Greatest Hits Of The 60's Vol 4*. (VJ/LBy)

Fourmyula

45:     Honey Chile/Come With Me   (Columbia DB 8549) 1969

This was a short-lived venture which covered a **Hendrix** classic on the 'A' side. (VJ)

The Four Pennies

Personnel:			
	ALAN BUCK	drms	A
	FRITZ FRYER	ld gtr, bs	A
	LIONEL MORTON	gtr, vcls	A
	MIKE WILSHER	gtr, piano	A

				HCP
ALBUMS:	1(A)	TWO SIDES OF THE FOUR PENNIES		
			(Philips BL 7642) 1964	R2 13
	2(A)	MIXED BAG	(Philips BL 7734) 1966	R3 -
	3(A)	JULIET	(Wing WL 1146) 1967	SC -

NB: (1) and (2) reissued on one CD (Beat Goes On BGOCD 345) 1997.

EPs:	1(A)	THE FOUR PENNIES	(Philips BBE 12561) 1964 SC
	2(A)	SPIN WITH THE PENNIES	(Philips BBE 12562) 1964 SC
	3(A)	THE SWINGING SIDE OF THE FOUR PENNIES	
			(Philips BBE 12570) 1964 SC
	4(A)	THE SMOOTH SIDE OF THE FOUR PENNIES	
			(Philips BBE 12571) 1964 SC

			HCP
45s:	Do You Want Me To/Miss Bad Daddy	(Philips BF 1296) 1963	47
	Juliet/Tell Me Girl	(Philips BF 1322) 1964	1
	I Found Out The Hard Way/		
	Don't Tell Me You Love Me	(Philips BF 1349) 1964	14
	Black Girl/You Went Away	(Philips BF 1366) 1964	20
	The Way Of Love/		
	A Place Where No-One Goes	(Philips BF 1398) 1965	-
	Until It's Time For You To Go/		
	Till Another Day	(Philips BF 1435) 1965	19
	Trouble Is My Middle Name/		
	Way Out Love	(Philips BF 1469) 1966	32
	Keep The Freeway Open/Square Peg	(Philips BF 1491) 1966	-
	No Sad Songs For Me/Cats	(Philips BF 1519) 1966	-
Reissue:	Juliet/(Flip by different artist)	(Old Gold OG 9251) 1982	-

From Blackburn in Lancashire this outfit was originally known as The Lionel Morton Four. Morton had been in the choir of Blackburn Cathedral, whilst Buck had previously played in several other bands including those of

Johnny Kidd and Joe Brown. They were certainly one of the more talented groups of this era and had the added advantage of being able to write most of their own material. There was also an American band of the same name who recorded on Stateside but this seemed to have escaped the band's attention.

The group had a wide musical range but in commercial terms certainly seem to have fared best with ballads. After enjoying minor success with their debut 45, *Do You Want Me To*, the 'B' side of their next 45, *Juliet*, was hastily flipped to the 'A' side after attracting airplay and proceeded to replace **The Searchers** at No 1 in May 1964. They may well be the only band to enjoy a No 1 in this way in Britain. This was to prove their only big hit, although the follow-up, a tearjerker, *I Found Out The Hard Way*, managed the UK Top 20. A cover of Leadbelly's *Black Girl*, was much more uptempo, and like their rework of Buffy St. Marie's *Until It's Time For You To Go*, achieved some chart success.

Rather like **The Fourmost** their Merseybeat sound had become passé by 1966 and after a final 45, Tom Springfield's *No Sad Songs For Me*, in October 1966, they split up.

Lionel Morton was first to depart to become a children's TV personality (he was also married to actress Julia Foster for a while). Fritz Fryer went on to form **Fritz, Mike and Mo** but rejoined **The Four Pennies** in April 1966. Later Fritz Fryer went into production with Motorhead and Squeeze. Buck worked in the music industry in various roles and tried unsuccessfully to reform the band to work the cabaret circuit in the seventies. All three of their albums are now quite collectable but *Mixed Bag* is a particularly expensive purchase nowadays.

In retrospect, along with **The Searchers**, they are seen as pioneers of the British folk-rock sound.

Juliet can also be heard on *Beat Merchants* (2-LP), *Nothing But No 1 Love Songs* (CD), *U.K. No. 1 Hits Of The 60's* (CD), *30 Years Of Number 1 Hit Singles - 1960/1989* (CD) and on *Hits of The 60's - Save The Last Dance For Me* (CD). (VJ)

Four Plus One

Personnel:			
	SIMON ALCOT	bs	A
	LES JONES	ld gtr	A
	KEN LAWRENCE	drms	A
	KEITH WEST	vcls	A
	JOHN 'JUNIOR' WOOD	gtr	A

45:	Time Is On My Side/		
	Don't Lie To Me	(Parlophone R 5221) 1964	R2

After recording this one 45 the band (minus Jones) evolved into **The In Crowd** with the addition of **Steve Howe** from **The Syndicats**. *Time Is On My Side* was an Irma Thomas soul number and the flip *Don't Lie To Me* rather bluesy.

FOX - For Fox Sake (LP).

Compilation appearances have included: *Time Is On My Side* and *Don't Lie To Me* on *Keith West - Excerpts From - Groups And Sessions 1965-1974* (CD); and *Don't Lie To Me* on *The Demention Of Sound* (LP) and *English Freakbeat, Vol. 5* (CD). (VJ)

The Four Sights

45:     But I Can Tell/And I Cry   (Columbia DB 7227) 1964

This beat group's sole vinyl offering was this 45. (MWh)

The Fox (1)

Personnel:	STEVE BRAYNE	gtr	A
	ALEX LANE	keyb'ds	A
	TIM REEVES	drms	A
	WINSTON WEATHERILL	gtr, sitar	A
	DAVID WINDROSS	bs, piano	A

ALBUM: 1(A) FOR FOX SAKE   (Fontana 6309 007) 1970 R2

NB: (1) issued in the US on Crewe (CR 1336) also reissued on CD (Flash 34) 1997, with the US sleeve. (1) reissued on CD again (RPM BC 254) 2003.

45:     Second Hand Love/Butterfly   (Fontana 6007 016) 1970 SC

A group of good musicians from Brighton who specialised in tuneful songs very much in the style of **Nirvana** or US bands like Phluph or Aorta and who deserved more success than they achieved. Their recordings are now very rare and sought-after, but *Butterfly*, which typified their style with some exquisite guitar and sitar work, later re-emerged on *Rubble Vol. 4: 49 Minute Technicolour Dream* (LP), *Rubble Vol. 3* (CD) and *Electric Psychedelic Sitar Headswirlers Vol. 6* (CD). Not all the tracks on the album work well, though. Some, like *Secondhand Love* or *Mr. Blank* have intriguing melodies and nice organ/guitar interplay, while there also are mistakes such as *Goodtime Music*, which sounds like a parody of **Them**, but certainly is not. The most psychedelic track is *Madame Magical (9'38")* with metre-changes and funny organ. If you want to hear this, buy the American issue in a much better cover and for a third of the price of the British one, or check out the recent reissue. (VJ/MK)

Fox (2)

45:     Hey! Mister Carpenter/Seek And You Find (CBS 3381) 1968 R2

This rare 45 may be by the previous band or a different one. The 'A' side is very poppy with a repetitive chorus and some catchy guitar. The flip is much heavier.

Compilation appearances have included: *Seek And You Find* and *Hey! Mr. Carpenter* on *Rubble, Vol. 17 - A Trip In A Painted World* (LP) and *Rubble, Vol. 10* (CD); *Hey! Mr Carpenter* on *We Can Fly, Vol 1* (CD) and *The Best Of Rubble Collection, Vol. 2* (CD); and *Seek And You Find* on *The Best Of Rubble Collection, Vol. 5* (CD). (VJ)

Fox (3)

Personnel:	HERBIE ARMSTRONG	gtr, vcls	A
	NOOSHA FOX		
	(SUSAN TRAYNOR)	vcls	A
	JIM FRANK	drms, perc, vcls	A
	JIM GANNON	gtr, vcls	A
	PETE SOLLEY	keyb'ds, vcls	A
	GARY TAYLOR	bs, vcls	A
	KENNY YOUNG	gtr, vcls	A

ALBUMS:	1(A)	FOX	(GTO GTLP 001) 1975 7
	2(A)	TALES OF ILLUSION	(GTO GTLP 006) 1975 -
	3(A)	BLUE HOTEL	(GTO GTLP 020) 1977 -

NB: (2) reissued on CD (Cherry Red CDM RED 263) 2004, with two previously unreleased bonus tracks.

			HCP
45s:	Only You Can/Out Of My Body	(GTO GT 5) 1974 -
	Only You Can/Out Of My Body	(GTO GT 8) 1975 3
	Imagine Me, Imagine You/	
	If I Point At The Moon	(GTO GT 21) 1975 15
	He's Got Magic/Love Ship	(GTO GT 37) 1975 -
	Strange Ships/Little Brown Box	(GTO GT 41) 1975 -
	S-ssingle Bed/Silk Milk	(GTO GT 57) 1976 4

The band's sound was moulded by the female vocals of Noosha Fox, an Australian who launched a solo career when they split. They enjoyed considerable commercial success in their relatively short lifespan, particularly with two of their 45s, *Only You Can* and *S-ssingle Bed*.

Their main songwriter/producer Kenny Young wrote most of the material for *Tails Of Illusion* on the beautiful Indonesian island of Bali. Noosha's unique dreamlike vocals provide special quality to songs like *Survival*, *Yuli Yuli* and *Strange Ships*. *Kupu Kupu* features lovely harmonies with Noosha's vocals hovering above. As well as the wonderful harmonies there is some lovely Balinese influenced instrumentation, making this an album well worth investigation.

Noosha Fox, she of the sexy voice, left the group in 1977 to go solo. Surprisingly, she achieved only one solo hit, *Georgina Bailey*. Nonetheless, her departure spelt the death knell of the group, which split after the mediocre *Blue Hotel* album. Irishman and ex-**Wheels** guitarist Herbie Armstrong and Kenny Young were later in Yellow Dog and Armstrong worked with **Van Morrison** in the late seventies and early eighties. (VJ)

Frabjoy and Runcible Spoon

Personnel:	KEVIN GODLEY	A
	GRAHAM GOULDMAN	A

45:     I'm Beside Myself/Animal Song   (Marmalade 598 019) 1969 SC

Future **10cc** members Godley and **Gouldman** were both with **The Mockingbirds** when they recorded this 45. *I'm Beside Myself* can also be heard on *Colour Me Pop, Vol 1* (CD) and *Animal Song* has resurfaced on *Fading Yellow, Vol 4* (CD). (VJ)

Frame

45s:	My Feet Don't Fit His Shoes/She	(RCA RCA 1556) 1966
	Doctor Doctor/I Can't Go On	(RCA RCA 1571) 1967 R2
	Rockin' Machine/One More Time	(Pye 7N 45213) 1970

A mod-influenced band judging by their two RCA 45s, of which the **Who**-influenced mod-beat song *Doctor Doctor* is the best known. Birmingham was the band's home. The third single on Pye may be the work of a different band.

Compilation appearances include: *My Feet Don't Fit His Shoes* on *Magic Spectacles* (CD); and *Doctor Doctor* on *Perfumed Garden, Vol. 1* (LP & CD) and *English Freakbeat, Vol. 3* (LP). (VJ)

Peter Frampton

				HCP
ALBUMS:	1	WIND OF CHANGE	(A&M AMLS 68099) 1972 SC -
(up to	2	FRAMPTON'S CAMEL	(A&M AMLH 68150) 1973 SC -
1976)	3	SOMETHING'S HAPPENING	(A&M AMLH 63619) 1974 -
	4	FRAMPTON	(A&M AMLH 64512) 1975 -
	5	FRAMPTON COMES ALIVE (2-LP)	
			(A&M AMLG 63703) 1975 6

NB: (4) reissued on CD (A&M 394 512-2) 1998. (5) reissued on CD (A&M 396 505-2) 1988, but deleted in 1991. (5) reissued again on CD (A&M 540 930 2) 1998. *Shine On* (Virgin CDMID 174) is a near perfect double-CD set which overviews his solo career. *Shows The Way* (Spectrum) is a mid-price compilation of his hits and *Greatest Hits* (A&M 540 557 2) 1998 is a more recent hits collection.

			HCP
45s:	It's A Plain Shame/Oh For Another Day	(A&M AMS 7025) 1972 -
(up to α	All Night Long/Don't Fade Away	(A&M AMS 7069) 1973 -
1976)	Show Me The Way/Crying Clown	(A&M AMS 7174) 1975 -

Show Me The Way/Shine On		
Baby I Love Your Ways/	(A&M AMS 7218) 1976	10
I'll Give You Money	(A&M AMS 7246) 1976	43
Do You Feel Like We Do/		
Penny For Your Thoughts	(A&M AMS 7260) 1976	39

NB: α as Frampton's Camel.

Peter Frampton was an example of a rock star made great by a live album. The 2-LP set *Frampton Comes Alive* made him one of the biggest arenas rock stars of the seventies, but in the eighties his career lost all direction.

Frampton was born on 22nd April 1950 in Beckenham, Kent, and blessed with very good looks which would be an asset throughout his career. He first caught the public eye as a member of the late sixties outfit **The Herd**. Later in 1969 he co-founded **Humble Pie** with ex-**Small Faces** singer **Stevie Marriott**. When he left **Humble Pie** in October 1971 he signed to A&M as a solo artist and recorded *Winds Of Change* with assistance from **Ringo Starr**, Billy Preston and other session men. However, later that year he formed his own band, Frampton's Camel (Mike Kellie (drms) (who was later in The Only Ones), Mickey Gallagher (keyb'ds), and Rick Wills (bs)). All three had previously left **Parrish and Gurvitz** although Kellie had also been in **Spooky Tooth**, Gallagher in **Bell and Arc** and Wills in **Cochise**. By the time of the *Frampton's Camel* album Kellie had been replaced by American John Siomos who'd beaten the skins for Mitch Ryder and a cult soul/funk group called Voices Of East Harlem. The album met with limited success in the States, where it peaked at No 110 but was largely ignored here in the UK. This probably led **Frampton** to target the lucrative US market, for the next album (which omitted the Camel from the band's title) and made No 25 in the US Album Charts but again passed largely unnoticed over here. After this album Gallagher left to join **Glencoe**. His replacement was **Alan Bown** (who'd also played with **Frampton** in **The Herd**). **Bown** shortly found himself playing bass as well as keyboards when Wills departed for **Roxy Music**. This new three-piece recorded *Frampton* which again did pretty well in the US climbing to No 32.

Frampton's really big breakthrough came with the double live set, *Frampton Comes Alive*, which was recorded at the Winterland in San Francisco. In fact, it became the most successful live album in rock history at that time, selling in excess of ten million copies. It made No 6 in the UK Album Charts. It topped the US Album Charts on four separate occasions during 1976 and was without doubt a stunning performance. It was also the subject of a phenomenal marketing hype. Most of its finest moments appeared on 45s and were consequently also hit singles. **Show Me The Way** (US No 6, UK No 10) featured his 'voicebox' guitar technique of forming words by channelling the sound through a mouthpiece; *Baby I Love Your Way* made No 12 in the US but only No 43 in the UK and *Do You Feel Like We Do* made No 10 in the US and No 39 in the UK.

Frampton Comes Alive was certainly his magnum opus although he continued to enjoy further spasmodic success during the rest of the seventies and the eighties, although his flirtation with acting (in Robert

PETER FRAMPTON - Frampton Comes Alive (LP).

Stigwood's film 'Sergeant Pepper's Lonely Hearts Club Band') was less successful.

In June 1978 he survived a serious car crash in the Bahamas in which he was concussed and suffered a number of broken bones and muscle damage, but then slipped into a drug problem. For most of the eighties his career was directionless although he continued to record.

Recently he's veered more towards session work and he recorded a solo album *Relativity* in 1994. In 1995, he recorded a new live album *Frampton Comes Alive II*. In the late nineties he recorded and toured with Bill Wyman and The Rhythm Kings and **Ringo Starr**'s All-Starr Band. In recent years he's recorded mostly live albums. (VJ)

Peter Franc

ALBUMS:	1	PROFILE	(Dawn DNLS 3043) 1972 SC
	2	EN ROUTE	(Dawn DNLS 3051) 1973 SC

45s:	I'll Move Along/Song For Every Season	(Dawn DNS 1033) 1972
	Ballad Of The Superstar/	
	Strange Kind Of Woman	(Dawn DNS 1039) 1973
	Flag Of Convenience/At Home With You	(Dawn DNS 1088) 1974

A singer/songwriter. (VJ)

Ritchie Francis

ALBUM:	1	SONGBIRD	(Pegasus PEG 11) 1971 SC

NB: (1) was also issued on Intercord.

This was a solo effort by **Francis**, who had earlier been a guitarist in **The Eyes Of Blue** and **Big Sleep**. (VJ)

Jackson C. Frank

ALBUM:	1	JACKSON C. FRANK	(Columbia 33SX 1788) 1965 R3

NB: (1) was later reissued as *Again* (B&C BCLP 4) 1978 R4.

45:	Blues Run The Game/	
	Can't Get Away From My Love	(Columbia DB 7795) 1965

This extremely rare and highly-rated downer folk album was produced by Paul Simon and featured **Al Stewart**. Tracks include *Blues Run The Game*, *Don't Look Back*, *You Never Wanted Me*, *Milk And Honey*, etc. The 45 has a completely different version of *Blues Run The Game* than is on the album with a folk-rock backing. (VJ/RMJ)

Frankie and Johnny

Personnel incl:	MAGGIE BELL	vcls	A
	BOBBY KERR	vcls	A

45s:	I'm Never Gonna Leave You/	
	I'll Hold You	(Decca F 22376) 1966 R2
	Climb Every Mountain/	
	I Wanna Make You Understand	(Parlophone R 5518) 1966

A short-lived duo notable for the inclusion of future **Stone The Crows** vocalist **Maggie Bell**. The combination was completed by ex-Rambler Bobby Kerr. The singles were spirited but lacking in subtlety. The first one is now very rare and sought-after, largely because the flip side was a top of the pile Northern soul rarity with a lovely lilting beat and soaring melody. It's been compiled on various Northern soul compilations. The duo split when Bobby Kerr left to pursue a solo career. (VJ)

Andy Fraser Band

Personnel:	ANDY FRAZER	vcls, bs	A
	NICK JUDD	keyb'ds	A
	MIKE KELLIE	drms	A

FRANKIE MILLER	vcls	A
HENRY McCULLOGH	gtr	A
KIM TURNER	perc	A

ALBUMS: 1(A) ANDY FRASER BAND   (CBS 80731) 1975
       2(A) IN YOUR EYES   (CBS 81027) 1975

NB: (1) reissued on CD in digipak.

45s: Don't Hide Your Love Away/Ain't Gonna Worry (CBS 3159) 1975
       Be Good To Yourself/Gotta Steal Away   (CBS 3725) 1975
       Listen To The Rain/Gotta Steal Away   (CBS 4004) 1976

This rock band was formed by ex-**Free** bassist after the demise of **Sharks**. Their debut album maintains a high quality throughout from the opening cut *Don't Hide Your Love Away* to the swirling finale *Baby Forever*. *Ain't Gonna Worry* is funky with lots of wah-wah guitar and another highlight is the mellow *Love Is All Around*. (BS/VJ)

The Frays

Personnel: CLIVE HOWES   lead gtr A
           MARTIN HUMM   drms   A
           BARRY LLOYD   bs   A
           JOHN PATTEN (MIKE PATTO) vcls   A

45s: Keep Me Covered/Walk On   (Decca F 12153) 1965 R3
       My Girl Sloopy/
       For Your Precious Love   (Decca F 12229) 1965 R1

This was an obscure group. *Keep Me Covered* is renowned as a pulsating R&B number and the second 45 featured session pianist **Nicky Hopkins** on piano. *My Girl Sloopy* was a McCoys song, which **The Yardbirds** also covered. The first 45 is now very sought-after and collectable and their second effort is also a minor rarity.

Mike Patto was later in **Timebox** before enjoying a solo career.

Keep Me Covered has been compiled on *Maximum R'n'B* (CD), *The R&B Scene* (CD), *Trans-World Punk Rave-Up! Vol. 2* (LP) and on *English Freakbeat, Vol. 3* (CD). (VJ/AD)

Freaks of Nature

45:    People! Let's Freak Out/
      Secret Police (Shadow Chasers)   (Island WI 3017) 1966 R2

Their 45 is sought-after not least because it included ex-**Them** members Pat and **Jackie McAuley** and the recording personnel amounted to the **Belfast Gypsies** under another name with American Kim Fowley at the production helm. (VJ)

Freddie and The Dreamers

Personnel: PETE BIRRELL   bs   A
           ROY CREWSDON   gtr   A
           BERNIE DWYER   drms   A
           FREDDIE GARRITY   vcls   A
           DEREK QUINN   ld gtr A

HCP

ALBUMS: 1(A) FREDDIE AND THE DREAMERS
                 (Columbia 33SX 1577) 1963 SC 5
       2(A) YOU WERE MAD FOR ME
                 (Columbia 33SX 1663) 1964 SC -
       3(A) SING ALONG PARTY   (Columbia SX 1785) 1965 -
       4(A) IN DISNEYLAND
           (mono/stereo)   (Columbia S(C)X 6069) 1966 R1 -
       5(A) KIND FREDDIE AND THE DREAMING KNIGHTS
                 (Columbia SX 6177) 1967 R1 -
       6(A) OLIVER IN THE UNDERWORLD
                 (Starline SRS 5019) 1970 -

FREDDIE AND THE DREAMERS.

COMPILATION:
ALBUMS: 7(A) BEST OF...   (EMI NUT 11) 1977 -
       8(A) THE BEST OF FREDDIE AND THE DREAMERS
                    (C5 503) 1987 -
       9(A) THE BEST OF THE EMI YEARS (CD only)
              (EMI 0777 99715 2 7) 1992 -

NB: They had an export only album issued, *See You Later Alligator* (Regal REG 1075) 1964. It came in a great sleeve and comprised an unusual fourteen-track selection. (1) reissued digipacked in both mono and stereo (EMI 499 4172) 1999. (6) a **Freddie Garrity** solo album.

EPs: 1(A) IF YOU GOTTA MAKE A FOOL OF SOMEBODY
              (Columbia SEG 8275) 1963 SC
     2(A) SONGS FROM "WHAT A CRAZY WORLD";
              (Columbia SEG 8287) 1964 SC
     3(A) YOU WERE MADE FOR ME
              (Columbia SEG 8302) 1964 SC
     4(A) OVER YOU   (Columbia SEG 8323) 1964 SC
     5(A) READY FREDDIE GO   (Columbia SEG 8403) 1965 SC
     6(A) FREDDIE AND THE DREAMERS
              (Columbia SEG 8457) 1965 SC

NB: They also contributed two tracks to *Just For You* (Columbia SEG 8349) 1965 (SC), which was shared with **Peter and Gordon**. Their EPs are compiled on *The EP Collection* (See For Miles SEE 299) 1990, also on CD (SEE CD 299) 1090, reissued again on CD in 1992.

HCP

45s: If You Gotta Make A Fool Of Somebody/
     Feel So Blue   (Columbia DB 7032) 1963 3
     I'm Telling You Now/
     What Have I Done To You? (Columbia DB 7086) 1963 2
     You Were Made For Me/
     Send A Letter To Me   (Columbia DB 7147) 1963 3
     Over You/
     Come Back When You're Ready (Columbia DB 7214) 1964 13
     I Love You Baby/
     Don't Make Me Cry   (Columbia DB 7286) 1964 16
     Just For You/Don't Do That To Me (Columbia DB 7322) 1964 41
     I Understand/I Will   (Columbia DB 7381) 1964 5
     A Little You/
     Things I'd Like To Say   (Columbia DB 7526) 1965 26
     Thou Shalt Not Steal/I Don't Know (Columbia DB 7720) 1965 44
     If You've Gotta Minute Baby/
     When I'm Home With You (Columbia DB 7857) 1966 -
     Playboy/Some Day   (Columbia DB 7929) 1966 -
     Turn Around/Funny Over You (Columbia DB 8033) 1966 -
     Hello, Hello/
     All I Ever Want Is You (Columbia DB 8137) 1967 -
     Brown And Porter's (Meat Exporters) Lorry/
     Little Brown Eyes   (Columbia DB 8200) 1967 -
  α Little Big Time/You Belong To Me (Columbia DB 8496) 1968 -
     It's Great/Gaberdine Mac (Columbia DB 8517) 1968 -
     Get Around Downtown Girl/
     What To Do   (Columbia DB 8606) 1969 -

Susan's Tuba/You Hurt Me Girl		(Philips 6006 098) 1970 -	
Here We Go/I Saw Ya		(Polydor 2059 041) 1978 -	
Reissue:	I'm Telling You Now/Just For You/		
	You Were Made For Me/Over You	(EMI EMI 2694) 1977 -	

NB: α flip side by **Freddie Garrity**.

Freddie and The Dreamers owed more to the variety show tradition than rock'n'roll and are better remembered for **Garrity**'s showmanship than their contribution to rock history.

Freddie Garrity worked as a milkman and had played in a series of local Manchester skiffle groups - The Red Sox, The John Norman Four and finally The Kingfishers - before the latter evolved into **Freddie and The Dreamers** in 1959. They appeared on BBC's 'Let's Go' and also on the 'Beat Show' radio programme in October of 1961. Then they followed this with a series of live appearances in the north of England and residencies at Margate's Dreamland and Hamburg, Germany's Top Ten Club. They were signed by EMI's Columbia label in the wake of **The Beatles** as record companies spread their antennae to root out other undiscovered talent. However, **Freddie and The Dreamers** were never in the same class. Their appeal was to the weenyboppers of the early and mid-sixties and their offbeat, slightly comic stage act made them the darlings of TV companies and parents everywhere. It was notable for Freddie's ungamely kicks and jumps around the stage.

They lacked any songwriting talent of their own but some carefully selected material ensured that they were rarely out of the charts in the 1963-65 era. Their revival of James Ray's *If You Gotta Make A Fool Of Somebody* made No 2. Then they turned to Mitch Murray (writer of some of **Gerry and The Pacemakers**' early hits) for their next two smashes - *I'm Telling You Now* and *You Were Made For Me*. Their first album also sold well, peaking at No 5 in the UK Album Charts. It commenced with their debut hit *If You Gotta Make A Fool Of Somebody* and, alongside a mixture of rock and novelty tunes, it also contains *I Understand* - a later hit single. In December 1965 they also appeared in 'What A Crazy World', a film in which Joe Brown played the lead role, performing 'Short Shorts' (dropping his trousers was another of Freddie's antics!).

In 1964 they enjoyed further hits with *Over You*, a cover of Paul Anka's *I Love You Baby* and a revival of the G. Clefs *I Understand*, which was to be their final Top Ten hit. An earlier release, *Just For You*, had already missed the Top 20.

1965 saw them break the lucrative US market, appearing on 'Hullaballoo' and 'Shindig' and seeing *I'm Telling You Now* (which had been reissued by Tower in the wake of the tour) top the US Charts for two weeks. Their stage act caused quite a stir and *Do The Freddie* was specially recorded for US release and fashioned a teen dance based on his stage movements. It gave them a Top 20 US hit. They enjoyed a couple of further UK hits with *A Little You* and *Thou Shalt Not Steal* and appeared in the low budget musical film 'Everyday's A Holiday' (it was titled 'Seaside Swingers' in the US) as singing chefs at a holiday camp.

None of their releases have subsequently excited collectors much. Some of their later releases were more overtly humorous as they moved increasingly into cabaret. In 1966 they recorded a whole album's worth of Disney film songs and their final album release *Oliver In The Underworld* was really a kiddies album. When they finally bowed out with **Graham Gouldman**'s *Susan Tuba* in 1970 Freddie starred in the successful ITV children's series 'Little Big Time'.

In 1976 **Garrity** put the band back on the road with a new line-up. It was short-lived, but they did oldies tours here, in the US and in Australia. Twelve years later he got his first serious acting role in a production of 'The Tempest'.

The Best Of Freddie And The Dreamers includes most of their UK hits, two flip sides and some better known and more obscure album tracks. It's as good an introduction to the band as any, though those of you who prefer CDs will want *The Best Of The EMI Years*.

Bernie Dwyer, who quit the music business to work as a commercial artist, when the original line-up disbanded, died of cancer, aged 62, in late 2002. **Freddie Garrity** still works the nostalgia circuit with a new line-up of the band.

Compilation appearances have included: *Things I'd Like To Say* and *A Little You* on *Liverpool '65* (LP); *Funny Over You* and *A Love Like You* on *Out Of Sight* (LP); *If You Gotta Make A Fool Of Somebody* on *Beat At Abbey Road* (CD); *I'm Telling You Now* and *What Have I Done To You* on *Freddie And The Dreamers - I'm Telling You Now* (LP); *I'm Telling You Now* on *20 Hits Of The 60's* (CD), *Beat Generation - Ready Steady Go* (CD), *Dizzy* (CD) and *Remember The 60's* (CD); *You Were Made For Me* on *Hits Of The 60's Vol 2* (CD) and on *The Swinging Sixties - 18 Classic Tracks* (CD); *If You Gotta Make A Fool Of Somebody* on the 2-CD set *Greatest Hits Of The 60's Vol 4*; and *If You Gotta Make A Fool Of Somebody* and *You Were Made For Me* on *Hits Of The Mersey Era, Vol. 1* (LP), *Hits Of The 60's - Save The Last Dance For Me* (CD) and *Everlasting Love* (CD). Finally, an alternate take of *You Were Made For Me* can be heard on the 2-CD set *Greatest Hits Of The 60's*. (VJ)

Free

Personnel:	ANDY FRASER	bs	A
	SIMON KIRKE	drms	ABC
	PAUL KOSSOFF	gtr	AB
	PAUL RODGERS	vcls	ABC
	JOHN 'RABBIT' BUNDRICK	keyb'ds	BC
	TETSU YAMAUCHI	bs	BC
	WENDELL RICHARDSON	gtr	C

				HCP
ALBUMS:	1(A)	TONS OF SOBS	(Island ILPS 9089) 1968	R1 -
	2(A)	FREE	(Island ILPS 9104) 1969	R1 -
	3(A)	FIRE AND WATER	(Island ILPS 9120) 1970	SC 2
	4(A)	HIGHWAY	(Island ILPS 9138) 1970	41

FREE - Tons Of Sobs (LP).

FREE - Fire And Water (CD).

FREE - Songs Of Yesterday (CD Set).

5(A)	LIVE!	(Island ILPS 9160) 1971 SC 4
6(A)	FREE AT LAST	(Island ILPS 9192) 1972 9
7(A)	HEARTBREAKER	(Island ILPS 9217) 1973 9
8(A)	THE FREE STORY (2-LP, with 4-page booklet, numbered)	
		(Island ISLD 4) 1974 SC 2

NB: (1) reissued on CD (Island IMCD 62) 1989 and again (Universal/Island IMCD 281) 2001, with bonus cuts. (2) reissued on CD (Island IMCD 64) 1989 and again (Universal/Island IMCD 282) 2001, with bonus tracks. (3) reissued on CD (Island IMCD 80) 1990 and again (Universal/Island IMCD 283) 2001, with bonus tracks. (4) reissued on CD (Island IMCD 63) 1989 and again (Universal/Island IMCD 285) 2001, with bonus tracks. (5) reissued on CD (Island IMCD 73) 1989 and again (Universal/Island IMCD 286) 2001, with bonus tracks. (6) reissued on CD (Island IMCD 82) 1990 and again (Universal/Island IMCD 287) 2001, with bonus tracks. (7) reissued on CD (Island IMCD 81) 1990 and again (Universal/Island IMCD 288) 2001, with bonus tracks. (8) reissued on CD (Island CID 9945) 1989. You may also be interested in *The Best Of Free - All Right Now* (Island ILPTV 2) 1991, also on CD, though it's marred by disappointing sound quality. *Molten Gold: The Anthology* (Island CRNCD 2) 1996 is a 2-CD set which draws on material from all of their six studio albums. *Songs Of Yesterday* (Island IBX CD 3) 2001 is an 80-track 5-CD set including alternate and unreleased mixes, live material and related bands. *Chronicles* (Universal 9822554) 2005 is a 2-CD collection and an excellent introduction to their material.

| EP: | 1(A) THE FREE EP (PS) | (Island IEP 6) 1978 11 |

NB: (1) also released as a 12" picture disc. It featured the following tracks:- *All Right Now*, *My Brother Jake* and *Wishing Well*. It was also reissued in October 1982.

		HCP
45s:	Broad Daylight/The Worm	(Island WIP 6054) 1969 -
	I'll Be Creepin'/	
	Sugar For Mr. Morrison (Some in PS)	(Island WIP 6062) 1969 -
	All Right Now/Mouthful Of Grass	(Island WIP 6082) 1970 2
	The Stealer/Lying In The Sunshine	(Island WIP 6093) 1970 -
	My Brother Jake/Only My Soul	(Island WIP 6100) 1971 4
	Little Bit Of Love/Sail On	(Island WIP 6129) 1972 13
	Wishing Well/Let Me Show You	(Island WIP 6146) 1973 7
	Travellin' In Style/Easy On My Soul	(Island WIP 6160) 1973 -
	The Hunter/Worry	(Island WIP 6351) 1976 -
Reissues:	Travellin' In Style/Easy On My Soul	(Island WIP 6233) 1973 -
α	Wishing Well/Woman (PS)	(Island IS 221) 1985 -
β	All Right Now (remix)/I'm A Mover	(Island IS 486) 1991 8
χ	My Brother Jake (remix)/	
	Wishing Well (remix)	(Island IS 495) 1991 -

NB: α Also issued in 12" format. β Also issued in 12" and CD single format with addition of *Get Where I Belong*. χ Also issued in 12" and CD single format with addition of *The Stealer* and *Only My Soul*.

Free lacked imagination but the power of much of their work is indisputable and they were one of the foremost rock/blues bands of the era.

Free formed in London in May 1968. The founder members **Paul Kossoff** (son of the actor David Kossoff) and Simon Kirke had both played together in a R&B outfit **Black Cat Bones**. They quickly recruited Paul Rodgers to the new band, after hearing him play in an outfit called Brown Sugar at a R&B club called The Fickle Pickle in London's Finsbury Park area. The four-piece was completed by the addition of Andy Fraser, who'd just been kicked out of **John Mayall's Bluesbreakers**. They were 'discovered' by **Alexis Korner** who suggested that they called themselves **Free** after his own Free At Last band. He also introduced them to Island Records who signed them up and got them their first concert in the Spring of 1968. All in all he seems to have been a very positive and significant influence at the early stage of their career.

In their early days they played a hard-hitting blend of blues and rock characterized by very catchy and upfront drumming from Kirke. Inevitable comparisons were made to **Cream**. Their debut album, *Tons Of Sobs*, was notable for some outstanding guitar work from **Kossoff** in what was only his second visit to a recording studio. One of its finest cuts was *I'm A Mover*, and its inclusion on Island's budget-priced *You Can All Join In* (LP) compilation introduced the band to a wider audience. Although it didn't sell particularly well and their debut 45, *Broad Daylight*, flopped, they build up a strong live reputation through constant gigging around the UK.

Their follow-up album entitled simply *Free* can be viewed as a definite progression on their debut. Coming hot on the heels of a US tour on which they'd supported the short-lived **Blind Faith** it added a funkier sound to the raw energy of their earlier effort and climbed to No 22 in the UK Album Charts. One of the album's standout tracks was *Woman* (indeed it was perhaps the best example of Kirke's very distinctive drumming) and its inclusion of Island's budget-priced *Nice Enough To Eat* (LP) compilation brought their unique and distinctive talent into new homes. In retrospect *I'll Be Creepin'* may have lacked sufficient commercial appeal to have been the best choice for a 45 release and unsurprisingly it failed to make much impact.

The band's big breakthrough came in 1970 with the commercial riff-based rock of *All Right Now*, a timeless party classic which shot to No 2 in the UK and later in the year made No 4 in the US. It was also included on their classic *Fire And Water* album which undoubtedly contained many of their other finest moments in the title track, *Heavy Load*, *Mr. Big* and *Be My Friend*. The only criticism I have of the band at this stage is that much of their material sounded similar. The release of the album coincided with the band's appearance at the 1970 Isle Of Wight festival, a factor which undoubtedly heightened its impact. The album climbed to No 2 in the UK and made it to No 17 in the US.

The group's follow-up 45, *The Stealer*, surprisingly failed in the UK, although it was a minor hit in the US. It was taken from their *Highway* album which was expected to consolidate their new found success. Its finest moments included the mesmerising *Soon I Will Be Gone* and a tender ballad *Bodine*. Much of the other material comprised more pedestrian rockers. The album's sales were disappointing and this undoubtedly left the band, which had not dealt well with its rapid rise to fame, dejected. They returned to the studio and recorded another vintage 45, *My Brother Jake*, which propelled them back to No 4 in the UK Charts, whilst the band was fantastically well received on tour in Japan. They headed on to Australia but disintegrated before this leg of the tour was

FREE - At Last (LP).

complete. The split seems to have been the result of inter-group friction, lack of consistent sales, with their lack of emotional maturity, on account of their youth an underlying factor.

In the aftermath of their split **Kossoff** and Kirke remained together and teamed up with Texan keyboard player John 'Rabbit' Bundrick and Japanese bassist Tetsu Yamauchi (ex-**Samurai**). The four of them recorded an album, with the somewhat predictable title of *Kossoff, Kirke, Tetsu and Rabbit*, which was well regarded. Meanwhile, Rodgers had formed a new band of his own called Peace and Fraser was in a band called Toby. Toby was an unsuccessful venture, but Peace did support **Mott The Hoople** on a UK tour. Eventually, through, both projects flopped and by January 1972 the band reformed for the *Free At Last* album. Although this was patchy overall it contained glimpses of the band at its best on tracks like *Little Bit Of Love* (which was also released as a 45 and comfortably made the UK Top 20); *Catch A Train, Travellin' Man*; the drug-influenced *Magic Ship* and *Guardian Of The Universe*. The album made the UK Top 10 and crept to No 69 in the US but the group's attempts to promote it on a US tour were hampered by **Kossoff**'s drug abuse problems and associated ill-health which meant many gigs were performed without him. Prior to their next major tour, this time to Japan in July 1972, Fraser left to form **The Sharks** and then **Kossoff**'s drug problems rendered him unfit for the engagement. Bundrick and Yamauchi were recruited prior to the Tour. **Kossoff** did rejoin the band for a subsequent UK tour in October 1972. He also made occasional appearances on their next album, *Heartbreaker*, which was one of their best. One of the finest tracks, *Wishing Well*, put them back in the 45 Chart Top 10 in the UK and the album made the Top Ten in the UK Album Charts and No 47 in the US. By now, though, **Kossoff** had left the band for good - see his solo entry for details of his subsequent exploits. His drug abuse eventually proved his downfall and he died of heart failure on a flight to London on 19 March 1976.

Immediately after Kossoff's departure, Wendell Richardson (of Osibisa) was recruited for future live engagements but the band split altogether in July 1973. Rodgers and Kirke then formed **Bad Company**, Tetsu replaced **Ronnie Lane** in **The Faces**. Bundrick joined **The Who** as a sideman. Inevitably, their most successful 45, *All Right Now*, was reissued and put the band back in the Top 20.

1974 saw the release of the double compilation, *The Free Story*, which climbed to No 2 in the Album Charts and is a good introduction to the band. *Wishing Well* and *Magic Ship*, were unfortunate omissions, but an interesting inclusion is *The Hunter*, later issued as a 45 in 1976, three years after their demise. In 1975 a *Best Of Free* collection peaked at No 120. *The Free EP*, released in 1978, put them back into the UK Top 20 and became a steady seller too. It charted again when it was reissued in October 1982.

In 2001, Universal repackaged all their albums, remastered and with bonus tracks. These bonuses comprise 45s which weren't originally on albums, out-takes, alternate mixes and BBC session material. Their 2005 2-CD collection *Chronicles* is an excellent introduction to their music and contains most of their finest moments.

THE FREEDOM - Nerosubianco (LP).

Compilation appearances have included *Oh I Wept* on *Bumpers* (2-LP); *I'm A Mover* on *You Can All Join In* (LP); *Woman* on *Nice Enough To Eat* (LP); *Little Bit Of Love* on *20 Star Tracks, Vol. 1* (LP), *Highway Song* on *El Pea* (LP); and *All Right Now* on *Wild Thing - Party* (CD). (VJ)

Freedom

Personnel:	BOBBY HARRISON	vcls, drms	AB
	ROGER SAUNDERS	vcls, gtr, keyb'ds	AB
	WALT MONAHAN	organ, cello, bs	A
	PETER DENNIS	vcls, bs, keyb'ds	B
	STEVE JOLLY	gtr	B

ALBUMS:	1(A)	FREEDOM	(Probe SPBA 6252) 1970 SC
	2(A)	THROUGH THE YEARS (US only)	(Cotillion SD 9048) 1971 R1
	3(A)	FREEDOM: THROUGH THE YEARS	(Vertigo 6360 049) 1971 R1
	4(B)	FREEDOM IS MORE THAN A WORD	(Vertigo 6360 072) 1972 R2

NB: (1) and (3) reissued on a 2-CD set (Angel Air SJP CD 027) 1999. (1) reissued on CD (Angel Air SJPCD 063) 2000. *Through The Years* was issued on CD (Repertoire REP 4226-WP) 1991, again on Italian import (Akarma AK 222) 2002 and more recently on CD (Angel Air SJPCD 177). (4) reissued on CD (Angel Air SJPCD 073) 2000 and again on Italian import (Akarma AK 219) 2002. In 1994 Tenth Planet released *Nerosubianco* (TP 011), a film Soundtrack previously only released in Italy (Atlantic ATL 08028) in 1969. It was reissued again (Moving Image Entertainment MIE 012) 2002 with additional out-takes and alternate versions and a revised running order. *Black On White* (Angel Air SJPCD 028) 1998 was originally conceived as a film soundtrack for a 1968 soft porn film by Dino De Laurentis and previously unreleased. *Freedom At Last* (Angel Air SJPCD 175) 2004 is a reissue of their second album, never originally issued in the UK.

45s:	Where Will You Be Tonight/Trying To Get A Glimpse Of You (Some PS)	(Mercury MF 1033) 1968 R1/SC
	Escape While You Can/Kandy Kay	(Plexium PXM 3) 1969 SC
	Frustrated Woman/Man Made Laws	(Probe 504) 1970
	Thanks/Little Miss Louise	(Vertigo 6059 051) 1971

This heavy rock group had a good live act but their albums were rather mundane. They were formed and fronted by drummer Bobby Harrison. He'd previously banged the skins for The Washington DC's and **Procol Harum**. Ray Royer had played also been in **Procol Harum**. They formed **Freedom** when they were given a generous out of court financial settlement to leave **Procol Harum** because they were considered to be incompatible with the rest of the band's sound.

During the Winter of 1967/8 **Freedom** (Harrison, Royer, Mike Lease (keyb'ds) and Steve Shirley (bs, vcls) were invited to contribute to the Soundtrack of the film 'Nerosubianco' ('The Attraction'), which was masterminded by noted Italian producer Dino De Laurentiis. The resulting album has now been issued in the UK by Tenth Planet and sounding similar to **Procol Harum** or instrumentally to early **Traffic** is worth a listen. Their debut 45 'B' side, penned by Roy Royer, is an excellent slice of psych-pop notable for some good mellotron, although the follow-up on the small Plexium label (which I haven't heard) is always regarded as disappointing.

Prior to their first UK album they put out an album called *At Last*, which was only released in Germany (Metronome MLP 15371) 1970 and in France on (Byg 529325) 1970. This is reputed to contain some good slices of psychedelia and changes hands for large sums of money now. This was followed by their eponymous album released on the Probe album. It was produced by Roy Thomas Baker who later found fame for his work with **Queen** and The Cars.

They secured a contract with Vertigo after supporting **Jethro Tull**, **Black Sabbath** and others on tour. The best track on *Through The Years* (the US edition) was *Freestone*, the opener. The title cut, *Get Yourself Together* and *London City* were competent but unexceptional heavy rock tracks, whilst *Thanks* was mellow and more mainstream. The final track, *Toe Grabber*, was based on boring guitar riffs.

Walt Monahan left after the first Vertigo album to join **Mick Abrahams Band**. He was replaced by Pete Dennis and second guitarist Steve Jolly. *Freedom Is More Than A Word* combined blues-rock, funk and piano-based

FRESH MAGGOTS - Fresh Maggots (LP).

pop. Tracks like *Brainbox Jam* are particularly funky, this one contains an instrumental segment recalling James Brown. *Sweaty Feet* is one of their more bluesy offerings with some great fuzz guitar. There's also a good heavy cover of *Going Down* on what is a decent album. However, sales were disappointing and the band split.

Bobby Harrison had and went on to perform vocal duties with **Snafu**. He later recorded a solo album *Funfest* that was only released in Germany and then joined jazz-rockers Mezzoforte. Now based in Southend he's still writing and performing. Roger Saunders became a session musician and formed a songwriting partnership with Scott English. He then joined **Medicine Head** and played in **Gary Glitter's** touring band during the eighties. He died in 2000.

Freedom also contributed two tracks, *Nobody* and *Frustrated Woman*, from their first album to Probe's *Handle With Care* (LP) sampler. *Where Will You Be Tonight* has resurfaced on *Jagged Time Lapse, Vol 1* (CD) and *Trying To Get A Glimpse Of You* can also be heard on *Psychedelia, Vol. 2* (LP) and *Hen's Teeth Vol. 1* (CD). (VJ)

Free Expression

Personnel:	RAY FEATHER	vcls	
	STEVE HUGHES		
	HOWARD McDERMOT-ROW		
	TERRY PEAKER	bs	A
	BRIAN WHITFIELD		

A Yorkshire-based group. They had one track, *Nightmares*, from 1970 on a very limited promo album, *Transworld* (generally known to collectors as *Samantha Promotions 2*). The album was recorded by two entrepreneurs who put an advert in 'Melody Maker' for young rock bands interested in getting recording contracts. Applicants were auditioned and the better ones selected to write a song to record. The album was sent to colleges and universities to get live work but with little success. Still *Nightmares* was a pretty good progressive rock song with good guitar but restrained vocals.

Feather and Peaker were later in a progressive rock outfit called Castle, who played a few festivals but didn't make it onto vinyl.

You'll also find *Nightmares* on *Syde Tryps, Vol. 1* (LP & CD), *The Best Of Rubble Collection, Vol. 3* (CD) and *The Best Of Rubble Collection, Vol. 6* (CD). (VJ)

Free Ferry

| 45s: | Mary, What Have You Become?/Friend | (CBS 4456) 1969 |
| | Haverjack Drive/Flying | (CBS 4647) 1970 |

A little known band. (VJ)

Free'n'Easy

| ALBUM: | 1 FREE'N'EASY | (Oak RGJ 628) 1968 R3 |

This was a rare private pressing, which has attracted little publicity to date. (VJ)

The Freewheelers

| 45: | Why Do You Treat Me Like A Fool/ | |
| | Ad Lib Blues | (HMV POP 1406) 1965 |

This short-lived folk trio came from London. The 'A' side was a **Donovan** song. (VJ)

Fresh

Personnel:	ROGER CHANTLER	drms	AB
	KEVIN FRANCIS	bs, vcls	AB
	BOB GORMAN	gtr, vcls	AB
	Plus The London Woodwind Ensemble		B
	and assisting musicians including		
	Paul Korda, Allan Gozzie		
	and Pete Whillshez (steel gtr)		

| ALBUMS: | 1(A) | FRESH OUT OF BORSTAL | (RCA SF 8122) 1970 SC |
| | 2(B) | FRESH TODAY | (RCA LSA 3027) 1971 |

| 45: | Stoned In Saigon/Just A Note | (RCA RCA 2003) 1970 |

A satirical rock trio whose first album was recorded in London. *Fresh Today*, their second album, was conceived, arranged and produced by Simon Napier-Bell (**John's Children**'s producer) and Ray Singer (Peter Sarstedt's producer). The same collaboration was responsible for **Forever More** and **Scaffold**. The album is basically mainstream and poppy. The best tracks are the version of **Marc Bolan**'s *Desdemona* and the bluesy Napier-Bell/Singer/**Paul Korda** composition, *Tricky Says We're Helpless*. *The Peasants Are Revolting* (one of Peter Sarstedt's songs on the album) is an interesting track with gypsy violin, harpsichord and percussion and *Stoned In Saigon* is a good pop song with a pre-World War II feeling. (CA)

Fresh Air

45s:	Running Wild/Stop, Look, Listen	(Pye 7N 17736) 1969 R2
	It Takes Too Long/Here Comes Summer	(Philips 6006 187) 1971
	Bye Bye Jane/It's All Over	(Columbia DB 8872) 1972

Nothing is known of this four-piece group, although they may have included songwriter Ian Holding. On *Running Wild* the vocalist certainly catches the ear and it's a pretty forceful song with some quite blistering guitar work too. Not surprisingly, this 45, unlike their other two is rare and sought-after. The other 45s listed on Columbia and Philips are thought to be by another band.

Compilation appearances include: *Stop Look Listen* on *Paisley Pop - Pye Psych (& Other Colours) 1966-1969* (CD); and *Running Wild* on *Rubble, Vol. 10 - Professor Jordan's Magic Sound Show* (LP) and *Hot Smoke & Sassafras - Psychedelic Pstones, Vol 1* (CD). (VJ)

Fresh Maggots

| Personnel: | MICK BURGOYNE | gtr, tamb, violin | A |
| | LEIGH DOLPHIN | acoustic gtr | A |

| ALBUM: | 1(A) | FRESH MAGGOTS | (RCA SF 8205) 1971 R3 |

NB: Two original pressings of (1) exist. One has a sharper cover image and a purple rear sleeve. The other has a paler cover and blue rear sleeve. (1) reissued on Fan Club (1988?) and on CD (Fan Club CD 8205) with two bonus tracks, *Car Song* and *What Would You Do*. Also reissued officially on CD in Korea (Si-Wan SRMC 1039) 1995 and on CD and LP in the UK, with two bonus tracks (Sunbeam SBR CD/LP 5002) 2005.

| 45: | Car Song/What Would You Do | (RCA RCA 2150) 1971 SC |

This teenage duo came from Nuneaton in Warwickshire, with its own individual brand of folk-rock. Their album, originally to be titled *Hatched*, was recorded at Radio Luxembourg's studios at the end of 1970. It's full of good songs like the exquisite *Rosemary Hill*, dealing with romance, and the fiery *Dole Song*, about signing on, which features some arresting guitar work. Other highlights include *Everyone's Gone To War*, a song of different moods with some good fuzz guitar work; *Who's To Die*, a lovely melodic song with a riff which sounded like early **Electric Light Orchestra** and the majestic finale *Frustration*. There are no weak links, though, on this consistent album which is thoroughly recommended. Numerous minor problems delayed its release (intended to be on RCA's Neon imprint) and, though it received acclaim in the music press when it finally appeared in November 1971, it simply didn't sell. When their (non-album) single fared no better in December 1971, they were dropped. They continued to play locally, eventually parting in the mid-seventies. (RMJ/VJ)

Fresh Meat

45:     Never Mind The Money/Candy Eyes   (Deram DMR 384) 1972

This was a short-lived venture. (VJ)

The Freshmen

Personnel:	BILLY BROWN	piano, sax	ABC
	MAURICE HENRY	sax	ABC
	SEAN MAHON	trombone	ABC
	TERRY McGAHEY	bs	ABC
	BARNEY McKEON	vcls	A
	DAVY McKNIGHT	drms	ABC
	DAMIEN McILROY	ld gtr	ABC
	TOMMY DRENNAN (TOMMY DEAN)	vcls	B
	DEREK McMENAMIN	vcls	C

ALBUMS:	1( )	MOVIN' ON	(Pye N(S)PL 18263) 1968 R2
	2( )	PEACE ON EARTH	(CBS 64099) 1970 R1

NB: *When Summer Comes* (Sanctuary CMRCD 271) 2001 is a 23-track compilation of their material.

45s:	Papa Oom Mow Mow/Let's Dance	(Pye 7N 17432) 1967
	Go Granny Go/Look At The Sunshine	(Pye 7N 17592) 1968
	Just To See You Smile/Indian Lake	(Pye 7N 17689) 1969
	She Sang Hymns Out Of Tune/	
	Mr. Beverly's Heavy Days	(Pye 7N 17757) 1969
	Halfway To Where/Time Hasn't Changed Her	(CBS 4842) 1970
	Banquet For The World/	
	Time Hasn't Changed Her	(CBS 5168) 1970
	One Bad Thing/Everywhere There Is Love	(CBS 7241) 1971
	Swanee River/Take The Time It Takes	(CBS 7694) 1972

This outfit had quite a prolific output despite their low UK profile. Their *Movin' On* album exudes a US West Coast sort of sound although the title track is a cover of a Raiders' song and the album includes covers of The Beach Boys' *The Little Girl I Once Knew*, Bread's *Make It With You*, *Close Your Eyes* and *Carpet Man*.

Formed in 1962, this highly-respected showband from Northern Ireland began recording in 1964 as Six Of One, before releasing a 45 as Dean and The Freshmen (*I Stand Alone*) the same year. In 1965 they scored a hit in Ireland with a cover of Johnny and Charly's *La Yenka* and were known throughout Ireland for their superb vocal harmonies.

Their 1967 Christmas hit, *Papa-Oo-Mow-Mow* reached the Irish Top 10, as did *Just To See You Smile* and *Halfway To Where*.

Movin' On is full of songs with complex harmonies like *Saturday and Sunday* and *Close Your Eyes*, whilst *Make It With You* recalls The Beach Boys circa *Pet Sounds*.

What was most extraordinary about **The Freshmen**, however, was their live sound and ability to master the intricate harmonies of their mentors the Beach Boys. They enjoyed chart success with a version of *The Little Old Lady From Pasadena*, (retitled *Go Granny Go*) and even included an ambitious version of *Good Vibrations* in their live act. **The Freshmen** survived the showband scourge of the early seventies and found Irish chart

success in 1976 with *And God Created Woman*. Meanwhile, original Freshman Billy Brown released successful chart covers of *Leaving Of Liverpool* and *Cinderella*. By the end of the decade, however, they disbanded, the victims of changing times and tastes.

Sanctuary's *When Summer Comes* compilation draws considerably from the *Movin' On* album and is full of harmony pop. It's a good introduction to the band.

Compilation appearances have included: *Look At The Sunshine* on *Ripples, Vol. 1* (CD); *Just To See You Smile* on *Ripples, Vol. 3* (CD); *Go Granny Go* and *Papa Oom Mow Mow* on *Ripples, Vol. 5* (CD); *Carpet Man* and *When Summer Comes* on *Ripples, Vol. 7* (CD); and *Make It With You* on *Ripples, Vol. 2* (CD). (MC/VJ)

Fresh Windows

45:	Summer Sun Shines/	
	Fashion Conscious	(Fontana TF 839) 1967 R2

The flip side to this 45 is an excellent mod number with great period lyrics, credited to a Barrett, though definitely not he of **Pink Floyd** fame! The 'A' side is a less interesting pop number.

Compilation appearances include: *Fashion Conscious* on *Chocolate Soup For Diabetics, Vol. 1* (LP) and *Jagged Time Lapse, Vol 3* (CD); whilst *Summer Sun Shines* can be found on *Jagged Time Lapse, Vol 1* (CD). (VJ)

Brian Joseph Friel

ALBUMS:	1	BRIAN JOSEPH FRIEL	(Dawn DNLS 3054) 1974
(up to	2	ARRIVEDERCI ARDROSSAN	(Dawn DNLS 3064) 1975
1976)	3	ASHES AND MATCHSTICKS	(Pye 12113) 1975

NB. (3) is a US pressing.

45s:	Rock And Roll In Me//Song For Ralph	(Dawn DNS 1050) 1974
	Mailbox Blues/Louise Is Loose	(Dawn DNS 1071) 1974
	Growing Stronger/Fat City	(Dawn DNS 1107) 1975

An obscure British singer/songwriter backed by Tim Renwick, **Andy Roberts**, Colin Allen, **Zoot Money** and Steve Thompson (of **Stone The Crows**). **Friel** would release another album, *Torc* in 1983 on BRM records. (SR/VJ)

Friends (1)

ALBUM:	1	FRIENDS	(Merlin HF 4) 1974 R6

NB: This is a white label test pressing.

Peter Howell of the BBC Radiophonic Workshop and his friend John Fernando were behind this album. It was one of a set of five he was involved with - the others being - **Agincourt, Ithaca**, **Tomorrow Come Some Day** and **Alice Through The Looking Glass**. *Friends* is the rarest of the four as the sole test pressing emanated from Howell himself. It's described as 'a folk-psychedelic gem' and according to the December 2004 edition of 'Record Collector', when Howell gave up his copy in the early nineties, it was sold to a Japanese collector for over £2,000! (VJ)

Friends (2)

45:     Piccolo Man/Mythological Sunday   (Deram DM 198) 1968 SC

This one-off project involved members of **The Ivy League** who were also the session artists behind **The Flowerpot Men**. The 45 is well worth a spin and *Mythological Sunday* can also be heard on *Deram Dayze* (LP). This is a fine effort with beautiful melodic harmonies. Both sides of this 45 can be heard too on **The Flowerpot Men**'s *Let's Go To San Francisco* (C5 526) compilation. (VJ)

CHOCOLATE SOUP FOR DIABETICS VOL. 1 (Comp LP) including Fresh Windows.

Friends O' Mine

ALBUM: 1   FRIENDS O' MINE   (Westwood WRS 021) 1972 R3

Only 250 copies of this album were released making it very difficult to locate now. (VJ)

Friendship

45:        Stop Living Alone/
           Friends Make Living What It Is   (B&C CB 163) 1971

This long-forgotten one-off 45 is of no interest to collectors at present. (VJ)

Fripp and Eno

Personnel:	ROBERT FRIPP	gtr	A
	BRIAN ENO	keyb'ds	A

ALBUMS:	1	NO PUSSYFOOTIN'	(Island HELP 16) 1973
(up to	2	EVENING STAR	(Island HELP 22) 1975
1976)			

NB: (1) and (2) released on Antilles in the US. (1) and (2) reissued on CD (Editions E.G. Records EEGCD 2 and EEGCD 3 respectively) 1987.

Robert Fripp, who was born in Wimbourne, Dorset, on 16 May 1946, was originally in **Giles, Giles and Fripp**, who formed in 1967 in Bournemouth. By 1969 the band had evolved into **King Crimson** and Fripp was their guitarist until they split in 1973.

In November 1973 *No Pussyfootin'*, the result of his collaboration with former **Roxy Music** member **Brian Eno** was released, but neither this nor *Evening Star*, the result of a later collaboration in 1975, sold particularly well, and both members concentrated on solo careers thereafter. Nonetheless, both albums were among the leading avant-garde recordings of the era. *No Pussyfootin'* is notable for the tape loop and layered guitar technique which became known as 'Frippertronics'. (VJ)

Fritz, Mike and Mo

Personnel:	MIKE DEIGHAN	A
	MAUREEN EVANS	A
	FRITZ FRYER	A

45s: Somebody Stole The Sun/

Let Me Hear Your Voice	(Philips BF 1427) 1965
What Colour Is A Man/	
So Now You've Gone	(Philips BF 1441) 1965

A little-known sixties folk act from Lancashire. They were formed by Fritz Fryer when he left **The Four Pennies** in April 1965. They split when he rejoined **The Four Pennies** a year later. (VJ)

Wynder K. Frog

See **Wynder K. Frog** entry. (VJ)

Raymond Froggatt

ALBUMS:	1	VOICE AND WRITING OF	(Polydor 583 044) 1969 SC
(up to	2	BLEACH	(Bell BELLS 207) 1972 SC
1976)	3	ROGUES AND THIEVES	(Reprise K 44257) 1974

NB: (1) reissued on CD in a digipak with 10 bonus tracks and a detailed booklet.

45s:	Callow-La-Vita/Lost Autumn	(Polydor 56249) 1968
(up to	Just A Little Bit Of Love/ABC Gold Fish	(Polydor 56274) 1968
1976)	The Red Balloon/Lost Autumn	(Polydor 56284) 1968
	Time Goes By/Rolly	(Polydor 56294) 1968
	Ring Ting A Ling/Anything You Want	(Polydor 56314) 1969
	Movin' Down South/It's Only Me	(Polydor 56334) 1969
	Lazy Jack/Hasn't The Lord Blessed You	(Polydor 56358) 1969
	Running Water/Rock 'n' Roll Song	(Bell BLL 1261) 1972
	Roadshow/Salt	(Reprise K 14328) 1974
	Try To Get You Into My Life/	
	This Could Last All Night	(Jet 749) 1975

Raymond Froggatt was a native of Birmingham. He formed his own band in the late sixties and they were a popular live act but failed to break into the big time. Their best known track was *Red Balloon*, an original (*), which got a lot of airplay on Radio One at the time. He was also in **Monopoly**. The CD reissue of his first album includes a mono single mix of *Callow-La-Vita*.

Froggatt continued to record spasmodically throughout the seventies and into the eighties, spending some time in America, where he developed an interest in country music. He eventually became a very popular figure in the international country music scene. He still writes his own songs and released *Here's To Everyone* on his own Red Balloon label in 1993. His autobiography 'Raymond Who' was published in 1995 and a further album *Moonshine* appeared in 1998.

Back in 1970 he had one cut, *Matter Of Pride*, on Polydor's *Pop Party* (2-LP) compilation.

NB: (*) Not to be confused with the Tim Hardin track. (VJ/WM)

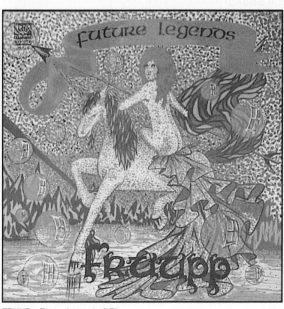

FRUUP - Future Legends (LP).

FRUUP - Seven Secrets (LP).

Frogmorton

Personnel:	DAVE HARDY	accordion, perc, vcls	A
	BILL LYNN	bs, double bs	A
	TERRY NEWBURY	drms	A
	LUCY SHARPE	gtr, perc, vcls, flute, mandolin	A
	MIKE SMITH	gtr, vcls	A
	CHRIS TULLOCH	keyb'ds, mandolin, vcls	A

ALBUM:	1(A)	AT LAST	(Philips 6308 261) 1976 SC

45:	White Swans/Uncivilised Man	(Philips 6006 506) 1976

This band played driving folk-rock with a lot of self-penned material. The combined male/female vocals are excellent throughout and though they tend to be a bit over-serious as well as over-joyous, most of the tracks are very listenable. *Judas and Mary* and *Wedding Day* have slight religious overtones. (VJ)

Frost Lane

ALBUM:	1	FROST LANE	(Cutty Wren MM 1) 1971 R1

This album was recorded by Southampton folk club members and is really a various artists album. (VJ)

Frugal Sound

Personnel:	MIKE BROWN	bs	AB
	ROSALIND RANKIN	vcls	AB
	BRIAN STEIN	gtr	AB
	CHRIS		B
	PETE		B

45s:	Norwegian Wood/Cruel To Be Kind	(Pye 7N 17062) 1966
	Just Outside The Door/I'm On Your Side	(Pye 7N 17129) 1966
	Backstreet Girl/Reason To Believe	(RCA Victor RCA 1556) 1966
	Abilene/Love Is A New Face	(RCA Victor RCA 1595) 1967
	All Strung Out/Miss Mary	(RCA Victor RCA 1659) 1968

A late sixties harmony folk group. Their first 45 also got a US release on Red Bird (10-052) in 1966. They came from Hampstead in North London. Their first 45 was a **Beatles** song, *Norwegian Wood*. Their third single, which coupled the **Jagger**/Richard number, *Backstreet Girl* with Tim Hardin's *Reason To Believe*, was arranged by **John Paul Jones** (later of **Led Zeppelin**).

Compilation appearances have included: *Norwegian Wood* and *I'm On Your Side* on *Ripples, Vol. 3* (CD); and *Norwegian Wood* on *Hippy Hippy Shake* (CD). (VJ)

Fruit Machine

Personnel incl:	ANDY 'CED CURTIS	gtr, vcls	A
	ANDY DEACON	drms	A
	STEVE GOULD	vcls, gtr	A
	CHRIS RANDALL	bs	A

45s:	Follow Me/Cuddly Toy	(Spark SRL 1003) 1969 R1
	I'm Alone Today/Sunshine Of Your Love (Some in title PS)	(Spark SRL 1027) 1970 R3/R1

NB: There was also a US-only 45: *The Wall/Willow Tree* (American Music Makers 0021) 1969.

An obscure band whose version of **Cream**'s *Sunshine Of Your Love* is very competent. *Follow Me* and *I'm Alone Today* are also both strong songs with considerable commercial potential. In particular, *I'm Alone Today* featured some good guitar and piano interplay but the la la la's are a bit of a turnoff.

Their second UK 45 was recorded in London. Chris Randall recalls:- "The recording of *I'm Alone Today* and *Sunshine Of Your Love* was made in the small basement studio below "Southern Music" in Little Newport Street, Soho. The tape machine was an old valve (tube) Ampex half-inch 4-track with a homebrew mixer. The recording engineer was Paul Holland and the producer was Barry Kingston. Paul used to get very agitated if anyone stood in front of the huge Altec Lansing monitors in the control room as it spoiled the sound! We didn't do all that many live gigs but spent our time writing stuff, being silly and worrying our parents almost to death!"

Steve Gould and Andy Curtis later played in **Rare Bird**.

Compilation coverage has included:- *Follow Me* and *I'm Alone Today* on *Circus Days, Vol. 2* (LP); *Follow Me* on *Circus Days Vol. 1 & 2* (CD); *I'm Alone Today* on *Circus Days Vol. 3* (CD); *The Wall* on *Rubble Vol. 10* (CD), *Rubble Vol. 18* (LP), *The Best Of Rubble Collection, Vol. 3* (CD) and *We Can Fly, Vol 1* (CD); *Willow Tree* on *Electric Sugar Cube Flashbacks, Vol. 4* (LP) and *Sunshine Of Your Love* on *Oddities, Vol 1* (CD). (VJ/BM/MW/CR)

Fruupp

Personnel:	PETER FARRELLY	gtr, bs, ld vcls	AB
	MARTIN FOYE	drms, perc	AB
	STEPHEN HOUSTON	keyb'ds, oboe, vcls	A
	VINCE McCUSKER	gtr, vcls	AB
	JOHN MASON	keyb'ds, vibes, vcls	B
	IAN McDONALD	sax	B

ALBUMS:	1(A)	FUTURE LEGENDS	(Dawn DNLS 3053) 1973 SC
	2(A)	SEVEN SECRETS	(Dawn DNLS 3058) 1974 SC
	3(A)	THE PRINCE OF HEAVEN'S EYES	(Dawn DNLH 2) 1974 SC
	4(B)	MODERN MASQUERADES	(Dawn DNLS 3070) 1975 SC

FRUUP - The Prince Of Heaven's Eyes (LP).

NB: Some copies of (3) with book (R1). (2) and (4) issued with lyric insert. (1) and (2) reissued on one CD (See For Miles C5HCD 645) 1997, with one track omitted from each album. (3) and (4) reissued on one CD (See For Miles C5HCD 646) 1997, again with one track omitted from each album. There's also two CD compilations, *Songs For A Thought* (Sequel NEX CD 203) 1992 and the 2-CD *It's All Up Now: Anthology* (Castle CMDDD 1019) 2004.

45:       Prince Of Heaven/Jaunting Car   (Dawn DNS 1087) 1974

McCusker put this techno-rock outfit together in Belfast in the early seventies although they later relocated to London. They were a popular band in the club/college circuit but never broke into the big league. Musically they were similar to **Yes** and **Genesis**, classically inclined progressive pop/rock. With a stronger vocal presence they would have gone further.

All titles on their first album were composed by McCusker and arranged by McCusker and Houston. It was produced by Denis Taylor. Farrelly was responsible for the beautiful cover painting. All the tracks on the album are good examples of classically-tinged progressive rock, with good string arrangements and often melodramatic keyboards.

Farrelly did the cover artwork for their *Seven Secrets* album too. This was similar in style, although some tracks had a hint of medieval-influenced instrumentation such as the opener, *Faced With Shekinah*, which was penned by Houston. There are more fine McCusker songs, too, notably *White Eyes*. *Elizabeth* is a predominantly instrumental number with some beautiful piano pieces, penned by Houston, though the final track, *The Seventh Secret* was a throwaway number.

Houston left after *Prince Of Heavens Eyes* (which he wrote most of the material for) failed to sell very well. This was probably their weakest album. John Mason joined as his replacement.

Produced by Ian McDonald, *Modern Masquerades* is a little less classically-influenced than their earlier efforts. McCusker's *Masquerading With Dawn* and *Mystery Might* are excellent tracks with some at times captivating instrumentation. John Mason contributed two tracks, too - the sad *Gormenghast* and the finale, *Sheba's Song*.

The Sequel CD compilation is a good introduction to their material. The recent Castle CD set compiles many of the best tracks from their four albums. *The Seventh Secret* has been compiled on the 3-CD box set *Ars Longa Vita Brevis: A Compendium Of Progressive Rock 1967-1974*. (VJ)

Mark Fry

ALBUM: 1   DREAMING WITH ALICE   (IT ZSLT 70006) 1972 R5
NB: (1) was an Italian-only release and has been reissued (Akarma AK 126) 2001.

Englishman **Fry** recorded this mystical folk-psych trip in Florence, and quite how it came to be released on RCA's Italian singer/songwriter label is a mystery. His soft voice is appealing and the instrumentation utilises sitar, mandolin, flute, acoustic and electric guitars as well as backwards tape effects, to good effect. The commanding title track is divided into eight sections. Other highlights include the Eastern-tinged *The Witch* and the haunting *Roses For Columbus*. Just a handful of copies were issued before it was inexplicably withdrawn. The album was **Fry**'s sole vinyl outing. He's now a successful painter based in Normandy. (RMJ/VJ)

Fuchsia

Personnel:	TONY DURANT	gtr, vcls	A
	MADELINE BLAND	cello, keyb'ds, vcls	A
	MIKE DAY	bs	A
	MICHAEL GREGORY	drms	A
	VANESSA HALL SMITH	violin, vcls	A
	JANET ROGERS	violin, vcls	A

ALBUM: 1(A)   FUCHSIA   (Pegasus PEG 8) 1971 R3
NB: reissued in Italy (Night Wings CD) 2005.

Vocalist, guitarist and songwriter Tony Durant was the creative force behind this obscure progressive folk act. Formed at Exeter University in 1970, the band was much influenced by cult writer and artist Mervyn Peake and had a distinctly classical sound, supplemented by lush violin and cello. Discovered by **Caravan's** manager Terry King, their album was produced by **Caravan** and **Mellow Candle** producer David Hitchcock, and recorded at Sound Techniques. They were unused to studios, perhaps accounting for the unusual combination of classical and electric influences. The front cover art, representing Peake's Gormenghast character Lady Fuchsia, was by Ann Marie Anderson, who also contributed cover art to **Caravan's** *In The Land Of Grey And Pink*. The use of two violins and one cello gave **Fuchsia** a very distinctive sound, near to classical baroque music. The tender lyrics lend a delicate atmosphere, like on *Shoes And Ships*:

"Above the morning grey sky rage scattered in confusion
Dispelled all thought of blame or praise, left me with its blessing
Oh she breathes, like she sighs, in sunshine and in shadow
And the day will come again my friend that she gave me a rainbow"

Sadly, the album bombed on release in October 1971 and, unable to find a deal elsewhere, the band was obliged to split.

Gone With The Mouse has been compiled on the 3-CD set *Ars Longa Vita Brevis: A Compendium Of Progressive Rock*. (RMJ/VJ/S)

Fumble

Personnel:	DAVE CHRISTOPHER	gtr, vcls	A
	MARIO FERRARI	bs, vcls	A
	DES HENLY	gtr, vcls	A

MARK FRY - Dreaming With Alice (CD).

FUSCHIA - Fuschia (CD).

319

| SEAN MAYES | vcls, piano | A |
| BARRY PIKE | drms | A |

ALBUMS: 1(A) FUMBLE (Sovereign SVNA 7254) 1972 SC
2(A) POETRY IN LOTION (RCA SF 8403) 1974

45s: Million Seller/Get Up (Sovereign SOV 118) 1973
Alexandra Park/
Mama I Can't Tell You (Sovereign SOV 121) 1973
Not Fade Away/After The Dance (RCA 2479) 1974
Don't Take Love/So Long Marilyn (RCA 2512) 1975
One Last Dance/Wishing (RCA 2628) 1975
Rock'n'Roll School/
On The Road To Fame (Decca F 13671) 1976
Carol Please Come Home/
Giving The Best Years Away (Decca F 13702) 1977

Fumble was previously known as The Balloons. This good-time "bryl-creem rock"; outfit's music was fast and frenetic and very different from the festival heavies of the era making them a sort of pub-rock version of **Showaddywaddy** or a UK version of Sha Na Na. (MW)

Funky Junction

Personnel:	ERIC BELL	gtr	A
	BRIAN DOWNEY	drms	A
	DAVE LENNOX	keyb'ds	A
	PHIL LYNOTT	bs	A
	BENNY WHITE	vcls	A

ALBUM: 1 A TRIBUTE TO DEEP PURPLE
(Stereo Gold MER 373) 1973 SC

A tribute album, recorded by the first line-up of **Thin Lizzy**, aided by Benny White and Dave Lennox... One track, *Palamatoon*, also appears on a similar **Jimi Hendrix** tribute (Purple Fox - *Tribute To Jimi Hendrix* (Stereo Gold MER 340) 1971), with possibly ficticious personnel. (JP)

Fusion Orchestra

Personnel:	DAVE BELL	drms	A
	DAVE COWELL	bs, hrmnca	A
	COLIN DAWSON	gtr	A
	STEN LAND	gtr, synth, perc, horns	A
	JILL SAWARD	gtr, synth, flute, vcls	A

ALBUM: 1(A) A SKELETON IN ARMOUR (EMI EMA 758) 1973 R1
NB: (1) reissued in Korea by Si-Wan.

45: When My Mama's Not At Home/
Nuthouse Rock (EMI EMI 2056) 1973

FUZZY DUCK - Fuzzy Duck (LP).

Fusion Orchestra was a short-lived progressive/hard-rock outfit. The album is now quite sought-after. *Except When My Momma's Not At Home*, which is essentially a mainstream rock 'n' rollin' piece with a brass arrangement, the remaining tracks, *Sonata In Z, Have I Left The Gas On?, A Skeleton In Armour* and *Talk To The Man In The Sky* are superb, especially the first two. Sophisticated compositions with astonishing and strong female vocals, superb manic guitar leads, powerful drumming, electric piano, flute and harmonica solos make this recommended listening. Jill Seward went on to record some jazz material in the eighties and nineties. (CA)

Fut

45: Have You Heard The Word/Futting (Beacon BEA 160) 1971 SC

This bizarre record was recorded by members of **The Bee Gees** and **The Marbles**. (VJ)

Fuzz Face

45: Mighty Quinn/Voices From The Sky (Page One POF 065) 1968

This short-lived combo covered **Manfred Mann**'s *Mighty Quinn* on the 'A' side of their sole single. (VJ)

Fuzzy Duck

Personnel:	PAUL FRANCIS	drms	A
	MICK HAWKSWORTH	bs	A
	ROY SHARLAND	organ	A
	GARTH WATT ROY	gtr, vcls	A

ALBUM: 1(A) FUZZY DUCK (Mam MAM 1005) 1971 R3
NB: (1) was reissued on Reflection (MM 05) in 1990 (SC) along with a booklet and a 45, *Double Time Woman/One More Hour* (MMS 01) and again (Aftermath AFT 1003) 1993 and (Repertoire REP 4352-WP) 1993 and again (Repertoire REP 4352-WP) 2000, with the 'A' and 'B' sides of their two 45s as bonus tracks.

45s: Double Time Woman/
Just Look Around You (Mam MAM 37) 1971 SC
Big Brass Band/One More Hour (Mam MAM 51) 1971 SC

This North London outfit included Mick Hawksworth who'd previously played with **Andromeda** and **Five Day Week Straw People**. Their organist Roy Sharland had previously been with Spice and **Arthur Brown**. Original copies of the album are expensive. Only 500 copies were originally pressed and are rumoured to have come with a free poster, though no one has actually ever seen one! The cover depicted an Afro-wearing duck. Musically it's in the heavy progressive genre. It does contain some pretty good organ-dominated instrumental passages and is worth investigation. The opening track *Time Will Be Your Doctor* is notable for a fine riff that gives way to guitar and organ solos.

The CD reissue on Repertoire comes with four bonus tracks: the 'A' side of the first 45, both sides of the second and *No Name Face*, a previously unissued song.

Garth Watt-Roy was also in **Greatest Show On Earth**. (VJ)

Fynn McCool

Personnel:	MICK CARTER	drms	A
	ALAN ESCOMBE	bs	A
	MICK FOWLER	keyb'ds, vcls	A
	CHRIS STONE	gtr, vcls	A

ALBUM: 1(A) FYNN McCOOL (RCA SF 8112) 1970 R1

45: U.S. Thumbstyle/Diamond Lil (RCA RCA 1956) 1970

This short-lived progressive underground rock outfit's album is now rare and sought-after. It contains some good instrumental interplay and maintains a high quality of material throughout. (VJ/RMJ)

GAGALACTYCA - Gagalactyca (LP).

Gagalactyca

ALBUM: 1 GAGALACTYCA
(Holyground HG 1135/Magic Mixture MM 3) 1990 SC

NB: (1) reissued on CD (Kissing Spell LKG 007) 2001 with bonus tracks from Thundermother.

Only 425 copies of this album were pressed and it came with a free booklet. Despite its late release date it's actually comprised of previously unreleased early seventies material by the two bands, Lightyears Away and Thundermother, who were responsible for the **Astral Navigations** album. Thunderrmother were a bluesy hard-rock quartet, led by freakbeat legend David John. Light Years Away played more thoughtful music and were assisted by **Bill Nelson** on one cut. The Thundermother bonus cut, *Pretty Anne* is one of the stronger offerings. (VJ)

Galactic Federation

45: March Of The Sky People/Moon Shot (Polydor 56093) 1966 R1

A forgotten sixties band, whose 45 is full of electronic and instrumental gimmicks. (VJ)

Gallagher and Lyle

| Personnel: | BENNY GALLAGHER | gtr, vcls | A |
| | GRAHAM LYLE | gtr, vcls | A |

				HCP
ALBUMS:	1	GALLAGHER AND LYLE	(A&M AMLS 68125) 1972	-
(up to	2	WILLIE AND THE LAP DOG	(A&M AMLH 68148) 1973	-
1976)	3	SEEDS	(A&M AMLS 68207) 1973	-
	4	THE LAST COWBOY	(A&M AMLS 68273) 1974	-
	5	BREAKAWAY	(A&M AMLH 68348) 1976	6
	6	LOVE ON THE AIRWAYS	(A&M AMLH 64620) 1976	19

NB: (5) reissued on Spot (SPR 8545) in 1984. (6) reissued on Music For Pleasure (MFP 50497) in 1981. There was also a *Best Of* (Warwick WW 5080) in 1980. (1) was originally issued on Capitol (21906) in 1972 in the UK. There's also a CD compilation, *Heart On My Sleeve (The Very Best Of)* (A&M 3971232) 1991.

				HCP
45s:	α	Trees/The In Crowd	(Polydor BM 56170) 1967	-
(up to		Desiderata/Comfort And Joy	(Capitol CL 15710) 1972	-
1976)		Give A Boy A Break/Joie Be Vivre	(A&M AMS 7013) 1972	-
		Jesus Save Me/Among The Birks	(A&M AMS 7063) 1973	-
		Sittin' Down Music/SS Man	(A&M AMS 7077) 1973	-
		Shine A Light/All I Want To Do	(A&M AMS 7087) 1973	-
		I Believe In You/Seeds	(A&M AMS 7099) 1974	-
		Song And Dance Man/Acne Blues	(A&M AMS 7134) 1974	-
		We/King Of The Silents	(A&M AMS 7142) 1974	-

	I Wanna Stay With You/		
	Fifteen Summers	(A&M AMS 7211) 1976	6
	Heart On My Sleeve/Northern Girl	(A&M AMS 7227) 1976	6
	Breakaway/Rock Writer	(A&M AMS 7245) 1976	35
Reissue:	I Wanna Stay With You/		
	Heart On My Sleeve	(Old Gold OG 9150) 1982	-

NB: α as Gallagher-Lyle.

This duo were from Largs, Ayrshire, in Scotland. **Gallagher and Lyle** began their songwriting career by writing *Mr. Heartbreak's Here Instead* for **Dean Ford and The Gaylords** in 1964. They also wrote songs for **James Galt**. They later moved down to London to secure a songwriting deal. Prior to signing to Apple in 1968 they released a 45 on Polydor as Gallagher-Lyle in 1967 but it attracted no notable interest. Whilst they were with Apple they wrote a couple of songs, *International* and *Sparrow*, which were covered by **Mary Hopkin** and Noel Harrison. When their contract expired they joined **McGuinness Flint** and wrote two Top Ten hits for the band, *When I'm Dead And Gone* and *Malt And Barley Blues*.

In September 1971 they left **McGuinness Flint** to strike out on their own. They proceeded to record a string of wimpish but admittedly melodic soft rock songs. After recording a debut album for Capitol they signed to A&M in March 1973, who proceeded to reissue their first album. Their first album proper for A&M was produced by Glyn Johns. After this they joined **Slim Chance**, who were **Ronnie Lane**'s touring group from the Spring of 1973 until May 1974, although during this time they recorded their *Seeds* album and contributed five songs to Dennis Coulson's Elektra album. After leaving **Slim Chance** they recorded *The Last Cowboy* album but this proved another flop in commercial terms.

The duo's big breakthrough came with their fifth album, *Breakaway*. It made No 6 in the UK Album Charts and provided them with two pretty insipid soft rock Top Ten hits:- *I Wanna Stay With You* and *Heart On My Sleeve* both peaked at No 6 in the UK and became minor hits in the US, where one would have thought their music would be ideally suited to FM Radio. The title track of the album was covered by Art Garfunkel whose version got to No 35 in the UK, but was much more successful in the States.

The duo split in 1980 to pursue independent careers but reformed in 1988 to release *Putting The Heart Back Into The City* on A&M to commemorate the opening of the Glasgow International Garden Exhibition. Concern for their native Scotland had been a theme in several of their songs. After this Gallagher moved into production and Lyle continued as a songwriter, most notably composing Tina Turner's No 1 *What's Love Got To Do With It* with Terry Britton.

Not a band who are of much interest to collectors, as yet. (VJ)

George Gallagher and White Trash

George Gallagher was the original vocalist with **The Poets**. *Rubble Vol. 13: Freakbeat Fantoms* (LP), *Rubble Vol. 7* (CD) and *The Best Of Rubble Collection Vol. 1* (CD) include a previously unreleased pop effort from 1967, *Dawn*, on which **The Pathfinders**, who later became **White Trash** back him. This is not a bad period piece. (VJ)

Rory Gallagher

				HCP
ALBUMS:	1	RORY GALLAGHER	(Polydor 2383 044) 1971 SC	32
(up to	2	DEUCE	(Polydor 2383 076) 1971 SC	39
1976)	3	LIVE IN EUROPE	(Polydor 2383 112) 1972 SC	9
	4	BLUEPRINT	(Polydor 2383 189) 1973 SC	12
	5	TATTOO	(Polydor 2383 230) 1973 SC	32
	6	IRISH TOUR 1974 (2-LP)	(Polydor 2659 031) 1974	36
	7	IN THE BEGINNING	(Emerald Gem GES 1 101) 1974	-
	8	AGAINST THE GRAIN	(Chysalis CHR 1098) 1975	-
	9	SINNER... AND SAINT	(Polydor 2383 315) 197	-
	10	THE STORY SO FAR	(Polydor 2383 376) 1975	-
	11	CALLING CARD	(Chysalis CHR 1124) 1976	32
	12	THE BEST YEARS	(Polydor 2664 303) 1976	-

NB: (1) and (2) originally issued on Atlantic in the US. (1) - (4) later reissued on Chrysalis in 1979. (2) reissued on CD (Capo CAPO 102) 1998. (4) and (5) reissued as a double set (That's Original TFOLP 021) in 1989, also on CD. (6) reissued on CD (Demon FIENDCD 120) 1988. (6) reissued again on CD (Sony/BMG Capo CAPO`106) 1998. (7) released on Springboard (4056) in the US. (8) reissued on CD

(Castle Classics CLACD 233) 1991. (11) reissued on CD (Essential ESSCD 143) in 1991, later on Castle (CLACD 352) 1994 and again (Sony/BMG Capo CAPO 109) 1998.

Also of interest is *Edged In Blue* (Demon FIENDCD 719) 1992, a selection of his work from 1972 onwards, and *G-Men-Bootleg Series, Volume One* (G-Men/Castle ESBCD 187) 1992, a 3-CD box set of bootleg recordings given legitimacy by **Gallagher** himself. *Big Guns - The Very Best Of* (Sony/BMG CAPO 705) 2005 is a 2-CD set to commemorate the 10 Year Anniversary of his death.

Born in Ballyshannon, County Donegal in Ireland, on 2 March 1949, **Gallagher** was still young when his family moved to Cork. He got his first guitar when he was just nine. The main local brand of music in Ireland at this time were showbands and when he left school at 15, having formed various local bands, he was in The Fontana Showband, which later changed its name to The Impact Showband. When it broke up in 1965 he remained with its bassist and drummer to form what evolved into the rock-blues band **Taste**. They went on to record several albums for Polydor between 1969-1971. Upon their demise he formed his own band with Gerry McAvoy (bs) and Wilgar Campbell (drms).

On his first two albums with this new band, **Rory Gallagher and Deuce**, he continued the blues-rock format of **Taste** but introduced several of his own compositions. He soon consolidated his reputation as one of the most talented guitarists in the second generation of British blues musicians. His third *Live In Europe* album reached the UK Top Ten. He was also honoured to contribute to the Muddy Waters' *Live In London* album.

In June 1972 Campbell left the band. His replacement, Rod de'Ath, and keyboardist Lou Martin, were both recruited to augment the line-up after leaving Irish band **Killing Floor**. The revitalised band embarked on a successful British tour and it became evident that Martin's keyboards were adding another dimension to the band's no nonsense driving blues-rock. The *Blueprint* and *Tattoo* albums are some of his finest and *Irish Tour 1974* was a double set incorporating material from an extremely successful tour to his homeland, which was also captured on film in a 90-minute documentary by film director Tony Palmer. It was premiered at the Cork Film Festival in 1974. *In The Beginning*, also released during 1974, comprised songs from the late sixties in Ireland prior to the formation of **Taste**. **Gallagher** went on playing right through the seventies, eighties and into the nineties and also recorded more albums.

Gallagher was a shy man who repeatedly turned his back on the glitsier side of showbusiness. An extremely powerful and talented guitarist (often known as "the people's guitarist") **Gallagher**'s albums are essential for fans of the blues-rock genre who don't already have them. **Gallagher** sadly died during a liver transplant operation in 1995. 10,000 people lined the streets of Cork for his funeral.

Big Guns - The Very Best Of is a worthwhile release and showcases his stadium blues rock and more acoustic traditional blues to commemorate the 10th anniversary of his death. It includes some rare live material from his time with **Taste** in the late sixties, his classic material like the title track, *Bullfrog Blues*, *Messin' With The Kid* and *Daughter Of The Everglades* and

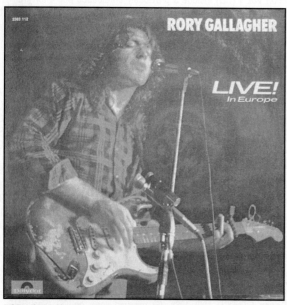

RORY GALLAGHER - Live In Europe (LP).

covers the period up to his posthumous *Wheel WithinWwheels* release. With extensive sleevenotes, it's a good introduction and retrospective of his career.

His performance of *Hands Off* at Reading Festival 1973, has been compiled on *Reading Festival 1973* (CD). (VJ)

Galliard

Personnel:	GEOFF BROWN	vcls	AB
	DAVE CASWELL	woodwind	AB
	RICHARD PANNELL	gtr	AB
	LESLIE PODRAZA	drms	AB
	(JOHN SMITH	woodwind	A
	HAROLD BECKETT	trumpet, flute, horn	B
	JOHN HUGHES	trombone	B
	LYLE JENKINS	sax	B
	JOHN MORTON	keyb'ds	B
	TONY ROBERTS	sax, flute	B
	TOMMY THOMAS	perc	B)

ALBUMS: 1(A) STRANGE PLEASURE
        (mono/stereo) (Deram Nova (S) DN 4) 1969 R3
     2(B) NEW DAWN (Deram SML 1075) 1970 R3

NB: (1) and (2) reissued on one CD (Two Of Us 002) 199?.

45: I Wrapped Her In Ribbons/
    Hermit And The Knight (Deram DM 306) 1970

Birmingham natives Geoff Brown and Richard Pannell had been members of **Craig**, responsible for one of the all-time great freakbeat 45s, *I Must Be Mad*. On *Strange Pleasure* **Galliard** established themselves as an extremely eclectic band, juxtaposing rural compositions with dissonant woodwind and brass, and starkly contrasting pastoral, even medieval songs with frenetic urban passages. It's an interesting but inconsistent debut. The A-side of the 45 was 'borrowed' from Ars Nova's *Wrapped Her In Ribbons* and credited to Brown. The B-side was non-album. *New Dawn* is even more schizophrenic. Most songs feature a tightly rocking backdrop, into which other parts are woven with varying degrees of success. The undisputed highlight is the funky electric sitar marathon *Ask For Nothing*, one of the great prog tracks of the era. Sadly *New Dawn* sold very poorly, and nothing more was heard from the band.

They also feature on the *Nova Sampler* (LP) playing *Skillet*. *I Wrapped Her In Ribbons* has been compiled on See For Miles' *Progressive Pop Inside The Seventies* (CD). (MK/VJ/RMJ)

James Galt

45s: Comes The Dawn/My Own Way (Pye 7N 15936) 1965
     With My Baby/Most Unusual Feeling (Pye 7N 17021) 1966 R1

From Largs in Scotland. **Gallagher and Lyle** were closely connected with this artist, writing at least one of these beat ballad 45s.

Compilation appearances have included: *Comes The Dawn* on *Ripples, Vol. 3* (CD); *In My Own Way* on *Doin' The Mod, Vol. 2* (CD); and *Comes The Dawn* and *In My Own Way* on *Footsteps To Fame, Vol. 2* (CD). (VJ)

The Gamblers

Personnel:	KEN BRADY	sax	A
	JIM CRAWFORD	gtr, vcls	A
	TONY DAMOND	trumpet, gtr	A
	ALAN GEORGE	keyb'ds	A
	ANDY MAC	drms	A
	ALAN SANDERSON	bs	A

45s: You've Really Got A Hold On Me/
    Can I See You Tonight (Decca F 11780) 1963
    Nobody But Me/It's So Nice (Decca F 11872) 1964 SC

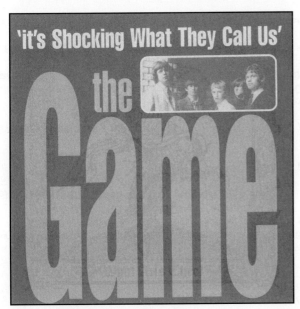

GAME - It's Shocking What They Call Us (CD).

Now I'm All Alone/			
Find Out What's Happening	(Decca F 12060) 1965 SC		
Doctor Goldfoot/It Seems So Long	(Decca F 12399) 1966 SC		
Cry Me A River/Who Will Buy	(Parlophone R 5557) 1967 SC		

A Geordie outfit who'd started life as Billy Fury's backing band (they also figured with him in the film 'I've Gotta Horse') but later went it alone. Their most successful record was *Now I'm Alone*, but somehow *Find Out What's Happening* found its way onto *The Garage Zone, Vol. 3* (LP). This 45 also got a US release on Press (9739) 1965 as did their final 45 on Coral (62525) in 1967. Their first 45, *You've Really Got A Hold On Me* was a Miracles' cover. Their final effort, *Cry Me A River*, was a Julie London song. (VJ)

Game

Personnel:	TONY BIRD	gtr, vcls	ABCD
	TERRY BOYES	vcls	A
	ALLEN JANAWAY	bs	ABC
	JIM NELSON	drms	AB
	TERRY SPENCER	ld gtr	ABCD
	RAY CHARLESLY	vcls	B
	TERRY GOODSELL	drms	CD
	(TERRY BROWN	drms	CD)
	STAN DECKER	bs	D

45s:			
	But I Do/Gotta Keep On Moving Baby	(Pye 7N 15889) 1965 R2	
	Gonna Get Me Someone/Gotta Wait	(Decca F 12469) 1966 R3	
α	The Addicted Man/		
	Help Me Mummy's Gone	(Parlophone R 5553) 1967 R6	
	It's Shocking What They Call Me/		
	Help Me Mummy's Gone	(Parlophone R 5569) 1967 R4	

NB: α withdrawn as a result of a negative review on 'Juke Box Jury'. The disc now commands four figure sums. There's also an Oak acetate of *The Addicted Man* dating from 3 December 1966. There's a CD *It's Shocking What The Call Us* (Dig) 199?, which compiles material from their 45s as well as unreleased material.

The Game formed in Mitcham, Surrey, in 1964. Terry Spencer and Allen Janaway had earlier played together in a group called The Secrets, along with future occasional member Terry Brown. Mod-popsters **Game** had a brief liaison with **Kenny Lynch** (the black Cockney entertainer) and then signed to the Original Sound Productions management agency and production company, which consisted of Mitcham songwriters Lesley Blake, Alan Gowing and Terry Brown.

Their debut for Pye, *Gotta Keep On Moving Baby*, was a reasonable beat-pop effort. Its sales were disappointing, though, and the band switched to Decca and was relaunched by that label for their promising **Who**-influenced mod-pop 45, *Gonna Get Me Someone*. The flip side, *Gotta Wait*, was basically a pop-art effort. Although the single didn't chart it impressed and they may have been on the brink of success when

Parlophone withdrew *The Addicted Man* after the song, which deals with heroin addiction, was voted a 'miss' on 'Juke Box Jury'. They recorded *It's Shocking What They Call Me* instead in a day and this was a great slice of psychedelia, but by now the momentum was lost. For me, though, their finest moment was *Help Me Mummy's Gone*, with it's great guitar riffs which recall **The Who** and **The Creation**. The song seemed to address the issue of divorce.

For the Parlophone 45s Tony Bird had switched from rhythm guitar to lead vocals. Tony Bird, who was only 14 when the group were formed, was later in an obscure seventies outfit **Kind Hearts and English** and may have also done some solo recordings. Terry Spencer and Stan Decker were later in **Lavender Grove**, who recorded an acetate for Oak. Later in 1969 they were in an Underground group called **Grail**, who recorded an album for the German Metronome label (MLP 15393) 1971 that was produced by **Rod Stewart**. The album, which was only issued in Germany and France, is now extremely collectable.

Game reformed in the nineties with a line-up of Tony Bird (vcls, gtr), Terry Brown (drms), Allen Janaway (bs) and Terry Spencer (lead gtr). A new 45, *Still On The Game*, their first since 1967, was released on Grass records. Thanks to Alan Gowing, who wrote the music to *Addicted Man* and *It's Shocking What They Call Me* for some of this info.

Compilation coverage has included:- *Gotta Keep On Moving Baby* on *Rubble, Vol. 10 - Professor Jordan's Magic Sound Show* (LP) and *The R&B Era, Vol. 1* (CD); *But I Do* on *Hippy Hippy Shake* (CD); *Gonna Get Me Someone* on *Rubble Vol. 5: The Electric Crayon Set* (LP) and *The Beat Scene* (CD); *Gonna Get Me Someone* and *Gotta Wait* on *Rubble Vol. 3* (CD); *Gotta Wait* on *Broken Dreams, Vol. 5* (LP), *Great British Psychedelic Trip, Vol. 2* (CD) and *British Psychedelic Trip, Vol. 4* (LP); *It's Shocking What They Call Me* on *Perfumed Garden, Vol. 1* (LP & CD), *Maximum Freakbeat* (CD) and *Electric Sugarcube Flashbacks, Vol. 2* (LP); *Help Me Mummy's Gone* on *Electric Sugarcube Flashbacks, Vol. 1* (LP), *Rubble Vol. 13: Freakbeat Fantoms* (LP), *Rubble Vol. 7* (CD), *The Best Of Rubble Collection, Vol. 5* (CD) and *Chocolate Soup For Diabetics, Vol. 3* (LP); *The Addicted Man* (acetate) on *Purple Heart Surgery Vol. 3* (LP), *Story Of Oak Records* (Dble LP)/*The Story Of Oak Records* (CD); and *The Addicted Man* on *Beat It* (3-CD). (VJ/AG)

Elmer Gantry's Velvet Opera

Personnel:	COLIN FORSTER	gtr	A
	JOHN FORD	bs	ABC
	ELMER GANTRY	vcls, gtr	ABC
	RICHARD HUDSON	drms	ABC
	JOHN JOYCE	vcls	C

ALBUMS:	1(A)	ELMER GANTRY'S VELVET OPERA	
		(Direction 8-63300) 1967 R1	
	2(C)	RIDE A HUSTLER'S DREAM	(CBS 63692) 1969 R1

ELMER GANTRY'S VELVET OPERA - Elmer Gantry's Velvet Opera (Mini LP).

ELMER GANTRY'S VELVET OPERA - Elmer Gantry's Velvet Opera (LP).

NB: (1) reissued on CD (Repertoire REP 4495-WP) with their six non-album 45 cuts and again (Akarma AK 297) 2005. (2) Credited to **Velvet Opera**. (2) reissued on CD (Akarma AK 306) 2005. Also of interest is *The Very Best Of* (See For Miles SEECD 437) compilation, which compiles tracks from both albums, alongside single tracks and four previously unreleased songs. Fans may also be interested in a mini-LP *Elmer Gantry's Velvet Opera* (Apothecary SORCERY 001), which contains a 1968 BBC 'Saturday Club' session alongside an acetate version of *Flames*.

45s:	Flames/Salisbury Plain	(Direction 58-3083) 1967 SC
	Mary Jane/Dreamy	(Direction 58-3481) 1968
	Volcano/A Quick 'B'	(Direction 58-3924) 1969

This London band is best remembered for hard-rock single, *Flames*, a cut from their first album which narrowly missed the charts in 1967. The track was also featured on *The Rock Machine Turns You On* (LP) compilation. Featuring Richard Hudson and John Ford of **The Strawbs** and **Hudson-Ford** fame the album was full of variety spanning Motown, pop-psych and harder rock genres. Other tracks which catch the ear include the laid back Oscar Brown song *I Was Cool*, the instrumental *Walter Sly Meets Bill Bailey*, the Eastern-influenced sitar-based *Air*, the Beatlesque *What's The Point Of Leaving*, the melodic *Long Nights Of Summer* and two tracks - *Dream Starts* and *Reactions Of A Young Man* - which veered towards psychedelia.

For the later single, *Volcano*, they shortened their name to **Velvet Opera** and also recorded a second album under that name. Although a popular underground band, commercial success eluded them. Ford and Hudson joined **The Strawbs** when **The Velvet Opera** disintegrated. In the seventies **Elmer Gantry** was in **Stretch**.

The Very Best Of Elmer Gantry's Velvet Opera (See For Miles SEECD 437) 1995 includes the 'best' of their first album alongside material from *Ride A Hustler's Dream*, their more progressive second effort recorded under the name **Velvet Opera** and four previously unissued cuts of which *Talk To The Devil* is a superb slice of freakbeat from an obscure movie of this name. This stands alongside *Flames*, their best known cut, as their finest moment on a CD which includes covers of *Statesboro Blues* and *Eleanor Rigby*.

Artefacts From The Psychedelic Dungeon CD also features two cuts from a session the band did on John Peel's 'Top Gear' around 1968: their best known number, *Flames*, and a version of **Hendrix**'s *All Along The Watchtower*. Other compilation appearances have included:- *Air* on *Electric Psychedelic Sitar Headswirlers, Vol. 2* (CD); and *Mother Writes, All Along The Watchtower* and *Mary Jane* on *Hard Up Heroes, Vol. 2* (CD). (VJ)

Garden Odyssey

| 45: | Joker/Have You Ever Been To Georgia | (RCA RCA 2159) 1972 |

This was a five-piece band, comprising two Canadians (the lead singers) and three Brits. The 'A' side was penned by **Graham Gouldman**. (VJ)

Garden Odyssey Enterprise

| 45: | Sad And Lonely/Sky Pilot | (Deram DM 267) 1969 SC |

A short-lived late sixties five-piece band. *Sky Pilot* was the **Eric Burdon** song. The 'A' side was written by **Graham Gouldman**, who oversaw this obscure project.

Sad And Lonely has been compiled on *The Psychedelic Scene* (CD). (VJ)

Col Garnett

| 45: | With A Girl Like You/Monday Monday | (Page One POF 002) 1966 |

This artist's solo pop single contained cover versions of hit songs by **The Troggs** and The Mamas and Papas. He also supervised Page One's recording sessions. (VJ)

David Garrick

ALBUMS:	1	A BOY CALLED DAVID	(Piccadilly NPL 38024) 1967 SC
	2	DON'T GO OUT IN THE RAIN, SUGAR	
		(mono/stereo)	(Piccadilly N(S)PL 38035) 1968 SC

NB: (1) reissued on vinyl (Marble Arch MAL 822) 1968. (1) reissued on Repertoire (RR 4091-WZ) 1991 with extra tracks. *The Pye Anthology* (Sequel NEECD 297) 1998 includes all his recordings between 1965 and 1969 (including the above two albums) along with 11 previously unissued songs.

| EP: | 1 | DAVID | (Piccadilly NEP 34056) 1967 R1 |

HCP

45s:	When The World Was Our Own/Go	(Piccadilly 7N 35231) 1965 -
	One Little Smile/	
	We Must Be In Love	(Piccadilly 7N 35263) 1965 -
	Lady Jane/Let's Go Somewhere	(Piccadilly 7N 35317) 1966 28
	Dear Mrs. Applebee/	
	You're What I'm Living For	(Piccadilly 7N 35335) 1966 22
	I've Found A Love/Broken Heart	(Piccadilly 7N 35371) 1967 -
	Certain Misunderstanding/	
	I'm Looking Straight At You	(Piccadilly 7N 35377) 1967 -
	Don't Go Out Into The Rain/	
	Theme For A Wishing Heart	(Piccadilly 7N 35402) 1967 -
	Ave Maria/Please Stay	(Pye 7N 17409) 1967 -
	Rainbow/I'll Be Home	(Pye 7N 17509) 1968 -
	A Little Bit Of This/	
	Flutter By Butterfly	(Pye 7N 17610) 1968 -
	Maypole Mews/	
	Like To Get To Know You Better	(Pye 7N 17685) 1969 -
	Poor Little Me/	
	Molly With The Hair Like Silver	(Pye 7N 17820) 1969 -

VELVET OPERA - Ride A Hustler's Dream (LP).

Bake Me A Woman/
House In The Heather   (Columbia DB 8680) 1969 -

Garrick's real name was Philip Darryl Core and he was a Liverpudlian who'd sung in a church choir and undergone operatic training for four years. He entered the world of pop in 1965 and enjoyed minor hits with his cover of **The Rolling Stones**' *Lady Jane* and the catchy *Dear Mrs. Applebee*. Aside from these two tracks his first album was comprised of other cover versions. Musically the material ranged from vaudeville pop to Motown and Stax material. Neither this nor any of his subsequent 45s have aroused much interest from collectors, although his EP is pretty scarce. He was a bit of a sex symbol at the time but has long since been forgotten.

The 1991 CD reissue of his debut album comes with five bonus tracks. *The Pye Anthology* includes all his recordings between 1965 and 1969 as well as 11 unissued songs, which were cover versions of songs ranging from **The Bee Gees**' *Spicks And Specks* to Sandie Shaw's *Monsieur Dupont*.

Compilation appearances have included: *Dear Mrs Applebee* on *Piccadilly Story* (CD), *Beat Generation - Ready Steady Go* (CD) and on the 2-CD set *We Love The Pirates: Charting The Big 'L' Fab 40*; and *Lady Jane* on *Beat Merchants* (CD) and *Radio Two: Sound Of The Sixties* (CD). (VJ)

Garrick's Fairground

Personnel incl: MICHAEL GARRICK   A

ALBUM: 1(A)   MR. SMITH'S APOCALYSE   (Argo ZAGF 1) 1971 R2

45:   Epiphany/Blessed Are The Peacemakers   (Argo AFW 105) 1971

Michael Garrick, who fronted this outfit, was a jazz musician who made several albums both on his own and as a quintet, a sextet and a trio. These are listed below:

ALBUMS:				
(up to	1	CASE OF JAZZ	(Airborne) 1963	R2
1976)	2	MOONSCAPE	(Airborne) 1964	R4
	3	POETRY AND JAZZ IN CONCERT (2-LP)	(Argo ZDA 26/27) 1964	R2
	4	OCTOBER WOMAN	(Argo (Z)DA 33) 1965	R1
	5	PROMISES	(Argo (Z)DA 36) 1965	R2
	6	BLACK MARIGOLDS	(Argo (Z)DA 88) 1968	R1
	7	JAZZ PRAISES AT St. PAULS	(Airborne NBP 0021) 1968	R1
	8	POETRY AND JAZZ IN CONCERT 250 (2-LP)	(Argo (Z)PR 264/5) 1969	R1
	9	HEART IS A LOTUS	(Argo ZDA 135) 1970	R1
	10	COLD MOUNTAIN	(Argo ZDA 153) 1972	R1
	11	HOME STRETCH BLUES	(Argo ZDA 154) 1972	R1
	12	ILLUMINATION	(Impulse AS 49) 1973	SC
	13	TROPPO	(Argo ZDA 163) 1974	R1

NB: (3) with Norma Winstone. (4) as Michael Garrick Quintet, with Joe Harriot. (5) as Michael Garrick Sextet, with Ian Carr. (6) as Michael Garrick Septet. (8) as Michael Garrick Quintet. (9) as Michael Garrick Sextet with Norma Winstone. (10) as Michael Garrick Trio. (13) as Michael Garrick Sextet.

EPs:	1	ANTHEM - MICHAEL GARRICK QUINTET		
		(mono/stereo)	(Argo EAF/ZFA 92) 1965	R1
	2	BEFORE NIGHT/DAY	(Argo EAF 115) 1966	R1

Garrick was born on 30 May 1933 in Enfield, Middlesex. He studied literature at London University and led a trio and quartet in the late fifties. In the early sixties he performed regularly mixing jazz and poetry in his concerts. He formed a sextet in 1965 and recorded profusely in the late sixties and early seventies as indicated in the discography above. In the seventies he began to teach as well as play and compose. He founded The Travelling Jazz Faculty in 1979, played with Chris Hunter in the early eighties and Dave Green's band in 1984. (VJ)

Nick Garrie

ALBUM: 1   THE NIGHTMARE OF J.B. STANISLAS
                                        (Disc AZ STEC 107) 1969 R2

NB (1) French only.

This youthful Englishman's 1969 debut originally appeared only in France, ensuring that originals change hands for three figures today. It's a competent assortment of orchestrated ballads and novelty songs whose dense arrangements frequently swamp the delicate material. The results are more reminiscent of Peter Sarstedt than the edgier work of, say, **Scott Walker**, though there are gems here such as the lush title track and eerie closer *Evening*. As a whole it isn't especially unusual or psychedelic, though. **Garrie** is now a French teacher in Slough.

His rather sugary pop composition *Wheel Of Fortune* from his album is on *Circus Days Vol. 1 & 2* (CD) and *Circus Days, Vol. 1* (LP). Another of his compositions, *Little Bird* can be found on *Spinning Wheel* (CD). (VJ/RMJ)

Freddie Garrity

ALBUM:	1	OLIVER IN THE UNDERWORLD (Soundtrack)	
(up to			(Starline SRS 5019) 1970 SC
1976)			

NB: (1) reissued on vinyl (CBS 70096) 1971.

45s:	Little Red Donkey/	
(up to	So Many Different Ways	(Columbia DB 8348) 1968
1976)	I Understand/I Know You Know We Know	(UK UK 55) 1973
	Hello Kids/It's Good For You	(Bus Stop BUS 1017) 1974
	The Chicken Song/Pooh Pooh Pooh	(Bus Stop BUS 1022) 1974

Freddie Garrity was born on 14 November 1940 in Manchester. He has led line-ups of **Freddie and The Dreamers** over five decades and still has a version of the band on the road. See the **Freddie and The Dreamers** entry for details of his career with them - these were a splattering of solo entries he had along the way. (VJ)

Gass

Personnel:	JUNIOR KERR		A
	ERROL McLEAN	congas	ABC
	GODFREY McLEAN	drms	ABC
	HUMPHREY OKAH	sax	ABC
	ALAN ROSKANS	lead gtr	ABC
	ROBERT TENCH		A
	FRANK CLARK	organ	BC
	IAN THOMAS		C
	PETER GREEN	gtr	

ALBUM: 1(-)   JUJU   (Polydor 2383 022) 1970 R1
NB: (1) featuring **Peter Green**.

45s:	One Of These Days/	
	I Don't Know Why	(Parlophone R 5344) 1965 SC
	The New Breed/In The City	(Parlophone R 5456) 1966 R1
	Dream Baby (How Long Must I Dream)/	
	Jitterbug Sid	(CBS 202647) 1967 SC
	Something's Got To Change Your Ways/	
	Mr. Banana	(Polydor 2058 147) 1971

Formed in London in May 1965, by Errol and Godfrey McLean (from British Guiana) and Robert Tench (from Trinidad), this group was managed by Rik Gunnell (**Georgie Fame / Zoot Money**) and their third 45 was produced by Mike Smith. **Peter Green** was also involved in **Gass** after leaving **Fleetwood Mac**. The band also featured in a cast recording, *Catch My Soul - The Rock Othello* (Polydor 2383 035) 1971 (SC). One cut, *Black Velvet*, was later featured on Polydor's 1970 compilation, *Supergroups, Vol. 2* (LP). (VJ/NR)

Gass Company

Personnel incl: BILL HURD
                  JOHN RICHARDSON

45:   Everybody Needs Love/Nightmare   (President PT 170) 1967 SC

One of a small batch of psychedelic-tinged goodies on this normally pop/soul label. It's *Nightmare* that hits the right spots. They came from Essex. Bill Hurd was later in **Wake** and **The Rubettes**.

Compilation appearances include: *Nightmare* on *Justavibration* (LP), *The Electric Lemonade Acid Test, Vol. 1* (LP), *Sometimes I Wonder* (CD) and *Oddities, Vol 1* (CD) and *Everybody Needs Love* on *Colour Me Pop, Vol 1* (CD). (VJ)

Gas Works

Personnel:
JOHN BROWN	gtr, vcls, bs	A
MICK DRAPER	violin, mandolin, hrmnca	A

ALBUM: 1(A) GAS WORKS   (Regal Zonophone SRLZ 1036) 1973 SC

45s: Standing Stiff/
Keep On Rolling   (Regal Zonophone RZ 3075) 1973
God's Great Spaceship/
Cider With Rosie   (Regal Zonophone RZ 3080) 1973

Well, it is on Regal Zonophone and it has got a nice back cover. Label completists must have this, of course. I would advise all others to steer clear of this self-indulgent live album by two funny Englishmen with a knack for wordplay and uninspired, er, folk music. One of the tracks is called *Verbalise Your Pre-orgasmic Tensions*. Enough said.

The album is an edited recording of a concert held at the Marquee club in London on 29 July 1972. (MK)

Gates of Eden

45s: Too Much On My Mind/
I'm Warning You   (Pye 7N 17195) 1966 SC
Snoopy Versus The Red Baron/
In Your Love   (Pye 7N 17252) 1967
One To Seven/Hey Now   (Pye 7N 17278) 1967 SC

Another forgotten sixties band. The first 'A' side was a **Kinks** song. The second had been done by US band The Royal Guardsmen and was later covered by **The Hotshots** in 1973.

Compilation appearances include: *Too Much On My Mind* on *Paisley Pop - Pye Psych (& Other Colours) 1966-1969* (CD); *1 To 7* on *Red With Purple Flashes, Vol. 1* (LP) and *Ripples, Vol. 5* (CD); *Yha Da Da* on *Red With Purple Flashes, Vol. 2* (LP); *Mini-Shirts, Too Much On My Mind, In Your Love* and *Yha Da Da* on *Sixties Years, Vol. 6* (CD); and *Hey Now* on *Doin' The Mod, Vol. 1* (CD). (VJ)

GENESIS - Trespass (LP).

GENESIS - Nursery Cryme (LP).

John Gaughan

45:     You Gotta Love Me/Motorcity Way   (CBS 1747) 1973

For further details see **Bobby Moonshine**. (VJ)

The Gaylords

45:     He's A Good Face But He's Down And Out/
You Know It Too   (Columbia DB 7805) 1966 SC

See also **Dean Ford and The Gaylords**. *He's A Good Face But He's Down And Out* later resurfaced on *Pop-In, Vol 2* (CD). (VJ)

Ron Geesin

ALBUMS: 1 RAISE OF THE EYEBROWS
(up to   (Transatlantic (S)TRA 161) 1967 R1
1976)   2 MUSIC FROM THE FILM THE BODY
                          (Harvest SHSP 4008) 1970
         3 ELECTROSOUND   (KPM KPM 1102) 1972 SC
         4 AS HE STANDS   (Ron Geesin RON 28) 1973 SC
         5 ELECTROSOUND, VOL. 2   (KPM KPM 1154) 1975 SC
         6 PATRUNS   (Ron Geesin RON 31) 1975 SC

NB: (2) with **Roger Waters**. (3) and (5) Library issues. (1) and (4) reissued on one CD (See For Miles SEECD 433).

EP: 1 MR. MAYOR STOMP YOUR HEAD (PS)
                          (RRG 319/320) 1965 R2

Born in Ayrshire in 1943 **Geesin** has been responsible for several avant-garde musical projects over the years. His first group was the Crawley-based Original Downtown Syncopators Jazz Band who made two EPs and a 10" album. Just before he left the band he recorded his own privately pressed EP of piano solos in 1965. Only 100 copies of the home-made EP were pressed and mostly sold in jazz clubs so they are practically impossible to find now and are his rarest item.

In the late sixties, he took his one-man show around the folk clubs and also appeared frequently on BBC folk programmes. His first Transatlantic album was also rare although one of the cuts, *Certainly Random*, got a further airing on Transatlantic's 1969 *Listen Here!* (LP) compilation. Another of his songs, *Agitation In Anticipation Of Offspring*, appeared the same year on BBC's *John Peel Presents Top Gear* (LP). Shortly afterwards he became friendly with **Pink Floyd**'s **Roger Waters** and this led to the two of them collaborating on *Music From The Film The Body*, which is notable for being **Waters**' first solo appearance on vinyl. The album is awful, a combination of depressing cello arrangements and body noises. It consists of several short tracks (12 on side one and 10 on side two) with titles like *March Past Of The Embryos* and *More Than Seven Dwarfs In Penis-Land*. Four or five of the songs are penned and sung by **Roger Waters** with acoustic guitar accompaniment. One of these, the closing track, *Give Birth To A Smile* has gospel-style vocals and features the rest of **Pink Floyd** albeit uncredited. **Geesin** went on to co-write much of the title-track music on Pink Floyd's *Atom Heart Mother*.

In 1972 he recorded the first of a series of music library albums which were pressed in quantities of 1,000 each. The following year he started his own label. Its second release, *Patrons*, was a series of piano solos.

He's continued to record until the present day. (VJ)

Gemini (1)

45:      Space Walk/Goodbye Joe   (Columbia DB 7638) 1965 R1

The 'B' side of this disc was a tribute to Joe Meek. It's rumoured to be The Tornados under a pseudonym. (VJ)

Gemini (2)

45:      Please Don't Let It Start/
         You Took Me By Surprise   (RCA RCA 1914) 1970

Rather typical uninspiring 1970s pop. (MWh)

Genesis

Personnel:

TONY BANKS	keyb'ds, vcls	ABCDEF G
(up to	PETER GABRIEL	vcls, flute	ABCD
1976)	ANTHONY PHILLIPS	gtr, vcls	ABC
	MICHAEL RUTHERFORD	bs, gtr, vcls	ABCDEF G
	CHRIS STEWART	drms	A
	JOHN SILVER	drms	B
	JOHN MAYHEW	drms, vcls	C
	PHIL COLLINS	drms	DEF G
	STEVE HACKETT	gtr	DEF G
	(BILL BRUFORD	drms	F)
	(CHESTER THOMPSON	drms	G)

HCP

ALBUMS: 1(B)   FROM GENESIS TO REVELATION (w/insert)
(up to   (mono/stereo)   (Decca LK/SLK 4990) 1969 R1 -
1976)   2(C)   TRESPASS   (Charisma CAS 1020) 1970 SC -
        3(D)   NURSERY CRYME   (Charisma CAS 1052) 1971 SC 39

GENESIS - Foxtrot (LP).

GENESIS - Live (LP).

4(D)   FOXTROT   (Charisma CAS 1058) 1972 12
5(D)   GENESIS LIVE   (Charisma CLASS 1) 1973 9
6(D)   SELLING ENGLAND BY THE POUND
                                   (Charisma CAS 1074) 1973 3
7(D)   THE LAMB LIES DOWN ON BROADWAY (2-LP)
                                   (Charisma CDS 101) 1974 10
8(C/D) GENESIS COLLECTION VOLUME 1 (2-LP)
                                   (Charisma CGS 102) 1975 R2 -
9(D)   GENESIS COLLECTION VOLUME 2 (2-LP)
                                   (Charisma CGS 103) 1975 R2 -
10(E) A TRICK OF THE TAIL   (Charisma CDS 4001) 1976 3
11G)   WIND AND WUTHERING   (Charisma CDS 4005) 1976 7

NB: Some copies of (1) were in mono. These are R4. There is one known test pressing of this in mono, valued at circa £1,850 in 'Record Collector'. Three stereo pressings are worth circa £1,250. (1) reissued on CD (Razor MACHK 11) 1988, but deleted in 1989 and by Music Club (MCCD 133) 1993 with the added bonus of their non-album Decca 45s. (2) reissued on CD (Charisma CASCD 1020) 1988 and (Virgin CASCDX 1020). Various test pressings of (3) exist. (3) reissued on CD (Charisma CASCD 1052) 1985 and (Virgin CASCDX 1052). (4) reissued on CD (Charisma CASCD 1058) 1986 and (Virgin CASCDX 1058). (5) reissued on CD (Charisma CLACD 1) 1985 and (Virgin CASCDX 1). (6) reissued on CD (Charisma CASCD 1074) 1986 and (Virgin CASCDX 1074). (7) reissued on CD (Charisma CGSCD 1) 1986 and (Virgin CGSCDX 1). (8) is a box set of (2) and (3) in original sleeves with poster. (9) is a box set of (4) and (6) with poster. (10) reissued on CD (Charisma CDSCD 4001) 1986. (11) reissued on CD (Charisma CDSCD 4005) 1986. (2), (3) and (4) are also available as a CD set (Virgin TPAK 1) 1990. *Three Sides Live* (Charisma GECD 2002) 1992 is also relevant as is *Genesis CD Box Set* (Virgin TPAK 17) 1991. *Genesis Archive 1967-1975* (Virgin CDBOX 6) 1998 is a 4-CD box set.

HCP

45s: The Silent Sun/That's Me   (Decca F 12735) 1968 R4 -
(up to α   A Winter's Tale/One-Eyed Hound (Decca F 12775) 1968 R4 -
1976) α   Where The Sour Turns To Sweet/
           In Hiding   (Decca F 12949) 1969 R4 -
       β   Looking For Someone/
           Visions Of Angels   (Charisma GS 1) 1970 R5 -
       χ   The Knife Part 1/
           The Knife Part 2 (Some in PS) (Charisma CB 152) 1971 R4/R1 -
           Happy The Man/
           Seven Stones (Some in PS)   (Charisma CB 181) 1972 R4/R1 -
           Twilight Alehouse (1-sided flexidisc free
           with 'Zig Zag' and later via fan club) (Charisma - no #) 1973 R1 -
           I Know What I Like (In Your Wardrobe)/
           Twilight Alehouse   (Charisma CB 224) 1974 21
           Counting Out Time/Riding The Scree (Charisma CB 238) 1974 -
           The Carpet Crawlers/
           Evil Jam (The Waiting Room live) (Charisma CB 251) 1975 SC -
           A Trick Of The Tail/Ripples   (Charisma CB 277) 1976 -

NB: A handful of one-sided test pressings of *The Silent Sun* exist on the blue Decca label. Their value is circa £1,750 according to 'Record Collector'. There are also one-sided acetates of *That's Me*, worth a similar value. There's also a one-sided test pressing of *In The Beginning* (1969), an unreleased UK single (which was released in a rare picture sleeve in Italy). α both sold poorly and are now very hard to find. β promo only, sent out to the press to market the *Trepass* album. Copies are now very

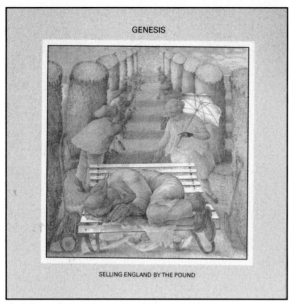

GENESIS - Selling England By The Pound (CD).

rare. χ was the first **Genesis** single with a picture sleeve - mint copies are very hard to find. *Your Own Special Way* (10" acetate) (Trident Studios CUT 1) 1976 is a very rare acetate on the Trident Studios label.

In the seventies **Genesis** was one of handful of groups spearheading progressive rock in the UK and the band also launched Peter Gabriel and Phil Collins as superstars. It remained a force for three decades and in the eighties became an arena-scale act in the States.

Genesis was formed out of the ashes of two groups formed at Charterhouse Public School, near Godalming in Surrey:- The Anon (Rivers Job (bs), Richard MacPhail (vcls), Rob Tyrell (drms), Anthony Phillips (lead gtr) and Michael Rutherford (rhythm gtr)) and The Garden Wall (Tony Banks (piano), Peter Gabriel (vcls) and Chris Stewart (drms)). The Anon seem to have been a **Beatles/Rolling Stones** covers band whilst The Garden Wall was more into flower-power. When Job (who later played for **The Savoy Brown Blues Band**) and MacPhail left the school in July 1966 The Anon continued as a trio but Phillips and Rutherford also supplemented The Garden Wall as The (New) Anon. This combo made a six-track demo of mainly Phillips/Rutherford songs which they sent to former Charterhouse pupil **Jonathan King**, who was already a pop star and working at Decca. He arranged for them to record a couple of demos and offered them a five year recording contract. With the band still at school, their parents objected and eventually they were signed on a one year contract with a further year's option. **King** also renamed the group **Genesis** in January 1967. In early 1968 they released two singles; *The Silent Sun* and *A Winter's Tale*, which attracted a little media attention but failed to sell. Naturally, both are now extremely rare and collectable. At this point Chris Stewart left the group to be replaced by John Silver.

Undeterred by the commercial failure of their first two 45s, **King** booked time in Regent Sound Studios during the 1968 Summer holidays to enable the band to record an album. The record company, having discovered the existence of an American band of the same name, put pressure on **King** to change their name, **King** refused but did agree to remove their name from their album calling it *From Genesis To Revelation*. **King** later added an orchestra to the original sessions as he sought to achieve a classical/rock fusion reminiscent of **The Moody Blues**. He failed, the end result being a rather messy production which only sold in small quantities. The album came with a lyric sheet and was released both in mono and stereo. Mono issues are particularly collectable now but mainly among **Genesis** completists. Also extremely hard to find (and expensive) now was a further 45 - *Where The Sour Turns To Sweet* - which simply didn't sell at the time. Their contract with Decca was allowed to lapse and they almost disbanded. Instead, all having left school, they decided to go professional but with John Mayhew, who'd been recruited via a Melody Maker ad. replacing Silver on drums.

After a few early gigs in youth and social clubs and colleges, the group retreated to a cottage near Dorking for five months to write songs for their second album and rehearse their stage act. In March 1970, they were signed by Charisma. Their debut album for the label, *Trespass*, wasn't entirely convincing and didn't sell in any large quantities. There was also a two-part single, *The Knife*, taken from the album, which didn't sell. Some copies came in picture sleeves and these are now extremely rare and collectable. After completing the album, Mayhew and Phillips left the band. They were replaced by Phil Collins, a childhood actor who'd played The Artful Dodger in the West End production of 'Oliver' and appeared in several TV and film roles, (Collins had responded to an advert in Melody Maker). Mick Barnard filled in briefly for Phillips but his permanent replacement was ex-**Quiet World** member **Steve Hackett**.

Nursery Cryme found the band gaining in confidence. The album was more adventurous than its two predecessors as they searched for the style which would eventually become their trademark. Peter Gabriel's outrageous stage costumes and the band's experimentation with visuals attracted some media attention but the album again failed to sell in significant quantities, as did the 45, *Happy The Man*. Again, some copies of these came in picture sleeves and are particularly rare and collectable.

Foxtrot was the album that brought them their big breakthrough, climbing to No 12 in the UK. The 24-minute track *Supper's Ready* won them considerable acclaim and became something of a live anthem. Hot on its success, they played their first US gig at Brandeis University in Boston followed by a charity gig in New York a couple of days later. After returning to the UK for a headlining tour with Tony Sratton-Smith, a promoter, taking over their management they returned to the US for a second more extensive US tour during November and December 1973. After filling Drury Lane Theatre for five nights in January 1974 they undertook a sell-out European tour and then returned to the US for a third tour in Spring 1974. They'd been slogging their guts out but their hard work was being repaid. *Genesis Live*, recorded during a UK tour in Leicester and Manchester, got into the UK Top Ten. Their relentless American touring also ensured it got a place in the lower echelons of the US Charts (No 105). Their next studio album, *Selling England By The Pound*, did even better, getting to No 3 in the UK and No 70 in the US. An edited version of one of the tracks, *I Know What I Like (In Your Wardrobe)*, was issued as a 45 and gave them their first UK hit single, peaking at No 21. A second 45, *Counting Out Time*, was culled from the album but failed to chart. With increasing interest in the band in the US, London Records released their debut album there and it crept to No 170.

The album that really established **Genesis** as a major rock band was the ambitious double concept album, *The Lamb Lies Down On Broadway*. After its release in November 1974 they embarked on a World Tour on which they performed the entire live album 102 times (God, they must have got bored)! To be fair it did contain some good progressive rock, not least the title track. It brought them further Chart success too, rising to No 10 in the UK and No 41 in the US, although *The Carpet Crawlers* 45 taken from it did not chart. Just when it seemed they had finally established themselves as superstars, Peter Gabriel stunned the rock world in May 1975, at the end of 'The Lamb Lies Down On Broadway' tour, by announcing that he was leaving for unspecified personal reasons. And leave he did, eventually enjoying a successful solo career. When Gabriel left **Genesis**, they hired a guy called Mich Strickland to sing lead vocals. However, he couldn't reach the high notes and was fired. Many rock pundits were already writing the

GENESIS - The Lamb Lies Down On Broadway (CD).

GENESIS - A Trick Of The Tail (CD).

GENESIS - Wind And Wuthering (CD).

band off when Phil Collins stepped up from behind the drums to take over the lead vocal role. He did so with remarkable success and their first album without Peter Gabriel, *A Trick Of The Tail*, was extremely well received. In fact, Collins played drums and sang lead vocals on the album. This was an arrangement which couldn't continue permanently and in March 1976 former **Yes** and **King Crimson** drummer, Bill Bruford, was recruited to augment their line-up on stage. After he left in November 1976 to fulfil other session commitments, Chester Thompson (formerly with Weather Report, Zappa, The Pointer Sisters, etc.), an American from Baltimore, Maryland, was recruited as a replacement.

As 1976 drew to a close, the band released another successful album, *Wind And Wuthering*, which they'd recorded in Holland in November. Their distinctive but often unexciting brand of music had undeniably established them as one of Britain's top progressive rock acts though for me at least they pale by comparison to bands like **Yes**.

Phil Collins also played with a second group, Brand X, whilst with **Genesis**, and **Steve Hackett** recorded solo albums in 1975 and 1978.

The group reconvened for 1980's *Duke*, which gave them their first UK No 1 album and they repeated the feat with *Abacab* in late 1981 as they became a massive attraction in the States too. 1983's *Genesis* was another UK No 1, but also became their second million-selling US album and spawned their first US Top Ten single *That's All*. 1985's *Invisible Touch*, another UK No 1, bettered this going platinum many times over in the States. They promoted it with their biggest tour to date which underscored their credentials as a mega arena-scale act in the States. Their 1991 album *We Can't Dance* was another UK No 1, but was Collins' last album with the band. Former Stiltskin vocalist Ray Wilson replaced him. 1997's *Calling All Stations* marked a return to their art-rock roots, but it was far less successful commercially than its predecessors as was the tour to help promote it and the group now seemed in terminal decline.

Genesis Archive is a 4-CD set with a booklet of photos, but rather lame liner notes. The first two CDs feature a live performance of *The Lamb Lies Down On Broadway* from the Shrine Auditorium, Los Angeles in 1975. CD 3 picks up a bit with their scarce singles *Happy The Man* and *Twilight Alehouse* along with more unreleased live material. CD 4 is the most interesting. It contains 20 tracks from the original line-up from 1967-1970. Some are rough mixes (before orchestration) from the final album. There are also three cuts from a BBC broadcast and several raw demos and unreleased cuts. Peter Gabriel's vocals are often the best thing about their early recordings. This is an essential release for hard-core Peter Gabriel fans, although there are a lot of jams and unreleased masters that could have been included in preference to a whole concert of *The Lamb Lies Down On Broadway*. *Genesis Archive, Vol. 2: 1976-1992* followed in 2000.

In The Beginning, a cut from their first album, was also given an airing on Decca's 1969 compilation, *Wowie Zowie! World Of Progressive Music* (LP). *That's Me* (the flip side to their now ultra-rare debut 45) appeared on *Broken Dreams, Vol. 3* (LP) and *Happy The Man*, an 'A' side from 1972, has resurfaced on *One More Chance* (LP). (VJ/CG)

Geneveve

45s: Once/Just A Whisper (Some PS)   (CBS 202061) 1966 SC/-
      Nothing In The World/Summer Days   (CBS 202096) 1966
      That Can't Be Bad/I Love Him, I Need Him   (CBS 202524) 1967

This was actually a teenager called Susan Hunt from Seddlescombe in Sussex. She sang ballads and was also known as an actress. (VJ)

The Gentiles

45:   Goodbye Baby/Madlene   (Pye 7N 17530) 1968

This is another forgotten sixties band. *Goodbye Baby* is a dreadful beat ballad. The flip, which had a slight fifties rock 'n' roll influence, is awful too. (VJ)

Tim Gentle and His Gentlemen

Personnel:	TIM GENTLE	ld gtr	A
	GRAHAM STEADY	drms	A
	STUART...	bs	A

45:   Without You/
      Someone's In The Kitchen With Dinah (Oriole CB 1988) 1965 SC

This beat group's 45 is now slightly sought-after. (MWh)

Gentle Folk

45:   That's My Song/In My Heart You Remain   (Pye 15859) 1965

A Seekers-like, female lead vocal, pop folk record. This is a fairly good example of its genre. (VJ)

Gentle Giant

Personnel:	GARY GREEN	gtr, vcls	ABCD
	KERRY MINNEAR	keyb'ds, vcls	ABCD
	DEREK SHULMAN	vcls, gtr, bs	ABCD
	PHIL SHULMAN	sax	ABC
	RAY SHULMAN	vcls	ABCD
	MARTIN SMITH	drms	A
	MALCOLM MORTIMORE	drms, vcls	B
	JOHN WEATHERS	drms	CD

NB: (3) released on Warner Bros in the US. (4) came out on CBS and (6) and (7) on Capitol in the US. (1) - (4) were all reissued on CD on Line during 1989. (1) reissued on CD (Vertigo 842 624-2) 1997 and again (Repertoire/Vertigo REPUK 1035) 2004. (1) reissued again on CD (Mercury 8426242). (2) reissued on CD (Vertigo 842 917-2) 1990 and again in 1997 and available on US import (Polydor 8429172). (4) reissued on CD (Vertigo 842 694-2) 1997 and again on CD (Polydor 8426942). There's also *Playing The Fool* (Chrysalis CTY 113) 1977, reissued by Essential/Castle Communications (ESSLP 006) on CD and LP in 1989. (5) and (6) reissued on CD (Road Goes On Forever RGF CD 1001 and 1002 respectively) 1992. (7) reissued on CD (Terrapin Trucking TRUCKCD 004) 1994. (9) reissued on CD (Terrapin Trucking TRUCKCD 005) 1994 and again (Glasshouse GLASS 103 CD) 2001. Vertigo has also released a compilation of their early albums, a 2-CD called *Edge Of Twilight* (Vertigo 534 101-2) and BBC sessions from 1970-75 are also available *Out Of The Woods* (Band Of Joy BOJCD 018) 199? *Out Of The Fire* (Hux HUX) 1998 is a 2-CD set of live concerts, one from 1973 featuring material from their fourth album and the other from 1978 (strictly outside this book's timeframe) contains selections from *Missing Piece*. *Totally Out Of The Woods* (Hux HUX 018) 2000 is a 2-CD issue of their BBC sessions plus a dozen songs from 1973/75 and a home demo of *Free Hand*. *Live Rome 1974* (Glass House GLASS 101CD) 2000 captures them at the peak, although the sound quality is not great. *In A Palesport House* (Glasshouse GLASS 102 CD) 2001 was mainly recorded in Italy in 1973 when the band was promoting material from (5) above. The recording quality leaves something to be desired. *Scraping The Barrel* (Alucard ALUGG 04) 2005 is a 4-CD collection.

This band formed in 1970 in the aftermath of **Simon Dupree and The Big Sound**, which had centred around the three Shulman brothers Derek (**Simon Dupree**), Ray and Phil. This time the brothers teamed up with Kerry Minnear, a multi-instrumentalist who'd just graduated from the Royal Academy of Music; lead guitarist Gary Green and former **Mojos'** drummer Martin Smith. The new band spent their first six months in hibernation in a cottage in Southampton rehearsing their new brand of progressive soft-rock (radically different from the blue-eyed soul/psych format tried and tested earlier as **Simon Dupree and The Big Sound**).

Having relaunched themselves into the wider world they teamed up with manager Gerry Bron who got them signed to Philips' new progressive label, Vertigo. Their first album used a wide range of instruments and drew upon hard-rock, classical and jazz elements into an unique style of music, although some have likened the sound to **King Crimson**. Certainly, the debut album met with some critical acclaim but failed to make any commercial impact.

GENTLE GIANT - Gentle Giant (LP).

GENTLE GIANT - Octopus (LP).

Their second album, *Acquiring The Taste*, was definitely one of their best. As the sleeve-notes explained, they were attempting to expand the frontiers of popular music and the result was an experimental, adventurous album with a number of good tracks, particularly *Pantagruel's Nativity, Wreck* and *Plain Truth*.

In commercial terms, they seemed to have established a better following on the Continent than in Britain. As with the first album, the second was well received by the critics, but once again, disappointing sales were registered.

Prior to the third album, their drummer Martin Smith left and was replaced by Malcolm Mortimore. Smith went on to run a musical instrument shop in Southampton and remained an active musical figure there for several years.

Their third effort, *Three Friends*, was produced by the group themselves. It was an attempted concept album about three old school friends who meet up later in life to reminisce about the old times and what had become of their old ambitions for the future. Unfortunately, whilst experimental, the disc was almost totally lacking in any excitement and was hardly a progression on what had gone before. It was notable for a couple of other reasons, though: it featured Ray's twelve-year-old-son Calvin on backing vocals and was their first album to get a US release. There was also a US promo-only single previewing three cuts from the album, *Prologue, Working All Day* and the title track (Columbia AE7 1059) which is now very sought-after. For me, though, *Schooldays* is by far the most interesting track with its echoed vocals and distinctive instrumentation. The band set about promoting the album on a tour which coupled them with the 'Hendrix Plays Berkeley' movie. Tragically Malcolm Mortimore was badly injured in a motorcycle accident during the tour which hospitalised him for some months. He was replaced by John Weathers, an experienced musician who'd also played with **Ancient Grease**, **Big Sleep**, **Pete Brown and Piblokto**, **Graham Bond**, **The Eyes Of Blue** and **The Grease Band**. When Mortimore recovered from his accident he joined G.T. Moore and the Reggae Guitars.

The new line-up returned to the studio and emerged with the band's magnum opus, *Octopus*. An imaginative effort issued in a memorable Roger Dean sleeve, it drew heavily on Minnear's knowledge of medieval music, particularly on *Raconteur Troubadour*. In contrast to earlier efforts *Octopus* was a great success both here and in the US.

Phil Shulman left the band after *Octopus*, having become fed-up with the continual touring. Their next effort, *In A Glass House* was not as bad an album as some (including Derek Shulman) say it is. Both *Runaway* and the title track featured fine instrumentation.

The most interesting thing about their next effort was probably the cover - it was only available as an import in the US. However, their next effort *The Power And The Glory* definitely put them back on the right track. It perfectly captured the post-Watergate mood of 1974 as many of its songs dealt with issues of political corruption. It should be noted that the 45, *The Power And The Glory*, was not on the album of the same name, but was released afterwards. It has subsequently become the most coveted of their singles.

After an extensive US tour during 1975, the band - now signed to Chrysalis - returned to the studio to work on their next album, *Free Hand*. This was their most commercial recording and became their best-selling album here in Britain. Two tracks, in particular, *Just The Same* and *On Reflection*, became big favourites in their stage repertoire. Their live reputation was also enhanced by a bootleg of a radio performance taped in LA, *Playing The Foole In Wonderland*, which was in circulation at the time.

1975 also saw the release of a decent double compilation, *Giant Steps (The First Five Years)*, which helped to keep them in the public eye. Yet their next studio effort, *Interview*, was a disappointment and as we leave the time span of this book, their days were clearly numbered, although they staggered on until 1980.

One of their most credible attributes was their ability to reproduce their sophisticated brand of music so effectively on stage and you may want to check out the live double-album package, *Playing The Fool*. This was originally released in 1977 on Chrysalis (CTY 113), complete with a booklet containing sleevenotes from Sounds' Phil Sutcliffe. It has been reissued by Castle Communications/Essential on album and CD (ESSLP/CD 006) in 1989. Collectors may also want to track down a US promo sampler, *Giant Edits*, which contains extracts from the album.

After the band's demise, only John Weathers remained regularly active in the music scene as a performer with the reformed **Man** until illness forced him to retire from the music business. Two of the Shulman brothers remained in the music business, Ray as a producer of several indie bands and Derek as Head A&R Executive at Polygram Records. Phil Shuman left the music business in the mid-seventies and was last reported running a gift shop. Gary Green later moved to the USA where he still plays in bands and does production work. Kerry Minnear is now involved in Christian music.

Scraping The Barrel is a 4-CD set, divided into three audio and one data disc. Two of the discs comprise demos, rehearsals and different mixes etc and are arranged in the order of the albums spanning 1970 - 1979 to which they relate. Disc 3 contains a previously unreleased **Simon Dupree** single and lots of post-**Gentle Giant** work. This should fascinate the band's fans. There was a brief re-union of four band members in 2004 to contribute four tracks to this 4-CD set, but a full re-union has been ruled out.

If soft, predominantly instrumental, experimental progressive rock is your niche you should like **Gentle Giant**, although many may find them an acquired taste. (VJ/PC)

Gentle Influence

45s:	Never Trust In Tomorrow/Easy To Know	(Pye 7N 17666) 1969
	Always Be A Part Of My Living/	
	Captain Reale	(Pye 7N 17743) 1969

From Witney in Oxfordshire, the flip side to their first 45, *Easy To Know*, is nearer to their live sound than the poppy 'A' sides which they were pressured into recording. The vocals are strong and appealing.

Compilation appearances have included: *Captain Reale* on *Paisley Pop - Pye Psych (& Other Colours) 1966-1969* (CD); *Easy To Know* on *Rubble, Vol. 17 - A Trip In A Painted World* (LP), *Rubble, Vol. 10* (CD), *The Best Of Rubble Collection, Vol. 2* (CD) and on *Hot Smoke & Sassafras - Psychedelic Pstones, Vol 1* (CD). (VJ)

Gentle People

| 45: | It's Too Late/Sea Of Heartbreak | (Columbia DB 8276) 1967 |

This was an obscure late sixties band. (VJ)

Geordie

Personnel:	BRIAN GIBSON	drms	A
	TOM HILL	bs	A
	BRIAN JOHNSON	vcls	A
	VIC MALCOLM	gtr	A

ALBUMS:	1(A)	HOPE YOU LIKE IT	(EMI EMC 3001) 1973
(up to	2(A)	DON'T BE FOOLED BY THE NAME	
1976)			(EMI EMA 764) 1974 SC
	3(A)	SAVE THE WORLD	(EMI EMC 3134) 1976 SC

NB: (1) and (2) reissued on CD (Repertoire REP 4033-WZ and 4124-WZ respectively) in 1991. There's also a vinyl compilation, *Featuring Brian Johnson* (Redbus RBMP 5001) 1981 and on CD check out *The Singles Collection* (Cherry Red GLAM CD 7) 2001.

HCP

45s:	Don't Do That/		
(up to	Keep On Rockin'	(Regal Zonophone RZ 3067) 1972	32
1976)	All Because Of You/		
	Ain't It Just Like A Woman	(EMI EMI 2008) 1973	6
	Can You Do It/Red Eyed Lady	(EMI EMI 2031) 1973	13
	Electric Lady/Geordie Stomp	(EMI EMI 2048) 1973	32
	Rock'n'Roller/Geordie's Lost His Liggy	(EMI EMI 2100) 1973	-
	She's A Teaser/We're All Right Now	(EMI EMI 2197) 1974	-
	Ride On Baby/Got To Know	(EMI EMI 2226) 1974	-
	Goodbye Love/She's A Lady	(EMI EMI 2314) 1975	-

This hard-rock group is most notable for the fact it included Brian Johnson, who was later in AC/DC. They came from the North-East of England and started off as a sort of poor man's **Slade**. Their first 45 for Regal Zonophone was a minor hit and on the strength of it, they were signed by EMI. Their first effort for EMI, *All Because Of You*, took them into the Top Ten. Two further but lesser hits followed and their albums sold solidly though not well enough to make the Charts.

The Singles Collection rounds up their A and B sides (though some of the latter are pretty forgettable) at an affordable price. It also features a Brian Johnson solo effort *I Can't Forget You Now*.

They lacked any real originality and with the onset of the punk era in 1976-77, their days were numbered. (VJ)

Denny Gerrard

| ALBUM: | 1 | SINISTER MORNING | (Deram Nova SDN 10) 1970 R1 |

Denny (Denver) Gerrard was in **Warm Sounds** and acted as producer for **High Tide**, who backed him on this solo album (which is nowhere near as heavy as either of their albums). A mixture of psychedelia and folk-rock, it features good songs like *Native Sun* and *Hole In My Shadow* but failed to take-off. **Gerrard** is thought to have emigrated to South Africa.

Native Sun can also be heard on the *Nova Sampler* (LP), and more recently on *Broken Dreams, Vol. 6* (LP). (VJ/RMJ)

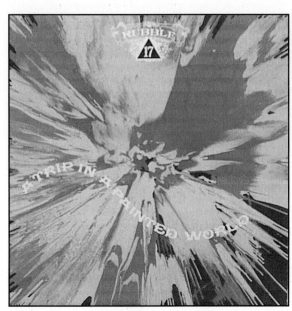

RUBBLE VOL. 17 (Comp LP) including Gentle Influence.

Gerry and The Pacemakers

Personnel:

LES CHADWICK	piano	A
LES MAGUIRE	bs, vcls	A
FREDDIE MARSDEN	drms	A
GERRY MARSDEN	gtr, vcls	A

HCP

ALBUMS:
- 1(A) HOW DO YOU LIKE IT? (mono/stereo) (Columbia 33SX 1546/SCX 3492) 1963 SC/R1 2
- 2(A) FERRY CROSS THE MERSEY (Soundtrack) (mono/stereo) (Columbia 33SX 1693/SCX 3544) 1965 SC/R1 19
- 3(A) BEST OF ... (EMI NUT 10) 1977 -

NB: (1) reissued as *You'll Never Walk Alone* (Music For Pleasure MFP 1153) in 1967. (1) reissued on vinyl (Beat Goes On BGOLP 57) 1989. (2) reissued on Beat Goes On (BGOLP 10) 1988. (2) reissued on CD, digitally remastered with both mono and stereo versions and presented in a digipak containing the original artwork (EMI DORIG 114) 1997. They had some US-only releases:- *Don't Let The Sun Catch You Crying* (Laurie 2027) 1964; *Second Album* (Laurie 2037); *I'll Be There* (Laurie 2030) 1965, *Greatest Hits* (Laurie 2031) 1965 and *Girl On A Swing* (Laurie 2037) 1966. (3) was issued on Capitol (11898) in the US. (1) reissued on CD (Repertoire REP 4422-WY) 1994, with 10 bonus tracks. (2) reissued on CD (Repertoire REP 4423-WY) 1994, with 14 bonus tracks. A recommended compilation is *The Very Best Of Gerry And The Pacemakers* (Music For Pleasure MFP 41 5654 1) 1984. There's also *The Hit Singles Album* (EMI EMS 1125) 1986, *The Singles Plus* (CD) (EMI CDP 746 602 2) 1987, *The EP Collection* (See For Miles SEE 95) 1987, issued on CD (SEE CD 95) in 1989, and *The Collection* (Castle CCSCD 247) 1990, which inevitably contains much material from the previous See For Miles set. *The Best Of The EMI Years* (EMI CDP 7 99030 2) 1992 is the most comprehensive CD compilation to date including all their Columbia 'A' sides from 1963-66 and their better album and EP cuts, plus a disappointing but previously unissued version of **John Lennon**'s *Hello Little Girl*. *At Abbey Road 1963 - 66* (CD ABBEY 102) 1997 will also interest their fans.

EPs:
- 1(A) HOW DO YOU DO IT? (Columbia SEG 8257) 1963 SC
- 2(A) YOU'LL NEVER WALK ALONE (Columbia SEG 8295) 1963 SC
- 3(A) I'M THE ONE (Columbia SEG 8311) 1964 SC
- 4(A) DON'T LET THE SUN CATCH YOU CRYING (Columbia SEG 8346) 1964 SC
- 5(A) IT'S GONNA BE ALRIGHT (Columbia SEG 8367) 1964 SC
- 6(A) GERRY IN CALIFORNIA (Columbia SEG 8388) 1965 R1
- 7(A) HITS FROM 'FERRY CROSS THE MERSEY' (Columbia SEG 8397) 1965 R1
- 8(A) RIP IT UP (Columbia SEG 8426) 1965 R1

HCP

45s:

How Do You Do It?/ Away From You	(Columbia DB 4987) 1963 1
I Like It/It's Happening To Me	(Columbia DB 7041) 1963 1
You'll Never Walk Alone/ It's Alright	(Columbia DB 7126) 1963 1
I'm The One/ You've Got What I Like	(Columbia DB 7189) 1964 2
Don't Let The Sun Catch You Crying/ Show Me That You Care	(Columbia DB 7268) 1964 6
It's Gonna Be Alright/ It's Just Because	(Columbia DB 7353) 1964 24
Ferry Cross The Mersey/ You You You	(Columbia DB 7437) 1965 8
I'll Be There/ Baby, You're So Good To Me	(Columbia DB 7504) 1965 15
Walk Hand In Hand/Dreams	(Columbia DB 7738) 1965 29
La La La/Without You	(Columbia DB 7835) 1966 -
Girl On A Swing/ A Fool To Myself	(Columbia DB 8044) 1966 -
Remember (The Days Of Rock And Roll)/ There's Still Time	(DJM DJS 298) 1974 -

Reissues:
- α Ferry Cross The Mersey/ Don't Let The Sun Catch You Crying (EMI EMI 2814) 1978 -
- Ferry Cross The Mersey/Don't Let The Sun Catch You Crying (Old Gold OG 9373) 1983 -
- You'll Never Walk Alone/ How Do You Do It? (Old Gold OG 9377) 1983 -
- Ferry Cross The Mersey/ How Do You Do It?/I'm The One (SMP SKM 8) 1984 -

NB: α Promo, picture sleeve release.

A pop group who enjoyed many of their biggest hits with ballads and almost totally lacking in pretentiousness, **Gerry and The Pacemakers** were one of Liverpool's finest and deserve a little flower in the tapestry of pop history.

The group originally came together as a part-time skiffle and rock outfit in 1959 known as The Mars Bars. If this was a ploy to gain them sponsorship it backfired horribly because the confectionary maker insisted that they changed the name, which they duly did to The Pacemakers. The Mars Bars originally consisted of Gerry and his elder brother Freddie, but with the addition of bassist Les Chadwick they became a trio and by 1960 they were using the name **Gerry and The Pacemakers**. After a late billing supporting Gene Vincent at a gig at the Liverpool Boxing Stadium in 1960 they found themselves thrust to the forefront of the new emerging Merseybeat sound. Like **The Beatles** they did a residency at a Hamburg club (in this case The Top Ten Club in late 1960/early 1961) where they belted out a mixture of R&B standards and mainstream pop classics.

By May 1961 Les Maguire (formerly of **The Undertakers**) had joined on piano (though he occasionally played the saxophone too) and the band had become a polished and respectable act fronted by a real Mr. Nice Guy. Later that year (on 19 October), they appeared with **The Beatles** at Litherland Town Hall in Merseyside as 'The Beatmakers' and both bands interchanged instruments and stage costumes on this occasion. In fact, the two bands were at the forefront of the Merseybeat boom and frequently appeared together at Liverpool venues like The Cavern Club during 1961 and 1962. It came as little surprise, then, when Brian Epstein, having already signed up **The Beatles**, became their manager in June 1962. A few months later, he persuaded EMI's **George Martin** to see them at Birkenhead's Empire Ballroom and this led to them getting a contract with EMI's Columbia subsidiary label.

They entered the recording studio in January 1963 and the first session produced *Pretend* (which appeared on their debut album); a **Gerry Marsden** composition, *Away From You*, and a Mitch Murray song, *How Do You Do It?*. This had become the showcase of the band's live act and was chosen as their first single, rocketing to No 1 in April 1963. In fact, **George Martin** had wanted **The Beatles** to record it but they'd rejected it, recording *Please Please Me* instead. A couple of months later, they shot back to the top of the UK Charts again with another Mitch Murray song, *I Like It*, and stayed there for four weeks. **The Dave Clark Five** had earlier recorded a demo version of this.

Their next 45, a revival of Rodgers and Hammerstein's *You'll Never Walk Alone*, became their best selling UK single. Its adoption as a crowd anthem by Liverpool Football Club not long after it became a No 1 hit has given the song a timeless quality. Indeed, it has been performed by **Gerry Marsden** on several occasions since then, most notably at the memorial service for Liverpool manager Bill Shankly. In June 1985, after the Bradford City Football Club fire disaster, he performed lead vocals on a muti-artists recording of the song organised by **Graham Gouldman** of **10cc**. Proceeds from the sales went into a fund for the victims' families. When the record hit the top spot back in 1963, it gave the band the distinction of becoming the

GERRY AND THE PACEMAKERS - EP Collection (CD).

first act to achieve No 1 with their first three singles, a record they held unrivalled for 21 years until it was equalled in 1984 by Frankie Goes To Hollywood.

You'll Never Walk Alone had been culled from their debut album, *How Do You Like It?*, which was also very successful, climbing up to No 2 in the UK Album Charts. It contained a fair splattering of R&B as well as more orchestrated numbers. By now the group's appeal as all round entertainers was so broad that they topped the bill on 'Sunday Night At The London Palladium' on 13 December 1963 and also appeared in the pantomime 'Babes In The Wood'.

1963 would prove to be the pinnacle of their career, although they remained in the public eye for another couple of years. For their fourth 45, they used a **Gerry Marsden** composition, *I'm The One*, which, although a strong song, lacked the magic of their earlier releases. It was kept off the top spot by another Liverpudlian band, **The Searchers**, and their version of *Needles And Pins*. This prompted an extensive series of tours first in the UK, then in Australia and New Zealand. In April they appeared on American TV in the 'Ed Sullivan' Show, performing their next 45, another **Gerry Marsden** song, this time a ballad, *Don't Let The Sun Catch You Crying*. It became their first US hit, peaking at No 4, but in the UK it only got to No 6.

On the strength of their 45 success in the US, a US-only album, *Don't Let The Sun Catch You Crying*, was put together from a collection of album tracks and UK singles, and rose to No 29.

Since June 1964, the band had been busy working on a feature film, written by Tony Warren (the man who created Granada's 'Coronation Street'). **Marsden**, though, wrote many of the songs for it. The group's next single, *It's Gonna Be Alright*, was a much more upbeat number, indeed, it was the film's finale. Given the band's previous commercial success, though, it was a disaster as it didn't even make the UK Top 20. Meanwhile, a second US-only album, titled precisely that - *Second Album* - was released. Again consisting of earlier album tracks and 45s it made No 129.

The film 'Ferry Cross The Mersey' was released in the UK at the beginning of 1965. The band played themselves (always a good ploy given the limited acting ability of many of these groups), winning a sort of Battle Of The Bands tournament. **The Fourmost**, **Cilla Black** and several lesser-known acts figured in the film. The title track of the soundtrack movie, *Ferry Cross The Mersey*, another **Gerry Marsden** ballad, gave the band their last Top 10 success on both sides of the Atlantic (No 8 in the UK, No 6 in the US). The Soundtrack album made No 13 in the US Album Charts and No 19 in the UK. Only the title track captured the band at its best but the rest of their material was OK. The soundtrack also featured *I Love You Too* by **The Fourmost**, *Is It Love* by **Cilla Black** and *All Quiet On The Mersey Front* by the **George Martin and His Orchestra**. After *You'll Never Walk Alone*, *Ferry Cross The Mersey* is probably the song people most closely associate with the band.

Prior to the release of *Ferry Cross The Mersey* as a 45, a cover of Bobby Darin's ballad had been put out in the US. It peaked at No 14. In the UK it was not released until after the *Ferry Cross The Mersey* 45, but the result was similar - again it made the Top 20.

In April 1965 they embarked on another US tour perhaps sensing that this was where their popularity now lay. They enjoyed minor US hits with *It's Gonna Be Alright, You'll Never Walk Alone* (when it was finally released as a single) and *Give All Your Love To Me* (another ballad and a US-only release). A US-only compilation album, *Greatest Hits*, also crept into the Top 50 over there.

Their final UK Top 30 entry came in December 1965 with a real tearjerker, *Walk Hand In Hand*, a revival of a fifties ballad and a pretty blatant attempt to court the Kop Choir once again.

By 1966, their sound was passé. A particularly naff, if more upbeat 45, *La La La*, didn't help their cause and their final 45, *Girl On A Swing*, squeezed into the US Top 30 and sold well in Europe, despite flopping here in the UK.

Their 1966 US-only album, *Girl On A Swing* included a number of songs (*Pretty Flamingo, Guantanamera,* and *Strangers In The Night*) they did not release in the UK. It was also released, with some track variations, in Canada as *Today* (Capitol (S)T6181).

GERRY AND THE PACEMAKERS.

After the band split, **Marsden** attempted to launch a solo career. Despite that failure, he's never been that far out of the public eye. At the start of 1968, he took over the lead role in the West End Musical 'Charlie Girl' from Joe Brown and enjoyed a couple of years in this capacity. By 1970 he'd become a prominent figure on children's television (he'd always wanted to become an 'allround entertainer'). During the seventies, he formed several Pacemakers groups for various nostalgia tours.

For those of you not familiar with their material, a good starting place is the 1984 compilation, *The Very Best Of Gerry And The Pacemakers*. This includes 11 of their Columbia 'A' sides, *It's Alright* (the flip side to *You'll Never Walk Alone*) and four songs not previously released in this country:- *Hallelujah I Love Her So, Come Back To Me, When Oh When* (which were recorded for a third album which was never released) and *Give All Your Love To Me*. A rival compilation is *The Hit Singles Album*, which includes the 'A' and 'B' sides of their eight hit singles. The problem here is that few of their 'B' sides were any better than mediocre and the 'A' sides can all be heard on the Music For Pleasure compilation anyway. *The EP Collection* consists of 22 cuts of Columbia material recorded between 1963 and 1965. The EPs included their first seven 'A' sides, a few 'B' sides and tracks from their two albums. All four tracks on the rare live EP, *Gerry In California*, on which they cover R&B material, are included but for some reason their cover of Little Richard's *Rip It Up* has been excluded. The collection will probably be of most interest to the band's fans for the seven tracks on the *Gerry In California* and *Rip It Up* EPs.

The German-based Repertoire label reissued their first album on CD in 1994, along with 10 bonus cuts. Six were from their 1965 US album, *I'll Be There* and the remaining four from their 1965 rock'n'roll EP, *Rip It Up*.

Repertoire have also reissued the *Ferry Cross The Mersey* film Soundtrack album, this time with 14 bonus tracks. Aside from some mid-sixties singles, these comprise the entire *Gerry In California* live EP, an outtake of the band covering **The Beatles'** *Hello Little Girl*, the film version of *It's Gonna Be All Right* and four songs from a mid-eighties Music For Pleasure collection.

Compilation appearances have included: *You Win Again, Rip It Up* and *Whole Lotta Shakin' Going On* on *Liverpool '65* (LP); *Ferry Cross The Mersey* and *Skinny Lizzie* on *Liverpool 1963-1968* (CD) and *Liverpool 1963-1968, Vol. 1* (LP); *I'm The One* and *Ferry Cross The Mersey* on *Mersey Beat* (2-LP); *I'll Wait For You* on *Beat At Abbey Road* (CD); *This Thing Called Love, Ferry Cross The Mersey, She's The Only Girl For Me, Baby You're So Good To Me, Think About Love, Fall In Love, Why Oh Why, It's Gonna Be Alright* and *I'll Wait For You* on *Ferry Cross The Mersey* (LP); *You'll Never Walk Alone* on *U.K. No. 1 Hits Of The 60's* (CD) and *Best of British Rock* (CD); *Don't Let The Sun Catch You Crying* on the 2-CD set *Sixties Summer Love*; *I Like It* on *Everlasting Love* (CD) and *Nothing But Number 1 Love Songs* (CD); *How Do You Do It?* on *60's Mix* (CD), *Beat Generation - Ready Steady Go* (CD), *Dizzy* (CD) and on the 2-CD set *60 Number Ones Of The Sixties*; an alternate take of *How Do You Do It?* on the 2-CD set *Greatest Hits Of The 60's*; *How Do You Do It* and *You'll Never Walk Alone* on *Hits Of The Mersey Era, Vol. 1* (LP); and *I Like It* (two versions), *I'm The One, Don't Let The Sun Catch You Crying* (two versions), *Ferry Cross The Mersey* (two versions), *My Babe, Why Oh Why* and *It's Gonna Be All Right!* on *Hard Up Heroes, Vol. 4* (CD). Finally,

Ferry Cross The Mersey has been compiled on the 2-CD set *Greatest Hits Of The 60's Vol 4* and *Brit Pop* (CD). (VJ)

Gervase

45:     Pepper Grinder/Visions   (Decca F 12822) 1968

Gervase was an Oxford University student whose folk-style 45 was produced by **Manfred Mann** member Tom McGuinness. (VJ)

Gethsemane

Personnel:	MARTIN BARRE	gtr, flute	A
	MIKE KETLEY	keyb'ds, vcls	A
	BRYAN STEPHENS	bs	A
	MALCOLM TOMLINSON	drms, flute, vcls	A

When Denny Alexandra left **The Penny Peeps**, the remaining members adopted a new moniker, In The Garden of Gethsame, which was soon shortened to **Gethsemane**.

This new look band, which incorporated blues and soul influences into its sound, soon attracted the interest of Robert Stigwood and Dick James Music, which recorded two tracks for a proposed album: a cover of **Tony McPhee**'s *Grease Monkey* and a cover of **Elton John**'s *Lady Samantha*. Disagreements between the various partners resulted in the tracks being shelved and the album was abandoned. Around this time, Tomlinson appeared on an **Elton John** radio session, which produced three tracks, including *Lady Samantha*.

Shortly after a date supporting **Jethro Tull** in Plymouth, Barre auditioned for the vacant guitar slot but failed to get the job. Following a Christmas concert at the Dundee College of Art with **Pink Floyd**, however, Barre auditioned again for **Jethro Tull** and was accepted.

At this point, Stephens dropped out of the music business to return to college and study surveying, while Ketley later played bass with Bognor Regis band The Concords during the early seventies. He now works for Yamaha keyboards.

Tomlinson helped out on an **Elton John** BBC session in October 1968 and then moved to Montreal, Canada early the following year where he played with a host of bands, including Milkwood. He also did a brief stint with Rhinoceros in early 1971 and later recorded with Bearfoot and Rick James (pre-Motown). He made two solo albums in the late 'seventies. (NW)

The Ghost

Personnel:	PAUL EASTMENT	lead gtr, vcls	AB
	CHARLIE GRIMA	drms	AB
	TERRY GUY	keyb'ds	AB
	DANIEL MACGUIRE	bs	AB
	SHIRLEY KENT	vcls, acoustic gtr	B

ALBUM: 1(B) WHEN YOU'RE DEAD - ONE SECOND

                                (Gemini GME 1004) 1970 R3

NB: (1) reissued as *For One Second* (Bam-Caruso KIRI 077) 1987 with one additional track, *I've Got To Get To Know You* which some original copies of (1) featured and on CD (Revolver BFTP 005CD) 1991.

45s: When You're Dead/Indian Maid   (Gemini GMS 007) 1969
             I've Got To Get To Know You/
             For One Second   (Gemini GMS 014) 1970

Ghost formed in Birmingham in the late sixties. They started out playing a heavish sort of blues-rock before they met up with singer **Shirley Kent** who'd already recorded two tracks on a charity EP, *The Master Singers And Shirley Kent Sing For Charec 67* (Keele University 103) in 1966. Paul Eastment had earlier played in **Velvett Fogg**.

They recorded their album at the end of 1969, spawning their first 45 at the end of the year. *When You're Dead* was a strong song with a clear US

West Coast influence. It was hardly Chart material, though, so predictably sales were poor. The album came out in January 1970. There's a clear contrast between the folk pieces that **Shirley Kent** sings on like *Hearts And Flowers* and *Time Is My Enemy*, which in style recall **Sandy Denny**'s heyday in **Fairport Convention**, and the blues-rock numbers contributed by the rest of the band, of which *For One Second* sounds the strongest. Also worth checking out is the powerful *Too Late To Cry*. The album has now become a major collector's item, partly on account of its rarity but also on account of the breadth of its appeal to fans of both blues-rock and folk.

The band returned to the studio in Spring 1970 to record *I've Got To Get To Know You*. Another track from their album, *For One Second*, was put on the flip, but when the 45 failed to sell the band slowly began to fall apart. **Shirley Kent** left to pursue a solo career and eventually released an album in 1975, *Fresh Out*, under the pseudonym **Virginia Tree**. I haven't heard it but it's reputedly folkier than **Ghost**'s output and featured former band members Paul Eastment and Terry Guy on three of the tracks. After **Kent**'s departure, the remaining band members soldiered on for a while using the name Resurrection but this later incarnation of the band didn't make it onto vinyl.

In 1987, Bam-Caruso reissued **Ghost**'s album under the title *For One Second* with the addition of the non-album 45 track, *I've Got To Get To Know You*. More recently the album has been reissued on vinyl and CD.

Danny Macguire sadly died in late 1998.

Compilation coverage has included:- *When You're Dead* on *It's Only A Passing Phase* (LP) and *Broken Dreams, Vol. 3* (LP); *The Castle Has Fallen* on *Rubble Vol. 14: The Magic Rocking Horse* (LP) and *Rubble Vol. 8* (CD). They also figured on one side of a Bam-Caruso promo release (Bam-Caruso 088), singing *Time Is My Enemy* (the flip side featured **The Poets**) and an extract from *When You're Dead* also appeared on a free flexi disc, *Psych-Out* (Bam-Caruso 092) which contained sound effects, sixties radio spots and other tracks from Bam-Caruso albums. (VJ)

Barry Gibb

45:     I'll Kiss Your Memory/This Time   (Polydor 2058 030) 1970

Barry Gibb was born on 1 September 1946 in Manchester, England. He emigrated to Australia with his family and that is where his career as a **Bee Gee** got underway. See **The Bee Gees** entry for details. The only solo recording he made within the time frame of this book was the 45 above. After the **The Bee Gees** first split, Barry concentrated mostly on songwriting. *Now Voyager* made No 85 in the UK album charts in 1984. He continues singing and writing today.

I'll Kiss Your Memory was also included on Polydor's 1970 compilation, *Pop Party* (LP). (VJ)

GHOST - When You're Dead One Second (LP).

Maurice Gibb

45:      Railroad/I've Come Back   (Polydor 2058 013) 1970

Maurice Gibb was born on 22 December 1949 on the Isle Of Man in England. He emigrated to Australia with his family and that is where his career as a **Bee Gee** got underway. See **The Bee Gees** entry for details. Again, 1970 was a year of solo projects for **The Bee Gees**. He worked on an album, which was never officially released, although parts of it have appeared on bootlegs over the years. This 45 was Maurice's sole vinyl offering in the time span of this book, but it sunk without trace. After this, he went into acting, married **Lulu** and battled with alcoholism. They later divorced. **Gibb** later married Yvonne Spencerley who helped him in his battle with recurring alcoholism over two decades.

He returned to solo recording in the eighties - he wrote and recorded the score to 'A Breed Apart' with arranger/conductor Jimmie Haskell and recorded a single *Hold Her In Your Hand*. He took the death of his younger brother Andy Gibb and his father both in 1988 badly, but came back to resume work with **The Bee Gees** on their 1989 album *One*. He died, aged 53, in January 2003 following a cardiac arrest while in hospital being treated for an intestinal blockage.

Railroad can also be found on Polydor's 1970 compilation, *Pop Party* (LP). (VJ)

Robin Gibb

ALBUM: 1   ROBIN'S REIGN   (Polydor 583 085) 1969

                                             HCP

45s: α Saved By The Bell/
        Alexandria Good Time   (Polydor 56337) 1969 SC -
        Saved By The Bell/Mother And Jack   (Polydor 56337) 1969 2
        One Million Years/Weekend   (Polydor 56368) 1970 -
        August October/Give Me A Smile   (Polydor 56371) 1970 45

NB: α withdrawn.

Robin Gibb (the twin brother of Maurice) was born on 22 December 1949 in Manchester, England. He emigrated to Australia with his family and that is where his career as a **Bee Gee** got underway. See **The Bee Gees** entry for details.

In 1969, **Robin Gibb** left his brothers in **The Bee Gees** to embark on a solo career. His quavering vocal style had considerable commercial appeal and he scored a big hit at the first attempt with the pop ballad, *Saved By The Bell*, which was ideally suited to his vocal style. After he'd achieved a minor UK hit with *August October*, the brothers reconciled their differences and reformed, which effectively ended this phase of his solo career.

Robin returned to solo work in the eighties, releasing *How Old Are You?* (1983), *Secret Agent* (1984) and *Walls Have Eyes* (1984) but none of them had much success. After Maurice died the brothers ceased using **The Bee Gees** name and, early in 2003 Robin released a solo single *Please* and later followed an album *Magnet*.

Mother And Jack can also be heard on Polydor's *Pop Party* (LP). (VJ)

Steve Gibbons

ALBUM: 1 SHORT STORIES   (Wizard SWZA 5501) 1971 R1

45:      Alright Now/Lay Some Lovin' Down   (Wizard WIZ 012) 1971

These were early efforts by Birmingham-based **Steve Gibbons** before he formed his Steve Gibbons Band. His album featured Albert Lee, **Trevor Burton**, Gary Wright, Mike Kellie, Pat Donaldson, Gerry Conway, Johnny Van Derek, Ian Whiteman, Larry Fallon and Alan White. Most of the material was written by **Gibbons** with three tracks being **Gibbons** / **Burton** compositions. The best track is probably *Leader Of The Band* about an innocent girl falling for a rock star. The gatefold album front and back covers featured a painting of the before and after scene of their liaison.

He was earlier in **The Uglys**. (VJ)

GILES, GILES AND FRIPP - Metaphormosis (LP).

Michael Gibbs

ALBUMS:	1	MICHAEL GIBBS	(Deram SML 1063) 1970 R1
(up to	2	TANGLEWOOD '63	(Deram SML 1087) 1971 R1
1976)	3	JUST AHEAD (2-LP)	(Polydor 2683 011) 1972 R1
	4	IN THE PUBLIC INTEREST	(Polydor 2383 252) 1974 R1
	5	ONLY CHROME-WATERFALL	
			(Bronze ILPS 9353) 197? SC

NB: (4) with Gary Burton.

Michael Gibbs was an innovative jazz artist in a progressive guise, who also arranged **Bill Fay's** debut. (VJ/RMJ)

Wayne Gibson (and Dynamic Sounds)

                                           HCP

45s: Linda Lu/Beachcomer   (Decca F 11713) 1963 SC -
(up to   Come On Let's Go/Pop The Whip (Decca F 11800) 1964 SC -
1976)   Kelly/See You Later Alligator (Pye 7N 15680) 1964 SC 48
       Portland Town/Please Baby Please   (Pye 7N 15798) 1965 -
       Ding Dong The Witch Is Dead/
       In The Night   (Parlophone R 5357) 1965 -
       One Little Smile/
       Baby, Baby, Baby Pity Me (Columbia DB 7683) 1965 SC -
   α Under My Thumb/
       It Always Happens (Icey) (Columbia DB 7911) 1966 R1 -
   α For No One/He's Got The Whole
       World In His Hands   (Columbia DB 7998) 1966 -
   α Under My Thumb/Game(Pye Disco Demand DDS 2001) 1974 17
   α Yesterday's Papers/
   α Don't Waste Time Following Me   (Pye 7N 45455) 1975 -
   α It's The Time Of The Year/
       Help The Night Away   (Pye 7N 45491) 1975 -

NB: α **Wayne Gibson** solo 45s.

A London-based group whose first four 45s were produced by Shel Talmy. **Jimmy Page** helped out on the second one and on their minor hit, a cover of Del Shannon's oldie *Kelly*. *Come On Let's Go* was done by Tommy Steele and their version had an instrumental 'B' side. **Gibson's** final 'A' side with Dynamic Sounds, *One Little Smile*, was a Carter-Lewis composition. The 45 was produced by Terry King, who'd been **The Fortunes'** manager. Most of these 45s were beat/R&B in style.

In 1966 **Gibson** went solo. On his first effort, he covered **The Rolling Stones'** *Under My Thumb*. His follow-up, **The Beatles'** *For No One* became the first record by a British male singer to get released on the Tamla Motown label in the States. In the mid-seventies, he returned to try his hand at disco music.

Compilation appearances include: *See You Later, Alligator* on *James Patrick Page: Session Man, Vol. 2* (LP & CD); *Kelly* on *Hippy Hippy Shake* (CD); *Kelly* and *See You Later, Alligator* on *Jimmy Page - Hip Young Guitar Slinger* (2-CD) and *Jimmy's Back Pages - The Early Years* (CD); *Under My Thumb* on *Go... With An All Star* (LP) and *Rare 60's Beat Treasures, Vol. 2* (CD); *Baby, Baby, Baby Pity Me* and *One Little Smile* on *Rare 60's Beat Treasures, Vol. 4* (CD); *Portland Town* on *The R&B Era, Vol. 1* (LP & CD); and *Baby, Baby, Baby Pity Me* on *Diggin' For Gold, Vol. 6* (LP) and *Hide & Seek Again (Vol. 2)* (LP). (VJ)

Gidian (and The Universals)

45s:	Try Me Out/There Isn't Anything	(Columbia DB 7826)	1966 SC
	Fight For Your Love/See If She Cares	(Columbia DB 7916)	1966
	Feeling/Don't Be Sentimental	(Columbia DB 8041)	1966
α	That's Love/We Are The Happiest	(UPC UPC 107)	1970

NB: α credited to **Gidian and The Universals**.

Gidian was a Scot called James Pollock who'd been discovered by Ken Dodd. His songs were mostly ballads and the final 45 may be by a different artist. (VJ)

Colin Giffin

45:	Changes In Our Time/		
	When We Were Young	(CBS CBS 4030)	1969

This was the outcome of a one-off venture by **Colin Giffin** after he left **The End**. It was produced by Kenny Lynch and arranged by Tony Visconti, but despite this pedigree it sank without making any impact. (VJ)

Gilded Cage

Personnel:	MAXINE	A
	PAULINE MORAN	A
	EILEEN WOODMAN	A
	ROBIN YORKE	A

45:	Long Long Road (For The Broken Heart)/		
	Baby Grumpling	(Tepee TPR 1003)	1969 R1

A late sixties girl group from Liverpool. Some of them were earlier in **She Trinity** and they were formerly better known as The Liverbirds. (VJ)

GILES, GILES AND FRIPP - The Cheerful Insanity Of... (LP).

Giles, Giles and Fripp

Personnel:	ROBERT FRIPP	gtr	A
	MIKE GILES	drms	A
	PETER GILES	bs	A
	(IAN McDONALD	woodwind, keyb'ds, vcls	A)
	(JUDY DYBLE	vcls, keyb'ds	A)

ALBUM:	1(A)	THE CHEERFUL INSANITY OF...	
		(mono/stereo)	(Deram DML/SML 1022) 1968 R2

NB: (1) reissued on (Deram SPA 423) 1970 (R1) and on CD (Deram 820 965-2) 1992 with bonus tracks. (1) also reissued on vinyl in a limited edition pressing of 500. *Metamorphosis* (Tenth Planet TP 049) 199? features an album of material not released at the time. This was later issued on CD with additional tracks as *The Brondesbury Tapes (1968)* (Voiceprint VP 235 CD) 2002.

45s:	One In A Million/Newly Weds	(Deram DM 188)	1968 R2
	Thursday Morning/Elephant Song	(Deram DM 210)	1968 R1

This outfit formed in Bournemouth in August 1967 after the **Giles** brothers had left **Trendsetters Limited**. In September of that year, they moved up to London but found gigs hard to come by. Eventually, they got a residency at a restaurant in Jermyn Street, backing an Italian singer but it only lasted a few days and they found themselves gigless again. In June 1968, Ian McDonald and former **Fairport Convention** singer Judy Dyble were recruited to their ranks. The same month, they put out their debut 45 but the punters just didn't seem interested in them. Both their 45s were decidedly weird and may well appeal to fans of freakbeat or psychedelia. Dyble only hung around for a month before moving on to **Trader Horne**, although, with her departure in July, Pete Sinfield became their lyricist. This and their second effort have become minor collectables, as has their album, which sold only in very small quantities at the time. It was actually quite a good amalgam of sunshine pop compositions like *North Meadow* and more offbeat tracks which owed more to **Syd Barrett**. There were also two narrations, Fripp's *The Saga Of Rodney Toady* and Giles' *Just George*. Their break-up was by now inevitable but Fripp went on to much greater things with **King Crimson** and the **Giles** brothers were both briefly involved in the band too. Robert Fripp later married Toyah.

The CD reissue of their album also includes both sides of their two previous non-album 45s and two previously unissued tracks:- *She Is Loaded* and *Under The Sky*.

The Brondesbury Tapes document the band when it was shortly to become **King Crimson**. Originally issued on Tenth Planet as *Metamorphosis* some additional tracks are added on this CD release. There are several cameo appearances from former **Fairport Convention** vocalist Judy Dyble. Included is an exquisite embryonic version of the future **King Crimson** classic *I Talk To The Wind* and *Why Don't You Just Drop In* contains a pulsating Fripp solo. This is recommended.

The See For Miles compilation *Psychedelia - Rare Blooms From The English Summer Of Love* (CD) also includes *Thursday Morning*. (VJ)

Gilgamesh

Personnel:	JEFF CLYNE	bs	A
	ALAN GOWAN	keyb'ds	AB
	PHIL LEE	gtr	AB
	AMANDA PARSONS	vcls	A
	MIKE TRAVIS	drms	A
	HUGH HOPPER	bs	B
	TREVOR TOMKINS	drms	B

ALBUMS:	1(A)	GILGAMESH	(Caroline CA 2007) 1975 SC
	2(B)	ANOTHER FINE TUNE YOU GOT ME INTO	
			(Charly CRL 5009) 1978

NB: (1) reissued on CD (Virgin CACD 2007). (2) reissued on CD (Spalax 1438). *Arriving Twice* (Cuneiform RUNE 140) 2000 features unreleased studio material that pre-dates their contract with Virgin.

A collection of talented and highly professional jazz musicians who created a modern jazz/jazz-rock sound typical of the mid-seventies period and including the likes of National Health, **Soft Machine** and Mirage. Mike Travis had earlier played with **Buzz** and **Atlantic Bridge**. Between albums Gowan toured with Soft Head (**Hugh Hopper**, **Elton Dean**, (sax) and Dave

GILGAMESH - Gilgamesh (CD).

Sheen (drms)) and recorded an album, *Rogue Element*, on Ogun records. After the second **Gilgamesh** album Gowan, **Hopper**, **Dean** and Pip Pyle recorded an album as Soft Heap, a rather inaccessible experimental jazz/rock album. **Hugh Hopper**, of course, was earlier in **Soft Machine** and he and Alan Gowan made an album together entitled *Two Rainbows Daily* in 1980 on Red Records. Gowan had previously played in Assegai and Sunship and later had a spell in National Health playing on their first album and was also involved in writing two tracks on it.

Following his death in 1981 the band produced an album solely of tracks written by Gowan in his memory, including tracks from the **Gilgamesh** albums. Phil Lee and Trevor Tomkins are still playing regularly on the jazz circuit.

Arriving Twice, which is available on US import, contains previously unreleased material predating their contract with Virgin. It is accompanied by a booklet which gives a full history of the band and previously unseen pictures. (VJ/MWh)

Dana Gillespie

ALBUMS:	1	BOX OF SURPRISES	(Decca SKL 5012) 1969 R1
(up to	2	WEREN'T BORN A MAN	(RCA APLI 0354) 1973 SC
1976)	3	AIN'T GONNA PLAY NO SECOND FIDDLE	
			(RCA APLI 0682) 1974 SC

NB: There's also a US-only album, *Foolish Seasons* (London 540) 1969.

45s:	Donna Donna/It's No Use Saying It	(Pye 7N 15872) 1965
(up to	Thank You Boy/You're A Heartbreak Man	(Pye 7N 15962) 1965
1976)	Pay You Back With Interest/	
	Adam Can You Beat That	(Pye 7N 17280) 1967
	You Just Gotta Know My Mind/	
	He Loves Me, He Loves Me Not	(Decca F 12847) 1968
	Weren't Born A Man/All Gone	(RCA RCA 0211) 1974
	Andy Warhol/Dizzy Heights	(RCA RCA 2466) 1974
	Really Love That Man/Hold Me Gently	(RCA RCA 2489) 1975
	Love Keeps No Season/Celandine's Blues	(EMI EMI 2453) 1976

Dana Gillespie was a folky singer, who was just 16 in 1965 when she first recorded. She was discovered by **Donovan** and was his girlfriend for a while. Her second 45, *Thank You Boy*, was written by **The Ivy League** and **Barry Mason**. The follow-up, *Pay You Back With Interest*, was a **Hollies** number. Her next effort, *You Just Gotta Know My Mind*, had been written by **Donovan** back in 1966. She made a comeback in the mid-seventies but has never achieved commercial success.

Dana Gillespie was a folky singer, who was just 16 in 1965 when she first recorded. She was discovered by **Donovan** and was his girlfriend for a while. Her second 45, *Thank You Boy*, was written by **The Ivy League** and **Barry Mason**. The follow-up, *Pay You Back With Interest*, was a **Hollies**

number. Her next effort, *You Just Gotta Know My Mind*, had been written by **Donovan** back in 1966. She made a comeback in the mid-seventies but has never achieved commercial success.

In the eighties she turned her attention to the blues, which were very dear to her heart. She recorded several albums in this era; including *I'm A Woman*, *Blue Job*, *Move Your Body Closer To Me*, *Below The Belt*, and *Sweet Meat*. She was also a prolific actress, appearing in stage shows like 'Jesus Christ Superstar' and in films like 'The Hound Of The Baskervilles'. She also appeared regularly on TV.

There's been no let up in the nineties as she has released a string of further blues albums: *Blue One*, *Hot Stuff*, *Have I Got The Blues For You*, *Big Boy* and *Back To The Blues*. She's also continued her acting career. Her 2003 album *Staying Power* shows her still to be a superb vocalist.

Pay You Back With Interest resurfaced on *Quick Before They Catch Us* (CD) and *Ripples, Vol. 4* (CD). (VJ)

Gordon Giltrap

ALBUMS:	1	GORDON GILTRAP	(Transatlantic TRA 175) 1968 R1
(up to	2	PORTRAIT	(Transatlantic TRA 202) 1969 SC
1976)	3	A TESTAMENT OF TIME	(MCA MKPS 2029) 1971 SC
	4	GILTRAP	(Philips 6308 175) 1973 SC
	5	VISIONARY	(Electric TRIX 2) 1976

NB: (1) and (2) reissued on one CD (Transatlantic).

An excellent acoustic and electric guitarist, **Giltrap** specialised in largely instrumental albums. He went on to film and television soundtrack work in the eighties and nineties and recorded several further albums. Much of his back catalogue was released on CD via Voiceprint. (BS)

Ginger Ale

45: In The Sand/Get Off My Life Woman

An obscure outfit whose *In The Sand* can also be found on *Colour Me Pop, Vol 3* (CD). (VJ)

Ginger Jug Band

Personnel:	GEOFF BEAUMONT	ba, jug, vcls	ABCDE	
	RICK HARPER	jug, washboard	A	F
	IVOR JONES	banjo	AB	
	HUGH LOUGHLIN	gtr	A	
	TONY PETTO	gtr	BCDEF	
	PETE BASTON	12-string gtr, hrmnca	CDEF	
	STEVE HORNE	jug, washboard	C	

GILGAMESH - Another Fine Tune You've Got Me Into (CD).

ROB JONES	gtr	C
MARK ABRAHAM	washboard	E
JOHN HURTLES	gtr, fiddle	E
CHARLIE JACOBS		F

ALBUM:1 (C)   GINGER JUG BAND

(Private Pressing GJB 001) 1970s SC

The group was from North West Kent. The roots of the band can be traced back to a one-off performance for a local charity by a folk band The Well Hill Billies in around 1967. Included in the band were brothers Geoff and Andy Beaumont and Ivor Jones. Geoff's brother Andy moved to North Wales and went on to form his own band Rub A Dub Jug Band, which recorded several cassettes. Geoff recruited two school friends, Rick Harper and Hugh Loughlin and along with Ivor Jones the first line-up of **The Ginger Jug Band** was formed. The idea for the name came from an earthware Lyle's Ginger Beer bottle they used as a jug. They were sometimes assisted by Mark Abraham on Spasmophone. This was a cobbled together musical intervention with a tuba mouthpiece connected by some random plumbing to a giant gramophone horn. Mark was a former member of Humber Jug, a band who included well-known washboard player John Pilgrim, who had featured in several successful skiffle bands.

After about three gigs Rick and Hugh departed to attend college and Tony Petto came in to form a new line-up. Some time later Ivor Jones had to leave due to family and work commitments and Pete Baston, Steve Horne and Rob Jones were recruited to what became the band's definitive line-up. In 1971, the band came second in Melody Maker's Folk-Rock competition and it was now a popular live attraction in North Kent and South East London folk clubs. In 1972 the band recorded their eponymous album. This was followed by more line-up changes when Steve Horne emigrated to South Africa with his family shortly after Jones left to concentrate on his graphics arts career. Mark Abraham rejoined for a while and John Hurtles stepped in on guitar and fiddle. Some time later Geoff left for new pursuits and Tony kept the band going for some years with Charlie Jacobs and Rick Harper who had returned from college and resurrected his washboard and jug.

In the late nineties there was talk of reforming the band and eventually in 2000 a revised line-up (Geoff Beaumont, Andy Beaumont, Tom Beaumont (Andy's son), Tony Petto and Rick Harper) played a few gigs at the Broadstairs Folk Festival. Interest in the original band was generated and a 2-CD set of its work was sold out within three gigs! (VJ)

Ginhouse

Personnel:	STEWART BURLISON	bs, vcls	A
	GEOFF SHARKEY	gtr, vcls	A
	DAVID WHITAKER	drms	A

ALBUM: 1(A)   GINHOUSE   (B&C CAS 1031) 1971 R1
NB: (1) reissued on CD (Green Tree).

A hard-rock trio from Newcastle whose album is now rare. They had a good reputation as a live act and wrote some strong material on their album, with the continuous track *The House/Sun In A Bottle* the highlight, alongside a cover version of **The Beatles**' *And I Love Her*. Geoff Sharkey had earlier played in **Sammy**. (VJ/CA)

Giorgio

45s:	Full Stop/Believe Me	(Page One POF 003) 1966
	How Much Longer Must I Wait/	
	Bla Bla Diddly	(Page One POF 028) 1967
	Happy Birthday/Looky Looky	(MCA MCA 1094) 1969

These were solo efforts by Giorgio Moroder who also fronted Marco's Men and recorded with Phil Oakey and Helen Terry. He became a top disco producer in the seventies. (VJ)

Giorgio and Marco's Men

Personnel incl: GIORGIO MORODER   A

| 45s: | Girl Without A Heart/Run Run | (Polydor 56101) 1966 |
| | Baby I Need You/Maureen | (Elektratone EP 1003) 1968 R2 |

Giorgio Moroder who fronted this outfit from Wolverhampton also recorded several solo 45s under his own name as well as a couple with Phil Oakey and one with Helen Terry. His best effort with this outfit is usually considered to be *Baby I Need You* but it's really nothing special.

Moroder's top achievements were as a disco producer with Donna Summer.

Baby I Need You has been compiled on *Psychedelia, Vol. 1* (LP), *Syde Tryps, Vol. 1* (LP & CD) and *Hen's Teeth Vol. 1* (CD). (VJ)

The Glass Menagerie

Personnel:	BILL ATKINSON	drms	A
	ALAN KENDALL	gtr	A
	JOHN MEDLEY	bs	A
	KEITH O'CONNELL	organ, piano, vcls	A
	LOU STONEBRIDGE	vcls, hrmnca	A

45s:	She's A Rainbow/	
	But That's When I Start To Love Her	(Pye 7N 17518) 1968
	You Don't Have To Be So Nice/	
	Let's All Run To The Sun	(Pye 7N 17568) 1968
	Frederick Jordan/	
	I Said Goodbye To Me	(Pye 7N 17615) 1968 R3
α	Somebody To Love/She's A Rainbow	(Metronome J 27014) 1969
	Have You Forgotten Who You Are/	
	Do You Ever Think?	(Polydor 56318) 1969
	Do My Thing Myself/	
	Watching The World Pass By	(Polydor 56341) 1969

NB: α was a Danish only release.

Originally from Lancashire, this group moved to London. They were managed by ex-**Animal** Chas Chandler. Their three singles for Pye were basically soft pop-psych. Their cover of **The Rolling Stones**' *She's A Rainbow* is quite interesting but to my ear their strongest composition for Pye, is *Frederick Jordan*. This is an excellent organ-led slice of heavy psychedelia, which is now very sought-after.

In 1969, they switched to Polydor recording two further guitar-driven progressive rock 45s. There's also an unissued album of their material on acetate. After their demise, Alan Kendall joined **Toe Fat** and Lou Stonebridge was in **Paladin** and later **McGuinness Flint** and Stonebridge McGuinness.

Compilation appearances have included: *Somebody To Love* on *Psychedelia, Vol. 3* (LP) and *Hen's Teeth, Vol. 3* (CD); *You Didn't Have To Be So Nice* on *Rubble, Vol. 7 - Pictures In The Sky* (LP); *Fredrick Jordan* and *She's A Rainbow* on *Rubble, Vol. 10 - Professor Jordan's Magic Sound*

HEN'S TEETH VOL. 3 (Comp CD) featuring The Glass Menagerie.

Show (LP) and on *Haunted - Psychedelic Pstones, Vol 1* (CD); *Frederick Jordan* can be heard on *We Can Fly, Vol 1* (CD) and on *Hot Smoke & Sassafras - Psychedelic Pstones, Vol 1* (CD) and finally *Do My Thing Myself* on *Jagged Time Lapse, Vol 4* (CD). (VJ)

The Glass Opening

| 45: | Silver Bells And Cockle Shells/ | | |
| | Does It Really Matter | (Plexium PXM 1236) 1968 R4 |

This ultra-rare and sought-after psychedelic 45 was recorded by an unknown band on an obscure label. The 'A' side is basically the nursery rhyme given a slightly psychedelic interpretation, but the flip mixing wah-wah guitar with a soulful lead vocal, is much closer to the genuine article. Curiously, the 45 also got a release in Canada on Polydor (540.006).

Does It Really Matter has been compiled on *Psychedelia, Vol. 2* (LP), *The Best Of Rubble Collection, Vol. 2* (CD) and *Hen's Teeth Vol. 1* (CD). (VJ/AGo)

Glencoe

Personnel:	STEWART FRANCIS	drms, vcls	A
	GRAHAM MAITLAND	keyb'ds, vcls	A
	JOHN TURNBULL	gtr, vcls	A
	NORMAN WATT-ROY	bs, vcls	A

| ALBUMS: | 1(A) | GLENCOE | (Epic 65207) 1972 SC |
| | 2(A) | THE SPIRIT OF GLENCOE | (Epic 65717) 1973 SC |

NB: (1) and (2) also released in the USA on Epic.

| 45: | Look Me In The Eye/Telephonia | (Epic EPC 8383) 1972 |

Glencoe was formed by Stewart Francis (ex-**Forever More**) and John Turnbull (ex-**Skip Bifferty**). On the second album, the American keyboardist Ben Sidran (ex-Steve Miller Band) guested, along with Kofi Ayivor and Gerald Johnson.

Norman Watt-Roy was also in **Greatest Show On Earth** and would later play in Ian Dury and The Blockheads, Graham Turnbull was in **Loving Awareness** and Graham Maitland went on to play with **Wishbone Ash**, **Bryn Haworth** and **Splinter**. (SR/CG)

Gary Glitter

				HCP
ALBUMS:	1	GLITTER	(Bell BELLS 216) 1972	8
(up to	2	TOUCH ME	(Bell BELLS 222) 1973	2
1976)	3	REMEMBER ME THIS WAY	(Bell BELLS 237) 1974	5
	4	ALWAYS YOURS		
			(Music For Pleasure SPR 90076) 1975	-
	5	G.G.	(Bell BELLS 257) 1975	-
	6	GREATEST HITS	(Bell BELLS 262) 1976	33

NB: (1) reissued on CD (Dojo DOJO CD 100) 1996. (2) reissued on CD (Dojo DOJO CD 200) 1996. Compilations have included *I Love You Love* (Hallmark SHM 916) 1977, *Golden Greats* (GTO GTLP 021) 1977, *Many Happy Returns: The Hits* (EMI 0777 7 80982 2 5) 1992 and *20 Greatest Hits* (Repertoire REP 4229 WG) 1993. *The Glam Years: Part 1* (Repertoire REP 4430-WO) 1995 is a two-CD set which concentrates on **Glitter**'s early years. It's accompanied by a 44-page booklet with details of his career including a discography and a Chart file. Without doubt this is the best **Glitter** collection around. *Greatest Hits* (Rhino) 199? is not recommended.

EP:	1	GARY GLITTER	(Bell REBEL 1) 1976
(up to			
1976)			

NB: (1) contains *Rock And Roll Part 2*/*Hello Hello I'm Back Again*/*Do You Wanna Touch Me*/*I'm The Leader Of The Gang I Am*.

			HCP
45s:	Rock And Roll Parts 1 & 2	(Bell BLL 1216) 1972	2
(up to	I Didn't Know I Loved You (Till I Saw You Rock 'n' Roll)/		
1976)	Hard On Me	(Bell BLL 1259) 1972	4

THE GLITTER BAND - Hey (LP).

Do You Wanna Touch Me?/		
I Would If I Could But I Can't	(Bell BLL 1280) 1973	2
Hello Hello I'm Back Again/I O U	(Bell BLL 1299) 1973	2
I'm The Leader Of The Gang/		
Just Fancy That	(Bell BLL 1321) 1973	1
I Love You Love Me Love/		
Hands Up! It's A Stick Up	(Bell BLL 1337) 1973	1
Remember Me This Way/		
It's Not A Lot	(Bell BLL 1349) 1974	3
Always Yours/		
I'm Right, You're Wrong, I Win	(Bell BLL 1359) 1974	1
Oh Yes! You're Beautiful/		
Thank You Baby For Myself	(Bell BLL 1391) 1974	2
Love Like You And Me/		
I'll Carry Your Picture	(Bell BLL 1423) 1975	10
Doing All Right With The Boys/		
Good For No Good	(Bell BLL 1429) 1975	6
Papa Oom Mow Mow/		
She Cat, Alley Cat	(Bell BLL 1451) 1975	38
You Belong To Me/		
Rock And Roll Part 1	(Bell BLL 1473) 1976	40
Reissues: α	Rock 'n' Roll, Part 2/	
I Didn't Know I Loved You (Till I Saw You Rock 'n' Roll)	(Old Gold OG 6132) 1989	-
Oh Yes! You're Beautiful/		
Remember Me This Way	(Old Gold OG 9880) 1989	-
I Love You Love Me Love/		
I'm The Leader Of The Gang	(Old Gold OG 6128) 1990	-

NB: α also issued as a 12" and CD single with two additional tracks:- *Rock 'n' Roll, Part 1* and *Do You Wanna Touch Me*.

Gary Glitter was the king of British glam-rock in the seventies when he recorded a string of anthemic hits, most notably *Rock and Roll*, which also became one of the national anthems of American football for many years, but several other timeless party classics like *I'm The Leader Of The Gang*, *Do You Wanna Touch Me*, *Hello Hello I'm Back Again* and *I Love You Love Me Love*. Even after his heyday he made several comebacks, but the child pornography revelation of the late nineties ended his career and worse was to follow.

Most people know that **Gary Glitter**'s real name was Paul Gadd. Many will also know that he was born on 8 May 1940 in Banbury, Oxfordshire. He has often tried to claim to be younger (well, why not if you can get away with it!). He's been playing in rock bands since the late fifties. His first outfit Paul Russell and The Rebels (Russell was his stepfather's surname) got a residency at The Safari Club in Trafalgar Square, London. Whilst working there he met Robert Hartford Davis, a film producer who became his manager and got him a recording contract with Decca. Now using the name **Paul Raven**, he recorded a 45 for Decca in 1960 (*Alone In The Night*) and two for Parlophone in 1961 (*Walk On Boy* and *Tower Of Strength*). All three flopped, but **Raven** soon resurfaced as a warm-up man for 'Ready Steady Go!' He also met Mike Leander (who would become his manager in his **Gary Glitter** days) and briefly became vocalist with The Mike Leander Orchestra. When they broke up he formed Paul Raven and Boston International (later The Bostons) who spent most of the early sixties in Germany.

Later, in 1968, when Leander became UK head of MCA Records, he signed **Paul Raven** to the label and using a pseudonym (**Paul Monday**), **Raven** recorded a Leander composition, *Musical Man*, but it made little impact and a cover version of **The Beatles**' *Here Comes The Sun* did little better. He reverted to the **Paul Raven** monicker for his next MCA 45 and then recorded a 45 as **Rubber Bucket**. He also appeared on MCA's million-selling *Jesus Christ Superstar* (LP).

In 1971, he renewed his relationship with Leander when he signed to Bell Records. With a complete change of musical style and another new pseudonym, **Gary Glitter**, he forced himself to the forefront of the 'glam-rock' movement. His debut 45, *Rock And Roll Parts 1 And 2*, took a while to take off but it paved the way for a whole series of one-riff smash hits which all sounded much the same. I'm not listing them all here but full details of his Chart attainments appear in the discography above. Despite his enormous success in the UK only two of his 45s were hits in the US:- *Rock And Roll Part 2* and *I Didn't Know I Loved You (Till I Saw You Rock And Roll)* got to No's 7 and 35 respectively during 1972. Of his albums, only the first, *Glitter*, had any success in the US and then it only crept to No 186. Still, over here, Gary 'did the business' outlasting many of his teenybopper contemporaries. In March 1974, his backing group, **The Glitter Band**, set out on their own and enjoyed several hits of their own.

In January 1975, Gary made a televised farewell performance, and for the next few years he seldom appeared in public, although he still continued to make records. In subsequent years, he made several 'comebacks' although it's undeniable that the early seventies were his heyday.

He returned initially to take a lead role in a New Zealand production of 'The Rocky Horror Show' and enjoyed minor UK hits with *It Takes All Night Long* and *A Little Boogie Woogie In The Back Of My Mind* in 1977. He began playing live again in 1980 and in 1981 recorded a dance medley of all his greatest hits entitled *All That Glitters*, which crept into the UK Top 50. Further singles followed and *Another Rock And Roll Christmas* returned him to the Top 10 in late 1984. In 1986, he guested on TV performances of Doctor and The Medics' re-work of *Spirit In The Sky* and in June 1988 returned to No 1 thanks to The Timelords' 'Dr Who' tribute *Doctoring The Tardis* which was set to samples of his *Rock And Roll* single. His autobiography 'The Leader' was a bestseller in 1991. Then in 1996 he played the godfather in **The Who**'s 'Quadrophenia' and successfully re-worked *The House Of The Rising Sun* to a Glitteresque beat. His classic *Rock And Roll* later found a new lease of life when it was one of the main tunes in the successful UK film 'The Full Monty'.

Then his world fell down in November 1999 when he was convicted of downloading child pornography and on his release from prison a few months later he fled the UK. In November 2005, he was arrested in Vietnam accused of having sex with underaged girls. (VJ)

ROGER GLOVER AND GUESTS - Butterfly Ball (CD).

GNIDROLOG - In Spite Of Harry's Toenail (LP).

The Glitter Band

Personnel:	HARVEY ELLISON		A
	TONY LEONARD		A
	PETE PHIPPS	drms	A
	GERRY SHEPHARD		A
	JOHN SPRINGATE		A

				HCP
ALBUMS:	1(A)	HEY	(Bell BELLS 241) 1974	13
(up to	2(A)	ROCK 'N' ROLL DUDES	(Bell BELLS 253) 1975	17
1976)	3(A)	LISTEN TO THE BAND	(Bell BELLS 259) 1975	-
	4(A)	GREATEST HITS	(Bell BELLS 264) 1976	52

NB: Also of interest may be *Paris Match* (CBS 81717) 1977, the compilation *People Like You, People Like Me* (Music For Pleasure MFP 50354) 1977, *20 Glittering Greats* (Music Club) 1998, *Best Of The Glitter Band* (Repertoire) 1998 and *The Bell Singles Collection* (7T's GLAMCD 1) 2000, which gives a further airing to all their Bell singles, complete with reproduced sleeves.

			HCP
45s:	Angel Face/		
(up to	You Wouldn't Leave Me Would You	(Bell BLL 1348) 1974	4
1976)	Just For You/I'm Celebrating	(Bell BLL 1368) 1974	10
	Let's Get Together Again/		
	Juke Box Queen	(Bell BLL 1383) 1974	8
	Goodbye My Love/		
	Got To Get Ready For Love	(Bell BLL 1395) 1975	2
	The Tears I Cried/Until Tomorrow	(Bell BLL 1416) 1975	8
	Love In The Sun/I Can Hear Music	(Bell BLL 1437) 1975	15
	People Like Me And People Like You/		
	Makes You Blind	(Bell BLL 1471) 1976	5

This was **Gary Glitter**'s backing band who branched out on their own in March 1974, but although they recorded and indeed toured on their own they still continued to work as **Glitter**'s backing band. They finally split in May 1977, although in 1981 they reunited with their old master for a UK tour. Their deployment of two drummers made them rather unique and, as you can see, they enjoyed a string of hits.

Peter Phipps later had a spell drumming with XTC. Compilation appearances have included: *Goodbye My Love* and *People Like You, People Like Me* on *70's Remembered* (CD); *Let's Get Together Again* on *The Seventies, Vol 2* (CD); and *Angel Face* on *Greatest Hits Of The 70's - cd3* and on *70's FAB FAV's - Classic 70's Hits* (CD). (VJ)

Global Village Trucking Company

Personnel:	JAMES LASCELLES	keyb'ds	A
	JOHN McKENZIE	bs	A
	MIKE MEDORA	hrmnca, gtr, vcls	A
	JON OWEN	gtr, vcls	A
	SIMON STEWART	drum set	A

ALBUM: 1(A) GLOBAL VILLAGE TRUCKING COMPANY
              (w/insert)   (Caroline C 1516) 1976 SC

This commune band was big on the festival circuit. The band also appeared on the compilation, *Greasy Trucker Live At Dingwalls* (LP). (VJ)

The Globe Show

45:       Yes Or No/Gettin' On Back   (Page One POF 128) 1969

This was an obscure late sixties band. (VJ)

Glory

45:       Sweet Old Letters/
          Hey, Hey, Here It Comes   (Penny Farthing PEN 722) 197?

The 45 was produced by **Honeybus** member Ray Cane, who also wrote the 'A' side. (VJ)

Roger Glover (and Guests)

ALBUM: 1 BUTTERFLY BALL   (Purple TPSA 7514) 1974 SC

NB: Issued on Oyster (1605) in the US and reissued on CD (Line LICD 900013) 1989. There's also a related CD, *The Butterfly Ball/Wizard's Convention* (1974) from a film musical (Connoisseur Collection VSOPCD 139) 1989.

45:       Love Is All/
          Old Blind Mole/Magician Moth   (Purple PUR 125) 1974
Reissue: Love Is All/
          Old Blind Mole/Magician Moth   (Safari SAF EP 1) 1984

Glover was born on 30 November 1945 in Brecon, Powys, in South Wales. He was bassist and backing vocalist with **Episode Six** from 1963-69, and from 1969-73 fulfilled the same role in what is generally reckoned to be **Deep Purple**'s best line-up. After he left, he embarked briefly on a solo career before ending up in Rainbow. He was commissioned to write the music to 'The Butterfly Ball' in 1974, which led to a film and a book. He was assisted on the album by David Coverdale, Glenn Hughes and Ronnie James Dio. He later recorded a couple of other solo albums, *Elements* (Polydor 2391 306) in 1978 and *The Mask* (Polydor POLD 5139) in 1984. The same year, both he and **Ritchie Blackmore** were active in a **Deep Purple** reunion.

Glover released a new solo album *Snapshot* in 2002 and still tours and records with **Deep Purple**. (VJ)

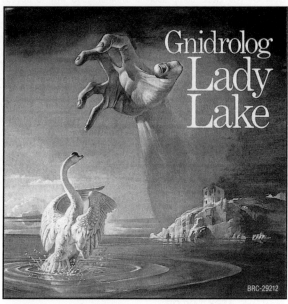

GNIDROLOG - Lady Lake (CD).

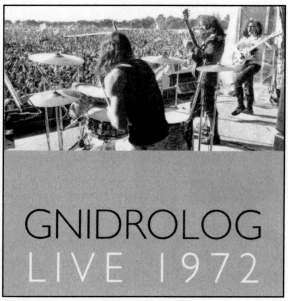

GNIDROLOG - Live 1972 (CD).

Gnasher

45:       Medina Road/Easy Meat   (Purple PUR 119) 1974

This was an ordinary pop/rock effort but with an obnoxious theme and lyrics. (VJ)

Gnidrolog

Personnel: PETER COWLING   bs, cello   AB
            COLIN GOLDRING   gtr, vcls, sax   AB
            STEWARD GOLDRING   gtr   AB
            NIGEL PEGRUM   drms, flute, oboe   AB
            JOHN EARLE   vcls, wind   B
            CHARLOTTE FRENCH   piano   B
            JOHN KNIGHTSBRIDGE   gtr   B

ALBUMS: 1(A) IN SPITE OF HARRY'S TOENAIL (RCA SF 8261) 1972 R1
        2(B) LADY LAKE (Some w/insert) (RCA SF 8322) 1972 R2/R1

NB: (2) reissued in Korea (Si-Wan SRML 1022) 1997. (1) and (2) reissued on one CD (BGO BGOCD 637) 2004. There's also a *Live 1972* CD (Audio Archives AACD 032) 1999.

These albums of progressive rock are sometimes dramatic, often disjointed, but in places contain some interesting and uncommercial music. This is epitomized by tracks like *Long Live Man Dead* on the first album, which also contains some pleasant woodwind accompaniment. As one might expect, they did not sell well and have become quite rare. Their unusual name is a near-anagram of Goldring.

The Goldrings later did session work, as did Pegrum (for John Otway among others) and Earle. Aside from doing session work, Cowling was later a member of The Pat Travers Band. Pegrum had a spell in **Steeleye Span** and the Ben Markus Band who had an album *Nocturn Gate* (Ooze 2002 BA) 1983, which he also produced.

A fourth album, *Gnosis*, with newly written material, has also been released. (VJ)

Gnomes of Zurich

Personnel: DICK ALLIX   drms   A
            TREVOR HEYWORTH   bs   A
            KEVIN LEAR   vcls   A
            JOHN McGURN   gtr   A

45s: Please Mr. Sun/
          I'm Coming Down With The Blues   (Planet PLF 121) 1966 R1
          Second Fiddle/Publicity Girl   (RCA RCA 1606) 1967 SC
          Hang On Baby/Blues For My Baby   (CBS 202556) 1967 SC
          High Hopes/Pretender   (CBS 2694) 1967 SC

Hailed from Gravesend in Kent. Their Planet 45 was produced by Shel Talmy, and they appeared on 'Juke Box Jury' to promote *Please Mr. Sun*. When they disbanded in August 1967 Dick Allix joined **Vanity Fair**.

Compilation appearances have included: *Second Fiddle* on *Yellow Elektric Years* (LP); and *Please Mr. Sun* on *The Best Of Planet Records* (CD). (VJ/IH)

Gobbledegooks

Personnel:	DAVE AMPLEFORT	A
	HENRY ANDREWS	A
	BARRY CONWAY	A
	HOWARD DAVIDSON	A
	JOHN SIMPSON	A

| 45: | Now And Again/ | |
| | Where Have You Been | (Decca F 12023) 1964 SC |

This band was originally known as The Seekers but changed names when the Australian band arrived here. They played beat ballads. (VJ)

Robert John Godfrey

| ALBUM: 1 | FALL OF HYPERION | (Charisma CAS 1084) 1974 SC |

Robert John Godfrey was the arranger for **Barclay James Harvest** and a future main man in Enid. Christopher Lewis performed vocals on this progressive rock album. (VJ)

The Gods

Personnel:	BRIAN GLASSCOCK	drms	A
	JOHN GLASSCOCK	bs, vcls	A C
	KEN HENSLEY	keyb'ds, gtr, vcls, perc	ABC
	JOE KONAS	gtr, vcls	ABC
	MICK TAYLOR	gtr	A
	LEE KERSLAKE	drms	BC
	GREG LAKE	bs, vcls	B
	PAUL NEWTON	bs, vcls	B

ALBUMS: 1(C)	GENESIS	(Columbia S(C)X 6286) 1968 R3
2(C)	TO SAMUEL A SON	(Columbia SCX 6372) 1970 R3
3(C)	GODS	(Harvest SHSM 2011) 1976 SC

NB: (3) is a compilation. (1) reissued on CD (Repertoire REP 4418-WY) 1994, with four bonus tracks. (2) reissued on CD (Repertoire REP 4555-WY) 1995, with one bonus track *Maria*. A further compilation is *The Best Of The Gods* (C5 537) 1989.

THE GODS - Genesis (CD).

THE GODS - To Samuel A Son (LP).

45s:	Baby's Rich/	
	Somewhere In The Street	(Columbia DB 8486) 1968 R1
	Hey! Bulldog/	
	Real Love Guaranteed	(Columbia DB 8544) 1969 R1
	Maria/	
	Long Time, Sad Time, Bad Time	(Columbia DB 8572) 1969 R1

Not to be confused with the American group of the same name, this **Gods** were formed in Hatfield in 1965 by Mick Taylor and the Glasscock brothers (all ex-**Juniors**). Taylor was a great **John Mayall** fan and left to join his Bluesbreakers in the Summer of 1967. He left behind a faltering blues band.

Line-up 'B' sought to revive their fortunes on the club/college circuit and relocating to London, secured a residency at the Marquee. The problem was that **Greg Lake** was too talented for the background role the rest of the band had in mind for him and in the Summer of 1968 he split to join **King Crimson**. The band had to re-group again but line-up 'C', with John Glasscock back in the fold, recorded a couple of interesting progressive rock albums and a few 45s. Of these *Hey! Bulldog*, the **Beatles** track, is their best known.

Their *Genesis* album is also certainly worth checking out, consisting as it does of an imaginative amalgam of psychedelia and progressive rock. Its better tracks like *Towards The Skies* and *Time And Eternity* are full of heavy ploughing Hammond organ and distorted guitar riffs and Ken Hensley's unique and rather dramatic vocals add a further dimension. The recent Repertoire reissues also includes bonus cuts.

The Best Of The Gods compilation is another good way to access their material which is for the most part pretty typical late sixties pop/rock, epitomised by songs like *Radio Show* and *Yes I Cry*. There are shades of Vanilla Fudge on their cover of 'West Side Story' extract *Maria* but only on a few tracks like *Candlelight* and *Real Love Guaranteed* is there an inkling of the heavier sound Hensley and Kerslake would propagate in their next venture, **Uriah Heep**.

Curiously it appears that the Glasscock brothers, Konas, Hensley and Kerslake were also responsible for the **Head Machine** album, recorded under pseudonyms in 1970. This too, is worth hearing.

Compilation appearances have included: *Baby's Rich* on *My Generation* (LP) and *Colour Me Pop, Vol 2* (CD); *Real Love Guaranteed* and *Hey Bulldog* on *Not Just Beat Music 1965-70* (LP), *British Psychedelic Trip, Vol. 2* (LP) and *Great British Psychedelic Trip, Vol. 3* (CD); *Hey Bulldog* on *Psychedelia At Abbey Road* (CD); and *Real Love Guaranteed* on *Harvest Heritage - 20 Greats* (LP). (VJ/MD)

The Gods (Thor, Hermes, Olympus, Mars)

Personnel incl: MICK TAYLOR

45:      Come On Down To My Boat Baby/
         Garage Man   (Polydor 56168) 1967 R3

This obscure 45 is most significant for including future **Rolling Stone** Mick Taylor.

Garage Man has appeared on *Echoes From The Wilderness - Sixteen UK R&B Freakbeat Trippers.* (LP & CD). (VJ)

The Go-Go's

45:      I'm Gonna Spend My Christmas With A Dalek/
         Big Boss Man (Some PS)   (Oriole CB 1982) 1964 R1/SC

Dr. Who and the daleks created quite a stir back in 1964 - hence this one-off novelty single. (VJ)

Herbie Goins (and The Night-Timers)

Personnel incl: HERBIE GOINS

ALBUM: 1 NUMBER ONE IN YOUR HEART
                                       (Parlophone PMC 7026) 1967 R3
NB: (1) reissued with a different title, *Soultime!* (See For Miles SEECD 362) 1992.

45s: Number 1 In Your Heart/Cruisin'   (Parlophone R 5478) 1966 R2
         The Incredible Miss Brown/
         Comin' Home To You   (Parlophone R 5533) 1966 R1
NB: (1) released as **Herbie Goins and The Night-Timers**.

Herbie Goins was one of Britain's best black soul singers; although resident here he was actually born in Florida. He started out guesting with **Alexis Korner's Blues Incorporated** but soon formed his own backing band, **The Night-Timers**, who also recorded a 45 under their own name. Their finest moment was *Number 1 In Your Heart*, which was also the title cut of their sole album. Both the album, which was comprised of quality cover versions of US soul classics, and the 45 have been significant collector's items for quite a while. The CD reissue package from See For Miles not only contains their original album but all their non-album 45s and a short recording of the band performing live. Herbie later moved to Italy.

Turn On Your Lovelight and *No 1 In Your Heart* have been compiled on *R&B At Abbey Road* (CD). (VJ/NR)

Golden Apples of The Sun

45s: α Monkey Time/
         Chocolate Rolls, Tea And Monopoly   (Decca F 12194) 1965 R2

HARVEST HERITAGE (Comp LP) featuring The Gods.

Monkey Time/
Chocolate Rolls, Tea And Monopoly (Immediate IM 010) 1965 R1
NB: α unreleased.

The band was managed by **Andrew Loog Oldham** and fashion photographer David Bailey. *Monkey Time* was a Curtis Mayfield number, recorded by Major Lance.

Compilation appearances have included: *The Monkey Time* on *Immediate Single Collection, Vol. 1* (CD); and *Chocolate Rolls, Tea And Monopoly* on *Immediate Single Collection, Vol. 5* (CD). (VJ)

The Golden Crusaders

Personnel: BILLY COLQUHOUN   baritone sax   A
              BOBBY JOHNSTON   bs   A
              BRIAN JOHNSTON   gtr   A
              JOHN LEE   drms   A
              DENIS MURPHY   vcls   A
              BRIAN SHERIDAN   lead gtr   A
              JACK TAYLOR   tenor sax   A
NB: Andy Doolan (trombone) is also thought to have been a member at some point.

45s: I'm In Love With You/
         Always On My Mind   (Columbia DB 7232) 1964 SC
         Hey Good Lookin'/
         Come On, Come On   (Columbia DB 7357) 1964 SC
         I Don't Care/
         That Broken Heart Is Mine (Columbia DB 7485) 1965 SC

Originally known as The Blackjacks from Bathgate in West Lothian, this seven-piece had formed back in 1960. Their live repertoire consisted of vintage rock'n'roll and covers of current hits. Their debut 45, *I'm In Love With You*, owed a lot to Merseybeat which was becoming passé by late 1964 and the two follow-ups were not innovative in any way. The band failed to outlive the beat boom, splitting up in 1965.

Hey Good Lookin' and *Come On, Come On* have resurfaced on *Rare 60's Beat Treasures, Vol. 5* (CD). (VJ/AD)

The Golden Fleece

45:      Athens 6 A.M./Gift From Syracuse   (Decca F 12669) 1967

This was a short-lived sixties band. (VJ)

Goldrush

45:      For A Few Dollars More/
         No More No More   (Decca F 13380) 1973

This group comprised four young guys from Bath. They twice competed in Melody Maker's National Rock and Folk contest but little else is known about them. (VJ)

Goliath

Personnel: ERIC EASTMAN   drms, perc   A
              MALCOLM GRUNDY   gtr   A
              JOSEPH ROSBOTHAM   woodwind   A
              LINDA ROTHWELL   vcls   A
              JOHN WILLIAMSON   bs   A

ALBUM: 1(A) GOLIATH   (CBS 64229) 1970 R1

45:      Port And Lemon Lady   (CBS 5312) 1971

This heavy progressive act's only album had a close-up of a cigarette butt on its sleeve. Judging from the album's back cover, they were a pretty gloomy bunch of hippies who played heavy jazz-prog reminiscent of **Room**

GONG - Magick Brother, Mystic Sister (CD).

but with less exciting musical interplay. The finest moment is probably their closing cover of **Davy Graham**'s *Maajun*, featuring some appealing Eastern flourishes. Linda Rothwell went on to make some solo 45s. (VJ/RMJ)

Gong

Personnel:	DAEVID ALLEN	gtr, vcls	ABCDEF
(up to	CARL FREEMAN	contrabass	A
1976)	DIETER GEWISSLER	contrabass	ABCDEF
	BURTON GREEN	piano, piano harp	A
	RACHID HOUARI	drms	AB
	DIDIER MALHERBE	sax, flute	ABCDEFG
	BARE PHILLIPS	contrabass	A
	GILLI SMYTH	whispered vcls	ABCDE
	TASMIN SMITH	vcls	A
	(KEVIN AYERS	vcls	B)
	GERRY FIELDS	violin	BCDEF
	DANIEL LALOU	horns, perc	BCDEF
	CHRISTIAN TRITSCH	bs	BCDEF
	LAURIE ALLEN	drms	CD
	FRANCIS MOZE	bs	CD
	TIM BLAKE	synth	DEF
	STEVE HILLAGE	gtr	DEF
	MIKE HOWLETT	bs, vcls	EFG
	PIERRE MOERLEN	drms	EF
	MIQUETTE GIRAUDY	keyb'ds	F
	MIREILLE BAUER	perc	G
	PATRICE LEMOINE	keyb'ds	G
	JORGE PINCHEVSKY	violin	G

NB: Unlike the other entries in this book, the discography that follows is not confined to UK releases.

ALBUMS:	1(A)	MAGICK BROTHER, MYSTIC SISTER	
(up to		(BYG Actuel 5 529 029) 1970 R1 France	
1976)	2(B)	CONTINENTAL CIRCUS (Soundtrack)	
		(Philips 6332 033) 1971 SC	
	3(B)	CAMEMBERT ELECTRIQUE	
		(BYG Actuel 45 529 533) 1971 R1 France	
	4(D)	THE FLYING TEAPOT	(Virgin V 2002) 1973
	5(E)	ANGEL'S EGG	(Virgin V 2007) 1973
	6(F)	YOU	(Virgin V 2019) 1974
	7(G)	SHAMAL	(Virgin V 2046) 1976

NB: (1) reissued in UK (Charly CRL 5025) 1977 on vinyl with a new sleeve, on CD (Decal CD LIK 31) 1986 with a booklet and again (Charly SNAP 199CD 43 48) 2004. (3) reissued in UK (Virgin VC 502) 1974 and (Charly CRM 2003) 1982 and on CD (Decal CD LIK 11) 1986, (Caroline C 1520) 1988 and (Decal CID LIK 64) 1990 and again on CD (Charly SNIP 405) 2004. (4) reissued (Charly CR 30202) 1982 and (Virgin OVED 14) 1984 and on CD (Decal CD LIK 67) 1990 with booklet and again on CD (Charly SNAP 025) 2004. (5) reissued (Charly CR 30219) 1982 and (Virgin OVED 15) 1984 and on CD (Decal CD LIK 75) 1990, (Virgin CDV 2007) 1989,

(Charly SNAP 015) 2004 and again (EMI/Virgin CDVR 2019CD) 2004. (5) and (7) reissued on a 2-CD set with individual booklets for each release. (6) reissued (Charly CR 30220) 1982 and (Virgin OVED 16) 1984 and on CD (Virgin CDV 2019) 1989, (Decal CD LIK 76) 1991, (Charly SNAP 148) 2004 and (EMI CDVR 200& CD) 2004. (7) reissued (Virgin OVED 17) 1984 and on CD (Virgin CDV 2046) 1989.

Also of relevance are two live albums- *Live Au Bataclan 1973* (Mantra 025) 1990 and *Live At Sheffield 1974* (Mantra 042) 1990 (both were only issued in France and were also available on CD). There are also three compilations:- *Gong Est Mort - Vive Gong* (Tapioca TP 10002/3 or 3/4) 1977, a double album issued in France and reissued on CD in France in 1993; *Live Etc* (Virgin VGD 3501), a double album and *The Mystery And History Of Planet Gong* (Demi Monde DMLP 1018) 1989, a double album compilation of rarities, which also came with a booklet. This has been reissued on CD twice (Thunderbolt CDTL 010) 1989 and (Thunderbolt CDTB 116) 1993. *Camembert Eclectique* (Gas A GAS CD 001) 1994 is a CD collection of material from circa 1970, some hitherto unissued, put out by the Gong Appreciation Society.

Fans of the band may want to investigate *The Best Of Gong* (Nectar Masters NTMCD 517) 1995 and the double CD set, *The Birthday Party* (Voiceprint VPGAS 101CD) 1995, which was the result of a two night reunion concert at The Forum, London, on 8-9th October 1994 to celebrate their 25th birthday. There's also *The Peel Sessions* (Strange Fruit SR CD 137) 1995, which includes some previously unreleased recordings from the early seventies, although some of the remaining material has appeared on other releases. Part three of their epic 'Radio Gnome' trilogy, *You* has also been the subject of a 2-CD re-mix album, imaginatively entitled *You Re-Mixed*, with the cream of the nineties psychedelic dance acts (The Orb, The Shamen, Astralasia, System 7, Glo, Global etc.) providing remixes of each of the albums original tracks (Gliss GLISSCD 001) 1997. *Gong On Radio* (1999) reproduces their jazzier and synthesiser-led works from 1973/1974 in a live setting. *Live In Sherwood Forest 1975* (CD) is a rare live and previously unreleased recording from a live radio set at Nottingham University on 25th November 1975. It comes with a 12-page booklet containing rare live photos and sleevenotes penned by the band. A new compilation is *Best Of Gong* (Kosmik Karma KAR 040901) 2004.

45:	Est-Ce-Que Je Suis/	
	Hip Hipnotize You (PS)	(BYG 129021) 1970 France

Despite being based in France and forming there **Gong** have sufficient British connections to justify their inclusion in this book. Their founding member was **Daevid Allen**, an Australian poet/composer/guitarist who'd first come to Britain in 1961. He'd formed the Daevid Allen Trio, a sort of free-form jazz group with **Robert Wyatt** and **Hugh Hopper**, which developed into **The Soft Machine**. After going on a European tour with them during 1967 he was refused re-entry to the UK because his visa had expired. He was briefly imprisoned and then returned to France spending time in Deya, one of the Majorcan islands, before settling in Paris. He put together various embryonic line-ups of what became known as **Gong** during 1968 and eventually recorded *Magick Brother, Mystic Sister* with line-up (A) for the French Byg label between September and October 1969. It was released in France only in 1970, but not released in the UK until Charly put it out in an entirely different sleeve in 1977. Indeed **Gong** were virtually unheard of here in the UK until Virgin signed them in 1973, except for a notable appearance at the 1971 Glastonbury Festival, which was subsequently documented on one side of the extremely rare *Glastonbury Fayre* (3-LP).

GONG - The Flying Teapot (LP).

GONG - Angel's Egg (LP).

In 1971 **Gong** recorded music for the Soundtrack to an obscure Jerome Lapperrousaz motorbike movie called 'Continental Circus'. They contributed four tracks:- *Blues For Findlay, Continental Circus World, What Do You Want* and an instrumental version of *Blues For Findlay.* This Soundtrack album was released in the UK on Philips. The same year **Daevid Allen** also cut a solo album *Banana Moon* with assistance from Pip Pyle, Christian Tritsch and **Robert Wyatt.**

By 1971 **Gong** had already undergone the first in what seems to have been an almost continuing series of line-up changes. *The Continental Circus* and *Camembert Electrique* albums were recorded by line-up (B). Originally only released in France in 1971 *Camembert Electrique* was later reissued in the UK at a budget price by Caroline 1974. Musically, it was an offbeat blend of jazz-influenced space-rock, unconventional psychedelia and bizarre experimentation. Indeed, with their communal lifestyle and blend of Eastern mysticism, this hippie band was definitely an anachronism from the sixties, but a welcome one in the more banal early seventies. The original French issue on Byg came in a gatefold sleeve and with a two-page lyric insert.

In November 1971 Pip Pyle left **Gong** to join **Hatfield and The North.** Laurie Allen replaced him briefly and former Magma bassist Francis Moze was also added to the line-up. However, in August 1972 **Daevid Allen** decided to disband **Gong** entirely and came to Britain in search of new musicians. The trip to Britain provided him with new inspiration. Whilst here he met Virgin chiefs Richard Branson and Simon Draper who offered the band a new record contract on their label, **Allen** returned to France with a new line-up which included former Uriel, **Arzachel**, **Egg** and **Khan** member **Steve Hillage**, who was playing for **Kevin Ayers'** band Decadence at the time.

At the start of 1973 **Gong** started work on the first part of what became known as their *Radio Gnome Invisible* trilogy, *Flying Teapot.* The recordings didn't go smoothly, Francis Moze didn't really fit in and eventually left but not before **Allen** had split to Deya with Gilli Smyth leaving the band to perform as Paragong with **Hillage** and Blake supervising things. *The Flying Teapot* album appeared in May 1973. It was an avant-garde collection of sound effects, sax, jazzy improvisation and comic vocals with titles like *The Pot Head Pixies, The Octave Doctors and The Crystal Machine* and *Zero The Hero and The Witch's Spell.* It marks a change in focus towards a more psychedelic, jazz-rock ensemble.

Gong spent most of the Summer and part of the Autumn of 1973 touring. Their appearance at London's Dingwall's club was partly captured on a side-long contribution to the double album, *Greasy Truckers - Live At Dingwalls Dance Hall.* Some of it later re-appeared on the *Live At Sheffield* CD.

Between the Summer and Autumn 1973 tours **Gong** recorded the second part of their *Radio Gnome Invisible* trilogy their *Angel's Egg* album, mostly in the back garden of their French residence. Early copies came with a booklet containing lyrics and explanations of the inhabitants of the Planet Gong. Uncharacteristically it contained one pop-orientated song, *Oily Way*

and **Steve Hillage**'s guitar-driven *I Never Gild Before*; but most of the remaining material consisted of the lengthy spaced-out, jazz-influenced jams that typified their sound in this era. The album was released in December 1973 and the compromising position of Zero The Hero's head on the cover in relation to the Moon Goddess meant early copies sported a sticker concealing this section of it. Although the weakest of the trilogy, it combines humour with good songwriting and features some trippy spacey synthesiser work.

Gilli Smyth left the band in February 1974. Her replacement was Miquette Giraudy. Pierre Moerlen quit temporarily too, but soon rejoined. This revised line-up (F) recorded *You,* the third part of the *Radio Gnome Invisible* trilogy, (although it wasn't credited as such). This was also one of their better albums, notable for *Master Builder*, which converted a gentle Buddhist chant into a frantic live favourite and the lengthy synthesiser-driven *A Sprinkling Of Clouds*, which had been composed by Tim Blake. Some regard this as one of the greatest space-rock albums.

After this **Daevid Allen** left the band in April 1975 during the latter half of a UK tour. Tim Blake had left a month earlier and the band would never be the same again. Tim Blake went on to record three solo albums in the post-1976 era and was later in **Hawkwind. Daevid Allen** moved to Spain with Gilli Smyth but he too went on to record further albums beginning with *Good Morning!* with Spanish group Euterpe in 1976.

The dominant forces in what remained of **Gong** were **Steve Hillage** and Pierre Moerlen, but the only vinyl output in this era seems to have been **Hillage**'s solo album *Fish Rising*, which included a lot of band material, and an outtake *Pentagramaspin*, which got an airing on Virgin's 1975 (2-LP) sampler *V*, credited to Paragong. **Hillage** left **Gong** too at the end of 1975 to concentrate on a solo career.

Still **Gong** soldiered on with a new line-up (G) recording *Shamal*, which was basically a jazz-rock album, released in February 1976. This was the final **Gong** release to fall within the time span of this book, but they carried on for a couple more years before evolving into Pierre Moerlin's Gong (Moerlin had been the band's dominant force since rejoining in 1976).

There was an outfit gigging in 1988 as Daevid Allen and Gong, although **Allen** was initially the only former **Gong** member to figure in this acoustic outfit. By 1989 this had evolved into Gong Maison and included former **Gong** member Didier Malherbe. A self-titled album emerged on Demi Monde in 1990. Meanwhile Gilli Smyth had put together her own Mother Gong outfit. **Daevid Allen** also collaborated with Graham Clarke and Mark Robson as The Magick Brothers resulting in one CD, *Live At The Witchwood 1991* in 1992 and earlier in the late seventies with the band Here And Now as Planet Gong. This aggregation produced one 1978 album (also available on CD) *Live Floating Anarchy 1977*. Then in 1979 he released *About Time*, an album credited to another of his outfit's New York Gong. Certainly it's hard to think of many bands whose history has been as confusing as **Gong**'s!

Aside from the band's studio output, collectors may be interested in the two Mantra releases in 1990. Both feature live material from the 'trilogy' era

GONG - You (CD).

band; *Live At Sheffield 1974*, the stronger of the two, contains material previously on the *Greasy Truckers* (LP). Virgin's 1977 *Live Etc* also concentrated on their 'trilogy' era combining a mix of live material, BBC sessions and other bits and pieces most notably their ultra-rare 1970 French-only 45 *Est-Que-Je-Suis*. *The Mystery and History of Planet Gong* was a double album compilation of rarities, which came with a 20-page booklet. It includes **Daevid Allen**'s 1964 Radio 3 spoken word performance of "Captain Shaw and Mr. Gilbert"; live, radio, and remixed versions of songs from the era when **Kevin Ayers** was their vocalist (from July 1971 - January 1972) and a French language version of **Allen**'s 1977 45, *Opium For The People*. They became Pierre Moerlen's Gong signing to Arista in 1979 for three studio albums.

A line-up of **Gong** was still gigging in the nineties. Their French-born drummer/composer Pierre Moerlen died on 3 May 2005.

I Never Glid Before recently resurfaced on the CD compilation, *The Age Of Enlightenment - Prog Rock, Vol. One.* (VJ)

The Gonks

Personnel:

PAUL BIRD	bs	A
GEOFF BRAY	lead gtr	A
MIKE BRAY	bs	A
TREVOR LEWES	drms	A

45:	The Gonk Song/		
	That's All Right, Mama	(Decca F 11984) 1964 SC

A beat group who were also **Twinkle**'s backing group until May 1965.

That's Alright Mama has been compiled on *Pop Inside The '60s, Vol. 2* (CD), *The Sixties Lost And Found, Vol. 2* (LP) and *Sixties Explosion, Vol. 1* (CD). (VJ/AD)

Good Earth

ALBUMS:	1	IT'S HARD ROCK AND ALL THAT		
			(Saga FID 2112) 1968 SC
	2	IN THE SUMMERTIME	(Saga FID 8157) 1970 SC
	3	RAY DORSET'S BEST	(Boulevard 4078) 1972

NB: (2) also includes tracks by **Macon Jug**. (3) contained four tracks by **Good Earth** and six by **Macon Jug**.

The title *It's Hard Rock And All That* just about sums up the music found on their plodding debut cash-in album. Tracks like *Stop Complaining*, *Same Song* and *My Own Country* sound vaguely similar to **The Kinks**, but this album should come very low down collectors' wish lists. **Ray Dorset** of

THE GOOD EARTH - It's Hard Rock & All That (LP).

Mungo Jerry was a member, and the band was actually dropped by Saga (a budget label) when he announced his new jug-band direction! Along with **The First Impression**, they supplied the music for *Swinging London* (Saga FID 2117) 1968, which maintains a respectable standard of pop/light rock throughout. They also shared a couple of albums with **Macon Jug**. (VJ/VL/RMJ)

Philip Goodhand-Tait (and The Stormsville Shakers)

ALBUMS:	1	REHEARSAL	(DJM DJLPS 411) 1971
(up to	2	I THINK I'LL WRITE A SONG	(DJM DJLPS 416) 1971
1976)	3	SONGFALL	(DJM DJLPS 425) 1972
	4	PHILIP GOODHAND-TAIT	(DJM DJLPS 432) 1973
	5	JINGLE JANGLE MAN	(DJM DJLPS 453) 1975
	6	OCEANS AWAY	(Chrysalis CHR 1113) 1976

45s:	α	I'm Gonna Put Some Hurt On You/		
(up to		It's A Lie	(Parlophone R 5448) 1966 SC
1976)	α	No Problem/	
		What More Do You Want	(Parlophone R 5498) 1966 SC
	α	You Can't Take Love/	
		J.C. Greaseburger	(Parlophone R 5547) 1966 SC
		Love Has Got Hold Of Me/	
		Too Pleased To Help	(Decca F 12868) 1969
		Jeannie/Run See The Sun	(DJM DJS 10230) 1971
		Oh, Rosanna/I Didn't Know Myself	(DJM DJS 10236) 1972
		Everyday/I Think I'll Write A Song	(DJM DJS 10261) 1972
		City Streets/Moon	(DJM DJS 10268) 1972
		You Are/Five Flight Walk Up	(DJM DJS 10278) 1974
		Almost Killed A Man/	
		Reach Out For Each Other	(DJM DJS 10295) 1974
		I Think I Can Believe/One More Rodeo	(DJM DJS 10319) 1974
		Jesus Didn't Only Love The Cowboys/	
		Sweet Emotions	(DJM DJS 10601) 1975
		Oceans Away/Can You Demonstrate	(Chrysalis CHS 2100) 1976

NB: α with The Stormsville Shakers.

Born in Hull on 3rd January 1945 **Goodhand-Tait** is a pianist and vocalist. He first attracted attention as composer for **The Love Affair** for whom his credits included *Gone Are The Songs Of Yesterday* (the flip to their No. 1 *Everlasting Love*) and *A Day Without Love*. Earlier in 1966 he'd recorded three 45s for Parlophone with The Stormsville Shakers which hadn't sold at all well, prior to the band renaming themselves **Circus** and recording an eponymous album for Transatlantic.

In the seventies, he was heavily promoted as a piano-playing singer/songwriter (a poor man's **Elton John**) but he failed to achieve anything like the latter's success. Some of his compositions were later recorded by **Roger Daltry**.

Philip Goodhand-Tait and The Stormsville Shakers also backed Larry Williams and Johnny Guitar Watson on a UK tour and an album, *The Larry Williams Show* (Decca), recorded prior to Larry's return to the USA.

I'm Gonna Put Some Hurt On You can also be heard on *Go... With An All Star* (LP). (VJ)

Good Ship Lollipop

45:	Maxwell's Silver Hammer/		
	How Does It Feel (Some PS)	(Ember EMBS 276) 1970

One of several band's to cover this **Beatles**' song. This version can also be heard on Ember's *New Faces For The 70s* (LP) compilation. Mike Warth tells me the compilation is awful, with only this and **Backstreet Band** being bearable, whilst the **Blonde On Blonde** track is outstanding. (VJ)

The Good Thing Brigade

This was actually an earlier version of **Jason Crest** who were from Tonbridge in Kent. In 1967 they recorded some demo tapes at R.G. Jones' Morden studios and after signing for Philips presented them with an acetate of a song called *My House Is Burning*, which can now be heard on *Syde Trips, Vol. 4* (LP). Whilst the label deliberated about whether to release it **The Move**'s similar *Fire Brigade* appeared and quickly became a hit ensuring that *My House Is Burning* remained in the can. (VJ)

Good Time Losers

Personnel:			
	JOHN DARBY	vcls	A
	COLIN DELANY	ld gtr	A
	CHRIS HUNT	drms	A
	TERRY TWIGGER	bs	A
	ALAN WAITES	gtr	A

45:    Trafalgar Square/Where Did My Heart Go(Fontana TF 791) 1967

From Tonbridge in Kent their 45 was a catchy soul-styled number. They once played at the Star Club in Hamburg. (VJ)

The Sam Gopal Dream

Personnel:			
	ANDY CLARK	keyb'ds, vcls	A
	SAM GOPAL	tabla, perc	A
	MICK HUTCHINSON	gtr	A
	PETER SEARS	bs	A

A legendary London underground band from 1967. Clark had previously been in The Fenmen and Hutchinson had been with **Sons Of Fred**. They played regularly at UFO, Middle Earth, Happening 44 etc. They are rumoured to have had a demo played on John Peel's 'Perfumed Garden' show on pirate ship Radio London in 1967. **Sam Gopal** was an Indian tabla player, which was most unusual in a band in 1967. In mid-1968 **The Sam Gopal Dream** played a farewell gig at the Middle Earth club under the name of "The exploding of the stereo phomi decibel" and were joined by **Viv Prince**. **Gopal** then left and the others carried on under the name **Vamp** and recorded *Floatin'* for Atlantic before Clark and Hutchinson formed **Clark-Hutchinson** and Pete Sears left for the West Coast of America where he joined Silver Metre, Copperhead and Stoneground, before ending up in Jefferson Starship.

Gopal and Clark were strongly rumoured to be recording in Berlin (1995) where **Gopal** lives. (VJ/JN)

Sam Gopal

Personnel:			
	ROGER D'ELIA	ld gtr, acoustic gtr, gtr	A
	PHIL DUKE	bs	A
	SAM GOPAL	tablas, perc	A
	IAN 'LEMMY' WILLIS	vcls, lead gtr, gtr	A

ALBUM: 1(A) ESCALATOR   (Stable SLE 8001) 1969 R2
NB: Reissued on CD (TTE 004CD) 199? and again on CD (Edsel EDCD 627) 2000.

EP: 1   Escalator/Cold Embrace/Sky Is Burning/Angry Faces
                                (Stable SLE 8001) 1969 R1

45:    Horse/Back Door Man   (Stable STA 5602) 1969
NB: Unissued.

This album, which was produced by Trevor Walters, is now very collectable. It contains a reasonable version of *Season Of The Witch* and a less impressive cover of Davidson's *Angry Faces*, but it's Lemmy's compositions which catch the ear. The best group compositions are *Cold Embrace, The Dark Lord* and *Midsummer Nights Dream*. All three are heavyish psychedelic rock with some good guitar work. Willis' contributions ranged from *Escalator*, another heavy, quite psychedelic number and probably the album's finest moment, to the mellower *The Sky Is Burning* and the sensitive, slightly Eastern-influenced *Yesterlove*. Four album tracks also appeared on a very limited DJ-only EP.

Lemmy was later in **Hawkwind** and Motorhead.

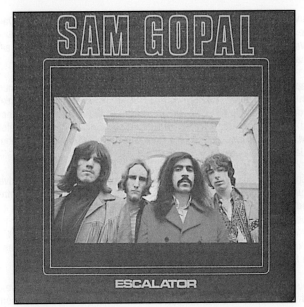

SAM GOPAL - Escalator (LP).

Psychedelic Salvage Co. Vol. 1 (LP & CD) includes *Horse*, which is well worth a listen. *Psychedelic Salvage Co. Vol. 2* (LP & CD) includes their reasonable stab at *Back Door Man*. Neither of these two cuts were on their album. *The Dark Lord* recently got a further airing on *Rock Of Ages, Four Decades Of Heavy Rock 1962-2002, Escalator* has resurfaced on the 4-CD box set *Acid Drops, Spacedust & Flying Saucers* and *The Sky Is Burning* has been compiled on the 3-CD box set *Ars Longa Vita Brevis: A Compendium Of Progressive Rock 1967-1974.* (VJ)

Trevor Gordon

ALBUM: 1 ALPHABET   (Polydor 2343 011) 1970

Gordon had previously recorded with **The Bee Gees**. He was then in **The Marbles** (with **Graham Bonnet**) and when they split in October 1969 he set about recording this album. (RMJ)

John Gorman

ALBUM: 1 (up to 1977)	GO MAN GORMAN	(DJM DJF 20491) 1977

| 45s: (up to 1977) | WPC Hodges/I Remember | (Island WIP 6151) 1973 |
| | Whole World In His Band/Poetry Rock | (DJM DJS 10777) 1977 |

John Gorman was born on 4 January 1937. He is best known as a member of **Scaffold**, but these were his solo efforts in the seventies. (VJ)

Gospel Garden

Personnel incl:			
	CRAIG AUSTIN	bs, vcls	A
	STEVE COX	drms	A
	GEOFF EATON TINDLE	ld gtr, vcls	A
	JOHN GLADWIN	vcls	A
	TERRY WINCOTT	gtr, vcls	A

45:    Finders Keepers/Just A Tear   (Camp 602 006) 1968

This act evolved out of **The Dimples** with a new drummer Steve Cox and guitarist Geoff Eaton Tindle (ex-**Primitives** / **Sutch**`s Savages / **Ian Hunter**). Heavily influenced by Jim Webb`s Magic Garden, Gospel, and Curtis Mayfield, they nonetheless developed a number of original material from John Gladwin.

Originally managed by Peter Stringfellow together with promoter Sid Hartess and a crazy American DJ "Chicken Fat" Charlie, their tight arrangements and complex harmonies soon attracted the attention of **Dave Dee** and the band's management was taken over by Jet Set producer Steve Rowlands of **Family Dogg** at Double-R Productions (who were also managing **The Herd** at the time).

Gospel Garden gigged extensively around London's "In Crowd" venues such as Speakeasy, Blazes, Sybillas, Scots of St James, Revolution, Marquee, Flamingo, 100 Club etc. in addition to the Universities, northern mod clubs like Twisted Wheel, Broken Wheel, Golden Torch Castleford Bowl, Jazz Workshop and endless other drug fuelled all-nighters throughout the land.

A short spell followed with Robert Stigwood negotiating a TV advert featuring the band being chauffeur driven in the ill-fated "Humber Sceptre". Needless to say this was a total flop and was hastily withdrawn from the screens with the Humber company almost immediately going bust. By this time, the band was pretty wild looking and was picked to share the bill on the first ever televised psychedelic flower-power festival up in Newcastle with **Robert Palmer**'s Mandrake.

Popular as the band was performing live, their 45 was unrepresentative of their live act, and consequently, record sales proved elusive. Shortly afterwards, the band's management decided that the **Gospel Garden** name wasn't commercial enough and ordered a total makeover. With that and a couple of changes of personnel, **Gospel Garden** became **Methuselah** and were soon signed to the highly prestigious Elektra record label. (VJ)

Gothic Horizon

| Personnel: | ANDY DESMOND | vcls, gtr, bs | A |
| | RICHARD GARRETT | vcls | A |

ALBUMS: 1(A) THE JASON LODGE POETRY BOOK
                                 (Argo ZFB 26) 1970 R2
         2(B) TOMORROW IS ANOTHER DAY (Argo ZDA 150) 1972 R2
NB: (1) and (2) also issued on CD.

45s:	The Jason Lodge Poetry Book/	
	Wilhelmina Before Sunrise	(Argo AFW 102) 1970 SC
	Marjorie/Song	(Argo AFW 104) 1971 SC
	If You Can Smile/Thoughts	(Argo AFW 107) 1972
	Girl With The Guitar/Can't Bear To	
	Think About You	(Argo AFW 108) 1972

This duo from Hertfordshire played bright and breezy folk music on their albums and 45s. The second album is rockier than the first with a more commercial edge. **Desmond** later recorded as a solo artist for the Konk label, which was owned by **The Kinks**. (VJ)

Dave Goulder and Liz Dyer

| Personnel: | DAVE GOULDER | A |
| | LIZ DYER | A |

| ALBUMS: 1(A) | JANUARY MAN | (Argo ZFB 10) 1970 R1 |
| 2(A) | RAVEN AND CROW | (Argo ZFB 30) 1971 R1 |

These are both rare folk albums, mostly with Liz Dyer's vocals and a mixture of traditional folk songs as well as original material. (VJ)

Graham Gouldman

ALBUM: 1 THE GRAHAM GOULDMAN THING (RCA SF 3954) 1968
NB: (1) a US-only release was reissued on CD (Edsel EDCD 346) 1992 and again on CD (BMG 82876 635272) 2004.

45s:	Stop! Stop! Stop! (Or Honey I'll Be Gone)/	
(up to	Better To Have Loved And Lost	(Decca F 12334) 1966 R2
1976)	Upstairs Downstairs/Chestnut	(RCA RCA 1667) 1968 SC
α	Windmills Of Your Mind/Harvey's Theme (Spark SRL 1026) 1969
	Nowhere To Go/Growing Older	(CBS 7739) 1972

NB: α credited to The Graham Gouldman Orchestra.

Graham Gouldman was born on 10 May 1945 in Manchester. His first band in 1964 were **The Whirlwinds**; later in February 1965, he formed **The Mockingbirds**. Their various singles flopped and in February 1966 he signed to Decca and attempted to launch a solo career. His first 45, *Stop! Stop! Stop! (Or Honey I'll Be Gone)* was a pleasant uptempo ballad which flopped but later that year he wrote *Pamela, Pamela* for **Wayne Fontana** and it became a hit.

In 1967 he wrote *Bony Maronie At The Hop* and set up a studio outfit called **Manchester Mob** to help him perform it. This turned out to be another commercially unsuccessful venture. His *Upstairs Downstairs* 45 is a light and charming pop offering. Yet later, he again proved he had what it took to write commercial material when he became a staff writer for the Kasenatz-Katz production team in New York in the Autumn of 1969. Whilst there, he wrote and sang lead vocals on The Ohio Express's *Sausalito (Is The Place To Go)*. He also penned *Have You Ever Been To Georgia*, which several artists have enjoyed hits with. Later in the year he wrote and sang on *Susan's Tuba* which **Freddie and The Dreamers** had an enormous hit with in France.

It's worth mentioning the calibre of the hits he wrote in the sixties which included *For Your Love*, *Evil Hearted You* and *Heart Full Of Soul* (all for **The Yardbirds**), *Bus Stop* and *Look Through Any Window* (**The Hollies**) and *No Milk Today* (**Herman's Hermits**).

Prior to his spell with Kasenatz-Katz, **Gouldman** signed a contract with RCA in 1968. This resulted in the above album, which he co-produced with **John Paul Jones** (later of Led Zeppelin), and another 45 but neither seemed to have interested the punters. The 2004 BMG reissue of this album on CD comes with some sleevenotes written by **Gouldman**.

Teaming up with future **10cc** members Lol Creme, Kevin Godley and Eric Stewart (who he'd earlier worked with for Kasenatz-Katz) they worked as **Hotlegs**, but also wrote material for **Ramases** and Neil Sedaka before eventually forming **10cc** early in 1972. He was with **10cc** until they split in 1983 and in 1980 released the animated feature album, *Animalympics*. He went on to play in Wax with Andrew Gold.

The 1969 Marmalade label sampler album, *Marmalade - 100 Proof*, includes **Graham Gouldman** singing *Late Mr. Late* and **Graham Gouldman** and Lol Creme teaming up on *To Fly Away*, which is erroneously credited to **Gouldman** and Lol Creme.

Other compilation appearances have included: *Stop! Stop! Stop!* on *The Mod Scene* (CD), *The Soul Of British R'n'B 1962-68* (LP) and *British R'n'B Explosion, Vol. 1* (CD); *To Fly Away* on *Rare Tracks* (LP); *Bus Stop* on *Pop-In, Vol 1* (CD); *The Impossible Years* on *Pop-In, Vol 2* (CD); *Upstairs, Downstairs* on *Colour Me Pop, Vol 2* (CD) and *Chestnut* on *Jagged Time Lapse, Vol 5* (CD). (VJ)

GRACIOUS - Gracious (LP).

Mick Grabham

ALBUM: 1 MICK THE LAD   (United Artists UAS 29341) 1972

NB: (1) reissued on CD (Angel Air SJPCD 012) 2002, with three bonus cuts.

45:     On Fire For You Baby/
      Sweet Blossom Woman   (United Artists UP 35391) 1972

In 1967 guitarist **Grabham** was in **Plastic Penny**. His next venture was the country-rock band **Cochise** and he recorded this album before his four year stint in **Procol Harum**, between 1972-76. On offer is melodious, laid-back rock. There are a lot of instrumentals and more vocals would have enhanced the album, but it will appeal to some **Procol Harum** collectors. The 2002 CD reissue features three additional cuts, *Diamonds*, *Hit And Miss* and a pretty average cover of *The Wanderer*. (VJ)

Grame Grace

ALBUM: 1 HAIL ME   (RCA SF 8418) 1975

45:     What Do You Do With My Sweetheart/
      Generation of Today   (RCA RCA 2472) 1974

Chrysalis had recently struck gold with Leo Sayer, so it's not hard to imagine lots of record labels searching for the next curly-haired, wacky singer-songwriter with a fetching smile and a touch of falsetto. In any event, RCA came up with **Mr. Grace** and his modestly-titled album of rock songs. There must have been some hype going on, as the sleeve reprints a review from that well-known musical journal "The Sun" in which he is called "the voice of tomorrow". To be fair, the tunes aren't bad and John Fiddy's arrangements are fine too. But the songs are lyrically odd, with words seemingly selected to make a rhyme, or near-rhyme, rather than mean anything. Then there's that falsetto. Approach with caution! (NM)

Gracious

Personnel:	ALAN COWDEROY	gtr, vcls	A
	PAUL DAVIS	gtr, vcls	A
	MARTIN KITCAT	keyb'ds, vcls	A
	ROBERT LIPSON	drms	A
	TIM WHEATLEY	bs	A

ALBUMS: 1(A) GRACIOUS   (Vertigo 6360 002) 1970 R2
       2(A) THIS IS...GRACIOUS (Philips 6382 004) 1972 R2

NB: (1) reissued by Beat Goes On (BGOLP 34) 1988 and on CD (Repertoire REP 4060-WP) 1991 and again (Repertoire REPUK 1033) 2004. (2) reissued on CD by Renaissance (RCD 1003) 1993. (1) and (2) reissued on CD (BGO Records BGO CD 256) 1995.

45s: Beautiful/What A Lovely Rain   (Polydor 56333) 1969 SC
      Once On A Windy Day/
      Fugue In D Minor   (Vertigo 6059 009) 1970

A heavy progressive outfit who came from Surrey. Its recordings all attract interest from collectors. Basically we're talking progressive symphonic rock here with a lush mellotron sound. The first album, which has been reissued on Beat Goes On with the original artwork and on CD by Repertoire, begins with a pretentious *Introduction*, which gives way to *Heaven*, an acoustic guitar and mellotron number followed by the heavier *Hell*, which is full of distorted vocals, unnerving keyboards and phased percussion. Side two kicks off with the more laid back *Fugue In 'D' Minor*, which features some pleasant guitar and harpsichord work. This is followed by the lengthy *The Dream* with frantic vocals, swirling keyboards and some thumping drum work.

Their second album *Blood Red Sun* was givena 6360 prefix but was eventually released the Philips International budget-priced This Is series, with a changed title. It included the majestic *Blood Red Sun*, but it didn't sell well and the band folded soon after its release.

Introduction, from their first album, can also be heard on *Vertigo Annual*, (2-LP) which appeared in 1970. *Once On A Windy Day* later resurfaced on *Fading Yellow, Vol 5* (CD).

Vocalist Paul Davis later guested on the *Jesus Christ Superstar* album and recorded a solo album as **Sandy Davis**. Bassist Tim Wheatley played in a mid-seventies band called **Taggett**. Cowderoy later went on to work for Stiff Records, Chrysalis and Go! Discs. (VJ)

Graded Grains

Personnel incl:	JOHN GREGORY	gtr	A
	TOMMY ?	drms	A

From the Exeter area this band evolved out of a **Who**-like mod band called The Spartans. They recorded acetate tracks which were subsequently included on *Chocolate Soup For Diabetics, Vol. 3* (LP). *Lucifer's Son* is really a rehash of **Syd Barrett**'s *Lucifer Sam* (from **Pink Floyd**'s *Piper At The Gates Of Dawn*) and *Animal Magic* is weaker, though still worth a hear.

Gabriel Says Yes, *Animal Magic*, *On The Dole* and *Harry The Hermit* have all been compiled on *Alphabeat (Pop, Psych and Prog 1967-1970)* (LP) and (CD). (VJ/AB)

Chick Graham and The Coasters

Personnel:	ARTHUR ASHTON	lead gtr	ABCDEF
	WILLIAM ASHTON	gtr, vcls	ABC
	GEORGE BRAITHWAITE	bs	ABCD
	BILLY FORDE	vcls	A
	TONY SANDERS	drms	ABCDE
	RAY DOUGHERTY	gtr, bs	BCDEF G
	GRAHAM (CHICK)		
	JENNINGS	vcls	DEFG
	ARTHUR RAYNOR	gtr	EFG
	JIMMY LACEY	drms	FG
	MIKE KONZLE	lead gtr	G

45s: Education/I Know   (Decca F 11859) 1964
      A Little You/Dance Baby Dance (Decca F 11932) 1964

This Liverpool group started out as Billy Ford and The Phantoms (line-up 'A'). After Ford left, Bill Ashton (aka **Billy J. Kramer**) took over on vocals and the band played as Billy Kramer and The Coasters (line-ups 'B' & 'C'). In 1962, **Billy J. Kramer** was snapped up by Brian Epstein who put him together with the Manchester-based **Dakotas**. The Coasters, then teamed up with 15-year-old vocalist Graham Jennings to record these two 45s. Neither made much impact.

Compilation appearances have included: *I Know*, *Dance Baby Dance* and *A Little You* on *Liverpool 1963-1964, Vol. 2* (LP); and *A Little You* and *Dance Baby Dance* on *Mersey Sounds* (2-LP). (VJ/AD)

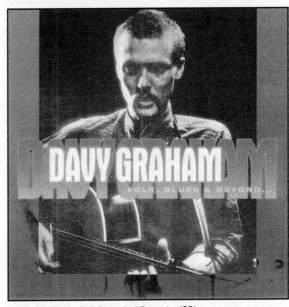

DAVY GRAHAM - Folk Blues And Beyond... (CD).

DAVY GRAHAM - After Hours At Hull University 4th February 1967 (CD).

Davy Graham

ALBUMS: 1 THE GUITAR PLAYER
(up to   (Golden Guinea GGL 0224) 1962 R1
1976)   2 FOLK, BLUES AND BEYOND   (Decca LK 4649) 1964 R1
         3 FOLK ROOTS, NEW ROUTES (some w/insert)
                           (Decca LK 4652) 1964 R3
         4 MIDNIGHT MAN   (Decca LK 4780) 1966 R2
         5 LARGE AS LIFE & TWICE AS NATURAL
           (mono/stereo)   (Decca LK/SKL 4969) 1968 R1
         6 HAT (mono/stereo)   (Decca LK/SKL 5011) 1969 R2
         7 HOLLY KALEIDOSCOPE   (Decca SKL 5056) 1970 R2
         8 GODINGTON BOUNDRY (President PTLS 1039) 1970 R1
         9 ALL THAT MOODY   (Eron ERON 007) 1976 R3

NB: (3) with **Shirley Collins**. He continued to record beyond the time frame of this book. (1) reissued as *The Guitar Player... Plus* (See For Miles SEECD 351) 1993 along with three tracks from the rare *3/4 AD* EP he recorded for the Topic label in 1962. (1) reissued again (Castle CMRCD 622) 2003 along with eight previously issued bonus cuts, many previously unissued photos and detailed sleevenotes, which concentrate on his early career and this album. (2) reissued on CD (Fledg'ling FLED 3050) 2005. (3) reissued on CD (Fledg'ling FLED 3052) 2005. (5) reissued on CD (Fledg'ling FLED 3054) 2005. (6) reissued on CD (Fledg'ling FLED 3051) 2005. (9) reissued on CD (Rollercoaster RCCD 3022) 1999, with six previously unavailable tracks added. Also relevant is *Folk Blues And All Points In Between* (See For Miles SEECD 47) 1990, also on LP (SEELP 48) 1990. *After Hours At Hull University, 4th February 1967* (Rollercoaster RCCD 3021) 1998 captures an impromptu performance in student quarters for his old friend John Pilgrim, which merges jazz, blues and folk.

EPs: 1 3/4 AD (with **Alexis Korner**)   (Topic TOP 70) 1962 R3
         2 From A London Hootenanny (split with the Thamesiders)
                           (Decca DFE 8538)1963 R3

NB: (1) exists in three pressings. The first and rarest is in a mauve sleeve with cream label. Later pressings have bronze or lilac sleeves and blue labels. These are R2.

45:     Both Sides Now/Tristano   (Decca F 12841) 1968

Born in 1940, **Davy** (sometimes Davey) **Graham** came from a Scottish-Guyanese background but grew up in London. Nomadic by nature, he travelled around Europe and North America in the late fifties and early sixties, soaking up a wide variety of exotic influences. When he added them to his experimental 'folk baroque' guitar style, the results inspired a whole generation of musicians. Though his albums sold respectably, however, they didn't chart and are not easy to acquire in decent shape today, probably because they tended to be played to death by fans attempting to decipher his tunings and finger-work.

His budget-label debut was an accomplished collection of folk, pop and jazz standards such as *Don't Stop The Carnival* and *Take Five*, accompanied by drummer Bobby Graham (no relation). **Graham** really found his stride a couple of years later, when he began a long association with Decca staff producer Ray Horricks on *Folk, Blues & Beyond*. One of the most influential albums of its time, it inspired countless people to take up the guitar.

Alongside his best-known song, *Anji* (famously appropriated by Paul Simon), it contained imaginative renditions of *Sally Free And Easy* and *Cocaine* as well as the Eastern-themed *Maajun*. His next release, *Folk Routes, New Routes*, was a fine series of collaborations with traditional vocalist **Shirley Collins**, and appeared almost simultaneously with its predecessor. It finds him on fine form on cuts like *Nottamun Town* and *Love Is Pleasin'*, and is the hardest of his Decca albums to find in decent shape today. A few copies came with an explanatory insert - these are especially rare.

For many his next effort, 1966's *Midnight Man*, is the most enjoyable he ever made. More aligned with the burgeoning folk-rock movement than his earlier work, it features excellent versions of *No Preacher Blues*, *Hummingbird* and *Walking The Dog* as well as covers of **The Beatles**' *I'm Looking Through You* and Charles Mingus' *Fire In My Soul*. Sadly 1967 saw no releases, though his next effort, 1968's *Large As Life...*, featured some superb material that reflected the psychedelic movement, principally *Sunshine Raga* and *Blue Raga*, the extended pieces that closed either side. The high point, however, was his stunning version of Joni Mitchell's *Both Sides Now*, which was extracted as a single to little effect.

In fact, **Graham**'s unreliability, lack of ambition and growing drug dependency conspired to prevent his ever becoming the star many believe he could have been. His singing (while never less than pleasant) is undistinctive and indeed his next two albums, 1969's *Hat* and 1970's *Holly Kaleidoscope*, feature the mediocre vocals of his American partner, Holly. Both are less consistent than their predecessors, though they contain excellent material. After a disappointing album for President, 1971's *Godington Boundry*, he disappeared from sight for a number of years, returning in 1976 with a very rare album on the Kent-based Eron label, *All That Moody* (which opens with another version of *Anji*). This is now very hard to find. He went on to record further albums on Sonet's Kicking Mule subsidiary that extend beyond the time frame of this book. To this day **Graham** continues to make sporadic live performances - some are transcendently brilliant and others are bitterly disappointing. Good luck! (RMJ/VJ/PL)

Ernie Graham

ALBUM: 1 ERNIE GRAHAM   (Liberty LBS 83485) 1971 R3
NB: (1) reissued on CD (Hux 032) 2002.

Graham was an Irishman who'd played guitar in **Eire Apparent**. He cut this rare solo set with backing from **Brinsley Schwartz** and **Help Yourself**. There's a strong Dylan and Band influence on tracks like *Sebastian* and *So Lonely*, but overall it is one of the more distinctive and memorable British solo albums of the period, and is very hard to locate indeed. When it failed to sell he briefly joined **Help Yourself**, then formed **Clancy**, who recorded two albums of funk-rock for Warner Bros. At the end of the decade he played with Nick Lowe and released a solo 45 on Stiff Records, both sides of which are included as bonuses on the Hux CD. In later years he developed health problems and became dependent on drink. **Graham** sadly died in April 2001.

He also contributed a track, *Don't Want Me Round You*, to United Artists' 1971 compilation, *All Good Clean Fun* (LP). (VJ/RMJ)

Grail

Personnel: PAUL BARRATT   ld gtr, clarinet, backing vcls   A
               DAVID BLAKE   cello, sitar, flute backing vcls   A
               STAN DECKER   bs, gtr, keyb'ds   A
               CHRIS PERRY   drms, talking drm   A
               CHRIS WILLIAMS   ld vcls, autoharp   A

ALBUM: 1 (A) GRAIL   (Metronome MLP 15393) 1971
NB: (1) only released in Germany. (1) reissued on CD (Second Battle SB 046) 1998 and the release reproduced the fantasy art work of the original cover and contained liner notes by Chris Williams.

45:     Grail/Sunday Morning   (Metronome) 1970

A psychedelic-influenced rock quintet. The album was produced by **Rod Stewart** and recorded in Tangerine Studios in London. Musically, it's in the heavy progressive category, although there are a couple of pleasant folky numbers, some Eastern music inflections and moody and flute passages. Chris Williams later joined the German group Abacus who released four albums between 1971-1974.

Grail later resurfaced on *Electric Psychedelic Sitar Headswirlers Vol. 6* (CD). (VJ)

Grand Union

45:	Slowly But Surely/She Said	(CBS CBS 3956) 1969

The flip side to the insignificant 'A' side is actually a cover of **John Lennon's** *She Said She Said* which appeared on **The Beatles'** *Revolver* album. This organ-based, lively rendition was produced by Peter Gage. (VJ)

Grannie

ALBUM:	1	GRANNIE	(SRT 71138) 1971 R5

NB: (1) reissued on Legacy (L 100) 1993.

This is one of these mega-rare privately-pressed albums which originally only appeared in demo form with just 99 copies being available in a home-made paste-on sleeve. Later a few stock copies found their way into collectors' hands. In its December 2004 edition 'Record Collector' valued this item at £850. The musical menu is guitar-dominated heavy progressive rock but with sufficient melody to make it worth a listen. It contains six cuts in all with *Coloured Armageddon Leaving*, the punchy *Saga Of A Sad Jester* and *Leaving*, which had some melodic guitar work, the pick of the bunch. (VJ)

Granny's Intentions

Personnel:	PETE CUMMINGS	bs, flute	A
	JOHNNY DUNCAN	vcls	A
	JOHNNY HOCKEDY	gtr, mandolin	A
	PAT NASH	drms	A
	JOHN RYAN	keyb'ds	A

ALBUM:	1(A)	HONEST INJUN	(Deram SML 1060) 1970 R1

NB: (1) reissued on CD (Lemon CDLEM 39) 2004.

45s:	The Story Of David/	
	Sandy's On The Phone Again	(Deram DM 158) 1967 SC
	Julie Don't Love Me Anymore/	
	One Time Lovers	(Deram DM 184) 1968 SC
	Never An Easy Thing/	
	Hilda The Builder	(Deram DM 214) 1968 SC
	Take Me Back/Maybe	(Deram DM 293) 1970 SC

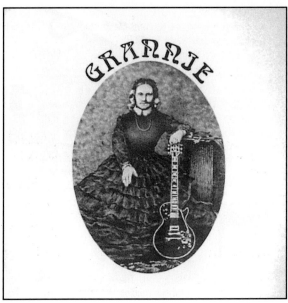

GRANNIE - Grannie (LP).

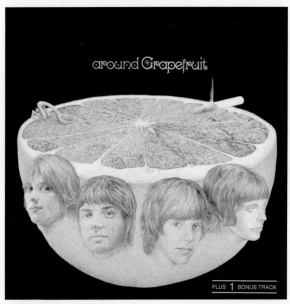

GRAPEFRUIT - Around Grapefruit (LP).

This Irish band's blues-based rock album hasn't enough spirit of its own to lift it above similar efforts. In fact, nothing on side one is very appealing. Side two is marginally better and has at least two interesting tracks: the instrumental *Nutmeg, Bittersweet*, which lives up to its title, and the folk-blues inspired *I'm Going*. Not a bad album, but nothing special at all.

A 17-year-old **Gary Moore** played on nine of the eleven album tracks and was briefly a member of the band.

Maybe can also be heard on *Progressive Pop Inside The Seventies* (CD) and *Broken Dreams, Vol. 6* (LP). (MK)

Erky Grant and The Earwigs

45:	I Can't Get Enough Of You/	
	I'm A Hog For You	(Pye 7N 15521) 1963 R1

Nothing is known about this band, although their sole 45 is now a minor collectable. You'll also find *I'm A Hog For You* on *Pebbles, Vol. 6 - The Roots Of Mod* (LP), *Rubble, Vol. 7 - Pictures In The Sky* (LP), *The R&B Era, Vol. 1* (LP & CD) and *English Freakbeat Vol. 6* (CD) but it's certainly nothing special. (VJ)

Lee Grant (and The Capitols)

45s:	Breaking Point/Don't Cry Baby	(Parlophone R 5531) 1966 SC
α	A Little Love And Understanding/	
	I Got To Get You Out Of My Mind	( ) 19??

NB: α Lee Grant solo.

The first single is a sought-after beat 45. (MWh)

Grantchester Meadow

45:	Candlelight/Winter Blues	(Amber ABR 004) 1971 SC

An obscure label 45 worth seeking out for its mellotron-drenched 'A' side. (MWh)

Grapefruit

Personnel:	GEORGE ALEXANDER	bs	A
	JOHN PERRY	ld gtr	A
	GEOFF SWETTENHAM	drms	A
	PETE SWETTENHAM	gtr	A

GRAPEFRUIT - Deep Water (CD).

ALBUMS: 1(A) AROUND GRAPEFRUIT (Stateside S(S)L 5008) 1969 R1
2(A) DEEP WATER (RCA Victor SF 8030) 1969 SC

NB: (1) and (2) reissued on CD (Repertoire REP 4363-WY and REP 4364-WY) 1993.

                                                                                        HCP
45s: Dear Delilah/The Dead Boot (RCA Victor RCA 1656) 1968 21
      Elevator/Yes (RCA Victor RCA 1677) 1968 -
      C'mon Marianne/Ain't It Good (RCA Victor RCA 1716) 1968 31
      Someday Soon/Theme For Twiggy (Stateside SS 8005) 1968 -
      Round Going Round/This Little Man (Stateside SS 8011) 1969 -
      Deep Water/
      Come Down To The Station (RCA Victor RCA 1855) 1969 -
      Lady Godiva/
      Thunder And Lightning (RCA Victor RCA 1907) 1969 -
      Sha Sha/Universal Party (Deram DM 343) 1971 -

NB: Readers may also be interested in a rare 45, *Dolce Delilah (Dear Delilah)* / *Mai Nessun (The Dead Boot)* (RCA 1541), sung in Italian and released in Italy.

The band was formed when the Swettenham brothers and Perry decided to form their own outfit after a brief spell with **Tony Rivers and The Castaways**, a harmony group who later evolved into a MOR vocal group, **Harmony Grass**.

Dear Delilah, an imaginative effort with a rich organ backing, attracted considerable publicity, reaching No 21 in February 1968. None of their subsequent work attained such success, despite the follow-up *Elevator* single benefiting from a promo film directed by **Paul McCartney**, which was made at Albert Memorial Hall in London. They did enjoy one further minor hit with *C'mon Marianne*, which peaked at No 31 in August 1968. Their albums contain some interesting music, with a psychedelic taint, but did not attract much attention. Their early songs were good harmony pop but later on they veered towards a very unappealing sort of funk. The group broke up soon after Pete Swettenham left in early 1969.

However, in 1971 Alexander reformed the group which included Harry Vanda and George Young from **The Easybeats**, but after one single, *Sha Sha*, for Deram it disintegrated.

George Alexander was the elder brother of George Young of **The Easybeats**, but passed over the chance to join the rest of his family when they emigrated to Australia. He'd earlier been in **My Dear Watson**.

Geoff Swettenham became an occasional session musician.

Of their two albums only the first is recommended.

Compilation appearances include: *Breakin' Up A Dream*, *Dear Delilah* and *Trying To Make It To Monday* on *Hard Up Heroes, Vol. 2* (CD); *Theme For Twiggy* on *Instro-Hipsters A Go-Go* (CD); *Dear Delilah* on the 4-CD box set *Acid Drops, Spacedust & Flying Saucers*; *Elevator* on *Pop-In, Vol 1* (CD);

Round Going Round on *Colour Me Pop, Vol 2* (CD) and *Yes* on *Colour Me Pop, Vol 1* (CD). (VJ)

Gravy Train

Personnel: NORMAN BARRETT vcls, gtr AB
            BARRY DAVENPORT drms A
            J.D. HUGHES woodwind, keyb'ds, vcls AB
            LES WILLIAMS bs, vcls AB
            RUSSELL CALDWELL drms B
            JIM FRANK drms B
            GEORGE LYNON gtr B
            PETE SOLLEY synth B
            MARY ZINOVIEFF synth, violin B

ALBUMS: 1(A) GRAVY TRAIN (Vertigo 6360 023) 1970 R1
        2(A) BALLAD OF A PEACEFUL MAN
                                (Vertigo 6360 051) 1971 R3
        3(A) SECOND BIRTH (Dawn DNLS 3046) 1973 R1
        4(B) STAIRCASE TO THE DAY (Dawn DNLH 1) 1974 R1

NB: (1), (2), (3) and (4) all reissued on CD by Repertoire (REP 4063-WP, 4122-WZ, 4164-WZ and 4133-WP respectively) 1991. (1) reissued again (Repertoire REPUK 1067) 2004. (3) reissued on CD (Sequel NEM CD 612) 1991 with one additional cut, *Good Time Girl*. (4) reissued on CD (Sequel NEM CD 613) 1991 with the bonus of both sides of their last 45.

45s: Strength Of A Dream/Tolpuddle Episode (Dawn DNS 1036) 1973
      Starbright Starlight/Good Time Thing (Dawn DNS 1058) 1974
      Climb Aboard The Gravy Train/
      Sanctuary (Dawn DNS 1115) 1975

Gravy Train was a Christian rock band originally from Manchester. Starting like your typical Vertigo act, their first album sounds faintly like early **Jethro Tull**, mainly due to similar flute lines, but without a dominating personality like Ian Anderson. Hard-rock riffing is alternated with quieter and melodic moments and the flute is high in the mix throughout. The tracks are not at all "folky" as some dealers' lists describe them. Some of the music sounds like any old power trio. A nice track is *Dedication To Syd* (**Barrett**), a quiet but highly atmospheric experimental piece.

Much better is the surprisingly rare second album for Vertigo. The solos are tighter and more controlled and the compositions are better. It is also less bluesy, very crisply produced and features good multi-part singing, greatly enriching their textures. They also try a track with a hook, the lovable *Home Again*.

Lack of commercial success drove them away from Vertigo into the arms of Dawn, while gigging all over the country to create a following. The result, *Second Birth*, is not very satisfying and actually sounds like a step backwards. Although more diversely instrumentated than either Vertigo album, the songs lack distinction and verve, making this sound like an attempt to please too many people simultaneously.

GRAVY TRAIN - Gravy Train (CD).

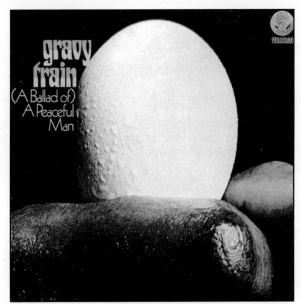

GRAVY TRAIN - (A Ballad Of) A Peaceful Man (CD).

Their swansong, housed in a Roger Dean cover and with a revised line-up, starts with the very best cut they made, *Starbright Starlight*, a blistering piece of melodious hard-rock, that sets the standard for similarly inclined music (though not many may have heard it, of course). The rest of the album isn't up to the same standard, but the title track with its Bach-derived intro and an unexpected foray into Greek folk, is good too. All in all, a band that plays well, but has too few original ideas to be of more than passing interest.

Norman Barrett formed his own band in the early eighties and drummer Russell Caldwell joined him. Pete Solley went on to a career as a session musician although he was in **Paladin** and **Fox**. Mary Zinovieff played with **Duffy Power**.

Starlight Starbright has been compiled on the 3-CD box set *Ars Longa Vita Brevis: A Compendium Of Progressive Rock 1967-1974*. (MK/BS)

Dorian Gray

HCP

45s:	Behind The Tears/		
	Walking Down A Backstreet	(Parlophone R 5612) 1967 -
	I've Got You On My Mind/	
	Move On	(Parlophone R 5667) 1968 36
	Love Is All It Should Be/	
	Let Me Go Home	(Parlophone R 5705) 1968 -
	Jingle Down A Hill/Get Going Baby	(Parlophone R 5732) 1968 -
	I've Got You On My Mind/Move On	(Parlophone R 5840) 1970 -

This name was presumably taken from the Oscar Wilde novel 'The Picture Of Dorian Gray'. The guy's best known song was *I've Got You On My Mind* but like him it's long since been forgotten. He came from Gravesend in Kent and his real name was Tony Ellingham. (VJ)

The Grease Band

Personnel:	JOE COCKER	vcls	ABCD
	FRANK MYLES	gtr	A
	DAVE MEMOTT	drms	A
	VERNON NASH	piano	A
	CHRIS STAINTON	bs	ABCDE
	TOMMY EYRE	keyb'ds	BC
	MICKEY GEE	gtr	B
	TOMMY REILLY	drms	B
	HENRY McCULLOGH	gtr	CDE
	KENNY SLADE	drms	C
	BRUCE ROWLANDS	drms	DE
	ALAN SPENNER	bs	DE
	NEIL HUBBARD	gtr, vcls	E
	MICK WEAVER	organ, vcls	E

NB: Line-ups (A) - (D) as **Joe Cocker and The Grease Band**. See **Joe Cocker** entry for details of recordings. The actual **Grease Band** line-up was (E).

ALBUMS:	1(E)	THE GREASE BAND	(Harvest SHVL 790) 1971 SC
	2(A)	AMAZING GREASE	(Goodear EAR 2902) 1975

NB: (1) issued on Shelter in the US. (2) reissued on Charly (30166) in the UK in 1979 and both albums reissued on Line in Germany in 1981.

45s:	Laughed At The Judge/	
	Jesse James/All I Wanna Do	(Harvest HAR 5052) 1972
	New Morning/Pont Ardawe Hop	(Goodear EAR 602) 1975

The Grease Band evolved out of Joe Cocker's Big Blues in Sheffield in 1966. They soon became **Joe Cocker**'s backing band. After they split from **Cocker** in 1970, Spenner, **McCullogh** and Rowlands joined the session band for 'Jesus Christ Superstar' and played on the resulting album. Spenner and McCullogh also worked briefly with **Spooky Tooth** but then, with the addition of Neil Hubbard (ex-**Juicy Lucy**), they reformed as **The Grease Band** in the Summer of 1975, recording one critically acclaimed album. They also toured the US a couple of times. After they split up at the end of 1971, Hubbard and Spenner played together in The Chris Stainton Band and were later in **Kokomo**; Rowlands went on to **Fairport Convention** and **McCullogh** and Weaver played together again in a later **Joe Cocker Band** line-up.

They reformed briefly in 1975 to record the *Amazing Grease* album and, of course, **McCullogh** was also later in **Wings** and did a solo album for Dark Horse. *Laughed At The Judge* can also be heard on the *Harvest Bag* (LP) compilation. (VJ)

Greasy Spoon

45:     Nova One/In My Life   (Penny Farthing PEN 920) 1976

Nothing else is known about this band. (VJ)

Great Expectations

45:     Midnight Man/Sky's The Limit   (Philips 6006 122) 1971

The 'A' side is very jerky, part chant, part heavy with a good bongo beat. (VJ)

Greatest Show On Earth

Personnel:	MIKE DEACON	keyb'ds	A
	DICK HANSON	horns	A
	COLIN HORTON-JENNINGS	vcls, gtr, drms	A
	TEX PHILPOTTS	sax	A

GRAVY TRAIN - Staircase To The Day (CD).

RON PRUDENCE	congas, drms	A
GARTH WATT-ROY	vcls, gtr	A
NORMAN WATT-ROY	vcls, bs	A

ALBUMS: 1(A) HORIZONS (Harvest SHVL 769) 1970 R1
2(A) THE GOING'S EASY (Harvest SHVL 783) 1970 R1
3(A) GREATEST SHOW ON EARTH (2-LP)
(Harvest SHSM 2004) 1975

NB: (1) reissued on CD (Repertoire REP 4484-WP) 1994 and vinyl (Si-Wan). (2) reissued on CD (Repertoire REP 4483-WP) 1994 with one bonus cut, *Mountain Song*. (1) and (2) reissued on one CD (See For Miles SEECD 473) 1997.

45s: Real Cool World/Again And Again (Harvest HAR 5012) 1970 SC
Tell The Story/Mountain Song (Harvest HAR 5026) 1970
Magic Touch Woman/Again And Again (Harvest HAR 5129) 1977

Greatest Show On Earth formed in 1968 as a soul band with a black vocalist called Ozzie Lane. However, when he headed back to the US and was replaced by Colin Horton-Jennings the band veered towards progressive rock. They were far more popular on the Continent than over here. Indeed, *Real Cool World* was quite a big hit in some European countries. Their two 1970 albums for Harvest are now minor collectables. *Horizons* was a consistent effort which appeared in one of the most distinctive Hipgnosis sleeves. The lengthy title track took up much of side two, but the finest moment was the finale, *Again And Again*.

The Going's Easy was much jazzier and not as good as the debut. A less characteristic track, *Magic Woman* Touch, was covered as a single by **The Hollies** in 1972 and later released as a 45 by Harvest in 1977, two years after they'd put out a double compilation of the band's material.

After they split up in 1971 Norman Watt-Roy joined **Glencoe** and was later in **Loving Awareness** before ending up one of Ian Dury's Blockheads. Garth Watt-Roy played with **Fuzzy Duck**, **East Of Eden**, **Marmalade**, Bonnie Tyler and Paul Young. Horton-Jennings joined **Taggett** and **Streetwalkers**, Deacon was later in **Vinegar Joe** and Darts. Hanson ended up with **Graham Parker**. The other three quit the music scene.

Compilation appearances include: *Again And Again* on *Picnic* (2-LP); and *Magic Woman Touch* on *Harvest Heritage - 20 Greats* (LP). (VJ)

Great Metropolitan Steam Band

ALBUM: 1 THE GREAT METROPOLITAN STEAM BAND
(MCA MNP/S 403) 1969 SC

NB: This album is dated 1970 on the sleeve and 1969 on the label.

This was a four-piece band featuring piano, vocals, brass and banjo. By the looks of them they probably played a mixture of jazz, ragtime and blues, but I have been unable to verify this. The album was released for a couple of weeks but got next to no record company support. (VJ/PC)

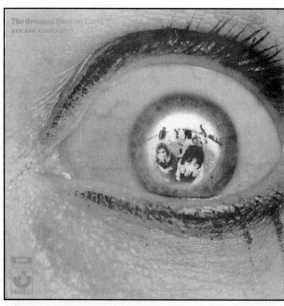

GREATEST SHOW ON EARTH - Greatest Show On Earth (2-LP).

Ian Green (Revelation)

Personnel:	MADELINE BELL	vcls	A
	IAN GREEN		A
	ROSETTA HIGHTOWER	vcls	A

ALBUM: 1(A) REVELATION (CBS 63840) 1970 SC

45s: α Last Pink Rose/Green Blues (Polydor 56194) 1967
When You Love A Man/Santa Maria (CBS 3997) 1969
Groover's Grave/Revelation (CBS 4623) 1969

NB: α as **Ian Green**.

Groover's Grave and *Revelation* are both brassy instrumentals. **Madeline Bell** was in **Blue Mink** and also recorded as a solo artist and Rosetta Hightower was a solo soul artist. (VJ)

Peter Green

ALBUM: 1 THE END OF THE GAME (Reprise RSLP 9006) 1970
(up to
1976)

NB: (1) reissued by Reprise (K 44106) in 1972. Credited to **Peter Green** and Nigel Watson. *Jumping At Shadows/The Blues Years* (Indigo/Sanctuary IGOXCD 2507) 2002 is a mid-priced 2-CD set.

45s: Heavy Heart/No Way Out (Reprise K 14092) 1971
(up to α Beast Of Burdon/Uganda Woman (Reprise K 14141) 1972
1976)

NB: α as **Peter Green** and Nigel Watson.

Green is a Londoner - he was born there as Peter Greenbaum on 29 October 1946 and played with Mick Fleetwood in **Peter B's** and **Shotgun Express**. He then replaced **Eric Clapton** in **John Mayall's Bluesbreakers** (in July 1966) but was sacked after just one month! In July 1967, he formed **Fleetwood Mac** with Mick Fleetwood. He recorded this album (with Nigel Watson) after leaving the band in 1970. It made no impression commercially and the album he recorded with **Gass** in 1970 met the same fate. Little was heard of him until the end of the decade when he returned to record six albums and 45s for PVK in the late seventies and early eighties. The first three of these *In The Skies*, *Little Dreamer* and *Whatcha Gonna Do?* have been reissued by Sanctuary in 2005.

Jumping At Shadows/The Blues Years is a 2-CD mid-priced collection, which is part of Sanctuary's 'Indigo Recording Blues' releases. Containing 36 tracks in all the collection draws from **Green's** 1968 recordings with the **Brunning Sunflower Blues Band**, the Kingston home tapes with **Duster Bennett**, the 1969 New York Studio sessions and the live 1970 Boston Tea Party tapes.

His version of *Loser Two Times* can also be heard on the 3-CD set *Guitar Heroes - Rock The Night Away*. (VJ)

The Green Angels

45s: Rockin' Red Wing/Let It Happen (Parlophone R 5390) 1965 SC
An Exile's Dream/Hannigan's Hooley (Parlophone R 5512) 1966

This was an Irish showband. (VJ)

The Greenbeats

45s: α If This Were Mine/You Must Be The One (Pye 7N 15718) 1965
So Sad/I'm On Fire (Pye 7N 15843) 1965
Pretty Woman/Thing (Spin SP 2007) 1967

NB: α demo only.

A beat/pop group. *If This Were Mine* is a forgettable ballad, but the 'B' side is a good beat record, which was penned by **Jagger**/Richard.

GREEN MAN - What Ails Thee? (LP).

Compilation appearances have included: *So Sad (To Watch Good Love Go Bad)* on *Ripples, Vol. 3* (CD); *You Must Be The One* on *English Freakbeat, Vol. 5* (CD); and *If This World Were Mine* and *You Must Be The One* on *Irish Rock - Ireland's Beat Groups 1964-1969* (CD). (VJ)

Green Bullfrog

Personnel:	ROD ALEXANDER	gtr	A
	TONY ASHTON	keyb'ds	A
	RITCHIE BLACKMORE	gtr	A
	MATTHEW FISHER	keyb'ds	A
	ROGER GLOVER	bs	A
	CHAS HODGES	bs	A
	EARL JORDAN	vcls	A
	ALBERT LEE	gtr	A
	IAN PAICE	drms	A
	BIG JIM SULLIVAN	gtr	A

ALBUM: 1(A)   GREEN BULLFROG   (MCA MKPS 2021) 1972 R1

NB: (1) reissued as *The Green Bullfrog Sessions* (Connoisseur NSPCD 503) 1991, also on LP (503) with three additional tracks. The original album was reissued by See For Miles (SEECD 227) in 1988, also on album (SEELP 227) 1988.

The above album was the work of a session group which comprised among others **Deep Purple** members, **Ritchie Blackmore**, **Roger Glover** and Ian Paice and Albert Lee and Big Jim Sullivan. It was masterminded by producer Derek Lawrence. It's basically R&B played in a hard-rock style. It's mostly comprised of cover versions, including **Creation**'s *Makin' Time*, and is notable for Earl Jordan's strong vocals.

The CD reissue on Connoisseur has been remixed and remastered from the original tapes and also includes the bonus of three previously unissued tracks:- *Louisiana Man, Ain't Nobody Home* and *Who Do You Love?*. The magnum opus remains *Bullfrog*, though, a fast instrumental which is full of some superb guitar work. It has a **Deep Purplish** sound, especially when **Ritchie Blackmore** plays the leads. (VJ/CA)

The Green Ginger Three

Personnel:	ALAN METCALFE	bass,vcls	A
	DAVID METCALFE	banjo, vcls	A
	DAVID KELLETT	gtr, vls	A

EP: 1(A)   FROM THE LAND OF GREEN GINGER
                                        (Decca DFE 8623) 1965

A folk trio from Lancaster, where they'd played for some years prior to making this rare EP, which appears to have been their sole recording and was produced by a young **Mike Vernon**. It comprises two originals (*Mournful Chimes* and *Can You Hold On Buddy*) and two standards (*Oh Miss Mary* and *Green Fields*). Pleasant but undistinctive. (RMJ)

Green Man (1)

ALBUM: 1   WHAT AILS THEE   (Private Pressing) 1975 R3

NB: (1) reissued on vinyl (Slightly Discoloured FADE 1).

This is a highly-rated home-made acid-folk album from four long-haired hippies with superb **Carolanne Pegg** - style lead female vocals, strange haunting three-part harmonies and some fine acid guitar heroics. There's a spooky live version of *Nottamun Town* and a fine amalgam of pure female vocals and an unnerving folk-rock backing on tracks like *Poor Sally Sat A-Weeping, Salisbury Plain* and *Pretty Polly*. Only a few dozen copies are likely to exist as both front and back are plain white with details individually stuck on. The labels on the disc are also pasted on to the record. If you like **The Trees, Mellow Candle, Spriguns Of Tolgus** and **Sandy Denny** era **Fairport Convention** this is in similar mould. (VJ)

Green Man (2)

Personnel ?:	DAVE	A
	DEREK	A
	PAUL?	A
	J? J?	A
	?	A

ALBUM: 1(A)   CHRISTMAS ROCK   (BWP) c1971

Pressed in the UK and released by and through Bob Wheatley Taverns Productions, this album contains four Christmas songs plus faithful covers of fifties rock (Jerry Lee Lewis, Ricky Nelson, etc), two **Stones** covers (*Honky Tonk Woman* and *Satisfaction*), **Free**'s *All Right Now*, a **Kinks** cover and more. It's good hard-rock style fare for the most part.

There are no artist credits on the sleeve, but the copy I've seen is autographed by five people. (RD)

Green Scarab

This band recorded two instrumental tracks, *Psychedelic Wilderness* and *Asariah's Dance* which were not released at the time. Both date from 1967 and the former in particular is an excellent Eastern-influenced slice of psychedelia.

Compilation appearances include: *Psychedelic Wilderness* on *Circus Days Vol. 1 & 2* (CD); *Asariah's Dance* on *Circus Days Vol. 3* (CD); and *Psychedelic Wilderness* and *Asariah's Dance* on *Circus Days, Vol. 2* (LP). (VJ)

Greenslade

Personnel:	DAVE GREENSLADE	keyb'ds	AB
	DAVE LAWSON	vcls, keyb'ds	AB
	ANDREW McCULLOCH	drms, perc	AB
	TONY REEVES	bs	A
	MARTIN BRILEY	gtr, bs, backing vcl	B
	(CLEM CLEMPSON	gtr	*)
	(GRAHAM SMITH	fiddle	*)

NB: * Guest performances on *Spyglass Guest* only.

				HCP
ALBUMS:	1(A)	GREENSLADE	(Warner Bros K 46207) 1973	SC -
(up to	2(A)	BEDSIDE MANNERS ARE EXTRA		
1976)			(Warner Bros K 46259) 1973	SC -
	3(A)	SPYGLASS GUEST	(Warner Bros K 56055) 1973	34
	4(B)	TIME AND TIDE	(Warner Bros K 56126) 1975	SC -
	5(B)	CACTUS CHOIR	(Warner Bros K 56306) 1976	-

NB: (5) credited to Dave Greenslade. Warner Bros have reissued all their albums on CD with original cover art (though their albums aren't hard to find). *The Pentateuch Of The Cosmogony* (EMI EMSP 332) 1980 was a 2-LP set issued as Dave Greenslade with a 47-page booklet. There is also a retrospective CD *Live* (Mystic MYS CD 136)1999. This is hard to find and was reissued (Beat Goes On BGOCD 170) 1997 as a CD-sized box set with a 48-page booklet reproducing the Patrick Woodroffe art.

GREENSLADE - Time And Tide (LP).

45s:
	Temple Song/An English Western	(Warner Bros K 16264) 1973	
	Catalan/Animal Farm	(Warner Bros K 16584) 1975	
α	Gangsters/		
	Rubber Face, Lonely Eyes	(Warner Bros K 16828) 1976	

NB: Flip to α credited to Dave Greenslade's Gangsters.

Formed by **Greenslade** and Reeves (both previously with **Colosseum**) in November 1972. Dave Lawson had earlier played with **Alan Bown** and **Episode Six**, whilst Andrew McCulloch had bashed the skins in **King Crimson**, **Crazy World Of Arthur Brown** and **Fields**. Their first two albums were critically acclaimed and successfully merged several different musical styles in a keyboard-driven format. Their album covers were illustrated and calligraphed by Roger Dean. Highly talented musicians, their albums were complex and rather elitist.

Before they recorded their third album, the line-up was supplemented by the addition of Dave Clempson (formerly with **Humble Pie**) and fiddler Graham Smith. After this album, Reeves quit (he later joined **Curved Air**) and was replaced by Briley (ex-**Mandrake Paddlesteamer**).

After their split in January 1976, **Dave Greenslade** recorded a solo album, *Cactus Choir* (Warner Bros K 56306), but it didn't sell well.

In 1977, the band reformed with a line-up of **Dave Greenslade**, another former **Colosseum** member Jon Hiseman, Tony Reeves and Mick Rodgers, but they only lasted for a tour. Their music was out of place in the emerging punk era. For the same reasons, **Dave Greenslade**'s lavish double concept album, *The Pentateuch Of The Cosmogony*, the result of his collaboration with fantasy writer and artist Patrick Woodroffe, also flopped. Still the package, which came with a 47-page book, is now a minor collectable (R1). During the eighties and nineties, **Dave Greenslade** made a good living composing theme music for British film and television.

Reading Festival 1973 (CD) includes their rendition of *Feathered Friends* from the festival of the same name. Following the release of a retrospective live CD in 1999 (which featured concerts from 1973 and 1974) the band reformed, with two original members (Greenslade (keyb'ds) and Reeves (bs)) joined by ex-Asia and Qango member John Young (keyb'ds, vcls) and John Trotter (drms). Trotter had been in **Manfred Mann's Earthband**. They released a new CD *Large Afternoon* (Mystic MYS CD 142). (VJ/JO)

Mick Greenwood

ALBUMS: (selective)
1	THE LIVING GAME	(MCA MDKS 8003) 1971	
2	TO FRIENDS	(MCA MKPS 2026) 1972	
3	MIDNIGHT DREAMER	(Warner Brothers K 56059) 1974	

Mick Greenwood was a multi-instrumentalist who recorded a series of albums in the seventies, including those listed above. On *Midnight Dreamer* he played a sort of commercial rhythm and blues. His backing bands over the years were a catalogue of well-known session musicians including Pat Donaldson, Gerry Conway and Jerry Donahue (ex-**Fotheringay**) and Barry de Souza (ex-**Tir Na Nog**, **Riff Raff** and **Schunge**). (BS)

Nick Greenwood

Personnel:
BUNK GARDNER	wind		A
NICK GREENWOOD	vcls, bs		A
DICK HENINGHEM	keyb'ds		A
BRYN HOWARTH	gtr		A
ERIC PEACHY	drms		A
CHRIS PRITCHARD	gtr		A

ALBUM: 1   COLD CUTS   (Kingdom KVLP 9002) 1972 R4

Housed in a suitably disgusting cover, the music on this album is organ-based, not unlike a mixture of **Arthur Brown** and **Norman Haines**, and strongly progressive in approach. Especially interesting are the extended track *A Sea Of Holy Pleasure* and the aptly titled *Melancholy*, both with inventive organ parts. The album is dense and hard to penetrate, as well as being heinously rare. It was also issued in Holland on Pink Elephant (PE 877.039-H) and France on Kingdom. Continental copies are slightly more common.

Greenwood was also in **Khan** and prior to that had played with **Crazy World Of Arthur Brown**. (MK/VJ/RMJ)

Greep

Personnel incl: COLIN FLETCHER   ld gtr   A

45:          Gemini/Tradition   (Charisma CB 237) 1974

This six-piece from Berkshire featured Fletcher who'd been in **The Troggs** and was later in Elandill. (VJ)

Gregory (and The Cadets)

45s:
	The Roman Spring Of Mrs Stone/Tears	(Fontana TF 778) 1966	
	Walk With Faith In Your Heart/		
	More Than Yesterday	(Pye 7N 17128) 1966	
α	The Best Part Of Loving You/		
	Harbour Lights	(Pye 7N 17270) 1967	
	Land Of Gingerbread/Girl Of My Dreams	(Pye 7N 17349) 1967	
	Girl Of Independent Means/		
	Young And Beautiful	(Pye 7N 17407) 1967	
α	C'mon Marianne/Angeline	(Pye 7N 17638) 1968	
α	Have I Told You Lately That I Love You/		
	Naughty Little Girl	(Pye 7N 17471) 1968	

GREENSLADE - Live (CD).

NB: α as **Gregory and The Cadets**.

A Dublin-based artist. (VJ)

Gremlins

45s:	The Coming Generation/		
	That's What I Want	(Mercury MF 981) 1966 SC
	You Gotta Believe It/I Can't Say	(Mercury MF 1004) 1967 SC

A band of this name have a cut called *The Only Thing* on My Mind on *Fading Yellow, Vol 1* (CD). (VJ)

Griffin

Personnel:	GRAHAM BELL	vcls	A
	KENNY CRADDOCK	organ	A
	COLIN GIBSON	bs	A
	PETE KIRTLEY	gtr	A
	ALAN WHITE	drms	A

45s:	I Am The Dark Noise In Your Head/	
	Don't You Know	(Bell BLL 1075) 1969 SC
	What Happens In The Darkness/	
	Calling You	(MGM 2006 088) 1972

A short-lived Newcastle-based venture. **Bell** and Gibson had both been in **Skip Bifferty** and **Heavy Jelly**. Kirtley and Craddock's last venture had been **Happy Magazine** and Alan White had played for **Alan Price**.

After their demise **Bell** was in **Every Which Way**. Craddock, Gibson and White all ended up in **Ginger Baker's Airforce**, but en route to there White was also in **Balls**.

One track from a John Peel session, *What A Day It's Been* has also resurfaced on *Mynd The Gap* (LP) and you'll also find *I Am The Noise In Your Head* on *Jagged Time Lapse, Vol 2* (CD). (VJ)

Carol Grimes (and Delivery)

ALBUMS:	1	FOOLS MEETING (WITH DELIVERY)		
			(B&C CAS 1023) 1970 R2
	2	WARM BLOOD	(Caroline CA 2001) 1974 SC
	3	CAROL GRIMES	(Decca SKL-R 5258) 1976 SC

NB: (3) reissued on CD (LC VP 126) 2001.

45s:	α	Harry Lucky/Homemade Ruin	(B&C CB 129) 1970
		You're The Only One/Southern Boogie	(Virgin VS 109) 1974
	β	Give It Everything You've Got/	
		Let's Do It Again	(Goodear EAR 105) 1974
		I Betcha Didn't Know That/Dynamite	(Goodear EAR 605) 1975
		I Betcha Didn't Know That/Dynamite	(Decca FR 13674) 1976
	χ	I Don't Wanna Discuss It/I'm Waking	(B&C BCP 2) 1977
		Ain't That Peculiar/	
		Fashion Passion (PS)	(Polydor POSP 417) 1982

NB: α with Delivery. β with London Boogie Band. χ with Red Price Band.

Carol Grimes started out with Delivery, which was basically a blues band. *Warm Blood* was recorded with an extensive array of session men, but it's really Carol's powerful vocals that stand out on the album, which blends a number of different influences, particularly country and blues. Indeed **Grimes** was a superb soul/blues singer much influenced by Janis Joplin.

Her eponymous album released in 1976 was recorded in Nashville and Memphis and featured Dick Dunn and The Memphis Horns, some of her music heroes. Her passionate vocals and their presence helped to make this a particularly successful venture.

She went on to record further albums, *Daydreams And Danger* and *Why Don't They Dance*. Her 45, *Ain't That Peculiar*, was a Marvin Gaye track.

She has continued to record and is a popular attraction on the Continent, releasing *Mother* (Irregular CG59) in 2005.

Blind To Your Light has been compiled on the 3-CD box set *Ars Longa Vita Brevis: A Compendium Of Progressive Rock 1967-1974*. (VJ/RMJ)

Grimms

Personnel:	ADRIAN HENRI		A
	NEIL INNES	keyb'ds, gtr, vcls	ABC
	MIKE McGEAR	vcls	AB
	MICHAEL GILES		A
	ROGER McGOUGH	vcls	ABC
	JOHN MEGGINSON	bs, vcls, keyb'ds	ABC
	ZOOT MONEY	keyb'ds	A C
	BRIAN PATTEN	vcls	AB
	OLLIE HALSALL	gtr	B
	DAVE RICHARDS	bs, vcls	BC
	ANDY ROBERTS	gtr	BC
	TIM DONNELL		C

ALBUMS:	1(A)	GRIMMS	(Island HELP 11) 1973
	2(B)	ROCKIN' DUCK	(Island ILPS 9248) 1973
	3(C)	SLEEPERS	(DJM DJLPS 470) 1976

NB: (1) issued on Antilles (7012) 1973 in the US. (1) and (2) reissued on one CD (Edsel EDCD 370) 1993.

45s:	Backbreaker/Masked Poet	(DJM DJS 10393) 1975
	Womble Bashers Of Walthamstow/	
	Worst Is Yet To Come	(DJM DJS 10679) 1976

A rock/comedy/poetry act from Liverpool incorporating former members of **Scaffold**, **Liverpool Scene**, former **Bonzo Dog Band** member **Neil Innes** and Ollie Halsall from **Patto**.

Their first album comprised poetry from **Roger McGough** and Brian Patten, with comedy routines and rather unexciting songs, including *Twyford's Vitromant*, a solo piano piece by **Neil Innes**; *Humanoid Boogie* (also by **Innes**), a slow boogie with pretty basic backing; *Following You*, a **Zoot Money** song with acoustic guitar and a band composition.

The second album is more song orientated although poetry, humour and satire have considerable place on the record. The music comprises **Neil Innes'** *Rockin' Duck*, a rock'n'rollin' novelty song with upfront piano; **Andy Robert's** country song *Songs Of The Stars*; the satirical *Policeman's Lot*, which is in **Scaffold's** mould; **McGough and McGear's** slow and melodic *Take It While You Can*; the short **Roberts-McGough** reggae track *Gruesome* and **Neil Innes'** *Oo-Chuck-A-Mao-Mao*.

The third album is more song-parody orientated but includes the usual mix of satire and humour that was expected at the **Grimms** live shows. Most of the material for the third album is composed by **McGough** and **Innes**. There are songs about a lady wrestler, a song about the *Womble Bashers Of Walthamstow* and the **Innes** penned *Randy Raquel*. **Grimms** was another act which was better live than on record and these albums are only really for **Liverpool Scene** and **Scaffold** fans. (VJ/CA/BS)

Gringo

Personnel:	CASEY SYNGE	vcls	A
	SIMON BYRNE	drms, vcls	A
	HENRY MARSH	gtr, keyb'ds, vcls	A
	JOHN G. PERRY	bs, vcls	A

ALBUM:	1(A)	GRINGO	(MCA MKPS 2017) 1971

NB: (1) reissued on CD (Audio Archives AACD 036).

45:	I'm Another Man/Soft Mud	(MCA MKS 5067) 1971

Evolving from student beat groups, Utopia / **Toast**, in sixties Bath, **Gringo** toured in Europe and even made a living with a club residency on the south coast of France. They were opening act on a UK tour featuring **Barclay James Harvest** and **Caravan**. Their recorded legacy is a quality album of pop-tinged progressive rock that still sounds fresh, with a lightness of touch and many distinctive twists. The song-within-a-song piece, *Emma And Harry*, is worthy of note, but all nine tracks are good. It is tempting to wonder if *Land Of Who Knows Where* may have been inspired by a certain **Caravan** album released the same year!

Gringo split and John Perry joined **Spreadeagle** but not in time to play on their only album. The **Caravan** connection reappeared and he joined that band in time for the *Girls Who Grow Plump* album. He played later with **Quantum Jump**, **Curved Air** and Aviator and did a host of session and solo work. Henry Marsh sampled chart success with **Sailor**, and Simon Byrne worked with **Brotherhood Of Man** among others. Casey went on to **Thunderthighs**. There you have **Gringo**, an overlooked band and album, worth discovering. The 'B' side of their single is a non-album track. (NM/BS)

Grisby Dyke

Personnel incl: DEREK FOLEY

45:      The Adventures Of Miss Rosemary La Page/
         Mary Ann She   (Deram DM 232) 1969

Grisby Dyke was one of several obscure acts who recorded for Deram in this era. Derek Foley had earlier played with **Paladin** and **Bond** and **Brown**. (VJ)

The Groop

Personnel: BRIAN CADD   organ   A
             RONNIE CHARLES   vcls   A
             DON MUDDIE   gtr   A
             MAX ROSS   bs   A
             RICHARD WRIGHT   drms   A

45s: Woman You're Breaking Me/Mad Over You (CBS 3204) 1968 SC
       Lovin' Tree/Night Life   (CBS 3351) 1968
       A Famous Myth/Tears And Joy   (Bell BLL 1070) 1969
       The Jet Song (When The Weekend's Over)/
       Nobody At All   (Bell BLL 1080) 1969

This **Easybeats**-type group of Australians moved to London in January 1968, so it's a marginal case for inclusion. (VJ)

The Groove

Personnel: JEFF BRIDGEFORD   A
             JAMIE BYRNE   A
             TWEED HARRIS   A
             ROD STONE   A
             PETER WILLIAMS   A

GROUNDHOGS - Scratching The Surface (LP).

GROUNDHOGS - Blues Obituary (LP).

45:      The Wind/Play The Song   (Parlophone R 5783) 1969 SC

These were also Australians who came to London in August 1968. *The Wind*, a slow slice of progressive pop, features dramatic vocals, but is not particlarly memorable.

Compilation appearances have included: *The Wind* on *Rubble, Vol. 14 - The Magic Rocking Horse* (LP), *Rubble, Vol. 8* (CD) and *The Best Of Rubble Collection, Vol. 4* (CD); and *Play The Song* on *Red With Purple Flashes, Vol. 2* (LP) and *Beat Us If You Can! Vol. 1* (LP). (VJ)

Luther Grosvenor

ALBUM: 1   UNDER OPEN SKIES   (Island ILPS 9168) 1971 SC

45s: Here Comes The Queen/Heavy Day   (Island WIP 6109) 1971
       All The People/Waiting   (Island WIP 6124) 1972

Luther Grosvenor was a member of **The Hellions** and later formed **Art** in 1967, who changed their name to **Spooky Tooth** in 1968. He left **Spooky Tooth** in the Autumn of 1970 and spent a while in Spain relaxing and songwriting.

He returned to the UK in 1971, recording the above solo efforts, and later joined **Stealer's Wheel** for their last few months. In August 1973, he joined **Mott The Hoople** under his assumed name of Ariel Bender and left a year later, eventually forming **Widowmaker** in 1976. (VJ)

Groundhogs

Personnel: DAVE BOORMAN   drms   A
             JOHN CRUICKSHANK   vcls, harp   A
             PETER CRUICKSHANK bs   ABCD
             BOB HALL   piano   A
             TONY McPHEE   gtr, bs, synth, vcls ABCDE
             KEN PUSTELNIK   drms   BC
             STEVE RYE   hrmnca   B
             CLIVE BROOKES   drms   D
             MICK COOK   drms   E
             MARTIN KENT   bs   E
             DAVE WELLBELOVED   gtr   E

                                                     HCP
ALBUMS: 1(B) SCRATCHING THE SURFACE
              (mono/stereo)   (Liberty LBL/LBS 83199E) 1968 R2/R1 -
        2(C) BLUES OBITUARY   (Liberty LBS 83253) 1969 R1 -
        3(C) THANK CHRIST FOR THE BOMB
                               (Liberty LBS 83295) 1970 SC 9
        4(C) SPLIT   (Liberty LBS 83401) 1971 SC 5
        5(C) WHO WILL SAVE THE WORLD
                               (United Artists UA 29327) 1972 SC 8

6(D)	HOGWASH	(United Artists UA 29419) 1972 SC -
7(D)	SOLID (w/insert)	(WWA 004) 1974 31
8(B/C)	BEST OF 1969-1972	
		(United Artists UA 60063/4) 1974 -
9(E)	CROSSCUT SAW	(United Artists UA 29917) 1976 -
10(E)	BLACK DIAMOND	(United Artists UA 29994) 1976 -
11(E)	HOGGIN' THE STAGE	(Psycho 24) 1984 SC -
12( )	RAZORS EDGE	(Landslide 102) 1985 -

NB: (1) issued on World Pacific in the US and (2) on Imperial. (1) reissued on Beat Goes On (BGOLP 15) 1988 also on Sunset (50376) in the UK. (2) reissued on CD (Beat Goes On BGOCD 6) 1989. (3) reissued on CD (BGOCD 67) 1990. (4) reissued on CD (Beat Goes On BEOCD 67) 1990. (5) reissued on CD (Beat Goes On BGOCD 77) 1992. (6) reissued on CD (Beat Goes On BGOCD 44) 1989. (7) reissued on CD (Castle CLACD 266) 1992. (8) reissued on CD (Beat Goes On BGODLP 1) 1988 and (EMI CDP 790 434 2) 1990. (9) and (10) reissued on one CD (Beat Goes On BGOCD 131) 1992. (11) reissued on CD (Hound Dog BUTCD 005) 1990.

There's also a CD compilation, *Groundhogs Best* (EMI CDP 7 90434 2) 1990. *Document Series Presents The Groundhogs* (Document CSAP CD 112) 1992 is a later CD compilation which concentrates on material from their strongest era (1968-1972). Also relevant is *Hogs On The Road* (CD CDTL 008) 1988 and (Thunderbolt CDTB 114) 1990, which is a collection of live material and *BBC Radio One Live In Concert* (Windsong WINCD 064) 1994, a 75 minute plus CD of BBC concert material from 1972 and 1974. *Four Groundhogs Originals* (EMI CDHOGS 1) 1996 is a four-album box set of their first four albums. The set comes with excellent graphics and notes. *The Best Of* (EMI Gold 7243 8 55504 2 3) 1997 is a CD mid-priced collection of material drawn from the band's albums from 1969 - 72. *On Air 1970-72* (Strange Fruit SFRSCD 053) 1998 captures them in fine fettle live. *Boogie With Us* (Mooncrest CRESTCD 049) 2000 comprises live material from three shows in 1971 and 1976. *BBC Live In Concert* (Strange Fruit SFRSCD 112) 2002 has been compiled from three sessions in February and December 1972, and May 1974.

45s:
	You Don't Love Me/Still A Fool	(Liberty LBF 15174) 1969 SC
α	BDD/Gasoline	(Liberty LBF 15263) 1969 SC
	Eccentric Man/Status People	(Liberty LBF 15346) 1970 SC
	Sad Go Round/Over Blue	(WWA WWS 6) 1973
α	Plea Sing Plea Sing/Dog Me Bitch	(WWA WWS 12) 1974
	Live A Little Lady/	
	Boogie With Us	(United Artists UP 36095) 1976
β	Pastoral Future/Live Right	(United Artists UP 36177) 1976

NB: α 'B' sides by **Tony McPhee**. β As Tony McPhee and Groundhogs.

The band first formed (line-up A) in 1963 and backed US blues artist John Lee Hooker as John Lee's Groundhogs for two years before disbanding in 1965. An album, *John Lee Hooker With The Groundhogs*, was recorded during this period.

The band reformed in 1968 with a new line-up (B), although Steve Rye left after their first album. They continued through their 'golden years' as a trio. *Scratching The Surface*, their debut, was a pretty mellow blues album. *Blues Obituary* was their final straight blues album and for the next few efforts they turned towards heavy rock with a certain degree of

GROUNDHOGS - Thank Christ For The Bomb (CD).

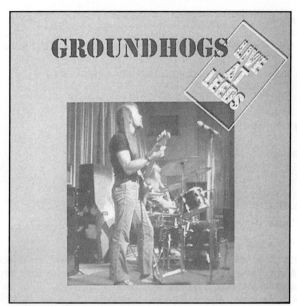

GROUNDHOGS - Live At Leeds (LP).

socio-political comment. *Thank Christ For The Bomb* was one of their more successful attempts and took them into the UK Album Charts for the first time.

For *Hogwash*, Ken Pustelnik was replaced by Clive Brooks, but after *Solid* the group disbanded, leader **Tony McPhee** having made a solo album, *The Two Sides Of Tony McPhee* (Worldwide Artists WWA 001) in 1973. However, in 1975 **McPhee** put the band back on the road with a new line-up (E).

The double compilation and free EP released by Psycho comprised live material from 1971 concerts in London and Leeds as part of a **Rolling Stones** tour, and material from a concert in Stockholm in 1976 shortly before the band split up. For diehard progressive blues fans only!

Best Of 1969-72 compiles material from their second, third, fifth and sixth albums. Originally issued on United Artists in 1974, the double set was reissued on Beat Goes On in 1988. Highlights include *Strange Town, Split Part 4* and *You Had A Lesson*, but it is recommended for blues and hard rock enthusiasts only.

Boogie With Us draws on three live dates in 1971 and 1976 and includes tracks from their classic *Thank Christ For The Bomb* and *Split* albums. **Groundhogs** and blues-rock fans generally will like this.

BBC Live In Concert compiles three sessions recorded in February and December 1972, and May 1974. The earlier tracks are **Hendrix**-influenced and the whole album showcases the band's talents.

Although they have achieved little commercial or critical acclaim since the early seventies a line-up of the band continues to tour and record and they still have a small following in the UK and Europe.

Compilation appearances have included *Cherry Red* on *All Good Clean Fun* (LP); *Still A Fool* on *Gutbucket* (LP), and *Mistreated* on *Son Of Gutbucket* (LP). More recently, *Break It* has appeared on *English Freakbeat, Vol. 1* (LP & CD), *Sad Go Round* on *Perfumed Garden Vol. 3* (CD), *Cherry Red* on *The Age Of Enlightenment - Prog Rock, Vol. One* (CD) and *Rock Resurrection*; and *Wang Dang Doodle* on *Classic Rock* (CD); whilst *Split, Part 1* can be found on the 3-CD set *Guitar Heroes - Rock The Night Away* and *Sad Go Round* can be found on the 3-CD box set *Ars Longa Vita Brevis: A Compendium Of Progressive Rock 1967-1974*. (VJ)

Group Two

| 45: | It's Raining Outside/ | |
| | Western Man, Eastern Lady | (Columbia DB 8374) 1968 |

This was a little known sixties band. (VJ)

Grumble

45:      Da Doo Ron Ron/Pig Bin An' Gone   (RCA RCA 2384) 1973

This obscure 45 was by **10cc** recording under a pseudonym. (VJ)

Jay Grunsky

Personnel:	ANNETTE BROX	vcls	A
	JAY GRUNSKY	vcls	A
	ALEXIS KORNER	gtr	A

ALBUM: 1(A)   TORONTO   (Kukuck 2375 002) c1972 SC
NB. German pressing.

A little known singer/songwriter whose album was arranged and produced by **Alexis Korner**. It is sought-after by some collectors as **Mick Taylor** (**Bluesbreakers**, **Rolling Stones**, etc) played guitar on four of the tracks. Mike Rosen also plays mellophone, trumpet and flugel on the album. Annette Brox was previously in **Sweet Pain**. (SR)

Grunt Futtock

45:      Rock'n'Roll Christian/
        Free Sole   (Regal Zonophone RZ 3042) 1972 SC

Grunt Futtock was an obscure early seventies band. The 'A' side is heavy rock with some unusual instrumentation. The flip is an attractive, rather dramatic, orchestrated instrumental. Both sides were produced by **Andrew Oldham**. (VJ)

Gryphon

Personnel:	BRIAN GULLAND	bassoon, crumhorns	AB
	RICHARD HARVEY	recorders, crumhorns, glockenspiel	AB
	DAVID OBERLE	vcls, perc	AB
	GRAEME TAYLOR	bs, gtr	A
	ALEX BAIRD	drms	B
	JON DAVIE	bs	B
	BOB FOSTER	gtr	B

ALBUMS: 1(A) GRYPHON   (Transatlantic TRA 262) 1973 SC
       2(A) MIDNIGHT MUSHRUMPS
                       (Transatlantic TRA 282) 1974 SC
       3(A) RED QUEEN TO GRYPHON THREE
                       (Transatlantic TRA 287) 1974 SC

GRYPHON - Midnight Mushrumps (CD).

GRYPHON - Raindance (LP).

    4(A)   RAINDANCE   (Transatlantic TRA 302) 1975
    5(B)   TREASON   (Harvest SHSP 4063) 1977

NB: (2) reissued on Conifer (CFRC 518) 1986. *The Collection* (Curio ITEM CD 1) 1991 is a compilation of their best material. (1) and (2) reissued on one CD (Essential! ESM CD 356) 1996. (3) and (4) reissued on one CD (Essential! ESSCD 460) 1997 and again (Essential! ESMCD 460) 2005. (4) reissued on CD (Curio ITEM CD 7*)*. (5) reissued on CD (See For Miles C5CD 602). *Crossing The Styles: The Transatlantic Anthology* (Sanctuary/Castle CMDDD 977) is a mid-price 2-CD compilation.

45:      Spring Song/Fall Of The Leaf   (Harvest HAR 5125) 1977

Harvey and Gulland (who formed the band) were both former students of the Royal College of Music. Indeed, **Harvey** was a first-class recorder virtuoso. Their musical roots were very much in medieval folk but after their first album, which achieved some minor Chart success, they experimented more with long instrumentals. Side two of *Midnight Mushrumps* consisted of one track commissioned by Peter Hall for a National Theatre production of 'The Tempest'.

Red Queen To Gryphon Tree is usually heralded as their masterpiece - it comprises instrumental, symphonic rock with folky twists and turns.

They went on to play film Soundtracks for 'Pope Joan' and 'Brother Sun, Sister Moon' and arranged the title theme for 'Glastonbury Fayre'. In 1975, **Harvey** recorded a solo album of recorder music, *Divisions On A Ground* (Transatlantic TRA 292). In 1975, when Graeme Taylor left, the group expanded from a quartet to a sextet. Baird had previously played with Contraband. If mid-seventies progressive/techno-rock is your scene the group may be for you.

Crossing The Styles is a 2-CD compilation of their material. It showcases their superb musicianship, especially on the many long instrumental passages. Material from all four of their Transatlantic albums is well-represented here, although not in chronological order. Overall, this package is a good introduction to the band's music.

Compilation appearances include *The Unquiet Grave* and *Raindance* on *The Transatlantic Story* CD box set and *Opening Move* on *Ars Longa Vita Brevis: A Compendium Of Progressive Rock 1967-1974*. (VJ)

Guggenheim

ALBUM: 1 GUGGENHEIM   (Indigo GOLP 7001) 1972 R2

This very rare privately-pressed progressive folk album sounds midway between **Bread Love and Dreams** and **Blue Epitaph**, but occasionally veers into the rural progressive mould of **Northwind** with some fine acid guitar leads. All twelve songs were penned by the band and the album is housed in an attractive cover design. (VJ)

Gulliver's People

Personnel:
BILL BUTLER	gtr		A
BRET COLLINS	bs, gtr		A
WENDY COLLINS	bongos		A
ANNE FRENCH	tambourine		A
JIMMY MacKINNON	piano, organ		A
BARRY MORGAN	drms		A

45s:
Splendour In The Grass/		
Took This Land	(Parlophone R 5435)	1966
Fi Fo Fum/Over The Hills	(Parlophone R 5464)	1966
On A Day Like This/My Life	(Parlophone R 5709)	1968
Somehow, Somewhere/I Found Love	(Columbia DB 8588)	1969

This outfit came from London. Morgan was later in **Blue Mink**. Their 45s were mostly fairly soft harmony-pop. (VJ)

Gulliver's Travels

Personnel incl: MIKE D'ABO

ALBUM: 1 GULLIVER'S TRAVELS (Instant INLP 003) 1969 R2

Instant was a subsidiary of Immediate and the **Gulliver's Travels** album appears to have been concocted by **Andrew Loog Oldham** and **Mike D'Abo** (although there are no credits on the album sleeve). The album includes snatches of other Immediate acts including P.P. Arnold and **The Small Faces** as well as the opening bars of Lovin' Spoonful's *You Didn't Have To Be So Nice*. (VJ)

Gun

Personnel:
ADRIAN CURTISS-GURVITZ	gtr		AB
PAUL CURTISS-GURVITZ	bs		AB
LOUIS FARRELL	drms		AB
PETE DUNTON	drms		B

ALBUMS:
1(A)	GUN	(CBS 63552)	1968 SC
2(B)	GUNSIGHT	(CBS 62683)	1969 SC

NB: (1) reissued on CD (Repertoire RR 4013-C) in 1990 and repackaged with three bonus tracks (Repertoire REP 4562-WY) 1995. (1) and (2) reissued on one CD (BGO BGO C 459) 2000.

			HCP
45s:	Race With The Devil/Sunshine	(CBS 3764)	1968 8
	Race With The Devil/		
	Three-Four In The Middle	(CBS 3764)	1968 -
	Drives You Mad/Rupert's Travels	(CBS 4052)	1969 -

GUN - Gun (CD).

GYGAFO - Legend Of The Kingfisher (CD).

Hobo/Don't Look Back	(CBS 4443)	1969 -
Hobo/Long Haired Wild Men	(CBS 4443)	1969 -
Runnin' Wild/Drown Yourself In The River	(CBS 4952)	1970 -
Reissues: Race With The Devil/Sunshine	(CBS 3764)	1979 -
Race With The Devil	(Old Gold OG 9193)	1982 -

From Ilford in Essex, this heavy rock band's finest moment was undoubtedly the frenetic *Race With The Devil*, which was subsequently reissued in 1979 and 1982. It also achieved some Chart success. The flip side *Sunshine* has a pleasing harmony vocal. The follow-up, *Drives You Mad*, was similar in style to *Race With The Devil*. Their first album's front cover was the first designed by Roger Dean and musically, it was very much part of the first wave of British hard-rock. Both their albums were psychedelic/progressive crossover items and could potentially also appeal to fans of either of these genres.

The Gurvitz brothers progressed to **Three Man Army** and **Baker Gurvitz Army** after **Gun**'s demise. Later on, Adrian Gurvitz recorded solo albums. Farrell also played with **The Bulldog Breed**. **Pete Dunton** went on to **T2** and also recorded a solo 45.

Jon Anderson was their vocalist in a pre-recording line-up.

They have one cut, *Situation Vacant*, on the *Psychedelic Dream* (2-LP) compilation, which captures them in one of their better moments. You can also find *Race With The Devil* and *Sunshine* on *Sixties Years, Vol. 2 - French 60's EP Collection* (CD); and *Race With The Devil* also appears on *Greatest Rock*. (VJ)

Jon Gunn

45s:	I Just Made Up My Mind/	
	Now It's My Turn	(Deram DM 133) 1967
	If You Wish It/I Don't Want To Get	
	Hung Up On You Babe	(Deram DM 166) 1967

This was a little known mid-sixties singer from Lancashire. Both sides of the first 45 have resurfaced on *Pop Inside The '60s, Vol. 1* (CD). (VJ)

Johnny Gustafson

45s:	Just To Be With You/Sweet Day	(Polydor 56022) 1965 SC
	Take Me For A Little While/	
	Make Me Your Number One	(Polydor 56043) 1965 SC

This Merseybeat artist is best known as a member of **The Big Three**. When he left them, he spent time in Germany and was later in **The Merseybeats**.

His short solo career comprised the R&B *Just To Be With You* and *Take Me For A Little While*, a Kim Westen Motown single which had been recorded by **The Kubas** shortly before. Neither disc made much impression.

In 1966, he was one half of **Johnny and John**. (VJ)

The Guys

Personnel:			
	JOHN BURNESS	vcls	A
	RICKY BURNESS	vcls	A
	BRIAN HAWKINS	bs	A
	IAN HORN	organ	A
	DICK MAYALL	drms	A
	RAY WASTLE	ld gtr	A

45: Go Your Own Way/Little Girl (Tepee TPR SP 1001) 1969

This group also backed singer John Burness on a solo 45 and toured Bulgaria with him. John and Ricky Burness had both been in **The Beat Six**. (VJ)

Gygafo

Personnel:			
	JOHN ATKINSON	lead vcls, gtr, mandolin, flute, glockenspiel	A
	PAUL KENT	bs	A
	PETE NICKSON	drms, perc	A
	CHARLIE SPEED	lead gtr, gtr, backing vcls	A
	EDDIE STRINGER	keyb'ds, piano, backing vcls	A
	(MIKE LEVON	sax, air guitar	A)

ALBUM: 1(A) LEGEND OF THE KINGFISHER
(Holyground HG 1155) 1989 R1

NB: (1) reissued on CD (Background HBG 122/2 CD) 1992.

Originally recorded in 1973, this progressive album remained in Holyground's domain until 1989 when, in the face of renewed interest in progressive rock and the Holyground label, it was released on an unsuspecting public. The original recordings were put out in a 1989 sleeve and the album, currently in the very rare category, is well worth seeking out. The band came from Leeds, and at one stage, a recording contract with DJM was rumoured but never became a reality. Their name was taken from a response to an audition, "Get Your Gear And Fuck Off"!!

It's not clear whether Paul Kent is the same **Paul Kent** who made solo albums.

You can also find *Nineteen Eighty Four* on *Loose Routes* (4-LP). (VJ)

Gypsy

Personnel:			
	JOHN KNAPP	vcls, gtr, keyb'ds	AB
	DAVID McCARTHY	bs, vcls	AB
	ROBIN PIZER	gtr, vcls	AB
	ROD READ	gtr, vcls	A
	MOTH SMITH	drms	AB
	RAY MARTINEZ	gtr, vcls	B

ALBUMS:	1(A)	GYPSY	(United Artists UAS 29155) 1971 SC
	2(B)	BRENDA AND THE RATTLESNAKE	(United Artists UAS 29420) 1972 SC

NB: *The Romany Collection* (CD) compiles their first album along with both sides of their debut 45 and six previously unreleased studio tracks.

45s: What Makes A Man A Man/
I Want To Be Beside You (United Artists UP 35202) 1971
Changes Coming/

Don't Cry On Me (United Artists UP 35272) 1971
Brand New Car/
You Know Better Than Me (United Artists UP 35462) 1972
Let's Roll/Without You (United Artists UP 35546) 1973

Leicester was this group's home town and they were originally known as **Legay** who released one now very rare 45 for Fontana before changing their name to **Gypsy** just prior to appearing at the 1969 Isle of Wight festival.

Their first album featured some tight harmonies and was well received. Rod Read left after this to be replaced by Ray Martinez. Their second album was disappointing and they split soon after its release. None of their recordings as **Gypsy** have interested collectors to date. *The Romany Collection*, which compiles their debut album along with both sides of their first 45 and some previously unreleased material could change that. It comes with a 8-page booklet containing sleevenotes which the band helped to write. You'll also find *Let Me Take You Home* from their first album on United Artists 1971 double compilation, *All Good Clean Fun* (LP). (VJ)

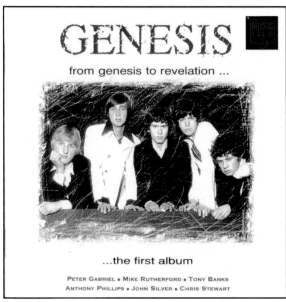

GENESIS - From Genesis To Revelation (CD)

GONG - Continental Circus (CD).

362

STEVE HACKETT - Voyage Of The Acolyte (LP).

Habibiyya

Personnel:	CONRAD ARCHULETTA		A
	SUSAN ARCHULETTA		A
	MIKE EVANS	bs	A
	ROGER POWELL	drms	A
	IAN WHITEMAN	piano, keyb'ds	A

ALBUM: 1(A) IF MAN BUT KNEW   (Island HELP 7) 1972 R1

All three members of this outfit had previously been in **Mighty Baby**. The album comprises Eastern-influenced hypnotic psychedelic music. In fact the album is based on Sufi music. All three members of the band had become converted to the Muslim Sufi faith. They are assisted on the album by two other musicians. (VJ/JRd/\E)

The Habits

Personnel incl:	BRIAN DAVIDSON	drms	A
	BRIAN SIMMONS	ld gtr	A

45:     I Need You/Elbow Baby   (Decca F 12348) 1966 SC

This obscure sixties band hailed from London. The R&B style 45 was produced by **Spencer Davis** and **Stevie Winwood**. Brian Davidson went on to play in the **Mark Leeman Five**, **The Attack** and **The Nice**.

Compilation appearances include: *Elbow Baby* on *The Mod Scene* (CD) and *Sixties Lost And Found, Vol. 3* (LP); and *I Need You* and *Elbow Baby* on *Made In England, Vol. 2* (CD). (VJ)

Hackensack

Personnel:	SIMON FOX	drms	A
	PAUL MARTINEZ	bs	A
	NICKY MOORE	vcls	A
	RAY SMITH	gtr	A

ALBUMS:	1(A)	UP THE HARD WAY	(Polydor 2383 263) 1974 R2
	2(A)	HERE COMES THE JUDGE	(Zel UZ 003) 1974 R3

NB: (1) also issued on CD. There have been other CDs: *Give It Some* (Audio Archives) 19??, which features 15 previously unreleased outtakes from 1969-1971 and *Live - The Hard Way* (Audio Archives) 19??, a 1973 show from Swiss radio. (2) was a privately pressed album credited to Hack and Sack.

45:     Moving On/River Boat   (Island WIP 6149) 1972

This hard-rock band is perhaps most significant for the inclusion of Nicky Moore who was later in **Tiger** and **Samson**. However, his growling vocal style was certainly not for all. Simon Fox went on to hit the skins for **Be-Bop Deluxe**. Paul Martinez went on to **Paice, Ashton and Lord**. He

was also in **Chicken Shack** and **Stretch** at various times. Ray Smith had previously been with **Heads, Hands and Feet** and **Poet and The One Man Band**. He went on to Flying Island. (VJ/MWh/CG)

Steve Hackett

HCP

ALBUM:	1	VOYAGE OF THE ACOLYTE	
(up to			(Charisma CAS 1111) 1975 26
1976)			

NB: Reissued on CD (Charisma CASCD 1111) 1987.

A Londoner, born on 12 February 1950, **Hackett** was involved in various little known bands like Canterbury Glass, Sarabande and **Quiet World** prior to joining **Genesis** as their guitarist in 1971. He was with them during their boom period but finally left after their live double album *Seconds Out* in 1977. The above solo album was recorded whilst he was still a **Genesis** member. After he left the group he went on to record a series of solo albums with which he achieved moderate success, but they are beyond the time span of this book.

In 1986 he linked up with **Yes** guitarist **Steve Howe** to form GTR, a progressive rock outfit who became a big MTV favourite in the States where they enjoyed a hit with *When Your Heart Rules The Mind* and a platinum selling album. In 1987 he resumed his solo career with added momentum and has continued to record into the new millennium, his latest album being *Metamorpheus* in 2005. (VJ)

Vernon Haddock's Jubilee Lovelies

Personnel:	DAVID ELVIN		A
	VERNON HADDOCK		A
	ALAN WOODWARD		A
	DAVID VAUGHN		A
	SID 'PILES' LOCKHART		A
	ALAN 'LITTLE BEAR' SUTTON		A

ALBUM:	1	VERNON HADDOCK'S JUBILEE LOVELIES	
			(Columbia SX 6011) 1965 R5

Recorded in one alcohol-fuelled session in summer 1965 and barely released, this must be about the rarest major label album release of the sixties. The 'Lovelies were proto-hippies from Southend, a sort of UK version of The Holy Modal Rounders or early Charlatans, adding a selection of weird and wonderful instruments and a stoned UK beatnik attitude to their basic jugband sound. Peter Eden (also a Southend native) and Geoff Stephens, red-hot from their discovery of **Donovan**, handled the album's production as part of a four-album deal with Columbia. Tracks include *Viola Lee Blues*, *Boodle-Am Shake*, *Stealin'* and even a manic version of *I Wish I Could Shimmy Like My Sister Kate*. A friend and sometime member of the band was **Vivian Stanshall** of **The Bonzo Dog Doo-Dah Band**, whose anarchic spirit can be detected throughout. Housed in a striking red, white and blue cover featuring a picture of the group posing with an Edwardian traction engine, very few copies of the album have ever surfaced. The other fruits of Eden & Stephens's production deal, incidentally, were by Bob Davenport & the Rakes and **Mick Softley**. A projected solo acoustic debut by **Eric Clapton** was reluctantly abandoned when he joined **John Mayall's Bluesbreakers**. (RMJ/VJ)

Haffy's Whiskey Sour

45:     Shot In The Head/Bye Bye Bluebird   (Deram DM 345) 1971

This one-off 45 involved former members of **The Easybeats** and The Paintbox. (VJ)

Norman Haines (Band)

Personnel:	NEIL CLARK	gtr	A
	NORMAN HAINES	keyb'ds	A
	ANDY HUGHES	bs	A
	JIMMY SKIDMORE	drms	A

ALBUM: 1(A)   DEN OF INIQUITY   (Parlophone PCS 7130) 1971 R4
NB: (1) reissued on CD by Shoestring and LP by Radioactive.

45s: Daffodil/Autumn Mobile   (Parlophone R 5871) 1970 SC
          Den Of Iniquity/Everything You
          See (Mr. Armageddon)   (Parlophone SPSR 338) 1971 R1
          Finding My Way Home / Rabbits (Parlophone R 5890) 1971 R1
          Give It To You Girl/Elaine   (Parlophone R 5960) 1972 SC
NB: (1) Credited to **The Norman Haynes Band**. (2) Promo only. (3) released as
Avalanche. (4) A **Norman Haines** solo 45.

This keyboardist's first significant band was a Birmingham-based pop outfit
called **The Brumbeats** (surprise, surprise) in which he played guitar. This
was not the same **Brumbeats** that issued a 45 on Decca in 1964. He was
soon offered a place in another Black Country outfit, **Locomotive**. When
they split in late 1969 **Haines** formed a new band called The Sacrifice,
which found it hard to get work. Their debut 45, *Daffodil*, was a Latin-style
45, which sounded like a commercial version of Santana but didn't sell. To
add insult to injury the record company didn't like the name Sacrifice and
credited the record to **The Norman Haynes Band** (even spelling Haines
wrongly!)

Their album, *Den Of Iniquity*, has gone on to become one of the most
sought-after collectors' items of the progressive era. The cover was striking
and pictured a huge creature giving birth to miniature human beings and
another huge creature chucking them through the air - presumably to their
deaths. It seems likely that some stores didn't stock the album at the time
on account of this artwork. Musically, the album boasted a very varied fare.
It included a re-recorded version of **Locomotive**'s classic, *Mr. Armageddon*,
but its finest moments were two lengthy instrumentals, *Rabbits* and **Haines**'
Life Is So Unkind. Curiously two tracks from the album (*Finding My Way
Home*/*Rabbits*) were also released as a 45 credited to **Avalanche**.

After a further solo 45, *Give It To You Girl*, they called it a day.

The *Den Of Iniquity* album was reissued on CD by an indie label,
Shoestring, with several bonus tracks (including the two 45s and the
previously unreleased *I Really Need A Friend*). (VJ)

Hair

ALBUM: 1   RAVE UP   (Pye NSPL 18314) 1969 R1

This outfit was also connected to **Hairband**. It featured **Alex Harvey**. (VJ)

Hairband

ALBUM: 1   BAND ON THE WAGON   (Bell SBLL 123) 1969 R1

45:      Big Louis/Travelling Song   (Bell BLL 1076) 1969

This outfit was connected to **Hair**. The 45 was produced by **Alan Price**. It
too, featured **Alex Harvey** and there may have been more albums. (VJ)

Halfbreed

Personnel: TOM FARMER   gtr   A
             FRANKIE GIBBONS   bs   A
             GEOFF HUTCHINSON   drms   A
             JIM LOWERY   keyb'ds   A
             MICK WHITAKER   vcls   A

ALBUM: 1 (A)   HALFBREED   (United Artists UAG 29877) 1975 SC

45s: Buttermilk/Rainmaker   (United Artists UP 56000) 1975
       Billy Dean/Change Your Mind (United Artists UP 56031) 1975

An obscure band whose hard to find album features rock with progressive
leanings. (BS)

Hallelujah

Personnel: KEITH FORSEY   drms, vcls   A
             RICK KEMP   bs   A
             PAUL VINCENT   gtr, vcls   A
             PETER WOOD   keyb'ds   A

ALBUM: 1 (A)   HALLELUJAH BABE   (Metronome LMLP 15805) 1971 SC

Hallelujah comprised four British session musicians who relocated to
Germany in the early seventies and recorded this German-only release. On
offer is early seventies rock with progressive/krautrock leanings and it's
recommended.

Rick Kemp was later in **Steeleye Span** and Peter Wood was in **Al
Stewart's** backing band. Keith Forsey re-emerged in Boney M. (BS)

The Halliard (and Jon Raven)

Personnel: NIC JONES   gtr, vcls   AB
             DAVE MORAN   vcls   AB
             NIGEL PATTISON   gtr, vcls   AB
             JON RAVEN   vcls, gtr   B

ALBUMS: 1(A)   IT'S THE IRISH IN ME   (Saga SOC 1058) 1967 R1
        2(B)   THE HALLIARD AND JON RAVEN
                                    (Broadside BRO 106) 1968 R2

This was a typical late sixties trad folk act. Jon Raven was involved in the
running of the Broadside label and just a few hundred of these early
independent releases were pressed. Their debut was entirely traditional in
material and execution, and its follow-up came in a black and white sleeve
made up of newspaper headlines. They are perhaps most notable for
featuring the young **Nic Jones**, who would later record a string of
well-regarded solo albums. (VJ/VZ/RMJ)

Ollie Halsall

Ollie Halsall is best known for his work with **Timebox** and **Patto**. *Caves*
(Market Square MSMCD 103) 2000 compiles self-penned three minute pop
songs. (VJ)

Halycon

Personnel incl: SIAN DANIELS / PERKINS

45:      Hey Friend (Won't Ya Join The Band)/
         Bored Brain Boogie   (Warner K 16390) 1974

A rock 'n' roll band featuring Sian Daniels who later joined **The Ralph
McTell** Band and **Kokomo**. (VJ)

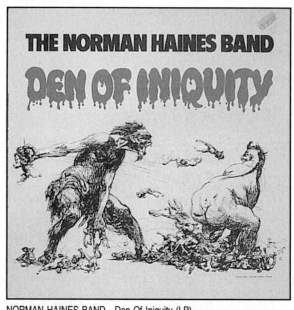

NORMAN HAINES BAND - Den Of Iniquity (LP).

OLLIE HALSALL - Caves (CD).

Claire Hamill

ALBUMS:	1	ONE HOUSE LEFT STANDING	
(up to			(Island ILPS 9182) 1971 SC
1976)	2	OCTOBER	(Island ILPS 9225) 1973 SC
	3	STAGE DOOR JOHNNIES	(Konk KONK 101) 1974
	4	ABRACADABRA	(Konk KONK 104) 1975

45s:	When I Was A Child/	
(up to	Alice In The Streets Of Darlington (PS)	(Island WIP 6122) 1972
1976)	Baseball Blues/Smile Your Eyes Away	(Island WIP 6133) 1972
	Speedbreaker/The Artist	(Island WIP 6154) 1973
	Geronimo's Cadillac/Luck Of The Draw	(Konk KOS 1) 1975
	Rory/One Sunday Morning	(Konk KOS 3) 1975

From Middlesbrough came this singer/songwriter who was quite popular on the folk circuit but failed to fulfil her earlier promise. **John Martyn** guested on her first album and the second was produced by Paul Samwell-Smith. She went on to record the first releases on the **Kinks**' Konk label.

She later enjoyed success in the late eighties as a new age artist. (VJ)

Gary Hamilton

45s:	Let The Music Play/Don't Ask	(Decca F 12697) 1967
	Easy Rider/Hare Krishna	(CBS 4674) 1969

These were solo efforts by **Hamilton** after the break-up of **Hamilton and The Movement**. His version of *Let The Music Play* can also be heard on *Colour Me Pop, Vol 3* (CD). (VJ)

Gavin Hamilton

45:	It Won't Be The Same/	
	Turn The Key Softly	(King KG 1067) 1967 R3

This seems to have been a one-off venture and you can also check out *It Won't Be The Same* on *Voyage Through The Sugarcube* (LP and CD). (VJ)

Hamilton and The Movement

Personnel incl: GARY HAMILTON
PAUL STEWART

45s:	Really Saying Something/	
	I Won't See You Tonight	(Polydor BM 56026) 1965 R2
	I'm Not The Marrying Kind/	
	My Love Belongs To You	(CBS 202573) 1967 R1

This was a nine-piece rather soulful outfit from London. *Really Saying Something*, a Marvelettes song, was a Tamla Motown favourite, but the flip side was a raw, bluesy number untypical of their usual style. **Gary Hamilton** went on to record a couple of solo 45s, as did **Paul Stewart**, though the second was credited to the **Paul Stewart Movement**. (VJ)

Hamilton Folk Four

45:	Ballad Of A Teenage Queen/	
	How Can I Tell Maureen	(Columbia DB 7557) 1965

The 'A' side is a great version of a Johnny Cash song. The flip side is pleasant pop penned by Russ Sainty and Rhet Stoller, which sounds more reminiscent of a few years earlier. (VJ)

Hammersmith Gorillas

Personnel:	ALAN BUTLER	bs	A
	GARY ANDERSON	drms	A
	JESSE HECTOR	vcls, gtr	A

NB: *Gorilla Got Me* ((Ace CDWIKD 185) 1999 compiles material from between 1974-1981.

45:	α	You Really Got Me/	
		Leavin' 'Ome	(Penny Farthing PEN 849) 1974 SC

NB: α reissued on Raw (RAW 2) in 1977 in company sleeve.

Some members of this band had earlier been in **The Clique**, who released a privately-pressed promotional EP and two 45s for Pye back in 1965. The 'A' side of this disc was a cover of **The Kinks**' classic sixties hit, produced by Larry Page. It's nowadays regarded as a classic pre-punk item.

The recent retrospective CD on Ace/Big Beat *Gorilla Got Me* includes both sides of Penny Farthing single, three unissued tracks from same session, the three later Chiswick singles, four later unissued and seven tracks live at Mont De Marsan 1976. (VJ/BD)

Peter Hammill

ALBUMS:	1	FOOL'S MATE	(Charisma CAS 1037) 1971 SC
(up to	2	CHAMELEON IN THE SHADOW OF THE NIGHT	
1976)			(Charisma CAS 1067) 1973 SC
	3	THE SILENT CORNER AND THE EMPTY STAGE	
			(Charisma CAS 1083) 1974 SC
	4	IN CAMERA	(Charisma CAS 1089) 1974 SC
	5	NADIR'S BIG CHANCE	(Charisma CAS 1099) 1975 SC
	6	OVER	(Charisma CAS 1125) 1976

HAMMERSMITH GORILLAS - Gorilla Got Me (CD).

NB: (1) reissued on Charisma (CHC 2) in 1983. (4) reissued on Charisma (9198 770) in 1980. (5) reissued on Charisma (CHC 19) in 1983. The following also appear on CD:- (1) on Charisma (CASCD 1037) 1988. (2) on Charisma (CASCD 1067) in 1989. (3) on Charisma (CASCD 1083) 1988. (4) on Charisma (CASCD 1089) 1988. (5) on Charisma (CASCD 1099) 1988. (6) on Charisma (CASCD 1125) 1991. There was also a US-only compilation, *Vision* (Charisma 9214 1016) in 1978. *The Peel Sessions* (Strange Fruit SFRCD 136) 1995 comprises material from sessions between 1974 and 1989. The inclusion of a rare solo album of *The Emperor In His War Room* (originally on **Van Der Graaf Generator**'s *H To He* album) will interest fans of his early work.

45:	Birthday Special/Shingle Shop	(Charisma CB 245) 1975
(up to 1976)		

Peter Hammill was the pivotal figure in **Van Der Graaf Generator** who formed in 1967 at Manchester University. He was also their principle songwriter. By the time this distinctive vocalist released his first solo album in 1971 **Van Der Graaf Generator** had already released four albums. They split up for the first time in the Summer of 1972.

Fool's Mate, his debut, was a collection of shortish and rather chirpy songs which were in marked contrast to the longer doom-ladened tracks **Van Der Graaf Generator** was producing at this time. By contrast, *Chameleon In The Shadow Of The Night*, which came almost two years later was a much angrier album.

1974 saw the release of *The Silent Corner And The Empty Stage* and *In Camera*, two more varied and experimental albums than his previous works. He had a home studio where much of the recording and production of these albums was done and he also played most of the instruments on them too. A man of many talents he also had his first book, 'Killers, Angels, Refugees', published that year. It contained the lyrics of all his songs to date together with some explanations of them alongside some poems and short stories.

His inventiveness was well illustrated by his 1975 album *Nadir's Big Chance*. This was full of fuzz-guitar driven songs completely in contrast to his earlier output and predating the 'punk rock' movement by a whole year. For the album **Hammill** adopted a new persona of 'Rikki Nadir', who as a loud, screaming guitar thrasher, seemed to represent his alter ego. Two tracks from this album were also put out on 45. A later 1979 45 was even credited to Rikki Nadir.

Van Der Graaf Generator reformed in the Summer of 1975 and went on to record three albums over the next eighteen months. During the final months of this second incarnation of **Van Der Graaf Generator**, **Hammill** released another solo album, *Over*. This is the hardest of his albums to locate and is notable for *Through The Looking Glass* on which he sings over an orchestral backing track for the first time.

After **Van Der Graaf Generator**'s final disintegration in early 1977, **Hammill** went on to record several further solo albums, worked with The K Group and also wrote a second book. 'Mirrors, Dreams and Miracles',

PETER HAMILL - Fool's Mate (LP).

which contained short-stories and all his lyrics from the 1974-80 era. **Hammill** is an interesting figure whose albums certainly merit investigation. (VJ)

Albert Hammond

ALBUMS:	1	IT NEVER RAINS IN SOUTHERN CALIFORNIA	
(up to 1976)			(Mum MUMS 65320) 1973
	2	FREE ELECTRIC BAND	(Mum MUMS 65554) 1973
	3	ALBERT HAMMOND	(Mum MUMS 80026) 1974
	4	99 MILES FROM LA	(Epic 80961) 1975

NB: There's also a compilation available on CD, *The Very Best Of Albert Hammond* (Collector's Choice 9022922) 1990.

HCP
45s:	Down By The River/The Last One To Know	(CBS 8304) 1972 -
(up to 1976)	It Never Rains In Southern California/	
	Anyone Here In The Audience	(Mum MUMS 8499) 1973 -
	The Free Electric Band/	
	You Taught Me To Sing The Blues	(Mum MUMS 1494) 1973 19
	Peacemaker/Who's For Lunch Today	(Mum MUMS 1759) 1973 -
	Everything I Want To Do/	
	Woman Of The World	(Mum MUMS 1834) 1974 -
	I'm A Train/Brand New Day	(Mum MUMS 2150) 1974 -
	We're Running Out/Fountain Avenue	(Mum MUMS 3045) 1975 -
	Lay The Music Down/	
	Life Is For The Living	(Mum MUMS 3272) 1975 -
	Good Old Days/Life Is For The Living	(Epic EPC 3071) 1975 -
	99 Miles From LA/Face Not The Image	(Epic EPC 3906) 1976 -
	Moonlight Lady/When I Need You	(Epic EPC 4558) 1976 -

Hammond was born in London on 18 May 1942 but grew up in Gibraltar. Prior to launching his solo career, which brought him hits on both sides of the Atlantic, he was in the **Magic Lanterns**. He was also a songwriter/producer, his credits including the **Mike Stuart Span**'s Fontana 45. His son Albert Jr. plays guitar in the Strokes. (VJ)

Hannibal

Personnel:	ALEX BOYCE	vcls	A
	JACK GRIFFITHS	bs	A
	BILL HUNT	keyb'ds, horns	A
	ADRIAN INGRAM	gtr	A
	JOHN PARKES	drms	A

ALBUM:	1(A)	HANNIBAL	(B&C CAS 1022) 1970 R1

45:	Winds Of Change/Winter	(B&C HB 1) 1974

A Birmingham act, which evolved out of the remnants of **Bakerloo** and were heralded by their management as the follow-up to **Black Sabbath**. Their album, like most releases on this label, has become a minor collectable and is a **Van der Graaf Generator**-style progressive, housed in an odd gatefold sleeve. The vocalist is strongly influenced by **Family**'s Roger Chapman whilst their music is strong, pleasant, jazz-rock.

Their guitarist Adrian Ingram later became a senior lecturer at Leeds Music School and was for many years the author of the jazz music column in 'Guitarist'. He also wrote an excellent instruction book for guitar "Cool Blues and Hot Jazz", a very good book on the history of the Gibson ES-175 guitar and he also released a CD under his own name. (VJ)

Junior Hanson

ALBUMS:	1	NOW HEAR THIS	(Manticore K 43507) 1973
	2	MAGIC DRAGON	(Manticore 66677) 1974

A good hard-psych black guitarist recording on a label founded by **Emerson, Lake and Palmer**. Produced by Mario Tedious and clearly inspired by **Hendrix**, the first (and best) album benefited from the backing of The **Jeff Beck Group** (without **Beck**) plus Chris Wood and Rebop Kwaku Baah from **Traffic**. Glen Le Fleur later played in Olympic Runners. Neil Murray went on to National Health, Whitesnake and **Black Sabbath**. (DMc/CG)

Happy Confusion

45:     Yes Sir/Hereditary Impediment   (Penny Farthing PEN 706) 1970

This was a short-lived pop group. (VJ)

Happy Magazine

Personnel: KENNY CRADDOCK   organ   A
            PETE KIRTLEY   gtr   A
            ALAN MARSHALL   vcls   A
            ALAN WHITE   drms, vcls   A

45s: Satisfied Street/
      Do Right Woman, Do Right Man   (Polydor 56233) 1968
      Who Belongs To You/Beautiful Land (Polydor 56307) 1969

This Newcastle band was managed by **Alan Price**, who was also their
producer and wrote *Satisfied Street*. Alan White had previously been in
Alan Price's backing group. Craddock, Kirtley and White were all later in
Griffin. *Who Belongs To You* later re-emerged on *Colour Me Pop, Vol 2*
(CD). (VJ)

Hapshash and The Coloured Coat

Personnel: MICHAEL ENGLISH   A
            GUY STEVENS   A
            NIGEL WEYMOUTH   A B
            TONY MCPHEE   gtr   B
            MIKE BATT   piano, accordion   B
            FREDDIE BALLERINI violin   B
            MICHAEL MAYHEW   gtr   B
            ANDY RENTON   drms   B
            EDDIE TRIPP   bs   B
            MICKEY FINN

ALBUMS: 1(A) FEATURING THE HUMAN HOST AND THE HEAVY
              METAL KIDS (w/insert)   (Minit MLS 40001E) 1968 R1
        2(B) THE WESTERN FLIER   (Liberty LBS 83212R) 1969 SC

NB: First pressings of (1) came on red vinyl (R2). Later reissued on vinyl (Drop-Out
DO SP 2001) 1987 and on CD (Repertoire REP 4404-WP) 1994. (2) reissued on CD
(Repertoire REP 4415-WY) 1994.

45:     Colinda/The Wall   (Liberty LBF 15188) 1969 SC

Basically a vanity project for the brilliant designers Michael English and
Nigel Weymouth, who traded as Granny Takes A Trip, the first album is
something of a freeform electric freakout, and has not stood the test of time

HAPSHASH AND THE COLOURED COAT - Featuring The Human Host And
The Heavy Metal Kids (LP).

HAPSHASH AND THE COLOURED COAT - The Western Flyer (CD).

well, though its sleeve is one of the most astounding of the period. Minit
was a short-lived subsidiary of Liberty. After the album's release the duo
continued to work as designers while producer Guy Stevens oversaw
albums by **Art** (later to become **Spooky Tooth**), **Mott the Hoople**, **Mighty
Baby** and others. In 1969 Weymouth revived the name for a second, far
less radical album on which he received assistance from **Tony McPhee** (of
Groundhogs) and precocious producer-arranger **Mike Batt**. Mickey Finn of
Tyrannosaurus Rex was also a member at some point, but the group
finally disintegrated late in 1969. Ken Kesey played bass on their 45.

They also have a track, *The Wall*, on the *Gutbucket* (LP) sampler. (VJ/RMJ)

Harbour Lites

Personnel: JOHN GIBB   A
            JOHN MERCER   A
            JOHN ROSS   A

45s: Come Back Silly Girl/Revenge   (HMV POP 1426) 1965
      I Would Give All/
      They Call The Wind Maria   (HMV POP 1465) 1965
      Run For Your Life/Lonely Journey (Fontana TF 682) 1966

The three Johns came to the UK from New Zealand in 1965. Their final 'A'
side was a **Beatles**' song. They mostly played harmony folk-orientated
music. *Ready Steady Win* (LP & CD) includes a version of *I'll Miss You*
taken from the TV series *Ready Steady Go*, originally broadcast as part of
a best unknown group competition. (VJ)

Hard Meat

Personnel: MICK CHARLESS   drms   A
            MICHAEL DOLAN   gtr, vcls   A
            STEVE DOLAN   bs, vcls   A

ALBUMS: 1(A) HARD MEAT   (Warner Bros WS 1852) 1970 SC
        2(A) THROUGH A WINDOW (Warner Bros WS 1879) 1970 SC

45s: Rain/Burning Up Years   (Island WIP 6066) 1969
      Ballad Of Marmalade, Emma And Ted/
      Yesterday, Today, Tomorrow   (Warner Bros WB 8010) 1970

The Dolan brothers were from Birmingham originally, although they moved
down to Cornwall with Mike Carless to get the band underway. They were
basically a hippie outfit who played a brand of progressive rock with some
cover versions thrown in. Their first 45, *Rain*, was a re-arrangement of **The
Beatles**' song. The flip side *Burning Up The Years* has been compiled on
Talking About The Good Times (CD). Steve Dolan was later involved with
Pete Sinfield's Under The Sky. (VJ)

Hard Stuff

Personnel:	JOHN CANN	ld gtr, vcls	A
	JOHN GUSTAFSON	bs	A
	PAUL HAMMOND	drms	A

| ALBUMS: | 1(A) | BULLETPROFF | (Purple TPSA 7505) 1972 SC |
| | 2(A) | BOLEX DEMENTIA | (Purple TPSA 7507) 1973 SC |

NB: (1) issued on Mercury (663) in the US.

| 45s: | Jay Time/The Orchestrator | (Purple PUR 103) 1972 |
| | Inside Your Life/How Do You Do It? | (Purple PUR 116) 1973 |

A heavy but melodic power trio with a good reputation. Paul Hammond had previously played in **Atomic Rooster**, **John Gustafson** had been in **Quatermass** and John Cann's previous band was **Atomic Rooster** and prior to that **Andromeda**. (VJ)

Hard Travellin'

| ALBUM: | 1 | HARD TRAVELLIN' | (Flams Ltd PR 1065) 1971 R3 |

Just 99 copies were pressed of this now ultra rare **Incredible String Band**-influenced effort. Unfortunately, the musical content is a big disappointment and its value is thought to be entirely due to the small number of copies originally released. (VJ)

Tony and Derek Hardman

| Personnel: | DEREK HARDMAN | A |
| | TONY HARDMAN | A |

| ALBUM: | 1 | TIGER MOTH | (UK UKAL 1019 SUPER) 1976 |

This folk duo's album is mainstream folk with some social comment and songs like *Orange Coloured Hankerchief* and *Goodbye Wishful Thinking*. Standard folk club fare, pleasant but not outstanding. (BS)

Colin Hare

| ALBUM: | 1 | MARCH HARE | (Penny Farthing PELS 516) 1971 R2 |

NB: Reissued as *March Hare Plus* (See For Miles SEE 261) 1989. This also includes his non-album 45 and was also available on CD (SEE CD 261) 1989.

| 45: | Didn't I Tell You/ | |
| | Seek Not In The Wide World | (Warner Bros K 16203) 1972 |

Colin Hare is best-known as a member of **Honeybus**. This album was recorded after they split for the first time, and contains a preponderance of ballads (*Bloodshot Eyes, Find Me* and *Grannie, Grannie*) and a number of country-rock tunes (of which *Get Up The Road* was the best). It is extremely rare but not especially good. The See For Miles reissue includes his 1972 45. (VJ/RMJ)

Harlan County

Personnel:	BARRY GUARD	sax, drums	A
	PETER SKELLERN	vcls	A
	STU LEATHERWOOD		A

| ALBUM: | 1 | HARLAN COUNTY | (Nashville 6336 002) 1970 |

| 45: | Dr. Handy's Dandy Candy/Big Heat | (Nashville 6076 002) 1970 |

Harlan County also operated under the name **March Hare**. As well as including **Peter Skellern**, Stu Leatherwood had been in **The Koobas**. (VJ/RMJ)

Harlem Jonns Reshuffle

| ALBUM: | 1 | HARLEM JONNS RESHUFFLE | |
| | | (mono/stereo) | (Fontana (S)TL 5509) 1969 R1 |

45s:	You Are The One I Love/	
	Good Loving	(Fontana TF 970) 1968 SC
	Everything Under The Sun/	
	Let Love Come Between Us	(Fontana TF 1004) 1969 SC

This six-piece band hailed from Lancashire. (VJ)

Harlem Speakeasy

Personnel:	DAVE ALLEN	baritone sax, vcls	A
	SAM EDDINGS	drms	A
	JOHN EDWARDS	ld vcls	A
	GEOFF GUNSON	bs	A
	PETE GURD	trumpet	A
	PHIL JONES	tenor sax	A
	JOHN LYTLE	organ	A
	KEITH SHILCOCK	gtr	A

| 45: | Aretha/Sights Of Pegasus | (Polydor BM 56270) 1968 |

An eight-piece 'soul-band' from Portsmouth - similar to **The Alan Bown Set**. The 'A' side of their 45 was a decent cover of a Drifters song and the flip's not bad either. The band developed a more progressive sound by the time it recorded a second single, *Life Is Not All*, but Polydor withdrew the second single before release. Their roadie, Richie Anderson, was the only one who went on to success, working with **Mott The Hoople**. Dave Allen went on to form a West Coast-influenced band called Rosemary with two other guys. They did record a single but Major Minor pulled it shortly before release. Allen later played in a skiffle/jug band called Reet Petite and Gone, which played a lot of folk festivals, occasional European dates and, released three albums and a CD. John Edwards and John Lytle played in a mid-seventies Isle of Wright band called The Pumphouse Gang, who cut one 45, *Motor City Fantasy / Cocaine* (Kitsch FAD 1) 1977.

Dave Allen has also written a book entitled 'Almost: 40 Years of Southsea Rock and Pompey Blues' (Minerva Press - ISBN 1 86106 773 9). He still does a fortnightly blues show on BBC Local Radio in Southern England and runs a degree called Entertainment Technology at University of Portsmouth. (VJ/PL)

Steve Harley (and Cockney Rebel)

Personnel:	JEAN PAUL-CROCKER	electric violin, gtr	A
(up to	STUART ELLIOT	drms	AB
1976)	STEVE HARLEY	vcls	AB
	PAUL JEFFREYS	bs	A
	MILTON REAME-JAMES	keyb'ds	A
	JIM CREGAN	gtr	B
	GEORGE FORD	bs	B
	DUNCAN MACKAY	keyb'ds	B

				HCP
ALBUMS:	1	THE HUMAN MENAGERIE	(EMI EMA 759) 1974	-
(up to	2	THE PSYCHOMODO	(EMI EMC 3033) 1974	8
1976)	3	THE BEST YEARS OF OUR LIVES		
			(EMI EMC 3068) 1975	4
	4	TIMELESS FLIGHT	(EMI EMA 775) 1976	18
	5	LOVE'S A PRIMA DONNA	(EMI EMC 3156) 1976	28

NB: (1) and (2) reissued as double set (EMI EDP 1546 773) in 1980. (1) reissued on CD (BGO BGOCD 616) 2004, with two bonus tracks. In 1990 the two albums were put out on CD with two bonus tracks each. (2) was also reissued on a budget label (Fame FA 4131351) in 1983 and on CD (BGO BGOCD 529) 2002. Other compilations are a retrospective double live album, *Face To Face* (EMI EMSP 320) in 1977; *The Best Of Steve Harley And Cockney Rebel* (EMI EMI 13345) 1979, which was later reissued on the budget priced Fame (FA 3007) label in 1981; *Greatest Hits* (EMI EM 1291) 1988, also put out on CD with three extra cuts; *The Collection* (Castle Communications CCSLP 197) 1988, which was expanded into a double set in 1990 and *Mr. Soft* (Connoisseur Collection VSOP LP 124) 1988, a budget-priced double set which includes several cuts from their first album as well as material from the full duration of their career, including a 1986 45, *Irresistable*. A later CD compilation is *Make Me Smile - The Best Of Steve Harley And Cockney Rebel* (EMI CDP 7 99062) 1992. Inevitably it duplicates most of the hits on the earlier compilations but it was compiled by **Harley** himself. There's also *Timeless*

Flight (EMI CDP 795 927 2) 1991. *Live At The BBC* (Windsong WINCD 073) 1995 features an 'In Concert' appearance from January 1974, some May 1974 session tracks for John Peel and four Nicky Campbell show recordings from 1992. *On Air* (Strange Fruit SFRSCD 0056) 1998 compiles a January 1974 'In Concert' set, a Peel session and five tracks from an acoustic Nicky Campbell session in 1992.

					HCP
45s:		Sebastian/Rock And Roll Parade	(EMI EMI 2051) 1973	-	
(up to		Judy Teen/Spaced Out	(EMI EMI 2128) 1974	5	
1976)	α	Psychomodo/Such A Dream	(EMI EMI 2191) 1974	-	
	β	Mr. Soft/Such A Dream	(EMI EMI 2191) 1974	8	
	χ	Big Big Deal/Bed In The Corner	(EMI EMI 2233) 1974	-	
		Make Me Smile (Come Up And See Me)/			
		Another Journey	(EMI EMI 2263) 1975	1	
		Mr. Raffles (Man It Was Mean)/			
		Sebastian (live)	(EMI EMI 2299) 1975	13	
		Black Or White/			
		Mad Mad Moonlight (live)	(EMI EMI 2369) 1975	-	
		White White Dove/			
		Throw Your Soul Down Here	(EMI EMI 2409) 1976	-	
		Here Come's The Sun/Lay Me Down	(EMI EMI 2505) 1976	10	
		(I Believe) Love's A Prima Donna/			
		Sidetrack One	(EMI EMI 2539) 1976	41	

NB: α withdrawn immediately after release. β released with two different label designs. χ **Steve Harley** solo.

Steve Harley was born in London on 27 February 1951 as Steven Nice. When he left school he became a local newspaper reporter in Colchester, but then moved to London to pursue his music career on the folk circuit. Before long, he changed his name to **Harley** and started to put together a band, who were snapped up amidst some competition by EMI.

Their first album, *The Human Menagerie*, was lavishly orchestrated but didn't sell in any great quantities. Early copies with a biographical booklet are extremely rare now. The prize cut, *Sebastian*, was also put out on 45. It was a big hit in many European countries but surprisingly failed to chart here in the UK. Before a follow-up album, *Judy Teen* was released as a stop-gap single. It shot to No 5 in the UK Charts.

Their second album, *The Psychomodo*, was a definite progression - theatrical and full of variety with some unnerving keyboard work. The band assumed a theatrical appearance and were the subject of considerable hype. They enjoyed an enormously successful tour in the Summer of 1974 but proceeded to split afterwards following internal friction. However, in *Mr. Soft* the album spawned another hit single and as a temporary measure **Harley** was supported by Francis Monkman (formerly of **Curved Air**), B.A. Robertson and Stuart Elliot as he promoted the 45, prior to putting together a new line-up (B) for a Rainbow Concert in October of that year. This new line-up included a guitarist, Jim Cregan (ex-**Family**), which had been a notable omission from the first line-up, but the move didn't go down too well with their fans. The new line-up soon worked on an album in November 1974 at EMI's Abbey Road studio and AIR studios in London. The band, which had previously been billed as Cockney Rebel, now operated under the monicker **Steve Harley and Cockney Rebel** leaving no-one in doubt who was in charge. Just prior to this **Steve** released his first solo record, *Big Big Deal*. Only Steve and Stuart Elliot played on it and it was pretty good but failed to sell at the time. Nowadays it's becoming a minor collectable as copies are hard to track down.

The Best Years Of Our Lives, which **Harley** co-produced with Alan Parsons, was their best album to date and climbed to No 4 in the Album Charts. It provided them with their biggest UK hit single, *Make Me Smile (Come Up And See Me)*, which rose to No 4, and with the superb *Mr. Raffles (Man It Was Mean)*, which narrowly missed the UK Top Ten. The flip to *Mr. Raffles* was a live recording of the band's 45, *Sebastian*, which had been recorded at the Hammersmith Odeon in April 1975. Another live track from the same concert, *Mad Mad Moonlight*, can be heard on the flip of the follow-up, *Black And White*, which didn't get any Chart action.

The *Timeless Flight* album was much more laid back than its predecessors, having a much more spiritual and religious feel to it. A second 45 to *Black And White*, *White White Dove* was also taken from this album but it too failed to chart.

By contrast, *Love's A Prima Donna*, was much more celebratory. The title track was also issued as a 45, as was a very spirited cover of **George Harrison**'s *Here Comes The Sun*. By contrast, *Love Compared With You*, a

fine love song, was issued as a US-only release.

Early in 1977 Steve went to live in the States and broke up the band. He embarked on a solo career but failed to achieve the same acclaim in this capacity as he had with Cockney Rebel. Neither of his initial solo albums *Hobo With A Grin* or *The Candidate* made much impression and aside from a couple of UK hits *Ballerina (Prima Donna)* (No 51 in 1983) and *The Phantom Of The Opera* (No 7 in 1986) he was mostly out of the public eye in the eighties. He assembled a new Cockney

STEVE HARLEY.

Rebel line-up and toured during the nineties, releasing a number of live albums culminating in 1999's solo acoustic set *Stripped To The Bare Bones*. In 2005 came the first studio Cockney Rebel album for 26 years - *The Quality Of Mercy*. This was released to some critical acclaim and it demonstrated on tracks like *Coast Of Amalfi* and *The Last Feast* that he still had the knack of writing a good tune.

In 2004, their debut album received a long overdue release on CD. The reissue comes with two bonus tracks; their second 45 *Judy Teen*, which wasn't included on an album at the time, and *Rock And Roll Paradise* (the 'B' side to *Sebastian*). The sleevenotes were penned by **Harley** himself.

Compilation appearances include: *Make Me Smile (Come Up And See Me)* on the 6-CD set *Best Of Driving Rock*, the 3-CD collection *Full Throttle - 60 Original Driving Classics*, *Brit Pop* (CD) and on the 3-CD set *Radio Caroline Calling - 70's Flashback*, along with *Sebastian*; whilst *Judy Teen* can be found on *Greatest Hits Of The 70's - cd3*. (VJ)

Harley Quinne

Personnel:	JED KELLY	drms	A
	PETER OAKMAN	bs, vcls	A
	STEVE SIMPSON	gtr, fiddle, vcls	A

45s:	New Orleans/In A Moment Of Madness	(Bell BLL 1255) 1972
	Rock And Roll Is Back Again/My Lady	(Bell BLL 1282) 1973
	Such A Night/We Go Down	(Bell BLL 1328) 1973

Steve and Peter first met while members of Joe Brown's Home Brew. The three came together again in 1969 and used the name Easy. After a while they broke up but then reformed again. A few demo tapes were recorded and having taken them to Roger Greenaway, he suggested the name **Harley Quinne**. The also recorded the old Gary U.S. Bonds number *New Orleans* at his suggestion. Oakman also used the name Peter Oakes. For further information see the **Country Fever** entry. (VJ)

Lee Harmer's Popcorn

45:	Love Is Coming/Hello Sunshine	(Page One POF 053) 1968

This was an obscure release on **Larry Page's** Page One label. The flip side is a restrained psych-pop number. (VJ)

Harmony Grass

Personnel:	RAY BROWN	bs	ABC
	BILL CASTLE	drms, vcls	AB
	TONY FERGUSON	ld gtr, vcls	A

TOM MARSHALL	gtr, piano, vcls	ABC
TONY RIVERS	ld vcls	ABC
KENNY ROWE	second bass, vcls	ABC
TONY HARDING	ld gtr, vcls	BC
BRIAN HUDSON	drms	C

ALBUM: 1(A) THIS IS US   (RCA SF 8034) 1969 R1

HCP

45s:	Move In A Little Closer Baby/		
	Happiness Is Toy Shaped	(RCA RCA 1772) 1968	24
	First Time Loving/What A Groovy Day	(RCA RCA 1828) 1969	-
	I Remember / Summer Dreaming	(RCA RCA 1885) 1969	-
	Cecilia/Mrs. Richie	(RCA RCA 1932) 1970	-
	Stand On Your Own Two Feet/		
	Sing On The Sunshine	(RCA RCA 2011) 1970	-

This group formed in Essex during 1968. Rivers, Brown and Rowe had all previously been in **Tony Rivers and The Castaways**. Signing to RCA, they enjoyed a Top 30 hit with *Move In A Little Closer Baby*, which was produced by **Chris Andrews**. Despite their second 45 being produced by Howard-Blaikley and their fourth being a very credible cover of a Paul Simon song, the harmony-pop outfit failed to repeat their early chart success and split up in 1970. The album is something of a harmony pop classic, echoing the work of US musicians such as Love and Curt Boettcher, with strong melodies and breathtaking vocal arrangements. Especially notable are the infectious *My Little Girl* and haunting *Mrs. Richie*. It's very hard to find in top condition!

Tony Rivers became a successful session singer. Tony Ferguson and Kenny Rowe went on to play in **Capability Brown**. (VJ/RMJ)

Jesse Harper

ALBUM: 1 GUITAR ABSOLUTION IN THE SHADE OF A
           MIDNIGHT SUN   (Kissing Spell KSLP 9203) 1992 SC

The above album was previously only available as an acetate from 1969. (VJ)

Roy Harper

HCP

ALBUMS: (up to 1976)	1	THE SOPHISTICATED BEGGAR		
			(Strike JHL 105) 1967	R4 -
	2	COME OUT FIGHTING GENGHIS SMITH (mono/stereo)		
			(CBS (S)BPG 63184) 1967	R1/SC -
	3	FOLKJOKEOPUS (mono/stereo)		
			(Liberty LBS 83231) 1969	R1 -

JESSE HARPER - Shades Of The Midnight Sun (LP).

4	RETURN OF SOPHISTICATED BEGGAR		
	(Youngblood SSYB 7) 1970	SC -
5	FLAT, BAROQUE AND BERSERK		
	(Harvest SHVL 766) 1970	SC -
6	STORMCOCK	(Harvest SHVL 789) 1971	SC -
7	RETURN OF SOPHISTICATED BEGGAR		
	(Birth RAB 3) 1972	-SC
8	LIFEMASK	(Harvest SHVL 808) 1973	SC -
9	VALENTINE	(Harvest SHSP 4027) 1974	SC 27
10	FLASHES FROM THE ARCHIVES OF OBLIVION (2-LP)		
	(Harvest SHDW 405) 1974	SC -
11	H.Q. (w/lyric insert)	(Harvest SHSP 4046) 1975	31

NB: (4) is a reissue of (1) and (7) was a reissue of (4). (1) reissued again on vinyl (Big Ben BBX 502) 1977 with different rear sleeve. (2) reissued on vinyl as *The Early Years* (Embassy EMB 31544) 1977 with a different sleeve. (3) reissued on vinyl (Sunset SLS 50373) 1975. (8), (9) and (10) were reissued on Awareness (AWL 1007), (AWL 1015) and (AWLD 1012) in 1987, 1989 and 1989 respectively. CD reissues have included: - (1) on Sundown (CDSD 051) 1989 and (2), (3), (6), (8), (9) and (10) appear on Awareness (AWTCD 1035, AWCD 1003, AWCD 2001, AWCD 1007, AWCD 1015 and AWCD 1012, respectively). (1) on (HUCD 007), (2) on (HUCD 006), (6) on (HUCD 004), (8) on (HUCD 005), (9) on (HUCD 015) and (11) on (HUCD 019). (5) reissued on CD (Hard Up HUCD 003) 1993 in a box with a 40-page booklet and signed poster (SC). There's also a compilation, *The Best Of Roy Harper* (EMI CDP 746 604 2) 1988, which was deleted in 1990. Two BBC session tapes capture him in fine form *The BBC Tapes - Volume 1 1969-73* (HUCD 022) and *The BBC Tapes - Volume 2 - In Concert 1974* (HUCD 023). *Counter Culture* (Science Fiction HUCD 039) 2005 is a 25-cut 2-CD compilation anthologising his career from the mid-sixties in chronological order.

45s: (up to 1976)	Midspring Dithering/Zengem	(CBS 203001) 1967	SC
	Life Goes On/		
	Nobody's Got Any Money In The Summer	(CBS 3371) 1968	SC
	Take Me In Your Eyes/Pretty Baby	(Strike JH 304) 1969	
	Banks Of The Dead/Little Lady	(Harvest HAR 5059) 1972	
	Forever/Male Chauvinist Pig Blues	(Harvest HAR 5080) 1974	
	Home (live)/Home (studio)	(Harvest HAR 5089) 1974	
	When An Old Cricketer Leaves The Crease/		
	Hallucinating Light (PS)	(Harvest HAR 5096) 1975	
	Grown-Ups Are Just Silly Children/		
	Referendum (Legend)	(Harvest HAR 5102) 1975	
α	Referendum/		
	Another Day (live)/Tom Tiddler's Ground	(EMI PSR 407) 1975	

NB: α Promo only.

Harper was born on 12 June 1941 in Manchester. In 1954 he played in a skiffle group with his brother Dave and in 1956 he joined the R.A.F; it's alleged he later faked mental illness to get out. This led to a spell of hospitalization and ECT treatment. He later spent time in Lancaster Moor Mental Institution and a year in prison in Liverpool. In 1964 he moved down to London and by 1965 he'd become a cult figure on the city's folk scene and also worked as a busker.

His debut album, *The Sophisticated Beggar*, contained the sort of highly personal songs that became his trademark. Indeed, one cut, *Committed*, recalled his ECT treatment. *Come Out Fighting Genghis Smith* and *Folkjokeopus* were in a similar mould and eventually led to him receiving a long-term contract with EMI's progressive Harvest label. The first product of this partnership was *Flat Baroque And Berserk*, which was fairly typical folk singer fare. Much of it is rather irritating but *I Hate The White Man* is a poignant sociopolitical song; *How Does It Feel* was similar but better; *Tom Tiddler's Ground* is typical druggy early seventies folk; and it also included a song called *Hell's Angels* about their life style.

Stormcock and *Lifemask* both featured Led Zeppelin's **Jimmy Page** on guitar. Indeed, their third album included a **Page/Plant** track, *Hats Off To Harper*, about him. In 1972, he made a none-too-successful acting debut in the film 'Made' and after an extensive British tour was taken seriously ill and hospitalised with a circulatory complaint. This led to speculation that he was dying and that *The Lord's Prayer* track on *Lifemask* was a final testament. However, he recovered, making his comeback at a packed Albert Hall and then playing at London's Rainbow with a lavish orchestra and all-star backing band on Valentine's Day, 1974, the same day as *Valentine* was intended for issue (in fact production difficulties prevented this and it was released a few days later). The same year, a double album retrospective of his career to date was released. *Flashes From The Archives Of Oblivion*, contained a selection of live recordings from 1973-74, as well as a studio version of *Home*. It was reissued again in the late eighties.

ROY HARPER - Flat, Baroque And Berserk (LP).

1975 saw the release of *H.Q.*, on which **Pink Floyd**'s Dave Gilmour guested (in return he sang lead vocals on *Have A Cigar* on their *Wish You Were Here* album). In the Spring, he toured the UK and put together a new support band which included Bill Bruford and **Chris Spedding** for this purpose. However, the punters were largely disinterested and they disbanded in July 1975. The following year, **Harper** relocated his operation to the States, where he put together a modified version of Trigger to help promote *H.Q.*

Compilation appearances have included *Living Here Alone* on *Harvest Bag* (LP); *Song Of The Ages* on *Picnic* (2-LP); *Nobody's Got Any Money In The Summer* on *The Rock Machine Turns You On* (LP); and *Sergeant Sunshine* on *Son Of Gutbucket* (LP). More recently *Mr. Station Master* has appeared on *The Youngblood Story Vol. 1* (CD); and *Bank Of The Dead* and *Highway Blues* on *Jimmy Page, Session Man* (CD). **Harper** has continued to record into the nineties.

If folk music is your niche **Harper** is essential; if it isn't, you can afford to give him a miss. (VJ)

Jet Harris

ALBUM:	1	ANNIVERSARY ALBUM	(Q LPMM 1038) 197? SC
(up to 1976)			

EP:	1	JET HARRIS	(Decca DFE 8502) 1962 R1

HCP

45s:	Besame Mucho/Chills And Fever	(Decca F 11466) 1962 22
(up to 1976)	Main Title Theme (To The Man With The Golden Arm)/	
	Some People	(Decca F 11488) 1962 12
	Big Bad Bass/Rifka	(Decca F 11841) 1964 -
	My Lady/You Don't Live Twice	(Fontana TF 849) 1967 -
α	Theme For A Fallen Idol/	
	This Sportin' Life	(SRT SRT 75355) 1975 -

NB: α For later pressings the 'A' side title was shortened to *Theme*.

Jet Harris was born on 6 July 1939 in London. He first came to attention as bassist with **The Shadows** (see entry) who were Cliff Richards' backing band at the time, but he left the band to go solo in April 1962 after differences with **Bruce Welch** to go solo. His singles after, made with frequent assistance by **Shadows** drummer **Tony Meehan** (see entry below) were relatively unusual in that they utilised the bass guitar as a lead instrument. His best solo single was *Main Title Theme (To The Man With The Golden Arm)* which had a menacing bass, but at their worst they were rather tame instrumentals. He enjoyed a few hits (some with **Tony**

Meehan) but a bad car accident and emotional problems halted his progress by 1964. He re-emerged in 1967 in the first **Jeff Beck** Group line-up, but didn't record with them. He recorded a couple more singles in the seventies (*Guitar Man* (1977) was strictly outside the time span of the book and there was a limited edition (2,500 copies) album too *Inside Jet Harris - The Last Concert* (Ellie Jay EJSP 8622) 1978 (SC). (VJ)

Jet Harris and Tony Meehan

ALBUM:	1	REMEMBERING	(Decca REM 1) 1976

EP:	1	JET AND TONY	(Decca DFE 8528) 1963 R1

NB: There was also an export issue EP *Diamonds* (Decca DFE 7099) 1963, which was reissued (Decca F 13892) in 1980.

HCP

45s:	Diamonds/Footstomp	(Decca F 11563) 1963 1
	Scarlett O'Hara/(Doing The) Hully Gully	(Decca F 11644) 1963 2
	Applejack/The Tall Texan	(Decca F 11710) 1963 4

These were recordings on which **Harris** was assisted by drummer **Tony Meehan**. His biggest hit *Diamonds*, which is rumoured to have featured a very young **Jimmy Page** on session guitar, competed with **The Beatles**' *Please Please Me* for the UK No 1 spot in early 1963. (VJ)

Pat Harris and The Blackjacks

Personnel incl: PAT HARRIS

45:	The Hippy, Hippy Shake/	
	You Gotta See Your Mama Ev'ry Night	(Pye 7N 15567) 1963 SC

A Welsh group from Llanelli was responsible for this version of *The Hippy Hippy Shake*. They recorded another 45 without **Pat Harris** later the same year (*The Red Dragon/Woo Hoo* (Pye 7N 15586)). Their version of *The Hippy Hippy Shake* was also included on Pye Golden Guinea's *1964 Package Tour* (LP) compilation and, more recently, on See For Miles' *Pop Inside The Sixties, Vol. 3* (CD) and Sequel's *Hippy Hippy Shake* (CD). (VJ)

Richard Harris

ALBUMS:	1	A TRAMP SHINING	
		(mono/stereo)	(RCA Victor RD/SF 7947) 1968 SC
	2	THE YARD WENT ON FOREVER	
		(mono/stereo)	(Stateside (S)SL 5001) 1969 SC

NB: (1) reissued on Stateside (SSL 5019) 1970. There's also a compilation CD, *MacArthur Park* (Half Moon / MCA HMNCD 002) 1997 which contains material from (1) and (2).

HCP

45s:	MacArthur Park/Paper Chase	(RCA RCA 1699) 1968 4
	In The Final Hours/Didn't We	(RCA RCA 1733) 1968 -
	How To Handle A Woman/	
	I Wonder What The King Is Doing	(Warner Bros 7215) 1968 -
	The Yard Went On Forever/	
	Lucky Me	(Stateside SS 8001) 1968 -
	The Hive/That's The Way It Was	(Stateside SS 8007) 1969 -
	One Of The Nicer Things/Watermark	(Stateside SS 8016) 1969 -
	Fill The World With Love/	
	What A Lot Of Flowers	(Stateside SS 8032) 1969 -
	Ballad Of A Man Called Horse/Morning Of	
	The Mourning For Another	(Stateside SS 8054) 1970 -
	Didn't We/My Boy	(Probe GFF 123) 1973 -
	I Didn't Have To Tell You/	
	How I Spent My Summer	(Probe GFF 583) 1973 -
Reissues:	MacArthur Park/	
	Yard Went On Forever	(Probe GFF 101) 1973 38
	MacArthur Park/	
	Yard Went On Forever	(Anchor ABC 4042) 1975 -
	How To Handle A Woman/	
	If I Would Ever Leave You	(Warner Bros K 16589) 1975 -
	MacArthur Park/Didn't We	(Old Gold OG 9216) 1982 -

Harris is best known as an actor and film star but the seven minute long *MacArthur Park*, written by Jimmy Webb, was a classic pop single. It gave him a massive hit but he was never able to equal this feat again.

Born in Limerick, Ireland, on 1 October 1930, he began acting in 1958. One of his most famous roles was his portrayal of King Arthur in the film version of 'Camelot'. In 1970 he sang the part of the Doctor in the orchestrated version of 'Tommy'. Acclaimed acting performances in the seventies included 'Juggernaut' (1974), 'Robin and Marion' (1976) and 'The Wild Geese' (1978). During this period he lived life in the fast lane, drank heavily and his health deteriorated as a result. So during the early eighties he withdrew largely from public life, gave up drinking, pursued a strict dietary regime and discovered religion. He then pursued a writing career but returned to film in the early nineties as star of the acclaimed 'The Field'. He died in London on 25 October 2002 of Hodgkin's disease. (VJ)

Bobby Harrison

Bobby Harrison was formerly with **Procol Harum**, **Freedom** and **SNAFU**. He recorded a solo album *Funkist* in 1972 before he joined **SNAFU**, which was only released in the USA at the time. The album blended funk and soul with blues-based rock and was subsequently reissued in the UK on CD (Angel Air SJPCD 056) in 2000. Micky Moody guested on the album and his slide guitar was prominent on *Thinking Of You*. Other guests included **Ian Paice**, Tony Iommi and Chris Stewart (of **Spooky Tooth**). (VJ)

George Harrison

			HCP
ALBUMS:	1	WONDERWALL MUSIC (mono/stereo)	
(up to		(w/insert) (Apple (S) APCOR 1) 1968	R3/R1 -
1976)	2	ELECTRONIC SOUND (Zapple ZAPPLE 02) 1969	R2 -
	3	ALL THINGS MUST PASS (3-LP)	
		(w/poster insert) (Apple STCH 639) 1971	SC 4
	4	CONCERT FOR BANGLADESH (3-LP)	
		(w/booklet) (Apple STCX 3385) 1972	1 SC -
	5	LIVING IN THE MATERIAL WORLD	
		(Apple PAS 10006) 1973	2
	6	DARK HORSE (Apple PAS 10008) 1974	-
	7	EXTRA TEXTURE (READ ALL ABOUT IT)	
		(Apple PAS 10009) 1975	16
	8	33 1/3 (Dark Horse K 56319) 1976	35
	9	THE BEST OF GEORGE HARRISON	
		(Parlophone 10011) 1976	-

NB: (1) reissed on vinyl (Apple SAPCOR 1) 1992 SC. (2) reissued on vinyl (Zapple ZAPPLE 2) 1996 SC. (3) reissued as a 3-LP set (Parlophone 5304741) 2001. (6) reissued on Music For Pleasure (MFP 50510) in 1980, and (9) reissued on Music For Pleasure (MFP 50523) in 1981. (8) reissued on CD (Dark Horse WPCD 4381) 1991. (5), (6) and (7) reissued on CD (Parlophone/Apple CD PAS 10006, 10008 and 10009) respectively. (1) reissued on CD (Apple CDP 7 98706 2) 1992. (3) reissued as a CD set (EMI CDS 746 688 8) 1987 and again remastered and repackaged as a

GEORGE HARRISON - Wonderwall Music (LP).

2-CD set (gn Records/Parlophone 7243 5 30474 2 9) 2001. (9) reissued on CD (Parlophone CDP 746 682 2) 1987. *Maximum George Harrison* (Chrome Dreams ABCD 107) 2002 is a spoken word biography.

			HCP
45s:	α	My Sweet Lord/What Is Life (PS) (Apple R 5884) 1971	1
(up to		Bangla Desh/Deep Blue (Some PS)(Apple R 5912) 1971	R2/- 10
1976)		Give Me Love (Give Me Peace On Earth)/	
		Miss O'Dell (Apple R 5988) 1973	8
		Dark Horse/Hari's On Tour (Apple R 6001) 1974	-
		Ding Dong Ding Dong/	
		I Don't Care Anymore (Apple R 6002) 1974	38
		You/World Of Stone (PS) (Apple R 6007) 1975	38
		This Guitar (Can't Keep From Crying)/	
		Maya Love (Apple R 6012) 1976	SC -
		This Song/	
		Learning How To Love You (Dark Horse K 16856) 1976	-

NB: α Later reissued in black and white picture sleeve, in 1976 (SC).

George Harrison was born on 25 February 1943 in Wavertree, Liverpool. In 1960 he joined **The Beatles** and, though he was slower to contribute material than **Lennon** and **McCartney**, his broad musical tastes and growing fascination with Eastern sounds and philosophy came to have a decisive impact on their work. By the end of the decade he was writing songs that were easily the equal of his bandmates', and was also the first **Beatle** to issue solo material.

In fact *Wonderwall Music*, the soundtrack to an underground film, was the first release on the Apple label late in 1968, and features the uncredited involvement of **Eric Clapton**. An instrumental album full of studio trickery, it developed **Harrison**'s interest in Eastern music, already apparent on his *Within You Without You* on *Sergeant Pepper*, and was partly recorded in Bombay. Despite its lack of commerciality, *Wonderwall* climbed to No 49 in the US. *Electronic Sound*, released on the short-lived Zapple imprint in May 1969, was even more avant-garde. Capturing **Harrison** experimenting rather self-indulgently on his new Moog synthesizer, it again fared better in the US, where it sneaked up to No 191 in the charts.

Among the Apple artists he produced were **Jackie Lomax** and **Radna Krishna Temple,** whose *Hare Krishna Mantra* made the UK Top 20 in 1969. Before the year was through **the Beatles** also enjoyed a massive hit with *Something*, the first 45 he'd written for them.

All Things Must Pass, his first album after **the Beatles'** split, was enormously successful and surprised many people musically and commercially. A triple album, it consisted of four sides of songs and two of an extended jam with several famous friends. Co-produced by **Harrison** and Phil Spector, it sold in excess of three million copies worldwide and spawned the classic 45, *My Sweet Lord*, which topped the singles charts on both sides of the Atlantic. It eventually sold more than five million copies worldwide, but Bright Tunes, owner of the copyright to the late Ronnie Mack's song *He's So Fine*, filed a law suit claiming that *My Sweet Lord* plagiarised it. As a result royalty payments were frozen, with **Harrison** claiming that the song was inspired by The Edwin Hawkins Singers' hit *Oh Happy Day*. After a battle lasting almost five years, a US District Court Judge ruled in favour of Bright Tunes, but recognised that **Harrison** may have subconsciously adapted the song. Bright Tunes were paid $587,000 in damages.

Harrison had considerable interest in Asia and its affairs and, after Ravi Shankar, a friend of his, sought his help, he organised two concerts to help the victims of the war and the resulting famine in Bangladesh. Held at New York's Madison Square Gardens, the concert included an array of stars including **Eric Clapton**, Bob Dylan and **Ringo Starr**, and raised several million pounds. It did much to enhance his reputation and has since been seen as a pioneering example of the rock community pulling together for charity. The 45 release *Bangla Desh* made the UK Top Ten and no 23 in the US. The triple box set album climbed to No 2 in the US and topped the UK album charts.

Living In The Material World was disappointing, particularly after the promise of *All Things Must Pass*. People still bought it in very large quantities, on the strength of his name, and it topped the US charts and made No 2 here in the UK. The *Give Me Love (Give Me Peace On Earth)* 45 taken from it became a US no 1 and made the Top 10 here, but the album is not recommended overall. The follow-up, *Dark Horse*, suggests that he was running seriously short of fresh ideas. A very mundane

GEORGE HARRISON - Dark Horse (LP).

offering, it failed to chart at all in the UK but achieved the No 4 slot in the US. The title track was a Top 20 hit in the US but failed to enjoy any chart action over here. The rather unimaginative *Ding Dong Ding Dong* also failed to make the Top 30 on both sides of the Atlantic. The album included a cover of The Everly Brothers' *Bye Bye Love*, which seems to have been a goodbye to his ex-wife Patti Boyd, who'd gone off with his friend **Eric Clapton**.

In the early seventies he developed an interest in film production, bailing out the Monty Python team when their Holy Grail project seemed in jeopardy, and eventually establishing the hugely influential Handmade Films. He also developed an interest in motor racing. In June 1974 he also set up his own Dark Horse label. Though he signed Ravi Shankar, the label's only real success apart from himself was the label's first release, **Splinter**'s *Costafine Town*, which he produced himself and became a top 20 hit in the UK. *Extra Texture* was an improvement on his previous two efforts but still devoid of the inspiration *All Things Must Pass* had exhibited. The label featured a partly-eaten apple core, and was his last for Apple. It made the Top 20 on both sides of the Atlantic, though the 45 culled from it did less well, only reaching No 38 in the UK.

Inevitably, **Harrison**'s career continued well beyond the time span of this book, and his untimely death from cancer on 29th November 2001 prompted a worldwide outpouring of nostalgia. A 'Concert For George' was held on 29 November 2002 at London's Royal Albert Hall, featuring **Paul McCartney**, **Ringo Starr**, **Eric Clapton**, **Jeff Lynne** and Ravi Shankar. In 2003 it was released as a double DVD/Video set. (VJ/RMJ)

Mike Harrison

ALBUMS: 1 MIKE HARRISON   (Island ILPS 9170) 1971 SC
         2 SMOKESTACK LIGHTNING   (Island ILPS 9209) 1972 SC
         3 RAINBOW RIDER   (Goodear 7002) 1975

45:     Somewhere Over The Rainbow/Easy   (Goodear EAR 603) 1975

Best known as one of the founding members of **The V.I.P.s** and **Spooky Tooth,** following the release of *The Last Puff* and the break-up of **Spooky Tooth**, vocalist/guitarist **Harrison** set off in pursuit of a solo career.

Recorded at Muscle Shoals Studios, 1972's *Smokestack Lightning* was co-produced by **Harrison** and Chris Blackwell. While it wasn't perfect, his sophomore release was far stronger than his debut effort. On the downside **Harrison** remained a singer of limited capabilities (an expansive vocal range wasn't one of his strengths) and on tracks such as *Paid My Dues* Harry Robinson's extensive string arrangements all but drown **Harrison's** lower register vocals. Those criticisms aside, backing from **Spooky Tooth** alumnus Luther Grosvenor (who turned in a couple of tasty guitar solos - check out *I Wanna Be Free*) and the cream of Muscle Shoals studio players (Barry Beckett, Clayton Ivey, Roger Hawkins, etc) certainly helped salvage material such as *Tears Behind My Eyes* and the self-penned *Turn It Over*. **Harrison** also proved deft working with the blues - *What A Price*

and the title track were both impressive, sounding like something off one of the early **Spooky Tooth** albums. To our ears it's probably the best of his three solo releases.

Unfortunately, with sales proving minimal, the following year **Harrison** reformed **Spooky Tooth** with **Gary Wright**. Although when the group disbanded again during 1974 he had another equally low key shot as a solo artist. (VJ/SB)

Harsh Reality

Personnel: CARL BARNWELL   gtr   A
            MARK GRIFFITHS   gtr   A
            CLIFF JENKINS   gtr   A
            STEPHEN MILLER   keyb'ds   A
            ROGER SWALLOW   drms   A

ALBUM: 1(A) HEAVEN AND HELL
              (mono/stereo)   (Philips (S)BL 7891) 1969 R2

45s: Tobacco Ash Sunday/How Do You Feel   (Philips PB 1710) 1968
        Heaven And Hell/
        Praying For Reprieve   (Philips PB 1769) 1969 SC

This heavy, organ-based progressive underground rock band's rare album is highly-rated. Released in June 1969 in a tasteless gatefold sleeve depicting the band covered in blood, its finer moments include the title cut and *Devil's Daughter*. Discovered and signed by Fritz Fryer of **The Four Pennies** (also responsible for **The Open Mind**'s classic *Magic Potion* 45), they're thought to have been Welsh and were involved with Terry Stamp from **Third World War**. Barnwell was later with **Matthews Southern Comfort**, Roger Swallow later went on to **Principle Edwards Magic Theatre** and the **Albion Country Band**. Other members went into session work.

How Do You Feel has been compiled on *Jagged Time Lapse, Vol 5* (CD). (VJ/RMJ)

Mike Hart

ALBUMS: 1 MIKE HART BLEEDS   (Dandelion 63756) 1969 SC
         2 BASHER, CHALKY, PONGO AND ME
                                      (Dandelion 2310 211) 1972 R1

NB: (2) credited to Mike Hart and Comrades. NB: (1) and (2) reissued on one CD (See For Miles SEECD419).

45s: Yawney Morning Song/
        Almost Liverpool 8   (Dandelion S 4781) 1970
        Son Son/Bad News Man   (Deram DM 409) 1974

HARSH REALITY - Heaven And Hell (LP).

A former member of **The Roadrunners**, **The Richmond**, Henry's Handful and **Liverpool Scene**, his debut album built him a cult following, which the 1972 release failed to consolidate. On his first album he was supported by members of the **National Head Band**. He rejoined **Liverpool Scene** for a reunion album in 1974.

The See For Miles' *Dandelion Rarities* (CD) includes *Nell's Song* and their *Dandelion Sampler 1969-1972* (CD) includes *Please Bring Back The Birch For The Milkman*. (VJ)

Tim Hart and Maddy Prior

ALBUMS: 1 FOLK SONGS OF OLDE ENGLAND, Vol. 1
                                 (Teepee TRPM 102) 1968 R2
           2 FOLK SONGS OF OLDE ENGLAND, Vol. 2
                                 (Teepee TRPM 105) 1969 R2
           3 SUMMER SOLSTICE   (B&C CAS 1035) 1971 SC

NB: (1) and (2) were very limited releases in gatefold sleeves. (1) reissued in a limited release in a single sleeve (Ad-Rhythm ARPS 3) 1969 R1. (1) later reissued on vinyl (Mooncrest CREST 23) 1976 and again (Mooncrest CREST 006) 1991 and on CD (Mooncrest CRESTCD 006) 1991. (2) reissued in a limited release in a single sleeve (Ad-Rhythm ARPS 4) 1969 R1. (2) later reissued on vinyl (Mooncrest CREST 26) 1976 and again (Mooncrest CREST 010) 1991 and on CD (Mooncrest CRESTCD 010) 1991. (3) reissued on vinyl (Mooncrest CREST 12) 1976 in a gatefold sleeve and later in a single sleeve and on CD (Mooncrest CRESTCD 023) 1996.

These two are well-known folk artists who were also members of **Steeleye Span** from January 1970 until its demise in March 1978. Prior to joining **Steeleye Span** they operated as a folk duo and these recordings are taken from that era. When **Steeleye Span** split, they both pursued solo projects. They also contributed to the *Rave On* (CD) compilation. (VJ)

Keef Hartley (Band)

Personnel incl:			
MILLER ANDERSON	gtr, vcls	ABC
IAN CUICKSHANK	ld gtr	AB
PETER DINES	organ	A
KEEF HARTLEY	drms	ABC
SPIT JAMES	gtr	A
GARY THAIN	bs	ABC
JOHNNY ALMOND	sax	B
JIMMY JEWEL	horns	B
HENRY LOWTHER	horns	B
MICK WEAVER	keyb'ds	B
DAVE CASWELL		C
LYLE JENKINS		C
HARRY BECKETT	trumpet, trombone	
JON HISEMAN	drms	

                                         HCP

ALBUMS:				
1(A)	HALFBREED	(Deram SML 1037) 1969 SC	-
2(B)	THE BATTLE OF NW6	(Deram SML 1054) 1970 SC	-
3(C)	THE TIME IS NEAR	(Deram SML 1071) 1970 SC	41
4( )	OVERDOG	(Deram SDL 2) 1971 SC	-
5( )	LITTLE BIG BAND	(Deram SDL 4) 1971 SC	-
6( )	SEVENTY SECOND BRAVE	(Deram SDL 9) 1972 SC	-
7( )	LANCASHIRE HUSTLER	(Deram SDL 13) 1973 SC	-
8( )	THE BEST OF.... (2-LP)	(Deram DPA 3011/2) 1974	-

NB: CD reissues include (1) on Deram (820 978-2) 1992; (2) on Deram (820 931-2) 1992; (3) on (Deram 820 979-2) 1995 and again on CD (Eclectic Disks ECLCD 1027) 2005; (4) on (Deram 820 974-2) 1995 and again on CD (Eclectic Disks ECLCD 1026) 2005 with both sides of the Deram *Roundabout* single as bonuses; (5) on (Deram 820 975-2) 1995 and (6) on (Deram 820 976-2) 1995.

45s:		
Leave It 'Til Morning/Just To Cry	(Deram DM 250) 1969
Waiting Around/Not Foolish, Not Wise	(Deram DM 273) 1969
Roundabout/	
Roundabout (different version)	(Deram DM 316) 1970
Dance To The Music/You And Me	(Deram DM 380) 1973

A Lancastrian - he was born in Preston during 1944 - **Hartley** first caught the public eye when he replaced **Ringo Starr** as drummer for **Rory Storm and The Hurricanes**. He later moved to London in 1964, hitting the skins first for **The Artwoods** and then for **John Mayall's Bluesbreakers** in April 1967. The following year, at **Mayall**'s suggestion, he formed his own **Keef**

Hartley Band. This had a rapidly fluctuating line-up but the personnel listed above were the nucleus of the band. They played a wide range of music but have tended to be most closely identified with the British blues scene. **Hartley** was a colourful figure who often dressed as an American Indian, sometimes with the head-dress and war-paint. All this helped make the band a popular attraction around the clubs. They were also one of the few British bands to appear at the Woodstock festival where they went down well.

On *Halfbreed*, they took the Chicago blues tradition and improvised mostly with their own compositions; relying quite heavily on solos. (The CD reissue on Deram also includes the non-album 45, *Leave It 'Til Morning*). By the time of *The Battle Of NW6* they'd veered more towards jazz musically. *The Time Is Near* came with a lyrics/picture booklet. **Miller Anderson** wrote all but one track on the album.

In 1971, *Hartley* formed a new combo, **The Keef Hartley Big Band**, which featured an enlarged brass section. This outfit recorded *Little Big Band* live at the Marquee Club. The band proved to be a very short-term venture, mostly due to conflict between **Hartley** and **Anderson**, and his *Seventy Second Brave* and *Lancashire Hustler* albums were really solo efforts with various session musicians lending assistance.

In 1974, **Hartley** met up with **Miller Anderson** again in the States. The two of them having settled their differences, they returned to the UK to form **Dog Soldier**, although once again this proved to be a short-term venture.

Keef Hartley Band can also be heard playing *Not Foolish, Not Wise* on Decca's *Wowie Zowie! World Of Progressive Music* (LP) compilation back in 1969 and the following year *World Of Blues Power! Vol. 2* (LP), included *Leavin' Trunk*.

There is also an acetate version of *Halfbreed* with Owen Finnegan on vocals. He was a good live vocalist but couldn't do it in the studio so he was ousted in favour of **Miller Anderson**.

Sinnin' For You (Live) has been compiled on the 3-CD box set *Ars Longa Vita Brevis: A Compendium of Progressive Rock*. (VJ)

Harverson Apricot

A five-piece outfit from Swansea who recorded a single-sided acetate in 1967, *Wax Candle*, which was a rather wimpy mod-rock derivative. It recently surfaced on *Syde Trips, Vol. 3* (LP). (VJ)

The Harvesters

ALBUM:	1	AT THE BOLDMERE	(Private Pressing) 1968 R3

A very rare album from a folk quartet with lead female vocals on songs like *Holy Ground*, *Flowers In The Rain*, *She Moves Through The Fair* and *Derby Ram* etc.. It comes in a black and white sleeve design with a group photo on the back sleeve. This is one for fans of female British folk. (VJ)

Alex Harvey (Soul Band)

Personnel incl:			
HOWIE CASEY	sax	A
ALEX HARVEY	vcls, gtr	AB
GIBSON KEMP	drms	A
KINGSIZE TAYLOR	gtr	A
BOBBY THOMPSON	bs	A
JIMMY GRIMES	bs	B
BILL PATRICK	sax, flute	B
BILLY LAW	drms	B
WALLY STEWART	vcls	B

NB: Line-up (A) 1964, line-up (B) 1965.

ALBUMS:	1( )	ALEX HARVEY AND HIS SOUL BAND	
			(Polydor LPHM 46424) 1964 R3
	2( )	THE BLUES	(Polydor LPHM 46441) 1964 R3
	3(-)	ROMAN WALL BLUES	(Fontana (S)TL 5534) 1969 R3

NB: (1) and (2) as **Alex Harvey and His Soul Band**.

45s:	α	I Just Wanna Make Love To You/		
		Let The Good Times Roll	(Polydor NH 52264) 1964 R1	
	α	Got My Mojo Working/		
		I Ain't Worried Baby	(Polydor NH 52907) 1964 R1	
	α	Ain't That Just Too Bad/		
		My Kind Of Love	(Polydor 56017) 1965 R1	
		Agent OO Soul/Go Away Baby	(Fontana TF 610) 1965 R1	
		Work Song/		
		I Can Do Without Your Love	(Fontana TF 764) 1966 SC	
		The Sunday Song/Horizons	(Decca F 12640) 1967 R1	
		Maybe Some Day/		
		Curtains For My Baby	(Decca F 12660) 1967 R1	
		Midnight Moses/Roman Wall Blues	(Fontana TF 1063) 1969 SC	

NB: α as **Alex Harvey and His Soul Band**.

Harvey was born in the Gorbals area of Glasgow on 5 February 1935. After leaving school, aged 15, he undertook numerous jobs but by 1954 had started playing in various skiffle groups. In 1959 he formed the **Alex Harvey Soul Band**. He also backed big name artists like Eddie Cochran and Gene Vincent on UK tours. He spent a lot of time playing with his band in Hamburg.

Musically **Alex Harvey's Soul Band** blended jazz and blues and used conga drums and other percussion instruments to give their music a unique texture. They were striking visually, too, often appearing in silver lame jackets, red shirts and trousers, white high-heeled boots and gold bow ties. Their first album was full of classic **Harvey** live standards like *Framed, Let The Good Times Roll, I Just Wanna Make Love To You* and *Mojo*. Their first two 45s were culled from it. It seems that this album didn't feature the Soul Band (despite its title); aside from **Harvey**, the remaining musicians were most of **Kingsize Taylor**'s backing group, The Dominoes. *The Blues* album only featured **Alex** and his younger brother Leslie on guitar, who was in a Glasgow group called The Ramblers. It was a very diverse collection of material and before a 'proper' Soul Band album could be released Alex split up the band in 1965.

He released a couple of solo 45s for Fontana; an Edwin Starr cover, *Agent OO Soul* and *Work Song*. The flip side to the first, *Go Away Baby* later appeared on Island's 1968 compilation *British Blue-Eyed Soul* (LP) and *Ain't That Just Too Bad*, a 1965 release on Polydor, later resurfaced on Polydor's 1977 *Rare Tracks* (LP) compilation.

In 1967 **Harvey** formed a short-lived psychedelic band Giant Moth, part of which appeared on his next two 45s for Decca. They were good singles but 'bummed' commercially and so he became part of the pit band of the London version of the musical 'Hair', appearing on the original cast album released on Polydor in 1969. Then, backed by his brother Lesley and members of the jazz group **Rock Workshop**, he recorded *Roman Wall Blues*, a progressive album which was quite unlike any of his earlier work. (VJ)

The (Sensational) Alex Harvey Band

Personnel:	ZAL CLEMINSON	gtr	A
	CHRIS GLEN	bs	A
	ALEX HARVEY	gtr, vcls	A
	HUGH McKENNA	keyb'ds	A
	TED McKENNA	drms	A

				HCP
ALBUMS:	1(A)	FRAMED	(Vertigo 6360 081) 1972 SC -	
(up to	2(A)	NEXT	(Vertigo 6360 103) 1973 37	
1976)	3(A)	THE IMPOSSIBLE DREAM	(Vertigo 6360 112) 1974 16	
	4(A)	TOMORROW BELONGS TO ME		
			(Vertigo 6360 120) 1975 9	
	5(A)	LIVE	(Vertigo 6360 122) 1975 14	
	6(A)	PENTHOUSE TAPES	(Vertigo 9102 007) 1975 14	
	7(A)	SAHB STORIES	(Mountain TOPS 112) 1976 11	

NB: (1) and (2) reissued as a 2-CD set (Mercury/Universal 586 696 2) 2002. (3) and (4) reissued as a 2-CD set (Mercury/Universal 586 697 2) 2002. (5) and (6) reissued as a 2-CD set (Mercury/Universal 586 698 2) 2002. (7) reissued as a 2-CD set along with *Rock Drill* (Mercury/Universal 586 699 2) 2002. *The Best Of The Sensational Alex Harvey Band* (Music Club MCCD 001) 1991 may be a good starting point for those not familiar with the band. Alternative CD compilations include *Collection* (Castle Collector CCSCD 149) 1986 and *The Best Of The Sensational Alex Harvey Band* (K-Tel NCD 5139) 1987. (1), (2), (4) (5) and (6) reissued on CD (Samurai SAMRCD 00119, SAMRCD 00114, SAMRCD 00111, SAMRCD 00117 and SAMRCD

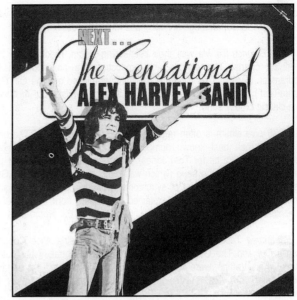

THE SENSATIONAL ALEX HARVEY BAND - Next (LP).

00112, respectively) 1986. *Delilah* (Spectrum) 1998 is a 14-track collection of their greatest hits. *The Gospel According To Harvey* (New Millennium Communications PILOT 45) 1998 is a 2-CD live collection from the BBC archives covering their career. *Faith Healer - An Introduction To The Sensational Alex Harvey Band* (Mercury 586 329 2) 2001 is a compilation which draws from some of their less well known but equally worthwhile material. *Considering The Situation* (Universal 065005 2) 2003 is a 2-CD compilation, which includes material by **The Alex Harvey Soul Band** as well as the better known and more commercially successful **Sensational Alex Harvey Band** material. *British Tour '76* (Major League Productions MLP 07 CD) 2004 captures the workmanlike band on the road.

HCP

45s:	There's No Lights On The Christmas Tree/		
(up to	Mother, They're Burning Big Louie Tonight/		
1976)	Harp	(Vertigo 6059 070) 1972 -	
	Jungle Jenny/Buff's Bar Blues	(Vertigo 6059 075) 1973 -	
	Giddy Up A Ding Dong/		
	Buff's bar Blues	(Vertigo 6059 091) 1973 -	
	The Faith Healer (edit)/St. Anthony	(Vertigo 6059 098) 1973 -	
	Sergeant Fury/Gang Bang	(Vertigo 6059 106) 1974 -	
	Anthem (edit)/Anthem	(Vertigo 6059 112) 1974 -	
	Delilah (live)/		
	Soul In Chains (live) (PS)	(Vertigo ALEX 1) 1975 7	
	Gamblin' Bar Room Blues/		
	Shake That Thing (PS)	(Vertigo ALEX 2) 1975 38	
	Runaway/Snake Bite	(Vertigo ALEX 3) 1976 -	
	Boston Tea Party/Sultan's Choice	(Mountain TOP 12) 1976 13	
	Amos Moses/		
	Satchel And The Scalp Hunter	(Mountain TOP 19) 1976 -	
α	Amos Moses/£25 For A Massage	(Mountain PSLP 183) 1976 -	

NB: α 12" promo only.

In 1972, whilst he was still based in Scotland, **Harvey** spotted Scottish rock group **Tear Gas** playing. He joined forces with them and brought them down to London where they became known as **The Sensational Alex Harvey Band**. They signed to Vertigo and gradually developed an enthusiastic following as they evolved a theatrical stage act and some offbeat songs. They recorded several albums but are best remembered for their cover of Tom Jones' 1968 hit, *Delilah*.

Framed was an energetic and enthusiastic debut. The sleeve had a box cut in the gatefold showing Alex behind bars - a play on its title and title track. This had been recorded ten years back by **Alex Harvey And His Soul Band**, but this version was much better. *Next* contained key songs from their live act like *The Faith Healer* (which effectively became their signature tune) , *Gang Bang* and *Swampsnake*. The title track was a Jacques Brel song about army brothels for which **Harvey** utlised a string quartet and interpreted it as a tango.

The Impossible Dream opens with the impressive *Hot City Symphony* and *The Tomahawk Kid* (which was inspired by 'Treasure Island') captures the band at its best. *Sergent Fury* was a 1920's style swing number inspired by his theatrical work in the sixties. Both *Sergent Fury* and *Anthem* were culled for 45 release, although neither made much impression.

Tomorrow Belongs To Me was their best-selling album, reaching No 9 in the Album charts. The playing and production are polished and the melodramatic *Give My Compliments To The Chef* (played on 'The Old Grey Whistle Test') and funky *Snake Bite* catch the ear, whilst *Soul In Chains* was a classic bluesy song.

Their 1975 *Live* album is often regarded as their magnum opus. The band tear through their best known numbers, including their Top Ten single *Delilah*, (previously a hit for Tom Jones), in a very professional power pop style. Halfway through the song (which was often played on 'The Old Grey Whistle Test') they did a bout of synchronised dancing prior to a passage of metallic guitar playing, which explained the cheers from the audience. They ended the year with a second hit single, *Gamblin' Bar Room Blues*.

The Penthouse Tapes is a collection of covers (including Alice Cooper's *School's Out* and The Osmonds' *Crazy Horses*) and outtakes put out by **Harvey** when Vertigo were wanting another studio album. It's certainly worth a listen, but was really a stop-gap album forced on them by the record company.

SAHB Stories is generally considered to be their last decent album. It includes their hit single *Boston Tea Party*, and *Sultan's Choice*, the amusing *$25 For A Massage* and *Jungle Rub Out* feature among its other highlights. It was also the first album to be released on Mountain. During the summer of 1976, their manager Bill Fehilly was killed in a plane crash and **Alex Harvey** collapsed on stage during a gig in Sweden. This was the result of stress and other health problems.

During his time away from the band Alex took his family on holiday to Scotland and interviewed many locals about sightings of the monster. These were included on *Alex Harvey Presents The Loch Ness Monster* (1977), which was released by K-Tel, who went bankrupt shortly after, leaving the album very hard to find now.

However, the band's fan base was affected by the onset of punk and when **Harvey** fell from the stage and almost broke his back it badly disrupted the band, who had to record the next album *Fourplay* without him. Hugh McKenna left and Tommy Eyre joined as a more than adequate replacement, but *Rock Drill* (with **Harvey** back in business) was disappointing and the band split soon afterwards. Their final single *Mrs Blackhouse* had been recorded a few years earlier and was targeted at Mary Whitehouse, who campaigned against many forms of social progression in the seventies.

The Best Of compilation issued by Music Club in late 1991 seems heavily weighted towards cuts from his *Penthouse Tapes* album, but it does contain his big hits *Delilah*, *Cheek To Cheek* and the long version of *Boston Tea Party*.

The Gospel According Harvey is a live collection from the BBC archives. The 2-CD set includes two versions of *Framed* and *Faith Healer*, but omits

GORDON HASKELL - Sail In My Boat (CD).

Next. A lot of the rest is mundane and only serves ot illustrate the lack of quality in much of their output.

Harvey sadly died on 4th February 1982. In 2002 his albums were lavishly re-packaged on a 2-on-1 CD basis. NB: There is a US country singer from Tennessee also called Alex Harvey, with one 45: *To Make My Life Beautiful / Tulsa Turnaround* (Capitol CL 15735) 1972. (VJ/MKu/WMc)

Richard Harvey

ALBUM: 1   DIVISIONS ON A GROUND
(up to   (Transatlantic TRA 292) 1975 SC
1976)

This was an early solo effort from **Harvey** whilst he was still with **Gryphon**. He went on to put out some privately pressed albums after the time span of this book. *Divisions On A Ground* is a poor album. (VJ)

Christine Harwood

ALBUM: 1   NICE TO MEET MISS CHRISTINE (Birth RAB 1) 1970 R3

Although this is an obscure album, some familiar names appear on it. The main support band consisted of Tommy Eyre (acoustic and electric piano, organ), Roger Sutton (bs, celli), Dave Lambert (gts) and J Kay Boots (drms). The album was produced by Mark Plummer and Mikki Dallon and arranged by Roger Sutton, Tommy Eyre and Dave Lambert. It was recorded at Pye Studios. Guest musicians include Geoff Matthews (gtrs), Mike Maran (acoustic grr), Ian McDonald (sax, flute), John Morgan (tamb), Pete Banks (gtr, acoustic gtr), Pete Yorke (drms, perc), and Johnny Van Derrick (violin) and The Designettes as backing vocalists, along with Jeff Stars and Richard Hart Walker. (VJ/PL)

Gordon Haskell

ALBUMS: 1   SAIL IN MY BOAT   (CBS 63741) 1969 R2
(up to   2   IT IS AND IT ISN'T   (Atlantic K 40311) 1972 SC
1976)
NB: (1) reissued on CD (Voiceprint VP 197 CD) 1997.

45s: Boat Trip/Time Only Knows   (CBS 4509) 1969
            Oo-La-Di-Doo-De-Day / Born Together   (CBS 4795) 1970

Gordon Haskell played with **League Of Gentlemen** and **The Fleur de Lys** in the mid-sixties, **Cupid's Inspiration** in the late sixties and was a member of **King Crimson** in 1970. He sang on *Cadence And Cascade* on *In The Wake Of Poseidon* and did all the vocal chores on *Lizard*, except for the exquisite *Prince Rupert Awakes* by **Jon Anderson**. The first album was recorded prior to his spell with **King Crimson** and is now hard to find. Musically it's MOR. *It Is And It Isn't* is a vast improvement and much-overlooked.

He also recorded at least two later albums, *Hambledon Hill* circa 1991 and *It's Just A Plot To Drive You Crazy* (Voiceprint VP 118CD) 1992. His solo albums are mostly in a folky, singer/songwriter vein. He performs live quite regularly in Hampshire and Dorset and *How Beautiful You Are* brought him back to the public eye in the winter of 2001 with *Harry's Bar* maintaining this new momentum the following year.

He can also be heard playing *Sitting By The Fire* on the *New Age Of Atlantic* (LP) compilation. (VJ)

Hat and Tie

Personnel: PATRICK CAMPBELL-LYONS
               CHRSITOPHER THOMAS

45s: Chance For Romance/
            California Jazz Club U.S.A.   (President PT 105) 1966 SC
            Finding It Rough/Bread To Spend   (President PT 122) 1967 R2

HATFIELD AND THE NORTH - The Rotters Club (CD).

Patrick Campbell-Lyons of **Nirvana** was the person behind this project. He teamed up with Christopher Thomas but *Chance For Romance* was an inconsequential single. *Finding It Rough* was a vast improvement on their debut with an incisive sitar-like guitar sound and powerful beat. Early copies of the flip side were just titled *Bread*, but it's another disappointing track.

Compilation appearances include: *Finding It Rough* on *Circus Days Vol. 3* (LP & CD), *The Electric Lemonade Acid Test, Vol. 1* (LP) and *Sometimes I Wonder* (CD). (VJ)

Hate

Personnel:	NEIL BRUCE	organ, piano, vcls	A
	LENNY GRAHAM	bs, vcls	A
	JIM LACEY	gtr	A
	RAB MONRO	vcls	A
	ALAN PRATT	drms, perc	A

ALBUM: 1(A) HATE KILLS (Famous SFMA 5752) 1970 R1

NB: (1) also issued in the US (Paramount PAS 5031).

This was a fairly obscure Scottish heavy-ish rock group. All the songs on their album are group originals. (VZ)

Hatfield and The North

Personnel:	PHIL MILLER	gtr	AB
	PIP PYLE	drms	AB
	DAVID SINCLAIR	keyb'ds	A
	RICHARD SINCLAIR	bs, vcls	AB
	DAVE STEWART	keyb'ds	B

				HCP
ALBUMS:	1(B)	HATFIELD AND THE NORTH	(Virgin V 2008) 1974	SC-
	2(B)	THE ROTTERS CLUB	(Virgin V 2030) 1975	SC 43
	3(-)	AFTERS	(Virgin VR 5) 1979	R1 -

NB: (3) was withdrawn soon after its release. (1) and (2) have been reissued on CD (Virgin CDV 2008) 1987 and (Virgin CDV 2030) 1988, both with additional CD-only tracks.

45: Let's Eat/Fitter Stroke Has A Birth (Virgin VS 116) 1975

This outfit came together in February 1972 and had a good pedigree. Sinclair had previously played with **Caravan** and **Wilde Flowers**; Phil Miller had been with **Matching Mole** and Pyle had drummed for **Carol Grimes and Delivery** and **Gong**.

They played a form of avant-garde music, as one would expect given their musical backgrounds. They signed to Virgin in 1973, after Dave Stewart (ex-Uriel, **Khan** and **Egg**) had replaced David Sinclair on keyboards when the latter headed for **Caravan**. Their albums were inevitably an acquired taste and they split up in mid-1975 having generated little interest. Still if you're into extended instrumental passages and clever keyboard work they could be for you. Their strange song titles suggest more than an air of pretentiousness though. **The Soft Machine** was clearly a strong influence on their music. The first album, although rather rambling in places, had some great moments with superb musicianship all round. Notable, too, is Richard's magnificent vocals and quirky lyrics. *Fol de Rol* is a highlight showcasing not only his vocals but his outstanding bass playing.

The second album is better and more melodic with Richard Sinclair again proving that his laid back vocal style was something special. Dave Stewart's keyboards dominate with his four-part epic *Mumps* the outstanding track.

Their 1975 single, another lyrical gem, is also non-album. The band also appear on the 1975 compilation (LP), *Over The Rainbow* - the last concert live playing *Halfway Between Heaven And Earth*, which does not appear on either of their albums.

After they split in June 1975, Stewart and Miller formed National Health. Pyle went into session work as a drummer and Richard Sinclair and his cousin David returned to **Caravan** in the late seventies, Richard having had a spell in **Camel** amongst other projects. He was later in Caravan Of Dreams in the early nineties. (VJ/MWh/MJs)

Hawkwind

Personnel:	DAVE BROCK	gtr, vcls, keyb'ds	ABCDEFG H I J K
	JOHN HARRISON	bs	A
	HUW LLOYD-LANGTON	gtr	A
	DIK MIK	keyb'ds	ABCDE
	TERRY OLLIS	drms	ABC
	NIK TURNER	flt, sax, vcls	ABCDEFG H I J K
	THOM CRIMBLE	bs	B
	DAVE ANDERSON	bs	C
	DEL DETTMAR	keyb'ds	CDEFG
	STACIA	dancer	CDEFG H I J
	IAN 'LEMMY' KILMISTER	bs	DEFG H I
	SIMON KING	drms	DEFG H I J K
	BOB CALVERT	vcls	EF K
	SIMON HOUSE	synth, keyb'ds, violin	HI J K
	ALAN POWELL	drms	H J K
	PAUL RUDOLPH	bs, vcls	J K

HAWKWIND - Hawkwind (LP).

HAWKWIND - In Search Of Space (CD).

NB: The first pressing of (1) was on the blue liberty label and is R3. (1) reissued on CD (Repertoire REP 4403-WY) 1994. Most of these albums have been reissued and repackaged, with the best being EMI's Premier series: (1) on (EMI/Premier HAWKS 1), (2) on (EMI/Premier HAWKS 2), (3) on (EMI/Premier HAWKS 3), (4) on (EMI/Premier HAWKS 4), (5) on (EMI/Premier HAWKS 5). What follows is a selection of their compilation and live albums: *Bring Me The Head Of Yuri Gagarin* (Demi Monde) 1985 consists of poorly recorded live material from 1972. It was later reissued as *Earlydaze (Best Of)* (Thunderbolt THBL 044) in 1987. In 1988 Virgin released *Spirit Of The Age* (Virgin COM CD 8), a CD-only compilation of their material with Charisma plus a booklet. *The Text Of Festival*, previously issued in 1983 and reissued (Thunderbolt THBL 2.068) in 1988 is a double side of live recordings from the 1970-72 era. There's also *Acid Daze, Vol. 1, 2 and 3* (Receiver RRLP 125/126/127) 1990, a three set anthology, which was earlier available back in 1986 on Samurai. *Stasis: The U.A. Years 1971-75* (EMI NTS 300) 1990 is a compilation of some of their rarer material from this period. This was reissued on Fame (CD FA 3267) 1992. *BBC Radio I Live In Concert* (Windsong WIND CD 007) 1991 is taken from a 1972 recording. It includes no new material but it does contain many old favourites. Also not recommended are a couple of CD/cassette-only 1991 compilations, *Masters Of The Universe* (Marble Arch CMA CD 129) and *Spirit Of The Age* (Elite ELITE 021 CD), which added little to what had gone before and should not be confused with similarly-titled compilations on United Artists and Virgin. *Anthology* (Essential ESBCD 168) 1992 is a three-CD compilation which is not quite all its name suggests. It's comprised of live material and studio material from later years but includes none of their (finest) songs recorded for United Artists. This 'anthology' is for diehard fans and completists only. *The Never Ending Story Of The Psychedelic Warlords* was a 30-minute CD of live material which came free with an Italian book of this name which was imported into the UK. *Lord Of Light* (Cleopatra CLEO 57732) 1993 is a short CD which compiles the band's material during the 1972-74 era. *Sonic Boom Killers: The Best Of The Singles, A's and B's, 1970-80* (Repertoire REP 4676 WY) 1999 compiles 'A' sides, rare 'B' sides and comes with rare pictures and sleevenotes from Chris Welch.

Hawkwind is unique in the tapestry of British rock. Rooted in the London underground with lyrics steeped in science fiction, they created their own unique brand of heavy metal music and developed a loyal fan base that has supported them over almost 40 years.

Hawkwind started up in the Notting Hill area of London and soon developed a strong reputation as a community-based group. Brock had previously played with Famous Cure and Mobile Freak-Out. They were initially known as Group X and later as Hawkwind Zoo, before becoming just plain **Hawkwind**.

Like San Francisco's Grateful Dead, they were willing to play for free almost anywhere in their early days (including an impromptu appearance at the 1970 Isle of Wight Festival) and specialised in long, acid-rock orientated sets. Indeed, the band's philosophy and life-style was very similar to that of the San Francisco bands. They strove to recreate all the trappings of this scene, specialising in light shows and visual effects and gimmicks, such as the use of speakers shaped like spaceships.

Their first album was preceded by a 45, the comparatively poppy *Hurry On Sundown*, which is now very rare and sought-after by **Hawkwind** collectors.

Their albums were influenced by the group's strong interest in science fiction and contained long, predominantly instrumental tracks, making liberal use of spacey sound effects. Their music could best be described as space rock, a musical strand which developed out of psychedelia as the range of electronic instrumentation available grew wider and more sophisticated. Aside from both sides of their earlier debut 45, the first album contained five **Pink Floyd**-style instrumental tracks. Their second album, released in October 1971, included a 24-page booklet, 'Hawklog', which was full of the sort of hippie mysticism with which the band was associated. The album reached No 18 in the UK album charts. The album's line-up included ex-Amon Düül bassist Dave Anderson and Del Dettmar, **Hawkwind**'s former sound engineer. The same year the band performed at the Glastonbury Fayre Festival and are featured on the now extremely rare (3-LP), *Glastonbury Fayre*, which was made to commemorate the event. **Hawkwind**'s input was a lengthy version of *Silver Machine* and the shorter *Welcome To The Future*. Nonetheless, they were something of an anachronism in an age of flash rock outfits like **T Rex** and **Gary Glitter**. They remained very much an underground band until the success of their *Silver Machine* single, a No 3 UK hit in the Summer of 1972. This won the band a younger following, and enabled them to go from strength to strength. Their third album, released in November 1972, made No 14 in the Charts. The original pressings included a free poster, designed by the now deceased Barney Bubbles, an artist/designer who was instrumental in planning the immensely ambitious *Space Ritual* project, which was financed out of the royalties of the sales of *Silver Machine*.

HAWKWIND - Doremi Farso Latido (CD).

HAWKWIND - Space Ritual (2-CD).

This next period was the band's most commercially successful with the double album, *Space Ritual*, which had been previewed during their earlier mammoth tour, climbing to No 9. It later got to No 179 in the US. In August 1973 Dik Mik left the band for good.

Their next 45, *Urban Guerilla*, climbed to No 39 but was then withdrawn because of an outburst of terrorist activity by the IRA. Clearly, it would have been a much bigger hit but for this. They completed 1973 with their first US tour.

In April 1974, following a full UK tour and a second US one during which they played a benefit for acid disciple Timothy Leary, Simon House joined on keyboards. A couple of months later, Dettmar, who had earlier withdrawn from the stage line-up, left the band to emigrate to Canada. In July 1974 the former **Chicken Shack**, **Stackridge** and **Vinegar Joe** member Alan Powell had to be drafted in when Simon King broke his ribs playing soccer. When King recovered though, Powell remained and the band simply operated with two drummers. Line-up (H) recorded *Hall Of The Mountain Grill*, which was released in September 1974 and rose to No 16 in the UK and No 110 in the US. A month earlier, *The Psychedelic Warlords* 45 was released. This line-up (I) recorded *Warrior On The Edge Of Time*, made two tours of America and played at the Harrow Free Festival. The album got to No 13 in the UK and No 150 in the US. On their second tour in May 1975 Canadian custom officials caught Lemmy with a small amount of amphetamine sulphate which they mistook for cocaine. As a result, he was jailed in a windowless cell and upon his release, was stunned to find that the band had sacked him rather than jeopardise the tour. Former **Deviants**, **Pink Fairies** and **Uncle Dog** member Paul Rudolph was flown out as a replacement. Lemmy, meanwhile, on his return to the UK formed Motorhead.

By now, **Hawkwind** had established themselves as a national rock institution - they were the top attraction at the August 1975 Reading Rock Festival. Former member **Bob Calvert**, who'd initially made a guest appearance, rejoined the band permanently. This line-up survived until January 1977 and recorded *Astounding Sounds And Amazing Music*. It got to No 33 in the UK. United Artists also released a compilation, *Road Hawks*, which had been compiled by Dave Brock. This album peaked at No 34 in the UK, but their accompanying 45, *Kerb Crawler*, failed to chart.

Although **Hawkwind** reached their peak in the mid-seventies, they continued to record and play spasmodically throughout the eighties, though by the middle of the decade, Dave Brock was the sole surviving member from their Group X days. Nik Turner was involved in Sphynx and Inner City Unit, after being fired from **Hawkwind**. In the late seventies, Brock, **Calvert** and King assumed a new name, The Hawklords, but the group reverted back to **Hawkwind** in 1979 by which time **Robert Calvert** resumed his solo career. Dave Brock had a couple of albums and 45s during the eighties. Michael Moorcock recorded a solo album, *New World's Fair* (United Artists UAG 29732) in 1975, whilst a member of **Hawkwind**. He later recorded a couple of 45s in the early eighties as Michael Moorcock and Deep Fix. Huw Lloyd-Langton formed The Huw Lloyd-Langton Group during the eighties and they released four albums and two more 45s (one of which was a 12").

They continued to release relatively successful albums throughout the eighties. One of the most ambitious was *Chronicle Of The Black Sword*, an adaptation of Michael Moorcroft's science fiction novels, although in common with all their eighties output it only spent a few weeks in the UK Album Chart. **Robert Calvert**, who left the band in the late seventies, died of a heart attack in 1988. **Hawkwind** embraced rave culture on their 1990 album *Space Bandits*, which introduced them to a much younger audience, but it didn't last long and the following year they were re-recording some of their earlier classics. They were reduced to a trio after internal friction on a 1992 US tour but in recent years have continued to enjoy a cult following here in Britain on the drug-fuelled dance/rave circuit.

In recent years their entire catalogue has been reissued on CD by various labels like Griffin, One Way, Magnum and Cleopatra.

Stasis: The U.A. Years 1971-75 includes the original 45 mix of *Silver Machine*; both sides of the *Urban Guerilla* 45, single mixes of *Psychedelic Warlords* and *You'd Better Believe It*; three live cuts and a few other odds and ends.

Compilation appearances have included an excerpt from *Be Yourself* on *All Good Clean Fun* (LP), as well as, *Born To Go* and *Master Of The Universe*, on the (2-LP) *Greasy Truckers Party* compilation and on the (3-LP) *Revelations - A Musical Anthology Of Glastonbury Fayre*. More recently, *The Age Of Enlightenment - Prog Rock, Vol. One* (CD) has included *Masters Of The Universe*, a space-metal anthem; *Silver Machine* can also be found on the 3-CD set *Full Throttle - 60 Original Driving Classics*, the 6-CD set *Best Of Driving Rock*; and the 3-CD set *Radio Caroline Calling - 70's Flashback*; *Urban Guerilla* can also be heard on *Greatest Rock* (CD); *Leviathan* on *Metal Gods* (CD); and the 3-CD set *Metal* includes live versions of *Silver Machine* and *Masters Of The Universe*. (VJ)

Bryn Haworth

ALBUMS: 1   LET THE DAYS GO BY   (Island ILPS 9287) 1974 SC
          2   SUNNY SIDE OF THE STREET   (Island ILPS 9332) 1975

Haworth was the guitarist with **The Fleur De Lys** - the man responsible for the stunning guitar work on many of their 45s. These solo albums were made long after the band's demise. (VJ)

Haydock's Rockhouse

Personnel:			
PETER AINSWORTH	vcls		A
IAN BROOKS	trumpet		A
TONY DANFORTH	organ, vcls		A
ERIC HAYDOCK	bs		A
BARRY WORTHINGTON	sax		A
HECTOR SMITH	drms		A

HAWKWIND - Warrior On The Edge Of Time (CD).

45s: Cupid/She Thinks (Columbia DB 8050) 1966 R1
Lovin' You/Mix A Fix (Columbia DB 8135) 1967 R1

This was a short-lived project of Eric Haydock's after he was sacked from **The Hollies** in 1966. *Cupid* was originally sung by Sam Cooke. *Lovin' You* was a Lovin' Spoonful number.

Cupid has been compiled on *R&B Scene, Vol. 1* (LP). (VJ)

Haystack

45s: A Letter To Josephine/Love You're
Making A Fool Of Me (United Artists UP 35024) 1969
Tahiti Farewell/
Pantomime People (United Artists UP 35035) 1969

The Carter-Lewis team were behind this group, producing the debut 45. The second 45 was a tribute to them and *Tahiti Farewell* can also be heard on the *Carter-Lewis Story* (CD). (VJ)

Justin Hayward

45s: London Is Behind Me/Day Must Come (Pye 7N 17041) 1965 R3
(up to I Can't Face The World Without You/
1976) I'll Be Here Tomorrow (Parlophone R 5496) 1966 R3

Two rare and sought-after 45s by this future **Moody Blues** member. He'd previously played with **The Wilde Three**, whose other two members were Marty and Joyce Wilde.

Hayward, who was born in Swindon on 14 October 1946, also recorded an album with former **Moody Blues**' member John Lodge, *Blue Jays* (Threshold THS 12) in 1975 which got to No 4 in the UK Album Charts and No 16 in the US. Its title also referred to the name of their duo. They also recorded two 45s:-

HCP
45s: I Dreamed Last Night/Remember Me (Threshold TH 19) 1975 -
Blue Guitar/When You Wake Up (Threshold TH 21) 1975 8

They were minor hits in the States, too, peaking at No's 47 and 94 respectively. He went on to a solo career which included a musical version of H.G. Wells' 'The War Of The Worlds'.

He went on to release a lively, acoustic-flavoured solo album *Songwriter* (1977), which climbed to No 28 in the UK Chart. 1980's *Night Flight* marked a significant departure towards a disco-oriented style and also entered the chart, peaking at No 41. He then concentrated on touring and recording with the revived **Moody Blues** and his 1985 album *Moving*

JUSTIN HAYWARD & JOHN LODGE - Blue Jays (LP).

Mountains marked a return towards their early seventies style. In later years, as well as recording and touring with **The Moody Blues** and writing new material, he has concentrated on reviving new solo versions of **Moody Blues** songs. His 1994 *Classic Blue* album, for example, contains some of their songs with orchestral accompaniment.

London Is Behind Me and *Day Must Come* can also be heard on *Footsteps To Fame, Vol. 1* (CD). (VJ)

Rick Hayward

ALBUM: 1 RICK HAYWARD (Blue Horizon 2431 006) 1971 R2

Rick Hayward had been in **The Accent** (when he was known as Rick Birkett), who'd produced a stunning 45 which is now sought-after by collectors of psychedelia. His solo album, a mildly psychedelic singer-songwriter effort, was released on the very collectable Blue Horizon label. Prior to recording it he'd done the guitar honours on **Christine Perfect**'s 1970 Blue Horizon album. These two rarities will appeal to very different collectors. (VJ)

Hayze

45: When Morning Has Come/
Long Lonely Road (Philips 6006 218) 1972

No other information available on this obscure project. (VJ)

Tony Hazzard

ALBUMS: 1 DEMONSTRATION (CBS 63608) 1969 SC
(up to 2 LOUDWATER HOUSE (Bronze ILPS 9174) 1971
1976) 3 WAS THAT ALRIGHT THEN? (Bronze ILPS 9222) 1973
4 TOGETHER (Warner Brothers K 56233) 1976

NB: (4) with **Richard Barnes**. *Go North - The Bronze Anthology* (Castle CMDDD 1094) 2005 is a 2-CD collection of his material.

45s: You'll Never Put The Shackles On Me/
Calling You Home (Columbia DB 7927) 1966
Sound Of The Candyman's Trumpet/
Everything's Gone Wrong (CBS 3452) 1968
Women In The West/Hangover Blues (Bronze WIP 6113) 1971
Blue Movie Man/Abbott Of The Vale (Bronze WIP 6123) 1972
Sweet Ruby Ruby Nite Time/Mrs. Q (Bronze BRO 4) 1973
I Think I'm Getting Over You/
Paul McCartney (Bronze BRO 5) 1973

A gifted songwriter who penned songs for the likes of **Herman's Hermits, The Hollies** and **Manfred Mann**. However, his own efforts as a recording artist were less commercially successful. The recent *Go North* anthology showcases his own solo work. The first disc comprises his *Loudwater House* album supplemented by a number of previously unreleased tracks and the second does the same centred around his *Was That Alright Then?* album. It's a good listen - the songs are melodic and sometimes amusing too. **Hazzard** continues to write music from his Cornish home and more releases are planned for the future. *Fade Away Maureen* later resurfaced on *Pop-In, Vol 1* (CD) and *Spinning Wheel* (CD) and you'll also find *Goodnight Sweet Josephine* on *Pop-In, Vol 2* (CD). (VJ)

Murray Head

ALBUMS: 1 NIGEL LIVED (CBS 65503) 1973 SC
(up to 2 SAY IT AIN'T SO (Island ILPS 9347) 1975
1976)

NB: (2) reissued on CD (Island IMCD 83) 1990.

HCP
45s: Alberta/He Was A Friend Of Mine (Columbia DB 7635) 1965 -
(up to The Bells Of Rhymney/
1976) Don't Sing No Sad Songs For Me (Columbia DB 7771) 1965 -

HEAD MACHINE - Orgasm (LP).

Someday Soon/You Bore Me	(Columbia DB 8102) 1967 -	
She Was Perfection/		
Secondhand Monday	(Immediate IM 053) 1967 R1 -	
Superstar/John Nineteen Forty One (PS)	(MCA MK 5019) 1969 -	
Say It Ain't So Joe/Don't Have To	(Island WIP 6252) 1975 -	
Someone's Rocking My Dreamboat/		
She's Such A Drag	(Island WIP 6304) 1976 -	
Reissues: Superstar/	(MCA MMKS 5077) 1972 47	
Superstar/	(MCA MK 5084) 1972 -	

Head is a singer/actor, originally from Scotland, who first started recording as a Dylan-inspired folk singer in the mid-sixties. *He Was A Friend Of Mine* and *The Bells Of Rhymney* were both Dylan songs. He appeared on the 1970 *Jesus Christ Superstar* rock concept album and also played a lead role in the 1971 film, 'Sunday Bloody Sunday'. He enjoyed a measure of commercial success with *Superstar*, which was taken from the *Jesus Christ Superstar* album.

After a lull in his recording career, whilst he concentrated on acting, he returned in 1975 with *Say It Ain't So Joe*. He went on to enjoy greater commercial success in the eighties.

Compilation appearances have included: *She Was Perfection* on *Justafixation II* (LP), *Justafixation* (CD) and *Immediate Single Collection, Vol. 1* (CD); and *Secondhand Monday* on *Immediate Single Collection, Vol. 4* (CD). (VJ)

Tony Head

ALBUM: 1 HEADS TO WIN AND TALES TO TELL (THE
            TRAVELLER)   (CBS 64572) 1972

The ex-**Fleur de Lys** and **Chocolate Frog** lead singer recorded this album for CBS in 1971, some years after the demise of the **Fleur de Lys**. He wrote all of the material with Richard Hill. It is pleasant enough and certainly displays his vocal prowess but it is full of mainstream ballads and is probably only of interest to **Fleur de Lys** completists, although it is difficult to dislike it. (BS)

Head Machine

Personnel:	JOHN LEADHEN		
	(JOHN GLASSCOCK)	bs	A
	KEN LESLIE (KEN HENSLEY)	vcls, gtr, keyb'ds	A
	BRIAN POOLE (JOE KONAS)	gtr	A
	LEE POOLE (LEE KERSLAKE)	drms	A

ALBUM: 1(A) ORGASM   (Major Minor SMLP 79) 1970 R3
NB: (1) also issued in France on Vogue with a different cover.

This album is now a rare collectors' item, not least because it appears to have been recorded by **The Gods** under pseudonym. Musically it veers towards heavy rock with most tracks being pretty heavy with driving guitar work. The title cut and *Climax* are the pick of the bunch, whilst *Make The Feeling Last* and *The Girl Who Loved, The Girl Who Loved* are softer and subtler numbers. Lyrically (if it isn't obvious from the titles) the album basically deals with sex...

Overall, this is a good example of the heavier rock genre which was quite prevalent in the late sixties / early seventies. Two tracks, *I Can't Believe* and *You Tried to Take it All* were later re-recorded for **Toe Fat**'s debut album. **Ken Hensley** and **Lee Kerslake** later joined **Uriah Heep**. (VJ/MD)

Headstone

Personnel:	MARK ASHTON	vcls, gtr	AB
	STEVE BOLTON	lead and acoustic gtr	AB
	CHILLI CHARLES	drms	A
	PHILIP CHEN	bs, donkey blankets	A
	JOE O'DONNELL	elec & acoustic violins,	
		8-string violin, violectra	B
	JEROME RIMSON	bs	B
	PETER VAN HOOKE	drms, perc	B

ALBUMS:	1(A)	BAD HABITS	(ABC DSD 50174) 1974
	2(B)	HEADSTONE	(20th Century T-483) 1975

These albums will interest fans of **Rare Bird** given the involvement of **Mark Ashton**. Two other **Rare Bird** members (Dave Kaffinetti and Steve Goulde) guested on the first album, which included two tracks - *High On You* and *Live For Each Other* - also recorded by **Rare Bird**. Steve Bolton came from **Atomic Rooster**. They are often confused with the US band of the same name. Both albums were produced by John Anthony - the second included two further crossover tracks also recorded by **Rare Bird**, *Turn Your Head* and *Hard Road*. **Mark Ashton** recorded an eponymous solo album in 1976. (VJ/BM/CG)

Head West

Head West was a very obscure outfit. *Circus Days, Vol. 1* (LP) and *Circus Days Vol. 1 & 2* (CD) includes a track taken from an album released on the French Vogue label, called *Someday*. Although poorly recorded, the vocals have a haunting quality and the song, which dates from 1970, has a certain charm. (VJ)

Heads, Hands and Feet

Personnel:	TONY COLTON	vcls	AB
	PETE GAVIN	drms	AB
	CHAS HODGES	bs	AB
	ALBERT LEE	gtr	AB
	MIKE O'NEILL	keyb'ds	A
	RAY SMITH	gtr	AB

ALBUMS:	1(A)	HEADS, HANDS AND FEET	(Island ILPS 9149) 1971 SC
	2(B)	ON THE TRACKS	(Island ILPS 9185) 1972 SC
	3(B)	OLD SOLDIERS NEVER DIE	(Atlantic K 40465) 1973

NB: (1) reissued on CD (See For Miles SEECD 458). (2) reissued on CD as *Tracks* (See For Miles SEECD 459). Also of interest is *Home From Home (The Missing Album)* (See For Miles C5CD 633). This is a CD of previously unreleased recordings, made in 1968 before they signed to Capitol Records.

45s:	Warming Up The Band/Silver Mine	(Island WIP 6115) 1971
	One Woman/Dirty Heavy Weather Road	(Atlantic K 10292) 1973
	Just Another Ambush/	
	I Won't Let You Down	(Atlantic K 10312) 1973
Reissue:	Warming Up The Band/Silver Mine	(Island WIP 6319) 1976

Fomed in 1968, they initially started with a repertoire of folk, soul and R&B. Tony Colton and Ray Smith were an established song-writing team before joining the group. Albert Lee was a much admired guitarist, he was the guy that eric Clapton would go to listen to in his pre-**Yardbirds** days. However

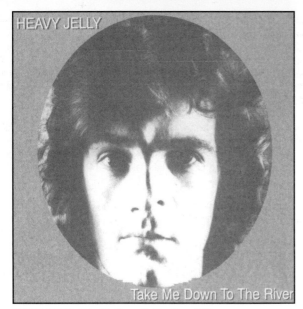

HEAVY JELLY - Take Me Down To The River (CD).

it took a couple of years for the band to gel with Colton, Gavin, Lee and Smith playing in **Poet And The One Man Band** around the same time. Upon the later's demise, they joined forces with Hodges and O'Neill to form **Heads, Hands and Feet** in 1970. Their debut album was issued as a double set in the US but as a single album here. It comprised a sort of country-influenced music which met with some critical acclaim. The follow-up, *On The Tracks*, made after Mike O'Neil had left, veered more towards rock than country but the group was by now plagued with interpersonal conflict and disintegrated before their final album was released.

Albert Lee later formed The Albert Lee Band, which included Gavin and Hodges. Hodges, incidentally, became half of the Chas and Dave duo and Albert Lee later played with **Eric Clapton**. He later moved to America where he became a sought-after country music session man and played for a number of years in The Emmylou Harris Hot Band. He returned to the UK in the eighties and has continued to play live.

Back in 1971, they could also be heard singing *Song For Suzie* on Island's *El Pea* (LP) compilation. (VJ/AH)

The (Purple) Hearts

Personnel:	JOE CUNNINGHAM	gtr	A
	JIMMY DUNCOMBE	vcls, gtr	A
	BARRY JEFFES	piano	A
	LAWRENCE "CURLY" SPECTOR	bs	A
	REGINALD "BUZZ" WASHINGTON	drms?	A

| 45: | Young Woman/Black Eyes | (Parlophone R 5147) 1964 SC |

Jimmy Duncombe was a Brit who moved to Germany in the early sixties in search of rock and roll stardom. By 1964 he was fronting a group called The Continentals, which soon relocated to England and signed a one-record deal with Parlophone. Someone at the label decided to re-name the band **The Purple Hearts**, although the name was banned (for the drug reference) and the record ended up being credited to just **Hearts**.

The 'A' side of their 45 was written by Gordon Mills, who also played harmonica on it and sang backing vocals. The 'B' side is a re-recording of an instrumental demo The Continentals had made earlier in the year. Shel Talmy produced both songs.

The single flopped, but later in 1964 a Continentals track, *My Soul*, made the charts in Germany. The group subsequently moved back to Germany and changed its name once again, this time to "Jimmy and The Rackets". They enjoyed moderate success on the Continent through the end of the decade, scoring numerous top-ten hits.

Duncombe is still active in the music business. (SS/VJ)

Heaven

| Personnel incl: | BRIAN KEMP | lead vcls |

A Portsmouth area band who played at The Isle of Wight festival and recorded for CBS, although no vinyl output resulted. Brian Kemp later played with Mark Andrews and The Gents. (DA)

Heavy Jelly

Personnel:	PETE BADFINGER	harmony	A
	TOM BADFINGER	harmony	A
	ALEX DMOCHOWSKI	bs	A
	BARRY JENKINS	drms	A
	MICHAEL KELLIE	drms	A
	BOBBY KEYS	tenor sax	A
	JACKIE LOMAX	vcls, gtr	A
	JOHN MOORHEAD	gtr	A
	JIM PRICE	trumpet, trombone	A

| ALBUM: | 1(A) | TAKE ME DOWN TO THE RIVER | (Psycho 30) 1984 |

NB: (1) is a reissue of a promo-only album issued in 1969 (Island HELP) (R3). Also reissued on CD.

45s:	I Keep Singing That Same Old Song/	
	Blue	(Island WIP 6049) 1968
	Time Out Chewn In/The Long Wait	(Head HDS 4001) 1969 SC

This name was originally used by **Skip Bifferty** who recorded one good rock 45, *I Keep Singing That Same Old Song*, for Island under this moniker after responding to an ad in 'Time Out'. At 7 minutes 49 seconds this was one of the longest singles ever made, yet it still made the Charts in some European countries. It's definitely recommended and if you can't find the 45 you'll also find it on the *Nice Enough To Eat* (LP) sampler or on *The Age Of Enlightenment - Prog Rock, Vol. One* (CD). The band used this name to avoid contractual problems, but quit when it was discovered that another band (line-up A, above) was using the same name. This blues-influenced outfit was put together by guitarist John Moorhead and, in addition, to the *Time Out* 45, recorded a promo-only album on Head Records, which is obviously extremely rare now. Psycho Records reissued this in 1984 although most of it is eminently forgettable.

Bobby Keys also played with **The Rolling Stones** and **Jackie Lomax** had previously been with **The Undertakers**. He also fronted **Lomax Alliance** and recorded for Apple in the late sixties.

I Keep Singing That Same Old Song has been compiled on *Jagged Time Lapse, Vol 2* (CD) and on the 3-CD box set *Ars Longa Vita Brevis: A Compendium Of Progressive Rock 1967-1974*. (VJ)

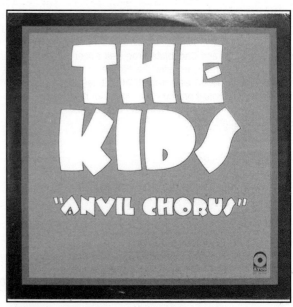

THE HEAVY METAL KIDS - Anvil Chorus (LP).

HEAVY METAL KIDS - Kitsch (LP).

The Heavy Metal Kids

Personnel:	KEITH BOYCE	drms	AB
	COSMO	gtr	A
	GARY HOLTON	vcls	AB
	DANNY PEYRONEL	keyb'ds	A
	RONNIE THOMAS	bs, vcls	AB
	BARRY PAUL	gtr	B
	JOHN SINCLAIR	keyb'ds	B

ALBUMS:	1(A)	HEAVY METAL KIDS	(Atlantic K 50047) 1974
(up to	2(A)	ANVIL CHORUS	(Atlantic K 50143) 1975
1976)			

NB: (2) credited to The Kids.

45s:	Rock And Roll Man/Hangin' On	(Atlantic K 10465) 1974
(up to	Ain't Nothing But A House Party/	
1976)	You Got Me Rollin'	(Atlantic K 10671) 1975
	She's No Angel/Hey Little Girl	(Rak RAK 234) 1976
	From Heaven To Hell And Back Again/	
	Boogie Woogie	(Rak RAK 239) 1976

Centred around former actor Gary Holton (who'd played Artful Dodger in 'Oliver' and appeared in 'Hair'), they came to public attention in 1974 conveying a strong Cockney and East End image. They were only ever a 'minor league' attraction but had a fanatical following. *Ain't Nothing But A House Party*, their second 45, was a cover of The Showstoppers' soul hit. On a US tour, they abbreviated their name to The Kids, but later reverted back to their original moniker. Mickie Most became their producer in December 1975 and they signed to the Rak label but were ripped apart by internal friction which resulted in Holton's departure in mid-1976. They managed a further 45 in 1977 and one further metal rock album, *Kitsch* (Rak SPAK 523).

Gary Holton later pursued an acting career, playing the streetwise Wayne in the TV series 'Auf Wiedersehen Pet' until he died of a drugs overdose during its filming. (VJ)

Dick Heckstall-Smith

ALBUM:	1 A STORY ENDED	(Bronze ILPS 9196) 1972 SC

NB: (1) reissued on CD (Sequel NEMCD 641) 1995.

Heckstall-Smith was born on 26 September 1934. He developed an appetite for music at school, where he played soprano saxophone, clarinet and led a traditional jazz band. When he finished school, he became a tenor saxophonist. Back in 1957 he fronted The Dick Heckstall-Smith Quintet, who recorded an EP, *Very Special Old Jazz* (Pye Jazz NJE 1057). He later played for **Graham Bond Organisation**, **John Mayall's**

Bluesbreakers and **Colosseum** and did session work prior to recording this album.

He co-wrote all six tracks, which are a mixture of progressive rock and jazz. Several well-known figures assisted him including former **Colosseum** members Jon Hiseman and Clem Clempson, **Graham Bond**, Gordon Beck, **Chris Spedding** and **Caleb Quaye** assisted him on the disc.

He made an album with **Duffy Power** in 1995, and sadly died early in 2005. (VJ)

Hector

Personnel incl:	PETE BROWN	gtr	A
	PHIL BROWN	vcls	A

45s:	Wired Up/Ain't Got Time	(DJM DJS 289) 1973
	Bye Bye Bad Days/Lady	(DJM DJS 303) 1974

This four-piece rock band didn't include "the" Pete and Phil Brown. (VJ)

Hedgehog Pie

Personnel:	MICHAEL DOONAN	flute	A
	JED GRIMES	gtr	A
	MARTIN JENKINS	violin, mandolin, vcls	A
	MARGI LUCKLEY	vcls	A
	STU LUCKLEY	bs, vcls	A

ALBUMS:	1(A)	HIS ROUND	(Rubber RUB 004) 1972 SC
(up to	2(A)	HEDGEHOG PIE	(Rubber RUB 009) 1975 R1
1976)	3(A)	GREEN LADY	(Rubber RUB 014) 1975 SC

NB: (2) reissued on CD (Rubber RUB 009).

EP:	1(A)	WONDERFUL WORLD OF LAMPTON	
(up to			(Rubber TUB 12) 197? SC
1976)			

45:	Well I Know/Go With The Flow	(Rubber ADU 88) 1976
(up to		
1976)		

A Geordie folk-rock band whose albums were produced by Rick Kemp of **Steeleye Span** and released on the small independent Newcastle-upon-Tyne-based Rubber label. Martin Jenkins had previously been with **Dando Shaft**. Their albums are now quite rare and conjure up a fresh and vibrant interpretation of the genre. They continued to play throughout the decade. (VJ)

Hedgehoppers Anonymous

Personnel:	LESLIE DASH	drms	A
	RAY HONEYBALL	bs	A
	ALAN LADD	gtr	ABC
	JOHN STEWART	ld gtr	ABC
	MICK TINSLEY	vcls	ABC
	KEITH JACKSON	bs	BC
	GLEN MARTIN	drms	BC
	TOM FOX	bs	C

			HCP
45s:	It's Good News Week/Afraid Of Love	(Decca F 12241) 1965	5
	Don't Push Me/		
	Please Don't Hurt Your Heart For Me	(Decca F 12298) 1965	-
	Baby (You're My Everything)/Remember	(Decca F 12400) 1966	-
	Daytime/That's The Time	(Decca F 12479) 1966	-
	Stop Press/Little Memories	(Decca F 12530) 1966	-
Reissue:	It's Good News Week/		
	Afraid Of Love (PS)	(EMI EMI 5271) 1982	-

This band formed in 1963 as The Trendsetters whilst all five were in the RAF at Leighton Buzzard. After a few months they changed name to The Hedgehoppers and when **Jonathan King** became their manager in 1965, he suggested a further name change to **Hedgehoppers Anonymous**. Written by **King**, their first 45 was a classic (and rather tongue-in-cheek) protest song. It also rests in the annals of one-hit wonders because the band was never able to equal this feat again and had disbanded by the end of 1966. Line-up (B) dates from December 1965.

It's Good News Week has inevitably featured on a number of hits compilations including Decca's *The World Of Hits, Vol. 2* (LP) back in 1969. It also includes **Jimmy Page** as a session guitarist. You can also find *Don't Push Me* on *Rare 60's Beat Treasures, Vol. 4* (CD). (VJ)

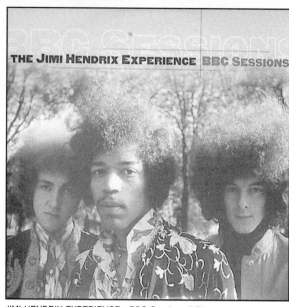
JIMI HENDRIX EXPERIENCE - BBC Sessions (LP)

Heinz

| ALBUMS: | 1 | TRIBUTE TO EDDIE | (Decca LK 4599) 1964 R2 |
| | 2 | REMEMBERING | (Decca REM 7) 1977 |

NB: (1) reissued on CD (Rollercoaster RCCD 3008) 1993, with some of his 45s included too and again on CD (Castle Communications CLC 5117) 1993. *Dreams Do Come True: The 45s Collection* (Castle CLC 5134-2) 1994 is a CD compilation of his Decca 45s and non-45 tracks from his two Decca EPs. *And The Wild Boys* (Rock Machine MACH 8) 1986 is an alternative compilation. *Heinz Burt - The Complete Heinz* (Rock In A Box RIB CD 027) 199? Is a Hungarian compilation. *Just Like Eddie/The Original Joe Meek* (Hallmark 300302) 1995 is a UK release and there's a 2-CD set *The Complete Heinz* (Repertoire REP 4718-WR) 1999.

| EPs: | 1 | HEINZ | (Decca DFE 8545) 1963 R1 |
| | 2 | LIVE IT UP | (Decca DFE 8559) 1963 R1 |

			HCP
45s:	Dreams Do Come True/		
	Been Invited To A Party	(Decca F 11652) 1963 SC -	
	Just Like Eddie/		
	Don't You Knock At My Door	(Decca F 11693) 1963 5	
	Country Boy/Long Tall Jack	(Decca F 11768) 1963 26	
	You Were There/		
	No Matter What They Say	(Decca F 11831) 1964 SC 26	
	Please Little Girl/		
	For Loving Me This Way	(Decca F 11920) 1964 SC -	
	Questions I Can't Answer/		
	The Beating Of My Heart	(Columbia DB 7374) 1964 SC 39	
α	Diggin' My Potatoes/		
	She Ain't Comin' Back	(Columbia DB 7482) 1965 R1 49	
	Don't Think Twice It's Alright/		
	Big Fat Spider	(Columbia DB 7559) 1965 SC -	
	End Of The World/		
	You Make Me Feel So Good	(Columbia DB 7656) 1965 R1 -	
	Heart Full Of Sorrow/		
	Don't Worry Baby	(Columbia DB 7779) 1965 R1 -	
	Movin' In/I'm Not A Bad Guy	(Columbia DB 7942) 1966 R1 -	
Reissues:	Just Like Eddie/		
	Don't Knock At My Door	(Decca F 13762) 1978 -	
	Just Like Eddie	(Old Gold OG 9353) 1983 -	

NB: α as Heinz and The Wild Boys.

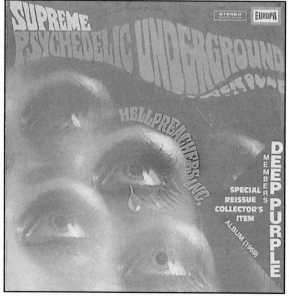
HELL PREACHERS INC. - Supreme Psychedelic Underground (LP).

Probably best remembered for his striking hair which he'd once dyed blond for a bet, Heinz Burt, which was his real name, first appeared in The Outlaws (1960/61) and had a two year stint in The Tornados (1961-63) (of *Telstar* fame) before rejoining The Outlaws briefly in early 1963 when mad genius Joe Meek wanted The Outlaws to be his in-house backing band. In the event, The Outlaws backed him on his early discs while a new outfit, The Saints (Tab Martin (bs), Roy Phillips (gtr) and Ricky Winters (drms)) was put together by Meek to support the singer, on a series of package and variety shows. **Heinz** didn't have a great voice but Meek found him some good material and he achieved three Top 30 hits, most notably with the Eddie Cochran tribute *Just Like Eddie*. The 45s were notable for Meek's good production and The Outlaws' backing.

In April 1964, he moved to EMI Columbia with a new backing band, The Wild Boys (Burr Bailey (organ), future **Deep Purple** member **Ritchie Blackmore** (gtr), Ian Broad (drms) and Brian Woods (bs)). They achieved a couple more minor hits but by the end of the year, The Wild Boys were no more. After a few more solo singles, **Heinz** descended into cabaret work.

And The Wild Boys is a worthwhile collection of his material. In fact, the composition and performances aren't all that strong; it's often Barry Tomlinson's excellent guitar work which catches the ear. His last hit, *Diggin' My Potatoes*, is included. It's notable also for the inclusion of **Jimmy Page** as a session guitarist (who also coincidentally plays on *Just Like Eddie*).

Heinz also figures on Decca's now rare 1964 *At The Cavern* (LP) compilation (which has been reissued by See For Miles) singing *Somebody To Love* and Ray Charles' *I Got A Woman*. He can also be heard on Decca's 1964 *Ready, Steady, Go!* (LP) collection singing *Just Like Eddie* and *Country Boy*. *Just Like Eddie* can also be heard on *Thank Your Lucky Stars, Vol. 2* (LP), *20 Hits Of The 60's* (CD), *Hits Of The 60's - Save The Last Dance* (CD), *Cruisin' Classics* (CD), *Dizzy* (CD) and on *Hits Of The Sixties - 20 Swinging Sounds* (CD). Other compilation appearances have included: *I Got A Woman* and *Somebody To Love* on *Original Liverpool Sound* (LP); *Big Fat Spider, I'm Not A Bad Guy* and *Movin' In* on *Ritchie Blackmore - Rock Profile, Vol. 1* (CD); *I Get Up In The Morning* on *Ritchie Blackmore - Take It!- Sessions 63 - 68* (CD); *Country Boy* on *Sixties Lost And Found, Vol. 3* (LP); *Movin' In* on *Beat Us If You Can! Vol. 1* (LP) and *Oddities, Vol 2* (CD); and *Questions I Can't Answer* and *The Beating Of My Heart* on *Freddie And The Dreamers - I'm Telling You Now* (LP). (VJ/KL)

The Hellions

Personnel incl:	JIM CAPALDI	drms	A
	LUTHER GROSVENOR	gtr	A
	DAVE MASON	gtr, vcls	A
	POLI PALMER	keyb'ds	A
	GORDON JACKSON	gtr	A
	DAVE MEREDITH	bs	A

45s:	Daydreaming Of You/		
	Shades Of Blue	(Piccadilly 7N 35213) 1964 SC	

Tomorrow Never Comes/		
Dream Child	(Piccadilly 7N 35232) 1965 SC
A Little Lovin'/Think It Over	(Piccadilly 7N 35265) 1965 SC

This Worcestershire group had some pedigree for it included in its ranks future **Traffic** members **Jim Capaldi** and **Dave Mason**, **Luther Grosvenor**, who later played with **Spooky Tooth**, and Poli Palmer, who turned up in **Bakerloo Blues Line** and then **Family** a few years later. They also released a fourth 45 as **Revolution**.

A Little Lovin' was a **Fourmost** track.

Compilation appearances have included: *Tomorrow Never Comes* on *Quick Before They Catch Us* (LP & CD) and *Ripples, Vol. 1* (CD); *Shades Of Blue* on *Rare 60's Beat Treasures, Vol. 5* (CD); *Daydreaming Of You* on *Ripples, Vol. 6* (CD) and *Brum Beat - Midlands Beat Groups Of The 60's* (CD); *Dream Child* on *Visions Of The Past, Vol. 3* (LP & CD); and *Think It Over* on *Beat Merchants* (CD). (VJ/JM)

Hello

Personnel:	JEFF ALLEN	drms	A
	BOB BRADBURY	gtr, vcls	A
	VIC FAULKNER	bs	A
	KEITH MARSHALL	gtr, vcls	A

ALBUM: 1(A) KEEP US OFF THE STREETS   (Bell BELLS 263) 1975

NB: There's a compilation which is also on CD, *The Glam Years 1971-79* (Biff BIFF 1 CD) 1988. A second CD compilation appeared in the nineties *The Early Years* (Dojo EARL D 17) 1993, *Best Of And Rarities* (Repertoire REP 4801 WG) 1999 and *The Glam Rock Singles Collection* (Cherry Red GLAM CD 5) followed in 2001.

			HCP
45s:	You Move Me/Ask Your Mama	(Bell BLL 1238) 1972 SC	-
(up to	C'mon/The Wench	(Bell BLL 1265) 1972	-
1976)	Another Schoolday/		
	C'mon Get Together (PS)	(Bell BLL 1332) 1973	-
	Tell Him/Lightning	(Bell BLL 1377) 1974	6
	Games Up/Do It All Night	(Bell BLL 1406) 1975	-
	Bend Me, Shape Me/We Gotta Go	(Bell BLL 1424) 1975	-
	New York Groove/Little Miss Mystery	(Bell BLL 1438) 1975	9
	Star Studded Sham/Jenny Dream	(Bell BLL 1470) 1976	-
	Teenage Revolution/		
	Keep Us Off The Streets	(Bell BLL 1479) 1976	-
	Love Stealer/Out Of Our Heads	(Bell BLL 1482) 1976	-
Reissue:	New York Groove/Tell Him	(Old Gold OG 9463) 1985	-

An unsophisticated glam-rock outfit from the North of England. Very uninteresting - they got into the Top 10 with a cover version of The Exciters/Billie Davis' *Tell Him*, but this was followed by two flops:- *Games Up*, a **Glitter Band** composition, and **Amen Corner**'s *Bend Me, Shape Me*. They made the Top 10 again with Russ Ballard's *New York Groove* but after switching to Arista for a couple of 45s, split in the late seventies.

Their album was a collection of poor cover versions and earlier 45s. They are one of those bands best forgotten. *Best Of And Rarities* includes their hits and other singles that 'might have been' and six previously unreleased tracks.

After their demise Keith Marshall embarked on a solo career and enjoyed a hit with *Only Crying* in 1981. (VJ)

Hell Preachers Inc.

ALBUM: 1 SUPREME PSYCHEDELIC UNDERGROUND
                        (Marble Arch MALS 1169) 1968 SC

NB: (1) counterfeited in the late 80s and later reissued officially in its original sleeve. It was also issued in Germany on the budget Europa label with a different cover.

It was rumoured that this budget album was made by **Ritchie Blackmore** (gtr), **Jon Lord** (keyb'ds) and Ian Paice (drms) in their pre-**Deep Purple** days, but all three have persistently denied this. The predominantly instrumental album does feature some good discordant guitar work, notably

JIMI HENDRIX - Live On The Killin' Floor (LP).

on *Spy In Space*, but it's best moment is probably the Bo Diddley derivative *Turn Turn*.

Hell Preachers Inc. can also be found on *Incredible Sound Show Stories, Vol. 2* (LP). (VJ)

Help Yourself

Personnel:	DAVE CHARLES	drms, vcls	ABC
	MALCOLM MORLEY	gtr, vcls	ABC
	RICHARD TREECE	gtr, vcls	ABC
	KEN WHALEY	bs	A C
	PAUL BURTON	bs, gtr	BC
	(JO JO GLEMSER	gtr	B)
	(ERNIE GRAHAM	gtr	B)

ALBUMS:	1(A)	HELP YOURSELF	(Liberty LBS 83484) 1971 SC
	2(B)	STRANGE AFFAIR	(United Artists UAS 29287) 1972 SC
	3(B)	BEWARE OF THE SHADOW	
			(United Artists UAS 29413) 1972 SC
	4(C)	RETURN OF KEN WHALEY	
			(United Artists UAS 29487) 1973
	5(C)	HAPPY DAYS	(United Artists UA FREE 1) 1973
	6(C)	RETURN OF KEN WHALEY/HAPPY DAYS	
		(2-LP box set)	(United Artists UDG 4001) 1973

NB: (1) Reissued on Beat Goes On (BGOLP 52) 1990. (1) and (3) reissued on one CD (Beat Goes On BGOCD) 1998. (4) and (5) available separately and as a double album, (6). 5 (CD) was to have been their fifth album, but the sessions were never completed and the album was never released.

45s:	Running Down Deep/Paper Leaves	(Liberty LBF 15459) 1971
	Heaven Row/Brown Lady	(United Artists UP 35355) 1972
	Mommy Won't Be Home For Christmas/	
	Johnny B. Goode	(United Artists UP 35466) 1972

A progressive outfit, formed in 1969 and who also have one track, *Street Songs*, on the *All Good Clean Fun* (LP) compilation and two live tracks, *Eddie Waring* and *Mona*, on *Christmas At The Patti* (2x10").

Their first album is rather mainstream progressive rock meets pub-rock, despite some excellent songs written by Malcolm Morley including the excellent *Deborah*. Most of the musicianship on the album is raw and derivative (with exception of Richard Treece's guitar) and consequently the punters weren't at all interested. After its release, Whaley departed for **Ducks Deluxe** and was replaced by Paul Burton.

Strange Affair exhibited a strong US West Coast influence with greater musical improvisation and some fine moments like *American Woman*. *Beware Of The Shadow* continued in much the same vein. Listen out for their magnum opus, *Reaffirmation*, on this one.

JIMI HENDRIX EXPERIENCE - Are You Experienced? (LP).

Ken Whaley rejoined the band in 1973, hence the title of their final album. *5*, which was to have been their fifth album but was never released at the time because the sessions were never completed, finally saw the light of day on a CD release. The cover features a Rick Griffin illustration and the set comes with a booklet including liner notes from Malcolm Morley and Phil McMullen of 'Ptolemaic Terrascope'.

After their demise, Malcolm Morley had a spell with **Man** (and Ken Whaley later joined him there). The rest of the band joined **Deke Leonard**'s Iceberg, and Treece was later in The Flying Aces. (VJ/MW/DR)

Hemlock

Personnel:
MILLER ANDERSON	gtr, vcls	A
ERIC DILLON	drms	A
PETER DINES	keyb'ds, gtr, vcls	A
JIM LEVERTON	bs, vcls	A
CHRIS MERCER	sax	A
BLUE WEAVER	keyb'ds, perc	A
PETE WILLSHER	steel gtr	A

ALBUM: 1(A) HEMLOCK (Deram SML 1102) 1973 R2

45: Mr. Horizontal/Beggar Man (Deram DM 379) 1973

The band's best known member was **Miller Anderson** who, apart from recording a solo album back in 1971, was also in **The Voice**, **At Last The 1958 Rock'n'Roll Show**, **Keef Hartley Band** and **Dog Soldier**. He now lives in Shoreham-By-Sea. More or less a vehicle for **Anderson**'s songwriting output (he wrote all the album's material), **Hemlock** sounds by no means artificial or put together. Rather, they were a typical British blues act, without the requisite posing. Naturally, the atmosphere is very serious and dominated by Weaver's passionate organ-playing. In fact, all the conditions for a good album would have been met, if **Anderson**'s bluesy songs had simply been a little more diverse. Some like *Mr. Horizontal* have intelligent lyrics, but none are musically very convincing. Good craftsmanship, little art. A case of more perspiration than inspiration.

Mr. Horizontal has been compiled on *Progressive Pop Inside The Seventies* (CD). (MK/VJ)

Brian Henderson

45: Folk's In A Hurry/
What Kind Of Woman (Columbia DB 8006) 1966

This was a folk/beat pairing produced by **Mark Wirtz**. The flip side is pleasant listening. A Scot from Edinburgh, **Henderson** had been in **Mark Five** and later played bass for **Nirvana**. (MWh)

(The) Jimi Hendrix (Experience)

Personnel:
JIMI HENDRIX	vcls, gtr	ABC
MITCH MITCHELL	drms	A C
NOEL REDDING	bs, vcls	A
BILLY COX	bs	BC
BUDDY MILES	drms	B

				HCP
ALBUMS: 1(A)	ARE YOU EXPERIENCED?	(Track 613 001) 1967	R1 2
(up to 2(A)	AXIS: BOLD AS LOVE	(Track 613 003) 1967	R1 5
1976) 3(A)	ELECTRIC LADYLAND (2-LP)		
		(Track 613 008/9) 1968	R2 6
4(A)	SMASH HITS (Compilation)	(Track 613 004) 1968	SC 4
5(B)	BAND OF GYPSIES	(Track 2406 002) 1970	SC 6
6(C)	CRY OF LOVE	(Polydor 2302 023) 1970	2
7( )	MONTEREY-OTIS REDDING AND THE		
	JIMI HENDRIX EXPERIENCE	(Reprise K 40430) 1970	-
8(C)	RAINBOW BRIDGE	(Reprise K 44159) 1971	16
9(-)	LIVE AT THE ISLE OF WIGHT		
		(Polydor 2302 016) 1971	17
10( )	HENDRIX IN THE WEST	(Polydor 2302 018) 1972	7
11( )	WAR HEROES	(Polydor 2302 020) 1973	23
12( )	JIMI HENDRIX (Compilation)	(Reprise K 64017) 1973	-
13( )	LOOSE ENDS	(Polydor 2310 301) 1974	-
14( )	CRASH LANDING	(Polydor 2310 398) 1975	35
15( )	JIMI HENDRIX (Compilation)	(Polydor 2343 080) 1975	35
16( )	JIMI HENDRIX (2-LP Compilation)		
		(Polydor 2343 086) 1975	-
17( )	MIDNIGHT LIGHTNING	(Polydor 2310 415) 1976	46

NB: Not included in the above discography are loads of records that suddenly appeared after he became successful containing material he'd recorded in the States prior to his discovery by Chas Chandler e.g. various albums supporting Curtiss Knight. Anyone thinking of buying them should remember they won't capture **Hendrix** the star but **Hendrix** the apprentice. Some copies of (1) came in a laminated sleeve - these are R3. (1) reissued at budget price in mono as *Backtrack 10* (Track 2407 010) 1970 (SC). (2) was issued in mono and stereo and some copies came with a gatefold insert, mono ones would be R3 and stereo ones R2. (2) reissued at budget price in mono as *Backtrack 11* (Track 2407 011) 1970 (SC). Some test pressings of (3) exist in a plain white, non-gatefold sleeve. This is the only mono pressing of the album and valued at £1,000 by 'Record Collector' in its December 2004 issue. (3) was also issued in stereo as two single albums: *Electric Ladyland Part 1* (Track 613 010) 1968 and *Electric Ladyland Part 2* (Track 613 017) 1968. (3) reissued again on vinyl as a 2-LP (Polydor 2657 012) 1973 and as two single albums: *Electric Ladyland Part 1* (Polydor 2310 271) 1973 and *Electric Ladyland Part 2* (Polydor 2310 272) 1973. (3) reissued again on vinyl as a 2-LP set (Polydor SPDLP 3) 1984. (4) was also issued in mono and stereo and mono releases are more collectable (R1). (4) reissued on vinyl (Polydor 2302 268) 1973 in stereo only. Original puppet sleeve pressings of (5) would be R2. There was a repressing in an Isle of Wight gatefold sleeve and a second repressing in a single sleeve. (5) reissued on vinyl (Polydor 2480 005) 1973 in a different gatefold sleeve. (5) reissued on vinyl (Classic/Capitol ST 472) 1997. Three factory custom, red vinyl pressings of (6) were produced in the 1970s and 'Record Collector' values them at circa £1,500 in its December 2004 edition. There was also a mail-order only Record Club release *Electric Jimi Hendrix* (Track 2856 002) 1971 (R6). What has appeared

JIMI HENDRIX EXPERIENCE - Axis: Bold As Love (LP).

JIMI HENDRIX EXPERIENCE - Electric Ladyland (2-LP).

above is only a selection, not a comprehensive list of the many releases of his material. CD reissues are not shown.

Friends From The Beginning (Ember EMBCD 3434) 1998 credited to **Jimi Hendrix** and Little Richard is misleading because the evidence now suggest (contrary to what was thought when the album was first released back in 1975) that **Hendrix** did not appear on this Little Richard album at all. *Original Soundtrack To The Motion Picture 'Experience'* (Charly CDGR 246) 1998 reissues what turned out to be his last UK show at The Royal Albert Hall on 24 February 1969 and unfortunately it captures him in self-indulgent mood. *Live & Unreleased The Radio Show* (Castle Communications LP HBLP100/CD HBCD 100) contains a lot of material from the proposed *First Rays Of The Rising Sun* album. Later the **Jimi Hendrix** estate put out what they claim to be the official authorised version of his unfinished recordings on two releases: *First Rays Of The Rising Sun* (MCA/C/D 11599) 199? and *South Saturn Delta* (MCA/C/D 11684) 199? *Live In Ottawa* (Dagger 088 112 737 2) 2002 captures a performance in March 1968 and *The Summer Of Love Sessions* (Jungle FREUD CD 067) 2002 is another new release of his material. *Live At Clark University* (Dagger DBRD 12033) 2002 is a previously unbootlegged portion of their second show at Clark University, Worcester, Massachusetts on 15 March 1968. *Live At Berkeley* (MCA/Experience Hendrix 9860752) 2003 is a release of his much bootlegged second show in Berkeley, California on 30 May 1970. *Drivin' South* (Jungle FREUD CD 065) 2000 showcases some tapes from 1965. *Axis Outtakes* (Purple Haze Records HAZE 002) 2003 is a mid-price 2-CD collection of alternate takes, unreleased songs and other bit and pieces. *Live At Woodstock* (Classic RTH 2014-140) 2005 is a vinyl box set version of the CD released in 2002. *Studio Out-Takes Volume 2 (1969)* (Radioactive RRLP 046) 2005 and *Studio Out-Takes Volume 3 (1969-1970)* (Radioactive RRLP 047) 2005 are both vinyl limited pressings of 3,000 and contain alternative versions of his songs, instrumental backing tracks and other oddities - these are for serious **Hendrix** fans only. *Hendrix* (Classics ST 472) 2005 is a vinyl 200gm 35th Anniversary edition of a recording from two nights he played at the Fillmore East, New York, when he was assisted by **Buddy Miles** and **Billy Cox**. *Winterland Night* (Purple Haze HAZE 008) 2005 is a collection compiled from six shows at San Francisco's Winterland Ballroom in October 1968.

			HCP
45s:	Hey Joe/Stone Free	(Polydor 56139) 1966	6
(up to	Purple Haze/51st Anniversary	(Track 604 001) 1967	3
1976)	The Wind Cries Mary/Highway Chile	(Track 604 004) 1967	6
	Burning Of The Midnight Lamp/The Stars That		
	Play With Laughing Sam's Dice	(Track 604 007) 1967	18
	All Along The Watchtower/		
	Long Hot Summer Night	(Track 604 025) 1968	5
	Crosstown Traffic/Gypsy Eyes	(Track 604 029) 1969	37
	Let Me Light Your Fire/Burning Of The		
	Midnight Lamp	(Track 604 033) 1969	-
	Voodoo Chile//Hey Joe/		
	All Along The Watchtower (Some P/S)	(Track 2095 001) 1970	1
	Angel/Night Bird Flying	(Track 2094 007) 1970	-
	Johnny B. Goode/Little Wing	(Polydor 2001 277) 1972	35
	Hear My Train A-Comin'/		
	Rock Me Baby	(Reprise K 14286) 1973	-
Reissues:	Angel/Night Bird Flying	(Track 2094 007) 1971	-
	Gypsy Eyes/Remember/		
	Purple Haze/Stone Free	(Track 2094 010) 1971	35
	Voodoo Chile/Hey Joe/		
	All Along The Watchtower (PS)	(Track 2095 001) 1978	-

All Along The Watchtower/		
Long Hot Summer Night	(Polydor 214 1279) 1980	-
All Along The Watchtower/Foxy Lady/Purple Haze/		
Manic Depression	(Polydor POSPX 401) 1981	-
Voodoo Chile/Gypsy Eyes/Hey Joe/		
Third Stone From The Sun	(Polydor POSP 608) 1983	-
Fire/Are You Experienced? (PS)	(CBS CBS A 2749) 1982	-
Hey Joe/Stone Free	(Old Gold OG 9429) 1984	-
Purple Haze/The Wind Cries Mary	(Old Gold OG 9430) 1984	-
Voodoo Chile/		
The Burning Of The Midnight Lamp	(Old Gold OG 9431) 1984	-
All Along The Watchtower/Foxy Lady	(Old Gold OG 9432) 1984	-

NB: Some time in the early seventies 'Rolling Stone' (the American magazine) had a special issue with a **Jimi Hendrix** flexi disc. It featured the previously released studio versions of *Red House* and *Spanish Castle Magic*.

The greatest rock guitarist of all time? This is certainly many people's view. Raised in Seattle, Washington, **Hendrix** found fame in England, hence his inclusion in this book. Born on the 27th November 1942, he left school early to join the army but was discharged after receiving a broken ankle and injured back and resolved to make a career in music. With a highly unusual style, owing to being left-handed and playing a right-handed guitar upside down (re-strung for left-handed playing), he toured the Southern States playing dives. His break came when the Isley Brothers heard him playing one night and offered him a place in their band. He made a few recordings with them, but did not stay for long.

Eventually, having toured with Little Richard and played on the West Coast with Ike and Tina Turner, he ended up fronting a group in New York's Greenwich Village, Jimmy James and the Blue Flames. Ex-**Animal** Chas Chandler discovered him playing at the Café Wha? one night and promptly brought him to London in September 1966. His dazzling musicianship almost immediately earned him an immense reputation, as well as the admiration and envy of players like **Eric Clapton**, **Peter Green**, **Jeff Beck** and **Pete Townshend**. Acting as manager, Chandler quickly put The Experience together. Drummer Mitch Mitchell had previously played with **Chris Sandford**'s backing group **The Riot Squad** and **Georgie Fame's Blue Flames**, and bassist **Noel Redding** had played with various little known groups before auditioning for The Experience.

1967 was quite a year for **Hendrix**. The Experience played their first gig at the Paris Olympia and, having been rejected by Decca, signed to Polydor. Their debut single, *Hey Joe*, hit the charts in January. Though it was one of the most recorded songs of the era, **Hendrix** completely reworked it, propelling it to no. 6 in the UK charts. Boosted by TV appearances on 'Ready Steady Go' and 'Top Of The Pops' and featuring brilliant psychedelic guitar work, his next single, *Purple Haze*, reached No. 3 in March. At the end of the month he embarked on a bizarrely incongruous national tour with the Walker Brothers, Engelbert Humperdinck and others, becoming a fixture in the music press. The slower, softer *The Wind Cries Mary* climbed to No. 6 in May, when his excellent, self-composed debut album *Are You Experienced?* also appeared. This was one of the strongest albums of the period; almost every track was a classic. Short, tight songs

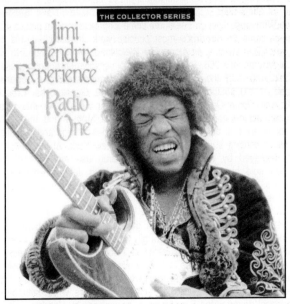

JIMI HENDRIX EXPERIENCE - Radio One (CD).

JIMI HENDRIX EXPERIENCE - Electric Ladyland Pt 1 (LP).

like *Remember*, *Foxy Lady* and *Can You See Me?* were mixed with the looser psychedelic haze of *May This Be Love*, *Third Stone From The Sun* and the outstanding title track, and the album climbed to No. 2, spending an impressive 33 weeks in the Charts.

In June **Hendrix** was included on the bill for the legendary Monterey Festival at **Paul McCartney**'s suggestion. Alongside Janis Joplin, he was the discovery of the festival. His mind-blowing act had all the sexuality of Joplin's and his guitar work was masterful. He was also a superb showman, playing the guitar behind his back and with his teeth, and even setting light to it at one stage. His performance is partly captured in the film 'Monterey Pop'. In July he embarked on a US tour with the Monkees, which he left early; at the time it was claimed he'd been thrown off it for his suggestive performances, but Chandler later admitted that this was a fabrication designed to stir up controversy. In August *The Burning Of The Midnight Lamp* reached number 18 in the UK, and much of the remainder of the year was spent recording his second album, *Axis: Bold As Love*, which appeared on December 1st. Another fine effort, it contained a mixture of the powerful psychedelic blues that had become the **Hendrix** trademark (*Up From The Skies*, *You've Got Me Floating* and *Bold As Love*) alongside slower, laid-back numbers like *Little Wing* and *Castles Made Of Sand*. Another track, *If Six Was Nine*, was featured in the soundtrack to 'Easy Rider'.

By 1968 he'd become a rock superstar, and was starting to show signs of strain. In January he was arrested in Sweden after smashing up his hotel room, and his relationship with **Noel Redding** became tempestuous. **Hendrix** began to spend more time in New York, where work began in April on his double album, *Electric Ladyland*, which appeared in October. More extravagant and self-indulgent than its predecessors, it featured a galaxy of guest stars including Al Kooper, Jack Casady, **Dave Mason** and **Stevie Winwood**. Though it features some long experimental pieces, it also captures some of **Hendrix**'s most concise work. In particular, his cover version of Bob Dylan's *All Along The Watchtower*, which climbed to No. 5 in the Autumn of 1968, is masterful. Two versions of *Voodoo Chile* are included, one short, the other extended. The former would give **Hendrix** his only No. 1 hit, posthumously. Other tracks like *Gypsy Eyes*, *Crosstown Traffic* and *Come On* typified his superb guitar work. Later that year he produced albums for **Eire Apparent** and Cat Mother and the All-Night Newsboys, as well as playing a punishing series of gigs and establishing his own recording studio, Electric Lady, in New York. At the end of the year, dismayed by **Hendrix**'s increasing drug use and loss of focus, Chandler sold his management interest to Mike Jeffery, whose role in **Hendrix**'s business affairs became the subject of fierce controversy in subsequent years.

1969 saw **Hendrix**'s downward turn gain momentum. Live performances became fewer, though one excellent gig was taped at the Royal Albert Hall in February. In May he was arrested at Toronto Airport for possession of heroin and, though he was subsequently acquitted, his drug use was increasing. In June, following abortive sessions in London's Olympic Studios, **Noel Redding** (who'd formed **Fat Mattress** whilst still with The Experience) departed the Experience, to be replaced by **Hendrix**'s old army

buddy Billy Cox. **Hendrix**, **Mitchell** and **Cox** spent much of the summer gigging and played a legendary set at the Woodstock Festival on August 14th. Though **Hendrix** is thought to have been tripping on especially potent LSD at the time, his ragged version of *Star Spangled Banner* came to symbolise the festival for many. At the end of the year, however, Mitchell also departed and, in response to considerable political pressure, **Hendrix** recruited drummer Billy Cox to create an all-black outfit he dubbed The Band Of Gypsies. This line-up recorded a live album at New York's Fillmore East on New Year's Eve, featuring an electrifying performance of *Machine Gun*. Ed Chalpin, manager of his former bandleader Curtis Knight, also recorded the best material from various New York shows for an album to be called *Get That Feeling*, but **Hendrix** claimed he didn't even know he was being recorded. Capitol agreed to pull the album only if **Hendrix** gave them another in its place, which transpired to be *Band Of Gypsies*. It features a lot of wah-wah pedal, but the material is mostly instrumental rock-funk jams and nothing special.

Hendrix was dissatisfied with the outfit and walked out in the middle of their second gig in Madison Square Gardens on January 28th 1970, reverting to Mitchell and Cox when work began on his final official release, *Cry Of Love*. Since returning to New York, **Hendrix**'s private life had become increasingly disorientated and his use of drugs ever more frequent. Having been subjected to increasing police harassment, he began to spend more time in London, where he contributed to album sessions by Stephen Stills and Love in March. In April he began the 'Cry of Love' tour, backed by Mitchell and Cox, and showcased a more radical musical style than before, which many fans found hard to take. For the remaining months of his life he tended to work in the week and gig at weekends. The quality of his gigs (much bootlegged) was variable, and his last live appearance in the UK (at the Isle Of Wight Festival in August) is generally considered disappointing. His final live performance was at the Fehmarn Festival in Germany on September 6th, where the atmosphere was ugly. After the show Cox returned to the States, but **Hendrix** remained in the UK, where he was found dead in his London apartment on the 18th September. An open verdict was returned, but the cause of death (inhalation of vomit due to barbiturate poisoning) was something of an indictment.

Hendrix's authorised recordings are essential to any proper understanding of the music covered in this book. Tragically, much of his early material and many unofficial live recordings which were not up to the standard of his authorised work, have also flooded the market since his death, mirroring the turmoil of his estate. **Hendrix** had loads of material "in the can" most of it was not finally mixed and some of it was not completely finished. He was supposed to have been working on a proposed double album to be called *First Rays Of The New Rising Sun*. The record company wanted product whilst he was still popular and put out *Cry Of Love*. Next came the live albums *Monterey*, *Rainbow Bridge*, *Isle Of Wight* and probably the best of the lot *Live In The West*. His version of Chuck Berry's *Johnny B. Goode* on the latter must rate as one of his all-time classic cuts. Then came three further albums, which revisited the vaults to dig out this legacy of unfinished recordings: *War Heroes*, *Loose Ends* and *Crash Landing*.

The Peel Session collection is way above the quality of most bootlegs of his material, and includes his earliest recording of *Hear My Train A Comin'*.

JIMI HENDRIX - Cry Of Love (CD).

JIMI HENDRIX - Loose Ends (CD).

The *Radio One* sessions were budget-priced album and CD issues containing 17 tracks from **Hendrix**'s various sessions. These capture him on top form and are absolutely vital purchases. *Calling Long Distance* was only available to subscribers of 'Univibes' magazine, but came with a superb 16-page booklet full of photos and information and will be of interest to **Hendrix** fans. *Live & Unreleased The Radio Show* contains a lot of interesting interviews with Mike Jeffries and **Noel Redding**. The music is good too, although sometimes spoilt by the announcer talking over tracks. The *Summer Of Love Sessions* were recorded in New York over four separate nights by his former bandleader Curtis Knight's manager Ed Chaplin.

Live At Clark University was recorded during a 1968 tour embarked on with **Soft Machine**. In addition to the music the CD features before and after gig interviews conducted by Tony Palmer. As with so many of these types of recordings, it is marred by poor sound quality and, in addition, by the tape cutting at unfortunate moments (such as the extended intro to *Purple Haze*). This is for completists only. Much of the material on *Axis Outtakes* can be heard on releases like *Studio Haze* and *Sotheby's Reels*. Despite the title, many tracks are from the early recording stages of *Electric Ladyland*. The unreleased material includes *Takin' Care Of No Business* (a ragtime ditty); two **Noel Redding** compositions - the psychedelic *Dream* and *Cat Talking To You* (with **Mitch Mitchell** on vocals), and finally *Little One* (with **Dave Mason** on sitar). This will only appeal to hardcore fans. *Live At Woodstock* is available on CD or as a 3-LP box set. Highlights include *Hey Joe* and *Star-Spangled Banner* and the vinyl box includes a 36-page book full of photos, interviews, a replica Woodstock ticket, a 7" colour vinyl single and a commemorative guitar pick.

An exhibition of 30 rarely seen photos of **Hendrix** was held at the Handel Museum between 20 November 2003 and 29 February 2004.

Winterland Night is a hit-filled package compiled from six gigs at San Francisco's Winterland Ballroom in October 1968. The collection captures him near to his peak with a superb early live version of *Voodoo Chile* and extended jams of classics like *Sunshine Of Your Love* and *Red House*.

Compilation appearances have included *Little Wing, If Six Was Nine* and *3rd Stone From The Sun* on Polydor's 1970 *Deep Overground Pop* (LP) compilation; *Changes* on Polydor's 1971 *Rock Party* (2-LP); *Little Miss Strange* on *Supergroups* (LP), a 1970 Polydor set; *All Along The Watchtower* on *Stardust* (2-LP); *Hey Joe, All Along The Watchtower* and *The Wind Cries Mary* on *Backtrack 1* (LP); *Purple Haze* and *Let Me Light Your Fire* on *Backtrack 2* (LP); *Voodoo Chile* on *Number 1 Hits Of The 70's & 80's* (CD) and *The Super 70's Vol 1* (CD); and *Dolly Dagger* on *Rare Tracks* (LP). (VJ/RMJ/AH)

Henry Cow

Personnel:	CHRIS CUTLER	drms, piano	AB
	FRED FRITH	gtr, violin, piano	AB
	JOHN GREAVES	bs, piano	AB
	TIM HODGKINSON	keyb'ds, sax, clarinet	AB
	GEOFF LEIGH	sax	A
	LINDSAY COOPER	woodwind, flute, piano	B

ALBUMS:	1	THE LEGEND	(Virgin V 2005) 1973 SC
(up to	2	UNREST	(Virgin V 2011) 1974 SC
1976)	3	IN PRAISE OF LEARNING	(Virgin V 2037) 1975 SC
	4	CONCERTS	(Caroline CAD 3002) 1976 SC

NB: (3) and (4) with **Slapp Happy**.

This experimental, left wing avant-garde group formed at Cambridge University in 1968. One of Virgin's earliest signings their music was totally uncommercial but tours with German band Faust and Captain Beefheart helped them build up a loyal cult following. Lindsay Cooper, formerly with **Comus**, replaced Leigh in 1974 and the band embarked on a collaboration with the avant-garde band **Slapp Happy**. This resulted in two interesting and highly individualistic albums. As a result of this collaboration, Dagmar Krause decided to join **Henry Cow**, leaving her two former colleagues in **Slapp Happy**, Peter Blegvad and Anthony Moore, to go their own way. The resulting album, *Western Culture*, in 1978 is beyond the time span of this book. When they finally split in the late seventies, Fred Frith went on to record a number of solo albums whilst most of the remaining members went on to form The Art Bears. (VJ)

Ken Hensley

ALBUMS:	1	PROUD WORDS ON A DUSTY SHELF	
(up to			(Bronze ILPS 9223) 1973
1976)	2	EAGER TO PLEASE	(Bronze ILPS 9307) 1975

NB: (1) and (2) reissued on Bronze (BRON 223 and 307 respectively) in the eighties. *The Anthology* (Essential ESM CD 824) 2000 compiles material from his six solo albums (four of which are outside this book's timeframe).

45: In The Morning/Who Will Sing For You (Bronze BRO 15) 1975

Hensley was a founder member of and organist in **The Gods** who later became **Toe Fat** shortly after his departure in November 1969 to **Uriah Heep**.

His debut solo album, *Proud Words On A Dusty Shelf*, featured **Uriah Heep** members Lee Kerslake and Gary Thain and was recorded whilst he was still with the band. It was nowhere near as heavy as the music he was playing with them at the time, though.

Eager To Please was made with **Colosseum** bassist Mark Clark, but it was poorly received. He was eventually sacked by **Uriah Heep** in 1980. He went on to record another poor solo album in 1981, and was later in Shotgun and US band Blackfoot before switching to session work.

The Anthology is a 16-track compilation taking material from his six solo albums up to 2000. The tracks come remastered and the package includes a self-penned 12-page booklet. (VJ)

JIMI HENDRIX - Concerts (2-LP).

Herbal Mixture

Personnel:
PETE CRUICKSHANK	bs		A
TONY McPHEE	gtr, vcls		A
MIKE MEEKHAM	drms		A

45s: A Love That's Died/Tailor Made   (Columbia DB 8021) 1966 R3
(up to   Machines/Please Leave My Mind   (Columbia DB 8083) 1966 R3
1976)

NB: There's also a retrospective compilation, *Please Leave My Mind* (Distortions 1012) 1993.

McPhee and Cruickshank had first played together back in 1962 in a group called The Dollarbills (which in late 1963 changed their name to **Groundhogs**). By January 1966 the first incarnation of the **Groundhogs** was falling apart and soon afterwards **McPhee** joined **Truth** shortly after they'd recorded Ray Davies' *I Go To Sleep*. He was only with them for about six months, before leaving to form **Herbal Mixture** with fellow ex-**Groundhog** Cruickshank and a young drummer, Mike Meekham, in the Summer of 1966. The name was derived from the fact Tony was a vegetarian who was also into alternative medicine, the resulting music reflected the burgeoning psychedelic era. *A Love That's Died* was an excellent psych-pop 45 with some good chopping riffs and some catchy fuzz guitar. The follow-up, *Machines*, was even better. A captivating psychedelic intro, some good changes of pace and compelling guitar work made this their magnum opus.

The retrospective *Please Leave My Mind* compilation includes both sides of the band's two 45s (and the flips which are similar in style and almost as good). It also includes two demo versions of *A Love That's Died* (one featuring an obscure Scottish vocalist who was given a trial with the band before **McPhee** decided to handle the vocals), along with demos of *Please Leave My Mind* and *Tailor Made*, and of two previously unreleased tracks:- *Something's Happening* and *Over You Baby*.

Herbal Mixture finally split in late 1967, having failed to achieve any commercial success. Early the following year, **McPhee** joined the **John Dummer Blues Band** before forming a new incarnation of the **Groundhogs**, which went on to achieve considerable success. He also recorded two albums with **Jo-Ann Kelly**, *Me And The Devil* and *The Same Thing On Their Minds*.

Both **Herbal Mixture** 45s are now very rare and sought-after.

Compilation appearances have included: *Please Leave My Mind* on *Perfumed Garden Vol. 3* (CD), *The Best Of Rubble Collection, Vol. 4* (CD); and *Machines* on *Beat It* (3-CD), *Electric Sugar Cube Flashbacks* (CD), *Electric Sugar Cube Flashbacks, Vol. 4* (LP), *Electric Sugarcube Flashbacks, Vol. 1* (LP) and the 4-CD box set *Acid Drops, Spacedust & Flying Saucers*. (VJ)

HERBAL MIXTURE - Please Leave My Mind (LP).

Herbie and The Royalists

Personnel:
BRIAN COOPER	drms		A
STEVE FIELD	bs		A
HERBIE HUNTE	vcls		A
DENIS LASCELLES	keyb'ds		A
IAN MILLER	gtr		A

ALBUM: 1(A) SOUL OF THE MATTER   (Saga FID 2121) 1968 SC

Unconnected to **Herbie Goins**, the **Herbie** in question here was a Barbados-born vocalist fronting a London-based quartet. The music is an uneasy marriage of soul, rock and pop with occasional psychedelic/prog leanings. (NR/VJ)

Herbie's People

Personnel:
LEN BEDDOW	ld gtr, vcls	AB
ALAN LACEY	drms	AB
HERBIE (DANNY ROBINSON)	ld vcls	AB
MICK TAYLOR	gtr, vcls	AB
PETER WALTON	bs, vcls	A
PETE STEVENS	bs, vcls	B

45s: Sweet And Tender Romance/
            You Thrill Me To Pieces   (CBS 200205) 1965 SC
            One Little Smile/You Never Know   (CBS 202058) 1966
            Residential Area/Humming Bird   (CBS 202584) 1967

Originally known as Danny Cannon and The Ramrods, **Herbie's People** came from Bilston, near Wolverhampton in the West Midlands. The band was managed by Bill Bates, whose brother in law was Ken Lewis of **The Ivy League**. Bill co-wrote *Sweet And Tender Romance* for P.J. Proby as well as *Will I What*, the novelty hit by Wendy Richard.

Sweet And Tender Romance, together with *I Wonder Why*, Pete Walton's *She's Crying* and the band's second single *One Little Smile* (1966) were played live on Brian Matthew's 'Saturday Club' radio show. This was followed by two headline shows at The Royal Albert Hall for the charity organisation Toc H.

For the third single, the band had lined up what they thought was a sure fire Carter - Lewis track. The song was a hit, but not for **Herbie's People**. Despite being pressed up and ready for the shops, the single was shelved when **Manfred Mann** heard it and decided to record it - the single in question was *Semi-Detached Suburban Mr. James* although it was originally *Mr. Jones* but changed due to the departure of **Paul Jones** from the **Manfreds**. The **Herbie's People** version, unknown to the band, came out on the American soul label Okeh (7265), whilst in England it was replaced by the song *Humming Bird* (1967) - both singles had the track *Residential Area* (written by the band) on the 'B' side. This song was featured as part of the soundtrack to the British film "Poor Cow".

Another Carter - Lewis track *Thank You For Loving Me* was recorded as the fourth single but was again shelved when it was used as an **Ivy League** single. An album had been planned around this time but a residency in Germany took its toll on the band and never materialised.

By 1968, Pete Walton had left the band to be replaced by Pete Stevens and the band had become **Just William** to record *I Don't Care* and the more psychedelic *Cherrywood Green* for Spark Records. A final single, back on CBS, as **The Bullring** followed. This was *Birmingham Brass Band / Lady Of The Morning Sun* and was featured on the British TV quiz show "The Golden Shot" in the musical part of the show, with the band filmed in Brass Band outfits at various points of local interest around Birmingham!

Various members continued to work in the music business for a few years but it wasn't until 1994 that the band played together again. This was after the chance discovery of one of the Okeh labelled *Semi-Detached...* 45's turned up, sparking an interest between the various members to do a re-union show for charity, with a second show in 1995.

Recently, *Semi-Detached...* was played by Brian Matthew on his current BBC Radio 2 version of 'Saturday Club'. Mick Taylor is now an author, writing romantic fiction.

Compilation coverage appears to have been limited to *Residential Area* on the U.S. garage/psych comp *Brainshadows Vol. 2* (LP & CD). (LB/VJ)

The Herd

Personnel:			
ANDY BOWN	keyb'ds, vcls	ABCD
TONY CHAPMAN	drms	A
TERRY CLARK	vcls	AB
PETER FRAMPTON	gtr, vcls	A C
LEWIS RICH	organ	AB
MIKE UNDERWOOD	drms	B
ANDREW STEELE	drms	A C
GARY TAYLOR	bs, vcls	A CD
HENRY SPINETTI	drms	D

HCP
ALBUMS:	1(C)	PARADISE LOST	(Fontana (S)TL 5458) 1968 R1 38
	2( )	NOSTALGIA	(Bumble GEMP 5001) 1972 SC -

NB: They also had one US-only album:- *Looking Thru You* (Fontana 67579) in 1968. There's a CD compilation, *Paradise Lost* (Fontana 842 760-2) 1989 of their material. However, the definitive **Herd** compilation is *Paradise And Underworld* (Repertoire REP 4257-WG) 1992, which includes all the material on the *Paradise Lost* compilation plus six additional 45 tracks and four previously unreleased cuts:- *Follow The Leader*, *Charlie Anderson*, *Bang!* and *Mother's Blue Eyed Angel*. *An Anthology* (Music Club MCCD 352) 1998 is a 27-track compilation. *Underworld* (Snapper SMD CD 439) 2004 includes everything they released, except their first three singles. *The Complete Herd* (Repertoire REP 5032) 2005 is a 2-CD set compiling all their material.

HCP
45s:	Goodbye Baby, Goodbye/		
	Here Comes The Fool	(Parlophone R 5284) 1965 R1 -
	She Was Really Saying Something/	
	It's Been A Long Time Baby	(Parlophone R 5353) 1965 R1 -
	So Much In Love/	
	This Boy's Always Been True	(Parlophone R 5413) 1966 R1 -
	I Can Fly/Diary Of A Narcissist	(Fontana TF 819) 1967 -
	From The Underworld/Sweet William	(Fontana TF 856) 1967 6
	Paradise Lost/Come On Believe Me	(Fontana TF 887) 1967 15
	I Don't Want Our Loving To Die/	
	Our Fairy Tale	(Fontana TF 925) 1968 5
	Sunshine Cottage/Miss Jones	(Fontana TF 975) 1968 -
	The Game/Beauty Queen	(Fontana H 1011) 1969 -
	You've Got Me Hanging From Your Lovin' Tree/	
	I Don't Want To Go To Sleep Again	(B&C CB 154) 1971 -
Reissues:	I Don't Want Our Loving To Die/	
	The Game	(Bumble GE 120) 1973 -
	From The Underworld/Paradise Lost/	
	On My Way Home	(Bumble GEX 1) 1973 -
	From The Underworld/Paradise Lost	(Old Gold OG 9236) 1982 -
	I Don't Want Our Loving To Die	(Old Gold OG 9245) 1982 -

THE HERD - Paradise Lost (LP).

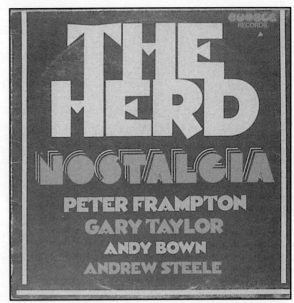

THE HERD - Nostalgia (LP).

Originally formed in 1965, this underground band was transformed into a pop-orientated outfit by songwriting duo Howard and Blaikley, who had earlier achieved success with **The Honeycombs** and **Dave Dee, Dozy, Beaky, Mick and Tich**. Although not psychedelic, their music was packaged to fit the flower-power era. Their first Fontana single, the catchy *I Can Fly*, failed to enter the charts, but the sombre orchestrated follow-up, *From The Underworld*, reached No 6 in 1967, and the excellent *Paradise Lost*, notable for its 'stripper music' intro and finale, and *I Don't Want Our Loving To Die*, reached No's 15 and 5 respectively in 1968. The group's teen appeal was largely attributable to **Peter Frampton**, voted 'the face of 1968' in 'Rave!'. However, their next single, *Sunshine Cottage*, failed to chart and when **Frampton** quit, appalled by some of the trappings of the music business, the band disintegrated. Of course, he later re-emerged to form **Humble Pie** - an early Supergroup - with **Stevie Marriott**, and later attained phenomenal success in the USA as a solo artist. **Bown** and Spinetti later joined **Judas Jump** and then formed the folk-rock group, **Storyteller**, although **Bown** wasn't actually a member. He also made solo albums and was later in **Status Quo**.

Compilation appearances have included: *So Much In Love* on *Rolling Stones Connection 1963-66* (CD); *This Boy Has Always Been True* on *Sixties Lost And Found, Vol. 1* (LP); *Echoes From The Wilderness - Sixteen UK R&B Freakbeat Trippers.* (LP & CD); *Miss Jones* on *Pop-In, Vol 1* (CD); *From The Underworld* on the 4-CD box set *Acid Drops, Spacedust & Flying Saucers*; *I Don't Want Our Loving To Die* on the 2-CD set *Greatest Hits Of The 60's Vol 4* and *I Can Fly* on *Colour Me Pop, Vol 2* (CD). (VJ)

Heritage

45:	Long Way Home/Sarah's Song	(Philips 6006 021) 1970

A folk 45, with girl lead vocals. (VJ)

Herman's Hermits

Personnel:			
KARL GREEN	bs, vcls	A
KEITH HOPWOOD	gtr, vcls	A
DEREK 'LEK' LECKENBY	gtr, vcls	A
PETER NOONE	vcls, gtr, keyb'ds	A
BARRY 'BEAN' WHITWAM	drms	A

HCP
ALBUMS:	1(A)	HERMAN'S HERMITS (Columbia 33SX 1727) 1965 SC 16
	2(A)	BOTH SIDES OF HERMAN'S HERMITS
		(Columbia SX 6084) 1966 SC -
	3(A)	THERE'S A KIND OF HUSH ALL OVER THE WORLD
		(mono/stereo) (Columbia S(C)X 6174) 1967 SC -

4(A) MRS. BROWN YOU'VE GOT A LOVELY DAUGHTER
                    (Columbia SCX 6303) 1968 -
5(A) THE BEST OF HERMAN'S HERMITS
                    (Columbia SCX 6332) 1969 -
6(A) THE MOST OF HERMAN'S HERMITS
                  (Music For Pleasure MFP 5126) 1971 14
7(A) THE MOST OF HERMAN'S HERMITS, VOL 2
                  (Music For Pleasure MFP 50008) 1972 -

NB: (4) reissued on CD (Repertoire REP 4424-WY) 1994 along with both sides of their early 'A' and 'B' sides and the content of their *Hermania* EP. Some compilations which may be of interest are:- *Twenty Greatest Hits* (K-Tel NE 1001) 1977 (No 37); *The Very Best Of Herman's Hermits* (Music For Pleasure MFP 41 5685 1) 1984; *The EP Collection* (See For Miles SEE 284) 1990, also on CD (SEECD 284) 1990; *The Collection* (Castle CCSCD 246) 1990, a 24-track compilation, only seven of which had been on the earlier See For Miles *EP Collection*; *The Best Of The EMI Years, Volume 1* (EMI CDP 7 97042-2) 1991 and *Volume 2* (EMI CDP 7 97043-2) 1992; and *Best Of Herman's Hermits* (Compacts For Pleasure CDB 792 192 2) 1989. *Singles Collection* (EMI/BR Music 7243 8 33288 2 6) 1997 is a definitive 2-CD set of their 45 output. *Retrospective* (ABKCO CD-92282) 2004 is a 21-track compilation which contains 16 Top Ten hits during the 1964-1969 era.

                                                        HCP
EPs: 1(A) HERMANIA   (Columbia SEG 8380) 1965 SC 19
      2(A) MRS. BROWN YOU'VE GOT A LOVELY DAUGHTER
                           (Columbia SEG 8440) 1965 SC 3
      3(A) HERMAN'S HERMITS HITS
                           (Columbia SEG 8442) 1965 SC 19
      4(A) A MUST TO AVOID   (Columbia SEG 8477) 1966 SC -
      5(A) MUSIC FROM THE SOUNDTRACK 'HOLD ON'
                           (Columbia SEG 8503) 1966 SC 4
      6(A) DANDY   (Columbia SEG 8520) 1967 SC -

                                                        HCP
45s: I'm Into Something Good/
(up to   Your Hand In Mine   (Columbia DB 7338) 1964 1
1976)   Show Me Girl/I Know Why   (Columbia DB 7408) 1964 19
         Silhouettes/
         Can't You Hear My Heartbeat (Columbia DB 7475) 1965 3
         Wonderful World/Dream On   (Columbia DB 7546) 1965 7
         Just A Little Bit Better/
         Take Love, Give Love   (Columbia DB 7670) 1965 15
         A Must To Avoid/
         The Man With The Cigar   (Columbia DB 7791) 1965 6
         You Won't Be Leaving/
         Listen People   (Columbia DB 7861) 1966 20
         This Door Swings Both Ways/
         For Love   (Columbia DB 7947) 1966 18
         No Milk Today/
         My Reservation's Been Confirmed (Columbia DB 8012) 1966 7
         East-West/
         What Is Wrong, What Is Right?   (Columbia DB 8076) 1966 37
         There's A Kind Of Hush (All Over The World)/
         Gaslite Street   (Columbia DB 8123) 1967 7

HERMAN'S HERMITS - Best Of Vol. III (LP).

Museum/Moonshine Man   (Columbia DB 8235) 1967 -
I Can Take Or Leave Your Loving/
Marcel's   (Columbia DB 8237) 1968 11
Sleepy Joe/Just One Girl   (Columbia DB 8404) 1968 12
Sunshine Girl/
Nobody Needs To Know   (Columbia DB 8446) 1968 8
Something's Happening/
The Most Beautiful Thing In My Life (Columbia DB 8504) 1968 6
No Milk Today/There's A Kind Of Hush
(white label promo)   (EMI SLES 15) 1968 SC -
London Look (white label promo) (EMI SLES 16) 1968 SC -
My Sentimental Friend/My Lady (Columbia DB 8563) 1969 2
Here Comes The Star/
It's Alright Now   (Columbia DB 8626) 1969 33
Years May Come, Years May Go/
Smile Please   (Columbia DB 8656) 1970 7
Bet Yer Life I Do/
Searching For The Southern Sun   (RAK 102) 1970 22
α Lady Barbara/Don't Just Stand There (RAK 106) 1970 13
β She's A Lady/Gold Mandela   (RCA RCA 2135) 1971 -
β The Man/Effen Curly   (RCA RCA 2265) 1972 -
   Train/Ride On The Water (withdrawn) (Buddah BDS 700) 1974 -
β Ginny Go Softly/
   Blond Haired, Blue Eyed Boy   (Private Stock 019) 1975 -
Reissues: Silhouettes/I'm Into Something Good (EMI G 45 26) 1984
          There's A Kind Of Hush/No Milk Today (RAK RR 8) 1986 -

NB: α credited to Peter Noone and Herman's Hermits. β credited to The Hermits (i.e. without **Peter Noone**).

Herman's Hermits were one of the more lightweight pop acts of the sixties but they were one of our most successful exports to the States and released several good three-minute pop singles.

Peter Noone (Herman) was born on 5 November 1947 in Manchester. His father was a semi-pro musician and keen that his son should follow in his footsteps, so Peter was sent to study singing and acting at the Manchester School of Music and Drama. He was something of a childhood star, playing Len Fairclough's son in the soap opera 'Coronation Street' as well as in the lesser-known 'Knight Errant' and 'Suki'. He combined this with local stage appearances, too. An acting career seemed inevitable but when he was offered a star role in a Judy Garland film when he was just 12 his parents vetoed it and this probably altered the course of his career - instead of becoming a film star he became a pop star.

In 1963, he joined a Manchester beat group, The Heartbeats, after their vocalist failed to show for a gig. He used the name Peter Kovak. The change to Herman came after the band's bassist Karl Greene had remarked on Peter's resemblance to the character Sherman in the TV cartoon 'The Bullwinkle Show', although he misheard the name as Herman. So the group, who by now were a popular dance hall and youth club attraction, and managed by Harvey Lisberg and Charlie Silverman, changed their name to **Herman and His Hermits**, although it soon became abbreviated to **Herman's Hermits**.

The band was soon signed by Mickie Most, who got them a deal with EMI's Columbia label. Most thought that **Peter Noone** resembled a young John F. Kennedy and resolved to make him the focus of the group. Most arranged for them to record a Gerry Goffin/Carole King number, which had recently been a minor hit in the States for Earl-Jean (the Cookies' vocalist). The song, *I'm Into Something Good*, shot up the charts and spent two weeks at No 1 in September 1964. The British public rapidly took **Peter Noone** into their hearts as the safe face of beat music, and the band soon became a household name. Delighted by the success of their earlier song, Goffin and King offered the band a follow-up. The group jumped at the chance, but in retrospect, *Show Me Girl*, which had the bounce but lacked the appeal of their debut disc, proved a poor choice and only just squeezed into the Top 20.

January 1965 saw the release of the group's first EP, *Hermania*, which contained a cover of *I Understand* (which had been a hit for The Four Tunes in 1954 and more recently for **Freddie and The Dreamers**; covers of Frankie Ford's *Sea Cruise* and Ernie K-Doe's *Mother-In-Law*, and a song called *I Think Of You*. The EP sold well and some people even spoke of 'Hermania' as a younger rival to 'Beatlemania'. The band made their first visit to the US, which was soon to prove a lucrative market for them. Whilst there, they made a cameo appearance in the teen movie 'When The Boys Meet The Girls'.

HERMAN'S HERMITS - Best Of (CD).

For their third UK single the group covered The Rays' 1957 hit *Silhouettes*, which climbed to No 3 and was undoubtedly one of their better singles. In the US they went one place better with a Carter/Lewis song, *Can't You Hear My Heartbeat*, outselling a rival version from **Goldie and The Gingerbreads** in the process. This gave them their second million-seller (*I'm Into Something Good* had been the first). Their next 45 was a slick revival of Sam Cooke's *Wonderful World*, which rose to No 7 here in April 1965 and No 4 in the US a month later.

Their really big breakthrough in the US came when an American DJ heard *Mrs. Brown You've Got A Lovely Daughter* on their first US album, *Introducing Herman's Hermits*, and persuaded their US record company, MGM, to release it as a 45. It sounded like an old music hall song (though it wasn't) with **Noone**'s George Formby-style vocals and the banjo guitar sound, and frankly sounded corny. Realising this the group prevented its release here, but in the US the song spent three weeks on top of the Charts, earning them another gold disc. It also topped the Australian Charts and sold 14 million copies worldwide. This success coincided with the group's first full US tour. Over the next two years, when the group faced strong competition from several rivals here in the UK, they enjoyed phenomenal success.

Their success seems to have been partly due to the fact that many of the first wave British invasion groups had already peaked in terms of sales (with only **The Beatles** and **Dave Clark Five** consistently selling vast quantities of vinyl) and partly because, fuelled by the success of *Mrs. Brown...*, they selected songs for US release that had a music hall and vaudeville edge to them. Not only did this set them apart from other UK beat acts of the time, it also fulfilled the American stereotype of what British life was like. So, whilst in the UK the band enjoyed another Top 20 hit with Kenny Young's bouncy *Just A Little Bit Better* (which later made it to No 7 in the US), across the Atlantic another US-only single, *I'm Henry The Eighth (I Am)*, a revival of a 1911 music hall song, extracted from their album *Herman's Hermits On Tour* gave them another No 1 and million-seller.

Their first UK album, simply titled *Herman's Hermits*, wasn't released until September 1965. It consisted of material from their first two US-only albums and included both their big US No1's, alongside beat material like **The Yardbirds**' *For Your Love* and Buddy Holly's *Heartbeat*. Climbing to No 16, it was to be their only UK Chart album until a budget-priced retrospective compilation in 1971 took them two places higher. Two EPs followed in the UK:- *Mrs. Brown You've Got A Lovely Daughter*, which became their best-selling EP, rising to No 3 in the EP Charts (and suggesting that, had the song been released as a single here, it would have done extremely well) and *Herman's Hermits Hits*, which got to No 19.

Their final 45 of 1965 was a fine, jangling P.F. Sloan/Steve Barri song, *A Must To Avoid*, which got to No 6 here and No 8 in the States. In the US, MGM issued another album, *The Best Of Herman's Hermits, Vol. 1*, which included most of the year's 45s and some earlier album tracks.

In March 1966, the band issued another US-only single. *Listen People* was a slow ballad and took them to No 3, earning another gold disc. Its flip *Got*

A Feeling, was taken from the Soundtrack to *Hold On!*, which reached No 14 in the US. This was a teen movie about naming a US spacecraft after a beat group to which the band contributed 11 songs. The album also included four Sloan and Barri tracks, such as *A Must To Avoid* and the title cut, *Hold On*. Here in the UK these two tracks were combined on an EP entitled *Hold On*, along with *Wild Love* and *The George And Dragon*. Meanwhile, *Listen People* appeared as the flip to a **Tony Hazzard** composition, *You Won't Be Leaving*, a folky number that just made it into the Top 20. The follow-up, *This Door Swings Both Ways*, was not one of their strongest 45s, but still took them to No 12 in the States and No 18 in the UK.

If it seemed that their fortunes were beginning to ebb when they were revitalised by **Graham Gouldman**'s *No Milk Today*. This was an excellent pop song and their first 45 to employ an orchestra. It gave them their first Top 10 hit in the UK for over a year and came with a good flip side too, *My Reservation's Been Confirmed*, a decent self-penned rocker. In the States, *No Milk Today* appeared on the flip side to a strong version of **The Kinks**' *Dandy*, which put them back in the US Top 5 and was every bit as good as the original. Here in the UK, *Dandy* became the title track of their sixth and final EP. In November 1966 **Peter Noone** also appeared in the US TV movie, 'The Canterville Ghost'.

Their next album, *Both Sides Of Herman's Hermits*, had different track listings in the UK and US. Whilst the British pressing appeared the more selective with fewer throwaway songs, it was the US one that enjoyed Chart action peaking, at No 48. Later, at the beginning of 1967, a US-only compilation, *The Best Of Herman's Hermits, Vol. 2*, just edged into the Top 20.

On the 45 front, their treatment of **Graham Gouldman**'s *East West* had failed to impress on either side of the Atlantic, but in late 1966, they bounced back with a beat ballad, *There's A Kind Of Hush*, a Les Reed/Geoff Stephens composition, which made No 4 in the US and No 7 in the UK. Definitely one of their best songs, it also became the title track of their next album, which for the first time had the same track listing on both sides of the Atlantic. It made the US Top 20 but failed to sell in large quantities over here. However, it was in America with the advent of The Monkees and the onset of the psychedelic era that their fortunes declined most rapidly. Kenny Young's *Don't Go Out Into The Rain*, which wasn't released in the UK because **The Swinging Blue Jeans**' version had already flopped, became their last US Top 20 hit. Their next UK 45 was a cover of **Donovan**'s *Museum*, which flopped here and only managed No 37 in the US. Their final album, *Blaze*, didn't even get a UK release, although it had its moments with the **Beatles**-like *Moonshine Man* and **Graham Gouldman**'s *Upstairs Downstairs*.

In their final years, the band concentrated on the mainstream pop market and enjoyed further big UK hits with *I Can Take Or Leave Your Loving*, *Sleepy Joe* and singalong ditties like *Sunshine Girl* and *Something's Happening*. They even reached No 2 with a 'weepie' Carter/Stephens song, *My Sentimental Friend*, which didn't even make the US Top 50. The one area of US success in this phase of their career was the group's appearance in the film 'Mrs. Brown You've Got A Lovely Daughter', in which **Noone** played a lead role. The Soundtrack album didn't chart at all in the UK but did get to No 182 in the US.

In November 1968, **Noone** married a French girl, Mireille Strasser, and the following month he formed a business partnership with **Graham Gouldman**, which led to the opening of a New York boutique called Zoo.

Whilst on tour in Australia they heard Ross D. Wylie's hit cover of Johnny Young's *Here Comes The Star*, and decided to record it for UK release. It was another 'weepie' but didn't enjoy the success of *My Sentimental Friend*, only managing No 33. Their final UK Columbia 45, *Years May Come, Years May Go*, did return them to the Top 10.

In mid-1970, Mickie Most launched his new RAK label and with their good track record, **Herman's Hermits** were an inevitable choice to help promote it. Their first 45 on this new label, the reggae-influenced *Bet Yer Life I Do*, which had been written by **Hot Chocolate**'s Errol Dunkley and Tony Wilson, marked a significant change of style and it did the trick for Most, giving him a Top 30 hit to help launch the label. The follow-up, another **Hot Chocolate** song, *Lady Barbara*, took things a step further putting them back in the Top 20. It was credited to **Peter Noone** and **Herman's Hermits** and soon proved to be his last with the band. **Noone** went solo, continuing to record on Mickie Most's RAK label whilst The Hermits relocated to the US where they signed to RCA. The band continued as a live act for several years and recorded the occasional single, none of which enjoyed any Chart action.

Inevitably, compilations were released after their split and there was also a brief reformation in June 1973 to top the bill at the 'British Invasion' nostalgia concert in New York's Madison Square Gardens. *The EP Collection* includes most of the band's hits from the 1964-66 period. The *Best Of The EMI Years* is a 2-CD set which includes all their hits. In 1980, **Noone** formed another rock band, The Tremblers, although they were short-lived.

Compilation appearances have included: *Wonderful World* and *Mrs. Brown, You've Got A Lovely Daughter* on *Mickie Most Presents: British Go-Go* (LP); *You Won't Be Leaving* and *This Door Swings Both Ways* on *Go... With An All Star* (LP); *Wings Of Love* on *Spinning Wheel* (CD); *It's Alright* on *Oddities, Vol 1* (CD); *I'm Into Something Good* on *U.K. No. 1. Hits Of The 60's* (CD), *Beat Generation - Ready Steady Go* (CD), *60's Mix* (CD), *Best Of British Rock* (CD), *Super Hits Of The 60s - Vol 1* (CD) and on *20 Hits Of The 60's* (CD); *Museum* on *Colour Me Pop, Vol 3* (CD); *Wonderful World* on *Super Hits Of The 60s - Vol 2* (CD); *My Sentimental Friend* on the 2-CD set *Sixties Summer Love*; *Something's Happening* (alternate take) on the 2-CD set *Greatest Hits Of The 60's*; *There's A Kind Of Hush* on *Love Songs* (CD), *Dizzy* (CD) and on *Hits Of The 60's Vol 2* (CD); *No Milk Today* on the 2-CD set *Greatest Hits Of The 60's Vol 4*; *Silhouettes* on *Super Hits Of The 60s - Vol 3* (CD) and *Moonshine Man* on *Colour Me Pop, Vol 5* (CD). (VJ)

Heron

Personnel:	ROY APPS	gtr, vcls	A
	GERALD T MOORE	gtr, pno, vcls	A
	STEPHEN JONES	keyb'ds	A
	TONY POOK	vcls, perc	A

ALBUMS:	1(A)	HERON (w/insert)	(Dawn DNLS 3010) 1970 R3
	2(A)	TWICE AS NICE AT 1/2 THE PRICE (2-LP)	
		(w/insert)	(Dawn DNLS 3025) 1972 R3

NB: (1) reissued on CD (Si-Wan SRMC 1031). There's also a compilation, *The Best Of Heron* (See For Miles SEE 242) 1988, also available on CD (SEECD 242).

45s:	Take Me Back Home/	
	Minstrel And A King	(Dawn DNS 1015) 1971
	Bye And Bye//Through Time	
	Only A Hobo/I'm Ready To Leave (PS)	(Dawn DNX 2509) 1971

Heron was formed in 1968 by Roy Apps and Tony Pook (both from Maidenhead) and with Bob Collins they got a deal with the Writers Workshop and joined Clearwater Productions with the likes of **Trees** and **Hawkwind**. In 1969 Roy and Tony joined forces with Steve Jones and Gerald T. Moore and recorded *Only A Hobo*, a maxi single at Pye studios, but it was not released until 1971. Their eponymous first album, released the following year was recorded in a field at Appleford in Berkshire (their second was recorded in the open air too).

In 1971 they went to the Black Dog in Devon and recorded their second album for the Dawn label. Called *Twice As Nice At Half The Price* it was intended to be part of the hippie 'good value for money' ethos they wanted to promote 'we're in it for the music not the money'. *Take Me Back Home* was culled from this album for 45 release.

A folk-based band their music also had tinges of pop and soul. Both albums were produced by Peter Eden with birdsong often clearly audible between tracks. Most of their material was self-penned, and their gentle love songs have aged well. The group has a devoted cult following, especially in Japan, and the albums have become very hard to find. They underwent several line-up changes after 1974/75. Gerald T. Moore left to form The Reggae Guitars. Big Tom Robinson joined and was then replaced by Terry Clarke, who left to record in the States with the likes of Levon Helm - and in 1997 Gerry Power joined. To celebrate their 30th anniversary Heron returned to the Black Dog in Devon - indeed to the same farm - to record two albums. The first *River Of Fortune* (Relax RH 001) 1998 is a trip down memory lane including songs from the first two albums and others from the late sixties not previously recorded. The second comprised mainly new songs. They have occasionally reformed in recent years and recently recorded a new album *Black Dog* in the village of Black Dog in Devon.

They also have a cut, *The Wanderer*, on the *Dawn Takeaway Concert* (LP) album. (VJ/RMJ/SJ)

Mike Heron's (Reputation)

Personnel:	DAVID BARKER		A
	GRAHAM FORBES	gtr	A
	JOHN GILSTON	drms	A
	MIKE HERON	vcls, gtr	A
	MALCOLM LE MAISTRE	vcls	A
	MIKE TOMICH		A

ALBUMS:	1	SMILING MEN WITH BAD REPUTATIONS	
(up to			(Island ILPS 9146) 1971
1976)	2(A)	MIKE HERON'S REPUTATION	
			(Neighbourhood NBH 80637) 1975

NB: (1) reissued on CD (Island IMCD 129) 1991.

45s:	Call Me Diamond/Lady Wonder	(Island WIP 6101) 1971
	Evie/One Of The Finest	(Neighbourhood NBH 3109) 1975

Mike Heron, who'd started out in The Saracens (harmony-pop), The Abstracts (Stones/R&B), and Rock Bottom and The Deadbeats (art-rock), was one of the founder members of **The Incredible String Band**. He recorded *Smiling Man With Bad Reputations* whilst still with the band, and in some respects it marked a return to the exuberance of the early **Incredible String Band** albums. Produced by Joe Boyd, it features guest appearances from various members of **Fairport Convention** and **Dr. Strangely Strange**, as well as **John Cale** and 'Tommy and the Bijoux' - a pseudonym for **Pete Townshend**, **Keith Moon** and **Ronnie Lane**.

Mike Heron's Reputation can also be heard playing *Feast Of Stephen* on Island's *El Pea* (LP) compilation. (VJ)

Hickory

45:	Green Light/Key	(CBS 3963) 1969 SC

Presumably the 'A' side was a cover of the song The American Breed enjoyed a US hit with. It was written by Eddie Grant. Northern soulish, it was big with the mods. A band of this name later became **Flaming Youth**. This could be the one. (VJ)

Hickory Stix

Personnel:	GRAHAM BAGSHAW	bs	A
	RENO GIANITTO	vcls	A
	GLYN HEWINES	gtr	A

HERON - Heron (CD).

| HOWARD RENSHAW | sax | A |
| KENNY THURSFIELD | drms | A |

45:    Hello My Darling/Feeling Blue   (Oak RGJ 149) 1964 R3

It's claimed that the vocalist on this disc sounded like a young **Robert Plant** but it was actually a Stoke-on-Trent singer called Reno Gianitto. Whatever, expect to pay in excess of £100 for a copy of this. Is it worth it? No, not unless you like early Cliff Richard singles. In any case, you can hear the 'A' side on *Story Of Oak Records* (2-LP)/*The Story Of Oak Records* (CD). (VJ)

The Hi-Fi's

Personnel:

BRIAN BENNETT	keyb'ds, vcls	AB
TED HARVEY	bs	A
MALCOLM LENNY	ld gtr, vcls	AB
MEL WRIGHT	drms	AB
MIKE DOUGLAS	gtr, vcls	B
GARY UNWINN	bs	B

NB: Line up 'A' up to 1965, and between 1965-67 Ted Harvey left, but new members Mike Douglas and Gary Unwinn joined.

45s:	Take Me Or Leave Me/I'm Struck	(Piccadilly 7N 35130) 1963
	Will Yer Won't Yer/She's The One	(Pye 7N 15635) 1964
	I Keep Forgettin'/	
	Why Can't I Stop Loving You	(Pye 7N 15710) 1964 R1
	Baby's In Black/Kiss And Run	(Pye 7N 15788) 1965
	It's Gonna Be Morning/	
	I Wanna Hear You Say Yeah	(Alp 595 010) 1966 R1

A London-based band whose music was generally soul-beat. They relocated to Germany where they recorded an album, *Snakes And Ladders* (German Starclub 15803 STY), which is reputedly well worth hearing and two 45s for the Star-Club label. The title track and *Tread Softly For The Sleepers* were also put out on a 45 over there.

I Keep Forgettin' was the Chuck Jackson classic and *Baby's In Black* was a **Beatles**' track.

Compilation appearances have included: *Tread Softly For The Sleepers* on *Psychedelia, Vol. 1* (LP), *The Star-Club Anthology, Vol. 3* (LP) and *Hen's Teeth Vol. 1* (CD); *I'm A Box* and *No Two Ways* on *The Star-Club Singles Complete, Vol. 10* (LP & CD); *Snakes And Ladders* and *Tread Softly For The Sleepers* on *The Star-Club Singles Complete, Vol. 11* (LP & CD); *I Keep Forgettin'* and *She's The One* on *Hippy Hippy Shake* (CD); *Odd Man Out* on *Incredible Sound Show Stories Vol. 11* (LP); *Baby's In Black* on *The Songs Of Lennon and McCartney* (CD); and *I Keep Forgettin'* on *The Songs Of Leiber and Stoller* (CD). (VJ)

High

45:    Long Live The High/Beggar Man Dan   (CBS 4164) 1969

This long forgotten pop combo produced a cheery sound on their 45. (VJ)

High and Mighty

45:    Tryin' To Stop Cryin'/
         Escape From Cuba   (HMV POP 1548) 1966 SC

Another obscure sixties band. (VJ)

High Broom

45:    Dancing In The Moonlight/
         Percy's On The Run   (Island WI 6088) 1970 SC

NB: (1) reissued on Columbia (DB 8969) 1973.

This is **Jason Crest** with **Mike Stuart Span**'s guitarist Brian Bennett. An album's worth of material was recorded for Island but was not released. (VJ)

INCREDIBLE SOUND SHOW STORIES VOL. 11 (Comp LP) including The Hi-Fi's.

High Noon

45s:	Old Fashioned Feeling/Drivin' Drivin'	(CBS 4972) 1970
	Dragonfly/Bring That Love Again	(CBS 5160) 1970
	Living Is A Loving Thing/Blind Alley	(CBS 7066) 1971

Nothing else is known about this band. (VJ)

The High Numbers

Personnel:

ROGER DALTREY	vcls	A
JOHN ENTWISTLE	bs	A
PETE TOWNSHEND	gtr	A
KEITH MOON	drms	A

45:    α I'm The Face/Zoot Suit   (Fontana TF 480) 1964 R4 -
Reissue: I'm The Face/Zoot Suit   (Back Door DOOR 4) 1980 SC 49

NB: α was later repressed with the same catalogue number in the same year with the sides reversed.

Townshend and **Entwistle** were school pals and formed a band called The Confederates whilst still at Acton Grammar School in 1959. **Townshend** was already determined to be a pop star and spent almost all his spare time studying guitar. **Entwistle** also played the french horn for the Middlesex Youth Orchestra and studied piano. When they left school in 1961, **Pete Townshend** went to art college and **John Entwistle** became a civil servant. However, a year later, **Roger Daltrey**, who'd also been at Acton Grammar School, invited them to join his band, The Detours, and an experienced drummer, Doug Sandom, was also recruited. The group didn't win a recording contract but built up a pretty strong live repertoire. In 1964 they met Pete Meaden, a freelance publicist, who remodelled them into the burgeoning 'mod' image and secured them a record contract with Fontana whilst renaming them **The High Numbers**. The resulting single, *I'm The Face*, a rewrite of Slim Harpo's *Got Love If You Want It* with mod-style lyrics provided by Meaden, was frankly rather ordinary but would cost you in excess of £200 today. It flopped at the time, although the band enhanced its reputation as a live act with flash interpretations of songs like *Mickey's Monkey*, *Shout* and *Heatwave*.

The band's big break came when a friend of Meaden's invited Kit Lambert, an entrepreneur, to a **High Numbers** gig - Lambert had been searching for a band to make a documentary on. However, Lambert and his business partner Chris Stamp (brother of actor Terence) liked what they saw and took over the band's management, paying off Meaden with £500. They shot a promo film of the band (which by now included the wild and theatrical **Keith Moon** on drums) and worked on their image, changing the name to **The Who** in November 1964. The rest, as they say, is history.

Compilation appearances include: *Zoot Suit* on *Rare Tracks* (LP). There's also two tracks, *Pretty Thing* and *Long Tall Shorty* on *Made In England, Vol. 2* (CD), though it's not confirmed that this is by the same band. (VJ/TF)

High Society

Personnel: FRIDAY BROWNE
               PETER COWAP
               CHRISTINE EBBREL
               GRAHAM GOULDMAN
               KEITH LAWLESS

45:     People Passing By/
        Star Of Eastern Street   (Fontana TF 771) 1966 SC

A one-off studio project comprised of Manchester singer **Friday Browne**, Cowap (formerly of **The Country Gentlemen**) and **Gouldman**. Clem Cattini, Phil Dennys and **John Paul Jones** were also involved in the recording session. It is largely due to the individuals involved in the recording that it's a minor collectable. The trio re-united the following year as **Manchester Mob**. (VJ)

High Street East

45:     Newcastle Brown/Everyone Knows   (Rubber One) 1970

This 45 is of some significance as the first release on the well respected Newcastle folk label, Rubber. (MWh)

High Tide

Personnel: TONY HILL   gtr, vcls   A
               SIMON HOUSE   violin, organ, piano   A
               PETER PAVLI   bs   A
               ROGER HADDEN   drms   A

ALBUMS: 1(A)   SEA SHANTIES   (Liberty LBS 83264) 1969 R2
(up to 2(A)   HIGH TIDE   (Liberty LBS 83294) 1970 R2
1976)

NB: (1) reissued (Psycho 26) 1984, (2) reissued (Psycho 27) 1984. (1) and (2) reissued on CD (Repertoire REP 4413-WY) and REP 4414-WY respectively) 1994. (1) and (2) also available on one CD (Liberty 7243 8 2971122) 1994. Also relevant are three retrospective CDs:- *Interesting Times* (Lobster 001) 1990, *Precious Cargo* (Cobra Records CD 003) 199? and *The Flood* (World Wide Records SPM-WWR-CD-0005) 1990. *Open Season* (Black Widow BWR 050) 2001 is an Italian import, which collects their rarities from 1969-90, plus a couple of fresh, previously unreleased tracks by Tony Hill.

Formed in 1969, **High Tide** were part of the wave of 'progressive underground' bands which grew up in Britain in the late sixties, and were probably the heaviest band in London when they started. Tony Hill had earlier played with **The Misunderstood**. Their albums, which were for the most part completely uncommercial, were characterised by elaborate, sometimes over-sophisticated guitar and electric violin work. The band were more popular on the Continent than in Britain. The strongest tracks on the

HIGH TIDE - Sea Shanties (LP).

HIGH TIDE - High Tide (LP).

first album are arguably *Walking Down Their Outlook* and *Pushed, But Not Forgotten*, which has a beautiful, mellowed vocal intro. *Futilist's Lament* was also melodic whereas *Missing Out* and *Nowhere* were high energy 'wall of sound' instrumentals with a mesh of violin and guitar. The album was produced by **Denver Gerrard** of **Warm Sounds**, who was backed by **High Tide** on his own solo album. Their second album was in a similar mould to the first and comprised just three tracks; the 14-minute *Saneonymous* which accounts for the whole of side 2, the eight-minute *Blankman Cries Again* and *The Joke*, which lasts for over nine minutes. All three are extended instrumental compositions with occasional vocal interludes. Despite their undoubted ability as musicians, **High Tide**'s music lacked sufficient interest to attain wide recognition. *Walking Down Their Outlook* was introduced to a wider audience via the *Son Of Gutbucket* (LP) compilation.

Simon House later played with **Hawkwind** and **David Bowie**. He also played with members of **The Third Ear Band** on the soundtrack to Roman Polanski's 'Macbeth'. Peter Pavli was later involved with House in several **Hawkwind** offshoot projects.

Of the recent CDs, the first to appear was *Interesting Times*, with ten tracks featuring Tony Hill and Simon House and a drum machine. This appeared first as a mail order cassette.

There have also been three later CDs. *Ancient Gates* (World Wide Records SPM-WWR-CD-007) 1990, is a reunion recording with Hill and Pavli teaming up with former **Crazy World Of Arthur Brown**'s Drachen Theaker, violinist Dave Tomlin and vocalist Sushi Krishnamurthi. The first track *Resonance* is brilliant, but gets worse with every subsequent track and I defy anyone to listen to it all the way through. Tony Hill also recorded a solo CD (on World Wide Records) and **Maggie Bell** released a single of the "Hazell" theme tune on Swan Song records in 1978. (VJ/JHo)

Highway

Personnel: IAN AITCHESON   gtr   A
               IAN BYRON   drms, vcls   AB
               JON ELSTAR   vcls, perc   AB
               JOHN GORDON   gtr, bs, vcls   AB
               JIM HALL   keyb'ds, vcls   AB
               RAY MINHINNET   gtr, vcls   AB

ALBUMS: 1(B)   SMOKING AT THE EDGES   (EMI EMI 2223) 1974 SC
        2(B)   HIGHWAY   (EMI EMC 3019) 1974 SC

45s: Ready/Steam Driving Man   (EMI EMI 2090) 1973
        Cell Block 4/Pisa (Peace)   (EMI EMI 2223) 1974

A Sunderland band. Aitcheson was in the original line-up but left in June 1973 to join **The Chris McClure Section**. They were apparently influenced by American bands such as The Eagles. **Highway**'s self-titled first album is pleasant enough without ever producing any outstanding moments. They were assisted on it by **Mick Grabham** and **B.J. Cole**. (VJ/BS)

Steve Hillage

			HCP
ALBUMS:	1	FISH RISING	(Virgin V 2031) 1975 33
(up to	2	L	(Virgin V 2066) 1976 10
1976)			

NB: (1) and (2) reissued on CD by Virgin (CDV 2031 and CDV IP 184) respectively). *BBC Radio One Live In Concert* (Windsong WIN CD 014) 1992 may also interest readers.

45:     It's All Too Much/Shimmer   (Virgin VS 161) 1976

Steve Hillage, who was born on 2nd August 1951, first played in an outfit called Uriel who later evolved into **Egg** but by then **Hillage** had departed for college. When he finished college he was first in **Khan** and then in **Kevin Ayers'** touring band Decadence before joining the French-based hippie outfit **Gong**.

He recorded his *Fish Rising* album with assistance from several **Gong** members, much of the material on it was co-written with his girlfriend Miquette Giraudy. He eventually left **Gong** in 1976. The same year he recorded another solo album, which was produced by Todd Rundgren in Woodstock, New York, and included members of Rundgren's band Utopia. It was critically acclaimed. His 45, *It's All Too Much*, was a **Beatles** cover.

He went on to record a series of solo albums in the late seventies with considerable recognition. In the eighties he became involved in production work. The nineties saw him recording again as leader of the loose knit dance music outfit System 7. (VJ)

Him and The Others

45:     I Mean It/
        She Got Eyes That Tell Lies   (Parlophone R 5510) 1966 R5

This 45 was a well respected slice of English garage band music. *She's Got Eyes That Tell Lies* is brilliant and one of the top five freakbeat rarities. The 'A' side is a pretty gritty number too. In 1967 they became The Hand.

I Mean It has been compiled on *Purple Pill Eaters* (LP & CD) and *Beat It* (3-CD). (VJ)

Rupert Hine

ALBUMS:	1	PICK UP A BONE	(Purple TPSA 7502) 1971 R1
(up to	2	UNFINISHED PICTURE	(Purple TPSA 7509) 1973 SC
1976)			

NB: (1) and (2) with David MacIver.

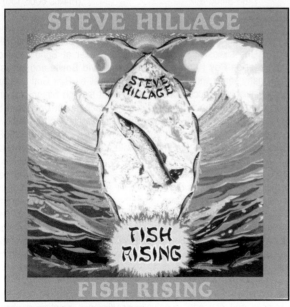
STEVE HILLAGE - Fish Rising (CD).

STEVE HILLAGE - Live In Concert (CD).

45s:	Hamburgers/		
(up to	Varlet Lad T'was Samuel Green	(Purple PUR 105) 1972
1976)	Snakes Don't Dance Fast/Hopi Smile	(Electric WOT 8) 1976

Rupert Hine had been half of **Rupert and David** (with David Iver) in the sixties. MacIver assisted him on these solo albums and the two of them later formed **Quantum Jump**. **Hine** continued to record well beyond the time-span of this book. (VJ)

The Hi-Numbers

45:     Heart Of Stone/Dancing In The Street (Decca F 12233) 1965 R1

A rare and sought-after R&B single, though the flip side is a disappointing version of a classic song.

Compilation appearances include: *Heart Of Stone* on *Purple Pill Eaters* (LP & CD) and *Broken Dreams, Vol. 4* (LP); and *Heart Of Stone* and *Dancing In The Street* on *The R&B Scene, Vol. 2 1986* (LP). (VJ)

Hipster Image

45:     Can't Let Her Go/Make Her Mine   (Decca F 12137) 1965 R4

This Sheffield band's superb 45 was produced by **Alan Price** and featured in a US advertisement for Levi's jeans. They also recorded a couple of tracks on a Keele University Rag Week EP, entitled 'Sounds Of Savile', which came out on flexidisc in 1965 and was introduced by Jimmy Savile himself. The two tracks they contributed were *A Little Piece Of Leather* and *All For You*. **Cooper** went on to form **The Climax Chicago Blues Band**.

Compilation appearances have included: *Make Her Mine* on *The Mod Scene* (CD) and *That Driving Beat* (CD); *Can't Let Her Go* on *The R&B Scene* (CD); and *Little Piece Of Leather* on *Incredible Sound Show Stories, Vol. 2* (LP). (MWh)

The Hitters

45:     Hypocrite/The Version   (United Artists UP 35530) 1973 SC

This was an offshoot of **Brinsley Schwarz**. (VJ)

Hobby Shop

45:     Why Must It Be This Way/Talk To Me (Columbia DB 8395) 1968

This was a short-lived pop band. (VJ)

Hobo

Personnel: STEVE BULL — drms — A
PAUL COBBOLD — bs, keyb'ds — A
COLIN DUGGAN — vcls, gtr — A
STUART HARRISON — vcls, acc gtr — A
JOHN MORRIS — vcls, gtr — A

ALBUM: 1(A) HOBO (United Artists UAS 29909) 1976

This is pleasant harmony rock with assistance from Kips (ex-**Blonde On Blonde**), Pick Withers (ex-**Spring** now Dire Straits) and Ray Martinez (ex-**Gypsy** and **Spring**). (BS)

Hoboken

ALBUM: 1 HOBOKEN (Oak no number) 1973 R5

Just six copies were pressed of this hopelessly obscure album. Sadly, no extracts figure on the *Story Of Oak* records (2-LP) compilation. It's a six-track acetate-only album housed in a gatefold sleeve. These comprise cover versions of **Yes**, **Capability Brown** and **Rare Bird** material. They were heavily influenced by the vocal harmonies of **Capability Brown**. (VJ)

Charles Hodges

45: Try A Little Love/
Someone To Love (Major Minor MM 654) 1969 SC

Originally with The Outlaws from 1960-65, and then **Cliff Bennett and The Rebel Rousers**, he recorded this 45 whilst with **The Roy Young Band** in 1969. In 1970 he played briefly with an outfit called Black Claw (basically **Young**'s old band after he left), he was then in **Heads, Hands and Feet** and The Albert Lee Band with Dave Peacock before he became the Chas and Peacock the Dave of Chas and Dave. (VJ)

Chris Hodge

45s: We're On Our Way/
Supersoul (Some in PS) (Apple APPLE 43) 1972 SC/-
Beautiful Love/
Sweet Lady From The Sky (RCA LPBO 5007) 1974
I Love You/Old James Dean (DJM DJS 10337) 1974

A budding pop star recorded these three 45s, and another for Apple, *Goodbye Sweet Lorraine/Contact Love*, which was only issued in the US. Perhaps that's why he decided to emigrate there in the mid-seventies. (VJ)

James Hogg (Band)

Personnel incl: JAMES HOGG

45s: Lovely Lady/Happy Sad (Regal Zonophone RZ 3054) 1972
California Blues/
Everybody Smile (Regal Zonophone RZ 3068) 1972
Gotta Be A Winner/
Everybody Smile (Regal Zonophone RZ 3078) 1973

The James Hogg (Band) hailed from Bridgend, Wales. *Lovely Lady Rock* is a guitar rocker of a Johnny Kidd song. They are still around on the club circuit. (VJ)

Hokus Poke

Personnel: CLIVE BLENKHORN — gtr, vcls — A
SMITH CAMPBELL — bs — A
ROGER CLARKE — gtr, steel gtr — A
JOHNNIE MILES — drms — A

ALBUM: 1(A) EARTH HARMONY (Vertigo 6360 064) 1972 R2
NB: (1) reissued on CD (Repertoire REP 4197).

Hokus Poke was the resident band at the Thomas A Beckett pub in London's Old Kent Road for a while. *Earth Harmony* is straight ahead rock, slightly bluesy, from a classic line-up of dual guitars, bass and drums. Mostly the sparse sound is topped by reasonably likeable vocals, here and there reminiscent of **Stevie Marriott**. The playing is flawless, but not very inspired, and gives the impression of being curtailed in the studio. It was produced by Kenny Lynch. Where the compositions are more thoughtful and melodious, there are some nice tracks like the beginning of *Sunrise Sunset* and *Big World Small Girl*, in which the vocals surprisingly enough sound like a mixture of CSN&Y and Split Enz. Still there probably isn't enough to set this apart from a lot of albums from the same era in the same vein. This is a pleasant but not outstanding album. It is now very hard to find, but is probably most sought-after by Vertigo collectors. (MK/VJ)

Ram Jam Holder

ALBUMS: 1 RAM BLUES GOSPEL AND SOUL
(Meledisc MLP 12-133) 1963 R1
2 BLACK LONDON BLUES (Beacon BEAS 2) 1974 R1
3 BOOTLEG BLUES (Beacon BEAS 17) 1974 R1
4 YOU SIMPLY ARE (Fresh Air 9299 470) 1975

45s: I Need Somebody/She's Alright (Columbia DB 8157) 1967
My Friend Jones/It Won't Be Long
Before I Love You (Columbia DB 8262) 1967 SC
I Just Came To Get My Baby/Yes I Do (Beacon BEA 108) 1971
Battering Ram/London Ghetto (Fresh Air 6121 103) 1973
Battering Ram/London Ghetto (Fresh Air 6121 124) 1975

This was an obscure blues artist. He'd earlier recorded a 45 in 1966 for Parlophone with The Ram Holder Brothers. More recently he's notable for acting on "Desmonds". (VJ)

Tim Hollier

ALBUMS: 1 MESSAGE TO A HARLEQUIN
(United Artists (S)ULP 1211) 1968 R1
2 TIM HOLLIER (Fontana 6309 003) 1970 R2
3 SKY SAIL (Philips 6308 044) 1971 R1
4 THE STORY OF MILL REEF (York YR 503) 1974

NB: There's also a CD compilation of his material *Tim Hollier*, which comes with a 12-page booklet with brilliant psychedelic sleeve art.

45s: In This Room/Love Song (Fontana TF 1080) 1970
Circle is Small//In a Corner of My Life/
Time Stood Still (Philips 6006 130) 1971

One of the period's more distinctive singer-songwriters, **Hollier** grew up in Cumberland but gravitated towards London as an art student and folkie at the end of the sixties. He soon became a regular at Soho's folk clubs, playing alongside **Roy Harper**, **Joe Cocker**, **David Bowie** and others, and co-wrote many songs with Rory Fellowes, as well as Rick Cuff and **Amory Kane**. His lavishly produced debut came about through Simon Napier-Bell, and varied from the heavily orchestrated title track (about **Donovan**) to the fragile and beautiful *Full Fathoms Five* (a setting of a song from Shakespeare's *The Tempest*). It appeared in the UK in October 1968 and was also issued in the US (on Imperial, with a slightly different sleeve).

His second album was distinguished by the excellent acid rock-influenced *Seagull's Song*, as well as *Llanstephan Hill* and *Evolution*, recorded at the same time by his friend **Kane**, and the moody ballad *Evening Song*. Several tracks were recorded live in single takes, and overall it perhaps benefited from being less elaborately-arranged than his other work. It appeared in a stunning psychedelic sleeve in July 1970, but also failed to sell. A single copy of an Apple acetate exists, comprising alternative versions of songs from the album as well as unreleased material.

Hollier undertook many BBC sessions at this time, as well as TV appearances and concerts, eventually headlining a prestigious showcase gig at the Queen Elizabeth Hall alongside **David McWilliams** and **Peter Sarstedt**, on whose early albums he played. Sky Sail was issued in March 1971, but when it too failed to sell he moved into jingle writing and set up a couple of small labels. In 1974 six new songs of his were included on the soundtrack to a Yorkshire TV film about a racehorse called Mill Reef. The album is padded out with spoken extracts by Albert Finney and racing commentaries. Eventually **Hollier** launched Filmtrax, which went on to become one of the UK's largest independent music publishers, specialising in providing film soundtracks. He's still very active in music publishing, as well as being a leading light of the British Academy of Composers and Songwriters. (RMJ/JM)

The Hollies

Personnel:	ALLAN CLARKE	vcls	ABCDE G
	ERIC HAYDOCK	bs	ABC
	GRAHAM NASH	gtr, vcls	ABCD
	DON RATHBONE	drms	AB
	TONY HICKS	gtr, vcls	BCDEFG
	BOBBY ELLIOT	drms	CDEFG
	BERNIE CALVERT	bs, keyb'ds	DEFG
	TERRY SYLVESTER	gtr, vcls	EFG
	MIKAEL RICKFORS	ld vcls	F

				HCP
ALBUMS:	1(C)	STAY WITH THE HOLLIES (mono/stereo)		
(up to		(Parlophone PMC 1220/PCS 3054) 1964 R1	2
1976)	2(C)	IN THE HOLLIES STYLE		
		(Parlophone PMC 1235) 1964 R1	-
	3(C)	THE HOLLIES (Parlophone PMC 1261) 1965 R1	8
	4(C)	WOULD YOU BELIEVE? (mono/stereo)		
		(Parlophone PMC/PCS 7008) 1966 SC/R1	16
	5(D)	FOR CERTAIN BECAUSE (mono/stereo)		
		(Parlophone PMC/PCS 7011) 1966 SC/R1	23
	6(D)	EVOLUTION (mono/stereo)		
		(Parlophone PMC/PCS 7022) 1967 R1	13
	7(D)	BUTTERFLY		
		(mono/stereo) (Parlophone PMC/PCS 7039) 1967 R1	-
	8(-)	THE VINTAGE HOLLIES (WRC ST 979) 1967 R1	-
	9(-)	STAY WITH THE HOLLIES (WRC ST 1035) 1968 R1	-
	10(-)	THE HOLLIES' GREATEST HITS		
		(mono/stereo) (Parlophone PMC/PCS 7057) 1968 SC	1
	11(E)	THE HOLLIES SING DYLAN		
		(mono/stereo) (Parlophone PMC/PCS 7078) 1969 SC	3
	12(E)	HOLLIES SING HOLLIES		
		(mono/stereo) (Parlophone PMC/PCS 7092) 1969 SC	-
	13(-)	REFLECTION (Regal Starline SRS 5008) 1969	-
	14(E)	CONFESSIONS OF THE MIND		
		(Parlophone PCS 7116) 1970 SC	30
	15(E)	DISTANT LIGHT (Parlophone PAS 10005) 1971 SC	-
	16(-)	STOP! STOP! STOP (Regal Starline SRS 5088) 1971	-
	17(C)	THE HOLLIES (Music For Pleasure MFP 5252) 1972	-
	18(-)	THE HOLLIES GREATEST HITS, VOL 2		
		(Parlophone PCS 7148) 1972	-
	19(F)	ROMANY (Polydor 2383 144) 1972 SC	-
	20(G)	THE HOLLIES (Polydor 2383 262) 1974 SC	38
	21(-)	I CAN'T LET GO (Music For Pleasure MFP 50094) 1974	-
	22(G)	ANOTHER NIGHT (Polydor 2442 128) 1975 SC	-
	23(-)	THE HISTORY OF THE HOLLIES (EMI EMSP 650) 1975	-
	24(G)	WRITE ON (Polydor 2442 141) 1976 SC	-
	25(G)	RUSSIAN ROULETTE (Polydor 2383 421) 1976 SC	-

NB: (8) (9) Record club issues. (8) was a reissue of (2), but this time in stereo. (9) was a reissue of (1) in stereo. (13) is a reissue of (3), but this time in stereo. (16) is a reissue of (5), this time in stereo. (17) is a reissue of (6) in stereo. (21) is a reissue of (4) in stereo.

They've also had a number of US-only albums. In their early days:- *Here I Go* (Imperial 12265) 1965, *Hear Here* (Imperial 12299) 1965, *King Midas* (Epic 26344) 1968; *Greatest Hits* (Imperial 12350) 1969; *Moving Finger* (Epic 30255) 1970 and *He Ain't Heavy* (Epic 26538) 1970.

(1) was reissued (Beat Goes On BGOLP 4) in 1987 and on CD (Beat Goes On BGOCD 4) 1989. (2) reissued (Beat Goes On BGOLP 8) 1988 and on CD (Beat Goes On BGOCD 8) 1989. (3) and (4) reissued on CD in 1991 on Beat Goes On (BGOCD 25 and 26) respectively. (4) reissued on CD (EMI 495 1502) 1998 in digipak format with both mono and stereo versions included. (5) reissued on Beat Goes On (BGOLP 9) 1988 and on CD (Beat Goes On BGO CD 9) 1989 and again (EMI 498 9522) 1999 on EMI digipak in both mono and stereo. (6), (7) and (14) all reissued in 1978 on vinyl in stereo, along with *The Other Side Of The Hollies* (Parlophone PMC 7176). (6) reissued (Beat Goes On (BGOLP 80) 1990, also on CD (BGOCD 80). (6) reissued again on CD (EMI 499 4272) 1999 in digipack. (7) reissued again (Beat Goes On BGOLP 79) 1990, also on CD (BGOCD 79) 1990 and again on CD (EMI 499 7712) 1999. *The Other Side Of The Hollies* was later reissued in 1990 on album and CD (See For Miles SEE LP 302/SEE CD 302) with two additional cuts:- *Open Your Eyes* and the first mix they recorded of Bob Dylan's *Blowin' In The Wind* as *The Other Side Of The Hollies Plus*. (11) reissued on vinyl (Parlophone PCS 7078) 1978 and on CD (EMI 0777 7 81330 2 5) 1993 with two bonus tracks. (11) reissued again on CD as an EMI digipak (EMI CD UK 520 1312) 1999. (12) reissued again on CD as an EMI digipak (EMI CD UK 520 1302) 1999. (14) reissued on Beat Goes On (BGOLP 96) in 1991, also on CD (BGOCD 96). (14) reissued again on CD as an EMI digipak (EMI CD UK 520 2232) 1999. (15) reissued on Beat Goes On (BGOCD 97) 1991 and again on CD as an EMI digipak (EMI CD UK 520 3972) 1999. *In The Hollies Style* (EMI DORIG 115) 1997 is another CD release coupling mono and stereo versions of all the tracks on the band's second album. Both the mono and stereo versions of their debut album *Stay With The Hollies* (EMI DORIG 111) 1997 have been coupled on one CD. *The Hollies* (EMI DORIG 117) 1997, originally from 1965, also gets the same treatment.

Of posthumous releases which may be of interest are *Hollies Live Hits* (Polydor 2383 428) 1977 (No 4); *20 Golden Greats* (EMI EMTV 11) 1978 (No 2) (later reissued on vinyl (EMI LP ATAK 38) 1988 and on CD (EMI CD CDP7 46238 2) 1987) and *The Best Of The Hollies EPs* (Parlophone PMC 7174) 1978, which was reissued on EMI (NUTM 30) in 1981. In 1987 it was reissued again with two extra tracks as *The EP Collection* (See For Miles SEE 94), or (SEE CD 94) 1989. *The Other Side Of The Hollies* (Parlophone PMC 7176) 1978 is a compilation of 'B' sides; *Up Front* (St. Michael LP 2102/0101) 1979 is a compilation produced exclusively for Marks and Spencer in the UK by Polydor; *Long Cool Woman In A Black Dress* (Music For Pleasure MFP 50450) 1979, *The Air That I Breathe* (Polydor 2384 115) 1980 and *The Hollies* (Music For Pleasure 41 5727 1) 1985 are further compilations. A 1986 compilation was *Not The Hits Again* (See For Miles SEE 63), which was later released on CD (See For Miles SEECD 63) 1989. *An Hour Of The Hollies* (Music For Pleasure HR 8153) 1987 was released as a boxed cassette - it was released on CD as *The Hollies* (Music For Pleasure CD CDB7) in 1988 and reissued again as *The Hollies* (EMI solo CBD7 52047-2) 1995, but with a different cover. The same year EMI put out a double compilation, *All The Hits And More* (EMI EM 1301) 1988 (No 51). *Rarities* (EMI LP EMS 1311) also on CD (EMI CDP 7 91297 2) 1988, combines a healthy dose of late sixties material with a couple of later tracks, including previously unreleased cuts, rarities and non-UK releases.

Early nineties compilations were *Love Songs* (EMI MFP 5883) 1990, issued on both vinyl and CD (it was later reissued on CD (EMI CDMFP 5883) 1996, but with a different cover); *The Air That I Breathe* (EMI EMTV 74) 1993, also on CD (CDEMTV 74) 1993; and *Singles A's & B's 1970-1979* (EMI CDMFP 5980) 1993. *Four Hollies Originals* (EMI HOLLIES 1) 1994 reissues (22), (25) and two post-1976 Hollies albums; *5317704* (from 1979) and *Buddy Holly* (from 1980) in mini, CD-sized facsimiles of their album packaging. The set also comes with a fold-out poster with pictures and sleeve-notes. *Legendary Top Ten 1963-1988* (Avon Cosmetics FFCD 822) 1994 was a compilation produced exclusively for Avon Cosmetics in the UK and Eire by Fastforward Music Promotions Ltd in association with EMI. *The Best Of The Hollies* (EMI CDMFP 6191) 1995 was a compilation produced by EMI exclusively for Woolworths in the UK. This was reissued again (EMI CDMFPE 6336) 1997. *Four More Hollies Originals* (EMI HOLLIES 2) 1995 is the second in a series of 5" box of miniature editions of **Hollies** albums. This time the albums featured are from the seventies:- *Romany, Hollies, Write On* and *A Crazy Steal*. *20 Classic Tracks* (EMI CDBTS3) 1996 is a compilation produced exclusively for Boots in the UK by EMI. *The Best Of The Hollies* (EMI CTMCD 311) 1997 is a poorly put together collection of their material which does include a selection of their later recordings: a live version of Prince's *Purple Rain* and Nils Lofgren's *Shine Silently*, along with their famous UK hits. It was produced to celebrate 100 years of EMI. *Special Collection* (Music For Pleasure CDTRBOX 280) 1997 is a 60-track budget-priced 3-CD set covering their material between 1963 to the nineties. It

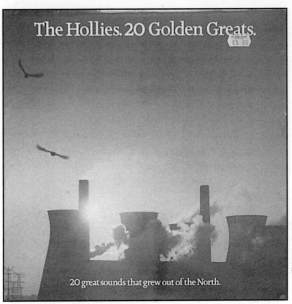

THE HOLLIES - 20 Golden Greats (LP).

includes about 75% of their hits, plus some 'B' sides, album tracks and near misses. *The Singles Collection* (EMI/BR Music 7243 8 33282 2 62) 1997 is a definitive 2-CD collection of their 45 output and includes some non-UK 45s. *Dear Eloise / King Midas In Reverse* (Sundazed SC 6123) 1997 is basically a CD reissue of their UK *Butterfly* album with the above two 45s added and giving it a new title. *Moving Finger* (Sundazed SC 6125) 1997 is a CD reissue of the US version of their UK *Confessions Of The Mind* album. Another restrospective, *A Special Collection* (EMI MFP CDTRBOX280) 1997 is a 3-CD box set compilation. *At Abbey Road* 1963 - 1966 (CD ABBEY 103) 1997 contains what the title suggests. *At Abbey Road: 1966 To 1970* (EMI 493 4502) 1998 concentrates on their ventures into harmony-pop and psychedelia. *At Abbey Road 1973-1989* (EMI 7243 496434 2 0) 1998 is the final part of their Abbey Road trilogy and includes four previously unissued cuts. *The Essential Collection* (Music For Pleasure CD MFP 6387) 1998 mixes 45s and album tracks - it's hardly a 'best of' but at mid-price is good value. *Orchestral Heaven* (EMI CD UK) 2000 is a compilation of original recordings that were augmented with strings. *Greatest Hits* (EMI 582 0122) 2003 is a 2-CD compilation celebrating 40 years of music by **The Hollies**. *The Long Road Home* (EMI 584 8562) 2003 is a 5-CD set spanning their 40 year career. *Collection* (HMV Easy HMV 594002) 2003 is a 22-track compilation exclusive to HMV. *Side By Side* (Marks & Spencer M7767 982) 2003 is a compilation of 10 original recordings by **The Hollies** and 10 by **Manfred Mann**. *A's, B's & EP's* (EMI Gold CD UK 596 8172) 2004 is a compilation of tracks from their singles (A and B sides) plus some from EPs. Phew!

EPs:				
1(C)	THE HOLLIES	(Parlophone GEP 8909)	1964	R1
2(C)	JUST ONE LOOK	(Parlophone GEP 8911)	1964	R1
3(C)	HERE I GO AGAIN	(Parlophone GEP 8915)	1964	R1
4(C)	WE'RE THROUGH	(Parlophone GEP 8927)	1964	R1
5(C)	IN THE HOLLIES STYLE	(Parlophone GEP 8934)	1965	R1
6(C)	I'M ALIVE	(Parlophone GEP 8942)	1965	R1
7(C)	I CAN'T LET GO	(Parlophone GEP 8951)	1966	R1

				HCP
45s: (up to 1976)	(Ain't That) Just Like Me/Hey, What's Wrong With Me	(Parlophone R 5030)	1963	SC 25
	Searchin'/Whole World Over	(Parlophone R 5052)	1963	12
	Stay/Now's The Time	(Parlophone R 5077)	1963	8
	Just One Look/ Keep Off That Friend Of Mine	(Parlophone R 5104)	1964	2
	Here I Go Again/Baby That's All	(Parlophone R 5137)	1964	4
	We're Through/Come On Back	(Parlophone R 5178)	1964	7
	(I'll Be True To You) Yes I Will/ Nobody	(Parlophone R 5232)	1965	9
	I'm Alive/You Know He Did	(Parlophone R 5287)	1965	1
	Look Through Any Window/ So Lonely	(Parlophone R 5322)	1965	4
	If I Needed Someone/ I've Got A Way Of My Own	(Parlophone R 5392)	1965	20
	I Can't Let Go/ Running Through The Night	(Parlophone R 5409)	1966	2
	Bus Stop/Don't Run And Hide	(Parlophone R 5469)	1966	5
	After The Fox (with Peter Sellers)/ BURT BACHARACH: The Fox-Trot	(United Artists UP 1152)	1966	R1 -
	Stop! Stop! Stop!/It's You	(Parlophone R 5508)	1966	2
	On A Carousel/ All The World Is Love	(Parlophone R 5562)	1967	4
	Carrie-Anne/ Signs That Will Never Change	(Parlophone R 5602)	1967	3
	King Midas In Reverse/ Everything Is Sunshine	(Parlophone R 5637)	1967	18
	Jennifer Eccles/ Open Up Your Eyes	(Parlophone R 5680)	1968	7
	Listen To Me/ Do The Best You Can	(Parlophone R 5733)	1968	11
	Sorry Suzanne/ Not That Way At All	(Parlophone R 5765)	1969	3
	He Ain't Heavy, He's My Brother/ 'Cos You Like To Love Me	(Parlophone R 5806)	1969	3
	I Can't Tell The Bottom From The Top/ Mad Professor Blyth	(Parlophone R 5837)	1970	7
	Gasoline Alley Bred/ Dandelion Wine	(Parlophone R 5862)	1970	14
	Hey Willy/ Row The Boat Together	(Parlophone R 5905)	1971	22
	The Baby/Oh Granny	(Polydor 2058 199)	1972	26
	Long Cool Woman (In A Black Dress)/ Cable Car	(Parlophone R 5939)	1972	32
	Magic Woman Touch/Indian Girl	(Polydor 2058 289)	1972	-
	The Day That Curly Billy Shot Down Crazy Sam McGhee/ Born A Man	(Polydor 2058 403)	1973	24

	The Air That I Breathe/ No More Riders	(Polydor 2058 435)	1974	2
	Son Of A Rotten Gambler/ Layin' To The Music	(Polydor 2058 476)	1974	-
	I'm Down/Hello Lady Goodbye	(Polydor 2058 533)	1974	-
	(Fourth Of July, Ashbury Park) Sandy/ Second-Hand Hangups	(Polydor 2058 595)	1975	-
	Boulder To Birmingham/ Crocodile Woman (She Bites)	(Polydor 2058 694)	1976	-
	Star/Love Is The Thing	(Polydor 2058 719)	1976	-
	Daddy Don't Mind/C'mon	(Polydor 2058 779)	1976	-
	Wiggle That Wotsit/Corrine	(Polydor 2058 799)	1976	-
	Hello To Romance/ 48 Hour Parole	(Polydor 2058 880)	1976	-
Reissues: β	Long Cool Woman In A Black Dress/ Carrie-Anne	(EMI EMI 2353)	1975	
	Look Through Any Window/ I'm Alive/Just One Look	(EMI 2813)	1978	-
	He Ain't Heavy, He's My Brother/ Yes You Like To Love Me	(Parlophone PMS 1001)	1982	-
	Just One Look/Here I Go Again	(EMI GG 1)	1984	-
	Bus Stop/Stop! Stop! Stop!	(EMI 1A 0065656)	1984	-
α	He Ain't Heavy, He's My Brother/ Carrie-Anne (PS)	(EMI EM 74)	1988	1
	The Air That I Breathe/ He Ain't Heavy, He's My Brother/ Bus Stop	(EMI EM 80)	1988	60
		(Old Gold OG 6170)	1983	-
χ	He Ain't Heavy, He's My Brother/ Carrie-Anne/On A Carousel	(Old Gold OG 6170)	1992	-
	I'm Alive/Just One Look	(Old Gold OG 6173)	1992	-

NB: α Also in 12" format with *The Air That I Breathe* added. β This was later repressed with the same catalogue number in the same year with the sides reversed. χ CD single. One US 45 of interest was: *Jesus Was A Crossmaker/I Had A Dream* (Epic 5-10989) 1973. The 'A' side was taken from the *Romany* album, but the flip, a nice ballad, wasn't issued in the UK.

The Hollies were Britain's third most popular sixties group with only **The Beatles** and **The Rolling Stones** ahead of them. Their consistency speaks volumes for them - between 1963 and 1974 they had only one single which failed to make the UK Charts. Undoubtedly they produced some of the finest harmony-pop singles to come out of the UK in this era.

The Hollies were formed in Manchester in 1961 by former schoolmates Allan Clarke and **Graham Nash**. These two were playing as The Two Teens duo but the addition of Eric Haydock and drummer Don Rathbone led to a change of names to The Fourtones, then The Deltas and by the end of the year, they'd changed names again to **The Hollies**.

In January 1963, Ron Richards of Parlophone Records saw them playing at Liverpool's Cavern Club and signed them up immediately. Their first single recorded by line-up (B) was a cover of The Coasters' *(Ain't That) Just Like Me*, which became a minor hit. For the follow-up they turned to another Coasters' song, *Searchin'* and it climbed to No 12. By the time it had

THE HOLLIES - Evolution (CD).

THE HOLLIES - Butterfly (CD).

reached the charts Don Rathbone had moved into a management capacity to make way for Bobby Elliot, an old pal of Tony Hicks who'd been playing in Shane Fenton and The Fentones on drums. This new line-up's first single was a revival of Maurice Williams and The Zodiac's *Stay*, which produced their first Top 10 hit. After this they worked on their first album, *Stay With The Hollies*, which certainly sold in large quantities. The hits continued to flow - first a revival of Doris Troy's *Just One Look* (which became their first single to enter the US Charts, albeit peaking at only No 98); *Here I Go Again* and then their first self-penned 'A' side, *We're Through*. Written by Clarke, Hicks and **Nash** using the pseudonym L Ransford it made the Top 10, yet despite all their 45 success their next album, *In The Hollies Style*, failed to chart at all.

By now the band had developed the distinctive three-part harmonies that would be their trademark for several years to come. 1965 was a particularly good year for them. They made the Top 10 with the Goffin/King song *Yes I Will*; topped the US Charts with Clint Ballard Jr's *I'm Alive* (undoubtedly one of their finest singles); took **Graham Gouldman**'s *Look Through Any Window* into the Top 5, and made the Album Charts Top 10 with a good third album, *The Hollies*, which featured a wide range of covers like *Mickey's Monkey* and *Fortune Teller* (R&B), *Lawdy Miss Clawdy* (rock'n'roll) and *Very Last Day* (folk-rock). The band also embarked on their first US tour, playing the New York Broadway Paramount with Little Richard and King Curtis. They enjoyed considerable US success in 1966 and 1967 but suffered undoubtedly from arriving a little later on the scene than **The Beatles**, **The Dave Clark Five** and **Herman's Hermits**.

Their least successful single of the sixties (after their debut) was their version of **George Harrison**'s *If I Needed Someone* and this was probably because **Harrison** slagged the band off, saying they sounded like sessionmen. The single peaked at No 20. To arrest any possible slide in their fortunes, they needed a strong follow-up and they certainly came up trumps with their version of a Chip Taylor's *I Can't Let Go* - this was harmony-pop at its very best and took them to No 2.

In April 1966, Eric Haydock was asked to leave the band after missing several gigs and Bernie Calvert (ex-Dolphins), who could also play keyboards, came in as a replacement. Haydock later formed **Haydock's Rockhouse**. Just prior to this the band had recorded the theme tune for a Peter Sellers movie, *After The Fox*, with **Jack Bruce** on bass and Burt Bacharach, who did the arranging, on slide piano. The first 45 Calvert played on was **Graham Gouldman**'s excellent *Bus Stop*, a song about a bus stop romance, and the result was another Top Ten hit. Their *Would You Believe?* album also made the Top 20.

Their next single, *Stop, Stop, Stop* was rather unusual for its distinctive six-string banjo riff. It was also a group-penned composition and it gave them another massive hit. It was also the closing track of their *For Certain Because* album, which saw them branching out beyond the beat format (still represented here by *What's Wrong With The Way I Live* and *Pay You Back With Interest*) with orchestrated numbers (courtesy of **The Mike Vickers Orchestra**) and several Graham Nash compositions, which were evocative of the emerging psychedelic era.

With the onset of the psychedelic era in 1967, the group continued to come up with new ideas and fresh sounding 45s. First there was *On A Carousel*, a slice of superb harmony-pop written by the band, which inevitably gave them another Top 10 hit (it also reached No 11 in the US) and then the Calypso-style *Carrie-Anne*, which had taken Clarke, Hicks and **Nash** almost two years to write and gave them another massive UK hit.

Work on their sixth album, *Evolution*, had begun at the start of 1967 but was disrupted when Bobby Elliot was hospitalised for a long spell, after suffering a burst appendix whilst on tour in Germany. The album had to be completed using session drummers Clem Cattini, Dougie Wright and Mitch Mitchell. The album peaked at No 13 in the UK and No 43 in the US. After this, US distribution switched from Imperial to Epic and Imperial released a US-only single, *Pay You Back With Interest*, which just made the Top 30. *Carrie-Anne*, their first Epic single fared better though, making it to No 9 in the US.

As 1967 progressed they became even more experimental. Heavily influenced by **The Beatles'** *Sergeant Pepper* they started work on a new album, *Butterfly*. Their next 45, *King Midas In Reverse*, was a taster of what was to come. Written largely by **Graham Nash** it featured an orchestra and was released against the advice of their producer Ron Richards who felt that its experimental structure wouldn't appeal to **Hollies'** fans. In fact, it did make the Top 20, but only just, by their standards it was a commercial flop. When it appeared *Butterfly* was a wholehearted venture into flower-power. It was probably their most interesting album. High points included *Dear Eloise*, which was released as a single in the US, *Lullaby To Tim* (which Allan Clarke had written for his son and **Nash** had added warbled vocals to) and *Elevated Observations*.

In late 1967, whilst in LA, the band were invited to a Mamas and Papas recording session. It was here that **Nash**, who was rapidly falling in love with the American lifestyle, met David Crosby - a meeting that was to prove very significant in a year's time.

Their first recording in 1968 was the beautiful and mildly psychedelic *Wings*, another Clarke/**Nash** composition, which wasn't released as a 45 but was included on the Word Wildlife Fund charity (LP), *No One's Gonna Change Our World*. Their next 45 was *Jennifer Eccles*, an unashamedly ultra-commercial pop song deliberately written by Clarke and Nash to contrast with the complexity of its predecessor, *King Midas In Reverse*. Inevitably it was a Top 10 hit over here (and it crept to No 40 in the US). In March they began work on another album but before it was completed **Graham Nash** had left both the band and his wife to start a new life in the States. This didn't come as a great surprise because there had clearly been friction in the band between **Nash** (who'd already been working on a solo album), who wanted the band to become more experimental and Tony Hicks who wanted the group to record the music their fans wanted. **Nash**'s last single with the band was the rather unadventurous *Listen To Me* and, just prior to his departure, they'd topped the Album Charts here in the UK for seven weeks with the compilation, *The Hollies Greatest Hits*.

Nash's replacement Terry Slyvester (formerly with **The Escorts** and **The Swingin' Blues Jeans**) was recruited in January 1969. His first recording

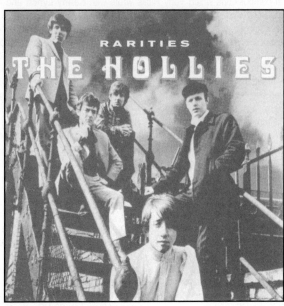

THE HOLLIES - Rarities (CD).

THE HOLLIES The EP Collection

THE HOLLIES - EP Collection (CD).

with the group was *Sorry Suzanne*, very much in their tried and tested formula, and it shot to No 3 in the UK but couldn't advance beyond No 56 in the US. They then recorded the *The Hollies Sing Dylan* album, which rose to No 3 in the UK Album Charts. **Graham Nash** had been very opposed to this project, indeed it seemed to have been a significant factor in him deciding to leave the band. However, **Nash**'s departure threw the band's songwriting partnership out of balance, so Tony Hicks set off in search of a new single. The one he eventually chose was a big ballad, *He Ain't Heavy, He's My Brother*. **Elton John**, who was by now on the verge of a commercial breakthrough, played keyboards on the song, which made the Top 10 on both sides of the Atlantic and sold a million copies worldwide. He also played piano on the follow-up single, *I Can't Tell The Bottom From The Top*, which also made the UK Top 10, but stalled at No 82 in the US.

For their next album project, *Hollies Sing Hollies*, the group recorded an album of their own material. It didn't sell particularly well but included some significant landmarks for the band. Bernie Calvert's *Reflections Of A Long Time Past* was the first instrumental they had recorded and *My Life Is Over Without You* was Allan Clarke's response to **Graham Nash**'s departure. Many of the tracks were orchestrated and the end product represented a significant progression away from their earlier teenage pop sound which continued on their next album, *Confessions Of The Mind*, which marked the emergence of Tony Hicks as the band's main songwriter. It peaked at No 30 in the UK whilst the US equivalent, *Moving Finger*, stuttered to No 183. They also enjoyed further hit singles in this period with *Gasoline Alley Bred* and *Hey Willy*.

In April 1971, they began recording the *Distant Light* album, which included several compositions which Tony Hicks wrote with **Kenny Lynch** and Allan Clarke's *Long Cool Woman (In A Black Dress)*, which was leaner than their usual harmony-pop sound. The album didn't chart at all in the UK and by the time it had reached the shops Allan Clarke had departed to record a solo album, basically he just wanted to record something that didn't sound like the group. His replacement was a Swedish singer, Mikael Rickfors, who'd previously been with Bamboo. They switched to the new Polydor label for their first single with Rickfors' lead vocals, which was Chip Taylor's *The Baby*. It made No 26 in the UK. Meanwhile in the States their *Distant Light* album had fared much better rising to No 21 and when *Long Tall Woman...* was belatedly released as a 45 over there it surpassed all expectations climbing to No 2 and going gold. Following re-promotion over here by EMI it also became a minor hit.

In the Spring of 1972, they began work on a new album, *Romany*. This veered more towards country-rock, with the title track and *Won't We Feel Good* among the highlights. Without Allan Clarke's distinctive vocals, it lacked that usual **Hollies** sound. With its country-rock leanings it's no real surprise that it sold better in the States, where it crept to No 84. It didn't make the UK Album Charts at all.

In November 1972, their fortunes nosedived when *Magic Touch Woman* became their first single to fail to enter the UK Top 40, although it did reach No 60 in the US, where it had been preceded by a Top 30 US-only 45 from

Distant Light, entitled *Long Dark Road*. They reached their lowest ebb when neither Polydor in the UK or Epic in the US would issue their next album, *Out On The Road*, which consequently only appeared in Germany. Perhaps its main significance was for the inclusion of a rare Bobby Elliot composition, *Transatlantic Westbound Jet*.

In an attempt to revive their fortunes it was decided to invite Allan Clarke to rejoin the band. Clarke's two solo albums had met with little success and finding himself in the wilderness, he accepted the proposition. He reached a new agreement which allowed him to make solo albums alongside the group's work. So in the Summer of 1973 he rejoined the band and Mikael Rickfors returned to Sweden where he subsequently became a successful solo performer. The search was on for an epic single to re-establish the band, which hadn't enjoyed a UK Top 20 hit for three years, as a commercial success. Allan Clarke's *The Day That Curly Billy Shot Down Crazy Sam McGhee*, a song very much in the mould of his earlier *Long Cool Woman...*, got the vote and reached No 24 in the UK. They started work on a new album titled simply *Hollies*, which included several re-recordings of songs from their earlier *Out On The Road* album, which hadn't been issued in the UK. It also included a song from a recent Phil Everly album, *The Air That I Breathe*, a powerful ballad which was ideally suited to their harmony vocal style. When they decided to issue it as a 45 it shot to No 2 in the UK becoming the epic single they had yearned for. The success of the single helped the album's sales and it reached No 38 in the UK and No 28 in the US, where *The Air That I Breathe* climbed to No 6 earning them another gold disk. However, their Chart comeback was to prove short-lived for their subsequent efforts, *Son Of A Rotten Gambler* (also in the *Long Cool Woman* mould) and *I'm Down* flopped. In the US they enjoyed minor hits with an edited version of Bruce Springsteen's *Sandy* (No 85) and the title track from their next album, *Another Night* (No 71). Both missed the UK Charts and neither of their 1976 albums (*Write On* and *Russian Roulette*) nor the singles from them charted anywhere at all!

Still this durable band went on and on... well beyond the time span of this volume. They enjoyed further successes in the late seventies - notably the live LP, *The Hollies Live Hits*, recorded live on stage in Christchurch, New Zealand, which was originally only issued in Europe and Australasia but reached No 4 when it got a British release in 1977. They recorded throughout the eighties, too, and in the Autumn of 1988 *He Ain't Heavy, He's My Brother* topped the UK Charts after it had figured in a UK Miller Lite Beer TV commercial.

EMI's 1988 double album anthology included all their hit singles as well as an album of rare tracks. Certainly many of those singles are well worth a listen.

The *At Abbey Road* set mixes hits, 'B' sides and album tracks, including three previously unaired tracks in the UK - *Man With No Expression*, *Sign Of The Times* and **Graham Gouldman's** *Schoolgirl*.

The Long Road Home is a 5-CD set which highlights some overlooked 'B' sides and album tracks at the expense of classics like *I'm Alive*, *On a Carousel* and *Look Through Any Window*, whilst many other hits are only

THE HOLLIES - Dear Eloise/King Midas In Reverse (CD).

represented by inferior live versions. Despite this there are lots of highlights although it is unlikely to become the definitive collection.

The band are still active on the sixties nostalgia circuit although in Spring 2000 Allan Clarke retired and was replaced by Carl Wayne of **The Move**.

Compilation appearances have included: *On A Carousel* on *Made In England, Vol. 2* (CD); *King Midas In Reverse* and *Maker* on *Psychedelia At Abbey Road* (CD); *Searchin'* on *Twist A La Star Club* (LP); *Come On Back* on *Beat At Abbey Road* (CD); *Searchin'* and *Stay* on *Hits Of The Mersey Era, Vol. 1* (LP); *Wings* on *No One's Gonna Change Our World* (Regal Starline) 1970; *Carrie-Anne* on *Stardust*; and *Dear Eloise* on *Psychedelic Dream*.

The Air That I Breathe and *Long Tall Woman In A Tall Black Dress* later resurfaced on the 3-CD box set *Radio Caroline Calling - 70's Flashback*; *He Ain't Heavy, He's My Brother* can also be heard on the 2-CD set *Sixties Summer Love*; *Wings* resurfaced on *Pop-In, Vol 2* (CD); *On A Carousel* can be heard along with *He Ain't Heavy, He's My Brother* on the 2-CD set *Greatest Hits Of The 60's Vol 4*; *The Day That Curly Billy Shot Down Crazy Sam McGhee* has been compiled on the 2-CD set *Stars And Stripes*; *Bus Stop* has resurfaced on *Beat Generation - Ready Steady Go* (CD) and you'll find *King Midas In Reverse* on the 4-CD box set *Acid Drops, Spacedust & Flying Saucers*. (VJ/BM)

Holy Mackerel

Personnel:	TERRY CLARK	vcls	A
	DEREK SMALLCOMBE	gtr	A
	ROGER SIGGERY	drms	A
	CHRIS WARE	gtr	A
	TONY WOOD	bs	A

ALBUM: 1(A) HOLY MACKEREL   (CBS 65297) 1972 SC

NB: *Closer To Heaven* (Tenth Planet TP 005) 1993 (SC), a numbered limited edition of 500, is taken from the acetate of a shelved follow-up album.

45s:	Rock-A-Bye/New Black Shoes	(CBS 8447) 1972
	We Got It Nailed Down/Rock On	(Santa Ponsa PNS 6) 1973
	Tennessee Waltz/Gemini	(Santa Ponsa DNS 11) 1974
	Ballad Of Joe McCann/	
	Girl Was Gone	(Santa Ponsa DNS 18) 1974

This group evolved from the late sixties psychedelic outfit **Jason Crest**, which Clark, Smallcombe and Siggery were all in. Both these albums are pleasant twin guitar-led melodic progressive rock with slight country influences. (VJ)

Home

Personnel:	MICK COOK	vcls, drms	ABC
	CLIVE JOHN	keyb'ds	A
	MICK STUBBS	keyb'ds, vcls, gtr	ABC
	JOHNNY WEIDER	violin	A
	CLIFF WILLIAMS	vcls, bs	ABC
	LAURIE WISEFIELD	gtr, vcls	ABC
	JIMMY ANDERSON	keyb'ds	C

ALBUMS: 1(A)	PAUSE FOR A HOARSE HORSE	(CBS 64365) 1972 R1
2(B)	HOME	(CBS 64752) 1972 SC
3(C)	ALCHEMIST	(CBS 65550) 1973

NB: (1) reissued as a mid-price CD reissue (Columbia 48440-2) 1996. (2) and (3) reissued on CD by Sony.

| 45s: | Fancy Lady, Hollywood Child/Shady Lady | (CBS 7809) 1972 |
| | Green Eyed Fairy/Sister Rosalie | (CBS 2362) 1974 |

Someone at CBS must have had very trustable ears. The development of **Home** within years from a competent but immature outfit to the makers of a minor masterpiece is nothing less than stunning. They started out as a surprisingly American-sounding progressive act. On the first album there are luckily no traces of self-indulgence or technical showmanship. There rather is an attempt to convey genuine emotion through well-contructed melody and tasteful arrangements. Yet, the results are more impressive for

HOLY MACKEREL - Closer To Heaven (LP).

their potentiality than for their immediate impact. Anyway, there is skill, courage and some excellent melodies as well. Already very noticeable is the fluent and "natural" sounding guitar of Wisefield.

The second album shows some progress. The aforementioned guitar reigns supreme on almost all tracks, the singing has improved and the sound is less derivative and swings effortlessly between different moods. The only flaw: the attempts to sound more controlled influence their emotional expressions unfavourably, resulting in a few compositions which are not on the usual level. Typically a transitory album.

They came to full bloom on *The Alchemist*. Suddenly all that previously only was suspected, springs into life. There are some incredible guitar parts, many highly emotional songs, dexterous but totally controlled playing and even inspired lyrics. While at times the music is strongly reminiscent of New Zealand band Dragon, thoughtful and gently powerful, on side two there is a unique and highly recommended apotheosis of most elements that make UK progressive rock worthwhile. The arrangements gain a hitherto only hinted at complexity, which is well-hidden, though, and only reveals itself after several spins. Don't let the fact that this is a concept album deter you from estimating its musical value.

Mick Stubbs and Mick Cook had earlier played in **The Blue Rondos**. Laurie Wisefield was later in **Wishbone Ash**. Cliff Willliams went on to be the bass player with AC/DC and has been with them for over 20 years. Test pressings exist for a 4th CBS album that was never released. (R3)

Mick Stubbs sadly passed away from cancer on 5 May 1999. (MK/VJ/NR)

Homer's Knods

45:     All She Said Was Goodbye/Mr. Rainbow   (Pye 7N 17731) 1969

A short-lived late sixties act whose *Mr. Rainbow* has been compiled on *Ripples, Vol. 7* (CD). (VJ)

Honeybus

Personnel:	RAY CANE	vcls, gtr, keyb'ds	AB
	PETE DELLO	vcls	A
	COLIN HARE	gtr, vcls, bs	AB
	PETER KIRCHER	drms	AB
	JIM KELLY	gtr, vcls	B

| ALBUMS: 1(A) | STORY | (Deram SML 1056) 1970 R2 |
| 2 (-) | RECITAL | (Warner Bros K46248) 1973 R5 |

NB: (2) was never released and is their rarest item by far. There's also a compilation, *At Their Best* (See For Miles SEE 264) 1989, which is also available on CD (SEE CD 264) 1997. This is a comprehensive set, which includes their 1969 album *Story* in full and showcases the superb and well-crafted material they produced. More recently *The Honeybus Story* (Repertoire REP 4733-WY) 1999 is a German import retrospective.

45s:	Delighted To See You/	
	The Breaking Up Scene	(Deram DM 131) 1967 -
	(Do I Figure) In Your Life?/	
	Throw My Love Away	(Deram DM 152) 1967 -
	I Can't Let Maggie Go/	
	Tender Are The Ashes	(Deram DM 182) 1968 8
	Girl Of Independent Means/How Long	(Deram DM 207) 1968 -
	She Sold Blackpool Rock/	
	Would You Believe	(Deram DM 254) 1969 -
	Story/The Right To Choose	(Deram DM 289) 1970 -
	She Is The Female To My Soul/	
	For Where Have You Been	(Bell BLL 1205) 1971 -
	For You/Little Lovely One	(Warner Bros K 16250) 1973 -
Reissues:	I Can't Let Maggie Go/Julie In My Heart	(Decca F 13631) 1976 -
	I Can't Let Maggie Go/	
	Tender Are The Ashes	(Decca F 13915) 1982 -
	I Can't Let Maggie Go/	
	(Flip by different artist)	(Old Gold OG 9347) 1983 -

A classic one-hit wonder act, this band will always be associated with the classic pop song *I Can't Let Maggie Go*.

The band formed in London in 1967. **Pete Dello** (real name Peter Blumsom) and Ray Cane (real name Raymond Byart) formed it as a vehicle for their songwriting aspirations. The other two original members were **Colin Hare** and drummer Peter Kircher, who'd previously played for the Folkstone-based **Loving Kind**. Signed to Decca's progressive Deram label, their debut 45 sunk without a trace but is worth checking out. The 'A' side was something of a novelty with a kazoo and birdwarbler, the flip a good slice of psychedelic pop with some fine fuzztone guitar and fast, upfront drumming. The follow-up, *(Do I Figure) In Your Life?*, was a rather wistful folksy ballad with intricate harmonies and a string accompaniment. Despite considerable airplay Chart action inexplicably eluded it, although several artists, including **Dave Berry**, **Joe Cocker** and Dana subsequently covered the song. Certainly it was one of the classics that got away. The flip was another strong electric composition with some fine guitar work.

It was a case of third time lucky for the band when **Dello**'s *I Can't Let Maggie Go* became their one and only Top 10 hit in April 1968. Another superb arrangement of strings and woodwind it echoed all the freshness and optimism of Springtime and its reputation was further assured when it was adopted as the theme tune by Nimble's TV bread advert. With the band on the brink of stardom **Dello** quit disillusioned with the music business - initially to study musical theory and to learn to play the violin. The band replaced him with Jim Kelly, a Scottish guitarist who they'd met whilst playing out in Germany.

Ray Cane now became their principal songwriter and his first 'A' side, *Girl Of Independent Means*, was quite catchy and the Cane, **Hare** and Kircher composition on the flip boasted fine harmonies. Sadly, the punters just weren't interested and over six months elapsed until their next 45, *She Sold Blackpool Rock*. Coming with a lush string arrangement, it lacked the magic of their second and third 'A' sides but was a fair attempt to emulate them. When it failed to make any impact the band split in the Summer of 1969 on the advice of their manager Terry Noon.

Deram released the *Story* album posthumously in 1970 and aside from an earlier 'B' side, *How Long*, it consisted of entirely new material. Much of it, like the title track, *She's Out There* and *He Was Columbus*, was accomplished pop with their by now characteristic string quartet arrangement but their harder side was well represented by *Under The Silent Tree*.

Deram also released the title cut as a 45 backed with a previously unreleased cut. **Colin Hare** and **Pete Dello** both embarked on solo careers after the band's demise (see their entries for details). Encouraged by the critical acclaim his solo album had received **Dello** reformed **Honeybus** in late 1971 with the original line-up. They recorded some tracks for the Bell label and one 45 resulted. In 1973 they recorded an album's worth of material for Warner Brothers, due to be called 'Recital'. Test pressings were produced, but its release was ultimately cancelled. Just one 45 emerged and the 'A' side featured the band's classic string arrangement plus a mandolin. Their final reunion came in 1976 and Decca put a product of it, *Julie's In My Heart*, on the flip to *I Can't Let Maggie Go*, the same year. Only Pete Kircher has remained active in the music business since then, initially as a member of R&B revivalists Shanghai, then in Original Mirrors and from 1983-86 in **Status Quo**.

I Can't Let Maggie Go inevitably went on to figure on several hits compilations including Decca's *The World Of Hits, Vol. 2* (LP). Other compilation appearances have included: *Story* on *Your Starter For Ten!!* (CD); and *(Do I Figure) In Your Life?* on *Hard Up Heroes, Vol. 2* (CD) and *Hard-Up Heroes* (2-LP). *Girl Of Independent Means* can also be heard on *Colour Me Pop, Vol 1* (CD).

The See For Miles compilation includes almost all of their *Stories* album, nearly all their Deram singles; *The Right To Choose*, a non-album 'B' side from 1970 and *Julie In My Heart*, which was put on the flip of *I Can't Let Maggie Go* when it was reissued in 1976. All in all a good purchase for fans of sixties pop. There's also a CD version which includes their remaining Deram singles.

More recently, *The Honeybus Story* kicks off with *I Can't Let Maggie Go* and includes many of their other singles along with the better tracks from *Story* and concludes with an Italian language version of *She Sold Blackpool Rock* and its 'B' side *Chi Sei Tu*. It certainly highlights that they were more than just a pure pop band. (VJ)

The Honeycombs

Personnel:	DENIS D'ELL	vcls, hrmnca	A
	ANN 'HONEY' LANTREE	drms	A
	JOHN LANTREE	bs	A
	MARTIN MURRAY	ld gtr	A
	ALAN WARD	gtr, keyb'ds	A

ALBUMS:	1(A)	THE HONEYCOMBS	(Pye NPL 18097) 1964 R1
	2(A)	ALL SYSTEMS GO!	(Pye NPL 18132) 1965 R2
	3(-)	MEEK AND HONEY	(PRT DOW 16) 1983

NB: (1) reissued on Golden Guinea (GGL 0350) in 1966 (SC) in a different sleeve. Also of interest is *The Best Of The Honeycombs* (PRT PYL 4009) 1988, and on CD, *It's The Honeycombs/All Systems Go* (Sequel NEXCD 125) 1990, which couples their two albums. Both (1) and (2) have also been reissued on CD by the German-based Repertoire label (RR 4098-WZ) 1990 and (RR 4121-WZ) 1990 respectively, along with bonus tracks plus *Live In Tokyo* (Repertoire RR 4180-WZ), a 12-track set previously only issued in Japan. There's also *The Honeycombs - The Best Of* (PRT PYC 4009) 1989, *The Honeycombs - The Best Of* (Marble Arch CMA CD 146) 1991 a 30-track CD compilation, *The Best Of The Honeycombs* (EMI CDEMS 1475) 1993, which, comprising all of (1), 11 cuts from (2) and 13 'A' and 'B' sides, contains all anyone unfamiliar with the band would need to hear and more besides.

EP:	1(A)	THAT'S THE WAY	(Pye NEP 24230) 1965 R1

45s:	Have I The Right/	
	Please Don't Pretend Again	(Pye 7N 15664) 1964 1
	Is It Because/I'll Cry Tomorrow	(Pye 7N 15705) 1964 38
	Eyes/If You've Got To Pick A Baby	(Pye 7N 15736) 1964 -
α	Don't Love You No More/	
	I'll See You Tomorrow	(Pye 7N 15781) 1965 R3

HONEYBUS.

404

Something Better Beginning/		
I'll See You Tomorrow	(Pye 7N 15827) 1965	39
That's The Way/		
Can't Get Through To You	(Pye 7N 15890) 1965	12
This Year, Next Year/		
Not Sleeping Too Well Lately	(Pye 7N 15979) 1965	-
Who Is Sylvia?/Wow Will I Know	(Pye 7N 17089) 1966	-
It's So Hard/I Fell In Love	(Pye 7N 17138) 1966	-
That Loving Feeling/Should A Man Cry	(Pye 7N 17173) 1966	-

Reissues:	Have I The Right/		
	Please Don't Pretend Again	(Pye 7N 17741) 1969	-
	Have I The Right/		
	Please Don't Pretend Again	(Pye 7N 45289) 1973	-
	Have I The Right/That's The Way	(Pye FBS 3) 1979	-
	Have I The Right/That's The Way	(Old Gold OG 9289) 1983	-
β	Have I The Right/	(Old Gold OG 6121) 1989	-

NB: α withdrawn. β CD single, other tracks by different artists.

This London-based group was formed in 1963 by Martin Murray, who'd worked as a hairdresser by day and played guitar in various skiffle and rock groups by night. Ann Lantree was a hairdressing colleague who played drums as a hobby. Murray persuaded her to join the band giving them the added novelty of a woman drummer. They weren't actually the first male band to use a woman drummer - this dubious honour belonged to The Ravens. Ann's brother John filled the bass slot after an earlier bassist had come and gone and Murray also recruited Nottingham-born Ward and vocalist **D'ell** (real name Denis Dalziel) on a friend's recommendation.

In their early days the band gigged around North London as The Sherabons but they soon opted for the catchier **Honeycombs** on account of Ann's nickname and their hair stylist background.

Their first big break came when they were spotted playing at the Mildmay Tavern in Islington by the Howard-Blaikley songwriting team. They took over the band's management, got them a record deal with Pye and the services of ace producer Joe Meek. The debut 45, *Have I The Right?*, a Howard-Blaikley composition with an infectious **Dave Clark**-style beat topped the UK Charts and later rose to No 5 in the US becoming a million-seller. A classic of the genre it's the type of record that you can't stand still to and was later covered by the Back Street Kids in the eighties. It was one of Meek's final offerings before his tragic suicide and arguably one of his best.

After this strong debut disc the group suffered a major setback when Martin Murray fell during a ballroom gig and suffered broken bones in his leg and right hand. Peter Pye, a sixteen year old, stood in for a while, as the group embarked on a major UK tour and this was followed not long after by a lengthy Australasian tour, which in hindsight took them away from base for too long during a crucial period. Their other problem was finding a strong follow-up to *Have I The Right?*. The faster Latin-tinged *Is It Because* failed to get into the Top 30 and the follow-up, *Eyes*, failed to make the Top 50 at all, despite an appearance on the Christmas 1964 edition of 'Thank Your Lucky Stars' to help promote it. Things were not much better in the US, where their follow-up to *Have I The Right?*, *I Can't Stop* peaked at No 48 becoming their only other US hit. Their debut US album, *Here Are The Honeycombs*, climbed to No 147.

Meanwhile back at base *Don't Love You No More* was selected as their next 45 release and then withdrawn when they decided to record Ray Davies' *Something Better Beginning*. This ensured that *Don't Love You No More* became their rarest and most sought-after disc. *Something Better Beginning* lacked the immediate appeal of their debut disc and fell short of being the classic they required but it did feature a strong vocal performance from **Denis D'ell**. The result was another minor hit.

Their final UK hit was *That's The Way*, which featured Honey duetting with **D'ell** and had some of the immediacy of their first 45. It had originally appeared on their patchy debut album (now a minor collectable) and was aided by lots of airplay on pirate radio. It climbed to No 12 in the UK but didn't lead to any longer-term improvement in their fortunes.

Their second album, *All Systems Go*, attracted little attention here in the UK, but it did include their earlier US-only 45, *I Can't Stop*. Retrospectively it's of interest to some collectors because of the inclusion of an otherwise unreleased Ray Davies composition, *Emptiness*. Only *Who Is Sylvia?* of their later singles attracted any interest, but not even the considerable airplay it enjoyed could propel it into the Charts.

THE HONEYCOMBS - The Honeycombs (LP).

The band ended its days on the cabaret circuit and **Denis D'ell** attempted to launch a solo career in the seventies with little success. Still, *Have I The Right?*, which inevitably gets reissued from time to time remains a classic of the beat era.

The Best Of The Honeycombs is a worthy compilation containing all the group's 'A' sides and a handful of album cuts. The 1991 CD reissue of their first album on Repertoire also includes the 'B' sides to their first four singles and a couple of German language versions. The reissue of their second album comes with *Something Better Beginning* and five 'B' sides.

Sequel's 2-CD set *The Joe Meek Story: The Pye Years* includes *Have I The Right?* and *Colour Slide*. Other compilation appearances have included: *Have I The Right?* and *That's The Way* on *The Sixties File* (2-LP); and *Have I The Right?* on *Watch Your Step* (LP & CD), the 2-CD set *60 Number Ones Of The Sixties* and *60's Mix* (CD). (VJ)

Honeyend

45:	Heartbreaker/Beautiful Downtown	(Spark SRL 1072) 1972 R2

This was a one-off disc by a very obscure band. (VJ)

Hookfoot

Personnel:	IAN DUCK	hrmnca, vcls	ABC
	DALE GLOVER	bs	AB
	ROGER POPE	drms, vcls	ABC
	CALEB QUAYE	gtr, vcls, keyb'ds	ABC
	PETER ROSS	hrmnca, vcls	A
	BOB KULICK	gtr, vcls	B
	FRED GANDY	bs, vcls	C

ALBUMS:	1(A)	HOOKFOOT	(DJM DJLPS 413) 1971 SC
	2(B)	GOOD TIMES A COMIN'	(DFM DJSLP 422) 1972
	3(C)	COMMUNICATIONS	(DJM DJSLP 428) 1973
	4(C)	ROARING	(DJM DJSLP 435) 1974
	5(-)	HEADLINES (2-LP Compilation)	
			(DJM DJMPS 28013) 1975

NB: (1) - (4) issued on A&M in the US.

45s:	Way Of The Musician/Hookfoot	(Page One POF 144) 1969
	Sweet Sweet Funky Music/The Opener	(DJM DJS 10265) 1972
	Freedom/Heart To Heart Talking/	
	Red Man	(DJM DJS 10272) 1972
	So You Want To Be A Rock And Roll Star/	
	Mr. Money	(DJM DJS 10293) 1974

This band had originally been session musicians for artists on the DJM label, including a certain **Elton John**. None of their albums attracted much attention and they split up in 1974. Their final 45 'A' side was a cover of The Byrds' *So You Want To Be A Rock And Roll Star*. Quaye (who'd earlier recorded as **Caleb**) moved to the US, where he continued to work as a session musician, and Pope went on to play in **Elton John**'s support band.

Duck, Glover and Pope were in **The Soul Agents** and **The Loot** together before forming this band. (VJ)

Hooky

Personnel:	EDDY LAMB		A
	JOHN LAMB		A
	TOM McKAY		A

ALBUM: 1(A) COLLECTED TALES OF HOOKY No. 1
(RCA SF 8247) 1972

This album presents a collection of average songs from this obscure three-piece. Acoustic guitar and piano - based harmonies with the occasional country-tinged number. The singing is not strong and the album never rises above the mediocre. (BS)

Hope Street

Personnel incl: CHRIS HARVEY   vcls   A

45s: Iron Sky/Never Mind   (Regal Zonophone RZ 3047) 1972
         Wait Until Tomorrow/Ladies (At
         The Bottom Of The Garden)   (Parlophone R 5982) 1973

This Scottish band's first 45 was withdrawn soon after release. Chris Harley moved down to London in the mid-seventies and started a solo career as Christopher Rainbow. (VJ)

Mary Hopkin

HCP

ALBUMS: 1 POST CARD (mono/stereo)
            (Apple (S)APCOR 5) 1969 SC 3
         2 EARTH SONG - OCEAN SONG
            (Apple SAPCOR 21) 1971 SC -
         3 THOSE WERE THE DAYS (Apple SAPCOR 23) 1972 R2 -
         4 THE WELSH WORLD OF MARY HOPKIN
            (Decca SPA 546) 1977 SC -

NB: (4) This album was recorded in 1968. (1) reissued on CD, cassette and vinyl (Apple SAPCOR 5) 1991 (SC) with bonus 12". (2) reissued on vinyl (Apple SAPCOR 21) 1992 SC and on CD (Apple CDP 7 98695 2) 1992. The CD compilation *Those Were The Days* (CD SAPCOR 23) 1995 covers material from her pop and folk eras.

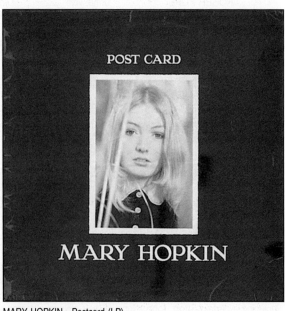

MARY HOPKIN - Postcard (LP).

NB: (2) with Edward Morris Jones.

HCP

45s: Those Were The Days/Turn Turn Turn (Apple APPLE 2) 1968 1
(up to   Goodbye/Sparrow   (Apple APPLE 10) 1969 2
1977) α Aderynilwyd/
         Y Blodwyn Gwyn (PS)   (Cambrian CSP 703) 1969 SC -
      α Pleserau Serch/Tyrd Yn Ol (PS) (Cambrian CSP 712) 1969 SC -
         Temma Harbour/
         Lontano Dagli Occhi (PS)   (Apple APPLE 22) 1970 6
         Knock, Knock Who's There?/
         I'm Going To Fall In Love Again (PS) (Apple APPLE 26) 1970 2
         Think About Your Children/
         Heritage (PS)   (Apple APPLE 30) 1970 19
         Let My Name Be Sorrow/
         Kew Gardens (PS)   (Apple APPLE 34) 1971 SC 46
         Water, Paper And Clay/
         Jefferson (PS)   (Apple APPLE 39) 1971 SC -
      β Mary Had A Baby/
         Cherry Tree Carol   (Regal Zonophone RZ 3070) 1972 -
         If You Love Me/Tell Me Now   (Good Earth GD 2) 1976 32
         Wrap Me In Your Arms/
         Just A Dreamer (Some PS)   (Good Earth GD 11) 1977 -

NB: α reissued in 1974. β repromoted in 1973. *Those Were The Days* was also released in French, German, Italian and Spanish with the same English 'B' side, *Turn, Turn, Turn*. She also had several singles which were only released outside the UK:- *Lontano Dagli Occhi/The Game* (APPLE 7) appeared in Italy and some South American countries. *Prince En Avignon/The Game* (APPLE 9) was a French-only release and *Que Sera Sera/Fields Of St Etienne* (APPLE 16) was released in France, Spain and the USA. The first four Apple 45s (including *Hey Jude*) were released in a presentation pack as *Our First Four* to celebrate Apple's launch. This set (the other discs were **Mary Hopkins**' *Those Were The Days*, *Sour Milk Sea* by **Jackie Lomax** and *Thingumybob* by the Black Dyke Mills Band) now fetches circa £1,000.

Mary Hopkin was born on 3 May 1950. She was 17 when she played in her first folk-rock band and when it split up she went solo. Her first break came when **Paul McCartney** invited her to sign a contract with the new Apple label after she'd appeared on 'Opportunity Knocks' and been recommended to him by **Twiggy**. He found her first song, *Those Were The Days*, produced the record and it climbed to No 1 not just here in the UK but in several other countries too. Thereafter, unfortunately, Apple created a ghastly sugary image for her, probably partly due to her naivety and the fact she was just out of school. One of her most banal songs was a Eurovision Song Contest entry, *Knock, Knock, Who's There*. Her only other half decent single was probably *Goodbye*.

Her *Post Card* album was produced by **Paul McCartney** and had its moments, including a few **Donovan** tracks. However, by the time of her final album, *Earth Song/Ocean Song*, which she recorded with **Ralph McTell**, Danny Thompson and **Dave Cousins**, she was beginning to assert herself and this is worth a spin, being nearer to the music she loved, British folk.

She parted company with Apple when her contract ended in 1972, having married Tony Visconti in 1971. She soon became pregnant and stepped back from the music business for a while aside from an awful 45 for Regal Zonophone in 1972, involvement in a 45, *Summertime, Summertime* as Hobby Horse for Bell in 1972 and a couple of 45s for her husband's Good Earth label in 1976 and 1977. Still she continued to record beyond the time span of this book. In 1980 she played in a trio called Sundance and in 1984 she was in the short-lived but commercially successful Oasis. She'll remain best remembered, though, as the angelic-looking Welsh teenager who had a massive international hit with *Those Were The Days*. (VJ)

Nicky Hopkins

ALBUMS: 1 REVOLUTIONARY PIANO   (CBS 62679) 1966 R1
         2 TIN MAN WAS A DREAMER   (CBS 65416) 1973 SC

NB: (1) reissued on Columbia (478502-2) 1995. (2) reissued on CD (Columbia 480969 2) 1995. He also recorded a US-only album, *No More Changes* (Mercury SRMI 1028) in 1975.

45s:	Mr. Big/Jenni	(CBS 202055) 1966 SC	
α	Mister Pleasant/Nothing As Yet	(Polydor BM 56175) 1967 SC	
	Top Pops No 1 (Medley: Cinderella Rockerfella,		
	Lady Madonna, Congratulations/Part 2)	(MGM MGM 1419) 1968	
	Speed On/Sundown In Mexico	(CBS 1328) 1973	

NB: α credited To Nicky Hopkins and His Whistling Piano.

Hopkins was undoubtedly one of the most talented piano players to have graced British rock during this era. A South Londoner, he was born there on 24th February 1944, he was playing piano before he went to school. He later trained at the Royal Academy of Music. His first big band was **Screaming Lord Sutch's Savages**, then in late 1962 he progressed on to Cyril Davies All Stars - a pioneering R&B band. You can hear him on piano on their *Country Line Special* album.

His career was often hampered by bad health and his spell with Cyril Davies culminated in a period of hospitalisation partly as a result of exhaustion. When he recovered he resumed his career working as a session-man rather than as a full-time group member in the hope that this would prove less exhausting. Top sixties bands he recorded with included **The Who** (on their *My Generation* album), **The Kinks**, **The Rolling Stones** and **The Easybeats**. In 1968 he joined **The Jeff Beck Group** after working with them on their *Truth* album. When he left them in the Summer of 1969 he moved to California (he'd already guested on Jefferson Airplane's *Volunteers* album whilst with **Beck**), first sessioning with The Steve Miller Band on *Your Saving Grace* then joining Quicksilver Messenger Service (though he continued to do session work for **The Rolling Stones** among others. Indeed he turned down an offer to join them in 1969).

Earlier in 1966 he'd recorded his *Revolutionary Piano* album and a couple of singles. Highlights of the *Revolutionary Piano...* album were cover versions of *Yesterday, Goldfinger* and *Satisfaction* as well as a rockin' rendition of Tchaikovsky's *Piano Concerto No 1*, on which he is assisted by The Mike Sammes Singers. The second, released in 1967, was produced by Shel Talmy and credited to Nicky Hopkins and His Whistling Piano. The 'A' side was a Ray Davies number and consisted of **Hopkins** on piano, a drummer and an anonymous whistler. He also collaborated on a one-off project called **Aquarian Age**. The *High On A Hill* 45 credited to him was actually by **Nigel Hopkins**.

In 1973 he not only put out his second solo album, on which he was assisted by **George Harrison**, **Mike Taylor** and Klaus Voormann. With the benefit of hindsight many now regard the album, which sold poorly, as a prototype power-pop album. He also recorded an album for CBS with several other musicians under the collective title, Sweet Thursday.

He continued to be a highly respected keyboardist whose individual achievements have in no way reflected his very considerable talent.

He recorded a third album, *Long Journey Home*, which remains unreleased. In 1974 he moved back to the UK from California, settling in Egham, Surrey. The following year, his final album, *No More Changes*, was released in the US.

HORSE - Horse (LP).

He died on 6th September 1994 after an operation for a stomach illness. At the time of his death he was working on his autobiography with Ray Coleman, which will hopefully appear in print soon.

Compilation appearances have included: *Piano Shuffle* on *Jimmy Page - Hip Young Guitar Slinger* (2-CD); and *Mister Pleasant* on *Rare Tracks* (LP). (VJ)

Nigel Hopkins

45s:	Chelsea Bun/Tea And Trumpet	(Decca F 12622) 1967	
α	High On A Hill/Trumpet Serenade	(Fontana TF 906) 1968	
	Afrikana/Little Pepito	(Fontana TF 1007) 1969	

NB: α wrongly credited to **Nicky Hopkins**.

Hopkins was a little known late sixties trumpeter. (VJ)

Hugh Hopper

ALBUMS:	1	1984	(CBS 65466) 1973 SC
(up to	2	CRUEL BUT FAIR	(Compendium FIDARO 4) 1976 SC
1976)			

NB: (1) reissued in France (Culture Press) and the same label has reissued *Monster Band* from 1974.

Hopper was part of the now legendary Canterbury scene. Initially bassist with **The Wilde Flowers**, he joined **The Soft Machine** in February 1969 and remained with them until May 1973 when he left to go solo. He went on to record other albums but the two listed were the only ones within the time frame of this book. He was also in the jazzy-rock band **Isotope**.

Hopper formed his own band The Hugh Hopper Band in 1985 and they released a CD *Meccano Pelorus* on the Cuneiform label in 1991 and further releases followed on Voiceprint and PONK as well. (VJ)

Hopscotch

Personnel:	STEWART FRANCIS	drms	AB
	ALAN KELLY	drms	AB
	NORRIE MACLEAN		AB
	OWEN 'ONNIE' McINTYRE		AB
	HAMISH STUART	vcls	A

45s:	Look At The Lights Go Up/		
	Some Old Fat Man	(United Artists UP 2231) 1969 R1	
	Long Black Veil/Easy To Find	(United Artists UP 35022) 1969	

This band was earlier known as **The Scots Of St. James** (and, prior to that The In Crowd). Hamish Stuart was recruited from **The Dream Police** when the band changed name to **Hopscotch**. It proved to be a short-lived venture, though. The first 45 was pleasant but ordinary pop and the second a cover of The Band's song. Hamish Stuart was the first to leave. After this they splintered into a group called **Forever More**. They were also linked to **Five Day Rain**.

Look At The Lights Go Up got fresh exposure on *Voyage Through The Sugarcube* (LP & CD). (VJ)

Horden Raikes

ALBUMS:	1	HORDEN RAIKES	(Folk Heritage FHR 026) 1972 SC
	2	KING COTTON	(Folk Heritage FHR 042) 1973 SC

An evocative English folk outfit whose album includes lovely versions of *Mad Tom Of Bedlam, Lord Franklin, The Seeds Of Love* etc. (VJ)

Horizontal

45:	Jennifer Generator/The Last Time	(RCA RCA 2140) 1972	

This remains an obscure early seventies 45. (VJ)

Horse

Personnel:
ADRIAN HAWKINS	vcls		A
RICK PARNELL	drms		A
ROD ROACH	gtr		A
COLIN STANDRING	bs		A

ALBUM: 1(A) HORSE (RCA SF 8109) 1970 R3

NB: (1) reissued on CD.

This was a short-lived hard-rock outfit. Rick Parnell was later in **Atomic Rooster**. The opening cut, *The Sacrifice*, is in the mould of **Black Widow**. Overall, it's only likely to be of interest to hard-rock fans.

Adrian Hawkins and Rod Roach later played in **Saturnalia**. (VJ)

Horslips

Personnel:
EAMONN CARR	drms, vcls		ABC
BARRY DEVLIN	vcls, bs		ABC
JIM LOCHART	flute, violin, keyb'ds		ABC
CHARLES O'CONNOR	violin		ABC
DECLAN SINNOTT	vcls, gtr		A
GUS GUIEST	vcls, gtr		BC
JOHN FEAN	vcls, gtr		C

ALBUMS: 1(C) HAPPY TO MEET... SORRY TO PART
(up to (Oats MOO 3) 1973 SC
1976) 2(C) THE TAIN (Oats MOO 5) 1973 SC
3(C) DANCEHALL SWEETHEARTS (Oats MOO 7) 1974
4(C) UNFORTUNATE CUP OF TEA (Oats MOO 8) 1975
5(C) DRIVE THE COLD WINTER AWAY (Oats MOO 9) 1976
6(C) HORSLIPS LIVE (Oats MOO 10) 1976
7(C) THE BOOK OF INVASIONS: A CELTIC SYMPHONY
(DJM DJF 20498) 1976

NB: (2) reissued on CD (Oats MOOCD 5) 1989. (1) reissued on CD (Edsel EDCD 661) 2000. (2) reissued on CD (Edsel EDCD 662) 2000. (4) reissued on CD (I Records CMOD 008) 1989. (5) reissued on CD (I Records CMOD 009) 1989. (7) reissued on CD (Edsel EDCD 667) 2000. Two vinyl compilations are *The Best Of Horslips* (Oats OASM 0021) 1982, reissued on I&B in 1989 or *Horslips' Story - Straight From The Horse's Mouth* (Homespun) 1989. There are also compilations available on CD:- *Best Of Horslips: Traditional Irish Rock Music* (I CMOD 021) 1989 and *Horslip's Story - Straight From The Horse's Mouth* (Outlet DHCD 802) 1989. *Tracks From The Vaults* (Edsel EDCD 669) 2000 is a 13-track album, originally released in 1977, which included their non-album material up until then. *The Best Of Horslips* (Edsel MEDCD 700) 2001 is a 2-CD compilation of their material.

45s: The High Reel/Furniture (Oats OAT 1) 1973
(up to Deary Doom/Shamrock Store (Oats OAT 2) 1973
1976) Fairy King/Green Gravel (Oats MOO 2) 1973

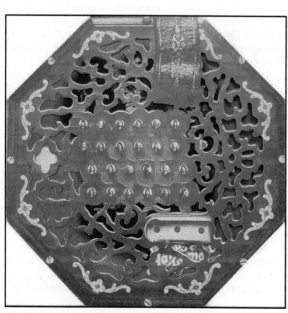

HORSLIPS - Happy To Meet... Sorry To Part (LP).

Nighttown Boy/We Bring Summer With Us (RCA 2452) 1974
King Of The Fairies/Sunburst (RCA 2505) 1975
That's What You Get/
Snake's Farewell To The Emerald Isle (RCA 2564) 1975

Horslips hailed from Dublin playing traditional Irish jigs and reels with rock undertones. They worked hard to establish themselves in their homeland enjoying hits with Irish-only singles *Johnny's Wedding* and *Green Gravel* during 1972. They then formed their own record company and pressed and distributed their first album themselves. Released in early 1973 it was enormously successful in Ireland and critically acclaimed over here when they signed a distribution deal with RCA. Housed in a beautiful concertina shaped sleeve, it is now much sought-after by some collectors. It is generally recognised as a unique and highly innovative debut which entered new territory in the Celtic rock genre.

The Tain was another strong album whose release followed a successful Autumn 1973 nationwide British tour on which they had supported **Steeleye Span**. A concept album it was based on an ancient Irish myth. Musically it blended traditional Irish airs and reels with self-penned progressive numbers. The vocal harmonies are appealing and the material is strong with *Cu Chulainn's Lament* and *More Than You Can Chew*.

Their subsequent albums were weaker and RCA ceased the distribution deal in 1975 meaning that *Drive The Cold Winter Away* and *Horslips Live* were originally only released on their Oats label in Ireland.

Their finest work was *The Book Of Invasions*, which was released over here by DJM. The album epitomised 'Celtic rock' from its superb opening track *Daybreak* (which was a very successful Irish-only single) and it contained three other post-1976 UK or US singles: *Warm Sweet Breath Of Love*, *The Power And The Glory* and *Trouble With A Capital T*. I have no hesitation in recommending this melodic rock album, which successfully interweaves traditional Irish music within its web. They continued to record until 1980 when they split after failing to conquer America. In 1999 they regained the recording rights to their material from a rogue ex-manager and supervised a remastering programme of their output.

Tracks From The Vaults, (originally released in 1977) include all their non-album material up to that point and one unreleased track, *Motorway Madness* from 1972. Both sides of their 1976 single under the pseudonym **Lipstick** are included too.

Edsel's *The Best Of Horslips* is a good introduction to their career. It was compiled by the group themselves and features tracks from their remastered original albums. (VJ)

Hot Chocolate

Personnel:
ERROL BROWN	vcls		ABCD
FRANKLIN DE ALLIE	gtr		A
LARRY FERGUSON	keyb'ds		ABCD
IAN KING	drms		AB
PATRICE OLIVE	bs		ABCD
TONY WILSON	bs, vcls		ABC
HARVEY HINSLEY	gtr		BCD
TONY CONNOR	drms		CD

HCP

ALBUMS: 1(C) CICERO PARK (RAK SRAK 507) 1974 R1 -
(up to 2(C) HOT CHOCOLATE (RAK SRAK 516) 1975 34
1976) 3(D) MAN TO MAN (RAK SRAK 522) 1976 32
4(-) 14 GREATEST HITS (RAK SRAK 524) 1976 6

NB: An alternative compilation is *The Very Best Of* (EMI EMTV 42) 1987, also on CD; the CD set *Their Greatest Hits* (EMI 07777 89068 27) 1993, *Twenty Hottest Hits* (EMI CDP 746 375 2) 1987 or *Greatest Hits: Hot Chocolate* (EMI CDB 752 014 2) 1987.

HCP

45s: α Give Peace A Chance/
(up to Living Without You Tomorrow (Apple APPLE 18) 1969 R1 -
1976) Love Is Life/Pretty Girls (PS) (Rak RAK 103) 1970 6
You Could've Been A Lady/
Everybody's Laughing (Rak RAK 110) 1971 22
I Believe (In Love)/Caveman Billy (Rak RAK 118) 1971 8
Mary-Anne/Ruth (Rak RAK 127) 1972 -

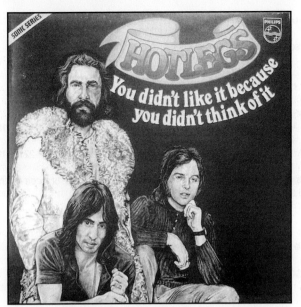

HOTLEGS - You Didn't Like It Because You Didn't Think Of It (LP).

You'll Always Be A Friend/Go-Go Girl	(Rak RAK 139) 1972	23
Brother Louie/I Want To Be Free	(Rak RAK 149) 1973	7
Rumours/Man Needs A Woman	(Rak RAK 157) 1973	44
Emma/Making Music	(Rak RAK 168) 1974	3
Changing World/Bump And Dilly Down	(Rak RAK 174) 1974	-
Cheri Baby/Sexy Lady	(Rak RAK 188) 1974	31
Blue Night/You Sexy Thing	(Rak RAK 199) 1975	-
Disco Queen/You're A Natural High	(Rak RAK 202) 1975	11
A Child's Prayer/		
Everything Should Be Funky	(Rak RAK 212) 1975	7
You Sexy Thing/Warm Smile	(Rak RAK 221) 1975	2
Don't Stop It Now/Beautiful Lady	(Rak RAK 230) 1976	11
Man To Man/Eyes Of A Growing Child	(Rak RAK 238) 1976	14
Heaven Is On The Back Seat Of My Cadillac/		
Sex Appeal	(Rak RAK 240) 1976	25
Reissues: You Sexy Thing/No Doubt About it	(EMI G 4512) 1984	-
β You Sexy Thing (remix)/Every 1's A Winner	(EMI 5592) 1987	10
χ Every 1's A Winner (remix)/		
So You Win Again	(EMI 5607) 1987	69
δ It Started With A Kiss/You Sexy Thing	(EMI CDEMCT 7) 1993	31

NB: α credited to The Hot Chocolate Band. β also as 12" with extra tracks. χ also as a 12". δ also as a CD single with *Every 1's A Winner* added.

Formed by Errol Brown in 1969 **Hot Chocolate** started out in Brixton as a reggae group. Indeed their first 45, a one-off for Apple, was a reggae adaptation of **John Lennon**'s *Give Peace A Chance*. In these early days Apple called them The Hot Chocolate Band. However, it wasn't a hit and the band left the label signing for Mickie Most's RAK Records in 1970.

Most shortened their name to **Hot Chocolate** and found them a strong single in *Love Is Life*. It took them into the Top Ten and the group became a regular Chart act for the rest of the decade. Brown's shaved head and distinctive pop/soul vocals gave them a unique sound which was supplemented by a commercial instrumental backing with upfront percussion. In the Autumn of 1970 Harvey Hinsley, who'd once been with **Cliff Bennett's Rebel Rousers** came in on guitar.

In the early seventies they concentrated very much on the singles market and didn't release an album until 1974. More notable 45s were *You Could've Been A Lady, I Believe (In Love), You'll Always Be A Friend, Brother Louie* and *Emma*. *Brother Louie* was a particularly poignant song about inter-racial love and racism, which gave them a Top Ten hit here (their biggest since *Love Is Life*), but in the US a cover version by Stories actually topped the Charts.

Emma was their first single to make the US Charts (No 8) and when their debut album, *Cicero Park*, finally emerged it fared better in the US (No 55) than in the UK.

Back in March 1973 former **Audience** and **Jackson Heights** member Tony Connor had replaced King on drums. In November 1975 Wilson departed for a solo career with Olive switching to bass. 1975 had been a good year

for the band with *Disco Queen*, with its superb beat, ideally tailored for the market at that time given the emerging disco scene, and the slow, sensitive *A Child's Prayer* providing an ideal contrast to its predecessor. They ended the year with their most successful 45 to date, *You Sexy Thing*, a powerful dance number, which climbed to No 2 in the UK and No 3 in the US, where it sold well over a million copies. On the back of this success their second album, *Hot Chocolate*, climbed to No 41 in the US, although they were always primarily a singles band.

By 1976 they were very big indeed - more distinctive hits - *Don't Stop It Now, Man To Man* and *Heaven Is The Back Seat Of My Cadillac* followed. Their *Man To Man* album was the first to make the UK Charts, peaking at No 32 over here, whilst it could only manage No 172 in the US. Their compilation album, *14 Greatest Hits*, was extremely successful, selling over half a million copies in the UK, where it climbed to No 6. *The Very Best Of...*, released in the mid-eighties, included 10 of their biggest hits.

As we leave them at the end of 1976 they were poised to go from strength to strength and carry on recording for several years well into the eighties. (VJ)

Hotlegs

Personnel:	LOL CREME	gtr, bs, vcls, keyb'ds	AB
	KEVIN GODLEY	drms, vcls	AB
	ERIC STEWART	gtr, bs, vcls	AB
	BAZ BARKER	violin	B
	GRAHAM GOULDMAN	bs	B
	MIKE TIMONEY	organ	B

ALBUMS:	1(A)	THINKS: SCHOOL STINKS	(Philips 6308 047) 1971 SC
	2(A)	SONGS	(Philips 6308 080) 1971 SC
	3(B)	YOU DIDN'T LIKE IT	(Sonic SON 009) 1976

NB: (2) and (3) are repackages of (1).

HCP

45s:	Neanderthal Man/You Didn't Like It Because		
	You Didn't Think Of It	(Fontana 6007 019) 1970	2
	Lady Sadie/Loser	(Philips 6308 140) 1971	-
Reissue:	Neanderthal Man /		
	(Flip by different artist)	(Old Gold OG 9245) 1982	-

Creme, Godley and Stewart had all been members of Manchester's beat scene. Creme's first group was The Sabres, Godley started out in Jerry Lee and The Staggerlees and was later in **The Mockingbirds**, which had been formed by **Graham Gouldman** in 1965. **Gouldman** was also a talented songwriter who wrote several hits for other artists and made several attempts at a solo career. Stewart first came to light in **Wayne Fontana and The Mindbenders**. When **The Mindbenders** broke away from **Fontana** Stewart stayed with them but when they finally split, Stewart and **Gouldman** bought a recording studio in Manchester. Godley and Creme, meanwhile, released a 45, *I'm Beside Myself*, under the pseudonym **Frabjoy and Runcible Spoon**, on which Stewart and **Gouldman** played as session musicians. Having done songwriting for the US Kasenetz-Katz production team, the group re-equipped their Manchester studio (now called Strawberry Studios) and wrote and recorded *Neanderthal Man*, a song with an extremely distinctive heavy rhythmic backing, which was released as a 45 under the name **Hotlegs** and became a massive worldwide hit, selling over two million copies. It peaked at No 22 in the US, but climbed to No 2 here in the UK. Subsequent recordings under this name failed but, as most of you know, a couple of years later the same personnel became **10cc**.

Their album, *Thinks: School Stinks* included the 45 and *To Fly Away*, a Godley/Creme composition, which had previously been recorded for a Marmalade sampler which never saw the light of day. Two other tracks from the album, *How Many Times* and *Run Baby Run* were released on an unsuccessful US-only 45 (Capitol 3043) 1971, but nothing more was heard of the band until September 1971 when a very ordinary 45, *Lady Sadie*, was released and predictably flopped.

Philips later repackaged the album as *Songs*, omitting *Neanderthal Man* and *Lady Sadie* in favour of *The Loser* and the previously unreleased *Today*. It sold poorly as did the subsequent repackaging, released on Sonic in 1976.

Just before they formed **Hotlegs** Godley and Creme supplied a couple of songs to promote a nightclub in Manchester called 'Blinkers' which were pressed up on a ltd edition single and given away to members, circa 1969. There is no artist credited on the 45 (Cat: 1C-1215) but the singers are clearly messrs Godeley and Creme. The two songs are *Going To Blinkers* (a rock number sung by Kevin Godley) and *Goodnight Blinkers* (a slow number sung by Lol Creme). (VJ/GCn)

Hot Potato

Personnel incl: PETE MURPHY   gtr, vcls

ALBUM: 1   HOT POTATO   (PMTB 1) 1973 R3

This was a rare privately-pressed album. All 10 cuts were written by guitarist and vocalist Pete Murphy. 500 copies were pressed of this electric folk album which has psychedelic tinges on cuts like *Bike Rider* and *Only Who You're With*. (VJ)

The Hotrods

45:   I Don't Love You No More/
      Ain't Coming Back No More   (Columbia DB 7693) 1965 R1

I've no information on the band but the 45 was produced by Joe Meek, which is no doubt why it's quite collectable now.

I Don't Love You No More and *Ain't Coming Back No More* got a further airing on *RGM Rarities, Vol. 2* (CD). (VJ)

The Hotshots

                                                     HCP
45s: Snoopy Versus The Red Baron/
       What Do You Say   (Mooncrest MOON 5) 1973 4
       Battle Of New Orleans/
       Knockin' On The Door   (Mooncrest MOON 12) 1973 -
       Yesterday Man/Jerusalem Rock   (Mooncrest MOON 20) 1973 -
       Caribbean/Together   (Mooncrest MOON 30) 1974 -
       Mellow Yellow/Come On Susie   (Gull GULS 25) 1975 -

A band of limited talent who made the Top Ten with a cover of The McCoy's hit *Snoopy Versus The Red Baron* but did nothing else of note. (VJ)

Hot Springs

45:   It's All Right/All I Know About Love(Columbia DB 7821) 1966 SC

This lone 45 was the work of a seven-piece soul/beat group from Bath. (VJ)

Hot Vultures

Personnel incl: IAN A. ANDERSON
                 MAGGIE HOLLAND

ALBUMS: 1   CARRION ON   (Red Rag Recordings RRR 005) 1975
          2   THE EAST STREET SHAKES
                             (Red Rag Recordings RRR 015) 1977 SC
          3   UP THE WINE   (Plant Life PLR 018) 1979

Formed by **Ian (A) Anderson** and his wife Maggie, the first **Hot Vultures** album was issued in 1975 entitled *Carrion On* (Best Seller 4C054-96947) and features a mix of folk and blues including versions of songs by The Holy Modal Rounders, Willie Dixon and Tucker Zimmerman but no self-penned numbers. John Pilgrim (ex-Vipers) and Dave Peabody also appears on the album.

Later **Anderson** projects included English Country Blues Band and Tiger Moth in the eighties. (VJ)

Household

Personnel: AVRIL JUMEL   A
             BARRY JUMEL   A
             TERRY JUMEL   A
             WAYNE JUMEL   A

45s: Guess I'll Learn How To Fly/
       Nothing You Can Do But Cry   (United Artists UP 1190) 1967
       Twenty First Summer/
       Winter's Coming On   (United Artists UP 2210) 1968

This obscure late sixties harmony pop outfit (comprised of three brothers and their sister) came from Coventry. (VJ)

The House of Lords

Personnel incl: ALAN PRATT

45:   In The Land Of Dreams/
      Ain't Gonna Wait Forever   (B&C CB 112) 1969 SC

A promising but short-lived Scottish progressive rock outfit, who included former **Three's A Crowd** member Alan Pratt. They moved down to England to work but only released this one promising 45. The 'A' side is similar to **The Clouds** ie mild progressive rock with a slight soul influence in the appealing vocals. Instrumentally the interplay is organ and piano, rather than guitar, and phasing.

In The Land Of Dreams can also be found on *Rubble Vol. 15: 5,000 Seconds Over Toyland* (LP), *Rubble Vol. 8* (CD) and *The Best Of Rubble Collection, Vol. 3* (CD). (VJ)

Brian Howard and The Silhouettes

Personnel incl: BRIAN HOWARD

45s: Somebody Help Me/
       Young And Evil   (Columbia DB 4914) 1962 SC
       The Worryin' Kind/Come To Me   (Columbia DB 7067) 1963 SC
       Back In The U.S.A./Hooked   (Fontana TF 464) 1964 SC

This outfit was from Mitcham in Surrey. Their best known song was their cover of Chuck Berry's *Back In The USA*.

Compilation appearances include: *Hooked* and *Back In The U.S.A.* on *Rare 60's Beat Treasures, Vol. 4* (CD); and *Back In The U.S.A.* on *Beat Im Star Club* (2-LP) and *Beat Merchants* (2-LP). (VJ)

STEVE HOWE - Mothballs (CD).

LINDA HOYLE - Pieces Of Me (CD).

Catherine Howe

ALBUMS: 1 WHAT A BEAUTIFUL PLACE
(Reflection REFL 11) 1971 R3
2 HARRY (RCA LPI 5091) 1975 SC
3 SILENT MOTHER NATURE (RCA RS 1041) 1976

45: Nothing More Than Strangers/
It Comes With The Breezes (Reflection HRS 11) 1971 SC

Howe was a folky singer/songwriter. Her debut album specialised in orchestrated ballads and came housed in a beautiful colour sleeve. On the *Harry* album she was backed by members of **Fairport Convention** and she continued to record throughout the seventies. She came from Halifax in West Yorkshire. (VJ)

Steve Howe

                                                          HCP
ALBUM: 1 BEGINNINGS (Atlantic K 50151) 1975 22
(up to
1976)
NB: Some copies of (1) were with embossed **Yes** logo. These are SC. *Mothballs* (r-p-m RPM 140) 1994 is a CD collection of singles and album tracks he played on.

Steve Howe was guitarist with **The Syndicats** (1963-65), lead guitarist with **The In Crowd** (1965-67), **Tomorrow** (1967-68) and **Bodast** (1968-69) prior to replacing **Pete Banks** in **Yes** in March 1970. He remained with **Yes** for the next decade and *Beginnings* was the first of two solo albums he recorded whilst with the band. *The Steve Howe Album* followed in 1979. When **Yes** split he formed the progressive rock supergroup Asia with Geoff Downes. He was in GTR in 1976, which also featured ex-**Genesis** member **Steve Hackett** and released one studio album. Later, in 1989 he teamed up with former **Yes** members in Anderson, Bruford, Wakeman and Howe for an eponymous album. Whilst they were working on a follow-up album, they became linked with other former **Yes** members to form an eight-piece and this recorded the *Union* album in 1991 and embarked on a successful world tour. When the tour was over he embarked on a solo career for the next few years, recording six albums before rejoining **Yes** in 1995. He continues to record and perform with them.

The r-p-m *Mothballs* (CD) compilation is an excellent introduction to his career. It includes the three Columbia mid-sixties 45s by **The Syndicats** he played on (he'd moved on to join **The In Crowd** by the time of *Crawdaddy Simone*, which is consequently omitted); the last two **In Crowd** 45s and their previously unissued version of Ike Turner's *Finger Poppin'*; six **Tomorrow** tracks, including *Real Life Permanent Dream*, *Revolution* and *My White Bicycle* and a previously unissued track *Come Over Stranger* from a post-**Tomorrow** power trio called Canto, which **Howe** was in. (VJ)

Linda Hoyle

ALBUM: 1 PIECES OF ME (Vertigo 6360 060) 1971 R3
NB: (1) reissued on CD (Repertoire 4473-WP) 1995, again (Angel Air SJPCD 117) 2002 and on Italian import (Akarma AK 220) 2003.

45: Eli's Coming/United States Of Mind (Vertigo 6059 018) 1970
NB: As **Linda Hoyle** and **Affinity**.

This album is now very rare. She was earlier in **Affinity** and **Nucleus**. She was certainly a dynamic vocalist - a mistress of the ballad. Her voice was equally suited to blues or hard-rock and she was backed by **Chris Spedding** and members of **Nucleus** on her album. The album contained strong covers of Nina Simone's *Backlash Blues* and Laura Nyro's *Lonely Women*. It was produced by Pete King the manager of Ronnie Scott's Club in London at the time who had encouraged her to go it alone.

She opted out of the music scene after this release and is now an art therapist in Canada. (VJ)

Wendy Hoyle

45: Coconut/
Best Thing That Happened To Me (Epic EPS 8123) 1972

This was **Linda Hoyle**'s sister. (VJ)

Hratch

45: Bare Back Rider/Ain't It Tough (Decca F 13007) 1970

This obscure 45 consisted of pleasant pop. (MWh)

Hudson-Ford

Personnel: RICHARD HUDSON gtr, vcls, perc A
JOHN FORD gtr, bs A

ALBUMS: 1(A) NICKELODEON (A&M AMLH 68208) 1973
(up to 2(A) FREE SPIRIT (A&M AMLH 68274) 1974
1976) 3(A) WORLDS COLLIDE (A&M AMLH 64535) 1975

                                                          HCP
45s: Pick Up The Pieces/
(up to This Is Not The Way (A&M AMS 7078) 1973 8
1976) Take It Back/Make No Mistake (A&M AMS 7088) 1973 -
Burn Baby Burn/Angels (PS) (A&M AMS 7096) 1974 15
Floating In The Wind/Reservations (A&M AMS 7116) 1974 35
Free Spirit/Dark Lord (A&M AMS 7130) 1974 -
When Love Has Overgrown/
What Day Is Without Love (A&M AMS 7179) 1975 -
95 In The Shade/Last In A World (CBS 4505/4045) 1976 -
Sold On Love/Daylight (CBS 4654) 1976 -

These singer/songwriters were originally in **Elmer Gantry's Velvet Opera** and later **The Strawbs**, writing their *Part Of The Union* single. Later in 1973 they embarked on a new career as a duet, after a bust-up with **Dave Cousins**. In commercial terms it was all downhill after their first hit, *Pick Up The Pieces*, which was an extremely accessible song which none of their subsequent efforts could equal. They split up in 1977.

John Ford's first band was **Jaymes Fenda and The Vulcans**. (VJ)

Hug

Personnel: MIKE HUGG keyb'ds, vcls A
MARCUS JAMES drms, vcls A
JOHN KNIGHTSBRIDGE gtr, vcls A
RON TELEMACQUE drms, vcls A

ALBUM: 1(A) NEON DREAM   (Polydor 2383 330) 1975

45:      Keep Pushing On/City   (Polydor 2058 553) 1975

A mostly unmemorable and short-lived pop outfit. **Hugg** had earlier pursued a solo career and prior to that been in **Manfred Mann** as their drummer.

The *Neon Dream* album is a bit of a conundrum. It has funky moments, laid-back moments and unashamed pop moments but it also contains a 10-minute track entitled *Star Traveller* that is well worth a spin as it contains some nice keyboards and guitar and will interest progressive rock music fans. Overall the album suffers from a lack of direction and weak vocals but **Hug** should not be dismissed as just a pop band.

Incidentally John Knightsbridge who played guitar on this album was previously in **Third World War**. (VJ)

Mike Hugg

Personnel:

MIKE HUGG	vcls, keyb'ds	AB
(ELTON DEAN	sax	AB)
(DAVE KING	gtr	AB)
(KEVIN PEEK	gtr	AB)
(ALAN TARNEY	bs	A)
(MICKEY WALLER	drms	AB)
(KIM GARDNER	bs	B)

ALBUMS: 1(A) SOMEWHERE   (Polydor 2383 140) 1972
       2(B) STRESS AND STRAIN   (Polydor 2383 213) 1973

45s: Blue Suede Shoes Again/Fool No More (Polydor 2058 265) 1972
       Wichita/No Love In The City   (Polydor 2058 805) 1976

These were solo ventures for the former **Manfred Mann** drummer who formed **Hug** in 1975 and **Mike Hugg Freeway** in 1976.

His two albums are a kind of who's who of the progressive scene, with participation by **Elton Dean**, **Manfred Mann**, **Caleb Quaye**, **Tom McGuinness**, Roger Pope, Ian Carr, **Andy Bown**, Gerry Beckley, Henri Spinetti etc.

In the early nineties he was reunited with former **Manfred Mann** colleagues **Paul Jones**, **Mike Vickers** and **Mike d'Abo** in what was initially intended as a one-off gig to promote a hits compilation but ended up as a part-time venture The Manfreds, who revived and expanded old **Manfred Mann** material. (VJ/SR)

Mike Hugg Freeway

Personnel incl: MIKE HUGG

45:      Same Old Fantasy/Those Days   (Polydor 2058 691) 1976

This was another short-lived **Hugg** venture. (VJ)

Alan Hull

                               HCP
ALBUMS: 1 PIPEDREAM   (Charisma CAS 1069) 1973 SC 29
(up to   2 SQUIRE   (Warner Bros K 56121) 1975 -
1976)

NB: (1) reissued on CD (Charisma CASCD 1069) in 1991. There's also a 2-CD anthology *We Can Swing Together Anthology 1965-1995* (Castle CMEDD 946) 2005.

45s: We Can Swing Together/Obidiah's Grave (Big T BIG 129) 1970
(up to   Numbers/
1976)   Drinking Song/One Off Pat (PS)   (Charisma CB 208) 1973
       Just Another Sad Song/Waiting   (Charisma CB 211) 1973
       Dan The Plan/
       One More Bottle Of Wine   (Warner Bros K 16561) 1975
       One More Bottle Of Wine/Squire (Warner Bros K 16599) 1975
       Crazy Woman/Golden Oldies (Warner Bros K 16643) 1975

Hull was born in Newcastle on 20th February 1940. He helped found the local beat group **The Chosen Few** before leaving to go into nursing. He also did some occasional folk singing. In 1967 he founded Downtown Faction which soon became **Lindisfarne**, the band he is best known as a member of, from 1967-74. When the band splintered in 1973 he embarked on a solo career. By this stage, though, the general public seemed largely to have lost interest in the band and its members. **Hull**'s first solo album, *Pipedream*, is well worth investigation. Much of the material dwelt with his earlier career working in a mental hospital. His 1973 45 *Numbers* later got a further airing on the *One More Chance* (LP) compilation. The follow-up, *Squire*, was relatively disappointing and he recorded infrequently thereafter until his sudden death in 1995.

We Can Swing Together Anthology 1965-1995 is a 40-track 2-CD set containing material from **The Chosen Few**, two tracks with **Skip Bifferty** and, of course much material from his days with **Lindisfarne** and his solo work. It comes with a detailed booklet.

We Can Swing Together resurfaced on *The Transatlantic Story* CD box set. (VJ)

The Hullaballoos

Personnel:

HARRY DUNN		AB
RICKY KNIGHT		AB
GEOFF MORTIMER		AB
ANDY WOONTON		AB
MICK WAYNE		B

45s: I'm Gonna Love You Too/
       Why Do Fools Fall In Love?   (Columbia DB 7392) 1964
       I'll Show You How To Love/
       Did You Ever?   (Columbia DB 7558) 1965
       I Won't Turn Away Now/Don't Stop (Columbia DB 7626) 1965

This rock outfit from Hull was notable for their bleached blond hair and actually achieved some success in the US, where they concentrated their operations. *I'm Gonna Love You Too* and *Did You Ever?* peaked at Nos 56 and 74 respectively in Billboard and a US-only release, *Learning The Game*, crept to No 121.

Mick Wayne, who was later in **The Bunch Of Fives**, **The Tickle** and **Junior's Eyes** joined after the 45s. (VJ)

Human Beans

Personnel:

DAVE EDMUNDS	gtr, vcls	A
TOMMY RILEY	drms	A
JOHN WILLIAMS	bs	A

45:      Morning Dew/It's A Wonder   (Columbia DB 8230) 1967 R2

HUMAN BEAST - Volume One (Instinct) (LP).

Originally from Cardiff, where he'd been in a local group called The Raiders, **Edmunds** moved up to London in 1966 and joined The Image before forming this band with Image drummer Tommy Riley in 1967. After releasing a cover of *Morning Dew* (made famous by Tim Rose but originally written by Canadian Bonnie Dobson in 1960) they became **Love Sculpture**. Both sides of this 45 can also be heard on the **Love Sculpture** compilation, *The Singles A's and B's* (Harvest SHSM 2032) 1980. (VJ/AH)

Human Beast

Personnel:
GILLIES BUCHAN	gtr, vcls	A
EDWARD JONES	bs, vcls	A
JOHN ROMSEY	drms	A
(DAVID McNIVEN	clarinet	A)

ALBUM: 1(A) VOLUME ONE (INSTINCT) (Decca SKL 5053) 1970 R3

This was the only release by a short-lived Edinburgh power trio, and is now rare and sought-after. They had earlier been known as Skin, and were signed to Decca by folk producer Ray Horricks on the recommendation of David McNiven from **Bread, Love and Dreams**. McNiven also contributed some lyrics to the album, which was recorded in London and alternates heavy psych tracks like *Mystic Man, Brush With The Midnight Butterfly* and *Reality Presented As An Alternative* with slower numbers like *Appearance Is Everything Style Is A Way Of Living* (which has fine Eastern-influenced guitar work) and a hypnotic cover of the **Incredible String Band**'s *Maybe Someday*. (CA/RMJ)

Human Instinct

Personnel:
MAURICE GREER	drms	A
DAVE HARTSTONE		A
FRANK HAYES		A
BILL WARD		A

45s:
Can't Stop Around/Want To Be Loved By You My Friend	(Mercury MF 951) 1965 R1
Rich Man/Illusions	(Mercury MF 972) 1966 R1
Go-Go/I Can't Live Without You	(Mercury MF 990) 1966 R1
A Day In My Mind's Mind/ Death Of The Seaside	(Deram DM 167) 1967 R1
Renaissance Fair/Pink Dawn	(Deram DM 177) 1968 R1

Originally from New Zealand, they arrived in England in September 1966 and since the above 45s were all recorded here I've decided to include them. They'd previously been known as The Four Fours back in New Zealand and were originally signed to Mercury. Indeed their first two 45s were leased to Mercury before they arrived here.

Human Instinct's best work however was for Deram. *A Day In My Mind's Eye* was quite a powerful song, notable for its electronic bleep. It's flip, *Death Of The Seaside* is poppier with summery harmonies which mourn the passing of Summer and has a few interesting tempo changes. The follow-up was a fine cover of David Crosby's *Renaissance Fair* to which they added a string arrangement. The flip side, *Pink Dawn*, sounds a little like **The Small Faces**.

The band later returned to New Zealand where they cut a series of albums, which are now rare and sought-after but that's another story, although the three albums concerned were repackaged on a three album set *1969-1971* (Little Wing LW 4002/3/4) 1988. The work of an entirely new line-up, assembled by drummer Maurice Greer, they fall very much into the power-rock category. Also repackaged with a booklet and poster is *The Zodiac Years* (Little Wing LW 4014/15) 1990, issued on a German label, which originally appeared on the Zodiac label. It's a double set.

Compilation coverage has included:- *A Day In My Mind's Eye* and *Pink Dawn* on *Rubble Vol. 12: Staircase To Nowhere* (LP); *A Day In My Mind's Eye* on *Rubble Vol. 6* (CD) and *The Psychedelic Scene* (CD); *Pink Dawn* on *Rubble Vol. 7* (CD) and *The Freakbeat Scene* (CD); *Death Of The Seaside* and *Renaissance Fair* on *British Psychedelic Trip, Vol. 3* (LP); *Death Of The Seaside* on *Great British Psychedelic Trip, Vol. 2* (CD) and *Psychedelic Unknowns, Vol. 7* (LP); *Renaissance Fair* on *Great British Psychedelic Trip Vol. 1* (CD) and *Deram Dayze* (LP) and *Rich Man* on *Jagged Time Lapse, Vol 4* (CD). (VJ)

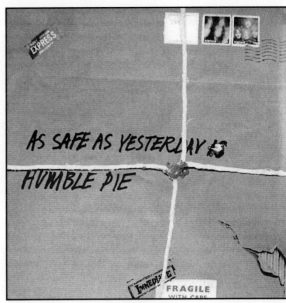

HUMBLE PIE - As Safe As Yesterday (LP).

Humblebums

Personnel:
BILLY CONNOLLY	ABC
TAM HARVEY	AB
GERRY RAFFERTY	BC

ALBUMS:
1(A)	A COLLECTION OF MERRIE MELODIES	(Transatlantic TRA 186) 1969 SC
2(C)	THE NEW HUMBLEBUMS	(Transatlantic TRA 201) 1969 SC
3(C)	OPEN UP THE DOOR	(Transatlantic TRA 218) 1970 SC
4(-)	THE COMPLETE HUMBLEBUMS	(Transatlantic TRA 288) 1974

NB: (4) is a box set of (1)-(3). (2) and (3) reissued on one CD (Castle ESMCD 498) 1997. There's also a CD *Humblebums* (Line TACD 900551) 1989. *Please Sing A Song For Us: The Transatlantic Anthology* (Sanctuary CMDD 1211) 2005 is a 2-CD compilation.

45s:
Saturday Roundabout Sunday/ Bed Of Mossy Green	(Big T BIG 122) 1969
Shoeshine Boy/My Appartment	(Big T BIG 130) 1970
Coconut Tree/Shoeshine Boy	(Big T BIG 520) 1972

This Glaswegian folk duo formed in the late sixties. Not surprisingly with Billy Connolly in their line-up they were known for their humorous songs. Their first album made quite an impact and after this **Gerry Rafferty** was asked to join them. They worked as a trio for six or seven months before Harvey was pushed out of the band. Connolly and **Rafferty** proceeded to record three more albums. The first of these, *A Collection Of Merrie Melodies*, was performed entirely on acoustic instruments, most notably the banjo and guitar and reflected Connolly's traditional folk inclinations.

The New Humblebums contained some good material, particularly *Please Sing A Song For Us* and *Her Father Didn't Like Me Anyway*. It was more melodic than the debut and featured some fine melodic woodwind and brass arrangements. *Open Up The Door* veered more towards pop and the duo used session musicians to achieve a fuller sound. The album featured **Barry Dransfield** and Bernie Holland of **Jody Grind**. However, this created difficulties for the duo in reproducing many of their songs on stage. Under pressure from their record company to form a backing group the two of them agreed to go their separate ways... not a bad decision as Connelly became a successful comedian and **Rafferty** a successful solo artist after first joining **Stealer's Wheel**.

If you missed **The Humblebums** first time around and think they sound interesting you may like to invest in their complete three album set which contained the album's original sleeve artwork and came in a nice outer slip case. However, this came out in 1974 and is not that easy to find now. Alternatively Sanctuary's recent compilation includes a BBC session and thorough sleevenotes from David Wells.

Why Don't They Come Back To Dunoon?, Everybody Knows That and *Patrick* were all later compiled on *The Transatlantic Story* CD box set. (VJ)

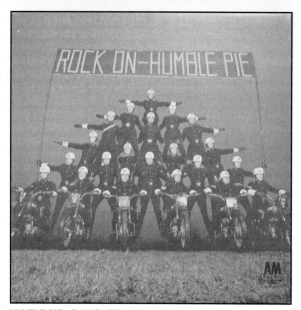

HUMBLE PIE - Rock On (LP).

Humble Pie

Personnel:	PETER FRAMPTON	gtr, vcls	A
	STEVIE MARRIOTT	gtr, vcls	ABC
	GREG RIDLEY	bs	ABC
	JERRY SHIRLEY	drms	ABC
	DAVE CLEMPSON	gtr	B

				HCP
ALBUMS: 1(A)	AS SAFE AS YESTERDAY IS			
(up to		(Immediate IMSP 025)	1969	SC 32
1976) 2(A)	TOWN AND COUNTRY	(Immediate IMSP 027)	1969	SC -
3(A)	HUMBLE PIE	(A&M AMLS 986)	1970	SC -
4(A)	ROCK ON	(A&M AMLS 2013)	1971	SC -
5(A)	PERFORMANCE - ROCKIN' THE FILLMORE (2-LP)			
		(A&M AMLH 63506)	1971	SC 32
6(B)	SMOKIN'	(A&M AMLS 64342)	1972	SC 28
7(B)	EAT IT (2-LP)	(A&M AMLD 6004)	1973	34
8(B)	THUNDERBOX	(A&M AMLH 63611)	1974	-
9(C)	STREET RATS	(A&M AMLS 68282)	1975	-

NB: (1) and (2) reissued on CD (Repertoire REP 4237-WY and 4231-WY respectively). (1) reissued on vinyl (Get Back GET 549) 1999 as an Italian import. (2) with extra tracks. (3) reissued on CD (Repertoire REPUK 1080) 2005. (4) reissued on Mobile Fidelity Sound (MFCD 847) 1988. (6) reissued on CD. (8) and (9) reissued on one CD (Beat Goes On BGOCD). *The Humble Pie Collection* (Castle CCSCD 104) 1994 may also be of interest. *Live On King Biscuit Hour* (King Biscuit Hour/Pinnacle KBFHCD 017) 1998 captures songs from the Winterland in 1973. There's also an earlier compilation on CD, *The Best Of Humble Pie* (A&M 393 208-2) 1988 and a 2-CD set *Natural Born Bugie - The Immediate Anthology* (Immediate CMDDD 054) 2001.

			HCP
45s:	Natural Born Bugie/Wrist Job	(Immediate IM 82)	1969 4
(up to	Black Coffee/Say No More	(A&M AMS 7052)	1973 -
1976)	Get Down To It/Honky Tonk Woman	(A&M AMS 7070)	1973 -
	Oh La De Da/Outcrowd	(A&M AMS 7090)	1973 -
	Rock'n'Roll Music/Scored Out	(A&M AMS 7158)	1975 -
Reissue:	Natural Born Boogie/	(Old Gold OG 9529)	1985 -

This outfit was formed in April 1969 and attracted considerable attention as **Stevie Marriott** had earlier been lead singer with **The Small Faces** and **Peter Frampton** had been vocalist and guitarist with **The Herd**. This combination gave them a 'supergroup' status and the other members had some pedigree too. Greg Ridley had been in **The V.I.P.'s**, **Art** and **Spooky Tooth** and Jerry Shirley was previously in **Apostolic Intervention**, as well as Wages Of Sin and Little Women. They were essentially a hard rock'n'roll band and enjoyed considerable success, embarking on over 20 American tours.

After forming in 1969 they soon hibernated to **Marriott**'s country cottage to work on their debut album. They were signed by Immediate but frankly the album, *As Safe As Yesterday*, was patchy, although it made No 32 in the Album Charts. One of its high points was *Natural Born Bugie*, which gave

them their only Top Ten hit when released as a 45. Also of note were the experimental *A Nifty Little Number Like You* and their cover of Steppenwolf's *Desparation*. Their follow-up album was more acoustic than its predecessor and flopped. It is best avoided. Thereafter they switched to A&M and started to embark on seemingly endless US tours, which slowly began to pay off.

In October 1971 **Frampton** quit to go solo being replaced by Dave Clempson (ex-**Colosseum**). The same month the band enjoyed a minor US hit with a US-only single, Ray Charles' *I Don't Need No Doctor*. It was in 1972 that the US breakthrough they had worked so hard for came when the double live album, *Performance-Rockin' The Fillmore* (which included **Frampton**) climbed to No 21 over there (it also put them back in the Album Charts here too). Featuring a much heavier brand of rock it marked a distinct change in musical direction. Their next album, *Smokin'*, developed this trend, peaking at No 6 in the US and No 28 in the UK, it was their best-selling album. To capitalise on its success their first two UK albums for Immediate were repackaged as a double set in the US and climbed to No 37 over there.

Eat It was another double album and signalled another change in musical direction - this time towards soul. Featuring the black trio The Blackberries, it again did better in the US rising to No 13 there compared with 34 over here.

After two further albums, which met with minor Chart success in the States, the band split in March 1975, weary of endless tours **Stevie Marriott** embarked on an unsuccessful solo career (Clempson having left to join **Greenslade** the previous year), then formed The Stevie Marriott All-Stars until **The Small Faces** reformed briefly in 1976.

Marriott reformed **Humble Pie** in 1980 although injury and ill health dogged this modified line-up, which had dissolved for good by the end of 1981. Like most so-called Supergroups **Humble Pie** didn't really fulfill their promise.

Their first two albums are now available on CD, the second with two previously unissued cuts, *Greg's Song* and *79th Street Blues*. In 2002, the band returned with a new album *Back On Track* (Sanctuary SANCD 106) and a new line-up including two of the original members Jerry Shirley and Greg Ridley.

Natural Born Bugie - The Immediate Anthology is comprised of material from their first two Immediate albums and supplemented with out-takes, backing tracks, demos and studio jams. It actually illustrates what a pale shadow his work with this band was compared to his time in **The Small Faces**.

Compilation appearances have included: *Song For Jennie* on *Come Together* (3-LP); *One Eyed Trouser Snake Rumba* on *Heads In* (LP); and *Natural Born Bugie* on *Immediate Single Collection, Vol. 2* (CD), on *Rock Of Ages, Four Decades Of Heavy Rock 1962-2002* and on the 3-CD box set *Ars Longa Vita Brevis: A Compendium Of Progressive Rock 1967-1974*. (VJ)

HUMBLE PIE - Performance - Rockin' The Fillmore (2-LP).

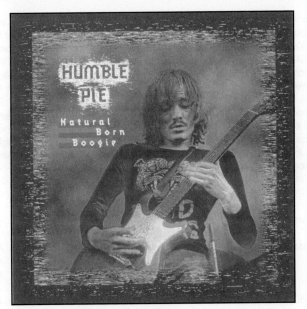
HUMBLE PIE - Natural Born Boogie (CD).

Hummingbird

Personnel:	CLIVE CHAPMAN	bs	AB
	BERNIE HOLLAND		A
	CONRAD ISIDORE		A
	MAX MIDDLETON	keyb'ds	AB
	BOB TENCH	gtr, vcls	AB
	ROBERT AHWAI	gtr	B
	BERNARD PURDIE	drms	B

ALBUMS:	1(A)	HUMMINGBIRD	(A&M AMLS 68292) 1975
(up to	2(B)	WE CAN'T GO ON MEETING LIKE THIS	
1977)			(A&M AMLH 68383) 1976
	3(B)	DIAMOND NIGHTS	(A&M AMLHI 64661) 1977

45s:	For The Children's Sake/	
(up to	You Can Keep The Money	(A&M AMS 7193) 1975
1977)	Trouble Maker/Gypsy Skies	(A&M AMS 7254) 1976
	Moodatcha/Anna's Song	(A&M AMS 7325) 1977

This band played a sort of soul/funk/jazz type pop!! The 'B' side of their second 45 was a superb keyboard piece that shows Max Middleton's credentials as a quality keyboard player.

Max Middleton and Bob Tench had both previously been in **Jeff Beck**'s backing band and Max Middleton was also in the brief incarnation of **Beck, Bogert and Appice**. Middleton and Ahwai later combined for a 1979 album. (MWh/JHx)

Humpy Bong

Personnel:	JONATHAN KELLY	gtr	A
	COLIN PETERSON	drms	A
	TIM STAFFELL	vcls, bs	A

45:	Don't You Be Too Long/	
	We're Alright Till Then	(Parlophone R 5859) 1970 R1

This band was formed in 1970 by ex-**Bee Gees** drummer Colin Peterson and was named after his first school in Australia. Tim Staffell was their lead vocalist and bassist until late 1970.

Their sole 45 has some country influences and it's rumoured that **Eric Clapton** played some guitar parts on the 'B' side. The single did nothing in spite of an appearance on "Top Of The Pops". **Jonathan Kelly** then decided to embark on a solo career whereas Tim Staffell joined the progressive band **Morgan**. (VJ/CSx)

Hungry Wolf

Personnel:	CLEM CATTINI	drms	A

JOHN EDWARDS	trombone	A
TONY FISHER	trumpet	A
HERBIE FLOWERS	bs	A
KEN GOULDIE	trombone	A
CLIFF HARDY	trombone	A
BOBBY HAUGHEY	trumpet	A
ALAN HAWKSHAW	keyb'ds	A
ALAN PARKER	gtr	A
PETER LEE STIRLING	vcls	A
DEREK WATKINS	trumpet	A

ALBUM:	1(A)	HUNGRY WOLF	(Philips 6308 009) 1970 R2

NB: (1) reissued on CD (HMP HMPCD 004).

This was the work of session musicians including future members of **Rumplestiltskin** and **Ugly Custard**. The album is now very rare. It featured vocals by **Peter Lee Stirling** who had a couple of dire pop hits in the early seventies as Daniel Boone. Guitarist **Alan Parker** later made a solo album entitled *Guitar Fantasy* on the Aristocrat label in 1970. (VJ)

Marsha Hunt

ALBUM:	1	WOMAN CHILD	(Track 2410 101) 1971 R1

NB: (1) also issued in Germany in 1971 and reissued in Germany as *Attention (Woman Child)* in 1974. Also of interest is *Walk On Gilded Splinters* (See For Miles SEE 209/SEE CD 209) 1988.

HCP

45s:	Walk On Gilded Splinters/	
	Hot Red Poppa	(Track 604 030) 1969 46
	Desdemona/Hippy Gumbo	(Track 604 034) 1969 SC -
	Keep The Customer Satisfied/	
	Lonesome Holy Roller	(Track 604 037) 1970 41
	Oh No Not The Beast Day/	
	Somebody To Love	(Vertigo 605 9080) 1973 -
	Medusa/Bop City	(Vertigo 605 9093) 1973 -
	Beast Day/City Bob	(Vertigo 605 9121) 1975 -
	C'est La Vie/	
	Do You Believe In Voodoo	(Electric WOT 1) 1976 -
	Best Kind Of Feeling/	
	Call Me Paradise	(Electric WOT 6) 1976 -
	Other Side Of Midnight/Heartache	(Magnet MAG 130) 1978 -

Actually an American, who came over to the UK after leaving Berkeley University, California. The rationale for her inclusion here is similar to **Hendrix**'s, though she found almost all of her success in the UK. Once here she played in **Alexis Korner**'s backing group and in **Ferris Wheel**. Her debut 45, a cover of Dr. John's *Walk On Gilded Splinters*, was powerful and distinctive and featured **Rick Wakeman** on keyboards. Also worth a spin was her version of **Marc Bolan**'s *Desdemona*, earlier a minor

HUNGRY WOLF - Hungry Wolf (CD).

hit for **John's Children**. The flip side *Hippy Gumbo* was also by **Bolan**. Both of these followed her first break - as part of the chorus of 'Hair' here in London in 1969.

Her album was a compilation of tracks from 45s. For most, her Afro-rock was an acquired taste, though, and when her initial commercial success tailed off she tried her hand at acting and broadcasting (a Capital Radio chat show). She briefly fronted a six-piece rock band, Marsha Hunt 22, in 1973, when she returned to record two 45s for Vertigo. She is also mother to **Mick Jagger**'s first child, Karis, born in November 1970.

The See For Miles compilation contains most of her *Woman Child* compilation, plus an early **Marc Bolan** composition, *Hippy Gumbo, Hot Rod Poppa*, and *Stacey Grove*. **Pete Townshend** and **The Faces** played on the final cut, *Wild Thing* and *My World Is Empty Without You* featured **Marc Bolan** on vocals.

Compilation appearances have included: *Keep The Customer Satisfied* on *Pop Party* (LP); *Walk On Gilded Splinters* on *Backtrack 1* (LP) and *Your Starter For Ten!!* (CD); whilst *Desdemona* received more exposure on *Backtrack 2* (LP). (VJ)

Hunter

| 45: | Some Time For Thinking/ | |
| | Coming On Strong | (RCA RCA 1995) 1970 |

An unknown band but Mike Warth tells me there's a great bit of guitar on the 'A' side. (VJ)

Ian Hunter

				HCP
ALBUMS:	1	IAN HUNTER	(CBS 80710) 1975	21
(up to	2	ALL AMERICAN ALIEN BOY	(CBS 81310) 1976	29
1976)				

NB: (1) reissued on mid-price budget label (Columbia Rewind 4773592) 1994. (1) reissued (Sony/BMG 519817) 2005 with six bonus cuts to commemorate its 30th Anniversary. There are also two compilations available on CD:- *The Very Best Of Ian Hunter* (CBS 467508-2) 1990 and *Collection: Ian Hunter* (Castle Collector Series CCSCD 290) 1991. An earlier vinyl compilation was *Shades Of Ian Hunter* (CBS 88476) 1978. This was also issued as a 2-CD set (Columbia 474782-2) 1993 in Germany. *Once Bitten Twice Shy* (Columbia 496284 2) 2000 is a 2-CD 38-track compilation set consisting of a 32-page booklet and several hard-to-find or previously unreleased tracks.

			HCP
45s:	Once Bitten Twice Shy/		
(up to	3,000 Miles From Here (PS)	(CBS 3194) 1975	14
1976)	Who Do You Love?/Boy	(CBS 3486) 1975	-
	All American Alien Boy/Rape	(CBS 4268) 1976	-
	You Nearly Did Me In/Letter To Britannia	(CBS 4479) 1976 SC	-

Hunter is best known as founder-member, vocalist and writer for **Mott The Hoople**, whom he left in acrimonious circumstances in late 1974. **Mick Ronson**, who left the band at the same time, produced, arranged and contributed to his first album, which made it to No 21 in the Charts and spawned a hit single in the shape of *Once Bitten Twice Shy*, its opening cut. Elsewhere on the album, *Boy* has a gentle orchestrated build-up culminating in a powerful opus, *It Ain't Easy When You Fall* represents the more acoustic dimension to **Mott The Hoople** and the final track *Shades Off* provides a poetical finale. Prior to this they had formed The Hunter-Ronson Band to promote the albums they were working on. Later in 1975 he toured extensively with **Mick Ronson** both here and in the US, billed as The Hunter-Ronson Show, although this proved a short-lived venture.

All American Alien Boy was a genuine 'solo' album and was well received charting here and making some impression in the US (No 177). It included contributions from several members of **Queen** as well as **Aynsley Dunbar**. He went on to enjoy a moderately successful solo career until 1983, becoming mostly based in the USA.

A man of many talents he also wrote of his experiences as a rock star in 'Diary Of A Rock'n'Roll Star', published by Star Books in 1973.

His heyday was very much in the seventies. Appearances were very spasmodic during the late eighties and nineties, but he did perform at the 1992 Freddie Mercury AIDS benefit and at tribute concerts for **Ronson** in 1994. He returned later with more solo albums *Artful Dodger* (1997) and *Rant* (2001), which was well received. In 2002, he performed a couple of semi-acoustic concerts in Oslo, Norway which were later released on CD and home video as *Strings Attached*. His latest release *The Truth, The Whole Truth And Nuthin' But The Truth* is a 2-CD set mostly showcasing his solo work but featuring some **Mott The Hoople** material too that was recorded on his recent Rant Band tour at London's Astoria. He's assisted on the release in delivering the old Mott material by his daughter Tracey, **Queen**'s Brian May and Joe Elliot (of Def Leppard). (VJ)

Hunter Muskett

Personnel:	CHRIS GEORGE	gtr, hrmnca, vcls	A
	TERRY HISCOCK	gtr, keyb'ds, vcls	A
	DOUG MORTER	gtr, vcls	A

ALBUMS:	1(A)	EVERY TIME YOU MOVE	(Decca Nova SDN 20) 1970	R3
	2(A)	HUNTER MUSKETT	(Bradley BRADL 1003) 1973	R1

NB: (2) reissued on CD.

45:	John Blair/Silver Coin (PS)	(Bradleys BRAD 303) 1973

This folk-rock band played at the original Isle of Wight festival in 1968 and their debut album is arguably the rarest on the Nova label. It successfully captured their three-pronged acoustic guitar work and mellow vocal harmonies. Their second effort was produced by **Keith Relf** and is an equally good starting point for folk fans wanting to investigate. Both albums feature multi-part harmonies, fluid electric guitar and a hint of West Coast rock.

Doug Morter later played on recordings by **Richard Digance**, **Maddy Prior** and **Magna Carta**. They also had three tracks on *Bradley's Roadshow*, a live album on Bradley Records, which also featured **Paul Brett's Sage**. (VJ)

Mike Hurst (and The Method)

Personnel incl:	MIKE HURST		
	(MIKE LONGHURST-PICKWORTH)	vcls	
	RAY SMITH	ld gtr	A

45s:	The Banjo Song/Any Chance For Me	(Philips BF 1295) 1963
	Carol Anne/Anytime That You Want Me	(Philips BF 1319) 1964
	Half Heaven Half Heartache/	
	Look In Your Eyes	(Philips BF 1353) 1964
	Last Time You'll Walk Out On Me/	

CHOCOLATE SOUP FOR DIABETICS VOL. 2 (Comp LP) including Hush.

	Something Told Me	(Philips BF 1389) 1965
	Show Me Around/I'm Running Away	(Philips BF 1424) 1965

Mike Hurst, whose proper name was Mike Longhurst-Pickworth, had already been in The Springfields, who predate the era of this book. They also featured **Dusty Springfield**. The Method were his backing group during 1964. These solo 45s are in the beat and/or folk mould and, aside from a cover of Gene Pitney's Carol Anne, were all written by **Hurst**, who went on to become a well-known producer/songwriter, especially for the Deram label. (VJ)

Hush

Personnel:	CHRIS ANGELO	vcls	A
	JOHN BEATTIE	ld gtr	A
	MAC POOLE	drms	A
	GEOFF SMITH	bs	A
	PETER 'TWIGGY' WOOD	organ	A

45:	Elephant Rider/Grey	(Fontana TF 944) 1968

This rare and sought-after 45 was the work of a five-piece band from Manchester. The flip side is an impressive slice of freakbeat/psychedelia with some good guitar work and strong vocals.

Compilation appearances include: *Elephant Rider* on *Magic Spectacles* (CD); whilst *Grey* can be heard on *Rubble, Vol. 1 - The Psychedelic Snarl* (LP), *Rubble, Vol. 1* (CD), *Chocolate Soup* (CD) and *Chocolate Soup For Diabetics, Vol. 2* (LP). (VJ)

Hush

Personnel incl:	MICK COX		A
	TONY HIGHTON		A

45s:	Everytime We Say Goodbye/	
	And Then There Was You	(Samantha SAMS 1) 1972
	White Christmas/Seasons Are Turning	(Samantha SAMS 2) 1972

This was a different outfit to the psychedelic sixties one. This band was in the studio in June 1972 and produced by Shel Talmy and Hugh Murphy.

Cox had previously been in **Eire Apparent** and Highton in Mother's Son. Highton was later in Stonehenge. (VJ)

Hustler

Personnel:	TONY BEARD	drms	A
	KENNY DAUGHTERS	keyb'ds	AB
	STEVE HAYNES	vcls	AB
	MICKEY LLEWELYN	gtr, vcls	AB
	KENNY LYONS	bs, vcls	AB
	HENRY SPINETTI	drms	B

ALBUMS:	1(A)	HIGH STREET	(A&M AMLS 68276) 1974 SC
	2(B)	PLAY LOUD	(A&M AMLH 33001) 1975 SC

45s:	Get Outa My House/Happy Days	(Firefly AM 5001) 1975
	Little People/	
	Why Do You Think Yer Fooling	(Firefly AM 5002) 1975
	Little People/	
	Why Do You Think Yer Fooling	(A&M AMS 5002) 1975
	Boogie Man/You Had It Coming To You	(Firefly AM 5003) 1975
	Boogie Man/You Had It Coming To You	(A&M AMS 5003) 1975
	Money Maker/Goin' Home	(Firefly AM 5004) 1975
	Money Maker/	
	Money Maker (different version)	(A&M AMS 5004) 1976

A heavy rock outfit with a good reputation. *High Street* is very much in **Free/Bad Company** mould. Tracks like *Just Leave A Good Man* and *Jack The Lad* are hard-rocking songs with strong melodies and good vocals and guitar work. There are some mellower moments on *Let The Wind Blow* and

Miranda, whilst *The Hustler* is reasonably orchestrated. *Get Outa Me 'Ouse*, the only track where Micky Llewellyn sings, is in a more pub-rock direction and *Pizanhas* has a long instrumental break with keyboard progressive overtones in a **Deep Purple** direction. A good example of this genre. (CA/VJ)

The Hustlers

Personnel:	DOUG DANIEL	bs	A
	ROY ENGLISH	gtr, vcls	A
	CHRIS JARVIS	drms	A
	GEOFF QUATERMAIN	ld gtr	A

45s:	Gimme What I Want/Not Much	(Philips BF 1275) 1963
	You Can't Sit Down/Be True To You	(Mercury MF 807) 1964
	Sick Of Giving/Easy To Find	(Mercury MF 817) 1964 SC

A beat group from Kent who failed to make much impact despite their name! *Sick Of Giving* later resurfaced on *Infernal World, Vol. 1* (LP) compilation. They used to dress in U.S. Civil War uniforms. (VJ)

Ashley Hutchings

ALBUMS:	1	MORRIS ON	(Island HELP 5) 1972
(up to	2	THE COMPLEAT DANCING MASTER	
1977)			(Island HELP 17) 1974
	3	RATTLEBONE AND PLOUGHBACK	
			(Island HELP 24) 1976 SC
	4	SON OF MORRIS ON	(Harvest SHSM 2012) 1976
	5	KICKIN' UP THE SAWDUST	
			(Harvest SHSP 4073) 1977 SC

NB: (1) was by various folk artists. *The Guv'nor, Vol. 1* (HTD CD 23) 1994 is a collection compiled largely from **Fairport Convention** outtakes. *The Guv'nor Vol 2* and *Vol 3* (HTD CD 38) 1995 contain material from, **Fairport Convention, Steeleye Span** and *The Albion Band*. *Vol. 4* (HTC CD 66) 1996 includes more material from his time with **Fairport Convention** and **Fotheringay**, but mostly contains material from the mid-seventies to mid-eighties Albion Band.

Hutchings was a founding member of **Fairport Convention** in 1967 but quit in early 1970 to form **Steeleye Span** and then The Albion Band. The *Morris On* album was recorded with Dave Mattacks, **Richard Thompson**, **Barry Dransfield** and **John Kirkpatrick** during 1972 whilst he was marking time between **Steeleye Span** and the **Albion Country Band**. After the latter's demise he recorded *The Compleat Dancing Master* and *Rattlebone And Ploughjack*, which were documentary albums, whilst playing in part-time dance bands Etchingham Steam Band and Albion Dance Band. The two Harvest albums were recorded during this time with the latter.

The Morris On and *Son Of Morris On* albums are notable for 'electrifying' Morris dancing. **Hutchings** has also worked for the BBC, writing and presenting programmes about folk music. He has been an interesting and key figure in the British folk-rock scene. Indeed, some view him as the father of British folk-rock.

Monck's March can also be heard on *Harvest Heritage - 20 Greats* (LP). (VJ)

Hygrades

45:	She Cared/We're Through	(Columbia DB 7734) 1965

The above 45 was this obscure beat band's sole vinyl excursion. They came from Harrow in North-West London. (VJ)

HAWKWIND - BBC Radio One Live In Concert (CD).

HAWKWIND - Masters Of The Universe (LP).

HAWKWIND - Hall Of The Mountain Grill (LP).

JIMI HENDRIX - Band Of Gypsies (CD).

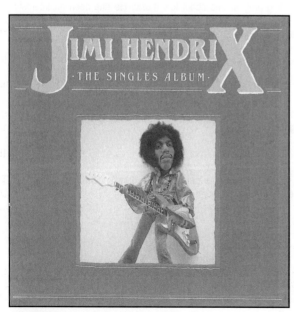

JIMI HENDRIX - The Singles Album (2-CD).

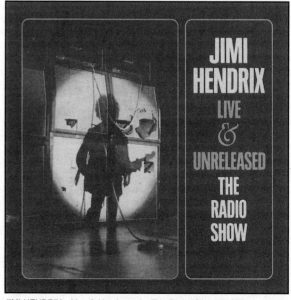

JIMI HENDRIX - Live & Unreleased - The Radio Show (3-CD).

Ian and The Zodiacs

Personnel:			
DAVE ?	sax	A	
JERRY GARAGHAN	piano	A	
PETER GRIFFITHS	lead vcls	A	
JOHNNY KENNEDY	gtr, vcls	A	
DAVE LOVEDAY	drms	AB	
PETE PIMBLETT	gtr, lead gtr	AB	
IAN EDWARDS	gtr, vcls	BCDEFG H I J KL M	
PETE WALLACE	lead gtr, bs	BCDE H I	
CHARLIE FLYNN	bs	CDEF I	
CLIFF ROBERTS	drms	C	
GEOFF BAMFORD	drms	D	
JOE WALSH	drms	E	
ARTHUR ASHTON	lead gtr	FG	
FREDDIE SMITH	drms	FG	
TONY COATES	bs	G	
JIMMY TUSHINGHAM	drms	H I	
COLIN FABB	bs	J KL M	
DAVE KENT	lead gtr	J K	
LES MAGUIRE	keyb'ds	J KL M	
PETER STEVENSON	drms	J	
CARL HARDIN	drms	K	
MAL LITTLE	lead gtr	L	
BARRY WOMERSLEY	lead gtr	L	

ALBUM: 1( ) GEAR AGAIN - 12 HITS (Wing WL 1074) 1965 R1

NB: They also made three German-only albums which have recently been reissued; *Star-Club Show 7* (Repertoire IMS 7006), *Just Listen To* (Repertoire IMS 7007) and *Locomotive!* (Repertoire IMS 7008) 1994. They also had another album, *Ian And The Zodiacs* (Phillips PH(M/S) 200-176) 1965, which was probably only released in the USA.

45s:
	Beechwood 4-5789/ You Can Think Again	(Oriole CB 1849) 1963 R1	
α	The Crying Game/Livin' Lovin' Wreck	(Philips 40277) 1964 R1	
α	Good Morning Little Schoolgirl/ Message To Martha	(Philips) 1965 R1	
β	Just The Little Things/ This Won't Happen To Me	(Fontana TF 548) 1965 R1	
	No Money, No Honey/ Where Were You?	(Fontana TF 708) 1966 SC	
	Wade In The Water/ Come On Along, Girl	(Fontana TF 753) 1966 R2	

NB: α US only releases. *Message To Martha* was a remake of Dionne Warwick's *Message To Michael*. β as Ian Edward and The Zodiacs.

One of the lesser-known Merseybeat groups who also featured on Oriole's *This Is Merseybeat* (LPs). *Vol. 1* featured a cover of Little Eva's *Let's Turkey Trot* and *Vol. 2* included *It Ain't Necessarily So* and *Secret Love*. Their UK album was a collection of cover versions of popular songs of the day.

ICARUS - The Marvel World Of (LP).

They also recorded two albums of cover versions of **Beatles**' songs as The Koppykats. One of these, *Beatlemania*, on the budget label Top Six, was released in Holland and in the UK and contained six tracks which also appeared in error on **The Searchers**' *Needles And Pins* album, released on Vogue in Germany.

Charlie Flynn also recorded a 45 as **Wellington Wade** and the band was managed for a time by Brian Epstein.

The three German-only albums, originally issued by the German Star-Club label and now reissued on Repertoire, mostly comprise cover versions of the hits of the day and R&B and soul standards. *Star Club 7* includes a dozen extra cuts, including the band's three contributions to Oriole's *This Is Merseybeat* (LPs). *Just Listen To* was a little better with a few good tracks whilst *Locomotive!* veered more towards soul covers than the previous two. These CDs include all the records they recorded for Oriole, Starclub and Fontana, but not the two Koppycats albums, nor their album for Wing.

Some of their music is poor, but *Wade In The Water*, a jazzy/R&B classic done by Ramsay Lewis and others, is brilliant, raunchy and very moddy with Hammond organ.

Peter Wallace, the band's lead guitarist, moved to New Zealand around 1970 and reformed the Zodiacs in Auckland. He returned to the U.K. a few years ago, where he still performs occasionally.

The Crying Game was a hit in Texas in 1965.

Compilation appearances have included: *Beechwood 4-5789* on *Let's Stomp!* (LP), *Mersey Beat* (2-LP), *Mersey Beat 1962-1964* (2-LP); *No Money, No Honey* on *Purple Pill Eaters* (LP & CD); *Take A Message To Martha* and *Spartacus* on *The Star-Club Singles Complete, Vol. 2* (LP & CD); *So Much In Love With You* and *All Of Me* on *The Star-Club Singles Complete, Vol. 5* (LP & CD); *Why Can't It Be Me, Leave It To Me, No Money, No Honey* and *Ride Your Pony* on *The Star-Club Singles Complete, Vol. 6* (LP & CD); *Na-Na-Na-Na-Na* and *Any Day Now* on *The Star-Club Singles Complete, Vol. 9* (LP & CD); *Come On Along Girl* on *Star-Club Show* (LP); *Take A Message To Martha* on *Sweet Beat* (LP); *All Of Me* on *Star Club Scene '65* (LP); *Why Can't It Be Me* on *The Star-Club Anthology, Vol. 1* (LP) and *Incredible Sound Show Stories, Vol. 9* (LP); *Get Out Of My Live, Woman* on *The Star-Club Anthology, Vol. 4* (LP); *That's Nice* and *Ride Your Pony* on *Bits And Pieces - Lost And Found* (LP & CD); *Clarabella* on *Beat Im Star Club* (2-LP); and *Let's Turkey Trot* and *It Ain't Necessarily So* on *The Exciting New Liverpool Sound* (LP). (VJ/DCe/JW/AD)

Icarus

Personnel:			
PETER CURTAIN	drms	A	
NORRIE DEVINE	sax, flute, clarinet	A	
JOHN ETHERIDGE	gtr	A	
STEVE HART	vcls	A	
IAIN HINES	keyb'ds	A	
JIMMY WILEY	bs	A	

ALBUM: 1(A) THE MARVEL WORLD OF ICARUS (Pye NSPL 28161) 1972 R2

NB: Repressed in 1997, and also issued on CD (Play Loud PL 28161) 1997.

45: The Devil Rides Out/You're In Life (Spark SRL 1012) 1968 R1

Each of the players on this fast-rocking album with a strong progressive touch presents themselves as comic character, ranging from Spiderman via Conan the Barbarian to the Hulk. The lyrics likewise deal with the vicissitudes of these heroes, lending the album a comparatively agreeable degree of fun. As the instrumental and vocal abilities of the band are no less than good, the only flaw is the lack of outstanding compositions, although a few highlights are present nonetheless. These include the scary intro to *Hulk*, the propelling rhythms of *Conan The Barbarian*, almost all flute parts, almost all of the opening track on the 'B' side, *Thor* and the slightly psychedelic *Silver Surfer*. All in all fun to listen to, though a bit overestimated.

The Devil Rides Out single is named after a Denis Wheatley novel. It's jazzy with lots of horns! Only Hines of the above line-up had earlier played on this - the other members were Les Karske, Roy Steadman and Glynn Havard.

Etheridge went on briefly to **The Soft Machine**. Iain Hines is the brother of Fraser Hines, who is known for his roles in 'Emmerdale Farm' and 'Doctor Who'.

Compilation appearances have included: *The Devil Rides Out* on *Rubble, Vol. 11* (CD) and *The Best Of Rubble Collection, Vol. 2* (CD); and *You're In Life* on *Voyage Through The Sugarcube* (LP & CD). (MK)

Ice

Personnel:	JOHN CARTER	bs	A
	GLYN JAMES	vcls	A
	LYNTON NAIFF	organ	A
	GRANT SERPELL	drms	A
	STEVE TURNER	gtr	A

45s: Anniversary (Of Love)/So Many Times (Decca F 12680) 1967 R2
Ice Man/
Whisper Her Name (Maria Laine)   (Decca F 12749) 1968 R2

NB: There's also a retrospective LP/CD *Ice Man* which includes their singles. The CD release comes with 12 bonus tracks to comprise their entire recorded output.

This London-based group was formed at Sussex University. Their debut 45, *Anniversary (Of Love)* was clearly influenced by **Procol Harum** around the time of *Whiter Shade Of Pale*. The follow-up, *Ice Man*, was more original, but rather restrained psych-pop. It's certainly the better of the two, with some unusual faltering guitar work and a catchy piano ending. The flip *Whisper Her Name* was more like their first 'A' side, being a keyboard-led ballad.

In addition to these 45s, they recorded six sessions for the BBC circa 1967/68, one with **Linda Hoyle**, who briefly joined the band before they changed name. When the band failed to create any sort of Icemania, they split, with Naiff, Serpall and **Hoyle** going on to **Affinity**.

Compilation coverage has so far included: *Anniversary (Of Love)* on *Rubble Vol. 6: The Clouds Have Groovy Faces* (LP) and *Rubble Vol. 4* (CD); *Ice Man* on *Rubble Vol. 11: Adventures In The Mist* (LP), *Rubble Vol. 6* (CD) and *The Psychedelic Scene* (CD); *So Many Times* (miscredited as *Anniversary (Of Love)*) and *Ice Man* on *The British Psychedelic Trip, Vol. 1* (LP) and *The Great British Psychedelic Trip* (CD); and *Whisper Her Name (Maria Laine)* on *British Psychedelic Trip, Vol. 4* (LP) and *The Great British Psychedelic Trip Vol. 2* (CD). (VJ/JH)

Ice Cream

Personnel:	JEFF BARNES	ld gtr	A
	JEFF BOLTZ	drms	A
	GARY DEANS	ld vcls	A

IDLE RACE - Idle Race (LP).

ROB NORMAN	keyb'ds	A
STEVE STROUD	bs	A
DAVE WELLS	gtr	A

45:     Shout It Out/Hold Ourself Tight   (Fontana 600.7039) 1974

A commercial band from South London. They were formed in late 1973 from three other bands: Love Country Music, Joe Roadster and Bronx. They started out as a pub band. In the Summer of 1974, they supported Leo Sayer on tour. *Shout It Out* was written by John Springate of **The Glitter Band**. (VJ)

The Ice Show

This group's pop-psych acetate *I Remember Susannah* (Oak, December 1967) with its whimsical lyrics and ethereal harmonies can now be heard on *Story Of Oak Records* (2-LP) compilation. (VJ)

Idle Race

Personnel:	JEFF LYNNE	gtr, vcls	A
	GREG MASTERS	bs	ABC
	DAVE PRITCHARD	gtr	ABC
	ROGER SPENCER	drms	ABC
	ROY CULLOM	vcls	B
	MIKE HOPKINS	ld gtr	BC
	DAVE WALKER	vcls	C

ALBUMS:	1(A)	THE BIRTHDAY PARTY		
		(mono/stereo)	(Liberty LBL/LBS 83132) 1968 R2/R1
	2(A)	IDLE RACE	(Liberty LBS 83221) 1969 R2
	3(C)	TIME IS	(Regal Zonophone SLRZ 1017) 1971 R3
	4(-)	ON WITH THE SHOW	(Sunset SLS 50354) 1973

NB: (1) reissued on Sunset (SLS 50381) in 1976 (SC) and on C5 (C5-536) in 1989. There's also a compilation, *Light At The End Of The Road* (See For Miles SEE 60) 1985, which was later issued on CD as *The Best Of The Idle Race Featuring Jeff Lynne* (See For Miles SEECD 60) 1990. In addition, *The Jeff Lynne Years 1968/1973: Message From The Country* (Harvest CDP 92585 2) 1983 includes seven cuts by **Idle Race**.

45s: The Imposters Of Life's Magazine/
Sitting In My Tree   (Liberty LBF 15026) 1967 R1
The Skeleton And The Roundabout/
Knocking Nails Into My House   (Liberty LBF 15054) 1968 SC
The End Of The Road/
Morning Sunshine   (Liberty LBF 15101) 1968 SC
α I Like My Toys/Birthday   (Liberty LBF 15129) 1968 SC
β Days Of Broken Arrows/
Worn Red Carpet   (Liberty LBF 15218) 1969 SC
Come With Me/
Reminds Me Of You   (Liberty LBF 15242) 1969 SC
Dancing Flower/Bitter Green   (Regal Zonophone RZ 3036) 1971
Reissue: The Skeleton And The Roundabout/
Morning Sunshine   (United Artists UP 36060) 1976

NB: α Unissued. β flipside credits 'Warm' mistakenly on the label.

This underground quasi-psychedelic band evolved from a local Birmingham group, **Mike Sheridan and The Nightriders**, which Masters, Pritchard and Spencer had all been in. They formed in May 1966 and their original guitarist was Johnny Mann (previously of **Carl Wayne and The Vikings**), but he was soon replaced by Jeff Lynne. Despite a series of fine singles, of which *Imposters Of Life's Magazine* and *The Skeleton And The Roundabout* were the most memorable, they failed to achieve commercial success. Lynne left to join **The Move** in 1970, having previously refused to join them in 1969. His replacement was Denny Laine and The Diplomats guitarist Mike Hopkins, but after one further album (along with Roy Cullom who was soom replaced by Dave Walker) the band fell apart. Of course, Lynne later achieved far greater fame with the **Electric Light Orchestra** and to cash in on this, *The Birthday Party* was re-issued in 1976. United Artists also issued a compilation album, *On With The Show*, on budget label Sunset. In 1986, See For Miles issued an 18-track compilation, *Light At The End Of The Road*, including several cuts previously unavailable on album, which is recommended. Although clearly influenced by **The Beatles**

420

and **The Move**, **Idle Race** also evolved their own unique style and their recordings are a 'must' for psych and progressive fans alike.

After *In The Summertime* had become a hit for **Mungo Jerry** in 1970, Liberty released the **Idle Race**'s version in Argentina, Australia, Germany, Italy, Japan, Netherlands, Singapore and Sweden. In Australia it appeared on a picture sleeve EP, that also included both post-Lynne **Idle Race** 45s: *In The Summertime*/*Told You Twice* and *Neanderthal Man*/*Victim of Circumstance*. *Neanderthal Man* was also obviously an attempt to get a hit off someone else's song and was similarly released in several countries.

Idle Race had three singles not issued in the UK (*Here We Go Round The Lemon Tree*/*My Father's Son* (Liberty LBF-15010 (UK cancelled)/Liberty 55997)(US); *Neanderthal Man*/*Victim Of Circumstance*(Liberty, Canada) and *In The Summertime*/*Told You Twice* (Columbia, Germany))

After their demise, Dave Pritchard went on to play for various local Birmingham-based bands. Dave Walker later played with **Savoy Brown**, **Chicken Shack** and **Fleetwood Mac**. Roger Spencer became comedian 'Ollie' Spencer and Mike Hopkins joined Quartz. Even after all these departures, the band staggered on with former **Tea and Symphony** members Dave Carroll and Bob Wilson, Bob Lamb (ex-**Locomotive**), Roy Cullom (briefly) and later **Steve Gibbons** (formerly of **Balls**). Indeed, after a few further line-up changes, it evolved into The Steve Gibbons Band.

Back in 1969, *Hurry Up John* appeared on *Son Of Gutbucket* (LP). Other compilation appearances have included: *Skeleton and The Roundabout* and *The Birthday* on *Not Just Beat Music 1965-70* (LP); *Imposters Of Life's Magazine* on *Psychedelic Visions* (CD), the 4-CD *Nuggets 11* box set and on the 4-CD box set *Acid Drops, Spacedust & Flying Saucers*; *Knocking Nails Into My House* on *Rubble, Vol. 2 - Pop Sike Pipe Dreams* (LP) and *Rubble, Vol. 2* (CD); *Days Of The Broken Arrows* and *Worn Red Carpet* on *Sixties Years, Vol. 5* (CD); *Imposters In Life's Magazine* and *The Lady Who Said She Could Fly* on *Artefacts From The Psychedelic Dungeon* (CD); *Skeleton and The Roundabout* and *Worn Red Carpet* on *British Psychedelic Trip, Vol. 2* (LP) and *Great British Psychedelic Trip, Vol. 3* (CD); *Skeleton and The Roundabout* on *In The Beginning* (LP); and *Days Of Broken Arrows* on the 4-CD *Nuggets 11* box set. (VJ/SBn/BM)

The Idols

Personnel:	GRAHAM BAILEY	drms, vcls	A
	MIKE SAX	ld vcls, gtr	A
	RAY SAX	bs, vcls	A
	JOHN SYKES	ld gtr, vcls	A

45:     Don't Walk Away/You Don't Care   (Mercury MF 840) 1965 SC

A beat group from Lancashire (Mike, Ray and Graham came from Rossendale and John from Bury). The group was originally called Mike Sax and The Vikings, with Mike, Ray, John and various other drummers.

IF - If (CD).

IF - If 2 (LP).

Graham joined them from The Beatmakers, and shortly after they had a publishing contract with DIX music and Harold Frantz; and a recording contract with Phillips, under the Mercury subsidiary.

They had no success with recording, although *My Little One*, their follow-up 45 as **Mike Sax and The Idols** was 'tip for the top' on Radio Caroline. The band folded in 1967 after a three month stint in Italy, with **The Casuals** and **The Riot Squad**. (VJ/GB)

If

Personnel:	DENNIS ELLIOT	drms	A
	J.W. HOGKINSON	vcls	A
	JOHN MEALING	keyb'ds	A
	DICK MORRISEY	sax, flute	AB
	DAVE QUINCY	alto sax	AB
	JIM RICHARDSON	bs	A
	TERRY SMITH	gtr	A
	CLIFF DAVIS	vcls, drms, synth	B
	GABRIEL MAGNO	keyb'ds	B
	WALT MONAHAN	bs, vcls	B
	GEOFF WHITEHORN	gtr	B

ALBUMS:	1(A)	IF	(Island ILPS 9129) 1970 SC
	2(A)	IF 2	(Island ILPS 9137) 1970 SC
	3(A)	IF 3	(United Artists UAG 29158) 1971 SC
	4(A)	IF 4	(United Artists UAG 29315) 1972 SC
	5(B)	NOT JUST A BUNCH OF PRETTY FACES	
			(Gull GULP 1004) 1974
	6(B)	TEA BREAK IS OVER	(Gull GULP 1007) 1975

European Releases:
	1	THIS IS IF	(Brain 201 005) 1973
	2	GOLDENROCK	(Brain 201 103) 1974
	3	WATERFALL	(Metromedia 1057) 1971
	4	DOUBLE DIAMOND	(Metromedia 10174) 1973

NB: (1) reissued on CD (Edsel EDCD 505). (2) reissued on CD (Edsel EDCD 506). (5) reissued on CD (Germanophon HF 9534). There's also a compilation CD *Forgotten Roads: The Best Of If* (Sequel NEM CD 773) 1995. Also of interest is *Europe '72* (Repertoire REP 4653) 1996.

45s: Raise The Level Of Your Conscious Mind/
         I'm Reaching Out On All Sides   (Island WIP 6083) 1970
         Far Beyond/Forgotten Roads   (United Artists UP 35263) 1971
         You In Your Small Corner/
         Waterfall   (United Artists UP 35356) 1972
         I Believe In Rock And Roll/Still Alive   (Gull GULS 5) 1974

A jazz-rock outfit who were originally formed in the late sixties by Morrisey and **Smith**. They toured relentlessly, particularly in the US, but never made much of a breakthrough here, although they attained considerable popularity in Europe. Their highly improvised, laid-back jazz-rock albums made good late night listening with red wine and a smoke.

IF - Not Just Another Bunch Of Pretty Faces.

Elliot, Mealing and Richardson all left in 1972. Elliot was later in Foreigner. Dick Morrisey put together an entirely new line-up to record their two albums for Gull, with Walt Monaghan (ex-**Rust** and **Mick Abrahams Band**). After **If**'s demise, saxophonist Morrisey linked up with guitarist Jim Mullen in quite a successful and enduring partnership. **Terry Smith** had earlier recorded a solo album, and together with Dave Quincy later formed **Zzebra**. Geoff Whitehorn later played on the reformed **Fantasy** album. Dave Quincey and **Terry Smith** (who also had a solo album) were also in **Zzebra**. Gabriel Mango is currently living and performing in Las Vegas.

Until recently completely neglected by CD compilers, but this is now rectified by *Forgotten Roads: The Best Of If*, which confirms them as one of Britain's best jazz-rock acts, who deserved a much higher profile than they achieved. Their dynamic live performances are also captured on *Europe '72*, which unearths material from the band's own personal archives. The set also includes an extensive interview with the band members.

They can also be heard playing *I'm Reaching Out On All Sides* on Island's 1970 *Bumpers* (2-LP) compilation. (VJ)

Kris Ife

45s:	Hush/The Spectator	(MGM MGM 1369) 1967 SC
	This Woman's Love/I Gotta Feeling	(MGM MGM 1390) 1968
	Give And Take/Sands Of Time	(Music Factory CUB 3) 1968
	Imagination/I'm Coming 'Round	(Parlophone R 5741) 1968 SC
	Haven't We Had A Good Time/ Will I Ever Fall In Love Again?	(Parlophone R 5770) 1969
	Out Of Time/ Crazy In Love With You Babe	(United Artists UAG 36010) 1975

This London-based artist was first in **The Quiet Five** but went solo when they split up during 1967. His solo efforts were mostly ballads. The first, *Hush*, was a Billy Joe Royal oldie. His second 45 was written and produced by **Mark Wirtz**. (VJ)

'Igginbottom

Personnel:	DAVE FREEMAN	drms	A
	ALLAN HOLDSWORTH	gtr, vcls	A
	STEVE ROBINSON	gtr, vcls	A
	MICK SKELLY	bs	A

ALBUM: 1(A) 'IGGINBOTTOM'S WRENCH (Deram SML 1051) 1969 R3

A promising but slightly inconsistent attempt to cross-fertilize rock and jazz without relying on tedious solos. It's also the recording debut of ace-guitarist Holdsworth, who effortlessly steals the show. Most songs alternate between the dreamy and driving, which works well on side 1, where the cuts are shorter and more concisely executed. The highlight is arguably the dreamy opener *The Castle*, though their unrecognisable rendition of *California Dreamin'* is also of interest. Only when the jazz takes over a bit too much on side 2 does one begin to wonder why so many small notes without meaning are being played. The band apparently hated the record, which was recorded in haste. Holdsworth was later in **Tempest** and recorded a solo album, *Velvet Darkness*, in 1977. (MK/VJ//RMJ).

Iguana

Personnel:	JOHN CARTWRIGHT	bs	A
	CHRIS GOWER	trombone	A
	PETE HUNT	drms	A
	DON SHINN	piano	A
	BRUCE ROBERTS	gtr, vcls	A
	RONNIE TAYLOR	sax	A

ALBUM: 1 (A) IGUANA (Polydor 2383 108) 1972 SC

This was a bluesy, hard-rock band with horns. Most of these musicians also played with **Jess Roden** and **Don Shinn** was previously in **Renaissance** and **Dada**. (SR)

Illusive Dream

45: Electric Garden/Back Again (RCA RCA 1791) 1969 SC

The flip side of this 45 was reputedly a bit unusual - in a typical 1969 psychedelic pop way. **Christine Perfect** was their organist in 1968, but then left to join **Chicken Shack**. The group came from Birmingham. *Electric Garden* has been compiled on *Spinning Wheel, Vol 1* (CD). (MWh)

I Luv Wight

Personnel:	DANNY BRIDGMAN	vcls, drms	A
	STEVE CLARK	bs, flute	A
	PETER DALTREY	vcls, keyb'ds	A
	EDDIE PUMER	vcls, keyb'ds, gtr	A

45: Let The World Wash In/ Medieval Masquerade (Some PS) (Philips 6006 043) 1970 R2/R1

This one-off 45 was recorded at the request of the promoters of the 1970 Isle Of Wight festival, who needed a theme tune for the event, by the former members of **Kaleidoscope**, who'd just changed their name to **Fairfield Parlour**. The 'A' side was a soft ballad, which Daltrey and Pumer had credited to the pseudonyms of Newnes and Baker in an attempt to hide their identify - but not everyone was fooled. The flip was a pleasant instrumental. In the end The Great Awakening's *Amazing Grace* became the festival's theme and this 45 passed by largely unnoticed. Partly as a consequence, it's now very collectable, particularly copies in its original art sleeve.

Let The World Wash In can also be found on *Kaleidoscope: The Fairfield Parlour Years* 2-CD retrospective and both sides of this single are included on the CD reissue of **Kaleidoscope's** second album *Faintly Blowing* (Repertoire REPUK 1047) 2005. (VJ)

Image

Personnel incl:	DAVE EDMUNDS	gtr		A
45s:	Come To The Party/ Never Let Me Go		(Parlophone R 5281) 1965 R1
	Home Is Anywhere/ I Hear Your Voice Again		(Parlophone R 5352) 1965 R1
	I Can't Stop Myself/ Let's Make The Scene		(Parlophone R 5442) 1966 R1

These singles are all quite rare and sought-after. The band came from Wales and are most notable for containing **Dave Edmunds**. *Come To The Party* and *I Can't Stop Myself* were Carter-Lewis compositions.

Creation (from a non-UK 45) has been compiled on *We Can Fly, Vol 1* (CD) and on *Talking About The Good Times*. (VJ)

The Images

Personnel incl: PETE BURFORD   bs   A

45:      I Only Have Myself To Blame/
         Head Over Heels   (Polydor 56011) 1965 SC

This obscure South London band recorded an equally obscure beat 45 which is now quite collectable. Burford was very briefly in **Manfred Mann**. (VJ)

Hamish Imlach

ALBUMS: 1   BEFORE AND AFTER
                                   (Transatlantic XTRA 1059) 1967 SC
          2   THE TWO SIDES OF HAMISH IMLACH
                                   (Transatlantic XTRA 1069) 1968 SC
          3   FINE OLD ENGLISH TORY TIMES
                                   (Transatlantic XTRA 1128) 1972 SC
          4   MURDERED BALLADS
                                   (Transatlantic XTRA 1131) 1973 SC

NB: There's also *The Definitive Transatlantic Collection* (Castle) 1997.

One of Scotland's best loved characters, **Imlach** was a traditional folk singer and humorist. He made use of guest musicians on most of his albums. For example, on *The Two Sides of Hamish Imlach* he was ably assisted by **Clive Palmer**, **Archie Fisher**, Ray Warleigh and John MacKinnon. (VJ)

Impac

45:      Too Far Out/Rat Tat Ta Tat   (CBS 202402) 1966 R2

This 45 is now rare and sought-after probably in part because the beat group's producer was Joe Meek.

You'll also find *Too Far Out* on *RGM Rarities, Vol. 2* (CD) and *English Freakbeat, Vol. 5* (CD). (MWh)

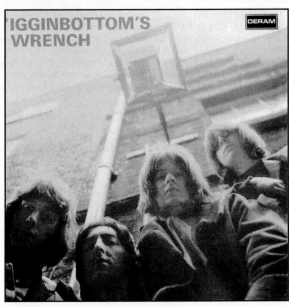

'IGGINBOTTOM - 'Igginbottom's Wrench (CD).

The Imp-acts

Personnel incl: LEE 'DAVE' COURTNEY   drms   A
                  BARRY HEYWOOD   bs   A

45:      The Dum Dum Song/
         If I Were The Only One   (Pye 7N 15911) 1965

This outfit from Romford in Essex also backed Adam Faith for a while. You can check out *The Dum-Dum Song* on *Ripples, Vol. 5* (CD). (VJ)

The Imposters

45:      Apache '69/Q Three   (Mercury MF 1080) 1969 SC

This is another one-off 45 by an obscure group. The 'A' side was originally done by **The Shadows**. (VJ)

The In-Be-Tweens (aka 'N Betweens)

Personnel: DAVE HILL   gtr   AB
              JOHNNY HOWELLS   vcls   A
              DAVE JONES   bs   A
              MICKEY MARSTON   gtr   A
              DON POWELL   drms   AB
              NODDY HOLDER   gtr, vcls   B
              JIMMY LEA   bs, piano, violin   B

45:      You Better Run/Evil Witchman   (Columbia DB 8080) 1966 R4

Yes, you've probably sussed it, this was an early version of **Slade**. They evolved out of a Woverhampton-based band, **The Vendors**, who didn't record commercially but did produce a four song demo, in 1965. Line-up (A) only released EPs in France on the Barclay label, but by 1966 Noddy Holder had joined from **Steve Brett and The Mavericks** along with Jimmy Lea and this later line-up (B) recorded a cover of The Young Rascals' *You Better Run*, which needless to say now costs an arm and a leg to purchase. **The In-Be-Tweens** continued on the Midlands circuit mostly doing cover versions before changing name to **Ambrose Slade** and the rest, as they say, is history.

60's Back Beat (LP) has included two previously unreleased cuts by the band:- *Hold Tight*, a marginally wilder version of the **Dave Dee** hit than the original and the rather oddball *Ugly Girl*, which was written by Noddy Holder and American Kim Fowley, who produced the session. Other compilation appearances have included: *Security* and *Delighted To See You* on *Made In England, Vol. 2* (CD); *You Better Run* on *Perfumed Garden Vol. 2* (LP & CD); *Delighted To See You* on *Psychedelia At Abbey Road* (CD); *Evil Witchman* on *English Freakbeat, Vol. 1* (LP & CD); and

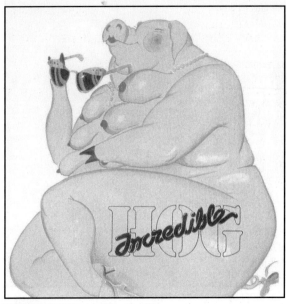

INCREDIBLE HOG - Incredible Hog (CD).

Can Your Monkey Do The Dog?, Respectable, I Wish You Would, Ooh Poo Pa Doo, Feel So Fine, Take A Heart, Little Nightingale, You Don't Believe Me, Security, You Better Run, Evil Witchman, Hold Tight, Ugly Girl and Need can all be heard on The Genesis Of Slade (CD). (VJ)

The Incas

45:     One Night Stand/
        I'll Keep Holding On   (Parlophone R 5551) 1966 SC

This band can also be heard contributing one track to the Keele Rag Record (EP) (Lyntone LYN 765/6) 1965 (R1), along with three other bands. A soulish mod group, they came from Birmingham. One Night Stand was written by **Small Faces Stevie Marriott** and **Ronnie Lane**. The flip side was a Marvelletes track.

You can check out One Night Stand on Rare 60's Beat Treasures, Vol. 5 (CD). (VJ)

The Incredible Hog

Personnel:	TONY AWIN	drms	A
	KEN GORDON	gtr, hrmnca, vcls	A
	JIM HOLMES	bs, vcls	A

ALBUM: 1(A) VOLUME 1   (Dart 65372) 1973 R3

NB: (1) also released on Telefunken in Germany. Reissued on CD (Repertoire REP 4511-WP) 199? and (Third Thunder TT 023).

45:     Lame/Tadpole   (Dart ART 2026) 1973

A heavy rock band from East London whose mediocre album, produced by Roger Watson (see under **Roger Denison**) is now extremely rare. Continental issues had a completely different cover. (VJ/RMJ)

The Incredible String Band

Personnel:	MIKE HERON	vcls, gtr, various	ABCDEFG
	ROBIN WILLIAMSON	vcls, gtr, various	ABCDEFG
	CLIVE PALMER	vcls, gtr, banjo	A
	LICORICE McKECHNIE	violin, keyb'ds	BCD
	ROSE SIMPSON	bs, perc	C
	MALCOLM LE MAISTRE	vcls	DEFG
	GERALD DOTT	clarinet, sax	EF
	STAN LEE	drms	FG
	JACK INGRAM	drms	FG
	GRAHAM FORBES	gtr	G

THE INCREDIBLE STRING BAND - The 5,000 Spirits Or The Layers Of The Onion (LP).

THE INCREDIBLE STRING BAND - The Hangman's Beautiful Daughter (LP).

HCP

ALBUMS:	1(A)	THE INCREDIBLE STRING BAND		
(up to			(Elektra EUK 254) 1966 - R1	
1976)	2(B)	THE 5,000 SPIRITS OR THE LAYERS OF THE ONION		
			(Elektra EUK 257/EUKS 7257) 1967 SC 26	
	3(C)	THE HANGMAN'S BEAUTIFUL DAUGHTER		
		(w/insert) (Elektra EUK 258/EUKS 7258) 1968 SC 5		
	4(C)	WEE TAM AND THE BIG HUGE (2-LP) (w/insert)		
			(Elektra EKL 4036/7 / EKS 74036/7) 1968 SC 34	
	5(C)	CHANGING HORSES (Elektra EKS 74057) 1969 SC 30		
	6(C)	I LOOKED UP (Elektra EKS 74061) 1970 SC 30		
	7(D)	BE GLAD FOR THE SONG HAS NO ENDING		
			(Island ILPS 9140) 1970 SC -	
	8(D)	U (2-LP) (w/insert) (Elektra 2665 001) 1970 SC 34		
	9(-)	RELICS OF THE INCREDIBLE STRING BAND		
			(Elektra EKS 74065) 1971 -	
	10(D)	LIQUID ACROBAT AS REGARDS THE AIR		
			(Island ILPS 9172) 1971 SC 46	
	11(E)	EARTHSPAN (Island ILPS 9211) 1972 SC -		
	12(F)	NO RUINOUS FEUD (Island ILPS 9229) 1973 -		
	13(F)	HARD ROPE AND SILKEN TWINE		
			(Island ILPS 9270) 1974 -	
	14( )	SEASONS THEY CHANGE - THE BEST OF THE		
		INCREDIBLE STRING BAND (2-LP)		
			(Island ISLD 9) 1976 -	

NB: (1) and (5) reissued on CD (Elektra 7559-61547-2 and 7559 61549-2 respectively) 1993. (1) and (2) reissued on 2-CDs (Elektra) 2004. (4) was also issued as two single LPs and almost all of the above sixties releases were reissued during the seventies. (6) reissued on CD (Warners 7559 627 602) 2002. (8) reissued on 2-CD set (Warners 7559 627 612) 2002. (10) reissued on CD (Island IMCD 130) 1991. (11) and (12) reissued on CD (Edsel EDCD 360 and 367 respectively) 1992.

On Air (Band Of Joy BOJCD 004) 1991 is a selection of their best songs taken from BBC Radio recordings in the early seventies. Live In Concert (Windsong WINCD 029) 1992 includes material from 1971, some of which was previously unreleased. The Chelsea Sessions 1967 (Pig's Whisker Music PWMD 5022) 2000 is a CD collection of demos recorded just prior to the sessions for their second album. The Circle Is Unbroken: Live And Studio 1967-1972 (Castle Music CMDDD 1210) 2005 is a 2-CD set which will appeal to their fans.

45s:	α	Way Back In The 1960s/	
		Chinese White	(Elektra EKSN 45013) 1967 R2
		Painting Box/No Sleep Blues	(Elektra EKSN 45028) 1968
		Big Ted/All Writ Down	(Elektra EKSN 45074) 1969
		This Moment/Black Jack Davy	(Elektra 2101 003) 1970
		Black Jack David/Moon Hang Low	(Island WIP 6145) 1972
		At The Lighthouse Dance/Jigs	(Island WIP 6158) 1973

NB: α White label promo-only.

With admirers including **the Beatles** and **the Rolling Stones**, **The Incredible String Band** produced some of Britain's best psychedelic folk and achieved significant commercial success in the process.

Londoner **Clive Palmer** and Scotsman **Robin Williamson** had formed a folk duo in Edinburgh in 1963. In 1965 they added **Mike Heron** (whose background lay more in rock and roll), named themselves **the Incredible String Band** at **Palmer**'s suggestion, and started Glasgow's Incredible Folk Club, which rapidly became a focal point for the local folk scene. Joe Boyd soon signed them to Elektra and flew them to London to record their May 1966 debut, which made considerable impact in folk circles. *October Song* (which got them signed) has a strong melody and spellbinding lyrics, while *Maybe Someday* has great energy and *Everything's Fine Right Now* exudes joy. **Palmer**'s sole contribution, the doleful *Empty Pocket Blues*, remains a highlight for many fans, but after its release he travelled to Afghanistan and India and on his return chose not to rejoin.

Without **Palmer**, **Heron** and **Williamson** (who had also been travelling) the band considerably extended their range and began to establish themselves in London's underground, regularly playing at Boyd's legendary UFO club. Their next album, 1967's *5,000 Spirits Or The Layers Of The Onion*, showcased the complex brand of psychedelic folk the duo had concocted, and has been called 'the folk *Sergeant Pepper*'. A radical deviation from their essentially traditional debut, it combined unheard-of instruments such as the oud, gimbri and tamboura with whimsical, quasi-philosophical lyrics and catchy melodies. Some songs were short and humorous (*Little Cloud*, *The Hedgehog Song*), while others were touching (*Painting Box* and the much-covered *First Girl I Loved*) or plain surreal (*No Sleep Blues*, *Way Back In The 1960s*). It reached No. 26 in the charts and was named 'album of the year' by **Paul McCartney**. They also made a considerable impression at the US Newport Folk Festival in the same year.

By 1968 they'd become the mouthpiece and inspiration for the artier end of Britain's hippie movement, and were widely-acknowledged to be highly original and unusual. Their next album, *The Hangman's Beautiful Daughter*, retained its predecessor's sense of fun and adventure while incorporating aspects of gospel, soul and burlesque, and still stands for many as the defining blend of folk and psychedelia. Its contents varied from **Williamson**'s stupendous mosaic of childhood memories *Koeeoaddi There* to the brilliant Gilbert and Sullivan pastiche *The Minotaur's Song* and an attractive ditty entitled *Witches Hat*. **Heron**'s highly ambitious *A Very Cellular Song* was a clever amalgam of several shorter compositions, and the hypnotic *Waltz Of The New Moon* and sitar-kissed closer *Nightfall* were also highly effective. The album was much acclaimed on its release in March and became their biggest seller, breaking out of the underground to reach No. 5.

Wee Tam And The Big Huge was patchy, as are many double albums, but still contained some excellent songs. On it the duo continued to experiment with obscure instruments and were supplemented by their girlfriends Licorice McKechnie and Rose Simpson. The pick of the material was **Williamson**'s nine-minute *Ducks On A Pond* and six-and-a-half-minute *Job's Tears*. The open-ended lyrics of his *The Half Remarkable Question* appealed to the (pseudo-) intellectuals of the era, and also worthy of note were **Heron**'s *You Get Brighter* and *Log Cabin Home In The Sky*. Despite wide acclaim, however, the disjointed nature of much of their material irritated some folk and rock fans and the album failed to repeat the commercial success of its predecessor.

The aforementioned albums captured the band at its best and are recommended. Their subsequent material was largely inferior. 1969's *Changing Horses* has its moments, but only in **Williamson**'s 16-minute *Creation* did they truly recapture the mysticism of their earlier work. Rose and Licorice sang on most tracks, and Ivan Pawle of **Dr. Strangely Strange** guested on organ and piano. *I Looked Up* was similar in style, and opens with **Heron**'s interesting interpretation of the traditional *Black Jack Davy*. Other cuts that shine through include *The Moment* and *When You Find Out Who You Are*. They memorably performed the latter at the Woodstock festival in August, though as a whole their set (delayed and then sandwiched between Creedence Clearwater Revival and Canned Heat) was not brilliant. For 1970's *U* they added dancer and vocalist Malcolm Le Maistre to the line-up. It was also a stage production, incorporating mime/dance troupe Stone Monkey, and not very successful creatively or commercially. The album marked the end of their association with Elektra, and they now signed to Island.

Be Glad For The Song Has No Ending was the soundtrack to their interminable film of the same name that briefly appeared at the time. *Liquid Acrobat As Regards The Air* included some traditional jigs and a strong anti-war song, *Dear Old Battlefield*. It recaptured some of their old magic, squeezing to No. 46 in the charts, but was to be their last hit. At this time **Heron** and **Williamson**'s musical ambitions were growing apart, which was reflected on their solo albums, **Heron**'s *Smiling Men With Bad Reputations* and **Williamson**'s *Myrrh*. In this period the band was moving towards a more mainstream rock sound, and 1971's excellent *Relics* compilation was a stark reminder of how much they'd changed since the early albums.

By this time the group's eclecticism had perhaps become a liability rather than an asset. Gerald Dott joined them for *Earthspan*, a mishmash of styles which spawned another 45, *Black Jack David* (a reworking of *Black Jack Davy*, the 'B' side of their previous 45), but neither release did anything to arrest their decline. *No Ruinous Feud* was their weakest album of all. It contained a number of throwaway numbers and jigs with only opening cut *The Explorer* and instrumental *Second Fiddle* (featuring **Williamson** and Dott backed by reggae band Greyhound) proving at all memorable. Dott departed after its release and was replaced by Forbes (formerly of **Powerhouse**), whose brash guitar work seemed bizarrely inappropriate. Former roadies Lee and Ingram were also drafted in at this time.

Their final album, *Hard Rope And Silken Twine*, appeared in April 1974. It included a decent live version of stage favourite *Cold Days Of February*, but the whole of side two was taken up by **Heron**'s lengthy *Ithkos*, which degenerated into a tedious heavy boogie. They appeared rehearsing and then performing *Ithkos* in the 1974 film 'Rehearsal', alongside the Wandsworth School Choir, the Band of the Scots Guards and the Royal Opera at Covent Garden. On 9th May they played at the Eternal Variety Show, a Scientology benefit, at London's Rainbow Theatre. Their poor performance was subsequently released on a US-only album of the event. Though they remained a popular live attraction, by this time they had lost much of their creative drive and the inevitable split came in autumn 1974.

THE INCREDIBLE STRING BAND - Wee Tam And The Big Huge (2-LP).

THE INCREDIBLE STRING BAND - Be Glad For The Song Has No Ending (CD).

INCREDIBLE STRING BAND - No Ruinous Feud (CD).

Williamson quit England for Los Angeles, later forming his Merry Band, who put out three albums (the first of which was a US-only release). In 1979 he published a book in poem form, 'Five Denials on Merlin's Grave', and during the eighties he worked as a solo artist. **Heron** flirted with Scientology before forming the promising theatrical rock outfit **Mick Heron's Reputation** in 1975. Sadly, they failed to break through commercially and disbanded after one album. With Le Maistre and Gilstron (drms) he then formed **Heron**, which met a similar fate after just one album, *Diamond Of Dreams*. They have occasionally reformed in subsequent years, and most recently **Heron** and **Palmer** have gone out under the group name.

Fans of the band will also relish the *Chelsea Sessions 1967* CD, which contains demos recorded just prior to the recording of *The 5,000 Spirits*, including some songs which hadn't been released in any form before.

Another CD set for their fans is *The Circle is Unbroken: Live And Studio 1967-1972*. The first disc features the *1967 Chelsea Demo Sessions* on which the songs and arrangements are often dramatically different from the final releases. There's also a bonus track from 1968 - a medley featuring *All Too Much, Take Your Burden To The Lord* and *Light From The Lighthouse*, which was recorded during the sessions for their fourth album. The second disc mostly comprises tracks from a concert in Calgary, Canada in 1972. Also included, though, are two bonus tracks *The Hag With The Money* and *Oh Did I Love To Dream*, which have never appeared on any of their studio albums.

1971's *Relics* compilation included two songs from their debut, seven from their second and four from their third, and is well worth obtaining. Better still was the US release, a double set which also featured five tracks from *Wee Tam And The Big Huge,* one from *Changing Horses* and two from *I Looked Up*. In 1976 Island put out a double compilation, *Seasons They Change*, which is a good selection of their work. They can also be heard on Elektra's 1969 *Begin Here* (2-LP) compilation, playing *Mercy, I Cry, City,* on Island's *El Pea* (2-LP), singing *Waiting For You,* and on *Select Elektra* (LP) performing *First Girl I Loved*.

Witches Hat later turned up on the 4-CD set *Acid Drops, Spacedust & Flying Saucers*. (VJ/RMJ)

The In Crowd

Personnel:	SIMON 'BOOTS' ALCOT	bs	ABC
	LES JONES	ld gtr	A
	KEN LAWRENCE	drms	AB
	KEITH WEST	vcls	ABC
	JOHN 'JUNIOR' WOOD	gtr	ABC
	STEVE HOWE	ld gtr	BC
	JOHN 'TWINK' ADLER	drms	C
			HCP

45s:	That's How Strong My Love Is/		
	Things She Says	(Parlophone R 5276) 1965 R2 48

	Stop! Wait A Minute/		
	You're On Your Own	(Parlophone R 5328) 1965 R1 -
	Why Must They Criticise/		
	I Don't Mind	(Parlophone R 5364) 1965 R1 -

This R&B / soul group had begun life as **Four Plus One**. They are best remembered, if at all, for their cover of Otis Redding's *That's How Strong My Love Is*, which was a minor hit. On the flip was the superb punkier *Things She Says*.

After the first 45, **Steve Howe** replaced Les Jones. Their second 45 had a beat-flavour and their final effort was a folk-styled protest number, that had originally been recorded by **George Bean**. All three of their 45s, particularly the first, are now rare and sought-after.

The band also recorded a version of Ike Turner's *Finger Poppin* which remained unreleased until r-p-m's recent *Mothballs* compilation, which also includes tracks by **Tomorrow** and **Steve Howe**.

Shortly after **Twink** left **The Fairies** to join **The In Crowd** they changed name to **Tomorrow**, abandoning its R&B style music for psychedelia.

Rumours of an unreleased **In Crowd** album are unsubstantiated.

Compilation appearances have included: *Why Must They Criticise* on *English Freakbeat, Vol 2* (CD); *Things She Says* on *English Freakbeat, Vol 4* (CD) and *I Don't Mind* on *Visions Of The Past, Vol 3* (CD). (VJ)

Incrowd

45:	Where In The World/		
	I Can Make Love To You	(Deram DM 272) 1969 SC

A different and very obscure act of this name, who came from Liverpool. (VJ)

Indian Summer

Personnel:	MALCOLM HARKER	bs, vibes, vcls	A
	PAUL HOOPER	drms, perc, vcls	A
	BOB JACKSON	keyb'ds, ld vcls	A
	COLIN WILLIAMS	gtr, vcls	A

ALBUM:	1(A)	INDIAN SUMMER	(RCA Neon NE 3) 1971 R1

NB: (1) has been counterfeited and also reissued on CD (Repertoire REP 4257-WP) 1993.

This keyboard-driven progressive band came from Coventry. Some tracks are quite pleasant but there is a tendency for them to be over-long and sometimes a little monotonous. Bob Jackson became a member of **Badfinger**. (VJ)

The Indians

ALBUM:	1	INDIAN COUNTRY	(Hawk) 1972

An Irish showband who released this strange album in April 1972. The tracks included *Indian Burial Ground, Wings Of A Dove, Polka Selection, Squawks Along The Yukon, Son Don't Go Near The Indians, Wigwam, Wiggle* etc. (VJ)

Indo-British Ensemble

ALBUM:	1	CURRIED JAZZ	(MFP 1307) 1969 SC

Made by a studio band featuring Indian players along side jazz stalwarts like Kenny Wheeler and Jeff Clyne, this is an enjoyable album housed in an attractive cover, and has attracted much attention from DJs for samples in recent years. Its producer, Victor Graham, describes it on the sleeve as 'happy exotic music', and that's just what it is. (RMJ)

Infantes Jubilate

45: Exploding Galaxy/Take It Now (Music Factory CUB 5) 1968 R2

The 'A' side of this unusual 45 was dramatic to say the least, heavily orchestrated and full of wailing trumpets and thumping tympani. The 'B' side is a soft-rock number minus the extras. Their identity remains a mystery.

Exploding Galaxy has been compiled on *Rubble, Vol. 11* (CD), *The Best Of Rubble Collection, Vol. 3* (CD), *We Can Fly, Vol 1* (CD) and on *Lovely Summer Days* (CD). (MWh)

Influence

Personnel:	VIV MALCOLM	gtr	A
	JOHN HERRINGTON (MILES)	keyb'ds, gtr, vcls	A
	PAUL THOMPSON	drms	A

45: I Want To Live/Driving Me Wild (Orange OAS 201) 1969 SC

This Newcastle group was most significant for containing **John Miles**, although he was still known by his original name of John Herrington. The 'A' side was a forgettable ballad, although the flip, *Driving Me Wild*, which has recently resurfaced on *Syde Trips, Vol. 4* (LP), is a more upbeat blues-tinged boogie with a good harpsichord intro which leads into some spirited vocals and lively guitar playing.

After their 45, when John Herrington embarked on a solo career as **John Miles**, the band split. Thompson later bashed the skins for **Roxy Music** and Malcolm was briefly in **Yellow**, who cut one 45 for CBS, before forming **Geordie** with future AC/DC member Brian Johnson. Other personnel included: Mick Golden, Chris Warren (who went on to **Pickettywitch**) and Arthur Rama (ex-**Beckett** and later a member of Les Humphries Singers). (VJ)

Information

45s:	Orphan/Oh! Strange Man	(Beacon BEA 121) 1968
	Lovely To See You/Face To The Sun	(Evolution E 24615) 1970

An obscure band, but *Oh! Strange Man* is reputed to be good.

Compilation appearances include: *Oh Strange Man* on *Justafixation II* (LP) and *Incredible Sound Show Stories Vol. 11* (LP); and *Face To The Sun* on *Incredible Sound Show Stories, Vol. 1* (LP & CD). (VJ)

Neil Innes

ALBUM:	1 HOW SWEET TO BE AN IDIOT	
(up to 1976)		(United Artists UAS 29492) 1973 SC

NB: (1) reissued as a budget-priced release on vinyl retitled *Neil Innes A-Go-Go* (Liberty LBR 1018) 1980 and on CD as *Re-cycled Vinyl Blues* (EMI 7248 8 30071 2 7) 1994 which includes the above album, the 1970 single by **The World** and some of his 1970s United Artists 45s.

45s:	How Sweet To Be An Idiot/	
(up to 1976)	The Age Of Desperation	(United Artists UP 35495) 1973
	Momma B/Immortal Invisible	(United Artists UP 35639) 1973
	Re-Cycled Vinyl Blues/	
	Fluff On The Needle	(United Artists UP 35676) 1974
	Lie Down And Be Counted/	
	Bandwagon	(United Artists UP 35745) 1974
	What Noise Annoys A Noisy Oyster/	
	Oo-Chuck-A-Mao-Mao	(United Artists UP 35772) 1975

Neil Innes is a first notch satirist who can also write catchy pop songs - something of a rarity among musical comedians.

He was born on 9 December 1944 at Danbury in Essex. Much of his childhood was in post-war Germany but he came to London to study at Goldsmith's College of Art where he became friends with the likes of **Vivian Stanshall**, Larry Smith and **Roger Ruskin Spear**. It was here that they formed The Bonzo Dog Dada Band, which became **The Bonzo Dog Doo Dah Band** when they graduated and turned professional in 1966.

After they split in 1970 he formed **The World**, but they only lasted for a few months. He then linked up with another former **Bonzo**, **Vivian Stanshall**, for a while and later toured as Neil Innes and Friends before joining **Grimms** in 1973.

In 1973, **Innes** also signed to United Artists as a solo artist, recording the above album and a series of humorous 45s. Both *How Sweet To Be An Idiot* and his second solo effort *Taking Off* in 1977 were evenly split between satire and pop in terms of content. In 1976, he worked on a 30-minute comedy programme with Eric Idle, 'Rutland Weekend Television'. This led to the Idle and Innes duo album, *The Rutland Weekend Songbook*, in 1976. Out of this came the **Beatles** parody project The Rutles, for which **Innes** is best known. As well as starring in Idle's film 'All You Need Is Cash' as Rutles leader Ron Nasty, **Innes** also penned 20 **Beatles**' parodies for the soundtrack. *The Innes Book Of Records* (1979) and *Off The Records* (1982) both compiled songs performed on his first TV show 'The Innes Book Of Records'. In 1996, **Innes** brought The Rutles together to record *Archaeology*, a parody of **The Beatles**' anthology CDs. (VJ)

The Innocents

Personnel:	DAVID BROWN	bs	AB
	ROGER M BROWN	lead gtr	A
	COLIN GRIFFIN	gtr, sax	AB
	DON GROOM	drms	AB
	BILLY KUY	lead gtr	B

45s:	Stepping Stones/Grazina	(Columbia DB 7098) 1963
	A Fine, Fine Bird/Spanish Holiday	(Columbia DB 7173) 1963 SC
	Stick With Me Baby/	
	Not More Than Every Day	(Columbia DB 7314) 1964

This Manchester beat band, were formed by Roger M. Brown at the request of Robert Stigwood/**Mike Berry**. Put together as **Berry**'s replacement backing band for The Outlaws, Roger M. Brown, Dave Brown and Colin Giffin had earlier played in The Tuxedos, who'd had a hit with *Baby Sittin'* backing Bobby Angelo. Don Groom was the original drummer with The Outlaws.

As **The Innocents** they played with John Leyton, **Jet Harris**, **Mike Berry**, Gene Vincent, The Four Seasons, B. Bumble and The Stingers, Johnny Burnette, **The Kinks**, **Hollies**, **Moody Blues**, **Yardbirds**, **Beatles** and **The Rolling Stones**. When their management company folded, Dave Brown and Colin Giffin formed **The End**, which later evolved into **Tucky Buzzard**. (VJ/AD/RB)

INDIAN SUMMER - Indian Summer (CD).

INSTANT SUNSHINE - Live At Tiddy Dols (LP).

Inquisitive People

45:    Big White Chief/Rhapsody Of Spring   (Decca F 12699) 1967

This short-lived pop combo's 45 is of little interest to collectors and attracted little attention at the time. (VJ)

Instant Sunshine

ALBUM: 1 LIVE AT TIDDY DOLS   (Page One POL 007) 1968 R1

45:    Here We Go Again/Methylated   (Page One POF 085) 1968

A three-piece music hall-style act. The sleevenotes just credit them as 'Sunny Alan', 'Sunny Peter' (Peter Christie) and 'Sunny David'. The album is a bizarre combination of inconsequential Swinging London pop and drunken music hall revelries. Originals are very hard to find, but one for the stouthearted. They are thought to have been Cambridge undergraduates led by Alan Marion-Davies, who has appeared on Radio One over the last few years as their resident doctor for phone-in programmes.

The band still performs today, with a new CD *Comes Of Age* under their belt. (VJ/DW)

The Intentions

45:    There's Nobody I'd Sooner Love/
       Hurry On Home   (Pye 7N 45123) 1970

This is another long-forgotten 45. (VJ)

The Interns

Personnel incl: MARK GOODWIN

45s: Don't You Dare/
       Here There Everywhere   (Philips BF 1320) 1964 SC
       Cry To Me/There's Love For You   (Philips BF 1345) 1964 SC
       Is It Really What You Want?/
       Just Like Me   (Parlophone R 5479) 1966 R1
       Ray Of Sunshine/
       Please Say Something Nice   (Parlophone R 5586) 1967

A Newport band who often appeared on stage clad in surgeon's outfits. Mark Goodwin was their founder member. Their first gigs often included backing Paul Raven and they played at The Star Club in Hamburg in 1963 under the name Rikki Allan Combo. *Is It Really Want You Want?* is now of most interest to collectors.

Their third 45 was recorded by Charles and Kingsley Ward at Future Sound (precursor to Rockfield Studios in Monmouth Wales). Dale Griffin, future **Mott The Hoople** drummer, played on the single as a session man. Goodwin joined Lonnie Donegan's band from 1967 - 1973.

Don't You Dare can also be heard on *Beat Merchants* (2-LP). (VJ/JPn/MG)

Ipsissimus

45:    Hold On/Lazy Woman   (Parlophone R 5774) 1969 R1

This four-piece band came from Barnet in North London. Their version of *Hold On*, which had previously been recorded by Sharon Tandy (assisted by **The Fleur de Lys**), can also be heard on *Rubble Vol. 3: Nightmares In Wonderland* (LP) and *Rubble Vol. 2* (CD). It's not bad but not essential either. It was also recorded by **Rupert's People**. (VJ)

Ironbelly

45:    Whoa' Buck/Wild About My Loving   (Parlophone R 5864) 1970

This is another of those obscure turn of the decade 45s. (VJ)

Iron Cross

45s: Little Bit O' Soul/Sunshine   (Spark SRL 1079) 1973
       Everybody Rock On/All Of The Time   (Spark SRL 1112) 1974

Their *Little Bit O' Soul* was an extremely raucous version of USA's Music Explosion's song. (VJ)

Iron Maiden

45:    Falling/Ned Kelly   (Gemini GMS 006) 1970

Not the Iron Maiden, but a much more obscure and earlier outfit with the same name. The 'A' side to their sole 45 is a brilliant lengthy guitar-led piece with a solo well beyond the length of a 1970 single. They were known as Burn Up until January 1970 and in March of the same year they toured Australia. (MWh)

Iron Virgin

Personnel: MARSHALL BAIN   bs   A
           STUART HARPER   ld vcls   A
           JOHN LOVATT   drms   A
           GORDON NICOL   gtr   A
           LAURIE RIVA   ld gtr   A

45s: Jet/Midnight Hitcher   (Deram DM 408) 1974
       Rebels Rule/Ain't No Clown   (Deram DM 416) 1974

A five-piece from Edinburgh who were originally known as Virgin. The 'Iron' appendage was added later to reflect their hard-rocking style. Gordon Nicol now lives in Dallas, Texas, where he owns his own recording studio.

Rebels Rule resurfaced on *Progressive Pop Inside The Seventies* (CD). (VJ/GN)

Jon Isherwood

ALBUM: 1 A LAUGHING CRY (mono/stereo)
                              (Decca LK/SLK 5051) 1970

45:    Old Time Movies/Apple Pie   (Parlophone R 5753) 1969

A pop singer whose inane *Apple Pie* recently got a further airing on *Circus Days, Vol. 4* (LP) and *Circus Days Vol's 4 & 5* (CD). Not recommended.

He went on to make several folk albums in the seventies. One of the best is *A Laughing Cry* (Decca 5051) in 1970. (VJ/BS)

Isolation

ALBUM: 1 ISOLATION (w/inset) (Riverside HASLP 2083) 1973 R4
NB: (1) reissued on Fanny (1994).

This is an extremely rare privately-pressed album. It came in a stamped plain white sleeve originally. A moody progressive folk album, it's somewhere between the second **Dr. Strangely Strange** album and **Ithaca**. Its recent reissue on the Belgian-based Fanny label means you no longer need to take out a second mortgage to get to hear it. Just 500 copies were pressed with a redesigned cover so these will soon become scarce. (VJ)

Isotope

Personnel:	GARY BOYLE	gtr	ABC
	JEFF CLYNE	bs	A
	BRIAN MILLER	keyb'ds	A
	NIGEL MORRIS	drms	ABC
	HUGH HOPPER	bs	BC
	LAWRENCE SCOTT	keyb'ds	BC
	ZOE KRONBERGER	vcls	C

ALBUMS: 1(A)	ISOTOPE	(Gull 1002) 1974
(up to 2(B)	ILLUSION	(Gull 1006) 1974
1976) 3(C)	DEEP END	(Gull 1017) 1976

NB: (1) and (2) reissued on one CD (See For Miles SEECD 432). There's also *The Best Of Isotope* (Gull 1024) 1979. Live *At The BBC* (Hux HUX 048) 2004 is also relevant.

A well-respected jazz-rock fusion outfit fronted by Indian-born guitarist Gary Boyle, who'd played with **Brian Auger**, **Keith Tippett** and Stomu Yamash'ta previously. Clyne and Miller returned to the jazz scene from whence they'd come after their first album and their replacements included former **Soft Machine** bassist **Hugh Hopper**. Vocalist Zoe Kronberger was added to the line-up for their third album. He also later guested on the first of Boyle's two solo albums recorded after **Isotope** split up in 1976.

Live At The BBC compiles material from a 1973 concert, a 1974 'Old Grey Whistle Test' appearance and a 1977 Peel session, when Boyle's band featured future Buggles and Asia member Geoff Downes. (VJ)

Ithaca

Personnel:	JOHN FERDINANDO	gtr, vcls, bs organ, harp	A
	PETER HOWELL	gtr, piano, organ, mandolin, perc, rec	A
	BRIAN HUSSEY	drms	A
	LEE MENELAUS	vcls	A

ALBUM: 1(A) GAME FOR ALL WHO KNOW
(w/insert) (Merlin HF 6) 1973 R4
NB: (1) reissued on CD (Background HBG 122/3) 1993 (SC).

A very rare privately-pressed demo-only album which is heavily influenced by the early seventies **Moody Blues** sound. In other words, we're talking progressive pop/rock with quasi-mystical lyrics. Some will love it, others will feel it typifies all that's bad in the genre. Among the better moments are *Dreams and Times*.

The individuals responsible for this had earlier been involved in **Agincourt**, **Alice Through The Looking Glass** and **Tomorrow Come Some Day**. In addition to the core band members, Robert Ferdinando played guitar on one track, Andrew Lowcock guested on flute on one track and Martin Garrett played 12-string guitar on some tracks.

The **Ithaca** album is a mega-rarity, but some further copies appeared on the market when the band were tracked down. According to 'Record Collector' the earlier market value (£1,500) was halved to £750.

The band was also responsible for an acetate album called *Friends* but this was never 'released'. This would definitely fall into the R5 category. (VJ/PM)

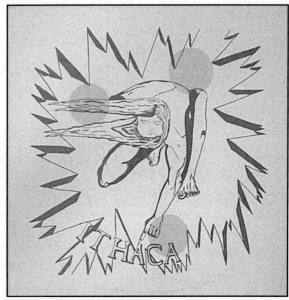
ITHACA - Game For All Who Know (LP).

Ivans Meads

Personnel incl:	ALAN JAY	A

45s:	The Sins Of A Family/	
	A Little Sympathy	(Parlophone R 5342) 1965 R2
	We'll Talk About It Tomorrow/	
	The Bottle	(Parlophone R 5503) 1966 R1

This Manchester band were managed by Mike Maxfield (of **The Dakotas**) and were the first band to record for **George Martin**'s production company, A.I.R.. Still, they failed to make an impact despite using a P.F. Sloan song for their debut 45. (VJ)

The Iveys

Personnel:	TOM EVANS	bs	AB
	MIKE GIBBINS	drms	AB
	RON GRIFFITHS	gtr	A
	PETE HAM	gtr, vcls	AB
	JOEY MOLLAND	gtr	B

ALBUM: 1( ) MAYBE TOMORROW (Apple SAPCOR 8) 1968
NB: (1) reissued on CD with bonus cuts (Apple CDP 7 98692 2) 1992 and again (Apple CD APCORP 8) 1992 and 2004.

45s:	Maybe Tomorrow/	
	And Her Daddy's A Millionaire	(Apple APPLE 5) 1968 R1
	Dear Angie/No Escaping Your Love	(Apple APPLE 14) 1969

NB: (2) released in Europe and Japan only.

From South Wales, this lot started life as **The Iveys**. **Paul McCartney** was sufficiently impressed by a demo tape they sent to him to have them signed to Apple in 1968. Their debut 45 didn't sell in the UK but did climb to No 67 in the States. Griffiths departed at this point and was replaced by Molland. Their second 45 also got released in Europe in 1969 but later that year, having recorded a **Paul McCartney** song, *Come And Get It*, they changed their name to **Badfinger**. UK test pressings of their album sell for predictably enormous sums on the rare occasions they turn up.

The *Maybe Tomorrow* album got an airing on CD in 1992 along with two 45 flip sides:- *And Her Daddy's A Millionaire* and *No Escaping Your Love* and three previously unissued tracks (*Mrs. Jones, Looking For Tomorrow* and *Arthur*). Some tracks on *Maybe Tomorrow* were in fact earlier resurrected on the first worldwide **Badfinger** album, *Magic Christian Music*. They also had a track, *Storm In A Tea Cup*, featured on a various artist promotional *Wall's Ice Cream* (EP) (Apple CT 1) 1969. It is also included on *Badfinger Rare Tracks* (Swingtime Records BF-01) 1989. More recently, *And Her Daddy's A Millionaire* has emerged on *Pop-In, Vol 1* (CD). (VJ/L)

429

The Ivy League

Personnel:
JOHN CARTER	vcls	A
PERRY FORD	vcls	AB
KEN LEWIS	vcls	A
TONY BURROWS	vcls	B
NEIL LANDON	vcls	B

ALBUMS:
1( ) THIS IS THE IVY LEAGUE
(Piccadilly NPL 38015) 1965 R1
2( ) SOUNDS OF THE IVY LEAGUE
(Marble Arch MAL 741) 1967
3( ) TOMORROW IS ANOTHER DAY
(Marble Arch MALS 821) 1969

NB: (1) reissued on CD (Repertoire RR 4094-WZ) 1991 with extra tracks. There's also *The Best Of Ivy League* (PRT PYL 4010) 1988. Alternatively you may prefer *The Best Of The Ivy League* (Sequel NEX CD 179) 1991.

EPs:
1 FUNNY HOW LOVE CAN BE
(Piccadilly NEP 34038) 1965 SC
2 TOSSING AND TURNING
(Piccadilly NEP 34042) 1965 SC
3 THE HOLLY AND THE IVY LEAGUE
(Piccadilly NEP 34046) 1965 SC
4 OUR LOVE IS SLIPPING AWAY
(Piccadilly NEP 34048) 1966 R1

HCP

45s:
What More Do You Want/		
Wait A Minute	(Piccadilly 7N 35200) 1964	-
Funny How Love Can Be/		
Lonely Room	(Piccadilly 7N 35222) 1965	8
That's Why I'm Crying/		
A Girl Like You	(Piccadilly 7N 35228) 1965	22
Tossin' and Turnin'/		
Graduation Day	(Piccadilly 7N 35251) 1965	3
Our Love Is Slipping Away/		
I Could Make You Fall In Love	(Piccadilly 7N 35267) 1965	-
Running Round In Circles/		
Rain Rain Go Away	(Piccadilly 7N 35294) 1966	-
Willow Tree/One Day	(Piccadilly 7N 35326) 1966	50
My World Fell Down/		
When You're Young	(Piccadilly 7N 35348) 1966 SC	-
Four And Twenty Hours/		
Arrivederci Baby	(Piccadilly 7N 35365) 1967	-
Suddenly Things/		
Tomorrow Is Another Day	(Piccadilly 7N 35397) 1967	-
Thank You For Loving Me/		
In The Not Too Distant Future	(Pye 7N 17386) 1967	-

Reissues:
Funny How Love Can Be/		
Our Love Is Slipping Away	(Pye 7N 45200) 1970	-
Funny How Love Can Be/Tossin' And Turnin'/		
Our Love Is Slipping Away/4 & 20 Hours	(Pye BD 111) 1977	-

Tossin' And Turnin'/(2 versions)/
Funny How Love Can Be   (Pye FBS 5) 1979 -

The Ivy League was a pleasant harmony-pop band that enjoyed a few hits in the mid-sixties. Carter and Lewis were involved in a number of other projects over the years.

Formed in 1964 when John Carter and Ken Lewis (real names John Shakespeare and James Hawker), previously of Carter-Lewis and The Southerners, joined forces with Perry Ford (real name Brian Pugh). All three were session singers with songwriting ability and a clear liking for high-pitched vocals, and decided to record under their own name of **The Ivy League**. After their initial 45 flopped, *Funny How Love Can Be*, a song with instant appeal and high-pitched vocals which typified their style, took them into the Top Ten. The sadder but otherwise similar *That's Why I'm Crying* was a minor hit, but was followed by their finest moment, *Tossin' And Turnin'*, which made No 3 over here and No 83 in the US. Their album, *This Is The Ivy League*, was a rather odd mixture of their own songs and other people's. During 1966 Carter and Lewis left and Burrows and **Landon** came in as replacements. Their final, if minor, hit was *Willow Tree* but the following year they returned as **The Flowerpot Men**.

During their hit period they used a backing group called Division Two (Clem Cattini (bs), Mickey Keen (gtr), Mike O'Neill (piano, organ), Dave Wintour (drms)), who also recorded a great instrumental beat/R&B album, *Discotheque* (Society SOC 1016) in 1965.

The eighties saw a band of this name working the night club circuit but it contained none of the earlier members.

The best introduction to their music is PRT's *Best Of...* compilation. It includes all their 'A' sides from the 1964-67 era, along with a couple of 'B' sides (including the Beach Boys/Four Seasons-inspired *Lonely Room*) and a few album tracks. A 'must' for harmony pop fans. Alternatively, the Repertoire CD reissue of their debut album in 1991 also includes most of their remaining Pye singles and all four tracks from their festive EP *The Holly And The Ivy League*. This was 26 tracks as opposed to the later Sequel 22-track compilation. Inevitably there is much duplication in material but the Sequel compilation included seven cuts not on the Repertoire set. The best of these was the exquisite *My World Fell Down*.

Compilation appearances have included: *Willow Tree* on *Pop Inside The Sixties, Vol. 3* (CD); *Tossin' and Turnin'* on *Piccadilly Story* (CD), *Hits Of The 60's - Save The Last Dance For Me* (CD), *Hits Of The 60's Vol 2* (CD), *Beat Generation - Ready Steady Go* (CD), *The Swinging Sixties - 18 Classic Tracks* (CD) the 2-CD set *We Love The Pirates: Charting The Big 'L' Fab 40* and there's an alternate take on the 2-CD set *Greatest Hits Of The 60's*; *My World Fell Down* on *Quick Before They Catch Us* (LP & CD), *Rubble, Vol. 7 - Pictures In The Sky* (LP) and on the 2-CD set *We Love The Pirates: Charting The Big 'L' Fab 40*; and *My World Fell Down* and *Graduation Day* on *Ripples, Vol. 1* (CD). Finally, *That's Why I'm Crying* has been compiled on *Hits Of The Swinging Sixties* (CD) and *Funny How Love Can Be* got a further airing on *Dizzy* (CD). (VJ)

INCREDIBLE STRING BAND - Hard Rope And Silken Twine (CD).

INCREDIBLE STRING BAND - The Chelsea Sessions 1967 (CD).

J.P. Sunshine

Personnel incl:	ROD GOODWAY	gtr, vcls	A
	ADRIAN RICKELL	ld gtr	A
	ADRAIN SHAW	bs, acoustic gtr	A

ALBUM: 1(A) J.P. SUNSHINE   (Uncle Glitch UG 001) 1995

This is a limited vinyl edition issue of 500 of a privately-produced recording from 1968, which was first distributed on the Acid Tapes label in the eighties. Basically we're talking a West Coast-influenced blend of folk and psychedelia and if that's your scene it's well worth investigating. The band is also of interest in that some of them went on to greater things. Goodway formed Magic Muscle, Rickell joined **Kingdom Come** under the pseudonym Android Funnel and Shaw later played in **Hawkwind**. (VJ)

J.S.D. Band

Personnel:	DES COFFIELD	gtr, keyb'ds, vcls, mandolin	ABCD
	JIM DIVERS	bs, cello, vcls	ABCD
	COLIN FINN	drms	ABCD
	CHUCK FLEMING	fiddle, mandolin	A C
	SEAN O'ROURKE	gtr, vcls, fiddle	ABCD
	LINDSAY SCOTT	violin, vcls	B
	IAIN LYON	violin	D

ALBUMS:	1(A)	COUNTRY OF THE BLIND		
		(Regal Zonophone SLRZ 1018) 1971 R1
	2(B)	J.S.D. BAND	(Cube HIFLY 11) 1972
	3(C)	TRAVELLING DAYS	(Cube HIFLY 14) 1973

NB: They also appeared on the Various Artists' compilation, *Take Off Your Head* (Rubber RUB 001) in 1972. (2) and (3) were also released in Germany.

45s:	Sarah Jane/Paddy Sticks (PS)	(Cube BUG 29) 1973
	Sunshine Life For Me/Reel Cool	(Cube BUG 40) 1974
	Hayes And Harlington Blues/Cuckoo	(Cube BUG 49) 1974

A Scottish traditional folk band from Glasgow. Their first album is by far the rarest, in fact it's very hard to find nowadays. It was a promising debut but didn't really capture them at their best. *J.S.D. Band* and *Travelling Days* were better, but their real reputation came as a live act. Centred around Chuck Fleming's frenetic fiddle playing, they played quite a captivating blend of jigs and pop. When Fleming left in 1974 the writing was really on the wall. They soldiered a little while longer with the addition of Iain Lyon from **My Dear Watson** but soon called it quits as Fleming's departure had deprived them of their focal point. (VJ)

Jackal

45:     The Year Of The Tiger/Big Star   (BASF BA 1009) 1974

This obscure outfit's 45 contains rather boring mid-seventies rock. The 'B' side is the better of the two. (MWh)

Gordon Jackson

ALBUM: 1 THINKING BACK   (Marmalade 608 012) 1969 R2
NB: (1) reissued on CD (Sunbeam SBRCD 5001) 2005.

45s:	Me And My Zoo/	
	A Day At The Cottage	(Marmalade 598 010) 1968
	Song For Freedom/	
	Sing To Me Woman	(Marmalade 598 021) 1969

Gordon Jackson had been a member Birmingham's **Hellions** alongside **Dave Mason**, **Jim Capaldi** and **Luther Grosvenor**. When the Hellions split he went on to play with **Capaldi**, **Grosvenor** and Poli Palmer in **Deep Feeling**. Though nothing was released, they did act as backing band for **Jimi Hendrix** at one of his earliest London performances. By the time of

J.P. SUNSHINE - J.P. Sunshine (LP).

Jackson's solo album, however, all his former bandmates had gone on to fame and fortune, leaving him somewhat in their shadow. The album, therefore, features **Mason, Capaldi, Steve Winwood** and Chris Wood of **Traffic**, Ric Grech, Poli Palmer and Jim King of **Family**, and other luminaries such as **Luther Grosvenor** (by now with **Spooky Tooth**), **Reg King** of **The Action** and **Julie Driscoll**. Despite this remarkable line-up, the album is intimate and mellow psychedelic folk, with a jazzy feeling to several songs. Both it and his second single were produced by **Dave Mason**, and all are now predictably tough to locate. In later years **Jackson** continued to work with **Winwood** in various capacities.

Compilation appearances have included: *Me And My Zoo* and *A Day At The Cottage* on *The Marmalade Record Co. Show Olympia 68* (LP); and *Journey*, a cut from the album, on the 1969 sampler, *Marmalade - 100% Proof* (LP). (VJ/RMJ)

Tony Jackson and The Vibrations

Personnel:	IAN BUISEL	ld gtr	ABC
	PAUL FRANCIS	drms	ABC
	TONY JACKSON	bs, vcls	ABC
	MARTIN RAYMOND	organ	A
	IAN GREEN	organ	B
	DENNIS THOMPSON	bs	C

			HCP
45s:	Bye Bye Baby/Watch Your Step	(Pye 7N 15685) 1964 SC 38
	You Beat Me To The Punch/	
	This Girl Of Mine	(Pye 7N 15745) 1964 R1 -
	Love Potion No 9/Fortune Teller	(Pye 7N 15766) 1965 R1 -
α	Stage Door/That's What I Want	(Pye 7N 15876) 1965 R1 -
α	You're My Number One/Let Me Know	(CBS 202039) 1966 R1 -
β	Never Leave Your Baby's Side/I'm The	
	One She Really Thinks A Lot Of	(CBS 202069) 1966 R1 -
β	Follow Me/Walk That Walk	(CBS 202297) 1966 R2 -
β	Anything Else You Want/	
	Come On And Stop	(CBS 202408) 1966 R1 -

NB: α as Tony Jackson Group. β **Tony Jackson** solo. There's also a compilation of his post-**Searchers** material available on vinyl and CD, *Just Like Me* (Strange Things STZ 5005) 1991 (SC) and also *Watch Your Step!* (Sanctuary CMQCD 892) 2004, is an alternative 24-track compilation of his post-**Searchers** material.

Jackson, a Liverpudlian born on 16 July 1940, first came to prominence as bassist and vocalist for **The Searchers** but left during the Summer of 1964 at the height of their success. He had a nose job and returned fronting the London-based Vibrations who, with Raymond's Vox Continental organ and girl background singers, sounded very different to **The Searchers**. The Vibrations were all Southerners. Martin Raymond had been with The Westminster Four, Ian Buisel (later Ian Leighton) joined from The Hot Rod Gang and Paul Francis had drummed for Rolf Harris and The Kangaroos. Their only hit was a superb cover of Mary Wells' *Bye Bye Baby* and

J.S.D. BAND - J.S.D. Band (CD).

gradually they faded from the public eye despite a series of 45s, including a re-recording of the old **Searchers**' song originally done by The Clovers, *Love Potion No 9*. Of their other 45s, *You Beat Me To The Punch* was also a Mary Wells song, produced by Larry Page.

By the time of Goffin/King's *Stage Door* the group had metamorphised into The Tony Jackson Group. In the States, this 45 was issued by Red Bird, a New York label better known for girl groups like The Shangri Las. They switched labels to CBS for **The Beatles** and **Searchers** hybrid *You're My Number One*, but this followed previous releases into the bargain bins. After this, Martin Raymond left the group. His replacement, Ian Green, had done session work with The Everly Brothers. *Follow Me*, a Warren Zevon song, got lots of airplay on pirate radio, but still failed to chart. The follow-up, *Anything Else You Want*, made no impression at all, although the 'B' side, a version of Bert Berns' *Come On And Stop*, contained some good fuzz guitar work. After this Pye failed to renew their contract, but the band (without Ian Green but with Dennis Thompson on bass and Tony concentrating on vocals) set off on a series of one night gigs across Europe ending up in Portugal. There, thanks to Ian Leighton's brother Jimmy's girlfriend, whose father ran a radio station, a Tony Jackson Group EP was issued. This is now one of the rarest EP's of the sixties and contains covers of *Shake* (with Ian Leighton handling vocals), the Byrds' *He Was A Friend Of Mine*, Paul Revere's *Just Like Me* and **The Small Faces**' *Understanding*. When the group returned to the UK, it disbanded.

Tony Jackson and The Vibrations reformed in 1991 at the instigation of Paul Francis, who'd done session work for **Bill Wyman** and Suzi Quatro in the interim. He'd also drummed for **The Luvvers**, **Tucky Buzzard** and **Cockney Rebel**. To coincide with this, Strange Things issued a mono version of **Tony Jackson**'s post-**Searchers** material, which is also available on CD. **Jackson** resurfaced on the nostalgia circuit in 1991 singing renditions of old **Searchers**' hits.

Tony Jackson died in August 2003, aged 63, after losing a long fight with liver cirrhosis and chronic arthritis. He was writing his autobiography at the time of his death.

Compilation appearances have included: *This Little Girl Of Mine* and *That's What I Want* on *Merseybeat Nuggets, Vol. 2* (CD); *Fortune Teller* and *Bye Bye Baby* on *Pop Inside The Sixties, Vol. 3* (CD); *Walk Walk Walk* and *Follow Me* on *Rare 60's Beat Treasures, Vol. 3* (CD); *Save A Dream For Me* on *Rare 60's Beat Treasures, Vol. 5* (CD) - although this may be a US singer by the same name.; *Fortune Teller* on *The R&B Era, Vol. 1* (LP & CD), *Freakbeat Freakout* (CD) and *Trans-World Punk Rave-Up!, Vol. 2* (LP); *Stage Door* on *Ripples, Vol. 4* (CD) and *Beat Merchants* (CD); *Stage Door* and *Bye Bye Baby* on *Some Other Guys* (2-LP); *Watch Your Step* on *Watch Your Step* (LP & CD); *This Little Girl Of Mine* and *That's What I Want* on *What About Us* (CD); *You're My Number One* on *Head Sounds From The Bam-Caruso Waxworks, Vol. 1* (CD); *Bye Bye Baby* on *It Happened Then* (EP); and *Just Like Me* on *It's Only A Passing Phase* (LP). (VJ/LBy)

Jackson Heights

Personnel:	CHARLIE HARCOURT	gtr, keyb'ds, vcls	A
	LEE JACKSON	vcls, gtr	AB
	TOMMY SLONE	drms, perc	A
	MARIO TAPIA	bs, gtr, vcls	A
	BRIAN CHATTON	keyb'ds, vcls	B
	MIKE GILES	drms	B
	JOHN McBURNIE	gtr, vcls, keyb'ds	B

NB: The above line-up is the nucleus of the band.

ALBUMS:	1(A)	KINGS PROGRESS	(Charisma CAS 1018) 1970 SC
	2(B)	5th AVENUE BUS	(Vertigo 6360 067) 1972 R1
	3(B)	RAGAMUFFIN'S FOOL	
		(Some w/poster)	(Vertigo 6360 077) 1973 R1/SC
	4(B)	BUMP AND GRIND	(Vertigo 6360 092) 1973 SC

NB: (1) was released on Mercury (SR 61331) in the US and they also had a US only release, *Jackson Heights* (Verve V6 5089) in 1973. (2) reissued on CD (Repertoire REP 4365-WP) 1993. (3) R1 copies came with a poster.

45:	Doubting Thomas/Insomnia	(Charisma JH1) 1970

Formed by former **Nice** bassist and vocalist Lee Jackson when **The Nice** split in 1969, **Jackson Heights** took their name from a district of New York. Musically they were more pop-orientated than **The Nice**, but they built up a good live reputation through relentless touring. Their debut album on Charisma made little impact although it did contain a fine version of an old **Nice** favourite *Cry Of Eugene* and another highlight was a similarly gentle, atmospheric song *Insomnia*. They re-emerged a couple of years later on Vertigo with *5th Avenue Bus*, an album of melodic, well constructed and somewhat orchestrated pop-orientated material. Brian Chatton had been in **Flaming Youth** and drummer Mike Giles was from **King Crimson**. They were also part of a Vertigo package tour with **Magna Carta** and **Jefferson**.

This format was repeated on *Ragamuffin's Fool*, which was housed in a poster sleeve. After a final effort, *Bump And Grind*, they disbanded, but in 1974 Jackson formed **Refugee**, who cut an album for Charisma. After this he disappeared from the music scene working as an interior designer until he was involved in a reformed **Nice** in 2002.

The **Aardvark**'s Dave Watts also had a spell in **Jackson Heights**. (VJ)

Jack The Lad

Personnel:	ROD CLEMENTS	bs	A
	SIMON CROWE	gtr, vcls	AB
	RAY LAIDLAW	drms	ABC
	BILLY MITCHELL	gtr, vcls	ABCD
	IAN 'WALTER' FAIRBAIRN	fiddle, vcls	BCD
	PHIL MURRAY	bs, vcls	BCD
	RAY JACKSON	hrmnca	CD

JADE - Fly On Strange Wings (LP).

432

ALBUMS: 1(A) IT'S JACK THE LAD   (Charisma CAS 1085) 1974 SC
(up to   2(B) OLD STRAIGHT TRACK (Charisma CAS 1094) 1974 SC
1976)   3(C) ROUGH DIAMONDS   (Charisma CAS 1110) 1975 SC
        4(D) JACKPOT   (United Artists UA 29999) 1976

NB: These were not released in the US, where a US-only compilation was put out:- *It's Jack* (Asylum 1014) 1975. (1), (2) and (3) reissued on CD on Virgin (CAS CD 1085, 1094 and 1110 respectively) in 1992. (1) reissued again on CD (Virgin CASCDR 1085) 2005.

45s: Why Can't I Be Satisfied/Make Me Happy   (B&C CB 128) 1970
(up to One More Dance/
1976)   Draught Genius (Polka) (PS)   (Charisma CB 206) 1973
        Why Can't I Be Satisfied/
        Make Me Happy   (Charisma CB 218) 1973
        Gentleman Soldier/
        Oakey Strike Evictions   (Charisma CB 253) 1975
        My Friend The Drink/Rocking Chair   (Charisma CB 264) 1975
        Eight Ton Crazy/Walters Drop   (United Artists UP 36162) 1976
        Trinidad/Let It Be Me   (United Artists UP 36180) 1976

Jack The Lad was a Geordie folk-rock band. Their second album is now the hardest to find; the first featured three **Lindisfarne** members, Ray Laidlaw, Rod Clement and Simon Crowe, along with Maddy Prior on one track.

Musically they played a sing-along amalgam of folk, pop and rock on their debut album. Clements left after this to be replaced by former **Hedgehog Pie** members Ian 'Walter' Fairburn and Phil Murray for the second effort, which contains a lot of traditional sounding folk-rock material.

For *Rough Diamonds*, Crowe was replaced by harmonica player Ray Jackson. Musically it seemed to mix the folky style of the second album with some of the pop/rock ingredients of the first. The CD reissue includes as a bonus an outtake of the standard *Baby Let Me Take You Home*.

They tended to drift from "traditional" electric folk to rock, never quite knowing where to stay. They disbanded in 1976 with occasional reformations since, most recently in 1993. (VJ)

Jade

Personnel: ROD EDWARDS   A
             MARIAN SEGAL   A
             DAVE WAITE   A

ALBUM: 1(A) FLY ON STRANGE WINGS   (DJM DJLPS 407) 1970 R3

45:     Alan's Song/Amongst Anemonies   (DJM DJS 227) 1970

An electric folk trio, all of whose songs were written by Marian Segal. Waite had played in a group called The Countrymen prior to forming a duo with

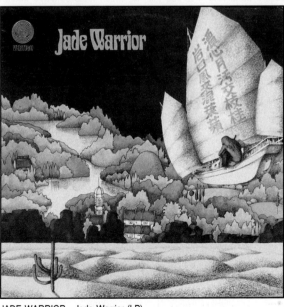

JADE WARRIOR - Jade Warrior (LP).

JADE WARRIOR - Eclipse (LP).

Segal. Edwards had been half of **The Piccadilly Line** and **Edwards Hand**. He joined **Jade** only briefly, to make the album and do live promotional work including an American tour. On the album they're augmented by a stellar supporting cast including Terry Cox of **Pentangle**, John Wetton of **Family** and session regulars like Clem Cattini and Pete Sears. It's a decent blend of driving folk-rock and mellow ballads, though too derivative (especially of **Fairport Convention** and **Sandy Denny**) to be especially convincing. On its release in June 1970 it was made Melody Maker's album of the month, but sold poorly, as did the single, which appeared in July. The album also appeared in the US the following year, as by 'Marian Segal with Silver Jade' (DJM 9100, 1971). That version is much easier to find, but has a single sleeve as opposed to the UK's gatefold.

Garry Edwards replaced Rod Edwards for a while, then Segal and Waite formed The Marian Segal Band, with Lee Oliphant on bass and Dave Morris on drums. They stayed together until 1975. Waite later joined **Country Fever**, Morris returned to working with Guys and Dolls and Oliphant returned to session work in Canada. Segal formed a new Marian Segal Band with musicians including Root Cartwright from **Principal Edwards Magic Theatre** but, though many live studio recordings were made, they didn't make it onto vinyl.

In 1980 Segal released a 45, *Love Amnesia/Ghosts Of Love* (Double Dee D DEE 4) and continues to write and do live work, with a new CD release *Hands Of Friendship*, 2002. (VJ/RMJ)

Jade Warrior

Personnel: TONY DUHIG   gtr, bs, keyb'ds   ABC
             JON FIELD   perc, gtr, keyb'ds, flute ABC
             GLYN HAVARD   bs, gtr, vcls   A
             DAVE DUHIG   gtr   B
             GRAHAM MORGAN drms   C

ALBUMS: 1(A) JADE WARRIOR   (Vertigo 6360 033) 1971 R1
(up to   2(A) RELEASED   (Vertigo 6360 062) 1971 R2
1976)   3(A) LAST AUTUMN'S DREAM (Vertigo 6360 079) 1972 R1
        4(B) FLOATING WORLD   (Island ILPS 9290) 1974 SC
        5(C) WAVES   (Island ILPS 9318) 1975 SC
        6( ) KITES   (Island ILPS 9393) 1976 SC

NB: (1) reissued on CD (Background HBG 123/11) and on CD (Repertoire REPUK 1019) 2004. (2) reissued on CD (Background HBG 123/12) and again on CD (Repertoire REPUK 1052) 2005. (3) reissued on CD (Background HBG 123/13). (4) reissued on CD (Island IMCD 99) 1990. Other CD releases have included, *Jade Warrior* (Line LICD 900548) 1989, *Way Of The Sun* (Island IMCD 100) 1990, *Eclipse* (Acme Deluxe ADCD 1021) was recorded in 1973, but never actually released until now. It would have been their fourth Vertigo album and finally there's *Fifth Element* (Background HBG 123/10), a further unreleased album from 1973.

45:     The Demon Trucker/Snake   (Vertigo 6059 069) 1972 SC

433

This band started out as an underground hard-rock band but their later albums were more progressive jazzy-rock in style. Founding members Tony Duhig and Jon Field had both previously played with **Tomcats**, **Second Thoughts** and **July**. The name came from a ballet Duhig and Field had completed based upon Japanese paintings, which they planned to call Jade Warrior. They then decided it was more suitable for a band so they formed a band and dropped the ballet idea.

Their debut album for Vertigo sought to create a heavy feeling of spirituality. It's very pleasant in places and certainly well worth a spin. Among the highlights are Jon Field's percussion playing. Both this and their follow-up were notable for some powerful bass playing from Glyn Havard. Their best effort was probably *Last Autumn's Dream* which spawned their only Vertigo 45, *The Demon Trucker*. They recorded a fourth album for Vertigo, *Eclipse*, which was withdrawn shortly prior to release. Bassist Glyn Havard quit circa 1973 but Duhig and Field, who were by now doing a lot of session work, continued the band, securing a new contract with Island. Havard re-emerged in the late seventies playing with The Yachts and Jane Aire and The Belvederes. Field also guested on *Tubular Bells*. Tony Duhig died in the early nineties but Jon Field keep the band alive and further small label albums were released.

Telephone Girl, from their first album, can also be heard on Vertigo's 1971 *Heads Together, First Round* (LP) compilation. *Mwenga Sketch* from their projected Eclipse album later resurfaced on the *Suck It And See* (LP) compilation. It has reappeared, along with *Bourne On The Solar Wind*, on the recent *Time Machine* (CD) compilation. (VJ)

Chris Jagger

ALBUM: 1 CHRIS JAGGER - YOU KNOW THE
NAME BUT NOT THE FACE (GM GML 1003) 1973 SC

NB: There was also an album, *The Adventures Of Valentine Vox* (Asylum 7E 1009) released in 1974 in the US.

45: Something New/Joy Of The Ride (GM GMS 53) 1973

As most of you will know, **Chris** is **Mick Jagger**'s younger brother. His two mid-seventies albums and his 1973 45 are only really of interest to **Rolling Stones** completists. In the early eighties, he wrote a swingtime musical 'It Ain't What You Do It's The Way That You Do It', but it was turned down by several producers, although the Fun Boy Three later enjoyed a hit with the proposed title track. He returned in 1994 with the CD *Atcha*, his first recording for 20 years, and put together an Atcha band (Ed Dean, Charlie Hart, Robbie McKidd and Malcolm Mortimore). His brother Mick and other celebrities like Leo Sayer and Dave Gilmour also assisted, but it's been hard for Chris who seems destined to remain over-shadowed by his famous elder brother.

Back in 1970, he starred in the Israeli cast production of the musical 'Hair', alongside other hired American and British, and some local stars. A soundtrack album was released on CBS Israel at the time, though this is now deleted. The Israeli production was translated and performed in the Hebrew language, with the foreign actors performing phonetically. One local Star featured, Shuki Levi, later emigrated to the States, where he collaborated with Haim Saban and composed the theme tune for 'Dallas', which made him multi-zillionaire, but that's another story. (VJ/MG)

Mick Jagger

HCP

45: Memo From Turner/Natural Magic
(Some in export PS) (Decca F 13067) 1970 R1/-32

A man who should need no introduction. See **The Rolling Stones** entry for details of his career. This single was his sole solo release during the 1964-76 period. The 'A' side was taken from the (LP) soundtrack to *Performance* in 1970, in which **Jagger** won much acclaim for his role as retired rock star Turner. It features some biting guitar work from Keith Richards and is as impressive as any contemporary work by **The Rolling Stones**. The flip side was a less interesting instrumental, but overall the single's chart placing was undeservedly low. There was also an export-only release of this 45 with a picture sleeve, which is much more collectable. An

JADE WARRIOR - Fifth Element (CD).

alternative version with **Steve Winwood** and **Jim Capaldi** of **Traffic** can be found on the **Stones**' 1975 out-takes collection *Metamorphosis*. **Jagger** also sings one track (*The Wild Colonial Boy*) on the rare (LP) soundtrack to his less successful film *Ned Kelly* in 1970. On it he is backed solely by a bamboo flute. He also undertook occasional production work in this period for artists such as **Chris Farlowe, PP Arnold, Marianne Faithfull** and even a young **Rod Stewart**. For true completists, the *Tonite Let's All Make Love In London* (LP) soundtrack features an interview with him discussing the pop business, as well as theorising about authority and the attitudes of the younger generation. (VJ/RMJ)

Jaghouse

45: Be My Guest/I'm Walking (Decca F 13342) 1972

No other information available. (VJ)

The Jaguars

Personnel: JIM CAPALDI vcls, drms A
MICHAEL MANN bs A
DAVID MASON lead gtr A
ROGER MOSS drms A

45: We'll Live On Happily/
Now You Wonder Why (Contest RGJ 152) 1965 R4

An obscure band who recorded this 45, which features **Dave Mason** and **Jim Capaldi**, at RG Jones' Morden studio but then issued it on their even more obscure Contest label. The 'A' side was very ordinary but the flip was more interesting - and seemingly influenced by the US garage bands which were appearing all over the States in this era. This 45 is hopelessly obscure and expensive, but you can now hear *Now You Wonder Why* on *Story Of Oak Records* (2-LP)/*The Story Of Oak Records* (CD). (VJ/AD)

Jake

45: And In The Morning/You And Me (Deram DM 350) 1972

Another obscure one! (VJ)

Jaklin

Personnel: TOMMY EYRE piano, organ A
JAKLIN ld gtr A
ANDY RAE bs A
JOHN PEARSON drms A

ALBUM: 1(A) JAKLIN   (Stable SLE 8003) 1969 R3

NB: (1) was issued on CD (SPM 52007) label in Germany. (1) reissued on vinyl (Abraxas 42073) and on CD by Earmark.

This is an extremely rare album. Musically, we're talking electric blues with some psychedelic touches especially on the track *Song To Katherine*. Most of the material is written by **Jaklin** aside from three traditionals:- *Rosie, Early In The Morning*, which has some jazzy piano improvisation and the heavier *Catfish Blues* and their **Cream**-like rendition of **Alexis Korner**'s *The Same For You*. Overall it's a varied blues album. (VJ/MWh/CA)

Calvin James

45:      Some Things You Never Got Used To/
         Remember   (Columbia DB 7516) 1965 SC

This was George Underwood of **The King Bees** using a pseudonym. He was also in **The Manish Boys** and was managed by Mickie Most, who produced the 45, which is an emotional ballad. (VJ)

Jimmy James and The Vagabonds

Personnel incl:
RUPERT BELGOBIN	drms		A
PHIL CHEN	bs		A
NAT FREDERICK	sax		A
JIMMY JAMES	vcls		A
MILTON JAMES	sax		A
COUNT MILLER	vcls		A
CARL NOEL	organ		A
WALLACE WILSON	gtr		A

ALBUMS: 1(A) NEW RELIGION   (Piccadilly NPL 38027) 1966 R1
(up to 2( ) OPEN UP YOUR SOUL (Pye NPL/NSPL 18231) 1968 R1
1976)   3( ) THIS IS JIMMY JAMES   (Marble Arch MAL 823) 1968
        4( ) YOU DON'T STAND A CHANCE IF YOU CAN'T DANCE
                                  (Pye NSPL 18457) 1975 SC
        5( ) NOW   (Pye NSPL 19495) 1976

NB: (1) reissued on Marble Arch (MAL 1244) 1970. There's also a *Golden Hour Of...* (Pye GH 679). They also contributed one side to *London Swings - Live At The Marquee Club* (Pye N(S)PL 18156) 1968. The other side featured **The Alan Bown Set**. *Where Your Music Takes Me* (Sequel NEMCD 978) 1998 combines their two mid-seventies albums for Pye with some singles from the same era.

EP: 1 JIMMY JAMES AND THE VAGABONDS
                                  (Piccadilly NEP 34053) 1966 R1

                                                              HCP
45s: α Bewildered And Blue/I Don't Want To Cry (Dice CC 4) 1962 SC -
(up to α Jump Children/Tell Me   (R&B JB 112) 1963 SC -
1976)   Shoo Be Doo You're Mine/
          We'll Never Stop Loving You   (Columbia DB 7653) 1965 SC -
       α Thinking Of You/Shirley   (Black Swan WI 437) 1964 SC -
          Your Love/Someday   (Ska Beat JB 242) 1966 SC -
          I Feel Alright/
          I Wanna Be Your Everything   (Piccadilly 7N 35298) 1966 -
          Hi Diddley Dee Dum Dum (It's A Good Good Feelin')/
          Come To Me Softly   (Piccadilly 7N 35320) 1966 -
          This Heart Of Mine/
          I Don't Wanna Cry   (Piccadilly 7N 35331) 1966 SC -
          Ain't Love Good, Ain't Love Proud/
          Don't Know What I'm Gonna Do (Piccadilly 7N 35349) 1966 SC -
       α I Can't Get Back Home To My Baby/
          Hungry For Love   (Piccadilly 7N 35360) 1967 -
          No Good To Cry/
          You Showed Me The Way   (Piccadilly 7N 35374) 1967 -
          Red Red Wine/
          Who Could Be Loving You   (Pye 7N 17579) 1968 36
       α Close The Door/Why   (Pye 7N 17719) 1969 -
          Better By Far/Give Us A Light (Pye 7N 17886) 1970 -
          Help Yourself/Why   (Trojan TR 7806) 1970 SC -
          A Man Like Me/Survival   (Stateside SS 2209) 1971 -
          Dancing To The Music Of Love/
          Suspicious Love   (Pye 7N 45402) 1974 -
          You Don't Stand A Chance/(2 versions) (Pye 7N 45443) 1975 -
          Hey Girl/I Am Somebody   (Pye 7N 45472) 1975 SC -

Whatever Happened To The Love We Knew/
Let's Have Fun   (Pye 7N 45524) 1975 -
I'll Go Where The Music Takes Me/
(2 versions)   (Pye 7N 45585) 1976 23
Now Is The Time/I Want You So Much (Pye 7N 45606) 1976 5
Do The Funky Conga/No Other Woman (Pye 7N 45641) 1976 -
Reissues: Help Yourself / Why   (People PEO 117) 1975 -
          Help Yourself / Why   (Miami MIA 404) 1976 -
          I'll Go Where The Music Takes Me/
          Now Is The Time   (Old Gold OG 9137) 1982 -

NB: α as **Jimmy James**.

Jimmy James was from Jamaica originally and really a marginal case for inclusion here. They were a very popular live act around the clubs but their only commercial success in the sixties was with *Red Red Wine*, a Neil Diamond track. They played R&B and soul and had a rapidly changing line-up. Of their other 45s, *Ain't Love Good, Ain't Love Proud* was a Tony Clarke R&B favourite.

The band went through several line-ups and got a second wind in the mid-seventies which was their most successful era.

Ain't Love Good Ain't Love Proud can also be heard on *Piccadilly Story* (CD). (VJ)

Nicky James (Movement)

ALBUMS: 1 NICKY JAMES   (Philips 6308 069) 1971 SC
         2 EVERY HOME SHOULD HAVE ONE
                                (Threshold THS 10) 1973 SC
         3 THUNDERTHROAT   (Threshold THS 19) 1976

45s: α Stagger Lee/I'm Hurtin' Inside (Columbia DB 7747) 1965 SC
          I Need To Be Needed/
          So Glad We Made It   (Philips BF 1566) 1967
          Would You Believe/Silver Butterfly (Philips BF 1635) 1968 SC
          Lookin' Through Windows/Nobody But Me (Philips BF 1694) 1968
          Time/Little Bit Of Paper   (Philips BF 1755) 1969
          Reaching For The Sun/No Life At All (Philips BF 1804) 1969
          Why / Foreign Shore   (Threshold TH 12) 1972
          Black Dream/She Came To Me (Threshold TH 16) 1973
          My Style/
          I Guess I've Always Loved You (Threshold TH 17) 1973
          Maggie/Bottle Of Cheap Red Wine (Threshold TH 25) 1976

NB: α as **Nicky James Movement**.

A Birmingham-based artist. Prior to fronting the **Nicky James Movement**, **James** had fronted a band called The Lawmen. He'd also been a member of **Denny Laine and The Diplomats**. He had a good voice and was responsible for a series of heavily orchestrated 45s. In the seventies, he

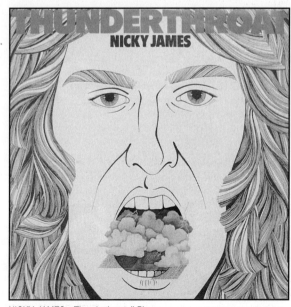

NICKY JAMES - Thunderthroat (LP).

435

was signed to **The Moody Blues**' Threshold label for whom he recorded two solo albums and four 45s. In 1974 he appeared on solo albums by **Moody Blues** members **Graeme Edge** and **Ray Thomas**.

One of his finest moments, *Silver Butterfly*, is a delightful piece of late sixties pop recorded with session player **Caleb Quaye**. Of his other songs, *Would You Believe* was a Jackie Lee track (which appears on **The Hollies**' *Butterfly* album) and *Nobody But Me* was a Human Beinz/Isley Brothers track.

Compilation appearances have included:- *Silver Butterfly* on *Rubble Vol. 17: A Trip In A Painted World* (LP), *Rubble Vol. 10* (CD) and *The Best Of Rubble Collection, Vol. 3* (CD); and *My Colour Is Blue* and *Take Me Back* on *Brum Beat - Midlands Beat Groups Of The 60's* (CD) and *Would You Believe* on *Pop-In, Vol 2* (CD). (VJ)

Stu(art) James (and The Mojos)

45s: α Wait A Minute/I Wonder If She Knows (Decca F 12231) 1965 SC
(up to β I Only Wish I Had The Time/
1976)   Back To Basingstoke, Pt. 1   (Bradley BRAD 7406) 1974
      χ I'm In The Mood For Love/Firefly (Bradley BRAD 7614) 1976

NB: α As **Stu James and The Mojos**. β As **Stu James**. χ As **Stuart James**.

James was in the **Mojos** and the first 45 was recorded with the band. He returned in the mid-seventies recording initially as **Stu James** and then as **Stuart James**. There were a couple of further post-1976 singles under the latter moniker too. (VJ)

James Boys

Personnel:	BRADLEY PALMER	vcls	A
	STEWART PALMER	vcls	A

45s:			HCP
	The Mule/The Horse	(Direction 58-3721) 1968	-
	Over And Over/		
	Same Old Way	(Penny Farthing PEN 806) 1973	39
	Shoog Shoog/		
	The James Boys Shuffle	(Penny Farthing PEN 813) 1973	-
	Hello Hello/Viva Maria	(Penny Farthing PEN 816) 1973	-
	Keep Moving/		
	Sally Don't You Run	(Penny Farthing PEN 831) 1974	-
	I Love You/		
	Pick A Bale Of Cotton	(Penny Farthing PEN 846) 1974	-
	Up Until Now/		
	Pick A Bale Of Cotton	(Penny Farthing PEN 857) 1974	-
	Don't Ever Leave Me/		
	Give Your Love A Chance	(Mam MAM 152) 1976	-

THE BEST OF RUBBLE VOL. 2 (Comp CD) including Nicky James Movement.

A vocal duo who briefly caught some attention with *Over And Over*. They were two brothers from Ilford in Essex. Stewart was just twelve and Bradley fourteen when they first recorded.

Some of the songs from the Penny Farthing 45s are included on *Here Come The James Boys* (Pye 12109) 1975, which may be a US retrospective collection. (VJ/VZ)

James Brothers

45s:	I Forgot To Give You Love/	
	The Truth About It	(Page One POF 077) 1968
	Does It Have To Be Me/	
	You Don't Really Love Me	(Page One POF 088) 1968

These "brothers" were actually Herbie Armstrong and Rod Demick, who'd been in the mid-sixties outfit **The Wheels**, who recorded four 45s for Columbia. (VJ)

Bobby Jameson

ALBUM:	1	TOO MANY MORNINGS	(Joy JOYS 193) 1969 R2

45s:	I Wanna Love You / I'm So Lonely	(London HL 9921) 1964 SC
	All I Want Is My Baby /	
	Each And Every Day	(Decca F12032) 1964 SC
	Rum-Pum / Please Mr. Mailman	(Brit WI 1001) 1965 SC

The recording career of this US singer-songwriter and all-round hipster is still somewhat confusing. Having travelled to England to visit his friends Kim Fowley and PJ Proby, he came to the attention of **Andrew Loog Oldham,** who produced his Decca single, which was co-written by Keith Richards and allegedly backed by **The Rolling Stones**. Despite being crowned 25th Best Newcomer in Record Mirror's 1965 poll, he returned to the States that year to record the much-admired psychedelic folk album *Songs Of Protest and Anti-Protest* for the tiny Surrey label, under the pseudonym 'Chris Lucey'. His next album, *Color Him In* (US Verve 5015, 1967) didn't appear in the UK, where his next release was in fact the belated appearance of the *Songs Of Protest* album, in a completely different sleeve (in the US it featured a close up of **Brian Jones** playing the harmonica; here it depicts a factory belching out smoke). How on earth it came to appear on these shores is yet another mystery about this most enigmatic of albums. (RMJ)

Stephen Jameson

ALBUM:	1 STEPHEN JAMESON	(Dawn DNLS 3044) 1973 SC

45s:	Margie Make It March/Happiness Road	(Pye 7N 45189) 1970
(up to	Don't Say/Back Together Once Again	(Dawn DNS 1035) 1973
1976)	Take Me To The Doctor/	
	Rocky Fitzroy Jameson	(Dawn DNS 1043) 1973

This was a little known solo artist. (VJ)

Jamie's People

Personnel:	JAMIE GUNN	vcls	A
	JERRY HOGAN	steel gtr	A
	BRIAN SHEPPARD	vcls	A

ALBUM:	1(A)	BRING BRITAIN TO NASHVILLE	(Gemini EM 2002) 1971

45s:	Hand Me Down That Can O'Beans/	
	Million Tears	(Gemini GMS 005) 1970
	Everybody Wants To Get To Heaven/	
	I'll Love Again	(Gemini GMS 015) 1970

Jamie's People was a country band. Their album features Kris Kristofferson's *Shadow Of Her Mind* and the Jim McGuinn arrangements of *Old Blue*. Jerry Hogan had been in **Country Fever**. (VJ)

Jan Dukes De Grey

Personnel: MICHAEL BAIRSTOW   flute, clarinet, sax,
                           trumpet, perc, keyb'ds   AB
            DEREK NOY   vcls, gtr, keyb'ds, bs, perc AB
            DENIS CONLAN   drms   B

ALBUMS: 1(A) SORCERERS   (Decca Nova (S)DN 8) 1969 R1
        2(B) MICE AND RATS IN THE LOFT
                                 (Transatlantic TRA 234) 1971 R2

NB: (1) reissued on CD (Wounded Nurse WN1). (2) reissued on vinyl (Earmark 42016) 2005 and on CD (Breathless 52001) 2005.

These are two totally uncommercial "folk" albums by a Yorkshire act. That doesn't mean they use any traditional songs. On *Sorcerers*, all tracks are composed and sung by Noy, with inventive but not always coherent accompaniment on wind instruments by Bairstow. Though some of the material is a bit bland, this album has its share of completely uncommon, yet strangely innocent melodies, put forward in a strongly self-willed way. Check out the strangely twisted *Dominique* on side two. There are no less than 18 tracks on this album, which producer David Hitchcock recalls being partially recorded inside a tent in the studio!

The second album continues in the same vein, yet sounds completely different. Their sound augmented with a useful drummer, they now presented three tracks instead of 18, one of them a side long. Instead of concise songs, we get long suited, still folky efforts but heavily spiced with dissonance and wild improvisations. None of the restraint is left, though few arrangements are very well executed. In spite of some overlong solos, this is highly interesting music made by minds that seem to be on the verge of disintegrating. Not for everyone's tastes, probably, but recommended nonetheless. Original copies came in an elaborate sleeve featuring a thin sponge layer designed to protect the record. Ironically, however, time has caused the reverse effect and clean copies are almost non-existent.

The title track of their first album was also included on the 1970 *Nova Sampler* (LP). More recently, *Mice And Rats In The Loft* has been compiled on the 3-CD box set *Ars Longa Vita Brevis: A Compendium Of Progressive Rock*. (MK/VJ)

Peter Janes

Personnel incl: PETER JANES (aka PETER HORGAN)   A

45s: Stage Door/People Say   (Reprise RS 20383) 1965
      Emperors And Armies/Go Home Ulla (PS)   (CBS 3004) 1967
      Do You Believe (Love Is Built On A Dream)/
      For The Sake Of Time   (CBS 3299) 1968

Peter Janes was a folk singer. His *Go Home Ulla* resurfaced on *Circus Days, Vol. 4* (LP) and *Circus Days Vol's 4 & 5* (CD), and was produced by **Cat Stevens** who he'd once played in a duo with. You can also check out *Do You Believe (Love Is Built On A Dream)* on *Fading Yellow, Vol 1* (CD).

His third 45 was also produced by Cat and he also played guitar and mellotron on it. (VJ/GBn)

Bert Jansch

ALBUMS: 1 BERT JANSCH   (Transatlantic TRA 125) 1965 SC
(up to   2 IT DON'T BOTHER ME
1977)   (Transatlantic TRA 132) 1965 SC
         3 JACK ORION   (Transatlantic TRA 143) 1966 R1
         4 BERT AND JOHN   (Transatlantic TRA 144) 1966 SC
         5 NICOLA   (Transatlantic TRA 157) 1967 SC
         6 BIRTHDAY BLUES   (Transatlantic TRA 179) 1968 SC
         7 THE BERT JANSCH SAMPLER
                                 (Transatlantic TRASAM 10) 1969 SC
         8 ROSEMARY LANE   (Transatlantic TRA 235) 1971 SC
         9 BOX OF LOVE - THE BERT JANSCH SAMPLER, VOL 2
                                 (Transatlantic TRASAM 27) 1972 SC
        10 MOONSHINE (w/lyric insert) (Reprise K 44225) 1973 SC
        11 L.A. TURNAROUND (w/lyric insert)
                                 (Charisma CAS 1090) 1974

BERT JANSCH - Box Of Love (LP).

        12 SANTA BARBARA HONEYMOON
                                 (Charisma CAS 1107) 1975
        13 A RARE CONUNDRUM   (Charisma CAS 1127) 1977

NB: (2) reissued as *Early Bert, Vol. 1* (Xtra 1163) 1976. (3) reissued as *Early Bert, Vol. 2* (Xtra 1164) 1976. (5) reissued as *Early Bert, Vol. 3* (Xtra 1165) 1976 and (8) as *Early Bert, Vol. 4* (Xtra 1170) in 1977. (1) reissued on Transatlantic (TRS 117) in 1979 and Transatlantic/Demon (TRANDEM 1) in 1988. (1) reissued again on CD (Castle CMRCD 204) with two bonus tracks and a booklet. (2) reissued on CD (Castle CMRCD 205). (1) and (3) reissued on one CD (Demon/Transatlantic TDEMCD 14) 1993. (3) issued on Vanguard (VSD 6544) in the US. There was also an US-only release - *Lucky Thirteen* (Vanguard VSD 79212) in 1966. (3) reissued on CD (Castle CMRCD 304) and on vinyl (Earmark 42007). (4) credited to **Bert Jansch** and **John Renbourn**. (5) reissued on CD (Transatlantic CMRCD 333) 2002, with the addition of two bonus cuts, *In The Game* and *Dissatisfied Blues*. (6), (9) and (11) released on Reprise in the US. (6) reissued on CD (Castle CMRCD 334) 2001. (8) reissued on CD (Wooden Hill HILLCD 2) 1996, in its original packaging and with informative liner notes by Colin Harper. (8) reissued on CD (Castle CMRCD 335) 2001. (10) reissued on CD (Castle CMRCD 112).

Readers may also be interested in *Anthology* (Transatlantic MTRA 2007) 1978, *The Best Of Bert Jansch* (Transatlantic TRA 333), *Strolling Down The Highway - The Essential Collection, Vol. 1* (on album and CD) (Transatlantic TRA 604/TRACD 604), and *Vol. 2* (on album and CD) (Transatlantic TRA 607/TRACD 607) 1987; *The Best Of Bert Jansch* (CD and cassette only) (Shanachie 99004) 1992; *The Gardener: Essential Bert Jansch 1965-71* (CD) (Transatlantic/Demon TDEMCD 9) 1992 and *Three Chord Trick* (1974-1979 (CD) (Virgin CDVM 9024) 1993. *Dazzling Stranger* (Castle Music CMEDD 009) 2000 is a 2-CD full career anthology. *The Pentangle Family* (Castle/Sanctuary ESACD 931) 2000 is a 2-CD set comprising **Bert Jansch** and **John Renbourn** solo material as well as **Pentangle** material from the 1965-1971 era. *Live At The 12 Bar - An Authorised Bootleg* (Essential ESMCD 921) captures their live sound. *Legend: The Classic Recordings* (Metro METRO 113) 2003 is a 20-track anthology, compiled mostly from his Transatlantic recordings. *The River Sessions* (River RIVERCD 006) 2004 contains material from the previously unknown Radio Clyde archives of a concert at Glasgow City Hall in November 1974.

EP: 1 NEEDLE OF DEATH (PS)
                                 (Transatlantic TRA EP 145) 1966 SC

45s: LIfe Depends On Love/
(up to   A Little Sweet Sunshine   (Big T BIG 102) 1967
1976)   Oh My Father/
           The First Time Ever I Saw Your Face   (Reprise K 14234) 1973
           In The Bleak Midwinter/One For Jo   (Charisma CB 240) 1974
           Dance Lady Dance/Build Another Band (Charisma CB 267) 1975

Born in Glasgow on 3 November 1943, **Jansch**'s formative years musically were as part of the Glasgow and Edinburgh folk scenes of the late fifties and early sixties.

His debut album, *Bert Jansch*, was recorded on borrowed guitars in the kitchen of freelance producer Bill Leader's Clapham home in 1964 and then sold extremely cheaply to the Transatlantic label as no-one else was interested. However, his innovatory guitar style quickly established him as one of the leading figures on the sixties folk scene, despite some very amateurish live performances in these early years. It was the folk album of the time.

He developed a close friendship with fellow guitarist **John Renbourn**, with whom he went on to share a number of flats. **Renbourn** appeared on a couple of tracks on **Jansch**'s *It Doesn't Bother Me* album. Since **Renbourn** was also signed to Transatlantic, it was simple for them to appear on each others albums. This album was more accessible and mainstream than his first effort.

The highpoint of **Jansch**'s partnership with **Renbourn** was reached on the *Jack Orion* and *Bert And John* albums. The former veered towards traditional folk with the nine-minute title cut and *Black Water Side* probably its finest moments. The latter was a largely instrumental and jazzy album.

One of **Jansch**'s most popular songs in these early days was anti-drug tale *Needle Of Death*, which was the title track for a 1966 EP. The other four cuts were *Running From Home, Tinker's Blues, Courting Blues* and *The Wheel*. **Donovan** was a great fan of Bert's, frequently performing his songs in his live act and dedicating two songs (*House Of Jansch* and *Bert's Blues*) to him.

The *Nicola* album marked a change of musical direction, experimenting with a live orchestra on half of the tracks. It was arranged by David Palmer, who later joined **Jethro Tull**. The end result was rather elaborate and it is generally considered one of his least successful albums, though it spawned his first single, *Life Depends On Love*, which made little impact. *Woe Is Love My Dear*, one of the stronger orchestral pieces, was also earmarked for 45 release, but never emerged in this format. Of the non-orchestrated cuts, *Go Your Way My Love* was recorded with **Anne Briggs** and particularly catches the ear.

In mid-1967, along with **John Renbourn** and Jacqui McShee, **Jansch** formed **Pentangle**, which was intended as an experimental outfit blending folk, blues and jazz. During this period, further solo albums were recorded. *Birthday Blues* showcased his songwriting, arranging and guitar playing admirably. **Pentangle** members Danny Thompson and Terry Cox assisted him on this album whereas his next effort - *Rosemary Lane* - was a genuinely solo and rather melancholic album. It mixed traditional English songs with baroque instrumentals and a small splattering of beautiful original compositions. During this period, Transatlantic also put out a couple of compilations - *The Bert Jansch Sampler* and *Box Of Love - The Bert Jansch Sampler, Vol. 2* - which helped to keep his profile as a solo artist alive. The second of these included a couple of previously unissued cuts:- *In This Game* and *Dissatisfied Blues*.

When **Pentangle** split in March 1973, **Jansch** resumed his solo career. His next album, *Moonshine*, had actually been recorded whilst he was still with the band. He was assisted on this by several musicians, including **Mary Hopkin**. A 45, *Oh My Father*, was also released but made little impression. After moving to Wales with his wife Heather, he was signed by the emerging Charisma label. The first album to result from this new collaboration was *LA Turnaround*. It was recorded in Sussex and Los Angeles and produced by Mike Nesmith. The same year saw the release of a non-album 45, *In The Bleak Midwinter*, produced by **Ralph McTell**. Ralph's brother, Bruce May, had now become his manager.

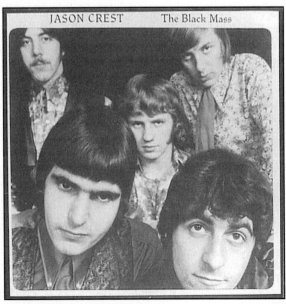
JASON CREST - The Black Mass (LP).

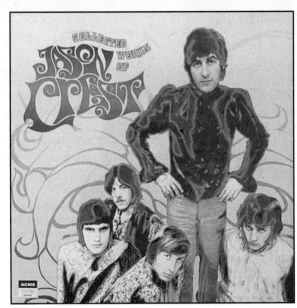
JASON CREST - The Collected Works (LP).

Santa Barbara Honeymoon was recorded in California and littered with LA session musicians. Many of the songs reflected on his separation from Heather. *A Rare Conundrum* was also unexceptional and veered towards a sort of country-rock. Although Bert would continue to record spasmodically into the nineties, his best work had certainly gone before him.

The album discography gives details of a selection of some of the reissues and compilations which may interest readers. Most of these come with detailed sleevenotes from his biographer Colin Harper.

Dazzling Stranger is a 2-CD anthology compiling key tracks from the vast majority of his solo albums plus a few **Pentangle** tracks. This is recommended to his fans.

Legend: The Classic Recordings is a 20-track anthology utilising mostly songs from his Transatlantic albums. It features many of his finest moments, including *The Time Has Come* (with **John Renbourn**) and *Needle Of Death*, an anti-drug song.

The River Sessions taped from a concert at Glasgow City hall in November 1974 includes seven numbers from his then current album *LA Turnaround*, his non-album single *In The Bleak Midwinter* and covers of two **Pentangle** songs.

Needle Of Death, Rosemary Lane and *After The Dance* (with **John Renbourn**) have all been compiled on *The Transatlantic Story* CD box set. (VJ)

Janus

ALBUM: 1 GRAVEDIGGER   (Harvest 29433) 1972 R2

NB: (1) reissued on CD (World Wide SPM-WWR-CD-0035) 1992.

This six man band only issued this album in Germany where they were based. Side one is comprised of heavy progressive rock with some psychedelic influence. The second extended side is in more of a US West Coast vein. A collectors' item, this is well worth tracking down. The band was active well beyond the timeframe of this book. (VJ)

Jasmin T

45:      Some Other Guy/Evening (PS)   (Tangerine DP 0013) 1969

An obscure band and label. The disc is recommended by '117' magazine. The flip side is an instrumental. (MWh)

Jason Crest

Personnel:
TERRY CLARKE	vcls		AB
TERRY DOBSON	gtr		AB
RON FOWLER	bs		A
ROGER SIGGERY	drms		AB
DEREK SMALLCOMBE	gtr		AB
JOHN SELLEY	bs		B

45s:
Turquoise Tandem Cycle/		
Good Life (Some in export PS)	(Philips BF 1633) 1968	R3/R2
Juliano The Bull/Two By The Sea	(Philips BF 1650) 1968	R1
(Here We Go Round) The Lemon Tree/		
Patricia's Dream	(Philips BF 1687) 1968	R1
Waterloo Road / Education	(Philips BF 1752) 1968	SC
A Place In The Sun/Black Mass	(Philips BF 1809) 1969	R3

NB: There's also been a CD compilation, *Collected Works Of Jason Crest* (Wooden Hill WHCD 006) 1998, which compiles all their recordings and comes with informative sleeve notes. There has also been an earlier counterfeit collection entitled *The Black Mass* (Scanner Jots). On vinyl only this was issued in the US in 1993 and just 300 copies were pressed initially, although the album was repressed in 1996. *Radio Session 1968-1969* (Tenth Planet TP041) features two daytime radio sessions taken from mastertapes featuring 11 previously unreleased performances.

Formed in Tonbridge, Kent, by Terry Clarke and Terry Dobson, this band were originally known as The Spurlyweeves and later as **The Good Thing Brigade**. In November 1967 they were spotted by former **Four Pennies** bassist, who was working as an A&R man for Philips at the time. He got them a recording contract just ahead of EMI, who were also interested.

A recent Clarke/Dobson composition, *The Collected Works Of Justin Crest*, proved the inspiration (with an adjustment to the Christian name) for a new name, **Jason Crest**. Their debut 45, *Turquoise Tandem Cycle*, was quite impressive - a slowish **Procol Harum**-like ballad with classical undertones, a steady beat and a sort of pipe organ throughout. With a little more power it could have been a hit, but is wasn't.

The follow-up, *Juliano The Bull*, a rather child-orientated pop song which isn't as good, met with the same fate. By now their record company was beginning to panic at their lack of commercial success and **Roy Wood** was brought in as a producer for their third 45, a cover of **The Move**'s (*Here We Go Round The) Lemon Tree* (which had been the flip side to *Flowers In The Rain* a year earlier). Despite **Wood**'s presence the single flopped.

For their fourth 45 the band were ordered to record a Fritz Fryer composition, *Waterloo Road*, which was so uninteresting that no-one's bothered to compile it. By now Philips had all but lost interest in them. One probable spin off is that they were allowed to select another Clarke/Dobson composition for what would be their final 45, *Black Mass*. A slow piece of heavier psychedelia, the vocals, in particular, reflect very much the emerging late sixties heavy rock style of bands like **Deep Purple**. The flip side was also pretty good.

Sadly, the 45 again met with indifference and the group broke up soon after its release. The band also recorded some other tracks in 1968 including:- *King Of The Castle, Collected Works Of Justin Crest, Teagarden Lane, You Really Got A Hold On Me* and *Charge Of The Light Brigade*. Of these the strongest are *Teagarden Lane*, another **Procol Harum**-type organ-led ballad with a fine ending and *You Really Got A Hold On Me*, which is given an interesting reinterpretation with more good organ work. The other three are pretty credible British whimsical pop-psych efforts which are well worth hearing.

After the band split Terry Dobson quit the music business. The remaining members splintered into **Orang Utan** (whose heavy psychedelic album was only released in the States), **High Broom** and **Samuel Proby**. Within a few months, though, Clarke, Siggery and Smallcombe teamed up in **Highway** who soon became **Holy Mackerel**. From 1983 onwards Terry Clarke fronted Vendetta with ex-**Mike Stuart Span** guitarist Brian Bennett.

Compilation coverage has included:- *Turquoise Tandem Cycle* on *Psychedalia - Rare Blooms From The English Summer Of Love* (CD), *British Psychedelic Trip, Vol. 3* (LP), *Rubble Vol. 15: 5,000 Seconds Over Toyland* (LP) and *Rubble Vol. 9* (CD); *(Here We Go Round The) Lemon Tree* and *Place In The Sun* on *Rubble Vol. 8: All The Colours Of Darkness* (LP); *(Here We Go Round The) Lemon Tree* on *Rubble Vol. 4* (CD); *Place In The Sun* on *Rubble Vol. 5* (CD); *Black Mass* on *Rubble Vol. 4: The 49 Minute Technicolour Dream* (LP), *Rubble Vol. 2* (CD) and on *Electric Sugarcube Flashbacks, Vol. 2* (LP); *King Of The Castle, Collected Works Of Justin Crest, Teagarden Lane, You Really Got A Hold On Me* and *Charge Of The Light Brigade* on *Syde Trips, Vol. 3* (LP); *Teagarden Lane* and *You Really Got A Hold On Me* on *Artefacts From The Psychedelic Dungeon* (CD); and *Juliano The Bull* on *Circus Days Vol's 4 & 5* (CD) and *Circus Days, Vol. 5* (LP). (VJ)

Jason's Generations

45:
It's Up To You/		
Insurance Co.'s Are Very Unfair	(Polydor 56042) 1966	R1

A Salford-based band whose *It's Up To You*, an organ-led pop-art number, is now quite collectable.

You can also check out *It's Up To You* on *Purple Pill Eaters* (LP & CD). (VJ)

Jasper

Personnel:
ALAN FELDMAN	keyb'ds		A
CHICO GREENWOOD	drms		A
NICKY PAYNE	vcls, hrmnca, flute		A
STEVE RADFORD	gtr		A
JON TAYLOR	bs		A

ALBUM: 1(A) LIBERATION   (Spark SRLP 103) 1969 R3

NB: (1) has been counterfeited on CD (Fingerprint) and issued officially (See For Miles SEECD 438) 1995. (1) reissued on CD again on Italian import (Akarma AK 217) 2002.

Strings (courtesy of Henry Lowther and at times disturbingly out of key), dissonant flutes, half-competent guitars and a confusing array of mostly blues-based styles are the ingredients on this one-off album for Spark. Where the blues come out on top, there is nothing very special to attract the ear, apart from the fact that blues are often used not to express a blue state of mind, but rather to attempt to reflect some lost region of childlike innocence. Tribal rhythms are used throughout the album, to good effect especially on *Confusion*, the best cut. Otherwise the sound is often amateurish with many useless jams and repeats. Considering the low-key performances it is not easy to understand, why this has been so intensively sought-after, apart from its sheer rarity. To be filed under unnecessary purchases. It did come in a wonderfully psychedelic cover, though. Alan Feldman went on to start **F.B.I.** (MK)

Jawbone

Personnel:
PIP BAKER		AB
TIM BARNSTON		AB
TAFFY DAVIS		B

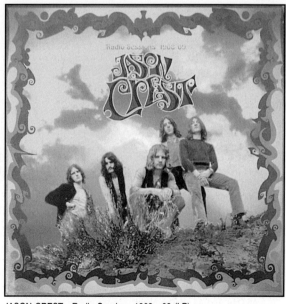

JASON CREST - Radio Sessions 1968 - 69 (LP).

COLIN HERRINGTON		B
PAUL JOHNSON		B
PETER MARCH		B
GRAHAM SHEPHARD		B
MALCOLM START		B

ALBUM: 1 JAWBONE (Carnaby CNLS 6004) 1970 R2

45s: How's Ya Pa/Mister Custer (Carnaby CNS 4007) 1970 SC
Way Way Down/
Bulldog Goes West (Carnaby CNS 4020) 1971 SC
Gotta Go/Automobile Blues (B&C CB 190) 1972

Jawbone were originally formed as a five-piece in 1966 by Baker and Branston. Their album, released in May 1970, combines originals with some **Beatles** covers. During 1971 their music veered from bluegrass to rock / delta blues / jug. In 1972, after several line-up changes, they re-emerged as an eight-piece. They spent a lot of time playing in the South of France.

Their final 45 *Gotta Go* was in a **Mungo Jerry** vein. It was produced by Jeremy Paul and Paul Lynton. Their album is mostly of interest to Carnaby label collectors. (VJ)

Peter Jay and The Jaywalkers

Personnel:			
	LLOYD BAKER	piano	A
	PETER JAY	drms	A
	JOHNNY LARKE	electric bs	A
	MAC McINTYRE	sax, flute	A
	PETER MILLER	ld gtr	A
	GEOFF MOSS	acoustic bs	A
	TONY WEBSTER	gtr	A

HCP

45s: Can Can 62/Redskins (Decca F 11531) 1962 31
Totem Pole/Jaywalker (Decca F 11593) 1963 -
Poet And Peasant/Oo La La (Decca F 11659) 1963 -
Kansas City/The Parade Of Tin Soldiers (Decca F 11757) 1963 -
You Girl/If You Love Me (Decca F 11840) 1964 -
Where Did Our Love Go/Caroline (Piccadilly 7N 35199) 1964 -
Tonight Your Going To Fall In Love/
Red Cabbage (Piccadilly 7N 35212) 1964 -
Parchment Farm/What's Easy For Two Is So
Hard for One (Piccadilly 7N 35220) 1965 -
Before The Beginning/Solitaire (Piccadilly 7N 35259) 1965 -

This East Anglian band pre-dated the beat boom and enjoyed a minor hit with *Can Can 62*. They were competent but stilted and seemed passé when compared with the emerging beat bands. Despite attempting a comeback with several R&B based releases and representing themselves as Peter Jay and The New Jaywalkers reduced to a quintet with the addition of Terry Reid on vocals they still didn't make a breakthrough and split in 1966.

Peter Miller later recorded as **Miller** and **Big Boy Pete**. (VJ)

The Jaybirds

Personnel:			
	ALVIN LEE	lead gtr	A
	LEO LYONS	bs	A
	DAVE QUICKMORE	drms	A

45s: Not Fade Away/Over You (Embassy WB 621) 1964
Tell Me When/You Can't Do That (Embassy WB 624) 1964
Can't Buy Me Love/(flip by Del Martin) (Embassy WB 625) 1964
Good Golly Miss Molly/
World Without Love (Embassy WB 626) 1964
Mockin' Bird Hill/
Hubble Bubble (Toil And Trouble) (Embassy WB 628) 1964
Baby Let Me Take You Home/
(flip by Bud Ashton and His Group) (Embassy WB 632) 1964
Juliet/Here I Go Again (Embassy WB 635) 1964
She's Not There/(flip by Paul Rich) (Embassy WB 651) 1964
All Day And All Of The Night/

JASPER - Liberation (LP).

Google Eye (Embassy WB 663) 1964
What Have They Done To The Rain/
(Flip by Bud Ashton and His Group) (Embassy WB 672) 1964
Go Now/(flip by Terry Brandon) (Embassy WB 673) 1965

This Nottingham-based beat-trio also spent time in Hamburg, Germany, and is most significant for including future **Ten Years After** members **Alvin Lee** and Leo Lyons. Embassy was a Woolworth's budget label, which specialised in cover versions of hits. You'll find among their singles covers of hits by **The Rolling Stones**, **The Beatles**, **The Swinging Blue Jeans**, **Manfred Mann**, **The Animals**, **The Four Pennies**, **The Zombies**, **The Kinks**, **The Searchers**, **The Moody Blues** and more.

The band evolved out of a band called The Jaycats. See the **Alvin Lee** entry for more details. (VJ/AD)

The Laurie Jay Combo

Personnel:			
	ROBIN BARNES	ld gtr	AB
	GRAHAM DEE	bs	AB
	MIKE FINNEY	organ	AB
	BRIAN GIBSON	vcls	AB
	STAN GORDON	gtr	A
	LAURIE JAY	drms	AB

45s: Shades Of Red/Nevada Sunsets (Ember JBS 710) 1962
Teenage Idol/Think Of Me (HMV POP 1234) 1963
Love In My Heart/'Til You're Mine (HMV POP 1300) 1964
Maybe/Be Good To Me (HMV POP 1335) 1964
A Song Called Soul/Just A Little Bit (Decca F 12083) 1965 SC

This was a London-based band. Perhaps **Laurie Jay**'s main claim to fame was that he once gave **Dave Clark** drum lessons. In the early sixties **Jay** had been in an instrumental combo called Nero and The Alligators and the *Shades Of Red* 45 was an instrumental. In 1964 they backed **Kenny Lynch** on a 45.

Stan Gordon was later in **Magna Carta**. (VJ)

Jeannie and The Big Guys

Personnel:			
	GEOFF DAWSON	gtr	A
	RITA (JEAN) HAYLES	vcls	ABC
	DAVID JONES	lead gtr	A
	TERRY LYNCH	drms	AB
	OWEN ROBERTS	bs	A
	PHIL BLACKMAN	keyb'ds	BC
	PETER JOHNSON		BC
	JOHN PICKETT	bs	BC
	GEORGE ROBERTS	drms	C

45s:	Don't Lie To Me/Boys	(Piccadilly 7N 35147) 1963
	I Want You/Sticks And Stones	(Piccadilly 7N 35164) 1964

An obscure group from Chester. *Jeannie* cut a solo 45 for Parlophone in 1965 and later recorded with **Jean and The Statesides**.

Compilation appearances include: *Boys* and *Sticks and Stones* on *Some Other Guys* (2-LP); *Don't Lie To Me* and *I Want You* on *What About Us* (CD); and *Don't Lie To Me* on *Merseybeat Nuggets, Vol. 2* (CD). (VJ/AD)

Jean and The Statesides

Personnel:
MICK BLOOMFIELD	bs		A
DAVE BROGEN	sax		A
JEAN HAYLES	vcls		A
DAVE HOVINGTON	gtr, vcls		A
BILL STEMP	sax, organ		A
JEFF STURGEON	lead gtr		A
IAN WALKER	drms		A

45s:	Putty In Your Hands/One Fine Day	(Columbia DB 7287) 1964 R1
	You Won't Forget Me/	
	Cold Cold Winter	(Columbia DB 7439) 1965 SC
	Mama Didn't Lie/Just Let Me Cry	(Columbia DB 7651) 1965 SC

This was a later girl group from Chester fronted by Jean Hayles. They mostly played pop and early Tamla covers. Indeed they were one of the first bands to play early Tamla live in the UK. Although their poppy records were never great sellers, they were a popular and busy live band around West London. They appeared with many of the great American soul artists of the day, such as Stevie Wonder and Ben E. King. They backed Wilson Pickett on his last UK tour in 1966. He arranged and tried out *Land Of 1000 Dances* with them before going back to record it in the US. The band split in 1967. Sadly, Jean died of a brain tumour some years ago. (VJ/IW)

The Jeeps

Personnel:
PAUL BIDWELL	bs, vcls		A
JULIAN FERRARI	drms, vcls		A
BOB MOORE	vcls		A
PIERRE TUBBS	gtr, vcls		A

45s:	He Saw Eesaw/The Music Goes Round	(Strike JH 308) 1966
	Ain't It A Great Big Laugh/	
	I Put On My Shoes	(Strike JH 315) 1966

Pierre Tubbs was the driving force behind **The Jeeps**. He was later in **The Silence** (not the early **John's Children** incarnation), **Our Plastic Dream** and **The Owl**. *Ain't It A Great Big Laugh* is a little like **The Kinks**, whilst the flip side is a pretty good beat song, a little in the Gary Lewis and The Playboys *Just My Style* mould. They also had a number of previously

JERUSALEM - Jerusalem (LP).

unreleased tracks: *Love Is A Sometime Thing, Don't Come Running Back, That Was The Good Life, Here's A Heart, Don't Do It, Come See Me* and *But It's Alright* compiled on *Pierre's Plastic Dream* (CD), along with both sides of their second single. *Love Is A Sometime Thing* is Dylanesque in its guitar style with a beaty chorus; *Don't Come Running Back* is strongly Four Season's influenced, but with a mad guitar solo added; *That Was The Good Life* is a surf-style song; and *Here's A Heart* and *Don't Do It* are delivered in a garage style. They also supported US singer J.J. Jackson on *Come See Me* (Strike JH 329) in 1966 and recorded a US 45 *Hey You Lolita/Wanda* (Red Bird RB 10-062) 1966 as **The Silence**. (VJ)

Jefferson

ALBUM: 1   THE COLOUR OF MY COLOUR
	(Pye NSPL 18316) 1969 SC

NB: (1) reissued on CD (Sanctuary CMRCD 268) 2001 with bonus tracks.

                                                  HCP

45s:	Montage/	
	Did You Hear A Heartbreak Last Night	(Pye 7N 17634) 1968 -
	The Colour Of My Love/	
	Look No Further	(Pye 7N 17706) 1969 22
	Baby Take Me In Your Arms/	
	I Fell Flat On My Face	(Pye 7N 17810) 1969 -
	Love And All The World/	
	I've Got To Tell Her	(Pye 7N 17855) 1969 -
	You Know How It Is With A Woman/	
	Are You Growing Tired Of My Love	(Pye 7N 17930) 1970 -
	Spider/Can't Get You Out Of My Mind	(Pye 7N 45022) 1971 -
	How Does It Feel Baby/Dish It Out	(Philips 6006 354) 1973 -
	Last Bus Home/	
	Baby You've Got Everything I Need	(Alaska 1009) 1975 -
	Working My Way Back To You/	
	Baby You've Got Everything I Need	(Alaska 1016) 1975 -

This is **Geoff Turton** (who recorded one 45 under his real name). He is best known as a member of the Birmingham-based **Rockin' Berries** and was also in **Sight And Sound**. In 1968 he embarked on a solo career. Most of his material was ballads. His most successful song, *The Colour Of My Love*, was written by Paul Ryan.

His *The Colours Of Love* album is mostly full of Gene Pitney-style ballads, although there is a beautiful version of Jimmy Webb's *Montage* and there's a decent version of *Are You Growing Tired Of My Love?* (also done by **Status Quo**). The Sanctuary compilation contains eight bonus tracks from a previously unreleased second album.

You can also check out *Montage* on *Ripples, Vol. 7* (CD). (VJ)

Jellybread

Personnel:
JOHN BEST	bs		AB
PAUL BUTLER	gtr, vcls		AB
CHRIS WATERS	drms		A
PETE WINGFIELD	keyb'ds, vcls		A
RICK HAYWARD	gtr		B
KENNY LAMB	drms, perc		B

ALBUMS:
1(A)	FIRST SLICE	(Blue Horizon 7-63853) 1969 R1
2(A)	65 PARKWAY	(Blue Horizon 2431 002) 1970 R1
3(B)	BACK TO THE BEGINNING AGAIN	
		(Blue Horizon 2931 004) 1972 R2

NB: (1) also issued in the US and reissued on Line (1983). (1) also reissued on CD (Walhalla WH 90351). (2) also reissued on CD (Walhalla WH 90350) with three bonus tracks. They also had a very rare (R3) mini-album, *Jellybread* (Liphook 1) issued on the sixties prior to (1). This has been reissued as a 10" LP (Akarma AK 2018LP).

45s:	Chairman Mao's Boogaloo/	
	No One Else	(Blue Horizon 573162) 1969
	Comment/Funky Wasp	(Blue Horizon 573169) 1970
	Rockin' Pneumonia/	
	Readin' The Meters	(Blue Horizon 573174) 1970

Old Man Hank/Faded Grace   (Blue Horizon 573180) 1970
Creepin' And Crawlin'/
The Loser/Clergyman's Daughter   (Blue Horizon 2096001) 1971
Down Along The Cove/Sister Lucy (Blue Horizon 2096006) 1971

This heavy blues-rock outfit had quite a prolific output. **Rick Hayward** also issued a solo album on Blue Horizon in 1971. Back in the late sixties he'd been in **The Accent** when he was known as Rick Birkett. On *First Slice*, which was produced by **Mike Vernon**, **Pete Wingfield's** piano dominates what is a pretty typical blues record. It includes some "revivals" by Percy Mayfield (*River's Invitation* and *Never Say No*) and Bobby Bland (*I Pity The Fool* and *I've Got To Forget You*), but all the other tracks were written by **Wingfield**. There are some instrumentals (*Chairman Mao's Boogaloo*, *Boogie Sandwich* and *No Bzag Just Facts*) and some classic blues numbers like *Rusty Blade* and *No One Else*. However, the stand-out track is *Evening*, an over seven-minute long slow blues number with a good melody line, strong vocals and guitar and some string arrangement. The album was produced by **Five Day Rain** guitarist John Holbrook. **Peter Wingfield** later embarked on a solo career. (VJ/CA)

Edward Jenkins

45:      I'm Going Home/Take A Seat   (Pye 7N 45158) 1972

Edward Jenkins was a **Cat Stevens** sound-alike from the Swansea area. Both songs were self-penned. He won the Duke of Edinburgh's Award in 1971. (VJ)

The Jensens

Personnel:	WALTER DAY	drms	A
	ROGER 'NEWTON' GREENWOOD	gtr	A
	JOHN HORNE	gtr	A
	LEONARD 'MICHAEL' HORNE	vcls	A
	BRIAN HOWE	bs	A

45:      Deep Thinking/Marguerita   (Philips BF 1686) 1968

This group later became **Tempus Fugit**. (VJ)

Jerusalem

Personnel:	BOB COOK	gtr	A
	PAUL DEAN	bs	A
	BILL HINDE	gtr	A
	RAY SPARROW	drms	A
	LYNDEN WILLIAMS	vcls	A

ALBUM: 1(A) JERUSALEM   (Deram SDL 6) 1972 R2

JETHRO TULL - This Was (LP).

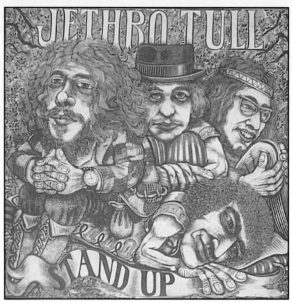

JETHRO TULL - Stand Up (LP).

45:      Kamakazi Moth/Frustration   (Deram DM 358) 1972 R1

From Salisbury comes this album's worth of bone-crunching hard-rock, played by immature teenies. Famous because it was produced by a young Ian Gillan, it doesn't offer anything musically that isn't available much more excitingly elsewhere. Skip this one.

In July 1972 their line-up was changed and in August they entered the studios to record a second album, again to be produced by Ian Gillan, but it was never released.

Kamakazi Moth also got an airing on *Circus Days, Vol. 4* (LP) and *Circus Days Vol. 3* (CD). This is similar in style to the album and also best avoided unless hard-rock is your scene. They were related to the band **Pussy**. (MK/VJ)

Jet

Personnel:	ANDY ELLISON	vcls	AB
	MARTIN GORDON	bs	AB
	DAVY O'LIST	gtr	A
	PETER OXENDALE	keyb'ds	A
	CHRIS TOWNSON	drms	AB
	IAN McLEOD	gtr	B
	TREVOR WHITE	gtr	B

ALBUM: 1(A) JET   (CBS 80699) 1975 SC

45s:	My River/Quandary	(CBS 3143) 1975
	Nothing To Do With Us/Brain Damage	(CBS 3317) 1975

Jet was formed in June 1974, after Martin Gordon placed an advert in 'Melody Maker', which former **John's Children** and **Jook** drummer Chris Townson replied to. **Andy Ellison**, who'd been vocalist with **John's Children**, was lured into the band, as was former **Misunderstood**, **Nice** and **Roxy Music** eccentric Davy O'List. Their album, which was produced by Roy Thomas Baker, was well received but didn't sell enough copies to make much impact. It was, however, a glitter-rock classic. O'List soon lost interest and left and Oxendale joined **The Glitter Band**. A couple of new members were recruited and line-up (B) did record demos but the writing was on the wall and by the Summer of 1976 the band had disintegrated. Six months later, Gordon, **Ellison** and McLeod re-emerged in Radio Stars. (VJ)

Jethro Tull

Personnel:	MICK ABRAHAMS	gtr, vcls	A
(up to	IAN ANDERSON	vcls, flute	ABCDEF
1976)	CLIVE BUNKER	drms	ABCD
	GLENN CORNICK	bs	AB

MARTIN BARRE	gtr	BCDEF
JOHN EVAN	keyb'ds	CDEF
JEFFREY HAMMOND-HAMMOND	bs	DE
BARRIEMORE BARLOW	drms	EF
JOHN GLASCOCK	bs	F

HCP

ALBUMS: 1(A) THIS WAS (Island ILP 985/ILPS 9085) 1968 R1/2 10
(up to 2(B) STAND UP (Island ILPS 9103) 1969 R1 1
1976) 3(C) BENEFIT (Island ILPS 9123) 1970 SC 3
4(D) AQUALUNG (Island ILPS 9145) 1971 SC 4
5(E) THICK AS A BRICK (Chrysalis CHR 1003) 1972 SC 5
6(-) LIVING IN THE PAST (2-LP) (Chrysalis CJT 1) 1972 SC 8
7(E) A PASSION PLAY
(w/theatre booklet) (Chrysalis CHR 1040) 1973 SC 13
8(E) WAR CHILD (Chrysalis CHR 1067) 1974 14
9(E) MINSTREL IN THE GALLERY
(Chrysalis CHR 1082) 1975 20
10(-) M.U. - THE BEST OF JETHRO TULL, VOL ONE
(Chrysalis CHR 1078) 1976 44
11(F) TOO OLD TO ROCK 'N' ROLL TOO YOUNG TO DIE
(Chrysalis CHR 1111) 1976 25

NB: (1) Withdrawn mono mix would be R2. Ist pressing in stereo would be R1. (1) reissued on vinyl (EMI 7243 4 99468 1 1) 1999. (1) reissued on CD (Chrysalis CCD 1041) 1986 and again (EMI 535 4592) 2001 with extra tracks. (2) reissued on CD (Chrysalis 7243 4 95400 2) remastered and with bonus tracks. (2) reissued on CD (Chrysalis CCD 1042) 1986, reissued again in 1989 and again (EMI 535 4582) 2001 with extra tracks. (2) reissued again on CD (Chrysalis 5354582) remastered and expanded. (3) reissued on CD (Chrysalis CPCD 1043) 1987 and again (EMI 535 4572) 2001 with extra tracks. (3) reissued again on CD remastered and with *Promise* and *Teachers* as bonus tracks. (4) reissued on vinyl (DCC Compact Classics LPZ 2030) 1997. (4) reissued on CD (Chrysalis CCD 1044) 1987 and again at mid-price with bonus tracks (Capitol 7243 4 9 5401 2 5) in 1996 and 2000. (4) has also been remastered and repackaged with an expanded booklet (Chrysalis) 1995. The new release includes an outtake from the original project *Lick Your Fingers Clean*, a different version of *Wind Up* and three late sixties recordings for the BBC:- *Fat Man*, *Song For Jeffrey* and *Bouree*. (4) reissued on CD (Chrysalis 495 4012) remastered in a deluxe edition with bonus tracks. *Aqualung Live* (R&M RAMCD 0015) 2005 revisits their 1971 album live for a 2004 US radio concert. (5) reissued on vinyl (EMI LPCENT 31) 1997. (5) reissued on CD (Chrysalis ACCD 1003) 1986 and on Mobile Fidelity (UDCD 510) 1989. (5) reissued again on CD (EMI 7243 4 95400 2) remastered with bonus tracks. (6) reissued on CD (Chrysalis CCD 1035) 1987 and again (Mobile Fidelity UDCD 2-708) 1998 as a deluxe, direct-from-the-masters of the original 1972 double-set. (7) reissued on CD (Chrysalis CCD 1040) 1989 and again (EMI 5815690) in 2003. (7) reissued on CD (Chrysalis 581 5690) remastered and with bonus tracks. (8) reissued on CD (EMI 5415712 7) 2002, with extra tracks, (9) reissued on CD (EMI 5415722 6), with extra tracks, (10) on reissued on CD (Chrysalis ACCD 1078) 1985 and (11) reissued on CD (Chrysalis CCD 1111) 1986 and again on CD (Chrysalis 541573 2).

Repeat - The Best Of Jethro Tull, Vol. Two (Chrysalis CHR 1135) followed in 1977 but is not recommended. Also relevant and on CD is *Original Masters* (Chrysalis CCD 1515) 1986. Provided you can afford it there is *Jethro Tull Compilation: Twentieth Anniversary* (Chrysalis), which is a five album, three cassette or three CD collection. It comes with a 12" format 24-page colour booklet, containing several photographs, a complete history of the group and a Pete Frame family tree. Sadly, though, the content leans towards their recent years rather than their early period,

JETHRO TULL - Aqualung (LP).

which was arguably their heyday. This was bettered by *25th Anniversary Box Set* (Chrysalis CDCHR 6004) 1993, which consists of a four-CD box set housed in a cigar-shaped package augmented by a full colour 48-page booklet which relates the band's history and contains lots of rare photos and memorabilia. Musically, what's on offer is a 1970 live concert from New York's Carnegie Hall, classic songs remixed, new versions of their old classics and a collection of various other live recordings. It was followed a few months later by *The Best Of Jethro Tull - The Anniversary Collection* (Chrysalis), a good double-set of their highlights which includes a cut from each of their 20 studio albums. Later in the year came *Nightcap - The Unreleased Masters 1972-1991* (Chrysalis) which comprised a number of previously unreleased tracks including the tapes from an unfinished double album recorded at Chateau D'Herouville in Paris, which was shelved prior to completion. *The Originals: This Was / Stand Up / Benefit* (Chrysalis 7243 8 56081 2 4) 1997 combines arguably their three most essential albums in a reasonably priced CD box set. *Nothing Is Easy: Live At The Isle of Wight 1970* (Eagle EAGCD 281) 2004 is an enjoyable extravaganza capturing the band on form. *Through The Years* (CD) is a good compilation that rounds up material like *Warchild*, *Living In The Past*, *Locomotive Breath*, *Acres Wild* and eight more tracks.

HCP

45s: α Sunshine Day/Aeroplane (MGM MGM 1384) 1968 R3 -
(up to Song For Jeffrey/
1976) One For John Gee (Island WIP 6043) 1968 R2 -
Love Story/A Christmas Song (Island WIP 6048) 1968 29
Living In The Past/Driving Song (Island WIP 6056) 1969 SC 3
Sweet Dream/Seventeen (Island WIP 6070) 1969 7
The Witch's Promise/
Teacher (Some PS) (Island WIP 6077) 1970 SC 4
Inside/Alive And Well And Living In (Island WIP 6081) 1970 -
Life Is A Long Song//Up The Pool/Dr Bogenbroom
From Later/Nursie (PS) (Chrysalis WIP 6106) 1971 11
Bungle In The Jungle/
Back Door Angels (Chrysalis CHS 2054) 1974 -
Minstrel In The Gallery/
Summerday Sands (Chrysalis CHS 2075) 1975 -
Living In The Past/Requiem (Chrysalis CHS 2081) 1976 -
Too Old To Rock'n'Roll Too Young To Die/
Rainbow Blues (Chrysalis CHS 2086) 1976 -
β Ring Out Solstice Bells//March Of The Mad Scientist
A Christmas Song/
Pan Dance (PS) (Chrysalis CXP 2275) 1976 28
Reissue: Living In The Past/
The Witch's Promise (Old Gold OG 9673) 1987 -

NB: α Early copies credited to Jethro Toe. β Reissued in 1979 (Chrysalis CHS 2443) 1979.

Jethro Tull was an unique band. An important part of the seventies progressive rock boom, they successfully blended folky melodies, hard-rock and blues with surreal and complex lyrics and were fronted by an eccentric flautist, guitarist and singer/songwriter who contributed immensely to their uniqueness. Few of their contemporaries surpassed their success.

The band's story began in Blackpool in 1963 when Ian Anderson, a Scot who'd been born in Edinburgh on 10 August 1947 but had relocated there, formed a group called The Blades (named after James Bond's club) with school friends Jeffrey Hammond-Hammond on bass and John Evan on drums. Brummie Barriemore Barlow was soon added to the line-up as drummer with John Evan switching to keyboards. Their main musical influence was the blues and they switched names to John Evan Band and John Evan Smash before heading for London to try their luck on the city's burgeoning blues scene in December 1967 by which time Glenn Cornick had replaced Hammond-Hammond on bass. After just a few days on the road they became disillusioned and split with only Anderson and Cornick remaining down South. After a couple of months these two teamed up with **Mick Abrahams** (gtr) and Clive Bunker (drums), playing under several different names like Bag Of Blues, until they stuck with **Jethro Tull** after the eighteenth century agriculturalist.

Their debut 45 was a **Mick Abrahams** demo, *Sunshine Day* with *Aeroplane* on the flip, which had been written by Anderson and recorded by John Evan Smash in Manchester circa 1966-67. Released by MGM original pressings were erroneously credited to Jethro Toe. An interesting single, it sold poorly and is now not at all easy to find.

The band started to assemble a cult following after securing a residency at the Marquee in June 1968 and this was further enhanced when they supported **Pink Floyd** at a free rock festival in London's Hyde Park on 29 June. Their first major breakthrough came after a storming performance at the Sunbury Jazz and Blues Festival in August 1968 won them widespread acclaim and was instrumental in Island Record's signing them up.

Their first album, *This Was*, was a fine debut. It mostly comprised originals of which Ian Anderson's *A Song For Jeffrey* (dedicated to ex-member Jeffrey Hammond-Hammond) was one of the best showcasing Anderson's flute playing which helped fashion the band's distinctive sound. A blues band with a flutist was pretty unique! Released as a 45 it flopped but this was because it wasn't commercial enough for the singles market. The single is not easy to track down but it was also included on Island's budget-priced compilation *You Can All Join In* (LP). The album also contained a couple of good cover versions:- *Cat's Squirrel*, which featured a strong performance from **Abrahams** on guitar and *Serenade To A Cuckoo*, with more stunning flute work from Anderson.

The band's rapid success led to inevitable pressure within the group and a rift emerged between Anderson and **Abrahams** which was resolved by the latters' departure to form **Blodwyn Pig**. The last recording **Abrahams** played on was *Love Story*, a superb disc which, despite its lack of commercialism, edged into the UK Top 30. Tony Iommi (later of **Black Sabbath**) and Davy O'List (of **The Nice**) both guested for them very briefly before Martin Barre (ex-**Gethsame**) was recruited as a permanent replacement, joining them on their first US tour. They attracted enough interest there for Reprise to reissue *This Was* and it climbed to No 62 in the US Album Charts.

Barre's first recording with the band was *Living In The Past*, which was undoubtedly one of their finest 45s, indeed one of those classic songs with a timeless quality. It made it to No 3 in the UK ensuring a 'Top Of The Pops' appearance. Both sides of the disc were non-album tracks.

Their next album fared even better, topping the Album Charts. Aside from one instrumental, *Bach's Bouree*, that Anderson had re-arranged, all the tracks were written by Anderson whose songwriting talents were further underscored. There's also lots of superb guitar work by Barre on the album typified by the fuzz guitar on *We Used To Know*, which can also be found on another of Island's budget-priced compilations, *Nice Enough To Eat* (LP). Another cut, *Fat Man*, was particularly unusual and featured some fine percussion and guitar work. The album, which came in a gatefold sleeve from which card figures of the band really did stand up, also rose to No 20 in the US.

Their next 45 was another excellent double-sided non-album single, *Sweet Dream/17*, which made No 9 in the UK Charts. It was also their first release on the new Chrysalis label, which had been formed by the band's management team of Terry Ellis and Chris Wright. **Jethro Tull** was at this time the label's prime attraction, although their next two albums still came out on Island.

The follow-up 45, *The Witches Promise/Teacher*, consisted of two of their finest songs and did even better, climbing to No 4. Again, both songs were written specifically for the singles market. They were subsequently included on the compilation *Living In The Past* (although the version of *Teacher* was different from the 45 release).

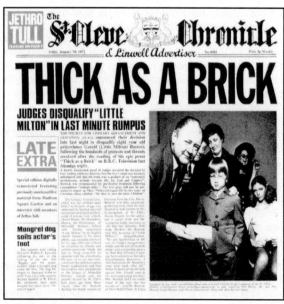

JETHRO TULL - Thick As A Brick (CD).

JETHRO TULL - A Passion Play (CD).

John Evan, who had been with the band in their pre-**Jethro Tull** days, guested on the band's next album, *Benefit*, although he soon joined on a permanent basis and stayed with them for 10 years. The album comprised mostly Anderson's songs but was different from its predecessor. It climbed to No 3 in the UK and after they'd been on their first headlining tour of the US it rose to No 11 there too. Their next 45 broke their previous practice of non-album 45s, though, coupling two tracks from the album, *Inside/Alive And Well And Living In*. It flopped! July 1970 saw the band consolidate its reputation in the US after playing at the Atlanta Pop Festival. Later on 4 November 1970 they played a benefit concert at New York's Carnegie Hall to raise funds for a drug rehabilitation centre.

Benefit was the last album Glenn Cornick appeared on. He left in December to form his own group **Wild Turkey**. His replacement was another former member from their early days, Jeffrey Hammond-Hammond.

Their next album, *Aqualung*, was probably their best of all. It's a skilful blend of heavy rock tracks and quieter acoustic songs. The title track, which became a stage favourite with the band's fans, concerned a tramp-type creature with a wheezing chest, who was pictured on the cover (and looked very much like Ian Anderson at the time!). The whole of side two concerned itself with Anderson's view on organised religion, which the God squad found offensive. In fact it contained some of their finest music - *Locomotive Breath* with its superb beat was outstanding, but *My God*, *Hymn 43* and *Wind Up* were also excellent musically and full of anti-(religious) establishment bantor.

There was a cancelled 45 shortly before *Aqualung*'s release - *Lick Your Fingers Clean*, so if demos were ever in circulation they would be extremely sought-after, by fans of the band at least. The track eventually resurfaced on the 25th Anniversary edition of the *Aqualung* album released in 1996. A different recording of the song was also included on the *War Child* album, retitled as *Two Fingers*.

Aqualung, which peaked at No 4 in the UK and No 7 in the US, was the last album to feature Clive Bunker, who departed to Jude in May 1971. Yes, you guessed it he was replaced by Barriemore Barlow, another old friend from their early days.

In the US, *Hymn 43* (from *Aqualung*), was released as a 45 and gave them their first (albeit minor) US hit, peaking at No 91. Here in the UK their next release was a five-track maxi-single. *Life's A Long Song* proved the most popular track and became their last UK hit until 1976, peaking at No 11.

If their first four albums are pretty essential much of what followed should be approached with definite caution. Despite its lavish packaging, *Thick As A Brick*, another concept album which dealt vaguely with the life of a young 'Gerald Bostock' was too self-indulgent and frankly boring. Not that this stopped it reaching No 5 in Britain and No 1 in the US. By now the band was due a compilation and a double package, *Living In The Past*, appeared in June 1972. Apart from one live side recorded at Carnegie Hall in New York, it comprised mostly previously unreleased cuts and 45s. It rose to No 3 in the US and No 8 in the UK.

Their next effort was another concept album (and a complex one at that), *A Passion Play*. In retrospect they made the mistake of premiering it live before the accompanying album was released. Many die-hard fans found it all too much and the critics savaged the show - the end result was so disastrous that Anderson announced the band would never play live again, though this proved not to be the case. Despite all this the album still got to No 13 in the UK and No 1 in the US. The higher US placing was probably because an edited version of the title track had already been a minor US hit, peaking at No 80. This was not released over here.

In 1974 they started work on a feature film, an orchestrated Soundtrack and an album. Only the latter survived, the other parts of the project were ditched due to lack of financial backing. The album, *War Child*, which was largely orchestral, saw the band return to a song-based format. They embarked on a long world tour to promote it, accompanied by a string quartet and playing sell-out concerts all over. The album sold pretty well, too, climbing to No 14 in the UK and No 2 in the US. It is worth checking out. It spawned a 45, *Bungle In The Jungle*, which didn't chart over here but made it to No 11 in the States.

If *War Child* was a step in the right direction, *Minstrel In The Gallery* marked a definite return to form. This was something of a novelty being mixed and recorded in the band's new mobile studio. Although the title track was rather weak and erroneously selected for 45 release (the non-album 'B' side, *Summerday Sands*, sounds much stronger), it did contain some of the band's best music in tracks like *One White Duck* and *Black Satin Dancer*. It deserved to do better than No 20 in the UK and No 7 in the US (where the title cut also made No 79 in the singles market). At the end of 1975 Hammond-Hammond left the band to concentrate on art and with no former members to call on John Glascock came in as a replacement.

M.U. - The Best Of Jethro Tull, Vol. One did contain one previously unreleased cut, *Rainbow Blues*, but otherwise has little to commend it to fans of the band and, in any case, this track turned up on the 'B' side to their next single.

Their next album, *Too Old To Rock'n'Roll, Too Young To Die*, came out of a planned play Anderson and David Palmer (who eventually joined the band in 1977) had been working on. The title track wasn't bad but much of the other material was weak and the production was flat. The storyline, that of an old rocker who refused to yield to new fashions, was particularly unfortunate with the onset of punk-rock all the more so since the character concerned looked very like Ian Anderson - the whole project became another milestone around his neck.

Still, by the end of the year the band bounced back with a Christmas hit single, *Ring Out Solstice Bells* (taken from an EP), which even earned them an appearance on 'Top Of The Pops'! As we leave the time span of this book the band was turning to folk-rock for new inspiration. They continued to record throughout the eighties and anyone not familiar with their music but wanting to seriously investigate them could seek out *Jethro Tull Compilation: Twentieth Anniversary*, a 65-track collection which traces their history in five albums, three cassette or three CD format. Warning: see the comment on the discography before purchasing.

1979 was a tragic year for the group as John Glascock died on 17 November from complications following heart surgery. With **Fairport Convention** having disbanded (albeit temporarily as it turned out) they acquired their long-term bassist Dave Pegg as a replacement.

Nothing Is Easy: Live At The Isle Of Wight 1970, released in 2004, captures the band in good form. The tracks include *My Sunday Feeling*, *Nothing Is Easy*, *To Cry You For A Song*, *Bouree*, *You There To Help Me* (with a lengthy piano piece) and *My God* (from their then forthcoming *Aqualung* album).

The band continued to record into the 21st century, largely returning to a blues and jazzy format. 2005 saw the release of a live version of their *Aqualung* album which was recorded for a US radio broadcast in 2004. Only Ian Anderson and guitarist Martin Barre remain from their 1971 line-up but the band sound in fine fettle and is clearly still going strong.

Compilation appearances have included: - *Nothing To Say* on *Bumpers* (2-LP); *Life Is A Long Song* on *20 Star Tracks, Vol. 1* (LP); *Mother Goose* on *El Pea* (2-LP); *A Song For Jeffrey* on *You Can All Join In* (LP); *We Used To Know* on *Nice Enough To Eat* (LP); *and Sunshine Day* and *Aeroplane* on *Rare Tracks* (LP). More recently, *A Song For Jeffrey* has resurfaced on *The Age Of Enlightenment - Prog Rock, Vol. One* (CD); *Sunshine Day* and *Aeroplane* have been compiled again on *Lovely Summer Days* (CD); *Aeroplane* also appears on *Jagged Time Lapse, Vol 5* (CD) and on the 3-CD set *Ars Longa Vita Brevis: A Compendium Of Progressive Rock 1967-1974*; and *Witch's Promise* got a further airing on the 3-CD box set *Radio Caroline Calling - 70's Flashback*. (VJ/TH)

Jigsaw

Personnel:			
BARRIE BERNARD	bs		A
TONY CAMPBELL	gtr		A
DES DYER	vcls, drms		A
CLIVE SCOTT	keyb'ds, vcls		A

ALBUMS:	1(A)	LETHERSLADE FARM	(Philips 6308 033) 1970 R2
(up to	2(A)	AURORA BOREALIS	(Philips 6308 072) 1971 R2
1976)	3(A)	BROKEN HEARTED	(BASF 29106-5) 1973 SC
	4(A)	I'VE SEEN THE FILM, I'VE READ THE BOOK	
			(BASF BAP 5051) 1974 SC
	5(A)	SKY HIGH	(Splash 1001) 1975

HCP

45s:	Mister Job/Great Idea	(Music Factory CUB 4) 1968 -
(up to	Let Me Go Home/Tumblin'	(Music Factory CUB 6) 1968 R2 -
1976)	One Way Street/Then I Found You	(MGM MGM 1410) 1968 R1 -
	One Way Street/	
	Coffucious Confusion	(Philips 6006 112) 1970 R1 -
	Lollipop And Goody Man/	
	Seven Fishes	(Fontana 6007 017) 1970 R1 -
	Jesu, Joy Of Man's Desiring/	
	No Questions Asked	(Philips 6006 131) 1971 -
	Keeping My Head Above Water/	
	It's Nice But It's Wrong	(Philips 6006 182) 1971 -
	That's Not What's It All About/I Like You	(UK UK 45) 1973 -
	I've Seen The Film, I've Read The Book/	
	Mention My Name	(BASF BA 1002) 1974 -
	You're Not The Only Girl/	
	Face The Music	(BASF BA 1010) 1974 -
	Baby Don't Do It/Stand Back To Me	(BASF BA 1013) 1975 -
	Sky High/Brand New Love Affair	(Splash CP 1) 1975 9
	Sky High/Brand New Love Affair	(Splash CP 11) 1975 -
	Love Fire/Your Lips Are Closed	(Splash CP 3) 1976 -
	Cry ('Till The Tears Run Dry)/	
	Low Life Love	(Splash CP 8) 1976 -
Reissues:	Sky High/Hard To Find	(Splash SP 2) 1979 -
	Sky High/If I Had To Go Away/	
	Who Do You Think You Are	(Slash CPS 1004) 1986 -
	Sky High/Fly Away	(Splash CPS 1006) 1986 -
	Sky High/Fly Away/	
	Shadows To Fall (12")	(Splash CPST 1006) 1986 -

JETHRO TULL - Too Old To Rock'n'Roll Too Young To Die! (CD).

This Rugby-based band was founded by Barrie Bernard. Some of their better moments can be heard on flip sides:- *Tumblin'* from 1968 and *Seven Fishes* from 1970 - the latter has a spacey electronic opening, which gives way to blistering wah-wah guitar before culminating in a high decibel crescendo. Prior to forming the band in 1966 Scott and Dyer had been successful songwriters (for Engelbert Humperdinck among others), Bernard had been in **Pinkerton's Assorted Colours** and Campbell had been with the **Mighty Avengers**. Their early seventies albums for Philips were quite interesting. Their big commercial success was *Sky High* - a Worldwide hit - but that didn't come until 1975.

Compilation appearances include: *Tumblin'* on *Justafixation II* (LP), *Rubble, Vol. 8 - All The Colours Of Darkness* (LP) and on *Lovely Summer Days* (CD); *Seven Fishes* on *Psychedelia, Vol. 3* (LP) and *Hen's Teeth, Vol. 3* (CD); *Let Me Go Home* on *Colour Me Pop, Vol 1* (CD) and *Lollipop And Goody Man* on *Colour Me Pop, Vol 2* (CD). (VJ)

Jill and Y'Verns

| 45: | My Soulful Dress/ | | |
| | Anything He Wants Me To Do | (Oak RGJ 503) 196? R2 |

This was one of the most obscure products of this very obscure but now collectable label. The 'A' side is a Sugar Pie De Santo Chess R&B favourite. (VJ)

Jody Grind

Personnel:	LOUIS CENNAMO	bs	A
	TIM HINKLEY	organ, keyb'ds	AB
	BARRY WILSON	drms	A
	IVAN ZAGNI	gtr	A
	PETE GAVIN	drms	B
	BERNIE HOLLAND	gtr, bs, vcls	B

| ALBUMS: | 1(A) | ONE STEP ON | (Transatlantic TRA 210) 1969 R1 |
| | 2(B) | FAR CANAL | (Transatlantic TRA 221) 1970 R1 |

NB: (1) reissued on CD (Akarma AK 058). (2) reissued on CD by Line in Germany. (2) reissued on CD (Akarma AK 065). (2) reissued on vinyl as *Far Canal (Jewel Case)* (GTR GTR 038) with two bonus tracks, *Rock'n'Roll Man* and *Paint It Black*.

Jody Grind was a progressive rock outfit. The first album is the more improvised of the two with more keyboards. The 18:43 minute title track is a long suite which dominates the album. Concluding side one is an epic, propulsive rendition of **The Rolling Stones**' *Paint It, Black*.

Far Canal is more varied instrumentally, with bluesy and jazzy material such as *Blues For Bridget*. A single edit of *Paint It, Black* was added as a bonus to the CD reissue of *Far Canal*.

JODY GRIND - One Step On (LP).

JODY GRIND - Far Canal (LP).

Pete Gavin went on to **Heads, Hands and Feet** and then **Vinegar Joe**. Louis Cennamo went on to an illustrious career as a session for the likes of **Al Stewart**, **Linda Lewis** and **James Taylor**. He was also in **Renaissance**, **Illusion** and **Steamhammer**. Tom Hinkley was in **Bo Street Runners** and **Beckett**. He later played on sessions for **Vinegar Joe**, **Alvin Lee**, **Mike Heron**, **Roger Chapman**, **Mickey Jupp**, David Coverdale and **Al Stewart** to name a few

Compilation appearances include *Bath Sister* on *The Transatlantic Story* CD box set. and on the 3-CD box set *Ars Longa Vita Brevis: A Compendium Of Progressive Rock 1967-1974*. (VJ/CB/BS)

Joe Jammer

Personnel:	REG ISODORE	drms	A
	JOE JAMMER	gtr	A
	TONY STEVENS		A

| ALBUM: | 1(A) | BAD NEWS | (Regal Zonophone SLRZ 8515) 1973 SC |

Joe Jammer was a short-lived heavy blues-rock trio. Tony Stevens had come from **Foghat** and Reg Isodore later played for **Robin Trower**. Joe was previously with **Paladin**. Reg Isadore also played on two of **Robin Trower**'s albums, *Twice Removed For Yesterday* (1973) and *Bridge Of Sighs* (1974). They have been likened to **Patto** and appeared on Day One of the 1970 Bath festival. (VJ/MWh)

Joe Soap

| ALBUM: | 1 | KEEP IT CLEAN | (Polydor 2383 233) 1973 SC |

This is actually Tennent/Morrison, so it's a mystery why it was issued as **Joe Soap**. Musically, it's very melodic - a rural progressive sound similar to **Northwind**. (VJ)

Joey and The Continentals

| 45: | She Rides With Me/Rudy Vadoo | (Polydor 56520) 1970 R1 |

A one-off 45 by a little known combo. (VJ)

Joey and Gentlemen

| 45s: | Like I Love You/I'll Never Let You Go | (Fontana TF 444) 1964 |
| | Dummy Dum Song/Goodbye Little Girl | (Fontana TF 485) 1964 |

These two 45s were this beat groups only vinyl offering. They played beat ballads and came from Cardiff. (VJ)

Andrew John

ALBUM: 1 THE MACHINE STOPS (CBS 64835) 1972

45: Streets Of London/Rick Rack (CBS 7017) 1971

This electric folk artist's album includes cover versions of songs by **Nick Drake**, **Roy Harper** and **Al Stewart** among others. He resided in Denmark, but came to Britain in April 1972 for gigs and recordings. On his album he was helped by Rick Lee and Clive Sarstedt. (MWh)

Clive John

ALBUM: 1 YOU ALWAYS KNOW WHERE YOU STAND WITH
A BUZZARD (United Artists UAS 29733) 1975

A solo effort by **John**, who is much better remembered as a member of **Man** and **Home**. He's assisted on this cult favourite by Martin Ace, Dave Charles, Tommy Riley and Phil Ryan. (MWh)

David John

45: Diggin' For Gold/She's Fine (Parlophone R 5301) 1965

This is a very rare and sought-after 45. **David John** was actually Miffy Charnley from Preston. He fronted The Mood but despite its value, **David Bowie** did not play on this single. (VJ)

David John and The Mood

Personnel:			
DAVID JOHN 'MIFFY' SMITH	vcls	A
PETE ATKINSON	gtr	A
JOHN BRIERLY	bs	A
PETE ILLINGWORTH	gtr	A
FREDDIE ISHERWOOD	drms	A

45s: Pretty Thing/To Catch That Man (Vocalion V 9220) 1964 R3
α Bring It To Jerome/
I Love To See You Strut (Parlophone R 5255) 1965 R3
Diggin' For Gold/She's Fine (Parlophone R 5301) 1965 R3

NB: α has been reproduced in a limited edition pressing of 500 from the original French Jukebox pressings.

A R&B outfit from Preston whose singles are extremely rare and sought-after. People have long (and incorrectly) assumed **John** was in fact **David Bowie** because of (i) the similarity between the names David John

and Davie Jones, (ii) the Vocalion connection (their singles for the label have consecutive catalogue numbers) and (iii) the titles of the first single. None of the singles feature **David Bowie** but they are still very collectable.

Brierly and Illingworth both went on to **Little Free Rock** and Smith was also involved in the **Astral Navigations Thundermother** project using the name David John.

Compilation coverage has so far included:- To Catch That Man on Broken Dreams, Vol. 2 (LP) and The R&B Scene (CD); Pretty Thing on Trans-World Punk Rave-Up!, Vol. 2 (LP); To Catch That Man and Pretty Thing on Maximum R'n'B (CD); I Love To See You Strut and Bring It To Jerome on Pebbles, Vol. 6 - The Roots Of Mod and Rare 60's Beat Treasures, Vol. 1 (CD); Diggin' For Gold on Diggin' For Gold, Vol. 1 (LP & CD); Diggin' For Gold (acetate) on Revenge Of The Amphetamine Generation (LP); I Love To See You Strut, Bring It To Jerome, Diggin' For Gold and She's Fine on RGM Rarities, Vol. 2 (CD); and Bring It To Jerome, I Love To See You Strut, To Catch That Man and Diggin' For Gold on English Freakbeat Vol. 6 (CD). (VJ)

Elton John

HCP

ALBUMS:	1	EMPTY SKY (mono/stereo)		
(up to			(DJM DJMLP 403/DJLPS 403) 1969	R2/SC
1976)	2	ELTON JOHN	(DJM DJLPS 406) 1970	11
	3	TUMBLEWEED CONNECTION	(DJM DJLPS 410) 1970	6
	4	17.11.70	(DJM DJLPS 414) 1971	20
	5	FRIENDS	(Paramount SPFL 269) 1971	-
	6	MADMAN ACROSS THE WATER		
			(DJM DJLPH 420) 1971	41
	7	HONKY CHATEAU	(DJM DJLPH 423) 1972	2
	8	DON'T SHOOT ME I'M ONLY THE PIANO PLAYER		
			(DJM DJLPH 427) 1973	1
	9	GOODBYE YELLOW BRICK ROAD (2-LP)		
			(DJM DJLPD 1001/2) 1973	1
	10	CARIBOU	(DJM DJLPS 439) 1974	1
	11	GREATEST HITS	(DJM DJLPH 442) 1974	1
	12	CAPTAIN FANTASTIC AND THE BROWN		
		DIRT COWBOY	(DJM DJLPX 1) 1975	2
	13	ROCK OF THE WESTIES	(DJM DJLPH 464) 1975	5
	14	HERE AND THERE	(DJM DJLPH 473) 1976	6
	15	BLUE MOVES (2-LP)	(Rocket ROSP 1) 1976	3

NB: He also appeared under his real name Reg Dwight on the Warlock Music Sampler (Warlock Music WMM 101/2) 1970. Copies are now valued at circa £1,000. (12) 2,000 copies came on brown vinyl. These would be R1 and those with signed covers R2. (1) - (3) and (6) - (14) all reissued by DJM in 1976. Some copies of (9) were put out in yellow vinyl and are now quite collectable. There was only a 2,000 limited edition pressing of (9) first time round in brown vinyl. (4) was reissued at a budget price with a new sleeve on Hallmark (SHM 942) in 1978. (14) was reissued at a budget price on Hallmark (SHM 966) the same year. Additionally, The Elton John Live Collection (Pickwick PDA 047) 1979 was a budget repackage of (4) and (14).

So far as CD reissues of his original albums are concerned:- (1) reissued on DJM (823 017 2) 1987, but deleted in 1988. Still available on import from USA (MCA 31000) 1988. (2) reissued on DJM (DJMCD 8) 1988 and available on import from USA (MCA 31105) 1988. (2) reissued again on CD (PolyGram 528 156-2) 1995 with three bonus cuts. (3) reissued on DJM (DJMCD 12) 1986 and available on import from USA (MCA 31103) 1988. (3) reissued again on CD (PolyGram 528 155-2) 1995 with two bonus tracks. (4) reissued on CD (PolyGram 528 165-2) 1995. (5) reissued (Anchor ABCL 5082) during the seventies. (6) reissued on DJM (DJMCD 5) 1981 and available on import from USA (MCA 31190) 1988 or Mobile Fidelity (UDCD 516) 1989. (6) reissued again on CD (PolyGram 528 161-2) 1995. (7) reissued on DJM (829 249-2) 1987 and available on import from USA (MCA 31104) 1988. (7) reissued again on CD (PolyGram 528 162-2) 1995 with one bonus track. (8) reissued on DJM (DJMCD 10) 1987 and DJM (827 690-2) 1988. Also on MCA (USA) (31077) 1988. (8) reissued again on CD (PolyGram 528 154-2) 1995 with four bonus tracks. (9) reissued on vinyl (Speakers Corner /DJM DJM 1001) 2005. (9) reissued on CD (DJMCD 2) 1987 and DJM (821 747-2) 1988. (9) reissued again on CD (PolyGram 528 159-4) 1995. (10) reissued on CD (DJMCD 6) 1987 and DJM (825 488-2) 1988. Also on MCA (USA) (31189) 1988. (10) reissued again on CD (PolyGram 528 158-4) 1995 with four bonus tracks. (11) reissued on CD (DJMCD 3) 1984. There's also Greatest Hits: Elton John, Vol. 2 (DJMCD 7) 1985. (12) reissued on DJM (DJMCD 1) 1983 and on MCA (USA) (31078) 1988. (12) reissued again on CD (PolyGram 528 160-2) 1995 with three bonus tracks. (13) reissued on DJM (DJMCD 9) 1987 and DJM (832 018-2) 1988, also on MCA (USA) (31001) 1988. (13) reissued again on CD PolyGram 528 163-3) 1995 with one bonus track. (14) reissued as a 2-CD set (PolyGram 528 164-2) 1995. (15) reissued on CD (Rocket 8228182) 1989.

On the compilation front Greatest Hits, Vol. 2 (DJM DJLPH 20520) appeared in 1977

ELTON JOHN - Tumbleweed Connection (LP).

and got to No 6. 1983 saw *The New Collection* (Everest CBR 1027) and *The New Collection, Vol. 2* (Everest CBR 1036), which were both reissued on Premier (CBR 1027 and 1036) respectively the following year.

Also of note are *Lady Samantha* (DJM ZCDJL 301) 1974, a cassette compilation, later reissued (DJM DJM 22085) 1980, when it got to No 56 in the charts. *Candle In The Wind* (St Michael 2094 0102) 1978, a compilation available exclusively via Marks and Spencer and now hard to find. *Elton John* (a five album boxed set) (DJM LSP 14512) in 1979, *The Very Best Of Elton John* (K-Tel NE 1094) in 1980 which got to No 24, *The Collection* (Pickwick PWKS 551) 1989, a CD collection and *To Be Continued* (Rocket 848 236-2) 1991, which is a lavish box of four CDs or cassettes, tracing his entire career. *Songbook* (Pickwick PWKS 4126) 1993 is a pretty random CD compilation of 16 of his tracks (by no means the best), which span the period 1969-1984. There's *Superior Sound Of Elton John 1970 - 1975* (DJMCD 4) 1984 and a CD set, *The Very Best Of Elton John* (Rocket 846 947-2) 1990, which got to No 1. *Elton John Greatest Hits 1970-2002* (Universal/Rocket 063 499-2) 2002 is a 3-CD set. There's also a deluxe version of *Goodbye Yellow Brick Road Limited Deluxe Edition* (Mercury 981 320 5) 2003 with a bonus DVD documenting the making of the album.

HCP

45s:			
(up to 1976)	I've Been Loving You/ Here's To The Next Time	(Philips BF 1643) 1968 R3	-
	Lady Samantha/ All Across The Heavens	(Philips BF 1739) 1969 R2	-
	It's Me That You Need/Just Like Strange Rain (Some in PS)	(DJM DJS 205) 1969 R2/R1	-
	Border Song/Bad Side Of The Moon	(DJM DJS 217) 1970 SC	-
	Rock And Roll Madonna/Grey Seal	(DJM DJS 222) 1970	-
	Your Song/Into The Dead Man's Shoes	(DJM DJS 233) 1971	7
	Friends/Honey Roll	(DJM DJS 244) 1971	-
	Rocket Man/ Holiday Inn/ Goodbye (Some gatefold PS)	(DJM DJX 501) 1972 SC/-	2
	Honky Cat//Lady Samantha It's Me That You Need (PS)	(DJM DJS 269) 1972	31
	Crocodile Rock/Elderberry Wine (PS)	(DJM DJS 271) 1972	5
	Daniel/Skyline Pigeon (PS)	(DJM DJS 275) 1973	4
	Saturday Night's Alright For Fighting//Jack Rabbit Whenever You're Ready (We'll Go Steady Again) (PS)	(DJM DJX 502) 1973	7
	Goodbye Yellow Brick Road/ Screw You (PS)	(DJM DJS 285) 1973	6
	Step Into Christmas/ Ho! Ho! Ho! (Who'd Be A Turkey At Christmas) (PS)	(DJM DJS 290) 1973	24
	Candle In The Wind/ Bennie And The Jets (PS)	(DJM DJS 297) 1974	11
	Don't Let The Sun Go Down On Me/ Sick City (PS)	(DJM DJS 302) 1974	16
	The Bitch Is Back/Cold Highway (PS)	(DJM DJS 322) 1974	15
	Lucy In The Sky With Diamonds (featuring Dr. Winston O'Boogie & His Reggae Guitars)/ One Day At A Time (PS)	(DJM DJS 340) 1975	10
α	Philadelphia Freedom / I Saw Her Standing There (PS)	(DJM DJS 354) 1975 SC	12
	Someone Saved My Life Tonight/ House Of Cards (PS)	(DJM DJS 385) 1975	22
	Island Girl/Sugar On The Floor (PS)	(DJM DJS 610) 1975	14
	Grow Some Funk Of Your Own/ I Feel Like A Bullet (In The Gun Of Robert Ford) (PS)	(DJM DJS 629) 1976	-
	Pinball Wizard/Harmony (PS)	(DJM DJS 652) 1976	7
β	Don't Go Breaking My Heart/ Snow Queen (PS)	(Rocket ROKN 512) 1976	1
	Bennie And The Jets/ Rock And Roll Madonna (PS)	(DJM DJS 10705) 1976	37
	Sorry Seems To Be The Hardest Word/ Shoulder Holster (PS)	(Rocket ROKN 517) 1976	11
Reissues:	Lady Samantha/Skyline Pigeon (PS)	(DJM DJS 10901) 1978	-
	Philadelphia Freedom / Lucy In The Sky With Diamonds (PS)	(DJM DJS 10911) 1978	-
	Candle In The Wind/ Bennie And The Jets	(DJM DJS EJS 15) 1988	-
	Your Song/Into The Old Man's Shoes	(DJM DJS EJS 14) 1988	-
x	Don't Go Breaking My Heart/ I Got The Music In Me	(Old Gold OG 9789) 1988	-
χ	Don't Let The Sun Go Down On Me/ Song For Guy	(Rocket EJS 26) 1991	-

NB: α as Elton John Band; B-side featuring **John Lennon** with Muscle Shoals

ELTON JOHN - Goodbye Yellow Brick Road (LP).

Horns. β 'A' side with **Kiki Dee**. χ Also on 12" and a CD single with the addition of *Sorry Seems To Be The Hardest Word* (Rocket EJS CD 26) 1991. x Flip side by **Kiki Dee**. The above list is not comprehensive. For example, in 1978, a 12 x 7" *Elton John Singles Collection* was released and each single was also available separately.

Elton John was the most successful pop star of the early seventies and has continued to prosper over four decades. He is now one of the richest pop stars in the world. Setting out as a singer/songwriter with a very attractive voice in his early days and boosted by a flamboyant stage act as his career developed, his recorded out put was extremely diverse - he could deliver ballads, rock, pop and even ventured into soul, country and disco too.

Reginald Kenneth Dwight (his real name, as many of you will know) was born on 25 March 1947 in Pinner, Middlesex, the son of an ex-Royal Air Force trumpeter. He began playing piano when he was just four and won a part-time scholarship to London's Royal Academy of Music at the age of 11. By the time he was 16 he was working as a messenger in music publishing by day and playing piano by night. In 1961 he joined **Bluesology**, who later became **Long John Baldry**'s backing group. He wrote **Bluesology**'s debut 45, *Come Back Baby*. By 1967 **Baldry** was moving into cabaret and Dwight decided the time had come to move on. He auditioned with Liberty Records, who, trying to establish a London office, had placed an advert for artists and writers in NME. He failed the audition but they put him in touch with lyricist Bernie Taupin and this new partnership ended up signing a new contract with the Tin Pan Alley publishing house. Dwight also changed his name by deed poll to **Elton John** (an amalgam of **Baldry**'s and **Bluesology**'s sax player Elton Dean's christian names).

Elton John's solo career commenced in March 1968. His first two 45s for Philips are now extremely rare. Neither charted, although the second got a lot of airplay at the time. Shortly after the second he auditioned for the vocal spot in **King Crimson** but didn't get selected. However, his reputation was enhanced the following month when **Lulu** performed his and Taupin's *I Can't Go On Without You* on her TV show, as one of the UK entries for the Eurovision song contest.

He switched to the DJM label for his May 1969 release, *It's Me That You Need*. This appeared in a collectable picture sleeve and is also very rare now. What is less well known is that the same year he also appeared as a session musician in an outfit put together by record producer Tony King. Other members were Bernie Calvert (**The Hollies'** bassist), Roger Pope (drms) and **Caleb Quaye** (gtr). An album of material was recorded but only one 45 (from the album tapes) was eventually put out, a humorous version of **Dick Barton** coupled with *Breakdown Blues* on the flip. The 45 was released as the **Bread And Beer Band** (Decca F 12891) in 1969 and reissued in 1973 (Decca 13354) after he'd become famous.

His debut album, *Empty Sky*, released in June 1969, was solid, if unexceptional. It was comprised entirely of **Elton John**/Bernie Taupin compositions. The same month he played piano on **The Hollies'** *He Ain't*

Heavy He's My Brother, (the following year he played piano on their *I Can't Tell The Bottom From The Top* single and organ on *Perfect Lady Housewife*, which figured on the group's *Confessions Of The Mind* album). He also did session work for labels like Pickwick and Music For Pleasure who did budget cover versions of popular songs.

In 1970 he appeared under his real name of Reg Dwight on the Warlock Music Sampler. The album was masterminded by producer Joe Boyd and recorded at Sound Techniques in Chelsea. It featured Pat Donaldson on bass and Gerry Conway on drums. On the album **Elton John** delivers straightforward renditions of **John Martyn**'s *Stormbringer*, **Mike Heron**'s *Go Out And Get It*, **Beverley Martyn**'s *Sweet Honesty* and four **Nick Drake** songs: *When The Day Is Done, Way To Blue, Time Has Told Me* and *Saturday Sun*. Although 100 copies were rumoured to have been pressed of this sampler, only around six are known to have survived, making it an extremely rare rock artefact.

His next 45, *Border Song*, which featured The Barbara Moore Choir, received a lot of airplay, although it failed to chart. It was later included on his second album, **Elton John**, which represented an enormous advance on his debut and was arguably his best. Produced by Gus Dudgeon with superb string arrangements by Paul Buckmaster it contained some of his finest moments. Songs like *Your Song, The King Must Die, I Need You To Turn To* and *First Episode At Hienton* showed him to be a romantic and sensitive performer, whilst *Take Me To The Pilot* characterised a brasher style that became an increasing part of his repertoire over the years. At this stage in his career he was also blessed with an extremely attractive voice. He was assisted on the album by **Caleb Quaye** (gtr), Dee Murray (bs) and **Nigel Olsson** (drms). The album climbed to No 11 in the UK and some months later to No 4 in the US, where he had signed to Uni and already got to No 92 in the Singles Chart with *Border Song*. He toured the States briefly in August 1970 and later, on 17 November, gave a concert in New York, which was broadcast live on W-PLJ FM and formed the basis of his 1971 *17-11-70* album. *Your Song*, from his second album, was an attractive ballad which made an ideal 45 and took him into the Top Ten on both sides of the Atlantic.

Also excellent was his third album, *Tumbleweed Connection*. This dealt with his obsession with the Wild West. Again all tracks except **Lesley Duncan**'s *Love Song* were **John**/Taupin compositions. He employed a wider range of musicians on this album and **Dusty Springfield** appeared as backing vocalist on two of its better tracks, *Ballad Of A Well-Known Gun* and *My Father's Gun*, which was arguably the albums finest moment. Another strong album overall, there were no weak cuts. Also noteworthy were *Amoreena* (on which he was assisted by the same musicians as his debut album), *Burn Down The Mission* and *Where To Now St. Peter?*. Surprisingly no 45s were taken from the album, which peaked at No 6 in the UK and No 5 in the US.

The live *17-11-70* (from the November 1970 New York concert) reached No 20 in the UK and No 11 in the US, and the Soundtrack from a Lewis Gilbert youth movie, *Friends*, made No 36 in the US.

ELTON JOHN - Blue Moves (LP).

Early in 1972 he enjoyed a couple of US hits with *Levon* (No 24) and *Tiny Dancer* (No 41), which weren't released here in the UK. Back home his next 45, *Rocket Man*, gave him a massive hit. His next album, the lavish *Madman Across The Water*, sold much better in the US, where it climbed to No 8 as against No 41 here. By this time ex-**Magna Carta** guitarist Davey Johnstone had joined his band, but really the album suffered from his over-exposure and wasn't particularly well received despite containing some doomy melodramatic arrangements.

Honkey Chateau, recorded in France, and his sixth in succession produced by Gus Dudgeon, was the first studio album recorded as an **Elton John** Group. Its direct, jaunty style ensured widespread popularity and it peaked at No 2 in the UK and topped the US Charts, where *Rocket Man* had also become a minor hit peaking at No 86. He embarked on a US tour and his next 45, *Honky Cat*, made it to No 9 there but couldn't quite make the Top 30 here.

A guest appearance in **Marc Bolan**'s movie 'Born To Boogie' and an appearance at the Royal Variety Show on 30 October 1972 continued to bolster his popularity and his next 45, the excellent *Crocodile Rock*, was the sort of song you can't keep your feet still to. It topped the US Charts for three weeks going gold and rose to No 5 in the UK.

Don't Shoot Me, I'm Only The Piano Player was another enormously successful album, topping the Charts here and in the US and **John** was very much at the peak of his popularity. *Daniel* (US No 2, UK No 4) earned him another gold disk and *Saturday Night's Alright For Fighting* (UK No 7, US No 12) wasn't far behind.

The double set, *Goodbye Yellow Brick Road*, was one of his best albums and his second in succession to top the Charts here and in the US. Arranged by Del Newman, it displayed a wide and credible range of musical styles. The title track was issued as a 45, earning him another gold disk in the US, where it spent three weeks at No 2. It peaked at No 6 over here. He ended what had been in every sense an excellent year for him by setting up his own Rocket label, which was initially intended to provide an outlet for other artists.

Bernie Taupin's *Candle In The Wind*, an exquisite song about Marilyn Monroe, gave him another big UK hit in the Spring of 1974. The flip side, *Bennie And The Jets* (a rather repetitive number) was issued as an 'A' side in the US and had the commerciality to reach No 1, becoming a million-seller. The follow-up, *Don't Let The Sun Go Down On Me*, became another US million-seller, peaking at No 2. It rose to No 16 in the UK.

His next album, *Caribou*, was hastily recorded at James William Guerio's studio (the Caribou Ranch) with assistance from The Beach Boys. Despite the fact that, at the peak of his popularity, it topped the Album Charts on both sides of the Atlantic, it is one of his weakest products and is best avoided.

His popularity at this stage of his career, in the States in particular, was enormous. In July 1974 he signed a new $8 million dollar contract with MCA, who were said to have taken out a $25 million dollar insurance policy on his life, making him one of rock's highest paid performers.

The hits continued to flow:- *The Bitch Is Back* (UK No 15, US No 4), a duet with **John Lennon**, *Whatever Gets You Through The Night* (UK No 36, US No 1) and a *Greatest Hits* compilation album, which topped the Album Charts on both sides of the Atlantic, all kept him in the public eye during the Autumn of 1974. His collaboration with **John Lennon** continued to blossom too. They sang *I Saw Her Standing There* together at a Thanksgiving concert on 28 November at New York's Madison Square Garden and his cover of **The Beatles**' *Lucy In The Sky With Diamonds* featured **Lennon** making a guest appearance. Although a pale imitation of the original, it gave him yet another US No 1 and million-seller and just edged into the UK Top 10.

Elton John had several leisure interests aside from his music. In June 1977, he achieved one of his life ambitions to become Chairman of Watford Football Club. Another love of his life was tennis and his next 45 release, *Philadelphia Freedom*, was written for his friend, the tennis player Billie Jean King, after the Philadelphia tennis team, The Freedoms. Arranged by Thom Bell and credited to The **Elton John** Band it gave him another US chart-topping single and climbed to No 12 in the UK. He also appeared in Ken Russell's movie version of **The Who**'s 'Tommy', singing *Pinball Wizzard* and, typically of his extravagant style, wearing giant boots.

His next album, *Captain Fantastic And The Brown Dirt Cowboy* was autobiographical, dealing with his and Taupin's early career. The songs were written on a cruise liner and it became the first album to go straight to No 1 in the US and climbed to No 2 in the UK.

Someone Saved My Life Tonight, a sensitive and moving 45, which partly related his recent unsuccessful suicide attempt, became his first 45 for a while not to top the US Album Charts, but it did reach No 4 and No 22 in the UK. His next single, *Island Girl*, another strong if brasher one, restored him to the top of the US Charts for three weeks and made No 14 in the UK.

His Rock Of The Westies album in retrospect was not one of his best, despite topping the US Album Charts and climbing to No 5 in the UK. So great was his popularity by now that great accolades began to be bestowed on him. Los Angeles declared 21 November 1975 "Elton John Day" as he received a star in Hollywood's Hall Of Fame. Then on 7 March 1976 he became the first rock star since **The Beatles** to have a wax effigy of him in Madame Tussaud's in London. In the interim he'd suffered a rare UK flop with double A-side, *Grow Some Funk Of Your Own/I Feel Like A Bullet (In The Gun Of Robert Ford)*, which could also only make it to No 14 in the US. However, a re-recorded version of *Pinball Wizzard* from the film 'Tommy' soon restored him to the UK Top Ten a couple of months later.

A poor live album, *Here And There* (his last for DJM), hinted at a wane in his fortunes but still got to No 6 in the UK and No 4 in the US, on the strength of his popularity, in May 1976. In fact in June 1976 he achieved his first UK No 1, which he had waited so long for, with *Don't Go Breaking My Heart*, a duet with **Kiki Dee**. It topped the UK Charts for six weeks and the US Charts for four weeks, going gold.

His final album release within the time span of this book, the double set *Blue Moves*, marked a return to his earlier more sensitive romantic style. It was the last on which all the tracks were the product of his collaboration with Taupin and the last to be produced by Dudgeon for a while. Like most double albums it was patchy but it did contain some fine tracks and one of the better, the sensitive ballad, *Sorry Seems To Be The Hardest Word*, climbed to No 6 in the US and No 11 in the UK, when released as a 45, whilst the album peaked at No 3 on both sides of the Atlantic.

The Very Best of Elton John and *Elton John Greatest Hits 1970-2002* are both pretty comprehensive guides to his hits, with the later covering the last decade and a half.

Elton John performed *Candle In The Wind 1997* at Princess Diana's funeral and with the profits donated to her favourite charities it became the fastest-selling hit of all times in both the UK and US, where it entered the charts in both countries at No 1. It was also his biggest ever hit.

Elton John continues to remain a superstar today several hit albums and singles, gold discs and sell-our tours since *Blue Moves*. One of his big strengths has been the range and diversity of his music and his showmanship. He's suffered his 'ups' and 'downs' in recent years and his

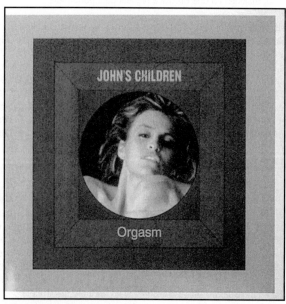

JOHN'S CHILDREN - Orgasm (LP).

JOHN'S CHILDREN - Midsummer's Night Scene (12").

voice may not be what it was but he is without doubt one of the most important singer/songwriters in rock. See the discography at the start of this article for details of the several repackages and compilations of his material.

David Johnstone, a member of Elton's backing band, also recorded albums in his own right, the first of which was *Smiling Face* issued on the Rocket Record Company label (owned by Elton) in 1973 (PIGL 2). He was assisted on this album by Elton himself, **Nigel Olsson**, Dave Henschell, **B.J. Cole** and Dee Murray and it included a version of **Bert Jansch** and **John Renbourn's** *After The Dance* as well as many of self-penned numbers. (VJ)

John's Children

Personnel:	ANDY ELLISON	vcls	ABC
	JOHN HEWLETT	gtr, bs	ABC
	GEOFF McCLELLAND	gtr	A
	CHRIS TOWNSON	drms, gtr	ABC
	MARC BOLAN	gtr, vcls	B
	CHRIS COLVILLE	drms	C

ALBUM: 1(B) ORGASM   (White Whale 7128) 1967 R1
NB: (1) reissued with four 45 tracks as Cherry Red (B RED 31) 1982 and on CD (CDMRED 31) 1988. (1) reissued on vinyl (Get Back GET 510) 2005. There have been a plethora of retrospective collections including: *A Midsummer Night's Scene* (Bam-Caruso KIRI 095) 1987 also issued on CD (Bam-Caruso MARI 095 CD) 1988, which included all their 'A' and 'B' sides plus *Arthur Green; Smashed Blocked* (New Millenium Communications PILOT 12) CD 1997 also issued on vinyl (Get Back 506) 1998 and *Jagged Time Lapse* (New Millenium Communications PILOT 18) CD 1997 also issued on vinyl (Get Back 507) 1998. Also relevant is *Playing With Themselves* (Zinc Alloy Records MLP 9001; album only) 1991 and *Vol. 2* (Zinc Alloy Records ZAR MLP 9002; album only) 1991. *Beyond The Rising Sun* was a vinyl issue comprising a partial reissue of *Orgasm* and a 1984 **Bolan** solo album. *Complete* (Voiceprint VP 465CD) is a recent 2-CD collection.

EP: 1   MIDSUMMERS NIGHT'S SCENE (12")
                  (Bam-Caruso PABL 059) 1988 SC

45s: The Love I'd Thought I'd Found/
       Strange Affair (Some PS)   (Columbia DB 8030) 1966 R4/R3
       Just What You Want, Just What You'll Get/
       But She's Mine   (Columbia DB 8124) 1967 R3
       Desdemona/Remember Thomas
       A' Beckett (Some PS)   (Track 604 003) 1967 R3/R1
   α   Midsummer Night's Scene/
       Sara Crazy Child   (Track 604 005) 1967 R6
       Come And Play With Me In The Garden/
       Sara Crazy Child (Some PS)   (Track 604 005) 1967 R3/R2
       Go Go Girl/Jagged Time Lapse   (Track 604 010) 1967 R1
NB: α withdrawn, but sold in small quantities at the John's Children's Club in Leatherhead, Surrey. Copies now sell for in excess of £3,000.

Simon Napier-Bell, who had earlier managed **The Yardbirds**, marketed this group to cash in on the flower-power era. Indeed, their publicity and personnel attracted more attention than their music. They had started playing in Surrey in 1964, and were earlier known as The Few and The Silence. Under the latter name, they got a residency at the Bluesette, a seedy coffee bar in Leatherhead. Eventually, the group were renamed **John's Children** by Napier-Bell after he saw them playing at a swimming pool dance at Hewlett's invitation.

Napier-Bell was also conscious of the fact that the original line-up (**Ellison**, Hewlett, McClelland and Townson) was very limited in its musical ability. So he travelled to Los Angeles and got some of California's top session musicians to record the backing track to a song he'd written, *Smashed Blocked*, and then added **Andy Ellison**'s vocals and spoken intro until it sounded like a melody. To hide **Ellison**'s own vocal deficiencies, a recording of the Arsenal football crowd was dubbed over the intro as well. It made for a rather unusual 45. Napier-Bell had to overcome an immediate setback when EMI refused to release the song because of its drug-inspired title, so it was changed to *The Love I'd Thought I'd Found* in the UK, although it remained *Smashed Blocked* for live gigs and overseas releases and after considerable hype the US release on White Whale sold well in California and Florida and edged into the national Charts, peaking at No 98. White Whale now wanted the band to record an album. Here in the UK, the single flunked completely.

Napier-Bell decided the best way to satisfy White Whale's expectations was to get the band to record a 'live' album. He put them in the studio and told them to play their 10 best songs as well as they could and then spend a few thousand pounds doctoring the tapes and overdubbing them with screams and shouts from the Soundtrack to the first **Beatles** movie 'A Hard Days Night', which he'd got hold of the tapes of for a few hundreds pounds. The end result was *Orgasm*, which still sounds like one of the worst albums ever recorded. Much of the music on this eminently forgettable item is drowned by screaming girls. The cuts included *Strange Affair*, the strange and unconventional flip side to their debut 45 and one of the very first slices of British psychedelia; *But She's Mine* (which sounded very similar in places to **The Who**'s *I Can't Explain*) and became the flip side to their second 45; and *Jagged Time Lapse*, which was eventually the flip to their final 45. The sleeve, with a girl on the cover, was flyposted across the USA and the album attracted advance orders of 35,000 but a few days before its projected release date in March 1967, a group of moral guardians, The Daughters Of The Revolution, took exception to the record's title and sleeve and plans to release it were shelved! Finally in 1971 White Whale resolved to release it in a new sleeve, blocking out the offending title, but after only a few promotional copies had slipped out they decided not to release it after all. Not until Cherry Red tracked down the original acetates in 1982 was it finally inflicted on the British public. Four additional cuts were added:- live and studio versions of *Smashed Blocked* and *Just What You Want Just What You'll Get*. With the cancellation of the album, an American tour scheduled for May 1967 was also scrapped and the band went to Paris for five weeks where they supported Jamaican reggae artist Jimmy Cliff every night at the Bus Palladium.

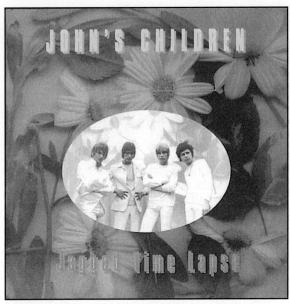

JOHN'S CHILDREN - Jagged Time Lapse (LP).

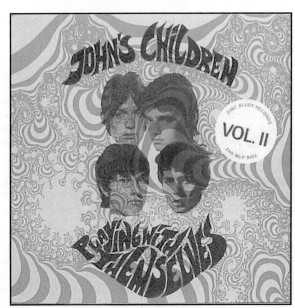

JOHN'S CHILDREN - Playing With Themselves Vol. 2 (LP).

A self-penned composition and a pretty awful one at that, *Just What You Want - Just What You'll Get*, was selected as the group's second 45. The band didn't even play on it, Napier-Bell hired sessionmen to do this. He did let the band play on **Who**-influenced 'B' side, *But She's Mine*, although he decided Geoff McClelland's guitar sound was too bad to be committed to vinyl and overdubbed it with one by **Jeff Beck**. Indeed, McClelland was perceived to be the weak link in the band and was replaced after this 45 by a certain **Marc Bolan**; he'd already recorded a few solo 45s and Napier-Bell had taken him under his wing. Napier-Bell brought him in as the band's backing vocalist and songwriter.

Back in late 1966 the band had bought The Bluesette Club in Leatherhead with the proceeds from their US hit, *Smashed Blocked*, and they renamed it The John's Children Club. It gave the group leverage because they could choose the artists that played there and it also brought them additional publicity. They were also featured in the 14-Hour Technicolour Dream Festival in 1967.

With **Marc Bolan**'s arrival, the band entered a more creative stage. **The Who**'s manager, Kit Lambert, signed them to his new Track label, after EMI had refused to allow them to issue another track from their album, *Not The Sort Of Girl (You'd Take To Bed)*, as a third single. Instead, a **Bolan** composition, *Desdemona*, was released and it is generally considered to be their finest moment. It attracted considerable airplay, although some stations banned it because of the line 'Lift up your skirt and speak'. The disc was later covered by **Marsha Hunt**. The flip side, *Remember Thomas A Beckett*, had been recorded whilst McClelland was still in the band. An interesting song about a guy who went mad and started playing funerals at the bottom of his garden, it was the first pop song of the time to mention flowers in the 'love and peace' type context.

Flowers figured in their next disc, too, *Midsummer Night's Scene*, in the form of a repeated chant of 'petals and flowers' which was superimposed with suitably surreal lyrics. A few promotional copies were pressed but then Track decided they weren't going to release it after all. **Bolan**'s subsequent fame and premature death (it was a **Bolan/Ellison** composition) has ensured that this slice of psychedelia is one of the most collectable items of British rock. **Bolan**, in any event, left the group at this point 'cos he wasn't happy with the band's treatment of the song. As you'll all know, he went on to form **Tyrannosaurus Rex** which later evolved into **T Rex** with whom he finally found fame and fortune.

The band's roadie, Chris Colville, was drafted in as **Bolan**'s replacement, but as he played drums Chris Townson switched to guitar. By now they had surrendered their earlier white suits for an out and out flower-power image and their next single, *Come And Play With Me In The Garden*, was marketed with a poster of the group nude, their modesty protected by flowers. The single was a remix of the 'B' side to *Desdemona* with different lyrics. It was a very poor recording, very muffled but it was an interesting disc and well received by most reviewers, although one complained that it had no real tune and some described the lyrics as inaudible in places. It kept the flip side that had been intended for *Midsummer Night's Scene*, **Bolan**'s *Sara, Crazy Child* - a much clearer recording about a seductive and sensual young woman. It got a lot of airplay on pirate radio (Radio London) but failed to happen.

Their final 45, *Go-Go Girl*, was released after a spell at Hamburg's Star Club, where they'd replaced **The Bee Gees**. The single was supposed to be based around their experiences with the Hamburg go-go girls. On the flip was *Jagged Time Lapse*, from their McClelland days; it had been one of the stronger tracks on their *Orgasm* album. It turned out to be their worst selling single of all. Not long after, the group broke up in 1968 after a furious row between Townson and Hewlett during a tour of the West Country.

In retrospect, the band seem to have been a plaything and challenge for producer Simon Napier-Bell. The challenge was to make it with (aside from **Bolan**) a bunch of extremely mediocre musicians. Whilst he didn't quite ever pull it off some of the tricks he tried say a lot for his ingenuity.

Inevitably *Desdemona* has resurfaced on several compilations:- *The House That Track Built* (LP), *Backtrack 7* (LP), *Rare Tracks* (LP) and *British Psychedelic Trip, Vol. 3* (LP). *Come And Play With Me In The Garden* later re-emerged on *Backtrack 2* (LP) and *Medium Rare* (LP). There have also been a couple of bootleg EPs, *The Smashed Blocked World Of John's Children* (*Go-Go Girl, Jagged Time Lapse, Come And Play With Me In The Garden* and *Sara Crazy Child*); and *Midsummer Night's Scene*, which aside from the title track included *Sara Crazy Child, Go-Go Girl* and *Cornflake Zoo*.

A recommended compilation is *A Midsummer Night's Scene* which contains most of their significant recordings, including the title track (a withdrawn single) and *It's Been A Long Time/Arthur Green*, the last single they recorded with **Andy Ellison** on vocals. Brian Hogg's sleevenotes provide a detailed history of the band. Alternatively, there's a more recent collection of their material *Smashed Blocked*, which includes many of their finest moments and features a classic Spring 1967 BBC session, alternate versions and out-takes. It's also superbly packaged with sleeve-notes by their singer **Andy Ellison**. *Jagged Time Lapse* from the same label is yet another introductory collection of their material, and both are recommended.

Collectors will also be interested in a six-track mini-album, *Playing With Themselves*, which is taken from old tapes and acetates. It includes instrumental versions of *Come And Play With Me In The Garden* and *The Perfumed Garden Of Gulliver Smith*, a different mix of *A Midsummer Night's Scene* and *Not The Sort Of Girl (You'd Take To Bed)*.

Playing With Themselves, Vol. 2 includes different outtakes of *A Midsummer Night's Scene* and *Not The Sort Of Girl (You'd Take To Bed)* from those which appeared on *Vol. 1* as well as different versions of *The Love I Thought I'd Found, Remember Thomas-A-Beckett* and an instrumental version of *Sally Was An Angel*. *Incredible Sound Show Stories, Vol. 2* (LP) also compiles three BBC recordings of *Daddy Rolling Stone, Perfumed Garden of Gulliver Smith* and *Hot Rod Mama*, it also features a short interview with John Hewlett.

JOHN'S CHILDREN - A Midsummer Night's Scene (LP).

Complete is a 2-CD collection, which includes *Hippy Gumbo* and *Mustang Ford*, along with instrumental takes, alternate versions, a few cover versions and BBC sessions. It's accompanied by a booklet detailing their career.

After their demise Hewlett went into management with Sparks and **Jook**, a popular London club band for whom Townson was drummer. When **Jook** split in 1975, Townson formed **Jet** with **Andy Ellison**, who'd recorded several solo singles in the meantime. **Jet** also included Chris White, who'd been due to join **John's Children** just before they'd split.

John's Children reformed in the nineties for sporadic one-off gigs. In 1999 they played the "66-99" event in San Diego, U.S.A., headlining on the 11th June at the Cashbah club - 33 years after they were first due to play America!!

Other compilation appearances include: *Just What You Want, Just What You'll Get* on *Head Sounds From The Bam-Caruso Waxworks, Vol. 1* (CD); *Hippy Gumbo* on *It's Only A Passing Phase* (LP) and *Desdemona* and *A Midsummer's Night Dream* on the 4-CD box set *Nuggets 11*. (VJ)

Johnny and John

Personnel:	JOHN BANKS	drms	A
	JOHNNY GUSTAFSON	bs	A

45:     Bumper To Bumper/Scrape My Boot   (Polydor 56087) 1966 SC

A short-lived duo formed by these two after they left **The Merseybeats**. After the 45, **Gustafson** went solo. He was later in **Quatermass** and **Roxy Music** among others. **Gustafson** had earlier played in a Liverpudlian beat band called **The Big Three** in the early sixties. The 'A' side was a soulish number and the flip was an instrumental. (VJ)

Duncan Johnson

45:     The Big Architect/Memories Of A Boy   (Spark SLR 1022) 1969

Johnson was actually a deejay. He'd been on the pirate ship Radio London and later worked for Radio One. *The Big Architect*, with mainly spoken lyrics, was so bad that it appeared on one of Rhino's *20 Worst Records* (LP) compilations.

The Johnstons

Personnel:	PAUL BRADY	AB
	ADRIENNE JOHNSTON	AB
	GAVIN SPENCER	B

ALBUMS:	1(A)	THE JOHNSTONS	(Transatlantic TRA 169) 1968 SC
	2(A)	GIVE A DAMN	(Transatlantic TRA 184) 1968 SC
	3(A)	THE BARLEYCORN	(Transatlantic TRA 185) 1968 SC
	4(A)	THE TRAVELLING PEOPLE	(Marble Arch MAL 808) 1969
	5(A)	BITTER GREEN	(Transatlantic TRA 211) 1970
	6(A)	THE JOHNSTONS SAMPLER	
			(Transatlantic TRASAM 16) 1970
	7(A)	COLOURS OF THE DAWN	(Transatlantic TRA 231) 1971
	8(B)	IF I SANG MY SONG	(Transatlantic TRA 251) 1972

NB: (8) as The New Johnstons.

45s:	Going Home/Travelling People	(Pye 7N 17144) 1966
	The Alamo/Life Of A Rover	(Pye 7N 17205) 1966
	The Curragh Of Kildare/Leaving London	(Pye 7N 17205) 1967
	I Never Will Marry/Banks Of Claudy	(Pye 7N 17430) 1967
	They'll Never Get Their Man/	
	Dublin Jack Of All Trades	(Transatlantic TRASP 17) 1967
	Both Sides Now/Urge For Going	(Big T BIG 113) 1968
	Give A Damn/	
	Walking Out On Foggy Mornings	(Big T BIG 116) 1968
	My House/The Wherefore And The Why	(Big T BIG 121) 1969
	Streets Of London/The Spanish Lady	(Big T BIG 132) 1970

A prolific folk-rock act, in terms of output anyway. Adrienne Johnston also released a solo album, *Adrienne Johnston Of The Johnstons* (RCA SF 8416) 1975. Gavin Spencer had earlier played with **Paul Kent**.

Compilation appearances include: *I Will Never Marry* and *Banks Of Claudy* on *Footsteps To Fame, Vol. 2* (CD); and *Brightness, She Came* and *Ye Jacobites By Name* on *The Transatlantic Story* CD box set. (VJ/JRy)

Jo Jo Gunne

45s:	Every Story Has An End/	
	Should Live Like That	(Decca F 12807) 1968
	Beggin' You Baby/Bad Penny	(Decca F 12906) 1969

Not to be confused with the better-known American seventies band of this name this was a much more obscure and short-lived British band. A seven-piece it was very much in the mould of **Amen Corner**.

Every Story Has An End was later compiled on *Colour Me Pop, Vol 3* (CD). (VJ)

Joker's Wild

Personnel incl:	DAVID ALTHAM	gtr, sax, keyb'ds	A
	DAVID GILMOUR	gtr	A
	JOHN GORDON	gtr, vcls	A
	TONY SAINTY	bs, vcls	A
	CLIVE WELHAM	drms	A

ALBUM: 1 JOKER'S WILD (Regent Sound RSLP 007) 1966 R6

NB: This was accompanied by a 7" *Don't Ask Me/Why Do Fools Fall In Love* (RSR 0031) 1966 (R5). This has been bootlegged on Eyetorn.

This one-sided 12" mini-album, which involved **Pink Floyd**'s Dave Gilmour is horrendously rare and sought-after. The group came from Cambridge and operated circa 1966/67. Just eleven minutes long, it features cover versions of Chuck Berry's *Beautiful Delilah*, Frank Lyman's *Why Do Fools Fall In Love*, Four Seasons' *Sherry* and *Big Girls Don't Cry* and one self-penned number *Don't Ask Me*. Only 50 copies were pressed and this, plus the presence of Dave Gilmour, in particular, has ensured a four figure valuation.

The band also had a demo-only 45 containing two cuts (*Don't Ask Me* and *Why Do Fools Fall In Love*) produced in similarly limited quantities which was given to family and friends. They attracted the interest of **Jonathan King**, who became their producer and took them into the studio to record a 45 (Sam and Dave's *You Don't Know What Love Is* backed by Otis Redding's *That's How Strong My Love Is*) but when pirate radio started to promote the original Decca shelved the plan.

Wills was later in **Cochise** in the early seventies and was in the reformed **Small Faces** in 1977. Wilson was later in **Quiver** and **The Sutherland Brothers and Quiver**. (VJ)

Jolly Tinkermen

45: Hold On To Me Baby/Shavin' Cream (Page One POF 121) 1969

This short-lived folk band's sole stab for stardom was this one 45. (VJ)

Jon

Personnel incl:	JONATHAN KELLY	vcls	A
	TONY THIERNEY		A
	JIM TOOMEY	drms	A

45s:	So Much For Mary/	
	Polly Sunday (Some PS)	(Parlophone R 5604) 1967 SC/-
	Is It Love/Sing Out	(Columbia DB 8249) 1967 R1

HEAD SOUNDS FROM THE BAM-CARUSO WAXWORKD (Comp CD) including John's Children.

An obscure four-piece group who included **Jonathan Kelly**, who'd previously recorded solo as John Ledingham and then under his own name. Thierney had been with **Lulu** and **The Luvvers** and Toomey went on to co-write a 45 for **Still Life**, **Titus Groan** and then **Colin Blunstone**'s backing group. Later still he was in The Tourists.

The first 45 is straightforward but excellent mid-sixties pop. Some copies came in a rare picture sleeve. The flip side is even better, nicely played and superbly produced. A good example of the genre, *Is It Love* is a hypnotic flower-pop offering and the flip side is a cover of the old spiritual *Sing Halllujah*, which was also recorded as *Sing Out* by **The Remo Four**.

You'll also find *Is It Love?* on *Fading Yellow, Vol 1* (CD) and *Jagged Time Lapse, Vol 1* (CD). (VJ/GB)

Jon and Alun

Personnel:	JON MICHAEL BURCHELL	gtr, vcls	A
	ALUN DAVIES	gtr, vcls	A
	(JUDD PROCTOR	banjo, gtr	A)
	(BIG JIM SULLIVAN	gtr, 12-string	A)
	(ARTHUR WATTS	bs	A)

ALBUM:	1(A)	RELAX YOUR MIND	
		(mono/stereo)	(Decca LK/SKL 4547) 1963 SC

This folk/skiffle duo later worked together in **Sweet Thursday** and the **Mark-Almond** band. **Alun Davies** later became **Cat Stevens**' backing guitarist and also recorded solo. Their album was produced by Shel Talmy. (GBn)

Al Jones

ALBUMS:	1(A)	ALUN ASHWORTH JONES	
			(Parlophone PCS7081) 1969 R2
	2 (B)	JONESVILLE	(Village Thing VTS19) 1973 R2

A leading figure on Bristol's thriving folk and blues scene from 1966 to 1968, **Al Jones** formed an acoustic blues trio with **Ian A. Anderson** and harmonica player Elliott Jackson, then began to focus on his own material. Moving to London, he performed in numerous clubs, where his fluid guitar playing and memorable songs marked him out as a future star. He was signed to Sandy Roberton's September Productions roster, home to **Shelagh McDonald**, **Keith Christmas**, **Steeleye Span** and many others, and got a deal on Parlophone. His debut, recorded in March 1969, was full of good songs but, just as he seemed poised for success, he decided to leave music behind and move to Cornwall. Predictably, the album failed to sell. Sessions for a follow-up were held in 1970, but it never appeared. In

1973 he was coaxed into making an album for **Anderson**'s Village Thing label, but declined to get properly involved again. Instead he focused on starting a business developing pick-ups for acoustic guitars, which went well and kept him connected to music. Guest appearances in the 1990s alongside luminaries such as **Wizz Jones** and **John Renbourn** eased him back into live work, and he started writing songs again, finally putting out a new album, *Swimming Pool* (Weekend Beatnik WEBE 9033) in 1998. (RMJ)

Casey Jones and The Engineers

Personnel:	DAVID COLEMAN	gtr	A
	ROGER COOK	gtr	A
	CASEY JONES (DUNCAN JONES)	vcls	A
	JIM REDFORD	bs	A
	PETE RICHARDS	drms	A
	ERIC CLAPTON	gtr	A

45:     One Way Ticket/I'm Gonna Love   (Columbia DB 7083) 1963 R1

Casey (whose real name is Duncan Jones) had started out playing in Liverpool as early as 1958 fronting Cass and The Casanovas, one of the earliest Merseyside bands who evolved into **The Big Three**, but by then **Casey** had headed for London where he formed The Engineers. **Eric Clapton** was with them only briefly. Tom McGuinness was with them for a couple of weeks too. They were more popular in Germany than here and subsequently **Casey** remained there forming a new outfit, The Governors, who gave old rock'n'rollers the beat treatment. **Casey Jones and The Governers** released several 45s and two albums on Golden 12, in Germany. Of these *Don't Ha Ha* re-emerged on *Pebbles, Vol. 24* (LP) and *Bumble Bee* (sung in German) can be heard on *A Prae-Kraut Pandaemonium, Vol. 2* (LP).

Later in 1968 **Jones** signed to Vogue/Pye, without the Governors. There's also been a CD on the Ruhrgebiet label with material originally released on the Golden 12 label.

Compilation appearances have included: *One Way Ticket* on *Liverpool 1963-1968* (CD) and *Liverpool 1963-1968, Vol. 1* (LP); and *One Way Ticket* and *I'm Gonna Love* on *Mickey Finn And The Blue Men / Jimmy Page - Keep Moving!* (CD). (VJ)

Davie Jones and The King Bees

Personnel:	BOB ALLEN	drms	A
	ROGER BLUCK	ld gtr, banjo	A
	'FRANK' DAVE HOWARD	bs	A
	DAVID JONES (DAVID BOWIE)	vcls	A
	DICK 'GEORGE' UNDERWOOD	gtr, hrmnca	A

45:     Liza Jane/Louie, Louie Go Home (Vocalion Pop V 9221) 1964 R6
NB: Reissued on vinyl (Decca F 13807) 1978.

THE GREAT BRITISH PSYCHEDELIC TRIP VOL. 3 (Comp CD) including Davy Jones and The Lower Third.

This R&B outfit formed in South London in 1963. They were a popular attraction around the R&B clubs of the era but in retrospect are much more significant for including **David Bowie** in their line-up. They also recorded as **The Manish Boys** and **Davy Jones**. In 1965 Jones left and joined **Davy Jones and The Lower Third**.

Both sides of the 45 were very brash, primitive R&B. The flip side is a Paul Revere and The Raiders track. Long established as one of the rarest singles of the sixties, expect to pay well in excess of £1,000 for an original - and beware counterfeits!

Compilation appearances include: *Liza Jane* on *Mod Scene, Vol. 2* (CD) and *Broken Dreams, Vol. 2* (LP); and *Louie Louie Go Home* on *The R&B Scene* (CD). (VJ)

Davy Jones (and The Lower Third)

Personnel:	DAVID JONES (BOWIE)	vcls	A
	PHIL LANCASTER	drms	A
	GRAHAM RIVERS	bs	A
	DENNIS 'T-CUP' TAYLOR	gtr	A

45:     You've Got A Habit Of Leaving/
        Baby Loves That Way   (Parlophone R 5315) 1965 R5
NB: This 45 was reissued in 1979 on EMI (EMI 2925) and Charly (CYM 1) in 1982 in a picture sleeve 10" format. More recently it has been issued on CD (SEACD 1) by See For Miles. On each occasion it has been coupled with two tracks by **The Manish Boys**.

David Jones (later to become **David Bowie**) recorded this brilliant, very mod 45 after fronting **Davie Jones and The King Bees**. It was basically in the beat mould with some good guitar bursts but failed to sell and is now practically impossible to find and consequently horrendously expensive for any **Bowie** collector able to trace a copy to purchase.

Compilation appearances have included: *You've Got A Habit Of Leaving* and *Baby Loves That Way* on *Not Just Beat Music 1965-70* (LP); *You've Got A Habit Of Leaving* on *British Psychedelic Trip, Vol. 2* (LP), *Great British Psychedelic Trip, Vol. 3* (CD) and *In The Beginning* (LP); and *Do Anything You Say* and *Good Morning Girl* on *Footsteps To Fame, Vol. 1* (CD). (VJ)

Davy Jones

| ALBUM: | 1 DAVY JONES | | (Pye NPL 18178) 1967 SC |

45s:	What Are We Going To Do/This Bouquet	(Colpix PX 784) 1965
(up to	It Ain't Me Babe/Baby It's Me (Some PS)	(Pye 7N 17302) 1967
1976)	Theme For A New Love/	
	Dream Girl (Some PS)	(Pye 7N 17380) 1967
	Rainy Jane/Welcome To My Love	(Bell BLL 1163) 1971
Reissue:	Theme For A New Love/	
	Dream Girl	(Pye International 7N 25432) 1967

Yes, this is he, that was later the Brit in The Monkees. Born in Manchester on 30 December 1946, on leaving school he'd became an apprentice jockey before utilising his good looks to launch an acting career, which had seen him play Ena Sharples' grandson Colin in TV soap 'Coronation Street'; appear in the first episode of 'Z Cars' and play The Artful Dodger in the London and New York productions of 'Oliver'. *It Ain't Me Babe* later resurfaced on *The Songs Of Bob Dylan*, a Sequel CD compilation.

He also recorded a 45 with fellow Monkee Mickey Dolenz, *Do It In The Name Of Love/Lady Jane* (Bell BLL 986) 1971, which was released in the UK. (VJ)

Heather Jones

| ALBUMS: | 1 MAE'R OLWYN YN TROI | (Sain SAIN 1008 M) 1974 R2 |
| | 2 JIAWL! | (Sain SAIN 1047 M) 1976 R2 |

EPs:	1 CANEUON HEATHER JONES (PS)	
		(Welsh Teledisc TEP 872) 1968 R3
	2 HEATHER (PS)	(Newyddion Da Recs ND 2) 1970 R3

| | 3 | COLLI IAITH (PS) | (Sain SAIN 20) 1971 R2 |
| | 4 | PAN DDAW'R DYDD (PS) | (Sain SAIN 30) 1972 R2 |

| 45: | Ddoi Di/Fe Ddaw | (Cambrian CSP 704) 197? R3 |

Heather Jones was a solo singer in the folk tradition, but not averse to rocking either. She was also a member of **Meic Stevens'** short-lived subversive folk trio Y Bara Menyn. She possessed a unique and captivating style of singing that distinguished her from many of her contemporaries including **Mary Hopkin**.

After a string of unsuccessful singles on the Cambrian label she struck gold with her rendition of a Harri Webb poem sung accapella *Colli Iaith*. Two excellent folk-rock albums on the Sain label followed plus a stint together with Annie Lennox (later of Eurythmics fame) in Red Brass. She still performs regularly in Wales today.

See the **Meic Stevens** entry for details of her recordings with Y Bara Menyn. (GM)

Janie Jones

| CD: | 1 | WE'RE IN LOVE WITH THE WORLD OF JANIE JONES |
| | | (rpm RPM 177) 1997 |

NB: (1) is a CD compilation of her 45s, which also includes some of The Clash's tributes to her.

			HCP
45s:	Witches Brew/Take-A My Tip	(HMV POP 1495) 1965 SC 46
	Gunning For You/		
	Go Go Away From Me	(HMV POP 1514) 1966 SC -
	Tickle Me Tootsie Wootsies/		
	High And Dry	(Columbia DB 8173) 1967 -
	Charlie Smith/Nobody's Perfect	(Pye 7N 17550) 1968 -
	Girl's Song/		
	I've Never Met A Boy Like You	(Major Minor MM 577) 1968 -
	Back On My Feet Again/Psycho	(President PT 309) 1970 -

Janie Jones was one of the socialites of the late sixties and early seventies. Her Kensington house parties for the pop and political establishment became legendary and then notorious, when in 1973 she was convicted for controlling three prostitutes and attempting to pervert the course of justice - charges which she has always denied. She also had a cabaret act performing at places like the Windmill Theatre and the exclusive Astor Club.

Her debut 45, *Witches Brew*, which was written by her sister (who issued several singles in the mid-sixties under the name Valerie Mitchell), was something of a novelty number with its distinctive bubbling sound and became a minor hit. Her follow-up, *Gunning For You* (also written by Valerie), sold quite well too.

She married John Christian Dee, a violent junkie, who wrote *Don't Bring Me Down* for **The Pretty Things**, *Daddy Was A Baddy* for **Keith West**'s *Teenage Opera* and recorded some songs with **Janie** that remain unreleased, as well as some solo 45s.

Upon her release from prison in 1977 she found she had become a punk heroine immortalised on The Clash's debut album. Later in the early eighties The Clash's Joe Strummer wrote a song for her, *House Of The Ju-Ju Queen*, and paid for it to be recorded with The Clash backing her billed as 'The Lash' for contractual reasons. In 1993 her autobiography 'The Devil And Miss Jones' related her prison friendship with Moors murderess Myra Hindley. Certainly Janie is one of the colourful characters of the British music scene. (VJ)

John Paul Jones

| 45: | Baja/A Foggy Day In Vietnam | (Pye 7N 15637) 1964 R2 |

NB: 'B' side by **Andrew Oldham Orchestra**.

From Kent in South-East England, **John Paul Jones** is best known as the bassist in **Led Zeppelin**. In the early part of the sixties, though, he was

RIPPLES VOL. 5 (Comp CD) featuring John Paul Jones.

quite a prolific songwriter, producer and arranger. He also recorded this instrumental 45, which is now very expensive. It was produced by **Andrew Loog Oldham**, whose orchestra is actually responsible for the B-side. Prior to this recording **Jones** had been the bassist in **The Tony Meehan Group**.

Compilation appearances include: *Baja* on *Ripples, Vol. 5* (CD) and *Watch Your Step* (CD); and *A Foggy Day In Vietnam* and *Baja* on *Footsteps To Fame, Vol. 1* (CD). (VJ)

Kenney Jones

| 45: | Ready Or Not/Woman Trouble | (EM GMS 027) 1974 |

This was a solo effort by **The Small Faces**, **Faces** and **Who** drummer. (VJ)

Nic Jones

ALBUMS:	1	BALLADS AND SONGS	(Trailer LER 2014) 1970 R1
(up to	2	NIC JONES	(Trailer LER 2027) 1971 R1
1976)	3	SONGS OF THE CHANGING WORLD	
		(Trailer LER 2083) 1973

A guitarist and fiddle player, **Nic Jones** was born in Orpington, Kent, on 9 January 1947. *Ballads And Songs* was a promising debut which contained folk standards like *Little Musgrave* and *Sir Patrick Spens*. In addition to the above albums, he backed Maddy Prior and June Tabor on *Silly Sisters* in 1976. He continued to record well-regarded albums in the late seventies, but his career was tragically interrupted by a car crash on 26 February 1982, which left him in a coma for six weeks and hospitalised for a further six months. He then had to re-learn how to play the guitar, but has never been able to resume music fully. (VJ)

Paul Jones

ALBUMS:	1	MY WAY (mono/stereo)	(HMV CLP/CSD 3586) 1966 SC
(up to	2	LOVE ME, LOVE MY FRIENDS	
1976)		(mono/stereo)	(HMV CLP/CSD 3602) 1967 SC
	3	PRIVILEGE (Soundtrack)	(HMV CLP/CSD 3623) 1967 SC
	4	COME INTO MY MUSIC BOX	
		(Columbia SCX 6347) 1969 SC
	5	CRUCIFIX IN A HORSESHOE	
		(Vertigo 6360 059) 1971 R1

NB: (1) reissued by EMI (DORIG 108) 1997. (5) reissued on CD (Repertoire REP 4196-WP) 1994. There are also two smartly packaged reissue CDs, one based around his first album and the other around his second, but each supplemented with bonus tracks taken from singles, EPs and previously unissued material. The two CDs - *The Paul Jones Collection: Volume One: My Way* (RPM RPM 168) 1996 and *The Paul Jones Collection: Volume Two: Love Me, Love My Friends* (RPM RPM

169) 1996 - cover a wide variety of styles from R&B to pop and blues to rock 'n' roll. On the compilation front there's also *Hits And Blues* (One Up 2231) 1980. *The Paul Jones Collection: Vol 3 - Come Into My Music Box* (RPM RPM 183) 1998 is based around (4) with some additional tracks.

| EPs: | 1 | PRIVILEGE | (HMV 7EG 8974) 1967 |
| | 2 | High Time/Thinking Ain't For Me/I've Been A Bad Bad Boy/Aquarius | (EMI EMI 2692) 1977 |

HCP

45s:	High Time/I Can't Hold On	
(up to	Much Longer	(HMV POP 1554) 1966 4
1976)	I've Been A Bad Bad Boy/	
	Sonny Boy Williamson	(HMV POP 1576) 1967 5
	Thinkin' Ain't For Me/	
	Softly (La Vita)	(HMV POP 1602) 1967 32
	Three Sisters/Sons And Lovers	(Columbia DB 8303) 1967 -
	And The Sun Will Shine/	
	The Dog Presides	(Columbia DB 8379) 1968 -
	You Have No Idea/	
	When I Was Six Years Old	(Columbia DB 8417) 1968 -
	Aquarius/Pisces	(Columbia DB 8514) 1968 45
	It's Getting Better/	
	Not Before Time	(Columbia DB 8567) 1969 -
	Life After Death/The Mighty Ship	(Vertigo 6059 053) 1971 -
	After All I Sacrificed/	
	City Summer Night	(Private Stock PVT 25) 1975 -
	Don't Gun Me Down/You Don't Know	(Buk BV 3025) 1975 -
Reissue:	I've Been A Bad Bad Boy/High Time	(HMV POP 2004) 1980 -

NB: **Jones** also recorded a one-sided demo of *Priviledge* on a white HMV label (PSRS 307), which was not officially issued on 45.

Jones' real name was Paul Pond and he was born in Portsmouth on 24 February 1942. He joined **Manfred Mann** in December 1962 but left them on 31 July 1966 to launch a solo career. His first 45, *High Time*, made quite an impression and took him into the Top 5, a feat matched by his follow-up, *I've Been A Bad Bad Boy*.

In May 1967 he starred with Jean Shrimpton in the Peter Watkins' film 'Privilege'. The resulting EP topped the UK EP Charts but couldn't make it into the Singles Chart.

It was all downhill from there. *Thinkin' Ain't For Me* couldn't quite make the UK Top 30 and *Aquarius* (from the musical 'Hair') was his last Top 50 hit. After a few more singles he dropped out of the music business to concentrate on his acting career, appearing in 'Conduct Unbecoming', 'Hamlet' and 'Joseph and The Amazing Technicolour Dream Coat' among others.

Crucifix In A Horseshoe was recorded in the US and released on the collectable Vertigo label. It attempted to re-establish his career. Comprising blues and country material, its highlights included his cover of Loudon Wainwright's *Motel Blues* and *The Mighty Ship*, which was included on a 45, but sank without trace.

Much later in 1979 the teamed up with Tom McGuinness to form The Blues Band and then made a name as a TV and radio presenter. He has also been involved in a re-formed **Manfred Mann** venture.

Compilation appearances have included: *It's Getting Better* on *Sixties Lost And Found, Vol. 1* (LP); *3 Sisters*, *The Sun Will Shine* and *The Dog Resides* on *Top Of The Pops No. 178* (LP) and, more recently on *Jagged Time Lapse, Vol 1* (CD). Finally he can also be heard singing *How Sweet It Is To Be Loved By You* on *Beat Generation - Ready Steady Go* (CD). (VJ)

Ronnie Jones

45s:	My Love/It's All Over	(Decca F 12066) 1965 SC
(up to	Anyone Who Knows What Love Is/	
1976)	Nobody But You	(Decca F 12146) 1965 SC
	Little Bitty Pretty One/Put Your Tears Away	(CBS 2699) 1967 SC
	In My Love Mind/Mama Come On Home	(Polydor 56222) 1967
	Without Love (There Is Nothing)/	
	Little Bitty Pretty One	(CBS 3304) 1968

WIZZ JONES - Right Now (CD).

Jones, like **Jimmy James**, was a black American who emigrated to Britain in the early sixties. The jazzy blues/soul artist first played for **Alexis Korner's Blues Incorporated** and later worked with **Georgie Fame** and **The Wes Minster Five**. He also recorded with The Blue Jays and **The Night-Timers**.

Satisfy My Soul got a further airing on *Ritchie Blackmore - Take It!- Sessions 63 - 68* (CD). (VJ)

Ronnie Jones with The Blue Jays

Personnel:	TONY ALLEN	sax	AB
	TONY BELL	bs	A
	ROGER DEAN	ld gtr	AB
	RONNIE JONES	vcls	AB
	JACK MAVERICK	organ	AB
	CLIVE THACKER	drms	AB
	PAT DONALDSON	bs	B

45: You're Looking Good/I'm So Clean (Parlophone R 5326) 1965 R1

This was **Jones**' backing band for this one 1965 single. Roger Dean recalls:- "Tony Allen was also a vocalist. He had a huge range, and used to sing the screaming girl part in *Night Time Is The Right Time*. I don't think Ronnie was too keen on the competition, so Tony wasn't around for long!! The first bass player, Tony Bell, was also replaced by Pat Donaldson. After PP Arnold joined the band, the rhythmn section split to do the Roy Orbison tour with her, and then split."

Roger Dean had previously played in **John Mayall's Bluesbreakers**. Pat Donaldson, later played in **Fotheringay**. (VJ/RD)

Ronnie Jones (with The Nightimers)

Personnel incl:	SPEEDY McACQUAYE
	HAROLD BECKETT
	MIKE CARR
	MICK EVE
	GEORGIE FAME
	DAVE MORSE

45:	Let's Pin A Rose On You/	
	I Need Your Loving	(Decca F 12012) 1964 SC

NB: *I Need Your Loving* was recorded with The Nightimers.

The Night-Timers also made solo recordings and their line-up changed a lot over the years. Saxophonist Mick Eve had previously played with **Georgie Fame**.

You can also find *I Need Your Loving* on *The Mod Scene* (CD). (VJ)

Wizz Jones

ALBUMS: (up to 1976)
1	WIZZ JONES	(United Artists (S)ULP 1029)	1969	R3
2	THE LEGENDARY ME	(Village Thing VTS 4)	1970	SC
3	RIGHT NOW	(CBS 64809)	1971	R2
4	WHEN I LEAVE BERLIN	(Village Thing VTS 24)	1974	SC

NB: (3) reissued on CD (Columbia 493337-2) 1999.

This influential and highly-rated guitarist was born Raymond Ronald Jones in Croydon, Surrey on 25 April 1939. He started out as a busker journeying around Europe and Africa with the likes of **Clive Palmer, Mick Softley, Ralph McTell** and others. When he returned to the UK in the mid-sixties he formed a bluegrass duo with **Pete Stanley**, recording an album together for Columbia. His solo albums merged folk and blues with Eastern touches, which are especially noticeable on *Right Now*, produced by **John Renbourn**. He went on to front **Lazy Farmer** alongside John Bidwell from **COB**, though their 1975 album appeared only in Germany.

In the late seventies and for most of the eighties, **Jones** played the festival and club circuit. He barely recorded himself, although he did appear on other artists' records. In the nineties there was renewed interest in his work. *The Village Thing Tapes* compiled his seventies material and *Dazzling Stranger* (1995) was a newly recorded compilation of his earlier music for the Scenes Of label. A well-regarded Milton Keynes performance has been captured on his *Through The Fingers* album and another Scenes Of release 2001's *Lucky The Man* included an array of guests including **John Renbourn, Jacqui McShee** and **Clive Palmer**. **Jones** still plays and records today.

You can also check out *One Grain Of Sand* on *Electric Psychedelic Sitar Headswirlers Vol. 4* (CD). (VJ)

Jonesy

Personnel:
PHIL CLARKE		A
JOHN EVAN JONES	gtr, vcls	ABC
JAMIE KALETH	keyb'ds, vcls	ABC
DAVID PAULL	bs, vcls	A
JIM PAYNE	drms	A
ALAN BOWN	trumpet, perc	BC
GYPSY JONES	gtr, vcls	BC
PLUG THOMAS	drms, vcls	BC
KEN ELLIOT	synth	C
BERNIE HAGLEY	sax	C
MORRIS PERT	perc	C

ALBUMS:
1(A)	NO ALTERNATIVE	(Dawn DNLS 3042)	1972	SC
2(B)	KEEPING UP	(Dawn DNLS 3048)	1973	SC
3(C)	GROWING	(Dawn DNLS 3055)	1973	SC

JONESY - Keeping Up... (LP).

NB: (1) reissued on CD (Progressive Line PL 557) with three bonus tracks. (2) reissued on vinyl (Get Back GET 582) and again on CD (Progressive Line PL 556) with three bonus tracks. (3) reissued on CD (Si Wan SRMC 1032) in Korea. Also relevant is *Sudden Progress Makes God Jump* (Night Wing NWRCD 01/NWRLP 01), a previously unreleased fourth album.

45:	Ricochet/Every Day's The Same	(Dawn DNS 1030)	1972

A progressive rock outfit whose albums were reputedly delicate, melodic affairs, somewhat similar to **King Crimson** and with a lot of mellotrons. *Ricochet*, their 45, was taken from the album *No Alternative* and was also included on the compilation *Has It Dawned On You?* (LP). It's a good melodic hard-rock number with keyboards, wah wah guitar and a circus music style finale.

Their *Keeping Up* album is basically of the progressive genre and in parts includes diverse ingredients; violins, harpsichord, harmony vocals and trumpet solos. Of its tracks *Duet* is more jazz/avant-gardish with strong vocals upon a minimal backing, trumpet á la Miles Davies and guitar improvisations. *Song* is a mellow, string-dominated number with a fine melody. The last track, *Children*, is probably the best. It's a good structured, progressive piece with strong vocals, brass, strings, viola and keyboards.

Growing was the final offering from the band at the time. It's a fusion of progressive and jazz-rock with lots of mellotrons, electric trumpets, saxes and flugelhorns spread over a few lengthy tracks. It has had a CD reissue on the Korean Si Wan label.

Sudden Prayers Make God Jump is a previously unreleased fourth album, now available in vinyl and CD format. A concept album, it deals with a guy who has had a mental breakdown and the stages and experiences he goes through in a mental hospital from the side-effects of the drugs he is treated with.

Alan Bown earlier had his own band and Morris Pert later made some solo albums. (VJ)

Jon-Mark

45s:
Baby I Got A Long Way To Go/ Night Comes Down	(Brunswick 05929)	1965
Paris Bells/Little Town Girl	(Brunswick 05052)	1966
All Neat In Black Stockings/Run To Me	(Philips BF 1772)	1969

This solo artist also wrote songs for **Marianne Faithfull**. Indeed, she also recorded *Paris Bells*, his second 45. *Night Comes Down* was written by Shel Talmy and also recorded by **Mickey Finn**. The first two beat - folk 45s were produced by Shel Talmy. **Jon-Mark** did guitar session work for **John Mayall**, among others, in the late sixties / early seventies. (VJ)

The Jonston McPhilbry

45:	She's Gone/Woke Up At Eight	(Fontana TF 663) 1966	R2

This Torquay band's 45 is pretty manic R&B. The wild 'B' side was penned by Phil Minton who presumably was in the band. This great record has become very collectable now. (MWh)

Jook

Personnel:
IAN HAMPTON	bs, vcls	A
RALPH KIMMETT	vcls	A
CHRIS TOWNSON	drms	A
TREVOR WHITE	gtr, vcls	A

EP:
1	Watch Your Step/La La Girl/Aggravation Place/ Everything I Do	(Chiswick SW 30) 1978

45s:
Alright With Me/Do What You Can	(RCA RCA 2279) 1972
Shame/City And Suburban Blues	(RCA RCA 2344) 1973
Oo Oo Rudi/Jook's On You	(RCA RCA 2368) 1973
King Capp/Rumble	(RCA RCA 2431) 1973
Bish Bash Bosh/Crazy Kids	(RCA RCA 5024) 1974

This was a sort of seventies mod band which operated from Autumn 1971 to Spring 1974. They never made an album at the time although Chiswick put out the retrospective *Watch Your Step* (Chiswick SW 30) in the late seventies. Upon their demise, Hampton and White joined Sparks and Townson (who'd earlier been in **John's Children**) helped form **Jet**. A recent CD release of their material *Different Class* may interest readers. (VJ)

Joyce's Angels

45:	Flowers For My Friend/Rodney Reginald		
	Smithfield Harvey Jones	(Major Minor MM 526) 1967	

The 'A' side of this 45 is a high-pitched flower-power number. (VJ)

The Joy Strings

Personnel incl:	SYLVIA CARR	vcls	A
	PETER DALZIEL	bs	A
	BILL DAVIDSON	lead gtr	A
	WYNCLIFFE NOBLE	drms	A
	CAPTAIN JOY WEBB	organ	A

ALBUMS:	1	WELL SEASONED		
		(Regal Zonophone LRZ/SLRZ 4016) 1966 SC		
	2	CAROLS AROUND THE WORLD		
		(Regal Zonophone LRZ/SLRZ 4018) 1967 SC		

EPs:	1	THE JOY STRINGS	(Regal Zonophone ERZ 8255) 1964
	2	THE SONG BOOK	(Regal Zonophone ERZ 8264) 1964

HCP

45s:	It's An Open Secret/We're Going To		
	Set The World	(Regal Zonophone RZ 501) 1964	32
	Million Songs/Joshua	(Regal Zonophone RZ 503) 1964	-
	A Starry Night/Now I Know	(Regal Zonophone RZ 504) 1964	35
	He Cares/All Alone	(Regal Zonophone RZ 505) 1965	-
	Only You/You're Welcome	(Regal Zonophone RZ 506) 1965	-
	Christmas Can Be Every Day For You/We Three		
	Kings Of Orient Are	(Regal Zonophone RZ 507) 1965	-

This was a Salvation Army beat group which took most pundits by surprise when *It's An Open Secret* and *Starry Night* sold enough copies to become minor hits. Thereafter the band seemed to concentrate on the Christmas market. Spurred on by their success Salvation Army beat groups sprang up all over the place for a while, but it proved to be a short-lived phenomenon as none of the others made any impact nationally. (VJ/AD)

Joy Unlimited

ALBUM:	1	TURBULENCE	(Page One POLS 028) 1970 R2

45s:	Daytime Night Time/	
	Mister Pseudonym	(Page One POF 147) 1969
	Oh Darlin'/Feeling	(Page One POF 160) 1969

The *Turbulence* album is now collectable and *Mr Pseudonym* has been compiled on *We Can Fly, Vol 2* (CD). (VJ)

Juan and Junior

45s:	The Chase/Nothing	(CBS 2949) 1967
	To Girls/Andurina	(CBS 3223) 1968 SC

This pop duo's orchestrated ballad, *To Girls*, can also be heard on *Circus Days Vol's 4 & 5* (CD) and *Circus Days, Vol. 4* (LP), whilst *Andurina* has resurfaced on *Fading Yellow, Vol 1* (CD). (VJ)

Judas Jump

Personnel:	ANDY BOWN	keyb'ds, gtr	A
	CHARLIE HARRISON	bs	A
	ALAN JONES	woodwind	A
	HENRY SPINETTI	drms	A
	ADRIAN WILLIAMS	vcls	A
	TREVOR WILLIAMS	gtr	A

ALBUM:	1(A)	SCORCH	(Parlophone PAS 1001) 1970 SC

NB: (1) also issued on Pride (0003) in the US in 1972.

45s:	Run For Your Life/	
	Beer Drinking Woman	(Parlophone R 5828) 1969
	This Feelin' We Feel/	
	Hangman's Playing	(Parlophone R 5838) 1969
	Beer Drinking Woman/	
	I Have The Right	(Parlophone R 5873) 1970

Something of a 'supergroup' since Jones came from **Amen Corner** and **Bown** and Spinetti from **The Herd**. Like most 'supergroups' they manifestly failed to live up to all the hype and only lasted for a couple of years. Their album was basically heavy progressive rock with lots of guitar, flute, sax and mellotrons.

Bown later joined **Storyteller** before embarking on a solo career. He later joined **Status Quo**. Spinetti went into session work although he was later in several other bands. (VJ)

Judas Priest

Personnel:	ALAN ATKINS	vcls	ABC
	K.K. DOWNING	gtr	ABCDEF
	JOHN ELLIS	drms	A
	IAN HILL	bs	ABCDEF
	ALAN MOORE	drms	B F
	CHRIS CAMPBELL	drms	C
	ROB HALFORD	vcls	DEF
	JOHN HINCH	drms	DE
	GLENN TIPTON	gtr	EF

ALBUMS:	1(E)	ROCKA ROLLA	(Gull GULP 1005) 1974 SC
(up to	2(F)	SAD WINGS OF DESTINY	(Gull PGULP 1015) 1976
1976)			

NB: (1) reissued on CD (Snapper SDPCD 124) remastered in a digipak with a 12-page booklet. (2) reissued on CD (Repertoire REP 4552 WY) 1995 and again on CD (Snapper SDPCD 120) remastered in a digipak with a 12-page booklet. *Metology* (Sony Music/Legacy) 2004 is a 4-CD box set.

45s:	Rocka-Rolla/Never Satisfied	(Gull GULS 6) 1974
(up to	The Ripper/Island Of Domination	(Gull GULS 31) 1976
1976)		

Judas Priest spearheaded a new wave of heavy metal bands in the late seventies and was one of the most influential bands of this genre between

JUICY LUCY - Get A Whiff Of This (LP).

1975 and 1985. Deploying two lead guitarists they also laid the foundations for the speed and death metal of the eighties.

Judas Priest was formed in Birmingham in 1970 by K.K. Downing and his friend Ian Hill. The early years were a struggle with much of their time spent 'on the road' and during this period they underwent several line-up changes. Gradually they built up a steady following and, after touring Germany and Holland in 1974 (their first tour abroad), they were signed to the small Gull label. Prior to the recording of *Rocka Rolla* Glenn Tipton, a second guitarist was added to flesh out their sound and make them into a five-piece. The resulting album was a disappointment to the band and their fans alike. An appearance at the Reading Festival in 1975 boosted their waning popularity and, with Moore having returned to the fold to replace Hinch, their second album was a big improvement and was greeted with good reviews. As we leave the time span of this book the band were on the verge of signing a worldwide contract with CBS which would see them go on to become one of the top heavy metal acts... but that's another story.

Metology is a 4-CD 65-track set housed in a metal-studded leather-trim box with a colour booklet, containing a discography, biography and rare photos. The first CD contains recordings from the time span of this book. The package is also available in a limited run with a bonus live DVD video.

They are still going strong today. The leather clad heavy metal legends embarked on a world tour in 2004 and released a new album *Angel Of Retribution* in 2005.

Compilation appearances include *United* on *Axe Attack Vol 2* (CD); *Breaking The Law* on the 2-CD sets *Greatest Rock*, *Rock Resurrection* and *The Best Heavy Metal Album In The World?Ever!*, whilst *Decapitate* resurfaced on *The Best Of Heavy Metal* (CD); and *Take On The World* can be found on the 2-CD set *Good Times - Best Of 70's*. (VJ)

Judd

Personnel:	MADELINE BELL	vcls	A
	ROGER FLAVELL	bs	A
	SUE GLOVER	vcls	A
	SUNNY LESLIE	vcls	A
	ROGER McKEW	gtr	A
	TAT MEAGER	drms	A
	DORIS TROY	vcls	A
	MARK P. WIRTZ	keyb'ds	A

ALBUM: 1(A) JUDD (Penny Farthing PEL 504) 1970 R1

45: Snarlin' Mama Lion/
Stronger Than A Man (Penny Farthing PEN 709) 1970

Mark Wirtz arranged and produced this album which was a mixture of soul and rhythm and blues. Doris Troy was a R&B singer and **Madeline Bell** was a solo artist, also in **Blue Mink** and **Seven Ages Of Man**.

The album included a version of Wilbert Harrison's *Let's Work Together*. (VJ)

Jude

The *Morgan Blue Town* (LP) and *Best And The Rest Of British Psychedelia* (CD) compilations include a previously unreleased song, *Morning Morgan Town*, by this artist whose real name was Judy Willey. Basically it's an unexceptional pop ballad. (VJ)

Jug Trust

Personnel:	BRIAN COOKMAN		AB
	TONY KNIGHT		AB
	JOHN REED		AB
	CHAS JOHNSON		B

45: Goodbye Train/Cat And Mouse (Parlophone R 5825) 1970

JUICY LUCY - Pieces (CD).

Setting out as a trio they worked the folk circuit and cut one 45 *Goodbye Train*, but it made no impact. They later added Chas Johnson to their line-up and changed their name circa September 1970 to **Bronx Cheer**. (VJ)

Juice

Personnel:	BRIAN 'BIZ' BINSTED	lead gtr	A
	EDDIE CRONEY	drms	A
	STEVE DAVIS	bs	A
	DAVE HOLDER	gtr	A
	BRIAN LEWIS	lead vcls	A

45: Not Enough Words/Girl (Amity) 1970

This group was a later incarnation of **The Millionaires**. *Circus Days, Vol. 5* (LP) and *Circus Days, Vol. 6* (CD) include a previously unreleased and potentially very commercial track, *The Elastic Band*. It's got strong vocals and a good beat but sadly wasn't released at the time.

Steve Davis recalls:- "The *Elastic Band* was a Demo recorded at 'Orange Studios' which was in the basement of former **Millionaire** vocalist Cliff Cooper's Orange Music Shop in Old Compton Street, London around 1969. The song was written by Robbie Fair, the lead vocalist for **Consortium**. **Juice** had another single release in 1970, *Not Enough Words*. (VJ/SD)

Juicy Lucy

Personnel:	LOUGHTY AMAO	perc	A
	GLENN CAMPBELL	gtr, vcls	ABC
	PETE DOBSON	drms	A
	KEITH ELLIS	bs	AB
	NEIL HUBBARD	gtr	A
	CHRIS MERCER	sax, keyb'ds	ABC
	RAY OWEN	vcls	A
	ROD COMBES	drms	BC
	MICK MOODY	gtr	BCD
	PAUL WILLIAMS	vcls, keyb'ds, perc	BCD
	JIM LEVERTON	bs	C
	RON BERG	drms	D
	ANDY PYLE	bs	D
	JEAN ROUSSEL	keyb'ds	D

			HCP
ALBUMS: 1(A)	JUICY LUCY	(Vertigo VO 2) 1969 R1 41	
2(B)	LIE BACK AND ENJOY IT		
		(Vertigo 636 014) 1970 R1 53	
3(C)	GET A WHIFF OF THIS	(Bronze ILPS 9157) 1971 SC -	
4(D)	PIECES	(Polydor 2310 160) 1972 -	

HCP

45s:	Who Do You Love?/		
	Walking Down The Highway	(Vertigo V1) 1970	14
	Pretty Woman/I'm A Thief	(Vertigo 6059 015) 1970 SC	44
	It Ain't Easy/Promised Land	(Polydor 200 1279) 1972	-
Reissue:	Who Do You Love?/		
	Chicago North Western (PS)	(Bronze BRO 72) 1979	-

Steel guitarist, Glenn Fernando Campbell, was the star behind this band. He'd joined them from **The Misunderstood**. Neil Hubbard has been in **Bluesology** and played with **Graham Bond**. Saxophonist Chris Mercer had played with **John Mayall**. Their vinyl zenith is usually considered to be their first album which contained a number of tight, well constructed songs, including a fine cover of Bo Diddley's *Who Do You Love?*, which also took them into the 45 charts. It came on the now highly collectable spiral Vertigo label in an attractive gatefold sleeve. **Ray Owen** departed to form his own band Moon after this and Neil Hubbard had joined **The Grease Band**.

Paul Williams, ex-**Zoot Money**, came in replacing **Ray Owen** on vocals on the second album, along with ex-**Tramline** guitarist Micky Moody and drummer Rod Coombes. The resulting album *Lie Back And Enjoy It* came with a six-fold poster sleeve. Highlights included a fine cover of Frank Zappa's *Willy The Pimp*, *Changes* and it spawned a strong single *Pretty Woman* (not the Roy Orbison song).

Get A Whiff Of This was a disappointing effort and none of the original line-up survived for their fourth and final effort, *Pieces*. The line-up for this included Andy Pyle, whilst he took a brief break from **Savoy Brown**. The final verdict must be that they failed to achieve their early promise.

Mickey Moody went on to **Snafu**. He worked with **Graham Bonnet**, David Coverdale and **Roger Chapman** amongst others. After 1976 he recorded an album with Bob Young entitled Young and Moody. In the nineties he made two blues albums under the band title Moody. Rod Coombes drummed with **The Strawbs**, **Trifle**, **Ro Ro**, **Stealers Wheel**, **Paul Brett**, **John Entwistle**, **Roy Young** and **Roger Morris**.

Neil Hubbard also played with **Wynder K. Frog**, **Grease Band**, **Kokomo**, **Miller Anderson**, **Henry McCullough** and **Pete Wingfield**. More recently he has worked with **Roxy Music**. Keith Ellis was in **The Koobas**, **Boxer**, **Van Der Graaf Generator** and played on some **Paul Williams** albums. Chris Mercer became a very popular session musician. He also played with **Hemlock**, Gonzales, **Coast Road Drive**, **Locomotive** and **Stretch** and he featured on albums by **Russ Ballard**, Mike Storey, **Paul Brett** and **Joe Jammer**. Keith Ellis died in 1978 while on tour in Germany with Iron

JULIAN'S TREATMENT - A Time Before This (2-LP).

JULY - Dandelion Seeds (LP).

Butterfly. Peter Hammill wrote a book 'Not For Keith' about his life. Glenn Fernando Campbell later reformed **The Misunderstood**. **Ray Owen** now lives in Crawley where we're told he is quite a character around town. **Juicy Lucy** reformed in 2004.

The Sequel compilation also includes a couple of previously unissued tracks, *I'm A Thief* and *Changed My Mind, Changed My Sign*.

The *Vertigo Annual 1970* (2-LP) included their own composition *Mississippi Woman*; *Voodoo Chile* has been compiled on *Classic Rock* (CD) *and Who Do You Love?* can also be found on the 3-CD set *Full Throttle - 60 Original Driving Classics*, *Hits Of The 70's Vol 2* (CD) and on the 3-CD set *Ars Longa Vita Brevis: A Compendium Of Progressive Rock 1967-1974*. (VJ/BS)

The Julian Kirsch

45:	Clever Little Man/		
	Adventures Of A Young Cuckoo	(Columbia DB 8541) 1969 SC

This was another of those countless forgotten sixties 45s. *Clever Little Man* later resurfaced on *Justavibration* (LP). (MWh)

Julian's Treatment

Personnel:	JOHN DOVER	bs	A
	JACK DRUMMOND	drms	A
	JULIAN JAY SAVARIN	keyb'ds	A
	CATHY PRUDEN	vcls	A
	DEL WATKINS	gtr, flute	A

ALBUM: 1(A) A TIME BEFORE THIS (2-LP)

(Youngblood SYB 2) 1970 R3

NB: (1) issued by Decca in the US. Reissued on vinyl (See For Miles SEELP 288) 1990, also on CD (SEECD 288). (1) reissued again (Akarma 192) in both CD and vinyl formats.

45:	Phantom City/Alda Dark Lady Of		
	The Outer Worlds	(Youngblood YB 1009) 1972 SC

Julian Jay Savarin wrote and directed this rare concept album, which is one for connoisseurs of progressive rock. It's full of dramatic keyboard playing and equally dramatic semi-spoken vocals from Cathy Pruden. Side one commences with the spoken *First Oracle*, which is followed by *The Coming Of The Mule*, an organ-led piece of progressive rock which is quite cosmic in places, with appealing vocals from Pruden. *Phantom City* is again keyboard-dominated but quite jazzy. *The Black Tower* is the weak link and previews the mediocre music which plagues much of side two. Pruden's melodramatic vocals introduce *Alda, Park Lady Of The Outer Worlds* and the side's final cut, *Altarra, Princess Of The Blue Women*, features some delightful, melodic vocals from Pruden rather in the style of US band The United States Of America. Side two begins with another spoken oracle but is weaker than the first side save for the album's finale and highpoint - the title cut which starts with some haunting keyboards and features more vocal melodramas from Pruden.

Savarin was born in Dominica and moved to Britain along with his family in 1962. Cathy Pruden was an Australian resident. A noted poet and writer, he also made a solo album, *Waiters On The Dance*. (VJ)

July

Personnel:
TONY DUHIG	gtr		A
JOHN FIELD	flute, keyb'ds		A
CHRIS JACKSON	drms		A
ALAN JAMES	bs		A
TOM NEWMAN	vcls		A

ALBUM: 1(A) JULY   (Major Minor MMLP/SMLP 29) 1968 R5

NB: (1) also issued in USA/Canada on Epic (BN-26416) and in Brazil (Musidisc Hi Fi 2.177). (1) reissued on vinyl (Essex 1011LP) 1997 (SC) with their second 45 as a bonus and on CD in original sleeve (Aftermath AFT 1004) 199? and by Acme on vinyl in the original sleeve, with the 45 cuts as a freebie bonus 45. Also of interest is *Dandelion Seeds* (Bam-Caruso KIRI 097) 1987 (SC), a reissue of their album with extra tracks and a different sleeve; and *The Second Of July* (Essex 1015) 1996 (LP) / (Essex 1008CD) 1995 (CD), which consists of all their previously unissued recordings from 1967.

45s:
My Clown/Dandelion Seeds	(Major Minor MM 568) 1968 R3
Hello, Who's There/The Way	(Major Minor MM 580) 1968 R2

They started out as a skiffle act from Ealing, called The Playboys and then became a R&B combo **The Tomcats**. **John (Speedy) Keen** was in them for a while. In 1966, **The Tomcats** went to Spain with a new line-up (the future **July** one). As Los Tomcats, they got in the Charts with four EPs, one of which was all in Spanish! They returned to the UK in 1968, still basing themselves in Ealing.

July recorded what has become one of the most sought-after British psychedelic sixties albums. 37 years on time has not been kind to all the tracks (e.g. *Jolly Mary*) but overall it's well worth purchasing for its eerie brand of psychedelia (on *Dandelion Seeds* and *My Clown*) and some fine psychedelic guitar work (*Crying Is For Writers*). More accessible are the Bam-Caruso reissue, which was put out in a different sleeve, and the Aftermath CD reissue. Both also include the second 45, which wasn't on the first album.

Duhig and Field went on to be in **Jade Warrior** and **Tom Newman** later released solo albums on Virgin and Decca. He also set up Branson's Manor Studios and engineered *Tubular Bells I* and *II*. Duhig was also later in Assagai. Alan James went on to play for **Cat Stevens**, **Duffy Power**, **Neil Innes** and **Kevin Coyne**. They were managed by **Spencer Davis**.

JULY - July (CD).

JUMBLE LANE - Jumble Lane (CD).

Compilation appearances have included: *Friendly Man* and *My Clown* on *Psychedelic Dream* (LP); *Friendly Man* and *I See* on *British Psychedelic Trip, Vol. 2* (LP) and *Great British Psychedelic Trip, Vol. 3* (CD); *My Clown* on *It's Only A Passing Phase* (LP); and *The Way* on *Electric Psychedelic Sitar Headswirlers, Vol. 1* (CD) and on the 4-CD box set *Acid Drops, Spacedust & Flying Saucers*. (VJ/AGo/ML)

Jumble Lane

ALBUM: 1 JUMBLE LANE   (Holyground HG 115) 1971 R5

NB: (1) reissued on CD (Background HBG 123/3).

Another of these ultra-rare privately-pressed albums, this was one of the rarest released on the Wakefield-based Holyground label but was recorded by a local college band. Only 99 copies were pressed and according to 'Record Collector', it begins with a couple of dull folk instrumentals before going through some wholly unexpected and bizarre changes; long before the end it becomes completely uncategorisable! (VJ)

Jumbo

Personnel incl:
BOB BENHAM	A
BILLY MAUDER	A

45s:
She Said/Wasting My Time	(CBS 7820) 1972
Round And Round/Sewing Circle	(Epic EPC 8057) 1972

This young band from Wales was, for a while, also known as Angelique. The four-piece was managed by **Tremeloes'** 'Chip' Hawkes and Alan Blakely. Bob Benham left them in December 1972 to join **The Tremeloes**. His replacement was Billy Mauder. They finally split up in February 1973, but **The Tremeloes** had them under their wing for two years. (VJ)

Junco Partners

Personnel:
CHARLIE HARCOURT	gtr	A
BOB SARGEANT	keyb'ds, vcls	A
DAVE SPROAT	bs	A
JOHN WOODS	drms	A

ALBUM: 1(A) JUNCO PARTNERS   (Philips 6308 032) 1970 R1

NB: (1) also issued in Europe on Barclay. There is also a live reunion CD *Almost Live- Full Steam R&B* ( ) 1996.

45: (up to 1976)
As Long As I Have You/ Take This Hammer	(Columbia DB 7665) 1965 R2

This progressive hard-rock outfit from Newcastle was most notable for including Bob Sargeant, who later played in several other outfits, including **The Mick Abrahams Band** and **Everyone**. Their album is reputedly very powerful and enjoyable. It's also rare and elusive but not as rare and sought-after as the 45 they recorded five years earlier for Columbia. At that time they were a mod band.

They've reformed several times and still gig today around Tyneside, but there's been no other recorded output. Charlie Harcourt was later in **Jackson Heights** and **Lindisfarne**. Bob Sargeant later went on to production work.

Take This Hammer later resurfaced on *Pebbles, Vol. 6 - The Roots Of Mod* (LP) and *English Freakbeat Vol. 6* (CD). (VJ)

Junction 32

ALBUM: 1 JUNCTION 32 (Holyground HGS 119) 1975 R5

Another horrendously rare privately-pressed album, indeed this was the rarest release from the Wakefield-based Holyground label. Like **Jumble Lane** this did not feature the label's house musicians, it was a case of a band using the label's studios and pressing facilities. Just 99 copies were pressed and according to 'Record Collector', it's a mixture of folk and jugband music. (VJ)

Juniors

Personnel:	MALCOLM COLLINS	vcls	A
	BRIAN GLASS (BRIAN GLASSCOCK)	drms	A
	JOHN GLASS (JOHN GLASSCOCK)	bs	A
	ALAN SHACKLOCK	lead gtr	A
	MICK TAYLOR	gtr	A

45: There's A Pretty Girl/Pocket Size (Columbia DB 7339) 1964 R1

An obscure mid-sixties beat group from Hatfield in Hertfordshire. All teenagers, they featured a 15-year old Mick Taylor, who went on to fame and fortune with **John Mayall** and **The Rolling Stones**. Alan Shacklock, who was just 14 at the time, was later with **Chris Farlowe**'s backing group and **Babe Ruth**, whilst Brian and John Glass' were later with **The Gods** and **Toe-Fat** amongst others.

There's A Pretty Girl and *Pocket Size* can both be heard on *Made In England, Vol. 2* (CD). (VJ/MD)

Junior's Eyes

Personnel:	STEVE CHAPMAN	drms	AB
	TIM RENWICK	gtr	ABC
	MICK WAYNE	gtr, vcls	ABC
	JOHN CAMBRIDGE	drms	BC
	GROM KELLY	vcls	BC
	JOHN REDFERN	organ	BC

ALBUM: 1(B) BATTERSEA POWER STATION
(Regal Zonophone SLRZ 1008) 1969 R1

NB: (1) reissued on CD (Worldwide Records SPM-WWR-CD-0025) 1991 and again on CD (Essential ESMCD 896) 2000 remastered and expanded.

45s: Mister Golden Trumpet Player/
Black Snake (Regal Zonophone RZ 3009) 1969 SC
α Woman Love/Circus Days (Regal Zonophone RZ 3018) 1969 SC
Star Child/Sink Or Swim (Regal Zonophone RZ 3023) 1969 SC

NB: α originally issued with a different 'B' side *White Light Part 2* (Regal Zonophone RZ 3018) 1969 but then withdrawn.

A rather short-lived heavy rock band, whose members backed **David Bowie** on his first album. Their album, which features some fine guitar work from Mick Wayne, is well worth hearing. They sound like they're enjoying themselves on this collection of imaginative songs with plenty of weirdness. Side one is the sidelong suite *Battersea Power Station*, actually more an unbanded collection of songs, that evokes a great amount of different

atmospheres and yet manages to sound quite coherent. Great guitar work is to be found on *Imagination*. Side two consists of four tracks, all with an interesting bend to them. Listen to the lyrics of the **Tyrannosaurus Rex** soundalike *I'm Drowning* and the musical diversity of *White Light*. Undoubtedly this comes recommended.

Wayne, who'd earlier been with **The Hullaballoos**, **The Bunch Of Fives** and **The Tickle** went on to **The Pink Fairies** briefly. Renwick was later in **Quiver** and then The Sutherland Brothers and Quiver, whilst John Cambridge went on to drum for **Dib Cochrane and The Earwigs**. Mick Wayne died in the USA in 1994.

An underrated band who deserve more credit. The CD reissue on Essential of their album has been expanded to include lots of outtakes and bonus tracks, including both sides of **The Tickle** single. The package includes a fold-out booklet with lots of liner notes.

Compilation appearances include: *Circus Days* on *Magic Spectacles* (CD); and *The Black Snake* on *Psychedelia, Vol. 1* (LP), *Visions Of The Past, Vol. 2* (CD) and *Hen's Teeth Vol. 1* (CD). (VJ/MWh)

Juniper Green

45: Dreams In The Sky/
Cascade Of Ice (Columbia DB 8809) 1971 SC

A one-off 45, this could be the sole UK release by a Scandinavian progressive outfit. (VJ)

The Just Four Men

Personnel:	LAWRENCE ARENDES	drms	ABCDEFG H
	HARRY J. BEAR	bs	AB
	DIMITRIOUS CHRISTOPHOLOS	vcls, gtr	ABCDEFG H
	PETER TURNER	gtr	ABCD
	JOHNNY KELMAN	lead gtr	BC EFGH I J
	LALLY STOTT	lead gtr	D
	KEITH SHEPHERD	bs	E
	BARRIE ASHALL	bs	FG H
	FRANK RENSHAW	lead gtr	H
	ARTHUR DAVIES	drms	I J
	FRANK GARLAND	gtr	I
	MAL HOYLAND	bs	I
	PETE HACKETT	vcls	J
	COLIN OWEN	bs	J

45s: α That's My Baby/
Things Will Never Be The Same (Parlophone R 5186) 1964 R2
That's My Baby/
Things Will Never Be The Same (Parlophone R 5208) 1964 R2

JUNIOR'S EYES - Battersea Power Station (CD).

There's Not One Thing/
Don't Come Any Closer   (Parlophone R 5241) 1965 R2

NB: α Issued as **Four Just Men** and withdrawn.

These 45s are now of interest to collectors largely because the band later became **Wimple Winch**. The band formed in Liverpool in 1961. They were originally known as Dee Fenton and The Silhouettes (Dee Fenton being Demetrius' stage name, naturally he was Greek by birth). The existence of local bands like Shane Fenton and The Fentones and **Mark Peters and The Silhouettes** led them to change names to **The Four Just Men**.

John Kelman left in 1963 to join **Freddie Starr and The Midnighters**. He was replaced by Lally Scott. They were signed to Kennedy Street Management who also looked after the likes of **The Hollies** and **The Merseybeats**. They recorded a demo for Decca, appearing on TV's 'Scene At 6.30' and wrote the theme music for TV's 'Friday Night'! A major label signing seemed assured and EMI snapped them up for Parlophone. However, with a debut 45 on the brink of release a court injunction from another band of the same name landed on EMI's desk. EMI's response was to change their name to **The Just Four Men**. Under this name they recorded two 45s which were both beat numbers with some good guitar pieces, but neither took off and they later opted for a new name, **Wimple Winch**, to signify a fresh approach.

Bam-Caruso did issue test pressings of an album entitled *The Wimple Winch Story '63-'65* (KIRI 104). 25 copies were made in all.

Compilation appearances have included: *Things Will Never Be The Same* and *That's My Baby* on *Freddie And The Dreamers - I'm Telling You Now* (LP) and *Rare 60's Beat Treasures, Vol. 2* (CD); and *Things Will Never Be The Same* on *Beat At Abbey Road* (CD) and *Beat Merchants* (2-LP). (VJ/AD)

Dave Justin

45s: For Brandy/What You Going To Do   (Polydor 56185) 1967
       Everybody's Gone Home/Lincoln Green (Polydor 56221) 1967
       You Outside/Thinking Twice   (Polydor 56253) 1968
       Rachel/Louise   (Polydor 56292) 1968

Dave Justin was a late sixties pop singer. *You Outside* is a pleasant 'sing-along' type pop song which can also be heard on *Circus Days, Vol. 6* (CD) and *Circus Days, Vol. 5* (LP). (VJ)

Justin and Karlsson

45:    Somewhere They Can't Find Me/
       What More Do You Want   (Piccadilly 7N 35295) 1966

This largely unknown band's quite highly-rated beat offering, *Somewhere They Can't Find Me* has been compiled on *Oddities, Vol 2* (CD). (MWh/VJ)

Justin and Wylde

Personnel: JUSTIN (LOUIS SEYHE)   A
            WYLDE (LARAY COLLINS)   A

45s: Maris Eternal Flight/Goodbye California   (Pye 7N 45224) 1973
       Living In A Dream World/
       It Doesn't Really Matter Now   (Pye 7N 45279) 1973
       Down On My Knees/Make It Again   (Pye 7N 45367) 1974

These were two former buskers. (VJ)

Justine

Personnel: KEITH TROWSDALE   vcls, gtr   A
            JOHN McBURNIE   vcls, gtr   A
            VALERIE COPE   vcls   A
            BETHLYN BATES   vcls   A
            LAURETTE STIVERS   vcls   A

ALBUM: 1(A)   JUSTINE   (Uni UNLS 111) 1970 R2

NB: (1) recently issued on CD (Elegy E 640/1).

45s   Leave Me Be / Clown   (Dot 121) 1969
       Right Now/Place Where Sorrow Hides   (Buffalo BFS 1001) 1969
       She Brings The Morning With Her /
       Back To Boulder   (Uni 528) 1970

This obscure pop outfit made some enjoyable music, with the emphasis very much on vocal harmonies. They sound more American than British, and it's possible that some members were from the US. Most of it is beautifully arranged, rather whimsical pop, but the closing track, *Unknown Journey*, veers off into something far more psychedelic. The album was produced by Hugh Murphy, who went on to work with **Jody Grind**, **Stray**, **Van Morrison**, **Gerry Rafferty**, **Clifford T Ward** and many others. Stivers made a couple of solo albums (for Warner Bros. and Chrysalis) as Laurie Styvers, also produced by Murphy. John McBurnie joined **Jackson Heights** and later collaborated with celebrated Swiss keyboardist and ex-**Yes** member Patrick Moraz. (RMJ)

SYDE TRYPS VOL. 2 (Comp LP) including Just Plain Smith.

Just Plain Smith

Personnel incl: CHRIS HATT   gtr, vcls   A
                 BILL HEATH   gtr, vcls   A
                 MIC READ   gtr, vcls   A
                 COLIN STANDRING   bs   A
                 JAKE WALTON   drms   A

45s: February's Child/
          Don't Open Your Mind (PS)   (Sunshine SUN 7702) 1969 R3
       α Crazy Crazy /
          Should Have Stayed With Mary (CBS CBS 7840) 1971

NB: α as Just Plain Jones.

This outfit is most significant for including one of Britain's most popular dee-jays, **Mike Read**. He played in various groups in the late sixties including **Amber** and **The Lost** and also recorded several cuts as singer/songwriter **Mike Read**. The only venture which made it onto vinyl at this time was **Just Plain Smith**/(**Just Plain Jones**). Their first 45 was released on a subsidiary of the Walton-on-Thames-based classical company Oryx. The 'A' side was a summer-pop song, the flip featured a certain Tim Rice among the backing vocalists and is more experimental. Both sides can now be heard on *Syde Trips, Vol. 2* (LP) along with other **Mike Read**-related projects.

After their second 45, released as Just Plain Jones, they became Saturday and then **Espirit De Corps**. (VJ)

Just William

Personnel:
LEN BEDDOW	ld gtr, vcls	A
ALAN LACEY	drms	A
HERBIE (DANNY ROBINSON)	ld vcls	A
MICK TAYLOR	gtr, vcls	A
PETE STEVENS	bs, vcls	A

45:    I Don't Care/Cherrywood Green   (Spark SRL 1018) 1968

A pop 45 with some psychedelic tinges, this was actually the work of **Herbie's People**. The flip side is the better of the two tracks and after this 45, they released another under **The Bullring** moniker. (MWh/LB).

Just Us

45:    I Can't Grow Peaches On A Cherry Tree/
       I Can Save You   (CBS 202068) 1966

This is an obscure pop 45. (VJ)

Jynx

45:    How/Do What They Don't Say   (Columbia DB 7304) 1964 R2

No other details known.

You can also check out *How* on *Rare 60's Beat Treasures, Vol. 3* (CD), *R&B Scene, Vol. 1* (LP) and *R&B At Abbey Road* (CD). (VJ)

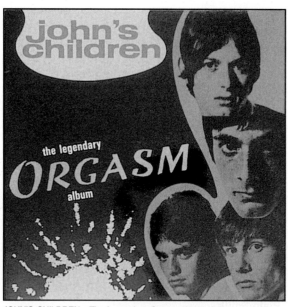
JOHN'S CHILDREN - The Legendary Orgasm Album (LP).

JULY - The Second Of July (LP).

JULIAN'S TREATMENT - A Time Before This (2-LP).

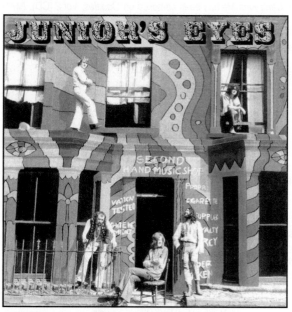
JUNIOR'S EYES - Battersea Power Station (Essential CD).

Moses K and The Prophets

Personnel incl:
KENNY McDOWELL (MOSES K)		A
BILLY WILLIAMSON	vcls, gtr	A

45: I Went Out With My Baby Tonight/
So Long   (Decca F 12244) 1965 SC

Moses K and The Prophets evolved from a Belfast band The Mad Lads who took over **Them**'s residency at Belfast's Maritime Club. The band was managed by Eddie Kennedy (who later managed **Taste**) and they also played The Rhythm & Blues Club and The Bastille Club in Dublin.

The Mad Lads were an excellent live band, with a tough Blues / R&B repertoire, much influenced by **Them**, Muddy Waters, John Lee Hooker and Sonny Boy Williamson. Both Billy and Kenny were members of the group and I remember Kenny telling me that they were going to make a record for Decca. I think Mervyn Solomons helped Eddie Kennedy secure the Decca deal as he was the Decca distributor for Ireland at the time. Presumably the band had to change its name to avoid problems with the Stax Records group of the same name.

Kenny McDowell was later in **Them**.

Compilation appearances have included: *I Went Out With My Baby Tonight*, (and as The Mad Lads) *I Can Tell, Strangers, Little Queenie* and *Answer Your Phone* on *Belfast Beat Maritime Blues* (CD). (TC/VJ)

Kajanus - Pickett

Personnel:
KAJANUS (GEORG JOHAN		
TJEGODIEV-SAKONSKI KAJANUS)	vcls	A
PHIL PICKETT	vcls	A

ALBUM: 1(A) HI HO SILVER   (Signpost) 1973

45: Movin' On/Cold Harbour Morning   (Signpost SGP 753) 1972

A folk act, **Kajanus**' real name is shown above. He was from Norway originally and had earlier been in Collection. Pickett also played in Blues United and both were later in **Sailor**. (VJ)

Kala

Personnel:
PETER ARNESEN	piano	A
JOHN BARHAM	cello	A
PAUL BENNETT	vcls	A
DAVE CODING	gtr, vcls	A
SID GARNER	bs, vcls	A
CAROL GRIMES	vcls	A
SHIVA SHANKAR JONES	keyb'ds, vcls	A
JOHNNIE MILES	drms, vcls	A
LES NICOL	gtr, vcls	A
PERRY SINCLAIR	gtr, vcls	A
DAVE SKINNER	piano	A
JACK STEVENSON	perc	A

ALBUM: 1(A) KALA   (Bradleys BRADL 1002) 1973 SC

45: Travelling Home/Still Got Time   (Bradleys BRAD 302) 1973

I haven't heard this album, but Shiva Shankar Jones and Dave Coding had previously been in **Quintessence**. **Carol Grimes** was with **Delivery**, **Uncle Dog** and also made solo recordings. (VJ)

Kaleidoscope

Personnel:
PETER DALTRY	keyb'ds	A
EDDIE PUMER	gtr	A
DANNY BRIDGMAN	drms	A
STEVE CLARK	bs	A

ALBUMS: 1(A) TANGERINE DREAM   (Fontana (S)TL 5448) 1967 R3
2(A) FAINTLY BLOWING   (Fontana STL 5491) 1969 R3

NB: (1) and (2) reissued on 5 Hours Back (Tock 005) and (006) 1987 (SC) and also pirated on CD (Fingerprint CDTD 2156 and CDTD 2166 respectively) 1994 with bonus tracks. There's also a legitimate compilation CD *Dive Into Yesterday* (Fontana 534 003-2) 1996. (1) reissued legitimately on CD (Repertoire PMS 7074-WP) with the following bonus tracks: *Flight From Ashiya* (Mono single version), *Holiday Maker* (Mono single mix), *A Dream For Julie, Please Excuse My Face* (Mono single mix), *Jenny Artichoke* and *Just How Much You Are*. Also worth seeking out is (2) reissued on CD (Repertoire REPUK 1047) 2005 with the 'A' and 'B' sides of three singles added as bonuses. *White Faced Lady* (UFO BFTPCD 001) 1991, is a previously unreleased album recorded after the band had changed its name to **Fairfield Parlour**. This was issued on CD originally by Kaleidoscope Records (KRC 001) 1991, with a different cover and as a double vinyl LP. *Please Listen To The Pictures* (Circle CPWC 104) is a lavishly packaged 22-track CD containing previously unreleased songs from BBC sessions and TV appearances by **Kaleidoscope** and their later incarnation **Fairfield Parlour**. There was also a very limited and beautiful numbered gatefold 2-LP format of this release (Circle CPWL 104) in a lavish sleeve with a LP-sized colour booklet. *White Faced Lady* also reissued as *Kaleidoscope: The Fairfield Parlour Years* (Burning Airlines PILOT 56) 2000, a 2-CD package, with the 2nd disc containing *From Home to Home*, All 'A' + 'B' sides of single releases as **Fairfield Parlour**, the previously unreleased film theme, 'Eyewitness', the **I Luv Wight** single, *Let The World Wash In* and a new recording of *Bordeaux Rose*.

45s:
Flight From Ashiya/	
Holiday Maker (Some PS)	(Fontana TF 863) 1967 R2/R1
A Dream For Julie/	
Please Excuse My Face	(Fontana TF 895) 1968 R1
Jenny Artichoke/	
Just How Much You Are	(Fontana TF 964) 1968 R1
Do It Again For Jeffrey/Poem	(Fontana TF 1002) 1969 R1
Balloon/If You So Wish	(Fontana TF 1048) 1969 R2

BBC Transcription discs:
45s:
Flight From Ashiya/	
The Murder Of Lewis Tollani	(Top Of The Pops 152) 1967
A Dream For Julie/	
Dive Into Yesterday	(Top Of The Pops 168) 1968
Music/Jenny Artichoke	(Top Of The Pops 203) 1968
Do It Again For Jeffrey/	
Snapdragon	(Top Of The Pops 232) 1969
Jump In My Boat/Balloon	(Top Of The Pops 248) 1969

Based in West London, this interesting psychedelic group started life in 1964 as The Side Kicks and later changed their name to The Key. Apparently, their drummer made an acetate of recordings from this era. By 1967, they had changed their name again to **Kaleidoscope** and signed to Fontana.

Their first 45, *Flight From Ashiya*, was an amalgam of pop and psychedelia, it told the story of the pilot of a crashing aeroplane. It picked up quite a lot of airplay but failed to chart. Some collectors seek out the Dutch release, which came with a different picture sleeve. After a further, equally good 45 (*A Dream For Julie*), sadly also flopped, the group were afforded the opportunity to record an album. The result, *Tangerine Dream* was a varied

KALEIDOSCOPE - Tangerine Dream (LP).

465

KALEIDOSCOPE - Faintly Blowing (LP).

collection of psychedelic pop with whimsical lyrics often delivered in that breathless style that characterised the UK genre. It featured both sides of their debut 45 and the flip of their second (*Please Excuse My Face*). The opening track was fittingly called *Kaleidoscope*. Other highlights were *Dive Into Yesterday*, a typical slice of whimsical pop psychedelia; *(Further Reflections) In The Room Of Percussion*, which had some great vocals and out of tune strings; *A Lesson Perhaps*, with its spoken lyrics; and *The Sky Children*, a fairytale dream, which was very much a preview of some of the material on their second album. *Tangerine Dream* came in a superb psychedelic sleeve.

The band appeared on several BBC radio shows for overseas broadcast which brought them into contact with deejay David Symonds who became their manager. BBC transcription discs of this material exist but are rarely offered for sale and are obviously expensive. There's also been a bootleg EP containing versions of *Flight From Ashiya*, *A Dream For Julie*, *The Murder of Lewis Tollani* and *Dive Into Yesterday* from these sessions, and the sessions also make up the bonus material included with the Fingerprint CD reissues.

Their next 45, *Jenny Artichoke*, was distinctly less psychedelic than the previous two. Its singalong style makes it less interesting too, but the fact it was not featured on either of their albums has made it collectable.

Their second album *Faintly Blowing* had a slightly more 'progressive' feel and contained psychedelic gems like *Music* with its liberal use of phasing and electronic sound effects, and *Snapdragon*, along with acoustic numbers like *Poems* and *I'll Kiss You Once*. Many of the songs had a story line or moral, none more so than *A Story From Tom Blitz*, the fictional story of an unfortunate traveller who tries to chat up a pretty female on a train journey in the USA. The girl slips him a potent liquid which gets him drunk and he ends up in the County Jail with a sentence of six months hard labour. Whilst in jail he pals up with an old cowboy, for whom he is caught trying to steal a horse and duly receives an extended sentence! The 2005 Repertoire CD reissue of this adds three singles 'A' and 'B' sides (including one recorded as **I Luv Wight**) as bonuses.

Their last two 45s, *Do It Again For Jeffrey* and *Balloon*, were very much in the style of *Jenny Artichoke* and were less interesting. The 'B' sides were from the *Faintly Blowing* album but the fact the 'A' sides were unavailable elsewhere has made them minor collectables.

With the decade at a close and a commercial breakthrough still eluding them the group agreed a change of name to **Fairfield Parlour** and with it came a different musical direction and label (Vertigo), although they also recorded a one-off 45 for the Isle of Wight festival (under the name **I Luv Wight**). Guitarist Eddie Pumer went on to become a broadcasting engineer and worked with **Paul McCartney** on his US radio 'Oobu Joobu' series. Peter Daltrey also had a solo album released on Voiceprint in 1995.

Sadly, on 1st May 1999, Steve Clarke was killed by a car as he walked across Chelsea Bridge in London.

Compilation appearances have included:- *Flight From Ashiya* on *Psychedalia - Rare Blooms From The English Summer Of Love* (CD), *Sgt. Salt And Other Condiments* and on the 4-CD box set *Acid Drops, Spacedust & Flying Saucers*; *Flight From Ashiya* and *A Dream For Julie* on *Rubble Vol. 4: 49 Minute Technicolour Dream* (LP), *Rubble Vol. 3* (CD) and on the 4-CD box set *Nuggets II*; *A Dream For Julie* on *Illusions From The Crackling Void* (LP); *Jenny Artichoke* on the *British Psychedelic Trip, Vol. 3* (LP) and the previously unreleased *Nursey Nursey* (later released as part of the *White Faced Lady* album) came on a disc (BOB 23) given away with the fanzine 'Bucketful of Brains No. 29'. (VJ)

Amory Kane

ALBUMS:
1 MEMORIES OF TIME UNWOUND (mono/stereo)
(w/insert)   (MCA MUP (S)348) 1968 R2
2 JUST TO BE THERE   (CBS 63849) 1970 R1

45s: Reflections Of Your Face/Four Ravens   (MCA MU1036) 1968
        You Were On My Mind/
        All The Best Songs And Marches   (UNI UNS 518) 1970
        Him Or Me/Forever Waiting   (CBS 5111) 1970

This US singer/songwriter/guitarist's pseudonym was a pun on 'American', though his two rare albums appeared in the UK only. His real name was Jack Daniel Kane, and he became a regular in London's folk clubs shortly after his arrival in 1967. Having come to the attention of producer Steve Rowland (of **Family Dogg**), he made his rare debut in 1968. A frustratingly convoluted mixture of rock, pop and ballads, it's bloated by excessive arrangements, some of which were by **John Paul Jones** just prior to joining **Led Zeppelin**. Despite extravagant praise at the time, it has not weathered at all well and is best avoided.

His second album, produced by Tony Cox (also responsible for albums by **Trees, Caravan** and others), is an altogether different proposal. Side one ('Heads') is a stark, dramatic suite of four songs linked by psychedelic effects from **Ron Geesin** and propelled by **Kane**'s fluid guitar work. Superbly subtle and atmospheric, it repays repeated listening. Side two ('Tales') is more conventional but still contains excellent material, especially the beautiful title track. **Kane** was friends with Peter Sarstedt and **Tim Hollier**, and some of the songs on *Just To Be There* were co-written with and also recorded by the latter, most notably the superb *Llanstephan Hill*. Dave Pegg (later of **Fairport Convention**) played bass. Overall this is an album deserving of a far wider audience.

You can also find *The Inbetween Man* on the CBS (2-LP) *Fill Your Head With Rock*. (NM/RMJ)

Kansas Hook

Personnel incl: CHRIS EVANS   A

45s: Echo Park/Manhattan Woman   (Uni UNS 5151) 1970
        Nervous Shakin'/Mr. Universe   (Decca F 13117) 1971

This band featured ex-**World Of Oz** member Chris Evans. (VJ)

Kaplan

45s: Do You Believe In Magic/I Like   (Philips BF 1636) 1968
        I Love It/Trousers Down   (Philips BF 1699) 1968

This was a short-lived pop outfit. *I Like* was later compiled on *Justavibration* (LP), *Psychedelic Voyage Vol. 1* (LP) and *Psychedelic Voyage* (CD). (VJ)

Kat

A very obscure band whose *Tell The World* was originally featured on a limited edition promotion (LP) from 1970 called *Transworld*. The band was never heard of again and having heard *Tell The World* I can't say I'm surprised.

Tell The World can also be found on *Syde Tryps, Vol. 1* (LP & CD). (VJ)

Katch-22

Personnel incl: PAUL BONNER
MARTIN WAYNE

ALBUM: 1 IT'S SOFT ROCK AND ALLSORTS
(Saga EROS 8047) 1968 SC

45s: Major Catastrophe/Hold Me (Fontana TF 768) 1966 SC
Makin' Up My Mind/While We're Friends (Fontana TF 874) 1967
The World's Getting Smaller/
Don't Bother (Fontana TF 930) 1968
100,000 Years/Pumpkin Mini (Fontana TF 984) 1968
Out Of My Life/Baby Love (Fontana TF 1005) 1969
Missus Jones/It's The Sunshine (CBS 4644) 1969

A straight-forward four-piece Midlands pop band whose best recording is generally considered to have been *Major Catastrophe*, which is notable for some frantic and loud guitar. Their album was offered at budget price and featured some nice harmony pop, including covers of Lefte Bank and Buffalo Springfield songs.

Paul Bonner and Martin Wayne who were the heart of the band went on to join **Paintbox**.

Major Catastophe has been compiled on *Voyage Through The Sugarcube* (LP & CD) and you'll also find *There Ain't No Use In Hanging On* on *Spinning Wheel* (CD); *Making My Mind Up* on *Colour Me Pop, Vol 1* (CD) and *While We're Still Friends* on *Colour Me Pop, Vol 2* (CD). (VJ)

Kate

Personnel incl: BARRIE EDWARDS drms A
HRAITON GARABALDIANNE vcls AB
CHRIS GILBY ld gtr AB
ROBERT GOLD organ AB
ALFRED TURNSTALL bs AB
VIV PRINCE drms B

45s: Strange Girl/I Don't Make A Sound (CBS 3631) 1968 SC
Hold Me Now/Empty World (CBS 3815) 1968 SC
Shout It/Sweet Little Thing (CBS 4123) 1969 SC

Kate originally formed in London with line-up (A). *Strange Girl* is rather ordinary, but *Don't Make A Sound* is much more interesting - a slice of pop-psych replete with organ, harpsichord and phasing. Despite this, they split late in 1968 after achieving little success.

They were reformed in 1969 by former **Pretty Things**' drummer **Viv Prince**. *Shout It* could easily have been a hit - powerful vocals, chorus girls and some good organ work, the production just let it down.

KALEIDOSCOPE - White Faced Lady (CD).

KALEIDOSCOPE - The Fairfield Parlour Years (CD).

Compilation appearances include: *Don't Make A Sound* on *Circus Days, Vol. 6* (CD); *Shout It* on *Circus Days, Vol. 3* (CD) and *Circus Days, Vol. 4* (LP); and *Strange Girl* on *Fading Yellow, Vol 1* (CD). (VJ)

The Kayes

45: It's No Secret/Remember Me (Major Minor MM 515) 1967

A long forgotten pop band. (VJ)

John (Speedy) Keen

ALBUMS: 1 PREVIOUS CONVICTIONS (Track 2406 105) 1971 SC
(up to 2 Y'KNOW WOT I MEAN (Island ILPS 9338) 1975
1976)

NB: (2) reissued on CD (Edsel EDCD 462) 1995.

45s: α Old Fashioned Girl/
(up to That's The Way It Is (Track 2094 103) 1973
1976) α Let Us In/Keep On The Grass (Track 2094 108) 1973
Someone To Love/
β Fighting In The Streets (Island WIP 6230) 1975
β Your Love/Heaven (Island WIP 6314) 1976

NB: α as **John Keen**. β as Speedy Keen.

In the sixties this guy was a songwriter and roadie for **John Mayall** among others. He was also the drummer in a pre-**July** outfit called **The Tomcats** for a spell. In 1969 he was in **Thunderclap Newman** and wrote their classic and timeless hit *Something In The Air*. After they split in 1970 he embarked on a solo career and his output in this capacity is highly-rated by those that know it. He also wrote *Armenia City In The Sky* for **The Who's** third album *Sell Out* and produced Johnny Thunders and The Heartbreakers' *L.A.M.F.* album. **Keen** died on 29 March 2002. (VJ)

Ace Kefford Stand

Personnel: DAVE BALL gtr A
DENNIS BALL bs A
ACE KEFFORD vcls A
COZY POWELL drms A

NB: *Ace The Face: The Lost 1968 Album?And More!* (Sanctuary CMQCD 799) 2004 gives an airing to material recorded for a solo album, which never got released at the time.

45: For Your Love/Gravy Booby Jamm (Atlantic 584 260) 1969 R1

Dennis Ball and **Cozy Powell** had earlier played in Cirencester outfit The Sorcerers who spent much time in Germany. The Sorcerers didn't make it onto vinyl and later changed their name to Youngblood, becoming **Ace Kefford Stand** when the former **Move** bassist joined their line-up in April 1968. The above 45 was their sole slab of vinyl - the 'A' side was an inferior cover of **The Yardbirds** hit. *Gravy Booby Jam* is better featuring a barrage of guitar and an enthusiastic vocal performance from **Kefford**. He also penned the psychedelic *William Chaulker's Time Machine*, which was a 45 for **The Lemon Tree**.

After its release, **Kefford** seems to have drifted out of the music business, whilst the remaining members (joined by ex-**Tintern Abbey** member Dave McTavish) went on to **Big Bertha** and were later in **Bedlam**. **Cozy Powell** was with **The Jeff Beck Group** in the early seventies for a while, then had his own band **Cozy Powell's Hammer** in the mid-seventies. He was later in Rainbow. Between **Big Bertha** and **Bedlam** John Ball was in **Procol Harum** and briefly played for **Long John Baldry** as did Dennis Ball.

Ace The Face has been compiled from sessions for a solo album, which was shelved. Aside from the 45 and *This World's An Apple* (a 45 for **Big Bertha**), the collection featured **Jimmy Page** on guitar for the cover of Paul Simon's *Save The Life Of My Child*.

Compilation appearances have included:- *For Your Love* on *Perfumed Garden Vol. 2* (CD) and *Rare 60's Beat Treasures, Vol. 3* (CD); and *Gravy Booby Jamm* on *Rubble Vol. 16: Glass Orchid Aftermath* (LP) and *Rubble Vol. 9* (CD). (VJ)

Kelly

45:        Mary, Mary/Reverend Richard Bailey   (Deram DM 277) 1969

On the 'A' side some promising opening guitar leads into more typical 1969 psych-pop. Surprisingly this 45 has been ignored by compilers so far. (VJ)

Dave Kelly

ALBUMS: 1   KEEP IT IN THE FAMILY (Mercury SMCL 20151) 1969 R2
(up to   2   BLACK BLUE KELLY   (Mercury 6310 001) 1971 R3
1976)
NB: (2) With **Jo-Ann Kelly** and **Brunning-Hall Sunflower Band**.

The brother of **Jo-Ann Kelly** he also recorded solo albums and 45s in the eighties, when he was also in The Blues Band.

He'd started out playing on the folk circuit and on a trip to America in 1966 played at Gerdes Folk City in New York. Whilst over there he saw people like Muddy Waters and John Lee Hooker. Upon his return to England he developed his interest in acoustic blues with his sister **Jo-Ann Kelly** and **Tony McPhee**. In the Summer of 1967 he joined the **John Dummer Blues Band** on vocals and slide guitar. He quit in August 1969, worn out after the incessant touring, to embark on a solo career, recording the two above albums. Then, after a brief spell in Rock Salt, which didn't really get off the ground, in 1972, he teamed up with **John Dummer** again the same year in the Ooblee Dooblee Band. He later played in The Dogs from 1974-75, The Wild Cats in 1978-79, The Blues Band and later still fronted his own band. (VJ)

Jo-Ann Kelly

ALBUMS: 1   JO-ANN KELLY   (CBS 63841) 1969 R3
(up to   2   SAME THING ON THEIR MINDS
1976)   (Sunset SLS 50209) 1972 R1
             3   DO IT   (Red Rag RRR 006) 1976 R1
NB: (1) issued on Epic in the US where she also made an album with Fahy, Mann and Miller (Blue Goose 2009) in 1972. (1) reissued on vinyl (Epic 26491). (1) reissued on CD (BGO BGOCD 429) 1999. (2) with **Tony McPhee**. (3) with Peter Emery. There's also a compilation, *Retrospect 1964-72* (Document CSAP LP 101) 1990, also on CD (CSAP CD 101) 1990. *Key To The Highway* (Mooncrest CREST CD 0372) 1999 subtitled *Rare And Unissued Recordings 1968-1974* is a mix of demos and home recordings *Takin' Low* (Mooncrest CRESTCD 045 2) 2000 comprises a collection of previously unreleased songs, alternate versions and live tracks.

PERFUMED GARDEN VOL. 2 (Comp LP) featuring Ace Kefford Stand.

EPs: 1   BLUES AND GOSPEL (live)   (GW EP 1) 1964 R3
             2   NEW SOUNDS IN FOLK
                                    (Harlequin HAL 1/HW 349) 1966 R2
NB: (1) released on CD (Blues Matters BMRCD 20041) 2005, with many bonus tracks. (2) with other artists.

Kelly came to the public eye as part of the British blues boom. The sister of **Dave Kelly**, she was a very powerful white blues singer. On her debut album she combined her own compositions with unique interpretations of traditional blues numbers. The album was critically acclaimed at the time but didn't sell and is now sought-after by blues collectors.

The two EPs were made prior to the above album; the first with other artists, the second recorded live at the Bridge House Club.

She also sang on **Dave Kelly**'s, **Tony McPhee**'s and **John Dummer**'s albums, on **Brunning-Hall Sunflower Blues Band**'s second album and Stefan Grossman's *Country Blues Guitar* album. She was in **Chilli Willi and The Red Hot Peppers** and later in **Tramp**. Sadly she died in 1990 of a brain tumour.

The compilation *Retrospect 1964-72*, compiled by **Jo-Ann Kelly** herself, includes 14 of this excellent blues singer's finest songs, including some from her ultra-rare *Blues And Gospel* EP.

Key To The Highway compiles rare and unissued recordings by her from the 1968-1974 era. It's a mixture of demos and home recordings. Its finer moments include folk-blues staples like *You've Got To Move* and *Make Me A Pallet On The Floor* and some brief interviews with her from 1988.

The Blues And Gospel EP was reissued on CD in 2005, with many bonus tracks added. Indeed eight of its 16 tracks get their first appearance on CD. The material is very varied, ranging from acoustic Delta blues songs like *Moon Going Down* to belting numbers like *Sweet Nuthins* where she is backed by the Quaggy Delta Blues Band. The collection certainly showcases her enormous talent, both as a blues vocalist and as a guitarist.

She can also be heard singing *Rollin' And Tumblin'* on *Gutbucket* (LP) and *Oh Death* (with **Tony McPhee**) on *Son Of Gutbucket* (LP). (VJ)

Jonathan Kelly

Personnel: GERRY CONWAY   A
             JONATHAN KELLY   AB
             DONAL LUNNY   A
             TIM RENWICK   A
             ROY BABBINGTON   B
             BARRY DE SOUZA   B
             RAY DUFFY   B
             MARK GRIFFITHS   B

```
        SUTHERLAND BROTHERS AND QUIVER        B
        PETER WOOD                            B

ALBUMS:  1  JONATHAN KELLY      (Parlophone PCS 7114) 1970 R1
         2(A) TWICE AROUND THE HOUSES (RCA SF 8262) 1972 SC
         3(B) WAIT TILL THEY CHANGE THE BACKDROP
                                  (RCA SF 8353) 1973 SC
         4  WAITING FOR YOU       (RCA LPL 15022) 1974
         5  TWO DAYS IN WINTER    (RCA SF 8415) 1975
```

NB: (2) and (3) reissued on CD (BGO BGOCD 533) 2001. (4) credited to **Jonathan Kelly's** Outside. (4) and (5) reissued on CD (BGO BGOCD 585) 2005.

```
45s:   Denver/Son John             (Parlophone R 5805) 1969
       Don't You Believe It?/Billy  (Parlophone R 5851) 1970
       Make A Stranger Your Friend/
       Daddy Don't Take Me Down Fishing (Parlophone R 5830) 1970
       Let The People Stay/Mother Moon   (RCA 2370) 1973
```

The young Irishman came from Drogheda, near Dublin. His real name was John Ledingham and he recorded two 45s: under this name: *Without An E / She's Got Me* (Pye 7N 17422) 1967 and *Love Is A Toy / Thank You Missus Gilbert* (Pye 7N 17488) 1968. He was spotted by Colin Peterson (of the **Bee Gees**) literally singing for his supper at a London restaurant. By then he'd already made three singles (two under the name **Jon**). He became a member of Peterson's band **Humpy Bong** and wrote their *Don't You Be Too Long*. Peterson produced his first solo album in 1970 and session men were used as back-up artists.

To promote his follow-up album *Twice Around The Houses* he toured with **The Strawbs**. The album had a strong **Donovan** feel. The songs concern fantasy adventures of a young man, presumably himself. His live performances at this time consisted simply of **Kelly** and his acoustic guitar. In December 1972 New Musical Express nominated him as the 'Best One Man Act' besides **Donovan**. From 1973 onwards he deployed a backing band.

Waiting for You was recorded with a backing band called The Outside who included future Blockhead Chas Jankel and Snowy White, who played with many bands including **Thin Lizzy**. His penchant for catchy folk-rock is represented by tracks like *Making It Lonely* and *I'll Never Find Another Love*, although the backing band format moved him away from his uncomplicated earlier folk style. His final album *Two Days In Winter* has a decidedly melancholic edge. (VJ/MWh)

Mike Kelly

```
45s:   Long Time Gone/Going Steady   (Decca F 13347) 1972
       Catalina/You Make My World    (Decca F 13397) 1973
```

This was a little-known singer. *Long Time Gone* was a Crosby, Stills and Nash track. (VJ)

Pete Kelly's Soulution

```
Personnel:  PETE (OLLIE) HALSALL   lead gtr   AB
            BILL LOVELADY          drms       A
            PETE KELLY             vcls       AB
            JOHN McCAFFREY         bs         AB
            JOHN SURGUY            sax        AB
            IAN McGEE              drms       B
```

```
45:   α  Midnight Confessions/
         If Your Love Don't Swing   (Decca F 12755) 1968 SC
```

NB: α The 'A' side was also coupled with **Bernie and The Buzz Band**'s *The House That Jack Built* on an Export issue (Decca F 22829) SC the same year.

This band was originally known as **Rhythm and Blues Incorporated**.

Compilation appearances have included: *If Your Love Don't Swing* on *The Mod Scene* (CD); *Midnight Confessions* on *Mod Scene, Vol. 2* (CD) and *British R'n'B Explosion, Vol. 1* (CD); and *Midnight Confessions* and *If Your Love Don't Swing* on *The Soul Of British RnB 1962-1968*. (VJ/AD)

Seymour Kelly

```
45:   Indian Scene/Worlds Apart   (Columbia DB 8445) 1968
```

A long forgotten singer. (VJ)

Paul Kelvin

```
45:   It's Easy/Anyone Can Move A Mountain   (Morgan MR 2) 1969
```

This was another long forgotten one-off venture. The 'A' side was a ballad. (VJ)

Linda Kendrick

```
ALBUM:  1  LINDA KENDRICK   (Philips SBL 7921) 1970 SC
```

```
45s:          It's The Little Things/
(selective)   When Your Love Is Warm     (Polydor 56076) 1966 SC
              I Fall Apart/Friend Of Mine (Polydor 56146) 1966
              Grey Sunny Day/In Need Of A Friend (Philips BF 1660) 1968
              Hold On/Fah La La          (Philips BF 1818) 1969
              Sympathy For The Devil/
              He Wrote Me A Letter       (Dawn DNS 1063) 1974
              House Of Cards/Music Brings Us Joy (Dawn DNS 1106) 1975
```

During the late sixties **Linda Kendrick** performed in the musical 'Hair'. Her seventies album is often compared to Barbara Streisend and features orchestral backing. When the album was released she was just 19 years old. Her cover of the '**Stones** *Sympathy For The Devil* is very good, and *House Of Cards* was the first recording of an **Elton John** composition. (VJ)

Kenny

```
Personnel:  RICHARD DRISCOLL       vcls      A
            CHRISTOPHER LACKLISON  keyb'ds   A
            CHRIS REDBURN          bs        A
            ANDY WALTON            drms      A
```

```
                                             HCP
ALBUM:  1(A)  THE SOUND OF SUPER K  (Rak SRAK 518) 1975 56
```
NB: Also relevant is *The Singles Collection Plus* (7T's GLAMCD 3) 2000 and repackaged (Anagram GLAD CD 3).

```
                                             HCP
45s:   The Bump/Forget The Janes, The Jeans And
       Might Have Beens          (Rak RAK 186) 1974 3
       Fancy Pants/I'm A Winner  (Rak RAK 196) 1975 4
       Baby I Love You, OK/Sound Of Super K (Rak RAK 207) 1975 12
       Julie Ann/Dancin' Feet    (Rak RAK 214) 1975 10
       Nice To Have You Home/Happy Melissa (Rak RAK 225) 1975 -
       Hot Lips/
       Bangin' My Head Against A Brickwall (Polydor 2058 705) 1976 -
       Red Heady Lady/Alone Together (Polydor 2058 770) 1976 -
Reissue: The Bump/Fancy Pants   (Old Gold 9718) 1987 -
```

Coming late onto the 'glam' rock scene these four had previously worked at a banana warehouse in Enfield, Middlesex, and were originally known as Chuff when they came together in 1974. After signing with manager Peter Walsh they changed name to **Kenny** and got a contract with Mickie Most's Rak label. With the assistance of some top songwriters and session men (including **Clem Cattini** and **Chris Spedding**) Most turned them into a hit machine with a series of inane but catchy tunes beginning with the dance craze *The Bump*. Their album, which didn't quite make the Top 50, was basically a collection of their hits and some other 'fillers'. They also provide the backing to Thames TV's 'Minder' series with Dennis Waterman doing the vocals. Despite their undoubted popularity at the time they are eminently forgettable.

The Singles Collection Plus includes all their hit singles and material from their *The Sound Of Super K* album. (VJ)

Kenny and Cash

Personnel: KENNY EVERETT   A
              DAVE CASH   A

45:       Knees/The B Side   (Decca F 12283) 1965 SC

A deejay record - **Kenny Everett** and Dave Cash were both working on pirate radio at the time. (VJ)

Kenny and The Wranglers

Personnel incl: KENNY BERNARD

45s: Somebody Help Me/
          Who Do You Think I Am?   (Parlophone R 5224) 1964 SC
          Doobie Doo/Moonshine   (Parlophone R 5275) 1965 SC

This beat group who played soul/R&B also turned up in the film 'Be My Guest' starring David Hemmings and **Stevie Marriott**. Also featured in film were **The Nashville Teens**, The Niteshades, **The Plebs** and **The Zephyrs**. (MWh)

Paul (PC) Kent

Personnel: PAUL KENT   vcls, keyb'ds   AB
              DAVE RICHARDS   bs   A
              GAVIN (SPENCER-)WATSON gtr, vcls   AB
              ??   A
              GERRY CONWAY   drms   B
              PAT DONALDSON   bs   B
              ROGER POWELL   drms   B
              TONY REEVES   bs   B
              TIM RENWICK   gtr   B
              ANDY ROBERTS   gtr   B
              CHRIS TURNER   hrmnca   B
              RAW WARLEIGH   sax, clarinet   B

NB: Gavin Watson changed names to Gavin Spencer after the first album.

ALBUMS: 1(A) P.C. KENT   (RCA SF 8083) 1970 SC
        2(B) PAUL KENT   (B&C CAS 1044) 1971 SC

45:       Do You/Helpless Harry   (B&C CB 165) 1971

This obscure folk-rock artist's albums are hard to track down now. His debut is pleasant, melodic pop-psych. The second featured **Andy Roberts**. Line-up 'A' was formed whilst all four members were at Ealing Grammar School in West London.

Gavin Spencer later played on **The Johnstons**' *If I Sang My Song* album. (VJ/JRy)

Richard Kent Style

Personnel incl: JOHN VERITY   vcls   A

45s: α No Matter What You Do/
         Go, Go Children   (Columbia DB 7964) 1966 R3
      α You Can't Put Me Down/
         All Good Things   (Columbia DB 8051) 1966 R2
         Marching Off To War/I'm Out (Columbia DB 8182) 1967 R1
         Love Will Shake The World Awake/
         Crocodile Tears   (MCA MU 1032) 1968 R1
         A Little Bit O'Soul/Don't Tell Lies (Mercury MF 1090) 1969 R1

NB: α have been reissued in limited editions pressings of 500 reproduced from the original French jukebox pressings with a large centre hole.

A Manchester-based mod band whose singles veered towards soul for the most part, the exception being *Go, Go Children*, the flip to their debut 45 which was really an amalgam of soul and experimental beat music.

KESTREL - Kestrel (CD).

This band featured a young **John Verity** as vocalist who was born in Bradford, Yorkshire on 3rd July 1949. He grew up there and played in various local bands between 1961 - 68. After **Richard Kent Style** (between 1967 - 69), he was in Tunnell (1969 - 70) before forming his own **John Verity Band** (1970 - 74).

Go Go Children has been compiled on *Yellow Elektric Years* (LP) and *Echoes From The Wilderness - Sixteen UK R&B Freakbeat Trippers.* (LP & CD). (VJ)

Shirley Kent

ALBUM: 1   FRESH OUT   (Minstrel 0001) 1975 SC

NB: (1) credited to **Virginia Tree** and reissued as *Forever A Willow* (Magic Spell 0001) in 1988 and again on CD (Akarma AK 086) with two bonus tracks housed in a miniature gatefold sleeve.

EP: 1   THE MASTER SINGERS AND SHIRLEY KENT
              SING FOR CHAREC 67   (Keele University 103) 1966 SC

Shirley Kent came from Birmingham. She'd been singing in Social Clubs since the age of 15 and later progressed onto Nightclubs eventually winning a residency at the Opposite Lock club in Birmingham. In this era she recorded two tracks on a charity EP issued by Keele University Students Union. Both songs, *One Day Old* and *Back*, were folk tunes recorded with just an acoustic guitar accompaniment.

In the late sixties she joined the progressive rock outfit **Ghost** but left the band in the early seventies to revert to a solo career, again securing a residency at Birmingham's Opposite Lock club. The *Fresh Out* album was recorded under a pseudonym, **Virginia Tree**. Apart from a cover of Jimmy Dorsey's *I'm Glad There Is You*, the remaining nine songs were self-penned and former **Ghost** members Paul Eastment and Terry Guy joined her on three of the tracks:- *Let Us Go Dancing*, *Hiding There*, and *Harlequin and Columbine*. Many of the songs were very folky with *Make Believe Girl* and *In My Garden* among the best. Only 1,000 copies were pressed and it soon became a collector's item. It was later reissued on Magic Spell in 1988 with a new title and two extra tracks, *A Dedication To Betram George Tipping, My Dad* and an orchestrated version of *In My Garden*.

Shirley gave up a full-time career in music in 1977 but has been involved in the formation of She Records and Tadpole Records and has written a book, 'A Guide To Popular Singing', which is also available as a cassette. (VJ)

Rik Kenton

45s: Bungalow Love/Lay It On You   (Island WIP 6214) 1974
          Libertine/Messin' Around   (EMI EMI 2443) 1976

Rik Kenton was very briefly in **Roxy Music** (he played on their *Virginia Plain* 45) before his short and unsuccessful solo career. Much earlier in 1967 he played for **Woody Kern**. Later he played on **Neil Harrison's** 1974 solo album. (VJ)

The Kerries

Personnel:	LENNY McILHONE	gtr, vcls	A
	RALPH OVERTON	gtr	A
	GILL THURLOW	vcls, penny whistle	A
	KERRY TODD	gtr, vcls	A
	GIBB TODD	vcls, banjo, tin whistle, mandolin	A

ALBUM: 1(A) THE KERRIES
(mono/stereo) (Major Minor MMLP/SMLP 9) 1967 SC

45: Coulter's Candy/A Gallon Of Whisky (Major Minor MM 541) 1967
NB: Both tracks from the LP.

This folk group played a mixture of traditional arrangements and originals. Based in Coventry, where they used to run their own folk club, they evolved out of family sing-alongs at the Kerry Todd's home and progressed to playing the local Irish Social Club for beer money. (TB)

Kestrel

Personnel:	DAVE BLACK	gtr, vcls	A
	JOHN COOK	gtr, synth	A
	TOM KNOWLES	vcls	A
	FENWICK MOIR	bs	A
	DAVE WHITAKER	drms, perc	A

ALBUM: 1(A) KESTREL (Cube HIFLY 19) 1975 R3

For unknown reasons, this progressive hard-rock outfit's album was barely released. Dave Black later played for the **Spiders From Mars**; David Whitaker was ex-**Ginhouse** and Tom Knowles was later with Johnny Cougar between 1978 - 79. (VJ)

Key Largo

Personnel:	LAURENCE GARMAN	hrmnca	A
	KENNY LAMB	drms	A
	PAT McAULIFFE	vcls	A
	LAURIE SANFORD	gtr	A
	BOB SAVAGE	keyb'ds	A
	TOM STEAD	bs	A

ALBUM: 1(A) KEY LARGO (Blue Horizon 7-63859) 1970 R1
NB: (1) reissued on Line (1983) and now on CD (Green Tree GTR 620).

45: Voodoo Rhythm/
As The Years Go Passing By (Blue Horizon 57-3178) 1971 SC

"**Key Largo** may best be described as a group of musicians seeking to create something fresh and unique within the supposed musical boundaries of what most people would simply term blues" state the sleevenotes to their album. In fact what's on offer is pretty typical British blues but with lots of harmonica, percussion and brass arrangements in places. The album includes lots of cover versions of W. Dixon, A. Toussaint, B.B. King and P. Mayfield songs. The better tracks include the soul/funk orientated *Give It Up* with a brass arrangement; the slow number *As The Years Go Passing By*, which features some good blues guitar work and *Come On And Get It, Baby*, written by thirties English pianist Stanley Black - an instrumental with jazzy electric piano, sharp guitar chords and percussion.

Savage and Garman went on to a pub-rock group formed in February 1974 called The Mitchigan Flyers. Walker joined Big Jim Sullivan's **Tiger** and Kenny Lamb went on to **Jellybread**. (CA/VJ/JM)

The Keys

45s: Sleep Sleep My Baby/Colour Slide (Oriole CB 1968) 1964 SC
Go Get Her/My Everything (CBS 201804) 1965

This North London duo sounds a bit Everly Brotherish on *Colour Slide*. (MWh)

Khan

Personnel:	NICK GREENWOOD	bs	A
	DAVE STEWART	guest organ	AB
	STEVE HILLAGE	gtr	AB
	ERIC PEACHEY	drms	AB
	DICK HENN	organ	A
	NIGEL SMITH	bs	B

ALBUM: 1(A) SPACE SHANTY (Deram SDL 11) 1972 R1
NB: (1) was later reissued in February 1977 (Deram SDL 11) to cash-in on **Hillage**'s fame. It was also issued in Germany on Brain back in 1972 and on PVC in the US in 1978. Also reissued on CD (Deram 844-008-2) 1993 and recently again remastered (Eclectic ECLCD)..

A London-based band formed by **Hillage** when he left college. Greenwood and Henn had both previously played with the **Crazy World Of Arthur Brown**. Musically the album offered a heavy spacey brand of jazz-rock which relied a lot on improvisational jams. It's worth investigation by ageing hippies everywhere. In the autumn of 1972 they embarked on a promotional tour with labelmates **Caravan** and **the Parlour Band**, but the band soon folded with Dave Stewart going on to play for **Hatfield and The North**. (VJ)

The Kids

Personnel:	KEITH BOYCE	drms, perc	A
	COSMO	gtr	A
	GARY HOLTON	lead vcls	A
	DANNY PEYRONEL	keyb'ds, vcls	A
	RONNIE THOMAS	bs, vcls	A

ALBUM: 1(A) ANVIL CHORUS (Atlantic K 50143) 1975

Produced by Andy Johns and recorded in London, *Anvil Chorus* is a rather good album in the style of **The Faces** or the British Lions. All their material was self-penned, with the help of Micky Waller (who's been **Rod Stewart's** drummer and bashed the skins for Silvermetre) on two tracks. Among the best cuts are *Hard At The Top*, *The Turk (An'Wot'e Smokes)* and *The Big Fire*.

Keith Boyce was previously in **Ashman Reynolds**. He later worked with Bram Tchaikovsky and **Savoy Brown**. (SR)

KHAN - Space Shanty (LP).

Kilburn and The High Roads

Personnel:

TERRY DAY	drms	AB
IAN DURY	vcls	ABCDE
RUSSELL HARDY	piano	ABCD
CHARLIE HART	bs	AB
TED SPEIGHT	gtr	A
GEORGE KHAN	sax	A
KEITH LUCAS	gtr	BCD
DAVEY PAYNE	sax	BCDE
DAVID ROHOMAN	drms	C E
CHARLIE SINCLAIR	bs	DE
GEORGE BUTLER	drms	D
LOUIS LAROSE	drms	D
ROD MELVIN	piano	E

NB: They also employed a few short-term bassists between Hart and Sinclair.

ALBUMS: 1(E) HANDSOME (Dawn DNLS 3065) 1975 SC
2(D) WOTABUNCH (Warners K 56513) 1978

NB: (1) later reissued on Pye (NSPL 18541) in 1978. (1) reissued on CD (Sequel NEX CD 144) in 1991. (2) was actually recorded in 1974 for the Raft label but never got released at the time 'cos WEA closed the label. It was later released after Ian Dury had become famous. There are also two compilations;- *Kilburn And The High Roads* (EP) (Bonaparte BONE 1) 1977 and *Upminster Kids* (PRT DOW 17) 1983.

45s: Rough Kids/Billy Bentley (Dawn DNS 1090) 1974
Crippled With Nerves/Huffety Puff (Dawn DNS 1102) 1975

In retrospect they are probably most significant as Ian Dury's first band but at the time they were one of London's most successful pub-rock bands.

Dury was born in Upminster, Essex on 12 May 1942. He contracted polio at the age of seven and went to a disabled school when he was nine. He formed **Kilburn and The High Roads** in November 1970 as a part-time combo - he was working as a lecturer at Canterbury College of Art in Kent at the time. They made their debut at Croyden School of Art in December 1971 and were by all accounts a pretty motley collection. Their early music was basically a humorous adaptation of rock'n'roll with lyrics which reflected Dury's cockney background.

They made their debut at the Tally Ho in Kentish, London in January 1973 and were soon working regularly on London's pub circuit and Charlie Gillett, a writer / broadcaster became their manager and he secured them a contract with Raft Records. Dury and Hardy began to write material for the band who hitherto relied on oldies and in October 1973 they toured the UK as support to **The Who**.

They recorded an album in January 1974, which was produced by Tony Ashton (of **Ashton, Gardner and Dyke**). It never saw the light of day when WEA closed the Raft label. The tapes were eventually released to Pye and the album titled as *Handsome* was put out on their Dawn label. It was released again in October 1978 to cash in on Dury's new found fame.

KILLING FLOOR - Killing Floor (LP).

After this blow Tommy Roberts became their manager and got them signed to Pye's Dawn label, but after a couple of unsuccessful 45s and the very disappointing *Handsome* album the group broke up in June 1975.

Towards the end of 1975, Dury returned, fronting a new six-piece band Ian Dury and The Kilburns, which disbanded in June 1976 when Dury's doctors advised him not to undertake any further live work. However, he continued to write songs with keyboardist Chaz Jankel, who'd joined the group in March. The fruits of their labours were well and truly reaped when Dury put together a new outfit, Ian Dury and The Blockheads, the following year, which elevated him to national and international fame for the first time.

Dury died on 27 March 2000 from cancer. (VJ)

John Killigrew

ALBUM: 1 KILLIGREW (Penny Farthing PELS 513) 1971 SC
NB: (1) with **Pete Dello**.

45: Just A Line/
Nothing's Impossible (Penny Farthing PEN 774) 1971

Killigrew is a native of Birmingham native whose sole album, a pleasant collection of folk-pop, barely ever shows up. The album was produced by **Pete Dello** following **Killigrew's** discovery by **Honeybus's** manager Terry Noon. (VJ)

Killing Floor

Personnel:

MICK CLARKE	lead gtr	ABC
LOU MARTIN	piano	A
STEWART MacDONALD	bs	AB
BAZ SMITH	drms	A
BILL THORNDYCRAFT	lead vcls, hrmnca	ABC
ROD DE'ATH	drms	BC
MICK HAWKSWORTH	bs, vcls	BC
ROY OWEN	vcls	BC
TONY FERNANDEZ	drms	C

ALBUMS: 1(A) KILLING FLOOR (Spark (S)RLP 102) 1969 R3
2(A) OUT OF URANUS (Penny Farthing PELS 511) 1970 R3

NB: (1) Also released on Sire in the US (R1). (1) reissued as *The Original Killing Floor* (Spark Replay SRLM 2004) 1973 (R1). Reissued on CD (See For Miles SEECD 355) 1992 as *Rock The Blues*. (1) reissued on CD (Repertoire REP 4532-WP) 1995 and again (Akarma AK 212) in both vinyl and CD format. (2) reissued on CD (Repertoire REP 4367-WP) 1993 and again (Akarma AK 232) in both vinyl and CD format.

45: Call For The Politicians/
Acid Bean (Penny Farthing PEN 745) 1970 SC

This blues-rock outfit's albums are now rare. Their power blues-rock was clearly influenced by **Cream** and certainly the CD reissues are worth a spin. The flip side to their sole 45 is quite good boogie-orientated music with some punk leanings (years before punk), and has subsequently resurfaced on *Syde Trips Vol. 5* (LP) along with *Soon There Will Be Everything* and *Lost Alone*.

In 1969 they supported **Yes** at the Marquee, backed Freddie King and toured Europe. Lou Martin left after the first album and a handful of BBC Radio Sessions (including a John Peel session) and later played with **Rory Gallagher**. McDonald left to join Peace in August 1971. He was replaced by ex-**Fuzzy Duck** member Mick Hawksworth. After the band split Death joined Martin in **Rory Galagher's** band. Fernandez, Hawksworth and Clarke joined **Toe Fat**. He went on to form The Mick Clarke Band and has released 10 albums since, touring all over Europe and the US. (VJ/CA/JN/JM/MC)

Kind Hearts and English

Personnel:

TONY BIRD	vcls	A
JOE BURT	bs	A
ELTON DEAN	sax	A

BRIAN GODDING	gtr	A
HUW GOWER	gtr	A
JOHN TIPPET	piano	A

ALBUM: 1 (A)	A WISH FOR A SEASON	(DJM DJF 20490) 1976
(up to 1976)		

45s:	Call Me Darling/I Still Believe In You	(DJM DJS 10615) 1975
(up to 1976)	Karen/Wish For a Season	(DJM DJS 10657) 1976
	Wish For A Season/	
	Call Me Darling/Karen	(DJM DJPI 00001) 1976

Kind Hearts and English was formed around the talents of Tony Bird and Brian Godding, who had previously been in **Blossom Toes**. (BS)

Kindness

45s:	Light Of Love/Lindy Lou	(RCA RCA 1942) 1970
	Let The Good Times Roll / Oh Yea	(Decca F 13318) 1972
	Oh, Julie/I Love You, Carolina	(Decca F 13338) 1972
	Make It Better/Lonely Long Lady	(Decca F 13429) 1973

Kindness was an early seventies pop outfit, previously known as The Elizabethans, who later became **Smokie**. (VJ)

Kinesphere

ALBUM:	1 ALL AROUND YOU	(Kinesphere KIN 5001) 1976 R2

This privately-pressed folk album has great male / female harmonies. It has been likened to midway between Friends Of Mine and **Tickawinda**. (VJ)

Kinetic

Personnel incl: ANDY MOBRAY   vcls

This English band recorded in France. It released an album, *Live Your Life* (French Vogue CLVLX 148) and EP (*Suddenly Tomorrow/Letter To Rosetta/Time Of The Season*) (French Vogue EPL 8520), both in 1967. Essentially they played straight pop material, but *Suddenly Tomorrow*, was a bit more inventive with some good guitar work and a catchy chorus. Their French album is now very rare. It has now been reissued (Disques SHOT12) in a limited edition of 500.

Compilation appearances have included: *Suddenly Tomorrow* on *Psychedelia, Vol. 1* (LP) and *Hen's Teeth Vol. 1* (CD); *Suddenly Tomorrow, Letter To Rosetta, Time Of Season, Live Your Life, Hall Of The Viking, Sunny Cloud,*

KILLING FLOOR - Out Of Uranus (CD).

The Train, Childs Song, Willy 'D' Fixer and *Jam Around* on *Sixties Years, Vol. 1 - French 60's EP Collection* (CD) and *The Train* can also be found on *Jagged Time Lapse, Vol 3* (CD). (VJ)

Danny King's Mayfair Set

Personnel:	DENNIS BALL	bs	A
	TREVOR BURTON	gtr	A
	ROGER HARRIS	keyb'ds	A
	DANNY KING	vcls	A
	KEITH SMART	gtr	A

45s:	α	Tossin' And Turnin'/Young Blood	(Columbia DB 7276) 1964 R1
	α	Pretty Things/Outside Of My Room	(Columbia DB 7456) 1965 R1
		Amen (My Teenage Prayer)/	
		It's Such A Shame	(Columbia DB 7792) 1965 SC

NB: α **Danny King** solo 45s.

A Birmingham-based act formed in 1964. **King**'s previous backing band had been The Royals. Burton was born on 9 March 1944. **King**'s first solo 45 was the Bobby Lewis track backed by The Coasters song. **Roy Wood** is rumoured to have played guitar on *Pretty Things* as was Trevor Burton making this disc quite a significant collectable. The flip side was an unexceptional ballad. **Wood** (who was never a member of the band) exited after this 45 but Burton remained to play on *Amen (My Teenage Prayer)* before joining **Wood** in **The Move**. The group split in January 1966. **Danny King** enjoyed a very good reputation locally as a vocalist and went on to several other groups. Ball joined The Sorcerers, Smart went to **Lemon Tree** and Harris became a painter.

Pretty Things was later compiled on *60's Back Beat* (LP). (VJ/JM)

Jonathan King

ALBUMS:	1	OR THEN AGAIN...	(Decca LK/SLK 4908) 1967 SC
(up to 1976)	2	TRY SOMETHING DIFFERENT	
			(Decca SKL 5127) 1972 SC
	3	PANDORA'S BOX	(UK UKAL 1004) 1973
	4	A ROSE IN A FISTED GLOVE	(UK UKAL 1010) 1975
	5	J.K. ALL THE WAY	(UK UKAL 1024) 1976

NB: There's also a CD compilation, *The Butterfly That Stamped* (Castle Communications JKDCD 001) 1989. It not only contains some of his own songs but several he wrote for his various creations.

HCP

45s:	Everyone's Gone To The Moon/		
(up to	Summer's Coming	(Decca F 12187) 1965	4
1976)	Green Is The Grass/Creation	(Decca F 12237) 1965	-
	Where The Sun Has Never Shone/		
	Don't Talk To Me Of Protest	(Decca F 12286) 1965	-
	Just Like A Woman/		
	Land Of The Golden Tree	(Decca F 12457) 1966	-
	Icicles/In A Hundred Years From Now	(Decca F 12517) 1966	-
	Seagulls/Take A Look At Yourself Babe	(Decca F 12540) 1967	-
	Round And Round/Time And Motion	(Decca F 12569) 1967	-
	Let It All Hang Out/Colloquial Sex	(Decca F 12988) 1969	26
	Million Dollar/City Of Angels	(Decca F 13009) 1970	-
	Cherry Cherry/Gay Girl	(Decca F 13069) 1970	-
	Lazy Bones/		
	I Just Want To Say Thank You	(Decca F 13177) 1971	23
	Hooked On A Feeling/		
	I Don't Want To Be Gay	(Decca F 13241) 1971	23
	Flirt/Hey Jim	(Decca F 13276) 1972	22
	It's A Tall Order For A Short Guy	(UK UK 1) 1972	-
	Mary My Love/Little Bit Left Of Right	(UK UK 35) 1973	-
	Kun Fu Anthem/Modest Proposal	(UK UK 56) 1973	-
	Help Me Make It Through The Night/		
	Colloquial Sex	(UK UK 75) 1974	-
	Free Man In Paris/		
	True Story Of Molly Malone	(UK UK 88) 1975	-
	Una Paloma Blanca/Impraiseofuk	(UK UK 105) 1975	5
	Baby The Rain Must Fall/		
	Very Very Melancholy Man	(UK UK 111) 1975	-

KING CRIMSON - In The Court Of The Crimson King (LP).

Happy People Song/		
I've Never Seen A Woman	(UK UK 122) 1976 -
Little Latin Lupe Lu/Sex Appeal	(UK UK 125) 1976 -
He's So Fine/King Of The Hooks	(UK UK 132) 1976 -
Mississippi/Little Greatest Love	(UK UK 146) 1976 -
When I Was A Star/Little Greatest Love	(UK UK 155) 1976 -
Reissues: Everybody's Gone To The Moon/		
Round Round	(Decca F 12950) 1969 -
Everybody's Gone To The Moon/		
Summer's Coming	(UK UK 47) 1973 -
Hooked On A Feeling/		
I Don't Want To Be Gay	(UK UK 62) 1974 -
Lazy Bones/I Just Wanna Say Thank You	(UK UK 142) 1976 -
Una Paloma Blanca/		
Everybody's Gone To The Moon	(Ariola ARO 199) 1979 -
Everybody's Gone To The Moon/		
Summer's Coming	(Old Gold OG 9104) 1982 -

NB: There was also a US only 45: *(A Message To the Presidential Candidates)/Colloquial Sex (Legend of Today)* (Parrot 3021) 1968.

Born Kenneth King on 6 December 1944 in London, **King** had a transatlantic hit with his pseudo-protest song *Everyone's Gone To The Moon*, whilst he was an undergraduate at Cambridge in 1965. He also wrote *It's Good News Week* for **Hedgehopper's Anonymous** the same year. On the back of these successes he became a personal assistant to Decca's founder Edward Lewis, signing and naming **Genesis**, as well as producing their debut. He also continued to record himself. At the start of the seventies he set up his own production company and recorded a series of one-off novelty songs, some of which were leased to record companies and became hits. His 1971 creations included:- *It's The Same Old Song* (The Weathermen) (No 19); a heavy metal version of The Archies' *Sugar Sugar (Sakkarin)* (No 12), which were recorded by **King** using a pseudonym, as well as *Johnny Reggae* for The Piglets and *Keep On Dancing* (originally a US hit for The Gentrys in 1965) for The Bay City Rollers.

In 1972 he formed UK Records - he continued to record under his own name, but enjoyed greater chart success under various pseudonyms:- *Loop Di Love* (Shag) (No 4) 1972; *(I Can't Get No) Satisfaction* (Bubblerock) (No 29) 1974; *Chick-A-Boom (Don't Ya Jes Love It)* (53rd and 3rd featuring The Sound Of Shag) (No 36) 1975; *In The Mood* (Sound 9418) (No 46) 1976; and *It Only Takes A Minute* (One Hundred Ton And A Feather) (No 9) 1976. He also got into the Top Five with his cover of George Baker's *Una Paloma Blanca*. The most successful act to record on his label was **10cc**. Other signings included **The Kursaal Flyers** and Ricky Wilde (son of Marty).

In the eighties he wound up UK Records and concentrated on being a pop 'expert' and radio and TV presenter. He also devoted much of his energy to grooming underage boys for sex, an activity which earned him a lengthy jail sentence in November 2001. (VJ/MM)

Paul King

ALBUM: 1   BEEN IN THE PEN TOO LONG
                    (w/lyric insert)   (Dawn DNLS 3035) 1972 SC

45:        Whoa Buck/Zoe   (Dawn DNS 1023) 1972

King was best known as a member of **Mungo Jerry** and sang and played guitar on their first three albums. When he left he was in **King Earl Boogie Band** as well as pursuing a solo career. This album, recorded whilst he was still a member of **Mungo Jerry**, is blues-based in a **Brett Marvin and The Thunderbolts** vein. He was assisted on the album by **Paul Brett**. (VJ)

Reg King

ALBUM: 1   REG KING   (United Artists UAS 29157) 1971 R1

45:        α   Little Boy/10,000 Miles   (United Artists UP 35204) 1971
NB: α as **Reg King** and **B.B. Blunder**.

King had sung in the mid-sixties R&B outfit **The Action** but left to pursue a solo career before they evolved into **Mighty Baby**. He co-produced Chris Barber's *Battersea Rain Dance* album, as well as appearing on Gordon Jackson's *Thinking Back* album (both were on Marmalade). Most of **Mighty Baby** played on his own album, which included a version of *Little Boy*, the abandoned last **Action** 45. **King**'s voice was as soulful and emotive as ever and the instrumentation from the **Mighty Baby** team had flashes of brilliance, but **King**'s heavy production made the overall sound too lumpen. Also appearing are members of **Blossom Toes**, as well as Mick Taylor of **The Rolling Stones** and **Brian Auger**. After making the album he sustained head injuries following a fall and made no further solo records, though he has occasionally teamed up with **The Action** for rapturously-received reunion gigs. (JRd/NR/RMJ)

King Crimson

Personnel:			
ROBERT FRIPP	gtr, keyb'ds	ABCDE
GREG LAKE	bs, vcls	AB
MIKE GILES	drms, vcls	AB
IAN McDONALD	sax, woodwind, keyb'ds	A
PETE GILES	bs	B
GORDON HASKELL	vcls, bs	BC
MEL COLLINS	sax, flute	BCD
(KEITH TIPPET	piano	BCD)
ANDY McCULLOCH	drms	C
BOZ BURRELL	bs, vcls	D
IAN WALLACE	drms	D
JOHN WETTON	bs, vcls	E
BILL BRUFORD	drms	E

KING CRIMSON - In The Wake Of Poseidon (LP)

KING CRIMSON - Lizard (LP).

DAVID CROSS	violin, flute, keyb'ds		E
JAMIE MUIR	perc		E

NB: (1)-(10) all reissued on Polydor in the 1977 (1979 in the case of (9)). (1) and (6) reissued as a double package by Polydor in 1980. . The following albums are also available on CD:- (1), (2), (3), (4), (6), (7), (8) and (10) on Virgin (EGCD 1, EGCD 2, EGCD 4, EGCD 5, EGCD 7, EGCD 12, EGCD 15 and EGCD 22, respectively) 1987. Also on CD are: - The Compact King Crimson (EGCD 68) 1986, and The King Crimson Box Set (which couples (1) and (6) (EGBC 6)) 1989. (2) reissued again on CD (Virgin CDVKCX 2) 2000 and again (DGM 0502) 2005. (3) reissued again on CD (Virgin CDVCX 3) 2000. (4) reissued on CD (Virgin CDVKCX 4) 2000. (5) reissued again on CD (Virgin CDVKCX 11) 2002 and again on CD remastered (Panegyric DGM 0511). (9) reissued again on CD (Virgin CDVKCX 12) 2002 and again (EG 724381 21202) with three bonus cuts including a mind-blowing version of 21st Century Schizoid Man.

In addition there's The Essential King Crimson: Frame By Frame, a comprehensive four boxed CD retrospective, the production of which was overseen by former member Robert Fripp. However, even this was upstaged by The Great Deceiver (Virgin/Discipline KC DLS 1) 1993, a 4-CD set of 47 tracks, almost five hours of live material, recorded in 1973 and 1974 by the Cross/Fripp/Wetton/Bruford line-up, in a limited edition of 20,000 complete with a 68-page booklet. Another live album from this period was released recently on Fripp's Discipline label called The Night Watch - Live at the Concertgebouw Amsterdam 23/11/1973 making their most bootlegged show officially available. Also of interest is the recently released Epitaph 4-CD set (Discipline Global Mobile DGM 9607) 1997, which brings together all the existing live and BBC recordings from the original 1969 band. Ladies Of The Road - Live, 1971-72 (Discipline Global Mobile DGM 0203) 2003 is a 2-CD set.

From the late sixties until the mid-eighties King Crimson was one of the country's top progressive rock groups. They avoided pop sensibilities, venturing into the realms of jazz and classical music and whilst this

probably cost them mass success they have enjoyed a strong cult following. They left behind a legacy of two or three albums of startlingly imaginative progressive rock.

King Crimson evolved out of Giles, Giles and Fripp, which Fripp had formed with the Giles brothers in 1967. Frustrated by lack of success Peter Giles left the band and with the addition of Greg Lake and Ian McDonald, King Crimson was born early in 1969. They debuted at London's Speakeasy Club, made their recording debut with a session for John Peel's 'Top Gear' and enjoyed a 12-week residency at the Marquee, but their big break came when they supported The Rolling Stones at their free concert in Hyde Park and made a big impression on the vast crowd.

Their debut album is usually regarded as their prime achievement and its best known track, 21st Century Schizoid Man, had a futurist feel and impulsiveness that made the listener sit up and take note. Its inclusion on Island's budget compilation, Nice Enough To Eat (LP), also helped bring it to a wider audience but strangely it was not released as a 45 at the time. The title track, a superb progressive number with harmonies and mellotron, was selected for 45 release but wasn't sufficiently commercial for the singles market. This debut album is recommended as one of the best by a UK progressive band.

After several UK gigs they toured America, where their debut album also enjoyed chart success peaking at No 28. At the time, a cover of Donovan's Get Thy Bearings was a pivotal part of their live act and featured solos from all the band's members. Indeed, Donovan joined them onstage to jam the song on at least one occasion and several versions have subsequently resurfaced on the Epitaph retrospective box set.

When they returned the first of many future line-up changes took place. Ian McDonald and Michael Giles departed (they later did an album together) and it was a semi-permanent line-up (B) that recorded their next rather uncommercial 45 and In The Wake Of Poseidon. Indeed whilst recording this album Fripp turned down the opportunity to replace Peter Banks in Yes and to join Blue Whale at Aynsley Dunbar's invitation. Shortly after work began on the album Greg Lake left to form Emerson, Lake and Palmer and Elton John was booked as a session musician to replace him, although when Lake agreed to sing on the album as a favour Elton's sessions were cancelled. Musically In The Wake Of Poseidon was very similar to their first effort and again one of the stronger tracks, Cadence and Cascade, was included on the 1970 compilation Bumpers (2-LP), taking it to a wider audience. Side one was full of first class harmonious progressive rock, but side two included an 18-minute instrumental piece, loosely based on Holst's Mars from the Planet's Suite, which wasn't always entirely convincing.

Singer/bass player Gordon Haskell and drummer Andy McCulloch were added to the line-up which started work on Lizard (apparently Bryan Ferry failed the audition for this one!). Haskell had previously played with Fripp in The League Of Gentlemen, but the result was a mostly inaccessible album which veered closer to avant-garde jazz than progressive rock and, unsurprisingly, it only managed a moderate placing in UK Album Charts.

KING CRIMSON - Red (CD).

KINGDOM COME - Galactic Zoo Dosier (CD).

There are a few redeeming features, though, guest vocals from **Jon Anderson** and the album does contain some of Pete Sinfield's most surreal and psychedelic lyrics. Sinfield also provided lyrics for many **Emerson, Lake and Palmer** tracks and for some of PFM's English albums, in addition to the first four **King Crimson** albums.

After recording the album **Haskell** left the band followed by McCulloch a few days later - he would later resurface in **Greenslade**. The ever resilient Fripp put together a new line-up, which embarked on a successful UK tour. Their next album *Islands* originally came with a gatefold bag including the lyrics but for the most part the vinyl inside does not include nearly enough of the actual core band playing together. The rhythm section are absent for over half the album and the overall sound is based too heavily on the contributions of **Tippett**, several members of his band and even a chamber orchestra! Most fans and critics have came down on it for being too lightweight and drummer Andy Wallace, after leaving the band, called it "an airy-fairy piece of shit".

After two further US tours most of the band had left leaving Fripp to form yet another version of **King Crimson**, which he immediately did. Meanwhile, Island released *Earthbound*, a budget-priced live album recorded on the second of the US tours which was let down by poor sound quality. The follow-up, *Larks' Tongue In Aspic*, is generally regarded as their best since their debut. It came with the lyrics printed on the inner bag and with far more structured, melodic songs than their recent efforts. *Starless And Bible Black* continued their renewed sense of purpose and contained lots of strong songs, particularly *The Night Watch*, which was also issued as a single.

Gradually, though, line-up E, fell apart. Jamie Muir had left after the *Lark's Tongue* album and reputedly spent a few years at the Samye Ling Tibetan Monastery in Eskdalemuir in the Scottish borders. Now David Cross left although the record *Red*, was another strong album with good material - the title track, for example, was a fine instrumental. However, a week before the album's release Robert Fripp announced that the band had split for good. John Wetton, formerly with **Family**, went on to join **Uriah Heep**, before forming UK with Bill Bruford who also made several solo albums. After their demise a live album, *U.S.A.*, was issued, recorded on their last American tour. A vast improvement on their previous live effort (*Earthbound*) this one captured the band at their best with masterful versions of *Larks' Tongues Part 2, U.S.A* and *21st Century Schizoid Man*.

The double compilation LP, *The Young Person's Guide To King Crimson*, compiled by Robert Fripp, contained tracks from all their studio albums (except *Lizard*), the demo of *I Talk To The Wind* (from their 1st album) and many tracks were remixed. Nicely packaged, with a booklet of photos, many reviews and a gig list, it had much to commend it, but surprisingly omitted the band's best known number, *21st Century Schizoid Man*. Later in 1981 Robert Fripp formed what effectively became a new **King Crimson**, recording three albums for the EG label. He also married Toyah Willcox in 1986. **King Crimson** reformed in the nineties recording albums like *Thrak* in 1994.

In 2000 they released a new studio album *ConstruKction Of Light* and a live box *Heavy ConstruKction* compiled from performances on the supporting European tour was released later in the year. For their 30th anniversary Fripp commissioned the remastering of their first 15 years catalogue.

The Essential King Crimson: Frame By Frame 4-CD boxed retrospective, released in 1991, comes with a comprehensive 64-page booklet largely made up of photos and a sample of the press commentary about the band over the years. This is recommended to those wanting to explore the band's music in depth.

An alternative is *The Great Deceiver*, a 4-CD set of live material recorded between 23 October 1973 and 30 June 1974. This also has a comprehensive booklet with key diary dates, commentary and photos.

Epitaph is a 2-CD box set, with two additional CDs available by mail order. The collection features five concerts plus their two sessions recorded for Radio 1. It provides more insight into their improvisational creativity during 1969 and the package also includes an informative 63-page booklet.

Ladies Of The Road - Live, 1971-72 includes a 55-minute version of *21st Century Schizoid Man* and fine versions of *The Sailor's Tale, Cirkus* and *Formentara Lady* but as with many albums of this type it's rather patchy overall.

The band has appeared on various compilations including *Bumpers* (2-LP) playing *Cadence and Cascade* and *Nice Enough To Eat* (LP) with *21st Century Schizoid Man*. (VJ/KB)

Kingdom Come

Personnel:

ARTHUR BROWN	vcls		AB
PHIL SHUTT	bs		AB
ANDY DALBY	gtr		AB
MICHAEL HARRIS	keyb'ds		A
MARTIN STEER	drms		A
VICTOR PERAINO	keyb'ds		B

ALBUMS:
1(A)	GALACTIC ZOO DOSSIER		
	(Some w/poster)	(Polydor 2310 130) 1971 R1/SC	
2(A)	KINGDOM COME	(Polydor 2310 178) 1972 SC	
3(B)	JOURNEY	(Polydor 2310 254) 1973 SC	

NB: (1), (2) and (3) reissued on CD (Voiceprint VP 135 CD, 136 CD and 137 CD) in 1993, each release coming with bonus material. *Jam* (Voiceprint VP 163 CD) 1995 contains material from a recently-discovered 1970 'jam'. There's also a 2-LP compilation with unreleased material, *The Lost Ears* (Gull GUD 2003/4) 1976.

45s:
General Messenger/	
I D Side To Be B Side The C Side	(Polydor 2001 234) 1971
Spirit Of Joy / Come Alive	(Polydor 2001 416) 1972

KINGDOM COME - Kingdom Come (CD).

KINGDOM COME - Journey (CD).

Galactic Zoo is an album of chaos and mayhem, with church - like mantras along the way. *Kingdom Come* is similarly demented. *Journey* is more song-based and there are some great guitar riffs on the closing track *Come Alive*. Many regard it as one of the best 'space-rock' albums of all time. *Jam*, however, is a spontaneous, rambling set, which veers between jazz and hippie-rock and is only for diehard fans.

The **Kingdom Come** live performance was as entertaining as that of **Brown**'s 'Crazy World' band. Arthur would come on resplendent in a set of traffic lights or would climb into a giant syringe on stage. For the band's *Journey* album they all wore gold paint and used a Bentley drum machine rather than a conventional drummer. Andy Dalby was only 16 when he joined the band having already had a stint with the **Spirit Of John Morgan**. He later played for **Kiki Dee**, Vapour Trails and went on to production work. **Arthur Brown** at his best possessed one of the great voices of rock music and his stage shows were never dull. (BS/VJ)

King Earl Boogie Band

Personnel:	RUSSELL JOHN BROWN	drms	A
	COLIN EARL	keyb'ds, vcls	A
	PAUL KING	vcls, gtr, banjo, hrmnca	A
	DAVE LAMBERT	gtr, vcls	A
	JOE RUSH	perc	A

ALBUM:	1(A)	TROUBLE AT MILL	(Dawn DNLS 3040) 1972 SC

45s:	Plastic Jesus/If The Lord Don't Get You	(Dawn DNS 1024) 1972
	Starlight/Goin' To Germany	(Dawn DNS 1028) 1972

A short-lived UK rock-boogie band. **Paul King** also made solo recordings and together with Colin Earl had earlier been in **Mungo Jerry**. Dave Lambert had been in **Fire**. Their debut 45 *Plastic Jesus* was produced by **Dave Cousins** (of **The Strawbs**). In June 1972 Brown and Rush were added to the line-up, around the time **Paul King** released his solo album (*Been In The Pen Too Long* for Dawn). Later that year the band put out *Trouble At The Mill*, with Dave Cousins again handling production duties. It was a disappointing effort, however and in September 1972 Lambert left to join **Dave Cousins** in **The Strawbs**. Earl departed to Ooblee Dooblee Band and **King** as 'P. Rufus King' released a 45 *Look At Me Now/Nobody Knows* (Dawn DNS 1031) 1973.

They later reformed in the late eighties and have toured on and off ever since. (VJ/JM)

Kingly Band

45:	Bitter And The Sweet/	
	Standing At The Crossroads	(Decca F 12926) 1969

This was a short-lived outfit. (VJ)

The Kingpins

Personnel:	HARVEY FROST	ld gtr	A
	LANCE HARVEY	vcls	A
	LES PROBYN	bs	AB
	DAVE STIRRUP	gtr, vcls	AB
	ROGER WOOD	drms	AB
	ROY GRANT	vcls	B
	KEITH TURNER	gtr	B

45s:	He's Telling You Lies/	
	How Do You Fix A Broken Heart	(Pye 7N 15647) 1964
	Two Right Feet/	
	That's The Way It Should Be	(Oriole CB 1986) 1965 SC
	Summer's Come And Gone/	
	Another Tear Falls	(Columbia DB 8146) 1967

At the end of 1965 Frost and Harvey left and Roy Grant (ex-The Saints) and Keith Turner came in as replacements. In 1966 they recorded a 45 in Germany on Star-Club, *Gotta Got A Good Thing Going / Willow Tree*. The same line-up recorded the 45 for Columbia in 1967.

Compilation appearances include: *Gotta Get A Good Thing Goin'* and *Willow Tree* on *The Star-Club Singles Complete, Vol. 9* (LP & CD); *Willow Tree* on *The Star-Club Anthology, Vol. 4* (LP); and *That's The Way It Should Be* on *Beat Us If You Can! Vol. 1* (LP). (WD/VJ)

The Kingpins

Personnel:	JIMMY BARNARD	drms	ABC
	TONY MARTIN	ld vcls	A
	RAY NEALE	ld vcls, gtr	ABCDE
	KEITH NEALE	bs	ABCDE
	GLYN STEPHENS	ld gtr	AB
	GEOFFREY COPPENS	ld vcls	B
	RED REECE	drms	D
	JOHN WOOLOFF	gtr	DE
	LES WARREN	drms	E

ALBUM:	1	THE KINGPINS FOR SALE	(Tenth Planet TP 016) 1995

NB: (1) limited numbered edition of 1,000.

This band came from New Addington in Kent. They were unconnected to the bands that recorded for Columbia or Oriole. They recorded several acetates at R.G. Jones' studio in Morden, South London:- *Diamond Girl / For Your Love* (Oak acetate); *Living In The Past* (Oak acetate one sided); *Hurting My Pride / Maybe Sometime* (Oak acetate); *You're My Girl* (Oak acetate one-sided); *You're My Girl/Maybe Sometime* (Oak acetate); *Baby I Need / Baby I Need (edited)* (Oak acetate) plus a four-track Oak acetate EP *Mysterious* (containing *Travelling Man, Mysterious, Do You Love Me* and *Raining In My Sunshine*).

KINGPINS - For Sale (LP).

They also recorded as **Those Fadin' Colours** and at the end of 1967 changed names to **Orange Seaweed**.

You can read all about **The Kingpins** and their related bands in the liner notes to Tenth Planet's release *The Kingpins For Sale*.

Compilation appearances have included: *Maybe Sometimes, You're My Girl* and *Baby I Need* (full length version) on *Purple Heart Surgery, Vol. 1* (LP) and *Hens Teeth Vol. 2* (CD); *Maybe Sometime* on *Story Of Oak Records* (2-LP); *You're My Girl* on *The Story Of Oak Records* (CD); and *Diamond Girl* on *Trans-World Punk Rave-Up!, Vol. 1* (LP). (VJ)

Charles Kingsley Creation

45:    Summer Without Love/
       Still In Love With You   (Columbia DB 7758) 1965 R2

Joe Meek handled the production duties on this beat ballad 45, which was the work of two brothers.

Summer Without Sun and *Still In Love With You* can both be found on *RGM Rarities, Vol. 2* (CD). (MWh)

The Kingstons

45:    Look Around/It Takes A Worried Man 'A
       Souvenier From Pontins'   (no label or cat. no.) 19??

How about this? A 45 from the holiday camp - obviously only available there! A folk ballad trio - Peter, Paul and Pam it would appear! The flip is a pretty ghastly sing-along effort. (VJ)

The Kinks

Personnel: MICK AVORY   drms   ABCD
             DAVE DAVIES   ld vcls, gtr ABCD
             RAY DAVIES   ld vcls, gtr ABCD
             PETE QUAIFE   bs   A
             JOHN DALTON   bs   BC
             JOHN GOSLING   keyb'ds   CD
             ANDY PYLE   bs   D

				HCP
ALBUMS:	1(A)	KINKS	(Pye NPL 18096) 1964 R2	3
(up to	2(A)	KINDA KINKS	(Pye NPL 18112) 1965 R2	3
1976)	3(A)	THE KINK KONTROVERSY	(Pye NPL 18131) 1965 R2	9
	4(A)	WELL RESPECTED KINKS (Budget Compilation)		
			(Marble Arch MAL 612) 1966 SC	5

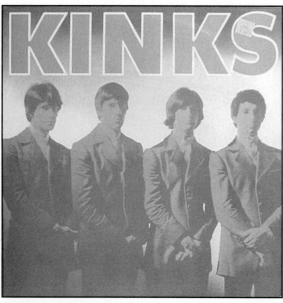
THE KINKS - Kinks (LP).

THE KINKS - Kinda Kinks (LP).

5(A)	FACE TO FACE (mono/stereo)		
		(Pye N(S)PL 18149) 1966	R2/R3 12
6(A)	LIVE AT THE KELVIN HALL (mono/stereo)		
		(Pye N(S)PL 18191) 1967	R2/R3 -
7(A)	SOMETHING ELSE BY THE KINKS (mono/stereo)		
		(Pye N(S)LP 18193) 1967	R3/R2 35
8(A)	SUNNY AFTERNOON (Budget Compilation)		
		(Marble Arch MAL 716) 1967	9
9(A)	KINKS ARE THE VILLAGE GREEN PRESERVATION		
	SOCIETY (mono/stereo) (Pye N(S)PL 18233) 1968	R3/R2	
10(B)	ARTHUR (mono/stereo) (Pye N(S)PL 18317) 1969	-	
11(A)	THE KINKS (2-LP compilation) 1964		
		(Pye NPL 18326) 1970	SC -
12(C)	LOLA VERSUS POWERMAN AND THE		
	MONEY-GO-ROUND VOL.1 (Pye NSPL 18359) 1970	SC -	
13(C)	PERCY (Soundtrack from film)		
		(Pye NSPL 18359) 1971	SC -
14(C)	MUSWELL HILLBILLIES	(RCA SF 823) 1971	SC -
15(C)	EVERYBODY'S IN SHOWBIZ, EVERYBODY'S		
	A STAR (2-LP)	(RCA DPS 2035) 1972	SC -
16(C)	PRESERVATION ACT 1	(RCA SF 8392) 1973	SC -
17(-)	ALL THE GOOD TIMES (4 album box set)		
		(Pye 11PP 100) 1973	R1 -
18(C)	PRESERVATION ACT 2 (2-LP)		
	(RCA LPLZ 5040) 1974 SC -		
19(C)	SOAP OPERA	(RCA SF 8411) 1975 -	
20(C)	SCHOOLBOYS IN DISCGRACE	(RCA RS 1028) 1975 -	
21(C)	CELLULOID HEROES - THE KINKS'		
	GREATEST	(RCA RS 1059) 1976 -	

NB: (1), (2) and (3); there were stereo versions of these, but probably for export only. (4) and (8) UK only releases. (1) reissued on vinyl (Earmark 42021) and also as *Kinks Size* (Abraxas 42062) with a Japanese cover. (1) reissued on CD (Essential/Castle ESM CD 482) 1998 with bonus tracks, new sleevenotes and rare photos and memorabilia and again CD (Sanctuary SMRCD 025) 2004, with many bonus tracks. (2) reissued on vinyl (Essential ESM LP 483) and on CD (Essential/Castle ESM CD 483) 1998 with bonus tracks, new sleevenotes and rare photos and again on CD (Sanctuary SMRCD 026) 2004, with many bonus tracks. (2) also reissued on CD with a German art cover (Abraxas 42069). (3) reissued on vinyl (Essential ESM LP 507) and on CD (Essential/Castle ESM CD 507) 1998 with bonus tracks, new sleevenotes and rare photos and reissued again on CD (Sanctuary Midline SMRCD 027) 2004, with many bonus tracks. (3) also reissued on vinyl as *United Kingdom The Kinks Kontroversy With Italia* (Abraxas 42063) with the original Italian sleeve. (1), (2) and (3) are also available as a 3-CD set (Sanctuary CMETD 1033). (5) reissued on vinyl (Essential ESM LP 479) and on CD (Essential/Castle ESM CD 479) 1998 with bonus tracks, new sleevenotes and rare photos and reissued again on CD (Sanctuary Midline SMRCD 028) 2004, with many bonus tracks. (6) reissued on CD (Sanctuary Midline SMRCD 061) and on vinyl (Akarma CMHLP 012). *Live At Kelvin Hall* (Essential/Castle ESM 508) 1998 comprises the entire original album in mono and stereo. (7) reissued on vinyl (Essential ESM LP 480) and on CD (Essential/Castle ESM CD 480) 1998 with bonus tracks, new sleevenotes and rare photos, then reissued on vinyl (Earmark 42005) 2003 and again on CD (Sanctuary Midline SMRCD 029) 2004, with many bonus tracks. Two stereo test pressings are known to exist of (9) with 12 tracks and these are valued by 'Record Collector' at in excess of £600. There is also a rarer blue label 15-track release of this album, in both mono and stereo. (9) reissued on CD (Essential/Castle ESM 481) 1998 as the 15-track U.K. mono album plus the 12-track stereo album listed overseas and the *Days* 45 in mono. (9) reissued on vinyl (Earmark 42006) and as an expanded 3-LP set in mono (Earmark 42047). (9) reissued again on CD (Castle CMTCD 319) and also as an expanded remastered 3-CD set (Sanctuary Midline SMETD 102) which contains both mono and stereo mixes of the original 1968 release with bonus mono and stereo singles and aborted songs on each disc. The third disc contains various cast-offs and oddities. (10) reissued on CD (Essential/Castle ESM CD 511) 1998 plus six mono and three stereo bonus tracks and the previously unissued *Mr Shoemaker's Daughter*. (10) also issued on CD (Castle CMTCD 322) and (Sanctuary Midline SMRCD 062), with many bonus tracks. (12) reissued on CD (Essential/Castle ESM CD 509) 1998 plus the mono 45 version of *Lola*, a demo version of *Apeman*, which was issued as a 45 in Denmark and an unissued demo of *Powerman*. (12) reissued on vinyl (Earmark 42010) and remastered on CD (Sanctuary Midline SMR CD 063). (13) reissued on CD (Essential/Castle ESM CD 510) 1998, plus *Dreams*, *Moments* and three unissued versions of *The Way Love Used To Be* (all unissued mono versions from the film). (13) remastered and reissued on CD (Sanctuary Midline SMR CD 064). (15) reissued on CD (Rhino RZ 70935) 1990. Rhino have combined (16), (18) and the subsequent double compilation and non-album 45 which completed the concept onto two CDs, but they were hardly **The Kinks** at their best and are only recommended for diehard fans who don't already have the original recordings. Full release details: - *Preservation (A Play In Two Acts)* (Rhino RZ 70523) 1991. (14), (19) and (20) reissued on CD in the US by Rhino.

The following were US only releases: - *Kinks Size* (Reprise 6158) 1965; *Kinks Kingdom* (Reprise 6184) 1966; *Kinks' Greatest Hits* (Reprise 6217) 1966; *The Kink Kronikles* (Compilation) (Reprise 6454) 1972 and *The Great Lost Kinks Album* (Reprise 2127) 1973. They also recorded a very rare German-only album, *In Germany* (Vogue LDVS 17 077) 1965.

As one would expect, their output has been subject to much repackaging. The more successful ones have included: - *Golden Hour Of The Kinks* (Golden Hour GH 501) 1971 (No 21); *The Kinks' 20 Golden Greats* (Pye/Ronco RPL 2031) 1978 (No 19); *Kinks Greatest Hits - Dead End Street* (PRT KINK 1) 1981 (No 96) and *The Ultimate Collection* (Castle Communications CTVLP 001) 1989 also issued on CD (CTVCD 001) 1990 (No 35). On CD there's *Hit Singles* (PRT PYC 4001) 1988; *Are Well Respected Men*, (PRT PYC 7001), a 2-CD which includes all the material from their Pye years not included on their original albums and *The Best Of The Kinks 1964-65* (Pickwick PWKS 527) 1989, which concentrates on their first two years with Pye and includes all their hits up to *See My Friends*. *The Very Best Of The Kinks* (Polygram TV 537 554-2) 1997, features twenty-five of their greatest songs, including all fourteen of their Top 10 singles, but no material recorded after 1970! *The Singles Collection / Waterloo Sunset* (Essential! ESS CD 592) 1997 runs through their hit singles on one CD and includes a collection of rarities, novelties and other odds and sods on the second. Castle, having acquired the PRT catalogue and in 1989/90, restored all of PRT's former CD reissues of all **The Kinks** Pye albums. There's also a 10-CD set *Pye Album Collection* (Sanctuary CMXBX 1125). *Fab Forty* (Decal CDLIK D 74) 1991, is a 2-CD set of all their original 45s for Pye. *The Kinks EP Collection, Vol. 2* (See For Miles SEECD 329) 1992, also on album and cassette, has been compiled from French EPs. *The Kinks EP Collection* (Box Set) (Essential ESFCD 667) is a 10-CD box set of all their UK EP tracks and includes miniature copies of the original sleeves. *The Kinks EP Collection* (Box Set) (Vol 2) (Essential ESFCD 904) 2000 again showcases their EPs, this time very rare ones from around the world. It's also a 10-CD box set with miniatures of their original EP sleeves. *BBC Sessions 1964-1977* (2-CD) (Sanctuary SANDD 010) is an exhaustive collection of their sixties sessions for the Beeb. *Kinks Remastered* (3-CD box set) (Essential ESBCD 268) is a superb collection drawing material from 10 of their albums. *Marble Arch Years* (3-CD) (Castle CMGBX318) is a reissue of their first three Marble Arch albums: - *Well Respected Kinks*, *Sunny Afternoon* and *Kinda Kinks*. *The Singles Collection* (2-CD) (Sanctuary Midline SMRCD 024) 2005 features 25 of their hit singles on the first disc and the second disc comprises rarities, demos, alternate

versions and live recordings - all taken from the archives of Ray Davies so this should interest **Kinks**' fans. *The Kinks Singles Collection 1964-1970* (2-LP) (Earmark 42040) 2005 compiles their hits and favourites from this period. *The Ultimate Collection* (2-CD) (Sanctuary SANDD 109) compiles their hits alongside some rarer tracks like *Do It Again*, *Celluloid Heroes* and *Starstruck*. *You Really Got Me - Best Of The Kinks* (CD) (Select SELCD 560) 2005 is a 20-track collection containing almost all of their big hits.

EPs:	1	KINKSIZE SESSION	(Pye NEP 24200) 1964 R1
	2	KINKSIZE HITS	(Pye NEP 24203) 1964 SC
	3	KWYET KINKS	(Pye NEP 24221) 1965 R1
	4	DEDICATED KINKS	(Pye NEP 24258) 1966 R2
	5	THE KINKS (SOMETHING ELSE)	
			(Pye NEP 24296) 1968 R3
	6	THE KINKS (export issue, red or blue vinyl)	
			(Pye Yesteryear AMEP 1001) 1975 SC
	7	YOU REALLY GOT ME (picture disc)	(PRT KBD 1) 1983

NB: (1)-(5) are compiled on *The EP Collection* (See For Miles SEE 295) 1990, also on CD (SEE CD 295) 1990 along with *The Dave Davies Hits* EP. (5) was actually called **The Kinks**.

HCP

45s: (up to 1976)	Long Tall Sally/ I Took My Baby Home	(Pye 7N 15611) 1964 R2 -
	You Still Want Me/ You Do Something To Me	(Pye 7N 15636) 1964 R3 -
	You Really Got Me/It's All Right	(Pye 7N 15673) 1964 1
	All Day And All Of The Night/ I Gotta Move	(Pye 7N 15714) 1964 2
	Tired Of Waiting/Come On Now	(Pye 7N 15759) 1965 1
	Everybody's Gonna Be Happy/ Who'll Be The Next In Line	(Pye 7N 15813) 1965 17
	Set Me Free/I Need You	(Pye 7N 15854) 1965 9
	See My Friend/ Never Met A Girl Like You Before	(Pye 7N 15919) 1965 10
	Till The End Of The Day/ Where Have All The Good Times Gone	(Pye 7N 15981) 1965 8
	Dedicated Follower Of Fashion/ Sittin' On My Sofa	(Pye 7N 17064) 1966 4
	Well Respected Man/ Milk Cow Blues (export only)	(Pye 7N 17100) 1966 -
	Sunny Afternoon/ I'm Not Like Everybody Else	(Pye 7N 17125) 1966 1
	Dead End Street/Big Black Smoke	(Pye 7N 17222) 1966 5
	Mr. Pleasant/ This Is Where I Belong (export only)	(Pye 7N 17314) 1967 -
	Waterloo Sunset/Act Nice And Gentle	(Pye 7N 17321) 1967 2
	Autumn Almanac/Mr. Pleasant	(Pye 7N 17400) 1962 3
	Wonderboy/Polly	(Pye 7N 17468) 1968 36
	Days/She's Got Everything	(Pye 7N 17573) 1968 12
	Plastic Man/King Kong	(Pye 7N 17724) 1969 31
	Drivin'/Mindless Child Of Motherhood	(Pye 7N 17776) 1969 SC -
α	Shangri-La/ Last Of The Steam-Powered Trains	(Pye 7N 17812) 1969 -

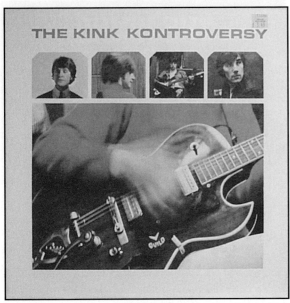

THE KINKS - The Kink Kontroversy (LP).

THE KINKS - Well Respected Kinks (LP).

479

KINKS - Face To Face (LP).

Shangri-La/		
This Man He Weeps Tonight	(Pye 7N 17812) 1969 SC -	
Victoria/Mr. Churchill Says	(Pye 7N 17865) 1969 33	
Lola/Berkeley Mews	(Pye 7N 17961) 1970 2	
Apeman/Rats	(Pye 7N 45016) 1970 5	
God's Children/Moments (export issue)	(Pye 7N 8001) 1971 -	
Percy (33rpm 4-track maxi single, PS)	(Pye 7NX 8001) 1971 -	
Supersonic Rocket Ship/		
You Don't Know My Name	(RCA RCA 2211) 1972 16	
Celluloid Heroes/Hot Potatoes	(RCA RCA 2299) 1972 -	
Sitting In The Midday Sun/		
One Of The Survivors	(RCA RCA 2387) 1973 -	
Sweet Lady Genevieve/		
Sitting In My Hotel	(RCA RCA 2418) 1973 -	
Mirror Of Love/Cricket	(RCA RCA 5015) 1974 -	
Mirror Of Love/He's Evil	(RCA RCA 5042) 1974 -	
Holiday Romance/		
Shepherds Of The Nation	(RCA RCA 2478) 1974 -	
Ducks On The Wall/Rush Hour Blues	(RCA RCA 2546) 1975 -	
You Can't Stop The Music/		
Have Another Drink	(RCA RCA 2567) 1975 -	
No More Looking Back/		
Jack The Idiot Dunce/The Hard Way (PS)	(RCA RCM 1) 1976 -	

Reissues:
Where Have All The Good Times Gone?/		
Lola	(Pye 7N 45313) 1974 SC -	
Sunny Afternoon/Dedicated Follower Of Fashion/Lola/		
Waterloo Sunset	(Pye BD 105) 1977 -	
You Really Got Me/		
All Day And All Of The Night	(Pye FBS 1) 1979 -	
You Really Got Me/		
All Day And All Of The Night	(RK RK 1027) 1980 -	
Lola/Celluloid Heroes	(Arista ARIST 404) 1981 -	
Waterloo Sunset/		
Dedicated Follower Of Fashion	(Old Gold OG 9140) 1982 -	
You Really Got Me/Misty Water	(PRT KD 1) 1983 47	
You Really Got Me 1 & 2/		
All Day And All Of The Night (pic disc)	(PRT KPD 1) 1983 -	
You Really Got Me/		
All Day And All Of The Night	(Old Gold OG 9408) 1984 -	
All Day And All Of The Night/		
I Gotta Move (pic disc)	(Prt KINKT 20) 1984 -	
Sunny Afternoon/		
Tired Of Waiting For You	(old Gold OG 9577) 1986 -	
Lola/Apeman	(old Gold OG 9579) 1986 -	
Dedicated Follower Of Fashion/		
Autumn Almanac	(PRT 7P 355) 1986 -	
Sunny Afternoon/Sittin' On The Sofa (PS)	(PRT PYS 2) 1987 -	
All Day And All Of The Night/I Gotta Move	(PRT PYS 4) 1988 -	
Dedicated Follower Of Fashion/		
Autumn Almanac (picture disc)	(PRT PYS 7) 1988 -	
β You Really Got Me/All Day And All Of The Night/		
Tired Of Waiting For You	(Old Gold OG 6102) 1988 -	
β Waterloo Sunset/Sunny Afternoon/		
Lola	(Old Gold OG 6117) 1989 -	

NB: α Unissued. β CD singles.

The Kinks are a British institution. They weren't as popular as **The Beatles**, **Rolling Stones** or **The Who** but they recorded several classic singles and a few good albums. Setting out as an R&B/blues band they were enormously influential in the States in the sixties as an important part of the British invasion sound. In later years, their material drew heavily on the British music hall tradition and traditional pop, but also incorporated aspects of country, folk and blues. They became the most English of bands and in Ray Davies they were fronted by a great showman and songwriter. Over the years their live act became increasingly professional and sophisticated from the drunken brawls into which some of their earlier live acts had degenerated. In the late seventies they relocated to the States and refashioned themselves as a hard-rock band for the remainder of the decade.

Ray and **Dave Davies** were born on 21st June 1944 and 3rd February 1947 respectively, and grew up in the Muswell Hill area of London. They started gigging in a local pub in 1958 but their first significant break came in 1963 when Ray met **Alexis Korner** after a gig and **Korner** introduced him to London's burgeoning R&B scene. Before long Ray was gigging in his brother Dave's R&B combo, The Ravens, and in a blues outfit called The Dave Hunt Band. Eventually The Ravens attracted the attention of Larry Page who arranged for them to record a five-track demo. This caught the attention of American producer Shel Talmy who got them signed to Pye. They became **The Kinks** early in 1963 when Mick Avory joined as drummer. It's said that in these early days their playing was so raw that on their debut 45, a cover of Little Richard's *Long Tall Sally*, the better parts of two takes had to be spliced together. Predictably it flopped as did the follow-up, *You Still Want Me*, a Ray Davies original from the same session. By this time, though, they'd been the subject of much music press hype and had an appearance on 'Ready Steady Go' under their belt.

The big breakthrough came with their third single, the *Louie Louie* influenced *You Really Got Me*. It's insistent riff powered what was a classic single to No. 1 in the UK in the Summer of 1964 and it also got to No. 7 in the US. Its style very much set the tone for all their singles in this early period. To cash in on this success they were pressured to put out an album which at the time rose to No. 3. In retrospect, though, it contained little of interest other than Ray Davies' *Stop Your Sobbing* and the instrumental *Revenge* (which session guitarist **Jimmy Page** would later re-record with lyrics added). The remaining material was mostly covers of R&B classics by the like of Bo Diddley and Chuck Berry, though another rehash of Slim Harpo's *Got Love If You Want It* had originally been on their five track demo.

The 45 follow-up, *All Day And All Of The Night*, was very much in the *You Really Got Me* mould, but it ensured another massive hit (No 2 UK, No 7 US). Hot on its heels came the laconic, cynical tone of *Tired Of Waiting* (No 1 UK, No 6 US), setting the scene for Ray Davies' writing style. Their next album *Kinda Kinks* peaked at No 3 here and No 60 in the US, where it had been preceded by a US-only album, *Kinks Size*, which had climbed to No 13.

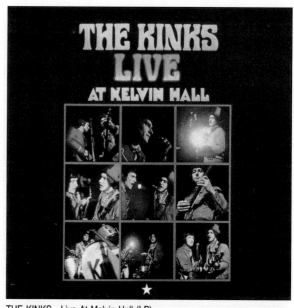

THE KINKS - Live At Melvin Hall (LP).

Their next 45, *Everybody's Gonna Be Happy*, represented a change of style from their earlier efforts, which didn't go down that well in that it could only manage No 17. Then **Dave Davies** was knocked unconscious a few weeks into their first UK tour at a London concert and the remainder of the tour had to be cancelled.

Another strong 45, *Set Me Free*, put them back on track making the Top 10 here and No 23 in the US. The following month they embarked on a US tour which turned out to be a disaster when they were banned for four years for 'unprofessional conduct' by the American Federation Of Musicians after failing to show up at a gig.

See My Friend, an almost psychedelic dreamy number, returned them to the Top 10 but only just, whilst in the States, *Who'll Be Next In Line* (an earlier 'B' side) was a minor hit (No 34). Their final single of the three chord variety was *Till The End Of The Day* (UK No 8, but only US No 50, where the touring ban was already beginning to hit them), which was among their best.

1966 marked the first in a series of changes of direction by the band, as Ray Davies chose to question first the prototype conservative with *A Well Respected Man* and then the whole 'Swinging London' scene with another softer song, *Dedicated Follower Of Fashion*. The former put them back in the US Top 20, whilst the latter reached No 4 in the UK, where it was supported by a promo film. It later rose to No 36 in the US. These two records were really transitional ones en route to the mellow melodic sound which marked the next stage of their development and was epitomised by *Sunny Afternoon* (UK No 1, US No 14), *Dead End Street* (UK No 5, US No 73) and *Waterloo Sunset* (UK No 2). These were unquestionably some of their finest moments. *Face To Face* also echoed this change of direction. Their first album to pursue particular themes it also had its moments with tracks like *House In The Country*, *Exclusive Residence For Sale* and *Session Man*. It sold quite well here peaking at No 12 but faltered in the US at No 135. It was full of social observation and sharp lyrical turns of phrase.

1966 also saw a change in personnel, albeit temporary, when John Dalton deputised for Pete Quaife, initially because the latter had broken his ankle. In fact he later formed a new group **Maple Oak** but rejoined **The Kinks** after they'd put out one flop single. In 1969, of course, John Dalton, who'd played with **The Mark Four**, replaced Quaife permanently when he left to pursue a career in commercial shops and buy a record shop in Copenhagen.

1967 was the year when **Dave Davies** paralleled his career in the band with a solo career after the two tracks from the band's *Something Else* album on which he performed lead vocals were put out on a solo 45. The 'A' side, *Death Of A Clown*, was written by his brother Ray and with the only other single to make much impression being *Susannah's Still Alive*, the experiment proved short-lived. *Something Else*, incidentally would prove to be their last original album to Chart in the UK. It peaked at No 153 in the US.

THE KINKS - Something Else By The Kinks (LP).

THE KINKS - Arthur (LP).

The hits soon dried up too: *Autumn Almanac*, another classic, proved to be their last Top Ten hit for a while with *Wonderboy*, *Days* and *Plastic Man* all selling disappointingly. To some extent, though, the band was beginning to leave their audience behind, as Ray Davies set out to pursue his own songwriting goals. Their next album, *The Village Green Preservation Society*, their first which was more than just a collection of songs, was really his homage to Old England. It sold poorly, but this didn't deter him from returning to the theme on the follow-up, *Arthur (Or The Decline And Fall Of The British Empire)*. This had begun life as a TV musical which he had written with Julian Mitchell. It was also the first on which Dalton replaced Quaife permanently (i.e. line-up B). Whereas the previous album had seen Old England as a haven, this time it was seen as a burden on the present generation with flight from town to country or Britain to Australia the only solution. Ray Davies was by now expanding his career well beyond that of the band's leader. Before the release of the *Arthur* album he'd produced the *Turtle Soup* album for The Turtles and written a song a week for the BBC TV Series, 'Where Was Spring?' Although *Arthur* had originally been commissioned as a UK Granada TV play it never met fruition in this form. Like its predecessor it failed to Chart in the UK but it did climb to No 105 in the US where the band embarked on their first US tour for four years as support to Spirit having finally resolved differences with the American Federation Of Musicians.

Their next album, *Lola Versus Powerman And The Moneygoround, Part One* marked a return to commercial success spawning as it did the excellent 45 *Lola* (UK No 2, US No 9), the story of a gender blurring encounter in an Old Soho Club, and *Apeman* (UK No 5, US No 45). The album's theme was the struggle of a rock band against the power of the music business. It was very much a description of the bands' own predicament as they prepared to leave the Pye label and their management. It was the first album to feature John Gosling on keyboards. Their final album for Pye, a film soundtrack called *Percy*, made little impression, but the commercial success of the predecessor helped them secure a new recording deal with RCA.

Their first album for RCA was the partly autobiographical *Muswell Hillbillies*, which addressed the issue of uprooting of inner-city communities. It also marked another change of direction towards a more theatrical 'live' presentation of the band. This was consolidated on the double album, *Everybody's In Showbiz, Everybody's A Star*, which consisted of a live and a studio set. The former portrayed the band as group of more theatrical entertainers supported by backing singers and a horn section. This approach seemed to lead to renewed enthusiasm for the band in the States, in particular, The stand-out track on the studio set was the gentle, melodic *Celluloid Heroes*, which became a minor UK hit but didn't fare as well as its predecessor *Supersonic Rocket Ship*. 1972 also saw the release of a US-only compilation in the States - *The Kinks Kronicles*. This reached No 94 in the US Album Charts helping to revive interest in the group. At the beginning of 1973 *The Great Lost Kinks Album*, another US-only package, was released and reached No 145.

At a time when their fortunes Stateside were reviving Ray Davies' own personal life was going through considerable turmoil. He left his wife and

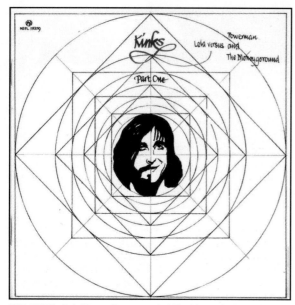

THE KINKS - Lola Versus Powerman And The Money-Go-Round Vol. 1 (CD).

children in July 1973, took two drug overdoses and then announced his retirement at the White City Pop Festival. This proved very temporary, however, lasting no more than a few days.

On the music front, the group set up Konk studios in Hornsey, London in May 1973 and, inevitably, a Konk record label followed in October 1974. They'd partly set up the label to spare other artists the hassles they'd undergone themselves. Its first release was **Claire Hamill**'s *Stage Door Johnies* and this and **Café Society's** debut album the following year were both produced by Ray Davies.

On record **The Kinks** took a character called *Flash* from their *Village Green Preservation Society* album and used him as the central character for *Preservation Act 1* and *2*. Neither album made much impression here but they climbed to No's 177 and 114 respectively in the US. Their next album *Soap Opera* (US No 51), stemmed from a TV musical Davies had been commissioned to write for Granada and told the story of a star played by Ray Davies searching suburbia for ideas for a new album and being lured into its values until he's not sure what he's about anymore. Like *Schoolboys In Disgrace* (US No 45) these albums lacked new ideas but each was accompanied by a stage presentation. This helped to enhance the band's reputation as a live and somewhat theatrical attraction in the States, particularly where their very Englishness proved an added bonus. Another hits compilation - *The Kinks Greatest - Celluloid Heroes* - which peaked at No 144 in the US proved to be their last album for RCA as in 1976 they moved their base to the States, signed a new contract with Arista Records and Andy Pyle came in as a temporary replacement for John Dalton.

On Arista they remodelled themselves as a hard-rock band enjoying major hit albums with *Sleepwalker* (1977), *Misfits* (1978) and *Low Budget* (1979) in the States, where they were soon filling arenas. *Give The People What They Want* (1981) and *State Of Confusion* (1983) brought further success in the early eighties. Ray Davies spent much of 1983 working on a film project 'Return To Waterloo' that caused some tension with his brother, but instead of breaking up they reshuffled their line-up and the main casualty was their long-serving drummer Mick Avory who was sacked and replaced by Bob Henrit (who was once with **Argent**). *Word Of Mouth* (1984) was similar in style to their recent albums but flopped commercially and marked a period of decline for the band. It was also their last album for Arista. In early 1986, they signed a new deal with MCA in the States and London in the UK. Their next album *Think Visual* was a moderate success. Their live album *The Road* (1987) was a US hit but *UK Jive* (1989) was their last studio album for MCA, who released a compilation of their recordings *Lost & Found (1986-1989)* in 1991. In 1991 they signed to Columbia, releasing an EP *Did Ya* which didn't chart and their first album for their new label *Phobia* received fair reviews but sold poorly. In 1994, they were dropped by Columbia and by now only Ray and Dave remained from their original line-up. However, they were never out of the public eye as many Brit-pop bands of the mid-nineties cited them as an influence and Ray had his autobiography 'X-Ray' published in 1995 and brother Dave's 'Kink' followed in 1996.

Compilation appearances have included: *Revenge* and *Bald-Headed Woman* on *Jimmy Page - Hip Young Guitar Slinger* (2-CD); *Waterloo Sunset* on *Maximum '65* (LP) and the 2-CD set *Sixties Summer Love*; *Lazy Old Sun* on *Quick Before They Catch Us* (CD) and *Hot Smoke & Sassafras - Psychedelic Pstones, Vol 1* (CD); *Got Love If You Want It* on *The R&B Era, Vol. 2* (LP & CD); *Milk Cow Blues* on *The R&B Era, Vol. 1* (LP & CD); *Sunny Afternoon* on *Ripples, Vol. 1* (CD), *No 1s & Million Sellers Vol 1* (CD) and on the 2-CD set *45s - 45 Classic No 1's* ; *Autumn Almanac* on *Ripples, Vol. 3* (CD); *Louie Louie* on *Ripples, Vol. 5* (CD); *All Aboard* on *Searching In The Wilderness* (LP & CD); *You Really Got Me* and *Waterloo Sunset* on *The Sixties File* (LP); *Something Better Beginning* on *Watch Your Step* (LP & CD); *Waterloo Sunset* on *Your Starter For Ten!!* (CD); *Harry Rag* on *Beat Merchants* (CD); *Louie Louie* on *The Best Of Louie Louie, Vol. 2*; *David Watts* on Sequel's *Radio Two: Sound Of The Sixties* (CD); *Phenomenal Cat* and *Wicked Annabella* on *Haunted - Psychedelic Pstones, Vol 2* (CD); *See My Friends* on the 4-CD box set *Acid Drops, Spacedust & Flying Saucers*; *You Really Got Me* and *Tired Of Waiting* on the 2-CD set *60 Number Ones Of The Sixties*; *Dedicated Follower Of Fashion* and *Waterloo Sunset* on *Hits Of The Swinging Sixties* (CD) and *You Really Got Me* on the 3-CD set *Rock Of Ages, Four Decades Of Heavy Rock 1962-2002* and on *No 1s & Million Sellers Vol 4* (CD). *Shangri-La* has been compiled on the 3-CD box set *Ars Longa Vita Brevis: A Compendium of Progressive Rock* and you can hear *Dedicated Follower Of Fashion*, *Tired Of Waiting For You* and *Sunny Afternoon* on the 2-CD set *We Love The Pirates: Charting The Big 'L' Fab 40*. **Kinks** fans may also be interested in *The Persuaders & Other Top Seventies TV Themes* CD on Sequel, which contains a very rare track written by Ray Davies. This track, *Nobody's Fool* by Cold Turkey was originally released on Pye and was the theme to the cult series 'Budgie' from 1972 onwards. (VJ/LBy)

Billy Kinsley

45s: Annabella / Blue Movies   (Epic EPC 1695) 1973
           You Make My Day/Make My Bed   (Epic EPC 2012) 1974

These were solo efforts by this former **Merseybeats** and **Rockin' Horse** member. (VJ)

The Kinsmen

45s: Glasshouse Green, Splinter Red/
           It's Started To Rain Again   (Decca 22724) 1968 SC
           It's Good To See You/Always The Loser   (Decca 22777) 1968

Originally known as **The Four Kinsmen** this band may not have been British. *Glasshouse Green, Splinter Red* starts out in a typical late sixties harmony-pop style but then slows down into a melancholic song. It was certainly their most inventive recording.

THE KINKS - Percy (CD).

KIPPINGTON LODGE - '67 - '69 (CD).

You can also find *Glasshouse Green, Splinter Red* on *Rubble Vol. 6: The Clouds Have Groovy Faces* (LP), *Rubble Vol. 4* (CD), *British Psychedelic Trip, Vol. 4* (LP) and *Great British Psychedelic Trip, Vol. 2* (CD). (VJ)

Kippington Lodge

Personnel:	BARRY LANDERMAN	keyb'ds, vcls	A
	NICK LOWE	bs, vcls	ABC
	BRINSLEY SCHWARZ	gtr, vcls	ABC
	PETER WHALE	drms	AB
	BOB ANDREWS	keyb'ds, vcls	BC

CD:	1(-)	KIPPINGTON LODGE '67-'69	(K 1P) 199?

EP:	1	Rumours/Lady On A Bicycle/And She Cried/ Shy Boy	(EMI NUT 2894) 1978

45s:	Shy Boy/Lady On A Bicycle	(Parlophone R 5645) 1967 R1
	Rumours/And She Cried	(Parlophone R 5677) 1968 R1
	Tell Me A Story/ Understand A Woman	(Parlophone R 5717) 1968 R1
	Tomorrow Today/ Turn Out The Light	(Parlophone R 5750) 1968 R1
	In My Life/I Can See Her Face	(Parlophone R 5776) 1969 R2

A late sixties pop group from Kent who evolved into **Brinsley Schwarz** in the early seventies. Lowe, **Schwarz** and Landeman all played together in school bands for several years and toured the airforce bases in Germany in the summer of 1964 as Sounds 4 + 1. This Tunbridge Wells - based venture was formed in 1967. Their most successful 45 was *Shy Boy*, a flower-pop **Tomorrow** song written by **Keith West**, but they never did get any hits. Their final 45, *In My Life* was a **Beatles**' track. Landerman departed to **Vanity Fare** and was replaced by Andrews but in October 1969 with a change of style came a change of name to **Brinsley Schwarz**. Whale dropped out of the music business at this stage but the other three stayed on in the new and much hyped band.

Musically they dished up pretty straightforward pop and two of their better efforts - *Lady On A Bicycle* and *Rumours* were both produced by **Mark Wirtz**.

Compilation appearances include: *Turn Out The Light* on *Justafixation* (CD); *Rumours* and *Lady On A Bicycle* on *Not Just Beat Music 1965-70* (LP), *British Psychedelic Trip, Vol. 2* (LP) and *Great British Psychedelic Trip, Vol. 3* (CD); *I Can See Her Face* on *Psychedelia, Vol. 3* (LP), *We Can Fly, Vol 1* (CD), *Hen's Teeth, Vol. 3* (CD) and *In The Beginning* (LP); *Tomorrow Today* on *Colour Me Pop, Vol 2* (CD); *Shy Boy* on *A Teenage Opera - The Original Soundtrack Recording* (CD) and *Pop-In, Vol 1* (CD), whilst *Tell Me A Story* has been compiled on *Pop-In, Vol 2* (CD). (VJ)

The Kirkbys

Personnel incl:	JIMMY CAMPBELL	gtr	ABCD
	KENNY GOODLASS	drms	AB D
	JOHN LLOYD	gtr	ABCD
	ALBY POWER	bs	ABCD
	GERRY SAVAGE	vcls	A
	JOE MAROOTH	vcls	BCD
	MERVYN SHARPE	drms	C

45:	It's A Crime/ I've Never Been So Much In Love	(RCA RCA 1542) 1966 R3

NB: This has been reissued (RCA RCA 1542) in a limited edition pressing of 500 taken from the original French jukebox release.

This Liverpool band was first known as The Panthers who revolved around **Jimmy Campbell**, who then formed **23rd Turnoff** (named after a motorway junction) before doing solo work. Bob Wooler of Cavern fame actually gave the band the name **Kirbys** during a live radio Luxembourg recording at the Cavern Club. He suggested that the band may gain support from all the people of Kirby if they used such a name. Actually at that time all the band members (except for Marooth) lived in Kirby, which is on the outskirts of Liverpool. The band also backed **The Merseys** after *Sorrow* became a hit in 1967.

Goodlass departed for **The Escorts** in early 1965 but later rejoined in late 1966 when Sharpe left to get married. The 45 is highly-rated, with *It's A Crime* being an experimental beat number with a good guitar break.

Line-up C visited Finland in 1965 and recorded two singles whilst there: *'Cos My Baby's Gone/She'll Get No Lovin' That Way* (RCA Victor FAS 942) 1965 and *Don't You Want Me No More/Bless You* (RCA Victor FAS 948) 1965. Both are very rare as only a few hundred copies of each were pressed.

The band still gig in the Liverpool area, but sadly without Jimmy Campbell, who is in poor health. Instead they now include Richie Routledge (ex-**Cryin' Shames**) and Brian Jones (ex-**Undertakers**).

It's A Crime has resurfaced on *Psychedelia, Vol. 2* (LP), *Rare 60's Beat Treasures, Vol. 3* (CD) and *Hen's Teeth Vol. 1* (CD). (VJ/JM/TR)

John Kirkpatrick and Sue Harris

ALBUMS:	1	JUMP AT THE SUN	(Trailer LER 2033) 1972 SC
(up to	2	THE ROSE OF BRITAIN'S ISLE	(Topic 12TS 247) 1974
1976)	3	AMONG THE ATTRACTIONS	(Topic 12TS 295) 1976
	4	PLAIN CAPERS	(Free Reed FRR 010) 1976

This is a respected folk duo. **Kirkpatrick** was born on 8 August 1947 in Chiswick, London and Harris at Coventry on 17 May 1949. Their first album is the rarest and for those into this genre it's essential. **Kirkpatrick** was a master of a wide range of instruments like the Anglo concertina and the button accordion - the album's full of finely crafted folk music but is now very hard to find. **Harris** was also a member of the English Country Blues Band for a while and was noted for her hammer dulcimer and oboe playing.

Kirkpatrick and Harris were also members of the **Albion Country Band** during 1973 and went on to record well into the next decade. (VJ)

Danny Kirwan

ALBUM:	1	SECOND CHAPTER	(DJM DJLPS 454) 1975

45s:	Ram Jam City/ Hot Summer's Day	(DJM DJS 10396) 1975
(up to	Misty River/Rolling Hills	(DJM DJS 10666) 1976
1976)	Angel's Delight/Ram Jam City	(DJM DJS 10709) 1976

Danny Kirwan was formerly with **Fleetwood Mac** and recorded this album after leaving the band with health problems. He went on to make two further albums; *Midnight In San Juan* and *Hello Big Boy*, and a couple more 45s beyond the time span of this book. (BS/VJ)

The Kittens

Personnel:
SUSAN CHASID	vcls		A
VIVIEN CHASID	vcls		A

45:     Round About Way/Don't Stop Now   (Decca F 12036) 1964

This girl duo hailed from Harrow in North-West London. (VJ)

Tony Klinger and Michael Lyons

ALBUM: 1   EXTREEMS   (Deram SML 1095) 1971 SC

This was actually a film Soundtrack featuring contributions by **Arc** and **Supertramp**. (VJ)

The Klubs

Personnel:
PADDY BREEN	vcls, bs	ABCDE
NORRIS EASTERBROOK	bs	ABC E
TREVOR GRIFFITHS	lead gtr	ABC E
KENNY MARSHALL	drms	AB
JOHN REID	gtr, vcls	ABCD
ALAN WALKER	vcls, hrmnca	A
PETER SINCLAIR-TIDY	drms	CDE

ALBUM: 1 (A/E) MIDNIGHT LOVE CYCLE   (Tenth Planet LP 046) 1999
NB. (1) also issued on CD (Wooden Hill WHCD011) 2001 with bonus tracks.

45:     I Found The Sun/
           Ever Needed Someone   (Cam CAM 681) 1968 R5

Formed in Birkenhead in 1964, they first came to notice as winners of 1965 beat competitions held on the Isle of Man. Although the line-up was initially fluid it had settled by the end of that year to (A) shown above. Building a reputation on Merseyside (they made more appearances at The Cavern than any other group except **The Beatles** and The Hideaways), they made sporadic appearances in London and elsewhere.

By late 1966 the group was moving away from R&B towards more original material and Alan Walker left without being replaced. The group started to be described as Merseyside's first with the psychedelic sound. They appeared on stage with painted faces, androgynous looks and a rudimentary light show. In February 1967 Peter Sinclair-Tidy from the Crazy Chains replaced Kenny Marshall, shortly before they cut a one-side demo for Chart Records - *Livin' Today*. Summer saw them in Abbey Road studio for an unsuccessful recording test.

THE KLUBS - Midnight Love Cycle (LP).

In 1968 they signed with Don Arden's Aquarius management company who arranged a deal with RCA Victor. They entered Decca's Hampstead studio to record four tracks: - *Midnight Love Cycle*, *Fire* (**Hendrix**), *Drive My Car* (**Beatles**) and *Ever Needed Someone*. The first was similar in style and content to *My White Bicycle* by **Tomorrow** and would have been the obvious single but when Don Arden asked them to change their name to Revolution, they refused, resulting in him dropping them and withholding the sessions.

The Klubs returned to Liverpool, where they took part in Kaleidoscope '68 along with **Pink Floyd** and **The Move** in December 1968. They finally released a single on the obscure CAM label the same month. Unfortunately, like so many groups of this era, weaker mainstream material was selected, instead of harder-edged originals. Unsurprisingly it failed to kick-start their career. Other material recorded at the sessions remained unreleased.

Easterbrook and Griffiths left the group in Spring 1969, and the remaining trio recorded two final demos for DJM. Some further line-up changes saw the group briefly revise their name to The Klubbs before becoming Wardog - a heavy metal band.

John Reid went on to join **Strife** in 1971. Paddy was also briefly a member. Trevor Griffiths recorded an album with The Lettermen in 1972.

There the story would have ended but for 'Record Collector' magazine who, after an appeal for information, published an article on the band leading to the posthumous releases on Tenth Planet and Wooden Hill and several reunion performances. Indeed the group are more famous now than they ever were at the time.

The Tenth Planet/Wooden Hill reissues include the band's demos, mainly recorded in 1968 from the band's tapes and acetates. Reviewing the CD in 'Record Collector' Andy Neill likens *Can't Ebenezer See My Mind?* to **The Attack** and **Elmer Gantry's Velvet Opera** and remarks that *Indian Dreams* features **Syd Barrett** style vocals overlaid with shimmering wah-wah. Another cut *The Stripper* uses abrasive double-tracked wah-wah. The prime cut is possibly *Livin' Today* - a powerful slice of freakbeat. *I Found The Sun* and *Ever Needed Someone* veer more towards mid-sixties harmony-beat. The CD contains bonus cuts from a 2000 gig at the Cavern and later incarnations of **The Klubs** in bands like **Strife** and The Lettermen. The recording quality leaves something to be desired but this is a significant release. (VJ/JM)

The Knack

Personnel:
TOPPER CLAY	drms		AB
PAUL GURVITZ	gtr		AB
BRIAN MORRIS	gtr		AB
MICK PALMER	bs		A
GERY KENWORTHY	bs		B

45s: She Ain't No Good/
           Who'll Be The Next In Line   (Decca F 12234) 1965 R1
           It's Love Baby (24 Hours A Day)/
           Time Time Time   (Decca F 12278) 1965 R1
           Did You Ever Have To Make Up Your Mind?/
           Red Hearts   (Piccadilly 7N 35315) 1966
           Stop! (Before You Get Me Going)/
           Younger Girl   (Piccadilly 7N 35322) 1966
           Save All My Love For Joey/
           Take Your Love   (Piccadilly 7N 35347) 1966
           (Man From The) Marriage Guidance And Advice Bureau/
           Dolly Catch Her Man   (Piccadilly 7N 35367) 1967

From Ilford originally, although they were based in London. This mid-sixties mod group were originally known as **The Londoners** who spent most of their time working in Germany.

Topper Clay left the band in Spring 1967 to join **New York Public Library**. He was followed by Brian Morris in 1968, after which Paul Gurvitz formed **Gun**.

Compilation appearances have included: *She Ain't No Good* on *Mod Scene, Vol. 2* (CD) and *That Driving Beat* (CD); *Time Time Time* on *Purple Pill Eaters* (LP & CD); *Younger Girl* and *Did You Ever Have To Make Up*

Your Mind on *Ripples, Vol. 1* (CD); *The Man From The Marriage Guidance Bureau* on *Ripples, Vol. 3* (CD) and *Quick Before They Catch Us* (CD); *Dolly Catcher Man* on *Ripples, Vol. 6* (CD); *Who'll Be The Next In Line* on *The Beat Scene* (CD); *Stop! (Before You Get Me Going)* and *Younger Girl* on *Footsteps To Fame, Vol. 1* (CD) and *Stop! (Before You Get Me Going)* on the 2-CD set *We Love The Pirates: Charting The Big 'L' Fab 40*. (VJ/TCy)

Knees

45:        Day Tripper/Slow Dance   (United Artists UP 35773) 1974 SC

This band had a **Brinsley Schwarz** connection. *Day Tripper* is best known as a **Beatles**' No 1. (VJ)

Jason Knight

45:        Love Is Getting Stronger/
           Standing In My Shoes   (Pye 7N 17399) 1967 SC
Reissue: Love Is Getting Stronger/
           Standing In My Shoes   (Pye 7N 45287) 1973

This is a collectable soulish 45. The 'A' side is a big Northern soul stomper, with a classic on-the-fours beat. (JR).

Tony Knight and The Livewires

Personnel:	TONY KNIGHT	vcls	A
	DAVE MALLETT	organ	A
	ROY MALLETT	bs	A
	JOHN NETTLES	lead gtr	A
	BOB SMITH	gtr	A
	COLIN TILLOTSON	drms	A

45:        Did You Ever Hear The Sound?/
           I Feel So Blue   (Decca F 11989) 1964 R1

As **Tony Knight and The Live Wires** they can be found performing *Did You Ever Hear The Sound?* on See For Miles *Ready Steady Win* (LP & CD) which compiles tracks taken from the 'Ready Steady Go' TV series, where the band was featured as part of a 'best unknown group' competition. In 1965 **Knight** put together a new band **Tony Knight's Chessmen**.

Other compilation appearances have included: *I Feel So Blue* on *R&B Scene, Vol. 2 - 1963-1969* (LP), *That Driving Beat* (CD) and *British R'n'B Explosion, Vol. 1* (CD). (VJ/JM)

Tony Knight's Chessmen

Personnel incl:	LOL COXHILL	sax	A
	TONY KNIGHT	vcls, drms	A
	TERRY MARTIN	bs	A

45:        How Sweet / Surfer Street   (Decca F 12109) 1965 R1

Tony Knight's Chessmen were most significant for having **Lol Coxhill** as their saxophonist. After this outfit he was in **Gass**, **Delivery** and **Kevin Ayers and The Whole World** before making several solo albums in the seventies. Knight went on to become drummer/singer with Sweetwater Canal, **Skin Alley**, etc. (VJ/JM)

Knocker Jungle

Personnel:	TONY COOP		A
	KEITH JONES		A

ALBUM: 1(A)   KNOCKER JUNGLE   (Ember NR 5052) 1971 SC

45:        I Don't Know Why/Reality (PS)   (Ember EMBS 293) 1970

A folky pop duo backed by Owen Finnegan, Dave Pegg and Dave Mattacks, though the latter two couldn't be properly identified on the album

RIPPLES VOL. 3 (Comp CD) featuring The Knack.

sleeve for legal reasons related to their belonging to **Fairport Convention**. The album was produced by Tony Cox, also responsible for records by **Caravan**, **Trees**, **Amory Kane** and others, and is mediocre. It appeared after the duo had split and sank like a stone. (VJ/RMJ)

Krysia Kocjan

ALBUM: 1   KRYSIA (Some w/insert)   (RCA LPLI 5052) 1974 SC/-

45:    α   Another Song/Wet Tuesday   (RCA RCA 2445) 1974
NB: α as Krysia.

Kocjan had been a member of the short-lived **Natural Acoustic Band** and also sang on albums by **Mike Heron's Reputation**, **The Kinks** and **Al Stewart**. This solo album is folk-rock. (VJ)

Kodiaks

45:        All Because You Wanna See Me Cry/
           Tell Me Rhonda   (Decca F 12942) 1969

Late sixties pop. (VJ)

Kokomo

Personnel:	DYAN BIRCH	vcls	AB
(up to	FRANK COLLINS	vcls	AB
1976)	MEL COLLINS	sax	AB
	NEIL HUBBARD	gtr	AB
	PADDY McHUGH	vcls	AB
	JIM MULLEN	gtr	A
	TONY O'MALLEY	vcls, keyb'ds	AB
	ALAN SPENNER	vcls, bs	AB
	TERRY STANNARD	drms	A
	JOHN SUSSEWELL	drms	B

ALBUMS:	1(A)	KOKOMO	(CBS 80670) 1975
(up to	2(B)	RISE AND SWINE	(CBS 69229) 1975
1976)			

45s:	I'm Sorry Babe/One Heart	(CBS 3063) 1975
(up to	I Can Understand It/Feeling This Way	(CBS 3379) 1975
1976)	Anytime/Kitty Sitting Pretty	(CBS 3706) 1975
	Use Your Imagination/Do It Right	(CBS 3917) 1976

Kokomo was a short-lived but tight, disciplined white soul band, which was unusual for its use of four vocalists. They were an important part of the seventies pub-rock scene.

They could also claim to be something of a supergroup. Birch, O'Malley and Frank Collins had all previously been with **Arrival**; Spenner and Hubbard had been with **Joe Cocker's Grease Band** and Mel Collins had played for **King Crimson** and **Streetwalkers**. Terry Stannard was from **Vinegar Joe**.

Their funky rhythms proved very popular with audiences during 1974. They signed to CBS and recorded two albums, but were never able to translate the energy and dynamism of their live act to vinyl, although they did reach the lower parts of the US charts.

They accompanied **Dr Feelgood** and **Chilli Willi and The Red Hot Peppers** on the Naughty Rhythms Tour in 1975 and also recorded cuts with Bob Dylan in New York for his *Desire* albums. These included a funky version of *Hurricane*, but never saw the light of day. They finally split in 1977, although they have played the odd reunion since. (VJ)

The Konrads

45:     Baby It's Too Late Now/I'm Over You   (CBS 201812) 1965 SC

This four-piece mid-sixties beat band came from Orpington in Kent. It toured with **The Rolling Stones** in 1965. (VJ)

The Koobas

Personnel:	KEN COCHRAN	drms	A
	STU LEATHERWOOD	gtr, vcls	AB
	ROY MORRIS	lead gtr	AB
	PETE WILLIAMS	bs	A
	KEITH ELLIS	bs	B
	TONY O'REILLY	drms	B

ALBUM: 1(B) THE KOOBAS   (Columbia S(C)X 6271) 1969 R5

NB: (1) reissued by Bam Caruso as *Barricades* (KIRI 047) 1988 (SC) and on CD (Essex ESSEX 10004 CD) 1994 with two additional tracks: - *Sweet Music* and *Face* from 1966. (1) reissued again on CD (BGO BGOCD 487) 2005, with eight bonus tracks.

45s:	Take Me For A Little While/	
	Somewhere In The Night	(Pye 7N 17012) 1965 R1
	You'd Better Make Up Your Mind/	
	Place I Know	(Pye 7N 17087) 1966 R2
	Sweet Music/Face	(Columbia DB 7988) 1966 R1
	Sally/Champagne And Caviar	(Columbia DB 8013) 1967 R1
	Gypsy Fred/City Girl	(Columbia DB 8187) 1967 R1
	The First Cut Is The Deepest/	
	Walking Out	(Columbia DB 8419) 1968 R2

They were formed in Liverpool in 1962 during the latter part of the Merseybeat boom and were managed by Brian Epstein. Ellis and O'Reilly had previously been with The Thunderbeats. Morris and Leatherwood (also known as Leithwood) were in The Midnighters. Despite appearing in *Ferry Across The Mersey* and touring with **The Beatles** in 1965, none of their numerous singles for Columbia and Pye reached the Charts. They cut two confident singles for Pye: the first was a Kim Weston Motown track. In Spring 1966 they switched to EMI Columbia. Their final 45 was a quasi-psychedelic version of **Cat Stevens**' *The First Cut Is The Deepest* - it's quite good fun. They also recorded an album, which was very rare and sought-after, prior to its reissue. It features some fine lead guitar work, and contains some competent and usually R&B influenced mid-sixties rock. One of the best tracks was the complex *Barricades*.

They also recorded as 45 as **The Kubas** in 1965 for Columbia.

The band split in late 1968. Keith Ellis went on to **Van der Graaf Generator** briefly. Stu Leatherwood was later in **March Hare** and O'Reilly went on to **Bakerloo.**

Compilation appearances include: *Gypsy Fred* on *Justafixation* (LP) and *Jagged Time Lapse, Vol 1* (CD); *The First Cut Is The Deepest* on *Liverpool 1963-1968* (CD), *Liverpool 1963-1968, Vol. 1* (LP), *Electric Sugarcube Flashbacks, Vol. 1* (LP), *Hard Up Heroes, Vol. 2* (CD) and on the 4-CD box set *Nuggets 11*; *Barricades* on *Psychedelia At Abbey Road* (CD), *Rubble, Vol. 3 - Nightmares In Wonderland* (LP) and *Rubble, Vol. 2* (CD); *You'd Better Make Up Your Mind* on *Rubble, Vol. 7 - Pictures In The Sky* (LP),

That Driving Beat (CD) and *The Sixties File* (2-LP); *Somewhere In The Night* on *Watch Your Step* (CD); *Take Me For A Little While* and *You'd Better Make Up Your Mind* on *What About Us* (CD) and *Merseybeat Nuggets, Vol. 2*; *A Place I Know* on *Doin' The Mod, Vol. 1* (CD); *Here's A Day* on *Illusions From The Crackling Void* (LP); *Royston Rose* on the 4-CD box set *Acid Drops, Spacedust & Flying Dust*; *Face* on *English Freakbeat, Vol. 2* (CD) and on *Twisted Teenage Screaming Fuzzbusters* (LP); and *Take Me For A Little While* on the 2-CD set *We Love The Pirates: Charting The Big 'L' Fab 40*. (VJ/AD/JM)

Kool

45s:	Look At Me, Look At Me/	
	Room At The Top	(CBS 203003) 1967
	Step Out Of Your Mind/Funny (What A Fool	
	A Man Can Be)	(CBS 2865) 1969 SC
	Lovin'/Baby's Out Of Reach	(MCA MU 1085) 1969

An obscure band who were brought to the attention of a slightly wider audience when *Room At The Top* was compiled on *Colour Me Pop, Vol 1* (CD). (VJ)

Tamara Koran and Perception

| 45: | Veils Of Morning Lace/ | |
| | Don't Throw Our Love Away | (Domain D7) 1968 R2 |

Circus Days, Vol. 2 (LP) and *Circus Days Vol. 3* (CD) include the organ-based *Veils Of Mourning Lace* (from 1968) by this band. It sounds very similar to **Julie Driscoll**. (VJ)

Paul Korda

| ALBUM: | 1   PASSING STRANGER | (MAM AS 1003) 1971 SC |

45s:	Go On Home/	
	Just Come Closer To Me	(Columbia DB 7998) 1966 SC
	Seagull (West Coast Oil Tragedy Of '68)/	
	Night Of The Next Day	(Parlophone R 5778) 1969
	Between The Road/	
	English Country Garden	(Mam MAM 20) 1971

Paul Korda's 45s were mostly soul-tinged ballads. His *Passing Stranger* album featured **Andy Roberts** (gtr), **Chris Spedding** (gtr), **Ray Russell** (gtr), **Mike Storey** (keyb'ds), Rob Tait (drms) plus the vocals of **Doris Troy** and **Madeleine Bell**. It also features Jonathan Coudrille on keyboards, who went on to win the 1974 Melody Maker Solo Rock/Folk Contest. **Korda** also recorded with **Tim Andrews** and wrote *Emergency 999* for **The Alan Bown Set**. In the seventies, he became a session vocalist and was also in **Dada**. (VJ)

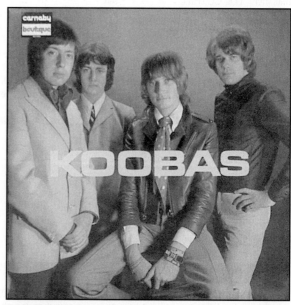

THE KOOBAS - The Koobas (LP).

Alexis Korner (and Blues Incorporated)

ALBUMS:	1	R&B FROM THE MARQUEE (live)		
(1960 -			(Ace Of Clubs ACL 1130) 1962	R3
1976)	2	RED HOT FROM ALEX	(Transatlantic TRA 117) 1964	R3
	3	AT THE CAVERN (live)	(Oriole PS 40058) 1964	R4
	4	ALEXIS KORNER'S BLUES INCORPORATED		
			(Ace Of Clubs ACL 1187) 1965	R3
	5	SKY HIGH (featuring **Duffy Power**)		
			(Spot JW 551) 1965	R4
	6	I WONDER WHO	(Fontana TL 5381) 1967	R3
	7	BLUES INCORPORATED	(Polydor 236 206) 1967	R2
	8	A NEW GENERATION OF BLUES		
			(Liberty LBL/LBS 83147) 1968	R2
	9	ALEXIS KORNER'S ALL STAR BLUES INCORPORATED		
			(Transatlantic TRASAM 7) 1969	R1
	10	ALEXIS	(Rak SRAK 501) 1971	R2
	11	BOOTLEG HIM (2-LP) (w/booklet)		
			(Rak SRAKSP 51) 1972	R2
	12	ACCIDENTALLY BORN IN NEW ORLEANS		
			(Transatlantic TRA 269) 1973	R1
	13	GET OFF MY CLOUD	(CBS 69155) 1975	R1

NB: (2) reissued on CD (Wooded Hill HILLCD 17) 1997, remastered and with the original artwork. (3) also reissued on CD. (5) reissued on CD by Indigo (IGOCD 2012) 1995 with two extra tracks. (7) was a reissue of (5) with less tracks. (8) later reissued as *What's That Sound I Hear* (Sunset SLS 50245) 1971. (12) remastered and reissued on CD. (13) reissued on CD (Sequel NEXCD 134) 199?.

EPs:	1	¾ A. D.	(Topic TOP 70) 1962	R3
	2	ALEXIS KORNER AND...	(Collector CCSLP 150) 197?	

NB: (1) was recorded with **Davy Graham**. First pressings in a mauve sleeve with a cream label are more expensive and sough-after. Later pressings came with a lilac or bronze sleeve and a blue label.

45s:	α	Blaydon Races/Up-Town	(Lyntone LYN 299) 1963	R3
(1963	β	I Need Your Loving/		
- 1976)		Please Please Please	(Parlophone R 5206) 1963	SC
	β	Little Baby/Roberta	(Parlophone R 5247) 1963	SC
	χ	See See Rider/Blues A La King	(King KG 1017) 1965	R1
		River's Invitation/		
		Everyday (I Have The Blues)	(Fontana TF 706) 1966	SC
		Rosie/Rock Me	(Fontana TF 817) 1967	SC
		Get Off Of My Cloud/Strange'n'Deranged	(CBS 3520) 1975	
		Ain't That Peculiar/Tree Top Fever	(CBS 3877) 1976	

NB: α Flexidisc, as Blues Incorporated With **Alexis Korner**. β As **Alexis Korner**'s Blues Inc. χ As **Alexis Korner**'s All Stars.

It should be said that despite his enormous influence on British rock, blues and R&B **Korner** wasn't actually British. He was born in Paris in 1928 to Greek/Turkish and Austrian parents. He relocated to England at the start of the Second World War and began his music career in 1948 in a blues group which was part of The Chris Barber Jazz Band. He then played in various skiffle and blues groups until he formed Blues Incorporated in late 1961 with Cyril Davies. They were among the first white electric blues bands in the world.

They began playing at Ealing Blues Club but later got a residency at The Marquee. This seminal band became a breeding ground for what were later to become some of Britain's top rock musicians. More a loose collection of musicians and vocalists than a tight-knit group, those who passed through their ranks included future **Rolling Stones**; **Mick Jagger**, Keith Richards, Charlie Watts and Brian Jones, as well as **Long John Baldry**, **Paul Jones**, **Graham Bond**, **Dick Heckstall-Smith**, **Eric Burdon** and **Ginger Baker** to name but a few.

In 1962 Blues Incorporated, whose blues sessions were legendary to blues fans throughout the country, recorded a live album *R&B At The Marquee*.

At The Cavern is now a very rare album, so the recent CD release is very welcome. For this live recording at Liverpool's famous Cavern Club, Blues Incorporated was minus '**Long**' John Baldry and Cyrille Smith. The sound is more of a big band one, although the blues is still evident, particularly on the slower numbers like *Hoochie Coochie Man* and *Whoa, Babe*.

Korner went on to record several other albums during the sixties, although he concentrated mainly on touring and session work. By the mid-sixties, future **Pentangle** members Danny Thompson and Terry Cox were a pivotal

part of his live band.

In 1967, he formed an outfit called Free At Last (Cliff Barton, Victor Brox, Gerry Conway, **Marsha Hunt**, Hughie Flint and Binky McKenzie) but it proved very short term and didn't survive the year. For the next year or so, he worked first with Victor Brox and then **Robert Plant** in duos.

He toured Scandinavia in 1968 with Peter Thorup, a Danish singer, then formed New Church with Thorup the following year. The band only lasted until late 1970, but **Korner** and Thorup continued to work together, teaming up with producer Mickie Most and director/composer John Cameron to form a big band **CCS** (Collective Consciousness Society) which had a few hits, including a cover of **Led Zeppelin**'s *Whole Lotta Love*, which became 'Top Of The Pops' theme tune.

In 1972, **Korner** formed another short-lived group, Snape, with Thorup (of **CCS**) and ex-members of **King Crimson**. Snape backed him on *Accidentally Born In New Orleans*. The album was recorded in San Francisco and London. It featured some interesting guests (**Stevie Marriott**, **Ollie Halsall** (of **Patto**), **Mike Patto** and Tim Hinkley). For the recent CD release, it has been remastered from the original tapes and comes with detailed liner notes from band member Ian Wallace.

On his final album, *Get Off My Cloud*, he was backed by an array of talent - **Peter Frampton**, Colin Hodgkinson, **Nicky Hopkins**, **Kokomo**, **Stevie Marriott** and Keith Richards.

The *Meets Jack Daniels* CD features seven tracks he recorded live with New Church in 1969, which include him telling his audience about the blues in the process and five tracks he recorded live in 1975.

In his later days, **Korner** worked more as a broadcaster, although he continued to work as a musician too. He made a well-received appearance at the Cambridge Folk festival in the early eighties. Clearly a man of many talents - he'd been instrumental in the formation of **Free** and had also played for a while in the house band for children's TV show 'Five O'Clock Club' - his premature death from lung cancer in early 1984 was a tragedy.

Compilation appearances include: *I Got My Mojo Working* on *The R&B Scene* (CD) and *Hard-Up Heroes* (2-LP); *Night Time Is The Right Time* on *The Soul Of British R&B 1962-68* (LP) and *British R'n'B Explosion, Vol. 1* (CD); *Early In The Morning*, *Night Time Is The Right Time* and *Jones* on *The Transatlantic Story* CD box set and *Built For Comfort* on *Broken Dreams, Vol. 7* (LP). (VJ)

Kossoff, Kirke, Tetsu and Rabbit

Personnel:			
	JOHN 'RABBIT' BUNDRICK	keyb'ds, vcls	A
	SIMON KIRKE	drms, vcls	A
	PAUL KOSSOFF	gtr	A
	TETSU YAMAUCHI	bs	A

ALBUM:	1(A)	KOSSOFF, KIRKE, TETSU AND RABBIT	
		(Island ILPS 9188) 1971	R1

NB: (1) reissued on CD (Repertoire REP 4529-WY) 1995.

This studio combo formed in May 1971 after **Free** split up for the first time. **Kossoff** and Kirke were formerly in **Free** and they'd met Tetsu on their Japanese tour and Bundrick had been working in Europe. After recording this one album **Kossoff** and Kirke rejoined a reformed **Free** in January 1972 and Tetsu and Rabbit followed in July.

Musically this is soulful blues-rock which pales in comparison with **Free**. (VJ)

Paul Kossoff

ALBUM:	1	BACK STREET CRAWLER	(Island ILPS 9264) 1973	SC
(up to				
1976)				

NB: (1) also issues on CD (Island IMCD 84) 1990 and (Repertoire REP 4528-WY) 1995. Also of interest to collectors will be *Koss* (a 2-LP compilation) (DJM DJE 29002) 1977, reissued on CD (Castle Classics CLACD 127) 1987; *Croydon June*

15th 1975 (2-LP) (Street Tunes STLP 1002) 1983 also on CD (Repertoire REP 4530-WY) 1995, which largely drew material from his solo album; and *Mr Big/Blue Soul* (Street Tunes SDLP 0012PD) 1983. *The Collection* (CD) (The Hit Label AHLCD 31) 1995 traces his career from 1969-1976. Finally, *The Best of Paul Kossof* (Track TRA 1034) 2003 chronicles his career.

Kossoff was born in Hampstead on 14 September 1950. He was the son of actor David Kossoff. His first band was **Black Cat Bones** but then having added Paul Rodgers and Andy Fraser to their line-up they were spotted by **Alexis Korner** playing at the Nag's Head, Battersea. He gave them the name **Free**, got them a recording contract with Island and 'coached' them in their early days.

When **Free** first split in May 1971 the guitarist formed **Kossoff, Kirke, Tetsu and Rabbit**, although this proved to be a short-term studio group because **Free** reformed at the start of 1972. After **Free** split for the final time in July 1973, **Kossoff** recorded the above solo album. By now, though, his drug addiction was having an adverse effect on his health and he spent the next couple of years trying to cure his addiction before assembling a new band **Back Street Crawler** (named after his debut solo album), in April 1975.

Sadly, though, his health was irreparably damaged. After suffering a serious heart attack in 1975, he was hospitalised for six weeks and his subsequent appearances were confined to just three further gigs that year. Then, having got the all-clear from his doctor the following year, he died in his sleep on 19 March 1976 on board a plane to New York. This was a tragic loss of a considerable talent.

The Best Of Paul Kossof traces his brief career and includes recordings from his days with **Free** and his two albums with **Back Street Crawler**, as well as cuts from his solo album. (VJ)

The Roland Kovac Set

ALBUM: 1   LOVE THAT   ( ) 1971

This privately-pressed album is a keyboard-dominated cosmic trip consisting of five lengthy tracks with lots of **Hendrix**-influenced axework. One of the best tracks, *Guru*, is a feast of **Hendrix** - styled guitar histrionics and feedback. The album was pressed in Germany, then exported to the UK for marketing purposes. Definitely only for those who like freaky guitar work!

Compilation appearances include: *Genesis* on *Psychedelic Salvage Co. Vol. 1* (LP & CD); and *Guru* on *Psychedelic Salvage Co. Vol. 2* (LP & CD). (VJ)

Billy J. Kramer

45s:			
(up to 1976)	You Make Me Feel Like Someone/ Take My Hand	(Parlophone R 5482)	1966 -
	Sorry/Going Going Gone	(Parlophone R 5552)	1967
	The Town Of Tuxley Toymakers/ Chinese Girl	(Reaction 591 014)	1967 SC
	1941/His Love Is Just A Lie	(NEMS 56-3396)	1968
	A World Without Love/Going Through It	(NEMS 56-3635)	1968
	The Colour Of My Love/ I'm Running Away	(MGM MGM 1474)	1969
	A Fool Like You/I'll Keep You Satisfied	(Decca F 13426)	1973
	Darlin' Come To Me/Walking	(Decca F 13442)	1973
	Stayin' Power/Blue Jean Queen	(BASF BA 1006)	1974

Kramer's real name was William Howard Ashton and he was born on 19th August 1943 in Bootle, Lancashire. This Liverpudlian began his musical career as a member of The Coasters, who were predominantly an instrumental band. The story goes that one night his guitar was stolen and rather than hanging around like a spare part he decided to sing... to such good effect that he became the group's vocalist, changing his name to **Billy J. Kramer**. In 1962, along came Brian Epstein who gave The Coasters the push, replacing them with **The Dakotas**. See the **Billy J. Kramer and The Dakotas** entry for details.

After splitting with **The Dakotas** in 1966, **Kramer** embarked on a solo career. Although a good looking lad, he lacked any real charisma and wasn't a particularly strong vocalist either, so it's no real surprise that he

was soon forced into the variety club circuit to make a living. None of his solo discs sold at all well. *Town of Tuxley Toymakers*, a **Bee Gees**' song, and *1941* were the strongest. Not even a cover of **Lennon/McCartney**'s *A World Without Love* in 1968 could put him back in the Charts.

In June 1971, he covered Neil Diamond's *And The Grass Won't Pay No Mind*, which was released under his real name of William Howard Ashton. Again it didn't sell, though **Kramer** continued to perform in clubs and on the cabaret circuit, joining the occasional major nostalgia concert and releasing a few more singles throughout the seventies and eighties.

Compilation appearances include: *Chinese Girl* on *English Freakbeat, Vol. 5* (LP & CD); *Do You Want To Know A Secret* on *The Swinging Sixties - 18 Classic Tracks* (CD); *The Town Of The Tuxley Toymaker* on *Pop-In, Vol 2* (CD) and you'll also find an alternate take of *I'll Keep You Satisfied* on the 2-CD set *Greatest Hits Of The 60's*. (VJ)

Billy J. Kramer and The Dakotas

Personnel:			
RAY JONES	bs	A	
BILLY J. KRAMER	vcls	AB	
TONY MANSFIELD	drms	A	
MIKE MAXFIELD	gtr	AB	
ROBIN MacDONALD	bs	AB	
FRANK FARLEY	drms	BC	
MICK GREEN	gtr	B	

HCP

ALBUMS:	1(A)	LISTEN TO (mono/stereo)		
		(Parlophone PMC 1209/PCS 3047) 1963	SC/R1	11
	2	BILLY BOY	(MFP MFP 1134) 1966	-

NB:(1) reissued on See For Miles (CM 107) 1983 and Beat Goes On (BGO LP 56) in 1989. They also had three US-only albums:-- *I'll Keep You Satisfied* (Imperial 9273/12273) 1964; *Little Children* (Imperial 9287/12267) 1964 and *Trains And Boats And Planes* (Imperial 9291/12291) 1965. The third one includes lots of songs not released in the UK at the time. Many of these are on the *CD Billy J. Kramer with The Dakotas at Abbey Road* (EMI 7243 4 93451 2 6) 1998. Of interest too is *The Best Of Billy J. Kramer* (EMI EG 26 0189 1) 1984. There's also been a CD compilation *Best Of The EMI Years: Billy J. Kramer* (EMI CDEMS 1392) 1991. *At Abbey Road: 1963 To 1966* (EMI 493 4512) 1998 is a 28-track compilation.

EPs:	1	THE BILLY J. KRAMER HITS		
			(Parlophone GEP 8885) 1963	SC
	2	I'LL KEEP YOU SATISFIED		
			(Parlophone GEP 8895) 1964	SC
	3	LITTLE CHILDREN	(Parlophone GEP 8907) 1964	SC
	4	FROM A WINDOW	(Parlophone GEP 8921) 1964	R1
	5	BILLY J. PLAYS THE STATES		
			(Parlophone GEP 8928) 1965	R1

HCP

45s:			
Do You Want To Know A Secret?/ I'll Be On My Way	(Parlophone R 5023)	1963	2
Bad To Me/I Call Your Name	(Parlophone R 5049)	1963	1
I'll Keep You Satisfied/I Know	(Parlophone R 5073)	1963	4
Little Children/ They Remind Me Of You	(Parlophone R 5105)	1964	1
From A Window/Second To None	(Parlophone R 5156)	1964	10
It's Gotta Last Forever/ Don't Do It No More	(Parlophone R 5234)	1965	-
Trains And Boats And Planes/ That's The Way I Feel	(Parlophone R 5285)	1965	12
Neon City/I'll Be Doggone	(Parlophone R 5362)	1965	-
We're Doing Fine/Forgive Me	(Parlophone R 5408)	1966 SC	-

The Dakotas were a Manchester-based group which formed back in 1962. It was Brian Epstein who provided them with their big break when he matched them up with **Billy Kramer** (whose name by birth was William Howard Ashton) and sent them all off to The Star Club in Hamburg, Germany for a three week slot to smarten up their stage act.

Their Epstein connection afforded them the opportunity to record **Lennon/McCartney** songs and, after EMI's **George Martin** rejected *She's My Girl* by Liverpool songwriter Ralph Bowdler as a debut disc, they recorded two **Beatles**' songs - *Do You Want To Know A Secret?* from their debut album and *I'll Be On My Way*. It climbed to No 2 in the UK and the 'J' was inserted on the record label to differentiate him from other singers

KRAYON ANGELS - Nineteen Sixty-Nine (LP).

called Billy. This was a bright idea of **John Lennon**'s and he was actually commissioned to write their next 45, *Bad To Me*, which topped the UK Charts for two weeks. The benefits of the Epstein link weren't confined to songwriting either. In the Summer of 1963 the group's popularity was further enhanced as they joined **The Beatles** on a UK tour. In August **The Dakotas** had a Top 20 hit in their own right with a **Shadows**-type instrumental, *The Cruel Sea*, which had been written 18 months earlier by Mike Maxfield, whose real name was Anthony Bookbinder!

Their third single, *I'll Keep You Satisfied*, was also written by **The Beatles**, enabling them to end the year on a high. This climbed to No 4 and was promoted by a 20-date UK tour, 'The Billy J. Kramer Pop Parade'. Inevitably an album was released to cash in on their recent successes and this sold well in the UK, too, peaking narrowly outside the UK Top Ten. As the year ended - and what a year it had been for the band - they took part in **The Beatles**' Christmas Stage Show at London's Finsbury Park Astoria.

Kramer was now so confident that he insisted upon Mort Shuman and John McFarlane's *Little Children* being the band's next single, against Epstein's advice and ending the tradition of using **Lennon/McCartney** compositions. How right he was, for it became their most successful record and the disc usually associated with the band after topping the UK Charts, climbing to No 7 in the States and selling over a million copies worldwide. Like its predecessors it didn't demand a strong vocal performance, which was as well because **Kramer** couldn't have given it, it was ideally suited to his more restrained sugary style.

In the States, *Bad To Me*, which had sunk without trace first time 'round, was reissued on the flip of *Little Children*; many deejays flipped the disc and it became a Top Ten hit in its own right.

At this point, Ray Jones left the band with MacDonald moving across to take over his bass duties and former Johnny Kidd and The Pirates' Mick Green coming in on rhythm guitar. Another **Lennon/McCartney** song, *From A Window*, was selected for their next 45 and it returned them to the Top Ten. In the States, the US-only album *Little Children* climbed to No 48 and *From A Window* peaked at No 23.

When their next 45, *It's Gotta Last Forever*, failed to chart in the UK it was apparent their fortunes were beginning to decline, though it fared a little better in the States climbing to No 67. Perhaps these US-only albums helped sustain interest in them a little longer Stateside, where they also recorded a live EP on stage at Long Beach, California, for UK release - though the punters showed only limited interest.

Their final hit was Burt Bacharach's *Trains And Boats And Planes* (UK No 12, US No 47), another song ideally suited to Kramer's vocal style, though the original outsold it here in the UK.

As 1965 drew to an end the Merseybeat sound on which the band had been so reliant was becoming passé and the band was forced onto the northern UK club and cabaret circuit to make a living. When their last three 45s failed to chart, **Kramer** resolved to go it alone. By now, Mansfield had

left **The Dakotas** with another former Johnny Kidd and The Pirates man, Frank Farley, replacing him on drums. **The Dakotas** soldiered on until March 1968 but then split. They are really one of several acts who enjoyed enormous popularity at the time but are really only of interest to Merseybeat fans now.

People wanting to investigate their music further may want to try *The Best Of Billy J. Kramer* which includes all his mid-sixties hits along with some more obscure tracks (*It's Up To You* and a live 1965 performance of *Sugar Babe* from a rare EP). It also includes modern material from the late seventies and others from 1984, which hitherto had only been released abroad. Material from their EP's has also been compiled on See For Miles' *EP Collection*.

The *At Abbey Road* set is a 28-track collection of hits, 'B' sides, rarities and album tracks. It includes two previously unissued tracks, *Listen* and Joe South's *Down In The Boondocks*.

Various artists compilation appearances have included: *Don't You Do It No More* on *Liverpool 1963-1968* (CD) and *Liverpool 1963-1968, Vol. 1* (LP); *Little Children* and *Bad To Me* on *Mersey Beat* (2-LP); *Bad To Me* on *U.K. No. 1 Hits Of The 60's* (CD), *Best Of British Rock* (CD), *30 Years Of Number 1 Hit Singles - 1960/1989* (CD), *Remember The 60's* (CD) and on *Super Hits Of The 60s - Vol 2* (CD); *Trains And Boats And Planes* on *Hits Of The Sixties* (CD) and *Beat Generation - Ready Steady Go* (CD); *From A Window*, *I'll Keep You Satisfied*, *Bad To Me* and *I'll Be On My Way* on *Songs Lennon And McCartney Gave Away* (LP); *When You Walked In The Room* on *Beat At Abbey Road* (CD); *Do You Want To Know A Secret* and *Little Children* on *Hits Of The Mersey Era, Vol. 1* (LP) and on *Hits Of The 60's - Save The Last Dance For Me* (CD); *Do You Want To Know A Secret?* on *60's Mix* (CD), *Hits Of The 60's Vol 2* (CD), *Super Hits Of The 60s - Vol 1* (CD) and *Love Is All Around* (CD); *I'll Keep You Satisfied* has resurfaced on the 2-CD set *Greatest Hits Of The 60's Vol 4* and on *Super Hits Of The 60s - Vol 3* (CD), whilst *I'll Keep You Satisfied*, *They Remind Me Of You*, *From A Window* and *Bad To Me* have all been compiled on *Hard Up Heroes, Vol. 4* (CD). (VJ)

Krayon Angels

ALBUM: 1   NINETEEN SIXTYNINE   (Dig The Fuzz DIG041LP) 200?

Dig The Fuzz has brought to our attention this 1968 power-pop band with psychedelic leanings that was only around for long enough to record this set of demos which captures the swinging sixties feel perfectly. (VJ)

Krimson Kake

45:     Feelin' Better/Waiter   (Penny Farthing PEN 707) 1970

A short-lived pop group, whose 'A' side was a soulish ballad. (VJ)

Sonja Kristina

45:     Let The Sunshine In/Frank Mills   (Polydor 56299) 1968

In the period covered by this book, sexy Sonja was best known as vocalist with **Curved Air**. Sonja was also in 'Hair', where she performed *Frank Mills*, the 'B' side to the above 45 prior to joining the band. She released a solo album *Sonja Kristina* (Chopper CHOPE 5) 1980 and a 45, *St. Tropez/Mr. Skin* (PS) (Chopper CHOP 101) in 1980 too. In the nineties, having been out of the limelight raising a family, she returned as a solo artist, and two of her albums were reissued in 1997 on CD by Mystic Records: *Songs From The Acid Folk* (with Tylor and Friends) and *Harmonies of Love* (with Cloud Ten). In 2002, *Songs From The Acid Folk* was reissued on CD again (Market Square) with extra tracks. (VJ)

The Kubas

45s: I Love Her/Magic Potion   (Columbia DB 7451) 1965 R1

This was basically **The Koobas**, a Merseybeat band, recording under a differently-spelt name. *I Love Her* was their own composition and a pretty good slice of Merseybeat it was too. It was coupled with an average cover of *Magic Potion*.

Compilation appearances include: *I Love Her* and *Magic Potion* on *Liverpool 1963-1968* (CD) and on *Liverpool 1963-1968, Vol. 1* (LP); *Magic Potion* on *Mersey Beat* (2-LP); and *I Love Her* on *English Freakbeat, Vol. 2* (LP & CD). (VJ)

Kubie

Personnel:
HARVEY BURNS	drms	A
GRAHAM JONES	keyb'ds, vcls	A
DAVID KUBINEC	vcls, gtr	A
CHRIS LAWRENCE	bs	A

ALBUM: 1(A) DAY OF THE MADMAN (Kuckuck 2375026) 1974
NB: (1) German release.

Kubinec had been vocalist in **World Of Oz** and made a solo 45. Harvey Burns had been in Shorty and played for **Cat Stevens**, as had Chris Lawrence. **David Kubinec** went solo again after this venture. (VJ)

Dave Kubinec

45: Schopi/Lady Loves (Parlophone R 5762) 1969

A solo effort by this former **World Of Oz** member. He later worked with **John Cale** and had more solo recordings (including an album) in the late seventies. (VJ)

The Kult

Personnel incl: BRENDAN BONASS
PAUL BRADY
JACKIE McAULEY
PETE O'DRISCOLL

45: No Home Today/Mr. No 1 (CBS 4276) 1969 R3

A very rare and sought-after single. The band formed in 1967 in Dublin out of the ashes of The Inmates and their earliest line-up included **Jackie McAuley** (formerly with **Them** and **Belfast Gypsies**), Brendan Bonass and Paul Brady. By the time of the CBS 45 all three had left but one member at least was Pete O'Driscoll. The 'A' side, *No Home Today*, in particular, was a good slice of psychedelia veering towards progressive notable for some fine guitar work.

No Home Today and *Mister Number One* can also be heard on *Perfumed Garden Vol. 2* (LP & CD). (MWh/VJ)

The Kursaal Flyers

Personnel: (up to 1976)			
WILL BIRCH	drms	A
RICHIE BULL	bs, vcls	A
VIC COLLINS	gtr, vcls	A
GRAEME DOUGLAS	gtr	A
PAUL SHUTTLEWORTH	vcls	A

ALBUMS: 1(A) CHOCS AWAY (UK UKAL 1011) 1975
(up to 2(A) THE GREAT ARTISTE (UK UKAL 1018) 1975
1976) 3(A) THE GOLDEN MILE (CBS 82253) 1976
NB. (1) and (2) reissued on one CD (On The Beach FOAMCD 3) 1991. There's also a compilation, *In For A Spin: The Best Of The Kursaal Flyers* (Edsel ED 149) 1985. *Hit Records: The Best Of The Kursaal Flyers* (On The Beach FOAMCD 6) 2002 is a CD compilation, which provides an overview of their career from 1975 to their short-lived 1988 re-union.

HCP
45s: Speedway/Chocs Away (UK 201 2001) 1975 -
(up to Hit Records/Brakeman (UK UK 116) 1975 -
1976) Groanin' For Love/Slim In For Women (UK UK 129) 1976 -
Little Does She Know/Drinking Socially (CBS 4689) 1976 14

Not a band to interest collectors yet, their roots lay in the pub-rock movement. They took their name from one of the most adventurous rides in Southend's Kursaal amusement park and Shuttleworth, Birch and Douglas

had originally been in an outfit called Surly Bird in 1970. They eventually won a residency at the Blue Boar pub in Southend and signed to **Jonathan King**'s UK Records. Birch could write a witty lyric and their first two albums veered towards a country-influenced brand of rock'n'roll, but didn't really portray the band at their best. In 1976 they left UK and signed to CBS. Their third album, *Golden Mile*, produced by **Mike Batt**, was similar in concept to The Turtles' *Battle Of The Bands*, a musical journey through a range of diverse musical styles including swing, ska and sixties pop. It is worth investigation and also produced a hit single, *Little Does She Know*. 1977 saw the departure of Graeme Douglas, his replacement was Barry Martin and a final album which was more punkish in style, *Five Live Kursaals*. Still, the band didn't survive the emerging punk-rock revolution.

After their demise Birch formed The Records with John Wicks (a guitarist who joined the band in their final days). They took their final song *Girls That Don't Exist* with them. Douglas became a key member and songwriter for Eddie and The Hotrods.

The 1985 Edsel compilation includes most of their singles, selected album tracks and five previously unissued songs. Similar material was also included on a 1982 compilation issued by the German Line label.

In 1988, **The Kursaal Flyers** reformed, minus Richie Bull. They recorded the excellently titled album *A Former Tour de Force Is Forced To Tour* (Waterfront WF 044 CD) but it once again failed to break them big and they returned to whence they came.

The 1991 CD was put together by former member Will Birch. The 2002 CD overview is the best introduction to their career.

Their albums had some good pop hooks but the careers of bands like this in the mid-seventies were cut short by the emergence of punk. (VJ)

The Kydds

45s: Sun Is A Laughing Child/
Touch Of The Sun (Nems 55-4095) 1969
Judas In Blue/Where Did I Go Wrong (President PT 289) 1970

This is another long forgotten band. (VJ)

The Kytes

45s: Blessed/Call Me Darling (Pye 7N 17136) 1966
Frosted Panes/I'll Give You Better Love (Pye 7N 17179) 1966 R1
Running In The Water/
The End Of The Day (Island WI 6027) 1968 R1

The Kytes started out as a melodic pop outfit judging by *Blessed*, their cover of Paul Simons folk-rocker and *Frosted Panes*. By their final release *Running In The Water* they were merging mod and psychedelia and featuring lots of backwards instrumentation. They once backed **Peter and Gordon**.

Compilation appearances have included: *Blessed* on *Paisley Pop - Pye Psych (& Other Colours) 1966-1969* (CD) and *Ripples, Vol. 6* (CD); *Frosted Panes* on *Rubble, Vol. 10 - Professor Jordan's Magic Sound Show* (LP) and *Ripples, Vol. 3* (CD); and *Running Through The Water* on *Voyage Through The Sugarcube* (LP & CD) and *We Can Fly, Vol 1* (CD). (VJ)

Kyttock Kynd

Personnel:
CYRUS LAURIE	A
JOHN YOUNG	A
HUGH CLARKE	A
BILL SHERRY	A

ALBUM: 1(A) KYTTOCK KYND (Dorian 4782) 1970 R2

A privately-pressed Glaswegian folk album housed in an attractive silver sleeve depicting the musicians dressed in monks' robes. The material is entirely traditional and acoustic, including standards such as *Baron O'Brackley* (the album's highlight) and *Let No Man Steal Your Thyme*. NB this never appeared on Decca, as previously stated. (VJ/RMJ)

Lace (1)

Personnel incl:	LLOYD COURTENAY	drms	A
	RONI DOUGLAS (PETE DELLO)	vcls	A
	JOHN LAWSON	bs	A
	TONY SINCLAIR	ld gtr	A

45: I'm A Gambler/Go Away   (Page One POF 135) 1969

Lace was a vehicle for the talents of **Pete Dello**, striving for anonymity after his controversial departure from **Honeybus**. The A-side later turned up on his solo album. Lawson had previously been with **The Universals** and **Gary Walker And The Rain**.

I'm A Gambler has been compiled on *Pop-In, Vol 2* (CD). (MWh/RMJ)

Lace (2)

Personnel:	ROGER BARBER		A
	JOHN BULLOCK	bs	A
	PETER PINCKNEY	vcls, gtr	A
	DICK KNOX RAY	drms	A

45: People People/The Nun   (Columbia DB 8499) 1968 SC

A different band, whose single was produced by Norman 'Hurricane' Smith - a former engineer for **The Beatles**. Peter Pinckney was later in **Aubrey Small**.

The Nun can also be heard on *Jagged Time Lapse, Vol 2* (CD). (VJ/PP)

Dave Lacey and Corvettes

Personnel incl: DAVE LACEY

45: That's What They All Say/
I've Had Enough   (Philips BF 1419) 1965

A beat-era band from Birmingham, whose sole vinyl offering was this long forgotten 45.

Clap Your Hands and *Unlucky I Am* resurfaced on *Brumbeat* (CD) and *Brum Beat, Vol. 2* (LP). (VJ)

La De Da Band

45: Come Together/Here Is Love   (Parlophone R 5810) 1969

The 'A' side is a cover of the **Lennon/McCartney** song. The 'B' side is very nondescript. (VJ)

The Ladybirds

45s:	Lady Bird/I Don't Care Any More	(Columbia DB 7197) 1964
	The White Cliffs Of Dover/	
	It's Not The Same Without A Boy	(Columbia DB 7250) 1964
	Memories/Try A Little Love	(Columbia DB 7351) 1964
	I Wanna Fly/O.K. Fred	(Columbia DB 7523) 1965

This was a girl duo, but nothing else is known of them. (VJ)

Lady June

Personnel:	LADY JUNE		
	(JUNE CAMPBELL-CRAMER)	vcls	A
	KEVIN AYERS	gtr, bs, synthesizer	A
	BRIAN ENO	keyb'ds, gtr, vcls	A
	JAKOB KLAASE	piano	A
	MARTHA	violin	A
	PIP PYLE	drms	A
	KIM SOLOMAN	piano	A

ALBUM: 1(A) LADY JUNE'S LINGUISTIC LEPROSY
(Caroline C 1509) 1974 SC

NB: (1) reissued on CD (See For Miles SEECD 350) 1992.

Lady June was the pseudonym of artist, model and eccentric June Campbell-Cramer, who was born in 1931. She grew up in Plymouth, but spent much of her youth (and most of the sixties) painting on the Continent. She befriended **Kevin Ayers** and **Daevid Allen** of the **Soft Machine** in Majorca in the mid-sixties, and gave them advice and financial help as they developed their music. When she returned to the UK at the end of the decade she quickly became a fixture of London's underground, playing concerts, giving talks and exhibitions and living in the heart of West London's hip Portobello area. It was at her birthday party, on June 1st 1973, that **Robert Wyatt** fell out of a window and became paralysed. Being old friends with many of the UK's leading avant-garde musicians, and having toured with **Henry Cow**, she made her only album for Virgin's budget offshoot Caroline in 1974. Supported by **Ayers** and **Brian Eno**, as well as Pip Pyle from **Hatfield and The North** and **National Health**, it's a highly eccentric blend of poetry and music. Only 5,000 copies were pressed, and it soon became something of a cult item. **Lady June** also contributed vocals to **GF FitzGerald's** *Mouseproof* album. Much of the rest of her life was spent in Majorca, though she frequently returned to Britain and participated in numerous avant-garde events as well as mounting solo art exhibitions. She died suddenly in June 1999. (RMJ/VJ/M\Wh)

Denny Laine

Personnel:	COLIN ALLEN	drms	A
(up to	DENNY LAINE	gtr, keyb'ds, vcls	A
1976)	PHOEBE LAOB	vcls	A
	MACEY McCREARY	vcls	A
	JOHN MOORSHEAD	gtr	A
	STEVE THOMPSON	bs	A
	LINDA McCARTNEY	keyb'ds, vcls	A
	PAUL McCARTNEY	bs, vcls, gtr, drms, keyb'ds	A

ALBUMS:	1(A)	AAH LAINE!	(Wizard SWZ 2001) 1973
(up to			
1976)	2(B)	HOLLY DAYS	(Capitol EMI 781) 1976

45s:	Find A Way Somehow/	
(up to	Move Me To Another Place	(Wizard WIZ 104) 1973
1976)	It's So Easy//Listen To Me	
	I'm Looking For Someone To Love	(EMI EMI 2523) 1976

Denny Laine, a Brummie, who was born as Brian Hines had been lead singer of **The Moody Blues**, but he left in August 1966 to go solo. Signing to Deram he later formed **Denny Laine's String Band**, a short-lived but interesting combo, and was then in **Balls**. In the seventies he was in **Ginger Baker's Airforce** before becoming a key member of **Wings**, which explains the involvement of Linda and **Paul McCartney** on his second solo album. (VJ)

RUBBLE VOL. 12 (Comp LP) featuring Denny Laine's String Band.

Denny Laine's String Band

Personnel:	CLIVE GILLINSON	cello	AB
	DENNY LAINE	gtr, vcls	ABC
	WILHELM MARTIN	violin	A
	BINKY McKENZIE	bs	A
	VIV PRINCE	drms	ABC
	JOHN STEIN	violin	AB
	CHRIS VAN CAMPEN	cello	A
	ANGUS ANDERSON	violin	B
	HALFLIDI HALYNISSON	cello	B
	ANDY LEIGH		BC

45s:	Say You Don't Mind/Ask The People	(Deram DM 122) 1967 SC
	Too Much In Love/Catherine's Wheel	(Deram DM 171) 1968 SC
Reissue:	Say You Didn't Mind/Ask The People	(Deram DM 227) 1969

A short-lived adventure for **Laine** who'd earlier fronted Denny and The Diplomats and, of course, been lead vocalist with **The Moody Blues**. Formed in December 1966, this act was notable for the use of amplified string instruments which was possibly an inspiration for the **Electric Light Orchestra**. With a string quartet recruited from the Royal Academy of Music, they were a frequent attraction on John Peel's 'Top Gear' and *Say You Don't Mind* was an excellent piece of 1967 art-pop.

In May 1967, 'Melody Maker' reported that **Laine** pulled out of the band's debut performance at London's Saville Theatre, one hour before the show was due to commence. McKenzie had left three days before and **Laine** simply didn't have enough time to rehearse a replacement.

Line-up 'B' apparently recorded an album due for release in December 1967 and then February 1968 release but it never appeared. A follow-up single *Why Did You Come?* was similarly shelved.

In December 1967, the string quartet left the UK for a tour of Russia, and the group carried on for a while as a trio (abetted by a conga player). Their follow-up 45, *Too Much In Love* sounds like it was recorded without the string quartet. The B-side, however, does feature them.

By February 1969, **Laine** had joined **Balls** and he was later in **Ginger Baker's Airforce**. **Viv Prince**, as many of you will know, had earlier been in **The Pretty Things**. His other bands included **The Bunch Of Fives**, **Vamp**, and **Kate**.

A cover of their first 45, *Say You Don't Mind*, was later a hit for **Colin Blunstone** in 1972.

Compilation appearances have included:- *Say You Don't Mind* and *Catherine's Wheel* on *Deram Dayze* (LP); *Say You Don't Mind* on *The Sixties Lost And Found, Vol. 2* (LP), *Sixties Explosion, Vol. 1* (CD), *Pop Inside The Sixties, Vol. 2* (CD) and on the 4-CD box set *Acid Drops, Spacedust & Flying Saucers*; *Catherine's Wheel* on *Psychedalia - Rare Blooms From The English Summer Of Love, Rubble Vol. 12: Staircase To Nowhere* (LP) and *Rubble Vol. 6* (CD); *Silly Love Songs* (with **Wings**) on *Love Is All Around* (CD); *Ask The People, Catherine's Wheel* and *Why Did You Come?* on *Hard Up Heroes, Vol. 2* (CD) and *Ask The People* on *Colour Me Pop, Vol 1* (CD). (NW/VJ)

Greg Lake

HCP

45:	I Believe In Father Christmas/	
	Humbug (PS)	(Manticore K 13511) 1975 2

NB: *The Greg Lake Retrospective: From The Beginning* (Castle ESDCD 552) 1997 is a 2-CD set, which covers his solo career as well as his days with **King Crimson** and **Emerson, Lake and Palmer**. It has been reissued again (Sanctuary CMEDD 1240) 2005.

Greg Lake has been a significant and influential figure in progressive rock initially as a founding member of the original **King Crimson** and later in **Emerson, Lake and Palmer**. He went on to enjoy a reasonably successful solo career.

Greg Lake was born on 10 November 1947 in Bournemouth, Dorset. He got his first guitar from his mum when he was 12 and took guitar lessons from a local teacher called Don Strike. One of Strike's other pupils was Robert Fripp and **Lake** formed a good friendship with him.

RONNIE LAINE'S SLIM CHANCE - ONE FOR THE ROAD (LP).

Greg Lake was in **Shame, The Shy Limbs** and **The Gods** before joining **King Crimson** at the start of 1969. Then in March 1970 he left to form **Emerson, Lake and Palmer**. *I Believe In Father Christmas* was, as its name suggests, a novelty Christmas 45 and a grandiose and commercially successful one which has gained much airplay at Christmas-time in subsequent years. It was a massive UK hit but only made No 95 in the US. Co-written with Pete Sinfield (lyricist for **King Crimson** and **ELP**) it also included an extract from Prokofiev's 'Sleigh Ride'. Later, as **Emerson, Lake and Palmer** began to falter **Lake** stepped up his solo career and he also temporarily replaced John Wetton in Asia for a Far East tour in the Winter of 1983/84.

He was also a producer for **Spontaneous Combustion** and **Stray Dog** among others.

Greg Lake fans will be interested in the 2-CD 32-track set *Retrospective From The Beginning* (Castle ESDCD 552) 1997, which encompasses his career from the early days with **King Crimson**, through to **Emerson, Lake and Palmer**, and his solo career. The first disc contains some well known songs like *In The Court of The Crimson King* and there's a live version of *21st Century Schizoid Man*. The second one features solo material and later **Emerson, Lake and Palmer** efforts. It features two previously unreleased solo tracks. It was reissued again in 2005 to coincide with his tour. (VJ)

Steven Lancaster

45:	San Francisco Streets/Miguel Fernando	(Polydor 56215) 1967

The 'A' side is an easy-going ditty produced by Shel Talmy. Pleasant enough but he was certainly no Scott McKenzie. (MWh)

The Lancastrians

Personnel:	TERRY BENSON	bs, vcls	A
	JOHN FLEURY	drms	A
	KEVIN HEYWOOD	gtr, vcls	A
	BARRY LANGTREE	lead gtr, vcls	A

HCP

45s:	We'll Sing In The Sunshine/		
	Was She Tall	(Pye 7N 15732) 1964 SC	47
	Let's Lock The Door (And Throw Away The Key)/		
	If You're Goin' To Leave Me	(Pye 7N 15791) 1965	-
	There'll Be No More Goodbyes/		
	Never Gonna Come On Home	(Pye 7N 15846) 1965	-
	Lonely Man/I Can't Stand The Pain	(Pye 7N 15927) 1965	-
	The World Keeps Going Round/		
	Not The Same Anymore	(Pye 7N 17043) 1966 SC	-
	The Ballad Of The Green Berets/		
	My Little Rose	(Pye 7N 17072) 1966	-

Their name is a bit misleading 'cos they were actually from Cheshire. In 1956 Kevin Heywood and Barry Langtree met at secondary school. They were both learning to play guitar. Kevin invited Barry back to his house and that's when it all started. 'The Garage' was their first venue. Teaming up with local friend Tommy Hart they were initially The Heartbeats, then Tommy Hart and The Heartbeats and they did a few radio gigs under this moniker. Tommy Hart left around the time Terry benson and John Fleury joined and they became Barry Langtree and The Lancastrians and eventually just **The Lancastrians**.

They are best remembered, if at all, for their debut 45, *We'll Sing In The Sunshine*, which was a very minor hit back in 1964. Another of their 45s, *The World Keep's Going Round*, was a Ray Davies' composition which flopped. Shel Talmy produced their six singles. He brought in **Jimmy Page** on sessions with them for *Was She Tall* and *The World Keeps Going Round*. **Nicky Hopkins** played on a couple of tunes too. They toured Germany and returned with less money than they set off with, so when they were asked to embark on another tour (this time to France) they declined and decided to disband.

The band reformed in February 2001 with three original members (Langtree, Heywood and Benson) plus ex-session man Steve Wilde on drums and vocals.

Compilation appearances have included: *We'll Sing In The Sunshine* on *The Hit Makers* Vol. 2 (LP); *The World Keeps Going Round* on *James Patrick Page: Session Man, Vol. 2* (LP & CD); *We'll Sing In The Sunshine*, *Was She Tall*, *The World Keeps Going Round* and *Not The Same Anymore* on *Jimmy Page - Hip Young Guitar Slinger* (2-CD) and on *Jimmy Page - Guitar For Hire* (CD); *Was She Tall* and *We'll Sing In The Sunshine* on *Jimmy's Back Pages - The Early Years* (CD); *We'll Sing In The Sunshine* on *Ripples, Vol. 1 - Look At The Sunshine* (CD); *Let's Lock The Door (And Throw Away The Key)* on *Ripples, Vol. 5 - Beach Bash* (CD) and *Hippy Hippy Shake - The Beat Era Vol 1* (CD); *Never Gonna Come On Home* on *Ripples, Vol. 7 - Rainbows* (CD); *Lonely Man* on *Ripples, Vol. 2 - Dreamline* (CD); *Was She Tall* on *Watch Your Step - The Beat Era Vol 1* (LP & CD); *The World Keeps Going Round* on *Ready, Steady, Stop! - Doin' The Mod Vol 4* (CD); *My Little Rose* on *Strung Out* (CD); *The World Keeps Going Round* on *Kinky: The Songs Of Ray Davies* (CD); and, finally, *We'll Sing In The Sunshine* on *200 Fab Sixties Favourites* (CD Box Set). (VJ/SW)

Neil Landon

45s: Waiting Here For Someone/
       I've Got Nothing To Lose   (Decca F 12330) 1966
       I'm Your Puppet/I Still Love You   (Decca F 12451) 1966

Neil Landon was part of **The Ivy League**, **The Flowerpot Men** and was later in **Fat Mattress**. *Waiting Here For Someone* was a Carter-Lewis composition. (VJ)

Ian Stuart Lane

45:    Don't Rock Me Baby/See What You Can Do With Your
     Life   (Greenwich Gramophone Company GSS 103) 1972

This outfit consisted of three girls and four guys. Several of them look familiar. On offer was rock 'n' roll. They were apparently assisted by superstars whose identity remains secret. Among those whose identity can be revealed were **B.J. Cole** (steel gtr), Tony Reeves (bs and producer) and **Caleb Quaye**'s sister Terri on congas. The 'A' side was penned by Andrew Hoy and David Stratten. They don't appear on the recording though which David's mother paid for. It has a strong melody with rolling piano. (VJ)

Ronnie Lane and Slim Chance

Personnel:			
BENNY GALLAGHER	gtr, vcls	A
JIMMY JEWELL	sax	AB
RONNIE LANE	gtr, vcls	ABC
BILLY LIVSEY	keyb'ds	AB
GRAHAM LYLE	mandolin, vcls	A
BRUCE ROWLAND	drms	AB
CHRISSIE STEWART	bs	A
KEVIN WESTLAKE	gtr	AB
BUDDY WHITE	bs	A
STEVE BINGHAM	bs	B
KEN SLAVEN	violin	B
ROBIN LUCAS	gtr, vcls	B
DREW McCULLOCH	gtr, vcls	B
BRIAN BELSHAW	bs	C
CHARLIE HART	keyb'ds, violin	C
COLIN DAVEY	drms	C
STEVE SIMPSON	gtr	C
RUAN O'LOCHLANN	sax, keyb'ds	C

NB: The band had a couple of drummers Jim Franks and Glen Le Fleur, between Bruce Rowland and Colin Davey.

HCP

ALBUMS:	1(A)	ANYMORE FOR ANYMORE (GM GML 1013) 1974 SC 48
(up to	2(B)	RONNIE LANE'S SLIM CHANCE
1976)		(Island ILPS 9321) 1975 SC -
	3(C)	ONE FOR THE ROAD (live) (Island ILPS 9366) 1976 SC -

NB: (1) reissued on CD (See For Miles SEECD 338) 1992, with bonus tracks. (3) reissued on CD (Edsel EDCD 464) 1995. The band also appeared on *Mahoney's Last Stand* (Atlantic K 50308) 1976 with Ron Wood and *Rough Mix* (Polydor 2442 147) with **Pete Townshend**. There's also a compilation: *Kuschy Rye: The Singles* (New Millennium Communications PILOT 19) 1997, which compiles all his solo singles (except his 1977 *Street In The City* recorded with **Pete Townsend**. The CD also includes two non-45 bonus tracks, a version of **The Rolling Stones**' *Sweet Virginia* and *Stone*, both recorded at Victoria Palace in 1975. It's a well-presented package with extensive liner notes and photos. There's also a 17-track retrospective from New Millennium Communications containing several alternative mixes from his time with **Slim Chance**, **Clapton** and **Townsend**, which is accompanied by a 20-page booklet. *You Never Can Tell* (New Millennium) 1997 compiles his mid-seventies BBC sessions with **Slim Chance**. *Anymore For Anymore* (New Millennium PILOT 15) 1998 adds another seven bonus tracks to the earlier release.

HCP

45s:	How Come/Tell Everyone Done	
(up to	This One Before (PS)	(GM GMS 011) 1973 11
1976)	The Poacher/Gonna See The King	(GM GMS 024) 1974 36
	Roll On Babe/Anymore For Anymore	(GM GMS 033) 1975 -
	What Went Down/Lovely	(Island ILPS 6216) 1975 -
	Brother Can You Spare Me A Dime/	
	Ain't No Lady	(Island WIP 6229) 1975 -
	Don't Try'n'Change My Mind/	
	Well Well Hello	(Island WIP 6258) 1976 -

Lane formed this outfit a few months after leaving **The Faces** in May 1973. **Kevin Westlake** had previously played guitar in **Blossom Toes**, drummer Bruce Rowland had banged the skins for **Joe Cocker** and **Terry Reid**. **Gallagher and Lyle** had previously been part of **McGuinness Flint** but went on to find fame and fortune as a duo. Soon after forming and going on a short trial tour, they undertook a massively ambitious tour, the Passing Show, which included a circus big top. The end result was that, after stretching its finances to the limit, the band had to split with just a debut album and three 45s to show for its troubles.

RON WOOD AND RONNIE LAINE - Last Stand (LP).

Later in 1974 **Lane** reformed the band, but with **Gallagher and Lyle** having gone solo and Chrissie Stewart gone off to play for **Joe Cocker**, it was with a very different line-up (C). This one signed for Island and put out a couple more albums and three more 45s. The line-up was pretty experienced because Steve Simpson had previously been with Tumbleweeds, Belshaw had been in **Blossom Toes**, Hart in The Kilburns and O'Lochlann in **Bees Make Honey**.

Musically their records veered towards a country sound but they were much better as a 'live' band and are remembered for their unpretentious, knees-up East End style live format.

In the eighties, **Ronnie Lane** had to retire from music, suffering from multiple sclerosis. Sadly he finally lost his battle and died on 4 June 1997, aged 51.

The Poacher has been compiled on *Your Starter For Ten!!* (CD). (VJ)

Gerry Langley

45:      Goodnight Sweet Lady/Write Me A Letter   (DJM 208) 1969

An Irish singer from Belfast, who'd earlier recorded as **Jerry Langley** and was part of **The Langleys**. (VJ)

Jerry Langley

45s:	Little Grey Man/Bitter Sweets	(Parlophone R 5325) 1965
	Joanna Jones/How Long	(CBS 2935) 1967

Jerry was also in **The Langleys** and later recorded as **Gerry Langley**. Jerry also had quite a lot of success as a songwriter and many famous people recorded his songs including **Sandie Shaw**, Val Donican, Peters and Lee, Russ Conway, Wayne Newton and even Brian Clough! Jerry is still very active in the music business. (VJ/JL)

Mary Langley

45s:	Stay In My World/Summer Love	(CBS 2862) 1967
	It Always Rains On Sundays/	
	All My Life Is You	(CBS 3032) 1967

Mary Langley, who'd earlier recorded as **Perpetual Langley**, was also in **The Langleys**. Mary ended up with her own TV show in Scotland and also supported Roy Orbison when he toured the UK. Sadly **Mary Langley** died in 1988 accidentally at the age of 38. (VJ)

LAST STRAW - Alone On A Stone (CD).

Perpetual Langley

45s:	We Wanna Stay Home/So Sad	(Planet PLF 110) 1966 SC
	Surrender/Two By Two	(Planet PLF 115) 1966 SC

A Belfast group containing **Mary Langley** who went on to a brief solo career and had earlier been in **The Langleys**. These 45s were produced by Shel Talmy.

We Wanna Stay Home, *So Sad*, *Surrender* and *Two By Two* can all be heard on *The Best Of Planet Records* (CD). (VJ)

The Langleys

Personnel incl: MARY LANGLEY
                 JERRY LANGLEY

45s:	Snakes And Ladders/	
	I Wander Everywhere	(Fontana TF 483) 1964
	Green Island/You Know I Love You	(Fontana TF 544) 1965

A Belfast group. After these two 45s, Jerry and Mary embarked on solo careers. Mary ended up with her own TV show in Scotland and also supported Roy Orbison when he toured the UK. The couple also did numerous Radio and TV shows together. Sadly Mary died in 1988 accidentally at the age of 38. Jerry had quite a lot of success as a songwriter and many famous people recorded his songs including **Sandie Shaw**, Val Donican, Peters and Lee, Russ Conway, Wayne Newton and even Brian Clough! Jerry is still very active in the music business. (VJ/JL)

Last Exit

Personnel:	JOHN HEDLEY	gtr	A
	RONNIE PEARSON	drms	AB
	GERRY RICHARDSON	keyb'ds	AB
	STING SUMNER	vcls, bs	AB
	TERRY ELLIS	gtr	B

CASSETTE: 1 FIRST FROM LAST EXIT (Wudwink WUD.C 101) 1975 R3
NB: This was sold at gigs.

45:      Whispering Voices/Evensong   (Wudwink WUD 01) 1975 R1

A short-lived Newcastle band who played their own amalgam of jazz, soul and blues from mid-1974 to early 1977 but were split on whether to move down to London in order to make it big. In 1977 Sting and Stewart were introduced to ex-**Animals** guitarist Andy Summers and **Gong** member Mike Howlett at a **Gong** reunion. It marked the first time that the three future Police stars played together as Strontium 90 and the rest is history as they say. (VJ)

Last Straw

Personnel:	PEYTE BURNAN	gtr	A
	STEVE GRIFIN	gtr	A
	GEOFF TAYLOR	vcls	A
	JACK TOOLE	drms	A
	PHIL TRUCKEL	bs	A

CD: 1(A) ALONE ON A STONE   (Kissing Spell KSCD 9591) 199?

This progressive rock outfit began recording circa 1972 and some of their output is collated on the above CD. They are sometimes likened to **Wicked Lady**. (PM)

Gene Latter

45s:	Just A Minute Or Two/Dream Lover	(Decca F 12364) 1966
	Mother's Little Helper/	
	Please Come Back To Me Again	(Decca F 12397) 1966 SC
	Something Inside Me Died/Don't Go	(CBS 202483) 1967
	Always/A Woman Called Sorrow	(CBS 202655) 1967

A Little Piece Of Leather/Funny Face Girl		(CBS 2843) 1967	
With A Child's Heart/Ways		(CBS 2986) 1967 SC	
A Tribute To Otis/			
Bring Your Love Home		(Direction 58-3245) 1968 SC	
α My Life Ain't Easy/Angie		(Spark SRL 1015) 1968	
Sign On The Dotted Line/I Love You		(Spark SRL 1022) 1969	
The Old Bell/Holding A Dream		(Spark SRL 1031) 1969	
Help Me Judy, Help Me/			
On The Highway		(Parlophone R 5800) 1969	
Tiger Bay/We Can Make Out		(Parlophone R 5815) 1969	
Someday You'll Need My Love		(Parlophone R 5833) 1970	
Catch My Soul/Happiness		(Parlophone R 5896) 1971	
Sing A Song Of Freedom/			
Too Busy Thinking About My Baby		(Parlophone R 5913) 1971	
Sign On The Dotted Line/			
I Love You (reissue)		(Spark SRL 1063) 1972	
All Over Now/Annie's Place		(Youngblood YB 1069) 1973	

NB: α as Gene Latter and The Detours.

This Arab R&B singer was born in Cardiff but later moved to London. He originally fronted a group called The Cousins. Despite a prolific 45 output commercial success always eluded him - his best known effort is probably a reasonable cover of **Jagger**/Richards' *Mother's Little Helper*, which you'll also find on *Rubble Vol. 5: The Electric Crayon Set* (LP) and *Rubble Vol. 3* (CD). In 1966, he was backed by Liverpool group The Anzacs (also known as The Aztecs). In 1967, he was backed by The Upsetters, another Liverpool group who included **Johnny Gustafson**.

Of his other songs, *A Little Piece Of Leather* is a Donnie Elbert R&B track; *A Tribute To Otis* is about Otis Redding, who'd recently died in a plane crash; *Tiger Bay* is in his home town of Cardiff; *Sign On The Dotted Line* is a popular Northern soul favourite and stomper and *Too Busy Thinking About My Baby* is a Marvin Gaye track.

My Life Ain't Easy (**Gene Latter** and The Detours) has been compiled on *Jagged Time Lapse, Vol 5* (CD). (VJ)

Laughing Gas

45:    All Shapes And Sizes/Opus No 1   (RCA RCA 2006) 1970

The above 45 was this outfit's sole platter. (VJ)

Lavender Grove

Personnel incl:	STAN DECKER	bs		A
	TERRY SPENCER	gtr		A

45:   α Lavender Grove/When I Was Young   (Oak) 1968 R4
NB: α Acetate.

Decker and Spencer formed this group upon the demise of the **Game**. They recorded this acetate in January 1968. The group and this 'A' side were named after the road in Mitcham where Spencer's girlfriend lived. Musically the 'A' side, *Lavender Grove*, was much in the style of the **Game**.

By 1969 **Lavender Grove** had become **The Grail**.

Compilation appearances include: *When I Was Young* and *Lavender Grove* on *Purple Heart Surgery Vol. 3* (LP); and *Lavender Grove* on *Story Of Oak Records* (2-LP)/*The Story Of Oak Records* (CD). (VJ)

Juliet Lawson

ALBUM: 1   BOO   (Sovereign SVNA 7257) 1972 R2
NB: (1) reissued on CD (Sunbeam SBRCD 003) 2005 with detailed sleevenotes.

45:    Only A Week Away/
        Weeds In The Yard   (Sovereign SOV 111) 1972

THE STORY OF OAK RECORDS (2-LP Comp) including Lavender Grove.

Juliet Lawson grew up in Bedfordshire and, after a brief stint at art school in Wimbledon, found work at London's Royal Court Theatre. A year spent singing in a rock group helped her find her feet as a songwriter, and she began to play solo club and college dates. Paul Samwell-Smith (ex-of **the Yardbirds**) helped her make demos, which earned her an offer from Island. She signed to EMI instead, however, and entered the studio with her friend David Costa (ex-**Trees**) producing. A superb collection of singer/songwriter material, *Boo* features **Trees**' bassist Bias Boshell as well as **Lol Coxhill** on sax. *Dear Fool, Igloo, Weeds In The Yard* and *Frog In The Jam* are among its finer moments, but there are no weak songs on this rare and highly-recommended album.

Ludicrously, its release was delayed by a week when the van leaving the pressing plant was car-jacked and all copies stolen. When it did appear the reviews were universally favourable, but it didn't sell. Its title, incidentally, was **Lawson's** nickname. Though a follow-up was recorded, it never appeared, perhaps owing to the failure of the Sovereign imprint. This is a great shame given that **Lawson** was a highly distinctive songwriter, in possession of a beautifully pure and expressive voice. She has continued to write and perform since *Boo*. (RMJ/VJ)

Ossie Layne Show

Personnel incl:	OSSIE LAYNE		A
	GARTH WATT-ROY		A
	NORMAN WATT-ROY		A

ALBUM: 1   MADDOX 2   (Spanish Edigsa) 1969 R?
NB: (1) was a Spanish-only release.

45:    α Come Back/
           Never Answer That 'Phone   (R&B MRB 5006) 1965 R1
NB: α credited to Ossie Lane.

In between their time in Newcastle pop-psych outfit **The Living Daylights** and the progressive underground outfit **Greatest Show On Earth**, Garth and Norman Watt-Roy were in this outfit. Their Spanish-only album was released in minute quantities. Taken from a live show in 1969, it features lots of swirling organ and frenzied fuzz guitars on cuts like *Rock My Plimsoul* and covers of Moby Grape's *Can't Be So Bad* and Spirit's *Fresh Garbage*. (VJ)

Lazy Farmer

Personnel incl:	JOHN BIDWELL	gtr, flute	A
	DON COGIN	banjo	A
	SANDY JONES	banjo	A
	WIZZ JONES	gtr, vcls	A
	JAKE WALTON	gtr, dulcimer	A

LEAF HOUND - Growers Of The Mushroom (CD).

ALBUM: 1(A)   LAZY FARMER   (Songbird C 062-31130) 1975 R2

NB: (1) German only. (1) reissued on CD (Sunbeam SBRCD 005) 2005 with detailed sleevenotes.

Wizz Jones had always been more popular abroad than at home, and by 1975 he was firmly-established on the German folk circuit. Having recruited his wife Sandy to back him on his 1974 *When I Leave Berlin* album, alongside former **COB** wizard Bidwell, banjo virtuoso Cogin and multi-instrumentalist Walton, things gelled and they decided to stay together. After touring Germany extensively, they made their only album in the German countryside for a local EMI subsidiary. Material ranges from the traditional (*Railroad Boy* and *Turtle Dove*) to **Ralph McTell's** *Standing Down In New York* and a reprise of **Jones**'s own *When I Leave Berlin*. The musicianship is superb and the production sophisticated. It was issued in an attractive gatefold sleeve, but failed to sell and is now a considerable rarity. (RMJ)

Lazy Lingo

45:    1st Floor, 2nd Floor/Race Against Time   (Deram DM 352) 1972

One of those obscure early seventies releases on Deram. (VJ)

Harry Leader Band

45:    Dragon Fly/Rush Hour   (Parlophone R 5386) 1965

This is another little known and long forgotten band. (VJ)

The Leaders

45:    Night People/Love Will Find A Way   (Fontana TF 602) 1965

More obscurities. (VJ)

Leading Figures

Personnel:	ROGER COULAM	keyb'ds	A
	RAY DAVIES	trumpet	A
	ERIC FORD	bs	A
	ARTHUR GREENSLADE	keyb'ds	A
	JOE MORETTI	gtr	A
	ALAN PARKER	gtr	A
	RONNIE VERRELL	drms	A
	ALAN WHALE	bs	A
	ANDY WHITE	drms	A

ALBUMS: 1(A)   OSCILLATION 67!   (Deram DML/SML 1006) 1967 SC
        2( )   SOUND AND MOVEMENT
                        (Ace Of Clubs SCL 1225) 1967 R1

The presence of **Mike Vernon** on production duties doesn't help much to save their debut album which is a useless exploitation effort. The music is an uninspired hotchpotch of instrumental and supposedly hip styles and should be included in a collection of "exotica"; rather than one of serious music. It's slick, technically competent, but utterly boring semi-orchestral pop. For Deram completists only.

The Ray Davies in this line-up is not **The Kinks**' frontman. Joe Moretti was a top session man. (MK)

Leaf Hound

Personnel:	DEREK BROOKS	gtr	A
	STUART BROOKS	bs	A
	PETE FRENCH	vcls	A
	MICK HALLS	ld gtr	A
	KEITH GEORGE YOUNG	drms	A

ALBUM: 1(A)   GROWERS OF MUSHROOM
                        (Decca SKL-R 5094) 1971 R5

NB: (1) also issued on Telefunken (14604) in Germany in 1971, but with fewer tracks. The German release has recently been pirated. The original German release included a poster of the band. The UK release was pirated in the early eighties on the US Discwaster label. The item is now a collectable too. Reissued on CD (See For Miles SEECD 403) 1994, with one bonus cut, *It's Gonna Get Better* (the 'B' side to their German-only 45 *Drowned My Life In Fear*) and on Repertoire (REP 4485-WY) 1994 with a second, previously unreleased bonus track (*Hip Shaker*) too. The See For Miles release was taken from the master tapes and has better sound quality, but the Repertoire one is better packaged and has one extra track. (1) reissued again on vinyl (Akarma AK 256) using the original British sleeve artwork (with the cover of the German release shown inside the gatefold) and on CD (Repertoire REPUK 1079) 2005, remastered in a digipak and with three bonus tracks: - *It's Gonna Get Better*, *Hipshaker* and one from a forthcoming album

Perhaps the most expensive major label album of the progressive era, *Growers of Mushroom* consists of competent hard-rock that is sure to disappoint those expecting a psychedelic classic from the title and cover.

Pete French, a South Londoner, had played with his cousin Mick Halls in various rock/blues outfits like Switch and Joe Poe before teaming up with Bob Brunning to form the **Brunning Sunflower Blues Band**. By 1969 he'd moved on to **Black Cat Bones**, in which Halls later joined him. In the latter half of 1970 they evolved into **Leaf Hound**, moving away from the blues towards the heavier sound of groups like **Led Zeppelin, Free** and **Black Sabbath**. Signed to Decca, they allegedly made *Growers of Mushroom* in 11 hours straight in Mayfair's Spot studios, late in 1970. Overseen by producer Paul Lynton, it features some incisive guitar work and raw, powerful vocals. The better numbers include *Drowned My Life In Fear, Stagnant Pool* and *Sad Road To The Sea*. All song titles are allegedly culled from horror story anthologies.

LED ZEPPELIN - Led Zeppelin (LP).

During their short time together **Leaf Hound** toured Germany, where their album was licensed to Telefunken before it appeared in the UK. Inexplicably the German release omitted two cuts, *Freelance Fiend* and the title track, though it did come with a poster of the band. Its sleeve was also completely different to the subsequent British pressing. Telefunken also issued *Drowned My Life In Fear* on a 45, backed by the non-album *It's Going To Get Better*, in a picture sleeve (Telefunken U 56 154) 1971. The Telefunken album was pirated a few years back. The UK release, which actually appeared early in 1972, is ultra-rare and very sought-after, though before spending a fortune on a copy some collectors might wish to ponder Disc's review of February 5th 1972, which called it 'a fairly passable impersonation of Deep Purple'.

After **Leaf Hound**'s demise French was briefly in **Big Bertha**, then joined **Atomic Rooster**. He later figured in US boogie band Cactus before returning to the UK to join Randy Pie. He played on their three German-only 1977 albums and put out a solo album and 45 the following year which were only released in Germany. (VJ/RMJ)

League of Gentlemen

Personnel:	JEFF BARTLEY	bs	A
	RON CLEAVE	lead gtr	A
	JOEL JAMES	sax	A
	JONATHAN KENT	vcls	A
	RAYMOND STEADMAN	drms	A
	RON THOMAS	gtr	A

45s:	Each Little Falling Tear/	
	And I Do Now	(Columbia DB 7666) 1965
	How Can You Tell/How Do They Know	(Planet PLF 109) 1966

A forgotten mid-sixties band, who were the backing group for various black American soul stars who toured the UK in the sixties.

We did think Robert Fripp and **Gordon Haskell** were in this act, but this now appears to be erroneous. (VJ/AD)

Leah

Personnel incl: PETE DELLO

| 45: | Arise Sir Henry/Uptight Basil | (GM GMS 10) 1973 |

This outfit was most notable for including ex-**Honeybus** member **Pete Dello**. (VJ)

Leapers Creepers Sleepers

| 45: | Precious Words/Ba Boo | (Island WI 275) 1966 SC |

This was another very obscure rock/pop act. (VJ)

Leather Head

| 45: | Gimme Your Money Please/Epitaph | (Philips 6006 3671) 1974 |

Leather Head was a pub-rock band. (VJ)

Led Zeppelin

Personnel:	JOHN BONHAM	drms	A
	JOHN PAUL JONES	bs, keyb'ds	A
	JIMMY PAGE	gtr	A
	ROBERT PLANT	vcls	A

			HCP
ALBUMS:	1(A)	LED ZEPPELIN	(Atlantic 588 171) 1969 SC 6
(up to	2(A)	LED ZEPPELIN II	(Atlantic 588 198) 1969 SC 1
1976)	3(A)	LED ZEPPELIN III	(Atlantic 2401-002) 1970 SC 1
	4(A)	LED ZEPPELIN IV	(Atlantic 2401-012) 1971 SC 1
	5(A)	HOUSES OF THE HOLY	(Atlantic K 40014) 1973 1

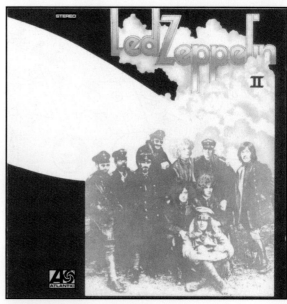

LED ZEPPELIN - Led Zeppelin II (LP).

6(A)	PHYSICAL GRAFFITI (2-LP)	
		(Swan Song SSK 89400) 1975 1
7(A)	PRESENCE	(Swan Song SSK 59402) 1976 1
8(A)	THE SONG REMAINS THE SAME (Soundtrack)	
		(Swan Song SSK 89402) 1976 1

NB: The earliest sleeves for (1) had turquoise lettering on the front and label credits to 'Superhype publishing'. These are R3 (4) is known under a number of other titles:- *The Fourth Led Zeppelin Album, Runes, The New Led Zeppelin Album*, and *The Four Symbols*. (1), (2), (3), (4), (5), (6) and (7) reissued again on CD (Atlantic 7567-82632-2, 7567-82633-2, 7567-82678-2, 7567-82638-2, 7567 82639-2, 7567-924 42-2 and 7567-92439-2 respectively) in 1994. (1) reissued on heavy vinyl (Atlantic SD 8216) 2000. CD collectors will be interested in a re-issue series of their albums in Japan, which duplicate in miniature their exact original album sleeves, including any die-cuts, paper bag etc. (1) (East West AMCY 2431), (2) (AMCY 2432), (3) (AMCY 2433), (4) (AMCY 2434), (5) (AMCY 2435), (6) (AMCY 2436), (7) (AMCY 2438), (8) (AMCY 2439), *In Through The Out Door* (AMCY 2441) and *Coda* (AMCY 2442). Other CD reissues include: - (3) on CD (Atlantic 7567-82678-2) and (4) on CD (Atlantic 7567-82638-2). There are also limited edition deluxe CD 35th Anniversary editions of (1) - (8).

BBC Sessions (Atlantic) 1997 is a 2-CD set of material from their radio broadcasts with the Beeb. *BBC Sessions* (Atlantic 8301 1) 2001 is a 4-LP box set available as a US import. It comprises radio sessions from 1969 and 1971. *Latter Days - The Best Of Led Zeppelin Volume 2* (Atlantic 7567 83278 2) 2000 is a 10-track selection. *Maximum Led Zeppelin* (Chrome Dreams ABCD 101) 2002 is a spoken word biography. *Early Days - Best Of Vol 1* (2-LP) (Atlantic 832681) compiles material from their first four albums. *How The West Was Won* (3-CD) (Atlantic 835872) contains material from performances in 1972 in Long Beach and Los Angeles, California to promote the *Houses of The Holy* album.

45s:	α	Communication Breakdown/	
(up to		Good Times, Bad Times	(Atlantic 584 269) 1969 R5
1976)	β	Whole Lotta Love (Edit)/Livin' Lovin'	
		Maid (She's A Woman)	(Atlantic 584 309) 1969 R6
	χ	D'Yer Maker/	
		Over The Hills And Far Away	(Atlantic K 10296) 1973 R4
	δ	Trampled Underfoot/	
		Black Country Woman	(Swan Song SSK 19403) 1975

NB: α & χ Unissued, promo-only. There was also an unissued one-sided acetate of α containing *Good Times, Bad Times* (Atlantic 584 268) 1969 (R4). β Withdrawn before release. One copy is known to exist with a solid centre with a small centre hole and 'Record Collector' valued this at circa £1,500 in its December 2004 edition. It is their most collectable release. Other versions exist with a large centre hole and these are valued at around £5,000. There is a white label test pressing of δ (R4).

Led Zeppelin were not only the most successful British rock act of the seventies, they were also the most influential. Each member was arguably the world's leading exponent of his instrument, and perhaps more than any other band in rock history demonstrated the awesome power and excitement that can be generated when virtuoso musicianship is allied to strong songwriting.

Their seeds lay in the ailing **Yardbirds**, who'd finally broke up in July 1968. Members **Jimmy Page** and Chris Dreja decided to form a new group, initially to play a 10-day tour of Scandinavia as The New Yardbirds. In the

LED ZEPPELIN - Led Zeppelin III (LP).

event Dreja left to pursue a career in photography, leaving **Page** to form an entirely new band. He promptly recruited session man, arranger, bassist and keyboardist **John Paul Jones**, whom he'd known for years. The vocal and drummer spots were more of a problem. **Terry Reid** and B.J. Wilson (of **Procol Harum**) turned the respective positions down, but Reid recommended an acquaintance of his, Midands-born R&B vocalist **Robert Plant**. **Page** went to see him live and, duly impressed, signed him up too. Plant then recommended his mate John Bonham, who was drumming for Tim Rose, to complete the quartet.

This new outfit completed **The Yardbirds**' contractual obligations in Scandinavia as The New Yardbirds, and played a couple of gigs back in the UK upon their return, at the Marquee on 18 October 1968 and Liverpool University on 19 October 1968, before changing their name to **Led Zeppelin**, supposedly at the suggestion of **Keith Moon**. Their first appearance under the new moniker was at Surrey University on Friday 25 October 1968. After a handful of gigs on the UK club circuit, the band recorded their stunning debut in a single day. There are no weak tracks on it, and two in particular - *Communication Breakdown* and *Dazed and Confused* - have served as templates for much subsequent rock music. With the album in the can, their legendary manager Peter Grant decided that the band should focus on the US market, and at his insistence a controversial decision was also taken not to make TV appearances or release UK singles. This inevitably led to a lack of airplay in their early days, but in the longer term created the sense of mystique that was to sustain them over the coming decade.

On Boxing Day 1968 they began their first US tour in Boston, Massachusetts, supporting the likes of Alice Cooper, Iron Butterfly and Vanilla Fudge. They were an immediate sensation, routinely blowing the headliners off the stage, and when their debut, *Led Zeppelin*, was issued in the US in February 1969 it climbed to No 10. On 21 March 1969 they made their only live UK TV appearance on a pilot BBC rock show, 'How Late It Is', and by the end of the month their album had climbed to No 6 in the UK. Over the Summer of 1969 they played a number of prestigious gigs - the London Playhouse Theatre for BBC Radio's 'In Concert' show (27 June), the Bath Festival (28 June), The Pop Proms (29 June) and The Newport Jazz and Blues Festival in the US during July, for example. Throughout this time they also played many BBC sessions, later compiled and released as the *BBC Sessions* boxed set. These show them to have been an act of almost superhuman intuition and power, rooted in the blues but effortlessly able to incorporate influences from folk, jazz and world music.

Led Zeppelin II, recorded in various locations as they criss-crossed the US during 1969, was the album which firmly established them as one of the world's biggest rock acts. Symbolically dislodging **The Beatles**' *Abbey Road* from the top of the charts on both sides of the Atlantic, it remained in the US Charts for 138 weeks and cemented their reputation as the world's most imaginative hard-rock act. Its finest moment was arguably *Whole Lotta Love*, which became a rock anthem and also appeared as a 45 in the US, where it rose to No 4 despite the group's reservations. Practically all of 1969 and the first few months of 1970 were spent touring, and they were

never far away from controversy. They were refused admission to Singapore because of their long hair, and tales of excess dogged them wherever they went.

Before recording their next album, **Page** and **Plant** spent a few idyllic weeks writing in a rundown Welsh cottage named Bron y Aur, later immortalised in two song titles. *Led Zeppelin III* was more folk-based than its predecessors, but still had a high quota of hard-rock songs such as *Immigrant Song*, which contains the line 'we are your overlords' - by now a simple fact where other bands were concerned. *Immigrant Song* was released as a 45 in the US, where it climbed to No 16. The album also contained some superb acoustic material, and appeared in a complex sleeve featuring a rotating wheel. Though reviews were typically sniffy, sales were again outstanding and it topped the charts on both sides of the Atlantic. Indeed by now, with **The Beatles** having split and **The Rolling Stones** in tax exile, **Led Zeppelin** were indisputably the world's top rock group.

Led Zeppelin IV continued the practice of coupling hard-rock songs like *Black Dog* and *Rock And Roll* (which climbed to Nos 15 and 47 respectively in the US) with subtler material such as *The Battle of Evermore*, which featured **Sandy Denny** and reflected Plant's ongoing preoccupation with Celtic folklore. The album also contained the band's magnum opus, *Stairway To Heaven*, whose opening chords have become many guitarists' first, faltering steps towards basic competence. It again topped the album charts in the UK, but only reached No 2 in the US, perhaps because of the radical decision not to list the band's name anywhere on the packaging.

1972 was largely spent touring. All 110,000 tickets for their 24-date December 1972-January 1973 UK tour sold out in just four hours. *Houses Of The Holy* was released in April 1973 and again topped the album charts on both sides of the Atlantic the same month. This was arguably their most diverse album, with tracks ranging from high energy rock to reggae, funk and folky ballads. The month after its release, the band's concert at Tampa Stadium, Florida, broke the US box office record, previously held by **The Beatles** for their 1965 Shea Stadium appearance. In July 1973 a concert at New York's Madison Square Gardens was filmed for possible inclusion in a movie. For their 1973 and 1975 American tours they rented a full-sized Boeing 720B jet, nicknamed 'the Starship'. On these jaunts the group effortlessly surpassed **The Rolling Stones**' reputation for debauchery.

At the start of 1974 the band and their manager formed their own Swan Song label and secured a distribution deal via Atlantic, signing acts including **The Pretty Things** and **Bad Company**. Big launch parties were thrown in London and in the States and then, in March 1975, a lavishly packaged double album was released entitled *Physical Graffiti*. Containing recordings stretching back to the start of the decade alongside new material, this again exhibited their extensive abilities, containing many fine songs, particularly the awesome *Kashmir* and funky *Trampled Underfoot*, which climbed to No 38 in the US. At one point *Physical Graffiti*, which topped the album charts on both sides of the Atlantic, was selling at the rate of 500 copies per hour in one New York record store alone and, in

LED ZEPPELIN - Led Zeppelin IV (CD).

LED ZEPPELIN - Houses Of The Holy (CD).

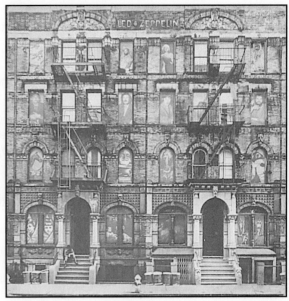

LED ZEPPELIN - Physical Graffiti (2-LP).

April 1975, 51,000 tickets for three concerts at London's Earls Court sold out in two hours. They ended up playing five four hour shows there the following month accompanied by a dazzling display of laser beams, lights and smoke.

By now, though, their astounding success was becoming almost counter-productive and in June they were forced into tax exile in Switzerland. A car crash in which **Robert Plant** and his wife were badly injured in August 1975 prevented any live appearances in the second half of the year, and the death of their young son Karac, coupled with **Page**'s increasing dependency on heroin and Bonham's alcoholism, further demoralised the band. The next album, *Presence*, was recorded in this time of turmoil, and again topped the album charts on both sides of the Atlantic on its release in April 1976. Though disappointing in comparison to their earlier work, it does contain at least two bona fide classics in the epic shapes of *Nobody's Fault But Mine* and *Achilles' Last Stand*.

Their long-awaited film 'The Song Remains The Same' eventually premiered in New York in October 1976. It featured lengthy live footage alongside toe-curling individual fantasy sequences. A double soundtrack album was released the same month and predictably topped the charts on both sides of the Atlantic, despite being far from the best testament to their onstage talents. Certainly by 1976 this great band had passed its heyday, and their final album, *In Through The Out Door*, was very different in style to its predecessors. Their final UK dates took place on 4 and 11 August 1979, when they attracted over 320,000 people to the Knebworth festivals. Their final tour was a 14-date hike around Europe, culminating at the Berlin Eissporthalle on 7 July 1980, where they closed with a longer-than-usual version of *Whole Lotta Love*. Their career was brought to an abrupt close when Bonham choked to death in his sleep after a heavy drinking bout during rehearsals for a US tour at **Page**'s Windsor home in September 1980. Widely acclaimed as the greatest rock drummer ever, Bonham was clearly irreplaceable and the remaining members instantly announced their dissolution. A career-spanning out-takes collection, *Coda*, appeared in 1982.

After the split **Plant** and **Page** concentrated on developing their solo careers, though there were a few one-off reunions too. On 13 July 1985 the three remaining members played a 20-minute set at the Philadelphia 'Live Aid' concert, but were under-rehearsed and underwhelming. There were subsequent reunions at Madison Square Gardens (14 May 1988), with Jason Bonham filling his father's shoes on drums, at Jason's wedding reception (28 April 1990) and for two invitation-only MTV Unplugged concerts on 25 and 26 August 1994. The success of the latter prompted **Page** and **Plant** to undertake a year-long world tour, comprising 115 concerts.

A lavish retrospective double DVD of **Led Zeppelin** was issued in 2003, and swiftly became the best-selling music DVD of all time. At the same time a double live CD, *How The West Was Won*, appeared and can be wholeheartedly recommended over *The Song Remains The Same*. It opens with the powerful *Immigrant Song* and contains a superb 24-minute version of *Whole Lotta Love* and many other classics from their first three albums.

Compilation appearances have included *Whole Lotta Love* and *Communication Breakdown* on *Age Of Atlantic* (LP); the non-LP *Hey, Hey, What Can I Do* on *New Age Of Atlantic* (LP); *Dazed And Confused, Whole Lotta Love* and *Stairway To Heaven* on *Classic Rock 1966-1998* (LP); *How Many More Times* on the film soundtrack *Homer* and *You Shook Me* on *Flying High* (a record club LP). Fans of the band will also be interested in **Plant** & Bonham's pre-**Led Zeppelin** act, **Band Of Joy** - acetate versions of *I Got To Find My Baby* by **Band Of Joy** have resurfaced on *Turds On A Bum Ride, Vol. 5* (CD), whilst *Vol. 6* (CD) includes the remaining two cuts from the acetate - covers of *Hey Joe* and *For What It's Worth*. (VJ/RMJ)

Alvin Lee

ALBUMS:	1	ON THE ROAD TO FREEDOM	(Chrysalis 1054) 1973 SC
(up to	2	IN FLIGHT (2-LP)	(Chrysalis 1069) 1974 SC
1976)	3	PUMP IRON!	(Chrysalis 1094) 1975 SC

NB: (1) with Mylon Lefevre.

45:     World Is Changing/Riffin'   (Chrysalis CHS 2020) 1974

Guitarist **Alvin Lee**'s career was transformed by his legendary appearance at the 'Woodstock' festival. He was born on 19 December 1944 in Nottingham and his first band was a beat outfit called **The Jail Breakers**. After **The Jail Breakers**, Alvin played with local Nottingham band The Atomites where he met Leo Lyons. They, along with lead singer Ivan Jay, formed Ivan Jay and The Jaymen which later became The Jaycats and finally **The Jaybirds**. In 1966, the band expanded its personnel and changed name to **Ten Years After**, one of the UK's top blues-rock groups. Having made a solo album with American Mylon Lefevre in 1973, whilst **Ten Years After** were still very much a going concern, **Lee** later formed his own **Alvin Lee Band** comprising Mel Collins (sax), Tim Hinkley (keyb'ds), Neil Hubbard (gtr) and Ian Wallace (drms). They recorded the live but almost inevitably patchy double album *In Flight*, at the Rainbow Theatre in London, one month before **Ten Years After**'s last UK concert at the same venue. Former **Blodwyn Pig** bassist Andy Pyle was recruited for *Pump Iron!* and Bryson Graham replaced Wallace on drums but the end result wasn't convincing. **Lee** has fronted various **Alvin Lee** Bands and **Ten Years After** reformations since but his finest moment remains that 'Woodstock' appearance. (VJ)

Barry Lee Show

Personnel:	MIKE DYBLE
	TONY DYBLE
	ANGUS JARVIS
	BARRY LEE
	ROGER REYNOLDS

45s:	Everybody Knows My Name/	
	Don't Call Me	(Columbia DB 8237) 1967

I Don't Want To Love You/		
Over And Over	(Columbia DB 8299)	1967
I Won't Cry Anymore/		
Kathy Come Home	(Columbia DB 8350)	1968
Wasn't It Good While It Lasted/		
One In A Million	(Parlophone R 5704)	1968

This band formed in 1963 in Aylsham, Norfolk as Barry Lee and The Planets. They played a range of music from pop to soul and ballads and changed their name to the **Barry Lee Show** around the time they signed to EMI. They later changed name again to The Performing Lees and Barry left them to go solo in 1972. The remaining members continued as The Brothers Lee.

You can also check out *I Don't Want To Love You* on *60's Back Beat* (LP). (VJ)

Fingers Lee (and The Upper Hand)

Personnel incl:	FINGERS LEE (FRED CHEESMAN)	piano	
	IAN PATTERSON	bs	A
	PETE PHILIPS	drms	A

45s:	The Friendly Undertaker/		
	Little Bit More	(Fontana TF 619)	1965 SC
	I'm Gonna Buy Me A Dog/		
	I Can't Drive	(Fontana TF 655)	1966 SC
α	Bossy Boss/Don't Run Away	(Columbia DB 8002)	1966 SC
β	Midnight Race/The Storm	(Columbia C23 852)	1966

NB: α as Fingers Lee and The Upper Hand. β as Fingers Lee and The Upper Hand. Only released in Germany.

Fingers Lee was actually Fred Cheesman, who'd earlier played with **Screaming Lord Sutch**. Ian Patterson was **Ian Hunter** who went on to play with **Mott The Hoople** and recorded solo material. **Lee** and Patterson also recorded as **At Last The 1958 Rock 'n' Roll Show**. These 45s were bluesy beat efforts.

Midnight Race from a French 45 has resurfaced on *Incredible Sound Show Stories, Vol. 9* (LP). (VJ)

Leapy Lee

ALBUMS:	1	LITTLE ARROWS	(Decca DL 75076)	1968
	2	LEAPY LEE	(Decca DL 75237)	1970

NB: (1) and (2) US only releases.

			HCP
45s:	It's All Happening/In The Meantime	(Pye 7N 17001) 1965	-
α	King Of The Whole Wide World/		
	Shake Hands	(Decca F 12369) 1966	R2 -
	The Man On The Flying Trapeze/		
	My Mixed-Up Mind	(CBS 202550) 1967	-
	Boiled Beef And Carrots/My Mixed-Up Mind	(CBS 3131) 1967	-
	Little Arrows/Time Will Tell	(MCA MU 1028) 1968	2
	It's All Happening/It's Great	(Pye 7N 17619) 1968	-
	Here Comes The Rain/		
	Three Little Words	(MCA MU 1054) 1969	-
	Little Yellow Aeroplane/Boom Boom	(MCA MU 1074) 1969	-
	Someone's In Love/Best To Forget	(MCA MK 5001) 1969	-
	Good Morning/Teresa	(MCA MK 5021) 1969	29
	Tupela Mississippi Flash/		
	Green Green Trees	(MCA MK 5040) 1970	-
	If I Ever Get To Saginaw/My Girl Maria	(MCA MK 5052) 1970	-
	Helena/Summer Rain	(Mam MAM 94) 1973	-
	Rub Your Nose/My Advise To You	(Mam MAM 110/111) 1973	-
	Every Road Leads Back To You/		
	Honey, Go Drift Away	(Bell BLL 1419) 1975	-
	Love On Borrowed Time/		
	Ode To A Friendly Toad	(Bell BLL 1456) 1975	-
	Our Sweet Precious Love/New York City	(Bell BLL 1475) 1976	-
	European Flowers Don't Grow In USA/		
	Jane	(Bell BLL 1486) 1976	-

INCREDIBLE SOUND SHOW STORIES VOL. 9 (Comp LP) including Finger Lee and The Upper Hand.

Reissues:	Little Arrows/Time Will Tell	(MCA MCA 167) 1974	-
	Little Arrows/	(Old Gold OG 9169) 1982	-
	Little Arrows/	(Old Gold OG 9794) 1987	-

NB: α This 45 featured **The Kinks**.

A comedian (his real name is Lee Graham) whose best remembered for his *Little Arrows* 45 which has been reissued on three occasions since. He was very friendly with **The Kinks** and his humour seems to have played a major role in soothing internal pressures in the group. He was almost offered the opportunity to record *Sunny Afternoon* before Ray Davies changed his mind and decided **The Kinks** should record it. Eventually Ray wrote, arranged and produced *King Of The Whole Wide World* for him and got **Dave Davies**, Pete Quaife and two of Goldie's Gingerbread's (Margo and Carole) to play on it. The song could easily have been a hit but it wasn't. In October 1968 **Pepper** became his backing group.

Little Arrows has been compiled on *The Swinging Sixties - 18 Classic Tracks* (CD) and you'll find *It's All Happening* on the 2-CD set *We Love The Pirates: Charting The Big 'L' Fab 40*. (VJ/VZ)

Mark Leeman Five

Personnel:	BRIAN 'BLINKY' DAVISON	drms	AB
	TERRY GOLDBERG	organ	AB
	DAVE HYDE	bs	AB
	MARK LEEMAN	vcls	A
	ALAN ROSKAMS	gtr	AB
	ROGER PEACOCK	vcls	B

45s:	Portland Town/		
	Gotta Get Myself Together	(Columbia DB 7452)	1965 SC
	Blow My Blues Away/		
	On The Horizon	(Columbia DB 7648)	1965 SC
	Forbidden Fruit/Goin' To Bluesville	(Columbia DB 7812)	1966 SC
	Follow Me/Gather Up The Pieces	(Columbia DB 7955)	1966 SC

NB: *The Memorial Album* (See For Miles SEE LP 317) 1991, also on CD (CD 317), is a recommended compilation of their material.

A popular mid-sixties act around the London clubs, they played a mixture of R&B and jazz and secured a deal with EMI's Columbia label. After their debut disc, *Portland Town*, which had been produced by **Manfred Mann**, **Leeman** was tragically killed in a car crash in June 1965. **Roger Peacock** came in as a replacement and the group retained **Leeman**'s name in tribute to him. Their second 45, *Blow My Blues Away*, had been recorded before **Leeman**'s death and featured him on vocals. Their subsequent releases aroused very little interest and the inevitable disintegration came in 1966. Brian Davison was later in **The Nice** and **Roger Peacock** later formed **Dave Anthony's Moods**.

Anyone interested in this band should seek out the See For Miles set which not only includes both sides of their four 45s (including alternate versions of both sides of their debut one) but 15 previously unreleased cuts including 11 from a tape of exciting R&B songs recorded back in 1963 which show what a major force this band would have become had **Leeman** survived. (VJ)

Lee Riders

Personnel:	MICHAEL CONNOR	piano, organ	A
	ROBERT LEE	lead vcls, gtr	A
	ROY O'TEMRO	drms, perc, slide gtr	A
	MATT PRESBY	gtr	A
	MIKE REILLY	bs, vcls	A

ALBUM: 1(A) THE LEE RIDERS   (United Artists UAS 29312) 1972

A little known band who deserved a better recognition. Their album which was recorded at Morgan Studios, with the help of the well known session musician **B.J. Cole** on steel guitar and dobro, is very U.S.-sounding, veering in a country-rock direction. It included some fine, very West Coastish bluesy tracks, somewhere between Hot Tuna and Grateful Dead, like *Phenomenological Blues*, *The Moment* and *Living With My Uncle Sam*. Robert Lee was the leader of the band and wrote all the material.

Roy O'Temro also played with **Cochise**. Mike Reilly and Michael Connor (or O'Connor) went to the U.S., where since 1975 they played with Pure Prairie League. (CA)

Brother Lees

Personnel:	MICHAEL LEE	A
	ROGER LEE	A
	TONY LEE	A

45s:	Why You Hesitating Mama/	
	Let's Do It Together	(Pye 7N 45138) 1972
	Night The Orchestra Sang/Tomorrow	(Jam JAM 59) 1973

In 1972 these brothers won the second prize in "Search For A Songwriter Contest" by the paper 'Disc And Music Echo'. They came from Adamhort in Norfolk. (VJ)

John Lee's Groundhogs

Personnel:	DAVE BOORMAN	drms	A
	JOHN CRUICKSHANK	vcls	A
	PETE CRUICKSHANK	bs	A
	BOB HALL	piano	A
	TONY McPHEE	gtr	A

| 45: | I'll Never Fall In Love Again/ | |
| | Over You Baby | (Planet PLF 104) 1966 |

A R&B band, whose only UK 45 was produced by **Bill Wyman** and Glyn Jones. Put together to back **John Lee Hooker** when he toured the UK, they also had a US only 45 *Shake It/Rock Me* (Interphon IN 7715), and recorded an acetate *Someone To Love/Hallelujah* (Regent Sound).

Compilation appearances include: *Shake It* on *Maximum R'n'B* (CD), *Beat It* (3-CD) and *English Freakbeat, Vol. 1* (LP & CD); *Someone To Love* on *Purple Heart Surgery, Vol. 1* (LP) and *Hens Teeth Vol. 2* (CD); and *I'll Never Fall In Love Again* and *Over You Baby* on *The Best Of Planet Records* (CD).

See also the **Groundhogs**. (VJ)

John Lees

| ALBUM: | 1 A MAJOR FANCY | (Harvest SHVL 811) 1973 SC |

45s:	Best Of My Love/You Can't Get It	(Polydor 2058 513) 1974 SC
	Child Of The Universe/	
	Kes (A Major Fancy)	(Harvest HAR 5132) 1977

John Lees is best remembered as the vocalist and guitarist with **Barclay James Harvest**. These were his solo recordings but they never made the same impact. (VJ)

Left Handed Marriage

Personnel:	JENNY HILL	A
	BILL RICHARD	A
	PETER TROUT	A

ALBUM: 1(A) ON THE RIGHT SIDE OF THE LEFT HANDED
              MARRIAGE   (Private Pressing) 1967 R4

NB: (1) reissued as a limited edition of 1,000 (Tenth Planet TP 022) 1995 (SC).

This mega-rarity was recorded by a student band and is significant for being one of the earliest-known privately pressed albums and one of the earliest amalgams of traditional folk and folk-rock. All the songs are self-penned but original copies are horrendously rare.

The band regrouped some years back without Trout but with Henry Deval and Terry Goulds to record a limited edition (500 copies only CD), *Crazy Chain* (LHM 1) 1993. It will be of great interest to **Queen** collectors since it includes three cuts:- *Appointment*, *She Was Once My Friend* and *I Need Time* from a July 1967 session which also featured a certain Brian May on guitar.

Their mega rare privately-pressed album has now been reissued in a limited edition, digitally remastered 1,000 copies vinyl-only format. The reissue includes three previously unissued alternate takes of album tracks, *Arthur*, *Happiness Is You-Shaped*, *Another Shoulder* and *That Was The Boy*, a previously unreleased cut. Most of the tracks are folk-influenced melodic pop penned by Bill Richards and those on which Jenny Rusbridge takes over lead vocals have the edge. (VJ)

Legay

Personnel:	JOHN KNAPP	gtr, keyb'ds, vcls	A
	DAVE McCARTHY	bs	A
	ROBIN PIZER	gtr, vcls	A
	ROD READ	gtr, vcls	A
	MOTH SMITH	drms	A

| 45: | No-One/The Fantastic Story Of The Steam | |
| | Driven Banana | (Fontana TF 904) 1969 R3 |

This outfit's 45 is now very rare and collectable. They later evolved into **Gypsy**. The 'A' side, written by Robin Pizer, is a superb slice of psychedelia with great guitar work and good drumming. The 'B' side is also a good pop-psych story song.

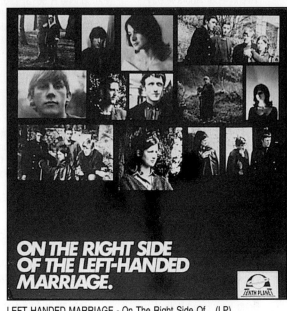

LEFT HANDED MARRIAGE - On The Right Side Of... (LP).

Compilation appearances include: *No One* on *Justafixation* (LP), *Justafixation* (CD), *Magic Spectacles* (CD) and *Red With Purple Flashes, Vol. 2* (LP) and *The Fantastic Of The Steam Driven Banana* on *Jagged Time Lapse, Vol 5* (CD). (VJ)

Legend

Personnel:	NIGEL DUNBAR	drms	A
	CHRIS EAST	gtr, vcls	A
	STEVE GEARE	bs, vcls	A
	MICKEY JUPP	gtr, keyb'ds, vcls	ABC
	JOHN BOBIN	bs	BC
	BILL FIFIELD	drms	B
	MO WITHAM	gtr	BC

ALBUMS:	1(A)	LEGEND	(Bell MBLL/SBLL 115) 1969 R2
	2(B)	LEGEND 'RED BOOT' ALBUM	
			(Vertigo 6360 019) 1971 R1
	3(C)	MOONSHINE	(Vertigo 6360 063) 1972 R2

NB: (1) reissued on CD (Repertoire RR 4061-CX). (2) reissued on CD (Red Bus 4061-CX) in 1990 and again on CD (Repertoire REPUK 1064) 2005, with four bonus tracks. (2) and (3) reissued on one CD (Mason MR 56437) 2005.

45s:	National Gas/Wouldn't You	(Bell BLL 1048) 1969
	Georgia George Part 1/July	(Bell BLL 1082) 1969
	Life/Late Last Night	(Vertigo 6059 021) 1971
	Don't You Never/Someday	(Vertigo 6059 036) 1971

Formed in Southend by Mickey Jupp, **Legend** are often regarded as the originators of the 'pub-rock' sound. They were also the first English group to feature on the Bell label. Indeed, *Cheque Book* from their second album was later covered by premier 'pub-rock' proponents **Dr. Feelgood**. Bill Fifield departed to **T Rex** prior to the *Moonshine* album, which was disappointing compared to the previous two. All three albums are now rare and quite sought-after and re-recorded versions from all three later emerged on *The Mickey Jupp Legend* album (Stiff GET 2) issued in 1978. The 1971 Vertigo album has recently been reissued on CD with four bonus tracks: - *Life*, *Late Last Night*, *Don't You Never* and *Someday*. The release comes with the original art work in a square CD digi-sleeve format.

Back in 1971 they had one cut, *Foxfield Junction* on Vertigo's *Heads Together, First Round* (LP) compilation. (VJ)

The Legends

Personnel incl: PETE WATKINSON   vcls

45s:	I've Found Her/	
	Something's Gonna Happen	(Pye 7N 15904) 1965 SC
	Tomorrow's Gonna Be Another Day/	
	Nobody Laughs Anymore	(Parlophone R 5581) 1967 R1
	Under The Sky/	
	Twenty-Four Hours A Day	(Parlophone R 5613) 1967 SC

The band had earlier released a 45 for Pye in 1965 as **First Impressions**. It was based in London. (VJ)

Andrew Leigh

ALBUM: 1   THE MAGICIAN   (Polydor 2343 034) 1970 SC

Leigh recorded this album whilst with **Matthews Southern Comfort**. Various **Action** and **Blossom Toes** members assist on this singer/songwriter folk-pop album, including Brian Godding, **Gary Wright**, **Gary Farr**, **Reggie King**, **Gordon Jackson** and **Kevin Westlake**, amongst others. (VJ)

The Lemmings

Personnel incl: MARTIN MURRAY

45s:	Out Of My Mind/My Little Girl	(Pye 7N 15837) 1965 SC
	You Can't Blame Me For Trying/	
	Bring Your Heart With You	(Pye 7N 15899) 1965 SC

This band's main significance seems to be that they included Martin Murray who was once in **The Honeycombs** and also made a solo single. (VJ)

Lemon

Personnel incl: LEM LUBIN   A

45:     Lady Eleanor/Lady Of The Evening   (Decca F 13192) 1971

The 'A' side of this 45 was a cover of the **Lindisfarne** classic, whilst the flip was written by Lem Lubin (ex-**Unit 4 Plus 2** and **Satisfaction**). Lubin joined **Christie** in 1972, so it's possible he was in **Lemon** in the interim. (VJ/RG)

Lemon Dips

ALBUM: 1   WHO'S GONNA BUY?   (De Wolfe DW/LP 3114) 1969 R2

This is a collection of great psychedelic / freakbeat vocal and instrumental tracks issued on this music library label. Three of them *Who's Gonna Buy, I Am Your Man* and *Unpack Your Bags* were featured in the film "Haunted House Of Horror". **Lemon Dips** weren't a band. All the De Wolf recordings comprised material penned by songwriters Peter Renno and Johnny Hawksworth, which was played by session musicians.

Compilation appearances include: *I Am The Man, Poor Lonely Woman, Who's Gonna Buy, Unpack Your Bags* and *Travelling Man* on *Freakout At The Facsimile Factory* (LP); and *Who's Gonna Buy* and *Poor Lonely Woman* on *Incredible Sound Show Stories, Vol. 3* (LP). (VJ)

Lemon Line

45:	For Your Precious Love/	
	You Made Me See The Light	(Decca F 12688) 1967

This was another short-lived pop outfit. The 'A' side is an Impressions track. (VJ)

Lemon Men

45:	I've Seen You Cut Lemons/	
	One Lemon Strip Two Lemon Walk	(Polydor 56365) 1969

This is an advert-linked novelty record. *I've Seen You Cut Lemons* was composed by Glyn Mason and Keith Miller. (VJ)

FREAKOUT AT THE FACSIMILE FACTORY (Comp LP) including Lemon Dips.

502

Lemon Tree

Personnel:
DEREK ARNOLD	bs		A
MIKE HOPKINS	gtr		A
KEITH SMART	drms		A
MICK TAYLOR	vcls		A
GARY WORTLEY	organ		A

45s: William Chaulker's Time Machine/
I Can Touch A Rainbow   (Parlophone R 5671) 1968 R1
It's So Nice To Come Home/
Come On Girl   (Parlophone R 5739) 1969 SC

A short-lived Birmingham group whose two singles are now minor collectables. The first, *William Chaulker's Time Machine*, a worthwhile slice of UK psychedelia comprising a catchy tune accompanied with brass and orchestration, was written by former **Move** member **Ace Kefford**. It was produced by another ex-**Move** man, Trevor Burton and **Amen Corner**'s **Andy Fairweather-Low**, who also produced the follow-up.

Smart had earlier been with **Danny King and The Mayfair Set** with Trevor Burton and Mike Hopkins had joined Denny (Laine) and The Diplomats. Hopkins was in the latter days of **Idle Race**; Gary Wortley moved to Canada; and Keith Smart was later in **The Uglys**, **Balls**, **Wizzard** and **Mongrel**.

Compilation appearances have included: *It's So Nice To Come Home* on *Not Just Beat Music 1965-70* (LP) and *British Psychedelic Trip, Vol. 2* (LP); *William Chalker's Time Machine* on *Rubble, Vol. 3 - Nightmares In Wonderland* (LP), *Rubble, Vol. 2* (CD) and *60's Back Beat* (LP); *William Chaulker's Time Machine* and *Hush* on *Top Of The Pops No. 178* (LP); *I Can Touch A Rainbow* on *Electric Sugar Cube Flashbacks* (CD); and *It's So Nice To Come Home* and *Wiliam Chaulker's Time Machine* on *Great British Psychedelic Trip, Vol. 3* (CD). (VJ)

John Lennon

HCP

ALBUMS:	1	UNFINISHED MUSIC No 1: TWO VIRGINS		
(up to			(Apple (S)APCOR 2) 1968 R5 -
1976)	2	UNFINISHED MUSIC No 2: LIFE WITH THE LIONS		
			(Zapple ZAPPLE 01) 1969 R3 -
	3	WEDDING ALBUM	(Apple SAPCOR 11) 1969 R4 -
	4	LIVE PEACE IN TORONTO 1969	
			(Apple CORE 2001) 1969 R2 -
	5	JOHN LENNON: PLASTIC ONO BAND	
			(Apple PCS 7124) 1970 11
	6	IMAGINE	(Apple PAS 10004) 1971 SC 1
	7	SOMETIME IN NEW YORK CITY (2-LP)	
			(Apple PCSP 716) 1972 11
	8	MIND GAMES	(Apple PCS 7165) 1973 13
	9	WALLS AND BRIDGES	(Apple PCTC 253) 1974 6
	10	ROCK 'N' ROLL	(Apple PCS 7169) 1975 6
	11	SHAVED FISH	(Apple PCS 7173) 1975 8

NB: (1) - (3) with Yoko Ono. Mono versions of (1), with blurb on the front sleeve can fetch £3,000 plus. (4) and (5) by The Plastic Ono Band. *Live In Toronto* (Apple 8743292) is a reissue of the US pressing of this album. (6) with The Plastic Ono Band and Flux Fiddlers. Later issued in Quadrophonic (Apple Q4 PAS 10004) 1974 (R3). (6) reissued on vinyl (EMICENT 27) 1997. (7) with Yoko Ono, Elephant's Memory and The Plastic Ono Band. (8) with Plastic UFOno Band. Vinyl reissues include: (8) on Music For Pleasure (MFP 50509) 1980 and again on CD (EMI LC 2009) 2005; (9) on EMI (7243 4 99464 1 5) 1999; (10) on Music For Pleasure (MFP 50522) 1981 and on CD (EMI 8743292) 2004, remixed and remastered; (4) on Parlophone (PCS 7301) 1986 and (5) on Fame (FA 41 3102-1) 1984. Of his albums the following are on CD: (2) (Apple/EMI CCP) 1995; (4) (Apple/EMI CCP 7904282) 1995; (5) (EMI CDP 746 770 2) 1988; (6) (EMI CDP 746 641 2) 1987; (7) (Apple/Parlophone 0946 3 40976) 2005 with bonus tracks. (8) (Parlophone CDP 746 769 2) 1987, again (EMI 7243 5 4245 2 6) 2002, with three bonus cuts and again (EMI LC 2099) 2005; (9) (Parlophone CDP 746 768 2) 1987 and again (Apple/Parlophone 0946 3 40971) 2005 with bonus tracks; (10) (Parlophone CDP 746 707 2) 1987 and (Apple 87433292); and (11) (EMI CDP 746 642 2) 1987.

Vinyl compilations include *The John Lennon Box* (Parlophone JCB 8) 1981, a 9-LP set; *The John Lennon Collection* (Parlophone EMTV 37) 1982 and *Imagine: John Lennon* (Parlophone PCSP 722) 1988, a 2-LP set.

In October 1990 a 4-CD boxed set with a photo/lyric booklet *Lennon* (Parlophone LENNON 1) was released. Several bootleg CDs and albums were also taken from 'The Lost Lennon Tapes' series which was broadcast on US Radio., along with *The John Lennon Collection* (Parlophone CDP 791 516 2) 1989 and *Testimony* (Thunderbolt CDTB 095) 1991. *Lennon Legend* (Parlophone CDPP 037) 1997 is a

JOHN LENNON - Imagine (LP).

hits collection, pretty similar to 1982's *The John Lennon Collection. Anthology* (EMI) 1998 is a 4-CD box set. *Acoustic* (Parlophone LCO148) 2004 is a 16-track set of the great man unplugged. *Working Class Hero: The Definitive Lennon* (Parlophone) 2005 has been released to commemorate what would have been his 65th birthday.

HCP

45s:	α	Give Peace A Chance/		
(up to		Remember Love	(Apple APPLE 13) 1969 SC 2
1976)	α	Cold Turkey/	
		Don't Worry Kyoko	(Apple APPLES 1001) 1969 SC 14
	λ	You Know My Name (Look Up The Number)/	
		What's The New Mary Jane	(Apple APPLES 1002) 1969 R6 -
	β	Instant Karma (We All Shine On)/	
		Who Has Seen The Wind? (PS)	(Apple APPLES 1003) 1970 5
	χ	Power To The People/	
		Open Your Box (PS)	(Apple R 5892) 1971 7
	δ	Woman Is The Nigger Of The World	(Apple R 5953) 1972 R6 -
	ι	Happy Xmas (War Is Over)/	
		Listen The Snow Is Falling (PS)	(Apple R 5970) 1972 4
	ε	Mind Games/Meat City (PS)	(Apple R 5994) 1973 26
		Whatever Gets You Through The Night/	
		Beef Jerky	(Apple R 5998) 1974 36
		No 9 Dream/What You Got	(Apple R 6003) 1975 23
		Stand By Me/Move Over Ms. L	(Apple R 6005) 1975 30
		Imagine/Working Class Hero (PS)	(Apple R 6009) 1975 6
		Stand By Me/Move Over Ms.	(Apple R 6005) 1981 -
		Love/Give Me Some Truth	(Parlophone R 6059) 1982 41
Reissues:		Give Peace A Chance/Cold Turkey (PS)	(EMI G 45 2) 1984 -
	φ	Imagine/Jealous Guy (PS)	(Parlophone R 6199) 1988 -
	γ	Imagine/Jealous Guy/	
		Happy Xmas (War Is Over)	(Parlophone 12R 6199) 1988 -

NB: α by The Plastic Ono Band. β with Yoko Ono. χ with The Plastic Ono Band. ι with Yoko Ono and The Plastic Ono Band. ε with The Plastic UFOno Band. φ also issued as a picture disc. γ also issued as a CD single with the addition of *Give Peace A Chance* (Parlophone CDR 6199). λ This 45 was withdrawn, but some test pressings got out and 'Record Collector' values them at £2,000 in its December 2004 edition. δ This was deemed to be too controversial and shelved, but test pressings fetch four figure sums. It was credited to **John Lennon**/Plastic Ono Band.

John Lennon was a special person. Arguably the most creative of **The Beatles** his solo career seems inconsistent by comparison, although it spawned timeless classics like *Imagine*. Yet **Lennon** was more than just an enormously influential rock musician, he was a writer, actor and political and social activist as well.

John Lennon was born on 9 October 1940 in Liverpool. In June 1957 he formed The Quarry Men along with **Paul McCartney**, which marked the beginning of his songwriting partnership with Paul. **George Harrison** joined the band the following August. The Quarry Men had regrouped by the following Spring, with **Pete Best** (drms) and Stuart Sutcliffe (gtr) as Long John and The Silver Beatles, although after a few weeks they were known as simply **The Beatles**. See **The Beatles** entry for details of John's years with the band.

JOHN LENNON - Mind Games (CD).

John launched his solo career in November 1968 when *Unfinished Music No 1 : Two Virgins* was released, although he made a film appearance, as Private Gripweed, in October 1967 in 'How I Won The War', directed by Richard Lester, who'd earlier directed 'A Hard Day's Night' and 'Help'. **Lennon** didn't contribute any music to the film, although a week before the premier to the film United Artists released a 45 of instrumental music from the film, along with various sound effects and snippets of dialogue. The single, which was credited to **Musketeer Gripweed and The Third Troop**, was clearly intended to exploit **Lennon**'s involvement in the film although any contribution he made to it would have been minimal. In fact it sold poorly but subsequently became a collectors' item. It can also be heard on the *Liverpool 1963-68* (LP) compilation.

Unfinished Music No 1: Two Virgins was an avant-garde collection of sound effects and disjointed music much more notable for its famous cover of John and Yoko Ono full frontal in the nude which EMI refused to distribute here in the UK - so it was put out by Track for retail. The album was counterfeited in 1974. Despite its lack of commercialism the album did get to No 124 in the US Album Charts.

Unfinished Music No 2: Life With The Lions contained an odd mixture of live recordings from Cambridge in early 1969 on one side and some avant-garde 'sounds' recorded on a cassette player during Yoko Ono's pregnancy, which ended in miscarriage. The opening piercing wails and John's atonal guitar feedback set the tone for the album that follows. It was originally issued on the Apple offshoot Zapple here and in the US. It was reissued on CD in late 1995.

John's first 45 *Give Peace A Chance* will be known to you all. It became the definitive peace anthem and rose to No 2 in the Charts here and No 14 in the US. Credited to The Plastic Ono Band (a loose collection of musicians he used for recording over the next few years), it was recorded during **Lennon** and Yoko Ono's bed-in at a Montreal hotel when they stayed in bed to protest for World Peace. The follow-up, *Cold Turkey*, which was (as its name suggests) about the trauma of drug withdrawal, also sold well peaking at No 14 in the UK and No 30 in the US. Still it seems **Lennon** had hoped for better for its failure to make the Top Ten was one of the reasons he gave, along with British involvement in the Biafra war and support of the US in Vietnam, for returning his MBE to Buckingham Palace. Not long after he emigrated to the US.

The third in his series of avant-garde albums with Yoko Ono was *The Wedding Album*, which was issued in a box with various souvenirs of their wedding on 20 March 1969 in Gibraltar - a reproduction of their marriage certificate, a book of press clippings and a photo of the wedding cake. This was also counterfeited later but without all of the related paraphernalia. The original release got to No 178 in the US Album Charts - presumably not on the strength of the music - because there wasn't any!

Lennon and Yoko also appeared on a flexidisc (Eva-Tone EV 330707) in April 1969 that came free with an art magazine called "Aspen". Side one featured *No Bed For Beatle John* (from *Life With The Lions*) and Yoko Ono's *Song For John*, but the flip contained a large chunk of the dire *Radio*

Play (also from *Life With The Lions*) which comprised Yoko turning a radio on and off whilst **John** made a phone call.

His next album *Live Peace In Toronto 1969* recorded with The Plastic Ono Band included highlights of a concert by a scratch group, including **Eric Clapton** and Klaus Voormann, he'd put together to play at a rock'n'roll revival festival in Toronto in September 1969. Musically it was certainly his best effort without **The Beatles** to date. It got to No 10 in the US but didn't sell too well here.

His next 45, *Instant Karma*, featured **George Harrison** on guitar and was produced by Phil Spector. Recorded in a day with instant commercial appeal it climbed to No 5 here and No 3 in the US.

John Lennon and The Plastic Ono Band was really his first proper solo album. He wrote much of the material for it whilst he and Yoko Ono were doing a six month course of primal scream therapy run by its founder Dr Arthur Janov. Lyrically very intense - it dealt with various topics from his turbulent adolescence - it was very stark musically. He was supported on the album by Klaus Voormann (bs), **Ringo Starr** (drms) and Yoko Ono (woodwind) and of course it was littered with primal screams. It got to No 11 here and No 6 in the US. The US-only 45 *Mother* got to No 43 there, whilst his next UK release *Power To The People* followed a similar format to his earlier 45s. It sold well, too, peaking at No 7 here and No 11 in the US.

JOHN LENNON - Shaved Fish (LP).

A little-known **Lennon** project from 1971 was a 45, *God Save Us/Do The Oz*, issued on Apple using the name **Bill Elliot and The Elastic Oz Band** to help raise money for the underground journal "Oz", which faced prosecution and closure after the publication of the "Schoolkids" issue. Bill Elliot, later with **Splinter**, who recorded for **George Harrison**'s Dark Horse label, sang on the 'A' side but the flip did feature **Lennon** on vocals assisted by Yoko Ono. Others featured on the record included **Ringo Starr**, soon-to-be NME journalist Charles Shaar Murray and Klaus Voormann. Sadly with **Lennon** not putting his own name on the record few people bought it at the time.

His next album marked a clear change of musical direction and was, in my view, his best. *Imagine* was full of tight, melodic pop-rock compositions but it was full of controversy - *How Do You Sleep?* and *Crippled Inside* were thinly-disguised attacks on **Paul McCartney**. Others like *Give Me Some Truth* were overt attacks on the political establishment. The title track was a gem - the best thing he'd written since his days with **The Beatles**. The album topped the Charts on both sides of the Atlantic. The title track was a US-only 45 peaking at No 3. It wasn't released as a 45 in the UK until November 1975, when it also made the Top 5.

Another US-only 45, *Woman Is The Nigger Of The World*, was a minor hit in June 1972, but the following month saw the release of the overtly political double album *Some Time In New York City*. The lyrics dealt with issues like Northern Ireland, the oppression of women and the Attica prison riots. They were attacked as simplistic and extremist and were certainly cliché-ridden, but musically the album had its moments with New York band Elephants's Memory providing powerful backing on one of the discs, though Yoko Ono's vocals, more frequent than on previous projects, were a counterbalancing negative factor. The second disc contained material from two live sessions with The Mothers Of Invention and a 1969 band, at London's Lyceum, which included **Eric Clapton** and **Keith Moon**. The album got to No 48 in the US and No 11 in the UK.

In August 1972 **Lennon** made his only concert appearance in New York's Madison Square Gardens for the One To One Charity. His closing number was predictably *Give Peace A Chance* and he was joined on stage for this by Stevie Wonder and Roberta Flack. He enjoyed a big Christmas hit that year in the UK with *Happy Xmas (War Is Over)*, which got to No 4. It had been released a year earlier in the US but had failed to chart.

In March 1973 **Lennon** was ordered to leave the States by the US Immigration Authorities because of a previous drug conviction in the UK. He began a long fight to remain in the States which was eventually won three years later when he received the necessary green card permitting him to remain permanently in the US.

His next album *Mind Games* was in a similar mode to *Imagine*, but more lightweight. The politicising of the previous album had given way to more melodic pop-rock, but, it was nowhere the standard of *Imagine*. The title track was undoubtedly the strongest commercially climbing to No 26 here and No 18 in the US.

1974 was a bad year for **Lennon**. He split temporarily from Yoko Ono and led a pretty debauched lifestyle in LA for a while. He produced Nilsson's album *Pussycats*, but since it comprised cover versions it didn't win either of them much credit artistically.

His next album *Walls And Bridges* was an improvement on *Mind Games* but by no means outstanding. It topped the US Charts and got to No 6 in the UK. It also spawned his first US No 1 45 in *Whatever Gets You Thru The Night*, which only got to No 36 in the UK. **Elton John** played on the disc and got **Lennon** to agree to appear in concert with him if it got to No 1. Sure that it wouldn't **Lennon** agreed and when it did he had to appear with **Elton John** at New York's Madison Square Gardens on 28 November 1974 for versions of *Whatever Gets You Thru The Night*, *Lucy In The Sky With Diamonds* and *I Saw Her Standing There*.

Early in 1975 he enjoyed a hit with *No 9 Dream* which got to No 23 here and No 9 in the US. The *Rock 'n' Roll* album represented the achievement of an ambition to record an album of his best-loved rock'n'roll songs. He'd begun the project two years earlier in 1973 with Phil Spector handling production duties, but this didn't work out too well and eventually **Lennon**, unhappy with the production, re-recorded the album himself. His stirring version of *Stand By Me* is a high spot and *Slippin' And Slidin'* is a real foot-tapper with fine vocals. There's a good cover of Chuck Berry's *You Can't Catch Me*, a less impressive rendition of *Sweet Little Sixteen* and an awful reggae version of *Do You Wanna Dance*. The album got to No 6 both

in the US and the UK. His cover of Ben E. King's *Stand By Me* just made the Top 30 here and the Top 20 in the US in April 1975.

On 9 October 1975 his first and only child by Yoko, Sean Taro Ono was born. For the next five years John effectively retired from the music business to look after their child. The month after Sean's birth the predictable 'Greatest Hits' compilation *Shaved Fish* appeared. It got to No 8 in the UK and No 12 in the US. To coincide with its release his finest moment *Imagine*, was released as a 45 for the first time in the UK. It got to No 6.

Of course, as you'll almost all know **Lennon** resumed his recording career with the *Double Fantasy* album, which marked a return to top songwriting form and topped the Charts in both the US and UK. Then disaster struck, having returned home from the recording studio with Yoko on 8 December 1980, he was assassinated by Mark Chapman having entered the courtyard to the Dakota building where they lived. One of rock music's most creative individuals had been struck down at a time when he again promised so much. Cruelly yet again in American society a person who preached peace had died by the bullet.

After **John Lennon**'s death people inevitably raced to buy his records. *(Just Like) Starting Over* (from *Double Fantasy*) topped the 45 Charts on both sides of the Atlantic in December 1980 and on 10 January 1981 *Imagine* topped the UK 45 Charts with *Happy Xmas (War Is Over)* at No 2.

In 1982 EMI released *The John Lennon Collection*, which they helped promote by remixing and releasing his 1970 song *Love* as a single. The album topped the UK Charts and got to No 33 in the States, whilst the single peaked at No 41 here in the UK. Subsequently Yoko Ono supervised the release of a studio album *Milk And Honey* featuring six songs recorded shortly prior to his death; the interview album *Heart Play*; and the live album *Live In New York City*.

For those of you wanting to collect **Lennon** on CD the 4-CD boxed set *Lennon*, released in October 1990, is comprehensive. The first three CDs include all of the *John Lennon: Plastic Ono Band* album, all but one track from *Imagine* and the better material from his other albums along with non-album 45s like *Cold Turkey* and *Instant Karma*. Also featured were the three songs he collaborated on with **Elton John** at Madison Square Gardens in late 1974 and four songs (*Blue Suede Shoes*, *Dizzy Miss Lizzy*, *Money* and *Yer Blues*) from the 1969 Toronto concert. The fourth CD collects all his vinyl output from his 1980 comeback.

The 4-CD *Anthology* box set was a long time coming and **Yoko Ono** acted as the package's Executive Producer. It's comprised of out-takes, off-cuts, live recordings, home demos and radio material. It was probably a fair representation of his music.

In 2002, EMI released *Mind Games* with three bonus cuts: home versions of *Aisumasen*, *Bring On Lucie* and *Meat City*. They make a useful addition to the package as do the lavish illustrations.

Acoustic (2004) contains seven previously unreleased tracks amongst its 16. Eight others had previously appeared on 1998's *Anthology* album. The highlights include *Working Class Heros*, *Love* (delivered with quivering emotional vocals), *John Sinclair*, *Luck Of The Irish*, a deranged version of *Cold Turkey*, the emotive rendition of *Real Love* and *Watching The Wheels*. This is a very welcome release.

Working Class Hero: The Definitive Lennon is a 38-track collection to commemorate what would have been his 65th birthday. (VJ)

Robin Lent

ALBUM: 1   SCARECROW'S JOURNEY (Nepentha 6347 002) 1971 R2
NB: (1) also issued in Germany on Global. Later reissued on See For Miles (SEE 270) 1989 on CD and vinyl.

Like **Amory Kane**, **Robin Lent** was an American guitarist / vocalist who'd settled in Europe. Close friends with **Marc Brierley**, he recorded this jazzy electric folk album in Holland with future Focus members Thijs Van Leer and Jan Akkerman. He's thought to have joined the Dutch cast of the musical 'Hair' too. After *Scarecrow's Journey* was released he left Holland for France, but returned in 1979 to form Robinson Cruiser. (VJ/GB/RMJ)

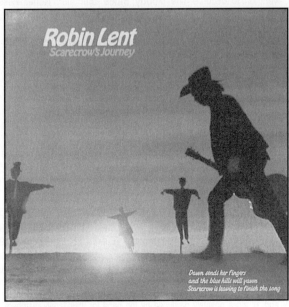

ROBIN LENT - Scarecrow's Journey (LP).

DEKE LEONARD - Iceberg (LP).

Van Lenton

45:     Gotta Get Away/You Don't Care   (Immediate IM 008) 1965 R1

This obscure singer's version of *Gotta Get Away* was produced by Shel Talmy. (VJ)

Deke Leonard

			HCP
ALBUMS:	1	ICEBURG	(United Artists UAG 29464) 1973 SC -
(up to	2	KAMIKAZE	(United Artists UAG 29544) 1974 SC 50
1976)			

NB: (1) and (2) reissued on one CD (Beat Goes On BGOCD 288) 1995 together with four non-album 45 cuts. *Wireless* (Hux HUX 064) 2005 is a collection of seventies radio sessions by the band.

45s:	Diamond Road/	
(up to	Circles And Squares	(United Artists UP 35494) 1973
1976) α	Nothing Is Happening/	
	She's A Cow	(United Artists UP 35556) 1973
	A Hard Way To Live/	
	The Aching Is So Sweet	(United Artists UP 35556) 1973
	Louisiana Hoedown/She's A Cow	(United Artists UP 35668) 1974
Later 45:	Map Of India/Hey There! (Lady In	
	The Black Tuxedo) (PS)	(United Artists UP 36488) 1979

NB: α Demo only. There was also a later 45: *Map Of India/Hey There! (Lady In The Black Tuxedo)* (PS) (United Artists UP 36488) 1979

When members of **The Bystanders** mutated into **Man**, 'Roger' **Deke Leonard** joined them from another South Wales group, The Dream. **Leonard** made these solo recordings after leaving **Man** in 1972. *Iceberg* was quite promising but *Kamikaze* was a big disappointment and he rejoined **Man** shortly after. After **Man** 'retired' in 1976, **Leonard** formed Iceburg. *Wireless* has been compiled from seventies radio sessions by the band. Two of the sessions in question were early seventies European ones and the other was a Peel one from 1978. It captures the band on form with some blistering guitar work. (VJ)

The Le Roys

45s:	Money/	
	Swinging On A Star (flexidisc)	(Give A Disc LYN 504/505) 1964
	Gotta Lotta Love (Ciribiribin)/	
	Don't Cry Baby	(HMV POP 1274) 1964
	Chills/Lost Out On Love	(HMV POP 1312) 1964 SC
	I Came On Smiling Through/	
	California GL903	(HMV POP 1368) 1964

Also a popular backing band, they backed Johnny Leyton, Mike Sarne, **Simon Scott** and Don Spencer on solo discs. These 45s were basically beat efforts. *Chills* is a Tony Orlando song and *I Come On Smiling Through* was written for them by **Mojos**' Nicky Crouch and Stu James. (VJ)

Levee Breakers

Personnel incl:	BEVERLEY KUTNER	vcls	
	JOHNNY JOYCE	gtr	A
	LES McCANN	gtr	A

45:     Babe I'm Leaving You/
        Wild About My Loving   (Parlophone R 5291) 1965 SC

This is quite a collectable 45. The group included **Beverley**. Joyce was later in **Velvet Opera** and McCann went on to **McGuinness Flint**. (VJ)

Levee Camp Moan

ALBUMS:	1	LEVEE CAMP MOAN	(County no #) 1969 R5
	2	PEACOCK FARM	(County no #) 1969 R5

NB: (1) and (2) reissued on CD (Audio Archives AACD 045) 2002 remastered and including six tracks from the Peacock Farm Free Concerts.

These are two privately-pressed raw heavy blues albums with splatterings of psychedelia and some strongly **Hendrix**-influenced guitar work by Ian Campbell and male/female lead vocals. On the first *I Just Can't Keep From Crying* and *Walking By Myself* catch the ear, but more profound is *Mr. Backlash*, which deals with racial prejudice. The second one was named after the farm where the band lived and commands a slightly higher three figure sum than the earlier one. (VJ)

Gerry Levene (and The Avengers)

Personnel:	GERRY LEVENE	vcls	A
	GRAEME EDGE	drms	A
	MIKE HOPKINS	gtr	A
	JIM ONSLOW	bs, vcls	A
	ROY WOOD	gtr	A

45:     α It's Driving Me Wild/Dr. Feelgood   (Decca F 11815) 1964
NB: α 'A' side is **Gerry Levene** solo.

This was one of the very early Birmingham beat groups which operated during 1963-64. In future **Mike Sheridan and The Nightriders**, **Move**, **ELO**, and **Wizzard** member **Roy Wood** they had a talented guitarist but even sharper was Mike Hopkins, who was later in **Idle Race**. **Graeme Edge**, went on to become **The Moody Blues**' drummer. Nonetheless, in spite of all this talent they made little impact at the time.

You'll also find *Dr. Feelgood* on *Rare 60's Beat Treasures, Vol. 3* (CD) and *Beat Merchants* (2-LP). (VJ)

Leviathan

Personnel incl:	BRIAN BENNETT	gtr	A
	STUART HOBDAY	vcls	A
	ROGER McCABE	bs	A
	GARY 'ROSCOE' MURPHY	drms	A

45s:	Remember The Times/		
	Second Production	(Elektra EKSN 45052) 1969 R1
	The War Machine/Time	(Elektra EKSN 45057) 1969 R1
	Flames/Just Forget Tomorrow	(Elektra EKSN 45075) 1969 R1

NB: *The Four Faces Of Leviathan* (Elektra EKSN 45052/EKSN 45057) 1969 was a special edition press pack, which comprised their first two singles, a biography, black and white photos in a white folder sleeve, some copies were overprinted with the Harrods logo (R3). *Elektra Daze* (no #) 1999/2000 was a six-track CD compilation of their 'A' and 'B' sides privately produced by the band for their family members. Just 25 copies were produced (SC).

This Brighton group evolved out of **Mike Stuart Span** and were one of the earliest British acts to be signed by Elektra. They were also featured in a BBC Documentary 'A Year In The Life' before splitting up late in 1969. *Second Production*, a superb psychedelic song with some excellent guitar work and phasing later resurfaced on *Echoes In Time, Vol. 2*. The group also recorded an album, which was never issued, for which acetates exist. These would fall in the R3 category. Its finest moments include *Time* and *Shades Of Autumn*.

After the group split in September 1969, Roger McCabe quit the music business completely. Brian Bennett joined **Jason Crest**, who almost immediately became *High Broom*. Stuart Hobday became a successful BBC music producer and Gary Murphy joined a bluesy band called Hellmet, who like **Leviathan** recorded an album's worth of material which didn't get beyond the acetate stage.

Tenth Planet's **Mike Stuart Span** compilation *Timespan* includes two studio outtakes by **Leviathan** - *Evil Woman* and *Through The Looking Glass* - from 1969.

Only Brian Bennett is still active in the music business, currently playing in a band called Calico as well as a Phil Collins tribute band, which also includes former members of **Jason Crest**. Gary Murphy had been in a rock/blues band Chameleon, which has now split.

Second Production has been compiled on *Oddities, Vol 1* (CD) and *Jagged Time Lapse, Vol 1* (CD). *The War Machine* has got a fresh airing on *Jagged Time Lapse, Vol 2* (CD), whilst *Remember The Times* can also be heard on *Jagged Time Lapse, Vol 3* (CD) and *Just Forget Tomorrow* has resurfaced on *Jagged Time Lapse, Vol 4* (CD). (VJ)

David Lewis

ALBUM: 1   SONGS OF DAVID LEWIS   (AX 1) 1970 R4

NB: (1) reissued on CD (limited pressing of 500) (Vinyl Japan UK ASKCD 141) 2003.

Lewis was the leader of **Andwella's Dream**. Just 50 copies of this privately-pressed effort were reputedly put out making it an ultra-rarity. Highlights include two tracks previously on **Andwella's Dream**'s *Love And Poetry* album (the psychedelic *Take My Road* and the heavier *Man With No Name*), much of the remaining material is starker with just an acoustic guitar and piano backing. Former **Andwella's Dream** members Nigel Smith and Gordon Barton play on some tracks. (VJ)

Linda Lewis

				HCP
ALBUMS:	1	SAY NO MORE	(Reprise K 44130) 1971	-
(up to	2	LARK	(Reprise K 44208) 1972	SC -
1976)	3	FATHOMS DEEP	(Raft 48501) 1973	-
	4	HEART STRINGS	(?) 1974	-
	5	NOT A LITTLE GIRL ANYMORE		
			(Arista ARTY 109) 1975	40

NB: There's are also some CD compilations, *The Best Of Linda Lewis* (Camden 74321431562) 1996, *Reach For The Truth - The Best Of The Reprise Years* (Warner) 2002 is an anthology of her seventies material, *The Best Of Linda Lewis* (BMG) 2003 is as its title suggests a 'best of' and *Legends* (?) 2005 is a 3-CD set .

			HCP
45s:	You Turned My Bitter Into Sweet/		
(up to	Do You Believe In Love	(Polydor 56173) 1967	R2 -
1976)	We Can Win/Hampstead Way	(Reprise K 14096) 1972	-
	Old Smokey/It's The Frame	(Reprise K 14209) 1972	-
	Rock A Doodle Doo/		
	Reach For The Truth	(Raft RA 18502) 1973	15
	Play Around/On The Stage	(Raft RA 18505) 1973	-
	Sideway Shuffle/Safe & Sound	(Raft RA 18507) 1974	-
	The Old School Yard/Cordon Blues	(Bell BL 1405) 1975	-
	It's In His Kiss/Walk About	(Arista ARIST 17) 1975	6
	Rock & Roller Coaster/Seeside Song	(Arista ARIST 25) 1975	-
	Rock A Doodle Doo/ Sideway Shuffle/		
	Play Around	(Reprise K14414) 1976	-
	Baby I'm Yours/Other Side	(Arista ARIST 43) 1976	33
	This Time I'll Be Sweeter/		
	So Many Mysteries To Find	(Arista ARIST 65) 1976	-
	Winter Wonderland/		
	All Comes Back To Love	(Arista ARIST 82) 1976	-

Linda Lewis is an immensely talented vocalist whose career lost its way in the second half of the seventies. As a consequence she was not as successful as she should have been.

Lewis was born in West Ham, East London, the oldest of six children. It was soon apparent that she was a talented singer and she often sang in public from an early age. Her mother sent her to a stage school when she was just three. She often performed alongside her mother and father in the East End clubs near to her home as a child. She was regularly cast in non-speaking TV and film roles. In 1961 she appeared in the film 'A Taste of Honey' and in 1964 she was a screaming fan in the **Beatles**' movie 'A Hard Day's Night'.

Her first band was The Q Set (named after a local nightspot, The Cue Club, where the group performed). The group played ska/blue beat and very heavy Jamaican-style music. Whilst studying 'O' levels with the intention of going to art school she had a chance meeting with John Lee Hooker on a weekend out with friends in Southend and he introduced her to Ian Samwell who produced **The Small Faces** and discovered **Elkie Brooks**. Samwell negotiated a one-off deal with Polydor for her to record *You Turned My Bitter Into Sweet*. It didn't make much impact at the time but is now a coveted collectors' item. It also led her to consider a career in music.

In 1970 she replaced **Marsha Hunt** in the soul-rock outfit **Ferris Wheel**. They were a popular live act in the UK who enjoyed modest success overseas. They undertook a succession of European tours but before the year was out they had disbanded.

At the start of the seventies she moved into a house run on the lines of a hippie commune in Hampstead. Whilst living there she began to play the guitar and write songs. A chance visit to the house by Ian Ralfini (then the head of Warner's in the UK) who overheard her playing guitar led to a contract with Warner's Reprise label in 1971. Ian Samwell produced her first recording sessions for the label, which were released as the album *Say No More*.

She also developed a career as a session vocalist and her stunning vocal range can be heard on albums by **David Bowie** (1973's *Aladdin Sane*), **Cat Stevens**, Al Kooper and others.

By the time of her second album *Lark*, **Lewis** was sufficiently confident to handle the production herself, assisted by her then boyfriend Jim Cregan (of **Blossom Toes** and later **Family**) who she would later marry. It marked her transformation into a fully-fledged composer and is usually regarded as one of her finest moments. The self-penned single *Rock-A-Doodle-Doo* gave **Lewis** her first UK hit, peaking at No 15. It showcased her five-octave

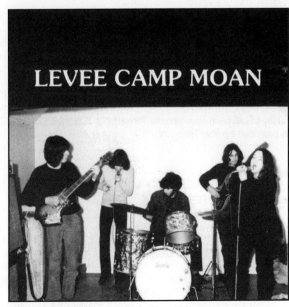

LEVEE CAMP MOAN - Levee Camp Moan (CD).

vocal range and contained an infectious chorus. She made her debut on 'Top Of The Pops' to promote it and embarked on a massive tour of the states headlined by **Cat Stevens**.

Her 1973 album *Fathoms Deep* was a successful amalgam of pop, folk, rock, funk and soul. The dreamy, orchestrated title track was co-written by **Lewis** and Cregan. Other highlights included the whimsical *Moles* and the funky *On The Stage*. The album was released on the UK-only Warner imprint Raft Records and her progress was jarred somewhat when the label went bust.

In 1974 Reprise released a compilation *Heartstrings* comprising tracks from *Lark* and *Fathoms Deep*. It also included *Rock-A-Doodle-Doo* and *Sideway Shuffle*, which had not been included on her albums before.

In 1975 she switched to Bell and recorded the **Cat Stevens**' song *The Old School Yard* with Jim Cregan producing. Clive Davis the head of Arista got to hear it and she was offered and accepted a deal with them. The resulting album *Not A Little Girl Anymore* included contributions from Alan Toussaint, Lowell George and The Tower of Power horn section. It also contained her disco-orientated cover of Betty Everett's US sixties R&B Top Ten hit *The Shoop Shoop Song* retitled *It's In His Kiss*, which became a big international hit and climbed to No 6 here in Britain. The song also gave **Lewis** her only US hit in July 1975. Two further excellent singles followed in 1976 - another upbeat disco-orientated offering *Baby I'm Yours* and the contrasting and beautiful *Winter Wonderland*, although the latter was not a hit.

As we leave the time span of this book her career flourished for a while. This was still the disco era and her next album 1977's *Woman Overboard* was suited to the times and was critically acclaimed. She also continued her session work in the late seventies appearing with **Rod Stewart**, **Rick Wakeman**, **Chris Spedding**, **Mike Batt** and **Steve Harley**. However, differences began to develop between **Lewis** and her record company as she increasingly disliked the pop-orientated material they wanted her to sing. She moved to Los Angeles with her husband Jim Cregan but returned to England in 1979, recording an album for Ariola *Hacienda View*, which was largely penned and produced by **Mike Batt**. At the start of the eighties she returned to Los Angeles and released an album *A Tear And A Smile* for Epic in 1983. She then opted out of the music business to concentrate on bringing up her son.

In the mid-nineties she moved back to England and released a trio of albums - *Second Nature* (1995), *Whatever* (1997) and *Kiss Of Life* (1999) for Turpin Records. In 2002, Warner Music released an anthology of her seventies output entitled *Reach For The Truth - The Best Of The Reprise Years*. A 'best of' collection of her work for BMG followed in 2003. She appeared at the Glastonbury Festival the same year and continues to write and record. Her most recent release has been a 3-CD compilation *Legends* in 2005. (VJ)

The Liberators

Personnel:	BARRIE BERNARD	bs	A
	SAM 'WIDGE' KEMP	vcls	A
	TOM LONG	lead gtr	A
	TONY NEWMAN	gtr	A
	JOHN WALLBANK	drms	A

| 45: | It Hurts So Much/You Look So Fine | (Stateside SS 424) 1965 |

This Rugby-based band later became **Pinkerton's Assorted Colours**. This 45 was produced by Shel Talmy. (VJ)

Lieutenant Pigeon

Personnel:	NIGEL FLETCHER	drms	A
	STEPHEN JOHNSON	bs	A
	ROBERT WOODWARD	piano	A

ALBUMS:	1(A)	MOULDY OLD MUSIC	(Decca SKL 5154) 1973
(up to	2(A)	PIGEON PIE	(Decca SKL 5174) 1974
1976)	3(A)	PIGEON PARTY	(Decca SKL 5196) 1974
	4(A)	THE WORLD OF LIEUTENANT PIGEON	
			(Decca SPA 414) 1976 SC

NB: There's also two compilations, *Mouldy Old Dough* (Emporio EMPRCD 782) 1998 and *The Best Of Lieutenant Pigeon* (Cherry Red GLAM CD 6) 2001 is a 16-track compilation. (4) was unreleased. Test pressings only.

			HCP
45s:	Mouldy Old Dough/The Villain	(Decca F 13278) 1972	1
(up to	Desperate Dan/Opus 300	(Decca F 13365) 1972	17
1976)	And The Fun Goes On/Opus 302	(Decca F 13403) 1973	-
	Oxford Bags/Creativity	(Decca F 13440) 1973	-
	Big Butch Baby/		
	I'll Take You Home Again Kathleen	(Decca F 13486) 1974	-
	You Are My Hearts/Love Inflation	(Decca F 13543) 1974	-
	Rockabilly Hot Pot/		
	Gosford Street Ragg	(Decca F 13602) 1975	-
	Goodbye/I'll Sail My Ship Alone	(Decca 13638) 1976	-

This Coventry-based band grew out of the little-known **Stavely Makepiece**. Their novelty 45 *Mouldy Old Dough*, which was basically an instrumental save for the intermittent refrain of the title, attracted considerable attention and went on to top the Charts here. It had been recorded in Woodward's front room and featured his mum Hilda on piano. The follow-up *Desperate Dan*, just made the Top 20 but after that it was a return to obscurity.

Almost inevitably *Mouldy Old Dough* kicks of their compilation, which includes a cover of **Mary Hopkins**' *Those Were The Days* and their big Aussie hit *I'll Take You Home Again Kahtleen*.

Rob Woodward had earlier recorded as **Shel Naylor**.

Mouldy Old Dough can also be heard on *Hits Of The 70's Vol 2* (CD), *Number 1 Hits Of The 70's & 80's* (CD), *30 Years Of Number 1 Hit Singles - 1960/1989* (CD) and *UK No 1 Hits Of The 70's* (CD); whilst you can check out their version of *Ziggy Stardust* on *Hits Of The 70's Vol 3* (CD). (VJ/MG)

Life

Personnel:	ROGER COTTON	keyb'ds, vcls, gtr	A
	IAN GIBBONS	keyb'ds, flute, vcls	A
	PAUL THORPE	drms, vcls	A
	RICHARD THORPE	vcls, bs	A

| ALBUM: | 1(A) | A LIFE AFTER DEATH | (Polydor 2383 295) 1974 R1 |

45s:	Hands Of The Clock/	
	Ain't I Told You Before	(Polydor 56778) 1969
	Woman/Bless My Soul	(Polydor 2058 500) 1974

This is a more or less straight rocking crew, not too fanciful, but with some niceties thrown in. The opening track *Riding Around* is exemplary. Starting out as a totally uninteresting average rock number, it comes up with a

LIGHT OF DARKNESS - Light Of Darkness (LP).

ENGLISH FREAKBEAT VOL. 2 (Comp CD) including The Limeys.

hardly related middle part, boasting symphonic tendencies and well developed extended structures. But even though this here and there may mollify the listener, too much time is spent among undistinguished bluesy rock riffs and boogie rolls. A pity, since the better parts of this album (produced by **Zombie** Chris White) sound promising. (MK)

Life

45:     Cat's Eyes/Death In The Family   (Philips 6006 280) 1973

This was a different band from the one who recorded on Polydor. The 'A' side is a keyboard driven predominantly instrumental number credited to Peter Shelley. The 'B' side, credited to Shelley and John Fidday, is a mellower instrumental. (VJ)

Life 'n' Soul

45s: Ode To Billy Joe/Peacefully Asleep   (Decca F 12659) 1967 R1
        Here Comes Yesterday Again/
        Dear Paul   (Decca F 12851) 1968 SC

Basically **Life'n'Soul** was a mainstream pop group, originally from Manchester, who later moved down to London. *Peacefully Asleep* was their most interesting recording, with its pleasant cello work and vocals epitomising the Summer of 1967. *Ode To Billy Joe* was a hit for Bobby Gentry. This version has bright harmonies and subdued guitar. It was produced by Steve Rowland who also fronted **Family Dogg** .

Peacefully Asleep has been compiled on *Rubble Vol. 6: The Clouds Have Groovy Faces* (LP), *Rubble Vol. 4* (CD), *British Psychedelic Trip, Vol. 4* (LP) and *Great British Psychedelic Trip, Vol. 2* (CD). (VJ)

Light Fantastic

45:     Jeanie/You Don't Care   (RCA RCA 2331) 1973

A Birmingham-based glam-rock outfit whose 45 was written and produced by **The Sweet** and is now quite collectable. (VJ)

Light Of Darkness

Personnel: MANFRED BEBERT   drms   A
             BYRON GRANT   gtr, violin   A
             JOHN LATIMER   vcls, keyb'ds, perc   A
             MIKE REOCH   bs, keyb'ds, perc   A

ALBUM: 1(A)   LIGHT OF DARKNESS   (Philips 6305 062) 1970 R1

NB: (1) German only release. Reissued on Zyx 1981 and (Second Battle SB 009) and on CD (Second Battle SB 019) 1991.

This sombre Scottish band with a German drummer specialised in moody progressive rock, though without too many niceties or frills. Most tracks are somehow based on a riff or else do not have any complicated harmonies or structures. There are quite a few long improvisations and these tend to get on your nerves after a while, because they mostly have very little direction and almost no dynamic variation. Probably this was deemed more fitting to the German public of the early seventies, but they likewise failed to make much of an impact over there. A few better spots notwithstanding, this is unfortunately nothing special and in places even sounds like listless variations on **Black Sabbath**. This is hardly a venture to warm your blood. (RR/MK)

Limelight (1)

45:     Baby Don't Get Hooked On Me/
        I'll See You On Sunday   (Deram DM 363) 1972

This 45 seems to have been their sole vinyl offering. (VJ)

Limelight (2)

45:     I Should Have Known Better/
        Tell Me Why   (United Artists 35779) 1975

This is another obscure group of the same name as the previous entry. The 'A' side is a **Beatles**' cover and there was a possible connection with **Brinsley Schwarz**. (VJ)

Limey

Personnel: DAVE BOWKER   bs, hrmnca   A
             BRIAN ENGEL   vcls   A
             IAN KEWLEY   keyb'ds, moog, french horn   A
             ROBIN LE MESURIER gtr, moog   A
             MAX McINERNEY   drms, perc   A

ALBUMS: 1(A)   LIMEY   (RCA SF 8463) 1975
         2( )   SILVER EAGLE   (RCA SF) 1976

An album of mainly soft melodic rock with the occasional country edge (**B.J. Coles**' steel guitar is evidenced on a couple of tracks). It's pleasant but not strong enough to be recommended. All the tracks are written by Brian Engel. A further album was issued in 1976 on RCA which featured Garth Watt-Roy and members of **Argent**.

Engel was previously in **Mandrake Paddle Steamer**. (BS)

The Limeys

45s: I Can't Find My Way Through/
        Don't Cry (My Love)   (Pye 7N 15820) 1965
        Some Tears Fall Dry/Half Glass Of Wine   (Pye 7N 15909) 1965
        Cara-Lin/Feel So Blue   (Decca F 12382) 1966 R1
        The Mountain's High/Lovin' Yourself   (Decca F 12466) 1966

A North London band who played a sort of Mersey-sounding music. Their best-known and most collectable 45 is *Cara-Lin*, which had been a minor hit in the States for The Strangeloves a year earlier. **The Limeys**' version was produced by **Mike Berry**.

You can also hear *Cara-Lin* on *English Freakbeat, Vol. 2* (CD), *Electric Sugarcube Flashbacks, Vol. 2* (LP) and *Electric Sugarcube Flashbacks, Vol. 3* (LP). (VJ)

Peter Lincoln

45:     In The Day Of My Youth/
        My Monkey Is A Junkie   (Major Minor MM 520) 1967

This is actually Peter Sarstedt using a pseudonym. (VJ)

Philamore Lincoln

ALBUM: 1   THE NORTH WIND BLEW SOUTH
                        (Epic BN 26497) 1970 R1 - US only.

NB: (1) reissued on vinyl (Epic BN 26497).

45s: Running By The River/Rainy Day   (NEMS 56-3711) 1968 R1
        Country Jail Band/You're The One   (CBS 55007) 1970

It's rumoured that **The Yardbirds** played on this mysterious artist's first 45, which is pretty inane pop. His intermittently superb album only got a US release. Its highlights include the spooky title track, funky *You're The One* and breezy *Plains Of Delight*, but it's marred by some pedestrian bluesy material, including the dreadful instrumental that closes proceedings. *Temma Harbour*, also from the album, later became a hit for **Mary Hopkin**. **Lincoln** later became a producer for **Paladin** and others.

Compilation appearances include: *You're The One* on *James Patrick Page, Session Man* (2-LP); *Running By The River* on *Rubble, Vol. 17 - A Trip In A Painted World* (LP), *Rubble, Vol. 10* (CD) and *The Best Of Rubble Collection, Vol. 5* (LP). (VJ/RMJ)

Lindisfarne

Personnel: ROD CLEMENTS   vcls, gtr, keyb'ds   A
                SIMON COWE   vcls, gtr, mandolin   A
                ALAN HULL   bs, vcls, keyb'ds, gtr AB
                RAY JACKSON   vcls, gtr, mandolin   AB
                RAY LAIDLAW   drms   A
                KENNY CRADDOCK   keyb'ds   B
                TOMMY DUFFY   bs   B
                PAUL NICHOLS   drms   B

			HCP
ALBUMS: 1(A)	NICELY OUT OF TUNE	(Charisma CAS 1025) 1970	8
(up to 2(A)	FOG ON THE TYNE	(Charisma CAS 1050) 1971	1
1976) 3(A)	DINGLY DELL	(Charisma CAS 1057) 1972	5
4(-)	LINDISFARNE LIVE	(Charisma CLASS 2) 1973	25
5(B)	ROLL ON RUBY	(Charisma CAS 1076) 1973	-
6(B)	HAPPY DAZE	(Warner Bros K 56070) 1974	-
7(-)	LINDISFARNE'S FINEST HOUR	(Charisma CAS 1108) 1975	55
8(-)	LADY ELEANOR	(Pickwick SHM 919) 1976	-

NB: Also of interest may be *The Singles Album* (Charisma BG 5), *The Peel Sessions* (Strange Fruit SFPS 059) 1988 and two CD compilations *Buried Treasures Vol. 1* and *Vol. 2* (Virgin CDVM 9012 and 9013 respectively) 1992, which piece together live rarities from BBC sessions and outtakes from their much loved debut album. (1) reissued on CD (Charisma CASD 1025) 1988 and again on CD remastered with two bonus tracks. (2) reissued on CD (Charisma CASCD 1050) 1988 and again on CD remastered with two bonus tracks. (3) reissued on CD

LINDISFARNE - Fog On The Tyne (LP).

(Charisma CASCD 1057) 1988 and again on CD remastered with one bonus tracks.

Compilations include: - *C'mon Everybody* (Stylus SMD 738) 1987 and *Best Of Lindisfarne* (Virgin VVIPD 103) 1989. There's also *Lindisfarne On Tap* (Castle Communications ESSCD 214) 1994 an 18-track hits and more collection. *Run For Home: Lindisfarne Collected* (Music Club MCCD 305) 1997 is a budget-priced CD collection of their material including live versions of *Lady Eleanor* and *Meet Me On The Corner*. *Lady Eleanor* (Recall) 1997 gives another airing to the *live Magic In The Air*, alongside studio material from the reformed line-up. *City Songs* (New Millennium Communications PILOT 34) 1998 presents four sessions taped for the BBC in 1971 and 1972 and includes versions of their well-known hits. *Anthology/Road To Kingdom Come* (Essential ESACD 884) 2000 provides an overview of the band's career. *Buried Treasure Vol 1* (CD) (Virgin 973425) contains early singles, obscure 'B' sides, rare live material and unreleased tracks from 1971-1990. *BT3 (Buried Treasures 3)* (Siren SRNC 202 CD) 2001 compiles live tracks, studio outtakes and radio recordings. *Very Best Of Lindisfarne* (EMI Gold 5925852) comprises the previously available 'best of' supplemented by four extra tracks and including two unreleased songs. *The Best Of LIndisfarne* (EMI 3 11845 2) 2005 is a new CD compilation of their material.

			HCP
45s:	Clear White Light Part II/		
(up to	Knacker's Yard Blues	(Charisma CB 137) 1970	-
1976)	Lady Eleanor/Nothing But The		
	Marvellous Is Beautiful (PS)	(Charisma CB 153) 1971	3
	Meet Me On The Corner/		
	Scotch Mist/No Time To Lose (PS)	(Charisma CB 173) 1972	5
	All Fall Down/		
	We Can Swing Together (live) PS	(Charisma CB 191) 1972	34
	Court In The Art/Don't Ask Me	(Charisma CB 199) 1972	-
	Taking Care Of Business/		
	North Country Boy	(Charisma CB 228) 1974	-
	Tonight/No Need To Tell Me	(Warner Bros K 16489) 1975	-
Reissues:	Lady Eleanor/Fog On The Tyne	(Charisma CB 266) 1975	-
	Clear White Light/		
	(Flip by different artist)	(Charisma CB 409) 1982	-

This seminal Geordie band originally called themselves Downtown Faction and were also called Brethren before they signed in 1968 as **Lindisfarne**. Basically a folk-rock act they were an increasingly popular attraction at festivals and clubs prior to the release of their debut album, *Nicely Out Of Tune*. In retrospect, although it didn't sell well at the time, it was their best album. **Alan Hull** proved himself to be a strong songwriter, in fact he'd written many of the songs whilst working as a nurse in a mental hospital before the band was formed. Among the album's finest moments were *Clear White Light* and *Lady Eleanor*, both issued as 45s, though neither made the Charts at the time.

Success came with their next album *Fog On The Tyne*. It was produced by Bob Johnston, a Nashville producer who'd worked with Bob Dylan and Simon and Garfunkel among others. It became the biggest selling UK album of 1971-72 and spawned a Top 5 hit with Clements' *Meet Me On The Corner*. In the wake of this success their earlier *Lady Eleanor* 45 was repromoted and did even better.

Thereafter it was all downhill. **Alan Hull** seemed to lose his songwriting flair and *Dingly Dell* cannot be recommended, although it did produce another minor hit single, *All Fall Down*. After a gruelling tour of the Pacific, Clements, Cowe and Laidlaw all left to form **Jack The Lad** early in 1973. **Hull** and Jackson remained and put together a new line-up (B) but the old flair and zeal just wasn't there. *Happy Daze* was an improvement on *Roll On Ruby* but by now the band had lost their audience and they disintegrated soon afterwards.

Alan Hull also made a couple of solo albums in 1973 and 1975 and pursued an intermittent solo career.

The original quintet were persuaded to reform for a series of Christmas concerts in 1976. The nostalgia that the reunion created gave the band a new lease of life and they went on to sign for Mercury, releasing further albums for them and LMP during the seventies and eighties.

Rod Clements also appeared on **Dando Shaft**'s reunion album *Kingdom* issued in 1977. *The Very Best Of Lindisfarne* is a good 20-track overview of their career. It includes their hits like *Lady Eleanor, Fog On The Tyne, Meet Me On The Corner* and *All Fall Down* alongside some of their classic album tracks. Also included are two previously unreleased songs (*Everybody Say Yeah* and *Love In A Cage*) penned by the late **Alan Hull** and recorded by the original line-up in the early eighties.

Buried Treasures 3 compiles live material, studio outtakes and radio recordings. Highlights include *100 Miles To Liverpool* (recorded at a school for a hospital radio session), *Newport Mount Rag* (recorded in 1974 with Mark Knopfler) and *Dragon Of Dreamland* (which actually dates form 1993).

They've also appeared on a few compilations. You'll find *Clear White Light* on *One More Chance* (LP) and *Lady Eleanor* on Ronco's *20 Star Tracks, Vol. 1* (LP) and *Run For Home* has been compiled on *Sunshine Day A Taste Of The 70's* (CD). (VJ)

The Lions

45:      Twisted Nerve/My Friend The Blackbird (Polydor 56757) 1969 R1

An obscure pop group of whom nothing is known. (VJ)

The Lions of Judah

Personnel:	HAIM ALGRANATI	gtr, vcls	A
	SHUKI ALGRANATI	gtr, vcls	A
	MOSHE BOYANJO	drms	A
	HAIM SABAN	bs	A
	DANNY SHUSHAN	ld vcls	A

NB: Line-up 'A' is that which recorded the UK 45.

45:      Our Love's A Growin' Thing/Katja   (Fontana TF 1016) 1969

Although *Katja* appears on *Rubble Vol. 11* (CD), they were in fact an Israeli band and the above 45 was also released in Germany.

The Lions of Judah were formed in Tel Aviv, Israel in 1965. Initially, they played covers and were active among the club scene, often sharing the same stage with The Churchills. They soon obtained a cult following and began writing original material.

In Israel they recorded numerous English-sung 45s. Being maligned by the local media that disapproved of any English material by local artists, their rising popularity among the record buying public in the Holy Land didn't transfer into air play, which was somewhat frustrating.

Being a smart entrepreneur, however, Haim Saban managed to re-locate the band to London and secured a three month residency for them at the Hatchett's Playground club in Piccadilly.

The lyrics for *Our Love's A Growing Thing* were penned by the famous songwriting team of Howard-Blaikley and composed by Haim Algranati. A poppy tune, it sounds somewhat pale, but is compensated by *Katja*, an all Algranati composition. This sizzling tune is a true progressive-pop workout with a generous helping of organ and typically late sixties rock guitar. The 45 sold dismally in the UK, but was popular enough to get released in Europe.

VISIONS OF THE PAST VOL. 3 (Comp CD) including Listen.

Failing to score any more single releases, the band returned to Israel, where they were surprised to see *Our Love* climbing the local chart, and... blowing the **Beatles'** *Get Back* off the top (!!!).

The band continued releasing English-sung 45s in Israel. In 1970, Danny Shushan left to join The Churchills/Jericho Jones, appearing on both their two European albums for A&M, as well as on two Israeli only 45s.

Today, The Algranati brothers still keep the band's name alive and working on the club circuit. Another vocalist, Jan Tajgan, went on to superstardom in Norway, whilst Haim Saban found fame and fortune in the States as a top producer and creator of children T.V. programmes. Among his creations are: The Ninja Turtles, Kidd Video, and the Power Rangers, to name but a few.

A retrospective CD of 20 songs was released in Israel (on Phonokol records) in 1998. (MG/VJ)

The Lion Tamers

45:      Speak Your Mind/Light   (Polydor 56283) 1968

Little is known about this band either, but the mildly unusual pop flip side has resurfaced on *Rubble Vol. 17: A Trip In A Painted World* (LP), *Rubble Vol. 10* (CD) and *The Best Of Rubble Collection, Vol. 2* (CD). Certainly it's nothing special though. (VJ)

Listen (1)

Personnel:	ROGER BEAMER	bs	A
	JOHN CRUTCHLEY	lead gtr	A
	ROBERT PLANT	vcls	A
	GEOFF THOMPSON	drms	A

45:      You'd Better Run/
         Everybody's Gonna Say   (CBS 202456) 1965 R4

This Birmingham-based band included **Robert Plant** who released a couple of solo singles the following year and was later in **Led Zeppelin**. *You'd Better Run* was a Young Rascals track, also done by **The In-Be-Tweens**.

Everybody's Gonna Say and *You Better Run* can also be heard on *Nowhere Men, Vol. 1* (LP & CD) and *Visions Of The Past, Vol. 3* (LP & CD). (VJ)

Listen (2)

Personnel:	PAUL ABRAHAMS	keyb'ds	A
	MIKE ANSCOMBE	drms	A
	ROGER CAIRNS	vcls	A
	ED DURBROW	gtr	A
	LINDA SUKENIC	vcls	A
	DAVE WARTH	bs	A

45:      Astral Boogie/
         All Your Rock 'n' Roll Is Dead   (Parlophone R 5977) 1973

Listen was an Anglo-American jazz-rock orientated band who won the 'Melody Maker National Rock/Folk Contest' in 1972. In November 1972, they entered the studio and recorded this 45. (VJ/BS)

Little Big Horn

45:      Another Man's Song/Just A Game   (Polydor 2058.042) 1970

A heavy mood based country pop band produced by Hugh Murphy. (VJ)

Little Darlings

45:      Little Bit O'Soul/Easy To Cry   (Fontana TF 539) 1965

This is a rare and sought-after 45. There was also a Bluebeat group of this name. This disc featured two Carter-Lewis compositions. The 'A' side was a well known song, the flip a powerful R&B number. (VJ)

Little Folk

ALBUM: 1 LEAVE THEM A FLOWER   (Studio Republic) 1971 R2

This privately-pressed album was recorded by a folk band who combine originals and Joni Mitchell, Paul Simon, Tom Paxton etc. covers on this album, which is housed in a home-made black and white sleeve. (VJ)

Little Frankie (and The Country Gentlemen)

45s: The Kind Of Boy You Can't Forget/
        I'm Gonna Do It   (Columbia DB 7490) 1965 SC
   α Make-A-Love/
        Love Is Just A Game   (Columbia DB 7578) 1965 SC
        It Doesn't Matter Any More/
        Happy, That's Me   (Columbia DB 7681) 1965 SC

NB: α as **Little Frankie and The Country Gentlemen**.

From Manchester, **Little Frankie** was just 16 when she recorded her first 45. On the second one, she was backed by **The Country Gentlemen**, who also recorded a solo 45. Her third 'A' side was a Buddy Holly song, both sides of this disc were produced by **Graham Gouldman**. She was also Denise in **Chimes**.

You can also check out *I'm Gonna Do It* on *Girls In The Garage, Vol. 7* (LP) and *Vol. 2* (CD). (VJ)

Little Free Rock

Personnel: PETER ILLINGWORTH   gtr, vcls   A
              FRANK NEWBOLD   bs, vcls, perc A
              PAUL VARLEY   drms   A

ALBUM: 1(A) LITTLE FREE ROCK   (Transatlantic TRA 208) 1969 R2

This group was a later version of Purple Haze who included ex-**David John and The Mood** guitarist Peter Illingworth. Their album is basically heavy psychedelia with some **Cream** influences. The songs are well structured with fine melodies and good guitar, with the best tracks being *Roman Summer Nights*, *Lost Lonely Castles In The Sky*, *Dream*, *Tingle* and *Evil Woman*.

Frank Newbold was later involved in the **Astral Navigations Thundermother** project. (VJ/CA)

Little Grants and Eddie

Personnel incl: EDDIE GRANT   A

45s: Rudy's Dead/Everything's Alright   (President PT 159) 1967
        Rock Steady '67/Bingo   (President PT 172) 1967

This mob was most significant for including Eddie Grant who was also in **The Equals**. (VJ)

The Lively Set

Personnel: TONY CARTWRIGHT   bs   A
              NORMAN HALE   organ   A
              JIM KENT   lead gtr   A
              MITCH MITCHELL   drms   A

45s: Don't Call My Name/What Kind Of Love (Pye 7N 15880) 1965
        Let The Trumpets Sound/
        The Green Years   (Capitol CL 15472) 1966

A London-based group, although the three members above were from Liverpool originally, where they played in **Chris Sandford**'s backing group, The Coronets. **Sandford** produced this 45. (VJ/AD)

The Liverbirds

A four-piece girl group, who were active in Liverpool's music scene from the early sixties onwards. They went to Germany where they recorded two rare albums on the Star-Club label: *Star-Club Show 4* (1964) and *More Of* (1965). The first one, which was reissued on Line in 1986, is full of cover versions of classics like *Johnny B. Goode*, *Love Hurts*, *Talking About You*, *Mona*, *Too Much Monkey Business*, *Money*, *Road Runner*, *Before You Accuse Me*, *Got My Mojo Working* etc. They had a raw, basement, but competent enough sound.

Compilation appearances have included: *Shop Around* and *It's Got To Be You* on *The Star-Club Singles Complete, Vol. 2* (LP & CD); *Diddley Daddy*, *Leave All Your Loves In The Past*, *Peanut Butter* and *Why Do You Hang Around Me* on *The Star-Club Singles Complete, Vol. 4* (LP & CD); *Loop De Loop* and *Bo Diddley Is A Lover* on *The Star-Club Singles Complete, Vol. 7* (LP & CD); *It's Got To Be You* on *Star-Club Show* (LP); *He Hardly Calls Me Honey Anymore* on *Sweet Beat* (LP); *Why Do You Hang Around Me* on *Star Club Scene '65* (LP); *Peanut Butter* on *The Star-Club Anthology, Vol. 1* (LP); *Loop De Loop* on *The Star-Club Anthology, Vol. 4* (LP); and *Talkin' About You* on *Beat Im Star Club* (2-LP). (CA/LBy)

Liverpool Echo

Personnell: MARTIN BRILEY   lead gtr   A
              KEITH BROWN   bs   A
              BRIAN ENGEL   vcls, hrmnca, acoustic gtr A
              DAVE JOHNS   drms   A

ALBUM: 1(A)   LIVERPOOL ECHO   (SPARK SRLM 2007) 1973
NB: (1) reissued on CD (Rev-Ola CRREV 131) 2005, with a booklet containing notes from Briley and Engel.

A four-piece fronted by ex-**Mandrake Paddle Steamer** men Briley and Engel who recorded an album for Spark in 1973. The album arguably attempted to 'get back to basics' three years before the onset of punk. It featured remakes of the Mersey sound but with extra twang added, like **Rockin' Horse**. All twelve tracks were originals and those of you who liked the mid-sixties Beatles should like this one. Briley was an in-demand session guitarist and Herbie Flowers and Clem Cattini were in this band for a while. (VJ/UF)

Liverpool Express

Personnel: DEREK CASHIN   drms   A
             TONY COATES   gtr, vcls   A
             ROGER CRAIG   keyb'ds   A
             BILLY KINSLEY   bs   A

ALBUM: 1(A) TRACKS   (Warner Bros K 56281) 1976
(up to
1976)

                                              HCP
45s: Smile My Smilers Smile/Lae Mei (Warner Bros K 16620) 1975 -
(up to   You Are My Love/
1976)   Never Be The Same Body   (Warner Bros K 16743) 1976 11
        Hold It Tight/Lost For Words   (Warner Bros K 16799) 1976 46
        Every Man Must Have A Dream/
        Call Me   (Warner Bros K 16854) 1976 17

Billy Kinsley had been with **The Merseybeats** back in the sixties but the remaining members of this scouser band were all new to the scene. They played a sort of accessible sixties style pop, very polished and very accessible. *You Are My Love* and *Every Man Must Have A Dream*, in particular, are well worth a spin.

Kinsley was a real veteran of Liverpool's music scene. On the demise of **The Merseybeats** he was in **The Merseys** and **The Swinging Blue Jeans**. A later venture was **Jimmy Campbell's Rockin' Horse** and after the demise of **Liverpool Express** he formed another Merseybeat combo, The Cheats. (VJ)

Liverpool Scene

Personnel incl:	BRIAN DODSON	drms
	MIKE EVANS	vcls, sax
	MIKE HART	vcls, gtr
	ADRIAN HENRI	vcls
	PERCY JONES	bs, hrmnca
	ANDY ROBERTS	gtr, vcls

ALBUMS: 1( ) THE INCREDIBLE NEW LIVERPOOL SCENE
  (CBS 63045) 1967 SC
2( ) THE AMAZING ADVENTURES OF LIVERPOOL SCENE
  (RCA SF 7995) 1968 SC
3( ) BREAD ON THE NIGHT (RCA SF 8057) 1969 SC
4( ) ST ADRIAN CO. BROADWAY AND 3RD
  (RCA SF 8100) 1969 SC
5( ) HEIRLOON (RCA SF 8134) 1970 SC
6(-) RECOLLECTIONS (Compilation) (Charisma CS 3) 1972
7(-) THE LIVERPOOL SCENE FEATURING ADRIAN HENRI &
  ANDY ROBERTS (Polydor 2310055) 1972

NB: (2) and (3) reissued on a 2-CD set (BGO BGOCD 538) 2002. (7) includes solo tracks by **Andy Roberts**.

| 45s: | Son Son/Baby | (RCA RCA 1762) 1968 |
| | The Woo-Woo/Love Is | (RCA RCA 1816) 1969 |

'The Liverpool Scene' was originally the title of a book featuring new Liverpool poets. From this came the idea to put out a record featuring two (possibly the best two) of these poets, **Roger McGough** and Adrian Henri, with **Andy Roberts** featuring on half of the tracks playing guitar accompaniment behind the poems and so *The Incredible Liverpool Scene* was recorded in a couple of hours at a studio in Denmark Street, London. John Peel liked it and, as a result, he produced their first full band effort, *The Amazing Adventures Of Liverpool Scene* and Sandy Robinson became their manager.

This was as much a mixed media project as a group comprised of leading Liverpool musicians and poets. Their act and songs were full of satirical humour. Their debut 45, *Son Son*, basically consisted of an inquisitive child asking a parent all the questions one doesn't want to be asked. John Peel soon became a fan and they were a popular band on the underground circuit - their reputation being aided by an acclaimed appearance at the 1969 Isle Of Wight Festival.

Bread On The Night was released the following year, when they toured the UK with **Led Zeppelin** and **Blodwyn Pig**. A gruelling 3-month US tour followed, but their format was far less successful there.

One side of *St Adrian Co, Broadway and 3rd* comprises the lengthy *Made In USA* suite and the other side was recorded live at Warwick University. The band finally split on stage at a London gig in May 1970.

Heirloon was a posthumous collection compiled by RCA after they had split. It consists of recordings from a live Warwick University gig (originally recorded for their *St Adrian Co* album) and including the non-album 'B' side *Love Is* as well as a selection of recordings of them supporting the show 'J'Emerveille', which was written by Adrian Henri and Michael Kustow, about the life of poet Guillaume Apollinaire. This was performed in late 1968 at the London Institute of Contemporary Art.

Roberts left in the early seventies to help form **Plainsong** and also put out some solo albums. **Hart** embarked on a solo career. **Roberts** and Henri later played together with **McGough** in **Grimms**.

There was a reunion tour in 1974 comprising **Andy Roberts**, Adrian Henri, Mike Hart, Dave Richards (bs) and Mike Kellie (drms). (VJ)

Ricky Livid and The Tone Deafs

45: Tomorrow/Nuts And Bolts (Parlophone R 5136) 1964 SC

A comedy style beat group from the South Coast were responsible for this dreadful 45. (VJ)

The Living Daylights

Personnel:	CURT CRESSWELL	gtr	A
	ROY HEATHER	drms	A
	GARTH WATT-ROY	gtr, vcls	A
	NORMAN WATT-ROY	bs, vcls	A

45s: α Let's Live For Today/I'm Real (Philips BF 1561) 1967 SC
  Baila Maria/Always With Him (Philips BF 1613) 1967 R1
NB: α 'B' side actually titled *It's Real*.

A Newcastle band whose debut 'A' side was a Top Ten hit in the US for The Grassroots. **The Living Daylights** enjoyed some success in Europe with their cover version of this harmony-pop song. Their follow-up, *Baila Maria* is not up to much, but *Always With Him*, the flip side is a lively beat song with a unusual wobbly guitar sound.

Their records were produced by **Caleb Quaye**. The Watt-Roy brothers were later in **Greatest Show On Earth** and later still Norman Watt-Roy played with **Glencoe** and then Ian Dury and The Blockheads.

Compilation coverage has included:- *Let's Live For Today* and *Always With Him* on *Rubble Vol. 1: The Psychedelic Snarl* and *Rubble Vol. 1* (CD); *Jane* (a previously unreleased cut from 1968) on *Circus Days Vol. 3* (LP & CD); and *I'm Real* on *Collecting Peppermint Clouds, Vol. 1* (LP). (VJ)

Liza and The Jet Sets

Personnel incl: LIZA STRIKE

45: How Can I Know?/Dancing Yet (Parlophone R 5248) 1965 SC

The Jet Set had recorded a 45 for Parlophone in 1964 prior to teaming up with **Liza Strike** (who made a solo 45 in 1968) for this effort which sank without trace. **Liza Strike** was also in **The Soulmates**. (VJ)

Llan

45: Realise/Anytime (CBS 202405) 1966 R1

A Welsh band who were previously known as **The Vogues**.

Realise can also be found on *That Driving Beat* (CD). (VJ)

LIVERPOOL SCENE - Bread On The Night (LP).

Gerry Lockran

ALBUMS:	1	HOLD ON I'M COMING	(Planet PLL 1002) 1966 R2
(up to	2	BLUES VENDETTA	(Waverley ZLP 2091) 1967 R1
1976)	3	BLUES AT SUNRISE	(Saga FID 2165) 1969
	4	THE ESSENTIAL GERRY LOCKRAN	
			(Spark SRLP 104) 1969 SC
	5	WUN	(Polydor 2383 122) 1972
	6	BLUES BLAST OFF	(Autogram ALLLP 201)1976
	7	NO MORE CANE ON THE BRAZOS	
			(Munich BM 150208)1976
	8	RAGS TO GLADRAGS	(Decca SKL-R 5257) 1976
	9	RALLY ROUND THE FLAG	
			(Autogram & Folk FLLP 50) 1976

NB. (3) was not a **Lockran** solo album. He played vocals and guitar on this with Dave Travis, Redd Sullivan and other musicians. (6), (7) and (9) were released on German labels.

45s:	Hey Jude/This Train	(Decca F 12873) 1969
	Standing On Your Own/You're Not There	(Decca F 12919) 1969
	Can't Get The Finger Pickin'/	
	Temptations Always Winning Through	(Goodear EAR 104) 1974

Gerald Cranston Frederick Loughran was born on the 19th July 1942 in the Yeotmal province of the central plains of India. However, after the death of his father, Gerry's family emigrated to England. Running the farm, as well as continuing to bring up a young family proved to be extremely difficult for Gerry's mother, especially in the face of the rapidly changing political climate in India.

The Loughran family arrived in London, England in 1953 and established themselves in the South London areas of Brixton, Tooting and Colliers Wood. Gerry was soon playing in a skiffle group called The Hornets. He spent three years with them playing such venues as the Skiffle Cellar (later known as the Les Cousins club). Gerry also appeared at the Finsbury Park Empire with Wally Whyton and The Vipers Into the early 1960s, Gerry and Royd Rivers worked as a duo, playing live in pubs and clubs throughout Southern England, including the Red Lion in Sutton, Surrey, one of England's first folk clubs. In 1961, Gerry took his musical obsession further when he bought a classic American acoustic guitar, a Martin D28 - the guitar played by his idol, Big Bill Broonzy. One of the earliest gigs Gerry played with his new Martin guitar was at a folk club in East Street, Brighton, West Sussex on 29 October 1961. Thankfully, this gig was put onto reel-to-reel tape by local club organiser Jim Marshall and the recording is still enjoyed by Gerry's family today.

Around April 1965 Gerry changed the spelling of his surname from Loughran to Lockran for stage purposes. His British live schedule at this time also included a package tour called 'Kings of the Blues' with **Long John Baldry, Alexis Korner** and **Duffy Power.**

The Half Moon pub in Putney, South West London, presented Gerry with his first major opportunity to run his own folk and blues club. It was on August 6th 1965, that Gerry, together with his old friends **Cliff Aungier** and Royd Rivers, first opened 'Folksville', a folk and blues club at the Half Moon. This music venue continues to thrive into the year 2005 - 40 years after being started by Gerry, Cliff and Royd!

In 1966 Gerry secured a recording contract which resulted in the release of his first album *Hold On - I'm Coming* featuring Danny Thompson on double bass.

Gerry followed this release with *Blues Vendetta* in 1967, which featured his powerful fingerpicking style on self-penned compositions like *Guitar Boogie* and *Jason's Blues* (written for his three year old son). In 1969 *The Essential Gerry Lockran* was released and Gerry also featured on *The Blues at Sunrise* compilation with Redd Sullivan and Dave Travis. In 1970 Gerry and Bobbi's second son, Jethro, was born. Young Jethro and his older brother Jason were immortalised in Gerry's song *Jonas and the Whale*, recorded on Gerry's 1976 album *Rags to Gladrags*.

During 1972 and 1973 Gerry toured the US, Canada and Europe as part of huge package tours featuring these artistes. After years of performing at the small clubs and pubs of the folk and blues circuit, Gerry was suddenly playing an opening set in front of crowds of tens of thousands of people. The US and Canadian tour headlined by **Joe Cocker** lasted three months and involved 40 concerts at venues, including Madison Square Gardens in New York and The Forum in Los Angeles. This was followed by a two-month European tour through France, Holland, Italy, Germany and England.

Being under the same management as **Joe Cocker, The Grease Band, Rod Stewart and The Faces** also resulted in Gerry recording two albums, featuring a stellar cast of accompanying musicians. These included: Ronnie Wood, Mick Ralphs, Henry McCulloch, Neil Hubbard, Alan Spenner, Philip Chen, **Pete Wingfield**, Mel Collins, Bruce Rowlands and his old friend **Cliff Aungier**, amongst others.

These albums, *Wun* (released in 1972) and *Rags to Gladrags* (released in 1976) represented a new direction for Gerry. His self-penned compositions came to the fore including introspective and family-inspired songs such as *Father To Your Children, My Brother, Temptations* and the chilling elegy *She Was A Very Good Friend Of Mine* (written about his late mother).

During the mid - 1970s Gerry's live work started to incorporate a PA system which enabled him to reach new audiences. Around this time he also started to use the relatively new Ovation Legend guitar (complete with built-in electric pick-ups) which was easier to play with amplification. This change from the classic Martin D28 may have caused slight consternation amongst folk and blues purists but Gerry considered his style had to develop further. And after all, he had already made a huge contribution to the world of acoustic blues guitar with his early albums and live work playing the Martin D28.

Gerry's developing style was captured on later albums including *Rally 'Round The Flag* (1976, live in Germany, featuring Matt Walsh), *The Shattered Eye* (1979, with Ian Hunt), *Total* (1980, with Ian Hunt), *Across The Tracks* (solo, 1981) and *Cushioned For A Soft Ride Inside* (with Hans Theessink, 1981).

His last solo album, 1981s *Across The Tracks* (self-produced and solo-performed) featured the blistering self-penned gospel-style blues, 'My soul is gonna rest with my God' with Gerry's vocal resembling Blind Willie Johnson and Howlin' Wolf. However, it was during this prosperous time that tragedy struck during late 1981. During a tour of Belgium and Holland Gerry started suffering heart problems, which culminated in a heart attack and stroke, depriving Gerry of the use of his left hand. This failure of his health effectively ended his career as a professional musician. After six years struggle he suffered a fatal heart attack on 17th November 1987. (VJ/GL)

Locomotive

Personnel:	NORMAN HAINES	keyb'ds, vcls	A
	MICK HINCKS	bs, vcls	A
	BOB LAMB	drms	A
	MIKE TAYLOR	trumpet	A
	(LYN DOBSON	sax	A)
	(DICK HECKSTALL-SMITH	sax	A)

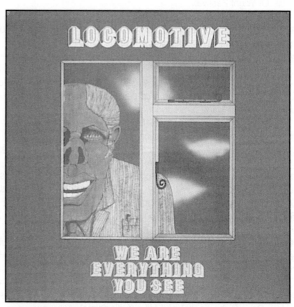

LOCOMOTIVE - We Are Everything You See (LP).

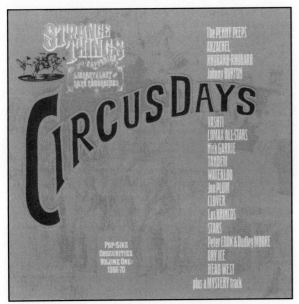

CIRCUS DAYS VOL. 1 (Comp CD) including Jackie Lomax.

(HENRY LOWTHER	trumpet	A)
(BILL MADGE	sax	A)
(CHRIS MERCER	sax	A)
(CHRIS WOOD	woodwind	A)

ALBUM: 1(A) WE ARE EVERYTHING YOU SEE
(Parlophone PCS 7093) 1969 R3

NB: (1) reissued on Zap! (ZAP 5) 1988 and on CD Shoestring (BL 003) 1995.(1) reissued on vinyl (Radioactive RRLP 042) and remastered from the original tapes.

EP: 1 Rudi's In Love/Mr. Armageddon/There's Got To Be A Way/
        Never Set Me Free (PS)   (EMI EMI 2960) 1979

HCP

45s: Rudy A Message To You/
      Broken Heart   (Direction 58-3114) 1967 SC -
      Rudi's In Love/
      Never Set Me Free   (Parlophone R 5718) 1968 SC 25
    α Mr. Armageddon/
      There's Got To Be A Way   (Parlophone R 5758) 1969 R1 -
      I'm Never Gonna Let You Go/
      You Must Be Joking   (Parlophone R 5801) 1969 SC -
      Roll Over Mary/
      Movin' Down The Line   (Parlophone R 5835) 1970 -
Reissues: Rudi's In Love/You Must Be Joking (Parlophone R 5835) 1971 -
      Rudi's In Love/Never Set Me Free (PS)   (EMI EMI 5033) 1980 -

NB: α some promo copies were issued with a picture sleeve (R2).

This Birmingham-based band included Chris Wood who was later a founder member of **Traffic**. They enjoyed a Top Thirty hit at the time with their ska-styled *Rudi's In Love*. Nowadays their rare album attracts interest from connoisseurs of progressive rock. Far and away the best track on it is *Mr. Armageddon*, a stunningly powerful slice of doomy psych/progressive crossover with brass (!), which deserved far more success than it achieved when issued as a 45.

The album, produced by Gus Dudgeon, also includes versions of *Coming Down* and *Love Song For the Dead Ché* (songs written by Joseph Byrd and performed with his band The United States Of America on their album). Certainly an album well worth investigating.

Locomotive member **Norman Haines** had earlier played in a mid-sixties beat band called The Brumbeats, but not the band who issued a 45. **Haines** soon became **Locomotive's** main songwriter, writing their first 45, *Broken Heart*, a soul-based number. The flip was a version of the bluebeat number, *Rudy, A Message To You*. The Jamaican influence remained with **Haines** when he wrote *Rudi's In Love*, a dance number which became a hit in the short-term but a millstone in the long-term since it prevented the group from being taken seriously as a progressive rock band which is what they really wanted to be. This was a great pity 'cos their next 45 was the excellent *Mr. Armageddon*, which was their finest moment and had the

potential in 1969 to be a hit, instead it flopped. Their fourth single was a cover of ? and The Mysterians' *I'm Never Gonna Let You Go*, a much more poppy offering, though the flip, *You Must Be Joking*, was a progressive rock number also featured on their album. When this too bombed the writing was on the wall and Mick Hincks and Bob Lamb soon departed to form **Dog That Bit People**. **Norman Haines** went on to form Sacrifice (who did not record) but after their demise EMI released an album of their material credited to the **Norman Haines' Band**. It is now one of the very rarest artefacts of UK progressive rock and much coveted by collectors.

The recent Shoestring CD reissue of their album comes with 12 bonus tracks, including both sides of their 1968 45 for Direction, all their non-album 45s for Parlophone, a 45 on Transatlantic they recorded under the pseudonym of Steam Shovel and two previously unissued tracks:- *Rudi Catch The Monster* and *My Girl Blue*.

Compilation appearances have included: *Mr. Armageddon* on *My Generation* (LP), *Not Just Beat Music 1965-70* (LP), *Psychedelia At Abbey Road* (CD), *British Psychedelic Trip, Vol. 2* (LP) and *Great British Psychedelic Trip, Vol. 3* (LP); *Rudi's In Love* on *20 One Hit Wonders* and *Colour Me Pop, Vol 1* (CD); whilst *Roll Over Mary* can be heard on *Pop-In, Vol 1* (CD). (VJ)

John Lodge

ALBUM: 1 NATURAL AVENUE   (London PS-683) 1973

This solo album by **Moody Blues** member **John Lodge** was recorded prior to the **Blue Jays** project. (VJ)

Jackie Lomax

ALBUMS:	1	IS THIS WHAT YOU WANT? (mono/stereo)	
(up to			(Apple (S) APCOR 6) 1969 R2/R1
1976)	2	HOME IS IN MY HEAD	(Warner Bros K 46091) 1971
	3	THREE	(Warner Bros K 46151) 1972
	4	LIVIN' FOR LOVIN'	(Capitol 11558) 1976

NB: (1) reissued on CD (Apple CDP 797512), cassette and vinyl (Apple SAPCOR 6) with a bonus 12" (SAPCOR 62) (SC) in 1991. (2) reissued on CD (Rhino/Warners 8122 78466 2) 2005 with bonus tracks and again on CD (Water WATER 153). (3) reissued on CD (Rhino/Warners 8122 78467 2) 2005 with bonus tracks and again on CD (Water WATER 154).

45s: Genuine Imitation Life/One Minute Woman (CBS 2554) 1968 SC
(up to Sour Milk Sea/
1976) The Eagle Laughs At You   (Apple APPLE 3) 1968 SC
      New Day/I Fall Inside Your Eyes (Apple APPLE 11) 1969 SC
      How The Web Was Woven/
      Thumbin' A Ride (Some PS)   (Apple APPLE 23) 1970 SC/-
      Helluva Woman/Higher Ground   (Warner Bros K 16104) 1971
      Peace Of Mind/Blue World   (Capitol CL 15897) 1976

Lomax was born in Wallasey, Merseyside, on 10th May 1944. His first band was a Wallasey group called Dee and The Dynamites. Then in early 1962 he joined **The Undertakers** until their demise in December 1964. He formed **Lomax Alliance** in 1967 and then embarked on a solo career which was interrupted by his involvement in 1969 in **Heavy Jelly**. Some references say he was also in **Balls**, but as he was still recording for Apple at the time, this is probably false.

Lomax then became one of Apple's first signings and **George Harrison** supervised his promising recordings with the label. *Is This What You Want?* was laid-back white-boy soul. With the demise of Apple he moved on to Warner Brothers for whom he recorded a couple of critically acclaimed albums before joining **Badger** in the mid-seventies.

Home Is In The Head was a definite advance on his first effort - a more confident album and it contained some nice bluesy riffs and nasal vocals. *Three* was funkier and featured Bernard Purdy (Aretha Franklin's drummer) and a horn section. Shortly after its release he was dropped by Warner, which was a shame because it was four more years before he made any further solo recordings.

515

He secured a contract with Capitol and returned with *Livin' For Lovin'* in 1976. After a further solo album, *Did You Ever*, in 1977 and he moved to the US.

Lomax based himself in Los Angeles and opted out of the music business for the remainder of the seventies and kept a very low profile in the eighties confining himself to a few appearances playing guitar locally. His career was boasted by the release of a CD compiling **The Undertakers'** output at the end of the decade and the reissue of his debut album on CD in 1981. In 2001 he issued a new solo album, *The Ballad Of Liverpool Slim*.

Compilation appearances include: *Honey Machine* a soul/R&B style number by the Lomax All Stars on *Circus Days Vol. 1 & 2* (CD) and *Circus Days, Vol. 1* (LP) and *One Minute Woman* on *Colour Me Pop, Vol 2* (CD). (VJ)

Lomax Alliance

Personnel:	JOHN CANNING	gtr	A
	JACKIE LOMAX	vcls, gtr	A
	BUGS PEMBERTON	drms	A
	TOM PETERS	bs	A

45:     Try As You May/See The People   (CBS 2729) 1967 SC

As the name suggests this Merseyside group was formed by **Lomax** who'd previously been with **The Undertakers**. After this one 45 (the flip side is a worthwhile specimen of psych-pop) he embarked on a solo career. Canning and Peters were Americans who'd previously played played together in US band, The Lost Souls.

Try As You May can also be heard on *Magic Spectacles* (CD).

Originally managed by Brian Epstein, the band was later managed by Robert Stigwood. (VJ)

The Londoners

Personnel:	PAUL GURVITZ	gtr	AB
	BRIAN MORRIS	gtr	AB
	MICK PALMER	bs	AB
	STAN ?	drms	A
	TOPPER CLAY	drms	B

45:   α   That's My Desire/Bring It On Home   (Star Club 148530) 1965
NB: α released in Germany.

From Ilford, this band formed in 1963 to play American bases in Germany. Upon returning to the UK, they played around London, before becoming the backing band for Gene Vincent. In May 1964, Topper Clay took over on drums and they continued as Vincent's backing group.

In spring 1965 they headed back to Germany to play the Star Club circuit around Bremen, Koln, Hanover and of course at Hamburg's Star Club, returning occasionally to the UK to gig and record. The 'A' side to their sole 45 was a slow, melodic Merseybeat version with harmony vocals and the 'B' side was Sam Cooke's classic covered in the UK by **The Animals** (1965) and **The Big Three** (1964) among others.

In 1966, they met and recorded with Larry Page, who renamed the band as **The Knack**.

Compilation appearances include: *That's My Desire* and *Bring It On Home To Me* on *The Star-Club Singles Complete, Vol. 4* (LP & CD) and *Beat Battle At The Star-Club, Vol. 1* (LP); *That's My Desire* on *Beat Im Star Club* (2-LP); *Bring It On Home To Me* on *Sweet Beat* (LP); and *Back In The USA* on *Star Club Scene '65* (LP). (VJ/TCy)

London Studio Group

ALBUM: 1   THE WILD ONE (10" LP) (De Wolf DW/LP 2974) 1966 SC

This project involved members of a fifties outfit the Ivor and Basil Kirchen Band who recorded on Parlophone. (VJ)

LONGDANCER - Trailer For A Good Life (LP).

London Underground

ALBUM: 1   LONDON UNDERGROUND   (Conroy BMLP 092) 1972

This is a sub-prog instrumental library album. Although credited to L Paul Phillips it is rumoured to be by Dave Brock of **Hawkwind**. (GCn)

London Waits

45:     Softly Softly/Serenadio   (Immediate IM 030) 1966 SC

Another rare and quite collectable instrumental 45.

Softly Softly can also be heard on *Immediate Single Collection, Vol. 5* (CD). (VJ)

Long and The Short

Personnel:	ALAN GRUNDY	bs	A
	BOB McKINLEY	vcls	A
	LES SAINT	gtr	A
	BOB TAYLOR	lead gtr	A
	GERRY WAFF	drms	A

HCP
45s: The Letter/Love Is A Funny Thing (Decca F 11964) 1964 SC 30
       Choc Ice/Here Comes The Fool   (Decca F 12043) 1964 SC 49

Considering they enjoyed two minor hits this outfit remains long forgotten. In fact all four songs were ordinary beat numbers, or worse, so it's understandable that they remain uncompiled. The first 45 was produced by Mike Leander. They also appeared in the film 'Gonks Go Beat'. (VJ/AD)

Longboatmen

45:   α   Only In Her Home Town/
          Take Her Any Time   (Polydor 56115) 1966 R5
NB: α has been repressed in a limited edition of 500 with a large centre hole.

This is an extremely rare freakbeat-style single. Originals (should you ever be lucky enough to find them) can change hands for over £500. (VJ)

Longdancer

Personnel:	BRIAN HARRISON	gtr, bs, vcls	AB
	KAI OLSSON	gtr, vcls	A
	STEVE SPROXTON	gtr, vcls	AB

DAVE STEWART	gtr, bs, vcls	AB
MATT IRVING	keyb'ds, gtr, bs, vcls	B
CHARLIE SMITH	drms, vcls	B

ALBUMS: 1(A)   IF IT WAS SO SIMPLE   (Rocket PIGL 1) 1973
        2(B)   TRAILER FOR A GOOD LIFE   (Rocket PIGL 6) 1974

45s: If It Was So Simple/Silent Emotions   (Rocket PIG 1) 1973
      Puppet Man/Cold Love   (Rocket PIG 11) 1974

This band is most significant for including future Tourists and Eurythmics member Dave Stewart. They grew out of a duo comprising Stewart and Harrison, which worked in the clubs around the northeast of England, recording an EP in 1971 for the local Multichord label. They became **Longdancer** when Olsson and Sproxton were added to make the band a four-piece. They signed to **Elton John**'s Rocket label in 1973 and became the first artists to record on the label, though the resulting album and 45 made little impression at the time. After touring with **Elton John** Olsson left and Irving and Smith came in to record a second album. Their brand of folk-rock with occasional country influences was rather passé by the mid-seventies. *Trailer For A Good Life* was pleasant enough but the music lacked excitement. The better tracks were *The Ship* with its bagpipe intro; the countryish *Country Song; Sweet Leaves* and *Mother Nature*. Dave Stewart's *Trailer* and *Cold Love* were among the weakest.

After **Longdancer** split up, Harrison and Smith played for folkies **Robin and Barry Dransfield**. Smith was also later in Blue. Olsson made a solo album for Chrysalis in 1979. In the eighties Irving was in Lords Of The New Church. Finally, as most of you will know, Dave Stewart formed The Tourists in 1977. Then in the eighties he was in Eurythmics. (VJ)

Claudine Longet

45s: Good Day Sunshine/The Look Of Love   (A&M AMS 708) 1967
      Claudine   (A&M AMS 903) 1967

In addition to the above she has a cut *Wanderlove* compiled on *Spinning Wheel* (CD). (VJ)

Long Hello

Personnel:	HUGH BANTON	bs	A
	CED CURTIS	gtr	A
	GUY EVANS	drms	A
	DAVID JACKSON	sax, flute, piano	A
	PIERO MESSINA	gtr, piano	A
	NIC POTTER	bs	A

ALBUM: 1(A)   THE LONG HELLO   (Private Pressing) 1973 SC

This was basically a **Van der Graaf Generator** offshoot. The privately-pressed album was for sale by mail order only. **Van der Graaf** regulars Banton, Evans, Potter and Jackson were joined by Curtis and Messina for this project, which was produced by Guy Evans and engineered by Hugh Banton to give it a real 'home demo' feel. Musically, it's long rambling jazz-rock tunes and improvisations were gentle and quite relaxing in their own way.

Later albums were made, beyond the time span of this book, which revolved around **Van der Graaf** members but they were a pretty fluid line-up. (MWh)

Looking Glass

45:     Can You Believe/Freedom In Our Time   (Philips BF 1837) 1970

This was a pick-up band featuring **Sunny and Sue**. (VJ)

Loose Ends

Personnel incl: ALAN MARSHALL   drms   A

45s: Send The People Away/I Ain't Gonna
      Eat My Heart Out Anymore   (Decca F 12437) 1966 SC

    Taxman/That's It   (Decca F 12476) 1966 R1

Loose Ends was from Birmingham. *Send The People Away* was a **Moody Blues** number and *Taxman* was a **Beatles**' cover.

Compilation appearances include: *That's It* on *The Mod Scene* (CD); *Send The People Away* on *Rare 60's Beat Treasures, Vol. 3* (CD); *I Ain't Gonna Eat Out My Heart Anymore* on *Twisted Teenage Screaming Fuzzbusters* (LP) and *Broken Dreams, Vol. 2* (LP); and *Taxman* on *The Freakbeat Scene* (CD). (VJ)

The Loot

Personnel:	CHRIS BATES	vcls	A
	JEFF GLOVER	bs	A
	ROGER POPE	drms	A
	BRUCE TURNER	ld gtr	A
	DAVE WRIGHT	gtr	A

45s: Baby Come Closer/Baby   (Page One POF 013) 1966
      Whenever You're Ready/
      I Got What You Want   (CBS 2938) 1967 SC
      I've Just Gotta Love You/
      You Need Someone To Love   (Page One POF 026) 1967 SC
  α   She's A Winner/Save Me   (Page One POF 095) 1968 R1
      Don't Turn Around/You Are My Sunshine Girl   (CBS 3231) 1968
      Try To Keep It A Secret/
      Radio City   (Page One POF 115) 1969 SC

NB: α originally issued with *Radio City* on the 'B' side but this was withdrawn. Demos also exist with *Save Me* on the 'A' side and *She's A Winner* on the flip. On some copies *Save Me* is mistyped as *Help Me*. *Singles As and Bs* (Radioactive RRCD 057) 2005 includes the above cuts as well as rare demos and French-only singles. It's also available in vinyl (Radioactive RRLP 057) 2005.

The band came from the Andover area of Hampshire where Wright had been an early member of **The Troggs**. Indeed they were signed by **Troggs** manager Larry Page to his Page One label and met with moderate success. *Don't Turn Around* and psychedelically-tainted *Radio City* are usually regarded as their most interesting efforts, but their best-known song was *Baby Come Closer*, which sounds very similar to **The Troggs**. The 'B' side was a very fine pop teaser, enhanced by one of Larry Page's ultra-compressed productions. The *She's A Winner* 45 was produced by Ronnie Bond of **The Troggs**.

Glover and Pope had earlier been in **The Soul Agents** and went on to play for **Hookfoot**. Ian Duck is also thought to have been in **The Loot** too and he was in **Hookfoot** as well. Later on Roger Pope became **Elton John**'s full-time drummer.

Singles As and Bs compiles their UK singles, as well as rare demos and some French-only singles. This is an attractive release for psych-pop fans.

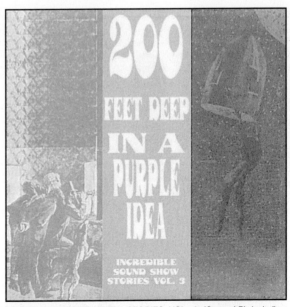

INCREDIBLE SOUND SHOW STORIES VOL. 3 (Comp LP) including The Loot.

Compilation appearances have included: *She's A Winner* on *Rare 60's Beat Treasures, Vol. 3* (CD); *She's A Winner* and *I Got What You Want* on *Red With Purple Flashes, Vol. 1* (LP); *Baby Come Closer, Whenever You're Ready, I Got What You Want, Try To Keep It A Secret, She's A Winner, Save Me* and *Radio City* on *Untamed And Innocent* (CD); *Try To Keep It A Secret* on *We Can Fly, Vol 1* (CD); *Baby Come Closer* on *English Freakbeat, Vol. 1* (LP & CD); *Radio City* on *Incredible Sound Show Stories, Vol. 3* (LP); *Whenever You're Ready* on *Jagged Time Lapse, Vol 3* (CD) and *Don't Turn Around* on *Jagged Time Lapse, Vol 5* (CD). (VJ/SP)

Jon Lord

ALBUMS:	1	GEMINI SUITE	(Purple TPSA 7501) 1971 SC
(up to	2	WINDOWS	(Purple TPSA 7513) 1974 SC
1976)	3	SARABANDE	(Purple TPSA 7516) 1976 SC

NB: (3) issued on CD (Line LICD 900124) 1989.

| 45: | Bouree/Aria | (Purple PUR 131) 1976 |

Lord is best known as a member of heavy rockers **Deep Purple** though he'd been a member of **The Artwoods** back in the mid-sixties and also played briefly with a band called **Roundabout** who evolved out of **The Loot** in early 1968, which didn't record but included Nick Simper and **Ritchie Blackmore** and evolved into the first **Deep Purple** line-up. Despite these solo efforts he didn't make much impact on his own and after being involved in a short-lived and very unremarkable supergroup **Paice, Ashton and Lord**, during 1976/77 he joined Whitesnake. (VJ)

Tony Lord

| 45: | World's Champion/It Makes Me Sad | (Planet PLF 102) 1966 SC |

This obscure solo artist's only vinyl offering seems to have been this one 45. A ballad, it was produced by Shel Talmy.

World's Champion has been compiled on *The Best Of Planet Records* (CD). (VJ)

Lords

| 45s: | Don't Mince Matters/No One Knows | (Columbia DB 8121) 1967 |
| | Gloryland/Gypsy Boy | (Columbia DB 8367) 1968 |

An obscure outfit whose *Don't Mince Matters* has been compiled on *We Can Fly, Vol 2* (CD). (VJ)

LORD SITAR - Lord Sitar (CD).

Lord Sitar

| ALBUM: | 1 | LORD SITAR | (Columbia SX/SCX 6256) 1968 R2 |

NB: (1) also released in the US (Capitol ST 2916). (1) reissued on CD (Zonophone 493616) 2005.

A minor collectable boosted in value by speculations that **Lord Sitar** was **George Harrison** whose interest in sitars and gurus was well-known. Competent instrumentals include covers of *Daydream Believer, I Am The Walrus, Eleanor Rigby, I Can See For Miles, Black Is Black* and more and make for pleasant if languid listening. The mystery person behind the album turns out to be U.K. session super-hero Big Jim Sullivan. (MW)

Gary and Jan Lorraine

| Personnel: | GARY LORRAINE | A |
| | JAN LORRAINE | A |

45s:	I'm Not To Blame/Alone Again	(Pye 7N 15836) 1965
	To Stay Alive/	
	They've Changed The Clouds	(Pye 7N 15898) 1965
α	Do You Want Me To Tell Him/	
	So Many People To Pity	(Pye 7N 15985) 1965

NB: α as Gary and Jan.

Gary and Jan were the children of composer/arranger Tony Osborne. The first 45 is pleasant pop. The second is more folky. Gary wrote both sides of that one. The third effort was arranged by Tony Osborne. Gary Lorraine was later in the UK **Chocolate Watchband**.

Do You Want Me To Tell Him has resurfaced on *Ripples, Vol. 4* (CD). (VJ)

The Lost

Personnel:	CHRIS HATT	ld gtr	AB
	MARTIN HATT	bs	AB
	BILL HEATH	ld vcls	AB
	JAKE WALTON	drms	AB
	PATRICK HANNAY	piano	B
	MIC READ	gtr	B

| ALBUM: | 1(-) | LOST IN ACTION | (Tenth Planet TP 009) 1994 |

NB: (1) is a numbered limited edition of 500.

Originally known as Paradise Lost this band were formed in 1964 by Bill Heath whilst he was at Uppingham Public School in Rutland. The early line-up fluctuated quite a bit but eventually stabilised into 'A' above. They started out playing R&B and in August 1966 visited R.G. Jones' recording studio in Mordon, Surrey. The session produced a cover version of *Neighbour, Neighbour*, a recent Stax single by Jimmy Hughes, which was also recorded by **The Spectres** (a pre-**Status Quo** act) and a **Rolling Stones**'-influenced Bill Heath/Chris Hatt composition, *Problems Of Day To Day Living*, but neither recording made it onto vinyl. They were augmented for this session by Stu Taylor, who'd been with The Tornadoes and The Savages (**Screaming Lord Sutch**'s band).

By 1967 they were known as simply **The Lost** and a seven-track single-sided acetate album was cut at a Birmingham studio. The featured tracks were four Bill Heath/Chris Hatt compositions:- *Problems Of Day To Day Living, Bread Van, The Times Are Gone* and *Something To Us*; covers of **The Rolling Stones**' *Spider And The Fly* and Chuck Berry's *Guitar Boogie* and a Chris Hatt instrumental *Lost In Paradise*. Of their originals *Something To Us* was arguably the most complete.

The Lost then augmented their line-up with the recruitment of pianist Patrick Hannay and ex-**Amber** guitarist **Mike Read**. This new line-up returned to R.G. Jones' studio cutting two new tracks - the raw and primitive *What's The Matter (With You Babe)* and *Don't Open Your Mind*, but still there was no record company interest. *Don't Open Your Mind* was a pulsating number which they later re-recorded as **Just Plain Smith**.

THE LOST - Lost In Action (LP).

In mid-1968 Heath and Walton departed to tour the world. The Hatt brothers teamed up with Charlie Adamson (who'd been one of the early drummers with Paradise Lost) and vocalist John Vaughan in a temporary band, Undergrowth Of Literature. Their tour manager was future Radio One disc jockey Peter Powell and they also cut an acetate album at R.G. Jones' studio.

The Lost had reformed by Autumn 1968, returning to R.G. Jones' studio to record a piece of pop-psychedelia, *Ernest Seymour, The Man From 66c*, but again it failed to secure a commercial release, although it was easily their most inventive recording. In mid-1969 they evolved into **Just Plain Smith**.

In 1994 Tenth Planet released a 14-track compilation of the band's material, *Lost In Action*, along with quite an extensive history of the band on the sleevenotes on which this article is based. Three of the finest moments:- *What's The Matter (With You Babe)*, *Don't Open Your Mind* and *Ernest Seymour, The Man From 66c* were also re-recorded by the band as a limited edition single in December 1993, which came with the Tenth Planet album. The original recordings of these songs also can be found on *Syde Trips, Vol. 2* (LP). (VJ)

Loudest Whisper

Personnel incl: BRIAN O'REILLY   A

ALBUM: 1(A) THE CHILDREN OF LIR (w/insert)   (Polydor) 1973 R5
NB: (1) released in Ireland and reissued again on vinyl in Ireland as *Loudest Whisper* (Polydor 2908 043) 1981 (R3). (1) reissued on CD by Kissing Spell with three bonus tracks. (1) reissued again on CD (Si-Wan SRMC 4039) on a Korean label. (1) has also been re-recorded with **Donovan** and released as *Brian O'Reilly (with Donovan)* (Si-Wan SRMC 2024). This version features narration and vocals by **Donovan**. Kissing Spell has also put out two previously unreleased albums: *11* (Kissing Spell KSCD 9501) and *Maiden Of Sorrow* (an unreleased album from 1975) (Kissing Spell KSCD 9507).

A very rare progressive folk album by an Irish band from Cork, *The Children Of Lir* recounts the myth of King Lir and his children, who are condemned to live as swans. The group had in fact been together for over a decade when the album was made. Employing acoustic and electric instrumentation as well as prominent string arrangements, its mellow and fragile one moment, jagged and rocking the next. The UK branch of Polydor rejected it, however, and it's thought that only 500 Irish copies were ever pressed. The band went on to record *Hard Times* (Fiona 011) (w/insert), which was another Ireland-only release in 1983. Both their albums are very rare and collectable, but *Lir* is generally considered their best and is certainly the most sought-after.

Compilation appearances have included: *She Moves Through The Fair* on *The History Of U.K. Underground Folk Rock 1968-1978 Vol. 1* (CD); and *Silent O'Moyle* on *The History Of U.K. Underground Folk Rock 1968-1978 Vol. 2* (CD). (BS/VJ/RMJ)

The Love Affair

Personnel:	MAURICE BACON	drms	ABCDE
	REX BRAYLEY	gtr	ABCDE
	STEVE ELLIS	vcls	ABCD
	MORGAN FISHER	keyb'ds	ABCDE
	MICK JACKSON	bs	ABCDE
	PETER BARDENS	keyb'ds	B
	LYNTON GUEST	keyb'ds	C
	GUS EADEN	vcls	E

ALBUMS: 1(C) THE EVERLASTING LOVE AFFAIR (CBS 63416) 1968 SC
        2( ) NEW DAY IN LA   (CBS 64109) 1970 SC
        3(-) GOLDEN ERA OF POP MUSIC (CBS 68255) 1973
NB: (1) reissued on CD as *Everlasting Hits* (Columbia 982828 2) 1992, with the *One Road* 45 added as a bonus. *Greatest Hits* (Autograph ASK 774) 1985 was a cassette-only release. *Everlasting Love* (Bear Tracks BTS 943 406) 1989 was a vinyl compilation available as a German import. *The Everlasting Love Affair* (Columbia 483673 2) 1996 is a mid-price reissue CD which captures their first two albums on one disc. *No Strings Every Now And Then* (Angel Air SJPCD 0071) 2000 is a compilation. *Singles A's and B's* (Arcadia 8031) 2002 also includes four previously unreleased 1966 efforts and some **Steve Ellis** solo tracks.

EP: 1(-) LOVE AFFAIR   (Scoop SR 5037) 1984
NB: This was available on 7" and 12" formats and featured all their hits.

HCP

45s:	She Smiled Sweetly/		
	Satisfaction Guaranteed	(Decca F 12558) 1967	R2 -
	Everlasting Love/		
	Gone Are The Songs Of Yesterday	(CBS 3125) 1967	1
	Rainbow Valley/		
	Someone Like Us (Some in PS)	(CBS 3366) 1968	SC/- 5
	A Day Without Love/I'm Happy	(CBS 3674) 1968	6
	One Road/Let Me Know	(CBS 3994) 1969	16
	Bringing On Back The Good Times/		
	Another Day	(CBS 4300) 1969	9
	Baby I Know/Accept Me For What I Am	(CBS 4631) 1969	-
	Lincoln County/Sea Of Tranquility	(CBS 4780) 1970	-
	Speak Of Peace Sing Of Joy/		
	Brings My Whole World Tumbling Down	(CBS 5017) 1970	-
	Wake Me I Am Dreaming/		
	That's My Home	(Parlophone R 5887) 1971	-
	Help (Get Me Some Help)/		
	Long Way Home	(Parlophone R 5918) 1971	-
	Let Me Dance/Love's Looking Out At You	(Pye 7N 45218) 1973	-
	Private Lives/Let A Little Love Come In	(Creole CR 146) 1977	-
Reissues:	Everlasting Love/		
	Bringing On Back The Good Times (PS)	(CBS CBS 1144) 1973	-
	Everlasting Love/		
	Bringing On Back The Good Times	(CBS CBS 3967) 1976	-
	A Day Without Love	(Stagecoach BANG 4) 1981	-

LOUDEST WHISPER - Children Of Lir (CD).

Everlasting Love/
A Day Without Love   (Old Gold OG 9194) 1982 -
Rainbow Valley/
Bringing On Back The Good Times   (Old Gold OG 9199) 1982 -

This London-based band was put together by Sid Bacon in late 1966 who was keen for his son Maurice to have a group to play in. They played at various London clubs and enjoyed a Marquee residency before going professional in mid-1967 when Fisher left to go to college and was replaced briefly by **Peter Bardens** from **Shotgun Express** but then by Lyton Guest.

After recording a cover of **Jagger**/Richards' *She Smiled Sweetly* for Decca they switched to CBS, recording a version of *Everlasting Love*, which had been a hit in the US for soul singer Robert Knight. Rather unexpectedly it shot to No 1 in January 1968 - it was one of those classic pop songs with immediate appeal. They covered another Robert Knight song, *Rainbow Valley*, for the follow-up and again it made the UK Top 10.

Lacking any real songwriting ability themselves they turned to Philip Goodhand-Tait material for their next three singles - *A Day Without Love*, *One Road* and *Bringing On Back The Good Times* - which were all competent and appealing pop singles. However, their longer-term prospects were damaged by revelations that they didn't play on their albums.

The Everlasting Love Affair album comprised their first three CBS singles, plus a selection of cover versions and originals. The former included *The First Cut Is The Deepest* (P.P. Arnold), *Tobacco Road* (**Nashville Teens**), *Hush* (**Deep Purple**), *Handbags And Gladrags* (**Mike D'Abo**) and a different pop/rock interpretation of the Hayes/Porter soul number *60 Minutes (Of Your Love)*. The originals were pop ditties like *Could I Be Dreaming*, *The Tree* and *Once Upon A Season* and the Cockney-laden *Tale Of Two Bitters*.

By early 1970 **Steve Ellis** had recorded a solo 45 and then departed to form **Ellis** and then **Widowmaker**. He was replaced by Gus Eaden. CBS dropped the group and they switched to Parlophone for now two hard-to-find 45s. By 1971 Bacon and Fisher left to form **Morgan**, though the latter went on to **Mott The Hoople**. Jackson left too soon after but the group soldiered on until Lynton Guest departed to form **English Rose**. Basically, **Love Affair** were a good pop group, no more and no less.

No Strings compiles material from their earlier incarnation as The Soul Survivors through their more successful days with some **Steve Ellis** solo songs and *It's A Love Affair* from a 1999 reunion. There are some cover versions too of *Hush*, *First Cut Is The Deepest* and *Handbags And Gladrags*. *Singles A's and B's* also includes four previously unreleased tracks, most notable a version of Philip Goodhand Tait's delightful *Do You Dream?*, which was recorded by his band **Circus** a couple of years later. There are also half a dozen **Steve Ellis** solo tracks from the early seventies, although they are not noteworthy.

Compilation appearances include: *Everlasting Love* and *Gone Are The Songs Of Yesterday* on *Sixties Years, Vol. 5* (CD); *Everlasting Love* on the 2-CD set *60 Number Ones Of The Sixties*; *The Tree* on *Jagged Time Lapse, Vol 5* (CD) and *Lincoln County* on *Pop-In, Vol 1* (CD). (VJ)

The Love Children

45s: Easy Squeezy/Every Little Step   (Deram DM 268) 1969
        Paper Chase/My Turkey Snuffed It   (Deram DM 303) 1970

A harmony-pop group whose *Paper Chase* could almost be mistaken for pure Los Angeles harmony-pop but for the British accents and the fact it's not quite the real McCoy.

Paper Chase has been compiled on *British Psychedelic Trip, Vol. 4* (LP) and *Great British Psychedelic Trip, Vol. 2* (CD). (VJ)

Love Sculpture

Personnel: TOMMY RILEY   drms, vcls   A
             DAVE EDMUNDS   gtr, keyb'ds, vcls   ABC
             JOHN WILLIAMS   vcls, bs, keyb'ds   ABC
             BOB JONES   drms, vcls   B
             TERRY WILLIAMS   drms   C
             MICKEY GEE   gtr   C

ALBUMS: 1(B)   BLUES HELPING (mono/stereo)
                              (Parlophone PMC/PCS 7059) 1968 R1
        2(B)   FORMS AND FEELINGS (Parlophone PCS 7090) 1969 R1
        3(B)   CLASSIC TRACKS   (One Up 2047) 1974

NB: (1) and (2) released in the US on Rare and Parrot respectively. Both reissued in UK on Parlophone in 1970. Both released in Germany on EMI Odeon. (1) reissued on CD (EMI 499 4162) 1999. (2) reissued on CD (EMI 4997682) 1999. A later compilation is *The Singles A's and B's* (Harvest SHSM 2032) 1980. *The Dave Edmunds Story, Vol. 1: The Love Sculpture Years* (EMI EMS 1127) 1986 is a repackage of the *Forms And Feelings* album with three bonus tracks. The 2-CD, *The Early Years* (EMI CDS 7 96717 2) 1991 documents his period with **Human Beans**, **Love Sculpture** and Rockpile.

HCP
45s: River To Another Day/
           Brand New Woman   (Parlophone R 5664) 1968 -
           Wang-Dang-Doodle/
           The Stumble   (Parlophone R 5731) 1968 -
           Sabre Dance/Think Of Love (Parlophone R 5744) 1968 5
           Seagull/Farandole   (Parlophone R 5807) 1969 -
           In The Land Of The Few/
           People People   (Parlophone R 5831) 1970 -
Reissues: α Sabre Dance/My White Bicycle   (Old Gold OG 9368) 1983 -
          β Sabre Dance/I Hear You Knocking   (EMI G 452) 1984 -

NB: α Flipside by **Tomorrow**. β Flipside by **Dave Edmunds**.

This Cardiff outfit had evolved out of **Human Beans** in 1968. Having put out *River To Another Day* on 45 Tommy Riley left to be replaced by Bob Jones. They were urged by EMI to record *Blues Helping* in an attempt to cash in on the UK late sixties blues boom, but neither this nor their next 45, a cover of Willie Dixon's *Wang Dang Doodle*, both sides of which were also included on the album, sold at all well. The album mostly included American R&B covers of songs from artists like Ray Charles, Willie Dixon and Elmore James, but their version of *Summertime* was very different to Gershwin's and their version of Freddie King's *Stumble* highlighted **Dave Edmunds'** ferocious guitar work. They will always be best remembered for their Top Ten instrumental hit with their seven-minute breakneck version of Khachaturian's Russian classical piece *Sabre Dance*, which was originally recorded for John Peel's 'Top Gear' Radio show.

Their second album, *Forms And Feelings*, included an 11-minute version of *Sabre Dance*, but the 45's flip side, *Think Of Love*, which featured some distinctive guitar work from **Edmunds**, wasn't featured on the album which was hastily put together to cash in on the singles success. Another album track, *Farandole*, another classic set to rock, was released as a 45 - a bad mistake, because it was too similar to *Sabre Dance*. A further track from the album, *In The Land Of The Few*, which **Edmunds** wrote with Mike Finesilver and Pete Kerr, who'd helped him produce the album, was then

LOVE AFFAIR - New Day (LP).

520

LOVE SCULPTURE - Forms And Feelings (LP).

released as a 45. This was a string-based number with an acoustic guitar intro more in the mould of **Electric Light Orchestra**. Again it flopped and it proved to be their final release. The band departed on a six-week US tour with a new line-up (C). Bob Jones was ousted but later appeared in **Sassafras**. He was replaced by former Dream drummer Terry Williams, and Mickey Gee, who'd briefly appeared in **Joe Cocker's Grease Band** in 1968, came in as a second guitarist. When they returned from America they split. Terry Williams was later in **Man**. **Love Scuplture**'s first drummer Tommy Riley formed The Memphis Band in the mid-seventies. They put out an album in 1972.

The US release of *Forms And Feelings* includes a version of Gustav Holst's *Mars* from *The Planets Suite*, which the Holst estate had prevented from being included on the British pressing. It was not available elsewhere.

Dave Edmunds subsequently enjoyed a successful solo career. The 1974 *Classic Tracks 1968-72* compilation also included four tracks from **Edmunds'** Rockpile era. The *Singles A's And B's* compiles all the **Love Sculpture** and Rockpile 45s as well as the **Human Beans** one.

Compilation appearances have included: *The Stumble* on *My Generation* (LP); *In The Land Of The Few* on *Not Just Beat Music 1965-70* (LP), *British Psychedelic Trip, Vol. 2* (LP) and the 4-CD *Nuggets II* box set; *Seagull* on *Sixties Lost And Found, Vol. 1* (LP); *In The Land Of The Few* and *Sabre Dance* on *Great British Psychedelic Trip, Vol. 3* (CD); *River To Another Day* on *In The Beginning* (LP) and *Jagged Time Lapse, Vol 5* (CD); and *Sabre Dance* on *20 One Hit Wonders* (LP) and on the 3-CD set *Guitar Heroes - Rock The Night Away*. (VJ)

Love Sounds

45: Ebb Tide/Sounds Of Love (Pye 7N 45437) 1975

The 'A' side of this obscure band's 45 was done by The Righteous Brothers. (VJ)

Love Story

45: Stay Awhile/Carrie McGuire (Rak RAK 115) 1971

This was another one-off project. (VJ)

Love Street

Personnel:			
	AIDAN CRANNY	vcls, bs	A
	BRAIN 'ROCKY' O'ROUKE	vcls, gtr	A
	REG WALKER	vcls, drms	A
	PETER YATES	vcls, gtr	A

45: Venus/Rock'n'Roll Woman (Pye 7N 17896) 1970

This was a four-piece from Dublin, playing rock covers from bands like The Lovin' Spoonful, Buffalo Springfield and The Byrds. Their single made it to No 6 in the Irish record charts, where it stayed for three weeks. The band was popular during their short 18-month existence playing to large crowds in the Dublin area. They recorded an album called *On The Way Home*, which was never released and the band broke up in the summer of 1970. (VJ/AC)

Lovin'

45s: Keep On Believin'/
I'm In Command (Page One POF 035) 1967 R1
All You've Got/Do It Again (Page One POF 041) 1967 R1

A good group whose 45s are both quite collectable now. They were produced by Larry Page and both *Keep On Believin'* and *All You've Got*, are appealing slices of pop-psych. *Do It Again* was more **Who**-influenced. The band later became **The Nerve**, releasing four further 45s for Page One.

Compilation appearances have included:- *Keep On Believin'* and *All You've Got* on *Rubble Vol. 16: Glass Orchid Aftermath* (LP) and *Rubble Vol. 9* (CD); *Do It Again* on *Circus Days Vol. 3* (LP & CD); *I'm In Command* on *Magic Spectacles* (CD); and *Do It Again* and *All You've Got* on *Red With Purple Flashes, Vol. 1* (LP). (VJ)

Loving Awareness

Personnel:			
	CHARLEY CHARLES	drms, vcls	A
	MICKEY GALLAGHER	keyb'ds	A
	JOHN TURNBULL	gtr, vcls	A
	NORMAN WATT-ROY	bs, vcls	A

ALBUM: 1(A) LOVING AWARENESS (w/two posters)
(More Love ML 001) 1976 SC

Put together by former Radio Caroline owner and pirate radio pioneer Ronan O'Rahilly and including former **Skip Bifferty**, **Arc** and **Bell and Arc** members Mickey Gallagher and John Turnbull (the latter had also been in **Glencoe** with Norman Watt-Roy), this outfit formed as early as March 1974 but it took a while before Charley Charles was recruited as a permanent drummer. They went to California for six weeks, recording this album whilst they were over there. Copies of the album apparently included two posters. Unfortunately John Turnbull broke a bone in his hand soon after they returned to the UK and the band soon lost momentum after that. Turnbull went on to form Ian Dury's backing band, The Blockheads, which contained Norman Watt Roy too. They have one cut, *Love To Know You* on the 3-CD box set *Radio Caroline Calling - 70's Flashback*. (VJ)

The Loving Kind

Personnel incl: NOEL REDDING gtr A

45s: Accidental Love/
Nothing Can Change This Love (Piccadilly 7N 35299) 1966 SC
I Love The Things You Do/
Treat Me Nice (Piccadilly 7N 35318) 1966 SC
Ain't That Peculiar/
With Rhyme And Reason (Piccadilly 7N 35342) 1966 SC

This soul-tinged beat group came from Folkestone in Kent. They are most notable for including **Noel Redding** before he joined **The Jimi Hendrix Experience**. *Ain't That Peculiar* was a Marvin Gaye song.

Compilation appearances include: *Ain't That Peculiar* on *Piccadilly Story* (CD); and *Accidental Love* and *Nothing Can Change This Love* on *Footsteps To Fame, Vol. 2* (CD). (VJ)

Henry Lowther Band

ALBUM: 1 CHILD SONG (Deram SML 1070) 1970 R2

Lowther was a jazz musician. This solo album is now very rare. He also played with **John Mayall's Bluesbreakers**, **Keef Hartley Band** and **Ricotti and Albuquerque**. (VJ)

Mark Loyd

45s:	I Keep Thinking About You/	
	Will It Be The Same	(Parlophone R 5277) 1965
	Everybody Tries/She Said No	(Parlophone R 5332) 1965
	When Evening Falls/	
	I'm Gonna Find Her	(Parlophone R 5423) 1965 R3

This obscure sixties singer's third single is very sough-after. (VJ)

Lem Lubin

45:	Oh Heartbreaks/Yesterday Don't Go	(Cube BUG 50) 1974

This was a solo effort from this vocalist / bass player who was in a few well known bands:- **Unit 4 + 2**, **Zoot Money**, **Satisfaction** and **Christie**. (VJ)

Lucas and Mike Cotton Sound

Personnel incl: BRUCE MacPHERSON LUCAS

45s:	α	I Saw Pity In The Face Of A Friend/	
		Dance Children Dance	(Polydor 56114) 1966
		Step Out Of Line/	
		Ain't Love Good, Ain't Love Proud	(Pye 7N 17313) 1967 R1
		Soul Serenade/	
		We Got A Thing Going Baby	(MGM MGM 1398) 1968 R1
		Jack And The Beanstalk/	
		Mother-in-Law	(MGM MGM 1427) 1968 SC

NB: α **Lucas** solo.

Bruce MacPherson Lucas was a black American serviceman, who was quite a showman and a good soul singer. He'd originally teamed up with a Norwich band, The Emperors, back in 1963, although their vinyl output was confined to a demo version of *Harlem Shuffle*. In the mid-sixties he joined **Mike Cotton Sound**, playing on several other of their discs aside from the ones specifically credited to him which are shown above. After leaving **Mike Cotton Sound** he put together several other backing groups before ending up on the cabaret circuit.

Ain't Love Good, Ain't Love Proud has been compiled on *Doin' The Mod, Vol. 1* (CD). (VJ)

Trevor Lucas

ALBUM:	1	OVERLANDER	(Reality RY 1002) 1966 R3

45:	Waltzing Matilda/It's On	(Reality RE 505) 1966 SC

Trevor Lucas recorded this album and 45 prior to joining **Eclection** back in 1967 and both are now ultra-rare and sought-after by collectors. He was assisted on the album by Alf Edwards (congas), George Gibbs (bs) and Cyril Harling (fiddle), but it is very much an acquired taste, consisting basically of Australian outback songs such as *Waltzing Matilda*.

An Australian by birth, **Lucas** had come to England to try and establish himself as a folk artist. When **Eclection** split at the end of the sixties, he joined the short-lived **Fotheringay** before becoming a producer for Island Records. In August 1972, he joined **Fairport Convention** remaining with them until the beginning of 1976 when he returned to production work. He married **Sandy Denny** in 1973. (VJ)

Lucifer

ALBUMS:	1	BIG GUN (w/poster/inserts)	(Lucifer LLP 1) 1972 R2
	2	EXIT (w/poster)	(Lucifer LLP 2) 1972 R2

45s:	Don't Care/Hypnosis	(Lucifer L 001) 1971
	Fuck You/Bad	(Lucifer L 003/004) 1972
	Prick/Want It	(Lucifer L 005/006) 1972

These were solo recordings by Peter 'Lucifer' Walker, who'd been in **The Purple Gang** in the late sixties. They were all private pressings and the albums were sold through 'Oz' magazine. Both 1972 singles were also presented as a double pack, black box set (R1). (VJ)

The Ludlows

Personnel incl: JIM McCANN

ALBUM:	1	THE WIND AND THE SEA	(Pye NPL 18150) 1966 SC

45s:	The Last Thing On My Mind/	
	Kisses Sweeter Than Wine	(Pye 7N 15946) 1965
	The Sea Around Us/The Butcher Boys	(Pye 7N 17050) 1966
	The Winds Thro' The Rafters/	
	That's My Song	(Pye 7N 17123) 1966
	Johnny Lad/Pack Up Your Sorrows	(Pye 7N 17221) 1966
	Enniskillen Dragoons/Foggy Dew	(Pye 7N 17319) 1967
	Plaisir D'Amour/Yesterday's Dreams	(Pye 7N 17384) 1967

This group was originally known as The Ludlow Trio and formed in Dublin in 1965. They soon became one of the most popular folk acts in Dublin. They were signed by Pye in 1966 and enjoyed an Irish No 1 with their version of Dominic Behan's *The Sea Around Us*. When they split the following year Jim McCann embarked on a solo career.

Yesterday's Dream can also be heard on *Troubadour's Of Folk: The '60s Acoustic Explosion* (CD). (VJ)

Lulu

			HCP
ALBUMS:	1	SOMETHING TO SHOUT ABOUT	
(up to		(Decca LK 4719) 1965 R2 -	
1976)	2	LULU! (Ace Of Clubs ACL 1232) 1967 R1 -	
	3	THE WORLD OF LULU (Decca PA/SPA 8) 1967 -	
	4	TO SIR WITH LOVE (Soundtrack)	
		(Fontana TL/STL 5446) 1967 R2 -	
	5	LOVE LOVES TO LOVE LULU	
		(Columbia SX/SCX 6201) 1967 R1 -	
	6	LULU'S ALBUM (Columbia SX/SCX 6365) 1969 SC	
	7	THE MOST OF LULU (MFP MFP 5215) 1969 15	
	8	NEW ROUTES (Atco 228 031) 1969 SC -	
	9	THE MOST OF LULU VOLUME 2 (MFP MFP 5254) 1970 -	
	10	MELODY FAIR (Atco 2400 017) 1970 -	
	11	THE WORLD OF LULU VOLUME 2	
		(Decca PA/SPA 94) 1970 -	

NB: (1) reissued on CD (Deram 820 616-2) 1989. (6) and (7) reissued on one CD (EMI 7243 538 850-2) 2002. Compilations on vinyl include: *The Very Best Of Lulu* (Warwick WW 5097) 1980 and *I'm A Tiger* (MFP MFP 5848) 1989. CD compilations include: *I'm A Tiger* (MFP CDMFP 6050) 1989 with three bonus cuts, *The Man Who Sold The World* (Start CHELD 1004), *The EP Collection* (See For Miles SEECD 452) 1994, *The Gold Collection* (EMI CDGOLD 1005) 1996, *The Best Of Lulu* (Spectrum 544 130-2) 1999, *The Best Of Lulu* (Crimson CIMCD 210) 1999, *The Lulu Collection* (HMV 540 506-2) 2002 and *The Greatest Hits* (Mercury 986 582-4) 2003. *The Mickie Most Years* (EMI 5603692) 2005 is a 2-CD set of her material for Coumbia.

EP:	LULU	(Decca DFE 8597) 1965 R1

			HCP
45s	α	Shout/Forget Me Baby	(Decca F 11884) 1964 7
(up to		Can't Hear You No More/I Am In Love	(Decca F 11965) 1964 -
1976)		Hear Comes The Night/	
		That's Really Some Good	(Decca F 12017) 1964 50
		Satisfied/Surprise Surprise	(Decca F 12128) 1965 SC
		Leave A Little Love/	
		He Don't Want Your Love No More	(Decca F 12169) 1965 8
		Try To Understand/	
		Not In This Whole World	(Decca F 12214) 1965 25
		Tell Me Like It Is/Stop Fooling Around	(Decca F 12254) 1965 -
		Call Me/After You	(Decca F 12326) 1966 -
		What A Wonderful Feeling/	
		Tossin' And Turnin'	(Decca F 12491) 1966 -

LULU - The Most Of Lulu (LP).

The Boat That I Row/			
Dreary Days And Nights	(Columbia DB 8169)	1967	6
Let's Pretend/To Sir With Love	(Columbia DB 8221)	1967	11
Love Loves To Love Love/			
You And I	(Columbia DB 8295)	1967	32
Me The Peaceful Heart/Lookout	(Columbia DB 8358)	1968	9
Boy/Sad Memories	(Columbia DB 8425)	1968	15
I'm A Tiger/Without Him	(Columbia DB 8500)	1968	9
Boom-Bang-A-Bang/March	(Columbia DB 8550)	1969	2
Oh Me Oh My/Sweep Around My			
Own Backyard	(Atco 226 008)	1969	47
Hum Your Song From My Heart/			
Mr Bojangles	(Atco 2091 014)	1970	-
Got To Believe In Love/			
Move To My Rhythm	(Atco 2091 049)	1971	-
Everybody Clap/			
After The Feeling Is Gone	(Atlantic 2091 083)	1971	-
Even If I Could Change/			
You Ain't Wrong,You Just Ain't Right	(Atlantic K 10185)	1972	-
The Man Who Sold The World/			
Watch That Man	(Polydor 2001 490)	1974	3
The Man With The Golden Gun/			
A Boy Like You	(Chelsea 2005 015)	1974	-
Take Your Mama For A Ride			
Parts 1 & 2	(Chelsea 2005 022)	1974	37
Boy Meets Girl/			
Mama's Little Corner Of The World	(Chelsea 2005 031)	1975	-
Heaven And Earth And The Stars/			
A Boy Like You	(Chelsea 2005 048)	1975	-

Reissue 45s:

Oh Me, Oh My (I'm A Fool For You Baby)/Sweep Around Your			
Own Back Door	(Atlantic K 10726)	1976	-

Reissues:	Shout/(different artist)	(Old Gold 9395)	1984	-
	Shout/Forgive Me Baby	(Decca SHOUT 1)	1986	8
	Shout/Forgive Me Baby/			
	Heatwave/Call Me (12")	(Decca SHOUX 1)	1986	-
	Shout/(acappella mix)/(New Shout mix)	(Jive LULU 1)	1986	8
	Shout/(acappella mix)/(single mix) (12")	(Jive LULUT 1)	1986	-

NB: α Credited to Lulu And The Luvvers. The newly recorded *Shout* entered the chart on 1986 and the next week the original Decca version by Lulu And The Luvvers also charted. For all subsequent weeks Gallup amalgamated both versions under one entry.

Lulu was born as Marie McDonald McLaughlin Lawrie (that's a mouthful!) in Lennox Castle, Lennoxtown, north of Glasgow on 3 November 1948. She seemed destined for show business from a very young age. She won her first singing contest whilst on holiday in Blackpool aged just five. She was spotted by Marian Massey (who became the greatest influence on her career) whilst singing with a local group The Gleneagles. She was invited to London for an audition and sang *24 Hours From Tulsa* but when she returned to record her first 45 the number selected was *Shout*. Her raucous, pulsating version of the song propelled her to No 7 in the UK charts and almost overnight she had become a new teenage sensation.

Her backing band on this disc The Luvvers included Jim Dewar (who was later in **Stone The Crows**). It's also rumoured that **Led Zeppelin's Jimmy Page** played on this disc as well as on *Satisfied* and *Surprise Surprise*. The Luvvers backed her on most of her Decca singles. Her strong version of Goffin-King's *I Can't Hear You No More* failed to chart and her rendition of *Here Comes The Night* lost out to **Them's** more gutsy rendition.

The 1965 *Lulu* EP contains versions of two Tamla classics *Heatwave* and *What's Easy For Two Is So Hard For One*. Her debut album *Something To Shout About* included several 'A' sides among its 16 tracks. Other songs of note are a version of Bobby Darin's *Dream Lover* and a lively rendition of *Can I Get A Witness*. Her final two Decca singles both failed. The first was *Call Me* (penned by Tony Hatch and Jackie Trent), but her rocky version lost out to Chris Montez's more subtle bossa nova treatment. To help promote the second *Oh What A Wonderful Feeling* the assistance of **Alan Price** was utilised but again to no avail.

In 1967 she switched to Columbia, but a compilation album *Lulu* was issued on Decca's Ace of Clubs label the same year. Alongside her popular songs like *Shout* it included previously unreleased tracks like *Lies* and *Stubborn Kind Of Fellow*. Now working with Columbia producer Mickie Most, her career really took off. Her first single for the label was one of the best records she ever recorded - a lively rocky interpretation of Neil Diamond's *The Boat That I Row*. She also took an acting part in the film 'To Sir With Love' which starred Sidney Poitier and was an enormous success in the States. The theme tune from the film gave her a million-selling US No 1 and topped the charts there for five weeks. In the UK it was placed on the 'B' side of *Let's Pretend*, which peaked at No 6. Her other song from the film *Stealing My Love From Me* could only be heard on the soundtrack album.

Her second album *Love Loves To Love Lulu* included six US/UK 'A' sides but her third one *Lulu's Album* was a varied collection that didn't contain any. The title track of her second album was released as a 45, but stiffed at No 32. She did enjoy considerable commercial success in this era though, notably with *Me The Peaceful Heart*, *Boy*, *I'm A Tiger* and *Boom-Bang-A-Bang*. *I'm A Tiger* was shamelessly commercial and she has later admitted that she couldn't stand the song. Also aimed at the lowest common denominator was *Boom-Bang-A-Bang*, which was selected to represent Britain in the 1969 Eurovision Song Contest. It tied with the Spanish entry for first place and became her biggest UK hit rising to No 2. She was also granted her own television series in this era.

Lulu had a great R&B voice and must have grimaced at some of the material she had to record with Mickie Most. After her marriage to **Maurice Gibb**, encouraged by him, she switched labels to Atlantic's Atco subsidiary. Her two albums for the label were recorded in the States with help from the Dixie Flyers and with Jerry Wexler, Tom Dowd and Arif Mardin handling production. *New Routes*, released in 1970, featured Duane Allman on guitar. *Oh Me Oh My* (her first single for the label) got to No 22 in the States and No 47 here, but otherwise this was a lean period for hits. **The Bee Gees** provided the title track for her next album *Melody Fair* (the song had originally appeared on their *Odessa* album). Her *Everybody Clap* 45 was co-written by her brother Billy Lawrie and **Maurice Gibb** and boasted an all-star line-up including John Bonham, but it too missed out. In the States it was renamed *Everybody's Got To Clap* and paired with a different 'B' side - a cover of **The Searchers'** hit *Goodbye My Love*. A number of additional 45s were released in the States in this period, including *Melody Fair* and *It Takes A Real Man*, which wasn't issued in the UK at all.

When her short marriage to **Maurice Gibb** ended **Lulu** switched again to Chelsea Records. She released a US-only single *Make Believe World* in 1973, but her UK debut for the company was issued on Polydor and rescued her fledgling career. The song in question was **David Bowie's** *The Man Who Sold The World* and he produced and arranged it whilst recording his *Pin-Ups* album in France. It gave her a No 3 hit here in the UK. Perhaps surprisingly, her follow-up *The Man With The Golden Gun* (a James Bond theme) was a commercial flop. Her next hit was 1975's disco-orientated cover of Kenny Nolan's dance song *Take Your Mama For A Ride*. In the States, her 1974 US-only album *Lulu* contained wide-ranging material from country to soul. A second US-only album *Heaven And Earth And The Stars* featured all her US 45s for Chelsea and both sides of her 45 collaboration was **David Bowie**.

In the mid-seventies, she appeared on stage in 'Peter Pan' and in 1976 she married hairdresser John Freida. After a one-off single for GTO, she switched again to **Elton John's** Rocket label and recorded material veering towards soul. In common with **Cilla Black** she developed more as an all round performer as her career developed. In the eighties, she appeared on stage in 'Guys and Dolls', Song and Dance' and as a comedy actress in ITV's 'The Secret Diary Of Adrian Mole' series. She returned to the UK Top Ten with a disco re-recording of *Shout* in 1986 and in November 1986 her autobiography was published by Grenada Books.

In 1993 she teamed up with Take That to record *Re-light My Fire* and the result gave **Lulu** her first No 1 hit. She also appeared on 'French and Saunders', the award-winning 'Absolutely Fabulous' and toured with Take That. She enjoyed a number of further hits in the nineties and when *Where The Poor Boys Dance* reached No 24 in 2000 she enjoyed the distinction of appearing on 'Top Of The Pops' in five consecutive decades - the sixties, seventies, eighties, nineties and two thousand. 2000 was a very significant year for her. It also marked her first festival appearance at Scotland's 'T In The Park', which was critically acclaimed. In June 2000 she was awarded the O.B.E. for her contribution to the Entertainment Industry and in December 2000 she received a Doctorate Of Music from the University of Westminster. She continues to record and perform today.

The Mickie Most Years is a 2-CD collection of her material for Columbia. It opens with *To Sir With Love*, but includes no less than three versions of *Boom Bang A Bang* sung in Italian, French and English! Don't let that put you off - overall it's a good collection of what was her most successful period.

She contributed *Just One Look* to *Fourteen* (LP), the title track and *Stealing My Love From Me* to *To Sir With Love* (LP) soundtrack and the title track to *The Man With The Golden Gun* (LP) soundtrack. (VJ)

Larry Lurex

45:     I Can Hear Music/Goin' Back   (EMI EMI 2030) 1973 R3
NB: There was also a demo of this (R4).

This is actually **Queen**'s Freddie Mercury using a pseudonym doing a revival of The Ronettes' *I Can Hear Music* shortly prior to the release of **Queen**'s debut 45. *Goin' Back* is a Burt Bacharach song. Inevitably the disc is now extremely sought-after and very expensive to obtain. It has also been counterfeited. (VJ)

Luv Machine

Personnel:	MICHAEL BISHOP	gtr, vcls	A
	BOB BOWMAN	gtr, vcls	A
	ERROL BRADSHAW	drms, vcls	A
	JOHN JEAVONS	bs, vcls	A

ALBUM: 1(A)   LUV MACHINE   (Polydor 2460 102) 1971 R3

45:     Witches Wand/In The Early Hours   (Polydor 2058 080) 1971

This is a rare album of heavy progressive rock from New Zealand. It appeared in a lurid sleeve that allegedly earned the album a ban in their homeland. It's included here to clarify the bands' origins. (VJ/RMJ)

The Luvvers

Personnel:	ALEC BELL	keyb'ds	A
	JIM DEWAR	gtr	A
	DAVID MILLER	drms	A
	ROSS NELSON	gtr	A
	JIMMY SMITH	sax	A
	TONY TIERNEY	bs	A

45:     The House On The Hill/
        Most Unlovely   (Parlophone R 5459) 1966 R1

The Luvvers became **Lulu**'s backing band in 1964 and recorded the above disc after splitting with her in 1966. It is now quite collectable. Some of them were also involved in making a privately-pressed album, *Three's Company* under the name Peter Ross Oliver, which mostly contained cover versions. Jim Dewar later played with **Robin Trower** in the seventies. (VJ)

Kenny Lynch

One of the more interesting characters of the sixties was this West Indian Cockney comedian, songwriter and producer for a string of groups, including **Game**. He appeared in the film 'Just For Fun' in 1962 and in the mid-sixties owned his own record store on Walkers Court in London. He released a series of solo 45s during the sixties, which are not listed here and also recorded a 45 in 1964, *Shake And Scream/Harlem Library* (HMV POP 1260) 1964 with **The Laurie Jay Combo**. A year earlier, in 1963, he'd recorded *I'm Not That Sort Of Girl/It Had Better Be A Wonderful Live* (HMV POP 1194), with Barbara Windsor and Harry Fowler. (VJ)

Sue Lynne

45s:	Reach For The Moon/All Alone	(RCA Victor RCA 1724) 1968
	You/Don't Pity Me	(RCA Victor RCA 1822) 1969 R3
	Baby Baby Baby/You lose Again	(RCA Victor RCA 1874) 1969

Both sides of her second 45 were written and produced by **Chris Andrews**. Despite the value attached to this 45, both are forgettable ballads. (VJ)

Lyons and Malone

45:     Dr. Gentle/She's Alright   (Jay Boy BOY 9) 1969

This is another forgotten late sixties disc.

Compilation appearances have included: *Dr. Gentle* on *Rubble, Vol. 10* (CD) and *The Best Of Rubble Collection, Vol. 6* (CD); and *She's Alright* on *Rubble, Vol. 11* (CD), *The Best Of Rubble Collection, Vol. 2* (CD) and *Beat Us If You Can! Vol. 1* (LP). (VJ)

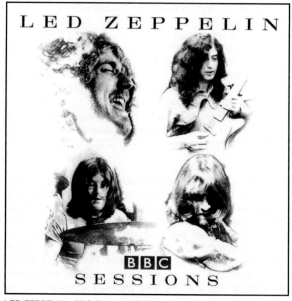

LED ZEPPELIN - BBC Sessions (CD).

MAGIC CARPET - Magic Carpet (LP).

Mabel Greer's Toyshop

Personnel:	JON ANDERSON	vcls	A
	PETE BANKS	gtr	A
	CLIVE BAILEY	gtr	A
	CHRIS SQUIRE	bs	A
	TUB THUMPER	drms	A

A mysterious, short-lived psychedelic group who gigged around London's clubs like Happening 44 and Middle Earth from late 1967 to mid-1968, when they became **Yes**. Their wild, psychedelic Ford Thames van was a welcome and regular sight around London's West End for a few brief months, but sadly their only recording date was for John Peel's 'Night Ride' broadcast on 3rd April 1968. It consisted of *Electric Funeral, Images Of Me And You, Janetta* and *Beyond And Before*, which later turned up in **Yes**. These tracks, minus *Electric Funeral*, have now surfaced on *Dustbin Full Of Rubbish* (LP) and reveal a rawer and less pompous version of early **Yes** in which **Jon Anderson**'s vocals stand out. (JN)

Spencer Mac

Personnel incl:	SPENCER MAC	A
	PAUL McCALLUM	A

45:	Better By You, Better Than Me/	
	Comuter	(Penny Farthing PEN 742) 1970 R1

The 'A' side of this obscure disc was presumably a cover of the **Spooky Tooth** song. **Spencer Mac** included Paul McCallum who was a member of **Mojo Hannah** during December 1972. (VJ)

Neil MacArthur

HCP

45s:	She's Not There/World Of Glass	(Deram DM 225) 1969 SC 34
	Don't Try To Explain/Without Her	(Deram DM 262) 1969 -
	It's Not Easy/12.29	(Deram DM 275) 1969 -

This was **Colin Blunstone** under a pseudonym. His first 45 was a re-recording of *She's Not There*, one of the finest moments of **Blunstone**'s earlier group **The Zombies**. This version is produced by Mike Hurst and comes with fuzz guitar. After this trio of 45s for Deram, **Blunstone** pursued a solo career under his real name. He also made guest appearances in several bands including The Alan Parsons Project in the seventies.

Compilation appearances include: *She's Not There* on *Collecting Peppermint Clouds, Vol. 1* (LP), *Deram Dayze* (LP) and *14 Groovy Sounds From The Blow Up* (LP); and *12.29* has been compiled on *Spinning Wheel* (CD). (VJ)

Freddy Mack Show

ALBUM:	1 THE FANTASTIC FREDDY MACK SHOW	
	(Rayrik TPLMP 142/143) c1966	

Recorded 'live' at Tofts Club, Folkestone. Freddy had previously been a world ranking light heavyweight boxer and had a nightclub in London in the late sixties. The album contains a great steaming R&B show, although it apparently wasn't exactly live, and some of **The Artwoods** are rumoured to have been brought in (uncredited) to bolster up the instrumentation..... The two bands shared Johnny Jones as manager. (Nr)

Andy MacKay

ALBUM:	1 IN SEARCH OF EDDIE RIFF	(Island ILPS 9278) 1974

45s:	Ride Of The Valkyries/Time Regained	(Island WIP 6197) 1974
(up to	Wild Weekend/Walking The	
1976)	Whippet (Some in promo PS)	(Island WIP 6243) 1975

A Londoner, **MacKay** started out as a classical musician but he took up rock whilst at Reading University, playing sax for a R&B band called Nova Express. He was offered a place in **Roxy Music**, in January 1971 and his sax work was influential in moulding their highly acclaimed style. He recorded his instrumental album, *In Search Of Eddie Riff*, whilst he was still a member of **Roxy Music**, with the assistance of a talented array of musicians including **Brian Eno**, Phil Manzanera and Eddie Jobson. It included his own interpretation of classics like **The Beatles**' *Long And Winding Road* and Jimmy Ruffin's *What Becomes Of The Broken Hearted?* and classical pieces like Wagner's *Ride Of The Valkyries*, which was also released as a 45. The blend was completed with a few originals, of which *Pyramid Of The Night* was the strongest.

He went on to compose the music for TV's 'Rock Follies' and he recorded a further album of sax instrumentals, *Revolving Contradictions*, in 1978, but that's really beyond the time span of this book. (VJ)

Judy MacKenzie

ALBUMS	1 JUDY	(Key KL 005) 1970 SC
	2 PEACE AND LOVE AND FREEDOM	
	(w/poster)	(Key KL 009) 1971 SC

A few years before the **MacKenzie and Cooke** duo, schoolteacher Judy made these two albums for the religious Key label. The first, in particular, is a fine achievement for a 21-year-old singer-songwriter, with a variety of styles from traditional to rocking. The lyrics certainly have a Christian flavour, but they are often subtle and nothing is rammed down your throat. The song *Sally Brown* is a critique of the empty consumerist society which many non-believers would find convincing, and there is much else to enjoy purely in musical terms, with a display of fine sincere singing. The second album adds string arrangements and continues in much the same vein. It comes with a big fold-out lyrics poster. Apparently these albums are now sought after in Japan for some reason, which can only add to their scarcity. (NM)

MacKenzie Cooke

Personnel:	DAVID COOKE	instruments	A
	JUDY MacKENZIE	vcls	A

ALBUM:	1(A) DAVE & JUDY THINKING IT OVER	(EMI EMC 3027) 1974

This was basically a pop duo. They co-wrote most of the music on their album, which is inoffensive but certainly unexceptional. It was produced by Walter J. Ridley.

Judy MacKenzie also made some solo recordings. (VJ)

Mackeral

45s:	Funny Fish/This Is Mine	(Columbia DB 8013) 1966

Trying Again/White Man's Burden   (Columbia DB 8388) 1968

This is another little-known late sixties band. (VJ)

Pete MacLaine and Clan

Personnel incl: PETE BROOKING   gtr   A

45:     Yes I Do/U.S. Mail   (Decca F 11699) 1963 SC

This beat group came from Manchester.

You'll also find *Yes I Do* on *Ready, Steady, Go!* (LP), *Sixties Lost And Found, Vol. 3* (LP) and *Beat Merchants* (2-LP). (VJ)

Robert MacLeod

Personnel: JOHN BACHINI   bs   A
              BRIAN HOLLOWAY   gtr   A
              ROBERT MacLEOD   vcls, gtr   A
              WIL MALONE   keyb'ds   A
              PETER WRIGHT   drms   A

ALBUM: 1(A) BETWEEN THE POPPY AND THE SNOW
                        (Charisma CAS 1114) 1976

Robert MacLeod is a singer / songwriter who recorded this album in Rome. Probable influences were people such as **Cat Stevens**. The album is full of pleasant love songs. **Wil Malone** of **Motherlight** assisted. (BS)

Macon Jug

ALBUMS: 1 IN THE SUMMERTIME   (Saga FID 8157) 1970 SC
         2 RAY DORSET'S BEST   (Boulevard BLVD 4078) 1972
NB: **Macon Jug** and **Good Earth** contributed tracks to (1). (2) contained four tracks from **Good Earth** and six from **Macon Jug**.

Ray Dorset of **Mungo Jerry** was a member of **Good Earth** who **Macon Jug** shared these two albums with. (VJ)

Made In Sheffield

45:    Amelia Jane/Right Satisfied   (Fontana TF 871) 1967 SC

MAGIC CARPET II - Once Moor (CD).

Some people rate this obscure 45 very highly. *Amelia Jane* has unusual rhythms and pleasing harmonies. It seems the driver behind the band was bassist and keyboardist Chris Stainton, who worked with **Joe Cocker** in the late sixties and early seventies. Indeed **Made In Sheffield** are thought not to be a real band at all - probably just a studio project put together by Stainton and mates of **Cocker**.

Right Satisfied has been compiled on *Jagged Time Lapse, Vol 5* (CD). (MWh)

Madrigal

45s: Blue Eyes In Paradise/Wendy   (Decca F 13110) 1971
        You Hear What You Wanna Hear/
        Guadalajara City   (Decca F 13184) 1971
        Time Of The Season/Tapestry   (Sovereign SOV 107) 1972

This **Madrigal** is a little known early seventies act. Their final 'A' side was a **Zombies** song. (VJ)

Madrigal

Personnel incl: JOHN COOK
                 PAUL DRISCOLL
                 ALLAN LOVE   vcls
                 JACOB MAGNUSSON   keyb'ds

ALBUM: 1 BENEATH THE GREENWOOD TREE (MAD 100) 1973 R3

This is a private pressing and is inevitably rare and expensive to purchase as only 99 copies were produced. A very English baroque folk album with pleasant male and female vocals it contains several cover versions and a few originals with *Madrigal Theme* and the title cut the finest moments. The band also recorded an acetate single, the two tracks being *Sun* and *Full Moon*, of which only seven copies were pressed. They also recorded a couple of cassettes in the eighties which were sold at gigs.

Magnusson left the band in October 1973 and later toured with **Kevin Ayers**. Allan Love had been in **Opal Butterfly** and **Referendum** previously. The band became **Merlin** in March 1974. (VJ/JM)

The Magic Carpet

Personnel: CLEM ALFORD   sitar, esraj, tamboura   A B
              JIM MOYES   gtr   A
              KESHAV SATHE   tabla, perc   A
              ALISHA SUFIT   vcls, gtr   A B
              PANDIT DINESH   tabla   B
              ESMAIL SHEIKH   tabla   B

ALBUMS: 1(A) MAGIC CARPET   (Mushroom 200 MR 20) 1972 R3
        2(B) ONCE MOOR - MAGIC CARPET II
                        (Magic Carpet Records MC 1004) 1996
NB: (2) as **Magic Carpet II**. (1) has been counterfeited and also reissued on CD (Essex 1005 CD) 1993, and on LP and CD (Magic Carpet MC 1001) 1995.

A mystical Eastern-sounding psychedelic folk album which was produced and engineered by Vic Keary at Chalk Farm Studios in the Winter of 1971/2. All the tracks are self-penned, half of them by the vocalist Alisha alone.

The band had formed at the beginning of the seventies. **Alisha Sufit** had a haunting voice ideally suited to the blend of Indian and Western music available on this album. **Clem Alford** was a classically-trained sitar player who'd travelled to India to learn more about Indian classical music. In 1971 they discovered Mushroom Records, which specialised in Indian-related recordings and has gone on to become a very collectable label. Sadly the band split up before the resulting album was released so it was never properly promoted. Mushroom was getting into financial difficulties in any case and could only afford to finance a limited pressing of 1,000 copies, which sold slowly over the next half dozen years.

MAGIC MIXTURE - This Is... (LP).

What of the album? Well, the tracks are basically of two types. There are the pleasant, Eastern-sounding instrumentals typified by the title track, *Alan's Christmas Card* and *Take Away Kesh* and the tracks that showcase **Alisha Sufit**'s delicate vocals like *The Phoenix, Black Cat, Peace Song* and *High Street*.

After the band's demise, **Clem Alford** went on to record a couple of solo albums and also issued an album as Sargam (misspelt as **Sagram** on the record). **Alisha Sufit** developed her interest in art but did eventually return to the recording studio in 1992 with some respected backing musicians to record *Alisha Through The Looking Glass* (Sufit 010 CD/MC), which was issued on CD and cassette.

Alisha Sufit and **Clem Alford** recorded a stylistically similar second album *Once Moor* as by **Magic Carpet II** in 1996.

Father Time can also be found on *Electric Psychedelic Sitar Headswirlers Vol. 5* (CD). (VJ)

The Magic Christians

Personnel incl: TREVOR BURTON   gtr   A

ALBUM: 1(A) THE MAGIC CHRISTIANS
                              (Major Minor SMLP 71) 1970 R1

45s:	Come And Get It/Nats	(Major Minor MM 673) 1970
Reissue:	If You Want It/Nats	(Major Minor MM 673) 1970

The full line-up of this band remains unknown. **Trevor Burton** had been in **The Move** and **The Uglys**. He was later in **Balls**, indeed this may have been a pseudonym for **Balls**. *Come And Get It* was a **Paul McCartney** song also done by **Badfinger**, who had recorded the soundtrack to the film The Magic Christian. It was produced by **Gary Wright** of **Spooky Tooth** and is of curio interest to Apple collectors. (VJ/RMJ)

The Magicians

45s:	Wet Your Whistle/Take The A Train	(Decca F 12361) 1966
	The Liars/Poggy Goes Pop	(Decca F 12374) 1966
	The Tarzan March/	
	What A Day For A Metamorphosis	(Decca F 12602) 1967
	Painting On The Wood/Slow Motion	(MCA MU 1046) 1968

This was a sixties pop band. *The Tarzan March* was also recorded by **Marty Manning and The Cheetahs**. The psychedelic *Painting On The Wood*, which combines medieval, rag-time and fuzz has also got a further airing on *Incredible Sound Show Stories, Vol. 6* (LP) - recommended. (VJ)

Magic Lanterns

Personnel:	JIMMY BILSBURY	vcls, piano	AB
	IAN MONCUR	bs	A
	PETER 'COCO' SHOESMITH	ld gtr	A
	ALAN WILSON	drms	A
	ALISTAIR 'BEV' BEVERAGE	gtr, vcls	B
	PETER GARNER	gtr, vcls	B
	MIKE 'OZ' OZBORNE	bs, vcls	B
	HARRY PAUL WARD	drms	B

ALBUMS: 1(B) LIT UP WITH THE MAGIC LATERNS
                              (CBS(S) 62935) 1969 SC
              2(B) ONE NIGHT STAND   (Polydor 2460 113) 1971

NB: They also had a US-only album *Shame Shame* (Atlantic SD8217) 1969 with following personnel: JIMMY BILSBURY (piano, vcls); "BEV" BEVERIDGE (gtr, vcls); MIKE "OZ" OSBORNE (bs, vcls); PETER GARNER (gtr, vcls); and HARRY PAUL WARD (drms). It's not known how this overlaps, content-wise with (1) above.

HCP

45s:	Excuse Me Baby/Greedy Girl	(CBS 202094) 1966 44
	Rumplestiltskin/I Stumbled	(CBS 202250) 1966 R1
	Knight In Rusty Armour/Simple Things	(CBS 202459) 1967 -
	Auntie Grizelda/	
	Time Will Tell (If I'm A Loser)	(CBS 202637) 1967 -
	We'll Meet Again/	
	What Else Can It Be But Love?	(CBS 2750) 1967 -
	Shame Shame/Baby I Gotta Go Now	(Camp 602 007) 1969 -
	Melt All Your Troubles Away/	
	Bossa Nova 1940 - Hello You Lovers	(Camp 602 009) 1969 -
	One Night Stand/Frisco Annie	(Polydor 2058 058) 1970 -
	Country Woman/You Ring A Bell	(Polydor 2058 202) 1972 -
	Stand For Your Rights/Pa Bradley	(Polydor 2058 322) 1972 -

They emerged in 1966 signing to CBS. They were originally known as The Sabres and came from Lancashire. They played ballads with four part harmonies in their early days. Their debut 45, *Excuse Me Baby*, was a minor hit. *Rumplestiltskin* was penned by **Graham Gouldman**. *Knight In Rusty Armour* was a **Peter and Gordon** song. *Auntie Grizelda* had been done by The Monkees and *We'll Meet Again* was a Vera Lynn oldie. The *Shame Shame* 45 was produced by Steve Rowland. They experimented with psychedelia on some of their 45s, but were basically a pop group.

Their U.S. only *Shame Shame* album has lead to some speculation that Ozzy Osbourne was involved with this band, due to confusion with Mike 'Oz' Osbourne. They are of course unconnected. Mike Osbourne also played with the US band Coven. They also had some US hits: *Shame Shame* got to No 29 in 1968; *One Night Stand* made No 74 in early 1971; *Let The Sun Shine In* got to No 103 later the same year and *Country Woman* made No 88. By now the band were The Magic Lantern. **Bilsbury** is thought to have gone on to play with the mysterious **Megaton**, as well as the Les Humphries Singers. He was found dead in his Bonn apartment in March 2003.

I Stumbled can also be heard on *Echoes From The Wilderness - Sixteen UK R&B Freakbeat Trippers*. (LP & CD). (VJ/VZ/RV/JM)

Magic Mixture

Personnel:	JIM THOMAS	gtr, vcls	A
	JACK COLLINS	drms	A
	STAN CURTIS	organ	A
	MELVYN HACKER	bs	A

ALBUM: 1(A) THIS IS   (Saga FID 2125) 1968 R2
NB: (1) reissued on Bat (4215) in Germany (1987), on CD Merlin (MER 1) 1993 and (Flash 61) 1998.

The above is a psychedelic classic of some repute, full of swirling guitar work and a heavy organ sound. It's now very rare and is worth investigation. Highlights include the opening cut, *(I'm So) Sad*, the mellow, rather jazzy *Urge To Leave*, the rocky *You*, the psych-pop of *Slowly The Day* and *New Man*, the frantic *When I Was Young* and the superb final track, *Moonbeams*. I found the vocals on the comedy number, *The Motor Bike Song*, extremely irritating. *Moonbeams* also crops up as a 'mystery track' on Bam-Caruso's *49 Minute Technicolour Dream* compilation.

Along with **Five Day Week Straw People**, this was one of the few decent albums on Saga. Sadly, like the others it was badly pressed on poor quality vinyl. Jim Thomas later did session work. (VJ)

Magic Valley

Personnel incl: PETE DELLO

45:     Taking The Heart Out Of Love/
        Uptight Basil   (Penny Farthing PEN 701) 1969

This is the sole vinyl offering by this band, which included **Pete Dello** of **Honeybus** fame. Both sides of the 45 are included as bonus tracks on **Pete Dello and Friends** See For Miles CD *Into Your Ears... Plus*. (VJ)

Magic Worms

A psychedelic pop outfit linked to **Angel Pavement**, who's *Green Mello Hill* typified the British variety of this musical genre.

Green Mello Hill has been compiled on *Morgan Blue Town* (LP) and *Best And The Rest Of British Psychedelia* (CD). (VJ)

Magna Carta

Personnel:			
	CHRIS SIMPSON	gtr, vcls	ABCD
	GLEN STUART	vcls	ABCD
	LYELL TRANTER	gtr, vcls	A
	DAVEY JOHNSTONE	gtr	B
	STAN GORDON	gtr	C
	(GRAHAM SMITH	bs	C)

				HCP
ALBUMS:	1(A)	MAGNA CARTA	(Mercury SMCL 20166) 1969	R1 -
(up to	2(A)	SEASONS	(Vertigo 6360 003) 1970	SC 55
1976)	3(B)	SONGS FROM WASTIES ORCHARD		
			(Vertigo 6360 040) 1971	SC -
	4(B)	IN CONCERT	(Vertigo 6360 068) 1972	SC -
	5(C)	LORD OF THE AGES	(Vertigo 6360 093) 1973	SC -
	6( )	PUTTING IT BACK TOGETHER		
			(GTO GTLP 012) 1976	SC -

NB: (1) reissued in remastered form by HTD (HTD CD 68) 1996. (2) reissued on CD (Si-Wan SRMC 0023) 2004. (3) reissued on CD (Repertoire REP 4447-WP) and again (Repertoire REP 0004447). (3) also issued on CD by Akarma and Pid. (5) reissued on CD (Vertigo 846 448-2) in 1990. (6) reissued on CD (Repertoire REP 4447-WP) 1994. (2) and (5) also issued as a 2-CD set (Recall SMDCD 481) and (2) and (3) reissued as a 2-CD set (Mercury 5388122). (6) also reissued on CD as *Took A Long Time* (Talking Elephant TECD 78). There's also a CD, *Live At The BBC*

(Pseudonym CDP 1022 DD) 1995. The 21-track CD *Old Masters and New Horizons* (Vertigo 510660-2) is a cheap introduction to their work. It has liner notes by Chris Simpson and contains some surprisingly decent tracks from 1991 as well. There's also a 30-track 2-CD compilation called *Milestones* and a 24-track 2-CD compilation *Gold* (Retro GOLD R2CD4256), which includes a 20-page booklet with rare photos.

45s:	Romeo Jack/Seven O'Clock Hymn	(Fontana TF 1060) 1969 SC
(up to	Mid-Winter/	
1976)	Spinning Wheels Of Time	(Mercury MF 1096) 1969 SC
	All My Life/Falkland Green	(Vertigo 6059 073) 1972
	Give Me Luv/Song Of Evening	(Vertigo 6059 092) 1973

This folk trio formed in the late sixties. In fact they were originally a duo - of Yorkshire-born Simpson and Australian Tranter. Glen Stuart, who'd been a child actor, joined them after they got a recording deal with Fontana. After what is now a very rare medieval-sounding album on Mercury, they recorded a series of fine progressive contemporary folk albums on Vertigo. *Seasons* is beautiful, its subject matter being as the title suggests. It got to No 55 in the UK Album Charts. Guitarist Davey Johnstone was added to the line-up for the third album which also featured a guest appearance from **Rick Wakeman**.

The *In Concert* album, which featured them live in Amsterdam was a live greatest hits set, but it was disappointing in comparison to *Songs From Wasties Orchard*, which many consider to be their magnum opus. It featured guest appearances from Tony Visconti, **Hookfoot** and **Rick Wakeman** and conjured up a medieval sound. Johnstone departed after these two albums to work with **Elton John** and **Kiki Dee**. He now lives in California with his wife and children.

Stan Gordon was added for *Lord Of The Ages*, which was well received. Bassist Graham Smith who'd done session work on the album joined the group shortly after. Within the year, though, Gordon and Smith had both departed, leaving Simpson and Stuart as a duo.

In the mid-seventies they briefly experimented with a more rock-based format, but this, like most of their subsequent line-ups, was short-lived. Stuart then quit the band for good in this era but Simpson remained to work with various line-ups over the next 15 years. He also recorded a solo album, *Listen To The Man*, in 1983. The band returned to record a new album *Heartlands* in 1992.

The BBC Radio Sessions CD contains three tracks from 1969, four from 1987, but concentrates on 1971, showcasing their distinctive brand of folk favourably.

Prior to recording for Vertigo **Magna Carta** made a record for the Road Safety Campaign. *When You're Young* put across a road safety message in the lyrics and featured pleasant harmonies and acoustic guitar. The 45 appeared on various labels credited to individual London boroughs including Enfield and Camden. In each case the 'A' side was a song about 'The Green Cross Code' performed by kids from Argyle School in Camden. None of the 45s had catalogue numbers.

MAGNA CARTA - Magna Carta (CD).

MAGNA CARTA - Songs From Wasties Orchard (CD).

MAHAVISHNU ORCHESTRA - The Inner Mountain Flame (LP).

You'll also find the band on Vertigo's 1971 compilation *Heads Together, First Round* (LP), playing *Good Morning Sun* and on *Vertigo Annual 1970* (LP), singing *Goin' My Way (Road Song)*. Retrospective compilation appearances include: *The Bridge At Knaresborough Town* on *Electric Psychedelic Sitar Headswirlers Vol. 6* (CD). (VJ/GCn)

Paddy Maguire

45:      Lay Me Down/Doin' The Best I Can   (Ember EMBS 292) 1970

Paddy Maguire is a folk artist from the Midlands. He's backed on this by **Stevie Winwood**, Phil Pickett, **Fotheringay, Sue and Sunny, Madeleine Bell** and Doris Troy. (VJ)

Mahavishnu Orchestra

Personnel:			
BILLY COBHAM	drms	A
JERRY GOODMAN	violin	A
JAN HAMMER	keyb'ds	A
RICK LAIRD	bs	A
JOHN McLAUGHLIN	gtr	ABC
RALPH ARMSTRONG	bs	BC
GAYLE MORAN	keyb'ds, vcls	BC
JEAN-LUC PONTY	violin	B
NARADA MICHAEL WALDEN	drms	BC
STU GOLDBERG	keyb'ds	C

				HCP
ALBUMS:	1(-)	THE INNER MOUNTING FLAME (w/insert)		
(up to			(CBS 64717) 1972	-
1976)	2(A)	BIRDS OF FIRE	(CBS 65321) 1973	20
	3(A)	BETWEEN NOTHINGNESS AND ETERNITY		
			(CBS 69046) 1973	-
	4(B)	APOCALYPSE	(CBS 69076) 1974	-
	5(B)	VISIONS OF THE EMERALD BEYOND		
		(w/insert)	(CBS 69108) 1974	-
	6(C)	INNER WORLDS	(CBS 69216) 1976	-

NB: Also of relevance is *In Retrospect* (2-LP) (Polydor 2675 091) 1976 and *Best Of Mahavishnu Orchestra* (CBS 84232) 1980. There's also a quadrophonic release of (2) (CBS CQ 31996) 1974. (2) reissued on CD (Columbia 4682242) 1992. There's also a more recent compilation, *The Collection* (Castle CCSCD 305) 1991.

45:      Can't Stand Your Funk/Eternity's Breath Pt 1   (CBS 3007) 1975

Mahavishnu's influence on a generation of fusion groups in the seventies and eighties was paramount.

This was the creation of guitarist **John McLaughlin**, who was born in Yorkshire on 4 January 1942. He formed the group in 1972 - **Mahavishnu** was the name given by his Hindu guru Sri Chimnoy. **McLaughlin** had been converted to the philosophy of this mystic while living in New York. Prior to

forming the band **McLaughlin** had made three solo albums, the third of which, *My Goals Beyond*, consisted of meditational solo acoustic and Indian music.

Mahavishnu Orchestra was soon noted for its successful and innovative fusion of jazz and rock and their first two albums were very positively received by the critics. On *Inner Mounting Flame*, **McLaughlin** was also assisted by several musicians, who'd played on his earlier solo albums. *For Birds Of Fire* he put together a new band which included former Flock violinist Jerry Goodman. This album successfully married some dazzling solo work within a tight musical framework and it is generally considered one of the finest of the jazz-rock genre. The album did well commercially, too, peaking at No 15 in the US Charts and No 20 here, where it was their only Chart album.

Between Nothingness And Eternity was recorded live in Central Park, New York in August 1973. It was noted for the long *Dreams* sequence and some superb interplay between **McLaughlin** and drummer Billy Cobham. It got to No 41 in the US. In 1974, this line-up disbanded but a year later **McLaughlin** reformed the group with a new line-up which included violin ace Jean-Luc Ponty. The four-piece band was supplemented further by a four-piece string quartet and for the new line-up's first album by The London Symphony Orchestra, conducted by Michael Tilson Thomas. The concept was ambitious but the vinyl output suggested the group was now over self-indulgent, although it sold quite well in the US, where it peaked at No 43. The follow-up, *Visions Of The Emerald Beyond*, failed to reverse this and only made it to No 68 in the US Charts. After this Ponty left and keyboardist Stu Goldberg played on the *Inner Worlds* album. Climbing to No 118 in the US, this failed to stem the spiral of decline and **McLaughlin** allowed the group to disintegrate, preferring to team up with an Indian instrumental group, Shakti, with whom he recorded the acoustic album, *Shakti With John McLaughlin* in 1976.

Morgan went on to play with Chick Corea's *Return To Forever* and Walden went into production work and had a massive disco hit in the late seventies.

There was an unsuccessful attempt to revive the band in 1982 with a line-up of Cobham, Bill Evans (sax), Mitchell Forman (keyb'ds), Jonas Hellborg (bs) and Danny Gottleib (perc), but only one album for Warner Brothers resulted. (VJ)

Mahogany

ALBUM: 1 MAHOGANY   (Epic BN 26898) 1969

Produced by Tony Clarke, this is an obscure but highly-regarded heavy blues-rock album, which only seems to have appeared in the US and Holland. (SR/RMJ)

Mitch Mahon and The Editions

45:      You Got What I Need/
         I've Thrown Our Love Away   (Pye 7N 17844) 1969

This was an obscure Irish late sixties band. You'll also find *You Got What I Need* on *Irish Rock - Ireland's Beat Groups 1964-1969* (CD). (VJ)

Mail

45:      Omnibus/Life Goes On   (Parlophone R 5916) 1971

Nothing is known about this band. (VJ)

Mainhorse

Personnel:			
BRYSON GRAHAM	drms	A
PETER LOCKETT	gtr, vcls, violin	A
PATRICK MORAZ	keyb'ds	A
JEAN RISTORI	bs	A

ALBUM: 1 (A)   MAINHORSE   (Polydor 2383 049) 1971 SC

NB: (1) issued in the US (Visa Import 1001) 1971.

Prior to his work with **Refugee, Yes** and **The Moody Blues**, Swiss-born Patrick Moraz fronted this early progressive/hard-rock band. Moraz went on to release several solo albums and Graham was later in **Spooky Tooth**. (CG)

The Majority

Personnel:			
	BARRY GRAHAM (WIGLEY)	vcls	A
	ROGER FRANCE	lead gtr	A
	DON LILL	drms	A
	ROB LONG	gtr	A
	KEN SMITH	bs	A

45s:		
	Pretty Little Girl/	
	I Don't Wanna Be Hurt No More	(Decca F 12186) 1965
	A Little Bit Of Sunlight/	
	Shut 'Em Down In London Town	(Decca F 12271) 1965 SC
	We Kiss In A Shadow/Ring The Bells	(Decca F 12313) 1966
	Simplified/One Third	(Decca F 12453) 1966 R1
	To Make Me A Man/Tears Won't Help	(Decca F 12504) 1966
	I Hear A Rhapsody/Wait By The Fire	(Decca F 12573) 1967
	Running Away With My Baby/	
	Let The Joybells Ring	(Decca F 12638) 1967
	All Our Christmases/People	(Decca F 12727) 1968

This outfit from Hull was a popular attraction at debutante balls in the mid-sixties and released several 45s of no particular merit. The band was initially known as Barry Graham and The Mustangs until Don Lill (who briefly managed **Mick Ronson's Rats**) joined on drums. *A Little Bit Of Sunlight* was a Ray Davies' composition. Their final 45, *All Our Christmases*, which was written by **The Bee Gees**, was a more light-hearted affair than their earlier harmony pop efforts. The band later backed **Barry Ryan** and played on *Eloise* and *Love Is Love* to name a few.

Lill quit the band sometime after they played on *Eloise* and they headed abroad continuing to record as Majority One. Particularly noteworthy is *Because I Love You*. In fact it's the fuzz-laden flip side *Get Back Home* that really excites collectors. They also issued an eponymous album in Italy on the Jolly label before finally disbanding in the mid-seventies.

Compilation appearances have included: *Time Machine Man* (from a crackly unreleased acetate) on *Psychedelia, Vol. 4* (LP) and *Hen's Teeth, Vol. 3* (CD); *One Third* on *Beat It* (3-CD), *Diggin' For Gold, Vol. 1* (LP & CD), *The Freakbeat Scene* (CD), *14 Groovy Sounds From The Blow Up* (LP) and on the 4-CD *Nuggets II* box set; *All Our Christmases* on *British Psychedelic Trip, Vol. 4* (LP) and *Great British Psychedelic Trip, Vol. 2* (CD) and *Charlotte Rose* and *Wait By The Fire* on *Fading Yellow, Vol 4* (CD). (VJ/JM)

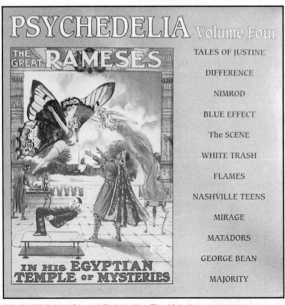

PSYCHEDELIA VOL. 4 (LP) including The Majority.

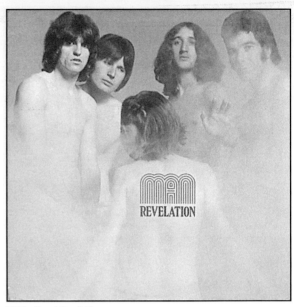

MAN - Revelation (LP).

Majority One

45:      Glass Image/Friday Man   (London 2534) 1970 R1

This was a one-off psychedelic 45. They also have a track called *I See Her Everywhere* compiled on *Fading Yellow, Vol 5* (CD). (VJ)

Mal and The Primitives

Personnel incl: MAL RYDER

45:	Every Minute Of Every Day/	
	Pretty Little Face	(Pye 7N 15915) 1965 R3

This is a rare and sought-after bluesy beat 45 by a Northampton outfit which also recorded as **The Primitives** and **Mal Ryder and The Spirits**. They also sang *Anyone Can Play*, which was the theme to the 1967 film 'Le Dolci Signore (Anyone Can Play)'.

Every Minute Of Every Day has been compiled on *Doin' The Mod, Vol. 1* (CD). (VJ/SB)

Maldoon

See **Curtiss Maldoon**.

Wil Malone

ALBUMS:	1	FUNNYSAD MUSIC	(Morgan MR112) 1968 R1
	2	WIL MALONE	(Fontana STL 5541) 1970 R4

NB: (1) credited to Wilson Malone Voiceband.

A multi-talented arranger whose work spanned easy listening, hard psychedelia and singer-songwriting, **Wilson Malone** was a member of **Orange Bicycle** (who'd released various singles and an album on Parlophone), and part of the in-house team at Morgan Studios. There he produced the *Funnysad Music* album (as The Wilson Malone Voiceband), which consists of harmony-laden arrangements of popular songs such as *Penny Lane* and *No Milk Today*, alongside a handful of originals such as *Nice Day For Monks*. Essentially an exercise in vocal arrangements, this is emphatically not for fans of psychedelia. His next project, 1969's legendary **Motherlight** album (recorded with Mike Bobak and Andy Johns) was in a completely different vein, and his hopelessly obscure 1970 solo effort (engineered by Bobak) is one of the rarest major-label releases of the period. Comprising guitar and piano ballads such as *Catherine Wheel* and *At The Silver Slipper*, all set to delicate string arrangements, it came in a wonderfully lurid psychedelic sleeve depicting a robed **Malone** reclining in some woodland. He went on to make yet another rare album as part of **Fickle Pickle** before forging a significant career as an arranger, collaborating on **Robert MacLeod**'s 1976 *Between The Poppy And The Snow* album and contributing music to cult late seventies kids' show 'The Bubblies', amongst many other projects. More recently he was responsible for the strings on The Verve's *Bittersweet Symphony*. (RMJ)

Man

Personnel:

CLIVE JOHN	keyb'ds, vcls	ABCD
JEFF JONES	drms, perc	AB
MICKY JONES	lead gtr, vcls	ABCDE
ROGER LEONARD	gtr, vcls	ABCDE
RAY WILLIAMS	bs, vcls	A
MARTIN ACE	bs, gtr, vcls	BC
TERRY WILLIAMS	drms, vcls	BCDE
PHIL RYAN	keyb'ds, vcls	D
WILL YOUATT	bs, vcls	D
KEN WHALEY	bs	E

HCP

ALBUMS: 1(A) REVELATION (mono/stereo)
(up to (Pye N(S)PL 18275) 1968 SC -
1976) 2(A) TWO OUNCES OF PLASTIC WITH A HOLE
IN THE MIDDLE (Dawn DNLS 3003) 1969 SC -
3(B) MAN (Liberty LBG 83464) 1970 SC -
4(B) DO YOU LIKE IT HERE NOW? ARE YOU SETTLING IN?
(United Artists UAS 29236) 1971 SC -
5(C) LIVE AT THE PADGET ROOMS PENARTH
(United Artists USP 100) 1972 SC -
6(D) BE GOOD TO YOURSELF AT LEAST ONCE A DAY
(United Artists UAG 29417) 1972 SC -
7(D) BACK INTO THE FUTURE (2-LP)
(United Artists UAD 60053/4) 1973 23
8(D) GOLDEN HOUR OF MAN (Pye GH 569) 1973 -
9(E) RHINOS, WINOS AND LUNATICS
(United Artists UAG 29631) 1974 24
10(E) SLOW MOTION (United Artists UAG 29675) 1974 -
11(E) MAXIMUM DARKNESS
(w/poster) (United Artists UAG 29872) 1975 SC 25
12(E) WELSH CONNECTION (MCA MCF 2753) 1976 40

NB: (1) and (2) reissued on See For Miles (SEE 274) and (SEE 273) respectively in 1989, also in CD format. (1) reissued on vinyl (Get Back GET 563) 2000 on Italian import. (2) reissued on vinyl (Get Back GET 585). (2) reissued on CD in Germany (Repertoire RR 4025-C) 1990. (3) later retitled *Man 1970* and reissued on Sunset (SLS 50380) in 1976. (5) reissued on CD (Beat Goes On BGOCD 365) 1998. (6) reissued on Beat Goes On (BGOLP 14) in 1988 and on CD in 1992. (9) and (10) reissued on CD by Beat Goes On (BGOCD 208 and 209 respectively) 1993. (11) reissued on Beat Goes On (BGOLP 43) 1989 and on CD (BGOCD) 1992. *Green Fly* (Latymer/Cherry Red D LATE 1) 1986 is a decent compilation. There's also a compilation of the United Artists years, *Perfect Timing 1970-75* (EMI EMS 1403) 1991, also available on CD. *Live At The Rainbow 1972* (World Wide Records

MAN - 2oz Of Plastic With A Hole In The Middle (LP).

MAN - Man (CD).

SPM-WWR-CD 0001) 1991 captures them live at the zenith of their career. *Greasy Truckers Party* (Point PNTVP 104CD) 1997 presents the two cuts from that compilation as a **Man** album. *Christmas At The Patti* (Point PNTVP 110CD) 1997 is a reissue of a various artists set taped at **Man's** 1972 Christmas Party. *To Live To Die For* (Point PVTVP 108CD) 199? is a bootleg quality recording from October 1970 upgraded. *The Dawn Of Man* (Recall SMDCD 124) is a 2-CD set which repackages their first two albums and adds three early cuts from their days as **The Bystanders**. The package captures some of their early material and demonstrates the strong influence of US West Coast acts like Quicksilver on their own blend of UK psychedelic rock. *The Definitive Collection* (Essential ESACD 917) 2000 provides an overview of their career. *And In The Beginning The Complete Early Man 1968-69* (Castle CMDDD 921) 2004 is a 2-CD set comprising their first two albums plus bonus tracks.

EP: 1(E) BANANAS (United Artists REM 408) 1976

45s: Sudden Life/Love (Pye 7N 17684) 1969 SC
(up to Daughter Of The Fireplace/
1976) Country Girl (Liberty LBF 15448) 1971 SC
Taking The Easy Way Out Again/
California Silks And Satins (United Artists UP 35703) 1974
Day And Night/
Hard Way To Live (United Artists UP 35739) 1974
Out Of Your Head/I'm A Love Taker (MCA MCA 236) 1976
Bananas/Bananas (United Artists UPS 408) 1976

One of the 'progressive' groups to develop out of the psychedelic era, **Man** evolved from a Swansea outfit, **The Bystanders**, with whom all but Leonard (previously with The Dream) had been involved. Despite their Welsh origins, like many other groups of their ilk, they based themselves on the Continent in the late sixties. During this period, they enjoyed only a very small following in England.

The music on their first two albums was strongly influenced by their connections with US West Coast Group, Quicksilver Messenger Service. The group is pictured largely nude on the cover of their debut album, which caused something of a stir at the time. A single from this album, *Sudden Life*, attracted considerable airplay, which won the band wider attention but did not enter the Charts. Nearly five minutes long, with its driving guitar and organ, and recorded screams superimposed upon sound effects, this was a little special at the time, whilst its flip side *Love* captured them in a laid-back mood. Also of note was the *The Future Hides Its Face*.

Another track off their second album, *Prelude/The Storm*, was a beautiful, flowing instrumental, complete with seagull sounds.

They became more improvisational on their Liberty album. The better tracks included *Alchemist* and the hard-rocker *Daughter Of The Fireplace*, which was put out as the group's second single.

Their fourth album won critical acclaim. Its prime cut, *Many Are Called But Few Get Up*, was a slice of psychedelic delirium. It was also the highlight of *Live At The Padget Rooms*, a budget release which also included *H. Samuel*, an improvised 20-minute jam.

The *Be Good To Yourself...* album is also a classic, coming in a gatefold sleeve featuring a hand-drawn map of Wales. *Bananas* became a dope-smokers' anthem and *C'mon* and *Life On The Road* were both great late sixties-style rock. In their live act, they were paying increasing homage to the Welsh choral tradition - the Gwalia Male Voice Choir backed them in an open-air concert at Kennington Oval in 1972 and again at the Roundhouse in 1973. An extended version of *C'mon* from the Roundhouse concert preceded by the traditional *Saspan Fach* by the Choir were used on the half live/half studio release, *Back Into The Future*. The budget price release made No 23 in the UK Album Charts and Pye capitalised on this by releasing the *Golden Hour* compilation of their first two albums. They also contributed two tracks, *Spunk Rock* and *Angel Easy*, to the *Greasy Truckers Party* (2-LP) in 1974.

The *Christmas At The Patti* set was taken from a concert at the Patti Pavilion in Swansea in 1972. *Slow Motion* was a relatively disappointing album. Guitar ace John Cipollina (ex-Quicksilver Messenger Service) was recruited for a 1975 tour. The resulting live album, *Maximum Darkness*, included versions of Buffy Sainte Marie's *Codine* (which was also covered by Quicksilver, among many others) and Quicksilver's *Babe I'm Gonna Leave You*. It made No 25 in the Album Charts but was their last for United Artists. Early copies came with a poster. **Man** went on to record a couple of albums for MCA and their career continued beyond the time frame of this book. So here we leave those loveable hippie-rockers, arguably one of Wales's best ever bands.

Terry Williams later rejoined **Dave Edmunds** in a revived Rockpile.

Green Fly is a double compilation of material from the 1972-75 era when their primary influence was progressive rock. The *Live At The Rainbow* 1972 set includes extended versions of stage favourites like *Bananas, Life On The Road* and *Love Your Life*, which fans should lap up.

And In The Beginning The Complete Early Man 1968-69 is a 2-CD set comprising *Revelation* on disc one plus three bonus singles. Disc two consists of *2ozs Of Plastic With A Hole In The Middle* plus an early version of their *Spunk Rock* anthem, two alternate takes of *My Name Is Jesus Smith* and the previously unreleased *Sad Song*. The set comes with thorough sleevenotes and photos.

Compilation appearances by the band have included: *Daughter Of The Fireplace* on *All Good Clean Fun* (LP); *Many Things Are Called But Few Get Up* on *The Age Of Enlightenment-Prog Rock, Vol. One* (CD); *It Is As It Must Be, Sudden Life* and *Spunk Box* on *Progressive Music* (LP); *Sudden Life* has resurfaced on the 3-CD set *Metal* and on *Rock Of Ages, Four Decades Of Heavy Rock 1962-2002* and you'll also find *Spunk Box* on the 3-CD box set *Ars Longa Vita Brevis: A Compendium Of Progressive Rock 1967-1974*. (VJ)

Manchester Mob

Personnel:	CLEM CATTINI	drms	A
	PHIL DENNYS	piano	A
	GRAHAM GOULDMAN	gtr	A
	JOHN PAUL JONES	bs, vcls	A

45: Bony Maronie At The Hop/
Afro Asian   (Parlophone R 5552) 1967 R1

Four session men who "just got together for a giggle" ('Beat Instrumental', March 1967), this studio combo was notable for containing future **10cc** member **Graham Gouldman**, **Led Zeppelin**'s **John Paul Jones** and Clem Cattini. The 45 flopped at the time but has now become quite collectable. More or less the same personnel had recorded a 45 the previous year as **High Society**. (VJ)

Manchester's Playboys

45: I Feel So Good/I Close My Eyes   (Fontana TF 745) 1966 R2

This is another rare and collectable 45 by a six-piece group. It's a big mod/soul favourite. (VJ)

MAN - Be Good To Yourself At Least Once A Day (LP).

Mandarin Kraze

45s: How Long Does It Take To Explain/
Magazine Cottage   (Carnaby CNS 4008) 1970
Blink Bonny Bluabora/Will You Ever   (President PT 332) 1971

How Long.... is a reasonable orchestrated pop ballad. The flip side is a pleasant pop song. (VJ)

Mandingo

ALBUMS:	1	MANDINGO 1: SACRIFICE	(EMI EMC 3010) 1973 SC
(up to	2	MANDINGO 2: PRIMEVAL RHYTHM OF LIFE	
1976)			(Studio Two TWO 400) 1973 R1
	3	MANDINGO 3: STORY OF SURVIVAL	
			(EMI EMC 3038) 1975 SC

NB: (2) also issued on quadraphonic (Studio Two Q4TWO 400) 1973 SC. They made a further album, *Mandingo 4: Savage Rite* (EMI EMC 3217) in 1977.

45s: Medicine Man/Black Rite   (EMI EMI 2014) 1973 SC
Fever Pitch/Cheater   (EMI EMI 2062) 1973 SC

These funky dance tunes were big in the clubs. They were actually played by the Geoff Love Orchestra! (VJ)

Mandrake Paddlesteamer

Personnel:	MARTIN BRILEY	lead gtr	A
	BRIAN ENGEL	vcls	A
	MARTIN HOOKER	keyb'ds	A
	BARRY NIGHTINGALE	drms	A
	PAUL RLORDEN	bs	A

ALBUMS: 1 MANDRAKE PADDLESTEAMER
(Forgotten Jewels FJ 001) 1991
2 OVERSPILL   (Scanner Jots) 199?

NB: (1) is a CD compilation of Engel / Briley compositions from the early seventies, which was also available on vinyl with gatefold cover. Taken from a poor quality cassette it also has some incorrect track titles. (2) is a vinyl compilation, containing five acetate cuts recorded in late '68/early '69 plus a recording of their appearance on 'Top Gear' on 6th April 1969.

45: Strange Walking Man/Steam   (Parlophone R 5780) 1969 R2
Reissue: Strange Walking Man/Steam (PS) (Bam-Caruso NRIC 033) 1988

Mandrake Paddlesteamer made one, now legendary, psychedelic 45 which inevitably interests collectors. The original release of *Strange Walking Man* is now very expensive to purchase but aside from the disc's reissue by Bam-Caruso in 1988, the 'A' side, *Strange Walking Man* has also been heavily compiled. It's unusual for a tempo change towards the end where the vocal parts end and the song culminates with an instrumental passage. The track also features some great understated guitar work, and superb trippy lyrics. The flip side, *Steam*, is a pretty decent keyboard-driven instrumental.

The band was formed around '67 / '68 when Martin Briley and Brian Engel met at Art School in Walthamstow, London. Brian recalls: "Martin knew a local businessman, John Lindsay who "had some money" and agreed to manage the band. He also knew a keyboard player, Martin Hooker who was playing James Brown/Booker T soul type stuff in a local "mod" band. He gave Hooker a couple of small parcels wrapped up in tin-foil and three days later Martin Hooker had become a committed underground music freak!! I still don't know what was in the small parcels!"

"Barry Nightingale's dad owned a rubber factory in Romford, next door to the Reslo mike factory where I worked for a while... he was a convenient drummer with a house out in the country where we could rehearse!! Anyway about a week later we found Paul Riordan who was working in an art studio in Gower St., W.1. and asked him to join. I was playing bass at the time, but I was crap and it was decided that I was a much better songwriter and lead vocalist, so that's what I became with Paul taking over on bass."

In order to prove that they were different from the other English "psychedelic" bands churning out rehashed Tolkein and second hand Timothy Leary they deliberately chose material which Brian thought would be politically incorrect: "Our songs tended to be based on authentic blood thirsty Viking sagas (as opposed to Bored Of the Rings), or Beowulf, or urban myths about East End sex criminals or circus dwarves... or anything outrageous. The closest we came to commerciality was a few songs using Ray Bradbury out of Shakespeare as our influence, *Something Wicked This Way Comes*, *The October Country* etc."

About this time the band were "discovered" by Shapiro Bernstein publishers, and together with Rob Finnis, (now a rock author) did a bizarre audition at EMI in Manchester Square. Originally their manager had arranged that we would be signed to the new Harvest label, but EMI were a bit wary about having such an unusual band on the label (Brian for instance, wanted to issue a pro-US press release saying that they hoped the U.S. would nuke the Vietcong!!) He recalls: "We predated the outrageous Punk excesses of 1977/8 by ten years!! Nobody ever knew how to categorise us. Our single, *Strange Walking Man* was the mildest of our songs, and our new label Parlophone couldn't see anything bizarre in it at all. It was, in fact, about a guy suffering from a very bad trip but maybe it was about a boy whose girlfriend had left him....."

Their second 45, *Sunlight Glide/Len* (Parlophone SD 6072) 1969, was only released in Sweden, though no-one seems to know quite how this came about. It was written by Clae Fellbom and Calvin Floyd, two film producers responsible for a minor Swedish film called 'Skottet', which the songs were included in. *Sunlight Glide* is a melancholic, slow number, quite unlike this first 45. The flip side, *Len*, is a fuzzy instrumental.

Brian Engel left **Mandrake Paddlesteamer** in around August 1970, in order to arrange exhibitions for Art degrees etc. and although the band carried on as a four piece instrumental for a few months (doing the first Isle Of White Festival, as Brian recalls), Briley then left and the band split up.

In late 1972 Briley and Engel joined forces again to form Prowler, which they intended to be a more commercial form of **Mandrake**, although the songs were just as bizarre.... Brian remembers: "There was one really good **Clapton**-esque riff based song called *Creeping Tom*, which I really liked and it contained the lines "I'm creeping round your house to find, What's going on behind your blind, I'm hiding there without a sound, To catch you with your sashcords down" which sounded like a really powerful **Cream**/Robert Johnson Blues unless you analysed the lyric and found it was about voyeurism.... I supposed it was a bit like *Arnold Layne*, now I come to think about it."

Prowler managed to release one 45 on Parlophone in 1973: *Pale Green Vauxhall Driving Man* about a South London pervert - molesting girls, etc, but which was musically a normal sort of family-oriented type pop song. The record company was worried about the word "Vauxhall" and deleted the word from the title on the 45 believing that it would be interpreted as advertising!! Never mind the fact that the lyrical content....

An album entitled *Liverpool Echo* was also intended for release on Spark, but Engel and Briley "fell out with the production team at AIR studios" and pulled the plug on the sessions "in disgust at their unhip, old fashioned approach". Brian remembers: "They wanted us to be like Tom Jones or someone. We said that if we were going to be old fashioned, then we'd be really old fashioned and so we retired to do Everly Brothers songs around the London pubs. However, as fate would have it, we were "discovered" again which resulted in us forming the early seventies band Starbuck, with songwriters/impresarios Howard and Blaikley who had at the time just lost **The Herd**."

After this brief period of pop stardom, Briley became disenchanted and joined **Greenslade** whilst Engel went off to "be artistic and sing on a million sessions". Eventually he was struck down with an acute bout of poverty and so joined a band on RCA which became the first credible English Country band, **Limey**. "After two albums I was then asked to join a very very commercial pop band which I did. I then discovered where the money disappears to in the music business and I have been chasing songwriter's royalties ever since...."

It should be pointed out that **Robert Palmer** was not in this group but in a Hull-based band called Mandrake.

Compilation appearances have included: *Len* on *Psychedelia, Vol. 3* (LP) and *Hen's Teeth, Vol. 3* (CD); *Strange Walking Man* on *Perfumed Garden, Vol. 1* (LP & CD), *Psychedelia At Abbey Road* (CD), *Illusions From The Crackling Void* (LP), *It's Only A Passing Phase* (LP) and on the 4-CD box set *Acid Drops, Spacedust & Flying Saucers*; and *Sunlight Glide* on *Psychedelia, Vol. 2* (LP), *The Best Of Rubble Collection, Vol. 3* (CD) and *Hen's Teeth Vol. 1* (CD). (VJ/BE)

Manfred Mann

Personnel:			
MIKE HUGG	drms	ABCD
PAUL JONES	vcls, hrmnca	ABC
MANFRED MANN	keyb'ds	ABCD
DAVE RICHMOND	bs	A
MIKE VICKERS	gtr	AB
KLAUS VOORMANN	bs	A
TOM McGUINNESS	bs, gtr	BCD
JACK BRUCE	bs	C
MIKE D'ABO	vcls	D

NB: Pete Burford and David Hyde each filled the bass slot for a couple of weeks each prior to **Jack Bruce** joining.

HCP

ALBUMS: 1(B) THE FIVE FACES OF MANFRED MANN
(HMV CLP 1731) 1964 R1 3

2(B) MANN MADE (mono/stereo)
(HMV CLP 1911/CSD 1628) 1965 R1 7

MANDRAKE PADDLE STEAMER - Overspill (LP).

3(B) MANN MADE HITS (Compilation)
                               (HMV CLP 3559) 1965 SC 11
4(D) AS IS (mono/stereo) (Fontana (S)TL 5377) 1966 SC/R1 22
5(D) SOUL OF MANN (Compilation)
      (mono/stereo)   (HMV CLP/CSD 3594) 1967 SC 40
6(D) UP THE JUNCTION - ORIGINAL SOUNDTRACK
      RECORDING   (Fontana (S)TL 5460) 1968 SC -
7(D) WHAT A MANN (Comp.) (Fontana STL 13003) 1968 SC -
8(D) MIGHTY GARVEY! (mono/stereo)
                               (Fontana (S)TL 5470) 1968 SC -

NB: (1) and (2) reissued as double set on EMI (EDP 1546363) 1983. (1) reissued on CD and in stereo (EMI DORIG 121) 1997. (2) reissued on Regal Starline (SRS 5007) 1969. (2) has been reissued on CD, but in stereo only (EMI DORIG 119) 1997. (5) reissued on See For Miles (SEE 52) 1983 and on CD digipack (EMI 498 9352) 1999 in mono and stereo. (6) reissued on Fontana (6852 005) 1970 and on CD (RPM RPM 189) 1998. (8) reissued as CD digipak (Umbrella BROLL CD2) containing both mono and stereo versions of the album. There have also been several compilations and hits collections which may interest collectors: - *The Greatest Hits Of Manfred Mann* (Music For Pleasure MFP 5269) 1971; *This Is... Manfred Mann* (Philips 6382 020) 1971: *Mannerisms* (Philips SON 016) 1976 (also reissued again on CD with detailed sleevenotes and a couple of tracks from a rare French EP); *The Best Of Manfred Mann* (EMI NUT 7) 1977; *Semi-Detached Suburban (20 Great Hits Of The Sixties)* (EMI EMTV 19) 1979 (No 9); *The R&B Years* (See For Miles CM 105) 1982, reissued in 1986; *The Very Best Of Manfred Mann 1963-1966* (Music For Pleasure MFP 41 5651 1) 1984; *The Singles Album* (EMI EMS 1121) 1986; *Instrumentals* (See For Miles SEE 52) 1986; *Hit Records 1966-1969* (Fontana PRICE 66) 1988; *The EP Collection* (See For Miles SEE 252) 1989 or (SEECD 252) 1989, *The Collection* (2-LP) (Castle CCSLP 245) 1990, also on CD, and *The Best Of The EMI Years* (EMI 0777 89490 2) 1993. *Four Manfred Mann Originals* (EMI CDMANFRED 1) 1995 is a 4-CD box set of American mid-sixties albums by the band: - *The Manfred Mann Album*, *The Five Faces Of..., My Little Red Book Of Winners* and *Pretty Flamingo*. These are bound to interest fans of the band because they include obscurities, which didn't figure on the British releases. There is also a 2-CD retrospective *The Ascent Of Mann* (Fontana 534 806-2) 1997 which surveys the material they recorded for Fontana. It also includes eleven previously unissued cuts, including a number of jazzy instrumentals. *At Abbey Road 1963 - 1966* (EMI CD ABBEY 101) 1997 will also interest fans of the band. *The Very Best Of Manfred Mann* (Spectrum) 1998 is a worthwhile compilation, as is *The Very Best Of Manfred Mann* (MFP CD MFP 6381) 1998, which omits early non-hit 45s to include more obscure 'B' sides and album tracks. *All Manner Of Menn: 1963-1969 And More?* (Raven RVCD-102) 2000 is a 2-CD set on Australian import, which includes the best of their Columbia and Fontana singles. *The Evolution Of Manfred Mann* (Creature MANFRED 1) 2003 is a 2-CD set plus a DVD containing all the hits of **Manfred Mann** and **Manfred Mann's Earth Band**.

                                                          HCP
EPs: 1(B) MANFRED MANN'S COCK-A-HOOP WITH 5-4-3-2-1
                               (HMV 7EG 8848) 1964 SC -
      2(B) GROOVIN' WITH MANFRED MANN
                               (HMV 7EG 8876) 1965 SC -
      3(B) THE ONE IN THE MIDDLE (HMV 7EG 8908) 1965 SC 7
      4(B) NO LIVING WITHOUT LOVING
                               (HMV 7EG 8922) 1965 SC -
      5(C) MACHINES   (HMV 7EG 8942) 1966 SC -
      6(D) INSTRUMENTAL ASYLUM (HMV 7EG 8949) 1966 SC -
      7(D) AS WAS   (HMV 7EG 8962) 1966 SC -
      8(D) INSTRUMENTAL ASSASSINATION
                               (Fontana TE 17483) 1966 -
      9(-) THE HITS OF MANFRED MANN (cassette EP)
                               (Philips MCF 5002) 1968 -
      10(-) THE HITS OF MANFRED MANN AND DAVE DEE,
            DOZY, BEAKY, MICK AND TICH (cassette EP)
                               (Philips MCF 5005) 1968 -

NB: (6) with **Jack Bruce**.

                                                          HCP
45s: Why Should We Not/Brother Jack (HMV POP 1189) 1963 SC -
      Cock-A-Hoop/Now You're Needing Me (HMV POP 1225) 1963 -
      5-4-3-2-1/Without You   (HMV POP 1252) 1964 5
      Hubble Bubble (Toil And Trouble)/
      I'm Your Kingpin   (HMV POP 1282) 1964 11
      Do Wah Diddy Diddy/
      What You Gonna Do?   (HMV POP 1320) 1964 1
      Sha La La/John Hardy   (HMV POP 1346) 1964 3
      Come Tomorrow/
      What Did I Do Wrong?   (HMV POP 1381) 1965 4
      Oh No Not My Baby/
      What Am I Doing Wrong   (HMV POP 1413) 1965 11
      If You Gotta Go, Go Now/Stay Around (HMV POP 1466) 1965 2
      There's No Living Without Your Loving/Tired Of Trying, Bored

MANFRED MANN - Groovin' With (7" EP).

      With Lying (demo-only EP sampler) (HMV 7TEA 2124) 1965 R1
      Pretty Flamingo/You're Standing By   (HMV POP 1523) 1966 1
      You Gave Me Somebody To Love/
      Poison Ivy   (HMV POP 1541) 1966 36
      Just Like A Woman/Wanna Be Rich (Fontana TF 730) 1966 10
      Semi-Detached, Suburban Mr. James/
      Morning After The Party   (Fontana TF 757) 1966 2
      Ha! Ha! Said The Clown/
      Feeling So Good (Some in PS) (Fontana TF 812) 1967 SC/- 4
      Sweet Pea/One Way   (Fontana TF 828) 1967 36
      So Long, Dad/Funniest Gig   (Fontana TF 862) 1967 -
      Mighty Quinn/
      By Request - Edwin Garvey   (Fontana TF 897) 1968 1
      Up The Junction/
      Sleepy Hollow (Some in PS)   (Fontana TF 908) 1968 SC/-
      My Name Is Jack/There Is A Man (Fontana TF 943) 1968 8
      Fox On The Run/Too Many People (Fontana TF 985) 1968 5
      Ragamuffin Man/A 'B' Side   (Fontana TF 1013) 1969 8
Reissues: Ha! Ha! Said The Clown/Mighty Quinn/Semi-Detached Suburban
      Mr. James/The 'B' Side   (Philips 6006 575) 1977 -
      Pretty Flamingo/The One In The Middle/
      Got My Mojo Working   (EMI 2644) 1977 -
      Mighty Quinn/
      By Request - Edwin Garvey   (Old Gold OG 9252) 1982 -
      Do Wah Diddy Diddy/
      What You Gonna Do?   (HMV PMS 1003) 1982 -
      Do Wah Diddy Diddy/
      What You Gonna Do?   (Old Gold OG 9369) 1983 -
      Pretty Flamingo / 5-4-3-2-1   (Old Gold OG 9376) 1983 -
      5-4-3-2-1 / Pretty Flamingo   EMI G45 15) 1984 -
      Pretty Flamingo/Come Tomorrow (Old Gold OG 9697) 1987 -

Manfred Mann was a very versatile band - although they recorded a string of successful pop singles, the band's range encompassed both jazz and R&B and they developed a large international following.

The band originally formed in London in December 1962 as The Mann-Hugg Blues Menn. **Manfred Mann**, whose real name was Manfred Lubowitz, was actually South African. He'd been born there on 21st October 1940 but left there in 1961 primarily because of his dislike of apartheid. He was very much into jazz, having been tutored by an American jazz pianist back in South Africa. He first met **Hugg**, who'd been born on 11th August 1942, in Andover, Hampshire at the Bull's Head Pub, an important jazz venue in Barnes, London and **Hugg** invited him to join his jazz quartet which was working at a holiday camp, having sacked their pianist. The Mann-Hugg Blues Menn was formed when the two of them had completed the Summer season at the holiday camp. They recruited **Paul Jones** (who'd been playing in a popular pub group called The Roosters, which included Tom McGuinness and had just broken up), **Mike Vickers** and Dave Richmond along with three horn players. They soon built up a strong reputation on London's burgeoning R&B circuit with a series of notable gigs including an appearance at the Marquee. By early 1963, the horns were dropped and shortly afterwards the band signed to EMI's HMV label who suggested a change of name to **Manfred Mann**.

Their first two singles - *Why Should We Not?*, a jazzy/R&B instrumental with some good harmonica playing from **Paul Jones**, and *Cock-A-Hoop*, a faster R&B number with vocals - made little impression. The group's next big break came when they were invited to write a new theme tune for the classic TV pop show 'Ready Steady Go'!! The result, *5-4-3-2-1*, a much poppier single than their first two, took them into the Top 5. After this Dave Richmond departed for session work, although he did later appear on the *Instrumental Assassination* EP, *Up The Junction* soundtrack and on an album cut *Autumn Leaves*. He was replaced by Tom McGuinness for their next effort, *Hubble Bubble (Toil And Trouble)*, an uptempo R&B number, which just missed the Top 10. The inevitable EP release followed: - **Manfred Mann**'s *Cock-A-Hoop With 5-4-3-2-1*, also included their first single and the flip to *5-4-3-2-1*.

One of their most memorable early songs was *Do Wah Diddy Diddy*. It had been written by Ellie Greenwich and Jeff Barry and first recorded by The Exciters. The **Manfred's** version gave them their first No 1 and also reached No 1 in the US, indeed it became their first recording to chart there.

Their debut album, *The Five Faces Of Manfred Mann*, was a classic R&B album of the era. It was comprised mostly of R&B covers but contained a few originals. It made No 3 in the Album Charts but was only issued in mono here in the UK, although it did appear in stereo in the US with a modified track listing to promote it, when a promo EP was also released, which is now scarce. It eventually climbed to No 141 in the US. The US release included two cuts, *Dashing Away With The Smoothing Iron* and *Sho*, which were unreleased in the UK.

Their next 45 was a revival of US girl R&B group The Shirelles' *Sha La La*, another strong R&B flavoured song, which made No 3 here and No 12 in the US.

Their first 45 of 1965 was the much slower cover of Marie Knight's *Come Tomorrow*. Its vastly different style contrasted with what had gone before and may have helped to ensure its UK Top 5 placing, though it fared less well in the States, where it only achieved No 50. January 1965 also saw the release of the *Groovin' With Manfred Mann* EP, which featured their earlier No 1 *Do Wah Diddy Diddy*.

Collectors may want to seek out a Canada-only release, which appeared in March 1965, *The Manfred Mann Return* (Capitol T 6102), which was essentially their first album with the two rare cuts on the US pressing plus a different take of *5-4-3-2-1* and *What Did I Do Wrong?*.

Their next 45 was a Maxine Brown soul ballad, *Oh No Not My Baby*, which just missed the Top 10 over here. This was rapidly followed by a four-track EP, *The One In The Middle*. It comprised new material, including a version of Bob Dylan's *With God On Our Side*, which attracted considerable airplay. It was their only EP to make the Charts, peaking at No 7.

They followed this with another EP, *No Living Without Loving*, in September 1965. Highlights included the orchestrated *Let's Get Stoned* (an Ashford

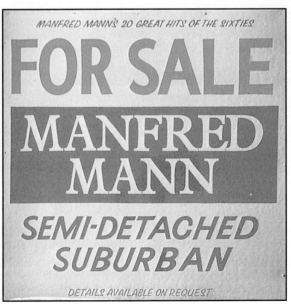

MANFRED MANN - For Sale (LP).

and Simpson composition) and the Screamin' Jay Hawkins classic, *I Put A Spell On You*.

Their final hit of 1965 was achieved with a (then) unreleased Bob Dylan composition, *If You Gotta Go, Go Now*. This powerful song had some suggestive lyrics leading to the inevitable bans from some radio stations.

Their *Mann Made* album effectively blended pop, R&B covers, originals and instrumentals. The punters liked it and it got to No 7 in the Album Charts.

In August 1965 they recorded *My Little Red Book*, a Bacharach-David song, for inclusion in the music score to *What's New Pussycat?* (United Artists UAL 4128/UAS 5128). Collectors may also be interested in a US-only album, *My Little Red Book Of Winners!* (Ascot ALM 13021/ALS 16021), which also included *My Little Red Book* along with *A Love Like Yours (Don't Come Knocking Every Day)*, which was not included on any UK releases.

In November 1965, **Vickers** left the band to record solo 45s, working once again with Dave Richmond in the **Mike Vickers Orchestra** and on several **Hollies** 45s. Tom McGuinness switched to guitar and Scot and ex-**Graham Bond** sidekick **Jack Bruce** came in on bass (with Pete Burford and David Hyde providing temporary cover whilst **Bruce** worked out his notice with **John Mayall**).

Their next 45, *Pretty Flamingo*, was a pop classic with vocalist **Paul Jones** in fine fetal and it gave the band its second UK No 1, topping the UK Charts for three weeks. It later climbed to No 29 in the US. Only a few months earlier, **Animals**' vocalist **Eric Burdon** had stood in for **Jones** at a London gig whilst he recovered from a minor car crash. The success of *Pretty Flamingo* made **Jones**' departure on 31 July 1966 all the more devastating, although to be fair, he'd given the band a year's warning of his intention to go solo. **Jack Bruce** also departed to join **Cream** whilst *Pretty Flamingo* was still in the Charts so after a couple of disappointing EPs - *Machines* and *Instrumental Asylum* - the band found itself seeking a new singer and new bassist and, dissatisfied with how EMI were promoting them, a new label too. On the vocal front, **Rod Stewart**, **Wayne Fontana** and **Long John Baldry** were all passed over in favour of **Mike D'Abo** from **A Band Of Angels**. German Klaus Voormann (previously of **Paddy, Klaus and Gibson**) was recruited on bass and they switched labels to Fontana, though once HMV got to hear of this they released two unfinished songs by the band on a 45 (*You Gave Me Somebody To Love/Poison Ivy*), which was also a minor hit. HMV also put out the inevitable *Mann Made Hits* album, which did include the previously unreleased *Spirit Level*; an EP, *As Was*, (which included four hitherto unreleased songs) and the *Soul Of Mann* album, a compilation of their instrumental tracks (save for *LSD*, a vocal blues number about money not the hallucinogenic drug), which included a version of their debut single in re-channelled stereo. *Mann Made Hits* rose to No 11 in the UK, but *Soul Of Mann* only got to No 40.

Their first Fontana single with **Mike D'Abo** on vocals was a pretty safe Dylan composition, *Just Like A Woman*, which was produced by Shel Talmy and gave them the Top 10 hit their flagging fortunes required. They

MANFRED MANN - The Singles Album (LP).

followed this with one of their better latter-day singles, *Semi-Detached Suburban Mr. James*, written by Geoff Stevens, which got to No 2 in the UK.

December 1966 saw the release of the *Instrumental Assassination* EP, which **D'Abo** didn't figure on but ex-member Dave Richmond did, on bass. It featured off-beat instrumental treatments of two **Troggs**' hits, *Wild Thing* and *With A Girl Like You*; **Georgie Fame**'s hit *Get Away* and Bobby Hebb's *Sunny*. The same month their *As Is* album was released (in two different covers - the 'alcove' pressing got to No 22, whilst the 'locomotive' cover is the rarer and more sought-after by collectors).

The first 45 of 1967 was the poppy (and disappointing) *Ha! Ha! Said The Clown*. Its commerciality took it into the UK Top 5 but it represented a regression on most of their earlier work. Their catchy instrumental revival of Tommy Roe's *Sweet Pea* could only climb to No 36 but their cover of Randy Newman's *So Long Dad* was their first single since *Cock-A-Hoop* back in 1963 to fail to chart. Once again they turned to a Dylan composition to get them out of a tight corner and *Mighty Quinn* did just that, topping the UK Charts for two weeks and climbing to No 10 in the US.

The group also supplied the music for the *Up The Junction* Soundtrack, which didn't chart. It was a rather diverse collection of musical styles, though, and is certainly worth a spin. *Walking Around*, *Just For Me* and *Sing Songs Of Love* (later covered by **Cherry Smash**) are examples of flower-pop.

The *What A Mann!* album was a compilation, which Fontana seem to have put out to retain interest in the band, until the *Mighty Garvey!* album was ready for release. This included their recent UK No 1, *The Mighty Quinn*, and three versions of *Happy Families*, one in a rock style, the second with a jazz flavour and the third as an Irish drinking song.

Their next single was a cover of John Simon's *My Name Is Jack*, from the film 'You Are What You Eat'. Another rather poppy song which certainly hasn't aged well, it saw them into the UK Top Ten at the time.

They charted again early in 1969 with a **Tony Hazzard** song, *Fox On The Run*. As well as reaching No 5 in the UK, it got to No 97 in the US. Their final hit single, Murray/Callander's *Ragamuffin Man*, was certainly their best since *The Mighty Quinn*. It got to No 8 in the UK, where its flip side, *A 'B' Side*, was used as the theme for a Mannekin Cigar commercial. By now, **Mann and Hugg** weren't interested in having a hit singles band and after a series of farewell gigs they split up in June 1969. By then, **Mann** and **Hugg** were already gigging under the name Emanon (no name spelt backwards) but they went on to form **Manfred Mann Chapter Three** with finance raised from making TV jingles. Tom McGuinness, meanwhile, formed **McGuinness Flint** and **Mike D'Abo** appeared on the *Jesus Christ Superstar* soundtrack album before launching a solo career. Klaus Voormann joined The Plastic Ono Band. When **Manfred Mann** split they left several unreleased songs in the can.

During his time with the **Manfreds**, **Manfred Mann** wrote the **Luvvers**' sole 'A' side, *House On The Hill*, and an unreleased **Mann/Hugg** composition, *House In The Country*, appeared on a 1969 45 by **Perfect People**. **Manfred Mann**'s production credits included both sides of a 1965 45 by **John Mantell**, a 1965 45 by the **Mark Leeman Five** and a 1968 45 by **Unit 4 Plus 2**. He also produced *Sweet Music* for **The Yardbirds**, a track which appeared on their US-only *For Your Love* album.

There was a re-union of **Mike D'Abo**, **Paul Jones**, **McGuiness**, **Hugg** and **Vickers** for a tour in 1992 to help promote *The Ages Of Mann* compilation, which collated their EMI and Fontana output using the name The Manfreds. Even Manfred Mann himself participated in some radio appearances with the reformed group. There were further Manfreds reunions over the next couple of years and they toured Europe and the US.

Inevitably several compilations have appeared since their demise and most are mentioned in the discography at the start of this article. Collectors may also be interested in *One Way* (Fontana 858 037 FPY), a now rare Dutch album from 1967, which included many of their 'B' sides.

Instrumentals, as its name suggests, compiles all their non-vocal material from the 1963-67 era. *All Manner Of Menn* is a worthwhile 2-CD compilation. It includes the pick of their Columbia and Fontana singles and adds key EP and album tracks like *There's No Living Without Your Love*, *My Little Red Book* and *Up The Junction*. *The Evolution Of Manfred Mann* contains the very best of **Manfred Mann** along with the finest moments of

the later incarnation **The Manfred Mann's Earth Band**. All the hits you would expect to find are there and there's also a bonus DVD, which features rarely archive footage of the band, including the extremely rare promo film for *Fox On The Run*. There's also a fold-out colour booklet, detailing the various Manfred's line-ups over the years, along with chart histories of the featured tracks.

They've also appeared on several Various Artists' compilations including: *The Mighty Quinn* on *Sixteen Star Tracks Of The Sixties* (LP); *Do Wah Diddy Diddy* on *Stardust* (2-LP) and on the 2-CD set *45s - 45 Classic No 1's*; *The One In The Middle* and *Watermelon Man* on *Liverpool '65* (LP); *Just Like A Woman* on *Made In England, Vol. 1* (CD); *Ha Ha Said The Clown* on *Made In England, Vol. 2* (CD); *Groovin'* and *I Put A Spell On You* on *R&B At Abbey Road* (CD); *5-4-3-2-1, Tired Of Trying, Bored With Lying*, and *Scared Of Dying* on *Beat At Abbey Road* (CD); *Nitty Gritty, You Don't Know Me, Semi-Detached Suburban Mr. James* and *Hound Dog* on *The Early Days Of Rock, Vol. 2 - Live In Concert 1964 - 1968* (CD); *If You Gotta Go, Go Now* on the 2-CD set *Stars And Stripes* and on the 2-CD set *Greatest Hits of The 60's Vol 4*; and *Pretty Flamingo* and *Long Haired Unsquare Dude Called Jack* on *Hard Up Heroes, Vol. 2* (CD). More recently, *54321* has resurfaced on the 6-CD box set *Best Of Driving Rock*; *Machines* can be found on *Colour Me Pop, Vol 2* (CD); *You're My Girl* on *Jagged Time Lapse, Vol 3* (CD); *Just Like A Woman* on the 2-CD set *Sixties Summer Love*; *She Needs Company* on *Colour Me Pop, Vol 3* (CD) and *Do Wah Diddy* on the 2-CD set *60 Number Ones Of The Sixties*. (VJ)

Manfred Mann and Mike Hugg

| Personnel: | MIKE HUGG | | A |
| | MANFRED MANN | | A |

45s:	Ski 'Full Of Fitness' Theme/		
	Baby Jane (Some PS)	(Ski SKI 1) 1971 SC/-
α	The Michelin Theme (Go Radial, Go Michelin) (PS)	
		(Michelin MIC-01) 1971 SC

NB: α is a one-sided 45.

Immediately after the break-up of **Manfred Mann**, their two founder members worked together on these advertising jingles prior to regrouping with the help of session musicians as **Manfred Mann's Chapter 3**.

In addition to the recordings listed above, they also recorded a flexi-disc commercial for Maxwell House coffee, *The Maxwell House Shake*. (VJ)

Manfred Mann's Chapter 3

Personnel incl:	BRIAN HUGG	gtr	A
	MIKE HUGG	vcls, electric piano	A
	MANFRED MANN	keyb'ds	A
	STEVE YORK	bs	A

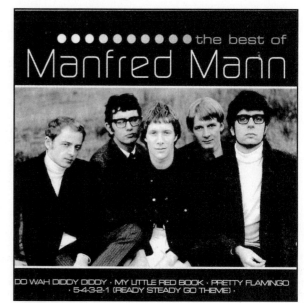

MANFRED MANN - The Best Of (CD).

MANFRED MANN'S EARTH BAND - The Roaring Silence (LP).

ALBUMS: 1(A)   MANFRED MANN CHAPTER 3, VOL 1
                                      (Vertigo VO 3) 1969 R1
         2(A)   MANFRED MANN CHAPTER 3, VOL. 2
                                      (Vertigo 6360 012) 1970 R1

NB: (1) reissued on CD (Cohesion MEMCD 14), (Cohesion MANN 001) and again (Creature 5000120573). (2) reissued on CD (Cohesion MFMCD 15).

45:      Happy Being Me/Devil Woman   (Vertigo 6059 012) 1970

This was a sort of free-form jazz group, which **Hugg** and **Mann** formed in 1969. Their two 'progressive' albums sold poorly at the time but they were able to finance them with income from their TV commercials. *Vol 1* had its moments on tracks like *One Way Glass* and *Devil Woman* and *Vol 2* was critically-acclaimed, although sales were disappointing. They also started a third album but disintegrated due to musical differences between **Mann** and **Hugg** before it could be completed. The line-up was supplemented by session singers, a wind section and drummers. Their next venture was **Manfred Mann's Earth Band**.

Manfred Mann's Chapter 3 had one cut, *One Way Glass*, included on *Vertigo Annual 1970* (LP) in 1970. (VJ)

Manfred Mann's Earth Band

Personnel: MIKE HUGG   drms   AB
              MANFRED MANN   keyb'ds   AB
              COLIN PATTENDEN   bs   AB
              MICK ROGERS   vcls, gtr   A
              CHRIS SLADE   drms   AB
              CHRIS THOMPSON   vcls   B
              DAVE FLETT   gtr   B

                                                        HCP
ALBUMS: 1(A)   MANFRED MANN'S EARTH BAND
(up to   (Philips 6308 086) 1972 SC -
1976)   2(A)   GLORIFIED MAGNIFIED   (Philips 6308 125) 1972 SC -
         3(A)   MESSIN'   (Vertigo 6360 087) 1973 SC -
         4(A)   SOLAR FIRE   (Bronze ILPS 9265) 1973 -
         5(A)   THE GOOD EARTH   (Bronze ILPS 9306) 1974 -
         6(A)   NIGHTINGALES AND BOMBERS
                                      (Bronze ILPS 9337) 1975 -
         7(B)   THE ROARING SILENCE (Bronze ILPS 9357) 1976 10

NB: Albums were released on Polydor in the US and (3) was entitled *Get Your Rocks Off* (Polydor 5050) 1973. Cohesion have reissued all of the above on CD except (2) and (4) along with a compilation, *20 Years Of Manfred Mann's Earth Band 1971-1991* (Cohesion COMME 1 CD) 1991, but as if this wasn't enough there was also a 13-CD collection, *Manfred Mann's Earth Band* (Cohesion MM Box 1) 1992 which came with a bonus CD featuring a 50-minute interview with **Manfred Mann**, a 40-page booklet of sleevenotes and a complete discography from 1971-1991. This must be the definitive statement of the band. *The Evolution Of Manfred Mann* (Creature MANFRED 1) 2003 is a 2-CD set plus a DVD containing all the hits of **Manfred Mann** and **Manfred Mann's Earth Band**.

45s: The Maxwell House Shake (one-sided flexi)
(up to   (Lyntone LYN 1981) 1970 -
1976)   Living Without You/Tribute   (Philips 6006 122) 1971 -
    α   Mrs. Henry/Prayer   (Philips 6006 159) 1971 -
        Meat/Glorified Magnified   (Philips 6006 251) 1972 -
        Let Your Rocks Off/Sadjoy   (Vertigo 6059 078) 1973 -
        Joybringer/Can't Eat Meat   (Vertigo 6059 083) 1973 9
        Father Of Day, Father Of Night/
        Solar Fire   (Bronze BRO 9) 1974 -
        Be Not Too Hard/Earth Hymn, Part 2A (Bronze BRO 13) 1974 -
        Spirits In The Night/
        As Above, So Below, Part 2   (Bronze BRO 18) 1975 -
        Blinded By The Light/Starbird No 2   (Bronze BRO 29) 1976 6
        Questions/
        Waiter, There's A Yawn In My Ear No 2 (Bronze BRO 34) 1976 -

NB: α as The Earth Band.

Mann formed this outfit in March 1972. Their first intended album, *Stepping Sideways*, was scrapped although half of its intended tracks later appeared on their eponymous debut album, which attracted little attention at the time here, though it did climb to No 138 in the States where they enjoyed an early hit single with *Living Without You* (No 69).

Glorified Magnified, which was full of incisive guitar riffs and frequent instrumental passages, represented a considerable advance on their debut effort. It was critically acclaimed but copies didn't shift in any considerable quantities. During 1973 they also toured the US and Europe extensively.

Their third album, *Messin'*, was spearheaded by a Dylan cover, *Get Your Rocks Off*, and in the US, where it climbed to No 196, this song name was used as the album's title.

The first significant commercial breakthrough came when *Joybringer*, which was based on *Jupiter* from Holst's *Planet's Suite*, took them into the Top 10. It remains a classic 45 and they were the first band granted permission by Holst's daughter to reinterpret his music.

In April 1974 they signed a new record contract with Bronze Records and rewarded them with their best album to date, *Solar Fire*. Very much in the space-rock mould its highlight was yet another Dylan song, *Father Of Day, Father Of Night*, which was turned into a nine-minute feast of moog and guitar riffs, superimposed by a lavish choir and melodramatic singers. Here in the UK an edited version was also put out on 45. The album got to No 96 in the States.

Avoid *The Good Earth* because it certainly wasn't as good as their previous two albums, though it still got to No 157 in the States, where the band had attracted quite a considerable following. The band came up with a pretty novel promotional scheme, though, whereby anybody who bought the album could remove the coupon on the inner sleeve to claim a square foot of land in Wales.

Nightingales And Bombers was their first album to include a cover version by emerging new US singer/songwriter Bruce Springsteen. In future years they became notable for their Springsteen covers. The song in question on this album, the excellent *Spirits In The Night*, was also put out as a 45 but failed to chart. After this album Rogers departed to help form Aviator. He was replaced by vocalist Chris Thompson and Dave Flett on guitar.

The new line-up's first release was another Springsteen cover, *Blinded By The Light*, which gave them a UK No 6 and a US No 1, becoming a million-seller. Another classic single it also opened (in an extended version) their *Roaring Silence* album. In fact it dominated the album, which also included a version of **Mike Heron**'s *Singing The Dolphin Through* and five originals. Of these, **Mann**'s *Waiter, There's A Yawn In My Ear*, was a rather boring instrumental; whilst *The Road To Babylon* and *Starbird* utilised the 'heavenly choir' approach earlier used on *Father Of Day, Father Of Night*; *This Side Of Paradise* was pretty standard progressive rock and *Questions*, a soft keyboard-dominated meander. **Mann** had written *Starbird* and *Questions* with Chris Slade. The album got to No 10 here (becoming their first UK Chart album). In the US, it gave them their only gold album.

The band lasted well beyond the time span of this book, until 1987 in fact. An offshoot of the Earthband, Colin Pattenden and Chris Slade together with Pete Cox, Chris West, Roy Shipston and Dare Fishel recorded as Terra Nova and issued a self-titled album in Europe in 1980 (BB 2010 13).

The album consists of mainstream rock. Back in 1973 **Manfred Mann's Earth Band** had one track, *Buddah*, included on the Vertigo compilation, *Suck It And See* (LP). In 1977, a Bronze promotional compilation, *The New Bronze Age* (LP), included edited versions of *Blinded By The Light, Father Of Day, Father Of Night, Spirits In The Night* and *Be Not Too Hard*. Also of interest may be a four-track 12" white label promo, which previewed their *Roaring Silence* album and is now hard to track down. Whilst he was with the band **Manfred Mann** wrote the music score to a film called 'Swedish Fly Girls' (Juno S-1003) 1975. The Soundtrack was only released in the States.

The Evolution Of Manfred Mann contains the very best of **Manfred Mann** along with the finest moments of **The Manfred Mann's Earth Band**. All the hits you would expect to find are there and there's also a bonus DVD, which features rarely archive footage of the band, including the extremely rare promo film for *Fox On The Run*. There's also a fold-out colour booklet, detailing the various **Manfred's** line-ups over the years, along with chart histories of the featured tracks. (VJ)

The Maniax

45:     Out Of Reach/
        The Devil's House   (White Label WLR 101/102) 1966

This very obscure five man band may be European in origin but their 45 was pressed in the UK. It was written by a Peter Green but not the famous one! The mid-paced flip side recently resurfaced on the excellent *Syde Tryps, Vol. 1* (LP & CD) and on *Visions Of The Past, Vol. 2* (LP & CD). (VJ)

The Manish Boys

Personnel: WOOLF BRYNE   sax   A
              DAVID BOWIE (DAVIE JONES)   vcls   A
              JOHNNY FLUX   ld gtr   A
              PAUL RODRIGUEZ   sax   A
              ROBERT SOLLY   organ   A
              JOHN WATSON   ld vcls, bs   A
              MICK WHITE   drms   A

45:     I Pity The Fool/Take My Tip   (Parlophone R 5250) 1965 R5

NB: (1) reissued with the addition of two **Davy Jones and The Third** tracks *You've Got A Habit Of Leaving* and *Baby Loves That Way* (EMI NUT 2925) 1979, again in a picture sleeve as a 10" (Charly CYM 1) 1982 and as a 12" (See For Miles SEA 1), also in 1982 and as a CD in a slimline or album jewel case (See For Miles SEECD 1) 1982.

This project from Maidstone, Kent involved **David Bowie** and this horrendously rare 45 (originals change hands for several hundred pounds) can also be found (much more cheaply) on *The Manish Boys/Davy Jones*

VISIONS OF THE PAST VOL. 2 (Comp CD) including The Maniax.

and The Lower Third (See For Miles SEA 1) 1985, a 12" single of some of his earliest recordings. Produced by Shel Talmy, the 'A' side is very bluesy. The flip is a groovy **Georgie Fame**-ish swinging sixties effort, later covered by **Janie Jones** on a 7"/10" EP. The single wasn't really commercial at all - and the saxes were overbearing! So **Davie Jones** joined **The Lower Third**. Paul Rodriguez and Bob Solly later worked as songwriters. Johnny Flux went on to work as a DJ, initially with pirate station Radio City (where **Davie Jones** contributed a series of jingles for his show) and Woolf Bryne also became a DJ with another pirate ship Radio London. Flux later joined Radio London too (working under the name John Edward), he also moved into record production with Canadian band The Guess Who and then he and Paul Rodriguez produced and co-wrote the **Edwick Rumbold** 45 *Specially When*. Flux also established the John Edwards Entertainment Agency, where he booked a range of psychedelic acts like **Mabel Greer's Toyshop** and **Magic Mixture**. Then in 1982, he wrote, arranged, produced and released *Save Your Love*, which became a No 1 for Renee & Renate. He was last reported working as a DJ on Radio Medway.

Compilation appearances include: *Take My Tip* and *I Pity The Fool* on *Sixties Lost And Found, Vol. 1* (LP); and *I Pity The Fool* on *In The Beginning* (LP). *Early On (1964-1966)* (CD) 1991 includes alternate versions of *I Pity The Fool* and *Take My Tip*. (VJ)

Marty Manning and The Cheetahs

45:     Tarzan March/Sunny   (CBS 2721) 1967

The Cheetahs, who came from Birmingham, had earlier recorded five 45s for Philips. *Tarzan March* was also recorded by **The Magicians**. (VJ)

John Mantell

45:     Remember Child/I'll See You Around   (CBS 201783) 1965 SC

Remember Child was a **Paul Jones** composition, produced by **Manfred Mann**. (VJ)

Phil Manzanera

                                                          HCP
ALBUMS: 1   DIAMOND HEAD   (Atco SD 36-113) 1975 40
(up to
1976)

Manzanera was a member of **Roxy Music**. Prior to his stints with **Quiet Sun** and 801 **Manzanera** cut this solo album. He went on to record two further albums for Polydor: *Listen Now* (1977) and *K-Scope* (1978). He then joined the revived **Roxy Music** for their best-selling US album *Manifesto* and remained with them for their final studio album *Avalon* in 1982. He later teamed up with former **Roxy Music** saxophonist Andy Mackay and recorded an album in 1986 with John Wetton. In the nineties he concentrated on live performances, appearing at the Guitar Legend and WOMAD festivals. At the close of the decade, he released a Latin-influenced album *Vozero*. (CG/VJ)

Maple Oak

Personnel: STAN ENDERSBY   gtr, vcls   ABC
              MARTY FISHER   keyb'ds, vcls   ABC
              PETE QUAIFE   bs   AB
              MICK COOK   drms   A
              GORDON MacBAIN   drms   BC

ALBUM: 1(C)   MAPLE OAK   (Decca SKL 5085) 1971 R3

NB: (1) reissued on CD with both sides of their earlier 45 as bonus tracks (Elergy E580/1) 2000.

45:     α   Son Of A Gun/Hurt Me So Much   (Decca F 13008) 1970 SC

NB: α non-LP.

RARE 60s BEAT TREASURES VOL. 2 (Comp CD) incuding The Marauders.

Maple Oak was formed by ex-**Kinks** bassist Pete Quaife. Canadian Stan Endersby (ex-Just Us) met Quaife on a trip to England in 1968, and Quaife suitably impressed with his guitar playing decided to form a band. It took six months to come to fruition with Endersby and Marty Fisher (ex-Flying Circus/Olivus) flying over to the UK from Toronto in April 1969. The band was revealed to the world in the centre spread of NME on 3rd April, and this came as a complete surprise to the other **Kinks**, who had no idea that Quaife had formed a new group!

Named after the two countries' national emblems, the band embarked on a tour of Denmark during May 1969. After the tour Cook left and the guys got their Canadian mate Gordon MacBain (ex-Flying Circus/Olivus) over from Canada as a replacement. Quaife departed in early 1970, shortly after the single and the others subsequently made the album as trio, with Fisher covering the bass slot on his keyboards. As with the 45, the album's release was delayed, this time until early 1971, by which time the group had split and returned to Toronto. The record itself, although often heavily criticised, is not that bad. It's one of the first country-influenced albums to be recorded in the UK, and features some early Bruce Cockburn songs that the writer never released himself.

Endersby later formed Heaven and Earth an interesting Toronto band that featured Ed Roth (ex-Just Us); Rick James and Denny Gerrard (ex-Paupers). Stan also played in Bruce Palmer and Dewey Martin's Buffalo Springfield Revisited during the eighties. He currently plays in a reformed Ugly Ducklings line up. Quaife also lives in Toronto and works as an airbrush artist. (NW/MWh)

Mike Maran

ALBUM:　　1　FAIR WARNING　　　　(Bronze ILPS 9221) 1972

This singer/songwriter often supported well-known bands in the early seventies. (BS)

The Marauders

Personnel:	DANNY DAVIS	gtr	A
	BRYN MARTIN	ld gtr	AB
	BARRY SARGENT	drms	AB
	KENNY SHERRATT	bs	AB
	CHRIS RENSHAW	gtr	B

			HCP
45s:	That's What I Want/		
	Hey What'd You Say	(Decca F 11695) 1963	SC 43
	Always On My Mind/Heart Full Of Tears	(Decca F 11748) 1963	-
	Lucille/Little Egypt	(Decca F 11836) 1964	SC -
	Baby I Wanna Be Loved/		
	Somebody Told My Girl	(Fontana TF 609) 1965	-

An R&B group from Stoke on Trent who achieved a minor hit with *That's What I Want*, a Carter-Lewis song but did less well with their later cover of Little Richard's *Lucille*. They were featured on Decca's 1964 *Saturday Club* (LP) compilation, playing *Greenback Dollar* and on *Thank Your Lucky Stars, Vol. 2* (LP) a year earlier with *That's What I Want*. They were also featured on *At The Cavern* (LP) playing *Dr. Feelgood* and *Keep On Rolling*. In May 1964 Davis left and was replaced by Renshaw.

Other compilation appearances have included: *Doctor Feelgood* and *Keep On Rolling* on *Original Liverpool Sound* (LP) and *Live At The Cavern* (CD); *That's What I Want* and *Hey Wha' D'Ya Say* on *Rare 60's Beat Treasures, Vol. 2* (CD); *Lucille* and *That's What I Want* on *Weekend Starts Here* (LP); and *That's What I Want* on *The Beat Scene* (CD) and *Beat Merchants* (2-LP). (VJ)

The Marbles

Personnel:	GRAHAM BONNET	vcls	A
	TREVOR GORDON GRUNNILL	vcls	A

NB: *The Marbles* (Repertoire REPUK 1014) 2004 is a reissue of their 1970 album (not released in the UK) with six bonus tracks.

			HCP
45s:	Only One Woman/		
	By The Light Of A Burning Candle	(Polydor 56272) 1968	5
	The Walls Fell Down/Love You	(Polydor 56310) 1969	28
	Breaking Up Is Hard To Do/		
	I Can't See Nobody	(Polydor 56378) 1970	-

This duo, originally from Skegness, had previously performed together in The Blue Sect. After that, Trevor Gordon emigrated to Australia, where he recorded with **The Bee Gees**. He returned to England with them, teamed up with **Bonnet** again and the resulting duo was signed up by Robert Stigwood. Their 1970 album included six **Bee Gees** songs, but by the time it was released they had split. The music is full of orchestration, vocal harmonies and acoustic guitar. It also contains covers of Bacharach and David's *A House Is Not A Home* and Greenfield and Sedaka's *Breaking Up Is Hard To Do*.

They had made an immediate impression when *Only One Woman*, one of those **Bee Gees**' compositions, burst into the UK Top 5 in 1968. The similar follow-up, *The Walls Fell Down*, also made the Top 30. They really could have been mistaken for **The Bee Gees** on that first 45. They also issued a single out in Australia with **The Bee Gees** (*House Without Windows/And I'll Be Happy* (Leedon LK-829) in 1965). Both sides of their first two 45s were written by the Gibb brothers. In addition to their three 45s they turn up on Polydor's *1970 Pop Party* (LP) compilation, playing *Breaking Up Is Hard To Do*. They also recorded a self-titled album released in Germany (Polydor 184 365) and in America (Cotillion SD 9029) in 1970.

After **The Marbles**' demise, in October 1969, **Bonnet** launched a solo career and then at the very end of the seventies became vocalist with **Ritchie Blackmore**'s Rainbow. **Trevor Gordon** issued an album, *Alphabet* (Polydor 2343 011) 1970.

Their 1970 album was reissued on CD in 2004, with six bonus cuts, including original mono versions of their other UK 45 releases.

Only One Woman has been compiled on *Pop-In, Vol 2* (CD). (VJ)

March Hare

Personnel:	BARRY GUARD	sax, drums	A
	PETER SKELLERN	vcls	A
	STU LEATHERWOOD		A

45s:	Cry My Heart/With My Eyes Closed	(Chapter One CH 101) 1968
	I Could Make It There With You/	
	Have We Got News For You	(Deram DM 258) 1969

This vocal harmony band also operated under the name **Harlan County**. They are most notable for having included **Peter Skellern**. Leatherwood had been in **The Koobas**. (VJ)

MARIE CELESTE - And Then Perhaps (CD).

The Mariane

45s: As For Marionettes/
          You Know My Name   (Columbia DB 8420) 1968
          You Had Better Change Your Evil Ways/
          Like A See Saw   (Columbia DB 8456) 1968

Originally from the States, **The Mariane** settled here in the UK. *Circus Days Vol. 3* (LP & CD) gives fresh exposure to *You Had Better Change Your Evil Ways*. **Mike Vickers** produced their 45s. (VJ)

Marianne and Mike

45s: α As He Once Was Mine/Go On   (Vocalion V 9218) 1964
          You're The Only One/
          One Good Turn Deserves Another   (Vocalion V 9225) 1964

NB: α 'B' side by Marianne only.

These records **do not** feature **Mick Jagger** and **Marianne Faithfull** as some have speculated and in collectable terms are near to worthless. **Marianne** appears to have been **Friday Browne**! (VJ).

Marie Celeste

ALBUM: 1 AND THEN PERHAPS   (Private Pressing) 1971 R4

NB: (1) reissued on CD (Audio Archives AACD 041).

Like most musically strong private pressings, this is ultra-rare and changes hands for vast sums of money. 200 copies were pressed originally and the album blends cover versions (Gershwin's *Summertime*, Paul Simon's *I Am A Rock* and Joni Mitchell and Tom Paxton compositions), traditional material and some originals with *Prisoner* the best of the small crop. Most tracks have an acoustic backing with twin female vocals. The band was from the Midlands. (VJ)

Marion

45:       I Go To Sleep/Abyssinian Secret   (Page One POF 042) 1967

This was wrongly included in earlier editions. Just to clear things up it was the first single (sung in English) by the German vocalist Marion Maerz who came from Hamburg and recorded over 20 singles and a few albums. The 'A' side is a **Kinks**' cover. (VJ/MS)

Mark-Almond

Personnel: JOHNNY ALMOND
              TOMMY EYRE   keyb'ds, flute, vcls,
                                perc, gtr
              JON MARK
              ROGER SUTTON   bs, vcls

ALBUMS: 1 MARK-ALMOND   (Harvest SHSP 4011) 1971 SC
         2 RISING   (Harvest SHVL 809) 1972 SC

Almond and Mark had both played together in **John Mayall's Bluesbreakers** previously. In addition to these albums, they can be heard playing *City, Part I (The Ghetto)* on the *Harvest Bag* (LP) compilation. It's a pleasant laid back bluesy number. The late Tommy Eyre had arranged **Joe Cocker's** *With A Little Help From My Friends* and later did sessions for people ranging from BB King to **Gerry Rafferty** and Wham. There are two further albums, which I don't have full details of. (VJ/DA)

Mark and John

Personnel: BEVERLY BROWN
              WILLIAM RAWLINSON

45:       Walk Right Back/Karen   (Decca F 12044) 1964

These two former members of the Merseybeat band The Mark Four were responsible for this rather undistinguished cover version of the Everly Brothers' hit.

Walk Right Back can also be found on *Mersey Sounds* (2-LP). (VJ)

Mark Five

Personnel: JOHN DALTON   bs   A
              JACK JONES   drms   A
              EDDIE PHILLIPS   gtr   A
              KENNY PICKETT   vcls   A
              MICK THOMPSON   gtr   A

45:       Baby What's Wrong/Tango   (Fontana TF 513) 1964 R1

With the addition of rhythm guitarist Mick Thompson **The Mark Four** briefly became **Mark Five** for the above 45. *Baby What's Wrong* was a rather ordinary uptempo song whilst *Tango* was rather unusual with a distinctive beat.

Baby What's Wrong has been compiled on *That Driving Beat* (CD). (VJ)

THE MARK FOUR - The Creation (LP).

The Mark Four

Personnel:

JOHN DALTON	bs	A
JACK JONES	drms	A
KENNY PICKETT	vcls	A
EDDIE PHILLIPS	ld gtr	A

ALBUM: 1(A) THE MARK FOUR THE CREATION (Eva 12005) 198?

EP: 1(A) LIVE AT THE BEAT SCENE CLUB
(Bam-Caruso OPRA 037) 1985

NB: Limited edition of 500.

45s:

Rock Around The Clock/Slow Down	(Mercury MF 815) 1964 R1
Crazy Country Hop/Try It Baby	(Mercury MF 825) 1964 R1
Hurt Me If You Will/I'm Leaving	(Decca F 12204) 1965 R2
Work All Day (Sleep All Night)/	
Goin' Down Fast	(Fontana H 664) 1966 R2

This group started out in Cheshunt, Hertfordshire, as the Blue Jacks back in 1963. They changed name to **The Mark Four** the following year.

Their debut 45 coupled a competent cover of rock'n'roll classic, *Rock Around The Clock*, with an up-tempo R&B Larry Williams track, *Slow Down*. The follow-up, *Crazy Country Hop*, had more of a country flavour about it as the title suggests and was pretty dire, though the flip, *Try It Baby*, was a more typical R&B offering. By the time of their third single, lead guitarist Eddie Phillips was experimenting with feedback and the next two 45s denoted a distinct change of style which leaned much more heavily towards the 'mod' sound of **The Who**. Indeed, **The Mark Four** became one of the most popular 'mod' groups on the British club circuit. They weren't also-rans, incidentally, they were innovators - Eddie Phillips went on to become the first guitarist to play guitar with a violin bow on *Makin' Time*, though by then the group had lost John Dalton to **The Kinks** and changed its name to **The Creation**.

The last two **Mark Four** 45s are recommended but quite expensive to acquire. Both sides of all four discs can be heard on Eva's *The Mark Four The Creation* compilation. Other compilation appearances have included: *I'm Leaving* and *Going Down Fast* on *Maximum Freakbeat* (CD); *Hurt Me If You Will* on *Mersey Sounds* (2-LP), *Rare 60's Beat Treasures, Vol. 3* (CD), *R&B Scene, Vol. 2* (LP) and *The Beat Scene* (CD); *I'm Leaving* and *Hurt Me (If You Will)* on *Rubble, Vol. 5 - The Electric Crayon Set* (LP), *Rubble, Vol. 3* (CD) and *The Demention Of Sound*; and *I'm Leaving* on *The Freakbeat Scene* (CD). (VJ)

Marksmen

45: Smersh/Orbit Three (Parlophone R 5075) 1963 SC

This band had previously backed sixties singers **Houston Wells** and **Mark Rogers**. (VJ)

Marlon

Personnel incl:

RAY FENWICK		A
ROGER GLOVER	drms	A

45: Let's Go To The Disco/Broken Man (Purple PUR 120) 1974

This was a one-off studio project featuring Ray Fenwick (of **Spencer Davis Group** etc) and **Roger Glover** of **Deep Purple** fame. (VJ)

Marmalade

Personnel:

JUNIOR CAMPBELL	lead gtr	AB
RAYMOND DUFFY	drms	A
PAR FAIRLIE	gtr	ABC
DEAN FORD	lead vcls	ABCD
GRAHAM KNIGHT	bs	ABCD
ALAN WHITEHEAD	drms	B
DOUGIE HENDERSON	drms	CD
HUGH NICHOLSON	lead gtr	C

MARMALADE - Kaleidoscope (LP).

JOE BREEN	bs	D
HOWIE CASEY	drms	D
MIKE JAPP	gtr, keyb'ds, vcls	D

ALBUMS: 1(B) THERE'S A LOT OF IT ABOUT (CBS 63414) 1968 SC
(up to 2(-) BEST OF THE MARMALADE (Compilation)
1976) (CBS SPB 36) 1969 SC
3(B) REFLECTIONS OF THE MARMALADE
(Decca LK/SKL 5047) 1970 SC
4(B) SONGS (Decca SKL 5111) 1971 SC
5(-) OB LA DI (Compilation) (Embassy 31032) 1973
6(D) OUR HOUSE IS ROCKIN' (EMI 3047) 1974
7(-) THE WORLD OF MARMALADE (Compilation)
(Decca SPA 470) 1976

NB: Other compilations include *Only Light On My Horizon Now* (Target TGS 501) 1977 and *Back On The Road 69/72* (Decca TAB 19) 1981. (3) entitled *Reflections Of My Life* in the US, where it was issued on London. (4) - (6) were UK-only releases. *Falling Apart At The Seams* (See For Miles) 1990 compiles their later material. There are also two CDs, *Reflections Of The Marmalade* (London 820 562-2) 1988 and *Falling Apart At The Seams.... Plus* (C5 C5CD 578) 1992, which is a reissue of the earlier See For Miles compilation of later material from 1976, but with two previously unissued bonus tracks. *The Definitive Collection* (Castle CCSCD 436) 1996 compiles material spanning their recordings for CBS and Decca onto one disc for the first time, now that the band has secured the rights to their back catalogue. The result is a nicely balanced collection of late sixties pop and more diverse seventies material. *The Definitive Collection* (Castle CCS CD 825) 1998 is a 2-CD set coupling the hits album released two years earlier with a reissue of their debut album, which does result in duplication of about seven tracks. *I See The Rain - The CBS Years* (Sequel NEM CD 463) 2000 is compilation, which concentrates on their sixties material. *Rainbow - The Decca Years* (Sequel NEMCD 335) 2000 is a 2-CD set concentrating on their seventies material. *Reflections Of The Marmalade* (Sanctuary CMEDD 281) 2001 is a 2-CD compilation of their Decca and CBS output and also includes the four 'A' sides of their earlier incarnation **Dean Ford and The Gaylords**. *Kaleidoscope: The Psych-Pop Sessions* (Castle Music CMRCD 636) 2003 is as its title suggests a collection of their more psychedelic moments of the early seventies. *BBC Sessions* (Castle CMQCD 940) 2004 is culled from several BBC sessions. *Ultimate Collection* (Sanctuary Midline SMETCD 182) is a 3-CD set of their CBS and Decca material.

HCP

45s: It's All Leading Up To Saturday Night/
(up to Wait A Minute Baby (CBS 202340) 1966 -
1976) Can't Stop Now/
There Ain't No Use In Hangin' On (CBS 202643) 1967 -
I See The Rain/Laughing Man (CBS 2948) 1967 SC -
Man In A Shop/Cry (CBS 3088) 1967 -
Lovin' Things/Hey Joe (CBS 3412) 1968 6
Wait For Me Marianne/Mess Around (CBS 3708) 1968 30
Ob-La-Di, Ob-La-Da/Chains (CBS 3892) 1968 1
Baby Make It Soon/Time Is On My Side (CBS 4287) 1969 9
Butterfly/I Shall Be Released (CBS 4615) 1969 -
Reflections Of My Life/
Rollin' My Thing (Decca F 12982) 1969 3
Rainbow/The Ballad Of Cherry Flavour (Decca F 13035) 1970 3
My Little One/Is Your Life Your Own? (Decca F 13135) 1971 15

Cousin Norman/Lonely Man	(Decca F 13214) 1971	6
Back On The Road/		
Love Is Hard To Re-arrange	(Decca F 13251) 1971	35
Radancer/Just One Woman/Sarah	(Decca F 13297) 1972	6
The Wishing Well/Engine Driver	(EMI EMI 2033) 1973	-
Our House Is Rockin'/		
Hallelujah Freedom Blues	(EMI EMI 2071) 1973	-
Come Back Joe/Way It Is	(EMI EMI 2131) 1974	-
Falling Apart At The Seams/		
Fly Fly Fly	(Target TGT 105) 1976	9
Walking A Tightrope/My Everything	(Target TGT 110) 1976	
What You Need Is A Miracle/		
Rusty Hands Of Time	(Target TGT 113) 1976	-
Hello Baby/Seafaring Man	(Target TGT 115) 1976	-

Reissues:
Ob-La-Di, Ob-La-Da/Lovin' Things (PS)	(CBS 83205) 1974	-
Ob-La-Di, Ob-La-Da/Lovin' Things	(CBS 5963) 1978	-
Reflections Of My Life/Rainbow/Radancer/		
Cousin Norman (PS)	(Decca F 13898) 1980	-
Ob-La-Di, Ob-La-Da/Lovin' Things	(Old Gold OG 9195) 1982	-
Reflections On My Life/Rainbow	(Old Gold OG 9334) 1983	-
α Ob-La-Di, Ob-La-Da/Shall I Be/Summer In The City/		
Lovin' Things/Baby Make It Soon/		
Wait For Me	(Scoop 7SR 5045) 1984	-
Lovin' Things/		
Ob-La-Di, Ob-La-Da	(Sounds Right MSSR 4) 1985	-

NB: α issued in 7" and 12" format.

The band formed in Scotland in 1963 as **Dean Ford and The Gaylords**, a soul and Tamla covers band who recorded three singles that deserved to do better. By 1967 they had signed to CBS and chosen a new name, **Marmalade**, which was more akin with the times. Despite being little more than a mainstream pop outfit at this time they managed to get gigs at 'underground' venues like the Marquee and were a regular attraction at jazz and blues festivals. Various publicity stunts were used to put them in the public eye, including a promotional film and the distribution of jars of marmalade to various radio stations. By now the group had relocated to London and set up communal home in Archway.

Their debut 45, *It's All Leading Up To Saturday Night*, had a harpsichord introduction and conveyed the imagery of weekend freedom pretty effectively. The flip was a rather lightweight composition written by the band. The follow-up, *Can't Stop Now*, was a pop/soul effort rather overshadowed by another group original on the flip. Their third release was a considerable advance - their first self-penned 'A' side. Notable for its tight harmonies, strong chorus and tuned-down lead guitar line, *I See The Rain* captured them at their most creative and together with the follow-up, *Man In A Shop*, which was full of gorgeous harmonies and swirling tapes, captured the feel of that memorable Summer of 1967, though sadly neither were hits here, though *I See The Rain* did get to No 23 in Holland.

Their breakthrough finally came with a cover of US band The Grassroots' *Lovin' Things*, a commercial, bubblegum-style song, which CBS pretty

MARMALADE - Rainbow (CD).

MARMALADE - I See The Rain (CD).

much forced upon them, as time was running out for the band. On the flip side they did a cover of *Hey Joe* - they'd earlier been on a tour with **Hendrix**. Having achieved a hit formula they stuck to it with *Wait For Me Mary-Anne* and a cover of *Ob-La-Di, Ob-La-Da* from **The Beatles'** *White Album*, which took them to No 1. Both songs were extremely commercial and destroyed any 'underground' credentials which some of their earlier recording had nurtured. They were a classic case of a band that had to compromise to achieve success. *Baby Make It Soon* gave them another Top 10 hit, though *Butterfly*, one of their more creative songs and their final release for CBS sadly flopped, as did their album, *There's A Lot Of It About.*

On 14 November 1969 they signed a new contract with Decca, which gave them complete freedom to write, arrange, produce and record whatever material they wanted free from record company interference - something they'd never enjoyed with CBS. The first result of this new arrangement was *Reflections Of My Life*, a ballad penned by Campbell and McAleese. It went down well climbing to No 3 in the UK and No 10 in the US. A new album inevitably followed, but *Reflections Of The Marmalade* failed to make much impact here in the UK, though it got to No 71 in the US, where it was issued as *Reflections Of My Life.*

Rainbow and *My Little One* gave them further UK hits and their next album, *Songs*, had its moments. *Rainbow* also made it to No 51 in the US. By now though **Junior Campbell** felt the band had gone as far as it could and departed (forming a new band Hallelujah Freedom the following year), to be replaced by Hughie Nicholson, who'd earlier played for another Scottish group, **The Poets**. Whitehead also left and was replaced by another ex-**Poet**, Dougie Henderson.

These changes gave the group a new injection of life in the short-term. A Nicholson composition, *Cousin Norman*, *Back On The Road* and *Radancer* were all pretty lively songs which made the Charts and kept the band in the public eye. Though, after the first of these hits, Fairley 'retired' from the group. The band received some adverse publicity, though, in 1972, when a popular Sunday newspaper accused the band of sexual debauchery in a typical tabloid-style groupie exposé and the promising *Radancer* became the revitalised line-ups final 45 and their final 45 for Decca.

Nicholson left to join **Cody** but in 1974 Ford, Knight and Henderson re-grouped and signed to EMI with a new six-piece line-up (D). This recorded the *Our House Is Rockin'* album and three 45s but Knight left almost as soon as the new line-up was put together and it was clear that the group was falling apart.

It was left to Knight and Whitehead to haul the band out of the ashes in 1976 and put together a new line-up. Signing to Target Records they enjoyed a further UK hit with *Falling Apart At The Seams* (which certainly described the band's predicament a few years earlier), which also climbed to No 49 in the US, where it was released on Ariola America. Subsequent singles and an album flopped and, in any case, they are beyond this book's remit. Still the band was certainly durable and recorded in various incarnations throughout the eighties.

A good introduction to the band's material is probably *The Best Of The Marmalade* (CBS) 1969. It surveys both their early hits and their psychedelic pop period. *Ob La Di* (Embassy) 1973 includes most of their late sixties hits. Their post-1972 recordings are not recommended.

The Reflections Of The Marmalade CD contains their 1970 album for Decca plus eight 45 cuts from 1970 onwards. Particularly noteworthy from the original album is *Kaleidoscope*, as its name suggests a fine slice of psychedelia.

There are two Sequel compilations, which may interest readers. *I See The Rain - The CBS Years* concentrates on their sixties tracks and showcases their impressive vocal harmonies. The hits like *Ob-La-Di, Ob La Da, Baby Make It Soon* and *Lovin' Things* figure of course, but they had some good misses too like the title track, *Man In A Shop* and *It's All Leading Up To Saturday Night. Rainbow - The Decca Years* is a 2-CD set, which includes songs like *Cousin Norman, Radancer* and *My Little One*. It also includes a couple of previously unissued tracks, including a strong version of Lorraine Ellison's *Stay With Me Baby*.

Sanctuary's later 2-CD set confusingly titled *The Reflections Of The Marmalade* presents most of their CBS and Decca output and their four A sides as **Dean Ford and The Gaylords**. There are 46 tracks in all and sleevenotes from original member Junior Campbell.

Ultimate Collection is a 3-CD box set compiling their CBS and Decca material. It also includes seven previously unissued demos as bonus tracks. It could well be the definitive work on the band.

BBC Sessions draws on their late sixties material and includes many of their hit singles, an alternative version of their psychedelic *I See The Rain* and covers of Crosby, Stills and Nash's *Judy Blue Eyes* as well as songs like *Carolina On My Mind* and *Seven Days Too Long*. There's also a pulsating version of *Sixty Minutes Of Your Love* and interviews with their English drummer Alan Whitehead.

Compilation appearances have included: *Falling Apart At The Seams* on *Your Starter For Ten!!* (CD); *I See The Rain* on *Electric Sugar Cube Flashbacks* (CD) and the 4-CD *Nuggets II* box set; *Reflection Of My Life* (alternate take) on the 2-CD set *Greatest Hits Of The 60's*; *Kaleidoscope* on *Haunted - Psychedelic Pstones, Vol 2* (CD); *Ob-La-Di Ob-La-Da* has resurfaced on the 2-CD set *60 Number Ones Of The Sixties, Brit Pop* (CD), *Hits Of The Swinging Sixties* (CD) and on *Hits Of The 60's Vol 2* (CD); and *Ob-La-Di Ob-La-Da* and *Lovin' Things* can also be found on *Here Comes Summer* (CD). (VJ)

Marquis of Kensington

45s:	Changing Of The Guard/	
	Reverse Thrust	(Immediate IM 052) 1967
	Flash/Sister Maria	(CBS) 1967

This was a Mike Leander concoction. *Changing Of The Guard* is a mock-genteel, whimsical effort. *Reverse Thrust*, which was by The Marquis of Kensington's Minstrels, is a backwards instrumental.

Changing of The Guard can also be heard on the *Tonite Let's All Make Love In London* (LP) soundtrack. (MWh)

Stevie Marriott

| ALBUM: | 1 MARRIOTT | (A&M AMLH 64572) 1976 SC |

NB: (1) reissued on CD (Lemon CDLEM 68) 2005. *It's All Too Beautiful* (3-CD set) (Castle CMEDD 935) contains all his big hits with **The Small Faces** and **Humble Pie** alongside many obscure and previously unavailable tracks by The Moments and his 1963 solo single for Decca. The sleevenotes are provided by Paolo Hewitt. *Rainy Changes (A Collection Of Rare Recordings) (2-CD)* (Darlings Of Wapping Wharf DWWLCD 003) contains 34 previously unreleased tracks but focuses on his later material including the last studio album he recorded before his death, tracks for a potential **Humble Pie** reunion, and *Tin Soldier* recorded with the Los Angeles Philharmonic orchestra in the mid-seventies.

45s:	Give Her My Regards/Imaginary Love	(Decca F 11619) 1963 R2
(up to	Star In My Life/Midnight Rollin'	(A&M AMS 7230) 1976
1976)		

TONITE LET'S ALL MAKE LOVE IN LONDON (Comp CD) including The Marquis Of Kensington.

Stevie Marriott was the best British white soul singer of this book's era.

Stevie Marriott was an Eastender, born in Bow, London, on 30 January 1947. He was a child actor and appeared in a London production of 'Oliver' and various TV and radio shows prior to releasing his now rare and sought-after *Give Her My Regards* 45 for Decca in 1963. He was working in a music shop in East Ham in June 1965 when he met the other three members of the embryonic **Small Faces** who were looking for a powerful singer or guitarist. **Marriott** fitted the bill perfectly and the rest is history as they say. They became one of Britain's top 'mod' bands and later experimented with psychedelia too. When **The Small Faces** disbanded in 1969, he formed **Humble Pie** with **Peter Frampton** and later had his own band, Stevie Marriott's All Stars, who had assisted in the 1976 recordings. *Early Evening Light* is easily the best of the few self-penned numbers on a disappointing album *Marriott* which retreads earlier ideas and is not much good. In 1976-77 he was involved in a **Small Faces** re-union. He was tragically killed in a fire in his Essex home in April 1991.

His 1976 album is not recommended but the recent 3-CD set *It's All Too Beautiful* is a fitting epitaph to this talented vocalist.

You can also find *Give Her My Regards* on *Pop Inside The '60s, Vol. 1* (LP) and *Hard-Up Heroes* (2-LP). (VJ)

Beryl Marsden

45s:	I Know/I Only Care About You	(Decca F 11707) 1963 SC
	When The Lovelight Starts Shining Through His Eyes/	
	Love Is Going To Happen To Me	(Decca F 11819) 1964 SC
	Who You Gonna Hurt?/	
	Gonna Make Him My Baby	(Columbia DB 7718) 1965 SC
	Music Talk/Break-A-Way	(Columbia DB 7797) 1965 SC
	What's She Got/	
	Let's Go Somewhere	(Columbia DB 7888) 1966 SC

This popular Merseybeat singer was originally backed by The Crew. She was one of Liverpool's best R&B vocalists in the Merseybeat era and had a powerful vocal style. She was unrelated to **Gerry (Marsden) and The Pacemakers** and was managed by Tony Stratton-Smith. *I Know* covered a Barbara George US R&B hit and *When The Lovelight...* suffered when it was released the same week as The Supremes' original version. *Who You Gonna Hurt?* was heavily orchestrated and marked a change of style, but a hit single eluded her and in 1966 she joined **Shotgun Express** alongside **Rod Stewart**, then on its demise, an all-girl combo **The She Trinity**. She was still going strong in the mid-seventies with a band called The Gamblers and was also a popular session vocalist.

She also figures on Decca's rare 1964 *At The Cavern* (LP). Retrospective compilation appearances include: *I Know (You Don't Love Me No More)* and *Everybody Loves A Lover* on *Liverpool 1963-1964, Vol. 2* (LP); *Breakaway* on *Liverpool 1963-1968* (CD), *Liverpool 1963-1968, Vol. 1* (LP) and *Beat At Abbey Road* (CD); *I Know (You Don't Love Me No More)* on *Mersey Beat* (2-LP) and *Mersey Beat 1962-1964* (2-LP); *I Know (You Don't Love Me No More)*, *I Only Care About You*, *Everybody Loves A Lover* and *Love Is Gonna Happen To Me* on *Mersey Sounds* (2-LP); *Everybody Loves A Lover* on *Original Liverpool Sound* (LP), *At The Cavern* (LP) and *Live At The Cavern* (CD); and *Breakaway*, *Love Is Gonna Happen To Me*, *Everybody Loves A Lover*, *I Know* and *All I Need Is You* can all be found on *Hard Up Heroes, Vol. 4* (CD). (VJ)

Gerry Marsden

45s:			
	Please Let Them Be/I'm Not Blue	(CBS 2784)	1967
	Gilbert Green/What Makes Me Love You	(CBS 2946)	1967
α	Liverpool/Charlie Girl	(CBS 3575)	1968
	In The Year Of April/Every Day	(NEMS 56-3831)	1968
	Every Little Minute/In Days Of Old	(NEMS 56-4229)	1969
	I've Got My Ukelele/What A Day	(Decca F 13172)	1971

NB: α as Gerry Marsden and Derek Nimmo.

One of Liverpool's famous music personalities, **Marsden** was born on 24 September 1942 and as you all know fronted one of that city's top Merseyside acts, **Gerry and The Pacemakers**. Along the way, he put out the occasional solo effort and when they split he made an unsuccessful attempt to launch a solo career. In the short-term, though, he attained greater success as an actor, playing the leading role in a London West End production of 'Charlie Girl' for two years in the late sixties. In 1970, he even appeared regularly on the children's TV programme 'Sooty and Sweep'! Later, he was involved in inevitable **Gerry and The Pacemakers**' reformations and in 1985, after the Bradford City F.C. fire killed several spectators, he organised a multi-artist recording of their classic hit, *You'll Never Walk Alone*, (which had been adopted as a football anthem by Liverpool F.C.), re-arranged by **Graham Gouldman** with proceeds of the sale contributing to a fund for the victims' families.

Gilbert Green has been compiled on *Pop-In, Vol 1* (CD). (VJ)

Marsupilami

Personnel:	MIKE FOURACRE	drms	AB
	FRED HASSON	vcls, hrmnca	AB
	LEARY HASSON	keyb'ds	AB
	RICHARD LATHAN HICKS	bs	AB
	DAVE LAVEROCK	gtr	AB
	JESSICA STANLEY CLARKE	flute, vcls	AB
	PETER BARDENS	perc	B
	MANDY RIEDELBANCH	woodwind	B
	BOB WEST	vcls	B

MARSUPILAMI - Arena (LP).

ALBUMS:	1(A)	MARSUPILAMI	(Transatlantic TRA 213)	1970 R1
	2(B)	ARENA	(Transatlantic TRA 230)	1971 R1

NB: (1) reissued on vinyl (Get Back GET 586) 2005 and on CD (Breathless 52012)) in digipak format in 2005.

This progressive rock outfit's albums are now collectable. Their first effort is full of atmospheric, moody, rambling songs which were typical of the progressive rock era. It's full of fine organ work and nice flute, though the guitar playing is a bit dodgy. **Pete Bardens** played on their second album. One track from this, *Prelude*, was later included on the Transatlantic 1970 compilation, *Heads and Tales* (LP). This progressive piece begins with wild vocals and manic guitar work which mellows into a keyboard solo with the wild vocals returning at the end. Certainly they were one of Transatlantic's most exciting outfits. However, aside from **Bardens**, their personnel was Italian so a very marginal case for inclusion.

Leary Hasson went on to the **Contemporary Music Unit**. *Prelude To The Area* has been compiled on the 3-CD box set *Ars Longa Vita Brevis: A Compendium Of Progressive Rock 1967-1974*. (VJ/MWh/CA)

Steve Martell

45:	When Comes The Time/		
	That Night With You	(Columbia DB 7777)	1965

Steve Martell is a Liverpudlian singer. The 'A' side of this 45 was written by Gary Osborne, who also recorded with his sister as **Gary and Jan Lorraine** and was in the UK **Chocolate Watchband**. (VJ)

George Martin and His Orchestra

ALBUMS: (up to 1976)	1	OFF THE BEATLE TRACK	(Parlophone PMC 1227/PCS 3057) 1964 R1
	2	PLAYS HELP!	(Columbia SX 1775 (mono)/Studio Two TWO 102 (stereo)) 1965 SC
	3	INSTRUMENTALLY SALUTES THE BEATLES GIRLS	(United Artists (S)ULP 1157) 1966 SC
	4	AND I LOVE HER	(Studio Two TWO 141) 1966 SC
	5	THE FAMILY WAY	(Decca (S)KL 4847) 1967 R2
	6	BRITISH MAID	(United Artists (S)ULP 1196) 1968 SC
	7	BY GEORGE!	(Sunset SLS 50182) 1970
	8	LIVE AND LET DIE (Soundtrack)	(United Artists UAS 29475) 1973
	9	BEATLES TO BOND AND BACH	(Polydor Super 2383 304) 1974

NB: (9) reissued on vinyl (St Michael IMP 105) 1978 exclusive to Marks and Spencer and on CD (Chrysalis CPCD 1604) 1987 and on Repertoire (REP 4142-WZ) 1991. *Produced by George Martin* (EMI) 2001 is a 6-CD box set profiling his production work.

EP:	1	MUSIC FROM 'A HARD DAY'S NIGHT'	(Parlophone GEP 8930) 1965 R1

45s: (up to 1976)	I Saw Her Standing There/		
	All My Loving	(Parlophone R 5135)	1964
	And I Love Her/		
	Ringo's Theme (This Boy)	(Parlophone R 5166)	1964
	All Quiet On The Mersey Front/		
	Out Of The Picture	(Parlophone R 5222)	1965
	I Feel Fine/The Niagara Theme	(Parlophone R 5256)	1965
	Yesterday/Another Girl	(Parlophone R 5375)	1965 SC
	By George! - It's The David Frost Theme/		
	Double Scotch	(United Artists UP 1154)	1966 SC
	Love In The Open Air/Theme From		
	"The Family Way"	(United Artists UP 1165)	1966 SC
	Theme One/		
	Elephants And Castles	(United Artists UP 1194)	1967 SC
	Pulp (Parts 1 and 2)	(United Artists UP 35423)	1972

George Martin, who was born on 3rd January 1926, is best known as a producer of most of **The Beatles**' songs. He'd studied oboe and composition at the Guildhall School of Music prior to joining EMI. From the mid-sixties onwards he was head of EMI's Parlophone label, where he supervised the recording of an enormous range of discs including comedy, cabaret, jazz and skiffle, as well as ballad singers like Matt Monro and **Shirley Bassey**.

He signed **The Beatles** to Parlophone in 1962 and produced all their records up to *Abbey Road* in 1970. It was at his instigation that their original drummer **Pete Best** was replaced by **Ringo Starr**, although he failed to persuade them to record Mitch Murray's *How Do You Do It?* as a 45 in 1963 and **Gerry and The Pacemakers** enjoyed a No 1 hit with it instead. The latter, along with **Cilla Black** and **Billy J. Kramer** were among the Liverpool acts managed by Brian Epstein which **Martin** acted as a producer for. In 1965 he left EMI to become an independent producer, setting up his own studios in London and on the Caribbean island of Montserrat. As **The Beatles** became more ambitious musically his knowledge of musical and studio techniques was enormously useful and masterpieces like *Strawberry Fields Forever* owe a lot to him.

Martin also recorded his own instrumental versions of **Beatles** songs on some of the albums and 45s listed earlier. He also wrote the instrumental Soundtrack score for their first film 'A Hard Day's Night' and some of this material was put out on a 1965 EP.

In the seventies, he worked with a wide range of artists, including **Ringo Starr** (on *Sentimental Journey*), America, **Stackridge** (on *The Man In The Bowler Hat*), **Jeff Beck** (*Blow By Blow* and *Wired*) and Neil Sedaka.

He continued to work with **The Beatles** after *Abbey Road*, producing the Soundtrack album to the 'Sgt. Peppers Lonely Hearts Club' film **The Beatles** had inspired. In the eighties, he worked with **Paul McCartney** on *Tug* and *Pipes Of Peace*.

He retired from the music business in 1998, following the release of *In My Life*, which featured a galaxy of stars, including Phil Collins and Celine Dion performing on songs he chose. In 2001 EMI released a 6-CD, 151-song box set *Produced By George Martin*, which covered a broad range of his production work.

You can also check out *All Quiet On The Mersey Front* on *Ferry Cross The Mersey* (LP). (VJ)

Martin's Magic Sounds

ALBUM: 1   MARTIN'S MAGIC SOUNDS
                        (Deram DML/SML 1014) 1967 SC

45:       Mon Amour, Mon Amour/Midem Melody   (Deram DM 141) 1967

This is a poor easy listening album. (VJ)

John Martyn

ALBUMS:	1	LONDON CONVERSATION	(Island ILP 952) 1967 SC
(up to	2	THE TUMBLER	(Island ILPS 9091) 1968 SC
1976)	3	STORMBRINGER	(Island ILPS 9113) 1970
	4	THE ROAD TO RUIN	(Island ILPS 9133) 1970 SC
	5	BLESS THE WEATHER	(Island ILPS 9167) 1971 SC
	6	SOLID AIR	(Island IPS 9226) 1973 SC
	7	INSIDE OUT	(Island ILPS 9253) 1973 SC
	8	SUNDAY'S CHILD	(Island ILPS 9296) 1975
	9	LIVE AT LEEDS (2-LP)	(Island ILPS 9343) 1975 SC

NB: (1) scheduled for reissue on CD (Island) 2006. (2) scheduled for reissue on CD (Island) 2006. (3) and (4) by John and **Beverley** Martyn. (3) reissued on CD (Island IMCD) remastered in a slipcase with bonus tracks. (4) reissued on CD (Island IMCD 318) remastered in a slipcase with bonus tracks. (5) scheduled for reissue on CD (Island) 2006. (6) has been coupled with a later album, *One World*, and reissued on one CD (Island ITSCD 2) 1992. (6) reissued on vinyl (Simply Vinyl SVLP 102). (6) also remastered and reissued separately on one CD (Cadiz/One World OW 119CD). (7) scheduled for reissue on CD (Island) 2006. (8) scheduled for reissue on CD (Island) 2006. (9) was recorded live at Leeds University in February 1975 as a 1,000 pressing mail order item for his fans. (9) reissued on Cacophony (SKELP 001) in 1987. (9) reissued on a 2-LP set (Turning Point TPM 02207) and also on CD (Cadiz/One World OW107CD). Vinyl compilations to date have been *So Far So Good* (Island ILPS 9484) and *The Electric John Martyn* (Island ILPS 9715) 1982. *Mad Dog Days* (Shakedown 125Z-UK) 2004 is a 3-CD set compiling various odds and ends, including mostly live acoustic work recorded with Danny Thompson at

Leeds in 1975, which falls into the time span of this book. The *Live In Nottingham 1976* (One World OW 124 CD) bootleg has now received an official CD release. *Patterns In The Rain* (CD) (Castle CMDDD 825), which was originally issued on Mooncrest, combines early studio recordings with live versions of standards like *Solid Air, Sweet Little Mystery* and *May You Never*.

45s:	α	John The Baptist/The Ocean	(Island WIP 6076) 1970
(up to		May You Never/Just Now	(Island WIP 6116) 1971
1976)			

NB: α by John and **Beverley** Martyn.

Glaswegian **Martyn** was born in 1948 and brought up by his grandmother and father. In the late sixties he moved down to London and built up a following on the London folk circuit. He signed to Island and in February 1968 his debut album, *London Conversation*, appeared. It stuck closely to the standard folk formula, but the follow-up, *The Tumbler*, was more adventurous. It's rumoured to have been recorded in an afternoon and was produced by **Al Stewart**. Of particular note was *Dusty*, which captured guest jazz flautist Harold MacNair in fine fettle. **Martyn** could have just consolidated on these two respected debuts but he was far more enterprising. The turning point came when he met and quickly married singer Beverley Kutner, who issued a couple of singles on Deram. The duo were signed by Warner Brothers, sent to Woodstock to rehearse and then, under Joe Boyd's production, recorded *Stormbringer*. The album was notable for the introduction of **Martyn**'s pioneering guitar sound and technique on a couple of tracks, *Would You Believe Me* and *The Ocean*, whilst another cut, *John The Baptist*, was issued on a 45, but it made no commercial impact.

The other album he made with his wife, *The Road To Ruin*, used jazz instrumentation in a rock format. It was also the first to feature **Pentangle** bassist, Danny Thompson, who was very influential in John's future development. At this point, the arrival of a second child halted **Beverley**'s musical ambitions, so for his fifth album, *Bless The Weather*, **Martyn** put together a backing band, including Danny Thompson and former **Fairport Convention** man **Richard Thompson**. The title track, in particular, became a long-time favourite with his fans and it featured him for the first time playing acoustic guitar through an echo unit which coupled with his unique vocal style made for a very distinctive sound.

Many regard his next album, *Solid Air*, as his finest. It developed the amplified guitar technique of the previous album further. He again put together an impressive array of talented individuals to assist him. Indeed, **Free**'s **Paul Kossoff** played drums and backing guitar on *May You Never*, a song he'd written for his son. It also includes a great cover of Skip James's *I'd Rather Be The Devil*, which utilises an Echoplex delay effect to give the guitar work an otherworldly feel. The highlight, though, was the hypnotic title track, written for his friend and tormented soul **Nick Drake**, who committed suicide within the year.

Inside Out found **Martyn** at his most experimental, playing a sort of free-form jazz with some typically inventive guitar work, supported by another talented array of musicians. It received much critical acclaim. By contrast, *Sunday's Child* returned to a more traditional folk format with songs like *Spencer The Rover*. Beverley sang vocals on *My Baby Girl*.

In 1975, he took to the road in earnest with a touring band which included Danny Thompson (bs), John Stevens (drms) and **Paul Kossoff** (gtr). On the course of the tour a vibrant appearance at Leeds University was recorded for a live album but when Island didn't want to release it, **Martyn** sold copies by mail order from his home. 1,000 were pressed and many were personally signed and numbered. Inevitably, it became a collector's item but is easier to obtain now by virtue of its reissue in 1987. It contains fine renditions of *Outside In, Bless The Weather* and *I'd Rather Be The Devil*. The Turning Point 2-LP reissue of this album is presented in a triple gatefold sleeve and contains a 12-page booklet with a biography/ discography and some stories from his time on the road.

Live in Nottingham 1976 is a live bootleg that has now received an official CD release. It contains very little from the album **Martyn** was promoting at the time (*Sunday's Child*) but it does contain many cuts from *Bless The Weather, Solid Air* and *Inside Out*, including *You May Never*, a much covered song. The bootleg was very popular with his fans so this official CD release is very welcome.

Martyn has continued to record until the present day. In the 1967-76 era, he figured on the following compilations: - *Dusty* on *You Can All Join In*

(LP), *Go Out And Get It* on *Bumpers* (2-LP); a live version of *Discover The Lover* appeared on *Over The Rainbow* (LP) in 1975; and the same year *Root Love* and *Spencer The Rover* figured on the promotional release *Summer '75* (LP).

Details of his compilations appear in the discography. In 1992, on *Couldn't Love You More (Best Of John Martyn)* (Permanent PERM LP/CD 9) he re-recorded several of his better-known songs but it didn't really work well. (VJ)

The Marvels

45:        Keep On Searching/Heartbeats   (Columbia DB 8341) 1968 SC

This was their sole vinyl offering. (VJ)

Brett Marvin and The Thunderbolts

Personnel:	PETE GIBSON	trombone, tin cans, vcls	ABCD
	GRAHAM HINE	slide gtr, mandolin, vcls	ABCD
	JIM PITTS	sax, banjo, bottleneck	
		mandolin, hrmnca, vcls	AB CD
	JOHN RANDALL	washb'd, drms	ABCD
	KEITH TRUSSEL		
	(aka KEEF TROUBLE)	zob stick, ironing board,	
		gtr, vcls	ABCD
	JOHN LEWIS (JONA LEWIE)	keyb'ds, vcls	BC
	DAVE ELLIS	gtr	CD
	TAFFY DAVIES	keyb'ds, vcls,	
		clarinet, accordion	D

ALBUMS: 1(B) BRETT MARVIN AND THE THUNDERBOLTS
                                (Sonet SNTF 616) 1970 SC
        2(C) TWELVE INCHES OF BRETT MARVIN AND
              THE THUNDERBOLTS   (Sonet SNTF 619) 1971
        3( ) BEST OF FRIENDS   (Sonet SNTF 620) 1971
        4( ) ALIAS TERRY DACTYL   (Sonet SNTF 630) 1972
        5( ) TEN LEGGED FRIEND   (Sonet SNTF 651) 1973

NB: (1) released on Metronome in Germany. *Vintage Thunderbolts* (Mooncrest CRESTCD 041 Z) 2000 compiles material from both their seventies albums and later ones too.

45s: Standing On The Platform/
(up to   Too Many Hot Dogs   (Sonet SON 2011) 1970
1976)   Thoughts Of You/Coming Back (Sonet SON 2015) 1971
           Southbound Lane/Little Red Caboose (Sonet SON 2017) 1971
           Hawaiian Honeymoon/
           If You Need Someone Call On Me (Sonet SON 2062) 1973

Formed in Sussex in 1969 **Brett Marvin and The Thunderbolts** were initially influenced by delta country blues, running 'Studio 51' on Sundays for four years with **Jo-Ann Kelly** and they played with, among others, Fred McDowell, Sonhouse, Howling Wolf, Arthur Bigboy Crudup, **Long John Baldrey**, **Dave Kelly**, **Medicine Head**, Steve Miller Band, **Lol Coxhill** and many others. Their first appearance on vinyl was in 1969 on Liberty's *Son Of Gutbucket* (LP) compilation, playing **The Beatles'** *I'm So Tired*.

When they recorded under the pseudonym **Terry Dactyl And The Dinosaurs** however, they enjoyed considerable commercial success with *Seaside Shuffle*, which got to No 2 in the UK. John Lewis (aka Jona Lewie) left at this point, being replaced by Taffy Davies. **Brett Marvin and The Thunderbolts** also toured Scandinavia, Holland and Belgium and they were very popular on the British university circuit. They also did British and European TV and radio shows.

On A Saturday Night gave them a minor hit climbing to No 45, whilst Jona Lewie later had a successful solo career. **Brett Marvin and The Thunderbolts** later recorded an EP in 1980, whilst **Graham Hine** recorded two solo albums, *Bottleneck Blues* (Blue Goose) 1971 and *Bowery Fantasy* (Blue Goose) 1973; and Keef Trouble recorded one, *Oasis* (Sun House Records) in 1994.

John Reed tells me Pete Gibson played on **Tom Newman**'s *Live At The Argonaut* unissued album. (VJ)

BRETT MARVIN AND THE THUNDERBOLTS - Alias Terry Dactyl (LP).

Hank (B.) Marvin

ALBUM: 1 HANK MARVIN (mono/stereo)
                        (Columbia S(C)X 6352) 1969 SC 14

NB: (1) originally pressed in a blue/black label. (1) repressed in 1970 with a silver/black label. These are not scarce. (1) reissued on CD as *Would You Believe It... Plus* (See For Miles SEECD 210).

45s: α   London's Not Too Far/
(up to   Running Out Of World   (Columbia DB 8326) 1968 SC
1976)   Goodnight Dick/Wahine   (Columbia DB 8552) 1969
         Sacha/Sunday For Seven Days (Columbia DB 8601) 1969
     α   Midnight Cowboy/
         Slaughter On Tenth Avenue (Columbia DB 8628) 1969 SC
     β   Break Another Dawn/
         Would You Believe It   (Columbia DB 8693) 1970 R3
         Break Another Dawn/Morning Star (Columbia DB 8693) 1970

NB: α 'B' sides were by **The Shadows**. β Demo only, unissued 'B' side.

Hank Marvin is best known as lead guitarist and a founder member of **The Shadows**. His real name is Brian Rankin and he was born on 28 November 1941 in Newcastle, England. He recorded these discs after **The Shadows** split in late 1968. He also did two duets with Cliff Richard: *Throw Down A Line* (Columbia DB 8615) 1969 got to No 7 in the UK and *Joy Of Living* (Columbia DB 8657) 1970 got to No 25 in the UK. (VJ)

Marvin and Farrar

Personnel:	JOHN FARRAR	A
	HANK MARVIN	A

ALBUM: 1(A) HANK MARVIN AND JOHN FARRAR
                            (EMI EMA 755) 1973 SC

NB: (1) with Olivia Newton-John. Reissued on CD (See For Miles SEECD 322) 199?

45s: a   Music Makes My Day/Skin Deep   (EMI EMI 2044) 1973
         Small And Lonely Light/
         Galadriel (Spirit Of Starlight) (EMI EMI 2335) 1975

NB: a with Olivia Newton-John.

When **Bruce Welch** left **Marvin, Welch and Farrar** the remaining two continued to record with Olivia Newton-John. They supported Cliff Richard and Olivia Newton-John on a Far East tour backed by bassist John Rostill, ex-**Shadow** Brian Bennett and keyboardist Alan Hawkshaw, who'd replaced **Welch** in **The Shadows** in mid-1969.

The *Hank Marvin and John Farrar* album, on which they were assisted by Olivia Newton-John, failed to chart and in November 1973 **The Shadows** reformed with a line-up of **Marvin**, **Welch**, **Farrar** and Bennett, to which Alan Tarney was added after a few weeks. (VJ)

Marvin, Welch and Farrar

Personnel: JOHN FARRAR   vcls   A
              HANK MARVIN   vcls   A
              BRUCE WELCH   vcls   A

                                                         HCP
ALBUMS: 1(A)   MARVIN, WELCH AND FARRAR
                        (Regal Zonophone SRZA 8502) 1971 SC 30
         2(A)   SECOND OPINION
                        (Regal Zonophone SRZA 8504) 1971 SC -

NB: (2) also issued in quadrophonic (4SRZA 8504) 1971. (1) and (2) reissued on CD (See For Miles SEECD 324 and 325).

45s: Faithful/Mr. Sun   (Regal Zonophone RZ 3030) 1971
        Lady Of The Morning/
        Tiny Robin   (Regal Zonophone RZ 3035) 1971
        Marmalade/Strike A Light (Regal Zonophone RZ 3048) 1972

This act formed in 1971 as a harmony vocal trio. **Marvin** and **Welch** had both played together in **The Shadows**. **Farrar** is Australian and had enjoyed great chart success out there with a band called The Stranglers who consistently got records into the Aussie Top 40 from 1963 - 1970. He is married to Pat Carroll, Olivia Newton-John's business and former singing partner. He was partially responsible for Olivia's recording success having produced/arranged/played/wrote on most of her recordings from 1971 - 1982.

The new trio tried a Crosby, Stills and Nash style venture. They made their debut on Cliff Richard's UK TV show. Then, in March, backed by another ex-**Shadow** Brian Bennett (drms) and Dave Richmond (bs) they toured West Germany, Switzerland, Belgium, Holland and Luxembourg, but it was old **Shadows** material rather than their new songs the fans wanted to hear. Their debut album made the UK Charts but their 45s didn't sell well. This combination was brought to an abrupt end when Olivia Newton-John broke off her engagement with **Bruce Welch**, which led him to attempt suicide and leave the trio. **Marvin and Farrar** continued to record together.

Tiny Robin has been compiled on *Fading Yellow, Vol 5* (CD). (VJ/JM)

Mary-Anne

ALBUM: 1   ME   (Joy JOYS 162) 1970 R3
NB: (1) reissued on CD (Sunbeam SBRCD 011) 2006 with detailed sleevenotes.

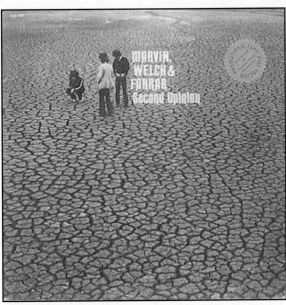

MARVIN, WELCH AND FARRAR - Second Opinion (LP).

On the back of her only album, Mary-Anne Paterson is described as 'a multi-talented young woman' - painter, teacher, actress and Scottish folk club regular. Joy was President's budget subsidiary, and the album was recorded in a single session over the New Year of 1969-70 in order to raise money for a nursery school she was involved with. Its contents vary from haunting treatments of traditional material (*Black Girl, The Water Is Wide*) to her own eerie compositions (*Love Has Gone, Reverie For Roslyn*), all sung in high, pure tones with basic acoustic backing, occasionally enlivened by understated electric guitar and bongos. Beautifully-recorded by in-house producer Mike Cooper, *Me* is superbly evocative but very rare. Paterson subsequently worked in children's television before moving into art therapy. (VJ/RMJ)

Masked Phantom

45:    These Clogs Are Made For Waltzing/
       Fried Scampi   (Parlophone R 5437) 1966

This is a novelty honky tonk piano 45. The identity of the singer remains unknown. (VJ)

Mason

Personnel incl: IAN 'TITCH' AMEY   A
                  JOHN 'BEAKY' DYMOND   A

ALBUM: 1(A)   MASON   (Dawn DNLS 3050) 1973 SC
NB: (1) export issue only.

45s: When Freedom Comes/It's All Gone Wrong(Pye 7N 45231) 1973
        Fading/It's Alright   (Dawn DNS 1040) 1973
        Follow Me/Peacefully   (Antic K 11505) 1974

Beaky and Tich of **Dave Dee, Dozy, Beaky, Mick and Tich** were in this band at the time of the Dawn single. They broke up in late January 1974. It's uncertain whether they reformed so the Antic 45 may have been another band. (VJ)

Barry Mason

45s: Misty Morning Eyes/Take Your Time   (Decca F 12401) 1966
        Over The Hills And Far Away/
        A Collection Of Recollections   (Deram DM 104) 1966 R1
        I'm In Love With You, Pom Pom/
        Mister D.J. Play Me A Sad Song   (Decca F 12895) 1969

An entertainer, dee-jay and songwriter, who worked a lot with Les Reed. He was most notable for writing ballads like *The Last Waltz, Release Me* (both for Englebert Humperdinck) and *Delilah* (for Tom Jones). He also recorded a 45 in 1966 with Les Reed as The Sound Of Les and Barry. *Over The Hills And Far Away* was a Gregorian-styled ballad co-written and produced by Paul Samwell-Smith. It has recently turned up on *Perfumed Garden Vol. 3* (CD) and *Justavibration* (LP). His final 'A' side was a waltz. Avoid his material unless you're into ballads. (VJ)

Dave Mason

                                                              HCP
ALBUMS: 1   ALONE TOGETHER   (Harvest SHTC 251) 1970 SC -
(up to   2   HEAD KEEPER   (Island ILPS 9203) 1971 SC -
1976)   3   DAVE MASON AND CASS ELLIOT
                                   (Probe SPBA 6259) 1971 49
           4   SCRAPBOOK   (Island ICD 5) 1972 SC -
           5   IT'S LIKE YOU NEVER LEFT   (CBS 65258) 1974 -
           6   DAVE MASON   (CBS 80360) 1975 -
           7   SPLIT COCONUT   (CBS 69163) 1975 -
           8   AT HIS BEST   (ABC ABCL 5122) 1975 -
           9   CERTIFIED LIVE (live 2-LP)   (CBS 88295) 1976 -

NB: (1) and (2) reissued on CD (BGO BGOCD 675) 2005. (3) recorded with Cass Elliot. (5) reissued on CD (Repertoire RES 2370) 2005. US-only albums were: - *Dave Mason Is Alive* (Blue Thumb BTS 54) 1972 and *Best Of Dave Mason* (Blue Thumb BTSD 6013) 1974. *Long Lost Friend: The Best Of Dave Mason* (Columbia Legacy CK 57165) 1995 is a CD compilation that draws on his early seventies studio work and offers little of excitement.

45s:	Just For You/Little Woman	(Island WIP 6032) 1968 SC
(up to	World In Changes/	
1976)	Can't Stop Worrying, Can't Stop Lovin' (Harvest HAR 5017) 1970	
	Only You Know And I Know/	
	Sad And Deep As You	(Harvest HAR 5024) 1970
α	Something To Make You Happy/	
	Next To You	(Probe PRO 513) 1971
	Lonely One/Misty Morning Stranger	(CBS 2153) 1974
	You Can't Lose It/	
	You Can't Take It When You Go	(CBS 3641) 1975
	Crying Waiting And Hoping/Save Your Love	(CBS 3893) 1976

NB: α recorded with Cass Elliot.

Dave Mason was born on 10 May 1947 in Worcester. His first appearance on vinyl was on a **Jaguars** 45 on Contest in 1965. He was a roadie with the **Spencer Davis Group** and had played in **The Hellions** (with **Jim Capaldi**) and **Revolution** before joining **Traffic** in April 1967. He was in and out of **Traffic** in the late sixties, departing in December 1967 and in October 1968, having rejoined in May 1968. The first 45 was recorded during his first absence from **Traffic**; after the second departure, he recorded the two solo albums. The first of these, the eight-song *Alone Together*, was pretty good. **Traffic** drummer Jim Capaldi, Jim Keltner, Rita Collidge, Delaine and Bonnie Bramlett, Leon Russell and The Flying Burritos' Chris Ethridge all appeared on this sweet acoustic rock album, whose highlights include *Waitin' On You* (an upbeat song), *Just A Song* (a lively banjo-backed number) and *Word In Changes*. *Head Keeper*, a half live/half studio affair, was similar in style. Highlights include the Hawaiian-flavoured *Here We Go Again*, *In My Mind* (notable for the dual lead vocals) and the harmony-laden tambourine-tinged *To Be Free*. The album got to No 51 in the US.

Next he worked with 'Mama' Cass Elliot and their album got to No 49 here. He also recorded with **Jimi Hendrix** and **The Rolling Stones** and later rejoined **Traffic** briefly during 1971. His US-only solo live album, *Dave Mason Is Alive!*, made No 116. In 1974, a US-only compilation of his Blue Thumb recordings, *The Best Of Dave Mason*, made No 183.

It's Like You Never Left, his fifth album is full of California harmonies with smacks of folk. He continued to enjoy greater success in the US, where he was now based, than in his UK homeland, earning a second gold disc in December 1974 when *Dave Mason* got to No 25 and peaking at No 27 with his *Split Coconut* album, which included guest appearances from Dave Crosby, **Graham Nash** and Manhattan Transfer. His earlier Blue Thumb compilation album was also revised and re-released with one additional track as *Dave Mason At His Best* and also got to No 133 in the US Charts. Certainly **Dave Mason** had come a long way from his days with **Traffic**.

He went on to work with Mama Cass Elliot, **Jimi Hendrix** and **The Rolling Stones**.

Compilation appearances include *Little Woman* on *Bumpers* (2-LP). (VJ)

DAVE MASON - Alone Together (LP).

Massed Alberts

45:    Blaze Away/Goodbye Dolly (Gray)   (Parlophone R 5159) 1964

This short-lived traditional jazz type group's sole vinyl offering was this one 45. (VJ)

The Masterminds

Personnel:	GEORGE CASSIDY	bs	ABC
	DOUGIE MEAKIN	lead gtr	AB
	JOHNNY JAY RATHBONE	drms	ABC
	CHRIS FINLEY	keyb'ds	BC
	JOEY MOLLAND	lead gtr	BC

45:	She Belongs To Me/	
	Taken My Love	(Immediate IM 005) 1965 SC

This Liverpool band was one of the first signings **Andrew Loog Oldham** made to his new Immediate label. Their version of Bob Dylan's *She Belongs To Me* made little impact, though, and they were never heard of again. Strangely, possibly by accident, they altered some of its lyrics.

Joey Molland later found fame in **Badfinger**.

Compilation appearances have included: *Taken My Love* and *She Belongs To Me* on *Jimmy Page Studio Works 1964-1968* (CD), *Jimmy Page - Hip Young Guitar Slinger* (2-CD), *Immediate Single Anthology, Vol. 1 - Rarities* (CD) and *Immediate Alternative* (CD); *She Belongs To Me* on *Immediate Alternative* (LP) and *Immediate Single Collection, Vol. 1* (CD); and *Taken My Love* on *Immediate Single Collection, Vol. 5* (CD). (VJ/AD)

The Master Said

The *Psychedelic Salvage Co. Vol. 2* (LP & CD) recently unearthed a whole side's worth of material by this obscure early seventies band whose music typified the more experimental strand of instrumental progressive rock. The cuts contained therein are the 10-minute *Birth Of A Saint* and *The Master Said Pt 1* and *Pt 2* and they clearly sound influenced by the likes of **Pink Floyd** and German bands like Tangerine Dream. This is strictly only for those of you who enjoy extended (and quite loosely structured) instrumental pieces.

The cuts are probably from the band's eponymous album, which was issued as part of a joint UK/German music library venture. Completely instrumental with some fine guitar work on the lengthy ten-minute plus cuts, it was housed in a plain white sleeve with a UK label sticker on the front and 'The Master Said - approval only' sticker on the back cover. (VJ)

Matching Mole

Personnel:	BILL McCORMICK	bs	AB
	PHIL MILLER	gtr	AB
	DAVID SINCLAIR	keyb'ds	A
	ROBERT WYATT	drms, vcls	AB
	DAVE McRAE	keyb'ds	AB

ALBUMS:	1(A)	MATCHING MOLE	(CBS 64850) 1972 SC
	2(B)	MATCHING MOLE'S LITTLE RED RECORD	
			(CBS 65260) 1973 SC

NB: (1) reissued on CBS (32105) in 1982 and on CD (Beat Goes On BGOCD 175) 1993. (2) reissued on CD (Beat Goes On BGOCD 174) 1993. *BBC Radio One Live* (Windsong WIN CD 083) 1994 consists of material from a short 25-minute session from July 1972, and will only appeal to fans of the band. *March* (Cuneiform RUNE 172) 2002 is US import featuring a 1972 live set.

45:    O Caroline/Signed Curtain   (CBS 8101) 1972 SC

Robert Wyatt formed this group soon after leaving **Soft Machine** in 1971. He'd cut a solo album, *The End Of An Ear*, prior to leaving **The Soft Machine**. David Sinclair had previously been with **Caravan**; Phil Miller with Delivery (and the short-lived DC The MBs, who didn't make it onto vinyl) and Bill McCormick had been in the obscure **Quiet Sun**. David Sinclair left during the recording of their debut album and Dave McRae came in as a replacement. The album contained considerable experimentation but it often

MATCHING MOLE - Matchine Mole (LP).

clicked, particularly on Side 1, on which *O Caroline*, *Instant Pussy* and *Signed Curtain* were the highlights. Indeed, *O Caroline* and *Signed Curtain* were so well-liked they were put out on a 45.

Their follow-up, **Matching Mole**'s *Little Red Record*, was another complex album but it had fewer highpoints than its predecessor. The track that really caught the ears was *God Song*, but by now personality rifts were pulling the group apart and it split just prior to Robert's tragic accident.

March, released in 2002, features material from a 1972 live set. It veers away from their usual studio material in favour of jazz-based improvised material. There's some nice guitar from Phil Miller on *Part Of The Dance* and Wyatt's scat singing is best showcased on *Instant Pussy*, but the release will only interest serious fans of this and the related bands.

Wyatt was planning to re-launch the band with a new line-up when he was seriously injured after falling from an apartment window. He was hospitalised for several months, but eventually returned paralysed from the waist down and confined to a wheelchair, to record further solo albums.

Of the remaining **Matching Mole** members, Sinclair and Miller went on to form **Hatfield and The North** with former **Caravan** member and David's brother Richard Sinclair; Bill McCormick went into session work; and Dave McRae joined an outfit called Pacific Eardrum, in the late seventies. (VJ)

Matchmakers

ALBUM:　1　BUBBLEGUM A GO GO　(Vogue CDMDINT 9796) 1970
NB: (1) released in Germany.

This British band's album was only released in Germany. It's rumoured that Thad Meager (of **Siren**) was featured on the album. (VJ)

Matchstick Men

Personnel incl:　RICK PARNELL　　　drms　　　　　A

45:　　Matchstick Men/Free Us Both　　(CBS 7124) 1971

This act was launched in April 1971 as a new progressive group by Rick Parnell. He'd previously played with Englebert Humperdinck, **Atomic Rooster** and **Horse**. (VJ)

Ian Matthews

ALBUMS:　1　IF YOU SAW THRU MY EYES
(up to　　　　　　　　　　(Vertigo 6360 034) 1971 SC
1976)　　2　TIGERS WILL SURVIVE　(Vertigo 6360 056) 1972 SC

3	VALLEY HI	(Elektra K 42144) 1973 SC
4	SOME DAYS YOU EAT THE BEAR, SOME	
	DAYS THE BEAR EATS YOU	(Elektra K 42160) 1974 SC
5	JOURNEYS FROM GOSPEL OAK (Compilation)	
		(Mooncrest CREST 18) 1974
6	GO FOR BROKE	(CBS 81316) 1976 SC

NB: (1) reissued on CD (Inbetweens IRCD 702) and also in Japan (UICY-9573) 2005 in a cardboard sleeve. (2) reissued on CD (Vertigo 5146172). (5) later reissued on Boulevard (BD 3009) in 1979.

45s:	Hearts/Little Known	(Vertigo 6059 041) 1971
(up to	Reno Nevada/Desert Inn	(Vertigo 6059 048) 1971
1976)	Da Doo Ron Ron/Never Again	(Philips 6006 197) 1972
	Devil In Disguise/Thru My Eyes	(Vertigo 6059 081) 1973
	Dirty Work/Wailing Goodbye	(Elektra K 12150) 1974
	Meet Her On A Plane/	
	Knowing The Game	(Mooncrest MOON 27) 1974
	I Don't Wanna Talk About It/	
	Keep On Sailing	(Elektra K 12197) 1976
	Brown Eyed Girl/Steam Boat	(CBS 4256) 1976
	Fool Like You/I'll Be Gone	(CBS 4526) 1976

Matthews was born in Lincolnshire in 1946. His first group was the short-lived London-based vocal harmony outfit, **The Pyramid**, in 1966. Between 1967-69, he was **Fairport Convention**'s lead vocalist. When he left them in January 1969 he formed his own band, **Matthews Southern Comfort**. Later at the end of 1970, he embarked on a solo career which has never equalled his considerable talent in terms of success.

He signed to Vertigo, releasing *If You Saw Thru My Eyes*, a highly regarded album on which he was assisted by several former **Fairport Convention** members. It includes *Reno Nevada*, which was originally covered by **Fairport Convention**.

His next Vertigo album, *Tigers Will Survive*, saw him backed by musicians of **Quiver** and the yet to be formed **Plainsong**. It crept into the US Charts, peaking at No 196. He also had a minor hit over there with his cover of The Crystals' *Da Doo Ron Ron*, which featured on the album.

In 1972 he formed **Plainsong**, which proved to be a short-lived venture. When they split, **Matthews** relocated to LA, teaming up with ex-Monkee Mike Nesmith, who produced his next solo album, *Valley Hi*. It reached No 181 in the US in 1973 where he formed a new support band to help promote it on tour as support to America. The following year, he put together a new touring band Ian Matthews and Another Fine Mess, which toured extensively in the US, where his next Elektra album failed to chart.

The Journeys From Gospel Oak album was a compilation of unreleased material from the 1971-72 era. Originally scheduled for release on Vertigo, it eventually appeared without his knowledge on Mooncrest in 1974, and was later reissued in 1979.

When his Elektra contract ended, **Matthews** signed a new contract for Columbia, after passing over Arista. He never did attain any substantial success as a solo artist and during the eighties worked as an A&R man first for Island Records and then Windham Hill, though he occasionally appeared with **Fairport Convention** and recorded another solo album in 1988. In 2000 he formed No Grey Faith (a **Sandy Denny** tribute band) with Jim Fogarty and Lindsay Gilmour. He still writes songs today and continues to record both as a solo artist and with **Plainsong**. He's also a regular at **Fairport Convention**'s Cropedy festivals. (VJ)

Matthews Southern Comfort

Personnel:	CARL BARNWELL	gtr	A
	RAY DUFFY	drms	A
	MARK GRIFFITHS	gtr	A
	GORDON HUNTLEY	pedal steel gtr	A
	IAN MATTHEWS	vcls	A

HCP

ALBUMS:	1(A)	MATTHEWS SOUTHERN COMFORT		
		(w/lyric insert)	(Uni UNLS 108) 1970 SC -
	2(A)	SECOND SPRING	(Uni UNLS 112) 1970 SC 52
	3(A)	LATER THAT SAME YEAR	(MCA MKPS 2015) 1970 SC -

NB: (1) issued by Decca in the US. There was also a *Best Of Matthews Southern Comfort* (MCA MCF 2574) 1975, which was reissued in 1982. Also of interest is

Meets Southern Comfort (See For Miles SEE 85) 1987. *Scion* (Band Of Joy BOJCD 7) 1994 compiles outtakes from (3) and some 1970 BBC sessions.

			HCP
45s:	Colorado Springs Eternal/The Struggle	(Uni UN 513) 1969	-
	Ballad Of Obray Ramsay/Parting	(Uni UN 521) 1970	-
	Woodstock/Scion	(Uni UN 526) 1970	1
Reissues:	Woodstock/(Flip by different artist)	(Old Gold OG 9168) 1982	-
	Woodstock/(Flip by different artist)	(Old Gold OG 9795) 1987	-

Best remembered for their classic cover version of *Woodstock*, the song commemorating the seminal sixties rock festival, this band was formed by **Ian Matthews** after he left **Fairport Convention** at the start of 1969. The material for their first album was written and produced by songwriters Howard and Blaikley. Characterised by **Matthews**' distinctive, crystal clear, high-pitched vocals and Huntley's fine pedal-style guitar work, their debut album was a fine amalgam of folk and country styles, which met with much critical acclaim. *Second Spring* sold better, getting into the UK Charts but it was their country-style cover of Joni Mitchell's *Woodstock*, which briefly made them a household name after bursting to No 1.

Sadly, the chemistry that made the band such a successful formula wasn't destined to remain and after one further album, **Matthews** left to go solo. The remaining members continued as **Southern Comfort**, but without **Matthews**' distinctive vocals were never able to attain the same heights and eventually fizzled out. This is emphatically demonstrated on *Meets Southern Comfort*, the 1987 See For Miles compilation, which featured material by **Matthews Southern Comfort** on side one and contained songs by **Southern Comfort** on side two. The **Southern Comfort** tracks are pleasant enough but without **Ian Matthews**' distinctive vocals sound very ordinary.

Woodstock can also be heard on *The Woodstock Generation* (LP) and the 2-CD set *Stars And Stripes*. (VJ)

Harvey Matusows Jews Harp Band

Personnel:	LESLIE KENTON	vcls, metronome	A
	CLAUDE LINTOT	auto jews harp	A
	ANNA LOCKWOOD	indian bells, gtr	A
	HARVEY MATUSOW	alto tenor harp, vcls	A
	ROD PARSONS	alto tenor, bs, jews harp	A
	CHRIS YAK	alto, tenor, jews harp	A

ALBUM: 1(A) WAR BETWEEN THE FATS AND THINS
(Head HDLS 6001) 1969 SC

NB: (1) also issued in the US on Chess in 1970.

45:	Afghan Red/West Socks	(Head HDS 4004) 1969

Harvey Job Matusow was born in the Bronx in 1926 and after the second world war worked for the FBI as an informer, eventually becoming an investigator for McCarthy's Un-American Activities Committee, spying on local trade unions and helping to undermine trust in 'The New York Times'. He was later tried and convicted for perjury and when released in 1960, he became involved with The East Village Other, discovered LSD and re-located to London in 1966. Whilst in the UK he helped to produce 'IT' and 'Frendz' underground magazines, and also made the above album. As an American this entry is a borderline case for inclusion, but the album may interest some readers. Recorded on acid, it largely consists of spoken word poetry and period weirdness. Leslie Kenton was the daughter of jazz musician Stan Kenton and Claude Lintot was then 79 years old! The single was the final release on the hippie Head label. **Matusow** later made bells and toys from old missile parts, became a children's entertainer on TV and ran the only public access TV station in Utah before his death in 2002. (MWh/GB/RMJ)

Maureeny Wishfull

Personnel incl:	JIMMY PAGE	gtr	A
	BIG JIM SULLIVAN		A
	JOHN WILLIAMS		A

ALBUM: 1(A) THE MAUREENY WISHFULL ALBUM
(Moonshine WO 2388) 1968 R2

NB: (1) has been counterfeited.

This is a very rare privately-pressed album, most notable for featuring **Jimmy Page** on guitar. Only 300 copies of the album were pressed originally. **John Williams** had earlier recorded a rare solo album and a couple of 45s. **Sullivan**, like **Page**, was one of London's top session guitarists. **Page**, of course, went on to form **Led Zeppelin**. Sullivan now has no recollection of this project and **Williams** seems to have vanished. Indeed, there is doubt as to whether any 'original' copies of the album exist, or whether all are 'counterfeits'. (VJ)

Maxwell Nicholson

45:	Trees And Things/Virgin	(Columbia DB 8811) 1971

An obscure 45, *Trees And Things* has been compiled on *Fading Yellow, Vol 5* (CD). (MWh/VJ)

John Mayall's Bluesbreakers

Personnel:	ROGER DEAN	gtr	A
	JOHN MAYALL	organ, vcls	ABCDEFG H I JKL
	HUGHIE FUNT	drms	ABCDE
	JOHN McVIE	bs	ABCDEFG H
	ERIC CLAPTON	gtr, vcls	B D
	JACK BRUCE	bs	C
	PETER GREEN	gtr	EFG
	AYNSLEY DUNBAR	drms	F
	MICKEY WALLER	drms	G
	MICK FLEETWOOD	drms	G
	MICK TAYLOR	gtr, vcls	H I JK
	CHRIS MERCER	sax	H I J
	KEEF HARTLEY	drms	H I
	RIP KANT	sax	H
	HENRY LOWTHER	trumpet	I J
	DICK HECKSTALL-SMITH		
		sax	I J
	JOHN HISEMAN	drms	J
	TONY REEVES	bs	J
	STEVE THOMPSON	bs	KL
	COLIN ALLEN	drms	K
	DUSTER BENNETT	gtr	L
	JOHNNY ALMOND	sax	L
	JON MARK	gtr	L
	ALEX DMOCHOWSKI	bs	L

HCP

ALBUMS: 1(A) JOHN MAYALL PLAYS JOHN MAYALL - LIVE
AT KLOOKS KLEEK   (Decca LK 4680) 1964 R2 -

JOHN MAYALL - The Turning Point (LP).

2(C)	BLUESBREAKERS WITH ERIC CLAPTON	(Decca LK/SKL 4804) 1965 R1 6	
3(F)	A HARD ROAD	(Decca LK/SKL 4853) 1967 R1 10	
4(H)	CRUSADE	(Decca LK/SKL 4890) 1967 R1 8	
5( )	RAW BLUES	(Ace Of Clubs ACL/SCL 1220) 1967 -	
6( )	THE BLUES ALONE	(Ace Of Clubs ACL/SCL 1243) 1967 SC 24	
7(I)	DIARY OF A BAND, VOL. 1	(Decca LK/SKL 4918) 1968 SC 27	
8(I)	DIARY OF A BAND, VOL. 2	(Decca LK/SKL 4919) 1968 SC 28	
9(J)	BARE WIRES	(Decca LK/SKL 4945) 1968 SC 3	
10(K)	BLUES FROM LAUREL CANYON	(Decca LK/SKL 4972) 1969 SC 33	
11( )	LOOKING BACK	(Decca LK/SKL 5010) 1970 SC 14	
12(L)	THE TURNING POINT	(Polydor 583 571) 1970 SC 11	
13(L)	EMPTY ROOMS (w/lyric insert)	(Polydor 583 580) 1970 SC 9	
14(-)	USA UNION	(Polydor 2425 020) 1970 SC 50	
15(-)	WORLD OF JOHN MAYALL, VOL. 1	(Decca PA/SPA 47) 1970 -	
16(-)	WORLD OF JOHN MAYALL, VOL. 2	(Decca PA/SPA 138) 1971 -	
17(-)	MEMORIES	(Polydor 2425 085) 1971 -	
18(-)	BACK TO THE ROOTS (2-LP)	(Polydor 2657 005) 1971 31	
19(-)	BEYOND THE TURNING POINT	(Polydor 2483 016) 1971 SC -	
20(-)	THRU THE YEARS	(Decca SKL 5086) 1971 SC -	
21(-)	JAZZ-BLUES FUSION	(Polydor 2425 103) 1972 SC -	
22(-)	MOVING ON	(Polydor 2391 047) 1973 SC -	
23(-)	TEN YEARS ARE GONE	(Polydor 2683 036) 1973 -	
24( )	TURNING POINT/EMPTY ROOMS	(Polydor 2683 039) 1974 -	
25 (-)	THE LATEST EDITION	(Polydor 2391 141) 1974 -	
26 (-)	NEW YEAR, NEW BAND, NEW COMPANY	(ABC ABCL 5115) 1975 -	
27 (-)	TIME EXPIRED, NOTICE TO APPEAR	(ABC ABCL 5142) 1975 -	
28 (-)	A BANQUET OF BLUES	(ABC ABCL 5187) 1976 -	

JOHN MAYALL - Empty Rooms (LP).

NB: (2) With **Eric Clapton**. (2) reissued on 180gm vinyl and mastered to perfection (Decca/Speaker's Corner LK 480) 2005. This discography is not comprehensive. There have been several repackages and the band continued to record throughout the seventies. Vinyl compilations include *Blues Roots* (Decca ROOTS 8) 1978, *Once Upon A Time* (2-LP) (Polydor 2664 436) 1980, (12) reissued (Polydor 2485 222) 1982, *Primal Solos* (Decca TAB 66), this was originally issued in the US (London LC 50003 in 1977), *The John Mayall Story Vol 1* (Decca TAB 72) 1983, *The John Mayall Story Vol 2* (Decca TAB 74) 1983, *Room To Move* (Polydor 2486 041) 1984, *The Collection* (2-LP) (Castle CCSLP 137) 1986, *Some Of My Best Friends Are Blues* (Decal LIK 1) 1986, *Roadshow Blues* (Thunderbolt THBL 060) 1988 and *Nightriding: John Mayall* (Knbight KNLP 10010) 1988. Many of these albums are now available on CD. (12) reissued on CD (BGO BGOCD 145). (26) and *Lots Of People* reissued on a 2-CD set (Beat Goes On BGO 492) 2000. (27) and (28) reissued as a 2-CD set (BGO BGOCD 495) 2000. *Hardcore Package/Last Of British Blues* (BGO BGOCD 493). A budget price CD compilation is *Waiting For The Right Time* (Elite 001 CDP) 1991. *Through The Years* (Deram 844 028-2) 1991 is a 14 -track archive collection from 1971 which has now been reproduced on CD. Among the 14 tracks are rare singles like *Crawling Up A Hill*, *Crocodile Walk* and *Suspicion*, as well as an excellent version of J.B. Lenoir's *Alabama Blues*. *London Blues 1964-1969* (Deram 844 302-2) 1992 is a 2-CD set. There's also *Life In The Jungle* (Charly Blues Masterworks Vol 4) (Charly CDBM 4) 1992. *Room To Move 1969-74* (Polydor 517 291-2) 1993 compiles some of the better material from his years with Polydor. *As It Began: The Best Of John Mayall and The Bluesbreakers* (Deram 844 785-2) 1998 should delight fans because it includes his own selection of tracks and the sleevenotes contain his memories of each choice. *Live At The Marquee 1969* (Eagle EAM CD 070) 1999 captures his live act effectively. *The Masters: Music From The Original Film Soundtrack The Turning Point* (Eagle EDM CD 071) 1999 is a 2-CD set, which does not capture the band at its best. *Rock The Blues Tonight* (Indigo GOXD CD 102 Z) 1999 is another 2-CD set compiled from Canadian performances during 1970/71. *Live 1969* is a 2-CD set features live recordings, including one track from the last performance by the *Laurel Canyon* line-up at Birmingham Town Hall on 9th May 1969 plus tracks recorded live in June 1969 with the line-up formed after he relocated to the USA. *Rockin' The Roadshow* (2-CD) (Castle CMDDD 639) compiles live cuts from his jazz-rock experiments from the early seventies and blues from his later 1981 band. *Rolling With The Blues - The Second Decade* (2-CD & DVD) (Recall/Snapper SBOX 027) features live performances from seven concerts between 1972-1982. The DVD contains an interview with **Mayall** recorded on his 2002.

EP:	1(F)	JOHN MAYALL'S BLUESBREAKERS WITH PAUL BUTTERFIELD	(Decca DFE 8673) 1967 R1

45s:

	Crawling Up The Hill/Mr. James	(Decca F 11900) 1964 R1	
	Crocodile Walk/Blues City Shakedown	(Decca F 12120) 1965 R1	
α	I'm Your Witchdoctor/ Telephone Blues	(Immediate IM 012) 1965 R1	
β	Lonely Years/Bernard Jenkins	(Purdah 45-3502) 1966 R4	
χ	Parchman Farm/Key To Love	(Decca F 12490) 1966 SC	
	Looking Back/So Many Roads	(Decca F 12506) 1966 SC	
	Sittin' In The Rain/Out Of Reach	(Decca F 12545) 1967 SC	
	Double Trouble/It Hurts Me Too	(Decca F 12621) 1967	
	Suspicions Pts 1 and 2	(Decca F 12684) 1967	
	Pictures On The Wall/Jenny	(Decca F 12732) 1968	
	No Reply/She's Too Young	(Decca F 12792) 1968	
	The Bear/2401	(Decca F 12846) 1968	
	Don't Waste My Time/Don't Pick A Flower	(Polydor 56544) 1970	
	Thinking Of My Woman/ Plan Your Revolution	(Polydor 2066 021) 1970	
Reissue:	Crocodile Walk/Sittin' In The Rain	(Decca 13804) 1978	

NB: α later reissued (Immediate IM 051) 1967 (SC). β With **Eric Clapton**. χ 'A' side was **John Mayall** solo.

John Mayall's Bluesbreakers were a highly respected bluesband and he was undoubtedly one of the most innovative and influential figures on the British blues scene in the sixties. He was probably most important of all as a trainer of other talents for rock stardom - **Eric Clapton**, **Jack Bruce**, John McVie, **Peter Green**, **Aynsley Dunbar**, Mick Taylor, **Keef Hartley**... the list is seemingly endless.

John Mayall was born in Macclesfield, Cheshire, on 29th November 1933. He grew up on American jazz, which his father was heavily into, and learnt to play piano and guitar. At 13, he went to a Junior Art School in Manchester and later advanced onto the city's Regional College of Art. He had his own band, called The Powerhouse Four, which included Peter Ward who was later in The Bluesbreakers. By now, he was in his element, having got himself a job in an art studio attached to an advertising agency.

Mayall's next band, Blues Syndicat, was inspired by **Alexis Korner's Blues Incorporated**. It was a raw R&B band which played mostly at Manchester's Twisted Wheel Club. In 1963, John decided to go down to London, get a day job (which he did as a draughtsman) and then put a band together. By early 1964, **Mayall** had signed a short-term contract with Decca, having got a semi-permanent band together. Line-up (A) recorded his debut album at an R&B dive, 'Klooks Kleek', in West Hampstead. **Mayall** had already released his first two 45s; the album contained a couple of cover versions (*Night Train* and *Lucille*) but the remaining 11 tracks were all originals.

Mayall's next coup was to recruit **Eric Clapton**, who'd left **The Yardbirds**, disenchanted with their movement away from the blues, but around the same time his Decca contract expired and they chose not to renew it. So line-up (B) recorded just two singles for Immediate and Purdah, but by early 1966, Decca seemed to acknowledge their mistake and took him back. However, in the Summer of 1965 **Clapton** headed for Greece and when he came back it was only for a short while. **Jack Bruce** (formerly of the **Graham Bond Organisation**) was with the band for a few weeks as a replacement for John McVie, who'd been sacked for boozing, but when **Bruce** left to join **Manfred Mann**, McVie was invited back into the fold.

In the Spring of 1966, line-up (C) recorded *Bluesbreakers*, which received wide acclaim and made **Eric Clapton** a star. It is recognised as the first classic British blues album. Indeed, before the year was out, he'd left to form **Cream** with **Ginger Baker**. Hughie Flint, who'd been with the band since 1964, left in September 1966. He later played with **McGuinness Flint** and **Savoy Brown**.

Aynsley Dunbar came in on drums and a new line-up made an EP with visiting American bluesmen Paul Butterfield, three 45s and another fine album, *A Hard Road*. **Dunbar** soon left for **The Jeff Beck Group** and Mickey Waller (ex-**Steampacket** and **Brian Auger's Trinity**) replaced him briefly. Next to fill in on skins was Mick Fleetwood but he was fired within a month for over drinking. In June 1967, **Mayall** expanded the band beyond a quartet, with **Keef Hartley** coming in on drums. However, this line-up didn't last beyond September when McVie, who'd been by far **Mayall's** longest-serving bandsman, decided to join the newly-formed **Fleetwood Mac**, which included Mick Fleetwood and **Peter Green**. The new line-up toured the US, which paid off in terms of record sales when their fourth album, *Crusade*, made No 136 in the US Album Charts as well as No 9 in the UK.

After McVie left, **Mayall** went through a series of bassists in quick succession. First **Paul Williams** (formerly of **Zoot Money**) then Keith Tillman and **Andy Fraser**, but line-up (I) recorded the *Suspicions* and *Jenny* 45s and *Diary Of A Band, Vols 1* and *2*, which included music, interviews and chat.

Mayall wanted to recruit Tony Reeves (New Jazz Orchestra) to fill the bass-player slot, but he would only join on condition that John Hiseman (ex-**Georgie Fame** and **Graham Bond**) would join as drummer. Consequently **Hartley** was sacked and went on to form his own band. **Mayall** then recruited **Dick Heckstall-Smith** (formerly of Blues Incorporated and **Graham Bond Organisation**) on sax, and with this new line-up (J) he recorded *Bare Wires*. His most successful album yet in terms of sales in the UK, it also sneaked to No 59 in the US Charts. He also put out a single, *No Reply*.

In September 1968 when Hiseman, Reeves and **Heckstall-Smith** all departed for **Colosseum**, **Mayall's** band, which now ceased to be called The Bluesbreakers and operated under his own name, reverted back to a quartet, as it had been for most of its early life. He found a new bassist in Steve Thompson and recruited Colin Allen (formerly of **Zoot Money** and **Stone The Crows**) on drums. *The Blues From Laurel Canyon* album recorded by this line-up actually sold better in the US, where it charted at No 68. Perhaps this was not surprising since it was **Mayall's** impression of a three week US holiday. This line-up survived until May 1969 when guitarist Mick Taylor joined **The Rolling Stones** and Allen departed for **Stone The Crows**. Now **Mayall** dispensed with a drummer altogether and switched labels to Polydor. Decca took the opportunity to issue *Looking Back*, a compilation of all the band's early singles. Line-up (L) was the last as a regular band. It put out the *Turning Point* and *Empty Room* albums. Thereafter, **Mayall** didn't bother to maintain a regular band, preferring to simply recruit suitable musicians whenever he needed them to tour or record. *Turning Point* veered much nearer to jazz than any of **Mayall's** earlier contributions and it featured some great sax playing from **Johnny Almond**.

On *U.S.A Union*, **Mayall** used American musicians for the first time. The album was full of social conscience and ecological protest songs but was musically disappointing as was *Back To The Roots*, despite the fact that **Mayall** assembled a plethora of illustrious musicians to appear on this lavish double set. Hereafter, he increasingly switched his base to America and his subsequent albums:- *Jazz Blues Fusion, Moving On* and *Ten Years Are Gone* were increasingly in a jazz-blues style. In 1975, he switched to ABC and used a female vocalist, Dee McKinnie, for the first time, but what followed falls outside the time frame of this book.

Mayall has appeared on numerous compilations over the years including Polydor's 1971 *Bombers* compilation, playing *Room To Move* and *Took The Car*, on Ace Of Clubs' *1967 Raw Blues*, playing *Burn Out Your Blind Eyes* and *Milkman Strut*; on the same compilation, he plays *Long Night* (with Steve Anglo who was **Stevie Winwood**); *Lonely Years* and *Bernard Jenkins* (with **Eric Clapton**) and *Evil Woman Blues* (with **Peter Green**); on

Polydor's 1971 *Rock Party* (2-LP) with *Thinking Of My Woman*; on Polydor's *Supergroups* (LP) (1970) singing *Room To Move*; then on *Supergroups, Vol. 2* (LP) later the same year playing *Saw Mill Gulch Road*; *The World Of Blues Power!* (LP), a Decca compilation from 1969 features **John Mayall's Bluesbreakers** with **Eric Clapton**, playing *All Your Love* and *Steppin' Out*, **John Mayall's Bluesbreakers** with **Peter Green** performing *Greeny* and *Out Of Reach* and they're joined by Chicago bluesman Paul Butterfield on *All My Life*; **John Mayall** pops up *The World Of Blues Power, Vol. 2* (LP) (1970), playing *Checkin' Up On My Baby* and *You Don't Love Me* and, finally, he was featured on another Decca compilation, *Wowie Zowie! World Of Progressive Music* (LP) with *Where Did I Belong*.

Important earlier compilation appearances include: *Crawling Up A Hill* on *Rhythm & Blues* (LP); *Burn Out Your Blind Eyes, Long Night, Milkman Strut, Lonely Years* and *Bernard Jenkins* on *Raw Blues* (LP); *I'm Your Witchdoctor* and *Telephone Blues* on *Blues Anytime Vol 1* (LP); *On Top Of The World* on *Blues Anytime Vol 2* (LP) and on the 2-LP set *Anthology Of British Blues Vol 1*. More recent compilation appearances include: *Telephone Blues* and *On Top Of The World* on *Jimmy Page Studio Works 1964-1968* (CD); *I'm Your Witchdoctor, Telephone Blues* and *On Top Of The World* on *Jimmy Page - Hip Young Guitar Slinger* (2-CD); *Looking Back* on *Mod Scene, Vol. 2* (CD); *I'm Your Witchdoctor* on *Maximum '65* (LP); *Crawling Up A Hill* on *The R&B Scene* (CD); *Have You Heard* on *Hard-Up Heroes* (2-LP); and *I'm Your Witchdoctor* and *Telephone Blues* on *Immediate Single Anthology, Vol. 1 - Rarities* (CD). More recently, *I'm Your Witchdoctor* resurfaced on the CD set *Rock Of Ages, Four Decades Of Heavy Rock 1962-2002*. (VJ)

May Blitz

Personnel:	KEITH BAKER	drms	A
	JAMIE BLACK	gtr, vcls	AB
	TONY NEWMAN	vibes, drms	AB
	TERRY POOLE	bs	A
	REID HUDSON	bs, vcls	B

ALBUMS:	1(B)	MAY BLITZ	(Vertigo 6360 007) 1970 R1
	2(B)	SECOND OF MAY	(Vertigo 6360 037) 1971 R2

NB: (1) issued on Paramount (5020) in the US. (1) later reissued on Beat Goes On (BGOLP 16) 1988 and on CD (Repertoire REP IMS 7026) 1994, again on CD (Repertoire/Vertigo) 2004 and also again on CD (Akarma 253). (2) has been repressed and reissued on CD (Repertoire REP IMS 7027) 1994 and again on CD (Repertoire/Vertigo) 2004 and (Akarma 1496454). (1) and (2) reissued on one CD (Beat Goes On BGOCD 153) 1993.

Tony Newman had previously played with **Sounds Incorporated** and **The Jeff Beck Group**. His powerhouse drumming suited this heavy rock act's loud aggressive sound which was liberally laced with echoed feedback guitar. They appeared on a Vertigo package tour with **Clear Blue Sky** and **Jimmy Campbell**. The first album is the better of the two, but is frankly

MAY BLITZ - May Blitz (LP).

over-rated and neither is good enough to justify the price originals sell for. The CD reissues are welcome because at least people that want to hear them or buy them can obtain them at a reasonable price now. Unless you're into heavy, rather lumbering progressive rock don't bother. The band also figured on the *Vertigo Annual 1970* (LP) compilation, playing *I Don't Know* from their debut album. Black went on to play with **F.B.I.** in the late seventies. Reid Hudson went back to Canada and **Tony Newman** went on to play with **Three Man Army**, **Boxer**, **Mick Ronson**, **Bowie**, **Whitesnake** and **T. Rex**. (VJ)

Mayfield's Mule

Personnel:	STEVE BRADLEY	bs	A
	SEAN JENKINS	drms	A
	CHRIS MAYFIELD	vcls	A
	PETE SAUNDERS	keyb'ds	A
	ANDY SCOTT	gtrs	A
	MIKE SMITH	sax, tamborine	A

45s:	Double Dealing Woman/(Drinking My)		
	Moonshine (Some PS)	(Parlophone R 5817) 1969 SC	
	I See A River/		
	"Queen" Of Rock'n'Roll	(Parlophone R 5843) 1970 SC	
	We Go Rollin'/My Way Of Living	(Parlophone R 5858) 1970 SC	

This North Wales group was formed by former **Amen Corner** roadie Chris Mayfield. Their producer was John Peel. Mike Smith had also been in **Amen Corner**, whilst Andy Scott had been in **The Elastic Band** and was later in **The Sweet**. (VJ/CSx)

The Maze

Personnel:	CHRIS BANHAM	organ	A
	ROD EVANS	vcls	A
	ERIC KEENE	bs	A
	ROGER LEWIS	gtr	A
	IAN PAICE	drms	A

| 45s: | Hello Stranger/Telephone | (Reaction 591 009) 1966 R2 |
| | Catari Catari/Easy Street | (MGM MGM 1368) 1967 R1 |

This mid-sixties group from Slough was originally known as **M.I. Five**, but their claim to fame is that in 1967 Evans and Paice both joined **Deep Purple**, although this spelt the death knell for **The Maze**. Evans soon departed to **Captain Beyond** but Paice remained with **Deep Purple** until their demise and was later with **Paice, Ashton and Lord** and then Whitesnake. Inevitably, these two singles are both quite sought-after, particularly by **Deep Purple** fans. *Hello Stranger* is a Barbara Lewis soul ballad.

THE MAZE - French 7" EP.

They also recorded an EP, released in France (Vogue INT 18136) 1967, which included: *Harlem Shuffle, What Now, The Trap* and *I'm So Glad*. The EP has also been reissued as a limited edition.

Compilation appearances have included: *Harlem Shuffle, What Now, The Trap* and *I'm So Glad* on *Sixties Years, Vol. 3 - French 60's EP Collection* (CD); *I'm So Glad* on *The Sound Of The Sixties* (2-LP), *Sixties Archive Vol. 1* (CD) and *Incredible Sound Show Stories, Vol. 1* (LP & CD); and *Harlem Shuffle, Aria Del Sud* and *Non Fatemi Odiare* on *Deep Purple - Odd Ditties* (CD). (VJ)

Jackie McAuley

| ALBUM: | 1 JACKIE McAULEY | (Dawn DNLS 3023) 1971 R1 |

NB: (1) reissued as *Jackie McAuley Plus* (See For Miles LP 315) 1991, also on CD (SEE CD 315). (1) reissued again on CD (Prog Line PL 598) plus two non-album tracks as bonuses.

| 45s: | Turning Green/It's Alright | (Dawn DNLS 1011) 1971 |
| | Rocking Shoes/One Fine Day | (Dawn DNLS 1020) 1971 |

McAuley, who grew up in Belfast, is best known as the piano player in **Them**, who relocated to LA without **Van Morrison** in 1967. Upon **Them's** demise, he formed **Belfast Gypsies** with his brother Pat (they also released a 45 under the name **Freaks Of Nature**) and he later moved to Dublin and formed a band called Cult, with Brendan Bonass and Paul Brady (who was later in **Planxty**). This proved to be a short-lived affair and before long **McAuley** was back in London, playing in a new band, **Trader Horne**, which he'd formed with **Fairport Convention's** original lead singer Judy Dyble. This interesting group fell apart when Dyble left to get married and **McAuley** then recorded this solo album with help from some of the best young jazz musicians of the time. All the material was self-penned except for a version of Leadbelly's *Poor Howard*. Highlights include *Away*, an autobiographical song which revisits his childhood in Belfast and *Country Joe*, a song about a fictional meeting with the legendary US West Coast star Country Joe McDonald. However, he didn't promote the album and both it and the 45 sold poorly, although *Rocking Shoes* was an N.M.E. single of the week. He recorded a follow-up which wasn't released, and co-wrote *Dear John* with **Johnny Gustafson**, which was a hit for **Status Quo**.

The 1991 See For Miles reissue also includes his non-album 45. *Country Joe* was also included on the 1971 compilation, *Dawn Takeaway Concert*. (VJ)

Cecil McCartney

| ALBUM: | 1 OM | (Columbia S(C)X 6283) 1968 SC |

| 45s: | Hey Aleuthia I Want You/Liquid Blue | (Columbia DB 8474) 1968 |
| | Orange And Green/Cloudy | (Columbia DB 8595) 1969 |

This obscure singer's odd (but rather dull) folk album contains frequent references to vegetarianism and associated beliefs. *Liquid Blue* resurfaced quite recently on *Circus Days, Vol. 5* (LP) and *Circus Days, Vol. 6* (CD) but it's nothing special. (VJ/RMJ)

Paul McCartney

HCP

ALBUMS:	1	McCARTNEY	(Apple PCS 7102) 1970 2
(up to	2	RAM	(Apple DAS 10003) 1971 1
1976)			

NB: (2) as Paul and Linda McCartney.

HCP

45s:	α	Another Day/Oh Woman, Oh Why	(Apple R 5889) 1971 2
(up to	β	The Back Seat Of My Car/	
1976)		Heart Of The Country	(Apple R 5914) 1971 39

NB: α reissued as a Japanese import (EMI/Toshiba TOCP 65500) 2000. β as Paul and Linda McCartney. β reissued as a Japanese import (EMI/Toshiba 65501) 2000. The above discography does not include recordings made with **Wings**.

Paul McCartney was born on 18 June 1942 in Liverpool. In June 1957 he met **John Lennon** and both became members of The Quarry Men. He began what would be an exceptionally fruitful songwriting partnership with **John Lennon**. The Quarry Men, whom **George Harrison** later joined during 1958, split up in November 1959, but by April of the following year John, Paul and George had formed Long John and The Silver Beatles with **Pete Best** and Stu Sutcliffe. The 'Long John' and 'Silver' were dropped in the first few weeks to leave **The Beatles**.

In March 1969 **McCartney** married American photographer Linda Eastman at Marylebone Registry Office. This seemed to pull him further away from **John Lennon** and, having announced on 11 April 1970 that he wouldn't record with **Lennon** again, he set about launching his own solo career. This concentrated on simpler pop music than much of the innovative work he'd been involved in as a member of **The Beatles**. His first solo album, *McCartney*, was homemade and, in many respects, unfinished. What it did have going for it was the promotion **McCartney** was getting as result of the break up of **The Beatles**. This and **McCartney**'s name and reputation enabled it to climb to No 2 in the Album Charts here and to top the US Charts. It did include one of his better compositions, *Maybe I'm Amazed*. Better than the album was his debut single, *Another Day*, a tuneful song about the routine of office life. It got to No 2 here and No 5 in the States.

Paul set about teaching Linda to play keyboards. His second album, *Ram*, was credited to Paul and Linda McCartney, although it's very doubtful whether she contributed much to it. Again it sold well (No 1 here, No 2 in the States) but musically it was very inconsistent. Paul and Linda enjoyed a minor hit with *Back Seat Of My Car* and a US-only 45, *Uncle Albert/Admiral Halsey*, topped the Charts over there. In retrospect, both releases were weak musically and seldom remembered now. After *Ram* he recorded an instrumental album in 1971, *Thrillington*, under pseudonym Perry 'Thrills' Thrillington. It wasn't released until 1977 (Regal Zonophone EMC 3175) along with a 45, *Eat At Home/Uncle Albert, Admiral Halsey* (Regal Zonophone EMI 2594). Both are now significant collectors' items. The album is in the R2 category. It was actually an orchestral version of *Ram* and is now available on CD, (Regal Zonophone 7234 8321 4525) 1995.

To enable him to perform live Paul formed a backing group, **Wings**, in 1971. He retained his undoubted ability to write catchy, melodic tunes with **Wings**, but sadly these were outnumbered by much inane rubbish. Rather than continuing to progress and push back musical frontiers as much of his work with **The Beatles** had, his career with **Wings** appeared to regress.

With half of **The Beatles** now dead Paul continues to thrive. He's recorded some good material since his days with **Wings** (1989's *Flower's In The Dirt* is a good example) and he's still touring and recording today. Most notably he headlined at the London 2005 Live 8 concert. Recently he's returned to basics and his *Chaos And Creation In The Back Yard* album has been likened to the *McCartney* album by those who have heard it. It was recorded in London and Los Angeles over a period of two years and comprised a set of memorable, melodic and simple songs. Paul plays most of the instruments on the album and described one of the highlights on the album a song called *Jenny Wren* as "daughter of *Blackbird*" in an interview with 'Record Collector' (October 2005 edition). (VJ)

Chris McClure (Section)

45s:	The Dying Swan/		
	The Land Of The Golden Tree	(Decca F 12346) 1966	
	Hazy People/I'm Just A Country Boy	(Polydor 56227) 1968 SC	
	Answer To Everything/Meditation	(Polydor 56259) 1968	
	Our Song Of Love/Weather Vane	(RCA RCA 1849) 1969	
α	You're Only Passing Time/Sing Our Song	(CBS 7646)1969	

NB: α As **Chris McClure Section**.

No other details known. (VJ)

Danny McCulloch

ALBUM:	1 WINGS OF A MAN	(Capitol E-(S)T 174) 1969 SC
45s:	Blackbird/Time Of Man	(Capitol CL 15607) 1969
	Colour Of The Sunset/	
	Smokless Zone	(Pye International 7N 25514) 1970

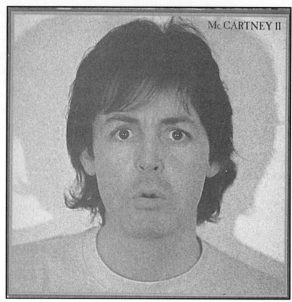

PAUL McCARTNEY - McCARTNEY II (LP).

London-born **Danny McCulloch** played bass with **Screaming Lord Sutch** before hooking up with **Eric Burdon and The Animals** from 1967-8. This solo effort, produced by Vic Briggs when both men were sacked by **Burdon**, comprises orchestrated popsike with occasional phasing. It came in a stupendous psychedelic sleeve but sold poorly. Both 45s were non-album. **McCulloch** later played bass on **Reg King**'s 1971 solo album.

Colour Of The Sunset has been compiled on *We Can Fly, Vol 2* (CD). (VJ/RMJ)

Henry McCullough

ALBUM:	1 MIND YOUR OWN BUSINESS	
(up to		(Dark Horse AMLH 22005) 1975 SC
1976)		

This Irish guitarist started off playing in an Enniskillen-based showband called The Sky Rockets. A 'phone call from an old friend, Chrissie Stewart, led to him crossing to the mainland to join a Blackpool-based band called The People, who later moved first to Dublin and then London. They'd started out playing soul, but later moved on to Mel Torme, Bobby Parker and R&B style numbers. **Hendrix** managers Chas Chandler and Mike Jeffries spotted them playing one night got them a record contract with Track and changed their name to the **Eire Apparent**. However, **McCullough** only played on their first 45 before returning to Dublin to join **Sweeney's Men**. He went on to play in **Joe Cocker's Grease Band** and was guitarist with **Wings** from 1972-73. After **Wings** he played around the London pub scene with people like **Frankie Miller** and recorded the above solo album which was released on **George Harrison**'s Dark Horse label. The label's subsequent demise hampered the further development of his solo career. In the eighties he was involved in various **Sweeney's Men** reunions and, more recently, he's accompanied English singer-songwriter Terry Clarke on tours. (VJ)

Shelagh McDonald

Personnel:			
	KEITH CHRISTMAS	gtr	AB
	GERRY CONWAY	drms	A
	PAT DONALDSON	bs	A
	MIKE EVANS		A
	TRISTAM FRY	vibes	A
	GORDON HUNTLEY	steel gtr	A
	SHELAGH McDONALD	gtr, vcls, keyb'ds	AB
	ROGER POWELL		A
	ANDY ROBERTS	gtr	A
	KEITH TIPPETT	piano	A
	IAN WHITEMAN	key'bds	A
	HARVEY BURNS	drms	B
	PAT DONALDSON	bs	B

KATHY KISSOON	bcking vcl	B
MAC KISSOON	bcking vcl	B
MIKE LONDON	bcking vcls	B
DAVE MATTACKS	drms	B
DAVE RICHARD	bs	B
JOHN RYAN	bs	B
DANNY THOMPSON	bs	B
RICHARD THOMPSON	gtr	B
RAY WARLEIGH	sax	B
IAN WHITEMAN	keyb'ds	B

ALBUMS: 1(A) THE SHELAGH McDONALD ALBUM
(B & C CAS 1019) 1970 R1
2(B) STARGAZER (B & C CAS 1043) 1971 R1

NB: (1) and (2) reissued as *Let No Man Steal Your Thyme: The Collection* (Castle CMDDD 1065) 2005, a 2-CD set, along with all her other known recordings, except her lost BBC Radio Session. *Album* (Mooncrest CRESTCD 059) 2000 is a retrospective that compiles material from the above two albums along with previously unissued items.

A Scottish singer, guitarist and pianist who mixed traditional and personal songs on her two albums, which feature a virtual A-Z of British folk-rock talent and are minor progressive folk classics.

Born and bred in Scotland, **McDonald** came to London in the late sixties and became close friends with **Keith Christmas**, who helped her find a record deal through his producer Sandy Roberton. Though there are songs by **Christmas**, **Andy Roberts** and **Gerry Rafferty** on her debut, it's hers that dominate. Numbers such as *Mirage* and *Ophelia's Song* are melodic and memorable, and feature impressive arrangements by Robert Kirby, who worked on both albums and rated her highly. The *Stargazer* album is almost entirely self-composed, and the two beautiful final songs, *Odyssey* and the title track, reach a level that could never have been anticipated from the 1969 recordings.

McDonald was a popular and much-admired feature of the early seventies folk circuit, so her abrupt departure from it following *Stargazer*'s appearance has given rise to much speculation. It's thought she may have suffered a bad drug experience and been hauled homewards by her concerned parents, but none of her friends in the industry have any real idea what became of her. She might have worked in a bookshop in Edinburgh for a while, and there are rumours that she later emigrated to California, but there have been no confirmed sightings of her since. None of her royalties have ever been collected, and if she is still alive it must be assumed she desires no publicity.

Let No Man Steal Your Thyme is a 2-CD overview of her career. The rare BBC live sampler *Dungeon Folk* (LP) contains unreleased material, as do the two Pegasus label samplers, *Club Folk Vol. 1* (LP) (Peg PS 2) and *Vol. 2* (LP) (Peg PS 3). *Let No Man Steal Your Thyme* is a 2-CD overview of her career, containing everything releasable (including her two contributions to *Dungeon Folk*, *Hullo Stranger* and *Street Walking Blues*, unavailable since their original release). She also had tracks on the *Rave On* (LP) compilation. (NM/BS/RMJ)

McDonald and Giles

Personnel: MIKE GILES drms A
IAN McDONALD keyb'ds, sax A

ALBUM: 1(A) McDONALD AND GILES (Island ILPS 9126) 1970 SC

NB: First pressing of (1) with pink label and 'i' logo is R1. (1) reissued on Polydor (2302 070) 1970 (SC) and later on CD (Virgin CDVKMG 1 X) 2002.

These two recorded this album whilst they were both members of **King Crimson**. **McDonald** was once the boyfriend of **Fairport Convention**'s Judy Dyble. It's full of whimsical vocal arrangements and one marathon track *Birdman*. This starts with a vocal introduction and culminates with full orchestra and chorus. This is an interesting album, which stiffed at the time. The 2002 reissue on Virgin is welcome.

McDonald later went on to form Foreigner and Giles worked extensively as a session musician.

One of the tracks, *Extract From Tomorrow's People*, was also included on Island's 1971 *El Pea* (LP) compilation. (VJ)

Mike McGear

ALBUMS: 1 WOMAN (Island ILPS 9191) 1972 SC
(up to 2 McGEAR (Warner Bros K 56051) 1974 SC
1976)

NB: (1) reissued on CD (Edsel EDCD 507) 1997. (2) was subject to a 6-track, signed and limited reissue in the eighties, which is now rare and collectable (R1). (2) also reissued on CD (See For Miles SEECD 339) 1992.

HCP
45s: Woman/Kill (Island WIP 6131) 1972 -
(up to Leave It/Sweet Baby (PS) (Warner Bros K 16446) 1974 36
1976) Sea Breezes/
Givin' Grease A Ride (Warner Bros K 16520) 1975 -
Dance The Do/Norton (Warner Bros K 16573) 1975 -
Simply Love You/What Do You
Really Know (Some PS) (Warner Bros K 16658) 1975 SC/-
Doing Nothing All Day/A-Z (EMI EMI 2485) 1976 -

These were solo ventures for **Paul McCartney**'s younger brother. Originally in **Scaffold** and later in **Grimms**, he also recorded an album with fellow Liverpudlian and poet **Roger McGough**. *Woman* contains some catchy pop tunes like *Witness* and *Roamin' A Road*. His second album features **McCartney** in a songwriting/producing capacity. (VJ)

McGough and McGear

Personnel: MIKE McGEAR A
ROGER McGOUGH A

ALBUM: 1(A) McGOUGH AND McGEAR
(Parlophone PCS 7047) 1968 R3

NB: Reissued on EMI (PCS 332) in 1990 (SC). Also on CD (Parlophone CDP 791 877 2) in 1989 (R2), but deleted in 1991.

Roger McGough was one of the country's top poets, and recorded this extremely rare and somewhat self-indulgent album with **Mike McGear** whilst both were members of **Scaffold**. The duo was actually signed to Apple for the project, but since the label hadn't been launched it was leased to Parlophone instead. Featuring anonymous contributions from **Jimi Hendrix**, **Spencer Davis**, **Dave Mason**, **Paul McCartney**, **John Mayall**, **Graham Nash**, **Gary Walker** and others, it's a mixture of **McGear**'s melodic pop songs and **McGough**'s poems, typified by *Summer With Monika*. Among the best cuts are the hypnotic *Yellow Book* and hard-rocking *Ex-Art Student*, which has **Hendrix** on guitar and sitar and **Nash** on vocals.

McGough also recorded an album of poetry with Brian Patten, *Read Their Own Verse - British Poets Of Our Time* (Argo ZPL 1190) in 1975, while he was a member of **Grimms**. **McGough** now lives in Barnes in South-west London. The 4-CD box set *Acid Drops, Spacedust & Flying Saucers* includes *So Much In Love* by this duo. (VJ)

McDONALD AND GILES - McDonald And Giles (LP).

McGOUGH AND McGEAR - McGough And McGear (LP).

McGuinness Flint

Personnel:			
DENNIS COULSON	keyb'ds, vcls	ABCD	
HUGHIE FLINT	drms	ABCDE	
BENNY GALLAGHER	gtr, vcls	AB	
GRAHAM LYLE	gtr, vcls	AB	
TOM McGUINNESS	gtr, bs	ABCDE	
PAUL RUTHERFORD	trombone	A	
JOHN BAILEY	gtr	C	
DIXIE DEAN	bs, harp	CDE	
NEIL INNES	piano	C	
JIM EVANS	gtr	E	
LOU STONEBRIDGE	keyb'ds, bs	E	

HCP

ALBUMS: 1(B) McGUINNESS FLINT (Capitol EA-ST 22625) 1970 SC 9
2(B) HAPPY BIRTHDAY RUTHIE BABY
(Capitol E-ST 22794) 1971 SC -
3(D) LO AND BEHOLD (DJM DJLPS 424) 1972 -
4(E) RAINBOW (Bronze ILPS 9244) 1973 -
5(E) C'EST LA VIE (Bronze ILPS 9302) 1974 -

NB: (3) issued on Sire (SAS 7405) in the US. There was also *Greatest Hits* (Sounds Superb SPR 80537) in 197?.

HCP

45s: When I'm Dead And Gone/
Lazy Afternoon (Capitol CL 15662) 1970 2
Malt And Barley Blues/Rock On (Capitol CL 15682) 1971 5
Happy Birthday Ruthie Baby/
Wham Bang/Back On The Road Again(Capitol CL 15691) 1971 -
α Let The People Go/Cheeky Chappy (Blue Mountain 1005) 1972 -
Ride On My Rainbow/Virgin Mary (Bronze BRO 8) 1973 -
C'est La Vie/Poppadaddy (Bronze BRO 12) 1974 -
Reissue: When I'm Dead And Gone/
Malt And Barley Blues (EMI G 4529) 1984 -

NB: α was on a short-lived subsidiary label of Island.

McGuinness Flint was formed by Tom McGuinness after the demise of his former band, **Manfred Mann**. Flint had earlier been in **John Mayall's Bluesbreakers**. They played a blend of good-time country and folk and enjoyed considerable success in the short-term with *When I'm Dead And Gone* and *Malt And Barley Blues*, both making the Top Ten here. The former was also a minor US hit (No 47). Their debut album sold well too, achieving No 9 here and No 155 in the US. By contrast, their second album did better in the US (No 198); it didn't chart here. They weren't much use as a live attraction, though, only doing a limited number of live gigs - they were very much a studio band. Their commercial decline seemed to stem from the departure of songwriters **Gallagher and Lyle** to embark on a solo career. Arguably, though, their recordings became more interesting.

Line-up (C) was very short-lived. **Innes**, of course, had once played for **Bonzo Dog Doo Dah Band**, but line-up (D) recorded *Lo And Behold*, an album of obscure Dylan songs, which was critically acclaimed but sold poorly.

When Dennis Coulson left early in 1973 to record a solo album, guitarist Jim Evans and keyboard player Lou Stonebridge were recruited and the new line-up was contracted to Bronze for a couple of country-orientated albums. This new line-up toured relentlessly in an attempt to re-establish them, but had little commercial success. In fact, *C'est La Vie* was an interesting set of originals produced by Big Jim Sullivan, a long-standing session guitarist.

The band split in February 1975 when Flint was hospitalised with a collapsed lung. After he'd recovered, he played with a traditional Irish group called Chanter, whilst Stonebridge and **McGuinness** soldiered on for another four years as a duo. **McGuinness** and Flint were later re-united in The Blues Band but that's beyond the time span of this book.

You can also check out *When I'm Dead And Gone* on *Greatest Hits Of The 70's - cd3*. (VJ/BM)

The McKinleys

Personnel:	JEANETTE McKINLEY	vcls	A
	SHEILA McKINLEY	vcls	A

45s: Someone Cares For Me/
Million Miles Away (Columbia DB 7230) 1964 SC
When He Comes Along/
Then I'll Know It's Love (Columbia DB 7310) 1964
Sweet And Tender Romance/
That Lonely Feeling (Parlophone R 5211) 1964 SC
Give Him My Love/Once More (Columbia DB 7583) 1965 SC

This girl duo hailed from Edinburgh. **Donovan** played on *Give Him My Love*, which also featured Perry Ford (then with **The Ivy League**), Clem Cattini and Licorice Locking. (VJ)

John McLaughlin

ALBUMS: 1 EXTRAPOLATION (Marmalade 608 007) 1969 R1
2 DEVOTION (Douglas DGL 65075) 1971 SC
3. MY GOAL'S BEYOND (Douglas DGL 69014) 1971 SC
4. WHERE FORTUNE SMILES (Dawn DNLS 3018) 1971

NB: (1) reissued on Marmalade (2343 012) in 1970 (SC) and also on CD. (2) reissued on CD (Rykodisc RCD 10051) 1992 and again (Snapper Music SNAP 232) 2005 in a rather ugly digipak sleeve. (3) issued on CD (Charly CPCD 8232) 1997. (4) Recorded with **John Surman** and reissued on CD (Beat Goes On BGO 191) in 1994. There are also some CD compilations, *Collection: John McLaughlin* (Castle Collector Series CCSCD 305) 1991, *The Collection* (Connoisseur/Sony VSOP CD 279) and *Greatest Hits: John McLaughlin* (CBS 4670102) 1991. This second one was only available on import.

McLaughlin is considered to be jazz-rock's greatest guitarist and fans of the genre not familiar with his work and that with **Mahavishnu Orchestra** should check it out.

Born in Yorkshire in 1942, **McLaughlin** first studied violin and piano, learning to play guitar at the age of 11. He moved to London in the mid-sixties and played with various jazz-rock outfits, most notable the **Graham Bond Organization** and **Brian Auger Trinity**. He also played with **Duffy Power** between 1965-67 and can be heard on the *Innovations* album.

His debut album showcased his virtuoso guitar playing which was a breakneck amalgam of blues, jazz and Eastern styles. In 1969 he relocated to New York, where he played on two Lifetime albums and on Miles Davis' *In A Silent Way* and *Bitches' Brew* albums. On the latter, he developed an interesting fusion of jazz/rock riffs with spiralling solos. The explosively psychedelic *Devotion* was recorded with Buddy Miles in France around the same time and is one of the heaviest albums of the period. His period in New York was to transform his musical career when he underwent conversion to the philosophy of Bengal mystic Sri Chinmoy. As a consequence, *My Goal's Beyond* was a mystical album of Indian-influenced meditation music comprised of solo acoustic pieces. He was supported on the album by violinist Jerry Goodman, who'd previously been in the US Chicago-based group Flock, and Billy Cobham on drums.

Aside from **Surman**, Karl Berger, Stu Martin and Dave Holland also played on *Where Fortune Smiles*. One track, *Hope*, is full of energetic bursts of electricity from **McLaughlin** on guitar. He later re-recorded it (in much briefer form) with the **Mahavishnu Orchestra**, which was to be his next project. Another track to preview **Mahavishnu**'s style was *Earth Bound Hearts* where a succession of picked guitar notes underlay **Surman**'s baritone sax work.

The Collection features his work with the jazz fusion **Mahavishnu Orchestra** as well as tracks from his solo career and his work with Shakti and its some of his best to date.

He also contributed *Pete The Poet* to the Marmalade label's 1969 label sampler *100% Proof* (LP) and played on **Bruce's** *Things We Like* album. (VJ)

The McLynns

Personnel: BARBARA McLYNN   A
              DONAL McLYNN   A
              PAULA McLYNN   A

ALBUM: 1(A) OLD MARKET STREET   (CBS S 63836) 1970 R2

This rare album was the work of an Irish trio comprising two sisters and a brother. The music is characterised by elegant vocal harmonies and clear, lucid instrumentation. The material is mostly traditional (*The Orange Maid of Sligo*, *Gaire Na Mon*) but there are also some good self-penned numbers, typified by the rueful *Sam's Return To Sam* and *Age Mood*. (VJ/RMJ)

Harold McNair

ALBUMS: 1 AFFECTIONATE FINK   (Island ILP 926) 1965 R4
         2 HAROLD MCNAIR   (RCA SF 7969) 1968 R3
         3 FENCE   (B&C CAS 1016) 1970 SC
         4 FLUTE AND NUT   (RCA INTS 1096) 1970 R1
         5 HAROLD MCNAIR   (B&C CAS 1045) 1971 SC

45:      The Hipster/Indecision   (RCA 1742) 1968 R1

This superb flute and sax player played on many sessions and was supported by the cream of British progressive and jazz-rock on his solo work. See **Seven Ages of Man**, **Cressida**, **John Cameron (Quartet)**, **CCS** and **Marc Brierley**. His albums are all good and the single is highly sought-after. He is perhaps best known to readers of this book for his contributions to **Donovan's** *Gift....* album. (VZ/RMJ)

David McNeil

45:      Don't Let Your Chance Go By/
         Space Plane   (President PT 212) 1968 SC

In addition to this single, **David McNeil** has a cut called *Linda* on *Fading Yellow, Vol 4* (CD). *Don't Let Your Chance Go By* can also be heard on *Jagged Time Lapse, Vol 5* (CD). (VJ)

Paul McNeill

ALBUMS: 1 CONTEMPORARY FOLK   (Decca LK 4699) 1965 R2
         2 TRADITIONALLY AT THE TROUBADOUR
                                   (Decca LK 4803) 1966 R2
NB: (1) with **Davy Graham**.

Paul McNeill's real name was Paul Jebb. He owned an impressive voice and was a regular on London's folk circuit in the mid-sixties, when these two albums were made. The first features a number of songs by his one-time flatmate Paul Simon, as well as guitar from **Davy Graham** throughout. The second was recorded live on stage at The Troubadour in

London, and produced by **Mike Vernon**. **Trevor Lucas** (later with **Fairport Convention**) played 12-string guitar on a few tracks. **McNeill** also sang with **Sandy Denny** on the 1967 *Alex Campbell And His Friends* album. The sleevenotes to that release state that **McNeill** 'was one of the stars of Rediffusion's 'Heartsong' series and has televised in various other regions. Something of a world traveller, he has sung all through Europe and as far as Israel, where he worked for a time on a kibbutz. He is a Lancastrian of Scottish Irish descent. He has made two films and co-starred with **Julie Felix** all over England. **McNeill** performed for a while in a duo with Linda Peters, who went on to marry and find fame with **Richard Thompson**. The duo released two 45s as **Paul and Linda** (including Bob Dylan's *You Ain't Goin' Nowhere* on MGM), but he vanished from the folk scene in the early seventies, settling in Switzerland, where he took a literary degree. He was spotted busking around Europe in the eighties, but died of lung cancer in Norway on Boxing Day 1989. (RMJ)

Paul McNeill and Linda Peters

45:      You Ain't Going Nowhere/
         I'll Show You How To Sing   (MGM MGM 1408) 1968

This was a one-off folk single that **Paul McNeill** recorded by with Linda Peters. *You Ain't Going Nowhere* was a Bob Dylan song. Peters (whose real name was Linda Pettifer) recorded a second single with **McNeill** in 1969 as **Paul and Linda**. After doing session work, singing jingles and performing in London folk clubs, she teamed up with **Sandy Denny** and various other folk figures to record *Rock On*, a collection of early rock and roll favourites using the name **Bunch**. She met **Richard Thompson** (guitarist and songwriter with **Fairport Convention**) in 1969 and they both performed on the *Rock On* record and on **Richard Thompson**'s debut solo album *Henry The Human Fly* in 1972. They married later that year and began a significant musical partnership that would last almost a decade. She had one of the best voices in rock and pop at the time. (VJ)

McPeake Family/Folk Group

ALBUMS: 1 IRISH FOLK!   (Fontana TL 5214) 1964 SC
         2 AT HOME WITH THE McPEAKES
                                   (Fontana TL 5358) 1965 SC
         3 PLEASANT AND DELIGHTFUL
                                   (Fontana TL 5433) 1967 SC
         4 WELCOME HOME   (Evolution Z 1002) 1969 R1
         5 IRISH TO BE SURE   (Windmill WMD 151) 1972 SC
NB: (1), (3) and (5) credited to **The McPeake Family**. (4) credited to **The McPeake Folk Group**.

This traditional Irish folk group from Belfast is reputedly in the top drawer of this genre. All of their albums are extremely elusive and have become very sought-after among fans of the genre. (VJ)

Tony (T.S.) McPhee

ALBUMS: 1 ME AND THE DEVIL   (Liberty LBL/LBS 83190) 1968 R1
         2 THE SAME THING ON THEIR MINDS
                                   (Sunset SLS 50209) 1971 SC
         3 TWO SIDES OF...
                                   (World Wide Artists WWA 001) 1973 SC

NB: (1) reissued on one CD with *I Asked For Water And She Gave Me Gasoline* (BGO BGOCD 332). (2) recorded with **Jo-Ann Kelly**. (3) reissued on CD (Castle CLACD 267) 1992 and again on CD (Talking Elephant TECD 065).

45:      α Someone To Love Me/
            Ain't Gonna Cry No More   (Purdah 45-3501) 1966 R3
NB: α recorded as **T.S. McPhee**.

Tony McPhee was probably better known as guitarist with the **Groundhogs** among others. He was also with **John Dummer's Blues Band** and flirted with psychedelia as a member of **Herbal Mixture**. **Tony** also cut these two 'solo' albums and recorded *Same Thing On Their Mind* (Sunset SLS 50209) with **Jo-Ann Kelly** in 1971.

His 45 for Purdah is very rare and sought-after and his 1968 album is quite a significant collectable too. That was recorded at home on a massive 16-track machine and a very large mixing desk.

His second album, a mixture of rural blues and electronic gymnastics, was recorded at his home studio in Suffolk.

He can also be heard playing on Liberty's 1968 *Gutbucket* (LP) sampler and on the sequel *Son Of Gutbucket* (LP) in 1969 - he has one track on each. He contributed four tracks; *Ain't Gonna Cry No More*, *Someone To Love*, *When You Got A Good Friend* and *You Don't Love Me* on the *Anthology of British Blues, Vol 1 & 2* (LPs) and on *White Boy Blues* (LP). *History Of British Blues* (LP) (from 1973) features previously unreleased tracks of his including *Blue Guitar* and *I B's Troubled*, which both date from 1965.

McPhee's been one of the most prolific performers on the blues circuit over the years and in 1993, he popped up supporting Paul Kantner's Jefferson Starship on a far from successful European tour. (VJ)

Gillian McPherson

ALBUM: 1 POETS AND PAINTERS AND PERFORMERS OF BLUES
(RCA Victor SF 8220) 1971 R2

45: It's My Own Way/Is Somebody In Tune
With My Song (RCA Victor RCA 2089) 1970

Gillian McPherson played support to **Ralph McTell** in 1971 (both artists shared the same manager as **Pentangle** and **Steeleye Span**) and was promptly signed by RCA who had been invited to the concert. Danny Thompson of **Pentangle** produced her album, which Colin Caldwell engineered at Marquee Studios in London. Jon Mark, **Johnny Almond**, Tommy Eyre, Spike Heatley, **Dave Cousins**, Brian Spring, Tony Carr, and Roy Babbington played on the album and it has attracted the attention of some collectors as a result. Beautifully arranged by Robert Kirby, the album consists of melodic folk ballads but is insufficiently distinctive to be called essential. Her 45 contains entirely different - and superior - recordings of the songs concerned from those on the album.

Gillian did one promotional tour which included the Cambridge Folk Festival and Reading Rock Festival. She recorded an album for John Reid who signed her to **Elton John's** Rocket Music Publishing Company, but the album was never released due to management problems. It was produced by Ken Scott who engineered **Bowie's** and **Elton John's** early albums. **McPherson** later performed on the wine bar circuit and also recorded the theme song for the film 'Dogs Of War' composed by Geoffrey Burgon. She also accepted an invitation to take part in another film called 'A Fella By The Name Of' by Nick Griffiths.

In the eighties she formed a duo, a trio, a seven-piece rock band and played on the London circuit, releasing a 45 on the Gee Whiz label, which she set up with her agent at the time. In 1989 they opened for **Joe Cocker** at the Hammersmith Odeon. **Alexis Korner** took an interest in her music in the late eighties and they shared concert work together and **McPherson** returned to her native Ireland to perform with him in Dublin and Belfast. **Korner** planned to sign her to a new label he was setting up with his manager shortly before he died of cancer.

In the nineties she turned to dance, becoming a freestyle dance teacher, but still continuing to write and compose. In 1993 she moved to France and released an album of new compositions with French musicians. They appear mostly at Celtic and Blues Festivals. (VJ/GMP/RMJ)

Ralph McTell

HCP

ALBUMS: 1 8 FRAMES A SECOND
(up to (Transatlantic TRA 165) 1968 SC -
1976) 2 SPIRAL STAIRCASE (Transatlantic TRA 177) 1969 SC -
3 MY SIDE OF YOUR WINDOW
(Transatlantic TRA 209) 1969 SC -
4 RALPH McTELL REVISITED (Compilation)
(Transatlantic TRA 227) 1970 SC -

5 YOU, WELL MEANING, BROUGHT ME HERE
(Famous SFMA 5753) 1971 SC -
6 NOT TILL TOMORROW (Reprise RSLP 2121) 1972 36
7 EASY (Reprise K 54013) 1973 31
8 STREETS (Warner Bros K 56105) 1975 13
9 STREETS OF LONDON
(Transatlantic TRASAM 34) 1975 -
10 RIGHT SIDE UP (Warner Bros K 56296) 1976 -

NB: (2) reissued on CD (Wooded Hill HILLCD 5). It comes with the original packaging and informative liner notes by Colin Harper. (9) reissued on CD (Repertoire RR 4764).

Vinyl compilations, apart from (4), have included: - *The Ralph McTell Collection* (Transatlantic TRASAM 39) 1977, reissued on Pickwick (PDA 040) 1978, *71/72* (Mays TG 001) 1982 and *At His Best* (Cambra CR 057) 1983.

CD compilations have included: - *The Very Best Of Ralph McTell* (Start SCD 17) 1988, *Love Songs Collection* (Castle Collector CCSCD 219) 1989, *Streets Of London* (RCA 295945) 1991, *Silver Celebration* (Castle Collector CCSCD 329) 1992, *The Definitive Transatlantic Collection* (Castle) 1997, *The Best Of Ralph McTell* (Essential ESACD 880) 2000 and *Definitive Transatlantic Singles Collection* (Essential ESMCD 527) 2005.

HCP

45s: (up to 1976)	Summer Comes Along	(Big T BIG 125) 1969
	Kew Gardens/Father Forgive Me	(Big T BIG 131) 1970
	Spiral Staircase/Terminus	(Big T BIG 134) 1970
	First And Last Man	(Famous FAM 105) 1971 -
	Teacher Teacher	(Famous FAM 111) 1971 -
	When I Was A Cowboy/ Small Voice Calling	(Reprise K 14214) 1972 -
	Zimmerman Blues	(Reprise K 14225) 1972 -
	Take It Easy/Sweety Mystery	(Reprise K 14325) 1974 -
	Streets Of London/ Summer Lightning (PS)	(Reprise K 14380) 1974 2
	El Progresso/Grande Affair	(Warner Bros K 16537) 1975 -
	Let Me Down Easy/ Would I Lie To You	(Warner Bros K 16633) 1975 -
	Dreams Of You/ Sweet Forgiveness	(Warner Bros K 16648) 1975 36
	Weather The Storm/First Song	(Warner Bros K 16843) 1976 -

One of the UK's leading folk singer/songwriters of the late sixties and seventies, **McTell** (real name Ralph May) was born in Farnborough, Kent on 3 December 1944 but grew up in Croydon. After a spell in the Army, he learnt guitar in 1965 and spent time in Europe (mostly busking in Paris) before returning to the UK and beginning to write songs. Having enrolled at Teacher Training College, he became a popular performer on the London folk club circuit, borrowing his stage name from Blind Willie McTell, a thirties blues player.

He was signed to Transatlantic in 1968 and released *8 Frames A Second*, a good debut which is now his rarest album. The follow-up, *Spiral Staircase*, included *Streets Of London*, which would later become a hit and the song with which he is most closely associated. This helped bring him wider acclaim and his third album, *My Side Of Your Window*, consolidated his reputation. In this period he spent much time in Cornwall, where he became firm friends with **COB**, whose two extraordinary albums he produced brilliantly.

His fourth album *You, Well Meaning Brought Me Here*, marked his real emergence as a singer-songwriter. Arranged by Tony Visconti, the songs recounted many of his life's experiences and dealt with issues such as racism (*Claudia*) and militarism (*Pick Up A Gun*). Visconti also produced his next album, *Not Till Tomorrow*, which included *Zimmerman Blues*, concerning the price of fame.

McTell only achieved real commercial success briefly, when a re-recorded version of *Streets Of London* climbed to No 2 in the UK Charts, but the song went on to become one of the most covered of all time. On the back of its success he embarked on a nationwide tour using a support band for the first time, and enjoyed a further minor hit with *Dreams Of You*. After this he withdrew from the limelight, going to America to write new material. He went on to make several further albums for Warner Brothers and set up his own Mays label in the early eighties.

The recent Castle CD compilation consists of 16 tracks including one previously unreleased (*Summer Girls*) track; three new recordings of old songs (*The Ferryman*, *Hand Of Joseph* and *Michael In The Garden*) and the inevitable *Streets Of London* hit.

Compilation appearances include: *Willoughby's Farm*, *Streets Of London* and *Summer Come Along* on *The Transatlantic Story* CD box set. (VJ)

Ray McVay Sound

45s: Raunchy/Revenge   (Pye 7N 15777) 1965 R1
        Kinda Kinky/Kingdom Come   (Pye 7N 15816) 1965 SC
  α Genesis/House Of Clowns   (Parlophone R 5460) 1966
        Destination Moon/Mexican Scavenger   (Mercury MF 1121) 1969
  β They Call Me Mr. Tibbs   (Philips 6006 083) 1971

NB: α credited to Ray McVay Band. β as Ray McVay & Orchestra.

A middle-of-the-road band that was popular on the Mecca ballroom and cabaret circuit. Understandably dreadful. (JN)

David McWilliams

                                           HCP
ALBUMS: 1 SINGING SONGS BY DAVID McWILLIAMS
(up to   (Major Minor MMLP/SMLP 2) 1967 SC 38
1976)   2 DAVID McWILLIAMS VOL. 2
                   (Major Minor MMLP/SMLP 10) 1967 SC 23
    3 THE DAYS OF DAVID McWILLIAMS (Compilation)
                    (Major Minor MCP 5026) 1967 SC -
    4 DAVID McWILLIAMS VOL. 3
                  (Major Minor MMLP/SMLP 11) 1968 SC 39
    5 DAYS OF PEARLY SPENCER (Compilation)
                   (Starline SRS 5075) 1971 -
    6 LORD OFFALY   (Dawn DNLS 3039) 1972 SC -
    7 THE BEGGAR AND THE PRIEST
                 (Dawn DNLS 3047) 1973 SC -
    8 LIVING'S JUST A STATE OF MIND
                 (Dawn DNLS 3059) 1974 SC -

NB: (6) released in the US (Pye 3302) 1972. There's also a compilation, *The Best Of The EMI Years* (EMI 0777 7 99732 2 4) 1992, also issued on CD (EMI CDEMS 1457) 1992. Later albums have included: *David McWilliams* (EMI EMC 3169) 1977, *Don't Do It For Love* (EMI EMC 3208) 1978, *When I Was A Dancer* (Crystal 26305) 1979, *Wounded* (Carmel CAR 1001 LP) 1981 and *Working For The Government* ( ) 1980's. A later CD compilation is *The Days Of David McWilliams* (RPM RPM 225) 2001 and *Days At Dawn* (Castle Music CMDDD) 452) 2002 is a 2-CD set which chronicles his early seventies recordings for Dawn. *Reflections Of David McWilliams* (RPM RPM 257) 2003 showcases his career.

45s: α God And My Country/Blue Eyes   (CBS 202348) 1966
(up to   The Days Of Pearly Spencer/
1976)   Harlem Lady   (Major Minor MM 533) 1967
        This Side Of Heaven/
        Mister Satisfied   (Major Minor MM 561) 1968

DAVID McWILLIAMS - David McWilliams Vol. 2 (LP).

        The Stranger/Follow Me   (Major Minor MM 592) 1969
        Oh Mama Are You My Friend?/
        I Love Susie In The Summer (Major Minor MM 616) 1969
        Love Like A Lady/
        Down By The Dockyard   (Dawn DNS 1044) 1973
        You've Only Been A Stranger/
        Ships In The Night   (Dawn DNS 1064) 1974

NB: α also issued in the US (CBS 43793) 1966. There's also two US 45s, *Days Of Pearly Spencer*/*There's No Lock Upon My Door* (Kapp 896) 1968 and *This Side Of Heaven*/*Can I Get There By Candlelight* (Kapp 952) 1968.

David McWilliams was born in Cregagh in Belfast, Northern Ireland, in 1945, a few months before the end of the war. He is best known for *The Days Of Pearly Spencer*, a beautiful pop song which deployed distorted vocals using a megaphone rather like **The New Vaudeville Band**'s *Winchester Cathedral*. Despite three releases it was never a hit, but it deserved better. The flip side, *Harlem Lady*, also won some recognition at the time, but despite considerable hype and plugging on Radio Caroline, he never broke through.

The 1992 compilation includes a few tracks from the late seventies as well as his better recordings from the sixties. His seventies material was much more folk-based. In 2001 RPM issued a new CD compilation of his material, *The Days Of David McWilliams*.

Days At Dawn, Castle's 2-CD set, chronicles his recordings for Dawn in the early seventies by which time he'd moved on to playing country/folk/pop backed by a range of session players. It's competent enough but not very lively and will only really attract completists.

The Days Of Pearly Spencer later got a further airing on *Sixties Lost And Found, Vol. 1 - 1964-1969* (LP) and on the 4-CD set *Acid Drops, Spacedust & Flying Dust*. A cover version of *The Days of Pearly Spencer* by Marc Almond (ex-Soft Cell) was a No. 2 hit in 1992.

Sadly, **David McWilliams** passed away on 8th January 2002. (VJ/NM)

Me and Them

Personnel: GEORGE DAVIES   vcls, ld gtr   A
             SPENCE GIBBONS   gtr   A
             ROY HARRIS   bs   A
             DENNIS HERRINGTON drms   A
             MICK TRACEY   sax   A

45s: Feels So Good/
        I Think I'm Gonna Kill Myself (Pye 7N 15596) 1964 SC
        Everything I Do Is Wrong/
        Show You Mean It Too   (Pye 7N 15631) 1964 SC
        Get Away/Tell Me Why   (Pye 7N 15683) 1964 SC

I Think I'm Gonna Kill Myself was done by Buddy Knox and *Tell Me Why* was a **Beatles**' song. For their final 45, they coupled **Georgie Fame**'s *Get Away* with **The Four Pennies**' *Tell Me Why*. Some of them played with **Chris Andrews** in Germany.

Show You Mean It Too has been included on *The R&B Era, Vol. 1* (CD) and *Beat Merchants* (CD). (VJ)

The Measles

Personnel incl: WYNDHAM DAVIS   gtr   A
                DAVE EARL   bs   A
                RED HOFFMAN   vcls   A
                RAY MONDELL   drms   A
                JOMO SMITH   ld gtr   A

45s: Casting My Spell/Bye Birdie Fly (Columbia DB 7531) 1965 R1
        Night People/Dog Rough Dan (Columbia DB 7673) 1965 SC
        Kicks/No Baby At All   (Columbia DB 7875) 1966 R1
        Walkin' In/Looking For Love (Columbia DB 8029) 1966 SC

This was a raw R&B style band from Manchester whose records never sold in any significant quantities. *Casting My Spell* was a Johnny Otis song and *Kicks* was a cover of the US band Paul Revere and The Raiders' classic.

Compilation appearances include: *Casting My Spell* and *Bye Birdie Fly* on *Rare 60's Beat Treasures, Vol. 4* (CD); and *Casting My Spell* on *Hide & Seek Again (Vol. 2)* (LP). (VJ)

Meddy Evils

45s: Find Somebody To Love/
  A Place Called Love   (Pye 7N 15941) 1965 R3
  It's All For You/Ma's Place   (Pye 7N 17091) 1966 R3

This was a mid-sixties male quartet from Southampton. They played very collectable freakbeat/R&B.

Compilation appearances have included: *Place Called Love* on *Justification* (LP) and *Doin' The Mod, Vol. 1* (CD); *Ma's Place* on *That Driving Beat* (CD) and *Doin' The Mod, Vol. 2* (CD); and *It's All For You* and *Ma's Place* on *Freakbeat Freakout* (CD). (VJ)

Medicine Head

Personnel: JOHN FIDDLER   gtr, vcls   ABCDEF
  PETER HOPE-EVANS   hrmnca, jews harp ABCDEF
  KEITH RELF   bs   B
  JOHN DAVIES   drms   B
  ROB TOWNSEND   drms   DE
  ROGER SOUNDERS   gtr   D
  GEORGE FORD   bs   D
  CHARLIE McCRACKEN bs   E

ALBUMS: 1(A) NEW BOTTLES, OLD MEDICINE
        (Dandelion 63757) 1970 R1
  2(A) HEAVY ON THE DRUM (Some w/lyric insert)
        (Dandelion DAN 8005) 1971 R2/R1
  3(B) DARK SIDE OF THE MOON
    (w/insert)   (Dandelion 2310 166) 1971 R1
  4(C) ONE AND ONE IS ONE (Polydor 2310 248) 1972 SC
  5(D) THRU' A FIVE   (Polydor 2383 272) 1974 SC
  6(C) MEDICINE HEAD   (Polydor 2384 069) 1975
  7(F) TWO MAN BAND   (Barn 2314 102) 1976 SC
  8(-) BEST OF...   (Vertigo 2485 204) 1981

NB: (1) reissued on CD (Repertoire REP 4080-WP) 1991 and as *New Bottles, Old Medicine... Plus* (See For Miles SEECD 411) 1994. The *Plus* being both sides of the *Pictures In The Sky* 45 and three live tracks. (1) reissued again on CD (Dandelion Super UICY 9439) 2005. (2) reissued on CD (Dandelion Super UICY 9440) 2005. (3) reissued on CD (Dandelion Super UICY 9441) 2005. (7) reissued on CD (Angel Air SJPCD 094) 2001, with extra tracks and sleevenotes. Also relevant is the CD compilation, *Best Of Medicine Head* (Polydor 8439 012) 1990. There's also a live 1975 recording from a Marquee Club concert on CD, *Timepeace: Live In London - June 1975* (Red Steel RMC CD 0201) 1995, which includes versions of a couple of their hit singles (*Pictures In The Sky* and *One And One Is One*) alongside versions of staple live numbers like *Blue Suede Shoes*, *Walking Blues* and samples of their original material. This was reissued again *Live At The Marquee 1975* (Angel Air SJPCD 091) 2001 with the addition of extensive sleevenotes and a discography, as well as a bonus track that featured **The Yardbirds' Keith Relf**. *Don't Stop The Dance* (Angel Air SJPCD 185) 2005 is a recently unearthed and uncompleted follow-up to (5) above, which will particularly interest their fans.

HCP

45s: His Guiding Hand/
(up to This Love Of Old   (Dandelion S 4661) 1970 SC -
1976) Coast To Coast/All For Tomorrow (Dandelion S 5075) 1970 -
  α Pictures In The Sky/
    Natural Sight (Some PS) (Dandelion DAN 7003) 1971 22
  α Pictures In The Sky/Natural Sight (Dandelion K 19002) 1972 -
    Kum On/On The Land   (Dandelion 2001 276) 1972 -
    Only To Do What Is True/
    Sittin' In The Sun   (Dandelion 2001 325) 1972 -
    How Does It Feel?/Morning Light (Dandelion 2001 383) 1972 -
    One And One Is One/
    Out On The Street   (Dandelion 2001 432) 1973 3
    Rising Sun/Be My Flyer   (Polydor 205 8389) 1973 11
    Slip And Slide/Cajun Kick (Polydor 205 8436) 1974 22
    (It's Got To Be) Alright/
    Part Of The Play   (Mercury 6008 009) 1974 -
    Mama Come Out/Come On Over (WWA WWS 15) 1974 -
    It's Natural/Moon Child   (Barn 2014 102) 1976 -
    Me And Suzie (Hit Floor)/Midnight (Barn 2014 103) 1976 -

NB: α are the same. They used two numbers; one for Warner Brothers, one for Dandelion.

This was one of many bands brought to prominence by DJ John Peel, after they sent him a tape, he signed them to his Dandelion label. They started out as a duo gigging in the Midlands. Their early albums conjured up a very sparse understated atmosphere and contained several love songs. A highlight of their debut album was *His Guiding Hand*, which was also issued as a 45. *Heavy On The Drum* was produced by ex-**Yardbird Keith Relf**. They enjoyed Chart success with *Pictures In The Sky* but then the eccentric Hope-Evans quit and they reformed as a trio (line-up B) with **Keith Relf** on bass. Before 1972 was over, Hope-Evans turned up again and they reverted back to a duo augmented by session musicians for *One And One Is One*. The title cut and *Rising Sun* brought them further Chart success and they expanded to a quintet for their next album, *Thru' A Five*. Thereafter they hit hard times, although former **Spencer Davis** and **Taste** bassist Charlie McCracken was involved in a later line-up. *Two Man Band*, however, was recorded by the original duo of Fiddler and Hope-Evans.

After their demise, Fiddler teamed up with former **Mott The Hoople** members in The British Lions and also worked and recorded as a solo artist. In the eighties he joined the ex-**Yardbirds** project The Box Of Frogs. Hope-Evans helped out **Pete Townshend** on his 1985 *White City Soundtrack* and played in a number of part-time groups.

Their bass player on *Thru' A Five*, George Ford later played with **Cockney Rebel**. *Don't Stop The Dance* is a recently uncovered and previously unreleased follow-up to *Thru' A Five*. It contains several live tracks (including the title track) and reinvigorated versions of earlier hits like *Rising Sun* and *One And One (Is One)*. Also included are a couple of rare (non-hit) singles: *Come On Over* and *(It's Got To Be) Alright*. The CD should interest their fans.

Only To Do What Is True is included on the *Dandelion Rarities* (CD) compilation, whilst the *Dandelion Sampler 1969-1972* (LP) features *Pictures In The Sky*. (VJ)

Meckenburg Zinc

45: Hard Working Woman/
  I'd Like To Help You   (Orange OAS 205) 1970

An interesting name but who were they? (MWh)

The Medium

Personnel: MIKE GOWER   A
  JOHN RICHARDSON   A
  ALAN WILLIAMS   A
  IAN WRIGHT   A

MELLOW CANDLE - Swaddling Songs (LP).

45:	Colours Of The Rainbow/		
	Edward Never Lies	(CBS 3404) 1968 SC	

This London band was originally known as Unsuited Medium. The 'A' side of this one-off 45 can also be heard on *Circus Days Vol. 3* (LP & CD). The 'B' side is a pop-psych tainted song, which may interest fans of this genre. Richardson and Williams later formed a songwriting duo, Baskin and Copperfield. They were later in **The Rubettes**. (VJ)

Jo Meek

45s:	You'd Better Believe It/	
	Too Good To Be True	(United Artists UP 35248) 1971
	It's Not Another Beautiful Day/	
	Tea Party	(United Artists UP 35290) 1971

This is not the Joe Meek but a woman from Norfolk. The first 'A' side is a Tom Paxton composition, the second is a Tom Paxton / **Ed Welch** song.

Jo Meek is the sister of Anna Meek, who was a member of **Catapilla**. (VJ)

Keith Meehan

45:	α Darkness Of My Life/	
	Hooker Street	(Marmalade 598 016) 1969 SC

NB: α The flip side was by **Tony Meehan**, but credited as by Keith.

Keith was the brother of ex-**Shadow Tony Meehan**. His only recorded output was *Darkness Of My Life*, which was a pretty dramatic song. Keith lives in the States now. On the flip is an instrumental of some quality by his brother Tony who also produced the 45.

Compilation appearances include: *Darkness Of My Life* on *Psychedelic Voyage Vol. 1* (LP) and *Psychedelic Voyage* (CD) and *Hooker Street* on *Jagged Time Lapse, Vol 2* (CD). (MWh)

Tony Meehan Combo

45:	Song Of Mexico/Kings Go Fifth	(Decca 11801) 1964 39

This was a one-off solo project by this former **Shadow** who also recorded with Jet Harris and **John Paul Jones** and worked with his brother Keith. The 'A' side was a Jerry London instrumental. He wrote the flip himself.

Meehan was born in Hampstead, London in March 1943 and was a co-founder of **The Shadows**. He was playing drums at the age of ten at dances in Willesden, north London. He later played with future colleague **Jet Harris** in The Vipers and, in 1958, joined Cliff Richard and The Shadows. He was with them between 1959 and 1961 and played on all their recordings in this period. He left for an A&R post with Decca linking up with **Harris** again. He also worked as a session musician for Billy Fury and Frank Ifield during the sixties and then produced **Roger Daltrey**'s solo work in the seventies. In later life he became interested in psychology and psychiatry. He died, aged 62, after a fall at his home on 27 November 2005. (VJ)

Megaton

ALBUM:	1	MEGATON	(Deram SML-R 1086) 1971 R4

NB: (1) released by Decca in Germany.

45s:	Out On Your Own Little World/Niagara (Deram DM 331) 1971 R1
	Sammy Is Dead / Aunt Sarah's Uncle
	George (Decca D 29114) 1971 [German-only]

This hard-rock album, one of the rarest and most sought-after issued by Deram, features good guitar work but is let down by some dreadful vocals. The band's origins remain a mystery. No credits are given on the sleeve, but the labels credit the songs to Bilsbury-Humphries. It seems likely, therefore, that the album features Jimmy Bilsbury (of **the Magic Lanterns** and Les Humphries Singers) and Humphries himself. However, as both

MELLOW CANDLE - The Virgin Prophet (LP).

men are dead, we will probably never know for sure. The album is commoner in Germany, where Humphries was a star, and for this reason it's thought to have been recorded there. The second 45 is non-album, and its 'B' side is said to be the best thing **Megaton** ever recorded. Another German-only 45, *Doctor Doctor/Gipsy's Kiss* by Jimmy & Co (Decca D 29100), is credited to Humphries & Bilsbury and appeared between the two **Megaton** singles, so may well be by the same musicians.

Both sides of their 45 can be heard on *Psychedalia - Rare Blooms From The English Summer Of Love* (CD). (VJ/RMJ)

Mellow Candle

Personnel:	CLODAGH SIMONDS	vcls, keyb'ds	A
	ALISON WILLIAMS	vcls	A
	DAVID WILLIAMS	gtr, vcls	A
	FRANK BOYLAN	bs	A
	WILLIAM MURRAY	drms	A

ALBUM:	1(A)	SWADDLING SONGS	(Deram SDL 7) 1972 R4

NB: (1) has been reissued on Zen (ZN 001) in Italy, and officially in Korea on Si-Wan and is also available on CD (See For Miles SEECD 404) 1994. Fans of the band will also be interested in *The Virgin Prophet* (Erewhon KSCD 9520) 1995, which contains early unreleased songs and songs which were later re-recorded for *Swaddling Songs*, and *My Lagan Love* (CD), which includes further rare and live performances. *Virgin Prophet* was also issued on LP (Kissing Spell KSF 004), but this version is as rare as their Deram album!

45s:	Feeling High/Tea With The Sun	(SNB 55-3645) 1968 R2
	Dan The Wing/Silversong	(Deram DM 357) 1972 R1

Mellow Candle's intricately-arranged album, full of imaginative psychedelic folk and featuring two excellent female singers, is now one of the most sought-after records on the planet.

Clodagh Simonds and Alison Williams were childhood friends and spent all their time at their Dublin convent school writing songs. They were still only 15 when their first 45, *Feeling High*, was recorded in London for Simon Napier Bell's SNB label in 1968. An orchestrated piece of whimsy, it failed to create much impact despite being distributed by CBS, and SNB folded soon afterwards. After a couple of years' separation, the girls regrouped and, following favourable responses to their live act, decamped to London. Following support from John Peel, who'd seen them live in Ireland, they signed to Deram on April 18th 1971. Initial demos were a disappointment, however, so at the suggestion of producer David Hitchcock they recruited bassist Frank Boylan (from Dublin beat group The Creatures) and Glaswegian drummer William Murray.

With a more solid, rock-based sound in place, they swiftly recorded *Swaddling Songs* at Decca's Tollington Park studio at Christmastime 1971. Less fragile than **Trees** and more mystical than **Fairport**, the sound is full of surprises and the songs are strong, especially the propulsive *Poet and* *the Witch* and hauntingly beautiful *Reverend Sisters*. In fact, the sheer quality of their performance makes it perplexing that the band didn't get more recognition at the time. But, despite favourable reviews and respectable airplay, both the album and the single culled from it sold very poorly.

The band, living in poverty in Hampstead, struggled to find live work and found that their management's attention was increasingly focused on **Thin Lizzy**. They did play occasional gigs supporting **Lindisfarne** and **Steeleye Span**, but left Deram and Ted Carroll's management. Shortly afterwards Boylan left, to be replaced by Steve Borrill (ex-**Spirogyra**), and they changed their name to **Grace Before Space**. A tour of Holland was planned, but they split up in the Summer of 1973.

After **Mellow Candle** split, Clodagh Simonds (who had also sung on **Thin Lizzy**'s *Shades Of A Blue Orphanage* album) worked with **Mike Oldfield** and **Jade Warrior** before relocating to New York, where she studied music and worked for Virgin. She later returned to Ireland, where she has recently returned to music, collaborating with musicians like **Brian Eno** on projects of a radically different sort to **Mellow Candle**. William Murray went on to play with **Richard and Linda Thompson**'s Sour Grapes band, and also toured with **Sandy Denny**. He too then headed for the States, where he formed The Same with Simonds, performing a Thursday night residency at New York's famous CBGB club. He sadly died in Dublin on 30th August 1998. David and Alison Williams headed for South Africa, and formed a band called Flibbertigibbet, whose charming, privately-pressed 1978 album, *Whistling Jigs To The Moon*, was reissued on CD in 1995 (Kissing Spell KSCD 9510-F). David Williams became head of light music with the South African Broadcasting Corporation in Capetown and also works as a record producer. Alison Williams currently lives in Brussels and, under the name Alison O'Donnell, performs contemporary and traditional music in an Irish style with her band Eishtlinn.

The *Virgin Prophet* and *My Lagan Love* releases consist of live performances and very early recordings made by Simonds and Williams, and were not released with the consent of the whole band.

Compilation appearances have included: *Dan The Wing* on *Progressive Pop Inside The Seventies* (CD); *Sheep Season* on *The History Of U.K. Underground Folk Rock 1968-1978 Vol. 1* (CD); *Silver Song* on *The History Of U.K. Underground Folk Rock 1968-1978 Vol. 2* (CD); and *Heaven Heath* on *Legends Of Ireland* (CD) (Rhino Records). (MK/VJ/RMJ)

Melody Fair

Personnel:	TED MARSH	drms	A
	ROY SHARLAND	organ	A
	MARTIN SLACK		A
	RICHARD WOOLF		A

| 45: | Something Happened To Me/ | |
| | Sittin', Watchin', Waitin' | (Decca F 12801) 1968 |

HISTORY OF UK UNDERGROUND FOLK VOL. 2 (Comp CD) including Mellow Candle.

This was another obscure and short-lived band. Roy Sharland went on to play for **Fuzzy Duck**. (VJ)

Memphis Band

Personnel:	LINCOLN CARR	A
	MICKY GEE	A
	TOM RILEY	A

| 45: | Louisiana Hoedown/Right String, But | |
| | The Wrong Yo Yo | (United Artists UP 35571) 1973 |

This rockabilly band came, not from the USA, but from Cardiff. Tom Riley had been in **The Grease Band**. Micky Gee went on to play for **Andy Fairweather Low**, **Dave Edmunds** and Shakin' Stevens among others. (VJ)

Men

Personnel:	TROY DANTE	AB
	DAVEY SANDS	A
	PETE KERSHAW	B

45s:	She Works In A Woman's Way/	
	I'll Just Wish You Luck And Say Goodbye	(Decca F 13083) 1970
	Candy/Leave A Little Light	(Decca F 13163) 1971
	Oh What A Naughty Man/	
	Rose Growing By The Sidewalk	(Bell 1294) 1973
	These Are Not My People/Yesterday Man	(Antic K 11508) 1974

This was a pop duo. Davey Sands quit to go solo in February 1971 and was replaced by former **Honeybus** member Pete Kershaw. Troy Dante later went solo too.

The Bell and Antic 45s could well be by different people. (VJ)

Merlin

Personnel:	ALAN LOVE	vcls	A
	JAMIE MOSES	lead gtr, vcls	A
	PAUL TAYLOR	bs	A
	BOB (SCULLY) WEBB	keyb'ds, gtr, vcls	A
	DAVE WHITWHICK	drms, vcls	A
	GARY STRANGE	bs, vcls	

| ALBUM: | 1(A) | MERLIN | (CBS 80338) 1974 |

Definitely not to be confused with the later funk outfit of the same name, **Merlin** produced a mixed album of progressive and glam sounds. They were earlier known as **Madrigal** and became **Merlin** in May 1974. Even the sleeve pictures reflect the schizophrenia; on the front they are laughing in red and white stage uniforms, decorations round their necks and covered in flashes and the letter "M", on the reverse they are more moody, clad in denim on fog-bound stone steps. The album itself displays progressive touches both lyrically and musically on the first three tracks, particularly *Taking Part* and *Gettin' Involved*. From track four onwards the album is a more straight-forward rocking affair, sounding a little like **Sweet** in places especially on (by coincidence) *Sweet Sweet Cheatin' Rita*. This is one of the two songs on the album jointly written by Roger Greenaway, who also produced. Elsewhere the songs are mainly band compositions. It's only a guess, but one gets the impression of the band coming from a prog direction, getting a record deal, and going all out for a hit with Cook and Greenaway production values. Ex-**March Hare** member Gary Strange joined the band in September 1974. (NM/JM)

The Merseybeats

Personnel:	JOHN BANKS	drms	ABC
	TONY CRANE	gtr, vcls	ABC
	BILLY KINSLEY	bs, vcls	A
	AARON WILLIAMS	gtr, vcls	ABC
	BOB GARNER	gtr, vcls	B
	JOHNNY GUSTAFSON	gtr, vcls	C

ALBUMS: 1(C) THE MERSEYBEATS (Fontana TL 5210) 1964 R2 12
2(C) THE MERSEYBEATS (Wing WL 1163) 1965 SC -
3(-) THE MERSEYBEATS GREATEST HITS
(Look LP 6160) 1977 -
4(-) BEAT AND BALLADS (Edsel ED 105) 1982 -

NB: (1) reissued on Fontana (842 761-1) 1990, also on CD. (2) is a reissue of (1).

EPs: 1(C) ON STAGE (Fontana TE 17422) 1964 R1 -
2(C) I THINK OF YOU (Fontana TE 17423) 1964 R1 -
3(C) WISHIN' AND HOPIN' (Fontana TE 17432) 1964 R1 -

45s: It's Love That Really Counts/
(up to The Fortune Teller (Fontana TF 412) 1963 24
1976) I Think Of You/Mister Moonlight (Fontana TF 431) 1963 5
Don't Turn Around/Really Mystified (Fontana TF 459) 1964 13
Wishin' And Hopin'/Milkman (Fontana TF 482) 1964 13
Last Night (I Made A Little Girl Cry)/
Send Me Back (Fontana TF 504) 1964 40
Don't Let It Happen to Us/
It Would Take A Long Long Time (Fontana TF 568) 1965 -
I Love You, Yes I Do/
Good Good Lovin' (Fontana TF 607) 1965 22
I Stand Accused/All My Life (Fontana TF 645) 1965 38
Reissues: I Think Of You/Wishin' And Hopin' (Fontana TF 1025) 1969 -
α Sorrow/I Think Of You (Philips 6006 258) 1973 -
I Think Of You/
(Flip by different artist) (Old Gold OG 9251) 1982 -

NB: α Sorrow by **The Merseys**.

The **Merseybeats** formed in Liverpool in 1961. Their original line-up comprised Crane, Kinsley, David Elias (drms) and Frank Sloane (gtr), although by 1962 Elias and Sloane had been replaced by Banks and Williams to give line-up (A) above. Crane and Kinsley had earlier played together in another local outfit called The Pacifics. In their early days they utilised Liverpudlian comedian Billy Butler and local beauty queen Irene Hughes as guest vocalists. Like most of the Merseybeat bands they also spent time in Hamburg.

They had a softer image than most of the Merseybeat bands, sporting frilly shirts, bolero jackets and lots of rings on their fingers. They were masters of the tearjerking ballad and this, plus their good looks and fancy clothes, guaranteed them a strong female following. Their first appearance on vinyl was on Oriole's 1963 *This Is Merseybeat, Vol. 1* (LP) compilation, playing *Our Day Will Come*.

They were signed by Fontana in 1963 and their debut 45, a cover of The Shirelles' *It's Love That Really Counts*, gave them a minor hit. The follow-up was an ideal ballad for their style, **Pete Lee Stirling**'s *I Think Of You* and it not only got into the Top Five but was raved about by **The Beatles** on 'Juke Box Jury'.

In February 1964, Kinsley left the outfit and was temporarily replaced by Robert Garner (who later joined **The Creation**) for a few weeks until **Johnny Gustafson** was recruited from **The Big Three**. The revised line-up enjoyed further significant hits in 1964 with *Don't Turn Around* and Burt Bacharach's *Wishin' And Hopin'*. The debut album also got to No 12. Even in their heyday, though, they failed to make any significant impression in the US where it was **Dusty Springfield** who scored a big hit with *Wishin' And Hopin'*.

By the end of 1964, there were signs of decline. *Last Night (I Made A Little Girl Cry)* and *Don't Let It Happen To Us* both flopped, although they achieved a minor hit in 1965 with *I Love You, Yes I Do*. By the end of 1965, the 'Merseybeat' sound had become passé and the writing was on the wall for the band that called it a day in January 1966. Their final 45, *I Stand Accused*, was among their more interesting, with some strange percussion effects. It was later covered by Elvis Costello in 1980.

Upon their demise Aaron Williams retired from showbusiness to try his hand (with little success) as a songwriter; Banks and **Gustafson** teamed up as **John and Johnny** and Johnny after a brief solo career later formed **Quatermass**; and Crane and Kinsley formed **The Merseys**.

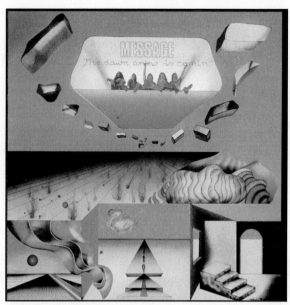

MESSAGE - The Dawn Anew Is Coming (CD).

Compilation appearances have included: *It's Love That Really Counts* on *Mersey Beat* (2-LP); *Really Mystified* and *Fortune Teller* on *Mersey Beat 1962-1964* (2-LP); *Last Night (I Made A Little Girl Cry)* on *Beat Merchants* (2-LP); *I Think Of You, Don't Turn Around, I'm Gonna Sit Right Down And Cry Over You, It's Love That Really Counts, I Think Of You* and *I'm Gonna Sit Right Down And Cry Over You* on *Hard Up Heroes, Vol. 4* (CD); *I Think Of You* on *Hits Of The 60's Vol 2* (CD) and *Super Hits Of The 60's - Vol 1* (CD); *I Think Of You* (alternate take) on the 2-CD set *Greatest Hits Of The 60's*; and *Wishin' and Hopin'* on *Remember The 60's (CD)* and *Cruisin' Classics* (CD). (VJ)

The Merseys

Personnel: TONY CRANE vcls A
BILLY KINSLEY vcls A

45s: Sorrow/Some Other Day (Fontana TF 694) 1966 4
So Sad About Us/
Love Will Continue (Fontana TF 732) 1966 -
Rhythm Of Love/Is It Love? (Fontana TF 776) 1966 -
The Cat/Change Of Heart (Fontana TF 845) 1967 SC -
Penny In My Pocket/
I Hope You're Happy (Fontana TF 916) 1968 -
Lovely Loretta/Dreaming (Fontana TF 955) 1968 -
Reissues: α Sorrow/I Think Of You (Philips 6006 258) 1973 -
Sorrow/(Flip by different artist) (Old Gold OG 9787) 1987 -

NB: α *I Think Of You* by **The Merseybeats**.

Formed by Crane and Kinsley earlier in 1966 after **The Merseybeats** had bitten the dust, they concentrated on two-part harmonies, using another Liverpool group, The Fruit Eating Bears (which usually had two drummers), as their backing band.

On their debut 45, *Sorrow* (which had previously been a 'B' side for US band The McCoys), they were assisted by **Jimmy Page**, **Jack Bruce** and Clem Cattini. It made the Top Five and was later covered and taken into the Top Five again (this time to No 3) by **David Bowie** in 1973. It proved to be their only success for all their subsequent singles flopped including a final one made in 1969 using the pseudonym **The Crackers**.

Crane formed a new **Merseys** in January 1973 when Philips re-released *Sorrow*. He was assisted by Phil Chiswick (drms) and Roger Craig (keyb'ds, mellotron). In 1974 Crane and Craig formed Crane and Chiswick went on to Supercharge. Crane recorded one 45 *American Dream* on Buk in November 1974. Shortly after, all members except for Crane went on to **Liverpool Express**. Kinsley joined **Jimmy Campbell's Rockin' Horse** before making the Charts again in 1976 with **Liverpool Express**. When they faded from the limelight he formed The Cheats in 1978.

Crane now works with a new **Merseybeats** doing cabaret.

Compilation appearances include: *Sorrow* and *Some Other Day* on *The Star-Club Singles Complete, Vol. 8* (LP & CD); *Sorrow* on *The Star-Club Anthology, Vol. 4* (LP) and *The Swinging Sixties - 18 Classic Tracks* (CD); and *So Sad About Us* on *Pop-In, Vol 1* (CD) and the 2-CD set *Sixties Summer Love*. (VJ/JM)

Message

Personnel incl:	GUNTHER KLINGEL	drms	A
	TOMMY McGUIGAN	sax, mellotron, vcls	A
	ALLAN MURDOCH	gtr	A
	HORST STACHELHAUS	bs	A

ALBUMS:	1	THE DAWN ANEW IS COMIN'	(Bellaphon) 1972
	2	FROM BOOKS AND DREAMS	(Bellaphon) 1973
	3	SYNAPSE	(Nova) 1976

NB: (1) reissued on CD (Bellaphon 288 09 111). (2) reissued on CD (Bellaphon 288 09 119).

Message was essentially a German-based British band with a German rhythm section. **Nektar**'s Allan "Taff" Freeman guests on mellotron and vocals on the first album. The second album is a minor masterpiece of psych-prog, with a haunting undercurrent of dark music and dream-state lyrics. (RR)

The Messengers

Personnel:	JOHN FRASER	bs	A
	RON KANE	gtr	A
	DON LEATHER	gtr	A
	SHINE LEATHER	vcls	A

45s:	I'm Stealin' Back/	
	This Little Light Of Mine	(Columbia DB 7344) 1964
	When Did You Leave Heaven/	
	More Pretty Girls Than One	(Columbia DB 7495) 1965

This Seekers-style folk group came from London. Don and Shine were husband and wife. (VJ)

Messengers Of The Cross

ALBUM:	1	MESSENGERS OF THE CROSS	(Emblem) 1969 R3

This is a strange garagey folk-rock album with both psychedelic and bluesy elements. Highlights include the bluesy *Watch Out*, dreamy electric folk with

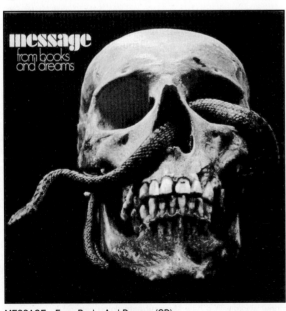

MESSAGE - From Books And Dreams (CD).

METHUSELAH - Matthew, Mark, Luke And John (LP).

female vocals *When Will I Learn* and *It Was You*, a Beau Brummels style *What Would You Say*, a R'n'B stomper with great mouth harp *This Concerns You* and two ace folky numbers with a psychedelic taint: *What Jesus Means To Me* and *Not Pie In The Sky*. In addition to their 13 self-penned songs there's a dreamy version of *Give Me Jesus* with female vocals, which was also recorded by Caedmon, who fall just outside the time span of this book. It's of much interest to collectors of British female folk and folk-rock / psychedelia. (VJ)

Method

Personnel:	MICK BRASSINGTON	vcls	A
	JOHN HUGHES	gtr	A

ALBUM:	1(A)	METHOD	(UK UKAL 1020) 1976

45s:	Hold On Tight/Run, Run, Run	(UK UK 98) 1975
	So Excited/Lonely Eyes	(UK UK 117) 1975
	Woman/Ask No Questions/0376	(UK UK 126) 1975
	Someone To Love/Sometimes You Win	(UK UK 138) 1976
	Passing Strangers/Don't Leave Me Baby	(UK UK 151) 1976
	Yorkshire Lad/Lonely Eyes	(UK UK 156) 1976

This duo was signed by **Jonathan King**'s UK Records label. (VJ)

Methuselah

Personnel:	CRAIG AUSTIN	bs, vcls	A
	MICK BRADLEY	drms	A
	JOHN GLADWIN	vcls, vibes	A
	LES NICOL	gtr, vcls	A
	TERRY WINCOTT	gtr, vcls	A

ALBUM:	1(A)	MATTHEW, MARK, LUKE AND JOHN	
			(Elektra EKS 74052) 1969

NB: (1) US only. A second album was recorded but remains unreleased.

This British hard-rock group made two albums for Elektra, of which only one was released. They evolved out of **The Dimples** / **Gospel Garden**, adding new drummer Mick Bradley (ex-**The Sorrows**) and whizzkid guitarist Les Nicol (ex-**ABC**). Having inherited **Gospel Garden**'s management contract with Steve Rowland, they promptly scored a three-album deal with Elektra. Label boss Jac Holzman drafted in songwriter Kenny Young (of *Under the Boardwalk* fame) to produce the first collection of Gladwin originals, which displayed folk, R&B, gospel and pop influences. Though uneven, at its best it was truly superb. In particular Nicol contributed some astonishing guitar leads (in a style reminiscent of another Elektra artist, John Echols of Love) and there were some gorgeous vocal harmonies. The decision to end proceedings with a protracted rendition of French nursery rhyme *Frere Jaques* was ill-judged, however. Inexplicably, the album was denied a UK release. Nothing daunted, the band proceeded to record a follow-up, but 'musical differences' split them before its release, which was then cancelled.

Gladwin, their main creative force, had grown sick of hard-rock and formed folk-rock stalwarts **Amazing Blondel** with Terry Wincott instead. Mick Bradley joined **Steamhammer**, and Craig Austin and Les Nicol joined ex-**Junior's Eyes** drummer Steve Chapman in psychedelic trio **Distant Jim**. Nicol also played on the second Pavlov's Dog album and was also in **Ray Owen's Moon**.

Compilation appearances have included: *High In The Tower Of Coombe* on *Rubble, Vol. 8 - All The Colours Of Darkness* (LP), *Rubble, Vol. 5* (CD) and *The Best Of Rubble Collection, Vol. 5* (CD). (VJ/CA/Can/RMJ)

Mick and Malcolm

45s: Little Venice/In A Game Of Chess (Piccadilly 7N 35344) 1966
Big Black Smoke/
Two Or Three Minutes Of My Time (Piccadilly 7N 35372) 1967

This was an obscure sixties duo. (VJ)

Mickey Finn (and The Blue Men)

Personnel: ALAN ANTHONY vcls A
RICHARD BRAND drms AB
JOHN BURKITT bs A
JOHN COOKE organ A
ALAN MARKS vcls AB
(JIMMY PAGE hrmnca, gtr A)
MICKY WALLER gtr AB
"Fluff" organ AB
MICK STANNARD bs B

NB: Line-up 'A' **Mickey Finn and The Blue Men**. 'B' The **Mickey Finn**

CD: 1 KEEP MOVING! (LCD 17-2) 1997
NB: (1) this retrospective CD compiles all their 45s, plus material recorded by **Mickey Finn and The Blue Men**. Also included are eight tracks by the **Jimmy Page All Stars**.

45s: Tom Hark/Love Me (Blue Beat 203) 1964 R1
Pills/Hush Your Mouth (Oriole 1927) 1964 R1
Reelin' And Rockin'/I Still Want You (Oriole 1940) 1964 R1
The Sporting Life/
Night Comes Down (Columbia DB 7510) 1965 R2
I Do Love You/If I Had You Baby (Polydor 56719) 1966 R1
Garden Of My Mind/
Time To Start Loving You (Direction 58-3086) 1967 R1

MICKEY FINN AND THE BLUE MEN - Keep Moving! (CD).

Ain't Necessarily So/
God Bless The Child (PS) (Noiseburger 3) 1995

NB: (1) - (2) as **Mickey Finn and The Blue Men**. The Columbia and Direction 45s have both been reissued in a limited edition pressing of 500 taken directly from the original French jukebox pressings. The Noiseburger 45 was a limited edition pressing of 1,000 - the first 500 copies were signed and it was presented with a fold around picture sleeve in a polythene bag.

Mickey Finn wasn't a person, but underworld slang for a spiked drink. From Bethnal Green in East London, **The Mickey Finn** emerged from an East London R&B band called The Strangers, who were active circa 1961. After developing a liking for ska, however, Brand and Waller formed **Mickey Finn and The Blue Men**, their new name indicating the shift to a more 'mod' sound.

Through their agent they got a deal with Blue Beat Records, and their first 45 led many to believe they were Jamaican. **Tom Hark** was originally done by Elias and Zig-Zag Jive Flutes. It was later copied by The Piranhas.

Their strong connection with the mod scene was also reflected in their next single, *Pills*, released just as the police discovered some purple hearts stashed in Waller's amp during a raid on a club. The 45 (which also featured **Jimmy Page**, an old friend of the band, on harmonica) was subsequently banned. For their next release they chose an old Chuck Berry number, *Reelin' And Rockin'*, which was tipped as a hit on "Juke Box Jury" before fading into oblivion. Burkitt then left, to be replaced by another ex-Stranger, Mick Stannard. At this point the band became known as simply **The Mickey Finn**.

In 1965 they supported **The Kinks**, **The Yardbirds** and **The Hollies** on tours through England, whilst Shel Talmy produced their next 45, *This Sporting Life*. It also featured **Jimmy Page** on the flip, *Night Comes Down*, and is very hard to obtain nowadays. The band spent the summer of 1966 in Southern France, where they had a residency at a club in St. Tropez, and were also invited to play at a private party for Brigitte Bardot. Their true claim to immortality however, came in the form of their final release; the brutal psych stomper *Garden Of My Mind*, with its incessantly-growling bassline and pounding guitar work.

The band soldiered on until 1971, after which each member continued to play on a semi-professional basis, with Waller and Fluff going on to **The Heavy Metal Kids**.

Compilation coverage has so far included: *Reelin' And Rockin'*, *Hush Your Mouth*, *I Still Want You* and *Pills* on *Mickey Finn And The Blue Men / Jimmy Page - Keep Moving!* (CD); *I Still Want You* on *Beat Merchants* (2-LP); *Reelin' And Rockin'* on *English Freakbeat, Vol. 4* (LP & CD); *Garden Of My Mind* on *We Can Fly, Vol 1* (CD); *Night Comes Down* on *James Patrick Page: Session Man, Vol. 1* (CD), *Beat It* (3-CD), *Electric Sugarcube Flashbacks, Vol. 1* (LP) and *Electric Sugarcube Flashbacks, Vol. 3* (LP); *This Sporting Life* on *James Patrick Page: Session Man, Vol. 2* (LP & CD); *Night Comes Down* and *Garden Of My Mind* on *James Patrick Page, Session Man* (2-LP); and *This Sporting Life*, *Night Comes Down*, *Ain't Necessarily So*, *God Bless The Child*, *I Do Love You*, *If I Had You Baby*, *Garden Of My Mind* and *Time To Start Loving You* on *Mickey Finn And The Blue Men / Jimmy Page - Keep Moving!* (CD). (VJ/CRr/RMJ)

Microbe

HCP
45: Groovy Baby/Your Turn Now (CBS 4158) 1969 29
NB: 'B' side credited to Microbop Ensemble.

This gimmick disc was probably a studio creation. The singers on the 'A' side have baby-like high voices. The flip side was an instrumental credited to The Microbop Ensemble. (VJ)

Middle of The Road

Personnel: KEN ANDREW (BALLANTYNE) drms, vcls, keyb'ds A
SALLY CARR vcls, percsn A
ERIC LEWIS bs, vcls, gtr, piano A
IAN LEWIS gtr, vcls, flute A

MIDWINTER - The Waters Of Sweet Sorrow (LP).

ALBUMS: 1(A) MIDDLE OF THE ROAD   (RCA International 8200) 1971
        2(A) BEST OF   (RCA SF 8305) 1972
        3(A) DRIVE ON   (RCA SF 8338) 1973
        4(A) CHIRPY CHIRPY CHEEP CHEEP/TWEEDLE
              DUM TWEEDLE DEE   (RCA SF 1433) 1973
        5(A) MUSIC MUSIC   (Road) 1974

                                                        HCP
45s: Chirpy Chirpy Cheep Cheep/
        Rainin 'n' Painin'   (RCA RCA 2047) 1971 1
        Tweedle Dee, Tweedle Dum/
        Give It Time   (RCA RCA 2110) 1971 2
        Soley Soley/To Remind Me   (RCA RCA 2151) 1971 5
        Sacramento/Love Sweet Love   (RCA RCA 2184) 1972 23
        Samson And Delilah/
        Try A Little Understanding   (RCA RCA 2237) 1972 26
        Bottoms Up/See The Sky   (RCA RCA 2264) 1972 -
        The Talk Of All The USA/Eve   (RCA RCA 2343) 1973 -
        Union Silver/Blind Detonation   (RCA RCA 2388) 1973 -
        Hitchin' A Ride In The Moonlight/
        Do You Wanna Be With Me   (DJM DJS 10361) 1975 -
Reissues: Chirpy Chirpy Cheep Cheep/Tweedle Dum Tweedle Dee/
        Soley Soley   (RCA RCA 2602) 1975 -
        Chirpy Chirpy Cheep Cheep/
        Soley Soley   (RCA GOLD 543) 1982 -
        Chirpy Chirpy Cheep Cheep/
        Tweedle Dum, Tweedle Dee   (old Gold OG 9632) 1986 -

This Scottish four-piece was originally known as Part Four, and it broke its teeth in Europe. Indeed the debut 45 was a novelty song from the Continent (also done by Mac and Katie Kissoon) which topped the UK Charts in the Summer of 1971. The band was always more popular on the Continent and *Tweedle Dee, Tweedle Dum* was a No 1 in Sweden, Denmark and Norway before it was even released in the UK, where *Soley Soley* completed their trio of smash hits. A couple more minor hits followed, but when the public lost interest the act ended up on the Europe cabaret circuit for many years. They were originally known as Los Caracas in Europe.

Chirpy Chirpy Cheep Cheep can also be heard on *UK No 1 Hits Of The 70's* (CD). (VJ/JM)

The Midnights

EP: 1 MIDNIGHTS   (MEP 101/MN 1/EAG-EP-134) 1963 R3

45:     Show Me Around/Only Two Can Play   (Ember EMB 220) 1966

This group's album is a private pressing. (VJ)

Midnight Shift

45:     Saturday Jump/Living Fast   (Decca F 12487) 1966 SC

The 'A' side of this disc was an instrumental tune for the 'Saturday Club' programme. (VJ)

Midwinter

Personnel: JILL CHILD   vcls, recorders, autoharp   A
            PAUL CORRICK   gtrs, recorder, mandolin, vcls A
            KEN SAUL   vcls, gtr, dulcimer, banjo   A
            (MICK BURROUGHS perc, jews harp   A)
            (DICK CADBURY   bs   A)

ALBUM: 1(A) THE WATERS OF SWEET SORROW
                                    (Porcelain PCN 001) 1973 R2
NB: (1) reissued on CD by Kissing Spell and on vinyl in the original sleeve.

A very pleasant early seventies hippie-folk offering very much in **The Trees**, early **Fairport Convention** and **Mellow Candle** mould. Tracks like *Sanctuary Stone*, *Winter Song*, *The Skater* and *Oak Tree Grove* are full of delightfully fragile female vocals. On a few others like *The Two Sisters* there are nice alternating female / male vocals. The album also contains a pretty good cover of *Scarborough Fair*. Paul Corrick, Ken Saul and Mick Burroughs went on to play in **Stone Angel**.

Compilation appearances include: *Winter Song* on *The History Of U.K. Underground Folk Rock 1968-1978 Vol. 1* (CD); and *Sanctuary Stone* on *The History Of U.K. Underground Folk Rock 1968-1978 Vol. 2* (CD). (VJ)

M. I. Five

Personnel incl: CHRIS BANHAM   organ   A
                 ROD EVANS   vcls   A
                 ERIC KEENE   bs   A
                 ROGER LEWIS   gtr   A
                 IAN PAICE   drms   A

45:     You'll Never Stop Me Loving You/
        Only Time Will Tell   (Parlophone R 5486) 1966 R2

This band is most significant for including Evans and Paice. Based in Slough, they were later known as **The Maze**. Then in 1967, Evans and Paice both joined **Deep Purple**. (VJ)

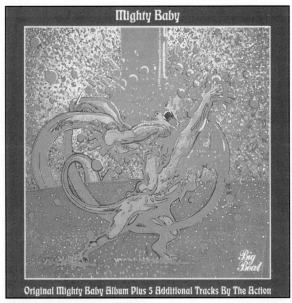

MIGHTY BABY - Mighty Baby (CD).

MIGHTY BABY - Jug Of Love (CD).

Mighty Avengers

Personnel:	BIFFO BEECH	drms, vcls	A
	TONY CAMPBELL	ld gtr, vcls	A
	MIKE LINNELL	bs, ld vcls	A
	TONY MACHON	gtr, hrmnca	A

			HCP
45s:	Hide Your Pride/Hey Senorita	(Decca F 11891) 1964 SC	-
	So Much In Love/		
	Sometime They Say	(Decca F 11962) 1964 SC	46
	Blue Turns To Grey/		
	I'm Lost Without You	(Decca F 12085) 1965 SC	-
	(Walkin' Thru The) Sleep City/		
	Sir Edward And Lady Jane	(Decca F 12198) 1965 SC	-

Rugby was home to this band and with **Andrew Loog Oldham** producing they developed a penchant for recording **Jagger**/Richard songs, though only *So Much In Love* sold in any significant quantities. Some of them were later in **Jigsaw**.

Compilation appearances have included: *Walking Through The Sleepy City* on *Pop Inside The 60s Vol. 1* (CD) and *The Beat Scene* (CD); *(Walkin' Thru The) Sleepy City* and *Blue Turns To Grey* on *Rolling Stones Connection 1963-66* (CD); *Blue Turns To Grey* on *Weekend Starts Here* (LP); and *So Much In Love* on *Hard-Up Heroes* (2-LP). (VJ)

Mighty Baby

Personnel:	MIKE EVANS	bs	ABC
	ALAN KING	vcls, gtr	ABC
	ROGER POWELL	drms	ABC
	PETE WATSON	gtr	A
	IAN WHITEMAN	woodwind	BC
	MARTIN STONE	gtr	C

ALBUMS:	1(C)	MIGHTY BABY	(Head HDLS 6002) 1969 R3
	2(C)	A JUG OF LOVE	
		(w/insert)	(Blue Horizon 2931 001) 1971 R3

NB: (1) reissued as *Egyptian Tomb* (Psycho 31) 1984 (SC) and on CD (Big Beat CDWIKD 120) 1994 along with some demos recorded in 1968 when they were still **The Action**. (2) reissued on CD (Flash 58) 199?, with one additional track - their, *A Blanket In My Muesli* from *Glastonbury '71*. *Live In The Attic* (Rolled Gold Productions no #) 2001 captures material from a live 1969 university tour.

45:	Devil's Whisper/Virgin Spring	(Blue Horizon 2096 003) 1971 SC

This superb underground act emerged from the ashes of mod heroes **The Action**, who had been joined late in 1967 by ex-**Savoy Brown** guitar ace Martin Stone. Initially calling themselves Azoth, they recorded some demos in 1968 which finally saw the light of day in 1985 as the mini-album *Action Speaks Louder Than Words* (Castle DOJOLP 3). These show the influence of US West Coast psychedelia, which also manifested itself on their debut album, made for the tiny independent Head label following months of hard gigging. Overseen by legendary producer Guy Stevens, it kicks off with the immortal *Egyptian Tomb* and highlights their improvisational approach on songs like *House Without Windows* and *Trials of a City*. Much of their unusual sound derived from the sophisticated interplay between the twin guitars of King and Stone, as well as Whiteman's woodwind accompaniment. Sadly, Head went bust shortly after the album's release, when its owner, John Curd, was jailed for drug offences, and it failed to sell in any significant numbers. He did, however, manage to secure the album a US release through Chess records first, and US copies are slightly easier to obtain today. The album appeared too late to capitalise on the psychedelic boom, and the group soon shed its acid-rock leanings.

Over the next two years they played innumerable sessions as well as becoming staples of the festival and club circuits, contributing an epic rendition of John Coltrane's *India* (renamed *A Blanket In My Muesli* after a complaint made by a hippie, accidentally captured on tape at the start of their set) to the *Glastonbury Fayre* (3-LP) compilation in 1972. They also developed a strong commitment to Islam, which was reflected in the more contemplative music they were starting to produce. When they finally returned to the studio in the summer of 1971, under the supervision of Blue Horizon head **Mike Vernon**, they'd replaced the blazing guitar leads and driving rhythms of their debut with an aura of calm and reflection. *A Jug Of Love* opens with the wistful title track and proceeds at a tranquil pace that allows the band to showcase their fluent, expressive musicianship and exquisite harmonies. Of particular note is *The Happiest Man In The Carnival*, a joyous entreaty to 'pick up on your good friends while you still have a moment'. Other tracks like *Virgin Spring* and *Slipstreams* continue the mellow mood, though there's one incongruous excursion into rock, *Keep On Jugging*. As a whole, however, the album is atmospheric and oddly moving, and deserved to sell much better than it did. Neither it nor the accompanying 45 (featuring an up-tempo rerecording of *Virgin Spring* alongside the country-rock-influenced *Devil's Whisper*) sold at all, and the band was forced to split shortly afterwards.

Notable amongst the sessions **Mighty Baby** played were recordings by **Robin Scott**, **Gary Farr**, **Shelagh McDonald**, **Reg King** and **Keith Christmas**. Whilst still with **Mighty Baby**, Stone also recorded a rare album called *Southern Comfort* (London SHK 8405) with American blues harmonica player Walter 'Shakey' Horton. This is principally notable for *Netti Netti*, the long psychedelic jam that ends proceedings. When **Mighty Baby** split, Stone sat in with **The Pink Fairies** and fronted **Chilli Willi and Red Hot Peppers** before going on to become one of the world's foremost experts on rare books. King was a founder member of **Ace,** while Evans, Powell and Whiteman were later in **Habibiyya**, who made an album for Island in a similar vein to *A Jug Of Love*. (VJ/RMJ)

The Migil Five

Personnel:	LENNY BLANCHE	bs	AB
	MIKE FELIX	drms, vcls	AB

MIGHTY BABY - Egyptian Tomb (LP).

RED LAMBERT	gtr	AB
GILBERT LUCAS	piano	AB
ALAN WATSON	sax, vcls	B

NB: Line-up (A) was **The Migil Four**.

ALBUM: 1(B) MOCKING BIRD HILL   (Pye NPL 18093) 1964 SC

NB: (1) reissued on CD (Repertoire REP 4188-WZ) with extra tracks. *Mockin' Bird Hill* (Sequel NEMCD 979) 1998 compiles their entire back catalogue.

EP: 1(B) MEET THE MIGIL FIVE   (Pye ????) 1964 SC

HCP

45s: α Maybe/Can't I?   (Pye 7N 15572) 1963 -
Mockingbird Hill/
Long Ago And Far Away   (Pye 7N 15597) 1964 10
Near You/Don't Wanna Go On Shaking (Pye 7N 15645) 1964 31
Boys And Girls/I Saw Your Picture (Pye 7N 15677) 1964 -
Just Behind The Rainbow/
Seven Lonely Days   (Pye 7N 15757) 1965 -
One Hundred Years/I'm In Love Again (Pye 7N 15874) 1965 -
Pencil And Paper/
Nevertheless (I'm In Love With You) (Pye 7N 17023) 1966 -
Together/Superstition   (Columbia DB 8196) 1967 -
If I Had My Way/
Somebody's Stolen The Moon   (Jay Boy BOY 4) 1969 -

NB: α as **The Migil Four**.

This outfit started out as a jazz trio consisting of Blanche, Felix and Lucas in 1961, but a couple of year's later guitarist Red Lambert was added and they veered towards pop, taking over the **Dave Clark Five**'s residency at the Tottenham Royal Ballroom. Then, at the suggestion of Kenny Ball, they added saxophonist, Alan Watson. Their first 45 as **The Migil Four** had flopped, but with the onset of ska their bluebeat-style revival of Ronald Ronalde's *Mocking Bird Hill* was particularly timely and shot them into the Top Ten, though they were never able to capitalise on this, enjoying only one more minor hit with the follow-up, *Near You*. Their album, EP and further 45s sold poorly and by 1967 they'd turned full circle back to their jazz roots.

The 1991 CD reissue of their album also includes all their Pye singles including *Maybe*, which was released when the band were still **The Migil Four**.

Compilation appearances include: *One Hundred Years* on *Ripples, Vol. 4* (CD); and *Mockingbird Hill* on *The Sixties File* (2-LP). (VJ)

Mike Stuart Span

Personnel:	STUART HOBDAY	vcls	ABCD
	NIGEL LANGHAM	gtr	AB
	ROGER McCABE	bs	ABCD
	GARY 'ROSCOE' MURPHY	drms	ABCD
	ASHLEY POTTER	organ	ABC
	GARY PARSLEY	trumpet	BC
	DAVE PLUMB	sax	BC
	JON POULTER	keyb'ds	BC
	BRIAN BENNETT	gtr	D

ALBUM: 1 TIMESPAN   (Tenth Planet TP 0014) 1995 SC

NB: (1) Limited numbered edition of 1,000, also released on CD (Wooden Hill WHCD003) 1996 with four bonus tracks, taken from a BBC Top Gear session from 26th May '68:- *Through The Looking Glass*, *Time*, *Children Of Tomorrow* and *My White Bicycle*. There's also a compilation, *The Story Of Oak Records* (Tenth Planet TP010) 1994 also on CD (Wooden Hill WHCD007) 1995.

EP: 1 EXPANSIONS   (117 CPAT 1171) 1993 SC

45s: Come On Over To Our Place/
Still Nights   (Columbia DB 8066) 1966 R1
Dear/Invitation   (Columbia DB 8206) 1967 R1
Children Of Tomorrow/
Concerto Of Thoughts   (Jewel JL 1) 1968 R3
You Can Understand Me/
Baubles And Bangles   (Fontana TF 959) 1968 SC

The band formed in Brighton in the mid-sixties, and centred on Stuart Hobday. Initially they played a soul/showband repertoire, and soon came to the attention of local manager/promoter Mike Clayton. On his advice the original quartet was expanded by three additional players into a seven-piece (line-up B). Sadly, soon after this Langham died after jumping out an upstairs window whilst tripping on LSD, thereby reducing them to a six-piece.

Early in 1966 they recorded an acetate for EMI, comprising a cover of The Drifters' *Follow Me* and Hobday's composition *Work Out*. It was good enough to earn them a contract, though EMI didn't actually release these songs. Instead they sent the band into the studio to record another Drifters song, *Come Over To Our Place*, and put another Hobday original, *Still Nights*, on the flip. It didn't sell, and nor did their next 45, an unadventurous cover of **Cat Stevens**'s *Dear*, backed by a version of **Mike D'Abo**'s soulful *Invitation*. The band was then dropped by EMI. As a result they abandoned the keyboards and horn section and advertised for a guitarist in 'Melody Maker'. Tunbridge Wells native Brian Bennett (who'd recorded a couple of solo 45s with **Tony's Defenders**) was thereby recruited. His aggressive guitar playing gave the band greater versatility, and they now veered towards psychedelia.

A Decca demo coupling the superb *Second Production* with an extended cover of Fontella Bass's *Rescue Me* was deemed too weird for release, so the band ended up funding the recording of their next single, Children *Of Tomorrow*, as an Oak acetate. They set up their own Jewel label to release it and pressed just 500 copies, making it an ultra-rarity. Punchy and powerful, with some great riffs, it is arguably their finest moment. In this period they also made a cameo appearance in the film 'Better A Widow' (for about 30 seconds), and composed and played *Cycle*, a 20-minute sci-fi fantasy, for the Brighton Arts Festival.

At this time the BBC invited them to feature in a documentary focusing on the life of a pop group on the way up. What could have been their big break, however, turned out to be a tour de force of unintentional comedy. 'A Year In The Life: Big Deal Group' (screened on Sunday, September 28th 1969) detailed their increasingly desperate efforts to make it in toe-curling detail. One of the most revealing films ever made about the realities of the music business, it's well worth tracking down a copy.

Meanwhile one final 45, *You Can Understand Me* (a sugary Howard-Blaikley pop song), was put by Fontana. Hardly an appropriate follow-up for a band that had recently recorded a song like *Children Of Tomorrow*, it flopped and by the start of 1969 the band had renamed itself **Leviathan**, at the insistence of new label Elektra. For their subsequent history, see the entry under that name.

The Tenth Planet compilation is a good starting point for anyone wanting to investigate **Mike Stuart Span**, though it's basically immediately pre-**Leviathan** recordings rather than earlier material. The 10-track set comprises two studio outtakes recorded by **Leviathan** in 1969, the lengthy *Evil Woman* (notable for extended guitar jams) and *Through The Looking Glass*, which features guitar ramblings characteristic of the progressive era.

MIKE STUART SPAN - Timespan (LP).

The remaining eight tracks have been taken from Oak acetates and include versions of *Children Of Tomorrow, Concerto Of Thoughts, Second Production* and *Rescue Me*. The retrospective is also available on CD with four tracks taken from a BBC Top Gear session - *Through The Looking Glass, My White Bicycle, Time* and *Children Of Tomorrow*.

In 1993 250 copies of the *Exspansions* EP were released. Co-ordinated by Gary 'Roscoe' Murphy and '117' fanzine, this coupled two previously unreleased Oak acetates (*Second Production/Rescue Me* and *Remember The Times/World In My Head*). The group recorded five acetates in all, and obviously these are very expensive to obtain now.

Only Brian Bennett is still active in the music business, currently playing in a band called Calico as well as a Phil Collins tribute band, which also includes former members of **Jason Crest**. Gary Murphy had been in rock/blues band Chameleon, which has now split.

Compilation coverage has included:- *Children Of Tomorrow* on *Chocolate Soup For Diabetics, Vol. 2* (LP), *Electric Sugar Cube Flashbacks* (CD), *Rubble Vol. 8: All The Colours Of Darkness* (LP), *Rubble Vol. 5* (CD) and *The Best Of Rubble Collection, Vol. 6* (CD); *Children Of Tomorrow* (BBC) and *Through The Looking Glass* (BBC) on *Artefacts From The Psychedelic Dungeon* (CD); *Concerto Of Thoughts* on *Story Of Oak Records* (2-LP)/*The Story Of Oak Records* (CD); *Still Nights* on *Purple Pill Eaters* (LP & CD); and *Children Of Tomorrow* and *Concerto Of Thoughts* on *Beat It* (3-CD). (VJ/RMJ)

John Miles

			HCP
ALBUMS:	1	REBEL	(Decca SKL 5231) 1976 9
(up to	2	STRANGER IN THE CITY	(Decca TXS 118) 1976 37
1976)			

NB: (1) and (2) released on London in the US. (1) and (2) reissued on CD (London 8200 802) in 1987 and (London 8205 182) in 1988. There's also a CD compilation *Anthology* (Connoisseur VSOPCD 191) 1993.

			HCP
45s:	Why Don't You Love Me?/		
(up to	If I Could See Through	(Amity OTS 508) 1971	-
1976)	Jose/You Made It So Hard	(Decca F 13196) 1971	-
	Come Away Melinda/		
	Walking With My Head Held High	(Orange OAS 207) 1972	-
	Yesterday (Was Just The Beginning)/		
	Road To Freedom	(Orange OAS 208) 1972	-
	Hard Road/You're Telling Me Lies	(Orange OAS 209) 1973	-
	Jacqueline/Keep On Tryin'	(Orange OAS 211) 1973	-
	One Minute Every Hour/		
	Hollywood Queen	(Orange OAS 213) 1973	-
	Fright Of My Life/Good Time Woman	(Orange OAS 220) 1974	-
	What's On Your Mind/		
	Rock'n'Roll Band	(Orange OAS 223) 1974	-
	What's On Your Mind/To Be Grateful	(Orange OAS 224) 1974	-
	High Fly/		
	There's A Man Behind The Guitar	(Decca F 13595) 1975	17
	Music/Putting My New Song Together	(Decca F 13627) 1976	3
	Remember Yesterday / House	(Decca F 13667) 1976	32
Reissues:	Music/Slow Down	(Decca MILES 1) 1982	-
	Music/Slow Down	(Old Gold OG 9339) 1983	-

The talented **Miles** was born in Jarrow in Tyne and Wear on 23 April 1949. His first band was **The Influence** in the late sixties, who cut a 45 for Orange. They also included future **Roxy Music** member Paul Thompson and Vic Malcolm, who was later in **Geordie**.

When **Influence** went their separate ways, **Miles** set up his own John Miles Band, which was popular in the north-east but attracted little wider attention. Several singles were released on the Orange label including a version of *Come Away Melinda*, but it wasn't until he relocated to London in 1975 with bassist Bob Marshall that he began to experience the success he'd worked so hard for. After signing to Decca and adding first Barry Black and then Gary Moberly to his line-up he scored his first hit with *High Fly*, which was produced by Alan Parsons. His finest moment, though, was the follow-up, *Music*, an excellent melodic rock ballad, also produced by Alan Parsons (**Miles** was a guest vocalist for The Alan Parsons Project), which peaked at No 3 here. Both songs were also minor hits in the US, where he

PETE MILLER - Summerland (CD).

toured with **Elton John**. He continued to record well into the eighties but had only two further hits with *Remember Yesterday* and *Slow Down* (No 10 in 1977) from his *Stranger In The City* album.

Subsequent albums like *Zaragon, More Miles Per Hour* and *Miles High* in the late seventies and early eighties failed to repeat his early successes. After releasing *Transition* in the mid-eighties he sang on projects with the Alan Parsons Project and **Jimmy Page** and toured with Tina Turner and **Joe Cocker**. It was eight years before his next solo project *Upfront* in 1993. Sadly, his epic *Music*, which some unfairly labelled pretentious, became a shackle he could never break free of. (VJ)

Robin Millar and Mick Taylor

45:	Catch As Catch Can/For My Life (PS)	(ION 821003) 1975

NB. French pressing.

Recorded at the Apple Studios, this single is interesting for the involvement of Mick Taylor (formerly with **John Mayall** and **The Rolling Stones**), who played guitar and produced these typical mid-seventies rock songs. (SR)

Miller

ALBUM:	1	SUMMERLAND	(Tenth Planet TP030) 1997

NB: (1) reissued on CD (Gear Fab GF-147) 2000.

45s:	The Girl With The Castle/	
	Baby I've Got News For You	(Oak RGJ 190) 1965 R4
	Baby I've Got News For You/	
	The Girl With The Castle	(Columbia DB 7735) 1965 R4

Baby I've Got News For You was arguably one of Britain's first psychedelic discs, originally recorded in limited quantities for the Oak label before it was picked up by Columbia for release the same year. **Miller** was actually Pete Miller from Norwich. He'd briefly been a member of two other Norwich acts, **The News** and **Peter Jay and The Jaywalkers**. The Oak recording of *Baby I've Got News For You* later resurfaced on *Story Of Oak Records* (2-LP)/*The Story Of Oak Records* (CD) and *Perfumed Garden Vol. 3* (CD) compilations and you'll also find the Columbia version of this catchy song, which was also written by **Miller**, on *English Freakbeat, Vol. 3* (LP). For the Columbia release the sides were reversed and *Baby I've Got News For You* was put where it belonged, on the 'A' side.

Miller went on to record another classic slice of psychedelia, *Cold Turkey* under the pseudonym **Big Boy Pete**, before heading for the States and continued obscurity. The *Summerland* retrospective compiles fourteen of **Miller**'s demo recordings from the same period. (VJ)

THE EARLY DAYS OF ROCK VOL. 2 (Comp CD) including The Mindbenders.

Frankie Miller

ALBUMS:	1	ONCE IN A BLUE MOON	(Chrysalis CHR 1036) 1973
(up to	2	HIGH LIFE	(Chrysalis CHR 1052) 1974
1976)	3	THE ROCK	(Chrysalis CHR 1088) 1975

45s:	Rock/Heartbreak	(Chrysalis CHS 2095) 1976
(up to	Loving You Is Sweeter Than Ever/	
1976)	I'm Old Enough	(Chrysalis CHS 2103) 1976

A Glaswegian, **Miller**'s first group was **The Stoics** in the late sixties, but he was then in the short-lived Jude which **Robin Trower** had formed shortly after leaving **Procol Harum**. Upon their demise, he recorded his first solo album, *Once In A Blue Moon*, supported by **Brinsley Schwarz**. It was on the follow-up, *High Life*, recorded in New Orleans that his throaty bluesy vocals were effectively showcased, with R&B legendary Allen Toussaint handling production duties. Neither album sold particularly well.

In 1975 **Miller** formed **The Frankie Miller Band** with a line-up of: - **Henry McCullogh** (gtr), Stu Perry (drms), Chrissie Stewart (formerly of **Spooky Tooth**) (bs) and Mick Weaver (gtr). They recorded *The Rock*, which was greeted quite positively by the critics but again sold only moderately. He has continued to record with various personnel since 1976 but remains embedded in the second division of white blues singers. (VJ)

Stephen Miller

ALBUMS:	1	MILLER AND COXHILL	(Caroline C 1503) 1974 R1
	2	THE STORY SO FAR... OH REALLY?	
			(Caroline C 1507) 1974 R1

Miller's first outfit seems to have been a blues band, Delivery, back in 1968. He was briefly with DC and The MBs, which never really got off the ground, before departing to **Caravan**, which he left in July 1972 to work with **Lol Coxhill** and go solo. These albums were recorded with **Lol Coxhill**. (VJ)

The Millionaires

Personnel:	'STASSY' ANASTASI	bs	A
	BRIAN 'BIZ' BINSTED	lead gtr	A
	CLIFF COOPER	lead vcls	A
	KEN COOPER	vcls	A
	ALAN HOLDER	drms	A
	DAVE HOLDER	gtr	A

45:	Wishing Well/Chatterbox	(Decca F 12468) 1966 R2

From Loughton, Newbury Park, Wanstead and North London, their sole 45

was produced by Joe Meek, but isn't especially adventurous. Cliff Cooper left in 1968 to found the famous 'Orange' Music Shop and Amplifier range, and his brother Ken left shortly after to manage **Consortium/West Coast Consortium**. The band later revamped themselves and made further recordings as **Juice**.

Wishing Well can also be found on *RGM Rarities, Vol. 2* (CD). (SD/VJ)

Johnny Milton and The Condors

Personnel:	MICK CLARKE	bs	A
	CLIVE GRAHAM	drms	A
	JOHNNY MILTON	vcls	A
	RIKKI SMITH	gtr	A

45s:	A Girl Named Sue/Something Else	(Decca F 11862) 1964
	Cry Baby/Hurt	(Fontana TF 488) 1964

This outfit evolved out of The Johnny Milton Band and later became **The Symbols**. They played at The Star Club in Hamburg. *Something Else* was an Eddie Cochran song and *Cry Baby* was written by their manager Geoff Stephens. Mick Clarke was later in **The Rubettes**.

A Girl Named Sue and *Something Else* have been compiled on *Rare 60's Beat Treasures, Vol. 5* (CD). (VJ)

The Mindbenders

Personnel:	BOB LANG	bs, vcls	ABC
	RIC ROTHWELL	drms	A
	ERIC STEWART	lead gtr, vcls	ABCDE
	GEORGE ROBERTS	drms	B
	PAUL HANCOX	drms	CDE
	CHARLIE HARRISON	bs	D
	JIMMY O'NEILL	gtr, keyb'ds	DE
	GRAHAM GOULDMAN	bs, vcls	E

HCP

ALBUMS:	1(A)	THE MINDBENDERS (mono/stereo)		
			(Fontana (S)TL 5324) 1966	R1 28
	2(A)	WITH WOMAN IN MIND		
		(mono/stereo)	(Fontana (S)TL 5403) 1967	R1 -

NB: (1) reissued on Fontana (SFL 13045) in 1968 (SC). (1) and (2) reissued on one CD (BGO BGOCD 389) 2002. They also appeared on the Soundtrack of *To Sir With Love* (Fontana STL 5446) 1967.

HCP

45s:	A Groovy Kind Of Love/Love Is Good	(Fontana TF 644) 1966	2
	Can't Live With You, Can't Live Without You/		
	One Fine Day	(Fontana TF 697) 1966	28
	Ashes To Ashes/		
	You Don't Know About Love	(Fontana TF 731) 1966	14
	I Want Her, She Wants Me/		
	The Morning After	(Fontana TF 780) 1966	
	We'll Talk About It Tomorrow/		
	Far Across Town	(Fontana TF 806) 1967	
	The Letter/My New Day And Age	(Fontana TF 869) 1967	42
	Schoolgirl/Coming Back	(Fontana TF 877) 1967	SC
	Blessed Are The Lonely/		
	Yellow Brick Road	(Fontana TF 910) 1968	
	Uncle Joe, The Ice Cream Man/		
	The Man Who Loved Trees	(Fontana TF 961) 1968	
Reissue:	A Groovy Kind Of Love/		
	(Flip by different artist)	(Old Gold OG 9266) 1982	

As you may know, **The Mindbenders** from Manchester started out as **Wayne Fontana**'s backing group in 1963. When they went their separate ways in 1965, it was rather surprisingly the backing group not the former lead singer who made the greatest impact. Their appealing ballad, *A Groovy Kind Of Love*, was a massive hit on both sides of the Atlantic. They developed a penchant for sob stories and enjoyed further hits with *Can't Live Without You* and *Ashes To Ashes*, both penned by Carole Bayer and Toni Wine. They also starred in the feature film 'To Sir With Love'. Then they went off the boil, despite recording a **Rod Argent** composition, *I Want Her, She Wants Me*, and covering Robert Knight's *Blessed Are The Lonely* with less success than **The Love Affair** achieved with his songs. Even a cover of The Box Tops' *The Letter*, produced by **Graham Gouldman**, could only get to No 42. Despite poor sales, *Schoolgirl* was a catchy commercial number with a lush string and wah-wah guitar backing. The flip side is a beautiful slice of pop-psych with superb vocals and three fade-outs. Their final 45 *Uncle Joe The Ice Cream Man* saw them return to a more commercial pop style.

Both their albums were fairly consistent post-beat boom offerings, which suffer from the lack of original material. Only four of the 24 tracks on the two albums were written by band members.

Rothwell left the band in 1968 to go into the antique business, although he was later in The Derek Quinn Band. His replacement George Roberts came from The Exchequers (a Chester-based band). Roberts only played on the last two singles. His replacement was ex-**Locomotive** man Paul Hancox, from Birmingham. Lang then went into the hi-fi business before ending up in **Racing Cars** in 1976. There was no further recording output but quite a few comings and goings. Harrison and O'Neill (ex-**Uglys**) joined, but Harrison soon departed again to Septimus who became **Judas Jump**. Finally, **Graham Gouldman** (ex-**Mockingbirds**) joined.

Their best known song, *A Groovy Kind Of Love*, was featured on Philips' *Sixteen Star Tracks Of The Sixties* (LP) compilation in 1971 and more recently on the 2-CD set *Sixties Summer Love*. *The Morning After*, a punchy flip side from 1966, has resurfaced on *Rubble Vol. 1: The Psychedelic Snarl* (LP) and *Rubble Vol. 1* (CD). Other compilation appearances have included: *My New Day And Age* on *Justafixation* (CD) and *Jagged Time Lapse, Vol 3* (CD); *Ashes To Ashes* on *Made In England, Vol. 1* (LP); *Can't Live With You, Can't Live Without You* and *One Fine Day* on *The Star-Club Singles Complete, Vol. 8* (LP & CD); *Tricky Dicky* on *Star-Club Show* (LP); *One Fine Day* on *The Star-Club Anthology, Vol. 3* (LP); *Groovy Kind Of Love* on *The Early Days Of Rock, Vol. 2 - Live In Concert 1964 - 1968* (CD); *Uncle Joe, The Ice Cream Man* on *Pop-In, Vol 1* (CD); *The Man Who Loved Trees* on *Colour Me Pop, Vol 2* (CD) and *Yellow Brick Road* on *Jagged Time Lapse, Vol 4* (CD).

After their demise, Eric Stewart and **Graham Gouldman** went into session work before later forming **Hotlegs** who developed into **10cc** with whom he enjoyed sustained success. **The Mindbenders**' cover of The Box Tops' *The Letter* was **Gouldman**'s first record production. Hancox joined **Chicken Shack**. (VJ/JM)

Ministry of Sound

45:      White Collar Worker/Back Seat Driver   (Decca F 12449) 1966

An obscure beat band. (VJ)

The Mint

45s: Luv/Simone   (Tangerine DP 14) 1969
          See If I Care/Penny   (Concord CON 011) 1970

An obscure pop group whose undistinguished, poppy *Luv* can also be heard as *Love By Numbers* on *Rubble, Vol. 16 - Glass Orchid Aftermath* (LP), *Rubble, Vol. 10* (CD) and *The Best Of Rubble Collection, Vol. 2* (CD). It's not confirmed that the Concord 45 is by the same act. (VJ)

The Mirage

Personnel:	RAY GLYNN	ld gtr, vcls	AB
	DAVE HYNES	drms, vcls	AB
	PAT HYNES	gtr	A
	PETE HYNES	ld vcls	AB
	DEE MURRAY	bs, vcls	A
	KIRK DUNCAN	keyb'ds	B
	JEFF PETERS	bs	B

45s:	It's In Her Kiss/		
	What Ye Gonna Do 'Bout It	(CBS 201772) 1965 SC
	Go Away/Just A Face	(CBS 202007) 1965 SC
	Tomorrow Never Knows/	
	You Can't Be Serious	(Philips BF 1534) 1966 R1
	Hold On/Can You Hear Me	(Philips BF 1554) 1967 SC

	The Wedding Of Ramona Blair/		
	Lazy Man	(Philips BF 1571) 1967 R2
	Mystery Lady/Chicago Cottage	(Page One POF 078) 1968
	Carolyn/World Goes On Around You	(Page One POF 111) 1969

This Hertford-based band had been playing together since 1960 when they started out as a skiffle group. Inevitably, they underwent many changes in style during their career. They made a couple of pop singles for CBS before hitting the right spots with a cover version of **The Beatles**' psychedelic classic *Tomorrow Never Knows* in 1967. Their later singles for Philips and Page One are highly regarded. *The Wedding Of Ramona Blair* is a whimsical slice of pop-psych.

They split in 1969 when Dee Murray and Dave Hynes joined **Spencer Davis Group** for a while. Later in 1970 Dave, Peter and Ray changed their name to **Portobello Explosion** with line-up (B) on joining the Carnaby label and later still became **Jawbone**. Dave Murray went on to play with **Elton John**.

Their recordings have been heavily compiled with *Psychedelia, Vol. 4* (LP) and *Hen's Teeth, Vol. 3* (CD) including an unreleased acetate track *I See The Rain*; *Circus Days Vol. 3* (LP & CD), featuring *Tomorrow Never Knows*, *And Life Goes On* and *My Door*, *Rubble Vol. 4: The 49 Minute Technicolour Dream* (LP) and *Rubble Vol. 3* (CD) including the popish story-song *The Wedding Of Ramona Blair* and the *Artefacts From The Psychedelic Dungeon* (CD) gives two previously unreleased cuts, *Ebenezer Beaver* and *Poor Mrs. Busby*, an airing. *Mystery Lady* has resurfaced on *Pop-In, Vol 1* (CD); *Hold On* gets an airing on *We Can Fly, Vol 2* (CD) and *Chicago Cottage* has been compiled on *Jagged Time Lapse, Vol 5* (CD). (VJ/MWh)

Mirkwood

Personnel:	DEREK BOWLEY	ld vcls	AB
	ANDY BROADBENT	bs	A
	JACK CASTLE	gtr, vcls	AB
	MICK MORRIS	gtr, vcls	AB
	STEVE SMITH	drms	AB
	DAVE EVANS	bs	B

ALBUMS: 1(B)   MIRKWOOD   (Flams Ltd PR 1067) 1973 R5

NB: (1) reissued on Tenth Planet (TP 003) 1993, limited edition of 500 copies (SC).

Mirkwood was formed in 1971 by Jack Castle and Mick Morris, who'd known each other since their days together at a Dover grammar school. In early 1972 Dave Evans replaced Andy Broadbent who moved away from the Dover area. Their album was recorded in early 1973 for the local Flams Ltd label. Only 99 copies were pressed and most of them ended up with family and friends. Six of its seven tracks were penned by Jack Castle, the remaining one, *The Leech*, was a Mick Morris composition. Musically the

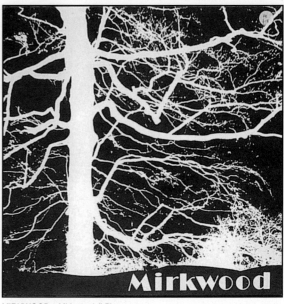

MIRKWOOD - Mirkwood (LP).

material is heavy rock with **Cream**-influenced harmonies and some inevitable guitar heroics. It's only likely to interest fans of this genre.

Up until their demise in June 1975 the band featured three further drummers after Steve Smith: - Nick 'Topper' Headon (who was later in The Clash), Terry Prior and finally Dave Blakey. They reformed briefly in 1978 and Bowley, Morris, Evans and Blakey were later in a band called Sprinter. A new version of **Mirkwood** was put together in 1985 featuring Morris, Castle and Bowley from the original line-up but when Castle moved to Wales, where he now performs as a solo artist, they renamed themselves Icebreaker. (VJ)

The Mirror

Personnel:	NICK BIGSBY	drms	AB
	CHRIS JEFFRIES	sax	AB
	BOB PIERCE	gtr	AB
	MIKE TRIEBWASSER	bs	AB
	CHRIS WARNETT	vcls	AB
	PETE FROLICH	gtr	B

45: Gingerbread Man/Faster Than Light (Philips BF 1666) 1968 R2

This is a rare and sought-after single. In addition, four previously unissued Eastern-influenced tracks by this band are compiled on an EP, *Reflected Glory* (Bam-Caruso PABL 042) 1986.

The band was one of Bath's finest, apparently. They formed in 1963 as The Spectres, changing their name to The Dreaded Spectres by 1965 and **The Mirror** in 1967 after securing a contract with Philips. The 'A' side of their sole 45 was straight-forward pop, but the flip, a Bob Pierce composition, is what might be termed freakbeat. Some good drumming and fuzz guitar is spoilt by a rather messy mix. Still the single was a minor hit in Germany and they got to appear on the German equivalent of 'Top Of The Pops'.

Pete Frolich joined their line-up in 1969 but within a year they'd disintegrated. Bob Pierce now runs a recording studio in Bristol and produced the new psychedelic sitar band Saddar Bazaar's debut album on Delerium.

You can also find *Faster Than Light* on *Rubble Vol. 1: The Psychedelic Snarl* (LP) and *Rubble Vol. 1* (CD) and *Gingerbread Man* has been compiled on *Colour Me Pop, Vol 2* (CD). (VJ)

The Misfits

45: Hanging Around/You Won't See
Men (Aberdeen Students Charities Campaign PRI 101) 1966

This Aberdeen band's sole vinyl offering was on this small independent Scottish label. *You Won't See Me* was a **Beatles**' song. (VJ)

The Mission Belles

45: Sincerely/
When A Girl Really Loves You (Decca F 12154) 1965 SC

A harmony beat girl group. (VJ)

Misty

45: Hot Cinnamon / Cascades (Parlophone R 5852) 1970

This sounds as if it ought to be an instrumental. (VJ)

The Misunderstood

Personnel:	RICK BROWN	vcls	A
	RICK MOE	drms	ABC
	GEORGE PHELPS	ld gtr	A
	GREG TREADWAY	gtr	A
	STEVE WHITING	bs	A
	GLENN CAMPBELL	steel gtr	BCD
	TONY HILL	gtr	C
	GUY EVANS	drms	D
	STEVE HOARD	vcls	D
	NEIL HUBBARD	gtr	D
	CHRIS MERCER	sax	D
	DAVY O'LIST	gtr	D
	NIC POTTER	bs	D

ALBUMS: 1(C) BEFORE THE DREAM FADED
(Cherry Red BRED 32) 1982
2(D) GOLDEN GLASS (Time Stood Still TSS LP 1) 1984

NB: (1) reissued on CD (Cherry Red CD BRED 32) 1992 and again (Cherry Red BRED 32) 1996. Fans of the band will also be interested in *The Legendary Goldstar Album* (Cherry Red CDBRED 142) 1997. This double CD package contains all the material featured on (2) plus previously unreleased material recorded at Gold Star in 1966. Only two of these 1966 cuts have surfaced before on the 'B' side to *Golden Glass* 12" single. However, to confuse matters further, (2) has also been reissued on CD in Italy (Get Back GET 4) 1996, also with the two 12" tracks recorded at Gold Star. This was reissued again as *Golden Glass* (Get Back GET 500) 2000 on vinyl as an Italian import. *The Lost Acetates 1965-1966* (Ugly Things UT 2201 CD) 2004/(Ugly Things UT 2201) 2004 in vinyl compiles newly discovered acetates belonging to drummer Rick Moe.

EP: 1 GOLDEN GLASS (Cherry Red 2 THYME 1) 1984

NB: (1) contains *Golden Glass* plus two tracks recorded at Gold Star studios in 1966: *Shake Your Money Maker/I'm Not Talking.*

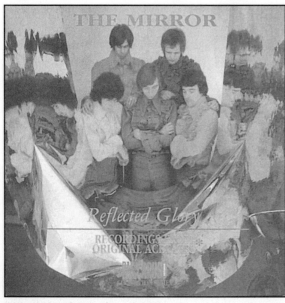

THE MIRROR - Reflected Glory (12" EP).

THE MISUNDERSTOOD - Before The Dream Faded (LP).

THE MISUNDERSTOOD - Golden Glass (LP).

45s: χ   I Can Take You To The Sun/
           Who Do You Love?   (Fontana TF 777) 1966 R2
      β   Children Of The Sun/I Unseen   (Fontana TF 998) 1968 R2
      α   You're Tuff Enough/
           Little Red Rooster (Some PS) (Fontana TF 1028) 1969 R2/R1
      α   Never Had A Girl (Like You Before)/
           Golden Glass   (Fontana TF 1041) 1969 R1
Reissue: Children Of The Sun/Who Do You Love?/I Can Take You
           To The Sun (PS)   (Cherry Red CHERRY 22) 1981

NB: α as Misunderstood featuring Glenn 'Fernando' Campbell. χ reissued (TF 777) in a limited edition of 500 based on the original French jukebox release. β reissued (TF 998) in a limited edition of 500 based on the original French jukebox release.

Something of an anomaly, in that they originated in California but recorded in London, **The Misunderstood** have two claims to fame: they were managed for a while by John Peel and recorded two of the best singles of the psychedelic era, *I Can Take You To The Sun* and *Children Of The Sun*.

The group started in Riverside, California, when Treadway, Moe and Phelps formed a surfing group, The Blue Notes. In 1965, by which time Brown and Whiting had been added to their line-up, they changed their name to **The Misunderstood**. Having recruited steel guitarist Campbell from another surfing band, The Goldstones, as a replacement for Phelps (who'd left), they cut two blues tracks, Jimmy Reed's *You Don't Have To Go* and Howlin' Wolf's *Who's Been Talkin'*, as a single. These can be heard on *Before The Dream Faded*, Cherry Red's 1982 compilation of the group's earlier material. They were evolving rapidly, however, and had started to play their own brand of proto-psychedelic R&B. After seeing them play at the opening of a shopping centre in Riverside, John Peel (then known as Ravenscroft and DJing locally) realised their potential and became their manager. They followed him back to London in mid-1966 and were swiftly signed to Fontana, for whom they recorded six songs in November. These recordings captured the band at their zenith, and showed Campbell to have been one of the most imaginative guitarists of the time.

The groundbreaking *I Can Take You To The Sun* appeared in December and was widely-praised in the music press. They'd also developed a mind-blowing stage act, and were making their presence felt on London's burgeoning psychedelic club scene when Treadway was called home to be drafted. He was replaced by Tony Hill, but when Moe was also drafted early in 1967 and other members were deported, the band fell apart. Fontana released the shattering *Children Of The Sun* in 1968, but their moment had passed.

In 1969 Campbell reformed the band with an entirely different line-up, recording two R&B influenced singles, *You're Tuff Enough* and *Never Had A Girl (Like You Before)*. They weren't bad, but certainly not as good as their predecessors. When they collapsed, Campbell and other members of the group formed **Juicy Lucy**. Tony Hill later formed **High Tide**. In the early eighties Rick Brown and Glenn Campbell formed an Eastern-influenced hard-rock outfit called The Influence, who recorded a one-sided flexidisc in 1982, *You're My Girl* (Bucketfull Of Brains BOB 2), which appeared with 'Bucketfull Of Brains' magazine.

The Misunderstood presaged acts like **Pink Floyd** and **Jimi Hendrix**, and had they not had such bad luck, could very possibly have attained the same level of success. As it is, the few songs they did record in their prime are among the very best psychedelic recordings of the period and essential listening.

The *Golden Glass* EP released by Cherry Red in 1984 contains material by the second line-up on the 'A' side. By then the band had veered towards blues-based progressive music. On the flip are two tracks by the earlier 1966 line-up:- *Shake Your Money Maker* and *I'm Not Talkin'*, recorded at the legendary Gold Star studios. The same year Cherry Red released a 45 containing *Shake Your Money Maker*, *I'm Not Talking* and *Golden Glass*. Other material recorded at these sessions was thought to have been lost. In 1998, however, *The Legendary Goldstar Album* appeared, which combined the later *Golden Glass* album with these earlier 1966 cuts. Of these, *I'm Not Talkin* remains the highlight, with a splendid feedback freakout section.

The *Golden Glass* album contains material by line-up (B), including both sides of their two singles, *You're Tuff Enough* and *Never Had A Girl Like You Before*. The remaining four tracks were a cover of the **Spencer Davis Group** hit *Keep On Running*, *Freedom*, *I'm Cruising* and the Little Richard track *I Don't Want To Discuss It*, which is laden with feedback. This isn't for psych heads, but many appeal to progressive fans who are into long, bluesy guitar solos..

The Lost Acetates has been compiled by Mike Stax (editor of 'Ugly Things' fanzine). It includes early versions of future classics like *I Unseen*, *Children Of The Sun*, *Find The Hidden Door* and *My Mind*. *She Got Me* has a menacing fuzzy riff, *Don't Break Me Down* is full of jingle-jangle guitar and there's a cover of Hoyt Axton's *Thunder'N'Lightining*. There's also a limited pressing of 1,500 copies of this on 180-gm vinyl.

Compilation coverage has included: - *I Can Take You To The Sun* on the 4-CD box set *Acid Drops, Spacedust & Flying Saucers*; *Children Of The Sun* on *Chocolate Soup For Diabetics, Vol. 1* (LP) and on the 4-CD *Nuggets II* box set; *Golden Glass* on *Rubble Vol. 4: 49 Minute Technicolour Dream*; and *Never Had A Girl Like You Before* (45 version) on *Rubble Vol. 1: The Psychedelic Snarl* (LP) and *Rubble Vol. 1* (CD). In addition a live track recorded by Line-up 'B' *Bad Hat*, has also resurfaced on *Turds On A Bum Ride, Vol. 4* (CD). (VJ)

Denny Mitchell Soundsation

Personnel: | MIKE BRESLIN | drms | A |
	PETE GOSLING	organ	A
	PETE LYNTON	bs	A
	DENNY MITCHELL	vcls	A
	HOWARD P. SANDON	lead gtr	A

45:   I've Been Crying/For Your Love   (Decca F 11848) 1964

An obscure beat group. (VJ/AD)

THE MISUNDERSTOOD - The Legendary Goldstar Album (2-CD).

Mixed Bag

Personnel:	JOHN COOK	vcls, organ	A
	MALCOLM PARRY	vcls, bs	A
	TERRY SAUNDERS	vcls, gtr	A
	BRYAN WILSON	vcls, drms	A

45s:	Potiphar/Million Dollar Bash	(Decca F 12880) 1969
	Round And Round/	
	Have You Ever Been In Love	(Decca F 12907) 1969

This obscure late sixties band also contributed to 'Joseph and The Amazing Technicolour Dreamcoat'. *Million Dollar Bash* is a Dylan song. *Round And Round* was a Chuck Berry number. They played cheerful beat music. (VJ)

Mixture

45:	One By One/Monkey Jazz	(Fontana TF 640) 1965

A harmony beat band from Manchester, who once played at The Star Club in Hamburg. (VJ)

The Mixture

Personnel:	IAN CAMPBELL	organ, piano	A
	HOWARD EDWARDS	drms	A
	DAVE GREATBANKS	ld gtr	A
	BOB HARRISON	vcls	A
	ROGER MYCOCK	bs	A

45:	Sad Old Song/	
	Never Trust In Tomorrow	(Parlophone R 5755) 1969

This was a different band. **Mike D'Abo** wrote the 'A' side of their 45. (VJ)

Mo and Steve

45:	Oh What A Day It's Going To Be/	
	Reach Out For Your Lovin' Touch	(Pye 7N 17175) 1966

This was a Manchester-based duo. The 'A' side was an obscure Ray Davies composition, never recorded by **The Kinks**, but it failed to sell at the time and hasn't aroused that much interest from collectors since. (VJ)

The Mockingbirds

Personnel:	BERNARD BASSO	bs	A
	KEVIN GODLEY	drms	A
	GRAHAM GOULDMAN		A
	STEVE JACOBSON	gtr	A

45s:	That's How It's Gonna Stay/	
	I Never Should Have Kissed You	(Columbia DB 7480) 1965
	I Can Feel We're Parting/	
	The Flight Of The Mockingbird	(Columbia DB 7565) 1965
	You Stole My Love/Skit Skat	(Immediate IM 015) 1965
	One By One/Lovingly Yours	(Decca F 12434) 1966
	How To Find A Lover/My Story	(Decca F 12510) 1966

A Manchester-based band formed by **Graham Gouldman** in February 1965. He'd earlier played in The Whirlwinds, another Manchester group with Jacobson and Basso. Drummer Kevin Godley had been in The Sabres, and **Gouldman** had also cut an unsuccessful solo disc for HMV prior to this. They signed to Columbia and in their early days had a regular slot as the warm up band for 'Top Of The Pops', which was transmitted from Manchester.

Gouldman wrote *For Your Love* during his lunch hour whilst working at Bargains Unlimited, a men's clothing shop in Salford, for their first single but Columbia rejected it and it was **The Yardbirds** who eventually got the

song - which became a bit hit for them. Surprisingly, none of the above singles he went on to write for **The Mockingbirds** did very well at all, although **Gouldman** continued to write several hits for other artists, including *Bus Stop* and *Look Through Any Window* for **The Hollies**; *Heart Full Of Soul* and *Evil Hearted You* for **The Yardbirds**; *Pamela Pamela* for **Wayne Fontana** and a string of hits for **Herman's Hermits**.

The Mockingbirds disintegrated in late 1966 and **Gouldman** concentrated on songwriting. For a while he became staff writer for the Kasenatz-Katz production team in New York during Autumn 1969 and sang lead on Ohio Express's *Sausalito*. He eventually joined **The Mindbenders**, then did session work until forming **Hotlegs** who became **10cc** in early 1972. **10cc** of course also included Kevin Godley.

As they didn't sell too well at the time, **The Mockingbirds**' 45s are inevitably sought-after and hard to find now. *You Stole My Love* featured **Julie Driscoll** on backing vocals and has some excellent twangy guitar work and some good harmonies. *One By One* is a fairly commercial freakbeat effort. *You Stole My Love* was later a hit in Australia for UK-born but Australian-based Mike Furber, who committed suicide in 1973.

Compilation appearances have included: *Lovingly Yours* on *The Mod Scene* (CD); *Lovingly Yours* and *One By One* on *Pop Inside The 60s Vol. 1* (CD); *One By One* on *The Beat Scene* (CD) and *English Freakbeat, Vol. 3* (LP & CD); *You Stole My Love* on *Electric Sugarcube Flashbacks, Vol. 2* (LP), *Immediate Alternative* (LP) and *Immediate Single Collection, Vol. 2* (CD); *You Stole My Love* and *Skit Skat* on *Immediate Alternative* (CD); *How To Find A Lover* on the 4-CD *Nuggets II* box set; and *Skit Skat* on *Immediate Single Collection, Vol. 4* (CD). (VJ/JM)

The Mode

Personnel:	ROGER FORBES	gtr	A
	JEFF HARRISON	drms	AB
	TONY JONES	ld gtr	AB
	DAVE MILLIDGE	bs	AB
	DEREK SHARPLING	vcls, clarinet	AB
	STEVE WEEKS	gtr	B

EP:	1(B)	THE MODE	(Private Pressing) 1967 R4

This school kid band came from the Thundersley area of Essex. They recorded a four-track privately-pressed EP in 1967, which is now extremely rare. The tracks were: - *Gone, She Won't Be Here Today, The Mode (Dance)* and *Girl*. The EP got some airplay on local pirate station Radio City. You can also check out the last of these on *Syde Trips, Vol. 4* (LP), although this is a live version of what is usually considered to have been their strongest song on the EP. Also on *Syde Trips, Vol. 4* (LP) were two previously unreleased tracks, the psychedelic *Eastern Music Back To Front*, which is a pale imitation of something like **Smoke**'s *My Friend Jack* and the light-hearted *Backing Britain* (both date from 1967). Who remembers the

RUBBLE VOL. 2 (Comp LP) featuring The Mode.

'I'm Backing Britain Campaign' then? It was started by a group of workers and its main tenet was more work for less pay. Musically this track, like the idea, was appalling!

In May 1967, they were spotted by a Decca talent scout and invited to Decca's London studio to record two tracks: - *Eastern Music* and *In This World Of Mine*, which the label subsequently decided not to release.

When Decca lost interest the band split soon after. Harrison, Millidge and Sharpling were briefly in a band called Rupert Bear soon after with guitarist Chris Rose, but it wasn't together long enough to make it onto vinyl.

Subsequently *Eastern Music* has reappeared on *Rubble Vol. 2: Pop-Sike Pipe-Dreams* (LP) and *Rubble, Vol. 1* (CD). This is a pretty commercial pop song vocally but interspersed with a sort of Eastern-influenced instrumental freak-out which the record company may have decided was too 'way out' to release, even in 1967. Considering their youth it's quite promising. Other compilation appearances include: *What You Been Doing* on *Incredible Sound Show Stories, Vol. 9* (LP). (VJ)

The Mods

45:     Something On My Mind/
     You're Making Me Blue   (RCA RCA 1399) 1964

This was another one-off 45 by an obscure band. The 'A' side is essentially Merseybeat pop. (VJ)

Mogul Thrash

Personnel:	ROGER BALL	sax	AB
	MALCOLM DUNCAN	sax, trumpet, flute	AB
	WILLIAM HARRIS	drms	A
	JAMES LITHERLAND	lead gtr	AB
	MIKE ROSEN	trumpet, gtr	AB
	JOHN WETTON	bs, vcls, keybids	AB
	BILL ATKINSON	drms	B

ALBUM: 1(B) MOGUL THRASH   (RCA SF 8156) 1971 R1

NB: (1) later reissued on CD (Discinforme SI DISC 1929 CD) and again (Won Sin WS 8856712).

45:     Sleeping In The Kitchen/St. Peter   (RCA RCA 2030) 1970 SC

This Scottish group was earlier known as The Dundee Horns. Litherland had been in **Colosseum** and Rosen in **Eclection**. William Harris left before their records were released and was replaced by ex-**Glass Menagerie** member Bill Atkinson. Their album is a brassy progressive offering, produced by **Brian Auger**.

The band split in February 1971. Litherland formed a trio called Million. He then toured and recorded with **Long John Baldry** (1971 -72), then with **Dick Heckstall-Smith** (helping to promote his solo album *A Story Ended* in 1972. He then formed a group called Manchild, toured with Leo Sayer in 1975 and joined Bandit in 1976.

Rosen, Ball and Duncan toured and recorded with The Pete York Percussion Band and then joined The Average White Band (Rosen rehearsed with them but didn't join).

Wetton did sessions for **George Martin**, and also went to Los Angeles and backed folksinger Marian Segal at the Troubadour. Returning to the UK, he rehearsed with **Renaissance** but decided to join **Family** in June 1971. (VJ/JM)

Mojo Hannah

Personnel incl:	MIKE FUDGE	violin	A
	PAUL McCALLUM	keyb'ds, violin	A
	MICK STEWART	gtr, vcls	A

ALBUM: 1(A) SIX DAYS ON THE ROAD (Kingdom KVL 9001) 1972 SC

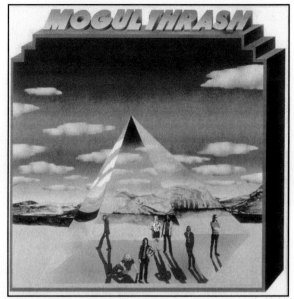

MOGUL THRASH - Mogul Thrash (CD).

45:     Six Days On The Road/
     Moon Dogs Gonna Howl Tonight   (Kingdom KV 8008) 1973

This five-piece country-rock band was formed by Mick Stewart, of **Sweet**, who also acted as a producer at the session. Paul McCallum had been in Spencer Mac. (VJ)

The Mojos

Personnel:	STU JAMES (STU SLATER)	vcls	ABCD
	KEITH KARLSON (KEITH ALCOCK)	bs	AB
	JOHN KONRAD	drms	AB
	TERRY O'TOOLE	piano	AB
	ADRIAN WILKINSON	gtr, vcls	A
	NICKY CROUCH	gtr, vcls	BCD
	LEWIS COLLINS	bs	CD
	AYNSLEY DUNBAR	drms	C
	STEVE SNAKE	drms	D

EP: 1(B) THE MOJOS   (Decca DFE 8591) 1964 R2

NB: There's also a compilation, *Working* (Edsel ED 110) 1982.

                                           HCP

45s:	Forever/They Say	(Decca F 11732) 1963 SC -
	Everything's Alright/	
	Give Your Lovin' To Me	(Decca F 11853) 1964 SC 9
	Why Not Tonight/Don't Do It Any More	(Decca F 11918) 1964 25
	Seven Daffodils/Nothin' At All	(Decca F 11959) 1964 30
	Comin' On To Cry/	
	That's The Way It Goes	(Decca F 12127) 1965 SC -
	Goodbye Dolly Gray/	
	I Just Can't Let Her Go	(Decca F 12557) 1967 SC -
	Until My Baby Comes Home/	
	Seven Park Avenue	(Liberty LBF 15097) 1968 R1 -

A Liverpool band who evolved out of another Liverpudlian band called The Nomads (Konrad and Wilkinson were members) who hadn't recorded any 45s but had had a track included on the *This Is Merseybeat* (LP) compilation. Professional actor Lew Collins was in the band before they recorded, which explains why they were managed by his dad and future **Iveys/Badfinger** manager Bill Collins.

They became **The Mojos** in August 1963 and, after winning a songwriting competition, got a contract with Carlin Music who leased their tapes to Decca. They got a residency at the Blue Angel and soon established themselves as one of the popular Merseybeat bands, particularly with the girls. James' real name was Stu Slater and Karlson was born Keith Alcock.

Wilkinson left after their first 45 to join The Mastersounds, who didn't make it onto vinyl. With his replacement Liverpudlian Nicky Crouch (ex-**Faron's Flamingos**), the remaining members headed for Hamburg, playing the Star

ZOOT MONEY'S BIG ROLL BAND - It Should've Been Me (LP).

Club and recording their second 45, *Everything's Alright*, whilst they were there. Regarded as a classic Merseybeat recording, this 45 took them into the Top Ten, a feat they were never able to repeat. They had a loud and lively stage act but most of their subsequent singles veered towards lightweight pop. They appeared as themselves in the 1964 movie 'Every Day's A Holiday'. They enjoyed a couple of further Top 30 hits with *Why Not Tonight* and *Seven Daffodils* before splintering in October 1964 due to differing views. Only **Stu James** and Nicky Crouch remained from the earlier line-up and they became known as Stu James and **The Mojos**. New members were Lewis Collins (ex-Gregorians) and **Aynsley Dunbar** (who'd been with **Freddie Starr** and The Flamingos). Dunbar left in September 1966 to join **John Mayall's Bluesbreakers**. He was replaced on drums by Southampton-born Steve Snake.

When the band called it quits, Collins became an actor - he appeared in the TV show 'The Professionals'. Stu James married singer Stephanie De Sykes and became a music publishing executive. Crouch quit the music business.

Compilation appearances have included: *Everything's Alright*, *Seven Daffodils* and *Forever* on *Liverpool 1963-1964, Vol. 2* (LP); *Everything's Alright* on *Mersey Beat* (2-LP), *Mersey Beat 1962-1964* (2-LP), *The Beat Scene* (CD) and *Hard-Up Heroes* (2-LP); *Don't Do It Anymore*, *Give Your Lovin' To Me*, *Forever* and *They Say* on *Mersey Sounds* (2-LP); *Forever* on *Ready, Steady, Go!* (LP) and *Beat Merchants* (2-LP) and *Until My Baby Comes Home* on *Oddities, Vol 1* (CD). (VJ/JM)

The Moles

45:     We Are The Moles/
        We Are The Moles (diff. version)   (Parlophone R 5743) 1968 R1

On its release this mysterious single, produced by **George Martin,** was rumoured to be by **The Beatles**. In fact it was **Simon Dupree and The Big Sound** playing under a pseudonym. Something of a novelty disc, it contained distorted vocals, phasing and heavy guitar. Despite some airplay it failed to achieve much commercial success.

Compilation appearances include: *We Are The Moles (Part 1)* on *My Generation* (LP), *Not Just Beat Music 1965-70* (LP), *Psychedelia At Abbey Road* (CD), *British Psychedelic Trip, Vol. 2* (LP), *Great British Psychedelic Trip, Vol. 3* (CD) and on the 4-CD set *Acid Drops, Spacedust & Flying Saucers*. (VJ)

The Moments

Personnel:	STEVIE MARRIOTT	gtr, vcls	A
	KENNY ROWE	drms	A
	JOHN WEIDER	gtr	A
	JIMMY WINSTON	bs	A

45:     α   You Really Got Me/Money   (World Artists) 196?
NB: α US only release.

This was a pre-**Small Faces Marriott** and **Winston** band. Weider was later in **Eric Burdon and The Animals** and **Family** and Rowe reappeared in **Capability Brown**.

Money, Money can also be heard on *Incredible Sound Show Stories, Vol. 9* (LP). (MWh/VJ)

Paul Monday

| 45s: | Musical Man/Wait For Me | (MCA MU 1024) 1969 |
| | Here Comes The Sun/Musical Man | (MCA MK 5008) 1969 |

These two 45s were recorded by a certain Paul Gadd. (At the time he called himself **Paul Raven**, but many of you will know him better by his later pseudonym, **Gary Glitter**).

Back in 1961 he'd met **Mike Leander** whilst working as a warm up artist on 'Ready Steady Go!' Following this he briefly fronted **The Mick Leander Orchestra** as a vocalist. In 1968 when **Leander** became head of MCA Records in the UK he signed Gadd (**Raven**) to the label and Gadd recorded these two 45s using yet another pseudonym - **Paul Monday**. *Musical Man* was written by **Leander** and, of course, *Here Comes The Sun* was a **Beatles**' song. Both flopped and Gadd reverted to the **Paul Raven** moniker for his next single. (VJ)

Money

45s:	Come Laughing Home/	
	Power Of The Rainbow	(Major Minor MM 620) 1969
	Breaking Of Her Heart/	
	Welcome My Love	(Major Minor MM 669) 1970

This soul-tinged harmony group hailed from Manchester. (VJ)

Zoot Money's Big Roll Band

Personnel:	ROGER COLLIS	gtr	AB
	JOHN HAMMOND	drms	A
	AL KIRTLEY	piano	A
	MIKE MONTGOMERY	drms	A
	ZOOT MONEY	organ, vcls	ABCDEF
	PETE BROOKS	drms	B
	KEVIN DRAKE	sax	B

ZOOT MONEY'S BIG ROLL BAND - Zoot! Live At Klook's Kleek (LP).

JOHNNY KING	bs	B
COLIN ALLEN	drms	CDE
NICK NEWELL	tenor sax	CDEF
ANDY SOMERS	gtr	CDE
CLIVE BURROWS	baritone sax	D
PAUL WILLIAMS	bs, vcls	DE
JOHNNY ALMOND	sax	E
JEFF CONDON	trumpet, flute, flugel horn	E
JOHN BEAUCHAMP	trombone	F
BERNIE BERNS	drms	F
MIKE COTTON	trumpet	F
LEM LUBIN	bs	F
MIKE MOODY	gtr	F

HCP

ALBUMS: 1(D) IT SHOULD'VE BEEN ME
(Columbia 33SX 1734) 1965 R2 -
2(E) ZOOT! - LIVE AT KLOOK'S KLEEK
(mono/stereo) (Columbia S(C)X 6075) 1966 R2 23
3( ) TRANSITION (Direction 8-63231) 1968 R1 -
4( ) ZOOT MONEY (Polydor 2482 019) 1970 SC -

NB: (3) was actually recorded by **Dantalion's Chariot** using **The Big Roll Band's** name and style. There's also a US-only album, *Welcome To My Head* (Capitol 318) 1969. (1) and (2) reissued on vinyl. (1) reissued on CD (Repertoire REP 5041) 2005 in a digipak with 10 bonus tracks and an extensive booklet. (2) reissued on CD (Repertoire REP 5004) remastered.

A's and B's Scrap Book (CD) (Repertoire REP 4796) is presented in a digipak and includes their A and B sides with an informative booklet. *A Big Time Operator* (2-CD) (Castle CMDDD 1219) 2005 is a detailed and expansive compilation of his work.

EP: 1(A) BIG TIME OPERATOR (Columbia SEG 8519) 1966 R3

HCP

45s: α The Uncle Willie/Zoot's Suite (Decca F 11954) 1964 R1 -
Good/Bring It On Home To Me (Columbia DB 7518) 1965 SC -
Please Stay/
You Know You'll Cry (Columbia DB 7600) 1965 SC -
Something Is Worrying Me/
Stubborn Kind Of Fellow (Columbia DB 7697) 1965 SC -
β The Many Faces Of Love/
Jump Back (Columbia DB 7768) 1965 SC -
Let's Run For Cover/
Self-Discipline (Columbia DB 7876) 1966 SC -
Big Time Operator/
Zoot's Sermon (Columbia DB 7975) 1966 SC 25
The Star Of The Show (The La La Song)/
The Mound Moves (Columbia DB 8090) 1966 SC -
Nick Knack/
I Really Learnt How To Cry (Columbia DB 8172) 1967 SC -
No One But You/Prisoner (Polydor 2058 020) 1970 -

NB: α as **Zoot Money**. β as **Paul Williams** and **Zoot Money Band**.

Zoot Money (real name George Bruno) was originally from Bournemouth, where he played in a band with John Henry Rostill prior to forming De Big Roll Band. This operated with line-up 'A' until 1963 but by the time they left Bournemouth to move up to London in 1964, when **Money** had been invited by **Alexis Korner** to play in **Blues Incorporated**, various personnel changes had led to a new line-up 'B'. Once in London Clive Burrows and **Paul Williams** were added to the line-up. They'd both been in The Blue Flames (**Georgie Fame**'s backing group) and **The Wes Minster Five**. Burrows was replaced by **Johnny Almond** in mid-1965 and Jeff Condon joined around the same time. **Paul Williams** recorded a couple of solo 45s in 1964 and 1965 on which he was backed by **The Big Roll Band**. Later, after leaving the band, he recorded a third 45 in 1968 on which he was backed by all **The Big Roll Band** members except **Zoot Money**.

They played a sophisticated form of R&B tinged with soul and a splatter of jazz. *It Should've Been Me* includes a great selection of R&B with a great mod/Hammond sound. Highlights include: - *Back Door Blues*, *Uncle Willie* and *The Cat*. They soon became a very popular live attraction, particularly on the London club circuit. **Money** was a great showman who loved dressing up and they became quite popular, yet despite this they only enjoyed one hit single, *Big Time Operator*.

In July 1967 the core of the band (**Money**, Somers and Allen) evolved into psychedelic outfit **Dantalion's Chariot**. **Paul Williams** went on to play for

John Mayall and **Juicy Lucy** and Clive Burrows played for **Alan Price**. Condon played trumpet for the Big Roll Band in its final days. The *Transition* album listed above was actually recorded by a **Dantalion's Chariot** line-up: **Zoot Money,** Andy Somers, Collin Allen, Nick Newell, Jeff Condon and Pat Donaldson were the performers on the album.

Zoot's Sermon, *The Mound Moves* and *I Really Learnt How To Cry* are all **Money**/Somers compositions that are utterly different from the group's regular output. *Zoot's Sermon* is a gospel-tinged instrumental; *The Mound Moves* is outrageously raw, powerful and at times aggressive psychedelic/jazz instrumental and *I Really Learnt How To Cry* is a quite powerful mod-psych tune.

Andy Somers was the Andy Summers (later of Police). He'd changed his surname to Somers for the second part of the sixties. Upon the demise of **Dantalion's Chariot**, **Zoot Money** went to LA in March '68 joining **Eric Burdon and The New Animals** in time to help record their *Every One Of Us Album*. Andy Somers later followed Zoot to the US the following Autumn and both appear on **Eric Burdon and The New Animals**' *Love Is* release. Whilst in the States **Zoot Money** recorded a US-only album, *Welcome To My Head*, with different session musicians not included in the personnel line-ups at the start of this article. These comprised David Cohen, Don Peake, (gtrs) Gary Coleman (perc), Vincent De Rosa, Bill Henshaw, Henry Sigismonti, Arthur Maebe (French horns), James Getzoff (concertmaster) Jim Gordon (drms), Lyle Ritz (bs) and Mike Rubini (keyboards). The album was produced by **Eric Burdon and The New Animals** guitarist Vic Briggs.

In late 1969 **Zoot Money** returned to London forming **Zoot Money's Music Band** '69 (line-up E).

Zoot Money was in **Centipede**, **Grimms** and **Ellis** in the seventies. He also played on various **Kevin Ayers** and **Kevin Coyne** albums and went on to record a solo album, *Mr. Money* (Magic Moon/MPL LUNE 1) 1980. He is now a bit of an actor. Sadly Kevin Drake, Johnny King and Mike Montgomery are all now dead.

A Big Time Operator is a 2-CD set. The first disc and the first 10 tracks of the second disc capture his r'n'b live in the London ballrooms during 1965 and 1966. The other tracks on disc 2 are from his solo career around 1972 and from the 1995 Alexis Korner Memorial Concert. The set is accompanied by liner notes and interviews conducted by David Wells. He's definitively in the same league as **Brian Auger** and **Georgie Fame** in the genre of jazzy R&B.

Compilation appearances have included: *Walking The Dog* on *The Mod Scene* (CD); *Zoot's Suite* on *Mod Scene, Vol. 2* (CD); *The Uncle Willie* on *Hard-Up Heroes* (2-LP), *Pop Inside The '60s, Vol. 2* (CD), *The R&B Scene* (CD), *Sixties Lost And Found, Vol. 2* (LP) and *Sixties Explosion, Vol. 1* (CD); *Get On The Right Track, Baby* and *Walking The Dog* on *British R'n'B Explosion, Vol. 1* (CD) and *The Soul Of British RnB 1962-68*; and *The Uncle Willie*, *Zoot's Suite*, *Walking The Dog* and *Get On The Right Track, Baby* on *Broken Dreams, Vol. 7* (LP). (VJ/VB/JO)

ZOOT MONEY - Transition (LP).

MONUMENT - First Monument (CD).

Mongrel

Personnel:	ROBERT BRADY	keyb'ds, vcls	AB
	MEGAN DAVIES	bs	AB
	TOM FARNELL	drms	AB
	CHARLIE GRIMA	perc	AB
	ROGER HILL	gtr	A
	RICK PRICE	bs, vcls	AB
	KEITH SMART	drms	AB
	STUART SCOTT	gtr, vcls	B

ALBUM: 1(A) GET YOUR TEETH INTO THIS
(Polydor 2383 182) 1973 SC

45s:	Lonely Street/Sing A Little Song	(Polydor 2058 813) 1972
	Last Night/Twist Her Hand	(Polydor 2058 347) 1973

This short-lived progressive outfit's sole album is now hard to find and hence a minor collectable. They originally formed as ex-**Move** man **Carl Wayne**'s backing band and included another former **Move** member, **Rick Price**, on bass and vocals whilst drummer Keith Smart had previously been with **Lemon Tree**. When Roger Hill departed to join **Fairport Convention** he was replaced by Stuart Scott.

Price, Grima, Smart and later Brady were all in **Roy Wood**'s **Wizzard**. (MWh)

The Mongrels

45s:	I Love To Hear/Everywhere	(Decca F 12003) 1964 SC
	My Love For You/Stewball	(Decca F 12086) 1965 SC

Ian Stewart of **The Rolling Stones** had some involvement on **The Mongrels**' second 45. (VJ)

Monopoly

Personnel:	LENNY ABLETHORPE	drms	A
	HARTLEY CAIN	gtr	A
	LOU CLARKE	bs	A
	RAYMOND FROGGATT	vcls	A

45s:	House Of Lords/Magic Carpet	(Polydor 56164) 1967
	We're All Going To The Seaside/	
	It Isn't Easy	(Polydor 56188) 1967
	We Belong Together/Gone Tomorrow	(Pye 7N 17940) 1970

This band came from Birmingham. *House Of Lords* was a **Bee Gees** song. This was **Raymond Frogatt**'s band. (VJ/AMH)

The Monotones

Personnel incl: BRIAN ALEXANDER

45s:	What Would I Do/Is It Right?	(Pye 7N 15608) 1964
	It's Great/Anymore	(Pye 7N 15640) 1964
	No Waiting/Like A Lover Should	(Pye 7N 15761) 1965
	Something's Hurting Me/A Girl Like That	(Pye 7N 15814) 1965

This mid-sixties group came from Southend.

Compilation appearances have included: *Something's Hurtin' Me* on *The R&B Era, Vol. 2* (LP & CD) and *Beat Us If You Can! Vol. 1* (LP); and *Is It Right?* on *Hippy Hippy Shake* (CD). (VJ)

The Montanas

Personnel:	JOHN ELCOCK	gtr	A
	WILL HAYWARD	ld gtr	A
	GRAHAM HOLLIS	drms	A
	JOHNNY JONES	vcls	AB
	TERRY ROWLEY	bs, flute, keyb'ds	AB
	GEORGE DAVIS	keyb'ds	B
	ROB ELCOCK	drms	B
	IAN LEES	gtr	B

45s: (UK)	All That Is Mine Can Be Yours/ How Can I Tell?	(Piccadilly 7N 35262) 1965
	That's When Happiness Began/ Goodbye Little Girl	(Pye 7N 17183) 1966 R1
	Ciao Baby/Anyone There	(Pye 7N 17282) 1967
	Take My Hand/Top Hat	(Pye 7N 17338) 1967
	You've Got To Be Loved/ Difference Of Opinion	(Pye 7N 17394) 1967
	A Step In The Right Direction/Someday	(Pye 7N 17499) 1968
	You're Making A Big Mistake/Run To Me	(Pye 7N 17597) 1968
	Roundabout/Mystery	(Pye 7N 17697) 1968
α	Ciao Baby/Someday	(Pye 7N 17729) 1969

NB: α reissue. *You've Got To Be Loved (Singles A & B)* (Sequel NEMCD 994) compiles all of their 45 tracks plus some outtakes and unreleased versions.

45s: (US)	That's When Happiness Began / Goodbye Little Girl	(Warner Bros 5871) 1966
	Anyone There / Ciao Baby	(Warner Bros 7021) 1967
	Anyone There / Ciao Baby	(Warner Bros 7208) 1968
	Take My Hand / Top Hat	(Independence 79) 1967
	You've Got To Be Loved / Difference Of Opinion	(Independence 83) 1967
	I'm Gonna Change / A Step In The Right Direction	(Independence 87) 1968
	Run To Me / You're Making A Big Mistake	(Independence 89) 1968/69
	Heaven Help You / Round About	(Independence 93) 1969
	Hey Diddle Diddle / Let's Get A Little Sentimental	(Decca 32682) 1969

This outfit formed in Dudley, Worcestershire and was essentially a mainstream harmony-pop band. Elcock had previously been in **Finders Keepers**. They issued a series of beautifully crafted mid-sixties singles that marked the development of beat into summer pop with even a hint of psychedelia, without getting the success they deserved. Their better efforts included *A Step In The Right Direction* and *Ciao Baby*, which both easily had the potential to be a hit. An earlier effort, *That's When Happiness Begins*, was an uncharacteristic pulsating garage rocker. *Syde Trips, Vol. 4* (LP) includes *Together* which was intended as their follow-up to *Roundabout*, but was shelved when the band split up early in 1969. *Together* shows that the band had by then developed quite a good melodic sound and had also discovered the mellotron. Somehow, though, the single really drags.

Apparently the band spent time soaking up the sun in California which may explain why their profile was high enough in the US to warrant so many 45 releases. One of these, *You've Got To Be Loved* was a big local hit in Chicago and the tiny Independence label pressed up thousands and thousands of copies - hoping it would break nationwide. It did see some action in some other US towns and did chart, but it was not the hit they were expecting. Another US 45, *Heaven Help You* was not released in the UK.

After their demise in early 1969 Terry Rowley and John Jones formed **Trapeze**. A new line-up was put together when the duo returned from **Trapeze**. This included another former **Finders Keepers** member Ian Lees and Rob Elcock, who'd been in **Sounds Of Blue**. The new line-up recorded three 45s on MAM: *Uncle John's Band, No Smoke Without Fire* and *Suzanne* before calling it a day for good. Rowley rejoined **Trapeze** and Less joined Light Fantastic.

Compilation appearances have included: *That's When Happiness Begins* on *Garage Punk Unknowns, Vol. 5* (LP), *Paisley Pop - Pye Psych (& Other Colours) 1966-1969* (CD) and *Freakbeat Freakout* (CD); *A Step In The Right Direction* on *Rubble, Vol. 10 - Professor Jordan's Magic Sound Show* (LP); *Take My Hand* on *Ripples, Vol. 3* (CD); *Ciao Baby* on *Ripples, Vol. 4* (CD) and on the 2-CD set *We Love The Pirates: Charting The Big 'L' Fab 40*; *Difference Of Opinion* on *Ripples, Vol. 6* (CD) and *We Can Fly, Vol 1* (CD); *You're Making A Big Mistake* and *I'm Gonna Change* on *Ripples, Vol. 7* (CD); *You've Got To Be Loved* and *Sammy* on *Ripples, Vol. 2* (CD); *Together* on *Syde Trips, Vol. 4* (LP); *That's When Happiness Began, Goodbye Little Girl, All That Is Mine Can Be Yours* and *How Can I Tell* on *Sixties Years, Vol. 6* (CD); *Hey Grandma, You've Got To Be Loved* and *Bend Me Shape Me* on *Top Of The Pops No. 178* (LP) and *Mystery* on *Colour Me Pop, Vol 1* (CD); and *The Roundabout* on *Haunted - Psychedelic Pstones, Vol 2* (CD). (VJ/SR/BM/MW/JM)

Monument

Personnel:	JAKE BREWSTER	drms	A
	MARVE FLETCHLEY	bs	A
	STEVEN LOWE	vcls, keyb'ds	A
	WES TRUVOR	gtr	A

ALBUM: 1(A) THE FIRST MONUMENT (Beacon BEAS 15) 1971 R2

NB: (1) reissued on vinyl (Black Widow BWR 041) 2000 and on CD (Audio Archives AACD 010).

This was a rather mystical progressive album, which is now rare and sought-after by collectors. All four of those listed above were members of **Zior** and the album was the result of a drunken all-night jam session, which is probably why it's such a mish-mash of tempo changes and different styles. The early seventies saw a rising interest in black magic in rock and this band was actually fronted by a coven member. So there are song titles like *Boneyard Bumne* and *Stale Flesh* on an album that is mostly keyboard-driven with operatic vocals. (VJ)

Mooche

Personnel:	JEFF DANN	drms	A
	IAN PEARCE	ld gtr, vcls	A
	DAVE SOARS	bs, vcls	A
	BRIAN 'SPUD' TATUM	organ, ld vcls	A
	DAVE WINTHROPE	sax, vcls	A

45: Hot Smoke And Sassafras/
Seen Through A Light (Pye 7N 17735) 1969 R1

This band operated from the Chelmsford/Sudbury area and enjoyed quite a following in East Anglia. Tatum had earlier played in The Baskervilles who did not make it onto vinyl and Winthrope went on to **Supertramp** in the early seventies.

The 45, which has a great version of Bubble Puppy's *Hot Smoke And Sassafras* on the 'A' side and a good workout on the flip, is really a bit special.

Compilation appearances include: *Seen Through A Light* on *Mynd The Gap* (LP), *Jagged Time Lapse, Vol 2* (CD) and on the 3-CD box set *Ars Longa Vita Brevis: A Compendium Of Progressive Rock 1967-1974*; whilst *Hot Smoke And Sassafras* is on *We Can Fly, Vol 1* (CD) and it was also the title track to *Hot Smoke And Sassafras - Psychedelic Pstones, Vol 1* (CD). (VJ/MWh/IP)

Mood Mosaic

Personnel incl:	KEITH WEST	A
	MARK WIRTZ	A

ALBUM: 1(A) MOOD MOSAIC (Columbia SX 6153) 1967 R1

NB: (1) also issued in stereo on Studio Two (TWO 160) in 1967 (SC).

45s:	A Touch Of Velvet, A String Of Brass/		
	Bond Street P.M.	(Columbia DB 7801) 1966 SC	
	Chinese Chequers/		
	The Real Mr. Smith	(Columbia DB 8149) 1967 SC	
	The Yellow Spotted Capricorn/		
	(Flip by different artist)	(Parlophone R 5716) 1968	
Reissues:	A Touch Of Velvet, A String Of Brass/		
	Bond Street P.M.	(Columbia DB 8618) 1969	
	A Touch Of Velvet, A String Of Brass/		
	Bond Street P.M.	(Soul Supply 755102) 1984	

Mood Mosaic was an instrumental pop outfit. **Keith West** was the vocalist in **Tomorrow** and **Mark Wirtz** was their producer. Their first 45 was used as a theme tune for 'Beat Club' in Germany and Dave Lee Travis brought it back with him and used it on his show. Great swinging sixties kitsch, it's also played on the Northern soul scene.

You can also check out *Why Can't There Be More Love* on *Justafixation* (LP). (VJ)

Mood of Hamilton

Personnel incl: HAMILTON KING

45: Why Can't There Be More Love?/
King's Message (Columbia DB 8304) 1967 SC

Soul man Hamilton King was responsible for this single whose 'A' side is described in the psychedelic fanzine '117' as 'a mindblowing psychedelic nugget', which is an exaggeration, although it does have a good guitar fade-out. (MWh/VJ)

The Moody Blues

Personnel:	GRAEME EDGE	drms	AB
	DENNY LAINE	gtr, vcls	A
	MIKE PINDER	keyb'ds, vcls	AB
	RAY THOMAS	horns, vcls	AB
	CLINT WARWICK	bs	A
	JUSTIN HAYWARD	gtr, vcls	B
	JOHN LODGE	bs, vcls	B

THE MOODY BLUES - Magnficent Moodies (LP).

ALBUMS: 1(A) THE MAGNIFICENT MOODIES
(up to   (Decca LK 4711) 1966 R1 -
1976) 2(B) DAYS OF FUTURE PAST
       (mono/stereo)   (Deram DML/SML 707) 1967 SC/- 27
    3(B) IN SEARCH OF THE LOST CHORD
       (mono/stereo)   (Deram DML/SML 717) 1968 SC/- 5
    4(B) ON THE THRESHOLD OF A DREAM (w/booklet)
       (mono/stereo)   (Deram DML/SML 1035) 1969 SC/- 1
    5(B) TO OUR CHILDRENS' CHILDREN (w/insert)
                                (Threshold THM/THS 1) 1969 2
    6(B) A QUESTION OF BALANCE   (Threshold THS 3) 1970 1
    7(B) EVERY GOOD BOY DESERVES FAVOUR
                                (Threshold THS 5) 1971 1
    8(B) SEVENTH SOJOURN   (Threshold THS 7) 1972 5
    9(B) THIS IS THE MOODY BLUES (2-LP Compilation)
                                (Threshold MB 1/2) 1974 14

NB: (2) - (5) released on London in the US. (2) and (3) were reissued on Deram in 1984. (1) reissued on CD (Decca 8207 582) 1988 and again (Repertoire REP 4232-WY) with seven bonus tracks. (2) reissued on CD (Threshold 820 006-2) 1986 and again on CD (Deram 844 767-2). (3) reissued on CD (London 8201 682) 1988 and again on CD (Deram 844 768-2). (4) reissued on CD (London 8201 702) 1986 and again on CD (Deram 844 769-2). (5) reissued on CD (London 8203 642) 1986 and again on CD (Threshold 844 770-2). (6) reissued on CD (Decca 8203 292) 1988 and again on CD (Threshold 884 771-2). (7) reissued on CD (London 8201 602) 1986 and again on CD (Threshold 844 772-2). (8) reissued on CD (Decca 8201 592) 1986 and again remastered on CD (Threshold 844 773-2). (9) reissued on CD (Threshold 820 007-2) 1989.

Later compilations comprise *Out Of This World* (K-Tel NE 1051) 1979, *Go Now* (AKA AKA 5) 1983 and *The Moody Blues Collection* (Castle CCSLP 105) 1985. Compilations available on CD include: - *Collection: Moody Blues* (Castle Collector CCSCD 105) 1986, *Greatest Hits: Moody Blues* (Polydor 840 659 2) 1990, *Blue* (Pickwick PWKS 4022 P) 1990 and *Voices In The Sky* (Decca 8201552) 1991. There's also a box set *Time Traveller* released in 1994. This is a retrospective from 1967 to 1992 with no real rarities. The fifth CD, a 'bonus', contains one new recording, *This Is A Moment* plus eight tracks from a 1992 concert. *The Singles +* (BR Music BS 8123 2) 2000 is a 3-CD set available as a Dutch import. *The Collection* (Universal 560 241 2) 2001 is a 2-CD set. *Moody Blues Caught Live + 5* (CD) (Threshold 820 161-2) is a 14-track combination of their classic songs recorded in 1977 plus five brand new studio tracks.

EP: 1(A) THE MOODY BLUES   (Decca DFE 8622) 1965 SC

NB: There's also an interesting French EP containing: *Boulevard De La Madeleine/People Gotta Go/This Is My House/Life's Not Life* (Decca 457.117M) Jun. 1966. The track *Life's Not Life* was not released in the UK until 1967, and *People Gotta Go* wasn't issued elsewhere, although it was covered by **Loose Ends** as *Send The People Away*.

45s: Lose Your Money/
(up to Steal Your Heart Away   (Decca F 11971) 1964 R1 -
1976)   Go Now!/It's Easy Child   (Decca F 12022) 1964 1
        I Don't Want To Go On Without You/
        Time Is On My Side   (Decca F 12095) 1965 33

THE MOODY BLUES - Days Of Future Past (LP).

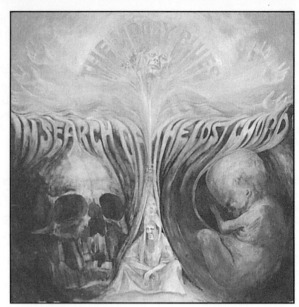

THE MOODY BLUES - In Search Of The Lost Chord (LP).

From The Bottom Of My Heart/
And My Baby's Gone   (Decca F 12166) 1965 22
Everyday/You Don't (All The Time)   (Decca F 12266) 1965 44
Boulevard De La Madelaine/
This Is My House (But Nobody Calls)   (Decca F 12498) 1966 -
α Life's Not Life/He Can Win   (Decca F 12543) 1967 R1 -
Fly Me High/
Really Haven't Got The Time   (Decca F 12607) 1967 SC -
Love And Beauty/
Leave This Man Alone   (Decca F 12670) 1967 SC -
Nights In White Satin/Cities   (Deram DM 161) 1967 19
Voices In The Sky/
Dr. Livingstone I Presume   (Deram DM 196) 1968 27
Ride My See-Saw/Simple Fame   (Deram DM 213) 1968 42
Never Come The Day/
So Deep Within You   (Deram DM 247) 1969 -
Watching And Waiting/Out And In   (Threshold TH 1) 1969 -
Question/Candle Of Life   (Threshold TH 4) 1970 2
Isn't Life Strange/After You Came   (Threshold TH 9) 1972 13
I'm Just A Singer/For A Lady   (Threshold TH 13) 1973 36
Reissues: Nights In White Satin/Cities   (Deram DM 161) 1972 9
Question/Candle Of Life   (Old Gold OG 9348) 1983 -
Nights In White Satin/Cities   (Old Gold OG 9349) 1983 -
Go Now!/
I Don't Want To Go On Without You (Old Gold OG 9509) 1985 -

NB: α withdrawn.

The Moody Blues, who started as an R&B band, are an essential band for fans of grandiose quasi-classical progressive rock. They were a very professional outfit and much of their music was extremely beautiful. Once they'd found a successful formula, though, their reluctance to change from it inevitably time-limited their success.

The Moody Blues formed in Birmingham in May 1964, an amalgam of various members of other Birmingham groups. **Denny Laine**, the founding member, had previously fronted Denny and The Diplomats. **Ray Thomas** and **Mike Pinder** had been with El Riot and The Rebels. **Graeme Edge** joined from **Gerry Levene and The Avengers** and only bassist Clint Warwick was new to the Birmingham music scene. The new band got Tony Secunda to be their manager and he negotiated them a contract with Decca Records.

In spite of an appearance on 'Ready Steady Go!' to help promote their first single, *Lose Your Money* was a pretty ordinary R&B number and it failed to sell in sufficient quantities to make the Charts. Their big breakthrough came with the follow-up, *Go Now*, a song which had been a R&B hit in the States for Bessie Banks. It was a very powerful song with some vibrant piano and captivating vocals, topping the Charts here and climbing to No 10 in the US. They followed this initial success with a series of more minor hits:- *I Don't Want To Go On Without You* (which had been a Drifters' 'B' side), *From The Bottom Of My Heart* (which as well as being a Top 30 hit here got to No 93 in the US) and Buddy Holly's *Everyday*. In the States *Stop!*

(which was not released as a 45 here got to No 98). Line-up (A) also recorded an album, *The Magnificent Moodies*. Musically it followed the same pop/R&B format as their early singles. Aside from *Go Now*, it is notable for **Ray Thomas**' version of Gershwin's *It Ain't Necessarily So* (which Bronski Beat later had a bit hit with) and a frantic version of Sonny Boy Williamson's *Bye Bye Bird*. It didn't sell too well and by the time **Denny Laine** and Clint Warwick decided to leave in August 1966 the band was sliding rapidly down a greasy pole. In the short-term **Laine** went solo but soon after he joined **Balls** and he was then in **Wings** from 1973. Clint Warwick turned his back on the music business for good.

The band's two new members were **John Lodge**, another Brummie who'd earlier been with **Thomas** and Pinder in El Riot and The Rebels. In the interim he'd been with other local bands, such as The Carpetbaggars, **The John Bull Breed** and The Falcons and **Justin Hayward**, who originated from Swindon. **Hayward** had released some solo 45s and been in **The Wilde Three**.

Their next 45, *Boulevard De La Madelaine*, had been recorded by the previous line-up. It was an exquisite French-style disc which deserved to do well but it failed to make the Charts at all. A similar fate befell their three following singles and even a new manager, Brian Epstein, seemed unable to arrest the trend.

In 1967 the band embarked on a drastic change of direction. They acquired a mellotron and started playing a form of quasi-classical music with deep, often poetic lyrics. Their next album, *Days Of Future Past*, was recorded with The London Festival Orchestra. This was one of the earliest concept albums based around the theme of different times of the day and night. The original intention had been for the band and orchestra to record Dvorak's *New World Symphony* together, but his was dropped early on. On what finally materialised the orchestrated passages were slotted between and around **The Moody Blues**' tracks; the band and orchestra didn't actually accompany each other. The album peaked at No 27 here and at No 3 in the US where it earned them a gold disc. One of its finest tracks, **Justin Hayward**'s beautiful, melodic *Nights In White Satin* was put out on 45. It got to No 19 in the UK registering their first Top 20 hit since *Go Now!* Another track, *Tuesday Afternoon* was issued as a 45 in the US, where it climbed to No 24. The significance of *Days Of Future Past* should not be underestimated - not only did it represent a drastic change of musical direction for the band it also helped encourage the avalanche of concept albums that followed.

In Search Of A Lost Chord was their next concept album. Out went the orchestra and they played all 33 instruments featured themselves. The many Eastern instruments and chanted vocals made it a typical period piece. Again sales were very good. It climbed to No 5 here and No 23 in the US, earning them a second gold disc. Among its finer moments were the delightful and melodic *Voices In The Sky* (which got to No 23 when issued as a single in the UK) and the more upbeat *Ride My See Saw* (UK No 42, US No 61). These placings could probably have been higher - most fans tended to buy their albums.

THE MOODY BLUES - On The Threshold Of A Dream (LP).

THE MOODY BLUES - To Our Children's Children's Children (LP).

1969 saw the release of *On The Threshold Of A Dream* - another excellent concept album. Indeed it was their best yet, topping the Charts in the UK and climbing to No 20 in the US where it earned them a third gold disc. Housed in a gatefold sleeve with lyric inset it was full of lovely melodic compositions for which the band had by now become renowned. The songwriting credits were shared pretty equally between the four members. There's not a naff track on the album, although arguably there wasn't an outstanding one either. A fact illustrated when **Justin Hayward**'s *Never Comes The Day*, the one selected for 45 release, failed to make the UK Top 50 and faltered at No 91 in the US.

In December 1969 the band relocated to Cobham in Surrey. Having already set up their own Threshold label they now proceeded to open a chain of Threshold Record Stores. Their first release on this label was the 45, *Watching And Waiting*, in October 1969. This didn't sell well but their album, *To Our Children's Children*, peaked at No 2 here and No 14 in the US, where it won them their fourth gold disc. It was another fine album in their now well tried and tested formula of grandiose rock songs with meaningful lyrics.

On 12 December 1969 the group performed at London's Royal Albert Hall. This appearance was recorded and later included as part of the album *Caught Live Plus Five*.

Justin Hayward's *Question*, released in Spring 1970, was another of his superb melodic pieces. It gave them their first UK Top 5 his since *Go Now!* and was only kept off the top by the England World Cup Squad's *Back Home*. In the US it got to No 21. It was culled from their *A Question Of Balance* album, another superb effort which spent three weeks on top of the UK Charts and got to No 3 in the US. It became their fifth gold disc. Other highlights on the album were **Ray Thomas**'s *And The Tide Rushes In* and **Mike Pinder**'s *Melancholy Man*.

Every Good Boy Deserves Favour was another excellent album. Another Chart topper in the UK, it got to No 2 in the US winning them their sixth consecutive gold disc. The opening cut, *Procession*, had a very Afro and Far Eastern ethnic flavour at times. It leads into **Hayward**'s *The Story In Your Eyes*, a rather up-tempo number for them which got to No 23 in the US, but was not released in the UK at the band's request. Particularly beautiful on this album is the sequence of tracks on the latter part of side 2 - *You Can Never Go Home* and *My Song*.

The band's next 45, *Isn't Life Strange*, was a **John Lodge** song. It sold quite well climbing to No 13 here and No 29 in the US in June 1972. Towards the end of what had been a quiet year for the band, *Nights In White Satin*, their finest moment on 45, was repromoted. It got to No 2 in the US where the album it was culled from, *Days Of Future Past*, peaked at No 3. Here in the UK it improved on its previous Chart placing by 10 places.

1972 also saw the release of *Seventh Sojourn*, which would prove to be their last studio album for six years. Once again sales were excellent. It got to No 5 here and topped the US Charts for five weeks, earning their

THE MOODY BLUES - A Question Of Balance (LP).

seventh consecutive gold disc. It contained some beautiful songs (*Now Horizons* and *For My Lady*) and spawned two hit singles: - *Isn't Life Strange* and *I'm Just A Singer (In A Rock And Roll Band)*.

Much of 1973 was occupied with a nine-month World Tour. Their final 45 release, *I'm Just A Singer (In A Rock And Roll Band)*, got to No 12 here and No 36 in the States. At the end of the tour the members decided to split, feeling they had achieved as much as they could. No formal announcement was ever made but the individuals concentrated on solo projects until they reformed in 1978.

This Is The Moody Blues was a double compilation of material from their second album onwards and would be a good introduction to the band for someone who hadn't heard their albums and wanted to investigate their music further.

An alternative compilation is *Out Of This World*, which contained their hits and was released to coincide with their first UK tour for six years. *Go Now* was a budget-priced compilation of material (mostly pop/R&B) by the band's first line-up. It's certainly better value than *The Moody Blues Collection*, a double budget-priced compilation of material from their first line-up, which only contains four more songs than *Go Now!*

The 4-CD overview of their work *Time Traveller* released in 1994 attracted more attention than their new albums, which attracted little attention at all.

Singles + is an excellent compilation of their pop singles and many of their finest album tracks over two CDs. This would be an excellent introduction for anyone wanting to investigate their music retrospectively.

The Collection is a 2-CD set. It contains 34 cuts covering most of the **Hayward/Lodge** era. Earlier classics like *Ride My See-saw*, *Voices In The Sky*, *Lovely To See You*, *Tuesday Afternoon* and *Question* are included.

Sadly, in the nineties the band was content to play their greatest hits dressed in tuxedos on the posh cabaret circuit. The 1997 upgrades of their seven original albums attracted far more attention than new releases like *Strange Times* (a studio effort) and the live *Hall Of Fame* at the turn of the century. In 2003, **Ray Thomas** retired although **Hayward**, **Lodge** and **Edge** continued as a core trio.

Clint Warwick (real name Albert Eccles) their original bassist died on 15 May 2004 in Birmingham, aged 63, having suffered liver damage, partly caused by heavy drinking following the death of his son Paul in 1996.

Compilation appearances have included: *Nights In White Satin* on *Wowie Zowie! World Of Progressive Music (LP)* and more recently on the 2-CD set *Sixties Summer Love* ; *Bo Diddley* and *Go Now* on *Made In England, Vol. 2* (CD); *Go Now* on the 2-CD set *60 Number Ones Of The Sixties*, *Greatest Hits Of The 60's Vol 4* (2-CD) and on *No 1s & Million Sellers Vol 4* (CD); *Love And Beauty* on *The Psychedelic Scene* (CD); *People Gotta Go* on *Rare 60's Beat Treasures, Vol. 2* (CD); *Lose Your Money, Go Now* and *I Don't Want To Go On Without You* on *Brum Beat - Midlands Beat*

Groups Of The 60's (CD); *Leave This Man Alone* on *Jagged Time Lapse, Vol 5* (CD). (VJ/BM/LBy)

Keith Moon

ALBUM: 1   TWO SIDES OF THE MOON (Polydor 2442 134) 1975 SC
NB: (1) reissued on CD (Repertoire REP 4635 WY) 1997, with some bonus tracks.

45:        Don't Worry Baby/Together   (Polydor 2058 584) 1975

Keith Moon was arguably one of the most talented rock drummers and his wild stage antics ensured he was visually one of the most exciting.

Moon, who was born on 23 August 1946 at Central Middlesex Hospital, Willesden, Middlesex, is best remembered as drummer of **The Who**. When he joined in 1964 they were The Detours but were on the verge of changing names to **The High Numbers**. He was earlier in Lee Stuart and the Escorts and in a band called The Beachcombers but not the band who issued singles.

These solo efforts were recorded after the other group members had concentrated on solo projects. Recorded in LA his album was littered with backing singers, session musicians and fellow travellers who drowned **Moon**'s vocals (though perhaps that was no bad thing). It included a new version of *The Kids Are Alright* alongside a number of cover versions like **Lennon**'s *In My Life* and *Move Over Ms. L.* and The Beach Boys' *Don't Worry Baby*, which was also selected for 45 release. Neither the album nor the single made much impression at the time though both are pretty scarce now.

His premature death - from an overdose of a drug prescribed to combat his alcoholism on 8 September 1978 - was a tragedy. (VJ)

Moonkyte

Personnel:	DAVE AMBLER	sitar, banjo, keyb'ds, flute	A
	DAVE FOSTER	gtr, hrmnca, vcls	A
	TREVOR GRAVEN	bs, vcls	A
	MICK HUMPHREYS	drms	A
	DAVE STANSFIELD	keyb'ds, vcls	A

ALBUM: 1(A)   COUNT ME OUT   (Mother SMOT 1) 1971 R3
NB: (1) has been counterfeited on vinyl and CD. (1) reissued officially on CD (Sunbeam SBRCD 006) 2005 with detailed sleevenotes.

This gentle psychedelic album has many fine moments and sounds like it was recorded in 1968. Its subject-matter is quite fantastic. One song,

THE MOODY BLUES - Every Good Boy Deserves Favour (LP).

KEITH MOON - Two Sides Of The Moon (CD).

Tapestry Girl, tells the tale of a rape which takes place amongst the figures inside an ancient goblin. Musically the songs are deceptively simple, but underscored with beautiful atmospheric touches of sitar and harmonium, sometimes recalling the best of **Bulldog Breed**. Unfortunately this album is very rare and very hard to find. Grab it whenever you come across it.

The band came from Bradford and the album came with a church spiral sleeve with an endorsement of the group by John Peel on the inner sleeve.

Compilation appearances include: *Jelly Man* on *Electric Sugar Cube Flashbacks* (CD); and *Where Will The Grass Grow* on *Electric Psychedelic Sitar Headswirlers Vol. 4* (CD). (MK)

Bobby Moonshine

45:      School Full/Strange One   (CBS 2572) 1974

Bobby Moonshine was a pseudonym for **John Gaughan**. He came from Leeds and was just nineteen when he recorded this. He was managed by Roger Greenaway and the single featured a fifties pop sound. He was in the reformed **Herman's Hermits** for a while and also cut a record under his real name. (VJ)

Moonstone

45s: Worlds Too Good For You/
         When The Moon Has Lost Its Stare   (Epic EPC 1426) 1973
         Place To Hide/Drinking Song   (Epic EPC 1961) 1973

The second 45 was produced by Chris White, who'd been in **The Zombies**.

All the songs were written by Roger Cotton (ex-**Rainbow People**) and it's possible that this band became **Life**. One of their songs was co-written with John Beecham, (ex-**Mike Cotton Sound**). (VJ/GB)

The Moonstones

Personnel: BILL HUSSEY   A
              BOB HUSSEY   A
              RUTH HUSSEY   A

45s: Heaven Fell Last Night/Little Roses   (Parlophone R 5331) 1965
         Violets Of Dawn/Power Of Decision   (Parlophone R 5497) 1966
         Louisville/How Many Times   (Mercury MF 1011) 1967

From a musical family background, **The Moonstones** consisted of two brothers and a sister. They did backing vocals for many artists including

Mike Leslie (their cousin who was also one of Joe Brown's Bruvvers and later with **Unit 4+2**). A recording contract with Columbia ensued, along with a management deal with Bryan Daly and various radio and TV work. Most of their recordings were made at Regent Sound in Denmark St, London.

In 2001, the group was preparing to return to the studio with a new album. (VJ/RH)

Moon's Train

Personnel: PETE 'FACE' ATTWOOD   bs   A
              ALEX BROWN   trumpet   A
              IAN DIBBEN   ld gtr   A
              PETER 'MOON' GOSLING   keyb'ds   A
              KEN LEAMON   sax   A
              MALCOLM PENN   drms   A

ALBUM: 1 (A)   MOON'S TRAIN   (Acetate, unissued) 1967
NB: (1) officially issued (Tenth Planet TP 037) 1999.

45:      Deed I Do/It's In My Mind   (MGM MGM 1333) 1967 SC

Moon's Train emerged out of The Preachers, a sixties R&B band who included **Peter Frampton** who left to join **The Herd**. Ex-Preachers Leamon and Attwood linked up with Brown, Dibben and Penn to form Beckenham-based **Moon's Train** and when they came to the attention of **Rolling Stone Bill Wyman** he sent them into the recording studio. In Autumn 1966 they recorded a raw amalgam of jazz and R&B. **P.P. Arnold** was invited as a guest vocalist on some of the tracks. The album was forgotten when **Stones** manager Allen Klein stopped **Wyman's** moonlighting. Gosling rejected an offer to join the embryonic **Fleetwood Mac** and ended up in the seventies kiddie's TV show 'Play School'. So, well done to David Wells' Tenth Planet label for giving this discarded album an airing 33 years later. It's no lost treasure but showcases Goslings' great voice and is worth a spin.

Back in 1967 **Moon's Train** did have a 45 released. The flip is best described as **Georgie Fame** style R'n'B with mostly fast (male) vocals but with slow beaty passages - well worth a listen. (VJ)

Anthony Moore

ALBUMS: 1   PIECES FROM THE CLOUDLAND BALLROOM
                                    (Polydor 2310 062) 1971 R1
          2   SECRETS OF THE BLUE BAG
                                    (Polydor 2310 079) 1972 R1

These obscure albums were recorded by **Moore** prior to his joining **Slapp Happy**. He also released several further solo recordings during the eighties. (VJ)

MOONKYTE - Count Me Out (CD).

Christy Moore

ALBUMS: 1   PADDY ON THE ROAD   (Mercury 20170 SMCL) 1969 R4
(up to   2   PROSPEROUS   (Tara 1001) 1972
1976)   3   WHATEVER TICKLES YOUR FANCY
                                       (Polydor 2383 344) 1975 SC
      4   CHRISTY MOORE   (Polydor 2383 426) 1976 SC

NB: (3) and (4) reissued on a 2-CD set (Raven RVCD 190) 2004, along with a non-album 'B' side *The Humours Of Ballymagash*.

This traditional folksinger came from Kildare in Eire. His first album is incredibly rare and much sought-after. Originally a bank clerk by profession, he came to England in 1966 and was working as a full-time musician who had built up a considerable following on the folk circuit by the time he recorded his first album. His disappointment when it didn't sell well led him to return to Ireland.

The second album was recorded in the vaulted cellars of Rynnes's stately Georgian house at Prosperous, Kildare. Donal Lunny, Andy Irvine and Liam O'Flynn assisted him on this album, which was instrumental in the formation of **Planxty**. It is highly-rated by fans of this music and launched him as a major force in Irish music.

The third album is also well thought of. On this **Moore** was assisted by Kevin Burke and Jimmy Faulkner. It includes a cover of *One Last Cold Kiss* by Mountain alongside lots of folk-rock material.

The fourth album was recorded with the same band, but is lower key. However, it will still interest folk and Irish music fans. (VJ)

The Gary Moore Band

Personnel: JOHN CURTIS   bs   A
                  PEARSE KELLY   drms   A
                  GARY MOORE   gtr, vcls   A
                  (JAN SCHELLHAAS   keyb'ds   A)

ALBUM: 1(A)   GRINDING STONE   (CBS 65527) 1973

NB: Reissued on CD (CBS 467449 2) 1990 and again on CD (Essential ESMCD 914) 2000. (1) reissued again in digipak format (Repertoire RES 2302) 2005.

Moore formed this short-lived outfit upon the demise of **Skid Row**. The album covered a range of musical styles from hard-rock (on *Time To Heal*) to progressivism (on the title track and *The Energy Dance*, on which keyboardist Jan Schellhaas guests) and the 17-minute guitar extravaganza *Spirit*. (VJ)

Moose

45:        Engine No 9/Do It   (Escort ERT 840) 1970

NB: 'B' side credited to Kurass.

This was a one-off project on a very obscure reggae label. (MWh)

The Moquettes

Personnel: TAGO BYERS   bs   A
                  KEITH NEVILLE   hrmnca, vcls   A
                  COLIN SHEAF   drms   A
                  RAY WHITEWORTH   gtr, organ   A

45:        Right String, But The Wrong Yo-Yo/
           You Came Along   (Columbia DB 7315) 1964 R2

This mid-sixties beat/mod outfit from Reading, Berkshire played a combination of beat and R&B. Their sole 45, which is hard to find, is now sought-after. They were a Mickie Most 'discovery' and he also produced the 45.

MOON'S TRAIN - Moon's Train (LP).

Compilation appearances include: *You Came Along* and *Right String, But The Wrong Yo Yo* on *Mickie Most Presents: British Go-Go* (LP); and *Right String, But The Wrong Yo Yo* on *Rare 60's Beat Treasures, Vol. 1* (CD) and *That Driving Beat* (CD). (VJ)

Morgan

Personnel: MAURICE BACON   drms   A
                  MORGAN FISHER   keyb'ds   A
                  BOB SAPSTEAD   bs   A
                  TIM STAFFELL   gtr, vcls   A

ALBUM: 1(A)   NOVA SOLIS   (RCA SF 8321) 1973 R1

Formed in November 1971, Maurice Bacon and Morgan Fisher had been in **The Love Affair** together. Their album was recorded in Rome and was available in the UK only on import. It tends toward complicated keyboard-dominated compositions which often became boring. A second album and a Morgan Fisher solo album were also recorded in Rome, shortly after this debut, but neither was released. Subsequently, the band split in mid-1973 with Fisher later playing in **Mott The Hoople**. **Morgan** made further albums in the late seventies and early eighties. (VJ)

Morgan and The Mark Seven

45:        I'm Gonna Turn My Life Around/
           Undercover Man   (Polydor BM 56083) 1966

A one-off 45 by an obscure band. (VJ)

David/Davy Morgan

45s: α   Tomorrow I'll Be Gone/
            Ain't Got Much More To See   (Columbia DB 7624) 1965 R1
       β   True To Life/Dawning   (Parlophone R 5692) 1968

NB: α as **Davy Morgan**. β as **David Morgan**.

The first 45 was folky, self-penned and produced by Joe Meek. Is the second by the same guy? (VJ)

John Morgan

ALBUMS: 1   KALEIDOSCOPE   (Carnaby 6302 010) 1972 R1
(up to   2   LIVE AT DURRANT HOUSE   (SWP 1007) 197? R3
1976)

Both albums are rare and sought-after, particularly the second one, which was a private pressing. He'd earlier recorded for Carnaby in the late sixties/early seventies as **The Spirit Of John Morgan**. (VJ)

Ray Morgan

			HCP
45s:	The Lord's Prayer/		
	I'll Walk With God	(Major Minor MM 640) 1969	-
	The Long And Winding Road/		
	Sweeter Wine	(B&C CB 128) 1970	32
	No More Tears/Wheel Keep Turning	(B&C CB 140) 1971	-
	Let's Fall In Love Again/		
	The Path Is Hard To Follow	(B&C CB 150) 1971	-
	Friend, Lover, Woman, Wife/		
	Burning Bridges	(B&C CB 167) 1971	-
	Wherever You Are/The Further You Look	(Decca F 13373) 1973	

-

Born in 1947, **Ray Morgan** began his singing career in 1955. He later enjoyed a minor hit in 1970 with his cover of **Lennon/McCartney**'s *The Long And Winding Road*. (VJ)

Ron Paul Morin and Wilson

Personnel incl:	RON PAUL MORIN	A
	LUKE P. WILSON	A

ALBUM: 1(A) PEACEFUL COMPANY (Sovereign SVNA 7252) 1972 SC

45: α Save The Country/
Down In The Valley To Pray (Sovereign SOV 102) 1972

NB: α as Morin and Wilson.

This album was also issued the following year with the same catalogue number but credited to **Peaceful Company**. (VJ)

Morning Glory

Personnel:	MALCOLM GRIFFITHS	trombone	A
	CHRIS LAURENCE	bs	A
	JOHN MARSHALL	drms	A
	TERJE RYPDAL	gtr	A
	JOHN SURMAN	sax	A
	JOHN TAYLOR	keyb'ds	A

ALBUM: 1(A) MORNING GLORY (Island ILPS 9237) 1973 SC

45: The Green Grass Is Dying/
Munday Street (Chapter One CH 140) 1971

The best known member of this jazz band was **John Surman**, who aside from making a number of solo recordings in the late sixties/early seventies also played with **John McLaughlin**, **Mike Westbrook** and **Trio**.

Their album was recorded live in Canterbury and produced by **Surman** and Peter Eden. (VJ)

Roger Morris

ALBUM: 1 FIRST ALBUM (Regal Zonophone SRZA 8509) 1972 R1
NB: (1) reissued on CD (Hux HUX 068) with four bonus tracks.

This rare album, produced by **Keith West** and Ken Burgess, is similar to The Band in style, with songs about the Old West. Musicians featured include **West**, John Weider, Tommy Eyre and Glenn Campbell. Originally known only to a handful of collectors and experts the album has recently been brought to the attention of a wider audience through the music press. (MWh)

Russell Morris

45s:	The Real Thing (Parts I & II)/		
	It's Only A Matter Of Time	(Decca F 22964) 1969	R1
	Rachel/Slow Joey	(Decca F 23066) 1970	

Russell Morris had nine top 40 singles in Australia between 1967 and 1972. After leaving **Somebody's Image** in 1968 he recorded the **Johnny Young** song *The Real Thing*. The single remained at No. 1 in Australia for weeks and was the largest selling single in Australia in 1969. The song itself was a 7-minute epic moving from an gentle beginning through full-on psychedelia with sound effects and phasing (ending with a Zeig Heil and a nuclear explosion!). After his follow-up, *The Girl That I Love/Part Three Into Paper Walls* also reached No. 1 in Australia he set off for the UK to promote his singles (unsuccessfully). While in England he recorded *Rachel* which also made No. 23 in Australia. He returned to Australia and released two more top ten singles. In 1973 he returned to the UK to record an album which eventually appeared as *Russell Morris* (but I don't think it got a UK release).

Compilation appearances have included: *The Real Thing* on *Rubble, Vol. 11* (LP); and *The Real Thing* and *Into Paper Walls Part 3* on *The Best Of Rubble Collection, Vol. 5* (CD). (TA)

Van Morrison

				HCP
ALBUMS:	1	BLOWIN' YOUR MIND	(London HA-Z 8346) 1967	R2 -
(up to	2	ASTRAL WEEKS	(Warner Brothers WS 1768) 1968	SC -
1976)	3	THE BEST OF VAN MORRISON (Compilation)		
			(President PTLS 1045) 1970	SC -
	4	MOONDANCE	(Warner Brothers WS 1835) 1970	SC 32
	5	HIS BAND AND STREET CHOIR		
			(Warner Brothers WS 1884) 1970	SC -
	6	TUPELO HONEY	(Warner Brothers K 46114) 1971	-
	7	ST. DOMINIC'S PREVIEW		
			(Warner Brothers K 46172) 1972	-
	8	HARD NOSE THE HIGHWAY		
			(Warner Brothers K 46242) 1973	22
	9	IT'S TOO LATE TO STOP NOW (dbl)		
			(Warner Brothers K 86007) 1974	-
	10	T.B. SHEETS (Compilation)		
			(London HSM 5008) 1974	-
	11	VEEDON FLEECE	(Warner Brothers K 56068) 1974	41

NB: (2) reissued on CD (Warner Bros K 246 024) 1987. (4) reissued on CD (WEA 246040) 1986. (5) reissued on CD (Warner Bros 7599-27188-2) 1993. (6) reissued on CD (Polydor 839 161-2) 1988. (7) reissued on CD (Polydor 839 162-2) 1988. (8) reissued on CD (Polydor 839 163-2) 1988. (9) reissued on CD (Polydor 839 166-2) 1988. (10) reissued on CD (Columbia 4678272) 1991. (11) reissued on CD (Polydor 839 164-2) 1988.

Also relevant is *Van - The Best of Van Morrison* (Polydor 841 970-2) 1990. *Payin' Dues: The Complete 'Bang Records' Sessions '67* (Fruit Tree FT 810) 2002 is a 2-CD Italian import of material he recorded for Bert Berns's label. *Bang Masters*

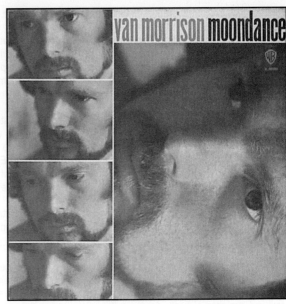

VAN MORRISON - Moondance (LP).

VAN MORRISON - Hard Nose The Highway (LP).

(CD) (Sony 468 3092) compiles his best recordings for the label. *Best Of Van Morrison* (Polydor 537 459-2) is a 20-track hits collection which includes his early hits with **Them** as well as many of his solo classics. *Complete New York Sessions 1967* (3-LP) (Get Back GET 501) is a special price set housed in a lavish front-fold sleeve. The sessions are also available as a 2-CD set (Pilot PILOT 6). *Midnight Special* (2-CD) (Pazzazz 2PAZZ002) is an excellent set which is accompanied by a four-page booklet.

45s:	Brown-Eyed Girl/		
(up to	Goodbye Baby (Baby Goodbye)	(London HLZ 10150)	1967
1976)	Come Running/Crazy Love	(Warner Brothers WB 7383)	1970
	Domino/Sweet Jannie	(Warner Brothers WB 7434)	1970
	Wild Night/When That Evening		
	Sun Goes Down	(Warner Brothers K 10120)	1971
	Jackie Wilson Said/		
	You've Got The Power	(Warner Brothers K 16210)	1972
	Warm Love/I Will Be There	(Warner Brothers K 16299)	1973
	Caldonia/What's Up, Crazy Pup	(Warner Brothers K 16392)	1974
	Bulbs/		
	Who Was That Masked Man	(Warner Brothers K 16486)	1974
Reissues:	Brown-Eyed Girl/		
	Goodbye Baby (Baby Goodbye)	(President PT 328)	1970 SC
	Brown-Eyed Girl/		
	Goodbye Baby (Baby Goodbye)	(London HLM 10453)	1974

An innovative and eccentric figure in the history of rock **Van Morrison** has drawn on a very diverse range of influences fusing R&B, jazz, blues and Celtic folk and enjoying a strong and flourishing cult following and periods of commercial success in his long and prolific career.

Van Morrison was born on 31 August 1945 in Belfast, Northern Ireland. He soon developed an interest in jazz and the blues, and played guitar and soprano sax with various local semi-professional groups, including country-rockers Deanie Sands and The Javelins. In 1961 he toured Britain and Europe with local R&B group The Monarchs, and recorded a European 45 with them (detailed in the **Them** entry). Then, in late 1963, he formed **Them** with members of The Monarchs and some old schoolfriends.

In 1967, **Morrison** left **Them** and returned to Belfast in a depressed state. This was altered when producer Bert Berns (who'd already worked with **Morrison** and **Them**) sent him an air ticket to New York. There he recorded several songs. First to be released was the classic *Brown-Eyed Girl*, which got to No 10 in the US Charts. Berns then released a whole album of **Morrison** material, *Blowin' Your Mind*, without the singer even knowing. It reached No. 14, and most of it later resurfaced on his *T.B. Sheets* compilation. A couple of months later Berns died of a heart attack. **Morrison**, free to negotiate himself a new deal, eventually signed to Warner Brothers.

Astral Weeks, his first solo album proper, showed a sharp change of musical direction. His earlier work had been R&B-based, but this contained much subtler material. Recorded in 48 hours in New York, the music was a finely textured backdrop of gently flowing guitars, flute, sax and drums for

Morrison's distinctive vocals. The lyrics are full of romanticism and wistfulness, but the album failed to produce a hit single and sales were slow. It never got into the charts on either side of the Atlantic, but many now consider it one of rock's top albums.

His follow-up, *Moondance*, was an effective amalgam of his earlier R&B work and the subtler sound of *Astral Weeks*. It climbed to No 32 here, becoming his first UK hit album, and No 29 in the US. It also spawned a hit single, *Come Running*, which climbed to No 39.

His Band And The Street Choir was disappointing, though it did get to No 32 in the US and spawned a hit single there, *Domino*, which got to No 9. By contrast, *Tupelo Honey*, a 1971 collection of love songs to his wife Janet Planet, marked a return to top form, peaking at No 27 in the US. Prior to its release **Morrison** had assembled the 11-piece Caledonia Soul Orchestra, which included guitarist John Platania, who had become pivotal to his studio work, and a string quartet. He also enjoyed three further US hit singles during 1971 - *Blue Money* (No 23), *Call Me Up In Dreamland* (No 95) and *Wild Nights* (No 28). Early in 1974 the title cut from *Tupelo Honey* was released on 45 in the US and climbed to No 47. The strength of material on this album is evidenced by the number of artists who covered its songs - Martha Reeves (*Wild Nights*), Richie Havens (*Tupelo Honey*) and **Dusty Springfield** and Jackie de Shannon (*I Wanna Roo You*). He also co-wrote *4% Pantomime* with The Band in 1971 and sang with Robbie Robertson on *Cahoots*.

St. Dominic's Preview (1972) was another of his better albums. It climbed to No 15 in the US and spent three months in the Charts. He turned in a barnstorming vocal performance on *Listen To The Lion*, and his lively tribute to soul singer Jackie Wilson, *Jackie Wilson Said (I'm In Heaven When You Smile)*, was put out on 45 and gave him another minor US hit, halting at No 61. *Hard Nose The Highway* (1973) was less consistent than his earlier offerings, but the mellow, ten minute-long *Autumn Song* was a tour de force alongside which some of the other tracks paled into insignificance. Here in the UK it proved to be his best-selling album yet, peaking at No 22, five places higher than it could manage in the US.

By 1973 **Morrison** was an established star, but his private life was in turmoil. He divorced Janet Planet and returned from the US West Coast to his native Ireland. The intensely personal songs he wrote upon his return appeared on the album, *Veedon Fleece*, which was released the following year. It wasn't one of his best, but did quite well commercially, rising to No 41 here and No 53 in the US. After his return to Ireland his career entered lean times, and his record companies did what they could to keep interest in him alive. London put out the *T. B. Sheets* compilation in January 1974, which consisted of tracks from the *Blowin' Your Mind* sessions. His much acclaimed live shows were well captured on the double album *It's Too Late To Stop Now*, which found **Morrison** and the Caledonia Soul Orchestra in fine fettle. It was therefore something of a surprise that **Morrison** chose to disband the latter in March 1974 and tour Europe with a five-piece band.

The mid-seventies were certainly a trough in **Morrison's** career, but he returned rejuvenated towards the end of the decade to take his flagging career to new heights. Today he remains extremely popular, with a very large and loyal following. Of his earlier recordings, *Astral Weeks* and *Moondance* are particularly recommended, and try to hear *Autumn Song* (on *Hard Nose The Highway*) if you haven't already.

Payin' Dues: The Complete 'Bang Records' Sessions '67 is a 2-CD Italian import, which will attract fans and collectors alike. It covers the period between his departure from **Them** and the release of *Astral Weeks*. Featured are his first US solo hit *Brown Eyed Girl*; the *Blowin' Your Mind* album, the start of a second album and 34 short compositions, mostly of under a minute long. Recommended. *Bang Masters* (CD) compiles his best recordings for that label and contains a hint of what was to follow with his solo hit *Brown Eyed Girl*, early attempts at *Beside You* and *Madame George* and the emotional *T.B. Sheets*. *Best Of* is a 20-track collection newly remastered which includes his early hits with **Them** alongside classics like *Brown-Eyed Girl*, *Moondance*, *Domino* and *Jackie Wilson Said*.

Complete New York Sessions is a lavish special price 3-LP set containing all of these legendary recordings. It includes *Brown Eyed Girl* and two whole sides entitled *Jamming*. Musically his garage sound with **Them** and more thoughtful, spiritual style showcased on *Astral Weeks* are both evident here. The set is also available as a 2-CD package.

His compilation appearances have included *Into The Mystic* on Warner Brothers' 1970 *Going Home* (LP) compilation and *I Wanna Roo You* on

Fruity (LP). *Brown Eyed Girl* can also be found on *The Best Summer Ever!* (CD). (VJ)

The Mosaics

45:    Let's Go Drag Racing/
       Now That You're Here   (Columbia DB 7990) 1966 SC

This group may have been connected to **Mood Mosaic**. (VJ)

Motherlight

Personnel:	MIKE BOBAK	gtr, vcls	A
	ANDY JOHNS	effects	A
	WILSON MALONE	keyb'ds, drms, vcls	A

ALBUM: 1(A) BOBAK, JONS, MALONE
                            (Morgan Blue Town BT 5003) 1970 R3

NB: (1) counterfeited - but easily identified as such (no fold-over back cover). (1) also reissued on CD (Edsel EDCD 690).

Known by the name of the album rather than the group, **Motherlight** was a studio project by three young men associated with London's Morgan label. Bobak was its chief engineer, Johns (whose name is mysteriously misspelt on the album) had cut his teeth working on **Jimi Hendrix** sessions and **Malone** was principally an arranger. The album they made together is an excellent, if slightly unsettling, collection of progressive psychedelia. *On A Meadow - Lea* has good fuzz guitar paired with pastoral lyrics, while *Mona Lose* bears overt traces of malice. *House Of Many Windows* comes close to conventional pop, while the country-flavoured *Burning The Weed* sounds surprisingly like US Kaleidoscope. Closing track *The Lens*, meanwhile, reprises all the preceding tracks and sounds like **Procol Harum** on a bad trip.

Malone was a member of **Orange Bicycle** when this album was recorded, and subsequently released an ultra-rare solo album on Fontana before going on to considerable success as an arranger. Bobak continued to work as an engineer, and Johns went on to work with **Free**, **The Rolling Stones**, **Led Zeppelin** and others. He also produced Television's classic *Marquee Moon* album.

House Of Many Windows, another of the band's songs, subsequently resurfaced on the *Morgan Blue Town* (LP) and *Best And The Rest Of British Psychedelia* (CD). (MW/VJ/RMJ)

Moths

ALBUM: 1 MOTHS   (Deroy no #) 1969 R5

NB: (1) reissued as *Heron's Daughter* (Erewhon 9470-f) 1994.

MOTHERLIGHT - Bobak, Jons, Malone (LP).

MOTIFFE - Motiffe (CD).

Moths recorded an ultra-rare and sought-after privately-pressed album of mellow folk-rock. It was originally issued in a plain white sleeve with an insert. In fact, only one copy of it was issued originally. There are lots of Bob Dylan and Tim Buckley covers and musically the framework is built around acoustic guitars, bongos and flutes. The only original song is *Heron's Daughter*, which lent its title to the 1994 reissue.

Heron's Daughter has been compiled on *The History Of U.K. Underground Folk Rock 1968-1978 Vol. 2* (CD). (VJ)

Motiffe

Personnel:	MICK AVERY	electric piano	A
	QUENTIN BRYAR	sax	A
	JOHN GRIMALDI	gtr	A
	MARK PASTERFIELD	drms, perc	A
	IAN WILSON	vcls, flute	A

ALBUM: 1(A) MOTIFFE   (Deroy 777) 1972 R6

NB: (1) reissued on CD by Ammonite Records, as a limited edition of 300 hand numbered copies in 1998.

A very rare album (possibly only one copy was ever made) by a St. Albans band who apparently split up by the time the end product was 'released'. Housed in a plain sleeve, it contained five tracks of progressive rock with typically pretentious titles: *Grotesque Piece*, *Analogy*, *Life Reciprocal*, *To George* and *Mind And Body* and is reputed to contain some superb guitar playing. **King Crimson**, **Jade Warrior**, **Jimi Hendrix** and early **Pink Floyd** were obvious influences. (VJ)

Motivation

Personnel:	MARTIN BARRE	sax	A
	MIKE KETLEY	keyb'ds, vcls	A
	JIMMY MARSH	gtr, vcls	A
	CHRIS RODGER	sax	A
	BRYAN STEPHENS	bs	A
	MALCOLM TOMLINSON	drms, vcls	A

When South African singer Mike Bush (aka Beau Brummell Esquire) parted company with his band The Noblemen in October 1965 following an appearance at The Piper Club in Rome, Italy, group members Ketley and Stephens (who had earlier played in Bognor Regis-based beat group, Johnny Devlin and The Detours) returned to England and formed a new version of The Noblemen with Marsh and Tomlinson. After advertising in 'Melody Maker' for a saxophone player, the group recruited both Rodger and future **Jethro Tull** guitarist Martin Barre for this position.

Signing up to the Roy Tempest Agency, the group supported Lee Dorsey at the Cavern in Liverpool before returning to the Piper Club in the Spring of 1966 to play as the house band for six months. Returning to England later in the year, the group provided support to visiting soul acts like The Vibrations, Ben E. King, Wilson Pickett, Alvin Robinson, The Drifters and Ike and Tina Turner.

In early 1967, the band took on a new moniker, **The Motivation** and supported the likes of **The Herd** and **Cream**. Marsh and Rodger both dropped out during the Autumn and the group returned to its base at the Shoreline Club in Bognor Regis where it took on a new guise, The Penny Peep Show (aka **The Penny Peeps**). **The Motivation** never got the opportunity to record and should not be confused with the band of the same name who issued a single for Direction in early 1968.

During the early sixties, Tomlinson had been a member of **Jeff Curtis and The Flames**, the house band at the Ealing Jazz Club. (NW)

Motivation

Personnel incl: LOUIS McKELVEY

45:	Come On Down/Little Man	(Direction 58-3248) 1968 R1

A little-known band who's 'A' side was a cover of *Come On Down To My Boat* (a US hit for Every Mother's Son). This lively version is organ-driven and was produced by Bernard Cochrane. The flip side *Little Man* is certainly nothing special, although it again features organ/guitar combination.

Compilation appearances include: *Little Man* on *Psychedelia, Vol. 2* (LP), *Circus Days, Vol. 6* (CD) and *Hen's Teeth Vol. 1* (CD); and *Delighted To See You* on *Incredible Sound Show Stories Vol. 11* (LP). (VJ/NW)

Motowns

Personnel:	TONY CROWLEY	drms	A
	LALLY "STOTT" MARCHELLE	vcls	AB
	DOUGIE MEAKIN	gtr	AB
	MIKE "SAINT" LOGAN	keyb'ds	AB
	ROBBIE "LITTLE" SCOTT	bs	AB
	DAVE SUMMER (SUMNER?)	drms	B

ALBUMS:	1	SI', PROPRIO I MOTOWNS	(RCA S 14) R2 1967
	2	MOTOWNS	(Cinevox 33148) 1971 R3

NB: These are Italian releases.

45s:	Prendi la chitarra e vai/	
	Per quanto io ci provi	(RCA PM 3374) 1966
	Prendi la chitarra e vai/Una come lei	(RCA PM 3414) 1967

CIRCUS DAYS VOL. 6 (Comp CD) including Motivation.

Sagamafina/Mr.Jones	(RCA PM 3420) 1967
Dentro la fontana/In un villaggio	(Durium LD 7585) 1968
Fuoco/In The Morning	(Durium LD 7594) 1968
Sogno sogno sogno/Hello To Mary	(Durium LD 7629) 1969
Na Na Hey Hey Kiss Him Goodbye/	
In The Morning	(Durium LD 7667) 1970
Lassu'/Sai forse ti amer	(Carosello 20254) 1970
Back To My Baby/Wings Of A Bird	(Cinevox MDF 026) 1971
I Want To Die/Back To My Baby	(Cinevox MDf 028) 1971

NB: These are Italian releases.

This band arrived in Firenze, Italy straight from Liverpool just in time to lose all their instruments and baggage in the disasterous 1966 flood. The sad story was told by notorious Italian TV presenter Mike Bongiorno and in a few weeks a beat charity collection enabled **The Motowns** to buy new gear and even to get a deal with the local RCA label. RCA promoted them as **Beatles'** relatives, coming from the same town and exploiting the striking resemblance of Robbie "Little" Scott to **Paul McCartney**.

They won the Cantagiro Festival in 1967 with *Prendi la chitarra e vai* (a cover of **David and Jonathan**'s *Lovers Of The World Unite*), then Stott and Meaking married two Italian models.

They band also appeared in four Italian movies, including Fellini's episode of "Tre Passi Nel Delirio"!

Their album is a sort of progressive effort written by Italian composers.

Stott later recorded as solo artist before joining **Middle Of The Road**, he sadly died in Liverpool in 1978, in a bike accident. Meakin formed the short-lived Godfather with Mark David and Dave Summer, before becoming an in-demand session musician. Dave Summer (ex-**Primitives**) later played with Sopwith Camel in 1969/70. Logan also stayed in Italy, forming Dhuo and also worked for Italian female singer, Mina. Mark David also played with Buggles. Today Summer is still playing in Italy with various singers and pop bands. (FB/CR/GB)

Mott The Hoople

Personnel:	VERDEN ALLEN	keyb'ds	A
	DAVE 'BUFFIN' GRIFFIN	drms	ABCDEFG
	IAN HUNTER	vcls, piano	ABCDEF
	MICK RALPHS	gtr	ABC
	PETER OVEREND WATTS	bs	ABCDEFG
	(STAN TIPPINS	vcls	A)
	LUTHER GROSVENOR	gtr	E
	MICK RONSON	gtr	F
	MORGAN FISHER	piano	CDEFG
	MICK BOLTON	organ	CDE
	RAY MAJOR	gtr	G
	NIGEL BENJAMIN	vcls	G

HCP

ALBUMS:	1(A)	MOTT THE HOOPLE	(Island ILPS 9108) 1969 R1 66
(up to	2(A)	MAD SHADOWS	(Island ILPS 9119) 1970 SC 48
1976)	3(A)	WILD LIFE	(Island ILPS 9144) 1971 SC 44
	4(A)	BRAIN CAPERS	(Island ILPS 9178) 1971 SC -
	5(A)	ROCK 'N' ROLL QUEEN	(Island ILPS 9215) 1972
	6(A)	ALL THE YOUNG DUDES	(CBS 65184) 1972 21
	7(C)	MOTT	(CBS 69038) 1973 7
	8(D)	THE HOOPLE	(CBS 69062) 1974 11
	9(E)	LIVE	(CBS 69093) 1974 32
	10(G)	DRIVE ON	(CBS 69154) 1975 45
	11(G)	SHOUTING AND POINTING	(CBS 81289) 1976 -
	12(-)	GREATEST HITS	(CBS 81225) 1976 -

NB: (10) and (11) credited to Mott. (1) - (5) released by Atlantic in the US. (1) and (2) reissued on one CD (Edsel EDCD 361) 1993. (1) reissued again on CD (Angel Air SJPCD 157) 2003, with bonus tracks and informative booklets. (2) reissued again on CD (Angel Air SJPCD 158) 2003, with bonus tracks and informative booklets. (3) reissued on CD (Angel Air SJPCD 159) 2003, with bonus tracks and informative booklets. (4) reissued on CD (Angel Air SJPCD 160) 2003, with bonus tracks and informative booklets. (7) reissued on CD (Castle Classics CLACD 138X) 1988. (8) reissued on CD (Columbia 498 2482) 2000 with three additional bonus tracks (two from the album sessions and the 45 cut *Foxy Foxy*). (9) reissued as an expanded 2-CD set (Columbia) 2004 to commemorate its 30th anniversary. (11) reissued on CD (Columbia) 1998.

Backsliding Fearlessly (Rhino R2 71639) 1994 is a US CD compilation which selects their best material from (2) - (5) and other unissued songs. Other compilations on CD include:- *Collection: Mott The Hoople* (Castle Collection CCSCD 174) 1988, *Greatest Hits: Mott The Hoople* (CBS CD 32007) 1989 and *Walking With A Mountain (Best Of 1969-72)* (Island IMCD 87) 1990. *The Ballad Of Mott: A Retrospective* (Columbia COL 474420 2)1993 is a 2-CD compilation with three previously unreleased tracks. *The Island Years 1969-1972* (Spectrum) 1998 is a mid-price compilation of their pre-glam-rock days. *All The Young Dudes: The Anthology* (Sony 491400 2) 1998 is a 3-CD anthology. *All The Way from Stockholm To Philadelphia - Live 71/72* (Angel Air SJPCD 029) 1998 is a 2-CD live set. *Friends And Relatives* (Eagle EDGCD 104) 1999 is a 2-CD compilation set, although only five cuts are by **Mott The Hoople**, the rest are by post-**Hoople** outfits. *Live - Over Here And Over There* (Angel Air SJPCD 025) 2002 is a 2-CD live set of material recorded in the UK and US during 1975-1976. *Two Miles Live From Heaven* (Angel Air SJPCD 099) 2001 features US recordings from 1971, 1973 and 1974. *Gooseberry Sessions And Rarities* (Angel Air SJPCD 054) 2002 will also interest collectors. *Two Miles From Heaven* (Angel Air SJPCD 161) 2003 is a 17-track collection of unreleased songs and outtakes. *Walkin' With The Hoople* (Recall SMDCD 518) 2004 is a 2-CD set of live recordings and *Hoopling - Best Of Live* (Angel Air SJPCD 121) is a single CD set drawing material from the 1971-74 period. *Family Anthology* (Angel Air SJPCD 196) 2005 is a 2-CD set compiling a mixture of their classics, rarities and a couple of previously unissued numbers as well as a new one by Overend Watts to provide new interest for their die-hard fans.

HCP

45s: (up to 1976)	Rock And Roll Queen/ Road To Birmingham	(Island WIP 6072) 1969 SC -
	Midnight Lady/The Debt (Some PS)	(Island WIP 6105) 1971 -
	Downtown/ Home (Is Where I Want To Be)	(Island WIP 6112) 1971 -
	All The Young Dudes/One Of The Boys	(CBS 8271) 1972 3
	Honaloochie Boogie/Rose	(CBS 1530) 1973 12
	All The Way To Memphis/Ballad Of Mott	(CBS 1764) 1973 10
	Roll Away The Stone/ Where Do You All Come From?	(CBS 1895) 1973 8
	Golden Age Of Rock'n'Roll/Rest In Peace	(CBS 2177) 1974 16
	Foxy Foxy/Trudi's Song	(CBS 2439) 1974 33
	Saturday Gigs/Lounge Lizard	(CBS 2754) 1974 41
α	Monte Carlo/Shout It All Out	(CBS 3528) 1975 -
Reissues:	All The Young Dudes/ Honaloochie Boogie	(CBS 13-33249) 1975 -
	All The Young Dudes/ Roll Away The Stone (PS)	(CBS 3963) 1976 -
	All The Young Dudes/ Roll Away The Stone	(Old Gold OG 9312) 1983 -
	All The Young Dudes/Honaloochie Boogie	(CBS A 4581) 1984 -
β	All The Young Dudes/Once Bitten Twice Shy/ Roll Away The Stone	(Columbus 6581772) 1992

NB: α as Mott. β CD single, also issued on vinyl 7" without *Roll Away The Stone*.

Mott The Hoople were a good live band who often struggled to do themselves justice on vinyl.

This Midland band evolved from **The Doc Thomas Group**, a Hereford-based pub rock/covers band which included Peter 'Overend' Watts, Dale 'Buffin' Griffin, Michael Ralphs and Terence Verden Allen, who played with very little acclaim around the Welsh borders circa 1966/67. They also spent some time in Milan, Italy, with vocalist Stan Tippins now added to their line-up, where they got to record an album and upon returning to Britain moved from Hereford down to London changing name to The Silence (which Watts and Griffin had used for an earlier combo after leaving school). They soon came to the attention of Guy Stevens who became their manager and producer. Tippins, who yearned for the warmer climate of Italy soon left and Stevens renamed the remaining members **Mott The Hoople** after a 1967 novel by Willard Manus. He also placed an advert in 'Melody Maker' for a new vocalist. It read, "Singer wanted, must be image-minded and hungry". He recruited Shrewsbury-born **Ian Hunter** whose real name was Ian Patterson. **Hunter** had previously been in **At Last The 1958 Rock 'n' Roll Show**.

In July 1969 the band hastily recorded a dozen songs for Island and these comprised their debut album, *Mott The Hoople*, released in December of that year. Stevens had originally wanted to name the album 'Talking Bear Picnic Massacre Dylan Blues' but this was overruled by Island who thought the title too stupid. It is rumoured that some white label copies were pushed out bearing this title. I can't confirm this but if any exist, they would be extremely collectable. The first 5,000 copies included the flip of their first 45, *The Road To Birmingham*, instead of the 'A' side (*Rock'n'Roll Queen*). These also sell for more than the correct pressings. **Hunter** was an avid Dylan fan and his similar vocal style was highlighted on the album, which

MOTT THE HOOPLE - Live (LP).

included covers of Sir Douglas Quintet's *At The Crossroads* and Sonny and Cher's *Laugh At Me*. Many find the album's organ-led sound reminiscent of Dylan's *Blonde On Blonde* period. Although the *Rock'n'Roll Queen* 45 failed to chart the album slowly climbed to No 66 in the UK and No 185 in the US the following year.

After touring both the UK and US the band began work on their *Mad Shadows* album, which was more inspired by **The Rolling Stones** than Dylan and captured **Hunter** in a more forceful mood. Released in mid-1970 it received quite good reviews but its sales were mediocre (it crawled to No 48 in the UK) and this put pressure on the group's finances. They therefore decided to produce the next album, *Wild Life*, themselves. It was recorded over a seven months period between February-September 1970 and severely hampered by the band's lack of finances and the band's lack of production experience. The end result was a mess. The only redeeming feature was a belting 10-minute version of Little Richard's *Keep A Knockin'*. Most of the remaining material sounded like a poor man's Bob Dylan. Understandably Island's promotion was half-hearted and after peaking at No 44 in the UK Charts it soon sank without trace.

In an attempt to salvage some credibility the band enlisted the services of George 'Shadow' Morton to help produce an unashamed assault on the singles Chart, a **Stones**-influenced original with a sing-a-long chorus called *Midnight Lady*. It got them a 'Top Of The Pops' appearance but failed to mount an assault on the Charts.

Their next album, *Brain Capers*, was more heavy-metal in style, successfully capturing the band's endless on-stage energy. Indeed they'd built up quite a reputation as a live act. One of their concerts at the Albert Hall had caused a minor riot leading to a ban on future rock concerts at the venue. Still the *Brain Capers* album didn't chart and this led to the band being dropped by Island. In retrospect its main significance was to attract the attention of **David Bowie**, who'd in any case been a long time fan of theirs. Hearing that they were going to dissolve after a concert in Zurich, Switzerland, he offered them one of his new songs to continue in business. After rejecting *Suffragette City* they choose *All The Young Dudes*. **Bowie** even set up a recording session and his manager, Tony de Fries, touted the resulting tape around the record companies until CBS picked it up and offered them a five year recording contract and considerable freedom provided they used **Bowie** as their producer.

So *All The Young Dudes* was the 45 that turned their career around. It got to No 3 here and No 37 in the US. The album of the same name, which included contributions from **Bowie** and his guitarist **Mick Ronson**, climbed to No 21 here and No 89 in the US. In the Summer of 1972 the band set off on a series of UK headline provincial gigs followed by a five week US tour designed to cash in on their new success and their relationship with **Bowie** who was hot in the US at this time. Upon their return home Allen quit to form an extremely unsuccessful outfit called Verden Allen's Soft Ground and the band continued as a quartet.

Their next album, *Mott*, was their best to date. It produced two hits, *Honaloochie Boogie* (UK No 12) and a song which soon became another of their anthems, *All The Way To Memphis* (UK No 10). It later appeared on the Soundtrack to 'Alice Doesn't Live Here Anymore' in 1975. The album got to No 7 here and No 35 in the US, but soon after their success guitarist Mick Ralphs, tired of his reduced vocal assignments, departed to form **Bad Company**. He was replaced by former **Hellions** and **Spooky Tooth** axeman **Luther Grosvenor**, who was now calling himself Ariel Bender. He filled in on a 'Top Of The Pops' slot to promote their next single, *Roll Away The Stone*. Another classic 45, which became something of an anthem for them, this got to No 8 in the UK.

January and February 1974 were mostly spent working on a new album, *The Hoople*. The band was supplemented by **Howie Casey** (sax) and backing singers **Barry St. John** and **Sue and Sunny** (who'd previously worked with **Dusty Springfield** and **T Rex**). The album certainly had its highlights. Aside from *Roll Away The Stone* it spawned *Golden Age Of Rock And Roll*, a glorious single which climbed to No 16 here and No 96 in the States. The album, meanwhile, rose to No 11 here and No 28 in the US.

June 1974 saw the publication of **Hunter**'s book, 'Diary Of A Rock'n'Roll Star', which gave a day by day account of their 1972 US tour. It was also serialised by 'N.M.E.' here and by 'Creem' in the US.

The band's next 45, *Foxy Foxy*, paid homage to sixties girls groups but its progress was arrested at No 33 in the UK Charts. The follow-up, *Saturday Gigs*, a tongue-in-cheek recital of the band's rise to fame, only managed No 41 and **Ian Hunter** suffered a nervous breakdown.

To keep interest in the band alive CBS released *Mott The Hoople - Live*, which was compiled from concerts recorded at London's Hammersmith Odeon in November 1973 and New York's Broadway in May 1974. It certainly didn't capture the band at its best, although it contained reasonable versions of some of their epic songs like *All The Way From Memphis*, *Rest In Peace* and *All The Young Dudes*.

With **Hunter** not having made a full recovery the band decided to split in December 1974. The following month **Hunter** and **Ronson** put together The **Hunter-Ronson** Band to promote the solo albums on which they were both working. Buffin, Watts and Fisher, meanwhile, re-grouped and with the addition of new members Ray Major (gtr) and Nigel Benjamin (vcls) continued playing as Mott. Under this moniker they recorded the dreadful *Drive On* and the somewhat better *Shouting And Pointing*. It soon became apparent, though, that the chemistry wasn't right and when Benjamin left in November 1976 Mott split.

Hunter and **Ronson** continued to work together from time to time until **Ronson**'s death in 1993. **Hunter** enjoyed a reasonably successful solo career with his eponymous 1975 solo album and *You're Never Alone With A Schizophrenic* in 1979. His *Ships* was covered by Barry Manilow in 1975 and Great White enjoyed a Top 10 hit with his *Once Bitten, Twice Shy* in the early nineties.

The *Greatest Hits* album, issued in 1975, contains many of the band's best songs and is probably the best starting point for someone who's not heard their music. Fans of the band may be interested in a six-track CD, *Featuring Steve Hyams* (See For Miles SEACD 7), which was recorded after Benjamin's departure, but before the band became The British Lions in May 1977. The interim vocalist was Steve Hyams. (The British Lions were basically the Mott line-up with Benjamin replaced by former **Medicine Head** member John Fiddler).

The 3-CD box set *All The Young Dudes: The Anthology* was released in 1998. It's a well assembled 62-track collection and includes much previously unreleased material (37 tracks, although 17 of them are 1998 mixes) that was re-mixed for this box set. The set comes with a 60-page booklet, which comprehensively surveys their history and discography, along with over 200 previously unseen photos.

All The Way From Stockholm To Philadelphia is a 2-CD live set. The first disc was recorded in Stockholm in February 1971 and mostly veers toward hard-rock material. The second disc was recorded at the Tower Theatre, Philadelphia in November 1972. **David Bowie** joins them on a version of *All The Young Dudes*, but this collection will have limited appeal beyond **Bowie** and **Mott The Hoople** fans. *Two Miles Live From Heaven* features material from live US recordings in 1971, 1973 and 1974 and is supplemented by a 24-page booklet. It's probably more of interest to serious rock fans than casual collectors.

Angel Air's *Live - Over Here And Over There* 2002 CD documents material recorded in the UK and US during 1975-1976. Despite poorish sound quality it captures the band in fine form, mixing later material with earlier classics like *All The Young Dudes* and *All The Way From Memphis*. *Two Miles From Heaven* is a 17-track collection of unreleased songs, out-takes, oddities and wilder versions of earlier material. *Walkin' With The Hoople* is a 2-CD set, which tries to cover all eras of their existence rather than concentrating on one or two good shows and as a result it's largely dispensable. *Hoopling - Best Of Live* draws material from the 1971-74 era. It contains 12 cuts in all, including superb versions of *All The Young Dudes*, *Original Mixed Up Kid*, *Golden Age Of Rock'n'Roll* and *Sucker*. The set comes with an interesting 16-page booklet. *Family Anthology* is a well-compiled 2-CD set comprising a nice blend of classics, rarities and previously unissued tracks, with a new song by Overend Watts added as well.

Fans of the band will be interested in *Original Mixed Up Kids: The BBC Recordings* (Windsong WINCD 084) 1996. This actually includes all their surviving BBC recordings - unfortunately lots of their output was wiped. On offer are five studio recordings from February 1970, March 1971 and November 1971 and a six-song live set taped at the BBC's Paris Theatre on 29th December 1971. Three songs are duplicated on each source; *Whiskey Women*, *The Moon Upstairs* and their surprisingly mellow cover of Jesse Colin Young's *Darkness Darkness*. The other three live cuts are *Your Own Backyard* (originally done by Dion), *Death May Be Your Santa Claus* and *The Journey* (which was one of the finest moments of the *Brain Capers* album).

Compilation appearances include *Thunderbuck Ram* on *Bumpers* (2-LP); *Original Mixed-Up* on *El Pea* (2-LP); *At The Crossroads* on *Nice Enough To Eat* (LP) and *Midnight Lady* on Ronco's *20 Star Tracks, Vol. 1* (LP). (VJ)

Mountain Ash Band

ALBUM: 1   THE HERMIT (w/insert)

(Witches Bane LKLP 6036) 1975 R4

NB: (1) reissued on CD (Vinyl Tap DORIS 2) 199?

This was a privately pressed album, originals of which are now extremely hard to find and expensive to purchase. Strongly influenced by **Fairport Convention**, the folk-rock gem, features some superb electric violin work and intelligent lyrics throughout. It is a concept album which tracks the birth, depressing life and death of a provincial folklore outcast whose value was only acknowledged after his death. It's impossible to find, but clearly well worth hearing if you ever get the opportunity. (VJ)

Mourning Phase

ALBUM: 1   MOURNING PHASE   (Private Pressing) 1971 R5

NB: (1) reissued in the eighties as *Eden* (R1) and again using its original title in 1991. Also reissued on CD (Erewhom KSCD 9440-f) 1994.

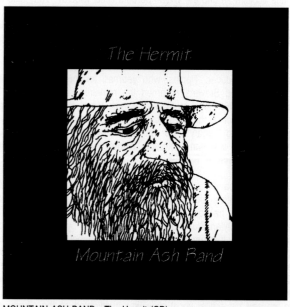

MOUNTAIN ASH BAND - The Hermit (CD).

MOURNING PHASE - Mourning Phase (CD).

This is a horrendously rare and expensive album to purchase now. Notable for some particularly vitriolic lyrics it relates the story of two lovers whose stars are at odds with one another and is reputedly told by the couple themselves within a folk-rock format. The better cuts musically are *Smile Song*, *Dross* and *August Song*. The reissue is certainly worth acquiring.

Ring Out The Bells can also be found on on *The History Of U.K. Underground Folk Rock 1968-1978 Vol. 2* (CD). (VJ)

Mouse

Personnel:	RAY RUSSELL	vcls, gtr	A
	AL CLARE	vcls, keyb'ds	A
	ALAN RUSHTON	drms	A
	JEFF WATTS	bs	A

ALBUM:	1(A)	LADY KILLER	(Sovereign SVNA 7262) 1973 R3

45s:	We Can Make It/	
	It's Happening To Me And You	(Sovereign SOV 122) 1973
	All The Fallen Teen Angels/	
	Just Came Back	(Sovereign SOV 127) 1974

Led by jazz guitarist and session regular **Ray Russell**, **Mouse** made an album of progressive rock that is sought-after for a number of reasons. **Russell's** soaring acid-guitar reigns supreme on *Ashen Besher* and *It's Happening To Me And You*, subdued sadness is to be found on *You Don't Know*, while an almost incredible use of strings in the tradition of Alban Berg highlights *East Of The Sun*. Given that all other tracks are at least listenable and at best marvellous, it's easy to see why progressive collectors consider this album a must. The sole cover is a good version of **Medicine Head**'s *All The Fallen Teen-Angels*. Great fun, this one, if somewhat disparate and short on playing time.

Ray Russell also produced and played lead on **Bill Fay's** *Time Of The Last Persecution* album, on which Rushton drummed. Jeff Watts was later in **Steel Mill**. The 45s are both scare too. (MK/VJ/RMJ)

Mousetrap

45:	Susie/Green Fields	(Aurora AU 5424) 1971

Susie is a decent slice of pop and *Green Fields* is a harder edged soulful song. (VJ)

The Move

Personnel:	BEV BEVAN	drms	ABCDE
	TREVOR BURTON	gtr, vcls	AB
	ACE KEFFORD	bs	A
	CARL WAYNE	vcls	ABCDE
	ROY WOOD	gtr, vcls	ABCDE
	RICK PRICE	bs, gtr, vcls	CD
	JEFF LYNNE	gtr, vcls, keyb'ds, bs	DE

HCP

ALBUMS:	1(A)	THE MOVE (mono/stereo)		
			(Regal Zonophone (S)LRZ 1002) 1967	R2/R1 15
	2(B)	SHAZAM	(Regal Zonophone SLRZ 1012) 1970	R1 -
	3(-)	BEST OF	(Fly TON 3) 1970	-
	4(D)	LOOKING ON	(Fly HIFLY 1) 1971	SC -
	5(-)	FIRE BRIGADE	(Music For Pleasure 5276) 1971	-
	6(E)	MESSAGE FROM THE COUNTRY		
			(Harvest SHSP 4013) 1972	SC -
	7(E)	CALIFORNIA MAN	(Harvest SHSP 4035) 1974	-

NB: (1) and (2) reissued as double set Cube (TOOFA 5/6) 1972. (2) released by A&M in the US. (4) and (6) released by Capitol in the US. (1) reissued on CD (Repertoire REP 4285-WY) 1992 and again remastered (Repertoire REP 4690). (2) reissued on CD (Repertoire REP 4296-WY) 1993 together with all five cuts from the *Something Else From The Move EP* and again remastered (Repertoire REP 4691). (4) reissued on CD (Repertoire REP 4281-WY) 1993 with the addition of their non-album singles from 1969 and again remastered (Repertoire REP 4692). (6) remastered and reissued on CD (EMI/Harvest 3302602) 2005 with nine bonus tracks, four of which were previously unreleased.

Compilations which may be of interest include: - *Greatest Hits, Vol. 1* (Hallmark SHM 952) 1978, *Platinum Collection* (Cube PLAT 1001) 1981 and *Off The Record With The Move* (Sierra FEDD 1005) 1984. CD compilations include: - *Collection: The Move* (Castle Collector CCSCD 135) 1986, *The Best Of The Move* (Music Club MCCD 009) 1991 and *The Early Years* (Dojo EARL D 7) 1992. The *BBC Sessions* (Band Of Joy BOJCD 011) 1995 includes several covers of US West Coast classics among its contents. *Movements* (??) 1997 is a 3-CD set that captures their career in fine detail, including all their singles, three albums, their rare EP, plus a few alternate mixes, foreign language versions and previously unissued cuts, excluding their later output for Harvest. *Looking Back: The Best Of The Move* (Music Club MCCD 345) 1998 is a fine mid-price compilation with their hits and a few album tracks - an excellent introduction to the band. *The Complete Singles Collection And More* (Crimson CRIMCD 233) 2000 includes all the hits but does omit some good 'B' sides. *30th Anniversary Anthology* (Westside WESX 302) is a 3-CD set. *Hits & Rarities - Singles A's & B's* (Repertoire REP 4665) includes all their singles and some withdrawn ones too.

EP:	1(A)	SOMETHING ELSE	
			(Regal Zonophone TRZ 2001) 1968 R1

HCP

45s:	Night Of Fear/The Disturbance	(Deram DM 109) 1966	2
	I Can Hear The Grass Grow/		
	Wave The Flag And Stop The Train	(Deram DM 117) 1967	5
	Flowers In The Rain/(Here We Go Round)		
	The Lemon Tree	(Regal Zonophone RZ 3001) 1967	2
α	Cherry Blossom Clinic/Vote For Me	(Regal Zonophone) 1967	-
	Fire Brigade/		
	Walk Upon The Water	(Regal Zonophone RZ 3005) 1968	3

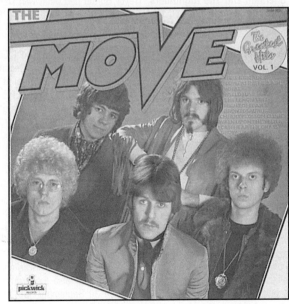
THE MOVE - Greatest Hits Vol. 1 (LP).

THE MOVE - The Move (LP).

Wild Tiger Woman/Omnibus (Regal Zonophone RZ 3012) 1968 -
Blackberry Way/Something (Regal Zonophone RZ 3015) 1968 1
Curly/This Time Tomorrow (Regal Zonophone RZ 3021) 1969 12
Brontosaurus/Lightnin' Never
Strikes Twice (Regal Zonophone RZ 3026) 1970 7
When Alice Comes Back To The Farm/
What? (Fly BUG 2) 1970 -
Tonight/Don't Mess Me Up (Harvest HAR 5038) 1971 11
Chinatown/Down On The Bay (Harvest HAR 5043) 1971 23
California Man/Do Ya/Ella James (Harvest HAR 5050) 1972 7
Do Ya/No Time (Harvest HAR 5086) 1974 -
Reissues: Fire Brigade/Night Of Fear/
I Can Hear The Flowers Grow (PS) (Fly ECHO 104) 1972 -
Flowers In The Rain/Blackberry Way (Cube BUG 85) 1979
Flowers In The Rain/Fire Brigade (Old Gold OG 9226) 1982 -
Blackberry Way/Brontosaurus (Old Gold OG 9227) 1982 -
Night Of Fear/
I Can Hear The Grass Grow (Old Gold OG 9228) 1982 -
I Can Hear The Grass Grow/Blackberry Way/Flowers In The
Rain / Fire Brigade (Archive 4 TOF 111) 1982 -

NB: α Unissued. Test pressings may exist.

The Move was basically a quality pop band who produced some innovative singles when they experimented with psychedelia. Later in their career they adopted a harder-edged approach.

Formed in Birmingham in February 1966, **The Move** comprised members of some of the city's best beat groups. **Roy Wood** had previously been with **Mike Sheridan and The Nightriders**, Trevor Burton had been with **Danny King and The Mayfair Set** and **Carl Wayne**, and **Ace Kefford** and Bev Bevan were previously with **Carl Wayne and The Vikings**.

In its early days the group gigged regularly at Birmingham's Cedar Club. Their first break came when they were signed by manager Tony Secunda, who brought them down to London and secured a residency for them at the Marquee club late in 1966. Taking over from **The Who**, they set out to be equally outrageous, and attracted considerable attention by demolishing TV sets on stage. Producer Denny Cordell soon secured them a recording contract with Decca's progressive Deram label, and they proceeded to release a string of catchy pop singles which successfully captured the atmosphere of London's underground.

Their debut, *Night Of Fear*, penned by **Roy Wood** and featuring a riff from the *1812 Overture*, climbed to No 2, laying the foundation for their subsequent success. The follow-up, *I Can Hear The Grass Grow*, consolidated their flirtation with psychedelia, which had been partly inaugurated by an appearance at the 14-Hour Technicolour Dream multi-media event at London's Alexandra Palace on 29 April 1967. The single peaked at No 5. Their next effort, *Flowers In The Rain*, was one of the definitive psychedelic pop singles of the era and also the first to be played on BBC Radio One when it opened on 30 September 1967, after the Labour government's Marine Offences Act had outlawed the exciting

era of offshore pirate radio. The 45 was publicised with a postcard of the then Prime Minister, Harold Wilson, naked in his bath. As a result of his successful legal action, all royalties from the record were donated to charity. The 'B' side, *(Here We Go Round) The Lemon Tree*, was superb too, and covered by **Idle Race** and **Jason Crest**.

The Move's next scheduled single, *Cherry Blossom Clinic*, was dropped since its lyrics, concerning a mental asylum, were thought to pose a risk of further adverse publicity. The scheduled flip side was *Vote For Me* and, if any test pressings exist, they are by far the band's rarest and most collectable items. In any event, both tracks were later included on their highly enjoyable debut album, *The Move*, their only one to make the charts, peaking at No 15. By the time of its release they had moved away from Deram and onto EMI's Regal Zonophone offshoot. The album spanned classy pop-rock (*Yellow Rainbow*, *Kilroy Was Here*), orchestrated ballads (*The Girl Outside*, *Mist On A Monday Morning*) and covers (Moby Grape's *Hey Grandma* and Eddie Cochran's *Weekend*). It was left to the mainstream pop 45, *Fire Brigade*, to propel the band back high into the Charts, however. The month after its release **Ace Kefford** left to pursue a solo career, forming the short-lived **Ace Kefford Stand**. Trevor Burton took over on bass and they continued as a four-piece, with Richard Tandy occasionally filling in on keyboards.

Their next 45 release, *Wild Tiger Woman*, was weak and failed to chart. Of more interest to collectors will be their live EP, *Something Else From The Move*, which featured covers of various songs including Love's *Stephanie Knows Who*. Early in 1969 they achieved their only No 1 with another straight-forward pop song, *Blackberry Way*, but Trevor Burton wanted to play more experimental music and left in February 1969, causing the cancellation of an imminent US tour. Indeed the group singularly failed to make an impression in the US. Burton joined **The Uglys** but later helped form **Balls** with **Denny Laine**. **Rick Price**, formerly of **Sight and Sound**, came in as his replacement.

Their next 45, the unexceptional *Curly*, climbed to No 12, but when they eventually got to the US (in Autumn 1969), the tour was a flop. They returned home to play the northern cabaret circuit, which caused friction between **Carl Wayne** and the other band members. In January 1970 **Wayne** left to embark on a moderately successful TV and cabaret career. Jeff Lynne (of **The Idle Race**), who'd originally been approached to join back in March 1969, came in as a replacement but **Electric Light Orchestra** was already being planned by **Roy Wood** and Lynne was more interested in this.

Their next album, *Shazam*, sold poorly although **Amen Corner**'s cover of one of the cuts, **Roy Wood**'s *Hello Susie*, made No 4 in the UK Charts. Other highlights were *Beautiful Daughter*, a well crafted pop ballad and their earlier shelved 45, *Cherry Blossom Clinic Revisited*. For their follow-up to *Curly* **The Move** chose an out-of-character heavy rocker, *Brontosaurus*, which provided them with their first Top Ten hit for over a year.

After the disappointing *Looking On* album, **The Move** signed to EMI's progressive Harvest label and their final album, *Message To The Country*, was recorded after **Price**'s departure. It contained parodies of Elvis Presley

THE MOVE - Shazam (CD).

THE MOVE - Looking On (CD).

(*Don't Mess Me Up*) and Johnny Cash (*Ben Crawley Steel Co.*). By the time *Chinatown* had climbed to No 23, plans were well advanced to convert **The Move** into the **Electric Light Orchestra**. They ended on a high, though, when *California Man* peaked at No 7. Ironically, the flip side, Jeff Lynne's frantic *Do Ya*, was released as the 'A' side in the States, where it gave them their only hit, albeit a minor one, peaking at No 93. Harvest reissued it here a couple of years later, but with the group already having evolved into **Electric Light Orchestra**, it unsurprisingly attracted little interest.

Although **The Move**'s *California Man* single wasn't released until September 1972, they'd ceased appearing live since October 1971 except to promote their singles on TV. The same month the *California Man* single was released, the **Electric Light Orchestra** played their first live gig at Croydon's Greyhound (16th April). This signified the demise of **The Move**. Initially the **Electric Light Orchestra** was an expanded version of **The Move**. The five additional members included Richard Tandy, who'd been a part-time member of **The Move** in any case. Then in August 1972 **Roy Wood** left to form **Wizzard**, leaving the **Electric Light Orchestra** to re-group and increasingly become a vehicle for Jeff Lynne's inventiveness.

30th Anniversary Anthology is a superb 54-track 3-CD box set comprising three complete albums, single and EP mixes and rare and alternate takes. It incorporates their big hits like *Flowers In The Rain*, *I Can Hear The Grass Grow*, *Blackberry Way* and *Fire Brigade* alongside more experimental sitar-laden psychedelia from their *Shazam* album. *Hits And Rarities* is a 2-CD set featuring all their 'A' and 'B' sides supplemented by rarities like *Vote For Me*, the Italian version of *Something* and the live *Something Else* EP. Housed in a slipcase it also contains interviews with **Roy Wood** and Bev Bevan.

Carl Wayne died of cancer aged 61 on 31 August 2004.

The band have made several appearances on compilations including: *Ella James* on *Harvest Bag* (LP); *I Can Hear The Grass Grow* on Decca's *The World Of Hits, Vol. 2* (LP) and on the 4-CD box set *Acid Drops, Spacedust & Flying Saucers*; *Stephanie Knows Who* and *Hey Grandma* (live radio broadcasts) on *Artefacts From The Psychedelic Dungeon* (CD); *Night Of Fear* and *I Can Hear The Grass Grow* on *A Whiter Shade Of Pale* (LP); *Fire Brigade* on the 4-CD *Nuggets II* box set; and *Night Of Fear, Sunshine Help Me, Stephanie Knows Who* and *Something Else* on *Brum Beat - Midlands Beat Groups Of The 60's* (CD). Finally, *Brontosaurus* resurfaced on the 3-CD box set *Radio Caroline Calling - 70's Flashback* and *California Man* got another airing on *Classic Rock - cd2*. (VJ)

The Movement

Personnel incl: DEAN KEARNEY   gtr

45s: α Something You've Got/Tell Her   (Pye 7N 17443) 1968 R2
          Head For The Sun/Mister Mann   (Big T BIG 112) 1968 R2

NB: α also issued in Ireland (Target 7N 17443) 1968.

Both of this Dublin band's 45s are extremely rare and collectable. *Tell Her* was a cover version of a soul number by Dean Parrish/Billie Davis. It featured **Jimmy Page** on guitar. The single was recorded in Eamonn Andrew's studio on Henry Street in Dublin and was done in a couple of takes. *Head For The Sun* was quite psychedelic. It has a driving beat, fuzz guitar and airplane noises which recall *Back In The USSR*, but the honky-tonk piano segments don't really fit.

Compilation appearances include: *Tell Her* on *Purple Pill Eaters* (LP & CD), *We Can Fly, Vol 1* (CD) and *Freakbeat Freakout* (CD); *Head For The Sun* on *The Electric Lemonade Acid Test, Vol. 2* (LP), *Incredible Sound Show Stories Vol. 4* (LP) and *Jagged Time Lapse, Vol 1* (CD); and *Tell Her* and *Something You Got* on *Irish Rock - Ireland's Beat Groups 1964-1969* (CD). (VJ/DMc)

The Movies

Personnel:	JON COLE	gtr, vcls	A
	JULIAN DIGGLE	perc, vcls	A
	GREG KNOWLES	gtr, vcls	A
	JAMIE LANE	drms, vcls	A
	DURBAN LAVERE	bs, vcls	A
	DAG SMALL	keyb'ds, vcls	A

ALBUM: 1(A)   THE MOVIES   (A&M AMLH 330002) 1975

There were two groups of this name. This progressive rock combo recorded a number of albums between 1975 - 81, but only the eponymous one falls within the time span of this book. (VJ)

The Moving Finger

Personnel:	ROY BELL	gtr	A
	CLIVE CLARE	organ	A
	GARRY FREEMAN	vcls	A
	HILSON HARLEY	drms	A
	AL THORN	bs	A

45s: Jeremy And The Lamp/
          Pain Of My Misfortune   (Mercury MF 1051) 1968 R1
      α   Higher And Higher/
          Shake And Fingerpop   (Mercury MF 1077) 1969
          So Many People/
          We're Just As Happy As We Are (Decca F 13406) 1973

NB: α has been reissued (Mercury MF 1077) in a limited edition pressing of 500 reproduced from the original French jukebox release.

This group evolved out of the Norwich-based Gary Freeman and The Contours who in 1966 became **The Anglians**. They became **The Moving Finger** in 1968. During the seventies they based their operation on the

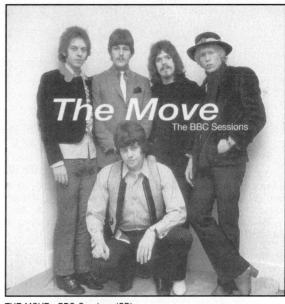

THE MOVE - BBC Sessions (CD).

Continent. *Jeremy The Lamp* was written by **Grapefruit**'s George Alexander. The flip side is quite psychedelic. Their second 45 was more soul-influenced. They played a residency at the Royal Ballroom in Tottenham, North London for a while and this led to another group of this name to rename themselves as **Secondhand**.

Compilation appearances have included: *Jeremy The Lamp* on *Justavibration* (LP); and *Pain Of My Misfortune* on *Rubble, Vol. 11* (CD), *We Can Fly, Vol 1* (CD) and *The Best Of Rubble Collection, Vol. 3* (CD). (VJ)

The Moving Finger

Personnel:	KEN ELLIOT	vcls, keyb'ds	A
	BOB GIBBONS	gtr	A
	KIERAN O'CONNOR	drms	A
	NICK SOUTH	bs	A

ALBUM: 1(A) REALITY   (Polydor 583 045) 1969 R3

This was really a band called **Secondhand**, although early copies of this album credit them as **The Moving Finger** on the record labels, but not on the sleeve. O'Connor went on to **Seventh Wave** and The Balham Alligators. (VJ)

Mr. Bloe

Personnel:	IAN DUCK	hrmnca, gtr	A
	DAVE GLOVER	bs	A
	ZACK LAWRENCE	keyb'ds, hrmnca	A
	ROGER POPE	drms	A

ALBUM: 1(A) GROOVIN' WITH MR. BLOE (DJM DJLPS 409) 1973 SC

			HCP
45s:	Groovin' With Mr. Bloe/Sinful	(DJM DJS 216) 1970	2
	Curried Soul/Mighty Mouse	(DJM DJS 229) 1971	-
	71 -75 New Oxford Street/Get Out	(DJM DJS 245) 1972	-
	Land Of A Thousand Dances/		
	Dancing Machine	(DJM DJS 346) 1975	-
	Anyway You Want It/One More Time	(DJM DJS 678) 1976	-
Reissue:	Groovin' With Mr. Bloe/Sinful	(Old Gold OG 9002) 1978	-

Pianist Zack Lawrence was the man behind the harmonica - driven instrumental whose novelty took it to No 2 in the Charts. The novelty soon wore off, despite **Elton John** helping out with some compositions and the project was eventually shelved. Except for Lawrence, all members of this studio group were in **Hookfoot**. (VJ)

Mr. Fox

Personnel:	ALUN EDEN	drms	AB
	BARRY LYONS	bs, dulcimer	AB
	ANDREW MASSEY	cello	A
	JOHN MYATT	woodwind	A
	BOB PEGG	vcls, gtr, bs, keyb'ds	ABC
	CAROLANNE PEGG	vcls, fiddle	AB
	RITCHIE BULL	bs	C
	NICK STRUTT	gtr	C

ALBUMS: 1(A)	MR. FOX	(Transatlantic TRA 226) 1970 R1
(up to 2(B)	THE GYPSY	(Transatlantic TRA 236) 1971 R1
1976) 3(A/B)	THE COMPLETE MR. FOX (dbl)	
		(Transatlantic TRA 303) 1975 R1

NB: (3) was a reissue of (1) and (2). (1) reissued (Get Back GET 590). (2) reissued (Get Back GET 591). (1) and (2) reissued on one CD (Castle) 1996, although some tracks are omitted and reissued again (Essential ESMCD 433) 2005. *Join In Our Game - The Anthology* (Castle CMRCD 1049) is a 2-CD set containing all their recorded output.

45:        Little Woman/Join Us In Our Game   (Big T BIG 135) 1970

An electric folk outfit from Leeds whose albums are now difficult to find and quite sought-after. **Ashley Hutchings** also wrote two of the songs on their first album and was clearly heavily involved in the band without actually playing in it. Their songs were often about Yorkshire nostalgia; closing lead mines etc. Most of the material was written by **Bob Pegg**, though, and a good standard is maintained throughout with *Salisbury Plain, Carolanne's Supernatural Gay Goshawk* and *The Hanged Man*, a gory tale of a hitch-hiker who slips to his death, particularly outstanding.

Massey and Myatt left after the first album reducing the group to a four-piece prior to *The Gypsy*. The title track, written and sung by **Bob Pegg** is a good traditional number with melodeon, electric fiddle, sopranino recorder and percussion. Still, it's outshone by *Mendle*, a long, slow and melodic song with floating organ backing and rather psychedelic electric guitar work, written and sung by **Carolanne Pegg**. After this album Eden and Lyons departed to join **Trees** in 1972 being replaced by Bull and Strutt. Then **Carolanne Pegg** left, leaving **Bob Pegg**, Bull and Strutt to soldier on - though not for long!

Carolanne Pegg has made a solo album as well as others with her ex-husband **Bob Pegg**, who himself made three albums with Nick Strutt. Richie Ball was later in **The Kursaal Flyers**.

The two *Mr. Fox* albums are masterpieces of contemporary folk music and the *Join In Our Game* anthology is recommended if you want to hear all their recordings. Their compilation appearances include *House Carpenter* on *The Transatlantic Story* CD box set. (VJ/CA)

Mr. Mo's Messengers

45:        Feelin' Good/The Handyman   (Columbia DB 8133) 1967

This is another of those bands about whom nothing is known, but the 45 is quite bluesy. (VJ)

Mucky Duck

45:        Jefferson/Psycho's On The Run   (Deram DM 314) 1970

An obscure one-off recording, which is typical of the label. (VJ)

Mud

Personnel:	ROB DAVIS	gtr	AB
	LES GRAY	vcls	AB
	PAUL GRAY	drms	A
	RAY STILES	bs	AB
	DAVE MOUNT	drms	B
	ANDY BALL	keyb'ds	

Mr. FOX - Mr. Fox (LP).

LINDSAY MUIR'S UNTAMED - It's All True (LP).

typical British flower-pop and the flip is a beaty number with a taint of psychedelia. They continued on a semi-professional basis until April 1968, when they turned professional and released their second and final single for CBS, *Up The Airy Mountain*, which like their follow-up single for Philips, *Shangri-La*, the following year, is not too easy to find either nowadays. By now an appearance on BBC's 'The Basil Brush Show' had introduced them to a wider audience, but it was really their link up with songwriters Nicky Chinn and Mike Chapman (the team behind **The Sweet**) which was their big break giving them a string of commercially successful (if ordinary often to the point of boring) pop singles beginning with *Crazy* in 1973. The most memorable of these were *Tiger Feet*, which topped the UK Charts for four weeks and led briefly to a new dance craze and *Lonely This Christmas*, an Elvis Presley pastiche, which became a classic Christmas record.

They split with Chapman and Chinn in 1975, but by then they were such a household name that their self-produced singles for Private Stock also made the Charts.

Post-1976 they signed to RCA for whom they recorded into the eighties, though in March 1977 Gray signed to Warner Brothers as a solo artist. As late as 1985 they were playing on the cabaret circuit when, in December of that year, a reissued version of *Lonely This Christmas* re-entered the UK charts, climbing to No 61. Gray still continues the group as Les Gray's Mud. In the late eighties Stiles joined **The Hollies**. Mount now works for a video company. Davis worked with The Darts for a while and is now retired.

Commercially they were extremely successful (in the UK, they never cracked the US market) but their significance in the evolution of rock is slight. However, *The Singles '67-'78* includes their UK 'A' and 'B' sides, German 'A' sides and singles issued under pseudonyms, such as **Dum's** *In The Mood*.

Their frontman and lead singer Les Gray died from a heart attack on 22 February 2004, having suffered from throat cancer for 12 years. He was 57.

Dynamite can also be heard on the 6-CD set *Best Of Driving Rock*, *Hits Of The 70's Vol 3* (CD) and *Seventies Legends 2* (CD); *Tiger Feet* and *Oh Boy* resurfaced on *The Best Summer Ever!* (CD); *Dynamite* and *Rocket* feature on *The Super 70's Vol 1* (CD); *Tiger Feet* and *The Cat Crept In* resurfaced on *The Super 70's Vol 2* (CD); *Oh Boy* can also be heard on *Number 1 Hits Of The 70's & 80's* (CD) and on *Seventies Legends* (CD); *Tiger Feet* gets another airing on *Greatest Hits Of The 70's - cd3*; *You're My Mother* has been compiled on *Jagged Time Lapse, Vol 3* (CD); *House On The Hill* got a further airing on *Jagged Time Lapse, Vol 5* (CD); *You're A Woman* has been compiled on *Sunshine Day A Taste Of The 70's* (CD) and *Latter Days* re-emerged on *Oddities, Vol 1* (CD). (VJ/NB/JM)

HCP

ALBUMS:	1(B)	MUD ROCK	(RAK SRAK 508) 1974	8
(up to	2(B)	MUD ROCK, VOL. 2	(RAK SRAK 513) 1975	6
1976)	3(B)	GREATEST HITS	(RAK SRKA 6755) 1975	25
	4(B)	USE YOUR IMAGINATION		
			(Private Stock PVLP 1003) 1976	33
	5(B)	IT'S BETTER THAN WORKING		
			(Private Stock PVLP 1011) 1976	-

NB: *The Singles '67-'78* (Repertoire REP 4657-WR) 1998 is a 2-CD set offered on German import. (1) and (2) reissued on one CD (BGO BGOCD 415). *Mud - A's, B's & Rarities* (EMI Gold 560 2222) is a 23-track collection with all their singles, including the one recorded as **Dum**. *Time & Again - Private Stock Collection* (Castle CMDDD 1016) is a 2-CD set which collects their hits from 1975-1978.

HCP

45s:	Flower Power/		
(up to	You're My Mother (Some PS)	(CBS 203002) 1967	R1/SC -
1976)	Up The Airy Mountain/Latter Days	(CBS 3355) 1968	SC -
	Shangri-La/House On The Hill	(Philips BF 1775) 1969	SC -
	Jumping Jehosaphat/Won't Let It Go	(Philips 6006 022) 1970	-
	Crazy/Do You Love Me	(Rak RAK 146) 1973	12
	Hypnosis/Last Tango In London	(Rak RAK 152) 1973	16
	Dyna-mite/Do It All Over Again	(Rak RAK 159) 1973	4
	Tiger Feet/Mr. Bagatelle	(Rak RAK 166) 1973	1
	The Cat Crept In/Morning	(Rak RAK 170) 1974	2
	In The Mood/Watching The Clock	(RAK 179) 1974	-
	Rocket/Ladies	(Rak RAK 178) 1974	6
	Lonely This Christmas/		
	I Can't Stand It (PS)	(Rak RAK 187) 1974	1
	Secrets That You Keep/		
	Still Watching The Clock (PS)	(Rak RAK 194) 1975	3
	Oh Boy/Watching The Clock	(Rak RAK 201) 1975	1
	Moonshine Sally/Bye Bye Johnny	(Rak RAK 208) 1975	10
	One Night//Shake Rattle And Roll		
	See You Later Alligator	(Rak RAK 213) 1975	32
	L'l'lucy/My Love Is Your Love	(Private Stock PVT 41) 1975	10
	Show Me You're A Woman	(Private Stock PVT 45) 1975	8
	Shake It Down/		
	Laugh, Live, Love (PS)	(Private Stock PVT 65) 1976	12
	Nite On The Tiles/		
	Time And Again	(Private Stock PVT 80) 1976	-
	Lean On Me/Grecian Lament	(Private Stock PVT 85) 1976	7
Reissue:	Tiger Feet//Oh Boy/Dynamite (PS)	(Rak RR 6) 1977	-

Mud was formed back in February 1966 out of The Mourners, a local Mitcham group put together by Les Gray and his brother Peter. After two members (Nigel Munt and Barry ????) were replaced by Rob Davis and Ray Stiles, the band changed its name to **Mud**.

Dave Mount, who came from Carshalton, Surrey, had played in several previous local groups. He soon replaced Paul Gray, and they recorded their first 45 for CBS, *Flower Power*, in 1967. Some copies came in picture sleeves and it is now their most collectable artefact. The 'A' side was

MU 5

| 45: | Rain Dance/Mrs. Watson | (Crystal CR 7015) 1971 |

This 45 was a total obscurity on a short-lived label of no distinction. (VJ)

Lindsay Muir's Untamed

| 45: | Daddy Long Legs/ | |
| | Trust Yourself A Little Bit | (Planet PLF 113) 1966 R2 |

NB: Copies were initially issued with the Planet company sleeve and these are slightly more collectable (R3). This 45 has been repressed in a limited edition pressing of 500 with a large centre hole. There's also a compilation *It's All True!* (Circle CPW C101), which is also on vinyl (Circle L101).

This was a later version of **The Untamed**, a mid-sixties freak-beat, mod, R&B group who never made the big time but whose singles (and the above one) are very collectable now. There's a recent compilation *It's All True* that collects their rare BBC Sessions and demos. The vinyl version is a numbered limited edition with a colour insert in a sixties style laminated sleeve.

Compilation appearances include: *Daddy Long Legs* and *Trust Yourself A Little Bit* on *Untamed And Innocent* (CD); and *Daddy Long Legs* on *The Best Of Planet Records* (CD) and *Echoes From The Wilderness - Sixteen UK R&B Freakbeat Trippers*. (LP & CD). (VJ)

The Muleskinners

Personnel incl:
TERRY BRENNAN	vcls		
PETE BROWN	bs	A	
MICK CARPENTER	drms	A	
IAN MacLAGAN	gtr, keyb'ds		
DAVE PETHER	ld gtr	A	
NICK TWEDELL	hrmnca		

EP: 1 MULESKINNERS (Keepoint KEE-EP-7103/4) 1965 R5

NB: (1) contained: *Why Don't You Write Back To Me / Back Door Man / Untie Me / Need Your Lovin'*

45: Back Door Man/Need Your Lovin' (Fontana TF 527) 1965 R3

This R&B group was formed at Twickenham Art School in South-West London. Their cover of Howlin' Wolf's *Back Door Man* is very rare and sought-after by R&B collectors and their privately pressed EP is one of the rarest and most expensive artefacts of the British early to mid-sixties R&B scene.

Their rendition of *Back Door Man* is one of the more credible versions of this Howlin' Wolf classic, whilst the flip side veers more towards punk. Incidentally, the band's vocalist Terry Brennan had earlier played with **Eric Clapton** and Tom McGuinness in a band called The Roosters. Ian MacLagan went on to replace **Jimmy Winston** in **The Small Faces** in late 1965.

The sleeve-notes to *Revenge Of The Amphetamine Generation* tell us that they also recorded *I Am The Giver Of All Things* as a flexi disc for "Oz" magazine in 1966, but all copies were destroyed and the group split shortly afterwards.

Compilation coverage has included:- *Need Your Lovin'* (from EP) on *Revenge Of The Amphetamine Generation* (LP); *Back Door Man* on *Maximum R'n'B* (CD) and on *English Freakbeat, Vol. 2* (LP); *Back Door Man* and *Need Your Lovin'* on *English Freakbeat, Vol. 2* (CD) and *Nowhere Men, Vol. 2* (CD); and *Need Your Lovin'* (from their 45) on *Garage Punk Unknowns, Vol. 4* and on *Rare 60's Beat Treasures, Vol. 3* (CD). (VJ)

Mungo Jerry

Personnel:
MIKE COLE	bs	A	
RAY DORSET	gtr, vcls, perc	AB	D
COLIN EARL	piano, vcls	AB	
PAUL KING	banjo, gtr, vcls	AB	
JOHN GODFREY	vcls, gtr, keyb'ds	B	
JOE RUSH	perc	C	
JON POPE	keyb'ds		D
TIM REEVES	drms		D

				HCP	
ALBUMS:	1(A)	MUNGO JERRY	(Dawn DNLS 3008) 1970	13	SC
(up to	2(B)	ELECTRONICALLY TESTED			
1976)			(Dawn DNLS 3020) 1971	SC	14
	3(C)	YOU DON'T HAVE TO BE IN THE ARMY			
			(Dawn DNLS 3028) 1971	SC	-
	4(D)	BOOT POWER	(Dawn DNLS 3041) 1972	-	
	5(-)	GREATEST HITS (Compilation)			
			(Dawn DNLS 3045) 1973	-	
	6( )	LONG LEGGED WOMAN	(Dawn DNLS 3501) 1974	-	
	7(-)	GOLDEN HOUR OF... (Compilation)			
			(Pye GH 586) 1974	-	
	8( )	IMPALA SAGA	(Polydor 2383 364) 1976	-	

NB: (1) issued on Janus in the US. (1) and (2) reissued on CD as *The Summertime* by Repertoire (REP 4177) 1991 with extra tracks. (1) reissued on CD (PRT GHCD 4) 1989. (2) reissued on CD (Repertoire REP 4179-WZ) 1991 and again on CD (Breathless 980124) more recently. (3) and (4) reissued on one CD (Beat Goes On BGOCD 292) 1995. The band continued to release albums on Polydor in the late seventies. A *Greatest Hits* album was released on Alstan (20001) in 1984. Alternatively *The Early Years* (Dojo EARL D 3) 1992 is a pretty good mid-price CD compilation of their earlier material. Other compilations on CD include:- *Golden Hour Of Mungo Jerry* (Knight KGHCD 116) 1990; *All The Hits Plus More* (Prestige CDPT 602) 1992; *Summertime* (Spectrum SSO 739-2) 1995; *The Best Of Mungo Jerry* (Music Club MCCD 292) 1997 which is a budget-priced, well-packaged CD set with good sleeve-notes which combines their early seventies hits with a selection of their better album tracks; *Baby Jump - The Definitive Collection* (Sanctuary Midline

SMETCD134) is a 3-CD set that covers their entire Dawn output and comes with a detailed booklet and *Baby Jump - The Dawn Anthology* (Essential ESACD 777) also covers their entire Dawn output and comes with interviews and as discography.

			HCP
45s:	In The Summertime/Mighty Man	(Dawn 7N 2502) 1970	-
(up to α	In The Summertime/Mighty Man/		
1976)	Dust Pneumonia Blues (PS)	(Dawn DNX 2502) 1970	1
	Baby Jump/The Man Behind The Piano	(Dawn 7N 2505) 1971	-
	Baby Jump//Midnight Special/Mighty Man		
	Maggie/		
	The Man Behind The Piano (PS)	(Dawn DNX 2505) 1971	1
	Lady Rose/Little Louis 1975	(Dawn 7N 2510) 1971	-
	Lady Rose//Have A Whiff On Me		
	Milk Cow Blues/Little Louis (PS)	(Dawn DNX 2510) 1971	5
	You Don't Have To Be In The Army/		
	We Shall Be Free (PS)	(Dawn 7N 2513) 1971	-
	You Don't Have To Be In The Army//The Sun Is Shining		
	O'Reilly/We Shall Be Free	(Dawn DNX 2513) 1971	13
	I Don't Wanna Go Back To School//Going Back Home		
	Open Up/No Girl Reaction	(Dawn DNX 2514) 1972	21
	My Girl And Me//It's A Goodie Boogie Woogie		
	46 And On/Summer's Gone (PS)	(Dawn DNX 2515) 1972	-
	Alright, Alright, Alright/		
	Little Miss Hipshake	(Dawn DNS 1037) 1973	3
	Wild Love/Glad I'm A Rocker	(Dawn DNS 1051) 1973	32
	All Dressed Up//Shake 'Til I Break		
	Too Fast To Live/Burnin' Up	(Dawn DNS 1092) 1974	-
	Longlegged Woman Dressed In Black/		
	Gonna Bop 'Till I Drop	(Dawn DNX 1061) 1974	13
	Can't Get Over Loving You/Let's Go	(Polydor 2058 603) 1975	-
	Hello Nadine/Bottle Of Beer	(Polydor 2058 654) 1975	-
	Don't Let Go/Give Me Bop	(Polydor 2058 759) 1976	-
Reissues:	In The SummertimeShe Rowed	(Dawn DNS 1113) 1975	-
	In The Summertime/Baby Jump	(Pye FBS 7) 1979	-
	In The Summertime/Mighty Man/Lady Rose/		
	Baby Jump	(Pye BD 114) 1977	-
	Baby Jump/Alright, Alright, Alright	(Old Gold OG 9139) 1982	-
	In The Summertime/Long Legged Woman Dressed		
	In Black	(Old Gold OG 9292) 1983	-
	In The Summertime/Baby JUmp/Long Legged Woman Dressed		
	In Black (CD)	(Old Gold OGCD 6139) 1989	-

NB: α There was a jukebox issue which is (SC).

Mungo Jerry was a big commercial success in the early seventies but is less significant in the history of rock. They are always associated with their anthem *In The Summertime*.

This was a group of skiffle revivalists within whom **Ray Dorset** was very much the dominant figure. Line-up (A) was originally known as **Good Earth** and made a big impression at the Hollywood Festival, Newcastle in 1970. They simply burst onto the scene with their summery ditty *In The Summertime*, which became a million-seller, topping the Charts here and climbing to No 3 in the US. They enjoyed further hits, most notably with *Baby Jump*, *Lady Rose* and *Alright, Alright, Alright*, but much of their music lacked diversity.

In The Summertime was also featured on their *Electronically Tested* album, which also contained their excellent nine-minute version of *I Just Wanna Make Love To You* that captures them in fine fettle with growling vocals and superb fuzz guitar work.

In the late seventies the band was signed to Polydor and original members Earl and Rush were back in the fold. They later formed Skeleton Crew. When the hits dried up, **Mungo Jerry** turned their focus abroad where they continued to attract audiences. **Dorset** tried to launch a solo career but couldn't shed the group's identity, which is perhaps why he still has a **Mungo Jerry** line-up on the road today.

They also appeared back in 1971 playing *Somebody Stole My Wife* on the *Dawn Takeaway Concert* (LP) compilation, whilst *In The Summertime* figured on Ronco's *20 Star Tracks, Vol. 1* (LP), *Seventies Legends 2* (CD), *Number 1 Hits Of The 70's & 80's* (CD), *Sunshine Day A Taste Of The 70's* (CD), *The Super 70's Vol 1* (CD), *Perfect Day* (CD), *Brit Pop* (CD) and *UK No 1 Hits Of The 70's* (CD); you can check out *Open Up* on *70's FAB FAV's - Classic 70's Hits* (CD) and *Baby Jump* has been compiled on *The Super 70's Vol 2* (CD) and on *No. 1s & Million Sellers Vol 4* (CD).

RAY DORSET from MUNGO JERRY.

Murgatroyd Band

Personnel:	RAY FENWICK	A
	EDDIE HARDIN	A
	PETE YORK	A

45:     Magpie/Twice A Week (Some PS)   (Decca F 13256) 1972 SC

Magpie was the title song to the great ITV challenge to 'Blue Peter'. **Spencer Davis Group** members Ray Fenwick, Eddie Hardin and Pete York helped perform the track, which was written by Fenwick with Tim Hardin and **Spencer Davis**.

The TV show 'Magpie' was presented by Mick Robinson who at the time was considered something of a superstar in the making. In fact, he even made a record in 1969 which was released in the early seventies.

Magpie can also be heard on Decca's *World Of TV Themes* (LP). (MWh)

Mister Murray

45s:	Down Came The Rain/	
	Whatever Happened To Music?	(Fontana TF 623) 1965
	I Drink To Your Memory/	
	I Was A Good Song	(Fontana TF 674) 1966

This was actually songwriter Mitch Murray. *Down Came The Rain* was a hit in Italy, as *Una Ragazza In Due* and has also resurfaced on *Turds On A Bum Ride, Vol. 5* (CD). See **Mitch Murray Clan** entry for more details. (VJ)

Mitch Murray Clan

Personnel incl: MITCH MURRAY

45:     Skyliner/Cherokee   (Clan 597 001) 1966

Mitch Murray, who was born on 30th January 1940 in Hove, Sussex, is best remembered as one of Britain's most successful sixties songwriters but he dabbled with recording himself first with **Mitch Murray's Monkeys** in the early sixties, then with **Mister Murray** and finally with this outfit. None of his recording exploits are memorable.

As a songwriter the story was very different. As early as 1963 he'd written two No. 1s: - *How Do You Do It?* and *I Like It* for **Gerry and The Pacemakers**. In 1965 he wrote *You Were Made For Me* for **Freddie and The Dreamers** and also co-wrote *I'm Telling You Now* with Freddie Garrity (Freddie of **Freddie and The Dreamers**). Then he began a songwriting partnership with Peter Callander which produced several hits including *The Ballad Of Bonnie and Clyde* for **Georgie Fame**, *Goodbye Sam, Hello*

Samantha for Cliff Richard, *I Did What I Did For Maria* for Tony Christie and a series of hits for **Paper Lace**. By the eighties he'd become a director of the Performing Rights Society and was working on TV jingles. He's now a speechwriter, after-dinner speaker and author of several books. (VJ)

Murray's Monkeys

Personnel incl: MITCH MURRAY

45:     Gipsy/I'll Be Here   (Pye 7N 15800) 1965

See **Mitch Murray Clan** entry for further details of **Murray**'s career. He was backed by a session group on this cheerful beat 45. (VJ)

Mushroom

| Personnel incl: | JOE O'DONNELL | |
| | PAT COLLINS | violin |

| ALBUM: | 1 | EARLY ONE MORNING | |
| | | (Some w/poster inner) | (Hawk HALPX 116) 1973 R4 |

NB: (1) reissued on Little Wing (LW 2027/28) 1992 and again on vinyl (Akarma AK 328) 2005. Later reissued on CD.

45s:	Devil Among The Tailors//Sun Ni Dhuibir	
	King Of Ireland's Daughter	(Hawk HASP 320) 1973 SC
	Kings And Queens/Met A Friend	(Hawk HASP 340) 1974 SC

This Irish group formed in Dublin in 1972. Their album is very rare and expensive to obtain. Some copies included a poster, and naturally these fetch a little more. Their 45s are minor collectables too. Their blend of progressivism and Irish folk music is well worth seeking out, so snap up the Little Wing reissue (which also includes both sides of their first 45) or the recent Akarma one if you can. (VJ)

Musical Theatre

| ALBUM: | 1 | A REVOLUTIONARY REVELATION | |
| | | | (Pye NSPL 28128) 1970 |

No other details known. (VJ)

Music Box

| ALBUM: | 1 | SONGS OF SUNSHINE | (Westwood MRS 013) 1972 |

This is a very pleasant electric folk album. Aside from a Dylan cover the material is self-composed. (VJ)

Music Motor

Personnel:	LES BRAID	bs	A
	RAY ENNIS	gtr	A
	KENNY GODLASS		A
	MIKE GREGORY		A
	TOMMY MURRAY		A

45:     Happy/Where Am I Going   (Deram DM 282) 1970

Recognise some of these names? Yes, this was Liverpool's **Swinging Blue Jeans** recording under another name. Soon after, of course, they reverted back to their old moniker. (VJ)

Musketeer Gripweed (and The Third Troop)

| 45: | How I Won The War/ | |
| | Aftermath | (United Artists UP 1196) 1967 R6/R3 |

NB: Both stock copies (R6) and demo copies (R3) exist: the stock copies are much rarer.

United Artists issued this 45 a week before the world premier of the film 'How I Won The War' in London. Gripweed was the character **John Lennon** played in the film and the record company obviously hoped this would help the disc sell as a **John Lennon** recording. The record consisted of instrumental music from the film overdubbed by sound effects and extracts from the dialogue, which probably included somewhere, though it's impossible to decipher **Lennon**'s voice. The record sold badly at the time but as is often the case, has subsequently become very collectable.

How I Won The War has been compiled on *Liverpool 1963-1968, Vol. 1* (LP). (VJ)

Mustang

45:     Why/Here, There and Everywhere   (Parlophone R 5579) 1967 SC

The 'A' side of this 45 was a Byrds' track and flip side a **Beatles**' song but it failed to propel the band beyond obscurity. (VJ)

Mustard

45:     Good Time Comin'/I Saw I Heard   (EMI EMI 2165) 1974

This was an obscure mid-seventies recording. (VJ)

Mutt 'n' Jeff

45:     Don't Nag Me Ma/Strolling The Blues   (Decca F 12335) 1966

This was another one-off project. This duo's 45 was produced by David Nicholson, who managed **Crispian St. Peters**. (VJ)

Tim Mycroft

45:     Shadra/Bournemouth Rock   (Parlophone R 5919) 1971

This 45 was produced by **Tony Ashton**. The backing was provided by Paul Buckmaster, **Chris Spedding**, Paul Curtis and **Tony Ashton** himself. The 'A' side comprised **Shadows**-style guitar with nonsensical Indian lyrics. **Mycroft** had earlier been in **Sounds Nice**. (VJ)

My Dear Watson

Personnel incl:	ALEX ALEXANDER		
	BILLY CAMERON	bs	A
	ROBERT CAMERON		
	IAIN LYON	gtr, drms, vcls	A
	JOHN STEWART	vcls, gtr, piano	A

45s:	Elusive Face/		
	The Shame Just Drained	(Parlophone R 5687) 1968 SC
	Stop! Stop! I'll Be There/		
	Make This Day Last	(Parlophone R 5737) 1968 SC
	Have You Seen Your Saviour/		
	White Line Road	(DJM DJS 224) 1970

From Buckie in Scotland, this band was earlier known as Johnny and The Copycats. The quartet's early influences were R&B. Stewart is thought to have been in a line-up of **Hedgehoppers Anonymous** prior to this band.

Their first two 45s are quite highly-rated pop but when they brought them no commercial success the band took off to work on the Continent. They returned in 1970 with a third country-influenced 45, but then split at the end of the decade. They also appeared on **The Easybeats**' *Vigil* album, issued in 1968. **The Easybeats**' Harry Vanda and George Young wrote *Elusive Face* and produced the group's second 45. Their final 45 was more country-ish and featured **Elton John** as a session man.

Alex Alexander is also known as George Alexander/Alex Young. He is the brother of George Young (of **The Easybeats**) and Malcolm and Angus Young (of AC/DC) and was later in **Grapefruit**. Lyon was later in the **JSD Band** and then with Lucas and McCulloch's Ragnorak. (VJ/JM)

My Kind of People

45:     Somebody's Coming/
        Nobody Knows Why The Butterfly Die   (CBS 5133) 1970

No other details are known about this 45. (VJ)

Rowland Myres

ALBUM: 1   JUST FOR THE RECORD   (Deroy DER 1063) 1974 R3

This is an obscure privately-pressed album, which is also listed as Music Sound Enterprise MSE 1. (VJ)

The Mysteries

45:     Give Me Rhythm and Blues/
        Teardrops   (Decca F 11919) 1964 SC

This 45 is now quite collectable. It was the work of a girl beat group. (VJ)

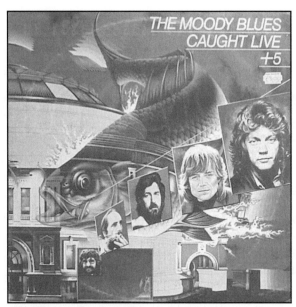

THE MOODY BLUES - Caught Live + Five (LP).

THE MOVE - Fire Brigade (LP).

Naked Truth

45:    Two Little Rooms/Rag Doll Boy   (Deram DM 287) 1970

This is one of the many obscure acts who recorded on Deram. (VJ)

The Name

The *Dustbin Full Of Rubbish* (LP) compilation first unearthed this previously unreleased 1966 acetate recording of *Hello Edythe*. Basically it is bad psychedelic pop, quite varied but badly put together and it is easy to see why it had remained unreleased. Subsequently, *Hello Edythe* and its flip, *What Do I Care?* resurfaced on *Syde Trips Vol. 6* (LP), but the band identity still remains mysterious. (VJ)

Nanette

ALBUM: 1 NANETTE   (Columbia SCX 6398) 1970 SC

45s:	Flying Machine/	
	You're Wastin' Your Time	(Columbia DB 8659) 1969
	Every Night When I Cry/Jamie	(Columbia DB 8673) 1969
	Let Me Be The One/To Be Loved	(Columbia DB 8733) 1970
	Everybody's Singing Like Now/	
	Could I Forget	(Columbia DB 8751) 1971

A Canadian female singer resident in the UK whose album was an orchestrated pop/folk effort. (VJ/GB)

Narnia

Personnel:	PETER BANKS	keyb'ds, gtr	A
	KENNETH DIXON	vcls, drms	A
	PAULINE FILBY	vcls	A
	TIM HAYWELL	bs, gtr	A
	JOHN RUSSELL	vcls, recorder, gtr	A

ALBUM: 1(A) NARNIA - ASLAN IS NOT A TAME LION
                          (Myrrh MYR 1007) 1974 R3

NB: (1) reissued on vinyl as a limited edition of 300 (Solar Circus SCR 003) and CD (NA NAR 1) 1997.

Hyped up by dealers worldwide as a masterpiece of acid-folk, this has a few arresting moments, but is generally overestimated. The main problem is the compositions, which do not render anything not heard before elsewhere. At worst they are trite and lacking in depth, at best they are agreeable as on *Agape* and on by far the best track *Living Water*. The playing is good, while the lyrics have strong religious undertones. **Pauline**

NARNIA - Aslan Is Not A Tame Lion (LP).

Filby sings very well, but often sounds uncomfortably like **Dusty Springfield**, while the overall sound is reminiscent of The Seekers. The most positive effect of this album could be that one may want to re-read C.S. Lewis's Narnia Cycle.

In June 1972 the band Agape formed featuring John Russell and **Pauline Filby**. **Filby** had been married for some time to Jack Filby, who was a vicar. They formed a folk duo after their marriage and lived in Cliff Richard's home in Essex, which was a Christian Arts Centre. Pauline had been a folk singer for a few years before she married.

You can also check out *Agape* on *Psychedelic Salvage Co. Vol. 2* (LP & CD). It's the wide-ranging female vocals that really catch the ear. Banks, Haywell and Russell were later in After The Fire. **Pauline Filby** also had solo albums. (MK)

Graham Nash

HCP

ALBUMS:	1	SONGS FOR BEGINNERS		
(up to			(Atlantic 2401 011) 1971 SC	13
1976)	2	WILD TALES	(Atlantic K 50025) 1973	-

NB: (1) reissued on Atlantic (K 40237) in 1972.

45s:	Chicago/Simple Man	(Atlantic 2091 096) 1971
(up to	Military Madness/	
1976)	I Used To Be A King	(Atlantic 2091 135) 1971
	On The Line/I Miss You	(Atlantic K 10425) 1974
	Grace Concern/Another Sleep Song	(Atlantic K 10470) 1974

Graham Nash has been one of the most significant figures in the history of rock and pop from the sixties. An attractive vocalist his voice was immediately recognisable and he enjoyed considerable success initially with **The Hollies** but later with Crosby, Stills, Nash and Young. He also wrote some memorable songs such as *Teach Your Children* and *Marakesh Express*, which encompassed the idealism of the 1960s.

Born in Blackpool on 2 February 1942, **Graham Nash** became friends with Allan Clarke whilst at school. In the mid-fifties they played together in a skiffle duo called The Two Teens, who later became known as The Levins and when they acquired Guytone guitars as The Guytones. Whilst playing a gig as The Fourtones, Clarke and **Nash** were approached by a group called The Deltas to join them and over the next few months they became the heart of **The Hollies** and within a relatively short time **Nash** discarded his rhythm guitar to become their singer and later a songwriter for the band. Gradually, though, he tired of their commercially successful, largely pop format and left in December 1968 to become part of Crosby, Stills and Nash. After their demise he emerged as a solo artist in his own right with *Songs For Beginners*, an easy-going folky album, which dealt with political issues of the day in songs like *Military Madness* and *Chicago*. However the stand-out track was *I Used To Be A King*, which contained some sensitive and personal lyrics. The album sold well climbing to No 13 here and No 15 in the US.

In December 1971 **Nash** toured Europe with David Crosby and the following year they recorded an album *Graham Nash and David Crosby* that achieved considerable success in the US, where it seemed to capture the mood of a nation dominated by the issues and morales of the Vietnam war and climbed to No 4. It spawned a single *Immigrant Man*, which brought him another US hit and the album also made the Top 15 here in the UK.

His second solo album *Wild Tales*, released after the murder of his girlfriend Amy Gosage, was understandably less upbeat than his first effort and met with a lukewarm response from critics and punters. After this he reverted to working with David Crosby and successful albums of new material *Wind On The Water* and *Whistling Down The Wire*, along with a live and greatest hits package, emerged in the second half of the decade. It was a partnership ended by Crosby's increasing drug problems and 1980's *Earth And Fire* which had started as a collaboration ended up as a **Nash** solo project, but the times had changed and the album was not well received. Later in 1982 **Nash** recorded with **The Hollies** again. 1986's attempt to utilise synthesisers and drum machines on a new solo album *Innocent Eyes* didn't work either. Since the mid-eighties, he has participated in various reunions with Crosby, Stills and Nash and Crosby, Stills, Nash and Young. (VJ)

The Nashville Teens

Personnel:

MICHAEL DUNFORD	gtr	A	
JOHN HAWKENS	piano	ABCDE	
ROGER GROOM	drms	A E	
PETE SHANNON	bs	ABCDE	
ARTHUR SHARP	vcls	ABCDE	
RAY PHILLIPS	bs, vcls	ABCDE	
JOHN ALLEN	gtr	BCDE	
PETE LACE	drms	B	
BARRY JENKINS	drms	CD	
(TERRY CROW	vcls	C)	

ALBUM: 1( )   THE NASHVILLE TEENS (New World NW 6002) 1975 R1

NB: There's three CD compilations: *The Best Of The Nashville Teens 1964-1969* (EMI O 777 7 81424 2 3) 1993, is marred by the inclusion of a weaker alternate take of their finest moment *Tobacco Road*; *Tobacco Road* (Repertoire REP 4858) 2000 contains their album plus 14 bonus tracks; and the pirate *Tobacco Road* (LCD LCD 1-2), is a 20-track retrospective.

EP: 1   THE NASHVILLE TEENS   (Decca DFE 8600) 1965 R2

			HCP
45s:	Tobacco Road/I Like It Like That	(Decca F 11930) 1964	6
	Goggle Eye/T.N.T.	(Decca F 12000) 1964	10
	Find My Way Back Home/Devil-In-Law	(Decca F 12089) 1965	34
	This Little Bird/Whatcha Gonna Do?	(Decca F 12143) 1965	38
	I Know How It Feels To Be Loved/		
	Soon Forgotten	(Decca F 12255) 1965	-
	The Hard Way/Upside Down	(Decca F 12316) 1966 SC	45
	Forbidden Fruit/Revived 45 Time	(Decca F 12458) 1966 SC	-
	That's My Woman/Words	(Decca F 12542) 1966 SC	-
	I'm Coming Home/Searching	(Decca F 12580) 1967	-
	The Biggest Night Of Her Life/		
	Last Minute	(Decca F 12657) 1967	-
	All Along The Watchtower/Sun-Dog	(Decca F 12754) 1968	-
	The Lament Of The Cherokee Reservation Indian/		
	Looking For You	(Major Minor MM 599) 1969 SC	-
	Ella James/Tennessee Woman	(Parlophone R 5925) 1971 SC	-
	Lawdy Miss Clawdy/		
	Let It Rock: Break Up	(Enterprise ENT 001) 1972	-
	You Shouldn't Have Been So Nice/		
	Tell The People	(Parlophone R 5961) 1972	-
Reissues:	Tobacco Road/		
	All Along The Watchtower	(Decca F 12929) 1969	-
	Tobacco Road/Chips And Peas	(Sky SKY 1007) 1977	-
	Tobacco Road (84)/Find My Way Home/		
	Born To Be Wild	(Butt FUNEP 4) 1984	-
	Tobacco Road/Goggle Eye	(EMI G 4543) 1987	-

The Nashville Teens were one of Britain's best sixties R&B acts and it's unfortunate that they didn't get the success they deserved.

THE NASHVILLE TEENS - Tobacco Road (LCD) (CD).

The Nashville Teens formed in Weybridge, Surrey in 1962. Founding members Arthur Sharp and Ramon Phillips had been lead singers in rival groups which joined forces in 1962. The group cut its teeth in Hamburg's clubs during 1963-64. This era saw a few personnel changes, with Dunsford and Groom being replaced by Woking guitarist John Allen and drummer Pete Lace, who was in turn replaced by Barry Jenkins. They also added a third vocalist, Terry Crow, but he decided to remain in Germany when their residency at the Star Club ended. During their time in Germany they backed Jerry Lee Lewis on a live album (*Live At The Star Club, Hamburg*, Philips BL 7646, 1965).

Returning to the UK in 1964, they were managed by Don Arden. Mickie Most (vocalist with The Minutemen at the time) became their producer after seeing them back Chuck Berry, who was over here on tour. For their debut 45 they chose a barnstorming R&B rendition of North Carolinan John D. Loudermilk's *Tobacco Road*. Sharp had come across the song whilst working in a record shop, and it proved the start of a close relationship between the group and composer. The single, notable for its strident piano, pulsating beat and twin vocals, climbed to No. 6 here and No. 14 in the US. It was a smash in several other countries too. They followed it up with another Loudermilk song, *Goggle Eye*, a folksy number about an unfortunate trout, which just made the Top Ten over here. Despite being supported by a promo film, the song made far less international impact than its predecessor.

Their opportunity to enhance their standing in the States was frustrated by visa restrictions, which meant a US tour with **The Zombies** couldn't go outside New York State. This deprived them of the publicity a trip to Nashville might have created. Whilst in New York, though, they recorded a third 45, *Find My Way Back Home*, which was a minor hit back in the UK. The fact they recorded it without producer Mickie Most soured their relationship with him.

Decca, their label, did little to help their cause by failing to grasp what a good R&B band they were, as evidenced by tracks like *Parchment Farm* and *I Need You Baby* on their 1965 EP. Then, in April 1965, they released both the group's and **Marianne Faithfull**'s versions of Loudermilk's *This Little Bird* - both, amazingly, produced by the same man, **Andrew Loog Oldham**. In the UK **Faithfull**'s version won the sales war (**The Nashville Teens**' version just scrapped into the Top 40), but it was a different story elsewhere, especially Japan and Australia.

The band's appearance alongside **The Animals** in the 1965 movie 'Pop Gear' was also significant, as the two groups forged a friendship and in 1966 Barry Jenkins defected to **The Animals**. Roger Groom rejoined **The Nashville Teens** as his replacement. Their final UK hit was *The Hard Way* in February 1966. Later they worked with producers including Shel Talmy, Mike Leander and **Roy Wood**, but could never come up with the right record at the right time. They failed to make much impact with a cover of Randy Newman's *Biggest Night Of Her Life*; their competent rendition of Dylan's *All Along The Watchtower* was upstaged by **Jimi Hendrix**'s and their good attempt at *Indian Reservation* was overshadowed by **Don Fardon**'s. They also recorded a 45 as the **Arizona Swamp Company**.

Later John Hawken departed for **Keith Relf's Renaissance**. Art Sharp left in 1972 to become Don Arden's assistant, but the band recorded throughout the seventies and into the eighties with different personnel. By 1982 only Ray Phillips survived from the original line-up.

A version of the band was working the nostalgia circuit well into the nineties and Repertoire's definitive CD compilation released in 2000 attracted some positive publicity in the band's direction.

Compilation appearances have included: *Last Minute* on *Justafixation II* (LP) and *Jagged Time Lapse, Vol 4* (CD); *Poor Boy* and *Indian Reservation* on *Made In England, Vol. 1* (CD); *I'm A Lonely One* on *Psychedelia, Vol. 4* (LP) and *Hen's Teeth, Vol. 3* (CD); *Poor Boy* on *Broken Dreams, Vol. 4* (LP) and *Rare 60's Beat Treasures, Vol. 3* (CD); *Revived 45 Time* and *Forbidden Fruit* on *Rare 60's Beat Treasures, Vol. 1* (CD); *Upside Down* on *Rare 60's Beat Treasures, Vol. 4* (CD); *Find My Way Back Home* on *Sound Of The Sixties* (2-LP) and *Sixties Archive Vol. 1* (CD); *High School Confidential* and *Lewis' Boogie* on *The Star-Club Singles Complete, Vol. 1* (LP & CD); *Born To Be Wild* on *Beat Merchants* (CD); *High School Confidential* on *Beat Im Star Club* (2-LP); *XK1LX* on *Broken Dreams, Vol. 1* (LP), *Incredible Sound Show Stories, Vol. 3* (LP) and *Jagged Time Lapse, Vol 1* (CD); *Whatcha Gonna Do?* on *Broken Dreams, Vol. 2* (LP); *Widdicombe Fair* on *Broken Dreams, Vol. 5* (LP) and *Jagged Time Lapse Vol 2* (CD); and *Tobacco Road* on *Hard-Up Heroes* (2-LP), *The World Of*

NASHVILLE TEENS - Tobacco Road (Repertoire) (CD).

Hits, Vol. 2 (LP), *Brit Pop* (CD), *Dizzy* (CD) and on *The Swinging Sixties - 18 Classic Tracks* (CD). (VJ)

Nasty Pop

Personnel:	JON FITZPATRICK	vcls	A
	STEVE GRACE	gtr, hrmnca	A
	KEITH WILKINSON	bs, vcls	A
	TONY WILMSHURST	gtr, vcls	A

ALBUM: 1 (A)	NASTY POP	(Island ILPS 9340) 1975

45s:	Crow/Gracie	(Island WIP 6253) 1975
	Crow/ Crow (alt version)	(Island NASTY 2) 1975

Nasty Pop was a mid-seventies rock band. A second album *Mistaken Identity* appeared in 1977. Keith Wilkinson was later in Squeeze. They released one further single for Polydor *You're Not The One/Track You Down* in 1977. (BS)

National Head Band

Personnel:	RUSTY FORD	gtr, vcls	A
	LEE KERSLAKE	drms, keyb'ds, vcls	A
	DAVE PAUL	bs, keyb'ds, gtr, vcls	A
	JAN SCHELHAAS	keyb'ds	A

ALBUM: 1(A)	ALBERT ONE	(Warner Bros K 46094) 1971 R1

A hard-rock/progressive outfit that formed in 1969 out of **Scaffold**'s backing group. Initially known as The Business, Lee Kerslake had joined from **Toe Fat**. Their varied album, which was produced by Eddie Offord, featured a laborious selection of introverted riffs and one song, *Too Much...*, which was very Beatle-ish.

They split in November 1971. Jan Schelhaas was later in **The Gary Moore Band** and **Caravan**, whilst Lee Kerslake went on to **Uriah Heep**. (VJ)

National Pinion Pole

45:	Make Your Mark Little Man/	
	I Was The One You Came In With	(Planet PLF 111) 1966 SC

This 45 was a tongue in cheek election bandwagon ditty from a little known band. The 'B' side is an even more tongue in cheek romantic beat song with some 'wonderful' guitar.

Make Your Mark Little Man has been compiled on *The Best Of Planet Records* (CD). (MWh)

Natural Acoustic Band

Personnel:	TOMMY HOY	gtr, vcls	ABCD
	KRYSIA KOCJAN	vcls, gtr	A
	ROBIN THYNE	gtr, vcls, flute, perc	ABCD
	AMIN MOHAMMED	bs	B
	GRAEME MORGAN	percsn	B
	JOANNA CARLIN	vcls, gtr	C
	DOUG BEVERIDGE	drms	C

ALBUMS: 1(A)	LEARNING TO LIVE	(RCA SF 8272) 1972 SC
2(C)	BRANCHING IN	(RCA SF 8314) 1974 SC

45:	Echoes/Is It True Blue	(RCA RCA 2324) 1973

This group formed as a folk duo in Milngarie, Glasgow, Scotland, in 1969. Tom Hoy was a Glaswegian by birth and Robin Thyne a Geordie. **Krysia Kocjan** who had a Flemish mum and a Polish dad, joined early in 1971. She was a talented vocalist who brought them a good degree of publicity - they were often billed as **The Natural Acoustic Band** featuring **Krysia Kocjan**.

Learning To Live was a good progressive folk effort notable for **Kocjan**'s vocals and similar to **Dando Shaft**. It came in a lovely gatefold sleeve. The follow-up was similar musically. Both albums were produced by Milt Okun, who had worked extensively with Peter Paul and Mary.

Kocjan left in December 1972. She went solo releasing an album in 1974 and did session work for Ray Davies, **Mike Heron** and **Robin Williamson** among others and now lives in the USA. Morgan left shortly after. Carlin and Beveridge were recruited as replacements but left not long afterwards with Mohammed. The band was soon reduced to a duo again with Thyne and Hoy.

The pair continued as a duo until 1975 when Hoy joined **Magna Carta**. Thyne followed him into **Magna Carta** a couple of years later, though in 1979 they both left to form Nova Carta, but that's another story. (VJ/JM)

Natural Gas

Personnel:	MARK CLARKE	bs	A
	JOEY MOLLAND	gtr	A
	JERRY SHIRLEY	drms	A
	PETER WOOD	keyb'ds	A

ALBUM: 1 (A)	NATURAL GAS	(Private Stock 2011) 1976

EP:	1(A)	NATURAL GAS (promo only)	(Private Stock PSS 1) 1976

45:	The Right Time/Miracle Mile	(Private Stock PVT 71) 1976

Mark Clarke came from **Tempest** and went on briefly to Rainbow. Joey Molland had been in **Badfinger** and Jerry Shirley had been with **Humble Pie**. Peter Wood joined from Quiver (when they were backing The Sutherland Brothers). So this was a minor supergroup, but it didn't set the world alight. (CG)

The Naturals

Personnel:	CURT CRESSWELL	gtr	A
	ROY HEATHER	drms	A
	BOB O'NEALE	hrmnca, vcls	A
	RICKI PORTER	vcls	A
	MIKE WAKELIN	bs	A

			HCP
45s:	Daisy Chain/That Girl	(Parlophone R 5116) 1964 -
	I Should Have Known Better/	
	Didn't I?	(Parlophone R 5165) 1964 24
	It Was You/Look At Me Now	(Parlophone R 5202) 1964 SC -
	Blue Roses/Shame On You	(Parlophone R 5257) 1965 SC -

This group came from Harlow in Essex and three members (Curt Cresswell, Roy Heather and Mick Wakelin) had earlier played in The

Cossacks. Their only hit was their cover of **The Beatles**' song *I Should Have Known Better*. They played in bowler hats and were managed by **The Beatles** song publisher, Dick James.

Another ex-Cossack, lead guitarist Richard Laws, went on to play with **The Couriers**.

Compilation appearances have included: *Shame On You* on *Liverpool '65* (LP); and *I Should Have Known Better* on *Beat At Abbey Road* (CD) and *20 One Hit Wonders* (LP). (VJ)

Shel Naylor

45s:	How Deep Is The Ocean/La Bamba	(Decca F 11776) 1963 SC
	One Fine Day/	
	It's Gonna Happen Soon	(Decca F 11856) 1964 R2

One Fine Day is generally considered the better of **Naylor**'s two singles. It was a cover of a Ray Davies song and both **The Kinks** and **Jimmy Page** played on it. **Naylor** later resurfaced in **Staveley Makepeace** and, under his real name Rob Woodward, in **Lieutenant Pigeon**.

Compilation appearances have included: *One Fine Day* on *Jimmy Page, Session Man* (CD), *Beat It* (3-CD) and *The Freakbeat Scene* (CD); *One Fine Day* and *It's Gonna Happen Soon* on *Nowhere Men Vol. 1* (LP & CD); and *It's Gonna Happen Soon* on *The Beat Scene* (CD). (VJ/MG)

Nazareth

Personnel:	PETE AGNEW	bs	A
	MANNY CHARLTON	gtr	A
	DAN McCAFFERTY	vcls	A
	DARRELL SWEET	drms	A

				HCP
ALBUMS:	1(A)	NAZARETH	(Pegasus PEG 10) 1971 SC	-
(up to	2(A)	EXERCISES	(Pegasus PEG 14) 1972 SC	-
1976)	3(A)	RAZAMANAZ	(Mooncrest CREST 1) 1973	11
	4(A)	LOUD AND PROUD	(Mooncrest CREST 4) 1974	10
	5(A)	RAMPANT	(Mooncrest CREST 15) 1975	13
	6(A)	HAIR OF THE DOG	(Mooncrest CREST 27) 1975	-
	7(A)	GREATEST HITS	(Mountain TOPS 108) 1976	54
	8(A)	CLOSE ENOUGH FOR ROCK 'N' ROLL		
			(Mountain TOPS 109) 1976	-

NB: (1) issued by Warner Bros in the US. (2) - (8) issued by A&M in the US. (1) and (2) reissued by Mooncrest in 1972. (1) - (6) later reissued by Mountain in 1975. (3) and (6) reissued by NEMS in 1982.

CD reissues have included: (2) reissued on CD (Castle Classics CLACD 220) in 1991. (3) and (4) reissued on CD (Castle Classics CLACD 173 and 174) respectively in 1990. (3) reissued on CD (Essential! ESMCD 370) 1996 with three 'B' sides added and their first recording of *Woke Up This Morning* from *Exercises*. (3)

NAZARETH - Hair Of The Dog (LP).

NAZARETH - At The Beeb (CD).

remastered and reissued again on CD (Eagle EAMCD 132) 2001. (4) reissued on CD (Essential! ESMCD 379) 1996 with US remixes of *This Flight Tonight* and *Go Down Fighting* plus an unedited take of *Hollis Brown*. (4) remastered and reissued again on CD (Eagle EAMCD 133) 2001. (5) reissued on CD (Castle Classics CLACD 242) 1992. (5) and (6) have been repackaged on one CD (That's Original TFOCD 13) 1988. (5) reissued on CD (Essential! ESMCD 551) 1997 with bonus tracks: - *Shanghai'd In Shanghai* (the US version), *Cat's Eye Apple Pie* (a 'B' side) and a seventies revival of **The Yardbirds**' *Shapes Of Things*. (5) remastered and reissued again on CD (Eagle EAMCD 134) 2001. (6) reissued on CD (Essential! ESMCD 550) 1997 with four bonus tracks *Morning Dew* from their debut album and four later LP tracks. (6) remastered and reissued again on CD (Eagle EAMCD 127) 2001. (6) reissued again on CD with bonus tracks (Snapper SDPCD 183) 2005. (7) reissued on CD (Essential! ESMCD 369) 1997 with bonus tracks. The Essential releases have been remastered with bonus tracks and detailed notes from the band themselves. (8) reissued on CD (Castle Classics CLACD 182) 1990. (8) remastered and reissued again on CD (Eagle EAMCD 138) 2002, with bonus cuts.

A good overview of their music can be obtained by acquiring *Anthology: Nazareth* (Raw Power RAWCD 039) 1989 and *Greatest Hits: Nazareth* (Castle Classics CLACD 149) 1989. Also relevant is *The Singles Collection* (Castle Communications CCSCD 280) 1990 or (CCSLP 280) 1990. *BBC Radio 1 Live In Concert* (Windsong WINCD 005) 1991 captures their live sound from a 1972 and 1973 concert well. *The Early Years* (Dojo EARL D 3) 1991 is, as its name suggests, a compilation of earlier material from 1971-74. . There's also *Nazareth - CD Box Set* (Castle Classics CLA BX 908) 1992. *From The Vaults* (Sequel NEM CD 639) 1993 is a rarities collection comprising songs which hadn't appeared on CD to date. It features some of their less successful early 45s, some German-only releases and four cuts from a double 7" live EP which dates from 1981. More recent compilations are *The Very Best Of Nazareth* (Eagle EAMCD 141) 2002, *The Collection* (Delta 47102) 2002 and *Love Hurts - The Rock Ballads* (Music Club MCC 486) 2002. *Back To The Trenches* (Castle CMEDD 725) 2003 is a 2-CD compilation of live and BBC performances from 1971-1984, which was originally issued in 2001.

			HCP
45s:	Dear John / Friends	(Pegasus PGS 1) 1972 SC	-
(up to	Morning Dew/Spinning Top	(Pegasus PGS 4) 1972 SC	-
1976)	If You See My Baby/		
	Hard Living	(Pegasus PGS 5) 1972 SC	-
	Broken Down Angel/		
	Witchdoctor Woman	(Mooncrest MOON 1) 1973	9
	Bad Bad Boy/		
	Hard Living (Some PS)	(Mooncrest MOON 9) 1973	10
	This Flight Tonight/		
	Called Her Name	(Mooncrest MOON 14) 1973	11
	Shanghai'd In Shanghai/		
	Love, Now You're Gone	(Mooncrest MOON 22) 1974	41
	Love Hurts/Down	(Mooncrest MOON 37) 1974	-
	Hair Of The Dog/		
	Too Bad, Too Sad	(Mooncrest MOON 44) 1975	-
	My White Bicycle/		
	Miss Misery	(Mooncrest MOON 47) 1975	14
	Holy Roller/Railroad Boy	(Mountain TOP 3) 1975	36
	Carry Out Feelings/Lift The Lid	(Mountain TOP 8) 1976	-
	You're The Violin/Loretta	(Mountain TOP 14) 1976	-
	I Don't Want To Go On Without You/		
	Good Love	(Mountain TOP 21) 1976	-

Reissues: α Love Hurts/This Flight Tonight/Broken Down Angel/
Hair Of The Dog (Pic Disc)   (Mountain NEP 2) 1983 -
This Flight Tonight/
Broken Down Angel   (Old Gold OG 9801) 1988 -

NB: α These four tracks also appeared on a *Special Edition* CD EP (Castle Communications CD 3-17) 1988.

Rarely ever critically acclaimed **Nazareth** proved to be an incredibly stable hard-rock outfit and one that certainly had staying power.

This band was originally from Dunfermline in Scotland and known as The Shadettes. Manny Charlton hadn't been with them nearly as long as the other three, having previously been guitarist for other local groups The Mark Five and Red Hawkes. The name change came shortly after Charlton joined in 1969. They took the name **Nazareth** from a line in The Weight by The Band. For the first couple of years they worked on a semi-professional basis establishing a reputation in Scotland as a no nonsense hard-rock band. After their first album *Nazareth*, they went full-time. Both this and the follow-up, *Exercises*, which also contained some acoustic tracks were recorded down in London, where they decided to move to. Their second 45, *Morning Dew*, covered a Tim Rose song.

Razamanaz, their third album, which was produced by **Deep Purple** bassist **Roger Glover** spawned two hit singles:- *Broken Down Angel* and *Bad Bad Boy*. The album, too, got to No 11 in the UK Album Charts and No 157 in the US. Their fresh interpretation of Joni Mitchell's *This Flight Tonight*, which was far removed from the original version, narrowly missed the Top Ten too, later the same year.

Glover also produced their *Loud And Proud* album, which was the first step to establishing the band internationally. It reached the higher echelons of the Charts in four European countries and got to No 150 in the US. Their next 45 UK hit was a self-penned composition *Shanghai'd In Shanghai*.

Their next two albums, *Rampant* (regarded by many as a great mix of rock'n'roll and hard-rock) and *Hair Of The Dog*, which were produced by guitarist Manny Charlton, built on their earlier success both here in the UK and internationally. *Rampant* yielded another Top 20 UK hit in the form of their cover version of **Tomorrow**'s *My White Bicycle*. *Hair Of The Dog* included *Love Hurts*, which had earlier flopped as a single in the UK, but gave them a surprise Top 20 hit in the US. Other highlights include their cover of Nils Lofgren's *Beggar's Day* and the extended *Please Don't Judas Me* is a prime example of heavy metal. *Close Enough For Rock and Roll's* finest tracks included *Telegram* and *Vancouver Shakedown*.

There are loads of compilations showcasing the band's material. *The Very Best Of Nazareth* (2001) edits many of their classics in order to squeeze 22 tracks onto one CD. *The Collection* (2002) is one of the latest and showcases many of their guitar-led hard-rock cuts from the seventies as well as their smoother eighties output, alongside the inevitable hits. *Love Hurts - The Rock Ballads* by contrast compiles the splattering of ballads that adorned their albums and of course some like *Love Hurts*, *Dream On*

NECROMANDUS - Orexis Of Death (LP).

and *Hearts Grown Cold* were really big sellers. *Back To The Trenches* is a 2-CD compilation of their live and BBC performances between 1972-1984. It was originally issued in 2001 and reissued again in 2003. The bulk of the material on offer is exclusive to this CD and the release comes with a family tree, extensive sleevenotes and an interview.

The band recorded well into the eighties and beyond. Dan McCafferty also recorded a solo album for Mountain in 1975 as well as a number of 45s. In the final analysis the band can only be recommended to fans of hard-rock. They're still on the road with only Manny Charlton missing from the original line-up - his place is taken by guitarist Billy Rankin.

Nazareth's version of *Ballad Of Hollis Brown* later resurfaced on Sequel's CD compilation, *The Songs Of Bob Dylan*. Other compilation appearances have included: a live version of *Broken Down Angel* on *Rock Of Ages, Four Decades Of Heavy Rock 1962-2002*; *Love Hurts* (live) on *No.1s & Million Sellers Vol 4* (CD); *My White Bicycle* on *Classic Rock - cd3*; *Bad Bad Boy* on the 2-CD set *The Best Heavy Metal Album In The World?Ever!* and on *Metal Gods* (CD), along with *Woke Up This Morning*. Finally, *Hair Of The Dog* resurfaced on *70's Arena Rockers* (CD). (VJ)

'N Betweens

See the **In-Be-Tweens** entry.

Johnny Neal and The Starliners

Personnel incl:	TERRY FRANKS	drms	A
	JOHNNY NEAL	vcls	
	ROGER 'MOON' SHAW	ld gtr	A

45s: And I Will Love You/Walk Baby Walk   (Pye 7N 15388) 1965
Put Your Hand On The Hand/Now   (Parlophone R 5870) 1970

A Birmingham band whose first 45 also got a US release courtesy of ABC. The 'A' side was a ballad but the flip was a pretty good bluesy R&B number.

Roger Shaw was later in **Storyteller** and Terry France had previously worked with **Mike Sheridan**.

You'll also find *Walk Baby Walk* on *Brum Beat - Midlands Beat Groups Of The 60's* (CD), *English Freakbeat, Vol. 1* (LP & CD) and *Freakbeat Freakout* (CD). (VJ)

Neat Change

Personnel incl: PETER BANKS

45:    I Lied To Auntie May/
Sandman (some PS)   (Decca F 12809) 1968 R1/SC

The Neat Change was discovered by **Spencer Davis**. This 45 is now quite collectable on account of **Peter Banks'** involvement in the band. **Banks'** other bands included **The Syn**, **Yes** and **Flash**. The 'A' side, *I Lied To Auntie May*, is a string quartet-laden piece of pop art. The track was written by **Andy Bown** and **Peter Frampton** of **The Herd**. Some demo copies of the single came in a fold-out promo sleeve.

I Lied To Auntie May has been compiled on *We Can Fly, Vol 1* (CD), *British Psychedelic Trip, Vol. 4* (LP) and *Great British Psychedelic Trip, Vol. 2* (CD). (VJ)

Necromandus

Personnel:	BILL BRANCH	vcls	A
	BARRY (BAZ) DUNNERY	gtr	A
	FRANK HALL	drms	A
	DENNIS McCARTEN	bs	A

ALBUM: 1(A) QUICKSAND DREAM   (Reflection MM 09) 1990 SC

NB: (1) was released in a limited edition of 500 and later reissued on CD as *Orexis Of Death* (Audio Archives AACD ?) 1994 and it was later followed by an anthology,

Necrothology (Audio Archives AACD 030) 1996. There's also a *Necromandus Live* CD (Audio Archives AACD 050).

Necromandus came from the Carlisle area and was heavily influenced by **Black Sabbath.** They originally gigged under the name Hot Springwater before changing name to **Necromandus** (which sought to blend Necrophilia with the 16th Century sect of Nostradamus). They opened for **Black Sabbath** on their 1973 tour. They also appeared at the Kendal Pop Festival the same year. Their sole album was recorded back in 1973 and was originally intended for release on Vertigo, along with a single. It was produced by Tony Iommi and allocated a Vertigo prefix (6360061). For some reason the release was delayed, along with their first intended single *Night Jar.* Eventually, Baz Dunnery became disheartened and left the band which wasn't viable without him so Vertigo cancelled both the album and the single.

When Ozzy Osbourne was sacked by **Black Sabbath** in 1978 he contacted Dunnery, Mc Carten and Hall to set up a new band Blizzard Of Oz. It rehearsed, but didn't work out. Only Dunnery remained in the music business in Violinsky (an **ELO** spin-off project).

Eventually in 1990 a South American re-issue label Reflection gave the album an official release. This 500 limited edition vinyl release and subsequent CD has brought it to the attention of a wider audience. Tony Iommi contributed some deft guitar to one track *Orexis Of Death* and the album was dark and moody. It later received a CD release. The anthology CD *Necrothology* was based around their studio album and supplemented by alternative versions and live material, including a tribute track by Spanish band The Tempter.

The *Live* CD is a private recording of a Blackpool gig by the band. It's dark and powerful as you'd expect and showcases Dunnery's guitar wizardry and Branch's doom-laden vocals. The set includes songs from their album and other previously unreleased tracks. The sound quality is good and the CD is accompanied by a poster sleeve detailing the band's history and containing many rare photos and memorabilia. (VJ)

Nektar

Personnel:	ROY ALBRIGHTON	gtr, vcls	A
	ALLAN 'TAFF' FREEMAN	keyb'ds, vcls	A
	RON HOWDEN	drms	A
	DEREK 'MO' MOORE	bs,mellotron, vcls	A

ALBUMS:	1(A)	JOURNEY TO THE CENTRE OF THE EYE		
(up to			(Bellaphon BLPS 19064) 1972 R1
1976)	2(A)	SOUNDS LIKE THIS (2-LP)		
			(United Artists UAD 60041/2) 1973 SC
	3(A)	A TAB IN THE OCEAN		
			(United Artists UAG 29499) 1974 SC
	4(A)	REMEMBER THE FUTURE		
			(United Artists UAS 29545) 1974 SC

NEKTAR - Journey To The Centre Of The Eye (LP).

NEKTAR - A Tab In The Ocean (CD).

5(A)	DOWN TO EARTH	(United Artists UAG 29680) 1974 SC
6(A)	LIVE AT THE LONDON ROUNDHOUSE	
		(Bellaphon BLPS 19182) 1974 R1
7(A)	RECYCLED	(Decca SKL-R 5250) 1975 SC

NB: (1) was a German-only release. (2) - (6) were also issued on Passport in the US and on Bellaphon in Germany. All their albums have been reissued on CD on Bellaphon. Details of the above are: (1) reissued on CD (Bellaphon 289 09 007) 2000. (1) reissued on CD (Dream Nebula DNECD 1203) 2004. (2) reissued on CD (Bellaphon 290 09 003) 2000. (3) reissued on CD (Bellaphon 289 09 002) 2000. (3) reissued on CD (Dream Nebula DNECD 1201) 2004. (4) reissued on CD (Bellaphon 289 09 001) 2000. There's now a CD release of 4 (Eclectic DNECD 1204) available in 5.1 Surround Sound. (5) reissued on CD (Bellaphon 289 09 006) 2000. (6) reissued on CD (Bellaphon 298 09 006) 2000. (7) reissued on CD (Bellaphon 289 09 003) 2000 (7) reissued on CD (Dream Nebula DNECD 1202) 2004 and again on CD (Eclectic DNECD 1202). They carried on recording until the end of the seventies releasing several further albums. *Live In New York* (Dream Nebula DNECD 1206/7) 2004 is a 2-CD set from a 1974 concert. *Sunday Night At The London Roundhouse* (Eclectic Discs DMECD 1208/9) 2005 is an expanded version of a 1973 Roundhouse concert.

45s:	What Ya Gonna Do?/Day In The Life Of	
	A Preacher Part One (PS)	(United Artists NEK 1) 1973 SC
	Fidgety Queen/Little Boy	(United Artists UP 35706) 1974
	Astral Man/Nelly The Elephant	(United Artists UP 35853) 1975

This British progressive, hard-rock outfit was based in Germany. *Journey To The Centre Of The Eye* was a sort of concept album with masses of electronic wizardry and some good progressive rock in between. The spacey keyboard sound came along a little too late to make much impression. Still *The Dream Nebula (Parts 1 & 2)* and *The Nine Lifeless Daughters Of The Sun* are fine examples of late sixties psychedelia.

A Tab In The Ocean veered away from the psychedelic progressivism of their debut album towards a more structured musical format. Its highlights include *King Of Twilight*, a 19-minute magnum opus of dreamy lyrics and sleek instrumentation. There is lots of pleasing guitar and keyboard interplay on this album.

Remember The Future became one of the best-selling albums in Germany when it was released. It made the US Top 20 and was released in quadrophonic as well as stereo. There's now a recent CD release of this album in 5.1 surround sound.

They toured the US relentlessly in the mid-seventies and *Down To Earth* was tailored to FM Radio and is often considered one of their finest. They also had an excellent light show in this era and *Saturday Night At The Roundhouse* album successfully captured their live act at this time.

Recycled, a concept album, used lots of state-of-the-art electronics and saw the band courting a more MOR sound. Its highlight is considered by many to be *It's All Over*. There's a CD release which includes the original mix of the album by **Beatles'** engineer Geoff Emerick (which was not used) as well as the current one.

All of their albums were reissued on CD by Bellaphon in 2000. Then, in 2004, some of their albums were reissued again and bonus tracks included alternative recordings of the album material. All reissues are attractively packaged.

Live In New York features a concert recorded at the New York Academy of Music in September 1974. There is lots of good guitar work and plenty of lengthy structured pieces. The set comes in a digipak with an eight-page booklet and authoritative sleevenotes by Mark Powell. (MWh/JK/VJ)

Bill Nelson

ALBUM: 1 NORTHERN DREAM

                (Smile LAF 2182/HG 116) 1971 R5/R1

NB: (1) originally released as a private pressing of 250 in a foldover gatefold sleeve and lyric sheet (R5). (1) repressed with a gatefold sleeve and lyric sheet with the same catalogue number in the mid-seventies (R1). (1) reissued with a different sleeve and minus the final track (Butt BUTT 002) 1980 and reissued on CD (Smiled SM 777CD) 1993.

Bill Nelson was best known for his superb guitar playing with **Be-Bop DeLuxe** in the seventies, but he also released more than 40 solo albums in various guises. Whilst at Wakefield Art College he played in various bands like The Teenagers and later the trio Purple Tangerine Snowflake (with Allan Quinn (bs) and Bryan Holden), who later became Global Village. Global Village recorded an acetate with covers of **Traffic's** *Dear Mr Fantasy*, **Fleetwood Mac's** *Long Grey Mare* and **John Mayall's** *You Don't Love Me Baby*. Holyground's *Loose Routes* compilation later included the **Traffic** cover, credited to Global Fantasy. Global Village toured around West Yorkshire playing psychedelic blues music and once supported **Geno Washington**. He also played on other Holyground albums, *A-Austr* and *Astral Navigations*.

After marrying he joined a church group named The Messengers, but he persuaded them to change name to Gentle Revolution, an acoustic outfit who played at church events, borstals and hospitals around the area. It was after this venture that he recorded *Northern Dream* at Holyground and just 250 copies were pressed on his own Smile label. These came with a lavish booklet, which a later unauthorised pressing omitted. The album is full of dreamy, acoustic, music and he was assisted on it by Gentle Revolution's keyboardist and drummer Richard Brown. Two local musicians Gareth Eilledge and Leom Arthurs played bass on one track each, but **Nelson** played all the other instruments. It was after this that **Nelson** formed a new band, which played some initial gigs as Flagship but then adopted the name **Be-Bop Deluxe** and the rest is history! **Nelson** also made several solo albums and 45s in the eighties. (VJ)

Peter Nelson

45s: Love Will Come Your Way/
            You're Not For Me   (Piccadilly 7N 35250) 1965

            Donna/I Want To Be Wanted   (Piccadilly 7N 35278) 1965
            Don't Make Promises/
            No Need To Cry   (Piccadilly 7N 35314) 1966
            A Little Bit Later On Down The Line/
            You're Not For Me   (Piccadilly 7N 35338) 1966

Peter Nelson was a Londoner, who was in **Peter's Faces** and later **The Flowerpot Men** and **White Plains**. These 45s were mostly folky ballads. Donna had been recorded by Ritchie Valens.

Compilation appearances include: *Don't Make Promises* on *Ripples, Vol. 3* (CD); *Please Please Me* on *Star-Club Show* (LP); and *Loop De Loop* on *Twist Im Star-Club Hamburg* (LP). (VJ)

Nemo

45s: Baby You've Been On My Mind/
            In The Summertime   (Parlophone R 5882) 1971
            Sun Has Got His Hat On/Ernie's Song (Parlophone R 5927) 1971
            Who's Been Polishing The Sun/
            Bo-Dee-O-Do   (Parlophone R 5945) 1972
            Kick A Tin Can/Attilah   (Decca FR 13539) 1974
            (It's Only A) Paper Moon/Paul's Song   (UK UK 58) 1974

The main man behind these singles was **Jonathan King** with a studio group. (VJ)

Neo Maya

45:       I Won't Hurt You/U.F.O.   (Pye 7N 17371) 1967 R2

This was a pseudonym for **Episode Six** guitarist Graham Carter-Dimmock at a time when the band decided that each member of the group could make a solo record whilst the group remained together. *I Won't Hurt You* had originally been recorded as an album track by US outfit the West Coast Pop Art Experimental Band. It is re-arranged on this single, which features Carter-Dimmock augmented by his sister Sheila, **Roger Glover**, Clem Cattini (formerly with The Tornados), and Alan Clark (on guitar) plus a 40-piece orchestra. It is a delightful slice of melancholic pop. The flip side *U.F.O.* features a megaphone distorted vocal recounting UFO sightings across the world accompanied by feverish drumming and a ghostly backing vocal. It proved to be their only single as Graham Carter-Dimmock remained with **Episode Six** and later settled in the Middle East before returning to the UK where he still resides.

I Won't Hurt You has been compiled on *Hot Smoke & Sassafras - Psychedelic Pstones, Vol 1* (CD) and *Jagged Time Lapse, Vol 1* (CD). (VJ)

NEKTAR - Live At The Roundhouse (CD).

NEKTAR - Recycled (CD).

CHIITRA NEOGY - The Perfumed Garden (LP).

Chiitra Neogy

ALBUM: 1   THE PERFUMED GARDEN (Gemini GMX 5030) 1968 SC

This London-based artist also crops up on the *Morgan Blue Town* (LP) and *Best And The Rest Of British Psychedelia* (CD) compilations playing *Leilla The Flatterer*, a pleasant Indian-style instrumental of a similar ilk to Ravi Shankar.

Indian by birth, she was born in Kampala, Uganda in 1946. In 1962 she left East Africa to continue her studies at the University of Calcutta, graduating from there with Honours Degrees in Psychology and the English Language. She also became an accomplished actress and dancer and also learned to play the sitar. Later she moved to England and side one of her album is a recitation of Sir Richard Burton's 1886 translation of *The Perfumed Garden* adapted by Marcus Harrison. On side two *The Blue Sari* was an Indian poem set to music; *Leilla The Flatterer* tells of an Eastern woman who knows how to please her man with honeyed words; *The Story Of Mocailama* and *Chedja* is an ancient tale of how a woman is outwitted by the resourcefulness of a man and *Krishna and The Lovely Cowgirls* is an erotic Bengali poem set to music. Unusual it may be but it's only possible interest is as a novelty item. Not recommended for its musical content. (VJ)

Neptune's Empire

ALBUM: 1   NEPTUNE'S EMPIRE   (Polymax PXX 01) 1971 R3

This is not too difficult to find in Scandinavia, where it was distributed, but is highly elusive in the UK. The music is unfortunately not on a par with its collectability. At best it sounds like **The Hollies** around 1966, but this only happens occasionally. Most of it is bland, nondescript pop, with nothing to keep the listener's attention. Forgettable.

The band was originally from Scandinavia and the album came in a particularly attractive green-and-blue Neptune cover design. (MK/VJ)

The Nerve

Personnel: IAN DAY   bs   A
              ROB DUFFY   gtr   A
              ROBIN HURST   vcls   A
              BARRY SATCHELLE   bs   A
              STEVE TAYLOR   ld gtr   A

45s: No 10 Downing Street/
        Georgie's March   (Page One POF 019) 1967
        Magic Spectacles/
        Come The Day   (Page One POF 055) 1968 SC
        It Is/Mystery Lady   (Page One POF 081) 1968 SC

Piece By Piece/Satisfying Kind   (Page One POF 097) 1968 SC

A Hampshire band. **The Troggs'** **Reg Presley** 'discovered' them and produced their last three 45s. The band was also known as **Lovin'** for a while and recorded two **Troggs**-influenced records under this name. *No. 10 Downing Street* is a **Troggs'** song and appeared on their *Troggloddynamite* album.

Compilation appearances include: *Come The Day* and *Magic Spectacles* on *Magic Spectacles* (CD); and *Piece By Piece* on *Rare 60's Beat Treasures, Vol. 3* (CD) and *Satisfying Kind* on *Pop-In, Vol 1* (CD). (VJ)

The Neutrons

Personnel: DAVE CHARLES   drms   A
              CAROMAY DIXON   vcls   A
              PHIL RYAN   keyb'ds   A
              MARTIN WALLACE   gtr, vcls   A
              RAY TAFF WILLIAMS gtr   A
              WILL YOUATT   gtr, bs   A

ALBUMS: 1(A)   BLACK HOLE STAR (United Artists UAG 29652) 1974 SC
        2(A)   TALES FROM THE BLUE COCOONS
                              (United Artists UAG 29726) 1975 SC

45:     Dance Of Psychedelic Lounge Lizard/
        Suzy And The Wonder Boy   (United Artists UP 35704) 1974

A short-lived progressive rock outfit. Phil Ryan and Ray Taff Williams had both been with **Man** and Dave Charles guested on their 1973 *Christmas At The Patti* 10 inch album. *Black Hole Star* is mostly a keyboard-driven amalgam of psychedelic, progressive and R&B influences with some good guitar leads. The better tracks are the keyboard-led progressive *Living In The World Today*, *Doom City*, a mid-tempo semi-progressive number with R&B influences and good guitar work and *Snow Covered Eyes*, a strong piece with a good melody. Overall a satisfying album. It's worth noting that the logo on the back cover was designed by Rick Griffin. John "Pugwash" Weathers who played on some of the tracks later joined **Gentle Giant** in 1973. (CA/VJ)

The New Breed

45:     Friends And Lovers Forever/Unto Us (Decca F 12295) 1965 R1

This 45 was the band's sole platter. Two of them were apparently of Greek origin.

Compilation appearances include: *Friends And Lovers Forever* on *Beat Us If You Can! Vol. 1* (LP); and *Unto Us* on *Broken Dreams, Vol. 2* (LP) and *The Freakbeat Scene* (CD). (VJ)

The Newcastle Big Band

Personnel incl: GORDON 'STING' SUMNER   bs   A

ALBUM: 1   NEWCASTLE BIG BAND (Impulse ISS NBB 106) 1972 R3

This album's collectability is solely due to the presence of a young Sting. It's full of uninspired cover versions of various jazz compositions and Sting's role is confined to bass. Only the most ardent Police completist ought to be interested in this, but just 2,000 copies were pressed. (VJ)

The New Dawn

ALBUM: 1   MAINLINE   (Private Pressing) 1969 R3

This heavy psychedelic group was responsible for the above privately issued concept album. The standout cut is *Hometown - Our Revolution*, which has sneering vocals, distortion and echo. Aside from a few pretty little folk songs, the music is powerful, organ-driven psychedelia with strange titles like *Depression - Doubting Castles*, *Drug Country* and *Journey - Sea Of Couldn't Care Less*. (VJ)

The New Dream

45:     Turn 21/Someone Like You   (Parlophone R 5946) 1972

Erroneously included in the earlier volume this was a UK release for an Australian band that had been around in one form or another since the early sixties. I've left it in to clear up any confusion. *Turn 21* is an undistinguished cheerie pop song and the flip is a dreadful pop ballad. Both tracks are in a New Seekers vein. (VJ/JM)

New Folk

45:     Today/Goodbye   (Decca 12482) 196?

This is a folk-pop 45. (VJ)

The New Formula

Personnel: BRUCE CAREY   bs   A
               RICKY DODD   vcls, sax   A
               MARTIN FALLON   ld gtr   A
               TOMMY GUTHRIE   drms   A
               MIKE HARPER   vcls   A

45s: Do It Again A Little Bit Slower/
        I'm On The Outside Looking In   (Piccadilly 7N 35381) 1967
        I Want To Go Back There Again/
        Can't You See That She Loves Me   (Piccadilly 7N 35401) 1967
        My Baby's Coming Home/
        Burning In The Background   (Pye 7N 17552) 1968
        Stay Indoors/Hare Krishna   (Pye 7N 17818) 1969 SC

A mainstream pop outfit from Corby, Northants, whose best effort *Stay Indoors*, certainly had some commercial potential. *My Baby's Coming Home* was written and produced by **Mike D'Abo**. In the seventies Dodd worked with **Roy Young**, **Tucky Buzzard** and **Kevin Coyne**.

Compilation appearances include: *Harekrishna* on *Rubble, Vol. 7 - Pictures In The Sky* (LP); *Stay Indoors* on *Rubble, Vol. 10 - Professor Jordan's Magic Sound Show* (LP) and *Hot Smoke & Sassafras - Psychedelic Pstones, Vol 1* (CD); whilst *Do It Again A Little Bit Slower* can also be found on *Ripples, Vol. 1* (CD) and *Burning In The Background Of My Mind* has resurfaced on *Oddities, Vol 2* (CD). (VJ)

A New Generation

Personnel: CHRISTOPHER KEMP   organ, vcls   A
               GAVIN SUTHERLAND   bs, vcls   A
               IAN SUTHERLAND   gtr, vcls   A
               JOHN WRIGHT   drms   A

RUBBLE VOL. 10 (Comp LP) featuring The New Formula.

45s: Sadie And Her Magic Mister Garland/
        Digger   (Spark SRL 1000) 1969 -
        Smokey Blues Away/
        She's A Soldier Boy   (Spark SRL 1007) 1969 38
        Police Is Here/Mister C   (Spark SRL 1019) 1970 -

This was actually The Sutherland Brothers. They scored a minor hit with *Smokey Blues Away* and the flip side *She's A Soldier Boy* was pleasant enough too. They also did sessions for the BBC which are highly thought of and issued one 45 in the US under the name UK Baby *Heartbreaker / Michael Blues* (Imperial Records 66409-S) c1969.

You can also find *She's A Soldier Boy* on *Rubble Vol. 17: A Trip In A Painted World* (LP) and *Rubble Vol. 10* (CD). (VJ/MWh/MRi)

New Hovering Dog

45:     Up On The Hills Where They Do The Boogie/
        I Know Now   (United Artists UP 35417) 1972

This was a pseudonym for steel guitarist **B.J. Cole** (of **Cochise** and **Greenslade**). Both songs were taken from a John Hartford album. They are best described as sing-a-long country-rock. The vocals were done by **Mick Audsley**. (VJ)

Andy Newman

ALBUM: 1   RAINBOW   (Track 2406 103) 1971 SC

Former Post Office engineer **Newman** is best known for his involvement in **Thunderclap Newman**. The above was a very offbeat solo album on which he played a number of strange instruments as well as some more usual ones. (VJ)

Dave Newman

45s: The Lion Sleeps Tonight/
        Mothers Gone Walking   (Pye 7N 45134) 1970 34
        She Taught Me How To Yodel/
        Three Score And Ten   (Pye 7N 45154) 1970 -
        Whispering Grass/Rose Marie   (Pye 7N 45216) 1970 -
        Monja/Leave Me Grievin'   (Pye 7N 45368) 1974 -

Despite being released in 1970 it was April 1972 before *The Lion Sleeps Tonight* made the Charts. It was originally a hit for US group The Tokens in the early sixties, but was later recorded by **Eno** and eventually taken to No 1 by Tight Fit in January 1982. Despite versions of other popular songs *The Lion Sleeps Tonight* proved to be **Newman**'s only hit. (VJ)

Tom Newman

ALBUMS: 1   FINE OLD TOM   (Virgin V 2022) 1975 SC
(up to   2   LIVE AT THE ARGONAUT   (Virgin V 2042) 1975 R2
1976)

NB: (2) was unreleased, but some test pressings did appear. (1) reissued on CD (Voiceprint VP 166 CD) 1995 with 10 additional tracks. (2) issued on CD (Voiceprint VP 168 CD) 1995. Also *Variations On A Rhythm Of Mike Oldfield* (Voiceprint VP 191 CD) 1995, incudes some pre-1976 demos. The lead track is by **David Bedford**, whose albums have been reissued by Voiceprint.

45s: Sad Song/Ali's Got A Broken Bone   (Virgin VS 120) 1975
(up to   Don't Treat Your Woman Bad/
1976)   Why Does Love Hurt So Bad   (Virgin VS 130) 1975
         Sleep/Darling Corey   (Virgin VS 133) 1976
         Ebony Eyes/Draught Guinness   (Virgin VS 141) 1976

Tom Newman had previously been in **July**. He later set up Manor Studios for Richard Branson. He recorded his first solo album with Jon Field of **July** and **Jade Warrior**, Fred Frith and Chris Cutler of **Henry Cow**, Neil Innes,

Lol Coxhill, Hughie Flint and **Mike Oldfield**. It's a genuinely eclectic album spanning a wide mixture of styles from traditional mid-seventies ballroom singalongs to downright eery, almost ambient passages. To say the least it's odd and rather disjointed. The recent CD reissue on Voiceprint comes with 10 additional bonus tracks.

Newman then fell out with Branson and taped *Argonaut* on his own studio barge. This album, which was unissued at the time but is now available on CD, also had Field and Frith on it. It's not as esoteric as his first album but like that contained some good songs and showcased his wide-ranging instrumental styles.

After 1976 he largely worked as a producer/engineer, although in 1977 he cut an album for Decca which included **Mike Oldfield**. (VJ/JRd)

Tony Newman

45:      Soul Thing/Let The Good Times Roll   (Decca F 12795) 1968

This was a solo instrumental soul effort by **Newman** who'd played drums for **Sounds Incorporated** and **Jeff Beck** in the sixties and **Driftwood**, **May Blitz**, **Kevin Ayers**, **David Bowie**, **Boxer**, **T Rex** and **Three Man Army** in the seventies. He shouldn't be confused with guitarist Tony Newman of **Pinkerton's Assorted Colours**. (VJ)

The New Overlanders

45:      Unchained Melody/Memories   (RCA RCA 1953) 1970

This was the reformed **Overlanders** still featuring **Paul Arnold**. (VJ)

The News

Personnel:	ANDY FIELDS	piano, vcls	A
	HARVEY PLATT	bs	AB
	DENNY ROYAL	drms	AB
	IVAN ZAGNI	gtr	AB
	PETER MILLER	vcls	B

45s:	The Entertainer/I Count The Tears	(Decca F 12356) 1966 SC
	This Is The Moment/Ya Ya Da Da	(Decca F 12477) 1966

The News hailed from Norwich. They had actually begun life as The Continentals in the early sixties, backing a black American serviceman Milton. When he returned to the States, they became **The News** with **Peter Miller** joining from Peter Jay and The Jaywalkers. After two unsuccessful singles they split up. *This Is The Moment* was from the TV series 'Adam Adamant'. Their second 45 was written and produced by **Chris Andrews**. Zagni later played for **Jody Grind** and **Aynsley Dunbar**. (VJ)

THE NICE - Thoughts Of Emerlist Davjack (CD).

The New Vaudeville Band

Personnel:	IAN GREEN	keyb'ds	A
	HENRI HARRISON	drms	AB
	BOB KERR	trombone, sax	AB
	NEIL KORNER	bs	A
	GEOFF STEPHENS	vcls	AB
	HUGH "SHUGGY" WATTS	trombone	AB
	MICK WILSHER	gtr	AB
	CHRISS EEDY	bs	B
	STAN HAYWOOD	keyb'ds	B
	ALAN KLEIN (aka Tristram, Seventh Earl of Cricklewood)	vcls	B

ALBUMS: 1(B)   WINCHESTER CATHEDRAL   (Fontana (S)TL 5386) 1967
2( )   FINCHLEY CENTRAL   (Fontana (S)TL 5430) 1967

NB: There are two compilations *Winchester Cathedral* (C5 C5 558) 1990 on CD and vinyl and a CD one (Philips 514 348-2) 1993.

EP: 1( )   NEW VAUDEVILLE BAND   (Fontana TFE 17497) 1967

HCP

45s:	Winchester Cathedral/Wait For Me Baby (Fontana H 741) 1966	4
	Peek-A-Boo/Amy	(Fontana H 784) 1966 7
	Finchley Central/Rosie	(Fontana H 824) 1967 11
	Green Street Green/ Fourteen Lonely Woman	(Fontana H 853) 1967 37
	The Bonnie And Clyde/Uncle Gabriel	(Fontana H 909) 1968 -
	Dear Rita Hayworth/There Was A Time	(Decca F 13370) 1973 -
	At Last/Own Up	(DJM DJS 10655) 1976 -

Harrison who formed the group had previously beaten the skins with **Cops 'n' Robbers**, though they were really the creation of composer / record producer Geoff Stephens. As their name implied **The New Vaudeville Band** concentrated on an old-time twenties/thirties jazz-styled music which had real novelty value for a while. Inevitably, though, when the novelty wore off the band's popularity nose-dived. They made a short-term impact in the US, too, where *Winchester Cathedral* was a No 1 and *Peek A Boo* a minor hit. The C5 compilation is full of novelty songs which sounded similar to their hits.

Although songwriter/producer Geoffrey Stephens used to claim he sang lead on *Winchester Cathedral* (and is credited as vocalist on the album liner notes), it's thought that he never actually sang with the group. The vocalist on their later hits, is still unknown, but it's now certain that the singer on *Winchester Cathedral* was John Carter of **The Ivy League**, **Flowerpot Men**, **First Class**, etc. He sang the track through his hands so that it would sound like he was singing through a megaphone. He also sang on Stephens's original demo of the song, where his voice is even more identifiable. Bob Kerr had earlier been in the **Bonzo Dog Band**

After the *Bonnie and Clyde* 45, Korner left to join **The Nashville Teens**. Green departed too for the Crabtree Comic Choir. Three new members (Eedy, Haywood and Klein) were recruited, but in March 1969 Kerr left to form Bob Kerr's Whoopee Band. Haywood left shortly and was part of a short-lived US based band with ex-**Animals** Hilton Valentine and Barry Jenkins. Klein went solo and then became a record producer.

Compilation appearances include: *Peek-A-Boo* on *Made In England, Vol. 2* (LP) and *Winchester Cathedral* on *The Swinging Sixties - 18 Classic Tracks* (CD). (VJ/DE/VZ/JM)

New York Public Library

Personnel:	DAVE BOWER	gtr	ABCD
	JOHN KIRBY WOLLARD	vcls	AB X
	PAUL SERVIS	bs	AB
	TERRY STOKES	gtr	ABCD
	?????	drms	A
	TOPPER CLAY	drms	BCDX
	BRIAN PARISH (MORRIS)	gtr, vcls	C
	PETE MORRISON	gtr, vcls	DX
	BOB DOWTY	bs	X
	DAVE RENG	gtr, pedal steel	X
	KARL RYELANDER	gtr, vcls	X

THE NICE - Ars Longa Vita Brevis (LP).

45s:　I Ain't Gonna Eat Out My Heart Anymore/
　　　Rejected　　　　　　　(Columbia DB 7948) 1966 SC
　　　Gotta Get Away/Time Wastin'　　(MCA MU 1025) 1968
　　　Love Me Two Times/Which Way To Go　(MCA MU 1045) 1968
　　　Whei Ling Ty Luu/Boozy Queen　　(B&C CB 176) 1972

This group's debut 45 was a Rascal's cover produced by Mickie Most yet it still failed to sell! They even covered The Doors' *Love Me Two Times* also to no avail. Nonetheless these 45s are worth tracking down and the first is now a minor collectable. *Gotta Get Away* is also quite good, but by 1968 this sound was possibly a little dated.

It's not totally clear if this band evolved out of **The Cherokees** or whether they were a later version of that band, but Dave Bower, John Kirby Wollard and Terry Stokes were all former **Cherokees**.

Topper Clay joined in Spring 1967 from **The Knack**. In 1968, John Kirby Wollard and Paul Servis left, and Brian Morris (ex-**The Knack**) joined.

Brian Morris had also played with **Earl Preston** and in 1970, left to pursue a solo career.

In 1971, the band masterminded the Buddy Holly tribute album under the **Raw Holly** pseudonym.

Incredibly, the band was still active in 2002 with line-up 'X' above.

Compilation appearances have included: *Love Me Two Times* and *I Ain't Gonna Eat Out My Heart Anymore* on *Nowhere Men Vol. 3* (CD); *Gotta Get Away* on *English Freakbeat, Vol. 5* (LP & CD); *I Ain't Gonna Eat Out My Heart Anymore* on *Go... With An All Star* (LP); *Love Me Two Times* on *Turds On A Bum Ride, Vol. 1* (2-LP) and *Turds On A Bum Ride, Vol's 1 & 2* (2-CD); *Which Way To Go* on *Jagged Time Lapse, Vol 2* (CD) and *Love Me Two Times* on *Jagged Time Lapse, Vol, 3* (CD). (VJ/TCy)

The Nice

Personnel:　BRIAN DAVIDSON　　drms　　　　ABC
　　　　　　KEITH EMERSON　　vcls, keyb'ds　ABC
　　　　　　LEE JACKSON　　　bs, gtr, vcls　ABC
　　　　　　DAVY O'LIST　　　gtr　　　　　A
　　　　　　GORDON LONGSTAFF　gtr　　　　　B

　　　　　　　　　　　　　　　　　　　　　HCP
ALBUMS: 1(A)　THE THOUGHTS OF EMERLIST DAVJACK
　　　　　　　(mono/stereo)　(Immediate IMLP/IMSP 016) 1967 SC -
　　　　　2(B)　ARS LONGA VITA BREVIS
　　　　　　　　　　　　　　(Immediate IMSP 020) 1968 SC -
　　　　　3(C)　THE NICE　　(Immediate IMSP 026) 1969 SC 3
　　　　　4(C)　FIVE BRIDGES SUITE　(Charisma CAS 1014) 1970 SC 2

　　　　　5(C)　ELEGY　　　　　(Charisma CAS 1030) 1971 SC 5
　　　　　6(-)　AUTUMN 67, SPRING 68　　(Charisma CS 1) 1972 -

NB: (4) and (5) released on Mercury in the US (SR 61295 and SR 61324 respectively). (1) and (2) reissued in 1978 on Charly (CR 300021) and (CR 30019) respectively. *Five Bridges/Autumn 67* reissued on Charisma (CASMC 163) on cassette and *Elergy* reissued on Charisma (CHC 1) in 1983. (1) reissued on CD (Line IMCD 900 228) 1988 and again (Essential! ESM CD 647) 1998, with bonus tracks. (2) reissued on CD (Castle Classics CLACD 120) 1986, again (Essential! ESM CD 646) 1998, with bonus tracks and again on CD (Essential! ESM CD 646) 2005. (3) reissued on CD (Essential! ESM CD 645) 1998, with bonus tracks and again on CD (Essential! ESM CD 645) 2005. (4) and (5) reissued on CD (Charisma CASCD 1014 and 1030 respectively) in 1991. (1), (2) and (3) reissued on CD (Repertoire REP 4238-WY, 4289-WY and 4290-WY respectively) in 1992. (1) is also supplemented by a 45 version of *America* and a couple of other cuts. (1) reissued again as a 2-CD set with lots of bonus tracks (Sanctuary CMQDD 790) 2003. (2) reissued again as a 2-CD set with lots of bonus tracks (Sanctuary CMQDD 791) 2003. (3) reissued again (just one CD) (Sanctuary CMQDD 792) 2003. *The Nice Collection* (Castle CCSCD 106) 1994 is a good introduction to their music which was originally available on vinyl in 1985. An earlier CD compilation was *20th Anniversary Of The Nice* (Bite Back BTECD 2) 1988. *The Best Of The Nice* (Essential! ESM CD 629) 1998 is good value and has been reissued in 2005. *Swedish Radio Sessions* (Castle CMRCD 349) 2001 captures the band in action back in 1967. *All The Best* (Repertoire REP 4822 VG) 1999 covers their 1967-1969 period with Immediate. *Here Comes The Nice - The Immediate Anthology* (Immediate CMETD 055) 2000 is a 3-CD set. *BBC Sessions* (Sanctuary CMFCD 457) 2002 suffers from inferior sound quality but features interesting material.

　　　　　　　　　　　　　　　　　　　HCP
45s:　Thoughts Of Emerlist Davjack/
　　　Angel Of Death　　　　　(Immediate IM 059) 1967 -
　　　America/Diamond Hard Apples Of
　　　The Moon (Some PS)　　　(Immediate IM 068) 1968 SC/- 21
　　　Brandenburger/Happy Freuds　(Immediate IM 072) 1968 -
　　　She Belongs To Me/
　　　She Belongs To Me　　　　(Immediate AS 4) 1969 -
　　　Country Pie/One Of These People　(Charisma CB 132) 1971 -

At its best **The Nice**'s music was unique, but it could also be pompous and overblown.

Emerson and Jackson had played with **Gary Farr and The T. Bones**. **Emerson** had also been in the short-lived **V.I.P.s** prior to the above quartet establishing themselves as P.P. Arnold's backing group in 1967. **The Nice** would play their own set prior to backing her own show, and went down so well that Immediate offered them a contract in October 1967. They soon became popular among British underground fans, as much for their flamboyant style as anything else, and were an integral part of the psychedelic scene. Musically they concentrated on re-vamping the classics, and were dominated by **Emerson**'s virtuoso keyboard playing.

Their well-received debut album included lengthy renderings of *Rondo* and *War And Peace*, fine psychedelia like *The Cry Of Eugene* and *Flower King Of Flies*, and straightforward rock like *Bonnie K*. Davy O'List departed soon after its release and was replaced for a while by Longstaff the following year. After his departure the band became more centred on **Emerson** and

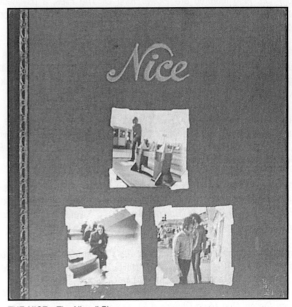

THE NICE - The Nice (LP).

THE NICE - Elegy (LP).

his highly theatrical keyboard playing. Their second album, *Ars Longa Vita Brevis*, is certainly worth investigation. It included **Emerson**'s interpretation of Leonard Berstein's *America* from *West Side Story*, which reached No. 21 in the UK when issued as a seven-minute single in the summer of 1968. The flip side, *Diamond Hard Green Apples Of The Moon*, was equally superb. That June they were banned from London's Albert Hall after setting fire to the stars and stripes during a rendition of *America*, and Bernstein prevented it from being from issued in the US.

Side two of the third album was recorded live at the Fillmore East, New York and included renderings of *Rondo '69* and Dylan's *She Belongs To Me*. It had its moments, but was frankly tedious at times. Their fourth album was their most ambitious to date. By this time Immediate had folded, and the band had switched to Charisma. However, by the time of their fifth album Jackson and Davidson were beginning to resent **Emerson**'s dominance of the group and they broke up amid considerable ill-feeling. Two of the four tracks (*America* and *Hang On To A Dream*) were new arrangements of earlier compositions, and the album is not really worth purchasing.

Emerson went on to achieve greater fame with **Emerson, Lake and Palmer**. O'List re-emerged in **Jet** in the seventies. Both Jackson and Davidson, however, were relatively unsuccessful in their attempts to launch their own bands, **Jackson Heights** and **Every Which Way**.

Numerous posthumous releases of **Nice** material have appeared, so readers who want to should experience little difficulty in tracking down their recordings. *Swedish Radio Sessions* opens with their cover of Bob Dylan's *She Belongs To Me* and contains an unreleased cover of *You Keep Me Hangin' On*. Also featured are *Flower King Of The Flies*, a psychedelic/progressive number, the jazzy *Sombrero Sam* and an extended version of *Rondo*.

All The Best is a compilation covering the 1967-1969 period. It includes the 'A' and 'B' sides of their four Immediate singles, a good selection of album tracks and the US edit of their classic *America* single. The lack of sleevenotes is a pity.

Here Comes The Nice is a 3-CD anthology of their recordings for Immediate and it's their earlier work like *The Thoughts Of Emerlist Davjack* and the organ-based psychedelia of songs like *The Diamond Hard Blue Apples Of The Moon* and *Flower King Of Flies* that catch the ear.

BBC Sessions, despite the second rate sound quality, contains sessions recorded between 1967-1969. There's the inevitable psych-pop (*Flower King Of Flies*), classical cuts (*Brandenburger*) and covers of Zappa's *Lumpy Gravy* and The Byrds' *Get To You*.

Compilation appearances have included: *Azrial (Angel Of Death)* on *Broken Dreams, Vol. 5* (LP) and *Immediate Single Collection, Vol. 4* (CD); *America* and *Brandenburger* on *Immediate Single Collection, Vol. 1* (CD); *The Thoughts Of Emerlist Davjack* on *Immediate Single Collection, Vol. 2* (CD); *Country Pie* on *One More Chance* (LP); *Flower King Of Flies* on *The Age*

Of Enlightenment - Prog Rock, Vol. One (CD). and on the 4-CD box set *Acid Drops, Spacedust & Flying Saucers*. Finally, *America* got a further airing on the CD set *Rock Of Ages, Four Decades Of Heavy Rock 1962-2002* and on the 2-CD set *Greatest Hits Of The 60's Vol 4* and you'll also find *America* and *The Thoughts Of Emerlist Davjack* on the 3-CD box set *Ars Longa Vita Brevis: A Compendium Of Progressive Rock 1967-1974*. (VJ/RMJ)

Paul Nicholas

HCP

45s: (up to 1976)	Where Do I Go/Here Comes The Clown	(Polydor 56285) 1968 -
	Who Can I Turn To/	
	Sing A Sad Song For Sammy	(Polydor 56322) 1969 -
	Freedom City/Run Shaker Life	(Polydor 56374) 1970 -
	D J Saturday Night/Lovely Lady	(Epic EPC 2174) 1974 -
	I Hit The Jackpot/	
	Falling In Love With You	(Epic EPC 2783) 1974 -
	Shuffling Tune/Hit Song	(RSO 2090 168) 1975 -
	Reggae Like It Used To Be/	
	Lamp Lighter	(RSO 2090 185) 1976 17
	Dancing With The Captain/?	(RSO 2090 206) 1976 8
	Grandma's Party//Flat Foot Floyd	
	Mr Sax and The Girl/Shufflin' Shoes	(RSO 2090 216) 1976 9

Paul Nicholas (real name Paul Beuselinck) was born in Peterborough on 3 December 1945. With his good looks he was well equipped for the acting career for which he is better known. After playing piano with **Screaming Lord Sutch and The Savages** in 1964 he was involved in **Oscar**, a mid-sixties outfit. Around the same time he moved into acting, playing the leading role of Claude in the London production of 'Hair'. He later played the title role in 'Jesus Christ Superstar' as well as a role in 'Grease'. In the seventies he became a film star appearing in 'Stardust', 'Tommy' and 'Lisztomania'. He eventually gained Chart success with ultra commercial novelty records like *Reggae Like It Used To Be*, *Dancing With The Captain* and *Grandma's Party*. He carried on recording until the mid-eighties and among his acting credits was an appearance as Billy Shears' brother in the film 'Sgt. Peppers Lonely Hearts Club Band' in 1978. He also recorded as **Paul Dean** and **Oscar**.

Lamp Lighter has been compiled on *Jagged Time Lapse, Vol 5* (CD). (VJ)

Billy Nicholls

ALBUM: 1 WOULD YOU BELIEVE (Immediate IMCP 009) 1968 R6

NB: (1) reissued on vinyl (Tenth Planet TP042) 1998 in a limited pressing of 1,000 numbered copies. *Snapshot* (Southwest SWCD 004) 2000 is a 22-track CD release, which includes his album, the withdrawn Immediate 45 and a series of demos taken from the original masters. *Forever's No Time At All - The Anthology 1967-2004* (Castle CMEDD 1120) 2005 is a 2-CD overview of his career.

THE NICE - Best Of (LP).

45s:	Would You Believe/Daytime Girl	(Immediate IM 063) 1968 R1
	Forever's No Time At All/	
	This Song Is Green	(Track 2094 109) 1973

NB: (1) features **Small Faces**. (2) with **Pete Townshend**.

Prodigal talent **Nicholls** was signed by **Andrew Loog Oldham** as Immediate's in-house songwriter straight from school. His first 45 was produced by **Ronnie Lane** and **Stevie Marriott** of **The Small Faces**. The *Would You Believe* album was **Oldham**'s attempt to concoct a British answer to The Beach Boys' *Pet Sounds*. Now firmly established as an ultra-rarity, it's an excellent collection of tuneful pop, set to muti-layered harmonies and baroque instrumentation, with superb production and backing from **The Small Faces, Denny Gerrard, Nicky Hopkins**, **John Paul Jones, Caleb Quaye**, Big Jim Sullivan and Immediate artists **Twice As Much** and Jerry Shirley (from **Apostolic Intervention** and **Humble Pie**).

Despite costing a fortune to record, its release was cancelled when Immediate hit dire financial straits. Only a few promo copies managed to leak out, though it's thought to have had a limited release in Scandinavia, and boxes of never-issued copies are said to have ended up as ballast for ships.

The 1998 Tenth Planet reissue, with customarily excellent liner notes from David Wells, brought this minor classic to a wider audience, and is in itself very collectable. **Nicholls** went on to contribute to **Townshend**'s early seventies solo album, which explains **Townshend**'s involvement on his 1973 45 for Track.

The 2-CD set *Forever's No Time At All - The Anthology 1967 - 2004* provides an overview of his career. The 43-track collection includes a lot of his more acoustic material as well as tracks from his rare album. This CD includes a version of *Can't Stop Loving You (Though I Try)* (which was a hit for Leo Sayer), the previously unissued and powerful *Heaven Come Quickly* (with **Pete Townshend** on bass and lead) and it closes with his recent recording of *Memory Lane*. This is a worthwhile set.

Compilation appearances have included: *Portobello Road* on *Justavibration* (LP) and *Justafixation* (CD); *London Social Degree* on *Maximum '65* (LP); *Would You Believe* on *Immediate Alternative* (LP); *Would You Believe* and *Daytime Girl* on *Immediate Alternative* (CD); *Daytime Girl* on *Immediate Single Collection, Vol. 5* (CD); *Girl From New York* on the 4-CD box set *Acid Drops, Spacedust & Flying Saucers* and *This Song Is Green* on *Fading Yellow, Vol 5* (CD). (VJ/RMJ)

Sue Nicholls

		HCP
45s:	Where Will You Be/Every Day	(Pye 7N 17565) 1968 17
	All The Way To Heaven/	
	I'll Be Waiting For You	(Pye 7N 17674) 1969 -

This was actually Audrey Roberts from 'Coronation Street'! As you can see she enjoyed a Top 20 hit with her first disc. (VJ)

Lea Nicholson

ALBUMS:	1	DEEP LANCASHIRE	(Topic) 1967
(up to	2	HORSEMUSIC	(Trailer LER 3010) 1972 SC
1976)	3	GOD BLESS THE UNEMPLOYED	
			(Transatlantic TRA 254) 1972

NB: There was also a further album *The Concertina Record* (Kicking Mule SNKF 165) 1980.

45s:	God Bless The Unemployed/	
	Piece Of Cake	(Transatlantic BIG 504) 1972
	Lazy Afternoon/	
	Sorry About The Phone Stephanie	(Virgin VS 149) 1976
α	Dam Busters March/Southampton	(Virgin VS 164) 1976

NB: α released as Rawtenstall Concertina Band, conductor Lea Nicholson.

Lea's first album, *Deep Lancashire* was also the first recorded outing for Mike Harding, who went on to become a well known comedian. Harry Boardman, one of the musicians on the album, and the guy who negotiated with the record company arranged that they would get a flat fee of £50 for doing the album!

Lea's second, *Horsemusic*, is a traditional folk album. **Tim Hart**, Maddy Prior, **Gay and Terry Woods** appear among the supported artists.

A further album, *The Concertina Record* features **Mike Oldfield**, **Rod Argent** and Nicholas Kraemer (now a well-known classical conductor!). A CD reissue of this is available from Lea Nicholson at: http://www.jamring-.com (VJ)

Nickelson

| Personnel incl: | HUGH McKENNA | A |

| 45: | Sitting On A Fence/Oh How Much | (Decca F 13328) 1972 |

A Scottish band was responsible for this little known early seventies 45. The 'A' side was a **Rolling Stones** song. Hugh McKenna later played with **Tear Gas** and **Sensational Alex Harvey Band**. (VJ)

Jimmy Nicol (and The Shubdubs)

Personnel incl:	TONY ALLEN	vcls
	ROGER COULAM	organ
	QUINCY DAVIS	sax

BILLY NICHOLLS - Would You Believe (LP).

BILLY NICHOLLS - Snapshot (LP).

BOB GARNER	bs
JOHN HARRIS	trumpet
JIMMY NICOL	drms

45s:
	Humpty Dumpty/Night Train	(Pye 7N 15623) 1964 SC
α	Husky/Don't Come Back	(Pye 7N 15666) 1964 SC
	Baby Please Don't Go/Shub Dubbery	(Pye 7N 15699) 1964 SC
β	Clementine/Bim Bam	(Decca F 12107) 1965

NB: α is a solo **Jimmy Nicol** release. β as Sound of Jimmy Nicol.

Liverpudlian **Jimmy Nicol** deputised for **Ringo Starr** in **The Beatles** during their tour of Sweden and Holland in 1964 when Ringo was ill. He'd earlier been in **Lee Curtis'** backing group and briefly backed **Georgie Fame** in June 1964. His own backing band, The Shubdubs featured some musicians who went on to better things:- Roy Coulam was later in **Blue Mink** and part of **Poet and One Man Band** and Bob Garner went on to play in **The Merseybeats** and **Creation**. **Nicol** himself was in **Peter and Gordon**'s backing group in 1965 and the following year he relocated to Sweden becoming part of The Spotnicks. *Humpty Dumpty* was a popular favourite and its flip side, *Night Train*, was a James Brown song. His third 45, *Baby Please Don't Go*, was popularised by **Them**.

Compilation appearances include: *Night Train* on *Doin' The Mod, Vol. 2* (CD); and *Husky* on *Instro-Hipsters A Go-Go* (CD). (VJ)

The Nightriders

Personnel:
GREG MASTERS	bs, vcls	AB
DAVE PRITCHARD	gtr, vcls	AB
ROGER SPENCER	drms	AB
JOHNNY MANN	lead gtr	A
JEFF LYNNE	gtr	B

45s:
Love Me Right Now/	
Your Friend (promo only)	(Polydor 56066) 1966 R2
It's Only The Dog/Your Friend	(Polydor 56116) 1966 R1

Formerly **Mike Sheridan and The Nightriders**, this Birmingham combo became **The Nightriders** when **Sheridan** left. Johnny Mann had previously been with **Carl Wayne and The Vikings**. They recorded just one 45, which is inevitably now rare and sought-after. Even more expensive and harder to find would be the promo-only recording of *Love Me Right Now* if you could track down a copy.

Mann left in May 1966 and the remaining trio teamed up with Jeff Lynne, who'd been born in Birmingham on 30 December 1947. They now became known as **Idle Race**.

You can also check out *It's Only The Dog* on *Electric Sugarcube Flashbacks, Vol. 1* (LP), *Electric Sugarcube Flashbacks, Vol. 3* (LP) and *Jagged Time Lapse, Vol 2* (CD). (VJ/JM)

Nightshift

45s:
Corrine Corrina/Lavender Tree	(Piccadilly 7N 35243) 1965 SC
That's My Story/	
Stormy Monday Blues	(Piccadilly 7N 35264) 1965 SC

An obscure mid-sixties band. The two 'A' sides were both old favourites. *That's My Story*, a perky beat number, was Tim Rice's first recorded song, and can also be heard on Sequel's *Hippy Hippy Shake* (CD). (VJ/RMJ)

The Night-Timers

45:
	The Music Played On/	
α	Yield Not To Temptation	(Parlophone R 5355) 1965 R1

NB: α featuring **Herbie Goins**.

This London club act, which was fronted by black vocalist **Herbie Goins** and Ronnie Jones, became known as **Herbie Goins and The Night-Timers** in 1966. (VJ)

9.30 FLY - 9.30 Fly (CD).

Bill Nile (and His Good Time Band)

45s:
Pashionella Grundy/Bric A Brac Man	(Decca F 12661) 1967
I Try Not To Laugh/	
Nobody Knows The Trouble	(Deram DM 290) 1970

Nothing else is known about this band. (VJ)

Nimbus

Personnel:
HENRY BAKER	bs	A
KIM CHESHIRE	lead vcls	A
PAUL KENDRICK	drms	A
TOM KING	gtr	A

45:
All For The Love Of Stephen/	
Let Me Go Home	(Polydor 2058.330) 1973

The above line-up is from mid-1974 - not the one responsible for the earlier 45. By mid-1974 their unknown pianist and original drummer had departed. From Kings Lynn, Norfolk, they played funky rock. (VJ)

Nimrod

45:
	The Bird/	
α	Don't Let It Get The Best Of You	(Mercury NCF 154664) 1969

NB: α was a French release that may have been a reissue of an earlier single (speculatively on Pathe).

This was a later version of **The State Of Mickey and Tommy** whose *The Bird* is a reasonable slice of UK psychedelia. The band backed Johnny Hallyday for a while in the late sixties.

Compilation appearances include: *Don't Let It Get The Best Of You* on *Psychedelia, Vol. 4* (LP) and *Hen's Teeth, Vol. 3* (CD); and *The Bird* on *Perfumed Garden, Vol. 1* (LP & CD), *Circus Days Vol. 1 & 2* (CD) and *Circus Days, Vol. 2* (LP). (VJ)

1984

Personnel:
MICK ERANDER	bs	A
BARRY HAYDON-PRICE	gtr	A
PETER HOWES	drms	A
PAUL PREWER	vcls	A
RAY STRICKSON	gtr	A

45s:
This Little Boy/Rosalyn	(Big T BIG 117) 1969
Got To Have Your Love/Here We Are	(Big T BIG 120) 1969
Little Girl/Laramee	(Decca F 23159) 1971

This outfit tended to specialise in gentle pop songs with just a tinge of psychedelia. *Little Girl* was a very good cover of the US Syndicate Of Sound track.

Compilation appearances have included: *This Little Boy* (raw acetate version) on *Mynd The Gap* (LP); *Rosalyn* and *This Little Boy* on *The Electric Lemonade Acid Test, Vol. 2* (LP); and *There Is Music All Around Me* can be found on *Incredible Sound Show Stories, Vol. 10* (LP) and *Talking About The Good Times, Vol 1* (CD). (MWh)

9.30 Fly

Personnel:	GARY CHARMAN	bs	A
	MIKE CLARK	drms	A
	LYN OAKEY	gtr	A
	MICHAEL WAINWRIGHT	vcls	A
	BARBARA WAINWRIGHT	keyb'ds, vcls	A

ALBUM: 1(A) 9.30 FLY   (Ember NR 5062) 1972 R3

NB: (1) reissued on CD (Repertoire REP 4355-WY) 1993.

This Cheltenham band's album of progressive rock is a mixed bag. The combination of female vocals and fuzz guitar has produced much fine music, but on this album the vocals lack emotion and the compositions are often below par. (MK/VJ/RMJ)

Ninette

45:     Push A Little Button/I Just Wonder Why   (Pye 7N 17039) 1966

This is a one-off 45 by a very obscure artist. (VJ)

Ning

Personnel:	JIMMY EDWARDS	organ, vcls	A
	JAMES PRYAL	drms	A
	MICK ROSS	bs	A
	DEREK WILSON	lead gtr	A

45:     Machine/More Ning   (Decca F 23114) 1971

This four-piece band came from Coventry. They played soul-rock and had a very energetic stage act. Their 45 was oriental with heavy overtones, although the 'B' side sounds like a psychedelic **Gary Glitter**! It's said that they played seven nights a week beneath a cafe because they had problems getting gigs. They also refused to give interviews or to give Decca any details with which to concoct a biography for fear of being predictable.

NIRVANA - The Story Of Simon Simopath (LP).

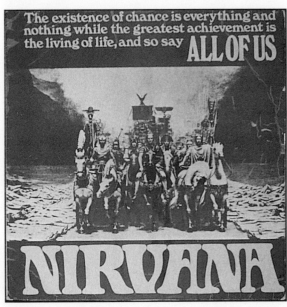

NIRVANA - All Of Us (LP).

Compilation appearances include: *Machine* on *Incredible Sound Show Stories, Vol. 3* (LP) and *More Ning* on *Jagged Time Lapse, Vol 2* (CD). (VJ)

Nirvana

Personnel:	PATRICK CAMPBELL-LYONS	AB
	ALEX SPYROPOULOS	A

ALBUMS: 1(A)	THE STORY OF SIMON SIMOPATH	
(up to		(Island ILPS 9059) 1967 R2
1976) 2(A)	ALL OF US	(Island ILPS 9087) 1967 R2
3(A)	DEDICATED TO MARKOS III	(Pye NSPL 28132) 1970 R3
4(B)	LOCAL ANAESTHETIC	(Vertigo 6360 031) 1971 R2
5(B)	SONGS OF LOVE AND PRAISE	
		(Philips 6308 089) 1972 R2

NB: (1) reissued on CD (Edsel EDCD 465) 1995 and again on CD (Universal IMCD 301) 2003. (2) reissued on CD (Edsel EDCD 466) 1995 and again on CD (Universal IMCD 302) 2003. (3) reissued on CD with two additional tracks (Demon) 1993 and again on CD (Universal IMCD 303) 2003. (3) also issued in Brazil on vinyl as a very limited promo edition (Continental/Metromedia MMLP 35007) 1970. (4) reissued on CD (Repertoire REP 4109-WP) 1991 and again on CD (Vertigo UICY 9536). (5) reissued on CD (Background HBG 123/9) 1995 with two previously unissued tracks: - the blues-tinged *On The Road* and reggae-influenced *OK For Kay*. Also of interest is *Black Flower* (Bam Caruso KIRI 061) 1987, a compilation of album cuts, singles and previously unreleased material. *Secret Theatre* (Edsel EDCD 407) 1997 is a compilation containing previously unreleased tracks. *Orange And Blue* (Edsel EDCD 485) 1996 contains marginally rockier and later material they recorded for Island, with a few more modern recordings thrown in. This is best avoided.

HCP

45s:	Tiny Goddess/I Believe In Magic	(Island WIP 6016) 1967 SC -
(up to	Pentecost Hotel/Feelin' Shattered	(Island WIP 6020) 1967 SC -
1976)	Rainbow Chaser/Flashbulb	(Island WIP 6029) 1968 SC 34
	Girl In The Park/	
	C Side In Ocho Rios	(Island WIP 6038) 1968 SC -
	All Of Us (The Untouchables)/	
	Trapeze	(Island WIP 6045) 1968 -
	Wings Of Love/	
	Requiem To John Coltrane	(Island WIP 6052) 1968 SC -
	Oh! What A Performance/	
	Darling Darlene	(Island WIP 6057) 1969 SC -
	The World Is Cold Without You/	
	Christopher Lucifer	(Pye International 7N 25525) 1970 SC -
	The Saddest Day Of My Life/	
	(I Wanna Go) Home	(Vertigo 6059 035) 1971 SC -
	Pentecost Hotel/Lazy Day Drift	(Philips 6006 127) 1971 -
	Stadium/Please Believe Me	(Philips 6006 166) 1971 -
	Rainbow/Chaser/Tiny Goddess (PS)	(Island WIP 6180) 1976 -
Reissue:	Black Flower/	
	(Flip by different artist)	(Bam-Caruso OPRA 45) 1988 -

In view of the commercial appeal of much of this multi-instrumental duo's music, it is surprising they did not achieve greater recognition.

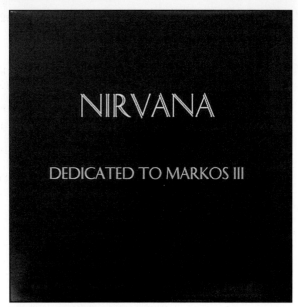

NIRVANA - Dedicated To Markos III (LP).

NIRVANA - Local Anaesthetic (CD).

Campbell-Lyons, who came from Ealing, but was born in Cork, Eire on 13 July 1945, had previously been in pre-**July** band Second Thoughts. Alex Spyrapoulous was born in Athens, Greece on 13 August 1943 and had sung vocals in various bands. They formed a backing band in 1967 comprising: Brian Henderson (bs, vcls) (ex-Soul Mates), Peter Kester (drms), and Sylvia Schuster (cello). They were managed by ex-**Spencer Davis Group** member Muff Winwood.

Their debut album *The Story Of Simon Simopath*, a science-fiction pantomime, was an early attempt at a rock concept album. It contained some finely constructed pop songs, including the harmonious *Pentecost Hotel* (later issued as a single), *We Can Help You* (issued as a single by the **Alan Bown Set**), the catchy *Satellite Jockey*, *Wings Of Love*, which was later issued as their sixth single and a couple of more mellow songs:- *Lonely Boy* and *Never Found A Love Like This Before*. The backing band was disbanded after this album was recorded.

The follow-up *All Of Us* was an even more poignant collection of often dreamy pop songs. Two tracks, the sad but beautiful *Tiny Goddess*, which was issued as the group's first single, and *Rainbow Chaser*, one of the early examples of phasing which actually climbed to No 34 in the UK in the Spring of 1968, were outstanding. This song was later included on *You Can All Join In* (LP), Island's 1969 sampler. Also of note were the heavily orchestrated *Melanie Blue*, *All Of Us*, and *Girl In The Park*.

The group increasingly became a vehicle for **Campbell-Lyon**'s musical journeys, with Spyropoulos eventually opting out in 1969 and going into TV and film work after the *Dedicated To Markos III* album, which only sold a few hundred copies and is consequently their hardest one to track down. It was originally leased to the US label Metromedia, but the label went bust before it could be issued, so only 500 copies of the album appeared here in promo-only form. One track, *The World Is Cold Without You* was culled for 45 release but met with a similar fate. The duo was supplemented on this by Billy Bremner (gtr) and Lesley Duncan (vcls) of **Spooky Tooth**.

Local Anaesthetic contained just two tracks *Modus Operandi* and *Home*. The latter can also be heard on *Heads Together, First Round* (2-LP), a compilation which **Campbell-Lyons** compiled for Vertigo in 1971.

Songs Of Love And Praise contained re-recordings of *Rainbow Chaser* and *Pentecost Hotel*, along with some fine new material, notably *Please Believe Me*, *I Need Your Love Tonight* and *Stadium*, which were all written by **Campbell-Lyons**. On this and all **Nirvana** albums, he was assisted by a flexible group of close friends. **Campbell-Lyons** later made a solo album *Me And My Friend* (Sovereign) in 1973, but this sold poorly and was quickly deleted.

Dedicated To Markos III was reissued on CD by Demon in 1993 and this release includes a re-recorded 1993 version of the second *Pentecost Hotel* single by **Campbell-Lyons** and Spyropoulos and one new song *Shine*.

They also had a couple of 45s released as **Pica** in 1970 and 1971. In 1973 **Campbell-Lyons** recorded a 45, *Queen Of Rock and Roll/Woman* as **Rock**

O'Doodle. The same year he recorded a solo album, *Me And My Friend* for Sovereign.

In 1976 a **Patrick Campbell-Lyons** and Alex Spyropoulos had a further 45, *Two Of A Kind (From The Musical 'Secrets')* (Bradley's BRAD 7602), which contained a grand ballad with choral backing in the style of early **Nirvana**.

In 1978 the pair reverted to the **Nirvana** name for another 45 called *Love Is/Pascale* (Pepper Records/United Artists UP 36461), which has a very strong tune and 'psychedelic' production. A second 45 followed the same year, (*Restless Wind/Thank You And Goodnight* (Pepper Records/United Artists UP 35638)1979. The pair also used the **Nirvana** name in the eighties. In 1992, Island released a CD, *Travelling On A Cloud*.

Orange and Blue is a collection of songs written in the Island Records 1968 era of **Nirvana's** history, except for a bizarre version of *Lithium* (from 1996) by the US Nirvana recorded just after Kurt's death.

Secret Theatre is a 21-track collection of songs by **Campbell-Lyons** and Spyropoulos, many of which are previously unreleased. There are also versions of their better known songs like *Rainbow Chaser* and *Tiny Goddess* and demos of several including *Girl In The Park*.

Other compilation appearances have included: *June* (prev unreleased) on *Rubble, Vol. 14 - The Magic Rocking Horse* (LP), *Rubble, Vol. 8* (CD) and *The Best Of Rubble Collection, Vol. 4* (CD); *Excerpt From The Blind and The Beautiful* on *Illusions From The Crackling Void* (LP); and *Satellite Jockey* on *It's Only A Passing Phase* (LP). (VJ/VG/CE/JM)

Nite People

Personnel:

PATRICK BELL	tenor sax	A
MARTIN CLARK	bs	A
BARRY CURTIS	keyb'ds, recorder	AB
CHRISTOPHER 'FERGY' FERGUSON	gtr	AB
FRANCIS GORDON	gtr	A
JIMMY WARWICK	vcls, gtr	AB
SCOTT FIRKPATRICK	bs	B

ALBUM: 1(B) P.M. (Page One POLS 025) 1969 R3

45s: Sweet Tasting Wine/Nobody But You (Fontana TF 747) 1966 SC
Trying To Find Another Man/
Stay As Sweet As You Are (Fontana TF 808) 1967 SC
Summertime Blues/In The Springtime (Fontana TF 885) 1967 R1
Morning Sun/Weird And Funny (Fontana TF 919) 1968 SC
Love, Love, Love/Hot Smoke And
Sassafras (Some w/insert) (Page One POF 149) 1969 SC/-
Is This A Dream/Cream Tea (Page One POF 159) 1969
Season Of The Rain/P.M. (Page One POF 174) 1969

NIRVANA - Songs Of Love And Praise (LP).

This progressive rock outfit from Bournemouth's music was characterised by a heavy organ and guitar sound. Ferguson and Gordon were both born in Cornwall; Bell was from Weymouth; Curtis was born in Farringdon, Berkshire and Jimmy Warwick was born James Shipstone in St Hellier in Jersey. So they originated from quite a wide catchment area! They released four 45s for Fontana and then Bell, Clark and Gordon left. Scott Kirkpatrick was recruited on bass and they switched to Page One for three further 45s and their album.

Their album included a rework of Frank Zappa's *Peaches en Regalia*, but their finest moment was their *Morning Sun* 45 for Fontana, which was written and produced by the **Spencer Davis Group** and can also be heard on *Jagged Time Lapse, Vol 2* (CD). Their version of *Hot Smoke and Sassafras* can also be heard on *Glimpses, Vol. 1*. They relied a lot on cover versions on their 45s; *Sweet Tasting Wine* (**Tony Colton**), *Trying To Find Another Man* (Righteous Brothers oldie) and *Summertime Blues* (Eddie Cochran). More recently, *Weird And Funny* has been compiled on *Colour Me Pop, Vol 2* (CD) and *Love, Love, Love, Love* also appears on *We Can Fly, Vol 2* (CD). (VJ/JM)

The Niteshades

| 45s: | Be My Guest/I Must Reveal | (CBS 201 1763) 1965 |
| | Fell So Fast/I'm Not Gonna Worry | (CBS 201 1817) 1965 |

This was a six-piece male group from Stevenage, Hertfordshire. They also appeared in the movie, 'Be My Guest'. The title track was a surf-sounding song. (VJ)

Nix-Nomads

Personnel incl: KEITH WYNNER   vcls   A

| 45: | You're Nobody (Till Somebody Loves You)/ | |
| | She'll Be Sweeter Than You | (HMV POP 1354) 1964 R2 |

This Ipswich R&B band's 45 is now very sought-after by R&B collectors. Keith Wynner was briefly in **The Fairies** in 1965 and then formed St. Willy Cool School. The 'A' side was an OK cover of a Ray Charles song, but it's the bluesy flip side that they're remembered for.

She'll Be Sweeter Than You can also be heard on *Maximum R'n'B* (CD), *English Freakbeat Vol. 6* (CD), *Electric Sugarcube Flashbacks, Vol. 2* (LP) and *Electric Sugarcube Flashbacks, Vol. 3* (LP). (VJ)

Rab Noakes

ALBUMS:	1	DO YOU SEE THE LIGHTS	(Decca SKL 5061) 1970 R2
(up to	2	RAB NOAKES	(A&M AMLS 68119) 1972 SC
1976)	3	RED PUMP SPECIAL	(Warner Bros K 46284) 1974
	4	NEVER TOO LATE	(Warner Bros K 56114) 1975

NB: (2) with **Stealer's Wheel**.

45s:	Drunk Again/Miles Away	(A&M AMS 7030) 1972
(up to	Wait A Minute/Travel Sickness	(A&M AMS 7043) 1972
1976)	Clear Day/Wrong Joke Again	(Warner Bros K 16361) 1974
	Branch/Sitting In The Corner Blues	(Warner K 16431) 1974
	Turn A Deaf Ear/I'll Be With You	(Warner Bros K 16531) 1975

Rab Noakes was a Scottish folk singer from Fife. Two of his songs, *Together Forever* and *Somebody Counts On Me* were included on *Thru' The Recent Years* (LP) in 1969, which was the result of a collaboration between **Archie Fisher** and **Barbara Dickson**. His debut album, which merged folk with rock and pop, is now very hard to find.

In 1972, he formed an embryonic version of **Stealer's Wheel** with fellow Scot **Gerry Rafferty** but left after a few months to go solo. **Gerry Rafferty** guested on his 1972 album. In 1974 he signed to Warner Brothers and recorded a couple of albums aimed very much at the American market. He never achieved much commercial success at all and eventually became executive producer for BBC Scotland. He continued to make records (including some on **Ringo Starr**'s Ring' O label) and play live well into the eighties. (VJ)

The Nocturnes

Personnel incl:	JOHN CAMP	drms
	EVE EDEN (EVE GRAHAM)	vcls
	ROSS MITCHELL	drms
	LYN PETERS (LYN PAUL)	vcls
	KEN TAYLOR	lead gtr
	NICKY WALLER	vcls, bs

| ALBUMS: | 1 | THE NOCTURNES | (Columbia S(C)X 6223) 1968 SC |
| | 2 | WANTED ALIVE | (Columbia S(C)X 6315) 1968 SC |

45s:	I Wish You Would Show Me Your Mind/	
	I Do, I Do	(Columbia DB 8158) 1967
	Why (Am I Treated So Bad)/	
	Save The Last Dance For Me	(Columbia DB 8219) 1967
	A New Man/Suddenly Free	(Columbia DB 8332) 1968
	Carpet Man/Look At Me	(Columbia DB 8453) 1968
	Montage/Fairground Man	(Columbia DB 8493) 1968

This Birmingham harmony-pop group was most notable for the inclusion of Camp, who was later in **Renaissance**; whilst Eve Graham and **Lyn Paul** were later in The New Seekers. The group was formed by drummer Ross Mitchell. *Save The Last Dance For Me* was a Drifters song. **Lyn Paul** also recorded solo.

Carpet Man can also be found on *Psychedelia At Abbey Road* (CD). (VJ/DB)

NITE PEOPLE - P.M. (CD).

The Nocturns

Personnel:	BRIAN COX	gtr	A
	KEITH DRAPER	lead gtr	ABCD
	BARRY ELMSLEY	vcls, piano	AB
	DAVE FOLEY	bs	ABCD
	FRANK SLOANE	drms	ABCD
	STEVE ALDO	vcls	BCD
	DAVE ELIAS	gtr	CD
	DAVE WILCOX	vcls	D
	ARTHUR McMAHON	piano	D

45:     Carryin' On/Three Cool Cats   (Decca F 12002) 1964

'Also-rans' from the Merseybeat era in Liverpool. Cox, Foley and Sloane had all been in Alby and The Sorrals previously. The band appeared in the stage musical 'Maggie May', which *Carryin' On* is from. The flip side was an old Coasters' hit. Elias and Sloane had both been in **The Merseybeats** and McMahon in **Gerry and The Pacemakers**. (VJ/AD/JM)

Noir

Personnel:	TONY COLE	keyb'ds	A
	BARRY FORD	drms, vcls	A
	GORDON HUNTE	gtr, vcls	A
	ROY WILLIAMS	bs	A

ALBUM: 1(A) WE HAD TO LET YOU HAVE IT
               (w/insert)   (Dawn DNLS 3029) 1971 SC

This is a low-key progressive album which does contain some good guitar work and is long on playing time. Barry Ford was later in **Clancy** in the mid-seventies and Merger in the late seventies, but neither of these was well known either. (VJ)

The Nomads

45:     The Singer Sang His Song/Lovin' Him   (Pye 7N 17906) 1970

No other details are known about this act. (VJ)

Peter Noone

			HCP
45s:	Oh You Pretty Thing/Together Forever	(Rak RAK 114) 1971	12
(up to	Right On Mother/Walnut Whirl	(Rak RAK 121) 1971	-
1976)	Shoo Be Doo Ah/Because You're There	(Rak RAK 129) 1972	-
	Should I/Each And Every Minute	(Rak RAK 136) 1972	-
	Getting Over You/All Sing Together	(Philips 6006 353) 1973	-
	Meet Me On The Corner At Joe's Cafe/		
	Blame It On The Pony Express	(Casablanca CBX 501) 1974	-
	We Don't Need The Money/		
	Love Don't Change	(Bus Stop BUS 1034) 1976	-

Peter Noone was born in Manchester on 5th November 1947. He studied at the Manchester School of Music and Drama and appeared in ITV Soap Opera 'Coronation Street' prior to joining the Manchester beat group The Heartbeats as vocalist in 1963 using the pseudonym Peter Kovak. They soon evolved into **Herman's Hermits** and his boyish looks won over many hearts. Over the next six years (1964-70) they became one of Britain's top British beat groups and one of its most successful exports to the States in this era. When they finally split in December 1970 The Hermits relocated to the States to work the nostalgia circuit whilst **Noone** remained in the UK, signing to Mickie Most's RAK label. Things went well to begin with when his cover of **David Bowie**'s *Oh You Pretty Thing*, with **Bowie** on piano climbed to No 12 in the UK Charts, but it proved to be his only hit. The follow-up, *Right On Mother*, another **Bowie** song failed to make any commercial impact as did all his subsequent releases. In 1973 he briefly reunited with The Hermits topping the bill at the "British Invasion" nostalgia concert at New York's Madison Square Gardens. In subsequent years he continued in cabaret and on the stage. He's continued to be one of the most consistent performers of the new millennium. (VJ)

Norman and The Invaders

45s:	α	Our Wedding Day/Stacey	(United Artists UP 1031) 1964
		Night Train To Surbiton/	
		Likely Lads	(United Artists UP 1077) 1965

NB: α reissued with sides reversed (United Artists UP 1058) 1964.

The 1965 45 was an instrumental. Both sides were used for a BBC TV series. The London band veered towards comedy in their material. (VJ)

Norman Conquest

Personnel incl: JOHN PANTRY

45:     Two People/Upside Down   (MGM MGM 1376) 1967 R2

A rare and sought-after single from a group who later became **Peter and The Wolves** and then **Factory**. **Pantry** is thought to be the lead vocalist on both sides of the single. *Two People* is pretty straightforward pop and *Upside Down* is dreamy flowery pop.

Compilation appearances have included: *Upside Down* on *Rubble, Vol. 8 - All The Colours Of Darkness* (LP), *Rubble, Vol. 5* (CD) and *Hard Up Heroes, Vol. 6* (CD); and *Two People* and *Upside Down* on *The Upside Down World Of John Pantry* (LP). (VJ)

North Stars

45s:	For My True Love/Nothing But The Best	(Fontana TF 581) 1965
	She's So Far Out She's In/	
	Eenie Meenie Minee Mo	(Fontana TF 726) 1966 SC

This four-piece mid-sixties band came from Manchester. An under-rated outfit, their songs are either beat ballads or folksy, whilst *She's So Far Out She's In* is a mid-fast tempo beat/mod dancer. (VJ)

Northwind

Personnel:	HUGH BARR	gtr	A
	TOM BRANNAN	bs, vcls	A
	(DAVE SCOTT	drms	A)
	COLIN SOMERVILLE	keyb'ds	A
	BRIAN YOUNG	gtr, vcls	A

ALBUM: 1(A) SISTER, BROTHER, LOVER
                (Regal Zonophone SLRZ 1020) 1971 R3

NORTHWIND - Northwind (CD).

Often advertised as "rural" progressive, this pleasant album full of gentle rock songs isn't that progressive at all. It's pleasantness is mainly due to the agreeable voice of the vocalists and the beautiful melodies on some of the tracks. There are no technical pyrotechnics, but instead a clever use of acoustic instruments provides a very listenable texture. Standing out is *Acimo And Noiram* with a lovely melodic line along with *Many Tribesmen*. The opening track *Home For Frozen Roses* wouldn't be out of place on a Paul Simon album! The other tracks are nice enough, but do not contain much substance. Worth a spin, but do not pay the astronomical prices asked nowadays.

A Scottish band, member Brian Young later set up the Ca Va Recording Studio. (MK)

Nosmo

45:     Goodbye (Nothing To Say)/Teenage Love   (Pye 7N 45383) 1974

This 45 is a British Northern soul favourite recorded by Nosmo King. (VJ)

The Notations

45:     Need Your Love/
        Just Nothing Left To Give   (Chapter One SCH 174) 1972 R1

This is a rare single by a UK group who should not be confused with the US soul group of the same name and era from Chicago. (VJ)

The Nothings

45:     At Times Like This/Love So Sweet   (CBS 201779) 1965

A six-piece male group out of Folkestone in Kent. The 'A' side is a beat ballad. The flip is more soulish. (VJ)

Now

45:     Marcia/
        The Hands Of My Clock Stand Still   (NEMS 56-4125) 1969 SC

This is an obscure one-off progressive/pop 45 of no particular merit. *Marcia* features acoustic guitar and orchestration with two lead vocals.

Marcia can also be heard on *Psychedelia, Vol. 3* (LP) and *Hen's Teeth, Vol. 3* (CD). (VJ)

Noy's Band

Personnel:	PAT DEAN	lead gtr	A
	FIONA	various	A
	MAURICE McELROY	drms	A
	DEREK NOY	vcls	A
	ALAN ROADES	bs	A

45:     Love Potion No 9/Eldorado   (Dawn DNS 1075) 1974

A one-off 45 reworking an the old Coasters' song, earlier covered by **The Searchers**. Derek Noy had been in **Jan Dukes De Grey** before forming **Noy's Band** in April 1974. The 45 was released in August 1974. The following August, Derek Noy played as a one-man band. (VJ/JM)

NSU

Personnel:	WILLIAM HUGH ALEXANDER	drms	A
	PETER GRANT NEGLE	bs, hrmnca	A
	JOHN GRAHAM PETTIGREW	vcls	A
	ERNIE REA	ld gtr	A

ALBUM: 1(A) TURN ON OR TURN ME DOWN
                                (Stable SLE 8002) 1969 R3

NB: (1) reissued on CD (Free Records FR 2012).

NUCLEUS - Elastic Rock (LP).

NSU was a heavy rock quartet from Scotland. This album is now very rare and expensive to acquire. The band also got to play at the Albert Hall but disappeared soon after. (VJ)

Nucleus

Personnel:	IAN CARR	trumpet	ABC
	KARL JENKINS	sax, keyb'ds	AB
	JOHN MARSHALL	drms	A
	CHRIS SPEDDING	gtr	AB

			HCP
ALBUMS: 1(A)	ELASTIC ROCK	(Vertigo 6360 008) 1970 SC 46	
(up to 2(A)	WE'LL TALK ABOUT IT LATER		
1976)		(Vertigo 6360 027) 1970 SC -	
3(B)	SOLAR PLEXUS	(Vertigo 6360 039) 1971 SC -	
4(C)	BELLADONNA	(Vertigo 6360 076) 1972 SC -	
5( )	LABRYNTH	(Vertigo 6360 091) 1973 SC -	
6(-)	ROOTS	(Vertigo 6360 100) 1973 SC -	
7( )	UNDER THE SUN	(Vertigo 6360 110) 1974 -	
8( )	SNAKE HIPS ETCETERA	(Vertigo 6360 119) 1975 SC -	
9( )	ALLEY CAT	(Vertigo 6360 124) 1975 -	
10(-)	DIRECT HITS	(Vertigo 9286 019) 1976 -	

NB: (4) an Ian Carr solo album. (1) reissued on vinyl (Beat Goes On BGOLP 47) 1989, also (1) and (2) reissued on CD (Beat Goes On BGOCD 47). (3) reissued on CD (Vertigo 1378150). (7) and (8) reissued on a 2-CD set (BGO BGOCD 568) 2004. (9) and (10) reissued on a 2- CD set (BGO BGOCD 565) 2004. Also relevant is *Pretty Redhead BBC Live Sessions 1971-1982* (Hux HUX 038).

Nucleus first attracted attention by winning first prize at the Montreux International Festival in 1970 for their improvised and integrated music which was an amalgam of jazz and rock. They were originally formed in 1969 by trumpeter Ian Carr. He was joined by ex-**Battered Ornaments** guitarist **Chris Spedding** and Karl Jenkins and John Marshall (who both went on to **Soft Machine**) on the first three albums. *Elastic Rock* was their most successful, actually climbing to No 46 in the Album Charts. Its cover was the first of many Roger Dean designed for the Vertigo label and its content was well received by jazz critics. All of the tracks were self-penned, apart from *Twisted Track*, which had been recorded by **The Battered Ornaments**. Keyboardist Karl Jenkins wrote the majority of the material on the second album *We'll Talk About It Later*. Ever restless Carr decided to opt for a change in direction after this and split up what was arguably the best **Nucleus** line-up. Their third album, *Solar Plexus*, was financed by Camden Arts Lab. It was originally intended as a solo album with **Spedding**, Jenkins and Smith all assisting They were supplemented by top notch jazz players Kenny Wheeler, Jeff Clyne and Harry Beckett. Carr reverted back to the **Nucleus** name at a late stage. This album is spacier than the two which preceded it and is particularly recommended. In 1972 Jenkins and Marshall both departed to join **Soft Machine**.

Belladonna was essentially an Ian Carr solo album, although he did enlist the services of guitarist Allan Holdsworth. Produced by Jon Hiseman (of

Colosseum fame) it is Carr's most sought-after work for Vertigo. Of the later albums *Snakes Hips Etcetera* is well regarded. *Alley Cat* boasts some good moments, particularly the interplay between Carr on trumpet and saxophonist Bob Berties on *Splat*.

Direct Hits is a retrospective album. Its highlights include *Crude Blues* (which features superb oboe playing from Karl Jenkins and *Bull Dance* (notable for Carr's soaring trumpet solos and whispered vocals). They eventually split up in the early eighties.

Nucleus is still considered to be one of Britain's top jazz-rock bands. Ian Carr now works as a session musician. **Chris Spedding** enjoyed some success as a solo artist and later worked with the Sex Pistols, and more lately with **Roxy Music**, **Jane Birkin** and Katie Melua. (VJ)

Number Nine Bread Street

Personnel:	BOB HART	A
	MIKE LEVON	A

ALBUM: 1 (A) NUMBER NINE BREAD STREET
(Holyground HG112/1109) 1967 R4

NB: (1) reissued on CD (Kissing Spell KSG 001) 2001.

This was the first album released on the Wakefield-based Holyground label which had been set up by Mike Levon and Dave Wood. Only 250 copies were pressed. The band comprised the label founder Mike Levon and Bob Hart, who wrote most of the songs. I've been unable to track down a copy but it's reputedly a collection of surreal folk music recorded at a local pub. The track list does include a cover version of Dylan's *Love Minus Zero* and a Pete Seeger tune *The Travelling People*. According to 'Record Collector' the better tracks make grim but humorous observations on satanic mills and miners.

Girl For All Seasons later resurfaced on *The History Of U.K. Underground Folk Rock 1968-1978 Vol. 2* (CD). (VJ/DS)

The Nu-Notes

Personnel:	ROGER DEAN	ld gtr	A
	BERNIE MARTIN	drms	A
	MEL MILLER	bs	A
	RUSS SAINTY	vcls	A
	ROY TOFT	gtr	A

45s:	Hall Of Mirrors/Fury	(HMV POP 1232) 1963 SC
	Kathy/Sunset	(HMV POP 1311) 1964 SC

This was the backing group of balladeer Russ Sainty, who made several 45s not listed in this book. These two 45s were quite beaty. *Fury* was written by Russ Sainty.

Roger Dean went on to play with **John Mayall's Bluesbreakers** and Ronnie Jones with The Blue Jays. Bernie Martin later achieved some success in Italy with **The Bad Boys**. (VJ/RD)

Nutz

Personnel:	MICK DAVENPORT	gtr, vcls	AB
	DAVE LLOYD	gtr, vcls	AB
	KEITH MULLHOLLAND	bs, vcls	AB
	JOHN MYLETT	drms	AB
	KENNY NEWTON	keyb'ds	B

ALBUMS:	1(A)	NUTZ	(A&M AMLS 68256) 1974
(up to	2(A)	NUTZ TWO	(A&M AMLS 68306) 1975
1977)	3(B)	HARD NUTZ	(A&M AMLS 64623) 1977
	4(B)	NUTZ LIVE CUTS	(A&M AMLS 68453) 1977

NB: (1) and (2) reissued on CD in Japan.

45s:	As Far As The Eye Can See/	
	Just For The Crack	(A&M AMS 7115) 1974
	Round And Round/Light Of Day	(A&M AMS 7128) 1974

Change's Coming/Long Ships	(A&M AMS 7160) 1975
Sick And Tired/Wallbanger	(A&M AMS 7272) 1977
One More Cup Of Tea/	
Down On My Knees	(A&M AMS 7281) 1977

This hard, but not heavy rock outfit from Liverpool, failed to achieve commercial success. Their debut was highly creative, filled with illustrious harmonies to synchopated drumming, incredible guitar and even soulful tunes such as *I Can't Unwind*. On it they were assisted on their first album by 'Rabbit' Bundrick (piano, organ) and on one track by Chris Hughes (brass). All the material on the album was written by Davenport or Lloyd.

The single *Change's Coming*, from their second album, was a cover of a **Gypsy** 45. The 'B' side, *Long Ships*, was a group composition and would appear to be non-album. They were supplemented on this album by Paul Carrack and Neil Kernon (both on keyboards). They recruited a permanent keyboardist Kenny Newton in April 1976. He played on *The Hard Nutz* album, released in February 1977, which was released as *Nutz 111* in the USA. After the *Live Cutz* album Newton left to join Lion and then Nightwing.

They later evolved into Rage. (MWh/AGl/JM)

Michael Nyman

ALBUM:	1	DECAY MUSIC	(Obscure No. 6) 1976

Long before *The Piano* and his success with Peter Greenaway film scores, **Michael Nyman** was featured on **Brian Eno**'s Obscure label distributed by Island Records. *Decay Music* can best be described as extremely minimalist. (VJ)

NUMBER NINE BREAD STREET - Number Nine Bread Street (CD).

OBERON - A Midsummer's Night Dream (LP).

Oak

Personnel:		
	TONY ENGLE	A
	DANNY STRADLING	A
	ROD STRADLING	A
	PETA WEBB	A

ALBUM: 1(A) WELCOME TO OUR FAIR (Topic 12TS 212) 1971 R2

Folk enthusiasts rate this album of traditional English folk music very highly indeed. Essential for any comprehensive folk collection, it is now very rare and hard to find. (VJ)

Oberon

ALBUM: 1 A MIDSUMMER'S NIGHT DREAM
(Acorn No number) 1971 R4
NB: (1) reissued on CD (Audio Archives AACD 035) in a limited run of 500. (1) reissued on vinyl (Akarma/Acorn AK 314) 2005.

A mega-rare privately pressed album recorded by an Oxfordshire folk band. Only 99 copies were pressed (the number being dictated by the tax man) making it one of the most obscure folk albums of the era. Acorn was a very small local label who also issued the first album by The Yetties. The recording was completed in a school hall. The music is delicate and improvised. Whilst predominantly folk it also embraces elements of jazz, progressivism and psychedelia. The reissue has made it accessible to a wider audience and whilst it's not a lost gold nugget it is worth obtaining. (VJ)

Object

Syde Trips, Vol. 4 (LP) features *Blue Skies And Green Green Grass*, a good piece of pop art with some pleasant jangling guitar work, from a four-track acetate EP the band had recorded at a Berkshire studio early in 1966. The EP also included a cover of **The Beatles**' hit *We Can Work It Out*.

Other compilation appearances include: *When She Told Me* and *She's Gone Away* on *Incredible Sound Show Stories, Vol. 10* (LP). (VJ)

Occasional Word Ensemble

Personnel:		
	JOHN BROWN	A
	GEOFF HILL	A
	MITCH HOWARD	A
	PETE ROCHE	A
	RICK SANDERS	A
	RICHARD SYLVESTER	A

ALBUM: 1(A) THE YEAR OF THE GREAT LEAP SIDEWAYS
(Dandelion 63753) 1970 SC
NB: (1) reissued on CD (See For Miles SEECD 420-D).

This now obscure release was the work of a group of beatnick poets from Sheffield. Long forgotten and completely oddball. You can hear *Missed My Times* on the budget *Dandelion Sampler 1969-1972* (CD), or go the full monty with the See For Miles CD reissue. (VJ/LBy)

Octopus

Personnel incl:			
	NIGEL GRIGGS	bs, gtr	AB
	PAUL GRIGGS	lead vcls, gtr, piano	AB
	BRIAN GLASCOCK	gtr	A
	RICK WILLIAMS	keyb'ds	A
	(TIM REEVES	drms	A)
	JOHN COOK	keyb'ds	B
	MALCOLM GREEN	drms	B

ALBUM: 1 (B) RESTLESS NIGHT (Penny Farthing PELS 508) 1970 R3
NB: (1) reissued on CD as *Restless Night... Plus* (See For Miles SEECD 328-A) 1991 and on vinyl (Essex 1013LP) 1996.

45s:	Laugh At The Poor Man/	
	Girlfriend	(Penny Farthing PEN 705) 1969 SC
α	The River/Thief	(Penny Farthing PEN 716) 1970 SC
	Hey Na Na/Future Feelings	(Mooncrest MOON 7) 1973

NB: α also issued in Argentina (Carmusic CM 3002).

This Hatfield, Hertfordshire band began life as **The Cortinas**, recording one 45 on Polydor under that moniker. They were discovered by Tony Murray of **The Troggs** and, having changed their name to **Octopus**, signed to Larry Page's newly-established Penny Farthing label. Line-up (A) recorded the melodic pop 45 *Laugh At The Poor Man*, which appeared in October 1969. Their album, recorded by line-up (B), was produced by Murray and is now extremely rare. Musically it's pretty commercial pop-rock with the occasional hint of psychedelia - for example, opening cut *The River* concludes with some good fuzz guitar and *Council Plans* has some nice organ touches. The title track has an unusual intro but is otherwise very ordinary. Arguably the best track is the finale, *Tide*. Most of the album is commercial pop, typified by songs like *Queen And The Pauper*. The See For Miles reissue includes their competent, poppish debut 45, and makes for a wiser expenditure than the now extremely rare original.

Reeves joined **Mungo Jerry** in March 1972, and Paul Griggs went on to Guys and Dolls. Nigel Griggs (as Nigel Smith) joined **Khan** in June 1972 and was in New Zealand group Split Enz from June 1977 to October 1984. Brian Glascock (who left during the album sessions) briefly joined **Toe Fat** before heading for the US , where he was later in The Motels.

OCTOPUS - Restless Night (LP).

Compilation appearances have included: *The River* and *The Thief* on *Rubble, Vol. 11* (CD); *The River* on *The Best Of Rubble Collection, Vol. 5* (CD); and *The Thief* on *The Best Of Rubble Collection, Vol. 6* (CD). (VJ/ML/RMJ)

Ann Odell

ALBUM: 1   A LITTLE TASTE   (DJM DJLPS 434) 1973 SC
NB: (1) reissued on CD (DJM).

45s: I Didn't Mean To/
         Every Girl Becomes A Woman   (DJM DJS 276) 1973
         Swing Song/Everything's Fine Sunshine   (DJM DJS 280) 1973

Ann Odell was later in a short-lived mid-seventies act called **Chopyn**. (VJ)

Odin

Personnel:	JEFF BEER	keyb'ds, perc, vcls	A
	RAY BROWN	bs, vcls	A
	STUART FORDHAM	drms, perc	A
	ROB TERSTALL	gtr, vcls	A

ALBUM: 1(A)   ODIN   (Vertigo 6360 608) 1972 R1
NB: (1) reissued on CD (Living In The Past LITP 1972-002).

A British progressive rock band but for some reason this album was only released in Germany, presumably they relocated to there. (VJ)

Odin's People

45s: From A Distance/I Need You   (Major Minor MM 501) 1967
         Tommy Jones/
         I Need Your Hand In Mine   (Major Minor MM 506) 1967

An Irish band. *From A Distance* was a P.F. Sloan composition. (VJ)

Rock O'Doodle

Personnel incl: PATRICK CAMPBELL-LYONS

45:     Queen Of Rock And Roll/Woman   (Decca F 13450) 1973

This was a pseudonym for former **Nirvana** member **Patrick Campbell-Lyons**. (VJ)

ODIN - Odin (LP).

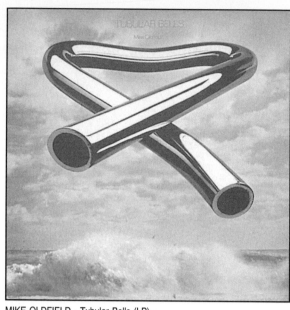

MIKE OLDFIELD - Tubular Bells (LP).

Odyssey

Personnel incl: DAVE PRESTON   drms   A

45:     How Long Is Time/Beware   (Strike JH 312) 1966 SC

This London band was first known as **Sons Of Fred**. Their 45 was produced by **Miki Dallon**. (VJ)

Oedipus Complex

Personnel:	IVAN CHANDLER	keyb'ds	A
	HUGH 'ULYSSES' McGAW		A
	PETER ROWLES		A
	FELIX TERRY		A

45s: Holding My Hands Out/
         Brought Me Such Confusion   (Philips BF 1716) 1968
         Up Down Round And Round/
         Empty Highway   (Philips BF 1771) 1969

This band formed in 1968. Chandler, who'd previously been in Echoes (**Dusty Springfield**'s backing group), was in **Daddy Longlegs** in 1972. (VJ)

John O'Hara and The Playboys/O'Hara's Playboys

Personnel incl:	BOBBY CAMPBELL	organ, vcls	A
	PETER GREEN	sax	A
	BARRY HERD	ld gtr, vcls	A
	BILL MATHIESON	bs	A
	DAVE McHARG	drms	A
	JOHN O'HARA	lead vcls, tenor sax	A

ALBUM: 1(A)   GET READY
                (mono/stereo)   (Fontana (S)TL 5461) 1968 R1
NB: (1) Credited to **John O'Hara and The Playboys**.

45s: α   Start All Over/I've Been Wondering   (Fontana TF 763) 1966
       α   Spicks And Specks/One Fine Lady   (Fontana TF 793) 1967
       α   Ballad Of The Soon Departed/
           Tell Me Why   (Fontana TF 872) 1967
       α   Island In The Sun/Harry   (Fontana TF 893) 1967
       α   In The Shelter Of My Heart/
           Goodnight Mr. Nightfall   (Fontana TF 924) 1968
       α   Voices/Blue Dog   (Fontana TF 949) 1968
       β   I Started A Joke/Show Me   (Fontana TF 974) 1968
       β   More Than Just A Woman/No No No   (Fontana TF 1043) 1969

NB: α as **O'Hara's Playboys**. β as **John O'Hara and The Playboys**.

These Glasgow bands were led by lead vocalist and tenor saxophonist **John O'Hara**. They did a couple of **Bee Gees** songs as 'A' sides; *Spicks And Specks* and *I Started A Joke* and some of their 45s were produced by **Dave Dee**. They also played a lot in Germany and made records over there, including an album *Playboys Party No 1* (Decca SLK/BLK 16295) 1964, and three 45s. Two of their songs were sung in German, and the album is reputedly a great party record.

Blue Dog has been compiled on *Oddities, Vol 2* (CD). (VJ)

Mike Oldfield

				HCP
ALBUMS:	1	TUBULAR BELLS	(Virgin V 2001) 1973 SC	1
(up to	2	HERGEST RIDGE	(Virgin V 2013) 1974 SC	1
1976)	3	THE ORCHESTRAL TUBULAR BELLS		
			(Virgin V 2026) 1975	17
	4	OMMADAWN	(Virgin V 2043) 1975	4
	5	V (2-LP compilation)	(Virgin VD 2502) 1975	-
	6	BOXED	(Virgin V BOX 1) 1976	22

NB: There was a quadrophonic version of (1) (Virgin QV 2001) 1974 (SC) and two different quadrophonic versions of (4) (Virgin QUQS 2043) 1975 and (Virgin QV 2043) 1976 (both SC). (6) was a boxed set of four albums. (1) reissued on CD (Virgin CDV 2001) 1983 and again remastered using High Definition Compatible Digital (HDCD) technology (Virgin 7243 8 49388 2 6) 2000. (2) reissued on CD (Virgin CDV 2013) 1986 and again remastered using HDCD (Virgin 7245 8 49369 2 1) 2000. (3) reissued on CD (Virgin V.I.P. VVIPD 101) 1989 and again remastered using HDCD (Virgin 7243 8 49369 2 1) 200. (4) reissued on CD (Virgin CDV 2043) 1986 and again remastered using HDCD (Virgin 7243 8 49370 2 7) 2000. *The Complete Mike Oldfield* is available on vinyl and CD (Virgin CDMOC 1) 1985. There's also *Mike Oldfield CD Box Set, Vol. 1* (Virgin TPAK 15) and *Vol. 2* (Virgin TPAK 16), both issued in 1990. (1) and (4) were also issued in quadrophonic. These are SC. There's also been another retrospective CD compilation the 4-CD box set *Elements - The Best Of Mike Oldfield* (Virgin VTCD 18) 1993, which was reissued again (Virgin CDBOXY 2) in 2002. *The Essential Mike Oldfield* (WEA) 1997 comprises excerpts from his most famous works.

			HCP
45s:	Tubular Bells Theme/Froggy Went A		
(up to	Courting (Some PS)	(Virgin VS 101) 1974 SC/-	31
1976)	Hergest Ridge excerpt/		
	Spanish Tune (promo only)	(Virgin VS 112) 1974 R2	-
	Don Alfonso/		
	In Dulce Jubilo (Some PS)	(Virgin VS 117) 1975 SC	-
	In Dulce Jubilo/On Horseback	(Virgin VS 131) 1975	4
	Portsmouth/		
	Speak (Tho' You Only Say Farewell)	(Virgin VS 163) 1976	3

Mike Oldfield was born on 15 May 1953 in Reading, Berkshire. His debut recording was an album, *Children Of The Sun*, made with his sister Sally as **Sallyangie** in 1968. This was strictly a short-term project which split up when its single *Two Ships* flopped. **Oldfield**'s next project was even shorter - he formed a group called Barefeet which never made it onto vinyl. Then

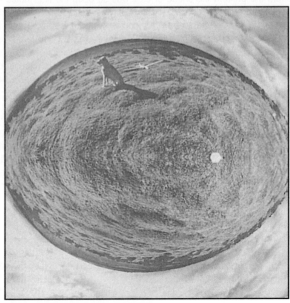

MIKE OLDFIELD - Hergest Ridge (LP).

MIKE OLDFIELD - Ommadawn (LP).

in March 1970 he joined **Kevin Ayers' Whole World** on bass but later switched to lead guitar, playing on their two albums. When they split in Summer 1971 he decided to go solo and with financial backing from Richard Branson, who was planning his own Virgin record label, he set about recording a 50 minute instrumental composition. The end result was *Tubular Bells*, a collage of melodic lines and various (mostly overdubbed) instruments (guitar, grand piano, bass, organ, mandolin) linked together by a bell motif. It wasn't entirely a solo album - he did get assistance from **Viv Stanshall** (ex-**Bonzo Dog Doo-Dah Band**) as an occasional narrator, Steve Broughton (drms) and ex-**July** member Jon Field (flute) and others. Critically acclaimed at the time, it was taken to a wider audience when part of side one was used as the main theme in 'The Exorcist' movie. An edited version was released as a 45 in the US peaking at No 7 in the Singles Charts. By this time the album had already climbed to No 3 in the US Album Charts earning a gold disc. (It would go on to become a mega-selling disc). Success was a little slower coming here in the UK but an edited 45 got to No 31 in the Singles Chart and (eventually) to No 1 in the Album Charts. Most of you will have heard this classic album, anyone who hasn't should certainly check it out for it was certainly one of the most significant of the seventies. It eventually spent 264 weeks in the UK Album Charts. It also won a Grammy Award for being the Best International Composition of 1974.

The follow-up *Hergest Ridge*, another collection of similarly compiled overdubs, was in retrospect too similar to his classic debut and this was reflected in its relatively disappointing sales. Although it entered the UK Charts at No 1 it was deposed by *Tubular Bells* after three weeks and it only got to No 87 in the US.

In 1975, **David Bedford** arranged an orchestrated version of **Oldfield**'s classic work (the *Orchestral Tubular Bells*) which was played by The Royal Philharmonic Orchestra with **Oldfield** on guitar. This also got to No 17 in the UK Charts.

His next album *Ommadawn*, another thematic work which incorporated Celtic and African influences and was full of more clever overdubs, countered any suggestion that his debut album was a one-off climbing to No 4 here in the UK and receiving widespread acclaim (though it didn't fare so well commercially in the US, where it peaked at No 146.)

The 1975 (2-LP) compilation *V* includes a long version of *Don Alfonso*.

As 1976 approached **Oldfield** was enhancing his status as a household name by achieving a Top 5 hit with a seasonal double A side which coupled the traditional *In Dulce Jubilo* (an instrumental) with *On Horseback* (which included vocals). At the end of the year he repeated this success with his own arrangement of another traditional tune *Portsmouth*, which eventually peaked at No 3 in the UK in January 1977.

The other **Oldfield** release in the time frame covered by this book was *Boxed*, as its name implies this was a (4-LP) boxed set, which consisted of remixed versions of *Tubular Bells*, *Hergest Ridge* and *Ommadawn* and various 45 releases. It climbed to No 22 in the UK in December 1976.

In the eighties **Oldfield** moved into pop with albums like *QE2* (1980), *Crises* (1983), *Discovery* (1984), and *Islands* (1987). Then in 1992, he linked with producer Trevor Horn to record *Tubular Bells II*, which took him to the top of the UK charts again. He enjoyed further success with *Songs Of Distant Earth* (1994) and a third version of *Tubular Bells* in 1998. Anyone not familiar with his work should start with the original *Tubular Bells* and progress from there.

The 4-CD box set *Elements*, first released in 1993 and again in 2002 offers a five hour journey through his career and includes the original and best *Tubular Bells* album in its entirety. It's an expanded alternative to the *Best Of Tubular Bells* album, released in 2001 and an excellent introduction to those not familiar with his career.

Tubular Bells can also be heard on the 3-CD box set *Radio Caroline Calling - 70's Flashback* and *Mrs. Moon And The Thatched Shop* has been compiled on the 3-CD box set *Ars Longa Vita Brevis: A Compendium of Progressive Rock 1967-1974*. (VJ)

Andrew Oldham (Orchestra)

ALBUMS: 1 16 HIP HITS   (Ace Of Clubs ACL 1180) 1964 R1
         2 LIONEL BART'S MAGGIE MAY (Decca LK 4636) 1964 SC
         3 THE ROLLING STONES SONGBOOK
                                     (Decca LK/SKL 4796) 1966 R2

NB: There's a CD collection, *Rarities* (See For Miles SEECD 394) 1993 which had originally been issued on vinyl by C5 in 1988. (3) reissued on Decca (820 186-1) 1982 and again on CD (Universal 9816711) 2004.

45s: α Funky And Fleopatra   (Decca F 11829) 1964
         365 Rolling Stones/Oh I Do Like To
         See Me On The 'B' Side   (Decca F 11878) 1964 SC
         We Don't All Wear D'same Size Boots/
         Right Of Way   (Decca F 11987) 1964 SC

NB: α credited to **Andrew Oldham** Group.

As manager of **The Rolling Stones**, **Andrew Loog Oldham** became one of the greatest influences on the direction on British pop culture in the sixties, his maverick, strutting image symbolising the glamour and arrogance of the newly-successful younger generation.

Oldham originally set out to establish himself as a teenage pop star under the name Sandy Beach, but he is not best remembered for his recorded output. He soon moved into publicity, working for Brian Epstein as an early publicist for **The Beatles**. He was casting around for an act of his own to manage, however, and in April 1963 became co-manager of **The Rolling Stones**. Having ousted their pianist Ian Stewart for not looking the part, he formulated their unruly image and was instrumental in their rapid rise. He also discovered and produced **Marianne Faithfull**, **Chris Farlowe**, **Duncan Browne**, **The Poets**, **Twice As Much**, **Billy Nicholls**, **Vashti Bunyan** and

OLIVER - Standing Stone (LP).

a host of lesser-known names such as **George Bean**, **Blues By Five**, **Bo and Peep** and **Charles Dickens**. The above recordings were made during his years with **The Stones**, and all are now collectable, though in truth he was never a great producer, relying too heavily on echo and attempts to recreate Phil Spector's 'wall of sound'.

In 1966 he launched his own record company, Immediate (which signed existing acts like P.P. Arnold, **The Nice**, **Humble Pie**, **Amen Corner** and **The Small Faces**) and in 1967 he parted company with **The Rolling Stones**. Whether he jumped or got the push is unclear, but by 1968 his vaulting ambition had put Immediate into severe financial difficulties. It finally went bankrupt in 1969, and he became a recluse in the States for a few years. Drug dependency reduced his capability in this period, though he re-emerged in 1973 to produce **Donovan**'s *Essence To Essence*, which led to further production work. In 1976 NEMS acquired the rights to the Immediate catalogue and he became their American director, helping to relaunch the label. **Marianne Faithfull**, who he'd discovered 12 years earlier, was one of his first signings.

His two volumes of memoirs, 'Stoned' and '2Stoned', are essential documents for anyone seeking to understand the pop world of the 1960s.

The 2004 CD reissue of *The Rolling Stones Songbook* contains an interview with **Oldham** in the booklet, along with rare photos.

Compilation appearances have included: *Memphis Tennessee, I Wanna Be Your Man, Oh, I Do Like To See Me On The 'B' Side, Da Doo Ron Ron (When He Walked Me Home), There Are But Five Rolling Stones* and *365 Rolling Stones (One For Every Day Of The Year)* on *Rolling Stones Connection 1963-66* (CD); and *Da Doo Ron Ron (When He Walked Me Home)* on *The Beat Scene* (CD) and *Hard-Up Heroes* (2-LP). (VJ/RMJ)

Oliver

Personnel: OLIVER CHAPLIN

ALBUM: 1 STANDING STONE   (Olive OL 1) 1974 R4/R3
NB: (1) initially issued in withdrawn blue sleeve (R4) and later in green sleeve (R3). (1) reissued on (Tenth Planet TP 001) 1992 in numbered edition of 500 (SC). (1) also available on CD with six additional tracks (Wooden Hill WHCD 001) 1995.

This ultra-rare and expensive privately pressed album by a certain Oliver Chaplin is an amalgam of folk, blues, progressivism and psychedelia. All the material was written by **Oliver**. Its highlights include *Freezing Cold Like An Iceburg*, which sounds very like Captain Beefheart; *In Vain*, which has been likened to **Pink Floyd**'s *More* Soundtrack; *Flowers On A Hill*, which has a sort of ragtime feel; *Cat And The Rat*, a length piece of guitar-driven progressivism and the folky *Primrose* and *Orbit Your Factory*. His brother Chris Chaplin had been employed as a BBC Sound Engineer and worked on the BBC's **Hendrix** sessions, which explains why the sound quality on the 50-minute album is so good. 250 copies of the album were issued originally in a plain blue cover with black letters. When the covers came back from the printers the shade of blue was so deep the liner notes were almost illegible and an olive green sleeve was substituted. Most copies were given to family and friends but copies were passed to Radio One deejays Brian Matthew and Alan Black. The latter was keen to feature it on his show but was reluctant to do so when it wasn't available in the shops. After refusing to sign a contract for the album to be distributed through Virgin Records because he considered the record industry corrupt Chaplin returned to his native Wales.

In the late eighties a copy of the album was purchased at a car boot sale and was transferred to the collectors' circuit. **Oliver** was contacted and a small number of other original copies of the album he made available circulated for increasing prices. In 1992 he authorised the Tenth Planet reissue of 500 further copies which should help satisfy the increasing demand for this album. (VJ)

Nigel Olsson (Drum Orchestra)

ALBUMS: 1 NIGEL OLSSON'S DRUM ORCHESTRA AND CHORUS
                                     (DJM DJLPS 417) 1971
         2 NIGEL OLSSON   (Rocket ROLL 2) 1975

45s:	α	Nature's Way/G.T. Over	(DJM DJS 239) 1971
	α	Alabama/Sunshine Looks Like Rain	(DJM DJS 206) 1972
		Only One Woman/In Good Time	(Rocket PIG 13) 1974

NB: α as **Nigel Olsson's Drum Orchestra**.

Olsson was **Elton John**'s drummer and had been in **Plastic Penny**. Most of the tracks on the album are self-penned with help from **Caleb Quaye** and **Mick Grabham**. On the album he's assisted by Dee Murray, **Mick Grabham**, **Caleb Quaye**, **B.J. Cole**, Doris Troy, **Liza Strike** etc. but it's a poor album.

In 1975 he recorded an eponymous album for Rocket, which featured **Elton John**. He recorded three further albums beyond the timespan of this book: *Drummers Can Sing Too* (1978), *Nigel* (1979) and *Changing Tides* (1980). (VJ/BS)

One

Personnel:	KEVIN FOGARTY	gtr	A
	BRENT FORBES	bs	A
	CONRAD ISADORE	drms	A
	NORMAN LEPPARD	woodwind	A
	ALAN MARSHALL	gtr, vcls, hrmnca	A
	BOBBY SASS	gtr, vcls	A

ALBUM: 1(A) ONE   (Fontana STL 5539) 1969 R2

A little known album whose participants were better known for session work. Brent Forbes, who was in Locust in the mid-seventies, also worked for **Bob Pegg** and The Surprise Sisters; Norman Leppard played with **Aynsley Dunbar** and Alan Marshall, who was in **Zzebra** in the mid-seventies, played for **Pete Bardens**. Conrad Isadore was most prolific of all - cropping up on several other artists albums. (VJ)

One and One

| Personnel: | TONY BURROWS |
| | ROGER GREENAWAY |

45:     I'll Give You Lovin'/It's Me   (Decca F 11948) 1964

A one-off project by these two session singers. Tony Burrows was later behind **The Ivy League**, **The Flowerpot Men** and **Edison Lighthouse**. Roger Greenaway was later in **David and Jonathan**, with Roger Cook, who he also formed a successful songwriting partnership with. (VJ)

One In A Million

Personnel:	BILLY FISHER	bs	A
	JACK McCULLOUCH	drms	A
	JIMMY McCULLOUGH	gtr, vcls	A
	ALAN YOUNG	gtr, vcls	A

| 45s: | | Use Your Imagination/Hold On | (CBS 202513) 1967 R3 |
| | α | Fredereek Hernando/Double Sight | (MGM MGM 1370) 1968 R4 |

NB: α has been repressed (MGM MGM 1370) in a limited edition of 500 reproduced from the original French jukebox with a large centre hole.

This Glasgow band was originally known as The Jaygars. Their first 45 is very collectable but the second is one of the jewels of British psychedelia - a superb double-sided disc with psychedelic guitar work out of the top drawer and a good vocal performance from Jimmy McCullouch, who later played in **Thunderclap Newman** (with his brother Jack), and with **John Mayall**, **Stone The Crows** and **Wings**. Jack McCullouch's future bands included **Wild Country** and **Andwella**.

Compilation appearances have included: *No Smokes* (from a one-sided Emidisc acetate also thought to have been by this band) on *Purple Heart Surgery, Vol. 1* (LP) and *Hens Teeth Vol. 2* (CD); *Use Your Imagination* on *Purple Pill Eaters* (LP & CD); and *Fredereek Hernando* and *Double Sight* on *Lovely Summer Days* (CD). (VJ)

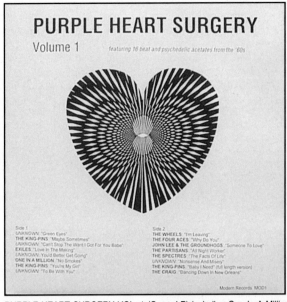

PURPLE HEART SURGERY VOL. 1 (Comp LP) including One In A Million.

One One Seven

Personnel:	PETE CARR	bs	A
	JAMES FRASER	vcls	A
	ALLAN GRIMLEY	gtr	A
	CHARLIE HART	keyb'ds	A
	JOHNNY SHIRREFF	drms	A

This obscure early psychedelic group who played at the legendary 14-Hour Technicolour Dream in April 1967 originally came from Cambridge where they were known as The Fix in 1966. Following gigs at Happening 44, and the Electric Garden in 1967 they were brought to the attention of **Andrew Loog Oldham** who cut a demo tape at Olympic Studios produced by Glyn Johns for Immediate Records. **Chris Jagger** was part of the social group around the band, and no doubt he was responsible for introducing them to his brother **Mick Jagger** and **Andrew Loog Oldham**.

The demo tracks they recorded included the memorable *Venusian Moonshine* and a lengthy dirge-like affair *Smokeless Zone*, which dealt with decriminalisation of cannabis. None of the tracks were ever officially released despite encouragement from **Mick Jagger** who was present at the recordings. (The recording session took place after **Mick Jagger** had received his infamous jail sentence and while his appeal was pending - as soon as the sentence was lifted he left the country).

They broke up soon after Charlie Hart joined **Pete Brown and His Battered Ornaments**.

The band also appeared in a Pathe Picorial documentary about "Flower Power", images from which regularly appear today as archive material in TV documentaries. The only recorded trace of the band to resurface has been roughly two minutes on the soundtrack, which of course has a commentary over it. Sadly there are no unedited rushes featuring the band.

We're not sure if Charlie Hart is the same chap who has played recently with **Chris Jagger** or the same guy who played with Ian Dury. (JN/TG)

One Two and Three

Personnel:	BILLIE LANEY	vcls	A
	MARTIN SHOBEN	gtr, vcls	A
	HARRY VALLINS	gtr, vcls, piano	A

ALBUM: 1(A) BLACK PEARLS AND GREEN DIAMONDS
                          (Decca LK 4682) 1965 R3

45:     Black Pearl/Bahama Lullaby   (Decca F 12093) 1965 SC

This folk-pop trio's rare album was overseen by Decca's in-house folk producer Ray Horricks, best known for his work with **Davy Graham**. It

THE OPEN MIND - The Open Mind (LP).

consists of traditional material (including a truly beautiful version of the folk ballad *All My Trials*, retitled *Bahama Lullaby*) alongside originals penned by Sri Lankan songwriter Nimal Mendis. Though reminiscent of earlier acts such as Peter, Paul and Mary, the group's complex harmonies and varied material also anticipated the work of later acts such as **Bread, Love & Dreams** and **Sallyangie**. Their album, in fact, sounds very similar to their American contemporaries The Goldebriars. (VJ/RMJ)

Onyx

Personnel:
DICK BLAND	bs	AB
STEVE COTTON	organ	AB
ROGER DELL	drms	AB
ALAN HODGE	gtr	A
TONY PRIEST	vcls	AB
BERNIE LEE	gtr	B

45s:
You've Gotta Be With Me/ It's All Put On	(Pye 7N 17477)	1968 SC
My Son John/Step By Step	(Pye 7N 17622)	1968 SC
Tamaris Khan/So Sad Inside	(Pye 7N 17668)	1969 R2
Time Off/Movin' In	(CBS 4635)	1969 SC
Our House/Air	(Parlophone R 5888)	1971
The Next Stop Is Mine/ What's That You Say	(Parlophone R 5906)	1971

Formed in Wadebridge, Cornwall, this band was originally known as Rick and The Hayseeds. They became **Onyx** around Christmas 1966 when guitarist Alan Hodge, who'd previously played with various local bands like The Buccaneers and The Fabulous Jaguars, was added to the line-up. They were a popular live attraction locally and also made a number of live appearances on 'Radio One'. Their material for Pye was pretty straight-forward pop with *Tamaris Khan*, being a story-song with some good guitar moments. In 1969 they switched to CBS recording *Time Off*, a good 45 which veered more towards progressivism, and a further 45 as **Salamander**, before switching again to Parlophone for a couple of final efforts in 1971. Hodge left to join Rogue and former **Cupid's Inspiration** member Bernie Lee replaced him on the two Parlophone 45s. Much of their material was written by Guy Fletcher and Doug Fleet, who during the seventies became a successful writing partnership and wrote hits for Cliff Richard and others.

Compilation appearances have included: *Tamaris Khan* on *Paisley Pop - Pye Psych (& Other Colours) 1966-1969* (CD), *Rubble, Vol. 10 - Professor Jordan's Magic Sound Show* (LP), *It's Only A Passing Phase* (LP) and *Hot Smoke & Sassafras - Psychedelic Pstones, Vol 1* (CD); *You Gotta Be With Me* on *Quick Before They Catch Us* (LP & CD); *So Sad Inside* and *You Gotta Be With Me* on *Rubble, Vol. 7 - Pictures In The Sky* (LP); *Time Off* on *Colour Me Pop, Vol 2* (CD) and *So Sad Inside* on *Haunted - Psychedelic Pstones, Vol 2* (CD). (VJ/JM)

Opal Butterfly

Personnel:
RICHARD BARDEY		AB
TOM DOHERTY	bs, gtr	ABCD
SIMON KING	drms	ABC
ALLAN LOVE	vcls	A
ROBBIE MILNE		AB
RAY OWEN	vcls, gtr	B
RAY MAJOR (SMITH)	gtr, vcls	CD
DAVID O'LIST	gtr	C
IAN WILLIS	gtr, vcls	D

45s:
Beautiful Biege/Speak Up	(CBS 3576)	1968 R1
Mary Anne With The Shakey Hand/ My Gration Or?	(CBS 3921)	1969 R2
You're A Groupie Girl/Gigging Song	(Polydor 2058 041)	1970 R2

Opal Butterfly's debut 45 was a pleasant psych-pop cover of a Cowsills' song, but sales were disappointing. It has been alleged that Lemmy was in this band, but he was still with **Sam Gopal** from mid-1968 to mid-1969 and then joined **Hawkwind** so I have been unable to verify this. However, the rumour has made their singles collectable and sought-after (particularly the second one). The 'A' side of this was a **Who** cover, which had been penned by **Pete Townsend**. The flip is an extremely ambitious song with different segments and an unconventional structure.

Love left the band in 1969 joining, first **Referendum** and then **Madrigal/Merlin**. Owen joined but departed later to **The Misunderstood**. Former **Nice** and **Jethro Tull** member David O'List joined briefly in March 1969, but soon departed to Cody's Glider. The **Sam Gopal's Dream** connection seems to have been provided when former member Ian Willis joined in 1970. This later line-up was responsible for the *Groupie Girl* 45, which became the title track for a 1970 'B' movie of the same name.

After the band split later that year, both Willis and King went on to join **Hawkwind** in August 1971 and January 1972 respectively. For the record Major was later with **Hackensack** and **Mott The Hoople**.

Compilation appearances have included: *Beautiful Biege*, *Gigging Song*, *Speak Up* and *Mary Anne With The Shakey Hands* on *Magic Spectacles* (CD); and *My Gration Or?* on *Electric Sugar Cube Flashbacks* (CD). (VJ/JM)

The Open Mind

Personnel:
TERRY MARTIN	gtr, vcls	A
MIKE 'BRAN' BRANCACCIO	gtr, vcls	A
TIMOTHY DU FEU	bs	A
PHILIP FOX	drms	A

ALBUM: 1(A) THE OPEN MIND (Philips SBL 7893) 1969 R4

THE OPEN MIND - The Open Mind (Bam-Caruso) (LP).

NB: (1) reissued on vinyl (Antar ANTAR 2) 1986 (SC) and again on vinyl with both sides of the *Magic Potion* 45 (Acme Deluxe ADLP 1038). Also reissued on CD in its original sleeve, with the 45 cuts *Magic Potion* and *Cast A Spell* as bonus tracks (Second Battle SB 024) 199?.

45s: Horses And Chariots/Before My Time (Philips BF 1790) 1969 R2
         Magic Potion/Cast A Spell   (Philips BF 1805) 1969 R3

The Open Mind's slender body of work is essential listening for anyone interested in the heavier end of psychedelia. The band, from London, started life as **The Drag Set**, under which name they released an extremely rare 45 on CBS subsidiary Go in early 1967. Having considered adding **Jon Anderson** from **the Syn** (and later **Yes**) to their line-up, they decided to continue as a quartet and renamed themselves **The Open Mind**. As 1967 progressed they undertook many club gigs around London, playing a heavier brand of psychedelic rock than was the norm and supporting acts such as **Pink Floyd**, **the Crazy World of Arthur Brown**, **Joe Cocker** and even the Electric Prunes. Their image was unusual too, in that they wore leather suits, anticipating the outfits of heavy metal bands by some years.

Veteran producer Johnny Franz signed them to Philips in 1968, but he was more used to acts such as the Walker Brothers and **Dusty Springfield** and perhaps mishandled them. Nonetheless, their album (recorded in the label's Stanhope Place studio in mid-1968) is excellent, and has gone on to become one of the most cherished artefacts of British psychedelia. It has a snappy, live feel to it and is characterised by particularly strong vocals and impressive psychedelic guitar work. Originally due to be called *Gestation*, the album crept out the following Spring, too late to capitalise on the psychedelic boom, and sank without trace, as did the extracted single, *Horses and Chariots/Before My Time*. They appeared in Philips's 'New Faces of 1969' promo film, miming to the former, but to no avail.

Managerial difficulties contributed to their gradual decline, though in the Summer of 1969 they returned to the studio to record what many regard as the finest heavy psychedelic single ever to emerge from the UK, the stunning *Magic Potion*. Produced by ex-**Four Pennies** man Fritz Fryer, it's a frantic fuzz guitar assault delivered at a breathtaking pace with twin lead guitars and thunderous drums. Before it had a chance to take off, however, radio stations picked up on its lyrics and banned it, making it one of the hardest 45s of the period to find today.

Early in 1970 Brancaccio left the band to concentrate more on classical guitar, and Fox soon followed suit. Martin and du Feu then formed Armada, who had an excellent reputation and supported the likes of **the Nice** and **Jethro Tull**, but made no recordings and split in 1973, after which they both left the music business.

Magic Potion has resurfaced on *Perfumed Garden, Vol. 1* (CD), *Psychedalia - Rare Blooms From The English Summer Of Love* (CD) and on the *Nuggets II* 4-CD box set. (VJ/RMJ)

Open Road

Personnel:	JOHN CARR	drms	A
	BARRY HUSBAND	gtr, vcls	A
	SIMON LANZON	keyb'ds	A
	MIKE THOMSON	bs	A

ALBUM: 1(A) WINDY DAZE   (Greenwich GSLP 1001) 1971 R1

45:     Swamp Fever/Lost And Found   (Greenwich GSS 102) 1972

Barry Husband had previously been with **The Warm Sounds**. **Open Road** were **Donovan**'s backing band for a short time. Their album is a melodic progressive effort.

After the demise of **Open Road**, Simon Lanzon and Barry Husband made a further album together as Lanzon and Husband entitled *Nostalgia* (Bradleys 1007) 1974. (VJ)

Opus

Personnel incl:	TOM WINTER junior	vcls, gtr	A

45:     Baby, Come On/Angela Grey   (Columbia DB 8675) 1969

ORA - Ora (CD).

Led by Tom Winter junior, this band's *Baby Come On* is not dissimilar to **Blind Faith** or **Led Zeppelin**'s *Whole Lotta Love*. Their finest moment may well have been an appearance on 'Top Of The Pops'.

Winter was the only British member of the band, the remainder being Dutch. In 1972 Tom returned to the UK to record two 45s and an album with Abi Ofarim.

Baby, Come On subsequently resurfaced on *Circus Days, Vol. 4* (LP) and *Circus Days, Vol's 4 & 5* (CD), although this is a slightly later take from 1970. *Angela Grey* can also be found on *Incredible Sound Show Stories, Vol. 11* (LP). (VJ/MWh)

Ora

Personnel:	MARK BARAKAN	gtr	A
	JULIAN DIGGLE	drms	A
	JAMIE RUBENSTEIN	vcls, acoustic gtr	A
	ROBIN SYLVESTER	bs, keyb's, gtr	A
	CHLOE WALTERS	gtr	A
	JON WEISS	ld gtr	A

ALBUM: 1(A) ORA   (Tangerine OPLOP 0025) 1969 R4

NB: (1) also issued in Germany under the name *Knick Knacks* (Metronome SMLR 332) 1971. Reissued on Background (HBG 122/14) 1993 with seven bonus tracks.

The key figure in this band seems to have been songwriter Jamie Rubenstein. Their album, effectively a collection of demos, was a mixture of pleasant, whimsical and haunting songs plus a frenzied piece of psychedelia, *Witch*. Though untypical of their sound, 25 years on it's the main reason for the album's collectability. All the other cuts have female vocals, with the best being *Fly*. This is based on a fast *Take Five* rhythm and has good electric guitar leads. *Are You Seeing* also has electric guitar leads but the other tracks are acoustic-based, with gentle melodies. *The Seagull and The Sailor*, *The Morning After The Night Before* and *Emma's Saga* have a samba feel, with sparse guitar accompaniment and discreet percussion only. Overall this was a good album of beautiful songs. Not many copies were pressed, ensuring its status as an ultra-rarity. The band later evolved into **Byzantium**, and Mark Barakan is part of Bruce Springsteen's backing band (under the name Shane Fontayne).

The recent CD reissue includes seven bonus cuts, mostly alternate versions of songs on the album. The accompanying booklet includes a band history which Jamie Rubenstein has contributed to. (VJ/CA/RMJ)

Orange Bicycle

Personnel:	JOHN BACHINI	bs	A
	KEVIN CURRY	drms	A
	BERNIE LEE	gtr	A

WILSON MALONE	keyb'ds, vcls	A
R.J. SCALES	vcls	A

ALBUM: 1(A) THE ORANGE BICYCLE (Parlophone PCS 7108) 1970 R2

NB: There's also a compilation, *Let's Take A Trip On...* (Morgan Bluetown MBT 5003) 1988 (SC) and a 2-CD set, *Hyacinth Threads: The Morgan Blue Town Recordings* (Edsel MEDCD 688) 2001.

45s:		
Hyacinth Threads/Amy Peate	(Columbia DB 8259) 1967 SC
Laura's Garden/Lavender Girl	(Columbia DB 8311) 1967 SC
Early Pearly Morning/	
Go With Goldie	(Columbia DB 8352) 1968 SC
Jenskadajka/Nicely	(Columbia DB 8413) 1968 SC
Sing This All Together/	
Trip On An Orange Bicycle	(Columbia DB 8483) 1968 SC
Last Cloud Home/	
Tonight I'll Be Staying Here	(Parlophone R 5789) 1969
Carry That Weight/	
You Never Give Me Your Money	(Parlophone R 5811) 1970
Take Me To The Pilot/	
It's Not My World	(Parlophone R 5829) 1970
Jelly On The Bread/Make It Rain	(Parlophone R 5854) 1970
Goodbye Stranger/	
Country Comforts	(Regal Zonophone RZ 3029) 1971

This rather lightweight vocal harmony outfit evolved out of **Robb Storme and The Whispers** and started playing quasi-psychedelic pop music in 1967. They had a No 1 in France with their debut single *Hyacinth Threads*, a fast-paced harmony-pop song with harpsichord, though this and their future singles (including a cover of **The Rolling Stones**' *Sing This All Together*) did not happen at home. *Laura's Garden* and its flip *Lavender Girl* represented the more benign end of psych-tainted pop, and *Jenskadajka* is simply dreadful. Their album was produced by John Peel and was largely comprised of cover versions, including **Elton John** material such as *Take Me To The Pilot*, which was also released as a single. It also included Dylan's *Tonight I'll Be Staying Here With You* and **Denny Laine**'s *Say You Don't Mind*.

In 1988 the revitalised Morgan Bluetown label produced the *Let's Take A Trip On...* album. Containing 16 tracks in all, it includes all the Columbia 'A' and 'B' sides (except the third), but none of the later Parlophone ones. Sadly there are no sleevenotes to clarify where the other tracks originated from. The 2-CD set *Hyacinth Threads* is a 33-track collection of their European hits, misses and outtakes. It's erratic, but tucked away within it are some gorgeous harmony-pop tracks like *LA*, *Amy Peate*, *Trip On An Orange Bicycle* and *Message For Mary*.

Wilson Malone was also in **Motherlight** and recorded a self-titled solo album as **Wil Malone** in 1970 for Fontana.

Laura's Garden can also be heard on *Morgan Blue Town* (LP), *Best And The Rest Of British Psychedelia* (CD) and on the 4-CD set *Acid Drops, Spacedust & Flying Saucers*. *Last Cloud Home* has been compiled on *Jagged Time Lapse, Vol 2* (CD) and *Competition* can also be found on *Fading Yellow, Vol 1* (CD). (VJ/RMJ)

Orange Blossom

ALBUM: 1 KEEP ON PUSHING (Westwood WRS 038) 1974 R3

This is a very rare album about which I have no further information. (VJ)

Orange Machine

Personnel:	ROBIN CROWLEY	ld gtr	A
	ERNIE DURKIN	ld vcls, gtr	A
	JIMMY GREELEY	drms	A
	TOMMY KINSELLA	bs	A

45s:		
Three Little Jolly Dwarfs/	
Real Life Permanent Dream	(Pye 7N 17559) 1968 R3
You Can All Join In/	
Dr. Crippen's Waiting Room	(Pye 7N 17680) 1969 R2

An Irish band who covered two **Tomorrow** songs on their first rare and collectable 45. The 'A' side was a little restrained compared to the original version, but *Real Life Permanent Dream* featured some good psychedelic guitar work, though its vocals lacked a cutting edge. *You Can All Join In* is a psyched-up version of the song **Dave Mason** wrote for **Traffic**. *Dr. Crippen's Waiting Room* is their finest moment, with superb fuzz guitar and vocals. They disbanded in mid-1969 when Kinsella and Durkin departed to join Blue (not the Scottish band of this name).

Compilation appearances have included: *Dr. Crippen's Waiting Room* on *Magic Spectacles* (CD), *Psychedelia, Vol. 3* (LP), *Hen's Teeth, Vol. 3* (CD), *Hot Smoke & Sassafras - Psychedelic Pstones, Vol 1* (CD) and on the 4-CD set *Acid Drops, Spacedust & Flying Saucers*; *Real Life Permanent Dream* on *Rubble, Vol. 7 - Pictures In The Sky* (LP), *Haunted - Psychedelic Pstones, Vol 2* (CD) and *We Can Fly, Vol 1* (CD); *You Can All Join In* on *Rubble, Vol. 10 - Professor Jordan's Magic Sound Show* (LP); *Three Jolly Little Dwarfs* on *Haunted - Psychedelic Pstones, Vol 2* (CD); whilst *Three Jolly Little Dwarfs*, *Real Life Permanent Dream* and *Dr. Crippen's Waiting Room* all feature on *Irish Rock - Ireland's Beat Groups 1964-1969* (CD). (VJ)

Orange Peel

45:	I Got No Time/	
	Searching For A Place To Hide	(Reflection HRS 5) 1971 SC

This seems to have been a one-off venture. *Searching For A Place To Hide* has also been compiled on *Talking About The Good Times, Vol 1* (CD). (VJ)

Orange Seaweed

Personnel:	RAY NEALE	gtr	AB
	KEITH NEALE	bs	AB
	LES WARREN	drms	A
	ANDY ROSNER	drms	B

45:	Stay Awhile/Pictures In The Sky	(Pye 7N 17515) 1968 R1

Some members had earlier been involved in **The Kingpins** (who recorded for Oak) and **Those Fadin' Colours**. This is an interesting, but not exceptional pop 45, which has become quite collectable in recent years. The recent **Kingpins** compilation *Kingpins For Sale* features both sides of this 45 plus their version of *Skinny Minnie*, which originally appeared on an acetate backed by *Sunshine In The Morning*.

Stay Awhile features a lavish orchestrated production and the flip *Pictures In The Sky* features superb guitar, although the arrangement could have been better. The band later evolved into The Ray Neale Band at the end of the psychedelic era. Neale later became lead guitarist with **Screaming Lord Sutch and The Savages**.

ORANGE BICYCLE - Let's Take A Trip On (LP).

Compilation appearances include: *Pictures In the Sky* on *Rubble, Vol. 7 - Pictures In The Sky* (LP), *It's Only A Passing Phase* (LP) and *Hot Smoke & Sassafras - Psychedelic Pstones, Vol 1* (CD); and *Stay A While* on *Rubble, Vol. 10 - Professor Jordan's Magic Sound Show* (LP) and on *Haunted - Psychedelic Pstones, Vol 1* (CD). (VJ)

Orang-Utan

NB: This album, originally only issued in the US in the early seventies has now been released in the UK on vinyl *Orang-Utan* (Dr Prog LP 7104DRPR) and on CD *Orang-Utan* (Lizard LR 0703-2).

This was the work of an obscure British act, although the album was only released in the US and it has that late sixties US feel to it. There's some good twin lead guitar work on the album and some compare it to **Leaf Hound** and early **Led Zeppelin**. (VJ)

Orbit Five

Personnel incl: KEIRAN FLOWERDEW   ld gtr   A

45:      I Wanna Go To Heaven/
         Walking (Some PS)   (Decca F 12799) 1968 R1/SC

Hailing from Hertfordshire came **The Orbit Five** and demo copies of their pop 45 *I Wanna Go To Heaven* were issued in a picture sleeve. (VJ)

The Orchids

45s: Gonna Make Him Mine/Stay At Home (Decca F 11743) 1963 SC
         Love Hit Me/Don't Make Me Mad   (Decca F 11785) 1963 SC
         I've Got That Feeling/Larry   (Decca F 11861) 1964 SC

The Orchids were three schoolgirls from Liverpool who Decca tried to turn (unsuccessfully) into a British version of The Crystals. Their third 45, *I've Got That Feeling*, was written by Ray Davies and produced by American Shel Talmy.

Compilation appearances have included: *I've Got That Feeling* on *Liverpool 1963-1964, Vol. 2* (LP); and *Love Hit Me* and *Don't Make Me Mad* on *Pop Inside The 60s Vol. 1* (CD). (VJ)

The Organisers

Personnel incl: HAROLD SMART

45:      Lonesome Road/The Organiser   (Pye 7N 17022) 1966 R3

A very rare and collectable instrumental 45, which was the work of sessionmen.

The Organiser resurfaced on *Doin' The Mod, Vol. 1* (CD). (VJ)

The Original Dyaks

45:      Got To Get A Good Thing Going/
         Would You Love Me Too   (Columbia DB 8184) 1967

The band hailed from Letchworth.

Gotta Get A Good Thing Going has been compiled on *60's Back Beat* (LP). (VJ)

The Originells (4)

Personnel incl: DAVE ALLAN
                 LES COATES

45s: My Girl/Kathy   (Columbia DB 7259) 1964 SC
       α Nights/I Can Make You Mine   (Columbia DB 7388) 1964 SC

NB: α as **Originells 4**.

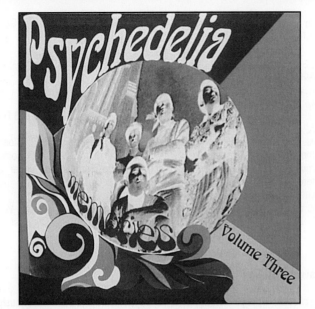

PSYCHEDELIA VOL. 3 (Comp LP) including Orange Seaweed.

A beat group. Dave Allen and Les Coates penned both sides of the first 45. (VJ)

Oscar (1)

45s: Club Of Lights/Waking Up   (Reaction 591 003) 1966 SC
         Join My Gang/Days Gone By   (Reaction 591 006) 1966 SC
         Over The Wall We Go/
         Every Day Of My Life   (Reaction 591 012) 1967 SC
         Holiday/Give Her All She Wants (Reaction 591 016) 1967 SC
         Open Up The Skies/Wild Ones   (Polydor 56267) 1968 SC

This mid-sixties singer (real name Oscar Beuselinck, better known as **Paul Nicholas**) attracted some publicity through the lyrics of his *Over The Wall We Go* 45. It had been written and produced by **David Bowie** who sang on one line of it. The chorus was 'Over the wall we go, all coppers are 'nanas'. To promote it, **Oscar** appeared on TV in a prisoner's uniform. His previous disc *Join My Gang* was a good version of a **Pete Townshend** composition (which wasn't recorded by **The Who** but was covered by **Creation**). Despite some strong material **Oscar** failed to achieve a breakthrough.

He also recorded as **Paul Dean** and played Claude in the British version of 'Hair' in 1969.

You can also hear *Club Of Lights* on *14 Groovy Sounds From The Blow Up* (LP). (VJ)

Oscar (2)

Personnel: TONY BAMFORTH   keyb'ds   A
              GARY McDOUGAL   bs   A
              BRIAN McGLADDERY   gtr, vcls   A
              KEVIN PARROT   gtr   A
              ROGER TWEEDALE   perc   A

ALBUMS: 1(A) OSCAR   (Buk BULP 2001) 1975
(up to   2(A) TWIGHLIGHT ASYLUM (DJM DJF 20494) 1976
1976)

45s: Well Known Lady/Feel Alright   (Buk BU 3001) 1974
(up to   Mad About The Boy/
1976)   Don't Care What Happens Tomorrow (Buk BU 3006) 1975
           Take Me Back To Them Good Old Days/
           Remember The Star   (DJM DJS 10724) 1976

A different **Oscar**. Their second album is a mixture of progressive / folk rock and is pleasant enough without ever hitting the heights. All songs were written by Brian McGladdery with assistance on one from Geoff Gill (ex-**Smoke**) who also produced the album.

They recorded a third album *Cobblestone Heroes* (DJM DJF 20516) 1977, which was poppier than previous efforts. (VJ)

Oscar Bicycle

45:	On A Quiet Night/		
	The Room Revolves Around Me	(CBS 3237) 1968 R1	

This 45 is now a minor collectable. The 'A' side is a P.F. Sloan composition. The flip is more interesting, a slice of freakbeat with some pumping guitar. The group would appear to be **Force West** under a different name.

You can also check out *The Room Revolves Around Me* on *Rubble, Vol. 17 - A Trip In A Painted World* (LP), *Rubble, Vol. 10* (CD) and *The Best Of Rubble Collection, Vol. 4* (CD). (VJ/MWh)

Oswald Slagge

Psychedelic Salvage Co. Vol. 2 (LP & CD) features this band's previously unissued **Hendrix**-inspired guitar freak-out, *Toke Joke*. From this description you should know whether you need to get to hear it or not. (VJ)

The Others

Personnel:	NIGEL BALDWIN	drms	A
	BOB FREEMAN	gtr	A
	IAN McLINTOCK	bs	A
	JOHN STANLEY	ld gtr	A
	PAUL STEWART	vcls	A

45:	Oh Yeah/I'm Taking Her Home	(Fontana TF 501) 1964 R2

Formed at Hampton Grammar School in Middlesex in the mid-sixties. Their *Oh Yeah*, written by Bo Diddley but a US hit for The Shadows Of Knight, became a minor R&B classic over here, although it made little commercial impact and is now rare and sought-after. They also recorded an acetate version of *Little Deuce Coupe* in 1966 and later became **Sands**. Brian May (of **Queen**) was also in the band but not on the 45.

Compilation appearances include: *Oh Yeah* on *Maximum R'n'B* (CD), *Twisted Teenage Screaming Fuzzbusters* (LP), *Beat It* (3-CD), *Beat Merchants* (2-LP) and *English Freakbeat, Vol. 4* (LP & CD); and *Oh Yeah* and *I'm Takin' Her Home* on *Made In England, Vol. 1* (CD). (VJ)

The Other Two

Personnel:	CAROLINE ATTARD	A
	JEMINA SMITH	A

45s:	I Wanna Be With You/Grumbling Guitar	(Decca F 11911) 1964
	Don't You Wanna Love Me/	
	Hold Back The Light Of Dawn	(RCA RCA 1465) 1965
	I'll Never Let You Go/Hot At Night	(RCA RCA 1531) 1966

A London-based band discovered by musical director Charles Blackwell. They once played at the Star Club in Hamburg, Germany and were also involved in **Moon's Train**. *Grumbling Guitar*, the flip of their first 45, was an instrumental. The 'A' side of the second was a Goffin-King composition.

Caroline Attard was later in **Storyteller**. (VJ)

Our Plastic Dream

Personnel:	PAUL BEDWELL	bs, vcls	A
	JULIAN FERRARI	drms, vcls	A
	BOB MOORE	perc, vcls	A
	PIERRE TUBBS	ld vcls, ld gtr	A

45:	A Little Bit Of Shangrila/	
	Encapsulated Marigold	(Go AJ 11411) 1967 R2

PIERRE'S PLASTIC DREAM (Comp CD) including Our Plastic Dream.

Originally known as **The Peeps**, this band came from Leatherhead in Surrey. Their leader Pierre Tubbs had also recorded demos for **The Silence** (not the early incarnation of **John's Children**). Their very rare and sought-after 45 was often played by John Peel on his 'Perfumed Garden' radio show. The 'A' side is quite mainstream vocally but very 1967 instrumentally. The flip side, a dreamy slice of psychedelia, is the real gem on the disc. They also recorded some other material, including *Someone Turned The Light Out*, *A Little Bit Of Shangri-La*, *Encapsulated Marigold*, *Paint Yourself* and *Rubber Gun*. *Someone Turned The Light Out* is a stomping slice of distorted pop which recalls **The Electric Prunes**, *Paint Yourself* is a beaty pop offering ladened with psychedelic effects and *Rubber Gun* was a slice of surf-psyche. All are included on the *Pierre's Plastic Dream* compilation CD. Tubbs was later in **The Owl** and produced **The Famous Jug Band** before becoming Creative Manager for United Artists records. (VJ/RMJ)

The Outer Limits

Personnel:	JEFF CHRISTIE	A
	STAN DROGIE	A
	GERRY LAYTON	A
	GERRY SMITH	A

45s:	α	When The Work Is Thru'/	
		(flip by different artist)	(Elephant CUR 100) 1967 R2
		Just One More Chance/	
		Help Me Please	(Deram DM 125) 1967 SC
		Great Train Robbery/	
		Sweet Freedom (demo only)	(Immediate IM 067) 1968 R2
		Great Train Robbery/Sweet Freedom	(Instant IN 001) 1968 SC
		The Dark Side Of The Moon/Black Boots	(Decca F 13176) 1971

NB: α Leeds Student Charity Rag disc.

A Leeds-based group who'd evolved out of a skiffle outfit, Three G's Plus One. After contributing one side to a Leeds Student Charity Rag disc, they signed to Deram, to record a mid-paced soul ballad *Just One More Chance*, which was written by Jeff Christie. The flip side had a US garage punk feel.

In 1968 they switched to Immediate to record *Great Train Robbery*. Although originally scheduled for release in May 1968 as IM 067 advance copies were rapidly withdrawn and the number was reallocated to P.P Arnold's *Angel Of The Morning*. The 45 eventually appeared on Immediate's Instant subsidiary label some five months later. It's much poppier than their earlier effort but had quite a grandiose production and good harmonies.

Jeff Christie was later in **The Epics** and **Acid Gallery**, but found some fame when he led **Christie** who enjoyed hits with *Yellow River* and *San Bernadino*.

Compilation appearances have included: *Just One More Chance* on *The Mod Scene* (CD), *Pop Inside The '60s, Vol. 2* (CD), *Sixties Lost And Found, Vol. 2* (LP), *Sixties Explosion, Vol. 1* (CD), *Great British Psychedelic Trip, Vol. 1* (CD) and *British Psychedelic Trip, Vol. 3* (LP); *Help Me Please* on *Rubble, Vol. 12 - Staircase To Nowhere* (LP), *Rubble, Vol. 7* (CD) and *The Freakbeat Scene* (CD); and *Great Train Robbery* on *Immediate Alternative* (LP & CD). (VJ)

Out of Darkness

Personnel incl: WRAY POWELL   gtr, vcls

ALBUM: 1   OUT OF DARKNESS   (Key KL 006) 1970 R3

NB: (1) reissued on *Little Wing* (LW 2008) 1990, also on CD. (1) also reissued on CD (Key Records KL006) with one live bonus track. *The Celebrated Club Session* (Plankton OCDN 138) 1994 was taken from a recording at the Celebration Club, Gillingham in 1972.

This Christian-influenced London-based outfit were good musicians, and the material on their rare album ranges from beat-psych to jazz-blues. Highlights include *Wings Of The Morning* and the **Hendrix**-influenced *Closing In On Me*, which resurfaced on *Psychedelic Salvage Co. Vol. 1* (LP & CD). Apparently it comes from a tape of the band when they appeared on a TV show. (VJ/RMJ)

The Outsiders

Personnel incl: MICK WAYNE

45:        Keep On Doing It/
           Songs We Sang Last Summer   (Decca F 12213) 1965 SC

This was a different UK band from the US outfit which recorded on Capitol and not the Dutch outfit either. Both of these songs were written and produced by **Jimmy Page**, but they are unexceptional beat efforts. More significantly the group included Mick Wayne, formerly of **The Hullabaloos**. He was later in **The Bunch Of Fives**, **The Tickle** and **Junior's Eyes**. (VJ)

Ovary Lodge

Personnel:			
ROY BABBINGTON	bs		A
FRANK PERRY	vcls, perc		AB
KEITH TIPPETT	keyb'ds		AB
HARRY MILLER	bs		B
JULIE TIPPETT	vcls		B

ALBUMS:	1(A)	OVARY LODGE	(RCA SF 8372) 1973 R2
	2(B)	OVARY LODGE	(Ogun OG 600) 1976 R1

Jazz musician **Keith Tippett** had played piano for **King Crimson** for a few months during 1970 and recorded several solo albums too. He was also a member of **Centipede**. **Ovary Lodge** were an early jazz-rock experiment in the grand British tradition. Julie Tippett, his wife, was **Julie Driscoll** before she married him. (VJ)

The Overlanders

Personnel:	PAUL ARNOLD (FRISWELL)	piano, gtr	AB
	PETER BARTHOLOMEW	gtr	ABC
	LAURIE MASON	vcls, piano, hrmnca	ABC
	DAVID WALSH	drms	BC
	TERRY WIDLAKE	bs	BC
	IAN GRIFFITHS	gtr	C

ALBUM: 1(B)   MICHELLE   (Pye NPL 18138) 1966 R1

NB: (1) reissued on Repertoire (RR 4095-WZ) in 1991 with extra tracks. *Michelle (The Pye Anthology)* (Sanctuary CMRCD 269) 2001 is a compilation.

EP: 1(B)   MICHELLE   (Pye NEP 24245) 1966 R1

OUT OF DARKNESS - Out Of Darkness (LP).

HCP

45s:	Summer Skies And Golden Sands/	
	Call Of The Wild	(Pye 7N 15544) 1963 -
	Movin'/Rainbow	(Pye 7N 15568) 1963 -
	Yesterday's Gone/Gone In The Rainbow	(Pye 7N 15619) 1964 -
	Sing A Song Of Sadness/	
	Don't It Make You Feel Good	(Pye 7N 15678) 1964 -
	If I Gave You/I Wonder Why	(Pye 7N 15712) 1964 -
	The Leaves Are Falling/Delia's Gone	(Pye 7N 15719) 1964 -
	Along Came Jones/	
	Walking The Soles Off My Shoes	(Pye 7N 15804) 1965 -
	Freight Train/	
	Take The Bucket To The Well	(Pye 7N 15883) 1965 -
	Room Enough For You And Me/January	(Pye 7N 15967) 1965 -
	Michelle/Cradle Of Love	(Pye 7N 17034) 1966 1
	My Life/The Girl From Indiana	(Pye 7N 17068) 1966 -
	Go Where You Wanna Go/	
	Don't Let It Happen Again	(Pye 7N 17159) 1966 -
Reissue:	Michelle/(Flip by different artist)	(Old Gold OG 9138) 1982 -

The Overlanders formed in 1963 as a folky trio recording several singles for Pye which made little impact except that *Yesterday's Gone* (an old Chad and Jeremy number) was a minor US hit (No 75) in 1964. In 1965 they were expanded to a quintet with the addition of Walsh and Widlake. *Along Came Jones* was a Coasters' oldie, but it didn't chart for them. Their big break came in December 1965, when under guidance from Tony Hatch (their producer), they cut an unsolicited cover version of **Lennon/McCartney**'s *Michelle*, which promptly shot to No. 1 here. This led to the release of their album but *Michelle* proved to be their only success and they've become a classic case of 'one hit wonders'. By the end of the year they'd split with Ian Griffiths replacing **Arnold**, who went solo, in their final weeks. Of their later singles *My Life* was worthy of some success.

Ex-Sherwoods member Terry Widlake was later in **Cuppa T** along with Vic Lythgoe, who was also in **The Overlanders** at some point. David Walsh went on to play for **Second City Sound**.

The CD reissue of their debut album on Repertoire also includes non-album tracks from the post *Michelle* 45s. The 'A' side of their first 45, *Summer Skies And Golden Sands*, can also be heard on the *1964 Package Tour* (LP) compilation.

Sanctuary's 2001 compilation includes all 12 of their 45s plus a few tracks from a joint album with The Settlers.

More recently, compilation appearances have included:- *Along Came Jones* on *The Songs Of Leiber and Stoller* (CD); *Michelle* on *Pop Inside The Sixties, Vol. 3* (CD), *No 1s & Million Sellers Vol 4* (CD), *Hippy Hippy Shake* (CD) and on the 2-CD set *60 Number Ones Of The Sixties*; *Go Where You Wanna Go* on *Ripples, Vol. 6* (CD); *The Leaves Are Falling* and *Don't Let That Happen* on *Ripples, Vol. 7* (CD); and *Call Of The Wild* on *Beat Merchants* (CD). (VJ)

Ray Owen('s Moon)

ALBUM: 1 RAY OWEN'S MOON   (Polydor 2325 061) 1971 R2

45s: α Tonight I'll Be Staying Here With You/
         Down, Don't Bother Me   (Fontana TF 1045) 1969
         Hey Sweety/Free Man   (Polydor 2058 095) 1971

NB: α as **Ray Owen**.

Prior to forming this outfit, vocalist **Owen** had recorded a solo 45 (whose 'A' side was a Dylan song) and been vocalist with **Juicy Lucy**. The album is an enjoyable hard-rock effort, featuring some wild guitar from Les Nicol (ex-**Methuselah**). Highlights include the driving *Talk To Me*, macho-posturing *Try My Love* and hard-riffing *Mississippi Woman* (whose riff is 'shared with' Creedence Clearwater Revival's *Pagan Baby*). Less impressive is their cover of **Jimi Hendrix**'s *Voodoo Chile*, which comes complete with badly-mistaken lyrics! The album is now hard to pin down. (VJ/RMJ)

Owl

Personnel: PAUL BEDWELL   bs   A
            VINCE EDWARDS   vcls   A
            ROB TAIT   drms   A
            PIERRE TUBBS   keyb'ds   A

45:   Run To The Sun/Shadows Of Blue And
      Green Water Flies   (United Artists UP 2240) 1968 SC

This band emerged out of the earlier **Our Plastic Dream** combo. Collectors now show some interest in this 45. The 'A' side is heavily orchestrated but none too special. An advert showed them dressed as owls to help promote it!

Rob Tait became a member of **Pete Brown's Battered Ornaments** and Vince Edwards recorded a number of solo singles throughout the sixties and seventies as J. Vincent Edwards. Pierre Tubbs was earlier in **The Peeps**, **The Silence** and **Our Plastic Dream**. After his time with **The Owl** he became Creative Manager for United Artists records.

Compilation appearances include: *Shades Of Blue And Greenwater Flies* and *Run To The Sun* on *Pierre's Plastic Dream* (CD). *Shades Of Blue And Greenwater Flies* is a powerful orchestrated ballad that recalls *The Worst That Happen* by The Brooklyn Bridge. The flip was equally as strong and similar in style. (VJ/MWh)

THE BEST OF RUBBLE COLLECTION VOL. 4 (Comp CD) including Oscar Bicycle.

WE CAN FLY VOL. 1 (Comp CD) including Orange Machine.

ENGLISH FREAKBEAT VOL. 4 (Comp CD) including The Others.

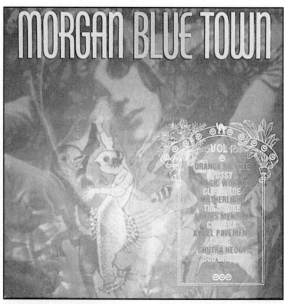

MORGAN BLUE TOWN (Comp LP) including Orange Bicycle.

Pacific Drift

Personnel:	LAWRENCE ARENDES	drms, perc, vcls	AB
	LARRY HARROP	bs	A
	GRAHAM HARROP	gtr, bs	AB
	BARRY REYNOLDS	violin, gtr, vcls	AB
	BRIAN SHAPMAN	keyb'ds, vcls	AB
	DAVE DAVANI	horns	B

ALBUM:	1(A)	FEELIN' FREE	(Deram Nova (S)ND 13) 1970 R1

45:	Water Woman/Yes You Do	(Deram DM 304) 1970 SC

A progressive blues-rock band. Lawrence Arendes (also known as Larry King) had earlier been with **Wimple Winch** and prior to them with **The Four Just Men**. Barry Reynolds had played with **Dave Berry** and The Cruisers. Though their album contains some clumsy blues-derived tracks, others are better and it's now a minor collectable. Highlights include the gentle *Tomorrow Morning Brings*, which is underscored with harpsichord, and the beautiful *Garden Of Love*, reminiscent of labelmates **Galliard**. William Blake poems form the lyrics for both that and the melodic *Grains Of Sand*, though he receives no credit for either. Their single was non-album and the rare US version of the album contains a different track listing.

When Larry Harrop left, Graham switched to bass and ex-**Dave Davani Four** leader Dave Davani joined on horns. After the band split Reynolds was in Blodwyn and Shapman joined **Chicken Shack.**

The Nova Sampler (1970) included one of the album's other cuts, *Just Another Girl*, whilst *Grains Of Sand* can also be heard on *Broken Dreams, Vol. 3* (LP). Lawrence Arendes (also known as Larry King), incidentally, had earlier been with **Wimple Winch** and prior to them with **The Four Just Men**. Barry Reynolds had played with **Dave Berry** and The Cruisers. After the band split Reynolds was in Blodwyn and Shapman joined **Chicken Shack.**

Water Woman (the Spirit song written by Jay Ferguson) also appears on the *Great British Psychedelic Trip, Vol. 2* (CD) and *British Psychedelic Trip, Vol. 4* (LP), whilst the 'B' side *Yes You Do* has resurfaced on *Progressive Pop Inside The Seventies* (CD). (MK/JM/VJ/RMJ)

The Pack

Personnel:	BOB DUCK	drms	A
	BOB GROADWAY	gtr, vcls	A
	BRIAN GREGG	bs	A
	ROGER HARTLEY	gtr	A
	ANDY RICKELL	hrmnca, gtr	A

45:	Do You Believe In Magic?/	
	Things Bring Me Down	(Columbia DB 7702) 1965 R1

Came out of Wiltshire in the mid-sixties and enjoyed some success with this cover of The Lovin' Spoonful song. Gregg had earlier played in Johnny Kidd and The Pirates and The Tornados. The 45, which was produced by Mickie Most, is now becoming hard to find and is quite collectable. (VJ)

Paddy, Klaus and Gibson

Personnel:	PADDY CHAMBERS		A
	GIBSON KEMP	drms	A
	KLAUS VOORMANN		A

45s:	I Wanna Know/I Tried	(Pye 7N 15906) 1965 SC
	No Good Without You Baby/Rejected	(Pye 7N 17060) 1966 R1
	Teresa/Quick Before They Catch Us	(Pye 7N 17112) 1966 SC

This outfit started out as **The Eyes** in Germany. Voormann was a German student who'd got to know **The Beatles** during their residency in Hamburg. His girlfriend was later engaged to Stuart Sutcliffe, the **Beatle** who died, and later still to Gibson Kemp. Voormann came to England in 1965. He also designed the cover to *Revolver*. When the trio split he replaced **Jack Bruce** as the bass player in **Manfred Mann**. Gibson had previously been with **Rory Storm and The Hurricanes**. Paddy Chambers had earlier been

in **Faron's Flamingoes** and then **The Big Three** for the last couple of months of 1963 and the first two or three of 1964. He left to join Dominoes, another Liverpudlian band but one which didn't make it onto vinyl. Paddy Chambers died of throat cancer on 28 September 2000.

Compilation appearances have included: *Quick Before They Catch Us* on *Quick Before They Catch Us* (LP & CD); *I Wanna Know* and *Hey Teresa* on *Some Other Guys* (LP); *I Wanna Know* on *The Sixties File* (2-LP); *Rejected* on *Doin' The Mod, Vol. 1* (CD); *No Good Without You Baby* on *Doin' The Mod, Vol. 2* (CD); *I Wanna Know* and *I Tried* on *Footsteps To Fame, Vol. 2* (CD); and *I Tried* on *Hippy Hippy Shake* (CD). (VJ)

Jimmy Page

45:	She Just Satisfies/Keep Moving	(Fontana TF 533) 1965 R5
(up to 1976)		

NB: *Hip Young Guitar Slinger* (Sequel NEECD 486) 2000 is a 2-CD 50-track chronically compilation charting his recordings with Pye and Immediate acts.

Jimmy Page has been one of the most influential, versatile and significant guitarists in the history of rock and he wasn't a bad songwriter either!

Jimmy Page (real name James Patrick Page) was born on 9th January 1944 at Heston, Middlesex. He joined **Neil Christian and The Crusaders** briefly, but did not record with them as a group member, though he later backed **Christian** on sessions. A former art student, he was briefly a member of **The Mickey Finn** and declined an invitation to join **The Yardbirds** in January 1965 because he was suffering from recurrent glandular fever and doing very nicely as a session guitarist.

In fact **Page** was probably the most prolific of all London's session men and it's been said, not entirely in jest, that he played on every 45 recorded in the UK during this period. The above 45 was his only solo release at the time. The 'A' side was similar to *Revenge*, credited to **Page**/Davies on **The Kinks'** first album, and features a rare vocal performance by **Page**. The flip featured **Page** on guitar and harmonica with backing vocals from his girlfriend Jackie De Shannon. It's not especially interesting, but - needless to say - is now an ultra-rare collectors' item, particularly among **Led Zeppelin** fans.

In 1965 he also worked for **Andrew Oldham**'s Immediate label, writing, playing on and producing numerous 45s. Eventually he joined **The Yardbirds** in June 1966, playing with them until they split in July 1968. He then formed The New Yardbirds who became **Led Zeppelin** in October 1968.

During his time with **Led Zeppelin**, **Page** also worked with folky **Roy Harper**, using the alias S. Flavius Mercurius on his *Stormcock* album. In the second half of the seventies **Page** got into heroin and other drugs and

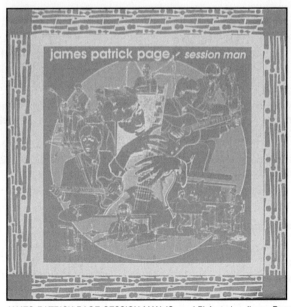

JAMES PATRICK PAGE SESSION MAN (Comp LP) featuring Jimmy Page!

he also developed an interest in the occult that disturbed some of his friends. When **Led Zeppelin** split in late 1980 **Page** opted out of the music scene for a while, returning in 1982 to compose and play on the motion picture soundtracks to *Death Wish* and *Death Wish II*. He also compiled *Coda* (a **Zeppelin** outtakes collection) and in 1983 teamed up with **Jeff Beck** and **Eric Clapton** as part of a tour to raise money for multiple sclerosis research. The following year he formed The Firm who included Paul Rodgers (ex-**Free** and **Bad Company**) on vocals and their debut self-titled album climbed to No 15 in the UK. However, they split when their follow-up *Mean Business* met with a less enthusiastic response. Since then he's been involved in various collaborations with former **Zeppelin** member **Robert Plant** and a separate one with David Coverdale.

Luckily you don't have to take a bank loan to hear his single now because it was reissued as a CD single as part of the 1991 Fontana box set, *Hits And Rarities Vol. 1* and on *Hip Young Guitar Slinger* (2-CD). The latter was compiled from the Pye and Immediate archives, and is a 50-track compilation including recordings made with the likes of **Carter-Lewis and The Southerners**, **The Kinks**, **Primitives**, **First Gear**, **Fleur de Lys** and others

Compilation appearances have included: *She Just Satisfies* and *Keep Movin'* on *Mickey Finn And The Blue Men / Jimmy Page - Keep Moving!* (CD), *James Patrick Page, Session Man* (2-LP) and *James Patrick Page: Session Man, Vol. 1* (LP & CD); *She Just Satisfies* on *Artefacts From The Psychedelic Dungeon* (CD); *When I Was 16* on *The Youngblood Story Vol. 1* (CD); *L.A. Breakdown* and *Down In The Boots* on *Jimmy Page Studio Works 1964-1968* (CD) and *Jimmy Page - Hip Young Guitar Slinger* (2-CD); *Stop The Drums, Coming Home Babe, Drum Stomp, Lord Byron Blues, L.A. Breakdown* and *Down In The Boots* on *Jimmy Page, Session Man* (CD); *Burn Up* and *Dixie Fried* on *Made In England, Vol. 2* (CD); and *Lord Byron Blues* and *Salvation* on *Nowhere Men Vol. 3* (CD). (VJ)

Page Five

45:      Let Sleeping Dogs Lie/
           I Know All About Her   (Parlophone R 5426) 1966 R1

This beat ballad 45 is now a minor collectable. (VJ)

Page Ten

45:      Boutique/Colour Talk   (Decca F 12248) 1965

A ten member band produced by Larry Page. Their 45 was an instrumental. (VJ)

Paintbox

45s: (up to 1976)	Get Ready For Love/ Can I Get To Know You Get Ready For Love/ Can I Get To Know You Come On Round/Take It From Here Let Your Love Go/Just Another Day	(Youngblood YB 1015) 1970 (Youngblood YB 1029) 1970 (President PT 284) 1972 (President PT 395) 1973

Their first single was a **Miki Dallon** production and was a typical British commercial soul number. The 'A' side was written by former **Grapefruit** member George Alexander. As George Alexandra wrote the 'A' side and Vanda and Young the 'B' side, **Paintbox** may have been formed by these three musicians, who also worked together in **The Easybeats**. The 45s on President could be by a different band. (VJ/SR)

Palace Court Brigade

45:      Whistlin' In The Sunshine/Girls Grow Up   (CBS 4643) 1969

An obscure one-off 45. (VJ)

ROBERT PALMER - Some People Can Do What They Like (LP).

Paladin

Personnel: PETE BECKETT   bs, vcls   AB
                 DEREK FOLEY   gtr, vcls   A
                 PETE SOLLEY   keyb'ds, vcls, violin   AB
                 LOU STONEBRIDGE   keyb'ds, vcls   A
                 KEITH WEBB   drms   AB
                 JOE JAMMER   gtr   B

ALBUMS: 1(A)   PALADIN   (Bronze ILPS 9150) 1971 SC
        2(A)   CHARGE   (Bronze ILPS 9190) 1972 R1
NB: (1) and (2) reissued as a 2-CD digi-pak set *Paladin-Charge!* (? RMCCD 0202), with extensive liner notes.

45s: Anyway/Giving All My Love   (Bronze WIP 6108) 1971
            Sweet Sweet Music/Get One Together   (Bronze BRO 3) 1973

A good progressive/hard-rock outfit, their first album was recorded live in the studio and their strength was really as a live act. Lou Stonebridge went on to play for **McGuinness Flint**. **Joe Jammer** also recorded as a solo artist. (VJ)

Clive Palmer

ALBUM: (1)   JUST ME (w/insert)   (Autogram) 1978 R1
NB: (1) German only.

Though he released no solo material within the time frame of this book, **Clive Palmer** was a vital figure in Britain's underground folk scene throughout it.

Born in Enfield, London on May 13th 1943, he suffered from polio as a child and mastered the banjo at an early age. As a teenage beatnik he was a regular performer in Soho's coffee bars, and after attending Hornsey Art College he travelled to Paris, busking with **Wizz Jones**, **Ralph McTell**, **Mick Softley** and others. On his return in 1963 he went to Edinburgh, forming a duo with **Robin Williamson** and playing alongside **Anne Briggs**, **Bert Jansch** and others. Having recruited **Mike Heron**, **Palmer** named the newly-formed trio **The Incredible String Band**, and they opened Glasgow's Incredible Folk Club, a now-legendary focal point for Britain's emerging folk musicians. Eventually Joe Boyd signed them to Elektra, for whom they recorded their debut in May 1966.

Palmer then travelled to India and Afghanistan, deciding on his return not to rejoin his former bandmates, who were going in a more overtly hippie direction. Instead he recorded a still-unreleased 1967 album with **Wizz Jones**, overseen by producer Peter Eden. Having become the first man in Scotland to be prosecuted for possession of LSD, he relocated to Cornwall, joining **The Famous Jug Band** for one album and forming **the Temple Creatures** and **the Stockroom Five**. Eventually these evolved into **COB**

(Clive's Original Band), who recorded two of the period's greatest folk albums. After **COB**'s dissolution early in 1973, **Palmer** became a musical instrument maker and teacher, though he has made sporadic recordings since and toured from time to time with **The Incredible String Band**. Now resident in Brittany, he is a much-revered figure and an important influence on the new generation of alternative folk acts. (RMJ)

Robert Palmer

				HCP
ALBUMS:	1	SNEAKING SALLY THROUGH THE ALLEY		
(up to			(Island ILPS 9294) 1974	-
1976)	2	PRESSURE DROP	(Island ILPS 9372) 1975	-
	3	SOME PEOPLE CAN DO WHAT THEY LIKE		
			(Island ILPS 9420) 1976	46

45s:	Which Of Us Is The Fool/Get Outside	(Island WIP 6250) 1975
(up to	Gimme An Inch Girl/Pressure Drop	(Island WIP 6272) 1976
1976)	Man Smart, Woman Smarter/	
	From A Whisper To A Scream	(Island WIP 6345) 1976

Palmer was born Alan Palmer in Batley, Yorkshire on 19 January 1949. He was just three when his service family moved to Malta and it was there he spent his childhood. When he returned to the UK he was in a semi-professional Scarborough-based band called Mandrake prior to moving down to London in 1969 to replace **Jess Roden** in **The Alan Bown Set**. In 1970 he replaced **Paul Korda** in avant-garde jazz-rock outfit **Dada** and when, in 1971, part of that band splintered to form **Vinegar Joe** he went with them and played with **Vinegar Joe** throughout their shortish career.

When **Vinegar Joe** split **Palmer** moved to Nassau and sought to launch a solo career employing ex-Little Feat member Lowell George to lead his support band. His first album *Sneaking Sally Through The Alley* was recorded in New Orleans and attracted a lot of airplay in the US where it eventually climbed to No 107 in July 1975. It didn't sell too well here. The title track and *From A Whisper To A Scream* were penned by Allen Toussaint (whose Sea Saint studios it had been recorded in). The album also included a version of Little Feat's *Sailing Shoes* with Lowell George on guitar. Musically the recipe was an amalgam of white-eyed soul and R&B - a formula he would develop further on his second album, *Pressure Drop*. Prior to its recording **Palmer** and his wife had moved to New York. **Palmer** had also been on an extensive US tour as support and back up singer with Little Feat. *Pressure Drop* was consequently recorded with assistance from all six Little Feat members and two Motown veterans James Jamerson (bs) and Ed Greene (drms). The album's title track was actually a reggae number previously recorded by Toots and The Maytals. Again the album was more successful in the US, where it climbed to No 136, than in the UK, where it failed to enjoy any Chart showing.

Some People Can Do What They Like, recorded in Los Angeles and released in 1976, included just two of **Palmer**'s own compositions. One

PANAMA LTD. (JUG BAND) - Indian Summer (LP).

track that caught the ear was his cover of Harry Belafonte's calypso-styled *Man Smart, Woman Smarter*. It was later released as a 45 and charted in the US (climbing to No 63) and attracted a fair amount of airplay here in the UK too though it didn't break into the Charts. His album did chart in the UK, though, peaking at No 46, which was better than its highest US placing (No 68).

For the rest of the decade and throughout the eighties, **Palmer** continued to make recordings, often with considerable commercial success. He also collaborated briefly with half of Duran Duran and half of Chic in Power Station during the mid-eighties. He died in Autumn 2003.

Compilation appearances include *Simply Irresistible* on the 3-CD set *Guitar Heroes - Rock The Night Away*; the 3-CD collection *Full Throttle - 60 Original Driving Classics*, and on the 6-CD set *Best Of Driving Rock*, along with *Mercy Mercy Me*. Finally, *Addicted To Love* has been compiled on *Wild Thing - Party* (CD). (VJ)

Panama Ltd. (Jug Band)

Personnel:	GARY COMPTON	hrmnca	AB
	LIZ HANN	ld vcls	A
	PETE HOZZELL	vcls	AB
	RON NEEDS	mandolin	AB
	DENNIS PARKER	ld vcls	AB
	BRIAN STRACHAN	gtr	AB
	ANNE MATTHEWS	vcls	B

ALBUMS:	1(A)	PANAMA LTD. JUG BAND	(Harvest SHVL 753) 1969 R2
	2(A)	INDIAN SUMMER	(Harvest SHVL 779) 1970 R2

NB: (2) reissued on CD (Mason MR 56413).

45s:	Lady Of Shallott/Future Blues	(Harvest HAR 5010) 1969 SC
	Round And Round/Rotting Wooden In	
	A White Collar's Grave	(Harvest HAR 5022) 1970 SC

This progressive outfit was based in the Richmond area of London and took its name from a 1930's Bukka White song. The first album was produced by John Peel. They'd earlier had two cuts on the Matchbox (LP) sampler, *Blues Like Showers Of Rain*. One of the finest moments on their first album, *Round And Round*, later appeared on Harvest's *Picnic* (2-LP) sampler. They shortened their name to **Panama Ltd.** for a better second album, by which time Liz Hann had left, to be replaced by Anne Matthews. On this their early jugband sound is replaced by a brand of Beefheart - influenced rock.

None of the band's members seem to have resurfaced in the music business since but Hozzell had been in **Screw**. (VJ)

Pandamonium

Personnel:	STEVE CHAPMAN		A
	MARTIN CURTIS		A
	MICK GLASS		A
	BOB PONTON	vcls, gtr	A

45s:	Season Of The Witch/Today I'm Happy	(CBS 202462) 1966 R1
α	No Presents For Me/	
	Sun Shines From His Eyes	(CBS 2664) 1967 R3
	Chocolate Buster Dam/	
	Fly With Me Forever	(CBS 3451) 1968 R1

NB: α has been reissued in a limited edition of 500, reproduced from the original French jukebox pressing. *The Unreleased Album* (Radioactive LP 070) 2004 and (Radioactive CD 070) 2004 gives a welcome airing to their unreleased 1970 album. *No Presents For Me - Singles & Rarities* (Radioactive LP 106) 2005 and (Radioactive CD 106) 2005 collects all three singles alongside numerous acetates and other recordings. Also relevant is *Thoughts And Words* (Radioactive RRCD 086) 2005, which is a collection of melodic and rather pensive Ponton and Curtis compositions from the era.

Originally from Kent, this psych-pop act's three singles are now rare and sought-after. Their version of **Donovan**'s *Season Of The Witch* predated his own recording of it. Their best is generally considered to be *No Presents For Me*, notable for some effective backwards guitar and distortion. Ponton and Curtis recorded a folk-pop album as **Thoughts and**

Words for Liberty in 1969, before regrouping as **Pandamonium** for further recordings in 1970, which remained unreleased until recently. Featuring support from members of **Fotheringhay**, their bright and breezy pop is at its best on *Sit Up And Watch The Sunshine* and the psychedelic *I Am What I Am*.

The *Unreleased Album* finally aired the psych-pop album they produced in 1970 with support from members of **Heads Hands And Feet** and **Fotheringay**. It's surprising that this set took so long to secure a release. The vinyl issue was numbered and on 180 gram vinyl. *No Presents For Me* is a collection of singles, demos, acetates and other rarities compiled from studio sessions between 1966 and 1972. Aside from the title track, other highlights include a cover of **Donovan's** *Season Of The Witch* and an alternate version of one of their live favourites *My Old Flame*.

Compilation appearances have included: *The Sun Shines From His Eyes* on *Magic Spectacles* (CD) and *Red With Purple Flashes, Vol. 2* (LP); *No Presents For Me* on *Electric Sugar Cube Flashbacks* (CD), *Electric Sugar Cube Flashbacks, Vol. 4* (LP), *Electric Sugarcube Flashbacks, Vol. 1* (LP) and on the 4-CD *Nuggets II* box set; and *Fly With Me Forever* on *Oddities, Vol 1* (CD) and *Jagged Time Lapse, Vol 1* (CD). (VJ/RMJ)

Panhandle

Personnel:	JON GOBIN	vcls	A
	HERBIE FLOWERS	bs	A
	MARTIN KERSHAW	gtr	A
	DENNIS LOPEZ	percsn	A
	DUDLEY MOORE	piano	A
	BARRY MORGAN	drms	A
	CHRIS SPEDDING	gtr	A

ALBUM: 1(A)   PANHANDLE   (Decca SKL 5105) 1972 SC

This studio band is notable to collectors for containing several well-known musicians. **Spedding** had recently toured/recorded with **Jack Bruce** and went on to join **Sharks** after this venture. Flowers and Morgan were members of **Blue Mink**. Gobin had been in **Selophane**. (VJ/JM)

John Pantry

| ALBUMS: | 1 | JOHN PANTRY | (Philips 6308 129) 1972 SC |
| | 2 | LONG WHITE TRAIL | (Philips 6308 138) 1973 SC |

NB: *The Upside Down World Of John Pantry* (Tenth Planet TP 040) 1998 (SC) is a vinyl anthology of his recordings from 1967-1969.

45s:	Sons Of A Thief/Jewel	(Philips 6006 241) 1972
	Net Of Concern/Words	(Philips 6006 250) 1972
	Sweet Lies/Where To Now	(Philips 6006 349) 1973
	Motor Car/Mary Go Round	(Philips 6006 379) 1974

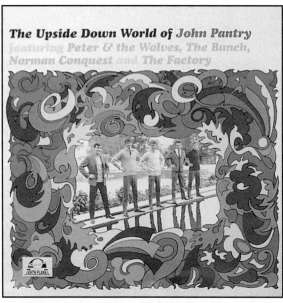

JOHN PANTRY - The Upside Down World Of (LP).

Obscure but not particularly collectable recordings by this former member of **Peter and The Wolves**, **The Bunch**, **Norman Conquest** and **Factory**.

Pantry was also involved with **Wolfe**, who released a US-only album.

Compilation appearances include: *Red Chalk Hill*, *Glasshouse Green, Splinter Red*, *Upside Down*, *Every Single Word*, *Smokey Wood Air* and *How It Is* on *The Upside Down World Of John Pantry* (LP); and a demo *Red Chalk Hill* on *Circus Days, Vol. 6* (CD). (VJ)

Paper Blitz Tissue

Personnel:	DAVE DuFORT		
	TERRY KEATLEY		
	BERNIE LEE	gtr, vcls	
	DEREK NEEDHAM		

45:   α   Boy Meets Girl/Grey Man   (RCA RCA 1652) 1967 R3

NB: α has been repressed in a limited edition of 500 (RCA RCA 1652) reproduced from the original French jukebox pressing with a large centre hole.

An ultra-rare and sought-after single. *Boy Meets Girl* was taken from the TV theme written by Ron Grainer. It has a great psychedelic intro, some fine guitar work and vocals which are ideally suited to this type of music. Recommended. They were particularly popular in London's clubs. Dave DuFort was later in **East Of Eden** and played for **Kevin Ayers**. Bernie Lee was in Polecat in 1976.

Compilation appearances include: *Grey Man* on *Magic Spectacles* (CD); *Locked In A Room* on *Voyage Through The Sugarcube* (LP & CD); and *Boy Meets Girl* on *Beat It* (3-CD), *Chocolate Soup* (CD) and *Chocolate Soup For Diabetics, Vol. 2* (LP). (VJ/MWh)

Paper Bubble

Personnel:	TERRY BRAKE	gtr, vcls	A
	BRIAN CRANE	gtr, vcls	A
	NEIL MITCHELL	bs	A

ALBUM: 1(A)   SCENERY   (Deram DML/SML 1059) 1970 R1

NB: (1) reissued on CD (Hugo Montes HMP CD-014) 2005 on a Korean label.

Paper Bubble came from Shrewsbury. Their album, produced by **Cousins** and **Hooper** from **The Strawbs**, is a pleasant, inoffensive collection of orchestrated, mildly psychedelic pop songs. At times it sounds like **World Of Oz**, due to similar arrangements, but lacks that band's commercial angle. The most psychedelic feature is the cover art, of which there are two variants - the rarer version is turquoise, whilst the commoner is purple.

Broken Dreams, Vol. 3 (LP) features the band's *Mother, Mother, Mother*. (MK/VJ)

The Paper Dolls

Personnel:	PAULINE 'SPIDER' BENNETT	vcls	A
	SUE 'COPPER' MARSHALL	vcls	AB
	SUZI 'TIGER' MATHIS	vcls	AB
	GLORIA 'RUSTY' RICHARDSON	vcls	B

ALBUM: 1(A)   PAPER DOLL'S HOUSE   (Pye N(S)PL 18226) 1968 SC

NB: There's now a CD anthology, *Paper Doll's House (The Pye Anthology)* (Castle CMRCD 342) 2005.

HCP

45s:	Something Here In My Heart/		
	All The Time In The World	(Pye 7N 17456) 1968	11
	My Life Is In Your Hands/		
	There's Nobody I'd Sooner Love	(Pye 7N 17547) 1968	-
	Someday/		
	Any Old Time You're Lonely And Sad	(Pye 7N 17655) 1968	-
	My Boyfriend's Back/		
	Mister Good Time Friday	(RCA RCA 1919) 1970	-

Remember December/Same Old Story (RCA RCA 2007) 1970 -
Reissue: Something Here In My Heart/
(Flip by different artist) (Old Gold OG 9470) 1985 -

This girl trio met whilst studying singing, dancing and acting at an Academy in Northampton. Pauline was born on 28 July 1948; Suzi on 4 April 1947 and Sue on 21 April 1948. Their records were soulful middle-of-the-road pop and they achieved a sizeable hit with their first 45. The hit songwriting team of Tony Macaulay and John Macleod provided several of their best songs. Suzi Mathis married Clive Lea of **The Rockin' Berries**. Bennett left after the third 45 and was replaced by Gloria Richardson, who was born in Middlesborough.

The CD *Paper Doll's House (The Pye Anthology)* features all their Pye recordings, including their album, rare single mixes and a previously unissued version of *Step Inside Love* (a hit for **Cilla Black**). It's the best way now to get to hear their music - if you want to.

Mathis later went solo as Tiger Sue and released a 45, *Burn Burn Burn/Tease Me* in 1971. A decade later Mathis returned as vocal coach to St. Winifred's School Choir who enjoyed a surprise No 1 with *There's No-One Quite Like Grandma*. *Something Here In My Heart* can also be heard on *Hits Of The Swinging Sixties* (CD). (VJ/JM)

The Paper Dragon

45s: April Fool/Get Something Going (Bell BLL 1054) 1969
At Last I've Found Somebody To Love/
Hushabye Boy (Bell BLL 1095) 1970
Julie Is Gone/Moonshine Mary (Bell BLL 2007) 1970

From Gibraltar, Steve Rowland put this band into a recording studio but I've no other details about them.

Paper Lace

Personnel:			
CLIFF FISH	bs, vcls	ABCD
CHRIS MORRIS	gtr, vcls	A C
MICHAEL VAUGHAN	lead gtr, vcls	ABC
PHILLIP WRIGHT	drms, lead vcls	ABCD
CARLO SANTANNA	gtr	BC
JAMIE MOSES	gtr, vcls	D
PETER OLIVER	gtr, vcls	D

ALBUMS: 1(A) PAPER LACE AND OTHER BITS OF MATERIAL
(Bus Stop BUSLP 8001) 1974
2(C) FIRST EDITION (Philips 6382 101) 1975
3(A-D) THE PAPER LACE COLLECTION (Compilation)
(Pickwick PDA 023) 1976

HCP

45s: Ragamuffin Man/
Martha Whatever Happened (Concord CON 27) 1970 -
Billy Don't Be A Hero/Celia (Bus Stop BUS 1014) 1974 1
The Night Chicago Died/
Can I Get It When You Want It (Bus Stop BUS 1016) 1974 3
Black Eyed Boys/Jean (Bus Stop BUS 1019) 1974 11
Hitchin' A Ride '75/
Love-You're A Long Time Coming (Bus Stop BUS 1024) 1975 -
So What If I Am/Himalayan Lullaby (Bus Stop BUS 1026) 1976 -
α I Think I'm Gonna Like It/Lost Love (EMI EMI 2486) 1976 -
Reissue: Billy Don't Be A Hero/
The Night Chicago Died (Old Gold OG 9028) 1979 -

NB: α as Lace.

This mainstream pop group formed in Nottingham in 1969; the lace manufacturing city was the inspiration for their name. Fish was born in Ripley, Derbyshire on 13 August 1949; Morris was born in Nottingham on 1 November 1954; Vaughan was born in Sheffield, Yorkshire on 27 July 1950 and Wright was born in Nottingham on 9 April 1948. Their route to commercial success came when they won ITV talent contest show 'Opportunity Knocks' with **Mitch Murray**'s and Peter Callender's *Billy Don't Be A Hero*. The follow-up *The Night Chicago Died*, topped the US Charts

CHOCOLATE SOUP (Comp CD) including Paper Blitz Tissue.

as well as climbing to No 3 here. Their final UK hit, *The Black-Eyed Boys*, was another Murray-Callender song.

Morris was sacked in late June 1974 but later rejoined in August the same year. In the interim Italian Carlo Santanna (born in Rome on 29 June 1947) had also been recruited.

Vaughan, Morris and Santanna all left in December 1975. Two new members: Jamie Moses (ex-**Merlin**) and Peter Oliver (ex-New Seekers) were recruited in their place. In May 1976 they shortened their name to Lace.

In 1978 they teamed up with Nottingham Forest F.C. to record *We've Got The Whole World In Our Hands*, which got to No 24, although the song's sentiments were an exaggeration for both parties.

Billy Don't Be A Hero can also be heard on *The Best Summer Ever!* (CD), *Hits Of The 70's Vol 2* (CD), *Number 1 Hits Of The 70's and 80's* (CD), *Seventies Legends* (CD), *UK No 1 Hits Of The 70's* (CD), *30 Years Of Number 1 Hit Singles - 1960/1989* (CD), *70's FAB FAV's - Classic 70's Hits* (CD) and *20 Hits From The 70's* (CD), whilst *The.Night Chicago Died* has resurfaced on *70's Remembered* (CD), *Hits Of The 70's Vol 3* (CD), *Super 70's Vol 2* (CD) and *Seventies Legends 2* (CD). (VJ/JM)

Paradise Hammer

Personnel:			
BILLY DAY	keyb'ds	A
CHRIS HUNT	drms	A
MIKE LESLIE	bs	A
TOMMY MOELLER	vcls	A

45s: You Get Me In/She Is Love (Polydor 2058 048) 1970
1 + 1 = 2 / To Live (Polydor 2058 084) 1971

Gary Brewer of Surbiton, Surrey worked with this band circa 1970/71. They had a concept album, which told of a travelling circus troupe, in the can which never saw the light of day. Essentially a vocal harmony-pop band, they formed in mid-1970. Tommy Moeller had previously been with **Unit 4 + 2**. (VJ)

Paradise Square

ALBUM: 1 NEVER THOUGHT I'D SEE THE DAY (no label) 1974
NB: This is a white label test pressing/promo.

A folky album by a Sheffield band, which is thought to have been a self-pressed vanity project. The female vocals are distinctive, but the male ones are a bit off key in places. (VJ)

PARAMETER - Galactic Ramble (LP).

Paradox

Personnel incl: DAVID WALKER

45:	Ring The Changes/		
	The Wednesday Theme	(Polydor 56275) 1968 R3	

David Walker also recorded a solo 45 the same year, which is a minor collectable. The **Paradox** 45 is very rare and hard to find. The 'A' side is a big mod/Northern soul dancer. (VJ)

Paraffin Jack Flash Ltd

ALBUM: 1 MOVERS AND GROOVERS (Pye NSPL 18252) 1968 SC

This album contains instrumental versions of hits of the era like *(I Can't Get No) Satisfaction*, *Green Onions*, *In The Midnight Hour* and *The Mighty Quinn*. Avoid it like the plague. (VJ)

Parameter

Personnel:	KEITH BARRETT	bs, vcls	A
	PAUL FAHY	gtr, 12-string gtr, vcls	A
	TONY MORTIMER	gtr, vcls	A
	LIONEL ?	drms	A

ALBUM: 1(A) GALACTIC RAMBLE   (Deroy no #) 1970 R6
NB: (1) reissued on vinyl (Kissing Spell CA 36003) and on CD (Kissing Spell KSCD 941) and the CD release includes studio outtakes too.

This album of previously unreleased material from 1970 is of an exceedingly crude calibre. It sounds like pre-demo quality, with verbal cues and background voices being clearly audible. The vocals on the first several songs range from flat to strained and might lead listeners to give up at that point - which would be a mistake.

The group includes three composers/singers, each of whom has several cuts on the CD issue. Keith Barrett's songs often have the cadence and feel of the more famous **Barrett**'s compositions, though his vocal phrasing is more reminiscent of Ian Anderson. Lyrically the most interesting of the band's songwriters, the following lines, from *Waves*, are an indication of Barrett's verbal evocations: "I wake this morning/Children with guns ruling/Telling us/How we may live/How we may die/They are the crown/Of all creation/Their God made them/In his image to rule".

One of Paul Fahy's songs, *Dear Johnny*, on the other hand, is in the vein of one of Ray Davies' song portraits from the mid-sixites.

Overall, listening to this CD makes one wonder what could have been done with this raw talent had someone taken them in hand. The music includes slight psychedelic touches such as space-rock type wah-wah guitar and cymbal phasing.

Compilation appearances include: *Emmeline* on *The History Of U.K. Underground Folk Rock 1968-1978 Vol. 1* (CD); and *Sun Gone* and *Virgin Childe* on *The History Of U.K. Underground Folk Rock 1968-1978 Vol. 2* (CD). (RR)

The Paramounts

Personnel:	GARY BROOKER	vcls, piano	ABCD
	MICK BROWNLEE	drms	AB
	CHRIS COPPING	bs	ABC
	BOB SCOTT	vcls	A
	ROBIN TROWER	gtr	ABCD
	BARRY J. WILSON	drms	CD
	DIZ DERRICK	bs	D

EP: 1(D)   THE PARAMOUNTS   (Parlophone GEP 8908) 1964 R3
NB: There's also a compilation *Whiter Shades Of R'n'B* (Edsel ED 112) 1983, later reissued on CD (Edsel ED CD 112) 1991.

			HCP
45s:	Poison Ivy/		
	I Feel Good All Over	(Parlophone R 5093) 1963 SC	35
	Little Bitty Pretty One/		
	A Certain Girl	(Parlophone R 5107) 1964 SC	-
	I'm The One Who Loves You/		
	It Won't Be Long	(Parlophone R 5155) 1964 SC	-
	Bad Blood/Do I	(Parlophone R 5187) 1964 SC	-
	Blue Ribbons/Cuttin' It	(Parlophone R 5272) 1965 SC	-
	You Never Had It So Good/		
	Don't Ya Like My Love	(Parlophone R 5351) 1965 SC	-
Reissue:	Poison Ivy/I Feel Good All Over/Blue Ribbons/		
	Cuttin' In	(EMI EMI 2834) 1978	-

The Paramounts were formed back in 1959 whilst Brooker, Copping and **Trower** were still at secondary school in Southend. With the addition of Brownlee and Scott they developed a good local reputation as a covers band gigging in local youth clubs. Eventually Scott dropped out and Brooker took over the vocal duties.

When they left school in 1962 they became semi-professional, acquired a manager Peter Martin and began to specialise in black American R&B covers of songs by artists like James Brown and Ray Charles. They also gained a residency at the Shades club in Southend.

At the start of 1963 Brownlee was replaced by Wilson and later that year Copping left to go to Leicester University with Diz Derrick joining in his place. They were signed by Parlophone the same year and one of their demos, a cover of The Coasters' *Poison Ivy* was put out as a 45. It had a lot of commercial appeal and sold pretty well. They were further boosted when **The Rolling Stones**, who'd they'd worked with on the 'Thank Your Lucky Stars' pop show, described **The Paramounts** as "the best R&B group in England". Although their follow-up 45, a revival of Thurston Harris' *Little Bitty Pretty One*, was plugged quite hard it failed to sell, as did their subsequent releases. In 1964 they were featured on a **Duffy Power** flip side, *Tired, Broke and Busted*.

By late 1965 they were clearly in decline (reduced to backing **Sandie Shaw** and **Chris Andrews** on European tours) and they split in September 1966. **Trower** and Wilson remained on the R&B circuit whilst Brooker concentrated on songwriting, linking up with lyricist Keith Reid. By Spring 1967 they'd written quite a few songs and needed a band to play them. After advertising in 'Melody Maker' **Procol Harum** was formed. Over the subsequent years all the old **Paramounts** (apart from Diz Derrick who left the music business) were recruited to its ranks. **Robin Trower** later embarked on a solo career.

The Edsel compilation includes all the band's recordings plus four previously unissued cuts including a very lively cover of **The Sorrows'** *You've Got What I Want* and a barnstorming rendition of Charlie Mingus's black liberation anthem *Freedom*.

Compilation appearances have includes: *Little Bitty Pretty One* on *R&B At Abbey Road* (CD); *Blue Ribbons* on *Sixties Lost And Found, Vol. 1* (LP); *I'm The One Who Loves You* and *Blue Ribbons* on *Beat At Abbey Road* (CD); and *Poison Ivy* has been compiled on *Beat Merchants* (2-LP), *20 One Hit Wonders* (LP), *Beat Generation - Ready Steady Go* (CD) and on the 2-CD set *Greatest Hits Of The 60's Vol 4*. (VJ)

Parchment

Personnel:

SUE McCLELLAN	vcls, gtr		A
JOHN PAC	mandolin, autoharp, gtr, vcls, sitar, nasal horn		A
KEITH RYCROFT	dobro, gtr, vcls		A

(Several additional musicians appear on individual tracks)

ALBUMS:	1(A)	LIGHT UP THE FIRE	(Pye NSPL 18388) 1972 SC
(up to	2( )	HOLLYWOOD SUNSET	(Pye NSPL 18409) 1973 SC
1976)	3( )	SHAMBLEJAM	(Myrrh MYR 1028) 1975 SC

HCP

45s:	Light Up The Fire/	
	Let There Be Light (PS)	(Pye 7N 45178) 1972 31
	Where Can I Find You/	
	Working Man	(Pye 7N 45214) 1972 -
	You Were On My Mind/	
	Rock'n'Roll Part Time	(Pye 7N 45233) 1973 -

A long forgotten group, though they did achieve a minor hit with the gospel-influenced *Light Up The Fire*. Prior to forming the trio had separately been part of a number of groups in Liverpool's folk scene performing in folk clubs. The trio wrote all the songs on the first album except *Love Is Come Again*, a traditional carol melody which was sung by Church choirs and *Pack Up Your Sorrows*, a Richard Farina song which was in their repertoire in Liverpool's folk circuit. Many of their songs are religious dealing with Jesus. For example, the sleevenotes tell us *Zip Bam Boom* "was written for a Good Friday session at Liverpool's Cavern. It aimed at bridging the communications gap through a free translation of the life of Jesus into the language of today. The result - a working class hymn"! It's certainly lively and, along with *Better Than Yesterday*, is one of the better tracks. The remaining material is softer, more mellow and acoustic-based. Of these *Love Is Come Again* has a beautiful melody sung by Sue McClellan, with strings and sitar. Very Eastern-influenced. The album was produced by Key Records, who also produced religious-orientated albums on their own label.

They recorded three further albums - the final one *Rehearsal For A Reunion* (Pilgrim GRAPEVINE 106) in 1977. (VJ/CA)

Paris

Personnel incl: RICK KENTON   A

45:	I've Lost The Way / Long Time	(Avalanche AV 67312) 1972

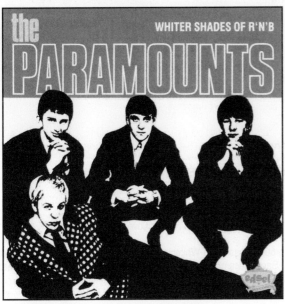

THE PARAMOUNTS - Whiter Shades Of R'n'B (CD).

A four-piece from Barking, Essex. They were the first British signing to Avalance, a subsidiary label of United Artists. Former **Roxy Music** member **Rick Kenton** joined after the 45 had been released. (VJ)

Alan Parker

ALBUMS:	1	GUITAR FANTASY	(Aristocrat AR 1022) 1970
	2	BAND OF ANGELS	(MCA MUPS 471) 1973

45:	Band Of Angels/Ain't It The Truth	(MCA MU 1178) 1972
(up to 1976)		

Parker was also involved in **Hungry Wolf** and **Ugly Custard**. *Band Of Angels* was essentially rock with a hint of country which typified his style.

David Parker

ALBUM:	1	DAVID PARKER	(Polydor Super 2460 101) 1971 R1

A strange and very obscure singer-songwriter effort, which veers from mediocre mainstream pop (*Right Now I'm Tired Of Running Away*) to decent introspective material (*Conclusions* and *Dark Eyed Lady*). **Parker** went on to become a music publisher. (RMJ)

Graham Parker and The Rumour

Personnel:

BOB ANDREWS	keyb'ds	A
MARTIN BELMONT	gtr	A
ANDREW BODNAR	bs	A
STEVE GOULDING	drms	A
GRAHAM PARKER	vcls, gtr	A
BRINSLEY SCHWARZ	gtr	A

HCP

ALBUMS:	1(A)	HOWLIN' WIND	(Vertigo 6360 129) 1976 -
(up to	2(A)	HEAT TREATMENT	(Vertigo 6360 137) 1976 52
1976)			

45s:	Silly' Going Thing/	
(up to	I'm Going To Use It Now	(Vertigo 6059 135) 1976
1976)	Soul Shoes/Wild Honey	(Vertigo 6059 147) 1976
	Hotel Chamberaid/	
	Don't Ask Me Questions	(Vertigo 6059 158) 1976

Graham Parker was a rhythm and blues singer who first came to prominence in the mid-seventies pub-rock boom. He put together a band "the Rumour" in 1975 from the ashes of **Ducks Deluxe** and **Brinsley Schwarz** singing a combination of his own material and some soul standards. His powerful gritty vocal style was showcased on songs like *Pouring It All Out* and *Hey Lord Don't Ask Me Questions*. The above discography only covers his 1976 output - he really belongs to a later period and he recorded several further 45s and albums. He tasted success in both the UK and US and went on to record solo albums well into the eighties and nineties eventually relocating to America. The Rumour also later recorded albums in their own right. This is not intended to be a detailed résumé of his career. (VJ/BS)

Parking Lot

45:	α	World Spinning Sadly/	
		Carpet Man	(Parlophone R 5779) 1969 R1

NB: α The 'A' side was reissued by Bam-Caruso (OCRA 060) on a split side 45 in 1988.

This 45, which was produced by Paul Samwell-Smith, is often touted as a collectable slice of psychedelia but some have their doubts. The 'A' side has also been compiled on both *Rubble Vol. 2: Pop-Sike Pipe-Dreams* (LP) and *Rubble Vol. 1* (CD) compilations and sounds much more like a reflective and pleasant ballad. The flip side was a Jim Webb song. (VJ/MWh)

THE PARLOUR BAND - Is A Friend? (LP).

The Parlour Band

Personnel:	CRAIG ANDERS	vcls, gtr	A
	MARK ASHLEY ANDERS	vcls, bs	A
	PETER FILLEUL	keyb'ds, vcls, gtr	A
	PIX	vcls, gtr	A
	JERRY ROBBINS	drms	A

ALBUM: 1(A) IS A FRIEND?   (Deram SDL 10) 1972 R3

The Parlour Band came from the Channel Islands and their rare album, produced by Nick Tauber, features well constructed progressive rock. The singing is mellow and the instrumentation largely acoustic. Highlights include the melodic *Pretty-Haired Girl* and epic *Home*, which concludes the album majestically. To promote *Is A Friend?* the band embarked on a nationwide tour alongside **Steve Hillage**'s **Khan**, supporting **Caravan**. It didn't help album sales, however, and they were dropped by the label soon afterwards.

Filleul joined **the Climax Blues Band**. The Anders brothers and Pix (short for Pickford) went on to form **A Band Called O**. (MK/VJ)

Parrish and Gurvitz

Personnel:	PAUL GURVITZ	gtr, vcls	A
	MIKE KELLIE	drms	A
	BRIAN PARRISH	gtr, vcls	A

ALBUM: 1(A) PARRISH AND GURVITZ
                 (Regal Zonophone SRZA 8506) 1971 SC

This was a one-off project for **Parrish and Gurvitz**, who were previously in **Gun** and **Baker-Gurvitz Army**. **Parrish** later went on to a solo career, recording an album, *Love On My Mind* (Barn 2314 101) in 1976. The title cut was also issued on a 45, followed by one the following year credited to simply **Parrish**. Kellie was also in **Spooky Tooth**.

Sam Parry

ALBUM: 1   IF SADNESS COULD SING   (Argo ZDA 155) 1973 R3
NB: (1) reissued on CD (Small Town CAMD 1).

Sam Parry was a singer/songwriter and his album is similar to early **John Martyn**, **Mick Softley** and **Roy Harper**. There's lots of acoustic instrumentation and a hippie counter culture feel to the album. (VJ)

Particular People

45:     Boys Cry/What's The Matter With Juliet   (Big T BIG 105) 1968

An obscure late sixties 45. The 'A' side was an Eden Kane song.

What's The Matter With Juliet can also be found on *The Electric Lemonade Acid Test, Vol. 2* (LP). (VJ)

The Partisans

EPs: 1   THE PARTISANS (Bulldog/My Babe/Perfidia/Sweet Little Sixteen)   (Eaglestone Recording Service) 1963 R2
      2   All Night Worker/Let The Winds Blow/Mr. Pitiful/ Why Can't You   (Modern Music Centre acetate) 196?

Purple Heart Surgery, Vol. 1 (LP) and *Hens Teeth Vol. 2* (CD) include this West London band's version of *All Night Worker*. The song had only appeared previously on a 10" acetate EP. Prior to that the band had recorded a four track EP of cover versions back in 1963. (VJ)

Don Partridge

ALBUM: 1   DON PARTRIDGE   (Columbia S(C)X 6280) 1968 SC

EP: 1   SINGING SOHO STYLE   (CFP CFP 001/002) 196?

                                                        HCP
45s: Rosie/Going Back To London   (Columbia DB 8330) 1968 4
        Blue Eyes/
        I've Got Something For You   (Columbia DB 8416) 1968 3
        We Have Ways Of Making You Laugh/
        Top Man   (Columbia DB 8484) 1968 -
        Breakfast On Pluto/Stealin'   (Columbia DB 8538) 1969 26
        Colour My World/Homeless Bones (Columbia DB 8583) 1969 -
        Going To Germany/Ask Me Why   (Columbia DB 8617) 1969 -
        We're All Happy Together/
        Following Your Fancy   (Columbia DB 8723) 1970 -

Don Partridge, who was born in Bournemouth in 1945, began life as a busker and his early records had something of a novelty value with *Rosie* and *Blue Eyes* the most successful. It's said that *Rosie* cost just £8 to record, but it became a Top Five hit. **Partridge** also supervised a Various Artists' compilation, *The Buskers* (LP). After a couple of years the novelty of his work wore off and he went back to busking, which he continued to do well into the nineties. He was briefly a member of **Accolade** in 1969, and before that, recorded as **Brotherhood**.

Pasha

45:     Someone Shot The Lollipop Man/
        Pussy Willow Dragon   (Liberty LBF 15199) 1969 R3

This 45 is now extremely rare and collectable. It was actually by **The Searchers** under a pseudonym, named after their producer's dog. The 45 was later included on **The Searchers** 3-CD box set.

Patches

Personnel:	MAX CHETWYN		A
	GERRY SAYER	vcls	A
	IAN WHITEMORE	bs	A

45:     Living In America/How Is Love   (Warner K 16201) 1972

This group's bassist Ian Whitemore went on to **Starry Eyed and Laughing**. Gerry Sayer became better known as **Leo Sayer**! Max Chetwyn is featured on his records.

The Pathfinders (1)

Personnel:	TONY ALDRIDGE	drms	A
	ROY BROCKLEHURST	bs	A
	TOM EARLEY	lead vcls, gtr	A
	BILLY MAY	lead gtr, vcls	A

NB: Above is the recording line-up. Previous personnel were:- Tony Berry (drms), Tommy Bennett (drms), Ritchie Prescott (lead gtr), John Hinton (piano), Kingsley Foster (piano), Frank Hopley (piano)

45s:	I Love You Caroline/		
	Something I Can Always Do	(Decca F 12038) 1964 SC	
	Don't You Believe It/		
	Castle Of Love	(Parlophone R 5372) 1965 SC	

The Pathfinders were formed by Tom Earley and Roy Brockhurst in Birkenhead in 1960. They remained as a performing and recording unit until 1966. The *Don't You Believe It* 45 sometimes credited to the Scottish band of the same name was recorded by this band at Abbey Road studios and engineered by David Gooch. The 'A' side was an original written by lead guitarist Billy May and Tom Earley and the 'B' side was written by a Mike Rooms. A third session was recorded but not released as lead guitarist and vocalist Billy May decided to quit the band and EMI cancelled its release a week prior to release. (VJ/AD/TE).

The Pathfinders (2)

Personnel:	IAN CRAWFORD-CLEWS	vcls	AB
	TIMI DONALD	drms	AB
	COLIN HUNTER-MORRISON	bs	AB
	RONALD LEAHY	organ	AB
	NEIL McCORMACK	lead gtr	A
	FRASER WATSON	lead gtr	B

A Glasgow-based band who included Fraser Watson (formerly of **The Poets**). He'd filled in when their founding member Neil McCormack had been ill and when McCormack became their manager a few months later he replaced him permanently. They specialised in soul (Tamala and Stax) covers. When they were later signed by Apple they took a dislike to the band's name changing it to **White Trash**. The BBC took exception to this so they eventually became known as **Trash**.

Compilation appearances include: *Pumpkin Lantern* (prev unreleased) on *Incredible Sound Show Stories, Vol. 10* (LP), whilst you'll also find *Pumpkin Lantern* and *To Love Somebody* on *Alphabeat (Pop, Psych and Prog 1967-1970)* (LP) and (CD). (VJ)

The Pathfinders (3)

45s:	What Do You Do/What'd I Say	(Hayton SP 138/9) 1964

A third group with this name, this time from Kent, produced this privately-pressed 45. (VJ)

Pathway To Your Mind

ALBUM:	1	PREPARING THE MIND AND BODY FOR MEDITATION
		(Major Minor SMLP 19) 1968 R1

This was a 'spoken word' album, which is now rare and hard to find. It sounds psychedelic from its title but wasn't. (VJ)

Bobby Patrick Big Six

Personnel:	ARCHIE LEGGATT	bs	A
	PETER McCRORY	lead gtr	AB
	BOBBY PATRICK	trumpet, vcls	A
	FREDDY SMITH	drms	AB
	JOHN A. WIGGINS	keyb'ds	AB
	ALEX YOUNG	tenor sax	AB
	IAN CAMPBELL	bs	B
	PETER R. CARTER	sax	B

EP:	1	TEENBEAT FROM STAR CLUB HAMBURG
		(Decca DFE 8570) 1964 R3

45s:	Shake It Easy Baby/Wildwood Days	(Decca F 11898) 1964 R1
	Monkey Time/Sweet Talk Me Baby	(Decca F 12030) 1964 R1

This act issued a handful of 45s in Germany on the Ariola and Star-Club labels and also appeared on one side of an album with **Kingsize Taylor**. Their EP was recorded live at the Star Club, Hamburg in 1964 and *Monkey Time* was a Major Lance soul track.

There's also a library music album credited to Bobby Patrick and Flash-Back (United Artists Recorded Music Library UAM 3), and subtitled *Music For Radio, Television and Films*. The album is undated, but sounds circa 1969/70. A decade later, and two 45s, containing versions of theme music for 'Dallas' and 'Knots Landing' also appeared on the Monza label, this time credited to the Bobby Patrick Band. Both feature original **John Mayall's Bluesbreakers** guitarist, Roger Dean, who has confirmed that these records are by the same Bobby Patrick.

Compilation appearances have included: *The Dog, Domino Twist, Roly Poly* and *Wildwood Days* on *The Beat Goes On, Vol. 1* (LP); *Fanny Mae, Green Onions, Shake It Easy Baby* and *Let The Four Winds Blow* on *The Beat Goes On, Vol. 2* (LP); and *New Orleans* on *The Beat Goes On, Vol. 3* (LP). (VJ/AD/GCn/RD)

The Patriots

45:	The Prophet/I'll Be There	(Fontana TF 650) 1966

The Prophet was a folk/protest style single. (VJ)

Patron of The Arts

45:	α	The True Patron Of The Arts/	
		Eleanor Rigby	(Page One POF 012) 1966 R1

NB: α The flip side was by the Queen City Show Band.

This **Beatles** cover version done as an instrumental on what is now a minor collectable. (VJ)

Brian Patten

ALBUMS:	1	BRIAN PATTEN	(Caedmon TC 1300) 1970 SC
(up to	2	VANISHING TRICK	(Tangent TGS 116) 1971 R1
1976)			

INCREDIBLE SOUND SHOW STORIES VOL. 10 (Comp LP) including The Pathfinders.

Patten also recorded with Liverpool poet **Roger McGough** who was a member of **Liverpool Scene**. Of these albums only the second interests collectors. He also recorded a third, *Sly Cormorant*, (Argo ZSW 607) in 1977. (VJ)

Pattern People

45:    Take A Walk In The Sun/?   (MGM MGM 1429) 1968

Circus Days, Vol. 5 (LP) and *Circus Days, Vol. 6* (CD) contain the pleasant harmony-pop ditty *Take A Walk In The Sun* by this obscure band, which is evocative of British summers in corn strewn countryside. (VJ)

Patterson's People

45:    Shake Hands With The Devil/
       Deadly Nightshade   (Mercury MF 913) 1966 SC

A one-off 45, which is now becoming collectable. This was a five man group from Aylesbury in Buckinghamshire.

Compilation appearances include: *Shake Hands With The Devil* on *Red With Purple Flashes, Vol. 2* (LP); and *Deadly Nightshade* on *Beat Us If You Can! Vol. 1* (LP) and *Oddities, Vol 1* (CD). (VJ)

Tuema Pattie

ALBUM: 1   IRISH AIRS   (Oak RG 1717) 1971 R4

A rare example of an album on the famous Oak custom label. On offer is female folk material including *She Moves Through The Fair* and *The Bold Unbiddable Child*. (VJ)

Mike Patto

45s: Can't Stop Talking About My Baby/
       Love   (Columbia DB 8091) 1966 R2
       Sitting In The Park/Get Up And Dig It   (Goodear EAR 106) 1974

Mike Patto (real name Michael Thomas McCarthy) first came to light as the vocalist in Norwich R&B outfit Mike Patto and The Breakaways. After several line-up changes The Breakaways became The Bluebottles, but soon after **Patto** headed for London to join The National Youth Jazz Orchestra. At the same time he had a spell with **The Bo Street Runners** and the **Chicago Line Blues Band** in 1966, before forming **Timebox**, which eventually evolved into **Patto.**

PATTO - Patto (LP).

The flip side to his first 45, *Love*, which was actually a leftover **Bo Street Runners'** track, later appeared on the *Pop-Sike Pipe-Dream* (CD) compilation. (RMJ)

Patto

Personnel:	CLIVE GRIFFITHS	bs	A
	OLLIE HALSALL	gtr, keyb'ds, vcls	A
	JOHN HALSEY	drms	A
	MIKE PATTO	vcls	A

ALBUMS:	1(A)	PATTO	(Vertigo 6360 016) 1970 R2
	2(A)	HOLD YOUR FIRE	(Vertigo 6360 032) 1971 R3
	3(A)	ROLL 'EM SMOKE 'EM, PUT ANOTHER LINE OUT	(Island ILPS 9210) 1972 R1

NB: (1) reissued on CD (Repertoire REP 4446-WP) 1994 and again on CD (Repertoire REPUK 1025/Vertigo) 2004 with a 15-minute bonus track and housed in a textured (as the original album was) mini gatefold sleeve. (2) reissued on vinyl (Akarma AK 189). (2) reissued on CD (Repertoire REP 4360-WP) 1993 and again on CD (Akarma 00017306). (3) reissued on CD (Edsel EDCD 510) 199?. *Warts And All* (Admiral ADM 001) 2001 is a live album, recorded during 1971 in Sheffield. There's also a double CD compilation, *Sense Of The Absurd* (Vertigo 528 696-2) 1995. Their unreleased fourth album, *Monkey's Bum*, finally appeared (Akarma AK 201) on vinyl and CD in 2001.

Patto has the dubious distinction of being known as the unluckiest band in British rock history.

Having released a string of superb but unsuccessful singles as **Timebox**, these four musicians decided to change both their name and direction as the seventies dawned. Their three albums of eccentric, jazz-tinged prog failed to catch on, however. *Patto* was a good jazz-rock fusion, featuring some fine vibraphone and guitar playing from **Ollie Halsall**, especially on the explosive *The Man* and fiery *San Antone*. *Hold Your Fire* was far jazzier. Its highlights included the rollicking title track and admonitory *You, You Point Your Finger*, though other numbers such as *Air Raid Shelter* strayed dangerously close to self-indulgence. A bungle at the pressing plant saw two separate mixes of the album appearing. Its cover, depicting a game of consequences, is nigh-on impossible to find in perfect condition.

After *Hold Your Fire* failed to sell, the band moved to Island and embarked on a major US tour supporting **Joe Cocker**. Their album for the label contained arguably their finest work, such as the funky *Singing The Blues On Reds* and energetic *Loud Green Song*, though it too was guilty of self-indulgence elsewhere. They recorded a further album for Island under the title of *Monkey's Bum*, which only appeared recently. By far their most commercial offering, it contained several excellent **Patto/Halsall** tracks (including the witty *Sugar Cube 1967* and a version of Randy Newman's *The Dream I Had Last Night*). It may well have been their breakthrough. Jaded from lack of success and heavy touring, the band folded in 1973.

Ollie Halsall, suffering from a serious drug addiction, left to join **Tempest**. Griffiths went on to Pure Chance, and Halsey joined **Zoot Money's Big Roll Band**. Both were seriously injured in a van crash, Griffiths permanently. **Patto** embarked on a brief solo career and also had spells in **Spooky Tooth** and **Boxer** (the latter venture re-uniting him with **Ollie Halsall**). His final solo 45, *Sitting In The Park* was a ballad done by Billy Stewart and **Georgie Fame**. Sadly, he died on 4 March 1979 of lymphatic leukaemia. He was buried in Hingham cemetery in Norfolk. His son Michael (who also uses the name Patto) is also a fine musician and record producer.

There's a double CD, *Sense Of The Absurd*, which collects their first two albums plus thirty minutes worth of bonus material (which includes four previously unissued cuts).

Warts And All is a live album, recorded in 1971 in Sheffield, but the sound quality leaves a lot to be desired because it was recorded on a mono cassette stage-side. (VJ/PM/JM/RMJ)

Paul

45:    Will You Follow Me/Head Death   (Polydor BM 56045) 1965 R2

Jimmy Page wrote, produced and played guitar on this obscure folky 45. (VJ)

Paul and Ritchie and Crying Shames

Personnel:
PETER BYRNE	organ	A
PAUL COMMERFORD	drms	A
PAUL CRANE	lead vcls, bs	A
MICHAEL ESTEL	lead gtr	A
BRIAN NORRIS	bs	A
RITCHIE ROUTHLEDGE	gtr	A

45: September In The Rain/
Come On Back (Decca F 12483) 1966 R3

An extremely rare and collectable disc. It's in many ways more akin to what American garage bands were playing in this era with its sneering vocals and tinny organ sound.

The band was the dying embers of **Cryin' Shames** with a modified line-up and name. See the **Cryin' Shames** entry for details of their earlier career. Paul Crane went on to play for **Gary Walker and The Rain**.

Compilation appearances include: *Come On Back* on *Maximum Freakbeat* (CD), *Broken Dreams, Vol. 5* (LP), *The Freakbeat Scene* (CD) and *The British Psychedelic Trip 1966 - 1969* (LP); *You* on *Mersey Sounds* (2-LP); and *You, September In The Rain* and *Come On Back* on *Nowhere Men, Vol. 4* (CD). (VJ)

Don Paul

45: Wise To The Ways Of the World/
Don't Let A Little Pride (RCA RCA 1666) 1968

He'd been in an early sixties group called The Viscounts. He later discovered **Don Partridge** busking in Berwick Street, London and became his manager. The 'A' side of this 45 was penned by McAuley/McLeod. (VJ)

Jason Paul

45: Shine A Little Light Into My Room/
Paradise Pudding (Pye 7N 17710) 1969

This London-based singer had earlier been one half of the duo **Svensk**. *Shine A Little Light Into My Room* can also be found on *Fading Yellow, Vol 4* (CD). (VJ)

Lyn Paul

ALBUM: 1 GIVE ME LOVE (Polydor 2383 340) 1975
(up to 1976)

HCP
45s: Sail The Summer Winds/
(up to Lay Me Down (Polydor 2058 472) 1974 -
1976) Who's Sorry Now/Sweet Lovin' Ways (Polydor 2058 514) 1974 -
Love/I Could Get Arrested (Polydor 2058 552) 1975 -
It Ought To Sell A Million/
Waiting Game (Polydor 2058 602) 1975 37
Here Comes That Wonderful Feeling/
How Long Will I Love You (Polydor 2058 655) 1975 -
Mam Don't Wait For Me/All By Myself (Polydor 2058 737) 1976 -

These were solo efforts by **Lyn Paul**, who was a member of The New Seekers. She was born on 16 February 1949 in Manchester and also played in **The Nocturnes** as Lyn Peters. *It Ought To Sell A Million* made the Top 40 in 1975. She had further post-1976 recordings. (VJ)

Paul and Linda

45: You're Taking My Bag/
When I Hear Your Name (Page One POF 140) 1969

This single was actually recorded by **Paul McNeill and Linda Peters**. See their entry for further details. (VJ)

PATTO - Roll 'em Smoke 'em Put Another Line Out (CD).

Paul's Disciples

Personnel:
ANDY CHISHOLM	bs	A
CHRIS CUNNINGHAM	lead gtr	A
TED (PAUL) HAMLYN	vcls	A
BRIAN JENKINS	piano	A
RAY SMITH	drms	A

45: See That My Grave Is Kept Clean/
Sixteen Tons (Decca F 12081) 1965

A hard-driving R&B group located in the St Albans/Watford area. They used to do fairly juiced up **Donovan** numbers as well. They supported artists such as Little Stevie Wonder, **Heinz** and **Screamin' Lord Sutch**. Jenkins was previously in a band called **Cops and Robbers**, which he named after the Bo Diddley track. He now plays for a band called Madison Blues band on the South London pub circuit.

See That My Grave Is Kept Clean has resurfaced on *The R&B Scene* (CD). (VJ/BJ)

Paul's Troubles

45: You'll Find Out/
You've Got Something (Ember EMB S 233) 1967 SC

Another minor collectable. This was a five-man beat group. (VJ)

Pax External

45: A Second Chance Mr. Jones/
You See Him As Your Brother (Decca F 13167) 1971

A short-lived early seventies act. (VJ)

Dave Peace Quartet

Personnel:
DAVE LLOYD	gtr	A
DAVE PEACE	gtr, vcls	A
DAVE PEGG	bs	A
MICK WALSH	drms	A

ALBUM: 1(A) GOOD MORNING MR. BLUES (Saga FID 2155) 1969 SC

A Birmingham-based blues band. They subsequently metamorphised into the band **Birmingham**. (VJ)

Peaceful Company

Personnel: RON PAUL MORIN   A
                    LUKE WILSON   A

ALBUM: 1(A)   PEACEFUL COMPANY (Sovereign SVNA 7252) 1973 SC

This album had been released the previous year but with the same catalogue number and credited to **Ron Paul Morin and (Luke P.) Wilson.** (VJ)

Roger Peacock

45s: Everybody's Talking 'Bout My Baby/
           Times Have Changed   (Columbia DB 7764) 1965
     α   Just A Lonely Man/Sun Was In Your Eyes (Joker M 7105) 1971

NB: α Italian only release, credited to **Peacock.**

When **The Cheynes** split in 1965, lead vocalist **Roger Peacock** recorded a solo 45 before joining **The Mark Leeman Five**. When the latter split, he formed **Dave Anthony's Moods**, who soon relocated to Italy.

When The Moods split, he stayed in Italy for some time, playing first with Mal of **Primitives** and then (Sopworth) Camel. In 1971 he released a further solo single, produced by Lally Stott of Motowns, before returning to England. (FB/CR/GB)

Peanut

Personnel incl: KATIE KISSOON

45s: Thank You For The Rain/I'm Not Sad   (Pye 7N 15901) 1965
           Home Of The Brave/
           I Wanna Hear It Again   (Pye 7N 15963) 1965 SC
           I'm Waiting For The Day/
           Someone's Gonna Be Sorry   (Columbia DB 8032) 1966 SC
           I Didn't Love Him Anyway/
           Come Tomorrow   (Columbia DB 8104) 1967 SC

A little known sixties soul band. Kissoon also recorded a solo 45, *Don't Let It Rain/Will I Never See The Sun* (Columbia DB 8525) 1969. She was also in The Marionettes in the mid-sixties, **The Rag Dolls** in the late sixties and Mac and Katie Kissoon. She later did backing vocals for **Roger Waters'** solo albums.

Compilation appearances have included: *Thank Goodness For The Rain* on *Ripples, Vol. 3* (CD); and *Home Of The Brave* on *Ripples, Vol. 2* (CD). (VJ)

The Peasants

45:      Got Some Lovin' For You Baby/
           Let's Get Together   (Columbia DB 7642) 1965 R3

This is a very rare and collectable freakbeat 45. The band was from High Wycombe, Buckinghamshire. (VJ)

The Peddlers

Personnel: TAB MARTIN   bs   A
             TREVOR MORAIS   drms   A
             ROY PHILLIPS   keyb'ds, gtr, vcls   A

                                             HCP
ALBUMS: 1(A)   LIVE AT THE PICKWICK
(up to   (Philips (S)BL 7768) 1967 SC -
1976)   2(A)   FREE WHEELERS (CBS (S)BPG 63183) 1967 SC 27
       3(A)   THREE IN A CELL   (CBS 63411) 1968 SC -
       4(A)   THE FANTASTIC PEDDLERS
                       (Fontana SFL 13016) 1968 SC -

THE PEDDLERS - Freewheelers (LP).

     5(A)   BIRTHDAY   (CBS 63682) 1970 16
     6(A)   THREE FOR ALL   (Philips 6308 028) 1970 -
     7(A)   GEORGIA ON MY MIND (Philips 6308 066) 1971 -
     8(A)   SUITE LONDON   (Philips 6308 102) 1972 -

NB: (5) also issued in the US (Epic 26529) 1970. (8) with The London Symphony Orchestra. (1) and (6) reissued on CD in 1998. (3) reissued on vinyl.

EP: 1(A)   SWINGING SCENE   (Philips BE 12954) 1966 SC

                                             HCP
45s: Let The Sunshine In/True Girl   (Philips BF 1375) 1964 50
(up to   Whatever Happened To The Good Times/
1976)   Song For The Blues   (Philips BF 1404) 1965 -
        Over The Rainbow/
        You Must Be Having Me On   (Philips BF 1455) 1965 -
        Adam's Apple/Anybody's Fool (Philips BF 1506) 1966 -
        I've Got To Hold On/Gassin'   (Philips BF 1530) 1966 -
        What'll I Do/Delicious Lady   (Philips BF 1557) 1967 -
        Irresistible You/Murry's Mood   (CBS 2947) 1967 -
        You're The Reason I'm Living/
        Nine Miles High   (CBS 3055) 1967 -
        Handel With Care/Horse's Collar   (CBS 3333) 1968 -
        Comin' Home Baby/Empty Club Blues (CBS 3734) 1968 -
        That's Life/Wasting My Time   (CBS 4045) 1969 -
        Birth/Steel Mill   (CBS 4449) 1969 17
        Girlie/P.S. I Love You   (CBS 4720) 1970 34
        Let Me Be Turned To Stone/
        True Girl   (Philips 6006 6110) 1970 -
        Back Alley Girl/Nothing Sacred (Philips 6006 6223) 1972 -
        Is There Anyone Out There/
        Just A Thought Ago   (EMI EMI 2106) 1974 -
        That Song Is Driving Me Crazy/
        Just A Thought Ago   (EMI EMI 2231) 1974 -

The Peddlers developed as a promising jazz-flavoured R&B trio in the mid-sixties. Phillips and Martin had earlier been with The Tornados and Morais had earlier drummed with **Rory Storm and The Hurricanes** and **Faron's Flamingoes**. They came from Manchester (meeting in a record shop) and were originally known as **The Song Peddlers**.

They achieved some commercial success, too, enjoying three minor UK hits. In their later years they veered more towards the cabaret circuit. After they split up Morais went on to play for **Quantum Jump**.

Three In A Cell opens with a frantic cover of *Comin' Home Baby* and *On A Clear Day (You Can See Forever)* is another highlight. Keith Mansfield provided the string arrangements on this album.

Their fifth album, *Birthday* is a strange psych/prog mix, with both originals and covers (*Little Red Rooster, Southern Woman*). The US sleeve depicted the front of a naked girl with their picture in a central frame. (VJ/SR/DS)

The Peelers

Personnel:
TOM MADDEN	vcls	A
JOE PALMER	vcls	A
JIM YOUNGER	concertina, violin	A

ALBUM: 1 (A) BANISHED MISFORTUNE
(Polydor Folk Mill 2460 165) 1972 R3

NB: (1) reissued (Barleycorn BACL 001) 1982 along with a 45. (1) also reissued on CD (Elergy E620/1).

This Irish folk group's rare and sought-after album appeared on the same short-lived imprint as **COB**'s Moyshe McStiff and **Barry Dransfield**'s solo album. The group mostly covered traditional songs like their album's title cut, utilising acoustic instruments like the dulcimer, banjo, Tin Whistle, guitar and concertina. When the band split in December 1972, Younger (who had earlier been in The Tinkers) went on to **The John Baldry Band**. Palmer and Madden joined Thady Quill. Palmer reformed **The Peelers** in 1984 and the new line-up released an album called *Dodger* on Etude. (VJ/JM)

Peenuts

45:        The Theme From "The Monkees"/The World's Been
Good To Me Tonight (some PS) (Ember EMB S 242) 1967 SC/-

Peenuts also have a cut called *Trouble* included on *Oddities, Vol 2* (CD) (VJ)

The Peeps

Personnel incl: PIERRE TUBBS

45s: Now Is The Time/Got Plenty Of Love   (Philips BF 1421) 1965
What Can I Say?/
Don't Talk About Love   (Philips BF 1443) 1965 SC
Gotta Get A Move On/I Told You Before (Philips BF 1478) 1966
Tra La La/Loser Wins   (Philips BF 1509) 1966

This band was also known as **Martin Cure and The Peeps**. *Now Is The Time* is quite a catchy beat number but their subsequent efforts were more soul-pop in style. They came from Coventry.

Compilation appearances include: *Now Is The Time* on *English Freakbeat, Vol. 5* (LP & CD); and *Gotta Get A Move On* on *Echoes From The Wilderness - Sixteen UK R&B Freakbeat Trippers.* (LP & CD). (VJ)

THE PEELERS - Banished Misfortune (CD).

THE PEEP SHOW - Mazy (LP).

The Peep Show

Personnel incl: PATRICK BURSTON

45s: Mazy/Your Servant, Steven   (Polydor BM 56196) 1967 R2
Esprit De Corps/Mino In A Mix-Up (Polydor BM 52226) 1968 SC

NB: *Mazy* (Tenth Planet TP 043) 1998 is a 16-track compilation of their material.

This obscure London-based four-piece group is best remembered for *Mazy*, a dreamy, rather haunting slice of flower-power pop. Apparently, their 45s were jointly produced by Peter Meadon, who'd helped mould **The Who** in their early days as **The High Numbers**, and Norman Jopling, who worked at 'Record Mirror'. *Your Servant, Steven* was also recorded by The Blues Magoos.

Mazy has been compiled on *Rubble Vol. 13: Freakbeat Fantoms* (LP), *Rubble Vol. 7* (CD), *Visions Of The Past, Vol. 2* (LP & CD), *We Can Fly, Vol 1* (CD) and *The Best Of Rubble Collection Vol. 1* (CD). (VJ)

Bob Pegg

ALBUMS: 1 BOB PEGG AND NICK STRUTT
(up to   (Transatlantic TRA 265) 1973 SC
1976)   2 SHIPBUILDER   (Transatlantic TRA 280) 1974 SC
3 ANCIENT MAPS
(w/insert)   (Transatlantic TRA 299) 1975 SC

NB: (1) and (2) recorded with Nick Strutt.

These were mostly pleasant and melodic albums, but little more. His compilation appearances include *Jesus Christ Sitting On Top Of A Hill In The Lake District* (recorded with Nick Strutt) on *The Transatlantic Story* CD box set. (VJ)

Bob and Carolanne Pegg

ALBUMS: 1 HE CAME FROM THE MOUNTAIN
(Trailer LER 3016) 1971 SC
2 AND NOW IT IS SO EARLY - THE SONGS
OF SYDNEY CARTER   (Galliard GAL 4017) 1972 R1

Bob and Carolanne Pegg recorded these two albums before they became **Mr. Fox**. I haven't heard them but they're reputedly pretty essential for folk fans. (VJ)

Carolanne Pegg

ALBUM: 1 CAROLANNE PEGG   (Transatlantic TRA 266) 1973 R1

NB: (1) reissued on CD (Pier PIER CD 503) 1999.

Carolanne (she changed her name from Carole after her marriage to **Bob Pegg** broke up) is backed by some top session musicians on this album, which saw her veering towards country and rock. *Winter People* is usually considered to be its best track and *The Sapphire* is a brooding harmonium-led piece. She later formed Magus with **Graham Bond**, though he met with an untimely death shortly after. (VJ)

Peggy's Leg

Personnel:	VINCENT DUFFY	bs	A
	JIMMY GIBSON	gtr, vcls	A
	DON HARRIS	drms	A
	JIMI SLEVIN	lead gtr, vcls	A

ALBUM: 1(A) GRINILLA (Bunch BAN 2001) 1973 R5

NB: (1) Reissued in 1995 by Kasoa Records, Italy. (1) issued officially on CD, digitally remastered with a bonus track, the live track *Son Of Grinilla* (Kissing Spell KSCD 915) 2001.

45: William Tell Overture (Bunch no #) 1973 R1

This is one of the rarest albums of the seventies. **Peggy's Leg** was an Irish classical rock outfit and their sole album was recorded in just 23 hours. 500 copies were pressed originally and as most were sold to local fans, originals are extremely difficult to locate nowadays, particularly with the inner lyric sheet. The album consisted of six tracks and, aside from an unadventurous cover version of **Love Sculpture**'s *Sabre Dance*, they comprised self-penned compositions which forged frantic heavy rock sections with soft dream-like passages into a series of well structured songs. They also recorded a pretty frantic and indeed demented version of the *William Tell Overture*, which was put out on a 45.

Jimi Slevin, the founder and leader of **Peggy's Leg** joined **Skid Row** when the band split. He later went on to record several solo albums. Don Harris went into session work and played with **David Bowie** in the early eighties. Vincent Duffy sadly committed suicide in 1983.

In 2001 *Grinilla* was reissued officially on CD, digitally remastered and with a bonus track *Son Of Grinilla,* which consists of a live recording featuring a drum solo by Don Harris. The album also contains a fine version of *Sabre Dance.*

Just Another Journey has got another airing on *Psychedelic Salvage Co. Vol. 1* (LP & CD). This is typical of their more melodic, well-structured songs and is very pleasant though too loose to have any commercial potential. *Sabre Dance* is featured on *Psychedelic Salvage Co. Vol. 2* (LP & CD). (VJ)

Pendlefolk

ALBUM: 1 PENDLEFOLK (Folk Heritage FHR 007) 1970 SC

Nothing else known. (VJ)

Penguin Cafe Orchestra

Personnel:	SIMON JEFFES	gtr, bs, ukelele	A
	HELEN LEIBMANN	cello	A
	NEIL RENNIE	ukelele	A
	GAVIN WRIGHT	violin, viola	A
	EMILY YOUNG		A

ALBUM: 1(A) MUSIC FROM THE PENGUIN CAFE (Obscure No. 7) 1976

NB: (1) reissued on CD (EG Records EEGCD 27).

Another group that first appeared on Obscure Records was Simon Jeffes' Orchestra. This album was recorded on location between 1974 - 76 and produced by Steve Nye and Simon Jeffes. It utilises a wide range of instruments including electric piano, ukele, bass, electric guitars, cello, violin, spinet, viola, cheng, cello, ring modulator and mouth percussion. The music is a blend of folk and jazz not easily articulated. (VJ)

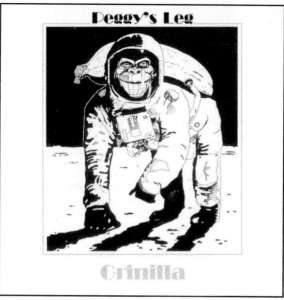

PEGGY'S LEG - Grinilla (CD).

Penny Peeps

Personnel:	DENNY ALEXANDER	gtr, vcls	A
	MARTIN BARRE	sax, flute	A
	MIKE KETLEY	keyb'ds, vcls	A
	BRYAN STEPHENS	bs	A
	MALCOLM TOMLINSON	drms, vcls	A

45s: α Little Man With A Stick/
Model Village (Liberty LBF 15053) 1968 R2
I See The Morning/
Curly, The Knight Of The Road (Liberty LBF 15114) 1968 SC

NB: α has been reissued in a limited edition of 500 and reproduced from the original French jukebox release.

This short-lived outfit was from the Brighton/Hove area of Sussex and had evolved from the mod/soul band **The Motivation** in late 1967. All were members except Alexander, who'd been in **The Clayton Squares**. Operating out of the Shoreline Club in Bognor Regis, they were managed by Mike Clayton, who played the same role for **Mike Stuart Span**, whom they supported at Oxford Street's 100 Club in February 1968.

Little Man With A Stick was a pure pop rendition of a Les Reed song, but *Model Village* was a much more interesting mod-influenced stomper with some good guitar work. A definite **Who** influence here. Their second 45, *I See The Morning*, marked a return to harmony-pop.

\When Alexander left in Spring 1968, the others changed name to **Gethsemane**.

Compilation appearances have included: *Model Village* on *Rubble, Vol. 3 - Nightmares In Wonderland* (LP), *Rubble, Vol. 2* (CD), *We Can Fly, Vol 1* (CD) and on the 4-CD box set *Acid Drops, Spacedust & Flying Saucers*; and *I See The Morning* on *Circus Days Vol. 1 & 2* (CD) and *Circus Days, Vol. 1* (LP). (VJ/NW)

Pentad

45s: Silver Dagger/Nothing But Love (Parlophone R 5288) 1965 SC
Don't Throw It All Away/
Too Many Ways (Parlophone R 5368) 1965
Something Other People Call Love/
It Better Be Me (Parlophone R 5424) 1966

A little known mid-sixties five man act from Surrey. *Don't Throw It All Away* was written by **Unit 4 + 2**'s Tommy Moeller and Brian Parker. (VJ)

Pentangle

Personnel:	TERRY COX	drms, perc	A

BERT JANSCH	gtr, vcls	A
JACQUI McSHEE	vcls	A
JOHN RENBOURN	gtr, vcls, sitar	A
DANNY THOMPSON	bs	A

ALBUMS:
(up to 1976)

HCP
1(A)	THE PENTANGLE	(Transatlantic TRA 162) 1968 SC 21
2(A)	SWEET CHILD (2-LP)	(Transatlantic TRA 178) 1968 SC -
3(A)	BASKET OF LIGHT	(Transatlantic TRA 205) 1969 SC 5
4(A)	CRUEL SISTER	(Transatlantic TRA 228) 1970 SC 51
5(A)	REFLECTION	(Transatlantic TRA 240) 1971 SC -
6(A)	SOLOMON'S SEAL (w/lyric insert)	
		(Reprise K 44197) 1972 R1 -
7(A)	HISTORY BOOK	(Transatlantic TRASAM 23) 1972 SC -
8(A)	PENTANGLING	(Transatlantic TRASAM 29) 1973 SC -
9(A)	PENTANGLE COLLECTION (2-LP)	
		(Transatlantic 85903/4) 1975 -

NB: (1) reissued on CD and (Castle Music CMRDD 132). (2) reissued on CD (Essential! ESM CD 354) 1996 and (Castle Music CMRDD 133). (3) was reissued on Demon/Transatlantic (TRANDEM 7) in 1988 and on again on vinyl (Abraxas 42053) 2005 and CD (Castle CMRCD 207) 2005. (4) reissued on CD (Castle CMRCD 206) 2005. (5) reissued on CD (Castle CMRCD 983) 2004, with excellent sleevenotes from Colin Harper. (6) reissued on CD (Castle CMQCD 555) 2005. A later compilation is *Pentangle, Vol. 1* (Transatlantic TRA 002) 1987 (released in 1986 on CD). *Vol. 2* followed in 1987 (TRA CD 606). There's also a 19-cut compilation CD *People On The Highway* (1968-71) (Demon TDEMCD 12) 1993 which draws on material from their Transatlantic albums in this era. Also relevant is *Collection: Pentangle* (Castle Collector CCSCD 184) 1988. *Live At The BBC* (Band Of Joy BOJCD 013) 1995 couples two BBC studio sessions (from 1970 and 1972) and a 1970 'In Concert' series, which includes a couple of gilt-eyed moments with *Train Song* and *In Time*. *On Air* (Strange Fruit SFRSCD 046) 1997 includes material from an August 1969 studio session for Radio One, a June 1970 'In Concert' session and a 1972 'Soloman's Seal' taped in a BBC studio in Summer 1972. *The Pentangle Family* (Castle/Sanctuary ESACD 931) 2000 is a 2-CD set comprising **Bert Jansch** and **John Renbourn** solo material as well as **Pentangle** material from the 1965-1971 era. Also relevant is *Pentangle Anthology* (Essential ESACD857) 2000 and *Lost Broadcast 1968-1972* (Hux HUX 049).

HCP
45s:	Travellin' Song/Mirage	(Big T BIG 109) 1968 -
(up to 1976)	Once I Had A Sweetheart/	
	I Saw An Angel	(Big T BIG 124) 1969 46
	Light Flight/Cold Mountain	(Big T BIG 128) 1970 43

Forming in 1967, they were something of a folk-rock 'supergroup'. **Bert Jansch** and **John Renbourn** were already highly-regarded soloists, Thompson had been a jazz sessionman and Cox had played a similar role in the blues world. Both had played in **Alexis Korner's Blues Incorporated**. Jacqui McShee was a well known figure in traditional folk circles.

Their debut album was noted for fine acoustic interplay between **Renbourn** and **Jansch** and contained an effective blend of originals and traditional folk material. The follow-up *Sweet Child* was a double set, which again

THE PENTANGLE - The Pentangle (CD).

included a very varied blend of material including two songs written by jazz bassist Charles Mingus, *Haitian Fight Song* and *Goodbye Pork Pie Hat*. *Light Flight* (from their third album *Basket Of Light*) was used as the title track to 'Take Three Girls', a TV drama. Other highlights from that album include a fine version of *Sally Go Round The Roses* and *House Carpenter*. Thereafter, they lost their way and seemed to be marking time on their early seventies albums. When the split came in 1972 **Jansch** and **Renbourn** continued with their solo careers. Danny Thompson went on to work with **John Martyn**, Cox did session work for Charles Aznavour, the French singer, and McShee sang for the **John Renbourn Band** between 1974-81. The original band reformed in 1982 and recorded three further albums in the eighties but that's another story.

The *Pentangle, Vol. 1* and *Vol. 2* compilations concentrate on material from their earlier albums. *Live Broadcasts 1968-1972* is a 2-CD 42-track collection of their BBC recordings and comprises primarily of rare and previously unheard tracks. It contains previously unreleased songs intertwined between classics from all six of their albums. The set is accompanied with a 12-page booklet containing comprehensive sleevenotes, rare photos and a full discography of their BBC recordings.

Various artists compilation appearances include: *Light Flight* on *Maximum '65* (LP) and *Sunshine Day A Taste Of The 70's* (CD); *Once I Had A Sweetheart* on *Electric Psychedelic Sitar Headswirlers Vol. 5* (CD); *Travellin' Song* and *Light Flight* on *The Electric Lemonade Acid Test, Vol. 2* (LP); and *Bells, Light Flight, Once I Had A Sweetheart* and *I Saw An Angel* on *The Transatlantic Story* CD box set. (VJ)

The People

45:     In Ancient Times/Glastonbury   (Deram DM 346) 1971

Basically a folk-rock group, though *Glastonbury* sounds like they picked up some of the vibes of the historic site and veers more towards pop. Pleasant but certainly nothing to get excited about.

Bands of this name also released 45s on Capitol, EMI and RCA.

You can also find *Glastonbury* on *Rubble Vol. 12: Staircase To Nowhere* (LP) and *Rubble Vol. 7* (CD). (VJ)

The People Band

Personnel incl:	LYNN DOBSON		A
	MIKE FIGGIS		A
	CHARLIE HART		A

ALBUM: 1(A)   THE PEOPLE BAND   (Transatlantic TRA 214) 1970 R1

The People Band had links originally to the very long-lived theatre group called the People Show. They had a residency at the North London Arts Lab for ages, and their album, which consists of free-jazz, was produced by **Rolling Stones**' Charlie Watts.

Lynn Dobson went on to play with **The Soft Machine**. Charlie Hart played with **Ronnie Lane** amongst many others, and Mike Figgis, later received an Oscar for best director of 'Leaving Las Vegas'. (GS/VJ)

People Like Us

Personnel:	GEORGE BOWSER	bs	A
	MARK HENSHALL	drms	A
	ROGER HODGSON	gtr	A
	CHRIS TOOKEY	piano	A

45:   α Duck Pond/Send Me No Answers   (Decca F12938) 1969
NB: α unreleased.

This act recorded the above 45, which was withdrawn before release. Hodgson was later in **Argosy** and **Supertramp**. (VJ)

Pepper

45: We'll Make It Together/
     I'm On The Way Down   (Pye 7N 17569) 1968

The six-piece group who recorded this 45 became **Leapy Lee**'s backing group in Autumn 1968. The 'A' side of this 45 was written by Vanda and Young of **The Easybeats**. (VJ)

Billy Pepper and The Pepperpots

ALBUM: 1 MORE MERSEYMANIA   (Allegro ALL 699) 1964
NB. (1) also issued on Hurrah (HUR-ALL 731).

This cash-in album, includes covers of **The Beatles**' *Please Please Me* and *She Loves You*, as well as originals by Bill Shephard and Jimmy Fraser. It was a product of Pickwick International and it's safe to assume that it was the product of a group of session men. No personnel are listed and the cover notes just talk about the Mersey scene (the cover shows screaming girls flashing a bit of underskirt).

The liner notes to the album, make reference to this album being the second in a series (the first being *Merseymania*), and as far as we can tell Allegro was a UK label. (VZ/KP)

Victor Peraino's Kingdom Come

Personnel:			
DAVID CHRISTIAN	gtr		A
HERMAN DALDIN	bs		A
EDWARD HOWLEHAN	drms		A
JOHN LA FLOTTE	flute, gtr, vcls		A
VICTOR PERAINO	keyb'ds, vcls		A
DAVID WILD	drms		A

ALBUM: 1(A) NO MAN'S LAND   (MKC 5121 NIO) 1975 R5

When **Arthur Brown** split his **Kingdom Come** band in 1974 for a solo career, his erstwhile keyboard player **Victor Peraino** formed an Anglo-American offshoot to tour the United States. Only 100 copies of their mellotron-dominated progressive rock album are thought to have been pressed. One of the rarest albums of the seventies, it now sells for well into four figures. (BS/RMJ)

Christine Perfect

Personnel:			
MARTIN DUNSFORD	bs		A
CHRIS HARDING	drms		A
RICK HEYWARD			
(aka RICK BIRKETT)	gtr		A
CHRISTINE PERFECT	piano, vcls		A
TONY 'TOP' TOPHAM	gtr		A

ALBUM: 1(A) CHRISTINE PERFECT   (Blue Horizon 7-63860) 1970 R2
NB: (1) reissued on vinyl (CBS 32198) 1982.

45s: When You Say/
      No Road Is The Right Road   (Blue Horizon 57-3165) 1969 SC
      I'm Too Far Gone/Close To Me (Blue Horizon 57-3172) 1970 SC

These were solo ventures by Christine, who is best known for her involvement in **Fleetwood Mac**. She'd played in a band called The Shades Of Blue, whilst at art college in Birmingham. Later she joined **Chicken Shack** but after marrying John McVie eventually left to become a 'housewife'. In fact in 1969 she'd been voted 'female vocalist of the year' in a 'Melody Maker' poll, which pressurised her to return to the public eye by forming this band. However, her solo career never really got going and by August 1970 she'd been drawn into **Fleetwood Mac**. Her support band included ex-**Yardbirds** member **Tony 'Top' Topham**.

After the band split in April 1970 Hayward joined **Jellybread**. Harding headed for Australia and joined a band called Queen in 1973. Nothing was heard of him after Queen split up. (VJ/JM)

Polly Perkins

ALBUM: 1 LIBERATED WOMAN   (Chapter One CMS 1018) 1973

45s: α I Reckon You/The Girls Are At It Again (Decca F 11583) 1963
         Sweet As Honey/I've Gotta Tell You   (Oriole CB 1869) 1963
         Young Lover/You Too Can Be A Beatle   (Oriole CB 1929) 1963
         Falling In Love Again/
         I Went By Your House Today   (Oriole CB 1979) 1963
NB: α 'A' side credited to Polly Perkins and Billy.

These were solo efforts by **Polly Perkins**, who was also a member of **Academy**. (VJ)

John Perry

45: Nancy Sing Me A Song/Crying Eyes   (Philips 6006 319) 1973

This was a one-off single by **Perry**, who was previously a member of **Summer Wine**. (VJ)

John G. Perry

ALBUM: 1   SUNSET WADING   (Decca SKL 5233) 1976
NB: (1) reissued on CD (Blueprint BP 288CD) 199?

John G. Perry (who had been bassist with **Caravan** and **Gringo**) recorded this largely instrumental tribute to mother earth aided by such luminaries as **Mike Giles** (ex-**King Crimson**) and **Roger Glover** (of **Deep Purple**). (BS)

Persimmon's Peculiar Shades

45: Watchmaker/Coplington   (Major Minor MM 554) 1968 SC

An obscure band whose 45 is now a minor collectable. The 'A' side, a whimsical **Keith West** style slice of 'flower pop' can also be heard on *Incredible Sound Show Stories, Vol. 6* (LP). (VJ)

The Persuasions

45s: I'll Go Crazy/Try Me   (Columbia DB 7560) 1965 SC
      Big Brother/Deep Down Love   (Columbia DB 7700) 1965 SC
      La, La, La, La, La/Opportunity (Columbia DB 7859) 1986 SC

There was also an American band of this name who had albums released over here on Straight and Island. The above three 45s are all minor collectables now. The first one, *I'll Go Crazy*, was a James Brown favourite.

CHRISTINE PERFECT - Christine Perfect (LP).

La, La, La, La, La can also be found on *Sixties Lost And Found, Vol. 1* (LP). (VJ)

Pesky Gee!

Personnel:	BOB BOND	bs	A
	CLIVE BOX	drms	A
	JIMMY GANNON	gtr	A
	KAY GARRETT	vcls	A
	CLIVE JONES	sax	A
	JESS TAYLOR	organ	A
	KIP TREVOR	vcls	A

ALBUM: 1(A) EXCLAMATION MARK　　(Pye NSPL 18293) 1969 R2

NB: (1) reissued on CD (Castle CMRCD 256) and on vinyl (Earmark 41043) 2005, with their Pye 45 as a bonus.

45: Where Is My Mind/
A Place Of Heartbreak　　(Pye 7N 17708) 1969 R1

This youthful act started in Leicester's soul clubs, playing alongside visiting American acts as well as emerging psych bands like **the Syn**. Malcolm Rabbit, who'd just had his song *Baby I Need You* recorded by the **Curiosity Shoppe** on Deram, spotted them playing in Warrington and introduced them to his manager, Patrick Meehan, who got them a deal on Pye. *Where Is My Mind* was a Vanilla Fudge cover. Their inconsistent album, which was recorded in four hours straight, consists of jazz-tinged progressive rock, and lyrics that hint at a preoccupation with the occult. Indeed in 1970 the band became **Black Widow**. The album contains a lengthy version of **Donovan's** *Season Of The Witch* as well as covers of *Born To Be Wild*, *Piece of My Heart* and *Dharma For One*. Much later in 1980 they made a 45 as Agony Bag. The **Pesky Gee!** album and 45 are both significant collectables now.

Where Is My Mind has been compiled on *Progressive Music* (LP) and on *Hot Smoke & Sassafras - Psychedelic Pstones, Vol 1* (CD). (VJ/RMJ)

Peter

45: Peace/Valves　　(Sonet SON 2012) 1970

This is Peter Gosling from Bermondsey, London. He'd previously played in **Denny Mitchel and The Soundsations**, **Preachers**, and **Moon's Train** and was later in **Renaissance**. He enjoyed a continental hit with this 45. (VJ)

Peter and Gordon

Personnel:	PETER ASHER	vcls	A
	GORDON WALLER	vcls	A

HCP

ALBUMS: 1(A) PETER AND GORDON
　　　　　　　(Columbia 33SX 1630/SCX 3518) 1964 SC 18
2(A) IN TOUCH WITH PETER AND GORDON
　　　　　　　(Columbia 33SX 1660/SCX 3532) 1964 SC -
3(A) HURTIN' N' LOVIN'
　　　　　　　(Columbia 33SX 1761/SCX 3565) 1965 SC -
4(A) PETER AND GORDON (Columbia S(C)X 6045) 1966 SC -
5(A) SOMEWHERE　　(Columbia S(C)X 6097) 1966 SC -
6( ) GORDON　　　　(Vertigo 6360 069) 1972 -

NB: (6) **Gordon Waller** solo album. (1) also in mono (33SX 1630). (2) also in mono (33SX 1660). (3) also in mono (33SX 1761). (2) reissued on CD and with both mono and stereo mixes on one disc (EMI DORIG 112) 1997. They released several albums in the US. Recommended compilations are:- *The Best Of* (EMI NUT 8) 1977 (also reissued in 1987), *World Without Love* (See For Miles CM 106) 1983, *The Hits And More* (EMI EMS 1146) and *The Best Of Peter and Gordon* (C5 202) 1987. They also had one track. *A World Without Love*, on the live compilation LP, *Tribute To Michael Holliday* (Columbia 33SX 1635) in 1964. A more recent compilation is *The Best Of Peter and Gordon* (Rhino RZ 70748) 1991. Also on CD there's *Best Of The EMI Years: Peter And Gordon* (EMI CDEMS 1409) 1991.

PESKY GEE - Exclamation Mark (CD).

HCP
EPs: 1 JUST FOR YOU　(Columbia SEG 8337) 1964 SC 20
2 NOBODY I KNOW　(Columbia SEG 8348) 1964 SC -

NB: (1) **Peter and Gordon** and **Freddie and The Dreamers** contributed two tracks each to this EP.

HCP
45s: A World Without Love/If I Were You (Columbia DB 7225) 1964 1
Nobody I Know/
You Don't Have To Tell Me　(Columbia DB 7292) 1964 10
I Don't Want To See You Again/
I Would Buy　　(Columbia DB 7356) 1964 -
I Go To Pieces/Love Me Baby　(Columbia DB 7407) 1964 -
True Love Ways/If You Wish　(Columbia DB 7524) 1965 2
To Know You Is To Love You/
I Told You So　　(Columbia DB 7617) 1965 5
Baby I'm Yours/When The Black Of
Your Eyes Turns To Grey　(Columbia DB 7729) 1965 19
Woman/Wrong From The Start　(Columbia DB 7834) 1966 28
Don't Pity Me/To Show I Love You　(Columbia DB 7951) 1966 -
Lady Godiva/Morning's Calling　(Columbia DB 8003) 1966 16
Knight In Rusty Amour/
The Flower Lady　　(Columbia DB 8075) 1966 -
Sunday For Tea/
Start Trying Someone Else　(Columbia DB 8159) 1967 -
The Jokers/Red, Cream and Velvet　(Columbia DB 8198) 1967 -
I Feel Like Going Out/
The Quest For The Holy Grail　(Columbia DB 8398) 1968 -
You've Had Better Times/
Sipping My Wine　　(Columbia DB 8451) 1968 -
I Can Remember (Not Too Long Ago)/
Hard Time Rainy Day　　(Columbia DB 8585) 1969 -
Reissues: Lady Godiva/Someone Ain't Right/
True Love Ways (PS)　　(EMI EMI 2645) 1977 -
A World Without Love/
Nobody I Know　　(Old Gold OG 9381) 1983 -
A World Without Love/Woman　(EMI Golden 45s G45 42) 1984 -

This was a pleasant, unassuming pop duo.

Peter Asher was born in London on 22nd June 1944, the son of a Wimpole Street doctor. Gordon was a doctor's son, too, although his mother had evacuated north to Braemer in Scotland during the war, where he was born on 4th June 1945. The two met at Westminster Boys' School. They eventually secured a recording contract with EMI and since **Paul McCartney** was going out with Peter's sister the duo pestered him to write them a song. The result was *World Without Love* and it gave them an instant No 1. They followed up with another **McCartney** composition, *Nobody I Know*, which also made No 10. However, their third **McCartney** composition, *I Don't Want To See You Again*, flopped completely. They wrote some of their 'B' sides and bounced back with a cover of Buddy Holly's *True Love Ways*, which made No 2 in the UK and No 14 in the

USA. They were enormously successful in the USA where Capitol issued ten albums of their material plus a 'Best Of' collection in just four years. In 1966 their version of *Lady Godiva* won them some notoriety, getting banned in Lady Godiva's home town of Coventry, but their music didn't really suit the psychedelic era and they split in the Autumn of 1968.

Peter became A&R manager at **The Beatles**' newly-formed Apple Records and later managed and produced **James Taylor**, whom he discovered. **Gordon Waller** embarked on a solo career and played Pharaoh in the 'Joseph and The Amazing Technicolour Dreamcoat' movie in the mid-seventies. Today Peter is an LA-based producer and Gordon, a South Midlands businessman.

Of their compilations *The Hits And More* concentrates on their biggest UK and US hits (as its title suggests). Among its 16 tracks are four not included on the earlier 17-track See For Miles compilation, but none are particularly good and the See For Miles one is marginally the better of the two. The C5 compilation has 19 tracks, including all their **McCartney** covers and some good versions of Everly Brothers' songs.

Various artists compilation appearances have included: *Nobody I Know* and *If You Wish* on *Liverpool '65* (LP); *Nobody I Know*, *Woman*, *A World Without Love* and *I Don't Want To See You Again* on *Songs Lennon And McCartney Gave Away* (LP); *Soft As Dawn* (1964) and *Tears Don't Stop* (1965) on *Outta' Sight* (LP); *A World Without Love* on the 2-CD set *Sixties Summer Love, Love Power* (CD), and on *Beat Generation - Ready Steady Go* (CD); and *I Feel Like Going Out* on *Colour Me Pop, Vol 3* (CD). (VJ)

Peter and The Headliners

Personnel:			
	BRIAN CORNWALL	gtr	A
	VIC GILLAM	sax	A
	DAVE GREEN	bs	A
	MARTIN JENNER	lead gtr	A
	PETER SENIOR	vcls	A
	CARL SIMMONS	drms	A

45s:	Don't Cry Little Girl/It Was Love	(Decca F 11980) 1964 SC
	Tears And Kisses/	
	I've Got My Reasons	(Decca F 12035) 1964 SC

This group also recorded as Count Down and Zeros. Peter Senior came from Brighton originally. A Peter-less Headliners also made at least two singles for Decca in 1965. Jenner and Green went on to session work and then joined **Deep Feeling**. (VJ/JM)

Peter and The Persuaders

Personnel:			
	ALAN BENNETT	bs	A
	LONNIE COOK	ld gtr	A
	GRAHAM COOPER	gtr	A
	PETER GROCOTT	vcls	A
	DAVID IONS	drms	A

EP:	1	The Wanderer/ Wine Glass Rock/Oh My Soul/	
		Cross My Heart	(Oak RGJ 197) 1965 R1

Stoke-on-Trent was this band's home patch and they specialised in cover versions of late fifties rock'n'rollers like *The Wanderer*, which was included on their four-track EP. *Cross My Heart*, which was written by local singer Jackie Trent who was married to Tony Hatch, was an uncharacteristic excursion into beat-pop territory.

David Ions went on to become general manager of DJM's publishing branch and Lonnie Cook works for BBC Radio Stoke.

Cross My Heart can also be heard on *Story Of Oak Records* (2-LP). (VJ)

Peter and The Wolves

Personnel incl: JOHN PANTRY

45s:	Little Girl/Lost And Found	(MGM MGM 1352) 1967 SC
	Lantern Light/	
	Break Up, Break Down	(MGM MGM 1374) 1968 SC

Julia/Birthday	(MGM MGM 1397) 1968 SC
Woman On My Mind/	
The Old And The New	(MGM MGM 1452) 1968 R1
Something In The Way She Moves/	
The Lady And Me	(UPC UPC 104) 1969

This group was later been known as **Factory** and also released a 45 using the monicker **Norman Conquest**. Their final 45 was also released on a US-only album as by **Wolfe**.

Pantry went on to release an album in 1972.

Little Girl is typical British pop-sike with a distinctive fairground organ backing, whilst *Lantern Light* is twee pop. They also recorded some **Beatles**' covers (*Julia/Birthday*) and their final 'A' side was a **James Taylor** cover.

Compilation appearances have included: *Birthday*, *Lantern Light* (two versions), *Woman On My Mind*, *Break Up-Break Down*, *Little Girl Lost And Found*, *The Old And The New* and *Julie* on *The Upside Down World Of John Pantry* (LP); *Smokey Wood* (previously unreleased) on *Circus Days, Vol. 6* (CD) and *Incredible Sound Show Stories, Vol. 6* (LP); *Little Girl Lost And Found* and *Lantern Light* on *Circus Days Vol's 4 & 5* (CD) and *Hard Up Heroes, Vol. 6* (CD); *Little Girl Lost And Found* on *Circus Days, Vol. 4* (LP) and on *Lovely Summer Days* (CD); and *Lantern Light* on *Circus Days, Vol. 5* (LP). (VJ/MJ)

Peter B's (aka Peter B's Looners)

Personnel:			
	DAVE AMBROSE	bs	AB
	PETE BARDENS	organ	AB
	MICK FLEETWOOD	drms	AB
	MICK PARKER	gtr	A
	PETER GREEN	gtr	B

45:	If You Wanna Be Happy/	
	Jodrell Blues	(Columbia DB 7862) 1966 R2

Following his work with **The Cheynes**, **Pete Bardens** put together this instrumental unit with Mick Fleetwood. Mick Parker left before the above 45 was recorded, to be replaced by the great **Peter Green**. Indeed the 45, which is now much sought-after, was **Green**'s recording debut. Prior to **The Cheynes**, **Bardens** had played with Hamilton King's Blues Messengers. Later he formed **Shotgun Express** and then he recorded two solo albums. He also worked with **Them** and numerous others. He released a single with the short-lived outfit **Village** before forming **Camel**. (MWh)

Peter's Faces

Personnel:	PETER COLEMAN	drms	ABC

INCREDIBLE SOUND SHOW STORIES VOL. 6 (Comp LP) including Peter and The Wolves.

TONY HALL	gtr, sax	ABC
JOHN McDONALD	lead gtr	A C
PETER NELSON	vcls, bs	ABC
ANTION MEREDITH	ld gtr	B

45s: Why Did You Bring Him To The Dance/
She's In Love (Piccadilly 7N 35178) 1964
Try A Little Love My Friend/
I Don't Care (Piccadilly 7N 35196) 1964
Just Like Romeo And Juliet/Wait (Piccadilly 7N 35205) 1964 SC
De-Boom-Lay-Boom/Suzie Q (Piccadilly 7N 35225) 1965

This beat outfit was fronted by **Peter Nelson** who later embarked on a solo career. He was also part of **The Flowerpot Men** and **White Plains**. *Just Like Romeo and Juliet* had been a US hit for The Reflections.

Antion Meredith (aka Vic Briggs) played with them from October 1964 to February 1965, before he left to join **Dusty Springfield**.

Compilation appearances include: *Suzie Q* on *The R&B Era, Vol. 2* (LP & CD); *(Just Like) Romeo and Juliet* on *Ripples, Vol. 5* (CD); and *I Don't Care* on *Hippy Hippy Shake* (CD). (MWh)

Mark Peters and The Silhouettes

Personnel:
MALLY ASTON	gtr	ABCDEF
KEN DALLAS	vcls	AB
DAVE MAY	bs	ABCDEF
ROD McCLELLAND	lead gtr	ABCDE
BOB O'HANLON	drms	A D
GEOFF LLOYD	drms	B
MARK PETERS (FLEMING)	vcls	CDEF
STEVE FLEMING	keyb'ds	CDEF
BRIAN JOHNSON	drms	C
TONY SANDERS	drms	EF

NB: Line-ups 'A' and 'B' as Ken Dallas and The Silhouettes.

45s: Fragile (Handle With Care)/Janie (Oriole CB 1836) 1963 R1
Cindy's Gonna Cry/Show Her (Oriole CB 1909) 1964 R1
Don't Cry For Me/I Told You So (Piccadilly 7N 35207) 1964 SC

A Merseybeat sextet. In addition to releasing these three 45s they also had a cut, *Someday (When I'm Gone From You)*, included on the 1963 *This Is Merseybeat* (LP) and Realm's *Group Beat '63* (LP) gave a further airing to their first 'A' side, *Fragile (Handle With Care)*.

Mark Peters was later in **The Rats**.

Other compilation appearances have included: *Someday (When I'm Gone From You)* and *Fragile* on *Let's Stomp!* (LP); *Someday (When I'm Gone From You)* on *The Exciting New Liverpool Sound* (LP) and *Mersey Beat 1962-1964* (2-LP); *Don't Cry For Me* on *Piccadilly Story* (CD); and *Don't Cry For Me* and *I Told You So* on *What About Us* (CD) and *Merseybeat Nuggets, Vol. 2*. (VJ)

Phase 4

Personnel incl: MIKE BATT — vcls, piano

45s: What Do You Say About That/
Think I'll Sit Down And Cry (Decca F 12327) 1966 SC
What Do You Say About That/
I'm Gonna Sit Down And Cry (Fab FAB 1) 1966
Man Am I Worried?/Listen To The Blues (Fab FAB 6) 1967 R1

This obscure Newcastle group who recorded on the Fab label is most notable for including **Mike Batt**, who was later behind The Wombles. *Listen To The Blues*, is an organ-driven R&B number.

Compilation appearances have included: *Think I'll Sit Down And Cry* on *That Driving Beat* (CD) and *Broken Dreams, Vol. 4* (LP); and *Listen To The Blues* on *Diggin' For Gold, Vol. 3* (LP & CD) and *Incredible Sound Show Stories, Vol. 1* (LP & CD). (VJ)

INCREDIBLE SOUND SHOW STORIES VOL. 1 (Comp CD) featuring Phase 4.

The Philadelphia Flyers

Personnel incl: LES WALKER

45: Hot Line/Oh Girl (GM GMS 020) 1974

A sort of J. Geils Band pub-rock outfit. Les Walker (ex-**Warm Dust**) joined after the 45 was released. (VJ)

Shawn Philips

ALBUMS: 1 I'M A LONER (Columbia SX1748) 1965 R3
(selective) 2 SHAWN (Columbia SX 6006) 1966 R3

45: Stargazer/Woman Mind (Parlophone R 5606) 1967 R1
(selective)

Itinerant American singer-songwriter **Philips** fetched up in Britain in the mid-sixties and made two very rare albums for Columbia's Lansdowne series, which was more usually associated with jazz. They're pretty uninspiring mixtures of traditional and contemporary folk material, though his guitar playing is superb. His equally rare 45 is very nice sitar-based psychedelia, especially the 'A' side, a cosmic song with tablas and good guitar. One of the first pop musicians to learn the sitar, he was great friends with **Donovan**, and the pair wrote several songs together. Philips later returned to America and recorded a string of well-regarded singer-songwriter albums.

Stargazer can also be heard on *Justafixation* (LP). (VJ/RMJ)

Gregory Phillips

45s: Angie/Please Believe Me (Pye 7N 15546) 1963
α Everybody Knows/Closer To Me (Pye 7N 15593) 1964
Don't Bother Me/
Make Sure That You're Mine (Pye 7N 15633) 1964
Down In The Boondocks/
That's The One (Immediate IM 004) 1965 SC

NB: α with **The Remo Four**.

Gregory Phillips was also a member of **The Remo Four**. Born in Greys, Essex in 1948, he was also a teenage film actor. His third single for Pye *Don't Bother Me* was the first **George Harrison** penned song ever released. *Down In The Boondocks* was a Billy Joe Royal song and featured backing tracks by **Jimmy Page**. The flip was written by **Jimmy Page** and **Andrew Loog Oldham**.

Compilation appearances include: *Down In The Boondocks* on *Jimmy Page Studio Works 1964-1968* (CD) and *Immediate Single Collection, Vol. 5* (CD); *Angie, Please Believe Me, Down In The Boondocks* and *That's The*

One on *Jimmy Page - Hip Young Guitar Slinger* (2-CD); *Please Believe Me* and *Angie* on *Jimmy's Back Pages - The Early Years* (CD); and *That's The One* on *Immediate Single Collection, Vol. 3* (CD). (VJ/MWn)

Warren Phillips and The Rockets

ALBUM: 1   THE WORLD OF ROCK 'N' ROLL
(mono/stereo)   (Decca (S)PA 43) 1969 SC

This album features covers of well known rock 'n' roll songs. The band was in fact **The Savoy Brown Blues Band** who used this pseudonym for a one album deal. (VJ)

Philwit and Pegasus

Personnel incl: JOHN CARTER   A
                  PETER LEE STIRLING   A

ALBUM: 1(A)   PHILWIT AND PEGASUS
                              (Chapter One CHSR 805) 1970 R1

NB: (1) reissued on CD (RPM BC 252) 2003.

45s: α   And She Came - Final Thought/
            Paupers Song   (Chapter One CH 130) 1970
            And I Try/Pauper's Son   (Chapter One CH 131) 1970
            The Elephants Song/
            Pseudo Phoney Mixed Up Croney (Chapter One CH 137) 1970

NB: α withdrawn.

A lovely orchestrated harmony-pop concept album, devised by **Mark Wirtz** with in-house Decca man Les Reed and similar to **The World Of Oz** album. John Carter, Roger Greenaway and **Peter Lee Stirling** appear among the featured vocalists on tracks like *Philwit's Phantasies* and *To Pegasus With Love*.

Elephant Song has been compiled on *Collecting Peppermint Clouds, Vol. 1* (LP). (VJ/AH)

Phoenix (1)

Personnel: LOUIS La ROSE   drms   AB
             MIKE PAICE   sax   AB
             ADRIAN PIETRYGA   gtr   AB
             ROY St. JOHN   AB
             CHARLIE SINCLAIR   bs   A
             STEVE WATERS   clarinet   AB
             DAVID BARKER   keyb'ds   A
             CHRIS BIRKIN   bs   B

45s: Pictures Of You/Thrill Me With Your Love (Dawn DNS 1110 1975
       Black Is Black/Beggin'   (Pye 7N 45511 1975

In addition to **Phoenix**, **Roy St. John** also made some recordings in his own right. Although from the U.S. he was mainly active in the U.K. circuit. (GB)

Phoenix (2)

Personnel: ROBERT HENRIT   drms   A
             JIM RODFORD   bs, keyb'ds   A
             JOHN VERITY   vcls, gtr   A

ALBUM: 1(A)   PHOENIX   (CBS 81621) 1976
(up to
1976)

Formed after **Argent** split, **Phoenix** played a melodious brand of hard-rock but split after a year. The band eventually reformed in 1979 without Jim Rodford but added Michael des Barres (ex-Silverhead), Ray Minhinnett (ex-**Highway**) and Bruce Turgeon and released the *In Full View* album. (BS)

Pica

45s: Take The Barriers Down/Insurance Man (Polydor 2058.056) 1970
       Rainbow Chaser/Ad Lib   (Philips 6006 129) 1971

The 'A' side of the first 45 was produced by **Patrick Campbell-Lyons** of **Nirvana**. He co-wrote the song with a certain Kelly and Ray (whoever they were). **Nirvana** had earlier recorded *Rainbow Chaser* and this project was **Nirvana** recording under another name. (VJ)

Pic and Bill

45s: All I Want Is You/It's Not You   (Page One POF 024) 1967
       This Is It/Nobody But My Baby   (Page One POF 037) 1967
       Sad World Without You/Just A Tear   (Page One POF 052) 1968

An obscure late sixties duo. (VJ)

Piccadilly Line

Personnel: ROD EDWARDS   vcls, gtr, keyb'ds   AB
             ROGER HAND   gtr, vcls   A
             KEITH HODGE   drms   A
             NORRIE McLEAN   bs   AB
             JAN BARBER   vcls   B
             GEORGE BUTLER   drms, vcls   B

ALBUM: 1(A)   THE HUGE WORLD OF EMILY SMALL
                           (CBS (S)BPG 63129) 1967 R2

NB: (1) reissued on CD (Lightning Tree LIGHT FLASH CD) 2005 with bonus tracks and on vinyl (Lightning Tree LIGHT FLASH LP) 2005 with bonus tracks.

45s: α   At The Third Stroke/
           How Could You Say (You're Leaving Me)   (CBS 2785) 1967
           Emily Small (The Huge World Thereof)/
           Gone, Gone, Gone   (CBS 2958) 1967 SC
       α   Yellow Rainbow/Evenings With Corrina   (CBS 3595) 1968
           Evenings With Corrina/My Best Friend   (CBS 3743) 1968

NB: α as Picadilly Line. Also issued as a demo with a different flip side *I Know, She Believes*.

Their much sought-after album has a superb 'period' cover and consists of whimsical toytown pop-psych, which some liken to **World Of Oz**, **Kaleidoscope** and early **Bee Gees**. The recent reissue is taken from the master tapes and includes bonus tracks, some of which are previously unreleased.

PIGSTY HILL LIGHT ORCHESTRA - Piggery Jokery (LP).

In the early seventies Edwards and Hand formed **Edwards Hand**. Of their 45s, *Yellow Rainbow* was written by **Graham Nash**. Keith Hodge later worked with **Duncan Browne**, Suzi Quatro and **Deke Leonard**.

Compilation appearances include: *Yellow Rainbow* on *Psychedelic Voyage Vol. 1* (LP) and *Psychedelic Voyage* (CD); *How Could You Say (You're Leaving Me)* on *Spinning Wheel* (CD); and *At The Third Stroke* on *Pop-In, Vol 1* (CD) and *Fading Yellow, Vol 4* (CD). (VJ/SR)

Nick Pickett

ALBUM: 1   SILVERSLEEVES
(Reprise/Warner Brothers K 44172) 1972 SC

45:    America/Lady Luck   (Warner Bros WB 14156) 1972

This was a later solo effort by violinist **Nick Pickett**, who is better-known as a member of **The John Dummer Blues Band**.

This solo album is a folk/blues offering. (VJ)

Pickettywitch

Personnel: POLLY BROWN   vcls   A
MAGGIE FARRAN   vcls   A
and various backing musicians.

ALBUM: 1(A)   PICKETTYWITCH   (Pye NSPL 18357) 1970
NB: *That Same Old Feeling* (CD) (Castle Music CMRCD 265) 2005 is the first CD release of their work and includes all their Pye recordings from 1969 to 1973.

			HCP
45s:	You Got Me So I Don't Know/		
	Soloman Grundy	(Pye 7N 17799) 1969	-
	That Same Old Feeling/		
	Maybe We've Been Loving Too Long	(Pye 7N 17887) 1970	5
	(It's Like A) Sad Kinda Movie/Times	(Pye 7N 17951) 1970	16
	Baby I Won't Let You Down/		
	Please Bring Her Back Home	(Pye 7N 45002) 1970	27
	Waldo P Emerson Jones/There He Goes	(Pye 7N 45035) 1970	-
	Summertime Feelin'/Dreamin'	(Pye 7N 45080) 1970	-
	Bring A Little Light Into My World/		
	Dream World	(Pye 7N 45096) 1970	-
	Number Wonderful/Point Of No Return	(Pye 7N 45126) 1970	-
	The Power And The Glory/		
	Living By The Gun	(Pye 7N 45254) 1973	-
	Love Me Just A Little Bit More/		
	Suddenly	(Penny Farthing PEN 879) 1975	-
Reissue:	That Same Old Feeling/		
	(Flip by different artist)	(Old Gold OG 9470) 1985	-

This group, which was named after a Cornish village, first caught the eye in 1969 when they appeared on ITV's 'Opportunity Knocks' singing *Soloman Grundy*, which was composed and arranged by Tony Macauley and John McLeod. The song appeared on the flip side to their debut 45, but it was the follow-up, *That Same Old Feeling*, that took them into the Charts. It also got to No 67 in the USA. A string of mostly Macauley-McLeod compositions followed but failed to attain the same commercial success and the group ended up on the cabaret circut, before splitting up. **Polly Brown** later went solo and got to No 43 in the UK Charts in 1974 with *Up In A Puff Of Smoke*. In the US it fared better climbing to No 16. She was later in a soul-reggae duo called Sweet Dreams.

That Same Old Feeling is the first time their recordings have been consigned to CD. On offer is a fully remastered collection of all their Pye recordings from 1969 to 1973 including the title track and *It's Kinda Like A Sad Old Movie*. The CD is accompanied by a booklet with sleevenotes from vocalist **Polly Browne** and rare memorabilia.

You'll also find *That Same Old Feeling* on *Hits Of The 70's* (CD), *Sunshine Day A Taste Of The 70's* (CD) and *Love Power* (CD); whilst *Sad Old Kinda Movie* has resurfaced on *Hits Of The 70's Vol 2* (CD). (VJ)

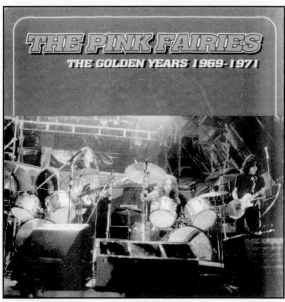

PINK FAIRIES - The Golden Years (CD).

The Pickwicks

Personnel incl: JIMMY PAGE

45s: Apple Blossom Time/
I Don't Wanna Tell You Again   (Decca F 11901) 1964 SC
You're Old Enough/Hello Lady   (Decca F 11957) 1964 SC
Little By Little/
I Took My Baby Home   (Warner Bros WB 151) 1965 R2

This Coventry band started as The Echo Four, but then Larry Page became their manager and changed their image. The group apparently wore Mr. Pickwick costumes and wigs on stage! The flip to their first 45, *Hello Lady*, is an R&B style song, but it's their Warner Brothers 45 which is now quite a significant collectable, probably partly because **Jimmy Page** played on it. *Little By Little*, was a **Rolling Stones** track and the flip, a **The Kinks** tune.

Compilation appearances have included: *Little By Little* on *James Patrick Page, Session Man* (2-LP) and *James Patrick Page: Session Man, Vol. 1* (LP & CD); *I Took My Baby Home* on *James Patrick Page: Session Man, Vol. 2* (LP & CD); *Little By Little* and *I Took My Baby Home* on *Nowhere Men, Vol. 4* (CD); and *Hello Lady* on *English Freakbeat, Vol. 5* (LP & CD). (VJ/MWh)

The Pigeon Flyers

45:    The Heaven We Shared Together/
Keep On Sayin'   (Columbia DB 8449) 1968

A very obscure five man act. (VJ)

Piggleswick Folk

ALBUM: 1   PIG IN THE MIDDLE   (Acorn CF 256) 1977 SC

A middle-of-the-road folk album. (VJ)

Pigsty Hill Light Orchestra

Personnel:	BARRY BACK	gtr, vcls, kazoo	AB
	DAVE CREECH	trumpet, vcls, jug	ABCDE
	ANDY LEGGETT	vcls, gtr, brass	ABC
	JOHN TURNER	vcls, bs	A
	BILL COLE	bs	B
	JOHN HAYS	perc, vcls	CDE
	DAVE PASKETT	vcls, gtr	C
	HENRY DAVIES	bs, brass	D

PINK FAIRIES - What A Bunch Of Sweeties (LP).

CHRIS NEWMAN	gtr, bs	D
ROBERT GREENFIELD	gtr	E
RICKY GOLD	bs	E

ALBUMS: 1(A) PHLOP!   (Village Thing VTS 1) 1970 SC
(up to   2(B) PIGGERY JOKERY   (Village Thing VTS 8) 1971 SC
1976)   3(E) THE PIGSTY HILL LIGHT ORCHESTRA (Phlo 001) 1976

This folk group formed at the start of 1968. Its members had all played previously in the UK folk groups. Back and Leggett had been together in The Alligator Jug Thumpers; Creech had played in The Elastic Band and Turner joined from The Downsiders. Basing their music loosely on twenties and thirties jazz and blues they used a range of unusual instruments to create a highly original sound. Their debut album *Phlop!* aroused much interest and considerable acclaim. They made their first of what what would be many appearances at the Cambridge Folk Festival the following year. Turner had left in 1970 and Bill Cole joined the group for a short while, playing on *Piggery Jokery*. *Sweet Miss Emmaline* from this album can also be heard on the *Us* (LP) sampler. Back left in 1972 and was replaced by Paskert and Hays. Indeed, they experienced several line-up changes in the mid-seventies, but still benefited from a very loyal following. In the final analysis, though, the lack of a stable line-up may account for why they failed to fulfil their initial promise. Later line-ups of the band were still active in the late eighties and early nineties. (VJ)

Pilot

Personnel: BILLY LYALL   synth, piano, flute, vcls   AB
            DAVID PATON   bs, vcls   ABC
            STUART TOSH   drms   ABC
            IAN BAIRNSON   gtr   BC

                                                      HCP
ALBUMS: 1(B) FROM THE ALBUM OF THE SAME NAME
(up to   (EMI EMC 3045) 1974 -
1976)   2(B) SECOND FLIGHT   (EMI EMC 3075) 1975 48
        3(C) MORIN HEIGHTS   (EMI EMA 779) 1976 -

NB: There's also *Best Of Pilots* (EMI NUT 29) 1980. (1), (2) and (3) reissued on CD (See For Miles C5CD 567, C5CD 568 and C5CD 569 respectively) in 1991. *The Best Of Pilot* is also available on CD (C5CD 563) 1991. *A's, B's and Rarities* (EMI Gold 72435 60224 23) 2005 is a good introduction to their material.

                                                      HCP
45s: Just A Smile/Don't Speak Loudly   (EMI EMI 2171) 1974 -
(up to Magic/Just Let Me Be   (EMI EMI 2217) 1974 11
1976)   January/Never Give Up   (EMI EMI 2255) 1975 1
        Call Me Round/Do Me Good   (EMI EMI 2287) 1975 34
        Just A Smile/Are You In Love   (EMI EMI 2338) 1975 31
        Lady Luck/Dear Artist   (EMI EMI 2377) 1975 -
        Running Water/First After Me   (EMI EMI 2457) 1976 -
        Canada/Mover   (EMI EMI 2490) 1976 -

        Penny In My Pocket/Steps   (EMI EMI 2530) 1976 -
Reissue: January/Magic   (Old Gold OG 9723) 1987 -

Pilot came together in Edinburgh, Scotland in 1973. Paton and Lyall had previously played in teenybop outfit **The Bay City Rollers**. They recorded a series of demos in London eventually getting signed up by EMI. A fourth Scotsman, Ian Bairnson, a session guitarist who came from the Shetland Isles, was added to the line-up at this stage.

They played a lightweight but well-crafted form of pop. Twenty years on they are remembered for good tunes like *Magic* and *January*, the latter was a No 1 here. In the States their biggest hit was *Magic*, which got to No 5. After a couple more minor hits - *Call Me Round* and *Just A Smile* (the latter was a reissue of their first 45) - their sales soon plummeted and they went their separate ways. A final album, *Two's A Crowd* (Arista SPARTY 1014) was released in 1977 along with three further 45s which made little impression. Bairnson and Paton both went into session work, Tosh joined **10cc** and Lyall recorded a solo album *Solo Casting*. Lyall later joiner Dollar but died in late 1989 of an A.I.D.S.-related illness.

More recently Ian and David have re-recorded their 1977 album *Two's A Crowd*. *A's, B's and Rarities* is a 22-track compilation that includes *Magic* and *January* as well as four tracks never issued before on CD and two rare David Paton solo tracks.

Magic and *Just a Smile* can also be heard on the 3-CD box set *Radio Caroline Calling - 70's Flashback.* (VJ/HM)

Mike Pinder

ALBUM: 1   THE PROMISE   (Threshold THS 18) 1976

45:    Carry On/I Only Want To Love You   (Threshold TH 23) 1976

A solo effort from **The Moody Blues** bass player. (BS/VJ)

Pineapple Chunks

45:    Drive My Car/Dream About   (Mercury MF 922) 1965

A London band who recorded a cover version of **The Beatles'** *Drive My Car* but with no success. The 45 was produced by Mike Hurst. (VJ)

The Pineapple Truck

A mysterious short-lived group that played at the Electric Garden (Middle Earth) during early 1967. It's thought that they lasted until 1969 and were probably Cambridge University students. David Frost, who had some involvement with booking bands at the University was the leader of the band. (JN/JA)

PINK FAIRIES - Live At Wheeley 1971 (LP).

PINK FAIRIES - Kings Of Oblivion (CD).

Pinkerton's Assorted Colours

Personnel:	BARRIE BERNARD	bs	A
	DAVE HOLLAND	drms	AB
	SAMUEL 'PINKERTON' KEMP	autoharp, vcls	AB
	TOM LONG	gtr	AB
	TONY NEWMAN	gtr	AB
	IAN COLEMAN	bs	B
	STEVE JONES	lead gtr	B

			HCP
45s:	Mirror Mirror/She Don't Care	(Decca F 12307) 1965	9
	Don't Stop Loving Me Baby/Will Ya?	(Decca F 12377) 1966	50
α	Magic Rocking Horse/It Ain't Right	(Decca F 12493) 1966	SC -
α	Mum And Dad/On A Street Car	(Pye 7N 17327) 1967	-
β	There's Nobody I'd Sooner Love/		
	Look At Me	(Pye 7N 17414) 1967	-
β	Kentucky Woman/Behind The Mirror	(Pye 7N 17574) 1968	-
Reissue:	Mirror Mirror / (Flip by different artist)	(Old Gold OG 9357) 1983	-

NB: α as Pinkerton's Colours. β as Pinkerton's. There is a double CD, *Flight Recorder*, which contains unreleased and, in some cases, unfinished Decca material on one disc and there's some late Pye material on the other.

This group were originally known as **The Liberators** and formed in Rugby in 1964. They were discovered by **The Fortunes**' manager Reg Calvert and signed to Decca. Calvert chose their name. As there was no colour TV he insisted on the 'assorted' tag, which the group particularly hated and hassled him to drop until the day he died, subsequently hassling his successors until they agreed.

They are best known for their first pop single, *Mirror Mirror*, which was something of a one hit wonder. **Tony Newman** had written it and Reg Calvert was doing all he could to revamp their image. Their success was very short-lived and, although *Don't Stop Loving Me Baby* was a much more minor hit, they could never shake off the 'one hit wonder' tag, a situation that a change of name to Pinkerton's Colours and then simply Pinkertons in their later days could do nothing to redress.

Magic Rocking Horse was later covered by Plasticland, a US new psych band from Milwaukee, Wisconsin, on their first album.

Pinkerton's Colours eventually became **Flying Machine**. Barrie Bernard was later in **Jigsaw**, whilst bassist Ian Coleman became a BBC London radio DJ in the late seventies/eighties, under the name Stuart Colman [sic], running the rock'n'roll show "Echoes". He became the record producer of all those Shakin' Stevens hits in the seventies. He also produced a Little Richard album and went on to become a big time operator in Nashville.

Sequel's 2-CD retrospective *Flight Recorder* compiles everything that they recorded for Pye between 1967 - 1971, including material as **The Flying Machine** (**Tony Newman** was vocalist) plus sixteen previously unreleased cuts including demos of their Decca hits (Sequel NECD 290) 1998.

Compilation coverage has included: *Strange Things* on *Relics Vol's 1 & 2* CD; *Magic Rocking Horse* and *Mirror Mirror* on *Pop Inside The '60s, Vol. 1*; *Magic Rocking Horse* on *Rubble Vol. 14: The Magic Rocking Horse* (LP) and *Rubble Vol. 8* (CD); *Mum And Dad* on *Petal Pushers* (LP); *Duke's Jetty* on *Doin' The Mod, Vol. 2* (CD) and there's an alternate take of *Mirror Mirror* on the 2-CD set *Greatest Hits Of The 60's*. (VJ/JRy)

The Pink Fairies

Personnel:	MICK FARREN	vcls	ABC	
	PHIL LENOIR	drms	A	
	STEVE TOOK	bs, drms	ABC	
	LARRY WALLIS	gtr, vcls	ABC	G H I J
	DAVE BIDWELL	drms	B	
	TWINK	drms, vcls	CD	H
	RUSSELL HUNTER	drms	DEFG	H I J
	PAUL RUDOLPH	gtr, vcls	DE	H
	DUNCAN SANDERSON	bs, vcls	DEFG	H I J
	MICK WAYNE	gtr, vcls	F	
	MARTIN STONE	gtr		J

					HCP
ALBUMS:	1(D)	THE NEVER NEVER LAND	(Polydor 2383 045) 1971	SC	-
(up to	2(E)	WHAT A BUNCH OF SWEETIES			
1976)			(Polydor 2383 132) 1972	SC	48
	3(G)	KINGS OF OBLIVION			
		(w/poster)	(Polydor 2383 212) 1973	R1	-
	4(-)	FLASHBACK (Compilation)	(Polydor 2384 071) 1975	SC	-
	5(H)	LIVE AT THE ROUNDHOUSE '75			
			(Big Beat WIK 14) 1982	SC	-

NB: (1) There was also a pressing of this album in a 3D cover, which is more collectable (R1). Also around 100 copies were pressed in pink vinyl and these are mega rarities (R3). (1) reissued on CD (Polydor 589 550-2) 2002, digitally remastered with bonus tracks. (2) reissued on CD (Polydor 589 551-2) 2002, digitally remastered with bonus tracks. (3) reissued on CD (Polydor 589 552-2) 2002, digitally remastered with bonus tracks. (5) This was recorded on 13 July 1975. Line-up (B) also recorded one side of *Glastonbury Fayre* (3-LP) (Revelation REV 1A-3F) 1972. There's also a 70-minute CD, which comprises *Live At The Roundhouse, Previously Unreleased* from 1984 and **Twink's** 1977 *Do It* (CD) as well all on one CD *Live At The Roundhouse / Previously Unreleased/Do It* (Big Beat CDWIKD 965). Other CD collections available include *The Best Of Pink Fairies* (Polydor 8438942) 1990, their re-union album *Kill Em 'N Eat 'Em* (Demon FIENDCD 105) 1990 and *The Golden Years '69 - '71* (Purple Pyramid CLP 0188-2) 1998, combines two tracks from **Twink's** solo album with versions of Jefferson Airplane's *Three Fifths Of A Mile In 10 Seconds*, **The Beatles'** *Tomorrow Never Knows*, Chuck Berry's *Lucille* and *Johnny B. Goode*, plus **Pink Fairies** originals. The highlight of the CD, however, is the 19-minute *Uncle Harrys Last Freak-Out* taken from their Glastonbury '71 performance. *Hams Volume 1* (UHCK UHCK 001) 2000, *Son Of Ham - Hams Volume 2* (UHCK UHCK 002) and *Hogwatch* (UHCK UHCK 003) 2000 are remastered recordings of what were previously subscriber-only cassettes taken from a variety of sources and eras. Also relevant is *Up The Pinks* (Polydor 589 553-2) 2002, a 12-track CD compilation and *Live At Weeley* (LP) (Get Back GET 27).

45s:	The Snake/Do It	(Polydor 2058 089) 1971	SC
(up to	Well, Well, Well/Hold On	(Polydor 2058 302) 1972	SC
1976)	Between The Lines/		
	Spoiling For A Fight (PS)	(Stiff BUY 2) 1976	

This was originally a very loosely knit band which came together as a sort of drinking gang/motorcycle club for **Steve Took** (after he was sacked from **T Rex**), **Twink** and **The Deviants**. They were also known as **Shagrat** at this time. Some of the early members soon drifted away. Their second drummer, David Bidwell, died of a heroin overdose. They eventually stabilised into line-up (D) and after a gig at The Roundhouse signed to Polydor. This line-up cut the first 45 and album. After this **Twink** left to spend a spell in Morocco. Meanwhile the band, along with **Hawkwind**, developed a reputation as one of Britain's top hippie bands invariably playing for free at key rock festivals in the era. They often did joint 'Pinkwind' sets with **Hawkwind**.

Flashback is probably the best introduction to their music, compiling some of the better tracks from their first three albums. *Live At The Roundhouse* was a recording of a one-off reformation gig, which was not officially released until seven years later. It includes lively versions of Little Richard's *Lucille*, Velvet Underground's *I'm Waiting For The Man* and the self-penned *Uncle Harry's Last Freakout*. This was later reissued on CD in 1991 along with *Previously Unreleased*, a set of mainly Larry Wallis' songs first issued in 1984 and **Twink's** *Do It '77* EP.

Up The Pinks: An Introduction To Pink Fairies is a 12-track compilation collecting material from their first three albums. It includes many of their fine moments like *The Snake*, *Uncle Harry's Last Freak Out*, *City Kids* and more. The compilation comes with a 12-page colour booklet.

Live At The Weeley (LP) captures them 'kicking out the jams' at the celebrated early seventies festival performing classic numbers like *Uncle Harry's Last Freak Out*, *The Snake*, *Riders In The Sky*, *Tomorrow Never Knows* and a long jam called *Why Does A Red Cow?*

Paul Rudolph builds and designs bicycles in Canada now. Russell Hunter is happily married, works in ICT and lives in West London. **Twink** is still in the music business and divides his time between the UK and US. Larry Wallis went on to be label producer for Stiff Records in their glory years and still records. Duncan 'Sandy' Sanderson is alive and well and living in London. (VJ)

Pink Floyd

Personnel:	SYD BARRETT	gtr, vcls	A
(up to	NICK MASON	drms	AB
1976)	ROGER WATERS	bs, vcls	AB
	RICK WRIGHT	keyb'ds, vcls	AB
	DAVE GILMOUR	gtr, vcls	B

HCP

ALBUMS:	1(A)	THE PIPER AT THE GATES OF DAWN			
(up to		(mono/stereo)	(Columbia S(C)X 6157) 1967	R3/SC	6
1976)	2(A/B)	A SAUCERFUL OF SECRETS			
		(mono/stereo)	(Columbia S(C)X 6258) 1968	R3/SC	9
	3(B)	MORE	(Columbia SCX 6346) 1969	R1	9
	4(B)	UMMAGUMMA (2-LP)	(Harvest SHDW 1/2) 1969	SC	5
	5(B)	ATOM HEART MOTHER	(Harvest SHVL 781) 1970	SC	1
	6(B)	MEDDLE	(Harvest SHVL 795) 1971	SC	3
	7(-)	RELICS	(Starline SRS 5071) 1971	SC	32
	8(B)	OBSCURED BY CLOUDS			
			(Harvest SHSP 4020) 1972	SC	6
	9(B)	DARK SIDE OF THE MOON			
			(Harvest SHVL 804) 1973	SC	2
	10(B)	WISH YOU WERE HERE	(Harvest SHVL 814) 1975	SC	1

NB: Original pressings of (1) in blue/black label (R3). Original pressings of (2) in blue/black label (R3). Both albums repressed in 1970 in silver and balck labels. (1) and (2) were reissued on EMI's Fame label in 1983 (FA 3065) and 1986 (FA 3163) respectively. They were also issued as a double set in 1973 *A Nice Pair* (Harvest SHDW 403) (No 21). *A Collection Of Great Dance Songs* (Harvest SHVL 822) 1981 consisted of remixes of *One Of These Days*, *Another Brick In The Wall (Part 2)*, *Wish You Were Here*, *Shine On You Crazy Diamond* and *Sheep*. It got to No 37 here and No 31 in the US and was later reissued in 1985 on Fame and in 1988 on CD (EMI CDP 790 732 2). (5) and (9) were also issued in quadrophonic (Harvest Q4 SHVL 781 and Q4 SHVL 804, respectively) in 1973 (R1). (1) reissued on CD (EMI CDP 746 384-2) 1987. (2) reissued on CD (EMI CDP 746 383 2) 1987 and again remastered (EMI CDEMD 1063). (3) reissued on CD (EMI CDP 746 386 2) 1987. (4)

PINK FLOYD - Piper At The Gates Of Dawn (LP).

PINK FLOYD - A Saucerful Of Secrets (LP).

reissued on CD (EMI CDP 746 404 8) 1987. (5) reissued on CD (Harvest CDP 746 381 2) 1987 and again remastered with a 22-page booklet. (6) reissued on CD (Harvest 746 034 2) 1984 and by Mobile Fidelity (USA) (UDCD 518) 1989. (8) reissued on CD (EMI CDP 746 385 2) 1987. (9) reissued on CD (Harvest CDP 746 001 2) 1984 and by Mobile Fidelity (USA) (UDCD 514) 1989. As if these albums haven't been reissued enough times on CD, in 1994 EMI have reissued (1) (EMI 7243 8 31261 2 5), (2) (EMI 7243 8 29751 2 0), (4) (EMI 7243 8 31213 2 8/31214 2 7), (5) (EMI 7243 8 31246 2 6), (6) (EMI 7243 8 27949 2 5), (9) (EMI 7243 8 29752 2 9) and (10) (EMI 7243 8 29750 2 1) on CD again. They've all been remastered and come with 16-24 page booklets, which are full of lyrics and rare photos. In 1995 this process was completed with (7) (EMI 7243 8 35603 2 5), (3) (EMI 7243 8 35631 2 8) and (8) (EMI 7243 8 35609 2 9). 1997's reissues include (1) (EMI 7243 8 59857 2 0) in mono and an EP CD *1967: The First 3 Singles* (EMI 7243 8 59895 2 0) 1997, which was issued separately at budget price or free to anyone buying two full price catalogue titles. It's also designed to fit into The Piper... box. For those of you who are still vinyl collectors, *'97 Vinyl Collection* (EMI/SIGMA 630) 1997 is a 7-LP box set comprising *The Piper At The Gates Of Dawn*, *Relics*, *Atom Heart Mother*, *The Dark Side Of The Moon*, *Animals*, *Wish You Were Here* and *The Wall*. This is the first time their digitally remastered versions have appeared on vinyl. Each album was also issued individually and most have new inner sleeves. *The Zabriskie Point* soundtrack has also been reissued as a 2-CD package by Rykodisc, with one CD containing the original soundtrack album and the other containing material recorded by **Pink Floyd** but not used in the film. There has recently been a further round of CD reissues: - (1) remastered with an expanded booklet (EMI CDEMD 1073), also on vinyl in mono (EMI CX 6157). (2) remastered with an expanded booklet (EMI CDEMD 1063), (3) remastered with an expanded booklet (EMI CDEMD 1084), (4) remastered as a 2-CD set with a booklet (EMI CDEMD ?), (5) remastered with a 22-page booklet (EMI CDEMD ?), (6) remastered with a 16-page booklet (EMI CDEMD 1061), (7) remastered with new cover art (EMI CDEMD 1082), (8) remastered with a booklet (EMI CDEMD 1083), (9) reissued as a 30th anniversary edition on vinyl (EMI 5821361) and on CD remastered with an expanded booklet (EMI CDEMD ?), (10) remastered with an expanded booklet (EMI CDEMD ?).

Compilations, on CD and vinyl, include *Collection: Pink Floyd* (Sony 32DP 363) 1988. 1992 saw the release of a 9-CD set, *Shine On* (EMI PFBOX 1), which came with eight postcards and a hardback book. This has been reissued (EMI CDS 7805572). There's also a collector's item, *The First XI* (Harvest PF 11) 1979. This consisted of their first eleven albums in their original sleeves with picture discs of *Dark Side Of The Moon* and *Wish You Were Here*. Just 1,000 copies were pressed and it's already extremely rare (R4). There's also a European album *Masters Of Rock* (054 04229) 1970, which was reissued in 1976 and widely imported into this country. It contained stereo early 45 cuts, which were all 'B' sides and had originally been released as *The Best Of The Pink Floyd* on the Dutch Columbia label (SC 054-04299) in 1970. *Maximum Floyd* (Chrome Dreams ABCD 061) 2000 is part of the label's 'talking book' series. *Echoes: The Best Of Pink Floyd* (EMI Chrysalis 7243 5 36111 2 5) 2001 is a 29-track collection of many of their finest moments. *Pink Floyd - 1967 Singles Sampler* (EMI 8598952) is a six-track EP/mini album that includes the 'A' and 'B' sides of their first three singles in mono housed in an attractive fold-out slipcase sleeve. *In London '66 & '67* (CD & CD-Rom) (Pucka PUC66) is an extremely rare 'Collectors Edition' housed in a slipcase sleeve, which features a 16-minute version of *Interstellar Overdrive*, a 12-minute previously unissued cut *Nick's Boogie* and a CD-Rom of the band live in the studio in 1967 and interviews taken from the 'Let's Make Love In London' film.

HCP

45s:	Arnold Layne/		
(up to	Candy And A Currant Bun	(Columbia DB 8156) 1967	R2 20
1976)	See Emily Play/Scarecrow	(Columbia DB 8214) 1967	R2 6

	Apples And Oranges/Paint Box (Columbia DB 8310) 1967 R3 -
α	It Would Be So Nice (Columbia DB 8401) 1968 R6 -
	It Would Be So Nice/Julia Dream (Columbia DB 8401) 1968 R3 -
	Point Me At The Sky/
	Careful With That Axe, Eugene (Columbia DB 8511) 1968 R2 -
β	The Narrow Way (EMIdisc acetate no cat no) 1969 -

Pink Floyd was unquestionably London's premier 1960s psychedelic band, and one of the very few to adapt their music and image to achieve subsequent success. Artistically uncompromising and relentlessly experimental, in *Piper At The Gates Of Dawn* and *Dark Side Of The Moon* they recorded what many regard as the ultimate achievements in psychedelia and progressive rock.

Barrett, **Waters** and Wright were old school pals from Cambridge. As students in London **Waters**, Wright and Mason formed a group called Sigma, which became The T-Set and finally **The Abdabs**, playing R&B. This band also included Clive Metcalf (bs) and two vocalists, Keith Noble and Juliette Gale, the last of whom later married Wright. When **Barrett** joined he swiftly established himself as their leader, and renamed them after a record he possessed by blues singers Pink Anderson and Floyd Council. In 1966, under his leadership, they won a residency at the Marquee Club and played gigs at the Roundhouse, accompanied by a San Francisco-style light show. On 23rd December they played their first gig at the legendary UFO Club, where they also secured a residency, consolidating their place at the vanguard of London's underground scene.

Their first single, *Arnold Layne*, the story of a pervert who steals ladies' underwear from washing lines, was the first truly psychedelic single to hit the charts, reaching No. 20 in March 1967 despite being banned by the BBC. In April they were the star attraction at the 14-Hour Technicolour Dream, and that June *See Emily Play* hit No. 6, establishing the band as a household name. At the time it represented a stunning advancement of musical frontiers, and their sensational debut album, *The Piper At The Gates Of Dawn*, established them as the most imaginative of Britain's psychedelic bands. Recorded at Abbey Road at the same time as **The Beatles'** *Sgt. Pepper's* album, it's dominated by **Barrett**'s compositions. Two long tracks, *Interstellar Overdrive* and *Astronomy Domine*, create a musical simulation of space travel, and are particularly significant as they point the direction in which the band's music developed without **Barrett**. Many of **Barrett**'s other compositions, like *Matilda Mother, The Scarecrow, Bike* and *Flaming*, are much shorter and characterised by surreal lyrics.

LSD had clearly provided much of **Barrett**'s musical inspiration, but unfortunately it started to take over. Their third single, the complex *Apples and Oranges*, failed to make the charts in November 1967 and by early 1968 he had begun to lose his sanity. At gigs he would sit onstage and stare into space, only playing the occasional note. He became increasingly unreliable and difficult to work with, and another Cambridge native, David

PINK FLOYD - Ummagumma (2-LP).

Gilmour, was drafted in to shore things up. Finally, after a disastrous visit to the US, **Barrett** left the group in April. Prior to his departure he recorded the legendary *Scream Thy Last Scream* and *Vegetable Man*, which went unreleased. In 1970 he recorded a pair of fragmentary solo albums, *The Madcap Laughs* and *Barrett*, with much support from Gilmour, and also undertook a session for 'Top Gear' which was released on a 12" EP in 1988. In 1972 he joined **Twink** (see **Pink Fairies**) and Jack Monck (ex-Delivery) in a Cambridge-based trio named **Stars**, which only managed three gigs before disbanding. **Pink Floyd** arguably never reached quite the same standards of inventiveness without him, and have always acknowledged his huge influence over their progress.

In the wake of his departure **Waters** took over as the group's central figure. April 1968 saw the release of *It Would Be So Nice*, their first 45 without **Barrett**, and their next album, *A Saucerful Of Secrets*, which appeared in June, indicated that they were coping well. As well as the light-hearted *Corporal Clegg*, **Waters** contributed the spacey *Let There Be More Light* and *Set The Controls For The Heart Of The Sun*, which evoke a sense of mystery and mysticism. The second side is dominated by the title track, written collectively by the group. It comprises three movements and is characterised by discordant keyboards, sound effects and relentless drums which eventually give way to an organ solo and orchestrated climax. Wright's contributions, *Remember A Day* and *See-Saw*, are more relaxed and less intense. The finale is a **Barrett** composition, *Jugband Blues*, which is in a similar vein to his nonsensical songs on their first album. Later that summer they contributed an otherwise unavailable version of *Interstellar Overdrive* to the soundtrack of the documentary 'Tonite Let's All Make Love In London'.

They spent the remainder of 1968 gigging and making occasional visits to recording studios, notably to tape the rare *Point Me At The Sky* 45, which came and went in November and was to be their last UK single for 11 years. Their next album, *More*, was a soundtrack for an obscure French underground film of the same name and appeared in June 1969. Though patchy, it contained some excellent material, notably *Cymbaline* and *The Nile Song*. Their fourth effort, *Ummagumma*, which appeared at the end of 1969, marked a downward trend. A double album, one record comprised live recordings of their old classics, and the other consisted of experiments by each member. Littered with studio trickery, the result was largely a self-indulgent mess. Dave Gilmour's lengthy two-part instrumental contribution, *The Narrow Way*, was recorded at Abbey Road. Around 30 copies were pressed onto 7" Emidisc acetates by his brother Peter, who gave some away to friends. Needless to say, these are now major rarities.

Compared with their earlier work their next album, *Atom Heart Mother*, was also a considerable disappointment. Ironically, though, it became their first to top the UK charts. Late in 1970 they also featured on the soundtrack (LP) to Antonioni's film *Zabriskie Point*. *Meddle*, however, represented a relative upsurge. One side was occupied by the melodic *Echoes*, part of which was used in the obscure film 'Crystal Voyager'. While containing some of the grinding organ work and sound effects that characterised their earlier albums, it was also full of powerful melodies and subtle electronica. The other side contained shorter, more structured rock songs, such as the

PINK FLOYD - More (LP).

PINK FLOYD - Atom Heart Mother (LP).

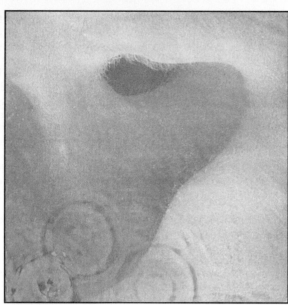

PINK FLOYD - Meddle (LP).

imposing instrumental *One Of These Days*, the relaxed *San Tropez*, which captured the group in laid-back vocal style, and *Fearless*, memorable for its recording of the Anfield Kop. 1972 saw the release of *Obscured By Clouds*, their soundtrack to Barbet Schroeder's movie 'La Vallée', which they recorded in France. The same year the band were filmed performing live at Pompeii.

1973 marked the release of what was for many their magnum opus, *Dark Side Of The Moon*. Expertly engineered by Alan Parsons, it made extensive use of tape effects and VCS-Z synthesizers and contained some of their finest moments in tracks like *Money, Us And Them, Brain Damage* and *Time*. The songs, all written by **Waters**, deal with the mental and emotional destabilisation brought about by poverty, ageing, solitude and fear of failure, with the spectre of insanity hovering menacingly in the background. Despite its sombre, pessimistic atmosphere the album was a massive commercial success, giving them their first US No 1 and spending 15 years in the Billboard chart. In the UK it reached No 2 and spent 301 weeks in the charts. One of the most successful recordings ever, the album eventually sold in excess of 20 million copies. *Money* was also released as a US single, and got to No 13.

In July 1975 they headlined at the Knebworth Festival in Hertfordshire, and staged one of the most spectacular shows of the decade. Their next album, *Wish You Were Here*, initially encountered a lukewarm response but went on to top the charts both here and in the US. One of its best known tracks was a tribute to **Syd Barrett**, *Shine On You Crazy Diamond*. **Roy Harper** occupied the vocal slot on *Have A Cigar*, and it also included more of **Waters**' gloom and doom with *Welcome To The Machine*.

They continued to record beyond 1976, of course, but later years were increasingly marked by internal strife. Particularly noteworthy in their later phase were *Animals* (influenced by Orwell's 'Animal Farm') and *The Wall* (which symbolised the lack of communication **Waters** found in the modern world). After almost twenty years of discord, by 2005 they had buried the hatchet sufficiently to perform a rapturously-received set at the Live8 concert in London.

Maximum Floyd charts the group's rise from their heady days in the sixties to the present. There are some brief interviews with Dave Gilmour, but mostly a female narrator relays their basic history over spiralling background music. *Echoes: The Best Of Pink Floyd* is a 29-track compilation which captures the band at their best.

Appearances on Various Artists' compilations have included *Embryo* on *Picnic* (2-LP); the previously unreleased *Scream Thy Last Scream* and an unreleased version of *See Emily Play* on the *Artefacts From The Psychedelic Dungeon* (CD); *Interstellar Overdrive* and *Nick's Boogie* on *Tonite Let's All Make Love In London* (LP) and *Come In No 51, Your Time Is Up, Crumbling Land* and *Heart Beat, Pig Meat* on the *Zabriski Point* (LP) soundtrack.

Undeniably they were one of the finest psychedelic acts of the sixties and they developed into one of the most creative progressive rock acts of the

seventies and, of course, in *Dark Side Of The Moon* they made one of the most successful recordings ever. It's sold in excess of 20 million copies. (VJ/RMJ)

Pink People

45s: Psychologically Unsound/
        Cow Catcher   (Philips BF 1355) 1964 SC
        Indian Hate Call/I Dreamt I Dwelt In   (Philips BF 1356) 1964 SC

This outfit were totally off the wall by all accounts. (VJ)

Pinky and The Fellas

Personnel: BOBBY BURNS   drms   A
              HUEY DEMPSEY   keyb'ds   A
              CAROLINE GARDNER (PINKY)   ld vcls   A
              JOHN GARDNER   gtr   A
              LES HUNTER   gtr   A
              JOHN STEVE   bs   A

45s: α Manchester And Liverpool/
         Come Back Again   (Decca F 12748) 1968
         Let The Music Start/
         Oh A Beautiful Day   (Polydor BM 56338) 1969

NB: α also issued in Japan (London) 1968.

This obscure UK act had a hit in Japan with *Manchester And Liverpool* which sold 310,000 copies there and reached No. 1 in 1969. The track was composed by Andrea Pop. The follow-up also reached No. 7 in Japan. (IS)

Pinnacle

ALBUM: 1 ASSASIN   (Stag HP 125) 1974 R3
NB: (1) reissued on CD as *Cyborg Assassin* (Kissing Spell KSCD 9409) 1994 with three additional tracks taken from a live cassette circa 1975. (1) also reissued on vinyl on Little Wing (SC).

This is a rare privately-pressed album by a Liverpool heavy rock band. The spelling of the title is theirs. Musically, this is a sonic assault with pounding drums and bass and frenzied keyboards. Powerful stuff indeed! A sort of prototype heavy metal album that was originally only available as a demo. This will clearly be of interest to heavy rock/metal fans. (VJ)

Pipes Of Pan

45:    Monday Morning Rain/
       Monday Morning Rain (instr mix)   (Page One POLS 038) 1967

This was an obscure one-off venture and the 'A' side has resurfaced on *Fading Yellow, Vol 4* (CD). (VJ)

Pipes Of Pan

ALBUM: 1   BRIAN JONES PRESENTS THE PIPES OF PAN
AT JOUJOUKA (w/fold-out insert)
(Rolling Stones COC 49100) 1971 R2

NB: Some copies had the album title misprinted on the cover as *Brian Jones Plays With The Pipes Of Pan*, these are more collectable but within the same banding as are copies with a 'Presents' sticker on the front cover.

This was one of two low profile projects that **Rolling Stones** member **Brian Jones** was involved in (the other was when he composed the soundtrack to the 1967 film 'A Degree Of Murder'). On the above project he recorded with traditional Moroccan musicians at the Rites Of Pan Festival in Morocco in 1968. Excerpts from these recordings were released on the above album, which is sought-after by his and some of the band's fans. (VJ)

The Pipkins

Personnel: TONY BURROWS   vcls   A
                ROGER GREENAWAY   vcls   A

ALBUM: 1(A) GIMME DAT DING!   (Capitol ST-483) 1970

NB: (1) US only. There was also a split album with **The Sweet**, *Gimme Dat Ding* (Music For Pleasure MFP 5248) 1971.

                                                   HCP
45s: α Gimme Dat Ding/To Love You   (Columbia DB 8662) 1969 6
        Yakety Yak/Sugar And Spice   (Columbia DB 8701) 1970 -
        Pipkins Party Medley/
        Pipkins Party Medley   (Columbia DB 8728) 1970 -
        Gonna Give Up Smokin'/
        Hole In The Middle   (Columbia DB 8824) 1971 -

NB: α also issued in the US (Capitol 2819) 1970. There was also a US EP: *Yakety Yak/Sugar And Spice/Are You Cookin'* (Capitol 2874) 1970.

Very good novelty records. Burrows was also involved (sometimes with Greenaway) with **The Brotherhood Of Man**, **The Flowerpot Men**, **One and One**, **First Class**, **Edison Lighthouse** and **White Plains**. In addition, he recorded a solo album for Bell in 1970.

Greenaway was a half of **David and Jonathan**. (VZ)

PINK FLOYD - Relics (LP).

PINK FLOYD - Obscured By Clouds (LP).

Pisces

Personnel: RICHARD DIGANCE   gtr, keyb'ds, vcls   ABC
                ALUN EDEN   drms, vcls   AB
                TIM GREENWOOD   bs, gtr, vcls   A
                BARRY LYONS   bs, vcls   AB
                JOHN O'CONNOR   gtr, bs, vcls   A
                FRANK McCONNELL   gtr, vcls   BC
                PAUL KARASS   bs   C

ALBUM: 1(A) PISCES   (Trailer LER 2025) 1971 R1

This folk-rock band was named after a solo album by **Richard Digance**. Eden and Lyons had both been with **Mr Fox** previously. Their album is now a minor collectable. It consists of self-penned soft folk-rock songs. Some, like *Jack O'Legs* are story songs. Others, like *The Ballad Of Benjamin Bratt* are very light-hearted. There are some nice melodies on this album, which is worth investigating for fans of this genre.

When O'Connor and Greenwood left to resume their solo careers, Frank McConnell was recruited as a replacement. In 1972 Eden and Lyons left to join **Trees.** Former **Rare Bird** member Paul Karass came in on bass, but he returned to **Rare Bird** in April 1972. When **Digance** resumed his solo career, McConnell retired.

Richard Digance went on to become a well-known humorous folk artist and TV personality. (VJ/JM)

The Plague

45:       Looking For The Sun/
         Here Today, Gone Tomorrow   (Decca F 12730) 1968 R2

A very rare and collectable 45. The band's personnel isn't known and this seems to have been their only release. *Looking For The Sun* is quite a mishmash of styles but the vocals stand out as being assertive.

Compilation appearances have included: *Here Today, Gone Tomorrow* on *The Psychedelic Scene* (CD) and *Voyage Through The Sugarcube* (LP & CD); and *Looking For The Sun* on *Rubble, Vol. 11 - Adventures In The Mist* (LP) and *Rubble, Vol. 6* (CD). (VJ)

Plainsong

Personnel: IAN MATTHEWS   gtr, vcls   A
                DAVE RICHARDS   keyb'ds, vcls   A
                ANDY ROBERTS   gtr, vcls   A
                BOB RONGA   bs, vcls   A

PINNACLE - Assasin (LP).

ALBUMS: 1(A)   IN SEARCH OF AMELIA EARHART
                                    (Elektra K 42120) 1972 SC
         2(A)   PLAINSONG II (promo only)
                                    (Elektra K 42136) 1973 R3

NB: There's also a 2-CD set *Plainsong* (Water WATER 149) which is a 40-track collection featuring (1) and (2) plus various live tracks.

45:      Even The Guiding Light/
         Yo Yo Man/Call The Tune   (Elektra K 12076) 1972

A 1972 outfit which **Ian Matthews** (of **Matthews Southern Comfort** fame) had first put together when he did a short US tour. By February 1972 they had evolved into **Plainsong**. Their only vinyl output was the above albums (and the second was never officially released). Upon their demise **Matthews** moved to California, where he started a solo career, Dave Richards moved to **Grimms** and Ronga and **Roberts** returned to session work. **Andy Roberts** was an underrated guitarist who'd earlier been in **Liverpool Scene** and **Everyone**. He also recorded solo albums and was later in **Grimms**, **Roy Harper's** and Hank Wangford's bands.

In 1990 **Plainsong** reformed and this resulted in a series of new albums and periodic tours. (VJ)

Robert Plant

45s: Our Song/Laughin', Cryin', Laughin'   (CBS 202656) 1966 R4
         Long Time Coming/I've Got A Secret   (CBS 202858) 1966 R4

These two singles by future **Led Zeppelin** member **Plant** are now very rare and sought-after by collectors (particularly **Led Zeppelin** ones) as you'd imagine. *Laughin', Cryin', Laughin'* is a Northern soul favourite. In 1966 he was backed by Band Of Joy who were part of **Alexis Korner's** backing group. He was also a member of **Listen**. (VJ)

Planxty

Personnel: ANDY IRVINE   gtr, mandolin, bouzouki, vcls ABC
            DONAL LUNNY   gtr, bouzouki, synth   A
            CHRISTY MOORE   gtr, vcls   AB
            LIAM O'FLYNN   uilleann pipes   ABC
            JOHNNY MOYNIHAN   bouzouki   BC
            PAUL BRADY   gtr, vcls   C

ALBUMS: 1(A)   PLANXTY   (Polydor 2383 186) 1973
(up to   2(A)   THE WELL BELOW THE VALLEY
1976)   (Polydor 2383 232) 1973
         3(B)   COLD BLOW AND THE RAINY NIGHT
                                      (Polydor 2383 301) 1974

         4(-)   PLANXTY COLLECTION   (Polydor 2383 387) 1976

NB: (2) and (3) reissued on CD (Shanachie Records (USA) SH 79010 CD and SH 79011 CD) in 1988 and 1990 respectively.

A popular Irish folk-rock band, whose albums are acknowledged to be fine examples of Celtic traditional music. **Christy Moore** also recorded as a solo artist. (VJ)

The Plastic Penny

Personnel: MICK GRABHAM   gtr   ABC
             BRIAN KEITH   vcls   A
             TONY MURRAY   bs   AB
             NIGEL OLSSON   drms, vcls   ABC
             PAUL RAYMOND   organ, vcls ABC
             CHRIS LAIN   bs   C

ALBUMS: 1(B)   TWO SIDES OF...   (Page One POL(S) 005) 1968 R1
         2(B)   CURRENCY   (Page One POLS 014) 1969 R1
         3(-)   HEADS YOU WIN, TAILS I LOSE
                                  (Page One POLS 611) 1970 R1

NB: (1) and (2) reissued on CD (Repertoire REP 4368-WP and REP 4369-WP) 1993. Also relevant is *Best Of & Rarities* (CD) (Repertoire REP 4766) which comes with an informative booklet.

HCP

45s: Everything I Am/
         No Pleasure Without Pain My Love (Page One POF 051) 1967 6
         Nobody Knows It/
         Just Happy To Be With You   (Page One POF 062) 1968 -
         Your Way To Tell Me Go/
         Baby You're Not To Blame   (Page One POF 079) 1968 SC -
         Hound Dog/Currency   (Page One POF 107) 1969 SC -
         She Does/Genevieve   (Page One POF 146) 1969 -
Reissue: Everything I Am/
         No Pleasure Without Pain My Love   (DJM DJS 10353) 1975 -

This band are best known for their only hit single, *Everything I Am*, on which Brian Keith, a former session vocalist, turned in a strong performance. The remaining material was recorded without Keith. Clearly *Everything I Am* is in no way representative for what this band could achieve, when no commercial forces were pushing them to record unfitting material. Significantly their debut album kicks off with this single, but then sets forth to produce some very fine psychedelic music. Short and mid-tempo pop songs prevail, but they convey a sense of drama seldomly equalled within this area. *Genevieve*, a mini-tragedy and *Wake Me Up*, a keen demasqué of the ego, with sly allusions to the name of the band, along with *So Much Older Now*, a painful story of a star growing old, are all examples of superb psych-pop. The climax is the epic *Mrs. Grundy* with cutting harmonies and great instrumental interplay, including a 'wrong'

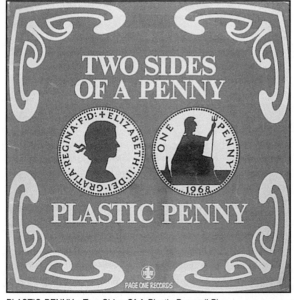

PLASTIC PENNY - Two Sides Of A Plastic Penny (LP).

PLASTIC PENNY - Currency (CD).

guitar solo. A cover of *Strawberry Fields Forever* is wasted, though. Two subsequent singles: *Nobody Knows It* and the lovely *Your Way To Tell Me Go*, which sounds like **The Move** wrapped in a tragic veil, failed to attract any sales.

A second album and a fourth single were released in 1969, the single being a psychedelic and slowed-down version of *Hound Dog!* The album still had its moments on *Baby You're Not To Blame* and the eight and a quarter minute *Sour Suite* with great organ and guitar, but also was left alone by the record-buying public. A big mistake was the awful cover of *MacArthur Park*. After they had called it a day, Page One released one more album with leftovers and some new tracks as well, which weren't saying anything new, but made for pleasant listening. All their albums are increasingly difficult to obtain.

Grabham and **Olsson** both played with **The Universals** in the early seventies. Many of the personnel went on to greater things. **Grabham** formed **Cochise** and then joined **Procol Harum** in 1973; Tony Murray joined **The Troggs**; Paul Raymond was with **Chicken Shack** and then **Savoy Brown**; **Nigel Olsson** was with the **Spencer Davis Group** for a while and later became the drummer in **Elton John**'s backing group and Brian Keith returned to session work.

Your Way To Tell Me Go has been compiled on *Pop-In, Vol 1* (CD). (MK/VJ)

Platform Six

45:     Girl Down Town/
        Money Will Not Mean A Thing   (Piccadilly 7N 35255) 1965 SC

A one-off 45 which is now becoming scarce to find. The group came from Reading.

Compilation appearances include: *Money Will Not Mean A Thing* on *Doin' The Mod, Vol. 1* (CD); and *Girl Down Town* on *Doin' The Mod, Vol. 2* (CD). (VJ)

Playground

45s: At The Zoo/Yellow Balloon   (MGM MGM 1351) 1967
        I Could Be So Good/
        The Girl Behind The Smile   (NEMS 56-4019) 1969
        Things I Do For You/Lazy Days   (NEMS 56-4442) 1969
        This Is The Place/
        The Rain, The Wind And Other Things (Decca F 13011) 1970

A harmony-pop band from Essex whose *The Girl Behind The Smile* has been compiled on *Fading Yellow, Vol 4* (CD). You'll also find *The Rain, The Wind And Other Things* on *Fading Yellow, Vol 5* (CD). (VJ)

The Playthings

45s: Stop What You're Doing To Me/Sad Songs (Pye 7N 45212) 1970
        Surrounded By A Ray Of Sunshine/
        Dance The Night Away   (Pye 7N 45399) 1974

Both these 45s are Northern soul favourites in a girlie pop vein. *Surrounded By A Ray Of Sunshine* was originally recorded by Samantha Jones. (VJ)

Please

Personnel: PETER DUNTON   vcls, drms, keyb'ds   ABC
            JURGEN ERMISCH   organ   A
            ADRIAN GURVITZ   gtr   A
            BERNIE JINKS   bs, backing vcls   ABC
            ROD HARRISON   gtr   B
            ROB HUNT   flute, vcls   B
            NICK SPENSER   gtr, backing vcls   BC

ALBUMS: 1(A/B) PLEASE 1968/69   (Essex) 1996
        2(C)   SEEING STARS   (Acme Deluxe ADCD 1028) (CD) 2001
NB: (1) reissued on CD (ACME Deluxe Series ADCD 1022) 2000.

Please were formed by Peter Dunton and Bernie Jinks in late 1967. They had just returned to Britain from Germany where they had played as Neon Pearl, which also included their third member Jurgen Ermisch. The fourth original member Adrian Gurvitz later co-founded **Gun**. Unfortunately this line-up left no vinyl legacy or unreleased recordings that have been located behind it. They disbanded in May 1968 when Peter Dunton joined **The Flies** for whom he wrote both sides of their *Magic Train* 45.

When **The Flies** split up at the end of 1968, Dunton reformed the band (line-up 'B'). Rob Hunt had also been in **The Flies**. They recorded all the cuts compiled on the *Please 1968/69* album.

Please split again in April 1969 when Peter Dunton joined **Gun**. The remaining members recruited a new drummer and renamed themselves **Bulldog Breed**. They later cut the *Made In England* album.

In the Autumn of 1969, Peter Dunton quit **Gun** to reform **Please** with Bernie Jinks and Nick Spenser (ex-Neon Pearl). This incarnation was relatively short-lived as they had difficulty recruiting a suitable keyboard player. This line-up recorded Seeing Stars, an undiscovered nugget with mellotrons, dreamy melodies and keyboards which recall **The Doors**.

In early 1970 Dunton, Jinks and a later **Bulldog Breed** member **Keith Cross** joined forces to form **T2**, who were responsible for the excellent *It'll All Work Out In Boomland* album. One of **T2**'s tracks, *No More White Horses* also crops up in a radically different form on **Please**'s *1968/69* retrospective. The stand-out tracks on this are the pulsating *Man With No Name* and *The Story*. (VJ/MM)

PLEASE - 1968/69 (LP).

PLEASE - Seeing Stars (LP).

The Pleasure Garden

45: Permissive Paradise/(Flip by Emperor Rosco
and **Jonathan King**)   (Sound For Industry SFI 31H/32H) 1968
NB: This flexidisc appeared in an art sleeve.

This London band's *Permissive Paradise*, was originally issued as a flexidisc to help promote a book called 'Young London', which was a pictorial account of Carnaby Street era London by photographer Frank Habicht. It really is rather good, with quite a catchy guitar riff and an appealing vocal arrangement.

You can also check out *Permissive Paradise* on *Syde Tryps, Vol. 1* (LP & CD) and *The Best Of Rubble Collection, Vol. 3* (CD). (VJ)

The Plebs

Personnel:	TERRY CROWE	vcls	A
	MICK DUNFORD	gtr	A
	DANNY McCULLOUGH	bs	A

ALBUM: 1(A)   THE PLEBS   (Oak no cat no) 1960s R6
NB: This was a one-sided private pressing.

45: α Bad Blood/
        Babe I'm Gonna Leave You   (Decca F 12006) 1964 R2
NB: α also issued in the U.S.A. (MGM K13320) 196?.

This beat group's version of *Bad Blood* has now become a minor collectable and their privately pressed album was valued at £1,000 in the December 2004 issue of 'Record Collector'..

Dunford was later in **Renaissance** and he and Crowe had been in **The Nashville Teens**. McCullough later played for **Eric Burdon and The Animals**. The band also turned up in the film 'Be My Guest' (see the **Kenny and The Wranglers** entry for further details) as Jerry Lee Lewis' backing band.

Compilation appearances include: *Babe I'm Gonna Leave You* on *The R&B Scene* (CD) and *That Driving Beat* (CD); and *Baby I'm Gonna Leave You* and *Bad Blood* on *Broken Dreams, Vol. 4* (LP). (VJ)

Simon Plug and Grimes

See under S.

Jon Plum

45s: Alice/Sunshine   (SNB SS 3971) 1969
     You Keep Changing Your Mind/
     An Apple Falls   (SNB SS 4317) 1969

Circus Days, Vol. 1 (LP) and *Circus Days Vol. 1 & 2* (CD) include *Alice*, a heavily orchestrated melancholic pop ballad from 1969. SNB was a small CBS subsidiary. (VJ)

Plus

Personnel:	MIKE NEWMAN	drms	A
	TONY NEWMAN	gtr	A
	MAX SIMMS	bs	A

ALBUM: 1(A)   THE SEVEN DEADLY SINS   (Probe SPB 1009) 1970 SC

A heavy progressive concept album produced by Ray Singer and Simon Napier-Bell. It has its moments with nice spoken passages, keyboard, strings and a choir. (VJ)

Pluto

Personnel:	PAUL GARDNER	gtr, vcls	A
	DEREK JERVIS	drms	A
	ALAN WARNER	gtr, vcls	A
	MICHAEL WORTH	bs	A

ALBUM: 1(A)   PLUTO   (Dawn DNLS 3030) 1972 R2
NB: (1) reissued as *Pluto Plus* (See For Miles SEE 265) 1989 with additional 45 tracks, also on CD (SEE CD 265) 1989. (1) reissued (Get Back GETLP 558) 2000 on Italian import and on CD again *Pluto Plus* (Breathless 52014) with bonus tracks in a 3-fold digipak.

45s: Rag A Bone Joe/
     Stealing My Thunder   (Dawn DNS 1017) 1971 SC
     I Really Want It/
     Something That You Loved   (Dawn DNS 1026) 1972 SC

A pretty clumsy progressive boogie rock outfit judging by their album. The playing is competent enough but the compositions are well below par with *Beauty Queen, Road To Glory* and the **Free**-like *Down And Out* the best of a poor pack. Only of interest to hard-rock completists. Their best song was a 1972 single, *I Really Want It*. Alan Warner had been in **The Foundations**.

The See For Miles reissue includes both sides of the 1972 Dawn 45. *I*

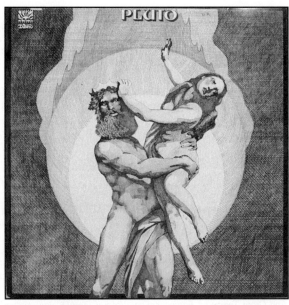

PLUTO - Pluto (LP).

Really Want It featured former **Cochise** member John Gilbert on vocals and some liken his voice to David Coverdale's. (VJ)

Pneumonia

45:     I Can See Your Face/All Your Love   (Oak RGJ 625) 1968 R3

An obscure and rather late R&B offering. *I Can See Your Face* has been brought to a wider audience recently by virtue of its inclusion on *Story Of Oak Records* (2-LP) compilation. The flip side *All Your Love* was also performed by **Mayall** and **Clapton** as the opening cut of their *Bluesbreakers* album back in 1966. (VJ)

Poet and The One Man Band

Personnel incl:			
SPEEDY ACQUAYE	congas	A
JOHN BELL	clarinet	A
TONY COLTON	vcls	A
WILLIAM DAVIES	organ	A
JERRY DONAHUE	gtr, vcls	A
PAT DONALDSON	bs	A
PETE GAVIN	vcls, drms	A
NICKY HOPKINS	piano	A
ALBERT LEE	gtr	A
BARRY MORGAN	drms	A
MIKE O'NEIL	keyb'ds	A
RAY SMITH	gtr, vcls	A

ALBUM: 1(A)   POET AND THE ONE MAN BAND
                                    (Verve SVLP6012) 1969 R1

NB: (1) also issued in the US (Paramount PAS 5010) 1969.

This group, which was home to some subsequently well-known musicians, was not able to survive the collapse of its record company, but eventually metamorphosed into **Heads, Hands and Feet**. Donahue was also a member of **Fairport Convention** and played for **Jaki Whitren**, **Andy Roberts** and **Richard and Linda Thompson**. Lee was in **Chris Farlowe (and The Thunderbirds)**, **Steve Gibbons Band**, **Green Bullfrog**, whilst Colton had previously fronted **Tony Colton's Big Boss Band**. (VZ)

The Poets (1)

Personnel:			
JOHN DAWSON	bs	AB
GEORGE GALLAGHER	vcls	AB
TONY MYLES	gtr	A
HUME PATON	lead gtr, vcls	AB
ALAN WEIR	drms	AB
FRASER WATSON	gtr	BC
JIM BREAKEY	drms	C
NORRIE MacLEAN	gtr	C
IAN McMILLAN	gtr	CD
ANDI MULVEY	vcls	C
DOUGIE HENDERSON	drms	D
JOHNNY MARTIN	organ	D
HUGHIE NICHOLSON	gtr	D

ALBUM: 1   THE POETS   (Immediate ZI2 52008) 1995

NB: (1) compiles their singles for Decca and Immediate. The version of *Baby Don't You Do It* is from a previously unreleased acetate rather than the 45 and there are also two previously unreleased acetates *I'll Keep My Pride* and *It's So Different Now*. (1) has also been released on CD as *In Your Tower* (Strike 901) 1995, with the addition of their Strike Cola 45. *Scotland's No. 1 Group* (Dynovox DYNOVOX 201) is a compilation covering from 1964 to 1968.

                                                        HCP

45s: Now We're Thru'/There Are Some (Decca F 11995) 1964 SC 31
        That's The Way It's Got To Be/
        I'll Cry With The Moon   (Decca F 12074) 1965 R2 -
        I Am So Blue/I Love Her Still   (Decca F 12195) 1965 R1 -
        Call Again/
        Some Things I Can't Forget   (Immediate IM 006) 1965 R2 -
        Baby Don't You Do It/
        I'll Come Home   (Immediate IM 024) 1966 R2 -
        Wooden Spoon/In Your Tower   (Decca F 12569) 1967 R4 -
        Heyla Hola/Fun Buggy   (Strike Cola SC 1) 1971 R2 -
Reissue: I Love Her Still/
        (Flip by different artist)   (Bam-Caruso OPRA 088) 1987 -

NB: The also contributed *I Love Her Still* (Bam Caruso OPRA 088) 1988 to a promo only 45. The reverse side featured a cut by **Ghost**.

This extremely popular Scottish beat group formed back in 1961, but they stabilised with the above line-up in 1963. They were managed by the owners of the Flamingo Ballroom in Scotland prior to being signed by **Andrew Oldham**. Their first 45, *Now We're Thru'*, introduced their distinctive minor key, acoustic 12-string sound to an unsuspecting world and gave them their only, albeit minor hit. The follow-up, *That's The Way It's Got To Be* was a pounding rocker, which could have really put them on the map but sadly it was under-promoted and flopped. The third 45 was much quieter and more in the style of their debut - unfortunately it met with the same fate. A change to **Oldham**'s new Immediate label failed to change their fortunes and by the end of 1966 most of their initial recording line-up had left or was on the verge of leaving. **Oldham**, too, lost any interest he might have had in the band and the crumbling outfit found themselves with no manager and no recording contract. Resilience proved to be one of their main qualities, though, they re-grouped with a new line-up (C), got signed to Decca and found a new manager and producer. *Wooden Spoon* was another fine single but in the true tradition of **Poets**' singles it flopped. It was written by their manager Eric Woolfson and **Unit 4 + 2**'s Tommy Moeller. Mulvey then left. He briefly sang with **Mustard** who later became **Tear Gas**. Breakey joined **Studio Six** and Fraser Watson departed for **The Pathfinders**, but **The Poets** still soldiered on, undergoing various line-up changes until they stabilised with line-up 'D'. This new line-up is thought to have recorded a 45 for Pye, *Alone Am I* (it's been suggested too that this was the work of a completely different Irish band). The band's death knell came in 1971 when Hughie Nicholson left to join **Marmalade**, Ian McMillan having originally departed to a short-lived act called **Cody**. The same year Tony Meehan, a Radio Scotland dee-jay used a band led by Dougie Henderson who called themselves **The Poets** to cut a 45 to promote Strike Cola, a sort of Scottish equivalent to Pepsi. Meehan was working as an advertising consultant at the time.

After they split in 1971 Nicholson joined **The Marmalade** and McMillan was in **Cody**, who splintered from **White Trash**. The two later re-united in **Blue**.

The Poets (Immediate ZI2 52008) 1995 compiles their singles for Decca and Immediate as does the *In Your Tower* CD (Strike 901) 1995. Either release is obviously a must for fans of the band who don't have all or most of their 45s.

Scotland's No. 1 Group is a good compilation which traces their development as a R&B band through their power-pop years to their flirtation with psychedelia. It features singles and demos (some of which are not of top notch sound quality).

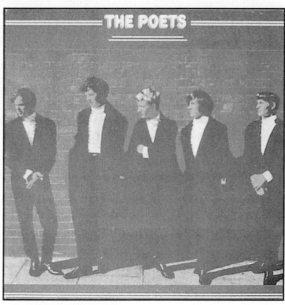

THE POETS - The Poets (LP).

Their original bass guitarist John Dawson died in Glasgow after a long struggle with oesophagal cancer.

Their recordings have been heavily compiled:- *That's The Way It's Gotta Be* on *The Mod Scene* (CD), *British Psychedelic Trip, Vol. 4* (LP), *Great British Psychedelic Trip, Vol. 2* (CD), *Illusions From The Crackling Void* (LP), *That Driving Beat* (CD) and the 4-CD *Nuggets II* box set; *Baby Don't You Do It* on *Maximum '65* (CD), *Immediate Single Collection, Vol. 3* (CD) and *Perfumed Garden Vol. 2* (LP & CD); *In Your Tower* on *The British Psychedelic Trip 1966 - 1969* (LP), *Great British Psychedelic Trip Vol. 1* (CD) and *The Psychedelic Scene* (CD); *That's The Way It's Gotta Be* and *I Love Her Still* on *Rubble, Vol. 5 - The Electric Crayon Set* (LP) and *Rubble, Vol. 3* (CD); *I Am So Blue* and *I'll Cry With The Moon* on *Rubble, Vol. 6 - The Clouds Have Groovy Faces* (LP) and *Rubble, Vol. 4* (CD); *Wooden Spoon* and *In Your Tower* on *Rubble, Vol. 11 - Adventures In The Mist* (LP) and *Rubble, Vol. 6* (CD); *Fun Buggy* and *Heyla Hola* on *Syde Tryps, Vol. 1* (LP & CD); *Locked In A Room* on *Beat It* (3-CD) and *Voyage Through The Sugarcube* (LP & CD); *I Am So Blue* on *Broken Dreams, Vol. 4* (LP); *I Love Her Still* on *The Beat Scene* (CD); *Wooden Spoon* on *Broken Dreams, Vol. 5* (LP), *Chocolate Soup* (CD), *Chocolate Soup For Diabetics, Vol. 3* (LP) and *The Freakbeat Scene* (CD); *Now We're Thru'* on *Hard-Up Heroes* (2-LP) and *A Journey To Tyme, Vol. 2* (LP); *Baby Don't You Do It, I'll Come Home* on *Immediate Alternative* (LP & CD); *I'll Come Home* on *Immediate Single Collection, Vol. 1* (CD); *Baby Don't You Do It, Call Again, I'll Come Home* and *Some Things I Can't Forget* on *Immediate Single Anthology, Vol. 1 - Rarities* (CD); *In Your Tower* on the 4-CD box set *Acid Drops, Spacedust & Flying Saucers* and *Locked In A Room* on *Haunted - Hot Smoke & Sassafras, Vol 2* (CD). (VJ/FM)

The Poets (2)

45:     Alone Am I/Locked In A Room   (Pye 7N 17668) 1968 R3 -

NB: This has been reissued in a limited edition of 500 reproduced from the French jukebox issue with a large centre hole.

This 45 was the work of a different Irish group. (VJ)

Poliphony

ALBUM: 1 POLIPHONY   (Zella no JHLPS 136) 1973 R3

This is a wholly instrumental privately-pressed album, which is consequently very rare. Its combination of rock, jazz and blues which suffers from a lack of structured song-based material is something of an acquired taste. (VJ)

Brian Poole

45s: Hey Girl/Please Be Mine   (Decca F 12402) 1966
        Everything I Touch Turns To Tears/
        I Need Her Tonight   (CBS 202349) 1966 SC
        That Reminds Me Baby/
        Tomorrow Never Comes   (CBS 202661) 1967
        Just How Loud/The Other Side Of The Sky   (CBS 3005) 1967
    α   Send Her To Me/Pretty In The City   (President PT 239) 1969
    α   What Do Women Most Desire/
        Treat Her Like A Woman   (President PT 264) 1969

NB: α as Brian Poole and The Seychelles.

Poole was born on 3 November 1941 in Barking, Essex, the son of a butcher. He formed an early version of The Tremiloes (as they were then known) with some ex-schoolfriends as long ago as 1959, and by January 1962, the group had signed to Decca as **Brian Poole and The Tremeloes**. When this successful aggregation split in January 1966 **Poole** embarked on a solo career, recording the discs listed above. The first four 'A' sides were orchestrated ballads. The second, *Everything I Touch Turns To Tears*, attracted some attention but none of them got into the Charts. By 1968 **Poole** was back working in the family butchers shop, although he still sang with local bands and made a couple more singles in 1969.

THE POETS - Scotland's No. 1 Group (CD).

In the eighties he returned briefly in 1983 to re-record new versions of *Do You Love Me?* and *Twist And Shout* with his old backing band and the following year he turned in a barnstormin' display at a celebration of thirty years of rock'n'roll at a Nottingham theatre.

Send Her To Me has been compiled on *Sometimes I Wonder* (CD); a solo version of *Do You Love Me?* can be heard on *Dizzy* (CD) and *Barefooting* has been compiled on *Perfect Day* (CD). (VJ)

Brian Poole and The Tremeloes

Personnel:	ALAN BLAKELY	gtr	ABC
	ALAN HOWARD	bs	ABC
	BRIAN POOLE	vcls	ABC
	GRAHAM SCOTT	gtr	AB
	DAVE MUNDEN	drms	BC
	RICK WEST	ld gtr	C

ALBUMS: 1(C) BIG BIG HITS OF '62 (Ace Of Clubs ACL 1146) 1963 SC
        2(C) TWIST AND SHOUT WITH BRIAN POOLE
              AND THE TREMELOES   (Decca LK 4550) 1963 R1
        3(C) IT'S ABOUT TIME   (Decca LK 4685) 1965 R2

NB: *Do You Love Me* (Deram 820 980-2) 1991 is a CD compilation of their career. *The Very Best Of Brian Poole and The Tremeloes* (Spectrum) 1998 documents their early years. *Twist And Twist/It's About Time* plus *Swinging On A Star/Time Is On My Side* EPs (Beat Goes On BGO 645) 2005 collects various EPs and albums on to two CDs.

EPs: 1(C) BRIAN POOLE AND THE TREMELOES
                                    (Decca DFE 8566) 1964 R1
        2(C) BRIAN POOLE AND THE TREMELOES
                                    (Decca DFE 8610) 1965 R1

                                                        HCP
45s: Twist Little Sister/Lost Love   (Decca F 11455) 1962 -
        That Ain't Right/Blue   (Decca F 11515) 1962 -
        Meet Me Where We Used To Meet/
        A Very Good Year For Girls   (Decca F 11567) 1963 -
        Keep On Dancing/Run Back Home   (Decca F 11616) 1963 -
        Twist And Shout/We Know   (Decca F 11694) 1963 4
        Do You Love Me?/
        Why Can't You Love Me?   (Decca F 11739) 1963 1
        I Can Dance/Are You Loving Me At All (Decca F 11771) 1963 31
        Candy Man/I Wish I Could Dance   (Decca F 11823) 1964 6
        Someone, Someone/
        Till The End Of Time   (Decca F 11893) 1964 2
        Twelve Steps To Love/Don't Cry   (Decca F 11951) 1964 32
        Three Bells/Tell Me How To Care   (Decca F 12037) 1964 17
        After A While/You Know   (Decca F 12124) 1965 -
        I Want Candy/Love Me Baby   (Decca F 12197) 1965 25
        Good Lovin'/Could It Be You   (Decca F 12274) 1965 -

Reissues: Do You Love Me?/Someone Someone   (Decca F 13815) 1978 -
Twist And Shout/Do You Love Me?/Candy Man/
Someone Someone (PS)   (Decca F 13893) 1980 -
Do You Love Me?/
Someone Someone   (Old Gold OG 9331) 19983 -

This band was formed in Dagenham, Essex by three ex-schoolfriends (**Poole**, Blakely and Howard) as long ago as 1959. They soon recruited Graham Scott to their ranks. In the original line-up **Poole** sang and played guitar, Blakely played drums and Howard was on sax, but when Dave Munden joined later in the year on drums the remaining members switched to the instruments shown at the start of this article, allowing **Brian Poole** to concentrate on vocals.

In their early days the band was strongly influenced by Buddy Holly, indeed **Brian Poole** was obsessed with the man and wore black framed spectacles just like those of his hero. Their act consisted of cover versions, more often than not of Buddy Holly and The Crickets' material. They played local dancehalls, US Airbases and even got a residency at a Butlins Holiday camp in Ayr, Scotland for a while. In these early days they were known as The Tremilos.

In 1961 Graham Scott had left the band to be replaced by another old classmate of the original trio, Richard Westwood, another Dagenham lad, who shortened his name to Rick West and played lead guitar.

The band's first break came when BBC Radio's Light Programme producer Jimmy Grant, having seen them at a gig in Southend, booked them for a stint on the popular 'Saturday Club' show, which often gave an airing to groups who had yet to record. In December 1961 they were offered an audition by Decca. The company's young A&R assistant Mike Smith only had budgetary provision to make one signing and at the Audition on New Years Day 1962 the choice between **The Beatles** (who'd travelled down from Liverpool the night before) and **Brian Poole and The Tremeloes** who had the advantage of an afternoon audition on New Years Day and a much shorter journey from Barking. The latter's proximity to Decca's West Hampstead recording studio and fresher performance got them the vote. Early appearances on record seems to have been as backing artists on Jimmy Saville's 1962 45 *Ahab The Arab* and The Vernon Girls cover version of *The Locomotion*.

Their debut 45 coupled *Twist Little Sister* with a cover of *Lost Love*, originally recorded by US vocal group The Superiors. Although it didn't chart it secured them a fair amount of airplay and an appearance on TV's 'Thank Your Lucky Stars'. Their next effort, *Keep On Dancing* sold slightly better and marked a change of direction for the group away from being Buddy Holly clones towards a rockier form of R&B music, which was becoming fashionable. They were also boosted by an appearance playing the song in a lightweight pop movie 'Just For Fun'.

Their first album, *Big Hits Of 1962*, was a budget-priced medley of songs from that years Top Twenty. Their 45 breakthrough finally came with a cover of The Isley Brothers *Twist And Shout*, a popular track from **The Beatles**' first album, which the Liverpudlians had not released as a 45. However, when **The Beatles**' *Twist And Shout* EP became a best-seller, sales of the Dagenham lads version soon fell away.

Their next effort a cover of The Contours' *Do You Love Me?* topped the UK Charts for three weeks. It was a very strong song and the band (with the advantage of a recent hit) was able to outsell a rival version from **The Dave Clark Five**. Decca made things easier for **Brian Poole and The Tremeloes** too by cancelling another version of the song by **Bern Elliot and The Fenmen**.

Then came the first big mistake - the release of a follow-up 45, *I Can Dance*, which was far too similar in style to the previous one. The disc staggered to No 31. Their reputation was damaged but they were far from dead as they proved when they bounced back with a rocky up-tempo revival of a Roy Orbison 'B' side, *Candy Man*, which climbed to No 6.

Their second album, *Twist And Shout*, was in truth hastily assembled to cash in on their 45 successes. Many of the tracks had appeared on a Canadian album, released the previous year. The remainder consisted of versions of early sixties standards and favourites from their live act like *Alley Oop*. The title cut, *Twist And Shout* and *Do You Love Me?*, two of their finest moments, were also included on Decca's *Ready, Steady, Go!* (LP) compilation in 1964. *Do You Love Me?* and *Twenty Miles* also figured on Decca's *Saturday Club* (LP) the same year. *Twist and Shout* can also

be heard on *Thank Your Lucky Stars, Vol. 2* (LP). *Someone, Someone*, their next 45, was a revival of a Cricket's 'B' side. It was their first ballad hit and their second biggest UK hit (rising to No 2) and they even got the song's composer and original producer Norman Petty to play piano on it. Moreover, it was their only disc to make any commercial impact in the States, which they had emphatically failed to conquer unlike rival bands like **The Dave Clark Five** and **Herman's Hermits**, by creeping to No 97.

During June 1964 they spent time in Ireland filming a lot in the movie 'A Touch Of Blarney'. Their next disc, *Twelve Steps To Love*, which became a minor hit, was taken from this 'B' movie. They followed this with another ballad, a revival of The Browns' autobiographical *Three Bells*, which restored them to the Top 20. Their final hit was one of their best, a real stompin' version of *I Want Candy*, which had been a US hit for The Strangeloves. This was later recorded again in 1982 by UK band Bow Wow Wow, who got to No 9 over here with it, but for my money **Brian Poole and The Tremeloes**' raw version remains the best.

The group's final 45, The Olympics' *Good Lovin'*, missed out (somewhat surprisingly when one considers that a year later The Young Rascals would enjoy a No 1 with the same song in the States). **Poole** then decided to embark on a solo career. Meanwhile **The Tremeloes** continued to record on their own with considerably more success than their former singer would enjoy. The split was formally announced in January 1966.

Other compilation appearances have included: *Twist And Shout, We Know* and *Do You Love Me?* on *Mersey Sounds* (2-LP) and, more recently on *U.K. No 1 Hits Of The 60's* (CD); *Twist And Shout* on *Wild Thing - Party* (CD); *Keep On Dancing* on *The Beat Scene* (CD); and *Silence Is Golden* on *Best Of British Rock* (CD) and *Brit Pop* (CD). (VJ)

The Poor Souls

Personnel:	JOHNNY CASEY	drms, vcls	A
	JOHNNY HUDSON	vcls	A
	DOUG MARTIN	bs	A
	CHICK TAYLOR	ld gtr	A

45s:	When My Baby Cries/		
	My Baby She's Not There	(Decca F 12183)	1965 SC
	Love Me/		
	Please Don't Change Your Mind	(Alp ALP 595 004)	1966 R1

The roots of this outfit lay in The Johnny Hudson Hi-Four, a Dundee-based combo who became **The Poor Souls** in 1964 when Casey, Martin and Hudson (real name Johnny Moran) were joined by Chick Taylor.

Their debut single *When My Baby Cries* was a ballad with piercing backing voices and a complex melody. An uncommercial but quite innovative disc it didn't get so much of a sniff at the Charts. The band spent a while in East Anglia playing at US bases in the area before returning for a fortnightly slot at Dundee's Top Ten Club. After being dropped by Decca they recorded a second single for the independent Scottish label Alp, which had a distribution deal with Polydor. *Love Me* was a considerable improvement on their first effort with complex chord and tempo changes and cutting harmonies. Sadly the sales were again disappointing and the subsequent collapse of the short-lived Alp label banished **The Poor Souls** to oblivion. (VJ)

The Poppies

45:	Lullaby Of Love/I Wonder Why	(Columbia DB 7879)	1966 SC

A one-off 45 by an obscure group which is beginning to interest collectors. (VJ)

Pop Workshop

45s:	Fairyland/		
	When My Little Girl Is Happy	(Page One POF 091)	1968
	Punch And Judy Man/		
	Love Is A One Way Highway	(Page One POF 129)	1969

These pleasant pop 45s were the work of a four-piece band from Harrow in North - West London. (VJ)

Porridge

45:        Do The Best You Can/Look At Yourself (Fontana 6007 037) 1974

This looks like a band quickly knocked together by **Mike Hugg** to make a title song for the TV series "Thick As Thieves". (VJ)

Portobello Explosion

45:        We Can Fly/
           Hot Smoke And Sasafras   (Carnaby CNS 4001) 1969 R1

A collectable 45 by a five-man band. The 'B' side was recorded by Texan band Bubble Puppy, among others, and is quite a good version. The group was previously known as **Mirage** and later became **Jawbone**.

We Can Fly can also be heard on *Rubble, Vol. 11* (CD), *We Can Fly, Vol 1* (CD) and *The Best Of Rubble Collection, Vol. 3* (CD). (VJ/MWh)

The Potatoes

45:        The Bend/Bend Ahead   (Fontana TF 756) 1966

Despite the fact that both sides of this disc were Howard-Blaikley compositions and they also managed the band it passed largely unnoticed at the time. It's rumoured that this band was **Dave Dee, Dozy, Beaky, Mick and Tich** under a pseudonym. (VJ)

Allen Pound's Get Rich

45:        Searchin' In The Wilderness/
           Hey You   (Parlophone R 5532) 1966 R5

This thumping slab of freakbeat is one of the mega-rarities from this era, and horrendously expensive to acquire.

Searchin' In The Wilderness resurfaced on *Maximum Freakbeat* (CD), *Searching In The Wilderness* (LP & CD) and on the 4-CD box set *Acid Drops, Spacedust & Flying Saucers*. (VJ)

Cozy Powell's Hammer

Personnel:			
FRANK AIELLO	vcls		AB
DON AIREY	keyb'ds		AB
CLIVE CHAMAN	bs		A
BERNIE MARSDEN	gtr		AB
COZY POWELL	drms		AB
NEIL MURRAY	bs		B

                                                              HCP

45s: Dance With The Devil/
(up to   And Then There Was Skin (instr)   (Rak RAK 164) 1973 3
1976)   The Man In Black/After Dark   (Rak RAK 173) 1974 18
            Na Na Na/Mistral   (Rak RAK 180) 1974 10

NB: There's also a 5-CD set (two of them are double CDs so the set contains three CDs) *The Early Years* (Majestic MAJCDBOX 2) 2005 which contains classic material which has been released individually on single or double CDs over the last year or so.

Cozy Powell was born in Cirencester on 29 December 1947. **Powell** began his career with The Sorcerers, who issued what is now an extremely rare and sough-after German-only 45 *Love Is A Beautiful Thing* in 1967. As a drummer who played in several groups including **Black Sabbath**, **Bedlam**, **Big Bertha**, **Jeff Beck Group**, **Ace Kefford Stand**, Rainbow and Whitesnake. He enjoyed considerable (and rather surprising) commercial success with these three 45s, which were produced by Mickie Most.

The first 45 was recorded whilst **Powell** was still with **Bedlam**. He formed a pub-rock backing group Hammer in May 1974. Frank Aiello had been with **Powell** in **Bedlam**. **Bernie Marsden** was in **Wild Turkey** and Chaman in **Hummingbird**. Don Airey had previously been in Unison and Escape. When Chaman rejoined **Hummingbird**, Neil Murray who'd been doing session work for Junior Hanson came in to replace him

MAXIMUM FREAKBEAT (Comp CD) including Allen Pound's Get Rich.

The band split in April 1975. **Powell** went motor-racing for Hitachi, until forming Strange Brew in July 1975. Aiello went on to session work. **Marsden** joined **Babe Ruth**. Airey and Murray headed for **Colosseum 11**.

Powell went on to record albums and several further 45s in the late seventies and early eighties. He was however tragically killed in a car accident on the M4 in April 1998. *The Early Years* CD Box set includes **Bedlam's** *Live In London 1972* which highlights Frank Aiello's superb vocals, the double *Bedlam Anthology* (which includes rare studio material, some from pre-**Bedlam** band **Youngblood** and some post-**Bedlam** material) and *Big Bertha Live* In Hamburg demonstrates what a fine live band **Big Bertha** was, but is marred by poor sound quality.

Dance With The Devil can also be heard on the 6-CD box set *Best Of Driving Rock*. (VJ/JM)

Jimmy Powell (and The Five Dimensions)

Personnel incl:		
DAVE FULLFORD	vcls	
RED GODWIN	ld gtr	
TONY LUCAS	bs	
JIMMY POWELL	vcls	
DUKE RUSSELL	drms	
ALAN SHEPHERD	tenor, flute	
ROD STEWART	hrmnca	

45s: α Sugar Babe Pts 1 and 2   (Decca F 11447) 1962
      α Tom Hark/Dance Her By Me   (Decca F 11544) 1962
      α Remember Them/Everyone But You   (Decca F 11570) 1963
         That's Alright/
         I'm Looking For A Woman   (Pye 7N 15663) 1964 R1
         Sugar Babe/I've Been Watching You   (Pye 7N 15735) 1964 SC
         I Can Go Down/Love Me Right   (Strike JH 309) 1966
      β Unexpected Mirrors/
         Time Mends Broken Hearts   (Decca F 12664) 1967
      β I Just Can't Get Over You/Real Cool   (Decca F 12751) 1968
         I Can Go Down/Captain Man   (Young Blood YB 1002) 1969
         House Of The Rising Sun/
         That's Love   (Youngblood YB 1006) 1969
      χ Sugar Man/Slow Down   (Youngblood YB 1008) 1969
         Witness To A War/
         Strangers On A Train   (Youngblood YB 1019) 1970
Reissue: αSugar Babe Pt's 1 and 2   (Decca F 12793) 1968

NB: α and α Solo. β with The Five Dimensions. χ as Jimmy and The Dimensions.

Jimmy Powell was an R&B singer who first attracted attention with two solo singles - fine versions of *Sugar Babe* and *Tom Hark*, which had been a No 2 hit for the South African instrumental group Elias and his Zigzag Jive Flutes back in 1958.

In 1963 he formed The Five Dimensions, who briefly included a young **Rod Stewart** on backing vocals and harmonica. The group were a regular attraction at the Crawdaddy Club but their 45s made little commercial impact and the band broke up in 1965.

Thereafter **Powell** formed various backing bands whom he called The Dimensions and undertook a lot of live work around the Midlands clubs.

There's also been a retrospective CD *The R'n'B Sensation* (See For Miles SEECD 337) 1992 which features the *I Can Go Down* 45 from 1966 and a number of **Miki Dallon** produced solo releases of his, which first appeared on the Young Blood label in the early seventies.

In 1994 the German label In Respect reissued **Powell**'s 1969 German album, *The R&B Sensation* plus eleven previously unissued tracks on CD, *The True Jimmy Powell* (In Respect 874 444) 1994.

Various artists compilation appearances have included: *Sugar Babe* on *Jimmy Page, Session Man* (CD); *Sugar Baby Pt 1* and *Sugar Baby Pt 2* on *Mod Scene, Vol. 2* (CD) and *The Soul Of British RnB 1962-68*; *Sugar Baby Pt 1* on *Weekend Starts Here* (LP) and *British R'n'B Explosion, Vol. 1* (CD); *That's Alright* and *Sugar Babe* on *The R&B Era, Vol. 2* (CD); and *I'm Looking For A Woman* on *The R&B Era, Vol. 1* (LP & CD) and *Beat Merchants* (2-LP). (VJ)

Keith Powell (and The Valets)

Personnel:

DAVE HOLLIS	drms		A
JOHNNY MANN	lead gtr		A
KEITH POWELL	vcls		A
TERRY WALLIS	gtr		A
CARL WAYNE	bs		A

45s:

The Answer Is No!/ Come On And Join The Party	(Columbia DB 7116) 1963 SC
Tore Up/You Better Let Him Go	(Columbia DB 7229) 1964 SC
I Should Know Better (But I Don't)/ Too Much Monkey Business	(Columbia DB 7366) 1964 R1
α People Get Ready/Paradise	(Piccadilly 7N 35235) 1965
α Come Home Baby/Beyond The Hill	(Piccadilly 7N 35249) 1965
α Goodbye Girl/ It Was Easier To Hurt Her	(Piccadilly 7N 35275) 1966
α Victory/Some People Only	(Piccadilly 7N 35300) 1966
α It Keeps Rainin'/Song Of The Moon	(Piccadilly 7N 35353) 1966

NB: α **Keith Powell** solo 45s. There's also a CD compilation of his material *The Keith Powell Story* (Sequel NEM CD 717) 1994.

A Birmingham-based beat group. **Powell** later went solo and recorded three 45s with Billie Davies. **Carl Wayne**, who'd already recorded a 45 in his own right as Carl Wayne and The Cheetahs in January 1964, left in September of that year to form **Carl Wayne and The Vikings**. He was later in **The Move**.

DUFFY POWER - Innovations (LP).

Victory was penned by former Viscounts member Don Paul. *Too Much Monkey Business* was an R&B standard. *People Get Ready* was an Impressions number and *It Was Easier To Hurt Her* was a Garnet Mimms ballad. Sequel's CD compilation *The Keith Powell Story* includes all of the 45 tracks listed above.

Various artists compilation appearances include: *It Keep Rainin'* on *Pop Inside The Sixties, Vol. 3* (CD) and *Piccadilly Story* (CD); *You Better Let Him Go* on *R&B Scene, Vol. 1* (LP); *The Answer Is No* on *Beat At Abbey Road* (CD); *Goodbye Girl, Some People Only* and *It Keeps Rainin'* on *Brum Beat - Midlands Beat Groups Of The 60's* (CD); and *Too Much Monkey Business* on *Beat Merchants* (2-LP). (VJ/AD)

Keith (Powell) and Billie (Davies)

45s:

α When You Move, You Lose/ Tastes Sour, Don't It?	(Piccadilly 7N 35288) 1966
You Don't Know Like I Know/ Two Little People	(Piccadilly 7N 35321) 1966
Swingin' Tight/ That's Really Some Good	(Piccadilly 7N 35340) 1966

NB: α as **Keith and Billie**.

See the **Keith Powell** entry for more details. *You Don't Know Like I Know* was a Sam and Dave single. Sequel's *The Keith Powell Story* (CD) includes the six 45 tracks listed above. Another Sequel CD, *Brum Beat - Midlands Beat Groups Of The 60's* gives a further airing to *Two Little People* and *Swingin' Tight*. (VJ)

Duffy Power

ALBUMS:	1	INNOVATIONS	(Transatlantic TRA 229) 1971 R2
(up to	2	DUFFY POWER	(GSF GS 502) 1973 SC
1976)	3	DUFFY POWER	(Spark SRLM 2005) 1973 SC
	4	POWERHOUSE	(BUK BULP 2010) 1976 SC

NB: (1) reissued on Rock Machine (MACH 5) 1986 and as *Little Boy Blue* (Edsel EDCD 356) 1992. (1) reissued (Get Back GET 551). (3) reissued as, *Blues Power* with extra tracks (See For Miles SEECD 356) 1992. (4) contained the same tracks as (2) but in a different order and without *Lilly*. There's also *Just Stay Blue* (RPM RETRO 802) 1995, which is a good value CD release with some of the best of his sixties output, the content of an unissued album from 1971 and both sides of a 1965 US-only 45. *Leapers And Sleepers* (RPM RPM D 240) 2002 is a 2-CD set that compiles both sides of his six Parlophone singles along with 12 previously unissued tracks.

45s:

(1963	It Ain't Necessarily So/ If I Get Lucky Someday	(Parlophone R 4992) 1963 SC
onwards)	α I Saw Her Standing There/ Farewell Baby	(Parlophone R 5024) 1963 R1
	Hey Girl/Woman Made Trouble	(Parlophone R 5059) 1963 SC
	Parchman Farm/ Tired, Broke And Busted	(Parlophone R 5111) 1964 SC
	I Don't Care/Where Am I?	(Parlophone R 5169) 1964 SC
	Davy O'Brien (Leave That Baby Alone)/ July Tree	(Parlophone R 5631) 1967 SC
	Hell Hound/Humming Bird	(CBS 5176) 1970
	River/Little Soldiers	(GSF GSZ 6) 1973
	Liberation/Song About Jesus	(GSF GSZ 8) 1973
Reissue:	Hummingbird / Hell Hound	(Epic EPC 7139) 1971

NB: α with the **Graham Bond Quartet**.

A British blues singer and a good one at that. He grew up in Fulham and released six mostly undistinguished singles for Fontana between 1959-61. Disillusioned he left the label in 1961, but after discovering the blues in a Soho basement he got a new contract with EMI in 1963. His debut 45 was a haunting version of *It Ain't Necessarily So*, which built into a dramatic climax and got a lot of radio play at the time but wasn't a hit. He recorded a follow-up, an early version of **The Beatles**' *I Saw Her Standing There* with the **Graham Bond Quartet** (which included **John McLaughlin** on guitar and **Jack Bruce** on bass). It featured some great Hammond organ work. His third 45, *Hey Girl* had a lush harp intro and showcased the power of his voice. He followed this with a frantic version of Mose Allison's *Parchman Farm*. The flip side to this, *Tired, Broke and Busted*, features **The Paramounts**. *I Don't Care* was a good R&B effort, but after a spell

Rare 60's Beat Treasures

King Size Taylor

VOL. 5

RARE SIXTIES BEAT TREASURES VOL. 5 (Comp CD) including The Presidents.

touring with The Fentones he found himself without a recording contract and a string of disappointments led to a spell of mental illness. He presented a demo of Love's *Gonna Go* to Decca, but they rejected it as being too jazzy. It was put out a little later on a small Philadelphia label Jamie, backed by *There's No Living Without Your Loving*, but because his manager didn't think Americans would go for the name **Duffy** the credit was changed to **Jamie Power**. He was then briefly in **Alexis Korner's Blues Incorporated** and had his own band **Duffy's Nucleus**. His *Innovations* album comprises R&B cuts from the mid-sixties. Released in 1971, it was recorded during 1965-67. There are powerful performances on cuts like *Rosie, There You Go* and *Comin' Round No More* and his band at the time included the likes of **John McLaughlin** and **Jack Bruce**. Most of his music consisted of him playing his acoustic style of guitar and harmonica. Musically good it lacked commercial appeal.

The promise of an album for Spark fell through, although it later appeared four years later in 1973 and is considered by many to be one of the best acoustic folk-blues albums of the period. His first contemporary solo album to appear was the self-titled effort on GSF, which was reasonable but failed to capture him at his best.

Of the two CD compilations *Little Boy Blue* is much the shorter: 37½ as opposed to 55½ minutes, but it's not a bad general introduction to his music. If you want to probe further go for *Blues Power* which comprises his album for Spark, three cuts from his *Innovations* album and his two tracks from Spark's *Firepoint* collection (*Halfway* and *City Woman*). The *Firepoint* album was originally issued on Music Man in 1969 and these releases are very rare (R3). **Power**, who was also a session harmonica player throughout the sixties, continued playing and had a new album out in 1995.

Leapers And Sleepers is a 2-CD set compiling both sides of his six Parlophone singles, 12 previously unreleased EMI and Marquis Music tracks and resequenced the relevant material from *Just Stay Blue*. The 34-track compilation comes with a colour fold-out, detailed sleevenotes and previously unpublished pictures.

Compilation appearances include: *I Saw Her Standing There* and *Farewell Baby* on *Rare 60's Beat Treasures, Vol. 1* (CD); and *I Saw Her Standing There* and *Tired, Broke And Busted* on *R&B At Abbey Road* (CD). (VJ)

Powerhouse

Personnel incl:			
GRAHAM ATTWOOD	sax		A
BERNIE BYRNES	drms		A
KEV CURTIS	vcls		A
PETER HEWITT	bs		A
BIFF KEEGAN	vcls		A
PETER TATTERSALL	lead gtr		A
T.D. BACKUS	vcls		B

JOHN FIRTH	drms		B
TERRY GIBBS	vcls		B
ALAN GREENHALGH	tenor sax		B
CALVIN 'SPUD' HUDSON	ld gtr		B
STUART MURRAY	baritone sax		B
JACK UNELL	bs		B
DARRYL OGDEN	keyb'ds		B

NB: Line-up 'A' formerly known as Ricky Adamas and The Steeltones. We previously also had Stuart Olsberg (gtr) listed as a member, which now appears to be incorrect.

45s:			
	Chain Gang/Can You Hear Me?	(Decca F 12471) 1966 SC	
	Raindrops/La Bamba	(Decca F 12507) 1966	

A soulish male sextet from Manchester. They were originally known as Ricky Adams and The Steeltones. Graham Attwood now plays with Pete Maclaines new Clan.

Compilation appearances include: *Can You Hear Me* on *Mod Scene, Vol. 2* (CD); and *Chain Gang* and *Can You Hear Me?* on *The Soul Of British RnB 1962-1968*. (VJ/DH/AD)

Power Pack

Personnel incl:			
TOMMY FROST	drms		A
BOBBY HARRISON	vcls		
ROBIN LUMSDEN	organ		

ALBUM:	1 SOUL CURE	(Polydor 583 057) 1969 SC

45s:		
It Hurts Me So/What You Gonna Do	(CBS 202335) 1966 R1
I'll Be Anything For You/	
The Lost Summer	(CBS 202551) 1967 SC
Hannibal Brooks/Juliet Simkins	(Polydor 56311) 1969
Oh Calcutta/Soul Searchin'	(Polydor 2001 077) 1970 SC

A soul-tinged R'n'B band from Birmingham. Bobby Harrish later played drums in **Procol Harum** and Lumsden later joined **Freedom**. (VJ)

The Preachers

Personnel:			
TONY CHAPMAN	drms		A
PETER FRAMPTON	gtr		A
PETER GOSLING	organ, vcls		A
KEN LEAMON	sax		A
PETE LINTON	gtr		A
ANDY BOWN	bs		A
STEVE CARROLL	gtr		A
GARY TAYLOR	gtr		A

45:		
Hole In My Soul/	
Too Old In The Head	(Columbia DB 7680) 1965 R2

NB: *Nod, Shake & Stomp With The Preachers* (Tenth Planet TP 053) 200? is a 16-track collection.

This London-based R&B group is perhaps best remembered for including **Peter Frampton** on guitar. They were managed by **Bill Wyman** (of **Rolling Stones**) and later evolved into **The Herd**. Line-up (A) played on the 45, but the three other members listed above were all in the band at some point. Along with **Frampton**, **Bown**, Chapman and Taylor were all later in **The Herd**. Peter Gosling had previously played in **Denny Mitchell Soundsation**.

Nod, Shake & Stomp With The Preachers is a 16-track collection comprising 14 live tracks and two studio demos. They were Tony Chapman's first band after leaving the embryonic **Rolling Stones** and the collection also showcases the superb guitar playing of Steve Carroll who died within a couple of weeks of these performances being recorded.

Compilation appearances include: *Hole In My Soul* on *R&B Scene, Vol. 1* (LP); and *Yesterday Today and Tomorrow* (from a US 45) on *Incredible Sound Show Stories, Vol. 9* (LP). (VJ)

The Precious Few

Personnel:	CHRIS BELL	drms, vcls	A
	BRIAN CROOK	ld gtr	A
	ROGER PYMER	bs	A
	PETE REYNOLDS	vcls	A

| 45s: | Young Girl/Little Children Sleep | (Pye 7N 17510) 1968 |
| | Pleasure Of You/Little Children Sleep | (Pye 7N 17641) 1968 |

Formed in Norwich in 1967. Bell, Crook and Pymer had all previously been with The Versions. They played a mixture of pop and Motown. Despite selling pretty well their 1968 cover of Gary Puckett and The Union Gap's *Young Girl* failed to chart and they disintegrated the following year.

Young Girl was later compiled on *Ripples, Vol. 4* (CD). (VJ)

Pregnant Insomnia

Personnel:	JOHN BOSWELL	drms	A
	TONY EDWARDS	organ	A
	ROCKY SHAN	vcls, bs	A
	NEVILLE WILLS	ld gtr	A

| 45: | Wallpaper/You Intrigue Me | (Direction 58-3132) 1967 R1 |

A rare and sought-after psychedelic 45 by a Dublin group. Boswell was later in **Samuel Proby**.

Compilation appearances include: *Wallpaper* on *Rubble, Vol. 11* (CD) and *The Best Of Rubble Collection, Vol. 3* (CD) and *You Intrigue Me* on *Colour Me Pop, Vol 1* (CD). (VJ)

Prelude (1)

| ALBUM: | 1 | PRELUDE | (Crochet CME 18 A/B) 197? R2 |

A privately pressed album, which is now a minor collectable. It consists of two girl singers with acoustic guitars singing mainly traditional material like *The Water Is Wide*. (VJ)

Prelude (2)

Personnel:	BRIAN HUME	gtr, vcls	A
	IRENE HUME	vcls, percsn	A
	IAN VARDY	gtr, vcls	A

ALBUMS: 1(A)	HOW LONG IS FOREVER	(Dawn DNLS 3052) 1973 SC
(up to 2(A)	AFTER THE GOLDRUSH	(Island ILPS 9282) 1974
1976) 3(A)	DUTCH COURAGE	(Dawn DNLS 3061) 1974 SC
4(A)	OWL CREEK INCIDENT	(Dawn DNLH 3) 1975 SC
5(A)	BACK INTO THE LIGHT	(Pye NSPL 19448) 1976

NB: (1) and (2) are the same album albeit in different packages. (3) also contains the same material, though the sleeve is only marginally different to (2). There's also a CD compilation, *Floating On A Breeze (The Dawn Anthology)* (Essential ESMCD 778) 1999.

HCP

45s:	Edge Of The Sea/Looking For Indians	(Decca F 13292) 1972	-
(up to	Out There/Three Months Gone	(Dawn DNS 1041) 1973	-
1976)	After The Goldrush/Johnson	(Dawn DNS 1052) 1973	21
	Here Comes The Sun/Follow Me Down	(Dawn DNS 1078) 1974	-
	Dear Jesus/Lady From A Small Town	(Dawn DNS 1089) 1974	-
	Fly/Rock Dreams	(Dawn DNS 1100) 1975	-
	Love Song/Me And The Boy	(Dawn DNS 1120) 1975	-
	Never Be Anyone Else But You/		
	Take It From Me	(Pye 7N 45612) 1976	-
	Feel Like Loving You Again/		
	Driven Out Of My Mind	(Pye 7N 45690) 1976	-
Reissue:	After The Goldrush/		
	I Have No Answers (picture disc)	(After Hours AFT 2) 1982	-

A Geordie folk trio (Brian and Irene were husband and wife) from Gateshead who first attracted attention when their cover of Neil Young's *After The Goldrush* made it to No 21 here in the UK and No 22 in the US.

This track was also included on their first album, which is well worth a spin and on the *Has It Dawned On You?* (LP) compilation. It is sung accepela (without instruments). Much of their material was melodic with harmony vocals and acoustic guitar. There are similarities to David Crosby and Steve Stills here, but their music was influenced by US country-rock too. Bassist Dave Peacock assisted on the *How Long Is Forever* album.

Floating On The Breeze is an anthology that draws from their four albums and non-album singles and showcases their fragile three-part harmonies and soft-rock sound effectively. (VJ/CA)

The Presidents

| 45: | Candy Man/Let The Sunshine In | (Decca F 11826) 1964 R1 |

A beat group from Cheam in Surrey, who had a shot at *Candy Man*, which had originally been a Roy Orbison 'B' side and which **Brian Poole and The Tremeloes** enjoyed a Top 10 hit with here in Britain.

Compilation appearances include: *Candy Man* on *Mod Scene, Vol. 2* (CD) and *Rare 60's Beat Treasures, Vol. 4* (CD); and *Let The Sunshine In* on *Rare 60's Beat Treasures, Vol. 5* (CD). (VJ)

Reg Presley

| 45s: | Lucinda Lee/Wichita Lineman | (Page One POF 131) 1969 |
| | 'S Down To You Marianne/Hey Little Girl | (CBS 1478) 1973 |

Reg Presley (born Reg Ball on 12 June 1943 in Andover) was, as most of you will know, lead singer with **The Troggs**, who originally formed as The Troglodytes in 1964. When they split in 1969 **Presley** recorded *Lucinda Lee* with little success so he later reformed **The Troggs** and recorded a further solo 45 for CBS along the way. (VJ)

Earl Preston and The T.T.'s/Realms

Personnel:	RITCHIE GALVIN	drms	A C
	DAVE GORE	gtr	A C
	EARL PRESTON	vcls	ABCDEF
	LANCE RAILTON	lead gtr	ABC
	WALLY SHEPHERD	bs	ABC
	CY TUCKER	gtr, vcls	ABC
	DON ALCYD	drms	B
	WENDY HARRIS	vcls	B
	JOHN CAULFIELD	bs	D
	TOMMY HUSKEY	sax	D
	TOMMY KELLY	drms	DEF
	TONY PRIESTLY	lead gtr	DEF
	BRIAN NORRIS	bs	E

NB. Line-ups A-C **Earl Preston and The T.T.'s**. Line-ups D-F **Earl Preston and The Realms**.

THE PRETTY THINGS - The Pretty Things (CD).

45s: α   I Know Something/Watch Your Step   (Fontana TF 406) 1963 SC
      β   Raindrops/That's For Sure   (Fontana TF 481) 1964 SC
NB: α as **Earl Preston and The TTs**. β as **Earl Preston and The Realms**.

This singer, whose real name was George Spurce, fronted a couple of popular Merseybeat groups in the early sixties. First he fronted The TTs, who were also featured playing pretty raucous versions of *Hurt* and *Thumbin' A Ride* on Oriole's *This Is Merseybeat, Vol. 1* (LP), *Vol. 2* (LP) of the same series includes *All Around The World* and he appeared with **The Realms**, on Ember's *Live At The Cavern* (LP) album.

He formed the T.T.'s (short for Tempest Tornadoes) in Liverpool in August 1961, having previously worked as Gene Day (with The Jango-Beats). Railton, Shepherd and Gore had all been in Faron and The Tempest Tornadoes. **Tucker** was ex-Cimarrons and Ritchie Galvin had fronted Ritchie Galvin and The Galvanisers. In April 1962, the group was about to tour France when Gore and Galvin left. Gore for family reasons and Galvin because his father wouldn't let him go to France. So Wendy Harris came in on vocals and another former Faron and The Tempest Tornadoes member Don Alcyd joined on drums. They toured US air bases in France until October 1962. Then Harris joined Groups Inc (who were touring France at the time) and Alcyd headed to **The Renegades**. This opened the way for Gore and Galvin to rejoin now the band was back in Britain. Gore later retired from the music business in April 1963 because he felt redundant. The same year the group backed Eden Kane on *Like I Love You* and Tucker released a solo 45, *My Prayer/High School Dance* on Fontana in November. The group split after an argument in December 1963. Railton, Shepherd and Galvin all went on to Vic and The T.T.'s and **Tucker** formed **Cy Tucker and The Friars**.

Earl Preston formed a new backing band The Realms with Tony Priestly (ex-Trends), Tommy Kelly (ex-Young Ones), Dave Tynan, Tommy Huskey and John Caulfield. After the Raindrops 45 Huskey left for The Times in 1965 and was later with The Houseshakers and The Hellraisers. Caufield also left in October 1965 and was replaced by ex-Bumblies member Brian Norris. In January 1966, Kelly departed to The Escosrts. In March *Hard Time Loving You/Certain Kind Of Girl* was released on CBS and credited to **The Realms**.

Norris left to join **The Cryin' Shames** in June 1966 and the band split early in 1967. Preston was still active in the business in the eighties and nineties. Lance Railton died on 24 december 1989 and a line-up played a benefit for his family.

Other compilation appearances have included: *Thumbin' A Ride* and *All Around The World* on *Let's Stomp!* (LP); *Watch Your Step* on *Mersey Beat* (2-LP) and *Beat Merchants* (2-LP); *All Around The World* on *The Exciting New Liverpool Sound* (LP); and *Thumbin' A Ride* and *All Around The World* on *Mersey Beat 1962-1964* (2-LP). (VJ/AD/JM)

The Pretty Things

Personnel:	PHIL MAY	vcls, hrmnca	ABCDEFG
	BRIAN PENDLETON	gtr	AB
	VIV PRINCE	drms	A
	JOHN STAX	bs, hrmnca	AB
	DICK TAYLOR	gtr	ABCD
	SKIP ALLAN	drms	ABC EFG H
	WALLY ALLEN	bs, vcls	CD
	JOHN POVEY	perc, vcls	CDEFG
	TWINK	drms	D
	PETER TOLSON	gtr, vcls	EFG H
	STUART BROOKS	bs, vcls	F
	GORDON EDWARDS	keyb'ds, gtr	FG H
	JACK GREEN	bs, vcls	H

HCP

ALBUMS:	1(A)	PRETTY THINGS	(Fontana TL 5239) 1965 R2 6
(up to	2(B)	GET THE PICTURE?	(Fontana TL 5280) 1965 R3 -
1976)	3(C)	EMOTIONS (mono/stereo)	(Fontana (S)TL 5425) 1967 R2 -
	4(D)	S.F. SORROW (mono/stereo)	
			(Columbia S(C)X 6306) 1968 R3/R2 -
	5(E)	PARACHUTE	(Harvest SHVL 774) 1970 SC 43
	6(E)	FREEWAY MADNESS	(Warner Bros K 46190) 1972 SC -
	7(G)	SILK TORPEDO (w/insert)	
			(Swan Song SSK 59400) 1974 SC -

PRETTY THINGS - Get The Picture? (LP).

8(G)   SAVAGE EYE   (Swan Song SSK 59401) 1976 SC -

NB: (1) reissued on vinyl in stereo (Wing WL 1167) 1967 (SC). (3) reissued on vinyl (Fontana Special SFL 13140) 1972 (SC). (4) reissued on vinyl in stereo (Columbia SCX 6306) 1970 (R1) with silver/black label. (5) reissued on vinyl (1,000 only) (G.I. WAX 6) 1982. (4) and (5) reissued as 2-LP set (Harvest SHDW 406) 1975. All the Fontana and EMI recordings have been repackaged and reissued several times. They also recorded five albums of incidental / background movie music under the "Electric Banana" pseudonym. During 1967 the band teamed up with the De Wolfe music library to record three of these. The first *Electric Banana* (de Wolf DW/LP 3040) 1967 was a 10" mini-album with five songs (three from the group and two from the songwriter Peter Reno). The second *More Electric Banana* (de Wolf DW/LP 3069) 1967 also includes two tracks from Peter Reno. Both of these were recorded by line-up C of the band. The third *Even More Electric Banana* (de Wolf DW/LP 3123) 1968 contains six tracks from the film 'What's Good For The Goose'. These were recorded by line-up D. Each album combined vocal tracks with their instrumental backing tracks and thanks to Tenth Planet you can hear these fascinating psychedelic artifacts on *The Electric Banana: Blows Your Mind* (Tenth Planet TP 031) 1997. The same material, with the addition of some later seventies library recordings, can also be found spread across two CD collections: *Electric Banana* (Repertoire RR 4088-WZ) 1990 and *More Electric Banana* (Repertoire RR 4089-WZ) 1990. There are also two other soundtracks by **The Pretty Things**: *Hot Licks* (1973) and *Return Of The Electric Banana* (1978).

(1) reissued on CD on Fontana (846 054-2) 1990 with their non-album 1964 singles added and again on CD (Snapper SMMCD 548) 1998, with bonus cuts and notes. (1) reissued on a limited edition gold CD (Snapper SDPCD 115) 2000 with a CD-ROM extra, which contains images of vintage press clippings and a black-and-white video of *Rosalyn*. (1) also reissued on vinyl (Norton ED 282). (2) reissued on CD (Phonogram 846 459-2) 1990 with five bonus tracks and again (Snapper SMMCD 549) 1998, with bonus tracks and notes. (2) reissued on a limited edition gold CD (Snapper SDPCD 115) 2000 with a CD-ROM containing some stunning mid-sixties film footage of the band and again on CD (Snapper SDPCD 114) 2004. (3) reissued on CD on Fontana (846 705-2) 1991, again on CD (Snapper SMMCD 550) 1998 and again on a limited edition gold CD (Snapper SDPCD 111) 2000. (4) was reissued on Edsel (XED 236) in 1987 in its original gatefold sleeve, again on CD (Edsel EDCD 140) in 1990. It was also reissued on CD by Snapper in 1998 with five bonus cuts, again on a limited edition gold CD (Snapper SDPCD 109) 2000 and again on CD (Edsel EDCD 109) 2004 in a digipak. (4) has also been reissued on mono on vinyl in a limited numbered edition (Rare Earth 506). (5) issued on CD (Edsel ED 289) 1988, again on a limited edition gold CD (Snapper SDPCD 110) 2000 and again on CD (Snapper SDPCD 110) 2004 in a digipak remastered with six extra tracks. (5) also reissued on vinyl in a gatefold sleeve. (6) reissued on CD (Medicine 74321 18967 2) 1995, again on a limited edition gold CD (Snapper SDPCD 117) 2000 and again as part of a 2-CD set with *Crosstalk* (Snapper SMDCD 390) 2002. (7) reissued on CD (Snapper SMM CD 559) 1999 and in a limited edition gold CD (Snapper SDPCD 112) 2000. (8) reissued on CD (Snapper SMM CD 560) 1999 and in a limited edition gold CD (Snapper SDPCD 113) 2000. (9) reissued on a limited edition gold CD (Snapper SDPCD 116) 2000.

Compilations include *Best Of The Pretty Things* (Wing WL 1164) 1967, *Let Me Hear The Choir Sing* (Edsel ED 139) 1984, *Cries From The Midnight Circus* (Harvest EMS 1119) 1986, *Closed Restaurant Blues* (Bam-Caruso KIRI 032) 1986, *The Pretty Things 1967-71* (See For Miles CM 108) 1982, reissued in 1986 and then on CD (SEE CD 103) in 1990 and *Live At Heartbreak Hotel* (Big Beat WIKA 24) 1984. *On Air* (Band Of Joy BOJ CD 003) 1992 is a disappointing set of their radio broadcasts with no information about where the tracks were recorded. Avoid! Other compilations include *Singles A's And B's* (Harvest SHSM 2022) 1977 and *The EP Collection... Plus* (See For Miles SEECD 476) 1997. Fans of the psychedelic era band will also be interested in a 12" EP, *1968 Radio Session*, (No label) 199? which contains live versions of *S.F. Sorrow Is Born*, *She Says Goodmorning* and *Balloon Burning*. Latest

Writs - The Best Of The Pretty Things Greatest Hits (Snapper SMACD 823) 2000 is a 19-track non-chronologically ordered compilation put out after the group acquired the rights to their back catalogue. *Defecting Grey* (Norton TED 1001) 2001 is an US import vinyl 10" EP containing four cuts originally included as bonus cuts on the 1998 Snapper reissue of *S.F. Sorrow*. *Singles As & Bs* (Repertoire REP 4937) 2002 is a 3-CD German import. *S.F.Sorrow/Resurrection* (Snapper SMDCD 415) 2003 is a 2-CD set comprising their classic album plus both sides of the *Defecting Grey* and *Talking About The Good Times* 45s on one disc and a live performance of the album to an invite-only audience at Abbey Road Studios on 6 September 1998 (to mark its 30th Anniversary) on the other disc. *Resurrection* (Snapper SDPCD 165) is also available as a single CD. **Dave Gilmour** guests on guitar and **Arthur Brown** provides the narration. *Still Unrepentant* (Snapper SMADD 888) 2004 is a 2-CD set plus a DVD, which compiles many of their 45 cuts. *Midnight To Six Man - 40th Anniversary Box Set* (Magoc MAG 3930442) 2005 is significant 7-CD retrospective. *Rhythm And Blues Years* (2-CD) (Snapper SMDCD 343) covers their entire life-span from 1964 to their 1999 reunion. *Psychedelic Years 1966-1970* (2-CD) (Snapper SMDCD 344) compiles the most overtly psychedelic tracks of their career. *Very Best Of The Pretty Things* (CD) (Repertoire REP 4990) is a 26-track 'best of' which covers many of the finest tracks from each stage of their creative development.

EPs:

1	THE PRETTY THINGS	(Fontana TE 17434) 1964	R2
2	RAININ' IN MY HEART	(Fontana TE 17442) 1965	R2
3	ON FILM	(Fontana TE 17472) 1966	R3

NB: *Midnight To Six Man* (7"EP) (Norton EP 504) is an exact reissue of a European picture sleeve 7" EP from 1965 with the title track backed with *Can't Stand The Pain*, *LSD* and *Me Needing You*.

HCP

45s:			
	Rosalyn/Big Boss Man	(Fontana TF 469) 1964	SC 41
	Don't Bring Me Down/ We'll Be Together	(Fontana TF 503) 1964	10
	Honey I Need/I Can Never Say	(Fontana TF 537) 1965	13
	Cry To Me/Get A Buzz	(Fontana TF 585) 1965	SC 28
	Midnight To Six Man/ Can't Stand The Pain	(Fontana TF 647) 1965	SC 46
	Come See Me/L.S.D	(Fontana TF 688) 1966	SC 43
	A House In The Country/ Me Needing You	(Fontana TF 722) 1966	SC 50
	Progress/Buzz The Jerk	(Fontana TF 773) 1966	SC -
	Children/My Time	(Fontana TF 829) 1967	SC -
	Defecting Grey/Mr. Evasion	(Columbia DB 8300) 1967	R2 -
	Talkin' About The Good Times/ Walking Through My Dreams	(Columbia DB 8353) 1968	R1 -
	Private Sorrow/Balloon Burning	(Columbia DB 8494) 1968	R1 -
	The Good Mr. Square/ Blue Serge Blues	(Harvest HAR 5016) 1970	-
	October 26/Cold Stone	(Harvest HAR 5031) 1970	-
	Stone-Hearted Mama/ Summertime/Circus Mind	(Harvest HAR 5037) 1971	-
	Over The Moon/ Havana Bound	(Warner Brothers K 16255) 1973	-
	Is It Only Love/Joey	(Swan Song K 19401) 1974	-
	Atlanta/I'm Keeping	(Swan Song K 19403) 1975	-
	Joey/Bridge Of Good	(Swan Song K 19404) 1975	-

PRETTY THINGS - Emotions (LP).

PRETTY THINGS - S.F. Sorrow (LP).

	Sad Eye/Remember That Boy	(Swan Song K 19405) 1976 -
	Tonight/It Isn't Rock'n'Roll	(Swan Song K 19406) 1976 -
Reissue:	Don't Bring Me Down/Honey I Need	(Old Gold OG 9237) 1982 -

The Pretty Things are best remembered as an R&B band which is what they set out as. Based in the Erith and Dartford area of Kent, **The Pretties** were considered even dirtier, scruffier and more outrageous than **The Stones** - so much so that they never achieved the public acceptance that would have made them as big as they should have been despite the success of their first three singles.

As the first phase of **The Pretties** chequered career drew to a close, the wildest of the bunch - **Viv Prince** - was sacked by the band following an Australasian tour in 1965 after being thrown off a plane for being drunk and disorderly and setting fire to a stage during the tour!

Their first two albums were basically R&B but *Emotions* was an unconvincing attempt to come to terms with the heady days of 1967. The album contained all original compositions, mainly credited to Taylor and May. *Children* is arguably the strongest track on the album, others like *Tripping* and *Growing In My Mind* were lyrically an attempt to come to terms with the changing times, although musically they lacked the imagination and creativity that characterised the better bands of this era. The band later claimed that they knew they had to complete the album to leave the label but had no control over the end product, which the producers laced with strings and brass. Stax and Pendleton quit the band soon after the album's release. Stax emigrated to Australia and Pendleton simply vanished. He reportedly suffered a nervous breakdown and his whereabouts remained a mystery until he resurfaced nearly 30 years later at the 100 Club in 1995, where he played on *Rosalyn* and was welcomed back into the band.

Meanwhile, Taylor and May made drastic changes bringing in Wally Allen and John Povey from **Bern Elliott and The Fenmen** and drummer **Twink** (alias John Alder) from **The Fairies**. This new line-up recorded *S.F. Sorrow* which was based on a short story by Phil May and is generally acknowledged to be the first rock opera giving **Pete Townshend** the inspiration to write *Tommy*. *S. F. Sorrow* was certainly one of the best things **The Pretties** did - an innovative and imaginative account of the life of an imaginary character - 'S. F. Sorrow'. Musically it represented a significant advance for **The Pretties**. It also may have influenced other artists of that era - for example, one of its tracks *Private Sorrow* sounded similar to subsequent **Jethro Tull** compositions on *Aqualung*. Despite its influence, it was largely unheralded at the time and did not sell well.

Around the time of *S.F. Sorrow*, the band recorded an album in France. The *Philippe De Barge* album, as it has become known, came into being when French millionaire Philippe De Barge wanted to finance something to do with swinging sixties London and he persuaded **The Pretties** to come over to his Chateau to record an album. The result was only transferred to one acetate and never pressed because he died shortly after. The album has subsequently been pirated on CDR, with some of the songs being different versions of titles which they also recorded as **Electric Banana**.

PRETTY THINGS - Parachute (LP).

Founder member Dick Taylor left near the completion of *S.F. Sorrow* and joined Clearwater Productions as house producer. Following the failure of *Parachute*, a hard-rock album, which was also highly acclaimed by the critics but sold badly, the band folded. However, they were later reformed in the mid-seventies by Skip Alan and manager Bill Shepherd and recorded three further albums *Freeway Madness* for Warner Bros. in 1973 and *Silk Torpedo* and *Savage Eye* for **Led Zeppelin**'s Swan Song label in 1974 and 1975. Line-up (H) was their final one - after six months they changed their name to Metropolis, but their fortunes remained on a downward spiral and at the end of 1977 they disbanded.

One curio from the early seventies and which is often ignored is *Monster Club*, a track which appears in the film/soundtrack (LP) "Monster Club" starring Vincent Price. In the film the band perform the track 'live' dressed in Monk's Robes, with both Tolsen and Taylor on guitar.

Along with **The Yardbirds**, the band were enormously influential on many US mid-sixties garage bands. They reformed in 1984 with a new line-up of May (vcls), Taylor (gtr) Joe Shaw (gtr), Dave Wintour (bs), John Clarke (drms) and Kevin Flanagan (sax).

The Pretty Things 1967-71 released in 1982 and again in 1986 is a collection of singles originally released for Columbia and Harvest during this period when the band advanced from R&B via art-rock to a heavier sound. Two other retrospective releases are *Let Me Hear The Choir Sing* (Edsel ED 139) 1984 and *Live At The Heartbreak Hotel* (Big Beat WIKA 24) 1984.

Of their compilations *Closed Restaurant Blues* is the most interesting documenting the period from mid-1965 to mid-1967, obviously a lean one for the band. The 18-track compilation includes strong mod-influenced 45s (*Come See Me, Midnight To Six Man, L.S.D.* and *Get The Picture*); some full blown psychedelia (*Can't Stand The Pain, Me Needing You* and *Buzz The Jerk*); several tracks from their *Emotions* album often with lush string arrangements or brass and a few attempts at soul (a previously unissued early version of *Progress*) and R&B (*Pretty Thing*). An interesting collection, this one. *Cries From The Midnight Circus* compiles material from their 1968-71 period including five tracks from their 1968 concept album *S.F. Sorrow*; four tracks from the more mainstream *Parachute* (including the heavy *Cries From The Midnight Circus*, which gives its name to the collection) and their singles from this era.

They later reformed in 1980, 1984 and 1992, but their most successful reunion started in 1998 with a live version of *SF Sorrow* recorded at Abbey Rd Studios. This featured guests David Gilmour and **Arthur Brown** and had a limited CD issue as *Resurrection* (Worldwidetribe 160042) 1998.

In 1999, **The Pretty Things** took to the road again, including a US tour and the recording of a new studio album *Rage.... Before Beauty*.

The CD reissue of their *Get The Picture* album comes with five bonus tracks:- three superb mid-sixties 45s, *Midnight To Six Man, Get A Buzz* and *Come See Me*; and excellent garage-rock flip side *L.S.D.* and *Sitting All Alone*.

The *Defecting Grey* 10" vinyl EP features a five-minute demo version of the title track, *Mr Evasion* (the 'B' side to the *Defecting Grey* 45) and two tracks from the follow-up 1968 single, *Talkin' About The Good Times* and *Walking Through My Dreams*. These four cuts were originally included as bonus cuts on the Snapper 1998 reissue of their *S.F. Sorrow* album.

Latest Writs - The Best Of Pretty Things Greatest Hits is a 19-track overview of their last 30 years with sleevenotes from Phil May. It's their R&B era (*Don't Bring Me Down* and *Rosalyn*) and their successful flirtation with psychedelia (*Defecting Grey* etc) that really catch the ear on this fine collection, although it does suffer from poor packaging.

Their original rhythm guitarist Brian Pendleton died, aged 57 during May 2001, after suffering from cancer.

Singles As & Bs is a 3-CD German import released by Repertoire in 2002. Disc One features their UK Fontana singles from 1964-1967 with several foreign releases added. Disc Two covers their EMI years up until the mid-seventies. Disc Three covers up until 1999. It's an impressive package with a booklet of rare sleeves and memorabilia and sleevenotes from 'Ugly Things' editor Mike Stax.

Very Best Of The Pretty Things is a 26-track 'best of' that compiles some of the best songs from different stages of their career. The R&B phase is represented by tracks like *Rosalyn* and *LSD*; psychedelia by *Defecting Grey, Private Sorrow* and *Death Of A Socialite* and heavy rock is represented by songs like *Havanna Bound* and *Cold Stone*.

Still Unrepentant compiles 45 tracks, ranging from R&B, rock'n'roll, psychedelia and even the odd attempt at heavy metal. The 2-CD and DVD set was released to celebrate their 40th birthday. The DVD contains an exclusive concert recorded in Brighton at the end of August 2004 as part of their 40th anniversary celebrations.

Most significant of their recent retrospectives is the 7-CD *Midnight To Six Man*. This set comprises two anthology CD discs, which essentially cherry pick from their albums. They also contain a few jewels, aside form the normal selections like *Children, Tripping, Private Sorrow* and *Balloon Burning*. There's an unreleased version of *Get Yourself Home* and an alternate version of *You'll Never Do It Alone* (from their second album) among the bonus tracks, as well as alternate takes of *The Sun* and *Progress*, for example. Their rather dodgy period around the *Silk Torpedo* and *Savage Eye* albums is fortunately underrepresented on this set. The third disc comprises the compilation *Midnight To Six Man* (originally issued in France in 1966). Here it is remastered and supplemented by 13 bonus tracks. The jewel in the crown of this retrospective is however their four French EP's (which differed slightly from their English counterparts) all with their original sleeves and mock vinyl CD artwork.

Compilation appearances have included:- *A House In The Country* and *Me Needing You* on *The Star-Club Singles Complete, Vol. 9* (LP & CD); *Alexander, Blow Your Mind* and *Grey Skies* on *Rubble, Vol. 9* (CD); *Bracelets* on *Electric Psychedelic Sitar Headswirlers, Vol. 1* (CD); *Buzz The*

PRETTY THINGS - Silk Torpedo (LP).

PRETTY THINGS - Midnight To Six (LP).

Jerk on *The Star-Club Anthology, Vol. 3* (LP); *Children* and *My Time* on *The Star-Club Singles Complete, Vol. 11* (LP & CD); *Children* and *Reincarnation* on *Made In England, Vol. 1* (CD); *Come See Me* on *Illusions From The Crackling Void* (LP) and *Psych-Out* (Bam Caruso flexi) 1987. *Come See Me* and *L.S.D.* on *The Star-Club Singles Complete, Vol. 8* (LP & CD); *Cry To Me* and *Get A Buzz* on *The Star-Club Singles Complete, Vol. 5* (LP & CD); *Death Of A Socialite* and *Photographer* on *The Star-Club Singles Complete, Vol. 12* (LP & CD); *Defecting Grey* on *Rubble, Vol. 1* (CD); *Defecting Grey* and *Walking Through My Dreams* on *Rubble, Vol. 2 - Pop Sike Pipe Dreams* (LP); *Don't Bring Me Down* on *Beat Im Star Club* (2-LP); *Eagle's Son* on *Rubble, Vol. 8* (CD); *Eagle's Son, Alexander* and *Blow Your Mind* on *Rubble, Vol. 15 - 5,000 Seconds Over Toyland* (LP); *Grey Skies* on *Rubble, Vol. 16 - Glass Orchid Aftermath* (LP); *Honey I Need* and *I Can Never Say* on *The Star-Club Singles Complete, Vol. 4* (LP & CD); *L.S.D.* on *Star-Club Show* (LP) and *Made In England, Vol. 1* (LP); *Progress* and *Buzz The Jerk* on *The Star-Club Singles Complete, Vol. 10* (LP & CD); *Raining In My Heart* on *The Star-Club Anthology, Vol. 4* (LP); *Raining In My Heart* and *Roadrunner* on *The Early Days Of Rock, Vol. 2 - Live In Concert 1964 - 1968* (CD); *S.F. Sorrow* on *Harvest Heritage - 20 Greats* (LP); *S.F. Sorrow Is Born* and *She Says Good Morning* on *Not Just Beat Music 1965-70* (LP), *S.F. Sorrow Is Born* and *She Says Good Morning* on *British Psychedelic Trip, Vol. 2* (LP) and *Great British Psychedelic Trip, Vol. 3* (CD); *Talkin' About The Good Times* and *Walking Through My Dreams* on *Psychedelia At Abbey Road* (CD); *The Good Mr. Square* on *Picnic* (2-LP); *Talking About The Good Times* and *Mr. Evasion* on *Rubble, Vol. 3 - Nightmares In Wonderland* (LP); *Turn My Head* and *Defecting Grey* ('Top Of The Pops' performances) on *Artefacts From The Psychedelic Dungeon* (CD); *Walking Through My Dreams, Talking About The Good Times* and *Mr. Evasion* on *Rubble, Vol. 2* (CD); *Midnight To Six Man, Rosalyn* and *Walking Through My Dreams* on the 4-CD box set *Nuggets II* and *Talkin' About The Good Times* resurfaced on the 4-CD box set *Acid Drops, Spacedust & Flying Saucers*.

In their later days they turned to the sideline of supplying music for film soundtracks, under the name **Electric Banana**. Their first album, a 10" *Electric Banana* recorded in early 1967, featured five songs, with various instrumental and vocal variations, and all of which featured brass accompaniment by Tilsley Orchestral. Two of the tracks, *Cause I'm A Man Free Love* were supplied by a resident songwriter at De Wolfe, but the remaining three songs, *If I Needed Somebody, Walking Down The Street* and *Danger Signs* were group compositions. By late 1967 they'd also completed a second album *More Electric Banana*, which included *Street Girl, Love Dance and Sing, I See You, A Thousand Ages From The Sun, I Love You* and *Grey Skies*. This last track was included in the Hammer film 'The Haunted House Of Horror'. Other recordings under the **Electric Banana** personna include *Eagles Son, Alexander* and *Blow Your Mind* - all are excellent. These date from 1968, and were originally released on *Even More Electric Banana*, along with *What's Good For The Goose, Rave-Up* and the epic *It'll Never Be Me*. This third album was recorded for Norman Wisdom's 'What's Good For The Goose' film, in which they also appeared. Collectors, need not fret too much however, as all the material featured on these three albums have now been compiled on *The Electric Banana Blows Your Mind* (Tenth Planet TP031) 1997, which also includes detailed sleeve

notes. Finally the last two **Electric Banana** albums, recorded in 1973 and 1978 featured harder rock material...

Wow, quite a band. (VJ/NL/JS)

(The) Alan Price (Set)

Personnel:			
CLIVE BURROWS	sax, flute	A
STEVE GREGORY	sax, flute	A
RAY MILLS	drms	A
ALAN PRICE	keyb'ds, vcls	A
RAY SLADE	bs	A
JOHN WALTERS	trumpet	A

HCP

ALBUMS:	1(A)	THE PRICE TO PLAY	(Decca LK 4839) 1966 SC -
(up to	2(A)	A PRICE ON HIS HEAD	(Decca LK/SKL 4907) 1967 SC -
1976)	3(A)	THE WORLD OF ALAN PRICE	(Decca SPA 77) 1970 -
	4(-)	O LUCKY MAN	(Warner Brothers K 46227) 1973 SC -
	5(-)	BETWEEN YESTERDAY AND TODAY	
			(Warner Brothers K 56032) 1974 9
	6(-)	METROPOLITAN MAN	(Polydor 2442 133) 1975 -
	7(-)	PERFORMING PRICE (2-LP)	(Polydor 2683 062) 1975 -
	8(-)	SHOUTS ACROSS THE STREET	
			(Polydor 2383 410) 1976 -

NB: NB: (4) - (8) **Alan Price** solo. (1) and (2) not released in the US where instead *Price Is Right* (Parrot PAS 71018) 1968 was released. (7) reissued on CD (Edsel EDCD 673) 2000. There are three 'hits' collections available on vinyl and CD (CD catalogue numbers are given):- *Greatest Hits: Alan Price* (K-Tel NCD 5142) 1987, *The Best Of And The Rest Of Alan Price* (Action Replay CDAR 1010) 1989 and *Greatest Hits In Concert* (Rialto CDRIA 2000) 1992. *Anthology* (Repertoire REP 4738-WY) 1999 is a German import covering two decades of his career. *I Put A Spell On You - The Decca/Deram Singles As & Bs* (Connoisseur VSOP CD 316) 2000 is the first time his early singles were compiled onto CD. A recent collection is *The House That Jack Built: The Complete 60s Sessions* (Castle Music CMEDD 1098) 2005.

EP:	1(A)	THE AMAZING ALAN PRICE	(Decca DFE 8677) 1967 SC

HCP

45s:	Any Day Now (My Wild Beautiful Baby)/	
(up to	Never Be Sick On Sunday	(Decca F 12217) 1965 -
1976)	I Put A Spell On You/Lechyd-Da	(Decca F 12367) 1966 9
	Hi-Lili, Hi-Lo/Take Me Home	(Decca F 12442) 1966 11
	Willow Weep For Me/	
	Yours Until Tomorrow	(Decca F 12518) 1966 -
	Simon Smith And His Amazing Dancing Bear/	
	Tickle Me	(Decca F 12570) 1967 4
	The House That Jack Built/Who Cares	(Decca F 12641) 1967 4
	Shame/Don't Do That Again	(Decca F 12691) 1967 45
	Don't Stop The Carnival/	
	The Time Has Come	(Decca F 12731) 1968 13

THE PRETTY THINGS - Electric Banana (CD).

When I Was A Cowboy/		
Tappy Turquoise (export issue)	(Decca F 12774) 1968 -	
Love Story/My Old Kentucky Home	(Decca F 12808) 1968 -	
Trimdon Garage Explosion/		
Falling In Love Again	(Deram DM 263) 1969 -	
α Sunshine And Rain/		
Is There Anybody Out There	(Decca F 13017) 1970 -	
α O Lucky Man/Pastoral	(Warner Brothers K 16266) 1973 -	
α Poor People/Arrival	(Warner Brothers K 16293) 1973 -	
α Jarrow Song/		
Look At My Face	(Warner Brothers K 16372) 1974 6	
α In Times Like These/		
O Lucky Man	(Warner Brothers K 16452) 1974 -	
α In Times Like These/		
Sell Sell Sell	(Warner Brothers K 16452) 1974 -	
α Mama Divine/It's Not Easy	(Polydor 2058 569) 1975 -	
α Papers/Little Inch	(Polydor 2058 613) 1975 -	
α Goodnight Irene/Spanish Harlem	(Polydor 2058 682) 1976 -	
α Kiss The Night/		
Ladybird/Hungry For Love	(Polydor 2058 806) 1976 -	

Reissues: Simon Smith And His Amazing Dancing Bear/
I Put A Spell On You   (Decca F 13764) 1978 -
α Jarrow Sng/Look At My Eyes   (Old Gold OG 9114) 1982 -
Simon Smith And His Amazing Dancing Bear/
I Put A Spell On You   (Old Gold OG 9594) 1986 -

NB: α **Alan Price** solo.

Alan Price was born on 19 April 1942 in Fairfield, County Durham. He formed this outfit upon his departure from **The Animals** in 1965. The albums featured a fair amount of bluesy material but the 45s were much more commercial with a happy-go-lucky air. Surprisingly, considering his talent as a songwriter, only *The House That Jack Built*, of his hits, was written by **Price**. He seemed to do just as well covering other artists' songs. The more noteworthy attempts included Randy Newman's *Simon Smith And His Amazing Dancing Bear*, US jazzmen Sonny Rollins' *Don't Stop The Carnival*, which **Price** covered in a calypso style, and Screamin' Jay Hawkins' *I Put A Spell On You*, which can also be heard on Decca's *World Of Hits, Vol. 2* (LP).

When the **Alan Price Set** broke up in 1968 **Price** teamed up with **Georgie Fame** with whom he achieved further success and he then went on to record several solo albums during the seventies. He also wrote the music score for the film 'O Lucky Man', immortalised the British Union movement with *The Jarrow Song* (which comprised a suite of melodies and analytical lyrics), and began an acting career in 'Alfie Darling'. **The Alan Price Set**'s trumpeter John Walters later became the producer of John Peel's Radio One show.

The *Performing Price* double album is taken from a live set in 1975 recorded at London's Royal Theatre. As you'd expect it includes hits like *I Put A Spell On You* and *Simon Smith And His Amazing Dancing Bear* (although *The Jarrow Song* is surprisingly omitted). It is the only place that *Take Me Back* can be heard.

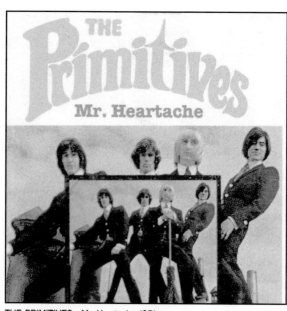
THE PRIMITIVES - Mr. Heartache (CD).

Price rejoined **The Animals** in 1975 and again in 1983.

The *I Put A Spell On You* collection covers his career with Decca and Deram and was the first time his early singles have been compiled onto CD. As well as all the hits, a few interesting 'B' sides were included like *Falling In Love Again*.

Simon Smith And His Amazing Dancing Bear has been compiled on the 2-CD set *We Love The Pirates: Charting The Big 'L' Fab 40*. (VJ)

Alan Price and Georgie Fame

| Personnel: | GEORGIE FAME | A |
| | ALAN PRICE | A |

| ALBUM: | 1(A) | FAME AND PRICE | (CBS 64392) 1971 |

| | | | *HCP* |
| 45: | Rosetta/Bonnie and Clyde | (CBS 7108) 1971 11 |

These recordings were the product of a collaboration between **Alan Price and Georgie Fame**. See their retrospective entries for details of their earlier careers. (VJ)

Bill Price

ALBUM: 1   THE FINE OLD YORKSHIRE GENTLEMAN
                            (Folk Heritage FHR 038) 1972 SC

This is an obscure folk album. (VJ)

Rick Price

ALBUM: 1   TALKING TO THE FLOWERS
                            (Gemini GME 1017) 1971 SC

| 45s: | Davey Has No Dad/Bitter Sweet | (Gemini GMS 012) 1970 |
| | Top Ten Record/Beautiful Sally | (Gemini GMS 017) 1971 |

Rick Price, who was born on 10 June 1944, in Birmingham had been guitarist and vocalist in **Sight'n'Sound** back in 1964 before leaving to join **The Move** as their bassist in March 1969. He made these records whilst he was with **The Move** and also recorded with **Mike Sheridan** (see **Rick Price and Sheridan** entry for album details). He also made recordings with fellow Brummie **Mike Sheridan** as **Sheridan-Price**.

In August 1971 he joined **Mongrel** which later expanded into **Wizzard**.

Daisy Farm Park and *Talking To The Flowers* have been compiled on *Sometimes I Wonder* (CD). (VJ)

Rick Price and Sheridan

ALBUM: 1   THIS IS TO CERTIFY THAT (Gemini GME 1002) 1970 SC

See **Rick Price** entry. This album is fairly sugary orchestrated pop, quite nice if you have a sweet tooth. *Lightning Never Strikes* has been compiled on *Sometimes I Wonder* (CD). (VJ)

The Primitives

Personnel:	GEOFF EATON	lead gtr	A
	ROGER JAMES	bs	A
	JAY ROBERTS	vcls, gtr	AB
	JOHN E. SOUL	gtr, keyb'ds	A
	MIKE WILDING	drms	A
	MAL (PAUL B. COULING)	vcls	B
	PICK WITHERS	drms	B
	DAVE SUMNER	lead gtr	B

| 45s: | Help Me/Let Them Tell | (Pye 7N 15721) 1964 R3 |
| | You Said/How Do You Feel | (Pye 7N 15755) 1965 R3 |

PRINCIPAL EDWARDS MAGIC THEATRE - Soundtrack (LP).

NB: (1) also released in the U.S. (Parkway 940) but this is almost impossible to find. *Maladjusted* (CD) (Castle CMPCD 051) is a chronological compilation containing their Pye 45s, unreleased demos and the whole of their Italian album *Blow Up. Mr Heartache* (CD) (LCD LCD 13-2) is a 20-track retrospective containing many of their Italian releases as well as their UK recordings.

This Oxford-based raw R&B group's 45s are now extremely rare and sought-after. They were originally known as The Cornflakes and also recorded a further 45 as **Mal and The Primitives**. Musically, comparable to the early **Pretty Things**, you won't need a second mortgage to get to hear these 45s. They're considered to be such definitive British R&B recordings that they've been heavily compiled and are well worth a spin.

They also recorded four acetates for Pye; one of which was the superb *Oh Mary*, a grinding R&B number. **Jimmy Page** is also said to have helped out on their second 45, whilst *Help Me* was also recorded by **The Rebounds**.

In 1965 Mal joined the band and they relocated to Italy as a quartet (at least according to the photo on their 1967 album). Aside from Mal, they comprised Jay Roberts (vcls, gtr) from the original line-up, Pick Withers (drms) and one other. Withers was later in **Spring** and Dire Straits. He stayed in Italy with **The Primitives** for three years. Line-up 'B' recorded two singles and the album *Blow-Up* which dates from 1967. This R'n'B/ soul-influenced album has been reissued in the nineties and the re-issue includes both sides of their debut Italian single *Yeeeh!.../L'Ombra Di Nessuno* (which is Dozier-Holland's *Standing In The Shadow Of Love*, with Italian lyrics) along with their follow-up Italian 45 *Johnny No* (Hoyt Axton's *Thunder 'n Lightnin'*) and other cover versions like **Stevie Winwood**'s *Gimme Some Lovin'*, The Strangeloves' *Cara Lin*, *Gina Gina* (which is Holland-Doziers' *Reach Out I'll Be There*), Don Covay's *Sookie Sookie*, which was later covered by Steppenwolf, Charlie Rich's *Mohair Sam* and an original penned by Jay Roberts *Mister Haertache* (which is misspelt like this on the sleeve). There's also an Italian song *Ma Beata Te*, penned by Cassia-Roberts, though from the soul style of the song the Roberts in question is probably Rocky Roberts, a black American singer also based in Italy at the time, who also recorded *Gina Gina*.

In 1968 came the Burt Bacharach-penned single *Bombolina*, credited to **Mal and The Primitives**, but in fact it was just by Mal. Then Mal parted from the group and started to record as **Mal dei (from the) Primitives** and later just as Mal. His recordings were MOR pop songs sung in Italian, including some covers of songs by **The Bee Gees** and Tom Jones. He even recorded a single in Greek when he visited Athens in 1970 with a backing rock group for a concert. The real surprise was that tucked away on the 'B' side was him singing a great version of **Deep Purple**'s *Black Night*. Mal remained in Italy at least until the mid-seventies and, in 1976, he released an album which contained four songs by professional Italian songwriters and six songs of his own, all in Italian.

Compilation appearances have included: *Yeeeeeeah* on *Pebbles, Vol. 18* (LP); *How Do You Feel* on *James Patrick Page: Session Man, Vol. 1* (LP & CD) and *That Driving Beat* (CD); *You Said* on *James Patrick Page: Session Man, Vol. 2* (LP & CD), *The Demention Of Sound* (LP), *Electric*

Sugarcube Flashbacks, Vol. 1 (LP), *The R&B Era, Vol. 1* (LP & CD) and on the 4-CD *Nuggets II* box set; *You Said* and *How Do You Feel* on *James Patrick Page, Session Man* (2-LP), *Footsteps To Fame, Vol. 2* (CD) and *Jimmy's Back Pages - The Early Years* (CD); *Help Me* on *Pop Inside The Sixties, Vol. 3* (CD) and *The R&B Era, Vol. 2* (LP & CD); *Help Me, Let Them Talk, You Said* and *How Do You Feel* on *Jimmy Page - Hip Young Guitar Slinger* (2-CD); *Help Me* and *You Said* on *Rubble, Vol. 7 - Pictures In The Sky* (LP), *Freakbeat Freakout* (CD) and *Maximum R'n'B* (CD); *Johnny No* on *Maximum Freakbeat* (CD), *English Freakbeat, Vol. 4* (LP & CD) and *Twisted Teenage Screaming Fuzzbusters* (LP); *I Ain't Gonna Eat Out My Heart Anymore* and *Ma Beata Te* on *Made In England, Vol. 1* (CD); *Oh Mary* on *The Sound Of The Sixties* (2-LP), *Incredible Sound Show Stories, Vol. 1* (LP & CD) and *Sixties Archive Vol. 1* (CD); *Help Me* and *Let Them Talk* on *English Freakbeat, Vol. 1* (LP); *Help Me, Let Them Tell, Cara-Lin* and *Forget It* on *English Freakbeat, Vol. 1* (CD); and *Every Minute Of Every Day* on *Incredible Sound Show Stories, Vol. 2* (LP). (VJ/CA)

Viv Prince

45:    Light Of The Charge Brigade/
      Minuet For Ringo   (Columbia DB 7960) 1966 R1

A solo outing for former **The Pretty Things**' drummer and rebel which is now quite rare. **Prince** was a classic UK rock nutter in the grand tradition of **Keith Moon** and Ozzie Osbourne.

Prince's first band had been The Dauphin Street Trad Band. He then progressed on to Carter-Lewis and The Southerners before joining **The Pretty Things** in 1963. Having been the first British rock star to become the victim of a drug bust he later managed to get sacked from what was one of the roughest bands around after getting chucked off a plane for being drunk and disorderly and setting fire to the stage during an Australasian tour.

After recording this single he formed **The Bunch Of Fives** and then joined **Denny Laine's String Band** and **Vamp**. He also played with **The Who** a few times as a stand in for **Keith Moon**. In 1969 he formed **Kate**.

Light Of The Charge Brigade also got an airing on *My Generation* (LP). (VJ)

Princess and Swineherd

ALBUM: 1 PRINCESS AND THE SWINEHERD
               (Oak RGJ 633) 1968 R3

A schoolchildren project only of interest to Oak collectors. (VJ)

Principal Edwards Magic Theatre

Personnel:			
BINDY BOURQUIN	violin, recorder, piano, organ	ABC
ROOT CARTWRIGHT	gtr, composer, arranger	AB
EVA DARLOW	dancer	A
LYN EDWARDS	perc	A
JEREMY ENSOR	bs	AB
GILLIAN HADLEY	choreographer, writer	A
JOHN HILL	dancer	A
DAVID JONES	writer, perc	ABC
VIVIENNE McAULIFFE	ld vcls	AB
MONICA NETTLES	dancer, speaking vcls	A
MARTIN STELLMAN	writer, ld vcls	AB
ROGER SWALLOW	drms	B
RICHARD JONES	vcls, bs	C
GEOFF NICHOLS	drms	C
NICK PALLETT	gtr, vcls	C

ALBUMS: 1(A) SOUNDTRACK   (Dandelion S 63752) 1969 R1
        2(B) THE ASOMOTO RUNNING BAND
                      (Dandelion DAN 8002) 1971 SC
        3(C) ROUND ONE   (Deram SML 1108) 1974 SC

NB: (1) and (2) reissued on one CD (See For Miles SEECD 412) 199? and they are back in print again.

45s: Ballad Of The Big Cow Girl And A Mere Boy/
Lament For Earth (Dandelion S 4405) 1970
Captain Lifeboy/Nothing (Deram DM 391) 1973
Weekdaze/Whizzmore Kid (Deram DM 398) 1973

Formed at Exeter University in the late sixties (their name was apparently inspired by the head of the university), **Principal Edwards Magic Theatre** were more a multi-media enterprise than a rock group, appearing with dancers and lightshows. John Peel signed them to his Dandelion label and helped produce their albums. They also appeared regularly on his 'Top Gear' show. One of the main assets was lead vocalist, Vivienne McAuliffe, whose crystal clear voice helped make them a little special. Their music was innovative and imaginative with a strong folk influence and an air of mysticism. This is typified by *The Death Of Don Quixote* and *Third Sonnet to Sundry Notes of Music* on their second album. However, arguably their best track was *Pinky: A Mystery-Cycle*. It's a melodramatic number with a thudding drumbeat, haunting lyrics and frequent changes of tempo.

However a loosely-knit outfit at the best of times, the group went their separate ways after three singles and a further album. The last one *Round One*, was made for Deram in 1974.

Compilation appearances have included: *Weekdaze* on *Psychedalia - Rare Blooms From The English Summer Of Love* (CD); *The Whizzmore Kid* on *Progressive Pop Inside The Seventies* (CD); *Autumn Lady Dancing* on *Dandelion Rarities* (CD); and *The Asmoto Running Band* on *Dandelion Sampler 1969-1972* (CD). (VJ)

Procol Harum

Personnel:			
(up to 1976)	GARY BROOKER	piano, bs	ABCDEF
	MATTHEW FISHER	keyb'ds	AB
	BOBBY HARRISON	drms	A
	DAVE KNIGHTS	bs	AB
	RAY ROYER	gtr	A
	ROBIN TROWER	gtr	BC
	B.J. WILSON	drms	BCDEF
	CHRIS COPPING	keyb'ds, bs	CDEF
	DAVE BALL	gtr	D
	ALAN CARTWRIGHT	bs	DE
	MICK GRABHAM	gtr	EF
	PETE SOLLEY	keyb'ds	F

HCP

ALBUMS: 1(B) PROCOL HARUM
(up to (Regal Zonophone LRZ 1001) 1967 R1 -
1976) 2(B) SHINE ON BRIGHTLY (mono/stereo)
(Regal Zonophone (S)LRZ 1004) 1969 R1/SC -
3(B) A SALTY DOG
(Regal Zonophone SLRZ 1009) 1969 R1 27
4(C) HOME (w/lyric sheet)
(Regal Zonophone SLRZ 1014) 1970 SC 49

5(C) BROKEN BARRICADES
(Chrysalis ILPS 9158) 1971 SC 42
6(D) LIVE (Chrysalis CHR 1004) 1972 48
7(E) GRAND HOTEL (Chrysalis CHR 1037) 1973 -
8(E) EXOTIC BIRDS AND FRUIT
(Chrysalis CHR 1058) 1974 -
9(E) PROCOL'S NINTH (Chrysalis CHR 1080) 1975 41

NB: (1) and (3) reissued as a double pack (Fly Double Back TOOFA 7/8) 1972. (No 26). (1) reissued as *1st Album Plus* (Westside WESM 527) 1998 with ten bonus tracks. (1) and (2) reissued as a 2-CD set (BGO BGOCD 556) 2002 and (1) features as bonus tracks their first two hits *A Whiter Shade Of Pale* and *Homburg* as well as the stray 'B' side *Lime Street Blues*. (1) reissued on CD (Repertoire REP 4666) in a digipak with four bonus tracks. (2) and (3) reissued as a CD set (That's Original TFOCD 5) 1988. (2) reissued again on CD (Repertoire REP 4667) 1997, with three bonus tracks (including a stereo version of *Hombourg*) and presented as a digipak including interviews with Gary Brooker and Keith Reid. (3) reissued on CD (Mobile Fidelity (USA) MFCD 823) 1986. (3) reissued again on CD (Repertoire REP 4668) 1997, with a seldom heard 'B' side *Long Gone Creek* (flip to the *A Salty Dog* 45) added to the end. (4) reissued on CD (Castle Classics CLACD 142) 1989 and again (Repertoire REP 4669) 1997 as a digipak with bonus tracks. (5) reissued on CD (Mobile Fidelity (USA) MFCD 846) 1990 and again (Repertoire REP 4980) 2002 as a digipak with a booklet and extra tracks. (6) reissued on CD (Chrysalis 252 675) 1988 and again (Repertoire REP 4981) 2002. (7) reissued on CD (Essential/Castle ESM CD 290) 1995 and again (Repertoire REP 4916) with two bonus tracks. (8) reissued on CD (Essential/Castle ESM CD 291) 1995 and again (Repertoire REP 4917) in a digipak with two bonus tracks. (9) reissued on (Essential/Castle ESM CD 292) 1995 and again (Repertoire REP 4919).

Compilations have included *The Early Years* (CD) (Dojo EARL D 6) 1992, *Collection: Procol Harum* (Castle Collector CCSCD 120) 1986, *Classics* (A&M CD 2515) 1988, *A Whiter Shade Of Pale* (Cube 853 007 CD) 1988, *Nightriding: Procol Harum* (Nightriding KNCD 10005) 1988, *Portfolio* (Chrysalis MPCD 1638) 1991 and *Procol Harum - CD Box Set* (Castle Classics CLA BX 910) 1992. *30th Anniversary Anthology* (Westside WESX 301) 1997 is a 3-CD set of the first four Regal Zonophone albums on two CDs supplemented by a third disc of 'A' and 'B' sides and outtakes, including a stereo version of *A Whiter Shade Of Pale*. There is also a booklet of information supplied by compiler Henry Scott-Irvine. More recently, there's another 'Best Of' - *The Best Of Procol Harum: Halcyon Daze* (Music Club MCCD 316) 1997. Repertoire's *The Best Of Procol Harum* (CD) 1998 concentrates on their singles from *A Whiter Shade Of Pale* to *A Salty Dog* and also includes three songs each from their *Whiter Shade Of Pale*, *Shine On Brightly*, *Salty Dog* and *Home* albums. *BBC Live In Concert* (Strange Fruit SFRCD 089) 1999 was recorded in Golders Green in 1974 and captures them around the time of the *Exotic Birds and Fruit* album. *Pandora's Box* (Westside WESA 821) 1999 features rare and previously unissued stereo versions of tracks from their first album. *A&B - The Singles* (Repertoire REP 4971) 2002 is a 3-CD set on German import with lots of rarities and alternate versions. *The First Four* (Metro Doubles METROCD 521) 2003 is a compilation of their first four albums as a 2-CD set. *Essential Collection 1967-1991* (CD) (Repertoire REP 4791) includes their best singles, including the original mono versions of cuts later available in stereo on albums. *30th Anniversary Anthology* (3-CD) (Westside WESX 301) brings to us their first four albums again remastered from the original tapes together with an extra disc of singles, outtakes and alternate mixes. This is likely to be the definitive set from this era.

HCP

45s: A Whiter Shade Of Pale/
(up to Lime Street Blues (Deram DM 126) 1967 1
1976) Homburg/

PROCOL HARUM - Procol Harum (CD).

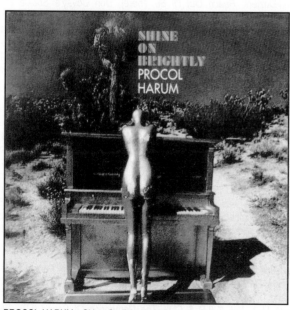

PROCOL HARUM - Shine On Brightly (CD).

Good Captain Clack	(Regal Zonophone RZ 3003)	1967	6
Quite Rightly So/In The Wee Small Hours Of Sixpence	(Regal Zonophone RZ 3007)	1968	50
A Salty Dog/ Long Gone Geek	(Regal Zonophone RZ 3019)	1969	44
Conquistador/Luskus Delph	(Chrysalis CHS 2003)	1972	22
Robert's Box/Rum Tale	(Chrysalis CHS 2010)	1973	-
Souvenir Of London/ Toujour's L'amour	(Chrysalis CHS 2015)	1973	-
Nothing But The Truth/ Drunk Again	(Chrysalis CHS 2032)	1974	-
Pandora's Box/Piper's Tune	(Chrysalis CHS 2073)	1975	16
The Final Thrust/Taking The Time	(Chrysalis CHS 2079)	1975	-
As Strong As Sansom/ The Unquiet Zone	(Chrysalis CHS 2084)	1976	-

Reissues:
Whiter Shade Of Pale/Homburg/ A Salty Dog (maxi) (PS)	(Fly Magni Fly ECHO 010)	1972	13
Conquistador/A Salty Dog	(Chrysalis CHS 2244)	1978	-
Homburg/A Salty Dog	(Cube/Dakota BAK 2)	1982	-
Whiter Shade Of Pale/Homburg	(Old Gold OG 9225)	1982	-
α Conquistador / Pandora's Box	(Old Gold OG 9692)	1987	-
α A Whiter Shade Of Pale/Homburg/Conquistador/ A Salty Dog	(Special Edition CD3-14)	1988	-

NB: α CD singles.

Procol Harum are best remembered for *A Whiter Shade Of Pale*, but we should not overlook their significance within the progressive rock genre and their reputation as a live festival act.

Brooker, **Trower** and Copping had first come together whilst still at secondary school in their native Southend as members of **The Paramounts**, an R&B group whose other members were Bob Scott (vcls) and Mick Brownlee (drms). The band went on to cut six singles for Parlophone between 1963-66, including a version of The Coasters' *Poison Ivy*, which was minor hit, climbing to No 35 in the UK. Indeed **The Rolling Stones** named the band their favourite UK R&B group after working with them on the 'Thank Your Lucky Stars' TV pop show. When **The Paramounts** finally split in September 1966, **Trower** and B.J. Wilson (who had replaced Mick Brownlee on drums back in 1963) continued to play in other R&B acts but Gary Brooker formed a songwriting partnership with lyricist Keith Reid. Having written a batch of songs they advertised in 'Melody Maker' for a band to play them and line-up (A) of **Procol Harum** was formed.

The band exploded onto the music scene in 1967 with their debut 45, *A Whiter Shade Of Pale*, a surreal poem of Reid's, which Brooker put to music adapting one of the movements of Bach's *Suite No 3 in D Major*. It was undoubtedly one of the classic progressive records of the era, topping the UK Charts for 6 weeks, rising to No 5 in the US and selling over 10 million copies worldwide. The drumming on this track was by session man Bill Eyden, although Harrison did drum on the 'B' side *Lime Street Blues*. Later that year their line-up was amended to bring in ex-**Paramounts**

PROCOL HARUM - Home (LP).

PROCOL HARUM - Broken Barricades (LP).

Trower and B.J. Wilson with Royer and Harrison having been asked to leave. They went on to form their own band, **Freedom**. Harrison went on to join **Snafu** in the seventies.

A follow-up single, *Homburg*, which was similar in style to their debut, climbed to No 6 in the UK (and 34 in the US) and their debut album appeared around the same time. Comprised almost entirely of Brooker-Reid compositions, this was more successful in America, where it reached No 47 in the Album Charts (perhaps because the American pressing, unlike the UK one, contained *A Whiter Shade Of Pale*). Often surreal in their lyrics, the band were by now becoming an important influence on subsequent art-rock acts like **The Nice** and **King Crimson**. Despite their early hits the band was essentially an album and live concert band.

Their debut album was impressive, but bombed here in the UK. Highlights include the psychedelic *Kaleidoscope*, the original version of their later hit *Conquistador* and the surreal *A Christmas Camel*.

The follow-up *Shine On Brightly* was even better. The magnum opus is the closing breathtaking 17-minute song suite *In Held Twas In I*, but the title track, *In The Autumn Of My Madness* and the rocky *Wish Me Well* all catch the ear.

After the release of *Shine On Brightly*, which again achieved Chart success in the US (No 24) but not in the UK, they played at the Miami Pop Festival on 28 December 1968 in front of 100,000 people on a bill which included Canned Heat, Chuck Berry, **Fleetwood Mac** and The Turtles.

In March 1969 Knights left the band to go into management and Fisher also departed for production, which opened the way for another ex-**Paramount**, Steve Copping, his university studies now complete, to rejoin his former **Paramount** co-founders on both bass and organ. This new line-up (C) played at The Palm Springs Pop Festival, California, on 6 April 1969, on a bill including Ike and Tina Turner and **John Mayall**.

They enjoyed further success with their next album, *A Salty Dog*, which reached No 32 in the US and went on to climb to No 27 in the UK, where the title track also reached No 44 in the Singles Chart. The album had actually been recorded by line-up (B) and produced by Matthew Fischer. *A Salty Dog* was another fine 45, much in the style of their earlier successes.

On 22 June 1969 they appeared at the Toronto Park Festival in Canada, alongside Steppenwolf, The Band, Blood Sweat and Tears and Chuck Berry. Then on 1 August they cemented their festival reputation further at the Atlanta City Pop Festival, New Jersey before well over 100,000 people on a bill that included Janis Joplin, Creedence Clearwater Revival and The Byrds.

Chris Thomas handled the production on their 1970 album, *Home*, which again achieved Chart success on both sides of the Atlantic. They played at the 3-day Atlanta Pop Festival in Byron, Georgia, before 200,000 people in July 1970, alongside **Jimi Hendrix**, The Allman Brothers Band, **Jethro Tull** and Captain Beefheart. Then on 28 August, they appeared on the second day of the Isle of Wight festival.

PROCOL HARUM - Exotic Birds And Fruit (LP).

In July 1971, they signed a new contract with Chrysalis Records in the UK and achieved more minor Chart success with their next album, *Broken Barricades*. Their guitarist, **Robin Trower**, who after the album departed for a lengthy solo career, was largely dominant on this album, which included, *Song For A Dreamer*, which he had dedicated to **Jimi Hendrix**. With his departure Dave Ball came in on guitar along with Alan Cartwright on bass. In this line-up (D) Chris Copping concentrated on keyboards. On 6 August they played a live concert in Edmonton, Canada, with the Edmonton Symphony Orchestra, which largely consisted of new arrangements of earlier album tracks. The concert was put out on a live album, *Procol Harum In Concert With The Edmonton Symphony Orchestra*, which made No 48 in the UK in May 1982. The same month a double reissue package combining their third and first (with *A Whiter Shade Of Pale* added) albums reached No 28 in the UK. Then in June, *A Whiter Shade Of Pale*, *Homburg* and *A Salty Dog*, were combined on a maxi single, which climbed to No 13. Meanwhile, as was often the case with their albums, their live album achieved greater success, going gold, climbing to No 5 and becoming their best-selling US album. It also spawned a new orchestrated version of *Conquistador*, which had first appeared on their debut album. Now, released on a 45, it became their most successful since *A Whiter Shade Of Pale*. When Ball departed in September 1972 to work with **Long John Baldry** his replacement was former **Plastic Penny** and **Cochise** member **Mick Grabham**.

This new line-up (E) recorded *Grand Hotel*, *Exotic Birds and Fruit* and *Procol's Ninth*, all of which lacked the creativity of their earlier efforts. *Procol's Ninth*, produced by Jerry Leiber and Mike Stroller, was the best of the brace. It included a revival of **The Beatles**' *Eight Days A Week* and a rather inventive cut, *Pandora's Box*, which was released as a 45 giving them their final UK Top 20 hit. They also headlined the 'Over The Rainbow' closing down concert at London's Rainbow Theatre along with **Kevin Coyne** and **John Martyn** on 16 March 1975. However, they couldn't stem the tide of their decline and split up in 1977 after one final album, *Something Magic*. With the emergence of punk-rock in the late seventies the brand of progressive rock they extolled had largely become a spent force. They did return in 1991 with *The Prodigal Stranger* album and again in 2003 - *The Well's On Fire*.

Gary Brooker went on to release three solo albums. The first *The Fear Of Flying* was produced by **George Martin** and certainly met with some critical acclaim. **Eric Clapton** and Phil Collins guested on the second *Lead Me To The Water* and *Echoes In The Night* was co-produced by his old band mate Matthew Fisher. In the late eighties he turned his attention to writing orchestral music mostly for ballet, but he also turned up to sing *A Whiter Shade Of Pale* at the 1990 **Fairport Convention** annual re-union at Cropredy in Oxfordshire. **Procol Harum**'s drummer B. J. Wilson died the same year.

The recent *The Early Years* compilation is a good starting point for those not familiar with their music. It includes all their hits, most of their 'B' sides and some of their best album tracks. *A&B - The Singles* is a 3-CD package form Repertoire on German import in 2002. Featuring their prolific 45 output with rarities and alternate versions added, this should interest the more serious fans of the band and comes with a good band history. As you'd expect, though, there are numerous other compilations which are detailed in the discography at the start of this entry.

The First Four is a 2-CD set of their first four albums, but inexplicably the title track of *A Salty Dog* is omitted from the package.

Inevitably, too, the band have appeared on a number of Various Artists compilations. *A Whiter Shade Of Pale* figured on *A Whiter Shade Of Pale* (LP), the 2-CD set *Sixties Summer Love*, and on the 2-CD set *45s - 45 Classic No 1's*; *Homburg* has been compiled on *Hits Of The Swinging Sixties* (CD); *Stardust* and *Conquistador* got a further airing on Ronco's *20 Star Tracks, Vol. 1* (LP) and *Shine On Brightly* resurfaced on the 4-CD box set *Acid Drops, Spacedust & Flying Saucers*. The band reformed in 1995 playing a string of gigs in the UK. (VJ/JM)

Mike Proctor

| 45: | Mr. Commuter/
Sunday, Sunday, Sunday | (Columbia DB 8254) 1967 R2 |

A psychedelic record quite highly-rated by some.

Compilation appearances include: *Mr. Commuter* on *14 Groovy Sounds From The Blow Up* (LP) and *Sunday, Sunday, Sunday* has resurfaced on *Colour Me Pop, Vol 3 (*CD). (VJ)

Profile

Personnel:	MILLER ANDERSON	gtr	A
	EDDIE HAMMILL		A
	JAMES MacDONALD		A
	JAMES McNALLY		A

45s:	Haven't They Got Better Things To Do/ Touch Of Your Hand	(Mercury MF 875) 1965
	Got To Find A Way/Don't Say Goodbye	(Mercury MF 981) 1965
	Politician Man/Where Is Love	(Philips BF 1757) 1969

An obscure male quartet who are thought to be Scottish, which also recorded as **Karl Stuart and The Profiles.** They later became **The Voice.** The Philips 45 may have been by a different band.

Haven't They Got Better Things To Do has re-emerged on *That Driving Beat* (CD). (VJ/SP)

Promise

Personnel:	PETER HICKS	A
	STEVE LAWSON	A
	ALAN MORGAN	A
	STEVE WEBBER	A
	PETER YOUNG	A

| 45: | Just For You/Nine Till Five | (Nems NEMS 56-4129) 1969 |

A harmony-pop group. Both sides of the 45 were written by Alan Morgan and Steve Webber, who were working at the time as songwriters for Apple Music. Morgan had previously been in **Felius Andromeda**.

Richard Hartley, the arranger on the 45 is now a successful film music composer.

Just For You has been compiled on *Colour Me Pop, Vol 1* (CD). (VJ)

Pros and Cons

| 45: | Bend It/No Time | (CBS 202341) 1966 |

The 'A' side of this disc was, of course, a massive hit for **Dave, Dee, Dozy, Beaky, Mick and Tich** the same year. The flip side was also a **Dave Dee etc.** song. These instrumental versions were the work of sessionmen. (VJ)

Brian Protheroe

ALBUMS:	1	PINBALL	(Chrysalis CHR 1065) 1974
(up to	2	PICK UP	(Chrysalis CHR 1090) 1975
1976)	3	I YOU	(Chrysalis CHR 1108) 1976
	4	LEAVE HIM TO HEAVEN	(Chrysalis CHR 1118) 1976

			HCP
45s:	Pinball/Money Love	(Chrysalis CHS 2043) 1974	22
(up to	Fly Now/Clog Dance	(Chrysalis CHS 2060) 1975	-
1976)	Running Through The City/		
	Back Away	(Chrysalis CHS 2077) 1975	-
	Good Brand Band Song/Soft Song	(Chrysalis CHS 2083) 1976	-
	Never Go Home Anymore/		
	Rock And Roll Is Our Business	(Chrysalis CHS 2096) 1976	-

From Salisbury in Wiltshire **Protheroe** was clearly a versatile sort of individual. He'd played folk music in the evenings whilst working as a trainee laboratory technician and when he recorded these albums he was pursuing a career in acting. **Protheroe**'s tuneful vocals and competent guitar and piano playing make them pleasant listening for those into singer/songwriter material. He was assisted by a backing band of Barry Morgan (drms) and Brian Odgers (bs). His best known song is *Pinball*, indeed it was his only UK hit and he's much better known as an actor now. He's appeared in productions of 'Leave Him To Heaven', 'The Beggar's Opera' and 'The Sound Of Music' (in Dublin) and in several TV drama roles and films. (VJ)

Providence

Personnel:	BOB BARRIATUA	bs, vcls	A
	BARTHOLOMEW BISHOP	lead vcls, keyb'ds	A
	JIM COCKEY	violin, vcls	A
	ANDY GUZIE	gtr, vcls	A
	TIM TOMPKINS	cello, vcls, recorder, percsn	A
	TOM TOMPKINS	viola, violin, vcls	A

ALBUM: 1(A) EVER SENSE THE DAWN (Threshold THS 9) 1972 SC
NB: (1) reissued on CD (Threshold) as a Japanese import.

45: Fantasy Fugue/Island Of Light (Threshold TH 14) 1973

An obscure US West Coast band who came to London to record on **The Moody Blues**' label. They sounded similar to **The Moody Blues**.

Their single was recorded in the US, again with the **The Moody Blues** producer.

Jim Cockey and Tim and Tom Tompkins were later in The Blue Jays, who cut an album for Threshold in 1975. (VJ/ND)

Ptolomy Psycon

An early seventies **Hawkwind** type progressive rock act from Birmingham. *Psychedelic Salvage Co. Vol. 1* (LP & CD) includes their previously privately-pressed *No One To Blame* and *Psychedelic Salvage Co. Vol. 2* (LP & CD) features the instrumental *Azreal*. The sleevenotes infer that both cuts were from a 33 1/3 EP called *Loose Capacitor*, which these sixth formers put out 50 copies of in sleeves they'd hand-painted themselves. (VJ)

Public Foot The Roman

Personnel:	SEAN BYRNE	gtr, vcls	A
	GREG KNOWLES	gtr	A
	JAMIE LANE	drms, vcls	A
	DAG SMALL	keyb'ds, vcls	A
	WARD	bs	A

ALBUM: 1(A) PUBLIC FOOT THE ROMAN
(Sovereign SVNA 7259) 1973 R1

A Cambridge progressive band whose album was housed in a striking Hipgnosis sleeve and whose odd name derived from a dilapidated road sign.

This group later became The Movies, though only Greg Knowles, Jamie Lane and Dag Small were still with them by that time. Sean Byrne was later in Legover, who made an album in 1978. He later wrote theme music for the BBC including 'The Rock'n'Roll Years'. (VJ)

The Pudding

45: The Magic Bus/It's Too Late (Decca F 12603) 1967 R2

Pete Townshend gave away *The Magic Bus* and **The Pudding** recorded this rather lightweight version. Later in 1968 **The Who** recorded the song and took a slightly heavier version to No 26 in the UK and No 25 in the US.

You can also find *The Magic Bus* on *Rubble Vol. 6: The Clouds Have Groovy Faces* (LP) and *Rubble Vol. 4* (CD). (VJ)

Peter Pumpkin

45: Would You Believe A March/
Don't Blow Your Mind (Page One POF 048) 1968

A catchy instrumental 45. (VJ)

Punchin' Judy

Personnel:	ALAN BROOKS	drms, vcls	A
	KEITH EVANS	bs, vcls	A
	ROBIN LANGRIDGE	keyb'ds	A
	BARBARA O'MEARA	vcls	A
	JOHN PHILLIPS	gtr, vcls	A

ALBUM: 1(A) PUNCHIN' JUDY (Transatlantic TRA 272) 1973 R1

A little known band. Alan Brooks also played with **Richard Digance** and Keith Evans played on Tony Kelly's 1972 album. The album sounds much like a combination of **Status Quo** and **Argent** (*Hold Your Head Up*), but without the former's enthusiasm and the latter's knack for melody. A Janis complex takes hold of the singer, who tries to bite and scratch, or else exploits an irritating vibrato in the obligatory ballads department. What's left is silly glam-rock with no appeal at all. Skip this. (VJ/MK)

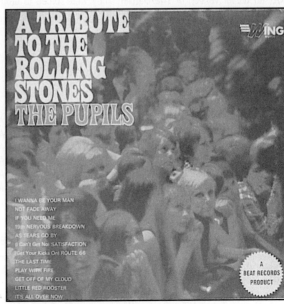

THE PUPILS - A Tribute To The Rolling Stones (LP).

The Pupils

ALBUM: 1   A TRIBUTE TO THE ROLLING STONES
                                    (Wing WL 1150) 1966 R2

NB: (1) reissued (Fontana SFL 13087) (R1) in 1969 and more recently (Beat Records BEAT 3) as a limited edition of 500 copies.

This was actually **The Eyes** using a pseudonym. As the title suggests it consists of **Rolling Stones** covers. (VJ)

The Puppets

Personnel: JIMMY 'WHITTLE' CARVEWOOD   bs   A
              DAVE MILLEN   gtr   A
              DES O'REILLY   drms   A

45s: Poison Ivy/Everybody's Talking   (Pye 7N 15556) 1963 R1
        Baby Don't Cry/Shake With Me   (Pye 7N 15634) 1964 R1

A Joe Meek-produced outfit. Indeed they were one of his few Merseybeat style groups. They were originally known as The Bobcats. Their version of *Poison Ivy* can also be heard on Sequel's *The Songs Of Leiber and Stoller* CD and *Baby Don't Cry* has resurfaced on Sequel's 2-CD set, *The Joe Meek Story: The Pye Years*.

Dave Millen was later in the **Astral Navigations Thundermother** project. (MWh/VJ.)

The Purge

45:    The Mayor Of Simpleton Hall/
       The Knave (PS)   (Corn CP 101) 1969 R3

A very rare and sought-after 45, which came in an attractive picture sleeve. This shows the band to have been a trio from Swindon in Wiltshire. The 'A' side isn't bad.

Compilation appearances have included: *The Mayor Of Simpleton Hall* and *The Knave* on *Syde Tryps, Vol. 1* (LP & CD); *The Mayor Of Stimpleton Hall* on *The Best Of Rubble Collection, Vol. 2* (CD); and *The Knave* on *The Best Of Rubble Collection, Vol. 3* (CD). (VJ)

The Purple Barrier

45:    Shapes and Sounds/
       Dawn Breaks Through   (Eyemark EMS 1011) 1968

This was an earlier version of **The Barrier**. They were forced to drop the 'Purple' due to confusion with **Deep Purple**.

See **The Barrier** entry for further details. (VJ)

The Purple Gang

Personnel: JAMES JOE BEARD   gtr   AB
              GEOFFREY BOURJER   piano, washb'd   A
              ANK LANGLEY   jug, banjo   A
              TONY MOSS   bs   A
              DEE JAY ROBINSON   mandolin, hrmnca   AB
              PETER 'LUCIFER' WALKER vcls   AB
              GEOFF BOWYER   keyb'ds   B

ALBUM: 1(A)   THE PURPLE GANG STRIKES
                                    (Transatlantic TRA 174) 1968 R1

NB: (1) reissued by Razor (RAZ 22) 1987 as *Granny Takes A Trip*. (1) reissued in original cover (Get Back GETLP 600) 1999 on Italian import. (1) reissued on CD with extra material (Essential ESMCD 636).

45s: Granny Takes A Trip/Bootleg Whisky   (Big T BIG 101) 1968

Kiss Me Goodnight Sally Green/
Auntie Monica   (Big T BIG 111) 1968

This group comprised a group of students from Stockport College of Art, Cheshire and are best remembered for their single, *Granny Takes A Trip*. Its title resulted in the single being banned by the BBC, although it was, in fact, the story of an old lady going to Hollywood to break into movies. Despite its lack of airplay, it was a popular club record and became the UFO Club theme song in 1967. Its humorous 'period' lyrics, and infectious melody still stand out as one of 1967's finest.

The band were formed as The Young Contemporaries Jugband in the winter of 1965/66 by Joe Beard and Peter Walker. A demo tape secured them a deal with Transatlantic, with Joe Boyd becoming their producer and manager. Joe, who was also working with **Pink Floyd**, also co-ran the UFO Club with John 'Hoppy' Hopkins, and helped integrate the band into the burgeoning hippie scene. Renamed as **The Purple Gang**, they got to play at the UFO, with **Pink Floyd** and **Tomorrow** and also appeared at the '14 Hour Technicolor Dream' festival.

Their gangster image and outrageous on-stage act (including on one occasion gunfire into the audience), endeared them to the early hippies, although Folk/Jug music was leagues away from the electric psychedelia of **Pink Floyd** or **The Softs**.

Granny Takes A Trip soon garnered play on John Peel's legendary 'Perfumed Garden' as well as other pirate shows, but the BBC ban, which was also partly due to Pete Walker (allegedly) being a witch, led to cancellation of a US deal amongst others.

Transatlantic, also refused to support the band financially beyond recording costs, and for most of their time in London they would live in their psychedelically decorated transit van, and later crashing at Joe Boyd's in a room next door to **The Incredible String Band**.

A follow-up 45, *Boon Tune* was written for the band by **Syd Barrett**, but not recorded (Syd later resurrected it as *Here I Go* on his *Madcap Laughs* solo LP). After the failure of their follow-up 45, *Kiss Me Goodnight Sally Green*, the group, frustrated by the lack of progress broke up.

Transatlantic, however, insisted on the band fulfilling their contractual obligations, so Joe Beard and Pete Walker put together line-up 'B'. The album, released in 1968, is now a minor collectable, but *Granny Takes A Trip* is it's high point. Most of the other material is pleasant enough, often with a comic feel to it, but it's mostly jugband music, and 'psychedelic' only in its context of the era.

Continued interest in their first 45, which became something of an anthem for the British underground, led to a reformation in 1969, although Peter Walker (who was popularly known as Lucifer) was replaced by George Janken (bs) and Irish Alex (washboard, drms). For this incarnation, the band re-appeared as a full electric band and quickly re-established itself on the college/university hall circuit - playing gigs with Love, **David Bowie**,

THE PURPLE GANG - Strikes (LP) (Reissue cover).

Captain Beefheart, **T. Rex**, **Yes**, **Ambrose Slade**, **The Kinks**, **Move**, **Family** and **The Pretty Things**. This time around they were managed by ex-Radio 1 DJ David Symonds, but no record company deal came to fruition.

The Purple Gang faded into obscurity for the next 25 years but in 1998 founder Joe Beard put together a new **Purple Gang**, reforming the band with three new members to record CD *Night Of The Uncool* and play live gigs again.

Compilation appearances have included: *Granny Takes A Trip* and *The Wizard* on *The Electric Lemonade Acid Test, Vol. 2* (LP); and *Granny Takes A Trip* on the 4-CD box set *Acid Drops, Spacedust and Flying Saucers* and on *The Transatlantic Story* CD box set. (VJ/JB)

Purple Scurf

This band's heavy progressive instrumental, *Heavy Switch*, from a previously unreleased 1971 private tape, has now been included on *Psychedelic Salvage Co. Vol. 1* (LP & CD), but is very tedious and not recommended. (VJ)

Pussy (1)

Personnel:	DEK BOYCE	vcls	A
	BARRY CLARK	gtrs	A
	STEVE TOWNSEND	drms	A
	JEZ TURNER	bs	A
	PETER WHITEMAN	keyb'ds	A

ALBUM: 1(A) PUSSY PLAYS (Morgan Bluetown BT 5002) 1969 R4

NB: (1) reissued on vinyl (Akarma AK 288LP). (1) reissued on CD (Background HBG 123/5) 1993, again (Edsel EDCD 689) 2001 mastered from the original tapes with sleevenotes and again (Akarma AK 288CD) digipaked in a gatefold sleeve.

This band was originally known as **Fortes Mentum**, and their album is one of the best British progressive rock ultra-rarities. It kicks off with a keyboard-driven rock number, *Come Back June*, which is followed by *All Of My Life*, notable for its unusual, melodramatic vocals and fine keyboard arrangements. In contrast, *We Built The Sun* is characterised by lovely melodic guitar work and eerie harmonies. *The Open Ground* is unusual and quite trippy, with partly spoken lyrics, while *Comets* is a maze of cosmic theremin-filled sound effects. Though there are also some less good instrumentals (*Tragedy In F. Minor*, which features a nice mellotron intro, and *G.E.A.B.*), if prog rock's your scene this is definitely one to check out.

The Edsel reissue features sleevenotes from the ever-dependable David Wells. The album has also been reissued on Akarma in both vinyl and CD formats.

All Of My Life has been compiled on *Morgan Blue Town* (LP) and *Best And The Rest Of British Psychedelia* (CD). (VJ/MH/RMJ)

Pussy (2)

45: Feline Woman/Ska Child (Deram DM 368) 1972 SC

This was a short-lived and later version of **Jerusalem**. The 45 was produced by Ian Gillan and is pretty nondescript with lots of guitars. (VJ)

Pussyfoot

Personnel:	TERRY "BARNYARD" BARFIELD	vcls	A
	TERRY "GOODMAYES" GOODMAN	drms	A
	DAVID OSBORNE	gtr	A
	DAVID "TURNIP" TOWNEND	bs	A
	JOHN "FINGERS" WILLIAMS	ld gtr	A

45s:	Freeloader/		
	Things That Still Remind Me	(Decca F 12474) 1966 SC
	Mr Hyde/Hasty Words	(Decca F 12561) 1967 SC
	Good Times/	

Till You Don't Want Me Anymore (Pye 7N 17520) 1968 SC

This London group was earlier known as **Rare Breed**. (VJ)

Natasha Pyne

45: It's All In Your Head/I'm A Dreamer (Polydor 56713) 1966

Natasha Pyne was an actress. The 'A' side of this folky 45 was penned by Hilton Valentine (of **The Animals**) and produced by Valentine and Ken Pitt. (VJ)

The Pyramid

Personnel incl: IAN MATTHEWS vcls

45: Summer Of Last Year/
Summer Evening (Deram DM 111) 1967 R1

A harmony group most notable for including a certain **Ian Matthews** who left to take up the vocal slot in the newly-formed **Fairport Convention** in November 1967. In January 1969 he left to go solo and soon formed **Matthews Southern Comfort**.

Both sides of this 45 are exquisite US West Coast-influenced harmony-pop and both can also be heard in all their glory on the *Deram Dayze* (LP) compilation. It was produced by Denny Cordell. (VJ)

The Pyramids

45: Baby's Gone Away/
Kiss And Dance With You (Polydor BM 56028) 1969

No other details known. (VJ)

Pythagoras Theorem

45s: Give A Damn/London Bridge (Pye 7N 17924) 1970
Our House/Free Like Me (Pye 7N 17990) 1970

A folksy pop group. There was also a Norwich band around at the same time with the same name - and the Norwich guys had to change it to Original Pythagoras Theorem. The second 'A' side *Our House* was a cover of the well known Crosby, Stills, Nash and Young song.

You can also check out *Give A Damn* on *Ripples, Vol. 6* (CD). (VJ)

PUSSY - Pussy Plays (LP).

PINK FLOYD - A Nice Pair (LP).

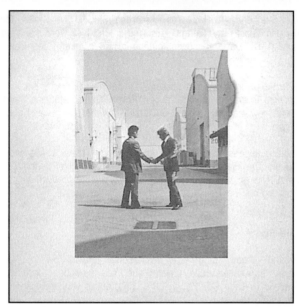

PINK FLOYD - Wish You Were Here (LP).

PRETTY THINGS - Phillipe de Barge (CD).

PROCOL HARUM - A Salty Dog (CD).

PURPLE GANG - Strikes (CD).

PROCOL HARUM - Grand Hotel (CD).

The Quakers

Personnel:
DAVE DENE	vcls	A
TERRY MUSE	bs	A
HOWARD PERKS	drms	A
MICK WHITE	ld gtr	A

45s: I'm Ready/Down The Road A Piece   (Oriole CB 1992) 1965 R3
        She's Alright/Talk To Me   (Studio 36 KSP 109/110) 1965 R4

Two extremely rare and sought-after 45s, especially the second, by a R'n'B duo from Melton, Leicestershire. *I'm Ready* is a bluesy number and *Down The Road A Piece* is a R&B track also done by **The Rolling Stones**. Their second 45 was issued on an obscure Northampton-based label.

Compilation appearances include: *She's Alright* on *Revenge Of The Amphetamine Generation* (LP); and *She's All Right* and *Talk To Me* on *English Freakbeat, Vol. 3* (CD). (VJ)

Johnny Quale and The Reaction

Personnel:
GEOFF DANIEL	gtr	A
MIKE DUDLEY	organ	A
RICKY PENROSE	bs	A
JOHNNY QUALE (aka JOHNNY GROSE)	vcls	A
JOHN "ACKER" SNELL	sax	A
ROGER TAYLOR	drms	A

EP: 1(A)   Bonna Serra/Just A Little Bit/What's On Your Mind/
          I'll Go Crazy   (Sound Studios D-105-10) 1966
NB: (1) acetate only.

This band from Truro is famous for the presence of future **Queen** member Roger Taylor. They played covers of **Swinging Blue Jeans**, Muddy Waters, Ray Charles, Billy Fury and Elvis Presley songs. The band split with **Johnny Quale** in 1965 and became **The Reaction**, but one year later **Johnny Quale** asked them to back him on an ultra-rare acetate recorded in Sound Studios, Wadebridge. This contained covers of: Acker Bilk's *Bonne Serra*, Rosco Gordon's *Just A Little Bit*, Shelley Smith's *What's On Your Mind* and James Brown's *I'll Go Crazy*. (CSx)

Quantum Jump

Personnel:
(up to 1976)
RAY COOPER	perc	A
RUPERT HINE	keyb'ds, vcls	A
TREVOR MORAIS	drms	A
JOHN G. PERRY	bs	A
MORRIS PERT	perc	A
MARK WARNER	gtr, vcls	A

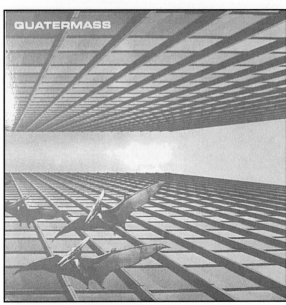

QUATERMASS - Quatermass (LP).

ALBUM: 1 (A)   QUANTUM JUMP   (Electric TRIX 1) 1976
(up to
1976)

45s: The Lone Ranger/Drift   (Electric WOT 2) 1976
(up to   No American Starship/Alta Loma Road/
1976)   Lone Ranger   (Electric WOT 9) 1976

Quantum Jump deserve a mention as their early recordings fall within the timeframe of this book. They were a sort of English Steely Dan and their music was tightly arranged and played, but with a sense of fun. They went on to record further albums beyond the timeframe of this book: *Barracuda* (Electric TRIX 3) 1977 and a compilation *Mixing* (Electric TRIX 11) in 1979. They also recorded further 45s and are best remembered for *The Lone Ranger* (Electric TRIX WOT 33), with its distinctive Maori introduction, climbed to No 5 and spent 10 weeks in the UK charts when it was re-released in 1979. (VJ/PC)

Quartet

Personnel:
TERRY BRITTEN	lead gtr, vcls	AB
KEVIN PEEK	gtr	AB
TREVOR SPENCER	drms	AB
ALAN TARNEY	bs	AB
DAVE McCRAE	keyb'ds	B

45s: Now/Will My Lady Come   (Decca F 12974) 1969
       Joseph/Mama Where Did You Fall   (Decca F 13072) 1970

The four original members of this band were from Australia originally but settled here in 1969. They soon became Cliff Richard's session band. Indeed **Terry Britten**, who had been a member of The Twilights, Australia's Number 1 group, between 1966-68, wrote *Devil Woman* for Cliff Richard (it was arguably one of the very best songs he ever recorded). Peek, Tarney and Spencer had all been in the Kevin Peek Trio.

Quartet set out as a semi-acoustic band playing classically-inspired songs. Dave McCrae was added to their line-up just prior to the release of their two 45s. They also cut an album for Decca, but it was never released. A tiny number of test pressings are known to exist, which show the band taking a mellow, Crosby, Stills & Nash-type direction.

They all became session musicians, playing for a lot of people including **Spirit of John Morgan** (on his *Age Machine* album, albeit uncredited), Tina Turner, **Mary Hopkin**, **Hank Marvin**, **Mike Hugg**, **The Hollies**, **Mike Vickers**, and Tony Cole. Spencer, Tarney and McCrae joined The Glenn Shorrock Group and later formed The Tarney-Spencer Band who issued some albums. Peek backed Cliff Richard, was later in Sky and also issued solo albums. **Britten** was also in a duo called Homer for a while. (CSx/VJ/JM/RMJ)

Quatermass

Personnel:
JOHN GUSTAFSON	bs, vcls	A
PETER ROBINSON	keyb'ds	A
MICK UNDERWOOD	drms	A

ALBUM: 1(A)   QUATERMASS   (Harvest SHVL 775) 1970 R2
NB: (1) reissued on *Harvest Heritage* (SHSM 2002) 1975 (SC) and on CD (Repertoire RR 4044-WZ) 1990 in Germany. (1) reissued as a 2-LP set (Akarma AK 175/2) beautifully packaged in a heavy duty version of the gatefold sleeve pressed on 180 gram vinyl with two bonus tracks.

This heavy rock band formed in September 1969. Mick Underwood's previous bands had included Jet Harris and The Jet Blacks, The Outlaws, an embryonic **Herd** and **Episode Six**. **John Gustafson** had been in **The Big Three** and **The Merseybeats**. They undertook a low cost US tour to help promote this album but it collapsed due to lack of finances.

Pete Robinson's organ work was very much to the fore on their album and musically they were influenced by bands like **The Nice** and early **Deep Purple**. One of its cuts, *Black Sheep Of The Family*, was later covered by Rainbow.

They were more popular on the Continent in countries like Germany and Italy than here. They had a German-only 45, *Three Blind Mice*, which is now very sought-after.

After they split in April 1971, Mick Underwood went on to play in Peace (who included Paul Rodgers of **Free** and **Bad Company** fame), Sammy, Strapps and Gillan. **John Gustafson** formed **Hard Stuff** with ex-**Atomic Rooster** members John Cann and Paul Hammond. He then did session work for **Bryan Ferry** and **Roxy Music** and was in The Ian Gillan Band and Pete Robinson went into session work before joining the jazz-rock act Brand X. Gustafson went on to **Bullet**.

Compilation appearances include: *Black Sheep Of The Family* on *Picnic* (2-LP) and *Harvest Heritage - 20 Greats* (LP) and *Good Day To Die* can be found on *Classic Rock* (CD). (VJ)

Queen

Personnel:

MIKE GROSE	bs		A
BRIAN MAY	gtr		A B C
FREDDIE MERCURY	vcls		A B C
ROGER TAYLOR	drms		A B C
BARRY MITCHELL	bs		B
JOHN DEACON	bs		C

				HCP
ALBUMS:	1(C)	QUEEN	(EMI EMC 3006) 1973	24
(up to	2(C)	QUEEN 2	(EMI EMC 767) 1974	5
1976)	3(C)	SHEER HEART ATTACK	(EMI EMC 3061) 1975	2
	4(C)	A NIGHT AT THE OPERA	(EMI EMTC 103) 1975	1
	5(C)	A DAY AT THE RACES	(EMI EMTC 104) 1976	1

NB: Also relevant is *Greatest Hits* (EMI TV 30) 1981, also on CD (CDEMTV 30) 1984. (1) and (2) reissued on Fame (FA 3040) 1982 and Fame (FA 3099) 1984 respectively. (1) reissued on CD (Fame CDFA 3040) 1988. (2) reissued on CD (Fame CDFA 3099) 1988. (3) reissued on CD (EMI CDP 746 206 2) 1988. (4) reissued on CD (EMI CDP 746 207 2) 1988 and also on vinyl (Hollywood Records LPZ 2072) 2000 as a stunning deluxe package . (5) reissued on vinyl (EMI LPCENT 29) 1997 and again (EMI 7243 99462) 1999. (5) reissued on CD (EMI CDP 746 208 2) 1988. If you've got lots of money and want to become a completist there's *The Complete Works* released in 1985 (a 13-LP box set which included an album's worth of non-album tracks, *Complete Vision*, two booklets and a map!). Also of interest may be *Twelve Inch Collection (Telstar Box Set)* (Parlophone CDQTEL 0001) 1992, but beware not all their hits are on it! *Crown Jewels* (EMI) 1998 was a box set repackaging the first eight albums.

			HCP
45s:	Keep Yourself Alive/		
(up to	Son And Daughter	(EMI EMI 2036) 1973	SC -
1976)	Seven Seas Of Rhye/		
	See What A Fool I've Been	(EMI EMI 2121) 1974	10

Killer Queen/Flick Of The Wrist	(EMI EMI 2229) 1974	2
Now I'm Here/Lily Of The Valley	(EMI EMI 2256) 1975	11
Bohemian Rhapsody/I'm In Love With My Car (Some PS)	(EMI EMI 2375) 1975	SC/- 1
You're My Best Friend/39	(EMI EMI 2494) 1976	7
Somebody To Love/White Man	(EMI EMI 2565) 1976	2

NB: When EMI was awarded the prestigious Queen's Award To Industry For Export Achievement it issued a special edition of *Bohemian Rhapsody* (EMI EMI 2375) in 1978 in blue vinyl. Copies are now very collectable and change hands for between £3,500 and £5,000.

Queen played a unique combination of pompous progressive rock and heavy metal often characterised by overdubbed vocals and layered guitars. In Freddie Mercury the band had one of the most dynamic and charismatic front men in rock history and the operatic *Bohemian Rhapsody* is definitely a top contender for the best single of all time.

Queen was formed in 1970 when Brian May and Roger Taylor (both formerly with **Smile** and prior to that May had been in a teenage band called **The Others**) teamed up with Freddie Mercury (real name Frederick Bulsara), who'd been born in Zanzibar on 5 September 1946. Bulsara had come to live in England with his family in 1959 at Feltham in Middlesex just a short walk from Brian May's home although the two didn't meet until 1970. Mercury's first band had been Sour Milk Sea and on 20 March 1970 they had a promotional page in the Oxford Mail to promote their gig in the town's parish hall. Bulsara had previously sung with Wreckage, who didn't make it onto vinyl. After some months of auditioning the line-up was completed by bassist John Deacon, a science graduate from Leicester. Their first concert as **Queen** was on 27 June 1970 at Truro City Hall. In late 1970, Mercury and Roger Taylor set up a fashion stall in London's Kensington Market. Brian May and Mike Grose completed the first line-up, but Grose was soon replaced by Barry Mitchell on bass. In February 1971 John Deacon joined, replacing Mitchell on bass, and this their classic line-up played their first gig at Hornsey Town Hall in London.

From hereon they picked up gigs whenever they could but continued to pursue their individual occupations. Their initial breakthrough came in November 1972 when they were signed by Trident Productions after some of the company's executives had attended a **Queen** concert on the recommendation of two of the firm's engineers who had heard a demo tape of the band.

Trident financed a debut album, produced by the two engineers who'd 'discovered' them (Roy Thomas Baker and John Anthony), which was leased to EMI. EMI launched **Queen** with a gig at London's Marquee on 9 April 1973. Whilst the debut album was awaited Freddie Mercury recorded a revival of The Beach Boys' classic *I Can Hear Music* using the pseudonym **Larry Lurex**. It didn't chart. The same fate befell **Queen**'s debut single *Keep Yourself Alive*.

Their first album veered towards the hard-rock of groups like **Led Zeppelin** although the style and posturings of frontman Freddie Mercury derived from the 'glam' rock era. It included their single, *Keep Yourself Alive* and other

QUEEN - Queen (CD).

QUEEN - Queen II (CD).

highlights were *The Night Comes Down*, *Liar* and *Great King Rat*. Sales were slow at first, but eventually as the band became better-known it peaked at No 24 in the UK and No 83 in the US the following year.

On 12 April 1974 **Queen** started a US tour as support to **Mott The Hoople**. Meanwhile, their second 45, *Seven Seas Of Rhye* got to No 10 in the UK. During the tour Brian May developed hepatitis and then a duodenal ulcer resulting in the tour eventually being abandoned in May 1974. This more or less coincided with the release of their second album *Queen II*, which got to No 5 in the UK and regenerated interest in their first album. Aside from *Seven Seas Of Rhye*, other highlights included *Father To Son* (with the stand-out vocal melody of the chorus), the short and simpler *Nevermore* and *Funny How Love Is*.

Their third album *Sheer Heart Attack* brought them international recognition, climbing to No 2 in the UK and No 12 in the US the following year going gold. Among its finer moments were the excellent *Killer Queen*, a dynamic song with some good harmonised vocals, which was released as a 45 and also got to No 2 in the UK and No 12 in the US; *Brighton Rock*, *In The Lap Of The Gods* and *She Makes Me* . The group toured the UK extensively to help promote their album and 45 during 1974. In February 1975 they turned their attention first to the States and later in the Spring they toured the Far East. Their next 45 *Now I'm Here* (also on the album) narrowly missed the UK Top Ten.

A Night At The Opera was their magnum opus with the seven-minute long lavishly produced and operatic *Bohemian Rhapsody* the jewel in its crown. By now the band had split amidst many recriminations from Trident Productions and were being managed by John Reid (**Elton John**'s manager). *Bohemian Rhapsody* was released as a 45 and was quite unlike anything ever released before. Each of the song's main sections contained a snippet of opera and the harmonies and production were superb. The single topped the UK Charts for seven weeks and got to No 9 in the US the following year. Definitely one of the top singles of the decade, it was also the first where success was closely related to a music video, directed by Bruce Gowers, which had been made to help promote it. The album, too, was in the UK Charts almost a year peaking at No 1. In the US it got to No 4. It had been one of the most expensive albums ever made, but it marked the pinnacle of Roy Thomas Baker's production skills and of Mercury's songwriting talents establishing the band as one of the foremost international rock acts in the world. *Death On Two Logs* was a barnstorming opener. *I'm In Love With My Car* boasted a powerful intro and luscious operatics. **Queen** ended 1975 'on top of the World' touring the UK in December 1975 and doing a live broadcast for BBC TV and Radio One from Hammersmith Odeon on Christmas Eve.

Perhaps inevitably their next album, *A Day At The Races*, was something of an anticlimax. Prior to its release they'd spent the first four months of the year touring the US, Japan and Australia. They'd also had a further hit with *Somebody To Love* (UK No 2, US No 13) (which like *Tie Your Mother Down*, a later single was included on the album). Other fine moments on this album include *Good Old Fashioned Lover Boy*, a well-crafted song, and *Drowse*, a swirling, druggy Roger Taylor composition. Such was their

QUEEN - A Night At The Opera (CD).

popularity by now that the album entered the UK Charts at No 1 and rose to No 5 in the US.

Queen went on to enjoy several more years of success becoming the archtypal stadium rock band until Mercury's tragic death on 24 November 1991 from A.I.D.S, which abruptly ended the group's career. *Bohemian Rhapsody*, probably their finest moment was re-released to raise money for A.I.D.S. research and topped the UK Charts. In the Spring of 1992 a large number of rock stars including **Elton John** and **David Bowie** performed a memorial concert for Freddie Mercury at Wembley Stadium.

After Freddie Mercury's death the remaining band members maintained low profiles. Brain May did release a second solo album *Back To The Light* in 1993 and Roger Taylor recorded with The Cross, who he'd been playing with since 1987. John Deacon opted out of the music business. The trio did re-unite in 1994 to record backing tapes for vocal tracks Mercury had recorded in his dying days and these were released in 1995 as *Made In Heaven*. Predictably they sold like hot cakes to **Queen** fans but met with mixed critical acclaim. In 2005 Paul Rodgers (ex-lead singer of **Free** and **Bad Company**) joined May and Taylor for some live concerts under the **Queen** name and one was captured on the 2-CD *Return of The Champions* release.

Compilation appearance include: *Sheer Heart Attack* on the 2-CD set *Rock Resurrection* and *We Will Rock You* on *The Best Heavy Metal Album In The World Ever!* (CD) (VJ)

The Questions

45:      We Got Love/Something Wonderful   (Decca F 22740) 1968 SC

This obscure 45 has become quite collectable. You'll also find *We Got Love* on *Mod Scene, Vol. 2* (CD). (VJ)

Tommy Quickly (and The Remo Four)

Personnel incl: TOMMY QUICKLY

HCP

45s:	α	Tip Of My Tongue/	
		Heaven Only Knows	(Piccadilly 7N 35137) 1963 R1 -
		Kiss Me Now/No Other Love	(Piccadilly 7N 35151) 1963 -
		Prove It/Haven't You Noticed	(Piccadilly 7N 35167) 1964 -
		You Might As Well Forget Him/	
		It's As Simple As That	(Piccadilly 7N 35183) 1964 -
		The Wild Side Of Life/	
		Forget The Other Guy	(Pye 7N 15708) 1964 33
		Humpty Dumpty/I'll Go Crazy	(Pye 7N 15748) 1964 SC -

NB: α **Tommy Quickly** solo.

QUEEN - Sheer Heart Attack (CD).

Brian Epstein dropped this Merseybeat era singer from Liverpool from his management. His real name is Thomas Quigley. Prior to going solo, he was vocalist with a band called The Challengers. After **Quickly** had recorded an appalling solo single, *Tip Of My Tongue*, for Piccadilly in 1963, which is now quite hard to find, Epstein recruited **The Remo Four** as his backing group. His only success in commercial terms was *The Wild Side Of Life*, a Hank Williams song, and Epstein soon realised that **Quickly** didn't have the talent to match his looks. His final 45, *Humpty Dumpty*, was recorded live at the Liverpool Empire. According to Derek Taylor's book, "Fifty Years Adrift" **Quickly** died after losing a fight against heroin addiction in the late sixties, however his nephew has pointed out that he's in fact alive and well and living in Merseyside!

Compilation appearances have included: *Kiss Me Now* on *1964 Package Tour* (LP); *The Wild Side Of Life* on *Mersey Beat* (2-LP) and *It Happened Then* (EP); *Tip Of My Tongue* on *Piccadilly Story* (CD) and *Songs Lennon And McCartney Gave Away* (LP); *The Wild Side Of Life* and *I'll Go Crazy* on *Some Other Guys* (LP); *Tip Of My Tongue* and *The Wild Side Of Life* on *The Sixties File* (LP); *The Wild Side Of Life*, *It's As Simple As That*, *Tip Of My Tongue* and *Heaven Only Knows* on *Sixties Years, Vol. 6* (CD); *Tip Of My Tongue*, *Humpty Dumpty* and *You Might As Well Forget Him* on *What About Us* (CD); and *Tip Of My Tongue* and *Heaven Only Knows* on *Merseybeat Nuggets, Vol. 2* (CD). (VJ)

Quicksand

Personnel:
ROBERT COLLINS	keyb'ds, vcls	AB
JIMMY DAVIES	gtr, vcls	AB
ANTHONY STONE	drms, vcls	AB
WILL YOUATT	bs, vcls	A
PHIL DAVIES	bs, vcls	B

ALBUM: 1(B) HOME IS WHERE I BELONG (Dawn DNLS 3056) 1974 R1

NB: (1) reissued on CD (Si-Wan SRMC 1030) 199? in Korea and again on CD (Breathless 52019).

45s:	Passing By/Cobblestones	(Carnaby CNS 4015) 1970
	Time To Live/Empty Street, Empty Heart	(Dawn DNS 1046) 1973

Another pair of Davies brothers, but this time with a very different kind of approach. Hailing from Wales, **Quicksand** played very melodious, guitar-based progressive rock, which is better than many of the sought-after rarities in this field. Youatt left to join **Piblokto** and Phil Davies was in the line-up that recorded the above album. He was also the chief songwriter.

Although nothing on this record may reach out for the sky, the tight playing, excellent vocals and above all else the exquisite melodies, makes this a worthwhile companion to all the £300+ discs in your collection. Nothing stands really out, but then again, nothing is less than good. Recommended.

QUICKSAND - Home Is Where I Belong (CD).

Collins left in May 1975. The Davies brothers joined **Alkatraz** and Stone headed for **Deke Leonard's** Iceburg. (MK/VJ/JM)

The Quiet Five

Personnel:
RICHARD BARNES	bs, vcls	A
JOHN GASWELL	sax	A
JOHN HOWELL	organ	A
KRIS IFE	gtr, vcls	A
ROGER MARSH	drms	A
ROGER McKEW	ld gtr	A

HCP

45s:	When The Morning Sun Dries The Dew/Tomorrow I'll Be Gone (Some PS)	(Parlophone R 5273) 1965	SC/- 45
	Honeysuckle Rose/ Let's Talk It Over	(Parlophone R 5302) 1965	-
	Homeward Bound/Ain't It Funny What Some Lovin' Can Do	(Parlophone R 5421) 1966	44
	I Am Waiting/ What About The Time For Me	(Parlophone R 5470) 1966	-
	Goodnight Sleep Tight/Just For Tonight	(CBS 202586) 1967	-

This London mid-sixties band enjoyed a couple of minor hits (including a cover of Paul Simon's *Homeward Bound*), but weren't so successful when they tried their hands at **The Rolling Stones'** *I Am Waiting* or the Fats Waller oldie, *Honeysuckle Rose*. **Richard Barnes** and **Kris Ife** both went solo later. Roger McKew was later in **The World**. They once backed **Patrick Dane**, **Whistling Jack Smith**, P.J. Proby, Bobby Vee and **Marianne Faithfull**. Indeed they were first known as Patrick Dane and The Quiet Five, but **Dane** left in early 1965. They recorded a version of *I Understand* for Decca, which was withdrawn because of **Freddie and The Dreamers'** success with it. **Kris Ife** later went solo. (VJ)

Quiet Melon

Personnel:
KIM GARDNER	bs	A
RON GARDNER		A
KENNEY JONES	drms	A
IAN McLAGEN	keyb'ds	A
ROD STEWART	vcls	A
ART WOOD	vcls	A

This short-lived 1969 band was the link between **The Small Faces** and **The Faces** and as you'll see had quite a star spangled line-up including ex-**Artwoods** vocalist Art Wood, **Rod Stewart**, former **Small Faces** Jones and McLagan and ex-**Birds** Kim Gardner and his brother Ron. No material was released at the time but you can now hear what they sounded like on a CD and 12" EP on the Lost Moment label. Both recordings feature the twin vocals of Art Wood and **Rod Stewart** on *Diamond Joe* and *Engine 4444* (both penned by Art) and the lengthy *Instrumental*, which was its name suggests. (VJ)

Quiet Sun

Personnel:
CHARLES HAYWARD	drms, keyb'ds, vcls	A
DAVE JARRETT	keyb'ds	A
BILL MacCORMICK	bs, vcls	A
PHIL MANZANERA	gtr, keyb'ds	A
DAVID MONAGHAN	alto, flute	A

ALBUM: 1(A) MAINSTREAM (Island HELP 19) 1975

NB. (1) reissued on Polydor/EG in 1977.

This band's roots lie in a series of **Soft Machine**-influenced groups from Dulwich College. Phil Manzanera was born as Phil Targett-Adams on 31 January 1951. The band formed in 1970 but later disbanded in February 1972 having found it hard to get gigs or a recording contract (Warner Brothers had financed some demos but nothing had come of them). In February 1972 Phil Manzanera joined **Roxy Music**, MacCormick went off to **Matching Mole** and then **Gong** and Hayward joined Mal Dean's Amazing Band (who didn't make it onto vinyl), **High Tide** (in their final months) and **Gong**. Jarrett now lectures in 'quantum physics'.

684

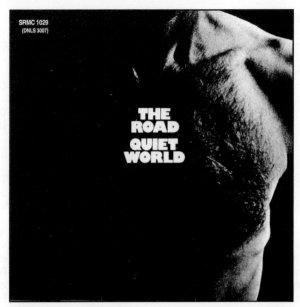

QUIET WORLD - The Road (CD).

The above album was recorded when Manzanera reformed the group in December 1974 on the strength of his success with **Roxy Music**. Mostly instrumental, it's essentially a jazz-rock orientated progressive album, which is unusual in both rock or jazz-rock terms. Its finer moments include *Sol Caliente*, which has a slightly Spanish feel and very good fuzz guitar leads by Phil Manzanera, and *Bargain Classics*, a very different dreamy number with floating keyboards. The album was issued on Antilles in the USA and re-issued on Polydor/EG in 1977.

MacCormick and Manzanera went on to play together as members of 801 (1976-77). (VJ/JM)

Quiet World

Personnel incl: STEVE HACKETT

ALBUM: 1( ) THE ROAD   (Dawn DNLS 3007) 1970 R2
NB: (1) reissued on CD (Essential ESMCD 776) and again on CD (Progressive PL 594) with rare bonus tracks.

45s: α Miss Whittington/
    There Is A Mountain   (Dawn DNS 1001) 1969 SC
    Love Is Walking/
    Children Of The World   (Dawn DNS 1005) 1970 SC
    Rest Comfortably/Gemima   (Pye 7N 45005) 1970
    Visitor/Sam   (Pye 7N 45074) 1971
NB: α as The Quiet World Of Lea and John.

This was one of a number of obscure groups Londoner **Steve Hackett** had been in prior to joining **Genesis** in August 1970. Musically, it was a Christian-based light progressive effort that mixes folk and rock with orchestrated pop, jazz and narration. After leaving **Genesis** in 1977 he recorded several solo albums. (VJ)

The Quik

45s: Love Is A Beautiful Thing/
    Bert's Apple Crumble   (Deram DM 121) 1967 R2
    King Of The World/My Girl   (Deram DM 139) 1967 R1
    I Can't Sleep/Soul Full Of Sorrow   (Deram DM 155) 1967 R2
NB: *Bert's Apple Crumble* (Klooks Kleek 60) 1998 issued on split single with a version of US band The Sonics' *The Witch*.

This late sixties soul/beat quintet's 45s are quite collectable. The flip to their first 45 is a massive mod club instrumental with some spectacular Hammond organ and a great beat.

Compilation appearances have included: *I Can't Sleep* on *Justafixation* (LP) and *Mod Scene, Vol. 2* (CD); *Bert's Apple Crumble* on *The Seventh Son* (LP) and *The Mod Scene* (CD); and *I Can't Sleep* and *Soul Full Of Sorrow* on *Psychedalia - Rare Blooms From The English Summer Of Love* (CD). (VJ)

Quincicasm

Personnel:	MALCOLM BENNETT	bs, flute	A
	JULIAN MARSHALL	keyb'ds, vibes	A
	MICHAEL ORMEROD	drms, perc	A
	NIGEL SMITH	drms, perc	A
	KAY ZESERSON	vcls	A

ALBUM: 1(A) QUINCICASM   (Saydisc SDL 249) 1973 SC

A marginal case for inclusion as the album is really progressive jazz, although side two may be of interest to progressive fans. The album is on the collectable Saydisc label. (BS)

Mike Quinn

45s: Someone's Slipping Into My Mind/
    I Know What You Know   (Fontana TF 761) 1966
    Apple Pie/There's A Time   (CBS 4506) 1969
    Toothbrush Neil/Fairy Cakes   (Jay Boy BOY 7) 1969

Mike Quinn was an important part of the Swinging London scene in the sixties. He ran a boutique in Carnaby Street where all the stars bought their gear and was a popular TV personality and deejay. His 45s were happy-go-lucky singalong numbers. *Someone's Slipping Into My Mind* was written and produced by Howard and Blaikey. (VJ)

Quintessence

Personnel:	SAMBHU BABAJI	bs, vcls	AB
	DAVE DODLING (aka MAHA DEV)	gtr	A
	PHIL JONES (aka SHIVA SHANKAR)	vcls, keyb'ds	A
	JAKE MILTON	drms	AB
	ALAN MOSTERT	gtr, vcls	AB
	RON ROTHFIELD (aka RAJA RAM)	flute, violin, perc	AB

                                           HCP

ALBUMS:	1(A)	IN BLISSFUL COMPANY	(Island ILPS 9110) 1969 R1 -
	2(A)	QUINTESSENCE	(Island ILPS 9128) 1970 R1 22
	3(A)	DIVE DEEP	(Island ILPS 9143) 1970 SC 43
	4(A)	SELF	(RCA SF 8273) 1971 SC 50
	5(B)	INDWELLER	(RCA SF 8317) 1972 SC -

QUINTESSENCE - Quintessence (LP).

NB: (1) reissued on CD (Repertoire REPUK 1009) digipaked with two bonus cuts and a detailed booklet. (2) reissued on CD (Repertoire REPUK 1016) digipaked with a detailed booklet. (3) reissued on CD (Repertoire REPUK 1063) digipaked with two bonus cuts and a detailed booklet. (4) and (5) reissued on one CD (Drop Out DOCD 1982) 1995 and the release includes a short biography, photos and more art reproduction. There's also a compilation CD from their first three albums, *Epitaph For Tomorrow* (Drop Out DOCD 1986), which reproduces some of the artwork. *Oceans Of Bliss: An Introduction To Quintessence* (Universal IMCD 300) 2003 is a recent compilation of their material.

45s:	Notting Hill Gate/		
	Move Into The Light	(Island WIP 6075) 1970	SC
	Sweet Jesus/		
	You Never Stay The Same (PS)	(Neon NE 1003) 1971	SC/-

This underground group was formed in April 1969 in response to an advert in 'Melody Maker' and after auditioning had been held in All Saints Hall, Notting Hill Gate. The guiding lights were Raja Ram (who'd been born Ron Rothfield in 1940 in Melbourne, Australia) and Sambhu Babaji, who was born in California. Canadian Jake Milton had been in **Junior's Eyes**. Phil Jones had fronted Phil Jones and The Unknown Blues, a Sydney, Australia band.

Their music was a fusion of jazz, rock and Eastern music which made great use of jazzy flute and rock guitars. At times they veered towards the pretentious but at their best they were able to achieve a high degree of spiritual union with their audience through the chanting of mantras.

In Blissful Company was recorded a few weeks after their formation following their rapid success in getting the audience to their feet at consecutive Implosion underground events at the Roundhouse in 1969. The self-titled *Quintessence* followed the next year. Very much a period piece it hasn't aged well. The opening track, *Jesus, Buddha, Moses, Gauranga* has a haunting quality and several other cuts like *High On Mt. Koilash, Shiva's Chant, Moho Mantra* and the finale, *Infinitum* are based around mantras and achieve a spiritual feel. Of the remaining material *Burning Bush* contains some good fuzz guitar and *Prisms* exudes an aura of freshness and optimism. The remaining cuts are rather tedious, mostly instrumental freak-outs.

Dive Deep is generally less spiritual (the exception being the final track *Sri Ram Chant*). It's comprised of pleasant, predominantly instrumental longer tracks (six in all), of which the title cut and *Sri Ram Chant* sound the best. Much of the material is too self-indulgent.

Jones and Dodling left after the partly live *Self* album. Jones went on to form the similar **Kala** and Dodling joined Midnight Wolf. After the *Indweller* album they split and Milton joined Blurt.

The recent Universal compilation *Oceans Of Bliss* is currently the best introduction to their career.

A compilation CD was issued on Demon in 1993. More recently, *Notting Hill Gate*, their debut 45, has been given another airing on the *Age Of Enlightenment - Prog Rock, Vol. One* (CD). They can also be heard playing *Jesus, Buddha, Moses, Gauranga* on *Bumpers* (2-LP); and *Dive Deep* on *El Pea* (2-LP) and *Gungamai* on *Nice Enough To Eat* (LP). More recently *Cosmic Surfer* has appeared on *Psychedelia and The Underground* (CD). (VJ/JM)

Daryl Quist

45s:	Thanks To You/Keep Moving (some PS)	(Pye 7N 15538) 1963
	Goodbye To You/All Through The Night	(Pye 7N 15563) 1963
	Above And Beyond/True To You	(Pye 7N 15605) 1964
	See The Funny Little Clown/	
	When She Comes To You	(Pye 7N 15656) 1964
	Put Away Your Teardrops/	
	Across The Street	(Decca F 12058) 1965

Daryl Quist was quite a prolific mid-sixties pop singer. He was Canadian but settled here and was "discovered" by Larry Parnes, who tried to push him into the big time with no success. (VJ)

Quiver

Personnel:	CAL BATCHELOR	vcls, gtr, keyb'ds	ABCD
	REG ISODORE	drms	A
	JOHN 'HONK' LODGE	bs	AB
	TIM RENWICK	lead gtr	ABCDE
	TIMI DONALD	drms	BC
	BRUCE THOMAS	bs	CDE
	JOHN WILLIE WILSON	drms	DE
	PHIL CROOKES	gtr	E

ALBUMS:	1(A)	QUIVER	(Warner Bros K 46089) 1971 SC
	2(A)	GONE IN THE MORNING	
			(Warner Bros K 46153) 1972 SC

| 45: | Green Tree/I Might Stumble | (Warner Bros K 16165) 1972 |

Quiver was formed by Tim Renwick and John 'Honk' Lodge (bs) who'd formerly been with **Junior's Eyes**, together with Cal Batchelor (ex-**Peter Bardens' Village**). The final part of the quartet was drummer Reg Isodore, who soon departed to **Pete Bardens'** On. Former White Trash/Trash member Timi Donald was recruited in his place. 'Honk' Lodge soon departed to **Uncle Dog** and the line-up was completed by Bruce Thomas (ex-**Pete Bardens' Village**) and John Wilson (formerly with **Cochise**), Donald having departed to **The Poets**.

Quiver's main claim to fame was to play the first set at The Rainbow in Finsbury Park, London, supporting **The Who**. Their albums hadn't really made much impression and lacked strong material. Dick Parry was drafted in on sax to add session support on the first one. So in 1972 all of them (except Batchelor, who'd joined 747)) amalgamated with folk-rock act **The Sutherland Brothers** with whom they went on to enjoy some success. Just prior to this Phil Crookes was briefly a member and he joined **Uncle Dog**.

Renwick and Thomas later played for **Bridget St. John**. Renwick was also in 747 and then formed Kicks, but both bands were short-lived. Renwick later played guitar in **Pink Floyd**'s live tours. Thomas was later in Elvis Costello's Attractions. (VJ/JM)

The Quotations

| Personnel incl: | JOHNNY GUSTAFSON | | A |
| | MICKEY WALLER | drms | A |

45s:		Alright Baby/Love You All Over Again	(Decca F 11907) 1964 SC
	α	Cool It/Mark Of Her Head	(CBS 3710) 1968
		Hello Memories/Pretend	(CBS 4378) 1969

NB: α has been reissued in a limited pressing of 500 reproduced from the original French jukebox pressing with a large centre hole.

This group from Liverpool was formed by former **Big Three** and **Merseybeats** bass guitarist **Johnny Gustafson**. They backed Carl Perkins on his 1964 live tour here and regularly supported The Walker Brothers during 1965 and 1966. They also supported **Cat Stevens** and were managed by Tito Burns. *Cool It* is an uptempo stomper. (VJ)

Rabbit

Personnel:

JOHN BUNDRICK	vcls, keyb'ds, gtr, bs	AB
PETE CARR	gtr	A
SIMON KIRKE	drms	A
SNUFFY WALDEN	gtr	A
TETSU YAMAUCHI	bs	AB
JANNE SCHAFFER	gtr	B

ALBUMS: 1(A)	BROKEN ARROW	(Island ILPS 9238) 1973
(up to 2(B)	DARK SALOON	(Island ILPS 9289) 1974
1976)		

NB: (1) Not issued.

45:	Broken Arrows/Blues My Guitar	(Island WIP 6161) 1973

A rock band which included former **Free** members John Bundrick and Simon Kirke and Snuffy Walden from **Stray Dog**. A different group, **Rabbitt** which included Trevor Rabin, was responsible for an album entitled *Boys Will Be Boys* (Jet JETLP 17) in 1976. (VJ)

Mike Rabin (and The Demons)

Personnel incl: MIKE RABIN

45s:	Head Over Heels/Leaving You	(Columbia DB 7350) 1964 R2
α	If I Were You/What Do You Do	(Polydor 56007) 1965 SC

NB: α as **Mike Rabin and His Music**.

From Manchester, **Rabin** was also briefly in The Troggery Five. *Head Over Heels* is punky beat.

Compilation appearances have included: *Head Over Heels* and *I'm Leaving You* on *Freddie And The Dreamers - I'm Telling You Now* (LP); and *Head Over Heels* on *Infernal World, Vol. 2* (LP). (VJ/BM/MW)

Racing Cars

Personnel:

RAY ENNIS	gtr, vcls	A
BOB LAND	bs	A
GARETH MORTIMORE	gtr, vcls	A
ROBERT WILDING	drms, vcls	A
GRAHAM HEADLEY WILLIAMS	gtr, vcls	A

ALBUM: 1 (A)	DOWNTOWN TONIGHT	(Chrysalis CHR 1099) 1976
(up to		
1976)		

NB: (1) reissued on CD (Lemon CDLEM 50)

Racing Cars played harmony-rock. Bob Land had been in **The Mindbenders** and Ray Ennis was earlier in **The Swinging Blue Jeans**. They went on to make two albums: *Weekend Rendezvous* in 1977 and *Bring On The Night* in 1978 and four 45s beyond the timescale of this book and enjoyed a hit with *They Shoot Horses Don't They?*

The CD reissue features a six-minute version of *They Shoot Horses Don't They?* (BS/VJ)

Radna Krishna Temple

ALBUM:	1 RADNA KRISHNA TEMPLE (Apple SAPCOR 18) 1971 R1

NB: (1) reissued on CD (Apple CDSAPCOR 18, also on vinyl) 1993 (SC) and again on CD (Apple CDP 7812552).

HCP

45s:	Hare Krishna Mantra/Prayer To The Spiritual	
	Masters (PS plus insert)	(Apple APPLE 15) 1969 SC/- 12
	Govinda/Govinda Jai Jai (PS)	(Apple APPLE 25) 1970 SC/- 23

NB: Only releases in picture sleeves are SC.

This was Indian spiritual music and both their 45s were unexpected hits resulting in a 'Top Of The Pops' appearance in 1969. The album, which was produced by **George Harrison**, largely comprised of hypnotic, spiritual chants and was widely listened to at the time - after all there were over two million members of the Krishna religion around the world. **Harrison** also played guitar on two tracks: - *Hare Krishna Mantra* and *Govinda*. The latest CD release on Apple comes with a bonus track and an informative 16-page colour booklet. It included the 'A' sides of their two hits, but the recent Apple reissue also features the non-album 'B' side, *Prayer To The Spiritual Masters*. (VJ)

Gerry Rafferty

ALBUMS:	1 CAN I HAVE MY MONEY BACK?	
(up to		(Transatlantic TRA 241) 1971 SC
1976)	2 GERRY RAFFERTY REVISITED	
		(Transatlantic TRA 270) 1974

NB: (1) reissued on CD (Wooden Hill HILLCD 3) 1996, in its original packaging with informative liner notes from Colin Harper. *Blood And Glory* (Demon TRANDEM 3) 1988 is a vinyl compilation of **Gerry Rafferty**'s best work for Transatlantic, both solo and as a member of **The Humblebums**. His best-known recordings of the seventies and eighties are compiled on *Right Down The Line - The Best Of Gerry Rafferty* (United Artists CDUAG 330333) 1989, including of course *Baker Street*. It was reissued again at mid-price (EMI) 1997. *Early Collection* (Transatlantic TRACD 601) 1987 compiles his earlier work. *Can I Have My Money Back? The Best Of Gerry Rafferty* (Essential ESMCD 879) 2000 is misleadingly titled as it only includes the' best of' his material for Transatlantic (and his early work with **The Humblebums**)

45:	Can I Have My Money Back/	
(up to	So Sad Thinking	(Transatlantic BIG 139) 1972
1976)		

Born in Paisley, Scotland, on 16 April 1947, **Rafferty**'s first group of any note was **The Humblebums**, whom he joined in 1968. Their two albums made little impact as did his first solo album, recorded in 1971. This was full of strong compositions which were an early indication of his potential. He then formed **Stealer's Wheel** but left them shortly after they'd recorded their debut album to return to his wife and baby in Scotland. However, when a 45 from their album, *Stuck In The Middle With You*, was a Top Ten hit on both sides of the Atlantic, he was persuaded to rejoin the band. A second solo album emerged largely unnoticed in 1974, whilst he was still with the band, but considerable commercial success awaited him at the end of the decade, though that story is beyond the time frame of this book.

Compilation appearances include: *Mr Universe* and *Can I Have My Money Back?* on *The Transatlantic Story* CD box set and *Get It Right Next Time* on *Greatest Hits Of The 70's - cd3*. (VJ)

The Rag Dolls

Personnel incl: KATHY KISSOON

RAINBOW FFOLLY - Rainbow Ffolly Sallies Forth (LP).

45: Never Had So Much Loving/
Any Little Bit   (Columbia DB 8289) 1967

This female vocal group came from Ealing in West London. They included Kathy Kissoon, who'd earlier been in The Marionettes and later went solo. (VJ)

The Ragtimers

			HCP
45s:	Sting Theme/Treat Me Gently	(Pye 7N 45323) 1974	31
(up to	Ragtime Dance/Pineapple Rag	(Pye 7N 45360) 1974	-
1976)			

This short-lived instrumental group enjoyed a minor hit with the theme to 'The Sting', a popular film of the era. (VJ)

Rainbow Cottage

Personnel:	BRIAN GIBBS	gtr	A
	GRAHAM HILL	bs	A
	TONY HOUGHTON	gtr, keyb'ds	A
	STEVE MORRIS	drms	A

ALBUM: 1(A) RAINBOW COTTAGE   (Penny Farthing PELS 553) 1976

45s: Seagull/
(up to   You've Gotta Make The Change (Penny Farthing PEN 906) 1976
1976)   Mam, Dad And Me/Walk Through Indiana (Decca F 13562) 1976
     It's A Real Nice Way To Spend A Day/
     Reach For The Sky   (Penny Farthing PEN 917) 1976

This mid-seventies pop band's album is not recommended. Brian Gibbs wrote most of the tunes although there is a version of the Jackson Browne / Glenn Frey song *Take It Easy*. (BS)

Rainbow Ffolly

Personnel:	JONATHAN DUNSTERVILLE	gtr, vcls	A
	RICHARD DUNSTERVILLE	vcls, gtr	A
	ROGER NEWELL	bs, vcls	A
	STEWART OSBORN	drms, vcls	A

ALBUM: 1(A) RAINBOW FFOLLY SALLIES FFORTH
                  (Parlophone PMC/PCS 7050) 1968 R3
NB: (1) reissued on CD (Golden Classics Rebirth GRC 008) 1997 and officially again as *Sallies Ffolly Plus* (See For Miles SEECD 493) 1998, with bonus tracks. (1) reissued again on CD (Rev-Ola CRREV 112) 2005 remastered with their rare Parlophone 45 in mono.

45:      Go Girl/Drive My Car   (Parlophone R 5701) 1968 R1

High Wycombe's **Rainbow Ffolly** had the misfortune to have their demos released as finished recordings. The resulting album is predictably patchy, though it does contain some inventive arrangements and imaginative material such as *She's Alright*, *Sun and Sand* and *The Sighing Game*. A large number of sound effects and inane chatter is employed between songs, which may grate on repeated listening and indicates that the group was not entirely serious in intent. Overall, a strong sense of British whimsicality is conveyed, making the album essential for some and near-unlistenable for others.

The A-side of their single was non-album, and the B-side was not the **Lennon/McCartney** song. When both it and the album flopped, no invitation to make further recordings was extended, though the album had apparently been "Saturday Club"'s album of the week on its release in July 1968. (MK/RMJ)

Rainbow People

Personnel:	CHAS O'BRIEN	drms, vcls	A
	PETE BUDD	vcls, gtr	A
	ROGER COTTON	gtr, vcls, piano	A
	DAVE HOLGATE	bs, vcls	A
	ANNE MALSROM	vcls	A

45s: The Walk Will Do You Good/
     Dreamtime   (Pye 7N 17582) 1968 SC
     The Sailing Song/Rainbows   (Pye 7N 17624) 1968
     Living In A Dream World/
     Happy To See You Again   (Pye 7N 17759) 1969

A late sixties group from Bristol of no real significance. Roger Cotton was later in **Life** and Chas O'Brien went into session work. *Living In A Dream World* is a Northern soul favourite.

Compilation appearances have included: *Dreamtime* on *Paisley Pop - Pye Psych (& Other Colours) 1966-1969* (CD) and *Ripples, Vol. 2* (CD); and *Rainbows* on *Ripples, Vol. 7* (CD). (VJ)

Rainbows

Personnel incl: MARTIN CURE

45s: Rainbows/Nobody But You   (CBS 3995) 1969
     New Day Dawning/Days And Nights   (CBS 4568) 1969

This was a very obscure band. *Circus Days, Vol. 5* (LP) and *Circus Days Vol's 4 & 5* (CD) gave another airing to *Rainbows*. It's quite appealing pop-psych with lots of orchestration and some good guitar at the end too. *New Day Dawning* has also been compiled on *Jagged Time Lapse, Vol 4* (CD). They included **Martin Cure** of **Peeps** fame. (VJ)

A Raincoat

Personnel:	ANDY ARTHURS	vcls, gtr	A
	PHILLIPPE CHAMBON	gtr, vcls	A
	ROD SYERS	bs, vcls	A
	DAVE HUDSON	keyb'ds, vcls	A

ALBUM: 1(A) DIGALONGAMACS   (EMI EMC 3090) 1975

An obscure album from an obscure band! The music is electric folk-rock based but clearly there is a joke somewhere centering on raincoats / mackintosh's and with song titles such as *You Can Heavy Breath On Me Now*, *I Love You For Your Mind (Not Your Body)* and *Who's A Mashed Potato Now?* they were clearly after laughs rather than admiration of their musical ability. Unfortunately the record misses the mark both in terms of humour and musical content. Perhaps you needed to have seen their live act to understand what it was all about. There are faint echoes of **Bonzo Dog Band** / Temperence Seven, but they are faint. One of their serious numbers *Making Me Nervous* does grow on you after one or two plays but all in all obscurity knocks. (BS)

The Raisins

Personnel incl:	BRANDIS	vcls	A
	HONEY DARLING	vcls	A
	DAVID GAMPORT	gtr	A
	KEITH GAMPORT	gtr	A
	PETER NELSON	organ	A
	LONDON STEEL	drms	A

ALBUM: 1(A) THE RAISINS   (Major Minor MMLP/SMLP 20) 1968 SC

45s: Ain't That Lovin' You Baby/
     Stranger Things Have Happened   (Major Minor MM 540) 1968
     I Thank You/
     Don't Leave Me Like This   (Major Minor MM 602) 1969

Produced by Tommy Scott and arranged by Peter Gage this black group's album consists of covers of popular soul numbers like *Jimmy Mack*, *When A Man Loves A Woman* and *Knock On Wood* - a marginal case for inclusion. Of their 45s, *Ain't That Lovin' You Baby* is an R&B favourite and *I Thank You* was a Sam and Dave track. (VJ)

RIPPLES VOL. 2 (Comp CD) including Rainbow People.

The Rally Rounders

45:     Bike Beat/
        Bike Beat Part 2 (PS flexidisc)   (Lyntone LYN 574) 1964 R2

This was actually a flexi-disc recorded by a later version of a prolific early sixties band called The Outlaws, who included **Ritchie Blackmore** among their personnel. They were based in London.

Bike Beat Pt. 1 and *Bike Beat Pt. 2* have been compiled on *Ritchie Blackmore - Take It! - Sessions 63 - 68* (CD) and *Visions Of The Past, Vol. 3* (LP & CD). (VJ)

Ramases

Personnel: LOL CREME   gtr, synthesizer   A
            KEVIN GODLEY   drms, flute   A
            GRAHAM GOULDMAN   gtr, bs   A
            MARTIN RAPHAEL   sitar   A
            SEL   AB
            ERIC STEWART   gtr, synthesizer   A
            BOB BERTLES   sax   B
            KAY GARNER   vcls   B
            SUE GLOVER   vcls   B
            ROGER HARRISON   drms   B
            PETE KINGSMAN   bs   B
            BARRY KIRSCH   keyb'ds   B
            SUNNY LESLIE   vcls   B
            JO ROMERO   gtr   B
            COLIN THURSTON   bs   B

ALBUMS: 1(A) SPACE HYMNS   (Vertigo 6360 046) 1971 R1
        2(B) GLASS TOP COFFIN   (Vertigo 6360 115) 1975 SC

NB: (1) was re-released in 1974 and also issued on Vertigo (9199 134) in Holland in 1980. It was issued on CD (Repertoire REP 4108-WP) 1991 in Germany and again on CD (Repertoire REPUK 1030).

45s: Ballroom / Muddy Water   (Philips 6113 001) 1971
        Jesus Come Back/Hello Mister   (Philips 6113 003) 1972

Ramases (real name Michael Raphael) was a central heating salesman from Sheffield who believed he was a reincarnation of an Egyptian god. The material for his first album, *Space Hymn*, was written by the future members of **10cc** (Creme, Godley, **Gouldman** and Stewart) who also played on it. The guitar riff from the opening cut *Life Child* later re-emerged on **10cc**'s *How Dare You* album. The album is housed in a superb Roger Dean poster sleeve. The duo recorded a further album *Glass Top Coffin*, which sank without trace.

Ramases, **Ramases and Seleka** and **Ramases and Selket** are all by the same artist - Sel was **Ramases**' wife.

You'll also find *Molecular Delusion* on *Electric Psychedelic Sitar Headswirlers, Vol. 1* (CD). (VJ/TA)

Ramases and Seleka

45:     Love You/Gold Is The Ring   (Major Minor MM 704) 1970 R1

This was an earlier single by **Ramases** and his wife who he renamed Selket after the ancient guardian of the sacred tomb in Egyptian mythology. In Europe the 'A' side appeared as *Screw You* which can be found on *Exploiting Plastic Inevitable, Vol. 2* (LP). It's a hypnotic piece with rather unnerving half-spoken lyrics and female climatic shrieks. (VJ)

Ramases and Selket

45:     Crazy One/Mind's Eye   (CBS 3717) 1968 R2

This ultra-rare, reputedly psychedelic 45, goes for well in excess of £80 in mint condition, when one finds a copy. This is Raphael and his wife again. The couple dressed in old Egyptian clothes and later recorded as **Ramases**.

In between this 45 and their **Ramases and Seleka** incarnation, they also had a German only 45, *Screw You* under the **Ram & Sel** monicker.

Compilation appearances have included: *Mind's Eye* and *Crazy One* on *Rubble, Vol. 11* (CD) and *The Best Of Rubble Collection, Vol. 3* (CD), whilst *Mind's Eye* can also be found on the 4-CD box set *Acid Drops, Spacedust & Flying*. (VJ)

The Ram Jam Band

45:     Shake Shake Senora/Akinia   (Columbia DB 7621) 1965 SC

After this 45 **The Ram Jam Band** became **Geno Washington**'s backing band. It included Ram Jam Holder. (VJ)

The Ramrods

45:     Overdrive/Stalker   (United Artists UP 1113) 1965

There had been an American band of this name in the early sixties but this 45 was the work of a long forgotten British instrumental band. The 'A' side was used in the TV series, 'Master Driving'. (VJ)

Randy

ALBUM: 1 LADY LUCK   (Transatlantic TRA 2909) 1975

A four-piece rock band about which little is known. (BS)

Peter Ransome

45:     Rainmaker Man/Saturday Morning   (York SYK 510) 1972

Peter Ransome was probably connected with **Ransome's Head**. (VJ)

Ransome's Head

45:     Sing/Wild Wide River   (York SYK 506) 1971

Sing is a good punchy rocker with lots of words per bar. (VJ)

Rare Amber

Personnel:	ROGER CAIRNS	vcls	AB
	JOHN DOVER	bs	AB
	GWYN MATHIAS	gtr, hrmnca, organ	AB
	DEL WATKINS	ld gtr	AB
	CHRIS WHITING	drms	A
	KEITH WHITING	drms	B

ALBUM: 1(B) RARE AMBER   (Polydor 583 046) 1969 R2

NB: (1) reissued on CD with their 45 as bonus tracks.

45:     Malfunction Of The Engine/
        Blind Love   (Polydor BM 56309) 1969 SC

A short-lived blues-rock quintet. The album sleeve depicts the band holding a black mass ceremony. The vinyl inside was a successful blend of originals and covers of compositions by blues kings like Otis Spann and B.B. King. It is now a significant collectable. Both sides of their sole 45 can also be heard on Polydor's 1970 *Deep Overground Pop* (LP) compilation.

The group also recorded a very gutsy mono album at Central Sound in Denmark Street on 4-track. Polydor then decided to re-make the album in 8-track for stereo, and the released album (regarded by the band as bland!). It was recorded at IBC studios in Portland Place, over the course of a few days. In fact they were slotted in the somewhat ridiculous hours of between 8.00am and 12 noon, as **The Who** were recording *Tommy* from noon to midnight, at the time! (VJ)

Rare Bird

Personnel:	MARK ASHTON	drms, vcls	AB
	GRAHAM FIELD	organ	AB
	STEVE GOULD	vcls, sax, bs, gtr	ABCDEFG
	DAVE KAFFINETTI	keyb'ds, synth	ABCDEFG
	KEVIN LAMB	organ, vcls	B E
	ANDY CURTIS	gtr	CD
	PAUL HOLLAND	perc	CD
	PAUL KARAS	bs	C
	FRED KELLY	drms, vcls	CDEFG
	NIC POTTER	bs	D
	ANDY RAE	bs	E
	MICK FEAT	bs, vcls	F

ALBUMS:	1(A)	RARE BIRD	(Charisma CAS 1005) 1969 SC
(up to	2(A)	AS YOUR MIND FLIES BY	(Charisma CAS 1011) 1970 SC
1976)	3(C)	EPIC FOREST	(Polydor 2442 101) 1972 SC
	4(D)	SOMEBODY'S WATCHING	(Polydor 2383 211) 1973
	5(E)	BORN AGAIN	(Polydor 2383 274) 1974
	6(G)	RARE BIRD	(Polygram 9299 008) 1975
	7(G)	SYMPATHY (Compilation)	(Charisma CS 4) 1976

RARE BIRD - Rare Bird (LP).

RARE BIRD - As Your Mind Flies By (LP).

NB: There was a free 45 (*Roadside Welcome (Four Grey Walls) / You're Lost* (PS)) with the original UK release of (3), which has a gatefold sleeve and poster. The US release had a single sleeve.

(1) and (4) reissued on one CD (Red Fox RF 603). (2) and (3) also reissued on CD. (2) reissued on CD (Red Fox RF 606). (3) reissued on CD (Red Fox RF 604) with three bonus tracks. (5) reissued on CD (Red Fox RF 625). (7) reissued in 1983 (Charisma CHC 6) and on CD (Virgin CDOVD 280) 1990.

There's also a compilation, *Rare Bird* (Polydor Special) (Polydor 2384 078) 1977. *Third Time Around: An Introduction To Rare Bird* (Universal 065 008 2) 2003 compiles material from their Polydor albums.

EP: 1   Sympathy/Devil's High Concern/What You Want To Know/
            Hammerhead (PS)   (Charisma CB 179) 1972

HCP

45s:	Sympathy/		
	Devil's High Concern (Some PS)	(Charisma CB 120) 1970	27
	What You Want To Know/		
	Hammerhead	(Charisma CB 138) 1971	-
	Roadside Welcome/		
	Four Grey Walls/You're Lost (PS)	(Polydor 2814 011) 1972	-
	Virginia/Lonely Street	(Polydor 2058 402) 1973	-
	Body And Soul/Redman	(Polydor 2058 471) 1974	-
	Don't Be Afraid/Passin' Through	(Polydor 2058 591) 1975	-
Reissues:	Sympathy/Beautiful Scarlet	(Charisma CB 262) 1975	-
	Sympathy/Beautiful Scarlet	(Old Gold OG 9040) 1979	-

NB: (3) was given away free with UK copies of their third album *Epic Forest*.

Rare Bird formed in London in October 1969 and began rehearsing in a room at organist's Graham Field's London apartment. Indeed Field and keyboardist Dave Kaffinetti played a key role in conceiving the group's then novel two keyboard sound. Gould (ex-**Fruit Machine**) proved to be a powerful vocalist and their drummer was former **Turnstyle** member **Mark Ashton**.

Within a few weeks the group was offered a residency at London's Marquee and before the end of the year they'd issued a much acclaimed debut album, which got to No 117 in the US Charts. This included the atmospheric *Sympathy*, which would prove to be a minor hit here in the UK, but it was very popular on the Continent too. The final cut, *God Of War*, was both atmospheric and innovative in its use of percussion, whilst *You Went Away* and *Beautiful Scarlet* featured powerful vocals and good keyboards. They were the first band to record for Tony Stratton's Charisma label, a cornerstone progressive label.

As Your Mind Flies By was another fine album of keyboard-driven rock punctuated by Steve Gould's often melodramatic vocals. The whole of Side 2 was taken up by the ambitious four-movement track, *Flight*, but the whole of Side 1 is recommended listening too. Kevin Lamb had joined the band to play on this album, but it split in March 1971 and **Mark Ashton** formed his own **Mark Ashton** Band.

The group reformed in April 1972 (line-up C) and signed to Polydor to release *Epic Forest* (which was varied ranging from the heavy riffing of *Hey Man* to mellower numbers like *House In The City* and *Fears Of The Night*) but somehow they failed to maintain any sort of momentum over here, although they remained very popular on the Continent. Fred Kelly had earlier been involved in the **Astral Navigations Thundermother** project.

Karas departed to **Stackridge** in December 1972 and ex-**Roy Young Band** member Nic Potter took his place. After the *Somebody's Watching* album and the *Birdman* and *Virginia* 45s, Potter joined **The Global Village Trucking Company**, Curtis joined **Van Der Graaf Generator** and Holland also left. Kevin Lamb rejoined the group and Andy Rae (aka Robinson) joined from **Kevin Ayers and The Whole World**. This line-up produced the *Body and Soul* 45 and the *Born Again* album. This contained the stunning track *Redman*.

Kevin Lamb left again to go solo. Andy Rae departed to **Savoy Brown** and former **Casablanca** member Mick Feat joined in August 1974, although he left quite soon to join **Blondel**. Line-up (G) recorded the *Don't Be Afraid* 45 and 1975 *Rare Bird* album. On *Sympathy*, released in July 1976, the line-up was supplemented by **Ashton** and Lamb.

When the final split came in 1976, Gould formed Runner and Kaffinetti departed to Fresh Start. A compilation was released on Polydor Special in 1977.

Third Time Around compiles material from their Polydor albums and does not capture the band at its prime.

Their second 45 'A' side, *What You Want To Know*, later resurfaced on the *One More Chance* (LP) compilation and *Sympathy* got a further outing on the 3-CD box set *Radio Caroline Calling - 70's Flashback*. (VJ/JM)

Rare Breed

45:     Beg, Borrow And Steal/Jeri's Theme   (Strike JH 316) 1966 SC

Erroneously included in the previous volume, this 45 was by the US band Rare Breed. I've included it here to put the record straight. (VJ)

The Rats (1)

Personnel:			
BRIAN BUTTLE	bs	A
FRANK INCE	lead gtr	A
ROBIN LECORE	keyb'ds	A
BENNY MARSHALL	vcls	ABCD
JIM SIMPSON	drms	AB
GEOFF APPLEBY	bs	BCD
JOHN CAMBRIDGE	drms	C
MICK RONSON	gtr	BCD
MICK 'WOODY' WOODMANSEY	drms	CD

RARE BIRD - Epic Forest (LP).

THE RATS - The Rise And Fall Of Bernie Gripplestone And The Rats From Hull (LP).

ALBUM: 1   THE RISE AND FALL OF BERNIE GRIPPLESTONE
                 AND THE RATS FROM HULL

                                        (Tenth Planet TPO 12) 1994 SC

NB: (1) Numbered limited edition of 1,000. It was later reissued on CD. *The Rise and Fall Of The Rats* (Angel Air SJPCD 165) 2004 is a reissue of a previous Angel Air package from 1998, but with a new cover and expanded sleevenotes. (1) also reissued on vinyl (Get Back 956884).

45s: Spoonfull (one-sided - some in PS) (Oak RGJ 145) 1964 R4/R3
         Spoonful/
         I've Got My Eyes On You Baby   (Columbia DB 7483) 1965 R3
         I've Gotta See My Baby Everyday/
         Headin' Back (To New Orleans)   (Columbia DB 7607) 1965 R2

The roots of this Hull-based R&B group lay in an outfit called Rocky Stone and The Stereotones who formed in Hull, Yorkshire in 1962. They consisted of David Barron (drms), Brian Buttle (bs), Joe Donnelly (gtr), Frank Ince (lead gtr) and Benny Marshall (vcls), who'd quickly replaced the original occupant of this slot and became the dominant force in the band. He ousted Barron and Donnelly in favour of Jim Simpson (drms) and renamed the band Peter King (Marshall's pseudonym) and The Majestics in 1964.

They were very much a Chart covers act at this time, but they linked up with Martin Yale, an agent from Grimsby, who coaxed them into a rawer R&B sound and persuaded them to change name to the rawer **Rats**. In September 1964 Yale arranged for them to record the Leiber/Stoller composition *Young Blood* and a version of **Chris Andrews'** *I Gotta See My Baby*, (featuring **Andrews** on backing vocals). Much to **Andrews'** displeasure the release was shelved in favour of a powerful rendition of Willie Dixon's *Spoonful*. Producer Bunny Lewis took the resulting tape to R.G. Jones' Morden, Surrey studio where 100 single-sided copies were pressed. Copies now change hands for £200. Some came in a fold-out picture sleeve and these fetch around £350. Lewis sent copies to record companies here and in the US and it was there where it was first picked up and released with a Marshall song, *I've Got My Eyes On You Baby* on the flip in December 1964 on Laurie (3276). The same coupling was put out a couple of months later in the UK on Columbia. They also participated in a 'Battle Of **The Rats**' contest with their namesakes from Lancashire.

The Rats' *Spoonful* was moderately successful locally and was subsequently re-aired on *Pebbles, Vol. 6 - The Roots Of Mod* (LP), though the sleevenotes wrongly contended that the track featured **Mick Ronson**'s aggressive guitar style. In fact **Ronson** was then with another Hull-based band, The Crestas. Prior to this he'd been in The Mariners and then The King Bees (not the **Bowie** backing group). This King Bees featured future **Steeleye Span** bassist Rick Kemp. He then moved to London replacing **Miller Anderson** in **The Voice** after they'd recorded their superb *Train To Disaster*. After an unproductive period in a soul combo called The Wanted he returned to Hull by which time **The Rats** had released their first recording *I Gotta See My Baby*, as a second 45. This flopped and the band disintegrated, but Marshall and Simpson put together a new line-up with

Ronson and Geoff Appleby (bs). Simpson soon quit, being replaced by John Cambridge from another local band, ABC.

In the Winter of 1967 line-up (C) recorded a group composition *The Rise And Fall Of Bernie Gripplestone*, which was full of **Ronson**'s storming backwards guitar and studio trickery. Sadly, it didn't even make it to the acetate stage. In 1968 **The Rats** briefly changed their name to Treacle (with temporary bassist Keith 'Ched' Chessman now in the line-up). They cut an acetate EP containing versions of Gladys Knight and The Pips' *Stop And Get A Hold Of Myself*, Tim Rose's *Morning Dew* and *Mick's Boogie*, which was laced with **Ronson**'s superb guitar work. Influenced by **Ronson**'s liking of Indian take-aways, **The Rats** recorded a second composition *Curry Bun*, but this doesn't seem to have made it to acetate stage. John Cambridge left the band in 1969 joining **Junior's Eyes** in London. His replacement was Mick 'Woody' Woodmansey, who'd previously been with a local blues band, The Roadrunners. Meanwhile, Cambridge had met **David Bowie** via his producer Tony Visconti (who was also the producer of **Junior's Eyes**). It was at Cambridge's instigation that **Ronson** was lured down to London to be the guitarist in **Bowie**'s newly formed backing band, The Hype, and of course he went on to play in Bowie's later and much better-known backing band, **The Spiders From Mars**. With **Ronson**'s departure **The Rats** petered out. Mick Woodmansey was also later in **The Spiders From Mars** and he subsequently formed U Boat.

Spoonful has subsequently been re-aired on *Pebbles, Vol. 6 - The Roots Of Mod* (LP), whilst the one-sided Oak version can now be heard on *Story Of Oak Records* (2-LP) and you'll also find *I Gotta See My Baby Everyday* on *A Journey To Tyme, Vol. 2*. The last-mentioned song's flip side, *Headin' Back (To New Orleans)*, a really raw-sounding R&B number, can also be heard on *English Freakbeat, Vol. 1* (LP & CD).

The best guide to **The Rats**' career is the recent Tenth Planet compilation, which comes with excellent sleevenotes from David Wells detailing the band's history. It includes all of **The Rats**' records and acetate recordings as well as the three tracks recorded using the name Treacle for the acetate EP in early 1969.

An alternative package is *The Fall And Rise - A Rat's Tale* traces their career as **Stones** and **Animals** influenced R&B artist, their foray into psychedelia (the highlight is *The Rise And Fall Of Bernie Gripplestone*, which is full of backwards guitar and phasing) and their later material when they changed name to The Treacle was more akin with **The Jeff Beck Group**. (VJ)

The Rats (2)

Personnel:	PETER KIRK	bs	A
	DAVE KUBINEC	vcls, gtr, keyb'ds,	A
	GRAHAM QUINTON - JONES	gtr, keyb'ds	A
	COLIN WHITE	drms	A

RAW MATERIAL - Raw Material (LP UK Sleeve).

ALBUM:	1(A)	RATS FIRST	(Goodear EARLH 5003) 1974

45s:	Turtle Dove/Oxford Donna	(Goodear EAR 101) 1974
	Don't Let Go/Dragon Child	(Mam MAM 113) 1974

This was a short-lived hard-rock band. **Kubinec** had earlier been in **World Of Oz**. When they split, **Kubinec** went solo; Kirke did session work and Quinton-Jones played for **Charlie** and Gizmo, before doing sessions too. (VJ/JM)

The Rats (3)

Personnel:	STEVE FLEMING	keyb'ds	A
	GERRY KENNY	bs	A
	JIMMY MARTIN	lead gtr	A
	DAVE RYLANCE	drms	A

NB: Other personnel included: - Mark Peters (vcls), Alan Parkinson (vcls), Mal Grundy (lead gtr), Dave Allen and Billy Geldard (lead gtr).

45s:	Parchman Farm/	
	Every Day I Have The Blues	(Oriole CB 1967) 1964 R3
	Sack Of Woe/Gimme That Wine	(CBS 201740) 1965 R2

These 45s were by a different **Rats** from Liverpool. They got a record deal with Oriole. The resulting single featured a cover of Mose Allison's *Parchman Farm* on the 'A' side and a rendition of Arthur Alexander's *Every Day I Have The Blues* on the flip. After the *Sack Of Woe* 45 for CBS they disappeared from the scene.

Parchman Farm and *Every Day I Have The Blues* can also be found on *Nowhere Men, Vol. 4* (CD). (VJ/AD)

Chris Ravel and The Ravers

Personnel incl: CHRIS RAVEL (CHRIS ANDREWS)

45:	I Do/Don't You Dig This Kind Of Beat	(Decca F 11696) 1963

After this debut project **Chris Andrews** went on to register hits under his own name and to become a fairly successful songwriter. This is another of the many sixties 45s **Jimmy Page** played guitar.

Don't You Dig This Kind Of Beat has resurfaced on *James Patrick Page: Session Man, Vol. 1* (LP & CD) and *James Patrick Page, Session Man* (2-LP). (VJ)

Raven

ALBUM:	1	RAVEN	(N/K) 1969

NB: (1) reissued on CD.

This is a very obscure progressive blues-rock band with a psychedelic taint. Highlights include *Bad News* and the opening cut *Feelin' Good*. Some liken the album to **The Spirit Of John Morgan**. (VJ)

Jon Raven

ALBUMS:	1	THE HALLIARD AND JON RAVEN	
			(Broadside BRO 106) 1968 R2
	2	KATE OF COALBROOKDALE	(Argo 2FB 29) 1971 R3
	3	SONGS OF A CHANGING WORLD	
			(Trailer LER 2083) 1973 SC
	4	BALLAD OF THE BLACK COUNTRY	
			(Broadside BRO 116) 1975
	5	HARVEST (w/book)	(Broadside BRO ST 117) 1976 SC
	6	THE ENGLISH CANALS	(Broadside BRO 118) 1976 SC

NB: (1) credited to The Halliard and Jon Raven. (2) as Jon and Mike Raven with Jean Ward. (3) with Nic Jones and Tony Rose. (6) with John Kirkpatrick and Sue Harris.

Jon Raven was an important part of the British folk scene in the late sixties and early seventies. (VJ)

RAW MATERIAL - Raw Material (LP - Spanish sleeve).

Paul Raven

45s:
Musical Man/Wait For Me	(MCA MU 1024)	1968
Soul Thing/		
We'll Go Where The World Can't Find Us	(MCA MU 1035)	1968
Stand/Soul Thing	(MCA MKS 5053)	1970

These 45s were the work of Paul Gadd, who became better known as **Gary Glitter** in the seventies. He also recorded as **Paul Monday** and **Rubber Bucket**. (VJ)

The Simon Raven Cult

Personnel:		
SIMON RAVEN (BUDDY BRITTON)		A
KID FREEDOM (NICK SIMPER)		A
RICHARD HONOUR		A
ROGER TRUTH (ROGER PINNER)		A

45:
I Wonder If She Remembers Me/		
Sea Of Love	(Piccadilly 7N 35301)	1966 R1

This was **Buddy Britten and The Regents** in disguise. After a batch of unsuccessful singles **Britten** adopted the name of author **Simon Raven**, whilst the band members became Roger Truth, Kid Freedom and Richard Honour. During their eight months existence they managed just one single release. Roger Truth (Roger Pinner) then joined Johnny Kidd and The Pirates six months before Kidd's fatal accident. With him followed Kid Freedom, better known under his original name of Nick Simper.

I Wonder If She Remembers Me has been compiled on *Diggin' For Gold, Vol. 1* (LP & CD) and *Freakbeat Freakout* (CD). (MWh)

Raw Holly

Personnel:		
DAVE BOWER	gtr	A
TOPPER CLAY	drms	A
PETE MORRISON	vcls	A
TERRY STOKES	gtr	A
(IAN CAMPBELL	vcls	A)
(ZED JENKINS	gtr	A)

ALBUM: 1(A) RAW HOLLY (MCA MAPS 4067) 1971

NB: (1) released in Germany. Also released in the USA (Coral 757515) 1971.

45s:
Raining In My Heart/		
Rock Me Baby/Not Fade Away	(Youngblood YB 1007)	1972
Raining In My Heart/		
Little Baby/Well Alright	(Youngblood YB 1022)	1972
Raining In My Heart/Maybe Baby	(Antic K 11512)	1974

This studio project was masterminded by **New York Public Library**. The album, which consists of covers of Buddy Holly songs, was only released in Germany and the USA, and was originally intended as a cash-in release for the Embassy label... (VJ/TCy)

Raw Material

Personnel:			
COLIN CATT	vcls, keyb'ds		AB
MIKE FLETCHER	sax, flute, vcls		AB
DAVE GREEN	gtr		AB
PHIL GUNN	bs, gtr		A
PAUL YOUNG	perc		AB
CLIFF HAREWOOD	lead gtr		B

ALBUMS:
1(A)	RAW MATERIAL ALBUM	(Evolution Z 1006)	1970 R3
2(B)	TIME IS	(RCA Neon NE 8)	1971 R3

NB: (1) reissued on vinyl with Spanish pop-art sleeve (Zel TZS 4015) 199? and again on vinyl (Wah Wah LPS 007). (1) also reissued on CD with four bonus tracks. (2) reissued on CD (SPM no Cat #) 199? and again (Abraxas AKCD 153). (2) reissued on vinyl (Abraxas AK 153).

45s:
Time And Illusion/Bobo's Party	(Evolution E 2441)	1969 R1
Hi There Hallelujah/		
Days Of The Fighting Cock	(Evolution E 2445)	1970 R1
Traveller Man Parts 1 and 2	(Evolution E 2449)	1970 R1
Ride On Pony/Religion	(RCA Neon NE 1002)	1972 SC

This progressive rock band's albums in particular are now very rare and sought-after. Mike Fletcher had earlier been in Steam and Cliff Harewood later joined from Welcome, but neither of these bands made it onto vinyl. Some members were later in **Shoot** and Dave Green was in **Deep Feeling**.

The 'A' side of their eponymous album includes three strong, long tracks: *Time And Illusion*, which had a long instrumental break and vibraphone on leading role; *I'd Be Delighted*, which featured strong vocals, good flute and sax work and *Fighting Cock*, which builds in strength after a mellow beginning. The 'B' side is not so good, although the finale, *Destruction Of America*, is a poetry recitation with unidentified orchestral backing.

Time Is Rare is better, with good progressive pieces based on heavy guitar and sax riffs or sax riffs and keyboard chords. *Ice Queen* includes frozen wind sounds and a slightly discordant flute solo. Its most sophisticated composition is *Empty Houses*, which has some inspired melodies and strong vocals. *Insolent Lady* has a slow, mellow beginning with acoustic guitar and flute. This gives way to a piano break which in turn evolves into progressive rock with guitar and sax riffs, although this becomes so repetitious as to be boring near the end. *Miracle Worker* is mainly based on Dave Brubeck's *Take Five* rhythm. *Religion* is based around more sax and guitar riffs. Finally, *Sun God* has some mellow, melodic moments with acoustic guitar, flute and electric guitar reminiscent of early **Pink Floyd**; a short heavy rock break and an instrumental part with some guitar leads in a more psychedelic vein. Overall it's a good album but not a great album.

RAW MATERIAL - Time Is... (LP).

You'll also find *Time And Illusion* on *Incredible Sound Show Stories Vol. 4* (LP). (VJ/CA)

Chris(tine) Rayburn

45s:	Slow Loving Woman/	
	Same Old Places	(Parlophone R 5098) 1963
	I've Cried My Last Tear/	
	You Forgot To Say When	(Parlophone R 5144) 1964
	I Wanna To Be In Love Again/	
	Another Light Alone	(Parlophone R 5422) 1966
	One Way Ticket/	
	Photograph Of Love	(Music Factory CUB 2) 1968
α	Skip A Rope/Starlight	(Pye 7N 17679) 1969

NB: α as Christine Rayburn.

One Way Ticket has been compiled on *Spinning Wheel* (CD). (VJ)

Mark Raymond and The Crowd

45:     Girls/Remember Me To Julie   (Columbia DB 7308) 1964

No other details known. (VJ)

Raymonde's Magic Organ

ALBUM: 1   SIXTIES HITS   (Deram SML 1032) 1969

As the name implies this album consisted of cover versions of the hits of the period and is best avoided. (VJ)

Martin Raynor and Secrets

Personnel incl: MARTIN RAYNOR
                    CLIFFORD T. WARD

45:     Candy To Me/
        You're A Wonderful One   (Columbia DB 7563) 1965 R1

This band later became **Secrets** and then **Simon's Secrets** and **Clifford T. Ward** embarked on a solo career in the seventies. *Candy To Me* was a Holland-Dozier song. The flip side was a Marvin Gaye track.

A remastered version of *Candy To Me* can be found on *Beat At Abbey Road 1963-66* (CD). (VJ)

INCREDIBLE SOUND SHOW STORIES VOL. 4 (Comp LP) including Raw Material.

Ray's People

45:     Run To The Park/I Spy   (Philips 6006 044) 1970

This was a short-lived pop act. (VJ)

The Reaction

Personnel:	GEOFF DANIEL	gtr	A
	MIKE DUDLEY	organ	A
	RICKY PENROSE	bs	A
	JOHN "ACKER" SNELL	sax	A
	ROGER TAYLOR	drms, vcls	A

45:     α   In The Midnight Hour/I Got You   (Sound Studios D-106-11) 1966
NB: α acetate only.

After the split with **Johnny Quale** in 1965, **The Reaction** recruited a new singer, Roger Brokenshaw and played a lot of soul material. In 1966, the band, minus Roger Brokenshaw, backed **Johnny Quale** on an acetate EP and also recorded during the same session an ultra-rare acetate with Wilson Pickett's *In The Midnight Hour* and James Brown's *I Got You*. Billed as the official "Champion group of Cornwall", **The Reaction** became a power-trio in 1967 with Roger Taylor (vcls, drms), Mike Dudley (gtr) and Ricky Penrose (bs). They then played cover versions of **Cream**, **Hendrix** and **Fleetwood Mac**.

In 1968, Roger Taylor moved to London and was recruited by Tim Staffell and Brian May to join **Smile**. (CSx)

Mike Read

It's not widely known that **Mike Read**, one of Britain's top radio DJs and some-time TV show host recorded a number of tracks for private release at the now legendary R.G. Jones studio in Morden, Surrey, which he cut for the studio's Oak label. Several of these tracks can now be heard on *Syde Trips, Vol. 2* (LP), but prior to this all had been unreleased. The material showcased is quite varied. There's a song about Edward E. James, the poet and enthusiast of surrealist arts; a couple of folk/pop ballads, *Nicola* and *If She's A Day*; the beatier *Charley Brewster's DJ Show*; his indictment of the Inspector of Taxes, *What The Dickens*, which featured **Atomic Rooster**'s Rick Parnell on drums and Keith Parnell (also of **Virgin Sleep**) on guitar; and the rather inane *Pictures On My Wall*.

Read was also in three other sixties bands: - **Amber**, **The Lost** and **Just Plain Smith**, whose exploits are detailed in their respective entries. (VJ)

Reality From Dream

ALBUM: 1   REALITY FROM DREAM
                    (Private Pressing CP 109) 1975 R3

Recorded as a school project, this is a folk-rock concept album, with lovely female vocals occasionally supplemented by a children's choir. Featuring all original material with titles like *Unknown Destiny*, *Forever Farewell* and *Free To Dream*. The unfinished nature of the sleeve suggests that just a few copies were pressed and distributed among friends. (VJ)

The Realm

45:     Hard Time Loving You/
        Certain Kind Of Girl   (CBS 202044) 1966 SC

This Liverpool band had previously been fronted by singer **Earl Preston** and had recorded as **Earl Preston and The Realms**. (VJ)

The Rebel Rousers

Personnel:	MICK BURT	drms	A
	JOHN GOLDEN	trumpet	A
	MOSS GROVES	sax	A

KEN HENSLEY	gtr	A
CHAS HODGES	bs	A
ROY YOUNG	keyb'ds, vcls	A

45:     Should I?/As I Look   (Fontana TF 973) 1968 R1

NB: This single has been reissued in a limited edition of 500 reproduced from the original French jukebox pressing with a large centre hole.

A transitional 45 recorded by **The Rebel Rousers** after they'd ousted **Cliff Bennett** but before becoming **The Roy Young Band.**

All six members co-wrote *As I Look*, a good soul number. **Ken Hensley** later formed **Uriah Heep.**

As I Look has been compiled on *Beat Im Star Club* (2-LP) and *Should I?* on *Colour Me Pop, Vol 3* (CD). (VJ)

The Rebels

45:     Hard To Love You/Call Me   (Page One POF 017) 1967 SC

This is quite a collectable 45 by a long forgotten band.

Call Me later appeared on *Purple Pill Eaters* (LP & CD). (VJ)

The Rebounds

Personnel incl:	SHAUN CORRIGAN	ld gtr	A
	PETE GILL	bs	A
	MICK SIMONS	drms	A
	DAVID WATTS	keyb'ds	

45:     Help Me/The World Is Mine   (Fontana TF 461) 1964 SC

Out of Essex, this band were originally known as The Searchers but had to pick a new name when they discovered Liverpool's **Searchers** had already bagged that name. They backed Johnny Burnette on his UK tour in November 1963.

Help Me, which is basically bluesy but with harmony-style vocals, can also be heard on *English Freakbeat, Vol. 1* (LP & CD). It was also recorded by **The Primitives**. (VJ)

The Redcaps

Personnel:	MICKEY BLYTHE	gtr	A
	MAC BROADHURST	sax	A
	ALAN MORLEY	drms	A
	DAVE WALKER	gtr, vcls	A
	MICK WALKER	bs	A

45s:	Shout/Little Things You Do	(Decca F 11716) 1963 SC
	Talkin' Bout You/Come On Girl	(Decca F 11789) 1963 SC
	Mighty Fine Girl/Funny Things	(Decca F 11903) 1964

A Walsall-based beat group who signed to Decca and recorded a fine version of The Isley Brothers' *Shout*, though it was beaten to the Charts by **Lulu and The Luvvers**. They followed this with a powerful rendition of Chuck Berry's *Talkin' Bout You* but just couldn't seem to get that vital breakthrough.

Alan Morley went on to play in **Chicken Shack** and Mick Walker is a comedian. Dave Walker was in **The Idle Race**, **Savoy Brown** and **Fleetwood Mac** as well as having a brief stint in **Black Sabbath** filling in for Ozzy Osbourne in late 1977.

Compilation appearances have included: *Talkin' Bout You* on *James Patrick Page: Session Man, Vol. 2* (LP & CD), *James Patrick Page, Session Man* (2-LP), *R&B Scene, Vol. 2 - 1963-1969* (LP), *The R&B Scene* (CD), *Weekend Starts Here* (LP), *British R'n'B Explosion, Vol. 1* (CD) and *Beat Merchants* (2-LP); and *Shout* on *Broken Dreams, Vol. 4* (LP). (VJ/SK)

Noel Redding Band

Personnel:	ERIC BELL	gtr, vcls	AB
	DAVE CLARKE	keyb'ds, vcls	AB
	NOEL REDDING	gtr, vcls, bs	AB
	LES SAMPSON	drms	AB
	ANDY KEELY	vcls, gtr	B

| ALBUMS: 1(A) | CLONAKILTY COWBOYS | (RCA RS 1030) 1975 SC |
| 2(B) | BLOWIN' | (RCA RS 1084) 1976 |

| 45s: | Roller Coaster Kids/Snowstorm | (RCA RCA 2662) 1976 |
| | Take It Easy/Back On The Road Again | (RCA PB 9026) 1977 |

Noel Redding (real name David Redding) was born on Christmas Day 1945. He first came into the public eye when he joined **The Jimi Hendrix Experience** in September 1966 on bass. At the time he was in a band called **The Loving Kind**. He played with **Lord Sutch and His Heavy Friends** in the early seventies and also with **Fat Mattress** before forming Road, a UK-US three-piece.

Road's eponymous album, which consists of decent rock has been reissued on CD (Free 9701) 1997. Redding then formed his own **Noel Redding Band**, which included former **Thin Lizzy** member Eric Bell and ex-**Stray Dog** member Les Sampson. Andy Keely was added to the line-up in May 1976 and played on their second album. Clarke remained with the band but was also in White Line from 1976.

After they split in 1977, Ball went solo and was later in Mainsqueeze. (VJ/JM)

Red Dirt

Personnel:	KEN GILES	bs	A
	STEVE HOWDEN	lead gtr, piano, lead vcls, bs	A
	STEVE JACKSON	drms	A
	DAVE RICHARDSON	steel gtr, piano, organ, hrmnca, ld vcls	A

ALBUM: 1(A)   RED DIRT   (Fontana STL 5540) 1970 R5

NB: (1) has been counterfeited. (1) also issued on CD, together with the *Diamonds In The Dirt* live material (Audio Archives AACD 033).

This blues-rock band's album is now an ultra-rarity. Produced by Geoff Gill, it mostly comprises heavy blues-rock which is unlikely to appeal much beyond fans of this genre. Some variation comes with opening cut *Memories*, the melodic *Song For Pauline*, the country-influenced *Death Of A Dream* and the final cut *I've Been Down So Long*, but don't spend a small fortune on it without hearing it first.

The band has also released a limited edition (300 copies) collection of live material, *Diamonds In The Dirt*. (VJ)

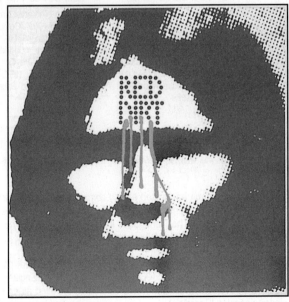

RED DIRT - Red Dirt (LP).

RED TELEVISION - Red Television (LP).

Red Herring

45:      I'm A Gambler/Working Class Man   (GMS GMS 007) 1973

As its name implies, **Red Herring** was a pseudonym for **Pete Dello**, who is principally known for his work with **Honeybus**. He also operated as **Magic Valley**, **Lace**, **Leah** and others, and released a much sought-after solo album under his real name in 1971. (VJ/RMJ)

The Red Squares

Personnel:	ANDY BELL	drms	ABC E
	DAVE BELL	gtr, vcls	A
	DAVID 'GEORDIE' GARRIOCK	ld vcls	ABCDEFG H I
	RONNIE MARTIN	ld gtr, vcls	ABCDEF
	PETE MASON	bs, vcls	ABCDEFG
	MICK ROTHWELL	ld gtr, vcls	BCDEFG H I
	HOWIE GEE (HOWARD GOLDMAN)	ld vcls (drms)	B D
	MICK MALONY	drms	F
	STEVIE McGHEE	gtr, vcls	G H
	DENNIS HASTINGS	bs, gtr	H I
	JAHN TEIGEN	gtr, vcls	I

ALBUMS:	1( )	RED SQUARES	(Columbia KSX 5) 1966
	2( )	IT'S HAPPENING	(Columbia KSX 6) 1967
	3(-)	POP FÓR SERIE (comp)	(EMI O54 38 110) 1974

NB: (1) - (2) one of the above catalog numbers is incorrect! Also of interest are the Dble CD anthology *Red Squares The Ultimate Collection 1966-1969* (Columbus CD.81536.2) 1996; and the retrospective LP *People Get Ready* (Elap 46519) 1994 and CD *It's Happening* (Elap 46513) 1994. Other recent releases have included, the live sampler CD, *Hit Hærg & Hentehår* (CMC ElaP 4936Cd) 1994; the CD *Red Squares Live + 3* ( ), a live concert recorded in Esbjerg, from 1st of July 1998, plus 3 new songs recorded in the studio; *Angel* (EMI 7946252.CD) 1990 and *Back On The Road* (EMI 7926372.CD.) 1989

| 45s: | Mountain's High/Pity Me | (Columbia DB 8160) 1967 |
| (UK) | True Love Story/Lollipop | (Columbia DB 8257) 1967 |

NB: One of their Danish 45s was *Pity Me/Any Other Girl* (Colubia DD 781) 1966.

This British beat/soul group epitomised a fairly common phenomenon in the 1960s - British bands who were far more popular abroad than at home; for **The Rokes** it was Italy, for **The Renegades** it was Finland, but in **The Red Squares'** case, Denmark that made them stars.

They formed in Boston, Lincolnshire in June 1964, and found work playing American bases in France. In July 1965 Dave Bell returned to England and was replaced by Mick Rothwell, with Howie Gee being recruited as an extra lead singer alongside 'Geordie'.

In December 1965 Howie Gee temporarily left the group to join his girlfriend in Denmark, where he discovered a fertile market for British groups and persuaded his bandmates to join him. Within six months they had become a big name and were breaking in Sweden. At gigs there was hysteria, and at one Swedish concert the crowd completely wrecked the stage.

In March 1966, Andy Bell returned to England to be a journalist and Howie Gee rejoined full-time as drummer and vocalist. He played on their two biggest Danish hits, *Sherry* and *People Get Ready*, but just as they were making their first album and preparing for a major tour of Sweden, he was thrown out of Denmark for want of a work permit.

Despite constant personnel changes, from 1966-1967 they were among Denmark's leading pop idols. Though inspired by US groups such as The Beach Boys and The Four Seasons, as well as soul acts, they wrote much of their own material and inspired many Danish acts. Few groups had the adulation they received wherever they went, and they were constantly in the press. **The Red Squares** split in December 1969 after a tour of Israel, as they had permit problems and no hope of returning to Denmark.

In 1971 Geordie went to Sweden, where he made four singles and an album in his own name. In 1975 he returned to Denmark and formed Squares, which broke up in the winter of 1977-78. Thereafter he sang with a variety of bands but, after a traumatic divorce, gave music up for a while. In the late 1980s Howie Gee proposed a **Red Squares** reunion, and the band was revived with numerous Danish musicians. The new **Red Squares** quickly became popular again in Denmark, enjoying a hit with *Goodbye My Love* from their album *Back On The Road*. Indeed the group did go back on the road, making many TV and radio appearances around the country.

The Red Squares are still on the road today, performing in Denmark with two original members and loving every minute of it.

You Can Be My Baby (from a Danish 45) has subsequently appeared on *Maximum Freakbeat* (CD), *Searching In The Wilderness* (LP & CD), *Incredible Sound Show Stories, Vol. 9* (LP) and on the 4-CD *Nuggets II* box set. (VJ/HG/RMJ)

Red Television

| ALBUM: | 1 | RED TELEVISION (w/insert) | (Brecht Times) 1971 R3 |

NB: (1) had a limited repress of 300 in 1995 on vinyl.

This is an extremely rare privately-pressed album, despite being pressed in relatively large quantities (2,000) and most copies being accompanied by a lyric sheet. It was another hippie-type commune project similar to **Everyone Involved**, but the folk material on the album owed as much to Bob Dylan as to **The Incredible String Band**. It included the 17-minute epic *Ghost Of Emile Zola*. (VJ)

The Reflections

| 45s: | Love And Affection/No More | (Purple PUR 124) 1974 |
| | Moon Power/Little Star | (Purple PUR 127) 1975 |

This was a short-lived mid-seventies group that should not be confused with the New York R&B band of the same name who released records in the UK in this era. (VJ)

Refugee

Personnel:	BRIAN DAVISON	drms	A
	LEE JACKSON	bs, vcls, gtr	A
	PATRICK MORAZ	keyb'ds	A

| ALBUM: | 1(A) | REFUGEE | (Charisma CAS 1087) 1974 SC |

Formed in August 1973 by former **Nice** members Brian Davison and Lee Jackson, this proved to be a short-lived jazz-pop experiment. Jackson's previous band had been **Jackson Heights** and Davison had been in **Every Which Way**. Patrick Moraz (who was Swiss) was previously in an outfit called Mainhorse, who released an eponymous album in 1971. He also released a solo album, *Patrick Moraz* (Charisma) 1975.

The *Refugee* album was very much in the style of **The Nice** but when keyboardist Patrick Moraz (also ex-**Jackson Heights**) left in August 1974 to replace **Rick Wakeman** in **Yes** the group collapsed. Brian Davison went into session work and later worked with **David Essex** and **Gong**. Lee Jackson went into production and was later in Stripjack. (VJ/JM)

Regency Kreem

| 45: | Little Lucy/Love Is Born | |
| | Again | (Liverpool Sound (Enterprises) Ltd. LS 1660) 1975 |

This may have been some sort of private pressing but is entirely forgettable. (VJ)

The Regents

| 45: | Bye Bye Johnny/Come Along | (Oriole CB 1912) 1963 SC |

This was a solo effort by **Buddy Britten**'s backing group. (VJ)

The Regents

| 45: | Words/Worryin' Kind | (CBS 202247) 1966 R1 |

This is a sought-after disc by a different band. (VJ)

Neil Reid

HCP

45s:	Mother Of Mine/If I Could Write A Song (Decca F 13264) 1971 2
	That's What I Want To Be/
	If Wishes Were Ships	(Decca F 13300) 1972 45
	End Of The World/Joanna, Marry Me (Decca F 13410) 1973 -
	Hazel Eyes/You're The Wine In My Life(Philips 6006 389) 1974 -
Reissue:	Mother Of Mine/
	(flip by different artist)	(Old Gold OG 9538) 1985 -

Neil Reid is now a forgotten sixties pop singer but he did enjoy a No 2 hit with *Mother of Mine*. (VJ)

Terry Reid

ALBUMS:	1	TERRY REID	(Columbia SCX 6370) 1969 R1
(up to	2	THE MOST OF TERRY REID	
1976)			(Music For Pleasure MFP 5220) 1971

REFUGEE - Refugee (LP).

TERRY REID - Seed Of Memory (CD).

| | 3 | THE RIVER | (Atlantic K 40340) 1973 SC |
| | 4 | SEED OF MEMORY (w/insert) | (ABC ABCL 5162) 1976 |

NB: Also relevant is *The Hands Don't Fit The Glove* (See For Miles SEE 50) 1985. (4) reissued on Edsel (EDCD 425) 1995.

45s:	α	The Hands Don't Fit The Glove/	
(up to		This Time	(Columbia DB 8166) 1967 SC
1976)		Better By Far/Fire's Alive	(Columbia DB 8409) 1968 SC
	β	Superlungs	(Columbia PSRS 323) 1969 SC
		Oooh Baby/Brave Awakening	(ABC 4137) 1976

NB: α credited to **Terry Reid and The Jaywalkers**. β promo-only. Credited to Terry Reid Is Superlungs.

Reid was born in Huntingdon, England, in November 1949. He joined a band called **Peter Jay and The Jaywalkers** in 1966 when he was just 15. They had been around for several years and he only stayed with them for a few months before going solo the same year. At the end of 1966, the band split up and he came under the influence of legendary hitmaker Mickie Most. His first 45, *The Hands Don't Fit The Glove*, was recorded whilst he was still with **The Jaywalkers** and was a fairly tame choice by Most for a debut, though he turns in a good soul-styled vocal.

After recording a further 45, in a poppier vein, **Reid** was invited to join **Led Zeppelin** by **Jimmy Page**, but declined owing to his commitment with Most, recommending **Robert Plant** instead. His debut album was a fairly gritty collection of material that showcased his precociously powerful vocals, as well as some powerful lead guitar from him on tracks like **Donovan**'s *Superlungs My Supergirl*. After its release **Reid** spent much of his time in America, where he recorded two further albums in quick succession, *Bang Bang You're Terry Reid* and *Superlungs*. The former album is full of cover versions like Cher's *Bang Bang*, Gene Pitney's *Something's Gotten Hold Of My Heart*, a long version of **Donovan**'s *Season Of The Witch* and Eddie Cochran's *Summertime Blues*, combined with his own composition *Writing On The Wall*.

He returned briefly to the UK as a member of **Arrival** in 1969, but spent most of the seventies in America, recording just three albums, *River*, *Seed Of Memory* and *Rogue Waves*. *River* prominently features David Lindley from the US Kaleidoscope and is one of the more unfairly overlooked singer-songwriter albums of the era. In particular the pensive title track and irresistibly funky *Dean* are classics. *Seed Of Memory*, produced by **Graham Nash**, has also been acclaimed, though some find it a little too slick. Like *River*, it's a moody collection with poignant lyrics. Unfortunately ABC Records went bust within a few days of its release, so it sank without trace.

The Hands Don't Fit The Glove retrospective contains his two 45s from 1967 and 1968 along with the whole of his first album. *Bang, Bang, You're Terry Reid* was reissued on CD (Beat Goes On BGOCD 164) in 1993. *The Hand Don't Fit The Glove* can also be heard on *My Generation* (LP), and *Superlungs My Supergirl* made it onto the *Psychedelic Dream* (2-LP) compilation. (VJ/JM)

THE REMO FOUR - Smile! (CD).

Reign

Personnel incl: JIM McCARTY
                  KEITH RELF

45:   Line Of Least Resistance/
      Natural Lovin' Man   (Regal Zonophone RZ 3028) 1970 R1

A short-lived collaboration involving former **Yardbirds** Jim McCarty and **Keith Relf** after they'd formed **Renaissance**. Needless to say the 45 is now rare and sought-after by some collectors.

McCarty went on to form **Shoot**, whilst **Relf** went on to **Medicine Head** and then formed a short-lived act, **Armageddon**, prior to his death during the formation of Illusion.

Line Of Least Resistance later turned up on *Perfumed Garden Vol. 3* (CD). (VJ)

Jane Relf

45:   Without A Song From You/
      Make My Time Pass By   (Decca F 13231) 1971 SC

Jane Relf was the sister of **Keith Relf**. She played with him in **Renaissance** and was later in Illusion with Jim McCarty. (VJ)

Keith Relf

                                                      HCP
45s: Mr Zero / Knowing   (Columbia DB 7920) 1966 R1 50
      Shapes In My Mind/Blue Sands   (Columbia DB 8084) 1966 R1 -

Relf recorded these three singles whilst he was lead vocalist with **The Yardbirds**. They were mellower and more laid back than the songs with **The Yardbirds** were producing. *Mr. Zero* was a Bob Lind song and *Blue Sands* was by **The Outsiders**.

Relf was later a founding member of **Renaissance**, then briefly in **Medicine Head**, prior to forming **Armageddon** in 1975. He tragically died from an electric shock at his home on 14th May 1976 during the founding of Illusion.

Mr. Zero and *Knowing* got a further airing on *Sixties Years, Vol. 5* (CD). (VJ)

The Remo Four

Personnel incl: DON ANDREWS   bs, gtr   A
                  ROY DYKE   drms   AB
                  COLIN MANLEY   gtr, vcls   AB
                  PHIL ROGERS   bs   AB
                  TONY ASHTON   piano, vcls B

45s: I Wish I Could Shimmy Like My Sister/
      Peter Gunn   (Piccadilly 7N 35175) 1964 SC
      Sally Go Round The Roses/
      I Know A Girl   (Piccadilly 7N 35186) 1964 SC
      Live Like A Lady/Sing Hallelujah   (Fontana TF 787) 1967 R2

An early to mid-sixties outfit from Liverpool. They sometimes backed singers **Johnny Sandon** and **Tommy Quickly** (indeed it was Brian Epstein who recruited them as his backing band). Their main significance was probably the inclusion of Tony Ashton and Roy Dyke who formed **Ashton, Gardner and Dyke** in the late sixties. Later still, Ashton was in **Family**. Ashton's earlier bands included The Mastersounds, **Chris Farlowe's Thunderbirds**, Tony Ashton Trio and Liverpool's Executives and College Boys.

They spent much of their time in Germany and had an album, *Smile* (Starclub 158 034) released there in 1967. This has been reissued again on CD (Repertoire IMS 7034) 1996. It's up there among the better British R'n'B records of the era. Highlights include covers of Mose Allison's *Seventh Son*, Chuck Berry's *No Money Down*, Dean Parrish's *The Skate* and Stevie Wonder's *Nothing's Too Good For My Baby*. This reissue comes with eight bonus tracks, of which four were previously unissued. They also appeared on a German-sampler album, *Attention* (Phonogram 6434 158) in 1973. Some of them also played on **George Harrison's** *Wonderwall Music* album.

In 1991 the German-based Repertoire label compiled a 22-track CD compilation of their 45s for Pye circa 1963/64, *The Pye Singles* (Repertoire REP 4186-WZ), most of which were supporting other vocalists like **Tommy Quickly**, Gregory Phillips and **Johnny Sandon**.

Their German-only album, *Smile* (Line/Conifer SCCD 9.00196 0) got a CD reissue in 1992. It's full of R&B and soul covers - they must have been a good live act in their heyday.

Colin Manley died of cancer on 9 April 1999, aged 57.

You can also find *Live Like A Lady* on *Rubble Vol. 16: Glass Orchid Aftermath* (LP) and *Rubble Vol. 9* (CD). It's an average mod-pop number which passed unnoticed at the time over here.

Other compilation appearances have included: *Whatcha Gonna Do About It* and *Like A Rolling Stone* on *Nowhere Men, Vol. 4* (CD); *Live Like A Lady* and *Sing Hallelujah* on *The Star-Club Singles Complete, Vol. 10* (LP & CD); *Peter Gunn* and *Mickey's Monkey* on *The Star-Club Singles Complete, Vol. 7* (LP & CD); *Peter Gunn* and *I Know A Girl* on *Some Other Guys* (LP); *Roadrunner* on *Star-Club Show* (LP); *Maybelline* and *The 7th Son* on *The Star-Club Anthology, Vol. 1* (LP); *Sing Hallelujah* on *The Star-Club Anthology, Vol. 3* (LP) and *That Driving Beat* (CD); and *Cry To Me* and *Peter Gunn* on *The Star-Club Anthology, Vol. 4* (LP). (VJ)

RENAISSANCE - Renaissance (LP).

RENAISSANCE - Turn Of The Cards (LP).

Renaissance (1)

Personnel:

LOUIS CENNAMO	bs	AB
JOHN HAWKEN	keyb'ds	AB
JIM McCARTY	drms	AB
JANE RELF	vcls	AB
KEITH RELF	gtr, vcls, hrmnca	AB
NEIL CORNER	bs	B
TERRY CROWE	vcls	B
DON SHINN	keyb'ds	B
TERRY SLADE	drms	B
JON CAMP	bs, vcls, gtr	C
MIKE DUNFORD	gtr, vcls	C
ANNIE HASLAM	vcls, perc	C
TERENCE SULLIVAN	drms, vcls	C
JOHN TOUT	keyb'ds, vcls	C

HCP

ALBUMS:	1(A)	RENAISSANCE	(Island ILPS 9114) 1969 SC 60
(up to	2(B)	ILLUSION	(Island HELP 27) 1972 R1 -
1976)	3(C)	PROLOGUE	(Sovereign SVNA 7253) 1972 -
	4(C)	ASHES ARE BURNING	(Sovereign SVNA 7261) 1973 -
	5(C)	TURN OF THE CARDS	(BTM 1000) 1975 -
	6(C)	SCHEHERAZADE AND OTHER STORIES	
			(BTM 1006) 1975 -
	7(C)	LIVE AT CARNEGIE HALL (2-LP)	(BTM 2001) 1976 -

NB: (1) and (2) reissued on CD set (Line LICD 921163) 1992 and individually: - *Renaissance First* (Line LICD 900421) 1991 and *Illusions* (Line LICD 900425) 1989. (1) also reissued on CD Repertoire (REP 4512-WY) 1995, with both sides of their 45 as a bonus. (2) also reissued on CD (Repertoire REP 4513-WY) 1995. (1) reissued as *Innocence* (Mooncrest CRESTCD 033) 1998, with four bonus tracks. (3) reissued on CD (Repertoire REP 4513-WY) and again (Repertoire REP 4574-WY). (3) and (4) reissued as double album (Sovereign CAPACK 3) 1979. (4) reissued on CD (Repertoire 4575-WY) (5) reissued on CD (Repertoire REP 4491-WY) 1994 and again (Timeless RRC 42). (6) reissued on CD (Repertoire REP 4490-WY) 1994 and again (HTD CD 59). (7) reissued as a double CD (Repertoire REP 4506-WL 2-CD) 1994 and (HTC CD 40) 1995. *Unplugged: Live At The Academy Of Music, Philadelphia* (Mooncrest CREST CD 056 Z) 2000 is a solid live recording. *BBC Sessions* (2-CD) (Wounded Bird WOU 1001) compiles their best seventies radio performances. *Innocents and Illusions* (2-CD) (Castle CMEDD 874) contains their first two albums, six bonus tracks and a detailed booklet and it's presented in a slipcase. *Live And Direct* (Kissing Spell KSCD 924) was recorded live at the Fillmore Auditorium during their 1971 tour of the US and it also includes some rare mid-seventies demos.

45:	Island/The Sea	(Island WIP 6079) 1970 SC
(up to		
1976)		

Renaissance initially set out as a progressive folk-rock band and enjoyed a strong following on the campus circuit. The band then underwent several line-up changes and its second incarnation fronted by Annie Haslam became a significant classically-influenced progressive-rock outfit throughout the seventies.

This band was originally formed by ex-**Yardbirds**' singer/harp player **Keith Relf** and drummer Jim McCarty in Surrey, England, in 1969. Their debut album was an experimental effort which sought to fuse classical, folk, jazz, blues and rock. It was full of melodramatic piano playing but the stand-out track was *Island*, which featured some gorgeous vocals by **Jane Relf**. Certainly an interesting album, it only achieved moderate success and **Relf** and McCarty left not long after. A second album, *Illusion*, was recorded for Island but it never got beyond the test pressing stage. It was only released in Germany prior to its reissue in the nineties. Whilst not a band member at the time, Michael Dunford wrote and performed on the track *Mr Pine* on this album. By the time they signed to Sovereign for the *Prologue* album none of the original line-up remained.

Prologue attracted far more attention in the US than in the UK and for the next couple of years the new line-up (C) made the US their base. Their aim remained the same - the fusion of classical music and rock - and they acquired two new assets, Annie Haslam's crystal clear vocals and the lyrics of poetess Betty Thatcher. They developed a cult following in the US.

Their finest moments were *Turn Of The Cards* and *Scheherazade And Other Stories*, which merged beautiful piano work and Annie Haslam's exquisite vocals. The stand-out track on *Turn Of The Cards* is *Mother Russia* with its melodramatic piano introduction, Annie Haslam's exquisite vocals and appealing orchestrated passages. *Running Hard* is similar with a nice piano intro. and heavy orchestration. *Things I Don't Understand* had more good piano work, several tempo changes and some lovely vocal passages, whilst *Cold Is Being* is sadder and more centred around Haslam's vocals.

Scheherazade.... is similar in style but better all round. The opener *A Trip To The Fair* had all the ingredients of *Mother Russia* but the end result is more polished, whilst *The Vultures Fly High* and *Ocean Gypsy* showcased Haslam's vocal abilities and Tout's keyboard dexterity. The whole of side two contained their interpretation of Rimsky-Korsakov's *Scheherazade*, which featured a stunning performance from Haslam augmented by an orchestra.

As 1976 eclipsed their best success was still to come (in 1978) with *A Song For All Seasons*, which featured more superb vocal harmonies and became their best selling UK album, peaking at No 35. It also spawned the hit single, *Northern Lights*, which got to No 10 here. They continued to record well into the eighties and Haslam also recorded a solo album, *Annie In Wonderland*.

Their eighties albums didn't attract much attention or acclaim and the band went their separate ways early in this decade. In 1995, both Haslam and Dunford attempted to revive the band but it seems certain that their finest days have passed.

Island was also included on the *Bumpers* (2-LP) compilation and, more recently, *Kings And Queens* has been compiled on the 3-CD box set *Ars Longa Vita Brevis: A Compendium Of Progressive Rock 1967-1974.* (VJ)

RENAISSANCE - Scheherazade And Other Stories (LP).

Renaissance (2)

45:      Mary Jane (Get Off The Devil's Merry Go Round)/
           Daytime Lovers   (Polydor BM 56736) 1968

A different act, *Mary Jane* is soulish, orchestrated number warning about the dangers of the evil weed. It has a slight American tinge in the vocals, and it could be that this was a UK release by an American act.

Check out *Mary Jane* on *Marijuna Unknowns, Vol. 1.* (BMF/IT)

John Renbourn

ALBUMS:	1	JOHN RENBOURN	(Transatlantic TRA 135) 1966 SC
(up to	2	BERT AND JOHN	(Transatlantic TRA 144) 1966 SC
1976)	3	ANOTHER MONDAY	(Transatlantic TRA 149) 1966 SC
	4	SIR JOHN ALOT OF MERRIE ENGLANDE'S MUSIC THYNGE AND YE GREENE KNIGHT	
			(Transatlantic TRA 167) 1968 SC
	5	THE LADY AND THE UNICORN	
			(Transatlantic TRA 224) 1970 SC
	6	JOHN RENBOURN SAMPLER	
			(Transatlantic TRASAM 20) 1971 SC
	7	FARO ANNIE	(Transatlantic TRA 247) 1971 SC
	8	SO CLEAR	(Transatlantic TRASAM 28) 1973 SC
	9	HEADS AND TAILS	(Transatlantic TRASAM 18) 1974
	10	THE HERMIT	(Transatlantic TRA 336) 1976

NB: He also recorded two now very rare albums with American folk singer Dorris Henderson: *There You Go* (Columbia SX 6001) 1965 and *Watch The Stars* (Fontana (S)TL 5385) 1967. (1) reissued (Castle Music CMRCD 359) 2001, with three bonus cuts. (2) was recorded with **Bert Jansch**. (3) reissued on CD (Castle CMRCD 436). (1) and (3) reissued on one CD (Essential ESMCD 408) 2004. (4) reissued on CD (Shanachie Records (USA) SHANCD 97012) 1992. (4) reissued again on CD (Wooden Hill HILLCD 1) 1996, in it's original packaging but with informative sleeve notes by Colin Harper. (5) reissued on CD (Transatlantic TRACD 224) 1987, by Shanachie Records (USA) (SHANCD 97022) 1992 and again (Castle Music CMRCD 625) 2003, with some live **Pentangle** material from 1968 and a version of *My Johnny Was A Shoemaker* (with Jacqui McShee on vocals) as a bonus. (5) and (10) reissued on one CD (Essential ESMCD 436) 2005. (7) reissued on CD (Castle CMRCD 534). *The Folk Blues Of John Renbourn* (Demon TRANDEM 2) 1988 combines the best tracks of his first two albums. *A Medieval Almanack* (Demon/Transatlantic TRANDEM 6) is an alternative collection of his songs. *The Essential John Renbourn (A Best Of)* (Demon TDEMCD 10) 1992 is an alternative guide to his music. Alternative compilations on vinyl and CD (CD catalogue numbers are given) are:- *Essential Collection, Vol. 1 (The Soho Years)* (Transatlantic TRACD 603) 1987 and *Essential Collection, Vol. 2 (Moon Shines Bright)* (Transatlantic TRACD 605) 1987. *The Definitive Transatlantic Collection* (Castle) 1997 includes a duet with **Bert Jansch** and two **Pentangle** tracks. It was later reissued (Essential ESMCD 569). *There You Go!* (Big Beat WIKD 186) 1999 is a reissue of a very rare album he recorded in 1965 with black American folk singer Dorris Henderson plus a non-album single in 1965. *Down On The Barge* (Delta 470 42) 2000 is a 19-track compilation drawing from seven of his ten Transatlantic albums. *The Pentangle Family* (Castle/Sanctuary ESACD 931) 2000 is a 2-CD set comprising **Bert Jansch** and **John Renbourn** solo material as well as **Pentangle** material from the

1965-1971 era. Also relevant is *John Renbourn Anthology* (Essential ESACD 858) 2000. *The Guitar Of John Renbourn* (Castle CMRCD 1124) 2005 gives a welcome CD release to an all-instrumental album recorded in 1976 for KPM as a library album.

Along with **Bert Jansch** (with whom he often played) and **Davy Graham**, **John Renbourn** was instrumental in evolving new acoustic guitar techniques in this period.

His career began in a folk band in Richmond, South-west London, but he soon drifted onto the club circuit and earned a reputation as an imaginative and dextrous guitarist. His debut featured some of the very best folk-blues playing of the era, but was impeded by his limited vocals and the unimaginative choice of material. Nonetheless, it is notable for some experimental bottleneck playing and is one of the key folk recordings of the period.

Like **Jansch** and **Graham**, he was never a strong vocalist, and often gigged with **Dorris Henderson**, whom he backed on her two ultra-rare albums. He also played with Jacqui McShee, and in 1968 they formed **Pentangle** along with **Jansch**, Danny Thompson and Terry Cox.

Renbourn continued to make solo recordings, however. *Sir John A Lot Of Merry England* explored his interest in medieval music and showed him to be a fine sitar player too. *The Lady And The Unicorn* was an instrumental album and contained re-interpretations of early English dances and 14th Century Italian pieces. Terry Cox and **Dave Swarbrick** help out on it.

After **Pentangle**'s demise he retreated to his Welsh farm for a couple of years, though he recorded further albums in the late seventies, including one with New Yorker Stefan Grossman. In the eighties he formed the John Renbourn Group and in the mid-eighties he teamed up with Stefan Grossman for a series of world tours. He later formed The Ship Of Fools and played music with a Celtic influence. **Renbourn** continues to tour both alone and with other guitarists.

The Guitar Of John Renbourn gives a welcome CD release to an all-instrumental album originally recorded in 1976 for KPM as a library album. **Renbourn** plays both acoustic and electric guitar on this album, and is assisted by Tony Roberts (on flute and clarinet) and Jacqui McShee. His fans will want this.

Any of the compilations listed in the discography provide a good guide to his solo career with a pleasant blend of instrumentals and vocal numbers. Appearances on various artists compilations include: *Plainsong*, *My Johnny Was A Shoemaker-Westron Wind-Scarborough Fair* and *After The Dance* (with **Bert Jansch**) on *The Transatlantic Story* CD box set. (VJ)

Renegade

45:      A Little Rock'n'Roll/My Revolution   (Dawn DNS 1067) 1974

One of several obscure outfits that recorded on this label. (VJ)

The Renegades

Personnel:	KIM BROWN	ld gtr, vcls	ABC
	DENYS GIBSON	gtr	A
	GRAHAM JOHNSON	drms	ABC
	IAN MALLET	bs	ABC
	JOE DUNNETT	ld gtr	B
	MICK WEMBLEY	ld gtr	C

ALBUMS:	1	UNA SERA AL PIPER	(Ariston ARLP 0119) 1966
(Italian)	2	HALF AND HALF	(Ariston ARLP 0162) 19??
	3	THE RENEGADES	(Oxford OX 3055) 1975
	4	LETTERE D'AMORE	(Emidisc - 048 51502) 19??
	5	L'INTERROGATORIO	(Ariston - 062 17638) 19??

NB: (3) and (4) were compilations. Two of their albums and a compilation have been released on CD in Italy. They also recorded an eponymous album in 1964 on a budget-priced label (Fidelio ALT 4108) as The Merseysound. It contained 12 tracks:- *Hippy Hippy Shake, She Loves You, What About Us, Love Me Do, Searchin', I Wanna Be Your Man, Can't Buy Me Love, Poison Ivy, You Can't Do That, Money, It's All Right,* and *Mashed Potatoes*.

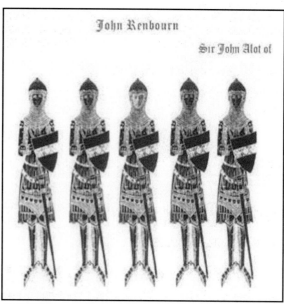

JOHN RENBOURN - Sir John Alot... (CD).

ALBUMS: 1 CADILLAC (Scandia SLP 600) 1964
(Finland) 2 THE RENEGADES (Scandia SLP 601) 1965
3 THE RENEGADES 3 (Scandia SLP 602) 1965
4 POP THE RENEGADES (Scandia SLP 603) 1966

NB: (1) also released in Germany. They also had other albums released in Europe including: *Have Beat, Will Travel* (Netherlands 1965), *Cadilac* (Netherlands 1965), *Take A Heart* (Netherlands and Germany 1966) and *Pop* (Netherlands 1966). There were other German albums on Hansa. *Renegades Story* (Scandia SLP 907) 1978 is a Finnish compilation. (1) and (2) reissued as a (2-LP) set *Cadillac/The Renegades* (Safir SAFLP 2054) 1990. *The Renegades* (Fazer 0630-12395-2) 1996 is a CD-only compilation.

EPs: 1 THE RENEGADES (PS) (Riviera 231 113) 1965 French
2 THE RENEGADES (PS)
(Supraphon 0.33 0414) 1968 Czech

45s: Cadilac/Every Minute Of The Day (Polydor BM 56508) 1966 SC
(UK) 13 Women/
Walking Down The Street (President PT 106) 1966 R2
Take A Message/
Second Thoughts (Parlophone R 5592) 1967 SC
No Man's Land/
Sugar Loaf Mountain (Columbia DB 8383) 1968 SC

45s: Cadillac / Bad Bad Boy (Ariston 0100 0101) 1966
(Italian) Un Giorno Tu Mi Cercherai /
Una Rosa Da Vienna (Ariston 0112) 1966
Thirteen Women / Don't Run to Me (Ariston 0123) 1966
Cadillac / Se morisse il Sole (Ariston 0137) 1966
This Song Really Knocks Me /
You're Gonna Lose Her Loving (Ariston 0163) 1966
John Fitzgerald Kennedy /
Il pi-?Grande Amico (Ariston 0167) 1967
Uomo solo / Take a Message (Parlophone QMSP 16406) 1967
L'Amore ? Blu / Mighty Queen (Columbia SCMQ 7090) 1968
Lettere D'Amore /
Vino E Campagna (Columbia SCMQ 7124) 1968
Era Settembre Un Anno Fa /
Piove Dentro Me (Columbia SCMQ 7151) 1969
Lola / Sun Arise (Columbia 062 17721) 1970

45s: Cadillac / Bad Bad Baby (Scandia KS 563) 1964
(Finland) Do The Shake / Seven Daffodils (Scandia KS 577) 1965
You Love Me Too / Matelot (Scandia KS 587) 1965
White Brown And Black /
Unchain My Heart (Scandia KS 598) 1965
Take A Heart / Broken Heart Collector (Scandia KS 607) 1965
Far From It / Every Minute Of The Day (Scandia KS 620) 1965
Walking The Street / Thirteen Women (Scandia KS 631) 1966
Un Giorno Tu Mi Cercherai /
Una Rosa Da Vienna (Scandia KS 644) 1966
Too Many Heartaches / Blue Eyes (Scandia KS 662) 1966
Can't You See / Never Get Married, Kid (Scandia KS 671) 1966

45s: Cadillac/Bad Bad Baby (PS) (Polar POS 1007) 196?
(Sweden) Thirteen Women /
Walking Down The Street (PS) (Polar POS 1020) 196?

This Birmingham beat group formed in the early sixties. At first they based their music on **The Shadows**. In 1963 they turned professional and changed their stage outfit radically; they began to use the cavalry costumes of the American Civil War. Their first recorded track was *Hungarian Rhapsody*, which appeared on the Birmingham compilation album *Brum Beat* (LP), which was released in February 1964. In Summer 1964 they toured Northern England and in Autumn 1964 they toured Finland, appearing on two Finnish TV shows ('Nuorten Tanssihekti' and 'Uudet Tuulet') and secured a recording contract with Scandia. They first 45 *Cadillac* was a Finnish No 1. They relocated to Italy in the mid-sixties and actually had several albums released out there, and in other countries such as Holland. They toured extensively around Europe. Obviously popular in Finland, as well, they also appeared in a film 'Topralli' ("Top Rally"), directed by Yrjo Tahtela in 1966.

In addition to the four UK 45s, which are all hard to find now, they also cut an acetate, *Bye Bye Johnny/She Lied* for Morden-based Oak records.

The main stay of the band Kim Brown never buried **The Renegades** completely and they continued to gig in Europe during the eighties and nineties and frequently appeared in "back to the sixties" events.

One of their more interesting releases was *13 Women*, a Bill Haley hit, originally released in Europe, which found its way onto President for a 1968 45. You can also check this one out on the *What A Way To Die* (LP) and *Songs We Taught The Fuzztones* (2-LP) compilations. Other compilation appearances include: *Cadillac* on *The Beat Goes On, Vol. 3* (LP); and *Hungarian Rhapsody* on *Brum Beat, Vol. 1* (LP). (VJ/MWh/HI/RB/TR)

Renia

Personnel: DAVE MATTHEWS drms A
JOHN ROBINSON gtr, vcls A
KENNY STEWART ld vcls A
MALCOLM SUTHERLAND bs, mellotron, vcls A
PETER SUTHERLAND keyb'ds, vcls A

ALBUM: 1(A) FIRST OFFENDERS (Transatlantic TRA 261) 1973 SC

This progressive rock quintet gave an early outing to Kenny Stewart, who was later in Dirty Tricks, a late seventies UK hard-rock quartet. Their album, as with many bands doesn't do justice to their live performance - they were capable of great keyboard and guitar work - but it is still impressive for a less than well known band. They were certainly underrated. (MWh/VJ)

Mike Reoch and The Tremors

Personnel: BYRON GRANT A
DENNIS MORRISON A
MIKE REOCH A
DON STUART A

ALBUM: 1(A) INTERNATIONALE EVERGREENS
(Elite Special SOLPS 246) 196?

This was a Scottish band who appeared to relocate to Germany. They do not appear to have released any recordings in the UK. There's a group photo on the back cover showing four clean cut Scottish lads and sleevenotes with a potted biography of each member in German! They came from Aberdeen and Dundee. The album, which was probably released some time between 1962-64 consists of MOR classics like *Mockin' Bird Hill, I Could Have Danced All Night, Summertime* and *Too Young*, given the gentle beat treatment. (MWh)

The Revellers

ALBUM: 1 REVELLERS AGAIN (Spin LP 1703) 1967

45s: Believe, Believe/
Love Is The Greatest Thing (Columbia DB 8093) 1966
Yasmin/When I Needed A Neighbour (Spin SP 2093) 1967
The Story/Lord's Prayer (Spin SP 62010) 1967

This gospel group was from Birmingham. (VJ)

The Revells

45: Mind Party/Indian Ropeman (CBS 7050) 1971 SC

The Revells were a short-lived early seventies act. *Indian Ropeman* was a **Brian Auger/Julie Driscoll** track. (VJ)

Revolution

Personnel incl: LUTHER GROSVENOR

45: Hallelujah/Shades Of Blue (Piccadilly 7N 35289) 1966 R2

This was a rare and sought-after 45 by a band that included the same members as **The Hellions**. The 'A' side was a gospel song, but the flip was beatier and the first composition by **Jim Capaldi** and **Dave Mason**.

Compilation appearances include: *Shades Of Blue* on *Watch Your Step* (LP & CD); *Hallelujah* on *Brum Beat - Midlands Beat Groups Of The 60's* (CD); and *Hallelujah* and *Shades Of Blue* on *Footsteps To Fame, Vol. 1* (CD). (VJ)

Revolver

| 45: | Frisco Annie/Imaginations | (Youngblood YB 1006) 1969 |

Miki Dallon produced this obscure 45. The 'B' side is highly-rated by many and **Small Faces**-influenced. It has been compiled on *Jagged Time Lapse, Vol 2* (CD). The band later evolved into Spiteri and they made an eponymous guitar progressive album (GML 1006) in 1973, which displayed Santana influences (CD). (VJ)

Rhubarb Rhubarb

Personnel:	PHIL CHILTON	gtr, vcls	A
	IAN SINCLAIR	bs, vcls	A
	PETER SMITH	gtr, vcls	A
	STEVE SMITH	drms	A

| 45: | Rainmaker/Moneylender | (President PT 229) 1968 R1 |

This Berkshire pop group's sole 45 came with a tinge of psychedelia.

Moneylender later emerged on *Circus Days Vol. 1 & 2* (CD), *Circus Days, Vol. 1* (LP) and on *Sometimes I Wonder* (CD), which also contains *Rainmaker*. (VJ)

Rhythm and Blues Inc.

Personnel:	PETER 'OLLIE' HALSALL	drms	AB
	PETE KELLY		AB
	JOHN McCAFFREY	bs	AB
	MIKE McKAY	gtr	A
	ALAN MENZIES	drms	A
	BARRY WOMERSLEY	ld gtr	A
	BILL LOVELADY	ld gtr	B
	IAN McGEE	drms	B
	JOHN SURGUY	sax	B

| 45: | Louie Louie/Honey Don't | (Fontana TF 524) 1965 R2 |

This Merseyside band from Southport, which included Pete Kelly (later of **Pete Kelly's Soulution**) recorded a cover version of The Kingsmen's classic *Louie, Louie*, which is now rare and collectable. On the reverse they turned Carl Perkins' *Honey Don't* into a wild rocker.

Ollie Halsall, who was only in the group for a few months in 1964, was later in **Timebox** and **Patto**. Barry Womersley went on to play for **Clayton Squares** and **Jasmin T**. Lovelady was also later in **Jasmin T**; McGee went on to play for **The Swinging Blue Jeans** and Surguy was in **Warm Dust**.

Honey Don't re-emerged on *Mersey Beat* (2-LP), *Pebbles, Vol. 6 - The Roots Of Mod* (LP) and *English Freakbeat Vol. 6* (CD). (VJ)

Tim Rice and The Webber Group

| Personnel: | TIM RICE |
| | ANDREW LLOYD WEBBER |

| 45: | Come Back Richard (Your Country Needs You)/ | |
| | Roll On Over Atlantic | (RCA RCA 1895) 1969 |

This was an early **Tim Rice and Andrew Lloyd Webber** project. They, of course, went on to considerable success in the seventies with 'Jesus Christ Superstar' and 'Evita'. Before finding fame in the seventies, both men had

dabbled in pop for some years. Rice had been Norrie Paramor's assistant at EMI, and had his songs recorded by acts such as **The Nightshift**, **Ross Hannaman** and **The Mixed Bag**, as well as producing sides for **The Shell**, **Murray Head**, **Tales of Justine** and others. Amongst **Lloyd Webber**'s efforts was the arrangement for **Marc Brierley**'s *Stay A Little Longer Merry Ann* 45. (VJ/RMJ)

Lewis Rich

45s:	Everybody But Me/	
	This Time It's Real	(Parlophone R 5283) 1965
	I Don't Want To Hear It Anymore/	
	Shedding Tears	(Parlophone R 5434) 1966
	I Keep It Hid/	
	If We Could Only Dance Together	(Philips BF 1715) 1968
	Prophet/Freedom City	(B&C 134) 1970

From Fulham in South-West London, **Rich** was only 21 when he recorded his first 45 in 1965. The vocalist and keyboardist went on to play for **The Herd**, **Moon's Train** and **Babylon** among others. (VJ)

Richmond

Personnel:	FRED ALEXANDER	cello	A
	CLIVE ANSTEY	cello	A
	TONI COOK	french horn	A
	ARTHUR COPPERSMITH	fiddle	A
	JEFF CLYNE	dbl bs	A
	STEVE HALL	vcls, gtr, flute, hrmnca	A
	JOHN MARSHALL	perc	A
	CHAS SEWARD	vcls, gtr	A
	TREVOR SPENCER	drms	A
	ALAN SKIDMORE	sax	A
	STAN SULZMAN	sax	A
	ALLAN TURNEY	bs	A
	DAVE WATKINS	keyb'ds, bells	A

| ALBUM: | 1 | FRIGHTENED | (Dart ARTS 65371) 1973 SC |

NB: (1) also issued in Europe on the Interchord label (26414-3U). This edition is a little easier to find.

45s:	Candy Dora/Willow Farm	(Dart ART 2008) 1971
	Frightened/Breakfast	(Dart ART 2025) 1973
	Raise Your Heads To The Wind/	
	All I Really Need	(Dart ART 2031) 1973
	Peaches/Work For My Baby	(Dart ART 2044) 1974

A folk duo (Hall and Seward), who put out a long forgotten album and four 45s on the Dart label. By all accounts much of their material contained some decent guitar work with a nice electric/acoustic balance. Some tracks sound similar to late sixties **Donovan**.

Steve Hall went on to join **Starry Eyed and Laughing** in 1973 but left again in November of that year. (MWh)

The Richmond Group

Personnel:	BARRY DAVID	lead gtr	A
	PETE DAVID	drms	A
	MIKE HART	gtr, sax	A
	HOWIE JONES	bs	A
	DAVE KERRIGAN	vcls	A

NB: Other personnel included: Eddie Cave (vcls), Terry Quinn (bs), Kenny Parry (lead gtr) and Billy Good (bs).

A post Merseybeat band from Liverpool who turn up on the Ember album, *Liverpool Today - Live At The Cavern* (LP) from 1965, playing *I Shall Not Be Moved*. (MWh/AD)

The Ricketts

This band recorded a superb psych/pop art/beat instrumental with some really freaky guitar work called *Action Painting*. They may have originated in Germany.

Action Painting has been compiled on *Maximum Freakbeat* (CD), *Visions Of The Past, Vol. 4* (LP & CD) and *Incredible Sound Show Stories, Vol. 1* (LP & CD). (VJ)

Frank Ricotti

ALBUM: 1   OUR POINT OF VIEW   (CBS 52668) 1969 SC

Ricotti was one of Britain's top session percussionists. He was assisted on this album by Chris Laurence (bs), **Chris Spedding** (gtr) and Bryan Spring (drms). (VJ)

Ricotti and Albuquerque

Personnel:	MICHAEL D'ALBUQUERQUE	gtr, vcls, keyb'ds	A
	CHRIS LAWRENCE	bs	A
	HENRY LOWTHER	trumpet	A
	FRANK RICOTTI	vibes, sax	A
	JOHN TAYLOR	keyb'ds	A
	TREVOR TOMKINS	drms	A

ALBUM: 1(A)   FIRST WIND   (Pegasus PEG 2) 1971

This was a jazz-rock band. **Frank Ricotti** had played in the **Georgie Fame** Band. For this album **Ricotti** teamed up with Michael D'Albuquerque, who made a couple of solo albums himself in the mid-seventies (*We May Be Cattle But We All Got Names* (RCA SF 8383) 1974 and *Stalking The Sleeper* (Warner Bros K 56276) 1976. He also released some 45s in 1969/70. Musically the format of *First Wind* was in the jazzy progressive genre. You'll note too that it was released on the collectable Pegasus label. In addition to the personnel listed above, session men Michael Keen and **Henry Lowther** (who made a solo album in 1970 and had also been with **John Mayall** and the **Keef Hartley Band**) assisted on trumpet.

After this project, **Ricotti** went to Gyroscope; Lawrence to El Skid and D'Alberquerque joined **The Electric Light Orchestra**. (VJ/JM)

Riff-Raff

Personnel:	AURERO DE SOUZA	drms	A
	TOMMY EYRE	keyb'ds, vcls	AB
	PETE KIRTLEY	gtr, vcls	AB
	ROGER SUTTON	bs, vcls	AB
	BUD BEADLE	sax	AB
	STEVE GREGORY	sax, flute	B
	JOANNA NEWMAN	vcls	B
	JOE O'DONNELL	viola	B

ALBUMS: 1(A)	RIFF RAFF	(RCA SF 8351) 1973 SC
2(B)	ORIGINAL MAN	(RCA LPLI 5023) 1974 SC

45:      Copper Kettle/You Must Be Joking   (RCA RCA 2396) 1973

A progressive rock outfit formerly known as Satyr, whose first album had soft passages similar to **Spring** as well as some heavy guitar parts. De Souza had been in **Nucleus** and Bud Beadle (formerly with **Ginger Baker's** Salt) assisted on sax on the first album and joined the band as a full-time member in August 1973, along with Steve Gregory.

When the project split, Beadle and Gregory went to Gonzales; Kirkly joined **Global Village Trucking Company**; De Souza's next venture was Bugatti & Muskett; Sutton headed for **Nucleus** and Eyre teamed up with **ZZebra**. (VJ/JM)

Rifkin

45:      We're Not Those People Any More/
         Continental Hesitation   (Page One POF 071) 1968 R2

A self-penned 45 produced by Colin Fletcher. *We're Not Those People Anymore* is a dreadful pop song, but *Continental Hesitation* is a superb slice of psychedelia, making it quite a collectable 45.

You can also hear *Continental Hesitation* on *Justafixation* (LP), *Oddities, Vol 2* (CD) and *Jagged Time Lapse, Vol 5* (CD). (VJ)

Rigor Mortis

Personnel:	TONY ASHTON	A
	HOWIE CASEY	A
	GRAHAM DEACON	A
	JOHN ENTWISTLE	A
	ALAN ROSS	A
	BRYAN WILLIAMS	A

NB: The Ladybirds also provide backing vocals.

ALBUM: 1(A)   RIGOR MORTIS SETS IN   (Track 2406 106) 1973 SC
NB: (1) reissued on CD (Repertoire 4621 WY) 1997 on German import and again on CD (Castle Music CMRCD 1154) 2005, with a plethora of bonus tracks.

45:      Made In Japan/Hound Dog   (Track 2094 107) 1973

This was essentially a solo project by **Who** member **John Entwistle**. The album got to No 174 in the US Charts. It was basically a tongue-in-cheek ode to the deah of Rock 'n' Roll and included renditions of *Lucille*, *Mr Bassman* and *Hound Dog* as well as the self-penned *Gimme That Rock'n'Roll*. The main attraction of the album was **Entwistle**'s humorous lyrics. It also included a re-make of *My Wife*, which many consider to be the best song **Entwistle** wrote for **The Who**.

Howie Casey had fronted **Howie Casey and The Seniors** in the early sixties. Tony Ashton had been in **Ashton, Gardner and Dyke**. Alan Ross went on to form **Ross**. (VJ)

Howard Riley (Trio)

Personnel:	BARRY GUY	bs	A
	JON HISEMAN	drms	A
	HOWARD RILEY	gtr, vcls	A

ALBUMS: 1(A)	DISCUSSIONS (w/insert)	(Opportunity CP 2499) 1968 R6
(up to 2	ANGLE	(CBS 52669) 1969 SC
1976) 3	THE DAY WILL COME	(CBS 64077) 1970 R1
4	FLIGHT	(Turtle TUR 301) 1971 R2
5	SYNOPSIS	(Incus INCUS 13) 1976 R2

NB: (1) credited to **Howard Riley Trio**. (2) - (4) **Howard Riley** solo projects. (5) credited to Howard Riley Trio with Tony Oxley and Barry Guy.

An historically significant jazz outfit. Just 99 copies were made of the privately-pressed *Discussions* album, which came with an information insert about the band's three members and were put out on the Opportunity label formed by one of **Riley**'s friends for this sole purpose. It is now one of the rarest and most expensive jazz albums to purchase and is in some demand as **Riley** went on to make a number of respected jazz albums; Hiseman went on to play in **Colosseum** and **Tempest** and Barry Guy became a member of **Spontaneous Music Ensemble**. (VJ)

Rings and Things

45:      Strange Things Are Happening/
         To Me To Me To Me   (Fontana TF 987) 1968 R2

This is a very rare and sought-after psych-pop 45. You'll also find the 'A' side on *Rubble Vol. 4: 49 Minute Technicolour Dream* (LP), *Rubble Vol. 3* (CD) and *Head Sounds From The Bam-Caruso Waxworks, Vol. 1* (CD), although it's certainly nothing to get excited about. It also gave its name to the splendid but short-lived magazine from Bam-Caruso Records. (VJ)

Bobby Rio (and The Revellers)

Personnel:			
	KEITH JENKINS	drms	A
	MIKE LUNT	bs	A
	BOBBY RIO	vcls	AB
	JOHN STILLITO	gtr	A
	TONY WARRELL	lead gtr	A
	ARTHUR DAVIES	drms	B
	DAVE ROSE	bs	B
	CHRIS WEBB	lead gtr	B

45s:	Boy Meets Girl/Don't Break My Heart	(Pye 7N 15790) 1965 R1
	Everything In The Garden/	
	When Love Was Young	(Pye 7N 15897) 1965 R1
	Value For Love/I'm Not Made Of Clay	(Pye 7N 15958) 1965 R1
α	Ask The Lonely/	
	Be Lonely Little Girl	(Piccadilly 7N 35003) 1966
α	Angelica/Lovin' You Girl	(Piccadilly 7N 35337) 1966

NB: α **Bobby Rio** solo 45s.

Bobby Rio's real name was Bobby Christo. The beat outfit came from Barking. Their 1965 singles were produced by Joe Meek. *Value For Love* was a Cook/Greenaway number. *Ask The Lonely* was a Four Tops song. When the band split **Rio** tried a couple of solo efforts.

Compilation appearances have included: *Boy Meets Girl* on *The Sixties File* (2-LP); *Boy Meets Girl* and *Value For Money* on *The Joe Meek Story: The Pye Years* (2-CD); and *When Love Was Young* on *Joe Meek: The Pye Years Vol. 2* (CD). (VJ/AD)

The Riot Squad

Personnel incl:			
	GRAHAM BONNEY	lead gtr	ABCD
	BRIAN DAVIES (aka BUTCH DAVIS)	bs	A
	BOB EVANS	vcls	ABCD
	MITCH MITCHELL	drms	AB
	MARK STEVENS	organ	ABCD
	MIKE MARTIN	bs	BCD
	BOB O'BRIEN	drms	D
	JON LORD	keyb'ds	

45s:	Anytime/Jump	(Pye 7N 15752) 1965 R1
	I Wanna Talk About My Baby/	
	Gonna Make You Mine	(Pye 7N 15817) 1965 R1
	Nevertheless/Not A Great Talker	(Pye 7N 15869) 1965 R1
	Cry Cry Cry/How Is It Done	(Pye 7N 17041) 1966 R1
	I Take It That We're Through/	
	Working Man	(Pye 7N 17092) 1966 R1
	It's Never Too Late To Forgive/	
	Try To Realise	(Pye 7N 17130) 1966 R1
	Gotta Be A First Time/	
	Bitter Sweet Love	(Pye 7N 17237) 1967 R1

NB: Bam-Caruso compiled the band's 'A' and 'B' sides in 1988 as did Repertoire on CD, *Anytime* (Repertoire REP 4192-WZ) 1991 in Germany. *Jump* (Castle CMRCD 703) is an alternative CD compilation.

This band underwent several personnel changes in their three year career and enjoyed quite a prolific 45 output, though no commercial success. They were usually a six-piece and their music was predominantly beat and R&B. Mitch Mitchell (later of **Georgie Fame and The Blue Flames** and **The Jimi Hendrix Experience**) was one of their drummers and **Jon Lord** was their keyboard player after leaving **The Artwoods** and prior to forming **Deep Purple**. **David Bowie** was also a member for a brief period in 1965, although he didn't take part in any of their recordings, and has only been connected with the band via a publicity shot from the period... Aside from these subsequent prestigious associations their other claim to fame was to have appeared on a couple of episodes of 'Emergency Ward 10' - not playing their songs, though!

All of their 45s are now minor collectables. *Cry Cry Cry*, *I Take It That We're Through* and *It's Never Too Late To Forgive* were Joe Meek productions. Curiously, another Meek produced track, *How Is It Done* was later ripped off almost note for note and word for word as *No Life Child* by **Keith Dangerfield**. They recorded several tracks at Joe Meek's studio in London's Holloway Road and were due to release *Knoxville Girl* - originally by The Louvin Brothers. However, it was rejected as being too bloodthirsty and it was not too long after that that Joe Meek killed himself and his landlady. There are thought to be copies of these recordings in the *Tea-Chest Tapes Collection*.

Davies left after the third 45 to join Silverhead and Mike Martin joined on bass. In December 1965 Mitchell departed to **Georgie Fame and The Blue Flames** and Bob O'Brien came in on drums. The band split in 1967 and O'Brien joined **The Casuals**.

Jump compiles their first seven Pye singles on CD along with alternate takes and previously unissued tracks. 15 of the cuts on the CD were produced by Joe Meek, which also includes a couple of tracks where they backed Glenda Collins.

Compilation appearances have included: *I Take It We're Through* on *Quick Before They Catch Us* (LP & CD), *It's Only A Passing Phase* (LP) and *The Joe Meek Story: The Pye Years* (2-CD); *Bitter Sweet Love* and *Try To Realise* on *Joe Meek: The Pye Years Vol. 2* (CD); *Gonna Make You Mine* on *The R&B Era, Vol. 2* (LP & CD); *Jump* on *The R&B Era, Vol. 1* (LP & CD); *Cry, Cry, Cry* on *The Sixties File* (2-LP) and on the 2-CD set *We Love The Pirates: Charting The Big 'L' Fab 40*; *I Wanna Talk About My Baby*, *Gonna Make You Mine*, *Anytime* and *Jump* on *Sixties Years, Vol. 6* (CD); *I Wanna Talk About My Baby* and *Gonna Make You Mine* on *Doin' The Mod, Vol. 1* (CD); *Nevertheless* on *Doin' The Mod, Vol. 2* (CD); and *Anytime* and *Jump* on *Footsteps To Fame, Vol. 1* (CD). (VJ/KL/MB/JM)

Twinkle Ripley

45:	Days/Caroline	(Bradley BRAD 7418) 1974

This was **Twinkle**, who recorded many singles in the sixties, including the big hit *Terry* as **Twinkle**. The above 45 was released later as **Twinkle Ripley**. Her real name was Marilyn Ripley. (VJ)

Tony Rivers and The Castaways

Personnel incl:			
	RAY BROWN	bs	A
	TOM MARSHALL	gtr, vcls	A
	JOHN PERRY	ld gtr	A
	TONY RIVERS	ld vcls	A
	KENNY ROWE	ld vcls, bs	A
	MARTIN SHAER	ld vcls	A
	GEOFF SWETTENHAM	drms	A
	PETE SWETTENHAM	gtr	A

TONY TIVERS AND THE CASTAWAYS.

45s:	Shake Shake Shake/		
	Row, Row, Row	(Columbia DB 7135) 1963 SC	
	I Love The Way You Walk/I Love You	(Columbia DB 7224) 1964	
	Life's Too Short/Tell On Me	(Columbia DB 7336) 1964	
	She/Till We Get Home	(Columbia DB 7448) 1965	
	Come Back/What To Do	(Columbia DB 7536) 1965	
	God Only Knows/Charade	(Columbia DB 7971) 1966 SC	
	Nowhere Man/		
	The Girl From New York City	(Parlophone R 5400) 1966	
	Girl Don't Tell/		
	Girl From Salt Lake City	(Immediate IM 027) 1966 SC	
	I Can Guarantee Your Love/Pantomime	(Polydor 56245) 1968	

Tony Rivers and The Castaways formed in Dagenham, Essex, in 1963. Their debut single was hard-hitting R&B originally done by Jackie Wilson, but over the next few years they developed into a harmony group, covering The Beach Boys' *God Only Knows* in 1966. They underwent several personnel changes over the years and briefly included the Swettenham brothers in 1966 before they formed **Grapefruit**. In late 1968 **Tony Rivers**, along with Ray Brown and Kenny Rowe, played for **Harmony Grass**.

Martin Shaer later replaced Kenny Rowe, joining the band at the same time as Perry and the Swettenham brothers and stayed with the band until 1970, when they performed their last gig as **The Castaways** in the "World" show at the Saville Theater as guests of the **Bee Gees**.

The group remain a favourite among surf/harmony group fans.

After the group's demise Martin Shaer did some writing and producing for Screen Gems/Columbia, and wrote the perennial *Reggae Christmas*, before emigrating to Canada in 1974. In Canada, he produced Sweeney Todd's No. 1 hit *Roxy Roller*, and was nominated twice as Producer of the Year at the Canadian Juno awards. Shaer was also responsible for recruiting 16-year-old Bryan Adams to Sweeney Todd, and produced their *If Wishes Were Horses, Beggars Would Ride* album.

Compilation appearances include: *Come Back* on *Liverpool '65* (CD); *God Only Knows* on *My Generation* (LP); *Shake Shake Shake* on *Rare 60's Beat Treasures, Vol. 3* (CD), *Beat At Abbey Road* (CD) and *Beat Merchants* (2-LP); *Girl Don't Tell Me* on *Immediate Alternative* (LP) and *Immediate Single Collection, Vol. 4* (CD); *Girl Don't Tell Me* and *Girl From Salt Lake City* on *Immediate Alternative* (CD) and *Immediate Single Anthology, Vol. 1 - Rarities* (CD); *Girl From Salt Lake City* on *Immediate Single Collection, Vol. 2* (CD); and *I Love You* on *Psychedelic Unknowns, Vol. 8*. (VJ)

The Roadrunners

Personnel incl:	DEREK SHULMAN
	RAY SHULMAN
	PHIL SHULMAN

A Portsmouth band formed by the Shulman brothers who became **Simon Dupree and The Big Sound** in 1966. (VJ)

The Roadrunners

Personnel:	DAVE BOYCE	drms	ABC
	MIKE HART	gtr, vcls	ABC
	PETE MACKEY	bs	ABCD
	JOHN PEACOCK	piano	ABCD
	DAVE PERCY	lead gtr	A
	NICK CARVER (LeCREC)	sax	BC
	JOHNNY PHILLIPS	sax	B
	BOB HARRISON	trumpet	C
	MIKE BYRNE	vcls	D
	MIKE KONZLE	lead gtr	D
	TERRY McCLUSKER	drms	D

ALBUMS:	1(A)	TWIST TIME IN THE STAR-CLUB	(Ariole 71224) 1964
	2(B)	STAR-CLUB SHOW 2	(Star-Club 148001) 1965

NB: (2) one side by **The Roadrunners**, the other by **Shorty and Them**. (2) reissued on CD together with tracks from the *Pantomania* EP below (Repertoire IMS 7014) .

EP:	1(B)	PANTOMANIA	(Cavern Sound 2BSNL 7) 1965 R1

NB: (1) also includes tracks by Chris Edwards and Clive Wood.

A Liverpool beat act who formed in 1962 and were originally known as The Tenabeats. They played the usual Liverpool club circuit, including the Cavern and Hope Hall on a regular basis. Like many Liverpudlian acts, they also spent a long time in Germany, headlining at the Star Club, where they recorded one and a half albums (the second being split with **Shorty and Them**).

The Roadrunners' earliest recorded output, *You Can Make It If You Try* and *Mary Ann* comes from the "First Annual R&B Festival" at Birmingham Town Hall on February 28th, 1964. Organised by Georgio Gomelsky, this one-night festival featured Sonny Boy Williamson backed by **The Yardbirds** and supported by **Long John Baldry and The Hoochie Coochie Men**, the **Spencer Davis Rhythm & Blues Quartet** and, of course, **The Roadrunners**. The gig was recorded by Gomelsky, and this somewhat low-fidelity album has subsequently been released by Charly Records and on CD by Repertoire (*Steampacket/First R&B Festival* (REP4090-WZ)). Incidentally, **Rod Stewart** (then roadie for **The Hoochie Coochie Men**) also makes an early appearance on the album and **The Roadrunners** also appear as part of the "All Star" jam through *Got My Mojo Working* which closes the album.

Around this time, the band was offered a deal by a major record label. However, **Mike Hart** seemed reluctant to get involved with "all this commercialism", and the deal fell through. The band returned to Liverpool and added two sax players:- Nick Carver and Johnny Phillips, becoming a James Brown style soul outfit.

Following the second Star Club album, the band returned from Hamburg and appeared on one more disc - the *Pantomania* - EP, which was made to raise money for the University rag week in 1965. It includes their version of the Bobby Bland classic *Cry, Cry, Cry* and a version of *The Leaving Of Liverpool*.

Mike Hart left shortly afterwards to pursue a solo career, and **The Roadrunners** carried on for a while under the leadership of Pete Mackey.

Pete and **Mike Hart** worked together again some years ago when Pete produced a demo tape for a proposed solo album by Mike. It never happened, but the demo tape still exists. Pete Mackey is now a marketing consultant.

Compilation appearances include: *Mary Ann* on *Beat Im Star Club* (2-LP); *Long Tall Sally* and *Beautiful Delilah* on *The Beat Goes On, Vol. 1* (LP); *You Better Move On* and *Rip It Up* on *The Beat Goes On, Vol. 2* (LP); *Slow Down* and *That's Alright* on *The Beat Goes On, Vol. 3* (LP); and *You Can Make It If You Try* and *Mary Ann* on *The First British R&B Festival, February 28, 1964* (LP). (DHs/MWh/AD)

The Roaring Sixties

45:	We Love The Pirates/	
	I'm Leaving Town	(Marmalade 598 001) 1966 R1

Their novelty pop ode to pirate radio, a crucial outlet for non-mainstream pop and rock in the mid-sixties, is now understandably quite collectable. It is probably not by the same **Roaring Sixties** that evolved into **Family**, though **Family** were very much part of the scene at Giorgio Gomelsky's Marmalade label.

Compilation appearances include: *I'm Leaving Town* on *Red With Purple Flashes, Vol. 1* (LP) and *We Love The Pirates* on the 2-CD set *We Love The Pirates: Charting The Big 'L' Fab 40*. (VJ)

Andy Roberts

ALBUMS:	1	HOME GROWN (w/insert)	(RCA SF 8086) 1971 R2/SC
(up to	2	HOME GROWN	(B&C CAS 1034) 1971
1976)	3	NINA AND THE DREAM TREE	(Pegasus PEG 5) 1971 SC
	4	URBAN COWBOY	(Elektra K 42139) 1973
	5	ANDY ROBERTS AND THE GREAT	
		STAMPEDE	(Elektra K 42151) 1973
	6	ANDY ROBERTS	(Charisma CS 6) 1973

NB: (1) also issued. (2) is a reissue of (1) with a different track selection, which omits several tracks and adds *Lonely In The Crowd* and other tracks remixed. (1) also released on Ampex in the USA, but with only eight tracks. It featured a compilation of four tracks from (1) plus four new ones, which later appeared on *Nina And The Dream Tree* in the UK. There's also a CD, *Best Of Andy Roberts* (Mooncrest CRESTCD 014) 1992 and more recently *The Andy Roberts Story* (Sanctuary) 2005.

45s: Baby Baby/
All Around My Grandmother's Floor (Elektra K 12109) 1973
53 Miles From Spanish Town/
Clowns On The Road (Elektra K 12127) 1973

Andy Roberts was born in Hatch End, East London on 12 June 1946. His dad was a music hall fan and his mum loved classical music. He started playing the violin when he was nine and bought his first guitar at 13. He played in a school band under various monikers, providing live music for a late night revue at the 1965 Edinburgh festival. Having accompanied **Scaffold**, he became guitarist with **Liverpool Scene** from 1968-1970.

His solo debut, *Home Grown*, is an excellent electric folk album, issued first on RCA (with 14 tracks) and then on B&C (with only ten tracks). There are five tracks exclusive to RCA's version (*Jello, Where The Soul Of Man Never Dies, Boris At The Organ, Autumn To May* and *The Praties Are Dug*) and one to B&C's (*Lonely In The Crowd*). The releases also came in different artwork. As if this wasn't confusing enough, *Home Grown* also appeared on Ampex in the USA with only eight tracks, four of which were brand new. These were later included on *Nina And The Dream Tree* in the UK.

Early in 1970 he guested on *The Shelagh McDonald Album*, and is thought to have produced several of its tracks uncredited. In March 1970 **Roberts** performed several tracks from *Home Grown* for John Peel's 'Top Gear', as well as *You're A Machine*, a non-album cut on which he is backed by **Mighty Baby**. A rehearsal of it, recorded shortly before the BBC Session, can be found on 2005's *The Andy Roberts Anthology*.

Next he formed his own band **Everyone** (1971) and was also in **Plainsong** (1972), alongside **Ian Matthews**, on whose early albums he had played. 1973's *...And The Great Stampede* album, which came in a gatefold sleeve and featured Gerry Conway, Pat Donaldson and **Zoot Money**, is recommended. **Ollie Halsall** makes a guest appearance on one track (*Speed Wall*). From 1973-76 he was a member of **Grimms**, appearing on their final two albums. When they split he played in **Roy Harper's** band and for **The Albion Band**. In 1978 he worked on the **Roger McGough** album *Summer with Monika*, and in 1980 he appeared in an enlarged version of **Pink Floyd** to perform *The Wall* at London's Earl's Court Theatre and in Germany. The same year he started a four year stint with Hank Wangford, also playing occasional gigs backing Adrian Henri's poetry. In the nineties he participated in a **Plainsong** reunion.

The Best Of Andy Roberts includes all of the *Nina* album, seven cuts from the RCA version of *Home Grown* and four tracks from the *Everyone* album.

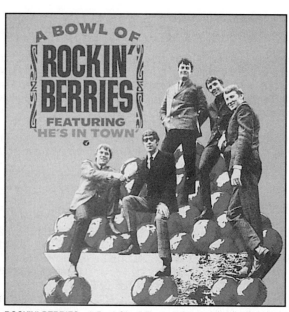

ROCKIN' BERRIES - A Bowl Of... (LP).

The Andy Roberts Anthology features tracks from all his solo albums (including both the RCA and B&C versions of *Home Grown*), the *Everyone* album and 14 previously unissued recordings. He also has a track *Richmond* on the Peg label folk sampler *Clogs* (LP). (VJ/RMJ)

Keith Roberts

ALBUM: 1 PIER OF THE REALM (Trailer LER 3031) 1972 SC

This was a humourous album of songs about Lancashire. **Roberts** is accompanied by Barry Halpin on whistle and banjo and Barrie Parkinson on mandolin. The album contains songs like *Blackpool Blues; A World Out Of Coal*, which attempts to trace the development of Lancashire from the first coal pits to the time of the album's release, when the final tracks of the coal mining industry were being erased from the scenery and *The Cage* and *Lament For Albert*, which were songs about the Lancashire mines. (VJ)

Rock Candy

Personnel:	MIKE LOVATT	A
	MARTIN O'MAHONY	A
	BUTCH OSBORN	A
	BOB STUART	A

			HCP
45s:	Remember/Don't Put Me Down	(MCA MK 5069) 1971	32
	Roly/Please	(MCA MK 5083) 1972	-
	Some Fine Day/Magic Horse	(MCA MK 5087) 1972	-

Their first 'A' side *Remember* is a song that all holiday makers to Spain seem to come back singing. The original Spanish version is by Los Diablos. They were helped by **Tremeloes'** Hawkes and Blakeley who knew the band was looking for a song and offered this one. They classified themselves as a harmony group and their aim was to succeed on the cabaret and ballroom circuit.

Magic Horse has been compiled on *Fading Yellow, Vol 5* (CD). (VJ)

Rockfield Chorale

45: Evensong/Amberley (Rockfield ROC 5) 1974

A one-off project by **Dave Edmunds** and various of his cronies. (VJ)

Rockin' Berries

Personnel:	ROY AUSTIN	bs	A
	TERRY BOND	drms	AB
	CHUCK BOTFIELD	ld gtr, vcls	ABC
	CHRIS LEA	ld vcls	ABC
	GEOFF TURTON	gtr, vcls	AB
	BOBBY THOMPSON	bs	BC
	KENNY REDWAY	drms	C
	PETE SPOONER	gtr	C

			HCP
ALBUMS:	1(A)	IN TOWN	(Piccadilly NPL 38013) 1964 R2 15
(up to	2(A)	LIFE IS JUST A BOWL OF BERRIES	
1976)			(Piccadilly NPL 38022) 1964 R2 -
	3(A)	BLACK GOLD	(Satril SATL 4002) 1976 -

NB: A later compilation is *A Bowl Of Rockin' Berries* (PRT PYL 4016) 1988, also on CD (PRT PYC 4016). (1) and (2) reissued on CD by Repertoire (RR 4099-WZ) and (REP 4181-WZ) in 1991 with bonus cuts. *The Best Of The Rockin' Berries* (Sequel NEX CD 180) 1991 is a CD compilation. *They're In Town* (Sequel NEECD 299) 1998 is a 2-CD set.

EPs:	1(A)	I DIDN'T MEAN TO HURT YOU	
			(Piccadilly NEP 34039) 1965 R1
	2(A)	NEW FROM THE BERRIES	
			(Piccadilly NEP 34043) 1965 R1
	3(A)	HAPPY TO BE BLUE	(Piccadilly NEP 34045) 1965 R1

THE ROCKIN' BERRIES - In Town (CD).

45s:			
(up to	Wah Wah Woo/Rockin' Berry Stomp	(Decca F 11698) 1963	SC -
1976)	Itty Bitty Pieces/The Twitch	(Decca F 11760) 1963	SC -
	I Didn't Mean To Hurt You/		
	You'd Better Come Home	(Piccadilly 7N 35197) 1964	43
	He's In Town/Flashback	(Piccadilly 7N 35203) 1964	3
	What In The World's Come Over You/		
	You Don't Know What To Do	(Piccadilly 7N 35217) 1964	23
	Poor Man's Son/Follow Me	(Piccadilly 7N 35236) 1965	5
	You're My Girl/Brother Bill	(Piccadilly 7N 35254) 1965	40
	The Water Is Over My Head/		
	Doesn't Time Fly	(Piccadilly 7N 35270) 1965	43
	I Could Make You Fall In Love/		
	Land Of Love	(Piccadilly 7N 35304) 1966	-
	Midnight Mary/		
	Money Grows On Trees	(Piccadilly 7N 35327) 1966	-
	Sometimes/Needs To Be	(Piccadilly 7N 35373) 1967	-
	Smiles/Breakfast At Sam's	(Piccadilly 7N 35400) 1967	-
	Dawn (Go Away)/She's Not Like Any Girl	(Pye 7N 17411) 1967	-
	When I Reach The Top/Pain	(Pye 7N 17519) 1968	-
	Mr. Blue/Land Of Love	(Pye 7N 17589) 1968	-
	Looking Glass/Boogaloo Pie	(Pye 7N 45362) 1974	-
	Rockabye Nursery Rhyme/		
	Long Time Ago	(Pye 7N 45394) 1974	-
	Black Gold/Eve	(Pye 7N 45439) 1975	-
	Lonely Summertime/Send Me No Letters	(Satril SAT 101) 1975	-
	I Didn't Know/Come On Sun	(Satril SAT 107) 1976	-

Formed in Birmingham in 1961, **The Rockin' Berries** spent much of the next two years in Germany, where they added two saxophonists to their ranks. As their name implied musically they took their inspiration from rock'n'rollers like Chuck Berry. Much of their music was harmony pop-rock.

When they returned to England they signed to Decca in 1963, though their first two singles flopped and there was a lapse of almost a year before they tried again, this time with Pye's Piccadilly label. Their label debut, *I Didn't Mean To Hurt You*, was a minor hit, but their big breakthrough came after they met Hollywood producer Kim Fowley who played them a song called *He's In Town* by an American band, The Tokens. Realising that this was a much more commercial offering they rushed out a cover version, which climbed to No 3 in the UK Charts, but at the same time halted the progress of their debut release. Turton's falsetto vocal style on this disc soon became the group's trademark.

The Ivy League wrote them *Funny How Love Can Be*, which was an ideal follow-up for **Turton**'s vocals but for some bizarre reason Piccadilly vetoed this idea in favour of a revival of Jack Scott's 1960 hit, *What In The World's Come Over You*. That was an OK song which gave the band a minor hit, though ironically the **Ivy League** took *Funny How Love Can Be* into the Top Ten themselves.

The Rockin' Berries had one more big hit with a good cover of US combo The Reflections' *Poor Man's Son*. This found Lea's low vocals vying with Turton's falsetto and was notable for an unusual guitar section. Thereafter it was all downhill commercially - they enjoyed just two more minor hits with *You're My Girl* and *The Water Is Over My Head*.

Their first album, *In Town*, sold pretty well and climbed quite high in the Album Charts. The follow-up, *Life Is A Bowl Of Berries*, was rather disappointing containing songs like *The Laughing Policeman* and *Iko Iko*.

Still the band seemed to have made contingencies for this eventuality for as early as in 1965 they made their debut in a pantomime season at Great Yarmouth. Subsequently they introduced comedy routines and impersonations by Clive Lea into their act. In 1967 Lea left to become a solo impersonator and by the late sixties the group were concentrating on comedy, TV and cabaret. **Turton** later went solo under the name **Jefferson** (as well as recording a 45 under his own name) but eventually ended up working in the hotel business. The remaining members continued as a popular cabaret act for the rest of the century with **Turton** back in the fold.

The best introduction to their material is probably PRT's *A Bowl Of Rockin' Berries*, which includes most of their finest moments, but the 1991 Repertoire CD reissues include lots of 45s. Indeed the reissue of (2) also includes all their non-album songs from their early Pye EPs and all their 'A' and 'B' sides until the end of 1968! Alternatively, the Sequel set *The Best Of The Rockin' Berries* includes 15 tracks by the band, including the previously unreleased *Yellow Rainbow* and seven by their lead singer **Jefferson**. A later Sequel collection *They're In Town* contains eight previously unissued songs, including covers of *Take A Giant Step* (a Goffin & King song recorded by The Monkees), **Donovan's** *Oh Gosh* and The Lefte Banke's *Barterers And Their Wives*. The collection also contains their 1964 albums: - *In Town* and *Life Is Just A Bowl Of Berries*.

The Water Is Over My Head was written by Al Kooper and Hank Levine.

Compilation appearances have included: *Poor Man's Son* on *Piccadilly Story* (CD) and *Dizzy* (CD); *The Water Is Over My Head* on *Quick Before They Catch Us* (LP & CD) and on the 2-CD set *We Love The Pirates: Charting The Big 'L' Fab 40*; *Itty Bitty Pieces* on *Ready, Steady, Go!* (LP), *Weekend Starts Here* (LP) and *The Beat Scene* (CD); *The Water Is Over My Head* and *Poor Man's Son* on *Ripples, Vol. 1* (CD); *Barterers And Their Wives* on *Ripples, Vol. 3* (CD); *Across The Street* and *Dawn (Go Away)* on *Ripples, Vol. 4* (CD); *You're My Girl* on *Ripples, Vol. 7* (CD); *He's In Town* and *She's Not Like Any Girl* on *Ripples, Vol. 2* (CD); *He's In Town* and *Poor Man's Son* on *The Sixties File* (2-LP); *He's In Town, Flashback, I Didn't Mean To Hurt You* and *You'd Better Come Home* on *Sixties Years, Vol. 6* (CD); *He's In Town* on *Watch Your Step* (LP & CD) and *20 Hits Of The 60's* (CD); *Funny How Love Can Be* on *Beat Merchants* (CD); *Flashback* and *Let's Try Again* on *Brum Beat - Midlands Beat Groups Of The 60's* (CD); *He's In Town* (alternate take) on the 2-CD set *Greatest Hits Of The 60's*; *He's In Town, Poor Man's Son* and *Follow Me* on *Hits From The Ivy League, The Rockin' Berries, And The Sorrows* (LP); *Brother Bill (The Last Clean Shirt)* and *He's In Town* on *Sounds Of The Sixties* (CD); and *He's In Town* on *Best Of British Rock* (CD) and *Yellow Rainbow* on *Haunted - Psychedelic Pstones, Vol 2* (CD). (VJ)

The Rocking Vickers

Personnel:	HARRY FEENEY	vcls	AB
	ALEX HAMILTON	gtr	A
	PETE MOORHOUSE	bs	A
	CIGGY SHAW	drms	AB
	KEN WHATSISNAME	gtr	A
	IAN 'LEMMY' KILMINSTER	ld gtr	B
	STEVE 'VICKERS' MORRIS	bs	B

45s:	I Go Ape/Someone Like You	(Decca F 11993) 1964
	It's Alright/Stay By Me	(CBS 202 051) 1966
	Dandy/I Don't Need Your Kind	(CBS 202 241) 1966

NB: There's also two CD compilations *The Complete Rocking Vickers Collection* (Retro 803) 1995 and *The Complete Rockin' Vickers: It's Aright!* (RPM RPM 196) includes all their singles and a plethora of previously unreleased tracks.

Originally known as Rev Black and The Rocking Vickers this was a wild beat era band from Blackpool. Their first 'A' side, *I Go Ape*, was recorded by line-up (A). *It's Alright* was a **Pete Townshend** track. Their final 45, *Dandy*, was a Ray Davies' composition, also recorded by **Herman's Hermits** among others.

In addition to the above 45s, they recorded another *Stella/Zing! Went The Strings Of My Heart* (Decca SD 5662) in 1965. It was considered too commercial for their raucous appeal and so it was decided not to give it a UK release. Instead, it was released in Finland and possibly some other European countries too.

In 1966 they switched to CBS and line-up (B), which included Lemmy whose subsequent bands were **Sam Gopal**, **Opal Butterfly**, **Hawkwind** and Motorhead, recorded a couple of further 45s. *Ciggy Shaw* went on to bang the skins for Soloman King.

Compilation appearances include: *I Go Ape* on *Hard-Up Heroes* (2-LP) and *I Don't Need Your Kind* on *Jagged Time Lapse, Vol 3* (CD). (VJ/TR)

Rockin' Horse

Personnel incl: JIMMY CAMPBELL
BILLY KINSEY

ALBUM: 1 YES IT IS   (Philips 6308 075) 1970 R1

NB: (1) reissued on CD (Rev-Ola CRREV 7) with six bonus tracks.

45s: Biggest Gossip In Town/You Say   (Philips 6006 156) 1971
Julian The Hooligan/
Stayed Out Late Last Night   (Philips 6006 200) 1972
I'm So Fed Up Part 1/Part 2   (Randy's RAN 535) 1973

A Billy Kinsey (ex-**Merseybeats**) and **Jimmy Campbell** project. Aside from his solo career, **Campbell** was in **The Kirkbys** and **23rd Turnoff**. This album was pop-rock and clearly influenced by the late sixties **Beatles**. **Rockin' Horse** backed Chuck Berry on a 1972 tour. They recorded a BBC 625 TV show which was subsequently issued on vinyl *Six Two Five* (Driving Wheel LP 1001) and also on CD (ARC CD 001), (PYCD 260) and (de Wolf CD 2010). (VJ/FR)

Rock Rebellion

45:    Let's Go/So Sorry Baby   (Santa Posa PNS 7) 1973

This outfit came from Wolverhampton. They had been the backing band for **Screamin' Lord Sutch** during 1972. (VJ)

Rock Workshop

Personnel:			
HAROLD BECKETT	horns	AB
BOB DOWNES	woodwind	AB
ALAN GREED	keyb'ds, vcls	AB
ALEX HARVEY	vcls	A
ROBIN JONES	drms	A
BRIAN MILLER	keyb'ds	AB
TONY ROBERTS	woodwind	AB
DARRYL RUNSWICK	bs	AB
ALAN RUSHTON	drms	AB
RAY RUSSELL	gtr	AB
DEREK WADSWORTH	trombone	AB
GINGER HARPER	vcls	B
BUD PARKES	horns	B
TONY UTER	perc	B
PHIL WAINMAN	perc	B

ALBUMS: 1(A) ROCK WORKSHOP   (CBS 64075) 1970 SC
2(B) THE VERY LAST TIME (2-LP)   (CBS 64394) 1971 SC

NB: (2) reissued on CD (Angel Air SJPCD 171)

45s: You To Lose/Born In The City   (CBS 5046) 1970
The Very Last Time/Light Is Light   (CBS 7252) 1971

This was a curious new-wave jazz collective which **Alex Harvey** co-ordinated on their debut album. Members of the collective had earlier appeared on **Harvey**'s 1969 album, *Roman Wall Blues*. The *Rock*

Workshop album was an uncomfortable mixture of covers and experimental originals which had its moments but failed to convince overall. *The Very Last Time* includes rehearsals of songs like *Ice Cold* and *Wade In The Water* with **Harvey** on vocals as well as live material recorded at London's Goldsmiths College. (VJ)

Jess Roden (Band)

Personnel:			
JOHN CARTWRIGHT	bs	AB
CHRIS GOWER	trombone	AB
PETE HUNT	drms, vcls	AB
BRUCE ROBERTS	gtr, vcls	AB
JESS RODEN	vcls, gtr	AB
STEVE WEBB	gtr, vcls	AB
BILLY LIVSEY	keyb'ds	B

ALBUMS: 1 JESS RODEN   (Island ILPS 9286) 1974
(up to   2 (A) YOU CAN KEEP YOUR HAT ON (Island ILPS 9349) 1976
1976)   3 (A) PLAY IT DIRTY PLAY IT CLASS   (Island ILPS 9442) 1976

NB: (2) as **The Jess Roden Band**. (1) reissued on CD (Island IMCD 143) 1991 and again on German import (Repertoire) 1998.

EP: 1 LIVE   (Island IEP 3) 1976

NB: Tracks included were *Can't Get Next To You, On A Winner With You* and *You Can Leave Your Hat On*.

45s: Under Suspicion/Ferry Cross   (Island WIP 6227) 1975
(up to   You Can Leave Your Hat On/
1976)   On A Winner With You   (Island WIP 6286) 1976
Stay In Bed/Me And Crystal Eve   (Island WIP 6358) 1976

Roden was in **The Alan Bown Set** in the sixties. In 1970 he formed **Bronco**, but this proved to be an unsuccessful venture. His next venture was The Butts Band with former Doors John Densmore and Robbie Krieger and whilst with them he recorded his 1974 'solo' album, assisted by Steve Webb and session men, which featured contributions from **Free's** Simon Kirke and Allen Toussaint. This inspired him to form his own band (The Butts Band were pretty unsuccessful too) and *You Can Keep Your Hat On* is quite highly thought of. This was recorded by line-up (A) above plus Billy Livsey on keyboards. Livsey (formerly of **Ronnie Lane's Slim Chance**) toured with the band in March 1976 and then became a full-time member until he joined **The Kevin Ayers Band** in August 1976. He guested on *Play It Dirty?Play It Class*. The band split in 1977.

In 1980 **Roden** joined The Rivits. He went on to make further solo albums, *The Player Not The Game* (November 1977) and *Stonechaser* (1980) and now lives in New York. (VJ/JM)

Mark Rogers and The Marksmen

45:    Bubble Pop/Hold It!   (Parlophone R 5045) 1963 SC

The Marksmen also recorded a 45. See their entry for details. (VJ)

Rogue (1)

Personnel:			
GUY FLETCHER	vcls, keyb'ds	A
ALAN HODGE	vcls, gtr	A
J.W. HODGKINSON	vcls	A
LES HURDLE	bs	A
BARRY MORGAN	drms	A

ALBUM: 1(A) FALLEN ANGELS   (Epic EPC 69235) 1976
(up to
1976)

45s: Cool Clear Air/Ohio Sun   (Epic EPC 3293) 1975
(up to   Dedication/Mother Nature   (Epic EPC 3642) 1975
1976)   Fallen Angel/Run For Shelter   (Epic EPC 3886) 1976
Dedication/Mother Nature   (Epic EPC 4332) 1976
Lay Me Down/Rosie   (Epic EPC 4626) 1976

Rogue was a group of session musicians who played harmony-pop. Guy Fletcher was a singer/songwriter who had composed the hit *Can't Tell The Bottom From The Top*. He also had an eponymous solo album released in 1971 (Philips 6303 013). Hodgkinson had been with **Daryl Way's Wolf** and **If**, whilst Morgan and Les Hurdle were session musicians who had been in **Blue Mink** and related projects. Their first 45 was a minor US hit, climbing to No 108 over there. They recorded two further albums, *Let It Go* (Epic, 1977) and *Would You Let Your Daughter* (Ariola, 1979), which are outside the time frame of this book. Fletcher was later in **Roxy Music**. (JM/BS)

The Rogues (2)

45:	Memories Of Missy/	
	And You Let Her Pass By	(Decca F 12718) 1967

This is a long forgotten sixties band. *Memories Of Missy* is a singalong pop song and the flipside is inconsequential pop too. (VJ)

The Rokes

Personnel inc:	JOHNNY CHARLTON	gtr, vcls
	BOBBY POSNER	bs, vcls
	NORMAN DAVID 'SHEL' SHAPIRO	gtr, vcls
	MIKE ROGER SHEPSTONE	drms, vcls

45s:	Let's Live For Today/Ride On	(RCA RCA 1587) 1967 SC
(UK)	Hold My Hand/Regency Sue	(RCA RCA 1646) 1967 R1
	When The Wind Arises/	
	The Works Of Bartholemew	(RCA RCA 1694) 1968 R1

45s:	Shake Rattle and Roll/Quando Eri Con Me	(ARC 4013) 1964
(Italian)	Un Anima Pura/She Ask For You	(ARC 4021) 1964
	C'e Una Strana Espressione Nei Tuoi Occhi/	
	Ci Vedremo Domani	(ARC 4046) 1965
	Grazie A Te/La Mia Città	(ARC 4067) 1965
	Ascolta Nel Vento/Il Primo Sintomo	(ARC 4075) 1965
	Che Colpa Abbiamo Noi/Piangi Con Me	(ARC 4081) 1966
	E La Pioggia Che Va/	
	Finche c'e Musica Mi Tengo Su	(ARC 4100) 1966
	Ride On/Che Mondo Strano	(ARC - Juke Box Only) 1966
	Bisogna Saper Perdere/Non Far Finta Di No	(ARC 4109) 1967
	Eccola Di Nuovo/Ricordo Quando Ero Bambino	(ARC 4122) 1967
	Cercate Di Abbracciare Tutto Il Mondo Come Noi/	
	Regency Sue	(ARC 4137) 1967
	Le Opere di Bartolomeo/Siamo Sotto Il Sole	(ARC 4142) 1968
	Lascia L'Ultimo Ballo Per Me/	
	Io Vivr Senza Te	(ARC 4152) 1968
	Qui non c'e Nessuno/	

THE ROLLING STONES - No. 2 (LP).

La Luna Bianca La Notte Nera	(ARC 4156) 1968
Baby Come Back/Hello Come Stai	(ARC 4169) 1969
Ma Che Freddo Fa/Per Te Per Me	(ARC 4172) 1969
28 Giugno/Mary	(ARC 4182) 1969
Ombre Blu/Sempre Giorno	(ARC 4194) 1970

ALBUMS:	1	THE ROKES	(ARC SA 4) 1965
(Italian)	2	THE ROKES VOL. 2	(ARC SA 8) 1966
	3	CHE MONDO STRANO	(ARC SA 15) 1967
	4	THE ROKES	(ARC 11006) 1968
	5	I SUCCESSI DEI ROKES (ANTHOLOGY)	
			(ARC KAN 27) 1969
	6	ANTHOLOGY	(RCA CD 71546) 1988
	7	DAL VIVO AL TEATRO PAIROLI 1969	
			(Raro/BMG 74321-12265-2) 1993

NB: (6) CD release with unreleased tracks. (7) Live 1969.

The Rokes achieved much more success in Italy, than they did in their homeland, but their UK 45s are now quite collectable and *When The Wind Arises* was quite psychedelic.

Norman Shapiro was born in London in 1943 and by the time he was seventeen was playing guitar and singing with Rob Storm & The Whispers (who later became **Robb Storme Group**). Norman then played for a while backing Gene Vincent's Blue Caps, followed by a stint in The Shel Carson Combo in 1961, touring Germany's clubs such as Top Ten Club in Hamburg, and supporting Tony "Colin" Hicks for a two month tour in Italy in 1963, where the band changed their name to "The Cabin Boys".

Spotted on tour by their (soon to be) new manager, they were renamed **The Rokes** and backed the young girl vocalist Rita Pavone before recording a demo for RCA Italiana. This led to the release of *Shake Rattle And Roll* on RCA subsidiary ARC Records, but this failed to create any impact.

A second 45 followed after they played at the "Festival Degli Sconosciuti" (Contest For Unknown) in Ariccia (Rome), performing *Un Anima Pura* sung in broken Italian. The song was received favourably, and although it was unsuccessful, it did point the way ahead for the remainder of the band's existence.

In 1965 **The Rokes** began writing original songs and had some hits: *Grazie A Te* (aka Clint Ballard Jr.'s *I'm Alive*) which reached No. 12 and *C'e Una Strana Espressione Nei Tuoi Occhi* (a version of Jackie DeShannon's *When You Walk In The Room*) which got to No. 11 in the Italian Charts. They also released their debut album *The Rokes*. The following year, the band had further success with *Che Colpa Abbiamo Noi* and *E La Pioggia Che Va*, both of which remained in the Top 20 for over 25 weeks, and they were also voted Second Best Beat Group in Italy at "Cantagiro 1966". Another track *Piangi Con Me* written by Shapiro/Mogul was released in the UK as *Let's Live For Today* and also covered by **The Living Daylights**. In the US, The Grassroots also covered the song, where it sold over two million records, although the band never received any money from the song.

In 1967 their first entry in the "Festival Di San Rem" *Bisogna Saper Perdere* was poorly received by the critics, but went to No. 2 in the Italian Charts, and remained in the Top 20 for fourteen weeks. They returned to the festival the next year where they performed *Le Opere Di Bartolemo* with US group Cowsills, and again the following year where they backed a little girl vocalist Nada with the song *Ma Che Freddo Fa* coming 5th for the journalists and critics.

1970 saw a decline in the group's fortunes, as the public taste changed, and they played their last concert in front of 3,500 people at the "Festival De L'Unità" on the 8th August. The concert was organised by the Communist Party!

The Rokes are still remembered fondly in Italy, although they never managed to recreate their success elsewhere. Shel Shapiro has remained active in the music business, as songwriter, producer and manager, and in 1977 founded Spaghetti Records in Milan, discovering new talent such as Luca Barbarossa. He now works in TV collaborating with music journalist. Gianni Minà. Mike Shepstone later played with Mick Brill (ex **Thane Russal Band**) in **Pax**, whilst Johnny Charlton became an Art expert, and now runs an Art Gallery in Rome. Bobby Posner returned to England and lives in Hastings.

Shapiro and Shepstone also released a single in 1966 under the name **Les and Kim** *La Mia Ispirazione/Unchained Melody* (ARC 4096).

Let's Live For Today later resurfaced on *Beat It* (3-CD); *When The Wind Arises* on *Incredible Sound Show Stories, Vol. 3* (LP) and *Ride On* can also be heard on *Jagged Time Lapse, Vol 3* (CD). (DZ/VJ/PV/AMj)

The Rolling Stones

Personnel:	MICK JAGGER	vcls, hrmnca	ABC
(up to	BRIAN JONES	gtr, vcls	A
1976)	KEITH RICHARD(S)	gtr, vcls	ABC
	CHARLIE WATTS	drms	ABC
	BILL WYMAN	bs, vcls	ABC
	MICK TAYLOR	gtr	B
	RON WOOD	gtr, vcls	C

ALBUMS: 1(A) THE ROLLING STONES   (Decca LK 4605) R2 1 HCP
(up to   2(A) THE ROLLING STONES No 2
1976)   (Decca LK 4661) 1965 R2 1
     3(A) OUT OF OUR HEADS
           (mono/stereo)   (Decca LK/SKL 4733) 1965 R2 2
     4(A) AFTERMATH
           (mono/stereo)   (Decca LK/SKL 4786) 1966 R2 1
     5(A) BIG HITS (HIGH TIDE GREEN GRASS)
           (mono/stereo)   (Decca TXL/TXS 101) 1966 R2 4
     6(A) BETWEEN THE BUTTONS
           (mono/stereo)   (Decca LK/SKL 4852) 1967 R2 3
     7(A) THEIR SATANIC MAJESTIES REQUEST
           (mono/stereo)   (Decca TXL/TXS 103) 1967 R2 3
     8(A) BEGGARS BANQUET
           (mono/stereo)   (Decca LK/SKL 4955) 1968 R2 3
     9(A) THROUGH THE PAST DARKLY (BIG HITS, VOL. 2)
           (mono/stereo)   (Decca LK/SKL 5019) 1969 R2 2
    10(B) LET IT BLEED
           (mono/stereo)   (Decca LK/SKL 5025) 1969 R1 1
    11(B) THE PROMOTIONAL ALBUM   (Decca RSM 1) 1969 R4 -
    12(B) GET YER YA-YA's OUT!   (Decca SKL 5065) 1970 SC 1
    13(-) STONE AGE (Compilation) (Decca SKL 5084) 1971 SC 4
    14(B) STICKY FINGERS   (Rolling Stones COC 59100) 1971 1
    15(-) MILESTONES (Compilation)   (Decca SKL 5098) 1972 14
    16(-) GIMME SHELTER (Comp.)   (Decca SKL 5101) 1972 19
    17(B) EXILE ON MAIN STREET (2-LP)
                                (Rolling Stones COC 69100) 1972 1
    18(-) ROCK 'N' ROLLING STONES (Compilation)
                                   (Decca SKL 5149) 1972 41
    19(-) GOLDEN B-SIDES (Comp.)   (Decca SKL 5165) 1973 R5 -
    20(B) GOAT'S HEAD SOUP
                                (Rolling Stones COC 59101) 1973 1
    21(-) NO STONE UNTURNED (Comp)(Decca SKL 5173) 1973 -

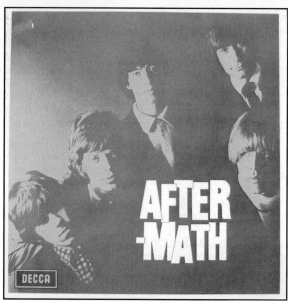

THE ROLLING STONES - Aftermath (LP).

    22(B) IT'S ONLY ROCK 'N' ROLL
                                (Rolling Stones COC 59103) 1974 2
    23(B) MADE IN THE SHADE
                                (Rolling Stones COC 59104) 1975 14
    24(-) METAMORPHOSIS   (Decca SKL 5212) 1975 45
    25(-) THE HISTORY OF THE ROLLING
           STONES (3-LP box set)   (Decca no cat no.) 1975 R5 -
    26(-) ROLLED GOLD   (Decca ROST 1/2) 1975 7
    27(C) BLACK AND BLUE   (Rolling Stones COC 59106) 1976 2
Later: 28(-) GET STONED   (Arcade ADEP 32) 1977 8
Comps: 29(-) TIME WAITS FOR NO-ONE: ANTHOLOGY 1971-77
                                (Rolling Stones COC 59107) 1979 -
    30(-) STORY OF THE STONES   (K-Tel NE 1201) 1982 24
    31(-) THE GREAT YEARS (4-LP set)
                                (Readers Digest GROLA 119) 1983 -
    32(A) THE FIRST EIGHT STUDIO ALBUMS (8-LP set
           with 192 page book)   (Decca ROLL 1) 1983 -
    33(-) REWIND 1971-1984 (THE BEST OF THE
           ROLLING STONES)   (Rolling Stones 4501991) 1984 23
    34(-) ROLLING STONES SINGLES COLLECTION/
           LONDON YEARS (4-LP set)   (Abkco 820900-1) 1989 -
    35(-) HOT ROCKS 1964-1971   (London 8201401) 1990 3

NB: Rarity ratings of (1) - (10) relate to first pressings. (5) Some copies came with a stapled 12" x 12"; picture booklet and these are now scarce. (10) A small number came with a promotional booklet advertising the rest of the band's catalogue. These are ultra-rare. (11) This was a promo-only release and is now one of their ultra-rare items, valued at around £800 in December 2004 by 'Record Collector'. (19) Unreleased, but some test pressings were produced and these are also ultra-rare. (25) This package was cancelled in favour of *Rolled Gold*, but some pink label pressings do exist and these are one of the band's rarest items, valued at around £800 in December 2004 by Record Collector'. They also recorded/released eight US-only albums:- *England's Newest Hitmakers* (London PS 375) 1964 (reissued remastered on vinyl Decca 8823), *12 x 5* (London PS 402) 1964, *The Rolling Stones Now* (London PS 420) 1965, *December's Children* (London PS 451) 1965 (reissued remastered on CD Abkco 94512), *Got Live If You Want It!* (London PS 493) 1966, *Flowers* (London PS 509) 1967, *Hot Rocks 1964-71* (2-LP) (London SPS 606/7) 1972 and *More Hot Rocks (Big Hits And Fazed Cookies)* (2-LP) (London 2PS 626/7) 1972. There are also some rare German-only albums: - *Beat, Beat, Beat* (10") (Decca HI FI 60 368), *The Best Of The Rolling Stones* (Decca BD 1080-C) (from a book club) and *In Action* (S*R HI FI 74 307). (14) reissued on vinyl (EMI LPCENT 38) 1997. The following albums have been reissued on CD: - (1) on London (8200472) 1985 and Decca (820 084-2) 1984. (2) on Decca (820 049-2) 1984, (3) on Decca (820 050-2) 1985. (5) on London (844-0882) 1991. (6) on Decca (820 138-2) 1985. (7) on London (820 129-2) 1986. (8) on Decca (800 084-2) 1983. (9) on London (844-0892) 1991. (10) on London (8200522) 1986. (12) on London (8201312) 1988. (14) on CBS (CDCBS 450195 2) 1989. (14) on (Virgin CDV 2730), (17) on (Virgin CDV 2731), (20) on (Virgin CDV 2735), (22) on (Virgin CDV 2733) and (27) on (Virgin CDV 2736). (17) on CBS (CDCBS 450196 2) 1989. (20) on CBS (CDCBS 450207 2) 1989. (22) on CBS (CDCBS 450202 2) 1989. (23) on CBS (CDCBS 450201 2) 1989 and again on CD digitally remastered. (27) on CBS CDCBS 450203 2) 1989. All of their US-only albums, except the first are on CD too.

Recent repackages of their original releases include: - (3) reissued remastered on CD (Abkco 822902). (4) reissued on vinyl (Decca 8823231). (5) reissued remastered on vinyl (Decca 8823221) and also on CD (Abkco 94512). (6) reissued remastered on vinyl (Decca 8823261. (7) reissued remastered on vinyl (Decca 8823291) and on CD (Abkco 8823002). (8) reissued remastered on vinyl (Decca 9539) and on CD

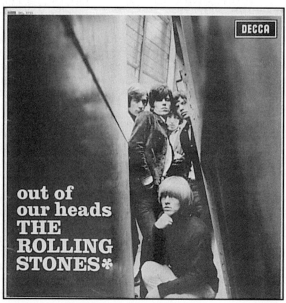

THE ROLLING STONES - Out Of Our Heads (LP).

(Abkco 8823012). (10) reissued remastered on vinyl (Abkco 88233321) and on CD (Abkco 90042). (12) reissued on vinyl and on CD (Abkco 88223042). (17) reissued on vinyl. (23) reissued remastered on CD (Virgin CDVX 2998). (24) reissued remastered on vinyl (Decca 8823441).

CD compilations have included CBS's *Collection 1971-1989* (a 15-CD box set with a bonus CD, 'Collectors Edition'), *Flashpoint/Interview 1990* (Sony 468 135-9/468 135-2) 1991, *CD Box Set* (Rolling Stones 4669 182) 1990, which is now deleted, and *Singles Collection: The London Years* (London 8209002) 1989, and *Jump Back*, a 2-LP, single CD compilation (Virgin CDV 2726) 1994, which is a mixture of hits and near misses. Another CD *Rock 'n' Roll Circus* (ABKCO 1268-2) 1995 contains six tracks by **The Rolling Stones** along with performances by **Jethro Tull**, **The Who**, Taj Mahal, **Marianne Faithfull**, Yoko Ono and The Dirty Mac (**John Lennon**, **Eric Clapton**, Keith Richards and Mitch Mitchell). Originally intended for a TV special at the end of 1968, the project was shelved at the time because the '**Stones** were unhappy with their performances. Abkco have also released a video and laserdisc, from the existing footage. *As It Happened: The Classic Interviews* (Chrome Talk CIS 2022) 2001 is a 4-CD spoken word biography of the band edited from press conferences and one-to-one interviews. One CD is allocated to each decade the band has been around. It comes with an informative and profusely illustrated booklet. *Live 1975: The Rolling Thunder Revue - The Bootleg Series Vol 5* (Columbia 510140 2) 2002 is a 2-CD set comprising material from an US East Coast tour in late 1975. *Four Flicks* (TGA/Warner Music Vision 747900122) 2003 is a 4-DVD box set with 10 hours of footage and most of the classics you'd expect are in the set. *Singles Box Set Volume 1, 1963-1965* (Decca) 2004 is a 12-CD set of their singles in this era, which also came with three photo cards and a 28-page booklet. *Singles Box Set Volume 2, 1965-1967* (Decca 9820985) 2004 is an 11-CD box set, which concludes with two US-only singles, *She's A Rainbow* and *2000 Light Years From Home*. Digitally remastered it came with a 28-page booklet, three collector's photo cards and a double-sided **Rolling Stones** poster. *Singles Box Set Volume 3, 1968-1971* (Universal) 2005 is the final set in the trio. It features nine CDs and a bonus DVD that includes the original *Jumpin' Jack Flash* promo film, their 1964 performance of *Time Is On My Side*, a live 1967 version of *Have You Seen Your Mother, Baby, Standing In The Shadow?* and the 2003 video of the Neptune's' remix of *Sympathy for The Devil*. Also relevant is *Singles Collection/The London Years* (3-CD set) (Abkco 8823072) which is presented in a fold-out digi pakage with a full colour booklet and each disc has been repackaged.

			HCP
EPs:	1(A)	THE ROLLING STONES (Decca DFE 8560) 1964 SC/-	19
	2(A)	FIVE BY FIVE (Decca DFE 8590) 1964 SC/-	9
	3(A)	GOT LIVE IF YOU WANT IT! (Decca DFE 8620) 1965 SC/-	7

NB: Only original copies with 'unboxed' as opposed to 'boxed' Decca logo are SC. (1), (2) and (3) reissued on Decca (DFEX 8560, 8590 and 8620, respectively) in 1983.

			HCP
45s:	Come On/I Want To Be Loved	(Decca F 11675) 1963 R1	21
(up to α	Poison Ivy/Fortune Teller	(Decca F 11742) 1963 R6	-
1976)	I Wanna Be Your Man/Stoned	(Decca F 11764) 1963 SC	12
	Not Fade Away/Little By Little	(Decca F 11845) 1964	3
	It's All Over Now/ Good Times, Bad Times	(Decca F 11934) 1964	1
	Little Red Rooster/Off The Hook	(Decca F 12014) 1964	1
	The Last Time/Play With Fire	(Decca F 12104) 1965	1
	(I Can't Get No) Satisfaction/		

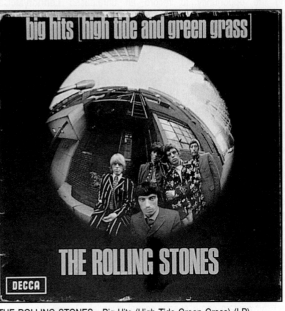

THE ROLLING STONES - Big Hits (High Tide Green Grass) (LP).

THE ROLLING STONES - Between The Buttons (LP).

The Spider And The Fly	(Decca F 12220) 1965	1
Get Off Of My Cloud/ The Singer Not The Song	(Decca F 12263) 1965	1
19th Nervous Breakdown/ As Tears Go By	(Decca F 12331) 1966	2
Paint It Black/Long Long While	(Decca F 12395) 1966	1
Have You Seen Your Mother, Baby, Standing In The Shadow?/ Who's Driving Your Plane	(Decca F 12497) 1966	5
Let's Spend The Night Together/ Ruby Tuesday	(Decca F 12546) 1967	3
We Love You/Dandelion	(Decca F 12654) 1967	8
Jumpin' Jack Flash/Child Of The Moon	(Decca F 12782) 1968	1
Honky Tonk Woman/ You Can't Always Get What You Want	(Decca F 12952) 1969	1
Street Fighting Man/ Surprise Surprise	(Decca F 13203) 1970	21
Brown Sugar/ Bitch/Let It Rock	(Rolling Stones RS 19100) 1972	2
Tumbling Dice/ Sweet Black Angel	(Rolling Stones RS 19103) 1972	5
β Everybody Needs Somebody To Love/ Surprise Surprise/Street Fighting Man	(Decca F 13195) 1972	-
Sad Day/ You Can't Always Get What You Want	(Decca F 13404) 1973	-
Angie/Silver Train	(Rolling Stones RS 19105) 1973	5
It's Only Rock'n'Roll/ Through The Lonely Nights	(Rolling Stones RS 19114) 1974	10
I Don't Know Why/ Try A Little Harder	(Decca F 13584) 1975 SC	-
Out Of Time/Jiving Sister Fanny	(Decca F 13597) 1975	45
Fool To Cry/Crazy Mama	(Decca F 19121) 1976	6
Reissues: Honky Tonk Women/ Sympathy For The Devil	(Decca F 13635) 1976	-
χ It's All Over Now/Paint It Black	(Decca F 13517) 1974	-
Brown Sugar/Happy/Rocks Off	(Rolling Stones K 19107) 1974	-
I Wanna Be Your Man/Come On	(Decca STONE 1) 1980	-
It's All Over Now/I Want To Be Loved	(Decca STONE 2) 1980	-
Satisfaction/Little By Little	(Decca STONE 3) 1980	-
Little Red Rooster/Not Fade Away	(Decca STONE 4) 1980	-
The Last Time/Paint It Black	(Decca STONE 5) 1980	-
Get Off Of My Cloud/Play With Fire	(Decca STONE 6) 1980	-
Jumpin' Jack Flash/As Tears Go By	(Decca STONE 7) 1980	-
19th Nervous Breakdown/Have You Seen Your Mother, Baby, Standing In The Shadow?	(Decca STONE 8) 1980	-
Let's Spend The Night Together/ You Can't Always Get What You Want	(Decca STONE 9) 1980	-
Honky Tonk Women/Ruby Tuesday	(Decca STONE 10) 1980	-
Street Fighting Man/Out Of Time	(Decca STONE 11) 1980	-
Sympathy For The Devil/ Gimme Shelter	(Decca STONE 12) 1980	-
δ Time Is On My Side (live)/ Twenty Flight Rock (live) (PS)	(Rolling Stones RSR 111) 1982	62
Let's Spend The Night Together (live)/		

Start Me Up (live) (promo only) (Rolling Stones RSR 112) 1983 -
χ Brown Sugar/Bitch (PS)   (Rolling Stones SUGAR 1) 1984 58
ε Jumpin' Jack Flash/
Child Of The Moon (PS)   (Decca F 102) 1987 -

NB: β Maxi single. α Withdrawn and it is now one of their rarest artefacts, valued at £1,000 in the December 2004 issue of 'Record Collector'. δ Also as a 12" (PS) with **Under My Thumb** added. χ Also as a shaped picture disc. ε Also as a 12" (PS) with *Sympathy For The Devil* added. They also recorded several export-only issue 45s which were manufactured in the UK. These are not included in the above discography. One US 45, *Street Fighting Man/No Expectations* (London 909) 1968, appears to have two masters. The standard mono mix appears with matrix XDR-43220-2C, but XDR-43220-A features a diferent vocal and instrumental mix.

After **the Beatles**, **the Rolling Stones** were the most successful and influential English group of the 1960s, turning out a string of brilliant singles and albums and virtually inventing the concept of the rock and roll band in the process. In leaders **Mick Jagger** and Keith Richard they had a uniquely charismatic double act, and in **Bill Wyman** and Charlie Watts arguably the finest rhythm section in rock history. Original guitarist Brian Jones, meanwhile, broadened pop music's instrumental vocabulary, and together they contributed an enormous amount to musical and cultural life in the late sixties and early seventies. In this period they very nearly lived up to their claim to be 'the world's greatest rock and roll band' and certainly no music collection can be complete without a decent selection of their material.

Jagger and Richards were both born in Dartford, Kent in 1943, and attended primary school together. They then lost contact until a chance meeting on a train in 1960, when Richards happened to be carrying some albums with him. They thereby discovered a common interest in R&B and records on the US Chess label. Before the year was through they were playing in R&B group Little Boy Blue and The Blue Boys with Dick Taylor (later of **The Pretty Things**), Allen Etherington and Bob Beckwith. A 13-track reel-to-reel tape of the band has recently been unearthed, containing two separate sets from 1961. It comprises several Chuck Berry covers (*Around And Around, Little Queenie, Beautiful Delilah, Down The Road Apiece* and *Johnny B. Goode*) as well as versions of Ritchie Valens' *La Bamba*, Billy Boy Arnold's *I Ain't Got You* and a couple of unattributed blues tunes, *On Your Way To School* and *Don't Want No Woman*. The remaining three tracks are second takes of *I Ain't Got You, Little Queenie* and *Beautiful Delilah*. It's said not to be great musically, but is of course an important artefact of British R&B.

Two years later, in early 1962, Brian Jones (born in Cheltenham on 28 February 1942) placed an advert in 'Jazz News' (under the pseudonym Elmo Lewis) for R&B musicians to form a band. Pianist Ian Stewart answered. **Jagger** and Richards became friendly with Jones after seeing him play with **Alexis Korner's Blues Incorporated** at the Ealing Blues Club, and an embryonic **Stones** line-up was therefore formed, comprising **Jagger** (vcls, hrmnca), Richards (lead gtr), Jones (gtr, vcls), Stewart (piano), Jeff Bradford (later in **The Hoochie Coochie Men**) (gtr), Dick Taylor (bs) and a succession of drummers, of whom Tony Chapman was the most regular. This embryonic **Stones** line-up played and rehearsed whenever they could, and **Jagger** also sang for **Alexis Korner's Blues Incorporated** in this period.

THE ROLLING STONES - Their Satanic Majesties Request (LP).

ROLLING STONES - Beggars Banquet (LP).

By late 1962 Bradford had left and Chapman decided to do likewise. Before doing so he introduced his friend **Bill Wyman** (real name William Perks) to the band. **Wyman** (from The Cliftons) took over on bass when Taylor left and, in January 1963, Charlie Watts (who'd been a regular drummer in Blues Incorporated) took over on drums. The group recorded a demo tape but was unable to win a record contract. They did, however, secure a Sunday residency at the legendary Crawdaddy Club (at the Station Hotel, Richmond, Surrey), and soon began to attract a considerable following. After seeing them play there one evening, **Andrew Oldham** (who had been working as a junior publicist for **The Beatles**) signed them to a management contract in partnership with the older Eric Easton. He soon decided that Stewart's looks didn't fit the image he had in mind for the group, so relegated him to the role of roadie and backing musician. Finally the band's seminal five-piece line-up was in place.

In May 1963 they were finally offered a deal by Decca, who were still stung by their rejection of **The Beatles**. A cover of Chuck Berry's obscure *Come On* was chosen as their debut 45. It failed to capture the full excitement of their live shows, but was still propulsive and hard-hitting. They made their UK TV debut on 'Thank Your Lucky Stars' to promote it, and instantly attracted bad press for declining to wave at the audience as the credits rolled. Though the song gained airplay, it narrowly missed the UK Top 20. A cover of The Coasters' *Poison Ivy* was recorded as a follow-up, but never released. Some copies did get into circulation, possibly for record clubs or export issue, making it by far the band's most expensive and collectable 45 to acquire (both *Poison Ivy* and its flipside, a cover of the Benny Spellman hit *Fortune Teller*, eventually got an airing on the *Saturday Club* (LP) compilation issued in early 1964). Instead, a chance meeting between **Oldham** and **Lennon** and **McCartney** resulted in **The Stones** getting the opportunity to record an unreleased **Lennon/McCartney** composition, *I Wanna Be Your Man*. By the time **Ringo**'s rendition appeared on *With The Beatles*, **the Stones** had taken it to No. 12 in the Charts. Some copies were pressed with the 'B' side *Stoned* misspelt as *Stones*, and are now minor collectables.

Although the band had started out as urban blues enthusiasts, they now found themselves caught in the burgeoning beat boom, and in their quest for success they became increasingly willing to compromise in their choice of material. This was evident on their first EP, which comprised covers of Barrett Strong's *Money*, Arthur Alexander's *You Better Move On* and Chuck Berry's *Bye Bye Johnny*. The quartet of songs was completed by a fresh recording of *Poison Ivy*, and the disc reached No. 19 in the UK singles chart. Their third 45 was a Buddy Holly song, *Not Fade Away*, which they performed in Bo Diddley style. This time they got to No. 3 in the UK. The flipside, incidentally, featured Phil Spector (who'd co-written the song with **Jagger**) on maracas.

As they began to climb the charts, **Andrew Oldham** was carefully fashioning their tough and surly image in direct contrast to **The Beatles**' cleaner cut appeal. He scored a direct hit with the headline-grabbing catchphrase 'would you allow your daughter to marry a Rolling Stone?' and indeed their debut album (which had no title or artist's name on the front sleeve) did contain some overtly sexual material. Overall, however, it was an enjoyable, somewhat predictable, blend of blues (*I'm A King Bee* and *I Just Want To Make Love To You*), rock'n'roll (*Carol* and *Route 66*) and contemporary black music (*You Can Make It If You Try* and *Can I Get A Witness*), along with their own *Tell Me*, which showed them to be unsophisticated songwriters. It still attracted advance orders of 100,000 and topped the charts.

In June 1964 they set off their first US tour with The Chiffons, Bobby Goldsboro, Bobby Vee and Bobby Comstock. Whilst there they fulfilled a major ambition by recording at the Chess Studios in Chicago, and meeting Chuck Berry, Muddy Waters and Willie Dixon, who'd been so influential on their music. The single they recorded there (*It's All Over Now*) went on to top the UK charts. Their first album was issued in the States with the addition of *Not Fade Away*, and retitled *England's Newest Hit Makers - The Rolling Stones*. It got to No 11. Their *Five By Five* EP contained more material recorded at Chess, including two of their best homages to Chuck Berry - *Around And Around* and *Confessin' The Blues*. It got to No. 9 in the UK, after 180,000 advance orders.

By now the group had gained the sort of notoriety **Oldham** always intended for them, and were rarely out of the news. Two days into a second US tour in October 1964 they were banned from the 'Ed Sullivan Show' after riots in the audience. Back in the UK the following month they were banned by the BBC after arriving late for 'Saturday Club' and 'Top Gear'. In the US their album *12 x 5* got to No. 3. In the UK they selected a revival of Willie Dixon's blues record *Little Red Rooster* for their next release and took it to No. 1, aided by some superb slide guitar from Jones. Meanwhile in the States they got to No. 6 with a cover of Irma Thomas' *Time Is On My Side*. As 1964 drew to an end, the quietest Stone, Charlie Watts, who'd got married on 14 October, had his tribute to jazz musician Charlie Parker, 'Ode To A High Flying Bird' published.

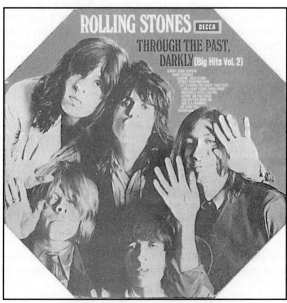

THE ROLLING STONES - Through The Past Darkly (LP).

Their second album, *The Rolling Stones No 2* (which, like their debut, had no text on the front cover), contained three self-penned songs - *Off The Hook* (the flip to their previous hit), *What A Shame* and *Grown Up Wrong*. There was also a version of Muddy Waters' *I Just Can't Be Satisfied*, but it was dominated by R&B covers like The Drifters' *Under The Boardwalk* and Solomon Burke's *Everybody Needs Somebody To Love*, and not a classic album by any means. Further controversy was courted by **Oldham**'s sub-Anthony Burgess sleevenotes, early printings of which referred to mugging a blind man and had to be withdrawn. As with **The Beatles**' later 'butcher cover', some recalled copies merely had the censored slick pasted over the offending one.

It was becoming increasingly urgent for **The Stones** to generate their own singles, and with this end in mind **Oldham** locked **Jagger** and Richard in the kitchen of their flat until they produced one. The result was their next UK 45, *The Last Time*, considered by most to be the first memorable **Jagger**/Richards composition. Complete with a sharp guitar riff, it was a milestone in their career (though it did in fact borrow from a Staple Singers gospel song of the same name!) Recorded at RCA's Hollywood studios with engineer Dave Hassinger (assisted by Phil Spector and Jack

THE ROLLING STONES - Let It Bleed (LP).

Nitzsche), it topped the UK charts after two weeks and later reached No. 9 in the US, where the album *The Rolling Stones, Now!* had climbed to No. 5.

In June 1965 they issued a live EP, *Got Live If You Want It*, which documented their UK tour (with **The Hollies** and **Dave Berry**) from March of that year. Successfully capturing their live act's excitement (assisted by much overdubbed screaming), it was their final EP and got to No. 7 in the UK. This delayed the release of their next 45, but when it was finally released, *(I Can't Get No) Satisfaction* instantly announced itself as a rock classic. Propelled by one of rock's definitive riffs, it was their first recording to top the charts on both sides of the Atlantic and made it clear that **Jagger** and Richard were blossoming into major songwriters.

Their notoriety continued when **Jagger**, **Wyman** and Jones were each fined £3 for urinating against a garage wall when a mechanic at the garage concerned refused to let them use a private toilet there. Their next album, the appropriately-titled *Out Of Our Heads*, was another weak effort blending modern soul covers with home-grown material. Nonetheless, it topped the US charts for three weeks and peaked at No 2 in the UK, where the band starred in their own edition of 'Ready Steady Go!' on 10th September 1965.

Commercially, **the Stones** were now at the pinnacle of their game, unleashing a succession of powerful and memorable 45s in rapid succession. *Get Off Of My Cloud* topped the charts here and in the US, *19th Nervous Breakdown* reached No. 2 both here and in the US, *Paint It, Black* made it to No. 1 in the UK and US, *Have You Seen Your Mother, Baby?* got to No. 5 in the UK and No. 9 in the US and *Let's Spend The Night Together* stalled at No. 3 here but was another US No 1. Over the course of these 45s **The Stones** firmly established a hip, world-weary image summarised in the brilliant *Mother's Little Helper* from their next album, *Aftermath* - 'what a drag it is, getting old.' No contemporary act other than **The Beatles** came close to matching their singles for sustained imagination and versatility, but - unlike **The Beatles** - **The Stones** had yet to master the album format. *Aftermath* was their first album comprised entirely of **Jagger**/Richards songs (including the notorious *Under My Thumb*), and still highly inconsistent. It did, however, showcase Jones's mastery of numerous unusual instruments and got to No 2 in the UK. It was also notable for the daringly long (if rather tedious) *Going Home*, which clocked in at 11 minutes and 35 seconds.

Their significance as a singles band was underlined by Decca's release of *Big Hits (High Tide and Green Grass)* shortly afterwards, which got to No. 3 in the US and No. 4 here. 1966 closed with their non-UK live album *Got Live If You Want It* climbing to No. 6 in the US. January 1967 saw the release of their next studio effort, *Between The Buttons*, which got to No. 3 here and No. 2 in the US despite being yet another curate's egg. The material was more pop-orientated than previously, and lacked focus despite containing a handful of fine **Jagger**/Richard songs including *Yesterday's Papers, My Obsession* and *Something Happened To Me Yesterday*. In its month of release Ed Sullivan finally lifted his ban on them, and they appeared on his show, though they had to change the chorus of *Let's Spend The Night Together* to 'Let's Spend Some Time Together'!

THE ROLLING STONES - Sticky Fingers (LP).

Life became increasingly complicated for them in 1967 after The News Of The World named **Jagger** in an article about drug-taking pop stars. In that heady Summer of 1967 he, Richard and Jones were all arrested for drug possession (following the legendary bust at Redlands, Richard's home in Sussex). **Jagger** and Richard both spent a short time in jail until their prison sentences were quashed on appeal, following a famous leader in The Times headlined 'Who Breaks A Butterfly On A Wheel?' July 1967 saw the release of an appropriately-named non-UK album, *Flowers*. A patchy compilation of 45s and studio outtakes, it was especially notable for an awful cover of Otis Redding's *My Girl*, but still got to No. 3 in the States.

Back in London **the Stones** were struggling to master psychedelia (and never really did). *We Love You* (which began with the sound cell doors being slammed and featured **Lennon** and **McCartney** on backing vocals) was not one of their best efforts and only reached no. 8 in the UK. A promotional film they made for it, based on the trial of Oscar Wilde, was predictably banned by the BBC. In the States the flip side *Dandelion* was put on the 'A' side, with *We Love You* on the reverse. Some copies of this release came in a picture sleeve and are quite collectable now.

During 1967 their relationship with **Andrew Oldham** became increasingly strained, and in September of that year he severed his links with the band and concentrated on his own Immediate label. November saw the release of their disappointing stab at a psych album, *Their Satanic Majesties Request*. Its complex 3-D sleeve went one step beyond **The Beatles**' *Sergeant Pepper* - but that was pretty much the only area in which their friendly rivals were trumped. Not only did the album lose out in the inevitable **Beatles** comparisons, it also suffered from appearing months after the so-called 'Summer of Love'. In fairness it did have its moments, most notably the stupendously trippy *2,000 Light Years From Home*, but much of it was dross. Also worthy of note was *2,000 Man* and **Wyman**'s *In Another Land* (which appeared as a single in the States under his name). The album did well enough commercially (peaking at No. 3 here and No. 2 in the US), but was too full of self-indulgent filler to qualify as much more than a wasted opportunity.

At the same time continual clashes with the authorities and increasing narcotic indulgence were placing increasing strain on Brian Jones' health. By mid-1967 he was barely contributing to the band's records, and indeed he is to be heard snoring on *Their Satanic Majesties Request*. In December he had to be hospitalised, and as 1968 dawned his future (and the band's) didn't look too rosy. *She's A Rainbow* was only a minor US hit (No. 25), and on 10 May 1968 Jones was again arrested for drug possession and placed on £2,000 bail to await trial (later in the year he was fined £50). In the face of this adversity the band proved its durability, teaming up with producer Jimmy Miller (who'd also worked with **Traffic**) to return to the straight-ahead R&B of their early days on the brilliant *Jumpin' Jack Flash*, which deservedly topped the charts in the UK and the US and effectively announced the end of their flirtation with flower-power.

The band wanted the sleeve of their next album, *Beggars Banquet*, to feature a graffiti-covered toilet wall, but Decca vetoed it. The album eventually appeared four months later, in December 1968, in a plain white sleeve in the form of an invitation (reminiscent of **the Beatles**' White Album, which appeared a month earlier). Produced by Jimmy Miller and including more acoustic guitar than any of their previous efforts, it was their strongest album to date, and many consider it their best of all. Its highlights included the epic *Sympathy For The Devil* (which saw **Jagger** casting himself as the Devil), *Stray Cat Blues* and *Jigsaw Puzzle*. The album rose to No. 3 in both the UK and US. *Street Fighting Man* had earlier been released as a non-UK 45, but only climbed to No. 48 in the US after radio stations banned it following concerns that the lyrics might incite civil disorder.

Beggar's Banquet proved to be the last album Jones would appear on, and his achingly beautiful slide guitar on the lazy acoustic blues *No Expectations* can be seen as his epitaph. He contributed precious little else to the album, in fact. **Dave Mason** played on some tracks in his place, and even **Eric Clapton** is rumoured to have guested. On June 9th 1969 Jones quit the group, maintaining that he could no longer support the band's musical policy. In fact years of drug and alcohol abuse had left him in poor mental and physical condition, and many believe he was fired because he wasn't capable of going back on the road. As Richard has remarked subsequently, no band can carry dead weight, which was what Jones had largely become by this stage. Following much speculation about a replacement (centring on candidates including Ry Cooder and **Mighty Baby**'s Martin Stone), Jones' place in the band was filled by **John Mayall**'s guitarist Mick Taylor.

Then, three weeks later (on 3rd July 1969) his girlfriend Anna Wohlin found Jones' body in the swimming pool of his Sussex home. The Coroner, found that he'd drowned after going for a midnight swim under the influence of alcohol and drugs, and recorded a verdict of 'death by misadventure', though conspiracy theorists have muttered about foul play ever since. He was buried a week later in his home town of Cheltenham, Gloucestershire. The new line-up (B) were scheduled to play their first gig at Rome's Coliseum on 25 June 1969, but it was cancelled and on 5 July 1969 they played their now-legendary free concert in front of 250,000 fans in London's Hyde Park instead. **Jagger** read an extract from a Shelley poem as a tribute to Jones, and 3,000 butterflies (many of them lifeless) were released in his memory. The occasion was filmed as 'The Stones In The Park' by Granada TV, and understandably shows the band on shaky form.

The following day **Jagger** flew to Australia with his pregnant girlfriend **Marianne Faithfull** to make a film entitled 'Ned Kelly'. After just two days **Jagger** announced that their relationship was over, causing **Faithfull** to make an unsuccessful suicide attempt. **Jagger** then changed his mind, and their jointly-written *Sister Morphine* hauntingly refers to the experience. **The Stones**' next single, *Honky Tonk Woman*, was another classic - and one of their most raunchy. It sped to the top of the charts both here and in America. A second hits selection, *Through The Past Darkly*, was also released. Dedicated to Jones' memory, it offered a good selection of material and climbed to No. 2 in both the UK and US.

Timed to coincide with their first US tour in three years, *Let It Bleed* was another of their stronger efforts. Highlights included the thrillingly intense

THE ROLLING STONES - 12 x 5 (LP).

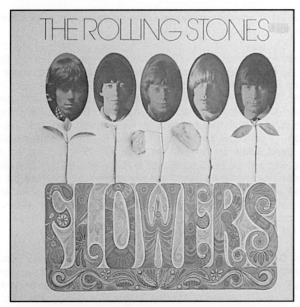

THE ROLLING STONES - Flowers (LP).

Gimme Shelter, the unsettling *Midnight Rambler* (about the Boston Strangler Albert de Salvo) and the rousing *You Can't Always Get What You Want* (which featured the London Bach Choir). The album also included a country-style arrangement of *Honky Tonk Women* entitled *Country Honk*, hinting at the direction they'd take in the near future. Sadly the accompanying US tour went disastrously wrong on 6 December 1969, when the Hell's Angels they'd rashly hired to act as security for their Altamont Speedway gig turned nasty. Fuelled by drink and drugs, the Angels were looking for trouble and erupted into violence when an 18 year-old black youth, Meredith Hunter, produced a gun (which later turned out not to be loaded). His murder was recorded on the Mayles brothers' 1970 film 'Gimme Shelter'. Still reeling from the Manson murders, many regarded Altamont as the final souring of the hippie dream. It certainly had a lasting impact on the band, who were relatively inactive in subsequent months.

July 28th 1970 saw 'Ned Kelly' premiered in Australia, to lukewarm reviews. Three days later 'Performance', (which **Jagger** had begun working on in September 1968) opened in London. Its release had been delayed because of worries about its violence and decadence, but **Jagger** won plaudits for his performance as Turner, a retired rock star, and even had his only UK solo hit with *Memo From Turner*, taken from the soundtrack. The **Stones'** next album, *Get Yer Ya-Ya's Out*, was recorded live at New York's Madison Square Gardens in November 1969. Another classic, it topped the UK album charts and climbed to No. 6 in the States.

In March 1971 the next phase in the band's career began when they relocated to France as tax exiles. Having finally escaped their increasingly fraught contract with Decca, they launched their own Rolling Stones Records label in April 1971, having arranged a distribution deal with Kinney and Warner Brothers. Over the next few years Decca was to release a series of badly put-together compilations, much to the band's irritation. The first release on the band's label was the classic *Brown Sugar* 45, which topped the US charts and got to No. 2 here despite highly risqué lyrics. Their new album, *Sticky Fingers*, perpetuated their depraved image. Its sleeve, designed by Andy Warhol, depicted a denim-clad male crotch, complete with a real zip fastener. Aside from *Brown Sugar*, its highlights included acoustic numbers like the moving *Wild Horses* and terrifting *Sister Morphine*. In May 1971 the album topped the charts here and in the US. The same month **Mick Jagger** married European jet-setter Bianca Rosa Perez-Mora, who was Nicaraguan by birth, and their daughter Jade was born on 1 October that year. *Cocksucker Blues* (which they'd offered Decca as a final 45 to complete their contract, knowing it to be unreleasable) remained in the can from these sessions, along with Chuck Berry's *Let It Rock*.

Following epic sessions at Richard's French villa, *Exile On Main Street* was finally released in June 1972. Their only double studio album, it was patchy but is now seen by many as their definitive statement. It made them the centre of controversy yet again when clean-up campaigner Mary Whitehouse tried (unsuccessfully) to get it banned from the BBC on account of its obscene lyrics. Among its best moments were the joyous opener *Rocks Off*, *Tumbling Dice* (which had been culled as a 45, peaking

at no. 5 here and no. 7 in the US), and the Richard-sung *Happy* (released as a 45 in the US, where it got to no 22). *Exile* featured more brass than previous efforts and, under the control of Peter Rudge (a Cambridge University graduate who'd become their manager in all but name), they embarked on an extensive North American tour with a full horn section and Stevie Wonder as support. The tour has gone down in history as a byword for excess, and the documentary of it, 'Cocksucker Blues', exposed the hollowness and squalor of their life on the road, as well as Richard's heroin dependency.

Though they remained an exciting live attraction, they were in creative decline by the mid-seventies. *Goat's Head Soup*, recorded in Kingston, Jamaica, suffered from poor material and slipshod production. It only really contained three decent tracks - the trippy *Can You Hear The Music*, the finale *Star Star*, and *Angie*, an acoustic love song about **David Bowie**'s wife which got to No. 5 in the UK and topped the US charts for a week. In the US the weaker *Doo Doo Doo Doo (Heartbreaker)* was also released, peaking at No. 15. August 1974's *It's Only Rock'n'Roll* was their first self-produced album since 1967, and not very impressive. In particular the vocals sounded too subdued in the final mix, and it contained too many ballads. It did harbour a few good cuts, though - notably the unnerving *Fingerprint File* and *Short and Curlies* (actually a *Goat's Head Soup* outtake). The album got to No. 2 in the UK and No. 1 in the US. Its title cut reached No. 10 here and No. 16 in the States. A revival of The Temptations' *Ain't Too Proud To Beg* was later taken from it as a US single, and got to No. 17.

Mick Taylor left **the Stones** in December 1974, and was eventually replaced by **Faces** guitarist Ron Wood. Wood had declined the original offer to join, but was persuaded to when the band was faced with a Summer 1975 American tour. He 'guested' for the tour and joined as a full member on 19 December 1975, by which time the **Faces** had disintegrated. 1975 saw a flood of new compilations, of which only the definitive hits collection *Rolled Gold* can really be recommended. A double compilation, it got to No. 7 in the UK. *Made In The Shade* was a collection of material from their own label, which will only be relevant if you don't have their previous four albums. It included their four previous UK singles. Three of the remaining six tracks (*Happy, Doo Doo Doo Doo (Heartbreaker)* and *Wild Horses*) had been US-only 'A' sides. *Metamorphosis*, an album compiled by Decca, comprising mostly **Jagger**/Richards songs demoed for other artists during the sixties, appeared against the band's wishes but is an interesting document.

1976's *Black and Blue* album, culled from various sessions between late 1974 and April 1975, saw them veer towards the contemporary black dance music scene, by now very influential. The material ranged from funk (*Hot Stuff*) and riffing rockers (*Crazy Mama*) to reggae (*Cherry Oh Baby*) and soul ballads (*Fool To Cry*). The last track was culled for 45 release, and got to No. 6 in the UK and No. 10 in the US. The album climbed to No. 2 here and gave them another US No. 1. 1976 was a particularly bad year for Keith Richards, who crashed his car near Stafford in May and was subsequently fined when drugs were found in it. Two weeks later his six week-old son Tara died from pneumonia in Geneva, Switzerland. That year **Bill Wyman** released his first solo album, *Stand Alone*, which met with limited success in the US, climbing to No. 166. On 21 August 1976 the

THE ROLLING STONES - Rock And Roll Circus (CD).

band headlined the Knebworth Festival in Hertfordshire, in front of an estimated 200,000 people.

The band continued to fill concert arenas in the eighties and nineties but their records didn't sell as well as in previous decades. After their 1991 live album *Flashpoint* **Bill Wyman** left the band and published his memoirs 'Stone Alone' a few years later. He wasn't immediately replaced but bassist Darryl Jones (who'd previously played with Miles Davis and Sting) emerged on 1994's *Voodoo Lounge* which enjoyed the best reviews for a **Stones** album for some years. It also won them their first Grammy for Best Rock Album in the States. Since then studio sets like 1997's *Bridges To Babylon* have been outnumbered by live sets like *Stripped* (1995), *The Rolling Stones Rock And Roll Circus* (1996), *No Security* (1998) and *Live Licks* (2004). However, 2005 has seen the release of a new studio album *A Bigger Bang*, which like *Voodoo Lounge* and *Bridges To Babylon* was produced by Don Was.

But were they 'the greatest rock'n'roll band in the world'? The quality of their live performances certainly made them prime contenders, but their studio performances were more questionable. Having started as enthusiastic R&B copyists, they undeniably forged their own hugely influential brand of rock'n'roll, writing some classic rock singles along the way. But the quality of their albums was variable, and it is to be regretted that their colossal success eventually smoothed away the rough edges that had once made them so thrillingly unpredictable. Still, it seems safe to say that for as long as rock and roll exists, **The Rolling Stones** will be regarded as icons.

Inevitably they've appeared on several Various Artists' compilations including: *Fortune Teller* and *Poison Ivy* on *Saturday Club* (LP); *Come On* on *Thank Your Lucky Stars, Vol. 2* (LP); *Come On* and *I Wanna Be Your Man* on *Ready, Steady, Go!* (LP); and *Surprise Surprise* on *Fourteen, Lord Taverners* (LP). (VJ/BM/RMJ)

Roll Movement

45:      I'm Out On My Own/Just One Thing   (Go AJ 11410) 1967 SC

This 45 appears to be this obscure band's sole vinyl offering. The 'A' side was a ballad, whilst the mid-tempo flip is worth a listen and it can also be heard on *Colour Me Pop, Vol 3* (CD). (VJ)

Ronno

Personnel incl:	TREVOR BOLDER		
	BENNY MARSHALL		
	MICK RONSON	gtr	A
	MICK 'WOODY' WOODMANSEY	drms	A

45:      Fourth Hour Of My Sleep/
         Powers Of Darkness   (Vertigo 6059 029) 1970 R2

A Hull-based group formed by **Ronson** and Woodmansey after they'd worked on **David Bowie**'s *The Man Who Sold The World* album. They signed to Vertigo and started work on an album of rock-blues material which was going to be produced by Tony Visconti. However, the project was curtailed when **Bowie** demanded the presence of all three in the backing band for his *Hunky Dory* album and only the above single ever emerged. It is now a minor collectable. (VJ)

Mick Ronson

				HCP
ALBUMS:	1	SLAUGHTER ON 10th AVENUE (RCA APLI 0353) 1974		9
	2	PLAY, DON'T WORRY (RCA APLI 0681) 1975		29

NB: (1) and (2) reissued on a 2-CD set *Only After Dark* (MainMan) 1994 along with three additional live cuts from **Ronson**'s gigs at London's Rainbow Theatre in February 1974 and two studio cuts. (1) reissued again on CD (Snapper SDPCD 121) 2003. *Just Like This* (Burning Airlines PILOT 50) was recorded in 1976 but not released until 1999 as a 2-CD set with demos and other mixes of the album.

45s:	α	Love Me Tender/Only After Dark	(RCA APBO 212) 1974
		Slaughter On 10th Avenue/	
		Leave My Heart Alone	(RCA LPBO 5022) 1974
		Billy Porter/Seven Days	(RCA RCA 2482) 1975

NB: α The 'A' side also appeared as a one-sided flexidisc (red or black vinyl) in press kits.

Ronson's early groups were in Hull. First The Marines, then The King Bees (not the **Bowie** backing group) and then The Crestas. He then moved to London replacing **Miller Anderson** in **The Voice** after they'd recorded their superb *Train To Disaster*. After an unproductive period in a soul combo called The Wanted he returned to Hull and joined **The Rats**. He was with them during part of 1967 and 1968. In 1969 he was lured back down to London to join **David Bowie**'s backing band The Hype. **Ronson** worked with **David Bowie** on *The Man Who Sold The World* but was not that enamoured with the music so returned to Hull to form his own band called **Ronno**. They signed to Vertigo and started work on an album but the project was rapidly curtailed when **Bowie** wanted the members of **Ronno** in his backing band for his *Hunky Dory* album. This backing band, of course, later became **The Spiders From Mars** and along with **Bowie Ronson**, his guitarist, won international fame in the *Ziggy Stardust* era.

When **David Bowie** dissolved **The Spiders From Mars** in 1973 **Ronson** resolved to launch a solo career. His debut 45 in early 1974 was a cover of Elvis Presley's *Love Me Tender*. On his debut album, *Slaughter On 10th Avenue*, he was assisted by **Aynsley Dunbar**, Mike Garson, Trevor Bolder and his sister Margaret Ronson added vocal harmonies. To help promote the album, which sold well enough to get into the UK Top Ten, he embarked on a UK tour for which the band was supplemented by a brass section. The title cut was also put out on a 45 but didn't chart.

When his follow-up album *Play, Don't Worry* was virtually complete he accepted **Ian Hunter**'s invitation to replace guitarist **Luther Grosvenor** in **Mott The Hoople** in September 1974, but when the album finally appeared in early 1975 it still managed to claw into the Top 30.

In 1999 *Just Like This* (which was recorded back in 1976) saw the light of day. The guitar work on *I'd Give Anything To See You* is cutting and *Taking A Train* is a tight track.

When **Ian Hunter** broke away from **Mott The Hoople Ronson** worked with him on and off over the next 15 years, initially to promote each others solo albums. He was also in Bob Dylan's backing band briefly in the mid-seventies and produced several albums during the seventies and eighties. In 1991 he was diagnosed as suffering from cancer. The following year he appeared with his old pal **Bowie** at the Freddy Mercury A.I.D.'S concert. Sadly he died prematurely on 29 April 1993 from liver cancer. (VJ)

Room

Personnel:	STEVE EDGE	gtr	A
	BOB JENKINS	drms	AB
	JANE KEVERN	vcls	AB
	ROY PUTT	bs	AB
	CHRIS WILLIAMS	gtr	AB
	JOHN HUTCHESON	keyb'ds	B

ROOM - Pre-Flight (CD).

ALBUM: 1(A)   PRE-FLIGHT   (Deram SML 1073) 1970 R4

NB: (1) reissued on CD in Korea (Si-Wan SRMC 0043) and again on CD (Prog Line PL 506).

A Blandford Forum band responsible for another extremely rare one-off album on Deram, **Room** won second prize in 'Melody Maker's' talent contest and earned a record deal as their prize. Recorded in a single day in the summer of 1970, *Pre-Flight* offers powerful progressive rock with strong bluesy overtones and some excursions into jazzy territory. The opener, *Pre-Flight Parts One and Two*, with its frantic drumming, stinging guitar leads and orchestral interludes, is a stunning example of how exciting progressive music can be when all the elements gel. Other highlights include the biting *Andromeda* and sinister *War*. The lengthy final track *Cemetery Junction*, with its unexpected foray into late 19th century symphonical, is also recommended. Its title in fact refers to the major traffic crossroads in central Bournemouth, where the band were resident.

Elsewhere on the album, however, somewhat less imaginative and complex fare is served, and Jane Kevern's powerful and unusual voice does not suit all of them. Additionally, the brass is a little obtrusive on some cuts. The album appeared in a memorable cartoon sleeve designed by their bassist, Roy Putt, but sold very poorly and is almost impossible to find nowadays. It comes as little surprise to learn that the band were disappointed by the material selected for release, and it is to be hoped that the other songs they recorded for Decca may come to light one day, especially their signature tune *Vehicle*.

Shortly after *Pre-Flight* was released John Hutcheson, who'd been in Ginger Man with drummer Bob Jenkins, joined the band on organ but, disillusioned by their experience, they went their separate ways soon afterwards. (MK/RMJ)

Room 10

45:      I Love My Love/Going Back   (Decca F 12249) 1965

Both sides of this disc were produced by Simon Napier-Bell. The 'A' side, a gentle pop ballad, was from the film 'Passion Flower Hotel'. The flip is more beaty. (VJ)

Ro Ro

Personnel:	ROD COOMBES	vcls, drms	A
	BRIAN ROGERS	orchestration	A
	ALAN ROSS	vcls, gtr, recorder	A
	NEIL SHEPPARD	vcls, keyb'ds	A
	ROSE WARWICK	bs	A
	JOHN WEIDER	gtr, violin	A

ALBUM: 1(A)   MEET AT THE WATER
                    (Regal Zonophone SRZA 8510) 1972 R3

45s: Here I Go Again/What You Gonna Do (Parlophone R 5920) 1971
       Goin' Round My Head/
       Down On The Road   (Regal Zonophone RZ 3056) 1972
       Blackbird/Feel It Coming   (Regal Zonophone RZ 3076) 1973

This group's album has a reputation for being highly interesting 'rural prog'. Well, if 'rural' means boring country-derived melodies played by a supple but uninspired band, then its reputation is fully justified. The title track sounds like a watered-down version of The Band's *The Weight*, and other tracks show even less character. Only *Something About Her* is good enough to play twice. Save your money for your holidays. The album was produced by **Keith West** of **Tomorrow** fame. (MK)

Tony Rose

ALBUMS: 1 YOUNG HUNTING   (Trailer LER 2013) 1970
(up to   2 UNDER THE GREENWOOD TREE
1976)   (Trailer LER 2024) 1971

Rose was born on 1 May 1941 in Exeter, Devon. He first became involved in folk whilst at Oxford and he worked semi-professionally whilst there in the early sixties. In 1965 he moved up to London and had a number of residencies at clubs like Cecil Sharpe House and the Mercury Theatre. In 1969 he became a full-time musician recording *Young Hunting* the following year. It's the follow-up, *Under The Greenwood Tree* for which he is best remembered. This featured songs about the West Country of England with **Rose** singing and playing guitar and concertina. It caused quite a stir in the folk press at the time of its release.

He's recorded spasmodically since 1976 and was involved in the short-lived group Bandoggs in 1978. In recent years he's reverted to performing part-time whilst working as a journalist. (VJ)

(Alan) Ross

ALBUMS: 1 ROSS   (RSO 2394 127) 1974
(up to   2 THE PIT AND THE PENDULUM   (RSO 2394 144) 1975
1976)

NB: (2) also issued in the US (RSO 4802) 1975.

45:      Alright By Me/Carolina   (RSO 2090 125) 1974
(up to
1976)

Essentially a session guitarist. Bands who **Ross** assisted included **The Who** and Sutherland Brothers and **Quiver** as well as **John Entwistle**. He went on to record two albums on the Ebony label and a few singles for Ebony and Good Earth, but they are beyond the timespan of this book. (VJ)

The Rothchilds

45s: You've Made Your Choice/It's Love   (Decca F 12411) 1966
       Artificial City/I Let Her Go   (Decca F 12488) 1966

A short-lived mid-sixties group. Arthur Greenslade was musical director on their second 45, which was pleasant mainstream pop. (VJ)

Linda Rothwell

45s: Dip-Dip-Dip-Chu-Chi-Face/
       Sweet And Sour   (Chapter One SCH 162) 1972
       Write Me A Letter/Tell Me   (Chapter One SCH 180) 1973

NB: (1) with Sweet and Sour.

These were solo efforts from **Linda Rothwell**, who was a member of **Goliath** in 1970/71. (VJ)

The Roulettes

Personnel:	RUSS BALLARD	gtr	AB
	BOB HENRIT	drms	AB
	JOHN RODGERS	bs	A
	PETE SALT	gtr	AB
	JOHN "MOD" ROGAN	bs	B
	(JOHN BEDDINGFIELD	drms)	

ALBUMS: 1(B) STAKES AND CHIPS   (Parlophone PMC 1257) 1965 R5
        2(B) RUSS, BOB, PETE AND MOD   (Edsel ED 113) 1983

NB: (1) was reissued on GI-Records in 1982 and also on CD (BGO BGOCD 130).

45s: Hully Gully Slip And Slide/La Bamba   (Pye 7N 15467) 1962 SC
       Soon You'll Be Leaving Me/
       Tell Tale Tit   (Parlophone R 5072) 1963 SC
       Bad Times/Can You Go   (Parlophone R 5110) 1964 SC
       I'll Remember Tonight/
       You Don't Love Me   (Parlophone R 5148) 1964 SC

Stubborn Kind Of Fellow/Mebody	(Parlophone R 5218) 1964 SC		
I Hope He Breaks Your Heart/			
Find Out The Truth	(Parlophone R 5278) 1965 SC		
The Long Cigarette/Junk	(Parlophone R 5382) 1965 SC		
The Tracks Of My Tears/Jackpot	(Parlophone R 5419) 1966 SC		
I Can't Stop (one-sided)	(Oak RGJ 205) 1966 R3		
I Can't Stop/			
Yesterday, Today and Tomorrow	(Parlophone R 5461) 1966 SC		
Rhyme Boy, Rhyme/Airport People	(Fontana TF 822) 1967 SC		
Help Me To Help Myself/			
To A Taxi Driver	(Fontana TF 876) 1967 SC		

This band originally started life as Adam Faith's backing band, appearing on several of his records and the *On The Move* album. They also had a pretty prolific vinyl output themselves. John Rodgers was killed in a car crash in 1964 being replaced by "Mod" Rogan. This line-up (B) remained in place until they split in 1967, although John Beddingfield replaced Henrit for a while in 1964/5. Beddingfield departed for Blues Roots in 1965. Thereafter **Ballard** and Henrit were briefly with **Unit Four Plus Two** before forming **Argent**. Henrit now plays with **The Kinks**.

Commercial success always eluded **The Roulettes** who were from Hertfordshie. One of their 45s was penned by fellow Hertfordshire group members Brian Parker, Tommy Moeller and Robert Henrit (of **Unit Four Plus Two**). They also spent a while in Europe during 1967 supporting French rocker Richard Anthony. Their *Stakes And Chips* album didn't sell in any significant quantities at the time but is now a mega-rarity.

Of their 45s, *Stubborn Kind Of Fellow* was a Marvin Gaye track and *The Tracks Of My Tears* was a Smokey Robinson and The Miracles number.

The Edsel album includes all the Parlophone 'A' sides and all the 'B' sides (except *Jackpot* and *Yesterday, Today and Tomorrow*). Two tracks from the *Stakes And Chips* album also appear - *This Little Girl* and *What You Gonna Do?*

Compilation appearances have included: *The Long Cigarette* on *My Generation* (LP); *La Bamba* on *Ripples, Vol. 5* (CD); and *Bad Time* on *Beat Merchants* (2-LP), *Sixties Lost And Found, Vol. 1* (LP), *Beat At Abbey Road* (CD). (VJ)

Roundabout

Personnel:	RITCHIE BLACKMORE	gtr	ABC
	CHRIS CURTIS	vcls	A
	JON LORD	keyb'ds	ABC
	NICK SIMPER	bs	A
	DAVE CURTIS	vcls	B
	BOBBY WOODMAN (aka CLARK)	drms	B
	ROD EVANS	vcls	C
	IAN PAICE	drms	C

Former **Searchers'** drummer **Chris Curtis** formed this outfit in late 1967, which saw him in a vocal role. **Jon Lord** was recruited from **The Artwoods** and **Ritchie Blackmore** from The Outlaws. Blackmore refused to play **Curtis'** original compositions and flew back to Germany. **Chris Curtis** was dumped and Lord flew to Germany to talk **Blackmore** into returning. **Blackmore** said he would be interested, if the band included Woodman. So Woodman (who'd been playing with Johnny Hallyday in France) was recruited along with Dave Curtis (who'd been fronting his own band called The Tremors) and **Blackmore** returned. However, Woodman and Dave Curtis left in March 1968 to form **Bodast**. Rod Evans and Ian Paice (both from **The Maze**) were recruited. This line-up headed for Denmark after a few rehearsals. They played a few gigs there and appeared on TV before returning to England and becoming **Deep Purple**. (VJ/JM)

Roundtable

ALBUM:	1	SPINNING WHEEL	(Jay Boy JSL 2) 1969 R1

45:	Saturday Gigue/Scarborough Fair	(Jay Boy BOY 18) 1970 SC

This was a reasonable pop outfit. (VJ)

The Roving Kind

Personnel:	SAM BECK	gtr, organ	A
	JIM BURNS	bs, sax	A
	GARY JAMES	vcls, drms, gtr	A

45s:	Ain't It True/Don't Tell Me The Time	(Decca F 12264) 1965
	Lies In A Million/How Many Times	(Decca F 12381) 1966

This little known group came from Plymouth. Gary James later made solo recordings for Polydor and Columbia in the second half of the sixties. (VJ/JM)

Normie Rowe

45s:	It's Not Easy/Mary Mary	(Polydor 56132) 1966
	Ain't Nobody Home/Ooh La La	(Polydor 56144) 1966
	Going Home/ Don't Care (Just Get Me There) (some PS)	(Polydor 56159) 1967

Mary Mary can also be heard on *Colour Me Pop, Vol 3* (CD). (VJ)

Roxy Music

Personnel:	ROGER BUNN	gtr	A
	BRIAN ENO	synthesizer	ABCD
	BRYAN FERRY	vcls, keyb'ds	ABCDE
	DEXTER LLOYD	drms	AB
	ANDY MACKAY	sax	ABCDE
	GRAHAM SIMPSON	bs	ABC
	DAVID O'LIST	gtr	B
	PAUL THOMPSON	drms	BCDE
	PHIL MANZANERA	gtr	CDE
	RIK KENTON	bs	D
	JOHN GUSTAFSON	bs	E
	JOHN WETTON	bs	E
	EDDIE JOBSON	violin, keyb'ds	E

				HCP
ALBUMS: 1(C)	ROXY MUSIC	(Island ILPS 9200)	1972	10
(up to 2(D)	FOR YOUR PLEASURE	(Island ILPS 9232)	1973	4
1976) 3(E)	STRANDED	(Island ILPS 9252)	1973	1
4(E)	COUNTRY LIFE	(Island ILPS 9303)	1974	3
5(E)	SIREN	(Island ILPS 9344)	1975	4
6(-)	VIVA! ROXY MUSIC	(Island ILPS 9400)	1976	6

NB: (1)-(6) reissued on Polydor (2302 048-053) in 1977. (1) reissued on vinyl (EMI LPCENT 37) 1997. All the above albums have been reissued on CD:- (1) on (EG EGLP 6) 1991, (2) on (EG EGCD 8) 1991, (3) on (EG EGCD 10) 1991, (4) on (EG EGCD 16) 1987, (5) on (EG EGCD 20) 1991 and (6) on (EG EGCD 25) 1991. (6) reissued again on CD (Virgin 7243 8 47436 2 8) 2002. Also of interest is *The First*

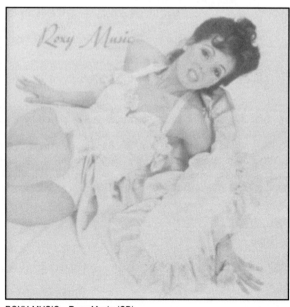

ROXY MUSIC - Roxy Music (CD).

Seven Albums (7-LP box set, plus insert) (Polydor/E.G. EGBS 001) 1981. You may want to investigate *Greatest Hits* (Polydor 2302 073) 1977 (No 20) and *The Atlantic Years 1973-80* (EG/Polydor EGLP 54) 1983 (No 23), which has also been released in CD format (EG 815 849-2) 1983. There's also *Streetlife* (a 2-LP compilation) (EG EGTV 2) 1986, also on CD, credited to Bryan Ferry and Roxy Music; *Greatest Hits: Roxy Music* (EG EGCD 31) 1988, a CD box set of their first seven albums (EGBC 1) 1981 and *Roxy Music Early Years Box Set* (EG EGBC 3) 1989, which covers their early albums and *Roxy Music Later Years Box Set* (EG EGBC 4) 1989. *The Thrill Of It All* (Virgin CDBOX 5) 1995 is a 4-CD box set which compiles most of their released material but very little in the way of rarities. Two further CD compilations are *Roxy Music / Bryan Ferry - Street Life - 20 Greatest Hits* (EG EGTV 1), and *Roxy Music / Bryan Ferry - The Ultimate Collection* (EG EGTV 2). *The Early Years* (Virgin CDV 2919) 2000 is a good guide to this phase of their career.

			HCP
45s:	Virginia Plain/The Numberer	(Island WIP 6144) 1972	4
(up to	Pyjamarama/The Pride And The Pain	(Island WIP 6159) 1973	10
1976)	Street Life/Hula Kula	(Island WIP 6173) 1973	9
	All I Want Is You/		
	Your Application's Failed	(Island WIP 6208) 1974	12
	Love Is The Drug/Sultanesque	(Island WIP 6248) 1975	2
	Both Ends Burning/		
	For Your Pleasure	(Island WIP 6262) 1975	25
Reissues:	Virginia Plain/Pygamarama (PS)	(Polydor 2001 739) 1977	11
	Do The Strand/Editions Of You	(Polydor 2001 756) 1978	-
α	Jealous Guy/Lover/Southdown	(Virgin CDT8) 1988	-
β	Love Is A Drug (live)/Editions Of You (live)/		
	Do The Strand (live)	(EG EGOCD 55) 1990	-

NB: α CD 3" single. β also issued on 7" vinyl minus *Do The Strand*.

Roxy Music was a stylish glam-rock band of the early seventies that played a unique brand of arty pop-rock which was to inspire many later acts. After **Brian Eno** left, in the mid-seventies, the band developed a sophisticated brand of soul-pop.

The pivotal figure in **Roxy Music** is **Bryan Ferry** who was born on 26 September 1945 in Washington, County Durham. His first group was **The Banshees**, a Sunderland-based band in Summer 1964, but he left in September of that year to study Fine Art at Newcastle University. Whilst there, he fronted a college band, The Gas Board, who played soul/R&B numbers.

After graduating in 1968 he worked in various jobs including a van driver, antiques restorer and ceramics teacher at a Hammersmith girls school. He was sacked from the last job for playing music in lessons, indeed he spent much of his time during these years writing songs and learning to play piano.

In November 1970 he decided to form a band with old university friend (and bassist) Graham Simpson. Andy MacKay and **Brian Eno** were added to the line-up in January 1971 and **Bunn** and tympanist Dexter Lloyd joined in response to adverts in 'Melody Maker'. This line-up (A) didn't play live but it did record demos which **Ferry** took around the London record companies - with little success initially.

In July 1971 **Bunn** and Lloyd both left the band and **Ferry** placed another ad in 'Melody Maker' to recruit drummer Paul Thompson, who'd played in several Newcastle bands including Smokestack and had also backed Billy Fury. He also headhunted former **Nice** guitarist Davy O'List, being an admirer of his style. This line-up did play a couple of gigs at Reading University's Union Ball and the Friends Of The Tate Gallery Christmas Show. More importantly deejay John Peel having been impressed by their earlier demo tape arranged for them to play a session at BBC's 'Sound Of The Seventies' which gave them national exposure.

O'List left the following month (he later re-emerged in **Jet**) and Phil Manzanera, who'd been the band's sound-mixer joined in his place. This line-up (C) signed with EG Management, who got them a record deal with Island. Their debut album *Roxy Music* was stunning. It rose to No 10 in the UK Charts.

Graham Simpson was pushed out in May 1972 and replaced by Rik Kenton, a friend of Pete Sinfield who'd produced their first album. This new line-up (D) recorded the classic *Virginia Plain* single with that unique **Roxy Music** sound. It made the Top 5 and the band embarked on a headlining UK tour to help promote it which had to be curtailed when **Bryan Ferry** was hospitalised to have his tonsils removed. When he recovered they toured the US in December 1972 but failed to conquer.

ROXY MUSIC - Stranded (CD).

The bassist slot in the band was always a problem. Kenton, who'd appeared on *Virginia Plain* was booted out at the beginning of 1973 and a session bassist John Porter was used for the second album sessions. Both this album (*For Your Pleasure*, which was promoted with the help of a successful UK tour), and their next 45, *Pyjamarama* (which wasn't included on the album), climbed to No 10 in their respective charts.

Brian Eno quit the band in July 1973 when **Bryan Ferry** made it clear he no longer wanted him in the band. **Eno**, of course, went on to assist a number of other artists on various projects as well as pursuing a solo career. His replacement was former **Curved Air** keyboardist and violinist Eddie Jobson, who had earlier assisted **Bryan Ferry** on his first solo album, *These Foolish Things*. In this new line-up Jobson assumed responsibility for all keyboards (**Ferry** and **Eno** had previously shared them) whilst **Ferry** fronted the band as a vocalist. Former **Big Three** bassist **John Gustafson** was brought in to fill the bass slot on their next album, *Stranded*. This climbed to the top of the UK album Charts and crept to No 186 in the US where, despite a further US tour in June 1974, the band had only achieved cult status. The album produced by Chris Thomas, also spawned another Top Ten UK hit, *Street Life*.

In Autumn 1974 the band embarked on a new 23-date UK tour on which **Ferry** attempted to conjure a new image clad in a US military style uniform. John Wetton was drafted in on bass for this tour but it was **Gustafson** who did the bass sessions for their next *Country Life* album, which was preceded by another significant UK hit, *All I Want Is You*. **Ferry** co-wrote most of the material on the album, which was produced by John Porter, with members of the band. It came in a controversial sleeve showing two scantily clad models, which was banned in the US but helped attract additional publicity. Indeed it was their first album to sell significantly in the US, where it got to No 37.

By the time the band toured the UK again in October 1975 Wetton had joined **Uriah Heep** and **Gustafson** played bass on tour for the first time. Wetton had filled this role on a Japanese promotional visit and a tour of Australia and New Zealand earlier in the year. Their new album, *Siren*, was again produced by Thomas and the sleeve bore a photo of Texas model Jerry Hall, with whom **Ferry** later became romantically involved. The album made the Top Ten here and climbed to No 50 in the US by the end of the year assisted by a further US tour. More significantly the album spawned two hits:- the excellent R&B dance number *Love Is The Drug* (No 2 here and No 30 US) and *Both Ends Burning* (No 25 here). After a further US tour in March 1976 it was decided to put the band to rest (temporarily). Andy MacKay wrote and produced the music for the 'Rock Follies' series, **Ferry** concentrated on solo work forming his own band, Manzanera formed 801 and Jobson went to play for Frank Zappa in the US.

During the band's lay-off Island assembled *Viva Roxy Music* from concert recordings during the 1972-75 period to maintain interest in the band. The material is taken from concerts in Glasgow, Newcastle and Wembley. It includes eight of their classic songs, including an extended *If There Is Something*, a funky *Both Ends Burning* and *Do The Strand*. This interest was rekindled too when EG Management transferred the band's music catalogue in late 1977 from Island to Polydor, who reissued all six of their albums and put out a *Greatest Hits* compilation. They also reissued their first two 'A' sides on one disc, which climbed to No 11 in the UK. This all helped to pave the way for a reformation of the band the following year.

Their comeback album *Manifesto* was a slick disco-influenced soul-pop album which captured the mood of the times well, climbing to No 7 in the UK and No 23 in the US. The follow-up *Flesh And Blood* in 1980 gave them a UK No 1 album and their non-album cover of **John Lennon**'s *Jealous Guy*, which they recorded as a tribute to **Lennon** became their only UK No 1 single. Their next album *Avalon* was even more successful. It climbed to No 1 in the Summer of 1982 where it stayed for three weeks. It spawned further hits with *More Than This* and *Take A Chance With Me*. In the US it became their only gold album and gradually reached platinum status. However, following a successful promotional tour a live EP *Musique/The High Road* was released and then the group split in 1983 as **Ferry** concentrated on a solo career. **Manzanera** and MacKay formed The Explorers in 1985 and went on to work together under various names as well as pursuing their own solo careers over the coming years. In 1990 a live album *Heart Still Beating* was released which documented a 1982 concert by the band.

The 1986 *Street Life - 20 Greatest Hits* compilation also included some of **Bryan Ferry**'s solo material. Various artists compilation appearances include *Love Is The Drug* on the 3-CD set *Full Throttle - 60 Original Driving Classics*. (VJ)

James Royal (and The Hawks)

ALBUMS:	1	CALL MY NAME	(CBS 63780) 1969 SC
	2	ONE WAY	(Carnaby CNLS 6008) 1970 R1
	3	THE LIGHT AND SHADE OF JAMES ROYAL	
			(Carnaby 6302 011) 1972 R1

45s:	α	She's About A Mover/	
		Black Cloud	(Parlophone R 5290) 1965 SC
		Work Song/I Can't Stand It	(Parlophone R 5383) 1965 R1
		Call My Name/	
		When It Comes To Me Baby	(CBS 202525) 1967 SC
		It's All In The Game/Green Days	(CBS 2739) 1967
		Take Me Like I Am/Sitting In The Station	(CBS 2959) 1968
		I Can't Stand It/Little Bit Of Rain	(CBS 3232) 1968
		Hey Little Boy/Thru' The Love	(CBS 3450) 1968 SC
		A Woman Called Sorrow/Fire	(CBS 3624) 1968 SC
		Time Hangs On My Mind/Anna-Lee	(CBS 3797) 1969
		House Of Jack/Which Way To Nowhere	(CBS 3915) 1969
		I've Something Bad On My Mind/	
		She's Independent	(CBS 4139) 1969
		Send Out Love/I've Lost You	(CBS 4463) 1969
		And Soon The Darkness/I'm Going Home	(CBS 5032) 1970
		Carolina/Big Heat On The Loose	(Carnaby CNS 4021) 1970

NB: α as James Royal and The Hawks.

Originally known as Jimmy Royal and The Hawks. **Royal** recorded a series of solo pop songs for CBS. *It's All In The Game* was the Tommy Edwards / Cliff Richard hit song.

I'm Leaving You can also be found on *Ready Steady Win* (LP & CD). (VJ)

Robbie Royal

| 45s: | Only Me/I Don't Need You | (Mercury MF 923) 1965 |
| | Within My Lonely Heart/When I Found You | (Decca 12097) 1965 |

When I Found You is a decent beat/pop song. (VJ)

Royalty

| 45: | That Kind Of Girl/ | |
| | Will You Be Staying After Sunday | (CBS 4181) 1969 |

This is a forgotten 45. (VJ)

Earl Royce and The Olympics

Personnel:	PETE (MELODY) COOK	lead gtr	A
	BRIAN DEE	bs	ABC
	KENNY HAZARD	gtr	ABC
	JIMMY JORDAN	drms	ABC
	BILLY (EARL) KELLY	vcls	ABC
	GEORGE PECKHAM	lead gtr	B
	FRANK BOWEN	lead gtr	C

NB: Other personnel included Eddie Forte (bs), Derek Nodwell (bs) and Rita Hughes (vcls).

45s:	Que Sera Sera/I Really Do	(Columbia DB 7433) 1964 SC
	Guess Things Happen That Way/	
	Sure To Fall	(Parlophone R 5261) 1965 SC

Out of Liverpool, this quartet's singles attracted little attention. **Royce** was also featured in the 'Ferry Cross The Mersey' movie playing *Shake A Tail Feather*.

Compilation appearances have included: *Que Sera Sera* and *I Really Do* on *Liverpool 1963-1968* (CD), *Liverpool 1963-1968, Vol. 1* (LP); and *Que Sera Sera* on *Mersey Beat* (2-LP) and *Beat Merchants* (2-LP). (VJ/AD)

The Rubber Band

Personnel:	JACK CHAPMAN	organ, vcls	A
	PHIL DREWERY	bs, vcls	A
	HARRY RIX	drms	A

ALBUMS:	1(A)	CREAM SONG BOOK	(Major Minor SMLP 5045) 1969 SC
	2(A)	HENDRIX SONG BOOK	
			(Major Minor SMLP 5048) 1969 SC

NB: (2) reissued on CD (GRT 10007).

Originally formed in 1965, this band backed several top singers, appeared on Radio One and toured extensively. On *Hendrix Song Book* they take the intricacies of his songs and add classical undertones utilising fine harmonies, guitar, violin, viola, oboe, celli, horns and various string instruments. They later changed their name to Skinn, finally disbanding in 1970. Chapman was sadly killed in a car accident in 1976. The 1993 compilation, *The Stars That Played With Dead Jimi's Dice*, included this band's version of *Manic Depression*. (VJ)

Rubber Bootz

| 45: | Joy Ride/Chicano | (Deram DM 134) 1967 SC |

This is another forgotten late sixties bands. (VJ)

Rubber Bucket

| 45: | We Are All Living In One Place/ | |
| | Take Me Away | (MCA MK 5006) 1969 |

This 45 was recorded by Paul Gadd (later **Gary Glitter**) using a pseudonym. It featured a chanting chorus of 3,000 people in front of the MCA offices watching the police evict squatters next door. Despite considerable hype it failed to sell and his next project was a version of **George Harrison**'s *Here Comes The Sun* under another pseudonym **Paul Monday**. He'd earlier recorded as **Paul Raven**. (VJ)

The Rubettes

Personnel:	PETER ARNISSON	keyb'ds	A
	MICK CLARKE	bs	A
	(PAUL DaVINCI	ld vcls	A)
	BILL HURD	keyb'ds, gtr	A
	JOHN RICHARDSON	drms	A
	TONY THORPE	gtr, keyb'ds, drms	A
	ALAN WILLIAMS	gtr, flute, keyb'ds	A

THE RUNNING MAN - The Running Man (LP).

				HCP
ALBUMS:	1(A)	WE CAN DO IT	(State ETAT 001) 1975	41
(up to	2(A)	RUBETTES	(State ETAT 004) 1975	-
1976)	3(A)	SIGN OF THE TIMES	(State ETAT 006) 1976	-
	4(A)	THE BEST OF THE RUBETTES	(State ETAT 008) 1976	-
	5(A)	WHERE IT'S AT	(Polydor 2383 306) 1976	-

NB: Later compilations include: *Impact* (Impact 6886 562) 1982 and *The Best Of The Rubettes* (Polydor 2384 111) 1982. On CD there's: *Best Of The Rubettes* (Polydor 843 896 2) 1990, an 18-track CD, *The Rubettes 20th Anniversary Compilation* (Dick RUBCD 15) 1995, *The Very Best Of The Rubettes* (Spectrum) 1998 and *The Master Series* (Polydor E 5336752) 199?

			HCP
45s:	Sugar Baby Love/I Can Do It	(Polydor 2058 442) 1974	1
(up to	Tonight/Teenage Dream	(Polydor 2058 499) 1974	12
1976)	Juke Box Jive/		
	When You're Falling In Love	(Polydor 2058 529) 1974	3
	I Can Do It/If You've Got The Time	(State STAT 1) 1975	7
	Foe-Dee-O-Dee/With You	(State STAT 7) 1975	15
	Little Darling/Miss Goodie Two Shoes	(State STAT 13) 1975	30
	You're The Reason Why/Julia	(State STAT 20) 1976	28
	Under One Roof/	(State STAT 27) 1976	40
Reissue:	Sugar Baby Love/I Can Do It	(Old Gold OG 9152) 1982	-

This unashamedly commercial teenybopper quintet scored considerable commercial success in the UK in the mid-seventies, although *Sugar Baby Love* was their only 45 to make an impact in the US where it got to No 37.

They are still going on the cabaret circuit. Paul DaVinci wasn't really in the band but sung on their first 45. Mick Clarke, the son of a Dagenham docker, was first in a band called The Teens, which included Rick Westwood, later of **The Tremeloes**, who Mick also joined briefly in 1966. Whilst with them he suggested they record *Silence Is Golden*, which they did and it became a million-seller after he left the band. His other bands were **Johnny Milton and The Condors**, who later became **The Symbols**. In the early seventies he became a session musician.

Bill Hurd played in a band called The Sneekers whilst at school in East London. In the R&B boom of the mid-sixties he formed The Diddly Daddies who didn't make it on to vinyl. In the psychedelic era, he formed the short-lived **Gass Company** with John Richardson. In 1969, he formed the progressive/psychedelic band **Wake**. Upon their demise in the early seventies he, too, did session work.

John Richardson and Alan Williams' first proper group was **The Medium**. They then later turned up as a songwriting duo in **Baskin and Copperfield**. Richardson was briefly one of **Mike Batt**'s Wombles in 1974. In 1968 he'd been in **The Three Sounds** with Tony Thorpe. Tony Thorpe's early bands were The Vibratones who later became the V.I.P.'s (not the pre-**Spooky Tooth** outfit). This was a Southend band. From 1965 he backed rock'n'roller, Wee Willie Harris, for three years. In 1968 he left to form **The Three Sounds** with John Richardson and ex-**Brian Auger** man Roger Sutton. Nowadays, Thorpe is the MC at a very professional Jam Night at

the Rhythm Station in Rawtenstall (owned by **Denny Laine** - ex-**Wings**) also at the Goodnight Club in Nelson, Lancashire. He gigs a lot and plays mainly blues and jazz these days and is considered a very able musician by the musicians around the North West.

Compilation appearances have included *Sugar Baby Love* on *The Best Summer Ever!* (CD), *Everlasting Love* (CD), *Number 1 Hits Of The 70's and 80's* (CD), *Wild Thing - Party* (CD), *Seventies Legends* (CD) and *20 Hits From The Seventies* (CD); *I Can Do* on *70's Remembered* (CD); *I Can Do* and *Juke Box Jive* on *The Super 70's Vol 2* (CD) and *Jukebox Jive* on *70's Remembered* (CD), *Hits Of The 70's Vol 3* (CD), *The Super 70's Vol 1* (CD) and *Seventies Legends 2* (CD). (VJ/RL)

Ruby

Personnel:	JOHN ABBOTT	gtr, vcls	A
	DAVE KNIGHTS	bs, vcls, gtr	A
	MIKE LENTON	gtr	A
	ROB MUNRO	vcls, drms	A
	GEOFF SWETTENHAM	drms	A

ALBUM: 1(A) RED CRYSTAL FANTASIES (Chrysalis CHR 1061) 1974

45: Someday I Will Return/Oh Woman (Chrysalis CHS 2025) 1974

This band formed in May 1973. Drummer Colin Fairley was also featured on their album.

Ruby also marked the return of David Knights who had played in the first two **Procol Harum** albums but left to pursue a management career. The album is quite varied with some rock and rhythm and blues influences in evidence as well as some harmony work but all in all is only average although the final track *Starshine* hinted at better to come, however this proved to be their only outing and the band folded. Drumming duties were largely performed by Colin 'Billy The Kid' Fairley of **String Driven Thing**. (VJ)

Rumble

Personnel incl:	STEVE CURRIE	bs	A

45: Rich Man, Poor Man/Let Me Down (Warner WB 8011) 1970

A Grimsby band who operated between 1966-72. They played jazzy music. Steve Currie was later in **T Rex**. (VJ)

Rumplestiltskin

ALBUMS:	1	RUMPLESTILTSKIN	(Bell SBLL 130) 1970 R1
	2	BLACK MAGICIAN	(Bellaphon 15145) 1972

NB: (2) was a German-only issue. Both albums have been reissued on CD on Repertoire.

45s:	Squadron Leader Johnson/Rumplestiltskin	(Bell BLL 1101) 1970
	Wimoweh/Through My Looking Glass	(Bell BLL 1157) 1971

Rumplestiltskin was a hard-rock band who included personnel from **Ugly Custard** and **Hungry Wolf**. (VJ/CG)

Running Man

Personnel:	HAROLD BECKETT	horns	A
	ALAN GREED	vcls, keyb'ds, bs	A
	ALAN RUSHTON	drms	A
	RAY RUSSELL	gtr, bs, keyb'ds, vcls	A
	GARY WINDO	sax	A

ALBUM: 1(A) THE RUNNING MAN (RCA Neon NE 11) 1972 R3

NB: (1) reissued on CD (Repertoire REP 4471-WP) 1994 and again (Akarma AK 111). (1) reissued again on CD (Angel Air SJPCD 199) 2005 with a bonus alternate take of one track.

It's **Ray Russell** time again, which means good savage progressive guitar. On this album typical seventies prog-rock tracks are effectively alternated with a few **Procol Harum**-like numbers, characterised by the plaintive voice of Alan Greed. The combination is only partly successful, sounding at times a bit too earnest, but on the whole it's quite listenable. Good, but not too good.

Ray Russell had been in **The Graham Bond Organisation, Georgie Fame's Blue Flames, Mouse** and was also a seasoned session guitarist. Many of the personnel were also in **Rock Workshop.** (MK/VJ)

Rupert and David

Personnel: RUPERT HINE
              DAVID MacIVER

45:    Sound Of Silence/
       Reflections Of Your Love   (Decca F 12306) 1965

The 'A' side was the Paul Simon song. There may have been other 45s under this name. **Hine** went on to record solo 45s in the seventies and an album with help from MacIver. They later formed **Quantum Jump**. (VJ)

Rupert's People

Personnel: CHRIS ANDREWS   vcls   A
              JOHN BANKS   drms   A
              GARY BROOKER   keyb'ds, vcls   A
              ADRIAN CURTIS   gtr, vcls   A
              TONY DANGERFIELD   bs, vcls   A
              RAY BEVERLEY   bs, vcls   B
              STEVE BRENDELL   drms   B
              DAI JENKINS   gtr, vcls   B
              ROD LYNTON   lead gtr, vcls B
              JOHN TOUT   keyb'ds   B

45s: Reflections Of Charles Brown/
       Hold On   (Columbia DB 8226) 1967 R1
       A Prologue To A Magic World/
       Dream In My Mind   (Columbia DB 8278) 1967 R2
       I Can Show You/
       I've Got The Love   (Columbia DB 8362) 1968 R2

NB: A CD compilation, *The Magic World Of Rupert's People* (Circle CPWC 103) 2002, also available as a deluxe vinyl album, features the above A and B sides and several in concert tracks from 1969 and a one-off re-union 30 years later.

A psychedelic outfit whose 45s are well worth seeking out, but are quite rare and sought-after. They seem to have had two entirely different line-ups. The Chris Andrews who fronted the first wasn't he of *Yesterday Man* fame but an actor-turned-singer who briefly fronted the **Fleur de Lys**. Bassist **Tony Dangerfield** had also been with **Gulliver's Travels, Neil Christian and The Crusaders** and **Lord Sutch's Savages** as had Adrian Curtis, who'd also played with **Crispian St. Peters**. Drummer John Banks had been with **The Merseybeats** and **Johnny & John**. Gary Brooker had been with **The Paramounts** and was busy getting **Procol Harum** together, but it was session man Pete Solley who supplied the *Whiter Shade Of Pale* style organ on the superb *Reflections Of Charles Brown*. The keyboard-driven ballad with strong vocals could easily have been a hit. Indeed, it was a sizeable hit all over Europe, but not in the UK. The flip side, *Hold On*, was covered by Sharon Tandy with **The Fleur de Lys** which led to rumours that the two groups were the same, which they weren't. *Hold On* had been written and recorded by **The Fleur de Lys** and Rod Lynton when producer/manager Frank Fenter had intended to metamorphise the band into **Rupert's People**. Of the band only Chris Andrews liked *Reflections*, the eventual 'A' side, which Lynton wrote, and only he remained with the project forming line-up (A). This was short-lived, with **Dangerfield** going on to **Crispian St Peter, Episode Six** and **Alan Bown**, etc; Banks also joined **Episode Six**; and Curtis went on to **Please** and then **Gun**.

Rod Lynton (formerly with **Sweet Feeling**) then comprised a new band (line-up B), which included two other former **Sweet Feeling** members Raymond Beverley and Steve Brindell. This line-up recorded two further 45s.

A Prologue To A Magic World wasn't quite as good as their debut 45, but the flip side *Dream In My Mind*, was a fairly typical slice of late sixties

pop-sike. Their third 'A' side *I Can Show You*, was also quite an appealing slice of pop-psychedelia, dominated by the vocals. Its flip side, culminates into some good phasing and guitar work, but it's a pity that it steals a riff from **The Beatles**' *Ticket To Ride* along the way.

Despite considerable airplay on pirate radio here in the U.K. they failed to breakthrough. They were very big in Germany, though, where their first 45 was released with a different 'B' side, *Love-Opus 193*, which was co-written by **The Smoke**'s Geoff Gill.

John Tout was later in **Renaissance** and **Wishbone Ash**. Lynton and Brendall went on to a studio band called Matchbox. There was a reformation in April 1999 which included three original members Rod Lynton (gtr,vcls), Ray Beverley (bs) and Steve Brendell (drms).

A CD compilation, *The Magic World Of Rupert's People* released in 2002, also available as a deluxe vinyl album, features their 45 A and B sides, a 45 by an earlier version of the band (**Sweet Feeling**), a previously unissued acetate and several in concert tracks from 1969 and a one-off re-union 30 years later. Not all the in-concert tracks appear on the vinyl version of this release.

Compilation appearances have included:- *Reflections Of Charles Brown* on *Perfumed Garden Vol. 2* (LP & CD) and on the 4-CD *Nuggets II* box set; *Hold On* on *Perfumed Garden Vol. 3* (CD) and *Yellow Elektric Years* (LP); *I've Got The Love* on *Rubble, Vol. 15 - 5,000 Seconds Over Toyland* (LP) and *Rubble, Vol. 9* (CD); *I Can Show You* and *Dream On My Mind* on *Rubble, Vol. 14 - The Magic Rocking Horse* (LP), *The Best Of Rubble Collection Vol. 1* (CD) and *Rubble, Vol. 8* (CD); *Love/Opus 193* on *Visions Of The Past, Vol. 3* (LP & CD); *I've Got The Love* and *Love/Opus 193* on *Beat It* (3-CD); *Dream In My Mind* on *English Freakbeat, Vol. 3* (LP) and on the 4-CD box set *Acid Drops, Spacedust & Flying Saucers*; and *Reflections Of Charles Brown, Hold On, Love/Opus 193, I Can Show You, Dream In My Mind* and *I've Got The Love* on *Hard Up Heroes, Vol. 6* (CD). (VJ)

Rush

Personnel: STUART ATTRIDE   gtr, keyb'ds, vcls   AB
              PETER HOLE   ld gtr, vcls   A
              CHAS WADE   drms, vcls   AB
              GERRY WADE   bs, vcls   AB
              STEVE MAHER   ld gtr, vcls   B

45s: Happy/Once Again   (Decca F 12614) 1967
       Make Mine Music/Enjoy It   (Decca F 12635) 1967

The Rush were formed in 1965, by brothers Gerry and Chas Wade and played mainly around the London scene as a pop harmony/surf band. Peter Hole left the band in 1967 after recording the first single and later emigrated to Sydney, Australia. His replacement was Steve Maher, and this line-up performed both sides of their second 45 on Granada TV Manchester for a "Top of the Pops" style program.

In late 1967, the band were given the new name **Tinkerbells Fairydust** by producer Vic Smith, for whom they recorded a further three 45s, and an unreleased album, although they rarely went on the road under that name.

Chas Wade left the band in 1968 to join **The Symbols**, who had a UK hit with *The Best Part Of Breaking Up* and toured the USA as support band to Vanilla Fudge and **Rod Stewart**. He was replaced by Drummer Barry Creasy and the band also briefly included vocalist Dave Church.

The Rush split up in 1970 with members going on to various bands. They reformed as **Rush** a couple of years later with most of the original line-up. Chas Wade later rejoined as front-man/vocalist and the band played the London scene as a comedy showband with various line-up additions until 1975 when Steve Maher left to take up a career as an Illustrator/cartoonist.

Rush were re-named as J.J. Foot in 76 and continued to play the London Pub/Club scene up until 1985. (VJ)

Thane Russal (and Three)

Personnel inc: DOUG GIBBONS (THANE RUSSAL)   vcls
                MICK BRILL

45s: α Security/
Love Is Burning In Me (some PS) (CBS 202049) 1966 R3
β Drop Everything And Run/I Need You (CBS 202403) 1966 R3

NB: α also issued in Italy. β **Thane Russal** solo release. **Russal** also had two further Italian 45s: *Adesso Tardi / If I Were A Carpenter* (CBS 2810)1967 and *Dopo Un Sogno / Dimmi Qualcosa* (CBS 3047) 1968.

Thane Russal's 45s are now very rare but some copies of the first one came in picture sleeves and these are now ultra-rarities. **Thane**'s real name was Doug Gibbons. He'd recorded a ballad under that name in 1965 then met up with **The Rolling Stones** which led to the deal with CBS for these two powerful 45s. When neither took off, he headed for Italy, where he recorded at least two further 45s. There are rumours of an Italian album too.

When in Italy, in 1968 his band was named Electric Heart and included Mick Brill (bs), Terry Slade (drms) and Chuck Fryers (keyb'ds, gtr). Slade had earlier played with **Jimmy Winston and The Reflections** and **Warren J.5**. He later went on to **Renaissance** and **Sunshine**. Fryers also played in **Warren J.5** and stayed in Italy with **The Sorrows**. Brill had been in Antonello Venditti and later played on Francesco DeGregori's *Theorius Campus* Italian-only album in 1972.

At the turn of the decade **Thane Russal** was assisted in Italy by another English band, Beggars Farm, who consisted: Bob Steel (keyb'ds, flute), Roger Munt(drms), Pete Dibbens(gtr) and Colin Gould (bs).

Security was a cover of the Otis Redding tune.

Compilation appearances have included: *Security* on *Perfumed Garden, Vol. 2* (LP & CD), *English Freakbeat, Vol. 4* (LP & CD) and *Twisted Teenage Screaming Fuzzbusters* (LP); *Your Love Is Burning Me* on *Voyage Through The Sugarcube* (LP & CD) and *Beat It* (3-CD); *Drop Everything And Run* on *Circus Days Vol. 3* (LP & CD); and *I Need You* on *English Freakbeat, Vol. 5* (CD) and *Echoes From The Wilderness - Sixteen UK R&B Freakbeat Trippers* (LP & CD). (VJ/GB)

Ray Russell Quartet

ALBUMS:	1	TURN CIRCLE	(CBS Realm 52586) 1968 SC
(up to	2	DRAGON HILL	(CBS Realm 52663) 1969 SC
1976)	3	RITES AND RITUALS	(CBS 64271) 1971 SC
	4	JUNE 11th 1971	(RCA SF 8214) 1971 SC
	5	SECRET ASYLUM	(Black Lion BLP 12100) 1973

A talented guitarist, **Ray Russell** played innumerable sessions in the sixties, seventies and beyond, as well as leading a jazz quartet and forming prog bands such as **Rock Workshop**, **Running Man** and **Mouse**. He also produced **Bill Fay**'s majestic 1971 album *Time Of The Last Persecution*, to which he contributed some truly stunning guitar work. (VJ/RMJ)

Rust

Personnel:	BRIAN HILLMAN		A
	WALT MONAGHAN	bs	A
	JONNY THOMAS		A

ALBUM: 1(A) COME WITH ME (Hör Zu SHZEL 59) 1969

NB: (1) only issued in Germany. (1) reissued on CD (Transcontinental).

A British psychedelic heavy rock pop trio, whose album was only released in Germany. Jonny Thomas was from Melbourne, in Australia, the other two were English. All the tracks are self-penned. Unfortunately the production is rather muddy and only some tracks are worth hearing: *You Thought You Had It Made*, *Delusion* and *Rust*. During the seventies, Walt Monaghan played with **Mick Abrahams** (1971/72), **If** (1972/74), **Bob Sargeant (1975)** and Ted Nugent (1979). (SR)

The Rustiks

Personnel:	DAVE GUMMER	bs	A
	WALLY MAINT	gtr	A
	JOE ROMAINE	drms	A
	ROB TUCKER	lead gtr, vcls	A

45s: What A Memory Can Do/Hello Anne (Decca F 11960) 1964
I'm Not The Loving Kind/Can't You See (Decca F 12059) 1965

This beat group from Paignton, Devon was signed up after winning a talent contest judged by Brian Epstein. He promised to record the winners and did so. Initially an instrumental band, they formed as The Vibros and were also known as The Fireballs before becoming **The Rustiks**. They did not prove to be the best of signings though. (MWh/JM)

Ruth

45s: Legs In The Wind/Society's Child (Columbia DB 8216) 1967
Cherish/
Until It's Time For You To Go (Columbia DB 8386) 1968

Ruth was a female pop singer. *Cherish* is an orchestrated ballad. The flip side is a Buffy St. Marie song. The 45 was produced by David Powell. (VJ)

Barry Ryan

ALBUMS:	1	SINGS PAUL RYAN	(MGM MGM-C(S) 8106) 1968 R1
	2	BARRY RYAN	(Polydor 583 067) 1969 SC
	3	ELOISE	(Polydor 2872 109) 1982

		HCP
45s:	Goodbye/I'm So Sad	(MGM MGM 1423) 1968 -
	Eloise/Love I Almost Found You	(MGM MGM 1442) 1968 2
	Love Is Love/	
	I'll Be On My Way Dear	(MGM MGM 1464) 1968 25
	The Hunt/Oh, For The Love Of Me	(Polydor BM 56348) 1969 34
	Magical Spiel/Caroline	(Polydor BM 56370) 1970 49
	Kitsch/Give Me A Sign	(Polydor 2001 035) 1970 37
	It Is Written/Annabelle	(Polydor 2001 154) 1971 -
	Can't Let You Go/	
	When I Was A Child	(Polydor 2001 256) 1971 32
	From My Head To My Toe/	
	Alimony Money Blues	(Polydor 2001 335) 1972 -
	I'm Sorry Susan/LA Woman	(Polydor 2001 362) 1972 -
	Do That/Summer's Over	(Dawn DNS 1109) 1975 -
	Where Were You/Making Do	(Private Stock PVT 70) 1976 -
	Brother/Life's So Easy	(Private Stock PVT 87) 1977 -
Reissue:	Eloise/Love Only Comes Tomorrow	(Polydor 2001 630) 1976 -
	Eloise/(Flip by different artist)	(Old Gold OG 9440) 1984 -

After several modest successes as a duo with his twin Paul, **Barry Ryan** went solo in 1968. See **Paul & Barry Ryan** entry for more information.

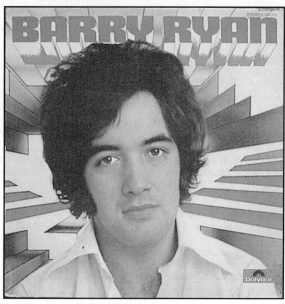

BARRY RYAN - Bary Ryan (LP).

Barry along with his brother, Paul, who were both identical twin sons of Marion Ryan, a fifties pop singer, were signed by Decca in 1965. With neat long hair and carefully selected fashionable clothes they were skilfully marketed by Decca although thankfully none of the slushy songs written for them (see **Paul and Barry Ryan** entry for details) met with much success. In 1968 **Barry Ryan** went solo and Paul took to songwriting. An early result of this new partnership was *Eloise*, a stunning single with its melodramatic vocal style and heavily orchestrated backing. This was certainly Barry's magnum opus and he soldiered on for several years after without achieving the same heights again.

Compilation appearances include: *There You Go* on *The Mod Scene* (CD), *Pop Inside The '60s, Vol. 2* (CD), *Sixties Lost And Found, Vol. 3* (LP) and *Sixties Explosion, Vol. 1* (CD); *Eloise* on *Brit Pop* (CD); *Gotta Go Out To Work* on *A Whiter Shade Of Pale* (LP); and *I Can't Make A Friend* on *Electric Sugar Cube Flashbacks* (CD). (VJ)

Kris Ryan and The Questions

Personnel:	STUART BRUBECK	bs	A
	JIMMY JEWELL	sax	A
	ALAN KENDALL	lead gtr	A
	KRIS RYAN	vcls	A
	GEOFF WILLS	drms	A

| EP: | 1(A) ON THE RIGHT TRACK | (Mercury 10024 MCE) 1965 R1 |

45s:	Miss Ann/She Told Me Lies	(Mercury MF 818) 1964
	Don't Play That Song/	
	If You Don't Come Back	(Mercury MF 832) 1964
α	Marie Marie/	
	I've Had Enough Of You Baby	(Mercury MF 852) 1965
α	Tell Me Who/She Belongs To Me	(Mercury MF 877) 1965

NB: α **Kris Ryan** solo efforts.

A male beat quartet from Manchester. When the band failed to take off **Ryan** recorded a couple of solo 45s, which were ballads, but these fared little better. *Don't Play That Song* is a Ben E. King number. The sax player Jim Jewell later played with **The Keef Hartley Band**, **McGuinness Flint**, **Gallagher and Lyle** and the first and second line-up of **Ronnie Lane's Slim Chance**. He also did session work for various artists, including **The Hollies** and is the featured sax player on *Love and Affection* by Joan Armatrading. (VJ/AD/CC)

Paul and Barry Ryan

| Personnel: | BARRY RYAN | vcls | A |
| | PAUL RYAN | vcls | A |

ALBUMS:	1	THE RYANS - TWO OF A KIND	
			(Decca LK 4878) 1967 R1
	2	PAUL AND BARRY RYAN	
			(MGM MGM-C (S) 8081) 1968 R1

HCP

45s:	Don't Bring Me Your Heartaches/		
	To Remind Me Of Your Love	(Decca F 12260) 1965	13
	Have Pity On The Boy/There You Go	(Decca F 12319) 1966	18
	I Love Her/Gotta Go Out To Work	(Decca F 12391) 1966	17
	I Love How You Love Me/		
	Baby I'm Sorry	(Decca F 12445) 1966	21
	Have You Ever Loved Somebody?/		
	I'll Tell You Later	(Decca F 12494) 1966	49
	Missy, Missy/Rainbow Weather	(Decca F 12520) 1966	43
	Keep It Out of Sight/Who Told You?	(Decca F 12567) 1967	30
	Claire/I'll Make It Worth Your While	(Decca F 12633) 1967	47
	Heartbreaker/Night Time	(MGM MGM 1354) 1967	-
	Pictures Of Today/Madrigal	(MGM MGM 1385) 1968	-

The Ryans were the identical twin sons of fifties pop singer Marion Ryan. Decca signed them in 1965 and carefully marketed them with neat long hair and carefully-selected fashionable clothes. Thankfully none of the slushy songs written for them met with much success, and in 1968 Barry went solo enjoying some success and Paul took to songwriting.

Keep It Out Of Sight later resurfaced on *Pop-In, Vol 1* (CD); *Pictures Of Today* has been compiled on *Pop-In, Vol 2* (CD) and *Madrigal* got a further airing on *Lovely Summer Days* (CD) and *Fading Yellow, Vol 1* (CD). (VJ)

Phil Ryan and The Crescents

Personnel:	BERNARD HIBBERT	vcls, gtr	A
	ROGER KEAYS	vcls, drms,	
		tenor sax	A
	DAVE MARTIN (DAVE BIRKENHEAD)	vcls, gtr, keyb'ds	A
	PHIL RYAN (PHILLIP RYLANCE)	vcls, drms, gtr	A

45s:	Mary Don't You Weep/Yes I Will	(Columbia DB 7406) 1964
	Gypsy Woman/	
	Be Honest With Yourself	(Columbia DB 7574) 1965 SC

A soul/beat group from Crewe, their records were produced by Norrie Paramor and engineered by Bob Barratt. The line-up remained the same throughout the group's life. They split during 1966.

They once backed **Cilla Black** and were frequent visitors to the Cavern and Iron Door in Liverpool. After they split, Phil Ryan moved to Germany after becoming a school teacher. Dave Martin (the same keyboard player who was with **The Times**) joined **Sandie Shaw** on keyboards six months before she won the Eurovision Song Contest and stayed with her for approximately four years. Eventually, in June 200 at the age of 53, he gained a degree in Music/Popular Music at Wolverhampton University and now lives in Stoke-on-Trent.

You'll also find *Gypsy Woman* on *R&B At Abbey Road* (CD). (VJ/DB)

Freddie Ryder

45s:	To Get Your Love Back/	
	A Little Thing Called Love	(Mercury MF 864) 1965
	Some Kind Of Wonderful/Slow Down	(Mercury MF 879) 1965
	Man Of The Moment/My Block	(Mercury MF 935) 1966
	Shadows (I Can't See You)/Airport	(Columbia DB 8335) 1968
	Worst That Could Happen/	
	World Of My Own	(Columbia DB 8427) 1968

Originally known as Freddie Self (he recorded one 45, *I Don't Cry/Why Should I* (Mercury MF 839) 1965) under that name. A Liverpudlian, he was a member of **The Fourmost**, when their vocalist Mike Milward was ill with leukaemia and he replaced him in the group for a week when Milward eventually died of the disease. He also worked with The Beatcombers, an early sixties instrumental group, and **The Trends**. *Some Kind Of Wonderful* was a Goffin-King composition and *Man Of The Moment* was a Greenaway/Cook number. (VJ)

Mal Ryder (and The Spirits)

Personnel incl: MAL RYDER

45s:	Cry Baby/Take Over	(Decca F 11669) 1963 SC
α	See The Funny Little Clown/	
	Slow Down	(Vocalion V 9219) 1964 R2
	Your Friend/Forget It	(Piccadilly 7N 35209) 1964 R1
α	Lonely Room/Tell Your Friend	(Piccadilly 7N 35234) 1965 SC

NB: α credited to **Mal Ryder**.

This was **Mal Ryder**'s band from early 1963 until mid-1965 when he formed **The Primitives**. The musical menu was pretty mundane R&B with *Forget It*, being one of their better efforts.

Compilation appearances have included: *Lonely Room* on *Piccadilly Story* (CD); *Forget It* on *Rare 60's Beat Treasures, Vol. 3* (CD) and *English Freakbeat, Vol. 4* (LP & CD); and *Your Friend* on *That Driving Beat* (CD). (VJ)

Park Sable and Jungle 'n' Beats

45:        Never Be Blue/Rave On   (Fontana TF 457) 1964 R1

An obscure, but quite collectable beat 45 with a rockabilly influence and lots of screams on *Never Be Blue*. (VJ)

The Sabres

Personnel incl: JOHN HUTTON   vcls   A
                    JIMMY KINGSLEY   drms   A
                    IAN NORMAN   bs, keyb'ds   A

45:        Roly Poly/Will You Always Love Me?   (Decca F 12528) 1966 SC

The Sabres came from Garndiffaith, a small mining community in what is now Torfaen, South Wales. A formidable covers band, they were well known and well respected on the Welsh and West of England circuit. Their 45 (which the band hated) was recorded after they'd won third place in a 'Melody Maker' contest, but it bombed and the group subsequently split. First place, in the contest, incidentally went to another Welsh band, **The Eyes Of Blue**.

It has previously been suggested that this act were related to **The Peeps**, but this is incorrect. (PW/VJ)

Sad People

45:        Lonely Man/Turn Around   (Chapter One CH 113) 1969

This was a male ballad duo. (MWh)

Sadie's Expression

45s: Deep In My Heart/My Way Of Loving   (Plexium PX 4) 1969
          Old Whitehall Number/Annie W   (Plexium PXM 13) 1970

This little known band recorded on the Plexium label.

Yesterday Was Such A Lovely Day (Elsie) has been compiled on *Nice* (LP). (MWh)

Saffron

ALBUMS: 1 SALISBURY PLAIN   (Mother Earth MUM 1001) 1974 R1
             2 FANCY MEETING YOU HERE
                                (Mother Earth MUM 1202) 1976 R2

NB: (2) reissued on Spectator in 1976.

45:        Charly/Come On Children   (Columbia DB 9040) 1974

Her real name is Saffron Summerfield. She started out as a solo folk artist in 1969 and had a spell with **Trader Horne** before resuming her solo career. In 1974, she formed her own Mother Earth label and recorded these two self-produced albums. All the material was original except for a cover of **The Beatles'** *Eleanor Rigby* on her second album. Another album appeared in Holland in the early seventies on Polydor.

Compilation appearances have included: *All Your Ambition* on *Electric Psychedelic Sitar Headswirlers, Vol. 3* (CD); and *Vision Is A Lonely Word* on *Electric Psychedelic Sitar Headswirlers Vol. 5* (CD). (VJ)

The Saffrons

45:        Give Me Time/
          Baby, Baby I Can't Let You Go   (Pye 7N 45236) 1973

This is a long forgotten early seventies act. (VJ)

Sagram

Personnel incl: CLEM ALFORD

ALBUM: 1 POP EXPLOSION SITAR STYLE
                              (Windmill WMD 118) 1972 R1

Clem Alford, who went on to record a couple of solo albums, was also a member of **Magic Carpet**, who released an acclaimed album of Eastern-influenced music the same year as this **Sagram** album. In fact the group was actually called Sargam. The budget label got the name wrong! **Clem Alford** was an excellent sitar player.

Heavenly Feeling can also be heard on *Electric Psychedelic Sitar Headswirlers, Vol. 2* (CD). (VJ)

Sailor

Personnel incl: GEORGE KAJANUS
                    (HULTGRIN)   bs, vcls   A
                    HENRY MARSH   gtr, keyb'ds, vcls   A
                    PHIL PICKETT   vcls   A
                    GRANT SERPELL   drms   A

                                            HCP

ALBUMS: 1(A) SAILOR   (Epic EPC 80337) 1974 -
(up to   2   TROUBLE   (Epic EPC 69192) 1975 45
1976)   3   THE THIRD STEP   (Epic EPC 81637) 1976 -

NB: (1) also isued in the US (Epic 33248) 1974. (2) also isued in the US (Epic 34039) 1975. (3) also isued in Holland (Epic EPC 81701) 1976. There's also a compilation *Greatest Hits* (Epic EPC 82754) 1978 and a CD, *Legacy - Greatest and Latest* (CMC CD6003-2)1996.

                                            HCP

45s: Traffic Jam/Harbour   (Epic EPC 2562) 1974 -
(up to   Blue Desert/Blame It On The Soft Spot (Epic EPC 2929) 1975 -
1976)   Sailor/Open Up The Door   (Epic EPC 3184) 1975 -
      α A Glass Of Champagne/Panama   (Epic EPC 3770) 1975 2
      β Girls, Girls, Girls/Jacaranda   (Epic EPC 3858) 1976 7
        One Drink Too Many/Melancholy   (Epic EPC 4804) 1976 35
        Stiletto Heels/Out Of Money   (Epic EPC 4620) 1976 -

NB: α also issued in the US (Epic 50194) 1976. β also issued in the US (Epic 50229) 1976. There was also a US 45 *Josephine Baker/Traffic Jam* (Epic 50094) 1975

Sailor's members had previously been in **Eclection**, **Gringo** and **Kajanus-Pickett**. **Kajanus** full name is Georg Johan Tjegodiev-Sakonski Kajanus. He was Norwegian. The first album is a pretty fine pop-novelty album. The drummer Grant Serpell had been in **The Ice** and **Affinity**. (VZ)

John St. Field

ALBUM: 1 CONTROL   (Movie Play) 1971 R4

NB: (1) was originally issued in Spain. It has been reissued on CD (Lost Vinyl LV-012) 1994 and (Cooking Vinyl - Cook 131 CD) 1997.

The above album, which only received a release in Spain originally, was the work of Scottish singer and guitarist Jackie Leven. Apparently, it was released after a period of intense experimentation with acid. The end result was a drug-inspired artistic album, which has been brought to a wider audience by virtue of CD releases in the nineties. Highlights include *I'm Always A Prinlaws Boy* , a song about a very poor working class area of a town called Leslie in which he lived as a child and *Raerona*, a song about a strange sprawling village he kept visiting in his sleep. (VJ/PL)

Barry St. John

ALBUM: 1 ACCORDING TO St. JOHN
                        (Major Minor MMLP/SMLP 43) 1969 R1

                                            HCP

45s: A Little Bit Of Soap/
        Thing Of The Past   (Decca F 11933) 1964 SC -
        Bread And Butter/Cry To Me   (Decca F 11975) 1964 SC -

Mind How You Go/			
Don't You Feel Proud	(Decca F 12111) 1965 SC -
Hey Boy/I've Been Crying	(Decca F 12145) 1965 SC -
Come Away Melinda/	
Gotta Brand New Man	(Columbia DB 7783) 1965 47
Everything I Touch Turns To Tears/	
Sounds Like My Baby	(Columbia DB 7868) 1966 R1 -
Cry Like A Baby/	
Long And Lonely Night	(Major Minor MM 587) 1968 -
By The Time I Get To Phoenix/	
Turn On Your Lovelight	(Major Minor MM 604) 1969 -

A female vocalist who scored a minor hit with her cover version of Tim Rose's *Come Away Melinda*. From Glasgow originally she sang in Hamburg's Star Club in the early sixties and returned there in 1965 when she was backed by **Bobby Patrick's Big Six**. In 1967 she married **Howie Casey**. Most of her recordings were either beat or ballads; *A Thing Of The Past* was a Shirelles song; *Bread And Butter* was the Newbeats song; *Mind How You Do* had been penned by **Chris Andrews**; *Cry Like A Baby* was the Box Tops track; *By The Time I Get To Phoenix* was done by Glen Campbell and *Hey Boy* was a Goffin-King number, produced by **Andrew Oldham**.

Bread And Butter has been compiled on *Original Liverpool Sound* (LP) and *Rare 60's Beat Treasures, Vol. 2* (CD). (VJ)

Bridget St. John

ALBUMS:	1	ASK ME NO QUESTIONS	(Dandelion 63750) 1969 R1
	2	SONGS FOR THE GENTLE MAN	
			(Dandelion DAN 8007/K 49007) 1971 R1
	3	THANK YOU FOR...	(Dandelion DAN 2310 193) 1972 R1
	4	JUMBLE QUEEN	(Chrysalis CHR 1062) 1974 SC

NB: (1) and (2) reissued on one CD, (See For Miles SEECD 408-D) 199? (3) reissued on CD with extra tracks (See For Miles SEECD 428-D) 199?. (4) reissued on CD (Beat Goes On BGOCD 260) 1995. An album released in 1995 called *Take The Fifth* (Road Goes On Forever RGF CD 026) includes unreleased material from 1975 to 1982, recordings made in Britain before she moved to the States and recorded with various groups of musicians over there. Seventeen songs in all are included, all of which are originals except one *Catch A Falling Star*.

| EP: | 1 | THE FIRST CUT | (Shagrat ENT 007 10") 1996 |

NB: A 10" EP with 4 tracks from **Bridget St. John**'s pre-Dandelion demo, plus one new track *Pig 'n' Peel*.

45s:	To Be Without A Hitch/Autumn Lullaby	(Dandelion K 4404) 1970
	If You've Got Money/Yep	(Warner Bros WB 8019) 1970
	Fly High/	
	There's A Place To Go/Suzanne (PS)	(Polydor 2001 280) 1972
	Nice/Goodbye Baby Goodbye	(Polydor 2001 361) 1972
	Passing Thru'/	
	The Road Was Lonely On My Own	(MCA MV 1203) 1973

A folkie who cut her teeth on the folk and college circuit prior to signing for John Peel and Clive Selwood's Dandelion label in 1969. Her debut album was the label's first release. Her best work is usually considered to be *Thank You For*, on which she was backed by **John Martyn** and members of **Quiver** and **Mighty Baby**. She stopped recording in 1974 and emigrated to the USA. Little has been heard of her since but she was a backing vocalist on **Mike Oldfield**'s *Anorak* album.

Another **Bridget St John** album was released in 1995 entitled *Take The Fifth*. It includes unreleased material from 1975 to 1982, recordings made both in Britain before she moved to the States and with various groups of musicians over there.

In 1996, *The First Cut* 10" EP compiled four tracks recorded in 1968, as demos for the Dandelion label, with a new song *Pig 'n' Peel*.

Compilation appearances have included: *The River, Song To Keep You Company, Night In The City* and *Lazarus* on *John Peel Presents Top Gear* (LP); *Fly High* and *Early Morning Song* on *Dandelion Rarities* (CD); and *Nice* on *Dandelion Sampler - 1969-1972* (CD). (VJ/NM)

Paul St. John

| 45: | Flying Saucers Have Landed/ | |
| | Spaceship Lover | (Pye 7N 45190) 1970 |

This is another obscure 45. (VJ)

Roy St. John

| ALBUM: | 1 | IMMIGRATION DECLARATION | (Caroline CA 2008) 1975 |

This US citizen spent considerable time living and gigging in the UK often as the band, **Phoenix**. Various personnel helped on the album, all British, but they included Mike Paice (hrmnca, sax) and Geraint Watkins (keyb'ds, accordion). On the musical menu, this is essentially pub-rock. (VJ)

St. Louis Union

Personnel:	TONY CASSIDY	vcls	A
	ALEX KIRBY	tenor sax	A
	KEITH MILLAR	gtr	A
	JOHN NICHOLS	bs	A
	DAVID TOMLINSON	organ	A
	DAVE WEBB	drms	A

			HCP
45s:	Girl/Respect	(Decca F 12318) 1966 SC 11
	Behind The Door/English Tea	(Decca F 12386) 1966 SC -
	East Side Story/Think About Me	(Decca F 12508) 1966 R2 -

This Manchester-based band whose dress was very mod won the Melody Maker Beat Contest in 1965, which led to them getting a contract from Decca. Their cover of **The Beatles**' *Girl* brought them initial Chart success, but when the follow-ups made little impression they quickly vanished from the scene.

Behind The Door was a pop-soul effort, whilst *East Side Story* achieved an unusual blend of freakbeat and soul.

Compilation appearances have included: *East Side Story* on *The Mod Scene* (CD), *The Seventh Son* (LP) and *Broken Dreams, Vol. 2* (LP); and *Behind The Door* on *Broken Dreams, Vol. 5* (LP). (VJ)

Crispian St. Peters

ALBUMS:	1	FOLLOW ME	(Decca LK 4805) 1966 R1
	2	SIMPLY.... CRISPIAN St. PETERS	
			(Square SQA 102) 1970 SC

NB: *The Anthology* (Repertoire REP 4608-WY) 1997 is a successful compilation of his hits, flops and album tracks.

SALLYANGIE.

726

EP: 1   ALMOST PERSUADED   (Decca DFE 8678) 1967 R1

                                                                HCP

45s: At This Moment/
           Goodbye, You'll Forget Me   (Decca F 12080) 1963 SC -
           No No No/Three Goodbyes   (Decca F 12207) 1965 SC -
           You Were On My Mind/
           What I'm Gonna Be   (Decca F 12287) 1965 2
           The Pied Piper/
           Sweet Dawn My True Love   (Decca F 12359) 1966 5
           Changes/My Little Brown Eyes   (Decca F 12480) 1966 47
           But She's Untrue/
           Your Ever Changin' Mind   (Decca F 12525) 1966 -
           Almost Persuaded/You Have Gone (Decca F 12596) 1967 -
           Free Spirit/I'm Always Crying   (Decca F 12677) 1967 -
           That's The Time/The Silent Times (Decca F 12761) 1968 -
           Carolina/That's Why We Are Through (Decca F 12861) 1968 -
           Monumental Queen/Soft As A Rose (Menlap MEN 002) 1969 -
    α   So Long/My Little Brown Eyes   (Decca F 13055) 1970 -
           Wandering Hobo/Love Love Love   (Square SQ 2) 1970 -
           Do Daddy Do/
           Every Time You Sinned   (Santa Ponsa PNG 17) 1974 -
           Carolina/Samantha   (Route RT 18) 1975 -
Reissues: You Were On My Mind/
           Glandular Fever (Traxter)   (Immediate IM 107) 1976 -
           The Pied Piper/You Were On My Mind (Virgin VS 342) 1980 -
           You Were On My Mind/
           The Pied Piper   (Old Gold OG 9203) 1982 -

NB: α withdrawn soon after release.

From Swanley, Kent, Peter Smith was this guy's real name and he first
came to attention with his cover of *You Were On My Mind*, which had been
a massive US hit for We Five. **St. Peters'** version reached No 2 in the UK
and he also enjoyed another big hit with the catchy *Pied Piper*. *Changes*
was a minor hit but most of his other recordings passed unnoticed.

The Anthology CD successfully tracks his career and his later attempts to
establish himself as a country and western entertainer. It came with
comprehensive sleevenotes from Chris Welch (of 'Melody Maker' at the
time).

Compilation appearances have included: *You Were On My Mind* on *20 Hits
Of The 60's* (CD), *Hits Of The Sixties - 20 Swinging Sounds* (CD), *60's
Love Songs* (CD), *Super Hits Of The 60s - Vol 2* (CD) and on *Remember
The 60's* (CD); and *The Pied Piper* on *Hits Of The 60's - Save The Last
Dance For Me* (CD), *Super Hits Of The 60s - Vol 1* (CD) and on *Hits Of
The 60's Vol 2* (CD). (VJ)

The St. Valentine's Day Massacre

Personnel: DEREK GRIFFITHS   gtr   A
            JON LORD   organ   A
            COLIN MARTIN   drms   A
            MALCOLM POOL   bs   A
            ART WOOD   vcls   A

45:     Brother Can You Spare A Dime/
        Al's Party (some PS)   (Fontana H 883) 1967

This was a later version of **The Artwoods** in 1967. The band wanted to
change their image and under this monicker they appeared in Bonnie and
Clyde style outfits with wide brimmed hats and pin stripe suits. The 45
flopped at the time and the group sank without trace but as so happens the
disc has now become rare and collectable, particularly the copies that
came in picture sleeves.

Jon Lord, of course, was later in **Deep Purple** and Whitesnake. Malcolm
Pool went on to play in Jon Hiseman's **Colosseum** and the **Don Partridge
Band**. Art Wood formed the short-lived **Quiet Melon** but then became a
graphic designer. Derek Griffiths played with the **Mike Cotton Sound**
before teaming up with former **Artwoods'** member **Keef Hartley** in **Dog
Soldier**. Griffiths was also later in **Satisfaction**.

Brother Can You Spare A Dime can also be heard on *Psychedalia - Rare
Blooms From The English Summer Of Love* (CD), *Rubble Vol. 16: Glass
Orchid Aftermath* (LP) and *Rubble Vol. 9* (CD). (VJ)

SAM APPLE PIE - Sam Apple Pie (LP).

The Saints

ALBUMS: 1   SAINTS (10" LP)   (MJB BEV 73/4) 1964 R4
          2   SAINTS ALIVE   (MJB BEVLP 127/8) 1964 R4

Both of these were private pressings and consequently are now extremely
expensive collectors' items. **The Saints** were a beat group clad in leather
waistcoats and white shirts. (VJ)

Bob Saker

45s: Still Got You/Imagination   (Polydor 56231) 1968
          Foggy Tuesday/Ooh Nana Na   (Parlophone R 5740) 1968

He also recorded as **Saker**. (VJ)

Saker

45s: Hey Joe/Constantly   (Parlophone R 5752) 1969 SC
          What A Beautiful World/City Of The Angels   (CBS 7010) 1971
          Even Though We Ain't Got Money/
          Wild Winds Are Blowing   (CBS 7399) 1971

Also recorded as **Bob Saker**. (VJ)

Salamander (1)

45:       Crystal Ball/Billy   (CBS 5102) 1970 SC

This 45 was recorded by **Onyx** using a different name. (VJ)

Salamander (2)

Personnel: A.B. BENSON   organ, vcls   A
            DAVE CHRISS   bs   A
            JOHN COOK   drms   A
            DAVE TITLEY   gtr, ld vcls   A

ALBUM: 1(A) TEN COMMANDMENTS (Youngblood SSYB 14) 1970 R3

This is a different band whose concept album is based on the Ten
Commandments. Each track deals with a different commandment. The
album, which was produced by **Miki Dallon**, was dominated by Bob
Leaper's orchestral arrangement, but there are also some good melodies,
strong vocals and organ work and powerful drumming. The best tracks are

those where the orchestral arrangements are more discreet:- *He Is My God*, on which the melody sounds like **King Crimson** in places; *Images*, which featured strong vocals, good drumming and organ work; the mellow and melodic *People* and *False Witness*, a good progressive piece with some fine guitar leads and powerful organ. (CA)

Sallyangie

Personnel:	MIKE OLDFIELD	gtr, vcls	A
	SALLY OLDFIELD	vcls	A

ALBUMS:	1(A)	CHILDREN OF THE SUN		
			(Transatlantic TRA 176) 1968 R1	
	2(A)	BEYOND A SONG	(Pilgrim PL 11) 1982	

NB: (1) reissued on Transatlantic (TRA 176) 1973 with a different cover (SC) and on CD by Line (TACD 900586) 1989. (1) reissued again as a 2-CD set (Castle CMDDD 545) in a slipcase that contains the original album and a second disc full of previously unreleased material.

45s:	Two Ships/Colours Of The World	(Big T BIG 126) 1969 SC
	Child Of Allah/Lady Go Lightly	(Philips 6006 259) 1973 SC

This folk duo with his older sister Sally provided **Mike Oldfield** with his first musical outing on vinyl. After an album and 45, in 1969, he left to play guitar and bass with **Kevin Ayers and The Whole World** before recording *Tubular Bells* in the studio, which became his magnum opus. His sister Sally continued her career as a folk singer and enjoyed some commercial success in 1979 with her 45, *Mirrors*.

The *Children Of The Sun* album remains a classic period piece of early recordings by the duo. It was produced by Shel Talmy who gave it a gentle contemporary British folk feel.

Compilation appearances include: *Lady Mary* on *The Electric Lemonade Acid Test, Vol. 2* (LP) and *Two Ships* on *The Transatlantic Story* CD box set. (VJ)

Sam Apple Pie

Personnel incl:	DAVE CHARLES	drms	A
	ANDY JOHNSON	gtr	ABC
	MIKE JOHNSON	ld gtr	A
	BOB RENNIE	bs	ABC
	SAM SAMPSON	vcls	ABC
	DENNY BARNES	gtr	B
	LEE BAXTER HAYES	drms	BC
	TINKERBELL SMITH	gtr	C

ALBUMS:	1(A)	SAM APPLE PIE	(Decca LK-R/SKL-R 5005) 1969 R2
	2(B)	EAST 17	(DJM DJLPS 429) 1973 SC

SAM APPLE PIE - East 17 (CD).

NB: (1) was pirated a few years back and officially reissued on CD (Repertoire REPUK 1017) 2004 with both sides of their two singles as bonus tracks and housed in a digipak with a detailed booklet.

45s:	Tiger Man/Sometime Girl	(Decca F 22932) 1969
	Call Me Boss/Old Tom	(DJM DJS 274) 1973

This blues-rock outfit came from the Walthamstow area of London.

Their debut album is competent heavy-duty blues-rock and the 2004 CD reissue includes mono versions of both sides of their Decca 45. They can also be heard on *Broken Dreams, Vol. 6* (LP) singing *The Hawk*, a 12-bar mid-tempo boogie. They split up in 1974, but reformed the following year. (VJ)

Sammy

Personnel:	KEITH GEMMELL	sax	A
	MIKE HODGKINSON	organ, vcls	A
	GEOFF SHARKEY	ld gtr, vcls	A
	PAUL SIMMONS	bs	A
	MICK UNDERWOOD	drms	A

ALBUM:	1(A)	SAMMY	(Philips 6308 136) 1972 SC

45s:	Goo Ger Woogie/Big Lovin' Woman	(Philips 6006 227) 1972
	Sioux-Eyed Lady/70 Days	(Philips 6006 249) 1972

This rock band was formed by Mick Underwood (previously of **Episode Six**, **The Herd** and **Quatermass** and later of Raw Glory) in 1972. There's lots of experience in this line-up. Keith Gemmell had been in **Audience** and was later in **The Roy Young Band** and **Stackridge**. Geoff Sharkey was in **Ginhouse**. Mike Hodgkinson and Paul Simmons were also members of **The Roy Young Band** and Hodgkinson had played with **Billy J. Kramer**. Their album was produced by Ian Gillan (of **Deep Purple**) and Louie Austin. The album cover features a colourful picture of an Indian squaw. (VJ)

Samson

Personnel:	IAN KEWLEY	keyb'ds, vcls	A
	EZ (LES) OLBINSON	bs, percsn	A
	JOHN PRITCHARD	trumpet	A

ALBUM:	1(A)	ARE YOU SAMSON?	(Instant INSP 004) 1969 R1

NB: Instant was a short-lived spin-off from **Andrew Oldham**'s Immediate label. (1) reissued on CD (Castle Music CMRCD 064) 2001 with detailed sleevenotes and a bonus track.

45:	Venus - Bringer Of Love And Peace/	
	Wool And Water	(Parlophone R 5867) 1970

Their concept progressive album came with various images of Victor Mature on the sleeve for no apparent reason. The band included Ian Kewley, who was subsequently involved with Paul Young and lived in a large house near the sea in Birchington, Kent. Musically it blends progressive rock with heavy psychedelia. The vocals are quite melodic and the instrumentation is a little spooky at times.

Both sides of their 45 were self-penned. Kewley and Olbinson went on to **Strider** and Pritchard joined **Trifle**. (VJ/JM)

Samuel Prody

Personnel:	JOHN BOSWELL	drms, vcls	A
	STEPHEN DAY	bs	A
	TONY SAVVA	gtr, vcls	A
	DEREK SMALLCOMBE	gtr, vcls	A

ALBUM:	1(A)	SAMUEL PRODY	(Phonogram 6306 906) 1971 R2

NB: (1) issued on Global in Germany in 1973, and reissued (Full Moon FM 69101) 1997, in a limited edition of 300 copies.

A short-lived blues-rock band, whose heavy and freaky album attracts rather more interest today than it did at the time. (VJ)

Samurai (1)

Personnel:			
KENNY BEVERIDGE	drms	A
JOHN EATON	bs	A
TONY EDWARDS	gtr, vcls	A
DAVE LAWSON	gtr, vcls	A
LENNIE WRIGHT	drms, perc	A

ALBUM: 1(A) SAMURAI   (Greenwich GSLP 1003) 1971 R3

NB: (1) reissued on vinyl (Dr. Prog LP 7103 DRPR) and on CD with five bonus tracks.

A heavy progressive band whose album, which is fairly similar to **King Crimson**, was released on this minor label. In addition to the line-up above, session men Don Fay and Tony Edwards assisted on sax and woodwind respectively. The music has some strong melodies, solid guitar and powerful vocals.

Beveridge, Eaton, Edwards, Lawson and Wright had all previously been with **The Web** and Dave Lawson was later in **The Alan Bown Set** and **Greenslade**. He now does TV work. Edwards went on to **Kilburn and The High Roads**. (VJ/JM)

Samurai (2)

Personnel incl:			
MIKI CURTIS	vcls, flute	A
JOE DUNNET	gtr	A
HIRO IZUMI	gtr, koto	A
JOHN REDFERN	organ	
TETSU YAMAUCHI	bs	A
MIKE WALKER	vcls, piano	A
GRAHAM SMITH	hrmnca	A
YUJI HARADA	drms	A

ALBUM: 1(A) GREEN TEA   (Phillips FX-8517) 1970

NB: (1) Japanese only release. (1) reissued on CD (Japanese PCD 155).

45:    Good Morning Starshine/
       Temple Of Gold   (United Artists UP 2242) 1969

Thanks to Hitomi Ishikawa for pointing out that this act was a different bunch to the act on Greenwich. This **Samurai** were from Japan, but came to Europe in November 1967, and recorded the above 45 whilst in the UK. Miki Curtis, the leader of the group, was the first Japanese ever to sing rock and roll in that country - the press labelled him "the howling mad dog".

SAMUEL PRODY - Samuel Prody (LP).

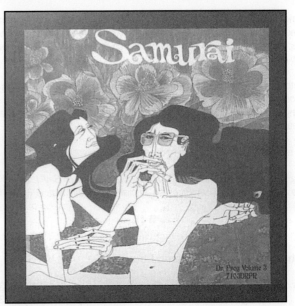

SAMURAI (1) - Samurai (LP).

He and Mike Walker were best friends when Walker was working in Tokyo as a Japanese-speaking journalist. Together they devised the idea of a rock band made up of Japanese, American and British players to achieve an unique sound that blended Eastern and Western musical influences. Walker became the band's manager, as well as one of its members. The 'B' side of their 45 is named after a famous temple in Kyoto, and the band had other releases in Japan (where the 45 was known as "Japanese Bands London Recording"), and an album on Metronome in Germany.

Their *Green Tea* album is reputedly a very strong effort sounding very much like **Andwellas Dream**/early **Traffic**. Standout cuts include the title track and the 9:47min *Four Seasons*, which is full of crashing guitar and Hammond organ.

The band may have also released another earlier album in 1969 (Phillips FX-8511).

Tetsu Yamauchi later played with **Free** and **The Faces**. Miki Curtis is still a well-known actor and singer in Japan. Mike Walker is the gossip columnist for America's biggest weekly, the National Enquirer. (VJ/HI/JSn/MW)

Alex Sanders

ALBUM: 1 A WITCH IS BORN   (A&M AMLS 984) 1970 R3

Alex Sanders was the most powerful witch and high priest in Britain. This album, which was released in a gatefold sleeve with a sticker on the cover saying "Record suitable for adults only" was rapidly withdrawn by A&M record company executives after its release and is consequently horrendously rare and obscure. The record consists of the initiation of a new member into the coven. (VJ)

Chris Sandford

Personnel: CHRIS SANDFORD   vcls

			HCP
45s:	Not Too Little - Not Too Much/		
	I'm Lookin	(Decca F 11778) 1963	17
α	You're Gonna Be My Girl/		
	Don't Leave Me Now	(Decca F 11842) 1964	-
	I Wish They Wouldn't Always Say I Sound Like		
	The Guy From The U.S.A. Blues/		
	Little Man, Nobody Cares	(Fontana TF 633) 1965	-
β	Listen To The Music/		
	The Man Who Lost His Smile	(Decca F 13348) 1972	-
χ	I'll Be Up Your Way Next Week/		
	My Love Is Going On The Rocks	(DJM DJS 10318) 1974	-

NB: α with The Coronets. β as Chris Sandford Friendship. χ as Chris Sandford Rag 'n' Bone Band.

Chris Sandford first caught the public eye as an actor on 'Coronation Street', that durable TV soap, in the early sixties. He cut his first 45, which was a minor hit, in 1963 and was backed on the second by The Coronets, who included Mitch Mitchell.

By the time of his funny **Donovan** spoof *I Wish They Wouldn't Always Say I Sound Like The Guy From The USA Blues* in 1965 he was working as a dee-jay on pirate radio (Caroline). This is worth a spin and also got a US release.

He resurfaced with various ad-hoc outfits in the seventies.

You can also check out *I Wish They Wouldn't Always Say I Sound Like The Guy From The USA Blues* on *English Freakbeat, Vol. 5* (LP & CD). (VJ)

Johnny Sandon (and Remo Four)

45s:			
α	Lies/On The Horizon	(Pye 7N 15542)	1963 SC
α	Magic Potion/Yes	(Pye 7N 15559)	1963 SC
	Sixteen Tons/The Blizzard	(Pye 7N 15602)	1964
	Donna Means Heartbreak/		
	Some Kinda Wonderful	(Pye 7N 15665)	1964
	The Blizzard/Legend In My Time	(Pye 7N 15717)	1964

NB: α credited to **Johnny Sandon and Remo Four**.

Sandon started out as frontman for **The Searchers** but then used **The Remo Four** as his backing group to record a couple of Merseybeat 45s. His later solo efforts were in a more country and western vein... ugh! *Sixteen Tons* was the 'Tennessee' Ernie Ford classic and *Some Kinda Wonderful* was a Joe Tex soul track.

You can also check out *Lies* on *Mersey Beat* (2-LP), *Mersey Beat 1962-1964* (2-LP) and *Beat Merchants* (CD). (VJ)

Sands (1)

Personnel:	NIGEL BALDWIN	drms	A
	BOB FREEMAN	gtr	A
	IAN McLINTOCK	bs	A
	JOHN STANELY	ld gtr	A
	PAUL STEWART	vcls	A

45s:	α	Mrs Gillespie's Refrigerator/		
		Listen To The Sky	(Reaction 591 017)	1967 R4

NB: α has had a limited repressing of 500 (Reaction 591 017) reproduced from the original French jukebox release with a large centre hole.

Originally known as The Tridents, this Middlesex act first recorded as **The Others**, but their finest moment was tucked away on the 'B' side to their first 45. *Listen To The Sky* commences in a pleasant but innocuous pop style but develops into a psychedelic haze with wailing siren sound effects before concluding with an interpretation of Holst's *Mars* from *The Planet Suite*. Mindblowing stuff and strongly recommended. Needless to say the 45 is particularly rare and expensive to purchase. The disappointing 'A' side was written by **Robin** and **Barry Gibb**.

Freeman and McLintock formed the duo **Sun Dragon** in 1968.

Compilation appearances include: *Listen To The Sky* on *Perfumed Garden, Vol. 1* (LP & CD), *Electric Sugar Cube Flashbacks, Vol. 4* (LP), the 4-CD *Nuggets II* box set and on the 4-CD box set *Acid Drops, Spacedust & Flying Saucers*; whilst *Mrs. Gillespie's Refrigerator* re-emerged on *We Can Fly, Vol 1* (CD) and *Beat It* (3-CD). (VJ)

Sands (2)

45:	Venus/Cara Mia	(Major Minor MM 681)	1970 SC

This single was by a different band from Ireland.

Sands (3)

Personnel incl:	FRAN BYRNE	drms	A
	TONY KENNY	vcls	A
	MURTY QUINN	vcls	A

45s:	Lend Me A Helpin' Hand/Sound Is Music	(RCA RCA 2136)	1971
	Salvation Sally/She Is Me	(RCA RCA 2210)	1972

These 45s were made by a Dublin showband. *Salvation Sally* was written by Steve Foley, a Machurian ex-cabaret star who once played with Irish progressive band Feather. The second 45 came out in late May 1972 but one week later the band decided to the drop the 'A' side in favour of the 'B' side *She Is Me*. This features the lead singer Tony Kenny.

Sands were formed a few years earlier by some deserted Miami showband members. Up until December 1972 **Sands** had two lead singers Kenny and Quinn. Fran Byrne was their drummer for five years. (VJ)

Davey Sands and The Essex

Personnel:	HOWARD ALEXANDER	lead gtr	ABC
	IAN BARRY	drms	A
	CHRIS DARYL	organ	ABC
	PETER JAMES	bs	AB
	DAVEY SANDS	vcls	ABC
	IAN WARNER	drms	BC
	LEN HAWKES	bs	C

45s:	Please Be Mine/All The Time	(Decca F 12170)	1965 SC
	Advertising Girl/Without You I'm Nothing	(CBS 202620)	1967 SC

A beat group who won a contest in 'Record Mirror' which got them a one-off deal with Decca. Ian Barry was born on 11 May 1943 in Karachi, India (as it was then), the remaining four were Londoners.

Barry left after the first 45 and Ian Warner replaced him. Shortly after, Peter James was replaced on bass by Len Hawkes.

After their demise **Sands** went on to session work and became a touring member of The Pipkins. Len Hawkes joined **The Tremeloes**. (VJ/JM)

Tony Sands and The Drumbeats

Personnel incl:	TONY SANDS		A

45:	Shame Shame Shame/		
	I Got A Feeling	(Studio 36 NSRS EP 1/22)	196? R3

This is a very valuable record on an extremely rare label. The 'A' side is a Jimmy Reed song, on the flip is the Ricky Nelson hit. (VJ)

PERFUMED GARDEN VOL. 1 (LP) including Sands.

The Sands of Time

Personnel:	DAVID BOOKER	gtr	A
	RON BROWN	drms	A
	PETE DURHAM	piano	A
	TOMMY McQUARTER	bs	A

45s:	Where Did We Go Wrong/		
	When I Look Back	(Pye 7N 17140) 1966	
	One Day/Every Time We Say Goodbye	(Pye 7N 17236) 1967	
	Spanish Harlem/		
	Love Found A Way To My Heart	(Pye 7N 17341) 1967	

Formed in Ealing in 1962. They were originally known as **The Four Macs** becoming **The Sands Of Time** in 1964. Jackie Trent saw them in a cabaret show in Manchester and introduced them to her husband Tony Hatch, who was a songwriter/producer for Pye at the time. This led to a recording contract. Musically they played harmony beat/ballads. Their final 45, *Spanish Harlem* was the Leiber/Stoller classic which was made famous by Ben E. King and Aretha Franklin.

Compilation appearances have included: *Where Did We Go Wrong* and *Love Found A Way To My Heart* on *Ripples, Vol. 1* (CD); and *Spanish Harlem* on *Ripples, Vol. 4* (CD). (VJ)

Bobby Sansom

45s:	Lady One And Only/		
	Handbags And Gladrags	(Decca F 13104) 1970	
	I Believe In Music/		
	The Valley Of The Shadows Of Tears	(Decca F 13151) 1971	

These were solo efforts by **Bobby Sansom** who in the sixties had fronted The Giants. (VJ)

Bobby Sansom and The Giants

Personnel:	TREVOR DUPLOCK	gtr	A
	MICK GRIMWADE	bs	A
	JOHN HILLS	drms	A
	BOBBY SANSOM	vcls	A
	BILL SMITH	lead gtr	A

45s:	There's A Place/Lucille	(Oriole CB 1837) 1963 SC
	Where Have You Been?/	
	Do You Promise	(Oriole CB 1888) 1963 SC

An early sixties act from Brighton, Sussex. They played rock and R&B. They played The Cavern in Liverpool and The Star Club in Hamburg during 1963 and 1964. They also toured extensively in Europe with acts like Jerry Lee Lewis and Johnny and The Hurricanes. *Lucille* was a Little Richard oldie and *There's A Place* was a **Beatles**' song. **Bobby Sanson** later went solo. (VJ/TD)

Saraband

ALBUM:	1 CLOSE TO IT ALL	(Folk Heritage FHR 050) 1973 SC

45:	This Moment/I'm Your Man	(Folk Heritage FHR 051) 1973

This is a gentle folk-rock 45. The 'A' side is a **Mike Heron** song. There's some pleasant woodwind on it. Both sides of this 45 and *Close To It All*, which it seems was originally intended as the 'A' side, appear on their album on Folk Heritage entitled *Close To It All*. (MWh)

Bob Sargeant

ALBUM:	1 FIRST STARRING ROLE	(RCA LPLI 5076) 1975

45:	Situation/Waiting Game	(RCA LPBO 5038) 1974

These were solo outings by this former **Junco Partners**, **Everyone** and **Mick Abrahams Band** member. His album was partly produced by **Mick Ronson**. (VJ)

Peter Sarstedt

ALBUMS:	1	PETER SARSTEDT (mono/stereo)	
(up to		(United Artists (S)ULP 1219) 1969 SC	
1976)	2	AS THOUGH IT WERE A MOVIE	
		(United Artists UAL 29037) 1969 SC	
	3	EVERY WORD YOU SAY	
		(United Artists UAS 29247) 1971 SC	

NB: Also relevant is *The Very Best Of Peter Sarstedt* (Object OR 0014) 1987.

HCP

45s:	I Must Go On/Mary Jane	(Island WIP 6028) 1968 R1 -
(up to	I Am A Cathedral/Blagged	(United Artists UP 2228) 1968 -
1976) α	Morning Mountain/	
	Step Into Candlelight	(United Artists UP 2262) 1969 -
	Where Do You Go To?/	
	Morning Mountain	(United Artists UP 2262) 1969 1
	Frozen Orange Juice/	
	Arethusa Loser	(United Artists UP 25895) 1969 SC 10
	As Though It Were A Movie/	
	Take Off Your Clothes	(United Artists UP 35041) 1969 -
	Without Darkness/	
	Step Into Candlelight	(United Artists UP 35075) 1969 -
	Every Word You Say/	
	What Makes One Man Feel	(United Artists UP 35369) 1972 -
	Tall Tree/Mellowed Out	(Warner Brothers K 16575) 1975 -
Reissues:	Where Do You Go To?/	
	Morning Mountain	(United Artists UP 355580) 1974 -
	Frozen Orange Juice/	
	Arethusa Loser	(United Artists UP 35895) 1975 -
	I Am A Cathedral/Blagged	(United Artists UP 36059) 1976 -
	English Girls/ Where Do You Go To?/	
	Frozen Orange Juice	(United Artists BP 396) 1981 -
	Where Do You Go To?/	
	Frozen Orange Juice	(Old Gold OG 9365) 1983 -

NB: α Unissued.

Peter Sarstedt set out as a solo artist enjoying a No 1 hit with *Where Do You Go To My Lovely?* in 1969. He drew on some folk roots but added a decidedly pop-conscious feel to his recordings, often with brassy orchestrations. He enjoyed a further Top Ten hit with *Frozen Orange Juice* the same year. His albums sound dated now, but were clearly aimed at both underground and mainstream audiences at the time. (VJ)

Robin Sarstedt

HCP

45s:	My Resistance Is Low/		
(up to	Love While The Music Plays	(Decca F 13624) 1976 3	
1976)	Let's Fall In Love/		
	So Long Lonely Nights	(Decca F 13662) 1976 -	
	Sitting In Limbo/Love Is All I Need	(Decca F 13677) 1976 -	

When the **Sarstedt Brothers** split up in September 1973 Clive Sarstedt recorded as **Robin Sarstedt** and achieved a No 3 hit with the Hoagy Carmichael song *My Resistance Is Low*. He continued to record quite extensively in subsequent years. (VJ)

The Sarstedt Brothers

Personnel:	CLIVE SARSTEDT	vcls	A
	PETER SARSTEDT	vcls, gtr	A
	RICHARD SARSTEDT	vcls	A

ALBUM:	1(A)	WORLDS APART TOGETHER	
		(Regal Zonophone SRZA 8516) 1973 SC	

45s:	Chinese Restaurant/		
	Beloved Illusions	(Regal Zonophone RZ 3081) 1973	
	Why Don't We Call It Quits/		
	Run Of Bad Luck	(Regal Zonophone) 1973	

This pop trio made up of hit-making brothers got together in 1973 to tour and record. Peter had enjoyed a No 1 UK hit with *Where Do You Go To My Lovely?* in 1969, followed by *Frozen Orange Juice*, which got to No 10 later the same year. Richard, born in Delhi, India on 29 March 1942, had worked as Eden Kane and was an UK teen idol in the era before **The Beatles**. His hits included *Well I Ask You* (No1, 1961), *Get Lost* (No 8, 1961), *Forget Me Not* (No 3, 1961), *I Don't Know Why* (No 7, 1962) and *Boys Cry* (No 8, 1964).

After they split in September 1973 they resumed their solo careers. Peter moved to the USA and recorded and toured there. Clive went on to record as **Robin Sarstedt**. He had a UK hit with the old Hoagy Carmichael song *My Resistance Is Low* (No 3, 1976) after meeting Carmichael in 1975. (JM)

Sasperella

45:         Spooky/Come Inside   (Decca F 12892) 1969

A one-off 45 covering the Classics IV US hit *Spooky*, which seems to have passed largely unnoticed. The five-piece group came from the North of England. (VJ)

Sassafras

Personnel:	TERRY BENNETT	vcls, perc	ABCDE
	RALPH EVANS	gtr, vcls	ABCDE
	RICKY JOHN HOLT	bs, vcls	ABC E
	ROB REYNOLDS	drms	A
	DAI SHELL	gtr	ABCDE
	BOB JONES	drms	B E
	CHRIS SHIRLEY	drms, vcls	CD
	STEVE FINN	bs, vcls	D

ALBUMS: 1(A/B) EXPECTING COMPANY   (Polydor 2383 245) 1973 SC
(up to   2(C) WHEELIN' AND DEALIN'   (Chrysalis CHR 1076) 1975
1976)   3(E) RIDING HIGH   (Chrysalis CHR 1100) 1976
NB: (2) and (3) reissued on one CD (Gott GOTTCD 026).

45s: Oh My Don't It Make You Want To Cry/
        Kansas City Wine   (Polydor 2058 497) 1974
        Wheelin' And Dealin'/Moonshine   (Chrysalis CHR 2063) 1975
        Small Town Talk/Long Shot Lover   (Chrysalis CHR 2098) 1976

A Welsh band who played a sort of boring boogie rock rather similar to **Status Quo** in this era. Ricky John Holt was born in Preston, Lancashire on 9 March 1950. He'd previously been with **Blonde On Blonde**. Ralph Evans, born in Cardiff on 6 June 1949, was last with Thank You. Terry Bennett, born on 3 November 1948 in Nottingham, was a former cabaret artist who had been in Exit. Bob Reynolds soon left and was replaced by

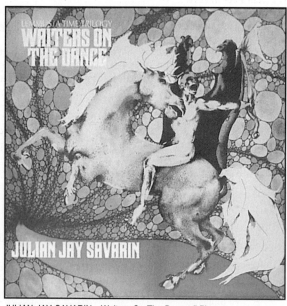

JULIAN JAY SAVARIN - Waiters On The Dance (LP).

ex-**Love Sculpture** drummer Bob 'Conga' Jones. Jones and Reynolds both featured on their debut album *Expecting Company*.

Jones left soon after and Chris Shirley came in on drums and vocals for the Polydor 45. Holt then left in August 1974 and Steve Finn (ex-Universe) replaced him. The band switched to Chrysalis and released the *Wheelin' and Dealin'* album - the title track was also put out on 45. Dick Raven played as a session drummer on this album. They appeared on 'The Old Grey Whistle Test' and toured extensively with **Stackridge**, Black Oak Arkansas, American Gypsy, **Ace** and **Ten Years After**.

Finn left in April 1975 and Shirley departed to **Hobo** sometime after. Ricky John Holt and Bob Jones both rejoined the band. The *Riding High* album and *Small Town Talk* 45 followed. Bennett eventually left to join Kracatoa which later included Ray Phillips from **Budgie**.

They toured relentlessly during the seventies and built up quite a loyal following but never made the big time. Live versions of *Wheelin' 'n' Dealin'* and *I Am The Walrus* can be heard on *Over The Rainbow - The Last Concert Live!* (Chrysalis CHR 1079) 1975.

A later line-up released a self-titled US album in 1978. (VJ/JM)

The Sassenachs

Personnel incl: NORMAN McGARRY   drms   A

45:       That Don't Worry Me/All Over You   (Fontana TF 518) 1964 SC

This Liverpool band's main claim to fame was the inclusion of the original **Searchers**' drummer Norman McGarry who was replaced by **Chris Curtis** before they made it onto vinyl. Prior to forming **The Sassenachs** McGarry had replaced **Ringo Starr** in **Rory Storm and The Hurricanes**.

The Sassenachs' sole 45 was a pretty routine beat/R&B offering. (VJ)

Satisfaction

Personnel:	JOHN BEECHAM	trombone	A
	MIKE COTTON	trumpet, flugal horn	A
	DEREK GRIFFITHS	gtr, vcls	A
	BERNIE HIGGINSON		
	(aka BYRNES)	drms, vcls	A
	LEM LUBIN	bs	A
	NICK NEWELL	sax, flute, vibes	A

ALBUM: 1(A) SATISFACTION   (Decca SKL 5075) 1971 R2

45s: Love It Is/Cold Summer   (Decca F 13129) 1971
        Don't Rag The Lady/Gregory Shan't   (Decca F 13207) 1971

This short-lived progressive-rock band is most notable for including **Mike Cotton**, who'd earlier had his own band **Mike Cotton Sound** in the early sixties. The band was formed by **Cotton** and Griffiths after **Lucas and The Mike Cotton Sound** split. Derek Griffiths had previously been in **The Artwoods** and **The St. Valentine's Day Massacre** and was also in **Dog Soldier**. All the remaining members had also been in **Zoot Money's Music Band**. Newell also worked with **The Keef Hartley Band**.

Their album is a brassy progressive effort. When they split, Griffiths went to **Alan Bown**. **Cotton** and Beecham went to session work, both also recorded and toured with **The Kinks**. Newell joined **Zoot Money's Big Roll Band** and Lubin headed for **Christie**. (VJ/JM)

Saturnalia

Personnel:	ALETTA	vcls	A
	TOM CROMPTON	drms	A
	ADRIAN HAWKINS	vcls	A
	RICHARD HOUGHTON	bs	A
	ROD ROACH	gtr	A

ALBUM: 1(A) MAGICAL LOVE   (Matrix TRIX 1) 1969 R2
NB: (1) reissued with same catalogue number in 1973 (SC) and again (Akarma AK 267) in both vinyl and CD format.

This picture disc album is now quite rare and sought-after by collectors. It was originally issued with a booklet and ticket. There were also a small number of test pressings on black vinyl which are particularly rare (R2). On offer is West Coast influenced psychedelia with fine female vocals and some searing guitar work. It was produced by **Keith Relf**. The album was also reissued in the same picture disc format in 1973. The Akarma reissue is an exact reproduction on picture disc vinyl with a booklet and extensive photos. The CD release on Akarma is housed in a mini card album style CD sleeve.

Adrian Hawkins and Rod Roach had earlier been in **Horse**. Roach later went into production work. (VJ)

Julian Jay Savarin

Personnel:	JOHN DOVER	bs	A
	NIGEL "ZED" JENKINS	gtr	A
	JO MEEK	vcls	A
	ROGER ODELL	drms	A
	JULIAN JAY SAVARIN	keyb'ds	A

ALBUM: 1(A) WAITERS ON THE DANCE
(Some w/insert) (Birth RAB 2) 1973 R3

NB: (1) Reissued on vinyl (Five Hours Back TOCK 002) in 1987 and again more recently (Akarma AK 161), in both vinyl and CD formats.

45: α I Am You/Kizeesh (Lyntone LYN 3426) 197?

NB: α issued as a Corgi Books sampler.

Savarin had written, directed and played on **Julian's Treatment**'s 1970 double concept album *A Time Before This*, which is worth checking out. By contrast I found *Waiters On The Dance* a tedious organ-led progressive. It's only saving grace being the vocals of Lady Jo Meek. It was apparently based on the book 'Lemmus, A Time Trilogy - Waiters On The Dance', which **Savarin** had written. **Savarin** was a poet and writer, as well as a musician. Avoid!

Odell came from **CMU** and **Meek** also had a solo career. (VJ)

Savoy Brown

Personnel:	RAY CHAPPELL	bs	A
	BOB HALL	piano	ABC
	LEO MANNINGS	drms	A
	JOHN O'LEARY	hrmnca	A
	BRICE PORTIUS	vcls	A
	KIM SIMMINDS	gtr	ABCDEFG H I J
	MARTIN STONE	gtr	A
	ROGER EARL	drms	BCDE
	RIVERS JOBE	bs	B
	DAVE PEVERETT	gtr, vcls	BCDE
	CHRIS YOULDEN	vcls	BCD
	TONE STEVENS	bs	CDE
	DAVE BIDWELL	drms	F G H
	PAUL RAYMOND	keyb'ds	F G H I
	ANDY PYLE	bs	F G H I
	DAVE WALKER	vcls	F G H
	ANDY SILVESTER	bs	G
	RON BERG	drms	I
	JACKIE LYNTON	vcls	I
	MILLER ANDERSON	gtr, vcls	J
	ERIC DILLON	drms	J
	JIMMY LEVERTON	bs	J
	STAN WEBB	gtr, vcls	J

HCP

ALBUMS:	1(A)	SHAKE DOWN		
		(mono/stereo)	(Decca LK/SKL 4883) 1967 R1	-
	2(B)	GETTING TO THE POINT		
		(mono/stereo)	(Decca LK/SKL 4925) 1968 R1	-
	3(C)	BLUE MATTER		
		(mono/stereo)	(Decca LK/SKL 4994) 1969 R1	-

SAVOY BROWN - Looking In (LP).

	4(D)	A STEP FURTHER		
		(mono/stereo)	(Decca LK/SKL 5013) 1969 R1	-
	5(D)	RAW SIENNA		
		(mono/stereo)	(Decca LK/SKL 5043) 1970 R1	-
	6(E)	LOOKING IN	(Decca SKL 5066) 1970 SC	50
	7(G)	STREET CORNER TALKING	(Decca TXS 104) 1971 SC	-
	8(G)	HELLBOUND TRAIN	(Decca TXS 107) 1972 SC	-
	9(H)	LION'S SHARE	(Decca SKL 5152) 1973 SC	-
	10(I)	JACK THE TOAD	(Decca TXS 112) 1973 SC	-
	11(J)	BOOGIE BROTHERS	(Decca SKL 5186) 1974 SC	-
COMPS:	12(-)	BLUES ROOTS	(Decca ROOTS 7) 1978	-
	13(-)	BEST OF	(Decca TAB 39) 1982	-
	14(-)	HIGHWAY BLUES	(See For Miles SEE 45) 1985	-

NB: (2) - (10) released on Parrot in the US. (11) released on London in US. US-only releases included: - *Wire Fire* (London PS 659) 1975, *Skin'n'Bone* (London PS 670) 1976, *Best Of* (London 50000) 1977, *Savage Return* (London PS 718) 1978, *Rock 'n' Roll Warrior* (Capitol 7002) 1981, and *The Best Of Savoy Brown* (C5 503) 1987, also on CD (C5 C5CD 504) In 1990. (1), (2) and (3) reissued on CD (Deram 820 921-2 -923-2 respectively) 1990. (4), (5), (6) and (8) reissued on CD (Deram 844 015-2, 016-2, 017-2 and 019-2 respectively) 1991. (3) and (4) reissued on one CD (BGO BGOCD 678) 2005. (5) and (6) reissued on one CD (BGO BGOCD 666) 2005. (11) reissued on CD (Deram 8454 022-2) 1992.

Also relevant is *Best Of Savoy Brown* (C5 C5CD 504) 1990, *Doin' Fine... An Anthology* (Deram 828 567-2) 1992 and *The Savoy Brown Collection* (2-CD) (Decca 8443 282) 199? There are some live CDs; *Archive Alive: Live At The Record Plant 1975* (Archive ACH 80014) *1998*, which is a US import release presenting a batch of radio shows in the style of the 'King Biscuit Flower Hour'. *Looking From The Outside - Live '69/'70* (Mooncrest CREST CD 051 Z) 2000, *Jack The Toad - Live '70/'72* (Mooncrest CREST CD 052 Z) 2000 and *Bring It Home* (Vickery Music 54213 2) 2000, which is available as a US import. *Hellbound Train 1969-1972* (2-CD) (Castle CMDDD 670) includes live material from this era when they were at their prime.

45s:	α	I Tried/Can't Quit You Baby	(Purdah 45-3503) 1966 R3
	α	Taste And Try Before You Buy/	
		Someday People	(Decca F 12702) 1967 SC
		Walking By Myself/Vicksburg Blues	(Decca F 12797) 1968
		Train To Nowhere/Tolling Bells	(Decca F 12843) 1969 SC
		I'm Tired/Stay With Me Baby	(Decca F 12978) 1969 SC
		A Hard Way To Go/	
		Waiting In The Bamboo Grove	(Decca F 13019) 1970 SC
		Poor Girl/Master Hare	(Decca F 13098) 1970
		Tell Mama/Let It Rock	(Decca F 13247) 1971
		So Tired/The Saddest Feeling	(Decca F 13372) 1973
		Coming Down Your Way/I Can't Find You	(Decca F 13431) 1973

NB: α credited to **Savoy Brown Blues Band**.

Savoy Brown are a prime example of a British band, who achieved enormous popularity in the States whilst attracting little attention at home.

Formed in 1966 in London they were part of the British blues boom. They were originally known as **The Savoy Brown Blues Band** and recorded four songs for Purdah (two of which were put out on a 45, which is now rare), before signing to Decca.

Kim Simmonds was the only ever present member in an ever-changing line-up and his brother Harry was the band's manager in those early days. After recording *Shake Down*, which was confined to a strictly blues format, Martin Stone departed to join **The Action** and **Mighty Baby** and Leo Mannings left to form the **Brunning Sunflower Blues Band**. **Chris Youlden** also replaced Brice Portius on vocals for the follow-up *Getting To The Point*.

Their finest moment is usually considered to be *Train To Nowhere* from the *Blue Matter* album, which augmented their earlier blues format with brass. Thereafter, with the British blues boom past its prime, the group's sound veered towards a kinda boogie-based rock with blues overtones. Having made little impression in the UK they also looked increasingly towards the US where constant touring brought them considerable success. By now Bob Hall had left to join Leo Mannings in the **Sunflower Blues Band** and after the release of the *Raw Sienna* album **Chris Youlden** also left to go solo recording two albums for Deram. The album mixed traditional blues with brassy material in the Blood, Sweat and Tears mould. Usually appearing on stage in a bowler hat and monacle (and later in topper and tails) **Youlden** had been the central tenet of their stage show in the late sixties. This role next fell to Dave Peverett for the *Looking In* album, but this album is marred by too much clumsy jamming. In December 1970 Peverett, Earl and Stevens all left to form **Foghat** and Kim Simmonds had to assemble an entirely new line-up (F). They embarked on a long US tour on which they were a bigger draw than **Rod Stewart** and **The Faces** and **The Grease Band**. This line-up (with some modifications) continued to record albums, which enjoyed considerable success in the US but passed largely unheralded in Britain.

After the release of Lion's Share, vocalist Dave Walker departed for **Fleetwood Mac** and Dave Bidwell died of a heroin overdose. Simmonds next vocalist, Jackie Lyndon, had been a sorta coffee bar rocker in the early sixties. This line-up (I) recorded *Jack The Toad* and lasted until January 1974. Then Simmonds put together yet another line-up (J) featuring three lead guitars. By now Simmonds had moved the entire operation to the US and three US-only releases were recorded in the mid-seventies with Ian Ellis (ex-**Clouds**) on bass and Tom Farnell (briefly of **Fairport Convention**) on drums.

Both the Decca and See For Miles compilations concentrate on their finer moments from their most successful 1968-71 period. The latter compilation has the bonus of detailed sleeve-notes from Roger Dopson. The C5 compilation covers the whole of their career with Decca from 1967-1974. It includes many of their finest moments like *Highway Blues, Hellbound Train* and *Train To Nowhere*.

A trio of CDs of live material were issued in 2000. Of these *Jack The Toad* was recorded in Canada.

Back in 1969 they appeared on Decca's *World Of Blues Power!* (LP) sampler singing *Taste And Try Before You Buy* and *Someday People* and they returned on *Vol. 2* (LP) of the same series the following year with *Don't Turn Me From Your Door* and *She's Got A Ring In His Nose, And A Ring On Her Hand*. *Train To Nowhere* also appears on *Wowie Zowie! World Of Progressive Music* (LP). More recently *Broken Dreams, Vol. 6* (LP) has given *Taste And Try Before You Buy, Someday People* and *Walking By Myself* a further airing and *Money Can't Save Your Soul* has been compiled on the 3-CD box set *Ars Longa Vita Brevis: A Compendium Of Progressive Rock 1967-1974*.

Dave Peverett died from cancer on 7 February 2000. Simmonds is still on the road with a version of the band in the States. (VJ)

Tom Sawyer

45:     Cookbook/Gates   (CBS 4243) 1969

This was former **Unit Four Plus Two** vocalist Tommy Moeller recording under a pseudonym. (VJ)

Mike Sax and The Idols

Personnel:	GRAHAM BAILEY	drms, vcls	A
	MIKE SAX	ld vcls, gtr	A
	RAY SAX	bs, vcls	A
	JOHN SYKES	ld gtr, vcls	A

45:     My Little One/Come Back To Me   (Mercury MF 886) 1965

This beat group came from Lancashire (Mike, Ray and Graham came from Rossendale and John from Bury). The group were originally called Mike Sax and The Vikings, with Mike, Ray, John and various other drummers. Graham joined them from The Beatmakers, and shortly after they had a publishing contract with DIX music and Harold Frantz; and a recording contract with Phillips, under the Mercury subsidiary.

They had no success with recording, although *My Little One*, was 'tip for the top' on Radio Caroline. The band, which also released a 45 as **The Idols**, folded in 1967 after a three month stint in Italy, with **The Casuals** and **The Riot Squad**. (VJ/GB)

Leo Sayer

				HCP
ALBUMS:	1	SILVERBIRD	(Chrysalis CHR 1050) 1973	2
(up to	2	JUST A BOY	(Chrysalis CHR 1068) 1974	4
1976)	3	ANOTHER YEAR	(Chrysalis CHR 1087) 1975	8
	4	ENDLESS FLIGHT	(Chrysalis CHR 1125) 1976	4

NB: (1) reissued on CD (RMG Universal Music AHL CD 34) 1996 and again (RPM RPM SB 1001) 2002 with both sides of the 1972 **Patches** single and **Sayer**'s spoken reminiscences added. (2) reissued on CD (RMG Universal Music AHL CD 34) 1996 and again (RPM RPM SB 1002) 2002 with bonus tracks and **Sayer**'s spoken reminiscences. (3) reissued on CD (Festival D20013) 1998 and again (RPM RPM SB 1003) 2002 with bonus tracks and **Sayer**'s spoken reminiscences. (4) reissued on CD (RMG Universal Music AHL CD 35) 1996. Compilations include *The Very Best Of Leo Sayer* (Chrysalis CHR 1222) 1979, *Leo Sayer* (Pickwick 8030) 1980, *The Very Best Of Leo Sayer* (CD) (Chrysalis CCD 1222) 1979, *The Definitive Hits Collection* (CD) (Universal Music TV 5471152) 1999 and *Original Gold* (2-CD set) (Disky HR 857702) 1999.

			HCP
45s:	Why Is Everybody Going Home/		
(up to	Quicksand	(Chrysalis CHS 2014) 1973	-
1976)	The Show Must Go On/Tomorrow	(Chrysalis CHS 2023) 1973	2
	One Man Band/Drop Back	(Chrysalis CHS 2045) 1974	6
	Long Tall Glasses/In My Life	(Chrysalis CHS 2052) 1974	4
	Moonlighting/	(Chrysalis CHS 2076) 1975	-
	Let It Be/Another Year	(Chrysalis CHS 2080) 1975	-
	You Make Me Fell Like Dancing/		
	There Is Someone Else	(Chrysalis CHS 2119) 1976	2
Reissue:	Moonlighting/ Long Tall Glasses	(Old Gold OG 9689) 1987	-

Leo Sayer was born on 21 May 1948 at Shoreham-on-Sea. Whilst an art school student in Sussex he fronted The Terraplane Blues Band in the late sixties. He later moved up to London and worked as an illustrator supplementing his income by working as a street busker and playing in local folk clubs.

In 1971, he formed **Patches** with drummer Dave Courtney (who'd played with pop singer Adam Faith). Courtney sought Faith's assistance in promoting **Patches** but Faith was unimpressed with them. He did, however, elect to promote **Sayer** and decided to promote him as a solo artist. With Courtney doing the writing **Sayer** set about recording some solo material at **Roger Daltrey**'s studio. His first effort *Why Is Everybody Going Home* missed out, but the follow-up, the invigorating *The Show Must Go On* (which he appeared on 'Top of The Pops' in a clown's costume to promote) gave him a UK No 1! (**Sayer** was denied a US hit because Three Dog Night covered it and themselves achieved a chart-topping hit in the States with the song). The clown image lasted into 1974 when he decided to end it following an American tour.

His first album *Silverbird* features some delightful string arrangements and poignant lyrics dealing with alienation, confusion, betrayal and more. His second *Just A Boy* was a more coherent album with **Sayer**'s voice more prominent and to promote it there was a complete change of image - he wore a suit called the 'Great Gatsby' his then wife Janice had designed, which was white with piping. It spawned two UK hit singles *One Man Band* and *Long Tall Glasses*, which went on to give **Sayer** his first US Top Ten hit in early 1975.

Another Year was his final UK-based album and his working relationship with Courtney also ended during the recording of this album. It spawned another big hit *Moonlighting* and *I Will Not Stop Fighting* and *Unlucky In Love* were sensitive ballads. Six months later **Sayer** relocated to the States and working with Ray Parker Jnr and producer Richard Perry and **Ringo Starr**'s co-writer Vini Poncia he soon became an international superstar.

While his cover of **The Beatles** *Let It Be* may have been unwise, 1976 saw him reach No. 2 in the UK and achieve a US No. 1 with the disco-oriented *You Make Me Feel Like Dancing*, which suited the times perfectly. His follow-up *When I Need You* topped the charts on both sides of the Atlantic. Both singles were culled from the *Endless Flight* album, which was co-written with ex-**Supertramp** member Frank Furrell.

A string of hits followed *How Much Love*, *Thunder In My Heart* (the title cut of his fifth album), *I Can't Stop Loving You (Though I Try)* and, he commenced the eighties, with a UK and US No. 2 *More Than I Can Say*, although this would prove to be his last big US hit single. His final US hit was *Living In A Fantasy* in 1981. His last UK Top Ten hit was 1982's *Have You Ever Been In Love*, but he went on to achieve modest commercial success with *Heart (Stop Beating In Time)* (1982), *Orchard Road* and *Till You Come Back To Me* (1983) and *Unchained Melody* (1986). By the late eighties he was without a recording contract and self-financing his UK tours, but following a legal dispute with his former manager Adam Faith he received reportedly well over £600,000 in lost royalties. In 1990 he attempted a revival with a new album *Cool Touch* but the punters weren't interested.

Recently **Leo Sayer**, now aged 57 and based in Australia, has staged a remarkable comeback, topping the UK charts with DJ Meck's *Thunder In My Heart Again* (a remix of his 1977 hit *Thunder In My Heart*). DJ Meck is a UK dance mixer who found the original version of the song whilst browsing in a second hand LA record shop. He loved the track and contacted **Sayer** about releasing it and the rest is history! (VJ)

Scaffold

Personnel:	MIKE McGEAR	vcls	ABC
	ROGER McGOUGH	vcls	ABC
	JOHN GORMAN	vcls	BC
	GERRY CONWAY	drms	C
	HELEN COX	vcls	C
	LOL CREAM	"gysmo"	C
	OLI HOUSAL	gtr	C
	BRIAN JONES	sax	C
	JOHN MEGGINSON	piano	C
	ZOOT MONEY	keyb'ds	C
	DAVE RICAHRDS	bs	C
	FRANK RICOTTI	perc	C
	ANDY ROBERTS	gtr	C
	ROB TOWNSEND	drms	C

ALBUMS:	1(A)	AN EVENING WITH THE SCAFFOLD		
		(mono/stereo)	(Parlophone PMC/PCS 7051)	1968 SC
	2(B)	LILY THE PINK		
		(mono/stereo)	(Parlophone PMC/PCS 7077)	1969 SC
	3(B)	FRESH LIVER	(Island ILPS 9234)	1973 SC
	4(C)	SOLD OUT	(Warner Bros K 56097)	1975

NB: There are also three compilations of interest: *Singles A's & B's* (See For Miles SEE CM 114) (LP) 1982; *The Best Of The Scaffold: The Songs* (EMI CDP 7 98502 2) 1992; and *The Best Of The EMI Years* (CD) (CDEMS 1436) 1992. *At Abbey Road: 1966-1971* (EMI 496 4352) 1998 includes all their hits and misses plus seven previously unissued tracks.

EP:	1	Lily The Pink/Thank U Very Much/Do You Remember/		
		Gin Gan Goolie	(EMI EMI 2690)	1977

				HCP
45s:	2 Day's Monday/3 Blind Jellyfish	(Parlophone R 5443)	1966	-
	Goodbat Nightman/			
	Long Strong Black Pudding	(Parlophone R 5548)	1966	-
	Thank U Very Much/Ide B The First	(Parlophone R 5643)	1967	4
	Do You Remember/Carry On Krow	(Parlophone R 5679)	1968	34
	1-2-3/Today	(Parlophone R 5703)	1968	-
	Lily The Pink/			
	Buttons On Your Mind	(Parlophone R 5734)	1968	1
	Charity Bubbles/Goose	(Parlophone R 5784)	1969	-
	Gin Gan Goolie/Liver Birds	(Parlophone R 5812)	1969	38

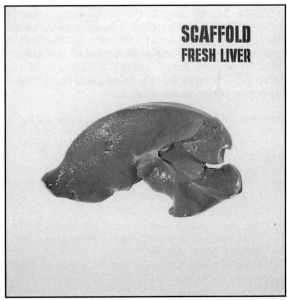

SCAFFOLD - Fresh Liver (LP).

	All The Way Up/Please Sorry	(Parlophone R 5847)	1970	-
	Busdreams/			
	If I Could Start All Over Again	(Parlophone R 5866)	1970	-
	Do The Albert/Commercial Break	(Parlophone R 5922)	1971	-
	Liverpool Lou/Ten Years After On			
	Strawberry Jam	(Warner Bros WB K 16400)	1974	7
	Mummy Won't Be Home For Christmas/			
	The Who Wind Is Blowing	(Warner Bros WB K 16487)	1974	-
	The Leaving Of Liverpool/			
	Pack Of Cards	(Warner Bros WB K 16521)	1975	-
	Wouldn't It B Funny/Mr. Noselighter	(Bronze BRO 33)	1976	-
	How Do You Do/Paper Underpants	(Bronze BRO 39)	1977	-
Reissue:	Lily The Pink/Do You Remenber/			
	Thank U Very Much	(EMI EMI 2085)	1973	-

This very individual trio formed in Liverpool in the mid-sixties. **McGough** was one of the country's top poets and **McGear** was found to be **Paul McCartney**'s younger brother. They gigged a lot at arts festivals and colleges in their early days and were signed to Parlophone in 1966. Their first two 45s flopped but they developed a merry singalong style which brought them massive hits with *Thank U Very Much* and *Lily The Pink*. In 1973 they joined up with some ex-members of the **Bonzo Dog Doo Dah Band** and other assorted odd characters in **Grimms**. **McGear** also cut a solo album produced by his brother **Paul McCartney** and **Roger McGough** made one too - featuring his poetry set to music - for Island in 1979 and **McGough and McGear** recorded an album together in 1968, originals of which, are extremely rare.

Reg Dwight (aka **Elton John**) is said to have been a session musician on *Lilly The Pink*.

The See For Miles compilation compiles all their 'A' and 'B' sides. The EMI CD set ten years later included most of the same material with a couple of album tracks substituted for the **Lennon/McCartney** produced *Liverpool Lou* 45.

Various artists compilation appearances include: *Do You Remember?*, *Yellow Book* and *Carry On Crow* on *Top Of The Pops No. 178* (LP), *Thank U Very Much* and *Lily The Pink* on the 2-CD set *Greatest Hits Of The 60's Vol 4*; *Do You Remember?* on *Beat Generation - Ready Steady Go* (CD) and *Charity Bubbles* on *Colour Me Pop, Vol 3* (CD). (VJ/MM/DK)

Scenery

Personnel:	MILLER ANDERSON		A
	IAN HUNTER (PATTERSON)		A
	JOHN VERNON SMITH	drms	A

A 1967 act who recorded a 45, *Thread Of Time/To Make A Man Cry* (France Impact 20.018) 1967, also released in Japan (Columbia LL-2258-IM). The A side also appears on the *Clap Hands Daddy Please* (LP) and *Red With Purple Flashes* (LP) compilations. It was recorded at

Regent Sound in Denmark Street, London with Bill Farley. *Thread Of Time* was probably a Bill Farley track credited to the band, but *To Make A Man Cry* is definitely a **Hunter/Anderson** collaboration. Johnny Banks (of **The Merseybeats**) played drums because band member John Vernon Smith was not at the sessions. Johnny Gustafson is reported to be a session musician on the recording as well. The picture sleeve for the single in both countries pictures **Hunter**, **Anderson** and Smith.

Thread Of Time can also be heard on *Jagged Time Lapse, Vol 3* (CD). (JP)

Schadel

ALBUM: 1   SCHADEL NUMBER 1   (United Artists UAS 29114) 1970

45s:		
	Stop Where You Are/	
	One Touch Of Your Hand	(Parlophone R 5509) 1966
	Flower Shop Girl/Man In The Making	(Parlophone R 5584) 1967
	With The Sun In My Eyes/	
	Goodbye Thimble Mill Lane	(Pye 7N 17528) 1968
α	Needle And Thread/	
	Little Red Watering Can	(United Artists UP 35113) 1970

NB: α both sides from the LP.

Schadel was an Australian who settled in Britain in late 1966. He was also briefly a member of **The Ivy League** during 1967/8. Future **Rolling Stones** guitarist Mick Taylor plays on the album, which is not recommended.

His final 'B' side, *Goodbye Thimble Mill Lane* also appears on *Paisley Pop - Pye Psych (& Other Colours) 1966-1969* (CD). (VJ/HK)

Janne Schaffer

ALBUM: 1   THE CHINESE   (Vertigo 6360 107) 1974

Schaffer was guitarist with **Rabbit** who recorded this instrumental album in which he displays his excellent guitar playing capabilities. The album is largely jazzy guitar and progressive with some flute and keyboards in evidence, some tracks are rhythms and blues influenced and there are some hard-rock moments. He was actually Swedish and I've left the entry in to make people aware of that. He played in Abba's backing band at one time. (BS/CG/VJ)

Schubert

45:	She Was A Woman/	
	Green Green Boy	(Major Minor MM 663) 1969

This was a folk 45. (VJ)

Schunge

Personnel:	ROY BABBINGTON	bs	A
	JEFF CLYNE	bs	A
	BARRY DE SOUZA	drms	A
	DAVE MACRAE	keyb'ds	A
	BOB RICARDO	vcls	A
	HAIM ROMANO	gtr, bouz	A
	SCHUNGE	gtr, vcls	A
	CHRIS SPEDDING	gtr	A

ALBUM: 1(A)   BALLAD OF A SIMPLE LOVE
                    (Regal Zonophone SLRZ 1033) 1972 SC

45s:	Misty/Joseph Demanio	(Regal Zonophone RZ 3066) 1972
	Ballad Of A Simple Love/	
	Enter The Violins	(Regal Zonophone RZ 3077) 1973

On the album **Mr. Schunge** gets backing from the cream of UK studio musicians to underscore his singer/songwriter ambitions with not too convincing results. Most tracks are about as average as you can get. More

often than not he reminds us of **Al Stewart**, but without the latter's drive and conviction. The very slyly arranged *Only A Midnight Train* is quite nice, though. It's a very long road from here to, say **Nick Drake** unfortunately. (MK)

Science Poption

Personnel:	OLA BRUNKERT	drms	A
	CLAES DIEDEN	vcls, gtr	A
	ANDERS GELLNER	vcls, gtr	A
	BJRN STOLT	vcls, bs	A
	ROGER WALLIS	vcls, gtr	A

45:	You've Got Me High/Back In Town	(Columbia DB 8106) 1967 R2

45s:	You're So Good/Back In Town	(Columbia DS 2301) 1966
(Swedish)	You've Got Me High/	
	Someone Will Come	(Columbia DS 2322) 1967

This Swedish band included one token Englishman, Roger Wallis, and consequently is a marginal case for inclusion here. Their rare U.K. single is now a significant collectable, culled as it is from two of their six Swedish 45s issued between 1966-67. The 'A' side is rather interesting - harmony pop vocals laced with strangely inappropriate backing. The flip side is orchestrated pop and utilises backing singers.

Ola Brunkert later went on to fame and fortune with Abba!!

You can also find *You've Got Me High* on *Rubble Vol. 14: The Magic Rocking Horse* (LP), *Rubble Vol. 8* (CD) and *The Best Of Rubble Collection Vol. 1* (CD). (VJ/MK/AO)

The Score

45:	Please Please Me/Beg Me	(Decca F 12527) 1966 R3

This band was responsible for an unusual cover of **The Beatles**' earlier classic, *Please Please Me* with chiming guitars, feedback, the lot. Not surprisingly it is now sought-after by collectors of this genre and is also very rare. The song borrows a few riffs from *Shapes Of Things* and *Satisfaction* along the way.

Compilation appearances include: *Beg Me* on *The Mod Scene* (CD) and *Yellow Elektric Years* (LP); and *Please Please Me* on *Rubble, Vol. 5 - The Electric Crayon Set* (LP), *Rubble, Vol. 3* (CD), *Chocolate Soup For Diabetics, Vol. 2* (LP) and *The Freakbeat Scene* (CD). (VJ)

The Scots of St. James

Personnel:	DIEGO DANALAISE	bs	AB
	ALAN KELLY	drms	AB
	GRAHAM MAITLAND	gtr	ABC
	HUGHIE NICHOLSON		A
	JIMMY OAKLEY	vcls	ABC
	OWEN 'ONNIE' McINTYRE		BC
	NORRIE MacLEAN	drms	C
	STEWART FRANCIS	bs	C

45s:	Gypsy/Tic Toc	(Go AJ 111404) 1966 R3
	Timothy/Eiderdown Clown	(Spot JW 1) 1967 R2

A Glasgow band originally known as The In Crowd. The debut 45 was a version of Ben E. King's *Gypsy*. After a second pop-psych 45 *Timothy* they toured Germany where they went down well, but by then there was a growing schism between Jimmy Oakley and the rest of the band and when he was ousted they changed name again to **Hopscotch** adding former **Dream Police** vocalist Hamish Stuart as a replacement for Oakley, who recorded one solo 45, *Little Girl* (United Artists) 1968 the following year. Graham Maitland was later in **Five Day Rain** and **Glencoe**.

Their first flip side, *Tic Toc*, was covered by Little Billy Dean on a 45 for Strike in 1967.

Compilation appearances include: *Tic Toc* on *Justification* (LP) and *Purple Pill Eaters* (LP & CD); *Timothy* on *Rubble, Vol. 11* (CD) and *The Best Of Rubble Collection, Vol. 5* (CD); and *Eiderdown Clown* on *Circus Days, Vol. 6* (CD) and *Incredible Sound Show Stories, Vol. 2* (LP). (VJ)

Nicky Scott

45s: Big City/
Everything's Gonna Be Alright (Immediate IM 044) 1967 SC
Backstreet Girl/Chain Reaction (Immediate IM 045) 1967 R1
Honey Pie/No More Tomorrow (Pye 7N 17688) 1968

This little known solo artist was managed by Simon Napier-Bell. *Backstreet Girl* was a **Jagger**/Richard composition. *Chain Reaction* was a **Twice As Much** song. This 45 was produced by **Mick Jagger** and **Andrew Oldham**. His final 'A' side *Honey Pie* was a **Lennon/McCartney** composition from the 'white' album.

Compilation appearances have included: *Backstreet Girl* on *Immediate Single Collection, Vol. 1* (CD); *Big City* on *Immediate Single Collection, Vol. 4* (CD); and *Everything's Gonna Be Alright* on *Immediate Single Collection, Vol. 5* (CD). (VJ)

Pete Scott

ALBUMS: 1 DON'T PANIC (Rubber RUB 003) 1971
         2 JIMMY THE MOONLIGHT (Rubber RUB 020) 1976

These are very rare, though as yet not expensive, folk-rock albums (there were almost certainly others) which were released on a small Newcastle-based label. The *Jimmy The Moonlight* album featured musicians connected with bands like **Lindisfarne**, **Prelude** and Whippersnapper. Fans of the genre rate these albums highly. (VJ)

Robin Scott

ALBUM: 1 WOMAN FROM THE WARM GRASS
           (w/insert) (Head HDLS 6003) 1969 R4

NB: (1) reissued on CD (Sunbeam SBRCD 009) 2006 with detailed sleevenotes.

45: The Sailor/The Sound Of Rain (Head HDS 4003) 1969

Croydon native **Scott** was at art college with Malcolm McLaren and Vivienne Westwood. His album, which is basically folk-rock with psychedelic touches, is very rare and much sought-after. On it he is backed by members of **Mighty Baby**. The 45, like the album, was produced by Sandy Robertson. **Robin Scott** later had hits with 'M', including the US number one *Pop Muzik*. (VJ/RMJ)

Simon Scott and The Leroys

Personnel: LENNY BROOKS gtr A
            MIKE BURGESS lead gtr A
            TONY COOK bs A
            MICKEY PORTER drms A
            SIMON SCOTT vcls A

                                              HCP
45s: α Move It Baby/
         What Kind Of Woman (Parlophone R 5164) 1964 37
      α My Baby's Got Soul/Midnight (Parlophone R 5207) 1964 -
      β Tell Him I'm Not Home/
         Heart Cry (Parlophone R 5298) 1965 SC -
         Brave New World/I'm The Universe (Polydor 56355) 1969 -
         Bethlehem/Every Mother's Son (Polydor 56364) 1969 -

NB: α Shown as by Simon Scott and The Leroys. β Shown as by Simon Scott and The All Night Workers.

Scott came to the UK from Darjeeling in India in 1962. He had dark good looks and when Parlophone signed him two years later he was the subject of a massive publicity campaign based around his good looks. *Move It Baby* was a minor hit, but his career never took off and he quickly became

an expensive flop. On the third Parlophone 45 **Goldie and The Gingerbreads** provided backing vocals.

Move It Baby can also be heard on *Rare 60's Beat Treasures, Vol. 3* (CD). (VJ/JM)

Screw

Personnel: NICK BROTHERHOOD drms AB
            PETE HOSSELL vcls, hrmnca AB
            ALISTAIR KINEAR gtr A
            STAN SCRIVENER bs AB
            CHRIS TURNER hrmnca, vcls AB
            GRAHAM gtr B

Managed by **The Rolling Stones**' 1969 tour manager Sam Cutler, this South London blues-rock band were given an early afternoon slot on **The Rolling Stones**' legendary Hyde Park concert in 1969. The best possible start a band could wish for. Eulogised in Richard Neville's book on the Underground, 'Play Power', they had a stunning show involving blood capsules and a twin harmonica attack. Inevitably though, like so many bands from this era, demos were cut, the main Underground clubs played and then nothing. "They played like they were disappearing through a meat grinder" as Neville so eloquently put it. (JN)

Scrubbers

Personnel incl: GREG RIDLEY
                 TIM HINCKLEY
                 STEVE MARRIOT

NB: The CD *Scrubbers* (Repertoire REP 4603-WP) 1996 available on German import compiles their material.

This excellent project, which comprised the three above artists and others, dates from 1974. (PM)

Scrugg

Personnel: PETE CLIFFORD lead gtr A
            CHRIS DEMETRIOU (aka CHRIS DEE) organ A
            JOHN KONGOS vcls A
            JACK RUSSELL bs, vcls A
            HENRY SPINNETTI drms A

45s: α Everyone Can See/I Wish I Was Five (Pye 7N 17492) 1968 SC
         Lavender Popcorn/Sandwichboard Man (Pye 7N 17551) 1968 R1
         Will The Real Geraldine Please Stand Up/
         Only George (Pye 7N 17656) 1969 SC

NB: α 'B' side by **John Kongos**.

This band derived from a group called The Echoes who had backed **Dusty Springfield** in South Africa, until she had been deported for refusing to play to segregated audiences. They returned to England with **John Kongos** among their ranks and initially adopted the name **Floribunda Rose**. They were signed by Pye and John Schroeder, their producer, suggested a name change to **Scrugg**. The name had been suggested by Jack Russell as having a basic Anglo-Saxon sound but was in fact a crib on the name of the famous banjo player Earl Scruggs, whom Jack admired.

Everyone Can See was a **John Kongos** song and **Kongos** had a solo effort on the 'B' side. The next 45 was a Scott English song called *Lavender Popcorn*. No-one in the band wanted to record the song because it was a teeny-bopper, bubblegum track, whilst on stage the band played a much more progressive style of music. The 'B' side was a dark, sad **Kongos** composition. Their final 45 *Will The Real Geraldine Please Stand Up And Be Counted* was another **Kongos** composition, which had great airplay and good publicity. John Peel opened his show with the song in the first week of its release and gave it a great plug. Sadly it wasn't a hit. Jack Russell left the band in the Autumn of 1969 and **Scrugg** never played live or in a studio again.

John Kongos went on to have two big hits with *He's Gonna Step On You Again* and *Tokoloshe Man*. Pete Cliffford is still working as a lead guitarist for vintage rock group The Bats in South Africa. Henry Spinetti (the younger brother of Victor Spinetti who had appeared in both the **Beatle** films as well as the *Magical Mystery Tour*) is a busy professional drummer who works regularly with Roger Chapman, **Bill Wyman** and **Eric Clapton**. He went on to **The Herd** on leaving **Scrugg** and later played long stints with **Eric Clapton**, Tina Turner, Cliff Richard and others as well as being the drummer on the **Gerry Rafferty** song *Baker Street*. Jack Russell went into advertising and has not played 1969 except one reunion concert in 2003. Chris Dee produced for **Mike D'Abo** and eventually became a pastor in an alternative church.

Compilation appearances include: *I Wish I Was Five* and *Lavender Popcorn* on *Paisley Pop - Pye Psych (& Other Colours) 1966-1969* (CD); *I Wish I Was Five* can also be heard on the 4-CD *Nuggets II* box set; *Lavender Popcorn* has been compiled on *Hot Smoke & Sassafras - Psychedelic Pstones, Vol 1* (CD) and *Only George* on *Haunted - Psychedelic Pstones, Vol 2* (CD). (VJ/JR)

The Sea-ders

45:       Thanks A Lot/Undecidedly   (Decca F 22576) 1967 R1

Originally from Lebanon this band relocated to the UK and I've decided to give them a mention. Their 45 had a Middle Eastern flavour to its frantic guitar work and vocals. In 1968 they changed name to **The Cedars**. The group also recorded a 4-track EP, *The Sea-Ders EP* (Decca DFE-R 8674) 1967, which was an export issue for the Lebanonese market (R3).

Compilation appearances have included: *Undecidedly* and *Thanks A Lot* on *Rubble, Vol. 16 - Glass Orchid Aftermath* (LP) and *Rubble, Vol. 9* (CD); and *Thanks A Lot* on *The Freakbeat Scene* (CD). (VJ/MG)

Phil Seaman

ALBUMS: 1 PHIL SEAMAN.... LIVE
            (mono/stereo)   (Verve (S)VLP 9220) 1968 R3
         2 MEETS EDDIE GOMEZ   (Saga OPP 102) 1968 R2
         3 THE PHIL SEAMAN STORY (Decibal BSM 103) 1974 R1
         4 PHIL ON DRUMS   (77 Records 77 SEU 12/53) 1974 R1

This legendary jazz drummer was also in **Ginger Baker's Airforce**. (VJ)

The Searchers

Personnel: CHRIS CURTIS   drms, vcls   AB
              TONY JACKSON   bs, vcls   A
              JOHN McNALLY   gtr, vcls   ABCD
              MIKE PENDER   gtr, vcls   ABCD
              FRANK ALLEN   bs   BCD
              JOHN BLUNT   drms   C
              BILLY ADAMSON   drms   D

                                                     HCP
ALBUMS: 1(A) MEET THE SEARCHERS   (Pye NPL 18086) 1963 SC 2
        2(A) SUGAR AND SPICE   (Pye NPL 18089) 1963 SC 5
        3(A) IT'S THE SEARCHERS   (Pye NPL 18092) 1964 SC 4
        4(B) SOUNDS LIKE THE SEARCHERS
                                   (Pye NPL 18111) 1964 SC 8
        5(B) TAKE ME FOR WHAT I'M WORTH
                                   (Pye NPL 18120) 1965 R1 -
        6(C) SECOND TAKE   (RCA SF 8289) 1972 SC -
        7(D) THE SEARCHERS   (Sire SRK 6086) 1980 SC -

NB: Their albums were issued, often with different titles and tracks by Kapp in the USA. (7) also reissued with some different tracks. All of their original UK albums were later issued by PRT at budget price in 1987 and on CD. (1) reissued on CD (PRT PYC 6014) 1987. (2) reissued on CD (PRT PYC 6015) 1987. (3) reissued on CD (PRT PYC 6016) 1987. (4) reissued on CD (PRT PYC 6017) 1987. (5) reissued on CD (PRT PYC 6018) 1987. In 1990 Castle also repackaged (1), (2) and (3) on CD (Castle CLACD 165-167 respectively). Also there's *German, French & Rare Recordings* (Repertoire RR 4102-WZ) 1990 which is available on German import. Then in 2001 Castle gave their first five albums a top-quality mid-price upgrade: *Meet The Searchers* (Castle Music CMRCD 155), *Sugar and Spice* (Castle Music CMRCD 156), *It's The Searchers* (Castle Music CMRCD 157), *Sounds Like Searchers* (Castle Music CMRCD 158) and *Take Me For What I'm Worth* (Castle

Music CMRCD 159). (6) reissued on CD (BGO BGOCD 512).

COMPILATIONS/REPACKAGES: HCP
ALBUMS: 1(-) SMASH HITS   (Marble Arch MAL(S) 640) 1967 -
        2(-) SMASH HITS, VOL. 2
                                  (Marble Arch MAL(S) 673) 1967 -
        3(-) NEEDLES AND PINS   (Hallmark HMA 203) 1971 -
        4(-) GOLDEN HOUR   (Pye GH 541) 1972 -
        5(-) GOLDEN HOUR, VOL. 2 (Pye GH 564) 1973 -
        6(-) NEEDLES AND PINS   (RCA Int. INTS 1480) 1974 -
        7(-) THE SEARCHERS FILE (Pye FILD 002) 1977 -
        8(-) GREATEST HITS   (Rhino RNLP 162) 1985 -
        9(-) SEARCHERS PLAY THE SYSTEM
                (Rarities, Oddities and Flipsides) (PRT PYC 6019) 1987 -
       10(-) SILVER SEARCHERS (CD Comp.)(PRT CDNRT 2) 1987 -
       11(-) HIT COLLECTION (CD Comp.)   (PRT PYC 4002) 1987 -
       12(-) COLLECTION
                    (Castle Communications CCSLP 208) 1989 -
       13(-) THE EP COLLECTION   (See For Miles SEE 275) 1989 -
       14(-) THE ULTIMATE COLLECTION(Castle CTVCD 003) 1990 -
       15(-) GOLDEN HOUR OF THE SEARCHERS (CD)
                                  (Knight KGHCD 101) 1990 -
       16(-) GOLDEN HOUR OF THE SEARCHERS, VOL. 2 (CD)
                                  (Knight KGHCD 102) 1990 -
       17(A/B) THE BEST OF THE SEARCHERS, 1963-64 (CD)
                                  (Pickwick PWKS 4076) 1991 -
       18(-) THE SEARCHERS - CD BOX SET
                                  (Castle Classics CLA BX 913) 1992 -
       19(-) THE SEARCHERS (CD)   (EMI CDMFP 5922) 1992 -
       20(-) 30th ANNIVERSARY COLLECTION (3 CD Set)
                                  (Sequel NXT CD 170) 1992 -
       21(-) THE EP COLLECTION, VOL. 2
                                  (See For Miles SEECD 359) 1992 -
       22(-) GERMAN, FRENCH AND RARE RECORDINGS (CD)
                                  (Repertoire RR-4102-WZ) 1991 -

NB: (9), (12 - 14) also released on CD. *Live At The Star-Club*, (CD) consists of their earlier *Sweets For My Sweet - Live Recordings At The Star-Club* and songs from other Philips albums. All of **Tony Jackson's** records, including the very rare Portuguese album, have also appeared on a private pressing CD. *The Searchers 30th Anniversary Collection* (Sequel NXT CD 170) 1992 is a 3-CD set. *Searchers Greatest: 20 Fabulous Hits Of The 60s* (Music Club MCCD 291) 1997 is another compilation. *The Definitive Collection* (Castle CCS CD 826) 1998 is a 2-CD set comprising a hits disc and a reissue of their debut album on the other disc. *The Pye Anthology 1963-1967* (Sequel NEECD 381) 2000 is a 2-CD anthology from this period. *The Swedish Radio Sessions* (Sanctuary CMRCD 394) 2002 chronicles their visits to Sweden between 1964 and 1967. *BBC Sessions* (Castle CMEDD 938) 2004 is a 2-CD set compiling every surviving the band recorded for the beeb. *1963-2003: 40th Anniversary Collection* (2-CD) (Castle CMEDD 726) 2005 is a 56-track collection drawing on material from every period of their history (except their two reunion albums for Sire in the early eighties). *Second Take - Complete RCA/UK Recordings* (Taragon TARCD 1055) compiles everything they recorded for the RCA and UK labels, including reworkings of their previous recordings and their comeback bid with *Desdemona*. *Definitive Collection + Meet The Searchers* (Rennaisance Collection CCSCD 826) is a 2-CD set which compiles some of the best of their sixties output, including their debut album in full. *Greatest Hits Collection* (CD) (Select SELCD 509) is self-explanatory and great value. *The Definitive Pye Collection* (3-CD) (Sanctuary Midline SMGTCD 005) is a 75-track collection of their best recordings on this label and includes rare singles.

EPs: 1 AIN'T GONNA KISS YOU   (Pye NEP 24177) 1963
         2 SWEETS FOR MY SWEET (Pye NEP 24183) 1963 SC
         3 HUNGRY FOR LOVE   (Pye NEP 24184) 1964 SC
         4 PLAY THE SYSTEM   (Pye NEP 24201) 1964 SC
         5 WHEN YOU WALK IN THE ROOM
                                 (Pye NEP 24204) 1964 SC
         6 BUMBLE BEE   (Pye NEP 24218) 1965 SC
         7 SEARCHERS '65   (Pye NEP 24222) 1965 SC
         8 FOUR BY FOUR   (Pye NEP 24228) 1966 R1
         9 TAKE ME FOR WHAT I'M WORTH
                                 (Pye NEP 24263) 1966 R2
        10 When You Walk In The Room/Don't Throw Your Love
            Away/Needles And Pins/Goodbye My Love
                                 (Pye BD 113) 1977

                                                     HCP
45s: Sweets For My Sweet/
         It's All Been A Dream   (Pye 7N 15533) 1963 1
         Sweet Nothins/What'd I Say (Philips BF 1274) 1963 48
         Sugar And Spice/Saints And Searchers (Pye 7N 15566) 1963 2
         Needles In Pins/Saturday Night Out (Pye 7N 15594) 1964 1

Don't Throw Your Love Away/		
I Pretend I'm With You	(Pye 7N 15630) 1964	1
Someday We're Gonna Love Again/		
No One Else Could Love You	(Pye 7N 15670) 1964	11
When You Walk In The Room/		
I'll Be Missing You	(Pye 7N 15694) 1964	3
What Have They Done To The Rain?/		
This Feeling Inside	(Pye 7N 15739) 1964	13
Goodbye My Love/Till I Met You	(Pye 7N 15794) 1965	4
He's Got No Love/So Far Away	(Pye 7N 15878) 1965	12
When I Get Home/		
I'm Never Coming Back	(Pye 7N 15950) 1965	35
Take Me For What I'm Worth/		
Too Many Miles	(Pye 7N 15992) 1965	20
Take It Or Leave It/		
Don't Hide It Away	(Pye 7N 17094) 1966	31
Have You Ever Loved Somebody/		
It's Just The Way	(Pye 7N 17170) 1966	48
Popcorn, Double Feature/Lovers	(Pye 7N 17225) 1967 SC	-
Western Union/I'll Cry Tomorrow	(Pye 7N 17308) 1967 SC	-
Secondhand Dealer/Crazy Dreams	(Pye 7N 17424) 1967 R1	-
Umbrella Man/Over The Weekend	(Liberty LBF 15159) 1968 R1	-
Kinky Kathy Abernathy/Suzanna	(Liberty LBF 15340) 1969 R1	-
Desdemona/		
The World Is Waiting For Tomorrow	(RCA RCA 2057) 1971 SC	-
Love Is Everywhere/And A Button	(RCA RCA 2139) 1971	-
Sing Singer Sing/Come On Back To Me	(RCA RCA 2231) 1972	-
Vahevala/Madman	(RCA RCA 2288) 1972 SC	-
Solitaire/Spicks And Specks	(RCA RCA 2330) 1973	-
Hearts In Her Eyes/Don't Hang On (PS)	(Sire SIR 4026) 1979	-
It's Too Late/		
This Kind Of Love Affair (PS)	(Sire SIR 4036) 1980	-
Another Night/Back To The War (PS)	(Sire SIR 4049) 1981	-
I Don't Want To Be The One/		
Hollywood (PS)	(PRT 7P 250) 1982	-

Reissues:
Needles And Pins/When You Walk In The Room/		
Come On Back To Me	(RCA RCA 2248) 1972	-
Needles And Pins/Sugar And Spice	(Pye 7N 45598) 1976	-
When You Walk In The Room/		
Don't Throw Your Love Away	(Pye 7N 46110) 1978	-
Needles And Pins/Sweets For My Sweet	(Pye FBS 4) 1979	-
Needles And Pins/		
Don't Throw Your Love Away	(Old Gold OG 9141) 1982	-
Sweets For Sweet/		
When You Walk In The Room	(Old Gold OG 9409) 1984	-
α When You Walk In The Room/		
Be My Baby (PS)	(PRT 7P 371) 1987	-

NB: α also issued as a 12".

After **The Beatles, The Searchers** were arguably the leading beat boom band and it's rather a shame that they never really stretched themselves beyond this to realise their full potential.

The Searchers formed in Liverpool in 1960. Founding member John McNally took their name from a John Ford epic Western movie. **Chris Curtis** and Mike Pender had been schoolmates of his and Pender had previously played with two other Liverpool groups, The Wreckers and The Confederates. The group soon started playing local clubs and, like **The Beatles**, also had a spell in Hamburg. They were soon discovered by Tony Hatch who provided them with *Sweets For My Sweet* from the hit-writing American Pomus/Schuman team and they soon became Liverpool's No 2 band to **The Beatles** with their faultless, crisp, vocal harmonies. Hatch followed their chart-topper with a composition of his own (written under the pseudonym Fred Nightingale), *Sugar And Spice*, which peaked at No 2 and was only kept off the top spot by **Gerry and The Pacemakers'** *You'll Never Walk Alone*.

Their next success *Needles And Pins* had been written by Jack Nitzsche and Sonny Bono (later of Sonny and Cher) and had been a minor US hit for Jackie de Shannon in 1963. **The Searchers** added their own unique vocal interpretation to the song and scored their second No 1. The follow-up, *Don't Throw Your Love Away*, gave them a third No 1 and also followed *Needles And Pins* into the American Top 20.

In early 1964, **Tony Jackson**, who often felt something of an outsider in the group since the other three had been at school together, left to form his own group, The Vibrations and Mike Pender took over the lead vocals with

THE SEARCHERS - EP Collection (CD).

Frank Allen, from **Cliff Bennett's Rebel Rousers**, coming in on bass. For their next single they covered Jackie de Shannon's *When You Walk In The Room*, which climbed to No 3 and they also enjoyed a Christmas hit with the haunting, *What Have They Done To The Rain?*, whilst *Love Potion No 9* was a big US hit for the team on the Kapp label.

In the Spring of 1965 they enjoyed another hit with *Goodbye My Love* and followed this with their first self-penned 'A' side, *He's Got No Love*. Their strength had previously come from adapting other artists' material but *He's Got No Love* was a strong song in its own right, but as the beat boom declined so did **The Searchers'** popularity. In mid-1966 **Chris Curtis** left the band, cut one solo single *Aggravation*, did some production work for Pye and then formed his own band **Roundabout**. John Blunt came in as his replacement. Their last Top 20 hit was with a P.F. Sloan song, *Take Me For What I'm Worth*. Thereafter they failed to keep pace with the rapidly changing musical scene but continued to record a string of technically faultless 45s of which, *Western Union*, a hit for The Five Americans in the States, and *Popcorn Double Feature*, were technically the best. Their dwindling popularity forced them increasingly onto the cabaret circuit but still they soldiered on... recording for RCA in the mid-seventies and then surprisingly signing to Sire in 1979 with a new line-up (D), which included Billy Adamson on drums. Mike Pendergast finally left in 1986. His replacement was Spencer James from **First Class**.

Castle's *Ultimate Collection* CD compilation, a 24-tracker, is as good a collection of the band's finest moments as one is likely to get.

German, French and Rare Recordings should delight real fans of the band. It includes both sides of **Chris Curtis'** extremely rare 1966 solo single *Aggravation*; French language versions of *Sugar And Spice* and *Saints And Searchers*; German language versions of hits like *Needles And Pins*, *Sugar And Spice* and *Goodbye My Love*; the band's two late sixties 45s on Liberty; a medley of some of their other hits and a 1983 comeback release on PRT *I Don't Want To Be The One*.

Sequel's *30th Anniversary Collection* is a recommended three CD set. The first CD covers their Pye singles from 1963-67 apart from two flip sides (*Saints And Searchers* and *Lovers*). The second CD selects the best tracks from their Pye albums. The third is a rarities CD, which includes *Needles And Pins*, *Sugar And Spice* and *Goodbye My Love* in German; some alternate takes and BBC session recordings; solo 45s from **Chris Curtis** and **Tony Jackson**; five cuts from 1983 and four previously unissued ones.

See For Miles' *The EP Collection, Vol. 2* has been compiled entirely from EPs issued in France and Germany and should excite the band's more fanatical fans.

The Pye Anthology 1963-1967 is a 2-CD set, which compiles all the singles, prime EP cuts and the best of their album tracks from this era.

In 2001 Castle repackaged The Searchers' first five Pye albums in a mid-price series. Each album was presented on CD in mono and stereo formats with out-takes, stray singles and foreign language singles.

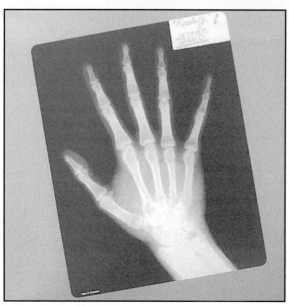

SECOND HAND - Reality (LP).

In 2002 Sanctuary released *The Swedish Radio Sessions*, which chronicles their visits to Sweden between 1964 and 1967. Their sound is professional and precise and many of their stage favourites can be heard here.

BBC Sessions compiles all the surviving material they recorded for the beeb. Sadly none of their early material was salvaged so this set begins with *When You Walk In The Room* (1964) and concludes with *I Don't Believe* (1967).

1963-2003: 40th Anniversary Collection is a 56-track 2-CD collection of hits, demos, album tracks, live tracks and unreleased material.

Various artists compilation appearances have included: *Sweets For My Sweet* and *Sugar And Spice* on *Mersey Beat* (2-LP); *Farmer John* and *Twist and Shout* on *Mersey Beat 1962-1964* (2-LP); *Popcorn Double Feature* on *Maximum '65* (CD) and *Beat Merchants* (CD); *Each Time* on *Quick Before They Catch Us* (LP & CD); *Have You Ever Loved Somebody* on *Ripples, Vol. 1* (CD) and on the 2-CD set *We Love The Pirates: Charting The Big 'L' Fab 40*; *Don't Throw Your Love Away, Needles And Pins* and *Sweets For My Sweet* on the 2-CD set *60 Number Ones Of The Sixties*; *Sugar And Spice* on *Love Power* (CD) and *Beat Generation - Ready Steady Go* (CD); *Sweets For My Sweet* and *Needles And Pins* on *U.K. No 1 Hits Of The 60's* (CD) and *60's Mix* (CD); *Sweets For My Sweet* on *No 1s & Million Sellers Vol 2* (CD); *Needles And Pins* on *Best Of British Rock* (CD), *Hits Of The Swinging Sixties* (CD), *Brit Pop* (CD) and *No 1s & Million Sellers Vol 4* (CD); *Take Me For What I'm Worth* on the 2-CD set *We Love The Pirates: Charting The Big 'L' Fab 40*; *Don't Throw Your Love Away* on the 2-CD set *Sixties Summer Love* and on *Dizzy* (CD) (credited to Mike Pender's Searchers); and *Second Hand Dealer* and *Goodbye My Love* on *Ripples, Vol. 3* (CD). *Everlasting Love* (CD) includes a version of *Needles And Pins* credited to Mike Pender's **Searchers**; *Crazy Dreams* has been compiled on *Haunted - Psychedelic Pstones, Vol 2* (CD) and *Umbrella Man* can also be found on *Jagged Time Lapse, Vol 4* (CD).

Tony Jackson died in August 2003, aged 63, after losing a long fight with liver cirrhosis and chronic arthritis. He was writing his autobiography at the time of his death. He was followed by **Chris Curtis**, who died in February 2005, also aged 63, after a lengthy illness. **The Searchers** continue to perform on the cabaret circuit. (VJ/LBy)

The Seashells

		HCP
45s:	Maybe I Know/Turning The Good Into Bad (CBS 8218) 1972	32
	(The Best Part Of) Breaking Up/	
	Play That Song (CBS 1023) 1972	-

A short-lived female vocal group who enjoyed a minor hit with *Maybe I Know*, which had originally been a Top 20 hit for US vocalist Lesley Gore back in 1964. Their follow-up, *(The Best Part Of) Breaking Up*, was a minor hit for **The Symbols** back in 1968, but was originally done by The Ronettes. (VJ)

Second City Sound (1)

Personnel incl: DAVE WALSH

			HCP
45s:	Tchaikovsky One/Shadows	(Decca F 12310) 1965	22
	Grieg One/In A Mist	(Decca F 12368) 1966	-
	Love's Funny/Tell Me Where I'm Going	(Decca F 12406) 1966	-
	Shopping List/Lover's Lament	(Decca F 12503) 1966	-

This instrumental group was from Birmingham. They narrowly missed the Top 20 with *Tchaikovsky One* in 1965. Dave Walsh had been in **The Overlanders**. By 1969 the group was a five-piece - four guys and one girl. (VJ)

Second City Sound (2)

Personnel:	POLLY BROWN	vcls	A
	DON CONBOY		A
	KEN FREEMAN	keyb'ds	A
	BILL GILBERT		A
	ALAN NICKLIN		A

		HCP
45:	Dream Of Olwen/	
	Touch Of Velvet, Sting Of Brass (Major Minor MM 600) 1969	43

Probably this 45 was by a different band. **Polly Brown** may have been Jeannie Darren because she recorded a cover of the Ike and Tina Turner oldie, *River Deep, Mountain High* backed by *Julie* for Major Minor (MM 611) 1969 a few weeks later. The 45 was credited to Jeannie Darren and The Second City Sound. Jeannie had previously recorded under the name of Jenny Wren in 1966, releasing a couple of singles, *Chasing My Dreams All Over Town* and *The Merry Go Round Is Slowing You Down*. In the 1970's she was known as Jenny Darren, signed to DJM and released four albums. Nowadays she works as a jazz singer and part-time teacher in Colchester, Essex.

Brown also played in **Pickettywitch** and Freeman went on to back **Elkie Brooks** in December 1977. (VJ/JM/MN)

Second Generation

45s:	Beyond The Sea/Suddenly	(Major Minor MM 610) 1969
	Ready Or Not There I Come/	
	House Of The Rising Sun	(Major Minor MM 692) 1970
	Day By Day/Gingerbread Man	(Philips 6006 182) 1971
	Take Up A Course In Happiness/	
	Walking On Air	(Philips 6006 228) 1972

This four-piece outfit comprised three guys and a girl. They specialised in uptempo harmony efforts but made little impact. (VJ)

Secondhand

Personnel:	KENNY ELLIOT	vcls, keyb'ds	AB
	BOB GIBBONS	ld gtr	A
	KIERAN O'CONNOR	drms	AB
	NICK SOUTH	bs	A
	ROB ELLIOT	vcls	B
	GEORGE HART	bs, violin, vcls	B
	MOGGY MEAD	gtr	B

ALBUMS:	1(A)	REALITY	(Polydor 583 045) 1968 R3
	2(B)	DEATH MAY BE YOUR SANTA CLAUS	
			(Mushroom 200 MR 6) 1971 R3

NB: Early copies of (1) credit **The Moving Fingers** on the disc! (1) reissued on vinyl (Essex LP 1006) and on CD (Essex 1006 CD) 1994. (2) reissued on CD (UFO BFTP 004CD) 1991 and (See For Miles SEECD 479) 1997.

45:	A Fairy Tale/?	(Polydor 56308) 1969

NB: There is a German issue in an art sleeve with *Steamtugs*, a track from their debut album on the flip.

The first album by this confused bunch of excellent musicians (who'd earlier worked as Next Collection and **Moving Finger**) still holds its ground after 37 years. Its unusual mixture of poetic psych with **Hendrixy** or **Arthur Brownish** heavy episodes and progressive (in 1968!) structures is inventive and only slightly flawed by not always strong vocals. Lovely arrangements and above average compositions make this recommended. Highlights: the opening cut *A Fairy Tale* (great mellotron), *The World Will End Yesterday* (an acid-drenched classic) and the trippy title track. Don't let the cover art fool you: it's meant to look "second hand".

The second album from a thoroughly revised line-up, of which two versions exist (one with and one without the funeral march), is much more complicated and even closer to **Arthur Brown**'s **Kingdom Come**. Fully developed progressive compositions and all kinds of keyboards dominate, often there are two or three different ones simultaneously, producing many very different textures. The rhythms are complex and unusual, enriched with odd time-signatures, at times drifting off towards inaccessibility, but always coming together. The atmosphere is sombre, yet not always completely serious (another **Arthur Brown** parallel). Not much easy listening here, nor are there any virtuoso passages. A very good record, though, definitely as recommended as the first one, albeit on different grounds.

They later recorded as **Chillum** and then evolved into **Seventh Wave**. They were also involved in a 1973 promo-only album under the name Fungus, which is now very collectable among progressive rock fans.

You can also find *The World Will End Yesterday* on *Rubble, Vol. 8 - All The Colours Of Darkness* (LP), *Rubble, Vol. 5* (CD) and *The Best Of Rubble Collection Vol. 1* (CD). (MK/VJ)

Secrets

Personnel incl: CLIFFORD T. WARD

45s:	I Suppose/Such A Pity	(CBS 202466) 1967 SC
	Infatuation/She's Dangerous	(CBS 202585) 1967 SC
	I Intend To Please/	
	I Think I Need The Cash	(CBS 2818) 1967 SC

This pop band originally recorded as **Martin Raynor and Secrets** and later became **Simon's Secrets**. *I Think I Need The Cash*, is a straight-forward pop effort.

Compilation appearances include: *She's Dangerous* on *Justafixation* (CD); and *I Think I Need The Cash* on *Circus Days Vol's 4 & 5* (CD) and *Circus Days, Vol. 5* (LP). (VJ)

The Seftones

Personnel:	DAVE STEPHENSON	gtr, vcls, organ	A
	YANNY TSAMPLAKOS	lead gtr	A
	MIKE BACON	drms, vcls	A
	DAVE EDMUNDS	bs	A

| 45: | I Can See Through You/Here Today | (CBS 202491) 1967 SC |

This beat group also recorded as The Perishers. They were managed by early **Beatles'** manager Alan Williams for a time in 1966. (VJ/AD)

The Selofane

Personnel:	ARNIE ARNOLD	sax	A
	ALEX GAVIN	organ	A
	JON GOBIN	vcls	A
	GEOFF HULME	drms	A
	JUD LANDER	ld gtr, hrmnca	A
	LES MARTIN	bs	A
	SPIDER	trumpet	A

| 45s: | Girl Called Fantasy/Happiness Is Love | (CBS 3413) 1968 |
| | Shingle I.A.O./Chase The Face | (CBS 3700) 1968 |

A little known late sixties pop group. (VJ)

The Senate

Personnel:	SOL BYRON (BILLY LOCHART)	vcls	A
	DAVIE AGNEW (MAK DAVID)	vcls, gtr	ABC
	ALEX LIGERTWOOD (ALEX JACKSON)	vcls	ABC
	BOB MATHER	sax	ABC
	TONY RUTHERFORD (TONY MIMMS)	trumpet	ABC
	BRIAN JOHNSTON	bs	B
	ROBBIE MacINTOSH	drms	BC
	MIKE FRASER	bs	C

ALBUM: 1(C)   THE SENATE SOCK IT TO YOU ONE MORE TIME
                  (mono/stereo)   (United Artists (S)ULP 1180) 1968 R1

NB: (1) reissued on CD by Line (RTCD 901146) in 1992.

| 45: | I Can't Stop/ | |
| | Ain't As Sweet As You | (Columbia DB 8110) 1967 SC |

A Glasgow R&B group who moved down to London. They originally formed to back Sol Byron. Some members used pseudonyms which are in brackets in the personnel listings above. Alex Ligertwood had earlier been in another Glasgow-based group The Quintones. Brian Johnston (previously of **The Golden Crusaders**) was later replaced by ex-**Viking** Mike Fraser.

The Senate split from singer Sol Byron in 1966 and quickly established themselves as a popular support act to visiting soul bands. Artists they supported included Ben E. King, who in turn produced their 45 in 1967. Indeed he wrote both of the songs the band recorded.

In 1967 **The Senate** supported Garnet Mimms on tour and they appeared on the later's 1967 in concert album. Their own album, released the previous year, was constructed from material taken from gigs at The Speakeasy and Sussex University. The end result was a lively collection of classic soul numbers like *What Is Soul?* and *Please Stay*. The band finally split up in 1968, having toured Germany. Fraser, MacIntosh and Ligertwood were all later in **The Primitives** at various times. This was a UK band that moved to Italy. MacIntosh and Ligertwood also played for **Brian Auger** and Mike Fraser became a session musician.

Can't Stop has been compiled on *R&B Scene, Vol. 1* (LP). (VJ)

The Senators

Personnel incl:	BOBBY CHILD	vcls	
	CHRIS MANDERS	ld gtr	A
	FRANK THIENAL	drms	A

45s:	When Day Is Done/Breakdown	(Oriole CB 1957) 1964 SC
	She's A Mod/I Know A Lot About You	(Dial DSP 7001) 1964 R1
	The Tables Are Turning/	
	Stop Wasting Time	(CBS 201768) 1965 SC

SECOND HAND - Death May Be Your Santa Claus (LP).

A five-piece beat group from Birmingham, who were originally known as The Rivals. Chris Manders had been with **Tony Rivers and The Castaways** and Frank Thienal had drummed for The Drifters. *The Tables Are Turning* was a **Unit Four Plus Two** song.

You'll also find *She's A Mod* on *Brum Beat, Vol. 1* (LP). (VJ)

The Sensations

45:	Look At My Baby/	
	What A Wonderful Feeling	(Decca F 12392) 1966

This 45 was this obscure outfit's sole vinyl excursion. The 'A' side was a Carter-Lewis composition. (VJ)

Sensory Armada

Personnel:	GEORGIE WOOD	gtr, vcls	A
	DAVEY McEWEN	drms, vcls	AB
	COLIN BROWN	gtr, vcls	B

This mysterious electric psychedelic duo played at the Middle Earth, Happening 44 and The Marquee late in 1967 to mid-1968. They featured a remarkable Byrds-like electric '12-string' guitar sound and were known for a heavily psychedelic version of **The Beatles**' *Eight Days A Week* - there's rumoured to be a demo of this somewhere. In 1968 they did a short Scandinavian tour with guitarist George Brown replacing Georgie Wood, after which they sank without a trace. **Sensory Armada** will always be remembered for having unbelievably long hair for the period and for introducing **Jimi Hendrix** to his legendary black stove pipe hat, that they both used to wear. (JN/DMc)

Serendipity

Personnel:	IAN BELLAMY	vcls	A
	TIM HUCKSTOPP	drms	A
	BILLY LANE	lead gtr	A
	PAT O'NION	keyb'ds	A
	GORDON SHAW	bs	A
	GRAHAM WALLER	organ	A

45s:	Through With You/I'm Flying	(CBS 3733) 1968 R2
	If I Could/Castles	(CBS 4428) 1969 R2

Both these 45s, particularly the first, are major collectors' items. The group came from Tunbridge Wells in Kent and were previously known as Abject Blues. They toured Germany for four months supporting Vanilla Fudge and **Paul Raven** (aka **Gary Glitter**) among others, before signing for CBS. Billy Lane had previously been with **The Tony Jackson Group**. Graham Waller had previously been in the short-lived **Ritchie Blackmore** project Mandrake Root.

RUBBLE VOL. 8 (Comp LP) including Serendipity.

Through With You is an abbreviated re-work of a Lemon Pipers song with swirling organ and much guitar wizardry. The 'B' side was penned by Tim Huckstepp and Pat O'Nion and it is also an organ-dominated psych-pop composition.

If I Could backed by *Castles* was a more straightforward pop single to whet the appetite for an album. They actually recorded half an album at CBS but split before it could be completed due to the lack of contractual agreement within the band.

Graham Waller later joined **Blodwyn Pig** and Ian Bellamy went on to the French progressive rock band Zoo.

Compilation coverage has included:- *I'm Flying* on *Rubble Vol. 8: All The Colours Of Darkness* (LP), *Rubble Vol. 5* (CD) and *The Best Of Rubble Collection Vol. 1* (CD); *Through With You* on *Perfumed Garden Vol. 3* (CD); *Castles* on *We Can Fly, Vol 1* (CD); and *Round And Round* (prev unreleased) on *Incredible Sound Show Stories Vol. 11* (LP). (VJ/MWh)

Seven Ages of Man

Personnel incl:	P.P. ARNOLD	A
	GORDON BECK	A
	MADELINE BELL	A
	COLIN GREEN	A
	ROSETTA HIGHTIWER	A
	HAROLD McNAIR	A
	BRIAN ODGERS	A
	DORIS TROY	A

ALBUM:	1	SEVEN AGES OF MAN	(Rediffusion ZS 115) 1972 SC

This melodic jazzy orchestrated concept album is similar to **Salamander** in style. **Beck** was a jazz musician and **Bell** was a black soulful singer. Both also recorded solo material. (VJ/VZ)

Seventh Wave

Personnel:	KEN ELLIOT	keyb'ds, vcls	A
	KIERAN O'CONNOR	perc	A

ALBUMS:	1(A)	THINGS TO COME	(Gull GULP 1001) 1974
	2(A)	PSI-FI	(Gull GULP 1010) 1975

45s:	Metropolis/Festival	(Gull GULS 3) 1974
	Fail To See/Things To Come	(Gull GULS 10) 1974
	Manifestations/	
	Only The Beginning (Part 1)	(Gull GULS 14) 1975

Elliot and O'Connor were in **Secondhand** in the late sixties/early seventies. Then, prior to forming **Seventh Wave**, they issued a privately-pressed 45 as Fungus in 1973, *Premonitions Pt's 1* and *2* (Fungus FUN 1). These albums are electronic rock. (VJ)

Severin

45:	Chance In Time/	
	Nothing Bad Can Be This Good	(CBS 7280) 1971

This is a forgotten early seventies 45. (VJ)

The Seychelles

45s:	Baker's Daughter/	
	Did You See Her Again?	(President PT 278) 1970
	And That Is Life/I Will Be There	(President PT 291) 1970

The Seychelles backed **Brian Poole** for a while but released these 45s in their own right. *Baker's Daughter* has been compiled on *Sometimes I Wonder* (CD). (MWh)

Denny Seyton and The Sabres

Personnel:
JOHN BOYLE	bs	AB
MIKE LOGAN	organ	A
EDWARD MURPHY	lead gtr	A
DAVE SAXON	drms	A
DENNY SEYTON (BRIAN TARR)	vcls	AB
JOHN FRANCIS	lead gtr	B
DAVE MAHER	gtr	B
BERNIE ROGERS	drms	B
TONY CROWLEY	drms	C
BLINK DRING	lead gtr	C
LALLY STOTT	bs, vcls	C

ALBUM: 1(C)   IT'S THE GEAR (14 HITS)   (Wing WL 1032) 1965 R1

HCP

45s: Tricky Dicky/
Baby What You Want Me To Do   (Mercury MF 800) 1964 SC -
Short Fat Fanny/
Give Me Back My Heart   (Mercury MF 814) 1964 SC -
The Way You Look Tonight/
Hands Off   (Mercury MF 824) 1964 SC 48
α   Just A Kiss/
In The Flowers By The Trees   (Parlophone R 5363) 1964 SC -

NB: α Credited to the Denny Seyton Group.

This early to mid-sixties showband, now long forgotten, actually scored a minor hit in 1964 with *The Way You Look Tonight*. **Denny Seyton** was a Liverpudlian and his real name was Brian Tarr. After the first two 45s, Murphy, Logan and Saxon all left. Francis, Maher and Rogers (ex-Memphis 3) replaced them and this line-up recorded the minor hit. They specialised in rough'n'ready covers of American R&B songs and on the first two 45s in particular strove to replicate a black American sound. They were the first British beat group to record on the American Mercury label. Their later recordings are more melodic as they tried to identify themselves more closely with the Merseybeat sound.

Prior to their album **Seyton** put together a new line-up, C above. Tony Crowley had previously been in Them Grimbles and Stott joined from **Four Just Men**. Their album was comprised of cover versions of 14 hits of the day and the name of the game was to sound as near to the originals as possible. Dave Saxon backed Eden Kane on most of his records. The band later became The Motowns and Stott went solo.

Tricky Dickie has been compiled on *Mersey Beat 1962-1964* (2-LP). (VJ/AD/JM)

Shade Joey and The Nightowls

Personnel:
BOB DOWNES	sax	A
RON EDGEWORTH	organ	A
SHADE JOEY	vcls	A
TONY MARSH	drms	A
DAVE RICHMOND	bs	A
RAY RUSSELL	lead gtr	A

45:   Bluebirds Over The Mountains/
That's When I Need You Baby   (Parlophone R 5180) 1964 R2

This obscure single has now become collectable, probably partly because Joe Meek produced the 'A' side, which was later recorded by The Beach Boys.

Bluebirds Over The Mountain has been compiled on *RGM Rarities, Vol. 2* (CD). (VJ/AD)

Shades of Blue

Personnel:
TONY GOODEN	drms	AB
COLIN (aka MICK) FULLER	bs	AB
COLIN RIGLER	vcls	A
ROY TONES	gtr	AB

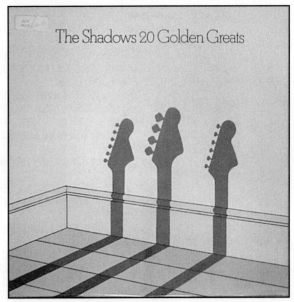

THE SHADOWS - 20 Golden Greats (LP).

PETER WARE	piano, organ	AB
JOHN BEECHER	anvil	B
DAVE BLAKE	vcls	B

45s: Where Did All The Good Times Go/
It Ain't No Use   (Pye 7N 15988) 1965
Voodoo Blues/Luceanne   (Parlophone R 5270) 1965 R1

There was also an American band of this name who had a 45 on Sue. This was a five-piece beat group from Newcastle who later recorded as **Toby Twirl**. Rigler was the vocalist on the first 45 and Blake on the second. Beecher played anvil on *Voodoo Blues*.

Voodoo Blues can also be heard on *R&B At Abbey Road* (CD). (VJ/JB)

Shades of Morley Brown

Personnel incl: MALCOLM BROWN   A
CHRIS MORLEY   A

45s: In Time/Walking Proud   (Mercury MF 896) 1966
Silly Girl/Pretty Blue Bird   (Mercury MF 1054) 1968

This was a short-lived duo. (VJ)

The Shadows

Personnel:
(up to 1976)
TERRY 'JET' HARRIS	bs	AB
HANK MARVIN	gtr	ABCDEF G
TONY MEEHAN	drms	A
BRUCE WELCH	gtr	ABCD FG
BRIAN BENNETT	drms	BCDEFG
BRIAN 'LICORICE' LOCKING	bs	C
JOHN ROSTILL	bs	DE
ALAN HAWKSHAW	gtr, keyb'ds	E
FARRAR	gtr	FG
ALAN TARNEY	bs	G

HCP

ALBUMS: 1(A)   THE SHADOWS (mono/stereo)
(up to   (Columbia 33SX 1374/SCX 3414) 1961 SC/R1 1
1976)   2(C)   OUT OF THE SHADOWS (mono/stereo)
(Columbia 33SX 1458/SCX 3448) 1962 SC 1
3 (-)   GREATEST HITS (mono/stereo)
(Columbia 33SX 1522/SCX 1522) 1963 SC 2
4 (D)   DANCE WITH THE SHADOWS (mono/stereo)
(Columbia 33SX 1619/SCX 3511) 1964 SC 2
5 (D)   THE SOUND OF THE SHADOWS (mono/stereo)
(Columbia 33SX 1736/SCX 3554) 1965 SC 4

6 (-)   MORE HITS (mono/stereo)
            (Columbia 33SX 1791/SCX 3578) 1965 -/SC -
7 (D)   SHADOW MUSIC
            (mono/stereo)   (Columbia 33SX/SCX 6041) 1966 5
8 (D)   JIGSAW   (Columbia 33S(C)X 6148) 1967 SC 8
9 (D)   FROM HANK, BRUCE, BRIAN AND JOHN
            (Columbia 33S(C)X 6199) 1967 SC -
10 (-) ESTABLISHED 1958* (Columbia 33S(C)X 6282) 1968 SC -
11 (-) WALKIN' WITH THE SHADOWS (MFP MFP 1388) 1970 -
12 (E) SHADES OF ROCK   (Columbia SCX 6420) 1970 SC 30
13 ( ) MARVIN, WELCH AND FARRAR
            (Regal Zonophone SZRA 8502) 1971 SC -
14 ( ) SECOND OPINION
            (Regal Zonophone SZRA 8504) 1971 SC -
15 ( ) MUSTANG (comp)   (MFP MFP 5266) 1972 -
16 (-) HANK MARVIN AND JOHN FARRAR
            (EMI EMA 755) 1973 SC -
17 (F) ROCKIN' WITH CURLY LEADS
            (EMI EMA 762) 1973 SC 45
18 (-) THE SHADOWS   (Ember SE 8031) 1975 -
19 (G) SPECS APPEAL   (EMI EMC 3066) 1975 30
20 (G) LIVE AT THE PARIS OLYMPIA   (EMI EMC 3095) 1975 -
21 (-) RARITIES   (EMI NUT 2) 1976 -

NB: (1) and (2) reissued on CD (EMI CDP 795732-2) 1991. (1) reissued on CD (EMI 7243 4 98937 2 6) 1999 in both mono and stereo in a digipak and again in a jewel case (EMI 7243 5 28239 2 5) 2000. (2) reissued on CD (EMI 7243 4 99415 2 6) 1999 in both mono and stereo and again in a jewel case (EMI 7243 52823622 8) 2000. (4) and (5) reissued on CD (EMI CDP 795733-2) 1991. (4) and (5) reissued as a 2-LP set (EMI EDP 1546323) 1983. (4) reissued on CD (EMI 7243 4 99418 2 3) 1999 in both mono and stereo in a digipak and again in a jewel case (EMI 7243 528238 2 6) 2000. (5) reissued on CD (EMI 7243 8 56566) 1997. (7) and (12) reissued on one CD (EMI 79 70332) 1992. (7) reissued on CD (EMI 7243 4 95151 2 3) 1998 in both mono and stereo in a digipak. (8) reissued on CD (Beat Goes On BGO 66) 1989. (8) reissued on CD (EMI 7243 4 99770 2 0) 1999 in both mono and stereo in a digipak. (9) reissued on CD (BGO BGOCD 20) 1997. (9) reissued on CD (EMI 7243 4 99767 2 6) 1999 in both mono and stereo in a digipak. (12) reissued on CD (EMI 7243 5 21033 2 6) 1999 in a digipak and again in a jewel case (EMI 7243 5 28240 2 1) 2000. (17) reissued on vinyl (Beat Goes On BGOLP 84) 1990 and on CD (Beat Goes On BGOCD 84) 1990 and again in 1997. (17) reissued again on CD (EMI 7243 5 20221 2 0) 1999 in a digipak and in a jewel case (EMI 7243 5 28240 2 1) 2000. (19) reissued on CD as Specs Appeal Plus (EMI 07777800422/6) 1992. (20) reissued on CD (EMI CDP 7985902) 1992.

Vinyl compilations have included: 20 Golden Greats (EMI EMTV 3) 1977 (No 1), The Shadows At The Movies (MFP 50347) 1978, Thank You Very Much (with Cliff Richard) (EMI EMTV 15)1979, Rock On With The Shadows (MFP 50468) 1980, The Shadows (6-LP set) (WRC ALBUM 72) 1981, The Shadows' Silver Album (2-LP) (Tellydisc TELLY 22) 1983, The Shadows' Vocals (EMI EG 26-0075-1) 1984, Hits Right Up Your Street (Polydor POLD 5169) 1984, At Their Very Best (Polydor 8415201) 1989 (No 12), The EP Collection (See For Miles SEELP 296) 1990, Relaxing With The Shadows (LP) (RDS 10709) 1990 was released as a free album with a Reader Digest Box Set Great Romantic Hits of the 70's and 80's, and The Shadows Collection (Readers Digest GSHAD A 219) is an 8-LP set. Finally, The Shadows Complete (Polydor 513449/1) was a 3-LP set also issued on CD (Polydor 513 449-2). The LP set was available by mail order only.

CD compilations have included: The EP Collection Vol 1 (See For Miles SEECD 246) 1988, Stepping To The Shadows (16 Great Tracks As Only The Shadows Can

THE SHADOWS - Rarities (LP).

Play Them) (Polydor 8393572) 1989 (No 11), The EP Collection Vol 2 (See For Miles SEECD 296) 1990, The EP Collection Vol 3 (See For Miles SEECD 375) 1993, At Their Very Best (Polydor 8415201) 1989 (No 12) and (Polydor 8415202) 1994, Relaxing With The Shadows (CD) (RD CD 157)1990 was released as a free CD with a Reader Digest Box Set Great Romantic Hits of the 70's and 80's, Dancing In The Dark (Pickwick PWKS 4031) 1990 and The Shadows, A Special Collection (Pickwick Box XD 8) 1990 contains three CDs The Shadows Collection/Dancing In The Dark and Diamonds.

The Early Years 1959-1966 is a 6-CD set: Vol 1 1959-1961 (EMI CDP 7971722) 1991, Vol 2 1961-1962 (EMI CDP 7971732) 1991, Vol 3 1962 (EMI CDP 7971742) 1991, Vol 4 1962-1964 (EMI CDP 7971752) 1991, Vol 5 1962-1964 (EMI CDP 7971762) 1991 and Vol 6 1964-1966 (EMI CDP 7971762) 1991. The Shadows Collection (Readers Digest RDCD 301-306) is a 6-CD set. The Shadows (Polygram PSPCD 299) 1993 was available by mail order only from Avon Cosmetics.

Further CD compilations are: Everything Of Value, Rarities Two (EMI 07777890412/0) 1993, The Best Of Hank Marvin And The Shadows (Polydor 5238212) 1994, Compact Shadows (Polydor 823/080-2) 1994, First 20 Years At The Top (75 Classic Recordings 1959-1979) (3-CD Box Set) (EMI CDSHAD 2) 1995, The Best Of The Shadows (MFP 7243835618/27) 1995, The Best Of The Shadows (MFP 7243835618-2/7) 1995 and The Shadows Gold Collection (MFP 7243 8 55319 2 7) 1995 (all three releases had the same track listing), The Shadows Collection (MFP 7243852621 2 6 - 7243852621 2 8) 1996 is a 3-CD set, The Shadows 20 Classic Tracks (EMI 7243852885 2 4) 1996 was exclusive to Boots Department stores, Into The Light - The Complete Shadows Collection (EMI CTMBOX 100 (8-54749-2) 1997 is a 4-CD set and The Shadows Vocals (See For Miles SEECD 475) 1997 compiles their vocal numbers. There's also Listen To The Shadows (EMI Sovereign 724359106 2 3) 1997, Thousand Conversations (The Best Of Hank Marvin & Bruce Welch/John Farrar/Marvin, Hank & Bruce Welch/John Farrar) (MFP CDMFP 6402) 1997, The Very Best Of The Shadows (MFP CDMFP 6385 - 7243 857467 2 7) 1997, At Abbey Road (EMI CDABBEY 104) 1997, The Shadows Shadtrax (See For Miles SEECD 494) 1998, The Shadows and The Ventures Back 2 Back (EMI 7243496846 21) 1998, The Very Best Of Hank Marvin and The Shadows: The First 40 Years (Polydor TV 559 211-2) 878662) 1997 is a 2-CD set comprising one album of **Shadows** material and one of **Hank Marvin** material and In The Seventies (EMI 7243 5 21729 2 4) 1999.

The Best Of Cliff Richard & The Shadows Collection (EMI B 99001BB3) 1999 is a 5-CD set which compiles many of their finest moments with Cliff and With Strings Attached (EMI 07243 526092 2 2) 2000 compiles some of their orchestrated numbers. More CD compilations include: The Shadows Fifty Golden Greats (EMI 7243 5 27586 2 3) 2000, The Shadows Collection (HMV EASY 7243-5-32794 2 4) 2001, The Hit Sound Of The Shadows (Connoisseur VSOP CD 341) 2001 contains the Polydor re-makes of the songs featured, and Live At Abbey Road & Live At The Liverpool Empire (See For Miles SEECD 732) 2001 captures their live sound. Live At The ABC Kingston 1962 was issued as an EMI label promo in a paper sleeve in 2002 and again (EMI 724353 793128) 2002 as a limited edition with an EMI label 7" size sleeve with a programme and four black and white photos and finally (EMI 7243 5373422 0) 2002 in a standard jewel case. Recent CD compilations include The Essential - Shadows (EMI 5818822) 2003, A's B's & EP's (EMI Gold 7243 5 83110 2 0) 2003 (which was initially issued as a promo in a paper sleeve), Life Story (CD LSI) 2004 was a promo CD which preceded Lifestory (EMI 9817819) 2004 and there was a promo version of this full release too, The Shadows Essential Collection (EMI 7243 5 77491 2 1) 2004 is a 2-CD set, More Hits - More Hits - More Hits (EMI 7243 578199 2 3) 2004 features their classic 'A' sides in mono and stereo, Complete A's & B's Complete Singles 1959-1980 (EMI 7243 578181 2) 2004 is a 4-CD set, Greatest Hits (EMI 7243578198 2 4) 2004 also contains many of their finest singles in mono and stereo, The Final Tour (Eagle EDG CD 283) 2004 is a 2-CD set that was preceded by a promo release housed in paper copy inside a PVC wallet, The Shadows 54 Guitar Hits (Crimson CRIM BX 51/1) 2004 is a 3-CD set exclusive to Tesco stores - the three CDs are split into three themes: CD 1 Classic Hits, CD 2 Classic Covers and CD 3 Classic Themes, The Ultimate Collection (Marks and Spencer MS 1004) 2005 is a collection of their classic singles exclusive to Marks and Spencer, Memories 36 Guitar Moods (Demon MCDLX014) 2005 features the band covering 36 classic songs and , finally, The Shadows Platinum Collection (EMI 0946 3349382-7) 2005 is a 2-CD set of their classic songs and it comes with a bonus DVD of them performing seven songs at the National Exhibition Centre in Birmingham in 1986 - the release was preceded by two promo versions of the CD.

EPs: 1 THE SHADOWS (mono/stereo)
(up to   (Columbia SEG 8061/ESG 7834) 1961 -/R1
1976)   2 THE SHADOWS TO THE FORE
                   (Columbia SEG 8094) 1961
        3 SPOTLIGHT ON THE SHADOWS
                   (Columbia SEG 8135) 1962 SC
        4 THE SHADOWS NO 2
                   (Columbia SEG 8148) 1962 SC
        5 THE SHADOWS NO 3
                   (Columbia SEG 8166) 1962 SC
        6 WONDERFUL LAND OF THE SHADOWS
                   (Columbia SEG 8171) 1962 SC
        7 THE BOYS (mono/stereo)
                   (Columbia SEG 8193/ESG 7881) 1962 -/R1
        8 OUT OF THE SHADOWS (mono/stereo)
                   (Columbia SEG 8218/ESG 7883) 1963 SC/R1
        9 DANCE ON WITH THE SHADOWS

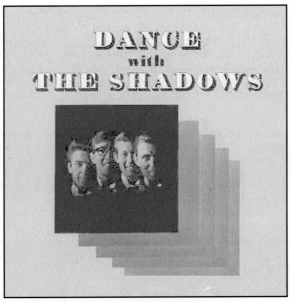

THE SHADOWS - Dance With The Shadows (LP).

	(Columbia SEG 8233) 1963 SC	
10	OUT OF THE SHADOWS NO 2 (mono/stereo)	
	(Columbia SEG 8249/ ESG 7895) 1963 SC/R1	
11	FOOT TAPPING WITH THE SHADOWS	
	(Columbia SEG 8268) 1963 SC	
12	LOS SHADOWS	(Columbia SEG 8278) 1963 SC
13	SHINDIG WITH THE SHADOWS	
	(Columbia SEG 8286) 1963 SC	
14	THOSE BRILLIANT SHADOWS	
	(Columbia SEG 8321) 1964 SC	
15	DANCE WITH THE SHADOWS	
	(Columbia SEG 8342) 1964 SC	
16	RHYTHM AND GREENS (mono/stereo)	
	(Columbia SEG 8362/ ESG 7904) 1964 SC/R1	
17	DANCE WITH THE SHADOWS NO 2	
	(Columbia SEG 8375) 1964 SC	
18	THEMES FROM "ALADDIN AND HIS WONDERFUL	
	LAMP"	(Columbia SEG 8396) 1965 SC
19	DANCE WITH THE SHADOWS NO 3	
	(Columbia SEG 8408) 1965 SC	
20	ALICE IN SUNDERLAND	(Columbia SEG 8445) 1965 SC
21	THE SOUND OF THE SHADOWS	
	(Columbia SEG 8459) 1965 SC	
22	THE SOUND OF THE SHADOWS NO 2	
	(Columbia SEG 8473) 1966 SC	
23	THE SOUND OF THE SHADOWS NO 3	
	(Columbia SEG 8494) 1966 SC	
24	THOSE TALENTED SHADOWS	
	(Columbia SEG 8500) 1966 SC	
25	THUNDERBIRDS ARE GO (with Cliff Richard)	
	(Columbia SEG 8510) 1966 R2	
26	THE SHADOWS ON STAGE AND SCREEN	
	(Columbia SEG 8528) 1967 R1	

NB: ESG prefixes are stereo releases. (1) - (6) were originally issued with turquoise labels; later blue/black label copies are worth two-thirds of the value of the turquoise label issues. (7) and (8) originally issued in stereo with turquoise and later with blue/black labels. (12) issued with two different sleeves.

HCP

45s:	α	Feeling Fine/		
(up to		Don't Be A Fool With Love	(Columbia DB 4263) 1959 -	
1976)	α	Jet Black/Driftin'	(Columbia DB 4325) 1959 -	
		Saturday Dance/Lonesome Fella	(Columbia DB 4387) 1959 -	
		Apache/Quartermasster's Stories	(Columbia DB 4484) 1960 1	
		Man Of Mystery/The Stranger	(Columbia DB 4530) 1960 5	
		F.B.I./Midnight	(Columbia DB 4580) 1961 6	
		The Frightened City/Back Home	(Columbia DB 4637) 1961 3	
		Kon-Tiki/36-24-36	(Columbia DB 4698) 1961 1	
		The Savage/Peace Pipe	(Columbia DB 4726) 1961 9	
		Wonderful Land/		
		Stars Fell On Stockton	(Columbia DB 4790) 1962 1	
		Guitar Tango/What A Lovely Tune	(Columbia DB 4870) 1962 4	
		Dance On!/All Day	(Columbia DB 4948) 1962 1	

Foot Tapper/The Breeze And I	(Columbia DB 4984) 1963 1	
Atlantis/I Want You To Want Me	(Columbia DB 7047) 1963 2	
Shindig/It's Been A Blue Day	(Columbia DB 7106) 1963 6	
Geronimo/Shazam!	(Columbia DB 7163) 1963 11	
Theme For Young Lovers/		
This Hammer	(Columbia DB 7231) 1964 12	
β	The Rise And Fall Of Flingel Bunt/	
It's A Man's World	(Columbia DB 7261) 1964 12	
Rhythm'n'Greens/The Miracle	(Columbia DB 7342) 1964 12	
Genie With The Light Brown Lamp/		
Little Princess	(Columbia DB 7416) 1964 17	
Mary-Anne/Chu-Chi	(Columbia DB 7476) 1965 17	
Stringray/Alice In Sunderland	(Columbia DB 7588) 1965 19	
Don't Make My Baby Blue/		
My Grandfather's Clock	(Columbia DB 7650) 1965 10	
The Warlord/I Wish I Could Shimmy Like My		
Sister Arthur	(Columbia DB 7769) 1965 18	
I Meet A Girl/Late Night Set	(Columbia DB 7853) 1966 22	
A Place In The Sun/		
Will You Be There?	(Columbia DB 7952) 1966 24	
The Dreams I Dream/		
Scotch On The Socks	(Columbia DB 8034) 1966 42	
Thunderbirds Are Go (one-sided		
advance promo)	(Columbia PSR 305) 1967 -	
Maroc 7/Bombay Duck	(Columbia DB 8170) 1967 24	
Maroc 7 (one-sided demo with spoken		
word intro)	(Columbia PSR 308) 1967 -	
Chelsea Boot/Jigsaw (demo only)	(Columbia PSR 310) 1967 -	
Tomorrow's Cancelled/Somewhere	(Columbia DB 8264) 1967 -	
Running Out Of World/		
London's Not Too Far+	(Columbia DB 8326) 1968 -	
Dear Old Mrs Bell/		
Trying To Forget The One You Love	(Columbia DB 8372) 1968 -	
χ	Slaughter On Tenth Avenue/	
Midnight Cowboy	(Columbia DB 8628) 1969 -	
The Shadows (flexi from WCR box set)		
	(Lyntone LYN 10099) 1972 -	
Turn Around And Touch Me/Jungle Jam	(EMI EMI 2081) 1973 -	
δ	Let Me Be A Man/Stand Up Like A Man	(EMI EMI 2269) 1975 -
Run Billy Run/Honourable Puff-Puff	(EMI EMI 2310) 1975 -	
It'll Be Me Babe/Like Strangers	(EMI EMI 2461) 1976 -	
Reissues: Apache/Wonderful Land/F.B.I.	(Columbia DB 8959) 1972 -	
Apache/Wonderful Land/F.B.I.	(EMI EMI 2573) 1977 -	

NB: α Released as The Drifters. β Some copies were mispressed with the 'A' side on both sides. χ 'B' side is a **Hank Marvin** solo number. δ This was also released with the sides reversed.

The Shadows were Britain's top instrumental band by miles. They were also one of the most famous groups in the history of popular music. Before **The Beatles** when people thought of groups it was **The Shadows** that most people thought of. Some describe them as Britain's answer to the Pacific North West band The Ventures, but **The Shadows** played a more polished, crisper sound. Their ability to write haunting melodies mostly neutralised their music's inherent sterile nature. Whilst the instrumental genre is not the focus of this book I've included them in this edition as they recorded throughout the years the book is concerned with and recorded many vocal numbers too.

Hank Marvin and **Bruce Welch** were pupils at Rutherford Grammar School, Newcastle-upon-Tyne. **Marvin's** interests lay in jazz and blues, whilst **Welch** was into rock'n'roll, but it was in skiffle that their interests merged. At the time they both played in their own groups, but **Welch** persuaded **Marvin** to join his band The Railroaders, who before long were playing rock as opposed to skiffle. By now the group had made it to the finals of a London talent contest, but when they only finished third they split up after the contest. **Marvin** and **Welch** remained in London working as The Geordie Boys at the 2 '1's covering Everly Brothers' material. In this era they met **Tony Meehan** and **Jet Harris**. As a result **Marvin** and **Welch** appeared on The Chesternuts' single *Jean Dorothy*.

In October 1958, Cliff Richard's manager needed a lead guitarist for Cliff's touring band. He came to the 2 '1's looking for **Tony Sheridan** but found **Hank Marvin** instead. He also took on **Bruce Welch.** Not only did they play for Cliff's touring band, they played for the other two acts The Kalin Twins and The Most Brothers who were on the tour as well. However, by the end of the tour Cliff Richard and The Drifters had taken top billing. **Tony Meehan** joined soon after and the classic line-up was formed.

THE SHADOWS - Best Of (LP).

Although they first backed Cliff at the Victoria Hall, Hanley on 5 October 1958 as The Drifters, they were obliged to change names to avoid confusion with the popular US R&B group of the same name. It was on their way to Ruislip Lido in July 1959 that **Jet Harris** had an idea - as they'd always be in Cliff's shadow whilst he was in the spotlight he suggested that they call themselves **The Shadows**.

At first they only backed Cliff live and session men were used on his early singles. However, they did back Cliff on *Livin' Lovin' Doll* and EMI's A&R manager Norrie Paramor was sufficiently pleased with what he'd heard to offer them a deal. Their first single (as The Drifters) recorded in February 1959 was a double vocal side *Feeling Fine/Don't Be A Fool With Love*, which tried to capture the authentic US sound of Buddy Holly and that ilk. In truth it was best forgotten. The 'A' side was penned by Ian Samwell and the flip by Pete Chester. In May 1959 they recorded their first instrumental *Chincilla* for the soundtrack to Cliff's film 'Serious Charge'. Their second single as The Drifters comprised two self-penned instrumentals. *Jet Black* was written by **Jet Harris** and featured his bass guitar as the lead instrument. The flip side *Driftin'* was scribed by **Hank Marvin**. It had a menacing tone and exuded a raw sound. Both tracks were covered by US band The Standells in the mid-sixties. In the US the single was released as by The Four Jets as *Feelin' Fine* had to be withdrawn when the US Drifters took out an injunction to prevent the duplication of their name. Both their 45s as The Drifters are hard-to-find and expensive now.

Their first single as **The Shadows'** *Saturday Dance* (a **Marvin**/Chester collaboration) was derivative of US styles, with doo-wop vocal harmonies and crisp guitar breaks. Released in December 1959, like its predecessors, it failed to chart. The same month the band appeared with Cliff in the pantomime 'Babes In The Wood' at Stockton. In January 1960, they toured the US supporting Cliff as part of a package which included Frankie Avalon, Freddy Cannon and Bobby Rydell.

On a UK tour in April 1960 the group met singer/songwriter Jerry Lordan who demonstrated his song *Apache* on his ukulele. The group recorded it with Cliff Richard on bongos and it became one of the instrumental classics, their first UK No 1 and went on to become a million-seller. It was later voted Record Of The Year in the New Musical Express. On 25th September 1960 **The Shadows** played their first concert without Cliff in Bristol.

Their next single was officially issued as a double 'A' side. *Man Of Mystery* was written by veteran Michael Carr as the theme for the Edgar Wallace film series. **The Shadows'** version utilised a heavily-tremeloed treble strings and there was a wrong note in the solo. The band preferred *The Stranger*, which was penned by Bill Crompton and 'Thunderclap' Jones, who they knew from their 2 '1's days, which is why the release (which rose to No 5) was plugged as a double 'A' side.

Their February 1961 release *F.B.I.*, which was notable for **Welch's** rapidly-changing rhythm patterns may have been credited to their manager Peter Gormley, but it was actually written by **Marvin**, **Welch** and **Harris** at **Hank's** flat. It climbed to No 6. In March 1961 the band toured southern

Africa, Australasia and the Far East with Cliff Richard. *The Frightened City*, which Paramor had written for his film score of the same name, was a moody, menacing number that took them to No 3 that Spring (their version didn't feature in the movie). They did, however, appear in 'The Young Ones' which they filmed with Cliff Richard in June 1961. Their debut album *The Shadows* was released in September 1961. It contained both new instrumental and vocal numbers and spent six weeks on top of the album charts.

Also released in September 1961 was *Kon-Tiki* which was notable for a dramatic opening with **Meehan** playing timpana and kettle drums, **Harris** dishing up some funky bass and **Welch** adding some jangly guitar. Penned by Michael Carr and named after Thor Heyerdahl's raft, it was one of their most successful singles and gave them a second No 1. Surprisingly **Tony Meehan** decided to leave the band when it was at the height of its success. He departed during their six week residency with Cliff Richard at Blackpool and became an A&R man for Decca as he wanted to move into record production. He was replaced by Brian Bennett a friend from their 2 '1's days, who'd been in Marty Wilde's Wild Cats and the instrumental group The Krew Kats.

The Savage released in November 1961 was a powerful rock'n'roll instrumental was thumping drums and pounding bass. Both this and the flip side *Peace Pipe*, a delightful ballad, were taken from the soundtrack of 'The Young Ones'. The single was really issued as a stop-gap because the band was touring heavily at the time. The band was far from happy about it, but it presented them with another Top Ten hit. They followed up in February 1962 with another all-time instrumental classic *Wonderful Land*. The track was penned by Jerry Lordan and unusual at the time because Paramor overdubbed the basic track with a soaring string arrangement. It topped the UK singles chart for eight weeks and went on to become another million-seller. Its jaunty flip side *Stars Fell On Stockton* marked Brian Bennett's debut with the band.

In April 1962 differences between **Harris** and **Welch** came to a head and **Harris** left to pursue a solo career. Brian 'Liquorice' Locking who had played with Bennett in groups backing Vince Taylor and Marty Wilde replaced him on bass. In May, they travelled to Greece to film 'Summer Holiday' with Cliff Richard. (**Welch** and Bennett penned the title song). Their next single *Guitar Tango* is notable for its all-acoustic sound with a dash of flamenco, which gave it a Spanish feel although it was written by two Frenchmen! The basic track was cut before **Jet Harris** left the band and Paramor added strings, cornets and castanets! It gave them another Top Five hit. **Harris** also contributed tracks to their second album *Out Of The Shadows*, which spent three weeks on top of the charts. Their November 1962 EP *The Boys* featured music the group had contributed to the movie of the same title and it too topped the UK EP charts.

Dance On! released at the end of 1962 topped the charts at the start of 1963 and they followed this with another chart-topper *Foot Tapper* (which had been included in 'Summer Holiday' at the last minute), although it was re-recorded for single release. On this version they utilised double-tracking for the first time. *The Shadows' Greatest Hits*, a compilation of their singles

THE SHADOWS - Mustang (LP).

to date climbed to No 2 in the album charts in May 1962. It was kept from the top by **The Beatles'** *Please Please Me*.

Their May 1963 release *Atlantis* was penned by Jerry Lordan and superbly arranged by Norrie Paramor to give the song a wistful feel and the band a No 2 hit. The flip side *I Want You To Want Me* is also of interest as it included a vocal and the end product was clearly influenced by the prevailing Merseybeat sound. That summer the group played a 16-week summer season 'Holiday Carnival' with Cliff Richard.

The brash, self-penned *Shindig* and **Marvin's** *Geronimo*, which successfully blended both powerful and menacing, quieter passages brought them two more hits and completed their singles output for 1963. *Los Shadows*, an EP recorded in Barcelona during the summer and containing four Spanish songs, climbed to No 42 in the singles chart. Locking meanwhile had become a Jehovah's Witness and left the band. John Paul Jones who was then bassist with **Harris** and **Meehan's** backing group (and who was later in **Led Zeppelin**) was considered but ex-Interns bassist John Rostill eventually got the nod.

Their first single of 1964 was a smoothly flowing, melodic **Bruce Welch** number *Theme For Young Lovers* from the 'Wonderful Life' soundtrack, which climbed to No 12. As he was recuperating from a nervous breakdown at the time the rhythm part was overdubbed on by **Hank Marvin**. The follow-up, a band composition *The Rise And Fall Of Flingel Bunt*, put them back in the Top Five. It was essentially an improvised 12-bar studio jam. In May they toured Europe and their latest album *Dance With The Shadows* made No 2. They also issued a 25-minute film that year - a pastiche history of British beaches from the Stone Age to the future. They appeared in various disguises whilst Cliff Richard was cast as King Canute. It was only shown as support to Dirk Bogarde's 'King And Country'. The title track *Rhythm'n'Greens*, another group composition, was intended as a send up of the R&B boom but was short on melody and became their first single since *Apache* not to make the Top 20. In Christmas 1964 Cliff and the band starred in 'Aladdin' at the London Palladium, which the band wrote the score for. Their next single *Genie With The Light Brown Lamp* was taken from the score and restored them to the Top 20. The flip *Little Princess* is a notable acoustic ballad based around musical dialogue between **Hank Marvin** and **Bruce Welch**.

Mary-Anne, written by Jerry Lordan and released in February 1965, was their first vocal 'A' side since *Saturday Dance* from five years earlier. The slow ballad was supplemented by acoustic and 12-string guitars with sandpaper blocks and Indian cymbals. It made the Top 20. The flip side *Chu-Chi* was another group composition from 'Aladdin'. They returned to a heavy instrumental sound with *Stingray* in May 1965, which scrapped in the Top 20. Some copies were pressed with G.Heigel wrongly credited as the composer instead of Klaus Ogerman and these interest some completists. Their latest album *The Sound Of The Shadows* climbed to no 4 in the album charts during July. *Don't Make My Baby Blue* also released in July 1965 was their most successful vocal single, but it would also be their last Top Ten hit for 13 years. Despite this they closed 1965 with another instrumental *The Warlord*. It was originally written by Jerome Moross as the theme to the film of the same name, starring Charlton Heston. It peaked at No 18.

In March 1966, they released another vocal track *I Met A Girl* which **Hank Marvin** had written, about double timing. It reached No 22 and their latest album *Shadow Music* climbed to No 5. In common with the follow-up *A Place In The Sun* (written by Jerry Lordan's wife Katrina), which was full of double-tracking, it stalled outside the Top 20. Their final single of 1966 was another **Marvin**-penned vocal track, *The Dreams I Dream*, a sad song with strong harmonies and a haunting melody, but it wasn't commercially successful and only reached No 42. In December, they wrote the music for and appeared in Cliff Richard's musical 'Cinderella' at the London Palladium. Gerry Anderson's movie 'Thunderbirds Are Go!' featured puppet likenesses to Cliff Richard and **The Shadows** and the band wrote and appeared on four tracks on the film soundtrack, which were also released on an EP. There is also a very rare one-sided promo release of the title track.

Maroc 7 released in April 1967 was the title track to a spoof spy thriller they had been approached to write the score to, but pressed for time they had commissioned composer Paul Ferris to do this. It restored them to the Top 20, but would prove to be their last hit for nearly eight years. Another **Shadows'** collectable is a very rare one-sided demo of *Maroc 7* with a spoken intro. Their next album *Jigsaw* peaked at No 6 in July 1967. The title track was demoed for 45 release on the flip to *Chelsea Boot* but it was

THE SHADOWS - Shades Of Rock (LP).

not officially issued and this is another highly collectable item. The following month they won the Split Song Festival in Yugoslavia with *I Can't Forget*. They then toured Australia and Spain without Cliff Richard. Their next single *Tomorrow's Cancelled* in September 1967 was a relaxed dreamy number composed by **Hank Marvin** and Brian Bennett. It was their first since *Apache* not to chart in the UK. A further album *From Hank, Bruce, Brian and John* was hastily released in December 1967 (only five months after its predecessor) and it showed. The album failed to chart at all!

On New Years Day 1968 **The Shadows** began a three week cabaret at the Talk of The Town - it was their first in London without Cliff Richard. It turned out a bit of a disaster as Rostill suffered a minor nervous breakdown after the first week and was ordered to rest and then Bennett was taken to hospital with appendicitis. Former members Locking and **Meehan** stood in for the remaining dates to complete the assignment.

The follow-up *Dear Old Mrs Bell* was the last single released by line-up (D) in March. In truth it was rather tame and the band was touring Japan so it wasn't here to help promote it. In May the band played a short season at the London Palladium with Tom Jones. In October, they celebrated their 10th Anniversary in the music business by releasing the album *Established 1958*. It contained an equal number of tracks on which the band backed Cliff Richard and of their instrumental numbers. By now though tiredness, lack of creativity and friction had set in and the band decided to split. Its final gig was fittingly with Cliff Richard at the London Palladium on 19 December 1968. **Marvin** and Bennett now concentrated on solo projects and the latter also played for seven days during March 1969 in The Washington DC's as Tom Jones's drummer.

During the summer of 1969, **Marvin**, Bennett and John Farrar re-united briefly as **The Shadows** with organist Alan Hawkshaw replacing **Bruce Welch**. They issued a patchy live album *Live At The Sankei Hall Japan* in October 1969 whilst touring Japan and a poor 1970 album *Shades Of Rock*, which is generally considered one of the worst **Shadows'** albums. It is comprised of rock'n'roll classics plus some **Beatles** and **Stones** numbers given instrumental treatment but it really doesn't work at all well. By contrast the line-up's 1969 cover of Richard Rodgers' *Slaughter On Tenth Avenue* was excellent and supported by a full orchestra. Although an artistic triumph, commercially the single was a disaster. The flip side *Midnight Cowboy* featured a **Hank Marvin** solo backed by session men and a full orchestra. After this the band split again for a second time. **Hank Marvin** and Brian Bennett embarked on solo careers, as well as doing some song writing and session work. John Rostill worked with Tom Jones and spent long periods in the US and **Bruce Welch** took some time out of the music business.

In 1970 the MFP label issued a compilation *The Shadows* that contained album, EP and some 'B' sides from the 1962-1967 era. Some fans may like to hear the stereo takes of *Les Tres Carabelas* (from their *Los Shadows* EP), *Running Out Of World* (the flip to **Marvin's** *London's Not Too Far*) and the humorous *What A Lovely Tune* (the 'B' side to *Guitar Tango*). The album was also issued in two sleeves. The rarer of the two is the first release, which features scrapbook-style photos of the band in lurid pink. It was quickly withdrawn and replaced with a sleeve containing a colour photo of the 1966 line-up. The sleeve shows the album title as *The Shadows*, but the label has the title as *Walkin' With The Shadows*.

In 1971, **Marvin**, **Welch** and Farrar (and later Brian Bennett) formed a new vocal harmony group, **Marvin**, **Welch** and **Farrar**. Despite the quality of their music the venture failed to equal the dizzy heights **The Shadows** had experienced. Their albums are included in the discography above. *Marvin, Welch and Farrar* (the first one) was issued in a gatefold sleeve designed by Hignosis. For the recording the trio was supplemented by Clem Cattini (drms, perc), Dave Richmond (bs), Alan Hawkshaw (organ) and Peter Vince (piano). Two tracks were written by the trio - the singalong-styled *My Home Town* and *Faithful*. Highlights include the opening track *Burning Bridges*, which features some crisp acoustic guitar work and a good solo from **Hank**; the brooding rendition of *Throw Down The Line*; the wistful *A Thousand Conversations* and luscious *Silvery Rain*. *Wish You Were Here* on side 2 features melancholic harmonies. The album did climb to No 30, but it could have been higher! The record company ran out of stock when it was first released and was unable to meet the initial demand. The follow-up *Second Opinion* was released in November 1971. The trio was supplemented by Bennett, Hawkshaw and Richmond and the blues spoof *All Day, All Night Blues* also featured **Duffy Power** on harmonica. The material was diverse with powerful tracks like *Black Eyes* and *Simplify Your Head* as well as a country and western send-up *Lonesome Mole*, a full scale ballad *Lady Of The Morning* and *Come Back To Nature*, which opens with an eerie, electronic wind, was an ecological song. Although critically acclaimed, the album failed to sell and was a commercial disaster. They appeared frequently on Cliff Richard's TV shows and also toured with Cliff billing themselves as Marvin, Welch and Farrar, featuring The Shadows! This was a bad time personally for **Bruce Welch** and after separating from his then wife Olivia Newton-John, he opted out of the band leaving **Marvin** and Farrar to continue as a duo. They toured the Far East with Cliff and released an album of predominantly love songs *Hank Marvin and John Farrar*. However, the sales were poor and Farrar left to work with Olivia Newton-John.

Mustang, their third budget compilation was released in October 1972. It included all four songs in stereo from *The Shadows* EP and a number of other songs, which had not previously been available in stereo.

In October 1973, **The Shadows** reformed. The line-up was **Marvin**, **Welch**, Bennett and Farrar. It was also intended to include John Rostill, but he was tragically electrocuted at his home recording studio, so session bassist Alan Tarney was recruited for future live appearances. Their new album *Rockin' With Curly* contained ten new compositions among its 12 tracks. It made the lower reaches of the Top 50. Two cuts, the wistful *Turn Around And Touch Me* and the heavier, almost progressive *Jungle Jam* were put out on a single, although it did not make the charts.

They made a few live appearances in early 1974; on **Cilla Black's** TV show and in March performing a mixture of old and new material on 'Sounds On Sunday'. When, in June, the 6-LP 84-track *Cliff Richard Story* was released, it contained 18 **Shadows** tracks, including an original stereo

THE SHADOWS - Rockin' With Curly Leads (LP).

take of *Foot Tapper*. Late in 1974, they played for a charity event at the London Palladium and Bill Cotton (then the Head of BBC Light Entertainment) offered them the chance to represent Britain at the 1975 Eurovision Song Contest. They accepted, and performed a Paul Curtis number *Let Me Be The One*, a typical Euro entry, it was a catchy bouncy song that eventually finished second in a close-run final to the Dutch entry - *Ding-A-Dong* by Teach-In. It sold well; giving them their first hit for eight years but didn't quite make the Top Ten. For six weeks they had performed a different song each week on **Lulu's** TV show and the runner-up *Stand Up Like A Man* was placed on the flip side of *Let Me Be The One*. All six of their potential Eurovision songs appeared on their 1975 *Specs Appeal* album, which had the highest proportion of vocal numbers of any **Shadows** album. It peaked at No 30 in the album charts.

In mid-1975 Ember reissued *Walkin' With The Shadows* with the same track listing but new sleevenotes and a full colour photo of line-up (D) of the band. *Live At The Paris Olympia*, released in November 1975, was the first live album **The Shadows** issued in the UK. In June 1975 possibly their worst single *Run Billy Run* was released. It was in the same mould as *Let Me Be The One*, but worse. Of more interest is the flip side *Honourable Puff-Puff*, a Bennett drum opus from the *Specs Appeal* album.

A June 1976 single, *It'll Be Me Babe* was a vocal effort penned by **Marvin** and Farrar. It was a punchy number but did not produce the hit they were seeking. The flip side *Like Strangers* was a hypnotic, haunting instrumental from their *Specs Appeal* album. In November 1976 a compilation *Rarities* was released on the budget NUT label. **The Shadows** side opens with *Scotch On The Rocks* (in mono) and features tracks from their *Thunderbirds* and *Aladdin* EPs. The highlight is *Slaughter On Tenth Avenue*. The other side is dedicated to **Hank Marvin** tracks and includes both sides of his first solo single *Goodnight Dick* and the wistful *London's Not Too Far*.

After the success of The Beach Boys' *20 Golden Greats* album, it was decided the group should do the same. Consisting entirely of 'A' sides **The Shadows'** album *20 Golden Greats* was a phenomenal success and rapidly rose to the top of the album charts. It spent six months in all in the charts and became a million-seller. To help promote it the group reformed (with Alan Jones on bass and Francis Monkman on keyboards) for a UK '20 Golden Dates' tour, which was mostly a sell-out. Encouraged by the audience response and the record sales from *20 Golden Greats*, the group decided to reform and split their time between the band and their respective solo ventures.

As we leave the time span of this book **The Shadows** were still seeking to relive their successes of the early sixties. Returning to the traditional band sound they recorded *Tasty* in 1977, but the album suffered from being recorded too quickly and the sales were disappointing. In August 1979, they released a new album *String Of Hits*, which consisted entirely of cover versions, except for their John Wayne tribute *Song For Duke*. It eventually climbed to No 1 aided by a TV advertising campaign. Whilst the group was delighted with its success they were disappointed with its lack of original material and wanted more say in what was issued, which led to them parting company with EMI and signing for Polydor in the summer of 1980. However, EMI continued to release their material commencing with *Another String Of Hot Hits* in 1983.

In the summer of 1981 World Records released a boxed set of **Shadows** material. The 6-LP, 84-track set covers their career from 1960 (*Apache*) to 1979 (*Cavatina*). Each disc comes with its own full colour sleeve and concentrates on a different theme. The package is accompanied with a small booklet with excellent notes by John Friesen and there's a flexidisc (LYN 10099) that edits sections of 13 songs and adds a voiceover describing the set.

Change Of Address was a new instrumental studio album and climbed to No 17. *Hits Right Up Your Street* was another new album of cover versions which reached No 15 and the band continued to record new albums at the rate of about one per year for many years to come.

Further compilations were released on the MFP label: *The Shadows At The Movies* contained stereo versions of both their *Rhythm'n'Greens* and *The Boys* EPs; *Rock On With The Shadows* is unlikely to include anything a serious fan of the band wouldn't already have; and the 2-LP set *The Shadows Live!*, which featured a straight reissue of *Live At The Paris Olympia* on one album and their *Live At The Sankie Hall, Japan* on the other (previously this had only been issued in Japan and later in Holland).

The 2-LP set *Shadows Silver Album* released by Tellydisc in 1983 during their 25th year in show business was promoted by an expensive TV advertising campaign. Only available through mail order it included 10 brand new recordings amongst its 25 tracks, 14 were previously available and the remaining track was a previously unreleased version of *Whiter Shade Of Pale*. Earlier in may that year the band won an Ivor Novello Award from the British Academy of Songwriters, Composers and Authors to mark 25 years of outstanding contributions to British music.

In March 1986 **Hank Marvin** played guitar on a new charity version of Cliff Richards's 1959 No 1 *Living Doll* on which Richards was accompanied by the comedy act The Young Ones. The recording, which was made in aid of comic relief, topped the UK singles chart for three weeks.

See For Miles have compiled their EPs over a series of three separate CD releases. Some of their other numerous compilations are listed in the above discography. In one form or another **The Shadows** continued to record well into the nineties. **Tony Meehan** died, after an accident at his home on 27 November 2005, aged 62. (VJ)

SHAGRAT - Pink Jackets Required (LP).

Shagrat

Personnel incl: STEVE TOOK   A
                  LARRY WALLIS   gtr   A

NB: *Nothing Exceeds Like Excess* (Shagrat ENT 001) was a numbered limited edition mini-album containing previously unreleased recordings from 1970 and 1971. *Pink Jackets Required* (Get Back GET LP/CD 607) is a collection of their demos from 1969/70 including some tracks that ended up on **Twink's** *Think Pink* album. *Lone Star* (CD) (Captain Trip CTCD 312) contains recordings from 1970 and 1971 by the band, which was previously released on the *Nothing Exceeds Like Excess* album.

Steve Took of **Tyrannosaurus Rex** fame formed this short-lived freak rock band in 1970 but it doesn't appear to have made vinyl at the time. However, a single was issued in 1990 - a more-or-less private pressing, '*Amanda/Peppermint Flickstick*' (Shagrat ORC 001). The flip is a killer with some impressive guitar work by Larry Wallis. The following year a mini-album of previously unreleased material was released and since there have been a couple of CDs revisiting their material. (VJ)

The Shakeouts

45:        Every Little Once In A While/
           Well Who's That   (Columbia DB 7613) 1965 R1

This was another Joe Meek - produced outfit. The 45 was beat with falsetto vocals.

Every Little Once In A While has been compiled on *RGM Rarities, Vol. 2* (CD). (MWh)

SHAGRAT - Nothing Exceeds Like Excess (LP).

The Shakers

ALBUM: 1   LET'S DO THE SLOP, TWIST, MADISON, HULLY
               GULLY WITH THE SHAKERS (Polydor 237 139) 1963 R2

45s: Money/Memphis Tennessee   (Polydor NH 52158) 1963 SC
         α Hippy Hippy Shake/Dr. Feelgood (Polydor NH 52213) 1963 SC
           Money/Hippy Hippy Shake   (Polydor NH 52258) 1963 SC
           Whole Lotta Lovin'/I Can Tell (Polydor NH 52272) 1964 SC

NB: α Also issued on (Polydor NH 66991) 1963.

This was Merseybeat group **Kingsize Taylor and The Dominoes** playing in disguise due to contractual problems. They were one of many groups in this era to record a version of Barrett Strong's *Money*. Their first two 45s were reissued under **Kingsize Taylor**'s name in 1964.

Money has been compiled on *Mersey Beat 1962-1964* (2-LP). (VJ/MWh)

Chris Shakespeare Globe Show

45:        Ob-La-Di, Ob-La-Da/Tin Soldier   (Page One POF 113) 1969 SC

This one-off project features cover versions of two big hits of the era. Given that **The Marmalade** took **Lennon/McCartney**'s *Ob La Di, Ob La Da* to No 1, this version inevitably remained in obscurity. (VJ)

Shakespeares

45:        Something To Believe In/
           Burning My Finger   (RCA Victor 1695) 1968 R1

An obscure outfit whose *Something To Believe* In has been compiled on *Oddities, Vol 1* (CD). (VJ)

Shakey Vick

Personnel: NED BALEN   drms   A
               BRUCE LANGMAN   gtr   A
               NIGEL TICKLER   bs   A
               GRAHAM VICKERY   hrmnca, vcls   A

ALBUM: 1(A) LITTLE WOMAN YOU'RE SO SWEET
                               (Pye N(S)PL 18276) 1969 SC

NB: (1) Reissued on CD (Forgotten Jewels FJ 002) 1991.

A late sixties blues band fronted by Graham Vickery. The album was recorded at Mothers, Birmingham, giving it a raw feel which suits the music, which consists of a selection of blues standards like *Good Morning Little Schoolgirl*, *Movin' To Chicago* and so on. For diehard blues fans only. (VJ)

Shalimar

45:     Kentucky River Line/Hobo's Hideaway   (Pye 7N 25527) 1970

This country-rock group was produced by Brian Bennett. (VJ)

Shame

Personnel: MALCOLM BRAISER   A
               JOHN DICKENSON   vcls, keyb'ds   A
               GREG LAKE   gtr   A
               BILLY NIMS   A

45:     Don't Go 'Way Little Girl/
        Dreams Don't Bother Me   (MGM MGM 1349) 1967 R2
NB: First 125 copies came with picture insert and although still R2 are more collectable.

A rare and sought-after 45. This group formed in Bournemouth in 1966. Their sole single emerged in September 1967. *Too Old To Go 'Way Little Girl* was a Janis Ian-penned psych-pop song with high-pitched guitar and splatterings of sitar. *Dreams Don't Bother Me* was a decent flip, although less notable than the 'A' side. They also recorded six or seven tracks for an album, which is still in the can.

The group later became **The Shy Limbs** (minus Braiser and Nims) and included **Greg Lake**, who was later in **The Gods**, **King Crimson** and **Emerson Lake and Palmer**. Malcolm Braiser was later killed in a motorbike accident.

Both sides of this 45 have been compiled on *Lovely Summer Days* (CD) and *Dreams Don't Bother Me* has also been included on *Colour Me Pop, Vol 3* (CD). (VJ)

Shanghai

Personnel: CHUCK BEDFORD   vcls, hrmnca   A
               MICK GREEN   gtr   AB
               PETE KIRCHER   drms, vcls   AB
               MIKE LE MAIN   vcls, keyb'ds   A
               BRIAN ALTERMAN   gtr   B
               CLIFF BENNETT   vcls   B
               PATRICK 'SPEEDY' KING bs   B

SHAPE OF THE RAIN - Riley Riley Wood And Waggett (CD).

ALBUMS: 1(A)   SHANGHAI   (Warner Brothers K 56093) 1974
(up to 2(B)   FALLEN HEROES   (Thunderbird THR 2000) 1976
1976)
NB: (2) came with lyric sheet.

45:     Shakin' All Over/Nobody's Fool   (Thunderbird THE 104) 1976
(up to
1976)

A short-lived Anglo-American rhythm and blues band who were more important for their personnel than the music they produced. Mick Green was ex-Pirates, **Dakotas** and **Cliff Bennett Band**. Bedford, Green and Le Main had all previously played in Fresh Meat and Kircher was in Compass. Bedford and Le Main left in June 1975 after the first album. Bennett (ex-**Hotshots**), Alterman and King (ex-**Trifle**) came in as replacements. They split following a second album. Green joined the reformed Pirates and Kircher departed to The Original Mirrors. Bennett retired and now works as a sales executive for an aviation firm. Pete Kircher was also ex-**Honeybus** and later in **Status Quo**. (BS/VZ/JM)

Shape of The Rain

Personnel: KEITH RILEY   gtrs, vcls   A
               LEN RILEY   bs   A
               TAG WAGGETT   drms   A
               BRIAN WOOD   gtr, vcls   A

ALBUM: 1(A)   RILEY RILEY WOOD AND WAGGETT
                                 (RCA Neon NE 7) 1971 R1

NB: (1) reissued on CD (Repertoire REP 4353-WP) 199? and *The Shape Of The Rain* (Background HBG 123/14) 2002 is a 19-track CD of their out-takes spanning 1966-1973..

45s: Woman/Wasting My Time   (Neon NE 1901) 1971
        α My Friend John/Yes   (RCA RCA 2129) 1971
NB: α as Shape.

A rare guitar **Badfinger**-style power-pop album that came in a gatefold sleeve and is very underrated. The band came from the Sheffield area. Brian Wood was the Riley brother' cousin. They wrote all the tracks on the album themselves, except *Rockfield Roll*, which they co-wrote with Eric Hine, who guests on electric piano on four of the tracks. The material on this album is excellent and there's some gorgeous guitar work. Recommended.

The 2002 release *The Shape Of The Rain* contains 19 tracks commencing with a double-sided acetate demo from 1966. There's some pleasant late sixties pop rock cuts, a hidden slice of psychedelia *Hello 503* featuring a Dalek-like vocal passage and a melodic rock backing and sleevenotes from the band's guitarist and vocalist Keith Riley. This release is a treat for collectors. (VJ)

Shapes and Sizes

45:     Little Lovin' Somethin'/Rain On My Face   (Decca F 12441) 1966

This was a short-lived mid-sixties act.

A Little Lovin' Somethin' can also be heard on *A Whiter Shade Of Pale* (LP). (VJ)

Helen Shapiro

                                                    HCP
ALBUMS: 1   TOPS WITH ME (mono/stereo)
(up to   (Columbia 33SX 1397/SCX 3428) 1962 SC/R1 2
1976)   2   HELEN'S SIXTEEN (mono/stereo)
                 (Columbia 33SX 1494/SCX 3470) 1963 R1/R2 -
         3   HELEN IN NASHVILLE (Columbia 33SX 1561) 1963 SC -
         4   HELEN HITS OUT (mono/stereo)
                 (Columbia 33SX 1661/SCX 3533) 1964 R1/R2 -

HELEN SHAPIRO - At Abbey Road (CD).

5   TWELVE HITS AND A MISS SHAPIRO
                          (Encore ENC 209) 1967 SC -
6   THE VERY BEST OF HELEN SHAPIRO
                          (Columbia SCX 6565) 1974 -

NB: (1) and (2) reissued as a 2-LP set (EMI EDP 1546343) 1963. (3) reissued on vinyl and CD (See For Miles C5CD 545) 1989. There's also a vinyl compilation *The 25th Anniversary Album* (MFP 41 57411) 1986. (1) reissued on CD (EMI DORIG 107) 1997. There are also some CD compilations: *Helen Shapiro* (Music For Pleasure CC 259) 1990, *Sensational* (RPM RPM 151) 1995, *The Essential Collection* (Music For Pleasure CDMFP 6400) 1997, *At Abbey Road* (EMI 4934522) 1998 and *The EP Collection* (See For Miles SEECD 272) 1998.

                                                              HCP

EPs: 1   HELEN (Goody Goody/The Birth Of The Blues/
           Tiptoe Through The Tulips/After You've Gone)
           (mono/stereo)
                   (Columbia SEG 8128/ESG 7872) 1961 - -/SC
       2   HELEN'S HIT PARADE (Don't Treat Me Like A Child/
           You Don't Know/Walkin' Back   To Happiness/When I'm
           With You)   (Columbia SEG 8136) 1961 SC -
       3   A TEENAGER SINGS THE BLUES (A Teenager Sings
           The Blues/Blues In The Night/St Louis Blues)
           (mono/stereo)   (Columbia SEG 8170/ESG 7880) - SC/SC
       4   MORE HITS FROM HELEN (Tell Me What He Said/I
           Apologise/Let's Talk About/Sometime Yesterday)
                          (Columbia SEG 8174) 1962 SC -
       5   EVEN MORE HITS FROM HELEN (Little Miss Lonely/
           I Don't Care/Keep Away from Other Girls/Cry My Heart
           Out)   (Columbia SEG 8209) 1962 SC -
       6   TOPS WITH ME NO 1 (Little Devil/Will Love Me
           Tomorrow/Because They're Young/The Day The Rain
           Came) (mono/stereo)
                   (Columbia SEG 8229ESG 7888) 1962 - SC/R1
       7   TOPS WITH ME NO 2 (Are You Lonesome Tonight/
           A Teenager In Love/Lipstick On Your Collar/Beyond The
           Sea) (mono/stereo)
                   (Columbia SEG 8243/ESG 7891) 1962 - SC/R1

                                                              HCP

45s: Don't Treat Me Like A Child/
(up to   When I'm With You   (Columbia DB 4589) 1961 3
1976)   You Don't Know/Marvellous Lie   (Columbia DB 4670) 1961 1
           Walkin' Back To Happiness/
           Kiss'N'Run   (Columbia DB 4715) 1961 1
           Tell Me What He Said/I Apologise   (Columbia DB 4782) 1962 2
           Let's Talk About Love/
           Sometime Yesterday   (Columbia DB 4824) 1962 23
           Little Miss Lonely/I Don't Care   (Columbia DB 4869) 1962 8
           Keep Away From Other Girls/
           Cry My Heart Out   (Columbia DB 4908) 1962 40
           Queen For Tonight/daddy Couldn't Get Me
           One Of Those   (Columbia DB 4966) 1963 SC 33
           Woe Is Me/I Walked Right In   (Columbia DB 7026) 1963 35

Not Responsible/No Tresspassing   (Columbia DB 7072) 1963 -
Look Who It Is/
Walking In My Dreams   (Columbia DB 7130) 1963 47
Fever/Ole Father Time   (Columbia DB 7190) 1964 SC 38
Look Over Your Shoulder/
You Won't Come Home   (Columbia DB 7266) 1964 -
Shop Around/
He Knows How To Love Me   (Columbia DB 7340) 1964 R2 -
I Wish I'd Never Loved You/
I Was Only Kidding   (Columbia DB 7395) 1964 -
Tomorrow Is Another Day/
It's So Funny I Could Cry   (Columbia DB 7517) 1965 -
Here In Your Arms/Only Once   (Columbia DB 7587) 1965 -
Something Wonderful/Just A Line   (Columbia DB 7690) 1965 -
Forget About The Bad Things/
Wait A Little Longer   (Columbia DB 7810) 1966 -
In My Calendar/Empty House   (Columbia DB 8073) 1966 -
Make Me Belong To You/
The Way Of The World   (Columbia DB 8148) 1967 -
She Needs Company/Stop And
You Will Become Aware   (Columbia DB 8256) 1967 R3 -
You'll Get Me Loving You/
Silly Boy (I Love You)   (Pye 7N 17600) 1968 -
Today Has Been Cancelled/
Facc The Music   (Pye 7N 17714) 1969 -
You've Guessed/Take Me For A While   (Pye 7N 17785) 1969 -
Take Down A Note Miss Smith/
Couldn't You See   (Pye 7N 17893) 1970 SC -
Waiting On The Shores Of Nowhere/
A Glass Of Wine   (Pye 7N 17975) 1970 -
The Prophet/Now Or Never*   (Phoenix SNIX 128) 1972 -
You're A Love Child/
That's The Reason I Love You   (DJM DJS 363) 1975 -
If You Feel He Cares/
It Only Hurts When I Love#   (Magnet MAG 65) 1976 -
Reissues: You Don't Know/
Walking Back To Happiness   (Old Gold OG 9370) 1983 -
Walking Back To Happiness/
Queen For Tonight   (EMI IA0065198) 1984 -

Helen Shapiro was one of the biggest and most successful singers of the early sixties who was notable for her rich, expressive voice. She soon developed a maturity that belied her tender years, but was a victim of the dominance of beat music in the charts in the mid-sixties, which cut short her period of ascendancy from what might have been.

Shapiro was born in Bethnal Green Hospital in London's East End on 28 September 1946. She showed a flair for music at a young age and performed with a ukulele when she was just nine as part of a group at her Clapton school that included a young Mark Feld (later to become **Marc Bolan**). They played their own versions of Elvis Presley and Buddy Holly songs. Next she played in her brother Ron Shapiro's traditional jazz group that developed into a skiffle band. She then enrolled in Maurice Burman's music school in London. He took **Shapiro** under his wing personally and once he thought she was ready to record he recommended her to top EMI producer Norrie Paramor, who had earlier signed Cliff Richard and The Shadows. Paramor was too busy to come and listen to her so he sent his assistant John Schroeder who was so impressed with her voice he arranged a recording test. When he first heard her singing *The Birth Of The Blues* Paramor refused to believe it was the work of a 14-year-old girl until she came to his offices and sang it to him there.

Her debut single *Don't Treat Me Like A Child* was produced by Norrie Paramor with a musical arrangement by Martin Slavin. Released in February 1961 the record was a slow burner not entering the charts until 23 March and even then its progress was uncertain until she appeared on 'Thank Your Lucky Stars'. It ended up spending 20 weeks in the Top 50 peaking at No 3. The follow-up *You Don't Know* was written by John Schroeder with help from Mike Hawker. The mature ballad climbed slowly up the charts to No 1 eventually selling ¼ million copies in the UK and a million worldwide. Next up was *Walkin' Back To Happiness* a catchy, more uptempo number penned by the same songwriting team. It was featured in a short film made at the Abbey Road Studio 'Look At Life' and when it went on general release it was a great boost for the song, which was another million seller worldwide and was a No 1 in both the UK and the US. Ironically, **Shapiro** had never wanted to record it feeling it to be hopelessly old-fashioned, but her interpretation added more depth to the song and helped make it such a success.

Her fourth single *Tell Me What He Said* climbed to No 2 in February 1962 but was kept off the top by **The Shadows'** *Wonderful Land*. The follow-up *Let's Talk About Love* only reached No 23, despite being included in her debut film 'It's Trad Dad', in which she co-starred with Craig Douglas. In July 1962, she scored her final Top Ten hit with *Little Miss Lonely*, another Schroeder/Hawker composition. She enjoyed subsequent minor hits, including *Keep Away From Other Girls* - the first Burt Bacharach song to make the UK Top 40.

She also released some very successful EPs in her early years. Her first one *Helen* featured versions of four standards and spent 30 weeks in the Top Ten EP chart rising to No 1. The second *Helen's Hit Parade*, which contained her first three singles and the flip side to the first one, also hit the top of the chart and spent 36 weeks in all in the EP chart. Her later EPs, whilst still worthy did not chart. Most notable was *A Teenager Sings The Blues* which previewed music that she would veer towards later in her career.

Her debut album *Tops With Me* was also extremely successful, climbing to No 2 during a 25-week chart residency.

Despite her tender age **Shapiro** was frequently appearing on TV and radio. She was voted Top British Female Singer in 1961 and 1962 and also won the best newcomer award from the Variety Club of Great Britain.

Her second album *Helen's Sixteen* blended standards and originals. It made play on her age and the number of tracks it contained, but it didn't emulate the chart success of its predecessor. Her third album *Helen In Nashville* was a landmark being the first time a British girl singer had recorded in the home of country music. In some respects it can be said to be a precursor for **Dusty Springfield's** *Dusty In Memphis* album some years later. In Nashville she recorded the first version of *It's My Party*, which was being lined up as a future UK single. However, Columbia chose to release *Woe Is Me* (a minor hit) and *Not Responsible* (her first miss) as singles first. Meanwhile Lesley Gore got to hear the song, recorded it and enjoyed an international hit with it!

She appeared in a second movie 'Play It Cool', which starred Billy Fury and was still a popular live attraction during 1963. She headlined **The Beatles'** first national tour and they loved her voice. She advised them to select *From Me To You* as their follow-up to *Please Please Me*. They, in turn, wrote *Misery* for her, but surprisingly EMI refused to let her record it and she never did record a **Lennon-McCartney** song despite being great mates with them. Then, ironically, as Beatlemania emerged and beat groups began to dominate the charts she was one of the earlier wave of artists that suffered.

Her 1964 album *Helen Hits Out* included decent cover versions of hits like *He's A Rebel*, *My Guy*, *Walk On By* and *It's In His Kiss*, but it was a commercial flop. She tried a number of further singles for Columbia but with no success and when her contract with EMI lapsed she switched to Pye, for whom she recorded five singles between 1968-1970. The deal re-united her with John Schroeder, who had originally arranged for her to record her first demo, but still no hits emerged.

When her contract with Pye ended she did record several one-off records. Of note is *The Prophet*, which she recorded under the name of Ella Stone & Moss with Al Saxon on the Phoenix label in 1972. She resumed recording under her own name releasing *You're A Love Child* for DJM in 1975, but then released *If You Feel He Cares*, which she co-wrote with her brother Ronnie Shapiro, under the pseudonym Swing Thing.

With her career as a pop entertainer in decline **Shapiro** moved into theatre. She played in West End musicals like 'The French Have A Song For It' and was Nancy in Lionel Bart's 'Oliver!' as well as appearing in UK soap operas. In 1983, she signed to Charlie Gillett's Oval label and released her first new album for 19 years, *Straighten Up And Fly Right*. Then, in 1985, she teamed up with Humphrey Lyttleton to record an album of songs by Duke Ellington called *Echoes Of The Dark*, which brought her much satisfaction. She made frequent concert appearances with him in this period. At least four CD compilations of her material were released in the eighties and a 'best of' CD of her material was released in Japan in the nineties.

Compilation appearances have included: *Walking Back To Happiness* on *Super Hits Of The 60s - Vol 2* (CD), *Hits Of The 60's, Vol 2* (CD), *Nothing But Number 1 Love Songs* (CD), *UK No. 1 Hits Of The 60's* (CD), the 2-CD set *60 Number Ones of The Sixties* and on the 2-CD set *Greatest Hits Of The 60's Volume 4*; and *Don't Treat Me Like A Child* has resurfaced on *Super Hits Of The 60s - Vol 3* (CD), *Hits Of The Sixties - 20 Swinging Sounds* (CD) and on *The Best Of British Rock* (CD).

The Sharades

45:	Dumb Head/Boy Trouble	(Decca F 11811) 1964 R2

A girl group who were better known as **The Breakaways**. (VJ)

The Sharks

Personnel:	ANDY FRASER	bs, piano	A
	MARTY SIMON	drms	AB
	SNIPS PARSONS	vcls, gtr	ABCD
	CHRIS SPEDDING	gtr	ABCD
	BUSTA CHERRY JONES	bs	BC
	NICK JUDD	keyb'ds	B
	STUART FRANCIS	drms	CD
	DAVE COCHRAN	bs	D

ALBUMS:	1(A)	FIRST WATER	(Island ILPS 9233) 1973
	2(B)	JAB IT IN YOUR EYE	(Island ILPS 9271) 1974

NB: (1) and (2) issued on MCA in the US.

This seventies heavy rock outfit included **Chris Spedding** (previously with **Jack Bruce and Friends**) and **Andy Fraser** (ex-**Free**). Snips Parsons had been in Nothing Ever Happens and Canadian Marty Simon in Mylon's Holy Smoke. **Free's** influence is very evident on tracks like *World Punk Junkies* on their *First Water* album, which is marred by lack of variety, but fine if you're into heavy rock. **Fraser** left owing to ill health in May 1973 and later went solo.

Jones (formerly with Isaac Hayes and Albert King) and Judd (previously with **Audience**) were recruited in their place. This line-up recorded the second album. Simon and Judd left in July 1974. Simon initially did session work and then joined Canadian band April Wine. Judd went on to **The Andy Fraser Band**. Ex-**Glencoe** member Stuart Francis came in on drums. Jones left for US band White Lightning and was later in Talking Heads and did session work. In the band's final weeks American Dave Cochran joined on bass.

The band finally split in November 1974. Parsons joined **The Baker-Gurvitz Army**; **Spedding** and Cockran worked with **Roy Harper** and Francis went into session work. (VJ/JM)

The Sharons

ALBUM:	1	SOMEONE TO TURN TO	(Emblem JDR 325) 1970 R3

This very rare album was only released in Ireland. (VJ)

HELEN SHAPIRO - Sensational (LP).

Sandie Shaw

				HCP
ALBUMS:	1	SANDIE	(Pye NPL 18110) 1965	SC 3
(up to	2	ME	(Pye NPL 18122) 1965	SC -
1976)	3	THE GOLDEN HITS OF SANDIE SHAW		
			(Golden Guinea GGL 0360) 1966	SC -
	4	SANDIE SINGS	(Golden Guinea GGL 0378) 1967	SC -
	5	PUPPET ON A STRING		
		(mono/stereo)	(Pye N(S)PL 18182) 1967	SC -
	6	LOVE ME, PLEASE LOVE ME		
		(mono/stereo)	(Pye N(S)PL 18205) 1967	SC -
	7	THE GOLDEN HITS OF SANDIE SHAW		
		(mono/stereo)	(Marble Arch MAL(S) 781) 1968	-
	8	THE SANDIE SHAW SUPPLEMENT		
		(mono/stereo)	(Pye N(S)PL 18232) 1968	SC -
	9	REVIEWING THE SITUATION		
		(mono/stereo)	(Pye N(S)PL 18323) 1969	R1 -
	10	GOLDEN HOUR PRESENTS SANDIE SHAW'S		
		GREATEST HITS	(Golden Hour GH 533) 1972	-
	11	PUPPET ON A STRING	(Hallmark HMA 217) 1972	-

NB: (8) reissued on vinyl (Marble Arch MAL(S) 1164) 1969. (1) and (2) reissued on one CD (See For Miles (SEECD 436) 1995. (6) reissued on CD (RPM RPM 124) 1994. (8) reissued on CD (RPM RPM 112) 1993. (9) reissued on CD (RPM RPM 101) 1993. Vinyl compilations include *The Sandie Shaw File* (Pye File FILD 007) 1977 and *20 Golden Pieces* (?) 1986. CD compilations include: *The EP Collection* (See For Miles SEECD 305) 1990, *Long Live Love* (Disky WMCD 5611) 1994, *The Collection* (Collection COL 067) 1995, *Long Live Love* (Disky DC869812) (containing her hits) 1996, *Greatest Hits Of Sandie Shaw* (Autograph MACCD 171) 1996, *Always Something There To Remind Me* (Tring QED 133) 1996, *Cover To Cover* (Emporio EMPRCD 625) 1996, *Puppet On A String* (Laserlight 21038) 1997, *Greatest Hits* (BR Music RM 1545) 1997, *Always Something There To Remind Me* (Disky WB 878602) 1997 and *Nothing Less Than Brilliant (The Best Of Sandie Shaw)* (Virgin CDVIP 183) 1997. *Pourvu Que Ca Dure* (EMI 5915762) is a French language version of her hits. *Nothing Comes Easy* (EMI 8660702) 2004 is a good 4-CD collection of her material.

EPs:	1	(THERE'S) ALWAYS SOMETHING THERE TO		
		REMIND ME	(Pye NEP 24208) 1964	SC
	2	LONG LIVE LOVE	(Pye NEP 24220) 1965	SC
	3	MESSAGE UNDERSTOOD	(Pye NEP 24236) 1966	SC
	4	TOMORROW	(Pye NEP 24247) 1966	SC
	5	NOTHING COMES EASY	(Pye NEP 24254) 1966	SC
	6	RUN WITH SANDIE	(Pye NEP 24264) 1966	SC
	7	SANDIE SHAW IN FRENCH	(Pye NEP 24271) 1967	R1
	8	SANDIE SHAW IN ITALIAN	(Pye NEP 24273) 1967	R1
	9	TELL THE BOYS	(Pye NEP 24281) 1967	SC

			HCP
45s:	As Long As You Are Happy/		
	Ya-Ya-Da-Da	(Pye 7N 15671) 1964	SC -
	(There's) Always Something There To Remind Me/		
	Don't You Know	(Pye 7N 15704) 1964	1
	Girl Don't Come/		
	I'd Be Far Better Off Without You	(Pye 7N 15743) 1964	3
	I'll Stop At Nothing/		
	You Can't Blame Him	(Pye 7N 15783) 1965	4
	Long Live Love/I've Heard About Him	(Pye 7N 15841) 1965	1
	Message Understood/Don't Count On It	(Pye 7N 15940) 1965	6
	How Can You Tell/If You Ever Need Me	(Pye 7N 15987) 196	21
	Tomorrow/Hurting You	(Pye 7N 17036) 1966	9
	Nothing Comes Easy/		
	Stop Before You Start	(Pye 7N 17086) 1966	14
	Run/Long Walk Home	(Pye 7N 17163) 1966	32
	Think Sometimes About Me/		
	Hide All Emotion	(Pye 7N 17212) 1966	32
	I Don't Need Anything/Keep In Touch	(Pye 7N 17239) 1967	50
	Puppet On A String/Tell The Boys	(Pye 7N 17272) 1967	1
	Tonight In Tokyo/		
	You've Been Seeing Her Again	(Pye 7N 17346) 1967	21
	You've Not Changed/Make Me Cry	(Pye 7N 17378) 1967	18
	Today/London	(Pye 7N 17441) 1968	27
	Don't Run Away/Stop	(Pye 7N 17504) 1968	-
	Show Me/One More Lie	(Pye 7N 17564) 1968	-
	Together/Turn On The Sunshine	(Pye 7N 17587) 1968	-
	Those Were The Days/Make It Go	(Pye 7N 17611) 1968	-
	Monsieur Dupont/Voice In The Crowd	(Pye 7N 17675) 1969	6
	Think It All Over/Send Me A Letter	(Pye 7N 17726) 1969	42
	Heaven Knows I'm Missing Him Now/		

So Many Things To Do	(Pye 7N 17821) 1969	-
By Tomorrow/Maple Village	(Pye 7N 17894) 1970	-
Wight Is Wight/		
That's The Way He's Made Me	(Pye 7N 17954) 1970	-
Rose Garden/Maybe I'm Amazed	(Pye 7N 45040) 1971	-
Power And The Glory/Dear Madame	(Pye 7N 45073) 1971	-
Where Did They Go/Look At Me	(Pye 7N 45118) 1972	-
Father And Son/Pity The Ship	(Pye 7N 45164) 1972	-

Reissues: Puppet On A String/Long Live Love/Girl Don't Come/(There's) Always Something There To Remind Me

	(Flashback FBEP 109) 1980 -
Puppet On A String/Long Live Love	(Old Gold OG 9133) 1982 -
Always Something There To Remind Me/	
Girl Don't Come	(Old Gold OG 9144) 1982 -

Sandie Shaw was one of the foremost British female singers of the sixties but she lost her way in the seventies and retired from the music business altogether between 1972-77. She has made occasional comebacks since.

Sandie Shaw was born as Sandra Goodrich on 26 February 1947 in Dagenham, Essex. When she left school she worked as a machine operator for IBM but always wanted to be a singer. When Adam Faith's package tour came to Essex in April 1964, she talked her way backstage and demonstrated her singing ability to his backing band The Roulettes by delivering a version of *Everybody Loves A Lover*. They were sufficiently impressed to fetch Adam and he, in turn, persuaded his manager and tour promoter Eve Taylor to take a listen. Taylor was initially quite ambivalent about Sandra Goodrich's talents but she decided to take her under her management wing, changed her name to **Sandie Shaw** and passed her over to producer Tony Hatch to make some demos. Her early demos were rejected but when they were offered her records as independent productions Pye added her to their impressive roster.

Her first single, *As Long As You're Happy* was issued on 10 July 1964 and some likened her to **Cilla Black**. The single failed to chart but under Eve Taylor's astute management, which exploited **Shaw's** links with Adam Faith to the full, her career soon blossomed. Taylor also decided that **Shaw** should always appear on stage barefoot, which was a gimmick to help her gain press attention. For her second release **Sandie** was given the classic Burt Bacharach/Hal David song *(There's) Always Something There To Remind Me*, which had been a big hit in the States for Dionne Warwick. The single, which entered the charts two weeks after it was released became a smash No 1. It was given a Stateside release on Reprise but so soon after Warwick's hit version of the song it understandably made little headway there.

Taylor then turned to songwriter **Chris Andrews** (who was already writing material for Adam Faith and The Roulettes). He had a penchant for sophisticated melodies and tricksy chord changes like Burt Bacharach and her next single *I'd Be Far Better Off Without Him* was in this mould. However, reviewers tended to prefer the catchy 'B' side *Girl Don't Come* and a couple of weeks after its release the single was flipped over in time to give her a No 3 hit for Christmas.

Her debut album *Sandie* was issued on Pye in February 1965. It comprised a selection of **Chris Andrews'** songs and cover versions, including *Downtown*, *Love Letters* and *Baby I Need Your Loving*. Also included was the song that had started it all for **Sandie**, *Everybody Loves A Lover*. To promote the album she toured as part of an Adam Faith package giving her first performance at the De Montfort Hall in Leicester on 21 February 1965. Her next single *I'll Stop At Nothing* had originally been written by **Andrews** for Adam Faith but was re-directed to her when it was released now that she had the greater commercial potential. In April she toured Canada and, after initially struggling to obtain a US work permit, eventually did so appearing on the 'Ed Sullivan Show'. *Girl Don't Come* (her third single) did become a minor US hit peaking at No 47, but her new single the catchy *Long Live Love* bombed there and she never did crack the US market. Here in Britain it gave her another big hit and it was also issued in Germany and France. Having failed to captivate fans in the US, Europe now became the main focus of her attention, outside of the UK.

With **Cilla Black** and **Lulu** moving into acting overtures were made in **Sandie's** direction too, but Eve Taylor turned them all down feeling that none of the roles were suitable. Parts rejected included ones in 'Half A Sixpence' (with Tommy Steele) and 'Mrs Brown You've Got A Lovely Daughter' (with Peter Noone). For now the hits continued, though and *Message Understood*, another catchy **Chris Andrews'** song reached No 6 in Autumn 1965.

Her second album *Me* contained no less than six **Andrews'** compositions, although its sales didn't match those of her first one. Her next 45, a flamboyant up-tempo **Andrews'** composition *How Can You Tell* failed to chart, but the follow-up *Tomorrow*, a much classier song put her back in the Top Ten.

In 1966 Pye put out a hits compilation on its mid-price Golden Guinea label and it re-appeared later on Marble Arch. The album was a good collection of her more successful songs to date. Early the same year Eve Taylor turned down the chance for **Shaw** to sing the theme tune to a new film called 'Alfie' which was written by Burt Bacharach. The film starred Michael Caine. **Cilla Black** later took *Alfie* into the Top Ten, while **Shaw's** next single *Nothing Comes Easy* stalled at No 14. Increasingly, in this period Taylor was making a conscious effort to push **Shaw** towards cabaret and to market her across Western Europe. In May 1966, she went to Italy to record an album - six tracks were actually completed and released as singles. When she returned to Venice in July to perform in the International Song Festival *Nothing Comes Easy* was an Italian No 1. Here in the UK, things were not going as well with *Run* and *Think Sometimes About Me* (her next two singles) again missing out on the charts. But her increasing cabaret commitments and growing success in Europe probably were influential in her selection to represent the UK in the 1967 Eurovision Song Contest.

1967 began slowly when *I Don't Need Anything* (her first single for three years not written by **Andrews'**) only crawled into the lower echelons of the Top 50. Her next album *Sandie Sings* was released on the mid-price Golden Guinea label not being considered worthy of a full-price release. But things rapidly changed when Martin and Coulter's *Puppet On A String* became the first British entry to win the Eurovision Song Contest on 8 April 1967. It became a No 1 all over Europe and the cabaret offers flooded in. An album *Puppet On A String* was rush-released - it contained many songs previously released as singles. She began work on an autobiography and The Daily Mirror's Don Short also started on her biography. She retained the Martin and Coulter partnership for her next single *Tonight In Tokyo* and it just missed the Top 20. Her final single of 1967, another **Andrews'** composition *You've Not Changed* peaked at No 18. The year's third album *Love Me, Please Love Me* was released in time for Christmas. This time containing just two **Andrews'** songs, it was dominated by a host of standards and she ended the year with an acclaimed Royal Command Performance.

In her private life 1968 was a good year for Sandie as she married fashion designer Jeff Banks. It was not a good year for her pop career, though as none of her five singles that year - *Today, Don't Run Away, Show Me, Together* and *Those Were The Days* - made the Top 20. Indeed, only *Today* (No 27) made the Top 50! The first three were **Andrews'** compositions. *Together* was a Harry Nillson number and had only been released a week after a hastily-recorded version of *Those Were The Days* was put out. It lost out to the **Mary Hopkins** version in record sales. By contrast she did get her own BBC TV series 'The Sandie Shaw Supplement'. An album of the same name was released and it was her rockiest to date. It featured versions of *Satisfaction, Route 66* and a couple of Simon and Garfunkel songs, but it didn't sell well.

Monsieur Dupont in early 1969 climbed to No 6. It was her last Top Ten hit. The follow-up *Think It All Over* made the lower reaches of the Top 50, but her subsequent efforts missed out completely. These included *Wight Is Wight* (a tribute to the Isle of Wight pop festival), a cover of Joe South's *Rose Garden* and a version of **Cat Stevens'** *Father And Son*. In late 1969 one final studio album *Reviewing The Situation* was issued. It was an attempt to review the happenings in rock music since **Sandie** had been singing and was a strange blend of rock and middle-of-the-road material.

Her contract with Pye ended in 1972 and she didn't record again until 1977, when two singles for CBS - *One More Night* and *Your Mama Wouldn't Like It* - flopped. In any case 1977 was probably not a good year for an older artist to attempt a comeback! She retired abroad, working as a waitress, until in 1982 a Heaven 17 side project the British Electric Foundation (BSF) lured her into the studio as part of their 'Music Of Quality and Distinction' project. A strong version of the old **Cilla Black** hit *Anyone Who Had A Heart* was released with **Sandie** handling the lead and backing vocals. It narrowly missed the singles chart but was included on BSF's album. Morrissey, The Smiths' lead singer then championed her cause and this culminated in her recording a version of the band's *Hand In Glove*, which did return her to the charts (after a 15 year absence) peaking at No 27. In 1986, she recorded a version of Lloyd Cole's *Are You Ready To Be Heartbroken*, which scraped into the bottom of the charts, rising to No 68.

SANDY SHAW - All The Hits (CD).

In 1988, she recorded an album of new material *Hello Angel*, which featured songs by The Smiths and The Jesus and Mary Chain, but it failed to make a significant impact.

Nothing Comes Easy is a 4-CD collection of her material and the fourth disc contains previously unreleased tracks and stereo mixes of her early singles.

Compilation appearances have included: *(There's) Always Something There To Remind Me* on *The Hitmakers* (LP), *The Hitmakers Vol 3* (EP) and on *Sixties Mix* (CD); *Girl Don't Come* on *Hitmakers Vol 2* (LP) and on *The Hitmakers No 1* (EP); *Long Live Love* on *Hitmakers Vol 3* (LP) and there's a live version of the song on *Here Come The Girls* (LP); *Gotta See My Baby* on *Stars Charity Fantasia* (LP); *Tell The Boys* on *A Galaxy Of Stars* (LP); and *Puppet On A String* on *Showcase* (LP) and on the 2-CD set *60 Number Ones Of The Sixties*. She also contributed two tracks each to *Hitmakers Vol 4* (LP), *Golden Hitmakers* (LP) and *Stars of '67* (LP) and four tracks to *Pye Presents Ten Years Of Golden Hits* (LP). (VJ)

The Sheep

Personnel:	MOLE BAKER	vcls, hrmnca, gtr	A
	LISA CAROTHERS	vcls, keyb'ds	A
	RICH HAAS	vcls, drms	A
	NICK MALHAM	drms	A
	REED MITTELSTEADT	vcls	A
	GREG NANCARROW	vcls, keyb'ds, gtr	A
	WILHELM PINNOW	bs	A

ALBUM: 1(A) SHEEP (w/insert)   (Myrrh Gold MYR 1000) 1973 R1

Although musically less overtly religious than most releases on Myrrh, this brand of straight-ahead organ dominated rock isn't very enticing. They play with enthusiasm and skill, but the compositions are clearly below par. Don't let any dealer seduce you into buying this as a masterpiece of progressive rock, because it isn't. Especially irritating is the children's choir on *Let All The Redeemed Of The Lord Say So*. This is a competent, but totally commonplace album. The best track by this band is to be found on the "Soundtrack" *Lonesome Stone* on the Reflection label. (MK)

Sheephouse

45:      Juicy Lucy/Ladder   (Decca F 13229) 1971

A male four-piece about whom nothing else is known. (MWh)

Sheep's Head Bay

45:      My Name Is The Wind/River Song   (Parlophone R 5897) 1971

This was an obscure early seventies act. (MWh)

The Sheffields

Personnel:	JOHN ALEXANDER	A
	DON ALLISON	A
	DAVE FAWCETT	A
	RICHARD SMITH	A

45s:	It Must Be Love/Say Girl	(Pye 7N 15600) 1964 R1
	I Got My Mojo Working/	
	Hey, Hey Lover Boy	(Pye 7N 15627) 1964 R2
	Bag's Groove (Skat Walking)/	
	Plenty Of Love	(Pye 7N 15767) 1965 R2

Yes this mid-sixties beat/R&B group were from Sheffield. Their records are now very rare and sought-after. *Bag's Groove*, was an odd jazz-pop song which had originally been a Milt Jackson instrumental. The band backed Memphis Slim on his 1964 tour here. They split in 1965.

Compilation appearances have included: *Got My Mojo Working* on *Maximum R'n'B* (CD), *Beat Merchants* (2-LP) and *The R&B Era, Vol. 1* (LP & CD); *Bags Groove (Skat Walking)* on *The R&B Era, Vol. 2* (CD), *Beat Merchants* (CD) and *Doin' The Mod, Vol. 1* (CD); *Plenty Of Love* on *English Freakbeat, Vol. 1* (LP & CD); and *It Must Be Love* and *Plenty Of Love* on *Freakbeat Freakout* (CD). (VJ)

The Sheiks

| 45: | Missing You/Tell Me Bird | (Parlophone R 5500) 1966 |

This little known four-piece band's sole disc was this 45, which had falsetto vocals. (VJ)

The Shell

| 45: | Goodbye Little Girl/ | |
| | Little Bit Of Lovin' | (Columbia DB 8082) 1966 |

A five-man band from Essex. The 45 is fast beat with harmony vocals and was produced by Tim Rice. Other acetates exist. (VJ/RMJ)

Shelley

45s:	I Will Be Wishing/	
	Why Won't You Say You Love Me	(Pye 7N 15711) 1964
	Stairway To A Star/I Heard A Whisper	(Pye 7N 15773) 1965
	Where Has Your Smile Gone/Paradise	(Pye 7N 15913) 1965

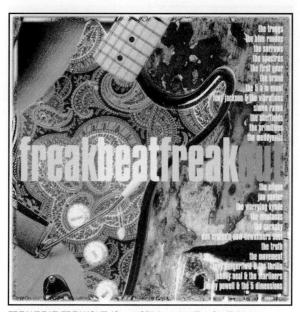

FREAKBEAT FREAKOUT (Comp CD) featuring The Sheffields.

This beat-era band came from Eastbourne in Sussex. In addition to these three 45s they have a cut, *The War* on the *Visions Of The Past, Vol. 2* (LP & CD) compilation. Their final 'A' side later resurfaced on Sequel's *Hippy Hippy Shake* (CD). (VJ)

Peter Shelley

		HCP
45s:	Gee Baby/I'm In Love Again	(Magnet MAG 12) 1974 4
(up to	Bye Bye/Storybook Ending	(Magnet MAG 18) 1974 -
1976)	Love Me Love My Dog/	
	My Sweet Deustch Friend	(Magnet MAG 22) 1975 3
	Little Julie/I'm Flying	(Magnet MAG 35) 1975 -
	Wisconsin/I'm Flying	(Magnet MAG 49) 1975 -
Reissue:	Love Me Love My Dog/Gee Baby	(Old Gold OG 9671) 1987 -

Considering he had two Top Ten hits **Peter Shelley** seems a very forgotten vocalist now. (VJ)

Shepperton Flames

| 45: | Take Me For What I Am/Goodbye | (Deram DM 257) 1969 R1 |

Both sides of this 45 were written and produced by **Mike Berry** and it had been suggested that this band were a studio creation for him. However, an Emidisc acetate has recently surfaced of **The Shepperton Flames** performing Brenton Wood's *Oogum Boogum Song*, which dates from 1968. This suggests that they were perhaps a Shepperton based act, who were spotted by **Berry** at some point.

Compilation appearances include: *Goodbye* on *Visions Of The Past, Vol. 3* (LP); and *Goodbye* and *Take Me For What I Am* on *Visions Of The Past, Vol. 3* (CD). (SP/VJ)

Sheridan

| 45: | Follow Me Follow/ | |
| | When Love Breaks Your Heart | (Gemini GMS 001) 1970 SC |

Mike Sheridan had fronted **Mike Sheridan and The Nightriders** and **Mike Sheridan's Lot** in the sixties. When he quit the latter to go solo he recorded this single - the first on the Gemini label and then linked up with **Rick Price** in **Sheridan-Price**. (VJ)

Mike Sheridan and The Nightriders

Personnel:	GREG MASTERS	bs	AB
	DAVE PRITCHARD	gtr	AB
	MIKE SHERIDAN	vcls	AB
	ROGER SPENCER	drms	AB
	ROY WOOD	gtr	B

| ALBUM: 1(A/B) | BIRMINGHAM BEAT | (Edsel ED 120) 1984 |

45s:	Tell Me Whatcha Gonna Do/	
	No Other Guy	(Columbia DB 7141) 1963 SC
	Please Mr.Postman/In Love	(Columbia DB 7183) 1963 SC
	What A Sweet Thing That Was/	
	Fabulous	(Columbia DB 7302) 1964 SC
	Here I Stand/Lonely Weekends	(Columbia DB 7462) 1965 SC

This was one of Birmingham's top bands who were joined by **Roy Wood** after the first couple of 45s. They met with no Chart success and in mid-1965 became **Mike Sheridan's Lot**. All their 45s are now quite collectable.

The most accessible guide to their music is the Edsel compilation which includes all eight 45 tracks, the two 'A' sides by **Mike Sheridan's Lot** (a later version of this band); two previously unreleased songs by **The Nightriders**: - covers of Vince Taylor's *Brand New Cadillac* and The

Shirelles' *A Thing Of The Past* and *Make Them Understand*, **Roy Wood**'s first published composition, which was pretty naff really. Overall, it's an album of solid but unexceptional beat music.

Compilation appearances have included: *What A Sweet Thing That Was* on *Sixties Lost And Found, Vol. 1* (LP); *Please Mr Postman* and *What A Sweet Thing That Was* on *Beat At Abbey Road* (CD); and *No Other Guy* on *Beat Merchants* (2-LP). (VJ)

Mike Sheridan's Lot

Personnel:	GREG MASTERS	bs	A
	DAVE PRITCHARD	gtr	A
	MIKE SHERIDAN	vcls	A
	ROGER SPENCER	drms	A
	ROY WOOD	gtr	A

45s:	Take My Hand/		
	Make Them Understand	(Columbia DB 7677) 1965 SC
	Don't Turn Your Back On Me, Babe/		
	Stop, Look, Listen	(Columbia DB 7798) 1966 SC

This was a later version of Birmingham-based **Mike Sheridan and The Nightriders** which carried on for one 45 as **The Nightriders** when **Sheridan** left in 1966 to go solo and **Roy Wood** departed to form **The Move**. **Sheridan** eventually formed a duo with **Rick Price**. With the addition of Jeff Lynne **The Nightriders** eventually became **Idle Race**.

The compilation *Birmingham Beat* (Edsel ED 120) 1984, credited to **Mike Sheridan and The Nightriders**, included both of this outfit's 'A' sides. *Don't Turn Your Back On Me Babe*, in particular, is a pretty good harmony vocal rendition of a Jackie De Shannon song. (VJ)

Tony Sheridan (and The Beat Brothers)

HCP

ALBUMS:	1	THE BEATLES FIRST	(Polydor 236 201) 1967 R2 -
(up to	2	THE EARLY YEARS - THE BEATLES FEATURING
1976)		TONY SHERIDAN	(Contour 2870111) 1971 3
	3	THE EARLY YEARS - THE BEATLES FEATURING
		TONY SHERIDAN	(CN 2007) 1976 -

NB: (1) reissued (Polydor 823701-2) 1984 and again (Polydor 9821323) as a deluxe 2-CD set.of material he recorded with **The Beatles** in Hamburg that was originally released in 1964. (3) is a reissue of (2). Also relevant is *Live! At The Star Club In Hamburg, Germany, 1962* (Lingasong LNL 1) 1977, *Beatles Live At The Star Club In Hamburg, Germany, 1962* (Smile 34001-2) 1977, *The Beatles Early Years Vol 1* (Phoenix PHX 1004) 1981, *The Beatles Early Years Vol 2* (Phoenix PHX 1005) 1981, *Historic Sessions* (Audiofidelity AFE LD 1018) 1981, *Rare Beatles* (Phoenix PHX 1011) 1982, *First Movement* (Audiofidelity PXS 339P) 1982 and again in 1983, *20 Great Hits* (Phoenix P20-629) 1983, *20 Greatest Hits* (Phoenix P20-623) 1983, *1962 The Audition Tapes* (Breakaway BWY 72) 1983, *Birth of The Beatles* (Valentine Records GSR 46) 1983, *The Hamburg Tapes Vol 1* (Breakaway BWY 85) 1983, *The Hamburg Tapes Vol 2* (Breakaway BWY 86) 1983, *The Hamburg Tapes Vol 3* (Breakaway BWY 87) 1983, *Birth of The Beatles Vol 2* (Valentine GSR 81) 1983, *The Beatles Historic Sessions* (box) (Audiofidelity PHX 3-1) 1984, *The Beatles Featuring Tony Sheridan Hamburg 1961* (Topline TOP 108) 1984, *Flashbacks* (Cambra CR 116) 1984, *The Beatles Words And Music* (Cambra CR 5149) 1985, *Live At The Star Club Hamburg Germany 1962 Vol 1* (Castle SHLP 130) 1985, *Live At The Star Club Hamburg Germany 1962 Vol 2* (Castle SHLP 131) 1985, *Just A Little Bit Of Tony Sheridan* (Import Music Service 831998-1) 1987, *Decca Sessions 1/1/62* (Topline TOP 181) 1987, *The Beatles Volume 11* (Baktabak BAK 2108) 1988, *Beatles At The Star Club* (Baktabak LTAB 5001) 1988 and *The Savage Young Beatles* (Get Back GET 570) 2000.

| EP: | 1 | TONY SHERIDAN WITH THE BEATLES (PS) |
| | | (Polydor EPH 21 610) 1964 R1 |

NB: First pressings in orange 'scroll' label. Second pressings in red label are (SC).

HCP

45s:	α	My Bonnie (English intro)/		
(up to		The Saints	(Polydor NH 66833) 1962 R2 -
1976)	χ	Sweet Georgia Brown/		
		Nobody's Child	(Polydor NH 52906) 1964 R2 -
	β	Jambalaya/		

		Will You Still Love Me Tomorrow	(Polydor NH 52315) 1964 SC -
β	Skinny Minny/		
	You'd Better Move On	(Polydor NH 52927) 1964 SC -
	Cry For A Shadow/Why	(Polydor NH 52275) 1964 R2 -
	Ain't She Sweet/		
	If You Love Me Baby	(Polydor NH 52-317) 1964 R2 -
	Lonely/I Should Have Stayed	(Buk BU 3026) 1975 -

NB: α Reissued with the same catalogue number in June 1963. β credited as **Tony Sheridan and The Beat Brothers**. *The Beatles' First* (Polydor 9821323) is a deluxe 2-CD set of material he recorded with **The Beatles** in Hamburg that was originally released in 1964. χ German import only. Unissued in UK.

Tony Sheridan was born as Andrew Esmond Sheridan McGinnity in Norwich. When he was 18 he appeared on the TV show 'Oh Boy' as a singer-guitarist and became the first musician to play an electric guitar on TV. He played in London with Eddie Cochran, Marty Wilde, Conway Twitty and Vince Taylor whilst still a teenager. His big break came when he was offered a contract at the 'Top Ten Club' in Hamburg, Germany. After a successful six-month residency there he was offered and accepted a one year contract at 'The Star Club', which quickly became Europe's most important rock'n'roll venue.

One of the back-up bands he used was The Beat Brothers (**Paul McCartney**, **John Lennon**, **George Harrison** and **Pete Best**) - this name was used because **The Beatles** did not translate in German, except as slang for the male sex organ. One night, following a backstage fray he sacked drummer **Pete Best** and replaced him with Richie Starkey (**Ringo Starr**), who had earlier worked with him, but not with **The Beatles**.

The first recordings ever made by **The Beatles** were with **Tony Sheridan** on his first album *Tony Sheridan and The Beatles*. The album sold well but when Brian Epstein offered **The Beatles** the chance of a new record contract which involved them returning to England they upped and went and **Sheridan** and **The Beatles** went their separate ways. His recordings with **The Beatles** were cut in June/July 1961 and April 1962. They backed him on six of the tracks and recorded two on their own: a raucous version of *Ain't She Sweet* with **John Lennon** on vocals and a twangy guitar instrumental written by **Lennon** and **Harrison**. The recent reissue of this album is lavishly packaged with a substantial booklet containing much memorabilia and with mono and stereo versions of the original album. There are also two bonus tracks, two versions of *My Bonnie* with German and English intros.

As the Vietnam war escalated **Tony Sheridan** took a troupe of musicians to entertain the American and allied troops in Vietnam. Whilst travelling in the military zone his crew came under fire and one member was killed. Reuters reported that **Sheridan** had been killed and his obituary appeared in papers around the world. In fact he remained in the Far East for a further two years entertaining the troops and for his services was made an honorary Captain in the US army.

When the Star Club reopened in 1978 **Tony Sheridan** was there to headline. He brought The TCB band as his support, but **George Harrison**,

TONY SHERIDAN - THE EARLY YEARS - THE BEATLES FEATURING TONY SHERIDAN (LP).

SHIDE AND ACORN - Under The Tree (LP).

John Lennon and **Paul McCartney** all made unannounced appearances to support him. Married with a large family, **Sheridan** now lives in Germany and performs around the world.

In the early eighties there was a plethora of releases of material recorded by **Sheridan** and **The Beatles** in Hamburg in the early sixties and a full discography is provided above. (VJ)

Sheridan - Price

Personnel:	RICK PRICE	gtr, bs, vcls	A
	MIKE SHERIDAN	vcls	A

ALBUM: 1(A) THIS IS TO CERTIFY THAT (Gemini GME 1002) 1970 SC

45: α Sometimes I Wonder/
Lightning Never Strikes Twice   (Gemini GMS 009) 1970 SC

NB: α 'A' side credited to **Sheridan and Rick Price**. 'B' side credited to **Sheridan**.

See the **Mike Sheridan** and **Rick Price** entries for more details of their careers. **Sheridan** had earlier released the first 45 on the Gemini label, *Follow Me Follow/When Love Breaks Your Heart* (Gemini GMS 001).

Compilation appearances have included: *Lamp Lighter Man* on *Rubble, Vol. 8 - All The Colours Of Darkness* (LP), *Rubble, Vol. 4* (CD) and *Sometimes I Wonder* (CD); *Tracy Smith* on *Circus Days, Vol. 6* (CD); *Lightning Never Strikes Twice* on *The Electric Lemonade Acid Test, Vol. 1* (LP) and *Sometimes I Wonder* provided the title track to the *Sometimes I Wonder* (CD) and can also be found on *Jagged Time Lapse, Vol 4* (CD). (VJ)

The She Trinity

Personnel incl:	SHELLY GILLESPIE	ABCD
	SUE KIRBY	AB
	ROBIN YORKE	ABCD
	PAULINE MONROE	BCD
	MARION HILL	CD
	BERYL MARSDEN	

45s: He Fought The Law/
The Union Station Blues   (Columbia DB 7874) 1966 SC
Have I Sinned/Wild Flower   (Columbia DB 7943) 1966
Wild Flower/The Man Who Took The Valise Off
The Floor Of Grand Central Station At Noon
(Columbia DB 7959) 1966
Yellow Submarine/
Promise Me You'll Never Cry   (Columbia DB 7992) 1966 SC
Across The Street/Over And Over Again   (CBS 2819) 1967
Hair/Climb That Tree   (President PT 283) 1969 R1

An all girl trio originally from Canada who came to London via New York. Marion Hill had been in **The Thoughts**.

Their 'A' sides also included covers of The Bobby Fuller Four's *He Fought The Law* and **The Beatles'** *Yellow Submarine*. *Wild Flower* with its abrasive guitar and Grace Slick-tinged vocals sounds a bit like an early Jefferson Airplane track. Also noteworthy was their final 'B' side *Climb That Tree*, which is full of frantic guitar and raging organ.

Beryl Marsden joined **Shotgun Express** in 1966 though the band struggled on with no success for a few more years.

Climb That Tree has been compiled on *The Electric Lemonade Acid Test, Vol. 1* (LP) and *Sometimes I Wonder* (CD). (VJ)

The Shevells

Personnel:	TREVOR LEWIS	piano	A
	GEOFF McCARTHY	vcls, bs	A
	MIKE STEVENS	gtr, vcls	A
	RAY STOCK	drms	A
	DENNIS ELLIOT	drms	A

45s: Ooh Poo Pa Doo/Like I Love You   (Oriole CB 1915) 1963 SC
I Could Conquer The World/How Would You
Like Me To Love You   (United Artists UP 1059) 1964 SC
Walking On The Edge Of The World/
Not So Close   (United Artists UP 1076) 1965 SC
Watermelon Man/
Taking Over Your Life   (United Artists UP 1081) 1965 SC
Come On Home/
I Gotta Travel All Over   (United Artists UP 1125) 1966 R1
Big City Lights/Coffee Song   (Polydor 56239) 1968 SC

This Welsh R&B outfit also acted as **Mike Stevens'** backing group. They backed several American blues artists when they came here on tour. After their debut recording on Oriole they switched to United Artists recording four 45s. These included *Watermelon Man*, the Herbie Hancock/**Manfred Mann** favourite. The last, their cover of Jackie Edwards' Northern Soul nugget *Come On Home* is the best and most collectable and it was backed by a strong R&B offering on the flip. They were also known as The Welsh Conquerors. Future **Ferris Wheel** member Dennis Elliot was also briefly a member. (VJ)

Shide and Acorn

Personnel incl:	JERRY CAHILL	gtr	A

ALBUM: 1 UNDER THE TREE   (Private Pressing) 1973 R4

SHIDE AND ACORN - Legend Of The Dreamstones (CD).

NB: (1) reissued on Acme (AC 8006 LP) 1994 as a limited edition of 500 (SC) and on CD by Kissing Spell (Erewhon KSCD 9400-f) 1995 and again on a Korean label (Si Wan SRMC 4028). There's also two CDs of archive material: *Princess Of The Island* (Erewhon KSCD 9640-f) 1994, is mostly recorded in Paris in 1970, and *Legend Of The Dreamstones* (CD) (Erewhon KSCD 9310-f) 1993, a collection of pre-album rehearsal tapes recorded in 1969.

Under The Tree is a mega rare privately-pressed album of mellow folk-rock. In an early incarnation of this band was Anthony Minghella (keyb'ds), now a world famous film director. The band also featured a very talented guitarist Jerry Cahill, and have been said to have played the 1970 Isle Of Wight festival - this is now known to be false.

You don't need to take out a second mortgage to buy a copy now as there was a limited (500) copies reissue in 1994 and CD reissue in 1995. Compilation appearances include: *Under The Tree* on *The History Of U.K. Underground Folk Rock 1968-1978 Vol. 1* (CD); and *I Used To Live Within A World* on *The History Of U.K. Underground Folk Rock 1968-1978 Vol. 2* (CD). (VJ/LV)

SHIDE AND ACORN - Princess Of The Island (CD).

Keith Shields

45s:	Hey Gyp/Deep Inside Your Mind	(Decca F 12572) 1967 R2
	The Wonder Of You/Run, Run, Run	(Decca F 12609) 1967 SC
	So Hard Living Without You/	
	Baby Do You Love Me	(Decca F 12666) 1967 SC

A now forgotten singer **Shields**, from Newcastle, had once played in The Wildcats, a Newcastle group, with Hilton Valentine, who when he left **The Animals** was, among other things, managing **Shields'** career.

Hey Gyp, was originally a **Donovan** song from his first album. **Shields'** version is rockier though, with some good guitar work, quite probably from the hand of Hilton Valentine. The flip side is a slow, rather brooding number with an enhanced vocal. His other two 45s made little impression and he drifted out of the music scene.

Compilation appearances have included: *Deep Inside Your Mind* on *The Psychedelic Scene* (CD) and *British Psychedelic Trip, Vol. 3* (LP) and *Hey Gyp* on *The Freakbeat Scene* (CD). (VJ)

Shillingford Mill

| 45s: | Thing Called Love/Walking Along | (Mama MAM 15) 1971 |
| α | Frightened/I Want To Know | (Mama MAM 28) 1971 |

NB: α as Shillingford.

This group came from the village of Shillingford between Oxford and Reading. They consisted of three boys. *Thing Called Love* was a rhythmic ballad featuring sitar. (VJ)

The Shindigs

| Personnel incl: | IAN PAICE | drms | A |

45s:	One Little Letter/	
	What You Gonna Do	(Parlophone R 5316) 1965 R1
	A Little While Back/	
	Why Say Goodbye	(Parlophone R 5377) 1965 R1

An obscure mid-sixties beat outfit from Oxford whose two 45s are now quite collectable. *A Little While Back* was a **Graham Gouldman** composition and Ian Paice went on to **MI 5**, and **Deep Purple**. (VJ)

Shine

| Personnel incl: | TONY RIVERS | | A |

| 45: | Candy Girl/I Wonder If Anything | (Fontana 600 7041) 1974 |

This mid-seventies act was most notable for featuring **Tony Rivers** who recorded a series of singles in the sixties with The Castaways. (VJ)

Don Shinn (& The Soul Agents)

Personnel:	DON SHINN	keyb'ds		AB
	BARRY MORGAN	perc		B
	TREVOR TOMKINS	drms		B
	STAN TRACY	keyb'ds		B

ALBUMS: 1(A)	TEMPLES WITH PROPHET	
		(Columbia SCX 6319) 1969 R1
2(B)	DEPARTURES	(Columbia SCX 6355) 1969 R1

| 45: | α | A Minor Explosion/ | |
| | | Pits Of Darkness | (Polydor BM 56075) 1966 R2 |

NB. α With **The Soul Agents**.

After forming **The Soul Agents**, **Shinn** recorded these two obscure albums, which are now hard to track down. He was later in **Renaissance**, **Dada** and **Iguana**. Trevor Tomkins later played with **Julie Driscoll** and **Neil Ardley**. Stan Tracy had previously played with **Georgie Fame** and became a member of **Keith Tippett's** group in the late seventies. (SR)

Shiralee

| 45: | I'll Stay By Your Side/Penny Wren | (Fontana TF 855) 1967 |

No other details are known about the band but *I'll Stay By Your Side* can also be found on *Psychdelic Voyage, Vol. 2* (LP) and *Psychedelic Voyage* (CD). (VJ)

Shoot

Personnel:	CRAIG COLLINGE	drms	A
	DAVE GREENE	gtr, vcls	A
	JIM McCARTY	keyb'ds, vcls	A
	BILL RUSSELL	bs	A

| ALBUM: 1(A) | ON THE FRONTIER | (EMI EMA 753) 1973 |

| 45: | On The Frontier/Ships And Sails | (EMI EMI 2026) 1973 |

A short-lived rock band. Dave Greene had previously played in **Raw Material** and Jim McCarty had been **The Yardbirds'** drummer. The album is a pleasant song-based melodic progressive offering. (VJ)

Glenn Shorrock

| 45s: | Let's Get The Band Together/ | |
| | Contemporary Cave Man | (Mam MAM 46) 1971 |

Rock And Roll Lullaby/
When God Plays His Guitar   (Mam MAM 65) 1972

Shorrock was originally from Australia. These were initial solo efforts for **Shorrock** who in 1972 joined **Esperanto**. (VJ)

Brian Short

ALBUM: 1 ANYTHING FOR A LAUGH
                                          (Transatlantic TRA 245) 1971 SC

From Gateshead, **Short** had earlier played in **Black Cat Bones**. His solo album comprises love songs, mainly for women but including one for Brother Paul. The only cover is Randy Newman's *I Think It's Going To Rain Today*. (VJ)

Shortwave Band

Personnel: STUART GORDON   strings, keyb'ds, vcls, gtr   A
              PHIL HARRISON   keyb'ds, gtr, flute, violin   A

ALBUM: 1(A) SHORTWAVE BAND   (RCA SF 8400) 1975

This duo formed in late 1974. Both came from the Merseyband Sticky George. Their sole album is a Zappa and Sparks mix. On it they were assisted by Pick Withers (perc) (ex-**Andy Fairweather-Low** and later of Dire Straits) and Paul Cobbold (bs). Both Gordon and Harrison were later in the **Stackridge** offshoot The Korgi's, who tasted chart success in the eighties. One of the Korgi's albums was entitled *Sticky George*. (VJ/BS)

Shorty and Them

45:       Pills Or Love's Labour's Lost/
          Live Laugh And Love   (Fontana TF 460) 1964 R1

This was a Newcastle-based R&B band. After this now acclaimed 45 they headed for Germany where they recorded a German-only album which they shared with Liverpool's **Roadrunners**. The album itself has recently been reissued on CD as *Star Club Show 2* (Star Club / Repertoire IMS 7014). It includes the Fontana single and other studio takes from both bands.

Compilation appearances have included: *Live, Laugh and Love* on *Justification* (LP); *Dimples* on *English Freakbeat, Vol. 4* (LP & CD); and *Pills* on *Exploiting Plastic Inevitable, Vol. 1* (LP). (VJ)

Shotgun Express

Personnel incl: PETE BARDENS   keyb'ds   AB
                 ROD STEWART   vcls   A
                 BERYL MARSDEN   vcls   AB

45s: I Could Feel The Whole World Turn Round/
          Curtains   (Columbia DB 8025) 1966 R1
          Funny Cos' Neither Could I/
          Indian Thing   (Columbia DB 8178) 1967 R1
NB: The two 45s were later reissued on a 10" release in a picture sleeve (See For Miles CYM 2) 1983 (SC).

A short-lived R&B touring show formed in London in late 1966 which worked the clubs and ballrooms. The two vocalists were backed by Dave Ambrose (bs), **Peter Bardens** (keyb'ds), Mick Fleetwood (drms), **Peter Green** (gtr), John Moorshead (gtr) and Phil Sawyer (gtr). **Bardens**, Fleetwood and **Green** had all previously been in the **Peter B's**. Although they only released two 45s in the UK an eponymous album of their material was released in France (Columbia ESRF 1864). Upon their demise **Rod Stewart** (who left in February 1967 before their second single) joined **The Jeff Beck Group**, **Beryl Marsden** had earlier been in **She Trinity** and also recorded as a solo artist. **Peter Green** and Mick Fleetwood joined **John Mayall's Bluesbreakers** briefly before forming **Fleetwood Mac**; Dave

Ambrose headed for **The Brian Auger Trinity** and **Peter Bardens** was with **The Love Affair** and **Mike Cotton Sound** before forming **Village**.

Indian Thing, a good Booker T type instrumental, which featured some fine organ work from **Bardens** and some meaty guitar from Phil Sawyer, is certainly worth a listen. *Curtains* is a good Hammond organ instrumental.

Compilation appearances have included: *I Could Feel The Whole World Turn Round* on *My Generation* (LP); *Indian Thing* on *Rubble, Vol. 2 - Pop Sike Pipe Dreams* (LP) and *Rubble, Vol. 1* (CD); and *Funny 'Cos Neither Could I* and *I Could Feel The Whole World Turn Round* on *Sixties Lost And Found, Vol. 1* (LP). (VJ)

Shotgun Wedding

45:       Thousand Year Old Man/Uptown Down   (Pye 7N 25524) 1970

A one-off project. (MWh)

The Shots

Personnel: GEOFF GILL   drms   A
              MALCOLM LUKER   gtr   A
              JOHN ZEKE LUND   bs   A
              PHIL PEACOCK   gtr   A
              MICK ROWLEY   gtr, vcls

45:       Keep A Hold Of What You've Got/
          She's A Liar   (Columbia DB 7713) 1965 R1

All members of this band (except Peacock) were later in **The Smoke**. This 45 is now quite rare and collectable. The 'A' side, *Keep Hold Of What You've Got*, is a pretty good R&B stomper. I've seen it suggested that they were managed by Ronnie and Reggie Kray, but I can't confirm this.

Compilation appearances include: *Keep Hold Of What You've Got* on *Morgan Blue Town* (LP), *That Driving Beat* (CD), *Best And The Rest Of British Psychedelia* (CD) and on the 2-CD set *We Love The Pirates: Charting The Big 'L' Fab 40*. (VJ)

The Shouts

45:       She Was My Baby/
          That's The Way It's Gonna Be   (React EA 1) 1964 R1

This single came out on the virtually unknown React label. (VJ)

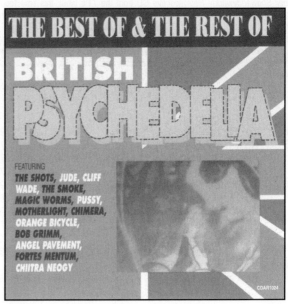

BEST AND THE REST OF BRITISH PSYCHEDELIA (Comp CD) including The Shots.

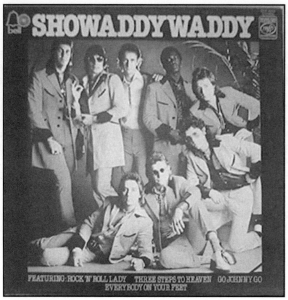

SHOWADDYWADDY - Showaddywaddy (LP).

Showaddywaddy

Personnel:	MALCOLM ALLURED	drms	A
(up to	DAVE BATRAM	vcls	A
1976)	ROMEO CHALLENGER	drms	A
	RUSS FIELDS	gtr	A
	BILLY GASK	vcls	A
	ALAN JAMES	bs	A
	TREVOR OAKES	gtr	A
	ROD TEAS	bs	A

				HCP
ALBUMS:	1(A)	SHOWADDYWADDY	(Bell BELLS 248) 1974	9
(up to	2(A)	STEP TWO	(Bell BELLS 256) 1975	7
1976)	3(A)	TROCADERO	(Bell SYBEL 8003) 1976	41
	4(A)	GREATEST HITS	(Arista ARTY 145) 1976	4

NB: (1) reissued on Music For Pleasure (MFP 50353) 1977 and again on CD (7T's GLAMCD 2) 2000. (2) reissued on CD (Cherry Red GLAM CD 4) 2001, with two bonus Christmas tracks. (3) reissued on CD (7T's GLAMCD 10) 2002. Compilations include: *Showaddywaddy* (Music For Pleasure MFP 50353) 1980, *Showaddywaddy* (Pickwick SHM 3105) 1981, *Rock On With Showaddywaddy* (Music For Pleasure MFP 50504) 1981, *The Very Best Of Showaddywaddy* (Arista SPART 1178) 1981 (No 33), *The Best Steps To Heaven* (Tiger SHCD 1) 1987 (No 90), Sweet Little Rock'n'Roller (Object Enterprises ONN 24) 1987, *25 Steps To The Top* (Repertoire REP 4171-WZ) 1991 on German import, *20 Greatest Hits* (Tring JHD 017) 1992, *The Very Best Of ...* (Summit SUMCD 4003) 1995 and *The Arista Singles, Vol 1* (7T's GLAMCD 12) focuses on both sides of their first nine singles for Arista so it's strictly beyond the timespan of this book.

Another Showaddywaddy Retrospective CD from the 7T's label, this time focussing on the Leicester glitterstompers' first nine singles (and 'B' sides) for Arista. All were UK top 50 hits (six making the Top 5), and several were also German chart smashes. Six of these have never appeared on LP or CD before - thus making this a must-have for all glam/rock'n'roll revival collectors. The lavish booklet contains notes (and pictures) for each release, plus ultra rare!! overseas sleeves. It includes "Dancin' Party" and "A Little Bit Of Soap".

			HCP
45s:	Hey Rock And Roll/		
(up to	You Will Lose Your Love Tomorrow	(Bell BLL 1357) 1974	2
1976)	Rock 'n' Roll Lady/I'm A Traveller	(Bell BLL 1374) 1974	15
	Hey Mr. Christmas/Rock 'n' Roll Man	(Bell BLL 1387) 1974	13
	Sweet Music/Windows	(Bell BLL 1403) 1975	14
	Three Steps To Heaven/The Party	(Bell BLL 1426) 1975	2
	Heartbeat/Lucy Jane	(Bell BLL 1450) 1975	7
	Heavenly/Smiling Eyes	(Bell BLL 1460) 1975	34
	Trocadero/Teenage Love Affair	(Bell BLL 1476) 1976	32
	Take Me In Your Arms/Go Johnny Go	(Bell BLL 1489) 1976	-
	Under The Moon Of Love/Looking Back	(Bell BLL 1495) 1976	1
Reissue:	αUnder The Moon Of Love/		
	Rock 'n' Roll Lady	(Genie GEN 7) 1986	-

NB: α also issued as a 12" with *When* and *Heartbeat* added.

A lighthearted rock 'n' roll revival band, **Showaddywaddy** formed in the Leicester area in 1973. They took their name from a chanted phrase in the backing vocals of *Little Darlin'*, a Maurice Williams song that the Canadian group The Diamonds enjoyed a No 3 hit with in 1957. Romeo Challenger had been in **Black Widow** at the start of the decade. They started off playing on the cabaret circuit but their first big break came in the form of a contract with Bell after appearing on TV's 'New Faces' programme.

Their early hits; *Hey Rock And Roll, Rock 'n' Roll Lady, Hey Mr. Christmas* and *Sweet Music* were self-penned and produced by Mike Hurst. By 1975, they found that cover versions of Eddie Cochran's *Three Steps To Heaven* and Buddy Holly's *Heartbeat* sold better than their own compositions, like *Heavenly*, and they increasingly covered late fifties and early sixties rock. As we leave the time span of this book they'd just enjoyed their only No 1 with a version of Curtis Lee's *Under The Moon Of Love*, but in the States they failed to register a single hit.

Their heyday was the 1976-78 period (seven consecutive Top Ten hits) but in the early eighties their popularity declined. They still work the cabaret and nostalgia circuit today, performing regularly with a line-up that includes five of the original eight members. (VJ)

The Showtimers

Personnel:	PAUL BENNETT	bs	A
	COLIN BOULTER	hrmnca, gtr	A
	ALAN REEVES	piano	A
	DAVE SEATON	vcls	A
	PETE TUFFIN	drms	A

EP:	1	4 BIG HITS AND 2 NEW ONES	(Showtime 1) 196?

NB: (1) contains *Everything's Alright, Don't Throw Your Love Away, Mockingbird Hill, Someone, Someone, Don't Say Goodbye* and *You Have The Right*.

45:	You Must Be Joking/Don't Say Goodbye	(HMV POP 1328) 1964

A little known beat group. Their original name was The Leons, a very popular group in the Catford area of Southeast London in the sixties. They were taken on and managed by The Rank Organisation who changed their name to **The Showtimers**, as this was the name of a magazine which was sold in Rank Cinemas. They were featured at all rank cinemas and their music was usually played at the interval. (VJ/LBy)

Shubert

45:	Until The Rains Come/		
	Let Your Love Go	(Fontana TF 942) 1968	SC

Circus Days, Vol. 4 (LP) and *Circus Days Vol's 4 & 5* (CD) gave *Until The Rains Come* a further airing recently. Very upbeat and quite heavily orchestrated, it inevitably featured some piano given their name. Quite commercial, if things had worked out differently it could have made the charts. The 45 was produced by **Mike Vickers**. (VJ)

Shusha

ALBUMS:	1	PERSIAN LOVE SONGS AND MYSTIC CHANTS		
(up to			(Tangent TNGS 108) 1971	SC
1976)	2	SONGS OF LONGTIME LOVERS		
			(Tangent TNGS 114) 1972	SC
	3	SHUSHA	(United Artists UAS 29575) 1974	
	4	THIS IS THE DAY	(United Artists UAS 29684) 1974	
	5	BEFORE THE DELUGE	(United Artists UAS 29879) 1975	

45s:	Baron Baruneh/Wild Flowers	(United Artists UP 35699) 1974
	Ev'ry Time We Say Goodbye/	
	Siren's Call	(United Artists UP 35759) 1974

Shusha was a Persian girl living in Chelsea. She moved to France from Persia when she was 16 and began singing. She came to England when the folk revival started. Her albums range from Persian folk to traditional Irish folk. She continued recording beyond 1976. A marginal case for inclusion. (VJ)

Shuttah

ALBUM: 1   IMAGE MAKER VOL 1 & 2 (2-LP)

                                 (Shadoks Music SHADOKS 030) 200?

This is a limited edition release (500 copies) from an acetate of an obscure atmospheric progressive rock album dating from 1971. It's well produced with lots of keyboards, harpsichord, bass, guitar and melodic vocals and is presented in a thick double gatefold sleeve. This should excite serious collectors of progressive rock. (VJ)

The Shy Limbs

Personnel:	ALAN BOWRY		A
	JOHN DICKENSON	vcls, keyb'ds, gtr	A
	GREG LAKE	bs	A
	ANDREW McCULLOCH	drms	A

45s:	Reputation/Love	(CBS 4190) 1969 R2
	Lady In Black/Trick Or Two	(CBS 4624) 1969 R2

The Shy Limbs came from Bournemouth and Lake and Dickenson had previously been in **Shame**.

Reputation is a superb organ-led song well sung by **Greg Lake** similar to **Procol Harum**'s *A Whiter Shade Of Pale*, which builds into an impressive crescendo. The flip side, *Love*, is rather disappointing by comparison, although the guitar on this track was courtesy of Robert Fripp. *Lady In Black* is a ballad with a beatier flip *Trick Or Two*, but this second single was nowhere hear as good as their debut.

Both their 45s are now hard to find and expensive. The first came out in Germany in a picture sleeve. **Greg Lake** later switched to keyboards and played with **The Gods** in 1968, leaving them to join **King Crimson** in late 1968/early 1969 and then **Emerson Lake and Palmer**. Drummer Andy McCulloch briefly joined **Lake** in **King Crimson**, but was later in **Greenslade**. John Dickenson and Alan Bowry later resurfaced in late seventies rock band King Harry.

Compilation appearances have included: *Reputation* on *Perfumed Garden, Vol. 1* (LP & CD) and on the 4-CD box set *Acid Drops, Spacedust & Flying Saucers*; and *Rick Or Two* on *We Can Fly, Vol 2* (CD). (VJ)

Shyster

Personnel:	KEITH GUSTER	drms	A
	GORDON HASKELL	bs	A
	BRYN HAWORTH	gtr	A

45:	α Tick Tock/That's A Hoe Down	(Polydor 56202) 1968 R3

NB: α has been reissued in a limited edition of 500 (Polydor 56202) reproduced from the original French jukebox pressing with a large centre hole.

This is an extremely rare and hence expensive single to acquire nowadays in its original format. This is partly because this was **The Fleur de Lys** recording under a pseudonym. *It's A Hoe Down* is nothing special but *Tick Tock* is a psychedelic interpretation of the 'Hickory Dickory Dock' nursery rhyme with lyrics about "a black-and-white mouse fight". Then two minutes into the song Haworth's guitar takes over and culminates in a psychedelic haze.

After this the trio resumed recording as **The Fleur de Lys**. **Gordon Haskell** also played in **Cupid's Inspiration** and **The Flowerpot Men**, recorded a solo 45 in 1969 and then joined **King Crimson**. **Bryn Haworth** issued a number of Christian-based religious albums during the seventies.

Tick Tock can also be heard on *Perfumed Garden Vol. 3* (CD) and it also appears on a **Fleur de Lys** CD retrospective. (VJ)

Sidan

Personnel:	CARYL	vcls, keyb'ds, gtr	A
	GAENOR	vcls, gtr	A
	GWENNAN	vcls	A
	MEINIR	vcls	A
	SIONED	vcls, gtr	A

ALBUM:	1(A) TEULU YNCL SAM	(Sain 1017 M) 1975 R2

EP:	1(A) LLIWIAU	(Sain 27) 1972

After having released an undistinguished EP with close harmony tracks, this five-piece female vocal band suprised with an excellent cut on the Sain sampler *Dafodau-tân* from 1973 (H 1007), called *William Morris*, an eclectic blend of traditional folk and dissonant harmonies, sung live and with great verve. Their sole album of two years later has some of both. A few tracks are a bit lifeless and bland, even though most have full band backing (credited by Christian names only). Others have a totally outworldly and serenely beautiful touch with five-part harmonies, rhythm changes, fuzz leads and whatever you could wish for. All tracks stay firmly in the Welsh tradition, but as most are co-written by Caryl, they have an original touch, especially obvious in the strange wriggling harmonies, which is sorely missing on most albums of this type. Try and find it. (MK)

Side By Side

45:	Wasn't It A Heavy Summer/	
	Ups And Downs In A Roundabout Way	(Pye 7N 45304) 1973

No other are known details. (VJ)

Sidekicks

This outfit from Harrow later became **Kaleidoscope**. The fanzine 'Ptolemaic Terrascope' included with one of its issues an EP (POT 14), which included a previously unreleased cut from 1964, *I'm Looking For A Woman*. Many further tracks were recorded and sent to record companies in an attempt to secure a recording contract. However, as an R&B combo they failed to generate interest and no tracks were released at the time. The 'Ptolemaic Terrascope' freebie remains their only vinyl epitaph. (VJ)

Sight and Sound

Personnel:	RICK PRICE	ld gtr	AB
	MIKE SHERIDAN	vcls	AB
	GEOFF TURTON	vcls, gtr	A
	JOE VALENTINE	drms	AB
	DAVE PRITCHARD	vcls, gtr	B

45s:	Ebenezer/	
	Our Love (Is In The Pocket)	(Fontana TF 927) 1968 SC
	Alley Alley/Little Jack Monday	(Fontana TF 982) 1968 SC

This Birmingham pop outfit's main significance was the involvement of **Rick Price** and **Mike Sheridan**. Dave Pritchard was the brother of **Fortunes** member Barry Pritchard. **Mike Sheridan** had previously fronted **Mike Sheridan and The Nightriders** and **Mike Sheridan's Lot** and, of course, he later teamed up with **Rick Price** in **Sheridan-Price**. **Geoff Turton** had been vocalist with **The Rockin' Berries** and later recorded as **Jefferson**. *Our Love (Is In The Pocket)*, their first flip side, was Darrell Banks' classic Northern soul side. They also have a cut *Gotta Get Out Of My Mind* on *Colour Me Pop, Vol 3* (CD). (VJ)

Signs

Personnel:	TONY BURNS	vcls	A
	PETE CONNELL	vcls	A
	DAVE KERRIGAN	vcls	A

45:	Ain't You Got A Heart/	
	My Baby Comes To Me	(Decca F 12522) 1966

This was a good-time Liverpool-based trio. (VJ/AD)

SILVER BIRCH - Silver Birch (CD).

The Silence

Personnel:	PAUL BIDWELL	bs, vcls	A
	JULIAN FERRARI	drms, vcls	A
	BOB MOORE	vcls	A
	PIERRE TUBBS	gtr, vcls	A

This was actually **The Jeeps** (not the early **John's Children's** incarnation). They ended up recording a US single *Hey You Lolita/Wanda* (Red Bird RB 10-062) 1966 after the pre-**John's Children's** combo's version had been so weak. (VJ)

The Silkie

Personnel:	IVOR AYLESBURY	gtr	A
	KEVIN CUNNINGHAM	bs	A
	MIKE RAMSDEN	gtr, vcls	A
	SYLVIA TATLER	vcls	A

ALBUM: 1(A) THE SILKIE SING THE SONGS OF BOB DYLAN
(Fontana TF 5256) 1965 R1

HCP

45s:	Blood Red River/		
	Close Your Door Gently	(Fontana TF 556) 1965	-
	You've Got To Hide Your Love Away/		
	City Winds	(Fontana TF 603) 1965	28
	Keys To My Soul/Leave Me To Cry	(Fontana TF 659) 1966	-
	Born To Be With You/So Sorry Now	(Fontana TF 709) 1966	-
Reissue:	You've Got To Hide Your Love Away/		
	(Flip by different artist)	(Old Gold OG 9787) 1987	-

These four Hull University students were signed up by Brian Epstein and achieved a Top 30 hit with their cover of *You've Got To Hide Your Love Away*, which was written and produced by **Lennon** and **McCartney**. Most of their songs were delivered in a folk format, indeed they recorded a whole album of Dylan songs. (VJ)

Mike Silver

| ALBUMS: | 1 | THE APPLICANT | (Fontana) 1969 R3 |
| | 2 | TROUBADOUR | (MCA 348) 1973 |

NB. (2) US catalogue number.

Cornishman **Mike Silver**'s debut was a peculiar folk concept album about the protagonist's desperate attempts to get a job. After a stint in **Daylight**, **Silver** released *Troubadour*, a mellow and quite interesting singer/songwriter album. In 1975, he played on *From Mighty Oaks*, the first solo album by **Ray Thomas** of **The Moody Blues**. (SR/RMJ)

Silver Birch

Personnel:	MARTIN BARTLETT	vcls, fiddle	A
	JAYNE CLARK	vcls, harmonium	A
	GEOFF LILES	vcls, harmonium, mandolin, autoharp, gtr, bells	A
	DEREK RUSHMER	vcls, gtr, autoharp, recorder, bells	A
	ANGIE SEAL	vcls, tambourine, bells	A
	DAVE WOODS	vcls, autoharp, gtr, bells, recorders	A

ALBUM: 1(A) SILVER BIRCH (Brayford BRO 2) 1973 R3
NB: (1) reissued on CD (Vinyl Tap DORIS 3) 199?

This privately-pressed album was recorded by a six-piece acoustic-based folk band. Originally a four-piece harmony group, they were led by Geoff Liles and were based in Grimsby. (VJ)

Silver Byke

45: I've Got Time/Who Needs Tomorrow (London HLZ 10200) 1968

A long forgotten pop act, who may have been American. There's lots of brass on *I've Got Time*. *Who Needs Tomorrow* is much more interesting with a cleverly arranged harmony ending. (VJ)

Silver Dollars

Personnel:	BOB BELL	organ	A
	BILLY FRENCH	gtr	A
	KEN MANNING	drms	A
	JOHN McNESTY	bs	A
	STAN NICHOLSON	ld gtr	A

45: Rainbow/If I Lost You (Mercury MF 835) 1964

This band formed in Newcastle back in 1962. *Rainbow* was a ballad. (VJ)

Silver Eagle

45: Theodore/True As A Brand New Lie (MGM MGM 1345) 1967 SC

A little known late sixties band whose *Theodore* can also be heard on *Lovely Summer Days* (CD). (VJ)

Silver Lining

45: Bye Goodbye/Writing On The Wall (Pye 7N 45242) 1973

This early seventies band made no impact.

Bye Goodbye has been compiled on *Ripples, Vol. 1* (CD). (VJ)

Silverhead

Personnel:	ROD DAVIES	perc, vcls, gtr	AB
	MICHAEL DES BARRES	vcls	AB
	STEVE FOREST	gtr, vcls	A
	NIGEL HARRISON	bs	AB
	PETE THOMPSON	keyb'ds, drms	AB
	ROBBIE BLUNT	gtr	B

ALBUMS:	1(B)	SILVERHEAD	(Purple TPSA 7506) 1972
	2(B)	SIXTEEN AND SAVAGED	(Purple TPSA 7511) 1973
	3(B)	LIVE AT THE RAINBOW	(Purple 80351) 1976

NB: (3) This was a Japanese release. (1) and (2) were issued by MCA in the US. (2) reissued on CD (Line LICD 9000325) 1989. (1) and (2) reissued as a CD set (Line LICD 921174) 1992.

| 45s: | Ace Supreme/Oh No No | (Purple PUR 104) 1972 |
| | Rolling With My Baby/In Your Eyes | (Purple PUR 110) 1973 |

A competent hard-rock band. Davies had been with **Riot Squad**; Forest was in Many Others and Harrison played with Champion Jack Dupree. Forest played on the 45s, but then departed to Buck. His replacement was ex-**Bronco** member Robbie Blunt.

Their first album includes some diverse influences. There are some boogie-orientated tracks like *Rock And Roll Band, Underneath The Light* (with good twin guitar work) and *Rolling With My Baby* (which had a brass arrangement). There are **Marc Bolan/T Rex** influences in *Long Legged Lisa* and *Sold Me Down The River*, some **Free** and **Deep Purple** influences in *Ace Supreme*, as well as slow and mellow tracks like *Wounded Heart* or the acoustic guitar-based *Johnny*. *In Your Eyes* is slow and mellow, at least in the beginning and in parts predates **Steve Harley's (Cockney Rebel)** vocal style, but also has some early seventies **Mick Jagger/Stones** influences too.

Michael Des Barres was later in the late seventies hard-rock band, Detective. They recorded on **Deep Purple**'s Purple label and their albums were notable for some good guitar leads. Harrison went on to play with Ray Manzarek. Blunt joined **Broken Glass** and Thompson went on to session work. (VJ/CA)

The Silvers

| 45: | What A Way To Start A Day/ | |
| | Blue Blue Eyes | (Polydor BM 56094) 1966 |

No other details known. (VJ)

Simon

45s:	I Like The Way/Little Tin Soldier	(RCA Victor 1609) 1967
	Dream Seller/Sweet Reflections Of You	(RCA Victor 1668) 1968
	Mrs Lillyco/There Is No More Of You	(Plum PLS 002) 1969 SC

An obscure group of whom little is known. Their final single *Mrs Lillyco* is a pleasant pop-psych offering, if with brass. (VJ)

Simon Plug and Grimes

Personnel incl: CAROL GRIMES

45s:	Is This A Dream?/I'm Going Home	(Deram DM 296) 1970
	Way In, Way Out/Long, Long, Summer	(President PT 310) 1970
	Pull Together/I'll Keep Smiling	(President PT 354) 1971

This was one of the many obscure acts who recorded on Deram in this era. **Carol Grimes** was later in **Uncle Dog**. See her entry for more details. (VJ)

Simon's Secrets

Personnel incl: CLIFFORD T. WARD

45s:	Naughty Boy/Sympathy	(CBS 3406) 1968 SC
	I Know What Her Name Is/	
	Keeping My Head Above Water	(CBS 3856) 1968 SC

This band had earlier recorded as **Martin Raynor and Secrets** and then as simply **Secrets**. As **Simon's Secrets** they recorded the commercially-orientated *Naughty Boy* and the punchy *I Know What Her Name Is*. After this **Ward**, by now at teacher training college in Worcestershire, signed for John Peel's Dandelion label and embarked on a solo career. He later switched to Charisma and enjoyed a Top Ten hit with *Gaye*. Sadly, he later developed multiple sclerosis, which hampered his later career and eventually claimed his life.

You can also check out *I Know What Her Name Is* on *Voyage Through The Sugarcube* (LP & CD). (VJ)

Simple Image

| 45: | Spinning, Spinning, Spinning/Shy Boy | (Carnaby CNS 4013) 1970 |

NB: *Spinning Spinning* (CD) compiles all of their sixties singles on the HMV label.

This 45, which was a No. 1 hit in New Zealand, was a UK release by the New Zealand **Simple Image**. The 'A' side was a cover of the Curt Boettcher track, and the flip a cover of **Tomorrow**. Most members are still working in the music business - two of them build sound systems. (VJ/GB)

Simpleside

| 45: | Feeling Alright/Gone Fishing | (Decca F 13198) 1971 |

This is another long forgotten early seventies act. Presumably *Feeling Alright* was a cover of the **Traffic** song. (VJ)

Simplicity

| 45: | Any Minute Of Your Life/ | |
| | The Sky's The Limit | (York SYK 501) 1971 |

The above 45 was this band's sole vinyl output. (VJ)

Sindelfingen

| ALBUM: | 1 ODGIPIG (w/insert) | (Medway no #) 1973 R5 |

NB: (1) reissued on Cenotaph (CEN 111) R1 as a 2-LP set, *Odgpig - Triangle*, with a live album in a limited edition of 300 in 1990 (SC) and on CD (Background HBG 122/10) 1992. (1) reissued again on CD (Kissing Spell KSCD 914).

This mega-rare privately-pressed album recently had a limited reissue (300 copies) as a double set (the second album is a live one) which should enable more people to get to hear it. Whether they should want to is another matter as its jerky, high-pitched rhythms have very limited appeal. Its best moment - *Perpetual Motion* which I've seen described as low budget **Van der Graaf Generator** - style rock. (VJ)

Sinewave

| 45: | Clochemerie / Star Trek | (Chapter One CH 172) 1972 |

This may have been a studio-based orchestra, given the 'A' side was the theme tune to 'Star Trek'. (VJ)

SINDELFINGEN - Odgipig (CD)

Pete Sinfield

ALBUM: 1 STILL (Manticore K 43501) 1973 SC

Greg Lake, Mel Collins and **Keith Tippett** were among an impressive array, many (as these) with **King Crimson** connections, who helped out on this album. **Sinfield**, too, had been an early member of **King Crimson** and wrote for them. (VJ)

Singing Folk

45: I Was Wrong/May The Road (Polydor BM 56018) 1965

This folk group came from London. (VJ)

Sir Alec and His Boys

45: I'm A Believer/
Green Green Grass Of Home (Deram DM 116) 1967

This was a one-off project covering these Monkees and Tom Jones' hits, which is completely dispensable. (VJ)

Siren

Personnel:	KEVIN COYNE	gtr, vcls	AB
	JOHN CHICHESTER	ld gtr	A
	DAVE CLAGUE	bs	AB
	NICK CODWORTH	piano	AB
	TAT MEAGER	drms	AB
	COLIN WOOD	keyb'ds, flute	A
	MICK GRATTON	gtr	B

ALBUMS: 1(A) SIREN (Dandelion 63755) 1969 SC
2(B) STRANGE LOCOMOTION (Dandelion DAN 8001) 1971 SC

NB: (2) issued by Elektra in the US. (1) reissued on CD (Repertoire REP 4202-WP) 1991 and again on CD (Green Tree GTR 013). (2) reissued on CD (Repertoire REP 4083-WP) 1991. (1) and (2) reissued on one CD (See For Miles SEECD 413) 199?. *Rabbits* (DJC Records DJCD 01) is a previously unreleased album which includes their Dandelion single. *Let's Do It* (CD) (DJC Records DJCD 02) presents 20 unreleased tracks from 1969/70. *The Club Rondo* ((DJC Records DJCD 03) presents previously unreleased material from the 1969-1970 era and is full of rarities to excite fans of the band. *Ruff Stuff* (DJC Records DJCD 022) features the original six-piece line-up playing rarities live and in the studio.

45: Strange Locomotion/I'm All Aching (Dandelion DAN 7002) 1971

Formed in Bradford in the late sixties they moved to London and signed for John Peel's Dandelion label. Mick Gratton replaced Chichester on lead guitar for the second album, but soon afterwards the group disintegrated. **Coyne** made a further album for Dandelion, *Case History*, and later a series of albums for Virgin, which did not attract the attention they deserved. Many of **Coyne**'s recordings were influenced by his experiences as a social therapist in a Preston psychiatric hospital and later, upon his move to London, as a social worker in Camden. Despite plugs by John Peel, neither **Siren** nor **Coyne**'s solo recordings sold well, although most are now sought-after by record collectors. They also recorded two 45s as **Clague**.

Rabbits is the first of four albums released by DJC Records containing previously unreleased albums. *Let's Do It* contains lots of interesting material and demonstrates the range of their music. *The Club Rondo* contains previously unreleased material from 1969/1970 including an alternate version of *Flowering Cherry* (a song from the *Rabbits* album), there are a trio of unreleased **Coyne**/Cudworth compositions and others are more improvisational and include spoken prose. *Ruff Stuff* also gives an airing to previously unreleased live and studio recordings.

Fetch Me My Woman and *The War Is Over* appear on *Dandelion Rarities* (CD), and *Strange Locomotion* is included on the *Dandelion Sampler 1969-1972* (CD).

Tat Meager was also in **Judd**. (VJ)

SKID ROW - Skid Row (LP).

Size Seven Group

Personnel:	ALAN BLACK	bs	A
	GEORGE CUMMING	piano, vcls	A
	BILLY GEARY	gtr, hrmnca	A
	BRIAN LYNN-DOWELL	vcls	A
	BILLY NICOL	drms	A
	JACK STEWART	ld gtr	A

45s: Crying My Heart Out/So How Come (Rendezvous PR 5020) 1964
Where Do We Go From Here/Till I Die (Mercury MF 845) 1965
In Time/Walking Proud (Mercury MF 854) 1965
It's Got To Be Love/
I Met Her In The Rain (Mercury MF 896) 1965

Despite the name the group had just six members. They played around the dance halls in the early sixties and specialised in harmony ballads. (VJ)

Pete Skellern

ALBUMS:	1	YOU'RE A LADY	(Decca SKL 5151) 1972
(up to	2	NOT WITHOUT A FRIEND	(Decca SKL 5178) 1974
1976)	3	HOLDING MY OWN	(Decca SKL 5191) 1974
	4	HOLD ON TO LOVE	(Decca SKL 5211) 1975
	5	HARD TIMES	(Island ILPS 9352) 1975

NB: (1) reissued on CD on London (8206 192) 1988 and on Pickwick (PWK 135) 1990. (2) reissued on CD on Deram (8206 202) 1990, but deleted in 1992.

HCP

45s: You're A Lady/Manifesto (Decca F 13333) 1972 3
(up to Our Jackie's Getting Married/
1976) I Don't Know (Decca F 13360) 1972 -
Roll Away/Somebody Call Me Tonight (Decca F 13392) 1973 -
Still Magic/Sleepy Guitar (Decca F 13465) 1973 -
Hold On To Love/
Too Much, I'm In Love (Decca F 13568) 1975 14
Make It Easy For Me/Lie Safely There (Decca F 13588) 1975 -
Hard Times/And Then You'll Fall (Island WIP 6235) 1975 -
Now That I Need You/
I Guess You Wish You'd Gone Home (Island WIP 6260) 1975 -
Reissue: You're A Lady/Hold On To Love (Old Gold OG 9350) 1983 -

Peter Skellern was born in Bury, Lancashire in 1947. In his youth he was an organist and choirmaster at a local church and also studied piano at the Guildhall Academy of Music in London. In 1968, he joined **March Hare** who also played under the name **Harlan County**, an album of whose material with **Skellern** was later released in 1970 *Peter Skellern With Harlan County* (Nashville 6336 002) after **Skellern** had become famous by virtue of his Top 5 ballad hit *You're A Lady*, which also rose to No 50 in the US.

His albums are evidence of his breadth of musical interest featuring ballads, ragtime and music hall comedy (on *Holding My Own*). *Not Without A Friend* was produced by Derek Taylor. It was good quality pop with progressive and folk influences. His only other hit in the time frame of this book was *Hold On To Love* in 1974, but **Skellern** seemed unconcerned by this as he developed a career as a stagewriter, composing the score for a revue and a musical. He continued to make records intermittently, though, throughout the seventies and eighties. (VJ)

Skid Row

Personnel:
NOEL BRIDGEMAN	drms	ABCD
GARY MOORE	gtr, vcls	A
BRUSH SHIELS (aka Brendan Shields)	bs, vcls	ABCDE
PHIL LYNOTT	vcls	A
PAUL CHAPMAN	gtr, vcls	B
ADRIAN FISHER	gtr, vcls	C
ED DEAN	gtr	DE
KEVIN McALEA	keyb'ds	D
JOHN WILSON	drms	E

				HCP
ALBUMS: 1(A)	SKID ROW	(CBS 63965)	1970	R1 30
2(A)	34 HOURS	(CBS 64411)	1971	R1 -
3(-)	ALIVE AND KICKING	(Release RRL 8001)	1976	-

NB: (1) reissued on CD (CBS 450623 1) in 1987 and also on CD (Columbia Rewind 4773602) 1994 and again on CD (Essential ESM CD 913) 2000. (2) reissued on CD (Repertoire REP 4073-WZ) 1991, (Columbia 480525-2) 1995 and again (Repertoire REP 4968) in a digipak with two bonus tracks. *Skid Row* (Snapper SMM CD 608) 2000 contains material recorded whilst **Gary Moore** was still with the band but which wasn't released until much later.

45s:			
α	New Places, Old Friends/?	(Song SO 0002)	1969
α	Saturday Morning Man/?	(Song SO 0003)	1969
	Sandie's Gone Part 1 / Part 2	(CBS 4893)	1970
	Night Of The Warm Witch/Mr. De-Luxe	(CBS 7181)	1971

NB: α contain instrumentals.

A very young **Gary Moore** fronted this Irish progressive and blues band who had a good live following but never really broke through with their vinyl. **Gary Moore** had previously been in an outfit called Platform Three and Lynott had been in Black Eagles. He soon left to become a folk singer and then joined Sugar Shack.

Although their first album sold well enough to get into the Album Charts, it was an average amalgam of mellow rock, heavy blues and even had a ragtime-style guitar piece. *34 Hours* veered more towards hard-rock than their debut. Moore was experimenting with the wah-wah pedal and *First Thing In The Morning* and *Night Of The Warm Witch* are two tracks which showcase his talent effectively. When **Moore** left in January 1972 to form

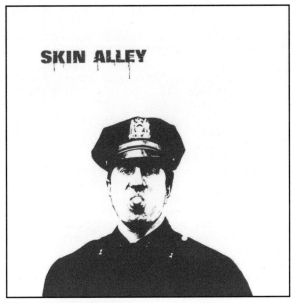

SKIN ALLEY - Skin Alley (CD).

SKIN ALLEY - To Pagham And Beyond (CD).

The Gary Moore Band, he was replaced by Paul Chapman, previously with South Wales band The Universe. This line-up cut an unissued album. Chapman then left to join Welsh bands Sad Sam and Kimla Taz. He was later in **UFO** (May 1974) and Lone Star. Adrian Fisher was then recruited, but the band was in its final days and soon split. Shiels joined Brush; Fisher went to Toby and Bridgeman joined an Irish band called The Gentry. **Moore** was later in **Thin Lizzy**, G-Force and recorded as a solo artist.

In May 1973, there was an attempted reformation (line-up D above). It only lasted in this form for three months. Bridman left in August 1973 and joined an Irish Showband called The Plattermen. In the late eighties he toured with The Waterboys. McAlea also departed at the same time for **Bees Make Honey**. Another former Brush man John Wilson joined on drums. *Dublin City Girls* was recorded, featuring Eamon Gibney. The band finally folded when Dean joined McAlea in **Bees Make Honey** and Wilson departed to Bitter Sweet.

Compilation appearances include *Youth Gone Wild* on *Kerrang! The Album* (CD) and on *The Best Heavy Metal Album In The World Ever!* (CD). (VJ/JM)

Skin Alley

Personnel:
THOMAS CRIMBLE	keyb'ds, bs, vcls	AB
BOB JAMES	sax, gtr	ABCD
KRZYSZTOF HENRYK JUSTKIEWICZ	keyb'ds	ABCD
ALVIN POPE	drms	AB
NICK GRAHAM	vcls, keyb'ds, bs, flute	BCD
TONY KNIGHT	drms, vcls	CD

ALBUMS: 1(A)	SKIN ALLEY	(CBS 63847)	1969	R2
2(B)	TO PAGHAM AND BEYOND	(CBS 64140)	1970	SC
3(C)	TWO QUID DEAL	(Big T TRA 260)	1972	SC
4(D)	SKINTIGHT	(Big T TRA 273)	1973	SC

NB: (3) and (4) issued on Stax in the USA. (1) reissued on CD and vinyl (Akarma 259). (2) reissued on CD and vinyl (Akarma 275). (3) reissued on CD.

45s:			
	Tell Me/Better Be Blind	(CBS 5045)	1970
	You Got Me Danglin'/ Skin Valley Serenade	(Big T BIG 506)	1972
	In The Midnight Hour/Broken Eggs	(Big T BIG 511)	1972

A progressive Anglo-American rock combo, who are probably best known for their track *Living In Sin* by virtue of its inclusion on CBS's popular 1970 budget-priced 2-LP compilation, *Fill Your Head With Rock*. This pleasant, melodic track was taken from their debut album and is arguably their finest moment. The first album is well worth seeking out, though. It contains *Tell Me*, a mellow song with a beautiful melody; *Mazsha*, a fast organ-dominated instrumental with a long sax solo; *Country Aire*, an instrumental folk piece with flute and harpsichord; *All Alone*, a slow, melodic song about

SKIN ALLEY - Two Quid Deal (LP).

loneliness with pleasant sax and a long organ solo; the mellow mid-tempo *Night Time* with lots of flute and jazzy piano improvisations and *Highway*, a fast R&B influenced progressive piece with long sax and organ solos.

An unreleased acetate album from this time also exists, recorded as a soundtrack to a German documentary about the supermodel Verushka and including tracks like *Shower Music*, *First Drug Scene* and *Cemetery Scene*, in a looser and funkier style than their debut.

To Pagham And Beyond had a West Coast vibe and there are three long jamming tracks which give the album a spacey hippie feel on each side.

By the time of *Skintight* in 1973 they were playing more commercial, mainstream rock with lots of orchestration and brass arrangements. Side A is disappointing but there are three decent tracks on Side B:- *Instermental*, a soul/funk orientated instrumental; *The Heep Turns Human*, which brings to mind **The Who** in the *Who's Next* period and the bluesy hard-rocker *Maverick Woman Blues*, which featured strong vocals and slide guitar. The album was produced by American Don Nix and remixed at Ardent Studios, Memphis.

Nick Graham was also in **Atomic Rooster**. The Nick Graham who was in **The End** and **Tucky Buzzard** was a different guy, later a record producer (including for BROS in the eighties) and now an executive at Sony Records. It's unconfirmed whether drummer **Tony Knight** was he of the Chessmen fame.

Compilation appearances include *If I Only Had Time* on *The Transatlantic Story* CD box set and *Skin Alley Serenade* on the 3-CD box set *Ars Longa Vita Brevis: A Compendium Of Progressive Rock 1967-1974*. (VJ/CA/BS/RMJ)

Skip Bifferty

Personnel:	GRAHAM BELL	vcls	A
	MICKY GALLAGHER	keyb'ds	A
	COLIN GIBSON	bs	A
	TOM JACKMAN	drms	A
	JON TURNBULL	gtr	A

ALBUM: 1(A) SKIP BIFFERTY (RCA RD/SF 7941) 1967 R3/R2

NB: (1) reissued on CD (Essex ESSEX 1003 CD) 1994 and on LP. *The Story Of Skip Bifferty/ BBC Sessions* (Sanctuary CMEDD 518) 2003 is a 2-CD compilation.

45s:	On Love/Cover Girl	(RCA RCA 1621) 1967
	Happy Land/Reason To Live	(RCA RCA 1648) 1967
	Man In Black/Mr. Money Man	(RCA RCA 1720) 1968

A fine underground band, **Skip Bifferty** was known as **The Chosen Few** until **Bell** arrived. Their new name was inspired by a cartoon character of

their own invention. They were discovered playing an early gig at the Marquee by manager Don Arden, who soon secured them a contract with RCA. Based in London, they regularly appeared on John Peel's 'Top Gear' and released a number of singles of which the hard-rocker *On Love* was the first and best, with a very catchy, insistent riff. The follow-up, *Happy Land*, was more flower-power orientated, but - despite a degree of airplay - neither entered the charts. Their final single, *Man In Black*, was taken from the album, which came in one of the most attractive psychedelic designs of all and featured sleevenotes by Peel. Alongside 45 cuts, it contained other fine tracks such as *Guru* (unusual for its sole drum backing) and the psychedelic *Time Track*, *Inside The Secret* and *Clearway 51*. *Man In Black* was produced by **The Small Faces'** **Ronnie Lane** and arranged by **Stevie Marriott**.

Despite having more commercial appeal than many underground acts, they failed to break through and after conflicts with Arden they answered an ad in 'Time Out' and recorded the seven-minute long *I Keep Singing That Same Old Song* under the name **Heavy Jelly**. The track received wide recognition after being featured on Island's *Nice Enough To Eat* (LP) sampler.

In the seventies **Bell** formed to **Bell and Arc**, which also included Gallagher and Turnbull. Gibson played with **Snafu** in the mid-seventies. Gallagher was in several other bands including **Parrish and Gurvitz**, Frampton's Camel and **Loving Awareness**.

Sanctuary's *The Story Of Skip Bifferty* is drawn from original master tapes. It also includes 45 cuts, a handful of previously unissued demos (including two with **Alan Hull**), live and studio material from post-Bifferty projects like **Heavy Jelly** and Griffin, and a few previously unreleased BBC recordings. Among these *Aged Aged Man* and *The Lion And The Unicorn* (both self-penned compositions) stand out.

Compilation appearances have included:- *On Love* and *Man In Black* on *Broken Dreams, Vol. 1* (LP); *On Love* on *Electric Sugar Cube Flashbacks, Vol. 4* (LP), *Electric Sugar Cube Flashbacks* (CD), *Rubble Vol. 8: All The Colours Of Darkness* (LP) and *Rubble Vol. 4* (CD); *Follow The Path To The Stars*, *When She Comes To Stay* and *Don't Let Me Be* on *Hard Up Heroes, Vol. 2* (CD) and *Round And Round* on *Talking About The Good Times* (CD). (VJ/RMJ)

Sky

Personnel incl: DINKY DIAMOND (NORMAN DIAMOND) drms A

45s:	Air-O-Plane Ride/	
	Weather Forecast	(United Artists UP 2234) 1968
	On Our Way/Singer Is Singing His Song	(Decca F 12971) 1969
	Long, Long Gone/Ballad Of Connie Judd	(Bell BLL 1133) 1970

A quintet from Aldershot who split up around July 1972. Their drummer Dinky Diamond later joined Sparks. (MWh)

SKIP BIFFERTY - Skip Bifferty (LP).

Skybird

ALBUM: 1   SUMMER OF '73   (Holyground HGS 118) 1974 R1
NB: (1) reissued on CD (Kissing Spell KSG 005) 2001.

Just 250 copies of this album were pressed making it an obvious rarity. It's also become quite collectable. They were a pleasant but unspectacular folk duo. The music is mellow and easy-going and utilises acoustic guitars and dobro.

Magdalena has been compiled on *The History Of U.K. Underground Folk Rock 1968-1978 Vol. 1* (CD). (VJ)

Sky Pony

45:        Jubeldown/Chubby   (Decca F 23082) 1970

This is an obscure one-off 45. (VJ)

Slack Alice (featuring Alice Springs)

Personnel: JOHN COOK   keyb'ds, vcls   AB
            PETE FINBERG   gtr, vcls   AB
            MIKE HOWARD   bs, vcls   AB
            DAVE RIDER drms   A
            ALICE SPRINGS (aka SANDRA BARRY) vcls   AN
            EDDIE LEACH   drms   B

ALBUM: 1(B)   SLACK ALICE   (Philips 6308 214) 1974 SC

This hard-rock band's recordings have yet to become collectable. The original drummer Dave Rider left before they recorded and ex-Jimmy McCulloch Band member Eddie Leach replaced him.

After the band folded, Alice Springs and Mike Howard joined Darling and Cook departed to **Ross**. (VJ/JM)

Slack Alice

Personnel: KEITH O'CONNELL   keyb'ds   AB
              MALCOLM CROSSLEY   bs   AB
              CHRIS DAY   drms   A
              ALAN PARKINSON   gtr, vcls   AB
              CLIFF STOCKER   vcls   AB
              WILGAR CAMPBELL   drms   B

45:        Motorcycle/Ridin' The Wind   (Fontana 6007 038) 1974

There were two bands called **Slack Alice** on the scene in 1974. This one came from Burnley in Lancashire. Alan Parkinson had played in an outfit called **The Beat Boys**. Keith O'Connell had been in **Geno Washington and The Ram Jam Band**. When the original drummer Chris Day left Wilgar Campbell (ex-Wilgar) joined. He'd previously played with **Rory Gallagher**. When they folded Campbell joined Dogs. (JM)

Slade

Personnel: DAVE HILL   gtr, vcls   A
              NODDY HOLDER   gtr, vcls   A
              JIM LEA   bs, vcls, keyb'ds, violin   A
              DON POWELL   drms   A

                                                          HCP
ALBUMS: 1(A) BEGINNINGS   (Fontana STL 5494) 1969 -
(up to 2(A) PLAY IT LOUD   (Polydor 2383 026) 1970 SC -
1976)   3(A) SLADE ALIVE   (Polydor 2383 101) 1972 2
        4(A) SLAYED?   (Polydor 2383 163) 1972 1
        5(A) SLADEST   (Polydor 2442 119) 1973 1
        6(A) OLD NEW BORROWED AND BLUE
                                  (Polydor 2383 261) 1974 1

SLADE - Sladest (LP).

7(A)   SLADE IN FLAME (Soundtrack)(Polydor 2442 126) 1975 6
8(A)   NOBODY'S FOOL   (Polydor 2383 377) 1976 14
NB: (1) reissued as *Beginnings Of Ambrose Slade* (Contour 6870 678) 1975. In the US (1) issued as *Ballzy* (Fontana SRF 67598) 1969. (1), (2) and (3) reissued on CD on Polydor (849 185-2), (849 178-2) and (841 114-2) respectively in 1991. (4), (5) and (6) reissued on CD on Polydor (849 180-2), (849 181-2) and (849 182-2) in 1992. (1) - (7) have also been available on mid-price CDs. (8) reissued on CD (Polydor 849 183-2) 1992. If you simply want to hear their hits go for one of the following: *Slade Smashes* (Polydor POLTV 13) 1980 (No 21); *Slade Greats* (Polydor SLAD1) 1984, (No 89); *Slade Story, Vol. 1* and *Vol. 2* (Bear Tracks BTCD 979411 and 979412 respectively) 1991 is a 2-CD collection of all their hits from a German-based label; *Wall Of Hits* (Polydor 5116122) 1991; *Crackers - The Christmas Party Album* (Castle CCSCD 401) 1993 or *Feel The Noize - Slade Greatest Hits* (Polydor 537 105-2) 1997 (No 16). *The Genesis Of Slade* (Cherry Red CDMRED 173) 2000 assembles 25 tracks recorded by three pre-**Slade** acts - **The Vendors**, **Steve Brett** and **The Mavericks** and by two different line-ups of the '**N Betweens**. *Greatest Hits* (Polygram 537 105-2) 2000 compiles 21 of their Top 30 hits. *The Very Best Of Slade* (2-CD) (Universal Music TV 9800715) 2005 features their seventies hits and a 1980 Reading Performance.

			HCP
45s:	Wild Winds Are Blowing/		
(up to	One Way Hotel	(Fontana TF 1056) 1969	R3 -
1976)	Shape Of Things To Come/		
	C'mon C'mon	(Fontana TF 1079) 1970	R3 -
	Know Who You Are/Dapple Rose	(Polydor 2058 054) 1970	R3 -
	Get Down And Get With It//Do You Want Me/		
	The Gospel According To Rasputin	(Polydor 2058 112) 1971	16
	Coz I Luv You/My Life Is Natural	(Polydor 2058 155) 1971	1
	Look Wot You Dun/Candidate	(Polydor 2058 195) 1972	4
	Tak Me Bak 'Ome/Wonderin'	(Polydor 2058 231) 1972	1
	Mama Weer All Crazee Now/		
	Man Who Speaks Evil	(Polydor 2058 272) 1972	1
	Gudbye T'Jane/		
	I Won't Let It Happen Again	(Polydor 2058 312) 1972	2
	Cum On Feel The Noize/		
	I'm Mee I'm Now An' Thats Orl	(Polydor 2058 339) 1973	1
	Skweeze Me Pleeze Me/		
	Kill 'Em At The Hot Club Tonite	(Polydor 2058 377) 1973	1
	My Friend Stan/My Town	(Polydor 2058 407) 1973	2
	Merry Xmas Everybody/		
	Don't Blame Me	(Polydor 2058 422) 1973	1
β	Everyday/Good Time Gals	(Polydor 2058 453) 1974	3
	The Bangin' Man/She Did It To Me	(Polydor 2058 492) 1974	3
	Far Far Away/		
	O.K. Yesterday Was Yesterday (PS)	(Polydor 2058 522) 1974	2
	How Does It Feel?/		
	So Far So Good (PS)	(Polydor 2058 547) 1975	15
χ	Thanks For The Memory (Wham Bam Thank You Mam)/		
	Raining In My Champagne	(Polydor 2058 585) 1975	7
	In For A Penny/		
	Can You Just Imagine (PS)	(Polydor 2058 663) 1975	11
	Let's Call It Quits/		
	When The Chips Are Down	(Polydor 2058 690) 1976	11

SLADE - Old New Borrowed And Blue (LP).

By 1974 they were becoming more ambitious. In an attempt to claim a higher level of public acceptability they made a movie 'Flame' about a mid-sixties band which **Slade** portrayed in the film. They made pretty decent acting debuts but the film failed to capture the public's imagination in a big way, although the accompanying Soundtrack did get to No 6 in the UK in December 1974 - the month the movie opened. In the States in particular, the movie made little impression and the band, which had been so hot in the first half of the decade, struggled to survive in the second half. To their credit, survive they did, not just the seventies but for most of the eighties too.

In the nineties, a Slade II was formed and on the road without either Holder or Lea, the former had become a popular TV personality through hosting a seventies rock radio show.

There are some good compilations if you weren't around in the seventies and want to hear their hits. You could try *Feel The Noize: The Very Best Of Slade* originally issued in 1997 and re-released again in 1999 under the simplified title of *Greatest Hits*. Or there's 2005's *The Very Best Of Slade*, a 2-CD set, which includes their 1980 Reading Festival performance too.

Naturally **Slade** have made several compilation appearances including *Shape Of Things To Come* on *Bombers* (LP). (VJ)

	Nobody's Fool/L.A. Jinx	(Polydor 2058 716) 1976 -
Reissues:	Merry Xmas Everybody/Okey Cokey/	
	Come Down And Get With It	(Cheapskate CHEAP 11) 1980 -
α	Cum On Feel The Noize/Take Me Back 'Ome/	
	Gudbye T'Jane	(Polydor POSP 399) 1981 -
	Merry Xmas Everybody/	
	Don't Blame Me	(Polydor POSP 780) 1985 48

NB: β Some copies were mispressed and played **The Hollies'** *The Air That I Breathe* on the 'A' side. χ There was also a promo-only version with altered lyrics on the 'A' side. α also issued on 12" format with one additional track, *Coz I Luv You*.

With their anthemic style **Slade** spearheaded the glam-rock movement of the early seventies. They achieved 11 Top Five hits (including five No 1s) during 1971-1974, when they were an important part of the nation's character.

The roots of **Slade** go back to a 1964 Wolverhampton-based band **The Vendors** who included Dave Hill and Don Powell and cut a four-song demo EP. By 1965 **The Vendors** had evolved into **The In-Be-Tweens**. The same year Noddy Holder was guitarist and backing vocalist in another Wolverhampton-based band, **Steve Brett and The Mavericks**. During 1966 **The In-Be-Tweens** split into two with only Hill and Powell remaining. They were then joined by Noddy Holder and another Wolverhampton lad Jimmy Lea. In early 1969 the foursome, who were now known as **Ambrose Slade** and playing Motown, **Beatles** and ska covers, moved down to London. They were spotted playing at Rasputin's Club by ex-**Animal** Chas Chandler who became their manager/producer, got them a record deal with Fontana and fashioned them in boots, braces and close-cut hair to cash-in on the skinhead movement. By the end of the year, he'd also persuaded them to shorten their name to **Slade**.

Their first hit came in 1971 with *Get Down And Get With It*, a cover of a Bobby Marchan song which had also been recorded by Little Richard. It climbed to No 16 in the UK Charts. What followed was a series of boot-stomping aggressive pop chants all written by Noddy Holder and Jimmy Lea and characterised by Holder's screaming vocals and deliberate misspellings of the English language - this was part of a deliberate ploy to promote them as a working class group. *Coz I Luv You*, which topped the UK Charts for four weeks, was the first of six Number One's and five years worth of Top Twenty hits - full details of their Chart exploits are given in the discography. The music was all very similar - direct, aggressive, unsubtle and ultra commercial. Their live act had guts, energy, aggression and enthusiasm - the sort of qualities so many punk bands would show a few years later. Despite their enormous success here they never really cracked the American market. Only four of their singles in this era made the lower echelons of the US Top 100 (*Take Me Bak 'Ome* (No 97), *Mama Weer All Crazee Now* (No 76), *Gudbye T'Jane* (No 68) and *Cum On Feel The Noize* (No 98)) and, although their albums sold relatively better, the story was similar (S*lade Alive* (No 158), *Slayed?* (No 69), *Sladest* (No 129), *Stomp Your Hands, Clap Your Feet* (No 168) and *Slade In Flame* (No 93)).

Slapp Happy

Personnel:	PETER BLEGVAD	gtr, vcls, clarinet	A
	DAGMAR KRAUSE	piano, vcls	A
	ANTHONY MOORE	piano, vcls	A

ALBUMS:	1(A)	SORT OF SLAPP HAPPY	
(up to		(w/insert)	(Polydor 2310 204) 1972 R3
1976)	2(A)	CASABLANCA MOON	(Virgin V 2014) 1974
	3(A)	DESPERATE STRAIGHTS	(Virgin V 2024) 1974
	4(A)	IN PRAISE OF LEARNING	(Virgin V 2027) 1975

NB: (1) reissued on Recommended (RRS 5) in 1986 (SC). (2) and (3) have been combined on one CD (Virgin CDOVD 441) 199?. (3) reissued and remastered on CD (ReR HCSH1) 2004. *Acnalbasac Noom* (RER REFSHCD1) is the version of their second album that Virgin rejected.

45s:	Casablanca Moon/Slow Moon's Rose	(Virgin VS 105) 1974
(up to	Johnny's Dead/Mr. Rainbow (PS)	(Virgin VS 124) 1975
1976)		

This experimental avant-garde jazz-rock outfit are included here on the strength of **Anthony Moore** being British. It was in fact a multi-national group. Blegvad was an American from New York and Dagmar Krause was German. Indeed the band formed in the Winter of 1971 whilst part of the circle of friends around the avant-garde German band Faust, who played on their first album, *Sort Of Slapp Happy*, which was recorded at Faust's Wumme studios, and on the second, *Casablanca Moon*.

SLADE - In Flame (LP).

SLADE - Smashes (LP).

The project remained dormant for a couple of years until signing for Virgin in 1974. They recorded three albums for Virgin - on the last two working with label-mates **Henry Cow**. The resulting music is not easy to classify, but certainly European-influenced and interesting.

The band folded when Blegvad left to return to New York and **Anthony Moore** went solo. Dagmar Krause then joined **Henry Cow**.

1996 saw the release of *Acnalbasac Noom*, a version of their self-titled second album which Virgin rejected. With German band Faust in support it's only a bit more rough 'n' ready than the sanctioned release which didn't feature Faust. Four additional tracks from a Recommended Records EP have been added along with a lyric booklet.

Slapp Happy were definitely an influence on the industrial/avant-garde music of the late seventies and eighties. (VJ)

Sleepy

Personnel incl: MICK FOWLER   organ

45s: Love's Immortal Fire/Is It Really The Same (CBS 3592) 1968 SC
Rosie Can't Fly/
Mrs. Bailey's Barbecue and Grill   (CBS 3838) 1968 SC

Both these 45s are now minor collectors' items. *Rosie Can't Fly* is superb - a dreamy fantasy-lyric song with perfect vocals. The 'B' side is good too, apart from the recitation of a recipe! Mick Fowler was later in **Grapefruit**.

Compilation appearances include: *Rosie Can't Fly* and *Love's Immortal Fire* on *Justafixation* (LP); *Rosie Can't Fly* on *Justafixation* (CD); *Loves Immortal Fire* on *Psychdelic Voyage, Vol. 2* (LP), *Psychedelic Voyage* (CD) and on *Jagged Time Lapse, Vol 1* (CD); and *Mrs. Bailey's Barbeque And Grill* has been compiled on *Jagged Time Lapse, Vol 4* (CD). (MWh)

Sleepy Hollow

Personnel incl: PAT CROWLEY   A
DECLAN PENDER   A
JOHNNY RICE   A

45s: Take Me Back/Roller Coaster Man   (Philips 607 8012) 1973
Come On Joe/Sad Affair   (Hollow Records HO 101) 1975

An Irish band, whose second 45 was recorded in Eamon Andrews Studios. (VJ/TG)

Slender Plenty

45:       Silver Tree Top School For Boys/I've Lost A
Friend And Found A Lover   (Polydor BM 56189) 1967 SC

This is a rare and sought-after 45. The 'A' side was a **David Bowie** song, also done by **The Beatstalkers**.

Silver Tree Top School For Boys has been compiled on *Justavibration* (LP) and *Justafixation* (CD). (VJ)

Slowbone

45:       Get What You're Given/Oh Man   (Rare Earth RES 119) 1974
NB: *Live At The Greyhound 1972* (CD) (Audio Archives AACD 003) was recorded live at the famous Greyhound pub in Fulham Palace Road during their heavy phase and is supplemented by two bonus tracks from an earlier gig. *Tales Of A Crooked Man* (LP) (Audio Archives PAM 1) comprises seven studio tracks recorded between 1972 and 1974 and side two captures them live in London and comes with an informative insert.

This was a heavy blues-rock outfit from London's East End, which formed out of the ashes of **Turquoise**. (VJ)

Slow Dog

Personnel:	CHRIS CURTIS	bs	A
	HANNIBAL NICK HEMERY	gtr	A
	SIMON JUDD	keyb'ds	A
	DEREK JEFFREY	vcls, gtr	A
	DAVE KELLY	reeds, woodwind, vcls	A
	JIM PRAGLIOLA	drms	A

45:       Walking Through The Blue Grass/
Ain't Never Going Home   (Parlophone R 5942) 1972

A Huntingdon band who formed in early 1970. (VJ)

Small Faces

Personnel:	KENNEY JONES	drms	AB
	STEVIE MARRIOTT	gtr, vcls	AB
	RONNIE 'PLONK' LANE	bs, vcls	AB
	JIMMY LANGWITH (WINSTON)	organ	A
	IAN McLAGAN	organ	B

			HCP
ALBUMS: 1(B)	SMALL FACES	(Decca LK 4790) 1966	R2 3
2(B)	FROM THE BEGINNING	(Decca LK 4879) 1967	R2 17

SLOWBONE - Live At The Greyhound (LP).

3(B) SMALL FACES
(mono/stereo) (Immediate IMLP/IMSP 008) 1967 R3 12
4(B) OGDENS' NUT GONE FLAKE
(mono/stereo) (Immediate IMLP/IMSP 012) 1968 R2 1
5(B) THE AUTUMN STONE (2-LP)
(Immediate IMAL 1/2) 1969 R1 -

NB: There was also an export-only single album version of (5) In Memoriam (Immediate IMLP/IMSP 022) 1969. (1) reissued on CD (Deram 844 634-2) 1996 and again (Essential ESMCD 476) 2005. (1) reissued a 2-CD set (Sanctuary CMDDD 533) 2002 to mark the 35th anniversary of their first 1967 album. (2) reissued on CD (Deram 844 634-2) 1996, which comes with liner notes and five bonus cuts. (3) reissued on CD in 1991 as Green Circles (The First Immediate Album) (Sequel NEX CD 163) with extra tracks and later on Repertoire (REP 4173-WY) 1993 in its original sleeve along with 14 bonus cuts (lots of 'A' and 'B' sides and several hitherto unissued tracks and alternate takes). (3) later reissued on 180 gram vinyl (Sequel LP 415) 1999 (plus both sides of their Itchycoo Park and Tin Soilder 45 and Here Comes The Nice) and on CD (Sunspots SPOT 506) 2002 in a limited 1,500 run miniature gatefold card sleeve with an insert and four bonus tracks. (3) reissued on CD (Castle ESMCD 476) 1997 with the reissued UK album combined with the equivalent US release - There Are But Four Small Faces. This was originally issued a few months later and included the singles Tin Soldier and Itchycoo Park (mini-LP sleeve) (CD) (Castle CMTCD 343). (3) reissued again on vinyl (Get Back GETLP 553) with four bonus tracks and as a 35th Anniversary Edition (2-CD) (Castle CMDD 553) which contains the mono and stereo edition of their 1967 output, including many rarities, outtakes and alternative mixes making it the definitive edition of this classic album. (4) reissued on vinyl (Immediate/NEMS IML 1001) 1975 (SC) in a round sleeve with a white label and again in 1977 with the same catalogue number in a square sleeve. (4) reissued on CD (Castle CLACT 016) 1991. Early copies came in a tobacco tin with five 'Ogdens' beer mats, a circular paper fold-out in the style of the original album cover and the CD has a bonus cut - a 'live' version of Tin Soldier. This CD was earlier available on Immediate (IMLCD 2001) 1986, but without the bonus cut. (4) reissued again on CD (Castle Music CMRCD 1192) 2005. (4) reissued on vinyl (Get Back GET550DL) - there's also a limited edition picture disc release (Get Back GET 550P). (4) reissued on CD repackaged and remastered (Jewel case edition) (Castle ESMCD 477) 1997, again in an exact miniature replica of the circular fold-out gatefold sleeve of the original album (Castle CMTCD 234) and also a 3-CD deluxe edition (Castle CMKTD 997) which includes both mono and stereo version of the original album and more. (5) reissued on CD (Castle Classics CLACD 114) 1986, on CD (Castle ESMCD 478) 1997, again on CD (Snapper SNIP 404CD) with four bonus tracks and again on CD (Essential ESMCD 478) 2005. The 1997 reissue includes the whole of the original album plus additional tracks recorded live at Newcastle and Donkey Rides, Penny A Glass. (3), (4) and (5) (Sanctuary CMETD 1035) is a 3-CD set of these classic albums.

The band's vinyl compilations include Live UK 1969 (Charly CR 300025) 1978, Big Hits (Virgin V 2166) 1980, For Your Delight The Darlings Of Wapping Wharf Launderette (Virgin V 2178) 1980 and Sha La La La Lee (Decca TAB 16) 1981. They also shared an album with Amen Corner (one side each) issued on New World (NW 6000) in 1980.

CD compilations include, The Singles A's and B's (See For Miles SEE CD 293) 1990, which contains exactly what the title suggests; The Ultimate Collection (Castle Communications CTV CD 004) 1990 and Collection: Small Faces (Castle Collector CLSCD 108) 1991. From The Beginning (London 820 766-2) 1989 is a pretty good CD compilation of material from their early days with Decca. The Decca Anthology 1965-67 (Deram 844 583-2) 1995, issued as a 2-CD set and 2-LP format, contains their Decca recordings lovingly packaged in chronological order of release, with superb sound quality and authoritative sleeve notes from their biographer Paolo Hewitt. The 4-CD box set, The Immediate Years (Charly CD IMM BOX 1) 1995,

contains 86 tracks, claiming to cover every Immediate recording made by the band and released in the UK, Germany and the USA and including many rarities and detailed liner notes. Another 2-CD compilation, The Definitive Anthology (Repertoire REP 4429-WO) 1995, duplicates the earlier See For Miles The Singles A's And B's exactly on one disc, and also includes Stevie Marriott's 1963 single, The Moments 45, and both Jimmy Winston's 45s amongst the assorted Small Faces tracks. Me You And Us Too: Best Of The Immediate Years (Repertoire REP 4818-WG) 1999 was available on German import. The Darlings Of Wapping Wharf - The Immediate Anthology (Sequel NEE CD 311) 1999 is a 2-CD 50-track set of their recordings for the label. The Immediate Singles Collection (Sequel ESB CD 725) 1999 is a limited edition of 7,500 6-CD box set of all six of their Immediate singles on mono. Nice (New Millennium NMC PILOT 66) 2000 compiles the group's German TV appearances between 1966-68 (with soundtracks) into an audio visual package. The BBC Sessions (Strange Fruit SFRSLP 087) 2001 is a limited vinyl edition of a set originally issued on CD (SFSR CD 087) in 1998 by the same label and reissued again in 1999. The Immediate Album Collection (Castle Music CMETD 1166) 2005 is a recent collection. Ultimate Collection (2-CD) (Sanctuary TDSAN 004) is a 50-track collection compiling their sixties material for Decca and Immediate that includes 12 hit singles. Nice (CD & CDR) (NMC PILOT 207) comprises 10 classic tracks from live German TV performances between 1966 and 1968 on the audio disc plus a CDR which shows the performances live and it's accompanied by a 12-page booklet. Here Come The Small Faces (2-CD) (Atom Music ATOM 2003) is a compilation including classics like Here Comes The Nice, Itchycoo Park and Tin Soilder.

HCP

45s:	What'cha Gonna Do About It?/		
	What's A' Matter, Baby?	(Decca F 12208) 1965	14
	I've Got Mine/It's Too Late	(Decca F 12276) 1965	SC -
	Sha La La La Lee/Grow Your Own	(Decca F 12317) 1966	3
	Hey Girl/Almost Grown	(Decca F 12393) 1966	10
	All Or Nothing/Understanding	(Decca F 12470) 1966	1
α	My Mind's Eye/I Can't Dance With You	(Decca F 12500) 1966	4
	I Can't Make It/Just Passing	(Decca F 12565) 1967	SC 26
β	Patterns/E Too D	(Decca F 12619) 1967	R1 -
	Small Faces (one-sided promo)	(Immediate AS 1) 1967	R2 -
	Here Comes The Nice/Talk To You	(Immediate IM 050) 1967	12
	Itchycoo Park/I'm Only Dreaming	(Immediate IM 057) 1967	3
	Tin Soldier/I Feel Much		
	Better (Some PS)	(Immediate IM 062) 1967	R1/SC 9
	Lazy Sunday/Rollin' Over	(Immediate IM 064) 1968	2
	The Universal/		
	Donkey Rides, A Penny A Glass	(Immediate IM 069) 1968	16
	Afterglow (Of Your Love)/		
	Wham Bam, Thank You Mam	(Immediate IM 077) 1969	36
Reissues:	Itchycoo Park/My Mind's Eye	(Immediate IMS 102) 1975	9
	Lazy Sunday/Autumn Stone	(Immediate IMS 701) 1975	-
	Lazy Sunday/		
	Have You Ever Seen Me	(Immediate IMS 106) 1976	39
	Tin Soldier/I Feel Much Better	(Immediate IMS 100) 1977	-
	Sha La La La Lee/What'cha Gonna Do About It/		
	All Or Nothing	(Decca F 13727) 1977	-
	Tin Soldier/Tin Soldier (live)/Renee	(Virgin VS 367) 1980	-
	All Or Nothing/My Mind's Eye	(Old Gold OG 9394) 1983	-
	Sha La La La Lee/		
	What'cha Gonna Do About It	(Old Gold OG 9344) 1983	-

SMALL FACES - Small Faces (LP).

SMALL FACES - From The Beginning (LP).

Lazy Sunday/Tin Soldier   (Old Gold OG 9465) 1985 -
Itchycoo Park/Here Comes The Nice (Old Gold OG 9466) 1985 -
Itchycoo Park/Lazy Sunday/Sha-La-La-La-Lee/
Here Comes The Nice (12" PS)   (Archive 4 TOF 103) 1986 -

NB: α US version (RCA Victor 47-9055) 1966, features a different take of *My Mind's Eye*. There's also an alternate demo mix (SC). β Some were released in export PS (R3).

The Small Faces started as one of the UK's foremost mod bands, before evolving into a superb hard-edged pop-psych act. **Stevie Marriott** is widely considered to have been our finest male soul singer of the sixties, and the band's influence in recent years has been enormous.

They formed in London's East End in June 1965. **Ronnie 'Plonk' Lane**, **Jimmy Winston** (born Jimmy Langwith) and Kenney Jones had started out as a pub trio. They met **Stevie Marriott** whilst he was working in a music shop in East Ham. **Marriott** was a former child actor who'd appeared in a London production and cast album of 'Oliver' as well as on various TV and radio shows. He'd also recorded a 45, *Give Her My Regards*, for Decca in 1963 and been on a US 45 by **The Moments**.

All four were all R&B fans and targeted their music at the emerging mod market. Their name was chosen because of their lack of height and their desire to be 'faces' in the mod sense (as in **The High Numbers**' song *I'm The Face*).

Though they were one of hundreds of British groups playing R&B and soul, it was apparent from a very early stage that they had 'the X factor' needed for success. They signed to Decca and recorded *What'cha Gonna Do 'Bout It?*, an Ian Samuel song which he also produced. Although the rhythm was lifted from Solomon Burke's *Everybody Needs Somebody To Love*, it was a punchy debut with unusual guitar work, and peaked at No 14 in the UK charts, though **Marriott** later admitted he could scarcely play at the time it was recorded.

After this 45 **Winston** departed to form a new group, **Jimmy Winston and His Reflections**. His replacement was Ian McLagan, who'd been keyboard-player with **The Muleskinners** and Boz and The Boz. Their next single, *I Got Mine* was written by **Marriott** and **Lane** for 'Dateline Diamonds', an uninspired movie about a jewel theft involving a pirate radio ship. By all accounts the band's live set was the film's highlight and should have guaranteed another hit, but due to a mix-up the film was released too late to assist the single, which already narrowly missed the charts.

They couldn't afford another flop, so at manager Don Arden's insistence their next 45 was *Sha La La La Lee*, a solid piece of commercial pop by **Kenny Lynch** and Mort Shuman. Released in late January 1966, it took them into the Top 3 but was one of their less interesting singles. By now, however, the band had undertaken a UK and European tour and built up a considerable live following in London, with a residency at the Cavern Club off Leicester Square in the West End.

Their next 45, *Hey Girl*, was another commercial number which **Marriott**

and **Lane** wrote themselves. It gave the duo their first self-penned Top Ten hit, but underscored their image as a teeny pop band when they really wanted to play rock and blues. Their debut album, *Small Faces*, allowed them to be a little more self-indulgent. Aside from the hits *What'cha Gonna Do 'Bout It* and *Sha La La La Lee*, it included little poppy material. Instead there was a number of **Marriott/Lane** compositions dating from their early Decca sessions. The album sold very well, staying at No. 3 for seven weeks and eventually spending six months in the charts.

All Or Nothing, was another **Marriott/Lane** composition and a landmark for the band for two reasons. It was their first and only No 1, and far more rocky than their previous material. By now they were planning to take the States by storm, but a short promotional visit (due to serve as a prelude for a full tour) had to be cancelled when it became known that McLagan had a drugs conviction which debarred him from entering the States. The group's inability to tour America was the major reason they sold relatively few discs there.

Meanwhile, in its impatience to follow their No. 1, Decca released an unpolished studio demo of *My Mind's Eye* without the group's knowledge; though (unbeknownst to the label) a far more polished recording was in existence. Though the 45 got into the Top 5, its release caused irreparable damage to the label's relationship with the group. When their seventh single, *I Can't Make It*, stalled at No. 26 in March 1967, the group announced it was leaving Decca to sign to **Andrew Oldham**'s Immediate label. A couple of months later Decca released *Patterns* without the band's agreement. Far from promoting it, they told their fans not to buy it and it flopped. Within a week Immediate rush-released *Here Come The Nice*, whose oblique drug references neatly captured the mood of the summer of 1967 and propelled it to No. 12.

Decca responded by rushing out a second collection of early material (including the *Patterns* 45) titled *From The Beginning*. In response Immediate released the self-produced **Small Faces** album, the first the band was happy with. Both labels splashed out on adverts in the music press to promote their albums. Immediate narrowly won the battle - *Small Faces* peaked at No 12 while *From The Beginning* only managed No 17.

Itchycoo Park, released in August 1967, was one of the first singles to use phasing and their most experimental to date. It was a major commercial success too, climbing to No. 3 in the UK and peaking at No. 16 in the States, giving them their first hit there. The group underscored its triumph by appearing at 'The Festival Of The Flower Children', a three-day event held over the August Bank Holiday on the Isle of Man. The next few weeks were spent feverishly touring, causing **Marriott** to collapse from nervous exhaustion during a tour of Ireland in November, the remainder of which had to be cancelled.

In December 1967 **Marriott** and the boys bounced back with another superb 45, *Tin Soldier*. They'd become a really tight musical unit by now, and the result was an early hard-rock sound with **Marriott**'s vocals at their punchy best. It reached No. 9 here and No. 63 in the States. In January 1968 McLagan married 20-year-old dancer Sandy Sargent in a secret

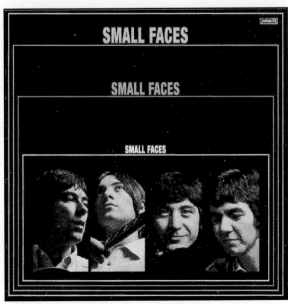

SMALL FACES - Small Faces (CD - Immediate).

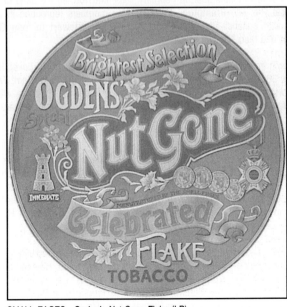

SMALL FACES - Ogden's Nut Gone Flake (LP).

SMALL FACES - The Autumn Stone (2-LP).

ceremony at Marylebone registry office. Unfortunately, their honeymoon plans were dashed when a lump of hash was found on him at the airport. Both were arrested and had to be bailed by the band.

Their next 45, the good-timey *Lazy Sunday*, was apparently about **Marriott**'s neighbours in Chiswick, who were always complaining about the noise he made. Sung in an exaggerated cockney accent by **Marriott**, it entered the charts at No. 2 and became their second biggest hit. Thrilled by this success, they embarked on a tour of Australia with **The Who** and **Paul Jones**, but were deported along with **The Who** after an in-flight disturbance, causing the local press to label them 'dirty, beer swigging ragamuffins'.

Ogdens' Nut Gone Flake appeared on 24 May and immediately topped the UK album charts, where it stayed for a remarkable six weeks. One of the key albums of the period, alongside **The Beatles**' *Sgt. Pepper*, **The Pretty Things**' *S.F. Sorrow* and **The Who**'s *Tommy*, it was full of superb songs such as *Afterglow (Of Your Love)*, *Rene* and *Song Of A Baker*, and one side was linked by surreal narrations by Stanley Unwin. Its circular cover, representing the lid of an Ogden's tobacco tin, was highly original too.

The Universal, released in June, was almost free-form and got to No. 16 in the UK.

In October 1968, the band embarked on a UK package tour with **The Who** and **Joe Cocker**. **Peter Frampton** guested on guitar on some of the dates and built up a friendship with **Marriott**. When the tour finished, **Marriott** and **Lane** produced **The Herd**'s next single *Sunshine Cottage* and **Frampton** helped **The Small Faces** with their work on **Skip Bifferty**'s album. A few months later, in February 1969, **Marriott** left the band to form **Humble Pie** with **Frampton**. The remaining members regrouped in June 1969 with guitarist Ron Wood and vocalist **Rod Stewart** to form **Quiet Melon** and then **The Faces**.

In March Immediate posthumously released *Afterglow (Of Your Love)*. It got to No. 36, though the band was now defunct. The flip, *Wham! Bam! Thank You Mam*, was a heavy rocker. The *Autumn Stone*, a double album, followed in November. Aside from the inevitable 45 and album tracks, it included live numbers from a concert at Newcastle City Hall. However, with the band no longer in the limelight, it failed to chart.

This wasn't the end of the story. In 1973 *Ogdens' Nut Gone Flake* was reissued in the States and got to No. 189. Then, in January 1976, *Itchycoo Park* was reissued and got into the Top Ten for a second time. This prompted the reissue of *Lazy Sunday*, which got to No 39, prompting the band to reform (though Rick Wills filled the bass slot in place of **Ronnie Lane**). Like most reunions, it was short-lived and unsuccessful.

The BBC Sessions, released on CD in 1998 and limited edition vinyl in 2001, includes a mixture of hit singles (*Sha-La-La-La-Lee*, *Hey Girl* and *All Or Nothing*), 'B' sides and album tracks like *E To D*, *Shake* and *Understanding*. **Jimmy Winston** sings vocals raucously on Marvin Gaye's *Baby Don't You Do It* and Rufus Thomas' *Jump Back*.

The Darlings Of Wapping Wharf is a 50-track, 2-CD anthology of their Immediate recordings. Remastered from original tapes, the collection includes their first two albums for the label in their entirety as well as the studio side of *Autumn Stone*, the singles and some rarities, including 35 seconds of an unissued backing track and a colourful sleeve insert, which displays rare memorabilia and excellent sleevenotes. This is probably the definitive compilation of their Immediate years.

Nice compiles their German TV appearances between 1966 and 1968 (including soundtracks) into an audio-visual package. It comes with a 48-page booklet containing interviews with band members taken from the out-of-print 'Quite Naturally' book.

Aside from the recordings listed in the earlier discography the band also featured on three of Decca's Various Artists EPs in the mid-sixties. *Hits, Vol. 5* included *Hey Girl*; *Hits, Vol. 6* included *All Or Nothing*; *My Mind's Eye* figured on *Hits, Vol. 7* and *All Or Nothing* featured on Decca's *The World Of Hits, Vol. 2* (LP). Other compilation appearances have included: *Grow Your Own* on *The Mod Scene* (CD); *Own Up Time* on *Mod Scene, Vol. 2* (CD); *Get Yourself Together* on *Maximum '65* (CD); *That Man* on *The Psychedelic Scene* (CD); *I Can't Make It* and *Hey Girl* on *A Whiter Shade Of Pale* (LP); *Here Come The Nice* on *Tonite Let's All Make Love In London* (LP); *Itchycoo Park* on *Juke Box Jive* (EP), *60's Mix* (CD) and *Your Starter For Ten!!* (CD); *Understanding* on *The Freakbeat Scene* (CD); *What'cha Gonna Do About It* on *Hard-Up Heroes* (2-LP); *Itchycoo Park* and *Afterglow (Of Your Love)* on *Immediate Single Collection, Vol. 1* (CD); *Lazy Sunday* on the 2-CD set *Greatest Hits Of The 60's Vol 4*; *Lazy Sunday* and *Wham Bam Thank You Man* on *Immediate Single Collection, Vol. 3* (CD); *Here Comes The Nice* and *Tin Soldier* on *Hits Of The Swinging Sixties* (CD); *I'm Only Dreaming* and *Talk To You* on *Immediate Single Collection, Vol. 4* (CD) and *All Or Nothing* on the 2-CD set *60 Number One Hits Of The Sixties*. More recently, *Wham Bam Thank You Mam* received fresh exposure on the CD set *Rock Of Ages, Four Decades Of Heavy Rock 1962-2002*; *Green Circles* got fresh exposure on the 4-CD box set *Acid Drops, Spacedust & Flying Saucers* and *My Mind's Eye* and *Here Comes The Nice* can be found on the 4-CD *Nuggets II* box set. You'll also find *Songs Of A Baker* on the 3-CD box set *Ars Longa Vita Brevis: A Compendium Of Progressive Rock 1967-1974* and *I Can't Make It* on the 2-CD set *We Love The Pirates: Charting The Big 'L' Fab 40*.

Ronnie Lane later became ill with multiple sclerosis and, after a long battle with the disease, died on 4th June 1997. **Marriott** was tragically killed in a fire at his home in April 1991. (VJ/BM/RMJ)

The Small Four

| 45: | One Up For Me/I'll Find Him | (Pye 7N 17191) 1966 |

An obscure folk group.

One Up On Me can also be heard on *Ripples, Vol. 2* (CD). (VJ)

SMALL FACES - There Are But Four Small Faces (LP).

John Small

45s: Can't Nobody See My Face/
        Woman Who Can Shake My Mind   (Famous FAM 101) 19?
        As I See You/Gently She Goes   (Famous FAM 106) 19?

John Small kicked off the short-lived EMI subsidiary (and not so) Famous label. He was from Yorkshire. (MWh)

Smile (1)

Personnel: BRIAN MAY   gtr   A
              TIM STAFFELL   bs, vcls   A
              ROGER TAYLOR   drms   A

ALBUM: 1(A) GETTIN' SMILE   (Mercury 18 PP-1) 1982

NB: (1) only issued in Japan. It includes the single from 1969 and four unreleased songs recorded the same year. Reissued on CD as *Ghost Of A Smile* (Pseudonym Records CDP 1049-DD) 1997.

45:   α   Earth / Step On Me   (Mercury 72.977) 1969

NB: α issued only in United States but it seems that some acetates, with handwritten notes, were pressed in the UK.

From London, this band was formed in summer 1968 by Brian May and Tim Staffell, who had previously been in a band called 1984 (not the same act who issued three singles) and Roger Taylor from **The Reaction**. Smile opened for a lot of acts, especially in London's Imperial College, as support to **Pink Floyd**, **Family**, **Yes**, **Tyrannosaurus Rex** and in a Benefit concert Festival at the Royal Albert Hall with **Free**, **Spooky Tooth** etc...

In April 1969, they were approached and signed for a one-off 45 by Lou Reizner, a talent scout for Mercury Records. The session took place at Trident Studios with producer John Anthony (**Van Der Graaf Generator / Rare Bird**). Three originals songs were recorded with *Doing Alright*, *Earth* and *Step On Me*, but the 45 was only released in the U.S.A. and inevitably flopped. *Earth* is a ballad with nice harmonies, and *Step On Me* a good uptempo number. The sound of the guitar is very strange and later became a trademark for Brian May.

Following the 45, Mercury booked another session at De Lane Lea Studios in Kingsway with producer Fritz Fryer, ex-guitarist of the **Four Pennies** and producer of **The Open Mind**'s *Magic Potion* 45, amongst others. Three further tracks were recorded: the hard *Blag*, a gentle ballad *Polar Bear* and a obscure cover titled *April Lady* in a **Beatles**' style. All these tracks were included in the Japan only album *Gettin' Smile* in 1982. *Doing Alriqht* was later re-recorded by **Queen** and featured on their first album.

Disillusioned by their lack of success (in spite of some good concerts as support for **Kippington Lodge** and **Mighty Baby**) Smile split at the beginning of 1970. After that, Tim Staffell joined **Humpy Bong**, **Morgan**, **Jonathan Kelly's Outside** and Tailfeather while Roger Taylor and Brian May formed **Queen** with a friend of Tim called Freddie Mercury. (CSx)

Smile (2)

Personnel incl: DAVE PRITCHARD   A
                 MIKE SHERIDAN   A

45:   Let Me Be Your Shadow/
      What Makes The World Go Round   (Philips 6006 396) 1974

There were several bands of this name. This particular outfit included Dave Pritchard, a veteran of **Idle Race** and Mike Sheridan who'd fronted **Mike Sheridan's Lot** and **Sheridan and Price**. (VJ)

Smile (3)

Personnel: BRIAN MAY   gtr   A
              TIM STAFFELL   vcls   A
              ROGER TAYLOR   drms   A

NB: A relevant release is *Ghost Of A Smile* (Pseudonym CDP 1049 DD) 1998.

THE SMALL FACES - BBC Sessions (CD).

The main significance of this group is that two thirds of them became **Queen**. They entered Trident studios in June 1969 for their first proper session and three tracks from this (*Earth* and *Step On Me*, with their harmony vocals and mock operatic singing) previewed the later **Queen** sound, whilst *Doin' Allright* was more pastoral in style. They returned to the studio in September 1969 to record three further tracks in more of a hard-rock vein. All six tracks plus a single, *The Man From Manhattan*, by Eddie Howell (which Freddie Mercury and Brian May sang on) are compiled on the above album, which is essential for any **Queen** fans. (VJ)

Gordon Smith

ALBUM: 1   LONG OVERDUE   (Blue Horizon 7-63211) 1968 R2

45:   Too Long/Funk Pedal   (Blue Horizon 57-3156) 1969 SC

Smith was from County Durham originally and had moved down to London in 1967. He was discovered busking in the Portobello Road and after a live appearance at the Blue Horizon club in Battersea, London, which was very well received, he was put in the studio to record demos the following day. **Peter Green**, Mick Fleetwood and John McVie, who were all members of **Fleetwood Mac**, appeared on various tracks on his now rare album and on his 45. (VJ)

Terry Smith

ALBUM: 1   FALL OUT   (Philips (S)BL 7871) 1969 R3

NB: (1) reissued on CD (Sunbeam SBRCD 008) 2005 with detailed sleevenotes.

Smith recorded this superb piece of jazz-rock shortly before joining **If** in 1969. Produced by **Scott Walker**, in whose band Smith had toured, it's almost impossible to find nowadays. In 1973 he played lead on Mike Carr's solo album. After **If**'s demise in 1975 he gigged with former **If** member Dick Morrissey in Sweden for a while, recorded with **Zzebra** and then recorded an album in 1977, *Terry Smith and The Tony Lee Trio* (Lambert LAM 002) (SC). (VJ/RMJ)

Whistling Jack Smith

ALBUM: 1   AROUND THE WORLD WITH WHISTLING JACK SMITH
                                    (Deram DML 1009) 1967 SC

                                                        HCP

45s: I Was Kaiser Bill's Batman/
       The British Grin And Bear   (Deram DM 112) 1967 5
       Hey There Little Miss Mary/

I Was Bizet's Carmen	(Deram DM 129) 1967	-
Ja Da/Sans Fairy Anne	(Deram DM 179) 1968	-
Only When I Larf/Early One Morning	(Deram DM 189) 1968	-
Battle Of Waterloo Love Theme/		
No Time For Punting	(Deram DM 411) 1974	-

Reissue: I Was Kaiser Bill's Batman/
The British Grin And Bear   (Decca F 13922) 1982 -

This guy's real name was Billy Moeller, a Liverpudlian born on 2 February 1946, whose brother Tommy was vocalist with **Unit Four Plus Two**. *I Was Kaiser Bill's Batman* was a novelty pop hit and Moeller wasn't even responsible for the whistling on the record - it was done by a session man. As well as getting to No 5 here, the disc got to No 20 in the US. It was a studio session production featuring the Mike Sammes Singers and Moeller was hired later to tour as **Whistling Jack Smith**. The disc proved to be a classic 'one hit wonder'! He also recorded as **Coby Wells**. (VJ)

Smithfield Market

ALBUMS: 1 LONDON IN 1665   (Gloucester GLS 0435) 1973 R5
      2 AFTER SHAKESPEARE GLOBE
        (w/insert)   (Gloucester GLS 0443) 1974 R5

This band was responsible for two very rare privately-pressed albums. The first is marginally rarer, and the second came in a die-cut sleeve with insert. (VJ)

The Smoke

Personnel:	GEOFF GILL	drms	A
	MAL LUKER	ld gtr	A
	ZEKE LUND	bs	A
	MICK ROWLEY	vcls	A

ALBUM: 1(A) IT'S SMOKE TIME (German only) (Metronome) 1966 R4
NB: (1) reissued as *My Friend Jack* (Gull 25114) in the late seventies (SC), again (Morgan Blue Town MBT 5001) 1988 (SC) and on CD by Repertoire (REP 4348-WZ) 1993 with 14 bonus tracks. A different *My Friend Jack* (Sin-Drome/Retroactive SD 8939) 2000 compilation was available on US import. There is also a 2-CD collection *High In A Room: The Smoke Anthology* (Castle CMEDD 516) 2002.

                                                    HCP

45s: My Friend Jack/
     We Can Take It   (Columbia DB 8115) 1967 R1 45
     If The Weather's Sunny/
     I Would If I Could, But I Can't   (Columbia DB 8252) 1967 R1 -
     It Could Be Wonderful/
     Have Some More Tea   (Island WIP 6023) 1967 R2 -

α Utterly Simple/Sydney Gill   (Island WIP 6031) 1968 -
  Dreams Of Dreams/
  My Birth   (Revolution Pop REVP 1002) 1970 SC -
  Ride Ride Ride/Guy Fawks   (Pageant SAM 101) 1971 -
  Sugar Man/
  That's What I Want   (Regal Zonophone RZ 3071) 1972 SC -
  Shagalagalu/Gimme Good Loving   (Decca FR 13484) 1974 -
  My Lullaby/Looking High   (Decca FR 13514) 1974 -

NB: α unreleased.

Setting out as R&B outfit **The Shots**, when this Yorkshire band changed their name to **The Smoke** they produced some of the better acid pop of the era. They're best remembered for their 1967 single *My Friend Jack*, which was inevitably banned by the BBC for its acid connotations, but nonetheless reached No 45. The flip side, *We Can Take It*, was a great power pop number. They were yet another act that attained greater popularity on the Continent than at home, and their *It's Smoke Time* album was issued only in Germany. Apart from the title track, *You Can't Catch Me* is notable for its fine psychedelic intro, *High In A Room*, was well-suited to the druggy days of 1967 and *Waterfall*, *If The Weather's Sunny* and *Wake Up Changeling* captured the group in a more laid-back mood. Their follow-up single, *If The Weather's Sunny*, was less successful.

The Smoke then recorded two singles for Island, *It Could Be Wonderful* and *Utterly Simple*, which was written by **Dave Mason** and produced by him and **Jeff Beck**. The latter was never released, but can now be heard in all its glory on *Psychedelia, Vol. 3* (LP) and *Hen's Teeth, Vol. 3* (CD). One of their most interesting and mature efforts, it's very different to **Traffic**'s version.

The 2000 *My Friend Jack* compilation inevitably kicks off with the title track, but there's a blend of originals (*High In A Room*, *Sydney Gill* and *You Can't Catch Me*) and some superb cover versions (**Traffic's** *Utterly Simple* and **Nirvana's** *Girl In The Park*) on offer too.

High In A Room is a 46-track 2-CD definitive anthology, which comes with excellent colour photos and comprehensive sleevenotes from David Wells. Attractions include no less than three versions of *My Friend Jack*, an alternate version of *Sydney Gill* and great covers of *Utterly Simple* (**Traffic**) and *The Girl In The Park* (**Nirvana**).

From their psychedelic era, *My Friend Jack* can also be heard on *Best And The Rest Of British Psychedelia* (CD), *Beat It* (3-CD), *Morgan Blue Town* (LP), a Bam-Caruso *Psych-Out* flexidisc, *Rock Of Ages*, the 4-CD box set *Acid Drops, Spacedust & Flying Saucers*; the 2-CD set *Greatest Hits Of The 60's Vol 4*, *Four Decades Of Heavy Rock 1962-2002* another CD-set; *Electric Sugarcube Flashbacks, Vol. 3* (LP), and on *Electric Sugar Cube Flashbacks* (CD). The latter two featuring a German demo version of the song, with different (and better) guitar work at the end, and some different lyrics. *My Friend Jack* and *Girl In The Park* have been compiled on *Made In England, Vol. 1* (CD); *Have Some More Tea*, one of their best 'B' sides, on *Chocolate Soup For Diabetics, Vol. 3* (LP); the previously unreleased

THE SMOKE - My Friend Jack (LP - Gull).

THE SMOKE - It's Smoke Time (CD - Repertoire).

and superb *Sydney Gill* on *Perfumed Garden, Vol. 1* (LP & CD); *Dreams Of Dreams*, the 'A' side of their one-off 45 on the Revolution label, on *Circus Days Vol. 1 & 2* (CD) and *Circus Days, Vol. 2* (LP); *Dream Of Dreams* and *My Birth* on *Psychdelic Voyage, Vol. 2* (LP) and *Psychedelic Voyage* (CD); *That's What I Want* on *We Can Fly, Vol 1* (CD); *High In A Room* on *Perfumed Garden Vol. 2* (CD) and *Thus Spake Alice* on *Talking About The Good Times, Vol 1* (CD).

They carried on recording into the mid-seventies with numerous personnel changes. Geoff Gill later became a producer and songwriter for Boney M. (VJ)

Smokestack Crumble

45:     Got A Bad Leg/Whisky Macaroni   (Dawn DNS 1013) 1971

The 'A' side was a good tightly structured composition with heavy percussion. The vocalist sounded like **Rod Stewart**. (VJ)

Smokey Circles

ALBUM: 1   THE SMOKEY CIRCLES ALBUM
                                    (Carnaby CNLS 6006) 1970 R2

45:     Long, Long, Love/
        Love Me While You Can   (Carnaby CNS 4011) 1970

A light pop album masterminded by impresario Mervyn Conn. Probably a group, but there has been speculation that this could be Tony Burrows and friends. Probably not, but Ralph Murphy and Schmulik Kraus wrote the twelve commercial bubblegum pop songs. The orchestra is by Ken Woodman and male/female vocals are deployed. (VJ)

Smokie and His Sister

45:     Creators Of Rain/In Dreams Of Silent Seas   (CBS 20604) 1967

Both sides of the 45 were written by Smokie. They sound like a pop / light folk duo. (VJ)

Smokie

Personnel: CHRIS NORMAN   vcls   A
               ALAN SILSON   bs   A
               PETE SPENCER   drms   A
               TERRY UTLEY   gtr   A

THE SMOKE - My Friend Jack (LP - Sin-Drome).

ALBUMS: 1(A)   PASS IT AROUND   (Rak SRAK 510) 1975 -
(up to   2(A)   CHANGING ALL THE TIME   (Rak SRAK 517) 1975 18
1976)   3(A)   MIDNIGHT CAFE   (Rak SRAK 520) 1976 -

NB: Also relevant is *Greatest Hits* (Rak SRAK 526) 1977 (No 6), later reissued on Fame (FA 41 3114 1) in 1984 and *The Very Best Of Smokie* (Rak SRAK 540) 1980 (No 23). (2) reissued on CD (Arista 261029) 1991, but now deleted. Also on CD is *The Best Of Smokie* (Telstar TCD 2455) 1990 and *Greatest Hits Live: Smokie* (Total WAGCD 3) 1990.

45s: Pass It Around/Couldn't Live   (Rak RAK 192) 1975 -
(up to   If You Think You Know How To Love Me/
1976)   Til Me   (Rak RAK 206) 1975 3
         Don't Play Your Rock'n'Roll To Me/
         Talking Her Round   (Rak RAK 217) 1975 8
         Something's Been Making Me Blue/
         Train Song   (Rak RAK 227) 1976 17
         Wild Wild Angels/Loser   (Rak RAK 23) 1976 -
         I'll Meet You At Midnight/Miss You (Rak RAK 241) 1976 11
         Living Next Door To Alice/Run To You (Rak RAK 244) 1976 5

This pop band formed in Bradford. Norman, Silson and Utley had previously been in a band called The Elizabethans. In 1968, with Pete Spencer also on board, they became **Kindness** and later Smokey, finally changing to **Smokie** in 1975. Their big break came when they joined Rak Records and Mickie Most introduced them to the songwriting partnership of Chinn and Chapman. Norman's distinctive vocals were quite appealing and with the likes of *If You Think You Know How To Love Me, Don't Play Your Rock'n'Roll To Me, Wild Wild Angels, I'll Meet You At Midnight* and *Living Next Door To Alice* they registered some good quality pop singles. They were still going strong as 1976 ended though they failed to make much impact on the lucrative US market, but competed well against the emerging punk scene for a while. When the hits dried up in the eighties Norman and Spencer, who'd been doing a greater share of the songwriting in **Smokie**'s later days, turned to songwriting for other artists in the Rak stable. They were also responsible for the England World Cup Squad's *This Time We'll Get It Right* in 1982. (VJ)

Des Smyth and The Collegemen

Personnel incl: DES SMYTH

45s: The Pillow That Whispers/Lonely Streets   (Pye 7N 15867) 1965
         Wedding Bells/All For The Love Of A Girl (Pye 7N 15996) 1965

This was a seven man showband from Eaton in Ireland who specialised in country ballads. (VJ)

Snake Hips

45:     Runaway/Tennessee Waltz   (Emerald MD 1173) 1974

Snake Hips was a Dublin rock group. (VJ)

Snafu

Personnel: COLIN GIBSON   bs   A
               BOBBY HARRISON   vcls, perc   A
               MICK MOODY   hrmnca, vcls, gtr   A
               TERRY POPPLE   drms, bs   A
               PETE SOLLEY   keyb'ds, violin, vcls A

ALBUMS: 1(A)   SNAFU   (WWA WWA 003) 1974 SC
        2(A)   SITUATION NORMAL (WWA WWA 013) 1974 SC
        3( )   ALL FUNKED UP   (Capitol 11473) 1975

NB: (1) reissued on CD (Repertoire REP 4391-WP) 1994. (2) reissued on CD (Repertoire REP 4466-WY) 1994. (1) and (2) reissued on one CD (Angel Air) 1998, with the addition of *Dixie Queen* and the previously unreleased *Sad Sunday*. (3) reissued on CD (Angel Air SJPCD 032) 2000.

45s: Dixie Queen/Monday Morning   (WWA WWS 007) 1974
         Lock And Key/Bar Room Tan   (Capitol CL 15838) 1975
         Are You Sure/Bloodhound   (Capitol CL 15858) 1976

This heavy rock band was formed by former **Freedom** vocalist Bobby Harrison in 1973. Moody, Gibson and Popple were all from the Northeast of England, but Solley like Harrison was a Londoner. The Northeast trio were all experienced session musicians and had also played on Harrison's 1970 solo album, *Funkest*.

Snafu, whose name came from an old RAF expression - Situation Normal - All Fucked Up - played a pretty repetitive form of heavy rock. *All Funked Up* is a sort of Little Feat-inspired blues-rock effort. It includes a cover of *Hard To Handle*, but the stand-out track is *Keep On Running*, with lots of **Hendrix**-style wah-wah and some nice psychedelic organ.

Pete Solley was later in **Fox** and **Procol Harum**. He did session work in the seventies and also worked as a producer in the late seventies and eighties.

Country Nest has been compiled on *Classic Rock* (CD). (VJ/CG)

Snake Eye

Personnel:			
KEN GILES	bs		A
RON HALES	gtr		A
STEVE JACKSON	drms		A
DAVE RICHARDSON	gtr, vcls		A

This early seventies rock band came from Hull. They toured with **Argent**, **Flash** and **Wishbone Ash** amongst others. They produced an interesting sound based on the interaction between guitar and violin, but no recorded output has emerged yet. (BS)

The Snappers

45:	Upside Down, Inside Out/Memories	(CBS 2719) 1967 SC

Another obscure one-off late sixties venture. The group was more popular in Germany than here in the UK.

Compilation appearances include: *Please Be Mine* (from *Pop Connection* LP) on *Rare And Raw Beat From The Sixties, Vol. 1* (CD) and *Upside Down, Inside Out* on *Colour Me Pop, Vol 2* (CD). (VJ)

The Sneekers

45:	I Just Can't Go To Sleep/	
	Bald Headed Woman	(Columbia DB 7385) 1964 R3

A very rare and sought-after 45, partly because the 'A' side was a Ray Davies composition produced by Shel Talmy, but also because it was one of several 45s from this era that a very young session guitarist, **Jimmy Page**, played on. The 'B' side, *Bald Headed Woman* is a Shel Talmy composition also recorded by **The Kinks** and **The Who**.

Compilation appearances have included: *I Just Can't Go To Sleep* on *James Patrick Page: Session Man, Vol. 1* (LP & CD); *Bald Headed Woman* on *James Patrick Page: Session Man, Vol. 2* (LP & CD), *Maximum R'n'B* (CD) and *R&B Scene, Vol. 1* (LP); and *I Just Can't Go To Sleep* and *Bald Headed Woman* on *James Patrick Page, Session Man* (2-LP). (VJ)

The Snobs

Personnel:	JOHN BOULDEN
	EDDIE GILBERT
	COLIN SANDLAND
	PETER YERRAL

45:	Buckle Shoe Stomp/	
	Stand And Deliver	(Decca F 11867) 1964 SC

This band wore buckled shoes and powdered wigs to deliver *Buckle Shoe Stomp* which had a pounding beat and raucous vocals. The group achieved a wider audience in Scandinavia than here; they were very big in Finland!

They relocated to Sweden where they issued a further gritty 45, *Ding Dong/Heartbreak Hotel*.

Compilation coverage has included: - *Buckle Shoe Stomp* and *Stand And Deliver* on *The Garage Zone, Vol. 2* (LP); *Buckle Shoe Stomp* on *Sixties Lost And Found, Vol. 2* (LP), *Sixties Explosion, Vol. 1* (CD), *Weekend Starts Here* (LP) and *Pop Inside The '60s, Vol. 2* (CD); *Ding Dong* on *English Freakbeat, Vol. 4* (LP & CD); and *Heartbreak Hotel* on *Searching In The Wilderness* (LP & CD). (VJ)

The Societie

Personnel incl:	DAVE DOUGALL	keyb'ds	
	DAVE STRUTHERS	bs	A

45:	Bird Has Flown/Breaking Down	(Deram DM 162) 1967 R2

A short-lived Glasgow band, originally known as A Certain Society, whose sole 45 was produced by **Hollies'** Graham Nash and Allan Clarke. The 'A' side sounded pretty much like **The Hollies** too - lots of pleasant harmonies. Dougall and Struthers were later in **Andwella**.

Compilation appearances have included: *Breaking Down* on *Mod Scene, Vol. 2* (CD); *Bird Has Flown* on *The Psychedelic Scene* (CD); and *Bird Has Flown* and *Breaking Down* on *Deram Dayze* (LP). (VJ)

Mick Softley

ALBUMS:	1	SONGS FOR SWINGIN' SURVIVORS	
			(Columbia 33SX 1781) 1965 R3
	2	SUNRISE	(CBS 64098) 1970 R1
	3	STREET SINGER	(CBS 64395) 1971 SC
	4	ANY MOTHER DOESN'T GRUMBLE	
			(CBS 64841) 1972 SC

NB: (1) reissued on CD (Hux HUX 043) 2003. (2) and (3) reissued on a 2-CD set (Beat Goes On BGOCD 660) 2005.

45s:	I'm So Confused/She's My Girl	(Immediate IM 014) 1965 R1
	Am I The Red One/	
	That's Not My Kind Of Love	(CBS 202469) 1967 R2
	Can You Hear Me Now/Time Machine	(CBS 5130) 1970
	Lady Willow/From The Land Of The Crab	(CBS 8269) 1972

A British Bob Dylan soundalike, whose 1965 album for Columbia is now very rare and difficult to track down. Like Dylan, many of his songs were in the protest vein - *All I Want Is A Chance*, *After The Third World War Is Over (Or How I Learned To Live With Myself)* and *The War Drags On*. Another protest folkie, **Donovan** (who shared management with **Softley**), included *The War Drags On* on his *Universal Soldier* EP. **Softley**'s debut also included a cover version of Woody Guthrie's *Plains Of The Buffalo* and versions of Dylan's *The Bells Of Rhymney* and *Strange Fruit*. Its 2003 reissue on CD finally brought it to the attention of a wider audience. Even harder to find is his one-off psychedelic single for CBS.

His early seventies albums are mildly easier to find, and electric rather than acoustic folk. *Sunrise* has some good acoustic numbers like *Waterfall* and *Birdie Birdie*, but a new rockier side is represented on tracks like *You Go Your Way, I'll Go Mine*. The album's best known song was *If You're Not Part of The Solution, You Must Be Part Of The Problem* and he's assisted by **Richard Thompson** on some cuts.

Street Singer has a bluesy feel, and features jazz musicians Frank Riccotti and Tony Carr. Highlights include *Just Flew In On A Jet Plane* and *Gypsy*. After 1972's *Any Mother Doesn't Grumble* he drifted out of the music business and now lives in Northern Ireland writing poetry.

Compilation appearances have included: *Am I The Red One* on *Fading Yellow* (LP) and on the 4-CD box set *Acid Drops, Spacedust & Flying Saucers*; and *Waterfall* on the 1971 CBS compilation *Together!* (LP). (VJ/RMJ)

The Soft Machine

Personnel:	DAEVID ALLEN	gtr	A
(up to	KEVIN AYERS	bs, vcls	ABC
1976)	LARRY NOLAN	gtr	A
	MIKE RATLEDGE	keyb'ds	ABCDEFG H I JKLM
	ROBERT WYATT	drms, vcls	ABCDEFG
	ANDY SUMMERS	gtr	B
	HUGH HOPPER	bs	DEFG H I J
	LYN DOBSON	sax, flute	EF
	ELTON DEAN	sax	EFG H I
	NICK EVANS	trombone	E
	MARK CHARIG	cornet	E
	PHIL HOWARD	drms	H
	JOHN MARSHALL	drms	I JKLM N
	KARL JENKINS	piano, sax	JKLM N
	ROY BABBINGTON	bs	KLM N
	ALLAN HOLDSWORTH	gtr	L
	JOHN ETHERIDGE	gtr	M N
	ALAN WAKEMAN	sax	N

				HCP
ALBUMS:	1(C)	SOFT MACHINE	(Probe CPLP 4500) 1968	-
(up to	2(D)	SOFT MACHINE, VOL. 2	(Probe SPB 1002) 1969 SC	-
1976)	3(F)	THIRD (2-LP)	(CBS 66246) 1970 SC	18
	4(G)	FOURTH	(CBS 64280) 1971 SC	32
	5(I)	FIFTH	(CBS 64806) 1972 SC	-
	6(J)	SIX (2-LP)	(CBS 68214) 1973 SC	-
	7(K)	SEVEN	(CBS 65799) 1973 SC	-
	8(L)	BUNDLES	(Harvest SHSP 4044) 1975	-
	9(N)	SOFTS	(Harvest SHSP 4056) 1976	-

NB: (1) and (2) reissued by Big Beat (WIKA 57 and 58) in 1987 and reissued again on one CD (Big Beat CD WIKD 920). (3) reissued by Decal (LIKD 35) in 1988 and on CD (Beat Goes On BGO 180) 1993. (3) reissued on CD (Columbia 471407 2) 1996 and again on vinyl and CD. (6) and (7) reissued on one CD (Demon/Edsel MEDCD 740) 2004. (8) and (9) reissued by See For Miles (SEE 283 and 285) 1990 respectively, also available on CD. (8) and (9) reissued on CD with their 1977 *Alive And Well* album in a 3-CD pack (See For Miles MAGPIE 2) 1992.

Also of interest is *Live At The Proms 1970* (Reckless RECK 5) 1970. *Giorgio Gomelsky Sessions* (Metro 380) 2001 is a CD of early 1967 sessions by line-up 'B'. *The Peel Sessions* (Strange Fruit SFRCD 201) 1990 contained material from the 1969-71 era, much of which later appeared on their *Third* album. *BBC Radio One Live In Concert* (Windsong WINCD 031) 1993 gives a 1971 Radio One 'In Concert' recording a further airing. It includes an 11-minute version of *Teeth* and concentrates on material from early seventies **Soft Machine**. A second Radio One 'In Concert' recording from the same year is featured on *BBC Radio One Live In Concert* (Windsong WINCD 056) 1994. Fans of the band will want *Live At The Paradise 1969* (Voiceprint VP 193CD) 1995, which is taken from an Amsterdam gig when they performed most of their second album live. Another live CD, *Virtually* (Cuneiform RUNC 100) 1998, compiles versions of songs from their third and fourth albums (many of which are reduced in length), originally recorded for a German radio broadcast. Another curio is a Dutch Soft Machine in the *Boek En Plaat* series (EMI-Stateside), this contains the first side of their 2nd album on side one, with the 1st side of their 1st album on side two... the cover uses the group picture taken from the round picture on original cover of the first album. *Live 1970* (Blueprint BP

THE SOFT MACHINE - Giorgio Gomelsky Sessions (CD).

290CD) 1998 is marred by poor sound quality on some of the recordings. *Kings Of Canterbury* (2-CD) (Recall SMDCD 456) compiles live material from the 1969-1970 era. *Noisette* (Cuneiform RUNE 130) 2000 is a release of a live performance from Croydon in January 1970. *Soft Machine Turns On Vol 1* (Voiceprint VP 231CD) 2001 and *Vol 2* (Voiceprint VP 234CD) 2001 are compiled from live sets in Amsterdam (10 December 1967) and Iowa (11 August 1968), but very much for completists only. *Backwards* (Cuneiform Rune 170) 2002 is an US import containing unreleased material from 1968 to 1970. *Facelift* (Voiceprint VP 233 CD) 2002 contains a live April 1970 performance featuring *Facelift, Moon In June* and *Esther's Nose Job*. *Somewhere In Soho* is another 2-CD set. This one was recorded in the legendary Ronnie Scott's Club in 1970 featuring line-up (G) above. The release is fully remastered and features sleevenotes written by Brian Hopper. *BBC In Concert 1971* (CD) (Hux HUX 067) is a CD release of a live concert recorded for the BBC at London's Paris Theatre on 11 March 1971. It was accompanied by a 12-page colour booklet which includes brief notes from **Robert Wyatt**, **Hugh Hopper** and Elton Dean all recording their memoirs of these recordings and the booklet also includes extensive liner notes. *Live In Paris May 2nd 1972* (Cuneiform RUNECD 195) is a 2-CD set made by line-up (I) above in their final days. The recorded concert is released in its entirety and contains tracks from *Third* and *5* (often in alternate versions) as well as songs not recorded elsewhere. *British Tour 1975* (CD) (MLP MLPCD 10) presents material originally recorded for a live radio broadcast at Nottingham University in October 1975. It contains 15 tracks - some from their *Bundles* and *Softs* albums - plus three improvisational numbers never recorded in the studio before. Mastered from the original tapes the sleevenotes are written by John Marshall and John Etheridge, who are accompanied by Karl Jenkins, Roy Babbington and Mike Ratlege, who was the only original member on this recording. *Breda Reactor* (2-CD) (Voiceprint VP 345CD) is recorded by line-up (F) in the Netherlands in 1971 and provides new improvised versions of classic songs like *Facelift, Moon In June, Out-Bloody-Rageous, Mousetrap* and *Esther's Nose Job*. Brian Hopper provides the sleevenotes on this remastered album. *Soft Stage - BBC In Concert 1972* (Hux HUX 070) is a concert recording made for the BBC at The Paris Theatre by line-up (K) showcasing material that eventually appeared on their *Six* album, and comes with an eight-page booklet with liner notes and photographs. *Spaced* (CD) (Cuneiform RUNECD 90) is a recently discovered 1969 recording commissioned for a swinging London multi-media psychedelic event and it's suitably weird and spacey.

BBC Radio 1967-1971 (Hux HUX 037) 2003 is a 2-CD set comprising their sessions for 'Top Gear' during their heyday. *BBC Radio 1971-1974* (Hux HUX 047) 2003 is a second volume completing the set and with the exception of the first two tracks none of these recordings have ever been released before. *Man In A Deaf Corner - Anthology 1963 -1970* (Castle/Sanctuary CMDDD 897) 2004 is a 2-CD selection of curios. *The Story Of Soft Machine* (Dejavu Retro R2CD 43-01) 2005 is a budget-priced 2-CD set, which is not what it purports to be! *Out-Bloody-Rageous: An Anthology 1967-1973* (Sony/BMG 5200392) 2005 is a 2-CD compilation. *British Tour 1975* (Major League Promotions MLP 10) 2005 releases a concert from Nottingham University.

45s:	Love Makes Sweet Music/		
	Feelin' Reelin' Squealin'	(Polydor BM 56151) 1967	R3
	Soft Space (two versions)	(Harvest HAR 5155) 1978	

The Soft Machine's early work is some of the most imaginative underground music of the sixites, but their continuing failure to compromise meant they were always cult favourites rather than chart stars.

Their roots lay in Canterbury, Kent, where a proto-hippie community had formed. **Robert Wyatt** had previously played with **The Wilde Flowers**, Mike Ratledge was a local youngster who'd got bored with life at Oxford University, **Kevin Ayers** came from the Herne Bay area, **Daevid Allen** was an Australian hippie and Larry Nolan (who was only in the band for its first few concerts) was a Californian. They used a variety of names (including The Four Skins) before settling on **The Soft Machine**, from a William Burroughs novel.

The group, which played free-form improvised rock, was based in London during this period and gigged regularly at the UFO club. They also appeared at the 14-Hour Technicolour Dream. They were discovered by Kim Fowley, who produced their first single and co-wrote its eccentric 'A' side with **Kevin Ayers**. The 'B' side was even more bizarre and, though the 45 made the lower reaches of the Radio London Chart, it failed to break through and is now extremely rare. The group cut several other demos in April 1967 which, though not intended for public consumption, subsequently (and much to their embarrassment) got a French release on *Rock Generation, Vols 7* and *8*. The group, who played a sort of free-form improvised rock, was based in London during this period and gigged regularly at the UFO club. They also appeared at the 14-Hour Technicolour Dream.

After the failure of their single, they went to France and became involved in a multi-media production of Picasso's play 'Desire Attrappé Par la Queue'. When they attempted to return to Britain, **Allen** was refused entry and returned to Paris to establish **Gong**. He was replaced for a short while by

THE SOFT MACHINE - Soft Machine (CD).

Andy Summers, previously of **Dantalion's Chariot** and later, of course, the Police, and the band set off on a long tour of America as support to **Jimi Hendrix**. In New York they recorded an album for Probe, produced by Chas Chandler and Tom Wilson. One of the key underground recordings of the period, it stands as fine testimony to the band's unique sound. Ranging from the mellow *Joy Of A Toy* to the funky *Lullabye Letter* and infectious *We Did It Again*, it's consistently inventive and takes many unusual twists, with an unusually distorted organ sound to the fore on many tracks and barely any guitar.

The album was inexplicably released in the US only in 1968, though it was heavily imported to the UK. Exhausted by their heavy touring schedule, the band disintegrated at its end, when **Ayers** moved to Ibiza before returning a year later to launch his solo career. One track on his excellent debut, *Joy Of A Toy*, featured a reunion with the band. **The Soft Machine**'s debut, meanwhile, attracted sufficient acclaim for them to re-form with **Hugh Hopper** (who'd also played with **The Wilde Flowers**) replacing **Ayers** on bass. Their second album was recorded early in 1969 by line-up (D), and produced by **Hendrix**'s controversial manager Mike Jeffrey. Winner of France's Meilleur Disque award for 1969, it's a superb piece of work and certainly their most psychedelic.

Then, augmented by four hornmen (one of whom, saxophonist **Elton Dean**, remained with the band until 1972), they embarked on an extensive European tour. In October 1969 they expanded to become a seven-piece, recruiting Dean and Charig from **Bluesology**. *Third*, regarded by many as their finest, includes **Wyatt**'s epic *Moon In June*, undoubtedly one of their best compositions.

Thereafter their sound became increasingly jazz-influenced and less rock-based. Founder member **Wyatt**'s vocals and influence also steadily diminished and, after their fourth album, he left the band to form **Matching Mole**.

Elton Dean left after recording *Fifth*. He'd cut a solo album, *Elton Dean* in 1971, whilst still with the band. He continued his involvement with a part-time outfit, **Just Us**, with whom he'd also played whilst with **The Soft Machine**.

Side one of *Six* is live and features tracks from two 1972 concerts. Side two was recorded in the studio. It lacks the experimentation of their previous efforts and **Wyatt's** input, but there's still lots of improvisation and complex interplay between musicians.

Hopper left the band in May 1973, after the release of *Six*, and he too went on to cut a solo album, *1984*, in 1973. He later played in **Isotope** and Stomu Yamashta's East Wind.

Seven was the band's last album for CBS. The opening track *Nettlebed* is notable for some swashbuckling keyboard playing from Ratledge, which is evident throughout the whole album.

They signed to Harvest to record *Bundles* with line-up (L), but, by now they were a shadow of their former selves. In March 1975 Allan Holdsworth left

to join **Gong** and in January 1976 Mike Ratledge, the last remaining founding member left. John Etheridge was recruited (he'd previously played with **The Global Village Trucking Company** and **Darryl Way's Wolf**) and the modified line-up (N) recorded a second album for Harvest, *Softs*. Their other new recruit Alan Wakeman was the cousin of **Rick Wakeman**.

The *Live At The Proms* 1970 album comes with sleeve notes by the then drummer **Robert Wyatt** and captures the band in pretty good form.

They soldiered on with different line-ups until the nineties but their subsequent feats are beyond the time frame of this book and were inferior efforts using the **Soft Machine** name.

Backwards is a CD release of 70-minutes of previously unreleased freeform progressive jazz fusion. The first half of the CD comprises tracks from May 1970 including *Esther's Nose Job* and *Moon In June*. *Hibou Anemone And Bear* and a shorter version of *Facelift* date from late 1969 and the album closes with a 20-minute demo of *Moon In June* in two parts, the first from Autumn 1968 and the second from a reconstituted **Soft Machine** session in Spring 1969.

The 2002 2-CD set *Facelift* captures the band performing in April 1970, but is marred by poor sound quality as it was only taped on a small cassette recorder. A better bet is *BBC Radio 1967-1971*, which comprises their sets for 'Top Gear'. These capture the band at the peak of their creativity. *BBC In Concert 1971* CD was recorded at London's Paris Theatre on 11th March 1971. The concert is introduced by John Peel, who refers to it as being by **Soft Machine** and their heavy friends. The CD also includes tracks by **The Elton Dean Group** (who later became **Just Us**) augmented by Mike Ratledge on electric piano. There's a 30-minute medley by line-up (G) containing some very jazz-oriented music. There's also a previously unreleased recording of *Slightly All The Time/Noisette*, which they performed as an encore. Ronnie Scott himself guested on some tracks on this release, which is accompanied by a 12-page colour booklet in which **Wyatt**, **Hopper** and **Dean** reminisce about the recording. The booklet also contains band photos and liner notes.

Man In A Deaf Corner - Anthology 1963-1970 compiles freeform jazz recordings from back in 1963 and material from live concert performances in 1969 and 1970.

Avoid the 2005 2-CD release *The Story Of The Soft Machine*, which is far from comprehensive! The first disc is comprised of early demos of variable sound quality, which have figured on other retrospectives previously; the second comprises solo performances by **Robert Wyatt**, **Daevid Allen** and **Hugh Hopper**. Whilst these are of interest they don't capture the band's story properly.

Out-Bloody-Rageous: An Anthology 1967-1973 is a 2-CD compilation. Disc one includes their debut 45 *Love Makes Sweet Music* and some of their classic album tracks from the **Kevin Ayers** era like *Hope For Happiness* and *Why Are We Sleeping*? Their jazz-rock era is glorified by 20-minute journeys like *Moon In June* and the title track. The second disc is entirely instrumental and includes influential numbers like *Teeth* and *Pigling Bland*.

THE SOFT MACHINE - Volume Two (LP).

SOFT MACHINE - Live At The Proms 1970 (LP).

British Tour 1975 gives a CD release to a Nottingham University concert by line-up (M). It's really one for their serious fans.

The Soft Machine are lovingly remembered, though, as one of the finest exponents of British underground and jazz rock.

Compilation appearances have included: *Love Makes Sweet Music* and *Feelin' Reelin' Squeelin'* on *Rare Tracks* (LP); *Feelin' Reelin' Squeelin'* on *Jagged Time Lapse, Vol 1* (CD); *Hibou, Anemone And Bear* on the 3-CD box set *Ars Longa Vita Brevis: A Compendium Of Progressive Rock 1967-1974*; *Love Makes Sweet Music* on *Jagged Time Lapse, Vol 3* (CD); *Esther's Nose Job* on *Canterburied Sounds Vol. 2* (CD); and *Teeth* on CBS's 1971 compilation (LP) *Together!*. The band was also featured on *Vols 7* and *8* of *The Roots Of British Rock* (LPs). (VJ/RMJ)

Soft Pedalling

45:     It's So Nice/Rolling On Home   (Decca F 23034) 1970

A little known 45, put together by a studio group. (MWh)

Solid British Hat Band

Personnel incl: KEN WILSON   A

| ALBUMS: | 1 | MISTER MONDAY | (Longman) 1971 R3 |
| | 2 | GOODBYE RAINBOW | (Longman LG 56712) 1974 |

NB: (2) as **Ken Wilson and The Solid British Hat Band**.

These were folk-rock offerings released via Longman, the famous publishers. Their debut was a folk-rock offering. **Pentangle**'s Terry Cox guested on drums and some later members of **Everyone Involved** were featured. There is some good original material on the album like *Tomorrow Will Be Wonderful* and *Present Continuous Baby* with alternating female / male vocals, superb harmonies and a good electric folk-rock band sound.

Ken Wilson was the band leader and composed all their material. (VJ/GC/RMJ)

Solid Gold Cadillac

Personnel:	ROY BABBINGTON	bs	A
	ALAN JACKSON	drms, perc	AB
	GEORGE KHAN	woodwind, keyb'ds	AB
	PHIL MINTON	vcls, trumpet	AB
	DICK MORCOMBE	gtr	A
	CHRIS SPEDDING	gtr	A
	FIACHRA TENCH	keyb'ds	A
	MIKE WESTBROOK	piano	AB
	BRIAN GODDING	gtr	B
	MALCOLM GRIFFITHS	trombone	B
	BUTCH POTTER	gtr, bs, keyb'ds, banjo	B

| ALBUMS: | 1(A) | SOLID GOLD CADILLAC | (RCA SF 8311) 1972 SC |
| | 2(B) | BRAIN DAMAGE | (RCA SF 8365) 1973 SC |

NB: (1) and (2) reissued as a 2-CD set (Beat Goes On BGOCD 471) 2000.

Solid Gold Cadillac mixed a blend of styles ranging from jazz and funk through to traditional Greek folk music on these albums. Unfortunately the result was a mess and there is nothing to recommend on these two albums.

Mike Westbrook also made several solo albums, whilst **Chris Spedding** played in several bands including **Pete Brown's Battered Ornaments**, **Sounds Nice**, **The Jack Bruce Band**, **Nucleus** and **Sharks**, as well as doing session guitar work and launching a solo career in the seventies.

Roy Babbington was later in **Soft Machine**, George Khan (earlier in **Khan**) and Brian Godding (ex-**Blossom Toes**) later teamed up in Mirage (1977), producing just one album, *Now You See It...* (Compendium Records FIDARO 9).

Someone's Band

Personnel:	CECIL JAMES	vcls, perc	A
	MELVIN BUCKLEY	gtr	A
	JOHN COXEN	gtr	A
	TERRY POWNEY	bs	A
	WOODY MARTIN	drms, perc	A

ALBUM: 1(A)   SOMEONES BAND   (Deram SML 1068) 1970 R3

NB: (1) reissued on CD (Rock-In-Beat RB 217).

45:     Story/Give It To You   (Deram DM 313) 1970

Formed from the ashes of **C Jam Blues** (who'd made one unsuccessful single for Columbia in 1966), this group got together via word of mouth and an advert in 'Melody Maker'. It centred on singer Cecil James and lead guitarist Melvin Buckley. At the recommendation of bandleader Cyril Stapleton they made a demo for Decca, who then sanctioned the album, which is now very rare. Given that it was recorded in the course of a single night, it's a surprisingly polished and varied collection of progressive blues and soul, ranging from the soulful *How It Began* to the funky *Country Ride*, poignant *Blues For Brother E* and heavy *Hands Of Time*. The influence of jazz, funk and African music is also in evidence. Though the group favoured an alternative track (*Fiddlesticks*), *Story* was culled from the album for 45 release and bombed. They recorded a session for BBC's 'Sounds Of The Seventies', but did little else to promote the album and split when their drummer headed for Sweden.

Two of their songs, *How It Began* and *Country Ride*, were included on *Broken Dreams, Vol. 6* (LP). (VJ/HL/RMJ)

Songbird

45:     Sweet Elaine/Spread The Word   (MAM R 12) 1971

Nothing else is known about this 45. (MWh)

The Song Peddlers

45:     Rose Marie/I'm Not Afraid   (Philips BF 1352) 1964

A folk group from Manchester who after this one 45 dropped the "Song" from their name and went on to greater success as **The Peddlers**. (VJ)

Sons of Fred

Personnel:
ALAN BOHLING	bs	A
TIM BOYLE	drms	A
MICK HUTCHINSON	gtr, organ, vcls	A
RAY REDWAY	gtr	A

45s:	Sweet Love/I'll Be There	(Columbia DB 7605) 1965 R3
	I, I, I (Want Your Lovin')/	
	She Only Wants A Friend	(Parlophone R 5391) 1965 R2
α	Baby What Do You Want Me To Do/	
	You Told Me	(Parlophone R 5415) 1966 R3

NB: α has been reissued in a limited edition pressing of 500 reproduced from the original French jukebox release.

This Great Yarmouth R&B band's singles passed largely unnoticed at the time but are now rare and sought-after. They also recorded a 45 as **Odyssey**. *Sweet Love*, an R&B effort, features some raucous garage-style vocals and farfisa organ backing. Their second 45, veered towards the poppy side of R&B particularly the flip which featured **Hollies**-style vocal harmonies. Their final 45, *Baby What Do You Want Me To Do*, leant more towards pop art.

The band later recorded as **Tandem**. It featured Mick Hutchinson on guitar, who went on to play in **The Sam Gopal Dream** and **Clark-Hutchinson**.

Compilation appearances have included: *I'll Be There* on *Maximum R'n'B* (CD) and *Trans-World Punk Rave-Up!, Vol. 1* (LP); *You Told Me* on *Magic Spectacles* (CD) and *Rare 60's Beat Treasures, Vol. 5* (CD); *Sweet Love* on *Rubble, Vol. 2 - Pop Sike Pipe Dreams* (LP) and *Rubble, Vol. 2* (CD); *Baby What You Want Me To Do?* on *R&B Scene, Vol. 1* (LP); *Baby What You Want Me To Do?* and *I'll Be There* on *R&B At Abbey Road* (CD); *I, I, I (Want Your Lovin')* and *She Only Wants A Friend* on *English Freakbeat, Vol. 3* (LP & CD); and *Baby What You Want Me To Do, Sweet Love* and *I'll Be There* on *English Freakbeat, Vol. 4* (CD). (VJ/JM)

Sons of Man

EP:	1	SONS OF MAN	(Oak RGJ 612) 1967 R4

An extremely rare and sought-after EP, which changes hands for in excess of £400. The identity of this band remains a mystery. Its four cuts consist of a couple of soulful numbers: *Invitation* (the **Band Of Angels/Mike D'Abo** track) and *I'm The One Who Loves You* (a Jackie Wilson number) and two others (*My Life With You* and **Skip Bifferty**'s *On Love* under the guise of *Our Love*) which merged beat music with psychedelia.

Compilation appearances have included: *Our Love* on *Purple Heart Surgery Vol. 2* (LP), *The Story Of Oak Records* (CD) and *Hens Teeth Vol. 2* (CD); and *My Life With You* on *Incredible Sound Show Stories, Vol. 10* (LP).

This group later became **Aubery Small** who were managed by Radio 1 DJ 'Whispering' Bob Harris and they went on to do several sessions for the BBC. (VJ)

The Sorrows

Personnel:
BRUCE FINDLAY	drms	AB
DON MAUGHN (FARDON)	vcls	A
PHILIP PACKHAM	bs	AB
WEZ PRICE	gtr	AB
PHILLIP WHITCHER	lead gtr	A
CHRIS FRYERS	organ, gtr	B

ALBUMS:	1(A) TAKE A HEART (mono/stereo)	
		(Pye N(S)PL 38023) 1965 R3/R4
	2(B) OLD SONGS, NEW SONGS	(Miura MIU 10011) 196?

NB: (1) reissued on vinyl (Piccadilly PDL 20834). (1) reissued as *The Sorrows* (Sequel NEXCD 165) in 1991 with two additional tracks. (1) also reissued on Raven (RVLP 1004) 1982. (1) reissued (Sequel NEECD 480) 2000. (2) only released in Italy. *Take A Heart* (Repertoire RR 4093-WZ) 1991 also includes their album, non-album 45s and a German-only 45 and its Italian equivalent. (1) also reissued on vinyl with various 7" bonus tracks. (2) has been reissued on CD (Rock-In-Beat RB 217) with bonus tracks. There's also another compilation, *Pink, Purple, Yellow and Red* (Bam-Caruso KIRI 089) 1987.

45s:	I Don't Wanna Be Free/	
	Come With Me	(Piccadilly 7N 35219) 1965 R1 -
	Baby/Teenage Letter	(Piccadilly 7N 35230) 1965 R1 -
	Take A Heart/	
	We Should Get Along Fine	(Piccadilly 7N 35260) 1965 SC 21
	You've Got What I Want/No, No,	
	No, No (Some export PS)	(Piccadilly 7N 35277) 1966 R1/SC -
	Let The Live Live/Don't Sing	
	No Sad Songs For Me	(Piccadilly 7N 35309) 1966 R1 -
	Let Me In/	
	How Love Used To Be	(Piccadilly 7N 35336) 1966 R1 -
	Pink, Purple, Yellow and Red/	
	My Gal	(Piccadilly 7N 35385) 1967 R2 -

45s:	Mi Si Spezza Il Cuore/Vivi	(Pye 45NP 5086) 196?
(Italian)	Verde Rosso Giallo Blu/No No No No	(Pye 45 NP 5122) 196?
	Per Una Donna... No!/Amore Limone	(Miura MIU 116) 196?
	Per Una Donna... No!/Amore Limone	(Miura MIU 117) 196?

NB: (10) as Chris & The Sorrows.

This mid-sixties R&B group hailed from Coventry and were originally known as **The Boys Blue**. Packham had previously been with **The Vampires**. Vocalist Don Maughn (who later changed his name to **Fardon** in 1967) sported a powerful voice, which was their main asset, and they made the Charts with *Take A Heart*, a pulsating R&B song, but then became rather tarred as 'one hit wonders'. Their UK album is now extremely collectable. As well as being reissued on CD, there has been a vinyl reissue which includes bonus tracks from various 45s including: - *You've Got What I Want*, *Let The Live Live*, *Pink, Purple, Yellow and Red* and *My Gal*.

After leaving Britain, because they were not able to repeat the success of *Take A Heart*, **The Sorrows** surfaced in Italy where they released an album and some singles to moderate success. Most of the 45s are remakes of UK tracks with Italian lyrics. The album is highly interesting, though. It features decent covers of **Traffic**, **Family** and **Small Faces** material as well as some excellent compositions by Chris Fryers like *Same Old Road* and *Mary J.*, which are much more psychedelic than any of the cuts on *Take A Heart*. This is very rare, but recommended. It has recently been reissued on CD with bonus tracks *6ft 7 ½* and *Hey Hey* plus tracks recorded with Italian lyrics.

Their 1967 single, *Pink, Purple, Yellow and Red* was an atmospheric single about depression. In the late sixties a revised line-up relocated to Italy and their Italian-only album *Old Songs New Songs*, which included **Family** and **Traffic** material, may interest some readers.

The Bam-Caruso compilation is recommended. Although on this evidence *Take A Heart* was clearly their magnum opus, they boasted some really raucous covers of Jerry Lee Lewis's *Teenage Letter*, Lovin' Spoonful's *My Gal* and The Strangeloves' *Cara-Lin*. *Don't Sing No Sad Songs For Me* with its wailing harmonica is a sixties punk ballad and by the time of their final

THE SORROWS - Pink, Purple, Yellow And Red (LP).

UK 45, *Pink, Purple, Yellow and Red* (the title track of the reissue) they'd veered towards freakbeat. The compilation comes with a detailed band history by sixties guru Brian Hogg and is well worth tracking down.

Compilation appearances have included: *Take A Heart* on *The Youngblood Story Vol. 1*, *Radio Two: Sounds Of The Sixties* (CD), *Maximum '65* (CD), *Pop Inside The Sixties, Vol. 3* (CD), *Watch Your Step* (LP & CD), *It Happened Then* (EP), *Piccadilly Story* (CD) and on the 2-CD set *We Love The Pirates: Charting The Big 'L' Fab 40*; *Let The Live Live* and *Phoenix* on *Made In England, Vol. 1* (CD); *Pink Purple Yellow and Red* on *Quick Before They Catch Us* (LP & CD), *It's Only A Passing Phase* (LP) and *Hot Smoke & Sassafras - Psychedelic Pstones, Vol 1* (CD); *Baby* on *The R&B Era, Vol. 1* (LP & CD); *Don't Sing No Sad Songs For Me* on *Ripples, Vol. 6* (CD); *Take A Heart, We Should Get Along Fine, Baby, Teenage Letter, Let Me In, How Love Used To Be, I Don't Wanna Be Free* and *No No No No* on *Sixties Years, Vol. 3 - French 60's EP Collection* (CD); *You've Got What I Want* on *The Demention Of Sound* (LP), *Sound Of The Sixties* (2-LP) and *Sixties Archive Vol. 1* (CD); *You've Got What I Want, No No No No, Take A Heart* and *Let Me In* on *Untamed And Innocent* (CD); *Let Me In* and *You've Got What I Want* on *Freakbeat Freakout* (CD); *Let The Live Live, You've Got What I Want* and *Take A Heart* on *Hits From The Ivy League, The Rockin' Berries, And The Sorrows* (LP); and *The Makers, Same Old Road* and *Old Songs, New Songs* on *Incredible Sound Show Stories, Vol. 7* (LP). More recently, *Take A Heart* got fresh exposure on the CD-set *Rock Of Ages, Four Decades Of Heavy Rock 1962-2002* and *Everything (That's Mine)* has resurfaced on the 4-CD *Nuggets II* box set.

Their debut album was reissued on CD in 1991 with two previously unissued covers of US soul songs *Gonna Find A Cave* and *Baby All The Time* added. Various other reissues are detailed in the discography.

Don Fardon later grabbed the limelight briefly as a solo artist with *Indian Reservation*. (VJ/MK)

The Soul Agents

Personnel:

JOHNNY (aka TONY) GOOD		gtr	A
JOHNNY KEEPING		vcls	A
ROGER POPE		drms	AB
JIM SACHS		bs	A
DON SHINN		organ	ABC
ROD STEWART		vcls	
IAN DUCK		gtr	BC
DAVE GLOVER	bs		BC
PETE HUNT		vcls, drms	BC

45s:		
I Just Wanna Make Love To You/		
Mean Woman Blues	(Pye 7N 15660) 1964 R1	
Seventh Son/Let's Make It Pretty Baby	(Pye 7N 15707) 1964 R2	
Don't Break It Up/Gospel Train	(Pye 7N 15768) 1965 R2	

This Southampton-based R&B group were a very popular club act. They had the gimmick of playing shows barefoot. When Keeping left **Rod Stewart** (ex-Hoochie Coochie Men became their lead singer throughout the winter of 1964-65 (as well as gigging with The Original All Stars). He then left to join **Steampacket**. Good and Sachs also left and a revised line-up (including Duck, Glover and Hunt) was put together by **Don Shinn**, their leader.

They should not be confused with a Jamaican band who recorded on Coxsone around the same time.

Their first 45, *I Just Wanna Make Love To You* was a R&B standard, also covered by **The Rolling Stones**. It's flip, a Bo Diddley-style arrangement of Roy Orbison's *Mean Woman Blues*, is unusual and worth hearing. For their second 45, the covered Mose Allison's *Seventh Son* backed by a dynamic interpretation of Lee Hooker's *Let's Make It Pretty Baby*. Their final effort, (recorded with line-up B) a Howard-Blaikley song *Don't Break It Up* was given a punk-pop treatment, backed by the excellent instrumental *Gospel Train*. The first two 45s were also released in the States, though both are very rare now.

When Pope left to join **The Loot**, Hunt took over on drums. After they split, **Shinn** went on to session work. He was later with **Renaissance, Da Da** and **Iguana**. Duck and Glover joined **Hookfoot**. Hunt became a session drummer, although he was later with **Iguana** (then **The Jess Roden Band**).

RUBBLE VOL. 15 (Comp LP) featuring The Sound Barrier.

Compilation appearances have included: *Let's Make It Pretty Baby* on *Pop Inside The Sixties, Vol. 3* (CD), *The R&B Era, Vol. 1* (LP & CD), *That Driving Beat* (CD) and *Beat Merchants* (2-LP); *Don't Break It Up* and *The Seventh Son* on *The R&B Era, Vol. 2 - Preachin' The Blues* (LP); *Don't Break It Up, The Seventh Son* and *I Just Wanna Make Love To You* on *The R&B Era, Vol. 2* (CD); *I Just Wanna Make Love To You* on *The Sixties File* (2-LP); *The Seventh Son* on *The Seventh Son* (LP); *The Seventh Son* and *Gospel Train* on *Doin' The Mod, Vol. 1* (CD); *Don't Break It Up* on *Doin' The Mod, Vol. 2* (CD); *Gospel Train* and *Let's Make It Pretty Baby* on *English Freakbeat, Vol. 2* (LP); *You've Got What I Want* on the 4-CD box set *Acid Drops, Spacedust & Flying*; and *Gospel Train* on *English Freakbeat, Vol. 2* (CD). (VJ/JM)

The Soul Brothers

45s:			*HCP*
	Good Lovin' Never Hurt/I Love Him	(Mercury MF 916) 1965	-
	I Keep Ringing My Baby/		
	I Can't Take It	(Decca F 12116) 1965	SC 42
	I Can't Believe It/		
	You Don't Want To Know	(Parlophone R 5321) 1965	SC -

There was also a Jamaican ska group of this name. This band scored a minor hit with *I Keep Ringing My Baby* in 1965. The Mercury 45 may have been by a US band. (VJ)

The Soulmates

Personnel:		
	BRIAN HENDERSON	A
	LISA STRIKE	A

45s:		
	Too Late To Say You're Sorry/	
	Your Love	(Parlophone R 5334) 1965
	Bring Your Love Back Home/	
	When Love Is Gone	(Parlophone R 5407) 1966
	Mood Melancholy/Sayin' Something	(Parlophone R 5506) 1966
	Is That You?/Time's Run Out	(Parlophone R 5601) 1967
Reissue:	Bring Your Love Back Home/	
	When Love Is Gone	(EMI EMI 2970) 1979

There was a Jamaican band of this name too, but this was a different outfit, a soulish duo, which was backed by The Jet Set. **Lisa Strike** also made solo recordings.

You can also check out *Bring Your Love Back Home* on *Sixties Lost And Found, Vol. 1* (LP). (VJ)

The Sound Barrier

Personnel: PHILIP GREENAWAY

KEITH HALL
JIM KNELL
PHILIP 'FRED' REEVES   vcls

| 45: | She Always Comes Back To Me/ | |
| | Groovin' Slow | (Beacon BEA 109) 1968 R1 |

This 45 is thought to have been the work of studio musicians. *Groovin'
Slow* is an interesting slice of psychedelic pop. It has a number of tempo
changes before culminating in a hazy, disorientated ending. The 'A' side is
good mod-pop.

Groovin' Slow can also be heard on *Beacon Brings It To You* (LP) (a 1969
sampler), *Rubble, Vol. 15 - 5,000 Seconds Over Toyland* (LP), *Rubble, Vol.
9* (CD) and *We Can Fly, Vol 1* (CD). (VJ)

Sound Network

| 45: | Watching/How About Now | (Mercury MF 944) 1965 SC |

Nothing else is known about this 45. (VJ)

Sound of Reflection

| 45: | Brave New World/ | |
| | Lord I Believe (PS) | (Reflection RS 6001) 1968 |

This is an obscure one-off religious 45. (VJ)

Sounds and Songs Of London

| ALBUM: | 1 | SOUNDS AND SONGS OF LONDON (Columbia) 1968 R1 |

This is a very obscure Swingin' London cash-in album that traces the
growth of sixties London via sound extracts from Petticoat Lane, a Carnaby
Street boutique, Big Ben and discotheques all interspersed with mostly
London-based pop songs, but including **The Koobas'** otherwise unavailable
City Girl. (VJ)

Sounds Around

45s:	What Does She Do?/	
	Sad Subject	(Piccadilly 7N 35345) 1966 SC
	Red White And You/One Of Two	(Piccadilly 7N 35396) 1967 SC

This was actually **John Pantry's Peter and The Wolves** under a
pseudonym who deserved better with *Red White And You*, which was a
good pop song with considerable commercial appeal. Despite considerable
airplay on pirate ship Radio Caroline the disc failed to chart. *Red White
And You* was also included on a US-only compilation *Petal Pushers* (LP) of
mostly UK psychedelia released in 1967 and, more recently on *Colour Me
Pop, Vol 2* (CD). (VJ)

Sounds Incorporated (Sounds Inc)

Personnel:	BARRIE CAMERON	keyb'ds	AB
	ALAN HOLMES	flute, sax	ABC
	WES HUNTER	bs	ABC
	TONY NEWMAN	drms	A
	JOHN St. JOHN		
	(aka JOHNGILLIARD)	gtr	ABC
	GRIFF WEST	tenor sax	ABC
	TERRY FOGG	drms	BC
	TREVOR WHITE	keyb'ds, vcls	C

ALBUMS:	1(A)	SOUNDS INCORPORATED (mono/stereo)	
		(Columbia 33SX 1659/SCX 3531) 1964 SC/R1
	2 (A)	RINKY DINK	(Regal SREG 1071) 1965 SC
	3 (A)	SOUNDS INCORPORATED	
		(Studio Two TWO 144) 1966 SC
	4 (A)	SOUNDS INCORPORATED (See For Miles CM 116) 1983

NB: (2) Export only. (1) and (3) reissued on one CD (Beat Goes On BGOCD 661)
2005, digitally remastered in a great slipcase with in-depth sleevenotes.

| EP: | 1 (A) | TOP GEAR | (Columbia SEG 8360) 1964 SC |

HCP

45s:	Mogambo/Emily	(Parlophone R 4815) 1961 SC -
	Sounds Like Locomotion/Taboo	(Decca F 11540) 1962 -
	Stop/Go	(Decca F 11590) 1963 -
	Order Of The Keys/Keep Moving	(Decca DB 11723) 1963 SC -
	The Spartans/Detroit	(Columbia DB 7239) 1964 30
	Spanish Harlem/Rinky Dink	(Columbia DB 7321) 1964 35
	William Tell/Bullets	(Columbia DB 7404) 1964 -
	Time For You/	
	Hall Of The Mountain King	(Columbia DB 7545) 1965 -
	My Little Red Book/Justice Neddi	(Columbia DB 7676) 1965 -
	On The Brink/I'm Comin' Thru	(Columbia DB 7737) 1965 SC -
	How Do You Feel/Dead As You Go	(Polydor 56209) 1967 -
α	Warmth Of The Sun/Apollo	(Decca 22883) 1969 -

NB: α Export only.

A very marginal case for inclusion here, this outfit backed touring American
rock singers (like Gene Vincent), and **Cilla Black**, but were also an
instrumental band with quite a prolific recording outfit in their own right.
Barrie Cameron was born in Erith, Kent on 25 October 1939. Alan Holmes
was born in Rotherhithe, London on 25 April 1940. Wes Hunter entered life
at Crayford on 17 December 1941. Drummer Tony Newman was born in
Southampton on 17 March 1943. John St John was born as John Gillard in
Dartford, Kent on 1 April 1940 and Griff West came to life in Barnhurst,
Bexley on 19 December 1940. They released a number of instrumental
singles, enjoying minor hits with *The Spartans* and *Spanish Harlem*.

In 1964 Brian Epstein signed them and the horn section played on *Good
Morning Sunshine* off **The Beatles'** *Sergeant Pepper* album. They also
opened **The Beatles'** famous concert at New York's Shea Stadium.

In 1967 the band shortened its name to **Sounds Inc**. Eventually the band
members drifted back into session work as instrumental bands were no
longer in vogue in the late sixties. **Tony Newman** later played with **The
Jeff Beck Group**, **David Bowie** and **Boxer**. **Newman** also recorded as a
solo artist, appeared on the *Tommy* soundtrack and was in **May Blitz**.
Terry Fogg joined in his place. Then Cameron left and Essex-born Trevor
White replaced him. This later line-up recorded two 45s for an Australian
label, *Maxwell's Silver Hammer/No I Never* (Festival) and *Holly-
Go-Lightly/Love Is A Happy Thing* (Festival). Most of the band emigrated to
Australia and took up a residency at the Currimbin Hotel on Queensland's
Gold Coast circa 1971-72. Some members returned to the UK. Fogg joined
the UK band **Taggett**. Trevor White, meanwhile, took up the role of 'Jesus'
in the Australian production of 'Jesus Christ Superstar'.

Compilation appearances have included: *William Tell Overture* and *Leichte
Kavallerie* on *Twist Im Star-Club Hamburg* (LP); and *William Tell Overture*
on *Beat Im Star Club* (2-LP). (VJ/LBy/JM)

Sounds Nice

Personnel:	PAUL BUCKMASTER	strings	AB
	TIM MYCROFT	keyb'ds	AB
	RICHIE DHARMA	drms	B
	TIM TAYLOR	bs	B
	LARRY WALLIS	gtr	B

| ALBUM: | 1(A) | SOUNDS NICE - LOVE AT FIRST SIGHT | |
| | | (Parlophone PMC/PCS 7089) 1969 R1 |

HCP

45s:	Love At First Sight/Love You Too	(Parlophone R 5797) 1969 18
α	Sleepless Night/	
	Continental Exchange	(Parlophone R 5821) 1969 -

NB: α shown as **Sounds Nice** featuring **Tim Mycroft**.

This session group briefly came to prominence when their less controversial
version of *Love At First Sight (Je T'aime... Moi Non Plus)* than the **Jane
Birkin and Serge Gainsbourg** one made it into the Top 20. As a
consequence it was featured on See For Miles' 20 *One Hit Wonders* (LP)
compilation. Tim Mycroft had previously been in **Gun** and Paul Buckmaster
was with **The Third Ear Band**. On the album the duo were assisted by

Herbie Flowers (bs), **Chris Spedding** (gtr), Brian Odgers (bs) and **Clem Cattini** (drms).

It proved to be a short-lived project, though. **Clem Cattini**, **Chris Spedding** and Herbie Flowers went on to solo projects and did session work and Paul Buckmaster was later in **Third Ear Band**. Tim Mycroft had previously been with **Gun**. Indeed, **Cattini** had once played with Johnny Kidd and The Tornados.

In late 1969 a tour band was put together (line-up B). Larry Wallis was in The Entire Sioux Nation at the time and Richie Dharma was working with **Mike Chapman**. After this, Wallis and Taylor joined **Shagrat**; Dharma headed for **Mick Abraham's** Wommet; Buckmaster rejoined **The Third Ear Band** and recorded the rare **Chitinous Ensemble** album, and Mycroft went on to back **Parrish and Gurvitz**. (VJ/JM)

Sounds Orchestral

Personnel incl:	KENNY CLARE	drms	A
	JOHN PEARSON	piano	A
	TONY REEVES	bs	A

HCP

ALBUMS: (up to 1976)	1	THUNDERBALL - SOUNDS ORCHESTRAL MEET JAMES BOND (some in gatefold sleeves) (Pye NPL 38016) 1965 SC/R1 -
	2	CAST YOUR FATE TO THE WIND (Piccadilly NPL 38041) 1970 17
	3	GOLDEN HOUR OF SOUNDS ORCHESTRAL (?) 1973 -

NB: (1) reissued on CD (Sequel NEBCD 908) 1996. (2) reissued on CD (Sequel NEMCD 617) 1991. There's also a 'best of' *The Best Of Sounds Orchestral* (Pulse PLSCD 225) 1997.

HCP

45s:	Cast Your Fate To The Wind/ To Wendy With Love	(Piccadilly 7N 35206) 1964 5
	Have Faith in Your Love/ Like The Lonely	(Piccadilly 7N 35226) 1965 -
	Moonglow/Scarlatti Portion No 9	(Piccadilly 7N 35248) 1965 43
	Boy & A Girl/Go Home Girl	(Piccadilly 7N 35268) 1965 -
	Thunderball/ Mr Kiss Kiss Bang Bang	(Piccadilly 7N 35284) 1966 -
	Hopping Dance/Summer Dance	(Piccadilly 7N 35305) 1966 -
	For Nashville With Love/Bugsy	(Piccadilly 7N 35313) 1966 -
	Image/Letter Edged In Black	(Piccadilly 7N 35325) 1966 -
	Pretty Flamingo/ Sounds Like Jacques	(Piccadilly 7N 35334) 1966 -
	Lara's Theme/When love Has Gone	(Piccadilly 7N 35357) 1966 -
	Our Love Story/El Malaga	(Piccadilly 7N 35410) 1967 -
	When Love Has Gone/ Fifth Avenue Walk Down	(Piccadilly 7N 17507) 1968 -
	Soul Coaxing/Love Story	(Piccadilly 7N 17687) 1969 -
	Porcelain/Gloria Gloria	(Piccadilly 7N 45081) 1970 -
Reissues:	Cast Your Fate To The Wind/ Romance Of The North Sea	(Pye 7N 17715) 1969 -
	Cast Your Fate To The Wind/Air For The G Strings/ Sleepy Shores/Pink Panther	(Pye PMM 105) 197?

Sounds Orchestral was a studio ensemble, which for a time was Pye's answer to EMI's **Sounds Incorporated**.

The group was the creation of Pye Records producer John Schroeder, who had earlier played a key role at Columbia in the rise of **Helen Shapiro**. Schroeder sensed that there was an audience looking for an alternative sound to the beat bands which had been dominating the charts for the previous couple of years. The group's leader was Londoner John Pearson, a veteran pianist born in 1925. Other key members in the ensemble of session musicians were former Johnny Dankworth drummer Kenny Clare and 21-year-old bassist Tony Reeves, who was later with **Curved Air**, **Greenslade** and **Colosseum**, among others.

The debut release, a cover of the Vince Guaraldi Trio's 1960 recording *Cast Your Fate To The Wind*, was timed to perfection because the melodic number with a jazzy feel sounded quite unlike anything in the last few years. The punters liked it and the song climbed to No 3 in the charts, also paving the way for subsequent instrumental singles by the likes of Marcello

Minerebi and Horst Jankowski. Surprisingly, it also made the US Top Ten. **Sounds Orchestral** went on to record a couple of albums and several further singles for Piccadilly for the remainder of the decade, although they failed to make the charts again.

They continued to record intermittently well beyond the time span of this book throughout the seventies and well into the eighties. (VJ)

Sounds Progressive

ALBUM: 1 KID JENSEN INTRODUCES SOUNDS PROGRESSIVE
(Eyemark EMCL 1009) 1970 R2

This record consists of cover versions of underground hits like *Race With The Devil* and *Paranoid*, recorded at the wrong speed. It was introduced by David 'Kid' Jensen and is very rare. (VJ)

Sound Sixty-Six

45:    Flight 4864/The Bouncer   (Decca F 12323) 1966

This instrumental group was in the same mould as **Sounds Orchestral**. (VJ)

Sounds Sensational

45:    Love In The Open Air/Night Cry   (HMV POP 1584) 1967 SC

A one-off 45. The 'A' side was written by **Paul McCartney**. (VJ)

Southern Comfort

Personnel:	CARL BARNWELL	gtr, vcls	A
	RAY DUFFY	drms	A
	MARK GRIFFITHS	gtr	A
	GORDON HUNTLEY	pedal steel gtr	A
	ANDY LEIGH	bs, vcls	A

ALBUMS:	1(A)	FROG CITY	(Harvest SHSP 4012) 1971 SC
	2(A)	SOUTHERN COMFORT	(Harvest SHSP 799) 1972 SC
	3( )	STIR DON'T SHAKE	(Harvest SHSP 4021) 1972 SC
	4(-)	DISTILLED (Compilation)	(Harvest SHSM 2009) 1976

NB: Also of interest is *Matthews Southern Comfort Meets Southern Comfort* (See For Miles SEE 85) 1987.

45s:	Willie Hurricane/Berkshire Berk	(Harvest HAR 5035) 1971
	I Sure Like Your Smile/ Return To Frog City	(Harvest HAR 5039) 1971
	Morning Has Broken/Cosmic Jig	(Harvest HAR 5047) 1971
	Wedding Song/Stir Don't Shake	(Harvest HAR 5054) 1972
	I Sure Like Your Smile/April Lady	(Harvest HAR 5115) 1976

This was basically a later version of **Matthews Southern Comfort** after **Ian Matthews** had left to sign to Vertigo as a solo artist.

Southern Comfort's three albums and the 45s from them were all quite good but eventually the band split through lack of public interest.

Carl Barnwell went on to form his own group, Ray Duffy played with **Gallagher and Lyle** and the rest went into session work.

The *Meets Southern Comfort* compilation which features **Matthews Southern Comfort** on side one and **Southern Comfort** on side two sorely demonstrated how anonymous **Southern Comfort** sounded deprived of **Ian Matthews'** quavering vocal style.

You can also hear *River Woman*, which captures their melodic guitar work at its best, on the *Harvest Bag* (LP) compilation. *I Sure Like Your Smile* also figures on *Harvest Heritage - 20 Greats* (LP). (VJ)

Southern Library Of Recorded Music

ALBUM: 1   SOUTHERN LIBRARY OF RECORDED MUSIC
(Southern) 196?

A late sixties music library issue with four superb mind-expanding sitar tracks - *Ganges Sunrise*, *Temple Courtyard*, *Rani's Wedding* and *Indian Festival*. (VJ)

Southern Sound

Personnel incl: ROBBIE BLUNT   gtr   A

45:   α   Just The Same As You/
I Don't Wanna Go   (Columbia DB 7982) 1966 R4

NB: α has been repressed in a limited edition of 500 (Columbia DB 7982) with a large centre hole.

Both sides of this very rare and sought-after 45 are pretty powerful. *I Don't Wanna Go*, in particular, features some fine guitar/drums interplay and is recommended. The 45 is a blend of freakbeat and pop art really.

Compilation appearances have included: *I Don't Wanna Go* on *Maximum Freakbeat* (CD) and *The Best Of Rubble Collection, Vol. 5* (CD); *Just The Sames As You* on *The Best Of Rubble Collection, Vol. 6* (CD); and *Just The Same As You* and *I Don't Wanna Go* on *Rubble, Vol. 13 - Freak Beat Fantoms* (LP), *Rubble, Vol. 7* (CD), *Electric Sugarcube Flashbacks, Vol. 1* (LP) and *Electric Sugarcube Flashbacks, Vol. 3* (LP). (VJ)

The Souvenirs

45:     How Many Teardrops/
Please Be Faithfull To Me   (Decca F 11731) 1963

This beat single is notable for falsetto vocals. (VJ)

So What

45:     Flowers/Tell Me Now   (CBS 5005) 1970

This was another obscure one-off project. (MWh)

Sparrow

Personnel:	JONATHAN BERGMAN	vcls, perc	A
	HELEN CHAPPEL	backing vcls	A
	MICKEY KEEN	gtr	A
	PETE KELLY	keyb'ds	A
	DIANE LANGTON	vcls	A
	KEN LEWIS	backing vcls	A
	ELAINE PAGE	vcls	A
	BILL SHEPHERD	string arr.	A
	LARRY STEELE	bs	A
	DEREK WADSWORTH	brass arr.	A
	LIZ WHITE	backing vcls	A
	PETE WOOLF	perc	A

ALBUM: 1(A)   HATCHING OUT   (Spark SPA-05) 1972 R2

A very rare album which has been reissued with additional cuts as *Hatching Out Plus*.. (See For Miles SEECD 434) 1995. Some of the members had previously appeared in 'Hair' and the album is a strange mixture of rock and MOR harmony pop. Not yet of much interest to collectors.

Pete Kelly had previously been in **Jonathan Swift**'s backing band, **Rhythm and Blues Inc.** and **Pete Kelly's Soulution**. Elaine Page sung in **The Colors Of Love**. Keen earlier played in a band called Division Two.

Spark was a subsidiary label of Peer-Southern Productions Inc., N.Y. It had no connection with the blues label Spark. (VJ/VZ)

Roger Ruskin Spear

ALBUMS:	1	ELECTRIC SHOCKS	(United Artists UAG 29381) 1972 SC
	2	UNUSUAL	(United Artists UAG 29508) 1972 SC

EP: 1   REBEL TROUSERS   (United Artists UP 35221) 1971

45s: On Her Doorstep Last Night   (United Artists UP 35683) 1974
I Love To Bumpity Bump/When Your Yuba
Plays The Rumba   (United Artists UP 35720) 1974

Roger Ruskin Spear is best known as a founding member of the **Bonzo Dog Doo-Dah Band** and he was responsible for many of the visual images which were very much a part of the band's act.

In 1970 he was briefly with **Viv Stanshall**'s biG GRunt but then he went solo. His two solo albums are weird. He was assisted on *Unusual* by **Help Yourself**, whilst *Electric Shocks* boasted a supporting roster which included San Francisco rock group The Flamin' Groovies and 'Melody Maker' journalists Chris Welch and Roy Hollingsworth. His eccentricity gave him something of a novelty value which wore off with time and by the mid-seventies he was no longer an attraction. (VJ)

The Spectres (1)

Personnel:	JOHN COGHLAN	drms	AB
	ALAN LANCASTER	gtr	AB
	ROD LYNES	keyb'ds	AB
	FRANCIS ROSSI	gtr	AB
	RICK PARFITT	bs	B

45s: I (Who Have Nothing)/
Neighbour, Neighbour   (Piccadilly 7N 35339) 1966 R4
Hurdy Gurdy Man/Laticia   (Piccadilly 7N 35352) 1966 R4
We Ain't Got Nothin' Yet/
I Want It   (Piccadilly 7N 35368) 1967 R4

Formed in South London back in 1962 and gradually developed playing local dates and backing visiting American singers. They were later joined by Rick Parfitt from The Highlifes, who they'd originally met at the Cafe Des Artistes in Earls Court. Signing to Piccadilly they covered a **Shirley Bassey** hit for their first 45, a song which **Donovan** later enjoyed a hit with for their second one and a song which had been a big American hit for The Blues Magoos for their third. In early 1967 they became **The Traffic Jam** who in turn evolved into **Status Quo**.

Neighbour Neighbour was a Jimmy Hughes R&B number also done by **Graham Bond**.

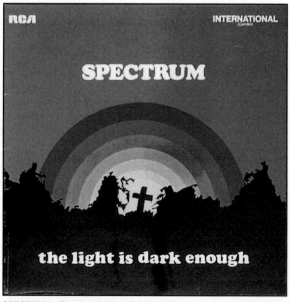

SPECTRUM - The Light Is Dark Enough (LP).

The three 45s can also be heard on two **Status Quo** compilations, *B Sides And Rarities* (Castle Collector CCSCD 271) 1990 and *The Early Works* (Essential ESBCD 136) 1990.

Various artists compilation appearances have included: *(We Ain't Got) Nothin' Yet* on *Maximum '65* (CD) and the CD set *Rock Of Ages, Four Decades Of Heavy Rock 1962-2002*; *Neighbour Neighbour* on *Beat It* (3-CD); *I Want It* and *(We Ain't Got) Nothin' Yet* on *Electric Sugarcube Flashbacks, Vol. 2* (LP); *(We Ain't Got) Nothin' Yet* on *Freakbeat Freakout* (CD); *Hurdy Gurdy Man* and *Laticia* on *Footsteps To Fame, Vol. 1* (CD); and *I (Who Have Nothing)* on *The Songs Of Leiber and Stoller* (CD). (VJ)

The Spectres (2)

45:    The Facts Of Life/Whirlpool   (Lloyd Sound UED QU 1) 1965 R4

This is a different group from Ulster whose 45 also commands three figure fees. The 'A' side was included on *Purple Heart Surgery, Vol. 1* (LP) and *Hens Teeth Vol. 2* (CD) which tells us that the flip side was a surf instrumental. (VJ)

The Spectrum

Personnel:			
	TONY ATKINS	ld gtr	ABC
	BILL CHAMBERS	organ	A
	COLIN FORSEY	vcls	ABC
	KEITH FORSEY	drms	ABC
	TONY JUDD	bs	AB
	JOHN BEATTIE	ld gtr	BC
	PETER WOOD	organ	BC

ALBUM: 1(-)   THE LIGHT IS DARK ENOUGH
                                (RCA International INTS 118) 1970 R2

NB: (1) has been reissued on CD.

45s:	Samantha's Mine/Saturday's Child	(RCA RCA 1589) 1967
	Portobello Road/Comes The Dawn	(RCA RCA 1619) 1967
	Headin' For A Heatwave/	
	I Wanna Be Happy With You	(RCA RCA 1651) 1967
	London Bridge Is Coming Down/	
	Tables And Chairs	(RCA RCA 1700) 1968
	Little Red Boat/Forget Me Not	(RCA RCA 1753) 1968
	Ob-La-Di, Ob-La-Da/	
	Music Soothes The Savage Beast	(RCA RCA 1775) 1968
	Free/The Tale Of Wally Toft	(RCA RCA 1853) 1969
	Glory/Nodnol	(RCA RCA 1883) 1969
Reissue:	Portobello Road/	
	Comes The Dawn	(RCA RCA 1976) 1970

NB: There's also an earlier 45, *Little Girl/Asking You* (Columbia DB 742) 1965. Can anyone confirm if this is by the same or a different act? *I'll Be Gone/The Launching*

CHRIS SPEDDING - Only Lick I Know (CD).

Place, Part II (Parlophone R 5908) 1971 was an UK release by an Australian band of the same name.

Formed in 1967 **The Spectrum** were one of a number of British bands who found more success on the Continent than in the UK. Here their best known song was *Portobello Road*, a song about London's then fashionable street market, which surprisingly failed to chart despite considerable airplay on pirate radio. In Spain, meanwhile, they enjoyed a No 1 with *Headin' For A Heatwave* and their cover of *Ob-La-Di, Ob-La-Da* made No 19 in Germany. By the time of its release Peter Wood had replaced Bill Chambers on organ. Later in the Summer of 1969, when Tony Judd left, Tony Atkins switched to bass guitar with Colin Forsey taking up rhythm guitar. Most of their better songs appear on their album, which is essentially a 'best of' and is now hard to track down and collectable. They also recorded tracks for two films and played a small screen role.

The Tale Of Wally Toft, a flipside from 1969, was given fresh exposure on *Broken Dreams, Vol. 6* (LP).

NB: *Portobello Road* is not the same song as recorded by **Cat Stevens**. (VJ/DS/GBn)

Chris Spedding

ALBUMS:	1	BACKWOOD PROGRESSION	
(up to			(Harvest SHSP 4004) 1970 R1
1976)	2	THE ONLY LICK I KNOW	(Harvest SHSP 4017) 1972 SC
	3	CHRIS SPEDDING	(Rak SRAK 519) 1976

NB: (2) reissued on CD (Repertoire REP 4411-WY). (3) reissued on CD (Fan Club FC 051 CD) 1990 and (Repertoire REP 4859). Also of interest is *Mean and Moody* (See For Miles SEE 40) 1985 a compilation of material from his first two albums. It was later reissued on CD (SEECD 372) 1993. *Motor Bikin': The Best Of* (EMI CDEMS 1425) 1991 compiled material from his early albums plus a couple of rare 'B' sides. *The Very Best Of Chris Spedding* (EMI 094633809420) 2005 compiles his finest moments.

                                            HCP

45s:	α	Rock and Roll Band/	
(up to		Goodbye We Loved You (Madly)	(Harvest HAR 5013) 1970 -
1976)		My Bucket's Got A Hole In It/	
		I Can't Boogie	(Island WIP 6225) 1975 -
		Motor Bikin'/Working For The Union	(Rak RAK 210) 1975 14
		Jump In My Car/Running Round	(Rak RAK 228) 1976 -
		New Girl In The Neighbourhood/	
		Rack Drivin' Man	(Rak RAK 232) 1976 -
		Guitar Jamboree/Sweet Disposition	(Rak RAK 236) 1976 -

NB: α The 'B' side was by **Battered Ornaments**.

Spedding was born on 17 June 1944 in Sheffield. He is best known as highly-rated session guitarist. He joined **Peter Brown's Battered Ornaments** in 1967 having previously been in various obscure dance and

CHRIS SPEDDING - Chris Spedding (CD).

jazz bands. After they split in 1969 he recorded his first two solo albums, though they made little impact. His debut album, produced by Andrew King, was a very disappointing effort influenced by Bob Dylan and The Byrds, but most of the material was directionless. The second was slightly better. There was also a third *Songs Without Words*, which only got released on the Continent. He was also with the short-lived **Sounds Nice** in 1969. In 1971 he joined **The Jack Bruce Band** playing on both his solo albums. He also had an eighteen-month spell with Ian Carr's **Nucleus** before concentrating on session guitar work with **Lulu**, **John Cale** and **Dusty Springfield** among others.

In Autumn 1972 he formed **Sharks** with ex-**Free** bassist **Andy Fraser** and enhanced his reputation as a rock guitarist considerably during his stay. After their demise in November 1974 he again returned to session work, touring with **John Cale** and **Roy Harper** before signing to Mickie Most's RAK label. This lead to a dreadful commercial punk-type single *Motor Bikin'*, which got into the Top 20 (there's no accounting for taste). This was followed by the inevitable solo album. He also played with **Bryan Ferry** in 1976. He went on to record further solo albums and was a 'member' of The Wombles!, but it was as a session guitarist that he performed best.

Mean And Moody, released in 1985, compiled material from his two Harvest albums. Eight tracks were taken from *Backwood Progression* including the opening instrumental 'overture' *For What We Are About To Hear* which leads into the title track itself. The remaining seven tracks are from *The Only Lick I Know*, including the rockin' title track, the country/soul influenced *Dark End Of The Street* and the upbeat *White Lady*. The album also came with a detailed appraisal of **Spedding**'s career written by Roger Dopson.

You'll also find *Motor Bikin'* on the 6-CD box set *Best Of Driving Rock*; *Classic Rock - cd3* and on *Greatest Hits Of The 70's - cd3*, whilst *Summertime Blues* can be found on *The Best Summer Ever!* (CD). (VJ)

Jeremy Spencer

ALBUMS: 1   JEREMY SPENCER   (Reprise RSLP 9002) 1970 R1
(up to   2   JEREMY SPENCER AND THE CHILDREN OF GOD
1976)   (CBS 65387) 1973

NB: (1) Catalogue number changed to (K 44105) in 1971, following the Warner Bros / Elektra / Reprise merger (SC).

45:        Linda/Teenage Darling   (Reprise RS 27002) 1970

These were solo ventures for **Spencer**, who'd played in a blues band called The Levi Set before becoming a founder member of **Fleetwood Mac** in 1967. He was well-known for his onstage parodies of various musical genres, and his debut (which was recorded while he was still with the band) is an affectionate collection of rock and roll pastiches whose drugged-up cover image belies its genial contents. In 1971, after having a

breakdown on tour in the US, he left to form his own band, Children Of God. Their debut is recommended. He recorded a third solo album, *Flee* (Atlantic K 50624) in 1979. (VJ/RMJ)

Spice

Personnel: MICK BOX   gtr, vcls   ABC
              DAVID BYRON   vcls   ABC
              ALEX NAPIER   drms   ABC
              PAUL NEWTON   bs, vcls   BC
              KEN HENSLEY   gtr, vcls   C

45s: What About The Music/In Love (United Artists UP 2246) 1968 R3

This Essex-based band had earlier been known as The Stalkers. Box and Byron had been in the original **Spice** line-up. Newton, who'd also been in **The Gods**, was in a later line-up of this band which eventually evolved into **Uriah Heep** with the addition of another former **Gods** and ex-**Toe Fat** member **Ken Hensley**.

Spice's 45 is now very collectable. It's the flip side, *In Love*, which really stands out with some superb psychedelic guitar work and Electric Prunes' style sound effects. Recommended. The 'A' side, a cover of a Billy Hamer single originally released on Kama Sutra, *What About The Music*, is a big Northern soul rarity.

Other early **Spice** members' included Barry Green (bs) who later became Barry Blue, and Nigel Pegram (drms) who later went on to **Gnidrolog** and **Steeleye Span**.

A 1994 CD compilation of early **Uriah Heep** material *The Landsdowne Tapes* includes 35 minutes of live material from **Spice** in late 1969. Musically this is much more akin to early **Uriah Heep** than the above 45.

There was also a Swedish band of this name who recorded a 45, *Union Jack/Delicious* (Olga OLE 013), the same year, which got a UK release.

Compilation appearances have included: *In Love* on *Magic Spectacles* (CD), *Rubble, Vol. 17 - A Trip In A Painted World* (LP), *Rubble, Vol. 10* (CD), *The Best Of Rubble Collection, Vol. 5* (3-CD) and *Beat It* (3-CD); and *What About The Music* on *Soul File* (CD). (VJ/KJ)

Spider

45:        The Comedown Song/Blow Ya Mind   (Decca F 12430) 1966 SC

This 45 is now a minor collectable. It was recorded by one guy who was a clothes designer and produced by Kim Fowley. Folky in style, the 'A' side was heavily influenced by Bob Dylan. The backing is notable for the

THE SPIRIT OF JOHN MORGAN - Spirit Of John Morgan (CD).

THE SPIRIT OF JOHN MORGAN - Age Machine (LP).

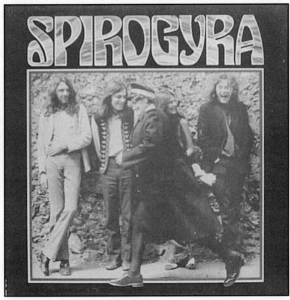
SPIROGYRA - St. Radigund's (LP).

prominent saxophone, organ and bustling percussion. *Blow Ya Mind* is similar in style although more uptempo and upbeat. The single would appear to be his only vinyl output.

The Comedown Song has been compiled on *Justafixation* (LP) and *Justafixation* (CD). (VJ)

The Spiders From Mars

Personnel:	DAVE BLACK	gtr	A
	TREVOR BOLDER	bs	A
	MIKE GARSON	keyb'ds	A
	PETE McDONALD	vcls	A
	MICK 'WOODY' WOODMANSEY	drms	A

ALBUM:	1(A)	SPIDERS FROM MARS	(Pye NSPL 18479) 1976

45s:	White Man Black Man/National Poll	(Pye 7N 45578) 1975
	(I Don't Wanna Do) Limbo/Can't Be Fair	(Pye 7N 45578) 1976

Woodmansey and Bolder had been in **David Bowie**'s backing band in his Ziggy Stardust days. **The Spiders From Mars** also made a few solo recordings in their own right. Their album got to No 197 in the US charts.

Mick Woodmansey had also been in the Hull-based **Rats** back in the mid-sixties. His previous band was Flight. Trevor Bolder had been in **The Mick Ronson Band**. Dave Black was in **Kestrel**. After this project, Garson joined **Fox**; Bolder headed for **Uriah Heep** and Woodmansey became a member of U-Boat. (VJ/JM)

Spiggy Topes

The *Dustbin Full Of Rubbish* (LP) compilation includes four tracks by this obscure band from a previously unreleased 1967 demo tape. The tape was discovered at a car-boot sale, without a title, and named by the compiler from the 'Private Eye' spoof, which had nothing to do with it. There's an unusual arrangement of Hellerman and Minkoff's *Come Away Melinda*, which Tim Rose recorded quite a well-known version of; but the other three tracks - *My Only Chance Is You, Love In The Wind* (an instrumental) and *Mr. Sullivan* - had little to commend them. (VJ)

Spiggy Topes and The Turds

Flexi disc cover mounted on Private Eye in 1967, "Hot Rod and Swinging Perve".

Originally suggested by Dudley Moore, **Spiggy Topes and The Turds** were a spoof group who regularly featured in 'Private Eye' during 1966/67, written by cartoonist and presenter of the proto-psychedelic art TV show 'Whole Scene Going', Barry Fantoni. This flexi disc featured Fantoni and was cover-mounted in 1967. They had nothing to do with the recently surfaced **Spiggy Topes**' demos. (JN)

The Spirit of John Morgan

Personnel:	JOHN FAGIN	lead gtr	A
	JOHN MORGAN	keyb'ds, vcls	ABC
	PHIL SHUTT (aka PHIL CURTIS)	bs	ABC
	MICK WALKER	drms, vcls	ABC
	DON WHITAKER	d gtr, vcls	B
	TREVOR THOMS		
	(aka THOMAS aka JAMES)	gtr	C

ALBUMS:	1(B)	SPIRIT OF JOHN MORGAN	
		(Carnaby CNLS 6002) 1969 R1	
	2(C)	AGE MACHINE	(Carnaby CNLS 6007) 1970 R1

NB: (1) later reissued by Carnaby (6437 503) 1971 (SC) and reissued on CD (Repertoire REP 4351-WP) 1993 and on vinyl with the original artwork reproduced. A subsequent limited vinyl edition of 500 copies of (1) was released in Spain (Wah Wah LPS 006) in 2001. (1) reissued on CD (Abraxas AK301CD) with a bonus track and thick card 'book' sleeve. (2) reissued on CD (Repertoire REP 4354-WP) 1994.

45s:	Ride On/Along Came John	(Carnaby CNS 4005) 1969
	Age Machine/Lost Nirvana	(Carnaby CNS 4019) 1970
	Floating Opera Show/Never Let Go	(RCA RCA 2085) 1971

This was a blues-rock band. Fagin left before they recorded and was replaced by Whitaker. The albums are now minor collectables. A couple of bar-room piano boogies popular during their live act are included but beyond these are some solid R&B numbers written by band members on the first album. *I Want You*, a **Graham Bond** number opens the album strongly and *She's Gone* is a definite highlight. *A Train For All Reasons* is a country-tinged harpsichord-led number, whilst *The Yodel* is a **Bond/Auger** style instrumental and *Yorkshire Blues* Is an emotive number.

Whitaker then left and Trevor Thoms (also known as Thomas and James) replaced him.

John Morgan went on to record solo albums. He was assisted by Shutt, Thoms and Walker on *Kaleidoscope*. Shutt and James (Thoms/Thomas) joined **The Steve Gibbons Band** and Walker headed for **Bond and Brown**. Shutt was later in **Arthur Brown's Kingdom Come**. (VJ/MWh/BM/JM/BS)

Spirogyra

Personnel:	STEVE BORRILL	bs	ABC
	MARTIN COCKERHAM	gtr, vcls	ABC
	JULIAN CUSACK	violin, keyb'ds	ABC
	BARBARA GASKIN	vcls	ABC
	DAVE MATTACKS	drms	ABC
	RICK BIDDULPH	mandolin	B
	ALAN LAING	cello	B
	STEVE ASHLEY	flute	C
	JOHN BOYCE	cello	C
	HENRY LOWTHER	trumpet	C
	STAN SULZMAN	flute	C

ALBUMS:	1(A)	ST. RADIGUND'S (w/inner)	(B&C CAS 1042) 1971 R2
	2(B)	OLD BOOT WINE	(Pegasus PEG 13) 1972 R2
	3(C)	BELLS, BOOTS AND SHAMBLES	
			(Polydor 2310 246) 1973 R4

NB: (1) and (3) reissued officially on vinyl, in Korea (Si Wan SRML 5005 and 5007 respectively) and later as a 4-CD set (Si Wan SRMC 5005/6/7) 1999. (1) also reissued on vinyl (Akarma AK 330). (3) has been reissued on CD (Repertoire RR 4137 WZ) 1991. *Burn The Bridges* (Si-Wan SRMC 5010) 2000 is a collection of unreleased demo tracks from 1970/71, available on vinyl as a Korean import. *A Canterbury Tale - The Collection* (2-CD) (Castle CMQDD 1258) 2005 includes all of their material anthologised on one CD.

45s:	Dangerous Dave/Captain's Log (PS)	(Pegasus PEGS 3) 1972
	I Hear You're Going Somewhere/	
	Old Boot Wine	(Polydor 2001 419) 1973

Though inconsistent, **Spirogyra**'s three albums contain some of the finest songs of the period.

Their roots lay in Bolton, where leader and principal songwriter Martin Cockerham had formed a folky duo with his friend Mark Francis in 1967, prior to enrolling at Kent University in Canterbury in 1969. There he teamed up with fellow student musicians Barbara Gaskin, Julian Cusack and Steve Borrill. Managed by their student union's entertainment secretary Max Hole (later to become a major figure in the UK music industry), they based themselves in a communal house in town, quitting studying to concentrate on the band and soon earning a contract with the UK's leading folk-rock entrepreneur, Sandy Roberton.

At its best, *St. Radigund's* (named after their street and produced by Robert Kirby, who also worked with **Nick Drake**, **Vashti Bunyan** and others) announced Cockerham as one of the period's best folk songwriters. In particular, the eerie *Captain's Log* and beautiful *Love Is A Funny Thing* put them towards the top of the folk-rock pack. The combination of Gaskin's crystal voice, Cusack's imaginative arrangements and Cockerham's strangely beautiful melodies sounds unique when it gels, but the material is variable in quality and all too often Cockerham sings his own songs in a voice too strained to convince. There is also a frenetic, dissonant quality to certain songs that not everyone can take.

Old Boot Wine found the band augmenting their sound with cello, mandolin and a fuller rock backing. It also gives more room to Gaskin's remarkably pure voice. Among the best tracks are the blistering *Dangerous Dave*, one of the most exciting folk-rock tracks ever recorded, the beautiful *Van Allen's Belt* and gloriously soothing *A Canterbury Tale*. Overall this is a more subdued album than its predecessor, though the good tracks are still brilliant and the bad ones plain irritating.

When *Old Boot Wine* didn't sell, Cusack and Borrill left. Reduced to a duo, Cockerham and Gaskin (now also a couple) moved to London, where Cockerham devised the magisterial *Bells, Boots and Shambles*. On it the promise of their first two albums is crystallised into a near-flawless progressive folk suite. The haunting sadness that permeated its predecessors is sustained in *Old Boot Wine* and *An Everyday Consumption Song*, while fuller rock arrangements define the epics that open and close the album, *The Furthest Point* and *The Western World*. On both these songs Lowther's trumpet works wonders. Elsewhere some marvellous flute and cello playing can be heard. Not every track is brilliant, but the album stands as a classic and is very difficult to obtain.

Though they'd played gigs alongside **Traffic**, **The Who**, **Rod Stewart** and **The Faces**, when it also failed to sell Cockerham decided to travel the world. He didn't settle in England again until very recently, but has continued to write and record.

Gaskin went on to guest with **Hatfield and The North** and National Health before spending over three years travelling. She then teamed up with Dave Stewart (who'd been in **Egg** as well as those bands), and together they scored a number one hit with a cover of Lesley Gore's *It's My Party* in 1980.

All three **Spirogyra** albums were also issued in Germany (on Brain). These are slightly less rare than their British counterparts. The Korean 4-CD box set contains their three original albums and the final disc contains the otherwise unavailable *I Hear You're Going Somewhere (Joe Really)*, along with three single cuts from the albums. The sound quality is excellent, and the discs are presented in high-gloss, thick card sleeve replicas. The package is accompanied by a booklet with lots of rare photos, full lyrics and sleevenotes from Barbara Gaskin herself. A year later came *Burn The Bridges*, a collection of previously unreleased demos from 1970/71, which lacked the input of Dave Mattacks on drums. The sound quality is rudimentary, but it's nicely packaged and the gatefold sleeve contains previously unseen pictures, lyrics and a selection of stickers.

The *Clogs* (LP) folk sampler features *Captain's Log*. (MK/VJ/MWh/RMJ)

Splinter

Personnel:	BILL ELLIOT	vcls	A
(up to	BOBBY PURVIS	vcls	A
1976)			

ALBUMS:	1(A)	THE PLACE I LOVE	(Dark Horse AMLH 22001) 1974
(up to	2(A)	HARDER TO LIVE	(Dark Horse AMLH 22006) 1975
1976)	3( )	SPLINTER	(Dark Horse DH 2) 1976 R2

NB: (3) promo only.

			HCP
45s:	Costafine Town/Elly May	(Dark Horse AMS 7135) 1974	17
(up to	α Drink All Day/		
1976)	Haven't Got Time	(Dark Horse AMS 5501) 1975	SC -
	China Light/Drink All Day	(Dark Horse AMS 5502) 1976	-
	Which Way Will I Get Home/		
	Green Bus Line	(Dark Horse AMS 5503) 1976	-
	Half Way There//What Is It If You		
	Never Ever Tried It Yourself	(Dark Horse AMS 5506) 1976	-

NB: α Withdrawn.

On their debut album, this duo were accompanied by some very well known musicinas including Klaus Voormann, Mike Kellie, **Alvin Lee**, Mel Collins, Billy Preston, Jim Keltrer and **Gary Wright**. **George Harrison**, who produced the album, plays various different instruments under a number of pseudonyms. All the songs were written by Bobby Purvis. Bill Elliot co-wrote the lyrics on two of them. Musically we're talking mellow, melodic, mainstream seventies rock. One track *Somebody's City* has interesting lyrics:

"The smokestacks pointing to the sky and oil forever floating on the river
Impairing all the beauty God created in this life for you and me
But what the hell do I care, I'll pretend it isn't there and keep on walking
It's somebody's city, it's somebody's life"
(CA)

SPIROGYRA - Old Boot Wine (CD).

SPIROGYRA - Bells, Boots And Shambles (LP).

SPIROGYRA - Burn The Bridges (CD).

The Splynters

45:      Don't Stop Me Dreaming/
         I Guess I Have To Love The Lady   (Philips 6006 059) 1970

A one-off 45. (MWh)

Spontaneous Combustion

Personnel: TONY BROCK   drms   A
             GARY MARGETTS   gtr, vcls   A
             TRISTIAN MARGETTS   bs, vcls   A

ALBUMS: 1(A)   SPONTANEOUS COMBUSTION
                                     (Harvest SHVL 801) 1972 R1
         2(A) TRIAD (w/insert)   (Harvest SHVL 805) 1972 R1

NB: (2) also released in the USA (Capitol ST-11095) 1972. (1) and (2) reissued on
one CD (See For Miles SEECD 472) 1997.

45s: Lonely Singer/200 Lives/Leaving   (Harvest HAR 5046) 1971 SC
         Gay Time Night/Spaceship   (Harvest HAR 5060) 1972
         Sabre Dance Pts 1& 2   (Harvest HAR 5066) 1973

This obscure outfit formed in 1971. **Greg Lake** spotted their potential and
produced their debut album, which was a pretty typical progressive offering
with lots of guitar and synthesizer. The follow-up *Triad* was more of the
same. They are classic examples of albums nobody much wanted at the
time becoming collectable - which is largely due to the label they appeared
on.

After their demise Tristian Margetts resurfaced playing and recording with
Greg Lake, but brother Gary quit the music business. Tony Brock was later
in **Strider** and The Babys. In the eighties he was in **Rod Stewart**'s backing
band. (VJ)

Spontaneous Music Ensemble

Personnel: DEREK BAILEY
             JOHN STEVENS

ALBUMS: 1   CHALLENGE   (Eyemark EMP L 1002) 1966 R3
         2   KARYOBIN... ARE THE IMAGINARY BIRDS SAID TO
             LIVE IN PARADISE   (Island ILP 979) 1968 R2
         3   SPONTANEOUS MUSIC ENSEMBLE
                                    (Marmalade 608 008) 1969 R1
         4   SOURCE FROM AND TOWARDS
                                    (Tangent TNGS 107) 1971 SC
         5   FACE TO FACE   (Emanem 303) 1973 SC
         6   SO WHAT DO YOU THINK   (Tangent TNGS 118) 1973

NB: (3) reissued on Marmalade (2384 009) in 1972.

An avant-garde jazz fusion outfit led by John Stevens. The first two albums
are very rare. Derek Bailey also recorded a privately-pressed album, *Duo*
(Incus INCUS 2) during the seventies with Tristan Hosinger. John Stevens
went on to record a couple of solo 45s during 1976 - *Annie Pt's 1 2*
(Vertigo 6059 140) and *Can't Explain Pt's 1 2* (Vertigo 6059 154) - under
the name John Stevens Away. (VJ)

Spooky Tooth

Personnel: MIKE HARRISON   piano, vcls   ABCDE
             LUTHER GROSVENOR   gtr   ABC
             GREG RIDLEY   bs   A
             MIKE KELLIE   drms   ABC EF
             GARY WRIGHT   organ, vcls   AB DEFG
             ANDY LEIGH   bs   B
             JOHN HAWKEN   keyb'ds   C
             STEVE THOMPSON   bs   C
             BRYSON GRAHAM   drms   D G
             MICK JONES   gtr, vcls   DEFG
             IAN HERBERT   bs   D
             CHRIS STEWART   bs   E
             MIKE PATTO   vcls   FG
             KEITH ELLIS   bs   F
             VAL MOORE   bs   G

ALBUMS: 1(A)   IT'S ALL ABOUT A ROUNDABOUT
               (mono/stereo)   (Island ILP 980/ILPS 9080) 1968 R1/SC
        2(A)   SPOOKY TWO   (Island ILPS 9098) 1969 R1
        3(B)   CEREMONY   (Island ILPS 9107) 1970 SC
        4(C)   THE LAST PUFF   (Island ILPS 9117) 1970 SC
        5(D)   YOU BROKE MY HEART SO I BUSTED YOUR JAW
                                   (Island ILPS 9227) 1973 SC
        6(E)   WITNESS   (Island ILPS 9255) 1973 SC
        7(G)   THE MIRROR   (Good Ear EARL 2001) 1974
        8(-)   THE BEST OF SPOOKY TOOTH (Island ILPS 9368) 1976

NB: (1) reissued on CD (Edsel EDCD 467) 1995, again on CD (Pline PL 585) and
again on CD (Repertoire REPUK 1074) 2005 in digipak with bonus singles and
sleevenotes compiled by Chris Welch containing first-hand reminiscences from **Mike
Harrison**. (2) reissued on CD (Repertoire REPUK 1061) 2005. (3) reissued on CD
(Edsel EDCD 565) 1998. (4) reissued on CD (Edsel EDCD 468) 1995 and again on
(CD) (Repertoire REPUK 1073) 2005 on German import in digipak with an
informative booklet and with four bonus tracks. (5) reissued on CD (Repertoire
REPUK 1059) 2005 on German import in digipak with an informative booklet and
one bonus track. (6) reissued on CD (Repertoire REPUK 1060) 2005 on German
import in digipak with an informative booklet. There was also an export issue of (7)
(Island ILPS 9292) 1974. (7) reissued on Charly (CR 30167) in 1979 in UK. There's
also *The Best Of Spooky Tooth* available on CD (Island IMCD 74) 1989. *That Was
Only Yesterday: An Introduction To Spooky Tooth* (Island IMCD 276) 2000 compiles
tracks from their 1968-1970 era.

45s: Sunshine Help Me/Weird   (Island WIP 6022) 1967
         Love Really Changed Me/Luger's Grove (Island WIP 6037) 1968

SPOOKY TOOTH - It's All About A Roundabout (LP).

The Weight/Do Right People	(Island WIP 6046) 1968
Son Of Your Father/	
I've Got Enough Heartache	(Island WIP 6060) 1969
All Sewn Up/	
As Long As The World Keeps Turning	(Island WIP 6168) 1973
Two Time Love/Hooser	(Goodear EAR 109) 1974
Fantasy Satisfier/Hoofer	(Goodear EAR 607) 1975

Spooky Tooth started life in Carlisle as **The V.I.P.'s**, before moving to London and changing their name to **Art**. After one unsuccessful album as such they changed name again in October 1967, adding American **Gary Wright**, a psychology graduate who'd been a child actor and led a band called New York Times back home.

Spooky Tooth's debut was an excellent collection of funky originals such as *Love Really Changed Me* and *Sunshine Help Me* and explosive cover versions, including their classic take on Janis Ian's *Society's Child*. *Spooky Two* is thought by many to be their best effort, and they toured the States to promote it, though they always remained a cult act there. The very rare US-only *Spooky Blow/Love Really Changed Me* 45 (Mala 12013) is perhaps their rarest item. The 'A' side never appeared in the UK. They also covered The Band's *The Weight* on a 45. Around this time they were frequently featured on John Peel's 'Top Gear' programme and were significant players in Britain's late sixties underground boom. Despite achieving critical acclaim, however, they never won over wider audiences, and in 1969 Ridley left to join **Humble Pie**.

In 1970 they teamed up with French electronics wizard Pierre Henry, the man behind **Les Yper Sound**, for their experimental third album *Ceremony*, which many considered a disastrous flop. They then split up for a while. **Gary Wright** left to form **Wonderwheel**, who recorded two albums, but later that year the rest of the band reformed with line-up (B). Steve Thompson had previously been with **John Mayall** and John Hawken with **The Nashville Teens** and **Renaissance**. However, neither had played on *The Last Puff*, on which **Harrison**, Kellie and **Grosvenor** had enlisted assistance from former **Grease Band** members, Alan Spenner and **Henry McCullough**. The album was well received in the States but made little impact here, so the band split again. Thompson went to **Stone The Crows** and Hawken to Illusion.

Harrison recorded an album, *Mike Harrison*, in October 1971, with the Carlisle band Junkyard Angel and later put out *Smokestack Lightning* in 1972 with assistance from members of Muscle Shoals. Neither was particularly successful, and nor was **Wright**'s **Wonderwheel**, so in September 1972 **Harrison** and **Wright** got together line-up (C), which recorded *You Broke My Heart So I Busted Your Jaw* and toured frantically around the States, where they built up quite a following though the album was mostly uninspired. *Times Have Changed* does have a haunting intro, though, and the guitar-driven *Wildfire* and keyboards on *Holy Water* are worthy of mention.

Mike Kellie rejoined the band in March 1973 and they recorded *Witness*, their final album for Island. Again it lacked the inspiration of their earlier

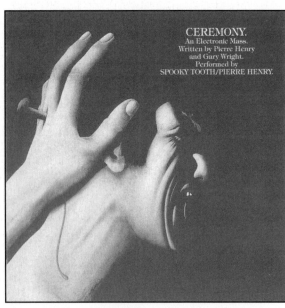

SPOOKY TOOTH - Ceremony (CD).

SPOOKY TOOTH - The Last Puff (CD).

work. There's some good guitar work on *Don't Ever Stray Away*, and *Wings On My Heart* is a successful power ballad. After its release there were further personnel changes, with Chris Stewart (who'd been in **Eire Apparent**) departing to join **Joe Cocker** and **Mike Harrison** departing to record another solo album, *Rainbow Rider* (Goodear EAR 7002) in 1975, and then joining The Chris Stainton Band.

In February 1974 ex-**Boxer** vocalist **Mike Patto** came in to replace **Harrison** and the band relocated to New York. Before the new line-up had much chance to stabilise, Kellie left (and later joined The Only Ones). **Spooky Tooth** managed one final album, the rather lame *The Mirror*, before disintegrating for good in September 1974.

Gary Wright went on to enjoy considerable solo success in his own country. Mick Jones eventually resurfaced in the enormously successful American band Foreigner, with another ex-Briton, former **King Crimson** member Ian McDonald, while **Mike Patto** reformed **Boxer** for a further album and tour. Thus **Spooky Tooth**, who'd enjoyed so many re-incarnations, were finally laid to rest with Island putting out the obligatory *Best Of* compilation in 1976.

That Was Only Yesterday compiles material from their 1968-1970 era. There are three cuts from their debut album, seven from *Spooky Two*, but only a brief extract from *Ceremony* - their collaboration with Pierre Henry.

They also appeared on Island's 1970 compilation *Bumpers* (2-LP) playing *I Am The Walrus* and a year earlier on *Nice Enough To Eat* (LP) with *Better By You, Better Than Me* and on *You Can All Join In* (LP) singing *Sunshine Help Me*. (VJ/GF/RMJ)

The Sportsmen

45:     I Miss You When I Kiss You/If It's Love   (CBS 202043) 1966

This seven-piece group came from Widnes in Lancashire. Their 45 is a ballad. (VJ)

Spreadeagle

Personnel:	ANDY BLACKFIELD	gtr, vcls	A
	JIM COPLEY	drms	A
	JON FIELD	perc	A
	SAM LLEWELLYN	bs, vcls, perc	A
	TIM PHILLIPS	gtr, vcls, keyb'ds	A

ALBUM: 1(A) THE PIECE OF PAPER   (Charisma CAS 1055) 1972 SC
NB. Also released in the USA on Charisma.

45s:	How Can We Be Lost/Nightmare	(Charisma CB 183) 1972
	Nightmare Lane (PS)	(Charisma BCP 7) 1972

A soft-rock band produced by Shel Talmy. Their songs are melodic with harmony vocals but not so strong on melodies. The better tracks on the album are three long ones, which have extended instrumental parts with very good guitar leads: *Brothers In The Sunshine*, *Piece Of Paper* and *Eagles*.

John Perry played with **Spreadeagle** after leaving **Gringo**, but he's not featured on the above album. (CA)

Spriguns (of Tolgus)

Personnel:	MANDY MORTON	vcls	ABC
	MIKE MORTON	vcls	ABC
	CHRIS RUSSON	gtr	ABC
	RICK THOMAS	fiddle	ABC
	TOM LING	fiddle	B
	DICK POWELL	keyb'ds	BC
	CHRIS WOODCOCK	drms	B
	DENNIS DUNSTAN	drms	C
	WAYNE MORRISON	gtr	C

ALBUMS:	1(A)	ROWDY, DOWDY DAY	(Private, cassette only) 1974 R1
	2(A)	JACK WITH A FEATHER	
			(Alida Star Cottage ASC 7755) 1975 R5
	3(B)	REVEL WEIRD AND WILD	(Decca SKL 5262) 1976 R2
	4(C)	TIME WILL PASS	(Decca SKL 5286) 1977 R2

NB: (1) Cassette only, reissued on vinyl by Kissing Spell (KSLP 002). (3) & (4) Credited to **Spriguns**. (2) reissued on Background (HBG 122/9) 1992. (3) reissued on vinyl (Acme ADLP 1045) 2005 in a limited edition of 500 and on CD (Acme ADCD 1945) 2005. (4) reissued on vinyl (Acme ADLP 1044) 2005 in a limited edition of 500 and on CD (Acme ADCD 1044). (3) and (4) reissued on one CD (Sunrise SR5 408112) and the set is accompanied by a 12-page colour booklet.

45s:	Nothing Else To Do/Lord Lovell	(Decca F 13676) 1976
	White Witch/Time Will Pass	(Decca F 13739) 1977

A Cambridge folk-rock band who started life playing Friday and Saturday nights at the Anchor pub in the city's Silver Street. Less than 50 copies of their privately released 1974 debut were produced, to be sold to students at gigs. The fact that it's a cassette, however, has meant that its value hasn't reached the epic proportions of the vinyl follow-up, *Jack With A Feather*, which boasted better sound quality and duplicated some material from the cassette. The playing on this album was good, and almost all the material was traditional.

Abbreviating their name to **Spriguns**, they recorded a couple of albums for Decca, which are also very rare. These moved away from their previously traditional folk style in favour of an electric folk-rock sound in the **Fairport Convention** mould. By now the band was almost totally a vehicle for

SPRIGUNS OF TOLGUS - Jack With A Feather (CD).

talented vocalist Mandy Morton, who went on to form The Mandy Morton Band and record for Banshee and Polydor. In the eighties she toured with a rock band and became a presenter on BBC Radio Cambridge.

Of the other members, Mike Morton sadly died, Rick Thomas is married and now lives in Italy, Tom Ling plays in a Cambridge-based band called Usual Suspects and Chris Russon has recently returned to the local music scene.

After the first Mandy Morton album *Sea Of Storms* (Polydor 2382 101), drummer Alex Cooper, Tom Ling and American guitarist Mark Boettcher left the group. Consequently Boettcher introduced Alex Cooper to some American musicians who then, together with ex-Soft Boy Kimberley Rew, formed Katrina and The Waves. The 'Waves later made a big splash with their hit *I'm Walking On Sunshine*. (VJ/RMJ)

Spring

Personnel:	KIPPS BROWN	keyb'ds, melltron	A
	ADRIAN MALONEY	bs, gtr	A
	RAY MARTINEZ	gtr, keyb'ds, mellotron	A
	PAT MORAN	vcls, keyb'ds, mellotron	A
	PICK WITHERS	drms	A

ALBUM:	1(A)	SPRING	(RCA Neon NE 6) 1971 R3

NB: (1) Reissued on CD (Repertoire REP 4472-WP) 1994 with three bonus tracks. (1) counterfeited on vinyl 198? with an out of focus cover and reissued officially on vinyl (Eclipse) 1999. (1) reissued again on vinyl (Akarma AK 213) housed in the original three-fold gatefold sleeve.

This sole album by a bunch of relative unknowns is a delight, with natural, moving melodies played over a tasteful mellotron background and supported by an able rhythm section whose drummer employs military rhythms in an unobtrusively effective manner. Side two doesn't quite reach the heights of side one, but it's still very enjoyable and never less than good. Strongly recommended. It came in a lavish triple fold-out cover that is predictably hard to find in top condition nowadays.

The recent Repertoire reissue includes three cuts: - *Fool's Gold, Hendre Mews* and *A World Full Of Whispers* from an unreleased second album.

Ray Martinez went on to **Gypsy** and Pique Withers later found fame and fortune with Dire Straits. Brown went on to **The Andy Fairweather Low Band** and Withers joined The Shortwave Band. (MK/VJ/JM)

Springboard

Personnel incl:	JEFF CLYNE
	TREVOR WATTS

SPRIGUNS OF TOLGUS - Rowdy, Dowdy, Day (LP).

SPRIGUNS - Time Will Pass (CD).

ALBUM: 1   SPRINGBOARD   (Polydor 545 007) 1969 R1

This is a progressive jazz album. (VJ)

Dusty Springfield

			HCP
ALBUMS:	1	A GIRL CALLED DUSTY	
(up to		(mono/stereo) (Philips (S)BL 7594) 1964 SC/R1 6	
1976)	2	EVERYTHING'S COMING UP DUSTY (mono/stereo)	
		(gatefold sleeve w/booklet)	
		(Philips (S)RBL 1002) 1965 SC/R1 6	
	3	GOLDEN HITS (mono/stereo)	
		(Philips (S)BL 7737) 1966 SC 2	
	4	WHERE AM I GOING	
		(mono/stereo) (Philips (S)BL 7820) 1967 SC 40	
	5	DUSTY SPRINGFIELD	
		(World Club Record WCR WRC ST 848) 1968 -	
	6	DUSTY.. DEFINITELY	
		(mono/stereo) (Philips (S)BL 7864) 1967 SC 30	
	7	STAY AWHILE (Wing WL 1211) 1968 -	
	8	DUSTY IN MEMPHIS (Philips SBL 7889) 1969 SC -	
	9	FROM DUSTY WITH LOVE	
		(Philips 6308 004) 1970 SC 35	
	10	THIS IS DUSTY SPRINGFIELD	
		(Philips 6382 016) 1971 SC -	
	11	STAR DUSTY (Audio Club Issue)	
		(Philips 6850 003) 1972 SC -	
	12	SHEER MAGIC (Audio Club Issue)	
		(Philips 6856 020) 1972 R1 -	
	13	SEE ALL HER FACES (Philips 6308 117) 1972 SC -	
	14	CAMEO (Philips 6308 152) 1973 SC -	
	15	THIS IS DUSTY SPRINGFIELD VOL 2: MAGIC GARDEN	
		(Philips 6382 063) 1973 SC -	
	16	DUSTY SINGS BURT BACHARACH AND CAROLE	
		KING (Philips 6382 105) 1973 SC -	
	17	YOU DON'T HAVE TO SAY YOU LOVE ME	
		(Contour CN 2016) 1976 -	

NB: (1) reissued on vinyl (Fontana 6438 024) 1970 and again (Contour 6870 555) 1972. (1) reissued on CD remastered (Mercury 5345202) 1997. (2) reissued on CD (Beat Goes On BGOCD 74) 1989 and again on CD remastered (Mercury 5368522) 1998. (4) reissued on CD remastered (Mercury 5369622) 1996. (7) reissued on vinyl (Fontana SFL 13189) 1970. (8) reissued on CD remastered (Mercury 5286872) 1995 and on vinyl (4 Men With Beards/Rhino 4M 112) 2005. (9) reissued on vinyl (Philips 6308 004) 1970. Vinyl compilations include: *Greatest Hits* (Philips 9109 629) 1979, *The Very Best Of Dusty Springfield* (K-Tel NE 1139) 1981, *Greatest Hits* (Philips 9279 305) 1981, *Greatest Hits* (Philips PRICE 45) 1983, *The Silver Collection* (Philips DUSTV 1) 1988, also on CD (Philips 83411282) 1988, with two extra tracks. Other CD compilations include the 4-CD set *Dusty (The Legend Of Dusty)* (Philips 5222542) 1994, *Goin' Back (The Best Of Dusty Springfield 1962-1994)* (Philips 8487892) 1994, *Something Special* (2-CD set) (Mercury 5288182) 1996 and *Hits Collection* (Spectrum 5375492) 1997. *Simply Dusty* (Mercury) 2000 is a 4-CD box set sequenced chronologically. *Heart And Soul* (Varese Sarabande 302 066 299 2) 2002, which was available as a US import, is a rarities collection

EPs:	1	I ONLY WANT TO BE WITH YOU	
(up to		(Philips BE 12560) 1964 SC	
1976)	2	DUSTY (Philips BE 12564) 1964 SC	
	3	DUSTY IN NEW YORK (Philips BE 12572) 1965 SC	
	4	MADEMOISELLE DUSTY (Philips BE 12579) 1965 R1	
	5	IF YOU GO AWAY (Philips BE 12605) 1968 SC	
	6	STAR DUSTY (Philips 6850 751) 1972	

NB: There was also a four-track cassette EP of Dusty's hits released by Philips in 1967 and one more EP *Dusty Springfield* (Philips CUT 111) was released in 1980.

			HCP
45s:		I Only Want To Be With You/	
(up to		Once Upon A Time (Philips BF 1292) 1963 4	
1976)		Stay Awhile/Something Special (Philips BF 1313) 1963 13	
		I Just Don't Know What To Do With Myself/	
		My Colouring Book (Philips BF 1348) 1964 3	
α		Losing You/Summer Is Over (Philips BF 1369) 1964 9	
		Oh Holy Child/Jingle Bells (PS) (Philips BF 1381) 1964 -	
		Your Hurtin' Kind Of Love/	
		Don't Say It Baby (Philips BF 1396) 1964 37	
		In The Middle Of Nowhere/	
		Baby Don't You Know (Philips BF 1418) 1964 8	
		Some Of Your Lovin'/	
		I'll Love You For A While (Philips BF 1430) 1965 8	
		Little By Little/	
		If It Hadn't Been For You (Philips BF 1466) 1965 17	
		You Don't Have To Say You Love Me/	
		Every Ounce Of Strength (Philips BF 1482) 1965 1	
		Goin' Back/I'm Gonna Leave You (Philips BF 1502) 1966 10	
		All I See Is You/Go Ahead On (PS) (Philips BF 1510) 1966 9	
		I'll Try Anything/The Corrupt Ones (Philips BF 1553) 1967 13	
		Give Me Time/The Look Of Love (Philips BF 1577) 1967 24	
		What's It Gonna Be/	
		Small Town Girl (Philips BF 1608) 1967 SC -	
		I Close My Eyes And Count To Ten/	
		No Stranger Am I (Philips BF 1682) 1968 4	
		I Will Come To You/	
		The Colour Of Your Eyes (Philips BF 1706) 1968 -	
		Son Of A Preacher Man/	
		Just A Little Lovin' (Philips BF 1730) 1968 SC 9	
		Am I The Same Girl/	
		Earthbound Gypsy (Philips BF 1811) 1969 SC 43	
		Brand New Me/	
		Bad Case Of The Blues (Philips BF 1826) 1969 -	
β		Morning Please Don't Come/Charley (Philips BF 1835) 1970 -	
		How Can I Be Sure/Spooky (Philips BF 1835) 1970 36	
		Yesterday When I Was Young/	
		I Start Counting (Philips 6006 214) 1972 -	
		Who Gets Your Love/Of All The Things (Philips 6006 295) 1973 -	
		Learn To Say Goodbye/Easy Evil (Philips 6006 325) 1973 -	
		What's It Gonna Be/Bring Him Back (Philips 6006 350) 1974 -	
		Yesterday When I Was Young/	
		The Look Of Love (Philips 6006 446) 1975 -	
Reissues:		Some Of Your Lovin'/ Son Of A Preacher Man/	
		You Don't Have To Say You Love Me (maxi single)	
		(Philips 6006 151) 1971 -	
		I Only Want To Be With You/You Don't Have	
		To Say You Love Me (Old Gold OG 9242) 1982 -	
		I Just Don't Know What To Do With Myself/	
		I Close My Eyes And Count To Ten (Old Gold OG 9763) 1988 -	

NB: α 'B' side was by The Springfields. β 'A' side was with Tom Springfield and the 'B' side was a Tom Springfield solo effort.

Dusty Springfield was the finest white soul singer of her era and one of Britain's very best (many consider the best) female singers. The variety of her material and the emotion of her performance make her special.

She was born as Mary O'Brien in Hampstead, London on 16 April 1939. Her elder brother Dion soon nurtured an interest in singing and they often rehearsed in their parents' garage. After leaving school she often performed with Dion in small clubs where they performed folk and latin songs. They also appeared at two Butlin's holiday camps in 1957. In 1958, Dusty joined a vocal trio known as The Lana Sisters, who recorded six singles for Fontana in the late fifties and early sixties, one whilst backing Al Saxon. The first four were released during the time she was with the band, the last two may have been by a later line-up.

In late 1959, she was back working with her brother Dion, having left The Lana Sisters. Dion meanwhile had teamed up with a new singer Tim Field. A few months later the three formed a trio called The Springfields (Dion got the idea from the combination of a pleasant Spring day and Tim's surname!). It was at this stage that the O'Brien's adopted the stage names Tom Springfield and **Dusty Springfield**. The group enjoyed a series of hits, including *Breakaway*, *Bambino* and *Say I Won't Be There* and soon became Britain's best-selling act. In September 1962, they gained their first US hit with *Silver Threads and Golden Needles*, which also entered the Australian charts at No 1. When they went to Nashville to record Dusty was so captivated by the emerging Motown sounds that she left the group to go solo and perform material more akin to the black American music she loved. This is where our story begins.

Her first single *I Only Want To Be With You* was co-written by her arranger Ivor Raymonde and Mike Hawker. It was a soulful song and her powerful vocals heightened its appeal. It climbed to No 4 here in Britain and climbed to No 12 in the States too. She wrote the 'B' side *Once Upon A Time* herself. Her second single *Stay Awhile* (also penned by Ivor Raymonde and Mike Hawker) was much weaker and stalled at No 13 in the UK and No 42 in the US. It also featured a 'B' side penned by **Dusty**, *Something Special*.

She toured the UK supporting **The Searchers** and went to the States to appear on the 'Ed Sullivan Show'. She then headed to Australia supporting **Gerry and The Pacemakers**. Returning to the UK she promoted her first album, *A Girl Called Dusty*. It had a raucous edge and featured rawish versions of R&B songs like *Don't You Know*, *Mockingbird* and *Mama Said*, as well as slightly more sophisticated material which Barbra Steisand and Dionne Warwick had recorded. It also contained two Bacharach/David compositions *Anyone Who Had A Heart* (a hit for **Cilla Black**) and *Wishin' And Hopin'*. The later gave Dusty her biggest US hit - here it was a hit for **The Merseybeats**. For her next single she recorded another Bacharach/David composition *I Just Don't Know What To Do With Myself*. This again showcased her powerful vocal style and made the UK Top 3.

In the States Philips released two American-only albums. The first *Stay Awhile* was a mixture of her early singles and tracks from her debut album. The second *Dusty* contained songs that gradually appeared here on EPs and 'B' sides, although *Guess Who* was never released here at all.

The pattern of issuing different singles in the UK and US continued. Her next US single was *All Cried Out* (it was released here on the *Dusty* EP). Here in Britain Tom Springfield's *Losing You* was selected as her next single and she gave another fine vocal performance. The single, which peaked at No 9, was also notable for its strong flip side *Summer Is Over*. Before 1964 was over a further single *Oh Holy Child* was released in time for Christmas to raise money for Dr Barnado's Childrens Homes. The hitherto unissued **Springfield**'s recording of *Jingle Bells* was selected as the 'B' side and unusually for this era the single was packaged in a picture sleeve. In December 1964, she toured South Africa, but was soon deported for refusing to perform before segregated audiences. She was voted Britain's top female vocalist of 1964 in an NME Poll.

SPRING - Spring (LP).

In 1965, she hosted the television special 'The Sound Of Motown', which did much to introduce new American music to the UK. He next UK/US singles paring both flopped - *Live It Up* could only manage No 90 in the States and *Your Hurtin' Kinda Love* stalled at No 37 here in Britain. The *Dusty In New York* EP, released in April 1965, showcased recordings from her earlier New York recordings. The remainder of the EP's songs were included on another US-only album *Oooooweeee!!!*, which again included two songs never issued here at the time - *Here She Comes* and *If Wishes Could Be Kisses*.

Alan Price and US soulstress Doris Troy assisted on the recording of her next UK single *In The Middle Of Nowhere* and it proved worthwhile because the bouncy number climbed to No 8, a position repeated by the Goffin/King follow-up *Some Of Your Lovin'*. Her second UK album *Everything's Coming Up Dusty* followed a similar format to her first combining new material with covers of American classics. It was lavishly packaged for an album at that time, coming with a fold-out sleeve and booklet containing photos and a biography of her career to date. UK 45 success followed with the uptempo Goffin/King song *Little By Little* (No 17) and the song that was arguably her magnum opus *You Don't Have To Say You Love Me*. This was a sublime rendition of an Italian ballad, which had been given English lyrics by Simon Napier-Bell and Vicki Wakeham. It gave Dusty her only UK No 1. Another classic Goffin/King song *Goin' Back* returned her to the Top Ten with an emotional arrangement - many of you will also recall The Byrds' excellent but slightly different interpretation. In 1966 she scored a further US hit with *You Don't Have To Say You Love Me* and an album of the same name comprised of her recent singles and the remaining tracks from her second UK album. Here in Britain Philips issued *Golden Hits*, which was her best-selling UK album.

In January 1967, Dusty recorded two film themes. *The Look Of Love* was recorded for the spoof James Bond movie 'Casino Royale'. It featured her vocals at their most exquisite. The second theme was *The Corrupt Ones*, which was recorded for the movie of the same name but released here as 'The Peking Medallion'. Both songs were included on the 'B' sides of her next two singles *I'll Try Anything* and *Give Me Time*, which peaked at Nos 13 and 24 respectively here in Britain. She embarked on a world tour in the summer of 1967 with cabaret seasons in London, San Francisco, New York, Chicago, Australia and Japan. When she returned to the UK in August she began work on her third UK studio album *Where Am I Going*, which was released in November 1967. It included some excellent covers, such as Aretha Franklin's *Don't Let Me Lose This Dream* and *Sunny*, but it only climbed to No 40 in the UK charts and her next 45 release *What's It Gonna Be* failed to chart at all. In the US the *Where Am I Going* track listing was changed and the album was re-titled *The Look Of Love*.

She struggled to find a suitable single for early 1968, with plans to record Jim Webb's *Magic Garden* being shelved. It did later appear on a 1968 EP *If You Go Away*. Eventually, after cabaret commitments in the US and Canada, she emerged with *I Close My Eyes And Count To Ten*, which was penned by Clive Westlake and became one of her most commercially successful singles, climbing to No 4. There were now clear grounds for believing that her career was in decline. She had been replaced as Top Female Singer by **Lulu** and her next single *I Will Come To You* was another flop. Her November 1968 album *Dusty Definitely* didn't fare much better either, although it is notable for her moving cover versions of *I Think It's Gonna Rain Today* and *This Girl's In Love With You*.

In autumn 1968 her recording contract switched Philips to Atlantic, which freed her up to record with the label's top session men. She travelled to Memphis to cut a single and ended up recording an album. The resulting single *Son Of A Preacher Man* was one of her commercial and artistic highs and rose to No 9. The *Dusty In Memphis* album was her artistic magnum opus. It featured four Goffin/King songs: *So Much Love* (both Steve Alaimo and Ben E. King had recorded this and enjoyed very minor hits in 1968 with it - in the UK it was a hit for **Tony Blackburn**), *Don't Forget About Me* (previously recorded by P.J. Proby and Barbara Lewis), *No Easy Way Down* (a soul-styled song) and *I Can't Make It Alone* (also recorded by P.J. Proby). The opening cut *Just A Little Lovin'* (Early In The Morning) was penned by Barry Mann and Cynthia Weil and hadn't been recorded by anyone prior to Dusty. There are also two Randy Newman songs: *I Don't Want To Hear It Anymore* (her favourite song on the album, which was released as a US 45 but only climbed to No 105) and *Just One Smile* (an earlier hit for Gene Pitney). The remaining tracks were *Son Of A Preacher Man* (which had been written by John Hurley and Ronnie Wilkins for Aretha Franklin originally), *Breakfast In Bed* (a strong beat ballad written by Eddie Hinton and Donnie Fritts) and *The Windmills Of Your Mind* (the love theme from the movie 'The Thomas Crown Affair', which Noel

Harrison, who sang it in the movie, enjoyed a US hit with).

Her two 1969 singles *Am I The Same Girl* and *Brand New Me* were relatively unsuccessful and the frequency of her 45 releases was slowing down too. Her final UK hit was *How Can I Be Sure* (which had been a US hit and would later be recorded by David Cassidy). She had several singles released in the States in this period but left Britain around this time and kept a relatively low profile throughout the seventies. She issued albums *See All Her Faces* and *Cameo* in 1972 and 1973 respectively, but they were under publicised here and weren't much more effective in the States. She commenced work on an album *Longings*, which was never released and effectively retired for a few years until she re-emerged in the late seventies with *It Begins Again* on United Artists.

She attempted further comebacks in the late seventies and early eighties, but it was only when she collaborated with the Pet Shop Boys in 1987 on *What Have I Done To Deserve This*? that she achieved real commercial success again climbing to No 2 in the UK charts. The partnership resumed two years later with *Nothing Has Been Proved* (the theme to the film 'Scandal' about the Profumo Affair that played a crucial role in bringing down the early sixties McMillan government). She also appeared in a Britvic TV advert (featuring sixties faces like **Scott Walker** and Simon Dee) in 1987 with a soundtrack of *I Only Want To Be With You*.

In 1993 Dusty did a duet *Heart And Soul* with **Cilla Black** on the latter's album *Through The Years*, which was recorded to celebrate 30 years in show business for Cilla. Two years later she recorded a duet with Daryl Hall on *Wherever Would I Be?* - a track on her final album *A Very Fine Love*. Whilst recording the sessions for this album she was diagnosed with breast cancer and after months of radiotherapy the illness was thought to be in remission, but by the summer of 1996 the cancer had returned.

In 1998 Dusty received an OBE in the New Year's Honours List. On 2 March 1999 she died aged 59 from the breast cancer, just weeks before what would have been her 60th birthday. A few days later she was also inducted into the Rock & Roll Hall Of Fame.

The Legend Of Dusty Springfield is a 4-CD box set released in 1994, which was arranged thematically rather than chronologically. Only a few thousand copies of the set were pressed and despite public demand there has been no repress as yet.

Something Special is a 2-CD set. CD One sub-titled Rarities contains 'B' sides, out-takes, a couple of Italian singles, a European single (*It Goes Like It Goes* from 1980) and two US singles (*I Am Your Child* - a 'B' side from 1977 and *Give Me The Night* - an 'A' side from 1978). CD Two is sub-titled Album Tracks, although tucked away in between are *The Look Of Love*, a 1977 'B' side, *Breakfast In Bed* (a 1969 US single) and *Let Me Love You Once Before You Go* (a 1977 US single). Overall this CD set will appeal to her fans, rather than the punter seeking an introduction to her career.

Simply Dusty is a 4-CD box set of her career sequenced chronologically. CD One covers the sixties. It opens with the 1970 tribute song *Dusty*

STACKRIDGE - Stackridge (LP).

Springfield by **Blossom Dearie**. There are a couple of tracks (*Ragtime Selection* and *Seven Little Girls*) from her period with The Lana Sisters and Al Saxon and four from her time with The Springfields. The remainder of the CD is taken up with her classic sixties singles, including remixed versions of *In The Middle Of Nowhere* and *Baby Don't You Know*. The remaining three CDs cover her later career and it culminates with her final recording ironically for a health insurance commercial - two short verses of *Someone To Watch Over Me*.

Heart and Soul, a 2002 US import, contains 20 rarities, including live-on-TV dubs of *Son Of A Preacher Man*, *The Look Of Love* and *A Brand New Me* as well as more obscure numbers like *Magnificent Sanctuary Band*. There is also a TV advert she did for milk shakes and duets with **Spencer Davis** and **Cilla Black**. Some diehard fans will be pleased about the inclusion of film themes *As Long As We Got Each Other* and *But It's A Nice Dream* and there's a forgotten eighties single *Sometimes Like Butterflies*.

Compilation appearances have included *You Don't Have To Say You Love Me* on the 2-CD set *60 Number One Hits Of The Sixties* and on the 2-CD set *Sixties Summer Love*. (VJ)

Springfield Park

Personnel:	MARTIN CROXFORD	piano	A
	TONY CURTIN	ld vcls	A
	ANDY GEE	vcls, ld gtr	A
	BOB SAPSTEAD	bs	A
	BARRY TUSTIN	drms	A

45:	Never An Everday Thing/		
	I Can See The Sun Shine	(CBS 3775) 1968	

NB: There's also a 10" mini-album *Fading Aka A Stroll Through* (Excalibur XCALMGO 505) which features a six-song demo that secured their contract with CBS.

This London-based group was put together by **The Love Affair**'s manager Sydney Bacon in an attempt to create a **Love Affair** Mark II, but it didn't happen. Gee went on to play with **Pete Bardens** and **Ellis**. Sapstead was in **Morgan**.

The band also recorded a one-sided Emidisc acetate. It has five tracks: *We Show You Paradise*, *Land Of Hope And Gloria*, *Halfway There*, *Loud As You Can*, *Battle-Cry* and *Love's Our Thing*. The tracks are all demos. but they are well recorded and recall bands like **The Kinks**, **Zombies** and Lefte Bank. Psych-pop fans will be interested. (VJ)

Springwater

ALBUM:	1	SPRINGWATER	(Polydor 2383 162) 1972

NB: (1) only released in Germany at the time. (1) reissued on CD (Angel Air SJPCD 105) 2002 with Phil Cordell's album *Born Again*, which was recorded many years later added as a bonus.

				HCP
45s:	α	I Will Return/Stone Cross	(Polydor 2058 141) 1971	5
		Listen Everybody/Guiding Light	(Polydor 2058 220) 1972	-
		Jerusalem/Amazing Grace	(Polydor 2058 271) 1972	-
Reissue:		I Will Return/(Flip by different artist)	(Old Gold OG 9434) 1984	-

NB: α also released in the US (Cotillion 44143) 1972 and (Polydor 15072) 1973.

Springwater was actually male instrumentalist Phil Cordell, who enjoyed a Top 5 hit with *I Will Return*. The album sold well at the time despite being entirely instrumental. On offer is an amalgam of seventies pop and folk. Versions of *Amazing Grace* and *Jerusalem* are included.

The CD reissue also includes his first solo album, recorded many years later, as a bonus. This is more mundane singer/songwriter pop with orchestration on some tracks. (VJ/VZ)

Spud

Personnel:	AUSTIN KENNY	gtr, vcls	A
	DON KNOX	vcls, fiddle	A

STACKRIDGE - Friendliness (CD).

DERMOT O'CONNOR	gtr, vcls		A
MIKE SMITH	bs, vcls		A

ALBUMS: 1(A)	A SILK PURSE	(Philips 9108 002) 1975 SC	
(up to 2(A)	THE HAPPY HANDFUL	(Philips 9108 003) 1975 SC	
1976)			

This Irish folk-rock group's albums are bound to be of interest to Celtic music lovers. Their debut album includes a competent version of the well-known traditional song *Blackleg Miner* amongst others. They also recorded a third album, *Smoking On The Bog* (Sonet SNTF 742) in 1977. This comes with a lyric sheet. By this time O'Connor had been replaced by Dave Gaynor (drms) and multi-instrumentalist Ken Wilson. This is generally regarded as their best album, a sorta good-time folk offering, but they've been dormant since. (VJ)

The Square Set

45:     That's What I Want/Come On   (Decca 13197) 1971

This is a little known early seventies band.

That's What I Want has been compiled on *14 Groovy Sounds From The Blow Up* (LP). (MWh)

Chris Squire

HCP

ALBUM: 1   FISH OUT OF WATER (w/poster)
(Atlantic K 50203) 1975 25

Chris Squire is a Londoner. He was in **Mabel Greer's Toyshop** in the late sixties with future **Yes** members **Jon Anderson** and **Peter Banks**. He was also in **The Syn** prior to being a founding member of **Yes** in June 1968. He released this solo album in 1975 when the band took a rest for most of the year. As well as selling quite well here in the UK it also climbed to No 69 in the US Album Charts. (VJ)

The Staccatos

45:     Butchers and Bakers/
        Imitations Of Love   (Fontana TF 966) 1968 SC

This was an obscure late sixties pop band. *Butchers and Bakers* is a very ordinary harmony-pop offering. It was written by Terry Dempsey and also recorded by **Chocolate Frog** (**The Fleur De Lys**' alter ego). There has been speculation that **The Staccatos** was a pseudonym used by **The Creation**.

You'll also find *Butchers And Bakers* on *Rubble, Vol. 16 - Glass Orchid Aftermath* (LP), *Rubble, Vol. 10* (CD) and *The Best Of Rubble Collection, Vol. 2* (CD). (VJ)

Stackridge

Personnel:			
BILLY BENT			
(aka BILLY SPARKLE)	drms, triangle		ABC
ANDY DAVIS (ANDY			
CRESWELL-DAVIS)	vcls, gtr, piano,		
	keyboards,		
	harmonium, bs		ABCDE
MIKE EVANS	violin, cello		ABC
MICHAEL 'MUTTER'			
SLATER	vcls, flute,		
	alto-flute		ABCDE
JAMES WARREN	vcls, gtr		ABC
JAMES (JIM) 'CRUN'			
WALTER	gtr, bs		BC E
BILLY SPARKLE	drms		B
JOHN WHITE	drms		C
ROD BOWKETT	keyb'ds		D
KEITH GEMMELL	saxophone,		
	clarinet, flute		DE
PAUL KARAS	vcls, bs		D
ROY MORGAN	drms		D
DAVE LAWSON	keyb'ds		E
PETER VAN HOOKE	drms		E

ALBUMS: 1(A)	STACKRIDGE	(MCA MDKS 8002) 1971 R1	
(up to 2(B)	FRIENDLINESS	(MCA MKPS 2025) 1972 SC	
1976) 3(C)	THE MAN IN THE BOWLER HAT		
		(MCA MCG 3501) 1974 SC	
4(D)	EXTRAVAGANZA	(Rocket PIG L 11-B) 1975	
5(E)	MR MICK	(Rocket ROLL 3) 1976	
6(-)	DO THE STANLEY	(MCA MCF 2747) 1976	

NB: (1) and (2) reissued by MCA in 1974. (1) reissued on vinyl (Beat Goes On BGOLP 65) 1990 and again on CD (Edsel EDCD 518) 1997. (2) reissued on CD (Edsel EDCD 487) 1996. (3) issued in USA under alternative title *Pinafore Days* (Sire SASD 7503 1974) with different tracks and different line-up as the group featured on (3) had split after recording it. A revised line-up subsequently toured the US. (4) was also issued in USA under the same title but with different track listing (Sire SASD 7509). (3) reissued on CD (Edsel EDCD 488) 1996. (4) reissued on CD (Nippon Phonogram PHCR 4211)1995. (5) reissued on CD (Nippon Phonogram PHCR 4212)1995. (5) also reissued as *The Original Mr Mick* (Dap DAP 103CD) 2000. (6) was a compilation of the 1971-74 period with one previously unreleased bonus track, *Let There Be Lids*, featuring Mike Evans, including *Do The Stanley*. *Radio One Live In Concert* (Windsong WINCD 019) 1992 is a collection of BBC 'In Concert' recordings from 1972, 1973 and 1975. *BBC Radio 1 In Concert* (Strange Fruit SFRSCD 40) 1997 compiles their Beeb recordings between 1973 and 1976.

45s:	Dora The Female Explorer/Everyman	(MCA MKS 5065) 1971	
(up to	Slark/Purple Spaceship Over Yatton	(MCA MK 5091) 1972	
1976)	Anyone For Tennis/Amazing Agnes	(MCA MK 5103) 1972	
	Do The Stanley/C'est La Vie	(MCA MU 1182) 1973	
	Galloping Gaucho/Fundamentally Yours	(MCA MU 1224) 1973	
	Dangerous Bacon/Lost Plimsoul	(MCA MCA 124) 1974	
	Spin Round The Room/Pocket Billiards	(Rocket PIG 15) 1975	
	Hold Me Tight/		
	Breakfast With Werner Von Braun	(Rocket ROKN 507) 1976	

NB: One additional single release of interest is *Dancing On Air/Solitude* (Rocket ROKN 510) 1976, by 'Mutter' Slater. Bboth sides were Bowkett-Slater compositions.

Stackridge emerged from the Bristol folk scene and their first two albums were folk-rock characterised by songs about strange characters/mythical beasts and instrumentals - threads that remained with them and which appear on all their albums.

On their debut, *Stackridge*, highlights were *Slark*, a ten-minute extrava-ganza about a mythical monster which perhaps extends a nod towards Greig's Norwegian dances and which was the cornerstone of their initial stage act, *Dora The Female Explorer*, a lively harmonica-driven piece and *The Three Legged Table*, a mixture of acoustic and soft-rock that works very well. Other tracks told the story of Percy the Penguin who had cucumber wings and who unfortunately came to a sticky end, and Marco Plod, the 'strangest man alive today', whose caricature was issued in badge form to members of the Stackridge Fan Club.

STACK WADDY - Bugger Off (LP).

Their second effort, *Friendliness*, continued in the same vein with *Syracuse The Elephant* (born and bred in Bristol Zoo, brought up on swedes, his keeper was a specialist who came down from Leeds), *Amazingly Agnes*, a reggae tune about a cow, a Charleston-type number entitled *Anyone For Tennis* featured **Pigsty Hill Light Orchestra**'s assistance and a song about factory farming established *Keep On Clucking*, which for **Stackridge** was quite a rocky number. It also featured the instrumental *Lummy Days*, which opened many a show.

The Man In The Bowler Hat was **Stackridge**'s attempt at serious music although it still had at its basis amusing story lyrics. **George Martin** produced it and it's probably their strongest album musically. Unfortunately it precipitated a split, as what was essentially a good time live folk-rock act full of dustbin lids, rhubarb thrashing antics (eat your heart out, Morrissey) and jokey tunes tried to become serious rock musicians. *The Last Plimsoul* is probably the best track but *Road To Venezuela*, *The Galloping Goucho*, and *Fundamentally Yours* are other highlights of what is a good album, not wholly out of character but definitely a progression from what had gone before. The album was recorded by what was the 'dream team' line-up of Andy Davis, James Warren, Mutter Slater, Mike Evans, 'Crun' Walter and Billy Sparkle. The band split almost immediately after and the USA version of the album has a different title, different track listings and shows pictures of different personnel.

Extravaganza was their first album for **Elton John**'s Rocket label. For this, Keith Gemmell (ex-**Audience**) and Paul Karas (ex-**Rare Bird**) joined. If anything the instructions to the new members of the group seem to have been "Let's go back to the good-time feel of previous albums". *The Volunteer*, a track left over from the *Man In The Bowler Hat* sessions is one of the strongest and there are several examples of Rod Bowkett's influence - particularly strong are the instrumentals *Pocket Billiards* and *Who's That Up There With Bill Stokes?*. *Benjamin's Giant Onion* has an old **Stackridge** feel about it and the band also recorded a version of **Gordon Haskell**'s *No One's More Important Than The Earthworm* (which they performed on the 'Old Grey Whistle Test'). The US version included *Do The Stanley*, a single previously released around the time of *The Man In The Bowler Hat*, a new dance inspired by Stan Laurel apparently! There is no doubt however that *Extravaganza* suffered as a result of James Warren's departure to join The Korgis. After this Morgan left and was replaced by former **Headstone** member Peter Van Hooke. Then Karas and Bowkett left, Jim Walters rejoined and former **Greenslade** member Dave Lawson was recruited too. So it was line-up E that was in place in February 1976 to work on *Mr Mick*, which was released the following month.

Dave Lawson, formerly of **Alan Bown**, **Episode Six** and **Greenslade** joined the line-up that recorded *Mr Mick*, their ill-fated attempt at a concept album. In truth the material was weak, opening with a **Beatles** cover version (*Hold Me Tight*), the best material being the instrumentals, one of which, *Coniston Water*, is quite good. Some tracks like *Mr Mick's Dream* and *The Cotton-Reel Song* had some sense of organisation, but the spoken parts and poetry are largely disjointed. By this time the band had lost the plot. Only Andy Davis seemed to have any real creative force left. Warren

had long since departed and Rod Bowkett did not appear on this album either. Time for bed, said Zebedee!! Mutter Slater recorded a solo album, *Dancing On Air* in March 1976 and Van Hooke went on to work with **Van Morrison**.

Do The Stanley (which refers to Stan Laurel) is a good compilation as it shows the band at their best (on record at least as really they were always better live than on record. Unfortunately the live CD is not representative of this). It contains a few single 'B' sides which are rather good, particularly the instrumental *Purple Spaceship*

Davis, who had played guitar on **John Lennon**'s *Imagine* album, made a solo album in the late eighties/early nineties entitled *Clevedon Pier* on the MMC label - it was 'new age' in style. He also played on Kim Beacon's two solo albums in 1979 and 1981, then with Julian Cope, **Bill Nelson** and he also toured with Tears For Fears. He was also a Korgi for their first two albums and featured on the next two as a musician and writer. He also issued a solo single entitled *Baby Good For You*.

Mutter Slater resurfaced in 1983 in a pub-rock band called Rave To The Grave, who recorded an album. He was no longer playing the flute, but did write a lot of material for the album. Mike Evans went on to join the trio of musicians who played at the Bath Pump Rooms and eventually sued the proprietors for wrongful dismissal!

The track, *The Volunteer*, on the 1975 album *Extravaganza*, which was produced by Tony Ashton, featured the line-up from *The Man In The Bowler Hat*, although this is not credited on the album.

An American fan compiled a bootleg CD in 1998 *Unearthed*, which features performances from the band or band members solo and includes some previously unreleased songs.

James Warren resurrected **Stackridge** in 1999 with Jim 'Crun' Walter and Mike Evans. A new album was released called *Something For The Weekend* and they played several low-key concerts. (VJ/BS/JM)

Stackwaddy

Personnel:	STUART BARNHAM	bs	ABCDE
	JOHN GROOM	drms	A
	JOHN KNAIL	vcls, hrmnca	AB
	MICK SCOTT	gtr	AB
	STEVE REVELL	drms	B
	NICK DAVIES	gtr	C
	JON LOWE	drms	C
	JOHN PARKER	piano	C
	MIKE SWEENEY	vcls	CDE
	ROBIN GOODWIN	drms	D
	WAYNE JACKSON	bs	DE
	KEVIN WILKINSON	drms	E

ALBUMS: 1(B) STACKWADDY (Dandelion DAN 8003/2310154) 1971 R2
2(B) BUGGER OFF (Dandelion 2310231) 1972 R2

NB: Both have been counterfeited but, unlike the originals, the counterfeits don't come in gatefold sleeves. (2) reissued on CD (Repertoire RR-4082 WP) 1992. (1) and (2) reissued on one CD (See For Miles SEECD 407) 1994 and again on one CD (Sunrise SR 502232).

45s: Roadrunner/Kentucky (Dandelion S 5119) 1970
You Really Got Me/Willie The Pimp (Polydor 2001 331) 1972

Stackwaddy set out as a wild and raucous R&B outfit (originally called New Religion) in Manchester in 1965. They built up a good reputation on the city's club circuit, but John Groom left in 1966 and Steve Revell came in on drums. Knail's tendency to throw bottles at or assault their audience when dissatisfied with their level of appreciation eventually led him to being jailed. Both albums are now rare and sought-after. The first one came in a gatefold sleeve and exhibited a strong Beefheart influence. Indeed it contained a cover of his *Sure Nuff 'N Yes I Do* alongside versions of **Jethro Tull**'s *Love Story* and standards like *Roadrunner* and *Susie Q*.

Bugger Off was withdrawn from sale in many record shops because of its title - obviously this hindered sales and it's the harder of their two albums to find. It included cover versions of **The Kinks**' *You Really Got Me* and Frank Zappa's *Willie The Pimp*, which were also put out on a 45, but these were just two among several cover versions.

The Repertoire CD reissue of *Bugger Off* includes *Mama Keep Your Mouth Shut*, a previously unreleased cut. *Girl From Ipanema* and *Mama Keep Your Big Mouth Shut* also feature on *Dandelion Rarities* (CD). *Roadrunner* has also surfaced on the budget *Dandelion Sampler 1969-1972* CD. The band split in 1972. Scott, Barnham and Revell all joined Jay Arthur.

Bamham reformed the band in 1973 with line-up (C) which lasted until 1976, but no new vinyl resulted. John Parker had been **in Long John Baldry's** Hoochie Coochie Men in the sixties and Jon Lowe was previously with **The Stylos**. When Davies, Parker and Lowe left, Jackson and Goodwin were recruited, although Goodwin soon made way for Kevin Wilkinson. The band finally split in 1976.

A line-up of the band is still gigging today. *Sex And Flags* (Angel Air SJPCD 205) 2005 rounds up most of their recent recordings, including material from their 1999 album *Something For The Weekend* and all of their 2003 mini-album *Lemon*. (VJ/JM)

Chris Stainton and Glenn Turner

Personnel:	CHARLIE HARRISON	bs	A
	HENRY SPINETTI	drms	A
	CHRIS STAINTON	keyb'ds,gtr	A
	GLENN TURNER	vcls, gtr	A

ALBUM: 1(A) TUNDRA (Decca SKL R 5259) 1976

A R&B/rock band featuring **Stainton** (ex-**Joe Cocker/Greaseband**) and Glenn Turner who used to play with Kim Fowley. (VJ)

Jo Stahl

45: Biding My Time/Beautiful Second Hand (Pathway PAT 101) 1971

This was the first release on the obscure Pathway label. (MWh)

Stamford Bridge

Personnel:	PETER BARNFATHER	vcls, gtr	A
	JOHN CARTER	vcls, gtr	A
	KEN LEWIS	vcls, keyb'ds	A

ALBUMS: 1(A) COME UP AND SEE US SOMETIME
(Penny Farthing) 1970
2(A) THE FIRST DAY OF YOUR LIFE (Penny Farthing) 1971

NB. (1) released as Stamford Bridge and Friends. (1) and (2) reissued on one CD (See For Miles SEECD 478) 1998.

HCP
45s:	α	Chelsea/Ossie	(Penny Farthing PEN 715) 1970	47
		Roly Poly/Little Boy Blue	(Penny Farthing PEN 731) 1970	-
		Rise Sally Rise/		
		Chaquita Maria	(Penny Farthing PEN 767) 1971	-
		World Of Fantasy/	(Penny Farthing)1971	-

NB. α released as Stamford Bridge and Friends. There's also a CD compilation, *Stamford Bridge - Come Up And See Us Sometime/The First Day Of Your Life* (See For Miles SEECD 478).

This group's members came from London/Birmingham area. Carter and Lewis were in **Carter-Lewis and The Southerners**, **The Ivy League** and **The Flowerpot Men**. They then worked as Scarecrow, **Dawn Chorus** and The Hooters. After that they started the vocal trio **Stamford Bridge** with Peter Barnfather and a backing group comprising John Ford (bs) and Richard Hudson (drms, washboard, percsn, sitar) (previously in **Elmer Gantry's Velvet Opera** and **The Strawbs**); Micky Keen (gtr) (he'd been in **The Ivy League's** backing group); Barry Kingston (keyb'ds); Russ Alquist (backing vcls) and Gillian Shakespeare (backing vcls), she was Carter's wife.

Their style ranged from folk to pop, sometimes very similar to **The Flowerpot Men**. *Face In The Crowd* on their first album is very similar to

this. In 1970 they enjoyed a No 47 hit with their football anthem *Chelsea* as the boys in blue headed for the 1970 Cup Final. This was intended as a Shed anthem, although the fans seemed to prefer *One Man Went To Mow*. After that they recorded two albums for Penny Farthing and a further 45. They all demonstrated that they reigned supreme in the field of the perfect three-minute pop song. The second album included the track *Let's Go Back To San Francisco*, which was incorrectly included on some compilations as **Flowerpot Men's** unreleased song. Their records were well received in Australia and South Africa, but they then split up. John Carter later joined **First Class**, who enjoyed a big hit with *Beach Baby*. (VJ/L)

Terry Stamp

ALBUM: 1 FAT STICKS (w/lyric insert) (A&M AMLH 63329) 1975 SC

This was a solo effort from ex-**Third World War** leading light **Terry Stamp**. Assisting on the album was former band mate Jim Avery plus **Ollie Halsall** (ex-**Patto** and **Boxer**), **Tony Newman** and Alan Spenner. (VJ)

Stampede

Personnel:	BRIAN APPLEYARD	drms	A
	MIKE BERG	bs	AB
	JOHN COLEMAN	piano	AB
	JESSE LINDSAY	lead violin	AB

45: Que Sera Sera/Harpsichord (United Artists UP 35111) 1970

Outside the studio they were known as Jesse Lindsay and Friends. In the studio they were joined by **Peter Frampton** (gtr, vcls) and **Andy Bown** (organ, vcls). When they became known in the press the single was soon withdrawn because **Frampton** and **Bown** had contracts with other bands **Humble Pie** and **Judas Jump**. *Que Sera Sera* was a cover of a well known song. Brian Appleyard, previously of **East Of Eden** and Cody's Glider and later of Bubastis, was only with the band briefly. (VJ)

Pete Stanley and Wizz Jones

ALBUM: 1 SIXTEEN TONS OF BLUEGRASS
(Columbia SX 6083) 1966 R2

45: The Ballad Of Hollis Brown/
Riff Minor (Columbia DB 7776) 1965 SC

This was a short-lived collaboration, which produced a very rare album. See the **Wizz Jones** entry for further details of him. (VJ)

Vivian Stanshall

ALBUM: 1 MEN OPENING UMBRELLAS AHEAD
(up to (Warner Brothers K 56052) 1974 R2
1976)

45s:	α	Labio-Dental Fricative/		
(up to		Paper Round	(Liberty LBS 15309) 1970 SC	
1976)	β	Suspicion/Blind Date	(Fly BUG 4) 1970	
		Lakongu/Baba Tunde	(Warner Brothers K 16424) 1974	
		Young Ones/		
		Are You Havin' Any Fun/Question	(Harvest HAR 5114) 1976 SC	

NB: α with Sean Head Show Band featuring **Eric Clapton**. β 'A' side with Gargantuan Chums. 'B' side with biG GRunt.

Stanshall, who was born in Shillingford, Oxfordshire on 21 March 1943, was a founding member of the **Bonzo Dog Doo-Dah Band**. When that seminal group began to disintegrate at the end of the sixties its members tended to pursue solo careers. **Stanshall** recorded a 45 for Liberty with a hastily-assembled outfit which incorporated **Eric Clapton**. The same year he assembled biG GRunt with ex-**Bonzos Roger Ruskin Spear**, Denis Cowan and Fred Munt. Their only vinyl output was *Blind Date*, which appeared on the 'B' side to a cover of Terry Stafford's *Suspicion* recorded by his Gargantuan Chums. biG GRunt may have gone on to better things but **Stanshall** suffered a nervous breakdown and was hospitalised bringing the outfit to a premature end.

When he re-emerged into society he recorded *Men Opening Umbrellas* with the assistance of a whole array of musicians including **Madeline Bell**, **Jim Capaldi**, Rich Grech, ex-**Bonzo Neil Innes** and **Stevie Winwood**. He later contributed to some of **Winwood**'s solo albums and performed 'Master of Ceremony' duties on **Mike Oldfield**'s *Tubular Bells* album.

Clearly a talented eccentric **Stanshall** not only continued to record spasmodically since 1976, he also worked for BBC Radio and more recently used his voice in advertising. He tragically died following a fire at his London Muswell Hill flat in March 1995.

Blind Date and *The Strain* can also be heard on *Hard Up Heroes, Vol. 2* (2-LP). (VJ)

Freddie Starr (and The Midnighters)

Personnel:

DAVE CARDEN	ld gtr	AB
KEEF HARTLEY	drms	A
JOHN KELMAN	gtr	AB
FREDDIE STARR	vcls	AB
BRIAN WOODS	bs	AB
IAN BROAD	drms	B

			HCP
45s:	Who Told You?/		
(up to	Peter Gunn Locomotion	(Decca F 11663) 1963	SC -
1976)	It's Shaking Time/Baby Blue	(Decca F 11786) 1963	R1 -
α	Never Cry On Someone's Shoulder/		
	Just Keep On Dreaming	(Decca F 12009) 1964	R1 -
α	Naomi/Free To Carry On	(A&M AMS 838) 1971	-
α	It's You/We Can't Make It Anymore	(Tiffany 6121 501) 1974	9
α	I Guess I'll Call You/You're The Fool	(GL GL 107) 1974	-
α	Ginny Come Lately/Teen Queen	(Tiffany 6121 504) 1974	-
α	Ape Call/I've Been Dreaming Again	(Tiffany 6121 508) 1975	-
α	White Christmas (2 versions)	(Thunderbird THE 102) 1975	41
α	Only Sixteen/Bad Boy	(Thunderbird THE 108) 1976	-

NB: α **Freddie Starr** solo efforts.

An early sixties Merseybeat group who failed to make it into the big time, but Freddie did as an impressionist on ITV's 'Who Do You Do'. He eventually got his own TV series and released a string of solo singles in the seventies of which *It's You* made the Top 10. These early efforts were very undistinguised, despite being produced by Joe Meek. They also released a German-only album, *Live At The Starr Club*, which featured **Keef Hartley** on drums.

Freddie Starr, who'd previously played with **Howie Casey**, later went solo enjoying some commercial success. **Keef Hartley** teamed up with future **Creation** bassist Bob Gardner in Blackpool and they went to London together. **Keef** then joined **The Artwoods** in 1964 but later had his own band. John Kelman's next outfit was **The Four Just Men** and Brian Woods played with **Heinz**.

Compilation appearances have included: *Peter Gunn Locomotion* and *Baby Blue* on *Liverpool 1963-1964, Vol. 2* (LP); *Who Told You?* on *Mersey Beat* (2-LP); *Baby Blue*, *Who Told You?* and *Peter Gunn Locomotion* on *Mersey Sounds* (2-LP); *Peter Gunn Locomotion* on *Mersey Beat 1962-1964* (2-LP); *Who Told You?* and *It's Shaking Time* on *RGM Rarities, Vol. 2* (CD); and *Peter Gunn Locomotion* and *It's Shaking Time* on *Rare 60's Beat Treasures, Vol. 5* (CD). (VJ)

Ringo Starr

				HCP
ALBUMS:	1	SENTIMENTAL JOURNEY	(Apple PCS 7101) 1970	SC 7
(up to	2	BEAUCOUPS OF BLUES	(Apple PAS 10002) 1970	SC -
1976)	3	RINGO	(Apple PCTC 252) 1973	7
	4	GOODNIGHT VIENNA	(Apple PCS 7168) 1974	30
	5	BLAST FROM YOUR PAST	(Apple PCS 7170) 1975	-
	6	RINGO'S ROTOGRAVURE	(Polydor 2302 040) 1976	-

NB: (3) reissued on CD (EMI CDEMS 1386) 1991 with extra cuts. (5) reissued on CD (Parlophone CDP 746 663 2) 1987, but deleted in 1989. (1) reissued on CD (Apple CDP 798 615 1) 1995.

			HCP
45s:	α	Steel	(ROR ROR 2001) 1971 -
(up to		It Don't Come Easy/	
1976)		Early 1970 (PS)	(Parlophone R 5898) 1971 4
		Back Off Boogaloo/Blindman (PS)	(Apple R 5944) 1972 2
		Photograph/Down And Out (PS)	(Apple R 5992) 1973 8
		You're Sixteen/Devil Woman (PS)	(Apple R 5995) 1974 4
		Only You/Call Me (PS)	(Apple R 6000) 1975 28
		Snookeroo/Oo-Wee	(Apple R 6004) 1975 -
		Oh My My/No No Song	(Apple R 6011) 1976 SC -
		A Dose Of Rock'n'Roll/Cryin'	(Polydor 2001 694) 1976 -
		You Don't Know Me At All/Cryin'	(Polydor 2001 695) 1976 -
		Hey Baby/Lady Gaye	(Polydor 2001 699) 1976 -
Reissue:		It Don't Come Easy/	
		Back Off boogaloo (PS)	(Old Gold OG 4513) 198? -

NB: α This was a one-sided promo-only interview disc for a reception at Liberty's store, which was available for one week only. It is valued by 'Record Collector' at £900.

Ringo always seemed the least likely of **The Beatles** to flourish when they embarked on their solo projects. He'd actually completed his first album before **The Beatles** split. Comprised of him singing showbiz standards using different producers for each track it made little impact. The second, recorded in Nashville was a considerable improvement utilising several carefully chosen musicians and specially commissioned ballads which were well-suited to his voice. He also achieved considerable commercial success with his first two singles, *It Don't Come Easy* and *Back Off Boogaloo*. Ringo had written *It Don't Come Easy* himself, but he got **George Harrison** to produce it and play guitar on it along with Stephen Stills. It peaked at No 4 in both the US and UK. His appearance at the **George Harrison**-arranged 'Concert For Bangladesh' on 1 August 1971 enabled him to remain in the public eye and in November of the same year he appeared in Frank Zappa's '200 Motels' in the dual role of Larry The Dwarf and Frank Zappa.

Alongside his burgeoning recording career, Ringo also continued to develop his film role. As early as 1969 he'd appeared, as a Mexican gardener, in the Italian/French film 'Candy' and in 1970 he'd played in a leading role with Peter Sellers in 'The Magic Christian'. In 1972 he played an outlaw called Candy in the spaghetti Western 'Blindman' and made his debut as a film director with 'Born To Boogie', a film of **T Rex** in concert. In early 1973 he starred as a teddy boy in 'That'll Be The Day'.

His next album, the lavishly-packaged *Ringo*, was produced by Richard Berry and included contributions from all **The Beatles**. It provided him with several hit singles - *Photograph* (which he'd co-written with **George Harrison**), which was actually a US No 1, as was his cover of Johnny Burnette's 1960 US hit, *You're Sixteen*, and *Oh My My*.

RINGO STARR - Sentimental Journey (LP).

Goodnight Vienna attempted the same formula. Using top LA sessionmen it was produced by Richard Perry but not on a par with his previous effort. It did, however, provide further hits, with Hoyt Axton's *No No Song* and a cover of The Platters' 1955 smash, *Only You*. He appeared as the Pope in Ken Russell's 'Lisztomania' the same month as he and his wife Maureen Cox were divorced. 1975 was rounded off nicely with the release of a *Greatest Hits* collection, *Blast From Your Past*. Having set up his own Ring' O Records label, he signed a new deal for himself with Polydor in the UK and Atlantic in the US.

In 1976 his *Ringo's Rotogravure*, produced by Arif Mardin, was released. Again, utilising several top session players, it brought him further commercial success and spawned a further US hit single, *A Dose Of Rock'n'Roll*. In November he appeared, along with several other stars, in The Band's 'The Last Waltz' farewell concert. As we leave the time frame of this book he continued to enjoy considerable commercial success both sides of the Atlantic but increasingly spent his time in America.

After **The Beatles** broke up in 1970, Ringo became friendly with interior designer Robin Cruickshank, who'd done work for Ringo at his house and at Apple's Saville Row headquarters. Ringo was so impressed with the results that he bought into the company and changed its name to Ringo Or Robin Ltd. (ROR). Based at a shop in Rathbone Street, the new firm produced fashionable mirrors, paperweights, dining tables and fireplaces, all made from shiny materials like glass, plastic, chrome and steel. To promote a ROR Exhibition Ringo recorded *Steel*, a one-sided seven inch single for Apple in 1971 (ROR 2001). The Exhibition was held at Liberty's in Regent Street from 14th - 25th September 1971 and copies of the single on which Ringo promoted the new company over a formless electronic backing track were given away free. Only two are known to have survived - it is not known how many were pressed. According to Record Collector these are now valued at £500 each.

The CD reissue of *Ringo* includes three extra cuts, both sides of his debut 45 and the non-album flip side from 1973 *Down And Out*.

I'm The Greatest can also be heard on *Songs Lennon And McCartney Gave Away* (LP). (VJ)

Starry Eyed and Laughing

Personnel:			
	ROSS McGEENEY	vcls, ld gtr	ABC
	TONY POOLE	vcls, 12 string gtr	ABCDE
	NICK BROWN	drms	B
	STEVE HALL	bs	B
	MICK WACKFORD	drms	CDE
	IAIN WHITMORE	bs, vcls	CD
	ROGER KELLY	vcls, lead gtr	DE

ALBUMS:	1(C)	STARRY EYED AND LAUGHING	(CBS 80450) 1974
(up to 1976)	2(C)	THOUGHT TALK	(CBS 80907) 1975

NB. (2) also released in the USA by Warner. *That Was Now And This Is Then* (Aurora AUR 02) 2004 is a 2-CD set reissuing both their albums and assorted bonuses.

45s:			
(up to 1976)	Money Is No Friend Of Mine/See Your Face	(CBS 2686) 1974
	Nobody Home/Closer To You Now	(CBS 3036) 1975
	Good Love/Down The Street	(CBS 3455) 1975
	Song On The Road/	
	Don't Give Me A Hard Time	(CBS 4577) 1976

Originally forming in Northampton in May 1973 with just McGeeney and Poole, they started out playing a Byrds-influenced jangling guitar-style rock. Line-up B was short-lived but the band soon stabilised with line-up C. Their debut album, which mostly comprised Poole/McGeeney material, was still very derivative of The Byrds. Still, it's underrated and included some fine guitar interplay - at its best on the track *Everybody*. This was less so on *Thought Talk* on which the orchestrated *Fools Gold* and *One Foot In The Boat* stand out.

After a US tour in Autumn 1975 McGeeney left with Roger Kelly coming in as a replacement. Whitmore was next to depart in Spring 1976. They abbreviated their name to Starry Eyed for a couple more singles but when the hoped-for Chart success didn't happen they quit. (VJ)

PSYCHEDELIA VOL. 1 (Comp LP) including State Of Mickey And Tommy.

The Stars

Circus Days, Vol. 1 (LP) and *Circus Days Vol. 1 & 2* (CD) include a track called *Auntie Annie's Place* from 1967 by this band. We're talking late sixties pop here, quite commercial, high-pitched vocals and some pleasant instrumentation, but obviously it didn't happen. (VJ)

The State Of Micky and Tommy

Personnel:	TOMMY BROWN	A
	MICK JONES	A

EPs:	1(A)	STATE OF MICKY AND TOMMY	
			(Mercury 152095 MCE) 196?
	2 (A)	FRISCO BAY	(Mercury 152102 MCE) 196?

NB: (1) and (2) were French releases. (1) contains: *With Love From One To Five/I Know What I Would Do/Sunday's Leaving/Quelqu'un Qui*. (2) contains *Frisco Bay/Nobody Knows Where You've Been/Julien Waits/Goodtime Music*.

45s:	α	With Love From One To Five/	
		I Know What I Would Do	(Mercury MF 996) 1967 R3
		Frisco Bay/	
		Nobody Knows Where You've Been	(Mercury MF 1009) 1967 R2

NB: α has been reissued (Mercury MF 996) in a limited edition of 500 reproduced from the French jukebox release with a large centre hole.

This duo comprised Mick Jones and Tommy Brown. They had played together in an early sixties instrumental group called Nero and The Gladiators and then as J & B, recording a soulish 45 for Polydor, before assuming this monicker. Their best known song *With Love From One To Five* is a great **Move**-influenced pop-psych number. It featured a superb string arrangement. The flip *I Know What I Would Do* is a tougher composition, introduced by manic laughter and including dual guitar/sitar leads with background organ. Whilst their follow-up *Frisco Bay* was nondescript its flip side is another hidden treasure. Both UK 45s (and the French EPs) are now very collectable. The duo also recorded as **Nimrod**.

They later backed Johnny Halliday (the French equivalent to Tom Jones) during the late sixties.

Unfortunately, Tommy Brown died in the mid-seventies, but Mick Jones later enjoyed success in Foreigner.

Compilation appearances have included:- *Grabbit The Rabbit* and *Mohamed Ali* (as Rosko with Mickey and Tommy) on *Made In England, Vol. 2* (CD); *I Know What I Would Do* on *Psychedelia, Vol. 1* (LP); *Nobody Knows Where You've Been* and *With Love From 9 To 5* on *Rubble, Vol. 15 - 5,000 Seconds Over Toyland* (LP); *Nobody Knows Where You've Been* on *Rubble, Vol. 8* (CD) and *The Best Of Rubble Collection, Vol. 3* (CD); *With Love From 9 To 5* on *Rubble, Vol. 9* (CD) and *Chocolate Soup For*

Diabetics, Vol. 2 (LP); and *I Know* on *Electric Psychedelic Sitar Headswirlers, Vol. 2* (CD). (VJ)

The Statesmen (1)

45s:	Look Around/I'm Wondering	(Decca F 11687) 1963
	I've Just Fallen In Love/	
	It's All Happening	(Fontana TF 432) 1964

This Manchester beat group once backed Little Richard and Fats Domino on a tour of the UK. Their music hasn't aged well, though. (VJ)

The Statesmen (2)

| ALBUM: | 1 | FIVE PLUS ONE | (Studio Republic) 1963 R3 |

A private label recording from September 1963, just as the beat boom was taking hold. It features a guest female singer on about half the tracks - the remainder have lead male vocals. The sound ranges from early beat group albums to Phil Spector's girl group sound. There are strong versions of Goffin/King's *One Fine Day* and *I Want To Stay Here* and the Carter/Lewis song *That's What I Want*. (VJ)

Static

| 45: | When You Went Away/ | |
| | Let Me Tell You | (Page One POF 039) 1967 |

An obscure late sixties pop 45. (VJ)

Status Quo

Personnel:	JOHN COUGHLAN	drms	AB
	ALAN LANCASTER	bs	AB
	ROD LYNES	organ, vcls	A
	RICK PARFITT	gtr, vcls	AB
	FRANCIS ROSSI	gtr, vcls	AB

HCP

ALBUMS:	1(A)	PICTURESQUE MATCHSTICKABLE MESSAGES	
(up to		FROM THE STATUS QUO	
1976)		(mono/stereo)	(Pye N(S)PL 18220) 1968 R2 -
	2(A)	SPARE PARTS (mono/stereo)	
			(Pye N(S)PL 18301) 1968 R2 -
	3(A)	MESSAGES FROM STATUS QUO	
			(Cadet LSP 315) 1968 -

STATUS QUO - Picturesque Matchstickable Messages From The Status Quo (LP).

STATUS QUO - Spare Parts (LP).

4(A)	STATUS QUO-TATIONS	
	(mono/stereo)	(Marble Arch MAL(S) 1193) 1969 R1/R2 -
5(A)	MA KELLY'S GREASY SPOON	(Pye NSPL 18344) 1970 -
6(A)	DOG OF TWO HEADS	(Pye NSPL 18371) 1971 -
7( )	BEST OF STATUS QUO	(Pye NSPL 18402) 1972 32
8( )	GOLDEN HOUR OF STATUS QUO	(Pye GH 556) 1973 -
9( )	PILEDRIVER	(Vertigo 6360 082) 1973 5
10( )	HELLO!	(Vertigo 6360 098) 1974 SC 1
11( )	QUO	(Vertigo 9102 001) 1974 2
12( )	ON THE LEVEL	(Vertigo 9102 002) 1975 1
13( )	GOLDEN HOUR OF STATUS QUO, 2 (DOWN	
	THE DUSTPIPE)	(Pye GH 604) 1975 20
14( )	THE REST OF STATUS QUO	(Pye PKL 5546) 1976 -
15( )	BLUE FOR YOU	(Vertigo 9102 006) 1976 1

NB: (1), (2), (5) and (6) reissued on PRT in 1987. (5) and (6) reissued on vinyl. (1) reissued on CD (Castle CLACD 168) 1990 and again on CD (Essential! ESM CD 620) 1998, with bonus cuts and enhanced packaging. (1) also reissued again as a remastered 2-CD set (Castle CMEDD 718) as an expanded edition containing the album in mono and stereo along with BBC sessions and early material from their days as **The Spectres** and **Traffic Jam**. (2) reissued on vinyl (Earmark 42032) 200? (2) reissued on CD (Castle Classics CLACD 205) 1990 and again as a 2-CD set (Castle CMEDD 717) in an expanded deluxe edition with mono and stereo versions of the songs and some previously unissued tracks. (5) reissued on CD (Castle CLACD 169) 1990. (5) reissued on CD (Essential! ESM CD 621) 1998, with bonus cuts and enhanced packaging. (5) reissued on vinyl (Earmark 42033) 200? and on CD (Castle Music CMQCD 754) remastered with 10 additional rare and previously unreleased tracks from 7" singles and BBC sessions and housed in an attractive slipcase with a detailed booklet. (6) reissued on CD (Castle Classics CLACD 206) 1990. (6) reissued on vinyl and on CD (Castle Music CMQCD 755) with five bonus tracks, including rough mixes, Peel sessions and 45 'B' sides housed in a tasteful slipcase with an expanded booklet. (8) reissued on CD (Knight KGHCD 110) 1990. (9) reissued on CD (Vertigo 88417 12) 1991 and (Repertoire REP 4119-WP), also in 1991. (9) reissued again on CD (Mercury 9825977) remastered with one bonus track and an informative booklet. (10) reissued on CD (Vertigo 8481722) 1991 and again on CD (Vertigo 9825942) remastered and with the non-album track *Joanne* added. (11) reissued on CD (Vertigo 8480892) 1991. (12) reissued on CD (Vertigo 8481742) 1991.

From The Beginning (PRT PYX 4007) 1988 is a reasonable hits collection from their Pye years divided equally between their pop and boogie years, it's also on CD (PYC 4007). Harder to find now is *The File Series* (2-LP) (Pye FILD 005) 1977, which was also issued the same year as *The Status Quo File Series* (2-LP) (PRT FILD 005) with a different sleeve. There are also loads of CD compilations. I'll just list some of them here:- *B Sides and Rarities* (Castle Collector CCSCD 271) 1990, which also includes tracks they recorded as **The Spectres** and **Traffic Jam** prior to becoming **Status Quo**; *Best Of 1968-71* (Pickwick PWKS 4080) 1991, *The Best Of Status Quo (The Early Years)* (PRT CDNSP 7773) 1986; *The Best Of Status Quo* (Pickwick PWKS 4087P) 1991; *C.90 Collector* (Legacy GHCD 3) 1989; *Collection: Status Quo* (Castle Collector CCSCD 114) 1988; the CD set *The Early Works* (Essential ESBCD 136) 1990, which also includes their recordings as **The Spectres** and **Traffic Jam**; *Introspective: Status Quo* (Baktabak CINT 5003) 1990; *Nightriding: Status Quo* (Nightriding KNCD 10018) 1990; *Quotations Vol, 1: The Early Years* (PRT PYC 6024) 1987; *Quotations Vol. 2 (Alternatives)* (PRT PYC 6025) 1987; *Twelve Gold Bars, Vol. 1* (Vertigo 800 062-2) 1984 and *Vol. 2* (Vertigo 822 985-2) 1984. *The Other Side Of Status Quo* (Connoisseur VSOP CD 213) 1995 compiles some of their Vertigo 45s from the 1973-1992 era, concentrating mostly on eighties material. So there's definitely no shortage of choice. *The Singles Collection 1966-1973* (Castle CCS CD 821) 1998 is an excellent compilation, which has been revamped again

(Castle Music CMDD 015) and documents the different styles of his era blending their some of their original singles with rare out-takes and alternate mixes. *Singles Collection 1968-1969* (7-CD) (Vertigo CMKBX 400) is the complete run of their sixties singles in a special collectors box - all individually numbered. Each CD comes in a replica picture sleeve and the package includes a fold-out poster booklet containing cuttings and pictures from the period. *Rockers Rollin' - Quo In Time, 1972-2000* (Universal) 2001 is a 4-CD set compiling their material for Vertigo. *The Technicolour Dreams Of The Status Quo* (Castle CMDDD 152) 2001 compiles their sixties output, including their rare early **Spectres/Traffic Jam** recordings, a few outtakes and more. *The 70s Singles Box* (Castle CMKBX 272) 2001 is a 6-CD box set. *Down The Dustpipe - 70s Pye Collection* (Castle CMRCD 273) 2001 is an anthology of material from the 1970-1971 era. *The Sixties Box Set* (Castle) 2002 comprises their seven Pye singles. *Complete Pye Collection* (3-CD) (Sanctuary Midline SMETD 003) anthologises their frantic five years at the label. *Matchstick Men (The Psychedelic Years)* (CD) (Select SELCD 555) is a 20-track collection of their psychedelic era recordings.

EP:	1 STATUS QUO LIVE!	(Vertigo QUO 13) 1975

			HCP
45s:	Pictures Of Matchstick Men/		
(up to	Gentlemen Joe's Sidewalk Cafe	(Pye 7N 17449) 1968	7
1976)	Black Veils Of Melancholy/		
	To Be Free	(Pye 7N 17497) 1968	SC -
	Ice In The Sun/		
	When My Mind Is Not Live	(Pye 7N 17581) 1968	8
α	Technicolour Dreams/		
	Paradise Flats	(Pye 7N 17650) 1968	R6/R4 -
	Make Me Stay A Little Longer/		
	Auntie Nellie	(Pye 7N 17665) 1969	SC -
	Are You Growing Tired Of My Love/		
	So Ends Another Life	(Pye 7N 17728) 1969	SC 46
	The Price Of Love/		
	Little Miss Nothing	(Pye 7N 17825) 1969	SC -
	Down The Dustpipe/		
	Face Without A Soul	(Pye 7N 17907) 1970	12
	In My Chair/Gergundula	(Pye 7N 17998) 1970	21
	Tune To The Music/Good Thinking	(Pye 7N 45077) 1970	-
	Paper Plane/Softer Ride	(Vertigo 6059 071) 1972	8
	Caroline/Joanne	(Vertigo 6059 085) 1973	5
	Mean Girl/Everything	(Pye 7N 45229) 1973	20
	Gergundula/Lakky Lady	(Pye 7N 45253) 1973	-
	Break The Rules/Lonely Night	(Vertigo 6059 101) 1974	8
	Down Down/Nightride	(Vertigo 6059 114) 1974	1
χ	Down Down/		
	Break The Rules (Some PS)	(Lyntone LYN 3145/5) 1975	SC/-
	Roll Over Lay Down/		
	Gergundula Junior's Wailing	(Vertigo QUO 13) 1975	9
	Rain/Is There A Better Way	(Vertigo 6059 133) 1976	7
	Mystery Song/Drifting Away	(Vertigo 6059 146) 1976	11
	Wild Side Of Life/		
	All Through The Night	(Vertigo 6059 153) 1976	9
Reissues:	Mean Girl/In My Chair	(Pye 7N 6095) 1978	-
	Pictures Of Matchstick Men/		

Ice In The Sun	(Pye 7N 46103) 1978 -
β Pictures Of Matchstick Men/	
Down The Dustpipe (PS)	Pye FBS 2) 1979 -
In My Chair/Gergundula (PS)	(Pye 7P 103) 1979 -
Caroline (live at the N.E.C.)/	
Dirty Water (PS)	(Vertigo QUO 10) 1982 13
Mean Girl/In My Chair	(Old Gold OG 9142) 1982 -
Pictures Of Matchstick Men/	
Down The Dustpipe	(Old Gold OG 9298) 1983 -
Caroline/Down Down	(Old Gold OG 9566) 1985 -

NB: α withdrawn (R6), demos are more common (R4). It's now very rare and sought-after by **Quo** collectors. It was valued at circa £1,000 in the December 2004 edition of 'Record Collector'. β On yellow vinyl. χ A Smiths Crisps flexidisc, a few with 'Smiths' PS.

Status Quo is one of Britain's best-loved and most durable bands. They started out as a psychedelic pop band and *Pictures Of Matchstick Men* in particular was a pretty memorable single but after a few lean years they remodelled themselves as a hard-rock boogie band in 1970 and fuelled by their reputation as an awesome live act have continued in this style ever since. In the period up to 1990 they chalked up 15 Top Five albums (including four No 1's) and 21 Top Ten singles.

Their origins lay in South London where they started life as **The Spectres** and later became **Traffic Jam**. They changed their name to **Status Quo** when they signed to Pye in November 1967. Starting life as a rather lightweight psychedelic pop group, they soon produced a string of 45s which featured Rossi and Parfitt's rather catchy guitar playing, of which *Pictures Of Matchstick Men, Ice In The Sun, Black Veils Of Melancholy, When My Mind Is Not Live* and *Are You Growing Tired Of My Love* were the best.

Their debut album, aside from their singles, included covers of The Lemon Pipers' *Green Tambourine*, **The Bee Gees** *Spicks And Specks* and Tommy Roe's *Sheila* yet surprisingly, perhaps couldn't break through into the Charts. Another of its tracks, *Technicolour Dreams* was issued as a single in November 1968 and then withdrawn shortly after, making it the rarest **Status Quo** recording.

Their second album *Spare Parts* registered disappointing sales considering their singles and several Radio 1 sessions meant they were well known. A notable moment on the album is the trippy *Mr Mind Detector*.

The release of *Ma Kelly's Greasy Spoon* in 1970 marked a distinct change in musical direction. Their by now passé psychedelic pop sound was replaced by an unimaginative 12-bar boogie sound which would bring them phenomenal success in future years. It included a cover of **Steamhammer**'s *Junior's Wailing*, which became one of their most popular live numbers. After their final album for Pye (excluding compilations), *Dog Of Two Heads*, was released in 1971 they signed to Phonogram's rock subsidiary label, Vertigo. *Dog Of Two Heads* was notable for the inclusion of *Mean Girl* and *Gergundula*.

By now they had built up a solid cult following with their no-nonsense 12-bar boogie sound and *Piledriver*, released in 1973, became the first of a string of phenomenally successful albums as the band became an archetype for the UK heavy metal movement. However boring their music might have become there's no denying that they were a helluva live band.

Hello entered the Album Charts at No 1. Indeed each of their seventies studio albums made the Top 5 and they enjoyed a number of hits, too, most notably with *Down Down* (a No 1), *Roll Over Lay Down*, *Paper Plane*, *Caroline*, the lengthy 10-minute *Forty-Five Hundred Times* and the touching *Softer Ride*. They have continued to enjoy commercial success throughout the decades. The CD reissue of *Hello* includes the non-album bonus track *Joanne*.

After the release of *Just Supposin'* in 1980 their drummer John Coughlan left the band to form his own group Diesel. His replacement ex-Original Mirror's drummer Pete Kircher appeared on 1981's *Never Too Late*. In the early eighties there was considerable friction between Alan Lancaster and Francis Rossi and Rick Parfitt and Lancaster left the band after performing with them at Live Aid. He later went to court to try to prevent them using the 'Status Quo' name but lost and Rossi and Parfitt put together a new line-up. Comprising keyboardist Andy Bown, bassist John Edwards and drummer Jeff Rich alongside Rossi and Parfitt the line-up continued to produce hit albums and Top Ten singles with the same aplomb as earlier ones.

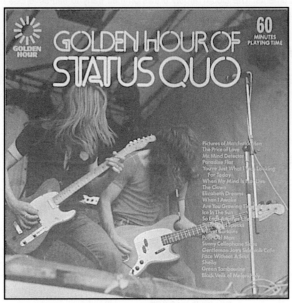

STATUS QUO - Golden Hour Of (LP).

The *Singles Collection* compiles all 26 songs from their 13 Pye singles, both sides of their five **Spectres/Traffic Jam** 45s and 13 previously unissued recordings.

The 4-CD box set issued by Universal covers their period with Vertigo from 1972 until 2000. The 68-song collection includes 17 previously unissued cuts as well as other rarities. Of course all their hits and classic album tracks are there too. It comes with a 48-page booklet containing many previously unpublished photos, memorabilia and a foreword by Francis Rossi and Mick Parfitt.

Down The Dustpipe - 70s Pye Collection compiles non-album minor hits, singles that might have been and significant later album tracks.

The 70s Singles Box is a 6-CD set which includes reproductions of six rare European picture sleeves and a poster.

The Sixties Box Set comprises their seven Pye singles, including the rare and withdrawn in the UK *Technicolour Dream*. The set is packaged in a five-by-five box with a fold-out poster booklet featuring press cuttings from the era. Each single came in a card repro of a rare European picture sleeve. This is a nice package for collectors.

The Techicolour Dreams Of The Status Quo will delight fans of their psychedelic phase. Alongside their two late sixties albums for Pye in their entirety and their late sixties 45s, you can also hear their rare **Spectres** and **Traffic Jam** incarnation releases alongside a few out-takes and new stereo mixes. Add to this sleevenotes by David Wells and a booklet full of rare covers and photos and you've got the definitive record of their sixties years.

Compilation appearances have included: *You're Just What I Was Looking For* on *Maximum '65* (CD); *Black Veils of Melancholy* on *Paisley Pop - Pye Psych (& Other Colours) 1966-1969* (CD); *Make Me Stay A Little Bit Longer* on *Pop Inside The Sixties, Vol. 3* (CD) and *Quick Before They Catch Us* (CD); *Pictures Of Matchstick Men* on *Psychedelic Visions* (CD) and *The Sixties File* (2-LP); The *Reading Festival 1973* (CD) also includes their performance of *Don't Waste My Time* from that particular event. More recently, *Mean Girl* resurfaced on the CD set *Rock Of Ages, Four Decades Of Heavy Rock 1962-2002*; *Forty Five Hundred Times* re-emerged on the 2-CD set *Rock Resurrection*; whilst *Down The Dustpipe* got fresh exposure on the CD set *Radio Caroline Calling - 70's Flashback* and *Sunshine Day A Taste Of The 70's* (CD), whilst *Mr. Mind Detector* and *You're Just What I Was Looking For Today* have been compiled on *Hot Smoke & Sassafras - Psychedelic Pstones, Vol 1* (CD); *Junior's Wailing* and *Down The Dustpipe* can be heard on the 3-CD box set *Ars Longa Vita Brevis: A Compendium Of Progressive Rock 1967-1974* and *Auntie Nellie* got fresh exposure on *Haunted - Psychedelic Pstones, Vol 2* (CD). *Pictures of Matchstick Men* and *Ice In The Sun* have been compiled on *Hits Of The Swinging Sixties* (CD). Finally, *When My Mind Is Not Live* re-emerged on the 4-CD box set *Acid Drops, Spacedust and Flying Saucers* and *Pictures of Matchstick Men* has resurfaced on the 4-CD *Nuggets II* box set. (VJ)

STEALER'S WHEEL - Stealer's Wheel (LP).

STEAMHAMMER - Steamhammer (CD).

Stavely Makepeace

Personnel:	NIGEL FLETCHER	drms	A
	STEPHEN JOHNSON	bs	A
	ROBERT WOODWARD	piano	A

45s:	(I Want To Love You Like A) Mad Dog/		
(up to	Greasy Haired Woman	(Pyramid PYR 6072)	1969
1976) α	Tarzan Harvey/Reggae Denny	(Pyramid PYR 6082)	1970
	Edna (Let Me Sing My Beautiful Song)/		
	Tarzan Harvey	(Concord CON 008)	1970
	Smokey Mountain Rhythm Review/		
	Rampant On The Rage	(Concord CON 013)	1970
	Give Me That Pistol/The Sundance	(Concord CON 018)	1970
	Walking Through The Blue Grass/		
	Swings And Roundabouts	(Spark SRL 1066)	1972
	Slippery Rock 70's/		
	Don't Ride A Pillion Paula	(Spark SRL 1081)	1972
	Prima Donna/Swings And Roundabouts	(Spark SRL 1085)	1973
	Cajun Band/Memories Of Your Love	(Deram DM 366)	1973
	Runaround Sue/		
	There's A Wall Between Us	(Deram DM 423)	1974

NB: α Unissued, but test pressings exist.

Stavely Makepeace is the alter ego of **Lieutenant Pigeon**. The band had no albums at the time but recorded several singles. In addition *The Scrap Iron Rhythm Review* (RPM RPM 280) collects the duo's experimental pop recordings which utilised tape loops, sound effects and assorted instruments. The album largely draws on their early to mid-seventies output. (VJ)

Staverton Bridge

ALBUM:	1 STAVERTON BRIDGE	(Saydisc SDL 266) 197? R1

No other details known. (VJ)

Stealer's Wheel

Personnel:	JOE EGAN	vcls, keyb'ds	ABCDE
	ROGER BROWN		AB
	RAB NOAKES		AB
	GERRY RAFFERTY	gtr, vcls	ABC E
	IAN CAMPBELL	bs	B
	ROD COOMBES	drms	CD
	PAUL PILNICK	gtr	CD
	TONY WILLIAMS	bs	C
	LUTHER GROSVENOR	gtr, vcls	D
	DELISLE HARPER	bs	D

ALBUMS: 1(C) STEALER'S WHEEL   (A&M AMLH 68121) 1973
(up to   2(E) FERGUSLIE PARK   (A&M AMLH 68209) 1974
1976)   3(E) RIGHT OR WRONG   (A&M AMLH 68293) 1975

NB: (1) reissued on CD (Lemon CDLEM 24) 2004. There was also *Best Of Stealer's Wheel* (Music For Pleasure 50501) 1981 and *The Best Of Stealer's Wheel* (Document CSAP LP 106) 1990, also on CD (CSAP CD 106) 1990. (2) reissued on CD (Lemon CD LEM 37) 2004. (3) reissued on CD (Lemon CDLEM 57) 2005.

			HCP
45s:	Late Again/I Get By	(A&M AMS 7033) 1972	-
(up to	Stuck In The Middle With You/Jose	(A&M AMS 7036) 1972	8
1976)	You Put Something Better Inside Me/		
	Next To Me	(A&M AMS 7046) 1972	-
	Everything Will Turn Out Fine/		
	Johnny's Song	(A&M AMS 7079) 1973	33
	Star/What More Could I Want	(A&M AMS 7094) 1973	25
	Right Or Wrong/This Morning	(A&M AMS 7152) 1975	-
	Found My Way To You/Wishbone	(A&M AMS 7170) 1975	-
Reissue:	Stuck In The Middle With You/Star	(Old Gold 9148) 1982	-

Stealer's Wheel was formed by two Scottish folk singers **Gerry Rafferty** and Joe Egan, who had previously sung harmonies on **Rafferty**'s 1971 solo album *Can I Have My Money Back?* **Rafferty** incidentally, had earlier played in **Humblebums**. Brown, **Noakes** and Campbell all left the band before any recordings were made. **Rafferty** and Egan then put together line-up (C), which included Paul Pilnick (once of **The Big Three** and later **Badger**).

The band's debut album was full of strong harmonies and was well received. Three of the **Rafferty**/Egan compositions on the album were issued as 45s and gradually one of them *Stuck In The Middle With You*, wound its way into the Top Ten. It also got to No 6 in the US. Ironically by then, though, **Rafferty** had left the band and Williams had been given the push. Harper and Grosvenor (later Ariel Bender in **Mott The Hoople**) were brought in to replace them, but when the song achieved commercial success **Rafferty** rejoined the band and everyone else (except Egan) was ousted.

The song received a second wind and a new audience when Quentin Tarantino used it in a 'Reservoir Dogs' torture scene. Apparently, Paul Simon described it as his favourite song ever.

Rafferty and Egan recorded *Ferguslie Park* (which was named after a district of their home town in Scotland, Paisley) with assistance from various session musicians. Like their debut this album was also produced by Leiber and Stoller and again it was full of strong harmonies. Unlike its predecessor it didn't produce a major hit though there were a couple of minor ones - *Everything Will Turn Out Fine* (also No 49 in the US) and *Star* (also No 29 in US). *Good Businessman* is a strong opening track, whilst *What More Could You Want* typifies their easy-going hit sound.

Favouring a change of approach **Rafferty** and Egan started working with a new producer, Mentor Williams. However, a series of problems with backing

STEAMHAMMER - Steamhammer Mk II (CD).

STEAMHAMMER - Mountains (CD).

musicians meant the duo couldn't make live appearances for some months and by the time their next album, *Right Or Wrong*, was released they didn't have much of an audience to receive it and in any case interpersonal relationships between **Rafferty** and Egan had reached an all time low. Despite this the album was solid. *Found My Way To You* has fine harmonies and *Benediction* and *This Morning* are also highlights. When the band split **Rafferty** embarked on a successful solo career. (VJ)

Steam Beating Association

This was an obscure band. The *Dustbin Full Of Rubbish* (LP) compilation includes the previously unreleased demo tape backtrack *Backstage Gold* from 1966 by them. This undistinguished effort need not detain the listener though. (VJ)

Steamhammer

Personnel:	STEVE DAVY	bs, vcls	ABCD
	MARTIN PUGH	gtr, vcls	ABCDEF
	MARTIN QUITTENTON	gtr	AB
	MICHAEL RUSHTON	drms	A
	KIERAN WHITE	hrmnca, gtr, vcls	ABCDE
	MICKY WALLER	drms	BCD
	HAROLD McNAIR	flute, sax	C
	STEVE JOLLIFFE	sax, flute, keyb'ds	D
	MICK BRADLEY	drms	E
	LOUIS CENNAMO	bs	EF
	IAN ELLIS	vcls, gtr	F
	JOHN LINGWOOD	drms	F

NB: Louis Cennamo played on their German *Speech* album and performed on a few tours.

ALBUMS: 1(A) STEAMHAMMER   (CBS (S) 63611) 1968 R1
        2(B) STEAMHAMMER Mk II (CBS (S) 63694) 1969 R1
        3(C) MOUNTAINS   (B&C CAS 1024) 1970 R1

NB: All their albums were issued on the Bellaphon label in Germany. (1) reissued on vinyl Reflection (RELF 1) 1970 (SC). (1) reissued on CD (Repertoire REP-4235-WY) 1992 and again on vinyl and CD (Akarma AK 234). (2) reissued on vinyl (Reflection RELF 12) 1970 (SC). (2) reissued on CD (Repertoire REP-4236-WY) 1992 with four bonus tracks. (2) reissued again on vinyl and CD (Akarma AK 243) - the CD version has one bonus cut *Blues For Passing People*. (3) reissued on Repertoire (REP 4066-WZ) 1991 and again on vinyl and CD (Akarma AK 203). *Speech*, their German only release, is also available on CD (Repertoire REP 4139-WZ) 1991 and again on CD (Akarma AK 263).

45s: Junior's Wailing/Windmill   (CBS 4141) 1969
       Autumn Song/Blues For Passing People (CBS 4496) 1969
       Junior's Wailing/You'll Never Know (Reflection HRS 9) 1971

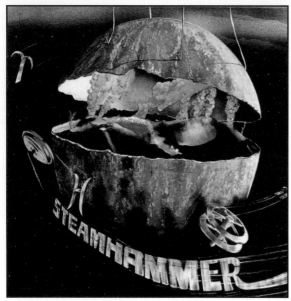

STEAMHAMMER - Speech (CD).

Steamhammer started out as a blues-rock band in Worthing, Sussex, but gradually developed into a more heavy progressive style. Their debut *Steamhammer* included the self-penned *Junior's Wailing*, which was later covered by **Status Quo**. Indeed it became an important part of **Status Quo**'s live act as they evolved into a 12-bar boogie band. Pugh and Quittenton assisted **Rod Stewart** on his first album and Quittenton stayed with **Stewart** co-writing *Maggie May* with him and playing mandolin on the million-selling disc. Harold McNair joined in July 1969 on flute and sax, but left the same month. When Steve Jolliffe (ex-Tangerine Dream) joined, their music on *Steamhammer Mk II* became jazzier and all the better for his harpsichord parts. At their best, as they proved on cuts like *Supposed To Be Free*, *Turn Around*, *Passing Through*, *Windmill* and *Autumn Song*, they were capable of melodic, progressive rock with some pleasant woodwind. Often, though, on tracks like *Johnny Carl Morten* and *6/8 For Amiran*, they over-utilised brass and ended up with some very messy arrangements. *Passing Through* was also included on CBS's very popular budget-priced (2-LP) *Fill Your Head With Rock* compilation. Former **Jeff Beck Group** member Micky Waller, who joined in March 1969, left after this album to join Silver Metre along with Joliffe (who joined Tangerine Dream) and Davy. Former **Methuselah** drummer Mick Bradley and ex-**Renaissance** bassist Louis Cennamo joined in their place. However, both Davy and Cennamo figured on their 1970 album *Mountains*.

Kieran White left in late 1971 and Martin Quittenton rejoined for recording only. The band suffered a further blow when Mick Bradley died of leukaemia on 8 February 1972. John Lingwood replaced him. Ex-**Clouds** member Ian Ellis joined at the same time.

They recorded a further album to these listed above, *Speech*, which was only released in Germany (Brain 1009) 1972 and was their magnum opus full of superb guitar work from Martin Pugh. Ian Ellis departed to the **Alex Harvey Band** and the band changed name to Axis in June 1973.

Brain also reissued *Mountains* and *Speech* as a double package, *This Is Steamhammer* (Brain 2/1043) in 1974. The CD reissue of *Steamhammer Mk II* on Repertoire also includes both sides of their two 1969 singles.

Levinia has been compiled on the 3-CD box set *Ars Longa Vita Brevis: A Compendium Of Progressive Rock 1967-1974*. This is certainly a band worth investigating. (VJ/JM)

The Steampacket

Personnel:			
	BRIAN AUGER	keyb'ds, vcls	A
	LONG JOHN BALDRY	vcls	A
	VIC BRIGGS	gtr	A
	RICHARD BROWN	bs	A
	JULIE DRISCOLL	vcls	A
	MICK FLEETWOOD	drms	A
	PETER GREEN	gtr	A
	ROD STEWART	vcls	A
	MICKEY WALLER	drms	A

ALBUM: 1(A)   STEAMPACKET - THE FIRST SUPERGROUP
(Charly CR 30020) 1977

NB: There were also two albums, *The Steampacket* and *Places and Faces* released by Byg Records in France. (1) was reissued on Decal (LIK 14) 1987 with the tracks in a different order. There's also a CD of their material, *Steampacket/First R&B Festival* (Repertoire REP 4090-WZ) 1991.

This was a short-lived R&B package show who played around the clubs and ballrooms between late 1965 and late 1966. As you can see they had a very distinguished membership. **Long John Baldry** returned to solo work after this venture. **Julie Driscoll**, who also worked as a solo artist during this period, teamed up with **Brian Auger Trinity** and **Rod Stewart** joined **Shotgun Express**. No recording output resulted at the time but Charly released a retrospective album of their material in 1977. This contains three instrumentals and **Brian Auger**'s organ work is very much to the fore on two of these. **Rod Stewart** takes the vocal slot on a version of Marvin Gaye's *Can I Get A Witness*, whilst **Long John Baldry** plays the same role on Julie London's *Cry Me A River*. Really, though, the record and band is more significant for its historical significance than the quality of its music.

The band was also featured on *The Roots Of British Rock, Vol 6*. (VJ)

Steeleye Span

Personnel:			
	TIM HART	gtr, vcls	ABCD
	ASHLEY HUTCHINGS	bs	AB
	MADDY PRIOR	vcls	ABCD
	GAY WOODS	vcls	A
	TERRY WOODS	gtr, vcls	A
	MARTIN CARTHY	gtr, vcls	B
	PETER KNIGHT	fiddle	BCD
	BOB JOHNSON	gtr, vcls	CD
	RICK KEMP	bs	CD
	NIGEL PEGRUM	drms	D
			HCP

ALBUMS:	1(A)	HARK! THE VILLAGE WAIT		
(up to		(w/insert)	(RCA SF 8113) 1970	SC -
1976)	2(B)	PLEASE TO SEE THE KING		
			(B&C CAS 1029) 1971	SC 45
	3(B)	TEN MAN MOP	(Pegasus PEG 9) 1971	SC -
	4(C)	BELOW THE SALT	(Chrysalis CHR 1008) 1972	43
	5(-)	INDIVIDUALLY AND COLLECTIVELY (Compilation)		
			(Charisma CS 5) 1972	SC -
	6(D)	PARCEL OF ROGUES	(Chrysalis CHR 1046) 1973	26
	7(-)	ALMANACK (Compilation)	(Charisma CS 12) 1973	-
	8(D)	NOW WE ARE SIX	(Chrysalis CHR 1053) 1974	13
	9(D)	COMMONER'S CROWN	(Chrysalis CHR 1071) 1975	21
	10(D)	ALL AROUND MY HAT	(Chrysalis CHR 1091) 1975	7
	11(D)	ROCKET COTTAGE	(Chrysalis CHR 1123) 1976	41

NB: (1) reissued on vinyl (United Artists UAG 29160) 1971, again on vinyl (Mooncrest CREST 22) 1974 and again on vinyl (Mooncrest CREST 003) 1991. (2) reissued on vinyl (Mooncrest CREST 8) 1974 and again on vinyl (Mooncrest CREST

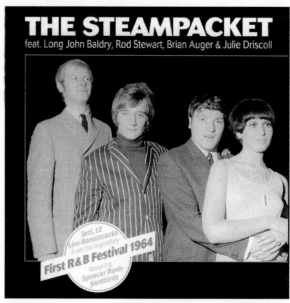

STEAMPACKET - First R&B Festival 1964 (CD).

STEELEYE SPAN - Parcel Of Rogues (LP).

005) 1991. (3) reissued on vinyl (Mooncrest CREST 9) 1974 and again on vinyl (Mooncrest CREST 009) 1991. (1) reissued on CD (Mooncrest CRESTCD 003) 1991. (2) reissued on CD (Mooncrest CRESTCD 005) 1991. (3) reissued on CD (Shanachie (USA) SH 79049 CD) 1988 and (Mooncrest CRESTCD 009) 1991. (4) reissued on CD (Chrysalis CCD 1008) 1991 and again (Beat Goes On BGOCD 324) 1997. (5) reissued on CD (Edsel EDCD 634) 2000. (6) reissued on CD (Shanachie (USA) SHAN 79045 CD) 1988 and (Beat Goes On BGOCD 323) 1996. (8) reissued on CD by Shanachie (USA) (SHMC 79060) 1991, also (Chrysalis CCD 1053) 1991 and (Beat Goes On BGOCD 157) 1992. (9) reissued on CD (Beat Goes On BGOCD 315) 1996. (10) reissued on vinyl (Music for Pleasure MfP 41 57061) 1975. (10) reissued on CD (Beat Goes On BGOCD 158) 1992, again on CD (EMI CDP 828 785-2) 1994 as a 25th anniversary edition and again (Chrysalis CDGOLD 1009) 1996. (11) reissued on CD (Chrysalis CCD 1123) 1991 and (Beat Goes On BGOCD 318) 1997.

There are also the following compilations: Steeleye Span Story (Chrysalis 2-1136) 1977 was a 2-CD retrospective of their career. Original Masters (2-LP) (Chrysalis CJT 3) 1977, Time Span (2-LP) (Mooncrest CRD 1) 1977, The Best Of Steeleye Span (LP) (Chrysalis CHR 1467) 1984, The Best Of Steeleye Span (CD) (Chrysalis CCD 1467) 1985; Portfolio (2LP) (Chrysalis CNW 7) 1988, Portfolio (CD) (Chrysalis MPCD 1647) 1988, which omits four tracks from the 2-LP set, Steeleye Span: The Early Years (2-LP) (Connoisseur VSOPLP 132) 1989, Steeleye Span: The Early Years (CD) (Connoisseur VSOPCD 132) 1989, which omits four cuts from the 2-LP set, Collection: Steeleye Span (CD) (Castle Collector CCSCD 292) 1991; Spanning The Years (2-CD) (Chrysalis 7243 8 32236 2 6) 1995; The King: The Best Of Steeleye Span (Mooncrest CD 022) 1996 and Original Masters (2-CD) (Beat Goes On BGOCD 322) 1997, which is a reissue of their 1977 release.

There have also been a number of budget compilations: Adam Catch Eve (LP) (Boulevard BD 3004) 1979, Steeleye Span (LP) (Pickwick SHM 3040) 1980, Steeleye Span (2-LP) (Cambra CR 5154) 1984, The Best And The Rest Of Steeleye Span (Action Replay CDAR 1012) 1990 (this is actually a reissue of the first 14 tracks of the Early Years CD from 1989) and A Stack Of Steeleye Span (CD) (Emporio 668) 1996. More recently, First Steps (Talking Elephant TECD 036) 2001 is a compilation drawn from their Mooncrest/B&C catalogue. The Best Of Steeleye Span (EMI 7243 5 41355 2 1) 2002 focuses on their mid-seventies output for Chrysalis.

			HCP
45s:	Rave On/Reels/Female Drummer (PS)	(B&C CB 164) 1971	-
(up to	Jigs And Reels (7-track maxi single)	(Peg PGS 6) 1972	-
1976)	John Barleycorn/Jigs	(Chrysalis CHS 2002) 1972	-
	Gaudete/		
	The Holly And The Ivy (PS)	(Chrysalis CHS 2007) 1972	14
	Thomas The Rhymer/		
	The Mooncoin Jig	(Chrysalis CHS 2026) 1974	-
	New York Girls/Two Magicians	(Chrysalis CHS 2061) 1975	-
	All Around My Hat/		
	Black Jack Davy	(Chrysalis CHS 2078) 1975	5
	Rave On/		
	False Knight On The Road	(Mooncrest MOON 50) 1976	-
	Hard Times Of Old England/		
	Cadgwith Anthem (Chrysalis CHS 2085) 1976		-
	Hard Times Of Old England/		
	Sum Waves (Tunes) (Chrysalis CHS 2085) 1976		-
	London/Sligo Maid	(Chrysalis CHS 2107) 1976	-
	Fighting for Strangers/		
	The Mooncoin Jig	(Chrysalis CHS 2125) 1976	-

Steeleye Span was the type of band you either loved or hated, but along with Fairport Convention they were at the pinnacle of British folk-rock in the seventies.

Steeleye Span formed in 1969 when Ashley Hutchings, former bassist with Fairport Convention, who'd originally wanted to call the group Middlemarch Wait, met up with Tim Hart and Maddy Prior, a popular folk duo who'd recorded three albums and Gay and Terry Woods, who'd played in an electric folk band called Sweeney's Men. This line-up rehearsed in Wiltshire and recorded a debut album in London but then split up without gigging when it became apparent that the Woods were incompatible with the rest. The Woods joined Dr. Strangely Strange in May 1970 and later formed The Woods Band whose albums were put out on Polydor. Mike Warth tells me that their first album is a real folk-rock masterpiece. If there was friction in the band it isn't reflected in the quality of the music. Apparently the shared vocals of Gay Woods and Maddy Prior are astonishing and the selection of traditional material is of the highest quality. The album was critically acclaimed and utilised electrical instruments - guitar, bass and dulcimer- which took its appeal beyond just folk clubs.

Martin Carthy, a significant figure on the traditional folk circuit and fiddle player Peter Knight were drafted into the new line-up. This incarnation gigged extensively and recorded two albums. Please To See The King was innovative and Hutchings' bass playing and Hart's electric dulcimer gave the band a driving rhythm section. Ten Man Mop was less popular being a mix of jigs and reels and electric settings of traditional songs. Still, the albums enhanced their growing reputation as part of the burgeoning UK folk scene but didn't break through commercially. This incarnation also released an acapella version of Buddy Holly's Rave On 45. In addition an 11-minute maxi-single Jigs And Reels, which compiled instrumental tracks from their second and third albums was released without their approval. They also got into theatrical work author Keith Dewhurst wrote 'Corunna' for them and they acted in the play as well as performing the music. They lasted until November 1971 when Ashley Hutchings left to do session work before eventually forming Albion Country Band. Martin Carthy also returned to his solo career. These changes marked a major upheaval in their development with their producer and manager Sandy Robertson leaving too and Jo Lustig taking over their management.

A new line-up was put together incorporating former accountant Rob Johnson and bassist Rick Kemp, who'd worked with Mike Chapman. They now embarked on the start of their most successful phase and their album Below The Salt spawned a hit single with their accapella version of the Latin hymn, Gaudete, Gaudete. Shortly after Charisma released Individually And Collectively, a compilation of material from their second and third albums, which included solo works from Carthy, Hart and Prior.

Nigel Pegrum, from Gnidrolog, was added to the band to give them a drummer for the first time, and they grew from strength to strength with Parcel Of Rogues. Highlights included Alison Gross, a Gothic tale utilising traditional material with veering towards harder rock. It also included two songs from another Keith Dewhurst/Bill Bryden stage production involving

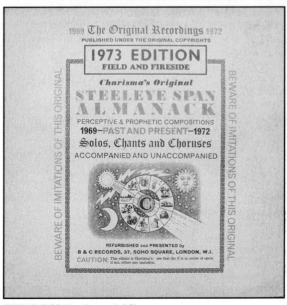

STEELEYE SPAN - Almanack (LP).

805

the band. The tracks were *Rogues In A Nation* and *Cam Ye O'er Frae France* and the production was an adaptation of Robert Louis Stevenson's 'Kidnapped'.

Now We Are Six (produced by **Jethro Tull**'s Ian Anderson, which spawned *Thomas The Rhymer*, one of their finest songs) was released in 1974 and an alternate version of this was also released as a 45. The album also included children's riddles and songs performed by the St Eleye Primary School Junior. **David Bowie** guested on saxophone for their cover of The Teddy Bears' 1958 hit *To Know Him Is To Love Him* as they veered more into pop territory. The BBC asked them to record a new version of the theme to 'Z Cars', the series had been conceived by **Maddy Prior's** father Alan and they also presented two series of six half-hour special 'Electric Folk' which captured the band performing in the stately homes and historic houses.

Commoner's Crown (which featured Peter Sellers playing ukelele on *New York Girls*) was notable for **Maddy Prior** singing the haunting *Weary Cutters* unaccompanied. However, when their contract with manager Jo Lustic ran out in May 1975 the band members chose to pursue separate projects.

They re-grouped the following year and with a new manager Tony Secunda and a new producer **Mike Batt** (of Wombles fame) they recorded *All Around My Hat*, their most successful album of all. The title track became a major British hit single and their first record to enter the US Charts. The album also included the harmony-laden *Cadgwith Anthem* and the though-provoking *Hard Times Of Old England*. Their second album under **Batt**'s production was the inconsistent *Rocket Cottage*, recorded in only one week in Hilversum, Holland. Its highlights were arguably the two tracks released as 45s the rocky *London* and slightly experimental *Fighting For Strangers*. They continued to record a couple more albums - *Storm Force Ten* and *Live At Last!* beyond this book's time span.

Maddy Prior and **June Tabor** teamed up for a solo album, *Silly Sisters* (Takoma 7077) in 1976. **June Tabor's** *Airs And Graces* (Topic 12TS 298) 1976 earned her the Top Female Singer Award for 1976 in 'Melody Maker' and should interest fans of **Steeleye Span**.

When the band eventually gave up the ghost in March 1978, **Tim Hart and Maddy Prior** both embarked on solo careers. There were a series of reformations throughout the eighties and nineties.

The Early Years compilation features material from their first three albums as well as their non-album 45 cut *Rave On* and four tracks from **Tim Hart and Maddy Prior**'s earlier career as a duo. This was a welcomed addition for **Steeleye Span** fans who didn't already have this material.

The 2001 compilation *First Steps* features material from their first two albums supplemented by **Maddy Prior/Tim Hart** and **Martin Carthy** releases from the same era. The packaging is basic, but the CD comes at mid-price and with brief sleevenotes from **Ashley Hutchings**.

EMI's 2002 *The Best Of Steeleye Span* focuses on their mid-seventies output but omits some of their better songs from this era.

They contributed to the *Rave On* (LP) compilation (including the title track). (VJ)

Steel Mill

Personnel:	JOHN CHALLENGER	woodwind	A
	CHRIS MARTIN	drms	A
	DAVE MORRIS	keyb'ds, vcls	A
	JEFF WATTS	bs	A
	TERRY WILLIAMS	gtr	A

ALBUM: 1(A) GREEN EYED GOD (Penny Farthing PELS 549) 1975 R3
NB: (1) reissued on CD (Essex ESSEX 1002 CD) 1994.

45s:	Green Eyed God/Zang Will	(Penny Farthing PEN 770) 1971
	Get On The Line/	
	Summer's Child	(Penny Farthing PEN 783) 1971
Reissue:	Green Eyed God/Zang Will	(Penny Farthing PEN 894) 1975

This band's album is now very rare and collectable. In the heavy progressive genre with elements of folk and ethnic music too, it got a German release on Bellaphon (BLPS 19105) in 1972 but had to wait three more years for a UK airing, by which time they'd split. The opening cut sounds **Pink Floyd**-influenced and the musical format is encouraging with some dramatic vocals and lots of improvised jazzy solos. The recent CD reissue comes with two bonus tracks.

Dave Morris later played in the Barratt band with Norman Barratt of **Gravy Train**. (VJ)

Steerpike

ALBUM: 1   STEERPIKE   (Private Pressing ADM 417) 1968 R5

An electric guitar-driven UK blues boom artefact, which is rawer and wilder than the material **Chicken Shack**, **Fleetwood Mac** and the other Blue Horizon acts were playing at the time. It's got plenty of crude fuzz guitar leads, especially on rousing versions of *Evil* and *Dust My Broom*. The album is housed in a home-made cover with the band's name sprayed on the front. (VJ)

Ewan Stephens

45s:	Queen Of The Good Times/	
	We Can Give It A Try	(Decca F 13219) 1971
	Brother, Surely We Can Work It Out/	
	Long, Long Summer	(Decca F 13299) 1972

These were solo efforts by Stephens, who'd been drummer with **Turquoise** back in the late sixties. (VJ)

Steve and Stevie

| Personnel: | STEVE GROVES | A |
| | STEVIE KIPNER | A |

ALBUM: 1(A)   STEVE AND STEVIE   (Toast TLP 2) 1968 SC

This album was the work of two Australians who like a number of their fellow musicians relocated to London in the sixties. Steve Kipner was the son of Nat Kipner, the owner of the Spin label, whose extensive roster included **The Bee Gees** among others. There is a distinctive **Bee Gees** influence on this obscure psych-pop album whose finest moment is the lushly orchestrated *Shine*, which came complete with harpsichord, dreamy passages and a catchy chorus.

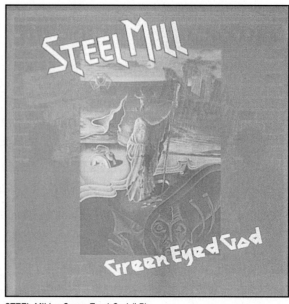

STEEL MILL - Green Eyed God (LP).

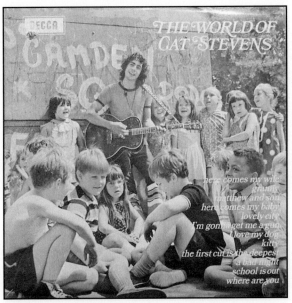

CAT STEVENS - World Of (LP).

Along with **Maurice Gibb** they were involved in the recording of the **Fut** single and re-emerged as **Tin Tin** in 1969. Steve Kipner became a successful songwriter in the eighties penning material for Cher and Olivia Newton-John among others.

Merry-Go-Round got a further airing on *Colour Me Pop, Vol 2* (CD) and *Shine* has been compiled on *Spinning Wheel* (CD). (VJ)

Cat Stevens

HCP

ALBUMS:	1	MATTHEW & SON		
(up to		(mono/stereo)	(Deram DML/SML 1004) 1967	SC 7
1975)	2	NEW MASTERS		
		(mono/stereo)	(Deram DML/SML 1018) 1968	SC -
	3	WORLD OF CAT STEVENS	(Decca SPA 93) 1970	-
	4	MONA BONE JAKON	(Island ILPS 9118) 1970	R2 63
	5	TEA FOR THE TILLERMAN		
			(Island ILPS 9135) 1971	SC 20
	6	TEASER AND THE FIRECAT		
			(Island ILPS 9154) 1971	SC 3
	7	CATCH BULL AT FOUR	(Island ILPS 9206) 1972	2
	8	FOREIGNER	(Island ILPS 9240) 1973	3
	9	BUDDAH AND THE CHOCOLATE BOX		
			(Island ILPS 9274) 1974	3
	10	NUMBERS	(Island ILPS 9370) 1975	-
	11	GREATEST HITS	(Island ILPS 9310) 1975	2

NB: Test pressings also exist for an unreleased 1967 album on Deram, *Cats And Dogs* (R1). (1) and (2) later issued as a double pack in the US and as *View From The Top* (Deram DPA 3019/20) in 1974 in the UK. His Island albums were released on A&M in the US. Deram released a US-only compilation *Very Young And Early Songs* in 1972. *New Masters* (Deram 820 767-2) 1989 is a CD collection of several of his Deram recordings including several tracks from the original *New Masters* album. (1) reissued on CD (Deram 820 560-2) 1988 with two additional cuts: *I'm Gonna Get Me A Gun* and *School Is Out*. (4) reissued on CD (Island IMCD 35) 1989 and again (Island IMCD 267/546 883 2) 2000. (5) reissued on CD (Mobile Fidelity (USA) UDCD 519) 1989, (Island IMCD 36) 1989 and again (Island IMCD 268/546 884 2) 2000. (6) reissued on CD (Island IMCD 104) 1990 and again (Island IMCD 269/546 885 2) 2000. (7) reissued on CD (Island IMCD 34) 1989. (8) reissued on CD (Island IMCD 72) 1989. (9) reissued on CD (Island IMCD 70) 1989. (10) reissued on CD (Island IMCD 277/546 890 2) 2001. *First Cuts* (Deram 820 561-2) 1989 is a CD 'greatest hits' collection of his material from the late sixties. (5) and (6) reissued on one CD (Island KSCD 12) 1992. *The Collection* (Castle CCSCD 127) 1993 compiles the best of his recordings for Deram between 1966-69. Earlier CD compilations have been *Greatest Hits: Cat Stevens* (Island CID 9310) 1987 and *The Very Best Of Cat Stevens* (Island 840 148 2) 1990. On The Road To Find Out ( ) 2001 is a US 4-CD set totalling 79 tracks, 21 of which are from previously unissued acetates, demos or other versions or mixes.

HCP

45s:	I Love My Dog/Portobello Road	(Deram DM 102) 1966	28
(up to	Matthew And Son/Granny	(Deram DM 110) 1966	2
1975)	I'm Gonna Get Me A Gun/School Is Out	(Deram DM 118) 1967	6

	A Bad Night/Laughing Apple	(Deram DM 140) 1967	20
	Kitty/Blackness Of The Night	(Deram DM 156) 1967	47
	Lovely City/Image Of Hell	(Deram DM 178) 1968	-
	Here Comes My Wife/		
	It's A Super Duper Day	(Deram DM 211) 1968	-
	Where Are You/The View From The Top	(Deram DM 260) 1969	-
	Lady D'Arbanville/		
	Time/Fill My Eyes (PS)	(Island WIP 6086) 1970	8
	Moon Shadow/Father And Son	(Island WIP 6092) 1971	22
	Tuesday's Dead/		
	Miles From Nowhere	(Island WIP 6102) 1971	-
	Morning Has Broken/		
	I Want To Live In A Wigwam	(Island WIP 6121) 1972	9
	Can't Keep It In/Crab Dance	(Island WIP 6152) 1972	13
	The Hurt/Silent Sunlight	(Island WIP 6183) 1973	-
	Oh Very Young/100 I Dream	(Island WIP 6190) 1974	-
	Another Saturday Night/		
	Home In The Sky	(Island WIP 6206) 1974	19
	Two Fine People/Bad Penny	(Island WIP 6238) 1975	-
Reissues:	I Love My Dog/Matthew And Son	(Deram DM 406) 1973	-
	Matthew And Son/I Love My Dog/A Bad Night/		
	I'm Gonna Get Me A Gun(PS)	(Deram DM 435) 1980	-
	Bad Night/		
	I'm Gonna Get Me A Gun (PS)	(Deam DM 435) 1980	-
	Matthew And Son/Granny	(Decca F 13909) 1981	-
	Mathew And Son/I Love My Dog	(Old Gold OG 9336) 1983	-
	Morning Has Broken/Moon Shadow	(Island IS 123) 1983	-

Cat Stevens (real name Steven Georgiou) was born on 21 July 1947 in Soho, London. His father ran a Greek restaurant and his mother was Swedish. He took up folk singing whilst studying at Hammersmith College, London and was heard performing there by ex-Springfields member, **Mike Hurst**, who had become a record producer. **Hurst** was sufficiently impressed to organise and finance a recording session which resulted in the self-penned *I Love My Dog*. Georgiou was quickly signed by Decca's Tony Hall (who changed his name to **Cat Stevens**) and promoted as the first act on the company's new Deram label, which had just been set up to promote young progressive British talent. Aided by considerable airplay on pirate radio the record made the UK Top 30 and **Stevens**' career was on its way. With his dark good looks he soon became a teen idol and enjoyed considerable commercial success with two orchestrally-arranged classic hits, *Matthew And Son* and *I'm Gonna Get Me A Gun*. He'd already established himself as a formidable songwriter with **The Tremeloes** covering his *Here Comes My Baby* and P.P. Arnold covering his *The First Cut Is The Deepest*. In February 1968 he contracted tuberculosis from which he spent the best part of a year recuperating. His unavailability to promote subsequent 45 releases inevitably affected their success and his popularity waned.

When he'd finally recovered from his illness **Stevens** signed to Island Records in July 1970. The songs he'd written during his convalescence were issued on *Mona Bone Jakon*. This, produced by ex-**Yardbird** Paul Samwell-Smith, heralded **Stevens** as a more serious singer-songwriter and

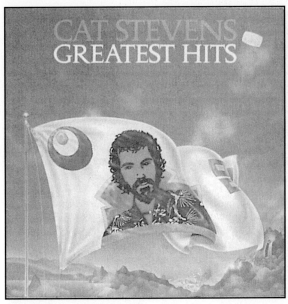

CAT STEVENS - Greatest Hits (LP).

its release conveniently coincided with the emergence of a number of singer-songwriters on both sides of the Atlantic. *Lady D'Arbanville*, taken from the album and dedicated to a former girlfriend, gave him another massive UK hit but in a significantly different style from those that had gone before.

His next album, *Tea For The Tillerman*, was enormously popular in Britain and spawned a further hit with *Wild World* on both sides of the Atlantic (his first in America). Jimmy Cliff had earlier enjoyed a UK Top 10 hit with his cover of **Stevens**' song. The album eventually went gold in America.

Teaser And The Firecat, his next album, built on his earlier success. Peaking at No 3 in the UK and No 2 in the US. It stayed in the album Charts for 93 weeks in the UK. The sleeve featured his own artwork and he produced a short animated film of the same name, which was later screened at gigs.

The album contained three more of his classic songs - *Moon Shadow*, *Peace Train* (a US-only 45, where it made the Top 10) and the classic, fresh *Morning Has Broken*, his interpretation of Eleanor Farjeon's childrens hymn, on which **Rick Wakeman** played piano, which made the UK Top Ten.

Catch Bull At Four topped the US Charts for three weeks giving him another gold disk. It peaked at No 2 in the UK. *Can't Keep It In* from the album gave him another UK hit, whilst *Sitting* made the US Top 20. One side of the *Foreigner* album was dedicated to *Foreigner Suite*, a rambling piece which evidenced his growing concern with religious and philosophical issues. *The Hurt* was less successful and he became increasingly reclusive, living in Brazil as a tax exile, donating the money he'd have otherwise paid to the taxman to UNESCO and other charities.

Buddha And The Chocolate Box and *Numbers* were both complex albums with elaborate orchestration in places. Lyrically and musically interesting they proved less accessible to many of his fans and *Numbers* was his first Island album not to chart in the UK. It's a light-hearted concept album based on a set of characters on the far-off planet of Polygor. The mood is playful, but it has its moments and *Monad's Anthem* is a weird spacey track recalling **Pink Floyd** circa 1968.

His next album *Numbers* failed to chart in the UK at all, but did make the US Top 20. He spent 18 months on *Izitso* his 1977 album but it paid off because it made the US Top 10 and No 18 in the UK. It also spawned the hit single *(Remember The Days Of The) Old School Yard*. On 23 December 1977 a very significant event occurred - **Stevens** converted to Islam and adopted the name Yusuf Islam. He recorded one final album *Back To Earth* in 1978 and then retired from the music business. He was part of an arranged marriage that produced five children. He auctioned his possessions and founded a Muslim school near London. He later shocked many of his fans when he supported the fatwa Ayatollah Khomeini placed on the writer Salman Rushdie for writing the book 'The Satanic Verses' and some radio stations ceased to play his records. Still his albums continued to remain popular and were inevitably reissued and remastered and in

MEIC STEVENS - Ghost Town (LP).

Spring 2000 he went on tour to promote these and a compilation *The Very Best of Cat Stevens.*

2001 saw the release of an American 4-CD set of his material, *On The Road To Find Out*. It features 79 tracks in all, of which 21 are from previously unissued acetates, demos or alternate versions and mixes. The third CD includes album and B-side rarities, while the fourth CD features in concert material from Virginia and Wembley in 1979 and the unreleased *Blue Monday*.

Compilation appearances have included: *The First Cut Is The Deepest* on *Hard-Up Heroes* (2-LP); *Maybe You're Right* on *Bumpers* (2-LP); the folky *Portobello Road* on *Deram Dayze* (LP); *Wild World* on *El Pea*; *I Love My Dog* on *The World Of Hits, Vol. 2* (LP); *Morning Has Broken* on *20 Star Tracks, Vol. 1* (LP); and *Matthew And Son* on *Stardust* (2-LP) and *A Bad Night* on *Pop-In, Vol 1* (CD). (VJ)

Meic Stevens

ALBUMS:
1	OUTLANDER		
	(w/insert)	(Warner Bros WS 3005)	1970 R3
2	GWYMON	(Wren WRL 536)	1972 R3
3	MEIC A'R BARA MENYN	(Wren WRC 702)	197?

NB: (1) counterfeited on vinyl in the eighties and reissued on CD (YSL 1063) 2001. *Dim Ond Cysgodion* (SAIN SCD 2001) 1992 is a compilation concentrating on the Welsh language material he recorded from 1971-1992. Also of interest is *Ghost Town* (Tenth Planet TP028) 1997, a collection of previously unreleased recordings, made in 1968 - 69. (3) was a cassette-only 'Best Of' plus material he recorded with Y Bara Menyn. *September 1965: The Tony Pike Sessions* (Tenth Planet TP 057) 200? a limited edition of 1,000 copies, unearths a long-lost debut album recorded shortly after his debut album for Decca but never issued.

EPs:
1	MIKE STEVENS (PS)	(Wren WRE 1045)	1968 R3
2	MIKE STEVENS RHIF 2 (PS)	(Wren WRE 1053)	1968 R3
3	MWG (PS)	(Wren 1073)	1969 R3
4	Y BARA MENYN (PS)	(Wren WRE 1065)	1969 R3
5	RHAGOR O'R BARA MENYN (PS)	(Wren WRE 1072)	1969 R3
6	Y BRAWD HOUDINI (PS)	(Sain SAIN 004)	1970 R3
7	MEIC STEVENS (PS)	(Newyddion Da NDI)	1970 R3
8	DIOLCH YN FAWR (PS)	(Sain SAIN 013)	1971 R3
9	BYW YN Y WLAD (PS)	(Wren WRE 1107)	1971 R3

NB: (4) with Y Bara Menyn. (7) is a mini-album.

45s:
α	Did I Dream/ I Saw A Field	(Decca F 12174)	1965 SC
	Nid Oes Gwydr Ffenestr/ Rhywbeth Gwell I Ddod (PS)	(Wren WSP 2005)	1970 R3
	Old Joe Blind/Blue Sleep	(Warner Bros WB 8007)	1970 SC

NB: α As Mike Stevens.

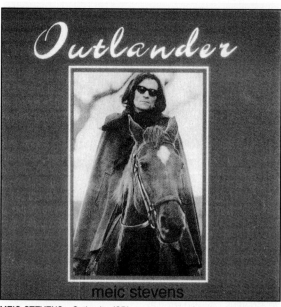
MEIC STEVENS - Outlander (CD).

A legendary folk singer who's been called 'the Welsh Dylan', **Stevens** was born in 1942 and grew up in Solva, West Wales. Having taught himself guitar and studied art in Cardiff, he paid his dues on London's folk circuit alongside **Davy Graham**, **Wizz Jones**, **Martin Carthy** and others before moving up to Manchester, where he was discovered by DJ Jimmy Savile, who wanted to make him into the next **Donovan** (of whom **Stevens** had never heard!) His debut 45, recorded for Decca in 1965, was arranged by **John Paul Jones** (later of **Led Zeppelin** fame) and is very much in that style. For the remainder of the decade **Stevens** divided his time between Wales, London and the continent, recording the first in a steady stream of now ultra-rare Welsh-language psych-folk EPs in 1968 and forming the tongue-in-cheek Welsh psychedelic group Y Bara Menyn. In London, meanwhile, he shared a house with the **Blossom Toes** and **Gary Farr**, on whose 1968 debut *Take Something With You* he played lead guitar.

In 1969 Warner Brothers paid him the then-huge advance of £50,000 for a five-year contract, but only one album and one single ever appeared. *Outlander* was a superb blend of plaintive, melodic folk, spiky psychedelia and Eastern jazz (the latter owing to arrangements from Indo-Jazz Fusions' John Mayer and tabla from **Magic Carpet**'s Keshav Sathe) but, like all his releases, is now very rare and collectable. The B-side of his Warners 45 is non-album.

When *Outlander* failed to sell, Warners lost interest in **Stevens**, and he happily returned to Wales to focus on Welsh language recordings for the local Sain and Wren labels, as well as backing other local musicians and writing music for TV and theatre. He's a major figure there, and has recently published a superb autobiography, *Solva Blues* (Y Lolfa, 2004), covering his childhood, youth, travels, experiences on the UK folk circuit and escapades with **Blossom Toes**, **Mighty Baby**, **Gordon Jackson**, **Traffic**, **Shawn Phillips**, **Gary Farr** and many others.

Dim Ond Cysgodion is a compilation concentrating on the Welsh language material he recorded from 1971-1992. *Ghost Town* is a vinyl-only limited pressing of an attractive set of English-language demos he recorded between 1968 and 1969, which have a mystical aura about them. *The Tony Pike Sessions* another 1,000 limited edition pressing, is a worthy companion to it. This long-lost demo album includes eleven previously unissued songs like *Winter Of The Clan* and *Not For Me Mister MP*.

Compilation appearances include: *The Sailor And Madonna* on *Electric Psychedelic Sitar Headswirlers, Vol. 2* (CD); and *Yorric* on *Electric Psychedelic Sitar Headswirlers, Vol. 3* (CD). (GM/VJ/RMJ)

Mike Stevens (and The Shevells)

45s: Cathy's Clown/Go-Go Train   (Pye 7N 17243) 1966 SC
      Guaranteed To Drive You Wild/Hog-Tied   (Polydor 56269) 1968

The Shevells also recorded 45s under their own name. **Mike Stevens** was also in The Squires and has nothing to do with **Meic Stevens**.

Go-Go Train has been compiled on *Maximum '65* (CD) and *Doin' The Mod, Vol. 1* (CD). (VJ)

Al Stewart

HCP

ALBUMS: 1 BEDSITTER IMAGES
(up to   (mono/stereo)   (CBS (S)BPG 63087) 1967 R2 -
1976)   2 LOVE CHRONICLES
             (mono/stereo)   (CBS (S) 63460) 1969 R1 -
         3 ZERO SHE FLIES   (CBS 63848) 1970 SC 40
         4 ORANGE   (CBS 64739) 1972 SC -
         5 PAST, PRESENT AND FUTURE   (CBS 65726) 1973 -
         6 MODERN TIMES   (CBS 80477) 1975 -
         7 YEAR OF THE CAT   (RCA RS 1082) 1976 38

NB: (1) reissued on CBS (64023) 1970 (SC) with different tracks. (5) onwards released by Janus in the US. (4) reissued on CD (Beat Goes On BGOCD 154) 1992 and (Columbia 48441-2) 1996. (7) reissued on CD by (Mobile Fidelity) (USA) MFCD 8039) 1986, by (RCA RCD 11749) 1988, on (Fame CDFA 3253) 1991 and again (EMI 535 4562) 2001, with two bonus cuts. (4), (5) and (6) all reissued on a 2-CD set (Edsel MEDCD 730) 2004 along with a non-album 'B' side. (6) also reissued (Beat Goes On BGO BGO CD 156) 2001, with three additional tracks.

Compilations include: *To Whom It May Concern: 1966-70* (EMI 7243 8 27709 2 3)

1993, a 2-CD set collection of his 1966 45 for Decca and his first three albums for CBS; *Chronicles - The Best Of Al Stewart* (EMI CDEMC 3590) 1991, which includes a couple of tracks not on the album equivalent; *The Best Of Al Stewart* (EMI CTMCD 310) 1997, a set of hotch pot CD compilation of his material which draws heavily on material from his *Year Of The Cat* and *Time Passages* albums. *Just Yesterday* (EMI 336 9362) is a 5-CD career retrospective box set.

HCP

45s: Turn Into Earth/The Elf   (Decca F 12467) 1966 R2 -
(up to   Bedsitter Images/Swiss Cottage Manoeuvres (CBS 3034) 1967 -
1976)   Electric Los Angeles Sunset/
         My Enemies Have Sweet Voices   (CBS 4843) 1970 -
         The News From Spain/Elvaston Place (CBS 5351) 1970 -
         You Don't Even Know Me/I'm Falling (CBS 7763) 1972 -
         Amsterdam/Songs Out Of Clay   (CBS 7992) 1972 -
         Terminal Eyes/Last Day Of June 1934 (CBS 1791) 1973 -
         Shallow Wind/Nostradamus   (CBS 2397) 1974 -
         Carol/Next Time   (CBS 3254) 1975 -
         The Year Of The Cat/Broadway Hotel (RCA 2771) 1976 31
Reissue: The Year Of The Cat/
         (Flip by different artist)   (Old Gold OG 9642) 1986 -

Born in Glasgow on 5th September 1945, **Stewart** played his first live gigs as lead guitarist in pop/rock band Tony Blackburn and The Sabres, who were fronted by the future dee-jay and based in Bournemouth. Later he relocated to London, began writing his own songs and performed at folk-club venues like Les Cousins and Bunjies. He recorded a one-off 45 for Decca in 1966 but it didn't sell. The 'A' side was a haunting **Yardbirds**' album track given a folkier rendition. The flip was a pleasant folk-pop number.

Having signed to CBS in 1967 his debut album, *Bedsitter Images*, was heavily orchestrated and full of introspective soft-rock songs. This and what followed was certainly typical bedsitter music. The title track to his next album, *Love Chronicles*, was an 18-minute autobiographical account of **Stewart**'s lost love. The inclusion of the word 'fucking' in the lyrics meant it got no airplay and it didn't sell in any quantities, but it further cemented his reputation in bed-sit land and on the college circuit and it was voted Album of the Year in Melody Maker's Annual Survey.

Zero She Flies again examined relationship breakdowns and the like. It became his first Chart album, whilst *Orange*, which wasn't one of his better efforts, marked a break from his earlier folk style. *Songs Out Of Clay* is a keyboard-driven number and *The News From Spain* also veered towards progressivism.

For Past, Present and Future **Stewart** worked with an electric band (mostly comprised of Tim Renwick, **B.J. Cole**, Francis Monkman, Bruce Thomas, **Rick Wakeman**, Tim Hinkley, Bob Andrews, Bob Sargeant and **Dave Swarbrick**). Inspired by the book, 'The Centuries Of Nostradamus', it was a concept album tracing historical events. It didn't chart in the UK but its release was almost simultaneous with his first US Tour, where he developed a strong cult following when his next effort *Modern Times*

AL STEWART - Year Of The Cat (LP).

expanded further. *Sirens Of Titan* has some delightful harpsichord, *What's Going On* has some catchy harmonica, and *The Dark And Rolling Sea* features traditional accordion and the eight-minute vandeviliian title track is another highlight. The Beat Goes On CD reissue of *Modern Times* includes three tracks from 1970/73 of which *News From Spain* is the pick.

As we leave the period of this book his magnum opus the album *Year Of The Cat* had just emerged. It also spawned his only hit single.

Stewart is still going strong in the 21st Century. *Just Yesterday* released in 2005 is a 5-CD boxed career retrospective. Disc One concentrates on his sixties material; Disc Two contains much of his most commercially successful work from seventies albums like *Modern Times* and *Year Of The Cat*; Disc Three covers the period from 1980-1993; and Disc Four covers the last ten years and includes several tracks from his 1995 *Between The Wars* album and three from 2005's *Beach Full Of Shells*. The fifth and final disc is a re-release of the live *Time Passages* album. Overall the collection provides a good chronological guide to his career and includes a few of his more obscure tracks for his diehard fans.

Stewart's first 45, *The Elf*, can also be heard on *British Psychedelic Trip, Vol. 3* (LP); It's flip *Turn Into Earth* can also be heard on *The Psychedelic Scene* (CD), *Beat It* (3-CD), *British Psychedelic Trip, Vol. 4* (LP), *Broken Dreams, Vol. 1* (LP) and *Great British Psychedelic Trip, Vol. 2* (CD). Back in 1970, *A Small Fruity Song* from his *Zero She Flies* album was included on the (2-LP) *Fill Your Head With Rock* budget-priced compilation. It was a short, simple, predominantly instrumental track. More recently, *Year Of The Cat* and *Time Passages* can be heard on the 3-CD box set *Radio Caroline Calling - 70's Flashback*. (VJ)

(Dave) Stewart and Harrison

| Personnel: | BRIAN HARRISON | A |
| | DAVE STEWART | A |

| EP: | 1(A) | GIRL | (Multicord MULT SH 1) 1970 |

| 45: | Deep December/? | (Multicord) 1970? |

Dave Stewart was born on 9 September 1952 in Sunderland. This short-lived project with **Brian Harrison** was **Stewart**'s first. In the early seventies he joined **Longdancer** and also developed a major drug problem. In the mid-seventies he met Annie Lennox and the two lived together for four years. In 1977 they joined a trio called The Catch, who had a minor hit in Holland with *Borderline*. The band expanded to become The Tourists. Lennox and Stewart also went on to play together in Eurythmics. (VJ)

Paul Stewart Movement

| 45: | Saturday Morning Man/Too Too Good | (Decca F 12577) 1967 |

A R&B band connected to **Hamilton's Movement**.

Too Too Cool has been complied on *English Freakbeat, Vol. 5* (CD). (VJ)

Rod Stewart

HCP

ALBUMS:	1	AN OLD RAINCOAT WON'T EVER LET YOU DOWN		
(up to			(Vertigo VO 4) 1970	SC -
1976)	2	GASOLINE ALLEY	(Vertigo 6360 500) 1970	SC 62
	3	EVERY PICTURE TELLS A STORY		
			(Mercury 6338 063) 1971	SC 1
	4	NEVER A DULL MOMENT	(Mercury 6499 153) 1972	SC 1
	5	SING IT AGAIN ROD	(Mercury 6499 484) 1973	1
	6	SMILER	(Mercury 9104 001) 1974	1
	7	ATLANTIC CROSSING		
			(Warner Brothers K 56151) 1975	1
	8	VINTAGE YEARS 1969/70	(Mercury 6672 013) 1976	-
	9	A NIGHT ON THE TOWN	(Riva RVLP 1) 1976	1

NB: (1) reissued on CD (Mercury 558 058-2) 1998. (2) reissued on CD (Mercury 558 059-2) 1998. (3) reissued on CD (Mercury 558 060-2) 1998. (4) reissued on CD

ROD STEWART - Gasoline Alley (LP).

(Mercury 558 061-2) 1998. (5) reissued on CD (Mercury 558 062-2) 1998. (6) reissued on CD (Mercury 558 063-2) 1998. (7) reissued on CD (Warners 7599 273 312) 2000. *Rod Stewart 1964-1969* (New Millennium Communications PILOT 44) 2000 is a 2-CD box set, which comes with a CD-ROM of photos from David Wedgbury. *A Little Misunderstood: The Sixties Sessions* (Yeaah YEAAH 44) is a 15-track CD compilation of demos, early singles and anonymous sessions from the sixties.

HCP

45s:	Good Morning Little Schoolgirl/		
(up to	I'm Gonna Move To The Outskirts Of Town		
1976)		(Decca F 11996) 1964	R3 -
	The Day Will Come/		
	Why Does It Go On?	(Columbia DB 7766) 1965	R3 -
	Shake/I Just Got Some	(Columbia DB 7892) 1966	R3 -
	Little Miss Understood/		
	So Much To Say	(Immediate IM 060) 1968	R2 -
	Reason To Believe/Maggie May	(Mercury 6052 097) 1971	19/1
	You Wear It Well/Lost Paraguayos	(Mercury 6052 171) 1972	1
	Angel/		
	What Made Milwaukee Famous	(Mercury 6052 198) 1973	4
	Oh No Not My Baby/Jodie	(Mercury 6052 371) 1973	6
	Farewell/		
	Bring It On Home To Me/		
	You Send Me	(Mercury 6167 033) 1974	7
	It's All Over Now/Joe's Lament	(Vertigo 6086 002) 1975	-
α	You Can Make Me Dance, Sing Or Anything/		
	As Long As You Tell Him (PS)	(Warner Bros K 16494) 1975	-
	Sailin'/Stone Cold Sober	(Warner Bros K 16600) 1975	1
	This Old Heart Of Mine/		
	It's All In The Name Of Rock'n'Roll	(Riva 1) 1975	4
	Tonight's The Night/The Balltrap	(Riva 3) 1976	5
	The Killing Of Georgie/Fool For You	(Riva 4) 1976	2
	Get Back/Trade Winds	(Riva 6) 1976	11
	Mandolin Wind//Girl From The North Country		
	Sweet Little Rock'n'Roller	(Mercury 6160 007) 1976	-
	It's All Over Now/		
	Handbags And Gladrags	(Mercury 6167 327) 1976	-
Reissues:	Sailin' /Stone Cold Sober		
	Maggie May/You Wear It Well/		
	Twistin' The Night Away (PS)	(Mercury 6160 006) 1979	31
	Maggie May/Reason To Believe	(Mercury CUT 201) 1984	-
	Maggie May/You Wear It Well	(Old Gold OG 9765) 1988	-
β	You Wear It Well/		
	I Would Rather Go Blind	(Mercury MER 379) 1992	-

NB: α As Rod Stewart and The Faces. β Also issued as a CD single with the addition of *Angel* (Mercury MERCD 379) 1992.

Rod Stewart is one of the most successful singer/songwriters in the history of UK rock and pop. Between 1971-1976 he had six consecutive No 1 albums and cartloads of hit singles, including six No 1's up to 1983. His music draws on folk, rock, blues and country influences but adds his own unique interpretation and throaty vocals. He made folk music rock, although as his career developed he sacrificed some of his roots in pursuit of stardom.

Stewart's parents were Scottish but they were living in Highgate, London on 10 January 1945 when he was born. He went to school in Hornsey with future **Kinks** members Ray and **Dave Davies** (they played in the same school football team) and Peter Quaife. He even had three weeks on the books of Brentford F.C. before heading for Europe where he made a living as a busker living rough beneath the arches of Barcelona's football ground until he was deported from Spain for vagrancy. These experiences later inspired his observations in *Every Picture Tells A Story*.

Returning to London in 1962, he attended the Aldermaston CND march on Trafalgar Square. He had a number of short-term occupations including a newspaper delivery boy, sign-writer, gravedigger(!), picture framer and fence erector.

He joined The Five Dimensions, a Birmingham-based R&B band in 1963 (but he didn't play on their Pye or Decca singles). The band enjoyed a residency at Ken Colyer's Studio 15 club

In 1964, **Long John Baldry**' recruited him as second vocalist/harmonica player with the Hoochie Coochie Men, after hearing him bawling and playing harmonica whilst the worst for booze on Twickenham station one freezing cold day. He duetted with **Baldry** on *Up Above My Head*, the 'B' side to **Baldry's** *You'll Be Mine*. The same year he left the Hoochie Coochie Men and appeared on 'Ready Steady Go' to promote his debut single *Good Morning Little Schoolgirl*. It didn't chart and is now his rarest and most sought-after 45. It was also recorded by **The Yardbirds**.

In 1965, after a stint leading Southampton's R&B outfit **The Soul Agents**, he joined **Steampacket** (with **Julie Driscoll** and **The Brian Auger Trinity**) and signed a solo deal with EMI, which resulted in the release of *The Day Will Come* on Columbia. When he was sacked from **Steampacket** in March 1966, he guested with the **Peter B's** (aka **Peter B's Looners**) and was then with the short-lived **Shotgun Express** (a revamped version of the **Peter B's**) playing on their first 45.

April 1966 saw the release of Rod's third single *Shake*, a Sam Cooke track as covered by Otis Redding.

Rod Stewart then joined **The Jeff Beck Group** as vocalist. They released three UK singles (*Hi Ho Silver Lining*, *Tallyman* and *Love is Blue*, although Rod only sang vocals on the last two 'B' sides, *Rock My Plimsoll* and *I've Been Drinking* and the two albums, *Truth* and *Beck Ola*. In 1968 he signed to Immediate Records for an unsuccessful single, *Little Miss Understood*, which was written by **Mike D'Abo**. Prior to this he recorded an unreleased single *Come Back Baby* (a duet with **P.P. Arnold**), which was produced by **Mick Jagger**.

In 1969 he signed a solo deal with Mercury and began work on his first solo album, *An Old Raincoat Won't Ever Let You Down*.

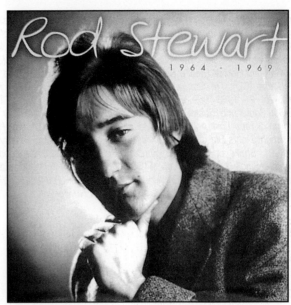
ROD STEWART - 1964-1969 (LP).

When **The Jeff Beck Group** split in October 1969 he turned down the chance to join the US group Cactus, opting instead for **Quiet Melon** and later **The Faces** (formerly **The Small Faces**). He also tried to step up his solo career at the same time. His first two albums helped establish him in the US although they made little impact in the UK. *Gasoline Alley* was arguably his finest album of the seventies. His gruff vocals set him apart from other singers and his songwriting ability was evidenced in compositions like *Jo's Lament, Lady Day* and the title track.

Every Picture Tells A Story elevated him to superstar status and contained the classic rock song *Maggie May*, which related a schoolboys dealings with a prostitute. It was, in fact, originally the 'B' side of *Reason To Believe*, a Tim Hardin number, which had earlier made No 19 in the UK, but deejays realising its potential flipped the disc. *Maggie May* topped the US and UK charts for five weeks (in fact one week he even topped the Album Charts both sides of the Atlantic too).

Never A Dull Moment was as successful as its predecessor, going gold and spawning another classic single, *You Wear It Well*. A double 'A' side *Angel* (a **Hendrix** song) backed by *What Made Milwaukee Famous* (which had been a hit for Jerry Lee Lewis) secured further Chart success for him during 1972.

In 1973 the compilation album *Sing It Again Rod* topped the UK Charts and made No 31 in the US, whilst his revival of **Manfred Mann**'s *Oh No Not My Baby* made the Top Ten.

The release of *Smiler* was delayed by a legal dispute between Mercury and Warner Bros as to whose album it should be but when it finally emerged it was hardly worth the wait save for *Farewell* and two Sam Cooke songs, *Bring It On Home To Me* and *You Send Me*, which were all included on a 45 (the last two in medley form) which gave him another Top Ten hit. In December 1974 he signed to Warner Brothers after a legal dispute between Warners and Phonogram about who had the rights to his solo releases.

Atlantic Crossing was recorded in Muscle Shoals following a widely publicised love affair with actress Britt Ekland, who apparently suggested that the album should have a fast and slow side. It provided another classic No 1, *Sailin'* and a revival of the Motown classic *This Old Heart Of Mine*, which climbed to No 4 in the UK and was his first release on Riva records. *Three Times Loser* was a decent disco tune and *All In The Name Of R&R* showcased his rockier side.

As we leave the time span of this book **The Faces** had split and Rod, now a megastar, announced he would concentrate exclusively on his solo career - one in which he would enjoy much further success in the coming years.

Rod Stewart 1964-1969 attempts to compile his pre-fame ventures with **Jimmy Powell and The Five Dimensions**, The Hoochie Coochie Men, **Steampacket, Shotgun Express, The Jeff Beck Group** and **Quiet Melon** plus his early solo 45s onto 2-CDs and there's a CD-ROM containing photos from Dave Wedgbury.

ROD STEWART - Atlantic Crossing (LP).

Compilation appearances have included:- *It's All Over Now* on *Dimension Of Miracles* (LP); *Handbags and Gladrags* on *Vertigo Annual 1970* (2-LP); *Shake* on *My Generation* (LP) and *Brit Pop* (CD); *Good Morning Little Schoolgirl* on *Pop Inside The '60s, Vol. 2* (CD), *Sixties Explosion, Vol. 1* (CD), *Hard-Up Heroes* (2-LP), *Sixties Lost And Found, Vol. 2* (LP) and *The R&B Scene* (CD); *I'm Gonna Move To The Outskirts Of Town* on *R&B Scene, Vol. 2 - 1963-1969* (LP) and *British R'n'B Explosion, Vol. 1* (CD); *I Just Got Some* and *Shake* on *R&B At Abbey Road* (CD); *The Day Will Come* on *Sixties Lost And Found, Vol. 1* (LP) and *Beat At Abbey Road* (CD); *Bright Lights Big City* on *The First British R&B Festival, February 28, 1964* (LP); *Shake* on *In The Beginning* (LP); *Little Miss Understood* on *Immediate Single Collection, Vol. 1* (CD); *Little Miss Understood* and *So Much To Say* on *Immediate Single Anthology, Vol. 1 - Rarities* (CD) and *You Wear It Well* on the 2-CD set *45s - 45 Classic No 1's*. (VJ)

Still Life (1)

Personnel incl:

GRAHAM AMOS		A
MARTIN CURE		A
TERRY HOWELLS		A
ALAN SAVAGE	drms	A

ALBUM: 1 (A) STILL LIFE (Vertigo 6360 026) 1971 R3

NB: (1) reissued on CD (Repertoire REP 4198-WP) 1991. (1) reissued again on vinyl and CD (Akarma AK 237).

Before he formed **Still Life** Martin Cure had played in The Sabres, **Martin Cure and The Peeps** and The Rainbow, where he met Graham Amos and Terry Howells. The three formed **Still Life** with drummer Alan Savage. Their organ-led progressive album is hampered by uninteresting lyrics. Coming with a gatefold sleeve and on the collectable spiral label it's now very rare and expensive to acquire, but whether it's worth the trouble and cost is another matter.

Martin Cure later played with **Cupid's Inspiration**, Chevy and Red On Red. He currently runs a PA company but still gigs from time to time with **Cupid's Inspiration** and The Rogues. (VJ/PS)

Still Life (2)

Personnel incl: STUART COWELL
                 JIM TOOMEY

45: What Did We Miss/
     My Kingdom Cannot Lose (Columbia DB 8345) 1968 R1

This was a completely different band. Jim Toomey and Stuart Cowell had previously played with a psychedelic pop outfit called **Jon**. They wrote *What Did We Miss*, an anti-war song with militaristic percussion, high-pitched harmonies and a catchy chorus. The flip by contrast is eminently forgettable. Cowell went on to play for **Titus Groan and Paul Brett's Sage** and Toomey later played in The Tourists (who later devolved into the Eurythmics).

Compilation appearances include: *My Kingdom Cannot Lose* on *Rubble, Vol. 11* (CD) and *The Best Of Rubble Collection, Vol. 5* (CD); and *What Did We Miss* on *Talking About The Good Times, Vol 1* (CD). (VJ/GB)

Peter Lee Stirling (and The Bruisers)

45s: α My Heart Commands Me/
         Welcome Stranger (Columbia DB 4992) 1963
      α I Could If I Wanted To/
         Right From The Start (Parlophone R 5063) 1963
      α Now That I've Found You/I Believe (Parlophone R 5112) 1964
      α Sad, Lonely And Blue/
         I'm Looking For Someone To Love (Parlophone R 5158) 1964
      α Everything Will Be Alright/
         You'll Be Mine (Parlophone R 5198) 1964
         The Sweet And Tender Hold Of Your Love/
         Everybody Needs A Someone (Decca F 12433) 1966
         Oh What A Fool/I'm Sportin' A New Baby (Decca F 12535) 1966
         You Don't Live Twice/
         8:35 On The Dot (Decca F 12628) 1967 SC

Goodbye Thimblemill Lane/Hey Conductor (Decca F 12674) 1967
Big Sam/Mr. Average Man (MCA MU 1093) 1969
Goodbye Summer Girl/Judes In Blue (MCA MK 5027) 1970

NB: α with **The Bruisers**.

Best remembered as a songwriter (with **The Merseybeats**' *I Think Of You* and *Don't Turn Around* among his credits), **Peter Lee Stirling** from Birmingham fronted **The Bruisers** in the mid-sixties and then recorded a string of solo pop singles. He continued to write and record into the seventies and later changed his name to Daniel Boone enjoying UK hits with *Daddy Don't You Walk So Fast* (No 17) and *Beautiful Sunday* (No 21) on the Penny Farthing label. In the seventies he was a member of **Hungry Wolf**.

You'll also find *8.35 On The Dot* on *British Psychedelic Trip, Vol. 4* (LP) and *Great British Psychedelic Trip, Vol. 2* (CD). (VJ)

The Stockingtops

Personnel incl: SUE GLOVER   vcls   A
                 SUNNY LESLIE vcls   A

45s: You're Never Gonna Get My Lovin'/
      You Don't Know What Love Is All About (Toast TT 500) 1968
      I Don't Ever Want To Be Kicked By You/
      The World We Live In Is A Lonely Place (CBS 3407) 1988

Glover and Leslie had originally been in The Myrtelles and then recorded as **Sue and Sunshine** and **Sue and Sunny**. (VJ)

The Stoics

Personnel:

JIM CASEY	drms	AB
JIMMY DORIS	gtr	AB
HUGH McKENNA	keyb'ds	AB
JOHN WYNN	bs	AB
FRANKIE MILLER	vcls, gtr	B

45: Earth, Fire, Air and Water/
     Search Of The Sea (RCA RCA 1745) 1968 SC

A Glasgow-based band whose sole 45 exhibited shades of progressivism and pop. It was recorded prior to **Frankie Miller** joining the group from another local band Westfarm Cottage. *Earth, Fire, Air and Water* was co-written by Graham Maitland (of **Scots Of St James**, **Hopscotch** and **Five Day Rain**) and is quite good. It is dwarfed, though, by the psych-pop flip *Search For The Sea*, which featured a strong vocal performance and pleasing guitar and flute interplay. They accompanied **Ten Years After** on a tour of Germany but split soon after. **Frankie Miller** embarked on a solo

STILL LIFE - Still Life (LP).

STONE ANGEL - Stone Angel (LP).

career and Jimmy Doris concentrated on songwriting particularly for fellow Scottish singer **Lulu**, but was later hit by a London bus and killed. McKenna was later in **Dream Police** and **The Sensational Alex Harvey Band**.

Search For The Sea has been compiled on *Jagged Time Lapse, Vol 3* (CD). (VJ)

Stone Angel

Personnel:	JOAN BARTLE	vcls, flute, recorder crumhorn	A
	MICK BURROUGHS	perc, bs, jew's harp	A
	PAUL CORRICK	gtr, bs	A
	DAVE LAMBERT	violin, mandolin, rebec	A
	KEN SAUL	vcls, gtr, dulcimer treble recorder	A

ALBUM: 1(A) STONE ANGEL (SSLP 04) 1975 R3

NB: (1) reissued on Acme (AC 8008 LP) 1995, numbered limited edition of 500 copies (SC), and by Kissing Spell on CD (Erewhon KSCD 9430) 1994. There's also a CD of material recorded as a three-piece late in 1975, *The Holy Road Of Bromholm* on Kissing Spell (Erewhon KSCD 9490-f) 1994.

An ultra-rare privately-pressed album which sells for big money. Corrick, Saul and Burroughs were previously in **Midwinter**. Guitarist Ken Saul also made a solo album before joining this Norfolk-based outfit. Musically we're talking acid-folk here with strong, brooding, dark material and unnerving, fragile vocals marred only by poor sound quality. It's not as hard to find as most private pressings but the original will still easily set you back a three figure sum. Consequently the Acme / Kissing Spell reissues are recommended.

The reputation of the album in later years encouraged the band back into the studios to record an album of new material *East Of The Sun* in 2001. Compilation appearances include: *Dancing At Whitsun* on *The History Of U.K. Underground Folk Rock 1968-1978 Vol. 1* (CD); and *The Bells Of Dunwich* on *The History Of U.K. Underground Folk Rock 1968-1978 Vol. 2* (CD). (VJ)

Stonefield Tramp

| Personnel incl: | TERRY FRIEND |
| | ROB VAN SPYK |

ALBUM: 1 DREAMING AGAIN (Acorn/Tramp CF 247) 1974 R3

This is an ultra-rare private-pressing. 200 copies of this were recorded and pressed at Acorn Studios. Very much of the folk genre with a tinge of psychedelia it comprised social commentary material with cuts like *Bitter World* and *Social State Blues*. **Van Spyk** and Friend both recorded

privately-pressed solo albums in the mid-seventies. *Friend's*, coming in 1977, was outside the timespan of this book. Titled *Comes The Day* it was a private pressing and just 100 copies were made (R2). Three years earlier **Stonefield Tramp** had recorded an unreleased acetate *Going Nowhere*, (R5) which had an anti-war theme. Just three copies were pressed. It comprised lovely guitar, flute and vocal work with *Lady Of The East*, *A Country Divided*, *Garbage Drama* (a poem similar in style to **Ithaca**) and *Peppermint Cream* and *Gooseberry Pie* among the best tracks. (VJ)

Stonehouse

Personnel:	TERRY PARKER	bs	A
	PETER SEARING	lead gtr, vcls	A
	JAMES SMITH	vcls	A
	IAN SNOW	drms	A

ALBUM: 1(A) STONEHOUSE CREEK (RCA SF 8197) 1971 R2

This was a progressive hard-rock outfit. The album is now rare and sought-after by collectors of this genre, apart from the acoustic title track it consists of bludgeoning hard-rock.

James Smith and Ian Snow joined **Asgard**. (VJ)

Stone's Masonry

Personnel:	MICHAEL RILEY	bs	A
	PETE SOLLEY (or SHELLEY)	organ	A
	MARTIN STONE	gtr	A
	KEITH TILLMAN	bs	A

45: Flapjacks/Hot Rock (Purdah 45-3504) 1966 R3

NB: Only 99 copies pressed.

Stone's Masonry recorded a very rare and sought-after blues-rock single. Martin Stone joined from Rockhouse and Pete Solley had been **Chris Farlowe's Thunderbirds**.

This group's life was ended when Stone departed to join **Savoy Brown**. He went on to play for **The Action** shortly before they became **Mighty Baby**.

The Pete Solley (or Shelley) listed above is not the guy who co-founded The Buzzcocks, but he went on to play with Terry Reid, produced the **Fable** album and may have been in **Julian Covey and The Machine**. Tillman was later in **Aynsley Dunbar's Retaliation**.

Compilation appearances include: *Hot Rock* on *Beat It* (3-CD); and *Flapjacks* on *Blues Anytime, Vol. 1* (Immediate IMLP 014). (VJ/JM)

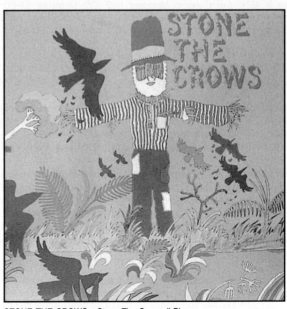

STONE THE CROWS - Stone The Crows (LP).

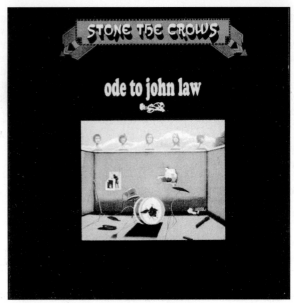

STONE THE CROWS - Ode To John Law (CD).

Stone The Crows

Personnel:	COLIN ALLEN	drms	ABC
	MAGGIE BELL	vcls	ABC
	JIM DEWAR	bs	A
	LES HARVEY	gtr	ABC
	JOHN McGINNIS	keyb'ds	A
	RONNIE LEAHY	keyb'ds	BC
	STEVE THOMPSON	drms	B
	JIMMY McCULLOCH	gtr	C

				HCP
ALBUMS:	1(A)	STONE THE CROWS	(Polydor 2425 017) 1970 SC	-
(up to	2(A)	ODE TO JOHN LAW	(Polydor 2425 042) 1970 SC	-
1976)	3(B)	TEENAGE LICKS	(Polydor 2425 071) 1971 SC	-
	4(C)	'ONTINUOUS PERFORMANCE		
			(Polydor 2391 043) 1972 SC	33
	5 (-)	STONE THE CROWS (Comp.)	(Polydor 2482 279) 1976	-

NB: (1) reissued on CD (Repertoire REP 4626 WY) 1997, again (River RIVERCD 045) and on vinyl (Akarma AK) 2005. (2) on CD (Repertoire REP 4624 WY) 1997 and on vinyl (Akarma AK 296) 2005. (3) reissued on CD (Repertoire REP 4625 WY) 1997 and on vinyl (Akarma AK 294) 2005. (4) reissued on CD (Repertoire REP 4627 WY) 1997, with new liner notes by veteran journalist Chris Welch and on CD (Akarma AK 300) 2005. (5) was reissued on Thunderbolt (THBL 070) 1989, also on CD (CDTB 070).

BBC Radio 1 Live In Concert (Strange Fruit SFRSCD 049) 1998 includes many of their early stage favourites and *BBC Radio 1 Live In Concert, Volume 2* (Strange Fruit SFRSCD) 1998 continues with tracks from 1971 and 1972. *Coming On Strong* (Snapper SNDCD 519) 2004 is a 2-CD live set comprising a live concert at Montreaux in 1972 and a **Maggie Bell** solo set recorded at London's Rainbow Theatre in 1974. *Live Crows In Montreaux 1972* (CD) (Angel Air SJPCD 116) features previously unreleased live material which comprises long tracks with lots of jamming full of acid guitar and keyboards. The set is also available on vinyl.

45s:	Mad Dogs And Englishmen/Sad Mary	(Polydor 2066 060) 1971
	Good Time Girl/On The Highway	(Polydor 2058 301) 1972

This Scottish group set out playing blues/heavy rock and were originally known as The Power. They were 'discovered' by **Led Zeppelin** manager Peter Grant whilst gigging at clubs and air bases in Europe. He renamed them **Stone The Crows** and they signed a record deal with Polydor.

The original line-up cut two tight soul-based albums. Les Harvey was a fine guitarist and **Maggie Bell**'s raucous vocals gave them a winning blend. Both albums are well worth checking out but didn't get the critical acclaim they deserved, a factor clearly instrumental in the departure of Jim Dewar and John McGinnis in February 1971. Leahy and Thompson came in as replacements. Thompson had previously played in **John Mayall**'s band as had Colin Allen.

The *Teenage Licks* album made a greater impression than their previous efforts. Highlights include *I May Be Right I May Be Wrong* and *Big Jim Salter* and, with **Maggie Bell** widely acclaimed as Britain's Top Girl Singer,

in 1972 things really seemed to be heading upwards for the band. Then Les Harvey was tragically killed on stage by a 'live' microphone during a gig at Swansea University. Jimmy McCulloch (ex-**Thunderclap Newman**) was drafted in as a replacement and their next album *'Ontinuous Performance* was completed by this new line-up. However, it was as if the band had had its heart ripped out. Sadly commercial success continued to elude them and they eventually called it a day during 1973. **Maggie Bell** launched a solo career but never achieved the success her talent suggested. Jimmy McCulloch joined Joe Soap and later **Wings**.

BBC Radio 1 Live In Concert captures them playing many of their early stage favourites at the Beeb like their rampaging rendition of Bob Dylan's *Don't Think Twice It's Alright*.

Coming On Strong collects **Bell's** live material from the seventies. The first CD features her playing with **Stone The Crows** at Montreal in 1972. It is poorly recorded and pretty heavy-going. The second CD is from London's Rainbow Theatre in 1974 after she has turned solo. This captures her at her best. The support band includes **Pete Wingfield** on keyboards and Brian Breeze on guitar. It includes superb versions of her *Suicide Sal* and **Free's** *Wishing Well* and culminates in a rousing gospel medley.

Jim Dewar went on to provide bass and soulful vocals (strong ones at that) for all **Robin Trower's** seventies albums. He suffered a crippling stroke in 1987. Colin Allen later played with the Dutch band focus from 1973 to 1975.

Stone The Crows can also be heard playing *Raining In Your Hearts* and *Sad Mary* on Polydor's 1971 compilation *Bombers* (LP) and *Fool On The Hill* on *Rock Party* (2-LP), which appeared the same year. (VJ)

Mike Storey

Personnel:	STEVE CHAPMAN	drms	AB
	WINSTON DELANDRO	gtr	AB
	CHARLIE HARRISON	bs	A
	NEIL HUBBARD	gtr	A
	MIKE STOREY	vcls, piano, organ, hrmnca	AB
	STUART BROOKS	bs	B

ALBUMS:	1(A)	STOREY	(MAM-AS 1011) 1974
	2(B)	WHO ARE YOU PLAYING TO?	(MAM-AS 1013) 1975

NB: (1) credited to Storey. (2) credited to Mike Storey Band.

Mike Storey was a singer / songwriter who composed rock tunes on the softer side with the occasional more up-tempo number rising above the mediocre. His second album is probably more up-beat than the first. He surrounded himself with some excellent musicians. Neil Hubbard had previously played in **The Misunderstood**, **Bluesology**, **Grease Band**, **Juicy Luicy**, **Wynder K. Frog** and **Kokomo**. Charlie Harrison was in

STONE THE CROWS - Teenage Licks (LP).

Judas Jump and Coast Road Drive along with Steve Chapman. Stuart Brooks was in Black Cat Bones and Leaf Hound and was also in a later line-up of The Pretty Things. Sadly the answer to the question posed by the title of his second album was 'not too many' and he disappeared from view. (BS)

Rory Storm and The Hurricanes

Personnel:			
TY BRIEN (O'BRIEN)	gtr	ABCDEFG H	
ALAN (RORY) CALDWELL	vcls	ABCDEFG H I J	
JOHNNY (BYRNE) GUITAR	lead gtr	ABCDEFG H I J	
RINGO STARR(KEY)	drms	AB	
LU WALTERS (EYMOND)	bs	A CDEFG	
BOBBY THOMPSON	bs	B	
GIBSON KEMP	drms	C	
BRIAN JOHNSON	drms	D	
IAN BROAD	drms	E	
TREVOR MORAIS	drms	F	
JIMMY TUSHINGHAM	drms	G H I	
VINCE EARL	bs	H	
DAVE MAY	bs	I	
CARL BRUCE	drms	J	
ADRIAN LORD	gtr	J	
KARL TERRY	bs	J	

45s:	Doctor Feelgood/I Can Tell	(Oriole CB 1858) 1963 R1
	America/	
	Since You Broke My Heart	(Parlophone R 5197) 1964 SC

This popular Merseybeat group missed out on the national stage but had a few claims to fame. Among their many members was one **Ringo Starr** before he joined **The Beatles**. Their second 45 was also the first record produced by Brian Epstein.

They'd started out as a skiffle group called The Raving Texans in the late fifties changing names to **Rory Storm and The Hurricanes** when they took up rock'n'roll in the early sixties. They were at the forefront of the Merseybeat scene but their 45s (the first was a pretty solid R&B coupling) only provided a glimpse of their live reputation.

In addition to the above two 45s, which are inevitably now sought-after, they can also be heard playing *Beautiful Dreamer* and *Dr. Feelgood* on Oriole's *This Is Merseybeat, Vol. 1* (LP) and *Vol. 2* (LP) of the same series includes *I Can Tell*. Other compilation appearances have included: *I Can Tell*, *Dr. Feelgood* and *Beautiful Dreamer* on *Let's Stomp!* (LP); *America* on *Liverpool 1963-1968* (CD), *Liverpool 1963-1968, Vol. 1* (LP) and *Mersey Beat* (2-LP); *I Can Tell* and *Dr. Feelgood* on *Mersey Beat 1962-1964* (2-LP); and *I Can Tell* on *The Exciting New Liverpool Sound* (LP).

Rory later killed himself in 1973 and drummer Gibson Kemp went on to play with **Paddy, Klaus and Gibson**. (VJ/AD)

STORYTELLER - Storyteller (LP).

Robb Storme Group

Personnel incl: ROBB STORME

45:	Here Today/Don't Cry	(Columbia DB 7993) 1966 SC

A Midlands beat group, previously known as Robb Storme and The Whispers. Indeed **Storme** had earlier released ten singles which were solo efforts or with The Whispers in the first half of the sixties for Pye, Piccadilly, Decca and Columbia. The 'A' side was a cover of a Beach Boys composition.

Compilation appearances include: *To Know Her Is To Love Her* on *Piccadilly Story* (CD); and *Love Is Strange* on *Hippy Hippy Shake* (CD). (VJ)

Storyteller

Personnel:			
CAROLINE ATTARD	vcls	AB	
RODNEY CLARK	bs, vcls	AB	
TERRY DURHAM	vcls	AB	
ROGER MOON	gtr, vcls	AB	
MICK RODGERS	steel gtr, vcls	A	
CHRIS BELSHAW	bs, vcls	B	
HENRY SPINETTI	drms	B	

ALBUMS:	1(A)	STORYTELLER	(Transatlantic TRA 220) 1970 SC
	2(B)	MORE PAGES	(Transatlantic TRA 232) 1971 SC

NB: (1) reissued on CD (Wooded Hill HILLCD 22) 1997 with six bonus tracks.

45:	Remarkable/Laugh That Came Too Soon	(CBS 7182) 1971

A progressive/contemporary folk group in which **Peter Frampton** and **Andy Bown** were closely involved without actually playing - they produced the first album. **Andy Bown** also wrote some of the songs on their albums. Their vocalist Caroline Attard had previously been with pop duo **The Other Two** and **Terry Durham** was **Judith Durham**'s brother. He'd recorded a solo album in 1969. The album contains no real highlights, although, *Ballad Of Old 3 Laps* tells an astonishing tale. The material is folk-inspired and there are lovely, often melancholic, harmonies, a soft-rock backing and restrained string section. The 1997 Wooded Hill reissue contains six bonus tracks taken from their second album. Rodgers left after their debut album and *More Pages* was recorded by line-up (B) but made little impact and so the story ended. They recorded several sessions for Radio 1, which remain unreleased. Henry Spinetti had earlier been in **The Herd** with **Peter Frampton**. He and Chris Belcher ended up playing with **Andy Bown**. Roger Moon went to the States where he recorded two albums but then drifted out of the music business.

Compilation appearances include *Remarkable* on *The Transatlantic Story* CD box set. (VJ)

The Storytellers

45s:	Deedle-um Song/Hey Lover	(Decca F 12336) 1966
	Let's Get Back On The Love Scene/	
	Just A Friend	(Decca F 12439) 1966

A mid-sixties beat group. (MWh/VJ)

Strange Days

Personnel:			
EDDIE McNEIL	drms	A	
EDDIE SPENCE	keyb'ds	A	
PHIL WALMAN	bs, vcls	A	
GRAHAM WARD	ld gtr, vcls	A	

ALBUM:	1(A)	9 PARTS TO THE WIND	
		(Retreat Records RTL-6005) 1975 SC	

45:	Monday Morning/Joe Soap	(Retreat RTS 263) 1975

A strange band this. The lyrics of their songs didn't fit well with the music and their sound was heavily influenced by *Selling England By The Pound* era **Genesis**. The band broke up shortly after the album was recorded. Keyboardist Eddie Spence also worked on some Gordon Giltrap albums. (VJ)

Strange Fox

45:      Bring It On Home/Time And Tide   (Parlophone R 5876) 1970

This five-piece band came from Stoke-On-Trent. *Bring It On Home* is a reasonable piece of rock/pop with a bit of life backed by an altogether more subtle flip, including a flute. Produced by Tony Hatch, only the vocals in places let it down. They recorded again in Abbey Road studios in April 1974 but nothing else emerged. (MWh)

Strange Fruit

Personnel: PETE KEELEY   gtr   A
              KEITH WARRINGTON   hrmnca, harp   A

45:      Cut Across Shorty/
         Shake That Thing   (Village Thing VTSX 1001) 1971 SC

This good-time blues/folk guitar/harmonica duo issued the first 45 on the folky Village Thing label. They came from the West Country and the disc was only available at their gigs. The 45 featured a version of *Cut Across Shorty* (also recorded by **Rod Stewart** among others) backed by *Shake That Thing*, a jug-band type song.

They broke up during 1971 due to musical differences, but reformed in September 1972. They were still together in July 1973. (VJ)

The Strangers (with Mike Shannon)

45s: α One And One Is Two/
          Time And The River   (Philips BF 1335) 1964 R1
          Do You Or Don't You/What Can I Do   (Philips BF 1378) 1964
NB: α credited to **The Strangers with Mike Shannon**.

The first of these two 45s is now quite sought-after, but the band's personnel remain unknown aside from **Mike Shannon**. They came from Birmingham.

Compilation appearances have included: *Do You Or Don't You* on *Rare 60's Beat Treasures, Vol. 4* (CD); *What Can I Do* on *Rare 60's Beat Treasures, Vol. 5* (CD); and *One And One Is Two* on *Songs Lennon And McCartney Gave Away* (LP). (VJ)

THE STRAWBS - Strawbs (CD).

STRAWBS - Dragonfly (CD).

The Strangers

45s: Look Out (Here Comes Tomorrow)/
         Mary Mary   (Pye 7N 17240) 1967 SC
         You Didn't Have To Be So Nice/
         Daytime Turns To Night   (Pye 7N 17351) 1967
         I'm On An Island/Step Inside (Pye 7N 17585) 1968
         Look Up And Around/Merry-Go-Round(Harvard HARV 003) 1970

An obscure late sixties act from Ireland. Both sides of their debut 45 were Monkees' tracks. The 45 on the short-lived Harvard label may be by a different band.

Compilation appearances have included: *Look Out (Here Comes Tomorrow)* and *You Didn't Have To Be So Nice* on *Ripples, Vol. 1* (CD); *Mary, Mary* on *Ripples, Vol. 7* (CD); and *Look Out (Here Comes Tomorrow)* and *Mary, Mary* on *Irish Rock - Ireland's Beat Groups 1964-1969* (CD). (VJ)

Strange Stone

ALBUM: 1   STRANGE STONE
              (w/insert)   (Private pressing DER 1399) 1977 R5

Although strictly outside the time frame of this book, the above album which had a limited pressing of 255 copies may interest some readers. (VJ)

Strapps

Personnel: JOE REED   bs, vcls   A
              NOEL SCOTT   keyb'ds, vcls A
              ROSS STAGG   gtr, vcls   A
              MICK UNDERWOOD   drms   A

ALBUM: 1(A) STRAPPS   (Harvest SHSP 4055) 1976
(up to
1976)
NB: (1) reissued on CD (Thunderbird CSA 118) 2004.

45:      In Your Ear/Rita B (PS)   (Harvest HAR 5108) 1976
(up to
1976)

Mick Underwood had been in **Quartermass** and Ross Stagg was a talented Australian vocalist. Their debut album was produced by **Roger Glover** and the band played a **Mott The Hoople** styled keyboard-dominated pop-rock. *School Girl Funk* will not go down well with feminists and the best cut is probably *Suicide*, one of the few to feature the guitar. They went on to record a couple more albums and two further 45s, which are beyond the time span of this book. (VJ)

The Strawbs

Personnel incl:

DAVE COUSINS	vcls, gtr, banjo, dulcimer	ABCDEFG
TONY HOOPER	gtr, vcls	ABCDE
ARTHUR PHILIPS	mandolin	A
RON CHESTERMAN	bs	BC
SANDY DENNY	vcls	B
CLAIRE DENIZ	cello	C
RICHARD HUDSON	drms	DEF
JOHN FORD	bs	DEF
RICK WAKEMAN	keyb'ds	D
BLUE WEAVER	keyb'ds	EF
DAVE LAMBERT	gtr, vcls	FG
CHAS CRONK	bs	G
ROD COOMBES	drms	G
JOHN HAWKEN	keyb'ds	G

HCP

ALBUMS:	1(B)	ALL OUR OWN WORK	(Hallmark SHM 813) 1973 SC -
(up to	2(B)	STRAWBS	(A&M AMLS 936) 1969 SC -
1976)	3(C)	DRAGONFLY	(A&M AMLS 970) 1970 SC -
	4(D)	JUST A COLLECTION OF ANTIQUES AND CURIOS	(A&M AMLS 994) 1970 SC 27
	5(D)	FROM THE WITCHWOOD	(A&M AMLS 64304) 1971 SC 39
	6(E)	GRAVE NEW WORLD	(A&M AMLS 68078) 1972 SC 11
	7(F)	BURSTING AT THE SEAMS	(A&M AMLS 68144) 1973 2
	8(G)	HERO AND HEROINE	(A&M AMLH 63607) 1974 35
	9(-)	STRAWBS BY CHOICE (comp.)	(A&M AMLH 68259) 1974 -
	10(G)	GHOSTS	(A&M AMLH 68277) 1975 -
	11( )	NOMADNESS (w/lyric insert)	(A&M AMLH 68331) 1976 -
	12(-)	DEEP CUTS (w/lyric insert)	(Oyster 2391 234) 1976 -

NB: (1) features recordings from 1968 credited to **Sandy Denny** and **The Strawbs**. (1) and (2) repackaged as a 2-LP set *Early Strawbs* (A&M SP 9014) 1974. (2) reissued on CD in Korea (Si-Wan SRMC 0088) and also (Progressive Line PL 527) with a lyric booklet. (3) reissued on CD in Korea (Si-Wan SRMC 0083) and also (Progressive Line PL 503) which comes with a booklet. (4) reissued on CD (A&M 540 938-2) 1998 remastered and with a few bonus tracks and again in 2005. (5) reissued on CD (A&M 032 Y35 578) 1988 and again on CD (A&M 540 939-2) 1998 and again remastered and with one bonus tracks and new sleevenotes (A&M 540 939-2). (6) reissued on CD (A&M 540 934-2) 1998 remastered and with a few bonus tracks. (7) reissued on CD (A&M 540 936-2) 1998 remastered and with a few bonus tracks. (8) reissued on CD (A&M 540 935-2) 1998 remastered and with a few bonus tracks. (10) reissued on CD (A&M 540 937-2) 1998 remastered and with a few bonus tracks. (11) reissued on CD (Progressive Line PL 517). (12) reissued on a 2-CD set with the 1977 album *Burning For You* (RGF WCDCD 027).

Compilations have included: *Classic Strawbs* (A&M SP 9800) 1977 a 2-LP retrospective of material from (3) through to (11), although it strangely omits their big hits *Lay Down* and *Part of The Union*; *The Best Of The Strawbs* (2-LP) (A&M AMLH 66005) 1978; *Preserve Uncanned* (2-CD) (Road Goes On Forever RGFCD 003) 1992; *A Choice Selection Of Strawbs* (CD) (A&M CD MID 173) 1992 and reissued again on CD with a 12-page fold-out booklet. *Greatest Hits Live* (CD) (Road Goes On Forever RGFCD 015) 1993; and *Halycon Days: The Very Best Of The Strawbs*

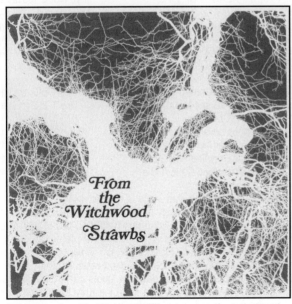

STRAWBS - From The Witchwood (CD).

STRAWBS - Grave New World (LP).

(CD) (A&M 540 662-2) 1997. Also of interest is *In Concert* (Windsong WIN CD 069) 1995, which comprises an 'In Concert' show from 1973 and five BBC cuts from 1974. *The Collection* (Spectrum 544 706 2) 2002 captures many of their finer moments. *Strawberry Music Sampler No 1* (Witchwood WRCD 2002) is a previously unheard demo which includes different versions of songs from their first three albums.

HCP

45s:	Oh How She Changed/	
(up to	Or Am I Dreaming	(A&M AMS 725) 1968 -
1976)	The Man Who Called Himself Jesus/	
	Poor Jimmy Wilson	(A&M AMS 738) 1968 -
	Forever/Another Day	(A&M AMS 791) 1970 -
	Witchwood//Keep The Devil Outside We'll Meet Again Sometime (live) (promo only)	(A&M AMS 837) 1971 -
	Benedictus/Keep The Devil Outside	(A&M AMS 874) 1971 -
	Lay Down/Backside	(A&M AMS 7035) 1972 12
	Part Of The Union/Will You Go (PS)	(A&M AMS 7047) 1973 2
	Shine On Silver Sun/And Wherefore	(A&M AMS 7082) 1973 34
	Hero And Heroine/Why	(A&M AMS 7105) 1974 -
	Hold On To Me/Where Do You Go	(A&M AMS 7117) 1974 -
	Grace Darling/Changes Arranged	(A&M AMS 7139) 1974 -
	Lemon Pie/Don't Try To Change Me	(A&M AMS 7161) 1975 -
	I Only Want My Love To Grow In You/ Thinking Of You	(Polydor 2066 705) 1976 -
	Charmer/Beside The Rio Grande	(Polydor 2066 744) 1976 -
	So Close And Yet So Far Away/ The Soldier's Tale	(Polydor 2066 751) 1976 -
Reissues:	Part Of The Union/Will You Go	(A&M AMS 7425) 1979 -
	Lay Down/Part Of The Union	(Old Gold OG 9149) 1982 -

One of the UK's better progressive bands **The Strawbs** drew their inspiration from English folk music rather than rock.

The group began life playing bluegrass music as The Strawberry Hill Boys in the mid-sixties. They took their name from the Strawberry Hill area of London where they originally rehearsed. **Cousins** and Hooper had been school mates and played together at various folk clubs. Their music gradually moved towards contemporary folk and in 1967 **Sandy Denny**, a talented female vocalist, joined their line-up. Shortly after this they took up a residency at the Tivoli in Copenhagen. Whilst there, they recorded *All Our Own Work* in 1968, although it was not actually released until the early seventies. The album included **Denny**'s *Who Knows Where The Time Goes?* which has been covered by several artists since.

In 1969 the band compiled *The Strawberry Music Sampler No. 1* a publisher's demo which did make it to the manufacturing stage, albeit just 100 copies and is now an ultra-rarity (R5). It contained some out-takes from an earlier abandoned version of their first album - *All I Need Is You, Just The Same In Every Way* and *How Everyone But Sam Was A Hypocrite* - along with some tracks from the album rejected by A&M *Stay Awhile, And You Need Me, And You Need Me/Josephine, Whichever Way The Wind Blows* and *Sweetling* and some demos and material from their unissued

1968 recordings with **Sandy Denny**. They distributed it to artists' agents and A&M chiefs but it passed unnoticed.

By the time they signed to A&M in 1969 **Denny** had moved on to **Fairport Convention**. All of the songs on their A&M debut album, which was produced by Gus Dudgeon, were written by **Cousins** and Hooper and one of the best was *The Man Who Called Himself Jesus*. The album was highly praised in folk music circles and Claire Deniz, a classical cellist, joined their line-up for their follow-up, *Dragonfly*, produced by Tony Visconti. In view of what had preceded it this particular album was a disappointment and **Cousins** and Hooper made more line-up changes of which the most significant was the recruitment of a highly talented keyboards wizard, **Rick Wakeman**, who was a graduate of the Royal Academy of Music, and John Ford and Richard Hudson, who'd previously comprised the rhythm section of **Elmer Gantry's Velvet Opera**. The line-up also gave the band a rock rather than folk sound. *Just A Collection Of Antiques And Curios* was the new line-up's first album, recorded live at the Queen Elizabeth Hall. It took them to a much wider audience and won **Wakeman** much coverage in the rock press. The recent remastered reissue includes a 10-minute version of *Vision Of The Lady Of The Lake*. The package comes with an eight-page booklet. *From The Witchwood* helped cement the new audience, but not long after this event **Rick Wakeman** left to join **Yes**. Blue Weaver (ex-**Amen Corner**) came in to replace him.

Grave New World was their first album to enter the Charts as their music became more commercial. This led to Hooper's departure not long after its release because he had become totally disillusioned by the band's move away from its folk roots. Nevertheless, it had its moments, particularly with **Dave Cousins**' *Queen Of Dreams*, which featured superb and quite psychedelic guitar work and the dramatic *New World*. John Ford's *Heavy Disguise* featured some pleasant woodwind and begged comparison to **Jethro Tull**. The most interesting cut on side two was Richard Hudson's *Is It Today, Lord?*

Dave Cousins brought in an old friend Dave Lambert to replace Hooper and released a solo album *Two Weeks Last Summer*. The band also enjoyed their first singles success with *Lay Down*, an excellent rock 45. **Hudson and Ford** wrote the follow-up, *Part Of The Union*, which was an attack on the power of Trades Unions and based on their earlier experience of working in a factory. *Bursting At The Seams* was another strong and extremely successful album.

Friction which had been building up between **Cousins** and **Hudson and Ford** boiled over during an American tour and soon after **Hudson and Ford** left to form their own band. **Cousins** put together another new line-up (G). John Hawken had previously played with **The Nashville Teens**, **Renaissance** and **Vinegar Joe**. Coombes the new drummer had been with **Stealer's Wheel**. The resulting album, *Hero And Heroine*, flopped badly in the UK, although the band continued to flourish in the US. Cellist Claire Deniz returned to the fold for the follow-up *Ghosts*, which also utilised the Charterhouse School Choir. John Hawken quit after *Ghosts* (resurfacing in **Illusion**) and they then utilised session keyboardists, particularly John Mealing (who had been with **If**) for their next few albums.

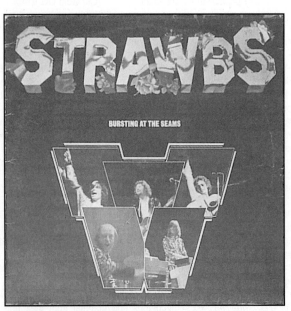

STRAWBS - Bursting At The Seams (LP).

Nomadness was an uneven album, although it had its moments. **Rick Wakeman** contributed keyboards on some cuts. *Deep Cuts* was a much stronger release and *I Only Want My Love To Grow In You* had a hit single written all over it, but failed to register. This underscores their strange lack of big success, which may had been partly due to whether or not the punters enjoyed **Cousins'** vocals in sufficient number. After *Burning For You* (1977) and the lacklustre *Deadlines* (1978) the ban finally called it a day. Dave Lambert released a solo album in 1979. An unreleased album from 1979 *Heartbreak Hill* was subsequently made available.

That would have been it if they hadn't been invited to play at the 1983 Cambridge Folk Festival. They (**Cousins**, **Hopper**, Hudson, Fords, Weaver and Willoughby) accepted and they were so popular that a tour was arranged and some further studio albums were released in Canada. The nineties were a quiet period for the band but the last two years has seen no less than four more albums released: *Blue Angel*, *Deja Fou*, *Live At NEARfest* and *Painted Sky*.

The 2-CD set *Preserves Uncanned* featured a selection of songs originally released on cassette by US magazine 'Dirty Linen'. It includes acoustic versions of songs like *The Battle* and *The Man Who Called Himself Jesus* from their first album, some demos, including *Martin Luther King's Dream*, from a 1970 Queen Elizabeth Hall live album and several bluegrass instrumentals. In 1992 A&M produced a mid-price collection of their material on CD, *A Choice Selection Of Strawbs*, which concentrated on the *Bursting At The Seams* and *Hero And Heroine* era. 1993 saw the release of *Road Goes On Forever's Greatest Hits Live*, a CD. The recording was made for Channel 4 and released on video by Castle. *The Collection*, a 2002 CD is an alternative collection of their studio material.

The Strawbs reformed in both the eighties and nineties to both record and tour. An interesting and rather unpredictable act - *Grave New World* and *Bursting At The Seams* are recommended. Compilation appearances included *Sheep* on *Come Together* (LP) and *Battle on Heads In* (LP). (VJ/CG)

Stray

Personnel:

DEL BROMHAM	gtr, vcls, keyb'ds	AB
RITCHIE COLE	drms	AB
STEVE GADD	hrmnca, gtr, vcls	A
GARY G. GILES	bs	AB
PETE DYER	gtr, vcls	B

ALBUMS:	1(A)	STRAY	(Transatlantic TRA 216) 1970 R1
(up to	2(A)	SUICIDE	(Transatlantic TRA 233) 1971 R1
1976)	3(A)	SATURDAY MORNING PICTURES	
			(Transatlantic TRA 248) 1972 SC
	4(A)	MUDANZAS	(Transatlantic TRA 268) 1973 SC
	5(A)	MOVE IT	(Transatlantic TRA 281) 1974
	6(A)	TRACKS	(Transatlantic TRA 3066) 1975
	7(A)	STAND UP AND BE COUNTED	(Dawn DNLS 3066) 1975
	8(B)	HOUDINI	(Pye NSPL 18482) 1976
	9(B)	HEARTS OF FIRE	(Pye NSPL 18512) 1976

NB: (1) reissued on CD (Castle Music CMRCD 1203) 2005 with four previously unreleased tracks as bonus tracks. (7) and (9) reissued on Repertoire (REP 4136-WZ and REP 4112-WZ, respectively) in 1991. Also relevant is *The Definitive Collection* (Essential ESACD 916) 2000. *Time Machine Anthology 1970-1977* (Castle CMDDD 607) 2003, a 2-CD anthology as its title suggest.

45s:	Our Song/Mamma's Coming Home	(Big T BIG 141) 1971
(up to	Hallelujah/Brand New Day	(Big T BIG 512) 1972
1976)	Move It/Crazy People	(Big T BIG 516) 1972
	Precious Love/Recover	(Dawn DNS 1101) 1975
	Smile/Stand Up And Be Counted	(Dawn DNS 1117) 1975
	Take It Easy/Fire And Glass	(Pye 7N 45564) 1976
	You Went Away/Take A Life	(Pye 7N 45642) 1976

Stray was a quartet who had quite a prolific output. The group of schoolboys from Shepherds Bush formed in 1967. They recorded their debut album, which is full of guitar-driven hard-rock, before any of them were 18. Tracks like the opener *All In Your Mind*, *Taken All The Good Things*, *Around The World In Eighty Days* and *Time Machine* are pretty tasty and at over 45 minutes playing time, good value. Its weakness is lack of variety and the musical quality definitely tapers off on side two. **Stray** were at one time managed by Charlie Kray, the Kray twins' brother. They were a rousing live act and gigged prolifically.

Time Machine Anthology is probably the best introduction to their music now. Disc one is taken mostly from their first four albums. *Around The World In Eighty Days* and *Time Machine* stand out.

Del Bromham lives in Milton Keynes and still regularly cobbles together a group to play under this name. He's also released singles under his own name in the past on the Gull label amongst others.

Compilation appearances include *All In Your Mind* on *The Transatlantic Story* CD box set and on the 3-CD box set *Ars Longa Vita Brevis: A Compendium Of Progressive Rock 1967-1974*; and *All In Your Mind* re-emerged on the 3-CD set *Metal* and on the CD set *Rock Of Ages, Four Decades Of Heavy Rock 1962-2002*. (VJ)

Stray Dog

Personnel:			
	ALAN ROBERTS	bs, vcls	AB
	LES SAMPSON	drms	AB
	SNUFFY WALDEN	gtr, vcls	AB
	LUIS CABAZA	keyb'ds, vcls	B
	TIM DULAINE	gtr, vcls	B

ALBUMS:	1(A)	STRAY DOG	(Manticore K 45306) 1974
	2(B)	WHILE YOU'RE DOWN THERE	(Manticore K 53504) 1974

NB: (1) reissued on CD (Renaissance RCD 1002) 1993. Also on CD, *Fasten Your Seat Belts* (Renaissance RCD 104) 1993.

Formed in early 1973 as a trio, Snuffy Walden and Al Roberts had earlier been in the Texas band Aphrodite, who toured the States but were relatively unsuccessful. On a short (two month) trip to the UK, they met **Emerson, Lake and Palmer**. After returning to the States, it was Snuffy's friendship with **Greg Lake** which led later to them signing to **ELP**'s own Manticore label.

Both albums were produced by **Greg Lake** and consisted of tedious hard-rock. It's eminently forgettable. (VJ)

Streetwalkers

Personnel:			
	ROGER CHAPMAN	vcls	ABC
	BOB TENCH	gtr	AB
	CHARLES WHITNEY	gtr	ABC
	NICKO McBRAIN	drms	B
	JON PLOTEL	bs	B
	DAVE DOWLE	drms	C
	MICHAEL FEAT	bs	C
	BRIAN JOHNSON	keyb'ds	C

				HCP
ALBUMS:	1(A)	STREETWALKERS		
(up to		(w/lyric sheet)	(Reprise K 54017) 1974	-
1977)	2(B)	DOWNTOWN FLYERS	(Vertigo 6360 123) 1975	-
	3(B)	RED CARD	(Vertigo 9102 010) 1976	16
	4(C)	VICIOUS BUT FAIR	(Vertigo 9102 012) 1977	-
	5(C)	STREETWALKERS LIVE (2-LP)	(Vertigo 6641 703) 1977	-

NB: (1), (3) and (4) released on Mercury in the US. (2) reissued on CD (BGO BGOCD 542) (3) reissued on CD (Repertoire REP 4147-WP) 1991. (4) reissued on CD as *Vicious But Fair... Plus* (See For Miles SEECD 352) 1992. (3) and (4) reissued on one CD (BGO BGOCD 669) digitally remastered and slipcased. (5) reissued on CD (BGO BGOCD 606). There's also *Best Of Streetwalkers* (Vertigo 846 661 2) 1991, although this is now deleted.

45s:	Roxianna/Crack	(Reprise K 14357) 1974
	Raingame/Miller	(Vertigo 6059 130) 1975
	Daddy Rolling Stone/	
	Hole In Your Pocket	(Vertigo 6059 144) 1976

Chapman and Whitney recorded the first **Streetwalkers** album after **Family**'s farewell tour in 1973 with help from ex-**Jeff Beck Group** guitarist Bob Tench, members of **King Crimson**, **Linda Lewis** and another former **Family** member John Wetton. At this stage **Streetwalkers** were a loose knit collection of individuals not a group in the real sense at all. After Chapman's work with **Family** the album was a real anti-climax.

STRAY - Stray (LP).

For the *Downtown Flyers* album Chapman and Whitney assembled a more stable line-up (B). John Plotel was previously with **Casablanca**. The album veered towards R&B and soul and Chapman's vocal style was much more mainstream than what he'd been doing with **Family**. Their most successful album commercially, though, was *Red Card*, which got to No 16 in the UK Album Charts. The group were popular on the Continent too, particularly in Germany. Their final 45 'A' side, *Daddy Rolling Stone* was a Derek Martin R&B track.

Internal friction ripped line-up (B) apart and line-up (C) recorded their remaining two albums to increasing public indifference. Inevitably, though Roger Chapman, a man of considerable talent, went on to make solo albums and he appeared in TV commercials. McBrain later worked for Pat Travers and was then in Iron Maiden. Tench and Feat worked for **Van Morrison** and Johnson and Dowle were in David Coverdale's Whitesnake.

Streetwalkers Live is worthy of mention. It features excellent versions of *My Friend The Sun*, *Can't Come In*, *Dice Man*, *Crazy Charade* and seven others. (VJ)

Stretch

Personnel incl:			
	STEVE EMERY	bs	AB
	ELMER GANTRY	gtr, vcls	AB
	KIRBY	gtr	AB
	JIM RUSSELL	drms	A
	JEFF RICH	drms	B

ALBUMS:	1(A)	ELASTIQUE	(Anchor ANCL 2014) 1975 SC
(up to	2(B)	CAN'T BEAT YOUR BRAIN FOR ENTERTAINMENT	
1976)			(Anchor ANCL 2016) 1976

NB: Also of interest is *Can't Judge A Book... The Peel Sessions* (Strange Fruit SFRCD 140) 1995, which comprises three sessions recorded for the BBC between 1973 and 1976.

			HCP
45s:	Why Did You Do It?/		
(up to	Write Me A Note	(Anchor ANC 1021) 1975	16
1976)	That's The Way The Wind Blows/		
	Hold On	(Anchor ANC 1027) 1976	-
	Love's Got A Hold On Me/		
	If The Cap Fits	(Anchor ANC 1034) 1976	-
Reissue:	Why Did You Do It?/		
	(Flip by different artist)	(Old Gold OG 9392) 1984	-

Featuring **Elmer Gantry** formerly of **Elmer Gantry's Velvet Opera** and Kirby, who went on to record a very rare album called *Composition* for Hot Wax in 1978, **Stretch** are best remembered for their sole hit, the catchy *Why Did You Do It?*. They recorded further albums, *Life Blood* (Anchor ANCL 2023) 1977 and *Forget The Past* (Hot Wax HW1) 1978 before splitting up. Kirby was later in **Curved Air**. (VJ)

STRING DRIVEN THING - String Driven Thing (Charisma) (LP).

William R Strickland

Personnel: PHILIP SPRINGER   orchestration, keyb'ds   A
WILLIAM R. STRICKLAND   vcls, gtr   A

ALBUM: 1(A)   ... IS ONLY THE NAME
(mono/stereo)   (Deram DML/SML 1041) 1969 SC

A whole album of singer/songwriter fare about troubled human relationships normally isn't my cup of tea, but this one occasionally makes me sit up and listen. Highly self-indulgent as these undertakings normally are, there is just enough originality to make this a little better than most of its kind. Also, the arrangements are very imaginative, and though they can't make a good song out of an ordinary one, it makes for a welcome addition. *World War 31/2* has very strange lyrics. Better than its haggard reputation would suggest.

He also contributed *Computer Love* on Decca's 1969 *Wowie Zowie! World Of Progressive Music* (LP) collection. (MK)

Strider

Personnel: GARY GRAINGER   gtr   AB
JIM HAWKINS   bs   A
IAN KEWLEY   keyb'ds, vcls   A
LEE STRELLEZYK   bs   AB
TONY BROCK   drms, vcls   B
ROB ELLIOT   vcls   B
(JENNY HAAN   vcls   B)

ALBUMS: 1(A)   EXPOSED   (GM GML 1002) 1973 SC
2(B)   MISUNDERSTANDING   (GM GML 1012) 1974 SC

NB. (1) also issued in the USA by Warner.

45s: Higher And Higher/Ain't Got No Love   (GM GMS 2) 1973
Esther's Place/Woman Blue   (GM GMS 12) 1973
Seems So Easy/Arthur Hydrogen   (GM GMS 23) 1974

A hard-rock band. *Higher And Higher*, their debut 45, was presumably the Jackie Wilson song. The *Reading Festival 1973* CD captures their performance of *Roadrunner* from that particular festival.

Jenny Haan was with **Babe Ruth** at the time of the *Misunderstanding* album. (VJ/MD)

Strife

Personnel: PAUL H. ELLSON   drms   A
JOHN REID   gtr, vcls   A
GORDON ROWLEY   bs, vcls   A

ALBUM: 1(A)   RUSH   (Chrysalis CHR 1063) 1975 SC
(up to 1976)

Strife was a progressive rock band formed in 1971, who gigged regularly by the end of that year. In February 1972, they recorded a live album at Wall City Club at Quaintways, Chester. It was never released. When an album finally emerged in 1975, it contained the most popular numbers from their stage act. They have been likened to **Tractor**. Gordon Rowley was later in the pomp-rock band Nightwing. They went on to record a second album *Back To Thunder* (Gull 1029) in 1978 (SC). (VJ/BS/CG)

Liza Strike

45:    All's Quiet On West 23rd/
Mr. Daddy-Man   (Parlophone R 5725) 1968

A solo effort by **Strike** who'd earlier fronted **Liza and The Jet Sets** in 1965 and was in **The Soulmates**. In the seventies she became a well-known backing vocalist. (VJ)

String Driven Thing

Personnel: CHRIS ADAMS   vcls, gtr   AB
PAULINE ADAMS   vcls, perc   AB
JOHN MANNION   12-str gtr, vcls   A
BILL HATJE   bs   B
GRAEME SMITH   violin   BC
COLIN WILSON   bs, gtr, banjo   B
KIMBERLEY BEACON   vcls   C
JAMES EXELL   bs, vcls   C
ALUN ROBERTS   gtr, vcls   C
COLIN FAIRLEY   drms, vcls   C

ALBUMS: 1(A)   STRING DRIVEN THING   (Concord CON 1001) 1970 R3
2(B)   STRING DRIVEN THING   (Charisma CAS 1062) 1972 SC
3(B)   THE MACHINE THAT CRIED
   (Charisma CAS 1070) 1973 SC
4(C)   PLEASE MIND YOUR HEAD
   (Charisma CAS 1097) 1974 SC
5(C)   KEEP YER 'AND ON IT   (Charisma CAS 1112) 1975 SC

NB: (1) reissued on CD. (2) reissued on CD (SPM-WWR-CD-0027). (3) reissued on CD (OZIT CD 0021) and there's also an extended version with the complete longer version of *River Of Sleep*, which was rejected by Charisma originally. There's also a 26-track CD collection, *The Early Years 1966-1982* and *Studio '72, Live Switzerland '73 & London '95* (OZIT CD 0022) comprises studio songs from 1972 with a bonus track, live material from 1973 when they were in Switzerland and a live bonus track from London in 1995.

45s: Another Night/Say What You Like   (Concord CON 7) 1970 SC
Eddie/Hooked ON The Road   (Charisma CB 195) 1972
Circus/My Real Hero   (Charisma CB 203) 1973
It's A Game/Are You A Rock'n'Roller   (Charisma CB 215) 1973
I'll Sing This One For You/To See You   (B&C CB 223) 1974
Mrs O'Reilly/Keep On Moving   (Charisma CB 239) 1974
Overdrive/Timpani For The Devil   (Charisma CB 247) 1975
But I Do/Stand Back In Amazement   (Charisma CB 276) 1976
Cruel To Feel/Josephine   (Charisma CB 286) 1976

An archetypal progressive rock outfit, formed in mid-1968 by husband and wife Chris and Pauline Adams. Although their debut album bears little resemblance to their subsequent work, being full of US West Coast-influenced breezy harmony-pop, only 100 copies were pressed and it's now inevitably rare and sought-after.

In 1972 they expanded the line-up, with Graeme Smith a classically trained violinist from the Scottish National Orchestra, Bill Hatje and Colin Wilson. The same year they signed to Charisma and released an eponymous album which enjoyed considerable critical acclaim. Characterised by Chris Adams' hard bitten lyrics and doomy vocals and Graham Smith's wailing violin playing, their 'sound' had built up a strong following on the club/college circuit. 1972 also saw them on tour in the U.S. with **Genesis**.

There is no doubt that *The Machine That Cried* although musically far stronger than their first Charisma release, was very doom-laden and apparently written while Chris Adams was hospitalised with a collapsed lung. The band too was suffering problems with Charisma. They recorded the album with a drummer against the express wishes of their label who thereafter insisted that the band demo all output for their final approval. Charisma also rejected the bands original title, *Heartfeeder*. The OZIT CD reissue of this album comes with three bonus tracks *If Only The Good*, *It's A Game* and *Part Of The City*. There's also an extended version of this album which features the complete extended version of *River Of Sleep*, which was rejected by Charisma originally.

Colin 'Billy the Kid' Fairley (ex-**Ruby** and **Beggars Opera**) also drummed on *The Machine That Cried*. Soon after the album's release, the Adams' left the band and Graham Smith took over its leadership assembling a new line-up (C). Apparently, however, an unreleased album exists featuring the Adam's, Graham Smith, Dave Mattacks and Dave Pegg. This was recorded just before the demise of the Adams-led band and examples from it are included on the *Discotomy* CD.

Their two subsequent albums were OK but never attracted the same attention as the previous two. One curious fact is their *It's A Game* 45, was later a hit for **The Bay City Rollers**! The link between the two was Shel Talmy who produced **String Driven Thing** and also produced/managed The Rollers. You can hear the original **String Driven Thing** version on the *One More Chance* (LP) compilation.

Chris and Pauline Adams made a single in 1975 after leaving the band, the 'B' side of which featured Grahame Smith on violin and this has become very collectable:

If Only The Good Die Young/	
The City At Night	(Charisma CB 24) 1975

After the band split Graham Smith went on to work with **Van Der Graaf Generator** in 1977 and later with **Peter Hammill** and Ascend. Colin Wilson went on to record a solo folk-rock album *Cloudburst* (Tabibla) 1975. Chris Adams too made a solo album *The Damage* 1992. Kimberley Beacon played with **Northwind**, although on a later line-up than the one featured on their collectable album. He also made some solo albums as Kim Beacon.

The Early Years 1968-1982 is a 26-track collection which consists of Chris Adam's personal favourites from their legendary first album, previously unissued demos from 1968 and **Dave Cousin's** demos from 1969 plus bonus material first released in 1993. The set is accompanied by a fold-out booklet that highlights the band's career.

Today Colin Fairley lives in Canada and runs a tartan import/export business, Colin Wilson works in computers in the Home Counties and Graham Smith teaches the violin. The most famous **String Driven Thing** song remains *Circus*. (VJ/BS)

STUD - September (CD).

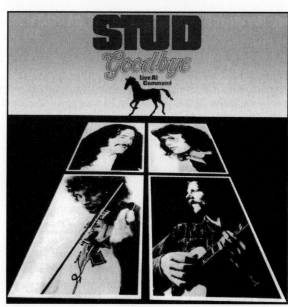

STUD - Goodbye Live At Command (CD).

Charles Stuart

An Englishman whose real name was Peter Chapwick, who recorded two singles in Finland, whilst living there in 1965-66. He was backed by the Finnish beat group The Esquires on both of them:

45s:	Stand By Me/Y'Arriva	(Parlophone PAR 979) 1966
	Some Other Guy/One Night	(Blue Master BLU 639) 1966

He made a couple of appearances on Finnish TV 1 and the Finnish music press gave him the nickname "the singing football player". (VJ)

Karl Stuart and The Profiles

Personnel incl:	MILLER ANDERSON
	KARL STUART

45s:	Love Of My Eyes/	
	Not A Girl In A Million	(Mercury MF 870) 1965
	Haven't They Got Better Things To Do/	
	The Touch Of Your Hand	(Mercury MF 875) 1965

The band had earlier recorded as **Profile**. Indeed a version of the second 45 listed here was recorded under this name. They later recorded as **The Voice**. (VJ)

Stud

Personnel:	JIM CREGAN	gtr, vcls	AB
	CHARLIE McCRACKEN	bs	AB
	JOHN WILSON	drms	ABC
	JOHN WEIDER	gtr, vcls	B
	ANDREW SNEDDON	bs	C
	SNOWIE WHITE	gtr	C

ALBUMS:	1(A)	STUD	(Deram SML-R 1084) 1971 R1
	2(B)	SEPTEMBER	(BASF 20 29054) 1972
	3(B)	GOODBYE LIVE AT COMMAND	(BASF 20 29117) 1973

NB: (2) and (3) were released in Germany only. (1) reissued on CD ((Red Fox RF 615). (2) reissued on CD (Germanophon HF 9514). (3) reissued on CD (Germaophon HF 9513). (2) and (3) reissued on one CD (Free Records FR 2007).

This outfit could never really get established in this country and its last two releases were German-only affairs. McCracken and Wilson had previously been in **Taste** (and Wilson had also been in **Them**). Cregan had cut his rock teeth in **Blossom Toes** and **Julian Covey and The Machine**. John Weider joined from **Family** after the first album had been recorded.

Jazz was a major musical influence on the band whose first album was released to enthusiastic critical acclaim. Like so many albums of this type the playing was good but the material and vocals were very average. They had a large German following though, largely 'cos they toured there regularly, and after their manager Eddie Kennedy had rowed with Deram, it was the German-based BASF label who released their next album. Again, despite some fine playing, the material and vocals were weak. Soon after the release of their third album Cregan left to join **Family**, Weider teamed up with **Keith West** in Moonrider and McCracken ended up in the reformed **Spencer Davis Group**. Wilson tried to keep the band alive with line-up (C), which included former **East Of Eden** member Andrew Sneddon, but the iron was no longer hot for them and they quickly fizzled out. (VJ)

Studd Pump

45:     Spare The Children/Floating   (Penny Farthing PEN 757) 1971

A one-off release on this quite collectable label. (MWh)

Studio Six

Personnel:	NEIL GRIMSHAW	ld gtr	A
	COLIN McCLURE	vcls	AB
	RICKY KERRY		AB
	RON MILNE	drms	A
	GERRY TEDESHI	bs	AB
	JIM BREAKEY	drms	B
	CHRIS McCLURE	gtr	A

45s: When I See My Baby/Don't Tell Lies   (Polydor BM 56131) 1966
         Times Were When/I Can't Sleep   (Polydor BM 56189) 1967
         Strawberry Window/Falling Leaves (Polydor BM 56219) 1967 SC
         Bless My Soul (I've Been And Gone And Done It)/
         People Say   (Polydor BM 56361) 1967

Formed in Glasgow in 1966, they signed to Polydor at the end of the year. A sextet they included ex-**Poet** Jim Breakey. Their first 45, *When I See My Baby* was a chirpy pop song. *Times Were When* was a ballad. *Strawberry Window* was psychedelic pop, full of sound effects, cellos, crashing drums and spoken passages. *Bless My Soul* was more in the mould of their first single. Perhaps they'd have done better if they'd chosen one particular style and persevered with it.

Strawberry Window has been compiled on *Justafixation II* (LP). (VJ)

The Stylos

Personnel:	TONY LOUIE	gtr	A
	JOHN LOWE	drms	A
	ROY LOWE	bs	A
	GREAME RENNIE	hrmnca, vcls	A
	JOHN YENDALL	ld gtr	A

45:     Head Over Heels/
        Bye, Bye, Baby, Bye Bye   (Liberty LBS 10173) 1964 R3

This Manchester-based beat group who had the distinction of being the first British beat group to record on the American Liberty label. Their 45 is ultra-rare and obscure. The 'A' side is a blues-based number, which opens with guitar and maracas building up to a wailing harmonica-led climax.

Compilation appearances have included: *Head Over Heels* on *Maximum R'n'B* (CD); *Bye Bye Baby, Bye Bye* and *Head Over Heels* on *Nowhere Men Vol. 1* (LP & CD) and *Rare 60's Beat Treasures, Vol. 2* (CD). (VJ)

Sue and Sunny

| Personnel: | SUE GLOVER | vcls | A |
| | SUNNY LESLIE | vcls | A |

ALBUM: 1(A) SUE AND SUNNY   (CBS 63740) 1970
NB: (1) also issued on Reflection (REFL 4) 1972 (SC).

45s: Every Ounce Of Strength/
         So Remember   (Columbia DB 7748) 1965
         You Can't By-Pass Love/
         I Like Your Style   (Columbia DB 8099) 1967
         Little Black Book/The Show Must Go On   (CBS 3874) 1968
         Runnin' Round In Circles/I Must Try   (CBS 4391) 1969
         Let Us Break Bread/
         Stop Messin' About With Me Heart   (CBS 4567) 1969
         You Devil Cotton Eyed Joe/Night In The City   (CBS 4757) 1970
         Ain't That Telling You People/
         Didn't I Blow Your Mind   (Deram DM 318) 1970
         Freedom/Break Up   (Deram DM 328) 1971
         Let Us Break Bread Together/
         Michael From The Mountains   (Reflection HRS 10) 1971
         I'm Gonna Make You Love Me/
         High On The Thought Of You   (Deram DM 355) 1972

This female duo had been in The Myrtelles who cut a single for Oriole in 1963. They'd earlier recorded as **Sue and Sunshine** and were also in **The Stockingtops**. They played a Swingin' London mixture of folk and baroque pop. Their final 'A' side, *I'm Gonna Make You Leave Me* was also recorded by The Supremes and The Temptations. (VJ/MWh)

Sue and Sunshine

| Personnel: | SUE GLOVER | vcls | A |
| | SUNNY LESLIE | vcls | A |

45s: Little Love/If You See Me Crying   (Columbia DB 7409) 1964
         We're In Love/Don't Look Behind   (Columbia DB 7533) 1965

This pop duo had previously been in The Myrtelles. They later recorded as **Sue and Sunny** and were also in **Stockingtops**. (VJ)

Alisha Sufit

CD: 1 LOVE AND THE MAIDEN
           (Magic Carpet MC 1002CD) 1994

Alisha Sufit was the vocalist in **Magic Carpet** who put out an album in 1972. It didn't sell and she took up busking in Portabello Market, where she was discovered by producer Nick Sykes. He arranged for her to record an album's worth of material at R.G. Jones' studios in 1974, but the project was later shelved as the singer wasn't happy with the results. Hot on the heels of the reissue of the **Magic Carpet** album and a freshly-recorded solo album, *Through The Looking Glass*, the 1974 tapes have been issued on the above CD, which typifies her high-pitched vocal style within a folk format. It's worth seeking out at the very least by folk fans. (VJ)

Summer Set

| Personnel incl: | DAVE BRIENT | vcls | A |
| | LES HUMPHRIES | | A |

45s: α Farmer's Daughter/
         What Are You Gonna Do   (Columbia DB 8004) 1966 R1
         Overnight Changes/It's A Dream   (Columbia DB 8215) 1967 R1
NB: α First issued with *Papa-Oom-Mow-Mow* on flip (R1).

This obscure five-piece surf band was managed by Bob Anthony. Their first 45, *Farmer's Daughter* was written by Les Humphries, who was later a member of Les Humphries Singers enjoying hits like *In My Father's House* and *Mexico*.

Their second 45, in particular, is becoming sought-after. *Overnight Changes* is a lively poppy composition. As was often the case in this era, it is overshadowed by the haunting psychedelic flip side *It's A Dream*.

They also had a US-only 45, with a terminally dull version of *(Let's Go To) San Francisco* backed by an original *Cos It's Over*. This is an effective amalgam of freakbeat and psychedelia with pounding drums and appealing double-tracked lead vocal.

Compilation appearances have included: *What Are You Gonna Do?* on *Red With Purple Flashes, Vol. 2* (LP); *Cos It's Over* on *Syde Trips Vol. 6* (LP); and *It's A Dream* on *Circus Days Vol. 3* (LP & CD). (VJ)

Summer Wine

Personnel:	RAY FENWICK		A
	MIKE HURST		A
	JOHN PERRY		A
	TONY RIVERS		A

45s:	Why Do Fools Fall In Love/		
	Ode To The Steel Guitar	(Philips 6006 217)	1972
	Take A Load Off Your Feet/		
	Sound Of Summer's Over	(Philips 6006 238)	1972
	She's Still A Mystery/Shanandoah	(Philips 6006 315)	1973
	Living Next Door To An Angel/		
	Sound Of Summer's Over	(Philips 6006 388)	1973

This studio band had some talented members. See the **Mike Hurst** and **Tony Rivers** entries for details of their careers. Ray Fenwick had been in **The Spencer Davis Group** among others and John Perry had been in **Grapefruit**. Despite the pedigree of their line-up, their 45s made little impression. (VJ)

Sun Also Rises

Personnel:	ANNE HEMINGWAY	vcls, dulcimer	A
	GRAHAM HEMINGWAY	gtr, vcls	A

ALBUM:	1(A)	THE SUN ALSO RISES	(Village Thing VTS 2) 1970 SC

NB: (1) reissued on CD (Progressive Line PL 565) with a bonus track and from the mastertapes.

A Cardiff duo, who were assisted by Andy Leggett (woodwind) and John Turner (bs) on their self-titled album, which was released on **Ian A. Anderson**'s Village Thing label. The duo were similar to **The Incredible String Band** with a penchant for doom-laden songs like *Tales Of Jasmine And Suicide*. They started work on a second album which was never completed, although one track found its way onto the Village Thing compilation *Us* (LP) in 1972. Back in 1970 they'd also contributed a track to Village Thing's *Great White Dad* four-track promotional EP, which was given away at gigs rather than sold through the label's normal retail outlets. (VJ)

Sunbird

45:	Brother Bird/Love Of The Free	(Philips 6006 046) 1970

ALISHA SUFIT - Love And The Maiden (CD).

Although *Brother Bird* was also featured on the Vertigo sampler *Heads Together* (2-LP), we haven't been able to dig up any further info on the band. (MWh)

Sunchariot

45s:	Rosemarie/Do You Wanna Know	(Decca F 13317) 1972
	All Your Love/You're Lovely	(Decca F 13368) 1973
	Firewater/Only Girl I Knew	(Decca F 13407) 1973

Sunchariot entered the Decca studios in November 1972 with **Mike Vernon** handling production duties. *You're Lovely* has been compiled on *Fading Yellow, Vol 5* (CD). (VJ)

Sundae Times

Personnel:	CONRAD ISIDORE	drms	A
	WENDELL RICHARDSON	gtr, vcls	A
	CALVIN SAMUELS	bs	A

ALBUM:	1(A)	US COLOURED KIDS	(Joy JOYS 159) 1970 SC

45s:	Baby Don't Cry/Aba - Aba	(President PT 203) 1968
	Jack Boy/I Don't Want Nobody	(President PT 219) 1968
	Live Today/Take Me Higher Baby	(President PT 285) 1970

A trio who were one of Eddie Grant's (of **The Equals**) protege groups. He also acted as their producer. They recorded a mixture of mildly progressive pop songs and reggae.

They were briefly known as The Tonics before splitting. Wendell Richardson was later in Osisbisa and **Free**. Conrad Isidore went on to **One** and **Manfred Mann Chapter 111**. Calvin Samuels was also in **One** and then with various mutations of Crosby, Stills, Nash and Young. (VJ/JM)

Sundance

Personnel:	BOB BOWMAN	gtr, vcls, banjo	A
	STEPHEN GRIFFIN	keyb'ds, vcls	A
	JOHN LYNAM	gtr, vcls, mandolin	A
	ALAN MOORE	drms, vcls	A
	PHIL SAVAGE	bs, vcls, hrmnca	A

ALBUMS:	1(A)	RAIN STEAM SPEED	(Decca TXS 111) 1973 SC
	2(A)	CHUFFER	(Decca SKL 5183) 1974 SC

45s:	Coming Down/Eagles	(Decca F 13428) 1973
	Stand By/Willie The Gambler	(Decca F 13461) 1973
	Loving You/Can You Feel It	(Decca F 13494) 1974

Sundance came from Birmingham and their sound was based on the US West Coast bands of the late sixties and early seventies. Their albums had train-related motifs; the first is named after a Turner painting showing a steam train. It was promoted by a college tour using the tag-line 'Who The Hell Are Sundance?' Well might they have asked. (VJ/BS/PC)

Sunday

Personnel:	JOHN BARCLAY	gtr, vcls	A
	JIMMY FOREST	keyb'ds, vcls	A
	DAVY PATTERSON	vcls, bs	A

ALBUM:	1(A)	SUNDAY	(Bellaphon BLPS 19066) 1971 R2

NB: (1) was a German only release. (1) reissued on CD (Black Rose BR 125).

Although recorded in London, this album of very atmospheric and melodic progressive rock by what seems to be a Scottish crew was only released in Germany. The music is generally very thoughtful and in quite a few places bluesy. Still there is your usual share of guitar solos and organ riffs, at times provoking **Beggars Opera** at their least arty. The album is undoubtedly as good as most in this class and it is hard to understand why they couldn't secure a UK release. The cover depicts a miraculous painting by Lyonel Feininger, a sure sign of good taste. (MK)

The Sundowners

Personnel:
STEVE ROBBINS	bs, vcls	A
DAVE SILVERMAN	multi-instruments	A
BARRY JOHN WEITZ	banjo, gtr, vcls	A

45s:
Baby Baby/		
House Of The Rising Sun	(Piccadilly 7N 35142)	1963
Come On In/		
Shot Of Rhythm And Blues	(Piccadilly 7N 35162)	1964
Where Am I/		
Gonna Make The Future Bright	(Parlophone R 5243)	1965
Dr. J. Wallace-Brown/		
Love Is In The Air	(Columbia DB 8339)	1968
Gloria The Bosom Show/		
Don't Look Back	(Spark SRL 1016)	1968

These three classical music students were Tommy Trousdale's backing group. They were the first British group to record *The House Of The Rising Sun*. Their third 45, *Where Am I*, was written by **Peter Lee Stirling**.

Compilation appearances have included: *A Shot Of Rhythm and Blues* on *Pop Inside The Sixties, Vol. 3* (CD) and *The R&B Era, Vol. 1* (LP & CD); and *Baby Baby* on *Rare 60's Beat Treasures, Vol. 5* (CD). (VJ)

Sun Dragon

Personnel:
ROBERT FREEMAN		A
ANTHONY JAMES (IAN McLINTOCK)		A

ALBUM: 1(A) GREEN TAMBOURINE   (MGM C(S) 8090) 1968 R3

HCP

45s:
Green Tambourine/		
I Need All The Friends I Can Get	(MGM MGM 1380) 1968	50
Blueberry Blue/Far Away Mountain	(MGM MGM 1391) 1968	-
Five White Horses/Look At The Sun	(MGM MGM 1458) 1968	-

This duo had previously recorded as **Sands**. When they split in late 1967, they recorded some demos which secured them a contract with MGM and released *Green Tambourine*, which was hampered by a pressing plant strike in its battle with The Lemon Pipers' version. **Sun Dragon** stalled at No. 50 and, of course The Lemon Pipers enjoyed a Top Ten hit. Their follow-up (another Lemon Pipers' cover) *Blueberry Blue* was another piece

SUPERTRAMP - Crime Of The Century (LP).

of orchestrated bubblegum with a psychedelic taint, although it didn't sell as well as their first effort.

Their album was attractive summery pop-psych in the vein of the first **Bee Gees** album, but rather short. **Deep Purple's Jon Lord**, Ian Paice and **Ritchie Blackmore** were recruited to fill out the sound and **Blackmore's** wah-wah guitar is much in evidence on their fine version of The Byrds' *So You Want To Be A Rock' n' Roll Star*. Other highlights include the pop-psych compositions *Peacock Dress* and *Seventeen* and the psychedelic *Five White Horses*, which was released as their final single in late 1968. Several other songs are bland, though.

Compilation appearances include: *Far Away Mountain* on *Justavibration* (LP) and on *Fading Yellow, Vol 1* (CD) and *Five White Horses* on *Lovely Summer Days* (CD). (VJ/RMJ)

Sunforest

Personnel:
ERIKA EIGEN	perc, vcls	A
FREYA HOGUE	gtr, banjo, vcls	A
TERRY TUCKER	vcls, keyb'ds	A

ALBUM: 1(A) THE SOUND OF SUNFOREST
(mono/stereo)   (Deram Nova (S)DN 7) 1969 R2

NB: (1) reissued on CD (Hugo Montes HMP 14).

This female trio was in fact American, but settled in London after travelling around Europe together. They attracted the attention of junior producer Vic Smith, who paid for them to record the album at Olympic Studios in London.

Their sound was influenced by medieval and renaissance music, but without being purist. Strong three-part vocal harmonies are present in nearly every song, as are oboes, bassoons, trumpets and interesting string arrangements. Songs include the superb psych-funk *Magician In The Mountain*, poignant *Where Are You?* and haunting *And I Was Blue*. Other tracks like *Peppermint Store* and *Mr. Bumble* have a definite sixties feel in being good-natured as well as intriguing.

The album appeared in January 1970 but didn't sell, perhaps a victim of its own variety. They played some small gigs and made some radio appearances to help promote the album, but Decca rejected their subsequent demos and eventually Eigen left the band.

One last break occurred, though - Stanley Kubrick was working on 'A Clockwork Orange' when the album was released, liked what he heard, and asked them to rerecord two tracks, *Overture To The Sun* and *I Want To Marry A Lighthouse Keeper*, for the soundtrack. *Give Me All Your Loving* also appeared on the *Nova Sampler* (LP) album.

They played some small gigs and made some radio appearances to help promote the album, but eventually Erika Eigen left the band and **Sunforest** became defunct. (MK/VJ/RMJ)

Sunshine

Personnel:
ETHEL COLEY	perc, vcls	A
GORDON EDWARDS	gtr, vcls, keyb'ds	A
JACK GREEN	gtr, bs, vcls	A
PETER OLIVER	gtr, vcls	A
TERRY SLADE	perc, drms	A
JOANNE WHITE	perc, vcls	A

ALBUM: 1(A) SUNSHINE   (Warner Bros WB K 46169) 1972

45: When Will I See The Light/
Sing Your Song   (Warner Bros K 16199) 1972

This was a lively gospel soul / funk / hard-rock band. Joanne White/Wight and Ethel Coley were with Edwards and Green in the London cast of 'Hair'. Oliver and Slade weren't in the original line-up, but replaced the original drummer and lead guitarist at an early stage. They backed **Geno Washington** in mid-1972 at gigs, but broke up in early 1973.

Jack Green was also a member of **The Pretty Things** and later in **T Rex**. Peter Oliver went on to play with Succubu, The New Seekers and **Paper Lace**. Terry Slade, who'd played with **The Nashville Teens** and **Rennaissance**, was later with **Kevin Coyne**. Gordon Edwards was an occasional member of **The Pretty Things**. (VJ)

Suntreader

Personnel:

MORRIS PERT	perc	A
PETER ROBINSON	keyb'ds	A
ALYN ROSS	bs	A
ROBIN THOMPSON	sax	A

ALBUMS:	1(A)	ZIN ZIN	(Island HELP 13) 1973
	2( )	THE MUSIC OF MORRIS PERT	(Chantry) 1976

A progressive / pompous rock outfit based around the percussionist Morris Pert. The *Zin Zin* album highlights his drumming and percussion expertise. Four lengthy tracks are present on which he is supported by Pete Robinson on saxophone. A jazzy progressive with the main emphasis on drums and piano and therefore an acquired taste. Pert had earlier played in a band called Come To The Edge with Robin Thompson and Andrew Powell. He went on to Stomu Yamashta's band. He also recorded some solo albums and was formerly in **Jonesey**. Peter Robinson was formerly in **Quatermass**, **Zakarrias** and **Three Man Army**. (VJ/BS)

Supertramp

Personnel:	RICHARD DAVIES	vcls, keyb'ds	ABC
(up to	ROGER HODGSON	bs, ld gtr	ABC
1976)	RICHARD PALMER	gtr	A
	BOB MILLER	drms	A
	KEVIN CURRIE	drms	B
	FRANK FARRELL	bs	B
	DAVE WINTHROP	sax	B
	JOHN HELLIWELL	sax	C
	DOUGIE THOMPSON	bs	C
	BOB SIEDENBERG (aka C. BENBERG)	drms	C

HCP

ALBUMS:	1(A)	SUPERTRAMP	(A&M AMLS 981) 1970	-
(up to	2(B)	INDELIBLY STAMPED	(A&M AMLS 64306) 1971	-
1976)	3(C)	EXTREMES (Soundtrack)	(Deram AML 1095) 1973	-
	4(C)	CRIME OF THE CENTURY	(A&M AMLS 68258) 1974	4
	5(C)	CRISIS? WHAT CRISIS	(A&M AMLH 68347) 1975	20

NB: (1) reissued on CD (A&M 393 149-2) 1989 and (Pickwick PWKS 543) 1989. (2) reissued on CD (A&M CDA 3149) 1988. (4) reissued on CD (A&M CDA 68258) 1982 and (Mobile Fidelity (USA) UDCD 505) 1989. (5) reissued on CD (A&M CDA 4560) 1988. There are also a couple of compilations, also on CD, *The Autobiography Of Supertramp* (A&M TRACD 1) 1986 and *The Very Best Of Supertramp* (A&M TRACD 1992) 1992. *Is Everybody Listening?* (2-LP) (Fruit Tree FT 816) is a live show from 1976, which includes nine cuts from their *Crime Of The Century* album and a further three from *Crisis? What Crisis?* It's pressed on 180 gram vinyl and presented in a gatefold sleeve.

HCP

45s:	Land Ho/Summer Romance	(A&M AMS 7101) 1974	-
(up to	Dreamer/Bloody Well Right	(A&M AMS 7152) 1974	13
1976)	Lady/		
	You Started Laughing When I Held	(A&M AMS 7201) 1975	-

Back in 1969 Richard Davies met Dutch millionaire Stanley August Miesegaes (commonly known as Sam) in Munich whilst playing in a band called The Joint. He offered to sponsor Davies if he formed a new group and Davies duly put together line-up (A) after advertising for players in a rock music paper. The new group was originally going to be named Daddy but after much correspondence between roadie Peter Viney and Richard Palmer, the band took its name from W.H. Davies' book, 'The Autobiography Of A Supertramp', published in 1910. Their first album, *Supertramp*, made little impact when released in 1970. It was full of lengthy and uninteresting solos and Bob Miller suffered a nervous breakdown soon afterwards.

The band regrouped in 1971 with new members Currie and Farrell and original bassist Hodgson switched to lead guitar. Their second album

Indelibly Stamped fared no better than the first and after their sponsor Sam paid off £60,000 worth of debts, all the band members quit except for Davies and Hodgson.

A new line-up (C) was put together. Helliweg and Thompson had both played with **The Alan Bown Set** previously. Bob Siebenberg (also known as C. Benberg) had been with **Bees Make Honey**. In a make or break gambit A&M installed the group in Southcombe (a farmhouse in Somerset) and assigned first rate producer Ken Scott to work with them. The resulting album, *Crime Of The Century*, a semi-concept affair, excellently produced, brought them into the big time. It developed what became a distinctive electric piano rhythm-based sound epitomised by *Dreamer*, which was taken from the album, put out on 45 and peaked at No 13 in the UK. In the US *(Bloody Well Right)* the flip side to *Dreamer* in the UK made it to No 35. The follow-up *Crisis? What Crisis* was very similar in style and achieved a comparable level of success. It also climbed to No 44 in the US. Indeed as we reach the end of 1976 the band's best days were still to come. *Breakfast In America* was their magnum opus spawning no less than four hit singles, but it was all down hill after that although they stumbled along into the nineties, when they continued to record sporadically.

Compilation appearances include *Remember* on *Come Together* (LP) and *Nothing To Show* on *Heads In* (LP). Dave Winthorp was later in Secret Affair. (VJ)

John Surman

ALBUMS:	1	JOHN SURMAN	(Deram DML/SML 1030) 1968 R2
	2	HOW MANY CLOUDS CAN YOU SEE?	
		(mono/stereo)	(Deram DMLR/SMLR 1045) 1969 R2
	3	ALORS!	(Futura GER 12) 1970 R1
	4	TALES OF THE ALGONQUIN	(Deram SML 1094) 1971 R2
	5	CONFLAGRATION	(Dawn DNLS 3022) 1971 R1
	6	WESTERING HOME	(Island HELP 10) 1972 SC
	7	MORNING GLORY	(Island ISLP 9237) 1973 SC
	8	LIVE AT WOODSTOCK TOWN HALL	
			(Dawn DNLS 3072) 1974 SC

NB: (4) with John Warren. (8) with Stu Martin.

45:	Obeah Wedding/	
	Can't Stop The Carnival	(Deram DM 224) 1969 R1

John Surman is one of Britain's most renowned and original saxophonists, but his roots include folk, ethnic and church music. In addition to these solo recordings **Surman** was also a member of **Morning Glory**, **The Trio** and he played with **Mike Westbrook**. His records were jazzy. He also did session work for several artists including **Pete Brown** and **Alexis Korner**. (VJ)

Screaming Lord Sutch

ALBUMS:	1	LORD SUTCH AND HEAVY FRIENDS	
(up to			(Atlantic 2400 008) 1970 SC
1976)	2	HANDS OF JACK THE RIPPER	
			(Atlantic K 40313) 1972 SC

NB: (1) reissued on vinyl (Sundazed LP 5152) 2005. (1) and (2) reissued on one CD (Waxin Gold SD 901549). *Screaming Lord Sutch and The Savages* (EMI CDP 7 98044 2) is a CD compilation of material which spans his entire career. *Rock And Horror* (CD) (Ace CDCHM 65) is a compilation of his more ghoulish numbers.

45s:		Till The Following Night/	
(up to		Good Golly Miss Molly	(HMV POP 953) 1961 SC
1976)		Jack The Ripper/	
		Don't You Just Know It	(Decca F 11598) 1963 SC
		I'm A Hog For You/	
		Monster In Black Tights	(Decca F 11747) 1963 SC
		She's Fallen In Love With A Monster/	
		Bye Bye Baby	(Oriole CB 1944) 1964 R1
		Dracula's Daughter/Come Back Baby	(Oriole CB 1962) 1964 R1
	α	The Train Kept A Rollin'/Honey Hush	(CBS 201767) 1965 R1
		The Cheat/Black And Hairy	(CBS 202080) 1966 R1
	β	'Cause I Love You/Thumping Beat	(Atlantic 584 321) 1970
		Election Fever/Rock The Election	(Atlantic 2091 017) 1970
		Gotta Keep A Rockin'//Flashing Lights	
		Hands Of Jack The Ripper	(Atlantic K 10221) 1972

Monster Ball/Rang-Tang-A-Lang   (SRT SRTS 76361) 1976
I Drink To Your Health Marie Pt's 1 and 2/
                            (SRT SRTS 76375) 1976
Reissue: Jack The Ripper/I'm A Hog For You   (Decca F 1369) 1977

NB: α as **Lord Sutch**. β also reissued on Atlantic (2091 006) in 1970.

This guy was one of the characters of the sixties. His act was a mixture of horror rock and slapstick humour. His usual decor was leopard skins, large bull horns and long black hair - in the early days his backing group The Savages carried him on stage in a black coffin which he'd crawl from screaming. This sequence was the subject of his first single. The group at this time drove to gigs in an ambulance with a large pink crocodile on top. There were various line-ups of The Savages during the sixties who included **Ritchie Blackmore** (gtr) (later of **Deep Purple**), Matthew Fisher (organ) (later of **Procol Harum**) and **Paul Nicholas** (piano).

His second single, *Jack The Ripper*, wasn't a hit but was popular on juke boxes of the era, where he could be seen in a top hat and long black cloak, carrying a butchers knife chasing young maidens. The flip side, was a cover of Clarence 'Frogman' Henry's *Don't You Just Know It*. Further 45s followed and this publicity-seeking individual was never far from the headlines throughout the era. His first six 45s were all produced by Joe Meek. They included some old favourites, like Little Richard's *Good Golly Miss Molly*, the classic *The Train Kept A Rollin'* and the R&B favourite *Honey Hush*. Their first 'A' side not produced by Meek in 1966, *The Cheat*, had a slow psychedelic feel. In 1965 he formed his own National Teenage Party and stood as a parliamentary candidate for Stratford-Upon-Avon on a manifesto of reducing the voting age to 18 and abolishing dog licenses. Later, of course, he made a point of standing in all by-elections with his Monster Raving Loony Party. He also attempted to start his own pirate radio station in the sixties.

His debut album *Lord Sutch And His Heavy Friends* features a potpourri of star names including **Jeff Beck**, **Nicky Hopkins**, **Noel Redding**, John Bonham and **Jimmy Page**. The music is raw and full of energy and **Sutch** well, screams a lot!

Much of his act was taken from black American singer Screamin' Jay Hawkins but Sutch lacked Hawkins' vocal power which is probably why real commercial success eluded him. Not even the backing and support of individuals like **Jeff Beck**, **Blackmore**, John Bonham, **Nicky Hopkins**, **Jimmy Page**, **Noel Redding** and **Keith Moon**, when he recorded a couple of albums in the seventies could compensate for this.

In 1970 he and his band were called Screaming Lord Sutch and His Whole Lotta Shakin'.

In 1973 to promote his appearance at a rock'n'roll revival concert at Wembley Stadium he dyed his hair green and paraded through London with a group of nude nubiles parading banners. The resulting court appearance achieved his publicity objectives admirably.

His *Rock And Horror* (CD) includes tracks like *Jack The Ripper*, *Monster Rock*, *Murder In The Graveyard*, *Screem And Screem*, *Rock-A-Billy Madman* and *Rock And Shock*.

Compilation appearances have included: *The Cheat* on *Justafixation* (LP); *Come Back Baby*, *Dracula's Daughter*, *She's Fallen In Love With The Monster Man* and *Bye Bye Baby* on *Jimmy Page, Session Man* (CD); *Honey Hush* and *The Train Kept A Rollin'* on *Ritchie Blackmore - Rock Profile, Vol. 2* (CD); *Don't You Just Know It* on *Sixties Lost And Found, Vol. 2* (LP) and *Sixties Explosion, Vol. 1* (CD); *Good Golly, Miss Molly* and *Till The Following Night* on *Twist A La Star Club* (LP); *The Train Kept A Rollin'* on *That Driving Beat* (CD); *I'm Still Raving* on *Beat Merchants* (CD); and *Black And Hairy* on *Turds On A Bum Ride Vol. 4* CD. (VJ)

Sutherland Brothers

Personnel:	GAVIN SUTHERLAND	gtr, vcls	A
	IAN SUTHERLAND	vcls, gtr, keyb'ds	A

ALBUMS:	1(A)	THE SUTHERLAND BROTHERS BAND	(Island) 1972
(up to	2(A)	LIFEBOAT	(Island) 1972
1976)			

NB: (2) reissued on CD (Columbia 4894502) 1998.

45s:	The Pie/Long Long Day (PS)	(Island WIP 6120) 1972
(up to	Sailing/Who's Crying Now	(Island WIP 6136) 1972
1976)	Lady Like You/Annie	(Island WIP 6147) 1972

The brothers signed to Island in 1972 and recorded two albums of melodic folk-based pop. Their debut single *The Pie* exemplified their style. They also wrote and recorded as their second single *Sailing*, which of course became a million-selling record for **Rod Stewart**. Their second album was made with the help of session musicians and their search for a permanent backing group resulted in them amalgamating with **Quiver** in 1973 to form **The Sutherland Brothers and Quiver**. (VJ)

Sutherland Brothers and Quiver

Personnel:	GAVIN SUTHERLAND	gtr, vcls, bs (in C)	A B C
(up to	IAN SUTHERLAND	vcls, gtr, keyb'ds	A B C
1976)	TIM RENWICK	gtr	A B C
	BRUCE THOMAS	bs	A
	WILLIE WILSON	drms	A B C
	PETE WOOD	piano	A B C
	TEX COMER	bs	B

			HCP
ALBUMS:	1(A)	DREAM KID	(Island) 1973 -
(up to	2(B)	BEAT OF THE STREET	(Island) 1974 -
1976)	3(C)	REACH FOR THE SKY	(CBS 69191) 1975 26
	4(C)	SLIPSTREAM	(CBS 81593) 1976 49
	5(-)	SAILING	(CBS) 1976 -

NB: (3) reissued on CD (Columbia 4805262) 1995.

		HCP
45s:	You Got Me Anyway/Not Fade Away	(Island WIP 6157) 1973 -
(up to	Dream Kid/Don't Mess Up	(Island WIP 6182) 1974 -
1976)	Saviour In The Rain/Silver Sister	(Island WIP 6209) 1973 -
	Ain't Too Proud/Mad Tril	(CBS 3769) 1975 -
	Arms Of Mary/We Get Along	(CBS 4001) 1976 5
	When The Train Comes/Lone On The Moon	(CBS 4336) 1976 -
	Secrets/Something's Burning	(CBS 4668) 1976 35
Reissue:	Arms Of Mary/ Secrets	(Old Gold OG 9402) 1984 -

This group formed out of the amalgamation of **The Sutherland Brothers** and **Quiver** in 1973. Their first album *Dream Kid* was well received and they had a US hit with their first 45 *You Got Me Anyway*. Prior to the sessions for *Beat Of The Street* Thomas departed and was later in Elvis Costello's Attractions. Tex Comer from **Ace** was a temporary replacement but Gavin Sutherland later assumed the bassist role himself. When **Rod Stewart** achieved his massive hit with *Sailing* the band was signed by CBS and soon registered a Top 5 hit with the wimpy pop ditty *Arms Of Mary*. They also enjoyed two hit albums *Reach For The Sky* and *Slipstream*. *Secrets* consolidated their commercial success, but although they recorded further singles and an album *Down To Earth* in 1977 they were a casualty

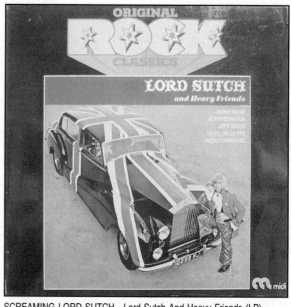

SCREAMING LORD SUTCH - Lord Sutch And Heavy Friends (LP).

of the punk era and by the end of the decade **Quiver** had departed and the two Sutherlands had reverted back to **The Sutherland Brothers** for their 1979 album *When The Night Comes*. Ian Sutherland recorded a solo album *Mixed Emotions* in 1983. (VJ)

Svensk

| Personnel: | ROGER HOPKINS | A |
| | JASON PAUL | A |

| 45s: | Dream Magazine/Getting Old | (Page One POF 036) 1967 SC |
| | You/All I Have To Do Is Dream | (Page One POF 050) 1967 SC |

A duo from Bournemouth. *Dream Magazine* was a pleasant song with a church organ (the organ of St. Giles Cripplegate) backing but the commercial success they anticipated eluded them. The flip side, *Getting Old*, is pretty unremarkable. Their second single wasn't as good and the duo soon disintegrated.

After their demise Roger Hopkins quit the music business, but **Jason Paul** made a solo single, *Shine A Little Light Into My Room/Paradise Pudding* (Pye 7N 17710) 1969, but when this made little impact he drifted out of the music scene too.

Compilation appearances have included: *Getting Old* on *Psychedelia, Vol. 1* (LP), *English Freakbeat, Vol. 3* (CD) and *Hen's Teeth Vol. 1* (CD); and *Dream Magazine* on *Electric Sugar Cube Flashbacks* (CD). (VJ)

Swan Arcade

Personnel:	JIM BOYES	gtr, vcls	A
	DAVE BRADY	vcls, synth, bs, concertina	AB
	HEATHER BRADY	vcls, dulcimer, cello	AB
	ROYSTON WOOD	concertina, vcls	B

ALBUMS: 1(A)	SWAN ARCADE	(Trailer LER 2032) 1973 SC
(up to 2(A)	MATCHLESS	(Shanachie MU 7428) 1976
1976)		

The group formed in Bradford, Yorkshire in 1970 and are noted for powerful unaccompanied vocals and harmonies of both traditional and contemporary arrangements. They got their name from a local landmark which was demolished during the city's radical redevelopment in this era. They were a popular folk festival attraction throughout the seventies and were also featured on John Peel's radio shows. Boyes left the band between 1972-74, having moved away from the area, he was replaced by former **Young Tradition** and **Albion Country Band** member Royston Wood. The band split in September 1973, but reformed later with an entirely new line-up comprising ex-Laggan and Great Fife Road Show member Brian Miller (gtr, vcls), Jack French (vcls, gtr, dulcimer), Kevin Hingston (bs, dulcimer, bazouki) and Chris Taylor (vcls, drams, percsn). This line-up was fairly short-lived. Miller left first in June 1974 to form a duo with Charlie Sloane.

The original line-up reformed in May 1975 and released a new album *Matchless* on Shanachie. The band went on to achieve greater recognition after 1976, recording throughout the eighties and into the nineties.

Dave Brady went on to work with the Scottish chamber orchestra as a roadie and much later played with Mr Mcfell's Chamber. Wood joined **The Young Tradition** but was later killed in a car accident in 1991. **Fairport Convention** covered **Swan Arcade**'s *Coal Not Dole* on their 1990 compilation benefit album *Hokey Pokey*. (VJ/JM)

Dave Swarbrick

ALBUMS:	1	RAG'S REELS AND AIRS	
(up to			(Polydor Special 236 514) 1967 R1
1976)	2	SWARBRICK	(Transatlantic TRA 337) 1976 SC

NB: (1) also issued on Bounty (BYI 6030) 1967 (R2). (1) and (2) reissued on one CD, (Essential! ESM CD 355) 1996. *Swarb! Forty-Five Years Of Folk's Finest Fiddler* (Free Reed FRQ CD 45) 2003 is a definitive 4-CD set, which overviews his career.

SWEENEY'S MEN - The Tracks Of Sweeney (CD).

Dave Swarbrick is one of the country's top fiddlers. He transformed **Fairport Convention** from a folk-rock band to one that concentrated on gigs and reels. He still performs at their annual reunion but has also enjoyed a successful solo career and lots of successful collaborations with **Martin Carthy**, Simon Nicol and others.

Swarbrick, who was born in New Malden, Surrey, on 5 April 1941, is a master fiddle player with a unique style. Early in his career, he played mandola and fiddle for the **Ian Campbell Folk Group**. He also toured with Simon Nichol and **Martin Carthy** and played on the latter's debut album in 1968. His first album, which was recorded with **Martin Carthy** and Diz Disley, was produced by Joe Boyd. It is now rare and sought-after by folk collectors and fans.

In September 1969 he joined **Fairport Convention**, but in the second half of the seventies he also began to make solo albums again. Only *Swarbrick* in 1976 falls within the time span of this book but this and his subsequent ones are pretty essential for folk music fans.

Swarbrick, who is now virtually deaf in one ear from constant playing of the electric violin, finally left **Fairport Convention** in 1984. He was then in Whippersnapper and subsequently recorded again with **Martin Carthy** in 1990 before joining the Keith Hancock Band, which **Carthy** is also in.

He celebrated his 50th birthday with a concert at Birmingham Town Hall on 6 April 1991 which included many musicians he'd played with over the years. The finest moments were later released on *Folk On 2* in 1996.

Swarb! Forty-Five Years Of Folk's Finest is a definitive 4-CD box set, which is lavishly illustrated with photos, rare record sleeves, memorabilia, and a clear discography and sleevenotes. This is a 'must' for his fans.

Compilation appearances include *Lord Inchiquin* on *The Transatlantic Story* CD box set and they also have tracks on the *Rave On* (LP) compilation. (VJ)

Sweeney's Men

Personnel:	ANDY IRVINE	mandolin, gtr, bouzouki	A
	JOHNNY MOYNIHAN	bouzouki	AB
	TERRY WOODS	gtr, mandolin, vcls	AB
	HENRY McCULLOUGH	gtr	B

ALBUMS: 1(A)	RATTLIN' AND ROARIN' WILLY	
(up to		(Transatlantic TRA 170) 1968 R2
1976) 2(A)	THE TRACKS OF SWEENEY	
		(Transatlantic TRA 200) 1969 R2

NB: (1) reissued as *Sweeney's Men* (Transatlantic TRASAM 37) in 1976 (SC) and (2) reissued (TRASAM 40) in 1977 (SC). (1) and (2) reissued on CD (Essential ESMCD 435) 2005. There's also a compilation, *The Legend Of Sweeney's Men* (Demon TRANDEM 4) 1988. (1) and (2) reissued on one CD, *Time Was Never Here: 1968-69* (Transatlantic/Demon TDEMCD 11) 1992. *Legend Of Sweeney's Men*

(Castle CMDDD 932) 2004 is a 2-CD compilation with informative sleevenotes from Colin Harper and is likely to be the definitive word on the band.

45s:	Old Maid In The Garrett/Derby Ram	(Pye 7N 17312) 1967
(up to	Waxies Dargle/Old Woman In Cotton	(Pye 7N 17459) 1968
1976)	Sullivan's John/	
	Rattin' Roarin' Willy	(Transatlantic TRASP 19) 1969

This legendary traditional Irish folk band were one of the prime forces in the resurgence of interest in Irish traditional music in the late sixties. They utilised a vast range of instruments on their albums, which made inspirational use of cross rhythms. Their albums were greeted with considerable acclaim in the British and Irish music press at the time. By the time they recorded *The Tracks Of Sweeney* Andy Irvine had left the band. His replacement was the electric guitarist **Henry McCullough**, who played with them at the Cambridge folk festival of 1968. His hippie-rock background was enormously influential on the band, although it was short-lived as this line-up only lasted for a couple of months and **McCullough** didn't play on the album. This consisted largely of self-penned material and arrangements of traditional pieces reworked in a modern style.

Terry Woods became an original member of **Steeleye Span** in 1969 but left in 1971. He worked with his wife Gay as **Gay and Terry Woods** in the early seventies and performed with **Ralph McTell** in 1975. He joined The Pogues in 1986. Andy Irvine and Johnny Moynihan went on to join **Planxty**.

The band paved the way for acts like **Fairport Convention** to electrify folk music. Both albums were reissued in the mid-seventies but even the reissues are now becoming difficult to find. Once again both are essential albums for folk fans.

The Demon compilation features nine cuts from their first album and eight from their second. It includes two **Terry Woods** compositions, *Dreams For Me* and *When You Don't Care For Me* and *Hall Of Mirrors*, which was co-written by **Henry McCullough** who was later in **The Grease Band**. However, the recent Sanctuary compilation is likely to be the definitive one and features excellent sleevenotes from Colin Harper. It includes rare material including the five Pye and Dolphin singles issued between 1966-1968 under various names like Capitol Showband, Paddy Cole and Des Kelly.

Compilation appearances include *The Handsome Cabin Boy* on *The Transatlantic Story* CD box set. (VJ)

The Sweet

Personnel:	BRIAN CONNOLLY	vcls	A B C
	STEVE PRIEST	hrmnca, vcls, bs	A B C
	MIKE TUCKER	drms, vcls	A B C
	FRANK TORPY	gtr	A
	MICK STEWART	gtr	B
	ANDY SCOTT	gtr, synthesizer, vcls	C

HCP

ALBUMS:	1(A)	GIMME DAT DING (side 1 only)		
(up to			(Music For Pleasure MFP 5248) 1971	-
1976)	2(A)	FUNNY HOW SWEET CO-CO CAN BE		
			(RCA SF 8288) 1971	SC -
	3(A)	SWEET'S BIGGEST HITS	(RCA SF 8316) 1971	-
	4(A)	SWEET FANNY ADAMS	(RCA LPL 1 5039) 1974	27
	5(A)	DESOLATION BOULEVARD	(RCA LPL 1 5080) 1975	-
	6(A)	STRUNG UP (2-LP)	(RCA SPC 0001) 1975	-
	7(A)	GIVE US A WINK	(RCA RS 1036) 1976	-

NB: (2) reissued on CD (RCA) 2005. (4) reissued on CD (RCA) 2005. (5) reissued on CD (Castle Classics CLACD 170) 1990 and again on CD (RCA) 2005. (7) reissued on CD (RCA) 2005.

Compilations have included: - *Sweet 16 - It's... It's... Sweet's Hits* (LP) (Anagram GRAM 16) 1984 (No 44); *The Collection* (LP) (Castle Communications CCS CT 230) 1991; *Blockbusters* (CD) (RCA ND 74313) 1989; *First Recordings 1968-1971* (CD) (Repertoire REP 4140-WZ) 1991; *Greatest Hits: Sweet (1971 Historic Original Re-Releases)* (CD) (Ariola 290 586) 1992; *Hit Singles* (2-CD) (Repertoire REP 4591-WL) 1995; *Ballroom Blitz - The Very Best Of Sweet* (Polygram TV 535 001-2) 1995. Also of interest are: - *Great Balls Of Fire* (Pseudonym CDP 1008DD) 1994, taken from a live radio appearance by the band on Swedish radio on 13 September 1971, when they were at the height of their bubblegum phase; *Platinum Rare* (Repertoire REP 4487-WP) 1995, which comprises outtakes which didn't make it onto vinyl at the time; and the retrospective CD *Electric Landlady* (Receiver RRCD

241) 1997, which was compiled by **Brian Connolly** a few weeks before his death. It contains previously unreleased material from his archives. *Solid Gold Sweet* (Snapper) 1998 is a 2-CD set, one studio and one live. *Teenage Rampage - The Alternative Anthology* (Essential ESACD 800) 2000 will be of interest. *Live At The Rainbow 1973* (RCA/BMG 74321 69859 2) 2000 has been digitally remastered from the original tapes. *Stairway To The Stars - Live And Rare!* (2-CD) (Castle CMDDD 521) is an alternative anthology. *Hell Raisers* (BeatRocket BR 215) 2000 is a vinyl US import which covers their 1971-1972 hits. *Hard Centres* (CD) (Zebra CDZEB 11) concentrates on hard-rock material from their *Sweet Fanny Adams, Give Us A Wink* and *Off The Record* albums.

HCP

45s:	Slow Motion/It's Lonely Out There	(Fontana TF 958) 1968	R5
(up to	The Lollipop Man/Time	(Parlophone R 5803) 1969	R2
1976)	All You'll Ever Get From Me/		
	The Juicer	(Parlophone R 5826) 1970	R1 -
	Get On The Line/		
	Mr. McGallagher	(Parlophone R 5848) 1970	R2
	Funny Funny/		
	You're Not Wrong For Me	(RCA RCA 2051) 1971	13
	Co-Co/Done Me Wrong Alright	(RCA RCA 2087) 1971	2
	Alexander Graham Bell/Spotlight	(RCA RCA 2121) 1971	33
	Poppa Joe/Jeanie	(RCA RCA 2164) 1972	11
	Little Willy/Man From Mecca	(RCA RCA 2225) 1972	4
	Wig-Wam Bam/New York Connection	(RCA RCA 2260) 1972	4
	Blockbuster/Need A Lot Of Lovin'	(RCA RCA 2305) 1972	1
	Hell Raiser/Burning	(RCA RCA 2357) 1973	2
	Ballroom Blitz/Rock And Roll Disgrace	(RCA RCA 2403) 1973	2
	Teenage Rampage/		
	Own Up, Take A Look At Yourself	(RCA LPBO 5004) 1974	2
	The Six Teens/Burn On The Flame	(RCA LPBO 5037) 1974	9
	Turn It Down/Someone Else Will	(RCA RCA 2480) 1974	41
	Fox On The Run/Miss Demeanour	(RCA RCA 2524) 1975	2
	Action/Sweet F.A.	(RCA RCA 2578) 1975	15
	Lies In Your Eyes/Cockroach	(RCA RCA 2641) 1976	35
	Lost Angels/Funk It Up	(RCA RCA 2748) 1976	-
Reissues:	All You'll Ever Get From Me/		
	The Juicer	(Parlophone R 5902) 1971	SC -
	Fox On The Run/Hell Raiser/Blockbuster/		
	Ballroom Blitz (PS)	(RCA PB 5226) 1980	-
	Blockbuster/Ballroom Blitz (PS)	(RCA PB 5226) 1980	-
	Blockbuster/Hellraiser (PS)	(RCA GOLD 524) 1981	-
	Ballroom Blitz/Wig-Wam Bam (PS)	(RCA GOLD 551) 1982	-
	Sixteens/Action (PS)	(Anagram ANA 27) 1984	-
	Blockbuster/Teenage Rampage/Hell Raiser/		
	Ballroom Blitz (PS)	(Anagram ANA 28) 1984	45
	Wig Wam Bam/Little Willy/Funny Funny/Sixteens/		
	Lost Angels (PS)	(Anagram ANA 29) 1985	-
	Blockbuster/Little Willy	(Old Gold OG 9797) 1987	-
	Fox On The Run/Ballroom Blitz	(Old Gold OG 9709) 1987	-
	Wig Wam Bam/Co-Co	(Old Gold OG 9760) 1988	-
	Teenage Rampage/Hell Raiser	(Old Gold OG 9762) 1988	-
	Wig-Wam Bam/Little Willy (PS)	(RCA PB 43337) 1989	-

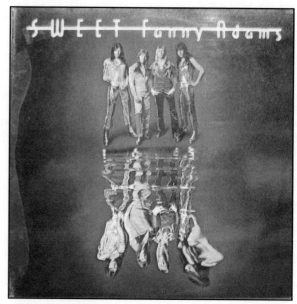

SWEET - Fanny Adams (LP).

828

Sweet was at the forefront of the early seventies glam-rock phenomenon. Most of their material was written by the songwriting duo of Nicky Chin and Mike Chapman who had the knack of writing catchy hooks which the band often merged with crunching, fuzzy guitars. The formula was enormously successful - ten UK Top Ten hits in the period between 1971 and 1978 and five of them were No 2's!

Formed in 1968 as Sweetshop, Tucker and **Connolly** had previously played in a Harrow-based band called Wainwright Children, which did not make it onto vinyl. Frank Torpy left after their first 45 and his replacement Mick Stewart played on the next three before Andy Scott joined from **Elastic Band**, who cut two albums and a 45 for Decca. Steve Priest seems to have had no prior professional experience. Their first 45 on Fontana and three others on Parlophone were unremarkable and made little impression although they all (especially the Fontana one), change hands for considerable sums of money now.

The band's big break came in late 1970 when they teamed up with songwriters Mike Chapman and Nicky Chinn. They got the group a deal with RCA and wrote their first hit, a bubblegum number, *Funny Funny* for them. Like most of what followed it was musically awful, but it proved popular with the potentially large teenybopper audience.

Their first album appearance was on one side of a Music For Pleasure album, with **The Pipkins** and their sole hit, *Gimme Dat Ding*, which the album was named after, filling the other side. **The Sweet**'s contribution consisted of their earlier recordings for Parlophone.

Their next 45 release *Co-Co* climbed to No 2 and prompted Parlophone to reissue *All You'll Ever Get From Me*, which proceeded to stiff for a second time. Next **The Sweet** recorded a less banal song *Alexander Graham Bell*, about the inventor of the telephone. The fact it could only stumble to No 33 clearly led Chapman and Chinn to return to the earlier successful teenybopper formula of banal lyrics and very basic music with *Poppa Joe*, which became the first in a long series of hits. They became very closely associated with the 'glam rock' movement appearing on TV shows like 'Top Of The Pops' (their hits made them a very regular feature over the next few years) in flamboyant costumes, make-up and glitter. Certainly their stage act brought its problems - they were taken to court in Belgium over an allegedly pornographic film clip and banned from the Mecca dancehall circuit in the UK for what was considered to be an overtly sexual act around the time of their *Little Willy* single.

To promote their *Wig-Wam Bam* 45, a song about love among the American Indians, they dressed in feathers and ponchos. *Blockbuster* coincidently used the same riff as **David Bowie**'s *Jean Genie* but kept it off the No 1 position and was possibly one of the finest examples of the band's music. Indeed it topped the UK Charts for five weeks. *Hell Raiser*, *Ballroom Blitz* and *Teenage Rampage*, which all reached No 2, helped maintain the band's momentum and in May 1974 *Sweet Fanny Adams* became their only UK Chart Album in the seventies. In contrast to their 45s it was entirely self-penned and proved that they were not limited solely to the three-minute pop song.

Over the next few years they tried to make the transition from a pop band to a serious hard-rock band and *The Six Teens* certainly was a pretty decent hard-rock single, but all this simply alienated the teenybopper audience which had been the key to their success. This identity crisis is evident on 1974's *Sweet Fanny Adams* album. If the glam-rock strand was represented by tracks like *Heartbreak Hotel* and *Rebel Rouser*, the more mature tracks were *No You Don't* and *Set Me Free*. In December 1974 they split from Chapman and Chinn to write and produce their own material and initially their first self-penned 45, *Fox On The Run*, was a big success. This and *The Six Teens* were both included on the *Desolation Boulevard* album.

Give Us A Wink was a failed attempt to court hard-rock and *Off The Record* (1977) was basically more of the same plus an ill-advised flirtation with disco (on *Funk It Up*). There was an inevitability about their decline, although they made several further 45s and albums before splitting in 1982.

In the years following their split **Sweet** reformed on various occasions and in 1989 Scott and Tucker reformed them to record a live album at London's Marquee Club.

There are several compilations of their material. As good as any is *Sweet It... It's, It's Sweet's Hits*, a 16-track compilation of all their Chart hits from the 1971-74 period except the dire *Funny Funny* and *Co-Co*. *Hell Raisers*

SWEET - Blockbusters (LP).

covers their successes from the 1971-1972 era with bubblegum pop like *Co-Co*, *Little Willy* and *Poppa Joe* and later glam-rock stompers like *Wig-Wam Bam*, *Blockbuster* and *Hell Raiser*. Also featured are four 'B' sides and two album tracks, *Spotlight* and *You're Not Wrong For Loving Me*.

Live At The Rainbow 1973 includes all their classic hits and contains a particularly pulsating version of *Hell Raiser* and the 13-minute *The Man With The Golden Arm* has a notable extended drum solo. *Teenage Rampage - The Alternative Anthology* is a 2-CD set that presents a selection of live and studio demo tracks that contain all their hits as well as some of their more popular album tracks. Another 2-CD anthology is *Stairway To The Stars*, which comprises vintage live recordings and demos, featuring their classic songs like *Ballroom Blitz*, *Blockbuster* and *Teenage Rampage*.

Compilation appearances have included: *Time* on *Electric Sugar Cube Flashbacks* (CD); *Poppa Joe* on *20 Star Tracks, Vol. 1* (LP); and *The Spider* on *The Beat Goes On, Vol. 3* (LP), although this may be by a different act. More recently, *Blockbuster* has figured on the 3-CD set *Full Throttle - 60 Original Driving Classics*; *Slow Motion* on *Colour Me Pop, Vol 1* (CD); *Little Willy* on *70's Remembered* (CD); *Fox On The Run* on *Brit Pop* (CD); *Action* and *Blockbuster* on *The Seventies Vol 2* (CD); *The Juicer* on *Jagged Time Lapse, Vol 4* (CD) and *Action* can be heard on *The Best Heavy Metal Album In The World Ever!*

Founder member Mick Tucker, one of the finest drummers of the glam-rock era, was diagnosed with leukaemia in the mid-nineties. He became ill again on 8th February 2002 and was admitted to hospital the following day. He died on 14 February 2002, aged 54.

The Sweet are best remembered as 'glam-rock' superstars. Between 1971 and 1976 they enjoyed 15 consecutive hit singles so their commercial success is undisputable. Over the course of time, their music which was so maligned at the time has won a greater measure of acceptability among rock pundits. (VJ)

Sweet Chariot (1)

ALBUMS: 1 SWEET CHARIOT AND FRIENDS
            (De Wolfe DWLP 3230) 1972 R2
         2 MEMOIR   (SRT) 1975

45:      When I'm A Kid/Mozart 73   (Columbia DB 8999) 1973

Their first album is library-only release in a late sixties style... An organ-based Swingin' London pop-psych effort, which is inevitably very rare but not worth the money you'd need to pay to acquire a copy. Their second, equally obscure album on the Grannie custom label, features cabaret/lounge lizard covers of sixties pop songs. Their 45 was recorded at Abbey Road studios. Sadly for them, *When I Was A Kid* was a huge hit all over Europe for Demis Roussos, who wrote the song! (VJ/PM)

Sweet Chariot (2)

45:      Heavenly Road/Wish I Were A Child   (MCA MCA 5010) 1969

The 'A' side of this 45 was penned by Carter-Lewis. It was a gospel harmony effort. (VJ)

Sweet Dreams

Personnel: POLLY BROWN   A
                TONY JACKSON   A

ALBUMS: 1(A)   WE'LL BE YOUR MUSIC   (Bradley's BRADL 1008) 1974

			HCP
45s:	Honey Honey/I Surrender	(Bradley's BRAD 7408) 1974	10
(up to	Best Of Everything/		
1976)	Only You Can Touch Me	(Bradley's BRAD 7502) 1975	-
	Let's Get Into Something/		
	I Could Conquer The World	(Bradley's BRAD 7522) 1975	-
	I'll Be Your Music/		
	I'm So Glad I've Gotcha	(Bradley's BRAD 7529) 1975	-
	Love Kiss And Run/		
	I'm So Glad I've Gotcha	(Bradley's BRAD 7604) 1976	-

This soul/reggae duo is a marginal case for inclusion here. **Polly Brown** had been lead singer of middle-of-the-road group **Pickettywitch**. She started her solo career in 1975. They achieved a Top Ten hit here with *Honey Honey*, which also got to No 68 in the US. (VJ)

Sweet Feeling

Personnel: RAY BEVERLEY   A
                STEVE BRENDELL   A
                ROD LYNTON   lead vcls   A

45:      All So Long Ago/Charles Brown   (Columbia DB 8195) 1967 R3

Sweet Feeling formed in 1966 and were quickly signed by Howard Condor (who had previously worked for Robert Stigwood). He oversaw the recording of this now rare and sought-after 45. With an expanded line-up the group later adopted the name **Rupert's People** and both sides of the 45 can be heard on the CD *The Magic World Of Rupert's People* (Circle CPWC 103), which is also available in a luxury vinyl version.

Compilation appearances include: *Charles Brown* on *Justafixation II* (LP); and *All So Long Ago* on *Voyage Through The Sugarcube* (CD) and (LP). (VJ)

Sweet Marriage

This Manchester group appeared at the Marquee in London on the same bill as **Yes** in 1969. They were noticed by a certain Germaine Greer and brought to the attention of John Peel. The resulting session for his "Top Gear" show is represented by two tracks on the compilation album *John Peel Presents Top Gear* (LP). *Mort* is a psychedelic workout with good guitar work while the more impressive *Titania* has atmospheric male/female vocals and lively tempo changes. It would have been good if more work by this band had survived. Their sound is a little reminiscent of **Eclection** and **Comus** among others. Other artists represented on the album concerned are **Bridget St. John**, **Ron Geesin** and **Welfare State**. (NM)

Sweet Pain

Personnel:	ANNETTE BROX	vcls	A
	STUART COWELL	gtr	A
	SAM CROZIER	perc, vcls	A
	JUNIOR DUNN	drms	A
	ALAN GREED	vcls	A
	DICK HECKSTALL-SMITH	sax	A
	JOHN O'LEARY	hrmnca	A
	KEITH TILLMAN	bs	A

ALBUM: 1(A)   SWEET PAIN   (Mercury SMCL 20146) 1969 R2
NB: (1) released in US as *England's Heavy Blues Super Session*.

45:      Timber Gibbs/
         Chain Up The Devil   (United Artists UP 35268) 1971

An all star blues session album. Annette Brox recorded a 45 in 1965 and an album in 1974, *Rollin' Back* with her husband Victor. **Dick Heckstall-Smith** recorded a solo album. He also played with **Graham Bond Organisation**, **John Mayall's Bluesbreakers** and **Colosseum**. (VJ)

Sweet Plum

45s: Lazy Day/Let No Man
       Steal Your Thyme   (Middle Earth MDS 103) 1969 SC
       Set The Wheels In Motion/
       Catch A Cloud   (Middle Earth MDS 105) 1969 SC

This girl singer was notable for being the only artist to release two singles on the Middle Earth label. Both sides of the second release also appeared on the sampler *Earthed* (LP). Her records were a mixture of Mama Cass and English folk.

Sweet Salvation

45s: Honey Man/Freedom City   (B&C CD 70) 1970
       Honey Man/Crucifix, Swastika And Star   (B&C CD 136) 1971

Honey Man conjured up a very strange and rather evil sound with a touch of **T Rex**. (VJ)

Sweetshop

Personnel incl: ROSS HANNAHAN

45:      Barefoot And Tiptoe/
        Lead The Way   (Parlophone R 5707) 1968 SC

This was a **Mark Wirtz**-related project. The 'A' side, *Barefoot And Tiptoe* sounds very much aimed at the school-aged audience.

Barefoot and Tiptoe has been compiled on *A Teenage Opera - The Original Soundtrack Recording* (CD), *Circus Days, Vol. 6* (CD) and *Circus Days, Vol. 5* (LP). (VJ)

JUSTAFIXATION II (Comp LP) including Sweet Feeling.

Sweet Slag

Personnel:	AL CHAMBERS	drms	A
	PAUL JOLLY	woodwind	A
	MICK KERENSKY	gtr, vcls	A
	JACK O'NEILL bs,	trombone	A

ALBUM: 1(A) TRACKING WITH CLOSE-UPS
                    (President PTLS 1042) 1971 R3

NB: (1) reissued on CD (Sunrise SR 4080101).

A very sombre lot, **Sweet Slag** cook their dissonant brand of jazzy prog-rock with more spices than many. Almost all tracks (written by Kerensky) are depressed, bitter and subtly menacing. There are also quite a few excellent and very discordant guitar solos to be found here. It may take some time and patience to explore this odd album, but it is rewarding to do so. (MK)

Sweet Thursday

Personnel:	HARVEY BURNS	drms	A
	ALUN DAVIES	gtr, vcls	A
	NICKY HOPKINS	keyb'ds	A
	JON MARK	gtr, vcls	A
	BRIAN ODGERS	bs	A

ALBUM: 1(A) SWEET THURSDAY   (Polydor 2310 051) 1969 SC
NB: (1) reissued on CBS (65573) 1973.

This short-lived venture was notable for the inclusion of **Nick Hopkins**, Jon Mark and **Alun Davies**. (VJ)

Sweet William's Ghost

| Personnel: | GEORGE DEACON | | A |
| | MARION ROSS | | A |

ALBUM: 1(A) SWEET WILLIAM'S GHOST (Xtra XTRA 1130) 1973 R3

Actually by Deacon and Ross but usually known by the above title, this is an atmospheric folk item with tales of murder and rape which bears some similarity to **Stone Angel**, particularly the use of harmonicum. George Deacon apparently spent many of the following years in mental hospitals. The album came with a lyric sheet. (VJ)

Swegas

ALBUM: 1 CHILD OF LIGHT   (Trend 6480 002) 1971 SC

45:    What'ya Gonna Do/
       There Is Nothing In It   (Trend 6099 001) 1970

This brass-rock outfit was a bit Blood, Sweat and Tears-ish, but with some decent guitar and organ work on their recordings. (MWh)

Jonathan Swift

| ALBUMS: | 1 | INTROVERT | (CBS 64412) 1971 |
| | 2 | SONGS (w/lyric insert) | (CBS 64751) 1972 |

45s: Haven't Got Anything Better To Do/
       Afraid Of Tomorrow   (MCA MU 1130) 1970
       Corrina/Just This Morn   (CBS 7931) 1972

Born in Baildon in the early sixties he was in Liverpool backing artists such as Marty Wilde and Gene Vincent. On *Introvert* he's backed by Steve Hammond (gtr), Colin Davey (drms) (who'd both played with **Chris Farlowe**), Jack Brand (bs) and Pete Kelly (piano, organ) but there's also an orchestral backing. His songs are typical mainstream singer/songwriter material, mostly mellow and melodic. One of his best tracks is *Who Is Who*, which didn't have an orchestral arrangement and came with interesting lyrics:-

"Somebody said we shall overcome
But tell me who we is!"
(from *Who Is Who*)

Others like *Blues Eyes* bring to mind **Elton John** or *What A Day It's Been* (Don McLean). By way of contrast *Clever Head Spell* is much rockier than the rest. The album's final track is written by the guitarist Steve Hammond who also wrote for **Quatermass**. The album's cover has a wonderful photo of a naked woman in a green field. (CA)

Steve Swindells

ALBUM: 1 MESSAGES (w/insert)   (RCA LPLI 5057) 1974 SC

45:    Shake Up Your Soul/Energy Circus   (RCA RCA 2454) 1974

Swindells had played with **Pilot** and **String Driven Thing** among others and was later keyboardist in The Hawklords (a **Hawkwind** spin-off). After the above solo recordings, which attracted little attention, he formed his own band Steve Swindell's Swallow in late 1974. He recorded a further album and a couple of 45s in 1980. (VJ)

The Swinging Blue Jeans

Personnel:	LES BRAID	bs, vcls	AB D
	RALPH ELLIS	gtr, vcls	A
	RAY ENNIS	lead gtr, vcls	ABCD
	NORMAN KUHLKE	drms	ABC
	TERRY SYLVESTER	gtr	BC
	MIKE GREGORY	bs	C
	JOHN LAURENCE	drms	D
	MIKE PYNN	lead gtr	D

ALBUMS:	1(A)	BLUE JEANS A' SWINGING	
(up to		(mono/stereo)	(HMV CLP 1802/CSD 1570) 1964 R2
1976)	2(A)	TUTTI FRUTTI	(Regal SREG 1073) 1964 R1
	3( )	LIVE AT THE CASCADE CLUB KÖLN	
			(Electrola SME 83 927) 1965
	4( )	DON'T MAKE ME OVER	(Capitol T 6159) 1966
	5(A)	BRAND NEW AND FADED	(Dart BULL 1001) 1974 SC

NB: (1) reissued on Music For Pleasure (MFP 1163) in 1967 (SC) and Beat Goes On (BGOLP 55) in 1989. (1) mono and stereo versions reissued on one CD (EMI DORIG 104) 1997. (2) Export-only release. (3) was a German-only release. (4) was a Canadian-only release, it includes songs like *This Boy* (**Beatles**), *Do You Believe In Magic* (The Lovin Spoonful) and *I'm Gonna Sit Right Down And Cry* and has been reissued on CD (Rock-In-Beat). A good compilation is *Shake* (EMI EMS 1123) 1986. A later 34-cut CD compilation is *The Best Of The EMI Years* (EMI CDP 7 99235 2) 1992, which includes nine previously unreleased tracks and should be the definitive compilation. An earlier effort had been *All The Hits Plus More* (Prestige (BBC) CDPT 003) 1992. *At Abbey Road: 1963 to 1967* (EMI 493 3272) 1998 captures them performing their hits and some foreign-only releases.

EPs:	1	SHAKE WITH THE SWINGING BLUE JEANS	
			(HMV 7EG 8850) 1964 R1
	2	YOU'RE NO GOOD MISS MOLLY	
			(HMV 7EG 8868) 1964 R1

HCP

45s:	It's Too Late Now/Think Of Me	(HMV POP 1170) 1963 30
(up to	Do You Know/Angie	(HMV POP 1206) 1963 SC -
1976)	Hippy Hippy Shake/Now I Must Go	(HMV POP 1242) 1963 2
	Good Golly Miss Molly/Shakin' Feelin'	(HMV POP 1273) 1964 11
	You're No Good/	
	Don't You Worry About Me	(HMV POP 1304) 1964 3
	Promise You'll Tell Her/It's So Right	(HMV POP 1327) 1964 -
	It Isn't There/One Of These Days	(HMV POP 1375) 1964 -
	Make Me Know You're Mine/	
	I've Got A Girl	(HMV POP 1409) 1965 -
	Crazy 'Bout My Baby/Good Lovin'	(HMV POP 1477) 1965 -

	Don't Make Me Over/		
	What Can I Do Today	(HMV POP 1501) 1966 31	
	Sandy/I'm Gonna Have You	(HMV POP 1533) 1966 -	
	Rumours, Gossip, Words Untrue/		
	Now The Summer's Gone	(HMV POP 1564) 1966 -	
	Tremblin'/		
	Something's Coming Along	(HMV POP 1596) 1967 SC -	
	Don't Go Out Into The Rain/		
	One Woman Man	(HMV POP 1605) 1967 -	
α	What Have They Done To Hazel?/Now That You've Got Me		
	(You Don't Seem To Want Me)	(Columbia DB 8431) 1968 -	
β	Hey Mrs Housewife/Sandfly	(Columbia DB 8555) -	
	Rainbow Morning/Cottonfields	(Dart ART 2035) 1973 -	
	Dancing/Baby Mine	(Dart ART 2046) 1974 -	
Reissues:	Hippy Hippy Shake/Baby Mine	(Dart ART 2058) 1976 -	
	Hippy Hippy Shake/Good Golly Miss Molly/		
	You're No Good/Don't Make Me	(EMI EMI 2693) 1977 -	
	Hippy Hippy Shake/You're No Good	(HMV POP 2020) 1980 -	
	Hippy Hippy Shake/You're No Good	(Old Gold OG 9374) 1983 -	
	Hippy Hippy Shake/Good Golly Miss Molly	(EMI G 4541) 1985 -	
	Hippy Hippy Shake/It's Too Late Now/		
	Long Tall Sally	(EMI EMI 83) 1989 -	

NB: α credited to Ray Ennis and The Blue Jeans. β credited to The Blue Jeans.

The Swinging Blue Jeans were one of the best of Liverpool's Merseybeat bands and whilst they are best remembered for their 1963 hit *Hippy Hippy Shake* they had some other strong songs too, including their interpretation of Betty Everett's *You're No Good* (later covered by Linda Ronstadt).

The origins of this group go back to 1958 and two Liverpool-based skiffle groups who came first and second in a talent contest and decided to regroup into the foursome listed under line-up (A) above. Renaming themselves The Bluegenes they held a series of residencies at Liverpool clubs like The Cavern, Mardi Gras and Downbeat. They adopted **The Swinging Blue Jeans** name in 1963 and gained a contract with EMI's HMV label in the Merseybeat boom that accompanied **The Beatles'** rapid success.

Their debut 45, *It's Too Late Now*, made the lower reaches of the UK Top 30, but the follow-up *Do You Know* failed to chart. Then, at the very end of 1963, the band got a number of breaks. A manufacturer of blue jeans sponsored their own 15-minute weekly show, 'swingtime', on Radio Luxembourg and they featured as a Merseybeat group in an episode of 'Z Cars'. Consequently, they were better known when their rousing revival of Chan Romero's *Hippy Hippy Shake* hit the Charts and climbed to No 2. This classic party record is the one most closely associated with the band. This is well illustrated by the number of times it's been reissued. A few months later it climbed to No 24 in the US. Next, they put out a raucous cover of Little Richard's *Good Golly Miss Molly*, which reached No 11 over here and No 43 in the US. After a more restrained cover of Betty Everett's *You're No Good* climbed to No 3 in the UK (and No 97 in the US) their fortunes ebbed dramatically. Ralph Ellis got tired of touring, left the band in February 1966 and quit the music business. His replacement was ex-**Big Three** and **Escorts** member **Terry Sylvester**. In July 1967 Braid switched to keyboards and Mike Gregory, who had earlier played with **Terry Sylvester** in a band called **The Escorts,** joined on bass and vocals.

As the Merseybeat sound became outdated their career declined because they didn't seem to have the flexibility to change with the times. The sales of their album, *Blue Jeans A' Swinging*, were disappointing. The 45, *What Have They Done To Hazel?*, credited to **Ray Ennis and The Blue Jeans**, failed to make an impression and **Terry Sylvester** joined **The Hollies** replacing **Graham Nash** in January 1969. Their next 45 *Hey Mrs Housewife* was credited simply to Blue Jeans. Kuhke left in 1969 and Gregory departed in 1973. The same year they had an album *Hippy Hippy Shake* released in Europe on Bellaphon.

In 1973 **Ray Ennis** reformed the band with a new line-up (D) above. They soon became a popular club and cabaret attraction and played a number of oldies tours in the UK and Europe, although a new album, *Brand New And Faded* and a couple of 45s made little impression. Clearly, like many other bands of their era, their future laid in cabaret and they worked this scene successfully for several years. Indeed Ennis and Braid gigged with the group throughout the nineties and until 2005.

The 1986 compilation *Shake* includes their three biggest hits:- *Hippy Hippy Shake*, *Good Golly Miss Molly* and *You're No Good* alongside a collection of other frantic rock'n'roll standards with a few less frenetic Merseypop numbers thrown in for good measure. Fans of psychedelia may warm to *Make Me Know You're Mine*, a tentative nod in the direction of sixties garage rock which became quite common in the States in this era.

At Abbey Road: 1963 To 1967 captures them performing their hits and songs like their versions of **The Beatles'** *This Boy* and The Lovin' Spoonful's *Do You Believe In Magic*, which only had overseas releases.

Their bassist Les Braid died in Liverpool on 31 July 2005, aged 68. He was the cornerstone of the band, playing with them from 1958 (on a part-time basis in the early days alongside his day job for Liverpool Corporation) until 2005.

Various artists compilation appearances have included: *It's So Right* and *One Of These Days* on *Liverpool '65* (LP); *Sandy, It's Too Late Now* and *You've Got Love* on *Liverpool 1963-1968* (CD); *Sandy* and *It's Too Late Now* on *Liverpool 1963-1968, Vol. 1* (LP); *The Hippy Hippy Shake* and *Good Golly Miss Molly* on *Mersey Beat* (2-LP); *You're No Good* on *Beat At Abbey Road* (CD) and on the 2-CD set *Greatest Hits Of The 60's Vol 4*; *The Hippy Hippy Shake* and *You're No Good* on *Hits Of The Mersey Era, Vol. 1* (LP); *Don't Make Me Over* on *Beat Generation - Ready Steady Go* (CD) and *Hippy Hippy Shake* on *Wild Thing* (CD), *The Swinging Sixties - 18 Classic Tracks* (CD) and *60's Mix* (CD). (VJ/LBy/JM)

Terry Sylvester

ALBUM:	1	I BELIEVE (w/insert)	(Polydor 2383 394) 1974

45s:	For The Peace Of Mankind/		
(up to	It's Better Off This Way	(Polydor 2058 482) 1974
1976)	I Believe/It's Too Late	(Polydor 2058 732) 1976
	At The End Of The Line/Make My Day	(Polydor 2058 769) 1976

Terry Sylvester's first band had been **The Escorts**, who'd recorded six 45s in the mid-sixties. Then in February 1966 he replaced Ralph Ellis in **The Swinging Blue Jeans**. Later in early 1969, after the latter had split, he came through an audition to join **The Hollies** remaining with them until 1981. These recordings were part of an unsuccessful attempt to launch a solo career. He recorded one further 45 in 1978. (VJ)

The Symbols

Personnel incl:	JOE BACCINI	bs	A
	MICK CLARKE	bs, vcls	A
	SEAN CORRIGAN	ld gtr	A
	CLIVE GRAHAM	drms	A
	JOHNNY MILTON	vcls	A
	RIKKI SMITH	ld gtr	A
	CHAS WADE	drms	A

ALBUM:	1	THE BEST PART OF THE SYMBOLS	
			(President PTL 1018) 1968 SC

NB: *The Best Part Of The Symbols - The President Recordings 1966-1968* (President PRCD 149) 2004 is the first UK compilation of their material.

			HCP
45s:	One Fine Girl/Don't Go	(Columbia DB 7459) 1965 -	
	You're My Girl/		
	Why Do Fools Fall In Love	(Columbia DB 7664) 1965 -	
	See You In September/		
	To Make You Smile Again	(President PT 104) 1966 -	
	Canadian Sunset/		
	The Gentle Art Of Loving	(President PT 113) 1966 -	
	You'd Better Get Used To Missing Her/		
	Hideaway	(President PT 128) 1967 -	
	Bye Bye Baby/		
	The Things You Do To Me	(President PT 144) 1967 44	
	(The Best Part Of) Breaking Up/		
	Again	(President PT 173) 1967 25	
	Lovely Way To Say Goodnight/		
	Pretty City	(President PT 190) 1968 -	
	Do I Love You/Schoolgirl	(President PT 216) 1968 SC -	

THE SYN - Spanish 7" EP.

This Essex group is best known for their cover of The Ronettes' *Best Part Of Breaking Up*, which was a minor hit. Originally known as **Johnny Milton and The Condors**, they had a distinctive four-part harmony sound. Their first 45, *One Fine Girl*, was a Van McCoy number produced by Mickie Most. *See You In September* was a lush song, whilst *Canadian Sunset* sounded similar to **The Newbeats**. Their other minor hit, was a cover of The Four Season's *Bye Bye Baby*. They caused a minor stir in the music press by disowning their album (a compilation of their material) when it came out. They felt it wasn't representative of their current sound, contained too many singles and had been recorded by an earlier line-up of the group. President records claimed they did not deliver enough new material for the proposed album so they had little choice but to fill it with earlier singles. Their final effort was an old Ronettes number.

Mick Clarke was later in **The Rubettes** and Chas Wade had been in **Rush / Tinkerbell's Fairydust**.

The 2004 President compilation collects all their albums and singles for the label, plus outtakes and demos including *Silence Is Golden* and *The Sun Ain't Gonna Shine Anymore*. This is the best way to discover more about this pleasant harmony-pop band. It includes a superb fold-out colour booklet.

Compilation appearances have included: *Don't Go* and *You Are My Girl* on *Mickie Most Presents: British Go-Go* (LP); and *(The Best Part Of) Breaking Up* and *Again* on *The Electric Lemonade Acid Test, Vol. 1* (LP) and *Sometimes I Wonder* (CD). (VJ)

Symon and Pi

45s:	Sha La La La Lee/Baby Baby	(Parlophone R 5662) 1968 SC
	Got To See The Sunrise/	
	Love Is Happening To Me	(Parlophone R 5719) 1968

This was a little-known late sixties duo. The first 45 was a Phil Spector tribute produced by **Mark Wirtz**. (VJ)

The Syn

Personnel:	GUNNER HAKANARSSON	drms	AB
	ANDREW JACKMAN	keyb'ds	ABCD
	STEVE NARDELLI	gtr, vcls	ABCD
	JOHN PAINTER	gtr	A
	CHRIS SQUIRE	bs	ABCD
	PETER BANKS	gtr	BCD
	CHRIS ALLEN	drms	C
	RAY STEELE	drms	D

45s:	Created By Clive/Grounded	(Deram DM 130) 1967 R3
	Flowerman/	
	14-Hour Technicolour Dream	(Deram DM 145) 1967 R2

NB: *The Original Syn* (LP) (Acme ADLP 1041) is a limited edition pressing of 500 featuring all their Deram singles and several studio tracks. *The Original Syn 1965-2004* (2-CD) (Umbrello UMBRCD 001) 2005 is a 2-CD collection of their material.

The Syn were from Wembley, Middlesex, and originally known as The Selfs. Renaming themselves **The Syn,** they set out as a Motown and white soul band, but soon became wrapped in the trappings of flower-power, recording two excellent singles for Deram.

Their debut 45 *Created By Clive* was also recorded by **The Attack**. Both versions are well worth a spin, but the flip *Grounded*, was a powerful self-penned slice of psychedelic R&B.

Their follow-up, *Flowerman* was a fine tongue-in-cheek English psychedelic pop composition. The 'B' side was even better - *14-Hour Technicolour Dream* was written to commemorate the multi-media event held at Alexander Palace on April 29-30, 1967. This is usually regarded as one of the highlights of British psychedelic pop.

The group had a Saturday night residency at The Marquee in London and performed their own pop operas like *Mr White's Flying Machine*, *Help I'm A Pop Star* and *The Gardener And The Flowers*. For the latter one they actually dressed up as flowers!

To sure their contract with Deram they recorded an audition acetate of the classic *Heatwave*, but this seems lost forever and there's no truth at all in the rumours of a **Syn** album reported in some music weeklies in early 1968.

Serious fans of the band should check out the recent *Original Syn* collection. Their Deram 45s are fleshed out with acetates and rehearsal tapes on the first disc, which includes two tracks from The Selfs (a pre-**Syn** incarnation of the band).

When the group split **Peter Banks** and **Chris Squire** became members of **Mabel Greer's Toyshop** and, of course, they were later both in **Yes**. They also both recorded solo albums. The group has recently reformed and released two new albums in 2005 *Cathedral of Love* and *Syndistructable*.

There's also a 2-CD release *The Original Syn* again containing all four sides of their two great singles, ultra-rare material by pre-**Syn** band The Selfs and unreleased material by **The Syn**. The second disc includes five bonus tracks and among them is a new recording of a previously unrecorded **Syn** classic *Illusion* by a reformed line-up (including **Chris Squire**). The set is presented in a jewel case with an informative 24-page booklet.

Compilation appearances have included: *Grounded* on *Perfumed Garden, Vol. 1* (LP & CD), *Rubble, Vol. 14 - The Magic Rocking Horse* (LP), *The Freakbeat Scene* (CD) and *Rubble, Vol. 8* (CD); *14-Hour Technicolour Dream* on *The Psychedelic Scene* (CD), *The Best Of Rubble Collection, Vol. 3* (CD), *Chocolate Soup* (CD), *Chocolate Soup For Diabetics, Vol. 2* (LP) and on the 4-CD *Nuggets II* box set; *Created By Clive* on *The Best Of Rubble Collection, Vol. 4* (CD); *Flowerman, 14-Hour Technicolour Dream, Created By Clive* and *Grounded* on *Sixties Years, Vol. 2 - French 60's EP Collection* (CD); *Grounded* and *14-Hour Technicolour Dream* on *Broken Dreams, Vol. 1* (LP) and *Flowerman* on *Jagged Time Lapse, Vol 3* (CD). (VJ)

The Syndicats

Personnel:	KEVIN DRISCOLL	bs, vcls	AB
	STEVE HOWE	gtr	A
	TOM LADD	vcls, bs	A
	JOHN MELTON	drms	AB
	RAY FENWICK	gtr	B
	JOHNNY LAMB	vcls	B

45s:	Maybellene/True To Me	(Columbia DB 7238) 1964 R3
	Howlin' For My Baby/What To Do	(Columbia DB 7441) 1965 R3
α	On The Horizon/	
	Crawdaddy Simone	(Columbia DB 7686) 1965 R5

NB: There are demo versions of α (R4). α has been reissued (Columbia DB 7686) in a limited edition pressing of 500 reproduced from the original French jukebox pressing with a large centre hole.

This North London R&B band formed in 1963 and were clearly influenced by Chuck Berry. Joe Meek produced these three 45s, which are all now very rare and sought-after, particularly the third one.

The Syndicats' finest moment was undoubtedly *Crawdaddy Simone*, which is one of the wildest slices of British R&B. Thankfully you don't need a second mortgage to get to hear it 'cos it has been heavily compiled.

Their debut 45 was a cover of Chuck Berry's *Maybellene* with *True To Me*, which **Howe** co-composed with Tom Ladd, on the flip side. Tom Ladd was the vocalist on this 45, but by the time of their second single, *Howlin' For My Baby*, a rawer brand of R&B, Kevin Driscoll had switched to vocals. EMI rejected their next 45, *Leave My Kitten Alone/Don't Know What To Do*, although both sides can now be heard on the recent **Steve Howe** CD compilation, *Mothballs*. After this, **Steve Howe** left to replace Les Jones in **The In Crowd**. The band's final 45, a cover of Ben E. King's *On The Horizon*, featured **Howe**'s replacement Ray Fenwick on guitar and Johnny Lamb on vocals. It got a lot of airplay on pirate radio but failed to chart. For a long time, many had wrongly assumed that the superb guitar work on its flip side *Crawdaddy Simone* was the work of **Peter Banks** who was in **The Syn**, but he was never in **The Syndicats**.

Steve Howe later played in **Tomorrow** and **Yes**. He also recorded a solo album.

Compilation appearances have included: *Crawdaddy Simone* on *Maximum Freakbeat* (CD), *Perfumed Garden, Vol. 1* (LP & CD), *The Demention Of Sound* (LP), *English Freakbeat, Vol. 4* (LP & CD), *Rare 60's Beat Treasures, Vol. 1* (CD) and on the 4-CD *Nuggets II* box set; *Howlin' For My Baby* on *English Freakbeat, Vol. 2* (LP & CD); *Roll Over Beethoven* and *Shame, Shame, Shame* on *Nowhere Men Vol. 3* (CD); *Maybelline, True To Me, Howlin' For My Baby, What To Do, Leave My Kitten Alone, Don't Know What To Do* and *On The Horizon* on *Steve Howe - Mothballs* (CD). (VJ)

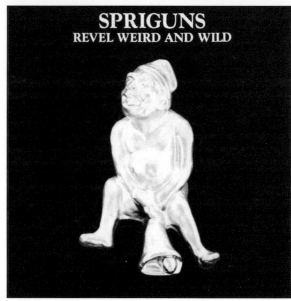

SPRIGUNS - Revel Weird And Wild (CD).

Synanthesia

Personnel:	LESLIE COOK	vcls, violin, mandolin, perc	A
	JIMMY FRASER	sax, flute, oboe, vcls	A
	DENNIS HOMES	gtr, vibes, vcls	A

ALBUM: 1(A) SYNANTHESIA   (RCA Victor SF 8058) 1969 R3

NB: (1) reissued on CD (Elegy E560/1) and again on CD (Sunbeam SBRCD 007) 2005, with full notes and a bonus track.

Synanthesia took their name from Cannonball Adderley's track of the same name, and formed when Londoner Homes placed an ad in Melody Maker early in 1968. Fellow Londoner Cook, a journalist on the paper, made contact before it went to press and Bolton native Fraser soon replied too. They were taken on by the Ellis-Wright agency (later Chrysalis), gigged widely and were soon signed up by ubiquitous folk entrepreneur Sandy Roberton.

Their album was recorded at Sound Techniques in February 1969 and is a typically classy product of Roberton's September Productions roster (alongside **Shelagh McDonald**, **Spirogyra**, **Keith Christmas** and others). It features an unusual lyrical preoccupation with classical mythology on memorable songs such as *Minerva*, *Morpheus*, *Vesta*, *Mnemosyne* and *Aurora*.

The arrangements are for vibes, oboe and saxophone, which lends a uniquely jazzy flavour to what is ostensibly a folk album. Sales were minimal when it appeared in the Winter of 1969, and Roberton decided not to issue a single. At the end of the year, however, Homes happened to play a new track for him in his office and the group was rushed into the studio to record it. The result, the stunning *Shifting Sands*, is their finest moment - but never did appear as a single. Instead it was slipped onto RCA's rare *49 Greek Street* (LP) folk compilation in July 1970, by which time the band had split. (VJ/RMJ)

THE SMALL FACES - Definitive Anthology (2-CD).

Syrup

45:	Gentleman Joe's Sidewalk Cafe/	
	Love Is Here	(Amity OTS 501) 196?

The 'A' side appears to be a cover of an early **Status Quo** 'B' side. (VJ)

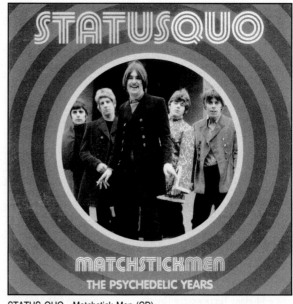

STATUS QUO - Matchstick Men (CD).

T2 - It'll All Work Out In Boomland (LP) (Reissue cover).

T 2

Personnel:
KEITH CROSS	keyb'ds, gtr, vcls	A
PETER DUNTON	drms, vcls	ABC
BERNARD JINKS	bs, vcls	AB
WILL KILLEEN	gtr, vcls	BC
JOHN WEIR	bs,vcls	C

ALBUM: 1(A) IT'LL ALL WORK OUT IN BOOMLAND
(Decca SKL 5050) 1970 R2

NB: (1) reissued on CD (World Wide Records SPM-WWR-CD-0032) 1992 with additional cuts, along with *Second Bite* (World Wide Records SPM-WWR-CD-0033) 1992, which was the product of a reformed line-up (C above) some years later. (1) also officially reissued on vinyl, in Korea (Si-Wan SRML 0022) 199?. Fans of the band will also be interested in, *T2* (Essex 1019 LP) 1997, which contains material originally intended for a second album and originally scrapped when they band split.

An obscure but now rare and quite sought-after album by a short-lived progressive rock trio. Formed in 1970, drummer **Peter Dunton** had previously been with **Gun** and Keith Cross and Bernard Jinks had been in **Bulldog Breed**. The band was originally known as Morning. Some likened Cross to **Eric Clapton** and the group made a successful appearance at the 1970 Isle Of Wight Festival and had a residency at the Marquee for a while. Their album contained an epic, 21-minute power-rock cut, *Morning*, and is certainly one of the better early seventies progressive rock efforts. Another of its cuts, *No More White Horses*, had a great freaky ending.

Cross departed to Sunburst and was replaced by Will Killeen. Cross later teamed up with Peter Ross in **Cross and Ross**. Then Jinks left and was replaced by John Weir. This reformed line-up recorded a CD *Second Bite* in 1992, but it suffers from the absence of Cross's dynamic guitar playing.

In 1992 their first album was reissued on CD with three bonus cuts that were recorded live for the BBC in October 1970. Of these, *CD* and *In Circles* are good power-rock offerings in the style of **Hendrix** and **Cream**. (VJ/JM)

Tages

45s:
Crazy 'Bout My Baby/In My Dreams	(Columbia DB 8019)	1966
So Many Girls/I'm Mad	(HMV POP 1515)	1966 R1
Treat Me Like A Lady/Wanting	(Parlophone R 5640)	1967
There's A Blind Man Playing Fiddle In The Street/		
Like A Woman	(Parlophone R 5702)	1967
Halycon Days/		
I Read You Like An Open Book	(MGM MGM 1443)	1968

Members of this Swedish band were later in **Blond**. *We Can Fly, Vol 2* (CD) includes a cut called *Fuzzy Patterns* by the band. They are only included here to clarify their nationality as they are sometimes wrongly mistaken as British. (VJ/RMJ)

Taggett

Personnel:
PETE ARNESEN	keyb'ds	A
TERRY FOGG	drms	A
TONY HICKS	gtr	A
COLIN HORTON-JENNINGS	lead vcls	A
TIM WHEATLEY	bs, vcls	A

ALBUM: 1(A) TAGGETT   (EMI EMC 3015) 1974

This short-lived group had quite some pedigree. Colin Horton-Jennings was previously lead vocalist with **Greatest Show On Earth**. Tim Wheatley had previously been with **Gracious**. Terry Fogg had been in **Sounds Incorporated** and Pete Arnesen was with **Cross and Ross**. (VJ)

Take Three

45:     Diane/Home   (Carnaby CNS 4003) 1969

This undistinguished group sang ballads. (VJ)

The 'Takers

Personnel:
CHRIS HUSTON	ld gtr	A
BRIAN JONES	sax, vcls	A
JACKIE LOMAX	bs, vcls	A
GEOFF NUGENT	gtr, vcls	A
BUGS PEMBERTON	drms	A

45:     If You Don't Come Back/Think   (Pye 7N 15690) 1964 SC

Yes, this was a slightly later version of **The Undertakers** from Wallasey.

After their 45, the band relocated briefly to the USA. **Jackie Lomax** went solo. Geoff Nugent went on to become a country and western singer and Brian Jones (not THE Brian Jones obviously) later played with **Gary Glitter**.

Compilation appearances have included: *If You Don't Come Back* on *Pop Inside The Sixties, Vol. 3* (CD), *The R&B Era, Vol. 1* (CD), *Some Other Guys* (2-LP), *Beat Merchants* (CD) and *The Songs Of Leiber And Stoller* (CD); and *Think* on *What About Us* (CD) and *Merseybeat Nuggets, Vol. 2* (CD). (VJ)

Tales of Justine

Personnel:
DAVID DALTREY	vcls, gtrs, bs, piano, mellotron, sitar, celeste	AB
BRUCE HURFORD	drms	A
PAUL MYERSON	organs, bs, celeste	AB
PAUL LOCKE	drms	B

T2 - T2 (LP).

ALBUM: 1(A) PETALS FROM A SUNFLOWER
(Tenth Planet TP 034) 1997 SC

NB: (1) documents the band's story and comes with label owner David Wells' usual extensive liner notes. 1,000 numbered copies only.

45: Albert/
Monday Morning (Some PS) (HMV POP 1614) 1967 R3/R1

The roots of this band lay in an outfit called The Court Jesters, who were formed in the wake of the British beat boom by a group of friends at Mount Grace School in Potter's Bar, Hertfordshire. By the end of 1966, they were galvanised by the new drug-inspired sounds from the States and, after various personnel changes, changed their name to **Tales Of Justine**. Now one of the first wave of authentic English psychedelic groups, they became a regular attraction at Happening 44 and The Electric Garden, which later became The Middle Earth club. One of their managers, Martin Wilcox, drew them to EMI employee **Tim Rice**'s attention (at that point he was an A&R man, trainee record producer and Norrie Paramor's assistant) and he arranged for them to record at EMI's Abbey Road studios.

Prior to this they made an impromptu appearance on stage at the International Love-in at Alexandria Palace (which was pretty much a repeat of the Fourteen Hour Technicolour Dream, which had taken place at the same venue three months earlier), when **Pink Floyd**'s set ended prematurely as **Syd Barrett** was barely functioning. Three days later they entered EMI's studios for a recording test. They put down five cuts: the inconsequential lightweight pop *Albert (A Pet Sunflower)*, three more idiosyncratic numbers *Sunday School*, *Music To Watch Us By* and *Obselete Incident* with suitably surreal lyrical observations, and the organ-driven *Evil Woman*, which is the one that really catches the ears. They returned about a fortnight later to record a less languid version of *Albert* backed by the far superior *Monday Morning*, which came with a superb arrangement and a David Daltrey sitar solo. Bizarrely, it became the penultimate pop release on EMI's decidedly unhip HMV label.

In the weeks following the recording Bruce Hurford had to leave the band and was later tragically killed in a road accident. He was replaced by Paul Locke. They recorded an acetate of *Sitting On A Blunestone*, a delightful slice of psychedelic pop with a guitar solo from David Daltrey, as a publishing demo at the offices of Southern Music. John Peel played it on his 'Top Gear' show but, incredibly, EMI refused to give what was the band's magnum opus an official release. By now, **Tim Rice** and Andrew Lloyd Webber were hard at work on "Joseph And The Amazing Technicolour Dreamcoat" and persuaded Daltrey to take lead part on the disc and show. This increasing attention on Daltrey distanced him from the rest of the group, though they returned to Abbey Road on 12th December 1968 to record four more appealing flower-pop songs - *Aurora*, *Morpheus*, *Pathway* and *Something Special* - which EMI unfortunately decided were too idiosyncratic for mass consumption. The omens were not good. Further sessions were held, but EMI's unwillingness to release any further material eventually led to the group's demise.

TALES OF JUSTINE - Petals From A Sunflower (LP).

Daltrey went on to record some singer-songwriter demos and later formed a band called Carillion, who played a Byrds-influenced brand of rock and supported **David Bowie** on his *Ziggy Stardust* tour. He departed when no record contract was forthcoming, and Carillion later evolved into **Starry Eyed and Laughing**.

All of **Tales Of Justine**'s studio recordings can now be heard on *Petals From A Sunflower*, which is recommended listening if you like flower-pop.

Compilation appearances have included: *Sitting On A Bluestone* on *Psychedelia, Vol. 4* (LP) and *Hen's Teeth, Vol. 3* (CD); and *Monday Morning* on *Psychedelia At Abbey Road* (CD) and on the 4-CD box set *Acid Drops, Spacedust & Flying Saucers*. (VJ/DW/HL)

The Talismen

45s: Masters Of War/Casting My Spell (Stateside SS 408) 1965 R1
You Break My Heart/The Wall (Acetate) 196?

One of many 'groups' American Shel Talmy produced for the Stateside label in this era. It probably wasn't a group at all but comprised of session men Talmy regularly used like **Jimmy Page** and drummer Bobbie Graham. **Page**'s involvement has inevitably rekindled interest in these recordings. *Masters Of War* was a Dylan song, whilst *Casting My Spell* was a Bo Diddley cover.

Compilation appearances have included: *Castin' My Spell* and *Masters Of War* on *James Patrick Page: Session Man, Vol. 2* (CD); *Casting My Spell* on *Bo Did It!*, *Parchment Farm* and *I Gotta Move* on *Nowhere Men Vol. 3* (CD); *You Break My Heart* on *Rubble, Vol. 2 - Pop Sike Pipe Dreams* (LP) and *Rubble, Vol. 1* (CD); and *You Break My Heart* and *What Kind Of Boy* on *English Freakbeat, Vol. 3* (CD). (VJ)

James Tamlin

45s: Is There Time/
Main Line Central Central Station (Columbia DB 7438) 1964
Now There Are Two/Yes I Have (Columbia DB 7577) 1965

The 'A' side of the second 45 with its sparse backing is a bit unusual but doesn't quite work. The flip is a more uptempo toe-tapper. (MWh)

Tandem

45: Song Of My Life/
Shapes And Shadows (Chapter One CH 102) 1968

Circus Days, Vol. 1 (LP) and *Circus Days Vol. 1 & 2* (CD) include a later version of *Shapes And Shadows*, from 1969 by this male duo, who were a later version of **Sons Of Fred** and based themselves in Great Yarmouth. The 'A' side was a ballad. (VJ)

Tangerine Peel

Personnel incl: MIKE CHAPMAN vcls A

ALBUM: 1(A) SOFT DELIGHTS (RCA LSA 3002) 1970 SC

45s: Every Christian Lion-Hearted Man Will Show You/
Trapped (United Artists UP 1193) 1968 SC
Solid Gold Mountain/Light Across The River (CBS 3402) 1968
Talking To No One/Wishing Tree (CBS 3676) 1968
Never Say Never Again/
Thousand Miles Away (MGM MGM 1470) 1969
Play Me A Sad Song And I'll Dance/
Wish You Could Be Here With Me (MGM MGM 1487) 1969
Move Into My World/In Between (RCA RCA 1936) 1970
Thinking Of Me/Soft Delights (RCA RCA 1990) 1970
What Am I To Do?/
Don't Let Me Be Misunderstood (RCA RCA 2036) 1970

HENS TEETH VOL. 1 (Comp CD) featuring Tangerine Peel.

Centred on singer and songwriter **Mike Chapman**, who later teamed up with Nicky Chinn to write hits, including songs for **Sweet** and **Mud**, **Tangerine Peel** were a product of the psychedelic era. Their best known single was *Never Say Never Again* in 1969. Their first 'A' side was an obscure **Bee Gees** composition, but which was also their most overtly psychedelic recordings. On the flip was *Trapped*, an excellent slice of psychedelic pop, dominated by distorted guitar and organ.

The best thing about their album was the psychedelic artwork on the sleeve. The contents were very disappointing. The title track, fuzz-driven *Cindy Lou* and *Long Long Ride* were the best of a poor bunch. The band consisted of five guys.

Compilation appearances include: *Every Christian Lion-Hearted Man Will Show You* on *Magic Spectacles* (CD); *Trapped* on *Psychedelia, Vol. 2* (LP) and *Hen's Teeth Vol. 1* (CD); and *Solid Gold Mountain* on *Oddities, Vol 1* (CD). (VJ)

Tapestry

45s: Carnaby Street/Taming Of The Shrew (London HLZ 10138) 1967
Like The Sun/Florence   (NEMS 56-3679) 1968
Heart And Soul/
Who Wants Happiness   (NEMS 56-3964) 1969 SC

Tapestry was a little-known late sixties group. It consisted of five guys who sang harmony ballads. *Who Wants Happiness* has been compiled on *Spinning Wheel* (CD). (VJ)

Taste

Personnel:			
NORMAN DAMERY	drms		A
RORY GALLAGHER	gtr, vcls		AB
ERIC KITTRINGHAM	bs		A
CHARLIE McCRACKEN	bs		B
JOHN WILSON	drms		B

			HCP
ALBUMS: 1(B)	TASTE	(Polydor 583 042) 1969 SC	-
2(B)	ON THE BOARDS	(Polydor 583 083) 1970 SC	18
3(B)	LIVE TASTE	(Polydor 2310 082) 1971 SC	-
4(B)	LIVE AT THE ISLE OF WIGHT	(Polydor 2383 120) 1972	41
5 (B)	IN THE BEGINNING	(Emerald/Jem) 1974	-

NB: (1) and (4) reissued on CD (Polydor 841 600-2 and 841 601-2 respectively) in 1992. (2) reissued on CD (Polydor 841 599-2) 1994. *The Best Of Taste* (Polydor 521 999 2) 2000 is a 16-track compilation. (5) and *In Concert* reissued on one CD.

45s: Blister Of The Moon/
Born On The Wrong Side Of Time   (Major Minor MM 560) 1968

Born On The Wrong Side Of Time/
Same Old Story   (Polydor 56313) 1969
Born On The Wrong Side Of Time/
Blister Of The Moon   (Major Minor MM 718) 1970
Reissue: Blister On The Moon/Sugar Mama/Cat Fish/
On The Boards   (Polydor POSP 609) 1983

Rory Gallagher was the leading light in this band which formed in Cork in Eire in August 1966. Prior to this he'd played in assorted showbands and skiffle groups. Damery and Kittringham were recruited from an R&B band, The Axels. **Taste** were pretty hot property over in Ireland and gigged a lot in London and Hamburg too. Kittringham and Damery left in May 1968. Former Cheese and Impact member Charlie McCracken came in on bass. John Wilson, who'd been with **Them**, **Misfits**, Cheese, Impact and **Boots**, was recruited on drums. Line-up (B) moved over to London where they soon became an important part of the blues boom. Their first album was basically a sparsely produced power blues effort. Their highlight was the *Live At The Isle Of Wight* album but in truth it hasn't aged too well. Their second 45 was produced by **Tony Colton**.

Taste were very much a vehicle for **Gallagher**'s blues playing and in late 1970 he went solo but continued in the same musical vein. McCracken and Wilson both joined **Stud**.

In addition to the albums listed above **Taste** had a number of non-UK albums: *First Taste* (BASF, Germany) 1971 (line-up B); *Greatest Rock Sensation* (Germany) 1977; *In Concert At The Marquee* (Ariola, Europe) 1977; *First And Best* (Bellaphon, Germany) (line-up B) and *The Story of Rory Gallagher* (Germany) (line-up B).

The Best Of Taste, a compilation released in 2000, is a 16-track selection ranging from doom-laden songs like *Catfish*, jazzy-blues numbers like *It's Happened Before?*, the wailing blues-rock of *Sugar Mama* and the heavy psych-tainted *Blister On The Moon*.

Taste appeared on several compilations in the early seventies including *Bombers* (LP) (playing *Sugar Mama* and *What's Going On*); *Deep Overground Pop* (LP) (playing *Born On The Wrong Side Of Time* and *Same Old Story*); *Rock Party* (2-LP) (with *What's Going On*); *Supergroups* (LP) (singing *Blister On The Moon*); *Supergroups, Vol. 2* (LP) (with *Morning Sun*) and *Way Into The 70's* (LP) (playing *Eat My Words*). More recently *Blister Of The Moon* and *Born On The Wrong Side Of Time* have resurfaced on *Nowhere Men, Vol. 2* (CD).

Gallagher died in 1995 during a liver transplant operation. (VJ/JM)

Taste of Honey

45s: Goody Goody Gum Drops/
Sunshine Raindrops   (Rim RIM 11) 1968
8.05/Charleston   (Rim RIM 19) 1969

This four-piece male harmony-pop group came from Liverpool. (VJ)

TASTE - On The Boards (LP).

John Taverner

ALBUMS: 1   THE WHALE   (Apple SAPCOR 15) 1970 R2
(up to   2   CELTIC REQUIEM   (Apple SAPCOR 20) 1971 R3
1976)

NB: (1) reissued on vinyl (Ring O' 2320 104) in 1977 (R1). (1) reissued again on vinyl (Apple SAPCOR 15) 1992, also on CD (SC). (2) reissued on Apple (CDSAPCOR 20, also on vinyl) 1993.

Both these albums are now very rare and sought-after, especially the second. The fact that they were avant-garde/contemporary classical music demonstrates how bizarre and full of variety Apple's catalogue was. **Taverner**, who was born in London in 1944 and studied at Highgate School and the Royal Academy of Music, first rose to prominence with 'The Whale' which he wrote in 1966. It was recorded for album release at the Church of St. John The Evangelist, Islington, London on 22, 23 and 24 July 1970. *Celtic Requiem*, despite its title, was a theatre piece for children, with a background of Irish and Latin words, scored for three instrumental groups, including Irish bagpipes. The music is a gigantic decoration of the chord of E flat major. His other main works in this era included 'In Alium' (commissioned by the BBC) and *Last Rites*. (VJ)

The Taverners

ALBUMS: 1   SELDOM SOBER   (Saga EROS 8146) 1969 SC
(up to   2   BLOWING SANDS   (Trailer LER 2080) 1973 SC
1976)   3   TIMES OF OLD ENGLAND
                         (Folk Heritage FHR 062) 1974 SC

This was a folk group. They made further recordings, including *Same Old Friends* (Folk Heritage FHR 101) in 1978. (VJ)

Taxi

This five-piece Irish progressive rock outfit from Ballymena contributed an instrumental version of *Summertime* and their bluesy *Counting Time My Way* to an Irish-only compilation album *Paddy Is Dead And The Kids Know* (LP) which came out on Pye's budget Golden Guinea subsidiary label in 1969. More recently, *Counting Time My Way* has been compiled on *Hot Smoke And Sassafras - Psychedelic Stones, Vol 1* (CD). (VJ)

Allan Taylor

ALBUMS: 1   SOMETIMES   (Liberty LBS 83483) 1971 SC
(up to   2   THE LADY   (United Artists UAG 29275) 1972
1976)   3   THE AMERICAN ALBUM
                        (United Artists UAG 29468) 1972

NB: (1) also issued on Liberty in the US. (3) later reissued on Mooncrest (CREST 28) 1977 and Rockburgh (ROC 19) 1978.

45s: Sometimes/Song For Kathy   (Liberty LBF 15447) 1971
        My Father's Room/Always You (United Artists UP 35541) 1973

A folk artist who was born in Brighton, Sussex, at the end of World War Two. **Dave Swarbrick**, Dave Pegg and Dave Mattacks guested on his first album, which came in a gatefold sleeve and is now hard to find. The second one, too, is pretty essential and equally rare. Featured with him on this one were **Andy Roberts**, Dave Mattacks, **Ian Matthews** and Royston Wood. The third album also came in a gatefold sleeve; by this time Taylor had moved to New York (he lived there from 1972-74) and several Nashville and LA session musicians assisted him on this album. Although quite sought-after, none of these albums are that expensive to obtain. In 1975 he formed **Cajun Moon**, a trio including Brian Golbey (fiddle) and Jon Gillespie (keyb'ds), which recorded an album, *Cajun Moon* (Chrysalis CHR 1116) 1976, that included Cajun, Appalachian and traditional music. All the material was self-penned and included *Lady Of Pleasure*, which has often been covered since.

In the late seventies **Taylor** recorded a couple of albums *The Traveller* (1978) and *Roll On The Day* (1980), for the independent Newcastle-based Rubber label. He's continued to record spasmodically since and is also a man of considerable intellect, having written novels, gained a BA from Leeds University and a PhD in Ethnomusicology. (VJ)

Kingsize Taylor (and The Dominoes)

Personnel incl: JOHN FRANKLAND   gtr, vcls   AB
                SAM HARDIE   piano, organ A
                GIBSON KEMP   drms   AB
                KINGSIZE TAYLOR sax, ld gtr, vcls AB
                BOBBY THOMPSON vcls, bs   AB
                HOWIE CASEY   sax   B
                BRIAN REDMAN   gtr   A
                DAVE LOVELADY   gtr   A
                DAVE WOODS   sax

EPs: 1   TWIST AND SHAKE   (Polydor EPH 21 628) 1963 R3
        2   TEENBEAT 2 - FROM THE STAR CLUB, HAMBURG
                          (Decca DFE 8569) 1964 R3

NB: There is a 4-LP box set *Kingsize Taylor and The Dominoes* (Merseyside's Greatest MGBOX 8001005-8).

45s: Memphis Tennessee/Money   (Polydor NH 66990) 1963 SC
        Hippy Hippy Shake/Dr. Feelgood (Polydor NH 66991) 1963 SC
        Stupidity/Bad Boy   (Decca F 11874) 1964 SC
    α Somebody's Always Trying/
        Looking For My Baby   (Decca F 11935) 1964 R1
        Thinkin'/Let Me Love You   (Polydor 56152) 1965 SC

NB: α a **Kingsize Taylor** solo release.

Taylor was a butcher by trade but this Merseybeat group spent much of the early sixties in Hamburg, where they perfected a popular live act. Signed by the German Philips label they recorded a series of singles none of which got an airing in Britain. They were also signed to Polydor in Germany as **The Shakers** and two of their singles were issued in the UK under this name. Their first 45 was a revival of Chuck Berry's classic *Memphis Tennessee*, backed by the Barrett Strong/**Beatles'** number *Money*. Their second 45, *Hippy Hippy Shake*, was later popularised by **The Swinging Blue Jeans**. He later signed to Ariola in Germany, who then leased his recordings to Decca in Britain. The first product of this collaboration was his magnum opus, the Soloman Burke track *Stupidity*, a really powerful song and one of the classics of the era. His second EP was recorded live at the Star Club in Hamburg as the second in a three part series of 'Teenbeat' releases. In 1967 **Taylor** returned to his former trade and Gibson Kemp, who was one of their drummers, was later with **The Eyes** and **Paddy, Klaus and Gibson**. **Howie Casey** went on to become the first Merseybeat recording artiste. Bobby Thompson went on to play for **Cliff Bennett** and **The Rockin' Berries**.

The 4-LP box-set *Kingsize Taylor and The Dominoes* includes two acetate albums from the late fifties as well as two EPs from the same era (the acetates were made by Lamba Records); a few tracks from their UK tour with Chuck Berry (1963) and an interview with **Taylor** from February 1987. The quality of the recordings is poor, but this collectors item will interest fans of the band.

SOUND OF THE SIXTIES (Comp 2-LP) featuring The T-Bones.

Kingsize Taylor and The Dominoes were enormously influential on all the Liverpool groups of their era, including **The Beatles**.

Compilation appearances have included: *I'm Late* and *I've Been Watching You* on *Mersey Sounds* (2-LP); *Stupidity* on *Mersey Beat 1962-1964* (2-LP); *Stupidity* and *Bad Boy* on *Rare 60's Beat Treasures, Vol. 5* (CD); *Fortune Teller* on *Star-Club Show* (LP) and *The Star-Club Anthology, Vol. 3* (LP); *Slow Down* on *Beat Im Star Club* (2-LP); *All Around The World, Down In The Valley* and *Stupidity* on *The Beat Goes On, Vol. 1* (LP); *Unchain My Heart, Hello Josephine, You Can't Sit Down* and *Bad Boy* on *The Beat Goes On, Vol. 2* (LP); and *Watussi* on *The Beat Goes On, Vol. 3* (LP). (VJ/L)

Mick Taylor

45:      London Town/Hoboin'   (CBS 201770) 1965 SC

This 45 was rumoured to be by **The Rolling Stones**' guitarist of this name, but this is not the case. This guy was a folk singer. *London Town* was later covered by **The Pretty Things**. (VJ)

Mike Taylor (Quartet/Trio)

Personnel:	JOHN HISEMAN	drms	AB
	TONY REEVES	bs	A
	MIKE TAYLOR	piano	AB
	DAVE TOMLIN	soprano, sax	A
	JACK BRUCE	bs	B
	RON RUBIN	bs	B

ALBUMS:	1	PENDULUM	(Columbia SX 6042) 1965 R3
	2	TRIO	(Columbia SX 6137) 1966 R3

NB: (1) as **Mike Taylor Quartet**. (2) as **Mike Taylor Trio**.

These ultra-rare albums of piano-led jazz feature Jon Hiseman (later of **Colosseum**) and Jack Bruce (later of **Cream**) alongside other stalwarts of Britain's avant-garde scene. Southend native **Taylor** was regarded as one of Britain's most original and promising jazz artists, and he went on to collaborate with **Ginger Baker** on tracks on **Cream**'s *Wheels Of Fire* album. In 1969, however, long before his potential had been fully realised, he drowned in the Thames. (RMJ)

The T-Bones

Personnel incl:	KEITH EMERSON	keyb'ds
	GARY FARR	vcls
	KEITH "LEE" JACKSON	bs
	DAVE LANGSTON	lead gtr
	ANDY McKECHNIE	gtr
	STUART PARKS	bs
	ANDREW STEELE	drms
	ALAN TURNER	drms
	WINSTON WEATHERALL	lead gtr

45s: How Many More Times/
      I'm A Lover Not A Fighter   (Columbia DB 7401) 1964
      Won't You Give Him (One More Chance)/
      Hamish's Express Relief   (Columbia DB 7489) 1965

Gary Farr formed the **T-Bones** in Worthing, Sussex, in 1963. They started out as a raw R&B outfit who were very popular in the clubs and made an appearance on 'Ready Steady Go'. Their debut 45 was a cover of Howlin' Wolf's *How Many More Times*, which was backed by a raw cover of the R&B standard, *I'm A Lover Not A Fighter*. Their second 'A' side was a cover of Soloman Burke's *Won't She Give Him (One More Chance)*, backed by another good R&B number, *Hamish's Express Relief*. After this **Gary Farr** went solo, although he used the **T-Bones** to back him on his initial recordings.

Future **Nice** and **Emerson, Lake and Palmer** member **Keith Emerson** was briefly with the **T-Bones** en route to **The V.I.P.'s**. Lee Jackson, previously of **Hedgehopper's Anonymous**, was also later in **The Nice**. Andrew Steele also went on to **The Herd** and **Doggerel Bank**.

TEA AND SYMPHONY - Tea And Symphony (CD).

Compilation appearances have included: *Hamish's Express Relief* on *Maximum R'n'B* (CD); and *I'm A Lover Not A Fighter* on *Sound Of The Sixties* (Dble LP) and *Sixties Archive Vol. 1* (CD).

Tea and Symphony

Personnel:	DAVE CLEM CLEMPSON	gtr	A
	JEFF DAW	flute, gtr, vcls	AB
	GUS DUDGEON	drms	A
	BOB LAMB	drms	A
	JAMES LANGSTON	gtr, vcls, woodwind	AB
	NIGEL PHILLIPS	vcls, keyb'ds, perc	A
	ANTON PHILLIPS		B
	PETE STARK		B
	BOB WILSON	keyb'ds, gtr, bs, perc	B

ALBUMS:	1(A)	AN ASYLUM FOR THE MUSICALLY INSANE	
			(Harvest SHVL 761) 1969 R2
	2(B)	JO SAGO	(Harvest SHVL 785) 1970 R2

45:     Boredom/Armchair Theatre   (Harvest HAR 5005) 1969

A progressive outfit from Birmingham who played some of the most esoteric and experimental music released on the Harvest label. They had some similarities with **Principal Edwards Magic Theatre** insofar as their act was a sort of travelling theatre incorporating music, drama and mime. They followed the above 45 with an album of interesting material which utilised a diverse range of instruments and some attractive vocal harmonies. They were assisted on this effort by members of **Bakerloo** and **Locomotive**. This is a pandemonium of wilful, oblique and obscure tunes, all filled with a manic musical magic that will either appall or take you by storm. Improbable instrumental combinations and unexpected barbed-wire dissonances are treated with excellent musical craftmanship. There is no sloppiness like **Dr. Strangely Strange**, nor any tendency to get mystical like **The Incredible String Band**. Instead the madness is musically and lyrically defined, which makes this album obligatory to anyone into this kind of style. A title like *Maybe My Mind (With Egg)* speaks for itself.

The follow-up, *Jo Saga*, was every bit as adventurous as their debut. The side-long title cut was an interesting attempt to relate the problems of a young Caribbean jazz musician living in Birmingham, but it pales in the company of the short tracks on the other side. These are more in the vein of the first album, but even better - ranking as among the best British acid-folk cuts. Sadly it was a bit too esoteric for wide public consumption and only sold a few hundred copies. It is now one of the label's rarest and most sought-after items. Both albums are recommended. The group split not long after its release but vocalist James Langston later resurfaced in the short-lived heavy rock outfit Mean Street Dealer in 1979.

They are also featured on Harvest's *Picnic* (2-LP) sampler singing *Maybe My Mind (With Egg)*. (VJ/MK)

TEAM DOKUS - Tales From The Underground (LP).

Tea Set

Personnel:	PETER BRIDGES	drms	A
	JOHN COUGHLIN	gtr	A
	MICHAEL COUGHLIN	ld gtr	A
	ANN CURTIN	vcls	A
	HARRY CURTIN	vcls	A

45:    Join The Tea Set/Ready Steady Go   (King KG 1048) 1966 SC

This group was formed especially for a contest in London. The groups had to write a song called *Join The Tea Set* and the winning group (this one) got the name **Tea Set** and the chance to make a record - in this case a catchy pop 45. They also won a car and a TV audition, but didn't get the chance to record again.

Team Dokus

ALBUMS: 1   TALES FROM THE UNDERGROUND

(Tenth Planet TP 007) 1994 SC

NB: (1) Limited edition of 500 numbered copies.

The members of this band are presently unknown but the above reissue is from a 1969 acetate, of which only one copy is known to exist. Essentially a concept album based on the theme of nuclear destruction it relates the tale of World War 3 and life after a nuclear holocaust. The music is lightish progressive rock with the opener, *Fifty Million Megaton Sunset*, the highlight musically and lyrically:-

"In the distance an orange sun burning through your eyes
The blisters burst on your body as the mushrooms rise!"
(from 'Fifty Million Megaton Sunset')

This cut had previously been included on *Psychedelic Salvage Co. Vol. 2* (LP & CD) and both *Psychedelia, Vol. 3* (LP) and *Hen's Teeth, Vol. 3* (CD) include the un-abbreviated version. Side one closes with another gem, the doom-laden, gently flowing and melancholic *On The Way Down*.

Side two opens with *Visions*, a pretty standard progressive rock offering, but *Tomorrow May Not Come*, which had previously got an airing on *Psychedelic Salvage Co. Vol. 1* (LP & CD), has some good extended instrumental pieces and *Big Red Beast* featured some promising guitar and vocals, but the other real gem was *Feel Your Fire*, a very effective blend of vocals, catchy drumming, guitar and keyboards which previews the finale, a reprise of *Fifty Million Megaton Sunset*. Recommended.

Tear Gas

Personnel:	EDDIE CAMPBELL	keyb'ds	AB
	ZAL CLEMINSON	gtr	ABC
	CHRIS GLEN	bs, vcls	ABC
	GILSON LAVIS	drms	A
	RICHARD MONRO	drms, vcls	ABC
	ANDY MULVEY	vcls	A
	DAVID BATCHELOR	keyb'ds, vcls	B
	HUGH McKENNA	keyb'ds, vcls	BC
	TED McKENNA	drms	BC

ALBUMS: 1(B)   PIGGY GO GETTER   (Famous SFMA 5751) 1970 R1
        2(C)   TEAR GAS   (Regal Zonophone SLRZ 1021) 1971 R3

NB: (1) reissued on CD. (2) reissued on CD (Renaissance RCD 1005) 1993 and also reissued on vinyl (Fist 'n' Egg FNE 001 LP) 199? as a limited edition of 1,000. (2) reissued on CD again (Red Fox RF 631) with a bonus track featuring **Alex Harvey** on vocals.

These Glasgow-based progressive/heavy rockers were originally known as Mustard. Their first vocalist Andy Mulvey had previously been with **The Poets**. However, he was soon replaced by David Batchelor and around the same time Gilson Lavis (their original drummer, who later played with Squeeze) was replaced by Richard Monro from **Ritchie Blackmore**'s Mandrake Root. This line-up recorded *Piggy Go Getter*, which made little impact. In 1970 Hugh McKenna took over Batchelor's vocal role and Ted McKenna (ex-**Dream Police**) relieved Monro on drums. They recorded a second album and tried to establish themselves on the underground scene but were going nowhere with their brand of tired boogie heavy rock, until they teamed up with **Alex Harvey** in August 1972 to become **The Sensational Alex Harvey Band**. (VJ)

Tears on The Console

ALBUM: 1   TEARS ON THE CONSOLE

(Holyground HG 120) 197? R3

NB: (1) reissued on Magic Mixture (MM 3) in 1990 (SC).

This album was actually by Chick Shannon and Last Exit. The Holyground issue came with a booklet and just 120 demo copies were pressed. The 1990 reissue, which had an insert, was also a limited pressing of 425. Expect this to become a mega-rarity in time like the original. The only problem is it's a rather dull bluesy pub-rock effort. (VJ)

Telegraph

Syde Trips, Vol. 3 (LP) included a track called *Putrefaction* by this band, which had originally appeared on a very limited promotional album from 1970, *Transworld* (known to collectors as Samantha Promotions 2). The bands who figured on the album had responded to an advert in 'Melody Maker' for young rock bands interested in obtaining recording/management contracts. The pick of the bunch appeared on the album, which was sent to universities and colleges in an attempt to gain live work. Sadly, none of the groups featured on the album were ever heard of again which sums up the success of the project. In fact, *Putrefaction* sounds pretty good - with some quite dramatic vocals which blend nicely with the keyboard-laden instrumentation. Worth a listen. (VJ)

Tempest

Personnel:	MARK CLARKE	bs	ABC
	JON HISEMAN	drms	ABC
	ALLAN HOLDSWORTH	gtr	AB
	PAUL WILLIAMS	vcls	A
	OLLIE HALSALL	gtr	BC

ALBUMS: 1(A)   JON HISEMAN'S TEMPEST (Bronze ILPS 9220) 1973 R1
        2(C)   LIVING IN FEAR   (Bronze ILPS 9267) 1974 R1

NB: (1) and (2) reissued on CD (Sequel NEX CD 159) in 1990. *Under The Blossom - The Anthology* (Castle Music CMQDD 1167) 2005 is a 2-CD anthology.

Tempest was formed by Mark Clarke and Jon Hiseman after the demise of jazz-rockers **Colosseum**. Their original vocalist, **Paul Williams**, had previously played with **Zoot Money**, **John Mayall** and **Juicy Lucy**. This line-up recorded Jon Hiseman's *Tempest* and toured mostly on the Continent and opened for **Rory Gallagher** in the U.S.A..

Williams left in June 1973 followed by Holdsworth a month later. Holdsworth went on to play for **Soft Machine** and was later part of Level 42. In the interim **Ollie Halsall** was brought in on guitar, and their first BBC live performance captured the change in line-up with **Williams**, Holdsworth and **Halsall** performing together. **Halsall** went on to play with John Otway.

Line-up (C) played at the Reading Festival in August 1973 and recorded *Living In Fear* before splitting in mid-1974. A year later Hiseman formed Colosseum II. Mark Clarke later was briefly in **Uriah Heep**.

These two albums show Hiseman moving away from the jazz-rock of **Colosseum** in favour of a sort of mundane and far less satisfying power-rock with **Tempest**. *Under The Blossom - The Anthology* is a 2-CD set that also includes two tracks *While You And Your Love* and *Dream Train* that were intended for a third album. Also of interest will be a BBC Radio One concert previously only available as a bootleg. The set comes with the usual superb sleevenotes from David Wells.

You'll also find their version of *Paperback Writer* on the CD set *Rock Of Ages, Four Decades Of Heavy Rock* and *Funeral Empire* has been compiled on the 3-CD box set *Ars Longa Vita Brevis: A Compendium Of Progressive Rock 1967-1974*. (VJ/KH)

Temple Creatures

Personnel:	JOHN BIDWELL	dulcitar, gtr, hand organ	A
	CLIVE PALMER	banjo, bazalaika, violin, vcls	A
	DEMELZA VAL BAKER	bongos, perc, tabla	A
	CHRISSIE QUAYLE	occasional vcls	A

Temple Creatures were formed by **Incredible String Band** founder Clive Palmer after he left **The Famous Jug Band**, and were based in Penzance, Cornwall. They gigged sporadically from 1969-70 before **Palmer** formed **C.O.B.** with Bidwell. Their music was a skilful blend of Eastern moods and folk roots, and a collection of unreleased recordings were released on the UK's Sunbeam label. (JN)

Temple Row

45s:	King And Queen/		
	One Of A Million Faces	(Polydor 2058 254) 1972 SC
	Walk The World Away/Mystery Man	(Polydor 2058 329) 1973

This band sound dead ringers for **The Moody Blues** on *King And Queen*, which later gained further exposure on *Circus Days, Vol. 4* (LP) and *Circus Days Vol's 4 & 5* (CD). So far as I know there was no Moodies involvement on the disc but it's a good imitation of the band in the early seventies. If you like them you could enjoy this. (VJ)

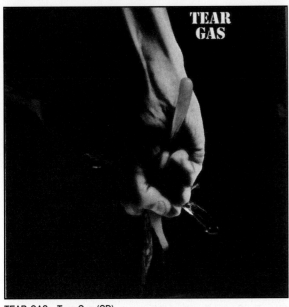

TEAR GAS - Tear Gas (CD).

Tempus Fugit

Personnel:	WALTER DAY	drms	A
	ROGER 'NEWTON' GREENWOOD	gtr	A
	JOHN HORNE	gtr	A
	LEONARD 'MICHAEL' HORNE	vcls	A
	BRIAN HOWE	bs	A

45:	Come Alive/Emphasis On Love	(Philips BF 1802) 1969 R1

Brian Howe and the Horne brothers were previously in sixties pop outfit **The Jensens** but changed name and style to **Tempus Fugit** when Roger Greenwood was recruited to the band. *Come Alive* is a light poppy number, which can also be found on *Rubble Vol. 4: 49 Minute Technicolour Dream* (LP) and *Rubble Vol. 3* (CD). **Four Pennies'** drummer Alan Buck played on the single, which was produced by Fritz Fryer.

They later became a seven-piece changing name to Reginald, but all to no avail. (VJ)

10cc

Personnel:	LOL CREME	vcls, gtr	A
	KEVIN GODLEY	vcls, drms	A
	GRAHAM GOULDMAN	vcls, gtr	AB
	ERIC STEWART	vcls, gtr	AB
	PAUL BURGESS	drms	B

				HCP
ALBUMS:	1(A)	TEN CC	(UK UKAL 1005) 1973	36
(up to	2(A)	SHEET MUSIC	(UK UKAL 1007) 1974	9
1976)	3(A)	100 CC	(UK UKAL 1012) 1975	-
	4(A)	THE ORIGINAL SOUNDTRACK	(Mercury 9102 500) 1975	4
	5(A)	GREATEST HITS OF 10 C.C.	(Decca UKAL 1012) 1975	9
	6(A)	HOW DARE YOU	(Mercury 9102 501) 1976	5

NB: (1) and (2) reissued as a double set, *The Collection* (Castle Communications CCSLP 214) in 1989 and also individually on CD (Castle CLACD 185 and 186) respectively in 1990. (4) reissued on CD again (Mercury 523964-2) 1996, but this time with copious sleevenotes and two 'B' sides - *Channel Swimmer* and *Good News* - added. Compilations have included: *Greatest Hits* (Mercury 9102 504) 1979; *10 Out Of 10* (Mercury 6359 048) 1981; *The Early Years* (CD) (Dojo EARL D 12) 1993, a CD compilation of the 'A' and 'B' sides of the seven 45s they recorded for UK Records; *The Very Best Of 10cc* (CD) (Mercury 534 612-2) 1997, (LP) (Polygram 5346124), an 18-track collection which includes all their No. 1's and four bonus tracks: Godley and Creme's *Under My Thumb*, *Wedding Bells*, *Cry* and **The Hotlegs'** *Neanderthal Man*. *Good News: An Introduction To 10CC* (Universal 548 521 2) 2001 is a rather inadequate overview fo their career.. *Dressed To Kill* (Spectrum/Universal 544 534 2) 2002 is a later collection. *Strawberry Bubblegum: A Collection Of Pre-10cc Strawberry Studios Recordings 1969-1972* (Castle CMRCD 751) 2003 should interest fans. *The Complete UK Recordings* (Varese 302 066 505) 2004 is a definitive collection of everything they recorded for the UK label.

			HCP
45s:	Donna/Hot Rock Sun	(UK UK 6) 1972	2
(up to	Johnny Don't Do It/4% Of Something	(UK UK 22) 1972	-
1976)	Rubber Bullets/Waterfall	(UK UK 36) 1973	1
	The Dean And I/Bee In My Bonnet	(UK UK 48) 1973	10
	The Worst Band In The World/		
	18 Carat Man Of Means	(UK UK 57) 1974	-
	Wall Street Shuffle/Gismo My Way	(UK UK 69) 1974	10
	Silly Love/The Sacroiliac	(UK UK 77) 1974	24
	Life Is A Minestrone/		
	Channel Swimmer	(Mercury 6008 010) 1974	7
	I'm Not In Love/Good News	(Mercury 6008 014) 1975	
	Art For Art's Sake/		
	Get It While You Can	(Mercury 6008 017) 1975	5
	I'm Mandy, Fly Me/How Dare You	(Mercury 6008 019) 1976	6
	Things We Do For Love/Hot To Tot	(Mercury 6008 022) 1976	6
Reissues:	Waterfall/4% Of Something	(UK UK 100) 1975	-
	I'm Not In Love/For You And I	(Mercury 6008 043) 1979	-
	I'm Not In Love/Dreadlock Holiday	(Old Gold OG 9475) 1985	-
	Rubber Bullets/Donna	(Old Gold OG 9786) 1987	-
	Wall Street Shuffle/The Dean And I	(Old Gold OG 9788) 1987	-
α	Worst Band In The World/Hot Sun Rock	(UK UK PZ) 1987	-
β	I'm Not In Love/Dreadlock Holiday/		
	I'm Mandy Fly Me	(Old Gold OG 6165) 1992	-

NB: α Also issued in 12" format. β CD single.

10cc - Sheet Music (LP).

Few would dispute that **10cc** were one of the most gifted and inventive new British bands of the seventies. Their songs were full of wit and polish and they successfully transcended the rock and pop market often with songs which were influenced by the music of the previous two decades.

Although **10cc** formed in Manchester in 1972 all four members had been involved on and off in the city's music scene since the early sixties. Back in 1963 Lol Creme was with a beat group, **The Sabres**. **Graham Gouldman** was with **The Whirlwinds** back in 1963 and, after releasing a 45, **Gouldman** formed **The Mockingbirds** in 1965 who also featured Kevin Godley on drums. Eric Stewart was a member of Jerry Lee and The Staggerlees back in 1963 and joined **Wayne Fontana and The Mindbenders** in 1964.

In the mid-sixties **Gouldman** was again attempting (unsuccessfully) to launch a solo career and in March 1968 he filled in as a temporary replacement for Bob Lang in **The Mindbenders**. When **The Mindbenders** split later that year Stewart and **Gouldman** purchased Inter-City recording studios in Manchester, which Stewart renamed Strawberry Studios after **The Beatles'** *Strawberry Fields Forever* song. Kevin Godley and Lol Creme were signed to Giorgio Gomelski's Marmalade label as **Frabjoy and The Runcible Spoon** for a while and **Graham Gouldman** was involved in various projects in this era. In 1966 he linked with **Friday Browne** to record *People Passing By* as **High Society**. Another obscure **Gouldman** project in 1969 was **Garden Odyssey Enterprise**. **Doctor Father**'s *Umbopo* in 1970 was a spin-off from **Gouldman**'s time with Kasenatz-Katz and in 1973 **10cc** released a 45 using the pseudonym **Grumble**.

In the late sixties **Gouldman** spent some time in the States as staff writer for bubblegum kings the Kasenatz-Katz production team but in late 1969 he and Stewart teamed up with Godley and Creme for a bout of writing, producing and recordings. **Gouldman**, for example, wrote and sang on **Freddie and The Dreamers'** *Susan's Tuba*, which became a massive hit in France whilst Godley and Creme wrote *There Ain't No Umbopo*, which was a minor US hit for Crazy Elephant.

In 1970 the four members recorded as **Hotlegs**, but the following year they concentrated on writing and producing, working with Neil Sedaka and **Ramases** (a central heating salesman from Sheffield) among others.

In 1972 they recorded demos of *Donna* and *Waterfall* and on the strength of these **Jonathan King** signed them to his UK label. He also named them **10cc**, adding 1cc to the average male sperm ejaculation of 9cc to indicate that they were above average! Godley and Creme's fifties parody single, *Donna*, got to No 2 in October 1972 and it seemed clear that the band was destined for big things. They overcame the setback of the follow-up, *Johnny Don't Do It*, another fifties pastiche but this time a teen death song, flopping, when the follow-up, *Rubber Bullets*, got to No 1 in June 1973. This was a superb pop song about a jail riot. It later got to No 73 in the US.

They set out on their first UK tour on 26 August 1973 to help promote their next 45, *The Dean And I*, which was a mini-classic and brought them another Top Ten hit, and their debut album, **10cc**, which climbed to No 36. Released to critical acclaim this album successfully bridged both the pop and rock markets - something the band would make a habit of doing with considerable success for some years to come.

In February 1974 **10cc** set off on their first US tour, although it had to be cancelled after just a few weeks when Godley was taken ill. The tour was rescheduled in May and helped to establish them with American audiences.

Their second album, *Sheet Music*, released in June 1974, was another diverse effort which further enhanced their reputation as songwriters. It got to No 9 here and No 81 in the US.

The second half of 1974 saw them embark on another UK tour and release two further hit singles:- *Wall Street Shuffle* and *Silly Love*.

In February 1975 they signed to Phonogram (Mercury) for a sum reputedly in excess of £1 million. They immediately set to work on what would be their most ambitious album yet, *The Original Soundtrack*. Hot on the heels of their *Life Is A Minestrone* Top Ten hit the album, which was further evidence of their increasing sophistication and inventiveness in the studio, spawned one of the classic pop singles of the decade, *I'm Not In Love*. Written and sung by Eric Stewart this exquisite ballad was layered by overdubbed backing vocals to create an atmosphere strongly evocative of that hot Summer of 1975. It topped the UK Charts and got to No 2 in the US. In July they topped the bill at Cardiff Castle backed by **Steeleye Span** and **Thin Lizzy**. They were at the apex of their career, a fact not lost on their old label, who put out a *Greatest Hits* compilation which got into the Top Ten here and climbed to No 161 in the US.

1976's *How Dare You?* was even more ambitious than *The Original Soundtrack*. It produced another Top 5 single, *Art For Art's Sake* (No 83 in the US) and got into the UK Album Top 5 (US No 47). *I'm Mandy Fly Me* was another classic pop/rock 45, in the style of *I'm Not In Love*, which narrowly missed the Top 5 here and got to No 60 in the US. In August 1976 **10cc** appeared at the Knebworth Festival in Hertfordshire with **The Rolling Stones**.

In October 1976 Godley and Creme left the group to concentrate on new projects. The original intention was to develop the 'Gizmo', a kind of guitar synthesizer that could hold notes and create orchestral sounds for long periods. The original idea was to record a 45 demonstrating its effect but what actually emerged was a triple album, *Consequences*, and the pair went on to record more discs together.

Gouldman and Stewart resolved to keep **10cc** going and added drummer Paul Burgess to make a trio. They also purchased a cinema in Dorking, Surrey, which they converted into a second studio, Strawberry Studio South. The first product of this new line-up was *Things We Do For Love*, a pop song with immediate appeal, which climbed to No 6 here and No 5 in the US early in 1977. They enjoyed several further hits without ever attaining the dizzy heights the band had enjoyed in the mid-seventies. **Gouldman** was still recording in the mid-eighties and the original line-up

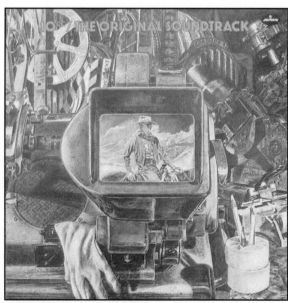

10cc - The Original Soundtrack (LP).

returned in 1992 with a new album, *Meanwhile*, but only Gouldman and Stewart remained for *Mirror Mirror* in 1993.

Good News: An Introduction To 10cc omits their two finest singles (*I'm Not In Love* and *I'm Mandy Fly Me*) but does include some of their better album tracks and a few good B-sides (*Good News* and *Get It While You Can*). Most of the material is taken from their better third and fourth albums, but this is far from a definitive collection.

The Complete UK Recordings is a reissue of their first two albums and all non-album 'B' sides, alternate versions and single mixes - in fact it contains everything they recorded for **Johnathan King's** UK label.

Rubber Bullets can also be found on the 3-CD box set *Radio Caroline Calling - 70's Flashback* and *I'm Not In Love* can also be found on the 2-CD set *45s - 45 Classic No 1's*. (VJ)

Ten Feet

45s:	Got Everything But Love/		
	Factory Worker	(RCA RCA 1544) 1966 SC	
	Shot On Sight/Losing Game	(CBS 3045) 1966 R1	

Both these mod/beat 45s are quite rare nowadays. *Factory Worker* is quite a snappy little song.

Compilation appearances include: *Factory Worker* on *That Driving Beat* (CD); and *Shoot On Sight* on *Echoes From The Wilderness - Sixteen UK R&B Freakbeat Trippers.* (LP & CD). (VJ)

Ten Feet Five

Personnel:	CHRIS BRITTON	gtr	A
	CHRIS PENFOUND		
	DAVE SMITH		
	PETE STAPLES	bs	A
	JOHNNY WALKER		

45:	Baby's Back In Town/		
	Send Me No More Lovin'	(Fontana TF 578) 1965 R1	

This Andover band's 45 is now quite sought-after because **Chris Britton** and Pete Staples went on to join **The Troggs**. Their 45 comprised two folksy ballads. (VJ)

Tennent-Morrison

Personnel:	DAVID MORRISON	gtr	A
	JEFF PEARCE	bs	A
	GUY SHEPHERD	drms	A
	JOHN TENNENT	gtr, vcls	A

ALBUM:	1(A)	TENNENT-MORRISON	(Polydor) 1972 R3

45:	Good For You/Tomorrow It Might Rain	(Polydor 2058 272) 1972

Despite their name, this was a four-piece acoustic rock band whose sole album is near-impossible to locate. When it failed to sell they changed their name to **Joe Soap**. (VJ/RMJ)

Ten Years After

Personnel:	CHICK CHURCHILL	keyb'ds	A
	ALVIN LEE	gtr, vcls	A
	RIC LEE	drms	A
	LEO LYON	bs	A

			HCP
ALBUMS:	1(A)	TEN YEARS AFTER	
		(mono/stereo)	(Deram DML/SML 1015) 1967 R1 -

TEN YEARS AFTER - Stonedhenge (LP).

2(A)	UNDEAD		
	(mono/stereo)	(Deram DML/SML 1023) 1968 R1 26	
3(A)	STONEDHENGE		
	(mono/stereo)	(Deram DML/SML 1029) 1969 R1 6	
4(A)	SSSSSH		
	(mono/stereo)	(Deram DML/SML 1052) 1969 R1 4	
5(A)	CRICKLEWOOD GREEN		
	(mono/stereo)	(Deram DML/SML 1065) 1970 SC 4	
6(A)	WATT	(Deram SML 1078) 1971 SC 5	
7(A)	ALVIN LEE & CO (Compilation)		
		(Deram SML 1096) 1972 SC -	
8(A)	A SPACE IN TIME	(Chrysalis CHR 1001) 1972 SC 36	
9(A)	ROCK 'N' ROLL MUSIC TO THE WORLD		
		(Chrysalis CHR 1009) 1972 27	
10(A)	RECORDED LIVE	(Chrysalis CTY 1049) 1973 36	
11(A)	POSITIVE VIBRATIONS	(Chrysalis CHR 1060) 1974 -	
12(A)	GOIN' HOME (Compilation)		
		(Chrysalis CHR 1077) 1975 -	
13(A)	ANTHOLOGY (Compilation)		
		(Chrysalis CHR 1104 ??) 1976 -	
14(A)	CLASSIC PERFORMANCES (Compilation)		
		(Chrysalis CHR 1134) 1977 -	

NB: (1) reissued on CD (Deram 820 532-2) 1988. (1) reissued again on CD (Decca 8828972) with bonus tracks and a 12-page booklet. (2) reissued on CD (Deram 820 533-2) 1988. (2) reissued on CD (Deram 8628992) with the four tracks originally omitted. (3) reissued on CD (Request RR 002) 1988, (Deram 820 534-2) 1989 and remastered (BGO BGO 356) 1997 and again remastered with bonus tracks and a 12-page colour booklet. (4) reissued remastered (BGO BGOCD 338) 1997 and again on CD (EMI 5789492). (5) reissued at mid-price (EMI Gold CDGOLD 1052) 1996. (5) reissued on CD (EMI 5330952) with two bonus track and a 10-page booklet. (6) reissued on CD remastered (BGO BGOCD 345) 1997. (7) reissued on CD (Deram 820 566-2) 1989 with additional cuts. (8) reissued on CD remastered (BGO BGO 351) 1997. (9) reissued on CD remastered (BGO BGO 348) 1997. (10) reissued on CD remastered (BGO BGOCD 341) 1997. (11) reissued on CD (BGO BGOCD 617). (14) reissued on CD (Chrysalis CCD 1134) 1987. (5), (6) and (8) reissued as a 3-CD box set (Chrysalis CDOMB 011) 1995.

Repackages included *Ten Years After* (Pickwick SHM 3038) 1980, *Hear Me Calling* (Decca TAB 24) and *Original Recordings, Vol. 1* and *2* (See For Miles SEE 80 and 90 respectively) 1987, reissued again in 1993. If you're looking for a compilation there's *The Classic Performances Of Ten Years After* (Chrysalis CCD 1134) 1987; *Universal* (Chrysalis VK 41580) 1988, *Portfolio - A History Of Ten Years After* (Chrysalis MPCD 1639) 1988, *The Collection: Ten Years After* (Castle Collector CCSCD 293) 1991, *Essential Ten Years After* (Chrysalis CDCHR 1857) 1992, *Love Like A Man* (Trad. Line TL 001327) 1993, *The Collection* (Cema-Griffin CGD 218-2) 1994, and *I'm Going Home* (Disky DC 868782) 1996 is a budget-priced collection. *Solid Rock* (Chrysalis) 1997 combines some of their vintage album tracks with later **Alvin Lee** solo efforts. *Live At The Fillmore East* (Chrysalis 7243 533297 23) 2001 is a 2-CD set, which captures them in form. *Best Of Ten Years After* (EMI 5284992) is a good compilation and comes with photos of the band's album covers and detailed sleevenotes.

			HCP
45s:	Portable People/The Sounds	(Deram DM 176) 1968 -	
	Hear Me Calling/I'm Going Home	(Deram DM 221) 1968 -	
	Love Like A Man (two versions)	(Deram DM 299) 1970 10	

TEN YEARS AFTER - Cricklewood Green (LP).

Reissues: α   Love Like A Man (two versions)   (Deram DM 310) 1970 -
               Love Like A Man/(Flip by Them) (Old Gold OG 9342) 1983 -
NB: α Deram DM 310 is a re-issue of DM 299.

Ten Years After is always going to be remembered for **Lee**'s flash, fast-fingered guitar playing as epitomised by their appearance in the 'Woodstock' movie. Ironically, this not only made them superstars, it also proved a straight-jacket for audiences' musical expectations of them which they were never able to shed in subsequent years.

The antecedents of this band were a mid-sixties band, **The Jaybirds**, who backed **The Ivy League** for a while. **Alvin Lee** formed the Nottingham-based rock'n'roll/R&B outfit in the early sixties with Leo Lyons and drummer Dave Quickmire. When Quickmire left in the Summer of 1965 Ric Lee came in as a replacement. The band became a popular live attraction in the Midlands and also, like so many of their contemporaries, spent time in Hamburg. In 1966 manager/agent Chris White took them on and they supported **The Bonzo Dog Band** at The Marquee as The Blues Yard for one gig before becoming **Ten Years After**. They soon became closely identified with the late sixties blues boom largely due to **Alvin Lee**'s lightning guitar work.

They signed to Decca in October 1967 who put out their recordings on their Deram subsidiary. Their debut album didn't chart but include the future band favourite *I Can't Keep From Crying* and the 10-minute *Help Me Baby*. There's a recent expanded CD release of this album which includes among it bonus tracks mono single versions of *Portable People* and *Sounds* along with four other bonus cuts *Rock Your Mama*, *Spider And The Web*, *Hold Me Tight* and *Woodhoppers Ball*.

The live follow-up, *Undead*, peaked at No 6 in the UK (and 61 in the US). This album was recorded in the tiny Klooks Kleek Club in London. It contained their trademark track *I'm Going Home* and the 10-minute epic *I May Be Wrong But I Won't Be Wrong Always*. Even if the music wasn't psychedelic the album sported a superb psychedelic sleeve. There's now a CD reissue of this album which contains the four tracks which were omitted from the original album.

1969 was the year they really made the big time. Their next album, *Stonedhenge*, made the UK Top Ten. It was in many ways their most experimental album utilising assorted sound effects and a variety of instruments. There's a recent remastered CD reissue of this album which includes as bonus tracks the 45 version of *I'm Going Home*, the US version of *Woman Trouble* and the 45 version of *Hear Me Calling* and a 14-minute version of *Boogie On*. On 3 July they became the first and only rock band to play the Newport Jazz Festival at Rhode Island in the USA. However it was their appearance at Woodstock in August of that year which transformed them into overnight stars, after **Lee**'s 11-minute guitar extravaganza on *I'm Going Home* was filmed for the movie.

Cricklewood Green was their most successful album in the UK. It spent 27 weeks in the Charts, peaking at No 4. It also spawned *Love Like A Man*,

their only UK Chart entry, which had the studio album cut on one side and a long live version which played at 33 rpm on the flip. It utilised studio effects alongside bluesy rhythms and **Alvin Lee**'s guitar histrionics. Highlights included *50,000 Miles Beneath My Brain* and *As The Sun Still Burns Away*. There's a CD reissue of this that includes two non-album bonus tracks and a 10-page colour booklet.

Their most successful US album was *A Space In Time*, notable for the use of electronics for the first time. It went gold in the US, but only managed No 36 in the UK, where their popularity was waning. This wasn't surprising since the band spent much of their time abroad, particularly in the US, where they also enjoyed a number of minor 45 hits like *I'd Love To Change The World* and *Baby Won't You Let Me Rock'n'Roll You.*

After recording *Rock And Roll Music To The World* in 1972, which met with modest Chart success, they took time out to pursue solo projects, although a double live album, *Recorded Live*, was released in the Summer of 1973. It utilised material from concerts at Amsterdam, Frankfurt, Paris and Rotterdam. In February 1973 **Alvin Lee** recorded a solo album, *On The Road To Freedom*, with Mylon Le Fevre, a US gospel singer. A number of famous rock personalities also guested on the album - **Stevie Winwood, Jim Capaldi**, **George Harrison** and Ron Wood. It peaked at No 138 in the US Charts. Chick Churchill also put out a solo album but this didn't sell in any great numbers.

TEN YEARS AFTER - Watt (LP).

In 1974, **Alvin Lee Co.** recorded *"In Flight"* live at the Rainbow Theatre in London, and the following month **Ten Years After** played a sell-out UK concert at the same venue. It was to be their final UK gig, although the band continued to tour the 'States through the summer of 1975 where their final album, *Positive Vibrations*, peaked at No 81 in the US Album Charts. This was a typical seventies blues-rock album which has also had a recent CD reissue.

After their demise, **Lee** continued to record some reasonably successful albums with his own band, **Alvin Lee Co**. In March 1976 he formed **Ten Years Later** and upon their demise in 1980 he put together the first of a series of **Alvin Lee** Bands which he worked with throughout the eighties.

They reformed in 1988 for European Concerts and released their first new album for 15 years, *About Time*, in 1989.

See For Miles have compiled a two-part epitaph of the band's recordings for Deram. *Vol. 1* includes both sides of their debut 45. *The Sounds*, a heavy psychedelic composition with plenty of distorted guitar and sound effects, which is definitely worthy of attention for connoisseurs of psychedelia. The remaining material is taken from their first three albums. This is more variable, sometimes degenerating into mundane heavy boogie rock. *Vol. 2* covers the 1969-71 period. It includes four tracks from *Sssssh* (including a good heavy rocker, *Stoned Woman*); two tracks a-piece from *Cricklewood Green* and *Watt* and 8½-minute live single version of *Love Like A Man*.

The 1990 Deram CD is a reissue of the earlier six-track retrospective, *Alvin Lee and Company*, which was dominated by *Boogie On*, a 15-minute *Stonedhenge* outtake, plus three additional cuts:- the bluesy *Spider In My Web* and a 1968 single, *Here Me Calling/I'm Going Home*.

Live At The Fillmore East is a deluxe slipcased version of a live performance on 27th/28th February 1970 shortly before the release of *Candlewick Green*. It includes a 12-minute version of *I'm Going Home*, which is similar to the rendition they gave it at Woodstock, *Love Like A Man*, *Working On The Road* and *50,000 Miles Beneath My Brain*. It also features rare live versions of Sonny Boy Williamson's *Help Me* and Willie Dixon's *Spoonful*, and a previously-unreleased rendition of Chuck Berry's *Roll Over Beethoven*.

A notable compilation appearance was, of course, *I'm Going Home* on the 3-LP set *Woodstock* in 1970 and *I'm Going Home* can also be heard on *The Woodstock Generation* (Nectar NTRCD 020) 1994. They also appeared on Decca's 1969 (LP) sampler, *World Of Blues Power!*, singing *Spoonful* and *Feel It For Me* and returned on *Vol. 2* (LP) of the same series in 1970 with *Going To Try* and *Speed Kills*. More recently, *Bad Scene* has resurfaced on *The Age Of Enlightenment-Prog Rock, Vol. One* (CD); *I'd Love To Change The World* has been compiled on the 2-CD set *Stars And Stripes*; *Love Like A Man* resurfaced on the 3-CD set *Guitar Heroes - Rock The Night Away*; and *I'm Going Home* on the 2-CD set *Rock Resurrection*. (VJ)

The Termites

45s: Tell Me/I Found My Place   (Oriole CB 1989) 1965 SC
        Every Day Every Day/
        No-One In The Whole Wide World   (CBS 201761) 1965

There was also a Jamaican band of this name who released several 45s, but these two discs were recorded by two teenage girls, who also recorded in Italy. *Everyday, Everyday* is a pop ballad, whilst *No-One In The Whole Wide World* is a gentle beat record.

Tell Me was also recorded by **The Rolling Stones** on their debut album. (VJ)

Jake Thackray

ALBUMS: 1   LAST WILL AND TESTAMENT
(up to   (Columbia SCX 6178) 1967 SC
1976)   2   JAKE'S PROGRESS   (Columbia SCX 6345) 1969
         3   LIVE PERFORMANCE   (Note NTS 105) 1971
         4   BANTAM COCK   (Columbia SCX 6506) 1972

45s: Remember Bethlehem/Joseph   (Columbia DB 8296) 1967
         Lah Di Dah/The Black Swan   (Columbia DB 8364) 1968
         Country/Old Molly Metcalfe (Columbia DB 8858) 1972
Reissue: Remember Bethlehem/Joseph   (Columbia DB 8949) 1972

Jake Thackray was born in 1938 and, after graduating from Durham University, became an English teacher. He worked in France and Algeria (and had his first poems published whilst working in Lille). Returning to Leeds he began to work as a singer/songwriter, writing short religious-based songs and performing in pubs and working-men's clubs. He also appeared on BBC's regional magazine programmes. In late spring 1967 he was signed by Columbia. Comedian Bernard Braden heard his debut album *The Last Will And Testament* and decided to invite him to perform one song a week on his newly launched magazine programme 'Braden's Week'. He deployed a band to support him on his second album *Jake's Progress*. When 'Braden's Week' ended he transferred to 'That's Life', its successor. After *Bantam Cock* in 1973 he assumed a lower recording profile and 1977's *On Again On Again* was his final studio album.

Thackray appeared on **Neil Innes**' *Innes Book Of Records* and a 1981 BBC broadcast was released in 1983 as the *Jake Thackray And Songs* album. He contributed one track *Tortoise* to 1986's *Where Would You Rather Be Tonight* benefit album and continued to play in local pubs until his death in December 2002. (VJ)

Thanksgiving

45:     Hanging By A Thread/
        Tomorrow Has Been Cancelled   (Parlophone R 5901) 1971

This was a little known 45. (VJ)

Thee

Personnel incl: ANDY MITCHELL

45:     Each And Every Day/There You Go!   (Decca F 12163) 1965

This mid-sixties Hampstead-based quartet was managed by Reg King, who was **Andrew Loog Oldham**'s chauffeur. The 'A' side of their sole 45 was a **Jagger**/Richard composition, which **The Rolling Stones** decided not to release because it wasn't much good. The flip, written by Andy Mitchell, was a raw beat number with a fine guitar break.

Compilation appearances have included: *Each And Every Day* on *Rolling Stones Connection 1963-66* (CD) and *The Beat Scene* (CD); and *There You Go* on *English Freakbeat, Vol. 3* (LP & CD). (VJ)

Them

Personnel: BILLY HARRISON   gtr   ABC
            ALAN HENDERSON   bs   ABCDEFG
            RONNIE MELLINGS   drms   A
            VAN MORRISON   vcls, hrmnca, sax ABCDE
            ERIC WRIXEN   piano   A
            JACKIE McAULEY   piano   B
            PAT McAULEY   drms   BC
            PETE BARDENS   piano   — CD
            JOE BONI   gtr   D
            TERRY NOON   drms   D
            JIM ARMSTRONG   gtr   EFG
            RAY ELLIOT   piano, sax   EF
            JOHN WILSON   drms   E
            DAVE HARVEY   drms   FG
            KENNY McDOWELL   vcls   FG

ALBUMS: 1(B) (THE ANGRY YOUNG) THEM (Decca LK 4700) 1965 R2
        2(E) THEM AGAIN   (Decca LK 4751) 1966 R2
        3(?) NOW AND THEM   (Tower ST 5104) 1967 R2
        4 (?) TIME OUT, TIME IN FOR THEM
                                     (Tower ST 5116) 1968 R3
        5(?) THEM   (Happy Tiger HT 1004) 1970 R1
        6(-) THE WORLD OF THEM (Compilation)
                                     (Decca (S)PA 86) 1970
        7 (?) IN REALITY   (Happy Tiger HT 1012) 1971 R2

THEM - (The Angry Young) Them (LP).

8 (-) THEM FEATURING VAN MORRISON LEAD
        SINGER (Compilation)   (Deram DPA 3001) 1973
9 (-) ROCK ROOTS   (Decca ROOTS 3) 1976

NB: (1) repressed with same catalogue number in 1970 (SC) on red label with boxed Decca logo. (2) repressed with same catalogue number in 1970 (SC) on red label with boxed Decca logo. (3), (4), (5) and (7) US-only. (1) reissued on CD as *The Angry Young Them Featuring Van Morrison* (Deram 844 824-2) 1998. (2) was issued on Parrot in the US. (2) reissued on CD as *Them Again Featuring Van Morrison* (Deram 844 825-2) 1998. (1) is available on CD (London 820 563-2) 1988, as is (2) (Deram 820 564-2) 1990. (3) reissued on CD (Zap! ZAP 6) 1988 and again on CD (Rev-Ola CRREV 29). (4) reissued on CD (Zap! ZAP 7) in 1988 and again on CD (Rev-Ola CRREV 52).

1992 saw the emergence of *The Collection* (Castle CCSCD 131), which compiled their material with **Van Morrison**. More recent UK repackages have included *Rock Roots: Them* (Decca ROOTS 3) 1976, *Them Featuring Van Morrison* (Decca TAB 45) 1982, *The Them Collection* (2-LP) (Castle CCSCP 131) 1986 and *Them* (See For Miles SEE 31) 1987. There's also a 13 track CD, *Them Featuring Van Morrison* (London 810 165-2) 1988. Their US albums on Happy Tiger, *Them* and *In Reality* have been reissued on one CD (Synton 1610973) 1997. *The Story Of Them Featuring Van Morrison* (Deram 844 813-2) 1998 is a 49-track 2-CD collection comprising most of their output for Deram.

EP: 1(B) THEM   (Decca DFE 8612) 1965 R3

NB: (1) was also issued in an alternative export sleeve. The export version is more valuable (R5).

			HCP
45s:	Don't Start Crying Now/		
	One Two Brown Eyes	(Decca F 11973) 1964	R2 -
	Baby Please Don't Go/Gloria	(Decca F 12018) 1964	10
	Here Comes The Night/All For Myself	(Decca F 12094) 1965	2
	One More Time/How Long Baby?	(Decca F 12175) 1965	-
	(It Won't Hurt) Half As Much/		
	I'm Gonna Dress In Black	(Decca F 12215) 1965	-
	Mystic Eyes/		
	If You And I Could Be As Two	(Decca F 12281) 1965	-
	Call My Name/Bring 'Em On In	(Decca F 12355) 1966	-
	Richard Cory/Don't You Know?	(Decca F 12403) 1966	-
	Gloria/Friday's Child	(Major Minor MM 509) 1967 SC	-
	The Story Of Them Parts 1 2	(Major Minor MM 513) 1967 SC	-
Reissues:	Gloria/Here Comes The Night	(Decca F 12875) 1969	-
	Baby Please Don't Go/Gloria	(Deram DM 394) 1973	-
	Here Comes The Night/All For Myself	(Deram DM 400) 1973	-
	Gloria/Baby Please Don't Go	(Decca F 13923) 1982	-
	Baby Please Don't Go/Gloria	(Old Gold OG 9341) 1983	-
	Here Comes The Night/		
	All For Myself	(Old Gold OG 9342) 1983	-
α	Baby Please Don't Go/Gloria	(London 292) 1991	65

NB: α also available as 12" and CD single with the addition of *Mystic Eyes*.

Them are likely to be best remembered as a launching pad for **Van Morrison** but their early line-up was also notable for some of the best Irish

THEM - Now And Them (LP).

THEM - Time Out Time In For Them (LP).

R&B recordings of the sixties and the later US-based line-up recorded some fine psychedelic artefacts.

This band originally came together in Belfast in 1963. They started a regular blues club at Belfast's Maritime Hotel and their mission was to convert the city to the blues to which vocalist **Van Morrison** added a soulful tinge. **Morrison** had previously played in an outfit called Georgie and The Monarchs, who had a 45, *Boo-Zooh (Hully Gully)/Twingy Baby* (CBS 1307), which was only released in Germany and Holland. **Them** soon established a good live reputation locally with a 15-minute version of Bobby Bland's *Turn On Your Lovelight*, their tour de force. A demo tape was also made of this.

In July 1964 Wrixen departed to join **The Wheels** and Mellings also left to become a milkman. Decca's Dick Rowe, having seen them perform at the Maritime, arranged a recording audition in London and to find a debut single. Seven songs were recorded - *Groovin', You Can't Judge A Book*, a shortened version of *Turn On Your Lovelight, Gloria, One Two Brown Eyes, Philosophy* and *Don't Start Crying Now*. This last frenetic number was chosen for their first 45. It failed to break through nationally but sold well in Belfast. It's now their most valuable and sought-after 45.

For their second single they covered the American blues classic, *Baby Please Don't Go*. With the stunning garage-punk standard, *Gloria*, on the flip, this was arguably one of the finest R&B 45s of the sixties. Both tracks featured fine vocal performances from **Morrison** but the remaining band members contributed little with Rowe utilising experienced sessionmen like **Jimmy Page**, who was responsible for the singles' fine guitar moments. *Gloria* was developed into a 20-minute jam in their live act and rapidly emerged as an anthem of America's garage-band phenomenon. It was covered by several American bands, most notably The Shadows of Knight. In the UK *Baby Please Don't Go* made the Top Ten.

American producer Bert Berns (whose earlier credits included *Hang On Sloopy, Twist And Shout* and *Under The Boardwalk*) wrote and produced their next 45, *Here Comes The Night*, which had been recorded by **Lulu** the previous year without much commercial success. This near-ballad featured another stunning vocal performance by **Morrison** and rose to No 2, becoming their biggest but last UK hit. Very poppy and mellow, it was uncharacteristic of their usual style.

In April 1965 the first in a series of line-up changes took place, which culminated in the death of the band. **Jackie McAuley** left, totally disillusioned by the continual involvement of sessionmen on the band's recordings. He was replaced by **Pete Bardens**. In July 1965, Jackie's brother Pat left (to be replaced by Terry Noon) and Billy Harrison was replaced by Joe Boni. In September 1965, **Morrison** and Henderson sacked **Bardens**, Boni and Noon and headed back to Belfast to look for new personnel. The McAuley brothers then formed **Belfast Gypsies**.

Them continued to record 45s which were never likely to break through commercially, although *Mystic Eyes* was musically very interesting. Their EP, released in February 1965 consisted of both sides of their first 45, alongside *Baby Please Don't Go* and *Philosophy*. A debut album, *Them* (sometimes referred to as *Angry Young Them* because that description appears on the back cover), came out in June 1965. Most of the backing was done by sessionmen although ostensibly it was recorded in the time span of line-up B. The opening cut, *Mystic Eyes*, was awesome and full of passion and excitement. The album also contained a few **Morrison** originals and a good re-work of John Lee Hooker's *Don't Look Back*.

In September 1965 **Morrison** and Henderson returned with line-up (E) who are credited with recording the *Them Again* album, which mixed R&B standards with some **Morrison** originals. However, the album was apparently made with the assistance of other session players. It sold badly.

Them finally split in June 1966 but later re-grouped in Los Angeles with Belfast vocalist Ken McDowell in **Morrison**'s place. This line-up cut two albums on Tower and continued, based in the US, into the seventies. The *Now And Them* album was a curious mixture of blues-rock and psychedelia. Most notable in the latter category was *Square Room*, a 10-minute Eastern-sounding group composition. This album is now highly collectable. Prior to the follow-up Roy Elliot departed and the band became a quartet.

By the time of their second Tower album, Them were a fully fledged psychedelic rock band. Like its predecessor it's recommended to fans of the psychedelic genre and now highly collectable. Sadly, it marked the end of this line-up who split in 1968, disillusioned by their financial situation. Armstrong and McDowell formed Sk'boo back in Belfast, but Henderson recorded two further albums on the Happy Tiger label. The first was *Them*, with respected LA sessionman Jerry Cole on guitar and vocals and an unnamed drummer. The album ranged from rock'n'roll through country to soul and Ry Cooder and Jack Nitzsche played uncredited on some tracks. However, the album was less interesting than what had preceded it and also failed to chart. Henderson's final effort, *In Reality*, is now their rarest album but was probably **Them**'s worst.

Van Morrison, of course, launched a successful solo career. What of the rest? Well, when the American-based line-up split, Henderson recorded a grandoise double Jesus-rock opera project with Ray Ruff (who'd produced all of **Them**'s US-only albums), entitled *Truth Of Truths* on Oak Records. It was a total disaster! He then spent several years on a Connecticut farm, but reformed **Them** with original members Eric Wixen and Billy Hamilton in the late seventies. They travelled to Hamburg (some of **Them**'s singles had successfully been reissued in Germany) to record *Shut Your Mouth*, a competent blues-rock album. After this reformation collapsed, Billy Harrison made a solo album, *Billy Who?* (Vagabond VRLPS 80001) 1980. After his time in the **Belfast Gypsies**, Pat McAuley withdrew from the music business and sadly drowned in Donegal in 1984. **Jackie McAuley** was later in Cult (who did not record), **Trader Horne** and also made a solo album in 1971. In the late seventies, Armstrong formed Light, whose 1978 album featured much of his fine guitar playing. John Wilson was later involved in **Taste** and **Stud** and **Peter Bardens**, who'd previously been in **Peter B's** and **Shotgun Express**, recorded three solo albums during the seventies as well as playing for **Camel**.

THEM - In Reality (CD).

There has been several compilations of **Them**'s material. See For Miles combined the 'A' and 'B' sides of all their Decca and Major Minor 45s and a very good EP track, *Philosophy*, which wasn't included on any of their albums. They also have two cuts, *I Can Only Give You Everything* (from the *Them Again* album) and the much rarer *Little Girl* (which had previously only appeared on the Lord's Taverner's Charity album, *Fourteen, Lord Taverners* (LP)), on *R&B Scene, Vol. 2* (LP) and *British R'n'B Explosion, Vol. 1* (CD). Other compilation appearances have included: *I Can Only Give You Everything* on *Mod Scene, Vol. 2* (CD) and on the 4-CD *Nuggets II* box set; *Gloria* and *Baby Please Don't Go* on *Made In England, Vol. 1* (CD); *Baby Please Don't Go* on *Sixties Lost And Found, Vol. 2* (LP) and *Sixties Explosion, Vol. 1* (CD); *Baby Please Don't Go* and *Little Girl* on *Weekend Starts Here* (LP); *Don't Start Crying Now* and *Philosophy* on *Belfast Beat Maritime Blues* (CD); *Black Widow Spider* on *Electric Psychedelic Sitar Headswirlers, Vol. 3* (CD); *The Story Of Them Pts 1 and 2* on *Hard-Up Heroes* (2-LP); *Here Comes The Night* on *World Of Hits, Vol. 2* (LP); and *Endless Journey, Phase Three* (LP) includes superb re-recordings of *Baby Please Don't Go* and *Gloria*, from the *In Reality* album.

Their move to America in 1966 has meant that many of their later recordings have resurfaced on American compilation albums and these are all well worth getting to hear. Compilation coverage has so far included: *Dirty Old Man/But It's Alright* on *Texas Punk From The Sixties* (LP); *Dirty Old Man* on *Boulders Punk (EP) Box, Vol. 2*; *Lonely Week* on *Mayhem And Psychosis, Vol. 2* (LP) and the excellent dope inspired *Walking In The Queen's Garden* on *Marijuana Unknowns, Vol. 1* (LP). (VJ)

Therapy

Personnel:	SAM BRACKEN	gtr, vcls	A
	DAVE SHANNON	keyb'ds, gtr, vcls	AB
	FIONA SIMPSON	gtr, vcls	AB

ALBUMS:	1(B)	ONE NIGHT STAND	(Indigo IRS 5124) 1973 SC
(up to	2(B)	ALMANAC	(CBS 69017) 1976
1976)	3(B)	BRINGING THE HOUSE DOWN	(CBS) 1976

Formed in 1970, this trio played a blend of folk, blues and ragtime. Bracken left in 1971 and these albums were recorded by the remaining duo of Shannon and Simpson. The first was privately-pressed and is now rare. The second, *Almanac*, based a song around each sign of the Zodiac. All the tracks were written by Shannon, but it was Fiona Simpson's vocals which accounted for much of their appeal. They were regulars on TV in this era and added comedy to their repertoire, which enabled them to open for acts like **The Barron Knights** and Jasper Carrot. They continued to record throughout the eighties, setting up their own Therapy record label and selling their albums at concerts. Shannon eventually became a BBC music producer and Simpson did solo and session work. (VJ)

They Bite

Personnel:	DAVE CLARKE	gtr, vcls	A
	MENNA DAVIES	vcls	A
	JON NEWEY	drms	A
	IAN RUTTER	bs	A

45: α I Wanna Screw With Jesus/The Pusher (Private Acetate) 1970

NB: α demo only.

A heavy rock band from South-West London formed from the remnants of Plasma and fronted by the rather risque performance of ex-folk singer Menna Davies. They played London's dwindling underground circuit in 1970/71. Rutter went on to **Crew**, Clarke to **England's Glory** and Newey to both **Crew** and **England's Glory**. The recording was never released due to problems with its lyrical content. (VJ)

These Fading Colours

See **Those Fading Colours**.

Thin Lizzy

Personnel:	ERIC BELL	gtr, vcls	A
(up to	BRIAN DOWNEY	drms	ABCD
1976)	PHIL LYNOTT	bs, vcls	ABCD
	GARY MOORE	gtr, vcls	B
	JOHN CANN	gtr, vcls	C
	ANDY GEE	gtr, vcls	C
	SCOTT GORMAM	gtr, vcls	D
	BRIAN ROBERTSON	gtr, vcls	D

HCP

ALBUMS:	1(A)	THIN LIZZY	(Decca SKL 5082) 1971 R1 -
(up to	2(A)	SHADES OF A BLUE ORPHANAGE	
1976)			(Decca TXS 108) 1972 SC -
	3(A)	VAGABONDS OF THE WESTERN WORLD	
		(Some w/inserts)	(Decca SKL 5170) 1973 SC -
	4(D)	NIGHT LIFE	(Vertigo 6360 116) 1974 -
	5(D)	FIGHTING	(Vertigo 6360 121) 1975 60
	6(D)	JAILBREAK	(Vertigo 9102 008) 1976 10
	7(A)	REMEMBERING - PART ONE (Compilation)	
			(Decca SKL 5249) 1976 SC -
	8(D)	JOHNNY THE FOX	(Vertigo 9102 012) 1976 11

NB: (1) reissued on CD (Deram 820 528-2) in 1989, along with the four tracks from the *New Day EP*. (2) reissued on CD (Decca 820 527-2) 1988. (2) counterfeited on vinyl 2001 and reissued on CD (Deram 8205272). (3) reissued on CD (Deram 820 969-2) in 1991. (4) reissued on CD (Vertigo 8380 292) 1989. (4) - (6) and (8) reissued in 1983. (6) reissued on CD (Vertigo 8227 852) 1989 and again on CD (Mercury 532 294-2). (8) reissued on CD (Vertigo 8226 872) 1990.

Compilations have included:- *Dedication - The Very Best Of Thin Lizzy* (LP/CD) (Vertigo 848 192-1) 1991; *Collection: Thin Lizzy* (Castle Collector CCSCD 117) 1987; *The Best Of Phil Lynott And Thin Lizzy* (Telstar TCD 2300) 1987; *The Peel Sessions* (Strange Fruit SFRCD 130) 1994, which largely consists of their better known material; and *Wild One: The Very Best Of Thin Lizzy* (Vertigo 528 113-2) 1995, which compiles most of their finest moments and a couple of previously unreleased tracks too - *Cold Sweat* and *Thunder And Lightning*. *Whiskey In The Jar 70-73* (Spectrum 552082) 1998 is a 16-track CD compilation of their early years. *Greatest Hits* (Universal 9821112) 2004 is a good 2-CD collection of their hits.

EP:	1(A)	NEW DAY (Dublin, Remembering, Old Moon, Madness,	
		Things Ain't Working Out Down On The Farm)	
			(Decca F 13208) 1971 R3

HCP

45s:	α	The Farmer/I Need You	(Parlophone DIP 513) 1970 R6 -
(up to	χ	Whiskey In The Jar/	
1976)		Black Boys On The Corner	(Decca F 13355) 1972 6
		Randolph's Tango/Broken Dreams	(Decca F 13402) 1973 SC -
		The Rocker/Here I Go Again	(Decca F 13467) 1973 -
		Little Darlin'/Buffalo Gal	(Decca F 13507) 1974 -
		Philomena/Sha La La	(Vertigo 6059 111) 1974 -
		Rosalie/Half Castle	(Vertigo 6059 124) 1975 -
		Wild One/For Those Who Love To Die	(Vertigo 6059 129) 1975 -

	The Boys Are Back In Town/Emerald	(Vertigo 6059 139) 1976 8
	Jailbreak/Running Back (PS)	(Vertigo 6059 150) 1976 SC 31
	Don't Believe A Word/Old Flame	(Vertigo LIZZY 1) 1976 -
Reissues:	Whiskey In The Jar/The Rocker	(Old Gold OG 9330) 1983 -
	The Boys Are Back In Town/	
	(Flip by Bachman Turner Overdrive)	(Old Gold OG 9764) 1988 -
β	The Boys Are Back In Town/Sarah	(Verigo LIZZY 15) 1991 63

NB: α Only released in Ireland and the band's name was mis-spelt as Thin Lizzie. χ Some demos issued in a picture sleeve (SC). β issued as a 7" and cassette single. There were also 12" singles, 12" picture discs and a CD single version with the above two tracks on the 'A' side and *Johnny The Fox, Black Boys On The Corner* and *Me And The Boys* on the flip.

Thin Lizzy was a popular hard-rock/heavy-metal act whose music was characterised by a ferocious twin lead guitar assault and lyrics that related working class sentiments. Their founder and singer/songwriter/bassist Phil Lynott was the band's creative force and something of an anomaly as a black man in the mostly white world of hard-rock.

Thin Lizzy first formed as a trio (line-up A) in Spring 1970. Lynott had first played with Brian Downey in The Black Eagles over in Dublin. He was also briefly with **Skid Row**, where he played alongside **Gary Moore**, before being reunited with Brian Downey in Orphanage, who took Tim Rose's *Morning Dew* into the Irish Charts.

In 1970, the recently formed band released an Irish-only 45 for Parlophone, *The Farmer*, which had a catchy chorus, is now a mega-rarity, valued by 'Record Collector' at £1,000! It's thought that just 500 copies were pressed and that only 203 were sold - the rest were melted down and recycled. Only five copies are known to have survived the seventies - hence the high price tag.

Late in 1970 they were signed by Decca and moved to London to play club gigs, although initially they certainly didn't pull in the crowds. They made their debut at The Speakeasy. Their first album, *Thin Lizzy*, lacked consistency. The excitement of many of their live performances at the time relied heavily on Eric Bell's celtic guitar. Many of Lynott's lyrics were rather obscure too and the story was no different on their second album, *Tales From A Blue Orphanage*.

In 1971 **Thin Lizzy** released the 4-track *New Day* (EP), which is now a legendary collectable. It was cut at Decca's Tollington Park studios over a two-day period in June 1971, shortly after they had moved to London from Ireland. Because their first album sold poorly Decca was reluctant to finance a picture sleeve and so their co-manager Ted Carroll financed it himself. No more than 2,000 were printed and they didn't all get out. The wonderful illustrations in pencil and watercolour were the work of a booking agent friend of the band. Tracks like *Dublin* and *Remembering Part 2* express quite a lot of nostalgia.

Late in 1972 they released their first 45 (having already released two albums, though this was not unusual for progressive bands), a rock version of a folk tune, *Whiskey In The Jar*, which had some very distinctive riffs.

SHADES OF A BLUE ORPHANAGE (LP).

THIRD EAR BAND - Alchemy (LP)

The retail version was five minutes long, but DJs were sent a special three-minute version. It was this 45 which gave them their big breakthrough, climbing to No 6 in the Charts. In the short-term, though, they didn't really capitalise on this. Their next 45, *Randolph's Tango*, missed out and their next album, *Vagabonds Of The Western World*, (which was in a heavier rock vein and omitted *Whiskey In The Jar*, which the band wanted to disassociate themselves with) made little commercial impact. However, it gave a clear indication of their future musical direction with strong heavy rock numbers like the title cut, *The Rocker*, *Little Darling* and *Gonna Creep Up On You*. When Deram reissued the album on CD in 1991, *Whiskey In The Jar* was added.

Disillusioned by their lack of progress, Eric Bell quit the band to return to Ireland in January 1974. **Gary Moore**, who'd earlier played with Lynott in **Skid Row**, was recruited as his replacement but by April the same year he'd moved on to Jon Hiseman's **Colosseum**. Just three tracks were recorded during this period:- the single *Little Darling; Still In Love With You*, which appeared on the *Nightlife* album and *Sitamoia*, which wasn't released until 1978. When **Moore** departed guitarist Andy Gee (formerly with **Steve Ellis**' band) and John (du) Cann (ex-Bullit, **Attack** and **Andromeda**), were brought in to play on a tour of West Germany, which the band were contractually committed to, in May 1974. The band then expanded to a four-piece with the addition of Glaswegian Brian Robertson and Scott Gorham, a Californian. These line-up changes coincided with a new record deal with Phonogram's progressive Vertigo label. The band worked very hard touring the UK extensively in 1975. They built up a burgeoning live reputation, headlining at London's Roundhouse in June 1975 and appearing at an open-air festival at Cardiff Castle the following month with **10cc**.

Their fourth album, *Nightlife*, made little impression but the fifth, *Fighting*, crept into the Album Charts, peaking at No 60. However it was on *Jailbreak* that they perfected their twin lead guitar assault with Lynott's songwriting talents. The album spawned two major hit singles:- *Jailbreak* itself and *The Boys Are Back In Town*, which peaked at No 8, and cracked the American market, climbing to No 12 there. A major UK tour capitalising on this success culminated in three nights at the Hammersmith Odeon.

So as we leave the time span of this book, **Thin Lizzy** were at the pinnacle of their career, and their success continued largely unabated until they split in August 1983. Lynott died on 4 January 1986 from heart failure and pneumonia. He'd collapsed at his home over Christmas 1985 and fallen into a coma following an overdose. The remaining members reunited to play a tribute gig for Lynott in Dublin on 17 May with Bob Geldof on vocals. To many people, Phil Lynott was **Thin Lizzy** so the band or any prospect of its successful reformation died with him.

Despite this there was a reformation in 1999 comprising Scott Gorman and John Sykes (gtrs), Darren Wharton (keyb'ds), Marco Mendoza (bs) and Tommy Aldridge (drms). They toured Europe and released a live album *One Night* in Summer 2000 which they promoted with a US tour. They were a pale imitation of the original band, though.

Universal's 2-CD *Greatest Hits* release is the best hits collection of the band to date. Aside from all their hits, it includes some solo Phil Lynott tracks, and a pair of unreleased live tracks. *Whisky In The Jar* is an excellent guide to their early folk-rock driven career. It includes their highly-touted 'B' side *Black Boys On The Corner*, the seven-minute mellotron-led title track from their second album, the full six-minute version of *Whiskey In The Jar* and 13 more tracks. (VJ)

Third Ear Band

Personnel:

RICHARD COFF	viola, violin	ABC
MEL DAVIS	cello	AB
PAUL MINNS	oboe	A
GLENN SWEENEY	perc	ABCD
DAVE TOMLIN	violin	AB
URSULA SMITH	cello	BC
DENIM BRIDGES	gtr	C
PAUL BUCKMASTER	cello, bs	C
SIMON HOUSE	violin, synth	C
NEIL BLACK	violin	D
MICK CARTER	gtr	D
LYN DOBSON	vcls, flute, synth	D

NB: There were numerous line-ups in between C and D. Ron Kort was a member around the time of their (unreleased) 4th album and Rod Goodway was in a 1977 line-up.

THIRD EAR BAND - Elements (LP).

HCP
ALBUMS: 1(A) ALCHEMY   (Harvest SHVL 756) 1969 R1 -
         2(B) ELEMENTS (AIR, EARTH, FIRE & WATER)
                                        (Harvest SHSP 773) 1970 SC 49
         3(C) MUSIC FROM MACBETH (Harvest SHSP 4019) 1972 SC -
         4(-) EXPERIENCES (Compilation)
                                (Harvest Heritage SHSM 2007) 1976 -

NB: (1) reissued on GI-Records in 1982, again on (Drop Out/Demon DO 1999) 1988 and on CD (Drop Out DOCD 1999) 1991. (2) reissued (Beat Goes On BGOLP 89) 1991, also on CD (BGOCD 89). (1) and (2) reissued on a two CD set (Gott Discs GOTTCD 010) 2004. (3) reissued (Beat Goes On BGOLP 61) 1990, also on CD. *The Magnus* (Angel Air SJPCD 173) 2004 brings to us their lost fourth album, which is also available on vinyl (Akarma AK 312).

Later releases include (D) *Live Ghosts* (Materiali Sonori MASO 33047 / MASO CD 90004) 1990, (D) *Magic Music* (Materiali Sonori MASO 33053 / MASO CD 90016) 1990, (D) (Materiali Sonori MASO CD 90045) 1995, *Radio Session* (Voiceprint VPR 017 CD) 1995, and *Magic Music Pt. 2* (Blueprint BP 257CD) 1997.

This hippie-rock band from Canterbury started out as a psychedelic act, The Giant Sun Trolley in 1967. Regulars at the UFO Club, they also used the name The Hydrogen Jukebox and East Of Eden before becoming **The Third Ear Band**. Musically, they had an oriental, druggy influence, and much of the material was improvised and hypnotic.

Of all the late sixties bands one might have predicted would survive for more than 25 years, the **Third Ear Band** would not have been amongst them. An an early signing to EMI's progressive Harvest label, the first album, *Alchemy* showcased the band's sound: entirely instrumental, acoustic and largely improvisational with strong oriental and experimental jazz influences.

The second album was in similar vein, although there were just four lengthy pieces, each named after an element. The opening track *Air* is full of light touches. *Earth* is a pipe-led piece. *Fire* is a predictably more manic before calm is restored with *Water*. This is a challenging and worthwhile effort.

The Third Ear Band had a rather unstable line-up and half of the 1970 band quit. Glen recruited other musicians to take their place, including Simon House, formerly of **High Tide** and later of **Hawkwind**. The film director, Roman Polanski, commissioned them to write the music for his version of 'Macbeth' and the band released the soundtrack as their third album. *Music From Macbeth* was the best of their early work, incorporating electric instruments for the first time along with medieval and folk elements.

Although very much an underground outfit, **The Third Ear Band** were quite successful and all of their early albums sold quite well. However, *Macbeth* was to be the band's final release for seventeen years. In 1972 Richard Coff and Ursula Smith quit the band on the eve of a major concert in Hyde Park and would later form the band Cosmic Overdose, leaving a fourth **Third Ear Band** album *Weird O'Clock* unfinished.

Glen soldiered on for another five years with various line-ups, including a 1977 line-up with Rod Goodway (ex-**J.P. Sunshine**/Magic Muscle), but the

THIRD EAR BAND - Music From Macbeth (LP).

band were increasingly an anachronism and little interest was shown in them. In 1976, Harvest released a compilation *Experiences* on their bargain priced Heritage label.

Nothing was heard of the band until a 1989 reunion with a completely new line-up. Lyn Dobson was a fairly well known player on the modern jazz scene and had been a member of **Soft Machine** amongst others. Part of the subsequent tour was recorded and released in Italy as the *Live Ghosts* album. All subsequent recordings were Italian releases. From what I've heard of the new line-up, they retain certain elements of the old band's sound, the druggy, improvisational, largely acoustic feel, but there is a much darker avant-garde undercurrent.

Denim (aka Denny) Bridges became an engineer/producer working for George Martin at Air Studios. In 1990 he moved to the USA where he's been producing about four albums a year, including *Live Under Brazilian Skies* by Annie Haslam of **Renaissance** fame. Paul Minns sadly died in 1997, but shortly before had recorded three new tracks with Ron Kort. Glenn who was ill at the time had to miss the sessions, which remain unmixed. The same year a reformed line-up released a new album *Magic Music (Part 2)*.

The Magnus brings to us their lost fourth album *Weird O'Clock*. Like its predecessors this was serious head music, but veered more towards **Moody Blues** spoken word territory on tracks like *The Phoenix*. There are some long experimental electronic passages and the overall feel is pretty trippy. It's offered at budget price and with thoughts from former band members. This is an essential artefact for fans of the band.

Compilation appearances include: *Water* on *Picnic* (2-LP) and *Stone Circle* on *Harvest Heritage - 20 Greats* (LP). (CW/VJ)

Third World War

Personnel:	TONY ASHTON	keyb'ds	A
	JIM AVERY	bs	AB
	BOBBY KEYS	sax	A
	MICK LIEBER	gtr	A
	PETER MARTIN	gtr	A
	JIM PRICE	horns	AB
	FRED SMITH	drms	A
	TERRY STAMP	gtr, vcls	AB
	CRAIG COLLINGE	drms	B
	JOHN HAWKEN	piano	B
	JOHN KNIGHTSBRIDGE	gtr	B

ALBUMS: 1(A) THIRD WORLD WAR (w/insert) (Fly HIFLY 4) 1971 R1
2(B) THIRD WORLD WAR II (Track 2406 108) 1972 R2

NB: (1) reissued on CD (Repertoire REP 4560-WP) 1995. (2) reissued on CD (Repertoire REP 4566-WP) 1995. (1) and (2) reissued on one CD as *Armageddon* (Eclipse ECCD 3) and again (Mason MR 56400).

45s: Ascension Day/Teddy Teeth Goes Sailing (PS) (Fly BUG 7) 1971
A Little Bit Of Urban Rock/
Working Class Man (Fly BUG 11) 1971

Though this political underground band played alongside **Arthur Brown**, **the Pink Fairies**, **Egg**, **Roy Harper** and **Gnidrolog** at the 'Oz Police Ball' obscenity trial benefit, they had a very different outlook. They were singing about the rebels, the poor and uneducated, the working class, the unskilled labourers and yobbos. They could write sensitive melodies, but in general their music and lyrics were ugly, brutish and short.

Their first album is essentially raw punk, with standouts including *M.I.5's Alive*, *Shepherd's Bush Cowboy* and *Preaching Violence*. It also contains two acoustic tracks, *Teddy Teeth Goes Sailing* (a nibbling satire on Prime Minister Edward Heath) and *Get Out Of Bed You Dirty Red*, while *Stardom Road Part 2* predates the eighties 'psychobilly' bands.

Their second album is better musically, though the ingredients are similar. There's good heavy rock with fine guitar leads (*I'd Rather Cut Cane For Castro* and *Hammersmith Guerrilla*), blues (*Coshing Old Lady Blues* deals with the Hell's Angel lifestyle, though not in any romantic way), and mellow balladry (*Factory Canteen Blues*, with its sensitive guitar licks, is a small masterpiece).

Third World War were too confrontational to have had any realistic prospect of commercial success, but their bludgeoning brand of political rock can now be seen as way ahead of its time and holds an exceptional place in early seventies music.

Terry Stamp, who had been involved with **Harsh Reality** prior to **Third World War**, went on to record a solo album, *Fatsticks*, for A&M (AMLH68329, 1975). (CA/RMJ/VJ)

Thirty-Second Turn-Off

ALBUM: 1 THIRTY-SECOND TURN-OFF (Jay Boy JSL 1) 1969 R1

This was Eddy Grant's attempt to come up with a **Hendrix**-style rock album. (VJ)

This Driftin's Gotta Stop

ALBUM: 1 THIS DRIFTIN'S GOTTA STOP
(Private Pressing) 197? SC

This rare privately pressed album is religious in tone and apparently not very good. (VJ)

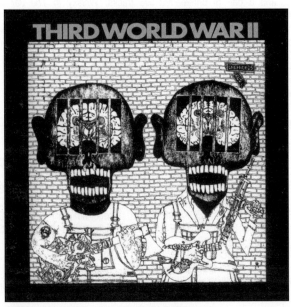

THIRD WORLD WAR - Third World War II (CD).

THIRD WORLD WAR - Armageddon (2-CD).

This 'n' That (1)

Personnel incl: CLEO
                 DERRY WILKIE

45:      Get Down With It/I Care About You   (Strike JH 310) 1967

This 14-person soulish outfit was based in London. Cleo also made solo recordings. They were managed by ex-boxer Freddie Mac and Peter Lloyd. (VJ)

This 'n' That (2)

Personnel: BILLY JOE ANDREWS
            BUZZ HALL

45:      Someday/Loving You   (Mercury MF 938) 1966 SC

This was a different London-based act. (VJ)

Jimmy Thomas

45s: α Beautiful Night/Above A Whisper (Parlophone R 5573) 1969 R3
         We Ain't Here Looking For No Trouble/
         Springtime   (Spark SRL 1035) 1971
         White Dove/
         You Don't Have To Say Goodbye   (Spark SRL 1040) 1971
         Where There's A Will/
         Just Trying To Please You   (Jay Boy JSL 67) 1972

NB: α Withdrawn. Demos are more common (R2).

Jimmy Thomas was a bluesy black soul singer. The first 45 was withdrawn and is consequently very rare. It's now worth a lot because it's a top Northern soul rarity. (VJ)

Ray Thomas

                                                        HCP
ALBUMS: 1 FROM MIGHTY OAKS   (Threshold THS 16) 1975 23
(up to   2 HOPES, WISHES AND DREAMS
1976)   (Threshold THS 17) 1976 -
NB: (1) reissued on CD (Threshold 820 782-2) in 1989. (2) reissued on CD (Threshold 820 783-2) 1989.

45s: High Above My Head/Love Is The Key (Threshold TH 20) 1975
(up to   One Night Stand/Carousel   (Threshold TH 24) 1976
1976)

Thomas, who was born on 29 December 1942 at Stourton-on-Severn, is best known as a member of **The Moody Blues**. He is one of a handful of well-known flute players in rock music. He was in several local groups in his teenage years, including Saint and Sinners and The Ramblers and for a while he was in El Riot and The Rebels (who also included **John Lodge**). In 1962, he was in The Krew Cats, with **Mike Pinder** and they had a spell in Hamburg. They split up in 1963 after returning to Birmingham and he and **Pinder** formed **The Moody Blues**, who were an R&B quintet in their early days. It was when the group advanced beyond its R&B roots that **Thomas** took up the flute. When their original bassist Clint Warwick departed, his old El Riot band mate **John Lodge** came in as a replacement. **Thomas'** flute was prominent on one of the group's defining moments *Nights In White Satin* and his harmony vocals were all over their records.

These solo efforts were recorded for the band's own label during a quiet period for the group from 1973-1978. The title track to *From Mighty Oaks* was orchestrated, there were also quite a few ballads on the album and some tracks like *High Above My Head* had commercial appeal. With often grandiose production the two albums feature **Thomas'** singing but not his playing.

Mike Pinder left **The Moody Blues** soon after they reformed in 1978 and **Thomas** became more prominent than before as a songwriter. He contributed three songs to 1981's *Long Distance Voyager* (*Painted Smile*, *Reflective Smile* and *Veteran Cosmic Rocker*) which completed the album and the live act to promote it. Subsequent to that, though his songwriting influence within the group gradually declined.

In recent years he has been plagued by ill health and was replaced by flutist Norda Mullen for **The Moody Blues** 2003 Winter tour and left the group soon after. (VJ)

Richard Thompson

ALBUMS: 1 HENRY THE HUMAN FLY   (Island ILPS 9197) 1972
(up to   2 GUITAR, VOCAL (2-LP Compilation)   (Island ICD 8) 1976
1976)
NB: (1) reissued on CD (Hannibal HNCD 4405) 1989. (2) reissued on CD (Hannibal HNCD 4413) 1989.

Richard Thompson is widely-regarded as the finest folk-rock guitarist of his generation, as well as one of the better singer-songwriters Britain has produced.

He was born on 3 April 1949 in London and, having dallied with becoming a glass-stainer, became a founding member of **Fairport Convention** aged just 17. His unusual songs and dazzling leads account for much of the appeal of the band's early output. Whilst with **Fairport** he also played a phenomenal number of sessions for artists including **John Cale**, **Sandy Denny**, **Nick Drake**, **Marc Ellington**, **Gary Farr**, **Mike Heron**, **John Martyn** and **Mick Softley**. He also played on *The Bunch* and *Morris On* albums.

In January 1971 he left the band to go solo, and the following summer he went on the road with his wife Linda (see below) as a duo to promote his highly-eccentric solo debut, which featured guest artists including **Sandy Denny**, Pat Donaldson, **Barry Dransfield**, **Ashley Hutchings** and **John Kirkpatrick**. It contained classic **Thompson** songs like *Roll Over Vaughan Williams* and *The Great Racehorse*, and is now a cult item.

Between October and December 1972 the pair (who had become Sufi Muslims) briefly joined the **Albion Country Band** but largely focused on their own recordings. Later, between November 1973 and March 1974, they played with Simon Nicol as a trio called Hokey Pokey.

The *Guitar, Vocal* album is a collection of unreleased and rare material from 1967-1976. It has long been deleted and was tricky to find prior to its reissue.

Thompson is still releasing idiosyncratic and critically-lauded albums to his devoted cult audience. (RMJ/VJ)

851

Richard and Linda Thompson

Personnel:	RICHARD THOMPSON	gtr, vcls	A
	LINDA THOMPSON	vcls	A

ALBUMS: 1(A)   I WANT TO SEE THE BRIGHT LIGHTS
(up to   (Island ILPS 9266) 1974
1976)   2(A)   HOKEY POKEY   (Island ILPS 9305) 1974
       3(A)   POUR DOWN LIKE SILVER   (Island ILPS 9348) 1975
       4(A)   OFFICIAL LIVE TOUR, 1975   (Island no #) 1975 R2
       5(A)   GUITAR/VOCAL (2-LP)   (Island ICD 8) 1976

NB: (4) Unreleased. There may have been some pressings. (1) reissued on CD (Island CID 9266) 1988 and again on CD (Island IMCD 304) remastered and expanded with a detailed booklet. (2) reissued on CD (Hannibal HNCD 4408) 1989 and again on CD (Island IMCD 305) remastered with a booklet. (3) reissued on CD (Hannibal HNCD 4404) 1988 and again on CD (Island IMCD 306) remastered and expanded with a new booklet. Also relevant is *End Of The Rainbow* (CD) (Island IMCD 270) which is compiled from their four studio albums (the fourth was *Henry The Human Fly* - a **Richard Thompson** solo album) for Island in the seventies. *The Best Of Richard And Linda Thompson* (CD) (Island) 2000 contains the pick of their recordings for Island.

45s: I Want To See The Bright Lights Tonight/
(up to   When I Get To The Border   (Island WIP 6186) 1974
1976)   Hokey Pokey/
         I'll Regret It All In The Morning   (Island WIP 6220) 1975

See above for details of **Richard Thompson**. **Linda Thompson** was born Linda Peters and had recorded two unsuccessful singles as a duo with folkie **Paul McNeill** as well as working as a prolific session vocalist.

The duo's first album, *I Want To See The Bright Lights*, included many of **Richard Thompson**'s best-known compositions with, aside from the title cut, *Calvary Cross* and *End Of The Rainbow* among its highlights. The duo then toured with Simon Nicol, resulting in the *Hokey Pokey* album, which was full of social comment as well as humour. *Pour Down Like Silver* was a more sombre affair, much influenced by their Muslim faith, and the duo didn't record again until 1978.

The Thompsons were often supported live by Danny Thompson, Dave Mattacks, Dave Pegg and **John Kirkpatrick**. They continued to record together into the new decade, but split in 1982 when their marriage ended. **Richard Thompson** pursued a much-acclaimed solo career, but until very recently Linda had recorded only one solo album, 1985's *One Clear Moment*. (RMJ/VJ)

Thor

Acetate: 1 Lindsay Davis/You're My Cream
                        (Brindwinnen Ent. Acetate) 196?

A Berkshire-based pop-psych outfit who recorded one acetate.

Compilation appearances include: *Lindsay Davis* on *Revenge Of The Amphetamine Generation* (LP); and *You're My Cream* on *Syde Trips, Vol. 3* (LP). (VJ)

Peter Thorogood

45:     Haunted/If No-One Sang   (Pye 7N 17577) 1968 R1

Peter Thorogood was a classically-trained violinist and played all the instruments on this single, which was written by the enormously successful Howard/Blaikley team. *Haunted* is an enchanting slice of psychedelic tainted pop with some good fiddle leads, but the flip is much less appealing, although it later emerged as the title track on an album by **Dave Dee, Dozy, Beaky, Mick and Tich** (who were probably one of the main vehicles for the Howard/Blaikley songwriting duo). He now works as a music teacher in Herefordshire and is involved in various local theatre productions.

Haunted later became the title track to *Haunted - Psychedelic Pstones, Vol 2* (CD). (VJ)

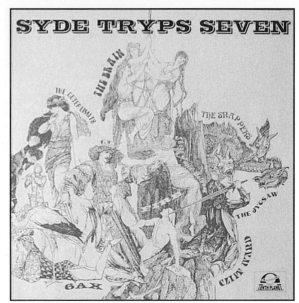

SYDE TRYPS VOL. 7 (Comp LP) featuring Those Fading Colours.

Those Fading Colours

Personnel incl:	GEOFF COPPINS	vcls	AB
	RON COCHRANE	gtr, vcls	B
	JOHN GILFOY	drms	B
	GRAHAM WRIGHT	bs	B

45:     (Just Like) Romeo And Juliet/
       Billy Christian   (Ember EMB S 229) 1966

This 45 was the work of **The Kingpins** (who recorded the acetates for Oak) recording under a pseudonym. They were recruited by Ember to record an album of cover versions (the sort of things Woolworth's Embassy label did), but the project was never completed although this 45 wrongly credited to **These Fading Colours** did emerge.

Early in 1966, before the 45 was released, Geoffrey Coppins and Glyn Stephens left and **The Kingpins** continued as a three-piece.

After Geoff Coppens departure, his Managers approached another band The Deckhands to see if they would, in an attempt to promote the 45, add Geoff to their line up, and rename themselves as **Those Fading Colours**.

The Deckhands agreed, and this line-up stayed together for nearly two years, playing mostly in London and South England. The new line-up also recorded two songs for Decca, *Blow Up* and *Try Me On For Size*, produced by **Mike Vernon**. Neither was released at the time.

(Just Like) Romeo And Juliet had been a US hit for The Reflections and was also recorded by US band Michael and The Messengers.

Compilation appearances have included: *Blow Up* and *Try Me On For Size* on *Return Of The Amphetamine Generation* (LP) and *Syde Trips Vol. 7* (LP). (VJ)

The Thoughts

Personnel:	PETE BECKETT	vcls, gtr	A
	PHIL BOARDMAN	ld gtr	A
	DAVE CROFT	drms	A
	ALAN HORNBY	bs	A

45:     All Night Stand/Memory Of Your Love (Planet PLF 118) 1966 R2

This band began life backing Liverpool acts like **Tiffany** (recording as **Tiffany and The Thoughts**), **Paul Dean** and **Johnny and John**, but in 1966 they moved down to London, where they recorded on their own as **The Thoughts**.

Their 45 which was produced by Shel Talmy, is now very rare and expensive. The 'A' side of their sole 45, *All Night Stand*, was a Ray Davies composition, which had never been recorded by **The Kinks**. The flip,

Memory Of Your Love, which was an original penned by Beckett and Boardman, is quite a catchy number. Both tracks are full of punch.

Pete Beckett was later in **Paladin**.

Compilation appearances have included: *If You Don't Come Back* and *Until You Love Someone* on *Untamed And Innocent* (CD); *All Night Stand* and *Memory Of Your Love* on *The Best Of Planet Records* (CD); *Memory Of Your Love* on *English Freakbeat, Vol. 3* (LP & CD); and *All Night Stand* on *Electric Sugarcube Flashbacks, Vol. 2* (LP), *Electric Sugarcube Flashbacks, Vol. 3* (LP), *Boulders, Vol. 9* and on the 4-CD *Nuggets II* box set. (VJ)

Thoughts and Words

| Personnel: | MARTIN CURTIS | A |
| | BOB PONTON | A |

ALBUM: 1(A) THOUGHTS AND WORDS   (Liberty LBL 83224) 1969 SC

45:      Morning Sky/Give Me A Reason   (Liberty LBF 15187) 1969

Curtis and Ponton had been the founders and mainstays of **Pandamonium** but, tired of record company interference, resolved in 1969 to proceed as a stripped-down duo. Duly signed to Liberty, their sole album was arranged and produced by **Mike Batt**. A dainty collection of earnest folk-pop, it has recently been reissued by Radioactive. Both 45 sides were from the album. Another album cut, *Charlie Gates*, is on *Pop-In, Vol 2* (CD) and *Morning Sky* has been compiled on *Fading Yellow, Vol 4* (CD). (VJ)

Eiri Thrasher

45s:	Roger/I Just Want O Say Thank You	(York SYK 511) 1972
	Old Rugged Cows/Yes Indeed	(UK UK 23) 1972
α	Help Me Make It Through The Night/	
	Colloquial Sex	(UK UK 75) 1974

NB: α With **Jonathan King**.

Eiri Thrasher was the lead singer of **Triban**. Both her solo 45s were **Jonathan King** productions (the second on his own label). Then two years later she recorded a 45 with him. (VJ)

Threads of Life

ALBUM: 1   THREADS OF LIFE   (Alco ALC 530) 1972 R5

A mega-rarity. The Hampshire band's name was actually **Alco** and the title of the album was *Threads Of Life*. It came in a beautifully-designed sleeve and its overall musical quality was high, aside from the final track. The first side included an orchestra directed by the band's music tutor. The second side is largely comprised of dreamy self-penned songs. An alternate version of one of the cuts, *Linda*, appeared on the flip side of an acetate-only version of **The Foundations**' hit *Baby Now That I've Found You*. The band also recorded an as yet unreleased second album. (VJ)

Three City Four

Personnel:	MARTIN CARTHY	A
	MARIAN McKENZIE	A
	LEON ROSSELSON	A
	RALPH TRAINER	A

ALBUMS:	1(A)	THE THREE CITY FOUR	(Decca LK 4705) 1965 R3
	2(A)	SMOKE AND DUST WHERE THE HEART	
		SHOULD HAVE BEEN	(CBS 63039) 1967 R2

A now-legendary folk outfit whose members were already accomplished solo performers prior to their formation. Their debut album is highly-rated and now very sought-after. It was a combination of Rosselson's own compositions and covers of folk protest songs by the likes of Dylan, Peter Seeger, Cyril Tawney and Sydney Carter. The second album is heading that way too.

A legend of British folk, **Martin Carthy** has recorded several solo albums to this day. (VJ)

Three Good Reasons

Personnel:	ANNETTE CLEGG	AB
	PETE CLEGG	AB
	RADIVOJ DANIC	A
	NOEL FINN	B

			HCP
45s:	Build Your Love/		
	Don't Leave Me Now (PS)	(Mercury MF 883) 1965	-
	Nowhere Man/Wire Wheels	(Mercury MF 899) 1965	47
	The Moment Of Truth/		
	Funny Kind Of Loving	(Mercury MF 929) 1965	-

This mid-sixties band from Bradford enjoyed a minor hit with their cover of **The Beatles**' *Nowhere Man*. Noel Finn replaced Radivoj Danic in 1966. *The Moment Of Truth* was penned by Marty Wilde and Mike Hawker. Their material was mostly folksy beat. (VJ)

Three Man Army

Personnel:	ADRIAN GURVITZ	gtr	ABC
	PAUL GURVITZ	gtr, vcls	ABC
	MIKE KELLIE	drms	A
	TONY NEWMAN	drms	B
	GINGER BAKER	drms	C

ALBUMS:	1(A)	A THIRD OF A LIFETIME	(Pegasus PEG 3) 1971 R1
	2(B)	THRE MAN ARMY	(Reprise K 44254) 1973 R1
	3(B)	THREE MAN ARMY 2	(Reprise K 54015) 1974 SC

NB: (1) reissued on CD (Repertoire REP 4071-QZ) 1991. (2) reissued on CD (Repertoire REP 4057-WZ) 1991. (3) reissued on CD retitled as *Mahesta* (Progressive Line PL 593). This is digitally remastered. *Soldiers Of Rock Anthology* (2-CD) (Castle CMDDD 941) brings together the above three albums and the package comes with a booklet.

45s:	What's Your Name/Travellin'	(Pegasus PGS 1) 1972
	Polecat Woman/	
	Take Me Down From The Mountain	(Reprise K 14292) 1974

This was a progressive rock band. The Gurvitz brothers had earlier played in **Gun** and **Baker-Gurvitz Army** and Adrian Gurvitz also made solo recordings. Drummer Mike Kelly had been in **Balls**. Their debut album *A Third of A Lifetime* was later issued in the States in 1974 with different tracks. The trio were assisted on the album by Buddy Miles (drms) and Brian Parrish (gtr) in a session capacity. Buddy Miles was an American artist, who made several recordings with his own band. The following year a 45 *What's Your Name* was recorded by Adrian and Paul Gurvitz with Carmine Appice on drums. Then Paul Gurvitz and Mike Kellie toured with **Parrish and Gurvitz** during May - June 1972.

After this the band reformed with the Gurvitz brothers but ex-Allan Clarke Band member **Tony Newman** on drums instead of Mike Kellie. **Tony Newman** also made solo recordings. When **Newman** joined **David Bowie** he was replaced on drums by **Ginger Baker** in September 1974. *Three Man Army 2* is a heavy rock album with a bluesy edge. The later line-ups also used backing vocalists Ruby James and Doris Troy. Doris Troy was born in New York City as Doris Payne on 6 January 1937. A R&B vocalist and songwriter she made several solo albums and singles. She also sang backing vocals on **Pink Floyd**'s *Dark Side Of The Moon*.

From late 1974 the band was known as **Baker-Gurvitz Army**. (VJ/JM)

The Three People

Personnel:	JOHN BROMLEY	A
	BRENDAN CLEMINSON	A
	PAULA COOPER	A

| 45s: | Have You Ever Been There/Good Times | (Decca F 12473) 1966 |
| | Suspicions/Easy Man To Find | (Decca F 12514) 1966 |

Got To Find A Reason/
Simple Thing Would Be For You To Start
Loving Me   (Decca F 12581) 1967

This group comprised three students from Manchester. Their material was folky. **John Bromley** went on to release solo recordings and also wrote *Come On Down* for Jackie deShannon and *This World's An Apple* for **The Ace Kefford Stand**. (VJ/JM)

The Three Quarters

45s: People Will Talk/
          Love Come A-Tricklin' Down   (Columbia DB 7467) 1965 SC
          The Pleasure Girls/Little People (Columbia DB 7576) 1965

This was a little known mid-sixties soul/beat trio. *Little People* later resurfaced on See For Miles' *60's Back Beat* compilation. They backed Roy Orbison on his 1965 tour. (VJ)

Three Valley Folk

ALBUM: 1   THREE VALLEY FOLK   (Westwood WRS 003) 1971 R2

This was a gentle three piece folk album with male / female harmonies. Two of the best tracks, *Ladies Go Dancing* and *When I Came To This Land* feature lead female vocals. There's also one acapella number *Kwa Heri*. It's one of the earliest releases on this short-lived label. (VJ)

Three's A Crowd

Personnel:	JIMMY BAIN	bs	A
	ALAN ?	drms	A
	BOB 'SMIGGY' SMITH	lead gtr, vcls	AB
	TOM BEVERIDGE	bs	B
	HARRY MacINTOSH	lead gtr	B
	IAIN McLEOD	drms	B

45:       Look Around The Corner/
          Living In A Dream   (Fontana TF 673) 1966 SC

This trio operated out of Edinburgh. Smith was previously with The Embers and later with **Blue**. Iain McLeod was later in the Clash. Jimmy Bain is still going strong. (VJ)

The Three Sounds

Personnel:	JOHN RICHARDSON	A
	ROGER SUTTON	A
	TONY THORPE	A

45:       Makin' Bread Again/Still I'm Sad   (Liberty LBF 15062) 1968

This 45 sank without trace but Richardson had been in **The Medium** and was later part of the songwriting duo, Baskin and Copperfield, with Alan Williams. In 1973, Richardson, Thorpe and Williams all joined **The Rubettes**. Roger Sutton had previously played with **Brian Auger**. (VJ)

Threshold of Pleasure

45:       Rain, Rain, Rain/
          He Could Never Love You Like I Do   (Decca F 12785) 1968

Well, someone had to record a 45 with a title like *Rain, Rain, Rain*, it's so much a part of British life. It's actually a good pop 45, well produced incorporating celeste and brass, and with a powerful lead vocal. The identity of the group remains unknown (some have speculated that the single could be the work of session musicians) but you'll also find it on *Circus Days Vol's 4 & 5* (CD) and *Circus Days, Vol. 5* (LP). (VJ)

THUNDERCLAP NEWMAN - Hollywood Dream (LP).

Percy 'Thrills' Thrillington

ALBUM: 1   THRILLINGTON   (Regal Zonophone EMC 3175) 1977 R3
NB: Also issued on cassette (Regal Zonophone TC-EMC 3175) 1977 R1.

45:       Uncle Albert-Admiral Halsey/
          Eat At Home   (Regal Zonophone EMI 2594) 1977 R2

Thrillington, who is credited as the producer of this album, is a non-existent personality as **Thrillington** was a pseudonym used by **Paul McCartney** for this instrumental version of his and Linda McCartney's 1971 album *Ram*. Although the sessions were recorded in June 1971, the project was not released until 1977. This was due to Paul and Linda's decision to form **Wings** in the summer of 1971. Although **McCartney** produced the album he did not appear on it and Richard Hewson was the arranger for the tracks. (VJ)

Thunder

Personnel incl: J.MYERS ?   A

45:       α   Money Honey/
              Get On The Telephone Martha   (Kingdom 45 K 4104) 1972
NB: α French release with PS.

Produced by Mike Stewart for Roc Productions, this was a little known group in the style of **Mungo Jerry** or **King Earl Boogie Band**. The 'A' side is the Jesse Stone R&B classic, the flip was written by J. Myers. (SR)

The Thunderbirds

45:       Your Ma Said You Cried In Your Sleep/
          Before It's Too Late   (Polydor BM 56710) 1966 R2

This was **Chris Farlowe**'s backing band. See **Chris Farlowe and The Thunderbirds**. (VJ)

Thunderclap Newman

Personnel:	JOHN 'SPEEDY' KEEN	gtr, vcls, drms	ABCD
	JIMMY McCULLOCH	gtr	ABC
	ANDY 'THUNDERCLAP' NEWMAN	keyb'ds	ABCD
	JIM AVERY	bs	B
	JACK McCULLOCH	drms	B
	ROGER FELICE	drms	C
	RONNIE PEEL	bs	C
	CHRIS HUNT	drms	D

ALBUM: 1(A) HOLLYWOOD DREAM (Track 2406 003) 1970 SC

NB: (1) reissued on CD Repertoire (REP 4065-WP) in 1991 and on Polydor (833 794 2) 1991. Later reissued on CD (Touchwood TWCD 2013) 1997 in the States with six bonus tracks: - the 45 version of *Something In The Air*, a shortened version of *Accidents* and *The Reason*, along with their 45 'B' sides.

			HCP
45s:	Something In The Air/Wilhelmina	(Track 604 301) 1969	1
	Accidents/I See It All	(Track 2094 001) 1970	46
	Wild Country/Hollywood	(Track 2094 002) 1970	-
	The Reason/Stormy Petrel	(Track 2094 003) 1970	-
Reissues:	Something In The Air/		
	Other tracks by other artists (PS)	(Track 2094 011) 1973	-
	Something In The Air/		
	Fire (**Arthur Brown**)	(Track 2094 017) 1975	-
	Wild Country/Hollywood (PS)	(Track 2095 002) 1979	-
	Something In The Air/Accidents	(Old Gold OG 9435) 1984	-

The Who's **Pete Townshend** put together this group as a studio outfit in the late sixties. Guitarist Jimmy McCulloch was just a sixteen at the time, '**Speedy**' **Keen** was an untried songwriter from the Ealing/Perivale area of London who'd previously been in pre-**July** act **The Tomcats** in 1965, as drummer and **Andy 'Thunderclap' Newman** was a plump ex-Post Officer engineer. The last thing they represented was a slick rock group, but their debut 45, *Something In The Air*, written by **Keen**, remains an all-time classic, a wonderfully atmospheric song which superbly captured the changing mood of the late sixties and simply boiled over with optimism. **Keen** played drums and **Townshend** bass on the 'A' side. It also made No 37 in the USA. The song was also used on the Soundtrack to the movie 'The Magic Christian' featuring Peter Sellers and **Ringo Starr**. When it rapidly climbed to No 1, Avery and McCulloch's younger brother Jack were rapidly added to the line-up for touring purposes, but after one minor hit with *Accidents*, further commercial success eluded them and they broke up in mid-1970, with Avery and McCulloch joining **Wild Country**.

Their *Hollywood Dream* album has become a minor collector's item, but is largely disappointing in comparison to the magic of *Something In The Air*. It has a few decent moments:- *Hollywood #1* has some good honky tonk piano playing; *The Reason* is certainly one of '**Speedy**' **Keen**'s stronger compositions and features a good vocal performance by him and more good piano from **Andy Newman**; Jimmy McCulloch's instrumental title track is a pleasant little ditty and *Wild Country* is worth a listen.

A new touring band was formed in early 1971 (line-up C). Felice and Peel had both previously been with Rockwell T. James and The Rhythm Aces, an Australian outfit. When McCulloch departed to **John Mayall's Bluesbreakers**, Felice and Peel returned to Australia. Jimmy McCulloch went on to join **Stone The Crows** and **Wings**. Chris Hunt (ex-**Paradise Hammer**) came in on drums to work with **Keen** and **Newman**.

Accidents was also included on Polydor's *Pop Party* (LP) sampler in 1970 and their classic *Something In The Air* resurfaced on *Backtrack 2* (LP) and more recently on the 2-CD set *45s - 45 Classic No 1's* and on the 2-CD set *60 Number Ones Of The Sixties*.

After the band split, **Newman** and **Keen** both made solo albums but with little success. Hunt went on to **BB Blunder**.

John 'Speedy' Keen died on 29 March 2002. Thunderclap returned in 2005 with a new album *Pick N Tell* with a special appearance by **Zoot Money**. The CD includes a fine re-make of *Something In The Air*. (VJ/JM)

Thunder Company

Personnel incl: BRIAN BENNETT

45:	Ridin' On The Gravy Train/	
	Bubble Drum	(Columbia DB 8706) 1970 R1

NB: There was also a demo issue of this 45 put out the same year with an edited version of the 'A' side (R1).

Brian Bennett also made several solo recordings, although he is best remembered as the drummer in **The Shadows**. (VJ)

Thunderthighs

Personnel:	KAREN DARI	vcls	A
	DARI LALLOU	vcls	A
	CASEY SYNGE	vcls	A

			HCP
45s:	Central Park Arrest/		
	Sally Wants A Red Dress	(Philips 6006 386) 1974	30
	Dracula's Daughter/Lady In Question	(Philips 6006 413) 1974	-
	Stand Up And Cheer/I'm Free	(EMI EMI 2276) 1975	-

Early seventies backing singers for the likes of Lou Reed, **Mott The Hoople** and **Mick Ronson**, who went on to form their own group under the supervision of producer Steve Rowland of **Family Dogg** fame. Their first single was penned by Lyndsey de Paul, but the venture proved short-lived. (BS/VJ)

The Thyrds

Personnel:	PAUL ELLIS	lead gtr	A
	MICK HUGHES	gtr	A
	JOHN MALCOLM	bs	A
	MIKE TEASDALE	drms	A

45s:	Hide And Seek/		
	I've Got My Mojo Working	(Oak RGJ 133) 1964	R3
	Hide And Seek/		
	No Time Like The Present	(Decca F 12010) 1964	R1

An R&B band who recorded the self-penned *Hide And Seek* for the Mordon, Surrey-based Oak label before they were signed to Decca, having made encouraging progress in a 'Ready Steady Go!' beat group competition. The Oak 45, which can also be heard on *Story Of Oak Records* (2-LP)/*The Story Of Oak Records* (CD), is rawer than the Decca version. It was backed by a rousing version of Willie Dixon's *I've Got My Mojo Working*. Both sides are well worth a listen. *Hide And Seek* is Bo Diddley-influenced and played at a rapid tempo. The See For Miles *Ready Steady Win* (LP & CD) includes another version of *Hide And Seek*, taken from the TV series *Ready Steady Go*, and originally broadcast as part of a unknown best group competition.

Other compilation appearances include: *Hide 'n' Seek* and *No Time Like The Present* on *Rare 60's Beat Treasures, Vol. 2* (CD); and *Hide 'n' Seek* on *Weekend Starts Here* (LP). (VJ/JM)

Tickawinda

Personnel incl: CLIVE GREGSON

ALBUM: 1 ROSEMARY LANE (Pennine PSS 153) 1975 R4

NB: (1) reissued on CD (Kissing Spell KSCD916).

A rare, privately-pressed folk album of interest since it featured Gregson who later played with Stiff band Any Trouble prior to working both solo and with **The Richard Thompson Band**. Characterised by two female vocalists, it includes an excellent cover version of the **Bert Jansch**-composed title track. (VJ)

The Tickle

Personnel incl: MICK WAYNE gtr

45:	Subway (Smokey Pokey World)/	
	Good Evening	(Regal Zonophone RZ 3004) 1967 R4

Mick Wayne had previously been in the Outsiders, The Hullaballoos and The Bunch of Fives, who became **The Tickle** at the start of the flower-power era. Their 45 is ultra-rare and very sought-after. It was culled from a five-track demo-session, though sadly the other three haven't materialised. The 'A' side features fine distorted vocals, guitars and effects,

THE BEST OF RUBBLE COLLECTION VOL. 6 (Comp CD) featuring The Tickle.

and the flip is arguably even better, with its compressed guitar and clumping piano. Both were co-written by Mick Wayne. It really is a double-sided gem, and one of the finer moments of British psychedelia.

The five-piece band later became **Junior's Eyes**. When they folded, Wayne played with **The Pink Fairies**, briefly appearing on their 1972 single, *Well Well Well*.

Compilation appearances have included: *Good Evening* on *Psychedelia, Vol. 2* (LP), *The Best Of Rubble Collection, Vol. 6* (CD) and *Hen's Teeth Vol. 1* (CD); and *Subway (Smokey Pokey World)* on *Beat It* (3-CD), *Chocolate Soup* (CD), *Chocolate Soup For Diabetics, Vol. 2* (LP) and on the 4-CD box set *Acid Drops, Spacedust & Flying Saucers*. (VJ/RMJ)

Tidal Wave

45s: With Tears In My Eyes/We Wanna Know (Decca F 22973) 1969
       Spider Spider/Crazy Horse   (Storm PD 9616) 1969 R1

This obscure South African band had at least one 45 issued in the UK. It's not clear whether Storm was an English or South African label, but their 45 on it comprised two excellent songs composed by Terry Dempsey (who also wrote *Butchers and Bakers*, as recorded by **Chocolate Frog** and **The Staccatoes**). *Spider Spider* is the stronger of the two. The band also released a rare progressive album back home. Compilation appearances include: *Spider Spider* on *Syde Tryps, Vol. 1* (LP & CD); and *Crazy Horse* on *Syde Trips, Vol. 3* (LP). (VJ/RMJ)

Peter Tierney and The Nighthawks

Personnel:	LENNIE BOYLE	drms	A
	DAVE EVANS	gtr	A
	MICK GILMORE	piano, bs	A
	EDDIE MADDOX	ld gtr	A
	PETER TIERNEY	vcls	A

45:   Oh How I Need You/That's Too Bad   (Fontana TF 547) 1965

This beat ballad outfit came from Birmingham. In October 1965 they changed their name to P.T. and The Fugitives, though we're not sure if this is the same act as **Tierney's Fugitives**. (VJ/DS)

Tierney's Fugitives

45:   Did You Want To Run Away?/
     Morning Mist   (Decca F 12247) 1965 SC

Another little-known beat 45. The band may have evolved out of **Peter Tierney and The Nighthawks**. **Peter Lee Stirling** was musical director on the 45 and also co-wrote both sides. The songs are pleasant but unexceptional.

Compilation appearances include: *Did You Want To Run Away* on *The Beat Scene* (CD). (VJ/DS)

Tiffany (and The Thoughts)

45s: I Know/Am I Dreaming   (Parlophone R 5311) 1965
   α Find Out What's Happening/
     Baby Don't Look Down   (Parlophone R 5439) 1966 R1
NB: α as **Tiffany with The Thoughts**.

Tiffany was an obscure Liverpool artist whose backing band was **The Thoughts**. This band later recorded in their own right and then included **Paul Dean**. (VJ)

Tiger

Personnel:	PHIL CURTIS	bs	A
	RAY FLACKE	gtr	A
	DAVE McCRAE	keyb'ds	A
	NICKY MOORE	vcls, hrmnca, gtr	AB
	BILLY RANKIN	drms	A
	BIG JIM SULLIVAN	gtr	AB
	LES WALKER	gtr	AB
	ANDY BROWN	bs, keyb'ds, vcls	B
	BILL McGILLIVRAY	vcls, gtr, keyb'ds	B
	ALAN PARK	keyb'ds	B

ALBUMS: 1(A) TIGER   (Retreat RTL 6006) 1976
       2(B) GOIN' DOWN LAUGHING   (EMI EMC 3153) 1976
NB: (1) also issued in the US (Warner Bros BS 2940) 1976. (1) reissued on CD by Line. (2) also issued in the US (EMI 11660) 1976.

45:   I Am An Animal/
     Stop That Machine   (United Artists UP 35848) 1976?

This short-lived rock band formed in February 1976 and was formerly The Big Jim Sullivan Band. Phil Curtis was ex-**Kiki Dee**; Dave McCrae ex-**Nucleus** and **Matching Mole**; Nicky Moore ex-**Hackensack**; Billy Rankin ex-**Ducks Deluxe** and **Brinsley Schwartz**; Les Walker ex-**Michigan Flyer**; and of course Big Jim Sullivan was one of the countries top session guitarists, who'd previously been the man behind **Lord Sitar** amongst others and played on the **Green Bullfrog** album.

The first album was produced by Derek Lawrence and Big Jim Sullivan. The heavy rock album often veers in a progressive direction and has a strong blues and country-rock flavour (particularly with Nicky Moore's vocal styling and writing contribution). The most progressive track *Tyger Tyger* takes its lyrics from the famous William Blake poem. After the first album, Flacke departed to Meal Ticket; McCrae went back to session work; Curtis rejoined **Kiki Dee**; and Rankin joined Terraplane. They were replaced by Bill McGillivray, Andy Brown and Alan Park (ex-Almanac and **Beggars Opera**), for a second effort but obscurity beckoned.

Nicky Moore later achieved some success in Samson, whilst Andy Brown and Alan Park went on to Bliss Band. Sullivan went on to produce the first two albums for US heavy metal band Angel.

In 1983, a further album surfaced, *Test Of Times* (Street Tunes). (JM/CG)

Steve Tilston

ALBUMS: 1 AN ACOUSTIC CONFUSION
(up to   (Village Thing VTS 5) 1971 SC
1977)   2 COLLECTION   (Transatlantic TRA 252) 1972
        3 SONGS FOR THE DRESS REHEARSAL
                 (Cornucopia CR 1) 1977 SC
NB: (3) recorded with **Rupert Hine** and **John Renbourn**. (1) reissued on CD (Scenescof SCOFCD 1002). (3) reissued on CD (Market Square MSMCD 132) 2005

with five bonus tracks from 1979. *Greening Wind* (CD) (Market Square HRCD 002) collects his instrumentals from 1971-1992. *Live Hemisphere* (CD) (Market Square HRCD 003) captures some of his live performances recorded in the UK and Australia.

Steve Tilston was an unknown singer-songwriter who sought out Village Thing on the advice of **Ralph McTell**. Impressed by a performance the singer gave at Bristol's Troubadour club, the label signed him and his debut album is a collection of simple but beautiful folk songs. On tracks like *Sleepy Time On Peel Street* and *Time Has Shown Me Your Face* the simple combination of **Tilston**'s vocals and guitar work well and sound mid-way between **Donovan** and **Nick Drake**. A few cuts, particularly *Green Toothed Gardener*, are reminiscent of **The Incredible String Band**. The album was well-received and he signed to Transatlantic for a follow-up. This featured orchestras, brass bands and rock musicians - a radical departure from his first effort. It didn't work and was savaged by the critics.

Tilston recorded a privately-pressed album, *Songs From The Dress Rehearsal* in 1977, with assistance from **Rupert Hine** and **John Renbourn**. The 11-track album showcases his airy acoustic guitar and vocals. He's assisted by ex-**King Crimson's** Mike Giles and **Quantum Jump's** John G. Perry. His subsequent efforts are beyond the remit of this book.

Greening Wind compiles his instrumentals from 1971-1992 and includes his favourites like *The Naked Highway, These Days* and *Tseste Fly Shuffle* as well as the title track. (VJ)

Time (1)

45s: Take A Bit Of Notice/
Every Now And Then   (Pye 7N 17019) 1966 R1
The First Time I Saw The Sunshine/
Annabel   (Pye 7N 17146) 1966 SC

Both 45s, particularly the first, are now quite collectable. The four-piece band came from Southampton. (VJ)

Time (2)

Personnel:	'JODE' LEIGH	drms, vcls	A
	ALEC JOHNSON	gtr, vcls	A
	GARY MARGETTS	gtr, vcls, keyb'ds	A
	TRISS MARGETTS	bs, vcls	A

ALBUM: 1(A) TIME   (Buk BULP 2005) 1975 R2

A short-lived, little-known band. Their album was produced by Conny Plank. It's reminiscent of early seventies **Yes** but with more emphasis on guitars than keyboards. Gary and Triss (Tristian) Margetts had both earlier been in **Spontaneous Combustion**.

Alec Johnson was later involved in Nightwing in the early eighties. (VJ/EK)

Timebox

Personnel:	CLIVE GRIFFITHS	bs	A
	PETE 'OLLIE' HALSALL	vcls, gtr, organ	A
	JOHN HALSEY	drms	A
	CHRIS HOLMES	piano	A
	MIKE PATTO	vcls	A

ALBUM: 1(A) ORIGINAL MOOSE ON THE LOOSE   (DCL 9016) 1976

NB: (1) US-only. There's also a CD compilation, *Timebox - The Deram Anthology* (Deram 844 807-2) 1998.

HCP

45s: I'll Always Love You/
Save Your Love   (Piccadilly 7N 35369) 1966 R1 -
Soul Sauce/I Could Jerk
Like My Uncle Cyril   (Piccadilly 7N 35379) 1966 R1 -
Walking Through The Streets Of My Mind/
Don't Make Promises   (Deram DM 153) 1967 SC -
Beggin'/A Woman That's Waiting   (Deram DM 194) 1968 SC 38

Girl Don't Make Me Wait/
Gone Is The Sad Man   (Deram DM 219) 1968 SC -
Baked Jam Roll In Your Eye/
Poor Little Heartbreaker   (Deram DM 246) 1969 SC -
Yellow Van/You've Got The Chance (Deram DM 271) 1969 SC -

Timebox was formed in Southport in 1966, named after US slang for a prison cell, and soon became one of the most popular acts on the British club scene.

After a couple of singles for Pye they moved to Deram, for whom they cut a number of increasingly eccentric singles. *Walking Through The Streets Of My Mind* is a good pop-soul number and well worth a spin. By far their best known song is their simply stunning cover of The Four Seasons' *Beggin'*, which has a great dance beat. It was confidently expected to shoot to the top of the charts, but it wasn't to be. Other gems include the more psychedelic *Gone Is The Sad Man*, with its gorgeous melody and backwards tapes, and *Baked Jam Roll In Your Eye*, a strange tale of alien invasion.

They were, however, increasingly unhappy with their musical direction, and in 1969 Chris Holmes left, prompting the others to change their name to **Patto**.

The best way to investigate their music is the *Deram Anthology* CD. There was also an earlier vinyl retrospective, *The Original Moose On The Loose* (Peter's Int'l 9016) 1976 and (Cosmos CCLPS 9016) 1977).

Mike Patto sadly died of throat cancer in 1979 and **Ollie Halsall** died in 1992 following a heart attack. Clive Griffiths was partially paralysed in a near fatal car crash. However, John Halsey escaped from the same crash without serious injuries and went on to become drummer with The Rutles.

The CD *Timebox - The Deram Anthology* features all their A and B sides for Deram along with 14 previously unissued tracks. These include the psychedelically-tainted *Barnabus Swain* and *Eddie McHenry*.

Compilation appearances have included:- *Girl Don't Let Me Wait* on *Pop Inside The 60s Vol. 1* (CD) and *The Mod Scene* (CD); *Beggin'* on *Mod Scene, Vol. 2* (CD) and *Hard-Up Heroes* (2-LP); *Soul Sauce* on *Maximum '65* (CD) and *Doin' The Mod, Vol. 2* (CD); *Gone Is The Sad Man* on *Psychedalia - Rare Blooms From The English Summer Of Love* (CD), *Illusions From The Crackling Void* (LP), *The Psychedelic Scene* (CD), *Rubble, Vol. 12 - Staircase To Nowhere* (LP), *Rubble, Vol. 7* (CD), the 4-CD *Nuggets II* box set and on the 4-CD box set *Acid Drops, Spacedust & Flying Saucers*; *I'll Always Love You* on *Piccadilly Story* (CD); *Baked Jam Roll In Your Eye* on *The British Psychedelic Trip 1966 - 1969* (LP); *Poor Little Heartache* on *Broken Dreams, Vol. 3* (LP) and *The Freakbeat Scene* (CD); *Walking Through The Streets Of My Mind* on *British Psychedelic Trip, Vol. 4* (LP) and *Great British Psychedelic Trip, Vol. 2* (CD); *A Woman That's Waiting* on *Broken Dreams, Vol. 5* (LP); *I Wish I Could Jerk Like My Uncle Cyril* on *Doin' The Mod, Vol. 1* (CD) and *Instro-Hipsters A Go-Go* (CD); and *I'll Always Love You* and *Save Your Love* on *Footsteps To Fame, Vol. 2* (CD). (VJ/VZ/RMJ)

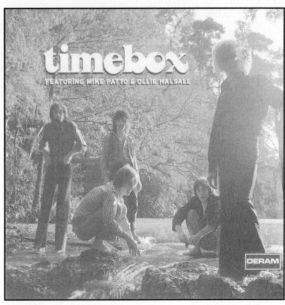

TIMEBOX - The Deram Anthology (CD).

The Times (1)

Personnel incl: TOMMY HUSKEY   sax
                 DAVID MARTIN   organ

EP: 1   Ooh Wee/Shepherd Blues/Suzie/
           Running And Hiding   (EMI/Columbia 7ES 24) 1965 R2
NB: (1) Demo only.

45s: Think About The Times/
       Tomorrow Night   (Columbia DB 7804) 1966 SC
       (She Can't Replace) The Love We Knew/
       Reconciled   (Columbia DB 7904) 1966 SC

This seven-piece from Manchester played in Germany a lot. All these
recordings are now quite collectable. Huskey had earlier been with **Earl
Preston and The Realms**.

(She Can't Replace) The Love We Knew has been compiled on *Red With
Purple Flashes, Vol. 1* (LP). (VJ)

The Times (2)

45s: Looking Thru' The Eyes/
       Flyin' High Feelin' Low   (Parlophone R 5855) 1970
       When I Look Around Me/
       Smile A Tender Smile   (Parlophone R 5956) 1972

This was a different early seventies act. (VJ)

Timon

45s: The Bitter Thoughts Of Little Jane/
       Ramblin' Boy   (Pye 7N 17451) 1968 R2
       And Now She Says She's Young/
       I'm Just A Travelling Man   (Threshold TH 3) 1970

These 45s were recorded by Tymon Dogg, a folk singer from Liverpool,
who had a brief solo career in the early eighties, when he also helped out
The Clash on vocals on their *Sandinista* and *Combat Rock* albums. *The
Bitter Thoughts Of Little Jane* is rather twee toytown popsike.

Compilation appearances include: *The Bitter Thoughts of Little Jane* on
Paisley Pop - Pye Psych (& Other Colours) 1966-1969 (CD), *Ripples, Vol.
1* (CD) and on the 4-CD *Nuggets II* box set. (VJ)

John Timpany and Audrey Smith

ALBUM: 1   COME ALL YOU TENDER HEARTED CHRISTIANS
                                    (Westwood) 1973 R3

This is a **Tickawinda** style folk offering with alternate male/female vocals
and a wide diversity of instrumentation. The title is misleading - the album
has no religious slant at all. (VJ)

Tinkerbell's Fairydust

Personnel: STUART ATTRIDE   A
              DAVE CHURCH   A
              BARRY CREASEY   A
              STEVE MAHER   A
              CHAZ WADE   A
              GED WADE   A

ALBUM: 1(A)   TINKERBELL'S FAIRYDUST
                                    (Decca LK/SKL 5028) 1969 R6
NB: (1) Unreleased but test pressings do exist (R5), from which a "reissue" has been
made on vinyl and CD (Carnaby Boutique X-0443276CD) 1998.

TINKERBELLS FAIRYDUST - Tinkerbells Fairydust (LP).

45s: Lazy Day/In My Magic Garden   (Decca F 12705) 1967 SC
       Twenty Ten/Walking My Baby   (Decca F 12778) 1968 SC
       Sheila's Back In Town/
       Follow Me Follow   (Decca F 12865) 1969 R1

Originally known as **The Rush**, producer Vic Smith renamed this popsike
band **Tinkerbell's Fairydust** for their *Lazy Day* 45. *Lazy Day* was a
Spanky and Our Gang song and its flip is a well-structured slice of
psychedelic pop. *Twenty Ten* is a amalgam of sunshine pop and
commercial psychedelic pop, and reached No. 2 in Japan in 1968.

All three 45s are rare and collectable.

The band recorded at regular Sunday sessions at Decca's Studio Two in
West Hampstead, with Smith at the helm. An album was recorded but not
released at the time. Test pressings of this are mega-rarities, as are the
absolute handful of stock copies in finished sleeves that have surfaced. It
included four of their six singles tracks and nine cover versions. Two of the
better covers were an attempt at **Joe Cocker**'s minor hit *Marjorine* and a
Vanilla Fudge-style arrangement of *You Keep Me Hanging On*. In 1998 the
album was finally released on vinyl and CD by 'Carnaby Boutique'.

The band also backed **Gene Latter** at a session at Lansdowne Studios,
Holland Park, resulting in his *Mother's Little Helper* 45.

Steve Maher later emigrated to Sydney, Australia, where he runs his own
recording studio. Chaz and Gerry Wade are in a band playing around
London, and Barry Creasy still drums in a band, but Dave Church and
Stuart Attride retired from the music scene.

Compilation appearances have included: *20-10* on *Rubble, Vol. 6 - The
Clouds Have Groovy Faces* (LP) and *Rubble, Vol. 4* (CD); *Majorine* and
You Keep Me Hanging On on *Syde Trips, Vol. 4* (LP); *In My Magic Garden*
on *British Psychedelic Trip, Vol. 3* (LP) and *Great British Psychedelic Trip,
Vol. 2* (CD); and *Lazy Day* on *British Psychedelic Trip, Vol. 4* (LP) and
Great British Psychedelic Trip, Vol. 2 (CD). (VJ/IS)

Tintern Abbey

Personnel: JOHN DALTON   drms   AB
              STUART MacKAY   bs   ABC
              DAVID MacTAVISH   vcls   ABC
              DON SMITH   ld gtr   A
              PAUL BRETT   ld gtr   B
              COLIN FORSTER   ld gtr   C
              JOHN 'WILLIE' WILSON drms   C

45:    Beeside/Vacuum Cleaner   (Deram DM 164) 1967 R6
NB: There's also a very limited edition 4-track picture sleeve EP featuring four
previously unreleased demos by the band: - *Do What You Want, How I Feel Today,
It's Just That The People Can't See* and *Naked Song*.

Tintern Abbey was a short-lived London-based psychedelic group who recorded arguably the finest one-off UK psychedelic 45 of all. It has now been hunted to extinction, and copies have been known to change hands for up to a thousand pounds.

The band was managed by Nigel Samuels, founder of underground newspaper IT. He installed them (and MacTavish's pet buzzard) in a mews in Sloane Square, where they rehearsed and played private gigs at all times of the night for him and his friends. Eventually a deal was signed with the recently-formed Deram records, and Jonathan Webber came in as producer. *Beeside* was a woozy slice of piano-led pop with mellotron parts, while *Vacuum Cleaner* is notable for propulsive drumming, electronic pulses and one of the finest fuzztone solos of the decade. Both sides were penned by MacTavish.

On 27 November 1967, three days after the single's release, the band was launched at London's Arts Lab Club in Drury Lane. Soon afterwards they returned to the studio (with **John Pantry** as engineer) to record a new song, *Snowman*, but the track was abandoned after the departure of guitarist Don Smith in January 1968. He was eventually replaced by **Paul Brett**, who'd been In **The Overlanders** and **Arthur Brown's** R&B band The South West Five.

The band then entered Tony Pike's studio in Putney to demo an upbeat MacTavish song called *How Do I Feel Today?*, which 'Record Mirror' announced as their new single in March 1968, suggesting it would be released the following month. Also recorded in the session was a spiky acid-pop number called *Do What You Must*, but neither song got beyond the studio. At this time Deram lost interest in the band, which therefore lost momentum.

Though the music weeklies also reported them to be working on an album, it's now known that one was not even started. In fact, Brett and Dalton both left soon after *How Do I Feel Today?* was aborted. Brett recently discovered a single acetate copy of the proposed second single, which has now been privately pressed alongside two other demos, *It's Just That The People Can't See* and *Naked Song*, on a limited edition EP.

Former **Elmer Gantry's Velvet Opera** guitarist Colin Forster and Cambridge-based drummer John 'Willie' Wilson then came in as replacements. The new line-up continued to write and demo new material for several months, finally quitting in early 1969. Wilson joined **Cochise** and **Quiver** before teaming up with his mate Dave Gilmour as an auxiliary **Pink Floyd** member. Forster and MacTavish resurrected **Velvet Opera** to record a 1970 single for Spark. MacTavish later played with **Big Bertha** and Smokestack Crumble. He also guested in a post-**Open Mind** combo called Armada. **Brett**, now a wealthy businessman, joined **Velvet Opera** and was then briefly in **Fire**, who (without Paul Lambert) evolved into **Paul Brett's Sage**.

Tantalisingly, prior to releasing *Beeside*, the band also recorded an acetate at R.G. Jones Oak records studio in Morden on 29th July 1967. This included a different 'B' side, *Black Jack*, which has yet to be resurface.

There's a four-track EP which compiles their earlier unreleased demos (see discography for details). On offer is sixties pop-rock with fuzz guitar and dreamy vocals.

Compilation appearances have included: *Vacuum Cleaner* on *Perfumed Garden, Vol. 1* (CD), *The Psychedelic Scene* (CD), the 4-CD *Nuggets II* box set and on the 4-CD box set *Acid Drops, Spacedust & Flying Saucers*. (VJ/AS/MB/DSh/RMJ)

Tin Tin

Personnel incl:
STEVE GROVES	vcls	A
STEVE KIPNER	vcls	A
??		A

ALBUMS:	1(A)	TIN TIN	(Polydor 2384 011) 1969 SC
	2(A)	ASTRAL TAXI	(Polydor 2382 080) 1971 SC

45s:
Only Ladies Play Croquet/	
He Wants To Be A Star	(Polydor 56332) 1969
Toast And Marmalade For Tea/	
Manhattan Woman	(Polydor 2058 023) 1970
Come On Over Again/Back To Winona	(Polydor 2058 076) 1970
Is That The Way/Swans On The Canal	(Polydor 2058 114) 1971
Talking Turkey/	
The Cavalry Are Coming	(Polydor 2058 283) 1972
I'm Afraid/Handle Me Easy	(Polydor 2058 366) 1973
It's A Long Way To Georgia/	
Can't Get Over You	(Decca F 13525) 1974

Tin-Tin was a vocal harmony duo/trio. Their debut album was produced by **Maurice Gibb**, the final member was either Billy Lawrie or Johnny Vallins. *She Said Ride* and *Toast And Marmalade For Tea* have both been compiled on *Spinning Wheel* (CD). (VJ)

Keith Tippett Group

Personnel:
MARC CHARIG	horns	AB
JEFF CLYNE	bs	A
ELTON DEAN	sax	AB
NICK EVANS	trombone	AB
GIORGIO GOMELSKY	bells	A
ALAN JACKSON	drms	A
KEITH TIPPETT	piano	ABCD
ROY BABBINGTON	bs	BC
GARY BOYLE	gtr	B
PHIL HOWARD	drms	B
ROBERT WYATT	drms	B
JULIE TIPPETT	gtr, vcls	C

ALBUMS:	1(A)	YOU ARE HERE, I AM THERE		
(up to			(Polydor 2384 004)	1970 R2
1976)	2(B)	DEDICATED TO YOU BUT		
		YOU WEREN'T LISTENING	(Vertigo 6360 024)	1971 R2
	3(C)	BLUE PRINT	(RCA SF 8290)	1972 R1
	4(-)	TNT	(Steam SJ 104)	1976 SC

NB: (2) reissued on CD (Repertoire REP 4449-WP) 1994 and again (Akarma AK 227) in both vinyl and CD format. (3) reissued on vinyl (Turning Point TPM 023220). (3) reissued on CD (BGO BGO BGOCD 485) 2004 and again on CD (BGO BGO BGOCD 634)2005.

Bristol-born **Keith Tippett** is best known as a modern jazz pianist. He appeared on albums by **Blossom Toes**, **King Crimson** and **Soft Machine** prior to his debut album for Polydor. Indeed his Vertigo album was named after a **Soft Machine** song. However, unless you're into avant-garde, avoid it! After this, **Keith**, who married **Julie Driscoll**, formed **Centipede**. His next solo album, *Blue Print*, was produced by Robert Fripp. In 1973 he was the man behind **Ovary Lodge**, whose album, also produced by Fripp, is quite collectable now. As the decade progressed he recorded further albums on obscure jazz labels and also created TV and film scores.

His group included such notable individuals as Marc Charig, who recorded a solo album in 1977, *Pipedream* (Ogan OG 710), which **Keith Tippett** played on, **Elton Dean**, **Robert Wyatt**, Giorgio Gomelski and his wife, who was **Julie Driscoll** before their marriage. He continues to perform regularly and collaborates with his wife. (VJ)

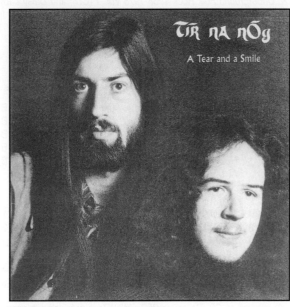

TIR NA NOG - A Tear And A Smile (CD).

Julie Tippetts

ALBUMS: 1 SUNSET GLOW   (Utopia UTS 601) 1975 SC
            2 ENCORE   (Warner Bros 3153) 1976

This was **Julie Driscoll**. Once she married **Keith Tippett**, the jazz and improvisational keyboard player, her music changed dramatically. She recorded one transitional album called *Sunset Glow*, which Alan 'Fluff' Freeman played a lot. This was progressive rock in which the personnel were nearly all the 'young turks' in the British free jazz scene - Mark Charig, **Elton Dean** etc. (VJ)

Tir Na Nog

Personnel: SCOTT CONDELL   gtr, vcls, perc   AB
               LEO O'KELLY   gtr, vcls, violin   AB
               BARRY DE SOUZA drms   B

ALBUMS: 1(A) TIR NA NOG   (Chrysalis ILPS 9153) 1971 SC
        2(B) A TEAR AND A SMILE (Chrysalis CHR 1006) 1972 SC
        3(B) STRONG IN THE SUN (Chrysalis SHR 1047) 1973

NB: (1) reissued on CD (BGO BGOCD 53) 1989. (2) reissued on CD (Edsel EDCD 334) in 1991. (3) reissued on CD (Edsel EDCD 336) 1992. (2) and (3) reissued on one CD (BGO BGO 653) 2005. *BBC Recordings 1972-73* (Hux HUX 021) features live recordings by the band.

45s: I'm Happy To Be/Let My Love Grow (Chrysalis WIP 6090) 1970
         Strong In The Sun/
         The Mountain And I   (Chrysalis CHS 2016) 1973

This Dublin band was at the forefront of the revival in Irish folk music in the early seventies. Although their music didn't really have that strong an Irish flavour, it was very much in the mould of gentle folky progressive rock that was so popular among underground audiences.

They signed to Chrysalis a day after being turned down by Island in 1970. Touring with **Jethro Tull**, **The Who** and **Emerson, Lake and Palmer** they built up a solid following across the country's colleges and clubs. Their first album set the tone for the rootsy folk-rock that was to characterise their three early seventies albums. On *A Tear And A Smile* the folk-rock on offer is typified by tracks like *When I Came Down* and *Come And See The Show*, whilst *Down Day* is notable for delicate string arrangements.

Their final album, produced by Matthew Fisher, is rockier and included a version of **Nick Drake**'s *Free Ride*, one of the very few covers of his songs to appear in his lifetime. Other tracks like *Teeside* and the Celtic-flavoured *The Wind Was High* are quieter, but *Love Lost* recalls the **Incredible String Band**. They can also be heard playing *Our Love Will Not Decay* on Island's 1971 *El Pea* (2-LP) compilation. They reformed in 1991 with a short-lived five man line-up.

Retrospective compilation appearances include: *Our Love* on *The History Of U.K. Underground Folk Rock 1968-1978 Vol. 1* (CD); and *Daisy Lady* on *The History Of U.K. Underground Folk Rock 1968-1978 Vol. 2* (CD). (VJ)

Titanic

Personnel: KENNY AAS   organ   A
               KJELL ASPERUD   drms   ABC
               JOHN LORCK   drms   AB
               JANNY LOSETH   gtr   ABC
               ROY ROBINSON   vcls   ABC
               HELGE GROSLIE   keyb'ds   B
               ANDREW RAILSTON drms   C
               JOHN WILLIAMS   gtr, bs, vcls   C

ALBUMS: 1(A) TITANIC   (CBS 64104) 1971 SC
(up to   2(B) SEA WOLF   (CBS 64791) 1972 SC
1976)   3(B) EAGLE ROCK   (CBS 65661) 1973
        4(C) BALLAD OF A ROCK 'N' ROLL LOSER
                      (CBS 80786) 1975 - Dutch

NB: Subsequent albums were *Return Of Drakkar* (Egg) 1978 in France and *Eye Of The Hurricane (Souplet)* in Holland. (1) reissued on CD (Repertoire REP 4151-WZ) 1991. (2) reissued on CD (Repertoire REP 4842-WZ) in a digipak with one bonus track. (3) reissued on CD (Repertoire REP 4881-WZ) in a digipak with four bonus tracks. (4) reissued on CD (Repertoire REP 4882-WZ) in a digipak with two bonus tracks.

                                      HCP

45s: Sultana/Sing Fool Sing   (CBS 5365) 1971 5
(up to   Santa Fe/Half Breed   (CBS 7278) 1971 -
1976)   Rain 2000/Blond   (CBS 8185) 1972 -
         Richmond Express/Heia Valenga (CBS 1670) 1973 -
         Macumba/Midnight Sadness   (CBS 2000) 1974 -

A part-Scandinavian (Norwegian) hard-rock outfit, who moved to Germany and had an English vocalist, which is why I've included them here. They are best remembered for their instrumental hit, *Sultana*, in 1971, though they proved to be 'one-hit-wonders' in this respect. This is included on their *Sea Wolf* album. (VJ)

Titus Groan

Personnel: STUART COWELL   keyb'ds, gtr, vcls   A
               JOHN LEE   bs   A
               TONY PRIESTLAND   sax, flute, oboe   A
               JIM TOOMEY   drms   A

ALBUM: 1(A) TITUS GROAN   (Dawn DNLS 3012) 1970 R2

NB: *Titus Groan Plus* (See For Miles SEE 260) 1989 is a reissue of their album plus three tracks from their single, also issued on CD (SEE CD 260) 1989. *Titus Groan Plus* (Breathless 52013) reissued again in a three-fold digipak.

45:      Open The Door Homer/
        Woman Of The World/Liverpool (PS) (Dawn DNX 2053) 1970 SC

Titus Groan took their name from the main character in Mervyn Peake's gothic fantasy cycle Gormenghast. Having played alongside **Comus**, **Trader Horne** and others in Dawn's 'penny concerts' promotional tour, they entered the studio with house producer Barry Murray early in 1970. Their early progressive style is laced with woodwind, which makes for interesting listening, but ultimately their moderate compositional skills make the wine too watery. Almost all the tracks on their album are over five minutes long, leaving room for elaborate instrumental passages which almost catch fire, but often fall short of generating the excitement they promise. By far the best cut is the versatile and passionate *Hall Of Bright Carvings* (whose title is also taken from Peake), though at 11'50, it's rather too long.

Jim Toomey had earlier been in **Jon**, wrote *What Did We Miss* for **Still Life** with Stuart Cowell and was later in The Tourists. He also did some session for for **Uriah Heep**'s **Ken Hensley** at the end of the seventies. (MK/GB/KJ/RMJ/VJ)

TIR NA NOG - Strong In The Sun (CD).

TITUS GROAN - Titus Groan (LP).

Toast

Personnel: SIMON BYRNE   A
              HENRY MARSH   A
              JOHN PERRY   A

45:     Flowers Never Bend With The Rainfall/
        Summer Of Miranda   (CBS 4768) 1970

A Somerset-based band who evolved out of an act called Utopia. When they started to write their own material and took on a girl singer in late 1970 they changed their name to **Gringo**. This 45, as **Toast** contains a fair version of the Paul Simon song - orchestrated inevitably.

Summer Of Miranda has been compiled on *Fading Yellow, Vol 5* (CD). (MWh)

Toby Jug (1)

ALBUM: 1   GREASY QUIFF   (Private Pressing) 1969 R4
NB: (1) reissued on CD (Kissing Spell LSCD 921) 2001.

An expensive ultra-rarity, largely comprised of jug band and electric blues material but also containing a **Hendrix** pastiche, *Elastic Landlady*, which is basically full of mayhem and noise. You can also check it out on *Psychedelic Salvage Co. Vol. 1* (LP & CD). The band, a three-piece, came from Cambridge and just 50 copies of this album were pressed. *Elastic Landlady* is only for fans of demented psychedelia. (VJ)

Toby Jug (2)

45:     Breakaway Man/Brotherhood   (Decca F 13173) 1971

Seemingly unconnected to the previous band, this was a little known and now long forgotten early seventies outfit. (VJ)

Toby Twirl

Personnel: DAVID HOLLAND   vcls   A
              JOHN REED   drms   A
              BARRY SEWELL   organ   A
              STUART SOMMERVILLE bs   A
              NICK THORBURN   ld gtr   A

45s: Harry Faversham/Back In Time   (Decca F 12728) 1968 SC
        Toffee Apple Sunday/
        Romeo And Juliet   (Decca F 12804) 1968 R2
        Movin' In/Utopia Daydream   (Decca F 12867) 1969 SC

A pop group originally known as **Shades Of Blue**, who came from Newcastle. They renamed themselves after a talking part in a popular children's comic. It's their second release, which usually attracts attention. *Toffee Apple Sunday* was an undistinguished pop song but the flip side, *Romeo And Juliet*, is stronger, veering toward psychedelic pop. The song was written by Tony Waddington and Wayne Bickerton - formerly of **The Pete Best Four**. After a third effort, *Movin' In*, failed to 'happen' they split up.

Compilation appearances include: *Movin' In* on *Mod Scene, Vol. 2* (CD), *British Psychedelic Trip, Vol. 4* (LP) and *Great British Psychedelic Trip, Vol. 2* (CD); *Romeo And Juliet* on *The Seventh Son* (LP) and *The British Psychedelic Trip, Vol. 1* (LP); *Toffee Apple Sunday* on *British Psychedelic Trip, Vol. 3* (LP); *Romeo And Juliet* and *Movin' In* on *Broken Dreams, Vol. 5* (LP) and *Harry Faversham* on *Pop-In, Vol 2* (CD); and *Back In Time* on *Colour Me Pop, Vol 1* (CD). (VJ)

Toe-Fat

Personnel: CLIFF BENNETT   vcls   ABC
              JOHN GLASSCOCK   bs   AB
              KEN HENSLEY   gtr, vcls   A
              LEE KERSLAKE   drms, vcls   A
              BRIAN GLASSCOCK   drms   B
              ALAN KENDALL   gtr   B
              MICK CLARK   gtr   C
              TONY FERNANDEZ   drms   C
              MICK HAWKSWORTH   bs   C
              LYNTON NAIFF   keyb'ds, vcls C

ALBUMS:1(A/B) TOE-FAT   (Parlophone PCS 7097) 1970 R2
       2(B)   TOE-FAT II   (Regal Zonophone SLRZ 1015) 1971 R2
NB: (1) and (2) reissued on one CD (BGO BGOCD 278) 199?.

45s: Working Nights/
        Bad Side Of The Moon   (Parlophone R 5829) 1970 SC
        Brand New Band/
        Can't Live Without You   (Chapter One CH 175) 1972 SC

Formed in June 1969 out of **The Cliff Bennett Band**, this outfit played progressive hard-rock. Vocalist **Cliff Bennett** came from Yiewsley, Middlesex and had previously achieved fame with **Cliff Bennett and The Rebel Rousers**. John Glasscock, Lee Kerslake and **Ken Hensley** had earlier been in **Gods** and **Hensley** had also previously played in **The Cliff Bennett Band**.

The band were signed by Tamla Motown subsidary Rare Earth in the US, but **Hensley** departed in November 1969 to join **Uriah Heep**. Lee Kerslake also left at the same time to join **The National Head Band**. They were replaced by Alan Kendall (ex-**Glass Menagerie**) and Brian Glassock (ex-**Gods**).

TOBY JUG - Greasy Quiff (CD).

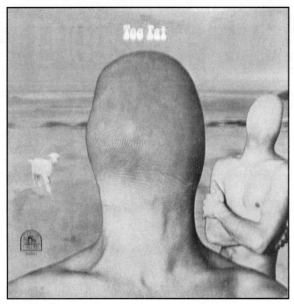
TOE-FAT - Toe-Fat (LP).

John Peel produced their two albums and the band toured the US a couple of times but it never quite happened for them. The band split, shortly before or shortly after the release of their second album, with members of **Killing Floor** backing **Cliff Bennett** for a short-lived third incarnation. His next port of call was Rebellion. Alan Kendall was later in **The Bee Gees'** backing band and John Glassock went on to **Chicken Shack** and was eventually in a **Jethro Tull** line-up. His brother, Brian joined Trouble and then a US act Motels.

Their albums now attract some interest from collectors. Two tracks on their debut, *You Tried To Take It All* and *I Can't Believe* were later versions of titles originally featured on the **Head Machine** album. (VJ/MD/JM)

Together

45:     Memories Of Melinda/Good Morning World   (Aurora 4278) 1969

A Scottish group was responsible for this whimsical poppy beat single. *Aurora* was a CBS subsidiary label.

Memories Of Melinda has resurfaced on *Circus Days, Vol. 6* (CD). (VJ)

Together

45:     Henry's Coming Home/
        Love Mum And Dad   (Columbia DB 8491) 1968 R2

Yardbirds' singer **Keith Relf** sang on this 45, which makes it valuable to some collectors. It was produced by another **Yardbirds'** member Paul Samwell-Smith and **Tony Meehan**. (VJ)

The Toggery Five

Personnel:	KEITH MEREDITH	gtr	A
	KEN MILLS	bs	ABCD
	FRANK RENSHAW	ld gtr	AB
	GRAHAM SMITH	drms	ABC
	PAUL YOUNG	vcls	ABCD
	ALAN DOYLE	gtr	B
	MICK ABRAHAMS	ld gtr	CD
	GRAHAM WALLER	keyb'ds	CD
	CLIVE BUNKER	drms	D

45s: Bye Bye Bird/I'm Gonna Jump   (Parlophone R 5175) 1964 R1
        I'd Much Rather Be With The Boys/
        It's So Easy   (Parlophone R 5249) 1965 R1

A Manchester-based R&B band. The 'A' side to the second 45 was a **Andrew Oldham**/Keith Richards number. Frank Renshaw later backed **Wayne Fontana** and joined **Herman's Hermits** in 1971. **Mick Abrahams**

and Clive Bunker went on to McGregor's Engine, and were later in **Jethro Tull**. Graham Smith joined Jet Black and Paul Young was later in Sad Cafe.

Mick Abrahams had previously played in **Neil Christian and The Crusaders**.

Compilation appearances have included: *Bye Bye Bird* on *Maximum R'n'B* (CD), *R&B At Abbey Road* (CD); *Bye Bye Bird* and *I'm Gonna Jump* on *Freddie And The Dreamers - I'm Telling You Now* (LP) and *Made In England, Vol. 2* (CD); *It's So Easy* on *R&B Scene, Vol. 1* (LP); *I'm Gonna Jump* on *Rare 60's Beat Treasures, Vol. 5* (CD); and *I'd Much Rather Be With The Boys* on *Rolling Stones Connection 1963-66* (CD), *60's Back Beat* (LP) and *Beat At Abbey Road* (CD). (VJ/AD/JM)

The Tomcats

Personnel:	TONY DUHIG	ld gtr, vcls	A
	JON FIELD	congas, perc, vcls	A
	ALAN JACKSON	bs	A
	CHRIS JACKSON	drms	A
	TOM NEWMAN	gtr, ld vcls	A

ALBUM: 1(A) THE TOMCATS   (Essex 1018 LP) 1997
NB: (1) came with a bonus EP.

Forming in London in the mid-sixties they were originally known as The Thoughts. In early 1965 they travelled to Madrid, Spain and got some gigs at the Consulate Club. The recordings they did out in Spain can be heard on the above restrospective album. They were taken from four EPs, which combine Spanish language songs like *Macarenas* and the fuzz-laden *A Tu Vera* with covers of hits of the day like **The Rolling Stones'** *Paint It Black*, *Get Off Of My My Cloud*, *Satisfaction* and *19th Nervous Breakdown*; **The Yardbirds'** *For Your Love* and **Spencer Davis Group**'s *Somebody Help Me*. It also includes an EP taped in 1964 by an earlier incarnation of the band, Second Thoughts.

The Tomcats later returned to Britain and changed name to **July**. (VJ)

Tomorrow

Personnel:	STEVE HOWE	gtr	A
	TWINK (JOHN ALDER)	drms	A
	KEITH WEST	vcls	A
	JOHN WOOD	bs	A
	(KEN LAWRENCE	drms	A)

ALBUM: 1(A) TOMORROW
        (mono/stereo)   (Parlophone PMC/PCS 7042) 1968 R3

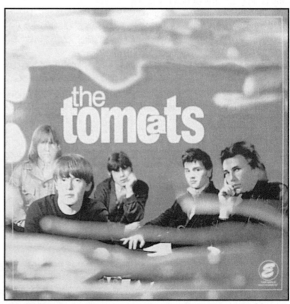
THE TOMCATS - The Tomcats (LP).

TOMORROW - Tomorrow (LP).

NB: (1) reissued as Harvest (SHSP 2010) 1976 in the UK, in 1978 on Visa (1002), in mono by Decal (LIK 2) 1987 and on CD in stereo (See For Miles SEE CD 314) 1991 and on CD again (EMI 7243.498819 2) 1999, with lots of bonus tracks including material by **Aquarian Age** and **Keith West**. There's also a CD, *50-Minute Technicolour Dream* (RPM RPM 184) 1998 and issued again in 2000, containing unreleased recordings, radio sessions and live material. *Christmas On Earth Continued* (Get Back GET 543) 2001 is a vinyl collection of live renditions of eight **Tomorrow** stage favourites from a 1967 show at the 'Freakout'. A sterling performance but the sound quality is poor.

45s:	My White Bicycle/Claremont Lake	(Parlophone R 5597) 1967 R1
	Revolution/	
	Three Jolly Little Dwarfs	(Parlophone R 5627) 1967 R1
Reissue:	My White Bicycle/Claremont Lake	(Parlophone R 5813) 1969 R1

Tomorrow was one of the leading psychedelic bands of the era. **West**, **Howe** and Wood had all earlier played with **The In Crowd**, a mid-sixties R&B group who released three singles, one of which, *That's How Strong My Love Is*, reached No 48 in May 1965. They changed their name to **Tomorrow** at the dawning of the psychedelic era in 1967. While playing with this band, **West** was working on the 'Teenage Opera' project with German producer **Mark Wirtz**. This was never actually completed, but two tracks from the projected album, *Excerpt From A Teenage Opera* and *Sam*, reached Nos 2 and 38 respectively in 1967.

Tomorrow appeared regularly at the UFO club in this era (indeed UFO owner Joe Boyd later described them as "the best group we had at the club"). They once shared the stage with **Jimi Hendrix** at the UFO club in 1967. They were invited to appear in two movies; Antonioni's 'Blow Up' and 'Smashing Time (a swinging London movie starring Rita Tushingham and Lynn Redgrave), although in neither case did their contributions make it onto the soundtrack album. The tracks they recorded for 'Blow Up' are assembled on RPM's *50-Minute Technicolour Dream* CD compilation.

Sadly, neither of **Tomorrow**'s singles - the fine psychedelic version of *My White Bicycle* and the psych-pop number *Revolution* broke through. Both were included on their album, composed largely of Hopkins/Burgess songs and produced by **Mark Wirtz**. Among the more interesting tracks on the album were *The Journey Of Timothy Chase*, *Auntie Mary's Dress Shop*, the Eastern-influenced *Real Life Permanent Dream* and a competent version of **Lennon/McCartney**'s *Strawberry Fields Forever*. This group failed to survive the psychedelic era, but **Howe** went on to form **Bodast** and later to play with **Yes**. **Twink**, meanwhile joined **Aquarian Age** and then **The Pretty Things**. John Wood was also in **Aquarian Age**. He later found fortune, if not fame, working as a croupé in Mediterranean casinos. Their second 'A' side, *Revolution*, was a highly experimental song in many respects but it had an element of commercial appeal. **Tomorrow** disbanded in April 1968.

50-Minute Technicolour Dream is a superbly packaged selection of studio out-takes plus eight tracks recorded at the December 1967 'Christmas On Earth Continued' show. This will delight psych-heads.

Compilation appearances have included: *Am I Glad To See You*, *Blow Up*, *Three Jolly Little Dwarfs*, *Revolution*, *Shy Boy* and *Colonel Brown* on *Keith West - Excerpts From - Groups And Sessions 1965-1974* (CD); *My White Bicycle* on *My Generation* (LP), on the 4-CD box set *Nuggets II*; and on *Harvest Heritage - 20 Greats* (LP); *My White Bicycle* and *Strawberry Fields Forever* on *Not Just Beat Music 1965-70* (LP), *British Psychedelic Trip, Vol. 2* (LP) and *Great British Psychedelic Trip, Vol. 3* (CD); *Revolution* on *Psychedelic Visions* (CD), *Rubble, Vol. 3 - Nightmares In Wonderland* (LP) and *Rubble, Vol. 2* (CD); *My White Bicycle* and *Why* on *Psychedelia At Abbey Road* (CD); *Real Life Permanent Dream*, *Claremont Lake*, *Revolution*, *Hallucinations*, *Three Jolly Little Dwarfs* and *My White Bicycle* on *Steve Howe - Mothballs* (CD); *Auntie Mary's Dress Shop* and *Colonel Brown* on *A Teenage Opera - The Original Soundtrack Recording* (CD); *Revolution* and *3 Jolly Little Dwarfs* (BBC live broadcasts 1967) on *Dustbin Full Of Rubbish* (LP); and *Real Life Permanent Dream* on *Electric Psychedelic Sitar Headswirlers Vol. 6* (CD). The 4-CD box set *Acid Drops, Spacedust & Flying Saucers* features the phased version of *Revolution*. (VJ/RMJ)

Tomorrow Come Some Day

ALBUM: 1   TOMORROW COME SOME DAY   (SNB 97) 1969 R4

An ultra-rare private pressing involving the musicians connected with **Agincourt**, **Alice Through The Looking Glass** and **Ithaca**. This was basically a late sixties underground folk album. (VJ)

Tomorrow's Children

45s:	You're My Baby/Maybe Today	(Plexium PXM 17) 1970
	Sing A Song/Don't Believe	(Plexium PXM 25) 1971
	Keep A Little Love In Your Life/	
	My Way Of Living	(Plexium PXM 26) 1971
	We Can Make Funtime/If It Could Be	(Plexium PXM 31) 1972

No other details known.

Tonton Macoute

Personnel:	PAUL FRENCH	keyb'ds, vcls	A
	CHRIS GAVIN	gtr, bs	A
	DAVE KNOWLES	woodwind, vcls	A
	NIGEL REVELER	drms	A

ALBUM: 1(A)   TONTON MACOUTE   (RCA Neon NE 4) 1971 R2

NB: (1) Reissued on Repertoire (REP 4467-WP) 1994. (1) reissued again on vinyl and CD (Akarma AK 149).

45:    α   Summer Of Our Love/Greyhound Lady   (RCA RCA 2190) 1972

NB: α As Tonton.

TOMORROW - Christmas On Earth Continued (LP).

TONTON MACOUTE - Tonton Macoute (LP).

This is a little-known band. Musically in the progressive-jazz genre, the album was released on RCA's now collectable Neon label. It's quite unusual and includes a number of woodwind solos. Despite being recorded under the supervision of Howard and Blaikley it's musically miles away from that duo's sixties pop format. Paul French went on to play in Voyager in the late seventies and early eighties. (VJ)

Tony and Tandy

Personnel incl: TONY HEAD
                 SHARON TANDY

45s: α Two Can Make It Together/
         The Bitter And The Sweet   (Atlantic 584 262) 1969 SC
         Two Can Make It Together/
         Look And Find   (Atlantic 2091 075) 1971

NB: α recorded with **The Fleur de Lys**.

The Fleur de Lys backed vocalist Sharon Tandy on some of her singles and this project was a collaboration between Tandy and **The Fleur de Lys'** vocalist **Tony Head**. In fact the group backed them on the first single. (VJ)

Tony's Defenders

Personnel incl: BRIAN BENNETT   gtr   A

45s: Yes I Do/It's Easy To Say Hello   (Columbia DB 7850) 1966
      Since I Lost You Baby/
      Waiting For A Call From You   (Columbia DB 7996) 1966

This band's guitarist Brian Bennett was later in the marginally more successful but considerably more significant, **Mike Stuart Span**. The band came from Tunbridge Wells.

Yes I Do can also be heard on *R&B Scene, Vol. 1* (LP) and *That Driving Beat* (CD). (VJ)

Steve Peregrine Took

Steve Peregrine Took was one half of **Tyrannosaurus Rex -** the other being **Marc Bolan** (see entry for more details of his career with them). The recently issued *Crazy Diamond* (CD) (Angel Air SJPCD 118) compiles previously unreleased solo material from the early seventies after his split with **Bolan**. For this he collaborated with **Twink** and Larry Wallis (of **Pink Fairies**) and it's also rumoured that **Syd Barrett** was involved too. He was also in **Shagrat**. (VJ)

Toomorrow

Personnel: KARL CHAMBERS   A
            VIC COOPER   A
            OLIVIA NEWTON-JOHN   A
            BEN THOMAS   A

ALBUM: 1(A) TOOMORROW (Soundtrack)
              (w/insert)   (RCA LSA 3008) 1970 R3

45s: You're My Baby Now/Goin' Back   (RCA RCA 1978) 1970 R2
      I Could Never Live Without Your Love/
      Roll Like A River   (Decca F 13070) 1970 R2

This group was put together by producer and Monkees mastermind Don Kirshner to star in a science fiction comedy movie of the same name. It flopped badly, however, as did the associated album and 45s, which are enjoyably frothy pop with 'space age' sound effects. Olivia Newton-John, of course, went on to enjoy a hugely successful acting and singing career. (VJ/RMJ)

David Toop / Max Eastley

ALBUM: 1 NEW AND REDISCOVERED MUSICAL INSTRUMENTS
                                    (Obscure No. 4) 1975 SC

NB: (1) reissued on Obscure (OBS 48) in 1978.

This strange album featured a side from each artist. Toop, who had earlier collaborated with **Simon Finn**, went on to much greater fame both as a journalist and ambient artist (his book / CD *Ocean Of Sound* was widely praised) while Eastley essentially makes sound sculptures and has been featured in the improvisational magazine 'Rubberneck'. (VJ/RMJ)

Tony 'Top' Topham

ALBUM: 1 ASCENSION HEIGHTS   (Blue Horizon 7-63857) 1970 R3

NB: (1) reissued on Line (OLLP 5314 AS) 1985. There's also a compilation, *Lookin' Down The Backtracks* (Sunflower SF-CD 103) 1992.

45: Christmas Cracker/
     Cracking Up Over Christmas   (Blue Horizon 57-3167) 1969 SC

Topham was lead guitarist in **The Yardbirds'** original line-up and also played in Christine Perfect / McVie's band. The album is entirely instrumental and features 10 self-penned numbers, together with *Tuxedo Junction* and *How Sweet It Is (To Be Loved By You)*. If moody and sometimes exciting blues guitar is your scene, this is one for you. Originals are now very rare and expensive, so the reissue in the mid-eighties was welcomed by many blues fans.

Fans might want the *Lookin' Down The Backtracks* set, which includes an acoustic rendition of *Sugar Babe* cut when he was just 15; four cuts from 1965 with **Duster Bennett**; four more from 1969, with **Topham** supporting vocalist Lloyd Watson, and nine instrumental guitar duets, also from 1969, with **Rick Hayward**, which were recorded as demos for his 1970 album. (VJ/RMJ)

The Tornados

Personnel: GEORGE BELLAMY   gtr   A
            HEINZ BURT   bs   A
            ALAN CADDY   gtr   A
            CLEM CATTINI   drms   A
            ROGER LAVERN (JACKSON)   organ   A

ALBUMS: 1(A) AWAY FROM IT ALL   (Decca LK 4552) 1963 R2
        2(A) THE WORLD OF THE TORNADOS
                                     (Decca SPA 253) 1972 SC
        3(A) REMEMBERING.... THE TORNADOS
                                     (Decca REM 4) 1976

NB: CD Compilations include: *The Original 60's Hits* (Music Club MCCD 161) 1994; *The EP Collection* (See For Miles SEECD 445) 1996; *The 60's French EP Collection*

(Magic 525732) 1997; *The Tornados Archive* (Rialto RMCD 228) 1998 and *Complete Tornados* (2-CD set) (Repertoire RR 4708) 1998.

EPs:	1(A)	THE SOUNDS OF THE TORNADOS		
			(Decca DFE 8510) 1962 SC	
	2(A)	TELSTAR	(Decca DFE 8511) 1962 SC	
	3(A)	MORE SOUNDS FROM THE TORNADOS		
			(Decca DFE 8521) 1963 SC	
	4(A)	TORNADO ROCK	(Decca DFE 8533) 1963 R1	

HCP

45s:	Love And Fury/Popeye Twist	(Decca F 11449) 1962 SC -
	Telstar/Jungle Fever	(Decca F 11494) 1962 1
α	Globetrotter/Locomotion With Me	(Decca F 11562) 1963 5
	Robot/Life On Venus	(Decca F 11606) 1963 17
	The Ice Cream Man/Theme From	
	'The Scales Of Justice'	(Decca F 11662) 1963 18
	Dragonfly/Hymn For Teenagers	(Decca F 11745) 1963 41
	Joystick/Hot Pot	(Decca F 11838) 1964 -
	Monte Carlo/Blue Blue Beat	(Decca F 11889) 1964 SC -
	Exodus/Blackpool Rock	(Decca F 11946) 1964 SC -
	Granada/Ragunboneman	(Columbia BD 7455) 1965 SC -
β	Early Bird/	
	Stompin' Through The Rye	(Columbia BD 7589) 1965 SC -
	Stingray/Aqua Marina	(Columbia BD 7687) 1965 R1 -
	Pop-Art Goes Mozart/	
	Too Much In Love To Hear	(Columbia BD 7856) 1966 SC -
	Is That A Ship I Hear?/	
	Do You Come Here Often?	(Columbia BD 7984) 1966 R1 -
Reissue:	Telstar/Globetrotter	(Old Gold OG 9327) 1983 -

NB: α Some 'B' sides credit *Locomotion With You*. β Credited to Tornados '65.

After **The Shadows** this was Britain's top early sixties instrumental band.

Producer Joe Meek assembled **The Tornados** in 1961 as the house band at his Holloway Road, North London recording studio. They backed artists like Billy Fury and John Leyton. Caddy and **Cattini** had previously played with Colin Hicks and His Cabin Boys. Lavern (real name Roger Jackson) and Bellamy were session musicians and Heinz Burt was discovered by Meek.

Their debut single flopped but he then got the band to play one of his own compositions, an instrumental called *Telstar*. It utilised futuristic studio techniques including distortion, a cheesy-sounding Clavioline (a two-octave battery-powered keyboard on which Geoff Goddard - one of his protégés deputised for Lavern), tape echo, beeping satellite sound effects and lots of tube compression and sounded both unique and original. It gave them a UK and US No 1, but an alleged copyright infringement tied up the royalties for six years and a contract employing them as a back-up group to Billy Fury prevented them from touring the States.

1963 was also a good year for the band and they enjoyed four further hits, but the departure of Heinz Burt seemed to weaken them. He embarked on a solo career as **Heinz**. More significantly, the emerging Merseybeat sound rendered their instrumental sound passé, particularly when in 1965 with songs like *Stingray* they were producing a similar sound to that of 1963. They underwent several line-up changes; **Clem Catttini** the last original member to depart became as significant session artist and worked a lot with producer Shel Talmy. Joe Meek's suicide in 1967 led to their disbandment. It happened after a row with his landlady which resulted in him shooting her and turning the gun on himself. He died penniless and yet if he'd survived a year longer when the copyright infringement suit was settled in his favour he'd have been a millionaire.

In the mid-seventies Bellamy, Burt, **Cattini** and Lavern reformed the band, re-recorded *Telstar* and worked the nostalgia circuit as The Original Tornados for a while. Later in 1989 Cattini put together a new **Tornados** line-up - this time with a female vocalist, but it didn't last. They can also be heard on several sixties hits compilations. (VJ)

Pete Townshend

HCP

ALBUM: 1 WHO CAME FIRST (Track 2408 201) 1972 SC 30

NB: *Scooped* (Redline/Wagram 3083972) 2003 is a 2-CD 'best of'. *Lifehouse Elements* (Redline/Wagram 3083962) 2003 features 11 tracks originally intended for

the abortive multi-media show 'Lifehouse', launched in 1970 There's also the 2-CD *Anthology* (Revisited SPVO89304292).

Pete Townshend was born on 19 May 1945 in London. He came from a musical background - his father played in a R.A.F. dance band The Squadronaires and his mother was a singer with the Sidney Torch Orchestra. His first band was The Confederates, which he formed with **John Entwistle** whilst they were still at Acton Grammar School. When he left school in 1961 he went to art college, but the following year along with **Entwistle**, he responded to another former Acton Grammar School pupil, **Roger Daltrey**'s invitation to join his band, The Detours. This later became **The Who** then **The High Numbers** then **The Who** again and **Pete Townshend** went on to enjoy several years of success with the band.

This solo album was made in 1972 during a spell when members of the group took a break from touring and recording to concentrate on solo projects. Aside from climbing to No 30 here it got to No 69 in the US.

Scooped is essentially a 'best of' CD. It includes early versions of *Pictures Of Lily*, *Substitute*, *Magic Bus*, *Pinball Wizard* and *You Better You Bet*, but there are 35 tracks in all and they are accompanied by detailed notes from the man himself.

Lifehouse Elements contains 11 tracks originally intended for the abortive multi-media show 'Lifehouse'. Their *Who's Next* period is particularly well represented by *The Song Is Over*, *Won't Get Fooled Again*, *Getting In Tune* and a new recording of *Behind Blue Eyes*. There are also two takes of *Barbara O'Riley* (one is orchestrated) and top notch renditions of *Who Are You* and *Let's See Action*.

The 2-CD *Anthology* is a 2-CD set covering tracks from his debut album and incorporating his musicals and more recent work. Highlights include one **Who** track *Pure And Easy*, *English Boy*, *Let My Love Open The Door*, *Rough Boys*, *Empty Glass* and *Face The Face*. (VJ)

Toyshop

Personnel incl: JOHN ASKEY   bs   A

45:       Say Goodbye To Yesterday/
          Send My Love To Lucy   (Polydor 56317) 1969

A melodic pop 45 by a Stoke-On-Trent band, *Send My Love To Lucy* can also be heard on *Fading Yellow, Vol 4* (CD). Askey had earlier been in **Hedgehoppers Anonymous**. (VJ)

Grant Tracy and The Sunsets

Personnel incl: GRANT TRACY   A
                  PETE DELLO
                  RAY CANE

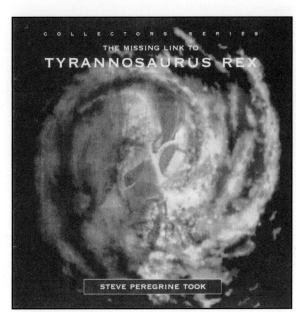

STEVE PEREGRINE TOOK - Crazy Diamond (CD).

ALBUM: 1(A) TEENBEAT   (Ember EMB 3352) 1964 R2

45s:	Say When/Please Baby Please	(Ember EMB S 126) 1961
	Pretend/Love Me	(Ember EMB S 130) 1961
	The Great Matchmaker/	
	Tears Came Rolling Down	(Ember EMB S 148) 1962
	Taming Tigers/The Painted Smile	(Ember EMB S 155) 1962
	Everybody Shake/	
	Turn The Lights Down, Jenny	(Decca F 11741) 1963 SC

This London group really belong to a previous era to that covered by this book, though *Everybody Shake* is a great beat record. They formed in the early sixties. Singer Grant Tracy (real name Roy Barker) and guitarist **Pete Dello** first met in the skiffle era playing at the 59 Club, which was actually convened in the St Mary of Eaton church hall in London which the vicar at the time (Father John Oates) opened up as a meeting place for young people. Musically they sounded something in between Cliff Richard and The Shadows and the US teen idols of the time. Their only single of distinction was *Everybody Shake*, which successfully captured the raucous early beat era sound. It was penned by **Dello** and Cane (indeed **Dello** wrote some of their other material). The group failed to manage a UK hit, but was more popular in Germany.

The 2-CD anthology *Everybody Shake! The Complete Collection* compiles all their sixties recordings as well as previously unreleased demos and unissued tracks.

Dello and Cane went on to form **Honeybus**. (VJ)

Tractor

| Personnel: | STEVE CLAYTON | keyb'ds, bs, drms, flute | A |
| | JIM MILNE | gtr, vcls, bs | A |

ALBUM: 1(A) TRACTOR   (Dandelion 2310 217) 1972 R2

NB: (1) reissued on vinyl (Thunderbolt THBL 002) in 1983 and on album and CD (Repertoire RR 4081-WP) 1991. (1) also reissued on one CD along with **The Way We Live** album (See For Miles SEECD 409) 1994. (1) reissued on CD again (Ozit OZITCD 217) 2002, with six extra bonus tracks from different phases of their career to celebrate their 30th Anniversary. There's also a compilation, *Worst Enemies* (Sunflower SFCD 102) 1991 and reissued (Ozit OZITCD OD 019) 1996 which draws on archive material from the 1971-91 era and *Original Masters* (World Wide Records SPM-WWR-CD-0036) 1992, which contains a number of early demos of variable standard, along with a few studio cuts. *Through To Deeply Vale And Beyond* (Ozit OZITCD 024) is a compilation of their work throughout the seventies and eighties featuring some early rarities and with packaging that celebrates the famous Deeply Vale festival.

45s:	Stony Glory/Marie/As You Say	(Dandelion 2001 282) 1972 SC
(up to	Roll The Dice/Vicious Circle	(UK UK 93) 1975
1976)		

TRACTOR - Tractor (LP).

TRADER HORNE - Morning Way (LP).

NB: **Tractor** also recorded two further 45s: *No More Rock And Roll/Northern City* (PS) (Cargo CRS 002) 1981 and *Average Man's Hero/Big Big Boy* (Roach RR 2) 1981.

This progressive duo was previously known as **The Way We Live** and came from Rochdale.

The album, which is now sought-after by collectors, is recommended. It's a nice mix of acoustic ballads and heavier material, but it's the latter that really catches the ear. The opening cut, *All Ends Up*, begins with strange sound effects which give way to a heavy futuristic sound (uncompromising vocals, intelligent lyrics and powerful fuzz guitar), which is undoubtedly one of the album's highlights. Another is the finale, *Make The Journey*, which again features distorted guitars and wild drums. Sandwiched in between are more complex heavy progressive cuts like *Little Girl In Yellow* and acoustic ballads like *The Watcher* and the album is spoilt only by the throwaway, *Ravenscroft 13 Bar Boogie*. (a tribute to label head John Peel, whose real surname was, of course, Ravenscroft).

The Repertoire reissue comes with the original artwork, an annotated booklet and a picture disc CD which contains three bonus tracks from 1973. The Sunflower release is a collection of previously unissued and rare material dating from 1971-91. Its highlight is *Peterloo*, a 21-minute cut in five movements, detailing the events of the 1819 massacre. The World Wide Records' CD will mainly interest archivists and **Tractor** fanatics due to the inclusion of a number of pre-album demos of which the Eastern-tinged *Siderial*, the inventive acoustic number, *Madrigel*, and the fuzzy *Willow* seem the pick.

They reformed to record 45s in the late seventies and early eighties, one under the moniker Jim Milne and Tractor.

See For Miles' *Dandelion Rarities* (CD) includes *All Ends Up*, whilst *Ravenscroft 13 Bar Boogie* appears on *Dandelion Sampler 1969-1972* (CD). (VJ)

Trader Horne

Personnel:	JUDY DYBLE	keyb'ds, vcls	A
	JACKIE McAULEY	keyb'ds, vcls, gtr	AB
	(SAFFRON SUMMERFIELD	gtr, vcls	B)

ALBUM: 1(A) MORNING WAY
          (w/photo & insert)   (Dawn DNLS 3004) 1970 R2

NB: (1) issued on Janus (3012) in the US. *Morning Way... Plus* (See For Miles SEE LP 308 or SEE CD 308) 1991. (1) reissued again on vinyl (Akarma AK 087) and on CD (Castle CMRCD 074).

45s:	Morning Way/Sheena	(Pye 7N 17846) 1969 SC
	Here Comes The Rain/	
	Goodbye Mercy Kelly	(Dawn DNS 1003) 1969

866

This short-lived late sixties folk-duo formed when Judy Dyble (ex-**Fairport Convention**) teamed up with **Jackie McAuley** (formerly of **Them** and **Belfast Gypsies**). Dyble, incidentally, also played with **Giles, Giles and Fripp** for about a month in 1968.

Trader Horne's superbly melodic first single is now very rare, and wasn't included on the album, which - if you like folk with crystal clear female vocals - comes highly recommended. An excellent standard is maintained throughout. Several tracks, including *Growing Man, In My Loneliness, Morning Way, Velvet To Atone* and *Luke That Never Was*, showcase Dyble's vocal talents and others, including *The Mixed Up Kind* and instrumental *Three Rings For Elven Kings*, feature lovely flute (by former **Them** member Ray Elliot) and harpsichord. Most of the material was penned by **McAuley**, but Dyble wrote the uniquely haunting title track and co-wrote *Velvet To Atone* with **Steamhammer**'s Martin Quittenton, who also penned *You Wear It Well* and *Maggie May* for **Rod Stewart**.

When Dyble departed, Saffron Summerfield took her place, but the new pairing didn't last long. Summerfield later recorded as a solo artist and ran the Mother Earth label.

Morning Way has been compiled on *Paisley Pop - Pye Psych (& Other Colours) 1966-1969* (CD). (VJ/RMJ)

Traffic

Personnel:	JIM CAPALDI	drms, vcls, keyb'ds	ABCDEF
	DAVE MASON	gtr, vcls	A D
	STEVIE WINWOOD	gtr, vcls, keyb'ds	ABCDEF
	CHRIS WOOD	wind	ABCDEF
	RIC GRECH	bs	CD
	JIM GORDON	drms	D
	REEBOP KWAKU.BAAH	congas	DE
	DAVID HOOD	bs	E
	ROGER HAWKINS	drms	E
	ROSKO GEE	bs	F

HCP

ALBUMS: 1(A) MR. FANTASY
(up to (mono/stereo) (Island ILP 961/ILPS 9061) 1967 R1/SC 8
1976) 2(A) TRAFFIC
(mono/stereo) (Island ILP 981/ILPS 9081) 1968 R1/SC 9
3(A) LAST EXIT
(mono/stereo) (Island ILP(S) 9097) 1969 R1/SC -
4(A) BEST OF TRAFFIC (Island ILPS 9112) 1969 SC -
5(B) JOHN BARLEYCORN MUST DIE
(Island ILPS 9116) 1970 SC 11
6(D) WELCOME TO THE CANTEEN (Island ILPS 9166) 1971 -
7(D) LOW SPARK OF HIGH HEELED BOY
(Island ILPS 9180) 1971 -
8(E) SHOOT OUT AT THE FANTASY FACTORY
(Island ILPS 9224) 1973 -

TRAFFIC - Mr. Fantasy (LP).

TRAFFIC - Traffic (LP).

9(E) ON THE ROAD (Island ISLD 2) 1973 40
10(F) WHEN THE EAGLE FLIES (Island ILPS 9273) 1974 31
11(-) HEAVY TRAFFIC (Comp.)
(United Artists LA 421) 1975 -
12(-) MORE HEAVY TRAFFIC (Compilation)
(United Artists LA 526) 1975 -

NB: (11) and (12) US only. Only pink label copies of (1), (2) and (3) are R1 others are SC. (1) reissued on CD (Island IMCD 43) 1989. (1) reissued again on vinyl (Simply Vinyl SVLP 099) and on CD remastered (Island IMCD 264). *Heaven Is In Your Mind* was the US edition of (1) and is now reissued on CD. (2) reissued on vinyl (Simply Vinyl SVLP 142) (2) reissued on CD (Island IMCD 45) 1989 and again remastered (Island IMCD 265) with four bonus tracks. (3) reissued on CD (Island CID 9097) 1989 and again on CD remastered (Island 842 787-2) 2002. (5) reissued on CD (IMCD 40) 1989 and again on CD remastered (Island 314548541-2) 2002. (6) reissued on CD (Island IMCD 39) 1989 and again (Island 314 586 847 2) 2002. (7) reissued on CD (Island IMCD 42) 1989 and again (Island 314 548 827 2) 2002. (8) reissued on CD (Island IMCD 44) 1989. (9) reissued on CD (Island 8000096FSU) 2002. (10) reissued on CD (Island IMCD 142) 1991.

Compilations have included *Hole In My Shoe* (Island IEP 7) in 1978, *Exit* (Island IMCD 41) 1989 and there's also a 2-CD compilation, *Smiling Phases* (Island IMCD 158) 1992. *An Introduction To Traffic* (CD) (Island IMCD 257) is an excellent 12-track introductory anthology which includes material from most of their albums. A more recent compilation is 2000's *Feelin' Alright: The Best Of Traffic*.

EP: 1 HOLE IN MY SHOE (Island IEP 7) 1978

HCP

45s: Paper Sun/
Giving To You (Some PS) (Island WIP 6002) 1967 SC/- 5
Hole In My Shoe/
Smiling Phases (Some PS) (Island WIP 6017) 1967 SC/- 2
Here We Go Round The Mulberry Bush/
Coloured Rain (Some PS) (Island WIP 6025) 1967 SC/- 8
No Face, No Name, No Number/Roamin' In The
Gloamin' With 40,000 Headmen (Island WIP 6030) 1968 40
Feelin' Alright/Withering Tree (Island WIP 6041) 1968 -
Medicated Goo/
Shanghai Noodle Factory (Island WIP 6050) 1968 -
Walking In The Wind/
Walking In The Wind (instr.) (Island WIP 6207) 1974 -
Reissue: Hole In My Shoe/No Face, No Name, No Number/Paper Sun/
Here We Go Round The Mulberry Bush (Island IEP 7) 1974 -

Traffic was an important late sixties/early seventies pop-rock group which produced some classic late sixties psych-pop singles (*Hole In My Shoe* and *Paper Sun*) and developed it own folk-pop sound characterised by talented singer/songwriter and keyboardist/guitarist's **Stevie Winwood**'s keyboards and Chris Wood's reed instrument, particularly his flute. In its later phase the band veered towards jazzy extended compositions and forged a unique sound.

Traffic was originally formed in April 1967 by **Stevie Winwood** after he left the **Spencer Davis Group**. **Mason** and **Capaldi** had previously played together in Birmingham-based group **Deep Feeling** (alongside **Gordon**

TRAFFIC - Last Exit (LP).

Jackson) and Wood had been in **Locomotive**. The four original members spent six months in a cottage in Aston Tirrold, Berkshire, where they got themselves together and partied long and hard.

Their debut single, *Paper Sun*, which featured some fine guitar runs from **Mason**, was an ideal summer single and climbed to No 5 in the UK chart. The follow-up, *Hole In My Shoe*, was another flower-power classic, based on a dream of **Mason**'s, and became one of anthems of 1967. A further single, *Here We Go Round The Mulberry Bush* (culled from the film of the same name), reached No. 8 in November 1967.

That December saw the release of their debut album, whose chart success crowned what had been a highly successful year for the band. It contained many fine tracks, such as the melodic *Dealer*, the mystical, Eastern-influenced *Utterly Simple*, the jazzy *Coloured Rain*, and the more commercial *Heaven Is In Your Mind*. The epic title track is, meanwhile, simply one of the classic recordings of the period.

Despite their success, there was friction within the band, mainly between **Mason**'s melodic, commercial impulse and the remaining members' jazz-orientated interests. **Mason** therefore departed in December 1967, but rejoined in May 1968. In his absence the band enjoyed a minor UK hit (No. 40) with the **Winwood-Capaldi** composition *No Face, No Name, No Number*. With **Mason** having rejoined, the band cut a second album which, whilst not as strong as their debut, is also well worth investigation. All four members also contributed to **Gordon Jackson**'s superb *Thinking Back* album, which was produced by Mason. He, however, quit **Traffic** again in October 1968, and they disintegrated six months later.

Last Exit, a part live and part studio recording issued in May 1969, was a rushed job which does not do them justice. Island also issued a *Best Of Traffic* compilation around the same time. Upon the demise of **Traffic**, **Mason**, **Capaldi**, Wood and **(Wynder K) Frog** retreated to another country cottage (Worcestershire this time) and formed an ill-fated outfit which lasted from January to March 1969 but did not record. **Winwood**, meanwhile, first became a member of short-lived supergroup **Blind Faith**, then joined **Ginger Baker's Airforce** for a short while.

In January 1970 **Winwood** began work on a solo album provisionally titled *Mad Shadows*. **Capaldi** and Wood came in to assist on the sessions and **Traffic** reformed as a trio. The resulting album, *John Barleycorn Must Die*, was a superb fusion of jazz, rock and traditional folk; indeed, the title cut dated back to the 15th century. All three cuts on side one - *Glad*, *Freedom Rider* and *Empty Pages*, are superb blends of jazz-influenced rock, though *Every Mothers Son* is uncannily similar to **Blind Faith**'s *Sea Of Joy*.

After that triumph, they headed, with the addition of Ric Grech, for Morocco to write the score for a movie, 'Nevertheless', that never became a reality. The dope there was too tempting and they spent most of their time getting stoned and sunbathing. When they returned in May 1971, the line-up was expanded to a sextet (D) incorporating Gordon, a US session man who'd played for **Derek and The Dominos** and Kwaku-Baah (ex-**Wynder K. Frog** and Airforce). Even **Mason** rejoined for half a dozen gigs after returning

from California. They toured both the US and UK and cut a couple of quite successful albums. The first, *Welcome To The Canteen*, included some live recordings which **Mason** played on. They also had a minor US hit with their live revival of the **Spencer Davis Group**'s *Gimme Some Lovin'* from it. This line-up's second album, *The Low Spark Of High Heeled Boys*, went gold in the US and from it *Rock'n'Roll Stew (Part I)* was a minor US hit.

In December 1971, Ric Grech departed (later joining KGB) and Gordon returned to session work in the USA. In January 1972, **Stevie Winwood** contracted peritonitis, which gave the band an enforced period of inactivity. **Jim Capaldi** recorded a solo album, *Oh How We Danced*. Whilst recording it at Muscle Shoals he befriended Hood and Hawkins, inviting them to Jamaica to help record the next **Traffic** album, *Shoot-Out At The Fantasy Factory*, which again went gold in the US but flopped in the UK. They went on a World Tour in 1973 and headlined at the Reading Rock Festival that year. The double live album *Traffic - On The Road*, which made No 29 in the US and No 40 in the UK, was recorded on this tour. When they returned from the tour Kwaku-Baah, Hood and Hawkins all departed for session work and the band's other players all took a couple of months rest. When they returned, former Gonzales bass player Rosko Gee augmented the remaining trio for some live UK engagements and played on *When The Eagle Flies*. This was another finely-crafted, jazz-influenced rock album - but it turned out to be their last because, after another successful tour in the US, where the album had become their fourth to go gold, they decided to split to concentrate on their solo careers.

Although **Traffic** didn't achieve the success their talent merited, they made some fine recordings. Sadly Chris Wood died on 12 July 1983 from liver disease. **Jim Capaldi** died of cancer on 28 January 2005, aged 60.

Compilation appearances have included *Every Mother's Son* on *Bumpers* (2-LP); *Empty Pages* on *El Pea* (2-LP); *Forty Thousand Headmen* on *Nice Enough To Eat* (LP); *Gimme Some Lovin'* on *20 Star Tracks, Vol. 1* (LP); *You Can All Join In* on *You Can All Join In* (LP); *Here We Go 'Round The Mulberry Bush*, *Utterly Simple* and *Am I What I Was Or Was I What I Am* on *Here We Go 'Round The Mulberry Bush* (LP); *Paper Sun*, *House For Everyone* and *Here We Go Round The Mulberry Bush* on *Hard Up Heroes, Vol. 2* (CD) and *Paper Sun* on the 4-CD box set *Acid Drops, Spacedust & Flying Saucers*. *Paper Sun* recently resurfaced on *The Woodstock Generation* (CD) though **Traffic** didn't play there! (VJ)

Traffic Jam

Personnel:	JOHN COGHLAN	drms	A
	ALAN LANCASTER	bs, vcls	A
	ROY LYNES	organ, vcls	A
	FRANCIS ROSSI	gtr, vcls	A

45:	Almost But Not Quite There/ Wait Just A Minute	(Pye 7N 35386) 1967 R4

TRAFFIC - John Barleycorn Must Die (LP).

TRAFFIC - When The Eagle Flies (LP).

Previously known as **The Spectres**, this outfit changed their name to Traffic in May 1967 but, threatened with legal action by **Traffic**, settled for **Traffic Jam** instead. By August they'd changed their name again to **Status Quo**, whose subsequent success has ensured that **Traffic Jam**'s mediocre 45 is now sought-after by many **Quo** collectors, changing hands for ridiculous sums. Thankfully you don't have to pay a small fortune to get to hear it anymore, because both sides also feature on two **Status Quo** compilations: - *B Sides And Rarities* (Castle Collector CCSCD 271) 1990 and *The Early Works* (Essential ESBCD 136) 1990. The 'A' side also appeared back in 1967 on a US-only compilation of UK material, *Petal Pushers* (LP).

Retrospective compilation appearances have included: *Almost But Not Quite There* on *Piccadilly Story* (CD); and *Almost But Not Quite There* and *Wait Just A Minute* on *Footsteps To Fame, Vol. 1* (CD). (VJ)

Phil Trainer

Personnel: BIAS BOSHELL   piano   A
             BARRY CLARKE   gtr   A
             ALAN EDEN   drms   A
             BARRY LYONS   dulcimer   A
             PHIL TRAINER   vcls, gtr, bs, hrmnca
                                 harmonium   A

NB: Main personnel only - additional musicians are featured on individual tracks.

ALBUM: 1(A) PHIL TRAINER   (BASF BAG 22-291073) 1972 SC

45:     Beautiful Jim/No No No   (BASF 05 19573-5) 1973

A New Yorker who had apparently travelled the world playing in groups and had tasted chart success in Japan, **Phil Trainer** turned up in England and somehow ended up joining forces with the revised line-up of the folk-rock band **Trees** on this album, one of only a small number which seem to have been issued on BASF (despite the ridiculously long catalogue number!).

All music and lyrics were by **Phil Trainer** himself, who was no beginner, having written the score for the film "The Road To Salina", and according to the sleeve notes, having nearly become a member of The Doors at one point. Indeed, one of the songs here, *Beautiful Jim*, is a farewell to Morrison, and not as mawkish as such efforts can be. Overall, the ten songs on the album are of mixed quality ranging from the horrible *Stud*, even if it is meant to be a satire on macho attitudes, to the sublime and wistful *Leave Me Alone*, which features what is accurately described as the "angelic vocal" of Celia Humpris, the **Trees**' singer. The sleeve notes ambitiously describe this as the "first of many fine releases" from **Trainer**; however, in the event it was the final bow on disc for the much-lamented **Trees**, whose playing is enjoyable throughout.

Phil Trainer is also thought to have recorded two later 45s:

45s: Carousel / Rose Coloured Sky   (Splash CP 17) 1977
        Wounded Eagle / Midnight Lover   (Splash SP5) 1979

He went on to form the band Clinic, who released an American album *Now We're Even* (Roulette 3010) 1973 with Gerry Murphy (drms), Alan Reeves (keyb'ds) and Phil Righam (gtr). (VJ/NM/BS)

Alan Trajan

ALBUM: 1 (A)   FIRM ROOTS   (MCA MKPS 2000) 1969 R3

45   Speak To Me, Clarissa /
        This Might Be My Last Number   (MCA MK 5002) 1969 SC

Keyboardist **Trajan** looks like a fierce Edwardian gamekeeper on the cover of his much sought-after album, which was overseen by Decca producer Ray Horricks (**Davy Graham**, **Bread Love & Dreams**, **Human Beast**). Aside from so-so covers of three Dylan tunes and David Ackles' *Down River*, it features some fairly heavy songs with a funky feel and fiery guitar licks, such as *Speak To Me, Clarissa* (about a girl who has OD'd), *Mental Destruction* and *This'll Drive You Off Your Head*. Other tunes such as *Thoughts* and *This Might Be My Final Number* are more downbeat. **Trajan**, a Scot, also played keyboards on **Bread Love & Dreams**'s ultra-rare *Amaryllis* album. He remained active on the Scottish music scene, but died a couple of years back. (RMJ)

Tramline

Personnel: JOHN McCOY   vcls, hrmnca   A
             MICKY MOODY   gtr   A
             TERRY POPPLE   drms   A
             TERRY SIDGWICK   bs, vcls   A

ALBUMS: 1(A) SOMEWHERE DOWN THE LINE
                                (Island ILPS 9088) 1968 R2
        2( ) MOVES OF VEGETABLE CENTURIES
                                (Island ILPS 9095) 1969 R2

This late sixties group's best known song was the **Winwood/Capaldi** composition *Pearly Queen*, by virtue of its inclusion on the *You Can All Join In* (LP) compilation.

Their albums are typical examples of second-rate blues boom albums, although the first one certainly has its moments. With Chris Blackwell on production duties, the first album relies strongly on Moody's sensitive guitar playing, which in places gets truly inspired and expressive. Nothing special, but at least passable white boy blues. The second effort is less good. The production (Guy Stevens) is a mess, the solos are flat and the tracks are too long. The vocals, on the first album are at least reasonable, but on the second are irritating. For hard-core blues boom fans only.

Micky Moody went on to enjoy greater fame as a member of Whitesnake, whilst Terry Popple went on to **Snafu**. (MK/VJ)

Tramp

Personnel: BOB BRUNNING   bs   AB
             MICK FLEETWOOD   drms   AB
             BOB HALL   keyb'ds   AB
             DAVE KELLY   vcls   AB
             JO ANNE KELLY   vcls   AB
             DANNY KIRWAN   gtr   AB
             DAVE BROOKS   sax   B
             IAN MORTON   perc   B

ALBUMS: 1(A) TRAMP   (Music Man SMLS 603) 1969 R3
        2(B) PUT A RECORD ON (Spark SRLP 112) 1974 R1

NB: (1) also available on Spark Replay (SRLM 2001) in 1969 (R1). (1) and (2) reissued on CD, *British Blues Giants* (See For Miles SEECD 354) 1992.

45s: Each Day   (Youngblood SBY 4) 1969
        Vietnam Rose/Each Day   (Youngblood 1014) 1970
        Put A Record On/You've Gotta Move (Spark SRL 1107) 1974

869

There was certainly a good blues pedigree behind this band with musicians like Mick Fleetwood (of **Fleetwood Mac**), Bob Brunning and Bob Hall (both of **Brunning-Hall Sunflower Blues Band**), **Jo-Ann Kelly**, **Dave Kelly** and Danny Kirwan (who was also in **Fleetwood Mac** and later made solo albums) involved, but the end results, two rather unimaginative bar-room blues albums, were frankly disappointing. On account of who played on them, both albums are expensive so the CD reissue, which comes with an information booklet, is welcome from this point of view.

Tranquility

Personnel:	PAUL FRANCIS	drms, perc	A
	BERNARD HAGLEY	bs	A
	TONY LUKYN	vcls, piano, organ	A
	KEVIN McCARTHY	vcls, gtr	A
	TERRY SHADDICK	vcls, ld gtr	A
	BERKELEY WRIGHT	vcls, ld gtr	A

ALBUMS:	1(A)	TRANQUILITY	(Epic EPC 64729) 1972
	2(A)	SILVER	(Epic EPC 31989) 1973

NB: (2) was a US only release.

45s:	Thank You/Saying Goodbye	(Epic EPC 7603) 1971
	Saying Goodbye/Happy Is The Man	(Epic EPC 8243) 1972
	Dear Oh Dear/Nice And Easy	(Epic EPC 1486) 1973
	Midnight Fortune/One Day Lady	(Island WIP 6192) 1974

Also featured on the first album are appearances on electric bass by John Perry and Jim Leverton, both members of **Caravan** at different points in the future, as well as playing on many other records. There was also an extra drummer called Eric Dillon. This odd balance of personnel creates the suspicion that **Tranquility** was not so much an established band as a vehicle for displaying the considerable talents of Terry Shaddick who composes, writes lyrics, sings, plays guitar and has his fingernails painted in different shades of blue! Every one of the eleven songs is written solely by him except for two joint efforts. This is a strong, quirky collection of songs in a vaguely progressive, vaguely pop direction, given a considerable weight in performance by the four multi-layered vocalists, probably heard at their best on *Saying Goodbye* and *Lady Of The Lake*. Their music recalls Crosby Stills and Nash, particularly the vocals, which sound like **Graham Nash** and in the country-rock flavour of many of the songs. Shaddick also co-wrote *Physical* by Olivia Newton John and many songs by America, including *You Can Do Magic*.

In January 1972 they were a support act to The Byrds at their Rainbow concert gigs. Thereafter, they joined them on a five week USA tour. They returned to England in mid-1972. In August 1972, they entered the CBS studios to complete a second album under the guidance of Ashley Koyaks. The album was only released in the USA, but it was available as an import. This is less folky and with more instrumental segments. Between 1971-74

TREES - The Garden Of Jane Delawney (LP).

they worked mainly in the States. The proceeds of their first single went to charity.

Kevin McCarthy had previously been in **Cressida** where he played bass; perhaps **Tranquility** didn't have a vacancy in that department at the time! Paul Francis had been in Buster and later played with **Maggie Bell**. (NM/VJ)

The Transatlantics

Personnel:	PETER BREWER	drms	A
	TONY CLOUT	bs	A
	JOHN EDMUNDS	ld gtr	A
	IAN SCOTT	gtr	A
	PETER WRIGHT	vcls	A

45s:	Many Things From Your Window/	
	I Tried To Forget	(Fontana TF 593) 1965 R1
	Stand Up And Fight Like A Man/	
	But I Know	(Fontana TF 638) 1965 SC
	Run For Your Life/It's All Over	(King KG 1033) 1966 SC
	Louie Go Home/	
	Find Yourself Another Guy	(King KG 1040) 1966 SC
	Don't Fight It/Look Before You Leap	(Mercury MF 948) 1966 R1

A harmony beat outfit from Grays in Essex. *Run For Your Life* was a **Beatles**' song and *Don't Fight It* a Wilson Pickett number, but despite this Chart success eluded them. The 45s may have been by one or more groups of the same name.

It's not known if Pete Brewer is the same guy who later founded **Zior**. (VJ/JM)

Trapeze

Personnel:	MEL GALLEY	gtr, vcls	ABCD
	DAVE HOLLAND	drms	ABCD
	GLENN HUGHES	bs, vcls	ABC
	JOHN JONES	vcls, trumpet	A
	TERRY ROWLEY	gtr, keyb'ds, flute	A
	PETE MACKIE	bs	C
	ROB KENDRICK	gtr	D
	PETE WRIGHT	bs	D

ALBUMS:	1(A)	TRAPEZE	(Threshold THS 2) 1970 R1
(up to	2(B)	MEDUSA	(Threshold THS 4) 1970 R1
1975)	3(B)	YOU ARE THE MUSIC WE'RE JUST THE BAND	
			(Threshold THS 8) 1972 SC
	4(B)	FINAL SWING (US-only)	(Threshold THS 11) 1974 SC
	5( )	HOT WIRE	(Warner Bros K 56064) 1974 SC
	6( )	TRAPEZE	(Warner Bros K 56165) 1975

NB: (1) reissued on CD (Lemon CDLEM 21) 2004. (3) reissued on CD (Lemon CDLEM 04) 2004. Later releases were *Hold On/Running* (Aura AUL 708) 1978 and *Live In Texas/Dead Armadillos* (Aura AUL 717) 1982. *Live At The Boat Club 1975* (CD) (MLP MLP04CD) is a live show from Nottingham that year and comes with an excellent booklet detailing their history.

45s:	Send Me No More Letters/Another Day	(Threshold TH 2) 1969
	Coast To Coast/Your Love Is Alright	(Threshold TH 11) 1972
	Sunny Side Of The Street/Monkey	(Warner Bros K 16606) 1975
	Don't Ask Me How I Know/	
	Take Good Care (PS)	(Aura AUS 14) 1979 SC
	Running Away/	
	Don't Break My Heart (PS)	(Aura AUS 16) 1980 SC

This hard/blues-rock band formed in Wolverhampton in 1968 and became the first band to sign to **The Moody Blues**' Threshold label. They are most significant for including Glenn Hughes before his spell with **Deep Purple** and Pete Goulby, who had been in **Fable** and later went on to **Uriah Heep**. Indeed **John Lodge** was their producer and his influence is evident on their first album, which combines melodic rock, subtle and psychedelia.

Jones and Rowley were forced out after the first album and rejoined their previous band **The Montanas**. Galley, Holland and Hughes recorded the next two albums as a three-piece. Their second album *Medusa* built on the promise of their debut and is probably their best.

The two Warner Brothers albums were recorded by a new line-up (D) after Hughes had left the band. Holland was later in **Judas Priest**.

Live At The Boat Club 1975 captured a live show from Nottingham. The 70-minute set features short numbers like *Medusa, You Are The Music* and *Way Back To The Bone* alongside beautiful long versions of *Jury* and *Black Cloud*. The set comes with a booklet with lots of period photos and the band's history. (VJ)

Trash

Personnel:			
	IAN CRAWFORD-CLEWS	vcls	A
	TIMI DONALD	drms	A
	COLIN HUNTER-MORRISON	bs	A
	RONALD LEAHY	organ	A
	FRASER WATSON	ld gtr	A

HCP
45s:	α	Road To Nowhere/Illusions	(Apple APPLE 6) 1969 SC -
		Golden Slumbers - Carry That Weight/	
		Trash Can	(Apple APPLE 17) 1969 SC 35

NB: α Early copies were credited to **White Trash** (R3).

This group (except for Hunter-Morrison) began life as **The Pathfinders** and were one of Scotland's top groups in 1968 when they were spotted by ex-**Shadow** and producer **Tony Meehan**. He persuaded them to go to London where they were signed by Apple's Richard DiLello, who renamed them **White Trash**. However, the BBC found the name offensive and refused to play their debut 45, so they shortened the name to **Trash**, eventually getting some airplay. Still, the various name changes hadn't helped and the pulsating version of a song, originally written and recorded by Carole King, didn't do as well as it deserved.

In 1969, they backed **Marsha Hunt** on a UK tour and had a minor hit with their cover of **The Beatles**' *Golden Slumbers/Carry That Weight*, but split up shortly after.

Donald was later in Blue and Leahy surfaced in **Stone The Crows, Alvin Lee & Co** and **The Jack Bruce Band**.

Compilation appearances have included: *Illusions* on *Psychedelia, Vol. 4* (LP) and *Hen's Teeth, Vol. 3* (CD); and *Trash Can* on *We Can Fly, Vol 1* (CD). (VJ)

Paul Travers

45:	Memories Of Melinda/Lullaby To Claire	(A&M AMS 785) 1970

This was an early solo outing for the man who became better known as Paul Da Vinci with **The Rubettes** and others. He later released several solo 45s as Paul Da Vinci. (VJ/DS)

Travis

ALBUM:	1	SHINE ON ME	(A&M AMLS 6182) 1973 R1

45s:	Band Of Heroes/Out In The Country	(A&M 7081) 1973
(up to 1976)	Band Of Heroes/Out In The Country	(A&M 7084) 1973

This outfit included **Paul Travis** and returned with further recordings in the mid-eighties. (VJ)

Dave Travis

45:	Button Nose/Patsy	(Tepee TPR 1004) 1968

This is actually the DJ Dave Lee Travis and oh dear he won't want to be reminded of this embarrassing effort! (VJ)

TREES - On The Shore (LP).

Paul Travis

ALBUM:	1	RETURN OF THE NATIVE	
		(w/lyric insert)	(A&M AMLS 68290) 1975 SC

45:	Bury Me Deep In The Ground/Valentine	(A&M AMLS 7149) 1975
(up to 1976)		

Paul Travis had earlier recorded as part of **Travis** and he made a further 45 for Decca in 1978. (VJ)

Treacy

45s:	Keep That Wheel A-Turnin'/	
	Road To Bandon	(Pye 7N 17328) 1967
	Murphy's Volunteers/Red-Haired Mary	(Pye 7N 17487) 1968

This was an undistinguished Irish folk group. (VJ)

Trees

Personnel:			
	BIAS BOSHELL	gtr, vcls, bs	AB
	UNWIN BROWN	drms, vcls	AB
	BARRY CLARKE	gtr	ABCD
	DAVID COSTA	gtr	AB
	CELIA HUMPHRIS	keyb'ds, vcls	ABCD
	(PETE CLARKE	drms	C
	ROBBIE HEWLETT	bs	C
	ALUN EDEN	drms	D
	CHUCK FLEMING	violin	D
	JOHN LIFTON	vcls, electronics	D
	BARRY LYONS	bs	D
	TONY COX	bs	B)
	MICHAEL JEFFRIES	harp	B)

ALBUMS:	1(A)	THE GARDEN OF JANE DELAWNEY	
			(CBS 63837) 1970 R2
	2(B)	ON THE SHORE	(CBS 64168) 1970 R2

NB: (1) and (2) reissued by Decal (LIK 15 and LIK 12 respectively), 1987 (both SC). (1) reissued on CD (Columbia 506064 2) 2002. (2) reissued on CD (BGO BGOCD 173) 1993 and (Columbia 484435-2) 1996.

45:	Nothing Special/Epitaph	(CBS 5078) 1970 SC

A superb folk-rock outfit, both of whose albums are now much sought-after.

Trees formed in London in 1969. All members were friends of friends and shared an interest in melding folk and rock in the style of **Fairport Convention**. They were soon signed to Clearwater, one of London's top underground management agencies, and were offered a deal with CBS after a triumphant gig at Notting Hill's All Saints Hall.

The Garden Of Jane Delawney was an excellent debut, if perhaps recorded too soon after their formation. Of special note was the title track, a delicate and mysterious song which showcased Humphris' lovely vocals, accompanied by sparse instrumentation. Other highlights include *Nothing Special*, which was also put out on 45, and a good arrangement of the traditional *She Moved Through The Fair*.

Though *On The Shore* was recorded only a few months later, it's better overall. Tracks like *Fool* and *Murdoch* showcase Boshell's unusual songwriting, and the instrumentation is fuller and more ambitious. *Streets Of Derry* and *Sally Free And Easy*, meanwhile, showcase Humphris' gorgeous vocals. The latter, in fact, is perhaps the band's magnum opus, and features a lovely piano intro. The final track, *Polly On The Shore* is well worth a listen too.

When *On The Shore* also failed to sell, and a support slot for the Byrds in America fell through at the eleventh hour, Costa, Brown and Boshell decided to leave the band. They were replaced by Robbie Hewlett (bs) and Pete Clarke (drms - ex-**Liverpool Scene**), but things fell apart in May 1971. Hewlett then went on to **Parrish and Gurvitz** and Clarke to **Stealer's Wheel**. The following November, Humphris and Clarke put together a new line-up with Chuck Fleming (ex-**JSD Band**), Barry Lyons and Alun Eden (both ex-**Pisces**), but this too was short-lived. In 1972, the band members backed **Phil Trainer** on an album he recorded for BASF.

Clarke was subsequently a session player and played with Vigrass and Osbourne. He and David Costa were also in **Casablanca**. Eden joined **Matthew Ellis** and together with Lyons later played with **Mr. Fox**; Unwin Brown achieved some success in Japan with **Capricorn**; Lyons went onto Spencer's Feet and Five Hand Reel; whilst Fleming later rejoined the **J.S.D Band**. Celia Humphris married Radio 1 DJ Pete Drummond.

In their heyday **Trees** are known to have recorded various other songs of Boshell's, as well as the theme for a TV sitcom pilot called '13a Adam & Eve Mews', a part-reggae, cross-rhythmic version of *Gipsy Davey* and another version of *The Great Silkie* that was more in keeping with their live rendition. Where any of these recordings are now, or indeed if they're still in existence, is unknown.

The Garden Of Jane Delawney was included on CBS's budget-priced (2-LP) compilation *Fill Your Head With Rock*, in 1970, whilst *Fool* from *On The Shore* got further exposure on *Together!* (LP). By accident, a totally different version of *Polly On The Shore* was included on the CBS sampler *Rockbuster* (LP). *Little Black Cloud* appears on *The History Of U.K. Underground Folk Rock 1968-1978 Vol. 1* (CD). (VJ/JM/RMJ)

The Treetops

45s:			
	Don't Worry Baby/I Remember	(Parlophone R 5628)	1967
	California My Way/Carry On Living	(Parlophone R 5669)	1968
	Mississippi Valley/Man Is A Man	(Columbia DB 8727)	1970
	Without The One You Love/		
	So Here I Go Again	(Columbia DB 8799)	1971
	Why Not Tonite/Funky Flop Out	(Columbia DB 8934)	1972
	Gypsy/Life Is Getting Better	(Columbia DB 9013)	1973

There was also a Jamican band of this name. This UK outfit were pop-orientated and sang high-pitched folk-beat compositions. Their first 'A' side, *Don't Worry Baby*, was a Beach Boys song. (VJ)

The Trekkas

Personnel:	RON BAIRD	bs	A
	MICK CASEY	ld gtr	A
	KEN CAYLOR	drms	A
	MARTYN DAY	gtr	A
	ANGELA PENKETH	keyb'ds	A
	MICK SIMMONS	ld vcls	A

45:			
	Please Go/I Put A Spell On You	(Planet PLF 105)	1966 R2

This is now quite a rare and sought-after single which was produced by Shel Talmy. The 'A' side is R&B, whilst the flip is a more punkish cover of

the Screamin' Jay Hawkins' classic. Based in and around Welwyn Garden City, most of the group were still at school when they recorded the 45, and they quickly found themselves supporting such artists as **The Who, The Small Faces, Zoot Money, Manfred Mann, Amen Corner**, Wilson Pickett and even **Elton John** when he was still Reg Dwight.

Please Go is reputed to have made No. 45 in the Radio London Fab 50. It later resurfaced on *The Best Of Planet Records* (CD).

The Tremeloes

Personnel:	ALAN BLAKELY	gtr, vcls keyb'ds	AB
	MICK CLARK	bs	A
	DAVE MUNDEN	drms	ABC
	RICKY WEST (WESTWOOD)	gtr	ABC
	LEN 'CHIP' HAWKES	bs, vcls	B
	AARON WOOLLEY		C
	BOB BENHAM		C

				HCP
ALBUMS:	1(B)	HERE COMES THE TREMELOES	(CBS (S)BPG 63017) 1967 SC	15
(up to	2(B)	SUDDENLY YOU LOVE ME		
1976)			(CBS (S)BPG 63138) 1967 SC	-
	3(B)	58/60 WORLD EXPLOSION	(CBS 26388) 1968	-
	4(B)	LIVE IN CABARET	(CBS 63547) 1969 SC	-
	5(B)	GREATEST HITS	(CBS 64206) 1970	-
	6(B)	MASTER	(CBS 64242) 1970 SC	-
	7(B)	REACH OUT FOR THE TREMELOES		
			(Embassy 31031) 1973	-
	8(B)	SHINER	(DJM DJLP 5441) 1974	-
	9(B)	SILENCE IS GOLDEN	(Embassy 31206) 1975	-
	10(C)	DON'T LET THE MUSIC DIE	(DJM DJF 20447) 1976	-

NB: (2) reissued on Repertoire (REP 4319-WY) 1993 with several bonus cuts. (6) reissued as *Master Plus* (Sequel NEMCD 470) 2000 with several bonus tracks. (3) had a US release on Epic (26388).

Compilations have included: - *The Best Of The Tremeloes* (Rhino R2 70528) 1992; *16 Greatest Hits* (CD) (BR Music BRCD 3) 1988; *Silence Is Golden* (CD) (Laserlight 15 067) 1992; *Silence Is Golden* (Spectrum 55074-2) 1995; and *Tremendous Hits* (Music Club MCCD 393) 1997. *The Very Best Of The Tremeloes* (Recall/Snapper) 1997 is a good value 2-CD set. *The Definitive Collection* (Castle CCS CD 827) 1998 is a 26-track hits collection. *Boxed* (BR Music Box 1011 2) 2000 is a 4-CD set available as a Dutch import. *Here Comes The Tremeloes (Complete 67 Sessions)* (Sequel NEMCD 468) 2000 is a 30-track CD coupling (1) and (2) together with 'B' sides and a previously unissued track. *Good Day Sunshine: Singles A's & B's* (Sequel NEECD 337) 2000 is a 2-CD collection. *May Morning* (Castle CMRCD 025) 2000 is a previously unreleased 1970 Soundtrack. *What A State I'm In: The Psych-Pop Sessions* (Castle Music CMRCD 637) 2003 is an anthology, which shows their pop-psych side. *BBC Sessions* (Castle CMEDD 939) 2004 compiles material from performances on 'Saturday Club', Happening Sunday' and 'The Jimmy Young Show' between August 1966-September 1969. *Greatest Hits* (CD) (Select SELCD 501) includes all their best 45s. *Here Comes My Baby: The Ultimate Collection* (3-CD) (Sanctuary Midline SMETCD 139) is their biggest retrospective covering from 1966 to the early eighties and includes all their hit 45s from *Here Comes My Baby* to *Hello Buddy*.

EP:	1	MY LITTLE LADY	(CBS EP 6402) 1968 SC

				HCP
45s:		Blessed/The Right Time	(Decca F 12423) 1966 SC	-
(up to		Good Day Sunshine/What A State I'm In	(CBS 202242) 1966	-
1976)		Here Comes My Baby/		
		Gentlemen Of Pleasure	(CBS 202519) 1967	4
		Silence Is Golden/		
		Let Your Hair Hang Down (PS)	(CBS 2723) 1967	1
		Hellule Hellule/Girl From Nowhere	(CBS 2889) 1967	14
		Even The Bad Times Are Good/		
		Jenny's Alright (PS)	(CBS 2930) 1967	4
		Be Mine/Suddenly Winter	(CBS 3043) 1967	39
		Suddenly You Love Me/As You Are	(CBS 3234) 1968	6
		My Little Lady/All The World To Me	(CBS 3680) 1968	6
		I Shall Be Released/I Miss My Baby	(CBS 3873) 1968	29
		Hello World/Up Down All Round	(CBS 4065) 1969	14
		Once On A Sunday Morning/		
		Fa La La, La La, La La	(CBS 4313) 1969	-
		(Call Me) Number One/Instant Whip	(CBS 4582) 1969	2
		By The Way/Break Heart Motel	(CBS 4815) 1970	35

THE TREMELOES.

	Me And My Life/Try Me	(CBS 5139) 1970	4
	Right Wheel, Left Hammer, Sham/		
	Take It Easy	(CBS 5429) 1971	-
	Hello Buddy/My Woman	(CBS 7294) 1971	32
	Too Late To Be Saved/If You Ever	(CBS 7579) 1971	-
	I Like It That Way/Wakamaker	(CBS 8048) 1972	-
	Blue Suede Tie/Yodel Ay	(Epic EPC 1019) 1973	-
	Ride On/Hands Off	(Epic EPC 1399) 1973	-
β	Make Or Break / Movin' On	(Epic EPC 1660) 1973	-
	Do I Love You / Witchcraft	(Epic S EPC 2047) 1974	-
	Good Time Band/Hard Woman	(DJM DJS 10336) 1974	-
	Someone Someone/My Friend Delaney	(DJM DJS 10348) 1975	-
	Be Boopin' Boogie/Ascot Cowboys	(DJM DJS 10406) 1975	-

Reissues: Here Comes My Baby/

Silence Is Golden (PS)	(CBS 1139) 1973	-
Silence Is Golden/Here Comes My Baby	(Epic 152265) 1975	-
Silence Is Golden/Here Comes My Baby	(CBS 5010) 1977	-
Silence Is Golden/Here Comes My Baby	(CBS 5965) 1978	-
Silence Is Golden/Here Comes My Baby	(CBS 7072) 1979	-
Silence Is Golden/		
Here Comes My Baby	(Old Gold OG 9200) 1982	-
Silence Is Golden/		
Even The Bad Times Are Good	(CBS A 4577) 1984	-
Silence Is Golden/The Last Word	(Meteor MTS 2) 1984	-
Here Comes My Baby/Me And My Life/		
Silence Is Golden	(Scoop 33 SR 75034) 1984	-

α Silence Is Golden/Silence
Is Golden (different version) (PS)   (Mojo MOJ 109770) 1984 -

NB: β Credited to The Trems. α Also released in 12" format. Some European 45s included: *You Can't Touch Sue / Story For The Boys* (Epic EPC 1972) 1972 (Germany & Holland Only) and *Say O.K. / Pinky* (Telefunken 6.11501 (AC)) 1974 (Germany Only).

The Tremeloes were originally Tommy Steele's and then **Brian Poole**'s backing band. At the start of 1966, **Poole** left to go solo and the **Trems** branched out on their own. Within a few months, **Poole** was back in the family butchers shop in Dagenham but **The Tremeloes** blossomed with a series of mostly bright and breezy pop songs, registering seven Top Ten hits between 1967 and 1970.

After *Blessed*, their debut 45 flopped, they switched to CBS. They didn't fare much better with their cover of **Lennon/McCartney**'s *Good Day Sunshine* (from **The Beatles**' *Revolver* album), but after Mick Clark left, his replacement, Len 'Chip' Hawkes, helped to develop a more distinct harmony vocal style that brought the band success.

Their big breakthrough came with their happy-go-lucky rendition of **Cat Stevens**' *Here Comes My Baby*. This catchy pop song got to No 4 in the UK and No 13 in the US and, in my view, was the best thing they did. The follow-up, a cover of a Four Seasons' 'B' side, *Silence Is Golden*, was a tortuous harmony ballad but sold like wildfire to become the band's best-selling single, topping the UK Charts for three weeks. It eventually climbed to No 11 in the US, where it became a million-seller. Its constant reissue throughout the early seventies meant we were seldom spared from hearing it for long. Their debut album, *Here Comes The Tremeloes* (it was titled *Here Comes My Baby* in the US) also sold well, although it was their only album that did, climbing to No 15 in the UK and No 119 in the US.

After the Latin-tinged *Helule Helule* stalled at No 14, they made the UK Top Five with the uptempo *Even The Bad Times Are Good*, which was very much in the happy-go-lucky style of *Here Comes My Baby*. The less commercial ballad, *Be Mine*, was a minor hit (tucked away on the flip side is *Suddenly Winter* - a song which exuded the flower-power era with waves of backwards guitar and appealing background harmonies) and then they returned to good-time harmony-pop to enjoy further Top Ten hits with *Suddenly You Love Me* and *My Little Lady*. Their final disc of 1968 did denote a change of style - a version of Bob Dylan's *I Shall Be Released*. It just made the Top 30.

They enjoyed further commercial success with *(Call Me) Number One* and *My And My Life*, but with the onset of the seventies, the emergence of several new teen acts made them seem distinctly unexciting. Perhaps the band sensed this; they dismissed their earlier work as "rubbish" in the early seventies and tried to win over rock audiences with their *Master* album, which predictably passed largely unnoticed. When this didn't work, they took refuge in the cabaret and the Northern club circuit.

Les Hawkes left in November 1974 to launch a solo country career with little success. Alan Blakely followed in January 1975 and Aaron Woolley and Bob Benham came in as replacements.

In the mid-seventies **The Tremeloes** (still featuring original members Dave Munden and Rick West) joined **The Searchers** and a few other surviving sixties bands on the cabaret circuit. They continued to record for DJM, Pye and Polydor and also recorded briefly for CBS in the early eighties. Munden and West were still involved in line-ups in the late nineties and the band remains active in the 21st century.

Tremendous Hits is a budget-priced 20-track collection complete with commentary by singer Chip Hawkes.

Boxed is a 4-CD box set available as a Dutch import. It includes a selection of hits, obscure 'B' sides, album cuts, solo and unissued tracks as well as foreign language recordings and yes their original version of *Yellow River* (later a hit for **Christie**).

Here Comes The Tremeloes (Complete 1967 Sessions) is a 30-track CD compiling their first two albums along with 'B' sides and a previously unissued track. Included here are massive hits like *Silence Is Golden*, *Here Comes My Baby* and *Even The Bad Times Are Good* plus some overlooked psychedelic-pop jewels.

Good Day Sunshine: Singles A's & B's is a 2-CD set that includes all of their singles except for their unsuccessful debut *Blessed* recorded for Decca before they switched to CBS. It also includes the Spanish-only *No Comprehende* (better-known to UK listeners as *Yellow River*, which **The Tremeloes** recorded before **Christie**, who went on to enjoy a No. 1 with this).

May Morning was a previously unreleased 1970 Soundtrack to an Italian cult film starring **Jane Birkin**. It was all part of their campaign to disown their pop history and court underground audiences, but on the evidence of this you can see why it didn't work.

What A State I'm In: The Psych-Pop Sessions will delight fans of this genre. Listen out for the experimental *Suddenly Winter*, the fuzz guitar on *What A State I'm In*, the freakbeat number *Gentlemen Of Pleasure* and their later hit *(Call Me) Number One*.

BBC Sessions compiles the cream of their sessions for 'Saturday Club', 'Happening Sunday' and 'The Jimmy Young Show' between August 1966 and September 1969. Whilst they dabbled with psychedelia in the studio, their live appearances seemed to concentrate on soul covers (*Two Many Fish In The Sea* (The Marvelletes), *Walk Away Renee* (Lefte Banke), *Angel Of The Morning* and *If You Think You're Groovy* (P.P. Arnold), and *Ain't Nothing But A House Party* (Showstoppers)).

Compilation appearances have included: *Here Comes My Baby*, *Gentlemen Of Pleasure*, *Silence Is Golden* and *Let Your Hair Hang Down* on *Sixties Years, Vol. 5* (CD); *Silence Is Golden* on the 2-CD set *60 Number Ones Of The Sixties* and the 2-CD set *Stars And Stripes* ; *Here Comes My Baby* on *The Swinging Sixties - 18 Classic Tracks* (CD) and on *Hits Of The Swinging Sixties* (CD); *Even The Bad Times Are Good* on *60's Mix* (CD), *No 1s & Million Sellers Vol 4* (CD) and on the 2-CD set *We Love The Pirates: Charting The Big 'L' Fab 40*; *Suddenly You Love Me* on *Love Power* (CD); *I Shall Be Released* on *The Songs Of Bob Dylan* (CD); *Instant*

Whip on *Rock Of Ages, Four Decades Of Heavy Rock 1962-2002* (CD) and *Suddenly Winter* on *Haunted - Psychedelic Pstones, Vol 2* (CD). In addition, back in the late sixties if you saved up lots of Coronet Yogurt tops and gave them to your friendly United Dairies Milkman he would give you an EP called *Four You* (CBS Special Products WEP 1138A). This featured tracks by Simon and Garfunkel, Gary Puckett, Johnny Mathis and *Good Day Sunshine* by **The Tremeloes**. (VJ/MRi)

Trend

45:	Boyfriends And Girlfriends/		
	Shot On Sight	(Page One POF 044) 1967 SC	

This was a little-known band whose one-off disc is now quite collectable. (VJ)

The Trends

Personnel:	MIKE KELLY	bs	AB
	TONY PRIESTLY	lead gtr	A
	FREDDIE (SELF) RYDER	gtr, vcls	ABC
	JOHN HAYES	drms	ABC
	FRANK BOWEN	ld gtr	BC
	HARRY SCULLY	bs	C

45s:	All My Loving/		
	Sweet Little Miss Love	(Piccadilly 7N 35171) 1964 SC	
	You're A Wonderful One/The Way		
	You Do Those Things You Do	(Pye 7N 15644) 1964 SC	

The Trends were a Liverpudlian band but very much an 'also-ran'. Their debut disc was a **Beatles** song also recorded by the masters themselves, which inevitably led to unfavourable comparisons with the original. They were switched to Pye's main label and recorded two Tamla Motown songs, produced by Billy Fury, but when they flopped their contract was ended. **Freddie Ryder**, who'd earlier been with The Beatcombers, later went solo.

Priestly left the band in February 1964 to join **Earl Preston's Realms**. He was replaced by Frank Bowen (ex-Bootleggers). The same year, Kelly left and was replaced by Harry Scully (ex-Lee Shondell and The Boys). Frank Bowen also later left the band to join **Earl Royce and The Olympics**. He went to Germany in 1966 and later died of pneumonia.

Compilation appearances have included: *All My Loving* on *Mersey Beat* (2-LP); *You're A Wonderful One* on *Pop Inside The Sixties, Vol. 3* (CD); *You're A Wonderful One, The Way You Do The Things You Do* and *All My Loving* on *Some Other Guys* (2-LP); and *Sweet Little Miss Love* on *What About Us* (CD) and *Merseybeat Nuggets, Vol. 2* (CD). (VJ/AD/JM)

The Trendsetters

45:	You Don't Care/My Heart Goes	(Silver Phoenix 1001) 1964 R1

This beat 45 by a Liverpool band is now rare and quite sought-after, possibly only because it's a novel label. (VJ)

The Trendsetters

EP:	1	AT THE HOTEL DE FRANCE	(Oak RGJ 999) 196? R1

Despite the recent publicity given to this label this band doesn't figure on the recent *Story Of Oak Records* compilation and their origins and members remain a mystery. A Greg Vandike discovery, I'm told the EP is dreadful. (VJ)

Trendsetters Limited

Personnel:	ALLAN AZERN	perc	A
	TRAM BLAKESLEY	trombone	A
	MIKE GILES	drms, vcls	A
	PETE GILES	bs	A
	BRUCE TURNER	ld gtr	A

45s:	In A Big Way/Lucky Date	(Parlophone R 5118) 1964 SC
	Hello Josephine/Move On Over	(Parlophone R 5161) 1964 SC
	Lollipops And Roses/Go Away	(Parlophone R 5191) 1964
	You Sure Got A Funny Way Of Showing Love/	
	I'm Coming Home	(Parlophone R 5234) 1965

This mostly instrumental outfit from Bournemouth included a brass section and often backed visiting American soul artists. They were the Giles brothers' first group. In August 1967, they linked up with Robert Fripp to form **Giles, Giles and Fripp**, who by January 1969 had evolved into **King Crimson**.

Turner went on to join **The Loot**. (VJ/JM)

Jackie Trent

ALBUMS:	1	THE MAGIC OF JACKIE TRENT	
(up to			(Pye NPL 18125) 1965 SC
1976)	2	ONCE MORE WITH FEELING	(Pye NPL 18173) 1967 SC
	3	STOP ME AND BUY ONE	(Pye NPL 18201) 1967 SC
	4	THE BEST OF JACKIE TRENT	(Pye) 1973
	5	GOLDEN HOUR OF JACKIE TRENT	
		ANDS TONY HATCH	(Pye) 1976

NB: Also relevant is *Golden Hour of Jackie Trent* (Knight KGHCD 120) 1990.

EP:	1	WHERE ARE YOU NOW	(Pye NEP 4225) 1965 SC

HCP

45s:	Pick Up The Pieces/In Your Heart	(Oriole CB 1711) 1961 -
(up to	The One Who Really Loves You/	
1976)	Your Conscience Or Your Heart	(Oriole CB 1749) 1962 SC
	Melancholy Me/So Did I	(Piccadilly 7N 35121) 1963 -
	If You Love Me/	
	Only One Such As You	(Piccadilly 7N 35165) 1964 SC -
	Autumn Leaves/Too Late	(Pye 7N 15649) 1964 -
	Somewhere In The World/	
	I Heard Somebody Say	(Pye 7N 15692) 1964 -
	Don't Stand In My Way/How Soon	(Pye 7N 15742) 1964 -
	Where Are You Now (My Love)/	
	On The Other Side Of The Tracks	(Pye 7N 15776) 1965 1
	When Summertime Is Over/	
	To Show I Love Him	(Pye 7N 15865) 1965 39
	It's All In The Way You Look At Life/	
	Time After Time	(Pye 7N 15949) 1965 -
	You Baby/Send Her Away	(Pye 7N 17047) 1966 SC -
	Love Is Me Love Is You/This Time	(Pye 7N 17082) 1966 -
	If You Ever Leave Me/There Goes My Love,	
	There Goes My Life	(Pye 7N 17158) 1966 -
	Open Your Heart/Love Can Give	(Pye 7N 17249) 1967 -
	Humming Bird/I'll Be With You	(Pye 7N 17286) 1967 -
	Your Love Is Everywhere/	
	It's Not Easy Loving You	(Pye 7N 17323) 1967 -
	That's You/Stop Me And Buy One	(Pye 7N 17415) 1967 -
	Bye Bye Love (German Version)/	
	Alles Okay (Send Her Away)	(Pye 7N 17437) 1967 -
	Hollywood/7.10 From Suburbia	(Pye 7N 17623) 1968 -
	I'll Be There/Close To You	(Pye 7N 17693) 1969 -
	Look At The Rain/When The City Sleeps	(Pye 7N 17882) 1970 -
	I'll Be Near You/Someone For Me	(Pye 7N 17918) 1970 -
	Come Home My Love/I'm Gonna Build My	
	World Around You	(Pye 7N 45347) 1974 -
	Send In The Clowns/	
	Warmth Of Our Love	(Pye 7N 45475) 1975 -
α	Can't Give It Up/Did I Say I Love You?	(Pye 7N 45536) 1975 -
Reissues:	Pick Up The Pieces/In Your Heart	(CBS 201776) 1965 -
	Where Are You Now (My Love)?/	
	(other side by different artist)	(Old Gold OG 9138) 1982 -

NB: α recorded with The Majestics.

Jackie Trent was born in Newcastle-under-Lyme in Staffordshire on 6 September 1940. She started singing in local bands when she was 13 and turned professional at 17. She toured Europe and the Middle East and played in cabaret before recording two 45s for Oriole in the early sixties. After successfully auditioning for Pye producer Tony Hatch the singer/

T. REX - T. Rex (CD).

songwriter recorded quite prolifically for Pye in the sixties, when in addition to the singles listed above she recorded a number of others with Tony Hatch, who became her songwriting partner and husband. Most of her efforts were middle-of-the-road and her finest moment was her 1965 No 1 *Where Are You Now (My Love)?* This knocked **The Beatles'** *Ticket To Ride* off the top.

Trent and Hatch also wrote a number of hits for Petula Clarke in the late sixties (Hatch was Clarke's producer too). These included: *Don't Sleep In The Subway, I Couldn't Live Without Your Love, Colour My World, My Love* and *The Other Man's Grass*. They also wrote **Scott Walker'**s 1968 hit *Joanna*.

After **Trent** married Hatch in 1967 they formed a double act for cabaret and gradually moved into the media and stage. She starred in the 1970 musical 'Nell' as Nell Gwynne (which Hatch co-produced and was the music director for) and in 1972 they wrote the score for Cameron Mackintosh's 'The Card'. Another project 'Rock Nativity' flopped in 1974.

They relocated predominantly to Australia in 1982 and in 1986 penned the theme song to the mega-soap opera 'Neighbours'. They have also composed numerous UK TV themes. *Where Are You Now (My Love)?* can be found on various sixties compilations. (VJ)

T Rex

Personnel:

MARC BOLAN	gtr, vcls	ABCDEF
STEVE CURRIE	bs	ABCDE
MICKEY FINN	bongos, vcls	ABCD
BILL LEGEND	drms	AB
JACK GREEN	gtr	BCD
GLORIA JONES	keyb'ds, vcls	CDE
DAVE LUTTON	drms	CDE
DINO DINES	keyb'ds	DE
MILLER ANDERSON	gtr	F
HERBIE FLOWERS	bs	F
TONY NEWMAN	drms	F

				HCP
ALBUMS:	1(A)	T REX	(Fly HIFLY 2) 1970	13
	2(B)	THE BEST OF T REX (Compilation)		
			(Fly TON 2) 1971	21
	3(B)	ELECTRIC WARRIOR	(Fly HIFLY 6) 1971	1
	4(B)	BOLAN BOOGIE	(Fly HIFLY 8) 1972	1
	5(-)	RIDE A WHITE SWAN (Compilation)		
			(Music for Pleasure MFP 5274) 1972	-
	6(C)	THE SLIDER	(EMI BLN 5001) 1972	4
	7(C)	TANX	(EMI BLN 5002) 1973	4
	8(D)	T REX GREAT HITS	(EMI BLN 5003) 1973	32
	9(D)	ZINC ALLOY AND THE HIDDEN RIDERS OF		
		TOMORROW	(EMI BLNA 7751) 1974	12
	10(-)	GET IT ON (Compilation)		
			(Sound Superb SPR 90059) 1974	-
	11(D)	BOLAN'S ZIP GUN	(EMI BLNA 7752) 1975	SC -
	12(E)	FUTURISTIC DRAGON	(EMI BLN 5004) 1976	50
	13(F)	DANDY IN THE UNDERWORLD	(EMI BLN 5005) 1977	26

NB: (1) reissued on CD (Castle Classic CLACD 287) 1992 and again on CD in an expanded edition (Universal 982 251-3) 2004. (3) reissued on CD (Castle Classic CLACD 180) 1990. (4) reissued on CD (Castle Classics CLACD 145) 1989. (6) reissued on vinyl (Edsel EDLP 390) 1997 and on CD (Edsel EDCD 390) 1997. (6), (7), (9), (11), (12) and (13) reissued on *Marc On Wax* (MARCL 503-508) respectively in 1989, also on CD. (6) reissued with bonus tracks in 1995 as part of a double package, *The Slider/Rabbit Fighter - The Alternative Slider* (Edsel REXLUX 1010) 1995. The second disc comprised out-takes and the whole package, which came in a deluxe fold-out sleeve, was only available by mail order and from Virgin stores.

Compilations have included (on vinyl and CD):- *The Singles Collection, Vol. 1* (Marc On Wax MARCD 510) 1986, *Vol. 2* (Marc On Wax MARCD 511) 1986 and *Vol. 3* (Marc On Wax MARCD 512) 1986; *The Very Best Of Marc Bolan And T Rex* (Music Club MCCD 030) 1991, which compiles material from the EMI years between 1972 and 1977; *Anthology* (Essential ESBCD 965) 1991, a 3-CD set charting his career from 1968 until his death in 1977. Discs two and three cover the **T Rex** years; *Born To Boogie* (Marc On Wax MARC LP 514, also on CD) 1991, a live recording from their March 1972 Empire Pool Wembley gig, The album comes with a 16-page photo booklet but the CD and cassette versions don't; *The Early Years* (Dojo EARL D 1) 1992, a very pointless compilation of material from 1970-71 which duplicates material already reissued; *Collection: T Rex* (Castle Collector 138) 1988; *Great Hits* (SMS Inc MD 32 5018) 1988; *Greatest Hits: T Rex* (Sierra CDTR 1) 1987; *Nightriding: T Rex* (Knight KNCD 10003) 1989; *Teenage Dream* (Pickwick PWK 040) 1987; Credited to Marc Bolan and T Rex *Great Hits 1972-77: The A-Sides* (Edsel EDCD 401) 1994; *Great Hits 1972-77: The B-Sides* (Edsel EDCD 402) 1994; and *Rabbit Fighter (The Alternative Slider)* (Edsel EDCD 403) 1994, an alternative version of *The Slider* compiled from demos and working tapes; Also credited to Marc Bolan and T Rex is *Messing With The Mystics* (Edsel EDCD 404) 1994, which was compiled from previously unissued songs. Really one for his fans only, it includes a vocal version of the previously instrumental-only *Bolan's Zip Gun (Theme For A Dragon)*; *Dirtysweet Volume Two* (Edsel FELD 2) 1994 was available only through Virgin Record stores. It includes a track each from *Rabbit Fighter* and *Messing With The Mystic*, along with many of their better known songs.

1995 saw the release of *Change (The Alternative Zinc Alloy)* (Edsel EDCD 440), which basically consists of 14 different versions of every song on the original album compiled from demos and out-takes plus five additional alternate versions; and *Unchained: Unreleased Recordings Volume 3: 1973 Part 1* (Edsel EDCD 441) and *Unchained: Unreleased Recordings Volume 4: 1973 Part 2* (Edsel EDCD 442) both compile unreleased songs from 1973. *A BBC History* (Band Of Joy BOJCD 016) 1995 compiles the material that has survived **Bolan'**s numerous sessions at the BBC chronologically beginning with his days with **Tyrannosaurus Rex** and it also features a sleeve note from John Peel. *Dazzling Raiment - The Alternative Futurist Dragon* (Edsel EDCD 522) 1997 contains 20 tracks of work-in-progress or demo versions of songs that eventually became *The Futurist Dragon* album including an alternate take of their *New York City* single. *Precious Star: The Alternate Bolan's Zip Gun* (Edsel EDCD 443) 1996 attempts to provide an insiders look at his *Bolan's Zip Gun* album of 1975. The bonus tracks includes covers of *Do You Wanna Dance?* and *Dock Of The Bay*. *Unchained: Unreleased Recordings Vol. 5: 1974* (Edsel EDCD 444) 1996, *Unchained: Unreleased Recordings Vol. 6: 1975* (Edsel EDCD 445) 1996, *Unchained: Unreleased Recordings Vol. 6: 1976 and 1977* (Edsel EDCD 523) 1997 continue the compilation series of previously unheard completed songs, interesting demos and rare outtakes from 1976 and 1977. *Unchained: Unreleased Recordings, Vol. 7* (Edsel EDCD 524) 1997 contains songs intended for his so-called opera at the end of 1975, as well as three unreleased cuts from 1977:- *Shy Boy, Love Drunk*

T. REX - Electric Warrior (LP).

and *Mellow Love* and six solo home recordings from 1976/77. *Unchained: Unreleased Recordings, Vol. 8* (Edsel EDCD 525) 1997 concludes this series with 35 tracks several of which also feature his then girlfriend Gloria Jones. If you want an introduction to this series there's *The Best Of The Unchained Series: Unreleased Recordings* (Edsel NESTCD 907) 1997.

The Best Of Marc Bolan And T. Rex 1972-77 (Edsel MEDCD 536) 1997 is another good introduction to their material and *Electric Boogie* (New Millennium Communications PILOT 13) 1997 includes material from their 1971 Electric Warrior tour. *The BBC Recordings 1970-1976* (New Millennium Communcations PILOT 17) 1997 is a 2-CD set. *Spaceball* (New Millenium Communications PILOT 21) 1997 is a 2-CD set which compiles his recordings for American radio between April 1971 and September 1972 when he was desperately trying to make it in the States. *Bump'n'Grind* (Thunderwing TEC 24004) 2000 contains rare and unreleased studio out-takes, demos and extended master recordings culled from sessions between 1972 and 1976. *Solid Gold* (Repertoire) 1999 is a 20-track import covering from 1972 to 1977. *Live At The Boston Gliderdrome 1972* (Diamondstar Productions LATBG 02) 2001 suffers from ropey sound quality. *Universal Love - A Tribute To Marc Bolan & T. Rex* (Egg Toss ETCY 1001) 2002 is a compilation of various artists performing **T Rex** songs, which are not a patch on the originals. *Boogie On* (Burning Airlines PILOT 147) 2002 is a 2-CD compilation of material, which is all available elsewhere. It does, however, include an US radio session from February 1972 containing an acoustic selection of songs from *Electric Warrior* and *The Slider*. *The Slider/Rabbit Fighter* (Edsel MEDCD 715) 2002 is a 2-CD digipak reissue of these two albums plus relevant singles and flip sides as bonuses. *Futuristic Dragon/Dazzling Rainment* (Edsel MEDCD 719) 2002 is a further 2-CD digipak release in the same vein. *Home Recordings - There Was A Time/Electric Warrior* (The Bolan Society no cat no) 2002 features acoustic demos from early 1971, including *Jeepster*, *Get It On* and *Electric Warrior* (then unreleased). *Wax Co. Singles Volume 1 (1972-1974)* (Edsel MARCBOX 101) 2002 is an 11-CD box set, as is *Wax Co. Singles Volume 2 (1975-1978)* 2002. *The T. Rex Wax Co. Singles As and Bs 1972-77* (Edsel MEDCD 714) 2002 is a 2-CD set but it doesn't include their four hits that appeared on Fly prior to **Bolan** forming his own label. *Home Recordings - Tanx* (The Bolan Society no cat no) 2002 contains material recorded in the summer of 1972 and *25th Anniversary Commemorative 1972 Interview* (The Bolan Society no cat no) 2002 is a previously unreleased interview disc. *20th Century Superstar* (Universal/A&M 493 452-2) 2002 is a definitive 4-CD box set. *The Tanx Recordings* (Thunderwing TPLCD 03) 2004 reveals the studio recordings for the 1973 *Tanx* album. *Bump And Grind* (Thunderwing TPLCD 4) 2004 comprises sessions from the 1972 to 1976 period. It was previously available as a Japanese import (Imperial TECI-24004) 2000. *Born To Boogie* (Sanctuary SMEDD 215) 2005 is a 2-CD reissue of a **Ringo Starr** documentary, which captured T. Rex live in their prime during 1972.

T. REX - Tanx (CD).

		HCP
EPs:	1 BOLAN'S BEST PLUS ONE (Ride A White Swan/The Motivator/Jeepster/ Demon Queen)	(Cube ANT 1) 1977 --
	2 RETURN OF THE ELECTRIC WARRIOR	(Rarn MBSF 0001) 1981 50

			HCP
45s:	α	Ride A White Swan/ Is It Love/Summertime Blues (PS)	(Fly BUG 1) 1970 2
		Hot Love/Woodland Rock/ King Of The Mountain Cometh	(Fly BUG 6) 1971 1
		Get It On/There Was A Time/Raw Ramp	(Fly BUG 10) 1971 1
	β	Jeepster/Life's A Gas	(Fly GRUB 1A) 1971 -

T. Rex - The Slider (CD).

Jeepster/Life's A Gas	(Fly BUG 16) 1971 2	
Telegram Sam/ Cadilac/Baby Strange	(T Rex Wax Co T REX 101) 1972 1	
Metal Guru/Thunderwing/Lady	(T Rex Wax Co MARC 1) 1972 1	
Children Of The Revolution/ Jitterbug Love/Sunken Rags	(T Rex Wax Co MARC 2) 1972 2	
Solid Gold Easy Action/ Born To Boogie	(T Rex Wax Co MARC 3) 1972 2	
χ Solid Gold Easy Action/ (Fifth Dimension track)	(T Rex Wax Co MARC 3) 1972 -	
χ Solid Gold Easy Action/ (Partridge Family track)	(T Rex Wax Co MARC 3) 1972 -	
δ Christmas Time//Wanna Spend My Christmas With You Christmas/Everybody Knows It's Christmas	(Fan Club) 1972 -	
20th Century Boy/Free Angel	(T Rex Wax Co MARC 4) 1973 3	
The Groover/Midnight	(T Rex Wax Co MARC 5) 1973 4	
Truck On (Tyke)/Sitting Here	(T Rex Wax Co MARC 6) 1973 12	
ε Teenage Dream/ Satisfaction Pony	(T Rex Wax Co MARC 7) 1974 13	
Light Of Love/ Explosive Mouth	(T Rex Wax Co MARC 8) 1974 22	
Zip Gun Boogie/Space Boss	(T Rex Wax Co MARC 9) 1974 41	
New York City/Chrome Sitar	(T Rex Wax Co MARC 10) 1975 15	
Dreamy Lady//Do You Wanna Dance? Dock Of The Bay	(T Rex Wax Co MARC 11) 1975 30	
χ Christmas Bop/ Telegram Sam/Metal Guru	(T Rex Wax Co MARC 12) 1975 -	
London Boys/Solid Baby	(T Rex Wax Co MARC 13) 1976 40	
Hot Love/Get It On	(Cube BUG 66) 1976 -	
I Love To Boogie/ Baby Boomerang	(T Rex Wax Co MARC 14) 1976 13	
Laser Love/ Life's An Elevator	(T Rex Wax Co MARC 15) 1976 41	
The Soul Of My Suit/ All Alone	(T Rex Wax Co MARC 16) 1977 42	
Dandy In The Underworld//Groove A Little Tame My Tiger (PS)	(T Rex Wax Co MARC 17) 1977 -	
Celebrate Summer/ Ride My Wheels (PS)	(T Rex Wax Co MARC 18) 1977 -	
Crimson Moon/ Jason B Sad (PS)	(T Rex Wax Co MARC 19) 197? -	
Reissues: Hot Love/Raw Ramp/ Lean Woman Blues (PS)	(Cube ANT 2) 1978 -	
Hot Love/Ride A White Swan	(Old Gold OG 9229) 1982 -	
Get It On/Jeepster	(Old Gold OG 9230) 1982 -	
20th Century Boy/Dreamy Lady/The Groover/ New York City (PS)	(EMI MARC 21) 1982 -	
Children Of The Revolution/I Love To Boogie/Solid Gold Easy Action/London Boys	(EMI MARC 20) 1982 -	
Children Of The Revolution/Jitterbug Love/ Sunken Rags	(EMI MARC 22) 1982 -	
Mellow Love/Foxy Boy/ Lunacy's Back (PS)	(Marc On Wax SBOLAN 13) 1982 -	

Jeepster/Get It On (PS)	(Cube BUG 90) 1983 -

Metal Guru/
Children Of The Revolution	(Old Gold OG 9505) 1985 -
Telegram Sam/I Love To Boogie	(Old Gold OG 9506) 1985 -
Solid Gold Easy Action/Groover	(Old Gold OG 9507) 1985 -

Get It On/There Was A Time/Raw Ramp/
Electric Boogie	(T Rex FED 12) 1985 -

Megarex 1/Chariot Choogie/
Life's An Elevator	(Marc On Wax TANX 1) 1985 72

Get It On/
Jeepster (remix) (PS)	(Marc On Wax MARC 10) 1987 54

I Love To Boogie/Hot Love/
Ride A White Swan (PS)	(Marc On Wax MARC 11) 1987 -
φ T Rex (EP) (Hot Love/Get It On/Telegram Sam/	
Metal Guru)	(Castle Special Edition CD3-13) 1988 -
γ Telegram Sam/Metal Guru/	
Children Of The Revolution	(Old Gold OG 6130) 1989 -
γ Solid Gold Easy Action/20th Century Boy/	
The Groover	(Old Gold OG 6134) 1989 -
γ 20th Century Boy/Dreamy Lady/The Groover/	
New York City	(Total CDMARC 501) 1992 13
γ Metal Guru / Thunderwing/Lady	(Total CDMARC 502) 1992 -

NB: There was an earlier unreleased version of α *Ride A White Swan/Summertime Blues/Jewel* (Octopus OCTO 1) 1970. Octopus was a working title for the record company that became Fly by the time the 45 was released with *Is It Love* substituted for *Jewel*. The two surviving copies with the OCTO 1 stamped in the run-off groove are worth circa £2,500. Some copies of β got out with GRUB 1A on the label and these are rarer. χ Mispressing. δ Fan club flexidiscs with letter in brown envelope. ε Credited to Marc Bolan and T Rex. φ issued on 12" and shaped picture discs. γ CD singles.

T Rex was one of the top UK pop/rock acts of the early seventies and at the forefront of glam-rock.

It was in October 1970, after Tony Visconti, his producer, shifted the label outlet for his productions from Regal Zonophone to Fly, that Visconti also persuaded **Marc Bolan** to abbreviate **Tyrannosaurus Rex**'s name to **T Rex**. The first **T Rex** 45, *Ride A White Swan*, was a pop song with immediate appeal. It was actually recorded by the final **Tyrannosaurus Rex** line-up and to help promote it the band embarked on an Autumn tour for which they set maximum ticket prices at 50p and billed themselves as 'the last of the great underground groups'. Early releases of this first 45 came in several variations because Fly, as a new record company, took a while to settle on a standard design. Reputedly only three test pressings were made of the record originally and these bore the catalogue number OCTO 1 because Fly was originally going to be called Octopus. They also contained *Jewel*, rather than *Is It Love* with *Summertime Blues* on the flip side. They are now the rarest and most sought-after **T Rex** items. The first batch of the 45s on the Fly label came in a light purple label. These are more sought-after than the later copies, which came in a mustard-coloured label. In any event, the 45 proved very popular and peaked at No 2 in the UK Charts, in which it enjoyed a lengthy 20 week spell.

T. REX - Bolan's Zip Gun (CD).

Following the Autumn 1970 **Bolan** had also decided to augment the duo into a four-piece to give it a fuller sound. So in December 1970 he recruited bassist Steve Currie and drummer Bill Legend (whose real name was Fifield, although **Bolan** knew him as Legend because he was recruited from the Mickey Jupp band of the same name). This line-up promoted the *T Rex* album, which was released the same month and only included *Is It Love* from the single. It had also been recorded by the final **Tyrannosaurus Rex** line-up and included new versions of **Bolan**'s earlier 45, *The Wizard*, and of **Tyrannosaurus Rex**'s *One Inch Rock*. Whilst songs like *Suneye* and *The Visit* were in the previous band's style more electric numbers like *Jewel* and *Childe* pointed the way to the fuller **T Rex** sound. It also utilised the falsetto harmonies of former Turtles Howard Kaylan and Mark Volman for the first time, a device which was repeated effectively on *Hot Love*, their next 45 and the first recorded by the new four-piece. This topped the UK Charts for six weeks. Early copies appeared with mustard coloured labels and are more sought-after than later ones which came with a label design featuring a large fly on a black background with silver lettering. A Greek pressing on multi-coloured vinyl is now extremely sought-after by **T Rex** fanatics. The *Hot Love* 45 also creeped into the US Charts at No 72, where the **T Rex** album, which had peaked at No 13 in the UK where it had spent 6 months in the Charts, also edged to No 188.

It was their next 45, the blatantly commercial *Get It On*, which saw **Bolan** turn his back on the underground, and became his first million seller. In the US, where it was known as *Bang A Gong*, it was **T Rex**'s only sizeable hit. Their next album, *Electric Warrior*, marked the band's transformation into a fully fledged electric rock quartet. In the US the album was preceded by a couple of promotional items. *The Electric Warrior Interview* (Warner Bros PRO 511), which consisted of nearly half an hours conversation between **Bolan** and Michael Cascarina and *Bolan Alley*, which contained a short interview, some album cuts and covers of *Blue Suede Shoes* and *Honey Don't*. In the UK an *Electric Warrior Preview Single* was issued coupling *Jeepster* with *Life's A Gas*. Under 500 were pressed and distributed among friends and DJs, making it a hard item for collectors to track down. When **Bolan** decided to leave Fly, in November 1971, the label released *Jeepster* (from the *Electric Warrior* album) as an official 45 and it climbed to No 2, although **Bolan** had never intended it to be released as a 45. In December 1971 *Electric Warrior* topped the UK Album Charts and stayed there for six weeks.

On 1 January 1972 **Bolan** signed a new deal with EMI to release his records in the UK on his own T Rex Wax Co. label, although it didn't apply in the US where his records continued to be put out on Warner Brothers until 1974. His first 45 on the new label, *Telegram Sam*, (a tribute to his then manager Tony Secunda) a sorta hard-rock glam-rock number, marked the first in a series of songs in this vein which included *Metal Guru*, *Children Of The Revolution*, *Solid Gold Easy Action*, *20th Century Boy*, *The Groover* and *Truck On (Tyke)*.

T-Rextasy, as it was known, was now at its peak and in March 1972, **T Rex** played two sell-out concerts to audiences of 100,000 at the Empire Pool, Wembley, while being filmed by **Ringo Starr** for Apple's documentary film, 'Born To Boogie', which unveiled the group's success. To capitalise on this a double reissue of two **Tyrannosaurus Rex** albums:- *My People Were Fair* and *Prophets, Seers And Sages* was put out and topped the UK Album Charts, whilst a reissue single coupling *Debora* and *One Inch Rock* made the UK Top 10.

In May 1972, Fly put out the album *Bolan Boogie*, which compiled their hits to *Jeepster* and topped the UK Charts for 3 weeks. 50% of the material on it came from their earlier incarnation as **Tyrannosaurus Rex**. Their newly-recorded album, *The Slider* (which had provisionally been titled *Rabbit Fighter*), is said to have sold 100,000 copies in four days, although it lacked the staying power of *Electric Warrior*, only climbing to No 4 and only spending 18 weeks in the Charts. It included the popular *Spaceball Ricochet* but lacked the variety of the earlier album and its limited popularity was perhaps the first indication that the band's popularity would soon decline.

December 1972 saw another double reissue album of **Tyrannosaurus Rex**'s, *Unicorn* and *Beard Of Stars*, climb to No 44 in the Album Charts. It also saw the release of a "T Rex Christmas Record", which was given away free to fan club members and is now another **T Rex** collectable.

March 1973 saw the release of another new album, *Tanx*, which displayed a mellower, slicker sound. *Highway Knees* is generally considered to be the stand-out track but the album was conspicuous for the absence of any hit singles to help boost its sales. **David Bowie** reputedly appeared on the

1966 composition, *Mad Donna. The Groover*, issued in the Summer of 1973, became **T Rex**'s tenth and final UK Top Ten hit.

The Great Hits album was, as its name suggests, a compilation which contained the 'A' and 'B' sides of the previous five singles (except *Free Angel*) plus *Shock Rock* from the *Tanx* album. It came with a free poster but surprisingly, perhaps, only peaked at No 32 in the UK Album Charts.

Much of 1973 was spent touring and in July the group were augmented by three female backing singers. *Truck On (Tyke)*, which failed to make the Top Ten (peaking at No 12), was the last 45 in the old **T Rex** style but the first with additional guitarist Jack Green.

In September 1973 **Bolan** issued a single, *Blackjack/Squint Eyed Mangle*, as **Big Carrot** in his desire to promote a new image, but it made little impression.

In January 1974 Davy Lutton came in for Bill Legend on drums and Gloria Jones began to play keyboards on stage. Again in his desire to change, the next 45, *Teenage Dream*, was credited to **Marc Bolan and T Rex**, but it lacked any originality and could only peak at No 13. Later pressings of the 45 were simply credited to **Marc Bolan**.

After the *Zinc Alloy* album peaked at No 12 in March **Bolan** parted company with his long time producer Tony Visconti and much the worse for food, drink and drugs became a tax exile with his girlfriend Gloria Jones in Los Angeles and Monte Carlo. Whilst he was away Track Records released material he'd recorded as demos back in 1966 and 1967 on the *Beginning Of Doves* album and the *Jasper C Debussy* maxi-single but neither charted.

By the time of the *Light Of Love* 45 Jack Green had also left to be replaced by the keyboard duo of Dino Dines and Gloria Jones. This seemed to give their material a distinct US MOR feel. *Light Of Love* missed the Top 20 and the follow-up, *Zip Gun Boogie*, couldn't even make the Top 40. Both were included on the album, *Bolan's Zip Gun*, which sold badly, failed to chart and **Bolan** later admitted, was his worst recording.

In the short-term his fortunes improved and he re-entered the Charts with the *New York City* 45. This was followed by one of his better compositions, *Dreamy Lady*, which was credited to the T Rex Disco Party and included a version of *Dock Of The Bay* by Gloria Jones and a cover of *Do You Wanna Dance?*. This was recorded by line-up (E), **Mickey Finn** having split with **Bolan** by now, which had been augmented by organist Billy Preston on this recording.

In September 1975 Gloria and Marc had a son, Rolan, which inevitably meant any live commitments had to be put on hold for a while. His next projected release was the *Christmas Bop* 45, which was scheduled for a November release but later shelved. When in 1976 the *London Boys* 45 and *Futuristic Dragon* album did appear both were disappointing below par efforts. *Futuristic Dragon* was intended to be a concept album but the end result was far from clear. **David Bowie** is rumoured to have played sax on it though.

His final Top 20 UK hit was *I Love To Boogie*, which climbed to No 13 in the Summer of 1976. It had been recorded as a demo by a four-piece but feeling its simplicity would be infectious, **Bolan** rushed to release the song in this form, which paid off.

Laser Love, released in September 1976, gave the band a minor hit. The 'band' was by now made up of line-up (F). This line-up also embarked on a UK tour with The Damned as a support band.

In January 1977 **Bolan** released a duet with Gloria Jones. The 'A' side was a cover of The Teddy Bears' *To Know Him Is To Love Him*. The flip was a **Bolan** composition, *City Port*. The 45 flopped and its poor sales have helped ensure its subsequent collectability. Despite this failure Marc made a sustained attempt to re-establish himself and the latest **T Rex** album, *Dandy InThe Underworld*, was the best for three years. Although, when the title track was re-recorded for 45 release, it failed to chart as did the follow-up, *Celebrate Summer*. Nonetheless, he was beginning to branch out in his career. In August 1977 he began a stint as guest journalist, writing a column in 'Record Mirror' and hosted a series of six Wednesday afternoon UK TV shows, called "Marc".

It was on 16 September 1977 that tragedy struck, as most of you will know. After a late night at a London club with Gloria, their car, driven by Gloria, crashed into a tree at a bend on Barnes Common at 5 am in the morning. **Bolan** was killed and Jones suffered a fractured jaw and other injuries. At the time Marc was working on a new album provisionally titled *Jack Daniels*, and there were plans to record more "Marc" shows. Inevitably a plethora of repackaged and posthumous releases followed his death.

The BBC Recordings 1970-1976 comprises well known sessions they did for 'Top Gear' and 'Sound Of The Seventies'; this set adds later oddities like reworked versions of *Teenage Dream* and *New York City* and slightly different takes of other songs like *The Groover, Rock On* and *Children Of The Revolution*.

Bump'n'Grind contains rare and unreleased studio out-takes, demos and extended master recordings from the 1972 - 1976 period. Highlights include the 12-minute jam version of *Children of The Revolution* and the master recording of *20th Century Boy*. The 15-track package came with highly detailed sleevenotes and very good sound quality.

In 2002 all the band's singles from 1972-1978 were released in two 11-disc box sets. *Volume One* starts with *Telegram Sam* and ends with *Zip Gun Boogie*. It includes the rare *Big Carrot* single from 1973. *Volume Two* commences with *New York City* and closes with *Crimson Moon*. The unreleased 12" single *Christmas Bop* is included on this one. The discs are presented in card sleeves, which feature reproductions of Japanese, German, French or Scandinavian picture sleeves.

Edsel's 2002 release *The T. Rex Wax Co. Singles As and Bs 1972-77* is a 2-CD set, but unfortunately doesn't include the four 45s they released on Fly before **Bolan** set up his own label. So no *Jeepster* or *Get It On* for example. The chronological approach highlights the patchiness of some of

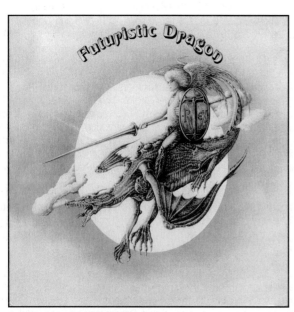

T. REX - Futuristic Dragon (CD).

T. REX - Dandy In The Underworld (CD).

T. REX - Off The Record With (2-LP).

his later releases, but there's still lots to interest punters who don't already have most of their hits.

Universal's 4-CD set released in 2002 is a must for all **Bolan/T Rex** fans. It contains 108 tracks, two previously unreleased songs (*Nickelodeon* from his **Tyrannosaurus Rex** days and *Ill-Starred Man*) and several new versions of his songs along with two live cuts and text from **Bolan** biographer and former 'Record Collector' journalist Mark Paytress.

TPL, the **Bolan** fans who acquired his master tapes have started releasing the studio recording sessions of some of his seminal releases, commencing with *The Slider*. *The Tanx Recordings* (2004) include an extended version of *20th Century Boy* (with extra guitar and sax) and a sparse version of *Children Of The Revolution*, but much of the other material is forgettable.

Bump And Grind is compiled from live recordings from 1972 to 1976 and, in contrast to many recordings of the type, the sound quality is excellent. **T Rex** fans and completists will love this.

Born To Boogie is a live 2-CD reissue of a **Ringo Starr** film that captured the band in their prime back in 1972. The first disc comprises the full soundtrack to the film plus some banter between **Bolan** and **Starr** and ending with an exclusive 10-minute interview with **Bolan**. The second disc features the band performing many of their classics for a packed audience.

Dines, who was keyboardist with **T Rex** from 1974 until **Bolan's** death in 1977, died of a heart attack in Spring 2004. He was 59 and had been teaching furniture design at a London College as well as touring with tribute band T. Rextasy.

Telegram Sam has resurfaced on the 2-CD set *45s - 45 Classic No 1's*.

Bolan's rise from underground status to teen idol in the early seventies had been rapid and **T Rex's** reputation as one of the top pop/rock acts of the early seventies has not diminished with time. (VJ/MP)

Triban

Personnel:	EIRI THRASHER	gtr, vcls	A
	BOB WILLIAMS	gtr, vcls	AB
	CARYL WILLIAMS	gtr, vcls	AB
	GILL JENKINS	gtr, vcls	B

| ALBUMS: | 1(A) | THE TRIBAN | (Cambrian MCT 592) 1969 SC |
| | 2( ) | RAINMAKER | (Cambrian MCT 218) 1972 SC |

45s:	Leaving On A Jet Plane/Night In The City	(CSP 707) 1969
	Black Paper Roses/One Paper Mirror	(Decca F 13115) 1970
	Listen To The Children/	
	Anything You Might Say	(Pye 7N 45372) 1974

A Cardiff folk trio, very much in the vein of Peter, Paul and Mary, but with skiffle influences. *Rainmaker* featured session men Clem Cattinni and **Chris Spedding** and they also recorded a number of Welsh language EP's and singles for Cambrian. The band still make occasional performances (GM/MWh)

Tribe

| 45s: | The Gamma Goochie/I'm Leaving | (Planet PLF 108) 1966 R2 |
| | Love Is A Beautiful Thing/Steel Guitar | (RCA RCA 1592) 1967 SC |

This was another little-known band. *I'm Leaving* is notable as a blues-influenced, organ-led number more in the style of American garage bands. This Planet 45 was produced by Shel Talmy. The RCA release is more soulful and could be by a different band. There was also a different American band of this name who released a 45 over here on Polydor in 1970.

Gamma Goochie and *I'm Leaving* are compiled on *The Best Of Planet Records* (CD). (VJ)

The Triffids

45s:	Lookin' Around/	
	She's No Longer Your Girl	(Columbia DB 7084) 1963
	Over Again/Lonely Boy	(Columbia DB 7177) 1963
	So Shy/Enough Of Your Love	(Columbia DB 7251) 1964

This was another long-forgotten beat era band. (VJ)

The Triffids

ALBUMS:	1	THE TRIFFIDS ARE REALLY FOLK	
			(Fontana TL 5231) 1965 SC
	2	STREETS OF LONDON	(DJM DJS 051) 1975

A folk group of no real consequence. (VJ)

Trifle

Personnel:	GEORGE BEAN	vcls	A
	ROD COOMBES	drms	A
	PATRICK 'SPEEDY' KING	bs	A
	BARRY MARTIN	sax	A
	JOHN PRITCHARD	trumpets	A

| ALBUM: | 1(A) | FIRST MEETING | (Dawn DNLS 3017) 1970 R2 |

45s:	All Together Now/Got My Thing	(United Artists 2270) 1969
	Old-Fashioned Prayer Meeting/	
	Dirty Old Town	(Dawn DNS 1008) 1970

Evolving out of **George Bean and The Runners**, this group was managed by Robert Stigwood. They also acted as a backing group for other artists. *Dirty Old Town* was a Dubliners track. **Bean** died in the early seventies, whilst drummer Rod Coombes went on to **Juicy Lucy**, **RoRo**, **Stealers Wheel** and **The Strawbs**.

Devil Comin' and *Old Fashioned Prayer Meeting* have been compiled on *Sixties Years, Vol. 5* (CD). (VJ)

Trilogy

This band appears on the *Hart Rock '71* EP with a harmony country/folk offering, *I Know You Well*, with a note 'by permission of Rubber records', which gives a hint to their origins up North. (MWh)

Trio

Personnel:
STU MARTIN	drms	A
BARRE PHILLIPS	bs	A
JOHN SURMAN	sax	A

ALBUMS:
1(A)	THE TRIO (2-LP with poster)	(Dawn DNLS 3006) 1970 R1
2(A)	CONFLAGRATION	(Dawn DNLS 3022) 1971 R1
3(A)	LIVE AT WOODSTOCK TOWN HALL	(Dawn DNLS 3072) 1976 SC

This band included jazz saxophonist **John Surman** who also recorded several solo albums and was a member of **Morning Glory**. In addition to these albums, **Trio** can be heard playing *Malachile* on the *Dawn Takeaway Concert* (LP) album. This is pure jazz with screaming horns, piano, drums and bass and was originally on their *Conflagration* album, which many people, including legendary US jazz-rock pianist Chick Corea, played on. (VJ)

Trisha

45:    The Darkness Of My Night/Confusion   (CBS 201800) 1965

Trisha was a 17-year-old girl from Weybridge. The 45 is folky: the 'A' side was penned by **Donovan**. (VJ)

Tristar Airbus

Personnel:
JOHN BAILEY	bs	A
JOHN KELMAN	lead gtr	AB
RIC ROTHWELL	drms	ABC
FRANK WORTHINGTON	vcls	ABC
BARRIE ASHALL	bs	BC
FRANK RENSHAW	lead gtr	C

45:    Travellin' Man/
       Willie Morgan On The Wing   (RCA RCA 2170) 1972

This was a post-**Wimple Winch** project linked to **10cc**. *Travellin' Man* was a pleasant **Graham Gouldman** composition. The flip side, a **Gouldman**-Smith number, was an ode to Manchester United's early seventies winger Willie Morgan and has some good fuzz guitar. (VJ/AD)

Marcus Tro

45:    Tell Me/What's The Matter Little Girl   (Ember S 203) 1965

Marcus Tor was a bluesy ballad singer. The 'A' side was a **Rolling Stones** song. (VJ)

The Troggs

Personnel:
(up to
1976)
RONNIE BOND (BULLIS)	drms	ABCD
CHRIS BRITTON	gtr	A
REG PRESLEY (BALL)	vcls	ABCD
PETE STAPLES	bs	A
BARRY LEE	gtr, keyb'ds	B
TONY MURRAY	bs	BCD
RICHARD MOORE	gtr	C
COLIN 'DILL' FLETCHER	gtr	D

HCP

ALBUMS:
(up to
1976)
1(A)	FROM NOWHERE - THE TROGGS (mono/stereo)	(Fontana (S)TL 5355) 1966 R1 6
2(A)	TROGGLODYNAMITE	(Page One POL 001) 1967 R1 10
3(A)	THE BEST OF THE TROGGS (Compilation)	(Page One FOR 001) 1967 R1 24
4(A)	CELLOPHANE (mono/stereo)	(Page One POL(S) 003) 1967 R1 -
5(A)	THE BEST OF THE TROGGS, VOL 2 (Compilation)	(Page One FOR 007) 1967 R1 -
6(A)	MIXED BAG	(Page One POLS 012) 1968 R3 -
7(A)	TROGGOMANIA	(Page One POS 602) 1969 R1 -
8(B)	CONTRASTS	(DJM Silverline DJML 009) 1970 SC -
9( )	THE TROGGS	(Penny Farthing PEN 543) 1975 -
10(-)	WITH A GIRL LIKE YOU (Compilation)	(DJM DJML 26047) 1975 -
11(D)	THE TROGG TAPES	(Penny Farthing PELS 551) 1976 -

NB: (1) reissued on CD (Fontana 8329572) 1989. (1) and (2) reissued on one CD (BGO BGOCD 340) 1997. (2) reissued again on CD (Repertoire REPUK 1020) with eight bonus tracks in a digipak sleeve. (4) and (6) reissued on one CD (BGO BGOCD 343) 1997. (4) reissued on CD (Repertoire REPUK 1021) more recently in a digipak with 12 bonus tracks. (6) reissued again as *Hip, Hip Hooray* (Repertoire REPUK 1062) 2005. *Wild Things* (See For Miles SEE 256) 1989 compiles material from their mid-seventies comeback albums (9) and (10). The comparable CD release (SEE CD 256) 1989 includes five additional cuts from 1976.

Compilations have included:- *14 Greatest Hits: Troggs* (Spectrum SPEC 85031) 1988; *Best Of The Troggs* (Big Time 2615262) 1988; they also share *Double Hits Collection* (Platinum PLATCD 3908) 1989 with **Dave Dee, Dozy, Beaky, Mick and Tich**; *Greatest Hits* (Polygram CD 5227392) features 27 tracks including all their big hits; *The EP Collection* (See For Miles SEECD 453) 1996 comprises material from UK and French EPs plus hits like *Love Is All Around* and *Night Of The Long Grass*. Beware of *The Best Of The Troggs* (Summit SUMCD 4002) 1995, which includes all their classic hits but re-recorded by a later eighties line-up of the band and to cap it all the photo on the front is of the seminal sixties line-up. Almost as bad is *Wild Thing* (Music De Luxe MSCD 30) 1995. This has the sixties combo on the cover too only this time the classic tracks from that era are redone by a seventies line-up! *The Singles Collection* (BR Music BX 5382) 2000 is a 26-track compilation of all their favourites. *The Troggs Double Album* (DJM DJM 66227) 1985 is a decent 2-LP compilation from the 1966-1969 era. *Singles A's & B's* (3-CD) (Repertoire REPUK 1028) is the definitive **Troggs** singles collection comprising 70 tracks covering from 1966 until the eighties.

EPs:
1	TROGGS TOPS	(Page One POE 001) 1967 SC
2	TROGGS TOPS VOLUME TWO	(Page One POE 002) 1967 R1

HCP

45s:
(up to
1976)
	Lost Girl/The Yella In Me	(CBS 202038) 1966 R1 -
	Wild Thing/From Home	(Fontana TF 689) 1966 2
	With A Girl Like You/I Want You	(Fontana TF 717) 1966 1
	I Can't Control Myself/ Gonna Make You	(Page One POF 001) 1966 2
	Any Way That You Want Me/ 66-5-4-3-2-1	(Page One POF 010) 1966 8
	Give It To Me/You're Lyin'	(Page One POF 015) 1967 12
α	My Lady/Girl In Black	(Page One POF 022) 1967 R1 -
	Night Of The Long Grass/ Girl In Black	(Page One POF 022) 1967 17
	Hi Hi Hazel/As I Ride By	(Page One POF 030) 1967 42
	Love Is All Around/ When Will The Rain Come	(Page One POF 040) 1967 5
	Little Girl/Maybe The Madman?	(Page One POF 056) 1968 37
	Surprise Surprise/ Marbles And Some Gum	(Page One POF 064) 1968 -

THE TROGGS - From Nowhere (LP).

THE TROGGS.

You Can Try If You Want To/
There's Something About You   (Page One POF 082) 1968 -
Hip Hip Hooray/Say Darlin'!   (Page One POF 092) 1968 -
Evil Woman/Sweet Madeline   (Page One POF 114) 1969 -
Easy Lovin'/Give Me Something   (Page One POF 164) 1970 -
Lover/Come Now   (Page One POF 171) 1970 -
The Raver/You   (Page One POF 182) 1970 -
Lazy Weekend/Let's Pull Together   (DJM DJM 248) 1970 -
Everything's Funny/Feels Like A Woman (Pye 7N 45147) 1970 -
Listen To The Man/Queen Of Sorrow   (Pye 7N 45244) 1973 -
Strange Movies/I'm On Fire   (Pye 7N 45295) 1973 -
Good Vibrations/
Push It Up To Me   (Penny Farthing PEN 861) 1975 -
Wild Thing (Reggae Version)/
Jenny Come Down   (Penny Farthing PEN 884) 1975 -
Summertime/
Jenny Come Down   (Penny Farthing PEN 889) 1975 -
(I Can't Get No) Satisfaction/
Memphis, Tennessee   (Penny Farthing PEN 901) 1975 -
I'll Buy You An Island/
Supergirl   (Penny Farthing PEN 919) 1976 -
Feeling For Love/Summertime   (Penny Farthing PEN 929) 1977 -
Reissues: Wild Thing/I Can't Control Myself   (Page One POF 126) 1969 -
Wild Thing/With A Girl Like You/
Love Is All Around   (Jam JAM 25) 1972 -
I Can't Control Myself/Give It To Me (Old Gold OG 9024) 1979 -
Love Is All Around/
Any Way That You Want Me   (Old Gold OG 9038) 1979 -
β Wild Thing/I Can't Control Myself/
Love Is All Around   (DJM DJS 6) 1984 -
χ Wild Thing/With A Girl Like You/
I Can't Control Myself   (Old Gold OG 6164) 1992 -

NB: α Withdrawn. Available in demo form only. β Also issued as a 12". χ CD single.

The Troggs were a versatile group who, as well as recording garage rock classics like *Wild Thing* and riffy hit singles like *I Can't Control Myself* and *With A Girl Like You*, were equally capable of producing well-crafted power-pop and ballads like the flower-power number *Love Is All Around*. In **Reg Presley** they possessed a charismatic front man and talented songwriter.

The group originally formed in 1964 as the Troglodytes. Andover in Hampshire was their home turf. The original line-up featured Tony Mansfield (gtr, lead vcls) and Dave Wright (gtr) as well as **Presley** (whose real name was Reg Ball) and Ronnie Bond. Early in 1965 Mansfield and Wright left to be replaced by **Chris Britton** and Pete Staples (both ex-**Ten Feet Five**). Since Staples was a bassist, Reg took up the lead vocal mantle in place of Mansfield.

The Troggs soon developed a very distinctive sound, brash and raw with suggestive lyrics. They were snapped up by **Kinks**' manager Larry Page after he heard their rendition of *You Really Got Me*, and he changed their name from The Troglodytes to **The Troggs**.

Their debut 45 flopped but for the follow-up, Page gave them a song written by US writer Chip Taylor, which had been recorded by an obscure outfit, The Wild Ones. The band gave *Wild Thing* a different arrangement with an ocarina solo in place of a whistling section on the original and it worked at treat. To coincide with its release, Ball changed his name to **Presley**, which won him considerable press coverage. Boosted by TV appearances on 'Top Of The Pops' and 'Thank Your Lucky Stars', it shot up the Charts, peaking at No 2 in the UK and topping the US Charts, where, because of a dispute about rights to the song, it was released on both Fontana and Atco, the latter 45 coupling it with *With A Girl Like You*, which was selected as the follow-up in the UK and cracked the No 1 spot.

When, in September 1966, Page launched his own Page One label, *I Can't Control Myself* was its debut release. Penned by **Presley**, this was probably their finest moment. The lyrics were risque for the era, 'Her slacks are low and her hips are showing', which guaranteed notoriety but limited airplay and the record was virtually banned in Australia. Their first two albums *From Nowhere - The Troggs* and *Trogglodynamite*, both made the UK Top Ten and the hits continued to flow. *Troggodynamite* showcased their pop credentials well. Its highlights included *Oh No, I Can Only Give You Everything* and *Cousin Jane*. This too has been reissued in a digipak sleeve with eight bonus tracks including a stomping version of the moody *Evil Woman*. The reissue comes with a 12-page colour booklet.

Cellophane was a 1967 album release which captured the spirit of the times perfectly. Its highlights included *Love Is All Around*, *My Lady* and *Little Red Donkey*. It has recently been reissued in a digipak with 12 bonus tracks including solo recordings by their drummer Ronnie Bond and vocalist **Reg Presley**. *Night Of The Long Grass* was different from the 45s that had preceded it - giving a nod and a wink to psychedelia both lyrically and musically but *Little Girl*, released in 1968, was their last UK Chart hit.

Mixed Bag (a 1968 album release) only contained one cover version and featured more snippets of psychedelia with *Purple Shades* and also contains the superb *Surprise Surprise*. It has recently been reissued in a digipak as *Hip Hip Hooray* with 11 bonus tracks (nine from the seventies and two **Presley** solo cuts). By now, **Britton** disillusioned with the whole pop scene, wanted to leave the group, but **Presley** persuaded him to stay and the band continued to work the club and college circuits until they eventually split in March 1969.

The following month, **Presley** released a solo 45, *Lucinda Lee*, as did Bond (*Anything For You*). **Britton** also cut an album, *As I Am*, but none of their solo ventures met with any success. Staples went on to become an electrician.

In 1970, the band reformed with Tony Murray (ex-**Plastic Penny**) and Barry Lee. The new line-up released further 45s and an album, *Contrasts*, but didn't achieve any great success. They worked the club and college circuit here in the UK and in Europe and a studio tape made during some of their later Page One sessions surfaced in bootleg form as *The Troggs Tapes* and revealed some laughably amateurish behaviour. Their live act was as strong and their lyrics as risque as ever as they continued to record.

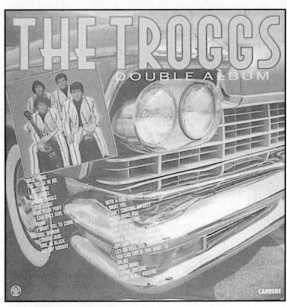

THE TROGGS - Double Album (2-LP).

In 1973, Barry Lee left, being replaced by Richard Moore and then in January 1975 by Colin 'Dill' Fletcher (ex-**Greep**).

At the start of 1975 they reunited with Larry Page and covered The Beach Boys' *Good Vibrations* for his Penny Farthing label. Typically they replaced the line, "I love the purple cloak she wears" with "I love the dress she almost wears" but although they attracted media attention they failed to chart with this or subsequent efforts, which included a cover of **The Rolling Stones'** *(I Can't Get No) Satisfaction*.

The *Trogg Tapes* album released by Penny Farthing was unconnected with the earlier bootleg but capitalised on the name because of its notoriety.

Towards the end of the seventies **Chris Britton** rejoined the group. In America in particular, the band still enjoyed a cult following. LA band, X, released a cover of *Wild Thing* and in 1979 **The Troggs** signed to Basement records releasing *Live At Max's Kansas City*. Several late seventies punk bands quoted them as an influence and they continued to gig on both sides of the Atlantic well into the eighties. Other later recordings include: *Black Bottom* (New Rose) 1982, *Every Little Thing* (10 Records) May 1984 and *Rock It Up* ( ) 1987. **Presley** also released a duet version of *Wild Thing* with Suzi Quatro in November 1986.

By March 1989 the band consisted of:- **Presley**, **Britton**, Peter Lucas (bs, ex-**Dozy Beaky Mick and Tich**) and Dave Maggs (drms); and a further album followed *Wild Thing* (Big Wave) October 1989. In 1992, REM collaborated with their heroes on a further album *Athens And Andover* (Page One) and two singles also resulted: *Don't You Know/Nowhere Road* (Page One) and *Together/Crazy Annie*.

Sadly Ronnie Bond died in November 1992. *The Singles* is a 26-track collection which combines their big hits like *Wild Thing* with lesser known tracks.

The band's finest moment, *Wild Thing*, has been heavily compiled, including on three US compilations:- *Frat Rock! The Greatest Rock'n'Roll Party Tunes Of All Time* (LP & CD), *Nuggets* (CD) and *Wild Thing* (LP); as well as on *The Best Summer Ever!* (CD); *20 Hits Of The 60's* (CD), *Wild Thing - Party* (CD), *Brit Pop* (CD), *Super Hits Of The 60s - Vol 2* (CD) and on *Remember The 60's* (CD). Other compilation appearances include: *Your Love* on *Turds On A Bum Ride, Vol. 6* (CD); *Lost Girl* on *Maximum Freakbeat* (CD) and on the 4-CD *Nuggets II* box set; *Wild Thing* and *With A Girl Like You* on *Made In England, Vol. 1* (LP); *Love Is All Around* was the title track to a CD of the same name and has also been compiled on *60's Love Songs* (CD) and *Super Hits Of The 60s - Vol 1* (CD); *I Can't Control Myself* can also be found on *Dizzy* (CD); *With A Girl Like You* on *U.K. No.1 Hits Of The 60's* (CD), *Best Of British Rock* (CD), *Super Hits Of The 60s - Vol 3* (CD) and on the 2-CD set *60 Number Ones Of The Sixties*; *Give It To Me* and *Mona* on *Made In England, Vol. 2* (LP); *Love Is All Around* on *Here Comes Summer* (CD) and on the 2-CD set *Sixties Summer Love*; and *Love Is All Around* (alternate take) on the 2-CD set *Greatest Hits Of The 60's*; *Everything's Funny* on *Beat Merchants* (CD); and *Feels Like A Woman* on *Freakbeat Freakout* (CD). Back in 1967 they also contributed the *Great Shakes Ad* to the *Great Shakes* (EP), which appears as *H.I.S. Spot* on *Great Shakes Shake-Out* (EP). Finally, *Feels Like A Woman* has resurfaced on *Rock Of Ages, Four Decades Of Heavy Rock 1962-2002*. (VJ/JM)

Robin Trower

Personnel:	JIM DEWAR	bs, vcls	AB
(up to	REG ISADORE	drms	A
1976)	ROBIN TROWER	gtr	AB
	BILL LORDAN	drms	B

HCP

ALBUMS:	1(A)	TWICE REMOVED FROM YESTERDAY		
(up to			(Chrysalis CHR 1039) 1973	-
1976)	2(A)	BRIDGE OF SIGHS	(Chrysalis CHR 1057) 1974	-
	3(B)	FOR EARTH BELOW	(Chrysalis CHR 1073) 1975	26
	4(B)	LIVE	(Chrysalis CHR 1089) 1976	15
	5(B)	LONG MISTY DAYS	(Chrysalis CHR 1107) 1976	31

NB: (1) and (2) reissued on CD (Beat Goes On BGOCD 339). (3) and (4) reissued on CD (Beat Goes On BGOCD 347). *Live* was originally recorded at Stockholm Concert Hall for the Swedish Broadcasting Corporation. (5) reissued on CD together with 1977's *In City Dreams* (Beat Goes On BGO 349) 1997. *BBC Radio One Live In Concert* (Windsong WINCD 013) 1992 includes material from a January 1975

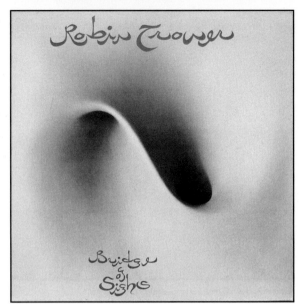

ROBIN TROWER - Bridge Of Sighs (LP).

concert. There are also some compilations: - *Anthology* (Connoisseur Collection VSOP CD 197) 1994 is a CD compilation of his recordings for Chrysalis between 1973-83; *Collection: Robin Trower* (Castle Collector CESCD 291) 1991 and *Portfolio* (The Classic Collection) (Chrysalis MFCD 1600) 1987. (2) reissued on Chrysalis (ACCD 1057) 1982, but now deleted. *Dreaming The Blues* (Snapper SNDCD 500) 2004 is a compilation, which concentrates on later material outside the time frame of this book.

45s:	Man Of The World/Take A Fast Train	(Chrysalis CHS 2009) 1973
(up to	Too Rolling Stoned/Lady Love	(Chrysalis CHS 2046) 1974
1976)	Caledonia/Messin' The Blues	(Chrysalis CHS 2124) 1976

Trower, who was born in Catford on 9th March 1945, had been in **The Paramounts**, **Procol Harum** and the short-lived **Jude** before launching his solo career in July 1971. He fronted his own band throughout the seventies and enjoyed big album sales in the United States and success well into the eighties.

His guitar style is very influenced by **Hendrix** but his albums have been particularly successful in the US where *Bridge Of Sighs*, *For Earth Below* and *Robin Trower Live!* all made the Top Ten. Briefly in the mid-seventies he was heralded as a guitar hero of almost **Hendrix** proportion.

By the eighties though, his fortunes faded. He briefly teamed up with **Jack Bruce** for *B. L. T.* in 1981 and *Truce* in 1982 and then returned to his solo career recording blues-rock based albums like *Passion* in 1987. He was involved in a brief **Procol Harum** reunion in 1991 and backed **Bryan Ferry** on 1993's *Taxi* and 1994's *Mamouna*, which he co-produced. He's still putting out solo albums like *Go My Own Way* (2000), *Living Out Of Time* (2004) and *Another Days Blues* (2005). He also worked with **Ferry** on *Frantic* (2002).

The recent album on Windsong includes live recordings of material from his first three albums.

Jim Dewar had previously played with **Jude**, and Reg Isadore with **Peter Barden's On**. Bill Lordan was ex-Sly and The Family Stone. (VJ/JM)

Truth

Personnel:	FRANK AIELLO	vcls	A
	STEVE GOLD	vcls	A

HCP

45s:	Baby Don't You Know/		
	Come On Home	(Pye 7N 15923) 1965	SC -
	Who's Wrong/She's A Roller	(Pye 7N 15998) 1965	SC -
	Girl/Jailer Bring Me Water	(Pye 7N 17035) 1966	SC 27
	I Go To Sleep/Baby You've Got It	(Pye 7N 17095) 1966	R1 -
	Jingle Jangle/		
	Hey Gyp (Dig The Slowness)	(Deram DM 105) 1966	R2 -

Walk Away Renee/Fly Away Bird	(Decca F 12582) 1967 SC -
Sueno/Old Ma Brown	(Decca F 22764) 1968 SC -

From North London, former hairdressers Frank Aiello and Steve Gold signed to Pye in 1965 and named themselves after the Ray Charles classic *Tell The Truth*. They are best known for their cover of **The Beatles**' *Girl*, which gave them a minor hit (although **St. Louis Union** enjoyed greater success with the song). Indeed, their 45s were mostly covers. For example, they recorded **The Kinks**' *I Go To Sleep*, The Left Banke's *Walk Away Renee*, **The Troggs**' *Jingle Jangle* (backed by a pulsating version of **Donovan**'s *Hey Gyp*) and The Young Rascals' *Sueno*. The latter was given a very British treatment.

Baby You've Got It was an uncharacteristically rough soul-rocker

Steve Gold (later recording as **Steve Jameson**) made several solo records and then called himself Nosmo King. In 1974 he enjoyed a hit with *Goodbye Nothing To Say*, which was a massive Northern soul favourite.

Compilation appearances have included: *Hey Gyp (Dig The Slowness)* on *Maximum Freakbeat* (CD) and *Beat It* (3-CD); *Girl* on *Pop Inside The Sixties, Vol. 3* (CD); *Sueno* on *Rubble, Vol. 14 - The Magic Rocking Horse* (LP) and *Rubble, Vol. 8* (CD); *Jingle Jangle* on *A Whiter Shade Of Pale* (LP); *She's A Roller* on *Doin' The Mod, Vol. 1* (CD); *Baby You've Got It* on *English Freakbeat, Vol. 5* (LP & CD) and *Freakbeat Freakout* (CD); *I Go To Sleep* and *Girl* on *Hippy Hippy Shake* (CD) and *Girl* and *I Go To Sleep* on the 2-CD set *We Love The Pirates: Charting The Big 'L' Fab 40*. (VJ)

Truth of Truths

Personnel:	HAL BLAINE		A
	LARRY CARLTON		A
	JERRY COLE		A
	JOHN GUERIN		A
	ALAN HENDERSON	bs	A
	JOE OSBORNE		A
	RAY RUFF		A
	JERRY SCHEFF		A

ALBUM: 1(A) TRUTH OF TRUTHS (2-LP)   (Oak OR 1001) 1971 SC

This lavishly-packaged double album was a Jesus rock opera, the brainchild of ex-**Them** bassist Alan Henderson and their former manager Ray Ruff. It came with a 20-page booklet but musically it was dreadful. Henderson didn't record again until the late seventies. (VJ)

Cy Tucker

Personnel:	PAUL DOYLE	ld gtr	A
	TOMMY HART	drms	A
	CHARLIE SMULLIN	bs	AB
	THOMAS (CY) THORNTON	vcls	AB
	LES CAVE	drms	B
	ARTHUR KERRIVAN	ld gtr	B

NB: Above personnel is **Cy Tucker Friars**.

45s:	α	My Prayer/High School Dance	(Fontana TF 424) 1963
		I Apologise/Let Me Call You Sweetheart	(Fontana TF 470) 1964
		My Friend/Hurt	(Fontana TF 534) 1965

NB: α with **Earl Preston and The TTs**.

A Merseybeat singer (and former village postman) who was guitarist/vocalist with **Earl Preston and The TTs**, one of Liverpool's finest groups. Indeed, the group are credited on his first 45. Sadly, both singles were naff ballads which are best forgotten. (VJ/AD)

Tucky Buzzard

Personnel:	DAVID BROWN	bs	ABCD
	PAUL FRANCIS	drms	A
	NICK GRAHAM	keyb'ds	A

JIMMY HENDERSON	vcls	ABCD
CHRIS JOHNSON	drms	ABCD
TERRY TAYLOR	gtr	ABC
PAUL KENDRICK	gtr, vcls	B
RON TAYLOR	gtr	B
PHIL TALBOT	gtr	C
VAL STEVENS		
(aka DICK HENNINGHAM)		D

				HCP
ALBUMS:	1(A)	TUCKY BUZZARD	(Capitol)1969 -
	2(A)	WARM SLASH	(Capitol E-ST 787) 1969 SC
	3(A)	COMING ON AGAIN	(Capitol ST-864) 1971 -
	4(B)	ALRIGHT ON THE NIGHT	(Purple TPSA 7510) 1973 SC
	5(C)	BUZZARD	(Purple TPSA 7512) 1973 SC

NB: (1) reissued on CD (Ripple RPICD 104) 2002. (2) reissued on CD (Ripple RIPCD 105) 2002. (1) and (2) reissued on one CD Sunrise 41020012. (2) reissued on CD (SPM SPMCD 004). (3) reissued on CD (Ripple RIPCD 106) 2002. (4) and (5) released on Passport in the US. (5) reissued on Line in 1983.

45s:	She's A Striker/Heartbreaker	(Capitol CL 15687) 1971
	Gold Medallions/Fast Bluesy Woman	(Purple PUR 113) 1973
	Gold Medallions/Superboy Rock'n'Roller	(Purple PUR 134) 1977

This hard-rock outfit was most famous for having been produced by **Bill Wyman**. Brown, Graham and Taylor had all previously been in **The End**.

Their eponymous debut album is a psych-progressive crossover album, typified by *Time Will Be Your Doctor* which merged psychedelia with a heavier progressive rock style.

Warm Slash was clearly influenced by **Led Zeppelin**. Finer moments include the riffy *Fill You In*, *Burnin* and *Sky Balloon*.

Coming On Again was recorded in Spain in 1972. It moves away from the hard-rock of their second album to a more melodic sound with baroque arrangements and lovely choral harmonies. The ambitious title track comprises the whole of one side.

One of **Tucky Buzzard**'s finest moments was *Bo-Bo's Hampton* on *Buzzard*, which mellows in the middle and ends with some good guitar work. Elsewhere on the same album there's some Southern USA influence on *Hanging On In There* and some good rock'n'roll with brass arrangements on *Super Boy Rock 'n' Roller 73*.

Paul Francis (ex-**Tony Jackson and The Vibrations**) left to join **Fuzzy Duck**. Further line-ups followed with Val Stevens being ex-**Khan**, and Paul Kendrick possibly being the **Czar** bassist. Nick Graham was later a record producer (credits include BROS in the eighties) and is now an executive at Sony Records. This is not the same Nick Graham who was in **Atomic Rooster** and **Skin Alley**.

Terry Taylor later played with Arrows. (VJ/JM)

TUCKY BUZZARD - Buzzard (LP).

Tudor Lodge

Personnel:

LYNDON GREEN	vcls, gtr		A
ANN STEUART	gtr, piano, vcls, flute		A
JOHN STANNARD	vcls, gtr		A

ALBUM: 1(A) TUDOR LODGE (Vertigo 6360 043) 1970 R3

NB: (1) reissued on Zap! (ZAP 4) in 1988 and again on vinyl (Akarma) 2005. (1) reissued on CD (Red Bus RR 4064-CX) 1990 and on Repertoire (REP 4064-CX) 1990. Recently, three new CD's have been released by the band. *It All Comes Back* (Scenescof SCOFD 1005) 1998, is a collection of previously unissued recordings from 1970 - 97, including their 1971 non-LP 'B' side. A reformed band have also released *Let's Talk* (Cast Iron CIRCD 010) 1998, and *Dream* ( ) 1999.

45: The Lady's Changing Home/
     The Good Times We Had (Vertigo 6059 044) 1970 SC

This progressive folk-influenced trio's album is now very rare and sought-after. They were named after a Reading pub and became a popular folk attraction, appearing at the 1971 Cambridge Folk Festival.

The album sleeve folds out into a striking poster, and is near-impossible to find in top condition. The 'A' side of their 45 was one of the better tracks from the album. The flip side was a not on the album making the 45 of interest too.

The group's vocalist was born in the States. The material on the album is rather delicate and whimsical. It contains nice vocal harmonies and its finer moments include a version of **Ralph McTell**'s *Kew Gardens*, John Stannard's *It All Comes Back To Me*, Lyndon Green's *Recollections*, the traditional instrumental *Madeline*, as well as the opening cut, *Willow Tree*, a fine slice of acid-folk which captures Steuart's vocals at their best. This last-mentioned track was also included on Vertigo's 1971 *Heads Together, First Round* (2-LP) compilation.

The Zap reissue only came in a single sleeve but more recently counterfeits have been in circulation with the original fold-out sleeve and poster.

Tudor Lodge are still going as a duo, and have recently been recording some new material. (VJ)

Tudor Minstrels

45: Love In The Open Air/
     The Family Way (Theme) (Decca F 12536) 1966 SC

These two instrumentals were written by **Paul McCartney** for the Hayley Mills film 'The Family Way'. (VJ)

Tuesday's Children

Personnel incl:

DENVER GERRARD	lead gtr		AB
DERRICK GOUCH	drms		A
BARRY YOUNGHUSBAND	bs, gtr, vcls		AB
LYNNE YOUNGHUSBAND	vcls		AB
JOHN CARR	drms		B
PHIL CORDELL	bs, vcls		
MIKE WARE	gtr, vcls		

45s: When You Walk In The Sand/
      High And Drifting (Columbia DB 7978) 1966 SC
      High On A Hill/
      Summer Leaves Me With A Sigh (Columbia DB 8018) 1966 SC
      A Strange Light From The East/
      That'll Be The Day (King KG 1051) 1967 SC
      Baby's Gone/Guess I'm Losing You (Pye 7N 17406) 1967 SC
      In The Valley Of The Shadow Of Love/
      Ain't You Got A Heart (Pye 7N 17474) 1968
      She/Bright-Eyed Apples (Mercury MF 1063) 1968

A harmony-pop group from Essex who made little impact but Barry Younghusband reappeared in the slightly more successful **Warm Sounds**. It's not certain that all these 45s were necessarily by the same band but one of the best was certainly the Eastern-influenced *A Strange Light From The East*. Another of their tracks, *She*, is a typically British slice of

TUDOR LODGE - Tudor Lodge (LP).

whimsical pop. They were originally a trio but became a quartet during 1968.

Barry and Lynne Husband must have left the band in 1967, but as Carr and Gerrard also played in **Warm Sounds**, the above line-ups are not conclusive. Cordell later went solo as **Springwater**; Gough and Ware joined **Czar** then Ware went on to a mid-seventies version of **Consortium**.

Compilation appearances have included:- *Strange Light From The East* on *Rubble, Vol. 15 - 5,000 Seconds Over Toyland* (LP), *Rubble, Vol. 8* (CD), *The Best Of Rubble Collection, Vol. 3* (CD) and *Incredible Sound Show Stories, Vol. 6* (LP); *She* on *Circus Days Vol's 4 & 5* (CD) and *Circus Days, Vol. 4* (LP) and *Mr. Kipling* and *In The Valley Of The Shadow Of Love* on *Haunted - Psychedelic Pstones, Vol 2* (CD). (VJ/AD/JM)

Tumbleweeds

45: All Of My Love/Confused (Pye 7N 17116) 1966

An obscure 45. Nothing is known about the band. (VL)

Tundra

Personnel:

CHARLIE HARRISON	bs, vcls		A
HENRY SPINETTI	drms		A
CHRIS STAINTON	keyb'ds		A
GLEN TURNER	vcls, gtr		A

ALBUM: 1(A) TUNDRA (Decca SKLR 5259) 1976

45s: They Don't Know/
      Love Is All You Have To Do (Goodear EAR 108) 1974
      All I Need Is Your Love/Northern Soul (Goodear EAR 610) 1975

This band featured Charlie Harrison (ex-**Judas Jump**), Henry Spinetti (ex-**Demick and Armstrong**), Glen Turner (ex-**Atlas**) and the ubiquitous Chris Stainton. By November '74, Harrison had left to join **Coast Road Drive** and Stainton had gone off to work with **Leo Sayer**.

Turner and Spinetti continued the band as Glen Turner's Tundra and their album appears to have been issued both as *Glen Turner's Tundra* in June 1975, and simply *Tundra* in October 1976.

Spinetti left the band in 1975 to join **Hustler**. (JM)

Tuppenny Two

45: Sugar Lump/Grass Is Turning Greener (Columbia DB 7701) 1965

A pop duo. (VJ)

Gordon Turner

ALBUM: 1 MEDITATION (Charisma CAS 1009) 1970 R1

This is a spoken word record giving tuition in **Mr Turner's** "Threefold Attunement" system of meditation and originally included a 12-page booklet. Musical content is virtually zero, consisting of a distant background of atmospheric but repetitive sitar sounds. Rare, yes, but probably only of interest to Charisma completists.

Before the release of the album he had studied the occult for 20 years. A second album was recorded in September 1970, produced by Shel Talmy for the Charisma label called *Sleep And Astral Projection*. The same month he worked on two further completed albums called *Sleep And Dreams* and *Entirely On Astral Projection*, produced by Shel Talmy and both released on Charisma. (NM)

Turnstyle

Personnel incl: MARC ASHTON drms A

45: Riding A Wave/Trot (Pye 7N 17653) 1968 R4

Turnstyle was a London band whose 45 is rare and sought-after. *Riding A Wave* is essentially experimental pop - the experimentation being evident in the instrumentation rather than vocals. During 1969 they were the support band of **The Nice**. In late 1969 **Mark Ashton** joined **Rare Bird**.

Compilation appearances include: *Riding On A Wave* on *Rubble, Vol. 10 - Professor Jordan's Magic Sound Show* (LP) and on *Hot Smoke & Sassafras - Psychedelic Pstones, Vol 1* (CD); and *Trot* on *Voyage Through The Sugarcube* (LP & CD). (VJ)

Turquoise

Personnel:			
	VIC JANSEN	bs	AB
	GUS PETERS	ld gtr, piano	AB
	EWAN STEPHENS	drms	AB
	GEOFF SYRETT	gtr	AB
	BARRY HART		B

45s:	53 Summer Street/		
	Tales Of Flossie Fillet	(Decca F 12756) 1968 R1	
	Woodstock/Saynia	(Decca F 12842) 1968 R1	

This Muswell Hill outfit was closely linked to Ray Davies - hence the strong **Kinks'** influence in some of their songs. **Keith Moon** and **John Entwistle** took a keen interest in them and they were produced and managed by Tom Keylock, **The Rolling Stones'** tour manager.

Both of their 45s are now quite sought-after and collectable. **The Kinks'** influence circa *Autumn Almanac* is evident on *Tales Of Flossie Fillet*, which is full of jangling acoustic guitars and appealing melodies and harmonies. *Woodstock* was similar in style, although with the addition of a fifth member, Barry Hart their sound had been filled with some punchier guitar work and a Hammond organ. (Incidentally *Woodstock* was not the Joni Mitchell song that **Matthews Southern Comfort** took to No 1.) The flip side, *Saynia*, was every bit as good - a melancholic psych-based ballad about a lost love with strong vocals and ideally suited harmonies and instrumentation.

The group deserved more success, but when it didn't emerge they evolved into a progressive/R&B act called **Slowbone** who in turn metamorphosed into The Roll-Ups.

Compilation appearances include: *Woodstock* on *The Psychedelic Scene* (CD), *Rubble, Vol. 11 - Adventures In The Mist* (LP), *Rubble, Vol. 6* (CD), *British Psychedelic Trip, Vol. 3* (LP) and *Great British Psychedelic Trip, Vol. 2* (CD); *Tales Of Flossie Fillet* on *Rubble, Vol. 6 - The Clouds Have Groovy Faces* (LP) and *Rubble, Vol. 4* (CD); *Tales Of Flossie Fillett* and *Saynia* on *The British Psychedelic Trip, Vol. 1* (LP) and *Great British Psychedelic Trip, Vol. 1* (CD) and *53 Summer Street* on *Jagged Time Lapse, Vol 1* (CD). (VJ)

Geoff Turton

45: Don't You Believe It/
I've Got To Tell Her (Pye 7N 17483) 1968

Turton is best-known as a member of **The Rockin' Berries**. In 1969, he commenced a solo career under the name **Jefferson**. Both sides of this 45 are dreadful ballads. The flip side was penned by **Turton** himself. (VJ)

23rd Turnoff

Personnel incl: JIMMY CAMPBELL

45: Michaelangelo/Leave Me Here (Deram DM 150) 1967 R1
NB: *The Dream Of Michaelangelo* (RPM BC 287) 2005 features their 45s (including one as **The Kirkbys**) with alternate recordings and several previously unreleased songs.

The band was named after the 23rd turnoff the M6, which goes to their home city, Liverpool. They had earlier recorded as **The Kirkbys**, when they mixed beat era **Beatles** with early jingly jangly Byrds sounds, but this disc was a big improvement and attracts considerable attention from collectors. *Leave Me Here* was an acoustic piece with just a hint of raga.

The RPM collection is very welcome compiling their recorded output as **The Kirkbys** and **23rd Turnoff** several alternate recordings of their songs (three in the case of *Michaelangelo*) with beefed up vocals and guitar, whilst the several previously unreleased tracks are experimental and will excite many who buy the CD. It's also nicely packaged, with lots of band photos and comprehensive sleevenotes.

Jimmy Campbell went on to record three solo albums and some 45s.

Compilation appearances include: *Michaelangelo* on *The Psychedelic Scene* (CD), *Rubble, Vol. 12 - Staircase To Nowhere* (LP), *Rubble, Vol. 6* (CD), *Deram Dayze* (LP) and on the 4-CD box set *Acid Drops, Spacedust & Flying Saucers*; and *Leave Me Here* on *The British Psychedelic Trip, Vol. 1* (LP) and *Great British Psychedelic Trip Vol. 1* (CD). (VJ)

Twice As Much

Personnel:	STEPHEN ROSE	A
	DAVID SKINNER	A

ALBUMS:	1(A)	OWN UP		
		(mono/stereo)	(Immediate IMLP/IMSP 007) 1966 R1	
	2(A)	THAT'S ALL (mono/stereo)	(Immediate IMCP 013) 1968 R1	

NB: (2) reissued in Germany on Out Line (OLLP 5257) in 1983. *Sittin' On The Fence - The Immediate Anthology* (Sequel NEM CD 413) 1999 is an 18-track compilation.

HCP

45s:	Sittin' On The Fence/		
	Baby I Want You	(Immediate IM 033) 1966	25
	Step Out Of Line/Simplified	(Immediate IM 036) 1966	-
	True Story/You're So Good	(Immediate IM 039) 1966	SC -
	Crystal Ball/Why Don't They All Go		
	And Leave Me Alone	(Immediate IM 042) 1967	SC -

Andrew Loog Oldham signed these two ex-public schoolboys to his Immediate label in 1966. Their debut 45, *Sittin' On The Fence*, a **Jagger**/Richard song was a minor hit, but that was the nearest they got to success.

Another **Oldham** discovered act, **Vashti**, sang on *The Coldest Night Of The Year*, on the *That's All* album.

The CD compilation *Sittin' On The Fence* includes their duet with **Vashti Bunyan** and *Night Time Girl* (which was included on the soundtrack to *Tonite Let's Make Love In London*). There's also a strong cover of **The Small Faces'** *Green Circles* too, but overall the CD plods through inferior covers of sixties classics like *We Can Work It Out* and *Help* and only goes to confirm their status as 'also rans' in this era.

Skinner resurfaced in the seventies on keyboards for **Uncle Dog**, a pub-rock group, and joined the reformed **Roxy Music** in 1979.

Compilation appearances have included: *Sittin' On A Fence* and *Step Out Of Line* on *Jimmy Page Studio Works 1964-1968* (CD) and *Jimmy Page - Hip Young Guitar Slinger* (2-CD); *Sittin' On A Fence* and *True Story* on the 2-CD set *We Love The Pirates: Charting The Big 'L' Fab 40*; *Night Time Girl* on *Tonite Let's All Make Love In London* (LP); *Sittin' On A Fence* and *You're So Good To Me* on *Immediate Single Collection, Vol. 2* (CD); *Crystal Ball* and *Step Out Of Line* on *Immediate Single Collection, Vol. 3* (CD); *True Story* on *Immediate Single Collection, Vol. 5* (CD); and *Sittin' On A Fence* on *Juke Box Jive* (EP) and *Radio Two: Sounds Of The Cities* (Sequel) (CD). (VJ)

Twiggy

			HCP
ALBUMS:	1	TWIGGY AND THE GIRL FRIENDS	
(up to		(Ember SE 8012) 1972 SC -	
1976)	2	THE BOYFRIEND (film soundtrack)	
		(Columbia SCXA 9251) 1972 -	
	3	TWIGGY	(Mercury 9102 600) 1976 33

NB: There was also a US-only TV soundtrack album *Cole Porter In Paris* (Bell Systems PH 365508) 1973. *A Snapshot Of Swinging London* (CD) (El ACMEM56CD) credited to **Twiggy** and Linda Thorson compiles both sides of **Twiggy's** sixties singles and all seven tracks Linda cut for Ember with Kenny Lynch producing.

			HCP
45s:	Beautiful Dreams/I Need Your		
(up to	Hand In Mine (Some PS)	(Ember EMB S 239) 1967 SC -	
1976)	When I Think Of You/		
	Over And Over (Some PS)	(Ember EMB S 244) 1967 SC -	
α	Zoo Do Zoo Song/		
	Little Pleasure Acre	(Bell BLL 1158) 1971 -	
	A Room In Bloomsbury/You Are My Luck Star/		
	All I Do Is Dream	(Columbia DB 8853) 1972 -	
	Here I Go Again/		
	In Love Together (PS)	(Mercury 6007 100) 1976 17	
	Vanilla Olay/Done My Crying Time	(Mercury 6007 105) 1976 -	

NB: α As **Twiggy** & Friends.

Now world-famous as a model **Twiggy** (real name Leslie Hornby) was a mod in the early sixties growing up in the North-West London suburb of Harrow. Justin de Villeneuve (real name Nigel Davies) transformed the hairdresser into an international celebrity and 'The Face of '66' was approached via de Villeneuvre (her manager) with a recording contract by the Ember label. The output was pretty forgettable, but she went on to star in Ken Russell's 'The Boyfriend'. In 1976 she recorded an album *Twiggy*, which contained several country tunes, and enjoyed a No 17 hit with a cover of Country Joe and The Fish's *Here I Go Again*. She continued to record beyond the time span of this book. (VJ)

Twink

ALBUM: 1   THINK PINK (Some w/insert)   (Polydor 2343 032) 1970 R2

NB: Some versions came in red vinyl with an insert. These would be (R3). (1) reissued on CD World Wide Records (SPM-WWR-CD-0031) 1991, and on vinyl and CD in a "25th Anniversary" edition by Twink (Twink Records TWK LP 4 / CD 7) 1996. (1) reissued again (Akarma AK 064) on vinyl and CD. *From The Vaults* (Get Back GET 526) 2000 is a vinyl Italian import compiling unreleased songs from the seventies. *The Lost Experimental Recordings 1970* (LP) (Get Back GET 572) 2000, is another vinyl set on Italian import compiling recordings made in a small basement studio in London. *Never Never Land & Think Pink Demos* (LP/CD) (Get Back GET 599) is a collection of previously unreleased late sixties acid head music. *Odds And Beginnings* (CD) (Captain Trip CTCD 118) compiles radio broadcasts, interviews and alternate mixes of some of his better-known tunes. This is also available in vinyl but with seven less tracks.

Twink's real name was John Alder. In 1963 he drummed for a Colchester band, Dane Stephens and The Deep Beats, who later changed their name to **The Fairies** in 1964, when they signed to Decca.

By 1967, Alder assumed the name **Twink** and resurfaced in **Tomorrow**. He was then involved in **The Pretty Things**, playing on their *S.F. Sorrow* album in 1968, but by 1969 he'd left them too to form an early **Pink Fairies** line-up with **Mick Farren** and **Steve Peregrin Took** (from **Tyrannosaurus Rex**). He'd also recorded the above solo album with assistance from

TWINK - Think Pink (LP).

several musicians, including **Took** and various members of **The Deviants**. **Twink** sings as well as drums on the album, which is a mixture of his own songs (including some instrumentals) and poems. It is a very significant disc in the wilderness of British psychedelia. Its highlights included the opening cut, *The Coming Of The Other One*, with its Eastern-sounding gongs, bongos, sitars, backward tapes and sighs and screams; *The Sparrow Is The Sign* and *Thousand Words In A Cardboard Box*. It wasn't actually released until 1970, though. It is now very collectable but some copies were pressed on red vinyl and these are now ultra-rare. In 1970, **Twink** also formed **Pink Fairies** as a more stable unit with **Mick Farren**, but by mid-1971 **Twink** had left the group and shortly afterwards left the country too.

In 1972, he formed an outfit called Stars with **Syd Barrett** and bassist Jack Monk (ex-Delivery). They only lasted for half a gig before **Barrett** wandered off the stage - indeed, they must be a contender for one of the shortest-lived bands in history. Having married in 1974, **Twink** returned to the music scene in the late seventies.

In 1977 he issued the solo EP *Do It (With The Fairies)*. After this he continued to tour and partake in the occasional **Pink Fairies** reunion. In 1989 he recorded *You Need A Fairy Godmother* with the neo-psych outfit Plasticland. *Mr. Rainbow* followed in 1990.

From The Vaults compiles previously unreleased songs from the mid-seventies onwards and *The Lost Experimental Recordings 1970* is put together from tapes recorded in a small London basement studio. It consists of spacey, low sound quality instrumentals and is for diehard fans only. *Never Never Land & Think Pink Demos*, which is available in both vinyl in a deluxe gatefold sleeve and on CD collects demos and previously unreleased late sixties material. Highlights include *Fluid*, *Gandalf's Garden* and *The Coming Of The Other One* and there's also a 2000 remix/remaster of *Ten Thousand Words In A Cardboard Box*. *Odds And Beginnings* compiles radio broadcast, interviews and alternate mixes from his times with **Tomorrow**, **Pretty Things** and **The Pink Fairies** and is available in vinyl and CD (with seven extra tracks). (VJ)

Twinkle

EP: 1   TWINKLE - A LONELY SINGING DOLL
                    (Decca DFE 8621) 1965 R2

NB: *Golden Lights* (RPM RPM 505) 2001 is a compilation.

			HCP
45s:	Terry/Boy Of My Dreams	(Decca F 12013) 1964 4	
	Golden Lights/		
	Ain't Nobody Home But Me	(Decca F 12076) 1965 21	
	Tommy/So Sad	(Decca F 12139) 1965 -	
	Poor Old Johnny/		
	I Need Your Hand In Mine	(Decca F 12219) 1965 -	
	The End Of The World/		

Take Me To The Dance	(Decca F 12305) 1965 -
What Am I Doing Here With You?/	
Now I Have You	(Decca F 12464) 1966 -
Micky/Darby And Joan	(Instant IN 005) 1969 -
α Days/Caroline	(Bradleys BRAD 7418) 1974 -
Reissues: Terry/Boy Of My Dreams	(Galaxy GY 104) 1976 -
Terry/Boy Of My Dreams	(Galaxy GY 154) 1978 -
Terry/Golden Lights	(Old Gold OG 9027) 1979 -

NB: All these 45s are on the *Twinkle* CD on RPM issued in 1992. α as Twinkle Ripley.

Twinkle's real name was Marilyn Ripley and she was just 16 when she wrote and recorded *Terry* - the teenbeat song about a boyfriend who crashes his motorbike after a row with his girl. The storyline had similarities to The Shangri-La's *Leader Of The Pack*, which was released in the States the same month. It was not quite a one hit wonder because *Golden Lights*, a P.F. Sloan/Barri number, was a minor hit. Most of her other songs were teenbeat ballads too. She was **Peter Noone**'s girlfriend in 1965, and was also the daughter of GLC Conservative Councillor Sidney Ripley. In 1975, she made a record with him, *Smoochy Smoochy/Always I Love You* (Bradley's BRAD 7513) 1975 under the name Bill and Coo!

Golden Lights compiles her 45s for Decca and Instant, along with a Bradley's single from 1974 and five other cuts, including a rare German language version of her third 45 *Tommy*. The collection comes with a fold-out history of her career.

Compilation appearances include: *Soldiers Dream* on *Immediate Single Collection, Vol. 2* (CD); *Darby And Joan* on *Immediate Single Collection, Vol. 5* (CD) and *Terry* on *The Greatest Sixties Album Of All Time Vol 2* (CD) and *Hippy Chick* (CD). (VJ)

Two and a Half

45s:	Midnight Swim/Faith	(CBS 202248) 1966
	Questions/In Harmony	(CBS 202404) 1966
	Walls Are High/Love You	(CBS 202526) 1967
	Suburban Early Morning Station/	
	Just Couldn't Believe My Ears	(Decca F 22672) 1967 SC
	I Don't Need To Tell You/	
	Christmas Will Be Around Again	(Decca F 22715) 1967 SC

The identity of this group remains unknown, but their best-known recording is *Suburban Early Morning Station*. The opening section is rather derivative of Simon and Garfunkel whilst subsequent passages recall **The Hollies**. After five 45s and no hits, they remained entrenched in obscurity.

Compilation appearances have included: *Suburban Early Morning Station* on *Rubble, Vol. 6 - The Clouds Have Groovy Faces* (LP) and *Rubble, Vol. 4* (CD); and *I Don't Need To Tell You* on *Fading Yellow* (LP). (VJ)

Two Much

| Personnel: | ANDREA GEROME | | A |
| | STEVE GEROME | | A |

45s:	Wonderland Of Love/Mister Money	(Fontana TF 858) 1967
	It's A Hip Hip Hippy World/	
	Stay In My World	(Fontana TF 900) 1968

This pop duo hailed from Middlesex. Their first 45 was produced by **Tony Meehan**. (VJ)

Two of Clubs

| Personnel: | BOB GRANT | | A |
| | MARTIN GRIFFIN | | A |

| 45: | The Angels Must Have Made You/ | |
| | True Love Is Here | (Columbia DB 7371) 1964 SC |

A beaty duo who came from the West Hampstead area of London. (VJ)

Two of Each

Personnel:	MEIK CASTRO	gtr, vcls	A
	JOHN CONRAN	bs	A
	JACQUI DANIELS	drms	A
	MOLLY PAGE	vcls	A

45s:	Every Single Day/I'm Glad I Got You	(Decca F 12626) 1967
	The Summer Of Our Love/	
	Saturday Morning	(Pye 7N 17555) 1968
	Trust/Trinity Street	(Pye 7N 17792) 1969
	Here Comes The Sun/	
	Who Wants Happiness	(NEMS 56-3964) 1969

This is a forgotten late sixties pop quartet - two guys and two girls. Their final 'A' side was a **Beatles** cover.

Molly Page was the sister of **Jackie Trent**, the singer/songwriter who had a UK No 1 with *Where Are You Now (My Love)?* in 1965. Later, with her husband Tony Hatch, she wrote many hits for the likes of Petula Clark. **Two Of Each** were later known as Sweet Corn.

Trust and *Summer Of Our Love* can also be heard on *Ripples, Vol. 7* (CD). (VJ/JM)

Two's Company

| 45: | Now That I Love You/As Before | (Polydor 56072) 1966 |

Another forgotten pop duo. (VJ)

2OW

Syde Trips, Vol. 4 (LP) has uncovered a previously acetate-only track, *What's It All About*, recorded at Pye Studios on 12 June 1967. It's very short and a bit amateurish, which may explain why it was never released. (VJ)

Toby Tyler

| 45: | The Road I'm On (Gloria)/ | |
| | Blowin' In The Wind | (Emidisc no cat no) 1964 R6 |

This is famous for being **Marc Bolan**'s first recording. The 'A' side was a Dion DiMucci song and the flip a Dylan cover. *The Road I'm On* is a simple blues-based strummer. 'Record Collector' in its December 2004 issue values this scratchy acetate at £1,800. *The Road I'm On (Gloria)* was officially issued for the first time when **Bolan** fan Marc Arscott pressed up 1,500 copies as a one-sided 45 in numbered picture sleeves, which were available by mail order. *The Maximum Sound Session* (Zinc Alloy ZAR CD 9006) 1993 (SC) is also relevant. (VJ)

Tyrannosaurus Rex

Personnel:	MARC BOLAN	gtr, vcls	ABC
	STEVE PEREGRIN TOOK	drms, bs, perc, piano	AB
	MICKEY FINN	perc, vcls	C

HCP

ALBUMS:	1(A)	MY PEOPLE WERE FAIR AND HAD SKY IN THEIR HAIR... BUT NOW THEY'RE CONTENT TO WEAR STARS ON THEIR BROWS	
		(Regal Zonophone SLRZ 1003) 1968 R1	15
	2(B)	PROPHET SEERS AND SAGES, THE ANGELS OF THE AGES	
		(w/inserts) (Regal Zonophone SLRZ 1005) 1968 R1	-
	3(B)	UNICORN (Regal Zonophone SLRZ 1007) 1969 R1	12
	4(C)	A BEARD OF STARS	
		(Regal Zonophone SLRZ 1013) 1970 R1	21
	5	MY PEOPLE/PROPHETS (Cube/Fly TOOFA 3) 1972	1

	6	UNICORN/		
		BEARD OF STARS	(Cube/Fly TOOFA 9) 1972	44
	7	BEGINNING OF DOVES	(Track 2410 201) 1974	-

NB: There have been many reissues of (1)-(4) since 1972. Most recently (1) reissued on CD in an expanded remastered edition (Universal 982 250-9) 2004. (2) reissued on CD in an remastered expanded edition (Universal 982 251-0) 2004. (3) reissued on CD in an expanded remastered edition (Universal 982 251-1) 2004. (4) reissued on CD in an expanded remastered edition (Universal 982 251-2) 2004. (1) and (2) reissued as a CD set (That's Original TFOCD 6) 1988, and (3) and (4) reissued as a CD set (That's Original TFOCD 15) 1988.

Most **T Rex** 'Greatest Hits' compilations also feature recordings from their **Tyrannosaurus Rex** days. In addition, *Anthology* (Essential ESBCD 965) 1991 is a 3-CD compilation of his career from 1968-1977. Disc one mostly contains **Tyrannosaurus Rex** material. *BBC Radio One Live In Concert* (Windsong WINCD 032) 1993 is a half an hour recording made for the BBC in January 1970, much of the material is from (4). The CD compilation, *The Definitive Tyrannosaurus Rex* (Sequel NEX CD) 1993 includes all the band's 45s, a couple of out-takes which previously appeared on the 1971 *Best Of T Rex* collection and the pick of their album tracks. *The Missing Link To Tyrannosaurus Rex - Steve Peregrin Took* (Cleopatra CLEO 9528-2) 1995 comprises rambling drugged jams **Took** recorded on an eight track in 1972. *Live At The Middle Earth* (CD) (T Rex Action TAG 200001) compile their earliest recordings from a late 1967 London gig. *Midnight At The Lyceum* (CD) (Burning Airport PILOT 28) captures a live concert from 1969.

					HCP
45s:	α	Debora/Child Star	(Regal Zonophone RZ 3008) 1968	34
		One Inch Rock/			
	α	Salamanda Palaganda	(Regal Zonophone RZ 3011) 1968	28
		Pewter Suitor/Crocodiles	(Regal Zonophone RZ 3016) 1968	-
	α	King Of The Rumbling Spires/			
		Do You Remember	(Regal Zonophone RZ 3022) 1969	44
		By The Light Of The Magical Moon/			
		Find A Little Wood	(Regal Zonophone TZ 3025) 1969	-
Reissues:		Debora/One Inch Rock/Woodland Bop/			
		The Soul Of Seasons	(Magic Fly ECHO 102) 1972	7
	β	Debora/Beltane Walk	(Old Gold OG 9234) 1982	-
		Debora/One Inch Rock	(Old Gold OG 9234) 1982	-

NB: α promos came with picture sleeves and are very rare and collectable. β Mispress.

After his departure from **John's Children Bolan** recorded material for the *Beginning Of Doves* album, although it was not released until 1974. He also tried to form a five-piece electric band which apparently failed when the hire purchase company repossessed their equipment. So eventually, he and **Took**, the only surviving members of their abortive venture, ended up as an acoustic duo in late 1967 and the first two **Tyrannosaurus Rex** albums are entirely acoustic and full of **Bolan**'s own compositions. They were produced by New York-born London-based Tony Visconti and the first was recorded on a budget of just £400. Both albums were well received. The first climbed to No 15. Their first two 45s - *Debora* and *One Inch Rock* - were also minor hits. The third album includes more instrumentation and is perhaps the best this underground act produced. After this, **Took** left the

band, being keen to branch out and write his own material and the final album *A Beard Of Stars* was made by a modified line-up and was transitional between the predominantly acoustic **Tyrannosaurus Rex** and the electric **T Rex**. **Bolan**, in fact, played electric guitar on many of its tracks. Highlights on this album include *Elemental Child*, *Pavilions Of Sun* and the title track. There is a digitally remastered CD reissue of this album, which contains 16 bonus tracks, a slipcase and a 14-page booklet. **Took** never got it together to record any material for release at the time, despite the fact Tony Secunda (**Bolan**'s manager) made available funds and gave him every encouragement to do so. However, he did record some tapes in 1972 which found their way onto CD in 1994, *The Missing Link To Tyrannosaurus Rex - Steve Peregrin Took*.

Tyrannosaurus Rex, being much a part of the 'progressive' underground of the late sixties, received considerable assistance from John Peel. They often appeared on his 'Top Gear' programme and he used his influence to secure several gigs for them. They also issued five singles and the first three were all minor hits. Promotional copies of the first two appeared in picture sleeves and these are now particularly collectable. Both 45s had particularly distinctive acoustic styles. Later in August 1969 *King Of The Rumbling Spiers* charted at No 44. Around 200 copies of these were issued in picture sleeves, which were used as promotional copies for reviewers. All are now extremely rare and very sought-after by **Bolan** collectors.

Tyrannosaurus Rex was unique in style and are worth investigating. Later, of course, **Bolan** formed the much more successful but much less interesting **T Rex**.

Steve Peregrin Took died in November 1980 choking on a cherry which lodged in his throat after a cocktail of morphine and magic mushrooms. **Marc Bolan** was killed on 16 September 1977, when his car, driven by singer and girlfriend Gloria Jones, hit a tree on Barnes Common.

Live At The Middle Earth Club captures their first ever gig at London's Middle Earth Club in late 1967. The tracks featured are *The Wizard*, *Hippy Gumbo*, *Hot Rod Mama* and *Lunacy's Back*. *Midnight At The Lyceum* features a 1969 concert and highlights include *Debora*, *The Wizard* and *One Inch Rock*.

One Inch Rock has been compiled on the 3-CD box set *Ars Longa Vita Brevis: A Compendium Of Progressive Rock 1967-1974*. (VJ/MP)

Lucas Tyson

Lucas Tyson was an unknown artist who appears on the *Hart Rock '71* EP with a reasonable, slightly heavy song, *Daylight Child*.

Daylight Child can also be found on *Beyond The Veil Of Time* (CD), *The Best Of Rubble Collection, Vol. 2* (CD) and *Incredible Sound Show Stories, Vol. 7* (LP). (VJ)

TYRANNOSAURUS REX - My People Were Fair... (LP).

TYRANNOSAURUS REX - Prophets Seers & Sages... (CD).

UFO - UFO I (LP).

UFO

Personnel:	MICK BOLTON	gtr	A
(up to	ANDY PARKER	drms	ABCDEFG
1976)	PHIL MOGG	vcls	ABCDEFG
	PETE WAY	bs	ABCDEFG
	LARRY WALLIS	gtr	B
	BERNIE MARSDEN	gtr	C
	MICHAEL SCHENKER	gtr	DEFG
	PAUL CHAPMAN	gtr	E
	DANNY PEYRONEL	keyb'ds	G

ALBUMS:	1(A)	UFO I	(Beacon BEAS 12) 1970 SC
(up to	2(A)	FLYING (ONE HOUR SPACE ROCK)	
1976)			(Beacon BEAS 19) 1971 SC
	3(A)	UFO: LANDED	( ) 1971
	4(D)	PHENOMENON	(Chrysalis CHR 1059) 1974 SC
	5(F)	FORCE IT	(Chrysalis CHR 1074) 1975
	6(G)	NO HEAVY PETTING	(Chrysalis CHR 1103) 1976

NB: (3) Japanese release, not originally issued in the UK. (1) and (2) reissued as double package (Decca SD 30311/2) in 1973. *The Decca Years* (Repertoire REP 4311-WF) 1993 is a collection of their recordings from the 1970-73 era. (1) and (2) reissued on Line (GACD 900691 and 900694) respectively in 1991. (4) reissued on vinyl (Chrysalis CHR 1059) 1978 and on CD (Episode WSCD 10) 1991. (4) and (5) reissued on a 2-CD set (Beat Goes On BGO BGO CD 227) 1994. (4) digitally remastered and reissued on CD (EMI EMI 7243 5 24628 2 7) 2000. (5) reissued on vinyl (Chrysalis CHR 1074) 1978. (5) digitally remastered and reissued on CD (EMI EMI 7243 5 24599 2 6) 2000. (6) reissued on vinyl (Chrysalis CHR 1103) 1978. (6) reissued on a 2-CD set with *Lights Out* (from 1977) (Beat Goes On BGO BGO CD 228) 1994.

Big Apple Encounters (Majestic MAJCD 008) 2003 was recorded live at New York's Record Planet in 1975 and features material from the *Force It* album. There have been several compilations of their material, including *Headstone - The Best Of UFO* (Chrysalis CTY 1437) 1983 a 2-LP set (No 39), which was later released as a 2-CD set (EMI TOCP 8029 30) in 1988; *The Collection* (2-LP) (Castle CCS LP 101) 1985; *Anthology - UFO* (LP) (Raw Power RAWCD 029) 1987; *Space Metal* (Line GACD 900 704) 1989; *Essential UFO* (Chrysalis CD CHR 1888) 1992; *The Early Years* (BMG CD EARL D) 1992; *Too Hot To Handle: The Best Of UFO* (Music Club MCCD 153) 1993, as its title suggests, includes the best of their studio work and three live cuts, *Doctor, Doctor*, *Only You Can Rock Me* and *Lights Out*.; *Rock And Pop Legends - UFO* (Disky RPCD 002) 1995; *The Michael Schenker/UFO Anthology* (2-CD) (Griffin CCD 235 2AB) 1995; *Champions Of Rock - UFO* (Disky CR 8622552) 1996; *The Best Of UFO* (EMI Gold 7243 8529 6727) 1996; *The X Factor: Out There And Back* (Snapper SMD CD 122) 1997; and *UFO: Original Hit Recordings* (Wise Buy WB 885 952) 1998.

On With The Action: Live At The Roundhouse 1976 (Zoom Club ZCRCD 1) 1998 captures an April 1976 gig in North London, most of the tracks came from their *Force It* album, although the three opening cuts were taken from *Heavy Petting*. *Live* (Repertoire REP 4698-WY) 1998 offers a live recording from 1972 on import. *On With The Action* (Zoom Club ZCR CD 1L) 1999 compiles a live concert from the Roundhouse in 1976 and captures them in form. *Flying: The Early Years 1970-1973* (Sanctuary CMQDD 996) 2004 is a compilation of their three Beacon albums squeezed onto two CDs plus tracks from their *Galactic Love* single from 1972.

45s:	Shake It About/Evil	(Beacon BEA 161) 1970 SC
(up to	Come Away Melinda/	
1976)	Unidentified Flying Object	(Beacon BEA 165) 1970 SC
	Boogie For George/	
	Treacle People (Some w/postcard)	(Beacon BEA 172) 1970 SC
	Prince Kajuka/	
	The Coming Of Prince Kajuka	(Beacon BEA 181) 1971 SC
α	Give Her The Gun/	
	Sweet Little Thing	(Chrysalis CHS 2024) 1973
	Doctor Doctor/Lipstick Traces	(Chrysalis CHS 2040) 1974
α	Shoot Shoot/Love Lost Love	(Chrysalis CHS 2072) 1975

NB: α Unissued.

UFO formed in the Wood Green/Enfield area of North London in August 1969. They played a unique amalgam of underground/progressive pop, R&B and folk-rock in those early days, which was augmented by more power and a little blues when Andy Parker joined the line-up in place of their original drummer.

In March 1970 they signed to the Beacon label and recorded *UFO I* in six evenings at Jackson Studios in Rickmansworth. It was produced by a South London car dealer on a four-track machine and licensed all over the world. Nobody really noticed it at all in Britain but it sold quite well in Germany and Japan. More important, two 45s from the album were released in Japan and became hit singles; in fact, *C'mon Everybody* got to No 1. Amazingly the group, which was surviving on a hand-to-mouth sort of existence in Britain, was in demand to visit Japan. A tour was arranged for them to support Three Dog Night, but when the latter pulled out, **UFO** found themselves headlining the tour and leading the lifestyle of superstars. Their second album, *Flying (One Hour Space Rock)*, will appeal to fans of the space-rock genre.

When Mark Bolton left the band to quit the music business in January 1972, they got Larry Wallis in as a replacement. Wallis had earlier been with **Shagrat** and **Blodwyn Pig**. He wasn't with them long but taught them how to move around and dress up, important considerations in the glam-rock era. By the time he left in October to join **Pink Fairies**, after a personality clash with Phil Mogg, the band had cultivated a distinct visual image, appearing on stage in snakeskin boots, tights, sequins, glitter, leather trousers, arm bands and so on.

Eventually they signed to Chrysalis and recorded a new album, *Phenomenon*, which they toured all over Britain and Scandinavia to promote. By now Schenker had been added to their line-up and Paul Chapman from **Skid Row** was added as a second guitarist around this time but was given the push before they set off on an American tour (he would later rejoin them). After the release of *Force It*, they spent several weeks in America, frenetically touring and establishing a live reputation, which paid off because the album eventually climbed to No 71 in the US Album Charts.

In September 1975, Danny Peyronel (ex-**The Heavy Metal Kids**) was recruited to augment their sound. This line-up recorded the *No Heavy Petting* album, which was also more successful in the US, where it climbed to No 169, but Peyronel didn't really fit in and left in Summer 1976.

They enjoyed a series of further hit albums in the first half of the eighties, with *Mechanix* (1982) the most successful, reaching No 8. Pete Way left the band later that year forming Waysted - his replacement was ex-Eddie and The Hot Rods bassist Phil Gray. They split following *Making Contact* (a No 32 in 1982/3 and the inevitable 'best of' collection *Headstone - The Best Of UFO* was released the same year and also charted. They reformed in 1985 and recorded a new album *Misdemeanour*, but when that only reached the lower echelons of the charts (No 74) they again split.

There was a reunion in 1993 featuring Mogg, Schenker, Way, Raymond and Parker which recorded a new album *Walk On Water* and toured to promote it, but the reunion didn't last long.

Big Apple Encounters is an 11-song set recorded live at New York's Record Planet in 1975 during the 'Force It' tour. The sound quality is good and fans should enjoy this.

Live available on import by Repertoire dates from 1971. Highlights include extravagant versions of Bo Diddley's *Who Do You Love?* and an expanded version of *Prince Kajuka*. The release does not capture them at their very best, though.

UFO - Flying (One Hour Space Rock) (LP).

In 2004 Sanctuary reissued their first three Beacon albums plus the 1972 Decca single on a 2-CD set entitled *Flying: The Early Years 1970-1973*. If you enjoy space-rock you should like this. These recordings capture the band when it had its blues influence and lots of acid guitar work which is evident on the extended tracks like the 20-minute *Star Storm*.

Compilation appearances include *Shoot Shoot* and *Only You Can Rock Me* on the 3-CD box set *Guitar Heroes - Rock The Night Away*; *Shoot Shoot* on the 3-CD set *Radio Caroline Calling - 70's Flashback* and on the CD compilation *Metal Gods*; *Doctor Doctor* on the 3-CD set *Full Throttle - 60 Original Driving Classics*; a live version of *Too Hot To Handle* on *Rock Of Ages, Four Decades of Heavy Rock 1962-2002*; *Doctor Doctor* on the 2-CD sets *Rock Resurrection* and *The Best Heavy Metal Album In The World... Ever!* and on *Axe Attack, Vol 1* (LP) and *Power Chords* (CD); *Mystery Train* on *Axe Attack, Vol 2* (LP); *Rock Bottom* on *Guitar Anthems* (CD); *Only You Can Rock Me* on the 2-CD set *Greatest Rock*; *Doctor Doctor* and *Only You Can Rock Me* on the 6-CD box set *Best Of Driving Rock*; *Lights Out* on *The Best Of Heavy Metal* (CD); *Borderline*, *Too Hot To Handle* (live) and *Shoot Shoot* on *Metal* (CD); *Too Hot To Handle* on *Arena Rocker* (CD); *Highway Lady* on *Harley-Davidson Road Songs* and *Follow You Home* on the 3-CD box set *Ars Longa Vita Brevis: A Compendium Of Progressive Rock*. (VJ/DS)

Ugly Custard

Personnel:	CLEM CATTINI	drms	A
	ROGER COULHAM	keyb'ds	A
	HERBIE FLOWERS	bs	A
	ALAN PARKER	gtr	A

ALBUM: 1(A) UGLY CUSTARD (Kaleidoscope KAL 100) 1971 R2
NB: (1) has been reissued on vinyl (WAH WAH SUPERSONIC SOU LP026).

This is an impressive crew of studio/session musicians, embarking on what could have been the umpteenth boring exploitation album. Luckily, it turns out to be surprisingly good. Side one of this all-instrumental album is made up of covers of songs like *Scarboro' Fair*, *My Babe* and Stephen Stills' *Hung Upside Down*, while side two comprises **Parker** originals. Strangely enough, side one is actually better, pairing imaginative arranging with expert playing. Not as good or disturbing as the similarly-inclined **Blue Phantom** on the same label, this is nonetheless listenable, though nothing very special. **Alan Parker** was also involved in **Hungry Wolf** and made a solo album in 1970 too. (MK/VJ)

The Uglys

Personnel:	BOB BURNETT	gtr	A
	STEVE GIBBONS	vcls	ABC
	JOHN GORDON	keyb'ds	A
	JIMMY HOLDEN	drms	AB
	JOHN HUSTWAYTE	bs	A
	ROGER HILL	gtr	B
	JIMMY O'NEIL	keyb'ds	B
	DAVE PEGG	bs	B
	WILLIE HAMMOND	gtr	C
	DAVE MORGAN	bs	C
	KEITH SMART	drms	C
	RICHARD TANDY	keyb'ds	C

45s:	Wake Up My Mind/Ugly Blues	(Pye 7N 15858) 1965 R1
	It's Alright/A Friend	(Pye 7N 15968) 1965 SC
	A Good Idea/The Quiet Explosion	(Pye 7N 17027) 1966 R1
	End Of The Season/	
	Can't Recall Her Name	(Pye 7N 17178) 1966 R1
	Real Good Girl/	
	And The Squire Blew His Horn	(CBS 2933) 1967 R2
α	I See The Light/Mary Cilento	(MGM MGM 1465) 1969 R6

NB: α Unreleased and credited to The Uglies. The disc was pressed as a demo, there are six known copies, but then it was recalled by MGM. *The Quiet Explosion* (Sanctuary CMQCD 919) 2004 is a long-awaited compilation of their material.

Formed as The Dominettes in Birmingham in 1962 by **Steve Gibbons**, **The Uglys** recorded several singles for Pye including Ray Davies' *End Of The Season*. Towards the end of the sixties they issued *And The Squire Blew His Horn* and *I See The Light*, which was an early example of progressive rock with a psychedelic taint. They evolved into **Balls** in April 1969, but never got it together. **Gibbons** went on to make a solo album, *Short Stories* (Wizard SWZ 45501), before forming **The Steve Gibbons Band**. Pegg had earlier left to form Way Of Life and later joined **Fairport Convention**. Hill later played in **Mongrel** and O'Neill joined a flagging **Mindbenders**.

The Quiet Explosion contains every studio recording they ever made and will be the definitive word on the band. It includes the mega-rare *I See The Light*, BBC Sessions and previously unreleased material, including the superb *This Is Your Mind Speaking*. The set comes with an informative booklet about the band's history, which details all the musicians who passed through their ranks.

Compilation appearances have included: *I See The Light* on *Perfumed Garden Vol. 2* (LP & CD); *The Quiet Explosion* and *A Good Idea* on *Paisley Pop - Pye Psych (& Other Colours) 1966-1969* (CD); *End Of The Season* on *Quick Before They Catch Us* (LP & CD), *Ripples, Vol. 3* (CD) and *Beat Merchants* (CD); *Ugly Blues* on *The R&B Era, Vol. 2* (CD); *Wake Up My Mind* on *Ripples, Vol. 6* (CD), *It Happened Then* (EP) and *Brum Beat - Midlands Beat Groups Of The 60's* (CD); *It's Alright* on *The Sixties File* (2-LP) and on the 2-CD set *We Love The Pirates: Charting The Big 'L' Fab 40*; *End Of The Season* and *Can't Recall Her Name* on *Footsteps To Fame, Vol. 2* (CD) and *I See The Light* and *Mary Cilento* can be found on *Lovely Summer Days* (CD). (VJ)

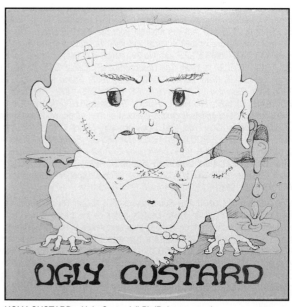

UGLY CUSTARD - Ugly Custard (LP) (Reissue cover).

U.K. Bonds

45s: The World Is Watching Us/
            I Said Goodbye To The Blues   (Polydor BM 56061) 1965
            Anything You Do Is Alright/
            The Last Thing I Ever Do   (Polydor BM 56112) 1966 SC

A mid-sixties band who are forgotten in the seeds of time. Originally known as Carl Dobson and The Meteors they were based in Birmingham. (VJ)

The U.K.s

45s: Ever Faithful, Ever True/
            Your Love Is All I Want   (HMV POP 1310) 1964 SC
            I Will Never Let You Go/I Know (HMV POP 1357) 1964 SC

Little is known about this band. Both sides of their first beat-styled single were written by someone called Tony Bailey. It also got a US release on the Cameo label. The flip of their second effort (*I Know*) is of some repute as a moody R&B style offering.

Your Love Is All I Want has resurfaced on *English Freakbeat, Vol. 3* (LP & CD). (VJ)

Ultrafox

45:      Nine By Nine/Stomping At Decca   (Deram DM 339) 1971

Ultrafox was one of many obscure bands who recorded on Deram in the early seventies. Not to be confused with Ultravox! (VJ)

Uncle Dog

Personnel:
PHILLIP CROOKS	gtr	A
CAROL GRIMES	vcls	A
SAM MITCHELL	gtr	A
JOHN PORTER	gtr, bs	A
DAVE SKINNER	keyb'ds, vcls	A
TERRY STANNARD	drms	A

ALBUM: 1(A) OLD HAT   (Signpost SG 4253) 1972 SC

45:      River Road/First Night   (Signpost SGP 752) 1972

This short-lived rock group included **Carol Grimes**, who fronted Delivery in 1970. She also made solo recordings. John Pearson played drums on four of the tracks and John 'Rabbit' Bundrick, who was later with **The Who**, played piano on a couple of tracks. Most of the songs were penned by Dave Skinner, although there are a few covers, including Dylan's *I'll Be Your Baby Tonight* and Sam C. Phillips/Hermann Parker's *Mystery Train*. **Carol Grimes**' vocals are the most appealing thing about this album. John Porter is a producer nowadays and produced The Smiths and John Lee Hooker's comeback album in 1989. (VJ)

The Undergrads

Personnel:
BARRY GUARD	bs	A
MIKE QUINN	lead gtr	A
GARY SULSH	gtr	A
TREVOR SULSH	bs	A
RICHARD THOMPSON	gtr, vcls	A

45:      Looks Like It's Gonna Be My Year/
            Calling You   (Decca F 12492) 1966

A short-lived mid-sixties band. Thompson was born in Worthing, Sussex on 3 April 1949; Sulsh was in Worcester Park, South London, and Guard in Esher, Surrey. When the band split, Thompson joined **Fairport Convention.** Guard went on to play in **March Hare** and then onto session work. (VJ/JM)

The Underground

Personnel incl: MADELEINE BELL

ALBUM: 1 BEAT PARTY   (Major Minor SMCP 5014) 1969 SC

Madeleine Bell featured on this album. (VJ)

The Underground Set

ALBUM: 1 THE UNDERGROUND SET (Pantonic PAN 6302) 1970 R1
NB: (1) also issued in Italy on Radio Records (RRS 134) 1970.

An obscure album which is now quite rare and collectable and came in a wonderfully colourful cover. The cover provides no clues or information about who was behind this swinging London keyboard-driven instrumental album with occasional backing vocals. In fact it appears that this album was the work of the well-known Italian maestro Giampiero Reverberi who issued another album *War In The Night Before* (Tickle TPLS 5002) 1971 and at least one 45. (VJ/GB)

The Undertakers

Personnel:
DAVE 'MUSHY' COOPER	bs	AB
BOB EVANS	drms	A
CHRIS HUSTON	ld gtr	ABCD
BRIAN JONES	sax, vcls	ABCD
JIMMY McMANUS	vcls	AB
GEOFF NUGENT	gtr, vcls	ABCD
BUGS PEMBERTON	drms	BCD
JACKIE LOMAX	bs, vcls	CD

CD: 1 UNEARTHED   (Big Beat CDWIKD 163) 1995

                                          HCP

45s: Everybody Loves A Lover/
           Mashed Potatoes   (Pye 7N 15543) 1963 SC -
           What About Us/Money   (Pye 7N 15562) 1963 SC -
           Just A Little Bit/Stupidity (Pye 7N 15607) 1964 SC 49

This was one of Merseyside's very first rock groups who formed in Wallasey in 1961. Some members had previously been in an even earlier combo, Bob Evans and The Five Shillings. Still fronted by Evans, they used nicknames (though 'Mushy' Cooper was the only one to survive the passage of time) and lived up to their name by turning up to gigs in a hearse, black frock coats, embalmers' trousers and black top hats.

Before the end of 1961, a kidney ailment forced Evans to leave and Bugs Pemberton was his replacement. The next few months were spent building

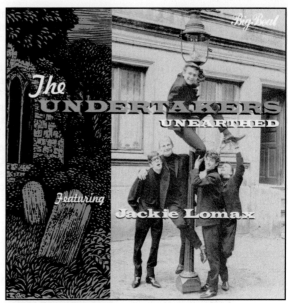

THE UNDERTAKERS - Unearthed (CD).

up a good live reputation playing powerful covers of US soul, R&B and rock'n'roll hits. Their most popular song seems to have been an obscure pounding dance number, originally recorded by Nat Kendrick and The Swans called *Mashed Potatoes*, which was also included on Pye's *Golden Guinea Package Tour* (LP) compilation.

Early in 1962, Cooper left to join **Faron's Flamingoes** and a certain **Jackie Lomax** came on board from another Wallasey group, Dee and The Dynamites. They sometimes backed **Beryl Marsden** and a black vocal group, **The Chants**, who did lots of Coasters songs.

After McManus left to join **The Renegades**, they had their first of a series of spells in Hamburg. They were also signed by Pye but none of their three 45s really captured their exciting live sound on disc, although *Just A Little Bit* was a minor hit. They were mostly cover versions. *Stupidity* was a Soloman Burke song.

They later abbreviated their name to **The 'Takers**, but despite an appearance on 'Thank Your Lucky Stars' failed to achieve a breakthrough.

In August 1965, **The Undertakers** went together with **The Pete Best Combo** to the USA, where they were managed by Bob Gallo and his partner in NYC. Over the following month, both bands recorded an album's worth of material each at their managers studio (Talentmasters on 42nd Street). Chris Huston Recalls: "Pete and his guys played on our stuff and we also played on theirs. We were then sent up to Canada, supposedly to play gigs while our immigration status was worked out. It soon got to be winter, with snow flurries, and we had no money or winter clothes. We all sneaked back across the border and back to NYC. Pete and his group then went home to Liverpool, along with Brian Jones, our saxophonist. Bugs Pemberton and **Jackie Lomax** joined two American musicians and became the Gypsy Wizards, whilst I stayed on at the studio and started producing and engineering. I guess I was lucky!". Chris got to work with The Rascals, James Brown, **The Who**, Van Morrison, Ben E. King, The Drifters, Solomen Burke, Patti La Belle, The Fugs, and Question Mark and the Mysterians to name but a few. He also discovered The Pigeons and got them a deal with Atlantic where their name was changed to Vanilla Fudge. Chris:- "In early 1969, I went to California, where I started a production company/studio called, Mystic. I worked with **Led Zeppelin** there on their *Zeppelin II* album also H.P.Lovecraft and **Screaming Lord Sutch**. In 1969, I also started a long relationship with the band War and have earned many gold and platinum records with them. We are finishing another album "as we speak". I also produced the first Robben Ford album and worked with David Clayton Thomas and BS&T and was VP in charge of production for Far Out Productions during the late seventies."

Jackie Lomax was later in **Lomax Alliance** and also launched a solo career. Chris Huston now runs a successful Recording Studio design company, whilst Dave 'Mushy' Cooper sadly died in 1998. Chris: "I did not know of the passing of Davey Cooper. I have fond memories of him. He worked for a coalman and we would have to follow the coal lorry to the end of its route in order to get Davey in time for a gig. He would go on stage, black streaks of sweat pouring down his face - good times and great music!!!"

In 1995, Big Beat released a retrospective CD, *Unearthed*, which contained the band's unissued album, which was cut live in the studio and comprised mostly of cover versions, in addition to their three singles.

Compilation appearances have included: *Just A Little Bit* on *Mersey Beat* (2-LP), *The Sixties File* (2-LP) and *It Happened Then* (EP); *Everybody Loves A Lover* and *Do The Mashed Potatoes* on *Mersey Beat 1962-1964* (2-LP); *Stupidity* on *Pop Inside The Sixties, Vol. 3* (CD); *Do The Mashed Potatoes* on *Ripples, Vol. 5* (CD); *Do The Mashed Potatoes, Stupidity, Everybody Loves A Lover* and *Just A Little Bit* on *Some Other Guys* (2-LP); *Money* and *What About Us* on *What About Us* (CD) and *Merseybeat Nuggets, Vol. 2* (CD); *(I Fell In Love) For The Very First Time* on *Diggin' For Gold, Vol. 2* (LP & CD); *Stupidity* and *Just A Little Bit* on *Footsteps To Fame, Vol. 1* (CD); and *Throw Your Love Away Girl* on *Incredible Sound Show Stories, Vol. 9* (LP). (VJ/JC/CH)

The Undivided

ALBUM: 1   LISTEN TO THE WORLD   (Decca SKL 5168) 1974

45:       Listen To The World/Harder They Come   (Decca F 13522) 1974

A mid-seventies band of little significance. The flip side of their 45 was a Jimmy Cliff song. (VJ)

The Unexplained

The now legendary (among collectors of psychedelia) compilation *Chocolate Soup For Diabetics, Vol. 1* (LP) included this band's organ driven instrumental, *A Walk Down Emily Lane*, from October 1966. (VJ)

Unicorn

Personnel:	KEN BAKER	gtr, vcls, keyb'ds	ABC
(up to	PAT MARTIN	bs, vcls, mandolin	ABC
1976)	TREVOR MEE	gtr, vcls, flute	A
	PETER PERRIER	drms, vcls	ABC
	KEVIN SMITH	gtr	BC
	CHRIS PIDGEON	keyb'ds	C

ALBUMS:	1(A)	UPHILL ALL THE WAY	(Transatlantic TRA 238) 1971 SC
(up to	2(B)	BLUE PINE TREES	(Charisma CAS 1092) 1974
1976)	3(C)	TOO MANY CROOKS	(Harvest SHSP 4054) 1976

NB: (1) reissued on vinyl (Breathless 52011) and on CD (Get Back GET 583). (2) and (3) issued on Capitol in US, with (3) under a different title as *Unicorn II*. There was one further album *One More Tomorrow* (Harvest) 1977, recorded with Howie Casey (sax) and Billy Livsey (keyb'ds). *Best Of Unicorn* (CD) (See For Miles SEECD 715) is a 20-track anthology.

45s:	Going Home/Another World	(Hollick and Taylor HT 1258) 196?
(up to	P.F. Sloan/Going Back Home	(Big T BIG 138) 1971
1976)	Cosmic Kid/All We Really Want To Do	(Big T BIG 509) 1973
	Ooh! Mother/Bogtrotter	(Charisma CB 321) 1974
	I'll Believe In You/Take It Easy	(Charisma CD 255) 1975
	Disco Dancer/Easy	(Harvest HAR 5105) 1976

Previously known as The Late, this was a pleasant country/folk band, who gradually became rockier and perhaps less interesting as a result. The *Going Home* 45 was a private pressing. The first Big T 45, *P.F. Sloan*, was a tribute to the American songwriter and, like flip side, is excellent. Dave Gilmour (of **Pink Floyd**) played on some of their albums and produced some of their material.

Ferrier later went on to Co-Co and Smith later played in Thumbs. Compilation appearances include *115 Bar Joy* on *The Transatlantic Story* CD box set. (MWh/JM)

Unit Four Plus Two

Personnel:	DAVID MEIKLE	gtr, vcls	AB
	TOMMY MOELLER	gtr, vcls	ABCD
	PETE MOULES	vcls	ABCD
	BRIAN PARKER	vcls	A
	HOWARD LUBIN	gtr, vcls	BCD
	ROD GARWOOD	bs	C
	HUGH HALLIDAY	drms	C
	RUSS BALLARD	gtr	D
	BOB HENRIT	drms	D

ALBUMS:	1(B)	UNIT FOUR PLUS TWO	(Decca LK 4697) 1965 R2
	2(C)	UNIT FOUR PLUS TWO	(Fontana SFL 13123) 1969 R2
	3( )	REMEMBERING	(Decca REM 6) 1977

NB: There's also a CD compilation, *Concrete And Clay* (Repertoire REP 4191-WY) 1993, which comprises their first two albums and six non-album 'A' and 'B' sides. *Singles As and Bs* (Repertoire REP 5016) 2004 compiles all the 45s below.

EP:	1(C)	UNIT FOUR PLUS TWO	(Decca DFE 8619) 1965 R1

HCP

45s:	The Green Fields/		
	Swing Down Chariot	(Decca F 11821) 1964 SC	48
	Sorrow And Pain/The Lonely Valley	(Decca F 11994) 1964	-
	Concrete And Clay/When I Fall In Love	(Decca F 12071) 1965	1

UNICORN - Uphill All The Way (LP).

(You've) Never Been In Love Like This Before/		
Tell Somebody You Know	(Decca F 12144)	1965 14
Hark/Stop Wasting Your Time	(Decca F 12211)	1965 -
You've Got To Be Cruel To Be Kind/		
I Won't Let You Down	(Decca F 12299)	1965 -
Baby Never Say Goodbye/Rainy Day	(Decca F 12333)	1966 49
For A Moment/Fables	(Decca F 12398)	1966 -
I Was Only Playing Games/		
I've Seen The Light	(Decca F 12509)	1966 -
Too Fast, Too Slow/Booby Trap	(Fontana TF 834)	1967 SC -
Butterfly/A Place To Go	(Fontana TF 840)	1967 -
α Loving Takes A Little Understanding/		
Would You Believe What I Say?	(Fontana TF 891)	1967 -
You Ain't Goin' Nowhere/		
So You Want To Be A Blues Player	(Fontana TF 931)	1968 -
3.30/I Will	(Fontana TF 990)	1969 -
Reissue: Concrete And Clay/When I Fall In Love	(Decca F 13478)	1973 -

NB: α credited to the Unit.

The roots of this Hertfordshire band lie with an instrumental combo The Hunters, from the Hertford/Cheshunt/Waltham Cross area. They recorded for Fontana in the early sixties. Their guitarist Brian Parker left the band early in 1962 and briefly joined **The Roulettes** but his ambition was to form a vocal group and after recruiting Moeller, Moules and Meikle, they began to gig in boys clubs and other local venues with sufficient success to turn pro. At this point, ill health forced Parker to leave and Howard Lubin stepped in to replace him. However, Parker remained the group's lyricist.

In 1963, they called themselves **Unit Four** (inspired by the fourth unit of Alan Freeman's 'Pick Of The Pops' show, Unit Four which played all the latest hits). Towards the end of 1963, they became Plus Two when a rhythm section of Garwood and Halliday was added to give their sound more meat.

Their debut single for Decca, *The Green Fields*, was folky with a gospel tinge and it was a minor hit. The follow-up, *Sorrow And Pain*, also had some pleasant vocal harmonies. But it was *Concrete And Clay*, with some nifty acoustic guitar work and a bossa nova drumbeat, which was their magnum opus. The song was one of the finest pop records of 1965. Not only was it a UK No 1, it was a worldwide hit. Incidentally, the band's usual rhythm section was discarded for this 45 in favour of two members of **The Roulettes**, Russ Ballard and Bob Henrit.

Decca quickly put out an album to capitalise on the 45's success, which was very diverse, ranging from Latin-flavoured folk to gospel-beat and more mainstream R&B and soul covers. Three of the tracks, *Wild Is The Wind*, *Cottonfields* (which was later covered by The Beach Boys) and *Cross A Million Mountains* appeared on an EP along with the gospel-influenced cut *To Be Redeemed*. Their next 45, *You've Never Been In Love Like This Before*, was more soul-tinged and mid-tempo. It failed to match the massive success of *Concrete And Clay* but did make the UK Top 20.

However, the group became a victim of its failure to move with the times. They seemed very straight in those trendy days of the mid-sixties. They did make a few other quality 45s, though:- *You've Got To Be Cruel To Be Kind* combined the soul influence of *You've Never Been In Love...* with the Latin guitar sound of *Concrete And Clay*; *Baby Never Say Goodbye* was a good song in the *Concrete And Clay* style and *I Was Only Playing Games* even gave a nod towards psychedelia with some unusual chord progressions and lavish orchestrated backing. The flip made interesting use of echoed guitar effects, too.

In 1967, they signed to Fontana for a few half-decent pop singles. By the end of the year Garwood left, as did Halliday (to return to acting) and Meikle. This conveniently coincided with the break-up of **The Roulettes** and enabled Ballard and Henrit to become a permanent part of the band, which, although now a five-piece, still used the name **Unit Four Plus Two**. In 1968, this line-up recorded a solid cover of Bob Dylan's *You Ain't Going Nowhere*, though it was outsold by the version by the more fashionable Byrds. In contrast, their final 45, *3.30/I Will*, released in 1969, is full of harpsichords and lavish orchestration. *3.30* is a beautiful orchestrated ballad with effective guitar and echoed vocals. *I Will* is a beat single with some quality guitar/organ interplay and effective percussion. By then, though, psychedelia was giving way to progressive rock, so again they missed out.

They split up in 1969 well and truly out of touch with the times. The same year, Fontana issued a compilation album, which contained many of their 45 tracks for the label and a wide variety of other material. The posthumous Decca album includes some tracks from their first album, their biggest hits and cover of Jimmie Rodgers' 1965 hit, *Woman From Liberia*.

The Singles As and Bs is a 20-track collection of 'A' and 'B' sides from 1964-1969 and the digipak set comes with a detailed booklet.

Concrete And Clay is the song they'll always be remembered for but some of their other more interesting 45s are well worth tracking down.

Compilation appearances include: *Baby Never Say Goodbye* on *Mod Scene, Vol. 2* (CD); *I Will* on *Rubble, Vol. 1 - The Psychedelic Snarl* (LP) and *Rubble, Vol. 1* (CD); *3.30 AM* on *Rubble, Vol. 4 - The 49-Minute Technicolour Dream* (LP) and *Rubble, Vol. 3* (CD); *So You Want To Be A Blues Player* on *Rare 60's Beat Treasures, Vol. 4* (CD); *Would You Believe What I Say* on *Voyage Through The Sugarcube* (LP & CD); *I Was Only Playing Games* on *The Beat Scene* (CD); *Women From Liberia* on *Fourteen, Lord Taverners* (LP); *Concrete And Clay* on *60's Mix* (CD) and on the 2-CD set *60 Number Ones Of The Sixties*; and *Booby Trap* on *Colour Me Pop, Vol 3* (CD). (VJ)

Unity

45:	We've Got To Get In To Get On/	
	Rainy Days	(Decca F 13200) 1971

This was an obscure one-off release. (MWh)

The Universals

Personnel:	TONY DANGERFIELD	bs	A
	BRIAN KEITH	sax	A
	CHRIS LAMB	vcls	A
	JOHN LAWSON	bs	A
	CARLO LITTLE	drms	A
	BILLY PARKINSON	lead gtr	A

45s:	I Can't Find You/Hey You	(Page One POF 032) 1967 R2
	Green Veined Orchid/	
	While The Cat's Away	(Page One POF 049) 1967 SC

This band had earlier recorded for Decca in 1965 as Chris Lamb and The Universals and then backed **Gidian** on his third Columbia 45 in 1966, before signing to Page One for these two efforts. Lawson was later in **Gary Walker and The Rain** and **Lace**.

Compilation appearances include: *Hey You* on *Echoes From The Wilderness - Sixteen UK R&B Freakbeat Trippers* (LP & CD) and on *Oddities, Vol 1* (CD). (VJ/AD)

893

ENGLISH FREAKBEAT VOL. 5 (Comp CD) featuring The Untamed.

The Untamed

45s:	So Long/Just Wait	(Decca F 12045) 1964 R2
	Once Upon A Time/	
	I'm Asking You	(Parlophone R 5258) 1965 R3
	I'll Be Crazy/My Baby Is Gone	(Stateside SS 431) 1965 R2
	It's Not True/	
	Gimme Gimme Some Shade	(Planet PLF 103) 1966 R2

All of these 45s have become collector's items and are worth finding. The London-based band's *I'll Be Crazy*, featured a young **Jimmy Page** on session guitar. Their final 45, *It's Not True*, was a Shel Talmy-produced attempt to sound like **The Who**.

They recorded a second 45 for Planet as **Lindsay Muir's Untamed**.

Compilation appearances have included: *I'll Go Crazy* on *James Patrick Page: Session Man, Vol. 2* (LP & CD), *The Demention Of Sound* (LP), *That Driving Beat* (CD) and *Once Upon A Time* on *R&B Scene, Vol. 1* (LP); and *It's Not True* on *The Best Of Planet Records* (CD) and *English Freakbeat, Vol. 5* (LP & CD). (VJ)

Upp

Personnel:	STEPHEN AMAZING	bs	AB
	ANDY CLARK	keyb'ds, vcls	AB
	JIM COPLEY	drms	AB
	DAVID BUNCE	gtr	B

ALBUMS:	1(A)	UPP	(CBS EPIC 80625) 1975
(up to	2(B)	THIS WAY UPP	(CBS EPIC 81322) 1976
1976)			

NB: (1) and (2) reissued on a 2-CD set *The Complete Upp* (Castle CMEDD 1031) 2005 set along with seven demos.

45:	Dance Your Troubles Away/	
(up to	I Don't Want Nothing	(Epic EPC 4204) 1976
1976)		

A progressive funk band formed in 1973 by Andy Clark and Stephen Amazing from **Clark-Hutchinson** and Jim Copley from **Spreadeagle**. Curiously described as **ELP** meets Isaac Hayes this inventive band's first album was produced by **Jeff Beck** who also played some of his best guitar work of the seventies on it. The second release again featured **Beck** but by now the original trio had expanded to include the **Beck**-influenced guitarist, David Bunce. **Upp** split around the time of the second album's release. During their time together they regularly sold out the Marquee with their steaming live shows, but disappeared when punk wiped out the scene in 1976/1977. Copley later turned up in Tears For Fears and Go West, and Andrew Clarke joined **Be-Bop Deluxe**.

The Complete Upp compiles their two studio albums as well as bonus demo tracks from a proposed third album. (JN/JM)

Urban

The compilers of *Syde Trips, Vol. 4* (LP) deserve credit for unearthing this band's *When My Train Comes In*, a strong song written by a Ron Roker with good vocals and stunning guitar. It deserved a better fate. (VJ)

Uriah Heep

Personnel:	MICK BOX	gtr, vcls	ABCDEFG
(up to	DAVID BYRON	vcls	ABCDEFG
1976)	KEN HENSLEY	keyb'ds, gtr, vcls	ABCDEFG
	ALEX NAPIER	drms	A
	PAUL NEWTON	bs, vcls	ABCD
	NIGEL OLSSON	drms	B
	KEITH BAKER	drms	C
	IAN CLARKE	drms	D
	MARK CLARKE	bs, vcls	E
	LEE KERSLAKE	drms, vcls	EFG
	GARY THAIN	bs, vcls	F
	JOHN WETTON	bs, vcls	G

HCP

ALBUMS:	1(B)	VERY 'EAVY VERY 'UMBLE		
(up to			(Vertigo 6360 006) 1970	R1 -
1976)	2(C)	SALISBURY	(Vertigo 6360 028) 1971	R1 -
	3(D)	LOOK AT YOURSELF	(Bronze ILPS 9169) 1971	SC 39
	4(F)	DEMONS AND WIZARDS	(Bronze ILPS 9193) 1972	20
	5(F)	THE MAGICIAN'S BIRTHDAY		
			(Bronze ILPS 9213) 1972	28
	6(E)	URIAH HEEP LIVE (2-LP)	(Bronze ILSD 1) 1973	23
	7(F)	SWEET FREEDOM	(Bronze ILPS 9245) 1973	18
	8(F)	WONDERWORLD	(Bronze ILPS 9280) 1974	23
	9(E)	RETURN TO FANTASY	(Bronze ILPS 9335) 1975	7
	10(-)	BEST OF URIAH HEEP (Compilation)		
			(Bronze ILPS 9375) 1975	-
	11(G)	HIGH AND MIGHTY	(Bronze ILPS 9384) 1976	55

NB: In 1977 Bronze reissued all of the above catalogue. Also (1) reissued on vinyl (Bronze ILPS 9142) 1971 and (2) reissued on vinyl (Bronze ILPS 9152) 1971. (1) - (6) was issued on Mercury in the US, where (7) - (11) appeared on Warner Bros. (1) - (5) were later reissued in the UK by Castle Classics in 1986, both on album and CD. (1) reissued on CD (Castle Classics CLACD 105) 1990, again (Castle CMTCD 327) 2001 and yet again (Castle/Sanctuary CMRCD 642) 2002, with even more previously unissued material as bonuses and most recently (Sanctuary SMRCD 048). (1) just reissued (2005) on vinyl by Earmark. (2) reissued on CD (Castle Classics CLACD 106) 1988, again (Castle CMTCD 327) 2001 and yet again (Castle/Sanctuary CMRCD 643) 2002, with even more previously unissued material as bonuses. (2) reformatted yet again on CD (Earmark 41025) 2004. (3) reissued on CD (Castle Classics CLACD 107) 1989. (1) and (3) reissued as a CD set (That's Original TFOCD 7) 1988. (4) reissued on CD (Castle Classics CLACD 108) 1986. (4) also reissued on vinyl. (5) reissued on CD (Castle Classics CLACD 109) 1988 and again (Castle CMRCD 771) 2003, with bonus tracks. (6) reissued on CD (Raw Power RAWCD 41) 1990 and again as a 2-CD set (Castle CMTCD 329) 2001 and again (Castle CMRCD 772) 2003, with the original double album sueezed onto one CD and with the second taken from the *Live At The Shepperton '74* set. (7) reissued on CD (Castle Classics CLACD 183) 1990. (8) reissued on CD (Castle Classics CLACD 184) 1990. (9) reissued on CD (Castle Classics CLACD 175) 1989 and again on CD (Essential ESMCD 381) 2005. (11) reissued on CD (Castle Classics CLACD 191) 1991. Most of their albums have now been digitally remastered and reissued on CD with at least two bonus tracks on each and accompanied by informative booklets. Here are the details:- (1) (Essential! ESMCD 316) 1995, (2) (Essential! ESMCD 317) 1995, (3) (Essential! ESMCD 318) 1995, (4) (Essential! ESMCD 319) 1995, (5) (Essential! ESMCD 339) 1995, (6) (Essential! ESMCD 320) 1995, (7) (Essential! ESMCD 338) 1995, (8) (Essential! ESMCD 380) 1995, (9) (Essential! ESMCD 381) 1995, and (11) (Essential! ESMCD 468) 1997 and again (Essential ESCMCD 468) 2005.

Other releases which may interest collectors include *Anthology*, a double album (Raw Power RAWLP 012) 1986, also on CD; *Live In Europe, 1979* (Raw Power RAWLP 030) 1987, also on CD; and *The Collection*, a double album (Castle CCSLP 226), released in 1989, also on CD. *Rarities From The Bronze Age* (Sequel NEXCD 184) 1991 was very welcome as it included a number of rare flip sides as does *The Lansdowne Tapes* (RPM 115) 1993 which includes seven tracks by **Spice**, an earlier incarnation of the band through to **Uriah Heep's** *Look At Yourself* 45. Rare photos and memorabilia, accompanied the sleeve-notes. Other compilations have included *Best Of Uriah Heep* (Starr 610 358) 1988; *Uriah Heep - Echoes In The Dark* (Pickwick ELITE 020 CD) 1991; the CD set, *Two Decades In Rock* (Essential

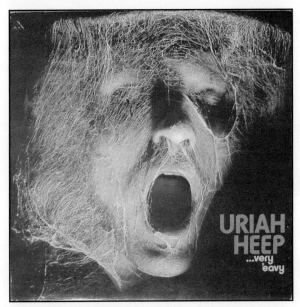

URIAH HEAP - Very 'Eavy Very 'Umble (LP).

ESRCD 022) 1990; *CD Box Set* (Castle Classics CLA BX 903) 1992; *The Uriah Heep Story* (EMI ROHACD 2) 1990; and *Lady In Black* (CD) (Spectrum 5507302) 1995. *Best Of ?. (Part 1)* (CD) (Essential ESMCD 418) compiles material from 1970 to 1976 and contains two bonus tracks.

There's a lovingly assembled compilation, *A Time Of Revelation 25 Years On* (Essential! ESFCD 298) 1995, a 4-CD set which traces the band's career from the late sixties until their demise. It comes with a 60-page colour booklet and the sound has carefully been remastered. *Travellers In Time - Anthology Volume 1* (Essential ESD CD 818) 2000 is a 2-CD anthology which compiles 30 tracks covering the period up to 1976. *Empty The Vaults: The Rarities* (Castle CMRCD 237) 2001 is as its name suggests a collection of rare material. *Come Away Melinda: The Ballads* (Castle CMRCD 238) 2001 compiles their lighter material from the seventies. *Remasters - The Official Anthology* (Classic Rock Legends CRL 0932) 2001 is a 2-CD set comprising re-recorded or remastered material spanning their 30 year careeer - many classics are included. The set includes a number of interesting out-takes and live recordings which are likely to whet the appetite of the band's fans. *You Can't Keep A Good Band Down* (Essential CMXBX 527) 2002 is an 8-CD box set. *The Very Best Of Uriah Heep* (BMG 82876 501942) 2003 seems an unnecessary compilation, given the others already on the market when it was released and the sleevenotes and sleeve hardly add to its appeal. By contrast *The Ultimate Collection* (Sanctuary Midline SANDD 189) 2003 is a well-compiled 2-CD anthology. *Chapter And Verse* (6-CD) (Sanctuary SMXBX 233) 2005 is an extremely comprehensive collection and it contains 12 unreleased tracks, alternate versions, demos and a whole disc featuring an unreleased concert from their 1979 'Fallen Angel' tour. *Classic Collection* (CD) (Collectables COL 84702) compiles many of their finest moments. Recently there have been two new live sets: *Live at Shepperton '74* (Essential ESMCD 590) 2005 and *Live In Moscow* (Essential ESMCD 611) 2005.

45s:	α	Lady In Black/Simon The Bullet Freak	(Vertigo 6059 037) 1970
(up to		Look At Yourself/	
1976)		Simon The Bullet Freak	(Bronze WIP 6111) 1971
		The Wizard/Gypsy	(Bronze WIP 6126) 1972
		Easy Livin'/Why	(Bronze WIP 6140) 1972
		Stealin'/Sunshine	(Bronze BRO 7) 1973
		Something Or Nothing/What Can I Do	(Bronze BRO 10) 1974
		Prima Donna/Shout It Out	(Bronze BRO 17) 1975
		One Way Or Another/	
		Misty Eyes (promo PS)	(Bronze BRODJ 1) 1976
		One Way Or Another/Misty Eyes	(Bronze BRO 27) 1976
Reissue:	β	Lady In Black/July Morning/	
		Easy Livin'	(Special Edition CD 3-16) 1988

NB: β CD single. α Not issued in the UK at the time.

Uriah Heep was one of the most popular hard-rock bands of the early seventies.

The roots of **Uriah Heep** lay in two late sixties bands. Byron and Box, who were both from Epping in Essex, originally played together in 1967 in a band called The Stalkers, which became **Spice**, whose later line-up also included Paul Newton. **Ken Hensley** had previously formed **The Gods** (which had also included Newton and drummer Lee Kerslake, who joined **Uriah Heep** in 1971). **Hensley** was also in **The Cliff Bennett Band** and **Bennett**'s subsequent **Toe Fat** en route to **Uriah Heep**. He may also have been a member of **Head Machine** under the pseudonym Ken Leslie.

Kerslake was also in **Toe Fat** and **National Head Band** before joining **Uriah Heep**.

Hensley, Box and Byron got together to form a heavy rock band in 1970 and took the name from the swindling accountant in the book 'David Copperfield'. 1970 was the centenary of Charles Dickens' death so there was a lot of interest in his books at the time.

They signed to the new Vertigo label and started work on an album, adding bassist Tony Newton and drummer Alex Napier to their line-up. Napier soon left and was replaced by Nigel Olsson, who'd earlier been with **Plastic Penny**, but he was only with them a short while too before departing for **Elton John**'s backing group.

The *Very 'Eavy Very Humble* album had some decent moments, particularly on *Gypsy*, which was adopted as the band's anthem and also appeared on *The Vertigo Annual* (2-LP) compilation in 1970, also included their acclaimed re-work of Tim Rose's *Come Away Melinda*.

Various drummers were tried but eventually Keith Baker (ex-**Bakerloo**) got the job on the *Salisbury* album, an important progressive recording which indicated a clear change of direction for the band. Church organ effects and operatic vocals were brought into play alongside Box's killer guitar riffs. On the 16-minute title track, a large brass and woodwind section was brought in too. Another song, *Lady In Black*, was issued as a 45. It was a No 1 twice in Germany. US copies of the album featured *Simon The Bullet Freak* (the flip side to their first two UK 45s, which was not on the UK album) in place of *Birds Of Prey* and this has made it sought-after by some collectors.

Baker quit soon after the album's release and Ian Clarke (ex-**Cressida**) came in to replace him. The band also signed a new record deal with Gerry Bron's new Bronze label, who reissued their first two albums.

Their next album, *Look At Yourself*, was accompanied by a sleeve with a transparent mirror effect, enabling the buyer to do just that. One of its finest numbers was *July Morning*, which featured a Moog synthesizer and featured members of Osibisa and **Manfred Mann**. This album climbed to No 39 in the UK Charts, but Clarke and Newton left, to be replaced by Lee Kerslake and Mark Clarke (briefly), then Gary Thain (ex-**Keef Hartley**).

Their next album, *Demons And Wizards*, is regarded as their magnum opus, climbing to No 20 in the Charts. It blended progressive rock, heavy metal and a sort of gospel folk style and its highlights included *The Wizard* which featured operatic vocal parts and very prominent organ-driven sound. By now, they had established a good reputation as a live touring band. Singles success still eluded them here in Britain; neither *The Wizard* nor *Easy Livin'* culled from the album were hits here, although the latter was a big hit on the Continent.

Another of their best songs was the title track to their next album, *The Magician's Birthday*. This 10-minute epic featured some fine guitar work from Box. There were plenty of other good tracks on this album, too, like

URIAH HEAP - Salisbury (LP).

Sweet Lorraine, Spider Woman and Sunrise. The 2003 reissue of this album comes with extra tracks and better sleevenotes.

Their *Live* album was taken from a concert recorded at Birmingham Odeon in 1973. It was lavishly packaged and came with an eight-page booklet. It starts with *Sunrise* and one Heep classic follows another with *Gypsy, Easy Lovin'* and *Look At Yourself* included. It concludes with a rock'n'roll medley, including *Roll Over Beethoven* and *Blue Suede Shoes*. Their live reputation was further enhanced when they appeared at London's Alexandra Palace in August 1973, headlining the British Music Festival.

Sweet Freedom, their sixth album, was another strong effort which made the Top 20. *Stealin'* was taken from it as a 45 - failed to chart, but remains one of their most popular songs. By contrast, the follow-up, *Wonderworld*, was weak. Then Thain took a fatal drug overdose, having been out of the band for several months after electrocuting himself on stage. John Wetton (ex-**Family** and **King Crimson**) replaced him.

Uriah Heep certainly demonstrated the resilience to reverse the recent downturn in their fortunes when their next album, *Return To Fantasy*, became their biggest album to date. It spawned another good 45, *Prima Donna,* but as with their previous efforts, the singles buying public just weren't interested.

Bronze put out a *Best Of Uriah Heep* compilation in 1975. By now, though, Byron had developed drink problems, which had disrupted the recording of their *High And Mighty* album. In June 1976, he left the band but went on to form his own outfit for a couple of solo albums in the late seventies. He met with a premature death, though, dying of a heart attack in February 1985, brought on by drug and alcohol over-indulgence. John Wetton went on to play with **Roxy Music**, U.K., **Wishbone Ash** and Asia. **Ken Hensley** remained with the band. He'd recorded a solo album back in 1973 and continued a solo career as a member of the band.

You Can't Keep A Good Band Down released in 2002 is an 8-CD box set repackaging seven of their albums (one a double) in miniature gatefold card sleeves with a booklet, containing sleevenotes, extra pictures and a discography. *The Ultimate Collection* is a 2-CD collection, which concentrates on their successful earlier years but includes some of their later material too. *Chapter And Verse* from 2005 is a 6-CD set (**Uriah Heep** has become one of the world's most compiled bands). The set was released to celebrate their 35th anniversary. The set includes some of the band's pre-history with tracks by **The Gods**, **Spice** and **Toe Fat** (from 1968). Otherwise the first disc concentrates on early **Uriah Heep** material - the highlights include the operatic *Birds Of Prey* and *Gypsy*. Disc two contains many of their seventies classics and will have a wide appeal. The third disc concentrates on more classic seventies driving rock from their David Byron years. Discs four and five concentrate on the late seventies and eighties with John Lawton as their vocalist. Disc six features some unreleased live material, including a previously unreleased set from their 1979 'Fallen Angel' tour with Lawton as vocalist. There's also a set from 1985 with Trevor Bolder shinning on guitar, more recent live tracks and a 12-minute interview. All in all this is a worthy release to excite their fans and collectors.

They may have enjoyed an indifferent press over the years but **Uriah Heep** were hard-working and durable. Very durable, in fact, for they not only recorded for the rest of the seventies, but were present throughout the eighties, nineties and are stilll going strong in the new millenium.

Compilation appearances have included *Easy Living* on the CD set *Rock Of Ages, Four Decades Of Heavy Rock 1962-2002* and on the 3-CD box set *Ars Longa Vita Brevis: A Compendium Of Progressive Rock 1967-1974; Gypsy* on the 2-CD set *Rock Resurrection; Easy Livin'* on *The Best Heavy Metal Album In The World... Ever!; July Morning* on the 3-CD box set *Radio Caroline Calling - 70's Flashback; Look At Yourself* and *Sweet Lorraine* on *Metal Gods* (CD); and, finally, *Easy Livin', Gypsy, Look At Yourself, Sweet Lorraine* (live) and *Love Machine* all figure on the 3-CD set *Metal*. (VJ)

VAN DER GRAAF GENERATOR - Aerosol Grey Machine (LP) (US cover).

VAN DER GRAAF GENERATOR - The Least We Can Do Is Wave To Each Other (LP).

VAN DER GRAAF GENERATOR - H To He, Who Am The Only One (LP).

Valentine

45:     Time/Leader Of The Band   (Track 2094 104) 1972

This was an obscure band comprising five guys. (VJ)

The Valkyries

Personnel:	JOHN ADAMS	drms	A
	ALLAN BURTON	bs	ABCD
	TONY CONWAY	sax	ABC
	IAN HUNTER	lead gtr	ABCD
	BILLY MAY	gtr	AB
	GORDON TEMPLETON	drms	B
	TERRY McCLUSKER	drms	CD
	BILLY BURTON	sax	D

45:     Rip It Up/What's Your Name?   (Parlophone R 5123) 1964 R1

This obscure beat recording is now of minor interest to some collectors. The 'B' side was a Little Richard song and the group was one of the least well known from Liverpool's Merseybeat era. McClusker was later in **The Roadrunners**.

What's Your Name? and *Rip It Up* can also be found on *Rare 60's Beat Treasures, Vol. 2* (CD). (VJ/AD)

Valley Of Achor

ALBUM: 1 A DOOR OF HOPE   (Dovetail DOVE 18) 1975 R1

This Christian progressive folk album features mostly female vocals and contains entirely self-penned material. The disc is housed in a great gatefold fantasy sleeve design. They went on to record albums outside the time frame of this book as Achor: *End Of My Day* (Cedar CEDAR 1) 1976 (R1) and *Hosana To The Son Of David* (Dovetail DOVE 54) 1978. (VJ/BS)

The Values

45:     Return To Me/
           That's The Way (some PS)   (Ember EMB S 211) 1966 R2/R1

This is a rare and sought-after single. (VJ)

Vamp

Personnel incl:	ANDY CLARK	organ	A
	MICK HUTCHINSON	ld gtr	A
	VIV PRINCE	drms	A
	PETE SEARS	bs	A

45s: Floatin'/Thinkin' Too Much   (Atlantic 584 213) 1968 R1
    α Green Pea/Wake Up And Tell Me   (Atlantic 584 263) 1969 R3
NB: α Unissued.

This band took its name from the initials of each member's Christian name. They included three former **Sam Gopal's Dream** members, Pete Sears, Andy Clark and Mick Hutchinson and former **Pretty Things'** and **Bunch Of Fives** drummer **Viv Prince**.

Vamp conjured up a laid back, hypnotic atmosphere on the reflective ballad *Floatin'*. Rumours of a 15-minute version of *Floatin'* abound. **Viv Prince** later played with **Denny Laine**. Andy Clark and Mick Hutchinson teamed up in **Clark-Hutchinson** and Clark was also in **Upp**. Pete Sears went on to US bands Silver Metre and Jefferson Starship.

Compilation appearances include: *Thinkin' Too Much* on *Magic Spectacles* (CD); and *Floatin'* on *Perfumed Garden, Vol. 1* (LP & CD) and *Electric Sugar Cube Flashbacks* (CD). (VJ)

The Vampires

45:     Do You Wanna Dance/My Girl   (Pye 7N 17553) 1968

A one-off pop 45. The 'A' side is a weak cover of The Beach Boys' hit with falsetto vocals. *My Girl* is given similar treatment on the flip side. The group were Irish and both sides of the 45 can also be heard on Sequel's *Irish Rock - Ireland's Beat Groups 1964-1969* (CD). (VJ)

Tommy Vance

45s: You Must Be The One/
          Why Treat Me This Way   (Columbia DB 7999) 1966
          Off The Hook/Summertime   (Columbia DB 8062) 1966

This guy was later a DJ for Radio London and Radio One. Generally in this era DJs were better deployed broadcasting than making records. Both 'A' sides were **Rolling Stones'** compositions. **Tommy Vance** is now dead. (VJ)

Harry Vanda

45:     I Love Marie/Gonna Make It   (Polydor 56357) 1969

Harry Vanda is best-known as a member of **The Easybeats**. This was a lone solo effort. (VJ)

Van Der Graaf Generator

Personnel:	PETER HAMMILL	keyb'ds, vcls, gtr	ABCDE
	NICK PEAME	organ	A
	CHRIS SMITH	drms	A
	HUGH BANTON	keyb'ds, gtr, bs	BCDE
	KEITH ELLIS	bs	BC
	GUY EVANS	drms	BCDE
	DAVE JACKSON	sax	DE
	NIC POTTER	bs	D

HCP

ALBUMS:	1(C)	AEROSOL GREY MACHINE	(Fontana 6430 083) 1969	
(up to	2(D)	THE LEAST WE CAN DO IS WAVE TO EACH OTHER		
1976)		(some w/poster)	(Charisma CAS 1007) 1970 R2/R1	47
	3(D)	H TO HE, WHO AM THE ONLY ONE		
			(Charisma CAS 1027) 1970	SC -
	4(E)	PAWN HEARTS		
		(some w/insert)	(Charisma CAS 1051) 1971	SC -
	5(-)	1968-71 (Compilation)	(Charisma CS 2) 1972	-
	6(E)	GOD BLUFF	(Charisma CAS 1109) 1975	-
	7(E)	STILL LIFE	(Charisma CAS 1116) 1976	-
	8(E)	WORLD RECORD	(Charisma CAS 1120) 1976	-

VAN DER GRAAF GENERATOR - Pawn Hearts (LP).

VAN DER GRAAF GENERATOR - Godbluff (LP).

VAN DER GRAAF GENERATOR - Still Life (CD).

NB: (1) was originally a US-only release until Fontana released it here in 1975. Original pressings of (2) R2/remix version R1. Original matrix reads: CAS 1007 A/B. (2) - (8) were all reissued by Charisma during the early eighties. (1) reissued on CD (Repertoire REP 4647-WY) 1997, and both sides of their debut 45 are tagged on the end. (1) reissued on vinyl (Mercury 61238) and on CD (FIE FIE 9116). (2) reissued on CD (Charisma CASCD 1007) 1987. (2) reissued again remastered and expanded with bonus cuts (Charisma CASCDR 1027) 2005. (4) reissued on CD (Charisma CASCD 1051) 1988 and again remastered and expanded with bonus cuts (Charisma CASCDR 1051) 2005. (6) reissued on CD (Charisma CASCD 1109) 1988 and again on CD (Charisma CASCDR 1109) in 2005 with two bonus tracks Forsaken Gardens and A Louise Is Not A Home, recorded live in Italy. (7) reissued on CD (Charisma CASCD 1116) 1987 and again on CD (Charisma CASCDR 1116) in 2005 with bonus tracks. (8) reissued on CD (Charisma CASCD 1120) 1988 and again (Charisma CASCDR 1120/EMI CASCOR 1120) 2005 with bonus tracks.

Also relevant is Time Vaults (Thunderbolt/Demi-Monde CDTB 106) 1993, a collection of demos and rehearsal tapes from the band's dormant era between 1971 and 1975 and I Prophesy Disaster (Virgin CDVM 9026) 1993, a compilation of some of their 45 and album tracks. Maida Vale (Band Of Joy BOYCD 008) 1994 compiles material from the BBC's archives. Other compilations have been First Generation (Virgin COMCD 2) 1987 and Second Generation (Virgin COMCD 3) 1987 and Now And Then (Thunderbolt CDTB 042) 1988, which is also on album. Maida Vale (Strange Fruit SFRSCD 064) 1998 collects BBC sessions (including two 1971 performances and ones from 1975 and 1976). Van Der Graaf Generator (4-CD box set) (Virgin VDGGBOX1) is a 34-track compilation which includes a lot of previously unreleased radio sessions and live material and comes with a lavishly illustrated and detailed 52-page book. An Introduction (CD) (Virgin CDV 2932) is what its title suggests and is a good one at that.

45s: α   People You Were Going To/Firebrand   (Polydor 56758) 1968 R3
(up to   Refugees/
1976)   The Boat Of Millions Of Years   (Charisma CB 122) 1970 R1
            Theme One/W (Some PS)   (Charisma CB 175) 1972 SC/-
            Wondering/Meurglys III   (Charisma CB 297) 1976
            Wondering (Song)/
            Wondering (Heroics) (Promo only) (Charisma PRO 002) 1976 SC

NB: α Withdrawn.

Van Der Graaf Generator is an interesting progressive band which was in many respects unique. As with so many bands of this ilk they were more successful on the Continent than in Britain, where they never developed more than a cult following. The Least We Can Do..., H To He and Pawn Hearts albums are particularly recommended.

Peter Hammill formed this band whilst studying at Manchester University in 1967. Line-up (A) was very short-lived, Peame left before any recordings took place. Line-up (B) included former Koobas' bassist, Keith Ellis, and recorded the People You Were Going To 45 for Polydor. The 'A' side centres around Hammill's dramatic vocals and is almost operatic rock. Firebrand is a more sinister song - characterised by haunting keyboards and Hammill's horror style vocals - it relates a tale of cod-Icelandic mythology. It was their only recording for that label and is now very rare and highly sought-after by fans of the band. Shortly after, they had all their equipment stolen and split up.

Hammill embarked on a solo career but soon invited Banton and Evans back to assist him on what eventually became the first Van Der Graaf Generator album, Aerosol Grey Machine. Originally released in the USA on Mercury it was only available as an import in the UK until Fontana released it here in 1975. There were also two versions of the album yet the catalogue numbers and track listings were identical. One version included Necromancer, the other Squid I, an instrumental. Necromancer was also released on a 45 with Afterwards. The 45, which was only released in the US, is now another sought-after item. This debut album certainly wasn't stunning and made little impression commercially but it is worth a spin. When Repertoire reissued this in 1997, they added both sides of the band's highly sought-after withdrawn debut 45 People You Were Going To/Firebrand as bonus tracks. Soon after its release Keith Ellis departed for Juicy Lucy and in the incestuous world of British rock Nic Potter, who had played with Guy Evans in the final version of The Misunderstood, replaced him. Dave Jackson (from Heebalob, who Chris Smith had left to form) also joined up on sax.

Their next album (which was their first proper UK release) was an important piece in the tapestry of UK progressive rock and it was well received by the critics. Early copies came in a gatefold cover and with lyrics printed on a poster. After The Flood and Refugees were the stand-out tracks and a different version of the latter was recorded for 45 release. This is now also very rare and sought-after by collectors.

Nic Potter left during the recording of H To He and Robert Fripp guested on this and their next effort, Pawn Hearts.

Pawn Hearts included A Plague Of Lighthouse Keepers, an extended 20-minute composition which may have been their finest moment. Full of changes in tempo, volumes and moods it ranges from quiet piano-dominated verses to Hammill's ranting vocals superimposed upon doomy organ work. The song builds up to an erupting crescendo at the end.

Their next 45, Theme One, was an instrumental written by George Martin. It came in a picture sleeve and originals were much sought-after, although it has resurfaced on a few Charisma compilations and on the One More Chance (LP) compilation. It was later used as the theme for Radio One's 'Friday Rock Show'. The group split up once again in 1972, while Hammill pursued a solo career. Charisma released the 1968-71 compilation to try to maintain interest in the band.

Banton, Jackson and Evans were never far away though, often supporting Hammill in his live appearances, and in 1975 Hammill reformed the band with line-up (E). This reformation is generally considered to have produced two decent albums, Godbluff and Still Life before running out of fresh ideas. The Repeat Performance compilation, which came out in 1980, may interest collectors.

Hammill continued to enjoy quite a prolific solo career. The former members of the band have appeared in various combinations on a series of records entitled, The Long Hello. The first of these was put out privately during 1975-76. David Jackson eventually became a school teacher and

Banton designs church organs. The remaining members remained in the music business in some form, in Smith's case in Iceland putting folk tunes on disc.

The group split up after the 1978 live set *Vital*, although many of them appeared on **Hammill**'s subsequent solo albums. They reunited a couple of times in the nineties for one-off gigs and again in 2005 to record a reunion album *Present*.

First Generation is an alternative compilation which showcases their finer tracks from the 1969-1971 period. The band is back together again and has recently put out a new album *Present*.

Killer, a melodramatic progressive piece, has recently resurfaced on *The Age Of Enlightenment - Prog Rock, Vol. 1* (CD). (VJ)

Van Doren Hawksworth Collection

| Personnel: | JOHN HAWKSWORTH | bs | A |
| | VAN DOREN | piano | |

| 45: | Pin-ball/Chief Inspectre | (Decca F 12105) 1965 |

This was an instrumental duo. (VJ)

Vanity Fair

Personnel:	DICK ALLIX	vcls, drms	AB
	TREVOR BRICE	piano, lead vcls	AB
	TONY GOULDEN	vcls, lead gtr	AB
	TONY JARRETT	vcls, bs	AB
	BARRY LANDERMAN	organ	B

ALBUMS:	1(A)	THE SUN, THE WIND AND OTHER THINGS	
		(Page One POLS 010) 1968 SC
	2( )	EARLY IN THE MORNING	(Page One) 19??

NB: (1) reissued on CD (Repertoire REP 4155-WZ) 1991. There's also a compilation *Hitchin' A Ride* (DJM/Silverline DJSL 043 or DJB 26043) 1971 or 1975 including unreleased cuts and a more recent CD compilation *Best Of Vanity Fayre* (Repertoire REP 5015) is a 26-track CD which includes their finest moments and comes with highly informative sleevenotes.

			HCP
45s:	I Live For The Sun/		
	On The Other Side Of Life	(Page One POF 075) 1968	20
	Summer Morning/Betty Carter	(Page One POF 100) 1968	-
	Highway Of Dreams/		
	Waiting For The Downfall	(Page One POF 117) 1969	-
	Early In The Morning/		
	You Made Me Love You	(Page One POF 142) 1969	8
	Hitchin' A Ride/Man Child	(Page One POF 158) 1969	16
	Come Tomorrow/Megown	(Page One POF 170) 1970	-
	Carolina's Coming Home/		
	On Your Own	(Page One POF 180) 1970	-
	Where Did All The Good Times Go/Stand	(DJM DJS 234) 1971	-
	Better By Far/Rock 'n' Roll Band	(DJM DJS 250) 1971	-
	Big Parade/Angel	(Jam JAM 2) 1972	-
Reissue:	Hitchin' A Ride/		
	Early In The Morning	(Old Gold OG 9039) 1979	-

This bright'n'breezy pop group, from the Medway Towns in Kent, enjoyed some minor hits in the late sixties with *I Live For The Sun* (a Carter-Lewis composition) and *Hitchin' A Ride* and a Top Ten song with *Early In The Morning*. Brice, Goulden and Jarrett had previously been in **The Avengers** and The Sages, whilst Allix had been with **Gnomes Of Zurich**. Barry Landerman joined from **Kippington Lodge** in January 1969.

The Best Of Vanity Fayre is a 26-track compilation featuring all their best moments including *I Live For The Sun*.

Man Child has been compiled on *Pop-In, Vol 1* (CD) and there's an alternate take of *Early In The Morning* on the 2-CD set *Greatest Hits Of The 60's*. *Hitchin' A Ride* can also be heard on *70's Remembered* (CD), *The Swinging Sixties - 18 Classic Tracks* (CD) and on *Hits Of The 60's Vol 2* (CD). (VJ/MGn/VZ)

Rob Van Spyk

| ALBUM: | 1 FOLLOW THE SUN | (Private Pressing) 197? R1 |

This folk-rock album is now quite a significant collectable. **Van Spyk** was also in **Stonefield Tramp**. (VJ)

The Variations

45s:	The Man With All The Toys/	
	She'll Know I'm Sorry	(Immediate IM 019) 1965 SC
	Crimson And Clover/	
	She Couldn't Dance	(Major Minor MM 638) 1969

This obscure group's first 45 is now quite hard to track down. It's a surf-styled novelty item.

Compilation appearances include: *She'll Know I'm Sorry* on *Immediate Single Collection, Vol. 3* (CD); and *The Man With All The Toys* on *Immediate Single Collection, Vol. 4* (CD). (VJ)

Vashti

See **Bunyan, Vashti**

The Vehicle

| 45: | Mr. Organ Grinder/Cloudy Day | (Deram DM 342) 1971 |

The Vehicle was one of many obscure bands who had one-off discs on Deram in the early seventies. The 'A' side has reappeared on *Psychedalia - Rare Blooms From The English Summer Of Love* (CD) and you can hear *Cloudy Day* on *Progressive Pop Inside The Seventies* (CD). (VJ)

The Velvet Frogs

Personnel:	JOHN CARROD	bs	A
	DENNIS MUCHMORE	vcls, gtr, violin	A
	ROLAND ROGERS	ld gtr	A
	CHRISTIAN STREBINGER	gtr	A

This band cut a few acetates for the highly collectable Oak label. The best of these was apparently *Jehovah*, penned by Dennis Muchmore, which includes some fine guitar work and tells a story of doom and destruction. You'll now find this on *Story Of Oak Records* (2-LP)/*The Story Of Oak Records* (CD), whose sleevenotes make reference to two other as yet unreleased acetates, *Archeology* (from the same session as *Jehovah*) and *Wasted Ground*. Recommended. Muchmore and Carrod later resurfaced in a late seventies act, The Method. (VJ)

Velvet Hush

Personnel:	DICK BLOOM	drms	A
	ANDY QUNTA		A
	TONY QUNTA		A

| 45: | Broken Heat/Lover Please | (Oak RGJ 648) 1968 R3 |

This now extremely rare 45 was written by the band members and released on the obscure Oak label run by R.G. Jones in Morden, Surrey. Musically it's one of the earliest and most obscure **Hendrix**-inspired discs. The flip side, *Lover Please*, has resurfaced on *Story Of Oak Records* (2-LP). It is **a Hendrix**-inspired slice of progressive rock with very prominent guitar.

They later returned to the studio as progressive blues-rockers Perfect Turkey and in 1967 as **Factory** (not the band on MGM). Andy Qunta later played in New Zealand band Icehouse. (VJ)

Velvet Opera

Personnel:	PAUL BRETT	vcls, gtr	A
	JOHN FORD	bs	A
	COLIN FOSTER	gtr	A
	RICHARD HUDSON	drms	A
	JON JOYCE	vcls	A

ALBUM: 1(A) RIDE A HUSTLER'S DREAM   (CBS 63692) 1969 R1

NB: (1) reissued on CD (Akarma AK 306) 2005.

45s:	Anna Dance Square/Don't You Realize	(CBS 4189) 1969
	Black Jack Davy/Statesboro Blues	(CBS 4802) 1970
	She Keeps Giving Me These Feelings/	
	There's A Hole In My Pocket	(Spark SRL 1045) 1970

This was a later version of **Elmer Gantry's Velvet Opera**. When **Elmer Gantry** left, he was replaced by **Paul Brett**, who was later in **Fire** and went on to form **Paul Brett's Sage**. Based in London, they finally split up in 1971. John Ford and Richard Hudson were later in **The Strawbs** and **Hudson-Ford**, Jon Joyce had earlier been in **Levee Breakers**. (VJ)

Velvett Fogg

Personnel:	PAUL EASTMENT		A
	MULLETT		A
	FRANK WILSON	organ	A
	POLLARD		A
	KEITH LAW		A

ALBUM: 1(A) VELVETT FOGG   (Pye NSPL 18272) 1969 R2

NB: (1) has been counterfeited and was also reissued as *Velvett Fogg Plus* (See For Miles SEE 259) in 1989 with the 45 added, also available on CD (SEE CD 259) 1989. (1) later reissued again on CD (Sanctuary CMRCD 619) 2002, with *Telstar '69* as a bonus track.

45: Telstar '69/Owed To The Dip   (Pye 7N 17673) 1969

Complete with sleeve notes from John Peel came **Velvett Fogg** with a blend of their own compositions, like *Yellow Cave Woman*, *The Delicate Wizard Of Gobsolob* and *Once Among The Trees*, the story of a chase with strong sexual overtones. *Plastic Man*, is a comment on politicians, and *Owed To The Dip*, an organ-dominated instrumental; and their own interpretative cover versions of **The Bee Gee**'s *New York Mining Disaster 1941* and Tim Rose's *Come Away Melinda*. It's worth a listen, but don't pay a lot for it.

Paul Eastment was later in **Ghost**. Organist Frank Wilson was a founding member of **Warhorse**.

VELVETT FOGG - Velvett Fogg (LP).

The See For Miles reissue includes the band's interesting version of *Telstar*. Two cuts from their album have also been compiled. The mildly psychedelic *Within The Night* can also be found on *Rubble, Vol. 7 - Pictures In The Sky* (LP) and *Lady Caroline*, an anguished story-song, got further exposure on *Rubble, Vol. 10 - Professor Jordan's Magic Sound Show* (LP). *Come Away Melinda* also appeared on *Progressive Music* (LP). (VJ)

The Vendors

Personnel:	DAVE HILL	gtr	A
	JOHNNY HOWELLS	vcls	A
	DAVE JONES	bs	A
	MICKEY MARSTON	gtr	A
	DON POWELL	drms	A

| 45: | Peace Pipe//Don't Leave Me Now | |
| | Take Your Time/Twilight Time | (Private Pressing) 1964 R5 |

A Wolverhampton band whose private pressing acetate is naturally now extremely rare, only 12 copies were made. As many of you will know in 1965 they became **The In-Be-Tweens** with Hill and Powell later regrouping with Noddy Holder and Jimmy Lea in a later line-up of that band which eventually became **Ambrose Slade** and then **Slade** during 1969.

Don't Leave Me Now, *Twilight Time*, *Take Your Time* and *Peace Pipe* can all be heard on *The Genesis Of Slade* (CD). (VJ)

John Verity Band

Personnel:	RON KELLY	drms	A
	GEOFF LYTH	horns, gtr	A
	GERRY SMITH	bs	A
	THUNDERTHIGHS	vcls	A
	JOHN VERITY	gtr, vcls	A

ALBUM: 1(A) JOHN VERITY BAND   (Probe SPB 1087) 1974

After this solo effort **Verity** joined **Argent** in November 1974 and dissolved his own Bradford-based band. (VJ)

Mike Vernon

ALBUM: 1 BRING IT BACK HOME
    (Blue Horizon 2391 003) 1971 R3

NB: He also had a US-only album, *Moments Of Madness*.

| 45: | Let's Try It Again/ | |
| | Little Southern Country Girl | (Blue Horizon 2096 007) 1971 |

Best known as a producer, **Mike Vernon** was an integral part of the blues scene in the sixties and seventies. Acts he produced included **Chicken Shack**, **Duster Bennett**, **Fleetwood Mac**, **John Mayall**, **Savoy Brown** and **Ten Years After**. He deserves much credit for raising the profile of the blues in this era.

Mike Vernon was born on 20 November 1944 in Harrow, North West London. After initially playing in the Mo Jo Men in 1963 he began working for Decca Records. Early production credits included albums by Curtis Jones (a Texan blues singer and pianist), Otis Spann and Champion Jack Dupree. He encouraged **John Mayall** to make an album with The Bluesbreakers with **Eric Clapton** as a guitarist *Bluesbreakers*, which is widely regarded as one of the very best British blues albums. He produced **Fleetwood Mac**'s early albums and their classic hit single *Albatross*. Many of the recordings he produced by bands like **Chicken Shack**, **Savoy Brown** and **Ten Years After** were released on his own Blue Horizon label or his other lesser known ones like Purdah and Outasite. Aside from his own recordings, he played percussion on albums by the likes of **Duster Bennett**, Jimmy Dawkins, Champion Jack Dupree and Freddie King. He also produced a plethora of other artists' recordings, including **David Bowie** and Focus. The 2-LP Sire compilation *History Of British Blues*, which contains mostly selections of his production work from the late sixties and early seventies, is a good introduction to the type of records he produced.

His 1971 solo album *Bring It Back Home* featured **Rory Gallagher** among the guest guitarists. He was in Diversions in the late seventies and recorded an album (*Soul Survivors*) for Polydor in 1977, which was never released.

He remained active as a producer in the following decades working with R&B based artists like **Dr Feelgood**, **Chris Farlowe**, Freddie King and Jimmy Witherspoon and with bands of other genres like Dexy's Midnight Runners, Level 42 and The Proclaimers. He re-established Blue Horizon in the late eighties and set up Indigo and Code Blue (two new blues labels) in the nineties. (VJ)

Mike Vickers

ALBUMS: 1   I WISH I WERE A GROUP AGAIN
                                    (Columbia S(C)X 6180) 1968 R1
          2   A DAY AT THE RACES   (DJM DJSLM 2034) 1976

45s: α   On The Brink/The Puff Adder   (Columbia DB 7657) 1965 R1
           Eleventy One/The Inkling   (Columbia DB 7825) 1966
       α   Morgan - A Suitable Case For Treatment/
           Gorilla Of My Dreams   (Columbia DB 7906) 1966 SC
       α   Air On A String/Proper Charles (Columbia DB 8171) 1967
           Captain Scarlet And The Mysterons/
           Kettle Of Fish   (Columbia DB 8281) 1967 SC

NB: α Credited To Mike Vickers and Orchestra.

Mike Vickers is best known as a multi-instrumentalist in the original **Manfred Mann** line-up, but he's been involved in several other recordings over the years and composed many film scores and TV tunes.

Vickers was born in Southampton on 18 April 1941. A talented instrumentalist from a jazz background, his guitar, sax and flute characterised much of their music until he left the band in October 1965. He recorded his first solo album *I Wish I Were A Group Again* with help from many **Manfred Mann** members and it sounds like one of their records. He also began writing film scores commencing with the comedy 'Press For Time' in 1966.

He worked with **The Beatles**, conducting the core orchestra that played on their live broadcast and recording of *All You Need Is Love* on 25 June 1967, and he later played synthesiser on their *Abbey Road* album. Since then he has worked with a broad spectrum of artists including **The Hollies**, **Cilla Black**, Ella Fitzgerald and **The Bee Gees**, but the list is endless. He also recorded several 45s (some with an orchestra) after leaving **Manfred Mann** and turned up playing synthesiser on the original 1971 recording of 'Jesus Christ Superstar'.

Later film score credits included 'Dracula AD 1972' and 'At The Earth's Core'. In the nineties he was involved in The Manfreds (which was essentially **Manfred Mann** without their co-founder **Manfred Mann** himself). (VJ)

The Vikings

Personnel: GRAHAM DUNCAN   drms   ABC
            ROY FLEMING   ABC
            ALAN GORRIE   bs   ABCD
            DOUGIE WIGHTMAN   ABCD
            IAN JACKSON   vcls   B
            JOHNNY TAYLOR (aka JOHNNY LITTLE)   C
            DONNIE COUTTS   D
            MIKE FRASER   vcls, gtr   D
            DREW LARG   vcls   D

45:   Bad News Feeling/What Can I Do   (Alp 595 011) 1966

The Vikings hailed from Perth in Scotland. They mostly played soul music, but after signing to the local Alp label recorded *Bad News Feeling*, which had been written by US folk singer Paul Simon, though it was by no means

one of his strongest compositions. The collapse of the Alp label was a factor in the band moving down to London, but it didn't work out and they split in 1967. They were known as Fancy Bred in their final days. (VJ)

Village

Personnel: PETE BARDENS   keyb'ds   A
             BILL PORTER   drms   A
             BRUCE THOMAS   bs   A

45:   Man In The Moon/
      Long Time Coming   (Head HDS 4002) 1969 R1

Bardens, whose previous bands had included **The Cheynes**, Pete B's Looners, **Shotgun Express** and **Them**, formed this band in 1969. They only managed the one 45, which is now rather obscure and sought-after. The highlight of their live career was to support the American band Chicago at the Royal Albert Hall. After they split in February 1970, former Roadrunner Thomas joined **Quiver** and was later in Elvis Costello's backing band, The Attractions. **Bardens** made a solo album before joining On and forming **Camel**. *Man In The Moon* is a long jazz-rock composition with lots of wah-wah guitars and a meaty keyboard backing. *Long Time Coming* is a **Nice**-influenced instrumental with lots of organ.

The single did not sell and despite a good live reputation (they supported US band Chicago at the Royal Albert Hall) their career soon faltered. After they split **Bardens** went solo and then formed **Camel**. Bruce Thomas was in Quiver and later became one of Elvis Costello's Attractions.

Man In The Moon has been compiled on *Electric Sugar Cube Flashbacks* (CD) and *Electric Sugar Cube Flashbacks, Vol. 4* (LP). (VJ)

The Village Idiots

45:   Laughing Policeman/
      I Know An Old Lady   (Piccadilly 7N 35282) 1966

This was a short-lived beat group. (VJ)

The Villagers/Parcel of Rogues

Personnel: (The Villagers)
             COLIN HARPER
             SHEILA SMITH
             JOHN STRIVENS

Personnel: (Parcel of Rogues)
             COLIN HARPER
             EILEEN MAWSON
             JEFF RADCLIFFE

ALBUM: 1   PARCEL OF FOLK (w/insert)   (Deroy no #) 1973 R3

An ultra-rare privately pressed folk album. This actually contains two bands. Both contain Colin Harper who I think is the rock journalist who has subsequently written many folk artists' biographies and who also writes for 'Record Collector'. Both groups play traditional English folk music. Tracks contributed by **The Villagers** are *Lykewake Dirge*, *Let All Mortal Flesh Keep Silent*, *John Riley*, *Byker Hill* and *The Holly Bears A Berry*. **The Parcels Of Rogues** contribute *A Soulin'*, *Marilyn Monroe*, *Old Pendle*, *The Weaver And The Factory Maid* and *Rave On*. The Deroy label operated from High Bank Studios in Carnforth, Lancashire. (VJ)

Ray Vince and The Vincents

45:   One Fine Day/Little Girl I'm Sad   (Piccadilly 7N 35211) 1964

The 'A' side of this beat combo's 45 was a Chiffons' number. (VJ)

Joey Vine

45:      Down And Out/The Out Of Towner (Immediate IM 017) 1965 SC

This single seems to have been a one-off venture. (VJ)

Vinegar Joe

Personnel:	ELKIE BROOKS	keyb'ds, vcls	ABC
	PETE GAGE	gtr, keyb'ds, vcls	ABC
	JOHN HAWKEN	keyb'ds	A
	TIM HINKLEY	keyb'ds	A
	ROBERT PALMER	gtr, vcls	ABC
	STEVE YORK	hrmnca, bs	ABC
	ROB TAIT	drms	A
	MIKE DEACON	keyb'ds, vcls	BC
	JIM MULLEN	gtr	B
	JOHN WOODS	drms	B
	PETE GAVIN	drms	C

ALBUMS: 1(A) VINEGAR JOE   (Island ILPS 9183) 1972 SC
2(B) ROCK 'N' ROLL GYPSIES (Island ILPS 9214) 1972
3(C) SIX STAR GENERAL (Island ILPS 9262) 1973

NB: (1) and (2) issued on Atco in the US. (1) reissued on CD (Edsel) 1998. (2) reissued on CD (Island IMCD 93) 1990 and again on CD (Lemon CDLEM 15) digitally remastered with a detailed fold-out booklet and fine pictures from the original album sleeve. (3) reissued on CD (Lemon LEMCD 3). *Speed Queen Of Ventura - An Introduction To* (Universal IMCD 292) 2002 is a CD compilation of material from their three albums.

45s: Never Met A Dog/
Speed Queen Of Ventura   (Island WIP 6125) 1972
Rock 'n' Roll Gypsies/So Long (Island WIP 6148) 1972
Black Smoke From The Calumet/
Long Way Round   (Island WIP 6174) 1973

This R&B based rock outfit was the launching pad for the careers of **Elkie Brooks** and **Robert Palmer**. Formed with much encouragement from Island Records boss Chris Blackwell it rose from the ashes of short-lived jazz-rock combo **Dada**. **Robert Palmer** had previously sung with **Alan Bown**; **Elkie Brooks** had previously had an unsuccessful solo career and Gage had been with **The Zephyrs** and then **Geno Washington and The Ram Jam Band**.

Their gutsy musical style ensured they were a popular live attraction, but although their records were solid enough they had difficulty translating their live sound onto vinyl. *Rock'N'Roll Gypsies* features the dual vocals **Brooks** and **Palmer** and is usually considered their best album. The stand-out track is *Charley's Horse* and **Keef Hartley** guested on drums. *Six Star General* was similar in style. They split up late in 1973 and **Palmer** and **Brooks** both went on to successful solo careers.

The 2002 Universal CD compilation is probably the best introduction to the band. (VJ)

The Vineyard

Personnel incl:	DICK WICKER-CHAIR	bs		A

45s: Ghost Train/Unicorns And Minotaurs (Decca F 13518) 1974
Myla/Charlemaine   (Deram DM 420) 1974

The Vineyard is now a forgotten mid-seventies band. Wicker-Chair became a member of the reformed **Sam Apple Pie** in December 1975. (VJ)

Violent Thimble

45:      Gentle People Parts 1 & 2   (Polydor 56217) 1967

This was an obscure late sixties band. (VJ)

Vipps

45:      Wintertime/Anyone   (CBS 202031) 1966 R2

This seems to have been a version of the Carlisle-based **V.I.P.s**. The 45 is now rare and sought-after. (VJ)

V.I.P.s

Personnel:	MIKE HARRISON	piano, vcls	AB
	JAMES HENSHAW	keyb'ds	A
	WALTER JOHNSTONE	drms	A
	FRANK KENYON	gtr	A
	GREG RIDLEY	bs	AB
	KEITH EMERSON	keyb'ds	B
	LUTHER GROSVENOR	gtr, vcls	B
	MIKE KELLIE	drms	B

45s: Don't Keep Shouting At Me/
She's So Good   (RCA RCA 1427) 1964 R2
I Wanna Be Free/Don't Let It Go (Island WI 3003) 1966 R1
Straight Down To The Bottom/
In A Dream   (Island WIP 6005) 1967 R1

NB: The first and third single has been reissued in a limited 500 copies edition based on the original French jukebox issue. There's also a retrospective album *VIPs* (Funtona V86001) containing material recorded in 1966. *VIP's* (CD) (Oxford OXFORD 4420) contains 16 studio recordings and seven tracks from a NDR radio session.

This mid-sixties four-piece from Carlisle also included **Keith Emerson** for a few weeks before he formed **The Nice**. Initially an R&B outfit line-up (A) they formed in 1963 and recorded the first two of three fine singles. They are also recorded a one-sided acetate for the Surrey-based Oak label, *How Many*, and a couple of other acetates on EMIDISC. In December 1966 Kenyon (later of Junkyard Angels), Johnstone and Henshaw all left and a new line-up (B) recorded the final 45 for Island and a US-only 45, *Mercy, Mercy*, a sterling cover of the Don Covey classic, before **Emerson** departed to form **The Nice**. A limited edition European EP on Kos Records has given another airing to both sides of the *Mercy, Mercy* 45 and *Sad Story* and *Blue Feeling*, two of the EMIDISC acetates. They changed their name to **Art** in 1967 and later became **Spooky Tooth**.

The retrospective *VIPs* album is a mixture of R&B, blues, rock'n'roll and includes covers of *Smokestack Lightning*, *Every Girl I See* and *Rosemarie*, along with a few numbers penned by their keyboardist James Henshaw. *The VIP's* CD includes 16 studio recordings dating from 1966 and ranges from blues, R&B, rock'n'roll and soul and a further seven tracks recorded at the Teen Club in 1966 including a 6-minute version of Ray Charles' *I Got A Woman*.

Compilation appearances have included: *Straight Down To The Bottom* on *Made In England, Vol. 2* (LP) and *Jagged Time Lapse, Vol 3* (CD);

VINEGAR JOE - Six Star General (LP).

THE V.I.P's - I Wanna Be Free (CD).

Smokestack Lightning and *I Wanna Be Free* on *British Blue-Eyed Soul* (LP) 1968; *I Wanna Be Free* and *Hold On, I'm Coming* on *Made In England, Vol. 1* (CD); *I Wanna Be Free* on *Rare 60's Beat Treasures, Vol. 3* (CD); and *She's So Good* and *Don't Keep Shouting At Me* on *Broken Dreams, Vol. 4* (LP). (VJ)

Virgil Brothers

45s:	α	Temptation 'Bout To Get Me/		
		Lock Away	(Parlophone R 5787)	1969 SC
		Good Love/When You Walk Away	(Parlophone R 5802)	1969

NB: α also issued in the US (Rare Earth 5006) 1969.

The Virgil Brothers are a marginal case for inclusion as they were three Australian brothers who stayed here in the UK for a while and were managed whilst here by ex-**Shadow Bruce Welch**. Indeed, *When You Walk Away* was a **Hank Marvin** composition.

Temptation 'Bout To Get Me was a James Leon Diggs composition and had earlier been a US hit for The Knight Brothers in 1965. (VJ/DS)

Virginia Tree

ALBUM:	1	FRESH OUT	(Minstrel 0001) 1975 R1

NB: (1) reissued on CD as *Forever A Willow* (Magic Spell 0001) in 1988 and again on CD (Akarma AK 086) with two bonus tracks housed in a miniature gatefold sleeve.

This was actually former **Ghost** vocalist **Shirley Kent**, under a pseudonym. See her entry for details. *Fresh Out* is a folk/jazz style album. (VJ)

Virgin Sleep

Personnel:	ALAN BARNES	A
	KEITH PURNELL	A
	RICK QUILTY	A
	TONY REES	A

45s:	Love/Halliford House	(Deram DM 146) 1967 R1
	Secret/Comes A Time	(Deram DM 173) 1968 R1

This psychedelic outfit came from the Richmond area of London and were originally known as The Themselves. *Love* was a **Troggs**-influenced 45 based on a Buddhist chant called "Om Mane Padme Hum" with a sitar plucking in the background. The flip side, *Halliford House*, is a delightfully sleepy arrangement (typically British psych-pop) with a period piece fade out ending.

Their second 'A' side, *Secret*, was more commercial with a string arrangement and mellotron. The band were definitely grade one psych-pop.

Compilation appearances have included:- *Halliford House* on *Psychedelia, Vol. 2* (LP) and *Hen's Teeth Vol. 1* (CD); *Secret* on *The Psychedelic Scene* (CD), *Rubble, Vol. 12 - Staircase To Nowhere* (LP), *Rubble, Vol. 6* (CD), *British Psychedelic Trip, Vol. 3* (LP) and *Great British Psychedelic Trip, Vol. 2* (CD); whilst *Love* can be found on *The British Psychedelic Trip, Vol. 1* (LP), *Great British Psychedelic Trip Vol. 1* (CD) and on the 4-CD box set *Acid Drops, Spacedrops & Flying Saucers*. (VJ)

Visitor 2035

ALBUM:	1	CAIN: A MODERN MYSTERY PLAY (2-LP)	
			(Private Pressing) 1976 R2

This is a very strange progressive concept double album. Musically, it's keyboard dominated with symphonic elements and there are some similarities to **Cirkus**. (VJ)

The Vogues

45:	Younger Girl/Lies	(Columbia DB 7985) 1966 SC

There was also a better-known US band of this name who had 45s released over here on London, King and Reprise, including their four US Top Ten hits:- *You're The One*, *Five O'Clock World*, *Turn Around Look At Me* and *My Special Angel*.

This **Vogues** also recorded a second 45 the same year as **Llan** and were based in Birmingham. The 45 listed above contains a mid-tempo beat / harmony song on the 'A' side, whilst the flip is a great uptempo beat / R'n'B number, which still manages to retain the harmony. (VJ)

The Voice

Personnel incl:	MILLER ANDERSON	A
	MICK RONSON	B
	DAVE BRADFIELD	B

45:	α	The Train To Disaster/Truth	(Mercury MF 905) 1967 R3

NB: α has been reissued in a limited edition of 500 (Mercury MF 905) reproduced from the French jukebox pressing with a large centre hole.

This London-based group evolved out of **Karl Stuart and The Profiles** and **Profile**. The five-piece band was backed by a Scientology splinter group called The Process (aka The Process Church). Their 45 is now an ultra-rarity, much sought-after by connoisseurs of psychedelia for its three minutes of guitar-driven mayhem. **Miller Anderson** was later in **Savoy Brown** and the **Keef Hartley Band**. When he left in early 1966, he was replaced by **Mick Ronson**. **Ronson** also brought drummer Dave Bradfield into the group. In June 1966, the cult left London for the Bahamas, so the three members who were in The Process left **Ronson** and Bradfield behind.

You'll also find *The Train To Disaster* on *Chocolate Soup* (CD)/*Chocolate Soup For Diabetics, Vol. 1* (LP), *Psychedelic Voyage, Vol. 2* (LP), *Psychedelic Voyage* (CD), *Beat It* (3-CD) and on the 4-CD box set *Nuggets II*. Its flip side, *The Truth*, has also resurfaced on *Magic Spectacles* (CD), but is nowhere near as good. (VJ/JP)

The Voids

45:	Come On Out/I'm In A Fix	(Polydor BM 56073) 1966 R2

The Voids came from Somerset. Their 45 is now collectable. The 'A' side is very much in the mould of **The Action**, whilst the flip was a pop-art offering.

Compilation appearances have included: *I'm In A Fix* on *Magic Spectacles* (CD), *Rare 60's Beat Treasures, Vol. 4* (CD), *Yellow Elektric Years* (LP), *Beat It* (3-CD) and *Echoes From The Wilderness - Sixteen UK R&B Freakbeat Trippers.* (LP & CD); and *Come On Out* on *Rare 60's Beat Treasures, Vol. 5* (CD). (VJ)

The Volunteers

Personnel incl: KAROL KEYES   vcls

45:        Farther Along/Little David   (Parlophone R 5088) 1963

This was a soft folk group from Essex. Karol Keyes later recorded solo 45s for Columbia and Fontana and worked as an actress and model. (VJ)

The Voomins

45:        If You Don't Come Back/
           March Of The Voomins   (Polydor BM 56001) 1965 SC

This is another very obscure and now forgotten band. The 'A' side was a Drifters' composition, the flip a bluesy instrumental. (VJ)

Vulcan's Hammer

ALBUM: 1   TRUE HEARTS AND SOUND BOTTOMS
               (w/insert)   (Brown BVH 1) 1973 R4

NB: (1) has had a limited reissue on vinyl and also reissued on CD (Kissing Spell KSCD 9502-F) 1995, along with *The Two Magicians* (Kissing Spell KSCD 9506-F) 1995, which is dogged by poor quality but includes unreleased sessions from 1973 and a radio broadcast from 1975. (1) has also had a limited edition release on vinyl (Porcelain PCN 002) in the original sleeve with the insert.

250 copies of this album were originally pressed by the band and sold at their local folk club making it another ultra-rarity. Some of the songs also appeared on the **Spriguns Of Tolgus** album. Some members of this band were later in an outfit called Mingled who had seven cuts on the 1975 album, *Good Folk Of Kent.*

Jamie has been compiled on *The History Of U.K. Underground Folk Rock 1968-1978 Vol. 1* (CD). (VJ)

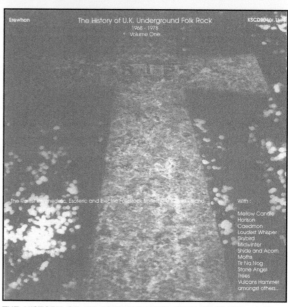
THE HISTORY OF UK UNDERGROUND FOLK ROCK VOL. 1 (Comp CD) including Vulcan's Hammer.

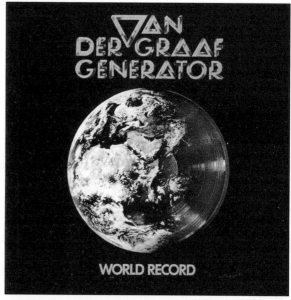
VAN DER GRAAF GENERATOR - World Record (CD).

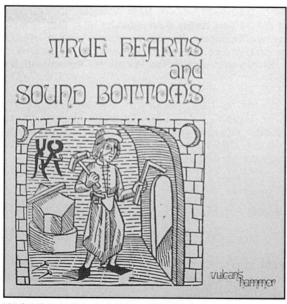
VULCAN'S HAMMER - True Hearts And Sound Bottoms (LP).

VAN DER GRAAF GENERATOR - Time Vaults (CD).

The Wackers

Personnel: TERRY ANTON   A
               DINO GRANT   A
               JOHN FOSTER   A
               JULIAN JOHNSTON   A
               BERNARD LEE   A

45s: I Wonder Why/
        Why Can't It Happen To Me   (Oriole CB 1902) 1964 SC
        Love Or Money/Hooka Tooka   (Piccadilly 7N 35195) 1964
        The Girl Who Wanted Fame/
        You're Forgetting   (Piccadilly 7N 35210) 1965

Although many people think they hailed from Merseyside, they actually came from Porthmadog in Gwynedd, Wales and decided to give people the impression they came from Merseyside, in order to appear cooler! **The Wackers** also appeared in a pop 'B' movie entitled 'Go Go Big Beat' in 1965. Their founder member Dino Grant is now a taxi driver in Porthadog. They are completely unrelated to the later American band of the same name.

Compilation appearances include: *The Girl Who Wanted Fame* on *Piccadilly Story* (CD) and *Ripples, Vol. 4* (CD); and *The Girl Who Wanted Fame* and *Love Or Money* on *Some Other Guys* (2-LP). (GM/VJ/JM)

Cliff Wade

45:     You've Never Been to My House/
        Sister   (Morgan Blue Town BT 1S) 1969 SC

An obscure vocalist, *Morgan Blue Town* (LP)/*Best And The Rest Of British Psychedelia* (CD) include two previously unissued pop compositions of his from around 1969, *Shirley* and *Look At Me I've Fallen Into A Teapot*. Both are great whimsical 'toy-town' psych tracks, in keeping with his rare 45. He also recorded material for an album which was never released.

Wade performed back-up singing duties and was responsible for orchestral arrangements on the second **Oscar** album *Twilight Asylum*. He later worked with singer Jenny Darren. (DC/VJ)

Wellington Wade (actually Charlie Flynn)

45:     Let's Turkey Trot/
        It Ain't Necessarily So   (Oriole CB 1857) 1963 SC

This 45 was actually recorded by **Ian and The Zodiacs**' bassist Charlie Flynn and has a song with his band on the flip. *Let's Turkey Trot* had been a hit for US vocalist Little Eva. (VJ)

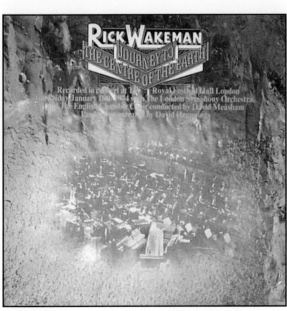

RICK WAKEMAN - Journey To The Centre Of The Earth (LP).

Waiting For The Sun

Personnel incl: IVOR TWYDELL

ALBUM: 1   WAITING FOR THE SUN   (Profile GMOR 167) 1978 R2
NB: (1) reissued on CD (Kissing Spell KSCD 9508).

This privately-pressed album by a Christian band would be expensive to acquire, if sighted. It was led by ex-After The Fire member Ivor Twydell.

Waiting For The Sun later turned up on *The History Of U.K. Underground Folk Rock 1968-1978 Vol. 2* (CD). (VJ)

Wake

Personnel incl: BILL HURD   A

ALBUM: 1   23.59   (Carnaby CNLS 6005) 1970 R2

45s: Angelina/So Happy   (Pye 7N 17813) 1969 SC
        Live Today Little Girl/
        Days Of Emptiness   (Carnaby CNS 4010) 1970 SC
        Boys In The Band/
        To Make You Happy   (Carnaby CNS 4014) 1970
        Noah/To Make You Happy   (Carnaby CNS 4016) 1971
        Linda/Got My Eyes On You   (Carnaby 6151001) 1971

Recording for the independent "swinging London" label Carnaby, **The Wake** actually got to appear on 'Top Of The Pops' to sing their *Boys In The Band* 45, which was chosen for them by concert promoter Mervyn Conn. It wasn't a memorable performance and the single flopped in the UK, as did their other 45s and album, which are best forgotten. The band had better fortune in Japan, however, where *Live Today Little Girl* was a smash hit.

Bill Hurd had earlier been in **Gass Company** and later did session work and was in **The Rubettes**. (VJ/IS)

Rick Wakeman

HCP

ALBUMS: 1   PIANO VIBRATIONS   (Polydor 2460 135) 1971 SC -
(up to   2   SIX WIVES OF HENRY VIII (A&M AMLH 64361) 1973 7
1976)   3   JOURNEY TO THE CENTRE OF THE EARTH
                                     (A&M AMLH 63621) 1974 1
          4   IN THE COURT OF KING ARTHUR
                                     (A&M AMLH 64515) 1975 2
          5   LISZTOMANIA   (A&M AMLK 64546) 1975 -
          6   NO EARTHLY CONNECTION (A&M AMLK 64583) 1976 9
          7   WHITE ROCK   (A&M AMLH 64614) 1976 14

NB: (2) reissued on CD (A&M 393 229-2) 1989. (3) reissued on CD (Mobile Fidelity (USA) MFCD 848) 1988. *Journey To The Centre Of The Earth Plus* (Voiceprint VPTCCD 7) is a rare set of alternative versions remastered, digitised and with choir accompaniment and sleevenotes from **Wakeman** himself. *King Biscuit Hour* (1998) reissued a live recording from the San Francisco Winterland in 1975, which was centred around (4) above, but included extracts from (2) and (3) as well. *Rick Wakeman: 20th Anniversary* (A&M RWCD 20) 1989 is a 4-CD set (R1). Only 1,000 copies were issued. *Classic Tracks* (The Store For Music SFMCD 003) 2001 features re-vamped re-workings of four of his classic tracks. *The Very Best Of Rick Wakeman - Recollections* (Polydor 490 7742) 2001 is a 14-track compilation. *Two Sides Of Yes* (Classic Rock Legends CRL 0857) 2002 captures his finest moments with **Yes**. *Tales Of Future And Past* (Purple Pyramid CLP 1043 2) 2001 is a 2-CD compilation.

45s: Catherine/Anne   (A&M AMS 7061) 1973
(up to Love's Dream/Orpheus Song   (A&M AMS 7206) 1975
1976) α Wagner's Dream/
        Love's Dream/Count Your Blessings (A&M LYN 3176/7) 1975

NB: α This was a flexi-disc recorded with **Roger Daltrey**, which was given away free with '19' magazine.

Rick Wakeman did successfully merge classical and rock music and many regard him as a master of contemporary light orchestral music, though an equal number would probably find much of his music tedious.

Born in Perivale, West London, on 18 May 1949, **Wakeman** went on to become a pupil at The Royal College of Music, playing pub gigs whilst he was there. After a spell as a session musician for artists like **David Bowie** and **Cat Stevens** he joined **The Strawbs** in 1970, playing on their first two albums. In 1971 he left for **Yes** and recorded *Piano Vibrations* whilst with that band. This is the only of his albums at present which is becoming hard to find.

The *Six Wives Of Henry VIII* was the next in a series of ambitious solo works. Inspired by a TV drama series it climbed to No 7 here and No 30 in the States and was the first in a series of commercially successful fusions of classical and rock music.

The follow-up, *Journey To The Centre Of The Earth*, which was based on a story by Jules Verne, was recorded live at the Festival Hall in January 1974. It topped the Charts here and climbed to No 3 in the US. He also gave a grandiose performance of the whole album at Crystal Palace 'Garden Party' in July of that year, a month after leaving **Yes**. All this clearly took its toll on him for he suffered a minor heart attack as a result and was sidelined for a while.

Wakeman's health problems did not deter him from future grandiose projects, though. The *Myths And Legends Of King Arthur And The Knights Of The Round Table* took his seeming desire for grandiose projects and performances to new levels, utilising a 45-piece orchestra and 48-piece choir. It was premiered on ice at Wembley Pool in May 1975 in a show involving **Wakeman**'s own group, The English Rock Ensemble, plus the orchestra and the choir, which must have cost him an arm and a leg. It's a pleasant enough progressive classical rock fusion piece and it again sold well achieving No 2 here and No 21 in the US. It contained passages of narration, several melodramatic arrangements and occasional vocals.

In 1975 he toured the States with a smaller version of his English Rock Ensemble and wrote the music score to Ken Russell's 'Lisztomania', although this did not make the Charts. *No Earthly Connections*, which was inspired by Science Fiction, put him back there (No 9 UK, No 67 US) and in 1976 he wrote the music for the Innsbruck Winter Olympics, *White Rock*, which consolidated on his previous success and reached No 14 here and No 126 in the US. He also rejoined the reformed **Yes** in 1976.

Tales Of Future And Past is a US import. The 2-CD compilation includes *Journey To The Centre Of The Earth*; *Merlin The Magician* and four other cuts from *The Myths And Legends Of King Arthur*, three tracks from *The Six Wives Of Henry VIII*; two **Yes** tracks (*Wum* and *Starship Trooper*) capturing him at his best and impressive cover versions of *Paint It Black* and *The Prisoner*. It's a good introduction to his music.

2001's *Classic Tracks* comprises re-vamped re-workings of *Journey To The Centre Of The Earth*, *Catherine Howard*, *Merlin The Magician* and *Umberto 11.*

The Very Best Of Rick Wakeman - Recollections includes keyboards classics like *Catherine Of Aragon*, *Catherine Howard* and *Anne Boleyn*

(from *Henry VIII*); edited versions of *The Battle* and *The Journey* (from *The Centre Of The Earth*) and *Arthur* and *Merlin The Magician* (from *King Arthur*). These are the tracks relevant to this book - the remaining material is drawn from his late seventies and early eighties recordings.

Released in 2002, *Two Sides Of Yes* captures some of his finest moments with the band and comes in a smart presentation box.

Wakeman went on to record several further albums though none of them achieved the same level of commercial success as his recordings of the mid-seventies.

David Measham, who conducted the London Symphony Orchestra on *Journey To The Centre Of The Earth* and the New World Symphony Orchestra on *The Myths And Legends Of King Arthur And The Knights Of The Round Table* died in Perth, Australia of pancreatic cancer on 6 February 2005.

Wakeman is still releasing records today. *Live At Lincoln Cathedral* (Hellopause HPVP 104CD) 2005 is a 2-CD set which captures recordings he made on the church organ in Lincoln cathedral back in 2001. (VJ)

Walham Green East Wapping Carpet Cleaning Rodent and Boggit Extermination Association

45:      Sorry Mr. Green/Death Of A Kind   (Columbia DB 8426) 1968 R2

This group, who had the longest name in pop, was responsible for a bizarre novelty record, which took a jibe at middle class businessmen, *Sorry Mr. Green*. Like most novelty records, you'll only want to play it a handful of times. It's the story of a randy office manager's search for a foxy nubile only to discover that his hideous wife has got the job. The flip side is a sombre song about severe depression.

The identity of the group remains a mystery. Paul Holland co-wrote both sides (was this the rare **Bird Bird** drummer?). His collaborator on the flip was Timothy Hill (whoever he was)!

Sorry Mr. Green has resurfaced on *Visions Of The Past, Vol. 2* (LP & CD) and *Electric Sugar Cube Flashbacks, Vol. 4* (LP). (VJ)

David Walker

45:      Ring The Changes/
         Keep A Little Love   (RCA RCA 1664) 1968 R1

David Walker was also a member of **Paradox**. This one-off solo effort is now quite collectable. (VJ)

Gary Walker (and The Rain)

Personnel incl: PAUL CRANE   gtr, lead vcls
                 JOHN LAWSON   bs
                 GARY LEEDS (WALKER)   drms, vcls
                 JOEY MOLLAND   lead gtr, vcls

ALBUM: 1 ALBUM No. 1   (Philips SFX-7133) 1968 R6
NB: (1) Japanese only release. (1) was pirated on vinyl with a black and white cover, reissued on CD with bonus tracks, and colour cover in 1997.

EP: 1 HERE'S GARY   (CBS EPS 5742) 1966 R1

                                                               HCP
45s: You Don't Love Me/Get It Right   (CBS 202036) 1966 SC 26
         Twinkie-Lee/She Makes Me Feel Better   (CBS 202081) 1966 26
      α Spooky/I Can't Stand To Lose You   (Polydor 56237) 1968 SC -
      α Come On In You'll Get Pneumonia/
         Francis   (Philips BF 1740) 1968 R1 -
         Hello How Are You/Fran   (United Artists UP 35742) 1974 -
NB: α as **Gary Walker And The Rain**.

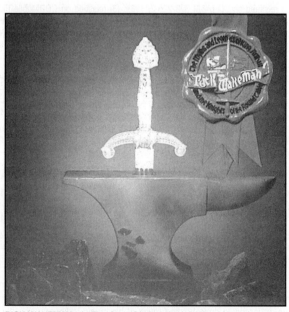

RICK WAKEMAN - In The Court Of King Arthur (LP).

This London-based US-born artist was backed by The Rain, a pretty typical beat-cum-psych late sixties outfit. More interesting than the above 45s is the album, *Gary Walker And The Rain Album, No 1*, which was only released in Japan and has long been established as one of the world's rarest records, with copies changing hands for several thousand pounds. It is thought to have been withdrawn from sale almost immediately because of Molland's contractual commitments to **The Iveys**. It includes some of the better 45 cuts but also contains a few psychedelic gems, particularly *If You Don't Come Back*, which is very psychedelic and has some great guitar work and an instrumental, *Thoughts Of An Old Man*. Two other cuts, *Magazine Woman* and *Market Tavern* are sort of mod/pop/psych, the latter with lots of phasing too. Recommended.

Gary Walker, incidentally, was one of The Walker Brothers, until he was ousted in 1967. As Gary Leeds he'd been in the early Standells. Then in 1966 frustrated at his limited role in the band he began a solo career. His first two efforts were minor hits and then he formed Rain with former **Cryin' Shames**' guitarist Paul Crane and ex-**Masterminds**' guitarist Joey Molland.

They kicked off with a cover of *Spooky*, which had been a big US hit for The Classics IV. They followed this with a cover of **The Easybeats**' *Come On In You'll Get Pneumonia*, which was backed by the self-penned *Francis*, a superb slice of pop-psych. **Gary Walker** sometimes went under the name Gary Leeds and his 45s are often credited as such.

The *Gary Walker And The Rain, No. 1* album has been bootlegged on vinyl, and has also been reissued officially on CD with three bonus tracks - *Francis, I Can't Stand To Lose You* and *Come In You'll Get Pneumonia*.

Joey Molland was later in **Badfinger**. Lawson (ex-**Universals**) went on to play in **Lace**.

Francis has been compiled on *Perfumed Garden Vol. 2* (LP & CD), *Rubble, Vol. 16 - Glass Orchid Aftermath* (LP) and *Rubble, Vol. 9* (CD). (VJ)

Howard Walker with The Bombthrowers

45:     Love Will Find A Way/Eat Me   (Decca F 12997) 1970

The 'A' side of their 45 has good opening vocals that suggest a promising obscurity, but all is lost on a terrible choir type chorus. The flip is a throwaway ditty about sweets. (VJ)

Scott Walker

				HCP
ALBUMS:	1	SCOTT	(Philips BL7816) 1967 SC	3
(up to	2	SCOTT 2 (Philips BL/SBL 7840) 1968 SC (with insert)		1
1976)	3	LOOKING BACK WITH SCOTT WALKER		
		(Ember EMB LP 3393) 1968 SC		-
	4	SCOTT 3	(Philips SBL 7882) 1969 R1	3
	5	SINGS SONGS FROM HIS TV SERIES		
		(Philips SBL7900) 1969 SC		7
	6	THE BEST OF SCOTT WALKER VOL 1		
		(Philips 7910) 1969 SC		-
	7	SCOTT 4	(Philips SBL 7913) 1969 R1	-
	8	TIL THE BAND COMES IN	(Philips 6308 035) 1970 R2	-
	9	THE MOVIEGOER	(Philips 6308 127) 1972 SC	-
	10	ANY DAY NOW	(Philips 6308 148) 1973 R1	-
	11	STRETCH	(CBS 65725) 1973 SC	-
	12	THE ROMANTIC SCOTT WALKER		
		(Philips 6850 013) 1973 R1		-
	13	TERRIFIC	(Philips 6856 022) 1973 R1	-
	14	THIS IS SCOTT WALKER VOL 2		
		(Philips 6382 052) 1973		-
	15	WE HAD IT ALL	(CBS 80524) 1974 SC	-
	16	SPOTLIGHT ON SCOTT WALKER (2-LP)		
		(Philips 6625 017) 1976 SC		-

NB: (12) is an Audio club issue. (13) is an audio club reissue of (2) with different tracks. (1) reissued on CD (Fontana 5108792) 1992. (2) reissued on CD (Fontana 5108802) 1992. (3) reissued on CD (Ember EMBCD 3393) 1998. (4) reissued on CD (Fontana 5108812) 1992. (7) reissued on CD (Fontana 5108822) 1992. (8) reissued on CD (Beat Goes On BGOCD 320) 1996. (11) and (15) reissued on one CD (Beat Goes On BGOCD 358) 1997. Much of his material is also contained on the CD box set *No Regrets (The Best Of Scott Walker/Walker Brothers)* (Fontana 5108312) 1992. A compilation of his early years is *It's Raining Today (The Scott Walker Story 1967-1970)* (Razor & Tie RE 21202) 1996. *In Five Easy Pieces* (Universal 981 0442)

GARY WALKER AND THE RAIN - Album No 1 (CD).

2003 is a 5-CD box set with each of the five separate discs representing a different theme. *Classics And Collectibles* (Universal/Mercury) 2005 is a 2-CD set which features 20 tracks not previously available on CD.

EPs:	1	SCOTT ENGEL	(Liberty LEP 2261) 1962 R2
	2	GREAT SCOTT	(Philips MCP 1006) 1967 SC

NB. (1) as Scott Engel. (2) is a cassette EP.

			HCP
45s:	Jackie / The Plague	(Philips BF 1628) 1967	22
(up to	Joanna/Always Coming Back To You	(Philips BF 1662) 1967	7
1976)	Lights Of Cincinatti/Two Weeks Since		
	You've Gone	(Philips BF 1793) 1967	13
	I Still See You/My Way Home	(Philips 6006 186) 1971	-
	The Me I Never Knew/This Way Mary	(Philips 6006 311) 1973	-
	A Woman Left Lonely/Where Love Has Died	(CBS 1975) 1973	-
	Delta Dawn/We Had It All	(CBS 2521) 1974	-

One of the most enigmatic figures in pop history, **Scott Walker** left The Walker Brothers in 1967 in order to pursue an increasingly esoteric solo career which steadily alienated his once-enormous fanbase. Though frequently overblown and obscure, his early albums all contain songs of remarkable ambition and complexity that show him to have been one of the more distinctive singer-songwriters of the period.

He was born Noel Scott Engel on the January 9th 1943, in Hamilton, Ohio, USA. He showed musical talent from early childhood, and by his early teens was releasing unsuccessful romantic singles under the name Scotty Engel. These are now considerable rarities. Aged 16 he moved to Hollywood and started to undertake session work (as a bassist) with arranger Jack Nitzsche, and in 1961 he joined The Routers as bassist, then The Dalton Brothers. In 1964 the latter evolved into The Walker Brothers, who found enormous success when they moved to England the following year. Always the dominant artistic influence in the band, **Walker** found pop super-stardom increasingly hard to bear, and left them in May 1967 following a mismatched and fraught tour with Engelbert Humperdinck and **Jimi Hendrix**. He made England his base which is why we've included him in this book.

His image had always been moody and withdrawn, characteristics which were amply demonstrated on his solo albums, which indicated a writer drawn to the darker sides of human nature and more intrigued by psychological detail than chart music usually permitted. With psychedelia raging all around, his debut was a defiantly unhip mixture of self-penned ballads (including the brilliant *Montague Terrace (In Blue)*), and covers of material by Tim Hardin, Mann/Weill and Jacques Brel, the last of whom would be a major influence on **Walker**'s own writing. Though gloomy, overblown and decidedly odd, the album sold very well and launched him as a major live attraction in his own right.

His second album featured three Brel compositions as well as work by Bacharach/David and Tim Hardin and superb originals like *Plastic Palace*

People and *The Amorous Humphrey Plugg*. Though equally as personal and uncommercial as his debut, it topped the UK charts on its release in 1968, and the extracted single, *Jackie* (whose 'B' side is non-album) reached the Top 20. With it lodged at No. 1 in the Spring of 1968, **Walker** was free to pursue his personal inclinations further on *Scott 3*, which appeared early in 1969. *Scott 3* was **Walker**'s final top ten album, and the first to be dominated by his own songs - all but three Brel covers are self-penned. *Big Louise* is a touching ode to a lonely prostitute, *30 Century Man* is an inscrutable ballad about cryogenics and *Copenhagen* is a touching ode to his girlfriend's home city. The string arrangements are overwhelming at times, but it is an odd and compelling album and came in a stunning psychedelic sleeve.

At this time, **Walker** hosted a television series, 'This Is Scott Walker', on which he sang and introduced musical guests (though no rock bands). Sadly the shows have been wiped in their entirety, but sound recordings survive. **Walker** was finding fame increasingly difficult to bear, faking a car accident in order to escape one live date, and going on a monastic retreat in order to avoid the attentions of his fans. His next album *Scott 4*, is unquestionably his finest, and one of the more varied and unusual singer-songwriter albums of its time. Produced, like its predecessors, by Johnny Franz, it demonstrates his ease with numerous styles and moods. *The Seventh Seal* is an unsettlingly jaunty existential meditation, *The World's Strongest Man* is straightforwardly romantic, *Hero Of The War* is sourly humorous and *Boy Child* is deeply personal. All are catchy, but **Walker**'s refusal to tour or give interviews to support the record, and his insistence on its being released under his real name, combined to ensure that it failed to chart. This represented a shocking fall from grace for a star of his magnitude, and perhaps shook his confidence, for there was a marked decline in quality on his subsequent albums, as cover versions crept back in.

His next effort, 1970's *Til The Band Comes In*, is an uneasy mixture of brilliant originals (*Little Things (That Keep Us Together)*, *Time Operator*, *Thanks For Chicago Mr. James*), and padding like a mediocre cover of Roy Orbison's *It's Over* and a solo number by guest Esther Ofarim. It sold even less well than *Scott 4* and is probably his hardest album to acquire in top condition today. Thereafter the seventies were a sorry waste of **Walker**'s singular talent. *The Moviegoer* was a collection of film themes, while its successors took him in a largely unconvincing Country and Western direction. All have their moments, but nothing beyond *Til The Band Comes In* is needed by anyone but completists.

Walker returned to prominence in the early eighties when Julian Cope oversaw the *Fire Escape In The Sky* compilation (subtitled 'The Godlike Genius Of Scott Walker'), and **Walker** released a much more interesting album for Virgin in 1983, *Climate Of Hunter*. In recent years he has been acknowledged as a significant influence by several major contemporary songwriters, and the handful of releases he has made have been avant-garde, especially 1995's bleak and demanding *Tilt* (on Fontana).

His 1993 5-CD set *In Five Easy Pieces* is the nearest to an anthology of his career. It is far from a chronological guide to his career, though. CD 1

WALRUS - Walrus (CD).

sub-titled *In My Room* features tales of tenement living; CD 2 *Where's The Girl?* contains songs about girls; CD 3 *An American in Europe* contains songs about America and Europe; CD 4 *This Is How You Disappear* rounds up the songs that don't fit on any of the other discs and CD 5 *Scott On Screen* features songs from films and avant-garde soundtracks.

Classics And Collectibles includes 20 tracks previously unavailable on CD. If you want to hear him singing *Speak Softly Love* from 'The Godfather', *The Impossible Dream* from 'The Man Of La Mancha' or *The Me I Never Knew* from 1972's 'Alice's Adventures In Wonderland' as well as some of his better known songs, this CD should interest you.

Still resident in London, he records only sporadically and entirely to his own specifications, and does not speak to the press, thereby fuelling the mystique that has always been his stock in trade. (RMJ/VJ)

Gordon Waller

ALBUM: 1   GORDON   (Vertigo 6360 069) 1972 R3
NB: (1) credited to Gordon.

45s: Rosencrans Boulevard/
         Red, Cream And Velvet   (Columbia DB 8337) 1968
         Every Day/Because Of A Woman   (Columbia DB 8440) 1968
         Weeping Annaeleah/The Seventh Hour(Columbia DB 8518) 1968
         I Was A Boy When You Needed A Man/
         Lady In The Window   (Bell BLL 1059) 1969
         You're Gonna Hurt Yourself/Sunshine (Bell BLL 1106) 1970

Gordon Waller, a public school educated doctor's son, was one half of **Peter and Gordon** and launched a solo career upon their demise. His album is one of the hardest of all Vertigo releases to find and reputedly only sold a minute number of copies. Musically it contains rather poor singer/songwriter material and after it got a comprehensive thumbs down from the record buying public **Waller** quit the music business to take up farming. He made a brief comeback in the mid-seventies appearing on the 'Joseph And The Amazing Technicolour Dreamcoat' Soundtrack but little has been heard from him since.

Rosencrans Boulevard later resurfaced on *Rubble Vol. 2: Pop-Sike Pipedreams* (LP) and *Rubble Vol. 2* (CD). Written by Jim Webb it's full of mood changes and has a complex orchestral arrangement with some sweeping piano work. It's a pop single which certainly could have achieved more success. (VJ)

Wally

Personnel:	PETE COSKER	gtr, bs, vcls	A
	PAUL GERRETT	gtr, harmonium, piano, harpsichord, mellotron, organ, vcls	A
	PAUL MIDDLETON	gtr, bs	AB
	ROGER NARRAWAY	perc	AB
	PETE SAGE	violin, bs, mandolin	AB
	ROY WEBBER	vcls, gtr	AB
	MADELINE BELL	vcls	B
	PETE COSHER	gtr, vcls	B
	JAN GLENNIE SMITH	vcls	B
	NICK GLENNIE SMITH	keyb'ds, vcls	B
	RAY WEHRSTEIN	sax	B

ALBUMS: 1(A)   WALLY   (Atlantic SD 18115 0698) 1974
        2(B)   WALLY GARDENS   (Atlantic K 50180) 1975

45s: I Just Wanna Be A Cowboy/
         Life Of Living
         (Atlantic K 10497) 1974
         I The Martyr/Sunday Walking Lady   (Atlantic K 10651) 1975
         Nez Perce/Right Me   (Atlantic K 10616) 1975

An obscure band, whose debut album of violin-led light progressive rock and country-influenced harmony rock was produced by Bob Harris and **Rick Wakeman**. Collectors have yet to show much interest in them. Sometimes they are likened to **Barclay James Harvest**. (BS/CG)

Walrus

Personnel:

NICK GABB	drms		A
NOEL GREENAWAY	vcls		AB
STEVE HAWTHORN	bs, vcls		A
BILL HOAD	sax, clarinet, flute		A
BARRY PARFITT	organ, piano		AB
DON RICHARDS	trumpet		AB
JOHN SCATES	lead gtr, gtr		AB
ROY VOCE	tenor sax		A
JOE BARSON	trumpet		B
ROY CARTER	tenor sax		B
IAN MOSLEY	drms		B
MARTINSTEPHENSON	bs		B

ALBUM: 1(A) WALRUS   (Deram SML 1072) 1970 R2

NB: (1) reissued on CD (Black Rose BR 140).

45s: Who Can I Trust?/
Tomorrow Never Comes   (Deram DM 308) 1970 SC
Never Let My Body Touch The Ground/
Why   (Deram DM 323) 1971 SC

A jazzy/bluesy progressive outfit. They utilised horns but it's some of the guitar leads which catch the ear. Roger Harrison guested on drums on the opening cut, *Who Can I Trust?* and their cover of **Traffic**'s *Coloured Rain*. Most of the material was written by bassist Steve Hawthorn. Aside from *Who Can I Trust?*, his better numbers include *Why*, which is quite mellow with lots of flute, the jazzy *Turning*, which starts with a spoken monologue from Hawthorn and the final track *Tomorrow Never Comes*. The album's front cover designed by David Ansley features his drawing of a walrus.

Gabb, Hawthorn, Hoad and Voce all left in April 1972 and line-up (B) was put in place; but had no recording output. Mosley departed to **Darryl Way's Wolf** in December 1972 and Harrison went on to **Ramases**.

Who Can I Trust? and *Never Let My Body Touch The Ground* have both been compiled on *Progressive Pop Inside The Seventies* (CD).

This act should not be confused with the US Walrus, who issued an album in the US on Janus. The American band, from LA, had a strong gospel influence. Their drummer, however, was English: Warren 'Bugs' Pemberton, who was also with **Lomax Alliance**, **Jackie Lomax** and **The Undertakers**. (VJ/JM)

Clifford T. Ward

                            HCP

ALBUMS: 1 SINGER SONGWRITER (Dandelion 2310 216) 1972 SC -
(up to 2 HOME THOUGHTS FROM ABROAD
1976)   (Charisma CAS 1066) 1973 SC 40
     3 MANTLEPIECES   (Charisma CAS 1077) 1973 42
     4 ESCALATOR   (Charisma CAS 1098) 1975 SC -

     5 NO MORE ROCK 'N' ROLL (Philips 9109 500) 1975 SC -
     6 WAVES   (Philips 9109 216) 1976 SC -

NB: (1) reissued on CD as *Singer Songwriter... Plus* with one bonus track, *Sidetrack* (See For Miles SEECD 418-D) 1995. (2) reissued on vinyl (Charisma CHC 56) 1985 and later on CD (Virgin CASCD 1066) 1992. (3) reissued on vinyl (Charisma CHC 37) 1985 and later on CD (Virgin CASCD 1077) 1992. (4) reissued on vinyl (Charisma CHC 57) 1985 and on CD (Cherry Red CDM RED 252) 2004 with bonus tracks and new sleevenotes. *Laugh It Off* (Ameless AME 001) 1992 is a collection of demos and outtakes from recent years. There's also a compilation, *Gaye And Other Stories* (Virgin COM CD 4) 1987, which was reissued again on CD (Virgin CDVM 9009) 1992, with a different cover, sleevenotes and an extra track. *Anthology* (Cherry Red CDM RED 210) 2002 is a poorly packaged and far from definitive attempt at what it purports to be.

                            HCP

45s: Carrie/Sidetrick   (Dandelion 2001 327) 1972 -
(up to Coathanger/Rayne   (Dandelion 2001 382) 1972 -
1976) Gaye/Home Thoughts From Abroad (Clarisma CB 209) 1973 8
Wherewithal/
Thinking Of Something To Do   (Charisma CB 212) 1973 -
Scullery/To An Air Hostess   (Charisma CB 221) 1973 37

Jayne (From Andromeda Spiral)/
Maybe I'm Right   (Charisma CB 233) 1974 -
Jigsaw Girl/Cellophane   (Charisma CB 248) 1975 -
No More Rock & Roll /Gandalf   (Philips 6006 490) 1975 -
Home Thoughts From Abroad/
Where Would That Leave Me   (Charisma CB 280) 1976 -
Ocean Of Love/Tomorrow Night   (Philips 6006 542) 1976 -
Reissue: Gaye/Scullery   (Old Gold OG 9008) 1978 -

Born in Kidderminster, Worcestershire, on 10th February 1944, **Ward** was soon singing and playing piano for local bands during his school days. He went on to play for various local groups including Cliff Ward and The Cruisers (formed in 1962) and **The Secrets** (who were also known as **Simon's Secrets** and **Martin Raynor and The Secrets** at various times). None of them had much success and **Ward** took a job as an English language teacher, continuing his songwriting as a sideline.

He was signed by John Peel's Dandelion label in 1970 and recorded *Singer Songwriter*. Peel had received a tape of **Ward's** songs and recommended him to Clive Selwood for their adventurous label. The album was trailed by a single *Carrie*, which was inspired by Theodore Dreiser's 'Sister Carrie', a favourite novel about the reality of the American Dream. The single is a different mix to the version that appeared on the album. His follow-up single was a melodic love song *Coathanger*, which had an appealing hook and a clever lyric which used a coathanger as a metaphor for developing a love affair. Somehow it worked and the single attracted a lot of airplay, nearly becoming a hit. He used three sessions for 'Top Gear' and daytime Radio 1 to showcase material from his debut album as well as forthcoming material from his next album. By then, Dandelion had collapsed and he switched to Charisma for his next album *Home Thoughts*, which included a Top Ten hit with *Gaye*.

His strength lay in his ability to write melodic and whimsical pop songs with social comment. His refusal to perform live may help explain why his commercial success was limited considering the potentially wide appeal of his material and the quite encouraging sales of his *Home Thoughts...* and *Mantlepieces* albums. On the latter he pays tribute to his disabled daughter on the heartfelt *For Debbie And Her Friends*.

Escalator was a strong album, which showcased his developing keyboard skills. It includes the infectious single *Jigsaw Girl* and one his very best numbers *A Day To Myself*, a moving anti-war song conceived during his time spent touring in France when he discovered a First World War cemetery during a break from touring. Six tracks from this album later figured on the *Gaye And Other Stories* CD compilation. `

No More Rock And Roll was recorded after his departure from Charisma with new musicians, including **Chris Spedding** and steel guitar king **B.J. Cole**. Its highlight is *Up In The World* (later covered by Cliff Richard on his *Every Face Tells A Story* album and Art Garfunkel) with **Ward's** vocals at their best and stunning strings arranged by Richard Hewson. The shimmering *Summer Solstice*, *Gentle* and *Secretary* are also worth a listen.

Waves was released in 1976 to a mixed reception. One highlight was the majestic, stirring single *Oceans Of Love*, although the version on the album was less piano-based than the earlier single version.

Sadly his recording career was prematurely ended by a particularly virulent form of multiple sclerosis and he sadly died on 18th December 2001.

Anticipation has been compiled on See For Miles' *Dandelion Rarities* (CD) and *Coathanger* similarly appears on their budget *Dandelion Sampler 1969 - 1972* (CD). *Scullery*, with an edited introduction, can also be heard on the (LP) compilation *Dynamite*; whilst *The Love Album* (LP) features a different version of *Lost Again*. Finally, *One More Chance* (LP) 1974 includes a different mix of *Wherewithal*. (VJ/DS)

Michael Ward

                            HCP

ALBUM: 1 INTRODUCING MICHAEL WARD
     (Philips 6308 189) 1974 26

                            HCP

45s: Let There Be Peace On Earth (Let It Begin With Me)/
Oh For The Wings Of A Dove   (Philips 6006 340) 1973 15
He/Jerusalem   (Philips 6006 375) 1974 -

This forgotten male vocalist enjoyed considerable success in his short-lived career. (VJ)

Wards of Court

Personnel:	TREVOR DANBY	lead gr	A
	BOB LEE	bs	A
	NIGEL SILK	drms	A
	ROB SMITHERS	gtr	A
	ROD SONES	vcls	A

45:	All Night Girl/		
	How Could You Say One Thing	(Deram DM 127) 1967 R1	

A soul/harmony beat group from Essex, named for their extreme youth. The 45, whose snappy B-side has made it much-sought-after, was produced by **Peter Lee Stirling**. They subsequently changed their name to The Latch, and Silk currently drums with **T.Rex** tribute band T. Rextasy.

How Could You Say One Thing has been compiled on *The Mod Scene* (CD) and *Echoes From The Wilderness - Sixteen UK R&B Freakbeat Trippers*. (LP & CD). (VJ/RMJ)

Warhorse

Personnel:	ASHLEY HOLT	vcls	ABC
	GED PECK	gtr	A
	MAC POOLE	drms	AB
	NICK SIMPER	bs	ABC
	FRANK WILSON	keyb'ds, synthesizer	ABC
	PETER PARKS	gtr	BC
	BARNEY JAMES	drms	C

ALBUMS:	1(A)	WARHORSE	(Vertigo 6360 015) 1970 R1
	2(B)	RED SEA	(Vertigo 6360 066) 1972 R1

NB: Both albums have been reissued on Thunderbolt in different sleeves. (1) and (2) also reissued on CD (Repertoire RR 4055-CC and 4056-CX) 1990 and again in 1997, with bonus tracks and sleevenotes. (1) also issued again on CD (Angel Air SJPCD 034) and again on CD (Akarma AK 205) with five bonus cuts. (2) also issued again on CD (Angel Air SJPCD 035) and again on vinyl and CD (Akarma AK 206). *The Warhorse Story Volume One* (RPM RPM 174) 1997 combines the first album, digitally remastered, with five bonus tracks - four live "in studio" recordings from an unbroadcasted BBC session plus *Miss Jane*, their original record. The set came with very detailed liner notes by Simon Robinson, with contributions from Nick Simper. *The Warhorse Story Volume Two* (RPM RPM) 199? combines their second album with six bonus tracks. *Outbreak Of Hostilities* is a CD compilation drawing from their two Vertigo albums.

45:	St Louis/No Chance	(Vertigo 6059 027) 1970 SC

Simper had earlier been involved with **Deep Purple** and prior to that, Johnny Kidd and The Pirates, although his previous group was **Lord Sutch** and Heavy Friends. Peck and Poole had both been in **The Marsha Hunt Group** and Frank Wilson joined from **Velvet Fogg**.

The *Warhorse* album sounded a lot like **Deep Purple** at the time but didn't make much impression. Their debut 45, *St Louis*, a cover of an **Easybeats'** song sold pretty well though.

Peck left in January 1971 and Peter Parks replaced him on the second album, *Red Sea*, which was much more guitar-orientated. There's a notable guitar solo on *Back In Time* and there's also a cover version of **Shirley Bassey's** *I (Who Have Nothing)*. Poole departed for **Broken Glass** (he later did session work) and ex-**Legend** member Barney James replaced him. The band built up audiences on the Continent but failed to stir many people here. They split in May 1974.

Simper and Parker formed Dynamite. At the end of the seventies Simper formed Nick Simper's Fandango. He also played with **Screaming Lord Sutch** and later emerged in Quartermass II. Wilson made an album with Melvyn Gale in 1980. Holt and James later worked with **Rick Wakeman**. Much later in 1980, Parker played with Dirty Looks. Ahsley Holt has his home recording studio and continues to record - *Gargle Of The Spartanites* is his latest effort. (VJ/JM/CG)

Ray Warleigh

ALBUM:	1	RAY WARLEIGH'S FIRST ALBUM	
		(mono/stereo)	(Philip (S)BL 7881) 1969 SC

Ray Warleigh is an Australian alto saxophonist (and also a talented flautist) who has lived in Britain since the early sixties. In his young days he developed a strong interest in jazz. He played with **Alexis Korner** and later with jazz icons such as **Mike Westbrook**, Ronnie Scott and Humphrey Lyttleton. His first album is not available on CD. Since then he's contributed to countless recordings by other artists including **Long John Baldry**, **John Mayall**, **Nick Drake** and **Georgie Fame**. In the seventies he was in **Spontaneous Music Ensemble** and also worked with guitarist Allan Holdsworth. In the eighties he was a member of the West Germany Radio Orchestra and Charlie Watts' big band. He worked with classical composer Gavin Bryars and flugelhornist Kenny Wheeler in the nineties. (VJ)

Warlord

CD:	1	WARLORD	(Audio Archives AACD 046) 200?

This CD presents extremely rare and previously unreleased recordings from this mid-seventies doom metal band. There's a strong **Black Sabbath** influence here with tormented vocals, brooding organ and blistering guitar. (VJ)

Warm Dust

Personnel:	PAUL CARRACK	vcls, keyb'ds	ABCDE
	TERRY 'TEX' COMER	bs	ABCDE
	DAVE PEPPER	drms	A D
	ALAN SOLOMAN	sax, keyb'ds, vcls	ABCDE
	JOHN SURGUY	sax, gtr, vcls	ABCDE
	LES WALKER	vcls	ABCDE
	JOHN BEDSON	drms	B
	KEITH BAILEY	drms	C
	CHRISTIAN FRANCIS	sax	E
	STEVE WITHERINGTON	drms	E

ALBUMS:	1(A)	AND IT CAME TO PASS (2-LP)	
			(Trend TNLS 700) 1970 R1
	2(C)	PEACE FOR OUR TIME	(Trend 6480 001) 1971 R1

NB: (1) reissued on CD (Red Fox RF 610). (1) also issued in Germany (Metronome 2/400002) 1979 and the US (Uni 73109) 1970. There was also a third, German only album *Dreams Of Impossibilities* (BASF 2229082-4) 1972. This has been reissued on CD, together with (2) as *Warm Dust* (Red Fox RF 611).

45:	It's A Beautiful Day/Worm Dance	(Trend 6099 022) 1970 SC

A jazz-rock fusion band. Paul Carrack was born in Sheffield on 22 April 1951 and Terry Comer entered the world in Burnley, Lancashire on 23

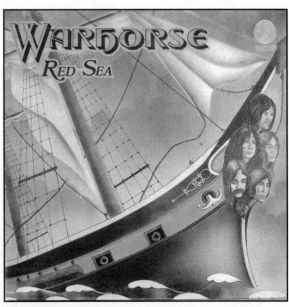

WARHORSE - Red Sea (LP).

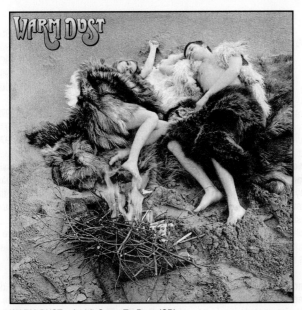

WARM DUST - And It Came To Pass (CD).

February 1949. Pepper left after the first album and was initially replaced by John Bedson on drums. When he left to join **Gnidrolog**, Keith Bailey (formerly of **Graham Bond's** Holy Magick) was recruited and played on the *Peace For Our Time* album. This is an excellent progressive album with strong vocals, long sax and flute instrumental sections and good organ work. Several tracks like *Rejection* and *Wind Of Change* veered towards jazz but one, *Wrote A Letter*, was an acoustic bluesy number with interesting lyrics.

When Bailey left to join **Brian Auger's Oblivion Express** Dave Pepper rejoined and figured on their third album, *Dreams Of Impossibilities*, which was a German-only release on the BASF label in 1972. Pepper then left for session work and ex-Mataya member Steve Witherington replaced him. Christian Francis also joined on sax.

Carrack, Comer and Witherington joined **Ace** in December 1972. Walker went solo and then joined The Mitchigan Flyers. Francis went on to join **Voice**. (CA/DS/VJ/JM)

The Warm Expression

45:    Let No Man Put Asunder/
      The Holy City   (Columbia DB 8672) 1970

Both sides of this 45 were arranged and conducted by **John Cameron** and produced by Bob Barrett. The 'A' side is orchestrated pop. The flip is a dreadful religious ballad. (VJ)

Warm Sensation

Personnel incl: PATRICK KERR

45:    I'll Be Proud Of You/The Clown   (Columbia DB 8568) 1969

This was probably a studio project which involved members of **The Ivy League**, including Patrick Kerr. It was produced by Allan Clarke of **The Hollies**. (VJ)

Warm Sounds

Personnel:	BARRY HUSBAND	gtr, bs	A
	DENVER GERRARD	gtr, vcls	A
	('CANDY' JOHN CARR)	drms	A

                                              HCP

45s:	Birds And Bees/Doo Dah	(Deram DM 120) 1967 SC 27
	Sticks And Stones/Angeline	(Immediate IM 58) 1967 SC -
	Nite Is A Comin'/Smeta Murgaty	(Deram DM 174) 1968 R1 -

This pop-orientated duo captured the 'Summer of Love' vibes with their single, *Birds And Bees*, which climbed to No 27 in June 1967. It actually reached No 1 in pirate ship Radio London's Top 40, the only single to do this and not make the UK Top 20! However, their other efforts, *Nite Is A-Comin'* and *Sticks And Stones*, despite being good examples of harmony-pop with the occasional tinge of weirdness, were less successful. Of their other tracks, *Doo Dah* is rather lightweight harmony-pop effort and *Smeta Murgaty* sees the band veer towards total dementia with a mayhem of backwards tapes and layered sound.

When the duo, which was sometimes assisted by 'Candy' John Carr, eventually split, Husband and Carr joined **Hapshash and The Coloured Coat** and were later in **Donovan's Open Road** band. **Carr** was also in **Junior's Eyes**. **Denver (Denny) Gerrard** went on to record a solo album for Decca's Nova label, *Sinister Morning*, with **High Tide** backing him, and also produced **High Tide's** debut album.

Compilation appearances have included:- *Nite Is A Comin'* on *The Psychedelic Scene* (CD) and on the 4-CD box set *Acid Drops, Spacedust & Flying Saucers*; *Nite-is-a-Comin* and *Smeta Murgaty* on *Rubble, Vol. 12 - Staircase To Nowhere* (LP), *Rubble, Vol. 7* (CD) and *Psychedalia - Rare Blooms From The English Summer Of Love* (CD); *Nite Is A Comin'* and *Doo Dah* on *Deram Dayze* (LP); *Angeline* and *Sticks And Stones* on *Immediate Alternative* (LP & CD) and *Immediate Single Anthology, Vol. 1 - Rarities* (CD); *Sticks And Stones* on *Immediate Single Collection, Vol. 2* (CD) and on the 2-CD set *We Love The Pirates: Charting The Big 'L' Fab 40*; *Angeline* on *Immediate Single Collection, Vol. 5* (CD) and *Birds And Bees* on *Pop-In, Vol 1* (CD). (VJ)

Warren J.5

Personnel:	CHUCK FRYERS	gtr	A
	COLIN MADELY	gtr	A
	JEFF PRIOR	bs	A
	JOHN WARREN REED	vcls	A
	TERRY SLADE	drms	A

ALBUM: 1(A) RHYTHM & BLUES   (Vedette VRMS 349) 1967 R3
NB: (1) Italian only.

45:       Sto Con Te/Se Hai Qualcosa Da Dire (Vedette VVN-33133 1967

Another English band that arrived in Italy via France and Germany. They had an Italian language 7", and then were allowed to record an entire album, all sung in English. It features only R&B covers, though.

Terry Slade had earlier been with **Jimmy Winston and The Reflections** and both he and Chuck Fryers went on to play with **Thane Russal**. (GB)

Warrior

Personnel:	ROGER BATCHELOR	bs	A
	HOWARD JONES	keyb'ds	A
	GRAHAM PITCHER	drms	A
	WILL PITCHER	gtr, bs, synth	A

ALBUM: 1(A) INVASION   (Private Pressing) 1972 R3

Warrior won the Oxford heat of the 1974 Melody Maker National Folk/Rock Group Competition. Their very rare progressive rock instrumental offering was never formally released but demo copies have turned up and change hands for three figure sums. It contained seven long tracks including *Warrior Suite*, *Nebula* and *The Pig*. Musically, there's a strong **Emerson, Lake and Palmer** influence. Howard Jones went on to fame and fortune in the eighties as a solo performer. (BS/VJ)

The Warriors

Personnel:	ANTHONY ANDERSON	vcls	A
	JON ANDERSON	vcls	AB
	MICHAEL BRERETON	lead gtr	A

DAVID FOSTER	bs		AB
RODNEY HILL	gtr		A
IAN WALLACE	drms		AB
BRIAN CHAPMAN	gtr		B

45: Don't Make Me Blue/
You Came Along   (Decca F 11926) 1964 R1

You've probably spotted that this Accrington beat group included **Jon Anderson**, who was later in **Yes**. As you can imagine their sole 45 is now an expensive purchase for **Yes** fans. However, **Anderson's** next band after this was **Mabel Greer's Toy Shop**. Anthony Anderson, Brereton and Hill left and Brian Chapman came in on guitar for a later line-up.

Wallace was also in **The World** and went on to become a popular session man with **Big Grunt** and **King Crimson** to name but two. Foster later resurfaced in **Badger**.

Compilation appearances have included: *You Came Along* on *Pop Inside The 60s Vol. 1* (CD) and *Hard-Up Heroes* (2-LP); and *Don't Make Me Blue* on *The Beat Scene* (CD). (VJ/JM)

Washboard Kings

Personnel incl: JEAN HART   vcls
                  BILL ODDIE   vcls

45: Five Feet Two/If You Knew Susie   (Rayrik LCR 1001) 1966

Bill Oddie does the vocals on the 'A' side, whilst female vocalist Jean Hart manages the flip. The key word here is 'washboard!!' (VL)

Geno Washington and The Ram Jam Band

Personnel:			
BUDDY BEADLE	tenor sax		A
PETE GAGE	lead gtr		A
LIONEL KINGHAM	baritone sax		A
HERB PRESTIDGE	drms		A
JOHN ROBERTS	bs		A
GENO WASHINGTON	vcls		A
JEFF WRIGHT	organ		A

			HCP
ALBUMS: 1(A)	HAND CLAPPIN', FOOT STOMPIN', FUNKY-BUTT... LIVE!	(Piccadilly NPL 38026) 1966	SC 5
2(A)	HIPSTERS, FLIPSTERS, FINGER-POPPIN' DADDIES! (mono/stereo)	(Piccadilly N(S)PL 38032) 1967	SC 8
3(A)	SHAKE A TAIL FEATHER! (mono/stereo)	(Piccadilly N(S)PL 38029) 1968	SC -
4(A)	LIVE! - RUNNING WILD! (mono/stereo)	(Pye N(S)PL 18219) 1968	SC -
5(A)	SITTERS, SHIFTERS, FINGER CLICK MAMA	(Marble Arch MAL 816) 1969	-
6(A)	UP TIGHT	(Marble Arch MAL 1162) 1969	-
7(A)	GOLDEN HOUR OF...	(Pye GH 594) 1975	-

NB: (1) reissued on Pye (NSPL 18618) in 1980. There's also a later compilation, *Hip Shakin' Soul Breakin' Earth Quakin' Live* (PRT PYL 4018) 1989. (1) and (2) reissued on one CD (C5 C5CD 581) 1992. (1) reissued on CD (Repertoire REP 4189-WZ) 1991 and (2) reissued on CD (Repertoire REP 4190-WZ) 1991. *Geno! Geno! Geno! Live In The 60s* (Sequel NXTCD 295) 1998 is a 3-CD box set. *My Bombers, My Dexy's, My Highs: The Sixties Studio Sessions* (Sequel NEMCD 973) 1998 is a 2-CD set.

EPs:	1(A)	HI	(Piccadilly NEP 34054) 1966 SC
	2(A)	DIFFERENT STROKES	(Pye NEP 24293) 1968 SC
	3(A)	SMALL PACKAGE OF HIPSTERS	(Pye NEP 24302) 1968 SC

			HCP
45s:	Water/Understanding	(Piccadilly 7N 35312) 1966	39
	Hi! Hi! Hazel/Beach Bash	(Piccadilly 7N 35329) 1966	45
	Que Sera Sera/All I Need	(Piccadilly 7N 35346) 1966	43
	Michael/Hold On To My Love	(Piccadilly 7N 35359) 1966	39
	She Shot A Hole In My Soul/ I've Been Hurt By Love	(Piccadilly 7N 35392) 1967	-
	Tell It Like It Is/ Girl I Want To Marry	(Piccadilly 7N 35403) 1967	-
	Different Strokes/You Got Me Hummin'	(Pye 7N 17425) 1967	-
	I Can't Quit Her/Put Out The Fire Baby	(Pye 7N 17570) 1968	-
	I Can't Let You Go/Bring It To Me Baby	(Pye 7N 17649) 1968	-
	My Little Chickadee/Seven Eleven	(Pye 7N 17745) 1969	-
	Alison Please/ Each And Every Part Of Me	(Pye 7N 45019) 1970	-
	Feeling Is Good/My Little Chickadee	(Pye 7N 45085) 1970	-
	Dirty Dirty/Give 'Em A Hand	(Pye 7N 45121) 1970	-

Geno Washington was a black serviceman, originally from Evansville, Indiana, who remained in the UK after his discharge to form a soul band. They became a very popular live act on the mid-sixties circuit with their dynamic renditions of classic soul numbers of the day. They achieved considerable commercial success, too, in their early days. Their first two albums soared high in the Album Charts and their first four 45s were all minor hits. The outfit, which used a wide array of supporting musicians, split up in 1970.

Geno Washington returned in 1975 with a shaven head to launch a new career with DJM Records, which lasted for the remainder of the decade. In 1981, he recorded a further album *Put Out The Cat* and he toured from time to time in the eighties and nineties and 2003 saw the release of *Return Of The G*.

Geno! Geno! Geno! Live In The 60s features his three live albums between 1966 and 1969 remastered and reproduced in their original sleeves plus a foldout booklet with an exclusive interview with the man himself as he tells the story of his early years.

My Bombers, My Dexy's, My Highs comprises one CD of his sixties singles, whilst the CD includes his *Shake A Tail Feather Baby* album plus eight previously unissued cuts, including a rock-steady version of *I Was Kaiser Bill's Batman*!

Compilation appearances include: *Que Sera Sera* on *Piccadilly Story* (CD) and *The Beat Goes On, Vol. 3* (LP); *Beach Bash* on *Ripples, Vol. 5* (CD); and *She Shot A Hole In My Soul* can be heard on the 2-CD set *We Love The Pirates: Charting The Big 'L' Fab 40*. (VJ/AD)

The Washington D.C.s

Personnel:			
GLEN DUKE	drms		A
BARRY FITZGERALD	gtr		A
GARY ILLINGWORTH	organ		A
BERNIE McCLEAN	bs		A
ROGER SAUNDERS	lead gtr		A

ALBUM: 1(A)	DAVE CLARK FIVE AND THE WASHINGTON D.C's	(Ember FA 2003) 1964

WATER INTO WINE BAND - Harvest Time (CD).

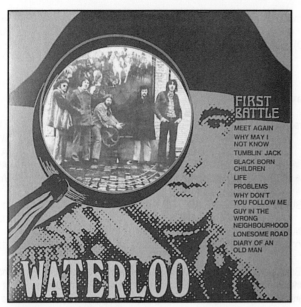

WATERLOO - First Battle (LP).

45s: Kisses Sweeter Than Wine/
Where Did You Go   (Ember EMB S 190) 1964 SC
32nd Floor/Whole Lot More   (CBS 202226) 1966 SC
Seek And Find/I Love Gerald Chevin
The Great (some in PS)   (CBS 202464) 1967 R2/R1
I've Done It All Wrong/Anytime   (Domain D 9) 1969 SC

A sixties pop outfit from London whose most sought-after 45 is *Seek And Find*, largely because it was produced by former **Yardbird** Paul Samuel-Smith. It has been compiled on *Jagged Time Lapse, Vol 4* (CD). Roger Saunders was later in **Freedom** and **Medicine Head**. (VJ)

Wasp

45: Melissa/Little Miss Bristol   (EMI EMI 2253) 1975

This single featured ex-**Shadows** drummer Brian Bennett. (VJ)

The Watch Committee

45: Throw Another Penny In The Well/
Now I Think The Other Way   (Philips BF 1695) 1968

An obscure band from Surrey whose sole recording was this 45. (VJ)

Waterloo

ALBUM: 1 FIRST BATTLE   (Vogue) 1969
NB: (1) Originally only issued in France. Reissued (Thorns WS 30150) 2001.

An obscure five-piece group whose keyboard/guitar driven progressive rock song, *Why May I Not Know*, from 1969, has resurfaced on *Circus Days, Vol. 1* (LP) and *Circus Days Vol. 1 & 2* (CD). It's well worth a listen and similar to **Jethro Tull** towards the end. It was originally released on a French album on Vogue in 1969. (VJ)

Water Into Wine Band

Personnel: PETER McMUM   A
             TREVOR SANDFORD   A
             WILLIAM THORP   A
             RAY WRIGHT   A

ALBUMS: 1(A)   HILL CLIMBING FOR BEGINNERS
             (w/insert)   (Myrrh MYR 1004) 1974 R3
           2(A)   HARVEST TIME   (Private Pressing CJT 002) 1976 R3

NB: (1) reissued as a 2-CD (Kissing Spell/Erewhon KSCD 918) which contains both the different US and UK mixes the album was mixed in. (2) reissued on CD (Kissing Spell/Erewhon KSCD 912).

This Christian-influenced acoustic folk-rock band's albums are now very rare and sought-after. They formed at Cambridge University in 1971. After going full-time in 1974 they were a popular attraction at colleges, folk clubs and festivals. The debut is the better of the two - it's a fine album of progressive acid-folk that doesn't have a bad track on it but is dominated by the 11-minute *Song Of The Cross*. The *Harvest Time* album isn't as consistently good but as a private pressing is extremely elusive and consequently sells for £200 plus. The title track takes up all of Side 2, whilst Side 1 contains several shorter compositions.

An accomplished violinist, Thorp went on to play for the Welsh National Opera and later the Royal Philharmonic Orchestra. More recently he's played in several chamber groups.

Waiting For Another Day later resurfaced on *The History Of U.K. Underground Folk Rock 1968-1978 Vol. 1* (CD). (VJ)

The Waterproof Sparrows

Personnel incl: STEVE PEREGRIN TOOK

This unrecorded 1967 psychedelic boogie band's main claim to fame was the inclusion of **Steve Peregrine Took**, who later linked up with **Marc Bolan** in **Tyrannosaurus Rex**. (VJ)

Roger Waters and Ron Geesin

Personnel: ROGER WATERS   A
               RON GEESIN   A

ALBUM: 1(A)   MUSIC FROM THE FILM "THE BODY"
                                (Harvest SHSP 4008) 1970 SC

NB: (1) reissued on CD (Harvest CDP 792 548 2) 1989 and again (EMI 0777 7 92548 2).

This was an extremely experimental collaboration between **Pink Floyd**'s bassist and **Geesin**, an avant-garde composer. It is notable for being **Waters**' first solo recording and little else. The 22 tracks are made up of depressing cello arrangements and body noises (burps, tummy rumbles, heartbeats, screams). Unless you're a **Pink Floyd** completist or a **Geesin** fan this is an album you can do without. Later in the eighties **Waters** went on to cut some more serious recordings. This one has little collectable value. (VJ)

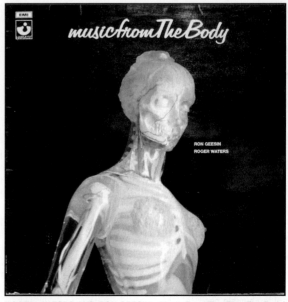

ROGER WATERS AND RON GEESIN - Music From The Film 'The Body' (LP).

The Watersons

Personnel:	LAL WATERSON	ABC
	MIKE WATERSON	ABC
	NORMA CHRISTINE WATERSON	ABC
	JOHN HARRISON	A
	BERNIE VICKERS	B
	MARTIN CARTHY	C

ALBUMS:	1(A)	NEW VOICES	(Topic 12T 125) 1965 SC
(up to	2(A)	FROST AND FIRE	(Topic 12T 136) 1965 SC
1976)	3(A)	WATERSONS	(Topic 12T 142) 1966 SC
	4(A)	A YORKSHIRE GARLAND	(Topic 12T 167) 1966 SC
	5(A)	THE WATERSONS SOUND	(Topic TS 346) 196? SC
	6(C)	FOR PENCE AND SPICY ALE	(Topic 12T 265) 1975

NB: (1) with Harry Boardman and Maureen Craik. (2) reissued on CD (Topic TSCD 136) 1990. (6) reissued on CD (Topic TSCD 462) 1993 along with extra cuts. *Mighty River Of Song* (Topic Records TSPCD 4002) 2004 is a 4-CD retrospective plus a DVD.

| 45: | Rubber Band/ | |
| | Red Wine And Promises | (Transatlantic BIG 507) 1972 |

This folk group should certainly be investigated by folk fans who don't know of them. They had a unique sound and their music is full of distinctive harmonies. They recorded into the eighties and Mike Waterson also recorded a solo album. The above discography may well be incomplete. *John Barleycorn* on their *Frost And Fire* album was the inspiration for **Traffic**'s later album of the same name.

Their most accessible recording is the CD reissue of (5), which also features tracks from Mike Waterson's later 1977 solo effort and Lal and Norma Waterson's later album, *A True Hearted Girl*.

John Harrison left the group in 1966 and they split up for the first time in 1968. They reformed in 1972 with Bernie Vickers replacing John Harrison in a new line-up (B), but Harrison was quickly replaced by **Martin Carthy**, who married Norma Christine Waterson.

Mighty River of Song is a well-compiled retrospective, which supplements their more commercial releases with a wide range of alternative takes and demos. The package also comes with detailed sleevenotes from Ken Hunt.

Lal Waterson died on 4 September 1998, aged 55. (VJ)

John L. Watson

ALBUM: 1 WHITE HOT BLUE BLACK (Deram SMLR 1061) 1970 R1

This guy was a black American singer (an ex-Serviceman, like **Geno Washington**) who had earlier fronted **John L. Watson and The Web** and **The Web**. This scarce album is basically overblown, bluesy horn-rock with a few decent riffs here and there. It was produced by **Mike Vernon** and features **Rick Hayward** on guitar. **Watson** still sings the blues today. (VJ/RMJ)

John L. Watson (and The Hummelflugs)

Personnel:	JEFF LEWINGTON	ld gtr	A
	ANDY MAGUIRE	bs	A
	PAUL MAGUIRE	organ, trumpet	A
	DUNCAN McCRACKEN	drms	A
	JOHN L. WATSON	vcls	A

45s:	Looking For You/Dance With You	(Pye 7N 15746) 1965
	Standing By/	
	I'll Make It Worth Your While	(Piccadilly 7N 35233) 1965
α	A Mother's Love/Might As Well Be Gone	(Deram DM 285) 1970
	Lonely For Your Love/	
	Into My Life You Came	(EMI EMI 2061) 1973

NB: α a **John L. Watson** solo disc.

This earlier outfit fronted by **John L. Watson** was more soul-based and a very marginal case for inclusion. 'Hummelflugs' incidentally is German for 'flight of the bumble bee'!

Compilation appearances have included: *Lookin' For Love* on *The Sixties File* (2-LP); and *I'll Make It Worth Your While* on *Doin' The Mod, Vol. 2* (CD). (VJ)

Wavemaker

Personnel:	KEN GALE	electronics	B
	BRIAN HODGSON	synthesizers	AB
	JON KELIEHOR	perc	A
	JOHN LEWIS	keyb'ds	AB
	ANTHONY McVEY	timpani	AB

| ALBUMS: | 1(A) | WHERE ARE WE CAPTAIN? | (Polydor 2383 331) 1975 |
| | 2(B) | NEW ATLANTIS | (Polydor 2383 434) 1977 |

| 45: | Tunnel Of Love/Micky Moonshine | (Polydor 2058 924) 1977 |

A British electronic project that had its roots in the BBC Radiophonic Workshop, where synthesizer techniques pioneer Brian Hodgson spent ten years, working, amongst other things, on the sound effects and music for the 'Dr. Who' series. Along with Delia Derbyshire, co-author of the absolutely astonishing 1963 theme tune of the series, Hodgson was invited to cooperate on David Vorhaus' groundbreaking **White Noise** project in 1968. This was after the closing-down of their Unit Delta Plus electronic band, a trio with Peter Zinovieff that barely lasted a year. Their most famous appearance was at the Million Volt Light and Sound Rave, a four-day electronic music event held in 1967 at the Chalk Farm Roadhouse. Canadian composer John Lewis studied with Hans Werner Henze in Rome. American-born percussionist Jon Keliehor was a member of The Daily Flash and Bodine in the mid-to-late sixties. He subsequently moved to Britain, finally settling in Scotland.

Wavemaker operated out of the Electrophon studios near Covent Garden (London) established by Hodgson after his departure from the Workshop in 1972 and filled with custom-designed synthesizer modules that also gave rise to other elusive items like *In A Covent Garden* (1973), *Zygoat* (1974) and *Further Thoughts On The Classics* (1975) (which is the same album as *In A Covent Garden* but with a different title). In 1973, Derbyshire and Hodgson also recorded the music to the film 'The Legend Of Hell House' there. The stated aim of *Where Are We Captain?* was "to explore the synthesizer as a sophisticated instrument in its own right, not as a substitute for conventional instruments". If you want comparisons, try *Timesteps*-period Walter Carlos, Mort Garson or Zorch (for the first album, that is). Their second effort, *New Atlantis*, is based on the same-titled visionary tale written by Sir Francis Bacon in 1624. It's a lot easier to find and it's a bit more accessible than its predecessor (imagine a slightly louder Bo Hansson). (LB)

Waygood Ellis

| 45: | I Like What I'm Trying To Do/ | |
| | Hey Lover | (Polydor 56729) 1967 R1 |

NB: This single has been reissued (Polydor 56729) in a limited edition pressing of 500 reproduced from the original French jukebox release with a large centre hole.

This 45 was actually recorded by **The Fleur de Lys** (see their entry for more details of them) and is consequently sought-after. The 'A' side is a strong rock/soul production similar to *Respect*. The 'B' side is a lousy ballad. (VJ)

Carl Wayne (and The Vikings)

Personnel:	DAVE HOLLIS	drms	A
	ACE KEFFORD	bs	AB
	JOHNNY MANN	gtr	AB
	TERRY WALLIS	gtr, vcls	AB
	CARL WAYNE	vcls	AB
	BEV BEVAN	drms	B

ALBUM: 1 CARL WAYNE (RCA SF 8239) 1972 SC

NB: (1) reissued on CD (BMG/Funhouse) 2001 in Japan.

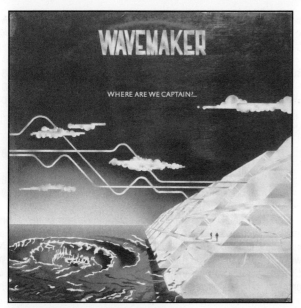
WAVEMAKER - Where Are We Captain? (LP).

45s:
What's A Matter Baby/		
Your Loving Ways	(Pye 7N 15702) 1964 R1
This Is Love/You Could Be Fun	(Pye 7N 15824) 1965 R1
Maybe God's Got Something Up His Sleeve/		
Rosanna	(RCA RCA 2032) 1970
Imagine/Sunday Kind Of Love	(RCA RCA 2177) 1972
Take My Hands For A While/		
Sweet Seasons	(RCA RCA 2257) 1972
You're A Star/Bluebird	(Pye 7N 45290) 1973

Carl Wayne was born on 18 August 1944 in Birmingham and had played with **Keith Powell and The Valets** before forming **Carl Wayne and The Vikings**, who played during 1964-65. A Birmingham-based beat group, they toured Germany. Both their 45s are now hard to find and collectable. They also had a US-only single, *My Girl/Shimmy Shammy Jingle* on ABC.

When Dave Hollis left he was replaced by former **Denny Laine and The Diplomats** drummer Bev Bevan. In February 1966 he became lead singer of **The Move,** along with **Kefford** and Bevan. Bevan was later in **The Electric Light Orchestra** and Johnny Mann subsequently joined **The Nightriders**.

The Move became major stars, but **Wayne** left them in January 1970 to pursue a career in cabaret and television. This was moderately successful, but not on record - these solo discs slipped by largely unnoticed. However the album included **Dusty Springfield** (uncredited) on four cuts. Latterly he sang with **The Hollies'** touring band, but sadly succumbed to cancer in August 2005.

Compilation appearances have included: *C' Mon Round To My Place* on *The Youngblood Story Vol.* 1(CD); You *Could Be Fun (At The End Of The Party)* on *Ripples, Vol. 4* (CD) and *Visions Of The Past, Vol. 3* (LP & CD); *What's A-Matter Baby (Is It Hurting You)* on *It Happened Then* (EP); *What's A-Matter Baby (Is It Hurting You)* and *Your Loving Ways* on *Footsteps To Fame, Vol. 1* (CD); *What's A-Matter Baby (Is It Hurting You), Your Loving Ways, This Is Love, You Could Be Fun (At The End Of The Party), My Girl* and *Shimmy Shammy Jangle* on *Brum Beat - Midlands Beat Groups Of The 60's* (CD). (VJ/JM)

Pat Wayne and The Beachcombers

Personnel incl: PETER COOK   organ
                PAT WAYNE   vcls

45s:
	Go Back To Daddy/Jambalaya	(Columbia DB 7121) 1963 SC
	Roll Over Beethoven/Is It Love?	(Columbia DB 7182) 1963 SC
	Bye Bye Johnny/	
	Strictly For The Birds	(Columbia DB 7262) 1964 SC
	Brand New Man/Nobody's Child	(Columbia DB 7417) 1964 SC
α	Come Dance With Me/	
	I Don't Want To Cry	(Columbia DB 7603) 1965
α	My Friend/Tomorrow Mine	(Columbia DB 7739) 1965
α	The Night Is Over/Hombre	(Columbia DB 7944) 1966

NB: α **Pat Wayne** solo 45s.

A Birmingham-based beat group who are best remembered (if at all) for their version of *Roll Over Beethoven*, which featured a very young **Jimmy Page** on session guitar. After he split from The Beachcombers in 1964 **Wayne** cut a trio of pop-orientated 45s, which were ballads.

Compilation appearances have included: *Roll Over Beethoven* on *James Patrick Page: Session Man, Vol. 1* (LP & CD), *James Patrick Page, Session Man* (2-LP), *Beat At Abbey Road* (CD) and *Beat Merchants* (2-LP); and *Bye Bye Johnny* on *R&B Scene, Vol. 1* (LP) and *R&B At Abbey Road* (CD). (VJ)

The Ways and Means

Personnel:
BARRY CLASS	drms, vcls	A
ROY DELLO	gtr	A
RAY FAIRBRASS	bs	A
LESLIE GEORGE GOSS-STANKOWKCH	ld gtr	A

45s:
Little Deuce Coupe/	
The Little Lady From Pasadena	(Columbia DB 7907) 1966 SC
Sea Of Faces/	
Make The Radio A Little Louder	(Pye 7N 17217) 1966 SC
Breaking Up A Dream/She	(Trend TRE 1005) 1968 SC

A long forgotten group whose output was largely undistinguished save for one song, *Breaking Up A Dream*, which has been salvaged on *English Freakbeat, Vol. 3* (LP & CD). This is a slice of energetic late sixties pop with some striking opening guitar notes, rather in the mould of **The Easybeats**. (VJ)

Darryl Way's Wolf

Personnel:
JOHN ETHERIDGE	gtr	AB
DEK MESSECAR	bs, vcls	AB
IAN MOSLEY	drms	AB
DARRYL WAY	violin, keyb'ds	AB
JOHN HODKINSON	vcls	B

ALBUMS: (up to 1976)
1(A)	SATURATION POINT	(Deram SML 1104) 1973 SC
2(A)	CANIS LUPUS (WOLF)	(Deram SDL 14) 1973 SC
3(B)	NIGHT MUSIC	(Deram SML 1116) 1974 SC
4(-)	DARRYL WAY'S WOLF	(London PS 644) 1974
5(-)	ANTHOLOGY	(King J 1008) 1976

NB: (1) and (2) later reissued as a 2-LP set on London, who issued most of their albums in Japan.

45s:
Wolf/Spring Fever	(Deram DM 378) 1973
Bunch Of Fives/Five In The Morning	(Deram DM 395) 1973
Two Sisters/Go Down	(Deram DM 401) 1973

Way was formerly with **Curved Air**. These albums provided him with further opportunities to showcase his superb violin playing. *Canis Lupus* is a good example of their work. It was produced by former **King Crimson** saxophonist Ian McDonald. Side one was vocal and side two instrumental. The lengthy *Cadenza*, which opens side two, is a good example of the band's instrumental prowess giving each member solo breathing space. *Chansons Sans Paroles* captures the band at its most relaxed and builds beautifully into a 'holocaust of sound' as Darryl describes it. The final cut, *McDonald's Lament*, which Darryl dedicated to Ian for his work on the album, featured a sensitive viola solo by Darryl. This band is worth investigation by fans of classically-influenced progressive rock.

Ian Mosley went on to fame and fortune with Marillion. He was also a member of the Dutch group Trace for their album *Birds* (Philips 6413 080) in 1975. He gave a good performance on this album, which will appeal to fans of **The Nice**, **ELP**, and **Ekseption**. **Daryl Way** also guested on the same album.

Two Sisters can also be heard on *Progressive Pop Inside The Seventies* (CD). (VJ)

THE WAY WE LIVE - A Candle For Judith (LP).

The Way We Live

Personnel: STEVE CLAYTON   perc   A
              JIM MILNE   multi-instrumentalist   A

ALBUM: 1(A) A CANDLE FOR JUDITH
                         (Dandelion DAN 8004/K 49004) 1971 R3

NB: (1) reissued on CD (Repertoire REP 4204-WP) 1991. Also reissued on one CD with the **Tractor** album (See For Miles SEECD 409) 1994. (1) reissued again (Ozit/Morpheus OZIT CD 216) 2003 with two previously unreleased bonus tracks from the same era as the album and nine further **Way We Live/Tractor** recordings covering the next 35 years. (1) reissued with the **Tractor** album as a 2-LP set entitled *Steve's Hungarian Novel* (Psygressive PG 8004).

This duo hailed from Rochdale. Clayton was a part-time painter and poet, while Milne was a physical education instructor and talented multi-instrumentalist. John Peel took them under his wing and helped bring out their album, which is now the most sought-after and expensive collectors' item associated with Peel's Dandelion label.

The album was a fine amalgam of folk, hard-rock and psychedelia. Highlights included the Eastern-influenced *Siderial* and the semi-epic *The Way Ahead*. There's also considerable musical contrast between the hard-rocker *Willow*, which has great vocals and guitars, and the gentle, acoustic style of *Angie*. This is recommended listening. Of the two period outtakes on the Ozit reissue, *Watching White Stars* would have fitted well on the album.

The band later evolved into **Tractor**. (VJ/IRMJ)

Weather

Personnel: PETER EDDLESTON   bs   A
              JIM HOPWOOD   ld gtr   A
              TONY JORDAN   piano   A
              HARRY L'ANSON   vcls   A
              PETER TAYLOR   drms   A

45s: Look In My Eyes/Running Forwards   (Philips BF 1734) 1969
        Jamboree Special/Two Peculiar People   (Philips BF 1819) 1969

This sixties pop outfit came from Blackburn in Lancashire. *Look In My Eyes* was written by Marty Wilde and Ronnie Scott. (VJ)

The Web

Personnel: KENNY BEVERIDGE   perc, drms   AB
              JOHN EATON   gtr, percsn, bs AB
              TONY EDWARDS   gtr, percsn   AB
              TOM HARRIS   sax, flute   AB
              DICK LEE-SMITH   bs   A

JOHN L. WATSON	vcls	A
LENNIE WRIGHT	drms, perc	AB
DAVE LAWSON	keyb'ds, vcls	B

ALBUMS: 1(A) FULLY INTERLOCKING   (Deram SML 1025)   1968 R3
         2(A) THERAPHOSA BLONDI   (Deram SML-R 1058) 1970 R2
         3(B) I SPIDER   (Polydor 2383 024) 1970 R3

NB: (3) has been reissued on CD.

45s: Hatton Mill Morning/Conscience   (Deram DM 201) 1968 R1
        Baby, Won't You Leave Me Alone/
        McVernon Street   (Deram DM 217) 1968 R1
        Monday To Friday/Harold Dubbleyew (Deram DM 253) 1969 R1

This outfit had earlier joined forces with black American singer **John L. Watson** to operate as a soul outfit **John L. Watson and The Web** after moving to London from the South Coast. Dave Lawson was earlier in **Alan Bown** and **Episode Six**. In 1968 they changed name again to **The Web** and whilst their 45s were in the bubblegum mould, their albums were very much of the progressive genre.

The first was an uneasy amalgam of orchestrated pop, soul, lounge jazz, tribal chanting, music-hall and - yes - psychedelia. The stand-out track is *East Meet West*, with an ominous melody and sparse but inventive instrumentation. Their penchant for musical suites manifests itself on *War Or Peace*, but overall it doesn't take itself seriously enough to be especially memorable. Its liner notes, contributed by sixties luminaries, are hilarious.

With the same line-up and the same producer (**Mike Vernon**), **Web** gave it another try on *Theraphosa Blondi*, which is in the same vein, but shows slight improvement. The musical suite now starts off side one and incorporates some superb mood changes as well as a cover of *Sunshine Of Your Love*. Overall the mood is more serious, more jazzy through intensive use of wind instruments and more mature, although there still is room for tribal gatherings and throwaway pop songs.

The departure of singer **Watson** to go solo (Dick Lee-Smith left around the same time) and his replacement by former **Almond Marzipan** member Dave Lawson (who wrote all the material on their third album), as well as the label-change, make **Web** sound like a completely different band on *I Spider*. There's still the suite (*Concerto For Bedsprings*), but the atmosphere is heavy and menacing, rather than lightweight. Lawson's dramatic voice and especially his assorted keyboards, inventively played, unify the sound remarkably well, while the production by drummer Wright suits the music much better. Harsh harmonies and some fuzzy episodes make for uncomfortable but interesting listening. Although still lacking coherence, this album is not to be missed - but those who hate horns would do better to leave it alone.

All the remaining members (except Harris) joined **Samurai** when the band spilt. Dave Lawson was later in **Greenslade** and **Stackridge**.

They also had one cut, *Love You*, on Polydor's 1971 *Bombers* (LP) compilation. (MK/VJ/JM/RMJ)

Peta Webb

ALBUM: 1   I HAVE WANDERED IN EXILE (Topic 12TS 223) 1973 R2

Webb was born in Woodford Green, Essex, in August 1946. She is a traditional ballad singer who also does Appalachian and women's songs. She started out singing in the mid-sixties at Oxford University's Heritage Folk Club and went on to sing with **Oak** between 1970-73. After recording *I Have Wandered In Exile* in 1973, she worked in duos: firstly, with John Harrison (ex-**Watersons**) and later (beyond the time span of this book) with Alison McMorland and then fiddler Pete Cooper. She's also sung in a jazz group, the Al Ward Band and in the nineties joined the capella women's group, Sisters Unlimited. She was a versatile performer. (VJ)

Sonny Webb and The Cascades

Personnel: BILLY DUNCAN   bs   A
              GERRY GILBERTSON   gtr   AB C

KENNY (SONNY) JOHNSON	gtr, vcls	ABC
JOHN STATE	gtr	AB
ROGER WILCOX	drms	AB
JOE BUTLER	bs	BC
BRIAN REDMAN	drms	C
FRANK WAN	lead gtr	C

45:	You've Got Everything/		
	Border Of The Blues	(Oriole CB 1873) 1964 R1
Reissue:	You've Got Everything/		
	Border Of The Blues	(Polydor NHS 52158) 1964

This was a Liverpool-based beat group. **Sonny Webb**'s real name was Kenny Johnson. They later recorded as The Hillsiders. *You've Got Everything* originally appeared with another song, *Who Shot Sam?* on Oriole's *This Is Merseybeat, Vol's 1* (LP) and *2* (LP).

Other compilation appearances have included: *Who Shot Sam?*, *You've Got Everything* and *Border Of The Blues* on *Let's Stomp!* (LP) and *The Exciting New Liverpool Sound* (LP); and *You've Got Everything* and *Who Shot Sam?* on *Mersey Beat 1962-1964* (2-LP). (VJ/AD)

The Wedgewoods

| Personnel incl: | BETTY TIVERINGTON | vcls | A |
| | DAVID TIVERINGTON | gtr | A |

45s:	September In The Rain/Gone Gone Away	(Pye 7N 15642) 1964
	Peace/Summer Love	(Pye 7N 15846) 1965
	Red Sky At Night/When Day Is Done	(Columbia DB 8459) 1968
	Cloudy/Cold Winds And Icy Rain	(Columbia DB 8535) 1968
	In Rainbow Valley/My Home	(Columbia DB 8619) 1969
	Flap Flap/Abracadabra	(Columbia DB 8690) 1969
	I Think It's Going To Rain Today/	
	Sunshine Of Your Smile	(Columbia DB 8855) 1972

Considering their considerable vinyl output surprisingly little is known of this group, other than that they were a folk trio. *Cloudy* is a Paul Simon song. Their version is quite pleasant and the flip side is a harmony-folk offering. Of their other efforts; *In Rainbow Valley* and *My Home* are reasonable folk-pop efforts; *Flap Flap* was a folk-pop cover of an inane Roger Whitaker song and the flip side *Abracadabra* is little better; more credible is their cover of *I Think It's Going To Rain Today*, a Randy Newman song which was also done by Judy Collins among others, and features pleasant female vocals. However, all of these recordings are dispensable.

Compilation appearances include: *September In The Rain* on *Ripples, Vol. 3* (CD); and *Summer Love* on *Ripples, Vol. 2* (CD). (VJ)

WEB - I Spider (CD).

WEED - Weed (CD).

Weed

Personnel:	PEET BECKER	drms	A
	KEN HENSLEY	vcls, gtr, keyb'ds	A
	BERND HOHMANN	flute	A
	WERNER MONKA	gtr	A
	RAINER SCHNELLE	keyb'ds	A
	REINHOLD SPIEGELFELD	bs	A

| ALBUM: | 1(A) | WEED | (Philips 6305 096) 1971 |

NB: (1) reissued on CD (Second Battle SB018) 1993.

In 1971, between the release of the **Uriah Heep** albums *Salisbury* and *Look At Yourself*, **Ken Hensley** went to Germany to record an album with a German band (from Recklinghausen) called Virus. The fruits of this project were released under the name **Weed**. (MD/DS)

Bruce Welch

| 45: | Please Mr. Please/Song Of Yesterday | (EMI EMI 2141) 1974 R1 |

Bruce Welch was born Bruce Cripps on 2 November 1941 at Bognor Regis. His main claim to fame was as a member of **The Shadows**. He worked with **Marvin, Welch and Farrar** from 1971-1973 and from March 1973, he and others were also recording/touring with Brian Bennett as **The Shadows**. His involvement with **Marvin, Welch and Farrar** ended after his failed suicide owing to the break-up of his engagement to Olivia Newton John. He released this now very rare solo 45 either after or while he was with **Marvin, Welch and Farrar**. It was written by himself and fellow **Shadow** John Rostill, who had accidentally electrocuted himself whilst playing guitar in his home studio the previous year. When the 45 failed to sell, **Welch** didn't repeat the experiment leaving this sole 45 as an expensive purchase, presumably for **Shadows**' fans. After his recovery, he produced recordings for Cliff Richard, including his biggest US hit to date *Devil Woman*. (VJ)

Ed Welch

45s:	Clowns/The Bird Song	(United Artists UP 35284) 1971
	It Ain't Easy/Fridays	(United Artists UP 35318) 1972
	What A Friend You Are/	
	Friend Of Mine	(Avalanche AV 67315) 1972
	Friend Of A Feather/	
	Goodbye Country Fever	(United Artists UP 35625) 1973
	Raining In My Heart/	
	Christmas Came A Litte Late	(Arista ARIST 11) 1975
	Crossed Lines/Ran Off With My Peter	(Arista ARIST 30) 1975
Reissue:	Clowns/Singer And The Song	(Arista ARIST 58) 1976

Basically this guy was a pop singer and *Clowns*, in particular, was a fine example of a beautifully crafted pop 45. (VJ)

Welfare State

These college freaks from Bradford, Yorkshire, are represented by a single track on the *John Peel Presents Top Gear* (LP) (BBC REC 52S) issued in 1969 and comprising selected sessions from his "Top Gear" radio show. The track in question is *Silence Is Requested In The Ultimate Abyss* and features backward vocals, hypnotic rhythms, psychedelic noise and a lyric, recited rather than sung, which seems to concern a body being seared and broken. The electronic treatment, under the direction of David Vorhaus, is by **White Noise** whose album *An Electronic Storm* (Island ILPS 9099) will be known to some. This mixture of "alchemists, an earth goddess, monsters, perspex lutes, poets and freaks" - to quote Peel from the sleeve notes - is weird but interesting.

You can also find *Silence Is Requested...* on *Visions Of The Past, Vol. 2* (LP & CD). (NM)

The Wellingtons

45s:	Savage Sam And Me/	
	Just Say Auf Wiedersehen	(HMV POP 1187) 1963
	Thomasina/Jesse James	(HMV POP 1319) 1964

A forgotten folky beat group. (VJ)

Coby Wells

| 45: | Venus de Milo/My Feet Ache | (Decca 12560) 1967 |

This ballad 45 was recorded by Billy Moeller, younger brother of **Unit Four Plus Two**'s Tommy Moeller. Billy also recorded as **Whistling Jack Smith**. (VJ)

Howard Werth and The Moonbeams

Personnel:	PHIL DUNNE		A
	FREDDY GANDY	bs	A
	MIKE MORAN	keyb'ds	A
	ROGER POPE	drms	A
	HOWARD WERTH	gtr, vcls	A
	BOB WESTON	gtr	A

| ALBUM: | 1 (A) | KING BRILLIANT | (Charisma CAS 11004) 1975 |

NB: (1) reissued on (Charisma CASCD 1104) 1992. (1) reissued on CD with one bonus track (Luminous Records).

45s:	Lucinda/Johan	(Charisma CB 225) 1974
	Cocktail Shake/Sammy Lee Lane	(Charisma CB 256) 1975
	Dear John/Roulette	(Charisma CB 269) 1975

Werth formed this short-lived outfit after the collapse of his previous band **Audience**. The album, which was produced by Gus Dudgeon, was a long time in the making but critically acclaimed when it finally arrived. He used members of **Hookfoot** to back him on the album. Sadly for **Werth**, though, the sales were disappointing.

Weston was ex-**Fleetwood Mac** and Ashton. Pope was ex-**Hookfoot**, **Loot** and **The Soul Agents** and he also played in the backing bands of **Elton John** and **Kiki Dee**. Gandy was ex-**Hookfoot**. (VJ)

Wes Minster Five

Personnel:	CLIVE BURROWS	baritone sax	
	DAVE GREENSLADE	keyb'ds	
	JON HISEMAN	drms	A
	WES MINSTER (aka BRIAN SMITH)	gtr	A
	TONY REEVES	bs	A
	PAUL WILLIAMS	vcls	

45s:	Shakin' The Blues/Railroad Blues	(Carnival CV 7017) 1964
	Sticks And Stones/	
	Mickey's Monkey	(Carnival CV 7019) 1964 SC

Guitarist Brian Smith, took the name **Wes Minster** from his favourite guitarist Wes Montgomery and his Austin Westminster car. He led this semi-pro London-based group through 1963 and 1964. Interval-slot regulars at The Flamingo Club, they had a similar jazz-influenced R&B repertoire as the others acts featured there. They also shared a very fluid line-up which included guest vocalists such as **Ronnie Jones**, **Duffy Power**, Bobby Breen, and Paul McDowell (of Temperance Seven fame). The group also did a few gigs with **Zoot Money** shortly after **Money** left **Alexis Korner's Blues Incorporated**.

In addition to the two singles released under their own name, the group also backed some of Carnival Records Jamaican vocalists on record. **Paul Williams** left the group before the singles were recorded (early 1964) to join **Zoot Money's Big Roll Band** as did Clive Burrows a few months later. Dave Greenslade left in the spring of 1964 to join **Chris Farlowe's Thunderbirds**.

Sticks And Stones is a great R'n'B number and *Mickey's Monkey* is the Motown number. One of the 45s they provided backing for was Maynell Wilson's:- *Hey Hey Johnny / Baby* (Carnival CV 7014) 1964. The 'A' side was a good R'n'B / beat number, whilst *Baby* is ska. (NR/MWt/VJ)

Keith West

| CD: | 1 | EXCERPTS FROM... GROUPS AND SESSIONS 65-74 |
| | | (RPM RPM 141) 1995 |

NB: *The Fantastic Story Of Mark Wirtz And The Teenage Opera* (RPM RPM 503) 2001 is a 2-CD documentary of the pre-, during and post- *Teenage Opera* works of the renowned producer **Mark Wirtz** and features a range of different artists.

HCP

45s:	α	Excerpt From "A Teenage Opera";/		
		Theme From "A Teenage Opera"	(Parlophone R 5623) 1967	2
	β	Sam (From "A Teenage Opera"/		
		Thimble Full Of Puzzles	(Parlophone R 5651) 1967	38
		On A Saturday/		
		The Kid Was A Killer	(Parlophone R 5713) 1968	R1 -
		Riding For A Fall/Days About To Rain	(Deram DM 402) 1973	-
		Havin' Someone/		
		Know There's No Livin' Without You	(Deram DM 410) 1974	-
Reissues:		Excerpt From "A Teenage Opera"/		
		Sam (From "A Teenage Opera"	(Parlophone R 5957) 1972	-
		Excerpt From "A Teenage Opera"	(Old Gold OG 9655) 1987	-

NB: α 'B' side by **Mark Wirtz** Orchestra. β 'B' side by **Mark Wirtz's Mood Mosaik**.

Keith West, who was born in Dagenham on 6 December 1946, first came to attention as vocalist with **The In Crowd** and later fronted **Tomorrow** in

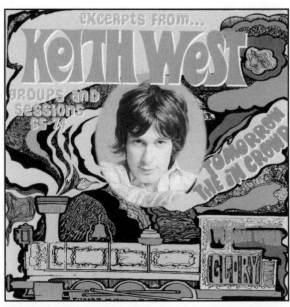

KEITH WEST - Excerpts From... Groups And Sessions 65 - 74 (CD).

1967. Around this time he started collaborating with composer **Mark Wirtz** on a teenage opera. An early product of this project, *Excerpt From A Teenage Opera*, proved a very catchy pop song all about "Grocer Jack" and it came complete with a childrens' chorus. The song shot to No 2 in the Charts and created a lot of interest in the project. This remains by far his best known song. The follow-up, *Sam*, was similar but not as good as *Excerpt...* and only became a minor hit and the teenage opera project never became a reality. Indeed, **West** later stated that the whole thing was a publicity hoax.

After one further under-rated 45, *The Kid Was A Killer*, he got into production work but still made the occasional recording. The 'B' side, *On A Saturday*, is characterised by acoustic guitar work and a catchy chorus. He recorded two further solo 45s in the mid-seventies and in an interview with him in 'Zig Zag Vol 6 No. 5' (1975) he made reference to an album he'd finished recorded (with Ken Burgess) in 1972, which was due to be released in Germany.

In 1975 he joined Moonrider who put out one album for Anchor and also included ex-**Animal** and **Family** member John Weider.

There's now an excellent CD *Excerpts From... Groups And Sessions 65-74*, which puts together a number of long-lost singles, a couple of **Tomorrow** album tracks, two tracks **Tomorrow** cut for possible inclusion in Michael Antonioni's 'Blow Up' (although they never made it into the film), two **Tomorrow** BBC recordings and some late sixties solo out-takes.

Compilation appearances have included:- *Excerpt From "A Teenage Opera"*, *Sam*, *On A Saturday*, *The Kid Was A Killer*, *The Visit*, *She*, *A Little Understanding*, *Power and Glory*, *West Country*, *Riding For A Fall* and *Having Someone* on *Keith West - Excerpts From - Groups And Sessions 1965-1974* (CD); *Excerpt From "A Teenage Opera"* and *On A Saturday* on *Not Just Beat Music 1965-70* (LP), *British Psychedelic Trip, Vol. 2* (LP) and *Great British Psychedelic Trip, Vol. 3* (CD); *Kid Was A Killer* on *Rubble, Vol. 2 - Pop Sike Pipe Dreams* (LP), *Rubble, Vol. 1* (CD) and *Steve Howe - Mothballs* (CD); *Excerpt From "A Teenage Opera"*, *On A Saturday* and *Sam* on *A Teenage Opera - The Original Soundtrack Recording* (CD) and *Excerpt From "A Teenage Opera"* on the 2-CD set *Greatest Hits Of The 60's Vol 4*. (VJ)

Mike Westbrook (Concert Band)

Personnel incl: MIKE WESTBROOK

ALBUMS:	1	CELEBRATION	(Deram DML 1013) 1967 R3
(up to	2	RELEASE	(Deram DML/SML 1031) 1968 R2
1976)	3	MARCHING SONG, VOL 1	(Deram SML 1047) 1969 R2
	4	MARCHING SONG, VOL 2	(Deram SML 1048) 1969 R2
	5	LOVE SONGS	(Deram SML 1069) 1970 R3
	6	TYGER: A CELEBRATION OF WILLIAM BLAKE	(RCA SER 5612) 1971 R3
	7	MIKE WESTBROOK'S METROPOLIS	(RCA Neon NE 10) 1971 R2
	8	LIVE	(Cadillac SGC 1001) 1972 SC
	9	CITADEL/ROOM 315 (2-LP)	(RCA SF 8433) 1975 SC
	10	LOVE/DREAM AND VARIATIONS	(Transatlantic TRA 323) 1975 SC
	11	PLAYS FOR THE RECORD	(Transatlantic TRA 312) 1976 SC

NB: (1) released as **Mike Westbrook Concert Band**. (9) with **John Surman**. (8) was a private pressing. (9) reissued on CD (Novus ND 74987) 1991.

45s:	A Life Of It's Own/	
	Can't Get It Out Of My Mind	(Deram DM 234) 1969 SC
	Requiem/Horray	(Deram DM 286) 1970 SC
	Magic Garden/	
	Original Peter (with Norman Winstone)	(Deram DM 311) 1970 SC

A jazz composer and arranger **Westbrook** got lumped in with the progressive boom of the late sixties. All his albums were jazzy. (VJ)

West Coast Consortium

45s:	Some Other Someday/Looking Back	(Pye 7N 17352) 1967 SC
	Colour Sergeant Lillywhite/	
	Lady From Baltimore	(Pye 7N 17482) 1967 R1

NB: *Looking Back The Pye Anthology* (CD) (Castle CMRCD 786) is a 27-track anthology that includes all their 45s (some as **Consortium**) and 11 previously unissued demo recordings.

A whimsical pop outfit whose songs were characterised by pleasant harmonies and quite inventive arrangements. After their second single they shortened their name to **Consortium**.

Compilation appearances include: *Looking Back* on *Ripples, Vol. 3* (CD); and *Some Other Sunday* on *Ripples, Vol. 7* (CD) and *Colour Sergeant Lillywhite* on *Haunted - Psychedelic Pstones, Vol 2* (CD) and *We Can Fly, Vol 2* (CD). (VJ)

West Coast Delegation

45:	Reach For The Top/	
	Mr. Personality Man	(Deram DM 113) 1967 SC

This short-lived act is thought to have come from Somerset. The 45 had cheerful harmonies. (VJ)

West Five

Personnel:	COLIN CHARLES	gtr	A
	MIKE LISTON	organ	A
	DON REGAN	bs	A
	BARRY SUMMERFIELD	lead gtr	A
	JERRY WOOD	drms	A

45s:	Congratulations/She Mine	(HMV POP 1396) 1965 R1
	Someone Ain't Right/	
	Just Like Romeo And Juliet	(HMV POP 1428) 1965 SC
	If It Don't Work Out/Back To Square One	(HMV POP 1513) 1966

This London band had earlier recorded as West Four (without Liston). Liston was later in **Ferris Wheel**. *Congratulations* got a further airing on *60's Back Beat* (LP). It was a **Jagger**/Richard composition. (VJ)

Kevin Westlake and Gary Farr

45:	Everyday/Green	(Marmalade 598 007) 1968

Gary Farr is better known for fronting **The T-Bones**, who also recorded as **Gary Farr and The T-Bones**. **Kevin Westlake** was a well-known songwriter who worked a lot with Mort Schuman. He also released some solo 45s and a mediocre album on Utopia in 1975. (VJ)

West Point

45:	Don't Know Why/Take What You Want	(Decca F 13050) 1970

This was an early seventies obscurity. (MWh)

Westwind

ALBUM:	1	LOVE IS	(Penny Farthing PELS 505) 1970 R3

NB: (1) reissued on CD (Elergy E600/1).

45:	Love Is A Funny Sort Of Thing/	
	Breakout	(Penny Farthing PEN 737) 1970

This obscure trio consisted of two guys and a girl. The female vocals are pleasant enough but the material is rather mundane folk-based pop. Rather mystifyingly, it's now very sought-after and expensive, perhaps for Penny Farthing completists. Still, it was housed in an attractive cover. (VJ/RMJ)

WESTWIND - Love Is (CD).

The We Talkies

45s: I Wanna Walk In Your Sun/I Order You   (CBS 202245) 1966
I've Got To Hold On/
What Are You Waiting For   (CBS 202457) 1967

This beat group is thought to have been a later version of The Avons, a late fifties/early sixties teen beat vocal group. Their first CBS 45 is MOR / light folk-pop. (VJ)

The Whales

45s: Come Down Little Bird/Beachcomber   (CBS 3766) 1968
Tell It To The Rain/Girl, Hey Girl   (CBS 4126) 1969

This was a short-lived and long forgotten sixties group. (VJ)

The Wheels

Personnel:	HERBIE ARMSTRONG	gtr	A
	VICTOR CATLING		A
	ROD DEMICK		A
	BRIAN ROSSI		A
	TITO TINSLEY		A

45s:		Gloria/Don't You Know	(Columbia DB 7682) 1965 R3
	α	Bad Little Woman/Road Block	(Columbia DB 7827) 1966 R3
		Kicks/Call My Name	(Columbia DB 7981) 1966 R3

NB: α some demos and a few versions had *Call My Name* on the flip side (R4). It has also been reissued in a limited edition pressing of 500. They also recorded an acetate for Regent Sound, *I'm Leaving/No One Told Me*.

This R&B combo formed in Belfast in the early sixties but later moved to Blackpool. They covered **Van Morrison**'s *Gloria* for their debut 45 which was every bit as gritty as **Them**'s but lost out in the Chart battle here and, although it got a US release, lost out there to The Shadows Of Knight. The flip, *Don't You Know*, which was a cover from **Them**'s first album, is more laid back.

Their follow-up, *Bad Little Woman*, was another raw R&B effort that builds up into a frantic climax. This was their own composition which was quickly snapped up by The Shadows Of Knight. The flip side was a rewrite of *Mystic Eyes*, which they called *Road Block*. Some copies of the 45, however, featured *Call My Name*, another **Them** song on the 'B' side.

Their final 'A' side, *Kicks*, was a Paul Revere song and like their first two 45s is now very rare and sought-after. **The Wheels** later changed names to Wheels-A-Way to avoid confusion with Mitch Ryder's Detroit Wheels.

Demick and **Armstrong** went on to record a couple of albums together and two 45s in 1968 as the **James Brothers**, before **Demick** joined **Bees Make Honey** and **Armstrong** went into session work (backing **Van Morrison** among others), though he was briefly with **Fox**. Rossi embarked on a solo career.

Compilation coverage has included:- *Gloria* and *Bad Little Woman* on *Maximum R'n'B* (CD), *Electric Sugarcube Flashbacks, Vol. 1* (LP) and *Electric Sugarcube Flashbacks, Vol. 3* (LP); *Roadblock* on *Maximum Freakbeat* (CD) and *Pebbles, Vol. 6* (LP); *I Don't Care* and *Ramble Boy* on *Made In England, Vol. 1* (CD); *Gloria* and *Road Block* on *Nowhere Men Vol. 1* (LP); *I'm Leaving* and *Bad Little Woman* on *Nowhere Men Vol. 3* (CD); *I'm Leaving* on *Purple Heart Surgery, Vol. 1* (LP) and *Hens Teeth Vol. 2* (CD); *I'm Leaving*, *Road Block*, *Send Me Your Pillow*, *Bad Little Woman*, *Call My Name*, *Don't You Know*, *You Got Me Dizzy*, *Kicks*, *Tell Me (I'm Gonna Love Again)*, *Mona (I Need You Baby)*, *Gloria* and *Bad Little Woman* on *Belfast Beat Maritime Blues* (CD); *Don't You Know* on *English Freakbeat, Vol. 2* (LP); *Don't You Know* and *Road Block* on *English Freakbeat, Vol. 2* (CD); *Call My Name* on *English Freakbeat, Vol. 4* (LP & CD) and *Bad Little Woman* on the 4-CD box set *Nuggets II*. (VJ)

The Wheels of Time

45:    1984/So Long   (Spin 62008) 1967 R2

Recorded on an Irish label, some have suggested that this was a later version of Belfast's **Wheels**. This certainly sounds very different. *1984* has good vocals but the slice of psych-pop is hampered by poor production.

1984 has been compiled on *Psychedelia, Vol. 2* (LP), *The Best Of Rubble Collection, Vol. 2* (CD) and *Hen's Teeth Vol. 1* (CD). (VJ)

Whichwhat

Personnel:	MICK BROWN	sax	A
	WAYNE FORD	lead gtr	A
	STEVE HARRIS	drms	A
	TERRY PENN	bs	A
	WALTER SAVAGE	keyb'ds	A
	EDDIE YOUNG	vcls	A

| ALBUM: | 1(A) | WHICHWHAT'S FIRST | (Beacon BEAS 14) 1970 R1 |

45s:	Gimme Gimme Good Lovin'/	
	Wonderland Of Love	(Beacon BEA 127) 1969 SC
	Why Do Lovers Break Each Other's Heart/	
	When I See Her Smile	(Beacon BEA 131) 1969
	In The Year 2525/Parting	(Beacon BEA 133) 1969
	I Wanna Be Free/It's All Over Again	(Beacon BEA 144) 1969
	Vietnam Rose/Shame And Solution	(Beacon BEA 169) 1969

Basically a hard-rock band, this album featured some belting sax, though with some quieter flute-filled moments. They came from Nottingham and were popular abroad, more so than at home. The album's opening cut, *Vietnam Rose*, was a Vanda/Young composition, later covered by a band called **Tramp** on Youngblood in 1970.

The band split in 1970, but reformed briefly in 1971 to record *The Wind Out Of Nowhere*, which has subsequently resurfaced on *Incredible Sound Show Stories Vol. 2* (LP). Eddy Young now lives in Melbourne, Australia. (MWh)

The Whirlwinds

Personnel:	BERNARD BASSO	bs	A
	GRAHAM GOULDMAN	lead gtr	A
	STEVE JACOBSEN	gtr	A
	MO STERLING	drms	A
	MALCOLM WAGNER	keyb'ds	A

| 45: | Look At Me/Baby Not Like Me | (HMV POP 1301) 1964 R2 |

This Manchester-based beat group was fronted by **Graham Gouldman**, later of **10cc** fame. They managed just this one 45, which is quite rare and inevitably quite sought-after, before he left to form **The Mockingbirds**, who included Basso and Jacobsen. *Look At Me* was an obscure Buddy Holly song and this version stuck pretty closely to the original. The flip was a Lol Creme composition - a pretty lightweight R&B number, though it did feature a promising guitar solo from **Gouldman**.

Compilation appearances have included: *Baby Not Like Me* on *R&B Scene, Vol. 1* (LP); and *Look At Me* on *60's Back Beat* (LP), *Beat At Abbey Road* (CD), *Beat Generation - Ready Steady Go* (CD) and *Beat Merchants* (2-LP). (VJ/AD)

The Whispers of Truth

Personnel incl: GRAHAM KENDRICK   vcls, gtr   A

This obscure group contributed four tracks to a 1969 Various Artists album, *Alive*, which appeared on the small gospel label Key. Two of them, *Sunday Afternoon With Emily* and *Reality*, were later included on *Syde Tryps, Vol. 1* (LP & CD). The latter, in particular, is a bizarre mixture of religious teaching augmented by screaming fuzz guitar. Quite interesting!

Another track, *Thoughts*, on *Electric Psychedelic Sitar Headswirlers, Vol. 3* (CD) is presumed to be the same act. (VJ)

Whistler

Personnel:			
	ERIC BELL	gtr	A
	TONY CARR	perc	A
	CLEM CATTINI	drms	A
	JOHN CHUTER	vcls, gtr, bs	A
	ANT GROUTH-SMITH	gtr, bs, sax, vcls	A
	JIMMY HASTINGS	flute	A
	GEORGE HOWE	vcls, gtr, keyb'ds	A
	GORDON HUNTLEY	steel gtr	A
	BARRY MORGAN	drms	A
	DOUGLAS WRIGHT	drms	A

ALBUM: 1(A)   HO-HUM   (Deram SML 1083) 1971 R2

Along with **Mellow Candle**, **Room** and **Zakarrias**, **Whistler** produced one of the very rarest albums on the highly-collectible Deram label. Collectors, however, would be well advised to hear the album before shelling out large sums for it. A London-based threesome comprising Chuter, Grout-Smith and Howe, they were backed by the cream of the UK's studio musicians and aided by a sympathetic and lush production courtesy of Peter Johnson, but the country-influenced acoustic pop they produced just wasn't very memorable. All three share songwriter's credits and sing nicely enough, but this is really for Deram completists only.

Grout-Smith designed the attractive cover, but tragically died young. Howe is better known today as the multi-Oscar-nominated composer George Fenton. (MK/RMJ)

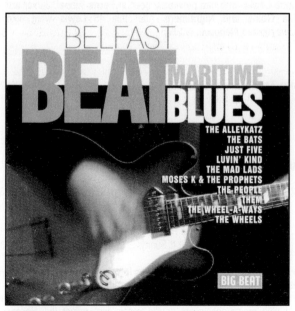

BELFAST BEAT MARITIME BLUES (Comp CD) including The Wheels.

Alan White

Personnel:			
	BUD BEADLE	sax, flute	A
	KENNY CRADDOCK	keyb'ds, vocals	A
	COLIN GIBSON	bs, perc	A
	STEVE GREGORY	tenor sax, flute	A
	PETER KIRTLEY	gtr, vcls	A
	HENRY LOWTHER	trumpet	A
	ALAN MARSHALL	vcls	A
	ANDY PHILLIPS	steel drum	A
	ALAN WHITE	drms	A

                                                  HCP
ALBUM: 1(A)   RAMSHACKLED   (Atlantic K 50217) 1976 41

This was the **Yes** drummer's solo effort and for it he surrounded himself with colleagues from former bands. **White**, Marshall, Gibson, Craddock and Kirtley had all been in **Happy Magazine**. **White**, Gibson and Craddock had been in **Ginger Baker's Airforce**. **White**, Craddock and Kirtley had been in **Griffen**. **White**'s career also spans **The Johnny Almond Music Machine**, **Bell and Arc** and **Balls**. Alan Marshall had been in **One** and **Zzebra**, Kenny Craddock had been in **Lindisfarne** and **Elcort**, Colin Gibson had been in **Skip Bifferty**, **Chosen Few** and **Snafu** and Pete Kirtley had also been in **Riff Raff**. The album is produced by **White** but largely written by Kirtley, Craddock and Gibson. **Jon Anderson** and **Steve Howe** of **Yes** appear on one track and the album is pleasant progressive rock with sax and flute much in evidence. (VJ)

Chris White

                                                  HCP
45s:	Spanish Wine/She's Only Dancing	(Charisma CB 272) 1976 37
(up to	Natural Rhythm/Another Little Miracle	(Charisma CB 282) 1976 -
1976)	Don't Look Now/Summertime,	
	Summertime	(Charisma CB 294) 1976 -

This forgotten vocalist had a hit with *Spanish Wine*. (VJ)

Kieran White

ALBUM: 1   OPEN DOOR   (Gull GULP 1011) 1975
NB: (1) reissued on CD (Repertoire REP 4361-WY) 1993.

This is an album of gentle, mellow and rather un-assuming rock from the former lead singer of **Steamhammer**. All the songs were written by **White** aside from his cover of J.J. Cale's *Cajun Moon*. The album was produced by Donal Lunney (whose one of six supporting musicians on it) and Dave Charles. (VJ)

Tam White

ALBUM: 1   TAM WHITE   (Middle Earth MDLS 304) 1970 R1

45s:	World Without You/	
	Someone You Should Know	(Decca F 12711) 1967
	Amy/Building My World	(Decca F 12803) 1968
	Dancing Out Of My Heart/	
	I'll Stay Loving You	(Decca F 12723) 1968
	Waiting Till The Night Comes Around/	
	Girl Watcher	(Decca F 128491) 1968
	That Old Sweet Roll/	
	Don't Make Promises	(Deram DM 261) 1969 SC
	Lewis Carroll/Future Thoughts	(Middle Earth MDS 104) 1970 R1
	What In The World's Come Over You/	
	After All We've Been Through	(Rak RAK 193) 1975
	Please Mister Please/Red Eye Special	(Rak RAK 203) 1975
	Cool Water/	
	Mister, I Don't Want Your Daughter	(Rak RAK 219) 1975

A folk singer from Edinburgh, who is still performing blues material today. He has guested with such people as Al Green, Robert Cray, Mose Allison, Dick Gaughan, Philip Walker and Boz Burrell to name a few.

He was also featured on the Middle Earth sampler. (VJ/GMe)

WHITE NOISE - An Electric Storm (LP).

White Line

Personnel:	DAVE CLARKE	bs, keyb'ds	A
	JACK McCULLOCH	drms	A
	JIMMY McCULLOCH	gtr, vcls	A

ALBUM: 1 (A) CALL MY NAME   (EMI) 1976

This band was put together by the McCulloch brothers when Jimmy was off the road with **Wings**. His brother Jack had been in **Andwella** and Dave Clarke was also in **The Noel Redding Band**. (JM)

White Lining

45:        Back In The Sun/Mon Amour   (Parlophone R 5768) 1970

No other details known. (MWh)

White Noise

| ALBUMS: | 1 | AN ELECTRIC STORM | (Island ILPS 9099) 1969 R1 |
| | 2 | WHITE NOISE (2-LP) | (Virgin V 2032) 1975 SC |

NB: (1) reissued on CD (Island 3D CID 1001).

This outfit featured members of the BBC Radiophonic Workshop and on their first album the act utilised a wide range of early electronics. Musically this is similar in style to Brainticket. (VJ)

White Plains

Personnel:	TONY BURROWS	vcls	A
	ROGER GREENAWAY	vcls	A
	PETE NELSON		AB
	ROBIN SHAW		AB

| ALBUMS: | 1(A) | WHITE PLAINS | (Deram SML 1067) 1970 R1 |
| | 2(B) | WHEN YOU ARE A KING | (Deram SML 1092) 1971 R1 |

NB: There's also a CD collection, *My Baby Loves Lovin'* (Deram 820 622-2) 1993.

HCP

45s:	My Baby Loves Lovin'/		
(up to	Julie Do Ya Love Me	(Deram DM 280) 1970 9
1976)	I've Got You On My Mind/		
	Today I Killed A Man I Didn't Know	(Deram DM 291) 1970 17
	Lovin' You Baby/Noises In My Head	(Deram DM 312) 1970 -
	Julie Do Ya Love Me/		
	I Need Your Everlasting Love	(Deram DM 315) 1970 8
	Every Little Move She Makes/		
	Caroline's Comin' Home	(Deram DM 325) 1971 -
	When You Are A King/		
	The World Gets Better With Love	(Deram DM 333) 1971 13
	Gonna Miss Her Mississippi/		
	I'll Go Blind	(Deram DM 340) 1971 -
	I Can't Stop/Julie Anne	(Deram DM 348) 1972 -
	Dad You Saved The World/		
	Beachcomber	(Deram DM 365) 1972 -
	Step Into A Dream/Look To See	(Deram DM 371) 1973 21
	Does Anyone Know Where My Baby Is?/		
	Just For A Change	(Deram DM 388) 1973 -
	Julie Anne/Sunny Honey Girl	(Deram DM 405) 1973 -
	Ecstasy/Simple Man	(Deram DM 415) 1974 -
	Summer Nights/Wildest Dream	(Bradley BRAD 7609) 1976 -
Reissues:	When You Are A King/		
	The World Gets Better With Love	(Decca F 13920) 1982 -
	When You Are A King/	(Old Gold OG 9531) 1985 -

A commercially successful studio group who included Tony Burrows whose other session groups included **The Ivy League**, **The Flowerpot Men**, The Kestrels, **Edison Lighthouse** and **Brotherhood Of Man**. Robin Shaw and Pete Nelson were also in **The Flowerpot Men**, whilst songwriter Roger Greenaway had previously been the David of **David and Jonathan**. He co-wrote their debut hit, *My Baby Loves Lovin'* with Roger Cook (Jonathan) and was also in **The Flowerpot Men**. After their second hit, another Greenaway/Cook composition, *I've Got You On My Mind*, Greenaway and Burrows both left to join **The Pipkins** and Nelson and Shaw brought in other session singers for further studio and live work. This revamped line-up enjoyed a couple more UK hits - *When You Are A King* and *Step Into A Dream* - but disbanded in 1974 by which time interest in them had waned.

The band scored a couple of hits in the US in 1970 with *My Baby Loves Lovin'* (No 13) and *Lovin' You Baby* (No 82).

Their musical format was pure and simple - early seventies style harmony-pop with orchestral backing. Their music director was Lew Warburton. Cook and Greenaway were involved in **Blue Mink** among others. (VJ)

White Rabbit

Personnel:	RON GOODWAY	vcls	A
	JUNIOR	organ	A
	LINDA LEWIS	vcls	A

45:    Ain't That Something/I'll Do The Rest   (NEMS 56-4165) 1969

This was a Darlington-based group. They are most notable for the inclusion of **Linda Lewis**, who had previously been in **Ferris Wheel**. Junior was with **Herbie Goins and Nightimers**. After this 45 **Lewis** went solo and Goodway joined Alehouse. (VJ/JM)

White Trash

See **Trash**.

Jaki Whitren

ALBUM: 1 RAW BUT TENDER (w/insert) (Epic EPC 65645) 1973 SC

45s:	Give Her The Day/		
	But Which Way Do I Go	(Epic EPC 1338) 1973
	Human Failure/Ain't It Funny	(Epic EPC 1715) 1973

Raw But Tender is a superb acoustic folk-rock album with country and blues overtones. Southampton-born **Whitren** was born in 1954, and was only nineteen when it was released. She plays banjo and guitar as well as contributing memorably gutsy soulful vocals that reflect the album's title, ranging from soft and sweet to powerful and angst-ridden. Her lyrics have a pastoral feel and effectively convey a sense of longing. She was managed by Stuart Cowell (ex-**Titus Groan**) but never recorded a follow-up.

Session personnel include numerous regulars of the period - Gerry Conway, Frank Ricotti and Pat Donaldson for example - and Henry 'VIII' Bartlett (ex-**Famous Jug Band**) contributes jug noises to one track. It's a rewarding album, and still not too costly.

Whitren later turned up as a vocalist (along with her partner John Cartwright) on one of **Jess Roden**'s Island label albums, and recorded an album with John Cartwright in 1983, *International Times* (Living Rec. LR1). She also sang on the Alan Parsons Project album *I, Robot*, and more recently has been involved in a project called Court of Miracles, as well as singing with French progressive band Minimum Vital. She is now resident in France. (NM/GB/RMJ)

The Who

Personnel:	ROGER DALTREY	vcls	A
(up to	JOHN ENTWISTLE	bs, vcls	A
1976)	KEITH MOON	drms, vcls	A
	PETE TOWNSHEND	gtr	A

					HCP
ALBUMS:	1(A)	MY GENERATION	(Brunswick LAT 8616) 1965	R3	5
(up to	2(A)	A QUICK ONE	(Reaction 593 002) 1966	R2	4
1976)	3(A)	THE WHO SELL-OUT			
		(mono/stereo)	(Track 613 002) 1967	R1	13
	4(A)	DIRECT HITS (Compilation)			
		(mono/stereo)	(Track 612 006) 1968	SC	-
	5(A)	TOMMY (2-LP)	(Track 613 013/4) 1969		2
	6(A)	LIVE AT LEEDS (w/12 inserts including poster)			
			(Track 2406 001) 1970	SC	3
	7(A)	WHO'S NEXT	(Track 2408 102) 1971	SC	1
	8(A)	MEATY BEATY BIG AND BOUNCY (Compilation)			
			(Track 2406 006) 1971		9
	9(A)	WHO DID IT?	(Track 2856 001) 1971	R4	-
	10(A)	QUADROPHENIA (2-LP) (original copies w/22 page			
		photo booklet)	(Track 2644 001) 1973		2
	11(A)	ODDS AND SODS (Comp.)	(Track 2406 116) 1974		10
	12(A)	THE WHO BY NUMBERS	(Polydor 2490 129) 1975		7
	13(A)	THE STORY OF THE WHO	(Polydor 2683 069) 1976		2

NB: (9) was sold by mail order only and then withdrawn, making it one of the rarest **Who** items. (5) also issued as two single albums, *Tommy Part One* (Track 2406 007) and *Tommy Part Two* (Track 2406 008) 1970. In 1975 a film Soundtrack version of *Tommy* was released (Track 2657 007), which got to No 30. (2) and (3) reissued as *Backtrack 8* (Track 2407 008) 1970 (SC) and *Backtrack 9* (Track 2407 009) 1970. (1) pirated on CD and reissued on vinyl (Virgin V2179) 1980. (1) reissued on vinyl as a 2-LP set (Brunswick 1139811) remastered with an extra album of bonus material comprising alternate takes, previously unreleased tracks, instrumental versions, 'B' sides and more. It comes in a fine gatefold sleeve with colour inserts

THE WHO - My Generation (LP).

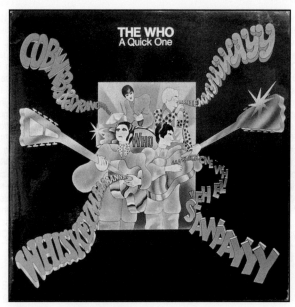

THE WHO - A Quick One (LP).

and reproduced Brunswick covers. (1) reissued on vinyl in mono (Classic/Brunswick LAT 8616) 2005. (1) also reissued as a 2-CD set (MCA 1129262) with the album remixed to stereo for the first time and a second disc of bonus material featuring alternate takes, instrumental versions, 'B' sides and six previously unreleased recordings. The package comes with a colour 28-page booklet. (2) reissued on CD (Polydor 835 728-2) 1988. (2) reissued on CD with bonus tracks from the *Ready Steady Who* EP, a handful of 'B' sides and three previously unreleased tracks:- an acoustic *Happy Jack*, a version of the Everly Brothers' *Man With Money* and a wild version of *My Generation* with *Land Of Hope And Glory*, (Polydor 527 758-2) 1995. (3) reissued on CD (Polydor 835 782-2) 1988. (3) reissued on CD with an additional 35 minutes worth of jingles, adverts and several other interesting nuggets (Polydor 527 759-2) 1995. (3) digitally remastered and reissued at mid-price (Polydor 527 759-2) 1996. (5) reissued on CD (Polydor 800 077-2) 1989 and the version with the London Symphony Orchestra on Essential (ESSCD 029) 1990. (5) reissued and remastered on CD (Polydor 531 043-2) 1996 and remastered and reissued again as a 2-CD set (Polydor/Universal 841 121 2) 2001. (5) reissued as a 2-LP set (Simply Vinyl SVLP 201) on 180 gram vinyl and with an exact reproduction of the original gatefold sleeve and again as a 2-CD (SACD) (Polydor 986 101-1) as a deluxe Super Audio Hybrid CD remixed in 5.1 surround and remastered in stereo. It plays on SACD in 5.1 surround and on CD players in stereo. (6) reissued on CD (Polydor 825 339-2) 1988 and (MCA (USA) 31196) 1988. (6) reissued on CD (Polydor 527 169-2) 1995, digitally remastered with extra tracks and a 24-page booklet. (6) reissued again as a 2-CD deluxe edition (Polydor 1126182) 2001 remixed and remastered with the *Tommy* segment extracted as a show in itself. (7) reissued on vinyl (MCA MCA-11164) 1997 and again (Simply Vinyl SVLP 088). (7) reissued on CD (Polydor 813 651-2) 1983. (7) reissued on CD (Polydor 527 760-2) 1995 with seven bonus tracks including a rousing version of *Pure And Easy* (better than the one on *Odds And Sods*), *Behind Blue Eyes* (with Al Kooper on organ), *Naked Eye*, *Water*, *I Don't Even Know Myself*, *Too Much Of Anything* (also from *Odds And Sods*) and a version of Marvin Gaye's *Baby Don't Do It*. (7) digitally remastered and reissued at mid-price (Polydor 527 760-2) 1996 and again in 1999. (7) reissued available as an US import as a 2-CD deluxe edition (MCA/Universal 088 113 056 2) 2003 and then in the UK (Polydor 1130562) remastered and with as bonus disc containing outtakes and remixed live tracks, most of which are previously unreleased. The package comes with a thick booklet full of information and photos and is housed in a fold-out digipak. (10) reissued on CD (Polydor 831 074-2) 1988 and remastered and reissued again (Polydor Universal 543 691 2) 2001. (10) reissued again as a 2-CD set (Polydor 531 971-2) remastered with enhanced sound quality and a 24-page booklet. (12) reissued on CD (MCA (USA) 31197) 1988 and on (Polydor 831 552-2) 1989. (12) reissued on CD (Polydor 533 844-2) 1996.

There are also several 'Best Of' and 'Hits Collections' including:- *Rarities Vol 1 1966-1968* (Polydor SPLEP 9) 1983; *Rarities, Vol 2* (Polydor SPELP 10) 1983 and on CD (Polydor 847 670-2) 1991; *The Singles* (Polydor WHOD17) 1984) 1984, also on CD (Polydor 815 965-2) 1985; *Who's Last* (2-LP) (MCA WHO1) 1984 is a live album, also on CD (MCA MCAD 19005) 1992; *Who's Missing* (Polydor 837 557-1) 1988, also on CD (Polydor SPECD 116) 1988 combines tracks that were rarities in the States (mostly 'B' sides with previously unreleased material (two studio out-takes from 1964 and 1965 and one live track in 1971)); *Two's Missing* (Polydor 837 558-1) 1988, also on CD (Polydor SPECD 117) 1988 follows a similar format to *Who's Missing* with two tracks from Shel Talmy sessions and two live cuts from a December 1971 San Francisco concert (*My Wife* and *Going Down*); *The Who Collection, Vol. 1* (CD/LP) (Impression IMCD 41) 1988 and *Vol. 2* (CD/LP) (Impression IMCD 42) 1988, which were also isusued as a double CD set, *Collection: Who* (Stylus SMD 570) 1988; *Who's Better Who's Best (The Very Best Of The Who)* (LP/CD) (Polydor 835 389-2) 1988; *Join Together* (LP/CD) (Virgin CDVDT 102) 1990 is culled from the mid-1989 Las Vegas Tour - a live version of *Tommy* was the masterpiece of this set; *Thirty Years Of Maximum R&B* (4-CD Box) (Polydor 521 751 2) 1994 came with a superb booklet and packaging and met with rave reviews; *My Generation - The Very Best Of The Who* (Polydor 533 150-2) 1996 is one of their definitive greatest hits collections; and *Live At The Isle Of Wight Festival 1970* (CD/LP) (Essential! EDF CD 326) 1996 is a good opportunity to hear a full live rendition of their *Tommy* album, which accounts for the bulk of the set. The remaining five songs comprised arse-kicking versions of *Summertime Blues, Shakin' All Over, Substitute, My Generation* and *Magic Bus. The Blues To The Bush* is a 2-CD Internet-only release containing 20-tracks recorded at Chicago's House Of Blues and the Shepherd's Bush Empire. *Live At The Isle Of Wight Festival 1970* (Sanctuary CMYTV 164) 2001 is a 3-LP set (which runs in the correct order) in an attractive gatefold sleeve with the original pictures and notes reproduced. This is also available on vinyl (3-LP) (Earmark 42043) and as a 2-CD set (Sanctuary Midline SMEDD 044). *Magic Bus* (CD) (MCA MCBBD 31333) is an undated release of their US-only album originally from 1968 which contained cuts from the *A Quick One* and *Sell Out* albums plus several early singles and 'B' sides, including the **Entwistle** composition *Dr Jeckyll and Mr Hyde*. It's also available in a limited edition picture disc album. *The Ultimate Collection* (Polydor 065 234 2) 2002 is a 2-CD 40-track collection and it's difficult to argue much with the choice of tracks. There's also a 2-LP set *BBC Sessions* covering performances, on-air interviews and radio jingles from the 1965-1973 period. Similar material is covered on CD - *BBC Sessions* (Polydor 547 727-2) a 26-track set featuring material recorded for 'Saturday Club', 'Top Gear', 'Dave Lee Travis Show' and 'The Old Grey Whistle Test' between 1965 and 1973.

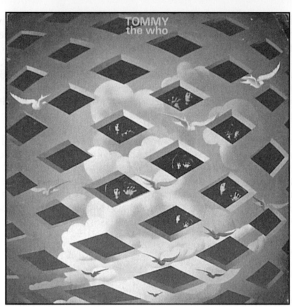

THE WHO - Tommy (2-LP).

| EPs: | 1(A) | READY STEADY WHO | (Reaction 592 001) 1966 R2 |
| | 2(A) | EXCERPTS FROM "TOMMY" | (Track 2252 001) 1970 SC |

NB: (1) reissued on Reaction (WHO 7) 1983 (SC), when it got to No 58.

			HCP
45s:	I Can't Explain/		
(up to	Bald Headed Woman	(Brunswick 05926) 1965 SC 8	
1976)	Anyway, Anyhow, Anywhere/		
	Daddy Rolling Stone	(Brunswick 05935) 1965 SC 10	
	My Generation/Shout And Shimmy	(Brunswick 05944) 1965 SC 2	
α	Circles/Instant Party	(Brunswick 05951) 1966 -	
β	Substitute/Instant Party	(Reaction 591 001) 1966 SC -	
	Substitute/Circles	(Reaction 591 001) 1966 R1 -	
χ	Substitute/Waltz For A Pig	(Reaction 591 001) 1966 SC 5	
	A Legal Matter/Instant Party	(Brunswick 05956) 1966 SC 32	
δ	The Kids Are Alright/The Ox	(Brunswick 05956) 1966 R1 -	
	The Kids Are Alright/The Ox	(Brunswick 05965) 1966 41	
	I'm A Boy/In The City	(Reaction 591 004) 1966 2	
	La-La-La-Lies/The Good's Gone	(Brunswick 05968) 1966 SC -	
	Happy Jack/I've Been Away	(Reaction 591 010) 1966 3	
	Pictures Of Lily/Doctor, Doctor	(Track 604 002) 1967 4	
	The Last Time/Under My Thumb	(Track 604 006) 1967 R1 44	
	I Can See For Miles/		
	Someone's Coming	(Track 604 011) 1967 10	
	Dogs/Call My Lightning	(Track 604 023) 1967 25	
	Magic Bus/Dr. Jekyll And Mr. Hyde	(Track 604 024) 1967 26	
	Pinball Wizard/Dogs Part Two	(Track 604 027) 1968 4	
	The Seeker/Here For More	(Track 604 036) 1970 19	
	Summertime Blues/Heaven And Hell	(Track 2094 002) 1970 38	
ε	See Me, Feel Me/		
	Overture From "Tommy"	(Track 2094 004) 1970 SC -	
	Won't Get Fooled Again/		

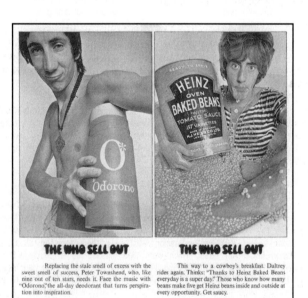

THE WHO - Sell Out (CD).

Don't Know Myself (PS)	(Track 2094 009) 1970 SC 9
Let's See Action/When I Was A Boy	(Track 2094 012) 1973 16
Join Together/Baby Don't You Do It	(Track 2094 102) 1973 9
Relay/Waspman	(Track 2094 106) 1973 21
5.15/Water	(Track 2094 115) 1973 20
ε Overture//See Me Feel Me	
Listening To You (PS)	(Polydor 2001 056) 1975 -
Squeeze Box/Success Story	(Polydor 2121 275) 1976 10
Reissues: Substitute/I'm A Boy/	
Pictures Of Lily (7" and 12")	(Polydor 2058 803) 1976 -
Twist And Shout/I Can't Explain	(MCA 927) 1984 -
φ My Generation/Substitute	(Polydor POSP 907) 1988 68
γ Won't Get Fooled Again/	
Boney Moronie (live)	(Polydor 917) 1988 -
η Join Together/I Can See For Miles	(Virgin VS 1259) 1990 -

NB: α Unreleased. β Withdrawn. χ 'B' side credited to Who Orchestra was by the **Graham Bond Organisation**. δ Mispressing with the wrong catalogue number. ε From the *Tommy* soundtrack. φ Also issued as 12" and CD single with two additional tracks: - *Baba O'Riley* and *Behind Blue Eyes*. γ Also issued as 12" and CD single with two additional tracks:- *Dancing In The Street* (live) and *Mary Ann With The Shaky Hand*. η Also issued as 12" with addition of *Behind Blue Eyes* and as a CD single with addition of *Behind Blue Eyes* and *Christmas*. Many of their earlier 45s were released with different flip sides in the US. One US 45, *Substitute/Waltz For A Pig* (Atco 45-6409) 1966 features a different recording of the 'A' side. In addition to the different lyric ("I try going forward, but my feet walk back", in place of "I look all white but my dad was black", the instrumental break follows the first verse and chorus, rather than the second. This Atco version was later reissued as Atco 45-6509. There was also a 7" acetate, *Acid Queen/Go To The Mirror* (Apple no #) 1969, which was part of a planned series of four promotional singles to help promote their rock opera *Tommy*. However, they were shelved when Polydor (Track's distributor) expressed a lack of interest in distributing them. *Singles Box* (12-CD) (Polydor 9866338) features 12 early singles that are representative of their career.

The Who was the premier mod band of the sixties and one of the best live bands in the history of rock. They possessed the most flamboyant drummer of the era in **Keith Moon** and in **Pete Townshend** had one of the finest songwriters of his era who wrote the teenager anthem *My Generation* and the ground-breaking rock opera *Tommy*.

The Who formed as The Detours in West London in 1962 (see individuals members' solo entries for details of their early years). In 1964 they met publicist Pete Meaden, who introduced them to London's burgeoning 'mod' scene. He transformed their image and changed their name to **The High Numbers**. Their original drummer, Dougie Sandon (who was 10 years older than the rest of the band) left around this time and was eventually replaced by **Keith Moon**. In July 1964 they recorded a rewrite of Slim Harpo's *Got Love If You Want It*, entitled *I'm The Face*. A pretty weak record, it flopped but is now a very expensive collector's item. Meanwhile the band was building a strong following in the pubs in Shepherd Bush, where they were based. This attracted the attention of Kit Lambert and Chris Stamp, who took over their management, changed their name to **The Who** and encouraged them to add more open aggression to their act.

They still found it hard to win a record contract, eventually gaining one with American Decca (no relation to the UK label) on the recommendation of expat US producer Shel Talmy, who'd produced a demo of **Townshend**'s *I Can't Explain*, which was released on the UK Brunswick label in January 1965. **Jimmy Page** was drafted in to augment **Townshend**'s guitar along with **The Ivy League** to handle the high-pitched vocals. Notable for its very distinctive opening chords, it remains one of their finest offerings and broke into the chart after the band appeared on TV's 'Ready Steady Go'. It took them into the Top 10 here and crept to No. 93 in the US.

The follow-up, *Anyway Anyhow Anywhere*, also made the UK Top Ten and was characterised by the crashing guitar riffs and high-pitched vocals that became their trademark for the next few years. Their early tour de force, however, was *My Generation*, on which **Daltrey**'s suggestive, stuttering vocals articulated the mod's incoherent rebelliousness and is still regarded by many as their finest moment. Brash and full of energy, it transcended the boundaries between pop and rock, and got to No. 2 here and No. 74 in the US (where, like their previous effort, it was released with a different flip side).

Their hastily-assembled debut album *My Generation* was a powerful, spontaneous amalgam of R&B standards like *I'm A Man, I Don't Mind* and *Please Please Please*, along with some fresh early **Townshend** songs. Aside from the stunning title track, other mini-classics were *La-La-La-Lies, The Kids Are Alright, It's Not True, The Good's Gone* (featuring great ringing guitar work) and *A Legal Matter*, along with group composition *The Ox* (**Entwistle**'s nickname), which showcased some wild, guitar-dominated instrumental passages. 30 years on, the album still sounds superb and is recommended listening. In the US it was titled *The Who Sing My Generation*.

After splitting from Brunswick to sign for Robert Stigwood's Reaction label in March 1965, they released *Substitute* the same month. Similar to its predecessors, but with cleverer lyrics, it climbed to No. 5 in the UK. The 'B' side on early copies was *Instant Party*, then *Circles*. After this, Talmy parted company with the band on acrimonious terms. Kit Lambert took over production duties, though subsequent legal action meant Talmy continued to benefit from their recordings for the next five years.

Relationships within the band were often tumultuous, making it all the more surprising that they stayed together so long. The first public evidence of this was on 20 May 1966, when **Townshend** and **Daltrey** appeared on stage at a Windsor Club with a substitute bassist and drummer when the other two didn't show. When they did eventually turn up, **Townshend** hit **Moon** over the head with his guitar, causing **Moon** to leave the band for a week.

Brunswick inevitably cashed in on the band's popularity by releasing three of the strongest songs from their *My Generation* album as 45s. The first two - *A Legal Matter* and *The Kids Are Alright* - were minor hits in the UK, but the third, *La-La-La-Lies* flopped.

Their next Reaction 45, **Pete Townshend**'s *I'm A Boy* (whose lyrics dealt with enforced transvestism) was another gem in their characteristically

THE WHO - Meaty Beaty Big And Bouncy (LP).

THE WHO - Quadrophenia (2-LP).

energetic style, and climbed to No 2. In October 1966 they appeared on a 'Ready Steady Go' special, and the following month their performance was re-recorded in the studio and released as the *Ready Steady Who* EP in tribute to the programme. It comprised a cover of The Beach Boys' *Barbara Ann, Bucket T* and *The Batman Theme* and is now a collector's item. *Happy Jack* (released in December 1966) got to No 3 in the UK, but wasn't one of their sharpest 45s. It was significant, however, for being their first to get into the US Top 30, peaking at No. 24.

Their second album, *A Quick One*, included songs by all four band members. Especially significant was **Townshend**'s lengthy *A Quick One While He's Away*, a mini-'rock opera' dealing with marital infidelity. It provided a glimpse of what was to come with *Tommy*. Another track of note was **John Entwistle**'s *Boris The Spider*, which typified his somewhat macabre style. The album sold well, peaking at No. 4 in the UK and No. 67 in the US (where it was titled *Happy Jack*).

1967 saw them sign to Polydor offshoot Track, which had been formed by Chris Stamp and Kit Lambert. Their next 45 was the superb *Pictures Of Lily*, in which **Townshend** dealt with sexual fantasies. Some fine guitar work and excellent vocals made this one of their best 45s, and it peaked at No. 4 here and No. 51 in the US.

1967 was also the year **The Who** cracked the lucrative American market. After making their US debut as part of an 'Easter Rock'n'Roll Extravaganza' package on 25 March, they played at the now-legendary Monterey Festival in June and then embarked on their first US tour in July as support to **Herman's Hermits**, who'd been one of the most successful British invasion bands in the States in the mid-sixties.

For their next 45 they covered **The Rolling Stones**' *The Last Time* and *Under My Thumb* after they were jailed for drug offences, vowing to continue releasing cover versions of **Stones** material until their release. Perhaps it's as well the pair were freed a few days later, as the record was not one of their best and only peaked at No. 44 in the UK.

They fared better with the brilliant *I Can See For Miles*, which perfectly conveyed their power and energy and put them back in the Top Ten here (though **Townshend** later expressed disappointment that it hadn't got to the top position, which it richly deserved). It also climbed to No. 9 in the US, where it was their first Top Ten hit.

Their next album, *The Who Sell Out*, is notable for having jingles linking its tracks, to mimic the atmosphere of offshore pirate radio broadcasts (which had been outlawed by the Wilson government's Marine Offences Act from August 1967). Though the Act did end one of the most exciting episodes in British radio, the band's jingles can become highly irritating on repeated listening and it is perhaps to be regretted that they chose to include them. Its musical content was varied, but the highpoints - *I Can See For Miles, Mary Anne With The Shaky Hand* and **Speedy Keen**'s *Armenia City In The Sky*, for example - rivalled anything most of their contemporaries were producing

Much of 1968 was spent touring America and Australasia, making it a quiet year in vinyl terms. *Dogs* was a minor hit here (No. 25), whilst its flip side, *Call Me Lightning*, was released as an 'A' Side with *Dr. Jekyll And Mr. Hyde* on the flip in the States and crept to no. 40. The absence of a new album led to the October 1968 release of a US-only album, *Magic Bus - The Who On Tour*, which got to No 39 and was not live, as is often assumed. Instead it comprised material from the last couple of years, including *Call Me Lightning, Pictures Of Lily, Doctor, Doctor* and the title track, which got to No. 26 here and No. 25 in the US when released as a 45 the same month. To keep interest alive in the UK, Track issued the *Direct Hits* compilation, which included all their significant hits from *I'm A Boy* onwards, and some of the flip sides too. The **Stones** covers were omitted, however.

Though the band seemed quiet, **Townshend** was in fact at work on his most ambitious work to date, which would be released the following year as *Tommy*. In 1968 he had also become fascinated by Meher Baba, an Indian Perfect Spiritual Master whose teachings influenced *Tommy*. To whet the public appetite, *Pinball Wizard* (arguably the project's strongest and most commercial song, with superb guitar work and vocals) was released as a 45 in March 1969. On the flip was *Dogs (Part 2)*, and it climbed to No. 4 here and No. 19 in the US.

On its release in May 1969, *Tommy* was hailed as a landmark in rock. The story of a deaf, dumb and blind boy who discovers a gift for pinball and is elevated to prophet status before being turned on by his disciples, it was the first successful 'rock opera', though **Townshend** readily acknowledged that he'd been influenced in its conception by **The Pretty Things**' *S.F.Sorrow*. It also saw them break forever with the three-minute pop song format. The album contained several superb compositions including *The Acid Queen, I'm Free* (later a US 45), *Underture* and *We're Not Going To Take It*, to name a few. Two songs (the distasteful *Cousin Kevin* and *Fiddle About*) were composed by **Entwistle** and one (the burlesque *Tommy's Holiday Camp*) by **Moon**. Not a fast seller initially, it rose to No. 2 here over the next few months and to No. 4 in the US.

To help promote it they embarked on a US tour, where songs from *Tommy* formed a major part of their act. They later toured Europe, but only performed the album in full twice - at a press launch in Ronnie Scott's club in London in May 1969, and at New York's Metropolitan Opera House on 7 June 1970. Sandwiched between these two performances were appearances at the Woodstock and Isle of Wight festivals in August 1969. Their performance at Woodstock was, in fact, substandard - their drinks had been spiked and by the time they took the stage they were out of their skulls

Their next single, *The Seeker*, had power and energy but only managed No. 19 here and No. 44 in the States. In hindsight, *Tommy* had marked the end of their success as a singles band - and also presented **Townshend** with the unwelcome problem of how to follow it. Whilst he pondered his dilemma, the *Live At Leeds* album (recorded at Leeds University) appeared in May 1970. It captured the excitement of their live act pretty favourably, and its highlights included punchy versions of classic songs like *Substitute*,

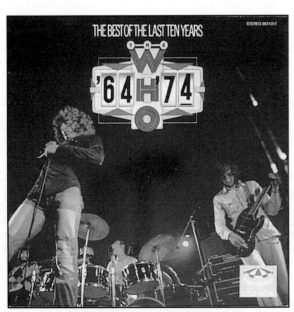
THE WHO - The Best Of The Last Ten Years (2-LP).

THE WHO - The Story Of The Who (2-LP).

My Generation (incorporating extracts from *Tommy*) and *Magic Bus* as well as old favourites like Eddie Cochran's *Summertime Blues* and Johnny Kidd and The Pirates' *Shakin' All Over*. The album sold well, climbing to No. 3 here and No. 4 in the US. *Summertime Blues* was also culled for 45 release and peaked at 38 here and 27 in the States.

Their next 45, *See Me Feel Me* (another track from *Tommy*) was only a hit (No. 12) in the States. In May 1971 **John Entwistle** brought out his debut album, *Smash Your Head Against The Wall*, and became the first band member to achieve solo success when it advanced to No. 126 in the US. After a dormant period, **The Who** returned to the charts (No. 9 UK, No. 15 US) with the energetic *Won't Get Fooled Again*, taken from their next album, *Who's Next*. Much of the album had in fact been salvaged by **Townshend** from an abandoned rock opera to have been called 'Lifehouse'. Unquestionably one of their best efforts, it included the full length version of *Won't Get Fooled Again, The Song Is Over* and *Baba O'Reilly* and topped the UK charts. In the US it got to No. 4. On 4 November 1971 they performed for three nights to mark the opening of The Rainbow, a new rock venue at London's Finsbury Park. The following month they released *Meaty, Beaty, Big And Bouncy*, a collection of their biggest hits to date (with an extended version of *I'm A Boy* and *Boris The Spider*).

'Best of' albums are often sign that a band is nearing the end of its life, and for a while this appeared to be the case with **The Who**. 1972 was spent with members concentrating on solo projects. **Townshend** issued his first solo album, *Who Came First*, which he'd made in his home studio. He went on to issue several more throughout the seventies and eighties. **Entwistle**'s second album, *Wistle Rhymes*, met with some success in the States, and in 1973 **Daltrey** made the singles charts with *Giving It All Away* from his self-titled debut album. In fact **The Who** only managed one 45 in 1972, *Join Together*. Though not one of their best, it got to No. 9 here and No. 17 in the States. The year ended with Lou Reizner's stage production of 'Tommy' in London, with **Daltrey** in the lead role. The inevitable all-star double soundtrack album got to No. 5 in the US when released soon afterwards.

By 1973, some were beginning to write the band off. The members seemed more interested in solo work and the *Relay* and *5.15* 45s were sub-standard. *Quadrophenia*, however, dispelled such doubts on its appearance in November 1973. This was another highly ambitious, thematic project, paying homage to the mods whose image had been such an inspiration to the band in their early days. Not all the music (much of which was heavily orchestrated) was up to standard, but the project was a success overall, climbing to No. 2 on both sides of the Atlantic and putting the band firmly back on the map. After promo tours of both the UK and US (where *Love Reign O'Er Me* and *The Real Me* were unsuccessfully extracted as 45s), they returned home and resumed their individual lives.

Odds And Sods, an album of previously unreleased **Who** recordings compiled by **Entwistle**, was released in October 1974 and climbed to No's 10 and 15 in the UK and US respectively. Two of its better tracks were also released on a US 45 (*Postcard/Put The Money Down*), but didn't chart.

Aside from **Entwistle**'s *Postcard* and Peter Meadon's *I'm The Face* (which, of course, they'd recorded as **The High Numbers**), the compositions were all by **Townshend**. Whilst not up to the standard of most of their previously released material, the album was of great interest to the band's fans.

Moon, who had cultivated an image as rock's most outrageous personality, appeared in the film 'Stardust' and became the final **Who** member to release a solo album, in April 1975. *Two Sides Of Moon* was pretty dire and sold poorly, but he found other things to do, such as promoting a road safety campaign.

Tommy, meanwhile, had developed a life of its own. 1975 saw the release of a film version directed by Ken Russell, which starred **The Who** and an all-star cast including **Elton John**, Oliver Reed, Jack Nicholson and Ann-Margaret. Its soundtrack got to No. 21 in the UK. 1976 saw them scrape into the Top Ten with *Squeeze Box* (No. 16 in the US). They gave the loudest performance by a rock group at Charlton Athletic Football Club on 31 May that year, getting into the Guinness Book Of Records as a consequence. In September the double compilation, *The Story Of The Who*, was released to keep interest in the band alive. It included most of their hits, but - surprisingly - omitted their first 45, *I Can't Explain*. Peaking at No. 2 here, it failed to chart in the US, where one of its less known tracks, *Slip Kid*, met with the same fate when released as a US-only 45. Side three of the album comprised some of the best songs from *Tommy*. A maxi single (also available in 12" format) containing three of their finest moments, *Substitute, I'm A Boy* and *Pictures Of Lily*, was released as part of the promotional campaign the following month and got to No 7 in the UK.

Eventually **Keith Moon**'s drinking and drug use caught up with him, and he died in bed on 8 September 1978 from an overdose of Herminevrin, which had been prescribed to counter his alcoholism. A month earlier, on 5 August 1978, their first manager Pete Meaden had committed suicide. In early 1979 former **Small Faces** and **Faces** member **Kenny Jones** took **Moon**'s place, and John 'Rabbit' Bundrick was added on keyboards for touring purposes. The film of 'Quadrophenia', which premiered in Spring 1979, created new interest in the band for a while - but they were never really as good after **Keith Moon**'s death in 1978. Their recording career continued until 1983, though they reformed several times for live work. In October 2001, they played at the concert for New York City benefit for families of the 11 September attacks. On 27 June 2002 **John Entwistle** died of a cocaine-induced heart attack at the Hard Rock Hotel, Las Vegas, aged 57, a day before a reconstituted **Who** were due to embark on an extensive US tour. **Daltrey** and **Townshend** gave a rousing performance at the 'Live 8' concert in Hyde Park in July 2005.

The 1994 4-CD box set *Thirty Years Of Maximum R&B* serves as a fitting epitaph. Though one might expect great songs like *Circles* and *Doctor Doctor* to have been included, their hits are there, along with rarities, some tracks which had previously appeared on bootlegs, some studio out-takes and a few **Keith Moon** comic interludes never featured in public before. It all comes with an excellent booklet carefully assembled by the set's co-compiler, Chris Charlesworth. Any serious fan of British rock should have this.

THE WHO - BBC Sessions (CD).

As one would expect, the band have featured extensively on Various Artists compilations, including:- *Pinball Wizard* on Polydor's *Deep Overground Pop* (LP); *Summertimes Blues* on Polydor's *Rock Party* (2-LP); *My Generation* on Stardust (2-LP); *I Can See For Miles* and *Call Me Lightning* on *Backtrack 1* (LP); *Under My Thumb, Magic Bus, Pinball Wizard* and *The Last Time* on *Backtrack 2* (LP) and other tracks on *Backtracks 3* (LP), *4* (LP) and *5* (LP).

Their 1970 Isle of Wight Festival set, which captured them at their prime, can be heard on Castle's 1996 2-CD set, or on Sanctuary's 2001 3-LP package.

Polydor's 2-CD *The Ultimate Collection* is a thorough, 40-track examination of their hits. There's also a limited pressing with a third CD, which includes an early take of *I'm A Boy*, the US 45 version of *Substitute*, an acoustic version of *Happy Jack* and the UK single take of *Magic Bus*. An enhanced section includes film of them playing *Substitute* and *Baba O'Riley* at their 1974 Charlton Athletic concerts. In recent years many of their albums have been reissued as deluxe 2-CD sets, with bonus cuts. These are recommended.

Recent compilation appearances include: live versions of *Substitute, Summertime Blues, Pictures Of Lily, A Quick One While He's Away, Happy Jack* and *My Generation* on *Monterey International Pop Festival* (LP); *Anyway, Anyhow, Anywhere* (diff. version) on *Artefacts From The Psychedelic Dungeon* (CD); *Great Shakes* on *Great Shakes Shake-Out* (EP); *Armenia City In The Sky* on the 4-CD set *Acid Drops, Spacedust & Flying Saucers*; and *Won't Get Fooled Again* on the 2-CD set *Rock Resurrection*. (VJ/BM/RMJ)

Wicked Lady

Personnel: BOB JEFFRIES   bs   A
            'MAD' DICK SMITH   drms   AB
            MARTIN WEAVER   vcls, lead gtr   AB
            DEL 'GERMAN HEAD' MORLEY bs   B

CDs: 1(A) THE AXEMAN COMETH (Kissing Spell KSCD 9307) 1994
        2(B) PSYCHOTIC OVERKILL (Kissing Spell KSCD 9499) 1994

NB: (1) and (2) reissued again in 2002. There's also a vinyl album *Blow Your Mind*.

This band was formed by guitarist and frontman Martin Weaver in 1968 as a three-piece heavy rock band. The band was notorious for their outrageous live performances often refusing to stop playing or walking off-stage mid-number leaving equipment to feedback until someone killed the power. They had a large biker following and several venues were trashed all in the name of fun. This line-up recorded material which has been released on CD by Kissing Spell, *The Axeman Cometh*. Drink and drugs caused the band to split for a while in 1970 'to get their heads together'. They reformed with a new bass player Del 'German Head' Morley

THE WHO - The Kid's Are Alright (2-LP).

who to begin with was a stabilising influence. Material this line-up recorded appears on *Psychotic Overkill*.

The band continued until 1972, by which time the music had turned into experimental noise (mainly because they could not concentrate long enough to play complete songs). At one gig they played one song over and over again until the management turned off the power.

The eventual end came because no venues would allow them to play. Weaver joined **Dark** just in time to record *'Round The Edges*. He later joined with keyboard player Dave 'Doc' Waddley and together under the name The Mind Doctors playing laid-back instrumental 'head' music *On The Threshold Of Reality* which was also issued by Kissing Spell.

Aside from a cover of **Hendrix**'s *Voodoo Chile* the *Psychotic Overkill* CD contains half a dozen guitar-driven blues-rock originals. Highlights include *I'm A Freak*, *Sin City*, *Passion* and 21-minute finale *Ship Of Ghosts*. (VJ)

WICKED LADY - Blow Your Mind (LP).

Widowmaker

Personnel:	ARIEL BENDER		
	(aka LUTHER GROSVENOR)	gtr, vcls	AB
	BOB DAISLEY	bs, vcls	AB
	STEVE ELLIS	vcls	A
	HUW LLOYD-LANGTON	gtr	AB
	JOHN BUTLER	vcls, keyb'ds	B

ALBUM:	1(A)	WIDOWMAKER	(Jet 2310 432) 1976 SC
(up to 1976)			

NB: *Straight Faced Fighters* (Sanctuary CMDDD 586) 2002 is a 2-CD set comprising their first album, six live cuts and six tracks from their second album *Too Late To Cry*, which falls outside the time span of this book.

45s:	On The Road/Pin A Rose On Me	(Jet JET 766) 1976
(up to 1976)	When I Met You/Pin A Rose On Me	(Jet JET 767) 1976
	Pin A Rose On Me/On The Road	(Jet JET 782) 1976

This hard-rock band formed in July 1975. Steve Ellis had been with **Love Affair** and **Ellis**; Bender with **Art**, **Spooky Tooth** and **Mott The Hoople**; Lloyd-Langton with **Leo Sayer**; Daisley with **Chicken Shack** and **Mungo Jerry**; and Nicholas with **Lindisfarne**. They recorded on Jet here in the UK and on United Artists in the USA.

Their eponymous debut album is a typically British blend of hard-rock and glam-rock. **Zoot Money** played session keyboards on this. There's also a strong southern-rock flavour on some cuts (which sound more akin to what Bob Seger was during at the time than a British band). Some tracks, such as *Pin A Rose On Me* and *Straight Faced Fighter* are quite commercial and, indeed, the former was selected for 45 release.

When **Steve Ellis** departed to re-form **Love Affair**, John Butler who'd been fronting his own band came in as a replacement. This line-up released a second album *Too Late To Cry* in 1977, which climbed to No 150 in the USA album charts.

After they split in July 1977, Daisley joined Rainbow and was later in Ozzy Osbourne's band and **Black Sabbath**, whilst Lloyd-Langton became a member of **Hawkwind**.

The 2002 Sanctuary 2-CD set comprises a reissue of their debut album on disc one, whilst disc two features six live cuts recorded for Bob Harris alongside six tracks from their superior second album.

They also contributed one cut, *Running Free* to the CD-set *Rock Of Ages, Four Decades Of Heavy Rock 1962-2002*. (VJ/JM)

Wigan's Ovation

Personnel:	ALF BROOKS	drms	A
	PETER PRESTON	gtr	A
	PHIL PRESTON	bs	A
	JIM MacCLUSKEY	vcls	A

ALBUM:	1(A)	NORTHERN SOUL DANCER	(Spark)1975

			HCP
45s:	Ski-ing In The Snow/	(Spark SRL 1122) 1975	12
	Per-So-Nal-Ly/	(Spark SRL 1129) 1975	38
	Super Love/	(Spark SRL 1133) 1975	41

A pop group who enjoyed some chart success. (VJ/JM)

Wild Angels

Personnel:	ROD COTTER	bs	A
	MAL GRAY	vcls	AB
	JOHN HAWKINS	gtr	ABCDE
	BILL KINGSTON	piano, vcls	ABCDE
	BOB O'CONNOR	drms	A
	GEOFF BRITTON	drms	BC
	KEITH READ	bs, vcls	BCDE
	MITCH MITCHELL	gtr, vcls	CDE
	GEOFF BROWNE	drms	D
	JIM	drms	E

ALBUMS:	1(A)	LIVE AT THE REVOLUTION	(B&C BCM 101) 1970 SC
	2(A)	RED HOT 'N' ROCKING	(B&C BCM 102) 1970 SC
	3(C)	OUT AT LAST	(Decca SKL 5134) 1972
	4(E)	LET'S GET BACK TO ROCK'N'ROLL	(Pye GH 614) 1975

45s:	Nervous Breakdown/	
	Watch The Wheels Go Round	(Major Minor MM 569) 1968 SC
	Buzz Buzz/Please Don't Touch	(B&C CB 114) 1970
	Sally Ann/Wrong Number Try Again	(B&C CB 123) 1970
	Three Night A Week/Time To Kill	(B&C CB 145) 1971
	Jo Jo Ann/My Way	(Decca F 13308) 1972
	Beauty School Dropout/Midnight Rider	(Decca F 13356) 1972
	Running Bear/Sussin'	(Decca F 13374) 1973
	Greased Lightning/Born To Hand-Jive	(Decca F 13412) 1973
	Clap Your Hands And Stamp Your Feet/	
	Wild Angels Rock And Roll	(Decca F 13456) 1973

A teddy boy rock'n'roll revival act from the Biggin' Hill area whose prolific output has to date failed to interest any of the reissue labels. The original line-up recorded two albums and three 45s. Then Cotter departed to Jaghouse and O'Connor left too. They were replaced by Keith Read and ex-**Gun** member Geoff Britton. Then, in August 1971 Gray left to form Mal Gray's Hurricane and Mitch Mitchell replaced him.

The new line-up recorded the *Out At Last* album and a number of 45s before Britton departed to **Paul McCartney and Wings**. Geoff Browne replaced him on drums for the *Clap Your Hands* 45, but then left himself and a drummer called Jim played on their final album. (VJ/JM)

Wild Country

Personnel:	TERRY KEYWORTH	gtr, trumpet, trombone, piano	A
	JACK McCULLOCH	drms	A
	JIM PITMAN-AVERY	gtr	A
	STUART WHITCOMBE	keyb'ds	A

45:     Silent Country/Too Bad   (Trafalgar TRAF 01) 1970

This one-off single is reputedly pretty good. Keyworth was born in Bournemouth and Whitcombe was originally from Lincolnshire. Pitman-Avery had been in **Thunderclap Newman**. After this 45 he joined **Third World War** and McCulloch departed to McCullochs, Struthers and Patterson. (MWh/JM/VJ)

The Wilde Flowers

Personnel:	GRAHAM FLIGHT	vcls	A
	BRIAN HOPPER	gtr, sax	ABCDE
	HUGH HOPPER	bs	ABCD
	RICHARD SINCLAIR	gtr	AB
	ROBERT WYATT	drms	ABC
	KEVIN AYERS	vcls	B
	RICHARD COUGHLAN	drms	CDE
	PYE HASTINGS	gtr, sax	CDE
	DAVE LAWRENCE	bs, vcls	CDE
	DAVE SINCLAIR	keyb'ds	E

NB: There's been a recent release of their original material on CD (Voiceprint VP 123 CD) 1994.

This now legendary Canterbury-based band later spawned both **Soft Machine** and **Caravan**. They formed in 1961. The original line-up all went to the Simon Langton School, an exclusive private school in Canterbury. Their original vocalist, Graham Flight, soon left to be replaced by **Kevin Ayers**, although in September 1965 he left and a year later helped form **Soft Machine**. Richard Sinclair left to go to college around the same time and later started **Caravan**. Line-up B did record a demo early in 1965 but it never saw the light of day. They had a few originals but much of their set consisted of Chuck Berry and **Beatles** numbers. Richard Coughlan and Pye Hastings came in as replacements for Ayers and Sinclair and **Robert Wyatt** switched to vocals. At the end of 1966 **Hugh Hopper** switched to sax by which time **Wyatt** had joined **Ayers** in **Soft Machine**. By now the band was mainly playing originals, which veered towards soul. In March 1967 **Hugh Hopper** also left (he also resurfaced a couple of years on in **Soft Machine**) and Dave Sinclair (Richard's cousin) and Dave Lawrence joined. A few months later Brian Hopper and Lawrence quit the music scene leaving Coughlan, Hastings and Sinclair dormant for a few months before they re-emerged in **Caravan**.

Ayers, **Hugh Hopper** and **Wyatt** all recorded solo albums.

Compilation appearances have included: *You Really Got Me* and *Thinking Of You Baby* on *Canterburied Sounds Vol. 1* (CD). (VJ)

The Wilde Three

Personnel:	JUSTIN HAYWARD		A
	JOYCE WILDE		A
	MARTY WILDE		A

45s:	Since You've Gone/Just As Long	(Decca F 12131) 1965 R1
	I Cried/Well Who's That	(Decca F 12232) 1965 R1

This short-lived trio's two 45s are hard to pin down now and hence collectable. *I Cried* is a dreadful sob sob ballad, with spoken vocal passages that could grace any '20 Worst Records' compilation.

Marty Wilde was a successful but dreadful British vocalist whose heyday had been in the late fifties and early sixties. Joyce, his wife, had been in The Vernons Girls, an early sixties female group who'd also had a number of hits. **Justin Hayward** went on to record a couple of solo 45s before becoming an influential member of **The Moody Blues**. (VJ)

Wild Honey

Personnel:	TINA CHARLES	vcls	A
	KIM KEENE	vcls	A
	MOLLY PAAGE	vcls	A

45s:	He's My Sugar/People Of The Universe	(Mam MAM 97) 1972
α	Baby Don't Know You Anymore/	
	He's My Sugar	(Mam MAM 154) 1972

NB: α 'B' side featuring Tina Charles.

This female vocal trio may have just been a studio group. Molly Page was **Jackie Trent**'s sister and had been in Sweet Corn. Tina Charles later enjoyed success with soul group 5000 Volts and as a solo artist. (JM)

Wild Oats

Personnel:	WILLY BROWN	vcls	ABC
	ROD GOLDSMITH	bs	A
	ROBIN HARE	ld gtr	ABC
	CARL HARRISON	vcls	ABC
	TREV ROLAND	ld gtr	AB
	STYKX SCARLETT	drms	ABC
	GRAHAM BALDRY	bs	BC
	MICK HUGHES	ld gtr	C

ALBUM: 1(A)   LIVE AT LEISTON   (Tenth Planet TP 013) 1995

NB: (1) Numbered limited edition of 500.

EP: 1(A)   WILD OATS (PS)   (Oak RGJ 117) 1963 R5

A Suffolk R&B band from Leiston to be precise, previously known as The Rebels, who'd cut an acetate for Oak (Put *The Blame On Me/Whole Lotta Woman*) prior to the above EP. This mega-rarity (£500 plus) featured energetic versions of *Can't Judge A Book By Its Cover* and *Walkin' The Dog* on side one and an uncharacteristic cover of The Shirelles' *Will You Still Love Me Tomorrow?* coupled with a bluesy version of Elvis Presley's *Put The Blame On Me* on side two.

In 1964 they recorded another acetate coupling *Soulful Dress* and *Bye Bye Baby* at the little-known City Of London studios. A further acetate coupling *Route 66* and *Fanny Mae* was made at Tony Pike's studio in early 1965, although the band were dissatisfied with the sound quality and their own performance. Rod Goldsmith left shortly afterwards due to musical differences. He was replaced by Graham Baldry. With Robin Hare switching from guitar to Farfisa organ the band's musical format veered more towards soul as they covered material by the likes of Lee Dorsey, Otis Redding and Wilson Pickett. Trev Rowland left the band in 1966 being replaced by Mick Hughes by which time they'd become **Crispian St. Peters**' live backing band. They finally split in 1967, but have reformed on several occasions since.

THE WILD OATS - Live At Leiston (LP).

Tenth Planet's posthumous *Live At Leiston* release is taken from a recently unearthed reel to reel tape of the band performing in May 1964 at the International Club in Leiston. It gives some insight into what a typical regional R&B act must have sounded like in this era as they work their way through standards like *You Better Move On, Poison Ivy, Sweets For My Sweet* and *Money (That's What I Want)*.

Compilation appearances have included: *You Can't Judge A Book By It's Cover* on *Story Of Oak Records* (2-LP) and *The Story Of Oak Records* (CD); and *Walking The Dog* on *The Demention Of Sound* (LP). (VJ)

The Wild Ones

ALBUM: 1   THE ARTHUR SOUND   (United Artists ULP 1119) 1965

45:    Bowie Man/Purple Pill Eater   (Fontana TF 468) 1964 R2

It's thought that this band backed ex-**Tornado Heinz** in 1964-65. *Purple Pill Eater* was about the mods appetite for "purple hearts".

Compilation appearances include: *Purple Pill Eater* on *English Freakbeat, Vol. 1* (LP & CD); and *Bowie Man* on *Pebbles, Vol. 6 - The Roots Of Mod* (LP) and *English Freakbeat Vol. 6* (CD). (VJ)

Wild Silk

Personnel:	BARNEY BEASLEY	bs	A
	ALLAN DAVIES	ld vcls	A
	DANNY MAIDMENT	gtr	A
	BILL SLANEY	drms	A
	JIM TURNER	piano	A

45s:	Poor Man/Stop Crying	(Polydor 56256) 1968
	(Visions In A) Plaster Sky/Toymaker	(Columbia DB 8534) 1969
	Help Me/Crimson And Gold	(Columbia DB 8611) 1969

This Luton-based band's three 45s were produced by Shel Talmy. The flip of their second 45, *Toymaker*, was a Ray Davies' song although not recorded by **The Kinks**. It's easy to see why **The Kinks** didn't bother as it's a rather juvenile song. The 'A' side, *(Visions In A) Plaster Sky*, was certainly the better track, being a typically whimsical pop effort. Curiously the 45 got a US-only release on the GRT label under the name Basil. They also had a US-only 45, *Monday Tuesday Wednesday/Jessie* (Kapp 974) in 1969.

Compilation appearances have included:- *Toymaker* on *Rubble Vol. 17: A Trip In A Painted World* (LP), *Rubble Vol. 10* (CD) and *The Best Of Rubble Collection, Vol. 5* (CD); and *(Visions In A) Plaster Sky* on *Rubble Vol. 3: Nightmares In Wonderland* and *Rubble Vol. 2* (CD). In addition as "Basil" *(Visions In A) Plaster Sky* is on *Magic Cube* (CD). (VJ)

Wild Turkey

Personnel:	JON BLACKMORE	gtr, vcls	AB
	GLEN CORNICK	gtr, bs, keyb'ds	ABCDE
	GARY PICKFORD-HOPKINS	gtr, vcls	ABCDE
	JOHN WEATHERS	drms	A
	GRAHAM WILLIAMS	gtr	A
	JEFF JONES	drms	BCD
	ALLAN 'TWEKE' LEWIS	gtr	BC
	MICK DYCHE	gtr, vcls	CDE
	STEVE GURL	keyb'ds	C
	BERNIE MARSDEN	lead gtr	DE
	KEVIN CURRIE	drms	E

| ALBUMS: | 1(B) | BATTLE HYMN | (Chrysalis CHR 1002) 1971 SC |
| | 2(C) | TURKEY | (Chrysalis CHR 1010) 1972 SC |

NB: (1) reissued on CD (Edsel ED CD 333) 1991 and again with two bonus tracks. (2) reissued on CD with bonus tracks. *Final Performance* (CD) (Audio Archives AACD 039) captures their final live performance at the Marquee on 24th June 1974 on CD. *Live In Edinburgh* (CD) (Audio Archives AACD 043) captures them on form and comes with a poster booklet full of previously unseen photos and sleevenotes by Gary Pickford-Hopkins. *Rarest Turkey* (CD) (Audio Archives AACD 048) features

the 'Chalfont' demos from 1974, both sides of their rare 1972 single, five bonus cuts and a few live cuts. The package comes with rare photos and memorabilia.

45:    Good Old Days/Life Is A Symphony   (Chrysalis CHS 2004) 1972

This was a mainstream rock outfit with progressive leanings, which included former **Jethro Tull** member Glen Cornick. They formed in 1971. Pickford-Hopkins had been with **The Big Sleep** and Graham Williams in **Pete Brown's Piblokto**. Before they recorded Williams and Weathers left to join **Graham Bond**'s Magick. They were replaced by former **Man** member Jeff Jones and Allan 'Tweke' Lewis from Just Felix.

Their albums are becoming harder to find now, but are they worth searching for? We're talking pretty run of the mill progressive rock here with nothing to distinguish them from the pack. The first one scraped into the lower reaches of the US charts, probably because of Cornick's connection to **Jethro Tull**. Blackmore left in September 1972 to join Panama Scandal. Dyche and Gurl were then both recruited to the band.

The better tracks on *Turkey* are *Telephone* and *A Universal Man*, hard-rock tracks with progressive leanings, strong vocals and fine guitar leads. Lewis joined **Man** in July 1973 and Bernie Marsden (ex-**UFO**), who was also in **Cozy Powell's Hammer** replaced him. In February 1974, Jones departed to **Sassafras** and ex-**Supertramp** member Kevin Currie joined.

After their demise, Marsden and Gurl joined **Babe Ruth**; Dyche was in Jack Straw; Currie joined Burlesque and Cornick ended up in a German band called Kathargo playing on their *Rock'n'roll Testament* album and later formed the hard-rock group **Paris** in 1975. (VJ/CA/JM/CG)

A Wild Uncertainty

Personnel:	GORDON BARTON	drms	A
	EDDIE HARDIN	keyb'ds	A
	TONY SAVVA	bs, vcls	A
	PETER LEE WALKER	gtr	A

45:    Man With Money/Broken Truth   (Planet PLF 120) 1966 R2

A rare and collectable 45, though the 'A' side was recorded by other bands in this era and originally written by The Everly Brothers. Planet was Shel Talmy's label and this group was named by **Andrew Oldham** and managed by **Reg King**. Their rendition of *Man With Money* is competent.

Gordon Barton was later in **Andwella's Dream** and Eddie Hardin went on to enjoy considerable success in the **Spencer Davis Group** and Hardin and York. Tony Savva was later in **Samuel Proby**.

Compilation appearances include: *A Man With Money* on *Rare 60's Beat Treasures, Vol. 3* (CD) and *English Freakbeat, Vol. 5* (LP & CD); and *Man With Money* and *Broken Truth* on *The Best Of Planet Records* (CD). (VJ)

WILD TURKEY - Final Performance (CD).

The Wildwoods

45:      It's No Sin/What Am I To Do   (Philips BF 1507) 1966

A long forgotten ballad 45. (VJ)

Wilfred

45:      Candle In The Wind/
            Between The Lines   (Parlophone R 5836) 1970

Wilfred was from the Isle of Wight, their producer was Alan Jones (of **Amen Corner** and **Judas Jump**). *Candle In The Wind* was written by Jack Winsley and Bob Saker. (VJ)

John Williams

ALBUM: 1   JOHN WILLIAMS   (Columbia SX 6169) 1967 R3

45s: She's That Kind Of Woman/
            My Ways Are Set   (Columbia DB 8128) 1967 SC
            Flowers In Your Hair /
            Can't Find Time For Anything Now (Columbia DB 8251) 1967 SC

Not to be confused with the classical virtuoso who later played in Sky, this obscure mid-sixties folk singer/songwriter from Bedford made one of the rarest major label UK folk releases of the sixties. His self-penned album consists of downbeat songs with cello accompaniment, and may well have featured involvement from **Jimmy Page.** No producer is listed, but the publishing is partly credited to **Page**, with whom **Williams** also played on the **Maureeny Wishfull** album. Somewhat bafflingly, on the back of the album shop-owners are instructed to 'File Under: Educational'. His second 45, a cheery hippie ditty backed with another gloomy ballad, is non-album.

Compilation appearances include: *Flowers In Your Hair* on *Fading Yellow, Vol 1* (CD) and *She's That Kind Of Woman* on *Talking About The Good Times* (CD). (VJ/RMJ)

Paul Williams Set

Personnel:	JOHNNY ALMOND	tenor	AB
	TEDDY CHILDS	piano, sax	A
	JEFF CONDON	trumpet	AB
	JIMMY CRAWFORD	lead gtr	AB
	ROY MILLS	drms	A
	ROD SLADE	bs	A
	PAUL WILLIAMS	vcls, gtr	AB
	ROGER SUTTON	bs	B
	ALAN WHITE	drms	B
	JOHN WIGGINS	piano	B

45s: α Gin House/Rockin' Chair   (Columbia DB 7421) 1964 SC
      β The Many Faces Of Love/
         Jumpback   (Columbia DB 7768) 1965 SC
         My Sly Sadie/Stop The Wedding (Decca F 12844) 1968 SC

NB: α as Paul Williams Big Roll Band. β released as **Paul Williams** and **Zoot Money Band.**

Surrey-born **Paul Williams** got his start by sitting in with **Georgie Fame and The Blue Flames** and later **Alexis Korner's Blues Incorporated** as a guest vocalist in 1963. By fall 1963 he had taken a job singing with the **Wes Minster Five**, another London-based R&B group. In early 1964, he accepted an offer to join **Zoot Money's Big Roll Band** as the group's bass guitarist and second vocalist. He also released two singles under his own name backed by The Big Roll Band during this period.

When Zoot dissolved the group; **Williams** was briefly a member of **John Mayall's Bluesbreakers**, replacing John McVie in August 1967 but leaving by November 1967. In early 1968, **Williams** began fronting the **Alan Price Set** which became the **Paul Williams Set**, allowing **Price** to focus more on studio and production work. Childs, Slade and Mills all left in 1968 (Mills

ROBIN WILLIAMSON - Myrrh (CD).

died in January 1971) and Sutton, Wiggins and White (another **Alan Price Set** man) were recruited. Slade, incidentally quit the music business to become an advertising executive.

After a year of club appearances and one single, the group broke up and **Williams** joined **Juicy Lucy**. The remaining members formed **Johnny Almond's Music Machine**. (NR/VJ/JM)

Rick Williams

45:      Cut Across Shorty/Pickin' My Way   (Famous FAM 104) 1971

The 'A' side of this one-off 45 was from **Rod Stewart**'s *Gasoline Alley* album. (MWh)

Tony Williams' Lifetime

Personnel:	JACK BRUCE		A
	JOHN McLAUGHLIN		A
	TONY WILLIAMS		A
	LARRY YOUNG		A

ALBUMS:	1(A)	EMERGENCY (2-LP)	(Polydor 583 574) 1969 R1
	2(A)	TURN IT OVER	(Polydor 2425 019) 1970 SC
	3(A)	EGO	(Polydor 2425 065) 1971

45:     α One Word/Two Worlds   (Polydor 2066 050) 1970

NB: α as Lifetime.

A distinctive and widely-respected drummer, **Tony Williams** played with Miles Davis for much of the sixties before forming this powerful, but short-lived, jazz-rock fusion outfit. This group also recorded as Lifetime. Sadly **Williams** died of a heart attack aged 51 in early 1997, following a gall-bladder operation. (VJ)

Robin Williamson

ALBUM: 1   MYRRH   (Island HELP 2) 1972 SC

NB: (1) reissued on CD (Edsel EDCD 366) and again on CD (Beat Goes On BGO BGOCD 647) 2004.

Williamson was born in Edinburgh, Scotland, on 24 November 1943. This was a 'solo' effort recorded with his Merry Band whilst he was with **The Incredible String Band** which was certainly better than anything the group was putting out by this time. Collectors are beginning to take an interest in it now. The stand-out track is *The Dancing Of The Lord Of Weir*, but also of note are *Cold Harbour*, a stark intense song, the rockier *Sandy Land* and *Through The Horned Clouds*.

When **The Incredible String Band** split in 1974 he headed for LA. In 1976 he formed Robin Williamson and His Merry Band (with harpist Sylvia Wood, Chris Carswell and Jerry McMillian). They released three albums between 1977 and 1979 *Journey's Edge*, *American Stonehenge* and *A Glint At The Kindling*. Upon their demise **Williamson** returned to a solo career releasing albums like *Songs Of Love And Parting* and *Legacy Of The Scottish Harpers*. He has continued to record into the new millennium. He's also produced books and story cassettes and provided Soundtracks for TV series and music for theatre. A man of many talents! (VJ)

Jimmy Wilson (and The Pets)

45s:	See That Girl/Dime A Dance	(Decca F 12372) 1966
	I'm Going Home/	
	All The Colours Of The Rainbow	(Decca F 12447) 1966
α	Edelweiss/Where We Belong	(Decca F 12564) 1967
	Walk Through This World With Me/	
	There Was A Time	(Major Minor MM 535) 1967

NB: α credited to **Jimmy Wilson and The Pets**.

A Londoner, who'd worked as a seaman prior to recording. Most of his output was quite beaty. *I'm Going Home* was written by U.S. singer Bobby Goldsboro. (VJ)

Wimple Winch

Personnel:	LAWRENCE ARENDES	drms	A
	BARRY ASHALL	bs	A
	DEMETRIUS CHRISTOPHOLUS	vcls, gtr	A
	JOHN KELMAN	ld gtr	A

ALBUM: 1(A) THE WIMPLE WINCH STORY PART TWO '66-'68
THE PSYCHEDELIC YEARS
(Bam-Caruso KIRI 104) 1988.

NB: (1) also on CD, *The Wimple Winch Story '63 – '68* (Bam Caruso KIRI 107 CD) 1988. *The Story Of Just Four Men* (CD) is a 16-track set which contains their complete 1966-1968 recordings.

45s:	What's Been Done/I Really Love You (Fontana TF 686) 1966 R3
	Save My Soul/
	Everybody's Worried 'Bout Tomorrow (Fontana TF 718) 1966 R3
α	Rumble On Mersey Square South/
	Typical British Workmanship (Fontana TF 781) 1966 R4
	Rumble On Mersey Square South /
	Atmospheres (Fontana TF 781) 1966 R3

NB: α Initial pressings came with a projected 4th single, *Atmosphere*. These are now particularly expensive to acquire. The second and third single have been reissued (Fontana TF 718) and (Fontana TF 781) in limited edition pressings of 500 reproduced from the French jukebox pressings with large centre holes.

Wimple Winch was one of Britain's finest freakbeat outfits, and their slender recorded output is essential for fans of the genre.

Liverpool natives, they were originally known as **The Four Just Men** and then **Just Four Men** (following legal action by another band). By 1966 they had released two unsuccessful 45s, so chose to adopt the odd name by which they are best-remembered (supposedly Old English for a ditch). Their manager, Mike Carr, owned a club named The Sinking Ship near Mersey Square South in Stockport and, having become the house band, it wasn't long before **Wimple Winch** secured a record contract with Fontana.

Their first 45, the Merseybeat-influenced *What's Been Done*, is a plodding number that fails to convey the excitement they were undoubtedly capable of. Its flip, *I Really Love You*, was more interesting, but still used a straight beat format. Their next effort, *Save My Soul*, however, is quite simply one of the most exciting singles ever recorded in the UK. A wild rave-up featuring unbearably intense fuzz guitar, ranting vocals and frenzied drumming, it was way ahead of its time and sold extremely poorly. The world just wasn't ready for that sort of thing in 1966 - the only other band doing anything comparable was the Monks, who suffered a similarly poor reception from the record-buying public. Its 'B' side, another plodding beat number, was nothing like as special.

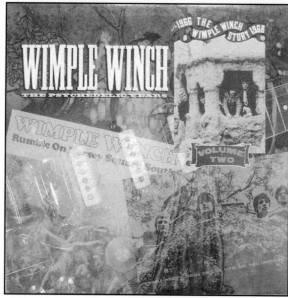

WIMPLE WINCH - The Wimple Winch Story Part Two (LP).

Their third 'A' side, *Rumble On Mersey Square South*, evoked a street fight with extraordinary vividness and was remarkably complex for its time. Again, it failed to sell. The version bootlegged on *Chocolate Soup For Diabetics, Vol. 3* is mastered considerably too fast, incidentally. Its 'B' side, the novelty-styled *Typical British Workmanship*, was another let-down by comparison - probably their weakest composition, in fact. However, a small number of copies were mispressed with a different song, *Atmospheres*, in its place. Another stunningly complex and punchy composition, it veered towards psychedelia and featured a highly melodic chorus. These mispressed copies are now extremely expensive, needless to say.

In 1967 the Sinking Ship caught fire, and all the band's gear was lost. They rallied to record some tracks that summer, but momentum was lost and they split soon afterwards. These tracks (including *Marmalade Hair*, *Lollipop Minds* and *Bluebell Wood*) have subsequently surfaced and are decent examples of British pop-psych, but nothing like the three **Wimple Winch** classics, for which you can expect to pay hundreds of pounds today.

When they disbanded in mid-1967, Lawrence Arendes joined Sponze, a jazzy progressive combo who backed **Dave Berry** on a 1969 45, *Huma Luma/Oh What A Life* (Decca F 12905). They later evolved into **Pacific Drift**, who recorded an album and single for Deram in 1970. Dee Christopholus went on to appear in several London stage shows, including 'Hair', 'Jesus Christ Superstar' and 'Joseph And His Amazing Technicolour Dream Coat'. He also appeared in BBC's 'Rock Follies' and recorded for G.T.O in the late seventies.

Compilation appearances have included: *Save My Soul* on *Maximum Freakbeat* (CD), *The Seventh Son* (LP), *Chocolate Soup For Diabetics, Vol. 3* (LP), *Head Sounds From The Bam-Caruso Waxworks, Vol. 1* (CD), *Chocolate Soup* (CD) and on the 4-CD *Nuggets II* box set; *Atmospheres*, *Rumble On Mersey Square South* and *Save My Soul* on *Rubble, Vol. 1 - The Psychedelic Snarl* (LP); *Marmalade Hair*, *Lollipop Music* and *Bluebell Wood* on *Rubble, Vol. 2 - Pop Sike Pipe Dreams* (LP); *Atmospheres*, *Rumble On Mersey Square South*, *Save My Soul*, *Marmalade Hair* and *Lollipop Music* on *Rubble, Vol. 1* (CD); *Bluebell Wood* on *Rubble, Vol. 2* (CD); *Rumble On Mersey Square South* on *Chocolate Soup For Diabetics, Vol. 2* (LP), *Electric Sugarcube Flashbacks, Vol. 1* (LP) and *Illusions From The Crackling Void* (LP); and *Pumpkin Pie* on *Incredible Sound Show Stories, Vol. 3* (LP). (VJ/RMJ)

Windmill

45s:	Big Bertha/Hey, Drummer Man	(MCA MU 1090) 1969
	Such Sweet Sorrow/I Can Fly	(MCA MK 5024) 1970
	Wilbur's Thing/Two's Company,	
	There's A Crowd	(MCA MK 5045) 1970

An obscure band whose *I Can Fly* has been compiled on *Colour Me Pop, Vol 3* (CD). (VJ)

Pete Wingfield

ALBUM: 1   BREAKFAST SPECIAL   (Island ILPS 9333) 1975

HCP

45s:	Eighteen With A Bullet/		
(up to	Shadow Of A Doubt	(Island WIP 6231) 1975	7
1976)	Whole Pot Of Jelly/Anytime	(Island WIP 6245) 1975	-
	Bubblin' Under/I Wanna Try	(Island WIP 6336) 1976	-

Pete Wingfield had been the keyboard/piano player with **Jellybread** and the session band Olympic Runners. He issued this solo album in 1975 on the back of a hit single *Eighteen With A Bullet*. A projected follow-up album was shelved, but he remained an in-demand session musician and also did some production work for the likes of Dexy's Midnight Runners. He is still active in the music business and was a member of Paul McCartney's 2000 backing band. (VJ/BS)

Wings

Personnel:	DENNY LAINE	gtr, vcls	ABCDE
	LINDA McCARTNEY	keyb'ds, backing vcls	ABCDE
	PAUL McCARTNEY	vcls, gtr, bs	ABCDE
	DENNY SEIWELL	drms, vcls	AB
	HENRY McCULLOUGH	gtr, vcls	B
	GEOFF BRITTON	drms	D
	JIMMY McCULLOCH	gtr, vcls	D
	JOE ENGLISH	drms	DE

HCP

ALBUMS:	1(A)	WILDLIFE	(Apple PCS 7142) 1971	11
(up to	2(B)	RED ROSE SPEEDWAY	(Apple PCTC 252) 1973	5
1976)	3(C)	BAND ON THE RUN	(Apple PAS 10007) 1973	1
	4(E)	VENUS AND MARS	(Capitol PCTC 254) 1975	1
	5(E)	WINGS AT THE SPEED OF SOUND		
			(Capitol PAS 10010) 1976	2
	6(E)	WINGS OVER AMERICA (live, 3-LP)		
			(Capitol PCSP 720) 1976	8

NB: (2) and (3) as Paul McCartney and Wings. (1) reissued on CD on Fame (CDP 752 017 2) 1987 with five additional cuts. (1) reissued on CD (EMI/Toshiba TOCP 65502) 2000 on Japanese import. (2) reissued on CD on Fame (CDFA 3193) 1987 with three additional cuts and available on Japanese import (EMI/Toshiba TOCP 65503) 2000. (3) reissued on vinyl (EMI LPCENT 30) 1997. (3) reissued on CD (Parlophone CDP 746 055 2) 1985 and available on Japanese import (EMI/Toshiba TOCP 65504) 2000. (4) reissued on CD (Fame CDP 746 984 2) 1988 and available on Japanese import (EMI/Toshiba TOCP 65505) 2000. (5) reissued on vinyl 1985 and on CD in 1989 (Parlophone CDP 748 199 2) 1989, on (Fame CDFA 3229) 1989 and on Japanese import (EMI/Toshiba TOCP 65506) 2000. (6) reissued as a CD set (Parlophone CDS 746 715 8) 1987 and on Japanese import as a 3-CD set (EMI/Tochiba TOCP 6055079) 2000. Also relevant is *Wings Greatest* (Parlophone PCTC 256) 1978, also on CD (Parlophone CDP 746 056 2) 1978 and later reissued in 1985. There is also a 2-CD anthology *Wingspan* released in 2001.

HCP

45s:	Give Ireland Back To The Irish/		
(up to	(instrumental version on flip side)	(Apple R 5936) 1972	16
1976)	Mary Had A Little Lamb/		
	Little Woman Love (PS)	(Apple R 5949) 1972	9
	Hi Hi Hi/'C' Moon	(Apple R 5973) 1972	5
α	My Love/The Mess	(Apple R 5985) 1973	9
	Live And Let Die/I Lie Around	(Apple R 5987) 1973	9
α	Helen Wheels/Country Dreamer	(Apple R 5993) 1973	12
α	Jet/Let Me Roll It	(Apple R 5996) 1974	7
αβ	Band On The Run/Zoo Gang	(Apple R 5997) 1974	3
αβ	Junior's Farm/Sally G	(Apple R 5999) 1974	16
	Listen To What The Man Said/		
	Love In Song (Some PS)	(Capitol R 6006) 1975	6
	Letting Go/You Gave Me The Answer	(Capitol R 6008) 1975	41
	Venus And Mars - Rock Show/		
	Magneto And Titanium Man	(Capitol R 6010) 1975	-
χ	Silly Love Songs/Cook Of The House	(Capitol R 6014) 1976	2
χ	Let 'Em In/Beware My Love	(Capitol R 6015) 1976	2

NB: α as Paul McCartney and Wings. β There were also demo versions of these singles with an edited version of the 'A' side on one side and a full version on the other (R2). χ There were demo versions of these in the same format at above (R1).

The problem with **Wings** was that no-one seemed to exercise any quality control over their output. **The Beatles** had challenged and pushed back

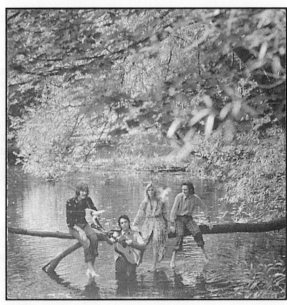

WINGS - Wildlife (LP).

musical frontiers in their illustrious career and influenced countless other bands. At their best **Wings** had marked time - sure Paul wrote and they performed some catchy songs (*Jet, Band On The Run, Listen To What The Man Said, Let 'Em In* etc.) - at their worst they recorded utter drivel and plenty of it.

The Beatles officially split on 11 April 1970, the month before their final album, *Let It Be*, was issued. The previous year on 12 March 1969 **Paul McCartney** had married American-born photographer Linda Eastman and just three weeks prior to the release of *Let It Be* he'd put out his first solo album, *McCartney*, which topped the US Album Charts and got to No 2 here in the UK where Simon and Garfunkel's *Bridge Over Troubled Water* kept it off the top spot. In truth the *McCartney* album was low key and many of the songs had an unfinished quality, it was his name and reputation which guaranteed the high Chart placing. The one track of real quality was *Maybe I'm Amazed*, which he later issued a live version of. Linda provided backing vocals on the album. After a melodic 45, *Another Day*, about the drudgery of office life, which got into the Top Five here and in the US but is now largely forgotten, he co-billed his wife Linda on his next album, *Ram*, and added Denny Seiwell on drums. An inconsistent album, its more memorable tracks included *Back Seat Of My Car* and the sprawling *Uncle Albert/Admiral Halsey*. The album again sold superbly - topping the UK Charts and climbing to No 2 in the US. It also spawned a couple of hit singles:- *Back Seat Of My Car* got to No 39 here and *Uncle Albert/Admiral Halsey* was a US No 1. Incidentally, the back cover of the album has a photo of two beetles copulating. Linda not only contributed backing vocals to this album she handled the keyboards, too, which Paul was teaching her.

Following *Ram* Paul recorded an instrumental album of songs and a 45, *Eat At Home*, under the pseudonym **Percy 'Thrills' Thrillington**. Neither were released until 1977 but both are now collector's items.

Paul launched **Wings** in Autumn 1971 adding former **Moody Blues**, **Balls** and **Uglys** member **Denny Laine** to the earlier trio of himself, Linda and Denny Seiwell. They rehearsed at Paul's farm in Campbeltown, Scotland, and made their vinyl debut in December 1971 with *Wild Life*, a hastily-made simple album which in *Mumbo* and *Bip Bop* included two of his worse songs (and since there were several candidates that's saying something). Its better moments included a version of *Love Is Strange*, which had once been recorded by Buddy Holly and Mickey and Sylvia. It was also earmarked for 45 release but cancelled when, angered by the Bloody Sunday Massacre, when 14 Irish civilians were killed by British soldiers, he recorded *Give Ireland Back To The Irish* instead. Guitarist and vocalist **Henry McCullough**, who'd previously been with **Joe Cocker** among others, was added to the line-up for this 45, which was banned by the BBC because they considered it 'inflammatory'. With little airplay it still got into the Top 20 here and to No 21 in the US. The flip side was simply an instrumental version of the 'A' side. Whatever the pros and cons of recording political songs of this type, it was weak and unadventurous musically. The follow-up, an updated version of the nursery rhyme, *Mary Had A Little Lamb* (recorded because his daughter liked hearing her name in a song), was inane. Nice for children but little else. Of course, such drivel did quite well commercially. It made No 9 here and No 28 in the States.

Wings made their formal concert debut at Chateauvillon, France, on 9 July, but the **McCartneys** were arrested for drug possession later that month in Sweden during a **Wings** European tour and they were arrested again for drug possession at their Scottish farmhouse in September 1972.

In December 1972 they released a good double 'A' side 45, *Hi Hi Hi/C Moon*, but *Hi Hi Hi* again fell foul of a BBC ban because of references to 'getting her' and for the segment "I want you to lie on your bed and get ready for my body gun". This resulted in *C Moon* being promoted and getting to No 5 here, but in the States *Hi Hi Hi* wasn't banned and got to No 10.

Paul could always write a good ballad and the follow-up, *My Love*, with Paul on electric piano and heavy orchestration, was just that. It got to No 9 here but topped the US charts. It was the first of a series of recordings through until the end of 1974 credited to Paul McCartney and Wings rather than simply **Wings**, presumably to try to ensure good sales.

The next album, *Red Rose Speedway*, was another weak one. Tracks like *Hands Of Love* and *Hold Me Tight* did little to enhance their reputation among rock fans and the best tracks were probably the live medley, which included a version of Tommy James and The Shondell's *Mony Mony* and their earlier 45, *My Love*.

Paul was asked by **George Martin** to write the title song for the 'Live And Let Die' movie, the film starring Roger Moore as James Bond 007 and it provided him with a US No 2 and a UK No 9. It was certainly one of the best Bond theme songs. The flip side, *I Lie Around*, featured **Denny Laine** on lead vocals - the only **Wings** 45 to do so. The follow-up, *Helen Wheels*, a song about **McCartney**'s Landrover jeep, peaked at No 12 here and No 10 in the US.

After this **Henry McCullough** went solo and Denny Seiwell switched to session work so *Band On The Run* - one of their finest albums, maybe their best - was recorded by the trio of Linda, Paul and Laine in Lagos, Nigeria. In *Jet* (named after his labrador puppy) it contained the best song he'd written since leaving **The Beatles**, which got to No 7 on both sides of the Atlantic. The title track, a song about musicians' oppression by bureaucrats, also captured **McCartney** near his best. The inspiration for one of the album's more throwaway tracks, *Piccasso's Last Words*, came when Dustin Hoffman, who was filming in Nigeria at the time, uttered them to Paul. *Bluebird* was a pleasant ballad and *Let Me Roll It* recalled much of the style of **The Beatles**' white album. *Mamunia* was the one track which had some African influence. The remaining tracks, *Mrs. Vandebilt, No Words* and *Nineteen Hundred And Eighty Five* were less distinguished but overall it was unquestionably **Wings**' best album to date.

The album sleeve was notable for the photo which featured the group escaping alongside celebrities (left to right) Michael Parkinson, **Kenny Lynch**, James Coburn, Clement Freud, Christopher Lee and John Conteh.

WINGS - Band On The Run (LP).

It spent 73 weeks in the UK Album Charts and topped them on both sides of the Atlantic. The US release included their earlier single *Helen Wheels*.

Wings were now on a high. Ex-**Thunderclap Newman** and **Stone The Crows** guitarist and vocalist Jimmy McCulloch and former **East Of Eden** drummer Geoff Britton were added to the line-up and they travelled to Nashville in 1974 to record *Junior's Farm*, a song about staying with sessionman Norbert Putnam and the flip side, *Sally G*, was about a country singer he met whilst in Nashville. It got to No 16 here and No 3 in the States. Britton soon departed and was later in Champion. Paul replaced Britton with American Joe English, who'd once been in Jam Factory. The revised line-up, now reverting to simply **Wings** rather than Paul McCartney and Wings recorded one of **McCartney**'s masterpieces, *Listen To What The Man Said*, which epitomised his ability to write simple but catchy songs. It also featured **Dave Mason** on guitar and Tom Scott on sax and got to No 6 here but was a No 1 in the US.

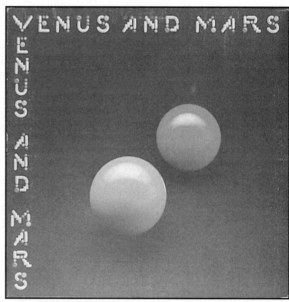

WINGS - Venus And Mars (LP).

Their next album, *Venus And Mars*, topped the Album Charts on both sides of the Atlantic but was very variable musically. It spawned two relatively unsuccessful 45s:- *Letting Go*, which only got to No 41 here and No 39 in the States, and *Venus And Mars: Rock Show*, which failed to chart at all here but got to No 12 in the US. Its flip side, *Magneto And Titanium Man* (also from the album) was inspired by Marvel Comics. Much of the album's music was easy listening and they even recorded the theme from "Crossroads", a long-running TV soap opera.

On 9 September 1975 they commenced a 13-month World Tour of 10 countries at the Gaumont, Southampton. It was largely based on *Venus And Mars* and their next album, *Wings At The Speed Of Sound*, which was definitely one of their better ones. Highlights on this were *Let 'Em In*, which began with door-chimes and was a song about Paul welcoming guests into his house. It mentioned various of Paul's friends and relations; *Beware My Love* and *Warm And Beautiful*, which all captured him on near top form. Paul also gave others the opportunity to write and sing on the album, so Jimmy McCulloch handled vocals on the mediocre *Wino Junko*, which McCulloch co-wrote; Linda handled the vocals on the lame jazz/blues number *Cook Of The House*; Denny sang lead vocals on *The Note You Never Wrote* and *Time To Hide*, which was certainly one of the better tracks; and Joe English handled vocals on the pleasant *Must Do Something About It*. Then, of course, there was *Silly Love Songs*, which when released as a 45 got to No 2 here and No 1 in the US. It was **McCartney** at his most inane and positively irritating to some (like me). *Let 'Em In* also got to No 2 when released as a 45 here but only managed No 3 in the States.

"The Wings World Tour" ended on 21 December 1976 with three nights at London's Empire Pool. *The Wings Over America* live triple album was a 30-track documentary of the US section of their tour. It included most of **Wings**' best known songs and five **Beatles**' songs **McCartney** had co-written with **John Lennon**:- *The Long Winding Road, Lady Madonna, I've Just Seen A Face, Blackbird* and *Yesterday*. It rose to No 8 here and to No 1 in the US.

WINGS - At The Speed Of Sound (LP).

After the tour **Wings** was put on hold during most of 1977, whilst **McCartney** released an instrumental version of *Ram* under the name **Thrillington** and also produced **Denny Laine**'s solo album *Holly Days*. **Wings** returned in Autumn 1977 with *Mull Of Kintyre*, a UK No 1 and one of the biggest selling singles of all time but the type of song you either love or hate. Their 1978 album *London Town* climbed to No 4 in the UK and became a platinum album. *Wings Greatest Hits* reached No 5 later the same year. **McCulloch** then departed for **The Small Faces** and 1979's *Back To The Egg* would prove to be **Wings**' final album. It became another platinum record but failed this time to spawn any big hits. **Wings** undertook a UK tour in the Spring of 1980 but **McCartney**'s next album was a solo effort *McCartney II*. **McCartney**'s reluctance to tour in the wake of **John Lennon**'s murder the following year resulted in **Denny Laine**'s departure from the band which in turn resulted in its demise.

The 2-CD anthology *Wingspan* is a must for both fans and anyone wanting an introduction to the band. The first disc includes many of their hits, often improved by sympathetic remastering. The second disc concentrates on lesser singles and album tracks.

As one might have predicted **Paul McCartney** had definitely been the most successful of the former **Beatles** after they split and he would go on to achieve considerable success after 1976 until the present (reverting to a solo career in late 1979). (VJ)

Wings of a Dove

45:     If You Jumbo Jet Me/Peaceful Life   (Plexium PXM 21) 1971

This was **The Barron Knights** recording a one-off protest single against a proposed airport in Wing, Bedfordshire under a pseudonym. (VJ/MWh)

The Winkies

Personnel:	MIKE DESMARIS	drms	A
	GUY HUMPHREYS	lead gtr	A
	PHIL RAMBOW	vcls, gtr	A
	BRIAN TURRINGTON	bs	A

ALBUM: 1(A)   THE WINKIES   (Chrysalis CHR 1066) 1975

This pub-rock band formed in mid-1973. Phil Rambow was originally from Canada via the USA, where he'd been in a band called Saturday Night. He'd also been in The Ronnie Hawkins Band. Guy Humphreys had been in Holy Rollers.

During February 1974 they toured with **Brian Eno** as his backing band. Soon afterwards they won a recording contract with Chrysalis. In July 1974, they recorded their first album, produced by Leo Lyons (of **Ten Years**

After). It also featured on keyboard Chick Churchill (also of **Ten Years After**) and even **Brian Eno** on one track. Eventually the album was scrapped and remained unreleased. Another, to be produced by Guy Steves, also failed to emerge. Eventually, an eponymous effort saw the light of day in March 1975.

After their demise, Rambow went solo; Humphreys went solo and then joined Fallen Angels in August 1976; Turrington headed for National Flag and Desmaris was in the Tyla Gang. (VJ/JM)

Jimmy Winston (and His Reflections)

45s:	Sorry She's Mine/It's Not What You Do (But		
	The Way That You Do It)	(Decca F 1240) 1966 R3	
α	Sun In The Morning/Just Wanna Smile	(Nems NEMS 12) 1976	

NB: α a **Jimmy Winston** solo effort.

Jimmy Winston was the **The Small Faces**' original organist, and appeared with them in the 1965 movie 'Dateline Diamonds', singing *I've Got Mine*. He formed this band after he left them. The 'A' side, *Sorry She's Mine*, was a good version of a song which also appeared on **The Small Faces**' debut album, and the single is now extremely expensive. The band later evolved into **Winston's Fumbs** (see below).

Compilation appearances include: *It's Not What You Do* on *The Mod Scene* (CD) and *Echoes From The Wilderness - Sixteen UK R&B Freakbeat Trippers* (LP & CD); *Sorry She's Mine* on *The Freakbeat Scene* (CD); and *Sorry She's Mine* and *It's Not What You Do* on *Nowhere Men, Vol. 2* (CD) and *Yellow Elektric Years* (LP). (VJ/RMJ)

Norma Winstone

ALBUM: 1   EDGE OF TIME   (Argo ZDA 148) 1971 R2

Born on September 23rd, 1941 in London, **Winstone** is a versatile singer and vocal improviser. She studied piano and organ for three years, then began singing with jazz groups in 1965. She joined The New Jazz Orchestra in 1966, and later became a member of Michael Garrick's group. *Edge Of Time* was produced by Peter Eden, renowned for his work with **Donovan**, **Bill Fay**, **Heron** and others. **Winstone** later married and worked with John Taylor, and has since performed with many of Europe's leading groups, orchestras, and combos. She formed the group Azimuth in the seventies, and has continued to tour and sing throughout Europe.

In her time she has worked with: Azimuth, Sarah Vaughan, **Nucleus**, **Henry Lowther**, **Mike Westbrook**, Tony Levin, Alan Skidmore and Ian Carr. She has also appeared on **Neil Ardley**'s *Harmony Of Spheres* (1979), and **Heads Hands and Feet**'s *Old Soldiers Never Die* (1973). (VZ/RMJ)

Winston's Fumbs

Personnel:	TONY KAYE	keyb'ds	A
	ALEX PARIS	bs	A
	RAY STOCK	drms	A
	JIMMY WINSTON	vcls, gtr	A

45:     Real Crazy Apartment/Snow White   (RCA RCA 1612) 1967 R4

Winston formed this outfit after splitting from **His Reflections**. Stock and Paris had been with **Casey Jones and The Engineers** and later **The Truth's** backing band, The Unknown. Tony Kaye had been in **The Federals**. Both sides of this rare 45 are highly recommended - *Real Crazy Apartment* is a manic rocker and *Snow White* is full of psychedelic undertones.

After their demise, **Winston** went on to appear in 'Hair'. He also made a solo 45 in 1976. Alex Paris briefly joined **Arthur Brown**, while Stock and Kaye linked up in the exotically-named Yellow Passion Fruit, who later renamed themselves Bitter Sweet. They spent weeks rehearsing in Scotland, but never performed, let alone recorded. Kaye later joined **Yes** and appeared on their first three albums.

Compilation appearances include: *Real Crazy Apartment* on *Yellow Elektric Years* (LP) and on the 4-CD *Nuggets II* box set; *Real Crazy Apartment* and *Snow White* on *Beat It* (3-CD); and *Snow White* on *Chocolate Soup* (CD) and *Chocolate Soup For Diabetics, Vol. 2* (LP). (VJ/RMJ)

Stevie Winwood

Though **Steve Winwood** didn't make his solo debut until 1977, his importance to British pop and rock in the era covered by this book is such that he merits an entry. One of Britain's foremost white soul/blues singers, he is also a superb songwriter and instrumentalist (especially keyboardist), and played on some of the most influential records of the period.

He was born on 12 May 1948 in Birmingham. Always musical, he was playing with his elder brother Muff and Pete York in The Muff-Woody Jazz Band in The Golden Eagle, a local pub, when they were spotted by **Spencer Davis**, who was playing an acoustic blues set at the same venue. He quickly recruited them and in August 1963 they became the **Spencer Davis Group**. A year later they secured a recording contract with Chris Blackwell's Island Records. **Winwood** was only in his teens at the time, but it was his superbly soulful vocals that gave the R&B band their special ingredient, on classic songs such as *I'm A Man* and *Keep On Running*.

He's also rumoured to have been involved in a 1965 45 by **The Anglos**, a R&B outfit (who may have been American) - no one seems sure. He also cut two songs with Powerhouse, a session band assembled by **Eric Clapton** for a 1966 Elektra session, using the name Steve Anglo.

At the start of 1967 he left the **Spencer Davis Group** to form **Traffic**, one of Britain's finer bands of the period. He also played on albums by **Jimi Hendrix**, **Gordon Jackson** and others. When **Traffic** disintegrated for the first time in early 1969, he formed **Blind Faith**, a short-lived supergroup which failed to fulfil their promise. He was then briefly in **Ginger Baker's Airforce**.

In 1970 **Winwood** began work on a solo album (provisionally titled *Mad Shadows*). **Jim Capaldi** and Chris Wood assisted him on the sessions, and **Traffic** soon reformed as a trio. The album was eventually released as *John Barleycorn Must Die*, and **Winwood** remained in **Traffic**'s various line-ups until their eventual demise in 1974. He went on to record six solo albums and several 45s, beyond the time span of this book.

There's a 4-CD set, *The Finer Things*, 1995 which includes material from his days with the **Spencer Davis Group**, **Traffic**, **Blind Faith** and his solo career. Only three previously unreleased cuts are featured, though, all from his time with **Blind Faith**. There's an electric version of *Can't Find My Way Home* and two cover versions from the band's Hyde Park Concert - **The Rolling Stones**' *Under My Thumb* and Sam Myers' *Sleeping In The Ground*. Alternatively *Keep On Running* (Island IMCD 224) 1995 compiles some of his first moments with **The Spencer Davis Group**, **Traffic** and **Blind Faith** plus some of his better solo material.

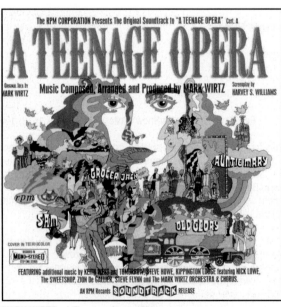

MARK WIRTZ - A Teenage Opera (CD).

Winwood is best remembered as one of Britain's foremost white blues singers and his vocal performances with **The Spencer Davis Group** knock the spots off any of his work in the last 25 years. (VJ/RMJ)

Wire Machine

Two cuts by this band: - *The Doves* and *Mind Fascination*, were recorded in 1969. Both are pretty standard guitar-led progressive rock.

Compilation appearances include: *The Doves* on *Circus Days Vol. 1 & 2* (CD); *Mind Fascination* on *Circus Days Vol. 3* (CD); and *The Doves* and *Mind Fascination* on *Circus Days, Vol. 2* (LP). (VJ)

Mark Wirtz

CD:	1	A TEENAGE OPERA: THE ORIGINAL SOUNDTRACK RECORDING	(RPM RPM 165) 1996

45s:	(He's Our Dear Old) Weatherman (From "A Teenage Opera")/ Possum's Dance	(Parlophone R 5668) 1968 SC
	Mrs Raven/Knickerbocker Glory	(Parlophone R 5683) 1968
	My Daddie Is A Baddie/I Love You Because	(CBS 4306) 1969
	Caroline/Goody, Goody, Goody	(CBS 4539) 1969

Composer **Mark Wirtz** first came to light when he collaborated with **Keith West** on the 'Teenage Opera' project, which was never completed. When **West** walked out after the *Sam* single flopped, **Wirtz** soldiered on releasing *Weatherman* (another 'excerpt' from the unfinished teenage opera project). This contained his usual mix of a good tune, children's voices and sound effects. It was **West**, however, who enjoyed the hits. He was later involved in **Philwit and Pegasus**. See also **Mood Mosaic** and **Sweet Shop**. **Wirtz** was German and settled in London early in 1965. I've included him because of his involvement in many British projects.

Wirtz also produced an album *Ten Again* (World Record Club T 452) by Belle Gonzalez and Russ Loader in 1964.

The retrospective CD *A Teenage Opera: The Original Soundtrack Recording* isn't quite as the original project (which never saw the light of day) might have appeared. However, compiled with **Mark Wirtz**'s help it's as close as anyone is likely to get to it. Superbly packaged and compiled it assembles **Keith West**'s singles, related tracks by **Tomorrow** and obscurities produced by **Wirtz** and recorded under various pseudonyms such as **Steve Flynn** (*Mr Rainbow*), Zion De Gallier and Astronaut Alan and The Planets (*Fickle Lizzie Anne*). Interspersed between all this are some inventive instrumental cuts by the Mark Wirtz Orchestra, which repeat and extend themes from the vocal tracks.

(He's Our Dear Old) Weatherman has been compiled on *Psychedelia At Abbey Road* (CD), *Rubble, Vol. 3 - Nightmares In Wonderland* (LP) and *Rubble, Vol. 2* (CD). (VJ)

Wishbone Ash

Personnel:	MARTIN TURNER	bs, vcls	ABC
	TED TURNER	gtr	AB
	GLEN TURNER	gtr	A
	STEVE UPTON	drms	AB
	ANDREW POWELL	gtr	BC
	LAURIE WISEFIELD	gtr	C

HCP

ALBUMS:	1(B)	WISHBONE ASH	(MCA MKPS 2014) 1970 SC 34
(up to	2(B)	PILGRIMAGE	(MCA MDKS 8004) 1971 SC 14
1976)	3(B)	ARGUS	(MCA MDKS 8006) 1972 SC 3
	4(B)	WISHBONE FOUR	(MCA MDKS 8011) 1973 SC 12
	5(B)	LIVE DATES (2-LP)	(MCA MCSP 254) 1974 SC -
	6(C)	THERE'S THE RUB	(MCA MCF 2585) 1974 16
	7(C)	LOCKED IN	(MCA MCF 2750) 1976 36
	8(C)	NEW ENGLAND	(MCA MCG 3523) 1976 22

NB: The band continued to record well into the nineties. (1) reissued on CD (BGO BGOCD 234). (2) reissued on CD (MCA DMCL 1762) 1991 and on vinyl (MCA

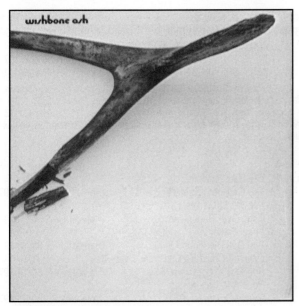

WISHBONE ASH - Wishbone Ash (LP).

10233). (3) reissued on CD remastered (MCA Decca 1128162) 2002 as a 30th Anniversary issue with three bonus tracks from the *Live At Memphis* promo EP. (4) reissued on CD (MCA MCAD 10350) 1991 and again (MCA MCLD 19149). (5) reissued on CD (BGO BGOCD 293). (7) reissued on CD (Repertoire REP 4557-WY) 1995. (8) reissued on a 2-CD set (along with *Front Page News* from 1977) (BGO BGOCD 405).

Compilation releases include *Wishbone Ash In Concert* (Windsong WINCCD 4) 1991; *Classic Ash* (LP) (MCA MCF 2795) 1977 and (CD) (MCA MCD 10578) 1977 (later reissued in 1981 and again in 1983 on Fame); *The Best Of Wishbone Ash* (MCA MCF 3134) 1981; *The Very Best Of Wishbone Ash:Blowin' Free* (Nectar NTRCD 014) 1994 and *Distillation* (Repertoire REP 4649-CX) 1997 is a 4-CD box set. *The Best Of Wishbone Ash* (MCA MCAD-11620) 1997 includes a previously unissued version of *Lorelei* from 1976 and an acoustic version of *Blowin' Free* (from 1997). *Tracks* (Talking Elephant TECD 045) 2002 is a 2-CD set containing previously unreleased live material from 1972-2001, which will interest fans and collectors. *Time Was - The Live Anthology* (Castle CMDDD 960) is a 2-CD set featuring recordings from 1970, 1973, 1976 and 1991 and it comes with a detailed illustrated booklet. *Lost Pearls* (CD) (Talking Elephant TEDCD 064) sometimes known as The Pig Sty Tapes contains 'lost' tapes from the seventies which have eventually been located and remixed by original member Martin Turner. *Backbones* (3-CD) (Talking Elephant TEDCD 071) compiles their better-known tracks on 2-CDs and the third bonus one has three previously unreleased live tracks and a 50-minute interview with Andy Powell. It's packaged in a lush triple digipak and features many previously unpublished photos of the band. *Warriors* (2-CD) (Snapper SMDCD 483) mixes their most popular numbers alongside some seldom heard nuggets.

45s:	Blind Eye/Queen Of Torture	(MCA MK 5061) 1971
(up to	Blowin' Free/No Easy Road	(MCA MKS 5097) 1972
1976)	So Many Things To Say/	
	Rock And Roll Widow	(MCA MU 1210) 1973
	Hometown/Persephone	(MCA MCA 165) 1974
	Silver Shoes/Persephone	(MCA MCA 176) 1975
	Outward Bound/Lorelei	(MCA MCA 261) 1976

Wishbone Ash was one of the most popular British hard-rock acts of the early and mid-seventies. It was also one of the most durable - still working in new millenium.

Martin Turner and Steve Upton formed **Wishbone Ash** in Torquay, Devon, in 1969 along with Martin's brother Glen. They'd earlier played together in various south-west groups. Glen Turner was soon forced to leave due to health problems and the band moved up to London with Ted Turner (no relation) and Andrew Powell, who'd come in as a replacement for Glen.

After signing to MCA they recorded their debut album in 1970. Essentially mainstream rock characterised by the twin guitars of Powell and Ted Turner some likened them to a British version of The Allman Brothers. It took them into the UK Album Charts peaking at No 34.

They began to build up a strong following in the UK, mostly around the clubs and colleges during the early seventies. Their next album, *Pilgrimage*, consolidated their earlier success, peaking at No 14 in the UK. This is full of instrumentation and some self-indulgent solos, but already their limitations vocally were becoming apparent. Tracks like *Vas Dis*, *The Pilgrim*, *Lullaby* and *Valediction* were pleasant enough but lacking in

excitement and, perhaps, imagination. They have not aged well. The lengthy *Where Were You Tomorrow* (which also features some melodic guitar work) and *Jail Bait*, were livelier and arguably the highlights. They have more vocals, too!

Their third album, *Argus*, is usually considered their definite offering. Rising to No 3 it was certainly their most successful commercially. This was their most varied album but somehow they failed to capitalise on its success reverting back to their earlier mainstream rock format for *Wishbone Four*. They failed to forge a distinctive identity and lacked real charisma on stage. Their albums also lack much musical excitement, although their double *Live Dates* album released in January 1974 is one of their better efforts.

Ted Turner, having got into religion, departed in June 1974 being replaced by former **Home** guitarist Laurie Wisefield. They also relocated to the East Coast of the USA which offered them a more favourable tax environment than the UK. *There's The Rub* was recorded in Miami and included the instrumental track, *F*U*B*B*, which stood for *Fucked Up Beyond Belief*.

By now they were almost adopted Americans. Their music became more country-ish (ugh!) and they toured the US frequently, but seldom came to the UK. *Locked In*, their seventh album, was produced by Tom Dowd and session man Peter Wood (formerly of **Sutherland Brothers and Quiver**) was featured on keyboards.

They continued to record well beyond the time span of this book. After 1979's *Just Testing* Martin Turner was replaced by John Wetton (whose former bands included **Family** and **King Crimson**). They continued to record in the eighties; initially on MCA (releasing albums such as *Number The Brave* and *Both Barrels Burning*) and later linked up with Stewart Copeland, releasing three albums on his new I.R.S. label. They worked throughout the nineties (with line-ups led by Andy Powell and Ted Turner) and continue to tour and record in the new millennium.

Distillation is a 4-CD, 56-track box set released by Repertoire in 1997. The first disc comprises 13 tracks from the 1970 to 1974 period and includes all their early favourites from their first line-up. Disc two covers from 1974 to their 1987 reunion. The third disc (subtitled Rarities) covers more recent material, obscurios and three later unreleased tracks. Finally, the fourth disc features live performances from their second line-up. It also came with a 30-page booklet including a lengthy history of the band and track-by-track analysis.

Tracks, a 2-CD set released in 2002, should excite fans and collectors as it contains previously unreleased live material. Anyone wanting to sample their sound could do no worse than to track down a copy of *Classic Ash*, which was originally issued in 1977 and reissued a couple of times in the early eighties. Generally, though, their early seventies music has not aged well.

Mystery Man has been compiled on *Classic Rock* (CD). (VJ/TV)

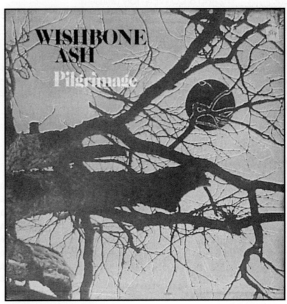

WISHBONE ASH - Pilgrimage (LP).

Wishful Thinking

Personnel:
BRIAN ALLEN	drms		ABCD
ROGER CHARLES	bs		AB
RAY DANIEL	vcls		AB
TERRY NEW	gtr, vcls		A
JOHN FRANKLIN	gtr		BCD
TONY COLLIER	bs, vcls		CD
KEVIN SCOTT	vcls		C
DANNY FINN	vcls, gtr		D

ALBUMS: 1(B) LIVE VOL 1   (Decca SKL 4900) 1967 R1
         2 (C) HIROSHIMA   (B & C CAS 1038) 1971 SC

NB: (1) has been issued on CD.

45s:
Turning Round/V.I.P.	(Decca F 12438)	1966
Step By Step/Looking Around	(Decca F12499)	1966
Count To Ten/Hang Around Girl	(Decca F 12598)	1967
Peanuts / Cherry Cherry	(Decca F 12627)	1967
Meet The Sun/		
Easter Said Than Loving You	(Decca F 22673)	1967
Alone/Vegetables (export issue)	(Decca F 22742)	1968
It's So Easy/I Want You Girl	(Decca F 12760)	1968
Lu La Le Lu/We're Gonna Change All This	(B & C CB 169)	1971
Clear White Light/Hiroshima	(B & C CB 184)	1972

Possibly from Birmingham, in 1966 **Wishful Thinking** signed to Decca, for whom they recorded various light popsike tunes and a scarce album (which is not live!). Terry New (formerly of **The Lively Set**) left in October 1966, and John Franklin replaced him for the album. They toured Scandinavia and were popular there.

Daniel and Charles then left and Scott and Collier joined in time to record the *Hiroshima* album. It's certainly rare, but those expecting to discover a neglected progressive gem will be disappointed. Most of the eleven tracks are conventional three-minute beat group fodder that could easily have originated back in Merseybeat days - not what one expects from the sleeve, with its blood-red storm clouds. The title track is indeed about the city destroyed by the atomic bomb, but it sits oddly with much of the other material. Two slightly more interesting and futuristic tracks are *The United States of Europe '79* and *1984*, with interesting phasing effects. Every song on the album is written by a Dave Morgan, whose connection with the band is not apparent. Eventually Scott left, and Danny Finn joined briefly before their demise.

Compilation appearances include: *Step By Step* and *Is She A Woman Now* on *Red With Purple Flashes, Vol. 2* (LP); and *V.I.P.* on *Beat Us If You Can! Vol. 1* (LP). (BM/VJ/JM/NM/DS)

Wizard's Convention

ALBUM: 1   WIZARD'S CONVENTION (w/insert)
                                              (RCA RS 1085) 1976 SC

NB: (1) Reissued on CD (Repertoire REP 4474-WY) 1994 with six bonus tracks.

This was a pop-orientated album inspired by **Roger Glover**'s *Butterfly Ball* project. It was stage-managed by Eddie Hardin and featured a plethora of guest musicians, including Tony Ashton, David Coverdale, **Mike D'Abo**, Ray Fenwick, **Jon Lord** and Henry Spinetti. (VJ)

Wizzard

Personnel:
MIKE BURNEY	sax		AB
CHARLIE GRIMA	drms		AB
NICK PENTELOW	sax		AB
RICK PRICE	bs, vcls		AB
KEITH SMART	drms		AB
BILL HUNT	keyb'ds		A
HUGH McDOWELL	cello		A
ROY WOOD	gtr, vcls		AB
BOB BRADY	keyb'ds		B

ALBUMS: 1(A)   WIZZARD BREW   (Harvest SHSP 4025) 1973 SC 29
         2(A)   INTRODUCING EDDY AND THE FALCONS
                                              (Warners K 56029) 1974 19
         3(B)   SEE MY BABY JIVE   (Harvest SHSP 4034) 1974 -

NB: (2) reissued on CD (Edsel EDCD 624) 2000 There's also a compilation, *The Best And The Rest of Roy Wood And Wizzard* (Action Replay CDAR 1009) 1989 and *You Can Dance The Rock 'n' Roll* (Roy Wood Years '71-73) (Harvest CZ 177) 1989 (on vinyl too but with fewer tracks) includes tracks by **Wizzard** as well as **The Move**.

45s:
Ball Park Incident/		
The Carlsberg Special	(Harvest HAR 5062)	1972 6
See My Baby Jive/		
Bend Over Beethoven	(Harvest HAR 5070)	1973 1
Angel Fingers/		
You Got The Jump On Me	(Harvest HAR 5076)	1973 1
I Wish It Could Be Christmas Every Day/		
Rob Roy's Nightmare (PS)	(Harvest HAR 5079)	1973 4
Rock And Roll Winter/		
Dream Of Unwin (PS)	(Warners K 16357)	1974 6
This Is The Story Of My Love (Baby)/		
Nixture	(Warners K 16434)	1974 34
You've Got Me Running/		
It's Just My Imagination	(Warners K 16466)	1974 -
Are You Ready To Rock/		
Marathon Man	(Warners K 16447)	1974 8
Rattlesnake Roll/Can't Help Me Feelings	(Jet JET 758)	1975 -

Reissues:
See My Baby Jive/Angel Fingers		
Ball Park Incident	(Harvest HAR 5106)	1976 -
I Wish It Could Be Christmas Every Day/		
Rob Roy's Nightmare	(Harvest HAR 5173)	1982 41
I Wish It Could Be Christmas Every Day/		
Rob Roy's Nightmare	(Harvest HAR 5173)	1984 23
α See My Baby Jive/Angel Fingers		
Ball Park Incident	(Old Gold OG 6180)	1992 -

NB: α CD EP.

Upon the demise of the Birmingham-based group, **The Move**, **Roy Wood** briefly collaborated with guitarist Jeff Lynne on what was originally known as The Wood-Lynne project, although it soon became known as the **Electric Light Orchestra**. However, despite their debut 45, *10538 Overture*, reaching the Top 10, **Roy Wood** soon lost interest in this concept and formed his own new band **Wizzard**. In many ways they were the antipathy of **ELO**, who were a disciplined outfit with considerable musical finesse. **Wizzard** were a fun band. **Wood**'s multi-coloured hair and clothes set the tone for the band whose gigs were a kind of bizarre circus. They became a leading glam-rock act. Their debut at a Wembley extravaganza on 5 August 1973 set the ball rolling and their ability to produce fine rock singles with wide commercial appeal ensured it never stopped. Their debut - *Ball Park Incident* - made the UK Top 10 and thereafter they produced a

WIZZARD - Introducing Eddy And The Falcons (LP).

938

string of memorable hits:- *See My Baby Jive, Angel Fingers, I Wish It Could Be Christmas Every Day, Rock And Roll Winter* and *Are You Ready To Rock* all made the UK Top Ten and the first two topped the Charts. Success in the US proved much harder to achieve. They embarked on an unsuccessful US tour in November 1974 and it was their management's refusal to even finance a second one in October 1975 when led to their demise. They were very much a 'singles' band, although their albums sold quite well over here at any rate. Their second one, *Introducing Eddy And The Falcons*, was rather unusual in that each of the tracks was in the style of a fifties rock'n'roll hero. People like Duane Eddy, Elvis Presley, Del Shannon, Neil Sedaka and Gene Vincent were all featured in this tribute.

Wizzard will perhaps be best remembered for producing one of the Christmas hits - *I Wish It Could Be Christmas Every Day*. This has been reissued at Christmas-time on several occasions and actually re-charted in 1981 and 1984, peaking at Nos 41 and 23 respectively.

Roy Wood also enjoyed a moderately successful solo career during his years with **Wizzard** and he continued it after they split. Later in 1977 he formed a new band The Wizzo Band, which also included **Rick Price**, although their story is beyond the time span of this book. Bob Brady, who'd earlier been in **The Applejacks** went on to play for **Fairport Convention**. Keith Smart joined a later line-up of **The Rockin' Berries** and Nick Pentelow went on tour with **Steve Gibbons**. Charlie Grima later became an actor. (VJ)

Wolfe

Personnel:
JOHN PANTRY	keyb'ds	A
JOHN RICHMOND	ld gtr, banjo, piano	A
NICK RYAN	bs	A
ROBIN SLATER	gtr, vcls	A
MIKE WADE	drms, vcls	A

ALBUM: 1(A) WOLFE (Rare Earth R451L) 1972
NB: (1) US only release.

Recorded at IBC Sound studios in the UK, this US-only album includes the final **Peter and The Wolves** 45, *Something In The Way She Moves* plus songs by Leslie Duncan, Chinn/Chapman, Wirtz/Ife, Scott (sic) English, Larry Weis and several **Pantry** originals. It was produced by Nick Ryan and **John Pantry**.

It's of marginal interest for the psych fan, as some songs do have a very sixties pop/bubblegum psych feel to them, and there is even a bit of fuzz, but there are also some dodgy synth sounds that are definitely early seventies. Not something to rush out and spend a fortune on. (MJ)

Wolfpack

English Freakbeat, Vol. 2 (LP & CD) includes the brief *We're Gonna Howl* by this outfit, which is rumoured to be **The Animals** under a pseudonym. I've no release details for it so it may have remained unreleased until its appearance on the 1989 compilation. (VJ)

Wolfrilla

45: Song For Jimmi/Come Tomorrow (Concord CON 015) 1970

This is a fine heavy rock single which has yet to attract interest from collectors. (MWh)

The Wolves

Personnel:
JOHN EADES	gtr	A
WILLIAM FEDER	bs, gtr	A
BOBBY HOLT	vcls	A
TREVOR LANGHAM	organ	A
CLIVE NICHOLLS	drms	A

JUSTAFIXATION (Comp LP) featuring Wonderland.

45s: Journey Into Dreams/
What Do You Mean (Pye 7N 15676) 1964 SC
Now/This Time Next Year (Pye 7N 15733) 1964 SC
At The Club/Distant Dreams (Pye 7N 17013) 1965 SC
Lust For Life/
My Baby Loves Them (Parlophone R 5511) 1966 R2

A Wolverhampton band which was managed by **Jonathan King**. *At The Club* was a Goffin/King number.

Compilation appearances include: *Lust For Life* on *Perfumed Garden Vol. 3* (CD); *At The Club* on *Ripples, Vol. 4* (CD); and *Now* on *Watch Your Step* (CD). (VJ/JM)

Wonderland

45: Poochy/Moscow (Polydor 56539) 1968

This was a one-off seventies venture. *Moscow* later resurfaced on *Justafixation* (LP). (VJ)

Wonderwheel

Personnel:
BRYSON GRAHAM	drms	A
MICK JONES	gtr, vcls	A
ARCHIE LEGGET	bs, vcls	A
GARY WRIGHT	keyb'ds, vcls	A

ALBUMS: 1(-) EXTRACTION (A&M AMLS 2004) 1971 SC
2(A) FOOTPRINT (A&M AMLS 64296) 1972 SC

45: Ring Of Changes/Somebody (A&M AMS 7034) 1972

When he left **Spooky Tooth Gary Wright** recorded *Extraction* as a solo album and then formed **Wonderwheel** to help promote it in the Spring of 1971. They then recorded *Footprint*, which aroused very little interest and by the end of Summer 1972 they'd quit. Graham, Jones and **Wright** all reformed **Spooky Tooth**, whilst Legget went on to play for **Kevin Ayers**. (VJ)

Hayden Wood

45s: The Lady Wants More/
The House Beside The Mine (Nems 56-4499) 1969
Sixty Years On/The Last One To Know (Nems 56-4803) 1970
That's A Mighty Road/Star Restaurant (Jam 3) 1972
The Spring Of '68/Where Are We All Going To (Jam 21) 1972
I Don't Wanna Lose You/Hand Me Down (Jam 46) 1973

The House Beside The Mine is a wonderful mid-tempo ballad with a fuzz-raga lead guitar and really cool phasing effects in the background rhythm section. His remaining singles are strictly folk-pop and are of little interest.

The House Beside The Mine has been compiled on *Justafixation* (LP), *Best Of Rubble Collection, Vol. 6* (CD), *Psychedelic Archives, Vol. 1* (cassette) and *Rubble, Vol. 11* (CD). (BM)

Ronnie Wood

ALBUMS:	1	I'VE GOT MY OWN ALBUM TO DO		
(up to			(Warner Bros K 56065)	1974 SC
1976)	2	NOW LOOK	(Warner Bros K 56145)	1975
	3	MAHONEY'S LAST STAND (Soundtrack)		
			(Atlantic K 50308)	1976 SC

NB: (3) with **Ronnie Lane**. (3) reissued on CD (Thunderbolt CDTB 067) 1988.

45s:	I Can Feel The Fire/		
(up to	Breathe On Me	(Warner Bros K 16463)	1974
1976)	If You Don't Want Me Love/		
	I've Got A Feeling	(Warner Bros K 16618)	1975
	Big Bayou/Sweet Baby Mine	(Warner Bros K 16679)	1976

Ronnie Wood showed an interest in guitar at a young age. He loved jazz but it was **The Rolling Stones** who got him interested in music. His brother Art Wood played with **Alexis Korner** and they developed his interest in R&B. **The Rolling Stones**' drummer Charlie Watts was in **Alexis Korner**'s original band with Art Wood.

Ronnie Wood's first band was The Thunderbirds, but when **Chris Farlowe and The Thunderbirds** came along they abbreviated their name to **The Birds**. When **The Birds** split he played in a studio band called Santa Barbara Machine Head which included **The Creation**'s Kim Gardner, and in 1968, **Wood** filled in for Eddie Phillips in **Creation** on a German tour when Diana Ross and The Supremes opened for them. He and Kim Gardner then joined **The Jeff Beck Group** and **Wood** played bass on *The Truth* and *Beck-Ola* albums. When the **Jeff Beck Group** split (two weeks before a scheduled Woodstock appearance) he went on to join **The Faces** who had an awesome live reputation in the seventies. He recorded his first solo album whilst with **The Faces** and continued a solo career after joining **The Rolling Stones** in April 1975 as lead guitarist. He continued with his solo projects, including a soundtrack with **Ronnie Lane** and he went on to record two albums *Give Me More Neck* (CBS 83337) 1979 and *1234* (CBS 85227) 1981 and further 45s beyond the time frame of this book.

In November 1990 he broke both legs in a car accident. (VJ)

Roy Wood

				HCP
ALBUMS:	1	BOULDERS	(Harvest SHVL 803)	1973 15
(up to	2	MUSTARD	(Jet JETLP 12)	1975 -
1976)	3	THE ROY WOOD STORY (2-LP Compilation)		
			(Harvest SHDW 408)	1976 -

NB: (1) was reissued on Harvest (SHSM 2021) 1977. (2) reissued on CD as *Mustard... Plus* (Edsel EDCD 625) 2000. Another vinyl-only compilation was *The Best Of Roy Wood (1970-1974)* (Music For Pleasure MFP 4156971) 1985. *The Singles* (Connoisseur VSOP CD 189) 1993 is an over 75-minute CD of all his finest 45s from his early days with **The Move** through to his mid-seventies work with **Wizzard**, originally issued on vinyl on Speed (SPEED 1000) in 1982, when it got to No 37. (3) reissued as *You Can Dance The Rock 'n' Roll (Roy Wood Years '71-'73)* (Harvest SHSM 2030) 1989 also includes **Move** and **Wizzard** material from this era. The CD edition (Harvest CDP 792 5862) includes four more tracks than the vinyl equivalent. *Outstanding Performer!* (Castle CMQCD 447) 2003 is an 18-track compilation of his seventies and eighties output.

			HCP
45s:	When Grandma Plays The Banjo/		
(up to	Wake Up	(Harvest HAR 5048)	1972 -
1976)	Dear Elaine/Songs Of Praise	(Harvest HAR 5074)	1973 18
	Forever/		
	Music To Commit Suicide By	(Harvest HAR 5078)	1973 8
	Going Down The Road/		
	The Premium Bond Theme	(Harvest HAR 5083)	1974 13

	Oh What A Shame/Bengal Jin	(Jet JET 754)	1975 13
	Looking Through The Eyes Of A Fool/		
	Strider	(Jet JET 761)	1975 -
α	Indiana Rainbow/		
	The Thing Is This (This Is The Thing)	(Jet JET 768)	1976 -
	Any Old Time Will Do/		
	The Rain Came Down On Everything	(Jet JET 785)	1976 -

NB: α credited to Roy Wood's Wizzard Single.

Roy Wood was one of the most influential rock musicians to come out of Birmingham in the era of this book. His early bands were **Gerry Levene and The Avengers** (1963-64) and **Mike Sheridan and The Nightriders** (1964-66) but he first came to the public eye in **The Move** who were the most successful sixties band to come out of Birmingham. **The Move** evolved into the **Electric Light Orchestra** (ELO) in 1971, but after a brief flirtation with **ELO**, **Wood** left in July 1972 to form his own band **Wizzard** whilst pursuing a solo career alongside this. His second solo 45, *Dear Elaine*, reached the UK Top 20. Indeed its 'B' side, *Songs Of Praise*, had just missed being the UK's Eurovision Song Contest entry the previous year.

His debut album, *Boulders*, made the UK Top 20 and reached No 173 in the US, which was something none of **Wizzard**'s albums could ever manage.

He enjoyed further hit singles with *Forever, Going Down The Road* and *Oh What A Shame*, but his second album, *Mustard*, which featured contributions from Phil Everly and his girlfriend, Annie Haslam (of **Renaissance**) was a flop. Despite epics like, *The Rain Came Down On Everything*, and *Any Time Will Do*; a Brain Wilson tribute (*Why Does A Pretty Girl Sing Those Sad Songs*) and the Spectre-influenced *Look Thru' The Eyes Of A Fool* no hit single emerged. Not even its repackaging as *Roy Wood The Wizzard* with the addition of two Top 10 **Wizzard** hit singles, *Rock And Roll Winter* and *Are You Ready To Rock* and his own hit single, *Oh What A Shame*, could reverse this.

By 1976 he'd run into managerial problems and committed himself to three different labels EMI/Harvest, Jet and Warner. The *Indiana Rainbow* 45 was taken from a projected album, *Wizzo*, which never saw the light of day as his solo career seemed to plummet with the demise of **Wizzard**.

He returned in 1977 with The Wizzo Band, although this proved a rather short-lived venture. He went on to write for and produce other acts including Darts and formed a live band, The Helicopters.

By the end of the seventies his best years, in musical terms, were well behind him but he popped up occasionally during the eighties doing interesting things. In 1983, for example, he sang *Message In A Bottle* on the album *Arrested*, a collection of The Police's songs performed by various rock musicians and the Royal Philharmonic Orchestra. In 1986 he played on Doctor and The Medics' cover of Abba's *Waterloo*, which made the lower echelons of the Top 50.

WOODEN HORSE - Wooden Horse II (CD).

Outstanding Performer! is a bit of a rag bag of his seventies and eighties output with **Wizzard,** as well as his solo recordings. It omits his Christmas hit (the song most people associate with him) and includes a selection of strong well-arranged material.

Dear Elaine can also be heard on *Harvest Heritage - 20 Greats* (LP). (VJ)

Wooden Horse

Personnel:	NEIL BROCKBANK	bs	A
	MALCOLM HARRISON	gtr, vcls	A
	STEVE MARWOOD	gtr, vcls	A
	DAVID MATEER	gtr, vcls	A
	SUSAN TRAYNOR	vcls	A

ALBUMS:	1(A)	WOODEN HORSE	(York FYK 403) 1972 R3
	2(A)	WOODEN HORSE II	(York FYK 413) 1973 R5

NB: (2) was scheduled for release and then withdrawn, making it extremely rare. In December 2004, 'Record Collector' valued this item at £900. (2) reissued on CD (Elegy E570/1).

45s:	Pick Up The Pieces/	
	Wake Me In The Morning	(York SYK 526) 1972 SC
	Wooden Horses/Typewriter And Guitar	(York SYK 543) 1973 SC

A pleasant-enough folk outfit whose sound was characterised by Susan Traynor's fragile vocals, which are similar to those in **Trees** and **Spriguns**, and some good guitar work. It seems the band was originally from Australia and was booked as a warm-up band at the Palladium with Raphael at the top of the bill. Back in Australia they'd had a successful cabaret career behind them, but they stayed in England after the Palladium Show. Their tight harmonies bore resemblance to Peter, Paul and Mary, but without such a professional finish.

The first album is rare enough, but the second is very difficult to track down, as it is alleged to have been withdrawn from sale.

Traynor later resurfaced as Noosha in pop/rock combo **Fox.** (VJ/JM)

Wooden O

Personnel:	HUGO D'ALTON	mandolin	A
	JAMES HARPHAM	recorder	A
	DAVID SNELL	harp	A
	CHRISTOPHER TAYLOR	recorder	A
	ARTHUR WATTS	bs	A

ALBUM:	1(A)	A HANDEFUL OF PLEASANT DELITES	
		(Middle Earth MDLS 301) 1969 R3	

NB: This has been counterfeited on vinyl.

Led by recorder player James Harpham, this crew of very British looking gentlemen play a completely unique all-acoustic kind of music, which manages to bend baroque classical themes into a frame of cool jazz with occasional flashes of total dementia. Evoking both the atmosphere of rural pastures and urban nervousness, this will appeal to anyone who is interested in distinctive and different sounds, but definitely not to those who feel that lead guitars and tight rhythm sections are indispensable ingredients to whatever music they are listening to.

They also recorded the title track on *Aries*, a Middle Earth compilation EP. The song was originally done by **Writing On The Wall.**

Toy Tune re-emerged on *Progressive Music* (LP). (MK)

The Woods Band

Personnel:	AUSTIN CORCORAN	gtr, bs	A
	ED DEANE	bs, gtr, keyb'ds	AB
	PADDY NASH	drms, vcls	A
	GAY WOODS		AB

THE WOODS BAND - The Woods Band (CD).

	TERRY WOODS		AB
	STEVE ASHE	bs	B
	TONY D'ARCY	drms	B
	JOE O'DONNELL	violin, mandolin	B

ALBUM:	1(A)	THE WOODS BAND	(Greenwich GSLP 1004) 1971 R2

NB: (1) reissued on Rockborough (ROC 102) in a different sleeve in 1977 (SC) and later on CD (Mooncrest CREST 29). (1) reissued on CD (Edsel EDCD 687) 2002 in the original sleeve with detailed information and photos. They recorded a further album *Tenderhooks* (Rockburgh ROC 104) 1978.

This is another album for folk-rock fans. They were a much respected group. Originals of this album are now rare and sought-after. It combined their own songs with traditional ballads. It didn't sell well, but received good reviews at the time.

Terry Woods had originally been in **Sweeney's Men**, an Irish folk group and both Gay and Terry were in the original **Steeleye Span** line-up in January 1970, though they left in April of that year to join **Dr. Strangely Strange** before forming **The Woods Band.** The line-up above worked live gigs and also appeared on *The Woods Band* album. Deane and Nash had previously been in **Granny's Intentions.** Nash and Corcoran left in April 1972 and O'Donnell, Ashe and d'Arcy were recruited for live work. Deane and session men worked on the *Backwoods* sessions.

In the mid-seventies as Gay and Terry worked as **Gay and Terry Woods.** Deane went on to **The Gentrys** and then **Skid Row** and O'Donnell joined **The Trees.** (VJ/JM)

Gay and Terry Woods

Personnel:	GAY WOODS		A
	TERRY WOODS		A

ALBUMS:	1(A)	BACKWOODS	(Polydor 2383 322) 1975 R1
(up to	2(A)	THE TIME IS RIGHT	(Polydor 2383 375) 1976 R1
1976)	3(A)	RENOWNED	(Polydor 2383 406) 1976 R1

See **The Woods Band** entry for further details of their career. They were assisted on these and subsequent albums by some of Britain's other top folk-rock artists. These are essential albums for fans of this genre. All three are quite rare and now minor collector's items. They comprised increasingly experimental singer/songwriter material with hypnotic Irish melodies. More recently **Terry Woods** has been a member of The Pogues. (VJ)

Woody Kern

Personnel:	STEVE HARRIS	drms	A
	RIK KENTON	gtr, keyb'ds	A

| JOHN SANDERSON | tenor sax, flute, violin | A |
| MIKE WHEAT | bs | A |

ALBUM: 1(A) THE AWFUL DISCLOSURES OF MARIA MONK
(Pye NSPL 18273) 1968 R1

NB: (1) reissued on CD (Castle CMRCD 515) 2002 with a fold-out information sheet and two bonus tracks.

45: Biography/Tell You I'm Gone (demo) (Pye 7N 17672) 1969 R3

This progressive outfit's album has a bluesy tinge. The title was inspired by a 19th Century book about the sexual abuse of nuns by clergymen at a convent in Canada. The album has been counterfeited. The opening cut *Biography* has some good flute and guitar bits; *Tell You I'm Gone* starts with Latin rhythms and goes through various tempo changes; *Fair Maiden* opens with some spiritual organ and has some nice flute parts in the middle and at the end; *Vile Lynn* has a choral opening, some good guitar runs and nice violin parts and the final cut *Vegetable* is a lengthier jazz-flavoured number with guitar, tenor sax, bass and drum solos. The album also contains covers of B. B. King's *That's Wrong Little Mama*, Little Walter's *Mean Old World* and Spirit's *Gramophone Man*. The CD reissue on Castle is welcome.

Rik Kenton was later (briefly) in **Roxy Music**. He also cut a couple of 45s in the mid-seventies and played on Neil Harrison's 1974 solo album.

Compilation appearances include: *Vile Lynn* on *Progressive Music* (LP); *Biography* on *Hot Smoke & Sasafras - Psychedelic Pstones, Vol 1* (CD) and *Xoanan Bay* on the 3-CD box set *Ars Longa Vita Brevis: A Compendium Of Progressive Rock 1967-1974*. (VJ)

Charlie Woolfe

Personnel incl:	MILLER ANDERSON		A
	IAN HUNTER (PATTERSON)		A
	FREDDIE 'FINGERS' LEE		A
	PETE PHILIPS		

45: Dance Dance Dance/Home (NEMS 56-3675) 1968

This project contained exactly the same personnel that had previously recorded a 45 as **At Last The 1958 Rock & Roll Show**. **Mott The Hoople**'s **Ian Hunter** played on both 45s. Miller Anderson was later with **Savoy Brown**, **Keef Hartley**, Hemlock and Broken Glass, among others. (VJ)

Woolly

45s:	Golden Golden/Sugar Daddy Song	(RCA RCA 2297) 1972
	Sunshine Souvenirs/	
	Living And Loving You	(Mooncrest MOON 10) 1973

This is a forgotten seventies pop act. (VJ)

Woolly Fish

45: Way You Like It/Sound Of Thick (Plexium PXM 16) 1970

A little known early seventies act. (MWh)

The World

Personnel:	DENNIS COWAN	bs	A
	NEIL INNES	vcls, piano, gtr	A
	ROGER McKEW	gtr	A
	IAN WALLACE	drms	A

ALBUM: 1(A) LUCKY PLANET (Liberty LBS 83419) 1970 SC

WOODY KERN - The Awful Disclosures Of Maria Monk (LP).

45: Angelina/Come Out Into The Open (Liberty LBF 15402) 1970

Neil Innes formed this group after the demise of the **Bonzo Dog Doo Dah Band** in 1970. McKew had been in **Quiet Five** and was also briefly a member of studio band **Judd**. Cowan and Wallace were previously in Big Grunt (a group formed by Stanshall, Spear and Cowan in early 1970). It did prove a very short-lived project - they even split up before the album was released which inevitably meant that it was not promoted and sank without trace. In any case it was pretty amateurish.

Innes and Cowan went on to Stanshall Innes and Freaks, McKew joined **Jackson Heights** and Wallace departed to **King Crimson**. (VJ/JM)

The World of Oz

Personnel:	TONY CLARKSON	bs	AB
	ROB MOORE	drms	A
	GEOFF NICHOLLS	gtr, organ	A
	CHRISTOPHER ROBIN EVANS		
	(TREVOR BEACHAM)	gtr, piano, vcls	ABC
	DAVID KUBINEC	gtr, organ	BC
	DAVID REA	drms	BC
	PETER BECKETT	bs	C

ALBUM: 1(B) THE WORLD OF OZ
(mono/stereo) (Deram DML/SML 1034) 1969 R2

NB: (1) was counterfeited in the late eighties, with white labels and reissued officially on CD by Si-Wan (SRMC 0077) in 1998

45s:	The Muffin Man/Peter's Birthday	(Deram DM 187) 1968 SC
	King Croesus/Jack	(Deram DM 205) 1968
	Willow's Harp/Like A Tear	(Deram DM 233) 1969 SC

This Birmingham-based band recorded some decent popsike amongst numerous other wimpy and juvenile efforts. Their leader Christopher Robin's real name is Trevor Beacham. He wrote or co-wrote many of their songs and also briefly deputised for the lead singer of **The Casuals** when he was ill in September 1969. Evans and Reay had previously played in **Denny King's Mayfair Set** and **David Kubinec** originated from Wales.

Their catchy debut 45, *The Muffin Man*, was an adaptation of a children's nursery rhyme. Its flipside, *Peter's Birthday*, was marginally better due to the fairground organ, which gave an additional dimension and prevented it being just another mundane pop single. Sadly this is just what their next two 'A' sides, *King Croesus* and *Willow's Harp*, were. Their finest moment was tucked away on the flip to their final 45 - the haunting Indian-flavoured *Like A Tear*, with its delightful whispered vocal backed by an acoustic guitar and gentle tabla. Their album, overseen by **Jonathan King**, was disappointing, though it did include *Like A Tear*.

Kubinec went on to record solo material in the late seventies and was later with **The Rats**, who recorded for Goodear in 1974. He'd earlier been in Pieces Of Mind. Tony Clarkson had been in **Nicky James Movement** and Zeus. Rea became a publicist. Peter Beckett replaced Clarkson and later joined **Paladin**.

Compilation coverage has included:- *The Muffin Man* on *The British Psychedelic Trip, Vol. 1* (LP) and *Great British Psychedelic Trip Vol. 1* (CD); *Peter's Birthday (Black & White Rainbow)* on *Psychedalia - Rare Blooms From The English Summer Of Love* (CD), *Rubble Vol. 6* (CD) and on the 4-CD box set *Acid Drops, Spacedust & Flying Saucers*; *Peter's Birthday* and *Like A Tear* on *Rubble Vol. 12: Staircase To Nowhere* (LP); and *Like A Tear* on *Rubble Vol. 7* (CD) and *The Psychedelic Scene* (CD). (VJ/JM/RMJ)

Worrying Kynde

Personnel incl: FIG FAGAN   gtr

45:       Call Out The Name/
          Got The Blame   (Piccadilly 7N 35370) 1967 R2

This is a rare and sought-after 45. *Got The Blame* was an up-tempo bluesy number. The previously unreleased *Sand And Water* from 1966 features good vocals and distinctive percussion.

Compilation appearances include: *Got The Blame* on *That Driving Beat* (CD), *Echoes From The Wilderness - Sixteen UK R&B Freakbeat Trippers* (LP & CD) and *Freakbeat Freakout* (CD); and *Sand And Water* on *Circus Days Vol's 4 & 5* (CD) and *Circus Days, Vol. 5* (LP). (VJ)

Worth

Personnel:	MIKE BARRON	A
	NORMAN BELLIS (ELLIS)	A
	DAVE STEPHENSON	A
	YANNY TSAMPLAKOS	A

45s:	Shoot Em Up Baby/	
	Take The World In Your Hands	(CBS 5309) 1970
	Let's Go Back To Yesterday/Let Me Be	(CBS 7460) 1971
	Don't Say You Don't/Polecat Alley	(CBS 7728) 1972
	I Ain't Backing Down/I'm Not Fooling	(CBS 1584) 1973

This Liverpool band originally formed back in 1963 and operated under the name The Perishers. In 1968, they moved down to London and started to play a strong Motown/soul sound. During the early seventies they were the backing band for many visiting Motown acts. (VJ)

The Wranglers

45:       Liza Jane/It Just Won't Work   (Parlophone R 5163) 1964 R2

Liza Jane is a very rare and sought-after R'n'B number. They later had two 45s for Parlophone with soul vocalist **Kenny Bernard** as **Kenny and The Wranglers**.

Liza Jane has been compiled on *Maximum R'n'B* (CD), *The Demention Of Sound* (LP) and *English Freakbeat Vol. 6* (CD). (VJ/MWh)

Gary Wright('s Wonderwheel)

ALBUMS:	1	EXTRACTION	(A&M AMLS 2004) 1970 SC
(up to	2	FOOTPRINT	(A&M AMLS 64296) 1971 SC
1976)	3	RING OF CHANGES	(A&M AMLH 64362) 1972 R2
	4	DREAM WEAVER	(Warner Brothers K 56141) 1976
	5	LIGHT OF SMILES	(Warner Brothers K 56278) 1976

NB: (3) as **Gary Wright's Wonderwheel**. Only test pressings were issued.

HCP

45s:	Get On The Right Road/	
	It Takes A Little Longer	(A&M AMS 812) 1971 -
	Get On The Right Road/Over You Now	(A&M AMS 826) 1971 -

	Stand For Our Rights/	
	Can't See The Reasons	(A&M AMS 852) 1971 -
α	I Know/Tonight It's Right	(A&M AMS 888) 1972 -
	Dream Weaver/Let It Out	(Warner Brothers K 16707) 1976 -
	Love Is Alive/Dream Weaver	(Warner Brothers K 16831) 1976 -

NB: α released as Gary Wright and Wonderwheel.

Gary Wright is a marginal case for inclusion here because he was actually an American, born in New Jersey, although most of his musical success was over here. He was something of a child actor appearing in a Broadway production of 'Fanny' for a couple of years. He had a lot going on between the ears too and, after achieving a degree in psychology, he formed an outfit called The New York Times, who covered soul/rock hits and toured Europe with them in late Summer 1967. Island boss Chris Blackwell spotted them playing in Scandinavia and persuaded them over to recording studios in London. The end result was that the band never made it onto vinyl but that at Blackwell's instigation **Wright** joined **Art**, who were on the verge of becoming **Spooky Tooth**. He played on their first three albums before departing in early 1970 to go into production work (he produced albums by **Splinter** and Tim Rose) and session work (for **George Harrison**, **Ringo Starr** and **Badfinger** among others).

In September 1970 he signed a solo contract for A&M cutting *Extraction* and then formed **Wonderwheel** as a road band to help promote it. His second effort, *Footprint*, was really a **Wonderwheel** album but made little impression and in September 1972 he disbanded **Wonderwheel** and embarked on a second stint in **Spooky Tooth**. Test pressings of *Ring Of Changes* do exist, but it was never released officially. The nine tracks consist of typical post-**Spooky Tooth** heavy organ/guitar progressive rock.

Upon **Spooky Tooth**'s eventual demise in September 1974, he signed a solo deal with Warner Brothers and went on to record a series of albums of which *Dream Weaver*, in particular, was very big in the States.

He also had one cut, *Love To Survive*, on A&M's 1971 compilation *Come Together* (LP). (VJ)

The Wrigleys

45:       A Little Bit/Come Down Little Bird   (Page One POF 118) 1969

This was a one-off sixties pop single. (VJ)

Writ

45:       Did You Ever Have To Make Up Your Mind? /
          Solid Golden Teardrops   (Decca F 12385) 1966

This was an undistinguished pop 45. The 'A' side is a John Sebastian (Lovin' Spoonful) song. They were managed by **Jonathan King**, who produced the 45 and wrote the 'B' side. (VJ)

THE WORLD OF OZ - The World Of Oz (LP).

Writing on The Wall

Personnel:
JIMMY HUSH	drms	ABC
LINNIE PATTERSON	vcls	A
BILL SCOTT	keyb'ds	ABC
JAKE SCOTT	bs	ABC
ROBERT 'SMIGGY'SMITH	gtr	A
WILLY FINLAYSON	gtr	B
ALBY GREENHALGH	wind	B

ALBUM: 1(B) THE POWER OF THE PICTS
(Middle Earth MDLS 303) 1969 R3

NB: (1) also issued in France (Vogue SLVXME 430) 1969. (1) had a limited reissue on Selector (German) and later on Repertoire (1992) with the addition of *Child On A Crossing*. (1) later reissued on vinyl and CD (Akarma AK 252) with two bonus cuts *Child On A Crossing* and *Lucifer Corpus*.

There's also been the following retrospective releases: *Rarities From The Middle Earth* (Pie & Mash PAM 003) 1995, a limited edition vinyl release of studio and live material; *Cracks In The Illusion Of Life* (Tenth Planet TP 017) 1995, which traces the history of the band and includes rarities from 1967 through to 1973; and *Burghley Road* (Tenth Planet TP 018) 1996, which consists of recordings made in their basement at their Kentish Town base in London during 1972.

45s: Child On A Crossing/
Lucifer Corpus (Middle Earth MDS 101) 1969 R1
Man Of Renown/Buffalo (Pye 7N 45251) 1973 SC

An Edinburgh band, who were originally known as The Jury. They moved down to London, changed their name to **Writing On The Wall** and were a popular attraction at London's Middle Earth Club. Patterson had previously been with **The Boston Dexters**. Robert Smith was in The Embers and **Three's A Crowd**. Patterson and Robert 'Smiggy' Smith then left and Finlayson and Greenhalgh replaced them. This new line-up recorded their album, which didn't capture them at their best. The sound was flat and it was poorly produced. *Bogeyman* catches the ear. With its maze of interlocking riffs and driving rhythm it was the natural choice for the Middle Earth sampler (LP) *Earthed*. *Child On A Crossing* was not included on the album but was added as an additional track when the album was reissued in Germany on Repertoire in 1992. Two of the better tracks on the album were a mad version of *Aries* and *Hill Of Dreams,* but also of note was the 'B' side to the single *Lucifer Corpus*, which had an excellent guitar solo and real menace.

Both sides of the Middle Earth 45 can also be heard on *Filling The Gap* (4-LP) and *Visions Of The Past, Vol. 2* (LP & CD). *Buffalo* has resurfaced on *Rubble, Vol. 10 - Professor Jordan's Magic Sound Show* (LP) and *Filling The Gap* (LP). It sounds pretty good to these ears. The band also signed to Tetragammaton in the US and they put out a live album, *Live At Middle Earth*, which is apparently better and much different to the UK release. It's also hopelessly rare. They also contributed *Aries* the title track to a Middle Earth label sampler (EP) 1969, which also contained tracks by **Wooden O** and **Arcadium**. Finally a version of **The Small Faces** *Sha La La La La Lee* recorded at a John Peel session has resurfaced on *Mynd The Gap* (LP), and *Ladybird* can be found on *Progressive Music* (LP).

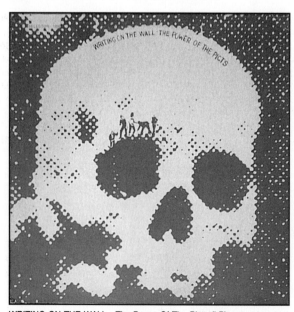

WRITING ON THE WALL - The Power Of The Picts (LP)

WRITING ON THE WALL - Cracks In The Illusion Of Life (LP).

Patterson left the band to join **Beggar's Opera**, but sadly died in the early nineties. Robert Smith joined **Blue**. Finlayson joined **Bees Make Honey** in Autumn 1974. The Scott brothers went on to The Rocky Rhodes Show in 1974.

Certainly **Writing On The Wall** was the best progressive rock outfit to come out of Edinburgh.

Of their retrospective albums, *Cracks In The Illusion Of Life* contains both sides of a 1967 45, *Words And Music / Peter Gunn*, issued originally as The Jury. Also featured are two promising pop-psych tracks from 1968; *Felicity Jane* and *Flight Of The Mind* plus the more mainstream *Katie's Been Gone*. From 1972 there's the keyboard-orientated *Fishers Of Men*, but sadly most of side two is taken up with rather unimaginative hard-edged rock. Of this both sides of their 1973 45 for Pye, *Man Of Renown*, are the pick of the bunch.

Buffalo has been compiled on the 3-CD box set *Ars Longa Vita Brevis: A Compendium Of Progressive Rock 1967-1974*. (VJ/MWh/MK/JM)

Robert Wyatt

ALBUMS: 1 THE END OF AN EAR (CBS 64189) 1970 R1
(up to 2 ROCK BOTTOM (Virgin V 2017) 1974 SC
1976) 3 RUTH IS STRANGER THAN RICHARD
(Virgin V 2034) 1975

NB: (1) reissued on CBS (31846) in 1980 and on CD (Sony 4933422). (2) and (3) reissued as a double pack on Virgin (VGD 3505) in 1981. (2) and (3) reissued on CD (Virgin CDV 2017 and 2034 respectively) in 1989. (2) and (3) reissued again on CD (Hannibal HNCD 1426 and 1427) 1998 and again in 2001. There are also two CD collections of his material, *Going Back A Bit: A Little History Of Robert Wyatt* (Virgin Universal CDVDM 9031) 1994, which is a double set and *Flotsam Jetsam* (Rough Trade R 3112) 1994. *Robert Wyatt & Friends - Theatre Royal, Drury Lane In Concert 1974* (Rykodisc HNCD 1507) officially releases on CD the first concert he performed after the accident that left him paralysed for life.

HCP
45: I'm A Believer/Memories (Virgin V 114) 1974 29
(up to
1976)

Robert Wyatt is one of those complex individuals whose music has considerable depth and originality. He's also appeared on several other artists' albums, including several of **Kevin Ayers'** early albums, **Syd Barrett**'s *The Madcap Laughs* and **Daevid Allen**'s *Bananamoon*.

Robert Wyatt grew up in Canterbury, Kent, attending an exclusive private school, The Simon Langton School, where he met the Hopper brothers and other important figures in what was to become the legendary Canterbury music scene. In 1962 he dropped out of school and headed for Spain where he met drummer George Niedorf, who as well as teaching **Wyatt** how to drum introduced him to **Daevid Allen**, who turned him on to psychedelics.

In 1963 **Wyatt** returned to Canterbury to form **The Wilde Flowers** before teaming up with Allen in the first **Soft Machine** line-up in August 1966. He remained with **Soft Machine** as their drummer and vocalist until 1971, when he left to form his own band, **Matching Mole**. He had cut his first solo album, *The End Of An Ear*, whilst still with **Soft Machine**. This was a musically complex album of fairly free-form jazz-rock. He was assisted on it by **Soft Machine** members Mark Charig and **Elton Dean** as well as David Sinclair. The end result wasn't that convincing but it was reissued in 1980 which means it is more accessible than it might have been because the original release was soon deleted.

In 1972 he was paralysed after a fall and spent several months in Stoke Mandeville Hospital, part of it writing songs for his next solo album, *Rock Bottom*. This was a very personal, emotional album, which had been produced by **Pink Floyd**'s drummer, Nick Mason. In 1974 he enjoyed a hit single with his cover of The Monkees' *I'm A Believer*, which had been recorded during the *Rock Bottom* sessions. It seems surprising that this uncharacteristic commercial success was never followed up. It was rumoured that the BBC had reservations about a man in a wheelchair appearing on programmes like 'Top Of The Pops'. In any event, his next projected single, a cover of **Chris Andrews**' sixties hit *Yesterday Man* was shelved but did get an airing on the double compilation, *V* (Virgin VD 2502) 1975. The projected single was eventually released in 1977 but by then as a commercial force **Wyatt** had lost his momentum and it passed largely unnoticed.

Wyatt recorded a second album for Virgin, *Ruth Is Stranger Than Richard*, in 1975. The result was a strange mixture of material not confined to his own compositions either. For example, Charlie Hayden's jazz composition, *Song For Che*, was included. After this **Wyatt** withdrew from the music scene for the rest of the decade. In 1980 he was persuaded to record a series of singles by Rough Trade and the following year his two Virgin albums were reissued as a double pack.

On *Theatre Royal, Drury Lane, 1974* (now officially consigned to CD) he is accompanied by a host of friends including **Ivor Cutler**, David Gilmour and Fred Firth. He performs the entire *Rock Bottom* album as well as **Soft Machine** and **Matching Mole** tunes and a barnstorming rendition of *I'm A Believer* which gave him a Top 40 hit.

Compilation appearances have included: *Mummie* and *Stop Me And Play One* on *Canterburied Sounds Vol. 1* (CD); *Instant Pussy, Moorish, Drum Solo* and *Love Song With Cello* on *Canterburied Sounds Vol. 2* (CD); and *Slow Walkin' Talk* and *Liu-Ba* on *Canterburied Sounds Vol. 3* (CD). (VJ)

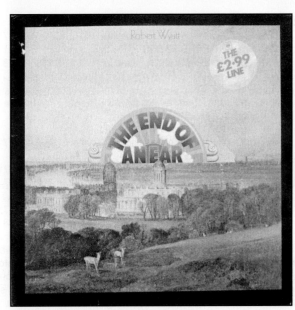

ROBERT WYATT - The End Of An Ear (LP).

Bill Wyman

ALBUMS: 1   MONKEY GRIP (Rolling Stones COC 59102) 1974 SC 39
(up to   2   STONE ALONE   (Rolling Stones COC 59105) 1976 SC -
1976)

45s: Monkey Grip Glue/What A Blow (Rolling Stones RS 19112) 1973
(up to   White Lightnin'/Pussy   (Rolling Stones RS 19115) 1974
1976)   If You Wanna Be Happy/
        Apache Woman   (Rolling Stones RS 19117) 1974
        Quarter To Three/
        Soul Satisfying   (Rolling Stones RS 19119) 1974
        Apache Woman/Soul Satisfying (Rolling Stones RS 19120) 1975

NB: There was also an earlier US 45, *In Another Land/*? (London 907) 1967, which reached No. 87. This was of course his contribution to the **Stones'** *Satanic Majesties Request* album.

Bill Wyman is regarded as one of rock's finest bassists.

Bill Wyman's real name is William Perks and he was born in Lewisham, London, on 24 October 1936. He was bassist with the band called The Cliftons before joining **The Rolling Stones** in December 1962. As with almost all megabands, various members made solo recordings along the way, and **Wyman** was no exception. His debut album charted both sides of the Atlantic (No. 39 in the UK and 99 in the US). *Stone Alone* did not chart in the UK, though it crept into the US charts, peaking at No. 166. He made occasional solo recordings after 1976, to little effect. His production credits include **The End** and **Tucky Buzzard**.

His next significant project was the 1985 covers band Willie And The Poor Boys (who included Charlie Watts, **Jimmy Page** and Paul Rodgers). In 1989 he attracted much media attention when he married model Mandy Smith, who he'd begun a relationship with when she was just 13. But it all ended in divorce the following year. After leaving the Stones in January 1993, he wrote a very factual autobiography, 'Stone Alone', and toured frequently with his rhythm and blues band The Rhythm Kings who he formed in 1997. They included guitarists **Peter Frampton** and Albert Lee and ex-**Procol Harum** keyboardist Gary Brooker. Their albums have included *Struttin' Our Stuff* and *Anyway The Wind Blows*. He also runs a successful restaurant business. (VJ/DS/RMJ)

Wynder K. Frog

Personnel incl:			
NEIL HUBBARD	gtr	A
CHRIS MERCER	sax	AB
BRUCE ROWLAND	drms	AB
ALAN SPENNER	bs	AB
MICK WEAVER	keyb'ds	AB
REBOP ANTHONY KWABAKU	congas	AB
MIKE LIBER	gtr	B

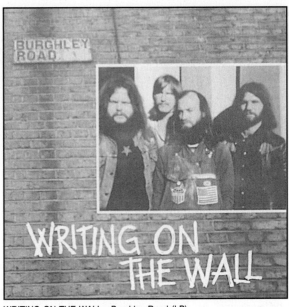

WRITING ON THE WALL - Burghley Road (LP).

ALBUMS: 1(A)   SUNSHINE SUPERFROG
              (mono/stereo)   (Island ILP 944/ILPS 9044) 1967 R2
        2(A) OUT OF THE FRYING PAN
              (mono/stereo)   (Island ILP 982/ILPS 9082) 1968 R1

NB: (1) reissued on CD (Walhalla WH 90352) with one bonus track *I'm A Man*. (2) issued on United Artists in the US and reissued on CD (Edsel EDCD 461) 1995 and again (Walhalla WH 90353). There was also an US-only release: - *Into The Fire* (UA 6740) in 1970, which has been reissued on CD.

45s: Turn On Your Lovelight/Zooming   (Island WI 280) 1966/7 R1
         Sunshine Superman/
         Blues From A Frog   (Island WI 3011) 1967 R1
         Green Door/Dancing Frog   (Island WIP 6006) 1967 R1
         I Am A Man/
         Shook Shimmy And Shake   (Island WIP 6014) 1967 R1
         Jumpin' Jack Flash/Baldy   (Island WIP 6044) 1968 R1

This blues and jazz influenced outfit was fronted by Weaver who'd previously been in **The Fairies**. Hubbard was previously with **Bluesology** and Mercer had been in **John Mayall's Bluesbreakers**. Their albums include several cover versions. *Sunshine Superfrog* features 12 mod-soul tracks including *Somebody Help Me, (Don't Fight It) Feel It, Hold On, I'm Coming* and an original *I Feel So Bad*.

Out Of The Frying Pan is an instrumental album and among others includes cover versions of *Jumping Jack Flash* (**Rolling Stones**), *Baby I Love You* (R. Shannon), *Willie And The Hand Jive* (Johnny Otis), *Alexander's Ragtime Band* (I. Berlin), *Tequila* (C.Rio), *The House That Jack Built* (**Alan Price**) and *Hi Heel Sneakers* (R. Higginbottom). Mick Weaver only wrote two tracks, *Gasoline Alley* and *Harpsichord Shuffle*, which is the best thing on the album. Very few British bands had such a strong Hammond organ sound, which is now big in the clubs. Their 45s included covers of Bobby Bland's *Turn On Your Lovelight*, **Donovan**'s *Sunshine Superman* and **The Spencer Davis Group**'s *I Am A Man*.

Compilation appearances include *Green Door* on *British Blue-Eyed Soul* (LP) and *Gasoline Alley* on *You Can All Join In* (LP), which is a good R&B instrumental with organ, guitar and sax in an early **Brian Auger** vein. The band also turn up in the 1968 film 'The Touchables' along with **Ferris Wheel**.

Upon their demise Weaver spent the first three months of 1969 in Mason-Capaldi-Wood-Frog (aka Wooden Frog), before becoming a session man. Hubbard left initially to join **Juicy Lucy** and was replaced by Mike Liber (ex-Phython Lee Jackson) who went on to **Ashton Gardner and Dyke**. Spenner and Rowland returned to **The Greaseband** from whence they'd come. Mercer joined **The Misunderstood** and Kwabaku went on to session work and **Traffic**. (VJ/JM)

THE YARDBIRDS - BBC Sessions (CD).

THE YARDBIRDS - Cumular Limit (CD).

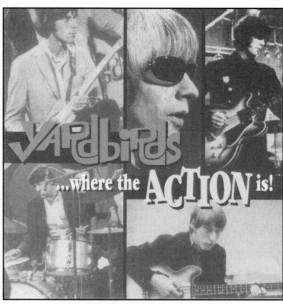
THE YARDBIRDS - Where The Action Is (CD).

THE YARDBIRDS - Can You Identify These Men? (10")

Xcalibres

45s: We Will Love/Swing That Chariot   (CBS 201805) 1965
          You'll Find Out/That's What Happens   (Mercury MF 941) 1965

A Lancashire band, who also recorded one 45 with Paul Newman, *Ain't You Got A Heart/Tears On My Pillow* (Mercury MF 969) 1967.

X-Caliburs

45:     We Will Love/That's What Happens   (Mercury MF 941) 1966

Five guys from Nottingham were responsible for this melodic ballad.

The Yaks

45:     Yakety Yak/Back in '57   (Decca F 12115) 1965 SC

A rock'n'roll band from Nottingham. *Yakety Yak* is the well-known Leiber/Stoller song and this is a fair version of it. Both sides were produced by Larry Page. (VJ)

Yamasukis

45:     Yamasuki/Aieaoa   (Dandelion DAN 7004) 1971

NB: (1) Reissued on UK (UK 72) in 1974.

The 'A' side of this 45 is an incredible East / West mixture of blood-curdling 'Hari Kiri' male yells and a sweet Japanese sound from a girl choir. The later reissue on **Jonathan King**'s label in 1974 suggests it could have been a one-off project of his. (VJ)

Yardarm

ALBUM: 1   YARDARM   (Folk Heritage) 1970

This album is a mixture of contemporary and traditional material with male / female vocals. (MWh)

The Yardbirds

Personnel:			
CHRIS DREJA	rhythm gtr	ABCDE
JIM McCARTY	drms	ABCDE
KEITH RELF	vcls, hrmnca	ABCDE
PAUL SAMWELL-SMITH	bs	ABC
TONY 'TOP' TOPHAM	lead gtr	A
ERIC CLAPTON	gtr	B
JEFF BECK	gtr	CD
JIMMY PAGE	gtr	DE

HCP

ALBUMS: 1(B)   FIVE LIVE YARDBIRDS
          (Columbia 33SX 1677) 1964 R3 -
      2(B)   SONNY BOY WILLIAMSON AND THE YARDBIRDS
          (Fontana TL 5277) 1965 R2 -
      3(D)   THE YARDBIRDS (mono/stereo)
          (Columbia S(C)X 6063) 1966 R1 20
      4(-)   REMEMBER THE YARDBIRDS (comp)
          (Starline SRS 5069) 1971 -

NB: (1) also had a later issue in 1969 with same catalogue number and black/silver label (SC). There's also a reel-to-reel tape of this album (SC). (1) reissued on CD (Charly CDCHARLY 182) 1979 and again on CD (Charly SNAP 407CD) with 10 bonus tracks recorded within a few months of this gig. (2) also had a later issue in 1969 with black/silver label (SC) and again in 1976 with a black silver label. Some copies were misprinted without the front cover illustration (SC). (2) reissued on CD as *Live At The Crawdaddy Club, Richmond* (Repertoire REP 4776 WY) 1999. Also relevant is *The Complete Crawdaddy Recordings* (2-LP) (Get Back GET 546) which is a reissue of (2) with three bonus tracks. *Roger The Engineer* (Diablo DIAB 852)

1998 is an enlarged CD release of their 1966 album in both mono and stereo with five bonus tracks. A complete replica of the original *Roger The Engineer* (Get Back GET 605) is also available in vinyl. *Roger The Engineer/Over Under Sideways* Down (CD) (Repertoire REP 4681) offers their 1966 album (also known as *Over Under Sideways Down*) along with five bonus tracks featuring **Jimmy Page** and **Keith Relf** solo singles.

Having A Rave Up With The Yardbirds was originally a US-only album in 1966. It has been reissued again on CD (Charly) 1993 and again on vinyl (Get Back GET 547) in 1999, with bonus tracks from 1966 era sessions. It was also issued on CD on German import (Repertoire REP 4758-WY) in 1999 plus 11 bonus tracks and housed in a digipak sleeve with a detailed booklet. *Over Under Sideways Down* (Get Back GET LP 559) 2001 is a vinyl reissue of the US mono version of this album. It includes harder-edged versions of *The Nazz Are Blue* and *Rackin' My Mind* than the UK version, with the addition of *Roger The Engineer* and the single *Happenings Ten Years Time Ago* and *Psycho Daisies*. *For Your Love* (Repertoire REP 4757-WY) 1999 reissues a US album with several bonus tracks. *Little Games* (EMI 7243 5 40813 2 3) 2003 is a further reissue of their US-only album from 1967 with 15 bonus tracks and a lavishly presented package.

Compilations and retrospective releases have included:- *Featuring Performances By Jeff Beck, Eric Clapton, Jimmy Page* (Epic EG 30135) (2-LP); *The Yardbirds* (2-LP) (Cambra CR 107) 1973; *Shapes Of Things* (Charly BOX 104) 1984 (SC) an LP box set; *Little Games* (LP) (EMI/Fame FA 41 3124 1) 1985; *Little Games* (CD) (EMI CDP 7 96064 2) 1991, a CD reissue of this earlier US-only album from 1967, with the six additional tracks that earlier appeared with it on the earlier 1985 UK release of this album and two additional tracks, a second version of *Goodnight Sweet Josephine* and *Together Now* by **Together**, who **Relf** joined when he left **The Yardbirds**; *On Air* (LP/CD) (Band Of Joy BOJLP 200) 1991; *Shapes Of Things* (Decal CD LIK BOX 1) 1991, a 4-CD set, largely based on a seven album set issued by that label in 1987. It also comes with a booklet written by the band's biographer, John Platt; *The Very Best Of The Yardbirds* (Music Club MCCD 023) 1991; *Over, Under, Sideways, Down* (Raven/Topic RVCD 12) 1991, a good 28-track CD compilation with material from the full duration of their career; *25 Greatest Hits* (Repertoire REP 4258) 1992, which in addition to their hits includes both sides of their German-only single, *Boom Boom/Honey In Your Hips*, and *Pafff...Bum*, their early entry into a 1966 Italian song contest; *Little Games Sessions And More* (EMI Ultra Set E2 98213, US import) 1992, a 32-track double set containing several rarities, a 28-page booklet, family tree and full discography; *Train Kept A-Rollin' - The Complete Giorgio Gomelsky Productions* (4-CD Set) (Charly CD LIK BOX 3) 1993, which comes with a 64-page booklet with lots of pictures and detailed track-by-track notes but it includes few of the band's recordings from 1966 onwards; *The Best Of The Yardbirds* (Rhino RZ 71025) 1994, a nine-track US compilation, which includes some of their early singles up to early 1966; *20 Greatest Hits: Yardbirds* (CD) (Spectrum SPEC 85005) 1988; *Classic Cuts* (CD) (Topline TOP CD 501) 1987; *Collection Yardbirds* (CD) (Castle Collector CCSCD 141) 1988; *Greatest Hits: Yardbirds* (CD) (Charly CDCHARLY 8) 1986; *Hits And More* (CD) (Instant CDINS 5012) 1989; *The Studio Sessions* (CD) (Charly CDCHARLY 187) 1989; *Good Morning Little Schoolgirl* (CD) (Pickwick PWKS 4273) 1995 and *Best Of The Legendary Yardbirds* (CD) (Nectar Masters NTMCD 527) 199? Fans of the band will also want to pick up *Where The Action Is* (New Millennium Communications PILOT 10) 1997, a 2-CD set which couples their BBC sessions alongside the tracks recorded on their 1967 Scandinavia tour. The package includes a 20-page booklet containing an interview with Chris Dreja and Jim McCarty.

The Complete BBC Sessions (Get Back GET 503) 1998 is a 27-track vinyl release of material recorded between 1965 and 1968 for 'Where The Action Is' digitally remastered from the original tapes. They mostly feature **Jeff Beck** on guitar, although a young **Jimmy Page** is on the later ones. *Can You Identify These Men?* (Get Back GET 567) 2000 is a mini-album of demos and alternate takes that will only interest their diehard fans. *BBC Sessions* (CD) (Repertoire REP 4777-WY) is a

THE YARDBIRDS - Five Live (CD)

33-track compilation of material recorded between 1965 and 1968 covering similar ground to the earlier release on Get Back. It includes a full interview with band members. By contrast *Cumular Limit* (NMC PILOT 24) 2000 is a 2-CD compilation (one CD and one CDR) accompanied by a very comprehensive booklet. The first disc compiles alternate and live versions of their catalogue from 1967/68 with **Jimmy Page** on guitar. The second one is an enhanced CD-Rom featuring footage of the band recorded for German TV. *Best Of* (2-LP) (Get Back GET 611) is a 24-track compilation of their biggest hits, outtakes, live tracks and rarities presented in a deluxe triple fold-out sleeve along with a 16-page booklet. *Eric (Slowhand) Clapton* (LP) (Charly 300012) compiles on vinyl a studio and live session at the Marquee, both recorded in London during 1964 when **Eric Clapton** was their lead guitarist.

Ultimate! (Rhino R2 79825) 2001 a US import is a 2-CD overview of their career. *Live! Blueswailing July '64* (Castle CMQCD 793) 2003 captures them in pretty good form and the set is also available on vinyl. *Early Yardbirds* (Get Back 300110) is a vinyl release showcasing material from the time they were known as The Metropolitan Blues Quartet. *Stroll With The Yardbirds* (2-CD) (Atom Music ATOM 2002) features many of their best songs and comes with an eight-page booklet. *The Yardbirds Story* (4-CD set) (Charly SNAB 905CD) is a book size set compiled by Giorgio Gomelsky, who managed them between 1963-1966. *London 1964-1965, New York, Memphis, Chicago 1965, London 1966* (LP) (Charly 300013) captures some of their finest live moments from the **Jeff Beck** era. *Shapes Of Things - The Very Best Of The Yardbirds* (Charly/Snapper 209 CD) 2005 compiles material mostly from 1965-1966. *The Very Best Of The Yardbirds* (Metro/Union Square Music METRCD 168) 2005 is a nicely balanced collection of material from the **Clapton** and **Beck** eras that goes as far as 1966.

EPs: 1 FIVE YARDBIRDS   (Columbia SEG 8421) 1964 R2
         2 OVER, UNDER, SIDEWAYS, DOWN
                                (Columbia SEG 8521) 1967 R3

NB: *Heart Full Of Soul* (EP) (CDEP) is an exact limited edition replica of a sixties French EP presented in a card picture sleeve.

			HCP
45s:	I Wish You Would/A Certain Girl	(Columbia DB 7283) 1964	SC -
	Good Morning Little Schoolgirl/		
	I Ain't Got You	(Columbia DB 7391) 1964	SC 44
	For Your Love/Got To Hurry	(Columbia DB 7499) 1965	3
	Heart Full Of Soul/Steeled Blues	(Columbia DB 7594) 1965	2
	Evil Hearted You/Still I'm Sad	(Columbia DB 7706) 1965	3
	Shapes Of Things/		
	You're A Better Man Than I	(Columbia DB 7848) 1966	3
	Over, Under, Sideways, Down/		
	Jeff's Boogie	(Columbia DB 7928) 1966	SC 10
	Happenings Ten Years Time Ago/		
	Psycho Daisies	(Columbia DB 8024) 1966	R1 43
	Little Games/Puzzles	(Columbia DB 8165) 1967	R1 -
	Goodnight Sweet Josephine/		
	Think About It	(Columbia DB 8368) 1967	-

NB: (6) Some copies were mispressed with *Still I'm Sad* on the flip side. These are rare and expensive (R1). (10) was unreleased and copies only exists in acetate form. They are ultra-rare and extremely expensive (R3).

The Yardbirds (like the less influential **Pretty Things**) will be remembered as one of Britain's best R&B bands, and for some interesting experiments

with pop and psychedelia. They are also noteworthy for having featured three of Britain's leading guitarists - **Eric Clapton**, **Jeff Beck** and **Jimmy Page**.

They evolved out of The Metropolitan Blues Quartet, and became **The Yardbirds** in 1963. Having replaced **The Rolling Stones** as resident band at Richmond's Crawdaddy Club, they won a Friday night residency at The Marquee. Before they won a recording contract **Topham** had been replaced by **Clapton**, though a bootleg EP of material from this era is rumoured to exist. Their first two singles, 1964's *I Wish You Would* and *Good Morning Little Schoolgirl*, were solid R&B, and their debut album captured the excitement of their live act convincingly.

Their third single, however, was to prove divisive. *For Your Love* pushed them into the public eye, reaching No 3 in March 1965, but **Clapton** was dismayed at the commercial direction it pushed them in and left to join **John Mayall's Bluesbreakers**. He was replaced by **Jeff Beck**. The group was now enormously popular and further hits followed - *Heart Full Of Soul* (No 2 in July 1965), *Evil Hearted You* (No 3 in October 1965), *Shapes Of Things* (No 3 in March 1966) and *Over, Under, Sideways, Down* (No 10 in June 1966).

In mid-1965 **The Yardbirds** had begun experimenting in the studio. *Still I'm Sad* was the first evidence of this, and their first self-penned single (it was in fact part of a double 'A' side). More significant testimonies of their experimental edge were *Shapes Of Things*, featuring stunning guitar work from **Beck**, and their first studio album, **The Yardbirds**, issued in the Summer of 1966 and entirely comprised of original compositions. This contained some superb early psychedelia, most notably *Over, Under, Sideways, Down* and *Happenings Ten Years Time Ago*. The latter, whilst less commercial than the former, was one of the most significant and ambitious recordings of 1966. Other impressive cuts were *Farewell*, *He's Always There* and the startling *Psycho Daisies*.

1966, however, also marked the departure of Paul Samwell-Smith (who went into production work with **Cat Stevens** and others). He was replaced by **Jimmy Page**, who soon took over on lead guitar whilst Dreja switched to bass. Although **The Yardbirds** lost much stability with Samwell-Smith's departure, they gained new significance as **Page**'s first outfit. **The Yardbirds** were enormously influential not only in Britain (especially on subsequent hard-rock outfits), but also in America, where countless garage bands emulated their style. Indeed they had no less than six albums released under different titles in the US, and with different tracks to the UK ones. The album with *Sonny Boy Williamson And...* came out on Mercury, but the other five were on Epic - *For Your Love*, *Have A Rave Up With...*, *Over Under Sideways Down*, *Little Games* and *The Yardbirds*. Avoid *Little Games*, which, aside from the title track, was a mish-mash of material that the group had not intended for public consumption.

A further album, *Live Yardbirds*, was apparently recorded on the understanding that the group could veto its release - which is exactly what they did when it appeared without their consent. It was rapidly withdrawn and is now a frequently-bootlegged collectors' item. It's of particular interest

THE YARDBIRDS - For Your Love (LP)

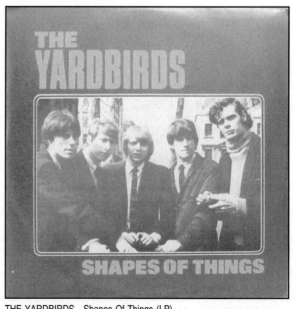

THE YARDBIRDS - Shapes Of Things (LP).

to **Led Zeppelin** fans as an example of **Page**'s guitar work, and even includes an early version of *Dazed And Confused*, which **Page** had copied from Jake Holmes, the band's support act at a New York club date.

Back in England their next single release was *Happenings Ten Years Time Ago*. Though superb, it lacked mass appeal and reached only No 43. At this stage **Beck**, who had earlier suffered a breakdown on a US tour, left the band for the last time. Their next effort, *Little Games*, flopped, and both 45s are now collectors' items. Their final single, *Goodnight Sweet Josephine*, exists only in acetate form and the handful of known copies change hands for huge sums among **Yardbirds**' collectors.

The Yardbirds also issued two EPs, *Five Yardbirds* and *Over, Under, Sideways, Down*, the second of which is now very rare. They also appeared in two films, 'Swinging London' and 'Blow Up'.

When their commercial success waned, **The Yardbirds** disintegrated. **Relf** and McCarthy formed **Together** and then **Renaissance**, which had some success. **Relf**, who had more recently played in **Armageddon**, died at his home in 1976 after electrocuting himself while playing guitar. Dreja became a photographer (shooting the rear sleeve of the first **Led Zeppelin** album, amongst other things) and **Page** formed the enormously successful **Led Zeppelin** (originally formed as The New Yardbirds, to fulfil outstanding European **Yardbirds** dates).

In 1985 EMI released the band's 1967 US-only album, *Little Games*, in this country along with six additional tracks which had previously only appeared on 45s. Highlights include **Jimmy Page**'s *White Summer* (an Indian-influenced acoustic number bearing considerable resemblance to **Davy Graham**'s arrangement of the traditional *She Moves Through The Fair*) and *Only The Black Rose*, a folky **Keith Relf** number which previewed his work with **Renaissance**. Of the additional tracks, *Think About It* takes the prize, largely for **Page**'s high energy guitar playing. The CD is not consistent, but worth acquiring.

EMI later reissued it again, this time with 15 bonus tracks. The best covers are of Nilsson's *Ten Little Indians* and *Good Night Sweet Josephine*. Of the originals, *Puzzles* ends with a blistering **Page** solo. *Think About It* also catches the ear, but the bonuses also include throwaway numbers. The set concludes with eight tracks from various BBC Sessions. It's a mixed bag overall.

On Air is a double album which contains BBC sessions recorded between 29 March 1965 and 16 March 1968. Several of their finest moments from this era are featured, including *For Your Love*, *Heart Full Of Soul*, *I'm A Man*, *You're A Better Man Than I*, *Shapes Of Things* and *Train Kept A-Rollin'*. Plenty of other compilations exist, and are detailed in the discography at the start of this article.

Roger The Engineer is an enlarged version of their second album, with the addition of five bonus tracks - *Mr Zero*, two mixes of the superb *Shapes Of Things*, and both sides of their ground-breaking *Happenings Ten Years Time Ago* single. It was offered at mid-price and accompanied by an excellent 16-page booklet.

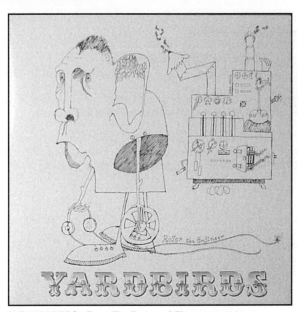

THE YARDBIRDS - Roger The Engineer (LP)

THE YARDBIRDS - Featuring Performances (LP)

The 2001 Rhino 2-CD import *Ultimate!* consists of two digipaks encased in a slipcase and accompanied by a 54-page booklet. It's currently the best overview of their career, and highly recommended.

The Yardbirds Story (a 4-CD set) is likely to be the definitive work - the music is ordered chronologically, with CD 1 subtitled *1963 - R&B roots*, CD 2 is *1964 - Early Studio & At The Marquee*, CD 3 is *1965/66 - Big Hits and America Calling* and CD 4 is *1966/67 - An Eye View Of Beat*. The book-size box set comes with a lavishly illustrated 52-page booklet.

2005's *Shapes Of Things - The Very Best Of The Yardbirds* is misleadingly titled, as it mostly contains material between March 1965 and October 1966, and therefore lacks several of their finest moments with **Clapton** and **Page** (though it does include some great stuff with **Beck** and *I'm A Man* with **Page**).

The CD *The Very Best Of The Yardbirds* is a nicely balanced collection between their **Jeff Beck** and **Eric Clapton** periods. It contains material from their R&B era with **Clapton** and then ventures into 1966 incorporating their hits up to *Shapes Of Things* (although only *Still I'm Sad* appears from their double 'A' side release and an alternate sitar version of *Heart Full Of Soul* is used). Also included is *Stroll On*, which features **Jimmy Page** as well as **Jeff Beck**!

The band reformed to play some gigs in Summer 1983.

Compilation appearances have included: *Little Games* (from 18 April 1967), *Most Likely You'll Go Your Way* (from 4 April 1967) and *I'm Confused* (by The New Yardbirds) from 1968 on *James Patrick Page: Session Man, Vol. 1* (LP); *Little Games* (from 18 April 1967) and *Most Likely You'll Go Your Way* (from 4 April 1967) on *James Patrick Page: Session Man, Vol. 1* (CD); *White Summer* on *James Patrick Page: Session Man, Vol. 2* (CD); *Train Kept A Rollin'*, *You Shook Me*, *Hot House Of Omagarashid* and *I'm Confused* on *James Patrick Page, Session Man* (2-LP); *Happenings Ten Years Time Ago* on *My Generation* (LP) and on the 4-CD box set *Acid Drops, Spacedust & Flying Saucers*; *Baby What's Wrong* (from 1964) on *The Sound Of The Sixties* (2-LP) and *Sixties Archive Vol. 1* (CD); *Goodnight Sweet Josephine*, *Think About It* and *My Baby* on *Top Of The Pops No. 178* (LP); *Shapes Of Things* and *Pafff...Bum* on *The Best Of Beat, Vol. 3* (LP); *Four Your Love* on *60's Mix* (CD); *Shapes Of Things* and *Happenings Ten Years Time Ago* on *The Early Days Of Rock, Vol. 2 - Live In Concert 1964 - 1968* (CD); *Slow Walk, Pontiac Blues, Lonesome Cabin, Bye Bye Bird* and *Got My Mojo Working* on *The First British R&B Festival, February 28, 1964* (LP); *Little Games* and *Puzzles* on *Great British Psychedelic Trip, Vol. 3* (CD); *Shapes Of Things* and *Over, Under, Sideways, Down* on *Go... With An All Star* (LP); *Shapes Of Things* and *Evil Hearted You* have been compiled on *Super Hits Of The 60s - Vol 1* (CD); *For Your Love* appears on *Super Hits Of The 60s - Vol 2* (CD); you can check out *Heart Full Of Soul* on *Super Hits Of The 60s - Vol 3* (CD) and you'll find *Great Shakes* on *Great Shakes Shake-Out* (EP). (VJ/RMJ)

Tom Yates

Personnel:	TOM YATES	acoustic gtr, lead vcls	AB
	DUNCAN BROWNE	gtr, bs, piano	B
	B.J.COLE	pedal steel gtr	B
	BARRY DE SOUSA	drms	B
	DAVID LIDDLE	bs, electric gtr	B
	CYNDY YATES	mandolin	B
	(DAVE BENTLEY	drms	B)
	(VIZ MISTRI	congas	B)

ALBUMS: 1(A) SECOND CITY SPIRITUAL (CBS BPG63094) 1967 R2
2(B) LOVE COMES WELL ARMED
(with booklet insert) (President PTLS 1053) 1973 R1

An obscure Mancunian folk-rock singer, whose albums are quite rare now. The first came in a lovely psychedelic sleeve and features plaintive folk. The second was co-produced by **Yates** and Alan Melina. **Yates** also wrote all the material except *Evangeline* and *Dear Life*, which were co-written with **Duncan Browne**. The album contains several songs with ambitious lyrics such as *Abyssinia (Kerouac's Song)*, *A Vision Of Einstein* and *Love's Philosophy*, and seems heavily influenced by American singer-songwriters such as Dylan and Arlo Guthrie, though **Yates** is not in their class.

He released a third album in 1977, *Song Of The Shimmering Way* (Satril SATR4007). (SR/RMJ)

Y Blew

See 'B' section filed under 'Blew'.

Year One

45: Eli's Comin'/
Will You Be Staying After Sunday (Major Minor MM 660) 1969

Year One was an obscure late sixties band. (VJ)

Yellow

Personnel incl: KENNETH JAMES MOUNTAIN gtr A

45: Roll It Down The Hill/Living A Lie (CBS 4869) 1970 SC

A South Shields band who played between 1969 - 70. After their demise Kenneth James Mountain was in various obscure bands. In 1972, he became a member of **Beckett** as Kenny Mountain.

The *Hart Rock '71* EP features a track called *The Hobo Song*, written and produced by Ken Mountain.

YELLOWSTONE AND VOICE - Yellowstone And Voice (LP) (French issue).

Other compilation appearances include: *Living A Lie* on *Rubble, Vol. 8 - All The Colours Of Darkness* (LP) and *Rubble, Vol. 4* (CD); and *Hobo* on *Beyond The Veil Of Time* (CD) and *The Best Of Rubble Collection, Vol. 2* (CD). (VJ)

Yellow Bellow Room Boom

| Personnel: | LOL CRÈME | vcls | A |
| | KEVIN GODLEY | vcls | A |

45: Seeing Things Green/Easy Life (CBS 3205) 1968 SC

10CC's Kevin Godley and Lol Crème wrote and were featured on this falsetto harmony 45. (VJ)

Yellow Pages

45: Here Comes Jane/Ring-A-Ding (Page One POF 090) 1968 R1

This band was completely unconnected to the Texan band who spelt Payges with a 'y'. (VJ)

Yellowstone and Voice

Personnel:	STEVE VOICE	vcls, gtr	A
	PETER YELLOWSTONE	vcls, gtr	A
	(TONY CAMPO		A)
	(CLEM CATTINI	drms	A)
	(MALCOLM GATES		A)

ALBUM: 1(A) YELLOWSTONE AND VOICE
(Regal Zonophone SRZA 8511) 1972 SC

45s: The Flying Dutchman/Philosopher (Parlophone R 5965) 1972
Thinking About You And Me/
Grandmother Says (Regal Zonophone RZ 3065) 1972
Memories/Well Hello (Regal Zonophone RZ 3073) 1973
Super Duper Star/Someday Someday (EMI EMI 2111) 1974
Do Me Good/Stay J (EMI EMI 2193) 1974

This outfit was really a duo. Yellowstone, a Scot with Italian parentage, had earlier written songs in Italian. Steve Voice came from Hounslow in West London.

Their album is a sorry collection of mediocre songs, partly **Casuals**, partly **McCartney**, brilliantly but too heavily orchestrated. It occasionally works on tracks like *Lady Rita*, but is mostly forgettable and regrettable. Avoid, unless you're heavily into orchestrated pop. (MK/VJ)

Yemm and The Yemen

45: Black Is The Night/Do Blondes Really
Have More Fun? (Columbia DB 8022) 1966 SC

An obscure beat outfit whose 45 is now a minor collectable. The 'A' side is quite good, the flip side is more lighthearted, as its title suggests.

The 45 was recorded by Charles and Kingsley Ward at Future Sound (precursor to Rockfield Studios in Monmouth Wales). Dale Griffin, future **Mott The Hoople** drummer, played on it as a session drummer. (VJ/JPn)

Yes

Personnel:	JON ANDERSON	vcls	ABCDE
(up to	PETE BANKS	gtr	A
1976)	BILL BRUFORD	drms	ABC
	TONY KAYE	organ	AB
	CHRIS SQUIRE	bs	ABCDE
	STEVE HOWE	gtr	BCDE

YES - The Yes Album (LP).

RICK WAKEMAN	keyb'ds	CD
ALAN WHITE	drms	DE
PATRICK MORAZ	keyb'ds	E

					HCP
ALBUMS:	1(A)	YES	(Atlantic 588 190)	1969	R1 -
(up to	2(A)	TIME AND A WORD	(Atlantic 2400 006)	1970	SC 45
1976)	3(B)	THE YES ALBUM	(Atlantic 2400 101)	1971	SC 7
	4(C)	FRAGILE	(Atlantic 2400 019)	1971	SC 7
	5(C)	CLOSE TO THE EDGE	(Atlantic K 50012)	1972	SC 4
	6(D)	YESSONGS (3-LP)	(Atlantic 60045)	1973	7
	7(D)	TALES FROM TOPOGRAPHIC OCEANS (2-LP)			
			(Atlantic K 80001)	1973	1
	8(E)	RELAYER	(Atlantic K 50096)	1974	4
	9(-)	YESTERDAYS (Compilation)			
			(Atlantic K 50048)	1975	27

NB: A further line-up recorded two further albums, *Going For The One* (Atlantic K 50379) 1977 and *Tormato* (Atlantic K 50518) 1978. (1) - (4) reissued on vinyl in 1972. (1) reissued on CD remastered (Elektra/Rhino 8122737862) with an 18-page booklet and six bonus tracks. (2) reissued on CD remastered (Elektra/Rhino 8122737872) with a 16-page booklet and four bonus tracks. (3) reissued on CD (Atlantic SD 191 312) 1988 and again on CD remastered (Elektra/Rhino 8122737882). (3) also issued on vinyl remastered (Rhino RHI 73788). (4) reissued on CD (Atlantic 250 009) 1986 and again on CD remastered (Elektra/Rhino 8122737892). (5) reissued on CD (Atlantic 250 012) 1986 and again on CD remastered (Elektra/Rhino 8122737902) with four bonus tracks. (6) reissued on CD (Atlantic 260 045) 1987. (7) reissued on CD (WEA 781 325) 1989 and again as a 2-CD remastered (Elektra/Rhino 8122737912). (8) reissued on CD (Atlantic 191 352) 1988.

Compilations include *Classic Yes* (Atlantic K 50842), which came with a free 45, *Roundabout/Your Move* (SAM 151) (SC). *The Yes Years* (Atco 7567-91 644-2) 1991 is a 4-CD set which covers the duration of their career. *Something's Coming (BBC Sessions) 1967-1970* (2-CD) (New Millennium Communications PILOT 25) is an 18-track set of BBC performances recorded in 1969 and 1970 along with live material from the same period. It comes with sleevenotes by **Peter Banks**. *Beyond And Before (BBC Recordings 1969-70)* (2-CD) (CLP CLP 0246-2) is a special deluxe edition of the *Something's Coming* session for the BBC with four bonus tracks and housed in a beautiful slip case sleeve with a poster insert and colour booklet. *In A Word* (Rhino/Warners R2 8122 871 862) 2002 is a 55-track 5-CD box set which includes six previously unreleased recordings, rare photos, extensive liner notes and state-of-the-art mastering. *The Ultimate Yes* (WEA 8122737022) 2003 is a well-balanced 2-CD set.

45s:			
(up to α	Sweetness/Something's Coming	(Atlantic 584 280)	1969 R1
1976)	Looking Around/Everydays	(Atlantic 584 298)	1969 R3
	Time And A Word/The Prophet	(Atlantic 584 323)	1970 R2
	Sweet Dreams/Dear Father	(Atlantic 2091 004)	1970 R1
	I've Seen All Good People/(a) Your Move/Starship Trooper		
	(b) Life Seeker (promo only)	(Atlantic 2814 003)	1971 R2
	Siberian Khatra/		
	And You And I (white label promo)	(6-A1/-B1)	1872 R1
	Roundabout/And You And I	(Atlantic K 10407)	1974
	Soon (from 'Gates Of Delirium')/		
	Sound Chaser	(Atlantic)	1975

NB: α unissued, but demos may have been made.

Yes seem certain to have secured a place in music history as one of the finest and certainly the most successful of the British progressive rock bands. At their finest they were one of the best two or three of the genre, but as their tracks became longer, more directionless and more self-indulgent, they slipped into the bad habits which are so closely identified with progressive rock.

Jon Anderson was born on 25th October 1944 in Lancashire. He met **Chris Squire** in a club in Soho, London, in June 1968. Prior to this **Squire** had been in **The Syn**, who'd recorded two good singles for Deram, whilst **Anderson** had been with a beat group called **The Warriors**, who'd cut one 45 for Decca and two solo 45s for Parlophone under the name **Hans Christian Anderson**. On the demise of **The Syn** their guitarist **Peter Banks** formed another group, **Mabel Greer's Toy Shop** in 1968, which also included **Anderson**, **Squire**, guitarist Clive Bailey and drummer Tub Thumper. It was a loose knit affair which played a combination of soul covers and West Coast-influenced acid-rock. After a few months Bailey and Thumper drifted off and the remaining trio formed **Yes** with the addition of organist Tony Kaye from a flower-power outfit called Bitter Sweet, which did not record, and London-born drummer Bill Bruford.

Soon after they'd began gigging **Yes** secured a residency at London's Marquee Club and a recording deal with Atlantic Records. Their first 45, *Sweetness*, was released in June 1969. A beautiful song, which exploited **Anderson**'s crisp appealing vocals, it lacked a strong commercial hook to be a successful 45 and only sold around 500 copies. The 'B' side, *Something's Coming*, was an adapted version of a song from 'West Side Story', which was never included on any of the band's albums, making this one of their most sought-after 45s. There is some doubt as to whether the follow-up, *Looking Around*, a more upbeat keyboard dominated number, was ever released other than in demo form. It never sold at all and is consequently the band's rarest 45 and the most sought-after by collectors.

Their debut album, released in November 1969, included beautiful re-workings of The Byrd's *I See You* and **The Beatles'** *Every Little Thing* and six originals, including *Sweetness* and *Looking Around*. It was an amalgam of different styles ranging from acoustic ballads to three-part harmonies and keyboard-driven compositions. The jewel of the album was the final track, *Survival*, a complex song with some beautiful vocal passages from **Anderson**, which in many respects combined all three styles. Perhaps the album didn't gel together as well as some of their later efforts but it showed promise and was well received by the critics.

Their follow-up album, *Time And A Word*, was more ambitious. It too contained a couple of covers:- Ritchie Havens' *No Opportunity Necessary, No Experience Needed* and Stephen Stills' *Everydays* (from his Buffalo Springfield era). Once again both were complexly rearranged. The former began with a melodramatic orchestrated introduction but then descended into a web of rather over-complex arrangements. *Everydays* suffered a little from the same problem, although the opening featured some exquisite vocals from **Anderson**. Many of the other tracks like *Clear Days* and *Astral Traveller* featured extensive keyboard doodlings. Two tracks were issued as 45s: *Sweet Dreams*, probably the album's tour de force by virtue of some

YES - Fragile (LP).

951

beautiful vocal harmonies. This featured a track called *Dear Father* on the 'B' side, which didn't appear on album until 1975. The second 45 coupled the title track with *The Prophet*. Neither was a hit but the album was well received and made No 45 in the Album Charts. A conscious decision seems to have been made not to bother with the singles market at this stage. Shortly before its release and following the making of a promotional film for the album in Switzerland, **Peter Banks** was asked to leave the band by **Jon Anderson**, who was in many respects its leader at this time. His replacement was **Steve Howe** who'd played with **The Syndicats**, **The In Crowd**, **Tomorrow** and **Bodast**. **Banks** meanwhile departed for **Blodwyn Pig** but later formed **Flash**. He also recorded a solo album in 1973.

The next album, *The Yes Album*, which was produced by Eddie Offord, was recorded in a Devon cottage. For the first time their sound really gelled together effectively and it represented a tremendous improvement on the two which had preceded it. All the material was self-penned and each side consisted of two extended compositions with a couple of short ones sandwiched in between. The longer tracks captured the band at its best. Indeed many of their finest moments are on this album in the form of tracks like *Yours Is No Disgrace*, the superb *Starship Trooper*, *I've Seen All Good People* and *Perpetual Change*. The first part of *I've Seen All Good People*, *Your Move* was issued as a 45 in the US where it peaked at No 40. The album reached No 7 in the UK Charts and now the group was really in the big time. However, it would be the last that Tony Kaye would play on. His Hammond organ was too limited in scope to achieve the sound that **Anderson** in particular sought and he left to form **Badger**. His replacement **Rick Wakeman** had been with **The Strawbs** and was able to give the band a much fuller keyboard sound making use of a much wider range of keyboard instruments like the moog synthesizer and mellotron.

Their next album, *Fragile*, consisted of nine tracks (four were group compositions, the other five were the individual ideas of each member of the band). *Cans And Brahms*, **Wakeman**'s piece was an adaptation of part of Brahm's *4th Symphony in E Minor Third Movement*. **Anderson** sang all the vocal parts on his composition *We Have Heaven*. On **Chris Squires'** *The Fish* each riff, rhythm and melody was produced using the different sounds of the bass guitar. *Five Percent For Nothing* was a sixteen bar tune by Bill Bruford and **Steve Howe's** *Mood For A Day* was a solo guitar piece. This policy gave the album a more disjointed appearance than its predecessor but certainly the group performances were among the best the band had recorded. The stand-out tracks here were *Heart Of The Sunrise* and the rather over-complex *Roundabout* but already there were glimpses of the self-indulgence that would plague the band in future years. Like its predecessor it climbed to No 7 in the UK Album Charts but it also broke through in the USA to become their first Top 10 album, peaking at No 4.

The follow-up, *Close To The Edge*, came with another Roger Dean designed sci-fi cover as *Fragile* had done. The title track accounted for the whole of side one, with another epic track, *And You And I* (which was released as a double-sided 45 in the US) and the darker *Siberian Khatru*. Shortly after the album a cover version of Paul Simon's *America* was released as a US-only single backed by *Total Mass Retain*. In the UK it

appeared on the budget compilation, *The New Age Of Atlantic* (LP) and was later featured on the *Yesterdays* album. After the 45's release Bill Bruford left to join **King Crimson** and he was replaced by Alan White, who'd played with The Plastic Ono Band.

In May 1973 Atlantic released a triple live album, *Yessongs*, of shows from the previous year. It came in another complex Roger Dean sleeve and included all of the *Close To The Edge* album and much of *Fragile* and *The Yes Album*. It also featured an excerpt from **Rick Wakeman's** solo album, *The Six Wives Of Henry VIII*. The album reached No 7 in the UK and No 30 in the US. A movie was later released with the same name.

January 1974 saw the release of the double album, *Tales From Topographic Oceans*, which found the band at their most self-indulgent. Consisting of just four tracks, one on each side of the album, its theme was based on the Shastric scriptures, which **Anderson** had read about in a book called 'Autobiography Of a Yogi'. The album had its moments, *Ritual*, was the strongest track, but for the most part it lacked much form or structure and was basically a directionless ramble. This didn't seem to affect the sales at the time, though, it climbed to No 1 in the UK Album Charts and stayed there two weeks (largely on the strength of their previous success). It also rose to No 6 in the USA. **Rick Wakeman** left after its release to concentrate on his solo career and a number of keyboard players were auditioned before Patrick Moraz from **Refugee** was offered the place.

Their next album, *Relayer*, continued their recent tradition of extended album tracks. *The Gates Of Delirium*, which was based on an adaptation of Tolstoy's 'War And Peace', accounted for all of side one, whilst *Sound Chaser* and *To Be Over* comprised side two. These two, in particular, were certainly more structured and melodic than much of the formless dross on their previous album. Again the album sold well, peaking at No 4 in the UK and No 5 in the US. The movie 'Yessongs' was also released in November 1974.

Although they were still at the zenith of their commercial success, there were signs that the band was losing a real sense of direction. After an US tour they took most of 1975 off to concentrate on solo projects. To maintain public interest in them Atlantic released the *Yesterdays* compilation, which contained a selection of tracks from their first two albums and two non-LP tracks, *America* and *Dear Father*. In view of the lack of new material, the album not surprisingly only reached No 27 in the UK. It fared a little better in the US, peaking at No 17.

As we leave the time frame of this book in 1976 all of **Yes** members solo projects had made the UK Top 50 and they re-grouped in November of that year with **Rick Wakeman** back in the fold in place of the discontented Moraz, who went on to join **The Moody Blues** in 1978. They went to Switzerland to start work on their *Going For The One* album and remained together successfully until April 1981.

Anderson and **Wakeman** both pursued solo careers in earnest after the band's demise. **Howe**, who also recorded solo albums, later joined Asia

YES - Close To The Edge (LP).

YES - Tales From Topographic Oceans (2-LP).

YES - Relayer (LP).

and **Squire** and White joined ex-**Led Zeppelin** members **Robert Plant** and **Jimmy Page** in what was meant to be a new project, although it never got off the ground. Later in 1980, of course, **Jon Anderson** teamed up with Greek keyboardist Vangelis Papathanassiou in what was to prove a fruitful partnership. Patrick Moraz also went on to record several solo albums in the seventies and eighties.

Yes reformed and continued to record throughout the eighties, nineties and into the new millennium. **Jon Anderson's** voice is as distinctive and strong as ever and they continue to record and tour in the face of growing indifference.

The *Yes Years* 4-CD box is, as one would expect, a fairly comprehensive guide to their career. Aside from many of their best known songs it includes some rare 'B' sides and some previously unreleased live cuts, including several instrumentals on disc three recorded in Switzerland.

In A Word, Rhino/Warners' 2002 5-CD box set contains 57 tracks and does justice to their illustrious career.

The Ultimate Yes is a well-balanced 2-CD set featuring many of their classics like *I've Seen All Good People*, *Survival*, *Yours Is No Disgrace*, *Starship Trooper*, *Roundabout* and *Ritual* on disc 1. The second disc comes up trumps too with *Awaken*, *Don't Kill The Whale*, *Big Generator*, *Wondrous Stories*, *Going For The One* and *You And I* all among the tracks included.

In A Word is a 5-CD box set. The 55-track collection includes six previously unreleased recordings, rare photos, and extensive liner notes and has benefited from state-of-the-art remastering.

Compilation appearances by the band (apart from *America* on *The New Age Of Atlantic* (LP)) were *Survival* on *The Age Of Atlantic* (LP); *Yours Is No Disgrace* and *Sound Chaser* on *By Invitation Only* (LP) in 1976 and *And You And I* on *Supertracks* (LP) in 1977. (VJ)

The Yetties

Personnel:	BOB COMMON	A
	MAC McCULLOCH	A
	BONNY SARTIN	A
	PETE SHULTER	A

ALBUMS:	1	FIFTY STONE OF LOVELINESS	
(up to			(Acorn CF 203) 1969 SC
1976)	2	WHO'S A-FEAR'D: SONGS AND MUSIC	
		FROM DORSET	(Acorn) 1970
	3	KEEP A'RUNNING - IT'S THE YETTIES	(Argo) 1970
	4	OUR FRIENDS	(Argo) 1971
	5	DORSET IS BEAUTIFUL	(Argo) 1972

45s:	Dorset Is Beautiful/Fling It Here	(Argo AFW 113) 1974
(up to	Bandy Bertha's Birthday's/	
1976)	One Morning In May	(Argo AFW 120) 1975
	Costa Del Dorset/ Fill Up The Cider	(Argo AFW 125) 1975
	Cigarettes & Whiskey & Wild Women/	
	She'll Be Comin' Round The Mountain	(Decca F 13654) 1976

This was a long-standing folk group which formed in the village of Yetminster, near Sherbourne in Dorset. They turned professional in 1967 and contributed two cuts *The Leaf* and *The Trashin' Machine* to the *Festival At Towersea* (LP) in 1968. Their debut album *Fifty Stone Of Loveliness* was released the following year and they went on to record a number of albums for Argo. One of their best was *Dorset Is Beautiful*, which included one of their best known songs *The Nutting Girl*. In 1976 they switched to Decca and recorded further albums and singles post-1976. The also had a long-running BBC Radio Show 'Cider And Song'. Bob Common left the band in 1979 and they became a trio. They continue to play in the 21st century and are one of the longest-lasting folk bands in Britain. (VJ)

Yoof

| 45: | It's Gotta Come Down/ | |
| | Take What You Want | (Decca F 13077) 1970 |

No other details known. (MWh)

Chris Youlden

| ALBUMS: | 1 | NOWHERE ROAD | (Deram SML 1099) 1973 SC |
| | 2 | CITY CHILD | (Deram SML 1112) 1974 SC |

| 45: | Nowhere Road/Standing On The Corner | (Deram DM 377) 1973 |

Chris Youlden had earlier played with **Savoy Brown** whom he left to go solo in May 1970. After these few recordings he vanished from the music scene.

Standing On The Corner has been compiled on *Progressive Pop Inside The Seventies* (CD). (VJ)

Johnnie Young

45s:	α	Step Back/Cara Lyn	(Decca F 22548) 1967
		Lady/Good Evening Girl	(Decca F 22636) 1967
		Craise Finton Kirk/I Am The World	(Polydor BM 56186) 1967
		Every Christian Lion Hearted Man/	
		Epitaph To Mr. Simon Sir	(Polydor BM 56199) 1967

NB: α as Johnny Young And Kompany.

This popster's 45 *Craise Finton Kirk* attracted a lot of pirate radio airplay at the time of its release but failed to break through commercially.

Tony Allen writes: The two Polydor singles are actually by 'Johnny Young', not **Johnnie Young** (was his name mispelled on the UK release?) as were the two Decca singles by Johnny Young.

Born as John De Jong in Djakarta, Indonesia on 12 March 1945, his parents were farmers and emigrated to Perth in Western Australia 1945. He had enjoyed a No. 1 Australian hit with *Step Back/Caralyn* (double 'A' side). This is still one of Australia's best loved singles. He was backed by Kompany until moving to England. *Step Back* was written by Stevie Wright and George Young of **The Easybeats**. He had two other Top 5 Australian singles before setting off for the UK for fame and fortune in June 1967.

The two Polydor singles were recorded in England (*Craise Finton Kirk* was written by the **Bee Gees** and had appeared on their debut album, but his version peaked at No. 14 on the Australian charts). The follow-up, *Every Christian Lion Hearted Man* was another **Bee Gees** album track. Performed by **The Bee Gees**, the song was quite psychedelic, but **Young** gave it a poppier interpretation, but to no avail. After this, he returned to Australia in January 1968 broke and disheartened. Once there, he resumed his career as a singer, songwriter and TV host. He had one other minor Australian hit (*It's a Sunny Day*) before turning his efforts to song writing for other Australian artists including *The Real Thing* by **Russell Morris** (No. 1 in Australia).

Through the seventies he concentrated on TV work, producing and comparing "Happening '70" and the long running "Young Talent Time". The theme song of "Young Talent Time" was a ballad version of **The Beatles'** *All My Loving* and was a source of derision whenever **Young** was discussed in the press or in private. He would have been laughing all the way to the bank. The series however, was responsible for kick-starting the careers of several well-known Australian entertainers, including Jamie Redfern, Debra Byrne, Danni Minogue (Kylie's sister) and Tina Arena.

All of his singles are pure pop. Twee cover versions, ballads and MOR pop. He is twice married with several children. *Caralyn* can be heard on Raven CD *60s Downunder Vol. 2* (RVCD-007). (VJ/JM)

Johnny Young

ALBUMS: 1 COUNTRY PRIDE   (Philips) 19??
          2 YOUNG'S BREW   (XTRA) 19??

45s: Always Thinking Of You/Dreaming Country   (RCA 1826) 1969
       Rockytop/Start Anew   (Orange OAS 206) 1970

The band was at one time the leading UK country band and backed several leading USA country and western singers on their UK tours, including George Hamilton and Slim Whitman. (VJ/RG)

Karen Young

ALBUM: 1 SING'S NOBODY'S CHILD AND 13 OTHER
            GREAT SONGS (mono/stereo)
                        (Major Minor MMLP/SMLP 66) 1969 SC

                                                    HCP

45s: Are You Kidding/
       I'm Yours, You're Mine   (Mercury MF 943) 1965 -
       We'll Start The Party Again/
       Wonderful Summer   (Pye 7N 15956) 1965 -
       Too Much Of A Good Thing/
       You Better Sit Down Kids   (Major Minor MM 584) 1968 SC -
       Nobody's Child/
       Oh How I Miss You   (Major Minor MM 625) 1969 6
       Allentown Jail/
       I Need Your Hand In Mine   (Major Minor MM 662) 1970 -
       Que Sera Sera/One Tin Soldier (Major Minor MM 691) 1970 -
       My Elusive Dream/

RIPPLES VOL. 1 (Comp CD) including Karen Young.

Ribbon Of Darkness   (Major Minor MM 699) 1970 -
Vaya Con Dias/Singing Of A Song (Columbia DB 8756) 1971 -
Reissues: Nobody's Child/Allentown Jail (Columbia DB 8746) 1971 -
Nobody's Child/
(Flip by different artist)   (Old Gold OG 9531) 1985 -

This pop singer from Sheffield is best remembered for her Top Ten hit, *Nobody's Child*. Another of her 45s, *Wonderful Summer*, later resurfaced on Marble Arch's 1970 *Hitmakers* (LP) compilation. *You Better Sit Down Kids* was a Sonny Bono song.

Other compilation appearances include: *Me And My Mini Skirt* on *Made In England, Vol. 1* (LP); *Wonderful Summer* on *Ripples, Vol. 1* (CD); and *Let's Start The Party Again* on *Ripples, Vol. 5* (CD). (VJ)

Roger Young

45s: Sweet, Sweet Morning/
       Whatcha Gonna Give Me   (Columbia DB 7869) 1966 R1
   α   It's Been Nice/No Address   (Columbia DB 8092) 1966 R3

NB: α has been reissued in a limited edition pressing of 500 reproduced from the original French jukebox pressing with a large centre hole.

The *It's Been Nice* single, a slice of classic sixties freakbeat, is extremely rare, so its recent reissue is very welcome. The single was produced by Chris Sanford (known to many via Coronation Street) when he was also working with **The Zombies**. (VJ)

Roy Young (Band)

Personnel:			
MICK BURT	drms	A	
JOHN GOLDEN	trumpet	A	
MOSS GROVES	sax	A	
HARVEY HINSLEY	gtr	A	
CHAS HODGES	bs, vcls	A	
ROY YOUNG	keyb'ds, vcls	ABCDEFG	
HOWIE CASEY	sax	B	
CLIFF DAVIES	drms	B	
JOHN LEE	trombone	B	
PAUL SIMMONS	bs	B	
ALAN TOWNSEND	trumpet	B	
DAVE WENDELLS	gtr	B	
ROD COOMBES	drms	C	
RICKY DODD	saxes, hrmnca	CDEFG	
ONNIE McINTYRE	gtr	CD	
NICK SOUTH	bs	CDE	
EDDIE THORNTON	trumpet	CDEFG	
DENNIS ELLIOT	drms	DEFG	
DAVE CASWELL	trumpet	E	
NIC POTTER	bs	FG	
KEITH GEMMEL	sax, flute	G	

ALBUMS: 1(A)   THE ROY YOUNG BAND   (RCA SF 8161) 1971 SC
        2 (B/C) MR. FUNKY   (MCA MKPS 2022) 1972

NB: (1) and (2) have been reissued on one CD.

45s: Granny's Got A Painted Leg/Revolution   (RCA RCA 2031) 1970
       Wild Country Wine/
       New Sun, New Horizon   (MCA MKS 5071) 1971
       Rag Mama Rag/Give It All To You   (MCA MKS 5080) 1972
       Bony Moronie/Back Up Train   (MCA MKS 5098) 1972
       Devil's Daughter/Roll It On   (MCA MUS 1175) 1973
       Dig A Hole/I'm A Loner   (MCA MUS 1214) 1973

Roy Young was the keyboard player in **Cliff Bennett's Rebel Rousers**. When they broke up in early 1970, he formed his own **Roy Young Band**. The entire first support band was with **Cliff Bennett** too, except for Harvey Hinsley who'd had a day job for three years after leaving The Outlaws. Golden left the band in December 1968. Based in England it toured Beirut, The Bahamas and Europe. When it split in December 1969, Hinsley, Hodges and Burt formed the country-rock band **Black Claw**.

In January 1970, **Young** put together a new line-up. Wendells had been with **Lulu and the Luvvers**; Lee with **Da Da** and Casey had been in Krew. This line-up split in August 1971. Wendells joined Mal Gray's Hurricane. Casey did session work before joining **Rigor Mortis**. Simmons departed to **Sammy** and Davies to **If**.

Young's third line-up included ex-**Forevermore** member Onnie McIntyre on guitar; Ricky Dodd (who'd been in **New Formula**) on saxes and harmonica; Eddie Thornton (who'd worked with **Georgie Fame**) on trumpet; Nick South (previously with **Moving Finger**) on bass; and former **Juicy Lucy** man Rod Coombes on drums.

The *Mr Funky* album includes tracks recorded by line-ups B and C. When Coombes departed to **Stealers Wheel**, he was replaced by ex-**If** member Dennis Elliot. McIntyre left to join The Average White Band in May 1972 and trumpeter Dave Caswell (ex-**Ashton Gardner and Dyke**) joined. Caswell and South then left, South joining **Vinegar Joe**. Former **Van Der Graaf Generator** member Nic Potter joined briefly, but then departed to **Rare Bird**. Keith Gemmel (ex-**Sammy**) was also briefly a member, but then left for **Stackridge**.

After they finally called it a day in July 1974 (owing to Lee's death at the time), never having really made it, Elliot went to work with **Hunter/Ronson**. Dodd worked with **Kevin Coyne**; Thornton returned to **Georgie Fame** and **Young** did sessions and also worked with **David Bowie** in 1977. (VJ/JM)

Young Blood

Personnel:	KENT ASHTON	lead vcls	AB
	ROY BLACK	bs	AB
	PETE BALL	organ, piano	AB
	CHRISTOPHER MOORE	lead gtr	AB
	COZY POWELL	drms	A
	MAC POOLE	drms	B

45s:	Green Light/		
	Don't Leave Me In The Dark	(Pye 7N 17495) 1968 SC
	Just How Loud/Masquerade	(Pye 7N 17588) 1968 SC
	Bang-Shan-A-Lang/I Can't Stop	(Pye 7N 17627) 1968 SC
	Continuing Story Of Bungalow Bill/	
	I Will	(Pye 7N 17696) 1969 SC

This Birmingham band was most notable for including **Cozy Powell**. They were earlier known as **The Sorcerers** and in this incarnation recorded an extremely rare single, a version of The Young Rascals' *Love Is A Beautiful Thing* on the Palletten label in Germany. They also toured in Turkey before returning to the UK and selecting the new moniker of **Young Blood**.

Green Light, which was their first single was an Eddy Grant song, originally recorded by **The Equals**. *Don't Leave Me In The Dark*, their first flip side, is quite psychedelic and was written by organist Pete Balls' brother Dennis. By contrast *Bang-Shang-A-Lang* was an Archies song and their final effort was a cover of **The Beatles'** *The Continuing Story Of Bungalow Bill* from *The White Album*. By now **Cozy Powell** had left to join **The Ace Kefford Stand**. His replacement Mac Poole's band **Hush** had just split up.

When **Young Blood** split early in 1969, Pete Ball joined his brother in **The Ace Kefford Stand** and Mac Poole ended up in **Warhorse**.

Compilation appearances have included: *Don't Leave Me In The Dark* on *Visions Of The Past, Vol. 2* (LP & CD); *Green Light* on *Brum Beat - Midlands Beat Groups Of The 60's* (CD); *Green Light* and *Don't Leave Me In The Dark* on *Footsteps To Fame, Vol. 2* (CD); and *The Continuing Story Of Bungalow Bill* on *The Songs Of Lennon and McCartney* (CD) and *Pop-In, Vol 2* (CD). (VJ)

Young Idea

Personnel:	TONY COX	piano, gtr, vcls	A
	DOUGLAS MacCRAE-BROWN	gtr, vcls	A

ALBUM: 1(A) WITH A LITTLE HELP FROM MY FRIENDS
(Music For Pleasure MFP 1225) 1968

45s:	The World's Been Good To Me/		
	It Can't Be	(Columbia DB 7961) 1966 -
	Gotta Get Out Of The Mess I'm In/	
	Games Men Play	(Columbia DB 8067) 1966 -
	Peculiar Situation/	
	Just Look At The Rain	(Columbia DB 8132) 1967 -
	With A Little Help From My Friends/	
	Colours Of Darkness	(Columbia DB 8205) 1967 10
	Mister Lovin' Luggage Man/	
	Room With A View	(Columbia DB 8284) 1967 -

A pop duo formed by two friends from London University. MacCrae-Brown was from Italy originally. Their first two 45s didn't make any impact, but then they toured with **The Hollies**, who gifted them their album track *Peculiar Situation* as a single. This didn't give them a hit, but their cover of **The Beatles'** *With A Little Help From My Friends* was a sizeable hit in 1967. The 'B' side *Colour Of Darkness* is an exquisite pop song with a string arrangement. Their final 45 was a Les Reed/Barry Mason song *Mr Lovin' Luggage Man*. The flip was a self-penned psychedelic pop song.

EMI released an album *With A Little Help From My Friends* on its budget Music For Pleasure label. It featured a number of their own songs (although *Colours Of Darkness* is unfortunately not included). Cox went on to production work.

Compilation appearances have included: *Perculiar Situation* on *Sixties Lost And Found, Vol. 1* (LP); *Mr. Loving Luggage Man* on *Collecting Peppermint Clouds, Vol. 1* (LP); *With A Little Help From My Friends* on on *20 One Hit Wonders* (CD); *Colours Of Darkness* on *Jagged Time Lapse, Vol 4* (CD) and *Room With A View* on *Colour Me Pop, Vol 2* (CD). (VJ)

The Young Ones

Personnel:	RICKY COBURN	lead gtr	A
	TOMMY KELLY	drms	A
	ALAN MOORHOUSE	gtr	A
	GEORGE VARCAS	bs	A
	DAVE WILCOX	vcls	A
	WILMA YORKE	vcls	A

45:	How Do I Tell You/Baby That's It	(Decca F 11705) 1963

This is a weak Merseybeat vocal 45 despite being produced by Shel Talmy. Kelly had previously been with **Earl Preston and The Realms**. (VJ/AD)

The Young Tradition

Personnel:	PETER BELLAMY	vcls, gtr	AB
	ROYSTON WOOD	vcls	AB
	HEATHER WOOD	vcls	B
	(DOLLY COLLINS	vcls	B)
	(ADAM SKEAPING	violin	B)
	(ROD SKEAPING	violin	B)
	(DAVE SWARBRICK	fiddle, mandolin	B)

ALBUMS:	1(B)	THE YOUNG TRADITION	
		(Transatlantic TRA 142) 1966 SC
	2(B)	SO CHEERFULLY ROUND	
		(Transatlantic TRA 155) 1967 SC
	3(B)	GALLERIES	(Transatlantic TRA 172) 1968 SC
	4(-)	THE YOUNG TRADITION SAMPLER (Compilation)	
		(Transatlantic TRASAM 13) 1969 SC
	5(-)	GALLERIES REVISITED	
		(Transatlantic TRASAM 30) 1973

NB: (3) with **Dave Swarbrick**. (5) is a reissue of (3). (1) and (2) reissued on one CD (Transatlantic / Essential! ESM CD 409) 1996. (3) reissued on CD with *No Tradition* a 1977 album by Royston and Heather Wood, the duo who were the heart of this band (Essential! ESMCD 461).

EP:	1	CHICKEN ON A RAFT	
		(Transatlantic TRAEP 164) 1968 SC

45:	The Boar's Head Carol/	
	The Shepherd's Hymn	(Argo AFW 115) 1974

Peter Bellamy and Royston Wood set out singing unaccompanied folk songs and sea shanties on the traditional folk circuit. Soon after Heather Wood (who was unrelated to Royston) joined they signed a record deal with Transatlantic. Their music was characterised by powerful harmonies and **Dave Swarbrick** and Dolly Collins both helped out on their first album. By contrast *Galleries* veered more towards medieval-style music with David Munrow's Early Music Ensemble guesting on a number of tracks. Their *Young Tradition Sampler* compilation includes all the tracks from their *Chicken On A Raft* EP, which is now very hard to find.

They split after a well publicised farewell concert at Cecil Sharpe House in Camden, London. **Peter Bellamy** then went solo recording several albums. Royston Wood initially went solo, too, but then joined the **Albion Country Band**. Heather Wood headed for the United States. Royston Wood later formed **Swan Arcade**. Both he and **Bellamy** are now dead. **Bellamy** committed suicide in 1991 and Royston Wood died in a car accident in April 1990 after being run over by a car in the USA.

Compilation appearances include *The Innocent Hare* on *The Transatlantic Story* CD box set. (VJ)

Young Turks

45:     Duel At Diablo/Our Lady From Maxim's   (CBS 202353) 1966

This is a forgotten sixties single. (VJ)

Youth

45:     Meadow Of My Love/
        Love Me Or Leave Me   (Deram DM 226) 1969 SC

This is a late sixties pop. The 1966 45 on Polydor was a soul effort by a Jamaican (Trevor Sutherland) who came to Britain in 1963. (VJ)

Les Yper Sound

Personnel: MICHEL COLOMBIER   A
               PIERRE HENRY   A

ALBUM: 1(A) MASS FOR THE PRESENT TIME
                          (Philips 4FE 8004) 1969 R2
NB: (1) credited to Pierre Henry. The French release was on Philips too (836 893 DSY) 1969.

45:     Too Fortiche/Psych Rock   (Fontana TF 880) 1967 R1

PIERRE HENRY - Mass For The Present Time (LP).

Although Pierre Henry was French he spent some time here in Britain collaborating with **Spooky Tooth** on their *Celebration* album. A marginal case for inclusion, I've varied my usual criteria in this case since it may interest collectors. The album comprises multi-textured electro-psych and the 45 was a hit in Scandinavia. In Germany *Psych Rock* was issued in a picture sleeve with a different 'B' side, *Jericho Jerk*. The French issue of the album has a scene on the front cover from the modern dance of the same name for Maurice Bejart in honour of Partick Belda, a brilliant dancer who was his tutor and was tragically killed in a car accident.

Psyche Rock the 'B' side of their 45, is a classic groovy instrumental with fuzz guitar, chimes, and oodles of electronic effects. It's resurfaced on *Incredible Sound Show Stories, Vol. 6* (LP). Another track, in similar style, *Teen Tonic* has also been compiled on *Turds On A Bum Ride, Vol. 6* (CD). (VJ)

YES - Something's Coming (2-LP).

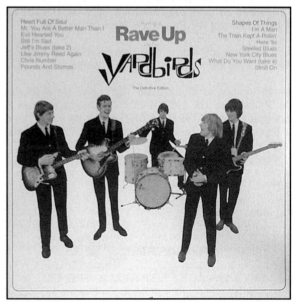

THE YARDBIRDS - Having A Rave-Up With (LP).

Zakarrias

Personnel: DON GOULD   keyb'ds, strings   A
            MARTIN HARRISON   drms   A
            GEOFF LEIGH   flute, sax   A
            PETER ROBINSON   keyb'ds   A
            ZAKARRIAS (ROBERT HAUMER) vcls, gtr, bs, kazoo A

ALBUM: 1(A) ZAKARRIAS   (Deram SML 1091) 1971 R4

NB: (1) reissued 199? with original catalogue number and on CD (Lady Eleanore LE 786).

Zakarrias was Robert Haumer, who came from Vienna in Austria, where he still lives. In 1968 he made a 45 with The Expiration, *It Wasn't Right/And The World Will Be A Bird.* (VRC 45-6266).

The album he made in London in 1971 has turned out to be arguably the rarest on Deram. Musically it's a strange blend of hard glam-rock and bluesy folk, with strongly romanticised hippie lyrics contributed by his wife, Eva. The accompanying band of session musicians plays tight enough, but most songs are a bit too commonplace to excite, and the absence of guitar solos becomes a drag as the album goes on. He's at his best on the slower tracks, when he doesn't rock out too much.

Decca did nothing to promote the album and quickly deleted it. The group played just one gig at Hampstead Country Club because Haumer did not have the relevant work permit. He became so short of money they had to start selling their equipment and the band fell apart.

Geoff Leigh went on to play in **Quiet Sun**, Mouseproof, Henry Cow and Radar Favourites. Peter Robinson had played with **Chris Farlowe** and went on to **Quatermass**, Curtis Maldoon, session work and a spell with **Al Stewart**. In the eighties, Haumer recorded a 45, *Modern/Zeit Bleibt* (Lemon 118 008) 1981 and a maxi 45, *Papa Was A Rolling Stone/Blue Wintermoon* (JMS 27001) 1987 with his own Bobby Hammer Band. He now works as a journalist.

Overall, *Zakarrias* can be taken as evidence that financial and musical value do not necessarily go hand in hand. (VJ/WZ/RMJ)

Zappo

45: Rock And Roll Crazy/Right On!   (Magnet MAG 2) 1973

This is an obscure early seventies 45. (VJ)

Zenith

45s: Face You Won't Forget/
      Just The Two Of Us In Mind   (Dawn DNS 1095) 1975
      Fool That Was In Love/Silent Words (Dawn DNS 1112) 1975

No other details known. (VJ)

The Zephyrs

Personnel: JOHN CARPENTER   drms   A
            JOHN HINDE   bs   A
            MARC LEASE   organ   A
            JOHN PEEBY   gtr   A

                                         HCP

45s: What's All That About/
      Oriental Dream   (Decca F 11647) 1963 R1 -
      I Can Tell/Sweet Little Baby (Columbia DB 7199) 1964 R1 -
      A Little Bit Of Soap/No Message (Columbia DB 7324) 1964 R1 -
      Wonder What I'm Gonna Do/
      Let Me Love You Baby   (Columbia DB 7410) 1964 R1 -
      She's Lost You/
      There's Something About You (Columbia DB 7481) 1965 R1 48
      I Just Can't Take It/She Laughed (Columbia DB 7571) 1965 R1 -

A London-based band whose 45s are now hard to find and quite collectable. Their producer was Shel Talmy who produced early hits for bands like **The Who** and **The Kinks** and launched his own Planet label. **Jimmy Page** played on some of their sessions. *She's Lost You* is a pretty good beat-punk offering with some good organ work from Marc Lease.

They appeared in the film 'Be My Guest' (1965) as 'Slash Wildly and the Cut-Throats', playing *She Laughed* from their then current 45.

Guitarist Pete Gage, who went on to play with **Vinegar Joe** in the early seventies, was in a later line-up.

Compilation appearances have included: *Sweet Little Baby* on *James Patrick Page: Session Man, Vol. 1* (CD); *I Can Tell* on *James Patrick Page: Session Man, Vol. 2* (LP & CD) and *Beat Merchants* (2-LP); *She's Lost You* on *Liverpool '65* (LP) and *The Garage Zone, Vol. 4* (LP); and *I Just Can't Take It* on *Fading Yellow, Vol 1* (CD). (VJ)

Zero Five

45: Dusty/Just Like A Girl   (Columbia DB 7751) 1965

This short-lived mid-sixties five-piece came from Staffordshire. (VJ)

Zig Zag

45: Keep On Bumping/Sleeping Blue Nights (Magnet MAG 17) 1974

This is a disco-influenced 45. Both sides were produced by Barry Blue. He co-wrote the mellow flip side with Lynsey De Paul. The 'A' side was promoting what was then a new dance 'The Bump'. (VJ)

Zior

Personnel: KEITH BONSOR   vcls, keyb'ds, bs, flute A
            PETER BREWER   drms, piano, hrmnca   A
            BARRY SKEELS   bs, vcls   A
            JOHN TRUBA   gtr, vcls   A

ALBUMS: 1(A) ZIOR   (Nepentha 6437 005) 1971 R2
        2( ) EVERY INCH A MAN   (Global) 197?

NB: (1) reissued as *Zior Plus* (See For Miles SEE 276) 1989, also on CD (SEE CD 276) 1989, with three extra tracks. (1) reissued on vinyl with bonus tracks (Akarma 313LP). (2) only issued in Germany. (2) reissued on CD (Germanophon HF 9553) and again on CD and vinyl (Akarma AK 242).

45s: Za Za Za Zilda/
      She's A Bad Bad Woman   (Nepentha 6129 002) 1971 SC
      Cat's Eyes/I Really Do   (Nepentha 6129 003) 1971 SC

ZAKARRIAS - Zakarrias (LP).

An obscure progressive/heavy-rock group whose debut album has few memorable moments but has become quite collectable because of the label it's on. The vocals are poor, the compositions weak and the playing is ponderous. The pick of a poor batch are *I Really Do*, *Za Za Za Zilda* (also released as a 45), *Love's Desire* and *Oh Mariya*, but all four were in a similar, rather flat, heavy-rock style.

The See For Miles album reissue includes five previously unreleased tracks from a second projected album which never saw daylight. The best of these was *Strange Kind Of Magic*, which had a good voodoo beat and some distorted guitar. Overall, they were stronger than the material on the original album. *Cat's Eyes* had some decent heavy rock guitar riffs. The CD featured three additional tracks to the album but I can only really recommend this to **Zior** and **Black Sabbath** fans.

Zior had their roots in Southend's early sixties R&B scene. Kevin Bonsor had previously been in a local R&B outfit, The Essex Five, and then classical/rock fusion outfit, **Cardboard Orchestra**. Pete Brewer had been in another Southend R&B band, The Night Riders. He and Bonsor were **Zior**'s founding members recruiting Truba and Skeels (who'd once played in a London band called The Bum) via a 'Melody Maker' advert.

Zior did have a reputation as a wild live band. They were heavily into Black Magic and Satanic Mass etc. They recorded an album on the Beacon label, later in 1971, which was credited to **Monument**, though in fact it featured all four members of **Zior**.

Pete Brewer eventually ended up a successful musical instrument/ equipment dealer in Southend. Skeels sells dress jewellery in his native Newcastle. Bonsor worked for many years as an engineer/producer at Tin Pan Alley Studios and also became a dee-jay in the late seventies, hosting 'Capital's Big Night Out' at 'The Lyceum' in London's Strand. (VJ)

Zipper

45:    Streak Up And Down/Funk '74   (Youngblood YB 1070) 1974

This obscure single is about streaking! (VJ)

The Zombies

Personnel:	ROD ARGENT	keyb'ds	AB
	PAUL ARNOLD	bs	A
	PAUL ATKINSON	gtr	AB
	COLIN BLUNSTONE	vcls	AB
	HUGH GRUNDY	drms	AB
	CHRIS WHITE	bs	B

ALBUMS:	1(B)	BEGIN HERE	(Decca LK 4679) 1965 R3
(up to	2(B)	ODESSEY AND ORACLE	
1976)		(mono/stereo)	(CBS (S) BPG 63280) 1968 R3
	3(B)	THE WORLD OF THE ZOMBIES	(Decca SPA 85) 1970
	4(B)	TIME OF THE ZOMBIES (2-LP Compilation)	
			(Epic EPC 65728) 1973 SC
	5(B)	ROCK ROOTS (Compilation)	(Decca ROOTS 2) 1976

NB: (3) is a reissue of (1). (2) was reissued on Rock Machine and *Meet The Zombies* (Razor RAZ 34) 1988, also on CD (MACH 6) 1986. (1) and (2) reissued on CD (Repertoire REP 4215 and 4214 respectively) 1992 with several additional tracks. (1) reissued (Big Beat CDWIKD 191) 1999, which includes both the stereo and mono version and the band's UK EP or you can reprogramme it and enjoy the US version of the album, *The Zombies*. (2) reissued on vinyl (Big Beat WIKD 181) 1998 and on CD (Big Beat CDWIKD 181), with the CD version including both mono and stereo versions of the original album plus three unissued tracks not included in the *Zombie Heaven* set. They also appeared on the Soundtrack *Bunny Lake Is Missing* (RCA RD 7791) 1965 (R2).

Also of interest is *Live On The BBC 1965-67* (Rhino RNLP 120) 1985, *She's Not There*, a compilation (Decca TAB 34) 1981 and *The Zombies* (See For Miles SEE 30) 1986, which compiled their 'A' and 'B' sides. This was also released on CD (SEE CD 30) 1988. Besides featuring their sole UK EP, *The EP Collection* (See For Miles SEECD 358) 1992 also draws material from their five French EPs as well as a cross-section of 45 and album tracks. *Zombie Heaven* (Big Beat ZOMBOX 7) 1998, is a 4-CD set which alongside their more familiar tunes includes mono single mixes, making their first appearance on CD, plus demos, outtakes, unfinished studio sessions and BBC recordings. Another CD, *The Zombies: 1964-67* (More Music MOCD 3009) 1995, contains 13 of their Decca recordings from the 1964-66 period (including their two hits, *She's Not There* and *Tell Her No*), three cuts from their classic *Odessey and Oracle* album and live renditions of four of the band's more popular numbers by Rod Argent from 1977. Other compilations include *Best Of The*

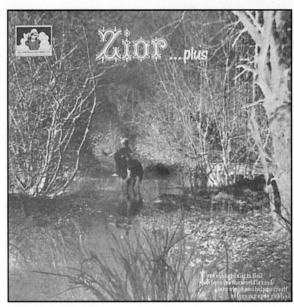

ZIOR - Zior... Plus (LP).

Zombies (Music Club MCCD 002) 1991; *Collection: Zombies* (CD/LP) (Castle Collector CCSCD 196) 1988; *Five Live Zombies* (CD/LP) (Razor RAZCD 41) 1989; *New World* (CD/LP) (Essential ESSCD 131) 1991; *Night Riding: Zombies* (CD) (Nightriding KNCD 10015) 1990; *The Zombies Collection, Vol. 1* (CD) (Impact IMCD 9 00691) 1989 and *Vol. 2* (CD) (Impact IMCD 9 00692) 1989; the 3-CD set, *The Zombies* (Razor RAZCDBOX 1) 1991; *Zombie Heaven* (Big Beat ZOMBOX 7) 1997 is a 4-CD box set and *The Decca Stereo Anthology* (Big Beat CDWIK 2 225) 2002 is a 2-CD set, containing all their output for Decca. *Live At The BBC* (CD) (Repertoire REP 4790) is a 28-track collection of tracks recorded in 1964-1968 and including a medley of jingles they recorded for the Kenny Everett Show. *Singles Collection: A's and B's* (Big Beat CDWIKD 200) presents both sides of the 14 singles they released in the UK in the sixties in mono and with an informative booklet. *The Singles As & Bs* (Repertoire REP 4985) 2002 is a 2-CD set available on German import. *The Zombies* (Vareses Sarabande 1394822) 2004 features recordings from their Decca and Parrot period.

EP:	1	THE ZOMBIES	(Decca DFE 8598) 1965 R2

HCP

45s:	She's Not There/		
	You Make Me Feel Good	(Decca F 11940) 1964	12
	Leave Me Be/Woman	(Decca F 12004) 1964	-
	Tell Her No/What More Can I Do	(Decca F 12072) 1965	42
	She's Coming Home/I Must Move	(Decca F 12125) 1965	-
	Whenever You're Ready/I Love You	(Decca F 12225) 1965	-
	Is This The Dream/Don't Go Away	(Decca F 12296) 1965	-
	Remember You/Just Out Of Reach	(Decca F 12322) 1966	SC -
	Indication/How Were We Before	(Decca F 12426) 1966	SC -
	Gotta Get Hold Of Myself/		
	The Way I Feel Inside	(Decca F 12495) 1966	SC -
	Goin' Out Of My Head/		
	She Does Everything For Me	(Decca F 12584) 1967	SC -
	I Love You/The Way I Feel Inside	(Decca F 12798) 1968	SC -
	Friends Of Mine/Beechwood Park	(CBS 2960) 1967	R1 -
	Care Of Cell 44/Maybe After He's Gone	(CBS 3087) 1967	R1 -
	Time Of The Season/I'll Call You Mine	(CBS 3380) 1968	R1 -
Reissues:	Care Of Cell 44/Maybe After He's Gone	(Epic EPC 2220) 1974	
	Time Of The Season/I'll Call You Mine	(Epic EPC 3380) 1975	
	Time Of The Season/Imagine The Swan	(CBS 2-1203) 1975	-
	She's Not There/Tell Her No	(Old Gold OG 9346) 1983	-
α	She's Not There/Time Of The Season/Tell Her No/		
	Got My Mojo Working	(Special Edition CD 3-12) 1988	-

NB: α CD single.

The Zombies never achieved the success their talent merited, especially in the UK, but have gone on to be acclaimed as one of the more unusual and gifted bands of the sixties. In particular their frequent use of jazzy keyboards in place of guitar, and **Colin Blunstone**'s uniquely breathy vocals, set them apart from the vast majority of their contemporaries.

They were formed by **Rod Argent**, **Colin Blunstone**, Hugh Grundy and Paul Atkinson whilst still at St Albans Grammar School, Hertfordshire, in 1963. Their original bassist was Paul Arnold, but he left the same year to concentrate on his studies and later qualified as a doctor. He was replaced by Chris White, whose father let them rehearse in a room above a store he owned. This accelerated their development, and before the year was through they'd undertaken a number of gigs around the Hertfordshire area.

In January 1964 they won a regional beat group competition organised by the London Evening News. The prize was an audition with Decca Records, who were impressed by **Argent** and White's songwriting and **Blunstone**'s unusual vocals. The group therefore found itself in possession of a long-term recording contract. The following month they left school with a collective total of 50 'O' and 'A' level passes, something Decca was quick to focus publicity on. The tag of 'Britain's brainiest beat band' never really left them.

With Decca staff producer Ken Jones at the helm, they proceeded to record a stunning debut 45, *She's Not There*. Its unusual, jazzy arrangement and dramatic vocal style gave them a worldwide hit. In particular it set a pattern of greater success in the US (where it made No 2) than here (where it made No 12) that was to continue throughout their career. Indeed, *She's Not There* sold over a million copies in the US and in December 1964 the band played a 10-day US tour with other leading stars of the era. Back in the UK, however, their fortunes were already waning. A follow-up 45, *Leave Me Be* (similar to *She's Not There* but less commercial), flopped and the superb *Tell Her No* just crept into the Top 30 here, though it made the US top ten.

Their debut album, 1965's *Begin Here*, was a mixture of originals and R&B standards like *I Got My Mojo Working* and *Roadrunner*. An undoubted highlight was their eerie version of George Gershwin's *Summertime*, but the whole collection was enjoyable and stands as one of the best British albums of its sort. It didn't chart, but they spent much of the year touring the USA (where their debut album had different contents), supporting **Herman's Hermits** and later **The Searchers**. Their next two 45s, *She's Coming Home* and *I Want You Back Again* were both minor US hits. The latter, in fact, wasn't even released in the UK.

In January 1966 they appeared very briefly in Otto Preminger's thriller 'Bunny Lake Is Missing', singing *Remember You*, *Just Out Of Reach* and the brilliant *Nothing's Changed*, but when the former two tracks were coupled on a 45 they failed to sell. The soundtrack is now very rare.

After a fraught tour of the Far East in the second half of 1966, they grew increasingly frustrated at Decca's reluctance to let them record a second album and generally disenchanted by the label's failure to promote them or assign them a more experimental producer. The final straw came when *Goin' Out Of My Head*, was mixed in their absence and released without their approval. They decided to split after having one more shot at making music on their own terms. As a result they signed to CBS early in 1967, receiving a meagre £1,000 advance and the promise of greater artistic freedom. Decca, meanwhile, issued two further 45s culled from leftovers.

Having spent a few weeks rehearsing in a village hall in their native Hertfordshire, the band entered Abbey Road studio that summer to make

The "Bunny Lake Is Missing" soundtrack album featuring The Zombies.

their belated second album. Not only were they the first non-EMI act to record there, they were also the first to use Studio Two after **The Beatles** finished making *Sgt. Pepper's*, and thus employed several of the innovations pioneered during their sessions. In particular they had two eight tracks rigged together, greatly increasing the number of overdubs possible. They also layered their vocals, creating breathtakingly dense and complex harmonies.

The album they recorded, *Odessey and Oracle*, is an exquisite delight. Full of lovely melodies, imaginative arrangements and **Blunstone**'s breathy vocals, every track's a winner. Highlights are hard to isolate, but opener *Care Of Cell 44*, *A Rose For Emily* (with its simple piano backing and lovely harmonies), *Beechwood Park* (another song of stunning simplicity), *Hung Up On A Dream* (more complex, even trippy, with gorgeous orchestration and lovely dreamy vocals), the happy-go-lucky *I Want Her She Wants Me* and *Butchers Tale* (Western Front 1914) with its ominous fairground-style organ, spring to mind. Perhaps its magnum opus, however, was the oddly unsettling *Time Of The Season*, their best 45 since *She's Not There*.

Despite the experimentation on show, it's interesting to note that, perhaps alone amongst their heavyweight contemporaries that year, drugs played no part whatsoever in **The Zombies**' creativity, and they've made it clear that they never regarded themselves as 'psychedelic' in any way.

With the sessions complete, they had every reason to expect another breakthrough, but when *Friends Of Mine* and *Care Of Cell 44* were issued as 45s that autumn and failed to sell, they became disillusioned and decided to split the following spring. CBS went ahead and issued *Odessey and Oracle* in April (the misspelling of Odyssey was the mistake of sleeve designer Terry Quirk) and *Time Of The Season* as a 45. Both were received rapturously in the UK. 'Disc's' review, which praised the album's 'outstanding creativity, originality, sensitivity and sheer dimension', was typical, but promotion was non-existent and it failed to chart. The album has gone on to be a significant collectors' item, especially in mono - unsurprising, given that Chris White remembers CBS's Head of A&R at the time telling him that that the total sales amounted to 800!

All seemed lost, but when US superstar Al Kooper heard *Odessey* on a visit to London he fell in love with it. Returning to the US with a cluster of copies, he badgered Columbia to issue it stateside. Eventually it was granted a release on CBS soul subsidiary Date, and *Time Of The Season* started to receive considerable airplay. Pulled as a single in March 1969, it became their second US million seller, rising to No 3. The only problem was the lack of a band to promote it. **The Zombies** came under enormous pressure to reform but, having not played live for two years, they refused to be resurrected. As a result a predictable host of bogus groups toured the US using their name, and the ex-members had to resort to law suits to halt them.

Argent and White had gone into production work after the band's demise, but **Argent**, who was in the throes of forming a new band (to be called **Argent**), did undertake some **Zombies** recordings with an interim line-up of

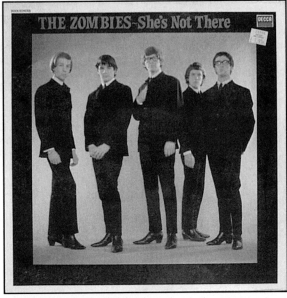

THE ZOMBIES - She's Not There (LP).

himself on vocals and keyboards, Jim Rodford (bs), Hugh Grundy (drms) and Rick Birkett (gtr). The aim was to make an album of unreleased material, but this fizzled out when two tracks, *Imagine The Swan* and *If It Don't Work Out*, were issued as US singles but failed to sell. **Colin Blunstone**, meanwhile, re-recorded *She's Not There* as **Neil McArthur** before embarking on a solo career. In recent years **Argent** and **Blunstone** have toured together under **The Zombies** name, but the prospect of a full reunion was scotched when Paul Atkinson succumbed to cancer in 2003. He had become a top A&R man in the US. Hugh Grundy, meanwhile, runs a pub in Hertfordshire.

Many compilations have appeared since their split, by far the most comprehensive of which was *Zombie Heaven*, a 4-CD box set compiled by Alec Palao. Disc one rounds up all their Decca albums and singles, while disc two includes the whole of *Odessey and Oracle* as well as leftovers for a third album which never emerged. Disc three concentrates on demos and rarities, and disc four expands on the collection of BBC Radio Sessions Rhino put out in 1985. The result is a very impressive package indeed, and the accompanying booklet is superb too.

THE ZOMBIES - Odessey And Oracle (LP).

Decca reissued *Begin Here* as *World Of The Zombies* in 1970, and put out a compilation of their early material as part of their *Rock Roots* series in 1976. CBS put out a *History Of...* compilation as well as the 2-LP *Time Of The Zombies* package. The *Live On The BBC 1965-67* collection on the US Rhino label includes 14 songs and studio chat from 'Top Of The Pops', 'Saturday Club' and 'The David Symonds Show', as well as some of their singles from this era (*Tell Her No*, *Whenever You're Ready* and *Going Out Of My Head*) and several covers of classic soul numbers performed in **The Zombies'** unique style. See For Miles' 1986 compilation is a fine collection of the 'A' and 'B' sides of their Decca singles and both sides of a rare US-only 45, *I Want Her Back/I Remember When I Loved Her*.

The Razor compilation includes their three most successful songs, *She's Not There*, *Tell Her No* and *Time Of The Season*. Much of the remaining material comes from their 1973 double compilation, *Time Of The Zombies*, which had included several previously unissued tracks. Two tracks get their first airing on this compilation:- *Girl Help Me*, with **Blunstone** on top form, and the disappointing *I Could Spend The Day*.

The Repertoire CDs take each of their original albums and add several additional tracks. *Begin Here* is supplemented by their 1964-66 singles, tracks from their rare Decca EP and the previously unissued blues number, *I'm Going Home*. *Odessey And Oracle* is supplemented by their remaining 45s and all their CBS material, including outtakes which earlier got an airing on the *Time Of The Zombies* compilation.

The Decca Stereo Anthology is a 2-CD set containing all their Decca output. They've been remixed to provide a more polished sheen courtesy of Alec Palao.

The Singles As & Bs compiles their 45 output in a fold-out 2-CD sleeve package, which contains a booklet of rare sleeves and memorabilia. Disc

One compiles their 1964-1967 Decca period and Disc Two covers the *Odessey And Oracle* period material, plus their Decca EP and the tracks from *Bunny Lake Is Missing*. This is an excellent package. *Singles Collection: A's and B's* contains both sides of their 14 UK singles recorded during the sixties. *Live At The Bloomsbury Theatre* (CD) captures them together on stage for the first time for 30 years performing their sixties hits and songs from a new 2004 CD *Out Of The Shadows*.

Compilation appearances have included: *I Love You* on *Made In England, Vol. 2* (CD); *Woman* on *Sixties Lost And Found, Vol. 2* (LP) and *Sixties Explosion, Vol. 1* (CD); *She's Not There* on *Your Starter For Ten!!* (CD), *60's Mix* (CD) and on *Everlasting Love* (CD); *Nothing's Changed* on *Fourteen, Lord Taverners* (LP); *Tell Her No* on *Hard-Up Heroes* (2-LP); and *Time Of The Season* on *The Rock Machine Turns You On* (LP). (VJ/RMJ)

Zuiderzee

Personnel incl: RAY HOPKIN   vcls

45s:	(You're My) Soul And Inspiration/	
	Please Don't Call Me	(CBS 202062) 1966
	Peace Of Mind/Provocative Child	(CBS 202235) 1966

This five-piece group from Wolverhampton specialised in soulish ballads. (VJ)

Zygoat

ALBUM:	1	ZYGOAT	(Polydor 2383 270) 1975 SC

45:	Catching A Thief/Letitia's Song	(Polydor 2058 124) 1975

This is reputedly an album of electronic music. (VJ)

Zzebra

Personnel:	LOUGHTY AMAO	perc, sax, flute, vcls	AB
	GUS EADON	piano, gtr, vcls	A
	LIAM GENOCKEY	drms, vcls	AB
	DAVE QUINCEY	sax	AB
	TERRY SMITH	gtr	A
	STEVE BYRD	gtr	B
	TOMMY EYRE	keyb'ds, flute, vcls	B
	ALAN MARSHALL	vcls	B
	JOHN McCOY	bs	B

ALBUMS:	1(A)	ZZEBRA	(Polydor 2383 296) 1974
	2(B)	PANIC	(Polydor 2383 326) 1975

45s:	Zardoz/Amusofi	(Polydor 2058 446) 1974
	Mr. J./Puts The Light On Me	(Polydor 2058 579) 1975

Zzebra was a jazzy progressive outfit. Four of the eight tracks on *Panic* are instrumentals: Tommy Eyre's *Death By Drowning*; Dave Quincey's *Karrola*; Amao/Quincey's *La Si Si-La So So* and Quincey and Eyre's arrangement of Spector and Mann's *You've Lost That Lovin' Feelin*. It's pleasant listening but certainly not essential.

Terry Smith also recorded as a solo artist and together with Dave Quincy were previously central members of **If**. Alan Marshall had earlier played on some **Pete Bardens** albums. Gus Eadon was previously in **Love Affair**. Both Liam Genochy and John McCoy previously backed Canadian folk singer Julie Felix. Loughty Amao had been in Osibisa. (VJ)

COMPILATIONS 1963 - 76

Here are the full details of the compilations released during the era which are relevant to this book. Many are referred to in the text of the book. Rarity ratings and chart placings, where applicable are also shown.

A

A Galaxy Of Stars	(Pye NSPL 9874)	1969	
The Age Of Atlantic	(Atlantic 2464 013)	1970	SC
Alive!	(Key KL 002)	1969	SC
All Folk Together	(Talisman STAL 5013)	1970	SC
All Good Clean Fun (2-LP)	(United Artists UDX 201/202)		
		1971	SC
Anthology Of British Blues, Vol. 1 (2-LP)			
	(Immediate IMAL 03/04)	1969	SC
Anthology Of British Blues, Vol. 2 (2-LP)			
	(Immediate IMAL 05/06)	1969	SC
At The Cavern	(Decca LK 4597)	1964	R2
Ayshire Folk (private pressing)	(Deroy DER 1052)	1974	R2

B

Backtrack One	(Track 2407 001)	1970	
Backtrack Two	(Track 2407 002)	1970	
Backtrack Six	(Track 2407 006)	1970	SC
Backtrack Seven	(Track 2407 007)	1970	
Bastards Of British Rock (2-LP)	(Charly CR 300017)	1975	
Battle Of The Bands, Vol. 1	(B&C BCM 103)	1971	SC
Beacon Brings It To You	(Beacon BEAB 1)	1969	SC
Beat	(Elite Special)	1965	
The Beat Merchants (2-LP)	(United Artists UDM 101/2)		
		1976	SC
Begin Here (2-LP) (mono/stereo)	(Elektra EUK 262/EUKS 7262)		
		1968	SC
The Best Of British Folk	(Xtra XTRA 103)	1965	SC
The Best Of Okeh, Vol 1	(Epic EPC 81224)	1976	SC
The Best Of Okeh, Vol 2	(Epic EPC 81532)	1976	SC
The Best Of President, Vol. 1	(President PTL 1016)	1969	SC
The Best Of President, Vol. 2	(President PTL 1036)	1969	SC
The Best Of Scottish Folk	(Xtra XTRA 1053)	1967	
The Big Folk	(Fontana SFXL 55)	1969	SC
Blues Anytime	(Immediate IMLP 014)	1968	No. 40
Blues Anytime, Vol. 2	(Immediate IMLP 015)	1968	
Blues Anytime, Vol. 3	(Immediate IMLP 019)	1968	
Blues At Sunrise	(Saga FID 2165)	1969	SC
The Blues Guitar Box (3-CD)	(Sequel NXT CD 185)	1992	
Blues Leftovers	(Immediate IMLP 024)	1969	SC
Blues Like Showers Of Rain	(Saydisc Matchbox SDM 142)		
		1967	R2

GREASY TRUCKERS PARTY Comp. CD.

Blues Like Showers Of Rain, Vol. 2	(Saydisc Matchbox SDM 167)		
		1968	R2
Bombers	(Polydor 2675 007)	1971	SC
British Blue-Eyed Soul (mono/stereo)	(Island ILP 966/ILPS 9066)		
		1968	R2
Brum Beat	(Decca LK 4598)	1964	R3
Brum Beat	(Dial DLP 1)	1964	R2
Bumper Bundle	(Decca LK 4734)	1966	SC
Bumpers (2-LP)	(Island IDP 1)	1970	
By Invitation Only	(Atlantic K 60112)	1976	

C

Christmas At The Patti (two 10" records)			
	(United Artists UDX 205/6)	1973	SC
Classical Heads	(Charisma CAS 1008)	1970	
Clogs (Folk Sampler) (w/insert)	(Pegasus PS 1)	1972	
Club Folk Volume One	(Pegasus PS 2)	1972	SC
Club Folk Volume Two	(Pegasus PS 3)	1972	SC
A Cold Wind Blows	(Elektra EUK 253)	1966	
Come Together (3-LP)	(A&M Mayfair AMLB 51028)		
		1971	
The Concert For Bangla Desh (3-LP box set)			
	(Apple STCX 3385)	1972	
			SC No. 1
The Contemporary Guitar Sampler	(Transatlantic TRASAM 14)		
		1970	
Contemporary Guitar Sampler	(Transatlantic TRASAM 15)		
		1970	
Conversation With The Blues	(Decca LK 4664)	1964	R2
Corby Catchment Area	(Wicksteed WCKLP 02)	1972	R4

D

Dawn Takeaway Concert	(Dawn DNLB 3024)	1971	
Deeper Into The Vaults	(United Artists UAS 29153)		
		1971	
Deep Overground Pop	(Polydor 2673 001)	1970	SC
The Deram Golden Pops Sampler	(Deram SML 1027)	1968	R3
Dimension Of Miracles	(Mercury 6641 006)	1970	SC
Disturbance (2-LP)	(Charisma)	1973	
A Drop Of The Hard Stuff	(Ember EMB 3413)	1970	
Dungeon Folk	(BBC REC 35S)	1969	
Dynamite	(K-Tel TE 298)	1973	

E

Earthed	(Middle Earth MDLS 20)	1970	R1
Edinburgh Folk Festival, Vol 1	(Decca LK 4546)	1963	SC
Edinburgh Folk Festival, Vol 2	(Decca LK 4563)	1963	SC
Electric Muse - The Story Of Folk Into Rock (4-LP set with booklet)			
	(Island/Transatlantic FOLK 1001)		
		1975	R1
El Pea (2-LP)	(Island IDLP 1)	1971	SC
The Exciting New Liverpool Sound	(Columbia)	1964	

F

Festival At Towersea	(Zeus CF 201)	1968	R1
Fill Your Head With Rock (2-LP)	(CBS PR 39/40)	1970	
Firepoint - A Collection Of Folk Blues	(Music Man no#)	1969	R3
Firepoint - A Collection Of Folk Blues (reissue)			
	(Spark SRLM 2003)	1973	R1
The First Great Rock Festivals Of The 70's: Isle Of Wight and Atlanta (3-LP)	(CBS 66311)	1971	SC
Flash Fearless vs The The Zorg Women Parts 5 & 6			
	(Chrysalis CHR 1081)	1975	SC
Folk At The Black Horse	(Eron ERON 012)	1976	
Folk At The Chequers	(Flams/Wounded WR 1068)		
		1976	SC
Folk Blues Song Fest	(Ember NR 5015)	1964	SC
Folk Favourites	(Waverley ZLP 2067)	1966	
Folk Festival (2-LP)	(Transatlantic TRA 324)	1976	SC

Folk Heritage	(Windmill WMD)	1973	R1
Folk Nottingham Style	(Nottingham Festival FEST 1)		
		1973	R3
Folk Now	(Decca LK 4783)	1965	SC
Folk Philosophy	(Talisman STAL 5019)	1971	SC
The Folk Scene	(Golden Guinea GGL 0265)		
		1963	SC
Folk Scene (Private Pressing)	(Folkscene SSP 001)	1966	R3
Fourteen - The Lord's Taverners' Album			
	(Decca LK 4695)	1965	R1
49 Greek Street	(RCA SF 8118)	1970	
From The Vaults	(Liberty LBS 83278)	1969	SC
Fruity	(Warner Bros WS 1874)	1970	

G

Glastonbury Fayre Revelations - A Musical Anthology (3-LP set, with poster, booklets and pyramid)	(Revelation REV 1/2/3)	1972	R3
Go!	(Columbia SX 6062) 1966		R2
Going Home	(Warner Brothers WS 1874)		
		1970	
Going Up The Country	(Decca LK 4931)	1968	SC
Good Folk Of Kent (w/insert)	(Eron 004)	1975	R1
Good Time Music (mono/stereo)	(Elektra EUK 260/EUKS 7260)		
		1967	R1
Greasy Truckers - Live At Dingwalls Dancehall (2-LP)			
	(Greasy Truckers GT 4997)		
		1973	SC
Greasy Truckers Party (2-LP)	(United Artists UDX 203/4)		
		1974	SC
Great Scots Sampler	(Transatlantic TRASAM 17)		
		1970	SC
Great Scots Sampler, Vol 2	(Transatlantic TRASAM 21)		
		1970	SC
Group Beat '63	(Realm RM 149)	1963	R1
Group '64	(World Record Club TP 444)		
		1964	SC
Guitar Workshop (2-LP)	(Transatlantic TRA 271) 1973		SC
Gutbucket	(Liberty LBX 3)	1969	SC

H

Handle With Care	(Probe SPSS 1)	1970	
Hard Up Heroes 1963-68 (2-LP)	(Decca DPA 3009/10)	1974	SC
Harvest Bag	(Harvest SHSS 3)	1971	
Harvest Sampler Of The Initial Four June Releases (promo-only)			
	(Harvest SPSLP 118)	1969	R2
Has It Dawned On You?	(Dawn DNSM 5001)	1975	
Heads And Tales (2-LP)	(Transatlantic TRASAD 18)		
		1970	
Headline News	(Polydor 582 701)	1966	SC

PICNIC Comp. 2-LP.

Heads In	(A&M Mayfair AMLB 1016)		
		1970	
Heads Together, First Round (2-LP)	(Vertigo 6360 045)	1971	SC
Here Come The Girls	(Pye NPL 18121)	1965	SC
History Of British Blues	(Sire)	1973	
Hit Machine	(K-Tel TE 713)	1976	No. 4
The Hitmakers	(Pye NSPL 18108)	1964	SC
Hitmakers	(Marble Arch MAL 1259) 1969		
Hits From The Ivy League, The Rockin' Berries and The Sorrows			
	(Marble Arch MAL 650) 1966		
Hits Of The Mersey Era - Volume One			
	(EMI NUT 1)	1976	
The House That Jack Built	(Track 613 016)	1969	R1
How Blue Can We Get (2-LP) (w/insert)			
	(Blue Horizon PR 45/46) 1969		R1

I

I Asked For Water... And She Gave Me Gasoline			
	(Liberty LBS 83252)	1969	R2
Immediate Lets You In	(Immediate IML YIN 1)	1969	SC
In Our Own Way (Oldies But Goodies)			
	(Blue Horizon PR 37)	1969	R1
Ireland's Greatest Sounds: Five Top Groups From Belfast's Maritime Club			
	(Ember FA 2034)	1966	R2
Irish Folk Night	(Decca LK 4633)	1964	SC
It's Dance Time	(Pye Golden Guinea GGL 0249)		
		1963	SC

J

John Peel Presents Top Gear	(BBC REC 525)	1969	R1
John Peel's Archive Things	(BBC REC 68 M)	1970	SC
Journey Through The Sixties	(Ronco RR 2007)	1974	
Juke Box Jive	(K-Tel NE 709)	1976	No. 3

L

Let Me Tell You About The Blues	(Blue Horizon LP 2)	1966	R4
Listen Here!	(Transatlantic TRASAM 2)		
		1968	SC
Liverpool Beat	(Embassy WLP 6065)	1964	SC
Liverpool Today - Live At The Cavern	(Ember NR 5028)	1965	R1

M

Marmalade - 100% Proof	(Marmalade 643 314)	1969	SC
Me And The Devil (mono/stereo)	(Liberty LBL/LBS 83190) 1969		R1
* Mersey Beat 1962-64 (2-LP)	(United Artists USD 305/6)		
		1975	
Mickie Most Presents: British Go-Go (mono/stereo)			
	(MGM E/SE 4306)	1965	
More From The Vaults	(Liberty LBS 83377)	1970	
More Rhythm And Blues	(Marble Arch MAL 813)	1968	
Morris On	(Island HELP 5)	1972	SC
The Mushroom Folk Sampler	(Mushroom 100 MR 16)	1971	R2
My Generation	(EMI NUT 4)	1976	

N

The New Age Of Atlantic	(Atlantic K 20024)	1972	
			SC No. 25
Nice Enough To Eat (mono/stereo)	(Island IWP(S) 6)	1969	
No Introduction	(Spark SRLM 107)	1968	SC
No One's Gonna Change Our World	(Regal Starline SRS 5013)		
		1969	SC
Nothing But The Blues (2-LP)	(CBS 66278)	1971	R1
Nova Sampler	(Decca Nova SPA 72)	1970	SC

O

Old Grey Whistle Test	(Super Beeb BELP 004) 1975		

THE WORLD OF HITS VOL. 3 Comp. LP.

One More Chance	(Charisma CLASS 3)	1973	
One Night Stand	(Columbia 33SX 1536)	1963	R1
On The Road Again	(Xtra XTRA 1133)	1973	R2
On The Scene	(Columbia 33SX 1662)	1964	R3
Our Folk Music Heritage	(Trailer LET SAM 2087)	1975	
Over The Rainbow	(Chrysalis)	1975	

P

Package Tour	(Golden Guinea GGL 0268)		
		1964	SC
Paddy In The Smoke	(Topic 12T 176)	1968	
Paddy Is Dead And The Kids Know	(Golden Guinea)	1969	
x Petal Pushers	(Chess LP-1520)	1967	R1
Picnic (2-LP)	(Harvest SHSS 1/2)	1970	
Pop Party	(Polydor 2682 001)	1970	
Pop Party (3-LP box set)	(Polydor 236 517/8/9)	1968	R1
Pop Power '69 (3-LP box set)	(Polydor 109601/2/3)	196?	R1
Progressive 60's (3-LP box set) (Dutch)			
	(Philips 6685 106)	196?	SC
Purple People	(Purple TPSS 1)	1973	SC
Pye Chartbusters	(Pye PCB 15000)	1971	No. 36
Pye Chartbusters, Vol 2	(Pye PCB 15001)	1971	No. 29
Pye Presents Ten Years Of Golden Hits (2-LP) (Aust)			
	(Astor GG 965/2)	19??	
Pye Sixties Sampler (99 copies only)	(Pye PSA 6)	1971	SC

R

Rags Reels And Airs	(Polydor 236 514)	1969	
Rare Tracks	(Polydor 2482 2740)	1975	
Rave (mono/stereo)	(United Artists (S)UX 1214)		
		1969	SC
The Mike Raven Blues Show	(Xtra XTRA 1047)	1966	SC
The Mike Raven Blues Sampler	(Transatlantic TRASAM 5)		
		1969	SC
Rave On	(Mooncrest CREST 17)	1974	
Raw Blues (mono/stereo)	(Ace Of Clubs ACL/SCL 1220)		
		1967	SC
Reading Festival '73	(GM GML 1008)	1974	
Ready, Steady, Go!	(Decca LK 4577)	1964	
		R1	No. 20
Ready, Steady, Win	(Decca LK 4634)	1964	R2
Recording The Blues	(CBS 52797)	1970	SC
Rhythm And Blues	(Decca LK 4616)	1964	R2
Rhythm And Blues	(Marble Arch MAL 726)	1967	
Rhythm And Blues, Vol. 1	(Golden Guinea GGL 0280)		
		1964	SC
Rhythm And Blues, Vol. 2	(Golden Guinea GGL 0351)		
		1964	
Rhythm And Blues Party	(Mercury MCL 20019)	1964	R2

Rhythm And Blues Party (reissue)	(Philips 643 6028)	1976	
Rock Generation, Vol. 7 (French)	(Byg 529 707)	1971	
Rock Generation, Vol. 8 (French)	(Byg 529 708)	1971	
The Rock Machine Turns You On	(CBS PR 22)	1968	No. 18
Rock Party (2-LP)	(Polydor 2682 002)	1971	SC
The Roots Of British Rock, Vol. 1 (Fr) (features **The Animals** and **Yardbirds**)	(Byg)	1971	
The Roots Of British Rock, Vol. 2 (Fr) (features **The Animals** and **Yardbirds**)	(Byg)	1971	
The Roots Of British Rock, Vol. 3 (Fr) (features Sonny Boy Williamson and **The Animals** and **Graham Bond**)	(Byg)	1971	
The Roots Of British Rock, Vol. 4 (Fr) (features Sonny Boy Williamson and **The Animals** and **Graham Bond**)	(Byg)	1971	
The Roots Of British Rock, Vol. 5 (Fr) (captures what it claims is the first English R&B Festival from Birmingham in Feb 1964 and includes **Spencer Davis Group**, Sonny Boy Williamson, **The Yardbirds** and **Long John Baldry** and The Hoochie Coochie Men)	(Byg)	1971	
The Roots Of British Rock, Vol. 6 (Fr) (features **Steampacket**)	(Byg)	1971	
The Roots Of British Rock, Vol. 7 (Fr) (features **Gary Farr with The T-Bones** and early **Soft Machine**)	(Byg)	1971	
The Roots Of British Rock, Vol. 8 (Fr) (features **Soft Machine** and an assortment of artists on side 2)	(Byg)	1971	
The Roots Of British Rock, Vol. 9 (Fr) (features **Jimmy Page**, Sonny Boy Williamson and **Brian Auger**)	(Byg)	1971	
The Roots Of British Rock, Vol. 10 (Fr) (features **Julie Driscoll** on side one and Sonny Boy Williamson and **Jimmy Page** on side two)	(Byg)	1971	

S

+Samantha Promotions (purple cover)	(Transworld SPLP 101)	1970	R5
+Samantha Promotions (orange cover)	(Transworld SPLP 102)	1970	R5
Saturday Club	(Decca LK 4583)	1964	R1
Scene '65	(Columbia 33SX 1730)	1965	R2
Screening The Blues	(CBS 63288)	1968	SC
Select Elektra (mono/stereo)	(Elektra EUK 261/EUKS 7261)		
		1968	SC
Shepway Folk (w/insert)	(Eron 003)	1974	SC
Showcase 21 (promo only)	(CBS SC21)	196?	
Sixteen Star Tracks Of The Sixties	(Philips 6300 039)	1971	
Some Folk In Leicester	(Lestar LLP 101)	1965	SC
Son Of Gutbucket	(Liberty LBX 4)	1969	SC
Son Of Morris On	(Harvest SHSM 2012)	1976	SC
Stardust (2-LP)	(Ronco RG 2009/2010)	1974	
Stars Charity Fantasia In Aid Of Save The Children Fund	(SCF PL 145)	196?	SC
Stars Of '67	(Marble Arch MAL 710)	1968	
Stars Sing Lennon And McCartney	(MFP MFP 5157)	1971	
Summer '75 (promo-only sampler)	(Island ISS 1)	1975	SC
Super Duper Blues (mono/stereo)	(Blue Horizon (S)PR 31)	1969	SC
Supergroups	(Polydor 2485 002)	1970	
Supergroups, Vol. 2	(Poldor 2485 003)	1970	
Swinging London	(Saga FID 2117)	1968	
Swinging Saga	(Saga FID 2136)	1968	SC

T

Take Your Head Off And Listen	(Rubber RUB 001)	1971	SC
Take One	(A&M Mayfair AMLB 51029)		
		1971	
Thank Your Lucky Stars	(Golden Guinea GGL 0190)		
		1963	SC
Thank Your Lucky Stars, Vol. 2	(Decca LK 4554)	1963	R1
There Is Some Fun Going Forward (some w/poster)	(Dandelion 2485 021)	1972	SC/-
This Is The Blues	(Island IWP 5)	1969	SC
This Is Folk, Vol. 1	(Pegasus PS 2)	1972	
This Is Folk, Vol. 1	(Pegasus PS 3)	1972	
This Is Merseybeat, Vol. 1	(Oriole PS 40047)	1963	
		R2	No. 17
This Is Merseybeat, Vol. 2	(Oriole PS 40048)	1963	R2
Together!	(CBS SPR 52)	1971	
Top Of The Pops	(Ember FA 2018)	1964	

Top 10 Hits, Original Artists	(Guinea Guinea GLL 0277)		
		1964	SC
Topic Sampler, No 1 - Folk Songs	(Topic TPS 114)	1964	SC
Topic Sampler, No 2 - Folk Songs	(Topic TPS 145)	1966	SC
Thru' The Recent Years	(Decca)	1969	
20 Flashback Greats Of The Sixties	(K-Tel NE 494)	1973	No. 1
20 Star Tracks, Vol. 1	(Ronco PP 2001)	1972	No. 2
Twist At The Star-Club, Hamburg	(Philips BL 7578)	1963	R2

U

| Us | (Village Thing CVTSAM 15) | |
| | | 1972 |

V

| V (2-LP) | (Virgin) | 1975 | |
| Vertigo Annual 1970 (2-LP) | (Vertigo 6499 407/8) | 1970 | SC |

W

Warlock Music Sampler (2-LP)	(Warlock Music WMM 101/2)		
		1970	
Way Into The 70's	(Polydor 218 006)	1970	
Weekend In Muisca	(Ricordi)	1968	
What's Shakin' (reissue of Good Time Music)			
	(Elektra EKS 7304)	1968	SC
Wizard's Convention (w/insert)	(RCA RS 1085)	1976	
Woodstock (3-LP)	(Atlantic 2663 001)	1970	
Woodstock II (2-LP)	(Atlantic 2657 003)	1971	
The World Of Blues Power (mono/stereo)			
	(Decca (S)PA-R 14)	1969	No. 24
The World Of Blues Power, Vol. 2 (mono/stereo)			
	(Decca (S)PA 63)	1970	
The World Of Blues Power, Vol. 3	(Decca SPA 263)	1973	SC
The World Of Contemporary Folk	(Decca SPA 156)	1971	
The World Of Folk	(Argo SPA-A 132)	1971	SC
The World Of Folk, Vol 2	(Argo SPA-A 307)	1973	SC
The World Of Hits, Vol. 2 (mono/stereo)			
	(Decca (S)PA 35)	1969	No. 7
The World Of T.V. Themes (mono/stereo)			
	(Decca (S)PA 217)	1972	
Wowie Zowie! - The World Of Progressive Music (mono/stereo)			
	(Decca (S)PA 34)	1969	
		SC	No. 17

Y

| You Can All Join In | (Island IWPS 2) | 1969 | |
| | | SC | No. 18 |

* This is a reissue of *This Is Merseybeat, Vol. 1 and 2.* + These were private pressings. x This is a US-only release of mostly UK material.

TONITE LET'S ALL MAKE LOVE IN LONDON Soundtrack. LP.

FILM AND TV SOUNDTRACK LPs
1963-1976
THAT ARTISTS IN THIS BOOK
APPEARED IN

A Hard Day's Night (featured **The Beatles**)			
	(Parlophone PMC 1230)	1964	R2
After The Fox (mono/stereo) (included **The Hollies**)			
	(United Artists (S)ULP 1151)		
		1966	R1
Blow Up (mono/stereo) (included **The Yardbirds**)			
	(MGM MGM-C(S) 8039)	1966	R2
The Boyfriend (included **Twiggy**)	(Columbia SCXA 9251)	1972	SC
Bunny Lake Is Missing (included **The Zombies**)			
	(RCA RD 7791)	1966	R2
Casino Royale (mono/stereo) (included **Dusty Springfield**)			
	(RCA Victor RD/SF 7874)	1967	R2
Catch Us If You Can (featured The **Dave Clarke Five**)			
	(Columbia SX 1756)	1965	R1
Confessions Of A Pop Performer (included **Three's A Crowd** and **Ed Welch**)			
	(Polydor 2383 350)	1975	
Continental Circus (featured **Gong**)			
	(Philips 6332 033)	1971	
Deadfall (mono/stereo) (included **Shirley Bassey**)			
	(Stateside (S)SL 10263)	1968	R1
Drake's Dream (featured **Paul Jones**)			
	(President PTLS 1068)	1970	SC
Easy Rider (included **Jimi Hendrix**)			
	(Stateside - Dunhill SSL 5018)		
		1969	SC
Experience - The Original Soundtrack (featured **Jimi Hendrix**)			
	(Ember NR 5057)	1971	
The Family Way (mono/stereo) (included **Paul McCartney** and **George Martin**)			
	(Decca LK/SKL 4847)	1967	R3
Ferry Cross The Mersey (mono/stereo) (included **Gerry And The Pacemakers**, **Cilla Black** and **The Fourmost**)			
	(Columbia 33SX 1693/SCX 3544)		
		1965	R1
Friends (featured **Elton John**)	(Paramount SPFL 269)	1971	
Goldfinger (mono/stereo) (included **Shirley Bassey**)			
	(United Artists (S)ULP 1076)		
		1964	SC
Gonks Go Beat (included **Lulu**, **Nashville Teens**, **Graham Bond** etc)			
	(Decca LK 4673)	1964	R3
Help! (mono/stereo) (featured **The Beatles**)			
	(Parlophone PMC 1255/PCS 3071)		
		1965	R1
Here We Go Round The Mulberry Bush (mono/stereo) (included **Traffic**, **Andy Ellison**, **Spencer Davis Group**)			
	(United Artist (S)ULP 1186)		
		1967	R1
Just For Fun (included **The Tornados**)			
	(Decca LK 4524)	1963	R1
Just For You (included **The Applejacks**, **Merseybeats**, etc)			
	(Decca LK 4620)	1964	R1
Kidnapped (included **Mary Hopkin**)	(Polydor 2383 102)	1972	SC
Let It Be (featured **The Beatles**)	(Apple PCS 7096)	1970	SC
The Liquidator (included **Shirley Bassey**)			
	(MGM MGM-CS 8029)	1966	R1
Live And Let Die (included **George Martin** and **Wings**)			
	(United Artists UAG 29475)	1973	SC
Loot (included **Steve Ellis**)	(CBS 70073)	1970	R2
The Magic Christian (included **Badfinger**)			
	(Pye International NSPL 28133)		
		1970	R1
Mahoney's Last Stand (included **Ronnie Lane** and **Ron Wood**)			
	(Atlantic K 50308)	1976	SC
The Man With The Golden Gun (included **Lulu**)			
	(United Artists UAS 29671)		
		1974	SC
Melody (included **The Bee Gees**)	(Polydor 2383 043)	1971	
Monterey International Pop Festival (2-LP)			
	(Reprise MS 2029)	1970	

ARTEFACTS FROM THE PSYCHEDELIC DUNGEON Comp. CD.

More (featured **Pink Floyd**)	(Columbia SCX 6346)	1969	R1
More Experience (included **Jimi Hendrix**)			
	(Ember NR 5061)	1972	
Mrs Brown You've Got A Lovely Daughter (mono/stereo)			
(featured **Herman's Hermits**)	(Columbia S(C)X 6303)	1965	SC
Music From Macbeth			
(featured **The Third Ear Band**)	(Harvest SHSP 4019)	1972	SC
Music From The Body (featured **Ron Geesin** and **Roger Walters**)			
	(Harvest SHSP 4008)	1970	SC
Music From Twisted Nerve And Les Bicyclettes De Belsize			
	(Polydor 583 728)	1969	
Ned Kelly (included **Mick Jagger**)	(United Artists UAS 29108)		
		1970	R1
Obscured By Clouds (featured **Pink Floyd**)			
	(Harvest SHSP 4020)	1972	SC
O Lucky Man! (featured **Alan Price**)			
	(Warner Bros K 46227)	1973	SC
Otley (included **Don Partridge**)	(RCA SF 8014)	1969	SC
Over The Rainbow		1975	
The Peking Medallion (mono/stereo) (included **Dusty Springfield**)			
	(Philips (S)BL 7782)	1966	R1
Performance (included **Mick Jagger**)			
	(Warner Bros WS 2554)	1970	R1
Poor Cow (included **Donovan**)	(?)	1967	
Privilege (mono/stereo) (featured **Paul Jones** and **Mike Leander**)			
	(HMV CLP/CSD 3623)	1966	SC
Rainbow Bridge (featured **Jimi Hendrix**)			
	(Reprise K 44159)	1971	
Slade In Flames (featured **Slade**)	(Polydor 2442 126)	1974	
Son Of Dracula (included **Ringo Starr**)			
	(Rapple/RCA APLI-0220)	1974	SC
Swedish Fly Girls	(Juno S-1003)	1975	
The Sweet Ride (mono/stereo) (included **Dusty Springfield**)			
	(Stateside S(S)L 10250)	1968	SC
The Swingin' Set (included **Dave Clarke Five**, **Animals**, etc)			
	(MGM MGM-C 8012)	1965	R1
Take A Girl Like You (included **The Foundations**)			
	(Pye NSPL 18353)	1970	SC
Thunderbirds Are Go! (mono/stereo)			
(includes Cliff Richard and **The Shadows**)			
	(United Artists (S)ULP 1159)		
		1967	R3
Time For Loving (included **Dusty Springfield**)			
	(RCA SF 8253)	1972	
Tonite Let's All Make Love In London (included **Pink Floyd**, **Chris**			
Farlowe, etc)	(Instant INLP 002)	1968	R3
Toomorrow (w/insert)	(RCA LSA 3008)	1970	R3
To Sir, With Love (mono/stereo) (included **Lulu** and **The Mindbenders**)			
	(Fontana (S)TL 5446)	1967	R1
The Touchables (mono/stereo) (included **Wynder K. Frog**, Nirvana, etc)			
	(Stateside S(S)L 10271)	1969	R1
Up The Junction (mono/stereo) (featured **Manfred Mann**)			
	(Fontana (S)TL 5460)	1968	R1

Up The Junction (reissue) (featured **Manfred Mann**)			
	(Fontana 6852 005)	1970	
What's New Pussycat? (included **Manfred Mann**)			
	(United Artists ULP 1096)	1965	SC
When The Boys Meet The Girls (mono/stereo)			
(included **Herman's Hermits**)	(MGM MGM -C(S) 8006)	1966	SC
Where's Jack? (included **Mary Hopkin**)			
	(Paramount SPFL 254)	1969	
Wonderwall Music (mono/stereo) (featured **George Harrison**)			
	(Apple (S)APCOR 1)	1968	R3/R2
Woodstock (included **Jimi Hendrix**, **The Who**, **Joe Cocker**, **Ten Years**			
After, etc) (3-LP)	(Atlantic 2663 001)	1970	SC
Yellow Submarine (mono/stereo)	(featured **The Beatles**)		
	(Apple PMC/PCS 7070)	1969	R3/R2
	(first pressings only)		
Zabriskie Point (included **Pink Floyd**)			
	(MGM MGM CS 8120)	1970	SC

EP COMPILATIONS RELEVANT TO THIS BOOK ARE LISTED BELOW:
(and many are mentioned in the book)

Aries	(Middle Earth MDE 201)	1969	SC
Great White Dap (4-track) (promo EP)	(Village Thing VTSX 1000)		
		1970	SC
Hart Rock	(Abreation ABR 001)	1971	R1
The Hitmakers No 1	(Pye NEP 24213)	1965	SC
The Hitmakers No 2	(Pye NEP 24214)	1965	SC
The Hitmakers No 3	(Pye NEP 24215)	1965	SC
The Hitmakers, Vol 1	(Pye NEP 24241)	1966	
The Hitmakers, Vol 2	(Pye NEP 24242)	1966	SC
The Hitmakers, Vol 3	(Pye NEP 24243)	1966	SC
The Hitmakers	(Piccadilly NEP 34100)	1966	
Hits Vol. 1	(Decca DFE 8648)	1965	
Hits Vol. 2	(Decca DFE 8649)	1965	
Hits Vol. 3	(Decca DFE 8653)	1965	SC
Hits Vol. 4	(Decca DFE 8662)	1966	
Hits Vol. 5	(Decca DFE 8663)	1966	SC
Hits Vol. 6	(Decca DFE 8667)	1966	SC
Hits Vol. 7	(Decca DFE 8675)	1967	SC
Just For You	(Columbia SEG 8337)	1964	R1
Keele Rag Record	(Lyntone LYN 765/766)	1965	
The Last Things On My Mind (99 copies)			
	(Holyground HG 111)	1966	R2
Maxwell House Presents Hitmakers	(Piccadilly NEP 34100)	1967	
Middle Earth Sampler (promo only)	(Middle Earth MDE 201)	1969	R3
On The Scene	(Columbia SEG 8413)	1965	R3
Our First Four (4x7" in presentation pack)			
	(Apple no #)	1968	R5

THE BEAT SCENE Comp. CD.

Popster Pack	(CBS Special Product. WEP 1135)	
		1968
Rag Goes Mad At The Mojo (33rpm in conjunction with Sheffield		
University Rag Magazine 'Twikker')	(Action ACT 002 EP)	1967 R2
Sheffield University Rag Record (Flexidisc)		
	(Lyntone LYN 738/739)	1964 R1
The Sound Of The Stars (Flexidisc with 'Disc and Music Echo')		
	(Lyntone LYN 995)	1966 SC
Sounds Of Savile	(Keele Rag/Lyntone LYN 951/952)	
		1965 R2
Teen Scene '64 (99 copies only)	(Ember EMB 4540)	1964 R1
Walls Ice Cream (some PS)	(Apple CT 1)	1969 R1/-

RETROSPECTIVE LP AND CD COMPILATIONS

Here are details of many retrospective compilations of music from the 1963-76 era several of which are referred to in the text of the book.

A

Absolute Anthology	(Albert Productions)	1980
Acid Drops, Spacedust & Flying Saucers: Psychedelic Confectionary From		
The UK Underground 1965-1969 (4-CD box set)		
	(EMI 5350782)	2002
Acoustic Routes (CD)	(Code 90 NINETY 7)	1993
Adventures In The Mist (Rubble Eleven)		
	(Bam-Caruso KIRI 069)	1986 SC
The Age Of Enlightenment - Prog Rock, Volume One (CD)		
	(Chrysalis 7243 8 32263 20)	1995
All The Colors Of Darkness (Rubble Eight)		
	(Bam-Caruso KIRI 051)	1991 SC
All You Need Is Covers: The Songs Of The Beatles (2-CD)		
	(Sequel NEECD 309)	1999
Alphabeat (CD)	(Top Sounds TSCD 001)	2005
Ambient: A Brief History of Ambient (2-CD)		
	(AMBT 1)	1993
And The Beat Goes On (CD)	(Deram 820 769-2)	1989
And The Beat Goes On (CD)	(Spectrum 9820120)	2005
And The Beat Goes On, Vol. 1 (2-CD)		
	(Debutante 535 693-2)	1995
And The Beat Goes On, Vol. 2 (2-CD)		
	(Debutante 535 668-2)	1995
And The Beat Goes On, Vol. 3 & 4 (4-CD)		
	(Debutante 535 ???-?)	1998
And Then She Kissed Me (2-CD)	(Debutante 535 672-2)	1996
And The Road Goes On Forever (CD)		
	(Debutante 535 717-2)	1996
And The Road Goes On Forever Vol. 2 (CD)		
	(Debutante 535 054-2)	1996
And The Times They Are A-Changin': Classic Covers Of Bob Dylan (CD)		
	(Debutante/Polygram)	1997
And Who Knows Where Time Goes (CD)		
	(Debutante 565 616-2)	1999
And Your Bird Can Sing: 36 Classic Interpretations Of Beatles Standards		
(not exclusively UK acts) (2-CD)	(Debutante 535 110-2)	1996
Anthems In Eden: An Anthology Of British and Irish Folk		
1955-1978 (CD box)	(Castle CMXBX 1030)	2006
A Shot Of Rhythm And Blues: The R&B Era, Vol. 1		
	(Sequel NEX 1062)	1994
A Shot Of Rhythm And Blues: The R&B Era, Vol. 1 (CD)		
	(Sequel NEXCD 1062)	1994
Arena Rocker (CD)	(K-Tel)	1998
Art School Dancing (CD)	(Harvest 538 7762)	2002
Artefacts From The Psychedelic Dungeon (Box of 7" singles)		
	(no label)	1990
Artefacts From The Psychedelic Dungeon (CD)		
	(Israphon ISR 007 CD)	1992
As Years Go By	(Deram 844 014-2)	1993
The Attack Of The Killer B's (2-LP)	(BBC REQ 739)	1990
At The Cavern	(See For Miles SEE 58)	1985
The Autumn Almanac: Ripples Volume 3 (CD)		
	(Sequel NEMCD 454)	1999

Axe Attack, Vol. 1	(K-Tel NE 1100)	1980
Axe Attack, Vol. 2	(K-Tel NE 1120)	1981

B

Baby Boomers: Greatest Hits Of The 60s & 70s (3-CD)		
	(Castle MBSCD 418)	1993
Back On The Road	(Stylus SMR 854)	1988
Back To The Sixties	(Telstar STAR 2348)	1989 No. 14
Bam Caruso Psych-Out (flexi sampler)		
	(Bam-Caruso BRAV 092)	1987
Dick Bartley Presents Collector's Essentials: The 60s (mostly US but		
includes tracks by **Crispian St Peters**, **Don Fardon** and **The Equals**) (CD)		
	(Varese Sarabande VSD-5705)	1996
Dick Bartley Presents Collector's Essentials: The 70s (mostly US but		
includes tracks by **Ian Matthews** and **Gallagher and Lyle**) (CD)		
	(Varese Sarabande VSD-5706)	1996
Baubles Vol. 1	(Big Beat WIK 72)	1988
Beat At Abbey Road (CD)	(EMI CDABBEY 100)	1997
Beat, Beat, Beat! Volume One: The Mersey Sound & Other Mop Top		
Rarities, 1962-63 (2-CD)	(Castle CMDDD 282)	2001
Beat, Beat, Beat! Volume Two: More Mop Top Rarities, 1962-63 (2-CD)		
	(Castle CMDDD 397)	2002
Beat, Beat, Beat! Volume Three: Mop Top Pop (2-CD)		
	(Castle CMDDD 517)	2002
Beat, Beat, Beat! Volume Four: 1-2-3-4! (2-CD)		
	(Castle CMDDD 728)	2003
Beat-Club Live Recordings (CD)	(Repertoire REP 4527-WR)	1995
Beat Generation - Ready Steady Go (CD)		
	(Disky)	2005
Beat It (3-CD) (not exclusively UK acts)		
	(Underworld UR 012/013/014)	1991
Beat Merchants (CD)	(See For Miles SEECD 430)	1996
Beat On The Krauts Im Star Club Hamburg (Ger) (not exclusively UK acts)		
	(Romulan UFOX26)	19??
The Beat Scene (CD)	(Deram 844 799-2)	1998
Beat Us If You Can, Vol. 1	(Liverpoodle LP 001)	199?
Beat Us If You Can, Vol. 2	(Liverpoodle LP 002)	199?
Belfast Beat Maritime Blues (CD)	(Big Beat CDWIKD 152)	1997
The Best Of And The Rest Of British Psychedelia (CD)		
	(Action Replay Records Ltd	
	CDAR 1024)	1991
The Best Of British Folk (CD)	(Castle CCSCD 222)	1989
The Best Of British Rock (CD)	(Centre Stage)	1999
The Best Of British Rock (2-CD)	(Fuel 2000 3020615072)	2005
Best Of Driving Rock (6-CD)	(EMI Gold 5347282)	2003
The Best Of Heavy Metal (CD)	(BMG 46841)	19??
The Best Heavy Metal Album In The World... Ever! (2-CD)		
	(Virgin VTDCD 598)	2004
Best Of Irish Folk (CD)	(Essential ESCD 768)	1999
+ The Best Of Louie Louie, Vol. 2	(Rhino R1 70515)	1989
The Best Of Planet Records (CD)	(RPM RPM 215)	2001

BEYOND THE VEIL OF TIME Comp. CD.

Best Of Scottish Folk (2-CD)   (Essential ESCD 769)   1999
The Best Of Strike Records (CD)   (RPM RPM 221)   2001
The Best Of The Rubble Collection Vol. One (CD)
                                      (Bam-Caruso BAMVP 1007CD) 1999
The Best Of The Rubble Collection Vol. Two (CD)
                                      (Bam-Caruso BAMVP 1008CD) 1999
The Best Of The Rubble Collection Vol. Three (CD)
                                      (Bam-Caruso BAMVP 1009CD) 1999
The Best Of The Rubble Collection Vol. Four (CD)
                                      (Bam-Caruso BAMVP 1010CD) 1999
The Best Of The Rubble Collection Vol. Five (CD)
                                      (Bam-Caruso BAMVP 1012CD) 1999
The Best Of The Rubble Collection Vol. Six (CD)
                                      (Bam-Caruso BAMVP 1013CD) 1999
Best Of The 60's (3-CD) (not exclusively UK acts)
                                      (Disky)   2005
Best Of The 60's (CD) (not exclusively UK acts)
                                      (Disky)   2005
Best Of The 70's (3-CD)   (not exclusively UK acts)
                                      (Disky)   2003
Best Of The 70's (CD) (not exclusively UK acts)
                                      (Disky)   2005
The Best Of Woodstock (CD)   (Atlantic 7567-82618-2)   1994
The Best One Hit Wonders Of The World... Ever! (not exclusively UK acts)
(2-CD)   (Virgin VTDCD 497 7243 8
                                      13207 2 3)   2003
The Best Rock Anthems... Ever! (2-CD)
                                      (Virgin VTDCD 215 7243 8
                                      46359 2 3)   1998
The Best Sixties Album In The World... Ever! (2-CD)
                                      (Virgin VTDCD 66)   1995
Beyond The Veils Of Time (CD)   (Kissing Spell KSCD 903)   199?
Richie Blackmore - Rock Profile, Vol. 2 (CD)
                                      (BGO BGOCD ??)   1992
Richie Blackmore - Take It!! - Sessions '63-'68 (CD)
                                      (RPM RPM??)   1998
Blockbuster! The Sensational 70's (2-CD)
                                      (Castle CTV CD 209)   1992
The Blue Horizon Story 1965-1970, Vol. 1 (3-CD box set)
                                      (Columbia 488992-2)   1997
The Blues Guitar Box (3-CD)   (Sequel TBB CD 47555)
(also on vinyl)   1990
The Blues Scene (CD)   (Deram 844 801 2)   1999
+ Bo Did It!   (Satan SR 2120)   1989
+ Brainshadows, Vol 2 (LP & CD)   (no #)   1994
Bring Flowers To The World (not exclusively UK)
                                      (Misty Lane MISTY 055)   2002
British Beat Before The Beatles (CD) (EMI CDBEAT 1)   1993
British Blues Heroes (CD) (contains material by **The Yardbirds** and
Steampacket)   1995
British Folk   (Castle CCSLP 222)   1989
The British Invasion Vol. 1   (Rhino R1 70319)   1988
The British Invasion Vol. 2   (Rhino R1 70320)   1988
The British Invasion Vol. 3   (Rhino R1 70321)   1988
The British Invasion Vol. 4   (Rhino R1 70322)   1988
The British Invasion - The History Of British Rock Vol. 5 (CD)
                                      (Rhino R2 70323)   1991
The British Invasion - The History Of British Rock Vol. 6 (CD)
                                      (Rhino R2 70324)   1991
The British Invasion - The History Of British Rock Vol. 7 (CD)
                                      (Rhino R2 70325)   1991
The British Invasion - The History Of British Rock Vol. 8 (CD)
                                      (Rhino R2 70326)   1991
The British Invasion - The History Of British Rock Vol. 9 (CD)
                                      (Rhino R2 70327)   1991
The British Psychedelic Trip 1966-1969
                                      (See For Miles SEE 66)   1986
The British Psychedelic Trip, Vol. Two 1966-1969
                                      (See For Miles SEE 76)   1986
The British Psychedelic Trip, Vol. Three
                                      (See For Miles SEE 86)   1987
The British Psychedelic Trip, Vol. Four 1965-1970
                                      (See For Miles SEE 206)   1987
The British R&B Explosion Vol. 1 (CD)
                                      (See For Miles SEE CD 224)   1988
British R&B Scene   (See For Miles SEE 33)   1985
Britpack (70's Innovations Of Pop) (CD)
                                      (Disky)   2004

BROKEN DREAMS VOL. 3 Comp. LP.

Broken Dreams, Vol. 1   (Line OLLP 5299 AS)   1983
Broken Dreams, Vol. 2   (Line OLLP 5316 AS)   1983
Broken Dreams, Vol. 3   (Line OLLP 5327 AS)   1983
Broken Dreams, Vol. 4   (Line OLLP 5395 AS)   1984
Broken Dreams, Vol. 5   (Line OLLP 5396 AS)   1984

Broken Dreams, Vol. 6   (Line OLLP 5397 AS)   1984
Brum Beat (CD)   (Merseybeat MBRCD 0002)   1992
Brum Beat: Midland Beat Groups Of The 60s (CD)
                               (Sequel NEXCD 251)   1993
Brum Beat: The Stody Of The 60s Midland Sound (2-CD)
                               (Castle CMEDD 1146)   2006
Bubble Oddities (20 UK Pop Oddities)(CD)
                               (RPM RPM 288)   2005
Buddy Buddy's (CD)   (Connoisseur VSOP CD 175) 1992
Buttercups & Rainbows - The Songs Of Macaulay & Macleod (2-CD)
                               (Sanctuary CMDDD 347)   2001
By Jingo It's British Rubbish (CD)   (Hux HUX 015)   1999

C

Canterburied Sounds, Vol. 1 (CD)   (Voiceprint VP201CD)   1998
Canterburied Sounds, Vol. 2 (CD)   (Voiceprint VP202CD)   1998
Canterburied Sounds, Vol. 3 (CD)   (Voiceprint VP203CD)   1998
Canterburied Sounds, Vol. 4 (CD)   (Voiceprint VP204CD)   1998
Capital Gold Sixties Legends (CD) (Virgin TV)   2002
The Carter-Lewis Story (CD)   (Sequel NEXCD 234)   1993
Chocolate Soup For Diabetics, Vol. 1 (Relics LSD 1)   1980 SC
Chocolate Soup For Diabetics, Vol. 2 (Relics ACID 1)   1981 SC
Chocolate Soup For Diabetics, Vol. 3 (Relics CSFD 3)   1983
Chocolate Soup For Diabetics, Vol. 4 (CD)
                                   (PCP 1 CD)   2002
Chocolate Soup For Diabetics, Vol. 5 (CD)
                                   (Tuinal 1 CD)   2002
Chocolate Soup (CD)   (Reverberation V)   1994
Circus Days, Pop-Sike Obscurities, Vol. 1 1966-70
                                   (Strange Things Are Happening
                                   STZ 5001)   1990
Circus Days, Pop-Sike Obscurities, Vol. 2 1966-70
                                   (Strange Things Are Happening
                                   STZ 5002)   1990
Circus Days, UK Psychedelic Obscurities, Vol. 3 1966-70
                                   (Strange Things Are Happening
                                   STZ 5006)   1991
Circus Days, UK Psychedelic Obscurities, Vol. 4 1966-72
                                   (Strange Things Are Happening
                                   STZ 5008)   1991
Circus Days, More Obscure Pop-Sike, Vol. 5 1966-70
                                   (Strange Things Are Happening
                                   STZ 5011)   1991
Circus Days, Psychedelic Obscurities, Vol. 6 1966-1972
                                   (Strange Things Are Happening
                                   STZ 50??)   199?

Title	Label / Cat. No.	Year
Circus Days, 1 and 2 (CD)	(Strange Things Are Happening STCD 10001)	1990
Circus Days 3 (CD)	(Strange Things Are Happening STCD 10004)	1990
Circus Days, 4 and 5 (CD)	(Strange Things Are Happening STCD 10006)	1990
Circus Days 6 (CD)	(Strange Things Are Happening STCD 10007)	1991
Circus Days Volume 6 (CD)	(Bam-Caruso BAMVP 1004CD)	1998
Circus Days Vols 1-6 (4-CD)	(Bam-Caruso BAMVP 1001-1004CD)	1999
Classic 60s (CD)	(Disky)	2003
Class Of '64 (CD)	(Cavern FAB 1964)	1989 SC
Clean Living Under Difficult Circumstances: The Mod Generation (CD)	(Castle CMFCD 684)	2003
The Clouds Have Groovy Faces (Rubble Six)	(Bam-Caruso KIRI 049)	1986 SC
The Clouds Have Groovy Faces (Rubble Six)	(Past & Present PAPR LP 006)	2000
Collecting Peppermint Clouds - Silky Psyche-Pop Sounds From The Lysergic Sixties	(Technicolor Dreams TDR 001)	1999
Collecting Peppermint Clouds Volume 2 - contains European psychedelia		
Collecting Peppermint Clouds Volume 3 - UK Psychedelia	(Technicolor Dreams TDR 003)	2002
Colour Me Pop, Vol. 1 (CD)	(Flashback Productions FBCD05)	200?
Colour Me Pop, Vol. 2 (CD)	(Flashback Productions FBCD06)	200?
Colour Me Pop, Vol. 3 (CD)	(Flashback Productions FBCD08)	200?
The Concert For Bangla Desh (2-CD box set)	(Epic EPC 468835 2)	1991
Cool Beat: 20 Rock Classics From The Sixties (CD)	(Renaissance REN CD 101)	1995

D

Title	Label / Cat. No.	Year
The Dandelion Sampler 1969-1972 (CD)	(See For Miles SFMD 96)	1996
Dawn Of A New Age (CD)	(Sequel NEM CD 608)	1991
Dawn Of Hawkwind (CD)	(Blueprint BP 309CD)	1999
Decade Of Instrumentals 1959-1967	(See For Miles SEE 204)	1997
The Demention Of Sound: British Beat And R&B From 1964-65	(Feedback LESSON 1)	1983 R1
Deram Dayze	(Decal LIK 9)	1986 SC
The Derek Lawrence Sessions: Take 1 (CD)	(Line 9.01118 0)	1992
The Derek Lawrence Sessions: Take 2 (CD)	(Line 9.01119 0)	1992
Diggin' For Gold	(Bat 1001)	1994
Diggin' For Gold, Vol. 3 (CD) (not exclusively UK)		

CANTERBURIED SOUNDS VOL. 1 Comp. CD.

Title	Label / Cat. No.	Year
	(Bat 3001)	1995
Diggin' For Gold, Vol. 4 (CD) (not exclusively UK)		
	(Bat 4001)	1995
Diggin' For Gold, Vol. 1 (CD) (not exclusively UK)		
	(Way Back MMCD 66071)	1997
Diggin' For Gold, Vol. 2 (CD) (not exclusively UK)		
	(Way Back MMCD 66072)	1997
DJC Collection (CD)	(DJC DJC 017)	2002
Dream Babes Volume 2 - Reflections (CD)	(RPM RPM 224)	2001
Dream Babes Volume 3 - Back'n'beat (CD)	(RPM RPM 233)	2002
Dreamtime (British Sunshine Pop) (CD)	(Sequel NEMCD 427)	1999
Drop Out - A Trip In Psychedelia (not exclusively UK) (CD)	(Renaissance RENCD 119)	1997
Dustbin Full Of Rubbish	(Grants GR-D 1974)	1993

E

Title	Label / Cat. No.	Year
The Early Days Of Rock, Vol. 2 - Live In Concert 1964-1968 (CD)	(Living Legend Records LLRCD 022)	1969
Early Morning Hush: Gather In The Mushrooms 2 - More British Acid Folk (CD)	(Castle CMQCD 1265)	2006
Early On (1964-1966) (CD)	(Rhino R2 70526)	1991
Easy Rider (2-CD)	(Hip-O 2115-02)	2004
Echoes From The Wilderness - Sixteen UK R&B Freakbeat Trippers (Limited Edition of 400)	(Paranoid Records 01)	1998
+ Echoes In Time, Vol. 2 (U.S. comp.) (numbered 500 only)	(Solar SR 2000)	1983 R1
Eiderdown Mindfog (Rubble 19) (25 test pressings only)	(Bam-Caruso KIRI 109)	1992 R3
Eiderdown Mindfog (Rubble 19)	(Past & Present PAPRLP 019)	2002
18 Rock Classics (CD)	(Connoisseur Collection VSOP CD 194)	1994
The Electric Crayon Set (Rubble Five)	(Bam-Caruso KIRI 044)	1986 SC
The Electric Crayon Set (Rubble Five)	(Past & Present PAPR LP 005)	2000
Electric Psychedelic Guitar Psychedelic Headswirlers, Vol. 1 (CD) (not exclusively UK acts)	(Purple Lantern Records)	199?
Electric Psychedelic Guitar Psychedelic Headswirlers, Vol. 2 (CD) (not exclusively UK acts)	(Purple Lantern Records)	199?
Electric Psychedelic Guitar Psychedelic Headswirlers, Vol. 3 (CD) (not exclusively UK acts)	(Purple Lantern Records)	199?
Electric Psychedelic Guitar Psychedelic Headswirlers, Vol. 4 (CD) (not exclusively UK acts)	(Purple Lantern Records)	199?
Electric Psychedelic Guitar Psychedelic Headswirlers, Vol. 5 (CD) (not exclusively UK acts)	(Purple Lantern Records)	199?
Electric Psychedelic Guitar Psychedelic Headswirlers, Vol. 6 (CD) (not exclusively UK acts)	(Purple Lantern Records)	199?
Electric Psychedelic Guitar Psychedelic Headswirlers, Vol. 7 (CD) (not exclusively UK acts)	(Purple Lantern Records)	199?
Electric Psychedelic Guitar Psychedelic Headswirlers, Vol. 8 (CD) (not exclusively UK acts)	(Purple Lantern Records)	199?
Electric Psychedelic Guitar Psychedelic Headswirlers, Vol. 9 (CD) (not exclusively UK acts)	(Purple Lantern Records)	199?
The Electric Lemonade Acid Test: An Anthology Of The President Label	(Tenth Planet TP 048)	2000
The Electric Lemonade Acid Test - Volume 2	(Tenth Planet TP 050)	2002
The Electric Lemonade Acid Test - Volume 3	(Tenth Planet TP 055)	2003
The Electric Lemonade Acid Test - Volume 4	(Tenth Planet TP 058)	2004
Electric Sugar Cube Flashbacks	(Archive International Productions AIP 10008)	1983 SC
Electric Sugar Cube Flashbacks, Vol. 2	(Archive International Productions AIP 10010)	1983 SC
Electric Sugar Cube Flashbacks, Vol. 3	(Archive International Productions AIP 10050)	1989
Electric Sugar Cube Flashbacks, Vol. 4	(Archive International Productions AIP 10052)	1989

Electric Sugar Cube Flashbacks (CD) (Archive International Productions
                                AIP CD 1054)   1993
Electrock The Sixties (4-LP) (not exclusively UK acts)
                                (Elektra 60403)   1985
The Ember Records Story (2-CD) (Ember EMBCD 506)   2000
The Ember Years, Vol. 3 (CD)   (Play It Again)   1995
Endless Journey - Phase Three (numbered 1,000 only)
                                (Psycho 19)   1983 SC
English Freakbeat, Vol. 1   (Archive International Productions
                                AIP 10039)   1988
English Freakbeat, Vol. 1 (CD) (Archive International Productions
                                AIP CD 1039)   1992
English Freakbeat, Vol. 2   (Archive International Productions
                                AIP 10047)   1989
English Freakbeat, Vol. 2 (CD) (Archive International Productions
                                AIP CD 1047)   1996
English Freakbeat, Vol. 3   (Archive International
                                Productions AIP 10048) 1989
English Freakbeat, Vol. 3 (CD) (Archive International
                                Productions AIPCD 1048) 1997
English Freakbeat, Vol. 4   (Archive International
                                Productions AIP 10051) 1989
English Freakbeat, Vol. 4 (CD) (Archive International
                                Productions AIPCD 1051) 1989
English Freakbeat, Vol. 5   (Archive International
                                Productions AIP 10049) 1992
English Freakbeat, Vol. 5 (CD) (Archive International
                                Productions AIPCD 1049) 1993
English Freakbeat, Vol. 6 (CD) (Archive International
                                Productions AIPCD 1055) 1996
Everlasting Love (CD)   (Sony TV)   2005
Exploding Plastic Inevitable, Vol. 1 - World Wildlife Foundation (includes
cut by **Shorty and Them**)   (Yahoo Records 009)   199?
Exploding Plastic Inevitable, Vol. 2 - Globular Lightning (includes cut by
Ram and Sel)   (Yahoo 11)   199?

F

Fading Yellow - Timeless Pop-Sike And Other Delights 1965-1969 (CD)
                                (Flower Machine FMRCD 1001)
                                                         2002
Fading Yellow Vols 2 & 3 contain US material
Fading Yellow Vol. 4 - "Light, Smack, Dab" Timeless UK Pop-Sike And
Other Delights 1967-1969 (CD)   (Flower Machine FMRCD 1004) 2003
Fading Yellow Vol. 5 - "Gone Are The Days" - Timeless UK Pop-Sike And
Other Delights 1970-1973 (CD)   (Flower Machine FMRCD 1005) 2003
The Fantastic Story Of Mark Wirtz And The Teenage Opera (2-CD)
                                (RPM RPM 503)   2001
Ferry Cross The Mersey (soundtrack) (Castle Showcase SHLP 102) 1986
Ferry Cross The Mersey (soundtrack) (BGO BGOLP 10)   1988
Ferry Cross The Mersey (soundtrack) (CD)
                                (EMI DORIG 114)   1997

CIRCUS DAYS VOL. 3 Comp. CD.

ELECTRIC SUGAR CUBE FLASHBACKS VOL. 4 Comp. LP.

A Festival Of Folk (2-CD)   (Emporio DEMCD 002)   1996
+ Filling The Gap (4-LP box set) (numbered 300 only)
                                (Obscure World 001)   1989 R1
Firepoint (CD)   (C5 C5CD 593)   1993
The First British R&B Festival (Decca LIK 54)   1989
5,000 Seconds Over Toyland (Rubble Fifteen)
                                (Bam-Caruso KIRI 984) 1991 SC
Flashback To The 60's (2-LP)   (Music For Pleasure CD-DL 1112)
                                                         1987
Flashback To The 70's (2-CD)   (Music For Pleasure CD-DL 1233)
                                                         1993
The Folk Collection (CD)   (Topic TSCD 470)   1994
Folk Rock And Faithful: Dream Babes Volume 5 (CD)
                                (RPM RPM 272)   2004
The Fontana Singles Box Set Volume 1 - Hits And Rarities
                                (Fontana FONT 1)
The Fontana Singles Box Set Volume 2 - Hits And Rarities
                                (Fontana FONT 2)
The Fontana Singles Box Set Vols. 1 & 2
                                (Fontana FONT 1/2)
Footprints In The Snow (2-CD)   (Sanctuary CMDDD 834)   2004
Footsteps To Fame, Vol. 1 (CD) (Repertoire)   1990
Footsteps To Fame, Vol. 2 (CD) (Repertoire)   1991
Forty 45s (2-LP)   (PRT PYL 7007)   1988
45 Classic No 1's (not exclusively UK acts) (2-CD)
                                (BMG Telstar TV TTVCD 3217) 2001
49-Minute Technicolour Dream (Rubble Four)
                                (Bam-Caruso KIRI 027)   1984 SC
49-Minute Technicolour Dream (Rubble Four)
                                (Past & Present PAPR LP 004) 2000
+Frat Rock! The Greatest Rock And Roll Party Tunes Of All Time
                                (Rhino RNLP 70136)   198?
+Frat Rock! The Greatest Rock And Roll Party Tunes Of All Time (CD)
                                (Rhino RNCD 75778)   198?
Freakbeat Fantoms (Rubble Thirteen) (Bam-Caruso KIRI 102) 1989
Freakbeat Freakout (CD)   (Sequel NEMCD 952)   2006
The Freakbeat Scene   (Deram 844 879-2)   1998
The Freakbeat Scene (CD)   (Decca 844 879-2)   2005
Freakout At The Facsimile Factory - de Wolf Library Recordings 1966-69
                                (Tenth Planet TP 036)   1999
Full Throttle - 60 Original Driving Classics (3-CD)
                                (Disky CB 901451)   2003

G

+ Garage Music For Psych Heads (U.S. cassette comp)
                                (Psych Out PSY 102)   198?
+Garage Punk Unknowns, Vol. 1   (U.S. comp) (original pressings with
pasted on sleeve)   (Stone Age SA-661)   1985 R1
+ Garage Punk Unknowns, Vol. 4
                                (U.S. comp) (original pressings with
pasted on sleeve)   (Stone Age no #)   1985 R1

+ Garage Punk Unknowns, Vol. 5

(U.S. comp) (original pressings with pasted on sleeve) (Stone Age SA 665) 1986 R1

+ The Garage Zone, Vol. 1 (U.S. comp)

(Moxie MLP 16) 1985

Gather In The Mushrooms: British Acid Folk Underground (CD)

(Castle CMQCD 840) 2004

The Genesis Of Slade (CD) (Cherry Red CDRED 173) 2000

+ Girls In The Garage, Vol. 7 (mostly US acts)

(Romulan UFOX17) 199?

Glam Slam (CD) (K-Tel NCD 3434) 1989

Glass Orchid Aftermath (Rubble Sixteen)

(Bam-Caruso KIRI 096) 1991 SC

+ Glimpses, Vol. 1 (numbered 500 only)

(Wellington 201085) 1982 R2

+ Glimpses, Vol. 3 (numbered 500 only)

(Wellington no #) 1983 R2

Glitterbest: UK Glam With Attitude 1971-1976 (CD)

(Cherry Red RPM 265) 2005

Glitter From The Litter Bin: 20 Junk Shop Glam Rarities From The 1970s (CD) (Castle CMQCD 675) 2003

Go Girl: Dream Babes Volume 4 (CD) (RPM RPM 259) 2003

The Go Go Train (Doin' The Mod, Volume 1) (CD)

(Sequel NEMCD 479) 2001

The Go Go Train: Doin' The Mod (CD)

(Castle CMRCD 1132) 2005

Golden Decade 1968-1969 (Decca SPA 481) 1977

Greasy Truckers Party (2-CD) (United Artists UDX 203/4) 199?

The Great British Psychedelic Trip, Vol. 1 (CD) (comprises Vol's 1 and 2 of the vinyl series)

(See For Miles SEECD 225) 1988

The Great British Psychedelic Trip, Vol. 2 (CD) (comprises Vol's 3 and 4 of the vinyl series)

(See For Miles SEECD 226) 1988

The Great British Psychedelic Trip, Vol. 3 (CD) (new material)

(See For Miles SEECD 365) 1993

Greatest Hits Of Rock (3-CD) (EMI Gold 8638492) 2004

Greatest Hits Of The 60's (3-CD) (Music) 2005

Greatest Hits Of The 60's, Vol. 1 (CD)

(Cosmopolitan 40259-2) 1999

Greatest Hits Of The 60's, Vol. 2 (CD)

(Cosmopolitan 40260-1) 1999

Greatest Hits Of The 70's cd3 (CD) (Platinum) 2005

Greatest Hits Of The 70's (3-CD) (not exclusively UK)

(EMI Gold) 2004

Greatest Hits Of The 70's (CD) (Marble Arch) 1996

Greatest Rock (3-CD) (EMI/Sony 7243 593053 2 5) 2004

The Greatest 70's Album (2-CD) (not exclusively UK)

(EMI Gold) 2004

The Greatest Sixties Album, Vol. 1 (CD)

(Metronome) 1995

The Greatest Sixties Album, Vol. 2 (CD)

(Metronome) 1999

The Great Glam Rock Explosion (Biff BIFF 3) 1988

Great Shakes (EP) (MO-DONNA EP#1) 1993

Guitar Heroes - Rock The Night Away (3-CD)

(Disky) 1995

Gutbucket (contains 25 tracks from two original Gutbucket samplers) (CD)

(EMI 7243 8 30712 2 7) 1994

H

Hang 11 - Mutant Surf Punks (Cherry Red RED 63) 1985

Harley-Davidson Road Songs (2-CD) (Cema/Capitol 31324) 1994

Harvest - 20 Greats (Harvest SHSM 2020) 1977

Harvest Showdown (CD) (Harvest/EMI 3302632) 2005

The Harvest Story Vol. 1 (Harvest EG 2600971) 1984

Haunted - Psychedelic Pstones Vol. 2 (CD)

(Castle CMRCD 514) 2002

Have A Nice Decade - 70s Pop Culture (not exclusively UK) (7-CD box set) (Rhino 0072919RHI) 1998

Head Sounds From The Bam-Caruso Waxworks Vol. 1 (CD)

(RPM RPM BC 203) 2000

Help! The Songs Of The Beatles, Vol. 2 (2-CD)

(Castle CMDDD 260) 2001

Hen's Teeth, Vol. 1 (CD) (contains material from Psychedelia, Vol's 1 and 2) (HEN 01CD) 1994

Hen's Teeth, Vol. 2 - Blocked! Rare Beat And Psychedelia (CD)

(Hen 02 CD) 199?

Hen's Teeth, Vol. 3 - Catherine On The Wheel (CD)

(Hen 03CD) 199?

A Hidden Secret Garden Found - Incredible Sound Show Stories Volume 10 (Dig The Fuzz DIG 039 LP) 2000

Hide And Seek Vol. 1 (contains two UK tracks)

(Moms Records DREAD 001) 199?

Hide And Seek Again (contains tracks by **Wayne Gibson and Dynamic Sound** and **Measles**) (Moms Records DREAD 002) 1996

Hippy Chick - The Girls Of The Sixties (CD)

(Metrodome) 2002

Hippy Hippy Shake - The Beat Era Volume 2 (Sequel NEXCD 218) 1992

History Of British Rock, Vol. 1 (CD) (Rhino/WEA) 1990

History Of British Rock, Vol. 2 (CD) (Rhino/WEA) 1990

History Of British Rock, Vol. 3 (CD) (Rhino/WEA) 1990

The History Of U.K. Underground Folk Rock 1968-1978, Vol. 2 (CD)

(Kissing Spell KSCD 905) 1998

Hits Of The Screaming 60's (Warwick WW 5124) 1982 No. 24

Hits Of The 60s (CD) (Music Club MCCD 028) 1991

Hits Of The 60s (CD) (EMI Gold) 1999

Hits Of The Sixties (CD) (Legacy) 2005

Hits Of The Sixties (CD) (Sony 15911) 1995

Hits Of The Sixties - Save The Last Dance For Me (CD)

(Delta 611862) 2005

The Sixties (CD) (Virgin) 1999

Hits Of The Swinging Sixties (CD) (Castle Pulse 501607378921) 2001

Hits Of?..65 + 66 (Polydor 515 001-2) 1992

Hits Of?..67 + 68 (Polydor 515 002-2) 1992

Hits Of?..69 + 70 (Polydor 515 003-2) 1992

Hits Reunion (Era BU 5004) 1978

Hoochie Coochie Men: A History Of UK Blues And R&B, 1955-2001 (4-CD box set) (Indigo IGOBX 2501) 2002

Hot Smoke And Sassafras - Psychedelic Pstones Vol. 1 (CD)

(Sequel CMRCD 255) 2001

House Of Many Windows - Psychedelic Pstones Vol. 3 (CD)

(Castle Music CMRCD 659) 2003

Steve Howe - Mothballs (CD) (RPM RPM 140) 2004

I

Illusions From The Crackling Void (Bam-Caruso MAHX 085) 1988

The Immediate Alternative (Sequel NEXLP 110) 1990

Immediate Lets You In (CD) (Sequel SEQ SAM 02) 1999

Immediate Mod Box Set (CD-box) (Castle CMETD 1078) 2005

Immediate Pleasure (2-CD) (Sanctuary/Castle Pulse CMDDD 425) 2002

Immediate R&B (CD) (Charly CDRB 8) 1994

The Immediate Record Company Anthology (3-CD box set)

(Dojo DO BOX 1) 1992

The Immediate Singles Collection (Castle CCSLP 102) 1985

The Immediate Singles Collection (CD)

(Castle CCSCD 102) 1986

JUSTAVIBRATION Comp. LP.

Immediate: The Singles Collection (6-CD)
(Sequel NXTCD 324)   2000
The Immediate Singles Story Episode 1 - Blitz Of Hits (CDBOOK)
(Charly CDBOOK 101)   2000
The Immediate Singles Story - Twenty By Ten (US album)
(Compleat 672 007-1)   1985
The Immediate Story   (Immediate/Virgin V 2165)   1980
Incredible Sound Show Stories, Vol. 1: The Technicolour Milkshake
(Dig The Fuzz DIG 001)   1995
Incredible Sound Show Stories, Vol. 2: When The Tangerine Strikes
Twelve   (Dig The Fuzz DIG 004)   1996
Incredible Sound Show Stories, Vol. 3: 200 Feet Deep In A Purple
Idea   (Dig The Fuzz DIG 007)   1996
Incredible Sound Show Stories, Vol. 4: A Trip On The Magic Flying
Machine   (Dig The Fuzz DIG 006)   1996
Incredible Sound Show Stories, Vol. 5: Yellow Street Boutique
(Dig The Fuzz DIG 009)   1996
Incredible Sound Show Stories, Vol. 6: Plastic And Rubber Lovers Of Life
(Dig The Fuzz DIG 010)   1997
Incredible Sound Show Stories, Vol. 7: Illusions of Alice In Black
(Dig The Fuzz DIG 013)   1996
Incredible Sound Show Stories, Vol. 8: Professor Potts Pornographic
Projector   (Dig The Fuzz DIG 0??)   199?
Incredible Sound Show Stories, Vol. 9: Clap Hands Daddy Come Home!
(not exclusively UK)   (Dig The Fuzz DIG 036LP)   1999
Incredible Sound Show Stories, Vol. 10: A Hidden Secret Garden Found
(Dig The Fuzz DIG 016)   1999
Incredible Sound Show Stories, Vol. 11: Crimson Valley Creatures In Your
Zoo (not exclusively UK)   (Dig The Fuzz DIG 033LP)   1999
Incredible Sound Show Stories, Vol. 12: Fuzz Pudding Factory
(Dig The Fuzz DIG 016)   1999
Incredible Sound Show Stories, Vol. 14: Candy Coloured Daydreams
(Dig The Fuzz DIG 042)   1999
Incredible Sound Show Stories, Vol. 16: Second Glance Through The
Looking Glass   (Dig The Fuzz DIG 046)   1999
The In-Crowd: The Ultimate Mod Collection From The Original Style
Movement 1958-1967 (4-CD)   (Universal 520 049-2)   2001
The In Crowd 2: Empire Made (CD) (RPM RPM 235)   2002
Infernal World, Vol. 1   (Martian R-1001)   1993
Infernal World, Vol. 2   (Martian R-1002)   1993
In My Imagination: Here Come The Boys Vol. 2 (CD)
(Sequel NEMCD 953)   1998
Instant Karma (CD)   (Castle CMRCD 426)   2002
Instrumental Gems Vol. 1 (CD) (Diamond GEMCD 008)   1997
In The Summertime: 20 Hot Hits (CD) (Crimson CRIMCD 245) 2000
Instrumental Nuggets Volume 1: 25 Rare Tracks From The 50s To The 80s
(CD)   (Repertoire REP 4330-WZ)   1994
Ireland's Beat Groups 1964-1969: Irish Rock (CD)
(Sequel NEXCD 262)   1993
Island Life (promo only)   (Island ISLAND MP 1)   1986
Island Life   (Island IBX 25)   1988
It Ain't Me Babe - The Songs Of Bob Dylan (CD)
(Sanctuary CMPCD 261)   2001
It Happened Then (EP)   (PRT DOW 451)   19??
It's Only A Passing Phase (contains **Tony Jackson's Group** version of
Just Like Me (side 2, track 5) but doesn't mention this in its track listing)
(Bam-Caruso MARX 100)   1988 SC
It's So Fine (2-CD)   (Castle CMDDD 1159)   2005
It's The Sensational 70s (CD) (Music Club MCCD 051)   1992

J

Jagged Time Lapse, Vol. One (CD)   (Flashback Productions FBCD01)
2005
Jagged Time Lapse, Vol. Two (CD)   (Flashback Productions FBCD02)
2005
Jagged Time Lapse, Vol. Three(CD) (Flashback Productions FBCD03)
2005
Jagged Time Lapse, Vol. Four (CD) (Flashback Productions FBCD04)
2005
Jagged Time Lapse, Vol. Five (CD) (Flashback Productions FBCD04)
2005
Jingle Jangle Mornings: Ripples Volume 6 (CD)
(Sequel NEMCD 388)   2000
Journey To The Edge (CD)   (Music Club MUSCD 018)   1994
A Journey To Tyme, Vol. 2 (numbered 500 only)
(Phantom PRS 1002)   1985 R1

MYND THE GAP VOL. 1 Comp. LP.

Juke Box Jive (2-CD)   (K-Tel NE 709)   1976
Jump And Dance - Doin' The Mod, Vol. 2
(Castle CMRCD 097)   2001
Justafixation (Limited Edition of 250) (FUNNY 1)   1996
Justafixation, Part 2 (Limited Edition of 250)
(FUNNY 3)   1996
Justafication   (FUNNY 2)   1996
Justavibration (Limited Edition of 250) (FUNNY 4)   1996
Justafixation (CD)   (FUNNYCD 001)   1998

K

Kerrang! The Album (2-CD)   (The Hit Label AHLCD 21)   1994
Kiss Yer Skull Goodbye   (Conifer CFRC 509)   1986

L

The Legendary Sixties   (Arcade ADEH 453)   19??
Legend Of A Mind (3-CD box set) (Decca/Universal 8829 312) 2002
Legends Of Ireland (CD)   (Rhino/WEA 75202)   1998
Legends Of The 70's (CD)   (Mix)   2005
Lennon And McCartney Songbook (Connoisseur Collection
VSOP LP 150)   1990
Let It Rock (CD)   (Deram 820 573-2)   1989
Let's Dance - Sound Of The Sixties Part One
(Old Gold OG 1702)   1990 No 18
Let's Go Get Stoned! The Songs Of Jagger/Richard (CD)
(Sequel NEMCD 377)   2000
Let's Stomp! Liverpool Beat (Edsel ED 103)   1983
Live And Heavy (CD)   (Nems NEL 6020)   1981
Live At The Cavern   (See For Miles SEE 58)   1985
Live At The Cavern (CD)   (See For Miles SEECD 385)   1994
Liverpool 1963-1968: Volume One (See For Miles CM 118)   1982
Liverpool 1963-1968: Volume One (CD)
(See For Miles SEECD 370)   1994
Liverpool 1963-1964, Vol. 2 (See For Miles CM 125)   1983
The London Look (CD)   (Castle CMQCD 1043)   2004
The London Sound (CD)   (London 820 489-2)   1988
Look At The Sunshine (British Summer Tyme Pop) (CD)
(Sequel NEMCD 426)   1999
Loose Routes (2-LP)   (Holyground HG 121)   1991 SC
Loose Routes: One - Musics From Holyground
(Kissing Spell KSG 008)   2002
Loose Routes: Two - Musics From Holyground
(Kissing Spell KSG 009)   2002
Lost And Found (2-LP)   (Decca DPA 3083/4)   1980
The Love Album   (K-Tel NE 1092)   1980
Love Power (CD)   (EMI)   2001
Love Songs Of The Sixties (CD) (not exclusively UK acts)
(MFP)   2001
Lovely Summer Days: Psych Treasures From The Vaults Of MGM

Records (100 numbered copies only) (Arc-Zen Records A-ZCD 2001) 2002

M

Made In England, Vol. 1: British Beat Special (CD)		
	(LCD 15-2)	
Made In England, Vol. 2 (CD)	(LCD 252)	
The Magic Rocking Horse (Rubble Fourteen)		
	(Bam-Caruso KIRI 106)	1988 SC
Magic Spectacles (CD)	(no label)	200?
Maximum R&B (CD)	(Reverberation V111)	199?
Maximum R&B - Doin' The Mod - Volume 3 (CD)		
	(Sanctuary CMRCD 283)	2001
Mayhem And Psychosis, Vol. 2	(Roxy XS-LP-101)	1986
Joe Meek's Groups - Crawdaddy Simone (CD)		
	(RPM RPM 227)	2001
Joe Meek Presents 304 Holloway (CD)		
	(Sequel 1038-2)	1997
Joe Meek Presents?.	(Castle CMWSE 1268)	2006
Joe Meek - Portrait Of A Genius: The RGM Legacy (4-CD box)		
	(Castle CMXBX 783)	2005
Joe Meek - RGM Rarities Vol. 1: The R'n'R Era (CD)		
	(Diamond GEMCD 012)	1997
Joe Meek - RGM Rarities Vol. 2: The Beat Group Era (CD)		
	(Diamond GEMCD 016)	2000
The Joe Meek Story (2-LP)	(Decca DPA 3035/3036)	1977 R1
The Joe Meek Story: The Pye Years (2-CD)		
	(Sequel NEDCD 171)	1990
The Joe Meek Story: The Pye Years, Vol. 2 (2-CD)		
	(Sequel NEXCD 216)	1992
Joe Meek The Alchemist Of Pop (2-CD)		
	(Sequel/Castle Music CMEDD 496)	
		2002
Meridian 1970 (CD)	(Forever Heavenly FB 214)	2005
Merseybeat Nuggets, Vol. 2 (CD)	(Sequel NEXCD 204)	1992
Mersey Beat: The Stody Of The 60s Liverpool Sound (CD)		
	(Castle CMEDD 1204)	2006
Message To Love: The Isle Of Wight Festival 1970 (2-CD)		
	(Essential! EDF CD 327)	1995
Message To Love: The Isle Of Wight Festival 1970 (2-CD)		
	(Sanctuary Midline SMEDDD 45)	
		2004
Midsummer Night Dreams	(Debutante 553 599 2)	1997
Millennium 1970-1979 (CD) (not exclusively UK acts)		
	(Disky)	1999
The Mod Generation (CD)	(Castle CMFCD 684)	2003
The Mod Scene	(Deram 844 549-2)	1998
Monterey International Pop Festival (2-LP)		
	(Rhino 70596-2)	199?
Monterey International Pop Festival (CD)		
	(Rhino R2 70596)	199?
Monterey International Pop Festival, Vol. 2		

(Living Legends		
LLR CD 019/020 030)		200?
More Greatest Hits Of The 70's (8-CD set) (not exclusively UK acts)		
	(Disky)	2005
More Greatest Hits Of The 60's (CD) (not exclusively UK acts)		
	(Disky)	2005
More Hits Of The 60s (CD)	(Music Club MCCD 193)	1995
Morgan Blue Town	(Morgan Blue Town MBT 5002)	1988
Morris On... The Road (CD)	(Talking Elephant TECD 083)	2005
Mr Straw's Hallway (2-CD)	(Terra Nova CD 019/020)	2000
Mr Toytown Presents Vol. 2: Nightmares At Toby's Shop (not exclusively		
UK acts) (CD)	(Toytown TT 1002)	2005
Music Of The Year - 1963 (CD)	(Spectrum)	2001
Music Of The Year - 1964 (CD)	(Spectrum)	2001
Music Of The Year - 1965 (CD)	(Spectrum)	2001
Music Of The Year - 1966 (CD)	(Spectrum)	2001
Music Of The Year - 1967 (CD)	(Spectrum)	2001
Music Of The Year - 1968 (CD)	(Spectrum)	2001
Music Of The Year - 1969 (CD)	(Spectrum)	2001
Music Of The Year - 1970 (CD)	(Spectrum)	2001
Music Of The Year - 1971 (CD)	(Spectrum)	2001
Music Of The Year - 1972 (CD)	(Spectrum)	2001
Music Of The Year - 1973 (CD)	(Spectrum)	2001
Music Of The Year - 1974 (CD)	(Spectrum)	2001
Music Of The Year - 1975 (CD)	(Spectrum)	2001
Music Of The Year - 1976 (CD)	(Spectrum)	2001
My Generation	(EMI NUT 4)	1977
Mynd The Gap	(no label no #)	1995
My 70's Valentine (CD)	(Disky)	2005

N

New Directions: A Collection Of Blue-Eyed British Soul 1964-1969 (CD)		
	(Past & Present PAPRCD 2052)	
		2005
New Directions, Vol. 2 (CD)	(Past & Present PAPRCD 2059)	
		2005
New Directions, Vol. 3: Floor Filler Killers (CD)		
	(Past & Present PAPRCD 2063)	2005
Nightmares In Wonderland (Rubble Three)		
	(Bam-Caruso KIRI 026)	1986 SC
Nightmares In Wonderland (Rubble Three)		
	(Past & Present PAPR LP003)	2000
94 Baker Street: The Pop Psych Sounds Of The Apple Era 1967-1969		
	(RPM RPM 270)	2003
1963: The Soundtrack (2-CD)	(Castle CMEDD 647)	2003
1964: The Soundtrack (2-CD)	(Castle CMEDD 655)	2003
1965: The Soundtrack (2-CD)	(Castle CMEDD 668)	2003
1966: The Soundtrack (2-CD)	(Castle CMEDD 705)	2003
1967: The Soundtrack (2-CD)	(Castle CMEDD 707)	2003
The Northern Soul Scene	(Deram 844 805-2)	1998
Not Just Beat Music 1965-70	(See For Miles CM 112)	1982

RUBBLE VOL. 3 - Nightmares In Wonderland Comp. LP.

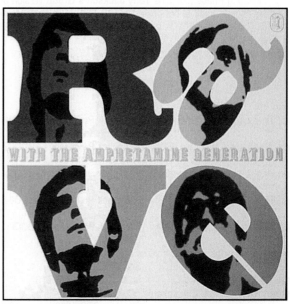

RAVE WITH THE AMPHETAMINE GENERATION Comp. LP.

Now Hear This (CD)	(Deram 820 774-2)	1990
Nowhere Men # 1	(no label)	1989
Nowhere Men # 1 (CD)	(LCD 7-2)	1993
Nowhere Men # 2 (CD)	(LCDoll - 2)	1993
Nowhere Men # 4: British Beat 1964-1968 (CD)		
	(LCD 29)	199?
Nuggets 11: Original Artyfacts from The British Empire And Beyond 1964-69 (4-CD)	(Rhino R2 76787)	2001
No. 1's Of The Sixties (CD)	(Spectrum 731454409629)	1999
Number 1 Hits Of The 60's (CD)	(Delux Music)	1990
Number 1 Hits Of The 70's and 80's	(Black Box BB 286)	2005

O

Oddities Volume One	(no label ODDS 001)	2002
Oddities Volume Two	(no label ODDS 002)	2002
One & Only: Twenty-Five Years Of Radio One (includes some acts in this book) (2-CD)	(Band Of Joy BOJCD 25)	1996
Original No. 1 Hits Of The Sixties (CD)		
	(Castle Pulse PLSCD 778)	2006
The Original 60s Album, 25 Passionate Hits From Across The Decade (CD)	(EMI Gold)	2004
Out Of Sight	(K-Tel 3627)	1996

P

Paisley Pop - Pye Psych (And Other Colours) 1966-1969 (CD)		
	(Sequel NEXCD 188)	1992
Pandemic Pop-Shyte (2-LP)	(Ancient twine no #)	1999
James Patrick Page: Session Man, Vol. 1		
	(Archive International Productions AIP 10049)	1989
James Patrick Page: Session Man, Vol. 1 (CD) (with slightly different tracks from the vinyl version)	(Archive International Productions AIP 1049)	1990
James Patrick Page: Session Man, Vol. 2		
	(Archive International Productions AIP 10053)	1990
James Patrick Page: Session Man, Vol. 2 (CD) (with slightly different tracks from the vinyl version)	(Archive International Productions AIP 1053)	1990
Jimmy's Back Pages - The Early Years (CD) (US release)		
	(Sony AK 52428)	1992
Jimmy Page - Hip Young Guitar Slinger (2-CD)		
	(Sequel NEECD 485)	2000
Peace And Love - The Woodstock Generation (CD) (not exclusively UK acts)	(WSM)	2004
Pebbles, Vol. 4 - Summer Means Fun (not exclusively UK acts)	(BFD Records BFD 5021)	1979
Pebbles, Vol. 6 - The Roots Of Mod (not exclusively UK acts)	(BFD Records BFD 5023)	1979

Pebbles, Vol. 12: The World (CD) (not exclusively UK acts)		
	(Archive International Productions AIP 5029)	1999
Pebbles, Vol. 18 (not exclusively UK acts)		
	(Archive International Productions AIP 10033)	1985
Pebbles, Vol. 19 (not exclusively UK acts)		
	(Archive International Productions AIP 10034)	1985
Pebbles, Vol. 20 (not exclusively UK acts)		
	(Archive International Productions AIP 10035)	1986
Pebbles, Vol. 24 (not exclusively UK acts)		
	(Archive International Productions AIP 10043)	1988
Pebbles, Vol. 28 (not exclusively UK acts)		
	(Archive International Productions AIP 10046)	1989
The Perfumed Garden	(Psycho 6)	1983 SC
The Perfumed Garden (CD with three extra tracks)		
	(Reverberation 1)	1994
The Perfumed Garden II	(Psycho 15)	1983 SC
The Perfumed Garden II (CD with two extra tracks)		
	(Reverberation 11)	1994
The Perfumed Garden III (CD)	(Reverberation VI)	1995
The Persuaders & Other Top Seventies TV Themes (CD)		
	(Sequel NEMCD 424)	1999
Pet Sounds: RPM Records 10th Anniversary Sampler (CD)		
	(RPM RPM 2001)	2001
The Piccadilly Story (2-CD set)	(Sequel NEDCD 240)	1993
Pictures In The Sky (Rubble Seven)	(Bam-Caruso KIRI 083)	1988 SC
Pictures In The Sky (CD)	(Demon DOCD 1997)	1993
Pierre's Plastic Dream (CD)	(Market Square MSMCD 101)	2000
Plastic Wilderness (Rubble Nine)	(Bam-Caruso KIRI 079)	1991 SC
Poison Ivy: The Songs Of Leiber/Stoller (CD)		
	(Castle CMRCD 827)	2003
Pop-In Volume One: Choice Cuts From The Other Side Of Mainstream U.K. Pop 1966-1970 (CD)	(Elevator Music Co.)	200?
Pop-In Volume Two: More Fizzy Pop Confectionery From The U.K. 1967-1970 (CD)	(Elevator Music Co.)	200?
Pop-In Volume Three (CD)	(Elevator Music Co.)	200?
Pop Inside The 60's	(See For Miles SEE 243)	1989
Pop Inside The 60's (CD)	(See For Miles SEECD 386)	1994
Pop Inside The 60's Vol. 2 (CD)	(See For Miles SEECD 399)	1994
Pop Inside The 60's Vol. 3 (CD)	(See For Miles SEECD 400)	1994
Pop-Sike Pipe-Dreams (Rubble Two)	(Bam-Caruso KIRI 025)	1986 SC
Pop-Sike Pipe-Dreams (Rubble Two)	(Past & Present PAPR LPOO 2)	2000
The Keith Powell Story (CD)	(Sequel NEMCD 717)	1994
Preachin' The Blues - The R&B Era Volume Two (CD)		
	(Sequel NEX CD 191)	1992
Pre-Purple Purple (CD)	(Purple PUR 325)	2002
Prime Cuts (10" special)	(RSO SINGL-1)	1975
Progressive Pop Inside The 70s (CD)	(See For Miles SEECD 424)	1995

PSYCHEDELIC VOYAGE VOL. 1 Comp. LP.

RETURN OF THE AMPHETAMINE GENERATION Comp. LP.

Professor Jordan's Magic Sound Show (Rubble Ten)
(Bam-Caruso KIRI 098)   1988 SC
Professor Jordan's Magic Sound Show (CD)
(Drop Out DOCD 1996)   1993
Psychedalia: Rare Blooms From The English Summer Of Love (CD)
(See For Miles SEECD 463)   1996
Psychedelia (CD)   (Music Club MUSCD 021)   1994
Psychedelia And The Underground (CD)
(Camden 74321628012)   1998
Psychedelia At Abbey Road 1965-1968 (CD)
(EMI 7243 496912 2 3)   1998

Psychedelia, Vol. 1: Oil Emulsion Slide
(Tiny Alice Records TA 002)   1992
Psychedelia, Vol. 2: The Fairy Fellers Master-Stroke
(Tiny Alice Records TA 003)   1993
Psychedelia, Vol. 3: Memories   (Tiny Alice Records TA 005)   1994
Psychedelia, Vol. 4: The Great Ramases In His Egyptian Temple Of
Mysteries   (Tiny Alice Records TA 006)   1996
Psychedelic Dream - A Collection Of 60's Euphoria (U.S. comp.) (2-LP)
(CBS 38026/7)   1982 R1
Psychedelic Dream - A Collection Of 60's Euphoria (U.S. comp.) (2-CD)
(Columbia C2 38025)   1982 R1
Psychedelic Dungeon (CD)   (Israphon ISR 007 CD)   1992
Psychedelic Frequencies (not exclusively UK acts) (CD)
(Temple TMPCD 027)   1996
Psychedelic Perceptions (not exclusively UK acts) (CD)
(Temple TMPCD 025)   1996
The Psychedelic Salvage Co., Vol. 1 (Ltd. Edition)
(Private Pressing no #)   1990 SC
The Psychedelic Salvage Co., Vol. 2 (Ltd. Edition)
(Private Pressing no #)   1990 SC
The Psychedelic Salvage Co., Vol. 1 (Ltd. Edition) (CD)
(Private Pressing SALVCD 1)   1998
The Psychedelic Salvage Co., Vol. 2 (Ltd. Edition) (CD)
(Private Pressing SALVCD 2)   1998
The Psychedelic Scene (CD)   (Deram 844 797-2)   1998
The Psychedelic Snarl (Rubble One)   (Bam-Caruso KIRI 024)   1984 SC
The Psychedelic Snarl (Rubble One)   (Past & Present PAPR LPOO 1)
2000
Psychedelic Unknowns, Vol. 6 (U.S. comp.)
(Scrap SCLP 1)   1985 SC
Psychedelic Visions (not exclusively UK acts) (CD)
(Temple TMPCD 026)   1996
Psychedelic Voyage, Vol. 1 (not exclusively UK acts)
(PV 001)   1995
Psychedelic Voyage, Vol. 2 (not exclusively UK acts)
(PV 002)   1998
The Psychedelic Years 1966-1969 (not exclusively UK acts) (3-CD)
(Knight PSDCD 47003)   1990
The Psychedelic Years Revisited 1966-1969 (3-CD)
(Sequel NXT CD 222)   1993
Psych-Out (flexi)   (Bam-Caruso BRAV 092)   1987

SYDE TRYPS VOL. 4 Comp. LP.

Puppet On A String - The Songs Of EUROVISION (CD)
(Castle CMRCD 498)   2002
Purple Heart Surgery, Vol. 1 (Ltd edition)
(Modern Records MOD 1)   1994
Purple Heart Surgery, Vol. 2 (Ltd edition)
(Modern Records MOD 2)   1994
Purple Heart Surgery, Vol. 3 (Ltd edition)
(Modern Records MOD 3)   1994
The Pye International Story (2-CD set)
(Sequel NEDCD 239)   1993

Q

Quick Before They Catch Us; Pop Vol. 1
(Sequel NEXLP 108)   1990
Quick Before They Catch Us; Pop Vol. 1 (CD)
(Sequel NEXCD 108)   1990

R

Radio Two: Sound Of The Sixties (CD) (not exclusively UK)
(Sequel NEMCD 693)   1994
Rainbow Thyme Winders (Rubble 18) (25 test pressings only)
(Bam-Caruso KIRI 101)   1992 R3
R&B At Abbey Road (CD)   (EMI 4934532)   1998
The R&B Scene   (See For Miles SEE 33)   1985
The R&B Scene, Vol 2   (See For Miles SEE 73)   1986
The R&B Scene   (Deram 844 798-2)   1998
Radio Caroline Calling - 70's Flashback (3-CD box set)
(Disky 648132)   2001
RAK's Greatest Hits (CD)   (EMI CDP 7 97486 2)   1991
The RAK Pack   (Connoisseur VSOP LP 117)   1988
Rare 60's Beat Treasures, Vol. 3   (Gone Beat BT-CD 77012)   1995
Rare 60's Beat Treasures, Vol. 4   (Gone Beat BT-CD 77013)   1995
Rare Tracks   (Polydor 2482 274)   1978
Rave On (folk) (CD)   (Edsel EDCD 685)   2001
Reading Festival '73' (CD)   (See For Miles SEECD 343)   1992
Reading Festival '73' (CD)   (Marquee MRCCD 001)   1990
Ready, Steady, Stop! - Doin' The Mod Vol. 4
(Sanctuary CMRCD 535)   2002
Ready Steady Win   (See For Miles SEE 202)   1987
Ready Steady Go + Win (CD)   (See For Miles SEE CD 202)   1992
Recorded Live At The Cavern (CD)   (See For Miles SEE CD 385)   1994
Red With Purple Flashes, Vol. 2 (CD)   2000
Rediscover The 60's: Sealed With A Kiss (CD)
(Old Gold OG 3207)   1993
Rediscover The 60's: Friday On My Mind (CD)
(Old Gold OG 3208)   1993
Rediscover The 70's: Emotions (CD)   (Old Gold OG 3209)   1993
Rediscover The 60's, 70's & 80's: 24 Rock Greats - Saturday Nights Alright
(2-CD)   (Old Gold OG 3220)   1992
Relics - Collectors Obscurities From The First Psychedelic Era
(DB DB 102)   1982 R1
Remember The Pirates   (EMI GO 2027)   1990
Remember The 60's (CD)   (Master Intercontine 1184)   1997
Return Of The Amphetamine Generation
(Dig The Fuzz DIG 032LP)   1999
Revenge Of The Amphetamine Generation
(aka Purple Heart Surgery Vol. 4)   (Dig The Fuzz DIG 023)   1997
Rewound (not exclusively UK acts) (CD)
(Columbia 48443-2)   1996
RGM Rarities, Vol. 2 (The Beat Group Era/The Joe Meek Collection) (CD)
(Diamond GGMCD 016)   2000
Rhythm And Blue Eyed Soul   (Kent 086)   1989
Ripples, Vol 1: Look At The Sunshine (CD)
(Sequel NEMCD 426)   1999
Ripples, Vol 2: Dreamtime (CD)   (Sequel NEMCD 427)   1999
Ripples, Vol 3: Autumn Almanac (CD)   (Sequel NEMCD 454)   1999
Ripples, Vol 4: Uptown Girls And Big City Boys (CD)
(Sequel NEMCD 455)   1999
Ripples, Vol 5: Beach Bash (CD)   (Sequel NEMCD 387)   2000
Ripples, Vol 6: Jingle Jangle Mornings (CD)
(Sequel NEMCD 388)   2000
Ripples, Vol 7: Rainbows (CD)   (Sequel NEMCD 431)   2000
Ripples, Vol 8: Butterfly (CD)   (Sequel NEMCD 554)   2002
The R'N'B Scene   (See For Miles SEE 33)   1986

The R'N'B Scene, Vol. II   (See For Miles SEE 73)   1986
Rock Instrumental Classics: Volume 2, The Sixites (CD)
                                  (Rhino R2 71602)   1994
The Rock Machine Turns You On   (not exclusively UK acts) (CD)
                                  (Columbia 484439 2)   1996
Rock Of Ages (CD)   (Renaissance REN CD 104)   1995
Rock Of Ages, Four Decades Of Heavy Rock 1962-2002 (CD)
                                  (Essential 448)   2002
Rock Resurrection (2-CD)   (X-Media)   2004
Rolling Thunder (CD)   (Renaissance/Castle RED CD 107)
                                                          1995
Round The Gum Tree - The British Bubblegum Explosion (CD)
                                  (Castle Music CMRCD 906)   2004
The Roxy London WC 2 (Jan - Apr 1977)
                                  (Harvest SHSP 4069) 1977   No. 24
The Rubble Collection, Vols 1-10 (10-CD box set) (Track listings as per
vinyl albums)   (Past & Present PAPRBOX 6)   2003
The Rubble Collection, Vols 11-20 (10-CD box set) (Track listings as per
vinyl albums)   (Past & Present PAPRBOX 7)   2003
Rubble, Vol. 1 (CD) (with different track listings to vinyl edition)
                                  (Bam-Caruso CD RUB 1)   1992
Rubble, Vol. 2 (CD) (with different track listings to vinyl edition)
                                  (Bam-Caruso CD RUB 2)   1992
Rubble, Vol. 3 (CD) (with different track listings to vinyl edition)
                                  (Bam-Caruso CD RUB 3)   1992
Rubble, Vol. 3 - Watch Your Step (CD) (new)
                                  (Past & Present PAPRCD 2067)
                                                          200?
Rubble, Vol. 4 (CD) (with different track listings to vinyl edition)
                                  (Bam-Caruso CD RUB 4)   1992
Rubble, Vol. 4 - Utopia Daydream (CD) (new)
                                  (Past & Present PAPRCD 2070)
                                                          200?
Rubble, Vol. 5 (CD) (with different track listings to vinyl edition)
                                  (Bam-Caruso CD RUB 5)   1992
Rubble, Vol. 5 - Scratch My Back (CD) (new)
                                  (Past & Present PAPRCD 2071)
                                                          2006
Rubble, Vol. 6 (CD) (with different track listings to vinyl edition)
                                  (Bam-Caruso CD RUB 6)   1992
Rubble, Vol. 6 - Painting The Time (CD) (new)
                                  (Past & Present PAPRCD 2072)
                                                          2006
Rubble, Vol. 7 (CD) (with different track listings to vinyl edition)
                                  (Bam-Caruso CD RUB 7)   1992
Rubble, Vol. 8 (CD) (with different track listings to vinyl edition)
                                  (Bam-Caruso CD RUB 8)   1992
Rubble, Vol. 9 (CD) (with different track listings to vinyl edition)
                                  (Bam-Caruso CD RUB 9)   1992
Rubble, Vol. 10 (CD) (with different track listings to vinyl edition)
                                  (Bam-Caruso CD RUB 10)   1992
Rubble, Vol. 11 (CD) (with different track listings to vinyl edition)
                                  (Bam-Caruso CD RUB 11)   1992

S

Scooter Rally Anthems (CD)   (Castle CMQCD 1195)   2005
Searching In The Wilderness   (Muziek Express ME 66)   1987
Seargant Salt And Other Condiments (CD)
                                  (Spectrum)   1993
Sensational 70's (CD) (not exclusively UK acts)
                                  (Disky)   2003
The Seventh Son (not exclusively UK acts)
                                  (Seventh Son 0001)   1999
The Seventies Volume 1 (CD)   (Telstar 1988)   19??
The Seventies Volume 2 (CD)   (APWCD 101)   19??
70's Arena Rockers Heavy Hitters: 1970-1974 (CD)
                                  (K-Tel 3985)   1998
'70s Blockbusters (not exclusively UK acts) (CD)
                                  (Camden 74321 449242)   199?
70's FAB FAV'S - Classic 70's Hits (CD)
                                  (Slam Music SLAM 0030)   1999
Sitar Celebrations, Vol. 01 (CD) (not exclusively UK acts)
                                  (SITCER-001)   200?
Sitar Celebrations, Vol. 02 (CD)(not exclusively UK acts)
                                  (SITCER-002)   200?
Sitar Celebrations, Vol. 03 (CD)(not exclusively UK acts)

SYDE TRYPS VOL. 5 Comp. LP.

                                  (SITCER-003)   200?
Sitar Celebrations, Vol. 04 (CD) (not exclusively UK acts)
                                  (SITCER-004)   200?
Sitar Celebrations, Vol. 05 (CD) (not exclusively UK acts)
                                  (SITCER-005)   200?
Sitar Celebrations, Vol. 06 (CD) (not exclusively UK acts)
                                  (SITCER-006)   200?
Sitar Celebrations, Vol. 07 (CD) (not exclusively UK acts)
                                  (SITCER-007)   200?
Sitar Celebrations, Vol. 08 (CD) (not exclusively UK acts)
                                  (SITCER-008)   200?
Sitar Celebrations, Vol. 09 (CD) (not exclusively UK acts)
                                  (SITCER-009)   200?
Sitar Celebrations, Vol. 10 (CD) (not exclusively UK acts)
                                  (SITCER-010)   200?
Sitar Celebrations, Vol. 11 (CD) (not exclusively UK acts)
                                  (SITCER-011)   200?
Sitar Celebrations, Vol. 12 (CD) (not exclusively UK acts)
                                  (SITCER-012)   200?
Sitar Celebrations, Vol. 13 (CD) (not exclusively UK acts)
                                  (SITCER-013)   200?
Sitar Celebrations, Vol. 14 (CD) (not exclusively UK acts)
                                  (SITCER-014)   200?
Sitar Celebrations, Vols. 1-14 (14-CD box set) (not exclusively UK acts)
                                  (SITCER-014)   200?
'60s Pop Classics (not exclusively UK acts) (CD)
                                  (Camden 74321 449232)   199?
Sixties Archive, Vol 1 - Sound Of The Sixties (CD)
                                  (Eva)   1994
The Sixties: A Decade In Sound (10-CD box set)
                                  (Dressed To Kill MOPTOP 1960)
                                                          2001
The Sixties: A Very Special Collection (3-CD box set)
                                  (Essential BOXD 51T)   1995
Sixties Backbeat   (See For Miles/Charly SEE 39) 1985
The Sixties Explosion (CD)   (See For Miles SEECD 223) 1988
The Sixties Lost And Found 1964-1969
                                  (See For Miles CM 113)   1982
The Sixties Lost And Found, Vol. II   (See For Miles CM 123)   1983
The Sixties Lost And Found, Vol. III   (See For Miles CM 126)   1983
The Sixties Lost And Found, Vol. 4   (See For Miles SEE 215) 1988
Sixties Teen Idols (3-CD) (CD 1 features **Billy J. Kramer**)
                                  (Pegasus)   2005
60's Apocalypse (CD) (not exclusively UK acts)
                                  (Age Of Panik)   1998
60's Mix (CD)   (Crimson CRIMCD 162)   1998
Sixties Party Megamix Album   (Telstar STAR 2307) 1987 No. 46
60's Summer Of Love (CD)   (Carlton)   1996
Sixties Summer Of Love (CD)   (Pickwick PWKS 4182)   1996
Sixties Summer Love (not exclusively UK acts) (2-CD)
                                  (Universal Music TV 564 271-2) 1999
60 Number Ones Of The Sixties   (Telstar STAR 2432)   1990 No. 7
60 Number Ones Of The Sixties (2-CD)

	(Warner Music WSMCD 017)	2000

Sixties Years, Vol. 1 - French 60's EP Collection (CD) (not exclusively UK acts) (no label 519382) 1996

Sixties Years, Vol. 2 - French 60's EP Collection (CD) (not exclusively UK acts) (no label 523302) 1996

Sixties Years, Vol. 3 - French 60's EP Collection (features material by **A Band Of Angels**, **The Maze** and **The Sorrows**) (CD) (Magic MAM 176162) 1997

Soft Rock Anthems (CD) (Sony TV) 2005

Soft Rock Classics (not exclusively UK acts) (CD) (Camden CD 74321 400252) 1996

Soft Rock Classics, Vol. 2 (not exclusively UK acts) (CD) (Camden CD 74321 400892) 1997

Something In The Air (CD) (Pickwick PWKS 577) 1990

Something In The Air: Rediscover The 60s: 1963-1969 (2-CD) (Old Gold OG 3204) 1989

Sometimes I Wonder: The Psychedelic Pop Sound Of President (CD) (President PRCD 154) 2004

Some Other Guys: 32 Merseybeat Nuggets (Sequel NED LP 102/NEWCD 102) 1990

Son Of Morris On (CD) (Talking Elephant TECD 051) 2003

Songs From The Underground (The Buskers) (2-CD) (Virgin VTDCD 668) 2004

The Songs Of Bob Dylan (CD) (Sequel NEBCD 655) 1993

The Songs Of Leiber And Stoller (CD)(Sequel NEBCD 656) 1993

The Songs Of Lennon And McCartney (CD) (Sequel NEBCD 654) 1993

Songs Lennon And McCartney Gave Away (EMI NUT 18) 1979

+Songs We Taught The Fuzztones (2-LP) (Way Back MMLP 66002) 1990

Sons And Lovers (CD) (Raven/Topic RVCD 27) 1993

The Soul Of British R&B 1962-1968 (See For Miles SEE 67) 1986

Sounds Of The Seventies (2-CD) (Castle CMDDD 464) 2002

Sounds Of The Sixites (2-CD) (Castle CMDDD 420) 2002

+The Sound Of The Sixties (contains one album of UK acts and one album of US ones) (2-LP) (Eva 12021/22) 1983 SC

Sounds Of The Sixties (CD) (Sequel NEM CD 693) 1994

Spinning Wheel Volume One: Soft Sike and Perfect Pop 1965-1970 (CD) (Sheroo) 2003

Staircase To Nowhere (Rubble Twelve) (Bam-Caruso KIRI 070) 1986 SC

Steampacket/First R&B Festival (Charly) 19??

Steampacket/First R&B Festival (CD) (Repertoire REP 4090 WZ) 199?

The Story Of Oak Records (2-LP) (numbered 1,000 only) (Tenth Planet TP 010) 1994 SC

The Story Of Oak Records (CD) (Wooden Hill WHCD 007) 1994 SC

Storytellers (CD) (Grapevine GRACD 298) 2001

Strange Things Free EP (includes two tracks each from Circus Days CDs 1 & 2 and given away free with Issue 7 of 'Strange Things Are Happening' magazine) (Strange Things STFREE 301) 1990

Strawberry Bubblegum: A Collection Of Pre-10cc Strawberry Studios

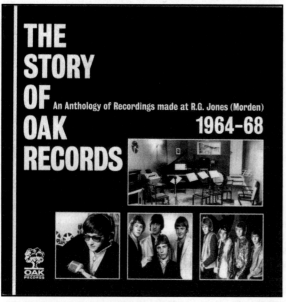

THE STORY OF OAK RECORDS Comp. CD.

Recordings 1969-1972 (CD) (Castle CMRCD 751) 2003

Sugar Lumps: A Psychedelic Selection Of Groovy Movers and Sweet Freakbeat (CD) (Acid Jazz AJXCD 161) 200?

The Sullivan Years: The British Invasion (LP & CD) (TVT 9428-2) 1991

The Sullivan Years: The Mod Sound (LP & CD) (TVT 9429-2) 1991

The Summer Of Love (CD) (Music Club MUSCD 022) 1994

Summer Of Love (CD) (not exclusively UK) (Dino) 1990

The Summer Of Love (3-CD) (Laserlight 55 624) 1997

Super Hits Of The 70s: Have A Nice Day Vols 1-5 (CD) (Rhino R 2 70921/5) 1990

Super Hits Of The 70s: Vol. 23 (CD) (Rhino R2 72297) 1996

Supernatural Fairy Tales The Progressive Rock Era (US import, not exclusively UK acts) (5-CD set) (Rhino RZ 72451) 1996

The Super 70's Volume 1 (CD) (Virgin TV VTDCD513) 2003

The Super 70's Volume 2 (CD) (Virgin TV VTDCD567) 2003

Supertracks (Vertigo SPORT 1) 1977

Sweets For My Sweet (CD) (Temple TMPCD 008) 1995

Syde Tryps One (numbered 500 only, w/insert) (Tenth Planet TP 002) 1993 SC

Syde Tryps Vol. 1 (CD) (Wooden Hill WHCD 002) 1995

Syde Tryps Two- From There To Uncertainty (numbered 500 only, w/insert) (Tenth Planet TP 004) 1993 SC

Syde Tryps Three (numbered 500 only, w/insert) (Tenth Planet TP 006) 1993 SC

Syde Tryps Four (numbered 500 only, w/insert) (Tenth Planet TP 008) 1994 SC

Syde Tryps Five: Instant Sound Productions (1,000 only) (Tenth Planet TP 020) 1996

Syde Tryps Six (numbered, 1,000 only) (Tenth Planet TP 024) 1996 SC

Syde Tryps Seven (numbered, 1,000 only) (Tenth Planet TP 052) 2002

T

Talking About The Good Times, Vol. 1 (not exclusively UK acts) (CD) (Arthur's Archives AA 101) 200?

A Teenage Opera - The Original Soundtrack Recording (CD) (RPM RPM 165) 2002

Telstar! - Instrumental Diamonds, '58-'77 (2-CD) (Sanctuary CMDDD 583) 2003

+Texas Punk From The Sixties, Vol. 2 (Eva 12053) 1986

There Is Some Fun Going Forward... Plus Dandelion Rarities, Vol. 1 (CD) (See For Miles SEECD 427) 1995

This Is Merseybeat (CD) (Edsel ED CD 270) 1991

30 Years Of Number Ones, Vol. 1 (Connoisseur Collection TYNO LP 100) 1989

30 Years Of Number Ones, Vol. 2 (Connoisseur Collection TYNO LP 101) 1989

30 Years Of Number Ones, Vol. 3 (Connoisseur Collection TYNO LP 102) 1989

30 Years Of Number Ones, Vol. 4 (Connoisseur Collection TYNO LP 103) 1989

30 Years Of Number Ones, Vol. 5 (Connoisseur Collection TYNO LP 104) 1989

304 Holloway Road: Joe Meek - The Pye Years Vol 2 (CD) (Sequel NEXCD 216) 1993

That's The 70's (2-CD) (EMI 7243 8 36519 24) 1995

This Is The Seventies (CD) (Disky) 2005

Those Pesky Kids! You Are Awful.... Vol. III (2-CD) (Castle CMDDD 231) 2001

Thrice Upon A Time: Rubble 20 (Past & Present PAPRLP 020) 2002

Time Machine (A Vertigo Retrospective) (3-CD) (Vertigo 9827982) 2005

Tonite Let's All Make Love In London... Plus (See For Miles SEE 258) 1990 (also on CD SEE CD 258 with two bonus **Pink Floyd** tracks)

Totally Number 1 Hits Of The 70's (CD) (EMI Gold) 2001

Totally Sensational 70's 1970-1973 (CD) (EMI Gold) 2001

Transatlantic Folk (3-CD) (Sanctuary Midline SMETCD 137) 2004

The Transatlantic Story (4-CD)   (Essential ESF CD 654)   1998
Trans-World Punk   (Crawdad TW 64)   1985
Trans-World Punk, Vol. 2   (Crawdad TW 65)   1987
Tremors: A Collection Of British Hard Rock Nuggets... Vol. 1 (CD)
                                    (Castle CMRCD 908)   2004
A Trip In A Painted World (Rubble Seventeen)
                                    (Bam-Caruso KIRI 099)   1991 SC
Troubadour (CD)   (Camden 82876 501982)   2003
Troubadours Of British Folk Volume 1 (CD)
                                    (Rhino R2 72160)   1995
Troubadours Of British Folk Volume 2 (CD)
                                    (Rhino R2 72161)   1995
Troubadours Of British Folk Volume 3 (CD)
                                    (Rhino R2 72162)   1995
Troubadours Of Folk: The 60s Acoustic Explosion (2-CD)
                                    (Castle CMDDD 638)   2003
+ Turds On A Bum Ride, Vol. 1 (2-LP or CD)
                                    (Anthology ANT 1.22)   1991
+ Turds On A Bum Ride, Vol. 5 (CD) (Anthology ANT 32.11)   199?
+ Turds On A Bum Ride, Vol. 6 (CD) (Anthology ANT 33.11)   199?
20 Instrumental Rarities   (See For Miles SEE 37)   1985
20 One Hit Wonders   (See For Miles CM 111)   1986
20 One Hit Wonders   (C5-529)   1988
20 One Hit Wonders (CD)   (C5 C5CD 607)   1993
20 Songs Of Love From The 70's (CD) (not exclusively UK acts)
                                    (MFP)   1993
21 Years Of Alternative Radio One   (Strange Fruit SFRLP 200)   1988
25 Hits From The British Invasion   (Varese Sarabande 302 066 333 2)
                                                                  2002
25 Years Of Rock'n'Roll : 1963   (Connoisseur Collection
                                    YRNR LP 63)   1988
25 Years Of Rock'n'Roll : 1964   (Connoisseur Collection
                                    YRNR LP 64)   1988
25 Years Of Rock'n'Roll : 1965   (Connoisseur Collection
                                    YRNR LP 65)   1988
25 Years Of Rock'n'Roll : 1966   (Connoisseur Collection
                                    YRNR LP 66)   1988
25 Years Of Rock'n'Roll : 1967   (Connoisseur Collection
                                    YRNR LP 67)   1988
25 Years Of Rock'n'Roll : 1968   (Connoisseur Collection
                                    YRNR LP 68)   1988
25 Years Of Rock'n'Roll : 1969   (Connoisseur Collection
                                    YRNR LP 69)   1988
25 Years Of Rock'n'Roll : 1970   (Connoisseur Collection
                                    YRNR LP 70)   1988
25 Years Of Rock'n'Roll : 1971   (Connoisseur Collection
                                    YRNR LP 71)   1988
25 Years Of Rock'n'Roll : 1972   (Connoisseur Collection
                                    YRNR LP 72)   1988
25 Years Of Rock'n'Roll : 1973   (Connoisseur Collection
                                    YRNR LP 73)   1988
25 Years Of Rock'n'Roll : 1974   (Connoisseur Collection
                                    YRNR LP 74)   1988
25 Years Of Rock'n'Roll : 1975   (Connoisseur Collection
                                    YRNR LP 75)   1988
25 Years Of Rock'n'Roll : 1976   (Connoisseur Collection
                                    YRNR LP 76)   1988
25 Years Of Rock'n'Roll Volume 2: 1963 (CD)
                                    (Connoisseur Collection RRT CD 63)
                                                                  1992
25 Years Of Rock'n'Roll Volume 2: 1964 (CD)
                                    (Connoisseur Collection RRT CD 64)
                                                                  1992
25 Years Of Rock'n'Roll Volume 2: 1965 (CD)
                                    (Connoisseur Collection RRT CD 65)
                                                                  1992
25 Years Of Rock'n'Roll Volume 2: 1966 (CD)
                                    (Connoisseur Collection RRT CD 66)
                                                                  1992
25 Years Of Rock'n'Roll Volume 2: 1967 (CD)
                                    (Connoisseur Collection RRT CD 67)
                                                                  1992
25 Years Of Rock'n'Roll Volume 2: 1968 (CD)
                                    (Connoisseur Collection RRT CD 68)
                                                                  1992
25 Years Of Rock'n'Roll Volume 2: 1969 (CD)
                                    (Connoisseur Collection RRT CD 69)
                                                                  1992

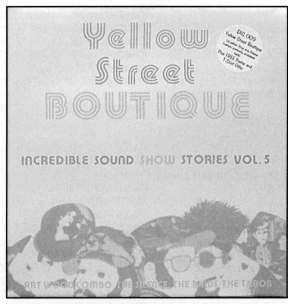

YELLOW STREET BOUTIQUE (I.S.S.S. Vol. 5) Comp. LP.

25 Years Of Rock'n'Roll Volume 2: 1970 (CD)
                                    (Connoisseur Collection RRT CD 70)
                                                                  1992
25 Years Of Rock'n'Roll Volume 2: 1971 (CD)
                                    (Connoisseur Collection RRT CD 71)
                                                                  1992
25 Years Of Rock'n'Roll Volume 2: 1972 (CD)
                                    (Connoisseur Collection RRT CD 72)
                                                                  1992
25 Years Of Rock'n'Roll Volume 2: 1973 (CD)
                                    (Connoisseur Collection RRT CD 73)
                                                                  1992
25 Years Of Rock'n'Roll Volume 2: 1974 (CD)
                                    (Connoisseur Collection RRT CD 74)
                                                                  1992
25 Years Of Rock'n'Roll Volume 2: 1975 (CD)
                                    (Connoisseur Collection RRT CD 75)
                                                                  1992
25 Years Of Rock'n'Roll Volume 2: 1976 (CD)
                                    (Connoisseur Collection RRT CD 76)
                                                                  1992
+ Twisted Teenage Screaming Fuzzbusters
                                    (Israphon ISR 004)   1990

U

Ugly Things, Vol. 1   (Raven RVLP-??)   198?
Ugly Things, Vol. 3   (Raven RVLP-20)   1987
The Ultimate Blues Collection (2-CD) (Castle Communications CTV CD
(also on vinyl)   206)   1990
The Ultimate 60s Collection   (Castle Communications) 1990 No. 4
UK No. 1 Hits Of The 70's   (Music 6423)   2003
Under The Silent Tree: Psychedelic Pstones IV (CD)
                                    (Castle CMRCD 893)   2004
Unearthed Merseybeat: From The Birth Of Merseybeat To Psychedelia
1957-1968 (CD)   (Viper VIPCD 016)   2003
Unearthed Merseybeat Volume 2: The Golden Age 1961-1966 (CD)
                                    (Viper CD 027)   2005
Unearthed Merseybeat Volume 3   (CD)
                                    (Viper CD032)   2005
The Upside Down World Of John Pantree
                                    (Tenth Planet TP 040)   1998

V

Vertigo - Classics And Rarities Vol 1 (Vertigo 846 522-1)   1990
Visions And Rarities from The 60TH and 70TH (not exclusively UK acts)
                                    (Red Fox RF 622)   200?
Visions Of The Past 1   (Disc-De-Luxe AS 711-250)   1991
x Visions Of The Past 2 (blue vinyl) (Disc-De-Luxe AS 711-251)   1991
Visions Of The Past 3 (orange transparent vinyl)

	(Disc-De-Luxe AS 711-252)	1991
Visions Of The Past, Vol. 1 (CD)	(Disc-De-Luxe AS 711-350)	199?
Visions Of The Past, Vol. 2 (CD)	(Disc-De-Luxe AS 711-351)	199?
Visions Of The Past, Vol. 3 (CD)	(Disc-De-Luxe AS 711-352)	199?
Voices (CD)	(Hannibal HNCD 8301)	1990
Voyage Through The Sugarcube	(Paranoid 02)	200?
Voyage Through The Sugarcube (CD)		
	(Paranoid CD 002)	200?

W

Watch Your Step: The Beat Era Vol. 1		
	(Sequel NEX LP 107/ NEXCD 107)	1990
We Can Fly, Volume 1 (CD)	(Past & Present PARCD 2004)	2000
We Can Fly, Volume 2 (CD)	(Past & Present PARCD 2037)	2003
We Can Fly, Volume 3 (CD) (not exclusively UK)		
	(Past & Present PARCD 2046)	2003
We Can Fly, Volume 4 (CD)	(Past & Present PARCD 2054)	2003
We Can Fly, Volume 5 (CD)	(Past & Present PARCD 2058)	2004
The Weekend Starts Here	(Big Beat WIKA 48)	1986
We Love The Pirate Stations	(BR Music BX 434-2)	1997
We Love The Pirates: Charting The Big 'L' Fab 40 (2-CD)		
	(Castle CMEDD 937)	2005
Keith West - Excerpts From Groups And Sessions 1965-1974 (CD)		
	(RPM RPM 141)	2003
What About Us (CD)	(Sequel NEX CD 204)	1992
What A Way To Die: 15 Forgotten Losers From The Mid-60's		
	(Satan SR 1313)	1983 SC
What's Shakin'	(Edsel ED 249)	1987
Where The Action Is (CD)	(London 820 490-2)	1988
While My Guitar Gently Weeps (2-CD)		
	(Universal 583 444 2)	2002
White Boy Blues (CD)	(Castle Pulse)	2001
A Whiter Shade Of Pale	(Disky)	199?
The Wildlife Album (CD)	(Market Square MSMCD 134)	2005
The Wildlife Album, Vol. 2 (CD)	(Market Square MSMCD 139)	2006
+Wild Thing	(Lake Shore Music OP 2521)	198?
Wizards And Demons: Music Inspired By The Writings Of J. R. Tolkien		
(CD)	(Castle CMRCD 635)	2003
Woodstock (CD)	(WEA ATL 60001)	1989
Woodstock (2-CD)	(Atlantic 7567-80593-2)	1994
Woodstock Diary (CD)	(Atlantic 7567-82634-2)	1994
Woodstock Generation (CD)	(Edel 0028612EDL)	1995
The Woodstock Generation (CD)	(Nectar NTRCD 020)	1994
Woodstock: Three Days Of Peace And Music (4-CD)		
	(Atlantic 7567-82636-2)	1994
Woodstock Two (CD)	(WEA ATL 60002)	1989
Woodstock Two (2-CD)	(Atlantic 7567-80594-2)	1994

Y

Yeh Yeh (CD)	(Temple TMPCD 007)	1995
You Can Be Wrong About Boys: Here Come The Girls, Vol. 4 (CD)		
	(Sequel NEXCD 238)	1993
The Youngblood Story, Vol. 1(CD)	(C5CD 549)	199?
Your Starter For Ten!!: The See For Miles 10th Anniversary Sampler (CD)		
	(See For Miles SEACD 5)	1992

Z

Zabriskie Point	(EMI GO 2029)	1990

+ These albums comprise mostly US material. For a detailed guide to retrospective compilations of U.S. material of this era see my earlier book, 'Fuzz, Acid and Flowers - Revisited'.

x This is an album of British psychedelia, although the front cover describes it as German Garage part II it isn't. Go by the back cover.

LIST OF OMISSIONS

The more significant (in terms of record sales) artists omitted from this book are listed below:-

MOIRA ANDERSON, THE ANGELETTES, MIKI ANTHONY, AVERAGE WHITE BAND, THE BACHELORS, KENNY BALL (AND HIS JAZZMEN), RICHARD BARNES, PETER E. BENNETT, BIDDU, ACKER BILK, (BAND OF THE) BACK WATCH, BABBITY BLUE, BARRY BLUE, BLUE HAZE, GRAHAM BONNEY, DANIEL BOONE, JOE BROWN, DORA BRYAN, MAX BYGRAVES, THE CADETS (with EILEEN READ), SUSAN CADOGAN, PAT CAMPBELL, JASPER CARROTT, CHAD AND JEREMY, THE CHANTER SISTERS, PETULA CLARK, COCKEREL CHORUS, JEFF COLLINS, BILLY CONNOLLY, JESS CONRAD, PETER COOK AND DUDLEY MOORE, BOBBY CRUSH, ADGE CUTLER AND THE WURZELS, DANA, PAUL DaVINCI, ALAN DAVID, BILLIE DAVIS, KARL DENVER, LYNSEY DE PAUL, STEPHANIE DE SYKES, NEVILLE DICKIE, KEN DODD, JOE DOLAN, VAL DOONICAN, ALAN DREW, THE DUBLINERS, CLIVE DUNN, RONNIE DYSON, BRIAN FAHEY AND HIS ORCHESTRA, ADAM FAITH, MARTY FELDMAN, MIKE FELIX, RAY FELL, PETER FENTON, CLINTON FORD, ANDY FORRAY, BILLY FURY, STUART GILLIES, THE GOODIES, JULIE GRANT, THE GRUMBLEW-EEDS, GUYS AND DOLLS, BOBBY HANNA, MIKE HARDING, ANITA HARRIS, NOEL HARRISON, TONY HATCH ORCHESTRA AND SINGERS, JIMMY HELMS, BENNY HILL, CHRIS HILL, VINCE HILL, LYNN HOLLAND, BILLY HOWARD, JOHNNY HOWARD BAND, FRANKIE HOWERD, ENGLEBERT HUMBERDINCK, DAVE HUNTER, GREG HUNTER, FRANK IFIELD, JOHN INMAN, THE JAVELLS, SALENA JONES, SAMANTHA JONES, SPIKE JONES, TAMMY JONES, TOM JONES, EDEN KANE, JOHNNY KEATING ORCHESTRA, CHARLES KENNEDY, DOUG KENNEDY, KENNY (Irish vocalist), KINCADE, JOHN KINCADE, KING SISTERS, KATHY KIRBY, MAC AND KATIE KISSOON, ALAN KLEIN, PETER KNIGHT ORCHESTRA, CLEO LAINE, JEANNIE LAMBE, JACKIE LEE, MICHAEL LESLEY, JOHNNY LEYTON, JOE LOSS (and HIS ORCHESTRA), GEOFF LOVE ORCHESTRA, MANUEL AND THE MUSIC OF THE MOUNTAINS, MARDI GRASS, JOY MARSHALL, LENA MARTELL, THE MASTER SINGERS, SUSAN MAUGHAN, SIMON MAY, DAN McCAFFERTY, KENNETH McKELLAR, TONY MERRICK, MIKI AND GRIFF, MILLICAN AND NESBITT, SPIKE MILLIGAN, GERRY MONROE, MONTY PYTHON'S FLYING CIRCUS, DUDLEY MOORE (TRIO), THE NEW FACES, NEW INSPIRATION, THE NEW SEEKERS, OLIVIA NEWTON JOHN, MAXINE NIGHTINGALE, DES O'CONNOR, BILL ODDIE, GILBERT O'SULLIVAN, SIMON PARK ORCHESTRA, PETERS AND LEE, THE PIGLETS, THE PIPKINS, GLYN POOLE, CLIFF RICHARD, CLODAGH RODGERS, JULIE RODGERS, ST. CECELIA, MIKE SAMMES SINGERS, HARRY SECOMBE, THE SETTLERS, TONY SHEVERTON, LABI SIFFRE, SLIK, HURRICANE SMITH, THE SPINNERS, DOROTHY SQUIRES, ALVIN STARDUST, STEVENSON'S ROCKET, PETER STRAKER AND THE HANDS OF DR. TELENY, FRANKIE VAUGHAN, THE VERNONS GIRLS, HOUSTON WELLS, DODIE WEST, ROGER WHITTAKER, DANNY WILLIAMS, EDWARD WOODWARD, THE WURZELS, MARK WYNTER, YIN AND YAN, JIMMY YOUNG, LENA ZAVARONI.

INCREDIBLE SOUND SHOW STORIES VOL. 12 Comp. LP.